The Oxford Handbook of School Psychology

OXFORD LIBRARY OF PSYCHOLOGY

Editor-in-Chief PETER E. NATHAN

The Oxford Handbook of School Psychology

Edited by

Melissa A. Bray

Thomas J. Kehle

OXFORD
UNIVERSITY PRESS

OXFORD
UNIVERSITY PRESS

Oxford University Press, Inc., publishes works that further Oxford University's
objective of excellence in research, scholarship, and education.

Oxford   New York
Auckland   Cape Town   Dar es Salaam   Hong Kong   Karachi
Kuala Lumpur   Madrid   Melbourne   Mexico City   Nairobi
New Delhi   Shanghai   Taipei   Toronto

With offices in
Argentina   Austria   Brazil   Chile   Czech Republic   France   Greece
Guatemala   Hungary   Italy   Japan   Poland   Portugal   Singapore
South Korea   Switzerland   Thailand   Turkey   Ukraine   Vietnam

Copyright © 2011 by Oxford University Press, Inc.

Published by Oxford University Press, Inc.
198 Madison Avenue, New York, New York 10016
www.oup.com

Library of Congress Cataloging-in-Publication Data

The Oxford handbook of school psychology / edited by Melissa A. Bray and Thomas J. Kehle.
p. cm. — (Oxford library of psychology)
ISBN: 978-0-19-536980-9
1. School psychology—Handbooks, manuals, etc. 2. Educational psychology—Handbooks,
manuals, etc. I. Bray, Melissa A., 1964- II. Kehle, Thomas J., 1943-
LB1027.55.O94 2011
370.15—dc22

2010011754

9 8 7 6 5 4 3 2 1

Printed in the United States of America on acid-free paper

SHORT CONTENTS

OXFORD LIBRARY OF PSYCHOLOGY

The *Oxford Library of Psychology*, a landmark series of handbooks, is published by Oxford University Press, one of the world's oldest and most highly respected publishers, with a tradition of publishing significant books in psychology. The ambitious goal of the *Oxford Library of Psychology* is nothing less than to span a vibrant, wide-ranging field and, in so doing, to fill a clear market need.

Encompassing a comprehensive set of handbooks, organized hierarchically, the *Library* incorporates volumes at different levels, each designed to meet a distinct need. At one level are a set of handbooks designed broadly to survey the major subfields of psychology; at another are numerous handbooks that cover important current focal research and scholarly areas of psychology in depth and detail. Planned as a reflection of the dynamism of psychology, the *Library* will grow and expand as psychology itself develops, thereby highlighting significant new research that will impact on the field. Adding to its accessibility and ease of use, the *Library* will be published in print and, later on, electronically.

The *Library* surveys psychology's principal subfields with a set of handbooks that capture the current status and future prospects of those major subdisciplines. This initial set includes handbooks of social and personality psychology, clinical psychology, counseling psychology, school psychology, educational psychology, industrial and organizational psychology, cognitive psychology, cognitive neuroscience, methods and measurements, history, neuropsychology, personality assessment, developmental psychology, and more. Each handbook undertakes to review one of psychology's major subdisciplines with breadth, comprehensiveness, and exemplary scholarship. In addition to these broadly conceived volumes, the *Library* also includes a large number of handbooks designed to explore in depth more specialized areas of scholarship and research, such as stress, health and coping, anxiety and related disorders, cognitive development, or child and adolescent assessment. In contrast to the broad coverage of the subfield handbooks, each of these latter volumes focuses on an especially productive, more highly focused line of scholarship and research. Whether at the broadest or most specific level, however, all of the *Library* handbooks offer synthetic coverage that reviews and evaluates the relevant past and present research, and anticipates research in the future. Each handbook in the *Library* includes introductory and concluding chapters written by its editor to provide a roadmap to the handbook's table of contents, and to offer informed anticipations of significant future developments in that field.

An undertaking of this scope calls for handbook editors and chapter authors who are established scholars in the areas about which they write. Many of the nation's and the world's most productive and best-respected psychologists have agreed to edit *Library* handbooks or write authoritative chapters in their areas of expertise.

For whom has the *Oxford Library of Psychology* been written? Because of its breadth, depth, and accessibility, the *Library* serves a diverse audience, including graduate students in psychology and their faculty mentors, scholars, researchers, and practitioners in psychology and related fields. Each will find in the *Library* the information they seek on the subfield or focal area of psychology in which they work or are interested.

Befitting its commitment to accessibility, each handbook includes a comprehensive index, as well as extensive references to help guide research. And because the *Library* was designed from its inception as an online as well as a print resource, its structure and contents will be readily and rationally searchable online. Further, once the *Library* is released online, the handbooks will be regularly and thoroughly updated.

In summary, the *Oxford Library of Psychology* will grow organically to provide a thoroughly informed perspective on the field of psychology, one that reflects both psychology's dynamism and its increasing interdisciplinarity. Once published electronically, the *Library* is also destined to become a uniquely valuable interactive tool, with extended search and browsing capabilities. As you begin to consult this handbook, we sincerely hope you will share our enthusiasm for the more than 500-year tradition of Oxford University Press for excellence, innovation, and quality, as exemplified by the *Oxford Library of Psychology*.

Peter E. Nathan
Editor-in-Chief
Oxford Library of Psychology

ABOUT THE EDITORS

Melissa A. Bray

Melissa A. Bray, PhD, is Professor of School Psychology at the University of Connecticut. She is a fellow of the American Psychological Association and the Association for Psychological Science, and is a licensed psychologist in the state of Connecticut. Dr. Bray's primary research interests include interventions in the areas of health, communication, and disruptive classroom behavior.

Thomas J. Kehle

Thomas J. Kehle, PhD, is Professor and Director of School Psychology at the University of Connecticut. He is a fellow of the American Psychological Association, the Association for Psychological Science, and the American Association of Applied and Preventive Psychology. He is also a member of the Council for the National Register for Health Service Providers in Psychology, and a licensed psychologist in the state of Connecticut. Dr. Kehle's primary research interests include individual differences, self-modeling, selective mutism, and psychological wellness.

CONTRIBUTORS

Angeleque Akin-Little
Behavioral, Educational, and Research
Consultants
Auckland, New Zealand

Laura B. Allen
Department of Pediatrics
David Geffen School of Medicine
University of California, Los Angeles
Los Angeles, CA

Nicole Alston-Abel
Department of Educational Psychology
University of Washington
Seattle, WA

Cynthia A. Austin
Therapeutic Assessment Project
University of Texas at Austin
Austin, TX

Stephen J. Bagnato
Department of Pediatrics
Department of Psychology
University of Pittsburgh School of
Medicine
Pittsburgh, PA

Carrie Ball
Department of Educational Psychology
Ball State University
Muncie, IN

Jennifer Bass
The May Institute
Randolph, MA

Jaime Benson
Center for Promoting Research to Practice
Lehigh University
Bethlehem, PA

Virginia W. Berninger
Department of Educational Psychology
University of Washington
Seattle, WA

Julie M. Bowen
Department of Educational
Psychology
University of Utah
Salt Lake City, Utah

Melissa A. Bray
Neag School of Education
University of Connecticut
Storrs, CT

Sandra M. Chafouleas
Neag School of Education
University of Connecticut
Storrs, CT

Allison Champion
Department of Educational
Psychology
University of Nebraska Lincoln
Lincoln, NE

Lauren Christian
The National Autism Center
Randolph, MA

Elaine Clark
Department of Educational Psychology
University of Utah
Salt Lake City, UT

Nathan Clemens
Department of Educational Psychology
Texas A&M University
College Station, TX

Alyssa Collaro
Department of Educational Psychology
University of Nebraska Lincoln
Lincoln, NE

Richard J. Cowan
School of Lifespan Development
& Educational Sciences
Kent State University
Kent, OH

Tony D. Crespi
Department of Psychology
University of Hartford
West Hartford, CT

Laura M. Crothers
School of Education
Duquesne University
Pittsburgh, PA

Jack A. Cummings
School of Education
Indiana University
Bloomington, IN

Rik Carl D'Amato
Center for Teaching and Learning
Enhancement
Department of Psychology
University of Macau
Taipa, Macau SAR, China

Angie Dahl
Department of Psychology
Utah State University
Logan, UT

Raymond S. Dean
Department of Educational Psychology
Ball State University
Muncie, IN

Beth Doll
Department of Educational Psychology
University of Nebraska Lincoln
Lincoln, NE

George J. DuPaul
School Psychology Program
Lehigh University
Bethlehem, PA

Tanya L. Eckert
Department of Psychology
Syracuse University
Syracuse, NY

Ruth A. Ervin
Department of Educational & Counseling
Psychology, and Special Education
University of British Columbia
Vancouver, BC

Michel Fayol
Université Blaise Pascal
Clermont-Ferrand, France

Jacquelyn N. Felt
Wisconsin Center for Education Research
University of Wisconsin, Madison
Madison, WI

Laura Fisher
The National Autism Center
Randolph, MA

Susan G. Forman
Graduate School of Applied and
Professional Psychology, Rutgers,
The State of University of New Jersey

Caryn Freeman
Los Angeles Unified School District
Los Angeles, CA

Michael K. Gardner
Department of Educational Psychology
University of Utah
Salt Lake City, UT

Maribeth Gettinger
Department of Educational Psychology
University of Wisconsin, Madison
Madison, WI

Caroline N. Racine Gilles
Wisconsin Center for Education Research
University of Wisconsin, Madison
Madison, WI

Rich Gilman
Department of Developmental and
Behavioral Pediatrics
Cincinnati Children's Hospital Medical
Center
Cincinnati, OH

Karen L. Gischlar
School Psychology Program
Rider University
Lawrence, NJ

Frank M. Gresham
Department of Psychology
Louisiana State University
Baton Rouge, LA

Robert M. Grom
Early Childhood Partnerships
Department of Pediatrics
University of Pittsburgh
Pittsburgh, PA

Barbara A. Gueldner
Parker Pediatrics & Adolescents, P. C.
Parker, CO

Chelsie Guerrero
Department of Educational Psychology
University of Nebraska Lincoln
Lincoln, NE

Sarah Harward
Department of Educational Psychology
University of Utah
Salt Lake City, Utah

Jocelyn R. Helwig
School Psychology Program
Lehigh University
Bethlehem, PA

Kathryn E. Hoff
Department of Psychology
Illinois State University
Normal, IL

E. Scott Huebner
Department of Psychology
University of South Carolina
Columbia, SC

Tammy L. Hughes
School of Education
Duquesne University
Pittsburgh, PA

William R. Jenson
Department of Educational
Psychology
University of Utah
Salt Lake City, UT

Kristin Jones
Department of Educational
Psychology
University of Nebraska Lincoln
Lincoln, NE

Randy W. Kamphaus
College of Education
Georgia State University
Atlanta, GA

Kenneth A. Kavale*
School of Education
Regent University
Virginia Beach, VA

Thomas J. Kehle
Neag School of Education
University of Connecticut
Storrs, CT

Thomas R. Kratochwill
Department of Educational Psychology
University of Wisconsin, Madison
Madison, WI

Lauren S. Krumholz
Therapeutic Assessment Project
The University of Texas at Austin
Austin, TX

Thomas Kubiszyn
Department of Educational Psychology
University of Houston
Houston, TX

Denise E. Laframboise
Department of Psychology
University of Hartford
West Hartford, CT

Cathryn Lehman
School of Education
Duquesne University
Pittsburgh, PA

Pui-Wa Lei
Department of Educational
Psychology, School Psychology,
and Special Education
The Pennsylvania State University
University Park, PA

Hongli Li
Department of Educational
Psychology, School Psychology,
and Special Education
The Pennsylvania State University
University Park, PA

Steven G. Little
School of Education
Massey University
Auckland, New Zealand

Jesse Logue
The National Autism Center
Randolph, MA

Ryan Macks
Department of Developmental and
Behavioral Pediatrics
Cincinnati Children's Hospital Medical
Center
Cincinnati, OH

*Deceased

May Matson
Therapeutic Assessment Project
University of Texas at Austin
Austin, TX

Kristen L. Mays
College of Education
Georgia State University
Atlanta, GA

Erica McConnell
University of Northern Colorado
Greeley, CO

David E. McIntosh
Department of Special Education
Ball State University
Muncie, IN

Kathleen M. McNamara
Psychology Department
Cleveland State University
Cleveland, OH

Natasha S. Medley
Graduate School of Education
University of California, Riverside
Riverside, CA

Kenneth W. Merrell
Department of Special Education and
Clinical Sciences
University of Oregon
Eugene, OR

Kristen Missall
College of Education
The University of Iowa
Iowa City, IA

Dipti Mudgal
The May Institute
Randolph, MA

Bonnie Kaul Nastasi
Department of Psychology
Tulane University
New Orleans, LA

Allison Osborn
Department of Educational Psychology
University of Nebraska Lincoln
Lincoln, NE

Gretchen Gimpel Peacock
Department of Psychology
Utah State University
Logan, UT

LeAdelle Phelps
Department of Counseling, School, and
Educational Psychology
University at Buffalo, SUNY
Buffalo, NY

Eric Pierson
Department of Educational Psychology
Ball State University
Muncie, IN

Janiece L. Pompa
Department of Educational Psychology
University of Utah
Salt Lake City, UT

Sally M. Reis
Neag School of Education
University of Connecticut
Storrs, CT

Joseph S. Renzulli
Neag School of Education
University of Connecticut
Storrs, CT

H. Jane Rogers
Neag School of Education
University of Connecticut
Storrs, CT

Jennifer L. Salaway
Early Childhood Partnerships
Department of Pediatrics
University of Pittsburgh
Pittsburgh, PA

Lisa M. Hagermoser Sanetti
Neag School of Education
University of Connecticut
Storrs, CT

Jessica Savage
Department of Psychological and
Social Foundations
University of South Florida
Tampa, FL

Clarissa J. Schienebeck
Department of Educational Psychlgy
University of Wisconsin, Madison
Madison, WI

Stephanie Seigel
Department of Educational Psychlgy
University of Wisconsin, Madison
Madison, WI

Jeffrey S. Selman
Graduate School of Applied and
Professional Psychology, Rutgers
The State University of New Jersey

Rohini Sen
Department of Statistics
University of Connecticut
Storrs, CT

Edward S. Shapiro
Center for Promoting Research
to Practice
Lehigh University
Bethlehem, PA

Lucinda S. Spaulding
School of Education
Liberty University
Lynchburg, VA

Brandi Simonsen
Neag School of Education
University of Connecticut
Storrs, CT

Peter M. Slay
School Psychology Program
Lehigh University
Bethlehem, PA

Mark W. Steege
Department of School Psychology
University of Southern Maine
Portland, ME

Hoi K. Suen
Department of Educational
Psychology, School Psychology,
and Special Education
The Pennsylvania State University
University Park, PA

Shannon M. Suldo
Department of Psychological and
Social Foundations
University of South Florida
Tampa, FL

Leslie Sutro
The National Autism Center
Randolph, MA

Hariharan Swaminathan
Neag School of Education
University of Connecticut
Storrs, CT

H. Lee Swanson
Graduate School of Education
University of California, Riverside
Riverside, CA

Amanda Thalji
Department of Psychological and
Social Foundations
University of South Florida
Tampa, FL

Deborah J. Tharinger
Therapeutic Assessment Project
University of Texas at Austin
Austin, TX

Lea A. Theodore
School of Education
The College of William and Mary
Williamsburg, VA

Jennie C. I. Tsao
Department of Pediatrics
David Geffen School of Medicine
University of California, Los Angeles
Los Angeles, CA

Cara A. Vaccarello
Wisconsin Center for
Education Research
University of Wisconsin, Madison
Madison, WI

Kris Varjas
Department of Counseling and
Psychological Services
Georgia State University
Atlanta, GA

Laura Vollmer
Department of Educational Psycholgy
University of Wisconsin, Madison
Madison, WI

Robert J. Volpe
Department of Counseling and Applied
Educational Psychology
Northeastern University
Boston, MA

Tonya S. Watson
Department of Educational Psychology
Miami University
Oxford, OH

T. Steuart Watson
Department of Educational Psychology
Miami University
Oxford, OH

Susan M. Wilczynski
The National Autism Center
Randolph, MA

Barbara Willard
Southwest Regional Key
YWCA of Pittsburgh
Pittsburgh, PA

Christina Zafiris
Jackson Memorial Hospital
University of Miami Medical School
Miami, FL

Victoria Zeiger
The National Autism Center
Randolph, MA

Lonnie K. Zeltzer
Department of Pediatrics
David Geffen School of Medicine
University of California, Los Angeles
Los Angeles, CA

Zheng Zhou
Department of Psychology
St. John's University
Queens, NY 11439

Sharon Zumbrunn
Department of Educational Psychology
University of Nebraska Lincoln
Lincoln, NE

CONTENTS

PART 1

Introduction and Overview

Introduction: On Such a Full Sea and We Continue to Flounder

Thomas J. Kehle *and* Melissa A. Bray

Abstract

"Science is built up of facts, as a house is built up of stones, but a accumulation of facts is no more a science than a heap of stones is a house" (Poincare, 1905, p. 101). The continual plea for scientifically based practice that affects measurable outcomes is laudable. However, with little or no consensus regarding the relationship between outcomes, the definition of an educated and psychologically healthy student is consequential in that there is a concomitant lack of noticeable incremental gains in educational and school psychological practice—a lack of accumulated knowledge (Kehle & Bray, 2005). If school psychology remains a discipline void of clear dependent variables other than the treatment of pathologies, we really do not know what defines an academically and socially competent student.

Keywords: school psychology, academic, social development

An obvious, but rarely publicly discussed, observation is that children are not appreciably better educated nor better behaved than they were 50 years ago. As a matter of fact, it could be argued that they are products of an educational system that is less efficient and substantially less civil than it was 50 years ago. It would seem that the phenomenal technological innovations over this period of time would have influenced the acquisition of knowledge and psychological functioning—it does not appear so. Further, the fields of education and psychology have done little to reach a consensus on what defines an educated and psychologically healthy individual (Kehle & Bray, 2005). It is not sufficient to say practice should be firmly based on the scientific method when one does not know the goal of that practice other than to address pathology.

In a very real sense, the most intellectually challenging task in life is to understand the functional relationship between oneself and one's environment—or, simply stated, to know where you are going. Similarly, institutions, including the discipline of school psychology, must either grapple with this complex task, or leave its future to what

Trachman (1981) characterized, almost three decades ago, as the bandwagon effect, faddism, and ill-conceived and scientifically anemic, politically motivated legal mandates. The latter do more harm than the fads, which eventually die out and in so doing lead to future abuse by what Hyman (1979) called the "panacea mongers" that have doomed education to be perpetually under reform. However, the passage of federal or state laws often seeps into the educational and school psychological mindset, where they are interpreted as moral and best practice.

The notion that the Gaussian curve and individual differences do not exist is fanciful. We believe that to make real and measurable progress in the education and psychological development of children, a cumulative knowledge must be built that is based on the scientific method and that embraces goals that are universally and culturally acceptable to all individuals, across all socioeconomic statuses, ethnicities, religious affiliations, and political ideologies.

To define an achievable goal that would be applicable to the broad diversity of students, socioeconomic status, psychological variables, ethnicity, gender, and other factors on which they differ, is a daunting task. We would like to propose the following, which is simply based on asking mothers what they would want their children to have as they are developing throughout the life span. Originally, this question was asked to mothers living in over 32 cultures throughout the world. Their responses were translated and factor analyzed. Obviously, there was considerable error when translating even across the Romance languages; further, there is subjective error when labeling the factors. However, this same question has been asked to students and others for over 30 years with remarkably similar results.

Based on this inquiry, we believe that our R.I.C.H. theory provides a definition of an educated and psychologically healthy person that has been shown to have broad cross-cultural acceptance. It appears that mothers want their children to grow up and have essentially the same four characteristics: Resources, Intimacy, Competence, and Health (Kehle, 1989; Kehle, 1999; Kehle & Barclay, 1979; Kehle & Bray, 2004; Kehle, Bray, Chafoulea, & Mcloughlin, 2002; Kehle, Clark, & Jenson, 1993). Furthermore, and of utmost importance, all children, regardless of their life's situation, can, in a relative sense, achieve the R.I.C.H. goals. Providing a clear definition of an educated and psychological healthy person that is universally and cross-culturally based, applicable across the life span and ability levels, would substantially promote goal-oriented research and ultimately result in a cumulative knowledge base to facilitate both further research and practice. Stated again: without doubt, the most challenging and complex task in life is to understand the functional relationship between oneself and one's environment, or, to know where you are going.

The acronym R.I.C.H. stands for these four characteristics: "R" for resources, "I" for intimacy, "C" for competence, and "H" for physical health. The four characteristics are interrelated to the extent that each can be defined by the other three (Kehle & Bray, 2004).

Resources. The appropriate allocation of resources results in a feeling of independence or professionalism, which is defined as being synonymous with a sense of individual freedom, or a sense of control over one's time and daily life.

Intimacy. Intimacy is defined as friendship. It involves empathy, appreciation, enjoyment of a friend's company, and ultimately the mutual learning that friendship allows.

Competence. The individual has feelings of competence. These feelings are, in fact, the consequence of being competent relative to some societal or personal standard. Competence is attributed to one's own abilities. The feeling of competence, in addition to being the consequence of some competent behavior, is also specific. Consequently, one may feel competent in some aspects of life, but not in others.

Health. In addition to being physically healthy, to the extent possible, the individual is aware of practices that are conducive to physical health and also has allegiance to them. (Kehle & Bray, 2004).

It is our belief that if schools embraced the R.I.C.H. characteristics by allowing students more individual freedom for what they want to learn, more opportunities for friendship formation, honest acknowledgement of competence, and increased time devoted to practices conducive to students' physical health, there would be a noticeable and enduring improvement in academic and social functioning. Allowing the student greater independence to assume responsibility for his or her decisions to learn would also promote the remaining R.I.C.H. characteristics. Ultimately, students should have a sense of "not working" in that they intrinsically enjoy their selections of school environments and their choices of what they learn relative to the R.I.C.H. characteristics.

What is implied here is that progression through life requires a series of decisions and, if made properly, students' decisions would promote movement toward the R.I.C.H. characteristics. The validity of the R.I.C.H. characteristics is evident in that they assume all possible human reinforcers—simply stated, one cannot envision a fifth characteristic to improve the four R.I.C.H. factors, since a given reinforcer promotes movement toward one of the characteristics and, therefore, also the remaining three. The R.I.C.H. characteristics appear to concur with Bertrand Russell's definition of happiness (Russell, 1930)—at least, that is our interpretation of his *Conquest of Happiness.*

Without a definable and measurable dependent variable that is achievable across the diversity of students, a cumulative knowledge base will probably not be realized, and 50 years from now we will still be asking whether or not our children are better educated and better behaved than they were in the 1950s. To the degree the reader considers the content of the *Handbook* relative to the R.I.C.H. characteristics, the more probable will be the formulation of a cumulative knowledge base to focus research and promote the practice of school psychology.

The chapters of this *Handbook* provide state-of-the-art knowledge relative to more than 43 areas that are germane to the science and practice of school psychology. We are immensely grateful to the 105 outstanding scholars in school psychology and related disciplines who contributed to this *Handbook*. We would like to express deep gratitude to our colleagues in school psychology, along with the Department of Educational Psychology within the Neag School of Education at the University of Connecticut, for providing a supportive scholarly environment conducive to inquiry and intellectual risk-taking. Our heartfelt thanks to our editor, Chad Zimmerman of Oxford University Press, who provided encouragement and support throughout the long process needed to bring the *Handbook* to completion. Finally, and most importantly, we thank our spouses, William Bray and Gretchen Kehle, and families (Adeline, Will, Clark, John, Kit, and Joe Bray, and Matthew Dwyer) who provided a safe haven and honest feedback.

References

Hyman, I. A. (1979). Psychology, education, & schooling: Social policy implications in the lives of children and youth. *American Psychologist, 34,* 1024–1029.

Kehle, T. J. (1989, March). Maximizing the effectiveness of interventions: The R.I.C.H.model. Paper presented at the National Association of School Psychologists, Boston, MA.

Kehle, T. J. (1999, August). R.I.C.H.-based interventions. Invited address at the annual meeting of the American Psychological Association, Boston, MA.

Kehle, T. J. & Barclay, J. R. (1979). Social and behavioral characteristics of mentally handicapped students. *Journal of Research and Development in Education, 12,* 45–56.

Kehle, T. J., & Bray, M. A. (2004). R.I.C.H. theory: The promotion of happiness. *Psychology in the Schools, 41,* 43–49.

Kehle, T. J. & Bray, M. A. (2005). Educing the gap between research and practice in school psychology. *Psychology in the Schools, 42,* 577–584.

Kehle, T. J., Bray, M. A., Chafouleas, S. M., & Mcloughlin, C. S. (2002). Promoting intellectual growth in adulthood. *School Psychology International, 23*(2),233–241.

Kehle, T. J., Clark, E., & Jenson, W. R. (1983). The development of testing as applied to school psychology. *Journal of School Psychology, 31,* 143–161.

Poincare, H. (1905). *Science and hypothesis.* New York: The Science Press.

Russell, B. (1930). *The conquest of happiness.* New York: W. W. Norton and Company, Inc.

Trachtman, G. M. (1981). On such a full sea. *School Psychology Review, 10,* 138–181.

PART 2

Historical and Contemporary Issues

The History of School Psychology: Understanding the Past to Not Repeat It

Rik Carl D'Amato, Christina Zafiris, Erica McConnell, *and* Raymond S. Dean

Abstract

Lightner Witmer has been credited with the underlying conceptualization of school psychology. He advocated a multidisciplinary approach to serving children through an individualized psychological examination which would lead to specialized interventions. This direct service model led to a long-term focus on *evaluations* in school psychology. The field has struggled to move from a focus on individual children to more evidence-based work with families, classrooms, home–school partnerships, learning, schooling, and consultation with systems like hospitals and the educational enterprise. The purpose of this chapter is to define school psychology, understand related definitions in psychology and education, and study past and present influences in the field, such as a consideration of the major school psychology conferences, professional organizations, publications, problem solving models, and related research advancements. This chapter attempts to understand where the field has been, recognize history makers, consider current issues, and help predict where the field should be moving in the future. Details concerning how to become a history maker are included.

Keywords: school psychology history, Lightner Witmer, change, evidence-based interventions, school psychology conferences, professional organizations, direct service model, publications

Be the change you want to see in the world

–Gandhi

Introduction to the History of Psychology

School psychology is obviously a complex, if not the most complex, area of study in all of psychology. This is because of the great number of clients that must be served effectively when working with children, and the complex relationships children have with parents, family, and peers (Reynolds & Gutkin, 1999). Certainly, parents, teachers, classroom peers, siblings, others living in the home, community members, and the children themselves must often be provided with psychological services. This has created what some have called the paradox of school psychology (Reynolds & Gutkin, 1999). If you want to facilitate change in a child, or in a child's life, you must work with *adults*. This can be quite different than other areas of clinical practice, where one might be able to work with a single client (Carlson & Christenson, 2005).

The need to focus on adults has created a quandary in the field, in that the main area of study, which started with a focus on individual children, has now grown to include a larger group of individuals including teachers, parents, and others. While the primary thrust of the field certainly included a focus on significant others in the child's life, the study of children was always paramount (e.g., see Witmer, 1907, 1911). During the last three decades, the field has struggled to move from a focus on individual children toward more work with families, learning, and systems like hospitals and the educational enterprise (Conoley, 1989, 1992/1997; Conoley & Gutkin, 1995; Plas, 1986). In light of this shift, how does one now decide what variables should be explored when studying the history of school psychology?

Should we focus on the children that need psychological services? Should we focus on school teachers or parents? Should we study the first school psychologist? Should the field focus on the research covered in its primary journals like *School Psychology Quarterly* and *School Psychology Review*? Should we focus on the associations that claim to guide the field, such as the Division of School Psychology (Number 16) of the American Psychological Association (APA), and/or the National Association of School Psychologists (NASP)? Should we study what practices are advocated by seminal books? Should we focus on individual authors rated as the most productive scholars in our field (e.g., C. Reynolds and M. Bray)? Should we consult leaders like journal editors, Fellows of Division 16, or diplomates of the American Board of Professional Psychology? Should we study the deliberations of the editorial board members that help decide what is published in our journals? Should we study the faculty and curriculum of popular longstanding school psychology programs? Actually, all of these lines of inquiry provide important information and a glimpse of how the past links to the future. The purpose of this chapter is to define school psychology, understand the definitions of other areas of psychology and education, study past and present influences in the field of psychology, recognize history makers, and understand where the field has been and where it is going. While space does not permit a comprehensive consideration of all these areas, we hope to mention the many influences that are leading us on our way to the future.

Lightner Witmer has often been credited with the underlying conceptualization of both school psychology and clinical psychology (Altmaier & Meyer, 1985; Brotemarkle, 1931; Eiserer, 1963; Magary, 1967; Reynolds, Gutkin, Elliott, & Witt, 1984). To understand his views, it is necessary to consider his background. Witmer's professional life began as an English and history teacher at Rugby Academy in Philadelphia (Brotemarkle, 1931). In this setting, Witmer was intrigued by the fact that some students did not learn, despite the fact that they seemed motivated and bright (Brotemarkle, 1931; Collins, 1931; Gray, 1963; Witmer, 1907). It was this paradox that stimulated his study of psychology, first at the University of Pennsylvania and later at the University of Leipzig. Under the direction of James Cattell, and later, Wilhelm Wundt, Witmer began to formulate his scientific approach to applied psychology (Boring, 1950; Brotemarkle, 1931; Garfield, 1985; McReynolds, 1987).

Wilhelm Wundt and the Importance of Selecting a Mentor

Despite the fact that Lightner Witmer is always credited with being the first school psychologist, few have asked the essential question: Who trained Lightner Witmer? Lightner Witmer (like all students today) had to make a decision about what to study and where to study, after he decided to pursue a doctoral degree. Just like many students today, he wanted to study people, especially children. Where should he go to study psychology? No accreditation system was in place, so he had to study the contributions of individual faculty to decide which program to select. Psychology was a new field, and only a few institutions offered such training. In addition, not many offered training with a clear focus on children—which appeared to be his key interest. But one faculty member in Germany, located at one of the largest and most celebrated universities in Europe at that time, had begun the study of psychology (Benjamin, Durkin, Link, Vestal, & Acord, 1992). His name was Wilhelm Maximilian Wundt. In 1879, Dr. Wundt founded a laboratory for the study of psychological research (Myers, 2010). *Interestingly, instead of devoting himself to the study of philosophy or physiology, he devoted himself to the development of a new science, the science of psychology* (Croog, 1947; Wundt, 2009). A physiology laboratory was already in place at the University of Leipzig, and so was a laboratory for the study of philosophy, so he could have joined either of these already established research centers. But he believed neither of the centers had the focus he thought was needed for empirical study. Thus, it is important to consider his background to understand his beliefs and future aspirations (Greenwood, 1999; Wundt, 2009).

Initially, Wundt studied medicine and graduated from Heidelberg in 1856 (Jastrow, 1935; Wundt, 2009). But then he made a major decision which was to influence his path and future research. Wundt studied briefly with Johannes Peter Muller, and then, in 1858, became an assistant to the prominent physicist and physiologist, Hermann von Helmholtz. Von Helmholtz initially was trained as a physician, but spent much of his free time studying mathematics and philosophy. He was a prolific author and published a number of important papers in a variety of subjects—these included work in mathematics of the eye, theories of vision, and sensation of tone. In the area of physics, he is known for his theories on the conservation of energy and mechanical thermodynamics. Von Helmholz also studied the philosophy of science, and the laws of perception (Helmholtz & Cahan, 1995; Herman von Helmholtz, 2009; Myers, 2010). The unifying element of all his activities was his focus on empirical research. In honor of his dedication to empirical research, a large German association of research institutions is named after him, the Helmholtz Association (Herman von Helmholtz). Thus, it seems, the importance of empirical research, an amazing dedication to broad-based work, and a strong work ethic were also major components of von Helmholtz's laboratory. Wundt published several important texts and papers while working with von Helmholtz; indeed, he published the first of what was to become his five-volume experimental psychology textbook. He also taught the first course ever offered in scientific psychology (Bringmann, 1975; Greenwood, 2003; Myers, 2010). Wundt spent around a decade working in von Helmholtz's laboratory, even though some indicated that the two did not get along well (Benjamin et al., 1992; Wundt, 2009)

It is obvious from this overview that Wundt learned many techniques from his mentor. While their relationship has been debated, Wundt went on to utilize most of what he learned from von Helmholtz. It should be clear that when future doctoral students select a mentor, they must realize that they are selecting more than an advisor. They are selecting an approach to psychology, a view of the psychological world, connections with other psychologists, and a network that includes other psychology laboratories. An old adage says, choose your mentor with care, because you become what they are. Numerous areas of emphasis are available to students, including areas like behaviorism, consultation, and clinical neuropsychology. A fun and important activity can be to trace the lineage from student to mentor or doctoral advisor. Figure 2.1 presents the lineage of the first author of this chapter.

The Founding of Applied Psychology

Wundt received an offer to move to the University of Leipzig. He viewed psychology as different from both philosophy and physiology; this was paramount, because if he had viewed it as similar to either of these disciplines, he might well have incorporated his work into the already functioning Leipzig laboratory of physiology, or into the department of philosophy. Wundt (1912) argued that psychology has to investigate that which we call *internal experience*—i.e., our own sensation and feeling, our thought and volition—in contrast to the objects of *external experience*, which form the subject matter of

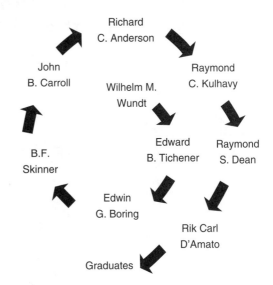

Fig. 2.1 Lineage table indicating who served as the major professor for each doctoral student

natural science (Boring, 1950; Leahey, 1980). These notions were in contrast to the physiological theories that were more biologically based, and the philosophical theories that had little or no empirical foundation (Myers, 2010). Wundt argued that only when we have psychology and physiology side by side, always beginning with a stimulus and always followed through to a response, can psychology be effective. Thus, the study of physiology without psychology was missing a major part of the total picture. Wundt was seen as the founder of the psychology of consciousness. He broke the elements of conscious experience into two main classes: (1) the sensations which seem to come to us from outside, and (2) the feelings which belong to ourselves. Interestingly, Wundt taught his students the need for the generation, dissemination, and preservation of new knowledge (Benjamin et al., 1992; Myers, 2010). His students have reported that he taught stringent research methods and a strict scientific attitude.

It is important to note, however, that although Wundt invented psychology, he continued to use physiological techniques in his laboratory, and his books certainly remained built on a physiological foundation. In this same fashion, he never truly gave up his fascination with philosophy. He continued for decades to work with students pursuing degrees in philosophy. Thus, while he clearly founded experimental psychology, he maintained interests in other areas, never giving up his drive for new knowledge across disciplines (Benjamin et al., 1992).

In fact, it was Wundt's yearning for new knowledge that seemed to compel him to train students,

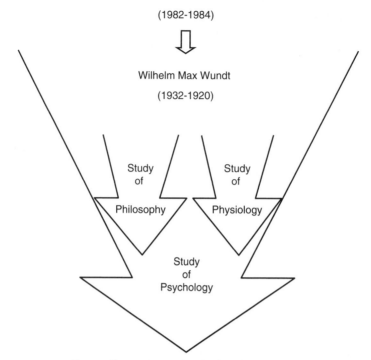

Herman Ludwig Ferdinand Von Helmholtz

(1982-1984)

Wilhelm Max Wundt

(1932-1920)

Study of Philosophy

Study of Physiology

Study of Psychology

Fig. 2.2 The First Step in the School Psychology Lineage

conduct research, and work impossibly long hours. Many of his evenings and weekends were dedicated to the study of psychology. His sharing of his quest for new knowledge gleaned from strong scientific study may have been the foundation of psychology, in particular (Myers, 2010). Wundt imbued his students with a scientific attitude that allowed them to frame questions in ways that created a science of mind that most of his predecessors had proclaimed would never be possible. This scientific attitude was spread by Wundt's students who returned to America after completing study with him (Benjamin et al., 1992).

Lightner Witmer's Approach to Psychology

Witmer's empirical approach to applied psychology was a departure from the introspective focus of the times (Leahey, 1980; Woodworth, 1948). In light of Witmer's experimental training with Wundt, it is surprising to find him continuing in his commitment to an unquestionably practical psychology (e.g., focusing on children's problems; Leahey, 1980; Witmer, 1907, 1911). Indeed, early in the twentieth century the union of experimental and applied psychology created the kind of cross-fertilization that Witmer (1896, 1897, 1907) had in mind.

With Witmer's leadership, psychology moved off the couch and into the laboratory. This was the opposite direction Freud seemed to be advocating in his book with Breuer in 1895, entitled *Studies on Hysteria* (Halberstadt-Freud, 1996).

Without doubt, it was Witmer's seminal work in the psychology laboratory at the University of Pennsylvania that provided the foundation for what we have come to know as the scientist-practitioner model. Witmer's (1907) first cases were children with school related difficulties. Specifically, one displayed difficulties with the English language (e.g., difficulties between verb tenses and missing word endings), and one had been labeled a chronic bad speller. These actual cases are currently available in Witmer's published journal. From this description, these children would most probably be diagnosed as learning disabled. In a systematic fashion (like Wundt), Witmer searched the literature and found that psychology had not investigated causes or treatments for these disorders (Witmer, 1907). He argued that there were no principles for him to follow and thus, he had to empirically and scientifically study these children before developing interventions. This procedure was the first step in the development of what we now call *evidence based interventions*. In 1896, Witmer integrated his rather novel ideas about applied psychology in a paper entitled, "The Clinical Method in Psychology and the Diagnostic Method of Teaching," presented at the annual meeting of the American Psychological Association (APA). This paper was an organizational plan for the role and structure of a specialty within applied psychology (Witmer, 1896, 1897).

The plan involved:

1. The investigation of mental development in children, as manifested by mental and moral retardation, by means of statistical and clinical methods.
2. A psychological clinic, supplemented by a hospital training school, for the treatment of children suffering from all defects interfering with school progress.
3. The offering of practical applied work to those engaged in the professions of teaching and medicine, in the observation and training of normal and retarded children.
4. The training of students for a new profession—the expert—who would work with the school, or in connection with the practice of medicine, treating mentally retarded children. (Brotemarkle, 1931; reprinted from Witmer, 1907).

Apparently, the only response Witmer got from his audience of predominantly experimental psychologists was "a slight elevation of the eyebrows on the part of a few of the older members" (Collins, 1931, p. 5). Whatever the reaction, this paper portrayed a practical specialty that evolved into school psychology. Perhaps the most intriguing aspect of the proposal was that it stressed *clinical* and *empirical* methods for the understanding and treatment of children who displayed psychological and developmental deficits. The plan stressed the study of normal and abnormal children, focused on a multidisciplinary problem-solving team approach, and used what seemed to be practicum and internship training. Witmer began what we more recently have called a problem solving process (like response-to-intervention), leading to evidence based interventions (Traughber & D'Amato, 2005). The techniques offered involved the assessment of the disorder, the development of hypotheses concerning an appropriate intervention and, finally, the provision and evaluation of the intervention. Training in Witmer's applied psychology was viewed as appropriate for professionals in varied careers (e.g., teachers, physicians, social workers), serving all types of children. Of interest to the present discussion, Witmer emphasized that psychologists trained as scientist-practitioners could expect to offer services in varied settings (Brotemarkle, 1931; Cutts, 1955; McReynolds, 1987). From its inception, then, it is clear that what has come to be known as school psychology was meant to define the *problems to be studied* and *not* the setting. This forces one to consider if the *school psychology* name we have come to embrace is really appropriate for services offered, since they are not location-linked. Indeed, counseling psychology and clinical psychology indicate services and not locations. From a historical perspective, it would seem that if one attempted to operationalize Witmer's model, *school psychology* is misnamed, and definitions of its areas of practice are overly limited.

Witmer (1907) viewed the psychological clinic as an institution for social and public service, for research, and for the instruction of students in psychology. From this point of view, practitioners needed to train in the *psychology orthogenics,* which included vocational, educational, corrective, hygienic, industrial, and social guidance. To this end, instruction in applied psychology was seen as a broad-based approach, reflecting contributions from a number of allied but related disciplines (Fernberger, 1931). Although much of this broad base is reflected in the common core psychology areas adopted by the APA, a number of elements (e.g., vocational, social guidance, etc.) are now also served by a multidisciplinary team approach (Brotemarkle, 1931; Reynolds, et al., 1984). Parenthetically, many of Witmer's notions seem in line with what has come to be called *community psychology*. However, few authors credit him with such a contribution (Spielberger & Stenmark, 1985).

Events and Conferences Impacting Applied Psychology

Before World War II, few distinctions were made between applied psychologists; however, there seemed to be two rather distinct components of psychological services. These were individuals who functioned using a psychotherapy/counseling/mental health focus, or those who followed a more actuarial/psychometric approach that stressed assessment *and* diagnosis (Gray, 1963). That is to say that prior to World War II, although psychologists could choose to emphasize one element over another, only *one* applied psychology existed. It could have been called *human service psychology*.

Table 2.1 Important conferences related to school psychology

Conferences
1948 Boulder Conference on Graduate Education in Clinical Psychology
1954 Thayer Conference held in West Point, New York
1973 Vail Conference on Professional Training in Psychology
1980 Spring Hill Symposium held in Wayzata, Minnesota
1981 Olympic Conference held in Oconomowoc, Wisconsin
2002 School Psychology Futures Conference held at Indiana University and video-televised to numerous sites around the world

The Clinical Psychology–School Psychology Split

A great deal of evidence supports the hypothesis that World War II had a major impact on our current conception of psychological specialties (Altmaier & Meyer, 1985; Reynolds, et al., 1984). With wartime stress came a considerable number of psychiatric casualties. However, few trained psychologists were available to meet these needs. In addition, because such a wide variety of psychological problems existed, the role of the service provider was quickly expanded to meet the needs of both diagnosis and ongoing treatment, often focusing on psychotherapy. To be sure, the needs of the Veterans Administration (VA) were instrumental in providing support for applied psychologists through both training grants and expanding employment opportunities immediately after the Second World War. Indeed, the VA was the major employer of what are now seen as clinical psychologists. It was at this time that the notion of "clinical psychology" began to be considered. The subspecialty can be followed most directly to a 1947 APA committee on training in clinical psychology (see Committee on training in clinical psychology, 1947). Table 2.1 displays school psychology conferences.

The Boulder Conference

The Boulder Conference in 1949 was a further attempt to refine the idea of "clinical psychology" (see Raimy, 1950). During this conference, the training model stressed for clinical psychology was that of a *scientist* (trained in the empirical tradition) linked with a *practitioner* (competent in dealing with psychopathology). Of interest here is the fact that this mix had been previously detailed by Witmer (1907). It is interesting that this movement has reemerged as "evidence based interventions" in the last few years. Activities at this conference

included the development of goals and policies for clinical psychologists, established by university trainers. In general, these factors solidified the role of the clinical psychologist, and moved "clinical psychology" further away from Witmer's early interpretation of "applied psychology." So too, with this move, clinical psychology became identified with the diagnosis and treatment of severe psychopathology. But, clearly, clinical psychology was now seen as a medically related, empirical science. Clinical psychology's move from child/family oriented services to more severe psychiatric disorders has been well detailed elsewhere (see Garfield, 1985; Harris, 1980). Harris (1980) has argued that school psychology is the applied specialty that "stayed at home," while clinical psychology "moved on to new neighborhoods" (p. 15). It seems obvious that applied psychologists working with children and families in community clinics, hospitals, and schools, providing counseling, consultation, assessment for intervention, and other mental health services, are far closer to Witmer's original notions that to what is generally thought of today as clinical psychology. Table 2.2 presents dates relevant to the development of applied psychology.

The Need for Psychology in the Schools

The demand for applied psychologists to provide services in the schools intensified after World War II (Eiserer, 1963). This need was related to the country's turn to domestic needs, the postwar baby boom, and notions of progressive, quality education for all children. During this period, it also became clear that many school children needed *individualized* instruction if they were to succeed in the traditional educational environment (Fagan & Wise, 2007). Consequently, psychologists contributed to these efforts by providing psychoeducational assessment and mental health services (Bower, 1955;

Table 2.2 Important dates relevant to school psychology

Dates
1879 Wilhelm Wundt founds **Psychology Laboratory** at the University of Leipzig for research and training
1892 Founding of the **American Psychological Association**
1895 **Freud** publishes his book, *Studies on Hysteria*
1896 Professor Lightner Witmer establishes first **psychological clinic** at the University of Pennsylvania to train students
1915 Gesell appointed as the first **school psychologist**
1928 New York University offers first **school psychology training program**
1945 APA reorganizes and **School Psychology Division 16** is founded
1947 Beginning of what will become the **America Board of Professional Psychology (ABPP)** to certify advanced psychological competence
1953 APA publishes its first **Code of Ethics**
1964 First examination in **professional psychological practice** used by state licensing boards
1967 ABPP Diplomate **specialty in school psychology** developed
1969 Founding of the **National Association of School Psychologists**
1971 APA accredits the **first school psychology program** at the University of Texas–Austin
1981 APA publishes **Specialty Guidelines**, including those for school psychology
1988 NASP begins the National School Psychology **Certification System**

Adapted from the American Psychological Association 2009a, Myers, 2010, and Fagan and Wise 2007.

Herron, Green, Guild, Smith, & Kantor, 1970; Reger, 1965). However, due to the limited number of trained applied psychologists, and the needs of the schools, the number of school psychologists was limited. In tandem with this shortage came questions about how to best meet the psychological needs of school-age children (Ysseldyke & Schakel, 1983). With the Boulder conference as a backdrop, some school psychologists (e.g., Newland, 1970) began arguing for a similar conference to outline elements of training and practice with school-age children (Cutts, 1955).

The Thayer Conference
Following in the steps of the Boulder Conference, Division 16 of the APA applied for money and received funding to establish the Thayer Conference in West Point, New York, to address the shortage of school psychologists who could meet the needs of children. Thayer was the name of the hotel where the conference was held. As a result of the conference, an outline was modeled of the guidelines for training and function of the school psychologist. The training recommendations established the necessity for two levels of school psychologists, one at the doctoral level and one at the master's level. Additionally, it provided a foundation for training with a dual orientation in psychology and education.

The objective of the Thayer Conference was to address the roles, goals, functions, and training of school psychologists, encourage the development of new training programs, and continue training psychologists as scientists/practitioners. Role definition issues were also addressed in an effort to establish school psychology as a distinct specialty in the APA. Although specific roles were detailed concerning the development and adjustment of children though assessment, consultation, remedial programming, research and the like, the conference proceedings stressed a rather broad definition of school psychology services:

> There are innumerable ways in which the school psychologist can apply his knowledge. The details of what he does and of how he does it will depend on the particular situation in which he finds himself, on the special needs for his service inherent in the situation, and upon his training and qualifications. (*Cutts*, 1955, p. 172).

With the definition of a specialty in mind, individual states were encouraged to set credentialing requirements, and the title *school psychologist* was thought to be best reserved for doctoral level psychologists. But, the need for two-year graduate training programs was seen as a necessary service component, although no title was agreed on for this level of training (Gray, 1963). Without a strong role statement, these two distinct levels of service (subdoctoral and doctoral) called for in this conference began, at once, to drift into a single level of service. Basically, in the shadow of the Boulder Conference, the Thayer Conference established school psychology as a separate and viable specialty within applied psychology. At this point in time, school psychology rested on a well documented foundation, albeit the foundation was built predominantly on *school property.* The fact that school psychology was not seen, like clinical and counseling psychology, as a doctoral *only* specialty, alienated the specialty and immediately created strife between school psychology practitioners and APA leadership. This eventually led to the establishment of the National Association of School Psychologists. Moreover, the nondoctoral issue continues to plague school psychology practitioners today.

Not surprisingly, little changed after the conference. Psychologists who practiced in the schools in the 1960s reported concerns about the efficacy and efficiency of their work, dissatisfaction with roles and relationships, problems developing multidisciplinary teams, few consultation opportunities, limited time for individual counseling, and dissatisfaction with the amount of time available for research (Bower, 1955; Eiserer, 1963; Gray, 1963; Hirst, 1963; Reger, 1965; Valett, 1963). In addition, it appears that some doctoral psychologists were inadequately prepared for the restricted school role, and overprepared for the daily public education routine (Bardon, 1981a, 1981b; Gray, 1963; Hynd, 1983; Mullen, 1981; Newland, 1981). Data indicate that many doctoral level practitioners left the schools after approximately five years of practice (e.g., see Reynolds & Gutkin, 1999).

The Vail Conference

While research as part of psychology training seems to have served the field well for decades, some individuals questioned why they should spend years learning how to conduct research studies when they wished to work directly with clients as psychotherapists, and did not wish to conduct research. Specialization in other professions was discussed, and it was noted, for example, that medical doctors were awarded an M.D., and lawyers were awarded a J.D. (juris doctor), and many other specialists also were awarded degrees specific to their disciplines. The Vail Conference was held to discuss if a training model should be developed that focused on clinical practice, and offered an alternative degree in accordance with this unique specialization. In 1973 the APA, at the Conference on Levels and Patterns of Professional Training in Psychology, decided to support the doctor of psychology (Psy.D.) degree. Since its inception, the awarding of the Psy.D. degree has received mixed reviews, especially in medical settings where research is an important part of daily practice and long-term outcomes.

The Spring Hill Symposium

The Spring Hill Symposium, held in 1980, was the first comprehensive examination and discussion of the future of school psychology since the Thayer Conference in 1954. The planning committee of the symposium invited 69 school psychologists from 22 states, the District of Columbia, and Alberta, Canada. The participants selected to attend and participate in the discussions held at the symposium consisted of leaders in school psychology, with a representative sample of males and females, including school psychology trainers and minority group members (Ysseldyke, 1982, p. 550). Efforts were made to have an equal number of practitioners and school psychology educators (Ysseldyke & Weinberg, 1981).

The participants were divided into three groups and questions concerning the "goals and roles for school psychology practice, ethical and legal issues, the professionalization of school psychologists, the content of training programs, and accountability" (Ysseldyke, 1982, p. 550) were addressed. Suggestions for growth were proposed by each group, even though resolution of the issues was not the main concern. Areas in need of ongoing attention included intra- and inter-professional communication, the need for a solid database of information, public policy, public relations, and professional control. Participants argued the importance of communicating with other professionals and professional organizations within the field of school psychology, rather than fighting or arguing against them, to include "increasing communication among NASP, Division 16, APA, and state and local groups" (Bardon, 1981a, p. 302). Furthermore, it was seen as important to work with other professionals outside of the field of school psychology in order to help children by solving common problems faced by all. Some of the suggestions included educators and practitioners working together in training school psychologists, forming standards committees to provide feedback to practitioners, providing review or retraining of basic skills, and teaching about educational policy and systems change at the preservice and inservice levels. Additional recommendations included establishing "a strong state organization, a strong state-level consultant, and good state training programs" (Rosenfield, 1981, p. 287), and documenting models of exemplary school psychological practices or best practices (Ysseldyke, 1982, p. 550), such as offering a clearinghouse that would identify evidence based interventions.

The Olympia Conference

The Olympia Conference was held in 1981, as a follow-up to the Spring Hill Symposium. Participants included the 69 practitioners and educators who participated in the Spring Hill Symposium, along with other leaders within NASP, Division 16, and APA and other state-level leaders, totaling 330 participants. The Olympia Conference was organized specifically to further address the major issues raised at the Spring Hill Symposium. One of the main goals was to provide skill-building opportunities, to be shared with others once the participants returned home (D'Amato, 2005a).

Some of the major themes at Olympia consisted of professional accountability, political action, public relations, collaboration, and research (Hart, 1982). The first and most pressing theme expressed the need for standards in the field, from the admission to graduate training programs to practice, including documentation and demonstration of competencies (Hart, 1982), and "a uniform set of credentialing standards linked to minimal competencies" (Brown & Cardon, 1982, p. 196). Along with the theme of competency, the issue of entry level for the practice of school psychology was also raised. Although it was agreed that the entry level would include specialist level practitioners, there was still debate between NASP and APA as to whether those with less than a doctoral degree could refer to themselves as school psychologists. The second theme, political action, focused on "political lobbying and other actions aimed at influencing laws, regulations, and policy" (Hart, 1982, p. 187). Public relations referred to educating others, parents, other laymen, and professionals, about the value of the services a school psychologist provides. Similarly, the collaboration theme emphasized working with parents and special interest groups to advocate for the needs of the child, adolescent, and family. The research theme focused on investigating the effects of the professional practices of school psychology, incorporating "university and practitioner collaboration, and developing models to improve our understandings and practices" (Hart, 1982, p. 187). Finally, the values theme highlighted the importance of living up to "our own personal and professional morals" (Hart, 1982, p. 188) and behaving appropriately to improve the education and mental health of all populations (i.e., children, adolescents, adults) (Brown & Cardon, 1982).

Some of the individuals attending the conferences were concerned about the loss of person power and money, fearing that the conferences would lead to little if any change. In a similar vein, D'Amato, Sheridan, Phelps, and Lopez (2004), the current editors (at that time) of *Psychology in the Schools, School Psychology Review, School Psychology Quarterly,* and the *Journal of Educational and Psychological Consultation* argued that:

> Although the Boulder conference clearly contributed to the science in our practice (Bardon, 1989; Reynolds & Gutkin, 1999), most of the issues considered at the Thayer conference (e.g., titles, roles, and services) were not resolved. The contributions of the "other" conferences, the Olympia Conference and the Spring Hill Symposium, remain even less obvious, and the outcomes are even more debated (Brown, Cardon, Coulter, & Meyers, 1982; Ysseldyke & Weinberg, 1981). Indeed, school psychology's track record with psychology conferences is filled with a great deal of conversation but little documented change (*Conoley & Gulkin*, 1995; *D'Amato & Dean*, 1989a, 1989b; *Sheridan & Gutkin*, 2000). (*D'Amato, Sheridan, Phelps*, and *Lopez*, 2004, p. 222).

Dean (1983) summed up the Olympic conferences most succinctly publishing a critique entitled, "The Emperor Had No Clothes and Olympia No Substance." Since the Futures Conference was recently held, it will be discussed near the end of this chapter.

Psychology Develops into an Empirically-Based Science

Numerous authors have outlined the development of the field, and some of these views are presented in Table 2.3. Cutts (1955), after attending the Thayer conference, highlighted many of the major issues discussed. Fagan, the NASP historian, is clearly our living expert and has written countless articles on the topic of school psychology history (Fagan, 1985a, 1985b, 1985c, 1986a, 1986b, 1996, 2005). He regularly

Table 2.3 Components related to the founding of school psychology

	Authors	
Cutts, 1955	**Fagan, 2007**	**Merrell, Ervin & Gimpel, 2006**
Development of Special Classes and Social/Cultural	Changing Status of Children and Youth	The Historical Context of School Psychology
The First Psychology Clinic	Compulsory Schooling	Philosophical, Intellectual, and Social–Cultural Foundations
Early Tests	Prevalence of Physical and Mental Defects	Classical Greek Influences
The First Department of Child Study	Emergence of Special Education	Modern European Influences
The Juvenile Delinquent	Emergence of School Psychological Services	The Emergence of Psychology
The Binet Schools		Developments in American Education
Group Tests	Rise of Clinics and Psychoeducational Testing	Beginnings of School Psychology
The Term *School Psychology*	Testing	Development and Professionalization of the Field
The Mental Hygiene Movement	School Psychological Roles and Functions	Recent History of School Psychology
The Guidance Movement	Early Literature, Organizations, and Training	Public Law 94 –142/ Individuals with Disabilities Education Act
The Needs of Youth	Training	Training Standards and Credentialing
	Important Contributors	APA Accreditation of Doctoral Programs
	Training and Credentialing	NASP Approval of Specialist Programs
	Literature	The NCSP Credential
	Role and Function and Employment	Growth through Tension and Opposition
	Opportunities	NASP and APA
	Organizational Development	Toward the Maturation of the Field
	Authors	
Bardon, 1989	**D'Amato & Rothlisberg, 1992/1997**	**Mischel, Shoda & Ayduk, 2008**
The Import of History and Development	A Behavioral Approach to Intervention	Psychodynamic–Motivational
What Might Have Been	A Psychoanalytic Approach to Intervention	Trait–Dispositional
The Reality	A Psychoeducational Approach to Intervention	Biological
Unifying and Diverging Forces Influencing School Psychology	A Person-centered / Humanistic Approach to Intervention	Phenomenological–Humanistic

(continued)

Table 2.3   (Cont'd) Components related to the founding of school psychology

Bardon, 1989	D'Amato & Rothlisberg, 1992/1997	Mischel, Shoda & Ayduk, 2008
Common Core Knowledge and Functions	A Neuropsychological Approach to Intervention	Behavioral–Learning
Differences From Other Specialties in Psychology	A Moral Developmental Approach to Intervention	Social–Cognitive
Applied Educational Psychology As a Way to Characterize School Psychology Practice in Any Setting	A Cognitive–Behavioral Approach to Intervention	Integration: The Person as a Whole
Schooling is More Than What Happens in Schools	An Ecological Approach to Intervention	
The Educational Psychology Knowledge Base	Integrating Psychological Approached to Intervention	
Implications of Applied Educational Psychology for Practice in Nontraditional Settings		

Please note that these terms have been liberally adapted and do not represent reprints that reflect all topics covered in related chapters. In fact, only selected headings from most chapters are reported from many of these books.

presents the major issues from our field. The Merrell, Ervin, and Gimpel (2006) text also overviews issues the authors believe should be highlighted. But a problem with many of these overviews is that they do not indicate how school psychology fits within the context of psychology overall. To this end, three additional authors are presented that show how school psychology links to the rest of the field (Bardon, 1982, 1989; D'Amato & Rothlisberg, 1992/1997; Mischel, Shoda, & Ayduk, 2008). For example, Bardon (1989) has focused on school psychology as a solution and not as a place, viewing schooling in a much broader context than what happens in schools. D'Amato and Rothlisberg (1992/1997) see school psychology falling into specific psychological paradigms, such as psychoeducational, behavioral, neuropsychological, or ecological. They argue that all school psychologists follow one or more of the discussed approaches when they practice. Mischel et al. take a similar approach, attempting to understand personality through an analysis of the major psychological schools of thought. It is fascinating that Michel et al. explain all approaches to psychology via a review of only six major schools of thought.

Journals and Books Related to School Psychology

During the time of the Thayer conference, individuals reported concerns that only a limited data base of child, parent, teacher, and school related issues

was available in the literature (Cutts, 1955). This same concern prompted Lightner Witmer to return to school, conduct interventions measuring outcomes, and begin his journal. But this concern has changed dramatically during the last few decades. The two primary journals with the largest circulations to individuals are *School Psychology Review*, related to NASP, and *School Psychology Quarterly*, related to APA Division 16. The *International School Psychology* journal is affiliated with the International Association of School Psychologists. Two older journals, not related to associations, are the *Journal of School Psychology* and *Psychology in the Schools*. Other journals often seen as related to the field are the *Journal of Psychoeducational Assessment,* the *Journal of Applied School Psychology,* and the *Journal of Educational and Psychological Consultation.* In a novel attempt to wed technology with journal usage, NASP began publishing an online journal available to members in November 2006, entitled *School Psychology Forum: Research in Practice.* Given the broad foundation of the profession, many individuals publish in journals not notably related to the field. For example, individuals working in the area of learning often publish in the *Journal of Educational Psychology,* whereas individuals working in clinical neuropsychology often publish in the *International Journal of Neuroscience.* Perhaps 50 additional journals are available in related areas, which makes tracking related research almost impossible.

Currently, some 100 books are available in school psychology or in a closely related field. Some of the seminal books are listed in Table 2.4.

Vital Research Questions

Sheridan and D'Amato (2003) believe that Conoley and Gutkin (1995) rooted out one of the most urgent problems in the field one and a half decades ago, but few have heeded their cry. They argued that perhaps the most critical quandary for those dealing with change in the field of school psychology is that:

> School psychology does not suffer from a lack of good science. It suffers from a science that is devoted almost exclusively to answering the wrong sets of questions. It is a science that is preoccupied with the problems of individuals rather than understanding the ecologies in which people function (p. 210).

It should be clear that if we do not change the direction of our research, we will not modify the evidence that forms the base of our practice (Carlson, & Christenson, 2005; Traughber & D'Amato, 2005). A great deal of practice is guided not by investigations but by enthusiasm, colorful and easy-to-use techniques, and mentor–mentee taught practices. Psychologists usually practice the way they were taught to practice. We need to reverse this trend, and use our knowledge to select interventions that are evidence based. A good example has been

Table 2.4   20 Influential books that continue to offer relevance today (by first year printed)

1. Bower, E. M. (1955). *The school psychologist.* Sacramento, CA: California State Department of Education.

2. Cutts, N. E. (Ed.). (1955). *School psychologists at mid-century.* Washington D.C.: APA.

3. White, M. A., & Harris, M. W. (1961). *The school psychologist.* New York: Harper & Row.

4. Eiserer, P. E. (1963). *The school psychologist.* Washington, D.C.: Center for Applied Research in Education.

5. Gray, S. W. (1963). *The psychologist in the schools.* New York: Holt, Rienhart and Winston.

6. Valett, R. E. (1963). *The practice of school psychology: Professional problems.* New York: Wiley.

7. Reger, R. (1965). *School psychology.* Springfield, IL: Charles Thomas.

8. Bardon, J. I., & Bennett, V. C. (1974). *School psychology.* Englewood Cliffs, NJ: Prentice-Hall.

9. Sattler, J. M. (1974). *Assessment of children's intelligence.* Philadelphia, PA: Saunders.

10. Reynolds, C. R., & Gutkin, T. B. (Eds.). (1982). *The handbook of school psychology.* New York: Wiley.

11. Hynd, G. W. (1983). *The school psychologist: An introduction.* Syracuse University Press.

12. Reynolds, C. R., Gutkin, T. B., Elliott, S. N., & Witt, J. C. (1984). *School psychology: Essentials of theory and practice.* New York: Wiley.

13. Thomas, A., & Grimes, J. (Eds.) (1985). *Best practices in school psychology.* Washington, DC: National Association of School Psychologists

14. Brown, D., Pryzwansky, W. B., & Schulte, A. C. (1987). *Psychological consultation: Introduction to theory and practice.* Boston, MA: Allyn & Bacon.

15. D'Amato, R. C., & Dean, R. S. (Eds.). (1989). *The school psychologist in nontraditional settings: Integrating clients, services, and settings.* Hillsdale, NJ: Erlbaum.

16. Ysseldyke, J.E., Reynolds, M.C., & Weinberg, R.A. (1984). *School psychology: A blueprint for training and practice.* Minneapolis, MN: National School Psychology In-service Training.

17. Jacob, S., & Hartshorne, T. S. (1991). *Ethics and law for school psychologists.* Brandon, VT: Clinical Psychology Publishing.

18. Fagan, T. K., & Wise, P.S. (1994*). School psychology: Past, present, and future.* White Plains, NY: Longman.

19. D'Amato, R. C., Fletcher-Janzen, E., & Reynolds, C. R. (Eds.). (2005). *Handbook of school neuropsychology.* New York, NY: Wiley.

20. Merrell, K. W., Ervin, R. A., & Gimpel, G. A. (2006). *School psychology for the 21st century: Foundations and practice.* New York: Guilford.

the federal government, and state education departments, pushing the implementation of the RTI model when little data has been collected to reveal if such an effort will be successful (Reynolds & Shaywitz, 2009a, 2009b; Witsken, Stoeckel, & D'Amato, 2008).

School Psychology Becomes a Specialty: Credentialing and Differentiation
APA Specialty and Reaffirmation Guidelines and the NASP Blueprint(s) and Standards
The APA was established in 1892. It views itself as a scientific and professional organization that represents psychology in the United States and Canada, and supports psychology around the world. Division 16, the Division of School Psychology, was formed in 1945 and is composed of scientific-practitioner psychologists whose major professional interests lie with children, youth, families, and the schooling process (Fagan & Wise, 2007; Reynolds & Gutkin, 1999). In contrast, because APA focuses mostly on doctoral level practitioners, NASP was established as a voice for nondoctoral level practitioners (Fagan & Wise, 1994). This is due, in part, to the fact that nondoctoral school psychology practitioners were treated a second-class citizens, in that they were not granted full membership in APA or in Division 16.

The APA advocates that due to the complexity of human beings, appropriate psychological services require doctoral level training. Any doctoral degree such as a Ph.D., Psy.D. or Ed.D. can offer suitable psychological training. For that reason, the APA accredits training programs, but only those offered at the doctoral level. According to NASP guidelines, doctoral requirements are not a necessary standard for the practice of a school psychologist, and the majority of NASP members do not posses a doctoral degree. For decades, this has been the major clash between APA "doctoral" and NASP "specialists, subdoctoral, or nondoctoral" school psychologists. In fact, APA struggles with allowing the use of the term *school psychology* for nondoctoral practitioners, and at times has considered attempting to revoke its support for NASP to use the title *school psychologist* at the nondoctoral level. Both NASP and APA have practice standards that have formed the foundation for the practice of the specialty since its inception. They both attempt to lead the way for practitioners at all levels. The APA has specialty guidelines that differentiate the areas of clinical practice within APA. For example, comparing and contrasting these guidelines allows one to understand the difference between a counseling psychologist, a

clinical psychologist, and a school psychologist. The Division 16 *Special Guidelines* are long and complex, and will not be repeated in detail here. They are summarized at the APA Division 16 website. The *Archival Description of the Specialty of School Psychology* is also available at the Division 16 website. Moreover, the petition for the reaffirmation for the specialty of school psychology is available from APA (see American Psychological Association, 1981). These comprehensive sets of guidelines, which seek to explain how school psychology is different from all other specialties, are extremely long. School psychologists are trained in 14 main domain areas including:

- biological bases (of behavior)
- affective bases
- cognitive bases
- social bases
- family/parenting process
- prevention
- effective instruction
- developmental psychopathology
- academic achievement
- history and systems
- psychological measurement
- research design and methodology
- scientific ethics and standards, and
- individual differences.

It is important to note that some of these basic skills domains would be covered in the training of all types of psychologists. For example, biological bases, affective bases, cognitive bases, and social bases of behaviors would usually be covered in all (human) clinical service areas. The guidelines present a list of essential, important, unique and shared activities that define the specialty area. Some of these skills include: social/emotional/behavioral assessment, neuropsychological assessment, determination of eligibility for special education services, educational and psychological test development, organization and operations of schools, systems-level intervention with schools, knowledge of child psychopharmacology, community collaboration, clinical interventions, teacher consultation, instructional consultation, parent consultation, pediatric consultation on educational issues, supervision, administration of school psychological services units, administration of testing programs in schools, research and inquiry, consumer protection, education law, professional development, and multidisciplinary team membership (e.g., see Carlson & Christenson, 2005). Perhaps the most illuminating (and unexpected by some) statement from these guidelines is the directive that professional training to be a school psychologist occurs at the doctoral level. To make clear how school psychology is unique, the *Petition for Reaffirmation of the Specialty of School Psychology* (2009), in its Petition Package available online, presented this definition on p. 2:

> Parameters that differentiate the specialty from other specialties. School psychology is differentiated from the other specialties in professional psychology by its focus on the application of psychological knowledge and methods to resolve problems or improve processes and outcomes within educational institutions or with individuals involved in the learning process. Thus school psychology is not defined simply by the setting where services are delivered but rather by the use of psychological theory and practice to improve educational outcomes for individuals and groups of learners across a variety of settings. One way to differentiate the specialties within professional psychology is by identifying the parameters that define professional practice in the specialty. As a general practice specialty, School Psychology is defined as a broad-based specialty that provides a range of psychological services to infants, children, youth; families with children; adult caregivers; learners of all ages; and organizations and agencies. Many of these services are provided in a broad array of educational settings (e.g., preschools, elementary, middle and high schools, post secondary educational institutions); between settings such as schools and hospitals or schools and employment settings; and in medical, social service and correctional facilities. The populations, problems, and procedures that define the specialty of school psychology are elaborated in Criterion V below.

In 1984, NASP offered what was to become the first School Psychology Blueprint for Training and Practice (Ysseldyke, Reynolds, & Weinberg, 1984). This blueprint was followed in 1997 by a revised NASP Blueprint II (Ysseldyke, Dawson, Lehr, Reschly, Reynolds, & Telzrow, 1997). These documents did much to broaden the role of school psychologists, and many practitioners distributed them widely to constituents, including principals. Blueprint II was especially popular with school psychologists in many districts. It was much more than a promotional flyer; it made clear how school psychologists were trained, and how the specialized training could be applied to the educational enterprise (e.g., school psychologists helping select new teachers). Given the practical nature of the Blueprint II, and the low cost of this publication, numerous positive advances were seen in the field based on the use of this document. This revised blueprint was also used as a platform for discussion of the future direction of the profession. The first author of this chapter was working fulltime as a school psychologist at the time in the schools, and school psychologists provided a copy of the Blueprint II to all principals (and some superintendents) in all of our school districts. This did much to improve the credibility of psychologists, and it also helped to increase our roles encouraging the provision of comprehensive services (Doll, 1996).

More recently, the NASP Blueprint III (Ysseldyke, Burns, Dawson, Kelley, Morrison, Ortiz, Rosenfield, & Telzrow, 2006) was developed, and includes several important changes. Four distinct areas of competency were noted. First, the foundation of training and practice is described as focusing on principles of psychology, education and scientific method. Further, the document entails eight integrated competency domains. Moreover, service delivery is described as a model involving a tiered system of training and practice. Finally, the interrelated academic and mental health factors are addressed in relation to student success. The Blueprint III makes clear the complexity of practice, and details many of the skills that are needed to be successful as a school psychologist. For example, domains of competence in training and practice include:

Foundational Competencies

- interpersonal and collaborative skills
- diversity awareness and sensitive service delivery
- technological application
- professional, legal, ethical, and social responsibility, and

Functional Competencies

- enhancing the development of wellness, social skills, and life competencies
- enhancing the development of cognitive and academic competencies
- systems-based service deliveries
- data-based decision making and accountability skills.

While many have argued both positively and negatively about the impact these documents have had in affecting the role of school psychologists and in forcing training programs to conform to NASP standards (if they valued accreditation), it seems apparent that these documents have served to help school psychologists expand roles, provide broader services in a wider context, and modify training curriculum to meet what some call contemporary standards (Fagan & Wise, 2007; Gutkin & Reynolds, 2008) . The Blueprint III from 2006 is available free online at: http://www.nasponline.org/resources/blueprint/FinalBlueprint Interiors.pdf

School Psychology Growth and Development

Concomitant with needs in the applied setting, some limited growth has occurred in programs that train school psychologists. Most of the growth seems to be in the development of specialist level programs. Fagan (1985a, 1985b, 1985c, 1986a, 2005) and Fagan and Wise (2007) report that there are approximately 35,000 school psychologists in the U.S. at present, and approximately 87,000 worldwide. About 24,000 hold membership in the National Association of School Psychologists, and about 2,500 belong to the American Psychological Association's School Psychology Division 16. The APA is an umbrella organizations with about 150,000 psychologists, most from the U.S. Members have the option of joining specialized divisions from a list of 56, including most areas of psychology, or even areas related to psychology. Many divisions publish newsletters and journals, and provide a forum for members to interact with each other. Moreover, training in school psychology is accomplished through 87 doctoral training programs and about 240 subdoctoral training programs (Brown & Minke, 1984; Brown, Sewall, & Lindstrom, 1977; Fagan, 1985b, 1985c, Fagan & Wise, 2007). Fifty-nine of the doctoral programs are accredited by the APA in school psychology (American Psychological Association, 2009b) and 10 programs are accredited in the area of Combined Professional-Scientific Psychology, for a total of 69 programs (American Psychological Association, 2009c). It is remarkable that *all* 10 of the programs featured in the combined psychology list focus on school psychology, as well as one or two other applied areas (Fagan, 1985c, 1986a).

It is apparent that the psychologist who practices in the schools has the potential of providing a unique view to the educational enterprise. By virtue of training and focus, the school psychologist brings the technical insight of the science of psychology to bear on problems that may hinder the full development of school-age children. While these services could be provided in a variety of settings, schools continue to dominate the employment picture. Although we are far from consensus on the specific role the school psychologist should play, there seems to be general agreement among educators that the

application of psychological principles and techniques in the educational setting is important to pedagogic pursuits (Conoley & Gulkin, 1986; Senft & Snider, 1980). Unfortunately however, assessment activities continue to cloud the original vision of school psychology (Bardon, Davis, Howard, & Myrick, 1982; Bennett, 1970, 1985; Benson & Hughes, 1985; Conoley & Conoley, 1981; Goldston, 1986; Stewart, 1986).

Although a wide variety of functions have been offered as appropriate for the school psychologist, numerous factors have combined to impede the growth of the specialty beyond an individual assessment focus. Owing, perhaps, to the fact that psychological personnel have been employed at only one level in the schools, the duties of the school psychologist have revolved around individual diagnostic assessments as a precursor to special class placement (e.g., D'Amato & Dean, 1987). Debate has continued for at least four decades concerning whether this is the proper role for the psychologist; however, it remains the primary function of most practicing school psychologists (e.g., Dean, 1980; Meacham & Peckham, 1978; Sattler & D'Amato, 2002a, 2002b). This expression of the specialty has been reemphasized by Federal legislation (e.g., P.L. 94-142) which has mandated even greater emphasis on formal child evaluation services by the public schools. With special education reimbursements tied to rather strict procedures in determining children's initial and continuing eligibility, and the fact that the bulk of the child assessment procedures are provided by psychological personnel, the school psychologist's role has become further solidified within the schools (Solly & Hohenshil, 1986). Therefore, although legislation has expanded the need for school psychological personnel, it has continued to narrow services to individual child assessment. The new *Response to Intervention* movement has narrowed services even further.

Doctoral versus Subdoctoral Training in Psychology

Confusion concerning the level of training necessary for entry into the profession has existed for some time, since before the Thayer conference. Unlike other applied psychology specialties, in school psychology, state standards for licensure, certification, and those offered by professional organizations are often at odds with each other. A case in point is the APA, which has continued to advocate that minimal competence as a psychologist, in any setting, can only be maintained at the doctoral level. Although this position has rarely been seriously challenged by other applied psychological specialties, it has led to controversy in school psychology (Dimond, Havens, Rathrow, & Colliver, 1977; Hilke & Brantley, 1982; Korman, 1974; Smith & Soper, 1978). The position of requiring less than a doctorate for entry into school psychology, although favored by some, is rather disturbing to many who feel that psychological practice in the schools is as demanding in its sophistication as any other applied specialty in psychology, regardless of the present reality of practice (Bardon, 1983, 1982, 1994; Dean, 1982a; Hilke & Brantley, 1982; National Association of School Psychologists, 1984). Historically, the interest in individual assessment, and relatively few trained psychologists, may have been responsible for the early entry, growth, and certification of paraprofessionals who served as testers and gatekeepers for special education entry (Cutts, 1955; Hall, 1949; Kennedy, 1971). This seems a benchmark, because this practice apparently is the antecedent of the certification of psychological personnel for work in the schools by the educational community (Bennett, 1985; Hall, 1949). Although the role frequently espoused for school psychology has been an expansion beyond diagnosis/placement functions (e.g., Alpert, 1985; Bergan, 1979), the profession has clearly remained dependent on this function, and hence on public education for direction (Gilmore & Chandy, 1973; Hartshorne & Johnson, 1985). Such dependency is in sharp contrast to the more broadly based service notions offered early on for school psychology (Cutts, 1955; Fernberger, 1931; Witmer, 1896, 1897, 1907, 1911).

Although an assessment emphasis may well be appropriate for subdoctoral trained specialists, doctoral level psychologists usually have expanded training that widens the scope of their skills and understanding (Fagan, 1985c, Matarazzo, 1987). In fact, some authors have argued for a distinction between doctoral- and subdoctoral-level psychological personnel, with names reflecting their level of training and expertise (Bardon, 1983, 1989). Thus, subdoctoral practitioners would be "school psychologists," whereas doctoral level psychologists would function under a title recognizing that they have the potential to offer services in a wider variety of settings (e.g., family service psychologist, child-community psychologist, or applied educational psychologist). Although these settings may include the schools, such applied psychologists would not be restricted to public education. After considering the level of services provided in most schools, some have questioned the need for doctoral level training in school psychology. In theory, it seems that additional

training should enable psychologists to perform functions not possible with less training. Obviously, different levels of training enable psychologists to perform varied types of activities. Although such service models have been articulated for decades (e.g., see Dean, 1982a), their application has not been realized in the schools. In essence, most doctoral level school psychologists perform duties identical to subdoctoral level school psychologists when they practice in the schools (Dean, 1982b; French & McCloskey, 1980; Gilmore & Chandy, 1973; Meacham & Peckham, 1978).

From this point of view, one wonders if acceptance of subdoctoral training as the level of entry might serve as a tacit acceptance of the services presently offered as "school psychology." In other words, are we prepared as a profession to accept psychological services now provided in the schools *as the definition of* school psychology? Bardon has made clear that this should not be the case. He has argued that school psychology is a *unique specialty*, not the current activities that are practiced banally in the schools, often on an as-needed basis under the Educational Specialist (Ed.S) umbrella provided by NASP (Bardon, 1983, 1989, 1994). Another question concerns the extent to which we are willing to accept the solidification of school psychology from forces outside of psychology. However, any argument counter to considering psychological services presently offered in the schools as defining *school psychology*. School psychology must come together with a resolve that the parameters of our practice must be defined by forces within the profession.

In what seems to be an effort to extend the role of the school psychologist, or to concretize role gains, a number of papers have appeared calling for expanded services (e.g., Alpert, 1985; Carlson & Christenson, 2005; Fagan, 1986b; Sheridan & D'Amato, 2003). These papers have come in the wake of other noteworthy attempts (e.g., Olympia and Futures conferences), to direct the future of school psychology (see Brown, Cardon, Coulter, & Meyers, 1982; Oakland, 1986; Sheridan & D'Amato, 2003; Ysseldyke et al., 2006). In each case, authors have portrayed the school psychologist as a provider of a full gamut of services. This position stands in sharp contrast to current training statements, which stress, or at least accept, subdoctoral level training. With this in mind, one must wonder if it is possible to accept a call for an increased role for school psychologists while retaining "a subdoctoral entry level." Nonetheless, authors who have argued for an expanded role have paid relatively little attention to how such additional elements could be integrated into training (e.g., see Sheridan & D'Amato, 2003). Although it is impossible to draw a line clearly separating appropriate services for doctoral-and nondoctoral-level psychological personnel, common sense establishes that we cannot continually expand services while advocating for less than doctoral level training. Evidence suggests that implicit in this role extension must be the need for doctoral level training (e.g., Bardon, 1983, 1989).

Certification versus Licensure in School Psychology

The difference between a certified school psychologist and a licensed school psychologist may be the person's level of education and professional credentialing. Training to become a school psychologist can be completed in two different ways. The first is by way of earning an Ed.S degree, or special graduate level certificate such as the S.S.P. (Specialist in School Psychology) or equivalent post-master's degree. Typically, this course of training takes approximately two years, with a full-year internship in the schools. These practitioners earn a degree in school psychology, and often go on to work in the schools. Credentialing for this type of practice is offered through state departments of education. For example, in Colorado the certificate is offered through the Colorado Department of Education.

The second course a person interested in becoming a school psychologist can take is through completion of a doctorate in school psychology. Generally, students on this track complete approximately four to five years of course work, and then a yearlong internship. Students who enter a doctoral level school psychology program, and who want the highest quality training possible, usually elect to complete an accredited program, and at the completion of coursework they often also choose to complete an APA-accredited internship (in or out of the schools). Internship information is available online at the APA website. If the internship is not located in the schools–for example, it is located in an adult hospital or adult clinic setting–training programs will often require school psychology doctoral students to complete an additional internship in the schools. Regardless of the doctoral student's internship experiences, these school psychologists have more options in placement or employment. Examples of employment options outside of the schools include hospitals, consulting firms, clinics, universities, private practice, and in state departments of education. These *nontraditional* employment opportunities are discussed in a later section of this chapter.

State Departments of Education. In regard to licensure and certifications, confusion abounds because many states use the words *licensure* and *certification* identically. However, there are basically two types of licenses or certification offered. The first, previously mentioned, is a license offered by a *state department of education* that allows a school psychologist to work in the *public schools*. Depending on the state, different requirements exist to earn licensure. Many times, states will require the completion of coursework and an internship, and some require the completion of a school induction program offered by the school district of employment. For example, one state requires the completion of a weekend class on child abuse. Others states require the addition of supervision in the schools for up to three years.

State Boards of Psychology. The other form of licensure is offered by the *state board of psychology* and offers licensure to *practice privately* or to work in an enterprise outside of education, such as in a hospital. This licensure is not specific to school psychologists, but rather applies to the practice of psychology in society including counseling, clinical, and school psychologists. Requirements for this licensure vary from state to state. However, typically, the practitioner must have a doctorate in psychology from an accredited university, two or more years of clinical training, a full-year accredited predoctoral internship, and many states also require two additional years of postdoctoral experience. So too, individuals must have passed the *Examination for Professional Practice in Psychology* (EPPP) test. Each state has its own criteria for granting a passing score on the EPPP. However, to earn this license, in almost all states the individual must be a doctoral level psychologist.

National Certification in School Psychology. National certification in school psychology is also available for Ed.S. and doctoral level practitioners who complete specified coursework, a school psychology internship, and achieve a state-specified score on a national examination. The certification is awarded by a division of NASP and allows one to be called a Nationally Certified School Psychologist (NCSP). Attending a NASP-approved program is the easiest way to meet many of these requirements. NASP is working diligently to encourage states to accept the NCSP credential, which allows individuals to move from one state to another more easily.

School psychologists with an Ed.S. degree are limited in their ability to offer private practice services, and few states allow school psychologists at this level to practice privately. However, doctoral level school psychologists in most states can achieve the private practice credential, although it may be time consuming because of the requirement of additional courses, clinical supervision, and/or professional psychology tests.

Major Movements Related to the Field of School Psychology

Assessment, Child Study, and Measurement

School psychology contributes uniquely to the study of psychology due to its focus on children and their educational, social, and emotional development. Some argue that child study, assessment, and measurement form the foundation of what has been seen as school psychology (D'Amato, Rothlisberg, & Leu, 1999; Fagan & Wise, 2007; Gutkin & Reynolds, 2008). In the middle to late 1800s, schools began to utilize uniquely trained teachers to serve children with learning and behavior problems. One attempt in 1871 occurred in New Haven, Connecticut, where classes were provided for children "who were running wild on the street and becoming a public nuisance" (Fein, 1974, p. 2). Because programs of this type were developing rapidly, specialists were in demand to identify students who would benefit from these special programs. The public school movement quickly adapted a psychometric emphasis, which followed in the wake of Binet and Simon's pioneering of standardized intelligence testing in Europe (Fein, 1974; Reynolds et al., 1984). It has been well established that the use of these tests, for the placement of deficient children, was well received by the public schools. This interpretation is consistent with the fact that the 1916 Stanford Revision of the Binet-Simon Intelligence Scale became the most popular test in the United States during the next 25 years (Fein, 1974). This instrument did much to crystallize the role of what was soon to become school psychology.

Intelligence testing is argued by some to have begun in the latter half of the 19th century, by Sir Francis Galton (Flanagan & Kaufman, 2004, Saklofske, Lynne-Beal, Weiss, & Coalson, 2003). Independently wealthy, Galton had an unlimited amount of time and funds to spend studying his interests. One such interest was that of measurement and statistics. Specifically, he concentrated on the area of correlation. He argued that anything could be measured with the right amount of drive. He attempted to measure the efficacy of prayer, beauty, and the relative worth of people. In 1884,

he established a laboratory at the International Exposition, where he pursued his interests in measuring skulls and bodies (Gould, 1996). Galton was said to have created the first comprehensive test of intelligence (Flanagan & Kaufman, 2004). Through his research, Galton measured sensory and motor abilities. However, although data gathered from these tasks were reliable, they were not found to relate to the construct of what we have come to call intelligence. At this time, there was a large movement toward establishing an objective method of differentiating groups of people based on intelligence. Further, the movement argued in favor of the need to classify individuals into separate groups (Flanagan & Kaufman).

Charles Spearman, an English psychologist, was educated in Germany at Leipzig and completed his Ph.D. with Wundt. However, he was greatly influenced by Galton and his theory of correlation and soon became known for his work in the factor analysis of intelligence. The G factor theory of intelligence (a concept of general intelligence), created by Spearman in 1904, "has been said to have been the birth of the psychometric research tradition" (Flanagan, McGrew & Ortiz, 2000, p. 18). The G-factor provides a theoretical model suggesting that a single factor g, or *general intelligence*, is responsible for an individual's ability or performance on all cognitive tasks. This notion has since been argued as narrow and invalid (Gould, 1996). Spearman eventually began to study *specific* cognitive abilities (s) and created the bi-factor model with Karl Holzinger.

Raymond Cattell, who earned his doctoral degree studying with Spearman, was also influenced by the work of Galton. In 1890, he coined the term *mental test* and adopted Galton's research to test American college students (Boake, 2002). As a result of his work with Spearman, and what he perceived as the incompleteness of the G-factor theory, Cattell's Gf-Gc theory, one of today's most prominent models of intelligence, emerged. He argued that intelligence was not a unitary trait, but a combination of two different types of general abilities. He believed that intelligence was made up of two general factors including fluid reasoning (Gf), the ability to solve novel problems, and crystallized reasoning (Gc), the ability to consolidate knowledge (Flanagan et al., 2000). Fluid intelligence is further described as inductive and deductive reasoning, influenced by a combination of biological and neurological factors, as well as incidental learning through exposure to environmental factors. Crystallized intelligence (Gc) is referred to as knowledge that is dependent on learning, and that reflects the influence of acculturation (Flanagan et al., 2000). In 1965, Horn expanded the Gf-Gc theory to include four additional factors, including: visual perception (Gv), short-term memory (Gsm), long-term storage and retrieval (Glr), and processing speed (Gs). In 1968, Horn added auditory processing ability (Ga) to the model.

In 1904, Binet was commissioned by the minister of public education to conduct a study that would develop a diagnostic system to identify students who would require special education (Roid & Barram, 2004). Shortly after the end of the nineteenth century, Binet and his colleagues had developed an intelligence measure assessing abilities that were language oriented, and emphasizing judgment, memory, comprehension, and reasoning. In 1908, Binet and Theodore Simon revised the scale and grouped tests into age levels. Administration to a child began with a task at the child's age level, and proceeded to either higher or lower age levels until finding the point where the student passed or failed the majority of the test items. The child's intelligence was quantified in terms of the intellectual level, or mental age. This was defined as the highest age level at which the student successfully completed the majority of problems (Boake, 2002).

H. H. Goddard, a research director at the Vineland Training School for Feeble-Minded Girls and Boys in New Jersey, is said to have been the first psychologist to popularize the Binet scale in America (Gould, 1996). He learned of the scale while on travels in Europe (Boake, 2002). He used the tests to measure limits, and refused to define his scores as "intelligence." A clear indication of the attitudes of the times was his stated wish to "not allow native morons to breed" (Gould, 1996, p. 195). To do this, in 1913 Goddard raised funds to use the Binet scales as an identifying factor of "mentally defective" immigrants at the New York harbor. This was carried out by stopping those who appeared feeble-minded and administering the test (Gould, 1996).

In 1916, Lewis Terman, a professor at Stanford University, adapted and translated the Binet-Simon Scales for use in the United States. He took Binet's last version from 1911, added tasks, and extended the age range of use. Additionally, he adapted the scales to the American culture, and revealed the importance of intelligence testing in children and adults (Saklofske, et al., 2003). He intended to use the test with everybody, and establish a degree of innate ability that could categorize children into "their proper stations in life" (Gould, 1996, p. 206).

To comprehensively and systematically evaluate recruits, Robert Yerkes, a Harvard University professor, proposed in 1915 that the U.S. Army test all its recruits. He hoped to transform psychology from a questionable art to an esteemed science. As a result, he brought together Terman, Goddard, and other colleagues to help develop the Army mental tests (Gould, 1996). In turn, as the United States entered World War I in 1917, the assessment of intelligence expanded for use in army identification procedures. The Army Alpha test was developed to select officers and place recruits through a group-administered IQ test, with verbal content similar to that of the Stanford-Binet. Those that failed the Alpha test would be given the Army Beta test, which was a pictorial test. Those that failed the two would be called in for an individual examination using a version of the Binet scales. It was estimated that 83,500 individual examinations were administered in the Army testing program (Boake, 2002).

David Wechsler began his work with the Army scales in Long Island under the supervision of Edwin Boring, and after graduating, it is estimated that he performed more than 300 individual examinations. He was convinced that the existing intelligence tests had critical shortcomings. Wechsler wanted to combine the verbal scale from the Stanford-Binet/Army Alpha scale, and the performance scale assessed from the Examination/Army Beta scale, to obtain dynamic clinical information. As such, the first of the Wechsler-Bellevue Intelligence Scales was developed (Flanagan & Kaufman, 2004). This measure was unique in that it offered an assessment of verbal and nonverbal intelligence. The Wechsler scales were highly influenced by Wechsler's theory that intelligence is an aggregate of multiple abilities and a broad construct. He believed that intelligence could not be described by an individual capacity, but rather by a multifaceted combination of abilities (Wechsler, 1950a, 1950b).

Most authors worked on developing the tests themselves and had less interest in researching interventions for remediating or compensating for intellectual abilities or disabilities (D'Amato, 2007; D'Amato, Crepeau-Hobson, Huang, & Geil, 2005b). Unlike Terman and Goddard, who believed in the biological nature of intelligence, Witmer posited that intelligence could either be retarded or enhanced based on environmental exposure and nurturance. From his perspective, if a child's intelligence was being thwarted by environmental factors, intervention could help a child. However, if cognitive retardation was due to biological aspects of development, Witmer argued that rehabilitation would not be successful.

The Mental Health Intervention Movement

Still another wave in the tide of psychology in the schools came with the mental hygiene/mental health movement. In this case, the applied psychologist working in the schools was seen as a good ally for providing mental health services to children (Magary, 1967; Tindall, 1964). Because this movement stressed prevention and early intervention services, the public schools became the ideal institution on which to focus (Balcerzak, & D'Amato, 2000a, 2000b; Cutts, 1955; Goldston, 1986). For some, schools appeared to have the potential of becoming what we view today as community mental health centers (Crawford & D'Amato, 2000; Tindall, 1964). This does make empirical sense, and the schools offer a way to reach *all* children and provide them with the many mental health (and physical health) services they need. Nevertheless, in many ways, this role ran counter to that of the more test-oriented psychometrists, who saw their role as diagnosing and placing "backward" children. Another great difference stemming from the mental health movement related to an understanding of the location of a child's problems (D'Amato & Rothlisberg, 1992/1997). Psychologists who were assessment specialists often offered solutions and recommendations related to changing the *child,* or the child's educational placement. Thus, problems were seen as mostly being related to, or originating within, the child. This is because early on, psychology followed the medical model. But the mental health intervention movement took issue with this belief, and sought to serve more than just the child (Carlson & Christenson, 2005; D'Amato, Crepeau-Hobson, Huang, & Geil, 2005b; D'Amato & Dean, 1989a; Gaddes & Edgell, 1994).

Many school psychologists became mental health experts and, in tandem, school counselors did the same. NASP has more recently published numerous documents, including the Blueprints (previously discussed in this chapter), stressing how school psychologists are mental health experts. APA Division 16 has followed suit with a similar publication entitled, *Making psychologists in schools indispensable: Critical questions and emerging perspectives* (Talley, Kubiszyn, Brassard, & Short, 1996). This model has been implemented in a few schools, and is discussed near the end of the chapter under the section titled "A Comprehensive School Psychologist Role Example from the Public Schools." In some states,

the shortage of school psychologists has also had an impact on the ability to implement such a full-service approach. The most serious problem with the model is the cost of placing a psychologist in every school building. Another problem is that little if any research has been done to validate such a role. In one study, referrals to the school psychologist's office for significant behavioral and emotional problems were reviewed before and after the implementation of this full-service model (Obrzut, Davis, & D'Amato, 2002). Referrals declined significantly when the school psychologist had taught peer counseling, and offered other services, to the students (Obrzut et al., 2002). This intervention validation research was entitled *Establishing caring school communities based on conflict resolution program outcomes.* Some of these notions are based on Fran Culbertson's idea of creating *Schools as a Haven* where students want to return to school because schools are safe, fun places where they can learn.

As expected, even during the formative years of the field, the diagnostic/remedial activities of psychologists in the schools often took precedence over the more preventive mental health oriented activities. From even a brief review of literature, it is evident that the practice of psychology in the public schools happened haphazardly, rather than developing from rational arguments for how psychology could be best applied to the educational enterprise (Cutts, 1955; Fagan & Wise, 2007). More recently, NASP has embraced this mental health movement, and has advocated that school psychologists are in a perfect place to help develop responsive psychological services. They have developed an informative and exciting in-service module on *School Psychologists as Mental Health Providers.*

Compulsory Schooling, Public Laws, and Legal Mandates

Historically, many children with physical, mental and emotional disabilities were shunned and placed in institutions away from society (Fagan & Wise, 2007). However, in 1975, President Ford signed the Education Act for All Handicapped Children Act, otherwise known as Public Law 94-142 (P.L. 94-142). The act stated that the federal government was responsible for providing funding for a free and appropriate public education for handicapped children. This began the movement of children from institutions into regular school buildings. The movement of "mainstreaming," or integrating children with disabilities into the regular education classroom, has been controversial for decades. However, mainstreaming in the 1970s and 1980s was rather different from today. Children with disabilities were then segregated into separate classrooms within the same school building. In many cases, less qualified teachers were assigned to these classrooms, and access to resources was limited.

In 1997, part B of IDEA was put into effect, providing a free and appropriate education for all children. Further, IDEA Part B required that children with disabilities be taught in the least restrictive environment (LRE). This was meant to ensure that children would receive "instruction in regular classes with supplementary services, special classes, special schools, home instruction, and instruction in hospitals and institutions" as necessary in order to meet their needs (Jacob & Hartshorne, 2003; p. 146). Several court hearings took place to reiterate the schools' responsibility to provide the least restrictive environment. However, in the Board of Education, Sacramento City Unified School District vs. Holland (1992) case and, Sacramento City School District vs. Rachel H. (1994) among other cases, led to consideration of the disruption on the teacher's ability to teach, and children's ability to learn (see Jacob & Hartshorne, 2007, for a listing of court cases). The Holland case considered two forms of disruptive behavior: (1) the child being disruptive and a behavioral concern, and (2) the impact of the behaviors on the other children's learning. Subsequently, an Individual Education Plan (IEP) team would be required to decide the appropriate placement of the student, also taking into consideration the extent of potential disruption for the teacher and the class.

Therefore, mainstreaming has been interpreted differently over time, and by different school districts. Today, many districts denote mainstreaming as a "push in" model, where children in regular and special education are integrated into the same classrooms for all subject areas. In these classrooms, special education services are provided within the general education setting. By contrast, other districts believe in a model of mainstreaming whereby children spend most of their day in the general education classroom, and are pulled out only in their area of need. Finally, other districts interpret mainstreaming as children being assimilated with the general education population only in classes such as art, physical education, and music. More recent legislation has extended services to infants and toddlers.

Multidisciplinary Teams

A multidisciplinary team is a team of professionals from different disciplines that provide comprehensive consultations, assessments, and, at times, direct services. The use of such teams originated with Witmer in 1896 (Fagan, 1996). The team may consist of, but is not limited to, a regular education teacher, special education teacher, school psychologist, school counselor, school social worker, speech therapist, school nurse, occupational therapist, physical therapist, the principal, and parents. Depending on the age of the child, he or she may also be part of the team. The team is involved in gaining informed consent from the parents, a comprehensive assessment of the student, if needed, collection and review of all materials, observations, collaboration in services provided, and, finally, decision making as a team. Traditionally, once the consent for evaluation is signed, each team member will independently assess the learner, and then the team will convene to discuss their results. As a team, a decision is then made, with the input of the parents, in regard to the ideal means of meeting the student's needs. At team meetings, issues may also be discussed if a particular area of concern exists. This could relate to classroom objectives such as use of a behavior plan or a behavior aide. Moreover, the team may be involved in making critical decisions regarding the student's current placement (considering other classrooms or schools), discussion of possible school expulsion, and/or a range-of-service decisions such as considering placing the student in a residential treatment facility. The team meeting is an opportunity for professionals from different disciplines to come together and combine their unique knowledge and skills to best serve the learner (D'Amato, Fletcher-Janzen, et al., 2005; Reynolds & Gutkin, 1999).

Psychological Consultation

This section highlights one of the most unique services provided by school psychologists. Consultation is a service that indeed is extremely distinctive, and oddly enough often is found only within school psychology training programs. The indirect service model is an integral part of the role of a school psychologist, because as a member of the school, teachers and parents often look to the school psychologist as a problem solver, and even at times as a child behavioral and emotional expert (Brown, Pryzwansky, & Schulte, 2006). Not only do school psychologists have unique access to children and their environment, they can also consult and provide indirect service to children through their parents and teachers, thus affecting the system that surrounds the child (Conoley & Conoley, 1981). Therefore, school psychologists offer a large scope of services, providing a comprehensive delivery model (Fagan & Wise, 2007; Reynolds & Gutkin, 1999).

The most well known and researched model of consultation was developed by Gerald Caplan (Caplan, 1970). His *mental health consultation* model involves consultee-centered case consultation. This form of consultation focuses on the consultee, usually a teacher, rather than a particular client, the student. In a school setting, a teacher may be having extreme difficulty with one of her students. Caplan's model involves working directly with the teacher to problem-solve, in an effort to empower the teacher with new skills (Caplan, 1970). The goal is to understand why a teacher is having difficulty with the student, and to recognize how the teacher may be contributing to the problem (Conoley & Conoley, 1981). The assumption of the model is that if we can help the teacher see how he/she is contributing to the problem, the teacher can then change his or her approach, thus promoting a more positive atmosphere for the students, as well as the class in general. Accordingly, the school psychologist works with the teacher to change the child's behavior, although the school psychologist may never see or work directly with the child being indirectly served (Brown et al., 2006).

A second form of consultation, *behavioral consultation*, focuses directly on behavior, and how the consultant can work to modify the behavior of the individual under consideration (Feldman & Kratochwill, 2003). Behavioral consultation involves the application of reinforcement principles to the consultee relationship, and is a problem-solving method. This is a more direct approach, in that the problem behavior is already visible. In the schools, the consultant, or school psychologist, focuses on working with the consultee to identify specific behavior problems (Conoley & Conoley, 1981). This should include identifying variables that could help understand the depth of the problem, developing a plan in concert with the teacher to begin solving the problem, and helping the teacher evaluate the intervention outcome through direct observation.

Another form of consultation takes a very different approach to problem solving. The *organizational development consultation* model is a form of consultation involving the application of behavioral science techniques for system change. It works to improve the interpersonal and group techniques utilized by each level of school personnel. Additionally, it aims to uncover the ways in which members of the group communicate, the underlying issues, and the

procedures by which decisions are developed. Indeed, the goal of the model is to create flexible, resilient schools that can evolve and change with students and the community, while meeting educational objectives.

The underlying goal of consultation in the schools is to be able to provide services indirectly to all students. As outlined in their article, "Problem solving consultation in schools: Past, present, and future directions," Feldman and Kratochwill (2003) present the advantages of school-based consultation including: (1) the "potential to enable psychologists to provide services to a greater number of clients than can be reached by traditional models of service delivery" (such as individual counseling); (2) its "capacity to be preventative"; (3) "it enables general education teachers to implement interventions targeting academic, social, emotional, and behavioral problems"; and (4) "it promotes teamwork and cooperative problem solving among school personnel."

Although an intervention may originally be set up to address a problem of an individual student, the teacher may find that this same intervention helps another student who is at risk for academic or behavior problems. Thus, school psychologists work with teachers and teach them how to identify a problem, implement an intervention effectively, and monitor student progress, all of which, hopefully, leads to student success. Empowering teachers to transfer these skills to other situations or students is the purpose of consultation. This is the basis of the idea of providing services to as many students as possible. Some say teaching teachers to help themselves can be called "giving psychology away" (Conoley & Conoley, 1981; D'Amato, 1985). Some of the challenges faced by school consultants may include: teachers who may be defensive or resistant to the intervention; lack of resources/money to implement an intervention; lack of the time needed to consult with a teacher; lack of time needed to monitor progress or follow up with the teacher; problems understanding the school culture; difficulties with time needed to teach a teacher the skills necessary to implement an intervention appropriately; and teachers and/or administrators not understanding the role of a school psychologist (Brown et al., 2006). All of these consultation models work well with cultures that value self-control and independence. Motivation and activity level must also be considered to make sure an intervention is successful. As a result of the potential cultural differences, it's important to consider the culture of the client, or even the consultee, to make sure the consultation is culturally sensitive. The consultant has to be able to adapt his or her expectations to match the culture of the consultee and client, in order to make sure that the intervention agreed upon and implemented is culturally appropriate (Brown et al., 2006; Crawford & D'Amato, 2000).

School Psychology's Connection to Education

In general, school psychology has remained intrinsically tied to a single institution—the school (Bennett, 1985; Dean, 1982b). This is not as trite a statement as it would appear; the ramifications of this fact may well be responsible for innumerable obstacles to the development of school psychology as a profession. This is not meant to paint public education with a brush of sinister motives, but rather a consideration of those factors that have shaped school psychology. Bardon (1983, 1989) has articulated a stance that recognizes our failure to fully develop as a field within the schools. Indeed, Bardon (1983, 1989), like many others, has questioned the heuristic value of the APA's Division 16 defining itself as school psychology when that entity has been associated with psychological applications which fall short of a distinct specialization within American psychology. Bardon's position, although rather disturbing to some, succinctly portrays the view held by many, that school psychology as presently practiced in the schools drastically lacks the sophistication envisioned for the specialty (Gray, 1963; Fernberger, 1931; Holt & Kicklighter, 1971; White & Harris, 1961).

The situation that exists is hardly surprising, because as psychologists who owe their existence to the schools, we are bound by the same political and economic forces which shape that institution. In fact, the many difficulties of the educational system have been well publicized (Education Commission of the States, Task Force on Education for Economic Growth, 1983; Goodlad, 1979; National Commission on Excellence in Education, 1983; National School Psychology In-service Training Network, 1984). Although a variety of problems have plagued public education, Hyman (1979a) succinctly portrays the overall picture:

> In fact, rather than accumulating wisdom and prestige, American education constantly appears to be deteriorating as it flaps and flutters in the changing winds of political and economic uncertainty. And the interface between psychology and education, whether it be at the experimental or the professional level, can never provide a solid base

for improvement in many children's lives until schooling becomes less susceptible to the whims of the many forces affecting it. (p. 1026)

Overall then, because certification, initial employment, and the ability to structure the role of psychological services are controlled by the educational community, acceptance by the APA of the practice of school psychology seems more a recognition of the realities of the specialty as practiced, than a reconceptualization of school psychology (Sewall & Brown, 1976). Hyman (1979a, 1979b) argues that the lack of effective contact between psychology and education is a problem of social policy and planning. Whatever the reason, it is a sad fact indeed that the influence the APA has enjoyed in the practice of school psychology is at best indirect, and at worst illusionary.

Nontraditional School Psychology

School psychology obviously has matured to the point where the specialty offers marketable, nonredundant skills that are in demand in a variety of settings (Levy, 1986). However, this fact is often obscured because of the institutional affiliation that the name "school psychology" designates. Indeed, a number of authors have argued convincingly that school psychologists have long utilized psychological skills that are appropriate in numerous settings (D'Amato, Dean, Hughes, Harrison, McCloskey, Pryzwanskv, & Hartlage, 1987; D'Amato, Fletcher-Janzen, & Reynolds, 2005; D'Amato & Rothlisberg, 1992/1997; Giebink & Ringness, 1970). By training, school psychologists are able to provide an understanding of the factors that influence children's cognitive and emotional functioning, notwithstanding settings (Alpert, 1985; Meacham & Peckham, 1978). Table 2.5 displays some of the nontraditional settings where school psychologists have successfully practiced, and lists some of the early articles where these practices were discussed. As reviewed previously, the roots of school psychology in settings other than the schools can be traced back to the very founding of the field (Fernberger, 1931; Witmer, 1896, 1897, 1907, 1911). With the expansion of psychology into new areas, a variety of alternative roles have continued to evolve for school psychologists. This approach stresses matching client needs with appropriate services, without putting undue emphasis on the settings in which the services are offered.

In general, over the last century two distinctive dimensions of applied service applications have evolved after melding clients, services, and settings. These two approaches seem to characterize the

Table 2.5 Nontraditional settings advocated for school psychologists

Evaluation Centers	Brantley (1971)
University Clinics	Witmer (1907); Hughes & Benson (1986)
Private Practice	Harries (1982)
Medical/Family Clinics	Hartlage & Hartlage (1978)
Neurology Departments	D'Amato & Dean (1988); D'Amato, 1990
Developmental Pediatric Centers	Hartlage & Hartlage (1978)
Medical/Neuropsychological Clinics	Dean (1982a)
Residential Treatment Facilities	Witmer (1897)
Community Mental Health Centers	Granowsky & Davis (1974); Klosterman (1974)

overall practice of school psychology. In fact, these two service dimensions were displayed rather dramatically before the clinical/school psychology split.

Consulting, Systemic, Family-Service Psychology. The first orientation is that of a consulting family-service psychologist. This specialist offers a holistic view of the child, who is interacting with the educational enterprise, in a context that includes their family, peers, and community (Carlson & Christiansen, 2005). Early on, anthropologists argued the importance of the relationship between individuals and their environment (e.g., Mead, 1961). Since that time, others have advocated for similar child/family services, with data suggesting both the effectiveness of this perspective and the scarcity of service providers (Hannah & Midlarsky, 1985; Hobbs, 1964, 1968, 1976; Montgomery & Paul, 1982; President's Commission on Mental Health, 1978; Pryzwansky, 1986; Rappaport, 1977; Smith & Hobbs, 1966). For instance, a Special Issue in *School Psychology Quarterly* (see Carlson & Christiansen, 2005), was offered from this view, and the recent revision of the APA School Psychology Specialty Guidelines also clearly integrated these features. From this ecological perspective, the psychologist is seen to interface, negotiate, and intervene after evaluating the needs of the client and the system/family (Lewin, 1936; Reynolds & Gutkin, 1999; Nelson, 1976). The state of affairs at present supports such an interactional/ecological view, in light of the forces that influence children and families on a daily basis (Crawford & D'Amato, 1999; Ysseldyke et al., 2006). Moreover, this community/family based approach to psychological services would seem to blend well with the more preventive mental health and social adjustment needs of school-age children (Alpert, 1985; Bardon, 1983; Conoley & Conoley, 1981; Hughes & Benson, 1986; Packard, 1983; Ruckhaber, 1970; Scarr, 1979; Spielberger & Stenmark, 1985). Services in this area may include educational activities for parents and children (e.g., parent training, marriage enrichment, self-concept development, communication classes), individual and family counseling and therapy (Conoley, 1989, 1992/1997), functional behavioral assessment, behavioral programming and management, (Morris & Morris, 1989) and support groups (e.g., assertiveness training, single parenting). The general focus of this area is on clinical services to children and families, with little consideration given to whether or not these services are offered outside of the educational enterprise (Pryzwansky, 1989). From a theoretical view, this wider service model makes both conceptual and practical sense, and is a good fit with the school psychologist's training and experiences.

Actuarial and Rehabilitation Psychology. In contrast, other authors have stressed psychodiagnostic and/or rehabilitation aspects of functioning in nontraditional settings (Anastasi, 1988; Cohen, Montague, Nathanson, & Swerdlik, 1988; D'Amato, Fletcher-Janzen, et al., 2005; Dean, 1982a; Sattler & D'Amato, 2002a; 2002b). For decades it has been argued that school psychologists have training and expertise that enables them to serve as assessment, compensatory, and remedial experts (Bardon & Bennett, 1974; Bower, 1955; D'Amato, Rothlisberg, & Leu, 1999; Gray, 1963; Reger, 1965; White & Harris, 1961; Valett, 1963). Although a number of these evaluative activities (e.g., standardized testing, patient/family interview) are similar to the traditional school assessment process (Sattler & D'Amato, 2002a, 2002b), when practiced in alternative settings a greater number of evaluative techniques are utilized, and the resulting data are interpreted quite differently (e.g., see D'Amato, Rothlisberg, & Leu, 1999). As would be expected, this actuarial approach (Cronbach, 1957; Meehl, 1954), finds easy expression inside and outside of the public school system (D'Amato, Crepeau-Hobson, et al., 2005; D'Amato, Fletcher-Janzen, & Reynolds, 2005). From this conceptualization, school psychologists may be involved in settings where comprehensive assessments are required, or they could work in the development and planning of rehabilitation programs (Stone, Gray, & Dean, 1989). With a psychometric background, school psychologists would also seem well positioned to spearhead test and product development, and serve as research and personnel consultants (Harrison & McCloskey, 1989).

For the most part, both service dimensions have the potential to contribute significantly to settings both inside and outside of the schools (Cummings, 1979; Hobbs, 1968, 1976, 1978). When one considers the political and economic forces that influence education, it is evident that school psychologists working outside of the educational enterprise may operate in a fashion *more* consistent with their training than psychologists providing services in the schools. It would also seem possible for the school psychologist working in nontraditional settings to offer a level of psychological services that authors have long argued ought to be an integral part of the school psychologist's role (Granger & Campbell, 1977; Granowsky & Davis, 1974; Hartlage, 1971; Hohenshil, 1974; Klosterman, 1974; Lambert, 1973; Reilly, 1973, 1974; Singer, Whiton, & Fried, 1970; Ysseldyke et al., 2006). To be sure, with employment in a number of nontraditional settings, the opportunity arises to practice and hone many school psychology skills that are rarely applied in educational settings. Apparently, the number of school psychologists attracted to alternative settings has grown significantly since opportunities outside of the public schools seem to be increasing (D'Amato et al., 1987).

It is appropriate to ask if school psychology training provides psychologists with the skills necessary to practice in both nontraditional and traditional settings. However, after a review of training requirements in school psychology doctoral programs, the breadth of the specialty becomes clear

(Fagan, 1985c; Goh, 1977; Reynolds et al., 1984). Students trained at the Ed.S. level are certainly at a disadvantage, and would be much more limited in practice areas when compared to the doctoral level graduates. Similar to other applied psychology specialties, school psychology training requires core coursework in the biological, social, individual difference, and cognitive–affective bases of behavior, as well as work in the general areas of assessment, interventions, consultation, and remediation (Fagan, 1985c; Goh, 1977). Specialized practicum and internship opportunities in clinical settings with children and families are also common training elements (Pryzwansky, 1971). In essence, it would appear that this training offers a solid foundation that could be applied across clients, services, and settings. Table 2.6 presents a list of professional activities that school psychologists are well prepared to offer.

Problem Solving Models and the Response to Intervention (RTI) Movement

Historically, individual or small-group student interventions have not significantly changed the gap between typically achieving students and low achieving students (D'Amato, Fletcher-Janzen, & Reynolds, 2005; D'Amato & Dean, 1987, 1989a). Special education services were initially developed with the idea that individualized instruction, tailored to meet the needs of students, could help low achieving students significantly increase academic achievement (Reynolds & Gutkin, 1999). However, this has not been the case. Often, children who enter special education programs do not exit these programs with increased academic knowledge or improved emotional status. Some have argued that special education was never very special at all (D'Amato & Dean, 1987), and that we never used our individual instructional knowledge base to truly offer children the type of services they needed (D'Amato, Fletcher-Janzen, & Reynolds, 2005). Whatever the case, a new movement was created to target children with academic/behavioral difficulties early on, and apply what some see as preventative measures. Called *Response to Intervention* (RTI), this is a multistep, preventative approach that systematically reviews data to make educational decisions targeting the curriculum, instruction, learner characteristics, and the student's environment to make changes and meet student needs (Witsken et al., 2008). Numerous authors have argued that this approach does not use current educational technologies and is in need of additional testing, but

Table 2.6   Human service activities with easy application to child, family, and educational settings

Assessment (Goh, 1977; Stewart, 1986)	**Neuropsychology** (Dean, 1982a)
Consultation (Pryzwansky, 1986; Ramage, 1979)	**Community Services** (Brantley, Reilly, Beach, Cody, Fields, & Lee, 1974; Granowsky & Davis, 1974)
Research (Dean, 1982b; Gray, 1963)	**Instruction** (National School Psychology In-service Training Network, 1984)
Counseling and Therapy (Hartshorne & Johnson, 1985)	**Mental Health Services** (Herman, Reinke, Parkin, Traylor, & Agarwal, 2009; Klosterman, 1974)
Systems Development (Dean, 1982b; Gray, 1963)	**Vocational Evaluations and Programing** (Hohenshil, 1974, 1979)
Behavioral Management (Gray, 1963)	**Multicultural Activities** (Gray, 1963)
Group Testing (Stewart, 1986)	**Personnel Development** (National School Psychology In-service Training Network, 1984)
Systemic Change (Plas, 1986; Talley et al., 1996)	**Group Interventions** (Kehle, Bray & Perusse, 2009)
Classroom Interventions (Work & Choi, 2005; Witsken et al., 2008)	**Problem-Solving/Response to Intervention** (Reynolds & Shaywitz, 2009a, 2009b)
Individual Program Planning (Stewart, 1986)	**Program Evaluation** (Granger & Campbell, 1977)

whatever the case, it is currently being implemented in hundreds of schools across the United States (Reynolds & Shaywitz, 2009a, 2009b).

The reauthorizations of IDEA 2004 focused much less on the need for psychological testing, stating that children would no longer be required to demonstrate an intelligence–achievement discrepancy to become eligible to receive some special education academic/learning services. Additionally, IDEA made clear that districts could use a problem solving process based on scientifically grounded interventions as part of the initial intervention plan for students. Thus, no formal psychological examination is now needed before these interventions can be implemented. These changes have caused districts to reexamine how they determine eligibility, and have sanctioned the use of an RTI approach in evaluation. As such, it seems like some districts have already abandoned the use of school psychologists to evaluate children and look for educational processing discrepancies. While some see this change as encouraging, freeing up school psychologists to perform other tasks, others worry that children with severe psychoeducational problems will not receive the psychological examinations required to help teachers and parents understand the child's unique, often biologically based, educational needs

(D'Amato, Fletcher-Janzen, & Reynolds, 2005; Reynolds & Shaywitz, 2009a, 2009b; Witsken et al., 2008).

As a result, current education services focus on intervention instead of evaluation for special education. An RTI model can be used schoolwide to improve student outcomes. The RTI model usually involves different steps, or tiers, based on the severity of student problems. These steps could include schoolwide universal screening, curriculum based reviews, and progress monitoring. A second tier focuses on identifying students who are below established cutoffs. Thus, monitoring becomes more targeted, and occurs regularly to track student learning growth. At this point, the first step of the problem solving model would be used, and groups might be formed according to intensive, strategic, and benchmark levels, thereby individualizing instruction to meet student needs.

The next tier involves a more focused plan for the children not responding to intervention. At this level, the team may want to meet to look at the student's progress in comparison to school/classroom norms, and review other data. Progress monitoring is conducted weekly, and a targeted, research-based intensive intervention should be implemented.

Now the team begins to look more deeply into the problem, analyzing it via an error analysis of work products, observations, and interviews with children and teachers. Also, communication with parents about expectations will help define the issue, analyze student difficulties, and individualize the intervention to student needs. The last level of the model is consideration of special education services. At this point the team often believes the student has significant issues that require a comprehensive psychological evaluation.

A Comprehensive School Psychologists Role Example from the Public Schools

Most typically, extremely comprehensive roles are demonstrated outside the public schools in nontraditional settings. But, in some cases, school districts have worked to offer the same comprehensive services in public schools. How such a role could be practiced in the public schools was detailed by Nelson, Hoover, Young, Obrzut, D'Amato, and Copeland (2006). In this model, school psychologists were trained in what might traditionally be seen as assessment, counseling, child protection, neuropsychology, systems change, conflict resolution, peer tutoring, social/emotional development, and community oriented services. This was accomplished by way of a partnership between a NASP-approved and APA-accredited school psychology Ed.S. and Ph.D. programs at the University of Northern Colorado, and the Greeley-Weld Independent School District #6. In this model program, individual school social workers and school counselors were retrained, and then a school psychologist was assigned to every school building in order to provide comprehensive within-building psychological services. These services included affective education, peer tutoring, and peer counseling, as well as a cluster of other mental health related services. The school psychologist spent a great deal of time in the regular education classroom, working on helping to develop healthy children. Over the years, numerous articles and papers/posters were presented about some of these unique services. Some examples of work with students and school psychologists in the district are presented in Table 2.7. Dozens of other projects and papers were also completed, but space permits listing only a few of them.

Human Service Psychology

What will the future bring? It has been argued that the distinctive forces that previously shaped applied specialties are no longer evident (Bardon, 1983; Goldstein & Krasner, 1987; Levy, 1984, 1986). For example, school psychologists often practice family therapy, clinical psychologists provide vocational assessment, and counseling psychologists are involved with psychotherapy in state hospitals (Altmaier & Meyer, 1985; Cummings, 1979; Fitzgerald & Osipow, 1986; Trickett, 1984). Further developing this notion, Matarazzo (1987) has claimed there is *one* psychology, with no specialties but many applications. Stated differently, Levy (1984, 1986) has argued that the traditional specialties, as once conceptualized, are in danger of extinction.

Table 2.7   Sample research activities reported from a university–school training partnership

- Understanding and preventing inhalant abuse among children and adolescents in schools. Communiqué, 25, 31–32. Newspaper of NASP. (Gunning & D'Amato, 1995).

- *Enhancing self-esteem and life competencies through affective education: THE SHOOTING STARS program.* (Crawford & D'Amato, 1999).

- *Changing society one classroom at a time: A school-wide approach to the development of social and emotional skills* (Balcerzak & D'Amato, 2000a).

- *Enhancing self-esteem and life competencies through family-school partnerships.* (Crawford & D'Amato, 2000).

- *Systemic change, it happens: Integrating character education and peer mediation into the curriculum* (Balcerzak & D'Amato, 2000b).

- *Establishing caring school communities based on conflict resolution program outcomes* (Obrzut, Davis, & D'Amato, 2002).

- *How to develop successful school and home interventions to service children and youth with TBI.* (Zafiris, Thomas-Duckwitz, & D'Amato, 2007)

- *Mary had a little impairment: Understanding and intervening with students who have traumatic brain injuries* (D'Amato, 2007).

They are so blurred that although current names remain (e.g., clinical psychology), the coherence and distinctiveness that may once have characterized these major areas is now absent (Levy, 1984, 1986; Fox, 1982; Trickett, 1984). This interpretation is consistent with the notion that clinical psychology, counseling psychology, and school psychology have all focused on role and guild issues instead of concerning themselves with an empirical foundation for training and practice (D'Amato & Dean, 1989b; Fox, 1982; Levy, 1986; Oakland, 1986; Routh, Schroeder, & Koocher, 1983). The issues within these specialty areas are further separated by distinct divisions within the APA. In place of integrated psychology services, we seem to have hybrids of specialty areas (e.g., clinical child psychology, pediatric psychology, clinical child neuropsychology). Keeping abreast of recent developments across related human service fields becomes a dilemma.

With this patchwork as a backdrop, Levy (1984) has argued convincingly for a merger of applied specialties into human services psychology. This reconceptualization would defined applied psychology "so as to include all professional psychology knowledge concerned with the treatment and prevention of psychological and physical disorders" (p. 490). The rationale here is to provide a wide band of services by clinically trained practitioners—which is, of course, consistent with Witmer's notions (Bardon & Bennett, 1974; Gray, 1963; Witmer, 1907). In concert with Levy's (1984) notion of human services psychology, recent occupational and employment analysis has shown the growth and development of some rather specialized areas (e.g., clinical neuropsychology, behavioral medicine) that cross traditional clinical, counseling, and school psychology boundaries in training and application (D'Amato, Fletcher-Janzen, & Reynolds, 2005; Dean, 1982a, 1986). A case in point is the considerable interest shown recently in clinical neuropsychology. Not only has there been growth in professional organizations, publications, and related training, but a concomitant increase has occurred in available positions (D'Amato & Dean, 1988; D'Amato, Fletcher-Janzen, & Reynolds, 2005; D'Amato & Hartlage, 2008). Of interest here is the fact that training in clinical neuropsychology can be found in clinical, counseling and school psychology programs. Thus, it seems that currently, the applied psychology specialties find it difficult to adapt *differently* to the unique needs of both individuals and systems. For example, Fagan (1985c) reported data from school psychology doctoral programs that offer specialization areas (e.g.,

behavioral medicine, clinical psychology, therapeutic intervention, research, organizational development) that would seem more closely aligned to programs in clinical or counseling psychology than to school psychology. Such confusion emphasizes either the need for further specialization areas within applied psychology, focusing on applied services in specific areas, or the need for a more general approach in the training of applied service psychologists.

Cross fertilization between traditional specialties (i.e., school, counseling, clinical) and other specialization/concentration areas would seem to offer a stronger applied psychology in general. It can be readily seen that growth in subareas like rehabilitation psychology and clinical neuropsychology offers promise for the development of effective school programs for students with emotional, physical, and learning disabilities. These skills would add much to the school psychologist's functioning. It would seem that applied psychology could first offer generic training for all human service psychologists, followed by more highly specialized training in specific areas. Stated differently, students could be trained in an Applied Psychology Ph.D. program, and then could specialize in a single focal area or a few areas. These areas could relate to *age groups* (e.g., perinatal/early childhood psychology, child/adolescent psychology, adult psychology, geriatric psychology), *specific areas of study* (neuropsychology, behavioral medicine, rehabilitation psychology, health psychology), and/or *areas of practice/application* (family psychology, community psychology, substance abuse psychology). Such distinctions would clarify which services psychologists would be trained to offer, and could be applicable to a variety of settings. Hynd and Reynolds (2005) have argued that it is time for school neuropsychology to become a specialty area. This would represent a merging of clinical child neuropsychology with school psychology. Thus, individuals would be fully trained in both disciplines. It seems like psychologists may need to become more specialized, following an approach similar to medical training. Should professional psychologists train for three years in general psychology and then select two from perhaps eight specialty areas (e.g., family psychology, school neuropsychology, health psychology, geriatric psychology)? Fagan and Wise (2007) have reported that the most popular subspecialty areas (specializations within doctoral school psychology programs) are (1) behavioral assessment and intervention, (2) consultation, (3) neuropsychology, (4) preschool and early childhood, and (5) prevention. This, and many other related discussions, led to the Futures Conference.

The Futures Conference

In 2002, a school psychology "Futures Conference" was held in Indianapolis and televised (via telecom video) to numerous sites, mostly across the United States. After so many years with no conferences, some school psychology leadership, including leaders from both Division 16 of the APA and leaders from NASP, believed it was time to reconsider many of the issues that had been previously discussed. Leaders also believed that the public schools were in dire need of direction, and that school psychologists could help lead the way for widespread, systemic school change. However, what was most unique compared to other school psychology conferences was the interactive e-conference, connecting indi-

viduals in real time who could listen to presentations, discuss present and future needs, set goals, and devise plans for the future of the field. Participants were able to ask questions from experts thousands of miles apart (D'Amato, Sheridan, Phelps & Lopez, 2004). Additionally, after the conference a leadership committee was created to continue collaboration and implementation (Dawson, Cummings, Harrison, Short, Gorin, & Palomares, 2003). Committees continue to work on these goals, and system change will be slow but, hopefully, forthcoming. Do you want to be part of the change? Elect to become a history maker. Table 2.8 presents 37 activities you could use to become a history maker.

Table 2.8   How to become a school psychology history maker

1. Complete your doctorate in school psychologist.
2. Change the life of a child, peer, parent, teacher, or school staff.
3. Restructure psychological services to make systemic district changes.
4. Partner with a university and school to impact your community.
5. Join APA, NASP, and your two state organizations affiliated with them.
6. Join a professional association related to an interest area you have (e.g., the *National Academy of Neuropsychology*).
7. Join a NASP interest group in an area of specialization (e.g., neuropsychology) and participate in the on-line discussion forum.
8. Become active in APA and NASP and join and work on professional committees.
9. Write an article for your *state association* newsletter.
10. Write an article for APA's *The School Psychologist* or NASP's *Communiqué* newspaper.
11. Serve in academia so you can train school psychologists.
12. Become director of a NASP-approved or APA-accredited school psychology program.
13. Work to start a new school psychology program.
14. Work to help a program become accredited or approved.
15. Volunteer to serve as an adjunct faculty or clinical supervisor for a local university.
16. Conduct research in your schools to develop empirically-validated interventions.
17. Present the results of your research at your state convention and/or APA or NASP.
18. Publish the results of your research.
19. Run for an office in APA Division 16 or NASP.
20. Publish articles in all school psychology journals.
21. Write a book.
22. Serve as the editor of a book.
23. Become an ad hoc reviewer for a school psychology journal.

(continued)

Table 2.8 (Cont'd) How to become a school psychology history changer

24. Serve on the editorial board of a school psychology journal.

25. Become an associate editor of a school psychology journal.

26. Become editor-in-chief of a school psychology journal.

27. Write a chapter in the *Oxford Handbook of School Psychology* or other classic school psychology books.

28. Train as an accreditation reviewer for APA in school psychology and review programs regularly.

29. Train as a program reviewer for NASP and review programs regularly.

30. Speak regularly to groups of parents in your community.

31. Provide in-services to teachers in your district.

32. Volunteer to write an article for your local parent-school organization or newspaper.

33. Apply to become a Fulbright Scholar to impact another country and yourself.

34. Become an APA Fellow in School Psychology.

35. Become a Nationally Certified School Psychologist.

36. Become a Diplomate (ABPP) in School Psychology.

37. Work overseas to change the world.

As part of the preservation of the Futures Conference, NASP and APA both published the convention proceedings in their respective journals (*School Psychology Quarterly* and *School Psychology Review*; see Sheridan & D'Amato, 2003) in an effort to reach *all* school psychologists. This represented a unique collaboration between two organizations, which had never been attempted before. Special issues were also published considering related issues in *Psychology in the Schools* and in the *Journal of Educational and Psychological Consultation* (see D'Amato, Sheridan, Phelps, & Lopez, 2004 for an introduction and overview).

In their introduction to the *School Psychology Quarterly/School Psychology Review* "Futures Special Issue," Sheridan and D'Amato (2003; the current journal editors at that time), stated what they believed needed to be done to help solve the many school, child, and family related issues that currently plague society. They stated that school psychologists could solve many of our pressing problems if they would:

(a) focus on prevention and youth development in place of assessment or diagnosis;

(b) increase collaboration with educators and other child service specialties;

(c) integrate computerized technology into prevention and intervention activities;

(d) increase home–school collaboration;

(e) develop culturally sensitive and culturally appropriate services;

(f) focus on problem-solving models and professional flexibility;

(g) focus on indirect psychological service models;

(h) work to enhance the development, health, and mental health of all children;

(i) decrease special education service involvement and increase regular education service participation;

(j) become educational curriculum and program evaluation experts;

(k) serve as safe school initiative coordinators;

(l) serve as performance assessment and outcome specialists;

(m) develop self-reflection and recursion; and

(n) become proactive in place of being reactive. (p. 353–354).

As mentioned several times before in this chapter, the role of the school psychologist should be ever-changing, since the needs of children, families, and teachers are fluid and increasing. As a result of the conference, strategies addressing several areas emerged and are presented in Table 2.9 as five main outcomes. Committees have been developed that are working to implement these plans and make these goals a reality. (Dawson et al., 2003).

Table 2.9 Futures conference 2002: priority goals

Outcome	Goal
Outcome 1: Improved Academic Competence for All Children	
Advocacy and Public Policy	Goal A: Advocate for universal early prevention and intervention programs that emphasize language, cognitive, and social/emotional development and are placed in the context of ethnicity, socioeconomic status, gender, and language.
Practice	Goal B: Ensure that assessment practices of school psychologists are empirically linked to strategies to improve academic performance and that those assessment practices account for the influence of ethnicity, SES, gender and language on learning outcomes.
Preservice Training Inservice Training	Goal C: Develop and implement preservice and inservice training for school psychologists related to universal early prevention and intervention programs.
Outcome 2 : Improved Social–Emotional Functioning for All Children	
Advocacy and Public Policy	Goal A: Promote the availability of a comprehensive range of services, from supportive and inclusive placements through interim alternative placements, for students with severe emotional and behavioral disorders.
Collaboration and Communication	Goal B: Educate all stakeholders about the importance of social/emotional competence for children.
Practice	Goal C: Ensure that school psychologists develop a systematic plan in all schools to reduce social/emotional barriers to learning.
Outcome 3: Enhanced Family–School Partnerships and Parental Involvement in Schools	
Research and Knowledge Base	Goal A: Identify evidence based models of effective family–school partnerships.
Practice	Goal B: Ensure that school psychologists engage in activities to change the culture of schooling by making families integral partners in the educational process of children.
Preservice Training	Goal C: Change preservice education and training of school psychologist candidates to infuse a focus on families as integral partners in the educational process.
Outcome 4: More Effective Education and Instruction for All Learners	
Research and Knowledge Base	Goal A: Identify key components of effective instruction of all learners, including evidence based approaches to prevention and early intervention for learning problems.
Inservice Training	Goal B: Provide inservice training for school psychologists in the use of a data-based problem solving model to implement evidence based instruction and interventions.
Preservice and Inservice Training	Goal C: Implement a national preservice and inservice training initiative for school psychologists regarding effective instruction.
Outcome 5: Increased child and family services in schools that promote health and mental health and are integrated with community services	
Practice	Goal A: Define and promote population-based service delivery in schools and school psychology.
Inservice Training	Goal B: Prepare current practitioners to implement a public health model.
Preservice Training	Goal C: Prepare future practitioners to implement a public health model.

Reprinted with permission of the American Psychological Association/National Association of School Psychologists from (Dawson et al., 2003).

Conclusions

School psychology has a strong and unique history, and may well be the first applied specialty area developed. So too, the original definition and vision for the field encompassed a full gamut of settings and services. That is not to say that school psychology does not hold promise for the future of education, but only that it is an appropriate specialty both in and out of the schools. School psychology has the ability to help the public schools succeed in our dynamic, changing, global community. Since its inception, school psychology has been defined as a specific approach to solving problems, and not as a setting-specific service. As such, it seems apparent that school psychology is a viable specialty in most environments. For decades, numerous school psychologists have successfully demonstrated how to apply their skills in various traditional and nontraditional settings.

In sum, little has changed since Gray (1963) issued a challenge to the field almost a half century ago, asserting that school psychologists "today often find themselves in a morass of unmet demands for service, but they may look beyond it to a future that will not be easy, but that is full of broad possibilities for the creative and productive use of psychology…" (p. 388). Today, more than ever before, individuals in society are displaying needs at an immeasurable rate, and the educational enterprise is in desperate need of leadership. These needs, taken together with recent advances in the science of psychology, suggest the paramount role that school psychologists must play both in our present and future. For this to happen, school psychologists will need to go well beyond the schools, and work with more than just children, in order to facilitate the emotional and educational adjustment of all individuals in our problem-saturated society.

Acknowledgments

Part of this chapter is adopted from an earlier work from 1989 by R. C. D'Amato and R. S. Dean entitled: The past, present, and future of nontraditional school psychology. In R. C. D'Amato and R. S. Dean (Eds.), *The school psychologist in nontraditional settings: Integrating clients, services, and settings* (pp. 185–209). Hillsdale, NJ: Erlbaum. Adapted with permission

The authors would like to express appreciation for the indispensable help provided by two University of Macau Graduate Assistants, Ms. Ka Man Fong and Ms. Ka Meng Hong for assistance with this chapter.

References

Alpert, J. L. (1985). Change within a profession: Change, future, prevention, and school psychology. *American Psychologist, 40,* 1112–1121.

Altmaier, E. M., & Meyer, M. E. (Eds.). (1985). *Applied specialties in psychology.* New York: Random House.

American Psychological Association (2009a) *Highlights of Psychology's Evolution as a Profession.* Retrieved March 9, 2009 from http://www.apa.org/crsppp/evolution.html.

American Psychological Association. (2009b). From the list of accredited programs in school psychology. Retrieved August 2, 2009, from http://www.apa.org/ed/accreditation/schoolpsy.html

American Psychological Association. (2009c). From the list of accredited programs in combined professional-scientific psychology. Retrieved August 2, 2009, from http://www.apa.org/ed/accreditation/proscipsy.html.

American Psychological Association. (1981). Speciality guidelines for the delivery of services by school psychologists. *American Psychologist, 36*(6), 640–681.

Anastasi, A. (1988). *Psychological testing* (6th ed.). New York: Macmillan.

Balcerzak, A., & D'Amato, R. C. (2000a). Changing society one classroom at a time: A school-wide approach to the development of social and emotional skills. *Communiqué,* 6–9. Newspaper of the National Association of School Psychology.

Balcerzak, A. & D'Amato, R. C. (2000b). Systemic change, it happens: Integrating character education and peer mediation into the curriculum Poster presented at the 25th Annual Convention of the Colorado Society of School Psychologists, Breckenridge, CO.

Bardon, J. I. (1981a). Small group synthesis, Group C. *School Psychology Review, 10*(2), 297–306.

Bardon, J. I. (1981b). A personalized account of the development and status of school psychology. *Journal of School Psychology, 19,* 119–210.

Bardon, J. I. (1982). School psychology's dilemma: A proposal for its resolution. *Professional Psychology, 13* (6), 955–968.

Bardon, J. I. (1983). Psychology applied to education: A specialty in search of an identity. *American Psychologist, 38,* 185–196.

Bardon, J. I. (1989).The school psychologist as an applied educational psychologist. In R. C. D'Amato & R. S. Dean (Eds.), *The school psychologist in nontraditional settings: Integrating clients, services and settings* (pp. 1–32). Hillsdale, NJ: Erlbaum.

Bardon, J. I. (1994). Will the real school psychologist please stand up: Is the past a prologue for the future of school psychology? The identity of school psychology revisited. *School Psychology Review, 23*(4), 584–588.

Bardon, J. I., & Bennett, V. C. (1974). *School psychology* Englewood Cliffs, NJ: Prentice-Hall.

Bardon, J. I., Davis, L.T., Howard, C., & Myrick, C. C. (1982). Raising standards of practice in school psychology through the use of field-based training. *Journal of School Psychology, 20,* 86–85.

Benjamin, L. T., Durkin, M., Link, M., Vestal, M., & Acord, J. (1992). Wundt's American doctoral students. *American Psychologist, 47,* 123–131.

Bennett, V. C. (1970). Who is a school psychologist? (and what does he do?). *Journal of School Psychology, 8,* 166–171.

Bennett, V. C. (1985). School psychology. In E. M. Altamier & M. E. Meyer (Eds.), *Applied specialties in psychology* (pp. 129–144). New York: Random House.

Benson, A. J., & Hughes, J. (1985). Perceptions of role definition processes in school psychology: A national survey. *School Psychology Review, 14*, 64–74.

Bergan, J. R. (1979). *Behavioral consultation* Columbus, Ohio: Charles E. Merrill.

Boake, C. (2002). From the Binet-Simon to the Wechsler-Bellevue: Tracing the history of intelligence testing. *Journal of Clinical and Experimental Neuropsychology, 3*, 383–405.

Boring, E. G. (1950). *A history of experimental psychology* New York: Appleton-Century-Crofts, Inc.

Bower, E. M. (1955). *The school psychologist* Sacramento, CA: California State Department of Education.

Brantley, J. C. (1971). Psycho-educational centers and the school psychologist. *Psychology in the Schools, 8*, 313–318.

Brantley, J. C., Reilly, D. H., Beach, N. L., Cody, W., Fields, R., & Lee, H. (1974). School psychology: The intersection of community, training institution and the school system. *Psychology in the Schools, 11*, 28–32.

Bringmann, W. G. (1975). Wundt in Heidelberg 1845–1874. *Canadian Psychological Review, 16*, 124–129.

Brotemarkle, R. A. (Ed.). (1931). *Clinical psychology: Studies in honor of Lightner Witmer to commemorate the thirty-fifth anniversary of the founding of the first psychological clinic.* Philadelphia: University of Pennsylvania Press.

Brown, D., Pryzwansky, W. B., & Schulte, A. C. (1987). *Psychological consultation: Introduction to theory and practice.* Boston, MA: Allyn & Bacon.

Brown, D., Pryzwansky, W. B., & Schulte, A. C. (2006). *Psychological consultation: Introduction to theory and practice* (6th ed.). Boston, MA: Allyn & Bacon.

Brown, D. T., & Cardon, B. W. (1982). Section III: Synthesis and editorial comment. *School Psychology Review, 11*(2), 195–199.

Brown, D. T., Cardon, B. W., Coulter, W. A., & Meyers, J. (Eds.). (1982). The Olympia Proceedings, [Special issue]. *School Psychology Review, 11.*

Brown, D. T., & Minke, D. M. (1984). *Directory of school psychology training programs* Washington, D.C.: National Association of School Psychologists.

Brown, D. T., Sewall, T. J., & Lindstrom, J. P. (1977). *The handbook of certification/licensure requirement for school psychologists* Washington, D.C.: National Association of School Psychologists.

Caplan, G. (1970). *The theory and practice of mental health consultation.* New York: Basic Books.

Carlson, C, & Christenson, S. L. (2005). Evidence-based parent and family interventions in school psychology [Special Issue]. *School Psychology Quarterly, 20*(4).

Cohen, R. J., Montague, P., Nathanson, L S., & Swerdlik, M. E. (1988). *Psychological testing: An introduction to tests & measurement.* Mountain View, CA: Mayfield Publishing.

Collins, J. (1931). Lightner Witmer: A biological sketch. In R. S. Brotemarkle (Ed.), *Clinical Psychology: Studies in honor of Lightner Witmer to commemorate the thirty-fifth anniversary of the founding of the first psychological clinic* (pp. 3–9). Philadelphia: University of Pennsylvania Press.

Committee on training in clinical psychology, American Psychological Association. (1947). Recommended graduate training program in clinical psychology. *American Psychologist, 2*, 539–558.

Conoley, J. C. (1989). The school psychologist as a community/family service provider. In R. C. D'Amato & R. S. Dean (Eds.), *The school psychologist in nontraditional settings: Integrating clients, services, and settings* (pp. 33–65). Hillsdale, NJ: Erlbaum. Republished by Prospect Heights, IL: Waveland Press.

Conoley, J. C., & Conoley, C. W. (1981). *School consultation: A guide to practice and training* Elmsford, NY: Pergamon.

Conoley, J. C., & Gutkin, T. B. (1986). Educating school psychologists for the real world. *School Psychology Review, 15*, 451–465.

Conoley, J. C., & Gutkin, T. B. (1995). Why didn't—why doesn't—school psychology realize its promise? *Journal of School Psychology, 33*(3) 209–217.

Crawford, E. N., & D'Amato, R. C. (1999). Enhancing self-esteem and life competencies through affective education: The Shooting Stars program. *Communiqué,* 34–35. Newspaper of the National Association of School Psychologists.

Crawford, E. N., & D'Amato, R. C. (1999, October). *Affective education is effective education: The Shooting Stars Program.* Poster presented at the 24th Annual Convention of the Colorado Society of School Psychologists, Vail, CO.

Crawford, N. A., & D'Amato, R. C. (2000). Enhancing self-esteem and life competencies through family-school partnerships. Poster presented at the 32nd annual convention of the National Association of School Psychologists, New Orleans, LA.

Crawford, N. A., & D'Amato, R. C. (2000). *Enhancing self-esteem and emotional development through affective education.* Poster presented at the Academic Excellence Week Research Conference, University of Northern Colorado, Greeley, CO.

Cronbach, L .J. (1957). The two disciplines of scientific psychology. *American psychologist, 12*, 671–684.

Croog, S. H. (1947). Wundt and the fork: an appraisal of Wundt's folk psychology. *Social Forces, 25*(3), 263–269.

Cummings, N. (1979). The undoing of clinical psychology. *APA Monitor, 2.*

Cutts, N. E. (Ed.). (1955). *School psychologists at mid-century.* Washington DC: American Psychological Association.

D'Amato, R. C. (1985). Teacher Assistance Teams: A problem solving system that creates interventions. Presented at the 17th annual convention of the National Association of School Psychologists, Las Vegas, NV.

D'Amato, R C. (1990). A neuropsychological approach to school psychology. *School Psychology Quarterly, 5*, 141–160.

D'Amato, R. C. (2003). School psychology is not what it used to be: Thoughts from the new editor concerning our "futures" and *School Psychology Quarterly. School Psychology Quarterly, 18*, 3–12.

D'Amato, R. C. (2005a). PowerPoint lecture on understanding the history of school psychology: Unit 2, Part B. Presented at the University of Northern Colorado, Greeley, CO. Available on-line to students via Blackboard. Retrieved September 5, 2005.

D'Amato, R. C. (2007). Mary had a little impairment: Understanding and intervening with students who have traumatic brain injuries. Presented to the Weld-Greeley #6 Public Schools Association of School Psychologists, Greeley, CO.

D'Amato, R. C., Crepeau-Hobson, F. C., Huang, L. V., & Geil, M. (2005b). Ecological neuropsychology: An alternative to the deficit model for conceptualizing and serving students with Learning Disabilities. *Neuropsychology Review, 15*(2), 97–103.

D'Amato, R. C, & Dean, R. S. (1987). Psychological reports, individual education programs, and daily lesson plans: Are they related? *Professional School Psychology, 2*, 93–101.

D'Amato, R. C, & Dean, R. S. (1988). School psychology practice in a department of neurology. *School Psychology Review, 18*, 416–420.

D'Amato, R. C, & Dean, R. S. (1989a). The past, present and future of school psychology in nontraditional settings. In

R. C. D'Amato & R. S. Dean (Eds.), *The school psychologist in nontraditional settings: Integrating clients, services and settings* (pp. 185–190). Hillsdale, NJ: Erlbaum.

D'Amato, R. C., & Dean, R. S. (Eds.). (1989b). *The school psychologist in nontraditional settings: Integrating clients, services, and settings.* Hillsdale, NJ: Erlbaum

D'Amato, R. C. (Chair), Dean, R. S., Hughes, J. N., Harrison, P., McCoskey, G., Pryzwansky, W. B., & Hartlage, L. C. (1987). Nontraditional activities for school psychologists. *Proceedings of the National Association of School Psychologists 19th Annual Convention*, (pp. 96–97). New Orleans, LA: The National Association of School Psychologists.

D'Amato, R. C., Fletcher-Janzen, E., & Reynolds, C. R. (Eds.). (2005). *Handbook of school neuropsychology.* New York, NY: Wiley.

D'Amato, R. C., & Hartlage, L. C. (Eds.). (2008). *Essentials of neuropsychological assessment: Rehabilitation planning for intervention* (2nd ed.). New York: NY: Springer.

D'Amato, R. C., & Rothlisberg, B. A. (Eds.). (1992/1997). *Psychological perspectives on intervention: A case study approach to prescriptions for change.* Republished by Waveland Press: Prospect Heights, IL.

D'Amato, R. C., Rothlisberg, B. A., & Leu Work, P. H. (1999). Neuropsychological assessment for intervention. In T. B. Gutkin and C. R. Reynolds (Eds.), *Handbook of school psychology* (3rd ed., pp. 452–475). New York: Wiley.

D'Amato, R., C., Sheridan, S., M., Phelps, L., & Lopez, E., C. (2004). Psychology in the schools, school psychology review, school psychology quarterly, and journal of educational and psychological consultation editors collaborate to chart school psychology's past, present, and "futures." *Journal of Educational and Psychological Consultation*, 233–238.

Dawson, M., Cummings, J.,A., Harrison, L., Short, R., J., Gorin, S., & Palomares, R. (2003). The 2002 multisite conference on the future of school psychology: Next steps. *School Psychology Quarterly*, 497–509

Dean, R. S. (1980). A comparison of preservice and experienced teachers' perceptions of the school psychologist. *Journal of School Psychology*, 18, 283–289.

Dean, R. S. (1982a). Neuropsychological assessment. In T. Kratochwill (Ed.), *Advances in school psychology (Vol. 2)* (pp. 171–201). Hillsdale, NJ: Lawrence Erlbaum Associates.

Dean, R. S. (1982b). Providing psychological services to school-age children. In G. D. Miller (Ed.), *Human support services for children* (pp. 98–123). St. Paul, Minnesota: State Department of Education.

Dean, R. S. (1983). The emperor had no clothes and Olympia no substance. *The School Psychologist*, 37(3), 3.

Dimond, R.E., Havens, R. A., Rathrow, S., & Colliver, J. A. (1977). Employment characteristics of subdoctoral clinical psychologists. *Professional Psychology*, 8, 116–121.

Doll, B. (1996). Becoming essential: Rethinking the practice of school psychology. In R. C. Talley, T. Kubiszyn, M. Brassard, & R. J. Short, (Eds.). *Making psychologists in schools indispensable: Critical questions and emerging perspectives*, pp. 23–29. Washington, DC: American Psychological Association.

Education Commission of the States, Task force on education for economic growth. (1983). *Action for excellence: A comprehensive plan to improve our nation's schools.* Denver, CO: Author.

Eiserer, P. E. (1963). *The school psychologist.* Washington, D.C.: Center for Applied Research in Education.

Fagan, T. K. (1985a). Sources for the delivery of school psychological services during 1890–1930. *School Psychology Review*, 14, 378–382.

Fagan, T. K. (1985b). The quantitative growth of school psychology programs in the United States. *School Psychology Review*, 14, 121–124.

Fagan, T. K. (1985c). Best practices in the training of school psychologists: Considerations for trainers, prospective entry-level and advanced students. In A. Thomas & J. Grimes (Eds.), *Best practices in school psychology.* (pp. 125–141). Kent, Ohio: The National Association of School Psychologists.

Fagan, T. K. (1986a). The historical origins and & growth of programs to prepare school, psychologists in the United States. *Journal of School Psychology*, 24, 9–22.

Fagan, T. K. (1986b). School psychology's dilemma: Reappraising solutions and directing attention to the future. *American Psychologist*, .41, 851–861.

Fagan, T. K. (1996). A history if division 16 (school psychology): Running twice as fast. In D. A. Dewsbury (Ed.), *Unification through division: Histories of the divisions of the American Psychological Association.* (Vol. 1, pp. 101–135). Washington DC: American Psychological Association.

Fagan, T. K. (2005). The 50th anniversary of the Thayer conference: Historical perspectives and accomplishments. *School Psychology Quarterly*, 20(3), 224–251.

Fagan, T. K., & Wise, P.S. (1994). *School psychology: Past, present, and future.* White Plains, NY: Longman.

Fagan, T. K., & Wise, P. S. (2007). *School psychology: Past, present and future.* Washington, D.C.: National Association of School Psychologists.

Feldman, E. S. & Kratochwill, T. R. (2003). Problem solving consultation in schools: Past, present, and future directions. *The Behavior Analyst Today*, 4(3), 271–366.

Fein, L G. (1974). *The changing school scene: Challenge to psychology.* New York: Wiley.

Fernberger, S. W. (1931). History of the psychological clinic. In R. A. Brotemarkle (Ed.), *Clinical psychology: Studies in honor of Lightner Witmer to commemorate the thirty-fifth anniversary of the founding of the first psychological clinic* (pp. 10–36). Philadelphia: University of Pennsylvania Press.

Fitzgerald, L. F., & Osipow, S. H. (1986). An occupational analysis of counseling psychology: How special is the specialty? *American Psychologists*, 41, 535–544.

Flanagan, D. P., & Kaufman, A. S. (2004). *Essentials of WISC-IV assessment.* Hoboken, NJ: Wiley & Sons.

Flanagan, D. P., McGrew, K. S., & Ortiz, S. O. (2000). *The Wechsler intelligence scales and Gf-Gc theory: A contemporary approach to interpretation.* Needham Heights, MA: Allyn & Bacon.

Fox, R. E. (1982). The need for a reorientation of clinical psychology. *American Psychologist*, 37, 1051–1057.

French, J. L., & McCloskey, G. (1980). Characteristics of doctoral and nondoctoral school psychology programs: Their implications for the entry-level doctorate. *Journal of School Psychology*, 18, 247–255.

Gaddes, W. H., & Edgell, D. (1994). *Learning disabilities and brain function: A neuropsychological approach* (2nd ed.). New York: Springer-Verlag.

Garfield, S. L (1985). Clinical psychology. In E. M. Altmaier & M. E. Meyer (Eds.), *Applied specialties in psychology* (pp. 19–44). New York: Random House.

Giebink, J. W., & Ringness, T. A. (1970). On the relevancy of training in school psychology. *Journal of School Psychology*, 8, 43–47.

Gilmore, G. E., & Chandy, J. M. (1973). Educators describe the school psychologist. *Psychology in the Schools, 10*, 397–403.

Goh, D. S. (1977). Graduate training in school psychology. *Journal of School Psychology, 15*, 207–218.

Goldstein, A. P., & Krasner, L. (Eds.). (1987). *Modern applied psychology.* New York: Pergamon.

Goldston, S. E. (1986). Primary prevention: Historical perspectives and a blueprint for action. *American Psychologist, 41*, 453–460.

Goodlad. J. I. (1979). Can our schools get better? *Phi Delta Kappan, 60*, 342–347.

Gould, S. A. (1996). *The mismeasure of man* New York, NY: W. W. Norton & Company, Inc.

Granger, R. C., & Campbell, P. B. (1977). The school psychologist as program evaluator. *Journal of School psychology, 15*, 174–181.

Granowsky, S., & Davis, L. T. (1974). Three alternative roles for the school psychologist. *Psychology in the Schools, 11*, 415–421.

Gray, S. W. (1963). *The psychologist in the schools.* New York: Holt, Rienhart and Winston.

Greenwood, J. D. (1999). From *VoÈ lkerpsychologie* to cultural psychology: the once and future discipline? *Philosophical Psychology, 12*(4), 503-515.

Greenwood, J. D. (2003). Wundt, Völkerpsychologie, and experimental social psychology. *History of Psychology, 6*(1), 70–88.

Gutkin T. G. & Reynolds, C. R. (Eds.) (2008). *Handbook of School Psychology* (4th ed.). New York: Wiley.

Gunning, M. P., & D'Amato, R. C. (1996). Understanding and preventing inhalant abuse among children and adolescents in schools. *Communiqué, 25*, 31-32. Newspaper of the National Association of School Psychologists.

Halberstadt-Freud, H. C. (*1996*). Studies on Hysteria, one hundred years on: A century of psychoanalysis. *International Journal of Psychoanalysis, 77*, 983–996.

Hall, M. E. (1949). Current employment requirements of school psychologists. *American Psychologist, 4*, 519–525.

Hannah, M., & Midlarsky, E. (1985, April). Assessing the child–classroom "fit"—an ecological approach to measurement Paper presented at the 17th annual convention of the National Association of School Psychologists, Las Vegas, NV.

Harris, J. (1980). The evolution of school psychology. Arizona State University, unpublished manuscript.

Harries, J. T. (1982). Perspectives on the private practice of school psychology. In C. R. Reynolds & T. B. Gutkin (Eds.), *The handbook of school psychology* (pp. 688–720). New York: Wiley.

Harrison, P. L., & McCloskey, G. (1989). School psychology applied to business. In R. C. D'Amato and R. S. Dean (Eds.), *The school psychology in nontraditional settings: Integrating clients, services, and settings* (pp. 107–137). Hillsdale, NJ: Erlbaum.

Hart, S. (1982). Section VII: Synthesis of Olympia Conference. *School Psychology Review, 11*(2), 186–188.

Hartlage, L. C. (1971). A look at models for the training of school psychologists. *Psychology in the Schools, 8*, 304–306.

Hartlage, L. C., & Hartlage, P. L. (1978). Clinical consultation to pediatric neurology and developmental pediatrics. *Journal of Clinical Child Psychology, 7*, 52–53.

Hartshorne, T. S., & Johnson, M. C. (1985). The actual and preferred roles of the school psychologist according to secondary school administrators. *Journal of School Psychology, 23*, 241–246.

Helmholtz von, H., & Cahan, D. (1995). *Science and culture: Popular and philosophical essays.* Chicago, IL: University of Chicago Press.

Hermann von Helmholtz (2009). In *Wikipedia, the free encyclopedia.* Retrieved June 13, 2009, from http://en.wikipedia.org/wiki/Helmholtz

Herman, K. C., Reinke, W. M., Parkin, J, Traylor, K. B., & Agarwal, G. (2009). Childhood depression: Rethinking the role of the school. *Psychology in the Schools, 45*(5), 433–446.

Herron, W. G., Green, M., Guild, M., Smith, A., &: Kantor, R. E. (1970). *Contemporary school psychology* Scranton, PA: Intext Educational Publishers.

Hilke, J. L., & Brantley, J. C. (1982). The specialist–doctoral controversy: Some realities of training, practice, and advocacy. *Professional Psychology, 13*, 634–638.

Hirst, W. E. (1963). *Know your school psychologist.* New York: Grune & Stratton.

Hobbs, N. (1964). Mental health's third revolution. *American Journal of Orthopsychiatry, 34*, 822–833.

Hobbs, N. (1968). Reeducation, reality and community responsibility. In J. W. Carter (Ed.), *Research contributions from psychology to community mental health.* New York: Behavioral Publications.

Hobbs, N. (1976). *Mental health, families, and children.* Austin: Hogg Foundation for Mental Health.

Hobbs, N. (1978). Families, schools, and communities: An ecosystem for children. *Teachers College Record, 79*, 756–766.

Hohenshil, T. H. (1974). The vocational school psychologist—a specialty in quest of a training program. *Psychology in the Schools, 11*, 16–18.

Hohenshil, T. H. (1979). Adulthood: New frontier for vocational school psychology. *School Psychology Digest, 8*, 193–198.

Holt, F. D., & Kicklighter, R. H. (1971). *Psychological services in the schools: Readings in preparation, organization and practice* Dubuque, IA: Brown.

Hughes, J. N., &: Benson, A. J. (1986). University clinics as field placements in school psychology: A national survey. *Professional School Psychology, 1*, 131–142.

Hyman, I. A. (1979a). Psychology, educational and schooling: Social policy implications in the lives of children and youth. *American Psychologist, 34*, 1024–1029.

Hyman, I. A. (1979b). Will the real school psychologist please stand up? A struggle of jurisdictional imperialism. *School Psychology Digest, 8*, 174–180.

Hynd, G. W. (1983). *The school psychologist: An introduction* Syracuse, NY: Syracuse University Press.

Hynd, G. W., & Reynolds. C. R. (2005). School neuropsychology: The evaluation of a specialty in School Psychology. In R. C. D'Amato, E. Flecher-Janzen, & C. R. Reynolds (Eds.). *Handbook of school neuropsychology* (pp. 3–14). Hoboken, NJ: Wiley.

Jacob, S., & Hartshorne, T. S. (1991). *Ethics and law for school psychologists.* Hoboken, NJ: Wiley.

Jacob, S., & Hartshorne, T. S. (2003). Ethical–legal issues in the education of pupils with disabilities under IDEA. In *Ethics and law for school psychologists* (4th ed., pp. 112–166). Hoboken, NJ: Wiley.

Jacob, S., & Hartshorne, T. S. (2007). *Ethics and law for school psychologists.* (5th ed.). Hoboken, NJ: Wiley.

Jastrow, J. (1935). Has psychology failed? *American Scholar, 4* (3), 261–269.

Kehle, T. J., Bray, M. A., & Perusse, R. (2009). Introduction to individual and group counseling in the practice of school psychology [Special Issue]. *Psychology in the Schools, 46*(3), 197–198.

Kennedy, D. A. (1971). A practical approach to school psychology. *Journal of School Psychology, 9,* 484–489.

Klosterman, D. (1974). The role of the school psychologist in a community mental health center. *Psychology in the Schools,* 11, 269–274.

Korman, M. (1974). National conference on levels and patterns of professional training in psychology: The major themes. *American Psychologist, 29,* 441–49.

Lambert, N. M. (1973). The school psychologist as a source of power and influence. *Journal of School Psychology, 11,* 245–250.

Leahey, T. H. (1980). *A history of psychology* Englewood Cliffs, NJ: Prentice-Hall.

Levy, L. H. (1984). The metamorphosis of clinical psychology: Toward a new charter as human services psychology. *American Psychologist, 39,* 486–494.

Levy, L. H. (1986). Reflections on "professional school psychology". *Professional School Psychology, 1,* 35–39.

Lewin, K. (1936). *Principles of topological psychology* New York: McGraw-Hill.

Magary, J. F. (1967). *School psychological services: In theory and practice* Englewood Cliffs, NJ: Prentice-Hall.

Matarazzo, J. D. (1987). There is only one psychology, no specialties, but many applications. *American Psychologist, 42,* 893–903.

McReynolds, P. (1987). Lightner Witmer: Little-known founder of clinical psychology. *American Psychologist, 42,* 849–858.

Meacham, M. L., &: Peckham, P. D. (1978). School psychologists at three-quarters century: Congruence between training, practice, preferred role and competence. *Journal of School Psychology, 16,* 195–206.

Mead, M. (1961). *Cooperation to competition among primitive peoples* Boston: Beacon Press.

Merrell, K. W., Ervin, R. A., & Gimpel, G. A. (2006). *School psychology for the 21st century: Foundations and practices.* New York: Guilford.

Meehl, P. E. (1954). *Clinical versus statistical prediction: A theoretical analysis and a review of the evidence* Minneapolis: University of Minnesota Press.

Mischel, W., Shoda, Y., & Ayduk, O. (2008). *Introduction to personality.* (8th ed.). Wiley.

Montgomery, M. D., & Paul, J. L (1982). Ecological theory and practice. In J. L Paul & B. C. Epanchin (Eds.), *Emotional disturbance in children* (pp. 213–241). Columbus, OH: Merrill.

Morris, R. M., & Morris, Y. P. (1989). School psychology in residential treatment facilities. In R. C. D'Amato and R. S. Dean (Eds.), *The school psychology in nontraditional settings: Integrating clients, services, and settings* (pp. 159–184). Hillsdale, NJ: Erlbaum.

Mullen, F. A. (1981). School psychology in the USA: Reminiscenses of its origin. *Journal of School Psychology, 19,* 103–119.

Myers, D. G. (2010). *Psychology* (9th ed.). New York, NY: Worth Publishers.

National Association of School Psychologists. (1984). *Standards for training and field placement programs in school psychology* Washington, D.C.: NASP.

National Commission on Excellence in Education. (1983). *A nation at risk: The imperative for educational reform.* Washington, DC: U. S. Government Printing Office.

National School Psychology In-service Training Network. (1984). *School psychology: A blueprint for training and practice.* Minneapolis, MN: Author.

Nelson, E. (1976). Interactional psychology. In D. Magnusson & N. Endler (Eds.), *Personality at the crossroads: Current issues in interactional psychology* (pp. 99–111). Hillsdale. NJ: Erlbaum.

Nelson, R. B., Hoover, M., Young, M., Obrzut, A., D'Amato, R. C., & Copeland, E. P. (2006). Integrated psychological services in the Greeley-Evans public schools. *School Psychology Quarterly, 21,* 445–467.

Newland, T. E. (1970). The search for the new: Frenzied, faddish, or fundamental? *Journal of School Psychology, 8,* 242–244.

Newland, T. E. (1981). School psychology—observations and reminiscence. *Journal of School Psychology, 19,* 4–20.

Oakland, T. D. (1986). Professionalism within school psychology. *Professional School Psychology, 1,* 9–27.

Obrzut, A., Davis, A. S., & D'Amato, R. C. (2002, February). Establishing caring school communities based on conflict resolution program outcomes. Poster presented at the 34th annual convention of the National Association of School Psychologists, Chicago, IL.

Packard, V. (1983). *Our endangered children: Growing up in a changing world.* Boston: Little Brown.

Petition for Reaffirmation of the Specialty of School Psychology. (2009). Retrieved March 23, 2009, from www.apa.org/crsppp/specialty_school.pdf

Plas, J. M. (1986). *Systems psychology in the schools.* New York, NY: Pergamon.

President's Commission on Mental Health. (1978). *Report to the president* (Vol. 1). Washington, D.C.: Government Printing Office.

Pryzwansky, W. B. (1971). Practicum training in the school setting. *Psychology in the Schools, 15,* 307–313.

Pryzwansky, W. B. (1986). Indirect service delivery: Considerations for future research in consultation. *School Psychology Review, 15,* 479–488.

Pryzwansky, W. B. (1989). Private practice as an alternative setting for school psychologists. In R. C. D'Amato and R. S. Dean (Eds.), *The school psychology in nontraditional settings: Integrating clients, services, and settings* (pp. 76–87). Hillsdale, NJ: Erlbaum.

Raimy, V. C. (Ed.). (1950). *Training in clinical psychology.* Englewood Cliffs, NJ: Prentice-Hall.

Ramage, J. C. (1979). National survey of school psychologists: Update. *School Psychology Digest, 8,* 153–161.

Rappaport, J. (1977). *Community psychology: Values, research and action* New York: Holt, Rinehart & Winston.

Reger, R. (1965). *School psychology* Springfield, IL: Charles C. Thomas.

Reilly, D. H. (1973). School psychology: View from the second generation. *Psychology in the Schools, 10,* 151–155.

Reilly, D. H. (1974). A conceptual model for school psychology. *Psychology in the Schools, 11,* 165–170.

Reynolds, C. R., & Gutkin, T. B. (Eds.). (1982). *The handbook of school psychology.* New York: Wiley.

Reynolds, C. R., & Gutkin, T. B. (Eds.). (1999). *The handbook of school psychology* (3rd ed.). New York: Wiley.

Reynolds, C. R., Gutkin, T. B., Elliott, S. N., & Witt, J. C. (1984). *School psychology: Essentials of theory and practice* New York: Wiley.

Reynolds, C. R., & Shaywitz, S. E. (2009a). Response to intervention: ready or not? Or, from wait-to-fail to watch-them-fail. *School Psychology Quarterly, 24*(2), 130–145.

Reynolds, C. R., & Shaywitz, S. E. (2009b). Response to intervention and remediation, perhaps. Diagnosis, no. *Child Development Perspectives, 3*(1), 44–47.

Roid, G. H. & Barram, R. A. (2004). *Essentials of Stanford-Binet intelligence scales (SB5) assessment* Hoboken, NJ: Wiley & Sons.

Rosenfield, S. (1981). Small group synthesis, Group A. *School Psychology Review, 10*(2), 285 – 289.

Routh, D. K., Schroeder, C. S., & Koocher, G. P. (1983). Psychology and primary health care for children. *American Psychologists, 38,* 95–98.

Ruckhaber, C. J. (1970). An elementary school mental health program: The stark school model. *Journal of School Psychology, 8,* 197–201.

Saklofske, D. H., Lynne-Beal, A., Weiss, L., & Coalson, D. (2003). The Wechsler scales for assessing children's intelligence: Past to present. In J. Georgas, (2003) *Culture and children's intelligence: Cross- cultural analysis of the WISC-III.* San Diego, CA: Academic Press.

Sattler, J. M. (1974). *Assessment of children's intelligence.* Philadelphia, PA: Saunders.

Sattler, J. M., & D'Amato, R. C. (2002a). Brain injuries: Theory and rehabilitation programs. In J. M. Sattler (Ed.), *Assessment of children: Behavioral and clinical applications* (4th ed., pp. 401–439). San Diego, CA: J. M. Sattler Publisher.

Sattler, J. M., & D'Amato, R. C. (2002b). Brain injuries: Formal batteries and informal measures. In J. M. Sattler (Ed.), *Assessment of children: Behavioral and clinical applications* (4th ed., pp. 440–469). San Diego, CA: J. M. Sattler Publisher.

Scarr, S. (Ed.). (1979). Psychology and children: Current research and practice [Special Issue]. *American Psychologist, 34.*

Senft, L. B., & Snider, B. (1980). Elementary school principals assess services of school psychologists nationwide. *Journal of School Psychology, 18,* 276–282.

Sewall, T. J., & Brown, D. T. (1976). *The handbook of certification/licensure requirements for school psychologists* Washington, D.C.: National Association of School Psychologists.

Sheridan, S. M., & D'Amato, R. C. (2003). (Eds.) Partnering to chart our futures: *School Psychology Review* and *School Psychology Quarterly* combined issue on the multisite conference on the future of school psychology. *School Psychology Quarterly, 18*(4), 352–357.

Singer, D. L., Whiton, M. B., & Fried, M. L. (1970). An alternative to traditional mental health services and consultation in school: A social systems and group process approach. *Journal of School Psychology, 8,* 172–179.

Smith, M. B., & Hobbs, N. (1966). The community and the community mental health center. *American Psychologist, 15,* 113–118.

Smith, R. G., & Soper, W. B. (1978). A survey of master's level staffing patterns and clinical roles. *Professional Psychology, 9,* 9–15.

Solly, D. C., & Hohenshil, T. H. (1986). Job satisfaction of school psychologists in a primarily rural state. *School Psychology Review, 15,* 119–126.

Spielberger, C. D., & Stenmark, D. E. (1985). Community psychology. In E. M. Altmaier & M. E. Meyer (Eds.), *Applied specialties in psychology* (pp. 75–98). New York: Random House.

Stewart, K. J. (1986). Innovative practice of indirect service delivery: Realities and idealities. *School Psychology Review, 15,* 466–478.

Stone, B. J., Gray, J. W., & Dean, R. S. (1989). The school psychologist in neurological settings. In R. C. D'Amato and R. S. Dean (Eds.), *The school psychology in nontraditional settings: Integrating clients, services, and settings* (pp. 139–157). Hillsdale, NJ: Erlbaum.

Talley, R. C., Kubiszyn, T., Brassard, M., & Short, R. J. (Eds.). (1996). *Making psychologists in schools indispensable: Critical questions and emerging perspectives.* Washington, DC: American Psychological Association.

Thomas, A., & Grimes, J. (Eds.) (1985). *Best practices in school psychology.* National Association of School Psychologists: Washington, DC.

Tindall, R. H. (1964). Trends in development of psychological services in the school. *Journal of School Psychology, 3,* 1–12.

Traughber, M. C., & D'Amato, R. C. (2005). Integrating evidence-based neuropsychological services into school settings: Issues and challenges for the future. In R. C. D'Amato, E. Fletcher-Janzen, & C. R. Reynolds (Eds.), *Handbook of school neuropsychology* (pp. 827–858). Hoboken, NJ: Wiley.

Trickett, E. (1984). Toward a distinctive community psychology: An ecological metaphor for the conduct of community research and the nature of training. *American Journal of Community Psychology, 12,* 261–279.

Valett, R. E. (1963). *The practice of school psychology: Professional problems* New York: Wiley.

Wechsler, D. (1950a). Intellectual development and psychological maturity. *Child Development, 21,* 45–50.

Wechsler, D. (1950b). Cognitive, connotative, and non-intellective intelligence. *American Psychologist, 5,* 78–83.

White, M. A., & Harris, M. W. (1961). *The school psychologist* New York: Harper & Row.

Wilhelm M. Wundt (2009). In *Wikipedia, the free encyclopedia.* Retrieved June 13, 2009, from http://en.wikipedia.org/wiki/WilhelmWundt

Witmer, L. (1896). Practical work in psychology. *Pediatrics, 2,* 462–471.

Witmer, L. (1897). The organization of practical work in psychology (abstract of APA paper). *Psychological Review, 4,* 116–117.

Witmer, L. (1907). Clinical psychology. *The Psychological Clinic, 1,* 1–9.

Witmer, L. (1911). *The special class for backward children* Philadelphia: Psychological Clinic.

Witsken, D., Stoeckel, A., & D'Amato, R. C. (2008). Leading educational change using a neuropsychological response-to-intervention approach: Linking our past, present and future. *Psychology in the Schools, 45*(9), 781–798.

Work, P. H. L & Choi, Hee-sook. (2005). Developing classroom and group interventions based on a neuropsychological paradigm. In R. C. D'Amato, E. Flecher-Janzen, & C. R. Reynolds (Eds.). *Handbook of school neuropsychology* (pp. 663–683). Hoboken, NJ: Wiley.

Wundt, W. (2009). In *Wikipedia, the free encyclopedia.* Retrieved June 13, 2009, from http://en.wikipedia.org/wiki/WilhelmWundt

Wundt, W. (1912). *An introduction to psychology* (Trans. Rudolf Pinter). London: George Allen & Unwin.

Woodworth, R. S. (1948). *Contemporary schools of psychology* New York: The Ronald Press.

Ysseldyke, J. E. (1982). The Spring Hill symposium on the future of psychology in the schools. *American Psychologist, 37*(5), 547 – 552.

Ysseldyke, J. E. & Schakel, J. A. (1983). Directions in school psychology. In G. W. Hynd (Eds.), *The school psychologist: An introduction* (pp. 3–26). Syracuse, NY: Syracuse University Press.

Ysseldyke, J. E., & Weinberg, R. A. (Eds.). (1981). The future of psychology in the schools: Proceedings of the Spring Hill symposium. *School Psychology Review, 10.*

Ysseldyke, J. E., Reynolds, M., & Weinberg, R. A. (1984). *School psychology: A blueprint for training and practice* Bethesda, MD: National Association of School Psychologists

Ysseldyke, J. E., Dawson, P., Lehr, C., Reschly, D., Reynolds, M., & Telzrow, C. (1997). *School psychology: A blueprint for training and practice II* Bethesda, MD: National Association of School Psychologists.

Ysseldyke, J. E., Burns, M., Dawson, P., Kelley, B., Morrison, D., Ortiz, S., Rosenfield, S., & Telzrow, C. (2006). *A blueprint for training and practice III*. Bethesda, MD: National Association of School Psychologists

Zafiris, C., Thomas-Duckwitz, C. & D'Amato, R. C. (2007). How to develop successful school and home interventions to service children and youth with TBI Poster/paper presented at the 27th annual convention of the National Academy of Neuropsychologists, Scottsdale, AZ.

The Expanding Role of School Psychology

Carrie Ball, Eric Pierson, *and* David E. McIntosh

Abstract

The impact of legislative changes on the traditional definition and role of school psychologists is discussed. Specifically, the influence of the No Child Left Behind Act (NCLB, 2001) and the reauthorization of the Individuals with Disabilities Education Improvement Act (IDEA, 2004) upon the practice of school psychology is reviewed. The potential impact of NCLB and IDEA on the employment outlook for the profession is considered. Finally, the dual standards and competing efforts of the National Association of School Psychologists (NASP) and Division 16 of the American Psychological Association (APA) have had on the field of school psychology is discussed.

Keywords: employment, NCLB, IDEA, standards, RTI, legislation, school psychology

Introduction

This chapter begins by discussing the traditional definition and role of school psychologists and, then, discusses the impact of legislative changes on these roles. Specifically, the influence upon the practice of school psychology of the No Child Left Behind Act (NCLB, 2001), and the reauthorization of the Individuals with Disabilities Education Improvement Act (IDEA, 2004) are discussed. An overview is provided on the potential impact NCLB and IDEA may have on the employment outlook for the profession. Finally, the chapter concludes by considering how the dual standards and competing efforts of the National Association of School Psychologists (NASP) and Division 16 of the American Psychological Association (APA) have influenced the field of school psychology.

Definition and Role of School Psychologists

Defining the profession of school psychology and describing the typical role of school psychologists is complicated, given the wide variability in training programs, degrees earned, and careers available. In general, school psychologists are professionals with specialized knowledge in both psychology and education. Graduate training programs include preparation in the areas of psychological assessment, intervention, consultation, human development, teaching and learning, and law and ethics; however, the relative emphasis placed on each area varies widely across programs (Merrell, Ervin, & Gimpel, 2006).

Doctorally trained school psychologists have historically had the most flexibility in employment options, and have successfully worked in a variety of settings, including universities, clinics, and hospitals, and private practices, as well as in school-based practice. Doctoral-level training in school psychology has long been recognized as one of the three primary postgraduate disciplines in professional psychology, and school psychology students have been able to compete successfully with students from clinical and counseling psychology programs for internships, postdoctoral fellowships, and professional practice opportunities.

School psychologists who choose school-based practice, however, have often been limited to very narrow roles. Despite their breadth of training, according to the National Association of School Psychologists (NASP) Standards for Training (2000) and the development and revisions of the NASP *Blueprint for Training and Practice* (1984, 1997, 2006), most school psychologists have not fulfilled roles that include significant involvement in prevention, intervention, or system-level change. Rather, they have served as key decision makers with regard to the eligibility of children for special education services (Sheridan & Gutkin, 2000). Their specialized knowledge of psychological assessment and special education law has typically made school psychologists a necessary part of the special education referral process, and has secured their role within school settings. Unfortunately, this gatekeeper role has limited the ability of school psychologists to interact with general education students, to become an integral part of school service delivery systems via intervention and consultation, or to be involved in systems change or program evaluation (Merrell et al., 2006). Thus, the specialized training of school psychologists has been underutilized in the context of traditional school psychological practice.

The Changing Educational Landscape

Significant changes in general and special education law over the past several years have contributed to rapid shifts in schoolwide practice, with major implications for the practice of school psychology. The most notable of these legislative changes are the No Child Left Behind Act (NCLB, 2001) and the reauthorization of the Individuals with Disabilities Education Improvement Act (IDEA, 2004).

With the passage of NCLB, schools that receive federal education funding are subject to requirements designed to ensure the quality of public education and successful student outcomes. The goals set forth in NCLB include (a) proficiency in reading and mathematics for all students by 2014, (b) high school graduation for all students, and (c) safe and drug-free schools (NCLB, 2001). Each of these goals has resulted in changes to school service delivery by shifting the allocation of resources, and increasing efforts to create positive school environments and prevent the development of learning and behavioral problems. Additionally, NCLB introduced a requirement that all students be assessed annually with respect to their progress toward grade-level standards, and that data be disaggregated to ensure that no group of students is systematically falling behind or failing to make adequate yearly progress (AYP; NCLB, 2001).

Despite the applicability of NCLB to general education and schoolwide programs, which has traditionally fallen outside the school psychologist's role, the new legislation has impacted school psychology by bringing the need for high-quality instruction, prevention, program evaluation, and data-based decision making to the forefront of educational discourse and practice.

The reauthorization of IDEA (2004) remained largely unchanged with regard to federal law governing eligibility for special education services; however, two important changes are far-reaching in their impact upon school psychology. First, local educational agencies are now allowed to allocate up to 15% of special education funds for early intervening services (IDEA, 2004). This provides an unprecedented opportunity for schools to devote financial resources to prevention efforts, and for school psychologists to become actively involved at the systems level. Second, the eligibility criteria for specific learning disability (SLD) were significantly revised in the new IDEA, such that schools are no longer required to use a traditional identification model, which depended on standardized psychological assessment to document a significant discrepancy between intellectual capability and academic achievement (IDEA, 2004). Rather, IDEA now encourages the application of a response-to-intervention (RTI) model to determine whether or not students qualify as having SLDs. RTI is conceptualized as a multi-tiered model of prevention and early intervention services that incorporates screening of all students three to four times per year, and provides increasingly intensive intervention and ongoing progress monitoring for students identified as at risk for failure. The introduction of RTI on a national scale has had two major effects on school psychology practice. First, with the reduced requirements for individual psychological testing when students are struggling academically, school psychologists are gradually conducting fewer assessments and are beginning to move away from their traditional gatekeeper roles. Second, school psychologists are often among the only professionals in school settings with postgraduate training in research, data management and analysis, and program evaluation. Inherent within RTI is an emphasis on prevention, early intervention, evidence based instruction, and data based decision making. This has provided school psychologists with opportunities to utilize their graduate training as they participate in developing and implementing large-scale changes to general and special education service delivery.

Increasing Diversity

Contemporary schools and school psychologists are also encountering rapid increases in cultural, socioeconomic, and linguistic diversity among students. The US Bureau of the Census (1992) projected that Caucasian individuals would comprise less than 50% of the total US population by the year 2050, with Latinos and African Americans representing the largest minority groups. Moreover, many new immigrants to the US are young, and some ethnic minority groups have higher birthrates than Caucasians, which has created a population of school-aged children even more diverse than the general US population (Merrell et al., 2006). Despite increasing diversity, however, over 90% of school psychologists are Caucasian, and there is a high need for practitioners from diverse cultural and linguistic backgrounds (Merrell et al., 2006). In addition to the need for recruiting and training a more diverse group of school psychologists, there is a need for all practitioners to develop and practice cultural awareness and cultural competence to establish strong working relationships with students, families, and colleagues in a school and community that may not share the perspective and priorities of the dominant culture.

One enduring challenge related to working with diverse populations lies in successfully opening and maintaining communication lines between the school system (which often represents the dominant culture) and the families of students from minority cultures (Ortiz, Flanagan, & Dynda, 2008). There also is a well documented and longstanding history of overrepresentation of minority students in special education, particularly in the categories of cognitive disability and emotional/behavioral disability (Jacob & Hartshorne, 2007). School psychologists continue to face these challenges, even as new ones emerge.

Among the fastest growing segments of students are those who are classified as English Language Learners (ELLs). The US Bureau of the Census (2002) reported that Latinos already comprise the largest ethnic minority group in the US (12.5%); that 11% of individuals are foreign born; and that 17.9% of the US population speaks a language other than English. School psychologists may receive more referrals to work with ELLs than for similarly sized other groups due to a lack of general understanding regarding the expected progression of language development and academic performance among students who are learning a new language. The delayed rate of academic language acquisition for students in this group may make it mistakenly appear to educators and parents that the student has a learning disability and is in need of a referral. The evaluation of students with ELL's for special education eligibility requires knowledge of appropriate assessment practices for students who are not fluent in English (Ortiz, 2008).

The following paragraphs outline more specifically the evolving expectations of contemporary school psychology practitioners, given the changing legal requirements and the ever-increasing needs of students and schools in the United States. Consistent with the traditional expectations of professional psychologists in most fields, the discussion is framed around three skill sets as they apply to school settings: assessment, intervention, and consultation. Implications for graduate training also are discussed.

Assessment

Assessment has historically been a primary role of school psychologists, and continues to be a central component of their training and expertise. In light of the recent introduction of RTI on a large scale, however, there is increasing disagreement among practitioners regarding the appropriate role of school psychologists related to assessment techniques in the context of both psychoeducational evaluations and whole-school programming (e.g., Gresham, Restori, & Cook, 2008; Reynolds & Shaywitz, 2009). School-based practitioners are likely to continue taking a leadership role in the area of assessment, although their specific responsibilities may be quite different from those to which they have historically been accustomed.

TRADITIONAL ASSESSMENT

School psychologists have a long history of expertise in individually administered standardized assessment, including IQ tests and academic achievement measures. These types of instruments have been an integral part of special education eligibility determinations since the original passage of the Education for All Handicapped Children Act in 1975. Essential to strong training in traditional assessment techniques, school psychologists also commonly have a thorough understanding of psychometric properties, including validity and reliability (Merrell et al., 2006). Despite recent changes in the legal requirements for identification of students with SLD, there is likely to be a continued need for school psychologists with expertise in psychometrics and traditional assessment. IQ tests are still required by law for determination of some disabilities, including cognitive disability and developmental delay (IDEA, 2004).

Although the professional debate continues regarding the appropriate role of cognitive assessment within an RTI framework (Hale, Kaufman, Naglieri, & Kavale, 2006), a sizable number of school psychologists continue to support the utility of IQ testing for educational decision making, even beyond the context of special education eligibility (see Braden & Shaw, 2009). Moreover, training in psychometrics provides school psychologists with a body of knowledge that is often quite unique in school settings. That is, the school psychologist may be one of only a few school personnel who understand issues of validity, reliability, standardization, standard scores, or test development. This expertise places school psychologists in a unique position to assist schools in systemwide projects, as will be discussed later.

NONTRADITIONAL ASSESSMENT

Even as school psychologists continue to fulfill their traditional roles with regard to psychological assessment, new legislation and the shift of school districts toward an RTI model necessitates development of an additional set of assessment skills. Increasingly, school districts have begun using curriculum based measurement (CBM), and other indicators of academic skills development to guide prevention, early intervention, and educational decision making. School psychologists have begun to take a leadership role in the application of CBM because of their background in assessment and data management. Nonetheless, there is a need for improved training of new school psychologists in using CBM and other informal measures to conduct screening and to monitor progress within the context of RTI (Kratochwill, Volpiansky, Clements, & Ball, 2007).

Additionally, the expansion of the evidence based practice literature, along with increasing emphasis on high quality instruction, have increased the need for school psychologists to demonstrate competence in assessment practices related to social, emotional, and behavioral functioning. In particular, systematic observation of students in classrooms and other settings must be learned and practiced in order to ensure that the analysis of maladaptive behavior adequately accounts for both student and environmental factors (Hintze, Volpe, & Shapiro, 2008). There is also an increasing need for school based professionals who are competent to conduct functional behavioral assessment (FBA), which incorporates the consideration of behavioral antecedents and consequences to facilitate effective intervention planning (Steege, & Watson, 2008). Training in

systematic observation and FBA has been incorporated into many graduate programs, and these added components represent a logical extension of the role of school psychologists given their traditional assessment training.

DATA COLLECTION AND MANAGEMENT

As noted above, school psychologists usually receive some graduate training related to data collection and management. This is especially true for graduates of doctoral training programs, although practitioners at the specialist level have typically completed courses in research methods and basic statistics. This training has become invaluable to school districts since the introduction of NCLB, which has forced schools to look closely at student achievement data to ensure they continue to meet AYP. Often, school psychologists are the only practitioners in their districts with adequate training and experience to interpret and make educational decisions based upon the data.

A second area in which the training of school psychologists has become increasingly valuable is in the use of CBM for screening and progress monitoring. Most districts attempting to implement RTI do not have any staff with expertise in prevention and early intervention systems (Kratochwill et al., 2007). Moreover, the empirical literature presently offers limited guidance for schools beginning to put effective and appropriate systems in place (Daly, Martens, Barnett, Witt, & Olson, 2007). This has opened the door for school psychologists, with their understanding of data management, to become an integral part of administering, collecting, and managing the screening and progress data needed to support RTI implementation. They may also be involved in helping schools establish and apply decision rules to guide intervention provision within RTI.

PROGRAM EVALUATION

Closely related to their knowledge regarding collecting and managing data, school psychologists are increasingly involved in changes at the systems level. Specifically, schools pursuing the NCLB goals of high school graduation and safe and drug-free schools (NCLB, 2001) are beginning to implement schoolwide prevention programs, which often require significant investments of time and money. Similarly, NCLB and IDEA requirements for high-quality academic instruction have resulted in costly curricular changes in many districts. Moreover, schools are now being held accountable for the outcomes of these programs, which necessitates the evaluation of program effectiveness. School psychologists are likely to play an important role in program evaluation in many districts; their prior knowledge of research methods, assessment options, and basic statistics allows them to facilitate decisions regarding how prevention programs should be implemented, monitored, and evaluated (Merrell et al., 2006).

NONDISCRIMINATORY ASSESSMENT

Finally, in all areas of assessment described above, school psychologists require sufficient training to ensure that they are practicing assessment in ways that do not unfairly disadvantage culturally or linguistically diverse populations. This is particularly important in the practice of traditional standardized assessment, which has long been criticized for overidentifying minority students as having disabilities, despite a lack of evidence that such instruments are psychometrically biased (Ortiz, 2008). Similar issues are also present in other assessment practices. Program evaluation and nontraditional assessments must be designed to consider preexisting variability and environmental factors that may adversely impact diverse populations, to ensure that any measures of effectiveness or non-effectiveness account for the possibility that certain ethnic and linguistic groups may respond to intervention differently than others. This requires that school psychologists not only understand the application of validity and reliability as it applies to the development of assessment tools, but also that they carefully consider psychometric issues when selecting the instruments to be used for traditional and nontraditional assessments and program evaluation activities (see Ortiz, 2008).

Intervention

Despite receiving graduate training in academic and social skill development (NASP, 2000), school psychologists historically have not been very involved in providing school-based interventions. Often, their intervention training is limited in application to a list of recommendations provided in psychoeducational reports (Merrell et al., 2006), and they provide little or no direct intervention to students. The introduction of evidence-based intervention within the context of NCLB and RTI provides unprecedented opportunities for school psychologists to become increasingly involved in direct service delivery in the schools with regard to prevention and early intervention in both academic and social/emotional domains.

ACADEMIC INTERVENTION

School psychology training programs typically provide instruction in academic skill development and effective teaching and learning strategies, in accordance with NASP *Domains of Training and Practice* (2000). School psychologists also typically have some training in how to select, implement, evaluate, and modify interventions that are appropriate for their clients. As schools face the need to provide evidence based interventions for all students, school psychologists may begin to take a more active role in helping administrators and teachers to select and evaluate empirically supported curricula. In addition, RTI requires a significant time investment on the part of all school personnel to shift from traditional to more prevention-oriented service delivery. School psychologists with training and experience in academic skill development are likely to have increased opportunities for direct academic intervention with individuals or small groups of students, since RTI implementation often overburdens the available teaching staff.

SOCIAL/EMOTIONAL INTERVENTION
AND PREVENTION

NASP also requires graduate programs to provide training related to the development of life skills, including social, emotional, and adaptive competence (NASP, 2000). Again, the federal impetus for schools to pursue prevention programs that ensure student safety and high school graduation has fueled an increased commitment to social/emotional learning (Collaborative for Academic, Social, and Emotional Learning, 2003). There also is research supporting a multi-tiered prevention model similar to RTI for addressing social, emotional, and behavioral problems in school settings (Crone & Horner, 2003). School psychologists, guidance counselors, and social workers may be among the school personnel who help to select and implement evidence-based prevention programs. School psychologists, however, are likely to have the strongest background among their colleagues in mental health, disability diagnosis, individual assessment and intervention techniques, FBA, and behavioral intervention planning (Merrell et al., 2006). This suggests that they will continue to play a pivotal role in designing, implementing, and evaluating interventions for children identified as at-risk for social, emotional, and behavioral difficulties. Again, schools attempting to implement multi-tiered prevention programs will probably turn to school psychologists for their training in intensive individual and small-group interventions.

NONDISCRIMINATORY INTERVENTION

As with assessment, school psychologists must understand issues of cultural and linguistic diversity as they relate to school-based intervention. Many interventions with empirical support, for example, have only been evaluated on Caucasian participants. To the extent possible, it is important for school psychologists to select interventions that have documented efficacy for populations that reflect the cultural and linguistic composition of their schools. Additionally, as they implement individual social/emotional interventions, school psychologists must strive to develop and utilize culturally competent therapeutic practices to improve their quality of service delivery, and the outcomes that are achieved (Ortiz et al., 2008).

CONSULTATION

School psychologists, perhaps even more than psychologists in other settings, have many opportunities to engage in consultation with administrators, teachers, families, and community agencies. Consultation represents a central role for school psychologists, and is likely to become increasingly important as their role in schools and districts continues to expand. Historically, school psychologists have tended to consult with teachers, parents, or other service providers to improve the services rendered to a single student (Kratochwill, 2008). Although certainly helpful, this type of consultation is often quite time consuming, fails to address the larger context within which problems are occurring, and does not ensure generalization of effective strategies among teachers (Coffee, 2007; Kratochwill, 2008). With the introduction of RTI and NCLB, however, school psychologists are beginning to encounter new opportunities for consultation at the systems and classroom levels. For example, school psychologists engage in systems consultation when they participate in efforts to select, implement, and evaluate schoolwide prevention programs or curricula. They also may be called upon to deliver professional development for teachers or administrators regarding the appropriate uses of screening and progress monitoring data. Additionally, classroom or group level consultation may be appropriate when teachers are struggling to meet the needs of a particular group of children, or if teachers are having difficulty with classroom management issues. Recent emphasis on accountability for students' learning outcomes is likely to result in teachers who are more willing to accept help from other professionals in the school.

Consultation at the individual level is likely to continue as it has in the past, although additional opportunities may also emerge. For example, many schools have some type of pre-referral problem-solving process in place for students who are demonstrating academic, social, emotional, and behavioral problems. School psychologists already participate in this process in some districts, and the experience can provide an opportunity to consult with teachers who are working with challenging students, and to gather valuable information as the problem-solving team collaborates to make students successful and prevent special education referrals (Burns, Ives Wiley, & Viglietta, 2008). School psychologists interested in expanding their role beyond the traditional gatekeeper responsibilities would do well to establish or participate in a pre-referral process in their schools.

Potential Impact of Legislation on the Employment Outlook of School Psychologists

Historically, there has been a shortage of school psychologists working within the schools (Curtis, Grier, & Hunley, 2004) and it is projected that this shortage will continue until the year 2020 (Curtis, Grier, & Hunley, 2004). These shortage estimates were based upon supply, retirement, and attrition estimates. Interestingly, these shortage estimates have not considered the impact changes in legislation may have on the profession. Even so, it would be difficult to accurately estimate what impact legislation like NCLB would have on the personnel needs of schools and the shortage of school psychologists. Fagan and Wise (2007) do begin to discuss how NCLB will impact school psychology, and how it might lead to changes within the profession. What is unclear is how NCLB and RTI *will* impact the profession.

Many within the profession have indicated that NCLB and RTI would result in an increased demand for school psychologists. This prediction makes sense, given the nature of RTI and the number of children who will need to be served. It also makes sense given the level of training and skills possessed by school psychologists. School psychologists are ideally prepared to meet the prevention, consultation, and evaluation demands of RTI, which is consistent with the expanding role of school psychologists (Fagan & Wise, 2007). However, NCLB and RTI may actually result in a decrease in the demand for school psychologists— yes, a decrease! While this perspective is sure to be unpopular, and some might see it as a threat to job security, it is important for a professional to consider alternative views.

While many schools will recognize that school psychologists are uniquely trained to help meet the requirements of NCLB and RTI, many schools now see school psychologists as assessment specialists. Redefining the role of school psychologists, and educating administrators and teachers on how school psychologists can contribute to RTI, will not be easy; history has shown this to be a challenge.

There already is a decreased need for traditional evaluations, with school psychologists conducting far fewer evaluations compared to two years ago. This decreased need has resulted in many school psychologists assisting with RTI, implementing prevention programs, and consulting more. However, schools also are beginning to utilize other professionals within the schools, such as those considered experts in reading, language, and math, to help implement RTI. Schools also are hiring behavioral specialists (e.g., Board Certified Behavior Analysts) and other professionals (e.g., evaluation specialists) and outsourcing many aspects of RTI. These professionals are often less expensive to hire compared to school psychologists, who (even when recently licensed) are often near the top of the school district payscale. As schools are increasingly forced to make hiring decisions based upon cost, it is not unrealistic for districts to opt against hiring a school psychologist when they could meet their needs through professionals or paraprofessionals who earn lower salaries. Schools may also cut costs by shifting internal employees (e.g., senior teachers, Title I teachers, administrators) to save money and address the needs of students. By shifting internally, schools can then hire recent graduates at a beginning teacher salary and save in salary costs.

Test companies also have been very astute about developing screening programs that are consistent with RTI. These systemwide measures are typically offered with a variety of additional services, if the school is willing to pay for them. Schools can now select from a wide range of screening measures and opt for support services that include administration, scoring, data analysis, and report generation. Many of these same services can be provided by school psychologists; however, it will be essential to assist schools in recognizing this fact. Also, while screening measures may identify children who are at-risk academically, school psychologists can be involved at the next level in conducting highly individualized assessments to assist in developing and implementing remediation programs. It will be important for schools to recognize this level of expertise and involve school psychologists in the RTI process.

Whether NCLB and RTI are current trends that will eventually disappear is difficult to determine (Fagan & Wise, 2007). However, they are here, and should not be ignored. Whether NCLB and RTI will positively or negatively impact the profession and the employment outlook for school psychologists is difficult to predict. But, as a profession, it will be important to consider all aspects related to personnel needs within the schools. Specifically, it will be important to look from the inside out. How do school administrators, other professionals (e.g., teachers, speech/language pathologists) within the schools, and other professional groups (e.g., behavior specialists) perceive and understand school psychologists' roles within the school? While school administrators may not deny that school psychologists would make significant contributions to their schools, is hiring school psychologists cost effective? Are there other professionals, within the schools, who are better suited to meet the needs within the RTI process? Lastly, other professional groups (e.g., board certified behavior analysts, clinical psychologists, social workers, statisticians) are beginning to see schools as an opportunity to expand their professional roles and gain additional revenue.

Professionalization and Advocacy

This section of the chapter will focus on how the dual standards and competing efforts of the National Association of School Psychologists (NASP) and Division 16 of the American Psychological Association (APA) have influenced the field of school psychology. The following paragraphs outline the development of the organizations and current points of tension that impact training and advocacy efforts.

Professional Organizations in School Psychology

For forty years, two distinguished professional groups have represented and advocated for the field of school psychology. The older of these two groups—the American Psychological Association (APA)—was founded in 1892 as a professional organization dedicated to promoting the field of professional psychology. Division 16 of APA was founded in the mid 1940s to advocate specifically for the field of school psychology (Fagan, 1993; Fagan & Wise, 2007). Currently, APA Division 16 has over 1200 full members and 170 associate members(www.apa.org/abut/division/division-16-2008), most of whom are individuals holding or pursuing a doctoral degree in school psychology. Division 16 views school psychology as a specialization within the larger family of professional psychology (Merrell, Ervin, & Gimpel, 2006). As such, school psychology training programs and internships share common accreditation with clinical and counseling psychology programs. The APA committee on accreditation also accredits postdoctoral programs in all areas, although there are currently no APA accredited, school based postdoctoral programs. Maintaining a common committee on accreditation helps maintain standards and requirements across areas of specialization. Although the full committee includes members of all specialty areas, site visitors reporting to the committee are typically assigned such that the visiting team is composed primarily of school psychologists when visiting a school psychology site during the accreditation or reaccreditation process.

APA has a longstanding history of endorsing as psychologists only those individuals with a doctoral degree in professional psychology. During the earliest part of the twentieth century, APA suggested that nondoctoral professionals use the term *assistant psychologist*; early history of school psychology indicates that many people also used job titles such as *psychometrist* or *mental tester* (Fagan, 1993). In 1939, however, the APA introduced an exemption, allowing the term *school psychologist* to be used by school based practitioners with specialist or masters level training. During the latter half of the twentieth century (after the inception of Division 16), APA again began advocating that the term *psychologist* be restricted to those having a doctorate, (Merrell, et al, 2006), in part to help place psychologists on a level of parity to medical physicians in hospital settings. APA officially codified their position in 1977, stating that the title "psychologist" should be reserved for those holding a doctoral degree (Fagan, 1993). APA did, however, retain a specific exemption allowing continued use of the title "school psychologist" by nondoctoral practitioners, to reflect the longstanding use of this title in the schools. As a result of APA taking an official position, full membership in the organization was restricted to individuals holding a doctoral degree; however, Division 16 continued to allow associate membership to individuals with nondoctoral training (Fagan, 1993). Today, APA continues to define psychologists as those with doctoral level training, and to advocate through its state organizations for the restriction of independent practice outside the schools to professional psychologists with a doctoral

degree. In fact, APA had recently moved further toward a universal requirement for doctoral level training in its proposed revisions to the Model Licensure Act (MLA, 2007) but later abandoned this effort. The MLA serves as a template for states' licensing laws regarding the practice of psychology, and the proposed changes do not include an exemption for use of the term "school psychologist" by non-doctoral practitioners.

The National Association of School Psychologists (NASP) was established in 1969, in part due to dissatisfaction among nondoctoral school psychologists with the efforts of Division 16 to advocate for the profession. Currently, it is estimated that NASP membership numbers are 25,245, with doctoral membership accounting for approximately 30 percent (A. Thomas, personal communication, December 8, 2009). In contrast to APA, NASP recognizes both nondoctoral and doctoral level school psychologists as full members, and allows them to receive national certification in school psychology. NASP has also worked closely with the National Council for Accreditation of Teacher Education (NCATE) to develop training standards, and accredit school psychology training programs at the nondoctoral level.

Since its inception, NASP has advocated for the continued acceptance of nondoctoral practitioners as professional psychologists. NASP continues to advocate—in opposition to APA —for specialist-level school psychologists to have private practice privileges. At the same time, however, doctoral-level school psychologists often feel underrepresented by the organization, as NASP devotes time and resources to recognition and privileges for its nondoctoral constituents. Although NASP officially maintains its position that school psychology is a specialization within the larger family of professional psychology, there have been some indications that NASP may be reconsidering this view (Short, 2002). That is, NASP may be considering a position that school psychology actually represents an entirely separate discipline.

Mounting Tensions
The relationship between APA and NASP has often been characterized as contentious (Fagan & Wise, 2007; Short, 2002), and tension between the two organizations continues to mount due to serious philosophical differences, and an apparent impasse regarding the training requirements for entry-level practice in professional psychology. It is typically only when outside forces such as the Department of Education require cooperation that the two groups can put aside differences. In 2002, after a two-decade

period of active communication, APA withdrew from the inter-organizational committee due to lack of progress on important issues. The release of APA's revisions to the MLA (2007) and removal of exemption for use of the term *school psychologist* has angered NASP and its contingent of nondoctoral practitioners. NASP has orchestrated continued efforts to block the recommended changes, which have been referred to by some state level leaders as the "greatest challenge facing children in the schools today" (personal communication).

A key part of the problem underlying the disagreement between NASP and APA revolves around the minimum level of training required for independent practice. NASP membership holds the view that APA fails to recognize the high quality work and extensive training that today's specialists receive. Moreover, NASP members often view the doctorate in school psychology as a degree relevant merely to those pursuing careers in academia, with doctoral students acquiring little additional knowledge beyond the specialist level that would help them in the schools. APA, however, firmly endorses its position, arguing that specialist level practitioners have not acquired training equivalent to their doctoral counterparts, such as research, advanced clinical training, and supervisory experiences that are often not available to graduate students at the specialist level. As is often the case, both views have merit.

Training programs that offer both specialist and doctoral degrees often find themselves pulled into the debate, as they actively train their students to enter the field at both levels. Although there have been attempts in the past to adopt a multilevel approach to the delivery of school psychological services (Dean, 1983), these efforts have met with insurmountable resistance from NASP. The continued training of school psychologists at both levels may serve to enforce the inter-organizational disagreement by creating cognitive dissonance on the parts of trainers, trainees, and institutions that view both groups as well prepared for practice. In addition, there is often very little difference in the role of school psychologists working in the schools, at either the specialist or the doctoral level (Fagan & Wise, 2007). It is critical to remember that the role of the school psychologist is often dictated by contextual factors such as legal standards or district policies, as opposed to client needs, professional philosophy, or psychologists' training (Pierson & McIntosh, in press).

In sum, the inability of either APA or NASP to effectively advocate for all professionals working to promote the delivery of school psychological services has negatively impacted the application of psychology in the schools. While both NASP and APA have participated in discussions regarding revisions to special and general education law, state licensure requirements, and private practice regulations, the two groups have at times produced adversarial messages. Today, given their intensifying differences, both entities risk compromising their effectiveness as advocates for the profession, and being perceived instead as competing guilds, claiming the same discipline as turf.

Advocacy

As we have outlined, there are legitimate concerns about the ability and desire of APA Division 16 to adequately represent the full range of school psychologists, especially given that full APA membership is denied to individuals without doctoral training, and that APA appears committed to its stance that the term *psychologist* should not apply to individuals without a doctoral degree. At the same time, doctoral-level practitioners often find the efforts of NASP to be inadequate in terms of advocating for their specific needs within the larger context of professional psychology. Moreover, some doctoral-level school psychologists from non-NASP-approved graduate programs may consider the additional requirements for obtaining an NCSP certification to be exclusionary. It is important to recognize that, despite sharp disagreement between the two organizations regarding the proposed revisions to the MLA, school psychologists are not necessarily divided based on training level. For example, most school psychologists at both the specialist and doctoral levels oppose removal of the exemption. Additionally, many doctoral-level school psychologists object to the MLA revisions for different reasons, including a lack of attention to the limited opportunities for postdoctoral training in school settings, and little recognition of school psychologists who do participate in formalized postdoctoral experiences.

Currently, neither APA nor NASP appears able or willing to provide adequate representation and advocacy for school psychologists at both the specialist and doctoral levels. If disagreement and tension continue, a new professional organization may emerge to advocate for a unified, or possibly more specialized, group of psychologists. Formation of a new organization may be even more likely if current leaders within NASP and APA remain entrenched in the debate and are unwilling to pursue resolution and compromise. Additionally, an increase in the number of school psychology training programs, and the number of young professionals interested in leadership opportunities, may provide a group of highly capable individuals who would be willing to assume leadership positions within a new organization. This would reflect a similar a movement that occurred in the 1970s, when the primarily nondoctoral leadership in NASP was gradually replaced by a large number of doctoral-level academicians (Fagan, 1993). Unlike previous trends in organizational leadership, however, the current technological age may provide alternatives to a permanent professional organization. For example, temporary organizations formed via social networking or electronic media may serve as catalysts for offsetting tensions and improving communication between APA and NASP members and leaderships. In any case, the development of a third professional organization dedicated to advocating for school psychology is unlikely to strengthen the profession or its reputation in the larger community of professional psychology. Just as NASP and APA have at times disagreed and provided divergent messages in their advocacy efforts, a third organization is likely to further divide the profession and dilute the advocacy message of both existing organizations. The membership of both organizations may find it easier to expand leadership to early and mid-career psychologists in an effort to improve inter-organizational communication and collaboration. Increased transparency regarding the process by which new leaders are recruited and selected may also improve the perception of each organization among its membership.

School Psychology: Discipline or Specialization?

Setting aside the contentious issue of entry level qualifications for practice as a school psychologist, there remains a fundamental question as to whether school psychology continues to represent a specialization within the larger community of professional psychology, or whether we have evolved into a separate discipline. While all branches of professional psychology trace a common heritage to the Witmer clinic, there is some historical evidence to suggest that Witmer himself was opposed to the development of special organizations for professional versus academic psychology. Later advocates for the development of the specialty in clinical psychology viewed the practice of working in a clinical fashion in schools as inherently problematic and too difficult (Fagan, 1993).

Indeed, the practice of psychology in the schools often differs significantly from practice in hospital,

clinic, and community settings. Legally, school psychologists in the schools may be required to follow standards for components of evaluations, supervision, payment, and diagnosis procedures that are different from those of their counterparts in other settings (Jacob & Hartshorne, 2007; Pierson & McIntosh, in press). School psychologists may find their professional practice to be guided more by due process and legal precedence than by medical necessity. The specific services provided by contemporary school psychologists also differ greatly from those of other areas of professional psychology, as described previously. While many practitioners and teachers may find the new activities more helpful for school-based practice than more traditional activities, professional psychologists outside the schools have little frame of reference to understand or appreciate the utility of the new instruments and techniques. As a result, school psychologists may be perceived by the larger community of professional psychology as being poorly prepared for work in non-school settings.

Historically, there is additional evidence that school psychology is increasingly viewed as a separate discipline from other areas of psychology, rather than a specialization within professional psychology. For example, there are longstanding differences in examination and licensure requirements for school psychology practice in school settings, as compared to the requirements for the independent practice of professional psychology. Second, previous attempts to consolidate Division 16 (School Psychology) and Division 12 (Clinical Psychology) of APA have failed, indicating that little common ground, and a lack of shared professional interest, exists between the two specialties. Third, the increasing divergence of training programs is evidenced by discrepancies between *Blueprint III* and the APA content areas as well as in overall lower performance of school psychologists on the Examination for Professional Practice in Psychology (EPPP) (Holcomb, Pierson, & Mazur-Mosiewicz, submitted manuscript). If the current trends continue, school psychology may come to be viewed as an entirely separate discipline, rather than as a specialization within professional psychology. For those who support the continued movement away from other established areas of professional psychology, we offer a reminder that there are costs associated with this move.

Implications for Training
Graduate Training

The rapidly changing educational landscape, and the evolving role of school psychologists, have unique implications for school psychology training programs. First, contemporary training programs may lack programmatic support for instruction in RTI, nontraditional assessment, prevention, systems consultation, and program evaluation. Many programs may need to revise or restructure course content, course sequence, or even program requirements to adequately meet the needs of trainees, as well as to recruit faculty with expertise in RTI and related skills. Second, and even more important, training programs are now faced with the need to train school psychologists with a much broader range of skills than have previously been expected of practitioners, as well as an increased level of competence in areas where basic knowledge has previously been sufficient. In addition to providing students with a firm foundation in psychometrics and standardized assessment, for example, students must also become competent to select, administer, and interpret nontraditional assessments. Whereas students in the past have needed only information regarding the basic development of social and behavioral competence, trainees now need a more thorough understanding of behavioral assessment and intervention techniques as they apply to school settings. Consultation courses, which have traditionally been focused on models of individual consultation, now need to introduce approaches and recommendations for system level consultation. These types of additional training needs are likely to place some programs under pressure to increase the number of

credit hours required to complete the specialist degree, and may even necessitate lengthening the number of semesters needed to finish the program.

Programs that offer both specialist and doctoral degrees also face additional challenges in maintaining high-quality programs for students working toward both degrees. APA and NASP, in addition to their disagreement over entry level training requirements, have also crafted separate guidelines for graduate training (see Table 3.1). Whereas clinical and counseling psychology programs adhere only to the guidelines set forth by APA, school psychology training programs that offer dual degrees must incorporate both APA and NASP training standards to ensure accreditation by both entities. This presents a challenge to trainers as they develop programs that adhere to competing sets of training standards. Generally speaking, dual degree programs provide similar training to both specialist and doctoral level candidates during the first two years of training. Programs may be adequately adapted to prepare both groups of students for school based practice during the first two years of graduate education, if some topics are covered in less depth to make room for new requisite skills sets. During the third year, specialist level trainees complete a school based internship, and doctoral students acquire additional training. This approach of parallel training during the first two years, however, must be supplemented for doctoral students to ensure that doctorally trained school psychologists remain competitive

Table 3.1 Training standards

Organization	
American Psychological Association	**National Association of School Psychology**
Breadth of scientific psychology	Data-based decision making
The scientific, methodological, and theoretical foundations of practice	Consultation and collaboration
Diagnosing or defining problems through psychological assessment	Effective instruction and development of cognitive/academic skills
Issues of cultural and individual diversity	Socialization and development of life skills
Attitude essential for lifelong learning	Student diversity in development and learning
	School and systems organization Prevention, crisis intervention, and mental health
	Home/school/community collaboration
	School psychology practice and development
	Information technology

Compiled from Fagan & Wise, 2007.

with graduates from other disciplines. The nature of training beyond the specialist level presently varies across programs, with many doctoral candidates receiving advanced instruction in research methodology, and some fulfilling requirements to specialize in an area of practice related to school psychology (e.g., counseling, educational leadership). Increased attention must now be devoted to ensuring that doctoral candidates in school psychology receive instruction that meets the APA competency areas, and provides adequate preparation for the EPPP (see Table 3.2) and for future independent practice. For example, the first two years of graduate education are likely to provide limited instruction in differential diagnosis, biological bases of behavior, clinical interviewing, psychopharmacology, and individual or group therapy (Holcomb, Pierson, & Mazur-Mosiewicz, 2009), which are important components of practice in clinical or counseling psychology milieus. It will be critical for programs to ensure that dual degree programs provide advanced training for doctoral candidates in the areas of assessment, intervention, and consultation that will prepare them for professional practice in the same variety of settings they have traditionally enjoyed.

Evidence from the EPPP, which assesses knowledge related to general practice in all areas of professional psychology, indicates that school psychology graduates have a lower passing rate than do graduates of either counseling or clinical psychology programs, regardless of the APA accreditation status of the programs (Ross, Holzman, Handal, & Gilner, 1991; Holcomb, Zimmerman, Mazur-Mosiewicz, & Pierson, 2010). While multiple factors may contribute to the differential passing rates, it seems possible that students trained according to the *Blueprint III* model are inadequately prepared for the examination when compared to their counterparts in clinical or counseling programs (Holcomb, Pierson, & Mazur-Mosiewicz, 2009). Continued difficulty on the EPPP by graduates of school psychology programs does nothing to improve the prestige or reputation of the specialty among the larger community of professional psychology, and may reflect a need to better incorporate the competencies set forth by APA into school psychology training programs.

The most basic difference in training standards reflects the amount of time necessary for entry-level proficiency to develop. Interestingly, this gap has begun to close in recent revisions by both organizations. NASP has historically advocated for a 60 semester-hour graduate training program and a 1200-hour internship as sufficient for entry level practice; however, there are hints that NASP now views this as insufficient. Recent changes indicate that NASP is placing increasing emphasis on the need for continuing education and mentorship in early career experiences (Ysseldyke et al., 2008). In addition, proposed revisions in the NASP training guidelines include an increase in the required length of internship from 1200 to 1600 hours. The changes proposed by NASP have resulted in a much narrower gap between the two sets of training guidelines. APA has historically encouraged a 2000-hour internship, and has included a period of postdoctoral residency as a prerequisite for independent practice. Notably, the Association of State and Provincial Psychology Boards recently supported a proposed policy revision that would allow appropriately supervised practicum experience to be substituted for the postdoctoral residency requirement on an hour-for-hour basis (ASPPB, 2009). The current narrowing of differences between NASP and APA regarding the requisite entry-level training for professional practice may represent an inroad toward better inter-organizational cooperation, although ongoing tension between the two groups does not bode well for the establishment of a compromise on training.

The requirements for training at the graduate level also differ as a result of discrepancies between the NCATE/NASP and APA accreditation standards. For example, APA allows individual programs to develop program goals and objectives as long as they demonstrate compliance with five broad competency areas (see Table 3.1), which are assessed prior to and as part of the EPPP. NASP/NCATE guidelines are typically more closely related to state

Table 3.2 Content areas of the examination for professional practice in psychology

Content Area	Percentage on Exam
Research Methods	6
Biology of Behavior	11
Social and Multicultural Bases of Behavior	12
Cognitive Affective Bases of Behavior	13
Growth and Lifespan Development	13
Assessment and Diagnosis	14
Ethical, Legal, and Professional Issues	15
Treatment and Intervention	16

As outlined in the *2006 Psychology Licensing Exam Scores by Doctoral Program*. Reprinted with kind permission of ASPPB.

licensure requirements. Similar to APA, programs are allowed to develop specific training goals and objectives, although they must document and evaluate student progress in 11 training domains (see Table 3.1). Competencies as required for state licensure or national certification, are assessed on the PRAXIS II exam for school psychology, which focuses on knowledge and skills needed for practice in school settings.

Continuing Education

Separate standards have also evolved regarding the ongoing maintenance of competency through mechanisms of continuing education. Both APA and NASP require continuing education with a particular emphasis on ethics and law. Both organizations also encourage a wide range of activities that can be used to gain continuing education credit. As was previously mentioned, NASP has begun to adopt a lifetime competency-building perspective that fits into the conceptual framework outlined in *School Psychology: A Blueprint for Training and Practice III* (Ysseldyke et al., 2008). This document urges school psychologists at all levels of training to view competency acquisition as a process occurring across the lifetime. The current expectation is that graduates will enter the field with a "novice" level of competence in all domains, and will acquire expertise in one or two domains after several years in practice (Ysseldyke et al, 2008). It is unclear how states may interpret this shift, or what changes, if any, may be made to training program requirements or licensing exams based upon the new model. The position of APA on the issue of competence is quite different, in that trainees are expected to demonstrate competency in the five broad content areas of psychology upon completion of their graduate training. Despite the fact that both organizations endorse the need for continuing education and ongoing development of competence, this emerging difference in semantics may become problematic in future attempts at cooperation.

It is important to recognize that school psychologists who obtain and maintain dual licensure and credentialing for private practice and practice in the schools must follow both sets of guidelines for continuing professional development. As a result, doctoral-level school psychologists may find themselves adopting a strategy of continuing education reflective of the *Blueprint III* model, despite identifying with the larger professional psychology community. While some may argue that this will not have a negative, or even a substantial, impact upon the continued training of school psychologists, there is

evidence that the five APA content areas are not sufficiently covered by training materials designed around the NASP standards (Holcomb et al., 2009). It appears, for example, that the application of the NASP standards as a guide for continuing professional development may lead to a de-emphasis on multiaxial diagnoses, psychopharmacology, and biological bases underlying human behavior. Instead, the focus of content surrounding best practices in school psychology has shifted to emphasize the use of curriculum based measurement tools, response to intervention, and behavioral consultation.

Summary

Whether NCLB, IDEA, and RTI will have a lasting impact on the profession of school psychology is difficult to predict. What is certain is that the recent legislation is impacting the professional in significant ways, and is resulting in rapid changes in how school psychologists are practicing in the schools. School psychologists are already starting to conduct fewer traditional assessments, as they become more involved in nontraditional assessment, prevention, and consultation. RTI also may have a potential impact on the future employment outlook of school psychologists. The profession will need to make concerted efforts to educate administrators regarding the expanding role of school psychologists. However, barriers may include the cost of hiring school psychologists compared to other professionals, and the current shortage may result in schools looking for other professionals to fulfill some of the roles of school psychologists. Finally, the profession will need to work through dual standards and competing efforts of the National Association of School Psychologists (NASP) and the American Psychological Association (APA) to strengthen the profession.

References

American Psychological Association (2007). Model Licensure Act. Washington, DC: Author.

Association of State and Provincial Psychology Boards. (2009). *Guidelines on Practicum experience for Licensure.*

Association of State and Provincial Psychology Boards (2006). *Psychology licensing exam scores by doctoral program.* Montgomery AL:Author.

Braden, J. P. & Shaw, S. R. (2009). Intervention validity of cognitive assessment: Knowns, unknowables, and unknowns. *Assessment for Effective Intervention, 34,* 106–115.

Burns, M. K., Ives Wiley, H., & Viglietta, E. (2008). Best practices for implementing effective problem-solving teams. In A. Thomas & J. Grimes (Eds.), *Best practices in school psychology V* (pp. 1633–1644). Bethesda, MD: National Association of School Psychologists.

Coffee, G. (2007). Generalization programming: An examination of the role of prevention in school-based problem-solving consultation. Unpublished dissertation, University of Wisconsin, Madison.

Collaborative for Academic, Social, and Emotional Learning (2003). *Safe and sound: An educational leader's guide to evidence-based social and emotional learning programs.* Chicago, IL: Author.

Crone, D. A., & Horner, R. H. (2003). *Building positive behavior support systems in the schools: Functional behavioral assessment.* New York: Guilford.

Curtis, M. J., Chesno-Grier, J. E., & Hunley, S. A. (2004). The changing face of school psychology: Trends in data and projections for the future. *School Psychology Review, 33*(1), 49–66.

Daly, E. J., Martens, B. K., Barnett, D., Witt, J. C., & Olson, S. C. (2007). Varying intervention delivery in response to intervention: Confronting and resolving challenges with measurement, instruction, and intensity. *School Psychology Review, 36,* 562–581.

Dean, R.S. (1983). Providing psychological services to school-age children. In G. Dean Miller (Ed.), *Human support service for children.* St. Paul: University of Minnesota.

Education for All Handicapped Children Act (1975). Pub. L. No. 94–142.

Fagan, T.K. (1993). Separate but equal: School psychology's search for organizational identity. *Journal of School Psychology, 31,* 3–90.

Fagan, T.K., & Wise, P.S. (2007). *School psychology: Past present and future* (3rd ed.). Bethesda, MD: National Association of School Psychologists.

Gresham, F. M., Restori, A. F., & Cook, C. R. (2008). To test or not to test: Issues pertaining to response to intervention and cognitive testing. *Communique, 37,* 5–7.

Hale, J. B., Kaufman, A., Naglieri, J. A., & Kavale, K. A. (2006). Implementation of IDEA: Integrating response to intervention and cognitive assessment methods. *Psychology in the Schools, 43,* 753–770.

Harrison, P.L. and Prus, J.S. (2008). Best practices in integrating Best practices V content with NASP standards. In A. Thomas & J. Grimes (Eds.), *Best practices in school psychology V* (pp. 71–100). Bethesda, MD: National Association of School Psychologists.

Hintze, J. M., Volpe, R. J., & Shapiro, E. S. (2008). Best practices in the systematic direct observation of student behavior. In A. Thomas & J. Grimes (Eds.), *Best practices in school psychology V* (pp. 319–335). Bethesda, MD: National Association of School Psychologists.

Holcomb, M. J., Mazur-Mosiewicz, A., Pierson E. E. (2009). Curriculum assessment: *Are we being served a look at curriculum and preparation for the EPPP in school psychology?* Presented at the 2009 Student Research Symposium, Ball State University, Muncie, IN.

Holcomb, M. J., Zimmerman, A.E., Mazur-Mosiewicz, A., & Pierson E. E. (2010). *Does the Blueprint Cover all the Training Bases.* Presented at the 2010 Annual Convention of the National Association of School Psychologists, Chicago, IL.

Holcomb, M.J., Pierson, E.E., & Mosiewicz-Mazur, A., (2010). Limitations of the NASP Blueprint III in preparing students for the EPPP Licensing Examination. (Manuscript submitted for review).

Individuals with Disabilities Education Improvement Act. (2004). Pub. L. No. 108–446.

Jacob, S., & Hartshorne, T. S. (2007). *Ethics and law for school psychologists* (5th ed.). Hoboken, NJ: Wiley.

Kratochwill, T. R. (2008). Best practices in school-based problem-solving consultation: Applications in prevention and intervention systems. In A. Thomas & J. Grimes (Eds.), *Best practices in school psychology V* (pp. 1673–1688). Bethesda, MD: National Association of School Psychologists.

Kratochwill, T. R., Volpiansky, P., Clements, M., & Ball, C. (2007). Professional development in implementing and sustaining multitier prevention models: Implications for response to intervention. *School Psychology Review, 36,* 618–631.

Merrell, K. W., Ervin, R. A., & Gimpel, G. A. (2006). *School psychology for the 21st Century.* New York, Guilford.

National Association of School Psychologists (2000). *Standards for training and field placement programs in school psychology.* Bethesda, MD: Author.

National Association of School Psychologists (2006). *School psychology: A blueprint for training and practice III.* Bethesda, MD: Author.

No Child Left Behind Act. (2001). Vol. Pub. L. No. 107–110.

Ortiz, S. O. (2008). Best practices in nondiscriminatory assessment. In A. Thomas & J. Grimes (Eds.), *Best practices in school psychology V* (pp. 661–678). Bethesda, MD: National Association of School Psychologists.

Ortiz, S. O., Flanagan, D. P., & Dynda, A. M. (2008). Best practices in working with culturally diverse children and families. In A. Thomas & J. Grimes (Eds.), *Best practices in school psychology V* (pp. 1721–1738). Bethesda, MD: National Association of School Psychologists.

Pierson, E.E. & McIntosh, D.E. (in press). Special education law and 504 plans In A. Davis (Ed.), *Encyclopedia of School Neuropsychology.* Springer: New York.

Reynolds, C. R., & Shaywitz, S. E. (2009). Response to intervention: Ready or not? Or, from wait to-fail to watch-them-fail. *School Psychology Quarterly, 24,* 130–145.

Ross, M. J., Holzman, L. A. Handal, P. J. & Gilner, F. H. (1991). Performance on the Examination for the Professional Practice of Psychology as a function of specialty, degree, administrative housing, and accreditation status. *Professional Psychology: Research and Practice, 5,* 347–350.

Sheridan, S. M., & Gutkin, T. B. (2000). The ecology of school psychology: Examining and changing our paradigm for the 21st century. *School Psychology Review, 29,* 485–502.

Short, R.J. (2002). School psychology as a separate profession: An unsupportable direction. *The School Psychologist, 56,* 111–117.

Steege, M. W., & Watson, T. S. (2008). Best practices in functional behavioral assessment. In A. Thomas & J. Grimes (Eds.), *Best practices in school psychology V* (pp. 337–347). Bethesda, MD: National Association of School Psychologists.

US Bureau of the Census (1992). *United States Census, 1992 Updated.* Washington, DC: US Government Printing Office.

US Bureau of the Census (2002). *Statistical abstract of the United States* (122nd edition). Washington, DC: US Government Printing Office.

Ysseldyke, J. Burns, M., Dawson, P. Kelley, B., Morrison, D., Ortiz, S., Rosenfield, S. and Telzrow, C. (2008). The blueprint for training and practice as the basis for best practices. In A. Thomas & J. Grimes (Eds.), *Best practices in school psychology V* (pp. 37–70). Bethesda, MD: National Association of School Psychologists.

PART 3

Theoretical
Perspectives

Individual Differences

Thomas J. Kehle *and* Melissa A. Bray

Abstract

Why individuals differ typically involves the study of practically inseparable influences of multiple dimensions of complex and confounded environmental, genetic, and epigenetic factors. With respect to the practice of school psychology within the context of historical, social, and political influences on education, studies dealing with individual differences, and the application of knowledge gained from these, are challenging and often controversial. It is difficult to simultaneously embrace both the values of individualism and egalitarianism—values that are deeply rooted in American education. The primary intent of this chapter is to present findings of replicated and recent research on individual differences, with emphasis on general cognitive functioning, genetic, and epigenetic factors that influence commonly desired life outcomes. Further, we suggest relevant educational and psychological applications of these findings to promote the design of optimal environments that facilitate individual functioning.

Keywords: general intelligence, g, general cognitive ability, intelligence, academic achievement, heterosis, epigenetics

General Cognitive Ability (g)

Individual differences in general cognitive ability, although vilified and dismissed by many, is arguably the most studied and singly the most powerful variable influencing individual differences in important life outcomes. It is indisputable that individual differences in general cognitive ability, or *g*, the common component of intellectual functioning, is a powerful predictor of many aspects of human behavior, including educational attainment, occupational status, and income (Hartmann, Larsen, & Nyborg, 2009). Similar to Lubinski (2004), we define *g* as the ability to grapple with complexity (Kehle & Bray, 2004a). The content of any particular task is irrelevant; it is the degree that the task is *g* loaded that affords predictive utility. In concert with Brody 's (1992) comments on Spearman's 1904 paper:

> Spearman surely would have thought that a
> definition of intelligence as that which the test

measures is bizarre. Since *g* was defined as a common intellective function that is variably estimated by any and all possible measures, including those that have not as yet been invented, it cannot be identified with any particular measure or subset of measures. All measures of intelligence are measures of a single common theoretical entity
(Brody, 1992, p. 5).

If differences are indicated amongst IQ tests, those differences are a reflection of the degree to which the tests are *g* loaded. Further, all thinking, decision making, grappling with complexity, and even tasks that involve little tuition such as choice reaction time, have some degree of *g* loading (Hemmelgran & Kehle, 1984).

As Lubinsky (2004, p. 97) cited:

> "The general mental test stands today as the most
> important technical contribution to the practical

guidance of human affairs" (Cronbach, 1970, p. 197); "[A general] intelligence test is the single most important test that can be administered for vocational guidance purposes" (Humphreys, 1985, pp. 210–211); "Almost all human performance (work competence) dispositions, if carefully studied, are saturated to some extent by the general intelligence factor *g*, which for psychological and ideological reasons has been somewhat neglected in recent years but is due for a comeback" (Meehl, 1990, p. 124); and "The great preponderance of the prediction that is possible from any set of cognitive tests is attributable to the general ability that they share . . . .'Empirical *g*' is not merely an interesting psychometric phenomenon, but lies at the heart of the prediction of real-life performance" (Thorndike, 1994).

Lubinski (2004, p. 100) stated, "*g* is clearly the most important dimension of individual differences uncovered in the study of cognitive abilities to date." This statement was buttressed by his citation of several studies (cf. Brand, 1987; Brody, 1992; Drasgow, 2002; Gottfredson, 1997; Jensen, 1998; Lubinski, 2000; Lubinski & Humphreys, 1997; Moffitt, Gabrielli, Mednick, & Schulsinger, 1981) indicating the relationship between *g* and commonly desired life outcomes including academic achievement (.70 – .80), work performance (.20 – .60), income (.30 – .40), unlawfulness (–.20), achieved socioeconomic status (.50 – .70), and assortative mating (.50), leading him to further state, "these correlations indicate that *g* is among the most important individual differences dimensions for structuring the determinants of Freud's two-component characterization of life, *lieben* and *arbeiten,* working and living (or resource acquisition and mating)" (p. 100).

As abstraction and fluidity in contemporary life increases, the need to grapple with complexity and change concomitantly increases (Lubinski, 2004). Consequently, as Gottfredson (2003) noted, the horizontal aspect of *g* enables the analysis of the psychometric properties of everyday life as an intelligence test. She credited Gordon (1997) for showing how daily life "mimics rather than departs from the properties of a reliable, valid test of intelligence and helps to explain the pattern of both *g*'s impact across life as well as people's likelihood of perceiving that impact" (p. 294). One's employment of *g*, or what we refer to as one's ability to grapple with complexity, permeates all aspects of one's life and provides understanding of "how individual differences in *g* shape our individual fates" (Gottfredson, p. 294).

She concluded, "life is a mental test containing subtests with a wide range of *g* loadings (p. 294)." Or, stated otherwise, life is a series of decisions which all require some degree of *g*.

> Further, the effort to dislodge *g* by use of the experimental method of investigating intelligence has not as of yet been conspicuously more successful than the attempt to dislodge *g* by psychometric methods. And, if anything, evidence that general intelligence is substantially related to ability to process information in relatively simple tasks that appear, on surface examination, to require minimal formal tuition, strengthens the need for a theoretical construct of general intelligence that is not restricted with respect to specific content (Brody, 1992, p. 125).

As Gottfredson asserted (2003), it was Jensen's influential work that refocused the study of intelligence back to Spearman's *g*. Since publishing his 1969 article, "How much can we boost IQ and scholastic achievement," Arthur Jensen has had an enormous influence on the study of individual differences in general cognitive functioning and, in so doing, has allowed crucial advances in the study of intelligence. Central to these advances is the unassailable notion that the *g* factor "emerges from diverse batteries of mental tests in diverse populations, together with the consequent option to derive scores for individuals on this common factor" (Gottfredson, 2003, p.293).

According to Nyborg (2003), "genes count for about 80% of the familial transmission of genes for intelligence in late adulthood (but seemingly much less in childhood!)" (p. 443); and in some analyses, they account for 90% of the variability in *g* in adulthood (Plomin, Pederson, Lichtenstein, & McClearn, 1994). In support of this, Davis, Haworth, and Plomin's (2009) summary of McGue, Bouchard, Iacono and Lykken's research (1993) was that "one of the most fascinating hints from research on the genetics of *g* is that heritability appears to increase during development" (p. 1301). The heritability estimate is defined as the proportion of variation in the phenotype caused by the variation in the genotype (Kranzler, 1999). It can be simply computed by subtracting the correlation of IQs of monozygotic (MZ) twins from the correlation of IQs of dizygotic (DZ) twins and multiplying by a factor of 2 or $2(r MZ - r DZ)$. In addition to heritability of intelligence increasing during development, "the same genes affect diverse cognitive abilities" (Plomin & Spinath, 2004, p. 112). Further, during the period between age 20 and 55, it appears "that virtually all of the genetic influences on cognitive performance expressed in young adulthood are still manifest 35 years later" (Lyons et al., 2009, p. 1151). Lyons et al.'s (2009) findings seriously challenge the popular notion that exposure to decades of environmental influences over the life span mitigate genetic factors.

Being able to grapple with complexity is an immense asset in individual functioning that is also quite difficult to appreciably and enduringly change; it does indeed appear that the degree of heritability in any human trait is inversely related to the modifiability of that trait. Further, according to Johnson, Turkheimer, Gottesman, and Bouchard (2009) "virtually every trait, from social attitudes to psychopathology, shows genetic influence." The fact that "genetic influences are involved in all aspects of psychology and behavior" (Johnson et al., 2009) can be considered as the "First Law of Behavior Genetics" (Turkheimer, 2000), which "underlies all of behavioral science." (Johnson et al, 2009).

"General cognitive ability is likely the most important dimension in the study of individual differences" (Lubinski, 2009). However, as Jensen asserted, "There is nothing at all 'intrinsic' or 'immutable' about human gene pools" (in Nyborg, 2003, p. 482), as research in heterosis and epigenetics has indicated.

Academic Attainment

Regardless the age, there is considerable evidence that individuals differ with respect to how they prefer information is to be presented to them. It is assumed that effective instruction requires the design of lessons that complement the preferences of the learner; i.e., the *meshing hypothesis* (Pashler, McDaniel, Rohrer, & Bjork, 2009). The idea of tailoring instruction to students' preferred learning styles is intuitively very appealing, and immensely influential in contemporary educational practice. "Although the literature on learning styles is enormous, very few studies have even used an experimental methodology . . . . Moreover, of those that did use an appropriate method, several found results that flatly contradict the popular meshing hypothesis" (Pashler, McDaniel, Rohrer, & Bjork, 2009, p. 105). Pashler et al. summarized their review by stating, "The contrast between the enormous popularity of the learning-styles approach within education and the lack of credible evidence for its utility is, in our opinion, striking and disturbing" (p. 117).

The lack of practical utility in designing instructional strategies that consider students' learning styles is in concert with the results of previous studies conducted over a considerable period of time. For example, Cronbach and Snow (1977) employed designs that examined aptitude treatment x instructional interactions and found no evidence that different instructional methods advantaged different types of learners. They were looking for effective instructional methods sensitive to individual student differences that were independent of general cognitive ability. However, such instructional methods were not found, and it is unlikely they will be. According to Jensen (1998), "the validity of *g* is most conspicuous in scholastic performance not because *g*-loaded tests measure specifically what is taught in school, but because *g* is intrinsic to learning novel materials, grasping concepts, distinctions, and meanings" (p. 270). Further, "the most critical tool for scholastic learning beyond the primary grades—reading comprehension—is probably the most highly *g*-loaded attainment in the course of elementary education (Jensen, 1998, p. 270). The ability to comprehend what one reads and what one hears are highly correlated (Jensen, 1998).

General cognitive ability, or *g*, as ascertained by most intelligence tests that measure essentially the same source of individual differences—as evidenced by the high correlations (approximately .80) amongst them—is overwhelmingly the strongest predictor of academic achievement (Kranzler, 1999). Furthermore, "there is relatively little evidence that the relationship between intelligence and academic achievement is substantially modifiable using present instructional interventions" (Brody, 1992, p. 270). This would be expected, given the definition of intelligence as grappling with complexity. Indices of academic achievement and general cognitive ability are essentially the same thing—both require one to think. It would be novel in the history of educational practices to evidence gains in general cognitive ability without commensurate gains in academic achievement, or vice versa. Without known exceptions, the level of students' general cognitive ability in any particular school predicts similar levels of academic achievement in that school. "The IQ that children bring to the school determines variations in what children learn in the schools" (Brody, 1992, p. 261). Further, according to Brody (1992), "virtually all of the relationship between IQ and grades and other indices of academic accomplishment in the schools is direct. That is, it is not diminished in path analyses that control for social class background (p. 260) . . . Schools do not make a large difference once one has accounted for the intellectual differences characteristic of children entering the schools" (p. 263). The popular argument that the socioeconomic status of the school predicts academic achievement is not credible if prediction models omit measures of general cognitive ability that are robust predictors of socioeconomic status (Gottfredson, 2003). General cognitive ability is a ubiquitous causal determinant in other common desired life outcomes, in addition to educational attainment, in that it is highly heritable and exists prior to these life outcomes.

> Further, with the possible exception of secular influences that are not clearly understood, there is little evidence that any single source of environmental influence is causally related with IQ. Variables as diverse as exposure to lead in air and water supplies, quality and quantity of schooling, and birth order may each exert a small but discernable influence on intelligence (Brody, 1992, p. 214).

General cognitive ability, income, physical health, and academic ability, on the basis of Gottfredson's (2003) argument, would all be highly intercorrelated. As stated previously, "life is a mental test containing subtests with a wide range of g loadings . . . g permeates all aspects of one's life and provides understanding how individual differences in g shape our individual fates (Gottfredson, p. 294)."

Pesta, McDaniel, and Bertsch (2010) suggested these variables of general cognitive ability, socioeconomic status, physical health, and educational attainment are components of a nexus that defines personal well-being. They also included the variables of religiosity and crime. Submitting these data to a hierarchical principal components analysis, they found that "a single general component of well-being emerged, explaining between 53 and 85% of the variance in the subdomains. General mental ability loaded substantially on global state well-being (.83)" (Pesta et al., 2010).

In concert with Johnson et al. (2009), the examination of what causes individual differences in educational attainment, and other desired life outcomes, is paramount. "Ironically, once we acknowledge the presence of genetic influences on behavior, the value of twin studies shifts from their ability to demonstrate genetic influences to their ability to illustrate causal environmental influences" (Johnson et al, 2009, p. 217). "Much gene expression is contingent on the presence of other gene products, environmental circumstances, and prior levels of gene expression, sometimes even in prior generations" (Johnson et al, 2009, p. 218).

Job Performance and Occupational Status

"Mental ability tests in general have a higher success rate in predicting job performance than any other variables that have been researched in this context" (Jensen, 1998, p. 282). Referencing Hunter (1989), Jensen summarized that mental ability tests " . . . in descending order of average predictive validity, were better than skill testing, reference checks, class rank or grade point average, experience, interview, education, and interest measures (p. 282)" in predicting job performance.

Gottfredson (2003) provided an excellent comprehensive summary of the research on the relationship between g and job performance (see Table 15.4, p. 310–311). She reported:

1. Higher levels of g lead to higher levels of performance in jobs, and along all dimensions of performance. The average correlation of mental tests with overall rated job performance is around 0.5 (corrected for statistical artifacts).
2. There is no ability threshold above which more g does not enhance performance. The effects of g are linear: successive increments in g lead to successive increments in job performance.
3. The value of higher levels of g does not fade with longer experience on the job. Criterion validities remain high even among highly experienced workers. That they sometimes even appear to rise with experience may be due to the confounding effect of the least experienced groups tending to be more variable in relative level of experience, which obscures the advantages of higher g.
4. g predicts job performance better in more complex jobs. Its (corrected) criterion validities range from about 0.2 in the simplest jobs to 0.8 in the most complex,
5. g predicts the core technical dimensions of performance better than it does the non-core "citizenship" dimension of performance.
6. Perhaps as a consequence, g predicts objectively measured performance (either job knowledge or job sample performance) better than it does subjectively measured performance (such as supervisor ratings).
7. Specific mental abilities (such as spatial, mechanical or verbal ability) add very little, beyond g, to the prediction of job performance. g generally accounts for at least 85%–95% of a full mental test battery's (cross validated) ability to predict performance in training or on the job.

8. Specific mental abilities (such as clerical ability) sometimes add usefully to prediction, net of *g*, but only in certain classes of jobs. They do not have general utility.

9. General psychomotor ability is often useful, but primarily in less complex work. Their predictive validities fall with complexity, while those for *g* rise.

10. *g* predicts core performance much better than do "non-cognitive" (less *g*-loaded) traits, such as vocational interests and different personality traits. The latter add virtually nothing to the prediction of core performance, net of *g*.

11. *g* predicts most dimensions of non-core performance (such as personal discipline and soldier bearing) much less well than do "non-cognitive" traits of personality and temperament. When a performance dimension reflects both core and non-core performance (effort and leadership), *g* predicts to about the same modest degree as do non-cognitive (less *g*-loaded) traits.

12. Different non-cognitive traits appear to usefully supplement *g* in different jobs, just as specific abilities sometimes add to the prediction of performance in certain classes of jobs. Only one such non-cognitive trait appears to be as generalizable as *g*: the personality trait of conscientiousness/integrity. Its effect sizes for core performance are substantially smaller the *g*'s, however.

13. *g* affects job performance primarily *indirectly* through its effect on job-specific knowledge.

14. *g*'s direct effects on job performance increase when jobs are less routinized, training is less complete, and workers retain more discretion.

15. Job-specific knowledge generally predicts job performance as well as does *g* among experienced workers. However, job knowledge is not generalizable (net of its *g* component), even among experienced workers. The value of job knowledge is highly job specific; *g*'s value is unrestricted.

16. Like job knowledge, the effect sizes of job-specific experience are sometimes high, but they are not generalizable.

17. In fact, experience predicts performance less well as all workers become more experienced. In contrast, higher levels of *g* remain an asset regardless of length of experience.

18. Experience predicts job performance less well, as job complexity rises, which is opposite the trend for *g*. Like general psychomotor ability, experience matters least where *g* matters most to individuals and organizations.

"In short, no other single personal trait has as large and as pervasive an effect on performance across the full range of jobs as does *g*" (Gottfredson, p. 311).

Based on an exhaustive review of the literature, it is undeniably evident that intelligent individuals earn more than less intelligent individuals (Lynn & Vanhanen, 2002). Jencks' (1972; 1979) study of the determinants of economic success was summarized by Brody (1992), who noted that "a 1-standard deviation increase in IQ is associated with a 14% increase in earnings with education and social class background held constant" (p. 255). Further, "a 1-standard deviation difference in IQ was associated with an 11% increase in earnings for individuals in the same occupation" (p. 255).

Hartmann, Larsen, and Nyborg (2009) comprehensively examined the predictive relationship between *g*, Eysenck's broad personality factors personality factors of P (psychoticism), E (extraversion), N (neuroticism), and L (lie scale), and individual socioeconomic status. Contrary to previous findings from numerous studies, they found almost no incremental validity to *g* by including broad personality factors in the regression analyses. They accounted for a minuscule amount of the variance—about 1%. "More importantly, *g* significantly predicted length of formal education, attained job status, and income" (Hartman et al., 2009). This is not dissimilar to what Jencks (1979) and Brody (1992) stated decades earlier, that "IQ is the most important single predictor of an individual's ultimate position in American society" (p. 255).

This irrefutable relationship is also evident in aggregates, as was documented by Kanazawa (2006), who noted that IQ, estimated by SAT scores, correlated with economic performance of American states accounting for approximately 25% ($r = .50$ when Washington DC, an extreme outlier, was omitted) of the variance in gross state product (GSP). The correlation is greater between state IQ and median family income. There was an inverse relationship ($r = -.35$) between the state IQ and the percent of its population that was living below the poverty level. "Across the states, the higher the mean intelligence of its population, the greater the GSP per capita, and the wealthier the state is" (Kanazawa, 2006, p. 596).

Further, the relationship between intelligence and the wealth of nations is apparent. National wealth or gross domestic product (GNP) can be predicted by knowing the mean IQ of the population. This is based on the assumption that because IQ is largely heritable, it can reasonably be considered causal. "Because the genotype pre-exists all behavior, . . . genetic influences have to be considered causal at some level" (Johnson et al., 2009). "The intelligence of the populations has been a major factor responsible for the national differences in economic growth and for the gap in per capita income between rich and poor nations" (Lynn & Vanhanen, 2002, p. xv). Whetzel and McDaniel (2006) essentially confirmed this statement; in addition, they addressed criticism of Lynn and Vanhanen's measurement of IQ in low IQ countries by truncating all IQ scores of these countries to equal 90. "In so doing, the relationship between IQ and wealth remained strong, and actually increased in magnitude ($r = .76$; p. 457)." In addition to measures of IQ of 181 countries, Whetzel and McDaniel used measures of economic freedom and democracy, as did Lynn and Vanhanen, but also included measures of public spending on health care and education in their regressions. "The multiple R for national wealth rose from .76 using the curvilinear truncated IQ distribution alone to .93 when public health spending per capita was added to the multiple R." (p. 456). Adding the variable of economic freedom to IQ, the multiple R was increased to .80. Spending on education did not add to the predictive value of IQ alone. In summary, using the curvilinear and truncated regression model of IQ, economic freedom, and per capital public health spending, the multiple R was .95 in the prediction of 121 countries' GNP (there were 121 countries that had no missing data on these 3 independent variables) (see Whetzel & McDaniel, 2006; Table 9, p. 455). According to Whetzel and McDaniel, "This suggests that almost all variance (90%) in the national prosperity of countries can be linked with IQ, health spending, and economic freedom" (p. 456). It is important to note that although IQ is the single most powerful variable in the prediction of the wealth of nations, there are two additional variables that add substantial incremental validity. One would think that these variables would contribute to longitudinal unreliability of nations' rankings over time. However, according to Kanazawa (2006), the "relative wealth and poverty of nations, with few exceptions, have remained more or less the same over the last 200 years" (p. 593).

In summary, "it appears that, just as some nations are wealthier than others because their populations have higher average intelligence, some American states are wealthier than others because their populations have higher average intelligence" (Kanazawa, 2006, p. 598).

Health

Lubinski (2009) presented a very cogent argument for considering general cognitive ability as an important variable in the study of epidemiological and

health care phenomena. In so doing, "cognitive epidemiology is placed in a broader context: just as cognitive epidemiology facilitates an understanding of *pathology*, it may also enrich our understanding of *optimal functioning*" (p. 625).

Lubinski and Humphreys (1992) compared intellectually gifted males and females, with an average IQ of approximately 140 and at the 86th percentile with respect to socioeconomic status, to "environmentally privileged" males and females with an average IQ of 115 and at the 99th percentile with respect to socioeconomic status. Their results indicated that the intellectually gifted group with a substantially lower socioeconomic status were physically healthier than the privileged participants with a high socioeconomic status.

Gottfredson (2004) noted that all indices of physical health are positively correlated with socioeconomic status (SES). It is a common assumption that lower socioeconomic status individuals are at risk for health related problems due to their relative lack of material resources. However, this assumption, and its accompanying theoretical explanations, cannot explain "why the relation between SES and health outcomes (knowledge, behavior, morbidity, and mortality) is not only remarkably general across time, place, disease, and kind of health system, but also finely graded up the entire SES continuum" (Gottfredson, 2004, p. 174). She posits that general cognitive ability is likely the fundamental cause of health inequalities across socioeconomic status.

Lubinski (2009) lamented the fact that given that these findings that have been accessible for years, there still exists the common practice to attribute positive influences on physical health to one's socioeconomic status. "Indeed, cognitive ability is frequently not even considered when modeling health behaviors and outcomes" (p. 627). A case in point was Gallo, Esinosa de los Monteros, and Shivpuri's (2009) statement that, "the powerful association between socioeconomic status (SES) and physical health has been recognized for many decades. Whether defined according to educational attainment, income, or occupational status, lower SES is associated with diverse disease endpoints and with premature mortality" (p.269). Their reserve capacity model does not include general cognitive ability as even a possible contributor in SES disparities in health outcomes. Rather, they suggest, "deficient psychosocial resources, such as low perceptions of control and social support, may be one of many factors that connect low SES with poor health" (p. 269). The most powerful predictor of educational attainment, income, and occupational status is general cognitive ability. To substitute a correlate of general cognitive ability in prediction models, such as educational attainment or social economic status, obscures reality and restricts formulations of tenable hypotheses and corrective interventions.

Examination of his Table 3 (Lubinski, 2009, p. 628) data derived from a "utopian" control design suggested possible outcomes of social policies designed to attenuate social problems, and to achieve explicit goals. The table allows comparison of the utopian subsample with the full population that comprised the National Longitudinal Study of Youth (NLSY) with respect to likely outcomes in educational attainment, employment and earned income, and childrearing characteristics, across 5 general cognitive classes ranging from very dull (< 10th percentile) to very bright (> 90th percentile). Omitted from the utopian subsample were participants raised in poverty or in single-parent homes. "The outcomes are strikingly similar between the full NLSY sample and the utopian subsample over the five ability gradients" (p. 629). Therefore, being raised in poverty and single parent status has little or no consequence with respect to health outcomes—but the 5 general IQ classes do, indeed.

Low intelligence is associated with lower income, more physical health problems, and shorter life span (Johnson et al., 2009). Johnson and Krueger (2005) provided a possible interpretation of these relationships that are somewhat similar to Gallo et al.'s (2009) "low perceptions of control"; however, g is the predictor variable. Those individuals that have genetically based personal characteristics, such as intelligence, tend to also have greater control over their lives and higher incomes, both of which are advantageous in maintaining physical health. Those individuals that have relatively lower intelligence, less control, lower incomes, and relatively poorer health, also experience greater psychological and environmental stress, which, according to Johnson and Krueger, "causes greater expression of genetic vulnerabilities unrelated to those personal characteristics" (p. 220).

With regard to psychological health, low cognitive ability in childhood is not only related to severe psychiatric disorders, it is also a risk factor for milder forms of psychological distress with regard to anxiety, and depression (Gale, Hatch, Batty, & Deary, 2009). Gale et al. (2009), after controlling for confounding variables such as parental social class, birth weight, parental divorce, and parental death, found that a standard deviation increase in childhood IQ was, in adulthood, related to a 39% reduction in psychological distress in one of their two cohorts studied, and a 23% reduction in the other.

Heterosis

The Flynn effect (1984; 1987) refers to the well documented, substantial rise (approximately 3.6 IQ points per decade) in mean IQ scores during the last century. The rise is not uniform across the distribution of IQ, apparently being most pronounced in the lower half of the distribution (Colom, Lluis-Front, & Andres-Pueyo, 2005). The Flynn effect is also variable across countries, and IQ indices. It is most evident in reasoning ability and problem solving, as measured by indices such as the Wechsler nonverbal subtests, and the Ravens Progressive Matrices, more than in subtests that measure acquired knowledge (Lynn, 2007). The theoretical explanations given for this dramatic rise in IQ have been varied and not without controversy. They range from nutritional, educational, economic and social, to genetic explanations—or a combination of all of these (Rodgers & Wänstrom, 2007). However, as Lynn noted, there is a zero correlation between the IQ scores of unrelated children raised by the same adoptive parents. This, together with the finding that the Flynn effect has also been observed in infants and preschool children, would for the most part diminish the credibility of educational, environmental, and economic explanations, and consequently suggest that genetics or nutrition (Lynn, 1998), or both, were tenable explanations for the increase in IQ.

However, an argument that most aligns itself with a genetically based explanation is that other human characteristics and traits have also increased in incidence rates, and these essentially parallel the secular rise in IQ. Furthermore, "it is actually difficult to find a heritable human trait that has not undergone large secular change in recent history..." (Mingroni, 2004; p. 68). A partial list of those with heritability estimates above 0.60 is sufficient to pose " . . . a paradox for environmental explanations for observed secular trends includes height, growth rate, myopia, asthma, autism (one of the most highly heritable of all the psychological disorders), attention deficit hyperactivity disorder, head circumference, and brain size" (Mingroni). Kehle, Bray, Theodore, Zhou, and McCoach (2004) have also suspected an increased secular rise in characteristics associated with emotional disturbance and social maladjustment in children, such as depression, anxiety, mood disorders, and aggression. The observation that both advantageous and disadvantageous genetically based phenotypic changes have occurred, and are in concert with the secular rise in IQ, would support the process of heterosis. "The condition that most probably causes heterosis to occur is the existence of microdifferentiation, or small-scale genetic heterogeneity between groups, that shifts to panmixia, or random mating throughout the larger population" (Mingroni). Heterosis, or hybrid vigor,

> results from the mating between persons from different ancestral lines. A purely genetic effect, heterosis enhances all polygenetic traits that involve genetic dominance. It is the converse of inbreeding depression. Heterosis results from decreasing the number of double-recessive genes that depress a polygenetic trait in relatively inbred populations; inbreeding depression results from an increase in double recessives. Heterosis shows up in the offspring of parents who each come from two separate regions that have long been relatively isolated from each other, and who have fewer ancestors in common than two persons from the same region would have. (Jensen, 1998, p. 327)

Mingroni (2004) also posited that heterosis offers a more tenable explanation for the cause of the Flynn effect, in that, "heterosis accounts for the high heritability and low shared environment effects seen in IQ, findings that are also difficult to reconcile with environmental hypotheses" (p. 65).

There is no evidence of secular changes in the IQ correlations of monozygotic twins raised apart, or in siblings. The degree that IQ is related to, or predicts, academic or occupational outcomes, has not in the slightest been affected by secular changes in IQ (Jensen, 1998). "Any explanation of the secular change in IQ test raw scores must take into account the fact that, unlike population means, there are certain properties of the IQ that have remained virtually constant across the past sixty or seventy years...." (Jensen, p. 322). These certain properties include "...its reliability, its correlations with measures of other psychometric abilities, its *g*-loading, and its external validity, as indicated by its correlations with variables such as SES, race, scholastic achievement, occupational status, and job performance." (p. 322)

"These findings suggest that any environmental factor(s) responsible for the IQ trend over time never varied among families at any single point in time." (Mingroni, p. 67) and therefore present strong support for heterosis. As a matter of fact,

"there would seem to be no plausible way to explain the IQ trend without positing genetic changes." (Mingroni, p. 67).

As stated previously, such a change could, according to Mingroni (2004), have a disproportionate effect on rare alleles, in that "even a small demographic change could have a very large effect on the phenotype under certain conditions" (p. 74). "On the basis of the assumptions underlying heterosis as a tenable cause for secular changes in many human traits, Mingroni's prediction that children who are more heterozygous than their parents should evidence higher intergenerational IQs" (Kehle et al, 2004, p.864), but would also evidence higher incidences of myopia, asthma, autism, attention deficit hyperactivity disorder, depression, anxiety, mood disorders, and aggression, along with all other heritable physical and psychological traits that are expressions of dominant alleles. "Whereas children who are less heterozygous than their parents should evidence a mean intergenerational decline in IQ, and supposedly other heritable traits with recessive alleles" (Kehle et al, 2004, p. 864).

As Mingroni (2004) has argued, there is no compelling environmental explanation for any one of these changes in several highly heritable physical and psychological traits, other than the occurrence of broad-based genetic change afforded through heterosis. "In scientific investigation, incorrect assumptions that go unquestioned are often a greater impediment to progress than frankly admitted ignorance" (Mingroni, p. 79).

Epigenetics

Epigenetics is an "emerging but fast growing field in the postgenomic era, involving the nonMendelian heritable changes in gene expression that are not mediated by alterations in Watson-Crick base pairing of the DNA sequence" (Devaskar, & Raychaudhuri, 2007, p. 1R). It is the new science of heritable biological adaptation (Devaskar, & Raychaudhuri, 2007). Epigenetics involves experientially based biochemical (methyl-CH_3) influences that result in the absence or occurrence of specific genetic expression. Champagne's (2009) research has indicated that environmental influences and experiences of one generation can enduringly alter behavior in subsequent generations. Developmental experiences, both in infancy and beyond, can influence the expression of DNA. Champagne and Mashoodh (2009) stated, "that it is becoming increasingly clear that creating a division between genes and environment limits our understanding of the complex biological processes through which individual differences are achieved" (p. 127). Their review focused on examples of gene–environment interactions that supported the argument that genetically based predispositions are realized within the context of particular environmental stimuli. For example, Caspi et al. (2003), in a longitudinal study, noted that depression could not be predicted by stressful life events or genetics alone. Depression appeared to be a consequence in individuals with certain genetic predispositions, who experience stressful life conditions. Champagne and Mashoodh believe that the results of the Caspi et al. study, and others, "illustrate the role of epigenetic mechanisms in shaping the activity of the genome in response to environmental cues and demonstrate the plasticity that is possible through shifts in DNA methylation" (p. 129). "Therefore, the transmission of traits across generations is not limited in scope to the inheritance of DNA" (Champagne & Mashoodh, 2009, p. 130). Genetic variation must be considered within a specific environmental context. The nutritional and social environment, as well as the process of learning and memory, can shape the likelihood that genetically based predispositions will be expressed.

Paul Kammerer, during the period 1906 to 1923, was probably the first to observe epigenetics, the process whereby behavioral and physical traits can be influenced by environmental conditions, and genetically transmitted to subsequent generations devoid of those environmental conditions (Begley, 2009; Vargas, 2009). In his experiments with the midwife toad, Kammerer demonstrated this inheritance of acquired traits.

Vargas (2009) summarized Kammerer's experimental procedure:

> Normally, the midwife toad mates on land and the male carries the fertilized eggs on his legs during embryonic development, which is spent exposed to air. By artificially exposing midwife toads to a heated, dehydrating environment, they could be made to spend most of their time in cool water, where they now copulated and fertilized their eggs. The eggs would cease to be carried by the male, but remained in the water. A few of these water eggs survived and developed into a generation of toads that innately preferred to mate and lay their eggs in water, even when normal non-arid conditions are restored. Kammerer bred up to six generations of "water" toads with this inherited preference. From the first generation onwards, both somatic and germ-line cells were exposed to water during embryonic development. "Water toads" developed a larger adult body size and from the third generation onwards, males developed nuptial pads in the reproductive season. (p. 668).

Apparently, the DNA of the midwife toads underwent a wave of methylation, resulting in some genes being "turned on" and others off (Begley, p. 32).

Further, as reported by Vargas, Kammerer produced hybrid crosses between the treated water toads and nontreated land toads and, in so doing, observed the phenomenon of dominance. The second generation had approximately a 3:1 ratio of water to land phenotypes.

Waterland and Jirtle (2003) showed that dietary supplements of folic acid, vitamin B_{12}, choline, and betaine alter the phenotype in mice with the agouri gene. This particular gene is responsible for the mice having yellow fur, obesity, diabetes, and, relative to other mice, shorter life spans. The dietary supplements given to the pregnant mice suppressed the expression of the agouri gene, resulting in the offspring having brown fur, and exhibiting normal life spans with an absence of diabetes. The suppression of the agouri gene continued in future generations of offspring without the dietary supplements.

The environmental toxicants, vinclozolin, (fungicide) and methoxychlor (pesticide), which do not cause genetic mutations, when given to pregnant rats resulted in approximately 85% of their pups, across four successive generations, developing breast and skin tumors, prostate and kidney disease, and immune abnormalities (Skinner, 2007a and 2007b). "What this means, then, is what your grandmother was exposed to when she was pregnant, could cause a disease in you—even though you've had no exposure—and you're going to pass it on to your great grandchildren" (Skinner, 2007a, p. 11). "The identification of novel epigenetic diagnostics and therapeutic strategies based on this unique disease etiology is anticipated to provide a significant advance in our understanding of disease phenotype transmission and development" (Skinner, 2007a, p.50).

Completion of the Human Genome Project in 2003 has resulted in incredible advances in our understanding of how genes and environmental factors interact. Rather than the expected 100,000 or more genes, the mapping revealed only approximately 25,000 genes—similar to that of a mouse, and less than what a plant has (Skinner, 2007a). It was hoped that after the mapping of the genome, it would be possible to read the "blueprint" and locate the genetic causes of diseases. It became apparent that something in addition to genes was being inherited, as evidenced by the human epigenome. Mapping the human epigenome will undoubtedly be difficult; however, as Mehler (2007, p. 11) stated, "it's crucial, it's essential. That's the way that the future is going to unfold. So in a sense, the human genome project was just the beginning."

This was noticed by Pembrey (2007) when he discovered that deletion of part of chromosome 15 would lead to the baby having either Angelman or Prader-Willi syndrome—two very different syndromes caused by the same damaged gene. "Although the DNA sequence is the same, the different sets of genes were being silenced depending on whether it came from the mother or from the father" (Pembrey, 2007, p. 3). If the partially deleted chromosome 15 was inherited from the father, the child will have Prader-Willi syndrome. If from the mother, the child will have Angelman syndrome.

There is considerable evidence in humans of transgenerational effects due to maternal experiences, and recent research has also documented transgenerational effects of paternal experiences. According to Pembrey et al. (2006) there is evidence to suggest that fathers' childhood experiences affect their sperm, and therefore influence their descendents' genetic makeup. Perhaps having a mechanism that controls the expression of genes relatively quickly, allows adaptation to deal with ancestral adversities. Pembrey et al. found that fathers' early onset of smoking, before puberty, was associated with their 9-year-old sons having greater body mass; however, this relationship was not apparent in their daughters. Such sex-specific effects were also noted in that paternal grandfathers' access to food was associated only with mortality risk ratios of their grandsons, not their granddaughters. If grandfathers experienced famine during their slow growth periods, between the ages of 9 and 12 and before puberty, their grandsons lived longer. Whereas, if the grandmothers experienced famine, both during their slow growth period and, to a more pronounced extent, during the time they were fetuses and infants, this affected their granddaughters' mortality risk ratios, but not their grandsons. On average, the granddaughters died far earlier. It is truly amazing that "the impact of famine can be captured by the genes, in the egg and sperm, and that memory of this event could be carried forward to affect grandchildren two generations later" (Ross, 2007, p. 10).

It have been postulated that "not only chemicals but also exposure to social behavior, such as maternal care, could affect the epigenome" (Szyf, 2007a, p. 7). The notion that being exposed to certain social behaviors could, through epigenetic programming, change one's behavior though life (Meaney & Szyf, 2005a; 2005b; Szyf, 2007a) is astonishing. Although epigenetic changes are very stable, Szyf's (2007a) research demonstrated they are also reversible. In animal models, they have shown that experiences alter the epigenome. Rats born to nurturing mothers were able to cope normally with stressful events, whereas rats born to non-nurturing mothers did not cope well with stress at all and, in addition, while under stress these rats increased their blood pressure and production of a stress hormone (Meany, 2007). When injected with a drug designed to remove epigenetic marks, the rats' behavior dramatically changed. They became less anxious and no longer screamed or tried to bite. "Also, they responded to stress like normally reared rats. And when we looked at the way that gene was marked in the brain, we saw that we actually changed the epigenetic marking of the gene" (Szyf, 2007b, p. 6).

In humans, according to Meany (2007), there is emerging evidence that the same phenomenon occurs. How a child is raised most likely can produce epigenetic marks that influence social behavior.

> If you grow up in a family that involves abuse, neglect, harsh and inconsistent discipline, then you are statistically more likely to develop depression, anxiety, and drug abuse. And I don't think that surprises anyone. But what is interesting is that you also are more likely to develop diabetes, heart disease and obesity. And the stress hormones' activity promotes the development of these individual diseases. (Meany, 2007, p. 6)

What is truly amazing is that it appears it is possible, as in Szyf's rats, to remove epigenetic marks. For example, myelodysplastic syndrome leukemia, a cancer of the blood and bone marrow, is usually fatal. However, treatment with the drug decitabine appears to eliminate methyl markers that prevent "tumor suppressor genes" from functioning. The results were "spectacular—complete disappearance of the disease—can be seen in almost half of the patients that receive this drug. And 20 years ago we wouldn't have dreamed that a drug that affects DNA methylation could have such a profound effect on patients" (Issa, 2007, p. 7). There is a likelihood that many complex diseases such as autism are caused by epigenetic triggers. The observation that monozygotic twins can exhibit different phenotypes, including one having autism and the other not, supports the possibility. Because they are genetically identical, there must be another mechanism causing the difference, such as epigenetic triggers. "We know environmental stimulation, sensory stimulation, auditory, visual stimulation, have an impact on brain development and brain function. And this impact we know now is mediated, at least in part, by epigenetic mechanisms" (Feinberg, 2007, p. 8).

Higher levels of cortisol are associated with a myriad of maladaptive social and psychopathological problems, and numerous physical health complaints. Children from low socioeconomic status, defined as families that have little savings and where the parents do not own their home, have higher longitudinal trajectories of cortisol output than children from higher socioeconomic status homes (Chen, Cohen, & Miller, 2009). These results were somewhat mediated by family chaos and children's perceptions of threat. It was assumed that low SES, and the often coexistent stressful environment, produces the hypothalamic–pituitary–adrenal axis that, in turn, produces the hormone cortisol.

Children who have been maltreated and raised in conditions of severe adversity are at risk for exhibiting psychopathology throughout their life spans. However, a subset of these children exhibit resilience that Kim-Cohen and Gold (2009, p. 138) defined as "a dynamic confluence of factors that promotes positive adaptation—defined as either the absence of psychopathology or the presence of competence—despite exposure to adverse life experiences." The most decisive influence on the development of an individual's psychopathology or competence may involve their " . . . subjective psychological reactions to social conditions, rather the properties of the external condition per se" (Kim-Cohen & Gold, 2009, p. 136). The child's perception of his or her social environment has the capacity to engender anxiety or reassurance. If the environment is perceived as unsafe and threatening, biological stress and concomitant alteration of gene expression may be realized (Kim-Cohen & Gold, 2009).

We are undoubtedly in the midst of the most phenomenal revolution in the history of human existence. The study of epigenetics will lead to the transformation of our understanding of how genetics and environment interact (Mehler, 2007). It does appear that genes interact differently with different environments (Ogren & Lombroso, 2008). The question becomes what kind of environment is most conducive to promoting optimal human functioning.

Applications to the Practice of School Psychology—The Optimal Environment

As stated in the abstract, the primary intent of this chapter was to present replicated and recent findings of research on individual differences, with emphasis on general cognitive functioning, genetic, and epigenetic factors that influence commonly desired life outcomes of academic attainment, occupational status, and physical health. And, to suggest relevant educational and psychological applications of these findings to promote the design of optimal environments that facilitate individual functioning. Ideally, these environments should be sensitive to individual differences, while maintaining allegiance to egalitarian goals.

Academic attainment, occupational status, and physical health are highly desired outcomes that are best predicted by g. Although it is considered by most school psychologists heretical to state, increasing g is not, to any major extent, afforded by environmental factors, including the child's family environment. "Wide ranges of between-family environmental variations encountered by children in Western societies have a vanishing small influence on post adolescent intelligence" (Brody, 1992, p. 173). We have no idea how to increase a person's general cognitive ability to an appreciable and enduring extent. Further, although academic attainment, occupational status, and physical health are highly desired outcomes, they are not the only important factors in life. In concert with Jensen (1998), "indeed it is the *interaction* between g and these other factors that accounts for much, probably most, of the enormous variance in the visible aspects of what most people regard as worldly success" (p. 573). For example, the personality constellation of conscientiousness is second only to g in predicting job performance (Jensen, 1998). Although its effect sizes for core performance are substantially smaller than g's, it is the only non-cognitive trait that is as generalizable as g (Gottfredson, 2003). More importantly, "worldly success" must include enjoyment of everyday life, or psychological well-being.

Psychological well-being is an enormously important aspect of enjoyment and happiness in one's everyday life (Kehle & Bray, 2004a; Lykken & Tellegen, 1996). Happiness interacts with g to some degree, but allows a broader and more inclusive definition of individual functioning, particularly if school psychological and educational practices are committed to fostering both individualism and the promotion of egalitarian goals. Unlike g, psychological well-being is more amenable to enhancement through carefully designed environments. This statement, on the surface, is in contrast to Lykken and Tellegen's (1996) research that suggested around 80% of the variation in psychological well-being is attributed to genetics. Further, based on data obtained from studying monozygotic twins raised apart, they concluded that the degree an individual enjoys happiness, although largely genetically based, may skip generations. That is, a very happy couple may have a very unhappy child; however, that unhappy child, may, in turn, give birth to a happy baby. They also stated that the degree of genetic influence on happiness is similar to the degree of genetic influence on one's eventual height. Consequently, Lykken and Tellegen concluded that attempting to increase your happiness is as futile as trying to make yourself taller and, furthermore, it may even be counterproductive.

Lykken and Tellegen's (1996) conclusions are most probably correct; however, what is most probably *incorrect* is their assertion that trying to increase psychological well-being is futile. That fact that they found psychological well-being skips generations would imply to us that it is not genetically but epigenetically based. As previously cited, phenotypical behavior that is epigenetically based is the consequence of environmental triggers. Further, there have been several studies, in both animal and human models reviewed in this chapter, that have showed elimination of methyl markers that, in essence, have turned on or off genes that are related to particular phenotypical expressions of dysfunctional behaviors and diseases (Issa 2007; Meaney & Szyf, 2005a; 2005b; Szyf, 2007a; Waterland and Jirtle, 2003). It is our contention that environments can be designed to positively influence, to some extent, phenotypical behavior including psychological well-being.

In order to get an idea of what are the components of beneficial environments, we considered what people want as outcomes of those environments. If you ask people the question, "What do you want your children to have when they grow up?" their responses are typically the same. A faithful interpretation of their responses to our single question was that they wanted their children to grow up to have (R.I.C.H.; Kehle & Bray, 2004a):

1. *R*esources to the extent that there is a sense of control over the allocation of their time, and to the degree that they have this control, they are credited with having professional status. That is to say, there is little bifurcation between their public and private lives—in a psychological sense, they do not "work." Further, and more definitively, they allocate their resources, to the extent possible, to initiating and maintaining friendships, to ensuring competence, and to maintaining physical health;

2. *I*ntimacy, or to be able to initiate and maintain friendships, and to enjoy social support. To learn from their friends and choose to allocate resources to them, particularly the resource of time;

3. *C*ompetence at something, relative to their peer group or a societal standard. Competence is defined as having resources, intimacy, and physical health; and,

4. *H*ealth, to the extent that they are aware of, and have allegiance to, the correlates of physical health that enables them to exhibit independence, intimacy, and competence.

The R.I.C.H. characteristics, on the basis of our understanding of Bertrand Russell's *Conquest of Happiness* (1930), form his definition of happiness. It is difficult to add a fifth characteristic to define a happy, or psychologically healthy person. However, challenging individuals to add a fifth characteristic usually involves the need for spirituality, which we believe is a component of intimacy. The lack of psychological health as depicted in the numerous definitions and theories of psychopathology typically include some aspect of anxiety, fear, or stress. The above four characteristics define life relatively devoid, but not absent, of these. It is assumed that these four characteristics are the foundation of environments that are most conducive to promoting optimal human functioning (Kehle & Bray, 2004a).

Briefly, the R.I.C.H. theory assumes that individuals intuitively strive toward acquiring resources, intimacy, competence, and health (Kehle, 1989; Kehle, 1999; Kehle & Barclay, 1979; Kehle & Bray, 2004a; Kehle, Bray, Chafouleas, & Mcloughlin, 2002; Kehle, Clark, & Jenson, 1993). The four characteristics are interrelated to the extent that they incorporate each other in their definitions, are relatively obtainable by all individuals, and the improvement or diminishment of any one of them results, to a degree, in improvement or diminishment of the remaining three.

Chesterton's description of Robert Browning's marriage to Elizabeth Barrett is a vivid example of this relationship amongst the four characteristics (Kavanagh, 1986). Elizabeth's riding accident left her with a diagnosis of a spinal injury; however, it was more likely hysteria. Her father, Edward Moulton Barrett, moved her from the country to a home in

London on Wimple Street. He "mounted a guard over his daughter's sickbed in a manner compounded of the pessimist and the disciplinarian . . . She was not permitted to stir from the sofa, forbidden to move, not even to cross two rooms to her bed, forbidden to see proper daylight, forbidden to receive a friend lest the shock should destroy her suddenly" (p. 11) and, most damaging, forbidden to write poetry. When Browning requested to see her, Elizabeth wrote back, "There is nothing to see in me; nor to hear in me . . . If my poetry is worth anything to any eye, it is the flower of me. I have lived most and been most happy in it, and so it has all my colours; the rest of me is nothing but a root, fit for the ground and dark (p. 16)."

The subjugation of Elizabeth's independence not only exacerbated her physical decline, it also eroded her ability to enjoy intimacy, and her sense of competence, even in her own poetry. Browning's reply was "I will call at two on Tuesday." (p. 16). On May 20, 1845, they met, fell in love, and eloped to Italy where in a brief period of time she was "toiling up the crests of maintains at four o'clock in the morning, riding for five hours on a donkey to what she called 'an inaccessible volcanic ground not far from the stars'." (p. 17). Mrs. Browning lived for 15 years after the marriage, "in infinitely better health than she had ever known before." (p. 17) (Kehle & Bray, 2004a, pp. 44)

As previously discussed (Kehle & Bray, 2004a), another example demonstrating the relationship between the four characteristics has been often observed in convalescent homes. When residents are allowed to promote their own independence, or friendship formation, their sense of competence and health improve. For example, if afforded greater independent choices in daily activities such as being able to plan their activities, trips, select their own menus, or decide to have a glass of wine at dinner, or choose to enjoy the companionship of a pet, psychological wellness improves.

We propose that psychological wellness or happiness should be the primary outcome of the educational process; however, it is most often relegated to secondary status below academic outcomes. It is our belief that psychological wellness would function as the foundation for promoting optimal academic and social functioning, in addition to fostering the values of individualism and egalitarian goals.

Decisions made by the school psychologist in the formulation of interventions, systemwide school policies, and students, should consider the R.I.C.H.

characteristics. In implementing change to promote movement toward the characteristics, the use of the processes of "chance" and "withdrawal." are important considerations.

Chance, similar to Darwin's (1859) function of mutation, allows change. Chance environmental events are specific and selective. "The individual does not go through life adapting to the changing environment; however, the individual does go through life being selected and affected by the changing environment" (Skinner, 1971). It is a daunting task to determine the functional relationship between the child's behavior and its consequences, given, according to Skinner (1971), that the environment acts in an inconspicuous and selective manner. "To understand the functional relationship between oneself and the environment, is perhaps the most challenging and intellectually difficult task in which an individual can engage—it is tantamount to knowing your own future" (Kehle & Bray, 2004b, p. 420). The procedure that perhaps best takes advantage of chance to facilitate movement toward the R.I.C.H. characteristics is affording the student diversity in his or her environment. Although it is alien to common educational and school psychological practice to assume that the environment acts selectively on the individual, if such is true, allowing greater diversity in the student's environment should increase the probability of selection by consequences. For example, individual students have a greater chance of initiating friendships if they have opportunities to come into contact with students similar to themselves, with respect to the predictors of friendship—proximity, similarity of values, and similar general cognitive ability (Kehle & Bray, 2004a).

Withdrawal from one's psychological or physical environment allows a greater opportunity to examine the functional relationship between oneself and one's environment, relative to promoting movement toward the R.I.C.H. characteristics. Withdrawal can be facilitated in countless ways; however, a timeless approach has been meditation. However, for some students, particularly young children and students who have highly resistant, dysfunctional behaviors, personal withdrawal is difficult to implement on their own. It is most likely that the teacher, or school psychologist, will implement a withdrawal strategy designed to help the student change what the R.I.C.H. theory refers to as his or her "ruts"—to change their psychological and/or physical environments. Ruts are the consequence of the individual's contingencies, value system, and reinforcement history.

What the individual child perseveres in and values may be quite detrimental to his or her academic and social functioning, and is typically quite resistant to intervention. One technique that has been employed to get children to withdraw from their dysfunctional environments and change to more R.I.C.H.-like psychological environments has been self-modeling (Kehle & Bray, 2009). In brief, self-modeling involves the video recording of the student in his or her typical dysfunctional psychological environment, editing the video to depict exemplary behavior within the context of a psychologically advantageous environment. Subsequently, the student, over a period of several weeks, repeatedly views the edited video of exemplary behavior.

Kehle and Bray (2009) have used video self-modeling to successfully treat (in approximately 70% of the cases) children with selective mutism. Bellini and Akillian's (2007) results of a meta-analysis of 23 studies of video modeling and/or self-modeling interventions designed for children with autism were quite beneficial in improving social communication skills, behavioral functioning, and functional skills. The meta-analysis indicated that video modeling and video self-modeling met the criteria for evidence based practices.

Bellini, Akullian, and Hopf (2007), using video self-modeling that targeted specific social deficits, substantially increased social engagement of two preschool children with autism. The intervention was four weeks in duration, where the children viewed 2-minute videos of themselves engaging in exemplary social interaction with their peers. The efficacious gains in the children's social engagement were maintained subsequent to the intervention. Several other investigators have also noticed maintenance of the gains shown in the video self-modeling results. Kehle and Bray (2009), with respect to children with selective mutism, are unaware of any child successfully treated reverting back to selective mutism. It has been suggested that the reason for the high maintenance effects of video self-modeling is that the intervention is based on learning principles, and therefore endures subsequent to the intervention. However, others have suggested video self-modeling actually changes the child's autobiographical memory of the previous dysfunctional behavior, which allows the maintenance of the newly acquired exemplary behavior (Kehle, Bray, Margiano, Theodore, & Zhou, 2002; Margiano, Kehle, Bray, Nastasi, & DeWees; 2009).

There are countless other strategies to promote psychological withdrawal, and consequently facilitate movement toward the R.I.C.H. characteristics. Some of these are predicated on changing the physical environment, and consequently altering the student's contingencies; i.e., changing the student's rut.

In summary, general cognitive ability is ubiquitous with respect to predicting important life outcomes, and historically it has been difficult to modify, if not immune to modification attempts. However, as stated previously, "it is the *interaction* between *g* and other factors that accounts for . . . most of the enormous variance in the visible aspects of what most people regard as worldly success" (Jensen, 1998, p. 573). More importantly, "worldly success" must include enjoyment of everyday life or psychological well-being. Individuals, if allowed access to optimal environments that are designed to promote movement toward the R.I.C.H. characteristics, will, to a degree, maximize their daily enjoyment of life.

References

Begley, S. (2009, September). What alters our genes? Was a 'fraud' really a discovery? *Newsweek*, 22.

Bellini, S., Akullian, J. (2007). A meta-analysis of video modeling and video self-modeling interventions for children and adolescents with autism spectrum disorders. *Exceptional Children*, 73, 261–284.

Bellini, S., Akullian, J., & Hopf, A. (2007). Increasing social engagement in young children with autism spectrum disorders using video self-modeling. *School Psychology Review*, 36, 80–90.

Brand, C. (1987). The importance of general intelligence. In S. Magil & C. Magil (Eds.). (pp. 251–265). New York: Falmer Press.

Brody, N. (1992). *Intelligence*. New York: Academic Press.

Caspi, A., Sugden, K., Moffit, T. E., Taylor, A., Craig, I. W., Harrington, H., et al. (2003). Influence of life stress on depression: Moderation by a polymorphism in the 5-HTT gene. *Science*, 301, 386–389.

Champagne, F. A. (2009). Nuturing nature: Social experiences and the brain. *Journal of Neuroendocrinology*, 21, 867–868.

Champagne, F. A., & Mashoodh, R. (2009). Genes in contest: Gene–environment interplay and the origins of individual differences in behavior. *Current Directions in Psychological Science*, 18, 127–131.

Chen, E., Cohen, S., & Miller, G. E. (2009). How low socioeconomic status affects 2-year hormonal trajectories in children. *This Week in Psychological Science*. Available from http://pss.sagepub.com/content/early/2009/11/30/0956797609355566.full. Accessed May 9, 2010.

Colom, R., Lluis-Front, & Andres-Pueyo, A. (2005). The generational intelligence gains are caused by decreasing variance in the lower half of the distribution: Supporting evidence for the nutrition hypothesis. *Intelligence*, 33, 83–91.

Cronbach, L. J. (1970). *Essentials of psychological testing* (3rd ed.). New York: Harper & Row.

Cronbach, L. J., & Snow, R. E. (1977). *Aptitudes and instructional methods*. New York: Irvington.

Darwin, C. (1859). *On the origin of species by means of natural selection, or the preservation of favoured races in the struggle for life*. London: John Murray.

Davis, O. S. P., Haworth, C. M. A., & Plomin, R. (2009). Dramatic increase in heritability of cognitive development from early to middle childhood. *Psychological Science, 20*, 1301–1308.

Devaskar, S. U., & Raychaudhuri, S. (2007). Epigenetics – A science of heritable biological adaptation. *Pediatric Research, 61*, 1R–4R.

Drasgow, F. (2002). Intelligence and the workplace. In W. C. Borman, D. R. Illgen, & R. J. Klimoski (Eds.). (Vol. 12, pp. 107–130). New York: Wiley.

Feinberg, A. (2007). NOVA Production. (produced by S. Holt & N. Paterson). *Ghost in your genes* [DVD]. Available from http://www.pbs.org/wgbh/nova/transcripts/3413_genes.html. Accessed May 9, 2010.

Flynn, J. R. (1984). The mean IQ of Americans: Massive gains 1932 to 1978. *Psychological Bulletin, 95*, 29–51.

Flynn, J. R. (1987). Massive IQ gains in 14 nations: What IQ tests really measure. *Psychological Bulletin, 101*, 171–191.

Gale, C. R., Hatch, S. L., Batty, G. D., & Deary, I, J. (2009). Intelligence in childhood and risk of psychological distress in adulthood: The 1958 National Child Development Survey and the 1970 British Cohort Study. *Intelligence, 37*, 592–599.

Gallo, L. C., Espinosa de los Monteros, K., Shivpuri, S. (2009). Socioeconomic status and health: What is the role of reserve capacity? *Current Directions in Psychological Science, 18*, 269–274.

Gordon, R. A. (1977). Everyday life as an intelligence test: Effects of intelligence and intelligence context. *Intelligence, 24*, 203–320.

Gottfredson (1997). Intelligence and social policy [Special issue]. *Intelligence, 24*(1).

Gottfredson, L. S. (2003). *g*, jobs and life. In H. Nyborg (Ed.), (pp.203–342). London: Pergamon.

Gottfredson, L. S. (2004), Intelligence: Is it the epidemiologists' elusive "fundamental cause" of social class inequalities in health? *Journal of Personality and Social Psychology, 86*, 174–199.

Hartmann, P., Larsen, L., & Nyborg, H. (2009). Personality as predictor of achievement. *Journal of Individual Differences, 30*, 65–74.

Hemmelgran, T. E., & Kehle, T. J. (1984). The relationship between reaction time and intelligence in children. *School Psychology International, 12*, 77–84.

Humphreys, L. G. (1985). General intelligence: An integration of factor, test, and simplex theory. In. B. B. Wolman (Ed.), (pp. 201–224). New York: Wiley.

Hunter (1989). *The Wonderlic Personnel Test as a predictor of training success and job performance*. Northfield, IL: E. F. Wonderlic Personnel Test.

Issa (2007). The dynamic epigenome and its implications in toxicology. *Toxicological Sciences, 100*, 7–23.

Jencks, C. (1972). *Inequality: A reassessment of the effect of family and schooling in America*. New York: Basic Books.

Jencks, C. (1979). *The determinants of economic success in America*. New York: Basic Books.

Jensen, A. R. (1969). How much can we boost I.Q. and scholastic achievement? *Harvard Educational Review, 39*, 1–123.

Jensen, A. R. (1998). *The g factor: The science of mental ability*. Westport, CT: Praeger.

Johnson, W., Turkheimer, E., Gottesman, I. I., & Bouchard, T. J. (2009). Beyond heritability: Twin studies in behavioral research. *Current Directions in Psychological Science, 18*, 217–220.

Johnson, W. & Krueger, R. F. (2005) Higher perceived life control decreases genetic variance in physical health: Evidence from a national twin study. *Journal of Personality and Social Psychology, 88*, 165–173.

Kanazawa, S. (2006). IQ and the wealth of states. *Intelligence, 34*, 593–600.

Kavanagh, P. J. (1986). *A G. K. Chesterton anthology*. San Francisco: Ignatius Press.

Kehle, T. J. (1989, March). *Maximizing the effectiveness of interventions: The RICH model*. Paper presented at the National Association of School Psychologists, Boston.

Kehle, T. J. (1999, August). *RICH-based interventions*. Invited address at the annual meeting of the American Psychological Association, Boston, MA.

Kehle, T. J. & Barclay, J. R. (1979). Social and behavioral characteristics of mentally handicapped students. *Journal of Research and Development in Education, 12*, 45–56.

Kehle, T. J., & Bray, M. A. (2004a). R.I.C.H.: The promotion of happiness. *Psychology in the Schools, 41*, 43–49.

Kehle, T. J., & Bray, M. A. (2004b). Current perspectives on school-based behavior interventions: Science and reality in the classroom. *School Psychology Review, 33*, 417–421.

Kehle, T. J., & Bray, M. A. (2009). Self-modeling. In A. Akin-Little, S. Little, M. Bray, & T. Kehle (2009). (pp. 231–244). Washington, DC: American Psychological Association.

Kehle, T. J., Bray, M. A., Chafouleas, S. M., & Mcloughlin, C. S. (2002). Promoting intellectual growth in adulthood. *School Psychology International, 23*(2),233–241.

Kehle, T. J., Bray, M. A., Margiano, S., Theodore, L. A., & Zhou (2002). Self-modeling as an effective intervention for students with serious emotional disturbance: Are we modifying children's memories? *Psychology in the Schools, 39*, 203–207.

Kehle, T. J., Bray, M. A., Theodore, L. A., Zhou, Z., & McCoach, D. B. (2004). Emotional disturbance/social maladjustment: Why is the incidence increasing? *Psychology in the Schools, 33*, 417–421.

Kehle, T. J., Clark, E., & Jenson, W. R. (1993). The development of testing and its influence on the practice of school psychology. *Journal of School Psychology, 31*, 1–19.

Kim-Cohen, J., & Gold, A. L. (2009). Measured gene–environment interactions and mechanisms promoting resilient development. *Current Directions in Psychological Science, 18*, 138–142.

Kranzler, J. H. (1999). Current contributions of the psychology of individual differences to school psychology. In C. R. Reynolds & T. B. Gutkin (Eds.), (3rd ed.) (pp. 223–246). New York: John Wiley & Sons, Inc.

Lubinski, D. (2009). Cognitive epidemiology: With emphasis on untangling cognitive ability and socioeconomic status. *Intelligence, 37*, 625–633.

Lubinski, D. (2004). Introduction to the special section on cognitive abilities: 100 years after Spearman's (1904) "'General intelligence,' objectively determined and measured." *Journal of Personality and Social Psychology, 86*, 96–111.

Lubinski, D. (2000). Scientific and social significance of assessing individual differences in human behavior: "Sinking shafts at a few critical points." *Annual Review of Psychology, 51*, 405–444.

Lubinski, D. & Humphreys, L. G. (1992). Some bodily and medical correlates of mathematical giftedness and commensurate levels of socioeconomic status. *Intelligence, 16*, 99–115.

Lubinski, D. & Humphreys, L. G. (1997). Incorporating general intelligence into epidemiology and the social sciences. *Intelligence, 24*, 159–201.

Lykken, D. & Tellegen, A. (1996). Happiness is a stochastic phenomenon. *Psychological Science*, *7*, 186–189.

Lynn, R.(1998). In support of the nutrition theory. In U. Neisser (Ed.), *The rising curve: Long term gains in IQ and related matters*. Washington, DC: American Psychological Association.

Lynn, R. (2007, March 2). What is intelligence? Beyond the Flynn effect. [Review of the book What is intelligence? Beyond the Flynn effect, by J. R. Flynn]. *Intelligence*, 515–516.

Lynn, R., & Vanhanen, T. (2002). *IQ and the wealth of nations*. Westport, CT: Praeger.

Lyons, M. J., York, T. P., Franz, C. E., Grant, M. D., Eaves, L. J., Jacobson, K. C., Schaie, K. W. (2009). Genes determine stability and the environment determines change in cognitive ability during 35 years of adulthood. *Psychological Science*, *20*, 1146–1152.

Margiano, S.G., Kehle, T. J., Bray, M. A., Nastasi, B. N., & DeWees, K. (2009), Examination if the effects of self-modeling on autobiographical memory. *Canadian Journal of School Psychology*, *24*, 203–236.

McGue, M., Bouchard, T. J., Jr., Iacono, W. G., & Lykken, D. T. (1993). Behavioral genetics of cognitive ability: A life-span perspective. In. R. Plomin & G. E. McClearn (Eds.), (pp. 59–76). Washington, DC: American Psychological Association.

Meany, M. J. (2007). NOVA Production. (produced by S. Holt & N. Paterson). *Ghost in your genes* [DVD]. Available from http://www.pbs.org/wgbh/nova/transcripts/3413_genes. html. Accessed May 9, 2010.

Meany, M. J., & Szyf, M. (2005a). Environmental programming of stress responses through DNA methylation: Life at the interface between a dynamic environment and a fixed genome. *Dialogues in Clinical Neuroscience*, *7*, 103–123.

Meaney, M. J., & Szyf, M. (2005b). Maternal care as a model for experience-dependent chromatin plasticity? *Trends in Neuroscience*, *28*, 456–463.

Meehl, P. E. (1990). Appraising and amending theories: The strategy of Lakatosian defense and two principles that warrant it. *Psychological Inquiry*, *1*, 108–141, 173–180.

Mehler, M. (2007). (NOVA Production, produced by S. Holt & N. Paterson). *Ghost in your genes* [DVD]. Available from http://www.pbs.org/wgbh/nova/transcripts/3413_genes. html. Accessed May 9, 2010.

Mingroni, M. A. (2004). The secular rise in IQ: Giving heterosis a closer look. *Intelligence*, *32*, 65–83.

Moffitt, T. E., Gabrielli, W. F., Mednick, S. A. & Schulsinger, F. (1981). Socioeconomic status, IQ, and delinquency. *Journal of Abnormal Psychology*, *90*, 152–156.

Nyborg, H. (2003). The sociology of psychometric and bio-behavioral sciences: A case study of destructive social reductionism and collective fraud in 20th century academia. In. H. Nyborg (Ed.), . (pp.441–502), London: Pergamon.

Ogren, M. P. & Lombroso, P. J. (2008). Epigenetics: Behavior influences on gene function, Part I. Maternal behavior permanently affects adult behavior in offspring. *Journal of the American Academy of Child and Adolescent Psychiatry*, *47*, 240–244.

Pashler, H., McDaniel, M., Rohrer, D., & Bjork, R. (2009). Learning styles: Concepts and evidence. *Psychological Science in the Public Interest*, *9*, 105–119.

Pembrey, M. E. (2007). NOVA Production. (produced by S. Holt & N. Paterson). *Ghost in your genes* [DVD]. Available from http://www.pbs.org/wgbh/nova/transcripts/3413_genes. html. Accessed May 9, 2010.

Pembrey, M. E., Bygren, L. O., Kaati, G., Evinsson, S., Northstone, K., Sjostrom, M. & Golding, J. (2006). Sex-specific, male-line transgenerational responses in humans. *European Journal of Human Genetics*, *14*, 159–166.

Pesta, B. J., McDaniel, M. A., Bertsch, S. (2010). Toward an index of well-being for the fifty U.S. states. *Intelligence*, *38*, 160–168.

Plomin, R., Pederson, N. L., Lichtenstein, P., and McClearn, G. E. (1994). Variability and stability in cognitive abilities are largely genetic later in life. *Behavioral Genetics*, *24*, 207–215.

Plomin, R., & Spinath, F. M. (2004). Intelligence: Genetics, genes, and genomics. *Journal of Personality and Social Psychology*, *86*, 112–129.

Rodgers, J. L., & Wänstrom, L. (2007). Identification of a Flynn effect in the NLSY: Moving from the center to the boundaries. *Intelligence*, *35*, 187–196.

Ross, N. (2007). NOVA Production. (produced by S. Holt & N. Paterson) (2007). *Ghost in your genes* [DVD]. Available from http://www.pbs.org/wgbh/nova/transcripts/3413_genes. html. Accessed May 9, 2010.

Russell, B. (1930). *The conquest of happiness*. New York: W. W. Norton and Company, Inc.

Skinner, B. F. (1971). *Beyond freedom and dignity*. New York: Random House.

Skinner, M. (2007a). NOVA Production. (S. Holt & N. Paterson) (2007). *Ghost in your genes* [DVD]. Available from http://www.pbs.org/wgbh/nova/transcripts/3413_genes. html. Accessed May 9, 2010.

Skinner, M. (2007b). Endocrine disruptors and epigenetic transgenerational disease etiology. *Pediatric Research*, *61*, 48R–50R.

Spearman, C. (1904). "General Intelligence" objectively determined and measured. *American Journal of Psychology*, *15*, 201–293.

Szyf, M. (2007a). The dynamic epigenome and its implications in toxicology. *Toxicological Sciences*, *100*, 7–23.

Szyf, M. (2007b). NOVA Production. (produced by S. Holt & N. Paterson) (2007). *Ghost in your genes* [DVD]. Available from http://www.pbs.org/wgbh/nova/transcripts/3413_genes.html. Accessed May 9, 2010.

Thorndike, R. L. (1994). *g* [Editorial]. *Intelligence*, *19*, 145–155.

Turkheimer, E. (2000). Three laws of behavior genetics and what they mean. *Current Directions in Psychological Science*, *9*, 160–164.

Vargas, A. O. (2009). Did Paul Kammerer discover epigenetic inheritance? A modern look at the controversial midwife toad experiments. *Journal of Experimental Zoology (Mol. Dev. Evol.)*, *312B*, 667–678.

Waterland, R. A. & Jirtle (2003). Transposable elements: Targets for early nutritional effects on epigenetic gene regulation. *Molecular and Cellular Biology*, *23*, 5293–5300.

Whetzel, D. L., & McDaniel, M. A. (2006). Prediction of national wealth. *Intelligence*, *34*, 449–458.

5

Theories of Intelligence

Michael K. Gardner

Abstract

This chapter reviews major theories of intelligence. The theories are grouped into four major theory types: (1) psychometric theories; (2) cognitive theories; (3) cognitive-contextual theories; and (4) biological theories. Psychometric theories derive from studying individual differences in test performance on cognitive tests. Questions about the structure of human intelligence, including the importance of general intelligence, have dominated the psychometric theories. Cognitive theories derive from studying the processes involved in intelligent performance. These processes range from the very simple (e.g., inspection time) to the fairly complex (e.g., working memory). Different theorists have focused on different processes (or aspects of these processes, such as processing speed). Cognitive-contextual theories emphasize processes that demonstrate intelligence within a particular context (such as a cultural environment). Major theories include Sternberg's triarchic theory, Gardner's theory of multiple intelligences, and Piaget's theory of development. Biological theories emphasize the relationship between intelligence, and the brain and its functions. Numerous relationships have been found, but none have been elaborated into a detailed theory of the neuropsychology of intelligence. The chapter concludes with several questions for future research in the area of intelligence.

Keywords: intelligence, individual differences, cognition

Introduction

The concept of intelligence and the tests developed to measure it have been considered one of psychology's greatest contributions to society (Hagen, 2007). However, the theories that attempt to explain intelligence are not all alike. They have emerged from different areas within psychology, and have emphasized different aspects of human performance. They have not necessarily agreed with each other concerning the number of abilities that constitute intelligence, or the organization of these abilities. Furthermore, the theories have evolved over time.

In this chapter I will review a number of the major theories of intelligence. For purposes of clearer exposition, I will group them into four major theory types: (1) psychometric theories; (2) cognitive theories; (3) cognitive-contextual theories; and (4) biological theories. As you will see, after 100 years of study, the concept of intelligence is still a subject of debate among those who attempt to understand it.

Psychometric Theories

Psychometric theories of intelligence are based upon the study of individual differences: in particular, individual differences in performance on tests that involve some cognitive component. In a typical investigation using this approach, a large number of people are administered a number of different tests of cognitive ability (e.g., vocabulary, number series, perceptual speed, general knowledge, analogies, etc.). These tests are scored, and the test scores are intercorrelated. The resulting correlation matrix can be further analyzed using mathematical techniques, such as factor analysis, to find underlying (i.e., latent) dimensions of cognitive ability (e.g., verbal ability, reasoning, etc.). These underlying dimensions usually form the basis of the resulting theory of intelligence.

It might seem that this approach to defining intelligence would lead to a single outcome on which all investigators could agree. However, nothing could be farther from the historical truth. This is due to a number of factors that were not immediately apparent, especially to the earlier investigators in the field.

First, the results of such an approach depend crucially on the sampling of tests used, and the sampling of individuals selected to perform the tests. Different selections of tests will lead to the uncovering of different sets of abilities. Further, different selections of individuals may also result in different abilities being discovered. This is because the technique depends upon individual differences in performance being present. The same tests given to a broad sample of the public will more readily show a profile of abilities than if these tests are given to Ivy League college students. The Ivy League students will have a restricted range of performance (due to ceiling effects), which will reduce the correlations among the tests. Also, similar tests given to individuals of different ages may reveal somewhat different profiles of abilities, as the distribution of individual differences in performance may change as a function of development.

Second, the results of the psychometric approach are, to some degree, intertwined with the mathematical techniques (i.e., factor analysis) used to analyze the correlational data. While factor analytic techniques were used to suggest the structure of mental abilities, some of the uncovered structure was the result of the technique rather than the data to which the technique was applied. When applied to non-cognitive data—or worse yet, random data—the techniques suggested similar structures to those obtained when applied to intellectual data. Once again, early investigators using the psychometric approach were less aware of this confound than were their later counterparts.

I now begin by describing a number of the psychometric theories that have been proposed for intelligence. I will follow the theories in historical order, because some of the later theories were, in fact, reactions to theories that had been proposed earlier.

Spearman's Two Factor Theory

English psychologist Charles Spearman was one of the first to develop a theory of intelligence based upon psychometrics. Spearman (1904a) had been critical of earlier correlational studies of intellectual performance, noting that the relationships they reported between cognitive measures underestimated the true relationships, because they failed to take into account the unreliability of the measures themselves (Brody & Brody, 1976). Spearman (1904b) performed his own experiment, in which he collected three measures of sensory discrimination (discrimination of pitches, shades of gray, and weights) and four measures of "intelligence" (school achievement, school achievement corrected for age, teachers' impressions of students, and "common sense" as evaluated by an interview). He then calculated the intercorrelations between the sensory measures (an average of 0.55), between the intelligence measures (an average of 0.25), and between the sensory measures and the intelligence measures (an average of 0.38) (Gardner & Clark, 1992). Spearman then made an assumption: that the measures of sensory discrimination and the measures of intelligence should, respectively, be perfectly intercorrelated, were it not for unreliability in the measures themselves. Using this assumption, he corrected the correlation between the measures of sensory discrimination and the measures of intelligence for unreliability, and found that the corrected intercorrelation was 1.00 (Brody & Brody, 1976)! This calculation was almost certainly an overcorrection for unreliability, but it led him to conclude "that all branches of intellectual activity have in common one fundamental function" (cited in Wiseman, 1967, pp. 56–57). Spearman termed this the "Universal Unity of Intellective Functions."

The Universal Unity of Intellective Functions forms the historical beginning of Spearman's two factor theory of intelligence (e.g., Spearman, 1927). According to the two factor theory, performance on any intellectual task is determined by two factors: g, or general intelligence, and s, a specific ability related to the particular task in question. The g factor is necessary for all intellectual tasks, though different tasks may call upon g in differing degrees. For instance, Spearman (1927) states, "At one extreme lay the talent for the classics, where the ratio of g to that of s was rated to be as much as 15 to 1. At the other extreme was the talent for music, where the ratio was only 1 to 4" (p. 75). The degree to which g is responsible for test performance is sometimes referred to as the "g loading" of a test.

It is fairly clear that of the two factors, g is the interesting one. There is only one g, but there is a separate s for every imaginable task. Furthermore, people can differ in the amount of *g* they possess. Thus, some students may have greater general intelligence than others.

But what is *g*? Spearman was not very clear on this point (Gardner & Clark, 1992). Occasionally, he claimed that *g* was simply that which was common to all tests of intellectual ability. This is an operational definition of how *g* was extracted or calculated, but it tells us very little about its underlying nature.

On other occasions, Spearman (1923) claimed that intelligence was the eduction of relations and correlates. The eduction of a relation is the ability to tell how two concepts are related: black and white are opposites. The eduction of a correlate is the ability to give a correct concept when presented with one concept and a relation: the opposite of black is white. Spearman proposed that all human cognition was dependent on three basic principles: the two eduction principles presented above, and a third, the apprehension of experience (the ability to learn from the environment). He therefore related *g* to his theory of the basic processes of human cognition.

On still other occasions, Spearman associated *g* with an individual's physiology. Spearman (1927) noted that *g* might be related to neural plasticity, or the blood. As we shall see, the idea that neural plasticity plays a role in intelligence is reflected in at least some of the biological theories of intelligence.

Finally, Spearman sometimes related *g* to mental energy (Brody & Brody, 1976; Gardner & Clark, 1992). The *g* factor represented some sort of mental potentiality on which individuals differed. Spearman even hypothesized that the output of this mental energy should remain constant, with new mental activities beginning when others ceased—a sort of "conservation of energy" law in the psychological realm. While the notion of "mental energy" is the most metaphoric description of *g*, it seems to be the one that has taken hold in the general public. According to this lay view, general intelligence, or g, is something people are born with. They possess it in differing degrees (i.e., they are "smart" or "dumb"), and it displays itself in many different intellectual tasks. Because it is innate, it is relatively immune to remediation or improvement.

Bond Theory

Bond theory was proposed, in slightly different forms, by Godfrey Thomson (Brown & Thomson, 1921; Thomson, 1951) in the United Kingdom, and by Edward Thorndike (1925) in the United States.

Thomson called his version of bond theory the "sampling theory." According to Thomson's theory, each mental test called upon some sample of mental operations, or bonds, for its solution. Correlations between mental tests arose due to the overlap in bonds necessary for each test's solution (Carroll, 1982). Thomson acknowledged that Spearman's derivation of a general factor was essentially correct mathematically. However, he felt it did not derive from an overarching causal *g* factor, but rather from the overlap of bonds, and the laws of probability and sampling (Brody, 1992).

Thorndike (1925; Thorndike, Bregman, Cobb, & Woodyard, 1927) also saw the mind as composed of a large number of bonds; namely, stimulus-response bonds. Again, tasks were correlated to the extent that they called upon the same stimulus-response bonds. For Thorndike, intelligence had both a genetic and an experiential basis: the number of bonds in an individual's mind reflected both the individual's ability to form bonds, and his or her experiences in the world that led the individual to link stimuli with responses (Carroll, 1982).

Thorndike's bond theory was also consistent with his "identical elements" view of positive transfer (Singley & Anderson, 1989; Thorndike, 1906; Thorndike and Woodworth, 1901). Training in one task would result in positive transfer to another task, insofar as the two tasks shared stimulus-response bonds (i.e., the identical elements). Practice alone, as suggested by the doctrine of formal discipline (Angell, 1908; Pillsbury, 1908; Woodrow 1927), was not enough. Practice must be focused on stimulus-response connections shared by the target task.

According to the bond theorists, Spearman's *g* factor was an index of the total number of bonds that an individual possessed. While Spearman's two factor theory and the bond theory produced very similar mathematical predictions, they painted very different pictures of the mind. Spearman's *g* presented an orderly view, with the mind dominated by a single factor. Bond theory presented an anarchistic view (Brody, 1992), with millions of bonds all having some small influence in an individual's mental ability.

Primary Mental Abilities

L. L. Thurstone was a psychologist and psychometrician at the University of Chicago who disagreed with Spearman about the existence of a single, overarching *g* factor (Gardner & Clark, 1992). In Thurstone's view, the mind was dominated by several "group" factors: factors responsible for certain aspects of mental activity (e.g., verbal ability or numeric ability). Once these factors were considered, there would be no need to postulate a "general" factor.

Spearman had pioneered the development of factor analysis, at least as it applied to the field of human abilities. To determine the g factor from a correlation matrix of cognitive ability tests, Spearman would extract a single, unrotated factor or component. This factor represented that which was common to all the tests in the battery. Thurstone (1931; Carroll, 1982), however, extended Spearman's factor analytic methods to include the possibility of multiple factors. Thurstone showed that a correlation matrix might require several factors to adequately account for the correlations present.

Armed with the methods of multiple factor analysis, Thurstone (1938) collected data from 240 students who completed 56 ability tests (Brody, 1992). These were factor analyzed, and seven to nine factors, or "primary mental abilities," were identified. The primary mental abilities were (Cronbach, 1970): (1) V, or verbal (e.g., vocabulary); (2) N, or number (e.g., arithmetic reasoning); (3) S, or spatial (e.g., paper folding); (4) M, or memory (e.g., digit span); (5) R, or reasoning (e.g., number series); (6) W, or word fluency (e.g., rapid word finding); and (7) P, or perceptual speed (e.g., comparing symbols quickly to detect differences). Occasionally, reasoning is split into deduction (D) and induction (I) (Cronbach, 1970), and arithmetic is split into numerical (N) and arithmetic reasoning (R) (Brody & Brody, 1976).

When the correlations among a set of ability tests are factor analyzed, the factors that result are not always readily interpretable. What emerges are a set of factors, and the loading of each test on each factor. The loadings indicate the relationship of the tests to the factors. When trying to interpret a factor, one looks at which tests load on it, and uses the nature of these tests to name the factor. But if all tests load on all factors, the interpretation process is hopeless.

This is the situation Thurstone (1938) found himself in. However, he proposed a solution to the problem. The factors that emerge from factor analysis are like axes of longitude and latitude. They are not fixed, but may be rotated around their center point. Certain orientations of the factors may be more interpretable than others. To find an interpretable orientation, Thurstone (1935, 1947; Gorsuch 1983, pp.178–179) proposed the criterion of "simple structure." Basically, simple structure seeks a solution in which tests either load high or near zero on a factor. Furthermore, the loadings should be distributed in such a way that all factors have some high loadings, and all factors have many zero loadings. This outcome leads to factors that are strongly associated with a few, and only a few, tests. The factors are then labeled according to what is common to those tests. Thus, Thurstone (1938) rotated his factor analysis solution to simple structure, and discovered the primary mental abilities.

Initially it appeared that Thurstone had disproven the notion of a single, overarching g factor and replaced it with a set of group factors. This led to a heated debate between Spearman (who claimed group factors did not exist) and Thurstone (who claimed g did not exist) (Brody & Brody, 1976). However, in later studies Thurstone (Thurstone & Thurstone, 1941) realized that in order to achieve simple structure, he would have to allow his primary mental abilities to correlate with each other (he had resisted this in 1938). He rationalized that many conceptually distinct entities (e.g., height and weight) were correlated with each other in the real world. Unfortunately, this led to the possibility that one could factor analyze the correlations among the primary mental abilities themselves, and this would lead to a general factor at the secondary level.

In the end, neither Spearman nor Thurstone succeeded in their original positions. Thurstone had demonstrated that an adequate sample of ability tests administered to a representative sample of individuals would require group factors to account for the high degree of correlation among them. But to achieve simple structure, these group factors would need to be correlated, allowing for a general factor above the group factors. How could these disagreements be resolved? We take up this question in the next section.

British Hierarchical Model

By the end of the 1940s, it became clear that neither Spearman's two factor theory nor Thurstone's group factor approach could adequately describe the correlations among cognitive ability tests. Psychologists in the United Kingdom (Burt, 1940; P. E. Vernon, 1950) proposed combining Spearman's and Thurstone's approaches into a single hierarchical description of human abilities. A typical example is given by Vernon (1950, p. 22). At the top of the hierarchy of abilities is a general factor (essentially Spearman's g) accounting for approximately 40% of the variance in ability tests. Below g are two major group factors: (1) v:ed or verbal/educational ability, and (2) k:m or spatial/mechanical ability. Under each of these major group factors are a number of minor group factors, which may emerge if there is a sufficient diversity of tests in the test battery. For instance, Vernon (1950, p. 23) states that the k:m factor may split into mechanical information, spatial, and manual subfactors. Under the minor group factor are specific factors (and error factors) related only to single tests. Thus, the hierarchical approach captures g and s factors at its top and bottom, and group factors in its middle. Exactly where Thurstone's abilities would lie depends greatly upon the specific tests being factor analyzed.

The British hierarchical model can be considered a "modal model" that combines and integrates many of the findings on human abilities that were discovered during the first half of the twentieth century. The British hierarchical model was wonderfully descriptive, but it did not lead to new avenues of research on human intelligence.

Fluid and Crystallized Ability

The theory of fluid and crystallized ability was originally developed by Raymond B. Cattell (1941, 1963, 1971), and later investigated more fully with his collaborator, John L. Horn (Horn; 1968, 1985; Horn & Cattell, 1966, 1967). Cattell and Horn's analysis begins by analyzing a set of ability tests into a group of correlated first order factors, similar to Thurstone's primary mental abilities. However, the number of first order factors extracted is somewhat larger, on the order of 30 (e.g., Horn & Cattell, 1966) to 40 (cited in Horn & Hofner, 1982). These correlated first order factors are then factor analyzed to produce a correlated second order factor solution. This solution has yielded between five (e.g., Horn & Cattell, 1966) and nine (e.g., Horn & Hofner, 1982) second order factors, the most interesting of which are g_f, or fluid intelligence, and g_c, or crystallized intelligence. The other second order factors are: g_q (quantitative knowledge), g_{sm} (short-term apprehension), g_{lr} (fluency of retrieval from long-term storage), g_v (visual processing), g_a (auditory processing), g_s (processing speed), and cds (correct decision speed).

Fluid intelligence is related to tasks such as inductive reasoning, deductive reasoning, understanding relations among stimuli, comprehending implications, and drawing inferences (Horn & Hofner, 1982). Horn & Cattell (1966) have associated fluid intelligence with the basic biological capacity to learn. Crystallized intelligence, on the other hand, is related to tasks such as vocabulary and cultural knowledge. It is related to experience in a culture, and exposure to formal schooling; that is, the knowledge acquired through experience with one's environment. Fluid and crystallized intelligence are not independent of one another; they are correlated approximately 0.4 to 0.5 (Brody & Brody, 1976). The distinction between fluid and crystallized intelligence is similar to the distinction made by Hebb (1942; see Brody & Brody, 1976, p. 32) between *intelligence A* (native ability) and *intelligence B* (realized potential).

The distinction between fluid and crystallized intelligence is more that just an academic distinction. Fluid intelligence is susceptible to decline due to central nervous system damage, while crystallized intelligence remains relatively intact after such damage (Horn & Hofner, 1982). Furthermore, the two intelligences display different patterns of growth and decline over the lifespan. Fluid intelligence peaks in the early to mid-20s and declines thereafter; crystallized ability peaks much later (in the early 40s), and in many cases remains high even into late adulthood (Horn & Hofner, 1982).

Horn (Horn & Hofner, 1982) clearly believes that each of the second order factors in his analysis represents a different form of intelligence. However, one must remember that these various "intelligences" are correlated, which leaves open the possibility of factoring the second order factors. This procedure could easily lead to a general factor at the top of the hierarchy, a result that would bring the fluid/crystallized intelligence theory more in line with the British hierarchical theory (for instance, see Carroll's (1993) "three stratum" model in the section below).

Three-Stratum Factor Analytic Theory of Cognitive Abilities

The three-stratum factor analytic theory of cognitive abilities was proposed by John B. Carroll (1993; 1997; see Sattler, 2008, for a summary). This model is similar to the British hierarchical model in that it is hierarchical; however, it proposes only three levels of hierarchy. At the top of the hierarchy is g. At the middle level of the hierarchy are eight broad group factors (Sattler, 2008): (1) fluid intelligence; (2) crystallized intelligence; (3) general memory and learning; (4) broad visual perception; (5) broad auditory perception; (6) broad retrieval ability; (7) broad cognitive speediness; and (8) processing speed. At the bottom of the hierarchy are 65 narrow abilities. The model bears similarity to Thurstone's theory of primary mental abilities (in that it contains broad group factors) and Horn and Cattell's theory of fluid and crystallized ability (in that it explicitly includes these as group factors).

Carroll was known as a consummate scholar. His model is based on reanalysis of a huge number of factor analytic studies in the literature. Whether one prefers his model or the British hierarchical model is probably a matter of taste. The British model can accommodate factors that shift in their importance according to the particular set of tests used in a study. Carroll's model is probably more descriptive of the true state of affairs when the sampling of tests and subjects is wide enough to approximate the universe of cognitive tests and the universe of normal subjects.

Structure of Intellect

The structure of intellect theory of human abilities was proposed by American psychometrician J. P. Guilford (1964; 1967; Guilford & Hoepfner, 1971). The model proposes that human abilities can be defined as the combination of one of five mental operations (cognition, memory, divergent production, convergent production, or evaluation) operating on one of four types of contents (figural, symbolic, semantic, or behavioral) to produce one of six kinds of products (units, classes, relations, systems, transformations, or implications). Thus, the model proposes 120 separate human abilities. The structure of intellect model is often presented visually in introductory psychology textbooks (e.g., Hilgard, Atkinson, & Atkinson, 1971, p. 370) as a cube, with each of the three dimensions of the cube representing mental operations, contents, and products.

Guilford (1977) later subdivided the figural category into auditory and visual categories (Brody, 1992), thereby increasing the total number of unique abilities to 150. Guilford spent a great deal of his career attempting to develop tests to assess each of the separate abilities implied by the theory. The major problem with the structure of intellect model is that it ignores the fact that virtually all cognitive abilities are positively intercorrelated: a finding known as the "positive manifold." Brody & Brody (1976) reexamined some of Guilford's own data and found evidence for the positive manifold, despite the fact that the structure of intellect model proposes that it does not exist.

By the end of his career, Guilford (1982) acknowledged that the abilities proposed by the model were indeed correlated. He modified the structure of intellect model by proposing a new,

hierarchical structure. At the first level of the hierarchy were the 150 abilities defined by the crossing of an operation, content, and product. At a second level of the hierarchy, he proposed 85 factors defined by pairs of abilities that shared one dimension (an operation, content, or product) but differed with regard to the other two. Finally, at the third level of the hierarchy, he proposed 16 factors defined by a single ability (an operation, content, or product) that shared the other two dimensions.

Guilford's theory of intelligence was a bold departure from those that preceded him. While his later modifications brought his model into better alignment with the data, it is the cube of 120 to 150 independent abilities that he will be most remembered for. Unfortunately, that incarnation of the structure of intellect did not account for the positive intercorrelations among cognitive abilities. The tests derived from it were often quite narrow, with little predictive validity beyond the test itself (Brody & Brody, 1976).

Conclusions

The psychometric approach to intelligence has been based on discovering underlying (i.e., latent) dimensions of communality by inspecting individual differences in test performance. Early debates concerned the importance of general intelligence as compared to group factors such as verbal ability or number ability. A rapprochement was found in a hierarchical model, with general intelligence at the top of the hierarchy, followed by major group factors at the next level, then minor group factors, and finally specific factors. Proposals such as the structure of intellect model, which hypothesized over 100 separate, independent abilities, have been shown to be inconsistent with existing correlational data.

Other proposals, such as the distinction between fluid and crystallized intelligence, have focused attention on important distinctions within intelligence. The distinction between fluid ability and crystallized ability can be thought of as the distinction between ability and achievement (or "realized potential"). These different aspects of intelligence show different developmental courses, and differing susceptibility to brain injury. Thus, while they may both represent intelligence, in many contexts it makes sense to distinguish between them so as not to confuse issues.

Cognitive Theories

While psychometric theories focus on the structure of human intelligence, cognitive theories have focused on the processes involved in human intelligence (Sternberg, 1985a). The cognitive processes investigated have spanned a continuum from extremely simple to reasonably complex. In my presentation, I will follow this continuum, beginning with research involving simple cognitive processes and concluding with research involving complex processes. Given the vast array of cognitive processes involved in intelligent behavior, there has been very little consensus on exactly which processes should be the center of attention in explorations designed to find the seat of intelligence.

Simple Sensory Testing

Advocates of simple sensory testing believed that more intelligent individuals were better able to make fine sensory discriminations, such as the discrimination of pitches, shades of gray, or weights of similar amount. This was apparent in the early work of Spearman (1904b). Others believed that more intelligent individuals would have superior physical stature and abilities (Terman, 1925).

Early interest in the simple sensory testing approach sprung from the work of Francis Galton. Galton was the cousin of famed English biologist Charles Darwin, whose book *On the Origin of Species* (Darwin, 1859) proposed the theory of evolution. Darwin had shown the importance of individual differences to environmental adaptation and reproduction. Galton's interest focused on individual differences in "natural ability" (Simonton, 2003). Galton (1869) felt that those with greater natural ability (roughly equated to a combination of intelligence and motivation [Simonton, 2003]) would be eminent in their fields of study, while those with lesser natural ability would fail to prosper.

Galton also made an important contribution to the notion of how intelligence is distributed in the population. He was intrigued by the work of the statistician Adolphe Quételet who had applied the normal distribution to human physical characteristics (Brody & Brody, 1976; Simonton, 2003). Galton extended this idea by applying the normal distribution to intelligence. To this day, tests of intelligence are assumed to be normally distributed (e.g., Roid, 2003).

Galton was a strong believer in the role of genetics in intelligence. He believed that intelligence was genetically transmitted by parents to children (Galton, 1874), although he allowed that environmental factors could play some role (Simonton, 2003). Galton also believed that races differed in

their intelligence, and that eugenics, or planned breeding, could be employed to improve the "intelligence" of a nation.

With regard to simple sensory testing, Galton (1883; see Brody & Brody, 1976) set up the "anthropometric laboratory" in the South Kensington Museum in London. He collected data on 17 variables (things such as strength and sensory acuity) from 9337 individuals. Unfortunately, he did not relate these to any criterion of intelligence, so his grand experiment ended without any proof of a conclusive relationship between simple sensory measures and intellect.

In the United States, Galton's ideas were championed by James McKeen Cattell. Indeed, it was Cattell (1890; see also, Brody & Brody, 1976) who first used the term "mental test" in describing simple sensory tests of the Galtonian type. Cattell had been a student of Wilhelm Wundt at Leipzig, and had had personal contact with Galton in Europe. While at Columbia University, he began a program of taking simple measurements from students in each year's freshman class (Cattell & Farrand, 1896). There were 21 measurements in all, and they included things such as strength of hand, visual acuity, cancellation of "A's", and reaction time. Cattell's graduate student, Clark Wissler, performed the validation study relating the simple sensory measures to students' grades at Columbia. Wissler's (1901) results were not very encouraging. He found that students' grades tended to correlate with each other, but not with the simple sensory test data that had been collected.

To a large degree, Wissler's validation study ended the early interest in simple sensory measures as an index of intelligence. Many years passed before interest in the relationship between simple measures and intelligence reoccurred. In the 1970s, however, several psychologists began to explore the relationship between cognitive measures (some simple, some complex) and intelligence. I begin by looking at one of the simplest measures: inspection time.

Inspection Time

In the inspection time paradigm (see Nettelbeck, 2003, for a complete description and review), participants are briefly shown two vertical lines, whose tops are connected by a horizontal line. The exposure is followed by a "backward mask" that overlays the original figure of the vertical lines. This prevents participants from further processing the original picture of the two vertical lines. The amount of time between the presentation of the picture of the two vertical lines and the presentation of the backwards mask is called the stimulus onset asynchrony (SOA). SOAs are varied over trials until, for each participant, the SOA is found with which the participant can respond correctly on 75% of the trials.

If processing time were not restricted, the procedure would result in virtually no errors, as one of the two vertical lines is clearly longer than the other. However, individuals differ with respect to this SOA parameter, and it is the relationship between participants' SOAs and intelligence that has been investigated. For simplicity's sake, I will simply refer to the SOA parameter as a participant's *inspection time* (IT). Nettelbeck & Lally (1976) were the first to report a relationship between IT and intelligence (defined as the performance IQ score from the Wechsler Adult Intelligence Scale): $r = -0.9$. This is an extremely strong relationship, but the Nettelbeck & Lally (1976) study used a very small sample (N = 10) with a very wide range of range of intelligence (72 points). This almost certainly exaggerated the size of the relationship, but it certainly piqued interest in IT as a measure of intelligence.

Several psychologists have attempted to estimate the true size of the relationship between IT and intelligence. Nettelbeck (1987), based on 16 studies, concluded that the size of the correlation was $r = -0.35$. These studies included only participants without mental retardation, since including the mentally retarded tends to inflate the size of the correlation. If the correlation is corrected for restriction of range, the estimate size of the relationship rises to $r = -0.50$.

Kranzler & Jensen (1989) performed a meta-analysis of 31 studies containing more than 1,100 participants (again, without mental retardation). They found a correlation between IT and intelligence of $r = -0.29$. With correction for restriction of range, the correlation rises to $r = -0.49$. Similar results were found in a meta-analysis by Grudnik & Kranzler (2001). In a sample of 92 studies with approximately 4,200 participants, they found a correlation between IT and intelligence of $r = -0.30$. Corrected for restriction of range, the correlation rises to $r = -0.51$.

The previous findings establish a relationship between IT and intelligence, but why does such a relationship exist? In particular, what is it that IT indexes? Several suggestions have been made, but there is little overall agreement among researchers. The earliest researchers in the field (Vickers, Nettelbeck, & Willson, 1972) felt IT reflected the rate at which the visual system could sample proximal stimulation, and therefore set a limit on speed of information processing. Later researchers (White, 1996) pointed out that the entire SOA function (essentially a psychophysical function) would include two stages: (1) an initial lag stage during which performance was essentially at chance levels, and (2) the SOA function portion, during which probability of correct decision improved with increased SOA. It was argued that the individual differences in the lag stage represented differences in focused attention or vigilance, while individual differences in the SOA portion represented the capacity to detect change in a briefly exposed visual array (Nettelbeck, 2003). Jensen (1998) referred to this second stage as "stimulus apprehension" or speed of perception.

What is clear is that IT, which was originally thought to be a simple task, indexing a simple information processing ability, is more complex than was initially thought. Further complicating the picture is the possibility that IT may reflect different cognitive processes for subjects with different levels of intellectual ability (e.g., retarded vs. normal) (Lally & Nettelbeck, 1980; Nettelbeck & Kirby, 1983) and for subjects of different ages (Kranzler & Jensen, 1989). While a relationship between IT and intelligence certainly does exist, it would be difficult to conclude that we can "explain" intelligence (or some part thereof) on the basis of IT.

Simple/Choice Reaction Time

Arthur Jensen has championed a slightly more complex paradigm for investigating the relationship between elementary cognitive operations and intelligence: simple/choice reaction time. In this task, a subject places his or her finger on a "home" button. A number of unlit lights are presented to the subject at an equal distance from the home button. In the simple reaction time condition, a single unlit light is presented. In the choice reaction time conditions, either two or four or six or eight unlit lights are presented. The subject's task is to watch for one of the lights to become lit. When this happens, the subject is to remove his or her finger from the home button and press a switch just below the light to turn it off. Subjects begin with approximately 30 trials in the simple reaction time condition. They then progress through approximately 30 trials in each of the choice reaction time conditions, beginning with the two-light condition and ending with the eight-light condition (e.g., Jensen & Munro, 1979; Hemmelgarn & Kehle, 1984). Time to response in this paradigm can be separated into response time (RT), the time between the light's illumination and the subject removing their finger from the home button, and movement time (MT), the time between the subject's finger leaving the home button and pressing the button to turn off the light. Theoretically, RT should represent decision time, while MT should represent the execution of the intended response.

Jensen (1982; see also Dreary, 2003) reminded the psychological community of a relationship between speed of response in the simple/choice reaction time task, and number of response alternatives known as Hick's law (Hick, 1952; Hyman, 1953): namely, that response time increases linearly as a function of the logarithm to the base two of the number of choice alternatives. This logarithm represents the number of bits of information in the stimulus display that the subject must deal with. The interesting finding with regard to intelligence is that the size of this slope of RT over bits of information is correlated with intelligence (first demonstrated by Roth [1964] and reported by Eysenck [1967]). More intelligent individuals have flatter slopes; they can deal with more information per unit of time.

Jensen and Munro (1979) replicated Roth's (1964) finding in a study with 39 teenage girls. The correlation between the RT slope and intelligence (measured by the Raven's Standard Progressive Matrices) was $r = -0.30$. Other measures also showed a relationship to intelligence: (1) the mean RT and intelligence, $r = -0.39$; (2) the standard deviation of RT and intelligence, $r = -0.31$; and (3) the mean MT and intelligence, $r = -0.43$. However, the standard deviation of MT did not show a substantial relationship to intelligence: $r = 0.07$.

Jensen continued research into the simple/choice reaction time paradigm and its relationship to intelligence over the following years. In a review chapter (Jensen, 1987; see also a summary in Dreary, 2003) he summarized the results of numerous studies with a total sample size of 2,317. He calculated the N-weighted correlations between the parameters from the paradigm, and the studies' various measures of intelligence. The results were: (a) RT slope, $r = -0.12$ (corrected for unreliability, $r = -0.32$); (b) RT intercept, $r = -0.12$ (corrected, $r = -0.25$); (c) mean RT, $r = -0.20$ (corrected, $r = -0.32$); (d) standard deviation of RT, $r = -0.21$ (corrected, $r = -0.48$); (e) mean MT, $r = -0.19$ (corrected, $r = -0.30$); and (f) standard deviation of MT, $r = -0.01$ (corrected, $r = -0.02$). Note that the individual parameters are based upon different total numbers of subjects (depending upon the designs of the individual studies), and thus the correction for unreliability may be different for different parameters.

What intrigued Jensen about the simple/choice reaction time task were its simplicity, and the fact that prior learning seemed to play no role in performance. In many ways it seemed like the ultimate "culture fair" measure of intelligence. However, several problems plagued research in this area. First, the slope of RT was the parameter theoretically related to intelligence; however, many of the other parameters correlated as high or higher with intelligence. Second, the mean MT correlated with intelligence, but this supposedly reflected only response execution. Finally, there was the issue of reliability, both split-half within a session, and test-retest over sessions. The various parameters demonstrated good split-half reliability (all above 0.66, with a median of 0.84), but the results were far more variable for test-retest reliability (range: 0.39 to 0.84, with a median of 0.63). Indeed, it was the RT slope that had the lowest test-retest reliability, of 0.39! Given that we think of intelligence as a stable aspect of human performance, it seemed hard to understand how an unstable parameter like RT slope could be used to explain intelligence.

Jensen had a biological theory to explain why RT slope was related to intelligence. I will leave this theory to the section on biological theories. However, suffice it to say that the theory was a distant extrapolation from the data, for which there was no direct biological support.

As with IT, the parameters derived from simple/choice reaction time paradigms show a significant relationship with psychometrically defined intelligence. The relationships are modest, but appear to show up reliably. However, the parameters from the task appear to be poorly understood from a cognitive processing perspective. MT mean correlates with intelligence, though theory predicts it shouldn't. Simple RT and MT means seem to correlate better with intelligence than the RT slope, though the RT slope is the theoretically most interesting parameter. If this doesn't shake one's confidence in the RT slope, consider the following: the RT slope of pigeons in an animal analog study (Vickery & Neuringer, 2000) would suggest they are more intelligent than humans! Apparently, we don't understand the simple/choice reaction time task and what it measures well enough to use it as an explanatory construct for intelligence.

Working Memory
Baddeley (1986; Baddeley & Hitch, 1974) introduced the concept of "working memory" to the cognitive psychology literature. Previously

(e.g., Atkinson & Shiffrin, 1968), the temporary storage of information was assumed to occur in a short-term store (or short-term memory). Storage of information was emphasized, while the processing of information was downplayed (with the possible exception of rehearsing information in short-term store to keep it "active"). Baddeley's proposal of a working memory emphasized both the storage of information and the processing or transformation of information being stored. According to Baddeley and Hitch (1974), working memory comprised a limited-capacity central executive that controlled two slave subsystems: the articulatory loop (for verbal material) and the visuospatial sketch pad (for visual and spatial material). The storage *and* processing aspects of working memory were proposed to be essential for learning, retrieval from long-term memory, language comprehension, and reasoning.

Kyllonen and Christal (1990) seized upon the importance of working memory for reasoning, and conducted a series of four experiments to determine the relationship between the two. The subjects in these studies were over 2100 U.S. Air Force recruits. In each experiment, the subjects completed a combination of paper-and-pencil tests and computerized tests, with the tests being somewhat different across the four experiments. However, the tests were selected to define the following four factors: reasoning (a combination of deductive, inductive, and quantitative reasoning, strongly related to fluid intelligence); general knowledge (a sort of crystallized intelligence measure); processing speed (a measure of the speed of performing simple perceptual/motor operations or the retrieval from memory of simple facts); and, of course, working memory. Data were analyzed using confirmatory maximum-likelihood factor analysis and structural equation modeling.

Kyllonen and Christal's (1990) finds were extraordinary. The correlations between the reasoning factor and the working memory factor in the four experiments were: 0.82, 0.88, 0.80, and 0.82! The title of their article neatly summarized their conclusion: reasoning ability is (little more than) working-memory capacity?!

Clearly, working memory capacity plays a central role in the information processing required to do well on tests of reasoning or intelligence, and this is what Kyllonen and Christal suggest. However, they note that the arrow of causation is not clear in correlational research such as their own. It could also be that those high in reasoning or intelligence

are better able to manage their limited working memory capacity. On this account, people high in reasoning ability have a more efficient central executive in their working memory system, perhaps due to their high reasoning ability. Either way, the relationship between working memory and reasoning/intelligence is very strong, and further research will be needed to flesh it out.

Cognitive Correlates

In the cognitive correlates approach (Sternberg, 1985b) to understanding intelligence and human ability, participants are tested using cognitive psychology experimental paradigms that are considered informative concerning basic information processes. Individual subjects' data are then modeled, processing parameters are derived, and these parameters are related to psychometrically defined abilities. Often, extreme ability groups (e.g., top quartile vs. bottom quartile) are used in an effort to more easily determine which parameters play roles in which psychometric abilities.

The foremost proponent of this approach has been Earl Hunt (1978; Hunt, Frost, & Lunneborg, 1973; Hunt, Lunneborg, & Lewis, 1975). He (Hunt, Frost, & Lunneborg, 1973) has tested undergraduate students at the University of Washington on a wide range of cognitive psychology experimental paradigms (e.g., Posner's [Posner & Mitchell, 1967] letter match/name match procedure; Wickens' [1970] release from proactive inhibition procedure; the Brown-Peterson [Peterson & Peterson, 1959] short-term memory procedure; Atkinson and Shiffrin's [1968, 1971] continuous paired-associates procedure; and others). These students were chosen so that they came from either the top or bottom quartile of a college entrance test for verbal ability, and either the top or bottom quartile of a college entrance test for quantitative ability. The crossing of these two dimensions produced four groups of students: (1) high verbal, high quantitative (N = 30); (2) high verbal, low quantitative (N = 25); (3) high quantitative, low verbal (N = 26); and low verbal, low quantitative (N = 23). Not all students participated in all experimental paradigms, but this total pool was constant throughout the many individual experiments.

Without digressing into the particular parameters estimated, and their correlations with verbal and quantitative ability, Hunt did come away with a set of generalizations from his studies. First, verbal ability appeared to be related to the rapidity of processes in short-term memory. Second, quantitative ability appeared to be related to resistance to interference in memory. These generalizations are based upon multiple findings over several experiments. Hunt expressed the hope that these findings could pave the way for a rapprochement between psychometric psychology and cognitive psychology, something called for by Cronbach (1957) decades earlier.

Unfortunately, the cognitive correlates approach has not progressed very far since Hunt's ambitious start. One reason is that testing large numbers of participants in cognitive paradigms is very costly and time consuming; yet, these large numbers are necessary to discover the correlational relationships between cognitive parameters and psychometrically defined abilities. A second reason that the cognitive correlates approach has stalled is that it is not particularly theoretical. While understanding psychometric abilities in terms of cognitive processes is a laudable goal, the cognitive processes chosen by Hunt and his colleagues were based primarily on the popularity of cognitive paradigms in the published literature. This popularity did not guarantee that the processes studied would be related to psychometrically defined abilities. The next approach I consider worked in much the opposite way: items from psychometric tests were analyzed to discover the underlying information processes.

Cognitive Components
During the late 1970s and early 1980s, Robert J. Sternberg (1977a; 1977b; Sternberg & Gardner, 1982, 1983; but see also Mulholland, Pellegrino, & Glaser, 1980; Whitely, 1980) pioneered the "cognitive components" approach to understanding intelligence. Sternberg (1977a, 1977b) investigated a task typically found on tests of intelligence: the analogy. Participants in his initial studies solved analogies while being timed. Error data were also collected. Sternberg used linear regression to decompose the total time necessary to solve an analogy into the time necessary to perform a set of information processes hypothesized to underlie analogy solution. The individual differences in the times necessary to execute the information processes were then related to paper-and-pencil tests of reasoning and perceptual speed. Error data were similarly modeled.

Sternberg's model of analogical reasoning consisted of seven information processing components: encoding, inference, mapping, application, justification, comparison, and response. *Encoding* set up an initial mental representation of the analogy. *Inference* discovered the relationship between the

A term and the B term. *Mapping* discovered the relationship between the A term and the C term. *Application* applied the A to B relation to the C term, to discover an ideal answer (D*). In multiple-choice analogies, *comparison* measured the process of discriminating the two answer options (D^T and D^F) from each other. The smaller the difference between D^T and D^F, the longer the comparison time required. Also, in multiple-choice analogies, *justification* involved justifying the better answer (D^T) as correct, even though it was not the "perfect" answer. Justification time increased as D* to D^T differences increased. Finally, *response* execution was measured by the regression constant. Not every analogy study modeled every component, due to differences in the analogies themselves (e.g., true-false vs. multiple-choice).

Sternberg (e.g., 1977a, p. 242) found substantial correlations (−0.54 to −0.56) between latencies for his basic reasoning components (inference and mapping) and a reasoning factor derived from his paper-and-pencil tests of reasoning. These component latencies, however, were not correlated with a perceptual speed factor, which indicates that the component latencies were not measuring simple speed of responding (consistent with Sternberg's hypotheses). Two other interesting correlational findings emerged from this research. Encoding was significantly correlated with reasoning, but in a positive direction (e.g., r = 0.63, Sternberg, 1977a, p. 242). This means that more intelligent individuals would spend more time on encoding, but less time on inference and application. Also, the response component was strongly correlated (negatively) with reasoning (e.g., r = −0.77, Sternberg, 1977a, p. 242). Because response was modeled using the regression constant, any constant processes (such as "planning") would be confounded with response. Sternberg (1982) interpreted these two findings as reflecting metacognitive processes he termed "metacomponents."

Metacomponents were information processing components, but they acted upon other components (rather than stimulus information) and governed things such as strategy selection and speed/accuracy trade-off. They were not directly estimated in much of Sternberg's early work, but their presence was suggested by the patterns of correlation of regular components (termed "performance components") and reasoning, just as the presence of a planet orbiting around a star might be suggested by the gravitational effects of the planet upon the star. Sternberg believed that much of what we termed "intelligence" could be accounted for by metacomponents.

Sternberg and Gardner (1983) extended Sternberg's (1977a; 1977b) earlier findings by developing information processing (i.e., performance component) models of two other tasks typically found on tests of intelligence: series completions, and classifications. These models included many of the same information processes found in the analogical reasoning model. Sternberg and Gardner demonstrated that information processes that were purportedly the same in different task environments (i.e., analogies, series completions, and classifications) would correlate more highly with each other than they would with processes that were purportedly different in different task environments. Thus, they provided evidence that the same information processes could underlie intelligent behavior across a range of tasks. Sternberg and Gardner (1983) also replicated Sternberg's (1977a; 1977b) findings of substantial correlations between component latencies and psychometrically defined reasoning, but not with perceptual speed.

The performance components approach offered a fairly direct link between performance on intelligence test items, and performance on cognitively-based information processes. Criticisms of this approach were based on its lack of generality. While one could explain psychometric performance in terms of the cognitive processes necessary to solve the individual items, how did these processes relate to other aspects of intelligent behavior in the real world—that is, beyond the testing environment? Questions such as these led Sternberg to develop his "triarchic theory of intelligence," which I will consider later in this chapter.

Processing Speed and Aging

Earlier I noted that fluid and crystallized intelligence display different developmental courses throughout adulthood. Fluid ability increases through adolescence, peaks in the early to mid-20s, and declines thereafter. In contrast, crystallized ability increases until the early 40s, and often remains high late into adulthood. Given that crystallized ability represents the products of education and acculturation, its slow growth may be understood as the gradual accumulation of knowledge. But what can explain the decline in fluid ability that occurs through middle age and later life?

Timothy Salthouse (1985, 1993, 1996) has proposed that the decline in fluid ability, and similar intellectual functions, is the result of a slowing of processing speed for cognitive processes with aging. He relates this slowing to two basic mechanisms of impaired performance: (1) the limited time mechanism, and (2) the simultaneity mechanism. According to the limited time mechanism, the time to perform later operations is greatly restricted when a large proportion of the available time is occupied by the execution of early operations. The simultaneity mechanism states that, due to slowing, the products of early processing may be lost by the time that later processing is completed. The result of both these mechanisms is a reduction in performance, not only in speed, but also in accuracy, as individuals age.

Salthouse (1996) found that nearly 75% of age-related variance in many cognitive measures is shared with measures of cognitive speed. This is strong support for the theory. Salthouse does not necessarily endorse that the reduction in speed with aging is due to a single factor (such as general slowing of nerve conduction); he believes there could be several common speed factors at work. He also believes that as individuals age, they adapt their strategies on cognitive tasks to try to compensate for the negative effects of slower processing. These strategic choices can mask the effects aging in everyday tasks.

While Salthouse's theory does not explain intelligence per se, it does offer an explanation for the decline in fluid ability during middle to later life. It also points out an important factor to consider when designing education and training for older adults: namely, speed of processing. When presenting information to older audiences, one must make accommodations for the slower speed with which stimuli can be encoded and analyzed, and for the possibility that older individuals may not have simultaneous access to as many different pieces of information as younger learners would.

Conclusions

Cognitive theories of intelligence have attempted to understand intelligence in terms of the cognitive processes that underlie it. In this sense, cognitive theories are analytic, attempting to break intelligence into its most basic components. The theories have differed greatly in positing just what those underlying components are. For Francis Galton and James McKeen Cattell, the components were elementary sensory and motor processes. Similarly, for IT researchers such as Nettelbeck, the components were some aspects of visual (and therefore sensory) apprehension (though, as I have said, the processes involved in IT may be more complex than the earliest IT researchers thought). For Arthur Jensen, the components involved the ability to process increasingly greater amounts (i.e., bits) of information and make a simple decision (i.e., which light to turn off). For Kyllonen and Christal, the components were those processes involved in working memory. For Earl Hunt and colleagues, the components were the processes involved in STM (for verbal ability) and the ability to resist interference in memory (for quantitative ability). For Sternberg and colleagues, the components were the information processes involved in solving intelligence test items such as analogies, series completions, and classifications.

Up to this point, I haven't mentioned the researchers who developed many of the actual assessment instruments in use today (or, at least, their historical forerunners). Binet's (Binet & Henri, 1896) initial conception of intelligence was based upon the psychology of faculties (Brody, 1992; Brody & Brody, 1976). This school of thought viewed the mind as composed of numerous independent abilities. The actual list of abilities, or faculties, came from philosophers such as Christian von Wolff, Thomas Reid, and Dugald Stewart. Binet believed that intelligence was based upon numerous quasi-independent abilities such imagination, attention, and comprehension. He also believed that a test of intelligence should sample these higher order cognitive processes (Brody, 1992; Brody & Brody, 1976; Sternberg & Jarvin, 2003).

By the time that Binet (Binet & Simon, 1905) actually developed his Metric Scale of Intelligence, he had moved away from using a theoretical model, and instead based his item and test selection on predictive validity: which items could differentiate retarded from nonretarded children. In his 1908 revision of the test (Binet & Simon, 1908), he extended the test so that it was able to differentiate among normal children, and the concept of mental age was introduced (Brody & Brody, 1976; Sternberg & Jarvin, 2003). A third revision of the test was produced in 1911 (Binet, 1911).

Binet did not actually introduce the notion of an intelligence quotient, or IQ (Brody, 1992). This innovation was produced by Stern (1912), who proposed dividing an individual's mental age by their chronological age, and multiplying by 100. This advancement allowed children of different ages to be compared in terms of their relative intellectual performances.

Binet's cognitive theory of intelligence, to the extent it existed, was tied to complex information processing. In a sense, Binet sought an average level of an individual's complex cognitive processing (Tuddenham, 1962, cited in Brody & Brody, 1976). David Wechsler, developer of the various Wechsler scales of intelligence (Wechsler, 1939; 1949; 1967), also felt that intelligence was a multifaceted construct tapping many complex processes (Wechsler, 1944). Not surprisingly, the tests that bear his name involve a number of cognitively complex subtests (e.g., vocabulary and object assembly).

My overall conclusion is that everyone recognizes that intelligence is based upon cognitive processing. However, researchers and theorists have differed with regard to the complexity of the cognitive processes that underlie intelligence. Successful assessment instruments have tended to emphasize the complex end of the continuum. Researchers from the field of cognitive psychology have to emphasize simpler processes (e.g., Nettelbeck, Jensen, and Hunt), though not exclusively (e.g., Sternberg).

Psychometric theories emphasize the structure of intelligence, while cognitive theories emphasize the processes involved in intelligence. In the next section, I discuss cognitive-contextual theories of intelligence, which emphasize the context in which intelligence in displayed.

Cognitive-Contextual Theories

Cognitive-contextual theories attempt to explain intelligent behavior in terms of the context in which it is displayed. While cognitive processing is certainly important within these theories, they tend to take a more biological approach: development of certain skills is determined (and encouraged) by fit to the environment or culture. Thus, there may be no such thing as universal intelligence; only intelligence or intelligences that are environmentally or culturally relevant. These theories also take a more "big picture" view than many of the cognitive theories discussed earlier. They tend not to focus on individual cognitive processes, but rather classes of processes, or types of intelligence.

Triarchic Theory of Intelligence

Sternberg's (1977a, 1977b) componential analysis of intelligence test items led him eventually to consider how information processing might interface with the environmental context in which it is displayed. By the mid-1980s, Sternberg (1985c, 1988) had proposed his triarchic theory of intelligence. This theory had three separate aspects: (1) the mechanics of intelligence; (2) the continuum of experience; and (3) the fit of an individual to the environment.

The mechanics of intelligence refer to the actual cognitive processes responsible for intelligent behavior. Three types of information processes (some of which I discussed earlier) were delineated by Sternberg. First, there were *performance components* (e.g., Sternberg, 1977a, 1977b; Sternberg & Gardner, 1983). These were cognitive processes that operated upon data and produced solution to problems. Second, there were *metacomponents* (e.g., Sternberg, 1980). These were cognitive processes responsible for performance component selection, organization, and strategic processing (e.g., speed/accuracy tradeoffs, self-terminating versus exhaustive processing, etc.). Third, there were *knowledge acquisition components* (Sternberg & Powell, 1983). These were components specifically involved with the acquisition of new information. They were highlighted in studies of the acquisition of vocabulary from surrounding context. Together, the three types of components (or information processes) were responsible for producing intelligence behavior in any particular context.

The continuum of experience refers to the fact that learning progresses from problems that are novel, to problems that are uncommon, to problems that are common, to problems that are routine. Speed and error rates for information processing components will correlate with intelligence, but only at two points along this continuum of experience: when problems are *novel* (Gardner & Sternberg, 1994) and when problems are so routine that they involve *automatic processing* (see Schneider & Shiffrin [1977] and Shiffrin & Schneider [1977] for a discussion of automaticity). According to the triarchic theory, when problems are novel, more intelligent individuals will display faster and less error prone componental processing. This is the typical finding on tests of fluid intelligence. With regard to automaticity (i.e., processing that is so routine that it consumes little to no attentional resources), more intelligent individuals are able to automate their componental processing more quickly than less intelligent individuals. Thus, with routine problems, more intelligent individuals are more likely to be fast and error free than less intelligent individuals, because more intelligent individuals are more likely to be relying on automatic processing.

The fit of the individual to the environment expands the triarchic theory, using the biological notions of adaptation and natural selection. According to Sternberg, more intelligent individuals fit into their environments better than less

intelligent individuals. This optimum fit can be accomplished in one of three ways: adaptation, selection, or shaping. In *adaptation*, the individual changes to better fit their environment. Thus, a student who arrives at graduate school with poor study skills may adapt to his new environment by improving his study skills. In *selection*, the individual may choose a new environment, if they are unable to fit into the current environment. Thus, a student who is unhappy in graduate school may choose a new occupation that doesn't require graduate study. In *shaping*, the individual attempts to change the environment to better match her or his abilities. Thus, a graduate student with poor verbal skill may try to convince professors that courses need to include a quantitative, statistical component. It just so happens that such courses would better align with this student's current skill set.

As you can see, the triarchic theory incorporates Sternberg's cognitive theory (the componental analysis of skills), but moves beyond it by delineating environmental variables that also influence performance. The theory is quite broad. However, like most broad theories, predictions in particular situations are not always well specified. Sternberg's more recent interests have included such wide ranging areas as practical intelligence (Wagner & Sternberg, 1985), creativity (Sternberg & Lubart, 1991, 1992), and wisdom (Sternberg, 1998).

Multiple Intelligences

Howard Gardner (1983, 1999) has proposed a "theory of multiple intelligences" that also strongly relies on the context in which cognitive processes are displayed. Gardner has long had an interest in the arts, and felt that the development of "artistic" skills was downplayed in theories of cognitive and developmental psychology. He later worked in the area of neuropsychology, and was struck by how brain injury could impair one skill while leaving others untouched. These experiences led him to propose (Gardner, 1983) seven relatively independent intelligences. The seven intelligences were: (1) *linguistic intelligence*, or the "sensitivity to spoken and written language" (Gardner, 1999, p. 41); (2) *logical-mathematical intelligence*, or the "capacity to analyze problems logically, carry out mathematical operations, and investigate issues scientifically" (Gardner, 1999, p. 42); (3) *musical intelligence*, or "skill in the performance, composition, and appreciation of musical patterns" (Gardner, 1999, p. 42); (4) *bodily-kinesthetic intelligence*, or the "potential of using one's whole body or parts of the body (like the hand or the mouth) to solve problems or fashion products" (Gardner, 1999. p. 42); (5) *spatial intelligence*, or "the potential to recognize and manipulate the patterns of wide space… as well as the patterns of more confined areas" (Gardner, 1999, p. 42); (6) *interpersonal intelligence*, or "a person's capacity to understand the intentions, motivations, and desires of other people and, consequently, to work effectively with others" (Gardner, 1999, p. 43); and (7) *intrapersonal intelligence*, or "the capacity to understand oneself, to have an effective working model of oneself—including one's own desires, fears, and capacities—and to use such information effectively in regulating one's own life" (Gardner, 1999, p. 43). Over time (Gardner, 1999), Gardner has added three new intelligences to the list: (1) *naturalistic intelligence*, or the "ability to discern patterns in nature" (Sattler, 2008, p. 234); (2) *spiritual intelligence*, or a "concern with cosmic or existential issues and recognition of the spiritual as an ultimate state of being" (Sattler, 2008, p. 234); and (3) *existential intelligence*, or a "concern with ultimate issues" (Sattler, 2008, p. 234).

In determining what does or does not constitute an intelligence, Gardner (1999) has relied upon eight sources of evidence derived from four different disciplinary backgrounds. From the biological sciences come the criteria of (1) the potential of isolation (or dissociation) by brain damage, and (2) an evolutionary history and evolutionary plausibility (does the intelligence serve a role in the evolution of our species?). From logical analysis come the criteria of (3) an identifiable core operation or set of operations (i.e., core cognitive operations), and (4) susceptibility to encoding in a symbol system (is the intelligence associated with its own symbol system?). From developmental psychology come the criteria of (5) a distinct developmental history, along with a definable set of expert "end-state" performances (i.e., ways of developing one's intelligence to serve a particular role in society), and (6) the existence of idiot savants, prodigies, and other exceptional people. From traditional psychology come the criteria of (7) support from experimental psychological tasks (i.e., is there evidence of independence of operations or interference among operations?), and (8) support from psychometric findings. The more evidence that can be found, and the more sources of evidence that can be adduced, the more likely a set of skills will be termed an "intelligence." As you can see from the list, context plays a major role in Gardner's theory, as intelligences may serve different functions in different

cultural contexts and at different points in both the individual's developmental history, and the species' evolutionary history.

Gardner's theory of multiple intelligences has not been well received by traditional psychologists (see Brody, 1996, for a critical review). However, it is extremely popular with educators (H. Gardner, personal communication, April, 9, 2008), who embrace the idea that we can all be talented, though perhaps in different ways. Multiple intelligences can be criticized on two grounds. First, it ignores the so-called positive manifold—the fact that traditional tests of cognitive abilities are positively intercorrelated. This should imply that at least linguistic and logical-mathematical intelligences would be correlated rather than independent. Second, it expands the definition of intelligence beyond its original meaning. When Binet was developing his original intelligence tests, intelligence was defined as the ability to do well in school (or school-like environments). Gardner's (1999) definition of intelligence is "a biopsychological potential to process information that can be activated in a cultural setting to solve problems or create products that are of value in a culture" (pp. 33–34). This is certainly a much broader definition of intelligence. Others have also expanded the use of the term intelligence, as in "practical intelligence" (Wagner & Sternberg, 1985) and "emotional intelligence" (Goleman, 1997; Salovey & Mayer, 1989–1990). But if intelligence can mean almost anything, does it mean anything at all? As Gardner has extended the meanings of intelligence, he also has diluted its meaning to a degree. In the end, the success of the theory of multiple intelligences will depend upon two things: (1) will new research support the distinctions it makes? and (2) will it inspire any new, successful applications (such as methods of instruction)?

Piaget's Stage Theory of Development
While Piaget's stage theory (Piaget, 1954, 1970, 1977; Piaget & Inhelder, 1969; see also Flavell, 1985 for a briefer review) is essentially a theory of child development, it is also a theory of the development of intelligence. It is both cognitive (it discusses thought processes) and contextual (it emphasizes the role of environment in stimulating cognitive growth). The theory is based in principles that Piaget derived from biology: namely, adaptation, assimilation, and accommodation. The child assimilates information from the environment using current ways of thinking about the world, which Piaget

called *schemes*. As new mental structures develop, the child will eventually find a mismatch between environmental stimuli and current schemes (i.e., cognitive disequilibrium). This can cause the child to accommodate to the stimuli by creating new, more advanced schemes that are a better match to the environment.

Piaget's model of the development of intelligence was qualitative, in that older children not only knew more than younger children, they knew *differently* than younger children. Children's thought progressed through four basic stages. During the *sensorimotor stage* (approximately ages birth to two years), children understand their environment through sensation and motor operations. By the end of the sensorimotor period, children understand that objects continue to exist when out of sight (object permanence) and they can remember and imagine ideas and experiences (mental representation). This second achievement allows the development of language.

During the *preoperational stage* (approximate age two years to six years), children use symbolic thinking (including language) to understand the world. Imagination flourishes during this period. The child begins the preoperational stage with an egocentric point of view (they think others will see and experience things as they do); however, over the course of this period, children gradually decenter (they become able to take the point of view of others). Children possess a quasi-logic at this stage: they can reason about things, but only in a qualitative way.

During the *concrete operational stage* (approximately age seven years to eleven years), children learn to apply quantitative, logical operations to specific experiences or perceptions. During this stage children acquire the concepts of conservation, number, classification, and seriation. Children also begin to appreciate that many questions have specific, correct answers that can be arrived at through measurement and logical reasoning.

During the *formal operational stage* (approximately twelve years onward) the adolescent or adult begins to be able to think about abstractions and hypothetical ideas. It is no longer necessary for individuals at this stage to manipulate objects to arrive at the solution to a problem. The capacities developed during the formal operational stage make subjects such ethics, politics, and the social sciences much more interesting to students. Piaget hypothesized that not all individuals achieve full, formal operational thought.

While Piaget's theory does not address psychometric *g*, it certainly addresses the development of the cognitive mechanisms that underlie much of formal reasoning and problem solving. It views the individual as someone who interacts with the environment, and who strives to have his or her thoughts (or *schemes*) in line with experience. It makes the strong claim that all individuals pass through the stages in the same order, with no one "skipping" any stages en route to higher stages. While many have criticized the exact ages given by Piaget for the attainment of specific skills, few have criticized his theory's ability to describe children's gradual acquisition of complex thought.

Conclusions

Cognitive-contextual theories attempt to embed cognitive processing in an environmental or cultural milieu. All of these theories go beyond the type of test performance studied by psychometricians, and some make strong claims (e.g., there are potentially 10 intelligences, or children pass through cognitive stages in a fixed order). All of the theories cited above make use of extensive evidence from many domains.

However, in most cases the link to the environment provides support for the theories without yielding testable claims. Sternberg's three types of fit (i.e, adaptation, selection, and shaping) between individual and environment are mostly supported by anecdotal reports. Gardner's theory of multiple intelligences makes use of neuropsychological and cultural evidence, but rarely makes predictions beyond the data adduced in support of theory. Piaget's theory is wonderful description, but fails to predict who will reach a particular stage at a particular time. Most of these theories seem to have educational implications, but, again, the theory developers have mostly distanced themselves from curricular development based on their theories. The cognitive-contextual theories are, in essence, a promissory note. Only the future can tell us if they are able to live up to their grand claims.

Biological Theories

Human intelligence clearly exists within the brain. Recent interest in cognitive neuropsychology has led to hopes that we will discover the particular biological and physiological mechanisms responsible for intelligence. I will review some of the biological theories put forward below; however, one needs to remember that the brain is an extremely complex organ, and our knowledge of its operation is still in its infancy.

Brain Size and Intelligence

Numerous studies have been conducted that have assessed the correlation between brain size and intelligence. In the early studies, brain size was measured via a more accessible surrogate such as head circumference (sometimes termed "perimeter"). In a review of 35 earlier studies comprising 56,793 individuals, Vernon, Wickett, Bazana, and Stelmack (2000) reported an n-weighted mean correlation of 0.191 between head size and intelligence. This correlation was not corrected for attenuation due to unreliability of measurement or restriction of range, so the theoretical relationship is likely higher.

Later studies substituted more accurate measures of actual brain volume (i.e., derived from CT or MRI scans) for head size measurements. The result was that the relationship between brain size and intelligence increased. In a review of recent brain volume and intelligence studies, Vernon, Wickett, Bazana, and Stelmack (2000) reported an n-weighted mean correlation of 0.381 based on 432 normal adults from 11 samples. Gignac, Vernon, and Wickett (2003) also report a review of 14 recent studies and find an n-weighted mean correlation of 0.37 between brain size and intelligence (note: these two reviews present overlapping studies). Again, these correlations are uncorrected for unreliability or restriction of range.

Clearly, brain size and intelligence are related. The size of the relationship increases when a more valid measure of brain size is substituted for a less valid one. Exactly how brain size determines intelligence is unclear from these studies. However, recent work suggests that genetics plays a role in the transmission of this relationship.

A study by Wickett, Vernon, and Lee (2000) examined the relationship between brain size and intelligence in 32 pairs of male, adult siblings. They found a within-family correlation of 0.229 between brain volume and g, and a between-family correlation of 0.366 between brain volume and g. This demonstrates that the relationship between brain size and intelligence exists within families, as well as between families. Such a within-family relationship is necessary to establish the influence of genetic factors. Correlations that exist only between families may be the result of environmental factors such as nutrition and socioeconomic status. The findings of Wickett, Vernon, and Lee (2000) are consistent with the hypothesis that both genetic and environmental factors are at play in the relationship between brain size and intelligence.

EEG String Length and Intelligence

Hendrickson and Hendrickson (1980; A. E. Hendrickson, 1982; see Brody, 1996, for a review) presented a theoretical model that linked intelligence to the electroencephalogram (EEG) complexity. Basically, the model posits that more intelligent individuals have fewer errors in synaptic transmissions, and that this will lead to a more complex EEG wave pattern. EEG wave pattern complexity is determined by the length of a "string" superimposed over the wave form; more complex EEGs lead to longer string lengths.

Blinkhorn and Hendrickson (1980) found correlations of approximately 0.45 between EEG string length (from an auditory listening task) and the Advanced Progressive Matrices (uncorrected for restriction of range) in a sample of 33 psychology undergraduates. The actual size of the correlation depended upon details of which portion of the EEG was measured. D. E. Hendrickson (1982) found a correlation of 0.72 between string length and WAIS total IQ in a sample of 219 school aged children (mean age = 15.6 years).

While the neural transmission errors theory and EEG string length provide interesting insights into intelligence, this research seems to be just beginning. Not all attempts to replicate these findings have succeeded (e.g., Stough, Nettelbeck, and Cooper, 1990). More research is clearly needed to sort out the various methodological issues (Brody, 1992), and to further elucidate the relationships between neural transmission errors and the actual EEG recordings provided by participants.

Glucose Metabolic Rate and Intelligence

Haier (2003; also reviewed in Vernon, Wickett, Bazana, & Stelmack, 2000) has presented evidence that the brain's rate of glucose metabolism (GMR), as measured through positron emission tomography, is negatively correlated with intelligence. For instance, Haier et al. (1988) found significant negative correlations between GMR and performance on the Ravens Advanced Progressive Matrices in a group of eight normal adults. These negative correlations between GMR and intelligence-related measures have been replicated by other investigators (Parks et al., 1988; Boivin et al., 1992).

Haier (2003) interprets these findings as resulting from brain efficiency: more intelligent individuals require less neuronal activity (and therefore less glucose metabolism) to solve intellectual problems than do less intelligent individuals. Haier et al. (1992) explored this theory further in a learning task.

Eight subjects underwent a PET scan while playing a computer game (i.e., tetris). At this point, the subjects were novice players. After four to eight weeks of practice, subjects underwent a second PET scan while playing the computer game. Results revealed that improvements in game play were related to decreases GMR. Haier et al. (1992) conclude that practice results in subjects learning what areas of the brain not to use, and this results in a decrease in GMR.

Haier's brain efficiency model of intelligence relates brain metabolism to performance; however, it must be noted that most of the studies involve very small sample sizes (primarily due to the cost of conducting PET scanning research). While the findings have been replicated, it would be desirable to see the results replicated in a large, representative sample of normal adults.

Jensen's Neural Oscillation Model

Jensen (1982, pp. 127–131) proposed a "neural oscillation model" to account for his finding that reaction time (RT) in a simple/choice reaction time task increases linearly with the bits of information in the stimulus display (see earlier in this chapter). Jensen hypothesized the nervous system used a hierarchical binary network to process information in the simple/choice reaction time task. To this, he coupled the assumption that each node in the network was subject to an oscillatory cycle between active periods (when the node could fire and thereby transmit information) and refractory periods (when the node could not fire). Brighter people were assumed to have shorter neural oscillation cycles, and, therefore, were able return to a "firing" state more quickly than less bright people. Jensen demonstrated that such a model could account for his basic findings: (1) linear increase in RT with increasing bits of information; and (2) increasing RT standard deviation with increasing bits of information.

Intriguing as Jensen's neural oscillation theory may be, it has no direct support in neurophysiological data. The theory was developed based on a mathematical model (the binomial expansion), and is a distant extrapolation from the experimental data. At best, it may be viewed as a physiological metaphor of performance on the task.

Conclusions

The various findings described above all provide evidence on relationships between aspects of the brain and intelligence or intellectual functioning. Not surprisingly, the findings are only loosely tied to the theories of intelligence proposed by the various researchers. Cognitive neuroscience is a relatively young field, and the causal links between brain structure and function, on the one hand, and intellectual performance, on the other, have not been fully elucidated. However, as the field progresses, the causal links are likely to become more clear, and I would expect to see progress on biological theories of intelligence.

I should caution that we live in time when reductionism is often equated with science. It is difficult not to be impressed when one sees a multimillion dollar fMRI machine. However, our understanding of intelligence is likely to progress on many levels. There is no one level of analysis that possesses a golden key to understanding.

Conclusion

In this chapter, I have reviewed four classes of theories of intelligence: psychometric, cognitive, cognitive-contextual, and biological. Psychometric theories of intelligence are relatively mature. The picture of structural relationships among abilities is best represented as a hierarchy, with g at the top, group factors in the middle levels, and relatively specific factors at the bottom. The choice between the British hierarchical model and Carroll's (1993, 1997) three stratum theory is primarily a matter of personal preference.

Cognitive theories of intelligence have attempted to elucidate the cognitive processing underlying intelligent behavior. To the extent that consensus exists, it is that intelligent behavior is related to broad processes implicated in a large number of tasks. Examples of these processes would be working memory, attention, rapidity of processes in STM, resistance to interference in memory, general reasoning components, and strategy selection and execution (i.e., metacomponents). Speed of information processing has also been shown to be important, though its importance may be highlighted only in certain special situations (e.g., during aging, and with novel problems). There is no single agreed-upon cognitive theory of intelligence as there is in the psychometric domain.

Cognitive-contextual theories expand cognitive theories by embedding them within a context, whether that context is environmental or cultural. These theories stress that cognitive processes can only be developed and valued within an environment that selects for them, supports them, or within a culture that values them. In this way, intelligence is an interaction between person and environment, with the environment shaping the individual's cognitive processes, and/or the individual molding his or her environment or culture. Although these theories emphasize the role of environment (broadly defined), they have not been very specific in terms of making forward-looking predictions. This can be seen as a weakness of this class of theory.

Biological theories attempt to explain intelligence in terms of brain structure and function. Numerous investigators have pointed out brain-related correlates of intelligence, but difficulties remain. Some of the relationships have been difficult to replicate. Furthermore, the theoretical explanations for the relationships are often ad hoc. Given the complexity of the brain, and the relative newness of the field of cognitive neuroscience, this is not surprising. Hopefully, as our knowledge of the brain expands, theories can be developed that explain several of the correlational relationships within a single framework.

The ability of intelligence tests to predict success in school and school-like environments is one of the great achievements of psychology. A great deal of time and effort has gone into developing the intelligence tests that educational institutions rely on. Psychology needs to spend at least as much time and effort to develop theories of intelligence that can accommodate the numerous influences of cognitive processes, biological processes, and environmental factors. Many parts of the picture are already in place, but a grand theory of human intelligence is still some ways off in the future.

Future Directions

In this last section, I will pose some questions for future research.

1. **Can cognitive theories account for the relationships displayed by psychometric theories?** Is it possible to show that tests which group together in psychometric theories do so because they share cognitive processes that are sources of individual differences in performance?

2. **Can cognitive-contextual theories make forward-looking predictions concerning which cognitive processes will be selected or valued in a particular context?** It would certainly help if this class of theories could be made specific enough so that they can make concrete predictions, rather than simply describe current situations after the fact.

3. **Can cognitive-contextual theories specify a mechanism by which cognitive processes are**

modified via context? This may simply be natural selection, but demonstrating how cognitive processes are modified by the environment would seem to be an important aspect of any cognitive-contextual theory.

4. **Can the numerous brain/intelligence correlations be unified under a single biological theory of intelligence?** Parsimony would dictate that we will eventually need a single biological theory of intelligence that is more specific than a statement such as "more intelligent individuals have more neurons or faster neurons."

5. **Can biological correlates of intelligence be tied to cognitive information processes?** Although the brain may be the physical substrate of intelligence, this intelligence must be manifest through cognitive information processes. Future theories will need to tie these two levels of analysis together.

Progress on any of these questions would constitute substantial progress toward a more comprehensive theory of human intelligence.

References

Angell, J. R. (1908). The doctrine of formal discipline in light of the principles of general psychology. *Educational Review, 36,* 1–14.

Atkinson, R. C., & Shiffrin, R. M. (1968). Human memory: A proposed system and its control processes. In K. W. Spence & J. T. Spence (Eds.), *The psychology of learning and motivation: Advances in research and theory* (Vol 2). New York: Academic Press.

Atkinson, R. C., & Shiffrin, R. M. (1971). The control of short-term memory. *Scientific American, 225,* 82–90.

Baddeley, A. D. (1986). *Working memory.* Oxford, UK: Clarendon Press.

Baddeley, A. D., & Hitch, G. J. (1974). Working memory. In S. Dornic (Ed.), *Attention and performance VI.* Hillsdale, NJ: Erlbaum.

Binet, A., & Henri, V. (1896). La psychologie individuelle. *L'Année Psychologique, 2,* 411–465.

Binet, A., & Simon, T. (1905). Méthods nouvelles pour le diagnostic du niveau intellectuel des anormaux. *L'Année Psychologique, 11,* 191–244.

Binet, A., & Simon, T. (1908). Le développement de l'intelligence chez les enfants. *L'Année Psychologique, 14,* 1–94.

Binet, A. (1911). Nouvelle recherches sur la mesure du niveau intellectual chez les enfants d'ecole. *L'Année Psychologique, 17,* 145–201.

Blinkhorn, S. F., & Hendrickson, D. E. (1982). Average evoked responses and psychometric intelligence. *Nature, 295,* 596–597.

Boivin, M. J., Giordani, B., Berent, S., Amato, D. A., Koeppe, R. A., Buchtel, H. A., Foster, N. L., & Kuhl, D. E. (1992). Verbal fluency and positron emission tomographic mapping of regional cerebral glucose metabolism. *Cortex, 28,* 231–239.

Brody, N. (1992). *Intelligence* (2nd ed.). New York: Academic Press.

Brody, E. B., & Brody, N. (1976). *Intelligence: Nature, determinants, and consequences.* New York: Academic Press.

Brown, W., & Thomson, G. (1921). *The essentials of mental measurement.* Cambridge, U. K.: Cambridge University Press.

Burt, C. (1940). *The factors of the mind.* London: University of London Press.

Carroll, J. B. (1982). The measurement of intelligence. In Sternberg, R. J. (Ed.). *Handbook of human intelligence.* Cambridge, U. K.: Cambridge University Press.

Carroll, J. B. (1993). *Human cognitive abilities: A survey of factor analytic studies.* Cambridge, U. K.: Cambridge University Press.

Carroll, J. B. (1997). The three-stratum theory of cognitive abilities. In D. P. Flanagan, J. L. Genshaft, & P. L. Harrison (Eds.), *Contemporary intellectual assessment: Theories, tests, and issues.* New York: Guilford.

Cattell, J. McK. (1890). Mental test and measurements. *Mind, 15,* 373–381.

Cattell, J. McK., & Farrand, L. (1896). Physical and mental measurements of the students of Columbia University. *Psychological Review, 6,* 618–648.

Cattell, R. B. (1941). Some theoretical issues in adult intelligence testing. *Psychological Bulletin, 38,* 592.

Cattell, R. B. (1963). Theory of fluid and crystallized intelligence: A critical experiment. *Journal of Educational Psychology, 54,* 1–22.

Cattell, R. B. (1971). *Abilities: Their structure, growth and action.* Boston: Houghton-Mifflin.

Cronbach, L. J. (1957). The two disciplines of scientific psychology. *American Psychologist, 12,* 671–684.

Cronbach, L. J. (1970). *Essentials of psychological testing* (3rd ed.). New York: Harper & Row.

Darwin, C. R. (1859). *On the origin of species by means of natural selection, or the preservation of favoured races in the struggle for life.* London: John Murray.

Dreary, I. J. (2003). Reaction time and psychometric intelligence: Jensen's contributions. In H. Nyborg (Ed.). *The scientific study of general intelligence: Tribute to Arthur R. Jensen.* Amsterdam: Pergamon.

Eysenck, H. J. (1967). Intelligence assessment: A theoretical and experimental approach. *British Journal of Educational Psychology, 37,* 81–97.

Flavell, J. H. (1985). *Cognitive development* (2nd ed.). Englewood Cliffs, NJ: Prentice Hall.

Galton, F. (1869). *Hereditary genius: An inquiry into its laws and its development.* London: Macmillan.

Galton, F. (1874). *English men of science: Their nature and nurture.* London: Macmillan.

Galton, F. (1883). *Inquiries into human faculty and its development.* London: Macmillan.

Gardner, H. (1983). *Frames of mind: The theory of multiple intelligences.* New York: Basic Books.

Gardner, H. (1999). *Intelligence reframed: Multiple intelligences for the 21ˢᵗ century.* New York: Basic Books.

Gardner, H. (April 9, 2008). Personal communication.

Gardner, M. K., & Clark, E. (1992). The psychometric perspective on intellectual development in childhood and adolescence. In Sternberg, R. J., & Berg, C. A. (Eds.). *Intellectual development.* Cambridge, UK: Cambridge University Press.

Gardner, M. K., & Sternberg, R. J. (1994). Novelty and intelligence. In Sternberg, R. J., & Wagner, R. K. (Eds.), *Mind in context: Interactionist perspectives on human intelligence.* Cambridge, UK: Cambridge University Press.

Gignac, G., Vernon, P. A., & Wickett, J. C. (2003). Factors influencing the relationship between brain size and intelligence. In H. Nyborg (Ed.). *The scientific study of general intelligence: Tribute to Arthur R. Jensen.* Amsterdam: Pergamon.

Goleman, D. (1997). *Emotional intelligence.* New York: Bantam Books.

Gorsuch, R. L. (1983). *Factor analysis* (2nd ed.). Hillsdale, NJ: Erlbaum.

Grudnik, J. L., & Kranzler, J. H. (2001). Meta-analysis of the relationship between intelligence and inspection time. *Intelligence, 29,* 525–537.

Guilford, J. P. (1964). Zero intercorrelations among tests of intellectual abilities. *Psychological Bulletin, 61,* 401–404.

Guilford, J. P. (1967). *The nature of human abilities.* New York: McGraw-Hill.

Guilford, J. P. (1977). *Way beyond the IQ: Guide to improving intelligence and creativity.* Buffalo: Creative Education Foundation.

Guilford, J. P. (1982). Cognitive psychology's ambiguities: Some suggested remedies. *Psychological Review, 89,* 48–59.

Guilford, J. P., & Hoepfner, R. (1971). *The analysis of intelligence.* New York: McGraw-Hill.

Hagen, J. (2007). The label mental retardation involves more than IQ scores: A commentary on Kanaya and Ceci (2007). *Child Development Perspectives, 1,* 60–61.

Haier, R. J. (2003). Positron emission tomography studies of intelligence: From psychometrics to neurobiology. In H. Nyborg (Ed.). *The scientific study of general intelligence: Tribute to Arthur R. Jensen.* Amsterdam: Pergamon.

Haier, R. J., Siegel, B. V., Nuechterlein, K. H., Hazlett, E., Wu, C. J., Peak, J., Browning, H. L., & Buchsbaum, M. S. (1988). Cortical glucose metabolic rate correlates of abstract reasoning and attention studied with positron emission tomography. *Intelligence, 12,* 199–197.

Haier, R. J., Siegel, B. V., MacLachlan, A., Soderling, E., Lottenberg, S., & Buchsbaum, M. S. (1992). Regional glucose metabolic changes after learning a complex visuospatial/motor task: A PET study. *Brain Research, 570,* 134–143.

Hebb, D. O. (1942). The effect of early and late brain injury upon test scores, and the nature of normal adult intelligence. *Proceedings of the American Philosophical Society, 85,* 275–292.

Hemmelgarn, T. E., & Kehle, T. J. (1984). The relationship between reaction time and intelligence in children. *School Psychology International, 5,* 77–84.

Hendrickson, A. E. (1982). The biological basis of intelligence. Part I: Theory. In H. J. Eysenck (Ed.), *A model for intelligence.* Berlin: Springer-Verlag.

Hendrickson, D. E. (1982). The biological basis of intelligence. Part II: Measurement. In H. J. Eysenck (Ed.), *A model for intelligence.* Berlin: Springer-Verlag.

Hendrickson, D. E., & Hendrickson, A. E. (1980). The biological basis of individual differences in intelligence. *Personality and Individual Differences, 1,* 3–33.

Hick, W. E. (1952). On the rate of information gain. *Quarterly Journal of Experimental Psychology, 4,* 11–26.

Hilgard, E. R., Atkinson, R. C., & Atkinson, R. L. (1971). *Introduction to psychology* (5th ed.). New York: Harcourt Brace Jovanovich.

Horn, J. L. (1968). Organization of abilities and the development of intelligence. *Psychological Review, 75,* 242–259.

Horn, J. L. (1985). Remodeling old models of intelligence: Gf – Gc theory. In B. B. Wolman (Ed.), *Handbook of intelligence.* New York: Wiley.

Horn, J. L., & Cattell, R. B. (1966). Refinement and test of the theory of fluid and crystallized intelligence. *Journal of Educational Psychology, 57,* 253–270.

Horn, J. L., & Cattell, R. B. (1967). Age differences in fluid and crystallized intelligence. *Acta Psychologica, 26,* 107–129.

Hunt, E. (1978). Mechanics of verbal ability. *Psychological Review, 85,* 109–130.

Hunt, E., Frost, N., & Lunneborg, C. (1973). Individual differences in cognition: A new approach to intelligence. In G. Bower (Ed.), *The psychology of learning and motivation: Advances in research and theory* (Vol. 7). New York: Academic Press.

Hunt, E., Lunneborg, C., & Lewis, J. (1975). What does it mean to be high verbal? *Cognitive Psychology, 7,* 194–227.

Hyman, R. (1953). Stimulus information as a determinant of reaction time. *Journal of Experimental Psychology, 45,* 188–196.

Jensen, A. R. (1982). Reaction time and psychometric g. In H. J. Eysenck (Ed.), *A model for intelligence.* Berlin: Springer-Verlag.

Jensen, A. R. (1987). Individual differences in the Hick paradigm. In P. A. Vernon (Ed.), *Speed of information processing and intelligence.* Norwood, NJ: Ablex.

Jensen, A. R. (1998). *The g factor: The science of mental ability.* New York: Praeger.

Jensen, A. R., & Munro, E. (1979). Reaction time, movement time, and intelligence. *Intelligence, 3,* 121–126.

Kranzler, J. H., & Jensen, A. R. (1989). Inspection time and intelligence: A meta-analysis. *Intelligence, 13,* 329–347.

Kyllonen, P. C., & Christal, R. E. (1990). Reasoning ability is (little more than) working-memory capacity?! *Intelligence, 14,* 389–433.

Lally, M., & Nettelbeck, T. (1980). Intelligence, inspection time, and response strategy. *American Journal of Mental Deficiency, 84,* 553–560.

Mulholland, T. P., Pellegrino, J. W., & Glaser, R. (1980). Components of geometric analogy solution. *Cognitive Psychology, 12,* 252–284.

Nettelbeck, T. (1987). Inspection time and intelligence. In P. A. Vernon (Ed.), *Speed of information processing and intelligence.* Norwood, NJ: Ablex.

Nettelbeck, T. (2003). Inspection time and g. In H. Nyborg (Ed.). *The scientific study of general intelligence: Tribute to Arthur R. Jensen.* Amsterdam: Pergamon.

Nettelbeck, T., & Kirby, N. H. (1983). Retarded-nonretarded differences in speed of processing. *Australian Journal of Psychology, 35,* 445–453.

Nettelbeck, T., & Lally, M. (1976). Inspection time and measured intelligence. *British Journal of Psychology, 67,* 17–22.

Parks, R. W., Loewenstein, D. A., Dodrill, K. L., Barker, W. W., Yoshii, F., Chang, J. Y., Emran, A., Apicella, A., Sheramata, W. A., & Duara, R. (1988). Cerebral metabolic effects of a verbal fluency test: A PET scan study. *Journal of Clinical and Experimental Neuropsychology, 10,* 565–575.

Peterson, L. R., & Peterson, M. J. (1959). Short-term retention of individual items. *Journal of Experimental Psychology, 58,* 193–198.

Piaget, J. (1954). *The construction of reality in the child.* New York: Basic Books.

Piaget, J. (1970). Piaget's theory. In P. H. Mussen (Ed.), *Carmichael's manual of child psychology* (Vol. 1). New York: Wiley.

Piaget, J. (1977). *The development of thought: Equilibration of cognitive structures.* New York: Viking.

Piaget, J., & Inhelder, B. (1969). *The psychology of the child.* New York: Basic Books.

Pillsbury, W. B. (1908). The effects of training on memory. *Educational Review, 36,* 15–27.

Posner, M. I., & Mitchell, R. (1967). Chronometric analysis of classification. *Psychological Review, 74,* 392–409.

Roid, G. (2003). *Stanford-Binet Intelligence Scales,* 5th *Ed: Technical Manual.* Itasca, IL: Riverside Publishing.

Roth, E. (1964). Die geschwindigkeit der verabeitung von information und ihr zusammenhang mit intelligenz. *Zeitschrift fur Experimentelle und Angewandte Psychologie, 11,* 616–622.

Salovey, P., & Mayer, J. D. (1989–1990). Emotional intelligence. *Imagination, Cognition, and Personality, 9,* 185–211.

Salthouse, T. A. (1985). *A theory of cognitive aging.* Amsterdam: North-Holland.

Salthouse, T. A. (1993). Speed mediation of adult age differences in cognition. *Developmental Psychology, 29,* 722–738.

Salthouse, T. A. (1996). The processing-speed theory of adult age differences in cognition. *Psychological Review, 103,* 403–428.

Sattler, J. M. (2008). *Assessment of children* (5th ed.). San Diego: Jerome M. Sattler, Publisher, Inc.

Schneider, W., & Shiffrin, R. M. (1977). Controlled and automated human information processing. I: Detection, search, and attention. *Psychological Review, 84,* 1–66.

Shiffrin, R. M., & Schneider, W. (1977). Controlled and automated human information processing. II: Perceptual learning, automatic attending, and a general theory. *Psychological Review, 84,* 127–190.

Simonton, D. K. (2003). Francis Galton's *Hereditary genius*: It's place in the history and psychology of science. In R. J. Sternberg (Ed.), *The anatomy of impact: What makes the great works of psychology great.* Washington, DC: American Psychological Association.

Singley, M. K., & Anderson, J. R. (1989). *The transfer of cognitive skill.* Cambridge, MA: Harvard University Press.

Spearman, C. (1904a). The proof and measurement of association between two things. *American Journal of Psychology, 15,* 72–101.

Spearman, C. (1904b). General intelligence objectively determined and measured. *American Journal of Psychology, 15,* 201–293.

Spearman, C. (1923). *The nature of "intelligence" and the principles of cognition.* London: Macmillan.

Spearman, C. (1927). *The abilities of man.* New York: Macmillan.

Stern, W. (1912). *Die psychologischen methoden der intelligenzprufung.* Leipzig: Barth.

Sternberg, R. J. (1977a). *Intelligence, information processing, and analogical reasoning: The componential analysis of human abilities.* Hillsdale, NJ: Erlbaum.

Sternberg, R. J. (1977b). Components of analogical reasoning. *Psychological Review, 84,* 353–378.

Sternberg, R. J. (1980). Sketch of a componential subtheory of human intelligence. *Behavioral and Brain Sciences, 3,* 573–584.

Sternberg, R. J. (1982). Reasoning, problem solving, and intelligence. In R. J. Sternberg (Ed.), *Handbook of human intelligence.* Cambridge, UK: Cambridge University Press.

Sternberg, R. J. (1985a). General intellectual ability. In R. J. Sternberg (Ed.), *Human abilities: An information processing approach.* New York: W. H. Freeman and Co.

Sternberg, R. J. (1985b). Introduction: What is an information-processing approach to human abilities? In R. J. Sternberg

(Ed.), *Human abilities: An information processing approach.* New York: W. H. Freeman and Co.

Sternberg, R. J. (1985c). *Beyond IQ: A triarchic theory of human intelligence.* Cambridge, UK: Cambridge University Press.

Sternberg, R. J. (1988). *The triarchic mind: A new theory of human intelligence.* New York: Viking.

Sternberg, R. J. (1998). A balance theory of wisdom. *Review of General Psychology, 2,* 347–365.

Sternberg, R. J., & Gardner, M. K. (1982). A componential interpretation of the general factor in human intelligence. In H. J. Eysenck (Ed.), *A model for intelligence.* Berlin: Springer-Verlag.

Sternberg, R. J., & Gardner, M. K. (1983). Unities in inductive reasoning. *Journal of Experimental Psychology: General, 112,* 80–116.

Sternberg, R. J., & Jarvin, L. (2003). Alfred Binet's contributions as a paradigm impact in psychology. In R. J. Sternberg (Ed.), *The anatomy of impact: What makes the great works of psychology great.* Washington, DC: American Psychological Association.

Sternberg, R. J., & Lubart, T. I. (1991). An investment theory of creativity and its development. *Human Development, 34,* 1–31.

Sternberg, R. J., & Lubart, T. I. (1992). Creativity: Its nature and assessment. *School Psychology International, 13,* 243–253.

Sternberg, R. J., & Powell, J. S. (1983). Comprehending verbal comprehension. *American Psychologist, 38,* 878–893.

Stough, C. K. K., Nettelbeck, T., & Cooper, C. J. (1990). Evoked brain potentials, string length and intelligence. *Personality and Individual Differences, 11,* 401–406.

Terman, L. M. (1925). *Genetic studies of genius, Vol. I: Mental and physical traits of a thousand gifted children.* Stanford, CA: Stanford University Press.

Thomson, G. H. (1951). *The factorial analysis of human ability* (5th ed.). London: University of London Press.

Thorndike, E. L. (1906). *Principles of teaching.* New York: A. G. Seiler.

Thorndike, E. L. (1925). *The measurement of intelligence.* New York: Columbia University, Teachers College.

Thorndike, E. L., Bregman, E. O., Cobb, M. V., Woodyard, E., & the staff of the Division of Psychology of the Institute of Educational Research of Teachers College, Columbia University. (1927). *The measurement of intelligence.* New York: Columbia University, Teachers College, Bureau of Publications.

Thorndike, E. L., & Woodworth, R. S. (1901). The influence of improvement in one mental function upon the efficiency of other functions. *Psychological Review, 8,* 247–261.

Thurstone, L. L. (1931). Multiple factor analysis. *Psychological Review, 38,* 406–427.

Thurstone, L. L. (1935). *The vectors of the mind.* Chicago: University of Chicago Press.

Thurstone, L. L. (1938). *Primary mental abilities.* Chicago: University of Chicago Press.

Thurstone, L. L. (1947). *Multiple factor analysis.* Chicago: University of Chicago Press.

Thurstone, L. L., & Thurstone, T. G. (1941). *Factorial studies of intelligence.* Chicago: University of Chicago Press.

Tuddenham, R. D. (1962). The nature and measurement of intelligence. In L. Postman (Ed.), *Psychology in the making.* New York: Knopf.

Vernon, P. A., Wickett, J. C., Bazana, G., Stelmack, R. M. (2000). The neuropsychology and psychophysiology of human intelligence. In R. J. Sternberg (Ed.), *Handbook of intelligence.* Cambridge, UK: Cambridge University Press.

Vernon, P. E. (1950). *The structure of human abilities.* London: Methuen & Co.

Vickers, D., Nettelbeck, T., Willson, R. J. (1972). Perceptual indices of performance: the measurement of "inspection time" and "noise" in the visual system. *Perception, 1,* 263–295.

Vickery, C., & Neuringer, A. (2000). Pigeon reaction time, Hick's law, and intelligence. *Psychonomic Bulletin and Review, 7,* 284–291.

Wagner, R. K., & Sternberg, R. J. (1985). Practical intelligence in real-world pursuits: The role of tacit knowledge. *Journal of Personality and Social Psychology, 49,* 436–458.

Wechsler, D. (1939). *The measurement of adult intelligence.* Baltimore: Williams & Wilkins.

Wechsler, D. (1944). *The measurement of adult intelligence* (3rd ed.). Baltimore: Williams & Wilkins.

Wechsler, D. (1949). *Wechsler intelligence scale for children.* New York: The Psychological Corporation.

Wechsler, D. (1967). *Manual for the Wechsler preschool and primary scale of intelligence.* New York: Psychological Corporation.

White, M. (1996). Interpreting inspection time as a measure of the speed of sensory processing. *Personality and Individual Differences, 20,* 351–363.

Whitely, S. E. (1980). Modeling test validity from cognitive components. *Journal of Educational Psychology, 72,* 750–769.

Wickens, D. D. (1970). Encoding categories of words: An empirical approach to meaning. *Psychological Review, 77,* 1–15.

Wickett, J. C., Vernon, P. A., & Lee, D. A. (2000). Relationships between factors of intelligence and brain volume. *Personality and Individual Differences, 29,* 1095–1122.

Wiseman, S. (Ed.). (1967). *Intelligence and ability.* Baltimore: Penguin.

Wissler, C. (1901). The correlation of mental and physical tests. *Psychological Monographs, 3,* 1–62.

Woodrow, H. (1927). The effect of the type of training upon transference. *Journal of Educational Psychology, 18,* 159–172.

PART 4

Research Methodology and Data Analysis

Research Methodology for Decision-Making in School Psychology

Hariharan Swaminathan, H. Jane Rogers, *and* Rohini Sen

Abstract

Sound and defensible decisions regarding the practice of education and psychology cannot be made without reliable and valid data. Data collection to inform decisions must be carefully planned within the framework of a rigorous research study designed to answer well-articulated research questions. Once collected, the data must be analyzed and summarized using appropriate procedures. The classical statistical framework for drawing inferences and making decisions, null hypothesis significance testing, has been severely criticized by prominent researchers in the field. The purposes of this chapter are to provide school psychologists with a clear description of how the statistical reasoning process is correctly applied to enable valid statistical inference leading to sound decisions; to describe the notion of effect size and power and provide tools for computing these; to describe procedures for testing hypotheses that incorporate tolerance limits on what differences between parameters are meaningful; and to provide an introduction to the Bayesian framework that permits probabilistic statements about parameters and hypotheses.

Keywords: Null hypothesis significance testing, school psychology, effect size, noncentral distributions, power, equivalence testing, range null hypothesis, cluster randomized design, Bayesian analysis, decision theory

It is axiomatic that sound and defensible decisions regarding the practice of education and psychology cannot be made without reliable and valid data. Data collection to inform decisions must be carefully planned within the framework of a rigorous research study designed to answer well-articulated research questions. Once collected, the data must be analyzed and summarized using appropriate procedures. Our goal in this chapter is to present a close examination of the fundamentals of research methodology for informed decisions. We aim to provide school psychologists with a careful analysis of the statistical reasoning underlying the process of drawing inferences from data, and making decisions based on those inferences. We will consider some of the concerns that have been raised about the application of inferential statistics in education and psychology, and highlight some of the new ways

in which researchers are beginning to address these methodological criticisms. We hope that this chapter will provide school psychologists with a richer insight into the role and proper use of statistics in research methodology for decision-making.

While data for decision-making can be either "qualitative" or "quantitative" in nature, we shall confine our discussion in this chapter to data that lend themselves to statistical analyses. Statistical analysis of data consists of both description and inference. Description of the data is an essential first step in the data analysis process, and in some cases can guide inferential analyses. Description involves providing detailed information of the distribution of the scores, appropriate summary statistics, and, whenever possible, appropriate graphical displays of the data. In some situations, descriptive data analysis may be all that is required for decision-making purposes; however, more often than not, inferential statistical analysis is required to allow generalizable conclusions to populations of interest.

Statistical significance testing, or more precisely, null hypothesis significance testing (NHST), remains the primary tool for researchers in the behavioral sciences. The practice of NHST is so entrenched in the behavioral sciences that often the hypotheses being tested are not even explicitly stated. The result of a statistical significance test, typically the p-value, is presented as the basis for conclusions and inferences. The problems associated with statistical significance testing have been well documented by prominent researchers in a variety of fields. Thompson (2001) provides a list of 402 references (by no means complete) from a broad spectrum of fields in science, medicine, business, psychology and education, all questioning the use of statistical significance testing. Several journals have published special sections or issues on the topic (for example, *Journal of Experimental Education*, 1993; *Psychological Science*, 1997, *Research in the Schools*, 1998). There has even been an effort in recent years to ban the practice of null hypothesis testing (see, for example, Schmidt, 1996; Schmidt and Hunter, 1997). Harlow, Steiger, and Mulaik (1997) present an entire book of arguments against and for hypothesis testing, and suggestions for alternatives. In the specific context of school psychology, Kehle, Bray, Chafouleas, and Kawano (2007) lamented the fact that researchers are either not cognizant of the arguments against significance testing, or are choosing to ignore them.

One of the major criticisms of NHST is that the information it provides is often misunderstood or misused by researchers. Recommendations that have been widely and repeatedly made to remedy this situation include requiring researchers to think in terms of effect sizes rather than statistical significance, to design studies so that they will have adequate power, and to interpret the findings not in terms of the dichotomous result of a hypothesis test, but in terms of confidence intervals for the parameters of interest. While procedures for implementing these recommendations have been in place almost since the introduction of null hypothesis testing in the 1920s, these procedures are still not routinely used in behavioral science research.

The requirement that the null hypothesis be stated with exact precision is a major flaw of the null hypothesis testing paradigm, and one that gives rise to misunderstanding and misuse. For example, if we want to determine the relative effectiveness of two interventions, the usual null hypothesis is that the difference in the means of the two groups that received the interventions is precisely zero. John Tukey, one of the most influential statisticians of our time, noted that it is foolish to ask if the effects of two treatments are different, since they will always be different to some degree of accuracy (Tukey, 1991). Rejection of the null hypothesis can always be achieved with sufficient sample size, and is no indication of the strength of an effect. It is more appropriate to ask if the means of two treatment groups on a specified variable differ by more than a prescribed amount. This gives rise to the notion of practical significance; that is, how different the effects should be before we consider the difference to be meaningful. Procedures are available for testing whether an effect is greater than some amount considered trivial, but those procedures are virtually unknown to researchers in the social sciences.

On the other side of this coin is the issue of what can be concluded if the null hypothesis is not rejected. Failure to reject the null hypothesis provides no evidence of its truth. In some cases, however, the usual null hypothesis is the hypothesis of interest. For example, we may hypothesize that two groups do *not* differ on a variable of interest. To obtain evidence of the *lack* of an effect, we must test an appropriate hypothesis directly. Once again, however, we would be better served by testing a hypothesis that the effect is approximately zero, or within a trivial difference of zero, rather than exactly zero. Procedures for equivalence testing are available, and are widely used in the biomedical field, but these procedures too have received little attention in the social sciences.

In addition to these problems, the logic of NHST often leads to misinterpretation of the outcomes. The NHST only permits us to answer questions concerning the probability of the observed data, given that the null hypothesis is true; however, the real question of interest concerns the probability that the null hypothesis is true, given the observed data. This question cannot be answered within the NHST paradigm. The confidence interval often leads to similar misinterpretation. A common misinterpretation is that the confidence level refers to the probability that the parameter lies in the confidence interval, an interpretation not permitted in the NHST framework.

Given these issues surrounding procedures for drawing inferences and making decisions, the purposes of this chapter are to provide school psychologists with a clear description of how the statistical reasoning process is correctly applied to enable valid statistical inference leading to sound decisions; to describe the notion of effect size and power, and provide tools for computing these; to describe procedures for testing hypotheses that incorporate tolerance limits on what differences between parameters are meaningful; and to provide an introduction to the Bayesian framework that permits probabilistic statements about parameters and hypotheses. While we expect that the basic statistical concepts are familiar to readers, it is safe to say that most researchers in the social sciences are inadequately versed in the topics to be covered in this chapter. We do not expect to be comprehensive in our coverage, but merely to introduce readers to some of the emerging statistical issues and techniques that they will encounter, sooner or later, in using research for decision-making in school psychology.

Overview of Basic Statistical Models and Procedures

Many researchers in the social sciences learn inferential statistics as a set of discrete, unrelated tests, appropriate for different types of variables and designs. However, inferential statistical procedures are unified if we view them as procedures for testing models. Parametric statistical data analysis begins with specifying a model that we believe explains the variability of interest in the population under consideration. For example, the simplest possible model is that observations on a variable vary randomly around the population mean. Here, the population mean is the parameter of the model. Once the parameters of the model are identified, we obtain a representative sample from the population, and estimate the parameters using appropriate procedures. These parameter estimates, or statistics, provide a description of the sample and give us a glimpse of the nature of the population from which the sample was drawn. However, since statistics will by their nature change from sample to sample, they cannot be used as a basis for making decisions. Instead, decisions must be made using the population parameters. Accordingly, the next step is to use the information provided by the statistics obtained in the sample to draw inferences about the unknown population parameters. We may wish to test hypotheses that the parameters take particular values. For example, in the simple model described above, we may hypothesize that the population mean has a certain value. The model then becomes a hypothesis about the population, and is subject to falsification. If falsified, a more suitable model must be found.

In other cases, we may wish to test whether a parameter is zero; in such cases, we are testing whether a simpler model is more appropriate than the one hypothesized.

In order to draw inferences about population parameters, we must know exactly how each parameter estimate, or a related quantity, fluctuates from sample to sample; i.e., we need to know the *sampling distribution of the statistic*. The sampling distribution of a statistic is the cornerstone of statistical inference. To make this idea concrete, suppose that we want to investigate the reading levels of a specified population of special needs children. We identify or devise a measure of the reading level of the children, and formulate a model for this variable at the population level. Denoting the mean of the population on this measure by μ, we formulate the simple model that observations y_i are distributed around μ, i.e.,

$$(1) \quad y_i = \mu + e_i, \ (i = 1, ..., n).$$

We further assume that over the population, the error e_i has a mean of zero and variance σ_e^2. Thus, our model states that observations are distributed normally around the population mean μ. To estimate this parameter, we will administer the reading measure to a random sample from the population. (Note that if we cannot obtain a random sample, we will have to provide justification for the inferences we draw about the population.) Let $y_1, y_2, ..., y_n$ denote the scores of n children in the sample on this measure. Given the model and the assumptions regarding the error, the best estimate of μ is the sample mean, $\bar{y}$, the simple average of the observations in the sample. This estimate is best in the sense that *over replications (samples)*, it is an "unbiased" estimator of μ. We can show that if the observations are independent draws from a normal distribution with mean μ and standard deviation σ_e, then *the sample mean* is normally distributed, with mean equal to the population mean μ, and variance equal to the error variance divided by the sample size. Symbolically, this fundamental result is expressed as

$$(2) \quad \bar{y} \sim N\left(\mu, \frac{\sigma_e^2}{n}\right).$$

From the model in (1), we see that the error variance is the same as the variance of our variable y in the population. The standard deviation of the sampling distribution (the square root of the variance) is referred to as the standard error of the statistic.

We have now obtained the *sampling distribution* of the sample mean. Once the sampling distribution is determined, it is possible to make statements regarding probabilities associated with any sample result $\bar{y}$ given a value of the parameter μ. With this information, we are in a position to test hypotheses about the population mean. Suppose that we wish to determine whether the mean reading level of this special needs population differs from that of an established reference population, known to be μ_0. In the NHST framework, which we will consider in more depth in the next section, we formulate a null hypothesis that states that the mean does *not* differ from the reference value, i.e., $\mu = \mu_0$. We then calculate the probability of observing a sample mean this different, or more different, from the hypothesized value μ_0 if the null hypothesis is true. If we find that this probability is very small (below a pre-specified limit), then we conclude that the sample did not come from a population with mean μ_0. Our conclusion is thus that this special needs population differs from the reference population with respect to mean reading level. In terms of our model, we conclude that the model $y_i = \mu_0 + e_i$ is not appropriate for the special needs population. Note that in order to compute probabilities using the distribution given above, we rescale $\bar{y}$ so that is has a standard normal distribution; i.e.,

$$(3) \quad Z = \frac{\bar{y} - \mu}{\sigma_e / \sqrt{n}} \sim N(0,1).$$

Normal tables are readily available for computing the required probabilities. If the population standard deviation is not known, then it must be estimated from the sample. If we replace σ_e by s, the sample standard deviation, in the expression given in (3), the resulting quantity is not distributed normally but instead is distributed (under the assumption that y is normally distributed) as the Student's t-distribution with $(n-1)$ degrees of freedom; i.e.,

$$(4) \quad t = \frac{\bar{y} - \mu}{s / \sqrt{n}} \sim t_{n-1}.$$

Tables of the t-distribution are required to calculate relevant probabilities.

The procedure described above, of specifying a model, deriving suitable estimators of the parameters in the model, determining the sampling distribution of the estimators, using the sampling distribution to arrive at a decision about the parameter, and testing the validity of a particular model is, in principle, generalizable. For example, if we have two populations, one made up of special needs

children who have received an intervention and another made up of similar children who did not receive the intervention, the model for the two populations may be written as follows:

$$(5) \quad y_{ij} = \mu_j + e_{ij}, \qquad (i = 1,...,n; \; j = 1,2)$$

The means of the two samples are unbiased estimators of the respective population means, and the difference between the sample means is an unbiased estimator of the difference in the population means. Once we determine the sampling distribution of the mean difference, we will be in a position to answer the question: What is the probability of observing a sample mean difference as large or larger than we have observed if there is no effect due to the intervention; i.e., if $\mu_1 = \mu_2$? If we find that the probability of observing a sample mean difference this large or larger is very small, then we conclude that the difference in sample means did not occur by chance, and therefore that the means of the populations are not equal. In other words, the model in (5) holds. If we fail to find support for this model, we retain the simple model in (1).

The model in (5) can be extended to the one-way analysis of variance (ANOVA) design, where the means of several interventions or treatments are compared with each other:

$$(6) \quad y_{ij} = \mu_j + e_{ij}, \quad (i = 1,...,n; \; j = 1,....,k)$$

The ANOVA model is conventionally rewritten as

$$(7) \quad y_{ij} = \mu + (\mu_j - \mu) + e_{ij}$$
$$= \mu + \tau_j + e_{ij}, (i = 1,...,n; \; j = 1,...,k)$$

where τ_j denotes the "effect" of treatment j. Here, we test the null hypothesis that the means of the k populations are equal, or, equivalently, that there are no treatment effects; i.e., $\tau_j = 0$. In the models given by (5), (6), and (7), we assume that the observations within each intervention group are *independent*. The errors e_{ij} are assumed to be normally distributed with mean 0 in each group, and variance σ_e^2 assumed to be equal across the groups.

The models in (1), (5), (6), and (7) may all be expressed as special cases of the *regression model* or the *general linear model* of the form:

$$y = \beta_0 + \beta_1 x_1 + \beta_2 x_2 + ... + \beta_p x_p + e,$$

where $x_1, x_2, ..., x_p$ are p *regressor* or independent variables. These regressors may be all discrete, or a combination of discrete and continuous variables. The model assumes that these regressors "explain" or account for the variability in the outcome variable y.

If we do not have any regressors, we have the simple model given by (1),

$$(8) \quad y_i = \beta_0 + e_i, \quad (i = 1,\dots, n)$$

where $\beta_0 \equiv \mu$. In the model given by (4), where we are interested in comparing the means of two groups, the parameter of interest is $\mu_1 - \mu_2$, and the model may be written as

$$(9) \quad y_{ij} = \mu_2 + (\mu_j - \mu_2) + e_{ij},$$
$$(i = 1,\dots, n; j = 1,2)$$

or equivalently, as $y = \beta_0 + \beta_1 x + e$, where if a person belongs to group 1, $x = 1$, and $x = 0$ otherwise. For example, if person i belongs to group 2, then $x = 0$, and $y_{i2} = \beta_0 + e_{i2}$. Comparing this with the model given in (1), we can identify β_0 with μ_2. If person i belongs to group 1, then $x = 1$, and $y_{i1} = \beta_0 + \beta_1 + e_{i1}$. Comparing this again with model (1), we conclude that $\mu_1 = \beta_0 + \beta_1$, which in turn implies that $\beta_1 = \mu_1 - \mu_2$. The indicator variable x (often called the "dummy" variable) enables us to rewrite the model in (5) as a regression model. The more general ANOVA model (6), (7) may also be written as a regression model,

$$y = \beta_0 + \beta_1 x_1 + \beta_2 x_2 + \dots + \beta_{k-1} x_{k-1} + e,$$

where $x_j = 1$ if a person belongs to group j and zero otherwise for $j = 1, 2,\dots, k - 1$. If a person belongs to group k (the last group), then $x_1 = x_2 = \dots = x_{k-1} = 0$. The parameters can then be interpreted as:

$$\beta_0 = \mu_k; \ \beta_1 = \mu_1 - \mu_k; \ \beta_2 = \mu_2 - \mu_k; \ \dots;$$
$$\beta_{k-1} = \mu_{k-1} - \mu_k.$$

In this form, rather than explicitly stating that the means of the groups differ, the model more generally states that group membership accounts for the variability in y. This general formulation of ANOVA models as regression models enables us to treat these models under one framework, making it easier to define effect sizes and carry out power analyses. It should be noted that the coding scheme employed above (1 or 0) is one of many. Different schemes for coding the regressors can be employed, depending on how we wish to interpret the parameters. An excellent account of the coding schemes and their effect on the meaning of parameters can be found in Cohen, Cohen, West, and Aiken (1983).

The general linear model formulation is applicable in a wide variety of situations. In the general regression framework, hypotheses are tested in terms of competing models of differing complexity. For example, if we compare the model in (9) to model in (1), we are testing the hypothesis that

$$\beta_1 = \beta_2 = \dots = \beta_p = 0.$$

In addition, hypotheses concerning subsets of parameters may also be tested. For example, it may be of interest to ask if the addition of a set of variables, such as socioeconomic status of the child (x_3) and the child's attendance record (x_4), is predictive of school achievement (as measured by some standardized test) beyond such variables as the child's performance in class (x_1) and achievement score in a previous year (x_2). This question translates into a comparison of two models:

$$\text{Model A: } y = \beta_0 + \beta_1 x_1 + \beta_2 x_2 + e$$

$$\text{Model B: } y = \beta_0 + \beta_1 x_1 + \beta_2 x_2 + \beta_3 x_3 + \beta_4 x_4 + e.$$

Equivalently, we are testing the null hypothesis

$$H_0 : \beta_3 = \beta_4 = 0.$$

If the data provide sufficient evidence to reject this hypothesis, Model B is the model of choice; otherwise, we retain Model A.

Specification of a model includes the assumptions that are necessary. For all the models given above, we assume that (1) the model holds; (2) the observations are independent; (3) the error variances across groups are equal, or, equivalently in the case of regression models, error variances are equal at all values of the regressors; and (4) for drawing inferences, the observations are normally distributed. Some or all these assumptions may be violated in specific situations. If the researcher feels that these assumptions are not tenable, then nonparametric or robust procedures provide a viable alternative (Wilcox, 2005; Erceg-Hurn & Mirosevich, 2008).

If we are comparing the effectiveness of k interventions by comparing the means on the outcome variable y of the groups that received the interventions/treatments, and we reject the null hypothesis, thus concluding that the means of the treatment populations are different, then the important question to be answered is whether the difference in the means was *caused* by the intervention. Since we can formulate the ANOVA model as a regression model, we can answer the question of whether treatment group membership, expressed by the indicator variables $x_1, x_2,\dots, x_p$, is *related* to the outcome variable. If there is a relationship, the hypothesis that $\beta_1 = \beta_2 = \dots = \beta_p = 0$ will be rejected. As is well known, however, a relationship between a variable or a set of variables and the outcome does not imply that these variables are causally related. This same argument applies to the means of the intervention groups; differences among the means merely implies that there is a relationship between treatment group membership and the outcome variable. Causality cannot be inferred.

The most direct way to answer the question of causality is to *randomly* assign individuals to the intervention conditions. With random assignment, we can assume that there are no systematic differences amongst groups prior to the interventions; hence any differences observed post-intervention can be attributed to the interventions. Unfortunately, random assignment is a process that is easier to conceptualize than to execute in school based research. Since, in most cases, children in a classroom cannot be randomly assigned to treatment or intervention conditions, one approach is to assign *classrooms* randomly to treatment conditions. This design, known as a *cluster randomized design*, is becoming widely used in large-scale school based studies. If the classrooms are sampled randomly from a population of classrooms, the ANOVA model given in (7) is known as a *random effects* model, where in the model

$$(10) \quad y_{ij} = \mu + \tau_j + e_{ij}, (i = 1,...,n; j = 1,....,k)$$

the variable τ_j that denotes the treatment effect is not a fixed variable, but a random variable with mean zero and variance σ_t^2. Thus, the variance of y_{ij} is not σ_e^2 but $\sigma_t^2 + \sigma_e^2$. In addition, it can be shown (see Swaminathan & Rogers, 2008) that the correlation ρ between the observations within a treatment condition, known as the intraclass correlation coefficient (ICC), is

$$(11) \quad \rho = \frac{\sigma_t^2}{\sigma_t^2 + \sigma_e^2}$$

This intraclass correlation must be taken into account in the analysis of cluster randomized designs.

The simplest cluster randomized design is one where schools drawn at random from a population are randomly assigned to either an intervention condition, or a control condition. It is conceptually simple to consider the model in two stages or levels. At the first level, we write a model for the observation y_{ij} of subject i in cluster j as in the model given in (6):

$$(12) \quad y_{ij} = \mu_j + e_{ij},$$

where μ_j represents the mean of cluster j and e_{ij} is a random variable with mean zero and variance σ_e^2.

Clearly, μ_j varies across clusters. It is necessary to model this variation; hence the second level of the model. One possible model is that which relates the variation in the means to treatment condition (experimental or control). As before, we define an indicator variable x_j where

$$x_j = \begin{cases} 1 & \textit{if a cluster belongs to} \\ & \quad \textit{the experimental condition} \\ 0 & \textit{if the cluster belongs to} \\ & \quad \textit{the control condition} \end{cases}$$

The model that relates the cluster means to treatment condition can then be expressed as

$$(13) \quad \mu_j = \beta_0 + \beta_1 x_j + u_j,$$

where u_j is a random error component with mean zero and variance denoted as σ_t^2. When $x_j = 1$ (the experimental condition), the mean of the cluster means is $\mu_E = \beta_0 + \beta_1$ (since the mean of $u_j = 0$), and when $x_j = 0$ (the control group condition), the mean of the cluster means is $\mu_C = \beta_0$. Thus, $\beta_1 = \mu_E - \mu_C$, and is a measure of the effect of the treatment. The models in (12) and (13) constitute a hierarchical linear model (HLM).

Combining the models in (12) and (13), we obtain the composite model

$$(14) \quad y_{ij} = \beta_0 + \beta_1 x_j + u_j + e_{ij}$$

The model in (14) is a *mixed model*, in that the component u_j is a random component, while the component x_j is a nonrandom, or fixed, component. As described above, the variance of y_{ij} in the model specified in (10) is:

$$Var(y_{ij}) = \sigma_t^2 + \sigma_e^2.$$

In terms of the mean of the observations in cluster j, the model is

$$\bar{y}_j = \beta_0 + \beta_1 x_j + u_j + \bar{e}_j$$

Since the variance of u_j is σ_t^2, and the variance of $\bar{e}_j$ is $\dfrac{\sigma_e^2}{n}$ from (2), we obtain

$$Var(\bar{y}_j) = \sigma_t^2 + \frac{\sigma_e^2}{n}.$$

Thus, in cluster randomized trials, the variance of the mean is larger than the variance of the mean in simple random sampling by a factor of σ_t^2. Furthermore, since the intraclass correlation given in (11) provides a relationship between σ_t^2 and σ_e^2, the variance of the mean within a cluster can be expressed in terms of the intraclass correlation as

$$Var(\bar{y}_j) = \frac{\sigma_e^2}{n(1-\rho)}\{1 + (n-1)\rho\}$$

This result shows that as ρ increases, the variance of the cluster mean increases. The variance is smallest when $\rho = 0$. In the ideal situation, the design is most efficient when the intraclass correlation is near zero. This will happen if the clusters are similar within the experimental and control conditions; i.e., the variation in the cluster means, σ_t^2, is very small in comparison with σ_e^2. Procedures for making inferences about parameters of the cluster randomized model are discussed in the next section.

The models described above provide a sampling of the models that may be considered in school based research. As outlined above, once the model is specified, its parameters are estimated and the sampling distribution of the estimators is determined. With this information, hypotheses about the parameters in the models can be tested. Conclusions about the adequacy of the model are then drawn. We now consider more closely the logic and procedure of hypothesis testing.

Null ypothesis Significance testing Hypothesis Significance Testing

In the early 1920s, Sir Ronald Fisher introduced the notion of hypothesis testing and experimental design in the now famous "Lady tasting tea" experiment. A lady in Rothamstead claimed that she could tell if milk was added to tea, or if tea was added to milk. To assess this claim, Fisher devised an experiment, wherein, in four cups milk was added to tea, and in four cups tea was added to milk. Fisher presented the cups in random order to the lady. Fisher used the term *null hypothesis* for the hypothesis that the lady guessed randomly. Under this hypothesis, Fisher calculated the probability that the lady would correctly identify one cup, two cups, and so on. If she was guessing randomly, the probability that the lady would identify n cups out of the eight correctly would decrease as n increased. For example, the probability that the lady would identify eight of the eight cups correctly if she guessed randomly would be very small. Fisher argued that if the probability of observing the event if the hypothesis is true is small, then it must be concluded that the hypothesis is false. Fisher's argument can be seen as a *modus tollens* argument of the form

If A, then not B; if B, then not A.

In this case, A is the proposition that the lady guesses randomly, and B is the event that the lady identifies many cups correctly. If the lady guesses randomly, she will not identify many cups correctly. If she does, she is not guessing randomly. Fisher used the term *null* hypothesis to indicate that by nullifying (rejecting) the hypothesis, you arrive at a conclusion.

One of the criticisms leveled against NHST arises out of the use of the *modus tollens* argument in this context. This logical argument is unimpeachable for deterministic events; however, when the event is probabilistic, the argument breaks down. Fisher's argument is more properly stated as follows: if the lady guesses randomly, she will *probably* not identify many cups correctly; if she identifies many cups correctly, she is *probably* not guessing randomly. Put in the *modus tollens* form, this argument is

A, then *most likely* not B;

if B, then *most likely* not A.

This argument can be shown to be seriously flawed (Cohen, 1994). We will discuss this issue in more detail in a later section.

In contrast to Fisher's notion of hypothesis testing, based simply on the null hypothesis, Neyman and Pearson introduced in the early 1930s the notion of testing the null hypothesis (H_0) against an alternate hypothesis (H_A) that must hold if the null hypothesis is rejected, and the notion of errors associated with *accepting* or *rejecting* the null hypothesis. They argued that two types of error, Type I and Type II, occur in testing hypotheses. These errors are displayed in the Table 6.1 below.

Let α, β denote the probabilities of committing Type I and Type II errors, respectively. Then

$$\alpha = \text{Probability}\left(\text{Type I error}\right)$$
$$= \text{Probability}\left(\text{Rejecting } H_0 \,|\, H_0 \text{ is True}\right),$$

Table 6.1 Type I and Type II errors in hypothesis testing

DECISION	True State	
	Null Hypothesis is True (H_0)	Null Hypothesis is False (H_A)
Reject	Type I Error	Correct Decision
Do Not Reject	Correct Decision	Type II Error

β = Probability (Type II error)

= Probability (Not Rejecting $H_0 | H_0$ is False).

It follows that

$1 - \beta$ = Probability (Rejecting $H_0 | H_0$ is False).

Neyman and Pearson used the term *Power* for this last probability, that of rejecting the null hypothesis when it is false:

Power = Probability (Rejecting $H_0 | H_0$ is False)

= $1 - \beta$.

Clearly, in testing hypotheses we want to minimize both Type I and Type II errors, or equivalently, minimize Type I error and maximize Power. Unfortunately, minimizing the errors simultaneously is not possible. Neyman and Pearson argued that it is more important to minimize Type I error, and this is the procedure that is followed when testing hypotheses using their approach. Usually, α is set to a small value (.05 or .01). It should be noted that there is an implicit relationship among α, β (or equivalently, $1 - \beta$), and sample size. Generally, with a fixed sample size, as α decreases, β increases; i.e., power decreases. On the other hand, with a fixed α, β decreases as sample size increases; i.e., power increases.

Fisher rejected outright the hypothesis testing paradigm of Neyman-Pearson. He objected to both a prespecified significance level, and the rigid reject/accept decision. The bitter dispute that ensued between Fisher and Neyman and Pearson is now legendary, and to the end, these researchers did not reconcile their differences.

To illustrate the principles of hypothesis testing, we shall consider a simple example where we want to investigate the creativity level of a population of home-schooled children. Suppose that it has been established that the national norm for scores on a creativity test, administered to conventionally schooled children in the age group of interest, is 80. We hypothesize that on average, our population of home-schooled children performs above the norm. In order to test this hypothesis, we administer the creativity test to a random sample of 36 home-schooled children and obtain a sample mean of 84. Using Fisher's approach, we ask: What is the probability of observing a sample mean of 84 or higher if the population mean is 80 (i.e., if the average creativity level of this population is the same as that of conventionally schooled children)? If this

probability is small, then we will conclude that this sample does not belong to a population with a mean of 80. In other words, we will conclude that the average creativity level of home-schooled children is higher than that of conventionally schooled children.

In order to determine this probability, we use the distribution of the sample mean given by (2). This probability can be stated as:

$$P(\bar{y} \geq 84 \,|\, \mu = 80).$$

In calculating this probability, we are operating under the assumption that the sample of home-schooled children came from a population with a mean creativity score of 80. We estimate the standard deviation from the sample, and find $s = 18$. The information we have thus far is as follows:

$$\mu = 80; \quad n = 36; \quad s = 18; \quad \bar{y} = 84.$$

Since the standard deviation was determined from the sample, we use the Student's t-distribution with $36 - 1 = 35$ degrees of freedom to compute the probability:

$$p(\bar{y} \geq 84 \,|\, \mu = 80) = p\left(t \geq \frac{84 - 80}{18 / \sqrt{36}}\right)$$
$$= p(t \geq 1.33) = .096.$$

If we define a small probability as .05, this probability is not small enough to warrant rejecting the null hypothesis. (The computation of the probability was carried out using the probability calculator provided in the website http://keisan.casio.com). However, this does not imply that the null hypothesis is true! According to Fisher, we should suspend judgment when we fail to reject the null hypothesis.

In contrast to the above "Fisherian" notion of testing only the null hypothesis, the Neyman-Pearson framework requires that we state complementary null and alternate hypotheses. In our example, appropriate null and hypotheses would be

$$H_0 : \mu \leq 80$$
$$H_1 : \mu > 80$$

The null hypothesis implies that the home-schooled children are, on average, no more creative than conventionally schooled children, while the alternate hypothesis states that they are. To reject the null hypothesis in favor of the alternate, we require a sample mean so much greater than 80 that it is unlikely to have come from a population with a mean of 80. The region of rejection for the test is, therefore, in the upper tail of the t-distribution. With $\alpha = .05$ and 35 degrees of freedom, the critical t-value is 1.69. We will reject the null hypothesis if the observed or computed t-value is greater than 1.69. Since the computed t-value, 1.33, does not exceed 1.69, we fail to reject the null hypothesis. The Neyman-Pearson approach is to accept the null hypothesis in this case.

For the one-way ANOVA model, the hypothesis of interest is that the means of the groups are equal. An alternative way to state this hypothesis is to state that the variation among the means is zero, or, equivalently, using the notation in (6),

$$H_0 : \sum_{j=1}^{k} \frac{(\mu_j - \mu)^2}{k} \equiv \sigma_t^2 = 0; \quad H_A : \sigma_t^2 \neq 0.$$

(The notation σ_t^2 is simply a shorthand notation, and should not be taken to indicate variance among the means, since these means are not realizations of a random variable.) The hypothesis for the regression model may be stated as $H_0 : \mathfrak{R}^2 = 0; \ H_A : \mathfrak{R}^2 \neq 0$, where $\mathfrak{R}^2$ is the population-squared multiple correlation. With the exception of the cluster randomized design, hypothesis testing procedures for the models described in the previous section are standard and can be found in basic statistics texts.

The analysis of cluster randomized designs is complex, and probably less familiar to most researchers in school psychology, so we will briefly describe the procedure for testing hypotheses for the case where the numbers of subjects are equal across clusters, known as the *balanced case*. The analysis of unbalanced designs is even more complex, and requires some knowledge of multilevel models or mixed models (Raudenbush & Bryk, 2002; O'Connell & McCoach, 2008).

The model for this design is given in (14) as $y_{ij} = \beta_0 + \beta_1 x_j + u_j + e_{ij}$. The parameter of interest, $\beta_1 = \mu_E - \mu_C$, provides a measure of the difference between the experimental and control groups. Its estimate is the difference between the means of the cluster means in the experimental condition, and the mean of the cluster means in the control condition; i.e., $\hat{\beta}_1 = \bar{\bar{y}}_E - \bar{\bar{y}}_C$, where $\bar{\bar{y}}_E$ and $\bar{\bar{y}}_C$ are the means of the cluster means for the experimental and control conditions, respectively. If there is a total of J clusters with $J/2$ clusters in the experimental condition, and $J/2$ clusters in the control condition, the statistic for testing the hypothesis $H_0 : \beta_1 = 0$ against $H_A : \beta_1 \neq 0$ is obtained using

the expression:

$$(15) \quad t = \frac{\bar{\bar{y}}_E - \bar{\bar{y}}_C}{\sqrt{\left[\frac{\widehat{\sigma_e^2}}{n} + \widehat{\sigma_t^2}\right]\left\{\frac{1}{J/2} + \frac{1}{J/2}\right\}}}$$

$$= \frac{\bar{\bar{y}}_E - \bar{\bar{y}}_C}{\sqrt{\frac{4}{J}\left[\frac{\widehat{\sigma_e^2}}{n} + \widehat{\sigma_t^2}\right]}} \sim t_{J-2}.$$

In the general case where the cluster sizes are unequal, computer software that is capable of analyzing multilevel or mixed model data is needed. The program HLM 6.0 (Raudenbush, Bryk, Cheong, Congdon, & du Toit, 2004) is suitable for carrying out this analysis. If the calculated t-value exceeds the critical value $t_{J-2, \alpha/2}$, we reject the null hypothesis and conclude that there is a difference between the means of the experimental and control conditions.

To illustrate this procedure, suppose that we have gathered data for 10 classrooms with 5 observations per classroom. The first five clusters belong to the experimental condition, and the last five belong to the control condition. It is expected that the intervention will result in lower scores on the outcome variable. The means of the classrooms in the experimental and control conditions are given below:

Experimental Class Means	34	40	38	36	46	Experimental Mean: 38.8
Control Class Means	44	70	60	60	68	Control Mean : 60.4

The difference between the experimental group mean and the control group mean is −21.6. Using HLM 6.0, we obtain $\widehat{\sigma_e^2} = 81$ and $\widehat{\sigma_t^2} = 46.8$. Substituting these values in the expression for t above, with $J = 10$, we obtain $t = 4.303$. The critical value of t with 8 degrees of freedom ($= 10 - 2$) for testing the hypothesis of no difference between the experimental and control conditions at $\alpha = .05$ is 2.306. Hence, the null hypothesis is rejected, and we conclude that there is a difference between the means of the experimental and control conditions. To complete the analysis, we need to compute the effect size, and construct a confidence interval for the population mean difference. We shall return to these procedures later.

When the cluster (classroom) sizes are equal, the analysis simplifies considerably. Carrying out a simple two-group comparison yields the same results as the sophisticated mixed model analysis! If we collapsed all clusters within each condition, the pooled variance would be 63.0, precisely the value of the term $(\widehat{\sigma}_e^2/n) + \widehat{\sigma}_t^2$ in (15). The mean difference between the two groups is, as before, -21.6. Thus, we would have arrived at the same conclusion using this simple analysis. In conducting cluster randomized experiments, keeping the cluster sizes the same, if possible, will result in an elegantly simple analysis.

Testing hypotheses about parameters of a model can be an important element of statistical inference, but by itself it provides a dangerously incomplete analysis of the data and yields an incomplete understanding of the variables under investigation in the population of interest. Confidence intervals for the parameters of interest, effect size measures, and a priori analysis of statistical power, must all be provided in the reporting of a study in order to provide a proper context for interpreting the results.

Confidence Intervals

A confidence interval for a population parameter encompasses all the values of the parameter that could reasonably give rise to the observed data, where "reasonably" is defined by the confidence level associated with the interval. Confidence intervals are often, although not always, based on the sampling distribution of the estimate of the parameter. For example, suppose we wish to establish a 95% confidence interval for the population mean. We use our knowledge of the sampling distribution of the mean to construct this interval. The sampling distribution tells us that the sample mean is distributed normally (or approximately so), with mean equal to the population mean and standard error equal to the population standard deviation σ divided by the square root of the sample size. Given a normal distribution, we know that in 95% of samples, the sample mean will be within 1.96 standard errors of the population mean. Conversely, in 95% of samples, the population mean will be within 1.96 standard errors of the sample mean. Thus, if we construct an interval with limits 1.96 standard errors either side of the sample mean, that interval will capture the population mean 95% of the time. The 95% confidence interval for the population mean μ is therefore

$$\bar{y} \pm 1.96\frac{\sigma}{\sqrt{n}}.$$

If we wish to use a lower or higher confidence level, we obtain the z-value associated with the corresponding central probability region in the normal distribution, and use it in place of 1.96. If we substitute the sample standard deviation for the population value, we use the t-distribution with $n-1$ degrees of freedom given in (4) to determine how many estimated standard errors we must allow around the sample mean to obtain the desired confidence level. In this case, the confidence interval is expressed as

$$\bar{y} \pm t_{n-1,.025}\frac{s}{\sqrt{n}}$$

where $t_{n-1,.025}$ is the upper .025 percentile of the t-distribution with $n-1$ degrees of freedom. More generally, for any confidence level denoted by $100(1-\alpha)\%$, the confidence interval is

$$\bar{y} \pm t_{n-1,\alpha/2}\frac{s}{\sqrt{n}}.$$

The notation α is used to indicate the close relationship between the confidence interval and the null hypothesis significance test. The $100(1-\alpha)\%$ confidence interval represents all values of the parameter for which the null hypothesis would not be rejected at the α significance level. Thus, a 95% confidence interval corresponds to a hypothesis test at the .05 significance level.

In the case of our earlier example of an investigation of the creativity levels of home-schooled children, we obtained a sample mean of 84, and sample standard deviation of 18, from a sample of 36 children. The 95% confidence interval for the population mean is

$$84 \pm 2.03\frac{18}{\sqrt{36}} = (84 \pm 6.1) = (77.9, 90.1).$$

We say we are 95% confident that the mean creativity level of the home-schooled population is between 77.9 and 90.1. We use the term "confidence" as a shorthand to refer to the *process* by which the interval was constructed, which produces intervals containing the true mean 95% of the time. Any value in the confidence interval could reasonably have produced the sample obtained. Note that a mean of 80 is in this interval; this was the hypothesized value that was tested in the example. Using the hypothesis testing procedure, the hypothesis that $\mu = 80$ was not rejected. The confidence interval corroborates this finding (as it must). The confidence interval, however, tells us much more; indeed, it makes very clear how little a failure to reject the null hypothesis means. Far from concluding that $\mu = 80$, all we can conclude is that 80 is one of the many possible values for the population mean. For example, suppose that the mean was at the lower limit, 77.9. Then the probability of observing a sample mean as high as 84 would be

$$P(\bar{y} \geq 84 \mid \mu = 77.9) = P(t \geq \frac{(84 - 77.9)}{18/\sqrt{36}})$$
$$= P(t \geq 2.03) = .025.$$

The t-value is right at the critical value used in testing the hypothesis in the example, so this value of μ is the lowest value for which the null hypothesis would not be rejected. Correspondingly, if the mean was at the upper limit of 90.1, the calculated t-value would be -2.03, at the lower critical value, making this the highest value for which the hypothesis would not be rejected at the .05 significance level.

A similar procedure is used to construct a confidence interval for the difference between two means. The sampling distribution of the difference between means from independent samples is

$$\bar{y}_1 - \bar{y}_2 \sim N(\mu_1 - \mu_2, \frac{\sigma_1^2}{n_1} + \frac{\sigma_2^2}{n_2}).$$

By the same logic as was used to derive the confidence interval for μ, a 95% confidence interval for $\mu_1 - \mu_2$ is

$$\bar{y}_1 - \bar{y}_2 \pm 1.96\sqrt{\frac{\sigma_1^2}{n_1} + \frac{\sigma_2^2}{n_2}}.$$

When we must substitute estimates of the population variances σ_1^2 and σ_2^2, the normal distribution can no longer be used for inferences. Instead, under the assumption of a normally distributed variable y, with equal population variances in the two groups, a t-distribution with $n_1 + n_2 - 2$ degrees of freedom is appropriate for making inferences about $\mu_1 - \mu_2$. The general $100(1 - \alpha)\%$ confidence interval for $\mu_1 - \mu_2$ is thus given by

$$(16) \quad \bar{y}_1 - \bar{y}_2 \pm t_{v,\alpha/2}\sqrt{s_{pooled}^2\left(\frac{1}{n_1} + \frac{1}{n_2}\right)}$$

where $v = n_1 + n_2 - 2$ and

$$s_{pooled}^2 = \frac{(n_1 - 1)s_1^2 + (n_2 - 1)s_2^2}{n_1 + n_2 - 2}$$ is the estimate of

the common population variance obtaining by pooling the two sample variances.

As an example of the two-group case, let us modify the example above. Suppose that the mean creativity level of conventionally schooled children is unknown, so we have no reference population mean with which to compare the mean of the home-schooled children. Instead, we take a random sample of conventionally schooled children of comparable age to the home-schooled group, and compare the means of the two samples. The usual null hypothesis would be $H_0 : \mu_1 - \mu_2 = 0$, tested against the alternate $H_1 : \mu_1 - \mu_2 \neq 0$. Suppose that in a sample of 36 conventionally schooled children, the mean and standard deviation are 82.5 and 16, respectively. The pooled variance estimate would be $(35(18^2) + 35(16^2))/70 = 289$ (a simple average in the case of equal sample sizes) and the degrees of freedom for the test are $v = 70$. The 95% confidence interval for $\mu_1 - \mu_2$ is

$$84 - 82.5 \pm 1.99\sqrt{289\left(\frac{1}{36} + \frac{1}{36}\right)} = 1.5 \pm 8.0$$
$$= (-6.5, 9.5).$$

Since this confidence interval contains zero, we would not reject the null hypothesis stated above. However, it is clear from the confidence interval that we cannot conclude that $\mu_1 = \mu_2$. The difference between means could be up to 6.5 points in favor of the conventionally schooled group, or up to 9.5 points in favor of the home-schooled group!

Several points should be noted about the confidence interval. First, it applies to the population parameter and provides an interval estimate of the parameter, rather than providing information about the sample. Second, the confidence interval varies from sample to sample, while the population parameter remains constant. Before the confidence interval is constructed, we can talk about the probability that the population parameter will be contained in the interval. Thus, we can say that there is a 95% chance that a confidence interval for the mean constructed using the procedure above will contain the population mean. By this, we mean that 95% of samples will yield 95% confidence intervals that contain the population mean. However, once the interval is constructed in a given sample, probability statements are no longer appropriate. The population mean is either in the constructed interval or not, although we don't know which is the case. A common misinterpretation of the confidence interval is that there is a 95% chance that the population parameter is in the interval. The population parameter is a constant; hence we cannot talk about the probability that it takes any particular value, or is in a particular interval.

Confidence intervals have traditionally been constructed as a follow-up procedure when the null hypothesis is rejected, in order to answer the question: If the parameter is not the hypothesized value, what is it? Clearly, however, the confidence interval obviates the hypothesis test, since it subsumes the test of the hypothesized value along with a great many other values. Thus, it is infinitely more informative than the hypothesis test. But the confidence interval tells us even more than what parameter values could have given rise to the data. It also tells us, through its width, how much we really know about the population parameter. When the interval is wide, it indicates that we have little specific knowledge about the parameter of interest; when it is narrow, it indicates that we have precise knowledge. The primary factor affecting the width of a confidence interval is sample size: the larger the sample size, the narrower the interval. In the case of confidence intervals for means, or differences between means, the variability in the population also plays a role: the greater the variability, the wider the confidence interval. In our first example above, the confidence interval $(77.9, 90.1)$ is wide, indicating that we know relatively little about the true value of the parameter. This width is a function of both the sample size and standard deviation.

Given the richness of the information provided by confidence intervals, it would be a misuse, indeed abuse, to use them merely as a means for testing hypotheses about parameters. While they permit the testing of specific hypotheses, they should be interpreted in a broader way as a statement of what we know about the population parameter, and how specific that knowledge is.

A confidence interval can be constructed for any parameter of interest. Confidence intervals for proportions, difference between proportions, variances, and regression model parameters, are all constructed in the manner described above. Procedures for constructing such intervals are available in most statistical texts. Other parameters such as population R^2 require a different approach; these confidence intervals are discussed in the next section.

Critics of the NHST paradigm recommend greater use of confidence intervals in place of NHSTs. The APA Task Force on Statistical Inference noted in its report that "it is hard to imagine a situation in which a dichotomous accept–reject decision is better than reporting... a confidence interval" (Wilkinson & Task Force on Statistical Inference, 1999, p. 599). They also noted that reporting confidence intervals allows stability of results across studies to be examined, and further helps in constructing "plausible regions" (p. 599) for population parameters. The American Psychological Association likewise strongly recommends reporting of confidence intervals (see the 2001 *Publication Manual of the American Psychological Association*, p. 22). Despite these recommendations, confidence intervals for any parameters have been rarely reported in the social sciences (Finch, Cumming, & Thomason, 2001).

Confidence intervals provide important information about population parameters, beyond that provided by NHST. Another, complementary approach to enhancing interpretability of results is to conceptualize and estimate the size of the "effect" obtained in a study. An effect size estimate is a way of quantifying how big a departure from the null hypothesis was obtained in a given study. Effect sizes are descriptive, and can be inferential if confidence intervals are provided for them. They can also be used prescriptively to determine a priori how large a sample is needed to detect a population effect of a certain size. Effect sizes provide a focus for answering questions about statistical power. Effect sizes and power analysis are discussed in the next sections.

Effect Size

The concept of effect size arises naturally from the Neyman-Pearson framework for hypothesis testing. The effect size is a measure of the discrepancy between H_o and H_A. While the concept of effect size has existed almost since the introduction of NHST (see Huberty, 2002, for an interesting history of effect sizes), effect size measures received little attention until meta-analysis came into vogue in the 1970s (Glass, 1976). Effect size measures have acquired even greater prominence with the introduction of power analysis (Cohen, 1988, 1992). Despite the extensive literature now available on these techniques, and despite the fact that effect sizes are simple to estimate, researchers still do not routinely report effect sizes. Pressure on researchers to report effect size in their studies has been steadily increasing over the last decade or so. In fact, editorial policies in several journals (Thompson, 1996; Fidler & Cumming, 2006; Kehle et al., 2006) have mandated the reporting of effect sizes.

In the single population case, where we want to determine if the mean of the population on a certain variable, μ_1, differs from some specified mean μ_0, the effect size is simply $\mu_1 - \mu_0$. Since this quantity is dependent on the units of the measured variable, a better indicator of effect size is the standardized effect size, defined as

$$\Delta = \frac{\mu_1 - \mu_0}{\sigma},$$

where σ is the standard deviation of the population. We will henceforth refer to the *standardized effect size* simply as *effect size*. Once the data are collected and analyzed, the effect size for the study can be estimated as

$$d = \frac{\bar{y} - \mu_0}{s}.$$

For the example provided earlier, the estimated effect size is $(84 - 80)/18 = .22$. The estimated difference between the home-schooled population mean on the creativity measure, and the reference population, is .22 standard deviations, considered a small effect using Cohen's (1988) rule of thumb.

In the case where two groups are to be compared, an obvious measure of effect size is

$$(17) \quad \Delta = \frac{\mu_1 - \mu_2}{\sigma},$$

where σ is the common standard deviation. The estimate of this effect size is computed as

$$(18) \quad d = \frac{\bar{y}_1 - \bar{y}_2}{s},$$

where s^2 is the pooled variance. In the example earlier where home-schooled and conventionally schooled children were compared, the effect size was $(84 - 82.5)/\sqrt{289} = .15$, a very small effect.

Estimated effect sizes provide a description of the extent to which statistics obtained in a sample depart from those expected under the null hypothesis. They are expressed in units that transcend the particular measurement scale used in a study, and consequently provide a common metric for combining the results of different studies. Like all estimates, however, they are subject to sampling fluctuations. Thus, confidence intervals are required if we wish to make inferences about population effect sizes.

For the two-group comparison of means example, we are easily able to construct a confidence interval for the difference between the means in the original metric; i.e., $\mu_1 - \mu_2$, using the t-distribution. The confidence interval, shown in (16), is based on the fact that for normally distributed y,

$$(19) \quad t = \frac{(\bar{y}_1 - \bar{y}_2) - (\mu_1 - \mu_2)}{s_{pooled}\sqrt{\dfrac{1}{n_1} + \dfrac{1}{n_2}}} \sim t_v$$

where $v = n_1 + n_2 - 2$ and $\mu_1 - \mu_2$ is the true value of the population mean difference. This t-distribution is referred to as the central t-distribution because it has a mean of 0. In testing a null hypothesis about $\mu_1 - \mu_2$, we assume that the parameter has a particular value; i.e, $H_0 : \mu_1 - \mu_2 = \delta_0$. Typically, we are interested in the case of $\delta_0 = 0$, but we could test any value of interest. Our statistic for testing the hypothesis would be

$$(20) \quad t = \frac{(\bar{y}_1 - \bar{y}_2) - \delta_0}{s_{pooled}\sqrt{\dfrac{1}{n_1} + \dfrac{1}{n_2}}},$$

which would have the central t-distribution. The concept and definition of effect size, however, is based on the notion that the true value of the parameter differs from that hypothesized. If this is so, $\mu_1 - \mu_2 \neq \delta_0$. We therefore have the wrong value for $\mu_1 - \mu_2$ in the expression above, and the central t-distribution in (19) does not hold. The mean of the distribution is no longer zero, but is shifted by an amount related to the discrepancy between the true mean difference and the hypothesized value. If we rewrite the t-statistic above as

$$t = \frac{(\bar{y}_1 - \bar{y}_2) - (\mu_1 - \mu_2) + [(\mu_1 - \mu_2) - \delta_0]}{s_{pooled}\sqrt{\dfrac{1}{n_1} + \dfrac{1}{n_2}}},$$

and compare it with the central t in (19), we see this shift. It can be shown that the t-statistic in (20) has a noncentral t-distribution with noncentrality parameter λ, where

$$\lambda = \frac{(\mu_1 - \mu_2) - \delta_0}{\sigma\sqrt{\dfrac{1}{n_1} + \dfrac{1}{n_2}}}.$$

This distribution would be appropriate for constructing a confidence interval for $(\mu_1 - \mu_2) - \delta_0$, or the effect size in raw units. (Note again that we typically take $\delta_0 = 0$). However, we are interested in a confidence interval for the standardized effect size. We can use the same argument to construct a confidence interval for Δ. The t-statistic in (20) can be written as

$$(21) \quad t = \frac{d}{\sqrt{\dfrac{1}{n_1} + \dfrac{1}{n_2}}},$$

given a hypothesized value of $\Delta_0 = 0$. This t-statistic has a noncentral t-distribution with $n_1 + n_2 - 2$

degrees of freedom and noncentrality parameter λ, where

$$(22) \quad \lambda = \frac{\Delta}{\sqrt{\dfrac{1}{n_1} + \dfrac{1}{n_2}}}$$

The noncentral t-distribution is a skewed distribution, centered approximately around λ. When $\lambda = 0$, as it would if the null hypothesis of no mean differences were true, the noncentral t reduces to the usual (central) t-distribution. It becomes more symmetric as λ decreases and degrees of freedom increase. The distribution with noncentrality parameter $-\lambda$ is the mirror image of the distribution with noncentrality parameter λ. Cumming and Finch (2001) provide a detailed description of the noncentral t-distribution. Unfortunately, they use the symbol Δ for the noncentrality parameter, whereas we have reserved it for standardized effect size.

To construct a confidence interval for Δ, we rely on the relationship between Δ and λ given above. A confidence interval is first constructed for λ, and then transformed according to the linear relationship to yield a confidence interval for Δ. Given that the confidence interval expresses all values of the parameter for which the hypothesis would not be rejected, we need to find the values of λ for which the calculated t would be at the edge of the region of rejection for the hypothesis. Thus, for a 95% confidence interval, we need the values of λ for which $P(t_{v,\lambda(L)} \geq t_{obs}) = .025$ and $P(t_{v,\lambda(U)} \leq t_{obs}) = .025$, where t_{obs} is the calculated value of the statistic using the data obtained in the sample. The value $\lambda(L)$ is the value for which the calculated t-value would be just on the upper edge of the region of rejection, and $\lambda(U)$ is the value for which the calculated t-value would be just on the lower edge of the region of rejection (Cumming & Finch, 2001). These values are difficult to compute, and require sophisticated computer routines that have not been widely available to users in the past. However, there are now freely available high-precision online calculators such as that previously mentioned, http://keisan.casio.com. Once the values of $\lambda(L)$ and $\lambda(U)$ are obtained, we convert them to Δ values using the relationship above. In our two-group example, no statistically significant difference was observed between the means, so the confidence interval for the effect size would symmetric around 0. For illustration purposes, suppose that the mean of the conventionally schooled children was 75.5. Then the calculated t-statistic would be

$$t_{obs} = \frac{84 - 75.5}{\sqrt{289\,(1/36 + 1/36)}} = 2.12$$

The value of λ for which this observed t is at the upper edge of the region of rejection is 0.12, and the value for which it is at the lower edge is 4.10. Converting these values to effect sizes, we obtain a 95% confidence interval for Δ of $(.03, 0.97)$. Despite the significant t-statistic, the true effect could have been as small as .03.

When several groups are to be compared (Analysis of Variance), an intuitive and simple measure of the effect size is the difference between the largest and the smallest treatment means, divided by the within-group standard deviation. An alternative measure is one that is expressed in terms of the differences among *all* the treatment means. The variance of the treatment means, σ_t^2, captures the differences among the means and is consistent with the null hypothesis. The standardized effect size for one-way ANOVA is therefore defined as

$$(23) \quad \Delta = \frac{\sigma_t}{\sigma_e} = \frac{\sqrt{\displaystyle\sum_{j=1}^{k}(\mu_j - \mu)^2 / k}}{\sigma_e} \equiv f,$$

where σ_e is the within-group standard deviation. This effect size is a key index in the computation of power for ANOVA designs, and has been widely used in the statistical literature. Cohen (1988, 1992) popularized this measure but used the symbol f to designate it. As a result, it is commonly known as Cohen's f. We prefer the notation Δ because it is more descriptive of the concept (that of difference). An alternate measure of effect size is ω^2, the index of strength of association in Analysis of Variance. This measure is defined as

$$\omega^2 = \frac{\sigma_t^2}{\sigma_t^2 + \sigma_e^2}.$$

The measure ω^2 is the ratio of the variance attributed to the treatment effects to the total variance, and hence is the proportion of variance explained by the treatment effects. It follows that

$$(24) \quad f = \sqrt{\frac{\omega^2}{1 - \omega^2}}.$$

Cohen (1988) suggested yet another measure, η^2, as the effect size measure. This measure is the *correlation ratio*, defined as

$$(25) \quad \eta^2 = \frac{\sigma_t^2}{\sigma_t^2 + \sigma_e^2}.$$

It follows that as with ω^2,

$$(26) \quad f = \sqrt{\frac{\eta^2}{1 - \eta^2}}.$$

It should be noted in the definition of f in (24) that for fixed effects models, the variation in the means should not be considered a variance, because in this case the number of treatment conditions (or units of comparison) is fixed and not a sample of units from a population, as in the case of the random effects model described earlier. In the random effects model, the effect size is the ICC coefficient ρ, defined in exactly the same way as ω^2 and η^2. Thus ρ, ω^2 and η^2 are identically defined, and are the same in the population. They differ, however, with respect to how they are estimated in samples.

The estimation of f (or Δ) is not straightforward. A simple estimate defined as

$$\hat{f} = \frac{\sqrt{\sum_{j=1}^{k} (\bar{y}_j - \bar{y})^2 / k}}{s_{within}}$$

may suffice in a pinch, but is not the correct estimate of f. A better estimate of ω^2 is given by

$$\hat{\omega}^2 = \frac{SSB - (k-1) MSSE}{SST + MSSE}$$

where SSB, SSE, SST are the Sum of Squares Between, Sum of Squares due to Error, and Sum of Squares Total; MSSE is the Mean Sum of Squares Error ($SSE/N\text{-}k$). The corresponding estimate of f is given by (24).

The measure of effect size often reported in commonly used statistical software packages is η^2, and is estimated as

$$(27) \quad \hat{\eta}^2 = \frac{SSB}{SST}.$$

This quantity is the usual *squared multiple correlation* coefficient R^2. In the case of a multifactor design, the proportion of variance explained by each factor in the design is termed Partial η^2, estimated a

$$(28) \quad \hat{\eta}^2_{PARTIAL} = \frac{SSB_{FACTOR}}{SSB_{FACTOR} + SSE}.$$

When there is only one factor, $\hat{\eta}^2_{PARTIAL}$ reduces to $\hat{\eta}^2$. As an estimate of effect size, $\hat{\omega}^2$ is preferred

to $\hat{\eta}^2_{PARTIAL}$ and $\hat{\eta}^2$, since the latter two are more biased than the former as estimators of the population parameter ω^2 (or η^2).

These measures are applicable in the general case of regression models. For the regression model, it is customary to define the measure of effect size as η^2 and use $\hat{\eta}^2$ defined in (27) or in (28) as its estimate.

In the case of association between two continuous variables, the Pearson product moment correlation serves as the effect size measure, and in the case of the multiple correlation, the effect size may be taken as $\eta^2/(1-\eta^2)$, with its estimate defined as $R^2/(1-R^2)$. Cohen (1988, 1992) has summarized these effect sizes and provided recommendations as to what may be considered small, medium, and large effect sizes. We provide some of these in Table 6.2 below.

As was pointed out earlier, all the parameters given in Table 6.2 can be defined in the context of models that are special cases of the general linear model or the regression model. In this sense, these effect size measures should all provide the same information. We could define one common effect size for all these seemingly different procedures. The f statistic provides this unified measure. As shown, the estimate of f can be expressed in terms of the estimates of ω^2 or η^2. Needless to say, it is important to clearly indicate which effect size measure was used, and provide the details.

Confidence intervals can be constructed for ω^2 and η^2 using the same approach as described for confidence intervals for mean differences. When the null hypothesis $H_0 : \eta^2 = 0$ (equivalently, $H_0 : \mathcal{R}^2 = 0$) is not true, the F-statistic for testing the hypothesis has a noncentral F-distribution with noncentrality parameter λ given by

$$\lambda = \frac{\eta^2}{1-\eta^2}(v_1 + v_2 + 1),$$

where v_1 and v_2 are the numerator and denominator degrees of freedom, respectively (Smithson, 2001). The confidence interval for λ is then constructed by finding $\lambda(L)$ such that the observed F is in the upper $\alpha/2$ tail, and $\lambda(U)$ such that the observed F is in the lower $\alpha/2$ tail. The interval is converted to a confidence interval for η^2 using the relationship $\eta^2 = \lambda/(\lambda + v_1 + v_2 + 1$. If a confidence interval for f is desired, it can easily be obtained using the same procedure.

To illustrate the computation of effect sizes, we consider a design where three interventions are to be compared with a control condition. This is a

Table 6.2 Effect sizes for various statistical tests

Departures from Hypothesis	Effect Size Parameter	Effect size Estimate	Recommended magnitudes		
			Small	Medium	Large
$H_0 : \mu = \mu_0$	$(\mu - \mu_0)/\sigma$	$(\bar{y} - \mu_0)/s$	.20	.50	.80
$H_0 : \mu_1 - \mu_2 = 0$	$(\mu_1 - \mu_2)/\sigma_e$	$(\bar{y}_1 - \bar{y}_2)/s^c$	.20	.50	.80
$H_0 : \rho = 0^a$	ρ	R	.10	.30	.50
$H_0 : \mu_1 = \mu_2 = ... = \mu_k$	f^c	$\hat{f}$	.10	.25	.40
	ω^2	$\widehat{\omega^2}$	.01	.06	.14
$H_0 : \mathfrak{R}^2 = 0^b$	$\eta^2/(1-\eta^2)$	$R^2/(1-R^2)$	.02	.15	.35

[a] Correlation
[b] Multiple Correlation
[c] Pooled Standard deviation
[d] Effect Size as defined by Cohen (1988)

one-way fixed effects ANOVA model. The analysis of this model may be found in any basic statistics text. In analyzing this data, it is customary to summarize the results in the form of an ANOVA Table that provides the partitioning of the variance into its components. Table 6.3 contains the results of the analysis.

From this table we obtain SSB = 42.393; SSE = 90.857; SST = 133.250; MSSB = 14.131; MSSE = 3.786. The number of observations in each condition is $n = 7$, and the number of conditions is $k = 4$. The effect size measures are:

$$\hat{\eta}^2 = \frac{SSB}{SST} = \frac{42.393}{133.250} = 0.318;$$

$$\widehat{\omega}^2 = \frac{SSB - (k-1)MSSE}{SST + MSSE}$$
$$= \frac{42.393 - 3*3.786}{133.250 + 3.786} = 0.226;$$

$$\widehat{f}_w = \sqrt{\frac{\widehat{w^2}}{1-\widehat{w^2}}} = \sqrt{\frac{0.226}{1-0.226}} = 0.540;$$

$$\widehat{f}_n = \sqrt{\frac{\widehat{n^2}}{1-\widehat{n^2}}} = \sqrt{\frac{0.318}{1-0.318}} = 0.683;$$

Obviously, the effect sizes are large. The last two columns of the table deal with the "observed" power and the noncentrality parameter of the noncentral F distribution. These quantities are critical for determining the power of the test; we shall describe them in the next section.

While the overall effect size for the ANOVA is informative, it is important that we provide effect sizes for comparing the means of the intervention conditions with the control condition, and also for making comparisons among the intervention conditions. Seldom are we interested simply in the result of the overall test of mean differences.

Table 6.3 Analysis of variance table for comparing the means of the interventions and control conditions

	Tests of Between-Subjects Effects							
Source	Type III Sum of Squares	df	Mean Square	F	Sig.	Partial Eta Squared	Noncent. Parameter	Observed Power[b]
Intervention	42.393	3	14.131	3.733	.025	.318	11.198	.738
Error	90.857	24	3.786					
Corrected Total	133.250	27						

[b] Computed by taking $\alpha = .05$.

Comparisons of the means are necessary to determine if the interventions are functioning the way they are expected to function. In our example, we need the means of the intervention and control conditions in order to determine specific effect sizes. The means for the first three intervention groups are 20.286, 19.143, and 21.429. The mean of the control group is 18.143. The pooled standard deviation is 1.948. With this information, we are in a position to calculate the effect sizes. The effect sizes for comparing each intervention condition with the control are: $(20.268 - 18.143)/1.948 = 1.10$; $(19.143 - 18.143)/1.948 = 0.51$; and $(21.429 - 18.143)/1.958 = 1.68$.

For the cluster randomized design, the effect size is given by

$$\Delta = \frac{\mu_E - \mu_C}{\sqrt{\sigma_e^2 + \sigma_t^2}} = \frac{\beta_1}{\sqrt{\sigma_e^2 + \sigma_t^2}}.$$

The estimate of this effect size is

$$\hat{\Delta} = \frac{\overline{y}_E - \overline{y}_C}{\sqrt{\left[\widehat{\sigma_e^2} + \widehat{\sigma_t^2}\right]}}.$$

For the example described earlier, with the values obtained for $\widehat{\sigma_e^2}$ (= 81) and $\widehat{\sigma_t^2}$ (= 46.8), and the difference in the classroom means of -21.6, the effect size is

$$\hat{\Delta} = \frac{21.6}{\sqrt{(81 + 46.8)}} = \frac{21.60}{11.31} = 1.91,$$

which is a very large effect size.

Power

As defined earlier, Power is the probability of rejecting the null hypothesis *when it is false.* Power tells us a great deal about the interpretability and value of the results of a study. If power is low, statistically nonsignificant results can be expected, and hence will have no meaning. If power is high, small effects will be detected and it will be important to consider estimated effect sizes in drawing conclusions and making decisions.

Power calculations are not easy, and in the past, this prevented researchers from carrying out a power analysis. Cohen (1988) has provided extensive "look-up" tables for determining power under various combinations of sample size, effect size, and α. Despite this, and his efforts to educate researchers on the importance of reporting effect sizes and conducting power analysis, Cohen (1992) lamented the fact that power analyses are not common in behavioral research. However, with major funding agencies (e.g., Institute of Education Sciences) and even internal institutional review boards that approve research projects within an institution, now demanding power analyses, it can be expected that power analysis will become routine. With the advent of such free computer software as G*Power (Faul, Erdfelder, Lang, & Buchner, 2007), which can be downloaded from the site http://www.psycho.uni-duesseldorf.de/abteilungen/, it is almost a trivial task to conduct a power analysis.

While the calculation of power may be difficult, the underlying concept is straightforward. In order to illustrate the concept of power, consider the problem of comparing two means to assess the efficacy of an intervention. Suppose two groups of children are assigned randomly to the intervention and control conditions. The hypothesis of interest may be stated as

$$H_0 : \mu_E - \mu_C = 0$$
$$H_A : \mu_E - \mu_C \neq 0,$$

where μ_E is the mean of the intervention group, and μ_C is the mean of the control group. With a common population variance for the two groups of σ^2, and a plan to collect data with equal numbers of subjects ($n = 20$) in each group, we can, under specified conditions, determine the probability of rejecting the null hypothesis when it is false; i.e., the power of the statistical test. When the null hypothesis is *true* (i.e., $\mu_E - \mu_C = 0$), the statistic t, defined as

$$(29) \quad t = \frac{(\overline{y}_E - \overline{y}_C)}{s_{pooled}\sqrt{\frac{1}{n} + \frac{1}{n}}}$$

has a central t-distribution with $2n - 2$ degrees of freedom. The hypothesis is rejected at the .05 significance level if the absolute value of the calculated t exceeds the critical value, $t_{2n-2,.025}$. For our example, $2n - 2 = 38$ and the critical value is $t_{38,.025} = 2.024$. But suppose that the null hypothesis is not true. What is the probability of rejecting the null hypothesis in this case? To answer this question, we need to specify the degree of departure from the null hypothesis, i.e., the difference in the population means, that we would like to be able to detect. Figure 6.1 shows graphically the distribution of the test statistic under the null hypothesis, and its distribution when the null hypothesis is not true for a specified difference in the means. As explained in the previous section, when the null hypothesis is not true, the test statistic for the effect given in (21)

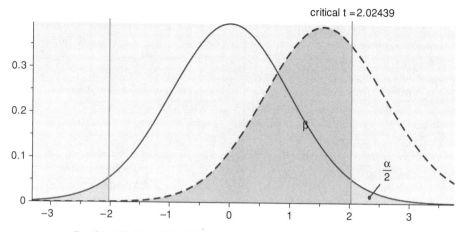

Fig. 6.1 Probability of Type II Error and Power Figure obtained from G*Power

has the *noncentral t*-distribution with *noncentrality* parameter λ defined in (22). For our example, suppose that we want to be able to detect an effect size of 0.5. The noncentrality parameter λ is therefore

$$\lambda = \Delta / \sqrt{\frac{1}{n_1} + \frac{1}{n_2}} = 0.5 / \sqrt{\frac{1}{20} + \frac{1}{20}} = 1.581.$$

In the figure, the probability of making a Type II error is shown as β. The power is $(1 - \beta)$.

To compute power, we must determine the area under the noncentral *t*-distribution, above the null hypothesis critical value of 2.024, and below -2.024. The required probability can be computed using computer routines available on the web. An accurate routine is available through http://keisan.casio.com. In order to calculate probabilities for the noncentral *t*-distribution, we need to provide the random variable ($+ 2.024$, in this case), the degrees of freedom for the *t*-distribution ($v = 38$), and the noncentrality parameter, which in this example is 1.581. The probability of interest is

$$p[t_{38;1.581} \geq 2.024] + p[t_{38;1.581} \leq -2.024]$$
$$= 0.338 + 0.000 = 0.338.$$

Thus, the power for detecting an effect size of 0.5 (a medium effect size), given our sample sizes, is 0.34. With a sample size of 20 in each group, we have little power to reject the null hypothesis even for medium-sized effects. Such results are generally surprising and shocking to the average researcher.

The purpose of this example was to provide a conceptual basis for computing power. This idea behind computing power generalizes to other hypotheses and distributions. In the case of Analysis

of Variance, we need to use the noncentral *F*-distribution for power calculations. Once the noncentrality parameter (again a function of the effect size) is specified, power can be computed. The noncentrality parameters for departures from various null hypotheses are given in Table 6.4. However, as mentioned earlier, all hypotheses listed can be framed as special cases of the general linear model, and hence the population effect sizes are subsumed under the effect size measure defined for regression analysis; that is, departures from $H_0 : \Re^2 = 0$.

The concept of noncentral distributions plays a key role in computing power. Noncentral distributions are required whenever the null hypothesis being tested is assumed to be false. A very readable account of noncentral distributions is provided in Cumming and Finch (2001). While it is straightforward to use these distributions and compute power, power calculation is nevertheless a daunting process. Computing sample size to achieve a given level of power is tedious. However, there are readily available free computer programs which take the stress out of computing power by hand. The software G*Power mentioned earlier is an ideal program for computing power. In using G*Power, the user chooses from the Test Family List, which contains the following tests: Exact *F* tests, *t* tests, χ^2 tests, and z tests. For each of these tests, G*Power provides the option of computing: (a) sample size given α, effect size, and power; (b) α and power given the ratio of β / α, sample size, and effect size; (c) α given power, sample size, and effect size; (d) power given α, sample size, and effect size; and (e) effect size given α, sample size, and power. The software is user-friendly and provides publishable quality graphics and tables.

Table 6.4 Noncentrality parameters corresponding to common effect size measures

Null Hypothesis	Effect Size Measure	Noncentrality Parameter
$H_0 : \mu = \mu_0$	$\Delta = (\mu_1 - \mu_0)/\sigma$	$\sqrt{n}\Delta$
$H_0 : \mu_1 - \mu_2 = 0$	$\Delta = (\mu_1 - \mu_2)/\sigma_{pooled}$	$\Delta / \sqrt{\dfrac{1}{n_1} + \dfrac{1}{n_2}}$
$H_0 : \mu_1 = \mu_2 = ... = \mu_k$	$f = \sigma_\mu / \sigma_e$	$N f^2$
$H_0 : \mathfrak{R}^2 = 0$	$f^2 = \dfrac{\eta^2}{1-\eta^2}$	$N f^2$

For the example worked out on determining the power for the comparison of two independent groups, we specify in G*Power the number of tails (= two), the effect size (= 0.5), α (= .05), and sample size in each group (= 20). G*Power outputs the noncentrality parameter, critical t, degrees of freedom, and power. These are shown in Figure 6.2 and agree with our "hand computations."

To determine the sample size required to achieve a power of 0.80 for the comparison of two independent groups, we specify in G*Power the number of tails, the effect size, α, power (= 0.80), and allocation ratio n_2/n_1 (= 1). The program outputs the noncentrality parameter, critical t, degrees of freedom, and the necessary sample size in each group. The required sample size is 64 subjects per group. Thus, to detect an effect size of 0.5 with a power of 0.8, we need a sample size of 128 (64 students in each group).

An important consideration in planning a study is the relationship between sample size, power, and effect size. G*Power can provide plots of the relationship between any two of these variables, when the third one is fixed at a certain value. For a given effect size, the relationship between sample size and power in a two-group study may be obtained by clicking on the x-y plot. This plot feature is flexible enough to provide plots for varying effect sizes. Figure 6.3 provides the relationship between sample size and power for effect sizes ranging from 0.3 to 0.7. Examining this chart, we confirm our statement that to achieve a power of 0.8 with an effect size of 0.5, we a need a total sample of about 125 subjects (it is difficult to determine precisely the sample size needed from the chart).

Charts of this nature are important in planning a study. They indicate the relationship between power and sample size, and allow the researcher to choose (and justify the choice of) a sample size to achieve a required level of power. Cohen (1992) recommends that a power level of .80 be used in power calculations to determine sample size. A smaller value will result in too large a Type II error rate, and a larger value will require sample sizes that may be beyond the reach of the researcher.

To calculate power in a one-way ANOVA design in G*Power, we choose the F test under the Family of Tests; select ANOVA: Fixed Effects, omnibus, one-way; and provide the information needed. In the example provided earlier, where three intervention conditions were compared with a control

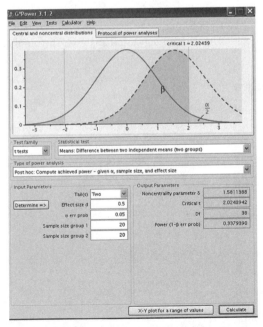

Fig. 6.2 Computation of Power for Comparing the Means of Two Groups for Sample Sizes of 20 in Each Group

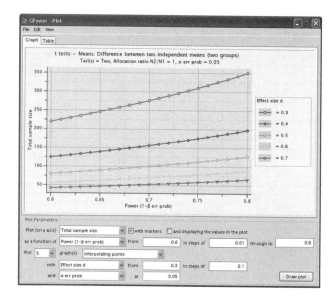

Fig. 6.3 Relationship between Sample Size and Power for Various Effect Sizes for the Comparison of Means of Two Groups

condition, to determine power for a medium effect size of 0.5 we need to input the effect size (= 0.5), $\alpha = 0.05$, the number of groups (= 4), and the total sample size (= 28). With this input, G*Power indicates that the power to detect an effect size of 0.5 with 4 groups and a sample size of 28 (seven in each group) is only 0.51. Rather than computing the sample size needed to achieve a given power for a specified effect size, we can examine the relationship between power and sample size for a range of effect sizes using G*Power. Figure 6.4 shows the relationship between sample size and power for effect sizes ranging from of 0.2 to 0.6.

If we want a power of 0.8 for a medium effect size of 0.5, we need a total of 50 subjects, or roughly 12 subjects per group. To be able to detect an effect size of 0.3 with a power of 0.8, we need a total sample size of about 140 subjects, or 35 subjects per group.

To calculate power in the regression model, we choose the F-test under the Family of tests. Under statistical tests, we choose Linear multiple regression: Fixed model, R^2 deviation from 0; and then specify the parameters necessary for the chosen power analysis. For example, to determine sample size for given power, the effect size, α, power, and the number of predictors must be specified. Note that the effect size here is f^2 and not f, as in ANOVA. It may be informative to recast the ANOVA power analysis in terms of regression analysis. The number

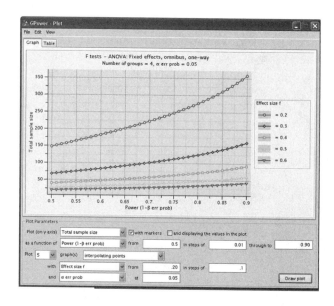

Fig. 6.4 Relationship Between Power and Sample Size in a One-Way ANOVA with Four Groups for Varying Effect Sizes

of regressors in the regression model corresponding to the ANOVA model above is three (since with four groups we need three dummy, or indicator, variables). The effect size in the regression analysis corresponding to an effect size of $f = 0.5$ is $f^2 = 0.25$. With this specification, we obtain the relationship between power and sample size for a range of effect size values. Figure 6.5 shows this relationship. Examining this chart, we find that for an effect size of 0.25, the power obtained with a sample size of 28 is approximately 0.5, the same value we obtained with the ANOVA model. This result demonstrates the equivalence of these procedures.

SPSS also provides a form of power analysis in which the probability of detecting the observed effect is calculated. For the ANOVA example provided earlier (Table 6.3), $\widehat{\eta^2} = 0.318$. The corresponding effect size measure $f = 0.683$. With this effect size, G*Power indicates a power of 0.80 while SPSS reports a power of 0.738. This discrepancy is due to the fact that SPSS computes the noncentrality parameter as $\{(N - k)\, f^2\}$ rather than $(N f^2)$ as defined by Cohen (1988). G*Power follows Cohen's convention; hence the discrepancy between SPSS and G*Power.

The analysis given above raises the question of whether we should we do a power analysis *after* collecting the data and rejecting (or not rejecting) the null hypothesis. In some situations, journal editors may ask that the researcher report the power of the study after it was conducted. Power analysis should be done *before* the data are collected by specifying the *population* effect size of interest, and not by using the sample effect size. Zumbo and Hubley

(1998) argued convincingly that the practice of reporting "retrospective" power is at best questionable, and they showed that retrospective power cannot be formally calculated. There is little value in trying to determine power after the null hypothesis is rejected by pretending that the effect size computed is the population effect size. If the null hypothesis was rejected, there was sufficient power. If the null hypothesis was not rejected, it was likely because there was insufficient power. Computing a probability after the data have been collected is similar to asking probability questions about a coin tossing experiment after it has been conducted. Once a coin has been tossed and the result recorded, the probability of the recorded outcome is one.

Power analysis in the cluster randomized trials design can be complex. In the balanced case (where cluster sizes are equal), the determination of power is straightforward when the analysis is carried out in terms of cluster means. In general, power in cluster randomized trials depends upon the ICC. Recall that the ICC is defined as

$$\rho = \frac{\sigma_t^2}{\sigma_t^2 + \sigma_e^2}.$$

Just as with ω^2, the ICC is the proportion of variance in the dependent variable explained by the independent variable or, in this case, the treatment classification, and hence has the same meaning. For the cluster randomized example provided earlier, $\widehat{\sigma_e^2} = 81$, $\widehat{\sigma_t^2} = 46.8$. Hence, the ICC is .366, indicating that schools account for 36% of the total variance.

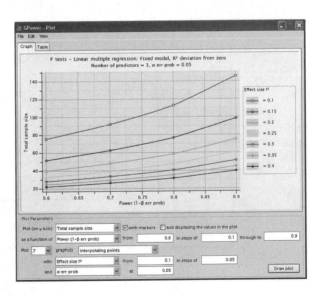

Fig. 6.5 Relationship between Sample Size and Power for Varying Effect Sizes for Three Predictors

As shown earlier, the variance of the cluster mean is

$$Var(\bar{y}_j) = \frac{\widehat{\sigma}_e^2}{n}\left\{\frac{1+(n-1)\widehat{\rho}}{(1-\widehat{\rho})}\right\}.$$

When $\widehat{\rho} = 0$, the variance of the cluster means is given by the usual expression, variance of the error divided by the sample size. As $\widehat{\rho}$ increases, the variance of the cluster means increases, and this increase in variance reduces the power to detect differences in the means when such differences exist. The term $\{1+(n-1)\widehat{\rho}\}$, known as the variance inflation factor, indicates the factor by which the correlation results in an increase in the variance of the cluster means. Since the ICC depends on the variance of the cluster means, the ICC will be high if the cluster means are widely different. Hence, in cluster randomized trials, it is important to ensure a low ICC to maximize power. Ideally, the schools within each condition should be as similar as possible.

Cluster randomized trials are expensive and difficult to conduct, and hence must be carefully planned. It is critical, therefore, that a power analysis be conducted *a priori* to determine the number of clusters, and the number of observations needed, to detect a specified effect size with a desired power. Since the ICC must be specified in order to compute power, it is important to know a priori the level of ICC one can expect. Typical ICCs in educational studies range from .17 to .25 (Hedges & Hedberg, 2007). While these values may or may not be applicable to the field of school psychology, they may be taken as ballpark figures in conducting power studies. In addition to the ICC, a factor that influences power is J, the number of clusters. Increasing the number of clusters is more important than increasing the number of subjects within a cluster.

Power analysis for the cluster randomized design is conveniently carried out using the free software, OPTIMAL DESIGN (Liu, Spybrook, Congdon, Martinez, & Raudenbush, 2006). A didactic on using this software is provided by Spybrook (2008). In using OPTIMAL DESIGN, the user specifies the ICC, the number of clusters, the sample size within a cluster, and the effect size of interest. To illustrate the calculation of power in a cluster randomized trial, we will examine power as a function of cluster size, ICC (0.1, 0. 2, .3), and effect size (0.2, 0.4).

Figure 6.6 shows that as the ICC increases, the power decreases rapidly. With 24 clusters and 40 subjects per cluster, and an effect size of 0.2, the power is 0.26 for an ICC of 0.10, and drops to 0.13 for an ICC of 0.3. With this information, it is possible to design a randomized cluster study and have a specified confidence of success.

The statistical issues of confidence intervals, effect size, and power, are all conceptualized within a framework of point null hypotheses; that is, null

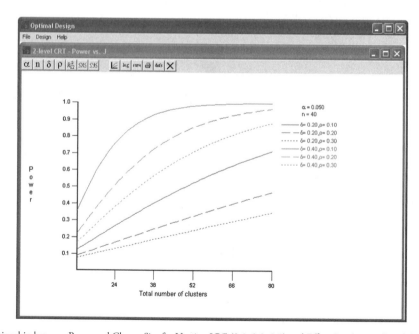

Fig. 6.6 Relationship between Power and Cluster Size for Varying ICC (0.1, 0.2, 0.3) and Effect Size (0.2, 0.4) and 40 Subjects Within a Cluster

hypotheses that specify that parameters take particular values. In the next section, we introduce the notion of range null hypotheses, which address some of the criticisms of NHST.

Range Null and Equivalence Hypothesis Testing

Among the many criticisms of null hypothesis significance testing is that the null hypothesis is always false in the strict sense, and can always be rejected with sufficiently large samples. For example, the null hypothesis that the means of two populations are exactly equal, i.e., $H_0: \mu_1 - \mu_2 = 0$, cannot be strictly true (Cohen, 1994). With large enough samples, even trivial differences between observed means will be statistically significant. Critics have long complained that statistically significant results are routinely interpreted as scientifically noteworthy or of "social significance" (Tyler, 1931). Of greater interest from theoretical and practical standpoints would be whether the difference between means is of "material significance" (Hodges & Lehman, 1954), as defined by either theoretical or practical considerations. One way of addressing this question is to replace the null hypothesis that states that the mean difference is exactly equal to zero (a "point null" hypothesis) with a null hypothesis that states that the mean difference is within some bounds of zero (a "range null" hypothesis). Serlin and Lapsley (1985, 1993) refer to this as the "good-enough" principle. For the case of inference about the difference between two means, the null and alternate hypotheses would be stated as follows:

$$H_o : |\mu_1 - \mu_2| \leq \delta_0$$
$$H_1 : |\mu_1 - \mu_2| \leq \delta_0$$

where δ_0 represents the mean difference considered to be of practical importance. More generally, we can test the hypothesis that any parameter θ is within stated bounds of a hypothesized value θ_0 (Serlin & Lapsley, 1985), in which case the null hypothesis would be stated as $H_0 : |\theta - \theta_0| \leq \delta_0$ or $H_0 : |\delta| \leq \delta_0$ where $\delta = \theta - \theta_0$. In the case of two-group mean comparison, the hypothesized mean difference is 0, so $\delta = (\mu_1 - \mu_2) - 0 = (\mu_1 - \mu_2)$.

Before continuing, we note that a variety of notations have been used in descriptions of range-null hypothesis and equivalence testing procedures, with none entirely satisfactory because of possible confusion of symbols with those used in other statistical procedures. We hope our choice of notation will not confuse the matter further.

The test of the range null hypothesis (referred to henceforth as RNHT) stated above is performed differently from the test of the point null hypothesis (PNHT) that the difference between the means is zero. In testing the point null hypothesis $H_0: \mu_1 - \mu_2 = 0$, the test statistic is the familiar t-statistic given in (19),

$$t = \frac{(\bar{y}_1 - \bar{y}_2) - (\mu_1 - \mu_2)}{s_{pooled}\sqrt{\frac{1}{n_1} + \frac{1}{n_2}}} = \frac{(\bar{y}_1 - \bar{y}_2) - 0}{s_{pooled}\sqrt{\frac{1}{n_1} + \frac{1}{n_2}}}$$

which, if H_0 is true, has a t-distribution centered at 0 with $n_1 + n_2 - 2$ degrees of freedom. The region of rejection for the test is $|t| > t_{v, \alpha/2}$ where $v = n_1 + n_2 - 2$ and $t_{v, \alpha/2}$ is the $100(1 - \alpha/2)$ percentile of the distribution. The range null hypothesis is $H_0 : -\delta_0 \leq \delta \leq \delta_0$. As noted earlier, this hypothesis states that $\mu_1 - \mu_2$ differs from the hypothesized difference of 0 by δ, which may be as much as δ_0. In this case, the t-statistic no longer has a central t-distribution. As explained earlier in the discussion of effect size, when the true value of $\mu_1 - \mu_2$ differs from the hypothesized value, the t-statistic has a noncentral t-distribution with noncentrality parameter λ, where λ is related to the difference δ by $\lambda = \dfrac{\delta}{\sigma\sqrt{\dfrac{1}{n_1} + \dfrac{1}{n_2}}}$ (negative when

δ is negative). Large absolute t-values are evidence against the null hypothesis. It can be shown (Anderson & Hauck, 1983) that symmetric critical values $-C$ and C can be determined such that

$$P(|t| > C) = \alpha.$$

Alternatively, a p-value can be computed:

$$\begin{aligned} p &= P(|t| > |t_{obs}|) \\ &= P(t < -|t_{obs}|) + P(t > |t_{obs}|). \end{aligned}$$

If $p \leq \alpha$, the null hypothesis is rejected. Serlin and Lapsely (1993) note that the square of the noncentral t-distribution with $n_1 + n_2 - 2$ degrees of freedom and noncentrality parameter λ is a noncentral F distribution with 1 and $n_1 + n_2 - 2$ degrees of freedom and noncentrality parameter λ^2. Since the F-distribution takes only positive values, it is more convenient for obtaining a critical value or p-value. The critical value for testing the range null hypothesis above is the $100(1 - \alpha)$ percentile of the distribution, and the p-value is simply the probability of obtaining an F-value larger than that observed.

To obtain a critical value or compute the p-value, we need to know the noncentrality parameter λ. However, λ depends on the unknown values σ and δ. We set δ at the value of the bound, i.e., $\delta = \delta_0$. Since this is the most extreme value of the parameter under the hypothesis, a Type I error rate of no more than α is assured. The obvious solution to the problem of the unknown value of σ is to substitute s_{pooled} for σ. Once λ is determined, the critical value or p-value can be obtained using tables or an online source.

Substituting s_{pooled} for σ will have an effect on Type I error and power, especially in small samples. Anderson and Hauck suggest that a better approach is to use a central t-distribution approximation by substituting s_{pooled} for σ, but then subtracting the estimated noncentrality parameter from the obtained test statistic and using the central t-distribution to test the hypothesis. The critical values are $-C - \hat{\lambda}$ and $C - \hat{\lambda}$ where C is the $100(1 - \alpha)$ percentile of the central t-distribution. Alternatively, the empirical significance level or p-value for the test is $p = P(|t| > |t_{obs}|)$. If $p \leq \alpha$, the hypothesis is rejected. The value of p is calculated as

$$P\left(t < -t_{obs} - \hat{\lambda}\right) + P\left(t > -t_{obs} - \hat{\lambda}\right).$$

Anderson and Hauck showed through simulations that this approximation leads to better control of Type I error, and greater power when testing the null hypothesis of nonequivalence (the converse of that tested in the range null hypothesis test). Our own simulations show negligible differences between the procedures for the kinds of sample sizes and effect sizes likely to be observed in the social sciences.

Serlin and Lapsley (1993) express the range null hypothesis in terms of effect size. In the case of comparison of means with independent samples, the effect size is, as defined earlier,

$$\Delta = \frac{\mu_1 - \mu_2}{\sigma}$$

where σ is the common population standard deviation. The hypotheses of interest would then be expressed as

$$H_0 : |\Delta| \leq \Delta_0$$
$$H_0 : |\Delta| > \Delta_0.$$

In this form, it may be easier to conceptualize the minimum tolerable difference between means, a value that must be specified before testing can be carried out. The estimate of Δ is as given in (18)

and the test statistic is as given in (21) with noncentrality parameter as in (22).

As in all good statistical practice, a confidence interval for δ (or Δ) is needed along with the hypothesis testing procedure. For this purpose, it is easier if the hypothesis is expressed in terms of standardized effect sizes, as then the unknown population standard deviation need not be estimated. The procedure for constructing a confidence interval for effect size was described earlier. A confidence interval is first constructed for λ, and then transformed according to the linear relationship between λ and Δ to yield a confidence interval for Δ. In constructing the confidence interval, we need only find one limit, given the way in which our hypothesis is expressed. Recalling that small absolute values of the test statistic are evidence in favor of the null hypothesis, the limit of the confidence interval for λ specifies the minimum value of the bound for which the hypothesis of "trivial" mean difference would be retained. Thus, the limit of the $100(1 - \alpha)\%$ confidence interval is the value of λ for which

$$P(|t_{v, \lambda}| \geq |t_{obs}|) = \alpha$$

This is the lowest value of λ for which t_{obs} would be in the region of acceptance. The confidence region for Δ is then

$$\Delta \geq \lambda \sqrt{\frac{1}{n_1} + \frac{1}{n_2}}.$$

The limit of this interval is the smallest definition of "trivial" that would result in retention of the null hypothesis, or, alternatively, the largest definition of "trivial" for which the conclusion of nontrivial mean difference could be reached. Denoting the confidence limit as Δ_L, the result above thus implies that $|\mu_1 - \mu_2| \leq \Delta_L$ (otherwise the null hypothesis of trivial mean difference would have been rejected).

One of the primary advantages of the RNHT procedure over the PNHT procedure is that for any value $|\Delta| \leq \Delta_0$, the probability of rejecting the null hypothesis is maintained at α regardless of sample size. Hence, using the RNHT procedure, rejection of the null hypothesis can never be attributed to large sample size. This is in contrast to the standard point null hypothesis of zero mean difference, where the nominal Type I error rate holds only for $\Delta = 0$. For any value of $\Delta > 0$, no matter how small, the probability that the null hypothesis will be rejected increases as sample size increases, bringing us back to the criticism of the procedure that motivated this discussion. Another conceptual advantage of the RNHT is that failure to reject the null hypothesis means that the null can be accepted (rather than merely "retained"), since the null is the true complement of the alternate. The range null hypothesis test is intuitively appealing and easy to implement, and hence should be more widely used. While the range null hypothesis is harder to reject than the point null hypothesis, there is correspondingly a lower probability that the null hypothesis will be rejected when the difference between means is trivial.

As an example of the RNHT procedure, consider a study employing a randomized trial design in which experimental and control groups are compared at post-test. Suppose two groups of participants, each $n = 25$, are measured on four variables, with results as shown in Table 6.5. The usual statistical analysis would involve a point null hypothesis test of zero mean difference on each variable, using a Type I error rate adjustment such as the Bonferroni procedure. Suppose we conduct a range null hypothesis test with a bound of 0.2 standard deviation units. That is, we will consider an effect of 0.2 or less as being of no practical importance. We wish to reject the null hypothesis of trivial mean difference only if the effect is greater than 0.2.

Table 6.5 shows that our estimated effects range from small (.21) to large (1.06). Table 6.6 contains the results of the PNHT and RNHT procedures. A Bonferroni adjustment based on four tested hypotheses was applied in interpreting all results. Hence, a p-value of $.05/4 = .0125$ was required for a conclusion of statistical significance at the .05 level. Based on the PNHT, we conclude that there is no statistically significant difference between the means of the two groups at the .05 level for Variables 1 and 2, but there is a statistically significant mean difference at the .05 level for Variables 3 and 4. Put more precisely, the difference between means is not statistically significantly different from zero at the .05 level for Variables 1 and 2, but is statistically significantly different from zero for Variables 3 and 4. The RNHT was conducted using the noncentral F-distribution as described above. The calculated t-value was squared to obtain the F-value in the table. The noncentrality parameter for the F-distribution is the square of that for the noncentral t-distribution, and was calculated by setting $\Delta = 0.2$, with the result

$$\lambda^2 = \frac{.2^2}{\frac{1}{25} + \frac{1}{25}} = 0.5.$$

The RNHT results indicate that for Variables 1, 2, and 3 we cannot reject the hypothesis that the difference between means is within 0.2 standard deviations of zero. Only for Variable 4 can we conclude that the mean difference is more than 0.2 standard deviations from zero (at an overall level of .05). For Variables 1 and 2, the PNHT and RNHT are in agreement that there is no statistically or practically significant difference between the means. For Variable 4, the PNHT and RNHT tell us that there is a statistically significant difference between means, and it is of practical interest. However, for Variable 3, the PNHT says that the mean difference is statistically significantly different from zero, but the RNHT says that mean difference is not of sufficient size to be of practical importance.

Interpretation of the confidence limits requires care, as the logic is somewhat different from that employed in PNHT. We really want to know how large we could have set the bound and still rejected the null hypothesis. For example, we would be more impressed with the conclusion that the mean difference is more than one standard deviation, than the conclusion that the mean difference is more than 0.2 standard deviations. The confidence limit tells

Table 6.5 Descriptive statistics for an example of a randomized trials design

Variable	Experimental		Control		Pooled SD	Estimated Effect	SE of Mean Difference
	Mean	SD	Mean	SD			
1	50.3	9.7	48.0	10.2	9.95	0.23	2.82
2	118.5	19.6	108.3	20.9	20.26	0.50	5.73
3	77.8	10.8	69.1	11.2	11.00	0.79	3.11
4	62.9	8.9	53.2	9.4	9.15	1.06	2.59

Table 6.6 Point null and range null test results for an example of a randomized trials design

Variable	NHST ($H_0 : \mu_1 - \mu_2 = 0$)				Range Null ($H_0 : |\Delta| \leq .2$)				
	t	p	95% CI	Decision	F	λ^2	p	Confidence Limit	Decision
1	0.75	.460	(−3.6, 7.8)	NR	0.67	0.5	0.520	N/A	NR
2	1.78	.081	(−1.3, 21.7)	NR	3.17	0.5	0.155	N/A	NR
3	2.80	.008	(2.4, 14.6)	R	7.82	0.5	0.023	0.303	NR
4	3.75	.000	(4.5, 14.9)	R	14.04	0.5	0.002	0.557	R

us how small a bound we can set and still retain the null hypothesis, so by implication it tells us how large a bound we can set and still reject. For Variables 1 and 2, there is no bound greater than zero for which the null hypothesis would be rejected. In other words, the difference between means is so small that any positive bound would satisfy the null hypothesis. This is consistent with the result that the PNHT was not rejected; i.e., the mean difference is not statistically significantly different from zero. Clearly, if we cannot reject the PNHT, we cannot reject the RNHT.

The confidence limit for Variable 3 is .30 (standard deviations units), which tells us that if we set our bound at .30 or greater, we would not reject the null hypothesis. Conversely, if we set the bound lower than .30, we will reject the hypothesis of trivial mean difference (which we did when we set the bound at .2). To restate, if we choose an effect size less than .3 as our definition of trivial mean differences, we can conclude from these data that there is a meaningful difference between the means of the groups. This result further indicates that the true effect is greater than .30, since any value larger than the bound is consistent with the data. This conclusion is in line with what the confidence interval for the mean difference indicates; the absolute value of the lower limit of the interval is 3.6, which corresponds to an estimated effect of .36. We do not expect exact agreement between methods, because of the differences in intention and methodology.

For Variable 4, the confidence limit is 0.56, indicating that we can conclude a meaningful difference between group means if we set our bound at 0.56 standard deviations or less. If our definition of "meaningful" is more stringent, i.e., greater than 0.56 standard deviations, we will not be able to reject the hypothesis of unimportant mean difference.

The range null hypothesis testing approach addresses criticisms concerning rejection of the null hypothesis in NHST. Another criticism of NHST concerns failure to reject the null hypothesis. The problem is that failure to reject does not indicate that the null hypothesis can be accepted as true. It tells us nothing more than that the data are consistent with a population parameter with the point value stated in the hypothesis. In a comparison of means, failure to reject the null hypothesis does not indicate that the means are equal. The $100(1 - \alpha)\%$ confidence interval makes it clear that the hypothesized mean difference is one of many possible mean differences that are consistent with the observed data. The often repeated statement that "absence of evidence is not evidence of absence" captures the issue succinctly.

In some cases, the question of interest is whether the two population means are equivalent rather than different. Failure to reject the null hypothesis in the usual test of mean differences does not answer this question satisfactorily. The researcher wants positive evidence of equivalence, rather than an absence of evidence of a difference. Here, equivalence is defined not as exact equality of means, but as means that differ by no more than a tolerable amount. For example, in a quasi-experimental situation, we may want to establish that the treatment and control groups are equivalent on relevant variables at pretest, even though randomization was not possible (Seamann & Serlin, 1998). Another case of interest would be when an intervention is designed to bring one group of underperforming or otherwise deficient individuals up to the same mean level as mainstream individuals. In another context, we need the assumption of equality of variances to perform the usual t-test of mean differences. We typically conduct a test of equality of variances, and take failure to reject the null hypothesis as evidence of equality—a conclusion we know to be faulty.

Tests of equivalence were developed, and have long been used, to establish the bioequivalence of drugs, where the question of interest is whether one drug formulation (such as a generic) is equivalent to another (such as a patented drug) with respect to mean absorption rates and extent. There is extensive literature on equivalence testing in the biomedical and pharmaceutical fields (see Chow and Liu [2000] for a comprehensive treatment of design and analysis of bioequivalence studies). However, just as range null tests are relatively unknown in education and psychology, so too are equivalence tests. Rogers, Howard, and Vessey (1993) introduced equivalence tests to social scientists, and a few authors have promoted the ideas and procedures behind both range null and equivalence tests (Serlin, 1993; Serlin & Lapsley, 1997; Mecklin, 2002; Wells, Cohen, & Patton, 2009).

Equivalence hypotheses are the converse of range null hypotheses. In the case of comparison of two means, the null hypothesis is that the means differ by more than a specified amount (the equivalence bound), and the alternate hypothesis is that the means differ by less than the bound. Thus, the hypotheses are

$$H_o : |\mu_1 - \mu_2| \geq \delta_0$$
$$H_1 : |\mu_1 - \mu_2| \geq \delta_0$$

Rejection of the null hypothesis is taken as evidence that the means are equivalent to the degree defined by the bound.

The equivalence test may be carried out using exactly the same statistics as the range-null test, merely reversing the regions of rejection and nonrejection. Indeed, most of the theory discussed above was developed in the context of equivalence testing, and has been merely reversed here to explain range null hypothesis testing procedures. However, other procedures have been suggested in the biomedical literature, and have been more widely used. The most commonly used procedure is the two one-sided test procedure (TOST) proposed by Schuirmann (1981, 1987), which breaks the composite null hypothesis into the two tests

$$H_0 : \mu_1 - \mu_2 \leq \delta_0 \text{ against } H_1 : \mu_1 - \mu_2 > \delta_0.$$

and

$$H_0 : \mu_1 - \mu_2 \geq \delta_0 \text{ against } H_1 : \mu_1 - \mu_2 < \delta_0.$$

Both hypotheses must be rejected in order for the composite hypothesis to be rejected. These two hypotheses are tested using ordinary t-tests. For each test, we need test the hypothesis only at the bound (since, if rejected, it will be rejected for any

more extreme value). For the first test, assuming that $\mu_1 - \mu_2 = -\delta_0$, the test statistic is

$$t_L = \frac{(\bar{y}_1 - \bar{y}_2) - (-\delta_0)}{s_{pooled}\sqrt{\frac{1}{n_1} + \frac{1}{n_2}}} = \frac{(\bar{y}_1 - \bar{y}_2) + \delta_0}{s_{pooled}\sqrt{\frac{1}{n_1} + \frac{1}{n_2}}},$$

which has a t-distribution with $n_1 + n_2 - 2$ degrees of freedom; and, for the second test, assuming $\mu_1 - \mu_2 = \delta_0$,

$$t_U = \frac{(\bar{y}_1 - \bar{y}_2) - \delta_0}{s_{pooled}\sqrt{\frac{1}{n_1} + \frac{1}{n_2}}},$$

with the same distribution. The first hypothesis is rejected if $t_L > t_{\alpha, v}$, and the second hypothesis is rejected if $t_U < -t_{\alpha, v}$. The difference between these tests and the noncentral t-test described earlier is that the two hypotheses are tested separately, with the true mean difference $\mu_1 - \mu_2$ assumed to be at the bound in each test.

While it may appear that both tests must be conducted, each at the $\alpha/2$ significance level in order to test the composite hypothesis at the α level, only one test is actually necessary. Since both tests must be rejected for the composite hypothesis to be rejected, we need only test the hypothesis that yields the smaller calculated t-value (Rogers et al., 1993). If this hypothesis is rejected, the other hypothesis will be rejected, since its t-value is larger. On the other hand, if the first hypothesis is not rejected, no further testing is necessary, as both must be rejected for the composite test. Thus the Type I error rate is controlled at α by performing only one test at the α level. The TOST is the standard procedure for testing bioequivalence, and is in fact required by the FDA (with $\alpha = .05$) (Berger & Hsu, 1996) in any application where evidence of bioequivalence is required.

An alternate approach to testing the hypothesis of nonequivalence with a t-statistic is to construct a $100(1-2\alpha)$ % interval around the difference between the observed means, i.e., $(\bar{y}_1 - \bar{y}_2) \pm t_{\alpha,v} SE$, where $SE = s_{pooled}\sqrt{\frac{1}{n_1} + \frac{1}{n_2}}$; $v = n_1 + n_2 - 2$; and $t_{\alpha,v}$ is the $100(1-\alpha)$ percentile point of the t-distribution (Westlake, 1976; 1981). If this interval is fully contained within the equivalence bounds, that is, in the interval $(-\delta_0, \delta_0)$, the hypothesis of nonequivalence is rejected at the α level. This is because in the region of rejection for the first hypothesis, where $t_L > t_{\alpha,v}$

$$t_L = \frac{(\bar{y}_1 - \bar{y}_2) + \delta_0}{SE} > t_{\alpha,v}$$

Rearranging terms,

$$-\delta_0 < t_{\alpha,v} SE + (\bar{y}_1 - \bar{y}_2),$$
$$-\delta_0 < (\bar{y}_1 - \bar{y}_2) - t_{\alpha,v} SE,$$

since $t_{\alpha,v} = -t_{1-\alpha,v}$ for a central t-distribution. In the region of rejection for the second hypothesis, where $t_U < -t_{\alpha,v}$,

$$(\bar{y}_1 - \bar{y}_2) + t_{\alpha,v} SE < \delta_0.$$

Put together, we have

$$-\delta_0 < (\bar{y}_1 - \bar{y}_2) - t_{\alpha,v} SE < (\bar{y}_1 - \bar{y}_2) + t_{\alpha,v} SE < \delta_0.$$

Thus, when both hypotheses are rejected, the interval

$$(\bar{y}_1 - \bar{y}_2) \pm t_{\alpha,v} SE$$

is fully contained within the equivalence bounds. This test produces identical results to that of the TOST.

Neither of these procedures provides a $100(1 - \alpha)\%$ confidence interval for the true value of δ (or Δ if expressed in standardized units). The equivalence interval above is an interval around the observed difference between the means, and is centered on that difference. While it produces equivalence tests results identical to those of the TOST with significance level α, its coverage as a confidence interval for δ is $(100 - 2\alpha)\%$ (Seamann & Serlin, 1998). Seamann and Serlin provide a procedure based on the central t-distribution in which they find, using simple algebra, the values of the bound (in standardized units) for which neither of the one-sided tests would be rejected. This is by definition a confidence interval for Δ. This equivalence confidence interval is given by

$$|\Delta| < |\bar{y}_1 - \bar{y}_2| + SE(\bar{y}_1 - \bar{y}_2)\, t_{v,\alpha}.$$

Seamann and Serlin regard this as a symmetric interval for Δ, that is, $-\Delta_{lim} < \Delta < \Delta_{lim}$ where Δ_{lim} is the value of Δ obtained from the expression above. However, given the form of the hypothesis, Δ_{lim} is better interpreted as the largest value of the equivalence bound for which the hypothesis of nonequivalence would be retained, or, alternatively, the smallest bound for equivalence that would lead to the conclusion of equivalence. In other words, it gives the most liberal definition of equivalence that would allow that conclusion.

As noted earlier, we can also construct an equivalence test analagous to that described for the range null hypothesis test, based on the noncentral t-distribution. Anderson and Hauck (1983) explicitly described this procedure. They showed that symmetric critical values $-C$ and C can be determined such that $P(|t| < C) = \alpha$. Alternatively, a p-value can be computed:

$$p = P(|t| < |t_{obs}|) = P(t < |t_{obs}|) - P(t < -|t_{obs}|).$$

If $p \leq \alpha$, the null hypothesis is rejected. The noncentral F-distribution is more easily used to compute the p-value, as previously described. In this case, the p-value is the probability of obtaining an F-value lower than that observed.

We can also find a confidence region for the equivalence bound based on the noncentral t-distribution. First, a confidence limit for λ is obtained, then transformed to a confidence limit for Δ. Recalling that small values of the test-statistic are evidence against the null hypothesis of nonequivalence, the confidence limit for λ is the value for which $P(|t_{v,\lambda}| \leq |t_{obs}|) = \alpha$, or alternatively, $P(F_{v,\lambda^2} \leq F_{obs}) = \alpha$. This is the lowest value of λ for which the computed value would be outside the region of rejection. The confidence region for Δ is then

$$\Delta \leq \lambda \sqrt{\frac{1}{n_1} + \frac{1}{n_2}}.$$

As an example of the application of equivalence testing procedures, consider an intervention designed to bring an underperforming population of children up to the same academic level as normal children of the same age. A sample of 50 underperforming children receives the intervention, while a sample of equal size from the regular school population is chosen as a control. Following the intervention, all children are measured on three variables of interest. We want to determine whether the means of the two groups are equivalent, where equivalence is defined as a standardized effect size of less than 0.2. Descriptive statistics for the two samples on the three variables are shown in Table 6.7; PNHT and equivalence test results are shown in Table 6.8.

Table 6.7 shows that our estimated effects are small, ranging from 0.02 to 0.39. A Bonferroni adjustment based on three tested hypotheses was applied in interpreting all results. Hence, a p-value of $.05/3 = .017$ was required for a conclusion of statistical significance at the .05 level. Based on the PNHT, we conclude that there are no statistically significant differences between the means of the two groups at the .05 level for any of the variables.

Table 6.7 Descriptive statistics for a two-group posttest comparison

Variable	Experimental		Control		Pooled SD	Estimated Effect	SE of Mean Difference
	Mean	SD	Mean	SD			
1	50.3	9.7	54.2	10.2	9.95	−0.39	1.99
2	118.5	19.6	122.7	20.9	20.26	−0.21	4.05
3	77.8	10.8	78	11.2	11.00	−0.02	2.20

The equivalence test was conducted using the noncentral F-distribution with an equivalence bound of 0.2 (standard deviations). Thus, the noncentrality parameter for the F-distribution was calculated by setting $\Delta = 0.2$. The equivalence test results in Table 6.8 indicate that for Variables 1 and 2, we cannot reject the hypothesis of nonequivalence. The difference between means is greater than is considered tolerable, even though it is not statistically significantly different from zero according to the PNHT. For Variable 3, however, we reject the hypothesis of nonequivalence, and conclude that the means are equivalent to within 0.2 standard deviations. Hence, for this variable we have positive evidence in support of the conclusion of equivalence, rather than merely absence of evidence of a difference, as indicated by the PNHT.

The confidence limit for Variable 1 indicates that we would have to define equivalence as a standardized mean difference of 0.72 or more in order to conclude equivalence. If our equivalence bound was anything less, we would retain the conclusion of nonequivalence. This result further indicates that the true effect is more than 0.72 with 95% confidence. For Variable 2, equivalence would have to be defined as an effect size of 0.54 or more. For Variable 3, the equivalence bound could be set as low as 0.17.

One of the major difficulties in using the range null and equivalence test approaches is determining what value to specify as the bound. In the biomedical field, where the variables are physical measurements such as absorption rate and extent, it is clearer what absolute quantities would constitute equivalence or difference and, hence, what value of δ_0 would be reasonable. A commonly used standard is that the test formulation mean is within 20% of the reference formulation mean. Chow and Liu (2000) list the decision rules that have been used by the FDA in establishing bioequivalence. In the social sciences, we typically specify effect sizes in terms of standard deviation units, rather than raw mean differences. One of the problems with the equivalence test approach, in particular, is that the power of the commonly used tests described above declines, as standard deviation increases relative to the difference between the means (Berger & Hsu, 2005). The effective result of this is that it requires large equivalence bounds (in terms of standardized effect sizes) for the hypothesis of nonequivalence to be rejected in favor of equivalence. In other words, only if equivalence is defined liberally will a conclusion of equivalence be possible. This makes the test very conservative. The procedure nevertheless makes it clear that failure to reject the point null hypothesis of no mean difference is not positive evidence of equivalence.

While the range-null hypothesis and equivalence testing approaches address some of the criticisms of null hypothesis significance testing, they nevertheless remain hypotheses tests with the attendant pitfalls of interpretation and the continued existence of

Table 6.8 Point null and equivalence test results for a two-group posttest comparison

Variable	NHST ($H_0 : \mu_1 - \mu_2 = 0$)				Equivalence Test ($H_0 : \|\Delta\| \geq .2$)				
	t	p	95% CI	Decision	F	λ^2	p	Confidence Limit	Decision
1	−1.96	.086	(−8.8, 3.0)	NR	3.84	1.0	0.826	0.72	NR
2	−1.04	.233	(−14.1, 9.8)	NR	1.08	1.0	0.492	0.54	NR
3	−0.09	.475	(−5.6, 7.4)	NR	0.01	1.0	0.043	0.17	R

Type I and Type II errors. Incorrect Type I error rate and low power are problems of some of these tests, notably the TOST. Berger and Hsu (1996) note that the Type I error rate of the TOST is less than α for all values of the null hypothesis except the bound. They also point out that the TOST is a biased test and, as noted above, lacks power, especially with increasing variance, a characteristic also noted by Muller-Cohrs (1990). Muller-Cohrs showed also that the Anderson and Hauck (1983) procedure for equivalence testing results in Type I error rates higher than the nominal value. Munk (1993), Berger and Hsu (1996), and Ennis and Ennis (2009) have all proposed modifications of the equivalence test to control Type I error and improve power, but none of these modifications are accessible to the average user. Our own simulations show that use of the noncentral t-distribution, rather than the central distribution, maintains the Type I error for the TOST and improves power somewhat for equivalence tests; however, power is still low, especially in small samples, a feature that is in common with NHSTs.

The procedures described above can be applied to the single group design for inference about a mean, or the paired sample design for testing mean differences. Serlin and Lapsley (1993) discuss the extension of range null and equivalence testing procedures to designs other than the simple two-group comparison of means. In designs where ANOVA and linear regression procedures are used, the range null hypothesis could be expressed in terms of $\Re^2$. For example, whereas the standard point null hypothesis for regression is $H_0 : \Re^2 = 0$, the range null hypothesis might be $H_0 : \Re^2 \leq 0.25$. The noncentral F-distribution can be used to formulate a test of this hypothesis.

Range null and equivalence hypothesis testing procedures are clearly a cogent response to criticisms of NHST. We believe that these procedures should be widely implemented, with accompanying confidence intervals for effect sizes. While specifying meaningful effects requires more of the researcher, it is no more than a researcher with adequate knowledge of the field should be able to provide.

Another response to some of the criticisms of the NHST can be found in Bayesian procedures. These procedures are discussed in the next section.

A Bayesian Framework for Statistical Inference

Some of the major criticisms facing NHST center around misunderstanding of the statistical concepts,

and misinterpretation of the results. For example, the statistical significance testing paradigm has been criticized because users misinterpret the p-value. The p-value, a "Fisherian" notion, is the probability of observing data as extreme or more extreme than that observed if the null hypothesis is true. The misunderstanding is that very small p-values signify that the null hypothesis is "probably" not true. The p-value is the conditional probability of the data, given that the null hypothesis true, $p = P\left[Data \mid H_0\right]$. It is neither the probability that the null hypothesis is true, i.e., $P\left[H_0\right]$, nor the conditional probability that the null hypothesis is true given the data, i.e., $P\left[H_0 \mid Data\right]$. The common misinterpretation of the confidence interval for a parameter is another example. For example, in interpreting a 95% confidence interval for the mean, the naïve researcher is tempted to conclude that the mean μ has a 95% chance of being in this interval; a somewhat more sophisticated researcher may conclude that the interval has a 95% chance of containing the population mean. These statements are seductive, but nonetheless wrong. But are they really wrong, or is it wishful thinking on the researcher's part? A researcher who does not read or grasp the reasoning that is put forward in fine print by the classical statistician intuitively wants to interpret the p-value as the probability that the null hypothesis is true (or at least make a statement about the likelihood of the null hypothesis), or interpret the confidence interval in terms of the probability that the parameter falls in that interval. When the statistician tells the researcher that the probability that the interval contains the true value is either one or zero, i.e., that the interval either contains the parameter or not, the reaction is one of puzzlement as to the usefulness of such an interval. While these interpretations are wrong, they show the wishful thinking on the part of the researcher.

In order to make a probabilistic statement about an entity, the entity must be a random variable. The researcher has been told repeatedly that a population parameter is fixed and immutable, and hence cannot be considered a random variable. This admonition is quickly forgotten when it comes to an intuitive interpretation of the confidence interval, or when it comes to an interpretation of the outcome of the null hypothesis testing. Can a parameter be a random variable? The answer lies in what *probability* means. The *frequentist* notion of probability, to which Fisher and Neyman subscribed, defines, loosely speaking, the probability of an event A in terms of the frequency with which A occurs in an infinite number of trials. While it is clear that the probability that a statistic takes on a particular value (in the discrete case) or falls within a range (in the continuous case) can be conceptualized from a frequentist point of view, probabilities with respect to parameters cannot. However, the frequency notion of probability does not apply in all situations. It clearly does not apply, for instance, in determining the odds in favor of a horse winning a race, since it is impossible to conceptualize this probability in the sense of the horse repeatedly running the race with the other horses. While the philosophical and mathematical foundation of probability is beyond the scope of this chapter, it suffices here to note that the Bayesian notion of probability, known as *inverse probability* until the 1950s, is not defined in terms of frequency but is interpreted as a measure of *a state of knowledge*. The Bayesian notion of probability is sometimes referred to as a "subjective" notion; however, as the word *subjective* has a negative connotation in objective science, the "better" description, *rational*, is often used. It is interesting to note that that the Fisher, Neyman-Pearson approach to statistics is now termed *classical* to distinguish it from the Bayesian approach, although the Bayesian approach is older and was formulated and developed during the classical period.

At the heart of the Bayesian notion of probability is the well-known theorem of the Reverend Bayes, whose paper on the subject was published posthumously in 1764. Bayes' theorem is well known, noncontroversial, and universally accepted. Bayes' theorem is simply an assertion regarding conditional probabilities. If A and B are two events, then

$$P[A \mid B] = \frac{P[B \mid A] P[A]}{P[B]}.$$

If we substitute H_0 for A and *Data* for B, Bayes' theorem yields

$$(30) \quad P[H_0 \mid Data] = \frac{P[Data \mid H_0] P[H_0]}{P[Data]}$$

In the above equation, $P[H_0 \mid Data]$ is known as the *posterior* probability, $P[Data \mid H_0]$ as the *likelihood*, and $P[H_0]$ as the *prior* probability. The probability $P[Data]$ is a constant, and hence equation (30) is often written as

$$(31) \quad Posterior \propto Likelihood \times Prior$$

Fisher outright rejected the Bayesian notion of probability. For Fisher, the most objectionable part about the Bayesian point of view was with respect to

the prior probability. He felt that prior belief has no place in objective scientific inquiry. Hence, in the Neyman-Pearson or the Fisherian hypothesis testing paradigms, only the likelihood, $P[Data \mid H_0]$, is used for drawing inferences.

To illustrate the difference between the Bayesian and the frequentist approaches to hypothesis testing, consider the following simple example. Let A be the event that the disease is not present and B the event that the result is positive. Suppose that it has been determined that the probability that a person who does not suffer from a serious disease will test positive, $P[B \mid A]$, is .046. This is a small probability. Hence the Fisherian paradigm will lead to the conclusion that if a person tests positive, we will reject the null hypothesis of no disease, and conclude that the person does suffer from the disease.

Suppose it has been found that the disease is rare, $P[A] = 0.98$, and that the probability of a positive test result $P[B] = .062$. We already know that $P[B \mid A] = 0.046$. Using Bayes' theorem, we can compute the probability that a person will not have the disease given a positive test result. For convenience, we represent this information in a 2 x 2 table, for 1000 people; $P[A]$ and $P[B]$ fix the marginals, and $P[B \mid A]$ fixes one of the elements in the table. With this information we can complete the table uniquely.

From Table 6.9, we can see that the probability that a person who tests positive will not have the disease is 45/62 = 0.73. Using Bayes' theorem, we can arrive at the same conclusion by computing

$$P[A \mid B] = \frac{P[B \mid A] P[A]}{P[B]} = \frac{.046 \times .98}{.062} = .73.$$

The probability is 0.73 that the person *does not* have the disease, although the person tested positive. We have in reality computed the probability, $P[H_0 \mid Data]$, the *probability that the hypothesis is true given the data*. By looking only at the likelihood, $P[Data \mid H_0]$, the Fisherian hypothesis testing paradigm led us to conclude that the person was

Table 6.9 Example of Bayes' theorem

	+ Result	− Result	Total
Disease	17	3	20
No Disease	45	931	980
Total	62	934	1000

suffering from the disease. This example also demonstrates the flaw in the Fisherian application of the *modus tollens* argument to a nondeterministic phenomenon. In this case the *modus tollens* argument is wrong.

In the Bayesian framework, when we test a hypothesis, we determine the posterior distribution, or the density function of the parameter of interest, in order to make probabilistic statements about it once we have observed the data. Based on this posterior distribution, we evaluate the null hypothesis. Evaluating the null hypothesis requires examining the relevant probabilities computed using the posterior distribution.

For example, if we want to draw inferences about the mathematics achievement level of a special needs child, we first assume that the child's *observed* achievement score y is a random variable distributed around the true value; e.g., normally with mean μ and standard deviation σ. Based on this, we can compute the likelihood function of the observation y. To specify the *prior* distribution of μ, we assume it is normally distributed with mean μ_p and standard deviation σ_p where the subscript p indicates that these are the parameters of the prior distribution. Once the prior distribution is specified, we multiply the likelihood by the prior as shown in (25) to obtain the posterior distribution of the child's true achievement level μ. Since the likelihood function and the prior distribution are normal, the posterior distribution of μ can be shown to be normal (Zellner, 1972) with mean and variance given by the expressions

$$
\begin{aligned}
\hat{\mu}_{post} &= \gamma\, y \;+\; (1-\gamma)\,\mu_p \\
(32)\quad \hat{\sigma}^2_{post} &= \frac{1}{(\sigma^2)^{-1} + (\sigma_p^2)^{-1}}
\end{aligned}
$$

where $\gamma = \dfrac{\sigma_p^2}{\sigma_p^2 + \sigma^2}$. Using this distribution, we can draw inferences about the child's true achievement level.

For example, suppose, based on the child's prior performance, we are 95% confident that the child's true achievement on a particular test is between 85 and 95, with our best "guess" at 90. We can construct from this belief a prior probability distribution. We deduce from this information that the standard deviation of the prior distribution is 2.5 ($85 = 90 - 1.96 * \sigma_p$). If we are willing to assume normality, we can state a priori that we believe that the child's true achievement μ is normally distributed with mean

$\mu_p = 90$ and standard deviation $\sigma_p = 2.5$. If we are not confident in our belief, we specify a larger standard deviation. In the limiting case, if we specify a standard deviation very large—large enough to cover the entire range of possible values—then we are saying a priori that we are "ignorant" about the achievement level of the child. In this case, the normal distribution will be flat and approach a uniform distribution, and the posterior distribution, obtained using equation (31), will simply be the likelihood; the results will be numerically identical with what would be obtained using classical statistics.

The posterior mean μ_{post} depends on σ, the standard deviation of scores on this test. To keep the analysis simple we shall assume it is known, say, from the test publisher (σ = 5). In this case, if we had observed a score for the child of y = 85, the posterior mean μ_{post} and standard deviation σ_{post} are, from (32),

$$
\gamma = \frac{2.5^2}{2.5^2 + (5^2)} = .0.2;
$$

$$
\hat{\mu}_{post} = .2 \times 85 + .8 \times 90 = 89; \quad \hat{\sigma}_{post} = 2.24.
$$

Note that the posterior standard deviation is smaller than the standard deviation σ, and the posterior mean of 89 has regressed towards the prior mean of 90. We can expect this phenomenon in general. The regression toward the prior mean is controlled by γ. If γ is close to zero, $(1-\gamma)$ dominates, and the posterior mean will regress towards the prior mean. If γ is close to 1, the observation will be weighted heavily and there will be less regression towards the prior mean. The quantity γ behaves like the reliability of the instrument; in fact, the form of γ is identical to the definition of the reliability coefficient in test theory (Lord & Novick, 1968). The posterior mean represents the true score of an individual from a test theory perspective.

If instead of measuring just one individual, we measure a group of n individuals, the variance σ^2 in equation (32) and in the definition of γ is replaced by σ^2/n, the variance of the mean. In this case,

$$
\begin{aligned}
\hat{\mu}_{post} &= \gamma\, \bar{y} \;+\; (1-\gamma)\,\mu_p \\
\hat{\sigma}^2_{post} &= \frac{1}{(\sigma^2/n)^{-1} + (\sigma_p^2)^{-1}}
\end{aligned}
$$

where $\gamma = \dfrac{\sigma_p^2}{\sigma_p^2 + (\sigma^2/n)}$. Here, γ resembles the expression for the intraclass correlation. In fact, we can write the model for the observation and the prior information as a simple multilevel model:

$$y_i = \mu + e_i$$
$$\mu = \mu_0 + u.$$

The variance of u is σ_p and the variance of e_i is σ^2; γ is therefore the intraclass correlation.

Historically, the expression for the posterior mean was first derived by Truman Kelley in the 1920s, in the context of predicting a person's true score from the observed score. Hence the posterior mean is generally called "Kelley's regressed estimate."

If we had observed a sample of 36 children and obtained a sample mean of 85, and assuming that $\sigma = 5$, then

$$\gamma = \frac{2.5^2}{2.5^2 + (5^2/25)} = .86;$$
$$\hat{\mu}_{post} = .86 \times 85 + .14 \times 90 = 85.7;$$
$$\hat{\sigma}_{post} = .93.$$

The posterior mean is less regressed towards the prior mean, since the data dominate the prior. The posterior variance is much smaller than the variance of the population from which the sample was drawn. Based on this information, we can construct the 95% probability interval, called the *credibility* interval, for the posterior mean μ_{post} :

$$[\hat{\mu}_{post} - \hat{\sigma}_{post} \times 1.96 \le \mu_{post} \le \hat{\mu}_{post} + \hat{\sigma}_{post} \times 1.96]$$
$$= [83.88 \le \mu_{post} \le 87.52]$$

We can conclude that the posterior mean lies in the interval [83.88, 87.52] with probability .95, a conclusion that we cannot draw with the classical 95% confidence interval. If we want to test the hypothesis that $\mu \ge 90$, we can compute the probability that the hypothesis is true; i.e.,

$$P\left[\mu \ge 90 \mid \bar{y}, \mu_p, \sigma_p, \sigma\right] = P\left[z \ge \frac{90 - 85.7}{.93}\right]$$
$$= P[z \ge 4.62]$$

We have calculated the probability that the null hypothesis is true given the data. This probability is so small that we can conclude that the hypothesis is not true.

It may be instructive to examine what happens when we are not confident about our prior belief about the parameter μ. In this case we specify a large value for σ_p to indicate that we have no prior information. As this value gets large, or as the prior distribution becomes flat, the posterior variance $\sigma_p^2 \to \sigma^2/n$, the usual variance of the mean. With no prior information, posterior standard deviation is $5/5/\sqrt{5} = 1$, and the 95% credibility interval for μ_{post} is

$$[83.74 \le \mu_{post} \le 87.66]$$

We obtain the same interval with the classical statistical procedure, except that with the Bayesian credibility interval, we can interpret the interval in terms of the probability that the mean is in the interval.

Despite the fact that he eschewed the Bayesian viewpoint, Fisher wanted to provide an interval with the probabilistic interpretation. He argued that the confidence interval contains all the possible values of the parameter for which the null hypothesis will not be rejected. With an argument that resembles sleight of hand, he concluded that the parameter μ behaves like a random variable in this case, and argued that a probabilistic statement about the parameter could be made. The advantage of his *fiducial* approach (from the Latin for faith, trust), Fisher argued, was that it avoided the notion of prior belief completely (Fisher, 1925). Fisher's fiducial argument bears close resemblance to the Bayesian perspective, albeit with a "flat" or uniform prior. Leonard Savage, a prominent Bayesian, noted that through the fiducial argument, Fisher "was making a Bayesian omelet without breaking the Bayesian egg." Neyman found the fiducial argument unconvincing, as did many other statisticians during Fisher's time, and this notion slowly disappeared from the statistical literature. (For a discussion of the fiducial argument and the debate between Fisher and Neyman, see Zabel, 1992).

The Bayesian example provided above is for the case where the population variance is treated as known. Bayesian counterparts for all classical statistical procedures are widely available (Box & Tiao, 1973; Zellner, 1972). However, it is not possible to discuss these in this chapter since, even for the simplest case, an understanding of statistical distributions is needed in order to specify the parameters of the prior distributions.

One of the most important aspects of the Bayesian approach is that it leads a decision-oriented approach to hypothesis testing. A decision-oriented approach requires that the researcher/decision-maker weigh the costs of making a decision. This is similar to the concept of Type I and Type II errors. If the researchers accepts H_0 and it is false (Type II error in the Neyman-Pearson paradigm), then the loss or cost incurred is C_2. Similarly if the researcher accepts H_A, then the loss incurred is (Type I error) C_1. If we denote the expected costs associated with accepting the null, and the alternate as $E(H_0|D)$ and $E(H_A|D)$ respectively, where D denotes data, then

$$E(H_0 \mid D) = 0 \times P(H_0 \mid D) + C_2 \times P\left(H_A \mid D\right)$$
$$= C_2 \times P\left(H_A \mid D\right)$$

and

$$E(H_A \mid D) = C_1 \times P(H_0 \mid D) + 0 \times P\left(H_A \mid D\right)$$
$$= C_1 \times P(H_0 \mid D).$$

Note that the expected losses are expressed with respect to posterior probabilities or distributions. The optimal decision is to accept the hypothesis for which the expected loss is smaller. If $E(H_0|D) < E(H_A|D)$, accept H_0; if not, accept H_A.

To better understand how the expected losses depend on the costs and prior beliefs, we use Bayes' theorem to arrive at the following result:

$$\frac{E(H_0 \mid D)}{E(H_A \mid D)} = \frac{C_2 \times P\left(H_A \mid D\right)}{C_1 \times P(H_0 \mid D)}$$
$$= \frac{C_2 \times P(D \mid H_A) \, P(H_A)}{C_1 \times P(D \mid H_0) \, P(H_0)}$$
$$= \frac{C_2}{C_1} \frac{P(D \mid H_A)}{P(D \mid H_0)} \frac{P(H_A)}{P(H_0)}.$$

If the prior probabilities are equal, and the costs are equal, then the decision is made by comparing the likelihoods. In determining the values of C_1 and C_2, we consider the seriousness of the possible errors. In our example, if we accept the hypothesis that the person does not have the disease given a positive result, and the person does in fact have the disease, how serious is the error? On the other hand, if we accept the hypothesis that the person has the disease given the positive result, and the person does not have the disease, how serious is this error? In part, the answer depends on what action we take as a result of the conclusion. If we decide not to follow up or do further tests after accepting the null hypothesis, and the person does have the disease, how serious is the consequence? On the other hand, if the person does not have the disease, but we conclude otherwise and do further tests, what are the consequences? Once we decide how serious one

error is compared to the other, we can include that in our decision rule; we just need the ratio of the two costs.

In our example (Table 6.9), we have used different prior probabilities for H_0 and H_1; hence we need to weight the posterior probabilities by the costs. We have $E(H_0|D) = C_2$ (17/62) and $E(H_A|D) = C_1$ (45/62). We accept H_0 if C_2 (17/62) $<C_1$(45/62). If the costs are equal, the inequality will hold, and we will accept H_0. If C_2 is three times the size of C_1, we will reject the null hypothesis. The "break-even" point is when C_2 is 2.6 times as large as C_1. Any C_2 larger than this will result in rejection of H_0. For example, if concluding that a person is disease free, when in fact the disease is present, is considered three times more serious than concluding that the disease is present when it is not, we will reject H_0 and treat the person as if the disease is present.

In all fairness, the decision–theoretic approach provided above was developed by Neyman and Pearson. However, their hypothesis testing procedure falls short, in that only Type I error is considered in accepting/rejecting the null hypothesis. The Bayesian framework provides the correct approach by taking into account both types of errors, and weighting the posterior probabilities of the hypotheses by the costs associated with Type I and Type II errors. It is easily seen that the costs can be set proportional to the probabilities of making Type I and Type II errors. It is better, however, to consider the entire decision-making procedure within a Bayesian framework, rather than hybridizing it with the classical approach to hypothesis testing.

Conceptually, Bayesian procedures have a clear advantage over classical procedures with respect to estimation, inference, and decision-making. The posterior distribution holds the key. The probability that a hypothesis is true can be computed once the data are obtained. Given the superiority of the Bayesian framework over the classical framework for inference, and the fact that it has found wide acceptance in the statistical community, it may seem surprising that Bayesian methods are not being more widely used in the social sciences. Part of the explanation is in the statistical sophistication required to implement these methods. To go beyond the simple example we described here would require a discussion of probability distributions and density functions, and an understanding of the parameters of these distributions. To carry out a Bayesian analysis, a more mathematical background and more advanced statistical knowledge is required than what is normally expected of researchers in the social sciences. The matter is further exacerbated by the fact that user-friendly software that can guide the user in specifying priors is not available. These two factors seriously limit the application of Bayesian procedures in the social sciences. However, progress is being made in education and medical fields with respect to the application of Bayesian methods. The wide use of hierarchical linear models is a positive sign; the estimation of random components in these models is carried out within the Bayesian framework, albeit with an *empirical Bayes* approach, where the priors are estimated using the data obtained (Raudenbush & Bryk, 2002; Swaminathan & Rogers, 2008). While the empirical Bayes procedure lacks the optimum properties that full Bayesian procedures enjoy, the empirical Bayes solution is a practical one. In our view, it is only a matter of time before Bayesian procedures become widely used in the social sciences.

Conclusion

Our goal in this chapter was to present a close examination of the fundamentals of research methodology for informed decisions. Our focus was on the statistical reasoning underlying the process of drawing inferences from data, and making decisions based on those inferences. That process begins with a model that describes the relationships among the variables of interest in the population under study. The parameters of the model are estimated, and inferences are subsequently drawn about the validity of the model. Those inferences are typically based, explicitly or implicitly, on the framework of null hypothesis significance testing. However, strict use of null hypothesis significance testing procedures, without regard for their limitations, often results in misinterpretation of findings and incorrect decisions. Yet, we cannot lay all the fault with the user. The null hypothesis significance testing procedure cannot provide a full answer to the researcher's questions. We have described the flaws of the NHST paradigm, and the errors of interpretation it engenders. More informed decisions can be made if the null hypothesis testing procedure is buttressed with complementary procedures that provide more information than mere rejection or nonrejection of the null hypothesis.

Confidence intervals for the parameters of interest should be provided, with attention to their interpretation. In addition to this information, effect size must be examined to assess the practical significance of the results. Effect size measures are relatively easy to compute, and yet are not routinely reported in

research studies. We have described effect size measures for a variety of research designs, and have provided a uniform treatment of effect size measures when the models belong to the same family.

Effect size measures are point estimates, and hence confidence intervals for them provide valuable interpretive information not only for the study being conducted, but also for later meta-analyses and small scale syntheses of research studies. While effect size measures are easy to compute, confidence intervals for them are more difficult. Confidence intervals for effect sizes require the use of noncentral distributions, which are unfamiliar to most researchers. We have therefore indicated how to work with these distributions, and have provided a link to a probability calculator that will make these computations easy and routine. Noncentral distributions are also key in conducting power analyses. While conducting a power analysis has been difficult in the past, and thus often ignored, the current availability of free software and noncentral probability calculators have put power analysis within the grasp of all researchers. With these tools, power analysis is a subject that can and should be taught in basic statistics and research methods courses.

While these tools provide valuable information for making better decisions within the NHST paradigm, the hypothesis testing procedure has a fundamental flaw. Statisticians have long recognized the foolishness of trying to test a precise null hypothesis. The range null hypothesis testing procedure allows the researcher to specify meaningful bounds for the parameter in stating the null hypothesis, so that it is not rejected in the presence of trivial effects. Likewise, equivalence testing procedures ensure that the absence of meaningful effects is tested directly, rather than through failure to reject a null hypothesis. The range null and equivalence testing procedures bring rationality (Serlin & Lapsley, 1985; 1993) to the hypothesis testing framework, and may prove useful for decision-making in school psychology.

Whenever a hypothesis test of any kind is performed, the question we would like to answer is: What is the probability that the null hypothesis is true, given what we have observed? This fundamental question cannot be answered within the classical frame of inference. Only in the Bayesian framework can such a question be entertained. We have described briefly the Bayesian philosophy, and the decision-making process that is a natural consequence of the Bayesian notion of probability. Unfortunately, Bayesian analysis requires some level of mathematical maturity and statistical sophistication.

This has hindered the use of Bayesian methods, not only in school psychology but in the social sciences in general. We believe it is only a matter of time before the efforts of software developers and teachers that have made classical statistical procedures accessible to researchers is applied to Bayesian methods, to enable these tools to be more widely used.

We have not attempted, nor is it possible to provide, a comprehensive treatment of research methodology for decision-making in school psychology. An issue not addressed here is that of violation of the assumptions of the models and procedures described. These models and methods require assumptions that may not be met in school psychology research. Robust statistical methods not discussed here may prove to be useful in situations where we suspect that the usual assumptions of underlying normality are not met. In their simplest form, robust statistical methods involve removing or resetting outliers to obtain "trimmed" means and "winsorized" standard deviations. The technique of bootstrapping can be used with these modified statistics to construct confidence intervals for the parameters of a model. Bootstrapping involves sampling with replacement from the observed data, to obtain an empirical sampling distribution from which a confidence interval is constructed. Another form of analysis to which more attention should be given is that of exploratory data analysis (Tukey, 1977). This type of analysis, combined with robust statistical procedures, can provide valuable information for decision-making when the assumptions underlying the analytic tools we have presented are not met. Whatever inferential procedures are used for decision-making, it is incumbent on the user to understand their proper use and limitations.

References

American Psychological Association. (2001). *Publication manual of the American Psychological Association* (5th ed.) Washington, DC: Author.

Anderson, S. & Hauck, W. W. (1983). A new procedure for testing equivalence in comparative bioavailability and other clinical trials. *Communications in Statistics – Theories and Methods, 12*(23), 2663–2692.

Berger, R. L. & Hsu, J. C. (1996). Bioequivalence trials, intersection-union tests and equivalence confidence sets. *Statistical Science, 11*(4), 283–302.

Box, G. E. & Tiao, G. C. (1973). *Bayesian inference in statistical analysis.* Reading, MA: Addison and Wesley.

Cao, L. & Matthew, T. (2008). A simple numerical approach towards improving the two one-sided test for average bioequivalence. *Biometrical Journal, 50*(2), 205–211.

Chow, S-C. & Liw, J-P. (2000). *Design and analysis of bioavailability and bioequivalence Studies.* New York, NY: Marcel-Dekker, Inc.

Cohen, J. (1992). A power primter. *Psychological Bulletin, 112,* 155–159.

Cohen, J. (1994). The earth is round ($p<$ .05). *American Psychologist, 49,* 997–1003.

Cohen, J. (1988). *Statistical power analysis for the behavioral sciences* (2nd ed.). Hillsdale, NJ: Lawrence-Erlbaum Associates.

Cohen, P., Cohen, J., West, S. G., & Aiken, L. S. (1983). *Applied multiple regression/correlation analysis for the behavioral sciences.* Mahwah, NJ: Lawrence-Erlbaum Associates.

Cumming, G., & Finch, S. (2001). A primer on the understanding, use, and calculation of confidence intervals that are based on central and noncentral distributions. *Educational and Psychological Measurement, 61*(4), 532–574.

Ennis, D. M. & Ennis, J. M. (2009). Hypothesis testing for equivalence defined on symmetric open intervals. *Communications in Statistics—Theory and Methods, 38,* 1792–1803.

Erceg-Hurn, D. M. & Mirosevich, V. M. (2008). Modern robust statistical methods: an easy way to maximize the accuracy and power of your research. *American Psychologist, 63*(7), 591–601.

Faul, F., Erdfelder, E., Lang, A.-G., & Buchner, A. (2007). G*Power 3: A flexible statistical power analysis program for the social, behavioral, and biomedical sciences. *Behavior Research Methods, 39,* 175–191.

Fidler, F. & Cumming, G. (2006). Lessons learned from statistical reform efforts in other disciplines. *Psychology in the Schools, 44*(5), 441–449.

Finch, S., Cumming, G., & Thomason, N. (2001). Reporting of statistical inference in the *Journal of Applied Psychology*: Little evidence of reform. *Educational and Psychological Measurement, 61,* 181–210.

Fisher, R. A. (1925). *Statistical methods for research workers.* Edinburgh, Scotland: Olive and Boyd.

Glass, G. V. (1976). Primary, secondary, and meta-analysis of research. *Educational Researcher, 5,* 3–8.

Harlow, L. L., Mulaik, S. A., & Steiger, J. H. (Eds) (1997). *What if there were no significance tests?* Mahwah, NJ: Lawrence-Erlbaum Associates.

Hedges, L. V. & Hedberg, E. C. (2007). Intraclass correlation values for planning group-randomized trials in education. *Educational Evaluation and Policy Analysis, 29,* 60–87.

Hodges, J. L. & Lehmann, E. L. (1954). Testing the approximate validity of statistical hypotheses. *Journal of the Royal Statistical Society. Series B (Methodological), 16*(2), 261–268.

Huberty, C. J. (2002). A history of effect sizes. *Educational and Psychological Measurement, 62,* 227–240.

Kehle, T. J., Bray, M. A., Chafouleas, S. M., & Kawano, T. (2007). Lack of statistical significance. *Psychology in the Schools, 44*(5), 417–422.

Lord, F. M. & Novick, M. R. (1968). *Statistical theories of mental test scores.* Reading MA: Addison-Wesley.

Liu, X., Spybrook, J., Congdon, R., Martinez, A., & Raudenbush, S. W. (2006). *Optimal design for longitudinal multilevel research.V1.77.* [Computer software]. Retrieved May 20, 2010 from http://sitemaker.umich.edu/group-based.

Mecklin, C. J. (2002). *The use of equivalence testing in conjunction with standard hypothesis testing and effect sizes.* Paper presented at the annual meeting of the American Educational Research Association, New Orleans, April.

Muller-Cohrs, J. (1991). An improvement of the Westlake symmetric confidence interval. *Biometrical Journal, 33*, 357–360.

Munk, A. (1993). An improvement on commonly used tests in bioequivalence assessment. *Biometrics, 49*(4), 1225–1230.

O'Connell, A. A., & McCoach, D. B. (Eds.) (2008). *Multilevel modeling of educational data.* Charlotte, NC: Information Age Publishing.

Raudenbush, S. & Bryk, A. (2002). *Hierarchical linear models: Applications and data analysis methods* (2nd ed.). Thousand Oaks, CA: Sage Publications.

Raudenbush, S., Bryk, A., Cheong, Y. F., & du Toit, M. (2004). *HLM6: Hierarchical linear and nonlinear modeling.* Chicago, IL: Scientific Software International.

Rogers, J. L., Howard, K. I., & Vessey, J. T. (1993). Using significance tests to eqaluate equivalence between two experimental groups. *Psychological Bulletin, 113*(3), 553–565.

Seamann, M. A. & Serlin, R. C. (1998). Equivalence confidence intervals for two-group comparisons of means. *Psychological Methods, 3*(4), 403–411.

Schmidt, F. L. (1996). Statistical significance testing and cumulative knowledge in psychology: Implications for the training of researchers. *Psychological Methods, 1*, 115–129.

Schmidt, F. L. & Hunter, J. E. (1997). Eight common but false objections to the discontinuation of significance testing in the analysis of research data. In L. L. Harlow, S. A. Mulaik, & J. H. Steiger (Eds.), *What if there were no significance tests?* Mahwah, NJ: Lawrence-Erlbaum Associates.

Serlin, R.C. (1993). Confidence intervals and the scientific method: A case for Holm on the range. *Journal of Experimental Education, 61*(4), 350–360.

Serlin, R. C. & Lapsley, D. K. (1985). Rationality in psychological research: The good enough principle. *American Psychologist, 40*(1), 73–83.

Serlin, R. C. & Lapsley, D. K. (1993). Rational appraisal in psychological research and the good enough principle. In G. Keren and C. Lewis (Eds.), *A handbook for data analysis in the behavioral sciences: Methodological issues.* Hillsdale, NJ: Lawrence Erlbaum Associates.

Schuirmann, D. J. (1987). A comparison of the two one-sided tests procedure and the power approach for assessing the equivalence of average bioavailability. *Journal of Pharmacokinetics and Biopharmaceutics, 15*, 657–680.

Schuirmann, D. J. (1981). On hypothesis testing to determine if the mean of a normal distribution is contained in a known interval. *Biometrics, 37*, 617.

Smithson, M. (2001). Correct confidence intervals for various regression effect sizes and parameters: The importance of noncentral distributions in computing intervals. *Educational and Psychological Measurement, 61*, 605–632.

Spybrook, J. (2008). Power, sample size, and design. In A. A. O'Connell, & D. B McCoach (Eds.), *Multilevel modeling of educational data.* Charlotte, NC: Information Age Publishing, Inc.

Swaminathan, H. & Rogers, H. J. (2008). Estimation procedures for hierarchical linear models. In A. A. O'Connell, & D. B McCoach (Eds.). *Multilevel modeling of educational data.* Charlotte, NC: Information Age Publishing, Inc.

Thompson, B. (1996). AERA editorial policies regarding statistical significance testing: Three suggested reforms. *Educational Researcher, 25*, 26–30.

Thompson, W. (2001). *402 Citations questioning the indiscriminate use of null hypothesis signficance testis in observational studies.* Retrieved January 10, 2010, from http://warnercnr.colostate.edu/! anderson/thompson1.html.

Tyler, R. W. (1931).What is statistical significance? *Educational Research Bulletin, 10*(5), 115–142.

Tukey, J. W. (1977). *Exploratory data analysis.* Reading, MA: Addison-Wesley.

Tukey, J. W. (1991). The philosophy of multiple comparisons. *Statistical Science, 6*, 100–116.

Volker, M. A. (2006). Reporting effect size estimates in school psychology research. *Psychology in the Schools, 43*(6), 653–672.

Wells, C. S., Cohen, A. S., & Patton, J. (2009). A range-null hypothesis approach for testing DIF under the Rasch model. *International Journal of Testing, 9*, 310–332.

Westlake, W. J. (1976). Symmetrical confidence intervals for bioequivalence trials. *Biometrics, 32*, 741–744.

Westlake, W.J. (1981). Response to T. B.L. Kirkwood: Bioequivalence testing—A need to rethink. *Biometrics, 37*, 589–594.

Wilcox, R. R. (2005). *Introduction to robust estimation and hypothesis testing.* New York, NY: Academic Press.

Wilkinson, L. & the APA Task Force on Statistical Inference. (1999). Statistical methods in psychology journal: Guidelines and explanations. *American Psychologist, 54*, 549–604.

Zabel, S. L. (1992). R. A. Fisher and the fiducial argument. *Statistical Sciences, 7*(3), 369–387.

Zellner, A. (1972). *An introduction to Bayesian inference in econometrics.* New York, NY: John Wiley & Sons.

Zumbo, B. D. & Hubley, A. M. (1998). A note on misconceptions concerning prospective and retrospective power. *The Statistician, 47*, 385–388.

7

Data Analysis for Effective Decision Making

Hoi K. Suen, Pui-Wa Lei, *and* Hongli Li

Abstract

Data analyses are statistical manipulations of numbers to help discern patterns in the data. As such, they need guidance from substantive theories in order to decide what patterns to look for, and to make sense of these patterns. The core outcomes of these manipulations are summary descriptors used to reduce the amount of information a researcher needs to digest. When such descriptors summarize data from a sample, and a researcher wishes to make inferences from the sample descriptors to the population, various inferential techniques are used. These techniques approach the inferential task from three different angles: significance testing, parameter estimation, and statistical modeling. For decisions regarding a single individual, reliability and validity of information need to be assessed. For the evaluation of the efficacy of intervention on an individual, however, the typical design used is that of an interrupted time-series analysis.

Keywords: theoretical guidance, statistical inferences, statistical modeling, measurement quality, single-subject data analyses

Data analyses are no more than statistical manipulations of numerical data to reveal patterns, trends and relationships otherwise not obvious from the original, often unwieldy raw data. Yet, interpretations of these trends and patterns, as well as the original raw data, are only as meaningful as the research process through which these data are collected. A random collection of facts rarely lead to any meaningful pattern that can be used for decisions. Therefore, prior to any data analysis, it is important to examine how the data are collected to begin with.

The Reciprocal Relationship Among Theory, Practice, and Data Collection

Research data collection activities, particularly in clinical and applied fields such as school psychology, do not exist in a vacuum. The purpose of research data collection in school psychology is most often to obtain information to guide real-life decisions regarding a child, a group, or a program. As such, clinical and educational concerns provide the guidance needed to pose the proper research or evaluation question. In order to provide answers to such a research or evaluation question, appropriate data or information needs to be gathered. Yet, a research or evaluation question alone provides no indication as to what data are most appropriate, nor directions for how to go about gathering the data. A model, theory, or even "hunch" is needed to provide some tentative conceptual structure for possible answers to the research questions. Through such theoretical structure, we are able to discern the type and manner of data to be collected. Therefore, a theory, no matter how informal or casual, "seat of the pants," is critical to data collection and data analyses. Results of data analyses provide empirical support for the tentative theoretical structure, which in turn provides evidence to support a particular clinical or educational decision. In this manner, practice, theory, and data analyses form an inseparable tripartite relationship, each providing guidance and support to another, and each a critical component of the overall process to guide decisions.

The need for guidance from theory and practice exists even for research or evaluation studies that are euphemistically called "exploratory" or "data driven." Performing data analyses and interpreting results without the guidance of a theoretical framework is not different from trying to read tea leaves to tell a fortune—with the results about as meaningful and useful. A case in point is the so-called "exploratory factor analysis" method. The name gives the impression that this is a data-driven analytic technique, and that the results will "uncover" the hidden structure among a number of unobserved constructs. In reality, both exploratory and confirmatory factor analyses start with a theoretical structure. The difference is that for the former, that structure is not entered as input into the analysis, while it is an integral part of the data input for the latter. For confirmatory factor analysis, the analytic steps involve evaluating mathematically whether the structure of the data is consistent with the theoretical structure that the researcher has input into the analysis. For exploratory factor analyses, the analytic steps produce the best and most reasonable and internally consistent structure, based on the data and a set of chosen numerical rules alone. The researcher makes the judgment as to whether the data-based structure thus produced is consistent with the theoretical structure. The actual data analysis itself is fundamentally a series of numerical transformations and manipulations, changing from one set of numbers to another set of numbers based on some mathematical or statistical rules—not totally unlike playing Sudoku, except much more complicated. Theories and structures of unobserved constructs do not magically appear from nothing through such numerical transformations. In other words, in both cases, an a priori theory is central to both data analysis and the interpretation of results.

Influenced by the U.S. federal government's preference for research and evaluation activities that use certain types of methodology in funding decisions in the past decade, the particular approach to research data collection design referred to as "evidence based" has been in vogue. It is important to clarify what constitutes evidence-based research; and not to confuse it with data-driven research. The central criterion of excellence for evidence-based research is strong internal validity. As such, randomized trial experimentation is viewed as the *sine qua non* of data collection designs. To further maximize internal validity, data reliability and statistical power are emphasized. These designs lend themselves to the use of numerical data and statistical analysis techniques. However, the use of empirical, quantitative data, and sophisticated statistical data analysis techniques, does not by itself constitute evidence-based research; nor should evidence-based research be confused with atheoretical, "empirical research," for which the common mantra has been "let the data speak for themselves." In reality, data do not speak at all; instead, theories speak through the language of data. Evidence-based research data collection without the proper guidance of theory and practice is essentially a manifestation of the now refuted radical epistemology of logical positivism, as was advocated by the Vienna Circle (Hahn, Neurath, & Carnap, 1929). As the great Hungarian philosopher Imre Lakatos cautioned us against:

> …patched up, unimaginative series of pedestrian "empirical" adjustments which are so frequent, for instance, in modern social psychology. Such adjustments may, with the help of so-called "statistical techniques," grant some "novel" predictions and may even conjure up some irrelevant grains of truth in them. But this theorizing has no unifying idea, no heuristic power, no continuity. They do not add up to a genuine research program and are, on the whole, worthless.
> (*Lakatos*, 1970, p. 176)

The officially sanctioned evidence-based approach to data collection is not without critics. Many feel that the approach is particularly not appropriate for field research, or for clinical program evaluation activities. The major objections have to do with the need for external validity, and the impracticality of randomized trials in many situations (see for example the debate among Brooks-Gunn, 2004; Cook, 2004; Cottingham, 2004; and McCall & Green 2004). However, few, regardless of their position about evidence-based research, challenged the need to guide research and evaluation data collection activities and analyses through theory and practice; in turn, results of data analyses help to clarify and revise theories.

Basic Data Reduction

Guided by theories and practice, school psychologists conduct research and evaluation activities by collecting and analyzing data. Data may be collected from a single individual, without any generalization to a larger population, or from a sample of people, with an intention to generalize results to a larger population. The data collected may be used as overt signs of some unobserved, covert psychological constructs. Alternatively, they may be no more than a sample of directly observable behaviors without further inferences to any latent traits or covert constructs. The nature of the data collected may be simple or complex, crossed or nested, single- or multileveled, univariate or multivariate. The theory or model that drives the data collection activities may involve a simple direct relationship, a complex set of direct and indirect relationships, or relationships among observed variables and unobserved theoretical constructs. In other words, school psychologists work with a very large variety of data types and structures, with a large array of different objectives. These require a large variety of data analytic tools. Additionally, some of these analyses are performed to help confirm larger, generalizable principles, while others are performed in order to provide information regarding the efficacy of a particular individual intervention.

Regardless of the nature, structure, and complexity of the data, and regardless of the goals, objectives, and underlying theories, the first and foremost purpose of statistical data analysis is to summarize an otherwise unwieldy set of raw sample data. That is, before we can make inferences about populations, about trends, about latent structures, about theories, or generalizations to other situations, we need first to obtain a clear picture of the actual, tangible, sample data in hand. However, sample data can be unwieldy, messy, idiosyncratic, and unorganized. The picture presented by sample data is, at first glance, murky and confusing. To understand this data, we need to reorganize the information so that we can characterize the data through manageably fewer pieces of information. To accomplish this, we use descriptive statistics. There are a number of fundamental descriptive statistics that will apply to most, if not all, sample data to help us gain a better understanding of the data at hand. Some combination of these descriptive statistics should be applied whenever feasible to the sample data, whether we end up reporting them or not, just so that we have a more complete perspective about the sample. First, it is often informative to summarize the data graphically through either a histogram, a polygon, a stem-and-leaf diagram, a boxplot, a scatterplot, or some other graphic format as appropriate. Basic univariate descriptive statistics such as mean, variance, median, and/or mode are usually informative. For data with more than one variable, there is a large array of descriptors of relationships, ranging from Pearson's r to Kendall's tau, Somer's d, Cohen's kappa, to various proportionate reduction in error (PRE) statistics.

One particularly important category of descriptive statistics is *effect size* statistics. The very first effect size statistic was Karl Pearson's r developed a century ago; but the concept of effect size was formally introduced through Jacob Cohen's d statistic in the 1960s. Since then, the concept of effect size has been much more broadly conceived as the magnitude of the effect that is attributable to the independent variable. This concept applies to describing the effect in a variety of experimental and quasi-experimental, as well as correlational studies, and is a central focus in meta-analytic studies. In addition to Pearson's r and Cohen's d, some common alternative effect size measures include the eta-square statistic in analyses of variance and r-square in regression. Effect size statistics are a particularly important category of sample descriptors, because the reporting of effect size has been required for over a decade for studies published in journals sponsored by the American Psychological Association, and many of those sponsored by the American Educational Research Association and other organizations.

Inferences About Population Parameters

The group of individuals from whom we collect the data is either the target population or a sample drawn from the target population. If these individuals constitute the entire target population, no legitimate inference beyond these individuals would be made. In this case, no inferential statistical analysis is necessary. At the same time, however, results of descriptive analyses cannot be extrapolated or generalized beyond the individuals actually studied. Except for some case studies and clinical, single-subject interventions, the majority of research studies in school psychology treat the individuals in the study from whom the data are collected as a sample of a larger population, to whom the results of the study are generalized. The reason for the use of a sample when the object of interest is a larger population is a practical one: it is much more economical to collect data from a small sample than it is from a large population. For this economical practice to be reasonable, the data collected from the sample need to be representative of those that we would have otherwise collected from the population; i.e., the sample data need to provide a microcosm of the larger population. Yet, samples almost never accurately represent populations. It is very rare that data from a sample form an exact microcosm of data from the population. The only exceptions are data collected via certain sampling procedures such as proportional stratified sampling; but even with these methods, the sample is a microcosm of the larger population only with respect to the stratifying variable(s) and nothing else. For example, if we were to draw a sample such that the sex ratio of the sample is the same as that of the population, the sample would be assured to be representative of the population only in terms of sex ratio, but nothing else.

If a sample is unlikely to be a microcosm of the larger population, how do we justify drawing conclusions about the population based on information from the sample? In statistical analyses, sample representation is treated as a probabilistic concept. When a scientific sample such as a simple random sample is drawn, there is some probability that the sample forms a microcosm of the population. It is somewhat less probable that the sample deviates slightly from the population; and even less probable that the sample deviates substantially from the population. However, even though there is a probability that the sample is a microcosm of the population, that probability can potentially be quite small. Since data from a sample may or may not be a microcosm of the population, what can we say about the population when all we have are data from a sample? The inference to the population is accomplished through some combination, or all, of three parallel approaches. These approaches are based on applications of probability theories.

The most fundamental approach is to develop descriptive statistics for the sample, such that these statistics are unbiased estimators of the corresponding quantities for the population. The objective here is not an accurate microcosm, but a fair and unbiased representation. These sample statistics may overestimate or underestimate the corresponding values in the population; but they are as probable to have overestimated as they are to have underestimated the corresponding population statistics (called *parameters*). Therefore, in the long run, under repeated estimations, the over- and underestimations would probably cancel each other out, resulting in the correct value of the population. Examples of these unbiased sample statistics include the arithmetic mean, and the adjusted variance calculated by dividing the sum of squared deviations by the degree of freedom of N-1.

Unbiased estimates from sample data are only fair in the long run. A single estimate calculated from a particular sample is most probably not an accurate or precise representation of the corresponding population parameter. To supplement the use of unbiased sample statistics, one or both of two approaches have been used.

Significance Testing

The first supplement is a negation approach developed by Ronald Fisher, commonly known as *significance testing*. With this approach, we postulate a worst-case scenario hypothesis that there is no relationship or difference in the population, and the sample statistic value is an artifact of random sampling fluctuation. If the sampling fluctuation hypothesis is incorrect, it removes the worst-case scenario of no relationship/difference from consideration. The sample statistic may still not represent the population parameter, but at least we know that the situation with the population is unlikely to be that of the worst-case scenario.

In practice, the methodology of significance testing will not determine whether the no relationship/difference scenario is true or not in the population. Instead, it determines whether it is plausible to obtain the sample statistics if there is no relationship/difference in the population. When it is implausible, we can safely rule out the idea that the observed sample statistics are a random sampling fluctuation artifact from a population of no relationship/difference. This situation is described as "statistically significant." Conversely, when it is plausible to obtain such sample statistics from a no-relationship/difference population, we are unable to negate the competing hypothesis of random sampling fluctuation. The results of the research are thus inconclusive, and the situation is described as "statistically not significant." There is no situation under which one can "prove" that there is no relationship/difference in the population, nor a situation in which one can conclude that the observed sample statistics accurately reflect the value in the population. As Ronald Fisher explained:

> … tests of significance, when used accurately, are capable of rejecting or invalidating (null) hypotheses, in so far as they are contradicted by the data; but they are never capable of establishing them as certainly true…
> (*cited in Salsburg*, 2001, p. 108)

The plausibility of the sampling fluctuation hypothesis is determined by evaluating a particular conditional probability value: the probability that, through random sampling fluctuations alone, one can obtain a sample statistic as large or larger than the one obtained by the researcher—given that the true difference/relationship in the population is zero (or equals some other meaningful value predetermined by the researcher). Note that this is a conditional probability of obtaining the sample statistics value or larger through random sampling fluctuation, given the condition of zero relationship/difference. It is not the probability that the population has a zero relationship/difference. That is a given condition for this conditional probability, and is therefore assumed to be true to begin with, prior to calculating probability values.

The threshold between a high and a low probability value is called the *alpha value*, and this threshold value is determined by conventional professional consensus. The most typical alpha value used is 5%, or .05. The alpha value is also referred to as the "Type I error rate" for certain decisions.

Dependent on the mathematical nature of the measurement metric used in the collection of sample data, the conditional probability value can be calculated directly or indirectly from the sample data. For certain data metrics such as frequencies, rates, and proportions, the conditional probability of obtaining the sample value by random sampling fluctuation can often be calculated directly. Some examples of methods used to calculate these conditional probabilities include the binomial test, the Poisson test, and the Weibull test. For situations other than the use of frequencies, rates, and proportions, however, the measurement metric is undetermined a priori and can be different from study to study. For example, the scoring metric used to measure reading ability may be different from instrument to instrument, and from study to study; or, the metric to scale "persistence" or "depression" may be a function of the instrument used, as well as the scaling technique employed. For these situations with a variable metric, a different approach is needed to calculate the conditional probability.

To calculate the conditional probability when the measurement metric is undetermined, we use an indirect approach. Instead of assessing the conditional probability of obtaining the sample descriptive statistic, such as the sample mean or the sample variance, we assess the conditional probability of obtaining the value of a ratio between the actual obtained sample statistic, and the typical random sampling fluctuation expected. One particular example of this approach is the chi-square test. The ratio used is called the *chi-square value,* and it is the ratio between observed frequencies beyond expectation and the frequencies expected under the random sampling fluctuation scenario. Another example is the two-sample independent *t*-test. The ratio, called *t*, is the ratio of the observed difference in mean scores between two samples, and the expected fluctuation of mean difference values under the random sampling fluctuation scenario. Other examples of such an approach include the F-ratio and the z-test.

It should be noted that in the attempt to negate various scenarios in the population, there are two alternatives to Fisher's significance testing scheme. One is the Neyman-Pearson approach, which pits one hypothesis against another and rejects the one that is less probable. Yet another is the Bayesian approach, which attempts to identify the most probable scenario inductively, through the sequential accumulation of data from many studies. These two approaches to significance testing, however, are rarely used in school psychology.

Parameter Estimation

The significance testing approach has clear limitations. Through the significance testing process, we can only ascertain that the worst-case null scenario is implausible and can be safely rejected. Yet, we gain no information as to what are the exact population parameters, and whether the sample statistics are accurate reflections of these population parameters. In contrast to Ronald Fisher's significance testing approach, Karl Pearson developed the "goodness of fit" approach in the early twentieth century, in the form of a chi-square goodness of fit test. The underlying idea for this approach is one of trying to estimate the population parameters directly, based on sample data. With Pearson's goodness-of-fit method, one postulates a set of possible population parameters, and then evaluates the probability that the sample data could have been drawn from such a population. If the probability is high, we would describe the data as fitting those parameters.

The general conceptual approach is thus one of first postulating some theoretical model regarding either the population parameters, or the relationship between sample statistics and population parameters. Based on these postulated models and relationships, we would estimate the population parameter values directly. Today, this general approach has been expanded to include a very large array of different inferential statistical techniques. These techniques can be categorized into those methods that use confidence intervals, and those that use statistical modeling.

CONFIDENCE INTERVAL APPROACH

Confidence intervals are built around a sample statistic to provide a range of values within which the true population parameter is likely to be.

Confidence intervals are calculated by the following generic form:

$$(1) \quad \text{Confidence interval} = \text{sample statistic}$$
$$\pm \text{ critical value}$$
$$\times \text{ standard error}$$

Population parameters of common interest include mean, proportion, and difference in mean or proportion. Standard errors are computed differently for sample estimates of different population parameters (see Appendix A for some common standard error formulas, and Glass & Hopkins, 1995, or Kirk, 1998, for an introductory text on statistics). Standard error gauges the magnitude of random sampling fluctuation of sample estimates, if different random samples are drawn from the population. Critical value is determined by the desired confidence level, and the sampling distribution of the sample estimates. The larger the desired confidence level (e.g., 95% vs. 68%), the larger the critical value is, and the wider the interval becomes. The most common sampling distribution used to form confidence intervals is probably the standard normal (z) distribution. Using the standard normal distribution is often adequate when sample size is large (i.e., large sample approximation).

Suppose that a research question is: Does depression affect reading comprehension? One way to tackle this question is to form two groups (e.g., depressed vs. not-depressed) based on scores on a depression inventory. A reading comprehension test can be administered to the two groups. Table 7.1 provides the simple descriptive statistics of reading comprehension for the two hypothetical groups.

Table 7.1 Descriptive statistics for reading comprehension scores

	Depressed	Not-depressed	Difference
N	28	174	
Mean	91.15	110.13	18.98
Standard deviation	13.29	16.31	15.93
Standard error (see equations 1 & 2 in Appendix A)	2.51	1.24	3.24
68% confidence interval	88.61, 93.70	108.90, 111.36	15.74, 22.21
95% confidence interval	86.00, 96.31	107.69, 112.57	12.58, 25.38

One can form a confidence interval around each of two means (using standard error calculated with equation 1 in Appendix A), and see if the two resulting ranges of possible population parameter values are far from each other. If the confidence intervals do not overlap, then there is evidence to suggest that the depressed sample and the not-depressed sample are drawn from different populations. One can then conclude that the mean comprehension scores are different between these two populations. In this example, neither the 68% nor the 95% confidence intervals for the two groups overlap. That is, the upper limits for the depressed group (93.7 and 96.31 respectively for 68% and 95%) are lower than the lower limits for the not-depressed group (108.9 and 107.69 respectively for the 68% and 95%). These hypothetical data suggest that the population mean of reading comprehension for the depressed group is generally lower than the population mean for the not-depressed group. Alternatively, one can take the difference between the two group means (18.98 in this example), which estimates the difference in population mean values. A confidence interval can be formed for that difference (using standard error calculated with equation 2 in Appendix A) to determine the range of likely differences in reading comprehension between depressed and not-depressed individuals. For the numerical example, the difference ranged from 15.74 to 22.21 68% of the time, and from 12.58 to 25.38 95% of the time[1].

Suppose an intervention program has been implemented to reduce incidents of depression. The investigator can establish a baseline level of depression for participants before program intervention. The baseline scores can be used to match respondents, to form pairs of treatment and control subjects. After intervention, all subjects are measured again on their level of depression. Due to the matching by baseline depression scores, post-intervention depression scores for the matched pair become dependent, because their scores are expected to be more similar to each other than to scores from respondents in different pairs. This dependence calls for a different estimate of standard error (equation 3 in Appendix A), which is usually smaller than the standard error estimate for independent group difference. Table 7.2 shows descriptive statistics for a hypothetical matched pair sample. In this example, subjects in the treatment condition had lower posttest depression scores than subjects in the control condition, and the estimated population difference ranged from 2.21 to 7.79 points 95% of the time.

Table 7.2 Descriptive statistics for reading comprehension scores for matched pairs

	Treatment	Control	Difference	Proportion (treatment < control)
N	101	101	101	101
Mean	45	50	−5	.634
Standard deviation	12	11	14.12	.484
Standard error (see equations 1, 3, & 4 in Appendix A)	1.194	1.095	1.405	.048
68% confidence interval	43.81, 46.19	48.91, 51.09	−6.40, −3.60	.586, .682
95% confidence interval	42.63, 47.37	47.83, 52.17	−7.79, −2.21	.538, .729

The intervention program can also be evaluated via a proportion estimation approach. That is, depression scores for treatment and control subjects in each pair are compared, and the proportion of the matched pairs in which the treatment subject had lower depression score than the control subject can be tabulated. If the estimated proportion is higher than .50, then there is an indication that subjects receiving the treatment have lower depression scores compared to subjects receiving no treatment. The estimated proportion for this example ranged from .538 to .729 95% of the time, suggesting that the proportion is generally higher than .50 and that the intervention program appeared to be somewhat effective in reducing depression. This proportion estimation approach arrived at the same conclusion as the paired mean difference approach in this example. However, the proportion approach only compares the paired values, and disregards the magnitude of difference. The loss of metric information renders the proportion estimates relatively less precise.

STATISTICAL MODELING

As opposed to finding a probable range of values for individual population parameters, statistical modeling is a general approach to estimating multiple population parameters simultaneously. Modeling starts with the postulation of a statistical model to describe relationships among variables in the population. Multiple parameters, representing various relationships of the postulated model, are estimated from sample data at the same time. Goodness-of-fit of the postulated model to sample data is evaluated by certain mathematical criteria. Different estimation methods employ different criteria. For example, the least square estimation method minimizes the sum of squared differences between observed and

fitted values. In contrast, the maximum likelihood method maximizes the likelihood of observed data given the model parameters, and the resulting parameter estimates will be the most probable among all possible parameter values for the observed data. The choice of estimation methods is often based on the properties of the resulting parameter estimates, such as unbiasedness, consistency, and efficiency. Under regular conditions, the least square estimation method is the best linear unbiased estimator for general linear models (GLM), and the maximum likelihood estimator is asymptotically unbiased (i.e., becomes increasingly unbiased as the sample size increases), consistent, and efficient, and is commonly used for more complicated models (e.g., generalized linear models with categorical outcomes and structural equation modeling).

Modeling Linear Relationships

When there is only one outcome variable with one or more independent variables, the model is considered univariate. One family of well known univariate models is the general linear model (GLM) in which the outcome variable is continuous. General linear models include analysis of variance (ANOVA) models and linear regression models. The question about whether depression affects reading comprehension in the population, in one of the previous examples, can be answered by fitting a GLM to the data. In this GLM model, reading comprehension score is a continuous outcome variable, and depression score on a depression measurement scale (not the depressed vs. not-depressed categories) is a predictor variable and is assumed to be linearly related to reading comprehension scores. Based on our data that generated the statistics in Table 7.1, the estimated regression model for this hypothetical example can be expressed as: predicted reading score = 148.94 – .87×(depression score). That is, reading comprehension score was expected to be .87 lower (or from .70 to 1.05 lower 95% of the time) for each score point increased in depression. Had all variables been standardized before fitting the regression model, the resulting regression coefficients would be on a standardized metric, and are customarily referred to as the *standardized coefficients*. For this example, the standardized regression coefficient was −.57, suggesting that reading score was expected to drop by .57 standard deviations for each standard deviation unit increased in depression score.

If the depression variable was dichotomously coded as 1 for "depressed" and 0 for "not-depressed," and was used instead as the predictor variable in the linear regression model, the estimated regression equation became: predicted reading score = 110.13 – 18.98 × (depressed/not-depressed indicator). That means the depressed group on average scored 18.98 points lower on reading comprehension than the not-depressed group. The estimated coefficients in both models suggested a negative effect of depression on reading comprehension in this hypothetical example.

Model assumptions for general linear models include independent residuals (i.e., prediction error), normal distribution of residuals, and same variance of residuals (i.e., homogeneity of variance for ANOVA models, or homoscedasticity for linear regression models) conditional on independent variables, as well as linear relationship between outcome and independent variables. When these model assumptions hold, estimates of model parameters from sample data will have such desirable properties as being unbiased, consistent, and efficient. In practice, the choice of model and estimator depends greatly on the satisfaction of model assumptions. When one or more of these assumptions are violated, Type I error (i.e., incorrectly rejecting a null hypothesis when null is in fact true) rate will be higher or lower than the alpha level used to make inference decisions, and confidence levels will be likewise incorrect.

Modeling Nonlinear Relationships
When the relationship between the outcome measure and predictor variables is nonlinear, but normality and homoscedasticity approximately hold, polynomial regression models can be used to model the nonlinear relationship. Power functions of predictor variables are used in polynomial regression models, but the models are still linear in model parameters (i.e., regression coefficients). Suppose that the relationship between reading comprehension score and depression score is nonlinear, in that the relationship is quite weak for low depression scores but becomes strong negative as depression score increases from a certain point. A hypothetical scatter plot of reading comprehension score on depression score is provided, with fitted linear and quadratic trends superimposed, in Figure 7.1.

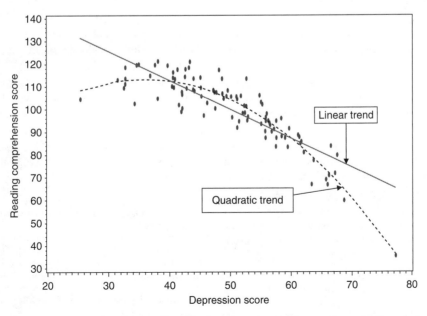

Fig. 7.1 A Hypothetical Scatter Plot of Reading Comprehension Score on Depression Score

The estimated linear equation is: predicted reading score = 163.75 − 1.28×(depression score), R^2=.72. R^2 indicates the proportion of accounted-for variance in the outcome variable, and may be used as a measure of predictive power of the model. The estimated quadratic equation is: predicted reading score = 55.22 + 3.23 × (depression score) − .045 × (depression score)^2, R^2 =.86. The incremental R^2 due to the quadratic term is .14, p < .0001, indicating that the estimated quadratic trend fitted the sample data better than the estimated linear trend. For this example, examination of residual plots for the quadratic model did not reveal substantial departure from normality or homoscedasticity. The quadratic model appeared to be adequate for the sample data.

When the normality assumption is violated (e.g., when the continuous outcome variable is skewed) or the residual variances are heteroscedastic, the outcome variable can be transformed to normalize the residual distribution, stabilize the residual variances, or both, as long as the relationship between the transformed outcome variable and the predictor variables remains linear. If the transformation results in an approximately normal distribution and stabilizes the variances, ordinary general linear models can be applied to the transformed outcome variable. Because transformation is more or less a trial-and-error exercise, we do not address this issue here. For more extensive discussion of nonlinear transformations, see Cohen, Cohen, West, and Aiken (2003, p.221–249).

When the outcome variable is categorical or discrete (e.g., binary outcome or count), however, using GLM on transformed outcome variable is usually not satisfactory. Non-normality and heteroscedasticity often remain problematic in these cases despite transformation, and the fitted values may go out of bound. Nonlinear models are generally more appropriate for categorical outcome variables, such as logistic regression for binary outcome and Poisson regression for count outcome. Nonlinear models are, by definition, not linear in model parameters in the original metric of the outcome variable. However, models belonging to the family of generalized linear models can be expressed as a linear function in model parameters by a suitable transformation (referred to as the *link function* that relates the predicted outcome to the original outcome variable), and different forms of probability distributions in the exponential family can be assumed for residuals, to allow for variances to vary as a function of the fitted value. In logistic

regression models, for instance, binomial distribution is assumed for the dichotomous outcome variable (e.g., event vs. nonevent) and the logit (or log odds transformation of the predicted probability of event) is modeled as a linear function of predictor variables (referred to as the *systematic component* of the model). As in ordinary regression, predictor variables for the systematic component of generalized linear models can be categorical or continuous, or nonlinear functions of the predictor variables, such as product terms for interactions or power functions for polynomial regression.

Suppose one is interested in the effect of depression on the proportion of students passing a difficult reading comprehension test, or making adequate yearly progress in reading. The outcome variable is dichotomized based on a cut point on the reading comprehension test (e.g., 1=passed, 0=failed). Because this outcome variable is binary, logistic regression can be used to model the relationship between the dichotomous passing score and the continuous depression score. Simple descriptive statistics for a synthetic data set are given in Table 7.3.

The estimated logistic regression equation for this example was: logit(passed) = 6.6 − .12 × (depression score). The estimated odds ratio for depression score was .889 (95% confidence interval was between .855 and .924). That is, the odds of passing for those who scored 1 point higher on depression was .889 times the odds for those who scored 1 point lower. Alternatively, the odds of passing for those who scored 1 point lower on depression was 1.125 (1/.889) times the odds for those who scored 1 point higher; the odds of passing was .125 higher for those who scored 1 point lower on depression. Fitted probabilities, along with the estimated 95% confidence interval, are plotted as a function of depression scores in Figure 7.2. The probability of passing appeared to drop quickly as depression score went above 40. The model seemed to fit the data quite well as indicated by the Hosmer and Lemeshow goodness-of-fit test (Hosmer & Lemeshow, 2000), chi-squared (df=8, N=202) = 9.41, p=.309.

Table 7.3 **Descriptive statistics by passed and failed categories**

	Passed	Failed
N (proportion)	137 (.678)	65 (.322)
Mean (SD) depression score	43.81 (10.22)	55.28 (9.39)

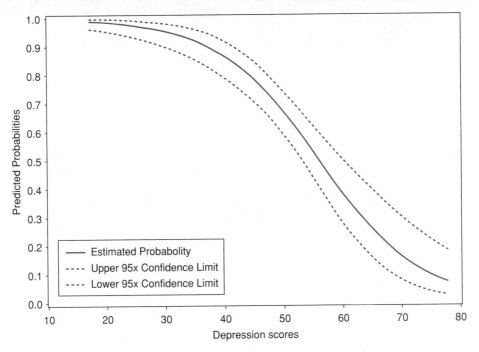

Fig. 7.2 Predicted Probabilities and 95% Confidence Interval

When the outcome or response variable is direct frequency count of the occurrence of some event, Poisson regression, also known as *loglinear modeling*, is appropriate. Poisson distribution is assumed for the count outcome variable (e.g., number of rare incidences in a period of time) and the natural logarithm transformation of count is modeled as a linear function of predictor variables.

Suppose the number of occurrences of a particular depression symptom within a week was measured as the outcome variable in the evaluation of program effect on depression, and that subjects were randomly assigned to a new intervention (treatment) and a traditional intervention (control) condition (coded 1 and 0 respectively). Because the number of symptom occurrences is discrete, and the occurrence of events is rare, the most frequent scores will concentrate at the low end, and the resulting frequency distribution will be highly positively skewed. The frequency distribution of number of symptom occurrences for a hypothetical sample is provided in Figure 7.3, and the associated descriptive statistics are given in Table 7.4. The observed variance was similar to the observed mean for each of the intervention conditions, suggesting that a Poisson regression model might fit the data well.

The estimated Poisson regression equation based on the hypothetical sample was: log(expected number of occurrences) = .425 − 1.070 × (treatment).

The coefficient of −1.07 indicates that the expected mean number of occurrences for treatment group subjects was .343 times that for control group subjects.

Loglinear models can also be used to model associations among two or more categorical variables. The response variable is frequency count for every combination of the categorical variables in the model, and it is assumed to have a Poisson distribution. Natural logarithm transformation of the expected frequencies is modeled as a linear function of the categorical variables. To determine the best fitting model, successive hierarchically less complicated models are usually fitted. The estimated models are compared by model fit indices. Simpler models with fewer model parameters are preferred for the sake of better interpretability and parsimony, if the loss in model–data fit is small.

To illustrate, in studying the relationship between depression, reading comprehension, and treatment effect, suppose that a pass or fail decision was made based on a subject's reading comprehension score, and a depressed or not-depressed classification was made based on a subject's depression test score. The relationship among treatment (1 = treatment condition, 0 = control condition), depression (1 = not-depressed, 0 = depressed), and passing reading comprehension (1 = passed, 0 = failed) can be examined by loglinear models. An example of the 2×2×2 frequency table

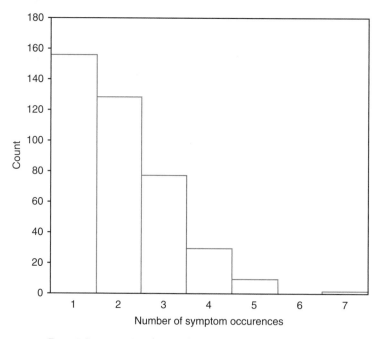

Fig. 7.3 Frequency Distribution of Number of Symptom Occurrences

for this hypothetical scenario is given in Table 7.5. Fit indices for the estimated hierarchical models are provided in Table 7.6.

According to the fit statistics (i.e., Δ deviance) in Table 7.6, the all 2-way associations model did not fit the data significantly worse than the 3-way association model, and the Passed x Treatment with Passed x Not-depressed model did not fit the data significantly worse than the all 2-way associations model. Because the other two models with two 2-way association terms fit the data significantly worse than the all 2-way associations model, the Passed x Treatment with Passed x Not-depressed model would be preferred. In addition, dropping one of the 2-way association terms from the Passed x Treatment with Passed x Not-depressed model significantly worsened the model fit to the data. As a result, the Passed x Treatment with Passed x Not-depressed model would be retained. The estimated equation for this model was: Log(expected frequency) = 2.8085 − 1.9855 × passed − 1.1192 × treatment + .6702 × not-depressed + 1.6106 × (passed × treatment) + 2.4133 × (passed × not-

depressed). Taking the exponentiation of the coefficients gives the multiplicative factors for expected frequencies. For instance, the value of exp(−1.9855) = .137 indicated that the expected number of passing was .137 times that of failing for depressed subjects in the control condition (i.e., when treatment=0 and not-depressed=0). The expected number of passing was exp(-1.9855+2.4133) = 1.53 times that of failing (or 53% higher than that of failing) for not-depressed subjects in the control condition. Estimated frequencies based on this model are quite similar to the corresponding observed frequencies (see Table 7.5). This was expected, as both the Pearson chi-squared (value=1.3163, df=2, p=.6581) and deviance (value=1.2824, df=2, p=.6412) tests for goodness of fit indicated good fit of the model to the data. The results for this hypothetical example suggested that treatment was associated with passing the reading comprehension test, but their association did not depend on depression status. Similarly, depression status was associated with passing the reading comprehension test, but their association did not depend on treatment condition.

Table 7.4 **Simple descriptive statistics for number of symptom occurrences by treatment condition**

Group	N	Mean	Variance	Min	Max
Treatment (New intervention program)	200	.525	.562	0	4
Control (Traditional intervention program)	200	1.53	1.215	0	6

Table 7.5 Frequency sistribution by categorical variables

Failed	Treatment (fitted frequency)	Control (fitted frequency)
Depressed	7 (5.42)	15 (16.58)
Not-depressed	9 (10.58)	34 (32.42)
Passed		
Depressed	3 (3.72)	3 (2.28)
Not-depressed	82 (81.28)	49 (49.72)

Multilevel Models

Another important assumption made by general linear models is independence of observations. This assumption is violated when random sampling occurs at the cluster level (e.g., classrooms, schools, districts), or subjects are measured repeatedly over time or by a set of related variables. In essence, the data will exhibit a nesting or multilevel structure. For example, subjects can be nested in classrooms in the cluster sampling case, and measures can be nested in subjects in the repeated measures case, regardless of whether the same instrument is administered at different points in time (e.g., growth models) or multiple measures are used to indicate the same general construct (e.g., item response models that account for measurement error). Dependence occurs among observations in the lower level of the multilevel structure. For instance, subjects sharing the same classroom and teacher are expected to be more similar to each other than to subjects in a different classroom with a different teacher. Likewise, scores measuring the same construct received by the same subjects are expected to be more similar to each other than to scores measuring the same construct received by other subjects. In these cases, estimators assuming simple random sampling or independence will provide underestimated standard errors and hence inflate Type I error in statistical inference. Multilevel models (also known as mixed, or hierarchical linear models (HLM)), are generally used to account for such dependence among observations sharing the same higher-level unit.

Suppose that a researcher wanted to evaluate the effectiveness of a reading program on improving reading comprehension, controlling for the effect of depression. Classrooms, instead of subjects, were randomly assigned to treatment (integrating the reading program into regular instruction) and control (regular instruction) conditions. Subjects are considered level-1 units and are nested within classrooms, which are considered level-2 units. Variables that are associated with level-1 units are distinguished from those that are associated with level-2 units. In this example, reading comprehension and depression were level-1 variables, while reading program treatment was a level-2 variable. Participating subjects were administered a depression scale prior to the experiment, and a reading comprehension test after the experiment. Using the multilevel notation, the level-1 equation is:

$$(2) \text{ Reading comprehension score}_{ij}$$
$$= \beta_{0j} + \beta_{1j}(\text{depression score}_{ij}$$
$$- \text{grand mean}$$
$$\text{depression score}) + e_{ij},$$

Table 7.6 Fit statistics for estimated hierarchical models

Model[a]	Deviance	df	Δ deviance	Δ df	p
3-way association	0	0			
All 2-way associations	1.0993	1	1.0993[b]	1	.294
Passed x Treatment, Passed x Not-depressed	**1.2824**	**2**	**.1831[c]**	**1**	**.669**
Passed x Treatment, Treatment x Not-depressed	28.7088	2	27.6095[c]	1	<.0001
Passed x Not-depressed, Treatment x Not-depressed	24.1842	2	23.0849[c]	1	<.0001
Passed x Treatment	31.3947	3	30.1123[d]	1	<.0001
Passed x Not-depressed	26.8701	3	25.5877[d]	1	<.0001
Independence	56.9823	4	-		

[a] Highest order term fitted along with all the lower order terms.
[b] Comparison model is the 3-way association model.
[c] Comparison model is the all 2-way associations model.
[d] Comparison model is the Passed x Treatment and Passed x Not-depressed model because it does not fit the data significantly worse than all 2-way associations model.

where the subscript i indexes subject, and j indexes cluster.

The level-2 equations are:

(3) Classroom average adjusted (for depression score at the grand mean) reading comprehension score (i.e., β_{0j})

$$= \gamma_{00} + \gamma_{01}(\text{treatment condition}) + r_{0j};$$

(4) The regression coefficient for depression (i.e., β_{1j}) $= \gamma_{10}$.

The two-level equations can be combined into a single equation as:

(5) Reading comprehension score$_{ij}$

$$= \gamma_{00} + \gamma_{10}(\text{depression score}_{ij}$$

$$- \text{grand mean}$$

$$\text{depression score})$$

$$+ \gamma_{01}(\text{treatment condition}) + e_{ij} + r_{0j}.$$

In the equations above, e_{ij} is a random error associated with student i in classroom j and r_{0j} is a random component associated with classroom j. These random components are usually assumed to be normally distributed and their variances are often assumed to be homoscedastic.

Compared to an ordinary regression model, the single equation for this two-level model (i.e., equation 5) has an extra random component that is due to classroom differences. The larger are the classroom differences on the outcome measure relative to the differences between individuals within classrooms, the larger will be the magnitude of dependence within classrooms. The level of dependence within classrooms is measured by an intra-class correlation, which is equal to the variance due to classrooms, divided by the sum of variance due to classrooms and variance due to individuals within classrooms.

Descriptive statistics by treatment condition and level for a synthetic data set are provided in Table 7.7. Parameter estimates and their associated standard error estimates by the ordinary regression and multilevel models are presented in Table 7.8. The OLS regression coefficient estimates were nearly identical to the corresponding estimates from the multilevel model, which supported the claim that parameter estimates were generally not biased when dependence due to clustering was ignored. As expected, standard errors estimated from the OLS model were smaller than standard errors estimated

Table 7.7 Descriptive statistics by treatment and level for the cluster sampling example

	Treatment	Control
Student level (N=500 for each group)		
Reading comprehension score	105.25 (19.78)	97.30 (19.30)
Depression score	49.49 (10.53)	50.51 (11.10)
Classroom level (N=25 for each group)		
Reading comprehension score	105.25 (6.69)	97.3 (5.26)
Depression score	49.49 (2.66)	50.51 (2.33)

Note. Table entries are means (standard deviations).

from the multilevel model, except for the depression score covariate. Intra-class correlation estimated based on the unconditional model was .08 [=32.38/(32.38+364.44)]. It could be interpreted as the estimated correlation between any two students in the same class. The estimated between-class variance was also statistically significant at the .05 level by a large sample z-test (see Table 7.8) indicating that the level of within-class dependence was not trivial. Hence, the effect of ignoring this level of dependence on standard error estimates was not small.

Dependence among observations due to repeated measurement of the same subjects, such as when the growth of individual child is modeled, can be handled in the same way as clustering in multilevel modeling.

In fact, the class of multilevel models subsumes general linear models, and is very broad and versatile. It is beyond the scope of this chapter to discuss the large variety of multilevel models in depth. Interested readers should consult Kreft and de Leeuw (1998), Snijders and Bosker (1999), or Raudenbush and Bryk (2002).

Structural Equation Modeling (SEM)[2]

When there are many dependent variables, including variables that are both independent and dependent, the Structural Equation Modeling (SEM) approach might be more convenient than the modeling approaches discussed hitherto. Like the class of multilevel models, SEM represents an extension of general linear models. One of the primary advantages of SEM (versus other applications of GLM) is

Table 7.8   Estimated model parameters for different models

Fixed effects	Ordinary regression model (Least Squares)	Unconditional multilevel model (Maximum likelihood)	Conditional multilevel model (Maximum likelihood)
Intercept	98.07 (.49)	101.27 (1.01)	98.07 (.86)
Depression score – grand mean	−1.50 (.03)	–	−1.49 (.03)
Treatment	6.41 (.69)	–	6.41 (1.22)
Random effects			
Variance of student level error	–	364.44 (16.72)	105.68 (4.85)
Variance of adjusted class outcome means	–	32.38 (10.15)	13.30 (3.73)

Note. Table entries are estimates (standard errors). All parameter estimates are significantly different from zero at the .05 level by large sample z-tests.

that it can be used to study the relationships among latent constructs that are indicated by multiple measures. It is also applicable to both experimental and nonexperimental data, as well as cross-sectional and longitudinal data. SEM takes a confirmatory (hypothesis-testing) approach to the multivariate analysis of a structural theory, one that stipulates causal relations among multiple variables. The *causal* pattern of intervariable relations within the theory is specified a priori. The goal is to determine whether a hypothesized theoretical model is consistent with data collected to reflect this theory. The consistency is evaluated through *model-data fit,* which indicates the extent to which the postulated network of relations among variables is plausible. SEM is a large-sample technique (usually *N*>200; e.g., Kline, 2005, pp.111, 178), and the sample size required is somewhat dependent on model complexity, the estimation method used, and the distributional characteristics of observed variables (Kline, pp.14-15). SEM has a number of synonyms and special cases in the literature, including path analysis, causal modeling, and covariance structure analysis. We briefly introduce the most common and basic SEM models in the following, and discuss some of the issues widely encountered in practice. Readers are referred to Kline (2005) for an accessible introductory text.

Path Models Path analysis is an extension of multiple regression, in that it involves various multiple regression models or equations that are estimated simultaneously. This provides a more effective and direct way of modeling mediation, indirect effects, and other complex relationships among variables. Path analysis can be considered a special case of SEM, in which structural relations among overt,

observable variables are modeled. Structural relations are hypotheses about directional influences or causal relations of multiple variables (e.g., how intervention will affect depression scores, which will in turn affect reading comprehension scores).

In SEM in general, a variable can serve both as a source variable (called an *exogenous* variable, which is analogous to an independent variable) and a result variable (called an *endogenous* variable, which is analogous to a dependent variable) in a chain of causal hypotheses. When a variable is both a source and a result, it is often called a *mediator.* As an example, suppose that depression has a direct effect on brain activity which, in turn, is hypothesized to affect reading comprehension. In this case, brain activity is a mediator between depression and reading comprehension; it is the source variable for reading comprehension, and the result variable for depression. Furthermore, feedback loops among variables (e.g., reading comprehension can, in turn, affect depression in the example) are permissible in SEM, as are reciprocal effects (e.g., depression and reading comprehension affect each other).

In path analyses, specific, observed variables are treated as if they are measured without error, which is an assumption that does not likely hold in most social and behavioral sciences. When observed variables contain error, estimates of path coefficients may be biased in unpredictable ways, especially for complex models (e.g., Bollen, 1989, pp. 151–178). Estimates of reliability for the measured variables, if available, can be incorporated into the model to fix their error variances (e.g., squared standard error of measurement via classical test theory, see later sections on *reliability* and on *parameter estimation in individual assessment*).

Measurement or Factor Analysis Model Alternatively, if multiple observed variables that are supposed to measure the same latent constructs are available, then a measurement (or factor analysis) model can be used to separate the common variances of the observed variables from their error variances, thus correcting the coefficients in the model for unreliability. The measurement of latent variables originated from psychometric theories. Unobserved latent variables cannot be measured directly, but are indicated or inferred by responses to a number of observable variables (indicators). Latent constructs such as depression or reading ability are often gauged by responses to a battery of items that are designed to tap those constructs. Responses of a study participant to those items are supposed to reflect where the participant stands on the latent variable. Statistical techniques such as factor analysis, exploratory or confirmatory, have been widely used to examine the number of latent constructs underlying the observed responses, and to evaluate the adequacy of individual items or variables as indicators for the latent constructs they are supposed to measure.

The measurement model in SEM is evaluated through confirmatory factor analysis (CFA). The number of factors in CFA is assumed known. In SEM, these factors correspond to the latent constructs represented in the model. Once the measurement model has been specified by the researcher, structural relations of the latent factors are then modeled essentially the same way as they are in path models. The combination of confirmatory factor analysis models with path models on the latent constructs represents the general SEM framework in analyzing covariance structures.

In general, every SEM analysis goes through the steps of model specification, model estimation, model evaluation, and, possibly, model modification, provided that the modification makes theoretical sense. A sound model is theory-based. Theory is based on findings in the literature, knowledge in the field, or one's logical deduction, or even educated guesses, from which causes and effects among variables within the theory are specified. Recall the above research interest in the relationship between depression and reading comprehension. Because depression and reading comprehension ability are not directly observed, but inferred from individuals' responses to a battery of items, they are considered latent variables. One can model the effect of the latent depression variable on children's latent reading comprehension ability by incorporating a

measurement model for each latent construct in the general framework of SEM, to take into account measurement error and unique variances of individual indicator variables. The structural relationship between the latent depression variable and latent reading comprehension ability would be of main interest.

SEM is a large-sample technique. That is, model estimation and statistical inference or hypothesis testing regarding the specified model and individual parameters are appropriate only if sample size is not too small for the estimation method chosen. The sample size required to provide unbiased parameter estimates and accurate model fit information for SEM models depends on model characteristics such as model size, as well as score characteristics of measured variables such as score scale and distribution. Larger models require larger samples to provide stable parameter estimates, and larger samples are required for categorical or non-normally distributed variables than for continuous or normally distributed variables. A general rule of thumb is that the minimum sample size should be no less than 200 (preferably no less than 400, especially when observed variables are not multivariate normally distributed) or 5 to 20 times the number of parameters to be estimated, whichever is larger (e.g., Kline, 2005, pp.111, 178). Larger models often contain a larger number of model parameters, and hence demand larger sample sizes.

A measurement instrument may be theorized to have hierarchically structured factors. Many published measurement instruments provide scores for several subscales, presumably based on factor analysis results of item level responses. Observed subscale scores are often sum, mean, or some other simple linear functions of item responses to the group of items that share a large amount of common variance. For instance, the Children's Depression Inventory (CDI; Kovacs, 1992) contains 27 items, from which 5 subscales (first order latent variables) are derived. The 5 subscales are *negative mood, interpersonal problems, ineffectiveness, anhedonia* (i.e., impaired ability to experience pleasure, including losing energy, sleep, and appetite), and *negative self-esteem* (Kovacs, 1992). The 5 subscales can serve as indicators for the general latent depression variable. Whether one should use the 5 subscales, or a single general scale of depression, depends on one's interest and the strength of correlation among the subscales. If the interest is in the effect of individual subscales, then it makes little sense to combine them into a single scale, especially if intercorrelations between subscales are not very high. On the other hand, if the subscales are highly correlated, and using 5 individual scales may make the model substantially more complicated, then it is more convenient to combine them into a single scale.

The CDI appears to have hierarchical factor structure. The question is whether one should include a hierarchical factor model in a full SEM model. A number of factors need to be considered before a decision can be made. If a hierarchical factor model is included, the lowest level observed indicator variables are item level responses. Most item level responses are categorical (e.g., dichotomous—correct or incorrect for achievement tests, 5- or 7-point Likert type scale). Categorical responses are, by definition, not normally distributed and require alternative treatment, as the normality assumption for common estimation methods is violated. Alternative estimation methods, such as weighted least squares or robust statistics, usually require larger sample sizes to provide unbiased parameter and standard error estimates (e.g., Boomsma & Hoogland, 2000). Compared to a simple CFA model using subscales as observed indicator variables for the latent depression construct, the hierarchical CFA model contains substantially larger number of parameters. Accordingly, sample size required will be larger for the hierarchical CFA model than for the simple CFA model, if one follows the 5–20 per parameter recommendation. That is, the answer depends at least partly on sample size.

Compared to simpler models with fewer parameters and continuous outcome variables, complex models and categorical outcome variables are more likely to encounter estimation problems such as nonconvergence or improper solutions (i.e., some parameter estimates are out of range; e.g., correlation greater than 1, negative variance). These problems may result if a model is ill-specified (e.g., the model is not "identified," indicating that there does not exist a unique solution), the data are problematic (e.g., sample size is too small, variables are highly correlated, etc.), or both. Standard error for individual parameters may not be properly estimated if multicollinearity (i.e., some variables are linearly dependent or strongly correlated) occurs. In any event, nonconverged solutions or improper solutions are not interpretable. In that case, it may be a necessity to deal with data problems prior to estimating the model of interest, or simplify the model if the problem does not appear to be related to data characteristics.

In the case of the CDI example, one can probably use observed subscale scores as indicators for the latent depression variable instead of using a hierarchical factor analysis model (see Figure 7.4 for the conceptual model of modeling the effect of depression on reading comprehension). This will not only simplify the model, but also alleviate the categorical indicator variable concern, because subscale scores are composites of item scores and have more unique score points. The publisher of CDI provides T-scores for each of the 5 subscales. Table 7.9 presents simple descriptive statistics for a hypothetical data set with 5 subscale scores of CDI, and reading comprehension scores on the T-scale (i.e., population mean = 50 and population standard deviation = 10).

The conceptual model of Figure 7.4 was fitted to the hypothetical data using maximum likelihood estimation. The overall model goodness-of-fit is reflected by the magnitude of discrepancy between the sample covariance matrix and the covariance

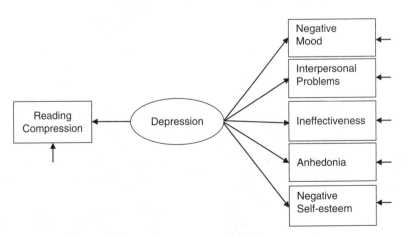

Fig. 7.4 Conceptual Model for Modeling The Effect of Depression on Reading Comprehension (Note. For illustration purpose, a simple model with one latent variable instead of two is used.)

Table 7.9   Sample correlation, mean and standard deviation for the model of figure 7.6

Variables	Variables					
	NM	IP	IE	AH	NS	RC
NM	1					
IP	.632	1				
IE	.515	.491	1			
AH	.494	.461	.382	1		
NS	.611	.554	.459	.451	1	
RC	−.173	−.192	−.152	−.189	−.183	1
MEAN	49.65	49.67	49.23	49.42	50.00	50.46
SD	10.26	10.98	10.62	10.11	10.15	10.69

Note. NM=Negative mood; IP=interpersonal problems; IE=ineffectiveness; AH= anhedonia; NS=negative self-esteem; RC=reading comprehension.

matrix implied by the model with the parameter estimates. When sample size is large, a chi-square test of model goodness-of-fit is often used. Unfortunately, this test statistic has been found to be extremely sensitive to sample size. That is, the model may fit the data reasonably well, but the chi-square test may reject the model because of large sample size.

A variety of alternative goodness-of-fit indices has been developed to supplement the chi-square statistic. Incremental fit indices measure the increase in fit relative to a baseline model (often one in which all observed variables are uncorrelated). Examples of incremental fit indices include Tucker-Lewis Index (TLI; Tucker & Lewis, 1973) and Comparative Fit Index (CFI; Bentler, 1989, 1990). Higher values of incremental fit indices indicate larger improvement over the baseline model in fit. Values in the .90s (or, more recently, $\geq$ .95) are generally accepted as indications of good fit. Absolute fit indices measure the extent to which the specified model of interest reproduces the sample covariance matrix. Examples of absolute fit indices include standardized root mean square residual (SRMR; Bentler, 1995) and the root mean square error of approximation (RMSEA; Steiger & Lind, 1980). Lower values of SRMR and RMSEA indicate better model–data fit.

It is generally recommended that multiple indices be considered simultaneously when overall model fit is evaluated. For instance, Hu and Bentler (1999) proposed a 2-index strategy; that is, reporting SRMR along with one of the fit indices (e.g., CFI or RMSEA). They also suggested the following criteria for an indication of good model-data fit using those indices: CFI $\geq$ .95, SRMR $\leq$ .08, and

RMSEA $\leq$ .06. For the hypothetical example, the model appeared to fit the data well. Chi-squared (df = 9, N = 500) = 3.334, p = .95, indicated that the discrepancy between observed and model-implied covariance matrices was not statistically significant. Using the 2-index strategy recommended by Hu and Bentler (1999), SRMR and RMEAS for the model were .01 (<.08) and .00 (<.06) respectively, which also support the good fit of the model to the data.

Individual parameter and standard error estimates of the model are provided in Table 7.10. All parameter and standard error estimates appeared to be reasonable in magnitude and direction. All standardized factor loading estimates for depression are higher than .60. The unstandardized estimate for the effect of the latent depression variable on the observed reading comprehension variable was −.306. That is, reading comprehension T-scores were expected to decrease by .306 for one unit increase in depression on the T-score scale. Note that the observed variables do not need to be on the same scale; the same T-score scale was used in this example for convenience. The corresponding standardized estimate was −.241, suggesting that reading comprehension scores were expected to decrease by .241 standard deviation units per each standard deviation increase in depression. Although the estimated effect was significantly different from zero at the .05 significance level (|−.306/.061| = 5.02 > 1.96), the standardized residual variance for reading comprehension indicated that 94.2% of the variance in reading comprehension scores was unaccounted for by depression.

Table 7.10 Parameter and standard error estimates for the model of figure 7.6

Model parameters	Standardized estimate	Unstandardized estimate	Standard error
Loadings on Depression			
NM	.822	1.00[a]	–
IP	.766	.996	.057
IE	.630	.793	.057
AH	.607	.727	.054
NS	.735	.884	.053
Effect on RC			
Depression	−.241	−.306	.061
Variances /Residual variances			
Depression	1.00	71.22	6.82
NM	.324	34.13	3.39
IP	.414	49.87	4.20
IE	.603	68.03	4.85
AH	.632	64.61	4.54
NS	.459	47.29	3.76
RC	.942	107.66	6.88

Note. Table values are Maximum Likelihood estimates. NM=Negative mood; IP=interpersonal problems; IE=ineffectiveness; AH= anhedonia; NS=negative self-esteem; RC=reading comprehension.
[a] Fixed parameter to set the scale of the latent variable.

Had the model failed to fit the data, post hoc modifications can be made based on the evaluation of modification indices and expected change in parameter estimates, provided that such modifications are supported by theory. However, it is often more defensible to consider multiple alternative models a priori. That is, multiple models (e.g., based on competing theories or different sides of an argument) should be specified prior to model fitting, and the best fitting model selected among the alternatives.

Other Models Current developments in SEM include the modeling of mean structures in addition to covariance structures, the modeling of changes over time (growth models) and latent classes or profiles, the modeling of data having nesting structures (i.e., multilevel models), as well as the modeling of nonlinear effects (e.g., interaction). Models can also be different for different groups by analyzing multiple sample-specific models simultaneously (multiple sample analysis). Moreover, sampling weights or design effects can be incorporated for complex survey sampling designs. See Marcoulides and Schumacker (2001) and Marcoulides and Moustaki (2002) for more detailed discussions of the more recent developments in SEM.

Pros and Cons of Various Approaches
All statistical models introduced here, including generalized linear models, HLM, and SEM, can estimate linear or nonlinear relationships between variables, as well as moderating and mediating effects. Because SEM can simultaneously estimate multiple equations, it can model mediating effects more directly, along with reciprocal and feedback effects. Moreover, latent variables can be specified explicitly in SEM models.

In general, more recently advanced modeling frameworks like SEM and HLM allow greater flexibility in model specification. Hence, a variety of models can be conceived to test different theoretical hypotheses. In fact, it can be shown that more conventional analysis approaches, such as GLM or generalized linear models, are merely special cases in these more advanced frameworks. In addition, new applications of these models are continually emerging. As an example, it has been demonstrated over the last few years that certain item response theory models, which were developed in the field of psychometrics and must be estimated using specialized software programs, can be modeled in both the SEM and HLM framework. Also, random coefficients of HLM models can be treated as latent variables in SEM. That is, conceptually equivalent models can be specified under different modeling frameworks.

However, parameter estimates obtained from different modeling frameworks as implemented in different software programs might be slightly different, because different estimation techniques might be used. For GLM models, estimation is usually more efficient and straightforward, as there are often closed form solutions (i.e., there are finite solutions that can be calculated through a formula). For other generalized linear models (e.g., logistic regression models, loglinear models), HLM, and SEM, iterative estimation procedures are required, as there are frequently no closed form solutions (i.e., solutions cannot be calculated directly, but are successively approximated in iterative steps). Consequently, the evaluation of modeling results is more complicated, and larger sample sizes are typically required, for iterative estimation procedures. The burden of making sure that the model parameters are properly estimated rests on the shoulders of modelers. Practitioners or researchers who are interested in statistical modeling should familiarize themselves with not only modeling procedures, but also their associated estimation issues and limitations.

As briefly illustrated in this section, the same research question can be examined in different ways. Many data collection decisions (e.g., the choice of measurement instruments, the selection of variables, the number of data collection times, etc.), once implemented, are irreversible in practice. Therefore, it is essential to consider data analysis options and their limitations before starting to collect data.

Decisions about Individuals

School psychologists are researcher-practitioners. On the one hand, they conduct research to help confirm principles and to develop theoretical models to understand child behaviors and other school-related issues, and to guide practice. On the other hand, they design and implement interventions and programs to help students and families to succeed in school. Data are collected to evaluate the efficacy of these interventions. School psychologists

also conduct educational and psychological assessments of individual children for placement and diagnostic purposes. While their research activities to test principles generally require the use of groups of participants as samples, their intervention evaluation and assessment activities most probably have only a single client or a few clients as the focus. For these activities, the "population" of interest is the single client or family, and no generalization is intended beyond that client or that family.

Even though no generalization to a larger population of people would be made for these individual assessments and/or interventions, this does not imply that no inference is to be made beyond the actual data obtained. In practice, these single-subject assessments and evaluations do involve sampling, and inferences are made beyond sample data. Specifically, for these situations, instead of drawing a sample of people from a larger population, we draw a sample of the child's performance or the parents' behaviors from all possible similar performances or incidents. That is, data are collected from within-subject sampling probes. Based on the data in this sample of performances or behaviors, we infer to other times, situations, conditions, and occasions. As such, inferential statistics do play a role in the analyses of these data. The general approach used in these single-subject situations depends on whether the decision to be made is one of assessing some trait of an individual, or one of evaluating the efficacy of an individual intervention program for a single person.

Individual Measurements

School psychologists routinely conduct individual assessments to evaluate a child's achievement, intelligence, preferences, compliance, and a host of other behaviors, traits, and psychological constructs. The results of these assessments are used either as baseline information for intervention, or to help diagnosis, placement, or classification, among other types of decisions. Individual assessments, whether in the form of a mental test, a series of naturalistic observations, interviews or other formats, are inherently a sampling process. Through these assessment activities, we draw a sample of either natural behaviors or responses to a sample of assessment probes. Inferences are made from sample statistics to population parameters, except that the sample statistic in this context is called the "observed score" of the individual, and the corresponding population parameter of interest is called the "true score" of that same individual.

For inferential analyses of group statistics, discussed earlier, we use a combination of several strategies: unbiased sample estimators, significance testing, confidence intervals, and modeling. Similar strategies are used in individual assessments to infer from observed scores to true scores, with one exception: the significance testing approach is not used in individual assessments. In its place, an evaluative index called the *reliability coefficient* is used to describe the extent to which the observed scores represent the true scores. Unbiased observed scores are not obtained via statistical adjustments; instead, they are obtained via procedural safeguards. Specifically, assessment procedures are standardized such that the process through which observed scores are obtained is as identical as possible from person to person, and from situation to situation. Steps include strict adherence to standard assessment environment, administrative procedures, rater training, scoring protocol, and so on; such that there is as little as possible systematic and random variation between the assessments of different clients.

RELIABILITY

In addition to attempting to obtain unbiased observed scores, a reliability coefficient is estimated for the observed scores. A reliability coefficient is the square of the correlation between observed scores and the corresponding theoretical true scores. The value of the reliability coefficient indicates the proportion of the variation in observed scores that is attributable to the variation in true scores. For example, a reliability coefficient of 0.8 indicates that 80% of the variance in observed scores among individuals assessed is due to variance in true scores. Reliability coefficients cannot be estimated directly. Instead, they are estimated indirectly through various strategies, under different mathematical or statistical assumptions, that would theoretically lead us to the values of the reliability coefficients. Most reliability coefficients today are estimated through strategies that are based on a set of assumptions called *classical parallel tests* assumptions. Under these assumptions, if we are able to identify two tests that meet a set of very restrictive statistical conditions (e.g., identical true scores, independence between true and error scores, identical variances), the correlation between the observed scores from these two tests is numerically equal to the reliability coefficient (i.e., square of correlation between observed and true scores) for either of the two tests. Strategies to obtain these parallel tests have included the test-retest method, equivalent forms method, and internal consistency methods. With the test-retest method, the same test is given to the same pilot sample of individuals at two points in time, generally several weeks apart. The correlation between the two sets of observed scores is an estimate of the reliability coefficient value. With the equivalent forms method, two interchangeable versions of the same test are administered to a pilot sample simultaneously, and the correlation between the two sets of observed scores is another estimate of the reliability coefficient value. Finally, with the internal consistency strategy, parallel tests are "created" internally within a single test. The most basic internal consistency strategy is the split-half method which takes half of the items within a single test as those of one parallel test, and the other items as those of another parallel test. The correlation between the observed scores of the two halves would be taken as an estimate of the reliability coefficients. This strategy provides an underestimation of the reliability coefficient. Generally, the Spearman-Brown prophecy formula (see Lord & Novick, 1968, pp. 112-114) is applied to correct for the underestimation. Another alternative internal consistency strategy is to treat a K-item test as if there were K parallel 1-item tests. The average inter-item correlation, after correcting for length via the Spearman-Brown prophecy formula, would then be taken as an estimate of the reliability coefficient value. The result of this internal consistency strategy is called *standardized item alpha*. The result is numerically equal to the average of all possible split-half estimates from a single test, estimated from splitting the same test repeatedly into two halves in every possible manner.

A very popular method that employs the internal consistency method is the Cronbach alpha method. It is conceptually similar to the standardized item alpha method, but is based on a set of slightly more relaxed statistical assumptions, called the *essentially tau-equivalent assumptions*. As such, it is a slightly more realistic method than the other internal consistency methods. In practice, if all item scores are converted to standard z-scores before calculation, the Cronbach alpha value equals that of the standardized item alpha. If item scores are not converted to z-scores, Cronbach alpha is expected to be less than or equal to the value of standardized item alpha. An earlier method to estimate reliability developed in the 1930s, called the Kuder-Richardson Formula-20 (KR-20), is in fact a special case of Cronbach alpha when items are scored dichotomously. It is, essentially, a computationally more convenient method to calculate Cronbach alpha when items are dichotomous. With computers today, KR-20 is essentially obsolete. Another index, called Kuder-Richardson Formula-21 (KR-21), is a computationally quick conservative estimate of KR-20. Again, with high-speed computers today, KR-21 is not needed.

The above methods are within a general theoretical approach called the *Classical Theory of Measurement*. Within this approach, true score is defined as the mean of all possible observed scores that would be obtained by the same individual in an undefined, infinitely large universe under a variety of unspecified conditions. In other words, true score is an ill-defined, rather nebulous concept. An alternative approach that is particularly suited for multifaceted assessments, such as naturalistic observations, authentic assessments, and performance assessments, is that of the Generalizability Theory (G-theory). With the G-theory, true scores are very circumscribed. Specifically, to assess reliability one needs to specify the dimensions to which the scores are to be generalized. For example, the observations of a child's behavior will be confined to only classroom behaviors during school hours, as observed by teachers or teachers' assistants and as recorded by the items on a particular behavior checklist. True score in this case is the average of all possible observations within this well-defined set of conditions. It is theoretically possible that the same child might have a different true score for other situations. For example, the true score might be different from observations made at home by parents in the evening.

Given a particular assessment method, a person can potentially have numerous different true scores—called *universe scores* in G-theory. Therefore, for a given assessment method, there are potentially many reliability coefficients, called G-coefficients; one for each generalization and application scenario. G-coefficients are "constructed" indirectly, rather than estimated directly, from data. Data are collected within the confines of the circumscribed dimensions of generalization. These data are analyzed via the general analysis of variance (ANOVA) approach. Instead of evaluating F-ratios to test for significance in its usual application, ANOVA is used to estimate the variances of the dimensions and their interactions within the circumscribed universe/population. These variances form the building blocks to "construct" G-coefficients. To estimate a G-coefficient, one needs to project a usage scenario in terms of a number of practical considerations. These include such considerations as whether the interpretation will be norm-referenced or criterion-referenced,

whether each dimension will be crossed or nested, random or fixed, how many items, raters, occasions, and any other relevant factors, will be used in the actual assessment. Based on these considerations, the variances estimated from the ANOVA are separated into those that may be considered components of the true variance, those that are components of the error variance, and those that are irrelevant to the situation. They are further adjusted by the projected sample size of each dimension in the application (e.g., number of observers used, number of items used during application under the usage scenario). G-coefficient is then calculated by:

(6) (Sum of all true variance components)/
[(sum of true variance components)+
(sum of error variance components)]

Increasingly, many standardized achievement and clinical assessment tools used by school psychologists are being scaled via the Item Response theoretic approach, particularly via the Rasch model. Item Response Theory methods, including the Rasch model, do not lead to a reliability coefficient per se. Instead, they produce an information function, which is a conceptual, though not statistical, analog to the reliability coefficient.

PARAMETER ESTIMATION IN INDIVIDUAL ASSESSMENT

Reliability and G coefficients are indices used to evaluate the precision of assessment scores. Assessment analogs to parameter estimations in individual assessment include the building of confidence intervals, and the direct estimation of true scores. Confidence intervals are built by identifying a margin of error around the observed score of the individual. This is accomplished via the standard error of measurement statistic, which is calculated by:

(7) Standard error of measurement
$$= \sigma_x \sqrt{1 - \text{reliability coefficient}}.$$

where σ_x is the standard deviation of the observed scores. We can build 68% confidence intervals by adding and subtracting 1 standard error of measurement from an observed score; or we can build a 95% confidence interval by adding and subtracting 1.96 standard errors of measurement from an observed score. The interpretation of these confidence intervals is that the true score of the individual is likely, with either a 68% confidence or a 95% confidence, respectively, to be within the range of scores encompassed by the confidence interval.

A more direct method is to estimate the true score of the individual via:

$$(8) \quad \text{estimated true score} = \rho_{xx}(x - \mu_x) + \mu_x.$$

where ρ_{xx} is the reliability or G coefficient, x is the observed score of the individual and μ_x is the mean observed score of the norm group. Note, however, that this estimated true score will effectively be a linear transformation of the original raw score.

One particular consideration for school psychologists is that the reliability coefficient and its corresponding standard error of measurement commonly reported by test publishers, including those discussed above, can be viewed as the average reliability and standard error across all score levels. Reliability and standard errors can vary substantially for different scores. Since school psychologists most often work with children closer to the extreme ends of score range, where reliability and standard errors are particularly different from the average, they should consider estimating their own reliability coefficients and standard errors for the particular scores that they use. Methods to estimate these can be found in such references as Haertel (2006, pp. 82-84) and Feldt and Brennan (1989, pp. 123–124).

RATER/OBSERVER INTERCHANGEABILITY

Many individual assessments used by school psychologists involve the use of raters or observers. One particular area of common data concern is rater/observer interchangeability. The issue of interest is whether the data obtained are independent of the particular rater/observer used in the assessment, which is taken to be a sign of data objectivity. To ascertain this, we calculate and evaluate inter-rater or inter-observer reliability, or agreement indices. These include correlations, proportion agreement indices, and/or kappa coefficients between the scores obtained by two independent raters or observers. It should be noted that inter-observer or inter-rater reliability is somewhat of a misnomer. Technically, reliability is a characteristic of scores, not raters/observers. The reliability coefficient value indicates the proportion of observed score variance that is due to true variance across subjects. Consistency between raters/observers does not assure score reliability. Therefore, inter-observer or inter-rater reliability is better described as rater/observer interchangeability. This interchangeability will enhance, but not guarantee, score reliability.

To evaluate score reliability by taking rater consistency, or the lack thereof, into account, one would need to conduct a multifaceted generalizability analysis in which raters are one of the facets of measurement. Brennan (2001) provides specific designs and procedures to accomplish this.

VALIDITY AND CLASSIFICATION DECISIONS

Validity in individual assessment refers to the adequacy of evidence to support the interpretation of assessment scores, and the decisions made on the basis of the scores. Validity evidence may be gathered from a variety of sources via different methodologies, which can range from qualitative to quantitative methods involving the analyses of objective, judgmental, or textual data. A variety of general statistical techniques can be applied for some particular pieces of validity evidence. Particularly common is the use of exploratory or confirmatory factor analyses to produce evidence that the internal structure of the response data from the assessment is consistent with the theoretical internal structure of the construct or trait being measured. Another cogent data analytic framework is the multitrait-multimethod matrix design (Campbell & Fiske, 1959) which can be implemented by a variety of statistical techniques, ranging from a correlation matrix, to analysis of variance, to confirmatory factor analytic procedures. The result is two particular compelling pieces of validity evidence, called *convergent* and *discriminant* validity, and is well within the conceptual frame of a cogent approach to validity known as the *nomological net* (Cronbach & Meehl, 1955). The Generalizability Theory approach can also be used to gathered validity evidence (see, for example, Kane 1982. Also see Kane (2006) and Messick (1989) for a comprehensive discussion of validity issues.)

One area of validity concerns that is particularly relevant to school psychologists is evidence to support the validity of classifications of children or other individuals. Examples include classifying a child as gifted, as mentally retarded, as having a learning disability, or as suffering from attention deficit hyperactive disorder. At least parts of these decisions are based on test scores being above or below certain cutoff thresholds (e.g., having an IQ score of higher than a cutoff score of 130 may be part of the criteria to classify a child as being gifted), or having a score profile similar to that of a particular known category of children. Evidence to support the validity of these classification decisions includes questions of classification accuracy and clinical utility.

Classification accuracy includes such statistics as hit rate, kappa coefficient, sensitivity and specificity. Clinical utility includes such statistics as positive predictive power, negative predictive power, false positive rate, and false negative rate. These statistics are estimated either through data gathered from a sample of subjects with known classifications, or those who can be classified through some alternative "gold standard" criterion. The test of interest is administered to the sample, and the individuals in the sample are classified into the categories based solely on their scores on the test, and whether the scores are above or below the predetermined cutoff score. The consistency between classifications based on test scores, and the known classifications based on the gold standard, would be evaluated from various angles to produce a set of classification accuracy and clinical utility statistics, which include hit rate, sensitivity, specificity, positive predictive power, negative predictive power, false positive rate, and false negative rate. Appendix B provides a summary of how each of these indices is calculated from sample data. The context for the table in Appendix B is one in which a child is classified as either learning disabled or not, based on a test, and the gold standard is determined by whether the child needs special help or not, after following the child for three years without actually classifying the child.

Efficacy of Single-Subject Interventions

In addition to individual assessments, school psychologists often implement individualized interventions. Since these interventions involve only one or few subjects, many of the group data analysis techniques discussed early in this chapter cannot be applied directly to evaluate the efficacy of the interventions. Instead, internally valid conclusions are drawn regarding intervention efficacy, based on a coordinated orchestration between the manipulation of interrupted time-series data collection designs and corresponding parametric or nonparametric statistical analyses.

The most basic of interrupted time-series designs is the A-B Design, which consists of a no-intervention baseline "A" phase, and an intervention "B" phase, over a period of time in which observations of some behavior of the single subject are made. Figure 7.5 shows the frequency of disruptive behavior exhibited by a child in a hypothetical A-B design single-case study. The child shows disruptive behaviors in the classroom, and after observing and recording the behavior without intervention for five days, a school psychologist attempts an intervention

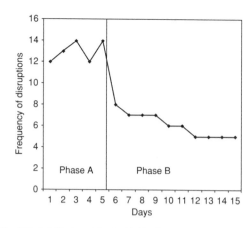

Fig. 7.5 A-B Design with a Stable Baseline

(e.g., giving warnings) and continues to observe and record for a number of days afterwards. The efficacy of the intervention is evaluated by comparing the frequency of disruptive behaviors in the A phase against that in the B phase. If the intervention is effective, one would expect a decline in frequency in the intervention phase, as is shown in the hypothetical example in Figure 7.5.

The A-B design is the most basic single-subject design. However, as a quasi-experimental design, it cannot eliminate some known potential threats to internal validity. Some of these threats may include maturation and autocorrelation. To control for additional threats to internal validity, features have been added to the basic A-B design, resulting in improved designs that may be applied in specific situations. One such improvement is the A-B-A design. In this design, a third phase is added, when feasible, to the end of the A-B design, by returning to a non-intervention phase from the intervention phase at some point. If there is a change in data (i.e., frequency or score returns to a level similar to that of the original baseline phase), the conclusion of intervention effectiveness is very cogent.

A particularly powerful alternative design is the multiple baseline design, which can be used if there are at least several subjects for whom the intervention can be appropriately implemented, individually and independently. For each subject, an A-B design is used and the same intervention is implemented. The A phase starts at the same time for all subjects. Observations are made at the same intervals and for the same duration for all subjects. The only difference across subjects is that the time point at which the intervention is initiated is staggered across subjects, each intervention starting at a different point. Ideally, the starting point of intervention for each subject is determined randomly, but after at least a certain number of baseline observations. Wolf and Risley (1971) recommended the use of 3 or 4 subjects with this design.

A design that is slightly more complicated than the A-B or the A-B-A design is the A-B-C-A-C-B design. This design is particularly appropriate when a second intervention, C, is attempted after the first intervention, B, shows little effect. A potential threat to the validity of conclusions regarding the effectiveness of C is multiple treatment interference; namely, that intervention C might be effective only with the prior help of intervention B. With the A-B-C-A-C-B design, at some point after the implementation of intervention C, we return to a no-intervention baseline phase. This non-intervention phase is then followed by the two interventions in a reversed order. By counterbalancing the order of the two interventions, the data would reveal whether multiple treatment interference has occurred.

In lieu of statistical analyses of these single-subject time-series data, visual inspections of graphic presentations have been widely used, and often advocated. Efficacy of intervention is determined by whether the data in the intervention phase are different from the data in the baseline phase. Although it has the merits of simplicity and convenience for use, there has been concern over whether judgment based on visual inspection is reliable and accurate. According to Brossart, Parker, Olson, and Mahadevan (2006), several studies found inter-rater consistencies of visual inspections to range from .40 to .60 (DeProspero & Cohen, 1979; Harbst, Ottenbacher, & Harris, 1991; Ottenbacher, 1990; Park, Marascuilo, & Gaylord-Ross, 1990). Park et al. (1990) found that even among expert raters, inter-rater agreements were 27% for graphs with statistically significant results, and 67% for graphs without significant results. Training did not seem to improve inter-rater agreements.

Statistical tests of significance seem to be a good alternative to mere visual inspections. Recently, there appears to be an increased interest in the use of statistical analysis in single-case studies. Kazdin (1982) suggests that statistical procedures may be used when (a) there is no stable baseline; (b) expected treatment effects cannot be well predicted, as with a new treatment; and (c) statistical control is needed for extraneous factors in naturalistic environments. Huitema (1986) further recommends that statistical analyses should be added whenever unambiguous results must be shared with other professionals.

However, the use of statistical tests for single-case study is still limited due to the problem of autocorrelation among errors, though it has been argued that this equally jeopardizes the validity of visual inspections. Autocorrelation refers to the dependence between observations at successive time points. Busk and Marascuilo (1988) computed lag-1 autocorrelations for 248 independent data sets from 44 studies in the *Journal of Applied Behavior Analysis,* published from 1975 to 1985. They found that 80% of the autocorrelations ranged from .10 to .49 for phases of size 5 to 18 observations; 40% of the baseline autocorrelations were greater than .25, and 59% of intervention phase autocorrelations were above .25. The existence of autocorrelation makes it inappropriate to use the traditional general linear model techniques, which assumes that residual errors are random, uncorrelated, normally distributed, and have constant variances (see earlier discussion on GLM). It has been found that when residuals in single-case data are positively autocorrelated, the standard errors for most traditional tests will be undesirably reduced, and the size of the resulting test statistics will be increased, as will the rate of Type I errors (Suen & Ary, 1987). Variations of general linear models have been proposed to compensate for autocorrelation; however, they did not necessarily remove or reduce the autocorrelation (Kazdin, 1976). One consequence of autocorrelation is that common significance testing techniques, such as t-test or F-ratios, cannot be used to analyze single-case study data.

Time-series analysis techniques, such as Box-Jenkins' Autoregressive Integrated Moving Average (ARIMA), provide a valid set of procedures to be used in single-case designs. Time-series analysis attempts to apply the General Linear Model to determine if there is a slope change between the baseline and intervention phases. This determination is made only after trends and autocorrelations have been removed from the original time-series data. A major limitation of time-series technique when applied to single-subject data is that time-series methods such as ARIMA require a large number of observations, usually difficult to obtain in typical single-subject intervention situations. The general recommendation is to have at least 35 to 40 observations (Box & Jenkins, 1970; Gottman & Glass, 1978) for each phase in order to justify the model. Consequently, time-series statistical techniques are not widely used in the evaluation of the efficacy of single-subject interventions. See Glass, Willson, and Gottman (1975) for detailed discussions of the application of time-series analyses in single-subject behavioral observation research. See Box and Jenkins (1970) for in-depth treatment of the subject.

Randomization tests are another important set of methods that have been recommended for analyzing time-series data from single-subject studies. Originally developed by Fisher (see Fisher, 1951) in the 1930s, randomization tests do not make prior assumptions about the form of distribution from which the data comes (Todman & Dugard, 2001), and they also ameliorate the dependency problem by randomly assigning treatments (e.g. A and B treatments) to different occasions. The basic approach is one of significance testing, rather than attempting to model the parameters. With the obtained data, we generate the probability distribution of the test statistic, which is then used to determine the probability that the observed sample value can be the artifact of randomization, instead of being the effect of intervention (Marascuilo & Busk, 1988). For instance, in a single-subject A-B design, there are N_A observations in the A Phase, and N_B observations in the B Phase. The mean difference $\bar{D} = \bar{Y}_A - \bar{Y}_B$ would be the statistic of interest. To generate the probability distribution of $\bar{D}$ values, we calculate all possible values of $\bar{D}$ when the B phase is initiated, at each of the possible points in the time series. By dividing the number of $\bar{D}$ values thus calculated that is equal to or exceeds the observed $\bar{D}$, by the total number of $\bar{D}$ values, we obtain the probability value for significance testing. If the probability is less than .05, the null hypothesis of the observed $\bar{D}$ being an artifact of random sampling fluctuation is rejected. Edgington (1967, 1969, 1975) provided a number of illustrative examples of how to implement this method.

The calculation of all the possible treatment assignments and their corresponding mean differences can be very labor-intensive. Marascuilo and Busk (1988) proposed to use rank tests, which is easier to perform and is available in some statistical software. Todman and Dugard (2001) have also provided detailed procedures for how to use SPSS, Minitab, and Excel respectively, to analyze randomization test data.

The above randomized A-B design is the simplest design, in which all A (baseline) treatment blocks precede all B treatment blocks. Wampold and Worsham (1986) developed a randomized multiple-baseline design, in which the experimenter employed a random selection of intervention times. The test statistic used in this design is based on the sum across S subjects of the difference in phase means.

$W = \bar{D}_1 + \bar{D}_2 + \bar{D}_3 + \bar{D}_4 + \ldots$ where $\bar{D}s. = \bar{Y}_{As} - \bar{Y}_{Bs}$ is the difference in phase means for subject S. For S subjects, there are a total of S! possible permutations for the random assignment of intervention time. We need to determine the proportion of these S! assignments in which the calculated W value is as large or larger than the W value obtained in the current data.

In the randomized multiple baseline design proposed by Marascuilo and Busk (1988), however, the random assignment of intervention to different subjects is different. If there are S subjects with T possible intervention points, the researcher would randomly select one of the T intervention points independently, for each of the S subjects. This allows for S^T possible configurations of intervention initiation points. For example, for 5 subjects each having 5 potential points of initiation, there are a total of $5^5 = 3125$ unique combinations of intervention arrangements. Compared to the Wampold-Worsham design, this design leads to more possible assignments, smaller p values and potentially more power (Ferron & Sentovich, 2002). In general, the principles and procedures for obtaining the probability value for significance testing for different designs are very similar. For more details about using randomization tests for multiple-baseline A-B and replicated A-B-A-B designs, see Marascuilo and Busk (1988).

In practice, randomization tests require that treatment be randomly assigned to occasions upon which the response measurements are obtained. The power of randomization tests varies depending on designs. Some empirical studies (Ferron, Foster-Johnson, & Kromrey, 2003; Ferron & Ware, 1995) show that it has an acceptable control over Type I error. Marascuilo and Busk (1988) also reported that risks of Type I error rates less than .05 could usually be generated with two or more subjects. In general, the power of the test can be increased by having a larger number of observations and experimental units (either individuals or groups) to which the intervention is applied.

Observations and Limitations

We are the beneficiaries of decades, and in some cases centuries, of creative and ingenious mathematical and statistical minds that have developed some very elegant, efficient, and powerful data analytic procedures to help us discern patterns, trends, and associations from otherwise unwieldy sample data. Without these analytical techniques, many statistical patterns and relations would have been otherwise buried deep in our data, obscured by the apparent chaos of the data. These analytic techniques have become increasingly sophisticated. They are now capable of extracting very complex patterns from our data that would not have been revealed by existing methods just a few decades ago. Yet, in spite of the sophistication of these methods, we cannot lose sight of the fact that they only point at patterns and associations in the existing data that we have collected. They are inherently incapable of providing explanations, interpretations, causal inferences, policy, or clinical implications. These necessarily need to come from the researcher and evaluator, based on theory and clinical considerations and guided by reason and experience.

The role of an a priori substantive theory, which is based on literature, experience, reasoning and practice, cannot be overemphasized. Increasingly, newer sophisticated modeling techniques are favored over the simpler conventional significance testing or confidence interval approaches for inferences from sample to the population. The logic of these modeling techniques in general is confirmatory in nature. One postulates one or several possible theory-based models in the population, and then examines whether sample data fit the model or which of several models fits the sample data best. This is the case whether the method used is one of general linear modeling, generalized linear modeling, hierarchical linear modeling, or structural equation modeling; whether there is an explicit statistic called a fit index or not; or whether the analysis is based on a least-squared criterion, or a maximum-likelihood criterion. The logic of this approach, however, can only work in one direction, not in the reversed direction. That is, the process is one in which, starting from theory or practice, we postulate a model. From the model, we decide what data to collect and then examine the data to see if the model is supported. However, we cannot start from data collection without a model, and then examine patterns and associations in the data in order to "find" a model. This is because, for any given set of sample data, there are many possible, some drastically different, models that will fit the data about equally well—including many models that the researcher has yet to imagine.

Results of data analysis may, in some limited situations, help to trigger insights toward the formulation of alternative theories, models, and explanations. This function becomes possible when data are from very large samples, and/or when the analyses have been replicated a number of times and all results have led to the same consistent pattern. These new insights would need to be confirmed via either a replication or, when appropriate, new data collection.

In general, for inferences to the population, large sample sizes are preferred when feasible, and in some cases are required. With larger sample sizes, parameter estimates will be more precise and statistical tests will be more powerful. More complex models require larger minimum sample sizes to provide adequate parameter estimates. Although simpler models such as GLM are more tolerant of smaller sample sizes, test statistics are generally more robust to violation of model assumptions with large samples.

There are practical limitations to data analysis techniques today, and not all theoretical relations or models can be analyzed. Scope of data collection for complex models is more extensive, and may require more resources than simpler models. Complex models are likely to have more variables and require more measures and larger sample sizes. Human and other resources are needed to administer measures, score responses, check and enter data. Lengthy questionnaires, tests, performances, or other measures that require extensive time to complete, may also diminish subjects' motivation to participate or provide complete, careful responses. Consequently, missing data or unusable data may result.

The use of the significance testing approach has been under persistent criticism over the last several decades, primarily due to the widespread misuses and misinterpretation of results from this approach. Books and numerous academic journal articles have been written, and are continually being written, on this controversy. Many have advocated for an end to the use of significance testing, while others have defended its role in data analysis. There is nothing inherently wrong with significance testing per se, and significance testing remains one of the useful tools in data analysis. The problem arises from widespread attempts, some misguided by textbook authors, to over-interpret the results of significance tests, which have led to many erroneous conclusions. The logic of significance testing is convoluted, and the proper interpretation of results is very narrow and restrictive. Very restrictively, "significance" means that it is reasonable to refute the competing explanation that the pattern (statistics) observed in the sample data is an artifact of random sampling fluctuation. Conversely, nonsignificance means that random sampling fluctuation remains a viable competing explanation for the sample pattern. Most attempts to interpret significance beyond the confines of this narrow meaning have led to misinterpretations.

The advantages of large sample sizes, as well as issues of inferences to a larger population, are moot in single-subject research. Results of single-subject research inherently cannot be generalized to other subjects; albeit, when the study has been designed properly, results may be generalized to the same subject in other occasions and situations. There does not exist any data analysis technique that would enable one to generalize the results of a single-subject study to a larger population or to any other subjects. Generalization to a larger population needs to be built over time through replications of the study with other subjects. Generalization to other occasions and situations may, however, be made in single-subject research via the significance testing approach, such as when one of the variations of the randomization test method is employed. However, the use of randomization tests requires the ability to randomize the time point for the initiation of intervention, which may be unrealistic in many clinical situations.

Given that data analysis methods are techniques to find patterns and associations in a set of existing numerical data, the results of data analyses can only be as trustworthy and as meaningful as that of the original data. Therefore, reliability and validity of the sample data are of foremost importance prior to data analyses. Of the two, validity is by far more critical. Poor reliability will reduce statistical power. However, it is possible to compensate for the reduced statistical power to some extent via other contributors of power, such as large sample sizes, large effect sizes, or homogenous population. When there is a lack of evidence to support valid interpretation or use of the scores or other forms of data in the study, however, data analyses may prove to be little more than numerical exercises.

Endnotes

1. These two approaches to comparing independent group means are not mathematically equivalent, and may occasionally result in different conclusions about population mean differences.

2. Part of the introduction is based on Lei (2006) and Lei and Wu (2007).

Appendix A
Formulas of standard errors for some common parameters

1. Standard error of the mean: $\hat{\sigma}_{\bar{x}} = \dfrac{s}{\sqrt{n}}$, where

$s = \sqrt{\dfrac{\sum\limits_{i=1}^{n}(X_i - \overline{X})^2}{n-1}}$, n is the sample size.

2. Standard error for independent group mean difference:

$\hat{\sigma}_{\bar{X}_1 - \bar{X}_2} = \sqrt{\dfrac{(n_1-1)s_1^2 + (n_2-1)s_2^2}{n_1+n_2-2}\left(\dfrac{1}{n_1}+\dfrac{1}{n_2}\right)}$, where

S_1 and S_2 are S for the two independent groups 1 and 2, respectively; n_1 and n_2 are sample sizes for groups 1 and 2, respectively.

3. Standard error for dependent group mean difference $(\bar{D} = \bar{X}_1 - \bar{X}_2)$: $\hat{\sigma}_{\bar{D}} = \dfrac{s_D}{\sqrt{n}}$, where

$s_D = \sqrt{\dfrac{\sum\limits_{i=1}^{n}(X_{1i} - X_{2i} - \bar{D})^2}{n-1}}$, and n is the number of pairs.

4. Standard error for proportion with large sample size: $\hat{\sigma}_p = \sqrt{\dfrac{p(1-p)}{n-1}}$, where p is the sample proportion.

Appendix B

		Gold standard		
		No help needed	Help needed	
Test	LD	A	B	A+B
	Not LD	C	D	C+D
		A+C	B+D	A+B+C+D

(B.1) $hit\ rate = p_0 = (B+C)/(A+B+C+D)$

(B.2) $kappa = \dfrac{p_0 - p_c}{1 - p_c}$

where p_0 is the hit rate and p_c is chance agreement, which can be calculated by:

(B.3) $p_c = \dfrac{(A+B)(B+D)+(C+D)(A+C)}{A+B+C+D}$

(B.4) $Sensitivity = \dfrac{B}{B+D}$

(B.5) $Specificity = \dfrac{C}{A+C}$

(B.6) $Positive\ predictive\ power = \dfrac{B}{A+B}$

(B.7) $Negative\ predictive\ power = \dfrac{C}{C+D}$

(B.8) *False positive rate*

$$= 1 - positive\ predictive\ power$$

(B.9) *False negative rate*

$$= 1 - negative\ predictive\ power$$

References

Bentler, P. M. (1989). *EQS structural equations program manual.* Los Angeles, CA: BMDP Statistical Software.

Bentler, P. M. (1990). Comparative fit indexes in structural models. *Psychological Bulletin, 107,* 238–246.

Bentler, P. M. (1995). *EQS structural equations program manual.* Encino, CA: Multivariate Software, Inc.

Bollen, K. A. (1989). *Structural equations with latent variables.* New York: Wiley.

Boomsma, A. & Hoogland, J. J. (2000). The robustness of LISREL modeling revisited. In R. Cudeck, S. H. C. du Toit, & D. Sörbom (Eds.). *Structural equation modeling: Present and future* (pp. 139–168). Lincolnwood, IL: Scientific Software International, Inc.

Box, G. E. P. & Jenkins, G. M. (1970). *Time-series analysis: Forecasting and control.* San Francisco: Holden Day.

Brennan, R. L. (2001) *Generalizability Theory.* New York: Springer-Verlag.

Brooks-Gunn, J. (2004). Don't throw out the baby with the bathwater: Incorporating behavioral research into evaluation. *Social Policy Report, 18*(2), 14–15.

Brossart, D. F., Parker, R. I., Olson, E. A., & Mahadevan, L. (2006). The relationship between visual analysis and five statistical analyses in a simple AB single-case research design. *Behavior Modification, 30*(5), 531–563.

Busk, P. L., & Marascuilo, L. A. (1988). Autocorrelation in single-subject research: A counter argument to the myth of no autocorrelation. *Behavioral Assessment, 10,* 229–242.

Campbell, D. T., & Fiske, D. W. (1959). Convergent and discriminant validity in the multitrait–multimethod matrix. *Psychological Bulletin, 56,* 81–105.

Cohen, J., Cohen, P., West, S. G., & Aiken, L. S. (2003). *Applied multiple regression/correlation analysis for the behavioral sciences* (3rd ed.). Mahwah, NJ: Lawrence Erlbaum Associates.

Cook, T. D. (2004). Beyond advocacy: Putting history and research on research into debates about the merits of social experiments. *Social Policy Report, 18*(2), 5–6.

Cottingham, P. (2004). Why we need more, not fewer, gold standard evaluations. *Social Policy Report, 18*(2), 13.

Cronbach, L. J. & Meehl, P. E. (1955). Construct validity in psychological tests. *Psychological Bulletin, 52,* 281–301.

DeProspero, A. & Cohen, S. (1979). Inconsistent visual analyses of intrasubject data. *Journal of Applied Behavior Analysis, 12,* 573–579.

Edgington, E.S. (1967). Statistical inference from N = 1 experiments. *Journal of Psychology, 65,* 195–199.

Edgington, E. S. (1969). Approximate randomization tests. *Journal of Psychology, 72,* 143–179.

Edgington, E.S. (1975). Randomization tests for one-subject operant experiments. *Journal of Psychology, 90,* 57–68.

Feldt, L. S. & Brennan, R. L. (1989). Reliability. In R. L. Linn (Ed.). *Educational measurement* (3rd ed., pp. 105–146). New York: Macmillan.

Ferron, J., Foster-Johnson, L., & Kromrey, J. D. (2003). The functioning of single-case randomization tests with and without random assignment. *The Journal of Experimental Education, 71,* 267–288.

Ferron, J. & Sentovich, C. (2002). Statistical power of randomization tests used with multiple-baseline designs. *The Journal of Experimental Education, 70*(2), 165–178.

Ferron, J. & Ware, W. (1995). Analyzing single-case data: The power of randomization tests. *The Journal of Experimental Education, 63,* 167–178.

Fisher, R. A. (1951). *The design of experiments* (6th ed.). New York: Hafner.

Glass, G. V. & Hopkins, K. D. (1995). *Statistical methods in education and psychology* (3rd ed.). Boston, MA: Allyn and Bacon.

Glass, G. V., Willson, V. L., & Gottman, J. M. (1975). *Design and analysis of time-series experiments.* Boulder: Colorado Associated University Press.

Gottman, J. M. & Glass, G. V. (1978). Analysis of interrupted time-series experiments. In T. R. Kratochwill (Ed.). *Single subject research: Strategies for evaluating change* (pp. 197–235). New York: Academic Press.

Haertel, E. H. (2006). Reliability. In R. L. Brennan (Ed.), *Educational measurement* (4th ed., pp. 65–110). Westport, CT: Praeger.

Hahn, H., Neurath, O., & Carnap, R. (1929). *Wissenschaftliche weltauffassung: Der wiener kreis* (A scientific world-view: The Vienna circle). Vienna: Ernst Mach Society.

Harbst, K. B., Ottenbacher, K. J., & Harris, S. R. (1991). Interrater reliability of therapists' judgments of graphed data. *Physical Therapy, 71,* 107–115.

Hosmer, D.W. Jr., & Lemeshow, S. (2000). *Applied logistic regression* (2nd ed.). New York: John Wiley & Sons, Inc.

Hu, L.-T. & Bentler, P. (1999). Cutoff criteria for fit indexes in covariance structure analysis: Conventional criteria versus new alternatives. *Structural Equation Modeling, 6,* 1–55.

Huitema, B. E. (1986). Autocorrelation in behavioral research: Wherefore art thou? In A. Poling & R. W. Fuqua (Eds.). *Research methods in applied behavior analysis: Issues and advances.* (pp. 187–208). New York: Plenum Press.

Kane, M. T. (1982). A sampling model for validity. *Applied Psychological Measurement, 6*(2), 125–160.

Kane, M. T. (2006). Validation. In R. L. Brennan (Ed.). *Educational measurement* (4th ed., pp. 17–64). Westport, CT: Praeger.

Kazdin, A. E. (1976). Statistical analyses for single-case experimental designs. In M. Hersen & D. H. Barlow (Eds.). *Single case experimental designs: Strategies for behavioral change* (pp. 265–316). New York: Pergamon Press.

Kazdin, A. E. (1982). *Single-case research designs: Methods for clinical and applied settings.* New York: Oxford University Press.

Kirk, R. E. (1998). *Statistics: An introduction* (4th ed.). New York, NY: Harcourt Brace College Publishers.

Kline, R. B. (2005). *Principles and practice of structural equation modeling* (2nd ed.). New York: Guilford Press.

Kovacs, M. (1992). *Children's depression inventory.* North Tonawanda, NY: Multi-Health System.

Kreft, I. & de Leeuw, J. (1998). *Introducing multilevel modeling.* London: Sage.

Lakatos, I. (1970). Falsification and the methodology of scientific research programmes. In I. Lakatos and A. Musgraove (Eds.). *Criticism and the growth of knowledge.* London: Cambridge University Press.

Lei, P.-W. (2006). Structural equation modeling (SEM). In N. J. Salkind & K. L. Rasmussen (Eds.). *Encyclopedia of measurement and statistics* (pp. 973–976). Thousand Oaks, CA: Sage.

Lei, P.-W. & Wu, Q. (2007). Introduction to structural equation modeling: Issues and practical considerations. *Educational Measurement: Issues and Practices, 26*(3), 33–43.

Lord, F. M. & Novick, M. R. (1968). *Statistical theories of mental test scores*. Reading, MA: Addison-Wesley.

Marascuilo, L.A. & Busk, P. L. (1988).Combining statistics for multiple-baseline AB and replicated ABAB designs across subjects. *Behavioral Assessment, 10,* 1–28.

Marcoulides, G. A. & Moustaki, I. (2002). *Latent variable and latent structure models*. Mahwah, NJ: Lawrence Erlbaum Associates.

Marcoulides, G. A. & Schumacker, R. E. (Eds.). (2001). *New developments and techniques in structural equation modeling*. Mahwah, NJ: Lawrence Erlbaum Associates.

McCall, R. B. & Green, B. L. (2004). Beyond the methodological gold standards of behavioral research: Considerations for practice and policy. *Policy Report, 18*(2), 1, 3–4, 6–19.

Messick, S. (1989). Validity. In R. L. Linn (Ed.). *Educational measurement* (3rd ed., pp. 13–104). New York: Macmillan.

Ottenbacher, K. J. (1990).When is a picture worth a thousand p values? A comparison of visual and quantitative methods to analyze single subject data. *Journal of Special Education, 23,* 436–449.

Park, H., Marascuilo, L., & Gaylord-Ross, R. (1990).Visual inspection and statistical analysis of single-case designs. *Journal of Experimental Education, 58,* 311–320.

Raudenbush, S. W. & Bryk, A. S. (2002). *Hierarchical linear models: Applications and data analysis methods* (2nd ed.). Thousand Oaks, CA: Sage.

Salsburg, D. (2001). *The lady tasting tea: How statistics revolutionized science in the twentieth century*. New York: Freeman

Snijders, T. & Bosker, R. (1999). *Multilevel analysis: An introduction to basic and advanced multilevel modeling*. London: Sage.

Steiger, J. H. & Lind, J. C. (1980, May). *Statistically based tests for the number of common factors*. Paper presented at the annual meeting of the Psychometric Society, Iowa City, IA.

Suen, H. K. & Ary, D. (1987). Autocorrelation in applied behavior analysis: Myth or reality? *Behavioral Assessment, 9,* 125–130.

Todman, J. B. & Dugard, P. (2001). *Single-case and small-n experimental design: A practical guide to randomization tests*. Mahwah,NJ: Lawrence Erlbaum Associates.

Tucker, L. R., & Lewis, C. (1973). A reliability coefficient for maximum likelihood factor analysis. *Psychometrika, 38,* 1–10.

Wampold, B. E., & Worsham, N. L. (1986). Randomization tests for multiple-baseline designs. *Behavioral Assessment, 8,* 135–143.

Wolf, M. M. & Risley, T. R. (1971). Reinforcement: Applied research. In R. Glaser (Ed.). *The nature of reinforcement.* pp. (310–325). New York: Academic Press.

PART 5

Assessment

Advances in Neuroscience and Reading Disabilities

Elaine Clark *and* Janiece L. Pompa

Abstract

Current neuroscience research suggests that with appropriate interventions of sufficient duration and frequency, struggling readers can access quicker, more efficient neurologic pathways for reading. Some research has indicated, however, that effective remediation may require 90 minutes of daily direct instruction in reading, for one to three years, before permanent structural changes in the brain are seen. In this chapter, the application of neuroscience research to reading interventions is discussed. Components of effective remedial reading interventions are reviewed, with examples given of research-supported Tier 3 and Tier 4 instructional programs. The authors raise questions, however, about the sufficiency of RTI methods alone to identify students with specific learning disabilities, and design interventions that can effectively meet their educational needs.

Keywords: neuroscience and reading disabilities, neuroscience and dyslexia, reading remediation, reading disabilities, neural plasticity and reading, RTI and reading disability, reading interventions, learning disabilities

"Change alone is eternal, perpetual, immortal."
                                    – Arthur Schopenhauer

The past few decades have seen an explosion of research with regard to the neurological underpinnings of human learning and brain development, which have upended the notion that brain structure is fixed and immutable by adulthood. Neuroscientists have long agreed that brain cells die, but new brain cells cannot be generated, because if so, "how could we remember anything? For that matter, how could we maintain a constant self-identity?" (Gage, 2003, p. 47).

These beliefs have led to the assumption that learning disabilities and other developmental disorders are essentially a function of brain damage, or anomalies in brain development that can only be treated through reducing academic demands and implementing techniques to compensate for such brain-based disabilities. However, the development of neuroradiological techniques such as functional MRI (fMRI) scans, careful study of brain structure and

organization in humans and animals with cognitive disorders, and outcome research with regard to interventions for learning disorders, suggest that considerable improvement in academic outcomes is possible with interventions of sufficient length and intensity. Moreover, learning-disabled students who have received effective interventions for disorders such as dyslexia demonstrate neurological changes on fMRI that indicate that their brains have "normalized" or come to more closely resemble normal brains, in terms of which cortical areas are activated during the act of reading (Shaywitz, 2003). These exciting results suggest that, with well-designed intervention of sufficient intensity, the struggling learner is capable of changing his or her brain structure to facilitate learning and continued cognitive growth through experience. This chapter will describe the neurological underpinnings of learning, discuss challenges facing psychologists and educators involved in reading assessment and instruction, describe components of effective remediation programs for learning disabilities that are consistent with the available literature regarding the neurological basis of learning in children, and review research on certain commonly used programs.

Neurological Underpinnings of Learning
Neural Development

Prior to birth, the human brain follows a predetermined program of development that occurs in a fixed sequence. *Neurons*, which are the brain cells that transmit information throughout the brain, and *glial cells*, which function as the support system for neurons, develop from stem cells prior to birth. Following neurogenesis, or the generation of these neural cells, each cell travels to the part of the cortex where it belongs. Disturbances in this process of migration will result in aberrant cellular organization within the cortex. For example, if migration stops prematurely, cells destined for more distant layers of the cerebral cortex will remain within the inner layers of cells, which may result in disorders such as dyslexia or epilepsy (Kolb & Whishaw, 2009).

Following neural migration and differentiation into different types of neurons, each neuron begins to grow and develop its *dendrites*, or small tube-like structures that radiate from the cell body and function to receive information from other neurons. The formation of *dendritic spines*, or small nubs that protrude from each dendrite, enhances its information-receiving ability by providing a larger receptive area for the neuron. The *axon* of each neuron acts as a microscopic "cable" that extends towards other neurons to pass information to them by transmission of neurochemicals over the *synapse*, or the space between the axon of one neuron and the dendrite of another. These chemicals, or *neurotransmitters*, and their release at neuronal synapses are the basis of information transmission in the brain. Each individual's pattern of neuronal and synaptic connections, formed through a combination of genetic programming and the individual's interactions with the environment throughout his or her lifetime, is unique to each person. The neuroscientist Joseph LeDoux, who advanced this thesis in his book, *The Synaptic Self*, has quipped, "you are your synapses" (LeDoux, 2002, p. ix).

After birth, axons in the human brain continue to grow at the rate of one millimeter per day, while dendrites grow at a slower rate (Kolb & Whishaw, 2009). Synapses also continue to grow very rapidly until perhaps 18 months of age, when their rate of growth plateaus (Kolb, 1995). According to Kolb,

synapses are generally thought to be either *experience expectant* or *experience dependent*. Experience expectant synapses occur when certain neuronal circuits "expect," or require, sensory experiences in order to develop, while experience dependent synapses are those that are unique to each individual, according to his or her experience in life. In short, the experience expectant synapses in some cortical circuits are hard-wired into the brain and are common to all humans, while experience dependent synapses are shaped through the unique events that occur in each individual's life every minute of every day. These synapses, which respond to experience, are evidence that not only does the brain drive behavior, but one's behavior and experience also causes physical changes in the brain.

CRITICAL PERIOD

Animal research and studies of feral children have suggested that there are critical periods of development for certain cognitive abilities. In 1981, Hubel and Wiesel received the Nobel Prize after demonstrating that kittens deprived from receiving visual input from one eye were never able to develop binocular vision, indicating a critical period in the development of ocular dominance columns. The discovery in 1970 of the feral, nonverbal child, Genie, and results of intensive attempts to teach her language, suggested that although she eventually was able to speak in short sentences, her linguistic development was "extremely slow" and never reached normal levels (Curtis, 1977). These studies illustrate the importance of sensory experience in the development of experience-expectant cortical circuits; if the organism is deprived of such experience, synaptic connections fail to develop, and normal competence will never be achieved.

NEURAL DEVELOPMENT THROUGHOUT LIFESPAN

It is well known that other cortical components continue to develop and change throughout one's lifetime. For example, glial cells, which provide support and maintenance functions with regard to neurons, are generated throughout one's lifetime. Neuronal myelination, or the development of the lipid covering around the axons that facilitates neuronal transmission, has also been shown to begin shortly after birth, and continue until approximately 18 years of age in some areas of the brain (Kolb & Whishaw, 2009, p. 687). Other areas are fully myelinated much earlier in childhood, and it has been hypothesized that the sequence of myelination corresponds to which brain areas are most active and necessary at various stages of human development. Areas involved in sensorimotor function, which are critical in the development of infants and young children, myelinate first; areas that elaborate and refine simple sensory and motor functions myelinate next; and areas involved in higher-order functions such as executive functioning and abstract reasoning myelinate last. Recent MRI studies indicate that children diagnosed with attention deficit hyperactivity disorder (ADHD) have brains whose myelination is approximately two years behind their age-mates (Shaw et al., 2007). In addition, their brains are an average of 3% to 4% smaller than the brains of children without ADHD. Those with more severe symptoms had smaller frontal lobes and less gray matter in the temporal lobes, caudate nucleus, and cerebellum.

PLASTICITY

The existence of experience-dependent synapses and continued myelination into adulthood are possible mechanisms for the expression of plasticity in the human brain. In its widest sense, the term *plasticity* can encompass any kind of change that occurs in the brain, including changes in neurochemical processes, the formation of new neurons, or rewiring of brain circuits. In its narrowest sense, plasticity refers to synaptogenesis, or the creation of new synapses among neurons, which occurs throughout the human lifespan and possibly until death (LeDoux, 2002). However, in the past, many believed that new neurons did not grow after birth. Recent research indicates that neurogenesis can in fact take place in the adult brain, specifically in the olfactory bulb and the hippocampus (Gage, 2003). Although questions have been raised with regard to how adaptive such neurogenesis might be, given that proper synaptic connections with other neurons must be made in order to facilitate rather than hinder cognition, intriguing research suggests that environmental factors have considerable influence on dendritic growth and synaptic connectivity in the developing brain.

Kolb and Whishaw (2009) report that rats exposed to complex environments, with different toys to play with and cognitive stimulation, show increased neocortical size when compared to rats raised in an impoverished environment. These animals display increases in glial cell density, length of dendrites, density of dendritic spines, and synaptic size. Kempermann, Kuhn, and Gage (1997) found that mice who were reared in an enriched environment developed significantly more new neurons in the dentate gyrus when compared with littermates housed in standard conditions. It was suggested that this finding confirms the importance of education in stimulating brain development, and goes against the hypothesis that neurogenesis can only occur early in life. It has also been reported that rats trained to solve more difficult spatial problems have more acetylcholine, a neurotransmitter that is important in learning, than rats trained to solve less difficult problems (Renner and Rosenzweig 1987 in Doidge, 2007). Life in enriched environments increased brain weight by 5 percent in the cerebral cortex of animals. Neurons that were stimulated developed 25% more branching, grew in size, and increased the number of connections per neuron and their blood supply (Kolb & Whishaw, 2009, p. 670). The authors even reported that pregnant rat mothers who experienced complex environments, or were given daily tactile stimulation, had offspring with larger brains, possibly due to a greater number of neurons and/or glia, or more synapses. These rat pups also performed better on cognitive and motor tasks, suggesting that exposure to stimulation may benefit animals prior to birth, as well as after. Van Praag has also discovered that mice who exercise in a running wheel can nearly double the number of dividing cells in the hippocampus, the brain structure critical for learning and memory (Gage, 2003).

As the human brain continues to grow and develop, a complementary phenomenon known as *pruning* also begins in childhood. Research has shown that the volume of gray matter, or neuronal cell bodies, begins to decline as early as 6–7 years of age, and continues to decline throughout adolescence, while the volume of white matter, or myelinated axons of neurons, continues to increase (Kolb & Whishaw, 2009). The process of pruning appears to represent the elimination of neurons and synaptic connections that are not being stimulated, because the individual is not using them. At the same time, neurons and synapses that are being used and stimulated continue to develop, depending on the individual's unique experiences in life. For example, studies have shown that infants up to approximately one year of age are auditorally responsive to a variety of phonemes, including those that do not occur in their native languages. However, after they reach six months to one year of age, infants' ability to perceive phonemes that are not represented in their native language is significantly reduced (Kuhl et al., 1992; Minagawa-Kawai, Mori, Naoi, & Kojima, 2007).

PLASTICITY AND AGE

As the brain shows considerable synaptic development following birth, it has long been surmised that plasticity is greatest in the young brain. In the 1930s, Margaret Kennard observed monkeys with lesions in the motor cortex and noted that the motor deficits of infant monkeys were less severe than those of adult monkeys. This led to the postulate known as the *Kennard principle*, or the hypothesis that the effects of brain lesions are less in infants compared to adults. However, subsequent research has suggested that, in some ways, outcomes for very young children with brain injuries (particularly those who are one year of age or younger), are often worse than outcomes for adults. Even though recovery of basic functions such as speech seems to be better in children, they frequently display higher-level deficits which do not become obvious until later in life.

Although it is generally believed that interventions to remediate the effects of in-utero brain injury, or anomalies of brain development such as learning disabilities, are most successful when implemented early in life, there is increasing evidence that experience can change brain structure and functioning, even in adulthood. For example, Maguire, Woollett & Spiers (2006) have found that London taxi drivers have a larger posterior hippocampus than London bus drivers, because that particular area of the hippocampus specializes in learning and using complex spatial information. While bus drivers follow fixed and presumably well-learned and familiar routes on a daily basis, taxi drivers must navigate throughout the city using different roads to reach a variety of destinations, an activity that is thought to stimulate neuronal growth in the hippocampus.

PLASTICITY AND INTERVENTION

In discussing individuals with brain injury, Spevack (2007) noted, "Although there is a high degree of unpredictability related to outcome following neural insult, the potential for sparing or recovery of function holds particular promise for intervention efforts" (p. 9). Through the promise of plasticity, it is also likely that children and adults with learning disorders may be able to rewire brain circuits to improve their cognitive functioning. It is obvious that plasticity in the form of synaptic growth, long-term potentiation, and perhaps even the formation of new neurons in certain parts of the brain throughout the lifespan, constitute the framework of the brain's ability to learn and remember information.

Inasmuch as any academic intervention generally results in the learning of new information, and increased competence in cognitive or motor skills, changes in cerebral structure result in changes in the individual's functioning, and vice versa. In the past, such interventions have been evaluated with regard to the degree of success in improving outcomes for individuals with learning disorders. However, at some point in the future, advances in neuroimaging may allow health care professionals and educators to evaluate progress through assessing whether brain changes after intervention result in functioning that is more typical of normal individuals.

NEUROIMAGING AND DYSLEXIA

Perhaps the most widely published research in reading disabilities is that of the neuroscientist Sally Shaywitz. In her book, *Overcoming Dyslexia* (2003), Shaywitz reports that there are several neural pathways for reading in the left hemisphere, one in the frontal lobe, and another in the parietotemporal region. The frontal lobe reading circuit appears to be important in analyzing the letters in a word and matching them to their sounds, which Shaywitz terms a "slower, analytic" pathway that is used primarily by beginning readers. The occipitotemporal pathway at the back of the brain, or "word form" area, is thought to be an "express route" that is utilized by proficient readers. In less than 150 milliseconds, the pattern of a whole word is identified and recognized very quickly in the occipitotemporal area. Shaywitz states that after analyzing and correctly reading a particular word several times, the brain encodes the word form, which includes its spelling, pronunciation and meaning, and stores it in the occipitotemporal area. After that, when the skilled reader reads the word, all the information associated with the word form is activated as well.

Shaywitz notes that, regardless of age, good readers show greater activation of posterior pathways in the brain while reading when compared to anterior pathways. She states that neuroimaging indicates that older dyslexic children show *overactivation* in more anterior brain regions in both left and right hemispheres while reading, in an attempt to compensate for an inability to use the more efficient posterior pathway. After a year of intervention with an experimental reading program, dyslexic children who underwent neuroimaging displayed greatly reduced activation in the right hemisphere, and increased activation in the left hemisphere. Shaywitz noted that these activation patterns were "comparable to those obtained from children who had always been good readers" (p. 86). She termed this improvement "brain repair," and suggested that through proper intervention the brain had rewired itself in order to perform the reading task in a more competent and efficient manner. Although the dyslexic child may have been born with neural anomalies that make it difficult for him or her to utilize the more efficient left posterior brain area during the process of reading, Shaywitz' research suggests that it is possible for him or her to rewire and "normalize" brain processing to resemble that of normal readers.

Other research that has demonstrated different patterns of activation in the brains of children with dyslexia, as well as brain plasticity, includes that of Michael Merzenich and Paula Tallal (e.g., Merzenich, Tallal, Peterson, Miller, & Jenkins, 1998; Tallal, 1999; Temple et al., 2003). According to their research, prior to intensive interventions, the brains of children with dyslexia were found to be under-activated in the left temporoparietal region and inferior frontal gyrus, areas that have been implicated in phonological processing in both children and adults. Following intensive intervention, these areas showed increased activation during reading, and the brain patterns for processing language resembled more closely those of children without reading disabilities. Further, the children with dyslexia showed significant improvement in their reading skills. Temple and colleagues concluded that it may be that the program's "major direct initial benefit...lies in enhanced phonological awareness, with benefits to reading as a secondary consequence" (Temple et al., 2003, p. 2864).

This line of neuroscientific research has brought into focus questions regarding what type and how intense an intervention must be to facilitate lasting positive change in learning. To remediate reading disability, for example, Shaywitz recommends early intervention and intense, high quality instruction of sufficient duration as essential components of an effective reading program. The prevention of reading problems, starting with scientifically based programs in kindergarten, is preferred. When this is not possible, then remediation beginning as early as possible, preferably in first grade, is highly recommended. Although Shaywitz does not describe details of the intervention program she has used, she recommends that the intervention be tailored to the student's needs, personality and behavior, and be delivered by a qualified teacher. The program should be of sufficient intensity and duration to produce lasting change, and the student's progress should be monitored regularly in order to adjust the program to his or her needs. For some children, this may mean as many as 150-300 hours of intensive intervention (approximately an hour and a half per day for one to three years), in order for them to catch up to their peers in reading.

The Practice Side of Learning Disabilities: Can Science Trump Politics?

For several decades, there have been concerns about the effectiveness of U.S. schools in providing reading instruction to students that will prevent serious reading problems in the future, and the efficacy of specific educational practices has been hotly debated. Although some argue that methods based on whole-word instruction are best, given the logic of putting emphasis on meaning, comprehension, and teaching reading in authentic contexts, the majority of the research indicates that direct instruction in phonics constitutes the necessary scaffolding for building reading skills. Chall, in his book the *Great Debate* (Chall, 1983), evaluated the effectiveness of direct versus whole-word instruction, and found that overall, direct phonics-based instruction results in higher reading achievement for students in first through third grade. Although Chall's data showed that in the first grade, whole-word instruction resulted in a higher reading rate and better comprehension, the benefit of direct instruction became increasingly apparent in the higher grades, where mastery of basic decoding skills allowed for greater success in word recognition, spelling and comprehension. However, translating research findings to improved educational practice in order to implement scientifically-based reading programs in schools takes time, and may result in lost opportunities for struggling readers to improve their skills, as well as their future educational and vocational outcomes.

The book *A Nation at Risk: The Imperative for Educational Reform* (National Commission on Excellence in Education, 1983) addresses issues related to setting standards in the schools. Their conclusions led to a number of initiatives for educational reform at the state level, including setting minimum test score standards expected of students, and competency testing for classroom teachers. In Texas, for example, the legislature implemented a "no pass, no play" rule that prevented students who did not receive passing grades from playing or participating in other extracurricular activities, and established an accountability system for school districts that was linked to students' scores on statewide performance tests (McNeil, 2000). In addition, Texas had, for many years, served as the model for textbook adoption across the nation; when Texas legislators mandated that first-grade reading texts be phonics-based, other states across the nation followed suit.

Not surprisingly, George W. Bush made reading a major focus of his gubernatorial campaigns in Texas and in his bid for the White House. His campaign pledge mandating that all students read at grade level by the third grade was ultimately realized when No Child Left Behind (NCLB) was signed into law during his presidency (NCLB, 2001). In addition, when the Individuals with Disabilities Education Act (IDEA) was reauthorized as the Individuals with Disabilities Education Improvement Act (IDEIA, 2004) during President Bush's administration, this special education legislation was aligned with NCLB. IDEIA-2004 required that states provide data demonstrating that quality instruction was being provided in the regular education classroom to all students, and that no student would be disadvantaged from being able to benefit from instruction because of limited English language proficiency (Batsche, Kavale, & Kovaleski, 2006). It was mandated that school districts collect data to demonstrate how many students were meeting state-approved grade level standards in core areas of reading and mathematics, including oral expression, listening comprehension, written expression, basic reading skills, reading fluency skills, reading comprehension, mathematics calculation, and mathematics problem solving (IDEA, 20 U.S.C. & 1414(b)(5) et seq.).

Before IDEIA-2004 was finalized and signed into law, the Bush administration convened the President's Commission on the Excellence of Special Education to study the status of special education in the United States. According to the their report, which was published as *A New Era: Revitalizing Special Education for Children and their Families* (2001), a number of changes had become necessary since the previous IDEA legislation had been signed into law by Congress (IDEA, 1997). Changes were recommended in the procedures to determine a child's eligibility for special education services, particularly in the category of Specific Learning Disability (SLD). The commission concluded that the primary method for classification of SLD students, the use of the IQ–Achievement (Ach) discrepancy, was of questionable validity, as data provided to the commission indicated that many students classified as SLD under IDEA-97 were not learning disabled at all, but were rather "casualties of instruction." The commission subsequently rec-

ommended that states no longer be required to use the IQ–Ach discrepancy, although they could still choose to do so. Instead, it was recommended that states be allowed to use a Response to Intervention (RTI) model to determine which students would be classified as having SLD.

The Logic of RTI in Identifying and Serving Students with SLD

The logic of using an RTI model for identifying students who are not benefiting from the regular education curriculum is clear. What is not clear is if RTI methods alone will reliably distinguish students who are unexpected underachievers, or truly learning disabled (Lyons et al., 2001), from those who are low achievers for other reasons. Obviously, research will be needed to determine whether RTI will prove itself to be a superior method to IQ–Ach discrepancy in identifying students early enough to make a difference in learning outcomes.

Proponents of the RTI model argue that the IQ–Ach discrepancy approach is based on a "wait to fail" system, and that RTI allows for much earlier identification of students with a true learning disability. As a result, under RTI, students with early reading difficulties should be identified early enough to prevent the emergence of serious problems later. However, it can be argued that the multiple components of RTI may increase the amount of time teachers spend experimenting with interventions, including some that are not sufficiently robust to impact students' learning. Further, the implementation of special education services for students who could benefit may be delayed. These delays may actually result in an increase in the number of students identified with a learning disability in the upper grades, where RTI has not been implemented as often. This is not meant to imply that early identification for special education services is the "answer" for all students with a reading disability or any SLD; however, schools should be doing much better than the 30% improvement in reading outcomes from elementary school to the 9th grade reported by Vellutino and his colleagues (Vellutino, Scanlon, & Lyon, 2000). Such findings have been used as an indictment against the educational system in the U.S. and to demand reform, with RTI as as a prime component.

According to a report by Torgesen (2007), schools in Florida that have implemented RTI and are using the Reading First program have dramatically reduced the number of students being identified with reading disabilities from kindergarten (K) to 3rd grade. There was a 67% drop in identified students from K to first grade, a 53% drop from first to second grade, and a 42% drop from second to third grade, for an overall decrease of 81% of students classified as SLD in the sample studied. It may be assumed that the reason for this drop is that RTI is working as intended, and the number of students with significant reading problems is decreasing. Data do show that the number of students performing below the 20th percentile on tests of pre-reading skills at the end of kindergarten, and on tests of reading comprehension at the end of first, second, and third grades, was reduced. However, as Torgesen points out, the reduction in the percentage of students classified as SLD was higher than the percentage of students who showed improvement on standardized testing, suggesting that a number of students who were not identified as having a learning disability continued to struggle on standardized testing. Torgesen's conclusion is that it is likely that part of the decrease in the number of students being classified as SLD is due to an increase in the level of confidence that teachers and schools have about their ability to meet student learning needs without making a referral for further diagnostic assessment and possible special education services, whether or not that confidence is warranted.

Making the wrong assumption about students with reading disabilities, or, for that matter, reading difficulties in general, can obviously interfere with students receiving critical services. With RTI there is also a very real possibility that school psychologists will not be involved in decisions regarding interventions, including special education services. Even if concerns arise about a particular student, there may be a tendency for the schools to turn for guidance to other school personnel who lack the educational backgrounds of school psychologists. School psychologists have been trained in psychometrics and diverse assessment methods, and possess knowledge of the wide range of conditions that may result in a student having serious reading difficulties. Reading problems may occur for a variety of reasons other than a "true" learning disability, such as problems with inattention and/or short-term memory, behavioral and emotional problems, and lack of English proficiency.

School psychologists are uniquely skilled in the knowledge of the appropriate measures to use to evaluate the wide range of possible explanations for a student's reading problems, to understand what each method's advantages and shortcomings are, and to know in which situations it would be helpful for a student to undergo a formal psychological and educational assessment. According to Fletcher et al. (Fletcher, Francis, Morris, & Lyon, 2005), students who are performing below the 25th percentile should be evaluated to determine what factors are responsible for their failure to meet age and/or grade standards. This includes ruling out competing explanations such as intellectual disabilities, serious emotional disturbance, etc. However, Fletcher and his colleagues argue that in order to determine if a student has a learning disability, the student's response to instructional interventions must also be assessed.

Assumptions and Adequacy of RTI

Inherent in the RTI model is the requirement that assessments be technically sound and sensitive to individual student growth (Busch & Reschly, 2007). IDEIA-2004 further requires that the evaluation of SLD include a variety of psychometrically valid assessment instruments to insure that "relevant functional, developmental, and academic information" is gathered [(Section 614(b) (2))]. Given this provision, as well as longstanding concerns that the IQ–Ach discrepancy model did not provide a consistent means to determine what constituted a "severe discrepancy," many expect the changes proposed in the IDEIA-2004 legislation to result in better identification of students in need of special education, as well as improved outcomes for students referred for these services (Busch & Reschly, 2007; Yell & Drasgow, 2007). One question that has arisen, however, is how to define the level and/or duration of nonresponsiveness to instruction in the general education classroom sufficient for a child to be identified as having a reading disability, or SLD, in the first place.

The first step in the RTI process assumes that regular education teachers are providing high-quality instruction in the classroom that should be effective for all non-disabled students, and that these teachers are able to reliably identify students who are at risk of being nonresponsive to their instructional efforts and may need further assistance. For students who are so identified, it is also assumed that additional instructional assistance, such as individualized tutoring at school, will be sufficiently effective to remediate the learning difficulties of all but the student with a true disability. Next, students who do not respond at the expected level are either automatically considered eligible for special education services under SLD, or undergo a comprehensive assessment involving standardized tests to evaluate the possibility of SLD and rule out other factors or disabilities, such as an intellectual disability. It may occur, however, that students with other serious problems that explain their nonresponsiveness to instruction in the regular classroom, such as students from different cultural backgrounds and/or disadvantaged situations, those who speak English as a second language, and so on, will either not be properly assessed or will be misdiagnosed.

IDEIA-2004 requires states to provide data that demonstrate quality instruction is being provided to all students in the regular education classroom, and that no student is disadvantaged from being able to benefit from instruction because of limited English language proficiency. Further, IDEIA-04 requires that decisions regarding special education eligibility be based on procedures that are nondiscriminatory and fair (Yell & Drasgow, 2007). It is, nonetheless, unclear how RTI methods, such as the selection of measures and interpretation of outcomes, can be defended as being objective and lacking bias, given the fact there are no objective criteria as yet for "nonresponsiveness" to instruction. Instead, the decision about "nonresponsiveness" is left up to educators who often do not have the tools to make the call. This is not to say that students with reading disabilities will not be identified for services; in fact, Reynolds (2008) warns that RTI may result in higher numbers of students with lower achievement and lower ability (e.g., IQs below 90) being classified as SLD. Reynolds argues that ability tracking is inevitable, given the fact that intelligence and learning ability are highly correlated. Another factor that may increase the probability of over-identification of certain groups of students as SLD is the fact that socioeconomic status (SES) has been shown to impact reading outcomes. For example, first grade students of lower SES have been found to have half the knowledge of vocabulary than same-age peers from upper SES families (White, Graves, & Slater, 1990).

Potential Benefits of Combining Models and Methods

Fletcher and his colleagues (2005) agree with many other researchers in the field that the RTI model, like the IQ–Ach discrepancy model, will not be sufficient for identifying students with SLD. However, unlike some researchers, Fletcher et al. do not see the value in "extensive assessments of cognitive, neuropsychological, or intellectual skills" (p. 519) for identifying learning disabilities. Instead, these researchers have proposed a hybrid method where RTI can be combined with standardized achievement testing for

SLD determination. A number of school psychologists and neuropsychologists have argued to extend the standard testing battery beyond achievement testing to include measures of cognitive skills found to be important for the process of reading, including phonemic processing, rapid naming, working memory, processing speed, visuospatial processing, and other critical reading skills identified by researchers.

Hale, Kaufman, Naglieri, and Kavale (2006), like others in the field, including Feifer and Della Tofallo (2007), Reynolds (2008), and Semrud-Clikeman (2005), recommend that comprehensive assessment be included in a process to identify students suspected of learning disabilities. This battery would include cognitive tests that are sufficient to address the deficits defined by IDEIA-2004 as being the essence of SLD, or "a disorder in one or more of the basic psychological processes involved in understanding or in using language, spoken or written"... (Public Law 108-446, Section 602 (30). To this end, various models have been proposed, including that of Hale et al. (2006) who have proposed a three-tiered identification model that combines RTI with traditional psychological testing.

According to the Three-Tier Identification Model for SLD, Tier 1 would involve the use of the standard RTI method, whereas Tier 2 would include more problem-solving approaches within the RTI framework. At Tier 3, a comprehensive assessment would be conducted that includes the administration of standardized tests of achievement and other cognitive skills that underlie the reading process. The reading literature is fairly consistent in demonstrating that individuals who are poor readers generally have problems reading because they have not mastered phonics (Stanovich & Siegel, 1994); and young children who are at risk for SLD often have specific problems with phonological processing and naming speed (Wills, 2007). As a result, it makes sense to insure that tests that evaluate the underlying processing deficits of children with reading disabilities be administered. Whether another goal of the three-tier identification model will be realized— to provide effective interventions based on skill deficiencies—will have to be determined by scientific investigations of aptitude–treatment interaction (ATI) in this model.

The merits of ATI have been debated for quite some time, due to literature that has found that matching interventions to student strengths does not result in improved outcomes with regard to academic performance (Cronbach & Snow, 1969; Snow, 1977; Tobias, 1976). However, researchers have continued to look for ways that might allow a match of ability to treatment to improve learning outcomes. According to Fuchs and Young's 2006 study that analyzed data from 13 different studies on 1,542 children with serious reading problems, IQ was shown to be predictive of different learning outcomes for different age groups of children receiving different reading interventions. Although IQ was not a perfect predictor, it was found to be a stronger and more reliable predictor for older students, who were receiving complex reading instruction that included orthographic pattern recognition, interpretation of meaning from written text, and writing, than it was for younger students receiving a less complex intervention, phonics awareness training. As the studies that Fuchs and Young analyzed did not use randomized control trials, further research is needed before drawing any firm conclusions about IQ as a variable in predicting ATI. However, this research serves as a reminder that further study is needed on the topic of ATI, and that models such as those being proposed by Hale and his colleagues (2006) are worth investigation to determine their effects. This may also stimulate research on how RTI methods— in particular, curriculum-based measurement (CBM) probe data—can be used to predict response to interventions specifically tailored to the cognitive strengths of students who are not responding to regular instructional methods.

How researchers and practitioners will judge the strength of the RTI model is yet to be determined, but it will undoubtedly be judged based on its claim that it screens students earlier, and identifies students who have a "true" learning disability sooner, so that students do not have to "wait to fail" before being referred for special education services. Given the multiple steps involved in the identification process, however, students still have to "wait to fail" to respond to the regular classroom curriculum, as well as more specialized interventions, before being considered eligible for special education. In most schools, this means a longer wait before initiating assessment to determine if the student has a reading disability, and a longer wait for additional remedial interventions to begin. Although not intended as a discrepancy model, the steps necessary for identification and service effectively constitute a "grade-level expectant discrepancy" rather than an IQ–Ach Discrepancy. Unfortunately, the model may also prove to discriminate between teachers who are capable of providing effective instruction for even the poorest of readers, and those who lack the knowledge and skill to teach readers with more difficult learning challenges.

Evidence for Effective Reading Interventions

Research by the National Research Council (NRC) in the late 1990s showed that many teachers lacked sufficient knowledge about the foundations of reading, and were not properly trained to implement programs that had been shown to be effective for instructing students in reading (Snow, Burns, & Griffin, 1998). Researchers have shown that phonetically-based instruction delivered via direct systematic instruction in kindergarten and first grade is the most effective method to reduce the chances of a child having serious reading problems. One study estimated that such instruction could reduce the number of children identified with reading problems to fewer than 10% of all students (Lyon, Fletcher, Fuchs, & Chhabra (2006; Torgesen, 2000).

Normally, during the first year of life, there is rapid development of the infant's auditory phonological processing abilities, as he or she refines skills to discriminate sounds in his or her native language during that period. It is not until direct instruction, however, that children begin to understand grapheme-phoneme correspondences, which helps them to understand more fully the phonological structure of words. Accordingly, children in kindergarten are more dependent on visual features of printed words, frequently identifying words by initial or final letter(s) rather than using the auditory properties of the letters to sound out words (Rayner, Foorman, Perfetti, Pesetsky, & Seidenberg, 2001). Not surprisingly, when children struggle to learn grapheme-phoneme correspondences despite receiving direct reading instruction, it can take a substantial amount of intensive instruction for them to learn to read. According to the National Reading Panel (NRP, 2000), reading instruction for children with reading difficulties must be explicit and systematic, organized to teach children to manipulate one or two types of phonemes at one time, and delivered in small groups of young children. Kindergarteners who receive these types of interventions showed significantly better reading and spelling skills, and first graders demonstrated improved decoding, spelling, and reading comprehension skills, when compared to baseline. The Reading Panel data also indicated that direct phonics instruction can yield some positive results in reading decoding, spelling, and fluency up until the sixth grade. However, little improvement was noted in reading comprehension, suggesting that different and/or additional interventions may be appropriate for older students with reading disability.

Despite NCLB's legislative mandate to use such empirically based instructional programs, many reading programs that are being used in the schools do not have strong empirical support. Even Reading First, which has been shown to be beneficial for students in Florida schools (Torgesen, 2007), has not received the high marks expected from researchers. According to results from an impact study by the National Center for Education Evaluation and Regional Assistance (NCEERA), despite the fact that data show that teachers in Reading First programs spent considerable instructional time on the program's core components, students did not demonstrate expected gains in reading comprehension (Gamse, Bloom, Kemple, & Jacob, 2008). Other studies of instructional programs have found similar results, which have been argued by some to be a function of philosophical differences of opinion on how students should be taught reading, rather than reflecting the science of reading (Foorman, Fletcher, Francis, & Schatschneider, 2000). Whereas some educators champion the progressive, student-centered learning approach of John Dewey, others prefer approaches that emphasize uniformity in methods and curriculum (Rayner et al., 2001) For those interested in using approaches based on scientific evidence, regardless of philosophical viewpoint, there are resources to help.

In 2002, the U.S. Department of Education's Institute of Education Sciences (IES) established the What Works Clearinghouse (WWC) in order to provide researchers, educators, policymakers, and the public with information about interventions that have been shown to be effective. There are other syntheses of research on educational programs, including the Best Evidence Encyclopedia (BEE) (www.bestevidence.org); however, the WWC is thought to have particular importance for policy, given the fact it has been endorsed by the U.S. Department of Education (Slavin, 2008). The WWC also has rigorous standards for selecting studies to evaluate, including the requirement that the research design employ randomized controlled trials, which have been described as "the most rigorous way of determining whether a cause–effect relation exists between treatment and outcome and for assessing the cost effectiveness of a treatment" (WWC, 2007). The WWC then analyzes studies based on research design quality, statistical significance of results, size of difference between intervention group participants and those in a comparison group, and consistency of findings across studies. Finally, the WWC rates intervention effectiveness

according to the following six categories: positive, potentially positive, mixed, no discernible effects, potentially negative, or negative.

Examples of Remedial Reading Program from What Works Clearinghouse

For the purposes of this chapter, three remedial reading programs were selected for review because they met WWC standards for investigation, and incorporated important components of instruction, especially the alphabetic principle.

READING RECOVERY

Reading Recovery (RR) is a short-term tutorial intervention program designed to support regular classroom instruction for the bottom 20% of readers in the first grade. The goal of the program is to reduce the number of first graders who struggle to read, and to promote literacy. The reading intervention consists of 30-minute lessons delivered daily for 12 to 20 weeks in an intensive one-on-one format. The lessons incorporate phonological awareness, visual perception of letters, word recognition, phonics/decoding skills, phonics/structural analysis, fluency/automaticity, and comprehension. According to a report from the Florida Center for Reading Research (FCRR), ample opportunities are provided for practice to increase reading fluency, and vocabulary and comprehension activities are infused throughout the lessons.

The program is considered a balanced literacy approach, as students are required to reread texts that reinforce word recognition and reading comprehension, while at the same time teachers provide immediate feedback regarding oral reading errors, and information about the alphabetic system. The program, however, is neither explicit nor systematic. Instead, teachers design daily lessons in accord with their assessment of student progress in the curriculum. Needless to say, Reading Recovery requires that teachers be knowledgeable about reading, and highly skilled as interventionists. The program requires teachers to receive multi-tiered training, starting with a full year of academic preparation, after which follow-up training sessions and coaching by expert RR teachers are provided.

Based on data from 700 first grade students, aggregated from five different studies, the WWC concluded that Reading Recovery had a positive effect on alphabetics and general reading achievement scores, and potentially positive effects on reading comprehension and fluency.

CORRECTIVE READING

Corrective Reading is a scripted, fast-paced direct instruction approach for students in the third through twelfth grades who have a reading disability and/or are behind one or more grade levels in reading. The goals of the program are to improve reading decoding, fluency, and comprehension. The instruction is typically offered in small groups of four or five students; however, it can be delivered in a classroom for up to 20 students. Instruction is provided 45 minutes a day for 4 or 5 days each week. Corrective Reading has 65 lessons of graduated difficulty. The first level teaches nonreaders basic decoding skills using rhyming, sounding out, sentence reading, and story reading, whereas the second level targets struggling nonfluent readers who confuse similar words. At the end of the first level, students are expected to read 90 words per minute, and at the end of the second level, 120 words per minute. The third level is for students who can competently decode words, but have below average vocabulary and skill in reading complex sentences.

Minimal teacher preparation is required, although teachers must undergo approximately seven hours of training on how to deliver the program. A tutorial CD-ROM is also available, as are coaches. Although Corrective Reading instructional components have been found to be consistent with the instructional reading research, most studies have been limited to investigations of program impact on decoding skills. Further, few have used random assignment of students to different instructional conditions.

Only one study reviewed by the WWC used a random control trial, Torgesen et al.'s (2006) study of 44 third grade students who received Corrective Reading, and 35 who received regular classroom reading instruction. Results showed that the group who received Corrective Reading had significantly higher scores on tests of phonics, sight word efficiency, and reading fluency compared to peers who received regular class instruction. The WWC concluded that Corrective Reading had potentially positive effects on alphabetics and fluency. Since only word-level skills were assessed by Torgesen and colleagues, no effects were reported for reading comprehension.

WILSON READING SYSTEM

The Wilson Reading System is a highly structured, fast-paced 12-step reading and writing program based on Orton-Gillingham's multisensory principles. The program was originally designed for second to twelfth grade students with dyslexia; however, it has been expanded to all learners in the second grade and up, who have difficulty learning to read. Core skills are taught in phonemic awareness, alphabetic principles, spelling, vocabulary, word fluency, and comprehension. A unique feature of the Wilson system is a "sound tapping" component to help students learn to discriminate phonemes in a word (by segmenting and sound blending) to help them decode and encode words. From the start of the program, comprehension skills are taught using visualization techniques, and children are exposed to tasks intended to build fluency, such as practice on word lists and sentences and timed drills.

The system can be implemented in a small group format with a reading specialist or regular classroom teacher, or, for students with a learning disability, in an intensive format with a Wilson-certified teacher (delivered individually or in small groups). Regardless of the format, the intervention involves continuous interaction between the teacher and student, and provides opportunity for instructional feedback and progress monitoring. Introductory workshops, online training, and follow-up tutorial sessions are provided. Certification is also available by Wilson, but involves more extensive training and a supervised practicum.

The Wilson Reading System lessons are explicit, and typically last 60 to 90 minutes. Instruction is also systematic, with 12 incremental steps. Students are not allowed to progress to the next step until the earlier steps have been mastered. Steps 1 through 6 provide instruction in the basic skills for decoding and encoding, and Steps 7 through 12 cover more advanced skills in word analysis, vocabulary, and comprehension. Regular monitoring of progress by teachers is required. Although the program is consistent with research on effective reading components, the design of most studies has been weak, as many studies fail to provide data on comparison groups.

According to the WWC, only one study they reviewed met their standard for use of a randomized control trial, that of Torgesen et al (2006). The study was of 53 third grade students receiving the Wilson Reading program, and 18 who received regular reading instruction. Both groups of students were assessed using tests measuring phonemic decoding/sight word efficiency, word identification/word attack, reading fluency, and comprehension. Results from the study demonstrated a small but potentially positive effect for learning alphabetics. There were no discernible effects for either fluency or reading comprehension.

SHARED PROGRAM COMPONENTS AND NEEDS

All three of these programs are intensive phonics-based programs intended for early elementary students who struggle with reading, including those with learning disabilities. The focus of each program is on improving skills in alphabetics, fluency, and reading comprehension; however, there seems to be less emphasis on actual text comprehension, with the primary emphasis on improving decoding skills essential for understanding written text (Feifer & Della Toffalo, 2007). Further, there was relatively little attention paid to writing in any of the programs, with only one incorporating a specific component to build writing skills, the Wilson Reading System. There is relatively little research on the pedagogy of teaching either writing or reading comprehension to students, and many programs lack sufficient components to build these skills (National Reading Panel, 2000). Reading comprehension requires readers to import information from outside the text they are currently reading, so it is easy to understand how struggling readers can lag so far behind their peers who are proficient readers (Rayner et al., 2001), as they presumably have had less access to information in print, which has been gained by their peers who are more competent readers.

All three programs employ skills of graduated difficulty, which are taught to individual students or small groups of no more than five students. The instruction for each program is provided daily (or a minimum of 4 days a week), and lessons typically last between 45 and 90 minutes each day. Methods for progress monitoring are included to determine whether students are making expected progress; if not, instruction is modified or repeated to insure mastery of prerequisite skills. Each program provides teacher training; however, each differs in terms of how extensive the training is. The more explicit and systematic the approach, the more extensive the training required to deliver the intervention with fidelity.

Other Programs Supported by Research

FAST FORWORD®

Fast ForWord® is an intensive computer-based intervention program designed to assist students who are having difficulty reading and perceiving language spoken at a normal rate. The program is based on research by Merzenich and Tallal and others who have demonstrated that developmental dyslexia is associated with difficulty processing phonological inputs (e.g., Temple et al., 2003).

In addition to behavioral deficits in phonological processing, studies of brain function have shown a neural deficit in dyslexia during phonological processing (5). Individuals with dyslexia have decreased activity (relative to controls) in left temporo-parietal cortex during phonological processing. This disrupted neural response has been shown in a number of studies (5), across different methodologies [positron emission tomography (PET; refs. 6–10) and functional MRI (fMRI; ref. 11)], with various analysis methods [whole-brain statistical parametric mapping (SPM; refs. 6–8 and 12) and region of interest (ROI; refs. 9–11)] in multiple tasks [letter rhyme (7, 11), pseudo-word processing (6, 8, 10, 11), and explicit and implicit (6, 8) tasks], across ability levels [compensated (6–8) and severely (10) dyslexic], and in different languages (8). The above results were initially reported in adults, making it uncertain whether they reflected an initial impairment or a long-term compensation. This disruption, however, is also evident in children with dyslexia (12, 13), which suggests that it is fundamental to the disorder.

To address this deficit, Fast ForWord® uses acoustically modified (or nonlinguistic) speech, with rapid frequency transitions slowed and amplified to improve auditory and language processing. There are two parts to the Fast ForWord® intervention: first, a language component that attempts to help children develop skills involving memory, attention, processing, and sequencing; and second, a reading component, which focuses on skills such as sound–letter comprehension, phonological awareness, and beginning word recognition.

There are seven separate sets of tasks in the program (Friel-Patti, Frome, & Gilliam, 2001). The first group of tasks, which train auditory discrimination, consist of exercises in auditory discrimination through identification of a two-sound sequence of pairs of frequency glides presented in rapid succession (Circus Sequence). The "Old MacDonald's Flying Farm" task trains the ability to distinguish between changes in initial phonemes of consonant-vowel syllables, and the "Phoneme Identification" task helps improve ability to distinguish phonemes by learning to identify a game character that produced a target sound. After successfully completing these exercises, the second group of tasks progresses to four exercises involving auditory processing of whole words. "Phonic Words" involves distinguishing between pairs of words whose initial consonants are different. "Phonic Match" resembles the card game "Concentration" and requires the child to identify two tiles in an array that are associated with the same word. The target words vary in either initial or final consonant, and contain the same vowel sound. "Block Commander" trains the child's listening comprehension and attention by requiring the child to follow increasingly long and complex commands to move different geometric shapes on a three-dimensional game board. "Listening Comprehension Builder" requires the child to match spoken sentences with pictures of actions, and complex relational themes involving increasingly more difficult phonological, syntactic and morphological sentence structures.

Children begin at the basic level in each of the games, and as they achieve proficiency, progress to more advanced levels. Throughout each module, the child's successful performance is rewarded by extra points, songs, and entertaining visual displays. A student generally spends 20 to 30 minutes working on each five of the seven modules (or a total of 100 to 150 minutes per day), five days a week, until 90% completion is reached for each module. The program typically takes 6 to 8 weeks for successful completion, which is defined as having undergone at least 20 days of training (although 30 days is preferred) and having completed at least 80 percent of a majority of the games (Rouse & Krueger, 2004). This typically takes 12 to 16 weeks; however, the intervention can be shortened to 4 to 8 weeks, if the amount of time students spend on the program increases to 90 to 100 minutes a day.

It should be noted that some researchers have found the Fast ForWord® program to be ineffective, or at least no more effective than other interventions available (Rouse and Krueger, 2004). There has also been criticism that the program may be training attention rather than language processing, as there have been no controlled studies comparing dyslexics who did not improve with those who did. Concerns have also been raised that the researchers' commercial interest in the program may render their research less than objective. Relatively few outcomes studies exist in the scientific literature that compare Fast ForWord® with regular classroom instruction or another reading intervention, or are not studies associated with the program's distributor, the Scientific Learning Corporation. According to the What Works Clearinghouse (WWC, 2007), however, the only study they reviewed that met their standard of using a randomized control trial was conducted by Scientific Learning. The WWC concluded that data provided by the distributor did not show a significant difference between first, second and third graders who received Fast ForWord® and their same-age peers who did not. Nonetheless, the WWC concluded that the program had a positive effect on phonics skills and a mixed effect on reading comprehension. Clearly, more high-quality independent research needs to be conducted on this program; however, Fast ForWord® remains one of the only remediation programs for learning disabilities that ties neuroscience research to direct interventions, and demonstrates change in the brain's processing of language. According to the data that are available, the brains of children who go through the Fast ForWord® program more closely resemble the brains of normal readers (Temple et al., 2003).

ARROWSMITH SCHOOL PROGRAM

This is another reading intervention that has received support, albeit via anecdotal report. Doidge (2007) reviews the account of Barbara Arrowsmith Young, who as a child had auditory and visual memory abilities that fell at the 99th percentile, but struggled with severe learning disabilities. She had difficulty pronouncing words, engaging in spatial reasoning, being aware of the location of her body in space, a narrowed field of vision, and difficulty associating and relating symbols. As a result, she had problems with grammar, math reasoning, logic, and comprehending cause-and-effect relationships. At age 28, while in graduate school, Ms. Young read about plasticity in the rat brain and determined to remediate her own disabilities, as she felt that relying on compensatory techniques had been less than satisfactory.

After intensive and exhausting self-intervention, Ms. Young founded the Arrowsmith School in Toronto, Canada, in 1980. Her intervention program involves up to 40 hours of assessment, geared towards identifying individual brain functions in need of remediation. With the aid of computerized exercises, foreign language study to improve the student's visual memory, the use of eye patches on the left eye to direct visual information to the left hemisphere, memorization of poems to improve auditory memory, and other techniques she has devised, Doidge reports that Dr. Young's program has helped students achieve significant improvements in their reading and mathematical abilities. However, no data was provided to support these claims or quantify the degree of improvement in academic skills or underlying cognitive processes.

Final Comments

Whether Fast ForWord®, the Arrowsmith School Program, or any others described in this chapter will fulfill their initial promise in the years to come is uncertain. What is more certain is that neuroscience will continue providing insights into the brains of learners, including the neural pathways used by learners with different abilities, and ways that the brain may "rewire" itself in response to interventions, and allow learners more efficient direct access routes for learning to read. A number of intriguing studies described in this chapter have shown that brain change can occur in individuals who engage in intense practice of certain activities. One of the studies demonstrated neuronal growth in the hippocampus of London taxi drivers who spend numerous hours and days driving all kinds of different routes to locations around the city (Maguire, Woollett & Spiers, 2006). Over the next several years, we can expect to learn a great deal more about how the young brain processes information, and what, if any, differences exist for children with reading disabilities and those without. Ultimately, it is hoped that studies such as these will lead to important insights about the best ways to teach children with different abilities in order to facilitate desired learning outcomes in an ATI model.

The type of research that needs to be conducted, however, including basic neuroscientific studies and investigations into the neuropsychology of reading, will require a substantial commitment by the government to fund studies. In a speech to the annual meeting of the National Academy of Sciences in April of 2009, President Barack Obama stated that he hoped to increase total spending on scientific research and development by government and industry to 3% of the gross domestic product of the United States, an increase of approximately $70 million (Aldhous, 2009). If fully realized, Mr. Obama's pledge of increased funding may provide the stimulus for research that will enable educators to find more efficient and productive ways to help struggling learners, including those who struggle to read, bringing us one step closer to the ambitious goals of quality instruction in reading and universal literacy mandated by No Child Left Behind. At the very least, we should expect that by the time the next IDEA is signed into law, poor readers with SLD will no longer be described as "casualties of instruction"; instead, they will be referred to as the "benefactors of interventions" selected based on science, not politics or philosophical viewpoint. To facilitate this outcome, whatever advances in the neuroscience of reading that are realized over the next several years must be widely communicated to the public, and efforts should be made to insure that legislators who are responsible for making policy, administrators who select programs, and teachers responsible for implementing these each day, are all informed as to "what works" in teaching reading.

References

Aldhous, P. (2009). *Obama vows to increase funding for basic science.*Retrieved on May 22, 2010 from http://www.newscientist.com/article/dn17037-obama-vows-to-increase-funding-for-basic-science.html.

Aylward, E.H., Richards, T.L., Berninger, V.W., et al. (2003). Instructional treatment associated with changes in brain activation in children with dyslexia. *Neurology, 22,* 212–219.

Batsche, G.M., Kavale, K.A., & Kovaleski, J.F. (2006). Competing views: A dialogue on response to intervention. *Assessment for Effective Intervention, 32,* 6–20.

Busch, T.W. & Reschly, A.L. (2007). Progress monitoring in reading. *Assessment for Effective Interventions, 32*(4), 202–213.

Chall, J.S. (1983). *Learning to read: The great debate, 2nd* edition. New York: McGraw-Hill.

Cronbach, L.J. & Snow, R.E. (1969). *Individual differences in learning ability as a function of instructional variability: Final report.* Washington DC: Office of Education, Bureau of Elementary and Secondary Education.

Curtis, S. (1977). *Genie: A psycholinguistic study of a modern-day "wild child".* Academic Press, New York.

Doidge, N. (2007). *The brain that changes itself: Stories of personal triumph from the frontiers of brain science.* New York: Penguin.

Feifer, S.G. & Della Toffalo, D.A. (2007). *Integrating RTI with cognitive neuropsychology: A scientific approach to reading.* Middlestown, MD: School Neuropsych Press.

Fletcher, J.M., Francis, D.J., Morris, R.D., & Lyon, G.R. (2005). Evidence-based assessment of learning disabilities in children and adolescents. *Journal of Clinical Child and Adolescent Psychology, 34,* 506–522.

Foorman, B.R., Fletcher, J.M., Francis, D.J., & Schatschneider, C. (2000). Response: Misrepresentation of research by other researchers. *Educational Researcher, 29,* 27–37.

Friel-Patti, S., Frome, L.D., Gillam, R.B. (2001). Looking ahead: An introduction to five exploratory studies of Fast ForWord. *American Journal of Speech-Language Pathology, 10*(3), 195–203.

Fuchs, D. & Young, C.L. (2006). On the irrelevance of intelligence in predicting responsiveness to reading instruction. *Exceptional Children, 73*(1), 8–30.

Gage, F. (2003). Brain, repair yourself. *Scientific American, 298*(3), 47–53.

Gamse, B.C., Bloom, H.S., Kemple, J.J., & Jacob, R. T. (2008). *Reading First impact study: Interim Report.* Retrieved on September 25, 2008 from http://ies.ed.gov/ncee/pubs/html.

Hale, J.B., Kaufman, A., Naglieri, J.A., Kavale, K.A., (2006). Implementation of IDEA: Integrating response to intervention and cognitive assessment methods. *Psychology in the Schools, 43*(7), 753–770.

Individuals with Disabilities Education Act of 1990, 20 USC 1400 *et seq.* (1990) (amended in 1997).

Individuals with Disabilities Education Improvement Act of 2004, 20 USC 1400 *et seq.* (2004) (reauthorization of IDEA of 1990).

Kempermann, G., Kuhn, H.G., & Gage, F.H. (1997). More hippocampal neurons in adult mice living in an enriched environment. *Nature*. 386, 493–495.

Kolb, B. (1995). *Brain Plasticity and Behavior*. New Jersey: Erlbaum.

Kolb, B. & Whishaw, I.W. (2009). *Fundamentals of human neuropsychology, 6th edition*. New York, Worth Publishers.

Kuhl, P. K., Williams, K. A., Lacerda, F., Stevens, K. N., & Lindblom, B. (1992). Linguistic experience alters phonetic perception in infants by 6 months of age. *Science, 255*, 606–608 [Citation as below: Linguistic Experience Alters Phonetic Perception in Infants by 6 Months of Age Author(s): Patricia K. Kuhl, Karen A. Williams, Francisco Lacerda, Kenneth N. Stevens, Björn Lindblom Source: Science, New Series, Vol. 255, No. 5044 (Jan. 31, 1992), pp. 606–608 Published by: American Association for the Advancement of Science Stable URL: http://www.jstor.org/stable/2876832 Accessed: 28/06/2010 16:35]

LeDoux, J. (2002). *The Synaptic Self: How Our Brains Become Who We Are*. New York, Viking.

Lyon, G.R., Fletcher, J.M., Fuchs, L.S. & Chhabra, V. (2006). Learning disabilities. In E. Mash & R. Barkley (Eds.), *The treatment of childhood disorders, 3rd* edition. New York: Guilford Press.

Lyon, G.R., Fletcher, J.M., Shaywitz, S.E., Shaywitz, B.A., Torgesen, J.K., Wood, F.B., et al. (2001). Rethinking learning disabilities. In C.E. Finn, R.A. Rotherham, & C.R. Hokanson (Eds.), *Rethinking special education for a new century* (pp. 259–287). Washington DC: Thomas B. Fordham Foundation and Progressive Policy Institute.

Maguire, E.A., Woollett, K., Spiers, H.J. (2006). London taxi drivers and bus drivers: A structural MRI and neuropsychological analysis. *Hippocampus, 16*, 1091–1101.

McNeil, L.M. (2000). Creating new inequalities: Contradictions of reform. *Phi Delta Kappan, 81*, 729–734.

Merzenich, M. M., Tallal, P., Peterson, B., Miller, S. L., & Jenkins, W. M. (1998). Some neurological principles relevant to the origins of—and the cortical plasticity based remediation of—language learning impairments. In J. Grafman & Y. Christen (Eds.), *Neuroplasticity: Building a bridge from the laboratory to the clinic* (pp. 169–187). Amsterdam: Elsevier.

Minagawa-Kawai, Y., Mori, K., Naoi, N., & Kojima, S. (2007). Neural attunement processes in infants during the acquisition of a language-specific phonemic contrast. *The Journal of Neuroscience*, 27(2):315–321.

National Commission on Excellence in Education (1983). *A nation at risk: The imperative for educational reform*. Washington DC: U.S. Department of Education.

National Reading Panel (2000). *Teaching children to read: An evidence-based assessment of the scientific research literature on reading and its implications for reading instruction*. Washington DC: National Institute of Child Health and Human Development.No Child Left Behind Act of 2001, 20 USC 70 6301 et seq. (2002)

President's Commission on Excellence in Special Education (2001). *A New era: Revitalizing special education for children and their families*. Retrieved May 30, 2010, from http://www2.ed.gov/inits/commissionsboards/whspecialeducation/reports/index.html.

Rayner, K., Foorman, B.R., Perfetti, C.A., Pesetsky, D., & Seidenberg, M.S. (2001). How psychological science informs the teaching of reading. *Psychological Science, 2*(2), 31–74.

Renner, M.J. & Rosenzweig, M.R. (1987). *Enriched and impoverished environments: Effects on brain and behavior*. New York: Springer.

Reynolds, C.R. (2008). *RTI, neuroscience, and sense: Chaos in the diagnosis and treatment of learning disabilities*. In E. Fletcher-Janzen & Reynolds, C.R. (Eds.). *Neuropsychological perspectives on learning disabilities in the era of RTI: Recommendations for diagnosis and intervention* (pp.14–27). New York: John Wiley.

Rouse, C. E. & Krueger, A.B. (2004). Putting Computerized Instruction to the Test: A Randomized Evaluation of a 'Scientifically-based' Reading Program. *Economics of Education Review, 23*(4), 323.

Semrud-Clikeman, M. (2005). Neuropsychological aspects for evaluating learning disabilities. *Journal of Learning Disabilities, 38*(6), 563–568.

Shaw, P., Eckstrand, K, Sharp, W., Blumenthal, J., Lerch, J.P., Greenstein, D., Clasen, J., Evans, A., Giedd, J., & Rapoport, J.L. (2007). Attention-deficit/hyperactivity disorder is characterized by a delay in cortical maturation. *National Academy of Sciences, 104*. 19649–19654.

Shaywitz, S.E. (2003). *Overcoming dyslexia: A new and complete science-based program for reading problems at any level*. New York: Alfred A. Knopf.

Slavin, R.E. (2008). Perspectives on evidence-based research in education what works? Issues in synthesizing educational program evaluations. *Educational Researcher, 37*(5), 5–14.

Snow, C.E., Burns, M.S., & Griffin, P. (1998). *Preventing reading difficulties in young children*. Washington DC: National Academy Press.

Snow, R.E. (1977). Individual differences and instructional theory. *Educational Researcher, 6*, 11–15.

Spevack, T.V. (2007). A developmental approach to pediatric neuropsychological intervention. In S.J. Hunter & J. Donders (Eds.), *Pediatric Neuropsychological Intervention* (pp. 6–29). New York: Cambridge University Press.

Stanovich, K. & Siegel, L.S. (1994). Phenotypic performance profile of children with reading disabilities: A regression based test of phonological-core variable difference model. *Journal of Educational Psychology, 86*, 24–53.

Tallal, P. (1999). Moving research from the laboratory to clinics and classrooms. In D. Drake (Ed.), *Reading and attention disorders: Neurobiological correlates* (pp. 93–112). Baltimore, MD: York Press.

Temple, E., Deutsch, G.K., Poldrack, R.A., Miller, S.L., Tallal, P., Merzenich, M.M., & Gabrieli, J.D. (2003). Neural deficits in children with dyslexia ameliorated by behavioral remediation: Evidence from functional MRI. *Proceedings of the National Academy of Science, 100*(5), 2860–2865.

Tobias, S. (1976). Aptitude Treatment Interaction. *Review of Educational Research, 46*(1), 61–75.

Torgesen, J.K. (2000). Individual responses in response to early interventions in reading: The lingering problem of treatment resisters. *Learning Disabilities Research & Practice, 15*, 55–64.

Torgesen, J.K. (2007). *Using an RTI model to guide early reading instruction: Effects on identification rates for students with learning disabilities: Florida Center for Reading Research Technical Report #7*. Retrieved on March 11, 2009 from http://www.fcrr.org.

Torgesen, J.K., Myers, D., Schrim, A., Stuart, E., Vartivarian, S., Mansfield, W. et al. (2006). *National assessment of Title 1 interim report-Volume II: Closing the reading gap: First year findings from a randomized trial of four reading interventions for striving readers.* Retrieved on November 2, 2008 from *www.air.org/files/closing_gap.pdf*

Vellutino, F.R., Scanlon, D.M., & Lyon, G.R. (2000). Differentiating between difficult to remediate and readily remediated poor readers: More evidence against the IQ-Achievement discrepancy definition of reading disability. *Journal of Learning Disabilities, 33*, 223–238.

What Works Clearinghouse (2007). *Intervention: Corrective Reading.* Retrieved October 3, 2008 from http://ies.ed.gov/ncee/wwc/reports/beginning_reading/cr/.

What Works Clearinghouse (2007). *Intervention: Fast ForWord®.* Retrieved April 2, 2009 from http://ies.ed.gov/ncee/wwc/reports/beginning_reading/fastfw/.

What Works Clearinghouse (2007). *Intervention: Reading Recovery®.* Retrieved October 3, 2008 from http://ies.ed.gov/ncee/wwc/reports/beginning_reading/reading_recovery/.

What Works Clearinghouse (2007). *Intervention: Wilson Reading System®.* Retrieved October 3, 2008 from http://ies.ed.gov/ncee/wwc/reports/beginning_reading/wrs/.

White, T.G., Graves, M.F., Slater, W. H. (1990). Growth of reading vocabulary in diverse elementary schools: Decoding and word meaning. *Journal of Educational Psychology, 82,* 281–290.

Wills, K.E. (2007). Remediating specific learning disabilities. In S.J. Hunter & J. Donders (Eds.), *Pediatric Neuropsychological Intervention* (pp. 224–252). New York: Cambridge University Press.

Yell, M.L. & Drasgow, E. (2007). Assessment for eligibility under IDEIA and the 2006 Regulations. *Assessment for Effective Interventions, 32*(4), 202–213.

Functional Assessment of Behavior

T. Steuart Watson, Mark W. Steege, *and* Tonya S. Watson

Abstract

Functional behavioral assessment (FBA) refers to a wide range of methodologies whose primary purposes are to identify the individual and environmental variables that directly influence behavior, and to derive an individualized treatment plan based on those variables.

The principles, assumptions, methodologies, and procedures that comprise an empirically valid FBA are drawn from applied behavior analysis. This chapter first provides a description of the SMIRC model that guides the functional assessment process. The basic principles, components, and procedures of FBA are described, to assist with methodology selection and implementation. A discussion of the five most common errors committed when attempting to assess function is presented in an attempt to reduce the likelihood of their occurrence. Finally, we address some of the most pertinent questions related to school based FBAs.

Keywords: functional assessment, brief functional analysis, SMIRC model, errors

Introduction

At some level, all fields of psychology are concerned with identifying the causes of behavior. For different specialties within psychology, however, the causes may be quite disparate. For instance, Freudian psychology is concerned with identifying the internal mechanisms (e.g., unconscious forces and conflicts) that drive human behavior, while humanistic psychologists seek to identify and correct the ways in which a person's ideal self differs from his/her real self. These "internal psychologies" represent one end of a philosophical continuum on which, at the opposing end, lies applied behavior analysis, or ABA. Psychologists who identify their specialty as behavior analysis look predominantly outside the organism to determine the causes of behavior. For behavior analysts, cause roughly translates to "under what conditions does the behavior occur, and what is the outcome of the behavior?" Answering these two general questions allows one to ascertain the function (i.e., purpose or motivation) of a particular behavior.

The primary reason for assessing variables outside the organism is that they are more amenable to observation and measurement than variables that are internal to the organism. Also notice that we said *predominantly* outside the organism as opposed to *exclusively* outside the organism. This distinction is critical because one of the common, albeit incorrect, criticisms of ABA is that it neglects variables that are only accessible to the person exhibiting the behavior. There are conditions that are internal to the organism that contribute to the responding of the organism. We further explain these variables in various sections throughout this chapter.

This chapter is certainly not meant to be a comprehensive treatment of functional assessment. Rather, it is a means by which we can convey some of the most salient information necessary to conduct empirically sound functional assessments in the school setting. Thus, in this chapter we are going to provide a very brief summary of the lineage of functional assessment, our conceptual model that guides not only the functional assessment process but also our understanding of human behavior, the wide range of procedures that one can use to determine function in an applied setting, the steps involved in conducting a functional behavioral assessment (FBA), the errors that often occur during school based functional assessments, and the more common limitations and criticisms related to the assessment of function.

A Brief History of Functional Assessment/Analysis

For most school psychologists, the term "functional assessment" has a rather recent history, as it was included in Public Law 105-17. The reauthorization of IDEA (IDEIA; PL 108-446) retained the requirement for Individualized Education ProgramsIEP teams to conduct functional behavioral assessments. Prior to being included in federal legislation, however, the notion that environmental variables contribute in a significant way to behavior has a rather long and storied history. Without going into undue detail, there are a number of important milestones in the development of what we now refer to as functional assessment methodology. Perhaps one of the first psychologists to experimentally examine the effect of consequences on behavior was Edward L. Thorndike (1898), who found that feline behaviors that resulted in escape from a box and subsequent access to food increased, while behaviors that did not result in these consequences decreased. Thorndike's experiment was a dramatic demonstration of the powerful effects that *consequences* can exert on behavior. From his experiments, Thorndike coined the term "Law of Effect" to refer the process by which behaviors that result in satisfying consequences are "stamped in" while behaviors that result in "annoying" consequences are "stamped out."

Following Thorndike, both Watson and Rayner (1920) and Pavlov (1927) conducted experiments that again demonstrated the powerful effects of variables outside the organism on behaviors that, at the time, were thought to be internally mediated. Because the work of Watson and Pavlov occurred in the early 1900s, their work was revolutionary at the time and directly challenged the internal psychologies that predominated. Early in the 1930s, B. F. Skinner (1938; 1953) began his long and illustrious career as the most influential psychologist of the twentieth century. Skinner's experiments on the effects of various reinforcement schedules on behavior literally established the field of operant conditioning, the science upon which applied behavior analysis was developed. ABA, which was the application of Skinner's scientific principles, began in earnest in the 1950s and 60s with such luminaries as Azrin (1960), Baer, Peterson, & Sherman (1967), Lindsley (1956), Goldiamond (1965), and Ayllon (1960), among others.

Perhaps the first formal "descriptive functional assessment" was recommended by Bijou, Peterson, and Ault in 1968. This type of assessment was particularly useful when conducting direct behavioral observations, and involved noting the antecedents and consequences temporally proximate to a target behavior. Thus, the A (Antecedent) – B (Behavior) – C (Consequence) recording procedure was born. Antecedents are those stimuli that occur just before a behavior that act as cues, or triggers. More formally, they are cues that indicate if a particular behavior occurs, reinforcement is usually available. Consequences were those events that immediately followed and reinforced a behavior.

From that point in time, the field of applied operant psychology flourished, and was used to solve a wide range of educational and social problems. Carr (1977) expanded on the descriptive procedures proffered by Bijou et al. by noting that, in some instances, an experimental analysis (i.e., a more rigorous type of methodology for ascertaining function) was needed to clearly identify the "motivation" of behavior; in this particular instance, self-injurious behaviors (SIB). Carr described a methodology for experimentally analyzing, or isolating cause–effect relationships, a methodology popularized by Iwata and colleagues. This rigorous methodology is known as *functional analysis*, and is typically regarded as the "gold standard" against which all functional assessment procedures are compared. At this point, it may prove beneficial to delineate terminology a bit. The term *functional assessment* refers to the broad range of assessment activities that are designed to ascertain function. *Functional analysis* is but one type of assessment strategy, albeit the only one that allows one to establish a cause–effect relationship. Since the seminal work of Iwata and colleagues (1982), hundreds of studies have been published in the educational (Ervin & Ehrhardt, 2000) and psychological literatures (e.g., *Journal of Applied Behavior Analysis*) whereby some type of functional assessment strategy was used to identify the cause of a behavior and the most appropriate treatment. As can be seen from this brief historical review, functional assessment is not a recent development, despite its recent emergence in federal legislation and the school psychology literature.

A Conceptual Model of Human Behavior for Guiding Functional Assessment

We have previously delineated our SMIRC model for conceptualizing the myriad variables that influence behavior and hence, the functional behavioral assessment process (Steege & Watson, 2009). The SMIRC model (Stimulus, Motivating operations, Individual variables, Response, Consequence) recognizes the often complex nature of human behavior by acknowledging the variables both within and external to the student. These variables rarely act in isolation; rather, they typically interact with each other, which results in an amalgamation of influences on any given response.

Some elements of the SMIRC model are fairly straightforward and easily understood. That is, "Stimulus" refers to a discriminative stimulus (a temporally proximate antecedent) and "Response" refers to the behavior being analyzed. Consequence refers to the outcomes following the behavior. Consequences can be further divided into three broad categories including socially mediated positive reinforcement, socially mediated negative reinforcement, and automatic reinforcement. Each of these can then be divided into additional categories (See Table 9.1). These categories are extremely important because they provide a conceptual map from which to work when seeking to identify the function (i.e., purpose) of a particular behavior.

Identifying Motivating operations and Individual variables can be a rather difficult enterprise, primarily because motivating variables may often be more temporally distant to the response than discriminative stimuli, and individual variables may, in some cases, not be readily accessible. When considering the effects of *motivating operations*, we look at both unconditioned motivating operations (UMO) and conditioned motivating operations (CMO). Each of these types of motivating operations can have reinforcer establishing/abolishing effects, as well as behavior evocative/abative effects. For instance, when someone is in pain (a UMO), reduction in pain as a negative reinforcer is increased (a reinforcer establishing effect) while, simultaneously, behaviors that have previously resulted in pain attenuation are more likely (a behavioral evocative effect). Conversely, for a student who has received noncontingent attention for a period of time (a CMO), the effectiveness of social attention as reinforcer is decreased (a reinforcer abolishing effect) and the

Table 9.1 Examples of categories and subcategories of reinforcers

Socially Mediated Positive Reinforcement	Socially Mediated Negative Reinforcement	Automatic Reinforcement
Attention from peers	Escape* from peer interactions	Automatic positive reinforcement
Attention from teachers	Escape from teacher interactions	Automatic negative reinforcement
Attention from staff	Escape from staff interactions	
Access to food	Escape from academic tasks	
Access to tangible items	Escape from activities	
Access to games/activities	Escape from commands	

* Note: Where escape is indicated, one may also substitute the term "avoidance" and be technically and pragmatically accurate.

likelihood of behaviors that would result in obtaining social reinforcement are also decreased (a behavioral abative effect). Likewise, consider the case of a student who exhibits verbal opposition when presented math assignments. In this case, math worksheets are a type of conditioned motivating operation (i.e., a warning stimulus) that evokes verbal opposition that results in task avoidance (negative reinforcement).

In short, discriminative stimuli, conditioned motivating operations, and unconditioned motivating operations are all antecedents that influence the probability of behavior. Motivating operations influence motivation (e.g., how much someone wants something) and discriminative stimuli influence the probability of obtaining the reinforcing stimulus (Steege &Watson, 2009).

Individual variables are those that are considered to be specific to a particular student. For instance, a student with severe articulation difficulties might be more prone to behavioral outbursts when asked to do something that requires a lengthy verbal response. Likewise, a student with noise sensitivity may be more likely to behave in a noncompliant fashion in a high-noise environment versus a low-noise environment. Other individual variables that need to be considered include: communication/language deficits, food/environmental sensitivities, altered physiological/cognitive states, illnesses, and other functional impairments. The implications for assessment and treatment planning will be discussed in subsequent chapters.

It is important to analyze the contribution of each of the variables within the SMIRC model when conducting a functional behavioral assessment. It is also important to recognize that this is a dynamic model, and the relative influence of the contributing variables may change. For example, motivating operations are temporary (i.e., motivation for food changes as a function of availability and metabolic rate), the availability of stimuli that occasion behavior may be transient, and the quality and quantity of reinforcing consequences may be quite variable. Therefore, one needs to continuously examine the interaction of both external and internal variables that contribute to occurrences of specific responses.

Basic Principles of Functional Behavioral Assessment

On the surface, functional assessment is a straightforward concept whose dual purposes are to identify the variables that are functionally related to a specific behavior, and to design an intervention based on those results. More specifically, FBA is a set of procedures whose primary purpose is to delineate the interactive relationship between environmental variables and the unique characteristics of the student that interfere with the acquisition, maintenance, and generalization of social, academic, adaptive, and other life skills.

We propose some fundamental principles that underlie every FBA conducted in the school setting. The first of these is that thoroughly conducted FBAs are composed of multi-source, multi-method, and multi-setting procedures. Essentially, we are seeking convergent validity from a variety of sources that all point to the same conclusion regarding function of the behavior. Second, the assessment process must include the consideration of a broad array of contributing variables (i.e., the SMIRC model). Third, topography of behavior has little to do with function. That is, how the behavior looks bears minimal impact on *why* the student is exhibiting the behavior. Fourth, the same behavior may serve different functions depending upon setting, people present, and other social variables. And fifth, the results of the FBA should lead to an intervention that is more effective than one based on topography, subjective opinion, or diagnostic criteria.

Essential Components of an FBA

The beginning of any FBA is an identification and unambiguous description of behaviors that are interfering with the student's academic, social, behavioral, or adaptive functioning. Most typically, the types of procedures used at this stage of the FBA process are indirect methods (interviews, record reviews) and direct descriptive methods (Steege & Watson, 2009). We advocate paying close attention to response classes during this phase, particularly for students who evidence a wide range of interfering behaviors. Briefly, response class refers to the principle that, although behaviors may look different (i.e., have different topographies) they may have similar antecedents and consequences. Typically, as one behavior in a response class is reinforced, there are similar effects for all members of that response class.

After the interfering behaviors have been operationally defined, the second step is to record the occurrence of the interfering behavior using some type of behavioral recording format (Skinner, Rhymer, & McDaniel, 2000). It is extremely important to note the antecedents and consequences that are temporally proximate to the interfering behavior, so that hypotheses about behavioral function may be made. The procedures most often utilized at this step are direct observation and other direct descriptive procedures. Some of the questions that should be answered, based on data collected at this point, include

- How often is the behavior occurring?
- To what extent does this behavior interfere with the student's learning and/or acquisition of academic, social, or adaptive skills?
- To what extent does this behavior interfere with classmates' learning and/or acquisition of academic, social, or adaptive skills?
- How intense is the behavior?
- To what extent does the behavior disrupt instruction?
- What are some possible antecedents, consequences, motivating variables, and individual variables that are impacting this behavior?

The third step in the FBA process is to identify and describe the antecedent, consequence, and individual variables that are related to the interfering behavior. This is sometimes difficult because one often must examine a host of potential antecedent variables that are present in the classroom at any given time (e.g., peer behavior, student behavior, and academic assignment) as well as the individual or motivating variables that may be influencing these antecedents. Although identifying consequences may seem relatively straightforward, and indeed it typically is, there are situations that make discerning the functional consequences difficult. For instance, behaviors that are on some type of intermittent schedule may preclude the direct observation of the application of some consequences. Consider the teacher who only attends to every 15th inappropriate comment from a particular student, and the observer leaves or discontinues the observation just after the 14th inappropriate comment. Missing the application of social attention may lead the observer to derive incorrect conclusions about the role that social attention plays in the maintenance of the inappropriate comments. Another difficulty may arise when seeking to determine if negative reinforcement is maintaining a behavior. Consider a student who only disrupts class when the teacher begins calling on individual students to answer questions. Because of the disruptions, the student is never called on. Thus, the hypothesis that disruptions are negatively reinforced by avoiding being called on to answer questions is a bit tenuous; because of the absence, the observer is *surmising* that not being called on is a negative reinforcer. Based on information that is collected in this step, one must then determine the function of the interfering behavior.

As we previously mentioned, one of the primary purposes of conducting an FBA is to design an individualized behavior support plan based on the information collected during the FBA. Too often, it seems that many school teams approach an FBA as merely a "documentation" process whereby legal requirements are filled, and the proper papers are completed. Designing an individualized behavior support plan is the final step in the FBA process. The main components are listed below:

- Consider antecedent manipulation as a means of preventing problem behaviors from occurring.
- Consider individual variables, so that socially valid replacement behaviors can be taught to the student.
- Consider manipulating consequence variables to avoid reinforcing interfering behavior while simultaneously reinforcing a more appropriate replacement behavior.
- Consider how motivating variables may be affecting other variables, and modify if possible.

Functional Assessment Procedures

Generally speaking, functional assessment procedures may be divided into one of four categories:

- Indirect procedures
- Direct descriptive procedures
- Brief functional analysis procedures, and
- Extended functional analysis procedures

Each of these procedures has merit in a broad based assessment process, and will be discussed in the paragraphs that follow.

Indirect Procedures

The procedures that are labeled *indirect* are done so because the information is collected from a variety of third party sources. The most typical procedures include record reviews, interviews, screening forms, rating scales, etc. Although these, by themselves, are not sufficient for determining function, they are useful for planning the types of procedures that will be helpful as the FBA process progresses, and for identifying potential variables for further evaluation. As such, indirect procedures are often a "first step" when beginning the FBA process.

There are a number of specific procedures that we recommend when using indirect methods as part of the FBA process. The first of these indirect procedures is the record review, which would include examining the student's attendance history, results from previous standardized assessments, medical and social histories, disciplinary referrals and patterns, results from previous idiographic assessments, and interventions that have been previously applied with the student. If the student has an IEP, it should be examined closely to determine the instructional goals and objectives, how they are being monitored, and any other data that indicates performance. It is not unreasonable to suggest that many worthwhile hypotheses regarding behavioral function are generated during the record review process.

When conducting interviews, three of the most valuable formats are the *Functional Behavioral Assessment Screening Form* (FBASF), the *Functional Assessment Informant Record for Teachers* (FAIR-T), and the *Behavioral Stream Interview* (BSI).

The FBASF is a semistructured interview procedure that is often used as a tool for determining areas of inter-individual and intra-individual strength, identifying interfering behaviors, identifying potential reinforcers, and broadly assessing the student's communication skills. We particularly like the FBASF because it forces an examination of the skills and strengths of the student, in addition to the interfering behaviors. An example of a completed FBASF is included in Appendix A. For further description and examples of the FBASF, please see Watson and Steege (2003) and Steege and Watson (2009).

In the example presented in Appendix A, the information collected for Frank from the FBASF has implications for both the remainder of the FBA process, and for treatment planning. With regards to functional assessment, some of the variables that would need to be explored include the role that Frank's articulation/language skills are antecedent to yelling at his teachers and refusing to complete academic work, and the relationship between these two behaviors. With regards to treatment planning, it would seem likely that improving literacy skills would be a major component of any intervention plan, along with teaching more appropriate means of accessing teacher attention/help and escaping from academic assignments.

The Functional Assessment Informant Record for Teachers (FAIR-T; Edwards, 2002) is used as an indirect measure to develop hypotheses about the function of interfering behaviors in the classroom setting. The FAIR-T is completed by the teacher, and consists of four sections: general referral information, information regarding problem behaviors, and two sections with questions seeking to identify antecedents and consequences. Although Edwards cautioned that the FAIR-T was not developed to be used in isolation, it is useful as a tool for structuring follow-up teacher interviews and indicating additional assessment procedures. A copy of the FAIR-T is reproduced in Appendix B.

The Behavioral Stream Interview (BSI) is a means of identifying the *interaction* between the myriad contextual variables that are often associated with interfering behavior, and capturing the nature of the ongoing interaction between a student and others in his/her environment. It is called a "behavioral stream" because it is not meant to reflect a snapshot of a behavioral interaction; rather, it is to reflect the dynamics of a *behavioral sequence* (i.e., how one event leads to another event, how that event leads to yet another, and so on). Instead of only noting the one immediate antecedent and the one immediate consequence that occurred for a behavioral incident, the goal of the interview is to uncover the *stream* of antecedents and the *stream* of consequences for an incident of the interfering behavior

The basic steps involved in conducting an effective BSI include:

- Identifying and operationalizing interfering behaviors

- Using a recent incident of the interfering behavior as a referent point
- Identifying antecedents to the interfering behavior, including activities, interactions, etc.
- Identifying contextual events that surrounded the specific antecedents
- As far back as is reasonable, identifying the antecedents to the antecedents
- Identifying consequences (e.g., teacher response) of the interfering behavior
- As far forward as is reasonable, identifying the flow of events that follow the immediate consequences

Using a BSI, one can capture the sequence of events that led up to, and followed, the incident of interfering behavior. This information should shed further light on the variables that seemingly trigger or cue the behavior to occur, and those that reinforce the behavior. It is important to mention that the behavioral stream method can be used during direct observations as well (see section below).

Finally, a third category of indirect procedures is a variety of checklist-type instruments that attempt to identify antecedents, individual variables, and consequences that are functional for that particular interfering behavior. These checklists include the Individual Variables Assessment Form (IVAF), the Antecedent Variables Assessment Form (AVAF), and the Consequence Variables Assessment Form (CVAF) (Steege & Watson, 2009). The first of these, the IVAF, is typically used during the early stages of the FBA process. Its primary purpose is not only to identify, but also to describe, the individual variables that are related to interfering behavior. The IVAF is critical for a number of reasons, not the least of which is that individual variables are an essential component of the SMIRC model. Briefly, individual variables are those that are specific to the individual, and that may impact the student's interaction with his/her environment. Some of the most salient individual variables that one should consider as part of a comprehensive FBA, and their potential role in contributing to interfering behavior, may be found in Table 9.2.

Although there certainly are additional individual variables that one may want to consider when conducting an FBA, the ones listed above represent a starting point for assessing the relative contribution of individual variables on interfering behavior.

Table 9.2 Selected individual variables and their potential contribution to interfering behavior

Individual Variable	Possible Role in Interfering Behavior
Communication skills	Both expressive and receptive language deficits may lead to difficulties with compliance, understanding directions, and misinterpreting social cues from peers.
Academic skills	Deficits in specific academic areas may lead to escape or avoidant motivated behavior when presented with those academic tasks.
Social skills	Deficits in social skills may lead to inappropriate responses to peers in play and other interactions.
Health/medical problems (including medication use)	Recurrent medical problems, such as headaches, may increase the likelihood of engaging in behaviors that result in escape from tasks and social interactions.
Sleep problems	Students who are sleep deprived and therefore feeling fatigued may be less tolerant of stimuli in their environment and less inhibited in their responding.
Personal sensitivities	Students who are especially sensitive to certain stimuli, such as noise, may be more likely to engage in interfering behavior as the noise level in the classroom increases.
Emotional states	Students who are experiencing emotional phenomena, like depression or anxiety, may be less responsive to reinforcers in their environment and more apt to engage in behaviors consistent with their affective state.

Both the Antecedent Variables Assessment Form (AVAF) and the Consequence Variables Assessment Form (CVAF) are used in the early stages of the FBA process to identify and describe variables for further evaluation. Some of the categories that are considered on the AVAF include:

- Environmental variables
- Instructional variables
- Social variables
- Transition variables

Categories for assessment that are included on the CVAF include:

- Gaining social attention from teachers/staff and peers
- Escaping/avoiding tasks, activities, settings, or social interaction with adults/peers
- Obtaining objects, activities, food
- Inducing or reducing arousal

When using these types of forms, it is unlikely that all categories will apply to a given student. Therefore, we advocate a flexible assessment process that includes those variables that are relevant for the student. In addition, because the variables that influence an interfering behavior may be highly idiosyncratic to that behavior, we recommend conducting separate analyses for each interfering behavior, instead of attempting to analyze all of them using a single form.

Among busy school based teams and practitioners, there is a temptation to exclusively use indirect methods to complete an FBA. Although they are time-efficient, cost effective, and may yield very useful findings, other, more direct procedures may need to be used to more clearly define the relationship between these variables and interfering behavior. Having said that, however, there may be instances in which the indirect procedures are sufficient for intervention planning. Consider a student who is exhibiting a high frequency, relatively discrete, interfering behavior; a number of indirect procedures have been used including record reviews, a behavioral stream interview, and the AVAF and CVAF. All of these point to the same set of antecedents and consequences for the interfering behavior. In this situation, it is probably safe to proceed with intervention planning based on these results. If the intervention is successful, then the indirect procedures have fulfilled not only their purpose, but the purpose of the FBA as well—an intervention designed specifically for the student that results in less of the interfering behavior, and more of the appropriate responding! If the intervention is not successful, or the information obtained through the indirect procedures is inconclusive, then one may proceed to the direct descriptive procedures.

Direct Descriptive Functional Assessment Procedures

Procedures that fall into this domain are characterized by direct observation of the student who is exhibiting the interfering behavior. In traditional behavioral assessment, this usually represents conducting observations where the primary purpose is to measure some dimension of the interfering behavior (i.e., frequency, intensity, duration, latency). Although measurement of these dimensions is important for determining problem magnitude, and for evaluating treatment effects, it tells us little about the functional relationship between environmental variables and interfering behavior. To do this, there are a number of procedures that are of value, including:

- A-B-C/Behavioral Stream Recording
- Task Difficulty Antecedent Analysis
- Conditional Probability Recording
- Functional Behavior Assessment Observation Form (FBAOF)
- Interval Recording Procedure (IRP)

Each of these has value for functional assessment, but may not be necessary for every assessment for every student. As the assessment unfolds, the school psychologist will need to determine which of these has particular salience for the target student.

A-B-C/BEHAVIORAL STREAM RECORDING

Antecedent-Behavior-Consequence (A-B-C) recording occurs when the observer, during an observation period, notes the antecedents and consequences that are temporally proximate to the interfering behavior. We have found it useful to use the principle of behavioral streams to augment and enhance the data collected from this type of recording. For instance, the following table illustrates the information from a typical A-B-C recording, and then the information in an expanded format taken from a behavioral stream observation.

From the above information, it appears as though the cue was the teacher asking the students to end one assignment and begin another, and the consequence was a verbal reprimand and a loss of money.

Table 9.3   Typical A-B-C recording

Antecedent	Behavior	Consequence
The teacher asked the students to put away what they were working on and get out their math worksheets.	Tyler shouted that he was not finished with his reading assignment and needed more time.	The teacher told Tyler that shouting was not acceptable in her class and "fined" him a dollar in their classwide token economy.

Indeed, the entire behavioral incident appeared to have a discrete beginning and end, with no other stimuli impacting the interaction. However, the behavioral stream recording indicated a much different picture:

> Tyler was working quietly at his desk on a reading assignment with his hand raised…The teacher assisted four students, and then went to the front of the class…Tyler put his hand down…The teacher asked the students to put away what they were working on and get out their math worksheets…Tyler looked up and shouted that he was not yet finished with his reading assignment and needed more time…The teacher looked at Tyler and told him that shouting was not acceptable in her class and fined him a dollar in their classwide token economy…Tyler got up from his desk and moved toward the teacher telling her it wasn't fair that he did not get enough time to finish his work…The teacher told him to sit back down or he would have to go see the principal…Tyler said he might as well go see the principal because he couldn't finish his work anyway…The teacher sent him to the principal's office with a disciplinary note.

When contrasting the information from the two observations, it appears that the A-B-C recording failed to capture some critical antecedent variables associated with this particular incident, most notably Tyler sitting with his hand raised for assistance, with none forthcoming. With regards to consequences, there was an escalation of the interfering behavior, as opposed to Tyler immediately exhibiting the most intense level of the behavior. Perhaps one of the most fundamental elements of behavioral stream recording is that a consequence can also serve as an antecedent for another behavior. Thus, it is unnecessary to label the events as antecedents or consequences, as they are occurring. Rather, the focus should be on describing the ongoing sequence of behaviors. Doing so allows one to capture a more complete understanding of the stimuli surrounding and contributing to the interfering behavior. A-B-C behavioral stream recording can be used for almost every functional assessment conducted in the school setting because it is brief, yet captures the rich interaction between the student, the interfering behavior, and a host of environmental variables.

TASK DIFFICULTY ANTECEDENT ANALYSIS

For some students, task difficulty may be hypothesized to be an antecedent for interfering behavior. This may be especially true for students whose skills in a particular academic area are at either the instructional or frustration levels. To test the "task difficulty as antecedent hypothesis," the school psychologist should follow these steps:

- Determine the academic subject during which interfering behavior is most likely to occur.
- With the assistance of the teacher, identify tasks from the selected academic area that are easy (greater than 90% accuracy), medium (70-80% accuracy) and difficult (< 70% accuracy) for the student.
- Present tasks to the student from each of the difficulty categories, while recording the occurrence of the interfering behavior. If task difficulty is an antecedent for interfering behavior, the rate should be higher in the difficult condition than the other conditions.
- If possible, conduct this measurement on a couple of occasions to determine if there is consistency across days, times, etc.

CONDITIONAL PROBABILITY RECORDING (CPR)

Stated simply, CPR involves recording the temporally proximate antecedents and consequences of the interfering behavior, and then computing the percentage of time that a particular antecedent or consequence occurs before or after the interfering behavior. For example, if a teacher-issued verbal command *precedes* 17/20 instances of interfering behavior, then one can state that the probability of interfering behavior is .85 following a teacher-issued verbal command. Likewise, if a teacher verbal reprimand *follows* 14/20 instances of interfering behavior, one can state that the probability of teacher attention following interfering behavior is .70. When examined this way, one can begin to make more definitive statements about the relative contributions to interfering behavior of different antecedents and consequences.

FUNCTIONAL BEHAVIORAL ASSESSMENT OBSERVATION

This procedure is useful when recording discrete behavioral episodes or events that involve a single interfering behavior. Seven primary variables need to be observed and recorded using this format:

- Date and time of day
- Contextual events including task, setting, activity, etc.
- Antecedents
- Interfering behavior

- Consequences
- Changes in the rate, intensity, or duration of the interfering behavior as a result of the consequence
- Staff present

Although other variables may be included, these are the ones deemed especially significant for making decisions about the function of discrete episodes of behavior, and for treatment planning.

INTERVAL RECORDING PROCEDURE (IRP)

The IRP is essentially a modified scatterplot assessment procedure, whereby an observer records interfering behavior and contextual variables at predetermined intervals (e.g., every 5, 10 or 15 minutes). As Steege and Watson (2009) noted, there are six uses of the IRP:

- Identifying specific settings/activities/tasks in which interfering behavior occurs
- Recording the magnitude of appropriate behaviors
- Recording the magnitude of interfering behaviors
- Identifying co-relationships among appropriate and interfering behaviors
- Identifying co-relationships among different interfering behaviors
- Identifying relationships between specific staff and both appropriate and interfering behaviors

Research using the IRP has shown it to be highly effective as an efficient and valid procedure for recording clinically relevant behavioral data (Steege, Davin & Hathway, 2001).

Brief Functional Analysis Model

As mentioned earlier, functional *analysis* is the gold standard by which all functional assessment procedures are evaluated, and is the only procedure that allows one to draw definitive statements about the cause–effect relationship between environmental variables and interfering behavior (Cooper et al., 2007; Shriver et al., 2001). Typically, traditional functional analysis involves repeated testing of four counterbalanced conditions to determine the functional relationship between a specific stimulus and interfering behavior. However, these extended, counterbalanced functional analyses may have very little social validity for use in schools, for a variety of reasons. The first of these reasons is that the length of time required to conduct such an analysis may be excessive for most school based teams. The second reason is that the school may be lacking personnel who are equipped to conduct an extended and methodologically rigorous functional analysis. Third, an extended functional analysis may not actually be required for a vast majority of problems that are referred for functional assessment, as the indirect and direct descriptive assessments have been shown to be both reliable and valid when properly conducted (Dufrene, Doggett, Henington, & Watson, 2007. And fourth, the temporal stability of the results from a functional analysis may be questionable, as function may change over time, situations, and people. For these reasons, we advocate a brief model of functional analysis, similar to that described by Steege and Northup (1998). The brief functional analysis is comprised of four sequential phases:

- A functional assessment consisting of indirect and direct descriptive methods
- Brief functional analysis
- Confirmatory functional analysis
- Contingency reversal

Within this brief model, both structural and/or consequence analyses may be conducted. A structural analysis consists of manipulating specific antecedent variables (e.g., gross vs. fine motor tasks, lengthy verbal instructions vs. brief verbal instructions, presence of specific teachers and/or peers), and recording the occurrence of interfering behavior in the presence of those specific variables. A structural analysis is an experimental method for evaluating the evocative effects of an antecedent variable on interfering behavior (O'Neill, et al., 1997). During a structural analysis, there is no contingent delivery of consequences. A consequence analysis consists of providing specific consequences (e.g., social attention, brief escape from task, tangible item/activity) contingent on the occurrence of a particular interfering behavior. This type of analysis is used to experimentally evaluate the variables that are thought to maintain (i.e., reinforce) interfering behavior.

Phase 1: Functional assessment. The purpose of Phase 1, indirect and direct descriptive procedures, is to identify antecedent and consequent variables to be evaluated in the brief function analysis. Because we have already addressed the procedures and steps involved in the first phase, we will focus on the subsequent three phases in this section.

Phase 2: Brief functional analysis. The brief functional analysis phase is intended to take about 30 minutes. During this phase, the variables identified from Phase 1 for further analysis are then systematically manipulated, while interfering behavior is observed and recorded. Once each of the variables has been tested, the results are then graphed so that a determination can be made about the relative influence of each on the interfering behavior (phase two).

Phase 3: Confirmatory analysis. Once the brief analysis is completed and the results indicate a clear pattern, a confirmatory functional analysis is conducted to assess the consistency of the interfering behaviors across specific conditions.

Phase 4: Contingency reversal. The purpose of the contingency reversal phase is to determine if the function identified through Phases 2 and 3 can be used to increase appropriate behavior. Essentially, this is an intervention validation phase.

Typical Errors Committed During FBA

Throughout this chapter, we have described numerous procedures of varying methodological rigor for evaluating the cues for interfering behavior and the consequences that maintain interfering behavior. Although these procedures are robust in and of themselves, there are a number of errors that may occur during any of these procedures (Steege & Watson, 2009; Watson & Steege, 2003). While not an exhaustive list of errors, psychometric or otherwise, these are the ones we have observed to be most common:

- Recency error of perception
- Primacy error of perception
- Error of misplaced precision
- Error of inaccurate functional behavioral assessment
- Error of association

Recency error of perception. This error occurs when the most recent instance of the interfering behavior is used as the basis for making judgments and hypotheses about the variables that are contributing to the interfering behavior. A basic assumption inherent in this error is that the variables present at this recent incident are/were present at all instances of the interfering behavior. This error is most likely to occur when collecting indirect data such as interviews, although it can occur during any of the indirect methods.

If one were to allow this error to go unchecked, the most likely adverse effect is on planning an intervention based on variables that may or may not be present when the interfering behavior occurs.

Perhaps the most effective procedure for avoiding this error is asking the teacher/staff to recall several incidents of the interfering behavior (across a wide time span, settings, etc) and indicate the variables present (or absent) at each of the incidents.

Primacy error of perception. This error is the opposite of the recency error of perception, in that it occurs when the first incident of the interfering behavior is recalled, and is used as the basis for making decisions about the salience of contributing variables. This error is based on the assumption that the extant variables present during the first episode of the behavior are present at all subsequent episodes of the behavior. Like the recency error, this error is most likely to occur during an indirect procedure such as an interview, when the interviewee recalls the very first time the interfering behavior occurred. Again, the primary method for minimizing this error is to examine several incidents of the interfering behavior across time, and recall the variables that were present/absent at each.

Error of misplaced precision. This error is perhaps one of the most common committed by school based teams. It occurs when considerable effort is expended in measuring some aspect of behavior that actually communicates very little about that behavior. As just one example, a teacher might go to great lengths to collect accurate frequency data on a high-frequency behavior that is occurring in the classroom. Collecting only frequency data tells little about patterns of responding, when the behavior occurs, the variables that are present when the behavior occurs, the response of individuals in the environment to the behavior, etc. When this error occurs, generating hypotheses about behavioral function and designing behavior support plans becomes more difficult. To avoid this error, which typically occurs during the direct descriptive assessment, one must carefully consider the data collection method, and whether it will answer questions or assist in generating hypotheses about behavioral function.

Error of inaccurate functional behavioral assessment. This error refers to those situations where the school based team has either failed to complete an FBA, or has used only indirect methods to do so (Dittmer-McMahon, 2001). In both cases, untenable hypotheses are likely to be generated, which will likely lead to ineffective interventions. This error is completely preventable if the team makes certain that they are using a variety of methods, including those that are more direct in nature.

Error of association. This error is based on the tendency to assume that variables that are merely present when an interfering behavior occurs are *functionally* related to the behavior. A host of variables are usually present at any given time an interfering behavior occurs. One of the primary purposes of an FBA is to determine which of those are functionally related to the interfering behavior. Preventing or minimizing this error typically involves using a variety of methods for assessing function, so that the team does not over-rely on a teacher's or parent's report of behavior, and carefully determining the variables that are present when the behavior occurs and when it does not.

Questions about Functional Assessment/ Analysis Procedures

In a special issue of *School Psychology Review*, Gresham, Watson, and Skinner (2001) provided a broad overview of the prevalent extant issues associated with school based functional assessments. A review of some of the most salient ones for school based teams is presented here.

The first issue concerns the degree of agreement between the various methods of functional assessment. That is, to what degree do results from well-conducted indirect and direct descriptive procedures match those from the gold standard criterion, the results of a functional analysis? Derby et al. (1992) provided some insight into this question by demonstrating that brief functional analysis procedures were effective for identifying function and leading to effective intervention. More recently, Dufrene (2005) and Dufrene, Doggett, Henington, and Watson (2007) demonstrated a high degree of consistency between well-conducted direct descriptive assessments and brief functional analyses. Thus, it appears that, in many instances, thorough direct descriptive procedures (which obviously involve indirect procedures to some degree) may be sufficient for ascertaining function in the school setting. The ultimate barometer is whether the results of the direct descriptive assessments result in effective intervention and more appropriate responding from the target student.

Given all of the emphasis on function, a reasonable question is whether interventions that are based on the identified function of a behavior are more effective than those that are derived from a solid foundation in applied behavior modification. The most concise and empirically correct answer is, "We don't know." That is, there are many published studies that demonstrate the effectiveness of intervention based on the results of a functional analysis. Some treatment procedures appear to be effective even though function has not been determined (Braden & Kratochwill, 1997). And, as Lalli et al. (1999) found, positive reinforcement was more effective for changing escape-motivated behavior (i.e., negatively reinforced behavior) than a negative reinforcement procedure. By all accounts, the negative reinforcement procedure should have been more effective than the positive reinforcement procedure, because it was based on the function of the behavior—but it wasn't. Thus, more research needs to be conducted to determine under what conditions, for whom, and for what kinds of problems function-based interventions should be applied.

Perhaps one of the most pressing issues related to functional behavioral assessment in schools is whether school based teams are sufficiently competent to perform these assessments. Research by Dittmer-McMahon (2001) suggests that even well-trained teams completed less than thorough assessments, and made incorrect conclusions about function. This may not be surprising in light of other research that shows experienced behavior analysts disagree about function approximately 54% of the time (Hagopian, Fisher, Thompson, & Owen-DeSchryver, 1997). A related question concerns the ability of school based teams to design effective positive behavior support plans, which is really the end goal of all FBAs. Two recent examples of statewide efforts in Utah and Maryland provide excellent strategies for ensuring that teams will have the necessary knowledge and skills to design meaningful behavior change plans (Hager, Slocum, & Detrich, 2007; Lewis-Palmer & Barrett, 2007). Left to their own devices and without proper training, coaching, and monitoring, it is unlikely that many school teams will inherently have the necessary expertise to accomplish this task.

Summary

The notion that all behaviors serve some sort of function has a rather lengthy history, dating back to the work of Thorndike and Skinner. Through literally hundreds of published studies, functional behavior assessment has been shown to be a robust tool for assessing behavior, and for deriving effective and meaningful positive behavior support plans for students exhibiting interfering behavior in the classroom. Although it is legally mandated in certain situations, the procedures described in this chapter can be used in a variety of circumstances where a student's behavior is in some way interfering with the educational process.

There are actually many tools available for conducting an FBA, among them indirect procedures, direct descriptive procedures, and functional analysis. We advocate a combination of indirect and direct descriptive procedures in all cases where a student's behavior is of sufficient concern to warrant closer scrutiny and possible direct intervention. In the small percentage of cases where these two procedures fail to clearly indicate the function of the interfering behavior, or do not lead to an effective intervention, we advocate using a brief functional analysis model to ascertain function.

The ultimate criterion for any assessment procedure or method is whether the results lead to effective intervention. A properly conducted FBA, using the procedures outlined in this chapter, will likely lead one to develop an intervention based on changing those variables found to be related to the student's interfering behavior. When the resulting intervention is delivered with at least a moderate degree of integrity (Watson, 2004), the outcome is likely to be beneficial for the student and the teacher.

A number of questions remain about the psychometric properties of FBA, the degree of convergence among the various procedures, the ability of school based teams to conduct thorough and accurate FBAs, and the relative effectiveness of function-derived interventions versus empirically derived interventions. Although these are certainly important issues for researchers to investigate, their existence does not diminish the value of conducting FBAs in those situations where they are required by law, nor in those situations where they are dictated by best practice considerations.

Appendix A
Functional Behavioral Assessment Screening Form (FBASF)

Name: <u>Frank</u>   Date of Birth: <u>12-4-2001</u>   Grade: <u>1</u>

School: <u>Chester Elementary</u>   Date Form Completed: <u>9-19-08</u>

Person(s) completing this form: <u>Wendy Colvard, School Psychologist</u>

Behavioral Strengths: Identify and briefly describe adaptive behaviors, skills, and characteristics that are functional and appropriate.

1. gross motor skills
2. fine motor skills
3. follows directions well
4. supportive family unit
5. helpful to others

Interfering Behaviors: Identify and describe priority problem behaviors.

1. angry outbursts (i.e.,screams and yells at teacher)
2. academic opposition (i.e., verbal refusal to complete tasks/assignments)
3. expressive language skills
4. basic literacy skills

Survey of Reinforcers: Describe events, activities, objects, people, foods, situations, or stimuli that appear to be preferred by this person.

1. one-on-one time with teacher
2. sports and physical activities
3. snacks/treats
4. social interactions with male classmates

Communication Skills: Describe the primary methods the person uses to communicate (e.g., speech, signs, gestures, symbols, electronic devices).

<u>Frank has difficulty articulating some speech sounds. He is often reluctant to speak in front of the class or when there are several classmates in the area. He has excellent receptive language skills and is quite adept at following even complex directions.</u>

Appendix B
Functional Assessment Informant Record for Teachers (FAIR-T)

If information is being provided by both the teacher and the classroom aide, indicate both respondents' names. In addition, in instances where divergent information is provided, note the sources of specific information.

Student: _____   Respondent(s): _____

School: _____   Age: _____   Sex: M   F   Date: _____

1. Describe the referred student. What is he/she like in the classroom? (Write down what you believe is the most important information about the referred student.)

2. Pick a second student of the same sex who is also difficult to teach. What makes the referred student more difficult than the second student?

3. a. On what grade level is the student reading?
   b. On what grade level is an average student in the class reading?
4. a. On what grade level is the student performing in math?
   b. On what grade level is an average student in the class performing in math?
5. a. What is the student's classwork completion percentage (0–100%)?
   b. What is the student's classwork accuracy percentage (0–100%)?
6. Is the student taking any medications that might affect the student's behavior?
   Yes   No   If yes, briefly explain:

7. Do you have any specific health concerns regarding this student?
   Yes   No   If yes, briefly explain:

8. What procedures have you tried in the past to deal with this student's problem behavior?

9. Briefly list below the student's typical daily schedule of activities.

Time	Activity
_____	_____
_____	_____
_____	_____
_____	_____
_____	_____
_____	_____
_____	_____
_____	_____

10. When during the day (two academic *activities* and *times*) does the student's problem behavior(s) typically occur?

Academic Activity #1 _____   Time _____

Academic Activity #2 _____   Time _____

11. Please indicate *good days* and *times* to observe. (At least two observations are needed.)

Observation #1	Observation #2	Observation #3 (Backup)
Date	Date	Date
Time	Time	Time

Problem Behaviors

Please list one to three problem behaviors in order of severity. Do not use a general description such as "disruptive" but give the actual behavior such as "doesn't stay in his/her seat" or "talks out without permission."

1. _____
2. _____
3. _____

1. Rate how *manageable* the behavior is:

a. Problem Behavior 1	1	2	3	4	5
	Unmanageable			Manageable	
b. Problem Behavior 2	1	2	3	4	5
	Unmanageable			Manageable	
c. Problem Behavior 3	1	2	3	4	5
	Unmanageable			Manageable	

2. Rate how *disruptive* the behavior is:

a. Problem Behavior 1	1	2	3	4	5
	Mildly			Very	
b. Problem Behavior 2	1	2	3	4	5
	Mildly			Very	
c. Problem Behavior 3	1	2	3	4	5
	Mildly			Very	

3. How often *does* the behavior occur *per day* (please circle)?

a. Problem Behavior 1	<1–3	4–6	7–9	10–12	≥13
b. Problem Behavior 2	<1–3	4–6	7–9	10–12	≥13
c. Problem Behavior 3	<1–3	4–6	7–9	10–12	≥13

4. How many *months* has the behavior been present?

a. Problem Behavior 1	< 1	2	3	4	entire school year
b. Problem Behavior 2	< 1	2	3	4	entire school year
c. Problem Behavior 3	< 1	2	3	4	entire school year

Antecedents: Problem Behavior # :		Yes		No
1. Does the behavior occur more often during a certain *type* of task?				
2. Does the behavior occur more often during *easy* tasks?				
3. Does the behavior occur more often during *difficult* tasks?				
4. Does the behavior occur more often during *certain subject areas?*				
5. Does the behavior occur more often during *new* subject material?				
6. Does the behavior occur more often when a request is made to *stop* an activity?				
7. Does the behavior occur more often when a request is made to *begin a new activity?*				
8. Does the behavior occur more often during *transition* periods?				
9. Does the behavior occur more often when a *disruption* occurs in the student's normal routine?				
10. Does the behavior occur more often when the student's *request has been denied?*				
11. Does the behavior occur more often when a *specific person is in the room?*				
12. Does the behavior occur more often when a *specific person is absent from the room?*				
13. Are there any other behaviors that usually *precede* the problem behavior?				

14. Is there anything you could do that would *ensure* the occurrence of the behavior?				
15. Are there any events occurring in the child's *home* that seem to precede occurrence of the behavior at school?				
16. Does the behavior occur more often in *certain settings*? (circle all that apply)				

large group	small group	independent work	one-to-one interaction
bathroom	recess	cafeteria	bus
other:			

Consequences: Problem Behavior # :

1. Please indicate whether the following consequences occur after the behavior is exhibited.

Consequence		Yes		No
Access to preferred activity				
Termination of task				
Rewards				
Peer attention				
Teacher attention				
Praise				
Ignore				
Redirection				
Interrupt				
Reprimand				

2. Is there any task you have stopped presenting to the student as a result of the problem behavior?
   Yes   No   If yes, describe:

3. Are there other problem behaviors that often occur after the behavior is exhibited?
   Yes   No   If yes, describe:

4. Does the student typically receive praise or any positive consequence when behavior occurs that you would like to see instead of the problem behavior?
   Yes   No

Comments:

References

Ayllon, T. (1960). The application of reinforcement theory toward behavior problems: The psychiatric nurse as a behavioral engineer. *Dissertation Abstracts, 20,* 3372.

Azrin, N. H. (1960). Use of rests as reinforcers. *Psychological Reports, 7,* 240.

Baer, D. M., Peterson, R. F., & Sherman, J. A. (1967). The development of imitation by reinforcing behavioral similarity to a model. *Journal of Experimental Analysis of Behavior, 10,* 405–416.

Bijou, S. W., Peterson, R. F., & Ault, M. H. (1968). A method to integrate descriptive and experimental field studies at the level of data and empirical concepts. *Journal of Applied Behavior Analysis, 1,* 175–191.

Braden, J. P., & Kratochwill, T. R. (1997). Treatment utility of assessment: Myths and realities. *School Psychology Review, 26,* 475–485.

Carr, E. G. (1977). The motivation of self-injurious behavior: A review of some hypotheses. *Psychological Bulletin, 84,* 800–816.

Derby, K. M., Wacker, D. P., Sasso, G., & Steege, M. (1992). Brief functional assessment techniques to evaluate aberrant behavior in an outpatient setting: A summary of 79 cases. *Journal of Applied Behavior Analysis, 25,* 713–721.

Dittmer-McMahon, K. I. (2001). *An evaluation of functional behavior assessments as implemented by teacher support teams after training.* Unpublished doctoral dissertation, Mississippi State University.

Dufrene, B. A. (2005). Functional behavior assessment: A preliminary investigation of convergent, treatment, and social validity. *Dissertation Abstracts International, Section A,* Vol. 66(4-A), p. 1272.

Dufrene, B. A., Doggett, R. A., Henington, C., & Watson, T. S. (2007). Functional assessment and intervention for disruptive classroom behaviors in preschool and Head Start classrooms. *Journal of Behavioral Education, 16,* 368–388.

Edwards, R. P. (2002). A tutorial for using the Functional Assessment Informant Record Teachers (FAIR-T). *Proven Practice: Prevention and Remediation Solutions for Schools, 4,* 31–38.

Ervin, R. A., & Ehrhardt, E. K. (2000). Behavior analysis in school psychology. In J. Austin & J. E. Carr (Eds.), *Handbook of applied behavior analysis* (pp. 113–135). Reno, NV: Context Press.

Goldiamond, I. (1965). Self-control procedures in personal behavior problems. *Psychological Reports, 17,* 851–868.

Gresham, F., Watson, T. S., & Skinner, C. H. (2001). Functional behavioral assessment: Principles, procedures, and future directions. *School Psychology Review, 30,* 156–172.

Hager, K. D., Slocum, T. A., & Detrich, R. (2007). No child left behind, contingencies, and Utah's alternate assessment model. *Journal of Evidence-Based Practices for Schools, 8,* 63–83.

Hagopian, L. P., Fisher, W. W., Thompson, R. H., & Owen-DeSchryver, J. (1997). Toward the development of structured criteria for interpretation of functional analysis data. *Journal of Applied Behavior Analysis, 30,* 313–326.

Individuals with Disabilities Education Act (IDEA), 20 U.S.C. § 1400 *et seq.* (1997).

Iwata, B., Dorsey, M. F., Slifer, K. J., Bauman, K. E., & Richman, G. S. (1982). Toward a functional analysis of self-injury. *Analysis and Intervention in Developmental Disabilities, 2,* 3–20. Reprinted in *Journal of Applied Behavior Analysis, 27,* 197–209 (1994).

Lalli, J. S., Vollmer, T. R., Progar, P. R., Wright, C., Borrero, J., Daniel, D., Barthold, C. H., Tocco, K., & May, W. (1999). Competition between positive and negative reinforcement in the treatment of escape behavior. *Journal of Applied Behavior Analysis, 32,* 285–296.

Lewis-Palmer, T., & Barrett, S. (2007). Establishing and sustaining statewide positive behavior supports implementation: A description of Maryland's model. *Journal of Evidence-Based Practices for Schools, 8,* 45–62.

Lindsley, O. R. (1956). Operant conditioning methods applied to research in chronic schizophrenia. *Psychiatric Research Reports, 5,* 118–139.

O'Neill, R. E., Horner, R. H., Albin, R. W., Sprague, J. R., Storey, K., & Newton, J. S. (1997). *Functional assessment and program development for problem behavior: A practical handbook* (2nd ed.). Pacific Grove, CA: Brooks/Cole.

Pavlov, I. P. (1927). *Conditioned reflexes: An investigation of the physiological activity of the cerebral cortex.* (W. H. Grant, Trans.). London: Oxford University Press.

Shriver, M. D., Anderson, C. M., & Proctor, B. (2001). Evaluating the validity of functional behavior assessment. *School Psychology Review, 30,* 180–192.

Skinner, B. F. (1938). *The behavior of organisms: An experimental analysis.* New York: Appleton-Century.

Skinner, B. F. (1953). *Science and human behavior.* New York: Macmillan.

Skinner, C. H., Rhymer, K. H., & McDaniel, C. E. (2000). Naturalistic direct observation in educational settings. In E. S. Shapiro (Ed.), *Conducting school-based assessments of child and adolescent behavior* (pp. 21–54). New York: Guilford Press.

Steege, M. W., Davin, T., & Hathaway, M. (2001). Reliability and accuracy of a performance-based behavioral recording procedure. *School Psychology Review, 30,* 252–261.

Steege, M. W., & Watson, T. S. (2009). *Conducting school-based functional behavioral assessments: A practitioner's guide* (2nd Ed.). New York: Guilford Press.

Steege, M. W., & Northup, J. (1998). Brief functional analysis of problem behavior: A practical approach for school psychologists. *Proven Practice: Prevention and Remediation Solutions for Schools, 1,* 4–11, 37–38.

Thorndike, E. L. (1898). Animal intelligence: An experimental study of the associative processes in animals. *Psychological Monographs, 2,* 1–109.

Watson, J. B., & Rayner, R. (1920). Conditioned emotional reactions. *Journal of Experimental Psychology, 3,* 1–14.

Watson, T. S. (2004). Treatment integrity. In T. S. Watson & C. H. Skinner (Eds.), *Encyclopedia of school psychology* (pp. 356–358). New York: Kluwer Academic/Plenum Publishers.

Watson, T. S., & Steege, M. W. (2003). *Conducting school-based functional behavioral assessments: A practitioner's guide.* New York: Guilford Press.

Academic Assessment

Edward S. Shapiro, Jaime Benson, Nathan Clemens, *and* Karen L. Gischlar

Abstract

The assessment of academic skills is an essential and critical component of the life of all schools. Like the assessment of other areas of functioning, assessment of academic skills needs to include multiple methods, multiple modalities, and multiple perspectives to obtain a comprehensive understanding of the nature of the problem. The process of assessment needs to cut across the range of direct and indirect approaches in order to capture a complete viewpoint of the academic skill problems that the student is experiencing. Included in the chapter are brief reviews of direct assessment methods built on observation, curriculum-based assessment, normative or criterion-referenced standardized tests, permanent product or portfolio review, as well as indirect methods built upon rating scales and interviews with teachers and students.

Keywords: academic assessment, curriculum-based assessment, direct observation

The assessment of academic skills is an essential and critical component of the life of all schools. Academic assessment can be aimed at an entire school district, grade, or school, as well as individual students. In particular, with the advent of the requirements of the No Child Left Behind federal law, school districts pay particular attention to school- and district-wide academic assessment, given the important role that statewide assessment measures play in determining high-stakes decisions. For example, statewide assessments may determine whether a parent will be given choices about sending their children to particular schools, or how the grading of schools based on student outcomes will be released for public consumption. Likewise, assessment of academic skills at the level of the individual student plays an important role in directing the nature of instructional interventions teachers will implement to address skill development, the nature of differentiated instruction within general education settings, and as a significant part of the high-stakes decisions related to special education eligibility.

School psychologists have always played a major role in the assessment process, including academic assessments. Early studies of the nature of referrals to school psychologists showed the highest percentage of problem referrals to be related to academic skills problems (Bramlett, Murphy, Johnson, & Wallingsford, 2002). The trend has continued into the current environment, where school psychologists are often viewed as having key roles in the implementation of Response-to-Intervention (RTI)—a process advocated as a schoolwide model of improvement, as well as an alternative to the ability–achievement discrepancy model for deciding the eligibility of a student for Specific Learning Disabilities (Batsche et al., 2005). Within an RTI model, school psychologists can assume roles around conducting, analyzing, and interpreting academic assessment for purposes of data management and instructional decision-making (National Association of School Psychologists, 2006).

Like the assessment of other areas of functioning, assessment of academic skills needs to include multiple methods, multiple modalities, and multiple perspectives. For example, in the area of assessing behavior or emotional difficulties, Shapiro and Kratochwill (2000) and Mash and Barkley (2007) along with many others, advocate that one needs to be using assessment methods that consider the broad perspective of parents, teachers, and the individuals themselves to fully understand the multiple factors that are impacting the observed behavior. One further needs to assess the problem using both direct methods, such as observation of the actual behavior in the setting where the problem was identified as occurring, as well as more indirect methods, such as rating scales completed by informants who may offer a more global sense of the behavior problem. Further, the assessment of the behavior problem needs to consider a systems perspective that examines how the family, school, community, and health systems are interacting in ways that contribute to the behavioral difficulties the student is experiencing (Mash & Terdal, 1997).

In a similar way, the assessment of academic skills also needs to consider multiple perspectives to obtain a comprehensive understanding of the nature of the problem. The process of assessment needs to cut across the range of direct and indirect approaches in order to capture a complete view of the academic skill problems that the student is experiencing. Based on the work of Cone (1978), Shapiro and Browder (2000) described a continuum of methods of academic assessment, ranging from direct to indirect, that mirror the range of methods utilized in a comprehensive assessment of behavioral difficulties.

The degree to which an assessment method is considered direct or indirect is based on the degree to which the data are collected at the same time as the actual behavioral occurrence. For example, observing and recording the behavior in the actual setting of the behavioral occurrence is considered the most direct form of assessment. Likewise, asking an informant (such as a teacher or parent) familiar with the problem to complete a rating scale at a time removed from the occurrence of the behavior is the most indirect form of assessment. The key to accurate assessment, however, is recognition that direct and indirect measures offer different, but equally important, perspectives on the behavior. Together, they represent comprehensive evaluation based on rich data sources, from which effective intervention and remediation strategies can be developed.

When children are having difficulties in academic skills, the problems develop in the context of an instructional environment, and require an assessment that fully examines the learning context as part of the assessment process, as well as assessing academic skill development. Lentz and Shapiro (1986) and Shapiro (2004) noted the importance and value in using both direct and indirect methods of assessment to conduct comprehensive evaluations of academic skills.

Figure 10.1 displays the methods of assessing academic behavior. Direct assessments of academic skills, or those that assess academic behavior at the same time as the behavior is actually occurring, include systematic observation of the student as he or she is completing academic tasks. Another method is curriculum based assessment (CBA), a method

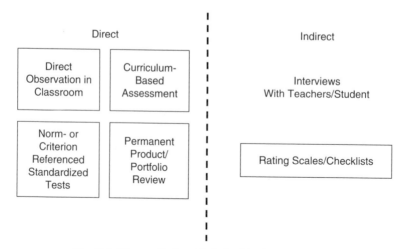

Fig. 10.1 Direct and Indirect Methods of Academic Assessment

that asks students to read passages or complete math problems under timed conditions. Other forms of direct assessment include norm- or criterion-referenced standardized tests, because the behavior of interest (e.g., student responses to academic problems) is being assessed at the same time as the data are being collected. These later forms of academic assessment are somewhat less direct than systematic observation or CBA, because the test measures may be less related to the actual information that the students have been taught (Shapiro & Lentz, 1985). Finally, permanent products, or examining worksheets produced by students during a period of academic work, also provide a direct measure of student performance. However, the measure is considered less direct than others, because the permanent product is collected at a time removed from its analysis. The indirect side of assessment would include the use of rating scales (i.e., informant or self), or interviews designed to obtain information on a student's academic skills. These measures are indirect because one is collecting data removed in time from the actual occurrence of the academic behavior, as well as potentially from individuals who are reporting their perspective about another's academic skill development. Various examples of direct and indirect measures utilized in academic assessment will be discussed throughout the remainder of this chapter.

Direct Measures
Direct Observation
Direct observation of student behavior is one of the most common assessment methods used by school psychologists, and is used frequently to screen students, assess emotional and behavior problems, evaluate classroom environment in the design of interventions, examine behaviors that support academic performance (e.g., on/off task), and monitor student academic and behavioral progress (Volpe, DiPerna, Hintze, & Shapiro, 2005). Two approaches to direct observation of student behavior are naturalistic, and systematic. In naturalistic observation, the school psychologist observes all behaviors occurring, with no preselected target behavior in mind. Typically, this type of observation is recorded in anecdotal form (Hintze, Volpe, & Shapiro, 2008). Conversely, systematic direct observation (SDO) entails recording and measurement of specific behaviors that have been operationally defined prior to observation. SDO is conducted under standardized procedures, at specific times, and in selected environments. Further, scoring and summary of observational data are stan-dardized and, thus, should not vary among observers (Salvia, Ysseldyke, & Bolt, 2007).

There are three types of SDO where occurrence of the target behavior is recorded. First, the practitioner should consider variables such as topography, context, and logistics of conducting the observation, in deciding which method to use (Shapiro & Clemens, 2005). Additionally, event/frequency recording involves counting the occurrences of a predetermined, operationally defined target behavior during a given period of time. This type of recording generally is used for behaviors that have an observable beginning and end, such as calling out or hitting, and that occur at a high frequency with a relatively short duration (Shapiro & Clemens, 2005). Further, duration recording, which is the amount of time between the start and end of a behavior, is useful for recording behaviors that continue for extended periods of time, such as tantrums or out-of-seat behaviors (Shapiro & Clemens, 2005). Latency recording is also used to measure the amount of time that lapses between a stimulus and the response, such as the amount of time it takes for a student to comply with teacher directions.

Although methods focused on recording the occurrence of behavior are useful, the methods can be cumbersome for behaviors that occur with high frequency or that do not have observable beginning and ending points. Time sampling, a fourth method of SDO, consists of dividing an observation period into equal portions of time, or intervals, and recording occurrence of the target behavior within each interval. For example, a 30-minute period could be broken down into 120 fifteen-second intervals. Each interval would be scored based upon the occurrence of the target behavior. Unlike the other methods described, time sampling provides only an estimate of behavior because every instance is not recorded (Shapiro & Clemens, 2005). For a more detailed description of methods of time sampling and observational recording, the reader is referred to Shapiro and Clemens (2005) and Hintze, Volpe, and Shapiro (2008).

Finally, permanent product recording involves the inspection of materials, such as worksheets, that the student has produced. This method does not enable the practitioner to observe behaviors directly, but it does allow for observation of the "results" of the behavior. This method can provide information regarding types of errors students make in completing work.

Additionally, the evaluator may examine the percentage of problems completed at the end of observations, in order to obtain an estimate of the child's work completion.

Direct observation methods are used frequently by practitioners. In a survey of more than 1,000 school psychologists, Wilson and Reschly (1996) found that the average practitioner completes at least 15 observations of student behavior per month. Likewise, Shapiro and Heick (2004) found, in their survey of methods used by practicing school psychologists in assessing students referred for emotional/behavioral problems, that systematic direct observation was one of the methods most frequently reported. Despite the common practice of direct observation in assessment, standard procedures for collecting observational data have not been adopted (Nock & Kurtz, 2005). Further, the most commonly used form of direct observation is the anecdotal record, or narrative, which lacks psychometric rigor. As with any psychological measure, direct observation data should be both reliable and valid (Hintze, 2005).

Hintze (2005) suggested that reliability and validity of direct observation data are not functions of the actual instrument used; instead, they refer to the outcomes of the observations. The reliability and validity of the data result from a particular observer, using a specific coding system, under specific conditions. Typically, direct observation codes have been assessed through inter-observer agreement (IOA) and inter-observer reliability. Inter-observer agreement is a class of techniques designed to demonstrate that data collected across multiple independent observers are consistent. Inter-observer reliability, on the other hand, estimates the consistency of data collected on a behavior multiple times by a single observer (Hintze, 2005).

Reliability of direct observation data is calculated through occurrence and nonoccurrence agreement indices, coefficient kappa, and coefficient phi. These three methods are used to establish the reliability of data recorded across multiple observers (i.e., inter-observer agreement). Coefficient phi also can be calculated to assess the reliability of data collected by a single observer (i.e., intra-observer agreement). Finally, an intraclass correlation coefficient can be used to determine the reliability of observations across multiple observers and subjects (Hintze, 2005).

Validity of direct observation methods should be determined through evaluating content validity (i.e., definitions accurately describe the behavior of interest), concurrent and predictive validity (i.e., data collected correlate with other known measures and can predict future behavior), and convergent and discriminant validity (i.e., the data correlate with other measures of similar content, and can discriminate among groups of known status). For a more in-depth discussion of the psychometrics of direct observation, the reader is referred to Hintze (2005).

In order to address concerns about the reliability and validity of observational data, the practitioner may want to use a standardized instrument. A number of authors have systematized the observational process for academic skills, and developed easily accessible products. Three representative observational codes designed for use in the elementary classroom are reviewed, that can be readily used by the practitioner with little training. Although other codes are available to school psychologists, these three were selected because of their ease of use and availability.

BEHAVIORAL OBSERVATION OF STUDENTS IN SCHOOLS

The Behavioral Observation of Students in Schools (BOSS; Shapiro, 2004) is a measure of student levels of academic engagement. On-task behavior is defined as either *active engaged time* (AET; e.g., completing a worksheet, reading aloud) or as *passive engaged time* (PET; e.g., listening to a lecture) for this instrument. Both AET and PET are recorded through momentary time sampling at the beginning of 15-second intervals. Throughout the remainder of each interval, the partial interval recording method is used to document off-task behaviors, including motor (e.g., walking around the room, throwing an object), verbal (e.g., talking to a classmate off-topic, making noises), and passive (e.g., staring out the window). The behavior of the target child is recorded for four of every five intervals. On the fifth interval, the behavior of a preselected peer is recorded for comparison purposes. Also, using the partial interval method, instances of teacher-directed instruction (e.g., lecturing or reading to the class, as opposed to sitting at the desk grading papers or conversing with a colleague at the classroom door) are recorded, which provides an estimate of the amount of time the teacher engages in instruction. Training to use this measure proficiently requires approximately 10 to 15 hours (Shapiro, 2004).

The BOSS (Shapiro, 2004) has demonstrated high levels of inter-observer agreement (IOA) in several studies. In one study, the BOSS was used to observe students with attention deficit hyperactivity disorder (ADHD) and their typically developing peers. Agreement across the measure's observation categories was consistently above 80%, with means ranging from 94% to 99% and kappa coefficients ranging from 0.77 to 0.92 (DuPaul, Ervin, Hook,

& McGoey, 1998). In a second study, the BOSS was used to observe students with ADHD who were using math software as a supplement to teacher instruction. Agreement for observations in this study ranged from 90% to 100%, with a mean of 94.7% (Ota & DuPaul, 2002). The BOSS also was used in a study that investigated the roles of teacher bias and behavioral differences, in the placement of minority students into special education categories. The IOA ranged from 97% to 99% across observation categories and academic subjects; kappa coefficients ranged from 0.89 to 0.96. Further evidence of the psychometric properties of the BOSS (Shapiro, 2004) is presented in a study by DuPaul, Volpe, Jitendra, Lutz, Lorah, and Gruber (2004) in which the measure's scores for PET and the off-task categories was able to discriminate between children with ADHD and their typically developing peers. Finally, a study that examined academic engagement in children with and without ADHD found that the participants with ADHD exhibited statistically significant lower rates of passive engaged time than peers. However, it should be noted that only the off-task motor variable of the BOSS consistently discriminated the groups (Junod, DuPaul, Jitendra, Volpe, & Cleary, 2006).

STATE-EVENT CLASSROOM OBSERVATION SYSTEM

The State-Event Classroom Observation System (SECOS; Saudargas & Lentz, 1986) was designed to quantify student behavior in order to assess the effectiveness of classroom interventions. The code uses momentary time sampling to derive an estimate of the time a student engages in the eight temporal "state" behaviors : (a) schoolwork (i.e., the student's head is oriented toward a worksheet); (b) out of seat (i.e., the student leaves seat without permission); (c) looking around (i.e., the student looks out window and is not engaged in activity); (d) motor behavior (i.e., the student engages in repetitive, stereotyped movements); (e) play with object (i.e., the student is repetitively playing with an object; (f) social interaction with another child (i.e., the student talks to one or more classmates); (g) social interaction with the teacher (i.e., the student interacts with the teacher); and (h) other activities (i.e., the student is engaged in activity not related to schoolwork). Further, "event" behaviors (frequency) are recorded in 15-second intervals: (a) raise hand (i.e., student has hand raised); (b) call out (i.e., the student calls out to teacher); (c) out of seat (i.e., student is out of his/her seat); (d) object aggression (i.e., student

aggresses against an object); (d) approach child (i.e., a classmate initiates contact with student being observed); (e) teacher approach to schoolwork (i.e., teacher initiates contact while student is engaged in schoolwork); (f) teacher approach to other activity (i.e., teacher initiates contact while student is not engaged in schoolwork); (g) direction-opposition (i.e., teacher gives direction which is followed by student noncompliance); (h) direction-compliance (i.e., teacher gives direction which is followed by student compliance); (i) approval (i.e., teacher praises student's behavior); and (j) disapproval (teacher disapproves of student's behavior). Approximately 12 hours of training are required to learn to use the SECOS (Saudargas & Lentz, 1986).

Inter-observer agreement in the few studies where the SECOS (Saudargas & Lentz, 1986) was used to collect data appears high. Fellers and Saudargas (1987) used the measure to examine behavioral differences between girls with an identified learning disability, and typically developing female peers. In this study, average total agreement was 81%. The SECOS was used in a second study that investigated the use of forced-choice and teacher identified reinforcers. Mean agreements for the four students who participated ranged from 96% to 98% (Damon, Riley-Tillman, & Fiorello, 2008). Furthermore, in the first study (i.e, Fellers & Saudargas) the measure discriminated between female students with and without identified learning disabilities, and in another study (Slate & Saudargas, 1986), it distinguished students with behavior disorders from their peers. However, it should be noted that in a study investigating the differences in behavior between males with and without learning disabilities, the findings suggested that the male students with learning disabilities did not exhibit keystone behaviors that were markedly different from peers, as observed with the SECOS.

ECOLOGICAL BEHAVIORAL (E-BASS)

The E-BASS is a group of observational codes designed to obtain data on the context of a student's academic instruction, as well as the situational and temporal factors related to child academic behavior (Greenwood, Schulte, Kohler, Dinwiddie, & Carta, 1986). One code, the Code for Instructional Structure and Student Academic Response (CISSAR; Stanley & Greenwood, 1981), is designed to assess typical performing students in typical classrooms. The MS-CISSAR is designed to assess students identified as having special education needs within general education settings. The third code, the ESCAPE, is designed to assess students in preschool environments. All codes follow a similar structure consisting of measures of classroom ecology, teacher behavior, and student behavior events within a single taxonomy, and are fully computerized (Greenwood, Carta, Kamps, Terry, & Delquadri, 1994).

Greenwood et al. (1986) reported that in a study of the reliability of the CISSAR, test-retest correlations at one month ranged from 0.35 to 0.93 (M = 0.88) across codes. Only 12 of the 53 codes resulted in mean values that were significantly different from test to retest. These same authors also reported that the CISSAR has contributed significant variance to the prediction of achievement, beyond that attributable to measures of intelligence. For example, in a study with inner city students, the measure accounted for 5% to 20% of the variance for achievement beyond intelligence (Greenwood et al., 1986). Graden, Thurlow, and Ysseldyke (1982), used the CISSAR to evaluate the nature of instruction and academic responding for students of high, middle, and low behavioral competence, as perceived by their teachers. Reliability was reported in terms of behavioral (i.e., observer agreement on a specific behavior under observation) and sequential (i.e., a measure of observer agreement on the sequence of items required by the observation system). The range for behavioral reliability was reported to be 60% to 100% agreement, and the reported range for sequential reliability was 85% to 99% agreement (Graden et al., 1982).

Practitioners have choices in the selection of observational codes. Deciding which code is best, is always a function of the nature of what needs to be learned about the student's academic performance. If one is interested primarily in the level of student engagement, then the BOSS is probably a good choice, given its simplicity and focus on behaviors related to student engagement during academic skill instruction. However, if one is more interested in the interactions between students and teachers, one might chose a code like the SECOS, which offers more information about the nature of the interactions within classrooms. If the real focus of the observation is on detailing the environmental context, the E-BASS codes would be a better choice. Of course, each of these codes has drawbacks in terms of simplicity, complexity, detail, and time available for observation. Each of these elements will need to considered by the clinician conducting the assessment.

Curriculum Based Assessment

Curriculum based assessment (CBA) is a direct method of assessing academic skills, where the student is asked to complete a set of academic tasks that mirror the type of academic tasks the student is expected to perform under naturalistic learning conditions. Focused primarily at the level of the individual student, these tasks are typically conducted under timed conditions, and the performance over time is used to represent the student's outcome. For example, in reading, a student is asked to read a brief passage at a specific grade level, and the *words correct per minute* serves as the outcome measure. In math, the student is asked to complete a set of math computation or concepts/application problems, with the number of digits correct per minute, or number of problems correct, represents the student's performance. There are several approaches to scoring written language tasks, but typically these include counting the number of words written in 3 minutes.

CBA has been categorized into two broad approaches, general outcome measurement (GOM) and specific subskill (SS) mastery (Fuchs & Deno, 1994). In a GOM, performance on the measure is a reflection of a student's overall performance across grade-level curriculum objectives. Curriculum-based measurement (CBM) is one of the most research-supported GOM approaches, with strong evidence of its applicability in assessing basic skills in reading (Wayman, Wallace, Hilda, Tichá, & Espin, 2007), mathematics (Foegen, Jiban, & Deno, 2007), and written language (McMaster & Espin, 2007). In an SS approach to CBA, each of the measures used is designed to assess a particular objective, with outcomes measured by the accumulation of objectives. Curriculum based evaluation (Howell, Kurns, & Antil, 2002) is an excellent, well developed example of SS mastery approach to CBA, applied across all basic skills areas.

Several key issues in the measurement of reading and mathematics skills must be considered in using this method of academic assessment. Research on the reliability, validity, and sensitivity to intervention outcomes for CBA is well established in the literature, especially for CBM (e.g., Foegen et al., 2007; McMaster & Espin, 2007; Wayman et al., 2007). CBM is the result of work by Deno and colleagues, who sought to develop a progress monitoring data collection system that could be used by special education teachers to evaluate the effectiveness of interventions with their students, and make instructional decisions (Deno, 1985; 2003a). Results of early experimentation found that tasks such as measuring the number of words a student read correctly in one minute from a basal reader were reliable and valid measures of student reading performance, related closely to student performance on standardized reading tests, and could be used to estimate performance for both decoding and comprehension (Deno, Mirkin, & Chiang, 1982). Most importantly, this research suggested that simply measuring the number of words a student read correctly in one minute, which would later be referred to as *oral reading fluency* (ORF), could validly and reliably indicate growth in that student's reading achievement across the elementary school years (Deno, 1985). This measurement could then be used to indicate a student's overall reading performance at a certain point in time, the student's level of proficiency within the curriculum, how changes in instruction impact student progress, or a student's performance relative to his/her peers administered the same measure (Deno, 1985).

Research revealed that when teachers used CBM frequently, to obtain feedback on student achievement and make adjustments to educational programs, students evidenced greater progress than when conventional methods of monitoring (i.e., periodic tests) were used. Teachers who used CBM were more realistic about their students' progress, demonstrated greater structure in their instruction, and their students were more aware of their own progress (Fuchs, Deno, & Mirkin, 1984). Research suggested, however, that simply collecting CBM data was not sufficient to observe gains in student performance—the greatest positive effects were observed when teachers used systematic data utilization rules to make instructional decisions based on the data (Fuchs & Fuchs, 1986). Subsequent experimentation confirmed this observation. Fuchs, Fuchs, and Hamlett (1989) found that students whose teachers used CBM with a system of data-based decision rules displayed superior achievement, over the students whose teachers used CBM without systematic evaluation procedures, or teachers who used only conventional means of measurement. Subsequent literature reviews on the impact of CBM on student achievement underscored these findings: teachers effected greater improvement in their students when they used CBM and made systematic decisions based on the data (Shinn & Hubbard, 1992; Stecker, Fuchs, & Fuchs, 2005).

A significant stage in the evolution of CBM involved the development of measurement materials independent of the curriculum of instruction. Like other methods of CBA, CBM involved drawing measures directly from the curriculum in which the student was instructed, such as sampling a reading passage from the student's reading textbook.

Several concerns with this practice emerged (Fuchs & Deno, 1994). First, passages within a reading textbook can vary a great deal in difficulty (Fuchs, Fuchs, & Deno, 1982), and passages drawn from literature-based versus basal readers can vary a great deal as well (Hintze, Shapiro, & Lutz, 1994). This variability can lead to measurement error, and a loss of sensitivity for measurement to reflect growth (Fuchs & Deno, 1994; Hintze et al., 1994). A second disadvantage to drawing CBM directly from student curriculum is the possibility of student familiarity with the passage or content, which may lead to inflated scores and inaccurate conclusions about student achievement (Fuchs & Deno, 1994). Third, some circumstances involve specialized student curricula that encompass a select range of reading skills. Sampling passages from a specialized curriculum may not reflect generalized reading skills, as the student's success within the specialized material may not generalize to naturally occurring reading materials, and would limit conclusions about the student's performance to that observed within the target curriculum (Fuchs & Deno, 1994).

With these concerns in mind, Fuchs and Deno (1994) determined that the sampling of CBM passages from the curriculum of instruction was not necessary, and in fact, use of passages independent of the curriculum, controlled for difficulty and reflecting year-end "general outcome" goals, may be preferred. Fuchs and Deno pointed out that passages of equivalent difficulty that reflect year-end reading levels can provide a better reflection of student growth over an extended time period (i.e., a school year).

These findings led to the exploration and construction of generic, curriculum-independent reading passages, controlled for grade-level readability, which reflected desired year-end reading outcomes. This facilitated a dramatic expansion of the uses of CBM, far beyond their original intent (Deno, 2003b). As Deno (2003a) reflects, this "uncoupling" of CBM from the curriculum of instruction made it possible for researchers and educators to use standardized stimulus materials that retained properties of validity and reliability for making instructional decisions. It also allowed student reading data to be aggregated across schools, thus allowing administrators to make district-level evaluations and decisions (Marston & Magnusson, 1998). It also allowed for the collection of local normative data to inform special education decisions (Shinn, 1988), and facilitated the screening of students to identify those who may be at risk for reading failure (Good, Gruba, & Kaminski, 2002; Stewart & Kaminski, 2002).

Later work expanded the uses of CBM to extend downward to the areas of early literacy, and as screening measures to predict performance on state-mandated high-stakes tests (e.g., Stage & Jacobsen, 2001; Good, Simmons, & Kame'enui, 2001; McGlinchey & Hixson, 2004; Shapiro, Keller, Lutz, Santoro, & Hintze, 2006; Shapiro, Solari, & Petscher, 2008). These extensions have provided schools with simple and cost-effective tools to identify early those students not meeting early literacy development targets, as well as those students at risk for failing statewide assessment measures, thus allowing them to allocate resources to provide intervention.

Despite their use in numerous studies, research on reliability and validity in mathematics and written language measurement is still developing, and more limited than in reading (Foegen et al, 2007; McMaster & Espin, 2007; Shapiro, 2004). However, research has shown that CBM of math results, evaluating both computation and concepts/applications, are strongly predictive of outcomes on norm-referenced standardized achievement tests, as well as state assessment of mathematics skills (Keller-Margolis, Shapiro, & Hintze, 2008).

CBM has become a standard part of the assessment of academic achievement in general, as well as response-to-intervention models specifically(Shapiro, Angello, & Eckert, 2004; Shapiro & Clemens, 2009), and is particularly valuable as a progress monitoring tool (Hosp, Hosp, & Howell, 2007). In addition to evaluating outcomes of individual students, CBM is useful to evaluate overall academic achievement of entire grades and districts (e.g., Deno, 2003a), as well as a method for program evaluation.

Standardized and Norm-Referenced Measures of Academic Achievement

Standardized measures of academic achievement have a long history of use in the assessment of eligibility for special education and performance. A wide range of tests have been developed over the years intended to evaluate overall academic achievement, as well as those designed to measure skills in specific sub-areas of achievement. Tests also vary with regard to the size of the population and specificity of the information generated for students; some tests have been designed to measure and summarize the achievement of groups of students, and others were developed to assess student skills on an individual basis.

INDIVIDUALLY ADMINISTERED TESTS— BROAD-BAND MEASURES

Approaching the assessment of academic skills, there are times when an evaluator may wish to gain a perspective of a student's overall levels of academic achievement. In these cases, the examiner may choose to use a measure designed to cut across several academic skill areas, such as reading, mathematics, spelling, and written expression. Tests such as these may contain several subtests within a particular academic area, from which scores on the subtests are combined to form composite scores. Tests that evaluate a range of skill areas can be described as "broad-band" measures, in that they are designed to assess skills across a broad range of skill areas and provide an index of student overall academic achievement.

Three commonly used broad-band assessment measures are the Woodcock-Johnson III Test of Achievement, Normative Update (WJ-III NU; Woodcock, McGrew, Schrank, & Mather, 2007), the Wecshler Individual Achievement Test, 2nd Edition (WIAT-II; Wechsler, 2001), and the Kauffman Test of Educational Achievement, 2nd Edition (KTEA-II; Kauffman & Kauffman, 2004). These norm-referenced measures are intended for individual student administration, and are designed to identify areas of academic strength and weakness, provide an overall picture of student academic performance, and evaluate students for the presence of learning disabilities. Now in their second and third editions, these tests are supported with strong psychometric properties and nationally standardized robust sample sizes. All tests are appropriate for prekindergarten students through adulthood, and each features an assessment battery that provides an index of achievement across academic areas, including reading, mathematics, written expression, and language (receptive and expressive). Several subtests are commonly available in each academic area, and composite scores can be generated for the individual academic areas, or as an overall achievement score. Table 10.1 displays the subtests utilized by each measure, as well as the composite scores they provide.

INDIVIDUALLY ADMINISTERED TESTS— NARROW-BAND MEASURES

Some circumstances call for a more specific assessment of student skills in a particular academic area. Possible reasons may include the need to identify more precisely the specific area in which a student is demonstrating skill deficiencies, or to provide some diagnostic information regarding possible reasons

Table 10.1 Areas assessed by the WJ-III NU test of achievement, WIAT-II, and KTEA-II

Test	Reading Subtests	Math Subtests	Writing Subtests	Language Subtests	Composite Scores
WJ-III NU*	*Standard Battery:* • Letter-Word Identification • Reading Fluency • Passage Comprehension *Extended Battery:* • Word Attack • Spelling of Sounds • Sound Awareness	*Standard Battery:* • Calculation • Math Fluency • Applied Problems *Extended Battery:* • Quantitative Knowledge	*Standard Battery:* • Writing Fluency • Spelling • Writing Samples *Extended Battery:* • Editing • Punctuation and Capitalization	*Standard Battery:* • Story Recall • Understanding Directions *Extended Battery:* • Picture Vocab • Oral Comprehension • Reading Vocabulary	• Total Achievement • Broad Reading • Broad Math • Oral Language • Broad Written Language • Academic Knowledge
WIAT-II**	• Pseudoword Decoding • Word Reading • Reading Comprehension	• Numerical Operations • Mathematics Reasoning	• Written Expression • Spelling	• Oral Language • Listening Comprehension	• Total Battery • Reading • Math • Written Language • Oral Language
KTEA-II***	*Standard Battery:* • Letter and Word Recognition • Nonsense Word Decoding • Reading Comprehension *Supplemental Tests:* • Phonological Awareness • Rapid Automatized Naming • Fluency-Semantic and Phonological • Timed Word Recognition • Timed Nonsense Word Decoding	• Math Concepts and Applications • Math Computation	• Written Expression • Spelling	*Supplemental:* • Listening Comprehension • Oral Expression	• Total Battery • Reading • Math • Written Language

*Woodcock-Johnson Test of Achievement, Third Edition, Normative Update; **Wecshler Individual Achievement Test, Second Edition; ***Kauffman Test Educational Achievement, Second Edition.

for a students' low achievement. Space does not permit an exhaustive list of all the measures that are available; however, descriptions of some more commonly used tests in the areas of reading and mathematics are described.

Several measures exist for evaluating student performance and areas of deficit in reading and early literacy skills. In order to decide the most appropriate measure, one should consider the reason for referral, and the types of difficulties exhibited on the more broad assessments. In the area of early literacy skill development, the Comprehensive Test of Phonological Processing (CTOPP, Wagner, Torgesen, & Rashotte, 1999) allows for the assessment of early and emergent literacy skills in phonological processing, including phonological awareness, phonological memory, and rapid naming. Similarly, the Test of Early Reading Ability, 3rd Edition (TERA-3; Reid, Hresko, & Hammill, 2001) is intended for students between ages 3 and 8 and is designed to measure skills in early developing areas of alphabet knowledge, print conventions, and constructing meaning from print.

The Woodcock-Johnson III Diagnostic Reading Battery (WJ-III DRB; Woodcock, Mather, & Schrank, 1997) is designed to provide diagnostic information in the areas of phonological awareness, phonics, oral language, and reading achievement. To assess skills related to reading fluency, the Gray Oral Reading Test, 4th Edition (GORT 4, Wiederholt & Bryant, 2001) provides an assessment of student reading rate, accuracy, and comprehension. To provide further assessment of reading comprehension, the Test of Reading Comprehension, 4th Edition (TORC-4, Brown, Hammill, & Wiederholt, 2009) is available.

Several measures are also available to assess mathematics skills more specifically. For evaluating early math skills, the Test of Early Mathematics Ability, 3rd Edition (TEMA-3, Ginsberg & Baroody, 2003) is designed to provide information on pre-counting, counting, formal and informal mathematics, and concepts skills in young students between ages 3 and 8. The KeyMath, 3rd Edition (Connolly, 2008) allows for the assessment of a range of mathematics skills that are typically targeted in kindergarten through ninth grade, with a greater emphasis on mathematics reasoning and problem-solving skills than in previous editions of the KeyMath tests. Similarly, the Test of Mathematical Abilities, 2nd Edition (TOMA-2, Brown, Cronin, & McEntire, 1994) is intended for students in grades 3 through 12, and is designed to assess computational and problem-solving skills, as well as the application of mathematics skills to everyday situations.

GROUP ADMINISTERED TESTS

Group administered tests of achievement are designed to provide information on how students are achieving as a group, in which results can be examined across grades, schools, districts, and states. Individual student scores can also be examined to provide an index of how the student performs on the test relative to peers. There are several major tests of achievement that are commonly used by schools across the country: The Terra Nova 2, Terra Nova 3, and the Terra Nova Comprehensive Test of Basic Skills, published by CTB/McGraw Hill; the Metropolitan Achievement Test, 8th Edition (MAT-8) and the Stanford Achievement Test Battery, 10th edition (SAT-10), published by Pearson; and the Iowa Tests of Basic Skills, published by Riverside Publishing. All of the previously mentioned tests are similar in structure and in the content sampled. All contain several subtests measuring skills in academic areas such as reading, mathematics, science, and social studies, as well as other areas such as language and vocabulary. Administration time is typically around 30 minutes per subtest; thus, total testing time will depend on the number of tests that are chosen. Some tests, such as the MAT-8 and SAT-10, are untimed. All tests involve standardized procedures for administration. Content for the tests was sampled using standards established by various states, and textbooks and curricula commonly used in schools (Wright, 2008). Scores are typically available in several formats, such as scaled or standard scores, percentile ranks, stanines, age and grade equivalents; scores can be obtained on a group or individual student basis.

STATE-MANDATED ACHIEVEMENT TESTS

Accountability in education under the No Child Left Behind Act (NCLB; No Child Left Behind Act, 2004) has mandated state-administered achievement testing for all students. NCLB requires that students achieve a level of proficiency in core academic areas, with a goal that all students are proficient in these areas by 2014. The U.S. Department of Education has allowed each state to develop its own academic standards, as well as the option for states to develop, or contract to develop, their own tests to measure student attainment of those standards (both of which must be approved by the federal government). Most states have opted to contract with a test development company or other organization to develop their state tests. For example, Pearson has developed the state test for Michigan, Minnesota, Mississippi, and Tennessee, among others (Wright, 2008). Other organizations that have developed tests for specific states include the American Institutes for Research, Educational Testing Service (ETS), Data Recognition Corporation, and Riverside Publishing.

Although there is some variation in the standards and tests across states, all share general characteristics with regard to the nature of the tests, grades and subjects tested, and when in the school year testing takes place. State tests are standards based and criterion referenced, meaning that student performance is compared to a predetermined standard indicating proficiency in an academic area. The requirement under NCLB is that schools should make annual yearly progress (AYP) toward having all students achieve proficiency; however, each state is allowed to determine what level of performance is considered "proficient" (Wright, 2008).

The Pennsylvania System of School Assessment (PSSA), for example, was developed through a contract with the Data Recognition Corporation. The PSSA program began in 1992, but it was not until 2000 that the PSSA became a standards based, criterion referenced measure, following the passage of state standards in 1999. Content of the PSSA underwent a process of development and field testing, with new items embedded within the test for field trials (Data Recognition Corporation, 2008). For the 2008/2009 school year, the PSSA involved tests in the areas of reading, mathematics, writing, and science. Assessment administration involved grades 3 through 8 and 11, with the exception of writing (grades 5, 8, and 11) and science (grades 4, 8, and 11). Tests were administered across February (writing), March (reading and math), and April (science). Based on their performance relative to the state standards, a student's score in each academic area fell within one of four categories: Below Basic, Basic, Proficient, or Advanced.

VALUE-ADDED ASSESSMENT

Several states have incorporated a new form of data analysis as part of the high-stakes testing process. Known as *value-added assessment*, the analysis involves an examination of student scores over time, to provide an index of growth. Each student's scores are compared to his or her previous scores, making it possible to measure the degree to which a student demonstrated growth in scores over previous years. Value-added assessment provides a new dimension to the analysis of student test scores. The traditional approach would involve looking at student test scores at a particular point in time. Scores would be compared to other students at that time only, and one would be able to see if the student's scores were lower, higher, or similar to the scores of other students at that time. This can be useful information; however, these scores do not provide information regarding the students' scores relative to prior years. Knowledge of a student's rate of growth is important in evaluating the achievement of individual students, as well as in summarizing the effectiveness of the instruction being delivered at the classroom, school building, district, or state level. Value-added assessment has been incorporated in several states including Tennessee, Arkansas, Colorado, Iowa, Minnesota, Pennsylvania, Florida, and Ohio (Wright, 2008).

There are several positive uses and implications of value-added assessment. First, on an individual student basis, value-added assessment allows one to determine if a student's score on a high-stakes test in one year is (a) similar to scores on previous years' tests, suggesting the student demonstrates expected growth; (b) higher than scores in previous years, suggesting greater than expected growth; or (c) lower than scores in previous years suggesting the student has made less than expected growth.

Second, value added-assessment can be used to evaluate the effectiveness of instruction and identify highly effective teachers (Wright, 2008). If students in a class make greater than expected gains over scores in previous years with a given teacher, it may indicate a highly effective teacher. On the other hand, if students make less than expected growth over previous years, it may suggest that the current teacher is less effective in delivering the curriculum or skills needed for the students to succeed.

Third, value-added assessment provides a more sensitive and descriptive picture of how schools or districts perform from year to year. This is particularly important for historically low-performing schools or districts. Value-added assessment provides information on the degree of growth these students are making from year to year, so although a high percentage of students may score below proficient levels, the value-added assessment can determine if students achieve expected levels of growth. Likewise, typically higher performing schools and districts can use value-added assessment to ensure that despite consistently high scores, students are still making expected levels of growth.

Fourth, value-added assessment allows school administrators to examine the growth of subgroups of students within a school or district (Wright, 2008).

In this way, schools can evaluate the growth of typically low achieving students relative to the growth made by average and high achieving students. This information is useful in evaluating the effectiveness of instruction for students of various achievement levels.

STANDARDIZED AND NORM-REFERENCED TESTS IN SCHOOL PSYCHOLOGY

The "paradigm shift" in school psychology (Reschly, 2008; Reschly & Ysseldyke, 2002), from a primary role as test administrator and special education gatekeeper to that of problem solver working to identify and proactively intervene on behalf of students, has meant a change in the way in which norm-referenced standardized tests (NRSTs) are used in the assessment of student academic skills deficits. Problem-solving approaches to academic assessment and intervention have emphasized the importance of using assessment measures closely aligned to the student's material of instruction; namely, curriculum based measures and assessments (e.g., Deno, 2005), and have deemphasized or discouraged the use of NRSTs (Shinn, 2005).

Difficulties with the use of NRSTs for purposes of problem-solving assessment are well documented, and include: a potential poor degree of overlap between the content of the test and material of instruction (Bell, Lentz, & Graden, 1992; Good & Salvia, 1988; Jenkins & Pany, 1978; Shapiro & Derr, 1987); failure on the part of NRST users to consider score variability and confidence intervals when interpreting discrepancies between student performance to that of the normative population (Brown-Chidsey, 2005); lack of sensitivity to small changes in performance; and an inability to effectively identify instructional strategies to address student skill deficits (Howell & Nolet, 2000; Shapiro, 2004). Concerns such as these have led many to advocate for the limited use of NRSTs, only under well-informed and well-reasoned conditions (e.g., Brown-Chidsey, 2005; Reschly and Grimes, 2002).

The influence of a problem-solving approach to academic assessment and intervention on the use of NRSTs is evident in the *Best Practices in School Psychology* series (Thomas & Grimes, 1995, 2002, 2008). The third edition of this series (BPIII, Thomas & Grimes, 1995) carried a strong emphasis on problem solving throughout, but it still contained a chapter on best practices in using standardized assessments (Stone, 1995). Chapters carefully emphasized that although important information can be obtained from the use of NRSTs, they should be utilized in conjunction with other methods of assessment. However, subsequent versions of *Best Practices* continued to emphasize a problem solving approach, and chapters on the use of standardized measures of academic achievement were missing from the fourth and fifth editions of *Best Practices in School Psychology* (Thomas & Grimes, 2002; 2008).

Studies have evaluated school psychologists' usage of certain types of NRSTs over the years. Hutton, Dubes, and Muir (1992) reviewed the assessment practices of school psychologists, compared their findings to a survey completed a decade earlier (Goh, Teslow, & Fuller, 1981), and found that, in general, usage of NRSTs had increased across that 10-year period. At the time of this writing, there have no studies published between 2000 and 2008 on usage of NRSTs by school psychologists in academic assessment. Thus, it is difficult to determine if the recent increase in popularity of problem solving approaches to assessment (e.g., Response to Intervention) and changes to federal regulations governing the use of NRSTs in identifying learning disabilities, have resulted in a decline in NRST usage and increase in the use of curriculum based forms of assessment and measurement.

Even when all of the disadvantages and potential pitfalls of using NRSTs are considered and understood, NRSTs hold value in certain situations. Certainly, state regulations mandate the use of measures to assess levels of academic achievement and evaluate the presence of a learning disability, requiring evaluators to use them as part of their assessment battery. Brown-Chidsey (2005) posited that NRSTs may be useful for screening purposes, and when students present with a mixed educational history. When little is known about a student, such as when students enter kindergarten, NRSTs may provide information on student achievement relative to a normative base, thus allowing for some preliminary decisions on students who may be in need of further attention. Similarly, when little is known about a student because of frequent transitions, absenteeism, or inadequate or inconsistent educational records, NRSTs may be helpful in providing information on a student's general levels of achievement and skills relative to peers (Brown-Chidsey, 2005). Particularly for students with incomplete or inconsistent records, it may be difficult for an evaluator to know where to begin in assessing a student's level of academic skills. In this case, careful use of an NRST may provide a starting point to suggest relative strengths and weaknesses, from which the evaluator can go forward with a more problem-solving type of assessment.

Fletcher, Lyons, Fuchs, and Barnes (2007) suggest that NRSTs of achievement be used within an RTI model. After a student demonstrates an inadequate response to instruction on progress monitoring measures, Fletcher et al. suggest that NRSTs of achievement can provide a sense of the student's level of achievement compared to normative rates, validate and confirm the results found on curriculum based measurements, and confirm that all academic skill domains have been assessed for the student. The use of NRSTs in this case would be to provide validation of poor academic achievement, and it is important to note that their use is in conjunction with a problem solving approach.

In addition to the areas identified above, NRSTs can assist in the assessment of academic achievement when the domain of interest may be less well known to the examiner. In some cases, curriculum based measures may not be readily available, or it may less apparent how to measure a particular area. For example, phonological processing abilities have been shown to be of substantial importance in the development of reading skills (e.g., Wagner, Torgesen, & Rashotte, 1994; Wagner et al., 1997); however, practitioners may not be aware of ways to measure them in a manner that is reliable and valid. In these cases, tests such as the CTOPP can be particularly useful.

In summary, current best practice recommendations minimize the role of NRSTs in the assessment of academic achievement, favoring a problem-solving type of assessment using measures that closely reflect the students' curriculum of instruction. This is justifiable, given the well-documented limitations or NRSTs and potential problems through their use. However, there are several situations in which the careful and informed use of a NRST of achievement might be necessary. If they are used, it is important that examiners consider them as a part of a multi-method evaluation, use them responsibly, and be aware of their limits.

Permanent Product, Performance Assessment, and Portfolio Evaluations

Academic products produced within the observation period, as well at other times, should be used to show performance under natural environment conditions. Examples of permanent products include workbooks, tests, quizzes, reports, other classroom activities. These types of products provide information related to student strengths and weaknesses in naturally occurring contingencies in the classroom. For example, an analysis of a writing sample of a second-grade student may reveal difficulty with grammar and punctuation, which can become direct targets for interventions. When combined with systematic, direct observation, permanent products are useful to determine work completion within the observation (Shapiro, 2004). For example, a student observed under systematic observation may be found to be engaged 80% of intervals. However, when examining the students' actual work produced during the observation, it showed that the student drew on the paper rather than actually answering any of the assigned problems. Thus, without an examination of the student's worksheet, it would appear that he was engaged in the activity while in fact, he was apparently off-task the entire interval.

Related to permanent product assessment, performance assessments present students with a task in which to apply their knowledge and skills, which is evaluated with clearly defined criteria (Niko & Brookhart, 2007). Performance assessments provide teachers with an opportunity to collect student work and analyze it for consistent patterns of difficulties, as well as areas of strength and level of support necessary to reach expectations for assignments. Scoring of performance assessment measures typically uses a rubric scoring method, where the response is judged on a scale with each anchor point defined for the evaluator.

When used as part of a comprehensive assessment of academic skills, performance assessment combined with permanent product reviews provides an opportunity to demonstrate educational growth and a student's best work. The combination of these methods is considered a form of portfolio evaluation, and offers an opportunity to examine student performance across a broad range of skills. For example, within a "best works" portfolio, students include sample work that provides evidence of meeting specific learning goals (Niko & Brookhart, 2007). Additionally, growth and learning progress portfolios include samples of student work with commentary about the progress of the student's learning. In contrast to the best works portfolio, progress portfolios focus on intermediate stages of learning, rather than final products. The teacher may use the portfolio to monitor the progress of individual studies, instruct the student, and help the student reflect on their knowledge and progress (Niko & Brookhart, 2007).

Performance assessments provide educators with an opportunity to specify meaning with complex learning goals, analyze the student's ability to integrate and apply knowledge and skills, and observe the process of learning, not simply the product (Hambleton & Murphy, 1992; Linn & Gronlund, 1995; Niko & Brookhart, 2007; Oosterhof, 1994; Stiggins, 1994). However, there are several disadvantages to using performance assessments. Performance tasks and scoring rubrics are not only difficult to develop, they are also time-consuming to create, and for teachers to score (Hambleton & Murphy, 1992; Linn & Gronlund, 1995; Niko & Brookhart, 2007; Oosterhof, 1994). While rubrics are one way to improve scorer reliability, the reliability of scores from performance assessments, and especially portfolios, may be problematic, since different teachers may have various levels of training, competence, expectations, and values for student learning (Baker, O'Neill, & Linn, 1993; Koretz, Stecher, Klein, & McCaffrey, 1994). Additionally, students may have different prior knowledge and experiences to rely on when creating portfolios. Further, performance on one task does not provide information about performance on other tasks (Niko & Brookhart, 2007), and portfolios may not adequately measure particular skills or concepts well.

In a review of one state's alternate assessment portfolio system, Johnson and Arnold (2004) indicated serious concerns in the content, response process, and structural validity of a portfolio assessment. Specifically, the content of the portfolios did not match well to state content standards, the scores were open to interpretation, and the content did not generalize to other skill areas (Johnson & Arnold, 2004). Additionally, construct underrepresentation, as well as instructional relevance, is a common concern, given the breadth and complexity of curriculum and content standards (Johnson & Arnold, 2007). Thus, portfolios may provide educators with more qualitative information about student learning in the classroom, including motivation and approach to complex tasks; however, the limitations of performance assessments, including portfolios, makes them problematic when designing instructional interventions and monitoring student progress.

Indirect Measures
Standardized Interviews

An important part of academic assessment is the assessment of the instructional environment. As a part of the assessment of the classroom ecology, Shapiro and Lentz (1985) encourage the use of structured teacher interviews and student interviews, along with other measures such as direct and systematic observation of the classroom, rating scales, and an examination of student-generated products, such as worksheets or homework assignments (Shapiro, 1990; 2004).

In general, teacher interviews should address general classroom instructional strategies, the curriculum, and methods of informal assessment used by teachers (Shapiro, 2004). The academic assessment of individual students typically begins with teacher interviews, which provide the most detailed information about the child and classroom. During the interviews, information regarding each of the basic skill areas, including reading (e.g, oral reading fluency and reading comprehension), math, spelling, and written language, is obtained. Interviews should provide clear definitions of academic problems and related environmental events (Lentz & Shapiro, 1986). Specifically, teacher interviews should include questions about placement within curriculum materials, expected levels in comparison to average performing peers, derivation of current placement in curriculum, instructional processes, types and frequency of feedback, contingencies for performance and accuracy, goal-setting procedures, and teacher planning strategies (Shapiro, 1990; 2004). The interview format is adapted from the behavioral consultation process (Bergan & Kraotchwill, 1990) in which problem identification interviews, tapping critical environmental variables that contribute to the defined problem, are utilized to design, implement, and evaluate interventions (Shapiro, 2004). A framework and format for conducting these interviews can be found in Shapiro (2004).

Student interviews should seek the student's perspectives regarding teacher instructions, self-efficacy, and performance, including his/her ability to meet expectations. These perspectives offer essential information when building intervention programs (Shapiro, 2004). For example, a student interview regarding a student's perceptions about reading revealed that he liked to read, and that there were a couple of books that he thought were good; however, he was unable to identify these books. The student stated that he did not like reading long books. Although he did not think reading was hard, the student stated he preferred to listen to stories, and liked working with classmates while reading stories. He also stated that he understands assignments and teacher expectations, but he does not think he is able to complete the assignments within the allotted time. When combined with other information, the student's perceptions of reading class may help to create interventions in which he can engage in shared reading with a peer (e.g., repeated reading and listening passage preview with a peer) in order to improve his oral reading fluency and help him complete assignments more efficiently.

Although teacher and student interviews are extremely valuable in the assessment process, they are considered indirect methods of assessment, since one is collecting information about the student at a time removed from when the behavior actually occurred. As such, the information obtained is primarily global perceptions of behavior, and subject to potential biases inherent in any form of indirect assessment (Shapiro & Kratochwill, 2000). Thus, multiple sources of information and multiple methods of assessment are essential in conducting a comprehensive assessment. However, teacher and student interviews may be useful for obtaining the perspective of teacher–student relationships, and the way they affect learning and behavior. Although these types of questions are typically included in more general interview formats (e.g., Goldstein, 1995; Sattler, 1997), the interviewer may modify questions directed at the family relationships, such as qualities the child likes and does not like about his or her parents, to target similar variables in the teacher (Goldstein, 1995; Pianta, 1999). Pianta (1999) suggested potential interview questions, such as "Does this teacher ever make you feel mad or sad? How does that happen?" and "What does this teacher do that's fun?" In addition, Pianta (1999) offered strategies to encourage the child to respond to these sometimes difficult questions, including posing the question about children in general, or about other children in their class, using affirmation of the child's view prior to the elicitation of specific examples, and gaining information about the child's representational models. The Student-Teacher Relationship Scale (STRS; Pianta, 1994), a standardized and validated measure, and the Teacher Relationship Interview (TRI; Stuhlman & Pianta, 2001) may also be utilized to assess teacher perspectives about his or her relationship with the child.

Rating Scales

The Academic Performance Rating Scale (APRS; DuPaul, Rapport, & Perriello, 1991) is a 19-item rating scale that assesses teacher perceptions of academic productivity and accuracy. Specifically, the teacher estimates student performance over the past week in a variety of subjects and types of instruction, which may be useful in quantifying students' performance on these academic tasks. Sample items include, "Estimate the accuracy of completed written language arts work (i.e., percent correct of work

done)" and "How quickly does this child learn new material (i.e., pick up novel concepts)?" (DuPaul et al., 1991). An analysis of the factors that contribute to a student's academic performance difficulties can assist in the decision making process, and the design and implementation of intervention strategies. Specifically, the inclusion of various indirect methods, such as rating scales and interviews, helps to triangulate data and either confirm or disconfirm hypotheses related to academic performance.

The APRS was developed on a sample of urban lower-middle-class elementary school children. Teachers were instructed to rate the academic performance over the past week of one boy and girl, randomly selected from the class list. The children ranged in age from 6 to 12 years, and 28.5% of the children were from diverse backgrounds including African American, Asian American, and Hispanic ethnicities. Validity was examined in a subsample of 50 children randomly selected from the larger study.

Results of a principal components analysis, followed by a normalized varimax rotation with iterations, revealed a three underlying factors that met retention criteria: *academic success* (i.e., achievement in various academic areas); *impulse control* (e.g., careless work completion or beginning work carelessly); and *academic productivity* (i.e., completion of academic-related assignments). These three subscales can be combined to produce an APRS total score. An examination of coefficient alphas revealed adequate internal consistencies for the total APRS (.95), academic success (.94), and academic productivity (.94) subscales; however, the internal consistency of the impulse control subscale was weaker (.72), which was attributed to the fewer number of items on the subscale. Test-retest reliability across a 2-week interval was uniformly high. More detailed descriptions of test development procedures and validation can be found in DuPaul et al. (1991).

The Academic Competence Evaluation Scales (ACES; DiPerna & Elliott, 1999) is another rating scale that may be used to gain additional information about teachers' perspectives of student performance, behavior, and academic enablers. The ACES yields reliable and valid scores in order to identify academic strengths and weaknesses in students (Elliott, DiPerna, Mroch, & Lang, 2004). The measure was nationally standardized, and three forms are available: teacher form for grades kindergarten to 12, student self-report for grades 6 to 12, and college student report. The ACES is composed of two subscales: *academic skills* (i.e., reading/language arts, mathematics, and critical thinking) and *academic enablers* (i.e., motivation, engagement, study skills, and interpersonal skills). A *total academic enablers* score is also available. Teachers respond to academic skills on a 5-point rating scale (i.e., far below, below, grade level, above, and far above). On the academic enablers scale, teachers respond on a 5-point frequency scale (i.e., never, seldom, sometimes, often, and almost always). Importance ratings (i.e., not important, important, and critical) are available for both subscales. Three levels of score interpretations are available: academic and academic enabling scales, subscale interpretation, and item analysis. The academic enablers of prior achievement and interpersonal skills have been shown to influence motivation, which influences study skills and engagement (DiPerna, Volpe, & Elliott, 2002).

The APRS and ACES are two examples of rating scales that may be useful in identifying intervention targets related to academic skill deficits. The measures show strong psychometric properties, and offer standardized scores that may be used to support information obtained from other assessment strategies (e.g., direct observation, curriculum based measurement).

Conclusions

Conducting assessments of academic skills requires evaluators to use a combination of methods that can effectively evaluate both the nature of the academic environment, and the academic skills of the student. Included are those assessment strategies that directly assess academic behavior as it is occurring in the natural environment of the classroom, such as direct systematic observation or curriculum based assessment, as well as indirect methods, such as interviews or completion of rating scales that assess academic behavior at a time and place removed from the actual occurrence of the behavior. Together, these methods of assessment offer a powerful combination to achieve a comprehensive examination of a student's academic skills.

Assessment of academic skills must determine how the student performs on tasks in basic skills, such as reading, mathematics, and written language, against a known criterion or standard (such as the expectations of a standards-based curriculum), as well as understanding how the student fares against same age/grade peers. When the evaluation process is aimed at an entire district, school, or grade, the evaluator is asking questions about an entire population's outcomes, against the expectations of a normative group. To effectively address the wide range of questions related to academic assessment, the

selected strategies to conduct the assessment must be well matched to the questions of interest.

Clearly, academic assessment is a crucial and critical part of evaluations within the school context. Outcomes of academic assessment significantly impact decisions about the future of individual students (i.e., those potentially eligible to receive remedial or supplemental educational services) as well as entire populations of schools (i.e., those schools achieving annual yearly progress). School psychologists play an essential role in helping to guide schools through the assessment process, recognizing that academic assessment requires a full understanding of student individual performance, as well as the context in which learning is occurring.

References

Baker, E. L., O'Neill, H. F., & Linn, R. L. (1993). Policy and validity prospects for performance-based assessment. *American Psychologist, 48,* 1210–1218.

Batsche, G., Elliot, J., Graden, J. L., Grimes, J., Kovaleski, J. F., Prasse, D., et al. (2005). *Response to intervention: Policy considerations and implementation.* Alexandria, VA: National Association of State Directors of Special Education.

Bell, P. F., Lentz, F. E., & Graden, J. L. (1992). Effect of curriculum–test overlap on standardized test scores: Identifying systematic confounds in educational decision making. *School Psychology Review, 21,* 644–655.

Bergan, J. R., & Kratochwill, T. R. (1990). *Behavioral consultation and therapy.* New York: Plenum Press.

Bramlett, R. K., Murphy, J. J., Johnson, J., & Wallingsford, L. (2002). Contemporary practices in school psychology: A national survey of roles and referral problems. *Psychology in the Schools, 39,* 327–335.

Brown, V., Cronin, M., & McEntire, E. (1994). *Test of Mathematical Abilities, Second Edition.* Austin, TX: Pro-Ed.

Brown, V. L., Hammill, D. D., & Wiederholt, J. L. (2009). *Test of Reading Comprehension, Fourth Edition.* Austin, TX: Pro-Ed.

Brown-Chidsey, R. (2005). The role of published norm-referenced tests in problem-solving-based assessment. In R. Brown-Chidsey (Ed.), *Assessment for intervention: A problem solving approach* (pp. 247–264). New York: Guilford.

Cone, J. D. (1978). The Behavioral Assessment Grid (BAG): A conceptual framework and a taxonomy. *Behavior Therapy, 9,* 882–888.

Connolly, A. J. (2008). *Key Math 3 Diagnostic Assessment.* San Antonio, TX: Pearson.

Damon, S., Riley-Tillman, T. C., & Fiorello, C. (2008). Comparing methods of identifying reinforcing stimuli in school consultation. *Journal of Educational and Psychological Consultation, 18,* 31–53.

Data Recognition Corporation (2008). *Technical report for the Pennsylvania System of School Assessment: 2008 Reading and Mathematics Grades 3, 4, 5, 6, 7, 8, 11.* Retrieved September 20, 2010 from http://www.portal.state.pa.us/portal/server.pt/community/technical_analysis/7447.

Deno, S. L. (1985). Curriculum-based measurement: The emerging alternative. *Exceptional Children, 52,* 219–232.

Deno, S. L. (2003a). Curriculum-based measures: Development and Perspectives. *Assessment for Effective Intervention, 28*, 3–12.

Deno, S. L. (2003b). Developments in curriculum-based measurement. *The Journal of Special Education, 37*, 184–192.

Deno, S. L. (2005). Problem-solving assessment. In R. Brown-Chadsey (Ed.), *Assessment for intervention: A problem solving approach* (pp. 10–40). New York: Guilford.

Deno, S. L., Mirkin, P. K., & Chiang, B. (1982). Identifying valid measures of reading. *Exceptional Children, 5*, 36–45.

DiPerna J. C., & Elliott, S. N. (1999). Development and validation of the Academic Competence Evaluation Scales. *Journal of Psychoeducational Assessment, 17*, 207–225.

DiPerna, J. C., Volpe, R. J., & Elliott, S. N. (2002). A model of academic enablers and elementary reading/language arts achievement. *School Psychology Review, 31*, 298–312.

DuPaul, G. J., Ervin, R., A., Hook, C. L., & McGoey, K. E. (1998). Peer tutoring for children with attention deficit hyperactivity disorder: Effects on classroom behavior and academic performance. *Journal of Applied Behavior Analysis, 31*, 579–592.

DuPaul, G. J., Volpe, R. J., Jitendra, A. K., Lutz, J. G., Lorah, K. S., & Grubner, R. (2004). Elementary school students with attention deficit hyperactivity disorder: Predictors of academic achievement. *Journal of School Psychology, 42*, 285–301.

DuPaul, G.J., Rapport, M.D., & Perriello, L.M. (1991). Teacher ratings of academic skills: The development of the Academic Performance Rating Scale. *School Psychology Review, 22*, 284–300.

Elliott, S. N., DiPerna, J. C., Mroch, A. A., & Lang, S. C. (2004). Prevalence and patterns of academic enabling behaviors: An analysis of teachers' and students' ratings for a national sample of students. *School Psychology Review, 33*, 302–309.

Fellers, G., & Saudargas, R. A. (1987). Classroom behaviors of LD and nonhandicapped girls. *Learning Disability Quarterly, 10*, 231–236.

Fletcher, J. M., Lyon, G. R., Fuchs, L. S., & Barnes, M. A. (2007). *Learning disabilities: From identification to intervention.* New York: Guilford Press.

Foegen, A., Jiban, C., & Deno, S. (2007). Progress monitoring measuring in mathematics: A review of the literature. *The Journal of Special Education, 41*, 121–139.

Fuchs, L. S., & Deno, S. L. (1994). Must instructionally useful performance assessment be based in the curriculum? *Exceptional Children, 61*, 15–24.

Fuchs, L. S., Deno, S. L., & Mirkin, P. K. (1984). The effects of frequent curriculum-based measurement and evaluation on pedagogy, student achievement, and student awareness of learning. *American Educational Research Journal, 21*, 449–460.

Fuchs, L. S., & Fuchs, D. (1986b). Effects of systematic formative evaluation: A meta-analysis. *Exceptional Children, 53*, 199–208.

Fuchs, L. S., Fuchs, D., & Deno, S. L. (1982). Reliability and validity of curriculum-based informal reading inventories. *Reading Research Quarterly, 18*, 6–26.

Fuchs, L. S., Fuchs, D., & Hamlett, C. L. (1989). Effects of instrumental use of curriculum-based measurement to enhance instructional programs. *Remedial and Special Education, 10*, 43–52.

Ginsberg, H. P., & Baroody, A. J. (2003). *Test of early mathematics ability* (3rd ed.). Austin, TX: Pro-Ed.

Goh, D.S., Teslow, J., & Fuller, G. B. (1981). The practice of psychological assessment among school psychologists. *Professional Psychology, 12*, 696–706.

Goldstein, S. (1995). *Clinical Interview Form.* Salt Lake City, UT: Neurology, Learning, and Behavior Center.Good, R.H., Gruba, J., & Kaminski, R.A. (2002). Best practices in using Dynamic Indicators of Basic Early Literacy Skills (DIBELS) in an outcomes driven model. In A. Thomas and J. Grimes (Eds.), *Best practices in school psychology IV* (pp. 699–720). Bethesda, MD: National Association of School Psychologists.

Good, R.H., & Salvia, J. (1988). Curriculum bias in published norm-referenced reading tests: Demonstrable effects. *School Psychology Review, 17*, 51–60.

Good, R. H., Simmons, D. C., & Kame'enui, E. J. (2001). The importance and decision-making utility of a continuum of fluency-based indicators of foundational reading skills for third-grade high-stakes outcomes. *Scientific Studies of Reading, 5*, 257–288.

Graden, J., Thurlow, M., & Ysseldyke, J. (1982). Instructional ecology and academic responding time for students at three levels of teacher-perceived behavioral competence. (Report No. IRLD-RR-73). Washington, DC: Office of Special Education and Rehabilitative Services. (ERIC Document Reproduction Service No. ED 224 189).

Greenwood, C. R., Carta, J. J., Kamps, D., Terry, B., & Delquadri, J. (1994). Development and validation of standard classroom observation systems for school practitioners: Ecobehavioral assessment systems software (EBASS). *Exceptional Children, 61*, 197–210.

Greenwood, C. R., Schulte, D., Kohler, F. W., Dinwiddie, G. I., & Carta, J. J. (1986). Assessment and analysis of ecobehavioral interaction in school settings. In R. J. Prinz (Ed.), *Advances in Behavioral Assessment of Children and Families* (Vol. 2, pp. 69–98). London, England: Jessica Kingsley Publishers.

Hambleton, R. K., & Murphy, E. (1992). A psychometric perspective on authentic measurement. *Applied Measurement in Education, 3*, 1–16.

Hintze, J. M. (2005). Psychometrics of direct observation. *School Psychology Review, 34*, 507 519.

Hintze, J.M., Shapiro, E.S., & Lutz, J.G. (1994). The effects of curriculum on the sensitivity of curriculum-based measurement in reading. *The Journal of Special Education, 28*, 188–202.

Hintze, J. M., Volpe, R. J., & Shapiro, E. S. (2008). Best practices in the systematic direct observation of student behavior. In A. Thomas & J. Grimes (Eds.), *Best Practices in School Psychology* (5th ed., Vol. 2, pp. 319–335). Washington DC: National Association of School Psychologists.

Hosp, M. K., Hosp, J. L., & Howell, K. W. (2007). *The ABC's of CBM: A practical guide to curriculum-based measurement.* New York: Guilford Press.

Howell, K. W., & Nolet, V. (2000). *Curriculum-based evaluation: Teaching and decision making* (3rd ed.). Belmont, CA: Wadsworth.

Howell, K. W., Kurns, S., & Antil, L. (2002). Best practices in curriculum-based evaluation. In A. Thomas & J. Grimes (eds) *Best practices in school psychology IV* (pp. 753–771). Washington, DC: National Association of School Psychologists.

Hutton, J. B., Dubes, R., & Muir, S. (1992). Assessment practices of school psychologists: Ten years later. *School Psychology Review, 21*, 272–284.

Jenkins, J. R., & Pany, D. (1978). Standardized achievement tests: How useful for special education? *Exceptional Children, 44*, 448–453.

Johnson, E., & Arnold, N. (2004). Validating an alternate assessment. *Remedial and Special Education, 25*, 266–275.

Johnson, E., & Arnold, N. (2007). Examining an alternate assessment: What are we testing? *Journal of Disability Policy Studies, 18*, 23–31.

Junod, R. E. V., DuPaul, G. J., Jitendra, A. K., Volpe, R. J., Cleary, K. S. (2006). Classroom observations of students with and without ADHD: Differences across types of engagement. *Journal of School Psychology, 44*, 87–104.

Kauffman, A. S., & Kauffman, N. L. (2004). *Kauffman Test of Educational Achievement* (2nd ed.). San Antonio, TX: Pearson.

Keller-Margulis, M., Shapiro, E. S., & Hintze, J. M. (2008) Long tern diagnostic accuracy of curriculum-based measures in reading and mathematics. *School Psychology Review, 37*, 374–390.

Koretz, D., Stecher, B., Klein, S., & McCaffrey, D. (1994). The Vermont Portfolio Assessment Program: Findings and implications. *Educational Measurement: Issues and Practice, 13*, 5–16.

Lentz, E., & Shapiro, E.S. (1986). Functional assessment of the academic environment. *School Psychology Review, 15*, 346–357.

Linn, R. L., & Gronlund, N. E. (1995). *Measurement and assessment in teaching* (7th ed.). Upper Saddle River, NJ: Prentice Hall.

Marston, D., & Magnusson, D. (1988). Curriculum-based measurement: District level implementation. In J. Garden, J. Zins, & M. Curtis (Eds.). *Alternative educational delivery systems: Enhancing instructional options for all students* (pp. 137–172). Washington D.C.: National Association of School Psychologists.

Mash, E. J., & Barkley, R. A. (Eds.) (2007). *Assessment of childhood disorders* (4th ed.). New York: Guilford Press.

Mash, E. J., & Terdal, L. G. (Eds.) (1997). *Assessment of childhood disorders* (3rd ed.). New York: Guilford Press.

McGlinchy, M. T., & Hixson, M. D. (2004). Using curriculum-based measurement to predict performance on state assessments in reading. *School Psychology Review, 33*, 193–203.

McMaster, K., & Espin, C. (2007). Technical features of curriculum-based measurement in writing. *The Journal of Special Education, 41*, 68–84.

National Association of School Psychologists (2006). *The role of the school psychologist in the RTI process*. Retrieved February 13, 2009 from http://www.nasponline.org/advocacy/RTIrole_NASP.pdf

Niko, A. J., & Brookhart, S. M. (2007). *Educational assessment of student* (5th ed.). Upper Saddle River, NJ: Merrill/Prentice Hall. No Child Left Behind Act (2001). Public Law 107–110.

Nock, M. K., & Kurtz, S. M. S. (2005). Direct behavioral observation in school settings: Bringing science to practice. *Cognitive and Behavioral Practice, 12*, 359–370.

Oosterhof, A. (1994). *Classroom applications of educational measurement* (2nd ed.). Upper Saddle River, NJ: Merrill/Prentice Hall.

Ota, K. R., & DuPaul, G. J. (2004). Task engagement and mathematics performance in children with attention deficit hyperactivity disorder: Effects of supplemental computer instruction. *School Psychology Quarterly, 17*, 242–257.

Pianta, R.C. (1994). Patterns of relationships between children and kindergarten teachers. *Journal of School Psychology, 32*, 15–32.

Pianta, R.C. (1999). *Enhancing relationships between children and teachers*. Washington, DC: American Psychological Association.

Reid, D. K., Hresko, W. P., & Hammill, D. D. (2001). *Test of early reading ability* (3rd ed.). Austin, TX: Pro-Ed.

Reschly, D. J. (2008). School psychology paradigm shift and beyond. In A. Thomas and J. Grimes (Eds.), *Best practices in school psychology, volume V* (pp. 3–15). Washington, D.C.: National Association of School Psychologists.

Reschly, D. J., & Ysseldyke, J. E. (2002). Paradigm shift: The past is not the future. In A. Thomas and J. Grimes (Eds.), *Best practices in school psychology, volume IV* (pp. 3–20). Washington, D.C.: National Association of School Psychologists.

Salvia, J., Ysseldyke, J. E., & Bolt, S. (2007). *Assessment in special and inclusive education*. Boston: Houghton Mifflin Company.

Sattler, J. (1997). *Clinical and forensic interviewing of children and families*. San Diego, CA: Sattler.

Saudargas, R. A., & Lentz, F. E. (1986). Estimating percent of time and rate via direct observation: A suggested observational procedure and format. *School Psychology Review, 15*, 36–48.

Shapiro, E. S., & Derr, T. F. (1987). An examination of the overlap between reading curricula and standardized achievement tests. *The Journal of Special Education, 21*, 59–67.

Shapiro, E. S. (1990). An integrated model for curriculum-based assessment. *School Psychology Review, 19*, 331–349.

Shapiro, E. S. (2004). *Academic skills problems: Direct assessment and intervention* (3rd ed.). New York: Guilford Press.

Shapiro, E. S., & Browder, D. M. (1990). Behavioral assessment: Applications for persons with mental retardation. In J. Matson (Ed.), *The handbook of behavior modification with persons with mental retardation* (2nd ed.) (pp. 93–122). New York: Plenum.

Shapiro, E. S., & Clemens, N. H. (2009). A conceptual model for evaluating system effects of response to intervention. *Assessment for Effective Intervention, 35*, 3–16.

Shapiro, E. S., Angello, L. M., & Eckert, T. L. (2004). Has curriculum-based assessment become a staple of school psychology practice? An update and extension of knowledge, use, and attitudes from 1990 to 2000. *School Psyhology Review, 33*, 243–252.

Shapiro, E. S., & Clemens, N. H. (2005). Conducting systematic direct classroom observations to define school-related problems. In R. Brown-Chidsey (Ed.) *Assessment for Intervention: A Problem Solving Approach* (pp. 175–199). New York: Guilford Press.

Shapiro, E. S., & Heick, P. F. (2004). School psychologist assessment practices in the evaluation of students referred for social/behavioral/emotional problems. *Psychology in the Schools, 41*, 551–561.

Shapiro, E. S., Keller, M. A., Lutz, J. G., Santoro, L. A., & Hintze, J. M. (2006). Curriculum-based measures and performance on state assessment and standardized tests: Reading and math performance in Pennsylvania. *Journal of Psychoeducational Assessment, 24*, 19–35.

Shapiro, E. S. & Lentz, F. E. (1985). Assessing academic behavior: A behavioral approach. *School Psychology Review, 14*, 325–338.

Shapiro, E .S., & Kratochwill, T. R. (Eds.). (2000). *Behavioral assessment in schools: Theory, research, and clinical foundations* (2nd ed.). New York: Guilford Press.

Shapiro, E. S., Solari, E., & Petcher, Y. (2008). Use of a Measure of Reading Comprehension to Enhance Prediction on the State High Stakes Assessment. *Learning and Individual Differences, 18*, 316–328.

Shinn, M. R. (1988). Development of curriculum-based local norms for use in special education decision-making. *School Psychology Review, 17*, 61–80.

Shinn, M. R. (2005). Identifying and validating academic problems in a problem-solving model. In R. Brown-Chidsey (Ed.), *Assessment for intervention: A problem-solving approach*. New York: Guildford Press.

Shinn, M. R., & Hubbard, D. D. (1992). Curriculum-based measurement and problem-solving assessment: Basic procedures and outcomes. *Focus on Exceptional Children, 24*, 1–20.

Slate, J. R., & Saudargas, R. A. (1986). Differences in the classroom behaviors of behaviorally disordered and regular class children. *Behavioral Disorders, 12*, 45–53.

Stage, S. A., & Jacobsen, M. D. (2001). Predicting student success on a state-mandated performance-based assessment using oral reading fluency. *School Psychology Review, 30*, 407–419.

Stanley, S. O., & Greenwood, C. R. (1981). *Code for Instructional Structure and Student Academic Response (CISSAR): Observer's manual*. Kansas City: Juniper Garden's Children's Project, Bureau of Child Research, University of Kansas.

Stecker, P. M., Fuchs, L. S., & Fuchs, D. (2005). Using curriculum-based measurement to improve student achievement: Review of research. *Psychology in the Schools, 42*, 795–819.

Stewart, L. H., & Kaminski, R. (2002). Best practices in developing local norms for academic problem solving. In A. Thomas and J. Grimes (Eds.), *Best practices in school psychology IV* (pp. 737–752). Washington, D.C.: National Association of School Psychologists.

Stiggins, R. J. (1994). *Student-centered classroom assessment*. Upper Saddle River, NJ: Merrill/Prentice Hall.

Stone, B. J. (1995). Best practices in the use of standardized assessments. In A. Thomas & J. Grimes (Eds.), *Best practices in school psychology* (3rd ed., pp. 841–848). Washington, D.C.: National Association of School Psychologists.

Stuhlman, M., & Pianta, R. C. (2001). Teachers' narratives about their relationships with children: Associations with behavior in classrooms. *School Psychology Review, 31*(2), 148–163.

Thomas, A., & Grimes, J. (Eds.) (1995). *Best practices in school psychology, Vol. I*. Washington: National Association of School Psychologists.

Thomas, A., & Grimes, J. (Eds.) (2002). *Best practices in school psychology IV*. Washington: National Association of School Psychologists.

Thomas, A., & Grimes, J. (Eds.) (2008). *Best practices in school psychology V*. Washington: National Association of School Psychologists.

Volpe, R. J., DiPerna, J. C., Hintze, J. M., & Shapiro, E. S. (2005). Observing students in classroom settings: A review of seven coding schemes. *School Psychology Review, 34*, 454–474.

Wagner, R. K., Torgesen, J. K., & Rashotte, C. A. (1999). *Comprehensive test of phonological processing*. Austin, TX: Pro-Ed.

Wagner, R. K., Torgesen, J. K., & Rashotte, C. A. (1994). Development of reading-related phonological processing abilities: New evidence of bi-directional causality from a latent variable longitudinal study. *Developmental Psychology, 30*, 73–87.

Wagner, R. K., Torgesen, J. K., Rashotte, C. A., Hecht, S. A., Barker, T. A., Burgess, S. R., Donahue, J., & Garon, T. (1997). Changing causal relations between phonological processing abilities and word-level reading as children develop from beginning to fluent readers: A five-year longitudinal study. *Developmental Psychology, 33*, 468–479.

Wayman, M. M., Wallace, T., Hilda, I., Tichá, R., & Espin, C. A. (2007). Literature synthesis on curriculum-based measurement in reading. *The Journal of Special Education, 41*, 85–120.

Wechsler, D. (2001). *Wechsler Individual Achievement Test (Second Edition)*. San Antonio, TX: Pearson.

Weiderholt, J. L., Bryant, B. R. (2001). *Gray Oral Reading Tests, Fourth Edition*. Austin, TX: Pro-Ed.

Wilson, M. S., & Reschly, D. J. (1996). Assessment in school psychology training and practice. *School Psychology Review, 25*, 9–23.

Woodcock, R. W., Mather, N., & Schrank, F. A. (1997). *Woodcock-Johnson III Diagnostic Reading Battery*. Rolling Meadows, IL: Riverside Publishing.

Woodcock, R. W., McGrew, K., Schrank, F. A., & Mather, N. (2007). *Woodcock-Johnson III Tests of Achievement (Normative Update)*. Rolling Meadows, IL: Riverside Publishing.

Wright, R. (2008). *Educational assessment: Tests and measurements in the age of accountability*. Thousand Oaks, CA: Sage.

The Development and Model of Therapeutic Assessment with Children: Application to School-Based Assessment

Deborah J. Tharinger, Lauren S. Krumholz, Cynthia A. Austin, *and* May Matson

Abstract

Therapeutic Assessment (TA) is a relatively new model of psychological assessment that, in addition to offering the benefits of a traditional assessment, also serves as a collaborative, short-term intervention. With variations, TA has been utilized with adults, adolescents, and children; research evidence on efficacy is encouraging. This chapter serves to introduce the model of TA with children to a wider audience, specifically school psychologists, as the use TA with children in schools stands to be a compelling and potent child–family–school intervention. In this chapter we review the development of TA, the rationale for and application of each step of the comprehensive model, and provide guidance to design meaningful feedback plans for parents, teachers and children. We also illustrate its use, with several examples of school-based special education assessment cases to demonstrate how including comprehensive or selected components of TA in school-based assessment of children can result in positive therapeutic change.

Keywords: therapeutic assessment, children, parents, school-based model, collaborative, feedback

Fortunately, in recent years much progress has been made in recognizing the large number of children who struggle with moderate to serious mental health and learning concerns. These children are in need of assessment, identification, and individual and systemic interventions to ameliorate the impact of their challenges. Given the number of children needing identification, and the shortage of resources to provide for assessment and treatment, we must make the best use of our available resources. Whenever possible, we need to utilize methods of assessment and intervention that are responsive to consumers and have proven efficacious. With these concerns at the forefront, this chapter raises the following questions: Can the psychological assessment of children offer more than identification/diagnosis and recommendations, and actually be an intervention in and of itself? And, if so, can this intervention involve and impact the child, as well as the child's support systems such as his or her family and school? And further, can the efficacy of such

efforts be documented? In this chapter, we suggest that the answer to all three of these questions is yes, and encourage assessment professionals to incorporate collaborative and therapeutic methods in their assessment practices with children and their parents. We also propose that these methods can be applied fruitfully in school-based assessment, and with diverse clients. Although the integration of these methods into assessment practice is perhaps most exciting for what it can offer the consumers of psychological services, it also stands to offer psychologists a satisfying experience and hopefully a renewed interest in assessment practice.

The psychological assessment of children has a long history (Kamphaus, 2001). Practices are well established for the assessment of children's functioning in cognitive/intellectual, academic, behavioral, and social/emotional/personality arenas. Psychological assessments of children take place primarily in (1) schools, where educational achievement and factors that may be hindering a child's learning are the focus, along with recommendations for educational and behavioral interventions; and (2) in clinics, hospitals, residential settings and juvenile justice facilities, where mental health/illness, its impact on behavior and development, and recommendations for psychotherapeutic interventions are the predominant focus. Regardless of setting, most assessments provide a diagnostic formulation and recommend educational and/or therapeutic interventions, but are not seen as interventions in and of themselves. However, the intervention or therapeutic potential of assessment has been noted by a number of clinicians who have advanced a new perspective on assessment, referred to generically as collaborative or therapeutic assessment.

A model that is gaining in prominence is Therapeutic Assessment (TA). TA, as developed by Finn and colleagues (Finn, 1996, 2007; Finn & Tonsager, 1997), is a relatively new application of psychological assessment that, in addition to offering almost all of the benefits of a traditional assessment, also serves as a collaborative, short-term intervention. TA is a semi-structured hybrid of assessment and intervention techniques, and requires assessors to possess and integrate competencies in both assessment and intervention. Fortunately, most psychologists are prepared with this foundation and, with additional training, can readily add TA to their repertoire. With variations in the model, TA has been utilized with adults, couples, adolescents, and children. Furthermore, TA has shown great promise clinically, and research studies and case studies have demonstrated its efficacy with adults and adolescents (Finn & Tonsager, 1992; Hilsenroth, Ackerman, Clemence, Strassle, & Handler, 2002; Hilsenroth, Peters, & Ackerman, 2004; Michel, 2002; Newman & Greenway, 1997). Recent research has also found TA with children (TA-C) to be an efficacious intervention (Tharinger, Finn, Gentry et al., (2009).

In TA-C, the assessor strives to provide the child with multiple opportunities and modalities to express his or her thoughts, feelings and behavior. The assessor also assists the parents in coming to a new understanding of their child, through active observation and collaboration. To accomplish these goals, the assessor uses an array of assessment and intervention tools. These include interviews with parents and children to co-construct and explore assessment questions (Tharinger, Finn, Wilkinson, & Schaber, 2007), along with parental observation and assisted processing of their child's testing sessions (for an example see Hamilton et al.,

2009), selected nomothetic and idiographic testing instruments (Finn, 2007), extended inquiry methods (Finn, 2007; Handler, 2008), features of play, playfulness and play therapy (Tharinger, Christopher & Matson, in press), family sessions (Tharinger, Finn, Austin, et al., 2008), oral and written consumer-friendly feedback for both the child and parents (Tharinger, Finn, Wilkinson, et al., 2008; Tharinger, Finn, Hersh, et al., 2008), and, finally, follow-up sessions.

The primary goal of TA-C is to help parents understand their child in new ways, become more empathic towards their child, and shift their interactions with their child to foster positive development in the child and the family. TA-C is designed to answer specific questions parents and children pose for the assessment, to form working alliances with parents and children, and to collaboratively engage children and their parents in the assessment process. As introduced above, in most instances parents are encouraged to observe their child's testing sessions and process the findings with the assessor along the way. In addition, parents and children receive interactive feedback that addresses their assessment questions and explores steps for change. Thus, TA-C is seen as a short-term family systems intervention (Finn, 2007). TA-C is particularly appropriate for challenging, multi-problem situations, with children who are difficult to understand, when previous interventions have failed, and with parents whose own projections or psychological difficulties keep them from being able to accurately perceive and appropriately respond to their children (Tharinger et al., 2007). TA-C also has the potential to be a child–family–school intervention, or child–school intervention, as will be addressed and illustrated later in this chapter.

The goal of this chapter is twofold. The first goal is to introduce TA-C to a wider audience, specifically school psychologists and psychologists who work with children in schools, and encourage them to consider how the model of comprehensive TA-C may be useful to their assessment practice. To accomplish this goal, we first briefly review the literature on the psychological assessment of children. We then proceed to describe the history and development of collaborative assessment and TA, including the philosophical and theoretical underpinnings and recent efficacy research. Following, we depict the rationale for, and application of, each step of the comprehensive model of TA-C, and refer to case studies where TA-C has been utilized. We also include a discussion of an underdeveloped aspect of training in child assessment: how to work with the information obtained, to reach a case conceptualization, organize the findings sensitively, and design a meaningful feedback plan for both the parents and the child.

We acknowledge the reality that using the comprehensive TA-C model will not be feasible in many practice settings, including schools. Thus, the second goal of this chapter is to propose a strategy for adopting selected components of TA-C, given the needs and constraints of a particular case and specific setting. To accomplish this goal, we highlight a sequential process for selecting and adapting components of TA-C for school-based assessment purposes. We discuss the major components of TA-C that appear to have the most value and transportability to assessment practice in the schools. We have organized these components into categories that can be conceptualized as four stages: (1) adopting a new foundational base, which includes embracing a collaborative stance toward assessment; (2) utilizing innovative assessment practices, which include constructing assessment questions with the child, parent and teachers; (3) integrating innovative practices of case conceptualization; and (4) planning and delivering feedback to parents, children, and teachers in meaningful and collaborative ways. We also propose the use of intervention sessions within the assessment as a potentially very useful component. Lastly, we illustrate a variety of protocols that adopt features of TA-C, using, as examples, school-based special education assessment cases conducted by graduate students under the instruction and supervision of the first author. Our intent is to demonstrate how including selected components of TA-C in school-based assessment can result in therapeutic change.

Psychological Assessment of Children

As introduced above, psychological assessment of children is usually used for diagnostic and intervention planning purposes. An assessment typically: (1) addresses a combination of cognitive, academic, social, emotional, behavioral and personality concerns; (2) determines if a psychiatric diagnosis or handicapping condition/disability is present that is impacting the child's functioning; (3) assists (if applicable) in school or other placement decisions; and (4) establishes the need for educational, psychosocial and/or psychiatric intervention/treatment. In addition, many assessments aim to understand the strengths and resources of the child's supportive systems, as these often impact access and response to treatment. And finally, assessment is sometimes used to evaluate whether an intervention has been successful. Thus, psychological assessment has usually been conceived of and recognized as a preamble to change, or as a way to document change, but not as a change agent in and of itself.

The traditional assessment model historically followed by psychologists has been labeled the "information gathering" model by Finn and Tonsager (1997). The goal of assessment from this model is to describe and diagnose individuals in order to make decisions and communicate about them among professionals. Also called the "medical model" (Mutchnick & Handler, 2002), this approach is characterized by a unidirectional flow of information in which the individual assessed (and, in the case of a child, his or her parents) typically has minimal input into the process of the evaluation. Moreover, depending on the particular evaluation circumstances, the individual being assessed may or may not understand the reasons for assessment, and may or may not be given the results. This may be particularly true if the individual being assessed is a child. In this model, the assessor follows the necessary standardized testing protocols, compares the data with appropriate norms, and determines relevant diagnostic categories, all with little collaboration with the client. In summary, in this approach, which has dominated assessment practice for decades, the "expert" assessor evaluates and diagnoses the patient or client, and then recommends a treatment to the patient or a referral source in order to "repair the problem" (Mutchnick & Handler, p. 75).

This information gathering, or medical model approach to psychological assessment, has been strongly associated with the area of personality assessment. Traditionally, personality assessment has been identified with psychodynamic theory and other depth psychology theories that seek to understand the underlying causes and mechanisms of an individual's patterns of behavior. The goal of this type of assessment has been to discover mechanisms that may account for, or influence, current behavior and patterns of the individual being assessed. This tradition of assessment has included a strong emphasis on using history, background information, responses to standardized tests, and responses to projective tests (also referred to more recently as *performance based tests*) to construct a formulation of how the individual may have come to develop his or her particular challenges, and how they are being maintained. This tradition has looked at the impact of early events and processes, as well as current concerns and themes (often not fully conscious or in awareness in the person being assessed) that may be affecting current emotional states, disordered behaviors and impaired relationships.

In personality assessment, projective tests have been viewed as useful in that they can offer alternative, less structured stimuli for clients to respond to (e.g., drawings, pictures, sentence stems, inkblots). These less structured stimuli are thought to allow many individuals, including children, to forego or lessen their protective layers or defenses, resulting in a less censored response. Thus, concerns and preoccupations that are useful to understanding the person and planning interventions may be revealed. More contemporary personality assessment utilizing projective measures has embraced an "experience-near" approach (Handler, 2008). As will become apparent in a later section, TA embraces and even heightens many of the experience-near features of personality assessment. This occurs through the use of process assessment techniques, as well as methods of interactive, collaborative discussion of findings.

Psychological assessment has also been influenced by the behavioral tradition (see chapter in this volume on behavioral assessment). Behavioral assessment, often referred to as *functional behavioral assessment* or *functional behavioral analysis*, has as its goal to determine the cause or function of a given behavior before an intervention is attempted. In this tradition, the resulting recommended intervention is based on the hypothesized cause of the behavior. Interviews, rating scales completed by multiple informants, naturalistic observations, and response to environmental manipulations are major tools of behavioral assessment. The scope of behavioral assessment typically is more circumscribed than that of personality assessment, as it focuses on specific behavior and patterns of behavior, in contrast to the more comprehensive focus of personality assessment. Furthermore, the behavioral assessment tradition has always been intervention focused. As will become evident, aspects of behavioral assessment are integrated into TA, and are perhaps most apparent in the use of intervention techniques within a testing session, or the inclusion of a complete session where intervention is the major focus.

Thus, as will be seen, TA-C utilizes aspects of contemporary personality and behavioral assessment, and also aims to gather accurate and useful information per traditional assessment models. TA-C is very compatible with the integrated perspective that is emerging in the literature, with its blending of personality and behavioral approaches, informed by multi-modal, multi-informant, multi-method techniques, and guided by an openness to understanding the findings from a multi-theoretical orientation. Contemporary assessment calls for the integration of the nomothetic and idiographic traditions, with clinical judgment valued along with statistic or actuarial judgment (Riccio & Rodriquez, 2007). This is all very encouraging.

However, from the point of view collaborative assessment and TA, psychological assessment still falls short of being optimally useful to the consumers of the assessments. Psychological assessment, particularly of children, has much more to offer than diagnoses, recommendations, and communication among professionals. It has been noted that the way in which assessment is typically practiced "profoundly undermines the usefulness of this potentially powerful diagnostic and therapeutic intervention" (Cohen, 1997, p. 254). In actual, day-to-day practice, assessments are often conducted quickly, without taking time to gather and integrate the perspectives of multiple individuals, including the child, parent, teachers, and others centrally involved in the child's life. Information from multiple informants, and the use of multiple methods, is essential if the assessor is to make sense of test data, which is not definitive alone (Cohen, 1997). Additionally, if parents, children, and teachers are not encouraged and given time to formulate the questions they hope the assessment might address, the assessment's meaning and utility are seriously limited. Furthermore, if the child, parents, and others involved are not helped to understand how the findings relate to the child's everyday life and their relationship and work with the child, an intervention opportunity is missed. The skills needed to provide meaningful feedback to stakeholders, including children themselves, have been underdeveloped, under-taught and under-practiced, in spite of ethical guidelines requiring or encouraging such practice (Tharinger, Finn, Hersh, et al., 2008; Tharinger, Finn, Wilkinson, et al., 2008).

As introduced earlier, the central question becomes: How can we maximize, or at least enhance, the usefulness and transparency of psychological assessments for consumers—in our case, children, parents and, in many cases, involved educators? Additionally, in this era of the call for evidence based practice in medicine and psychology, can we provide empirical evidence for the efficacy and effectiveness of psychological assessment *and* assessment as an intervention? We now endeavor to address these questions.

Development of Collaborative and Therapeutic Assessment Models

In the 1960s and 1970s, many psychologists with interpersonal and humanistic theoretical perspectives called for a reevaluation of the purposes and practices of psychological assessment (Fischer, 1985/1994). Some psychologists, disenchanted by the traditional and medical models, rejected the practice of assessment altogether. Others independently began to adjust the ways they interacted with individuals they were assessing, including both adults (Fischer, 1985/1994; Mosak & Gushurst, 1972; Richman, 1967) and children (Colley, 1973; Fischer, 1970, 1985/1994), after incidentally noticing benefits from more humanistic and interpersonal techniques. For example, Mosak and Gushurst discovered that simply the act of giving clients their assessment results signified that the clinician had "a genuine belief in the patients' strength" and in their ability to handle undesirable information (p. 542), which then had a noticeable effect on clients' mood and engagement in treatment. Richman noted similar improvements in difficult inpatient populations, concluding that a "skillful sharing of test results with the patient is often beneficial, *especially* for the very disturbed, when conducted by a psychologist trained in both testing and psychotherapy" (p. 63). Fischer explained the advantages of collaborating with children in her assessments, and described a successful collaborative assessment approach in which she observed a child in the context of his family's home environment, and also processed portions of the testing that were difficult for him at the time they occurred.

Paralleling these movements in the field of psychology, the medical research literature has reflected a shift in the medical model of diagnosis, and in the traditional attitudes toward the doctor–patient relationship. Approaches such as shared decision-making (Quill & Brody, 1996) and patient-centered medicine (Laine & Davidoff, 1996) emphasize the importance of medical providers collaborating with patients by projecting an empathic, attentive attitude, in order to facilitate disclosure of concerns, increase participation in treatment planning, and improve compliance with recommendations (Pegg, Auerbach, Seel, et al., 2005). Indeed, engaging clients in a relationship and giving them information tailored to their personality and life can convey "respect and consideration for their autonomy and capability," and indicate that the clinician sees them "as an integral component in their own treatment" (Pegg et al., p. 373). Thus, a more collaborative approach to client–provider interaction, influenced by a common desire to make the experience more "humane, respectful, and understandable" to consumers (Finn, 2007, p. 5), has emerged in both the medical and psychological fields.

In psychology, these collaborative approaches aim to help clients directly, and to provide transformative experiences during the assessment process itself, rather than waiting until testing is complete to indirectly help clients by drawing up treatment recommendations (Finn, 2007). Numerous therapeutic and collaborative models and techniques have been developed. Although all share the goals of helping clients have a positive experience of the assessment, and experience positive change (Finn), and many techniques overlap, there are some important differences between the approaches. We review two prominent models: Fischer's model of collaborative, individualized assessment, and Finn's semi-structured Therapeutic Assessment model.

Fischer's Model of Collaborative Assessment

Collaborative assessment embraces the belief that clients and their families are the experts on their own lives, and brings that knowledge to the assessment process, while assessors are the experts on psychology and on the assessment instruments (Fischer, 2000). Thus, clients and assessors must work together, drawing on their different areas of expertise, in order to fully understand the client's challenges and develop ideas about the kinds of intervention needed. The goal of Fischer's approach is to describe the client as an individual— that is, his or her "particular situation" and "life comportment"—and to provide individualized recommendations that have already been tested, to some extent, during the assessment process (Fischer, 1985/1994). In this model, testing methods and responses, rather than reflecting an absolute truth, are viewed as tools that may help illuminate the client's life and challenges; the client's life experiences themselves are regarded as the primary data (Fischer, 2000). For Fischer, the value of tests lies not necessarily in their normative data or resulting scores based on client responses, but in their ability to produce experiences that bear similarities to situations the client likely faces in everyday life. For example, taking a reading achievement test may evoke behaviors and emotions that the client regularly demonstrates when reading in school. For this reason, in some cases tests may be used in idiographic ways, or standardized procedures may be deviated from when opportunities arise to explore experiences in greater depth. Tests are tools that are "used by" the assessor and client as they work together to learn about the client's situation; they are not simply "administered to" the client (Fischer, 1985/1994).

In Fischer's model, collaborative dialogue between the client and assessor is essential to understanding how test findings and experiential information fit together. Reports are written in very accessible language, in the first person, and include detailed narrative descriptions of the client's behavior and the assessor's impressions of the client. Fischer discusses with the client what will be included in the report, and notes in the report itself any disagreements between herself and the client about the picture presented. She also invites clients to write annotations on the actual copies of reports to be sent to other professionals, expressing their evaluation of, and reactions to, what she has written (Fischer, 1985/1994). Outlined in her ground-breaking book, *Individualizing Psychological Assessment*, this "human-science" model follows six guiding principles: (1) primary emphasis is on life events, rather than on test scores and theoretical constructs; (2) events that occur in session are processed as they occur, and are considered as important data; (3) collaboration occurs with the client; (4) it is expected that clients will react in different ways, and these reactions are processed with the client; (5) assessors consider all data as behavior *in context*; and (6) the goal is to practice "authentically," which means to strive for what is possible, while acknowledging the necessary limits and requirements of clinical reality (Fischer, pp. 46-48). Fischer's work has provided an excellent foundation for conducting psychological assessment from a collaborative stance.

Finn's Model of Therapeutic Assessment (TA)

Therapeutic Assessment (TA), a form of collaborative assessment developed by Finn and colleagues (Finn, 1996, 2007; Finn & Tonsager, 1997), is a brief, semi-structured therapeutic intervention informed by psychological testing. It is based on the premise that psychological assessment, when practiced in a collaborative and interpersonal manner, can produce benefits beyond its typical information gathering purposes. It can serve as a kind of short-term intervention in and of itself (Finn & Tonsager). In contrast to traditional assessment (discussed earlier), which focuses on collecting accurate information about the client that can be used to make placement or treatment decisions, the goal of TA is not only to collect accurate information, but to use that data to help the client (or child client and parents) learn new ways of understanding and addressing the client's current challenges in living (Finn & Tonsager). According to Finn (1996), the traditional approach to psychological assessment "ignores the interpersonal context of clients' test responses and promotes a mechanistic, de-humanized approach to psychological testing" that is possibly "harmful to clients and at best benefits them only indirectly" (p. 83). Moreover, the traditional approach has been described as imparting stress, anxiety, anger, and confusion to clients (Handler, 2007), especially children. In contrast with this traditional, "information gathering," model of assessment, Finn (2007) describes "therapeutic assessment" as an attitude and respect about the relationship with the client, where:

> [T]he goal of the assessor is more than collecting information that will be useful in understanding and treating the patient. In therapeutic assessment, in addition, assessors hope to make the assessment experience a positive one and to help create positive changes in clients and in those individuals who have a stake in their lives. (p. 4)

Whereas traditional assessment's intent is to help clients indirectly through the recommendations that follow, therapeutic assessment's intent is to help directly (Finn, 2007). The process of TA itself is intended to be transformative (Handler, 2007) and to leave clients "positively changed at the end of an assessment" (Tharinger et al., 2007, p. 297). Although aspects of TA are likely practiced by many gifted clinicians without their even knowing it (Finn, 2007), this idea that psychological assessment can be a therapeutic intervention is a "major paradigm shift in how assessment is typically viewed" (Finn & Tonsager, 1992, p. 286). However, it is important to clarify and emphasize that collaborative/therapeutic techniques in TA do not replace standardized testing; rather, they augment the diagnostic process by engaging clients more honestly and respectfully. Simply by making "minor changes" in evaluation procedures, "assessors can enhance the therapeutic effects of an assessment without compromising in any way the valid and reliable test information that is collected" (Finn & Tonsager, 1997, p. 382).

TA originally differed from other forms of collaborative assessment in its explicit goal of leaving clients positively changed at the end of an assessment, although other collaborative assessment techniques have now adopted this goal as well. This goal is achieved through an ongoing focused dialogue between the client and assessor, which can lead to the "co-authoring" of a "new story" about the client and his or her strengths, significant relationships, and problems in living. By providing an experience of empathic attunement and accurate mirroring, assessors help support clients in grasping and assimilating these new conceptualizations, and in trying out next steps in their growth process (Finn & Tonsager, 1997, 2002). Although the techniques used in TA are drawn from a number of different interventional approaches, one strong underpinning is *collaborative empiricism* as practiced in cognitive-behavioral therapy. In this approach, the clinician and client work together to set up different "experiments" to test mutually generated theories about why the client experiences certain problems in living, and what will ameliorate them (Beck, 1995). In TA, as contrasted with cognitive therapy, these "experiments" often make use of results from psychological tests.

THEORETICAL UNDERPINNINGS OF TA

Like other forms of collaborative assessment, the principles of TA are rooted in intersubjective, phenomenological, and interpersonal theories of human behavior (Finn, 2007). TA also incorporates concepts and techniques from a variety of other psychological orientations, including behavioral, social learning theory, cognitive-behavioral, object relations, attachment, narrative, humanistic, and family systems. Interpretation and inference involve an integration of nomothetic and idiographic methods. Data is interpreted in the context of the reason for the assessment, and the client's relationship with the assessor. The tests and methods used are an opportunity for the client to communicate with the assessor, and responses reflect the quality of the developing relationship. Assessors use clients' test responses and descriptions of their test experiences to "get in their shoes" and empathically comprehend their experiences and perspectives. This is the philosophical foundation of the collaboration and working alliance established with the child and parents. In addition, the assessor's experience, affect,

and counter-transference reactions are essential pieces of information that are understood to illuminate potentially important case dynamics, but are also considered as potential sources of bias in interpretation and communication about the findings (Fowler, 1998; Handler & Meyer, 1998; Smith, 1998). Thus, the assessor's active self-awareness is a key tool in TA. It is our experience that assessors who also have training and expertise in therapy models that involve the use of the self (such as interpersonal and attachment-based models) easily transfer these abilities to their work with TA.

Three characteristics of personal motivation are thought to account for the therapeutic value of a collaborative/therapeutic assessment: (a) self-verification; (b) self-enhancement; and (c) self-efficacy/self-discovery (Finn & Tonsager, 1997). Self-verification theory posits that a person aspires to have his or her self-concept and reality affirmed by others, regardless of whether that self-concept is positive or negative (Swann, 1990). TA specifically attends to clients' self-verification needs through a deliberate organization of feedback findings, in which the first testing results revealed are always those that are consistent with, and thus reaffirm, the client's self views (Finn, 2007; Finn & Tonsager). Self-enhancement can be conceived of as the desire to be appreciated and loved by others, and to feel good about oneself (Finn & Tonsager). This construct is reflected in TA by the collaborative, interpersonal nature of the process in which assessors strive to be respectful, open, and humane with their clients (Finn). The third variable proposed by Finn and Tonsager is self-efficacy/self-discovery, which refers to the need to feel in control over one's environment, in addition to an individual desire for knowledge and personal growth. The collaborative nature of therapeutic assessment addresses this construct by including the client in all phases of the process, as well as by the practices of soliciting clients' assessment questions, and asking clients to confirm or deny assessment results. It is theorized that when the assessor acknowledges and attends to these three constructs during the course of an assessment, clients become positively changed and experience more beneficial effects than they would from an assessment conducted following the "information gathering" model (Finn).

RESEARCH ON TA

A number of case studies attest to the success of collaborative and therapeutic assessment methods with adults and adolescents (Finn, 1994, 1998,

2003; Finn & Kamphuis, 2006; Michel, 2002). Additionally, controlled studies of TA and collaborative assessment with adults have found positive effects including decreased symptomatic distress, increased self-esteem, and greater hopefulness (Finn & Tonsager, 1992; Newman & Greenway, 1997). A study comparing traditional and collaborative assessment also found that adults who received a therapeutic assessment felt a stronger alliance with their assessor, and were less likely to terminate follow-up treatment against medical advice, than those who received a traditional assessment (Ackerman, Hilsenroth, Baity, & Blagys, 2000).

Findings also are accumulating for the efficacy of TA-C and collaborative assessment with children. Numerous supportive clinical case studies have been published (Fischer, 1985/1994; Hamilton et al., 2009; Handler, 2007; Mutchnick & Handler, 2002; Purves, 2002), as well as empirical case studies (Smith & Handler, 2009; Smith, Nicholas, Handler & Nash, 2009; In these case studies, parents report gaining a better understanding of their children's problems, feeling more effective in their parenting and being more motivated to pursue appropriate services. Parents also indicate decreased behavioral problems, and improved mood and social functioning in their children.

Furthermore, the Therapeutic Assessment Project (TAP) conducted a study of the efficacy of TA-C with 14 children and their parents (Tharinger, Finn, Gentry, et al., 2009. They found high treatment acceptability, significantly decreased child symptomatology, and enhanced family functioning as reported by children and mothers following a TA-C. In addition, mothers demonstrated a significant increase in positive emotion, and a significant decrease in negative emotion, pertaining to their children's challenges and future. These findings support assertions from published single case studies that TA-C is likely an efficacious child and family intervention. Tharinger and students also have several new research studies underway in child populations that are investigating the comparative efficacy of assessment practice as usual, versus assessment infused with selected components of TA-C. These studies, being conducted in schools and independent assessment practice sites, are addressing the impact of enhanced parent collaboration and feedback in two studies—child feedback in one study, and child collaboration in another. Findings from these studies will inform the transportability of TA-C components into real world practice.

STEPS OF TA

Finn (1996, 2007) has proposed a semi-structured, six-step generic model for TA. There is variation in the phases as applied to children, adolescents, adults, and couples. Each of the steps of TA, according to Finn, is important in its own right; and yet, in our experience, the whole is greater than the sum of the parts. In TA-C the steps include: (1) the assessment question gathering phase, typically an initial interview with the parents and a brief interview with the child and parents together; (2) the standardized testing phase, ranging from two to eight sessions, where the child is tested while the parents observe and discuss the ongoing process and findings; (3) the family intervention phase, where the child and parents are engaged together to test out both typical and new ways of relating; (4) the summary/discussion phase, where the assessor and parents meet to collaboratively discuss the feedback and plans for the future, and a subsequent session where the child is presented with feedback (verbally and in written form), usually with parents present; (5) the written communication phase, where individualized written feedback for parents and standardized reports for referral sources, if required, are prepared; and (6) a follow-up phase, where the child and parents return for a final discussion of progress, one to three months later. Finn acknowledges the reality of client, setting, assessor, and resource variables that may preclude adopting all six phases, and encourages assessors to adapt the model to their particular needs and circumstances. We discuss adopting components of TA, short of a comprehensive TA, in a later section. We now provide the comprehensive TA-C model.

Comprehensive TA-C Model

The comprehensive TA-C model as used in TAP (see Tharinger, Finn, Gentry, et al., 2009; Tharinger et al., 2007) is now described, session by session, and a rationale is provided for many of the methods, particularly the construction of assessment questions, collaboration, the use of tests, and communication of findings (feedback) in both oral and written forms. Case studies that have used this model can be found in Hamilton et al. (2009), Tharinger et al. (2007), Tharinger, Finn, Austin, et al. (2008), and Tharinger, Christopher, and Matson (in press).

TA-C typically involves 8 to 10 weekly sessions that take place over a 3-month period (although these sessions can be condensed over a much shorter time period). We have found that weekly sessions allow parents, in particular, time between sessions to process what they are learning and begin to construct a new story about their child. The weekly schedule also allows assessors time to absorb the findings and plan the next session. In this way, the typical pacing of TA-C is more like a therapy or counseling schedule than a traditional assessment. Weekly sessions of an hour and a half each are usually sufficient.

Although TA-C can be provided by a single assessor (discussed below), in TAP the TA-C is conducted by a team of two assessors (referred to as the *assessment team*). When there are two assessors, they work together with the child and parents at the initial and final sessions of the assessment (interviews, family session and feedback). However, during the testing phase, one assessor administers the testing and creative procedures with the child, while the other supports the parents in their observation of their child's testing. The following description of comprehensive TA-C assumes a two-person assessment team.

Initial Phone Contact with Parents to Discuss Referral

In the initial conversation with parents to explore contracting for a TA-C, the assessor explicitly expresses to parents the intention that the assessment be a *collaborative process* and the conviction that parents' input is essential to the success of the TA-C. This assertion is then put into practice by asking parents to start thinking about their questions for the assessment, in preparation for their first session. This process lets the parents know from the beginning that they have the opportunity to direct where the assessment will go.

First Session with Parents: Interview to Generate Assessment Questions/Related Background

TA-C assumes that parents' concerns and questions about their children can be best addressed if the assessors are able to elicit specific assessment questions at the beginning of the assessment process (Finn, 2007). This exemplifies the *collaborative stance in action*. It is sometimes difficult for parents to translate their concerns into questions, and many parents are surprised even to be asked what they would like to learn. The assessment team helps parents understand the purpose of asking questions, and actively helps them generate useful assessment questions. While gathering background information, the assessment team remains alert to any

implicit questions, confusions, or concerns in the parents' narrative, and asks if these are areas they would like the assessment to focus on and be able to answer. Assessment questions are most useful when they are phrased in colloquial rather than technical language. Inquiring about the events or circumstances that led up to the referral often leads to a more complete description of what it is the parents (or referring person, through the parents) are wondering about the child, and why. Asking parents what decisions they need to make about their child further contextualizes the referral concern, and provides information as to what parents really want to learn from the assessment (Fischer, 1985/1994). For instance, parents asking if their child has ADHD may be wondering how to manage the child's oppositional behavior at home, wondering whether the child would benefit from a different school environment, or wondering why the child's academic performance has recently declined. Each of these concerns would call for a different kind of recommendation, and perhaps even a different selection of tests. Choosing tests based on clients' assessment questions is more efficient than administering a standard battery, increases diagnostic accuracy, and leads to more useful answers to the clients' concerns (Brenner, 2003).

An additional benefit of gathering specific assessment questions is that it provides an opportunity for assessors to learn parents' expectations for the assessment, and to provide information to parents about what the assessment may or may not realistically be able to address. Gauging parental expectations prior to the assessment is important, in light of studies that have shown relatively low parent satisfaction with the degree to which assessments met their expectations for providing help (Bodin, Beetar, Yeates, et al., 2007). Well-formulated assessment questions can serve as a "contract" of what parents can expect from the assessment. Parents typically formulate questions about a broad range of topics including etiology, diagnosis, causes of specific behaviors, parent or family influences on the child's problem, how to help, prognosis, what the child thinks and feels, and triggers or contributing factors. In addition, the content and phrasing of assessment questions may provide illuminating information about the parents' existing "story" about their child, the parent–child relationship, the parents' openness to certain kinds of feedback or recommendations, and the parents' fears and hopes for their child (Finn, 2007). This information can later be used to inform decision-making about how best to organize and frame feedback to parents about the assessment findings.

Thus, in the initial meeting with the parents, the assessment team verbally reviews the procedures of the assessment, and answers parents' questions about the process. The team explores the parents' goals for the assessment, and co-constructs individualized assessment questions that capture the concerns, puzzlements, and challenges the parents have about their child and family. Initial background information is obtained to inform the context for each assessment question (often, an additional interview is conducted later in the assessment process to further flesh out relevant history, background, etc.). The obtained questions (e.g., "Why is my child having a hard time getting along with other kids?"…"What is the source of my son's stress and sadness?") guide the assessment from this point on. Finally, the assessment team coaches the parents on preparing their child for his or her upcoming first session.

First Session with Parents and Child Together: Beginning Testing with the Child and Parent Observation

The second session, typically a week following the initial meeting with the parents, begins with a brief check-in between the assessment team and the parents, after which the child is invited to join. These steps again underscore the foundation of active collaboration. The parents are asked to introduce the child to the assessment team, explain a bit about their understanding of the process of the assessment, and verify that the child understands the reasons for the assessment, and is willing to participate. The parents and assessment team work together to address any questions and concerns raised by the child, and the parents share with their child one or two of their assessment questions (the parents have been coached on this, in the previous session). The parents are encouraged to share a question that is systemic in nature (e.g., "How can we all learn to control our anger and talk together about what bothers us?"), so as not to single out the child. The child also is invited to contribute his or her own assessment questions, at this time or at any time during the assessment. In our experience, it is hard for most children to generate their own questions at this time. They may feel overly self-conscious during this first meeting with the assessment team, as so much attention is being focused on them. However, we have found that more outspoken or parentified children are sometimes able to construct

initial questions. Examples from recent cases in TAP include, "Why do I get blamed every time something goes missing at home?" from one child, and "Why won't my parents help me more?" from another.

After this joint introduction, the session continues with the parents leaving the room with one member of the assessment team, and going to an observation room—either behind a one-way mirror, or in an adjacent room with a live video feed—to observe as the other member of the assessment team begins to engage the child in the assessment process. The child is aware that the parents will be observing, and that there is a video camera and/or one way mirror in the testing room. The opportunity for the parents to observe the child assessment sessions with the support of an assessment team member is a variation on the practice originally proposed by Finn (2007). Finn described inviting parents to observe assessment sessions from the corner of his office, and then talking with the parents after each session to ascertain their reactions, respond to their questions, and make small interventions in relation to the way they perceive their child. This method can be used successfully when TA-C is conducted by a single assessor. However, in TAP, the use of an assessment team allows one assessor to conduct these conversations "in the moment" rather than at the conclusion of the session. In our experience, this practice significantly advances the collaborative experience of the parents, and also helps them to digest the information their child is providing through the tests and creative methods.

It is important to acknowledge that inviting parents to observe all or some of their child's testing sessions is a controversial feature of TA-C. The practice of inviting parents to observe testing may raise significant concerns for some assessment professionals, as test security may be compromised to some extent. However, parents only view the testing materials briefly, and they do not take the tests themselves. Inviting the parents to observe is done in the spirit of collaborative empiricism as practiced in cognitive-behavioral therapy (Beck, 1995). The opportunity for parents to observe and discuss their reactions is thought to affect the process and outcome of the therapeutic assessment in significant ways (Tharinger et al., 2007). For example, when parents are given the opportunity to watch their child's testing, it can foster their curiosity about their child, engage them as active participants, demystify psychological assessment, and educate them about psychological tests and the assessment process.

Furthermore, by discussing parents' perceptions of the testing sessions, the assessor can help them discover answers to their questions about their child, and can help them begin to shift their "story" about why their child has problems. The assessor emotionally supports the parents as they reach new understandings, or confirm their existing beliefs, about their child. This process also allows the assessor to ascertain parental readiness and resources for change, thus informing the subsequent sessions involving the parents, including the upcoming family intervention session and feedback sessions. In working with the observing parents, the assessor maintains a collaborative stance by adopting the terms the parents use, actively and empathically listening to their concerns, and encouraging the parents' questions and comments about the process. In our experience with the parents in TAP, many indicated that the observation piece was one of the most central aspects of their coming to a new understanding of their child.

It is also important to acknowledge that some assessors may be concerned about the willingness of children to disclose with their parents observing. As discussed in Tharinger et al., (2007), we have found in TAP that most pre-adolescent children not only willingly accept their parents observing the assessment, but with the support of their strong collaborative alliance with the assessor, use this setup as an opportunity to communicate to their parents either directly or indirectly through some of the tests and methods. However, there are likely children who would not be comfortable or feel safe with this setup. In this case, it may be that TA-C is not indicated, or that the assessor will instead need to work more intensely with the parents outside of the observational context. In fact, when using TA with adolescents, the parents do not observe any of the adolescents' sessions. This differentiation is based on adolescents' developmental need for privacy and some individuation from their parents.

It is also important to note that there are cases and circumstances when parental observation of their child's testing sessions is not helpful, and can even be overwhelming and possibly detrimental. We are aware of cases where parents with backgrounds of severe trauma have been overwhelmed and traumatized while watching their children, even with good support from the assessor. In these cases, it might be best to videotape the child sessions and show excerpts to the parents later, carefully choosing what might be useful for the parent to view.

With the parents situated behind the mirror or watching the video feed with one assessor, the child and the other assessor begin to form their unique relationship. The assessor and the child typically talk more about the process, and discuss any further questions the child may have. Depending upon the child, this discussion may be lengthy or short. Next, it is common practice to invite the child to do a series of drawings (Tharinger & Roberts, in press). Standard instructions are used, and questions follow each drawing, with selective "extended inquiry" (Finn, 2007; Handler, 2008) that may include asking the child to tell a story about one of the drawings. This initial child session often ends with free play, to provide the child with the opportunity to engage in unstructured activity that may reveal aspects of his or her personality and life themes (Tharinger, Christopher, & Matson, in press), as well as to allow the child a chance to express reactions to the experience of the session.

Child Testing Sessions and Continued Parent Observation

The subsequent two to six (or more) sessions consist of child testing activities, with parents continuing to observe. Again, the number of sessions is determined by the nature and extent of the questions guiding the assessment. Test selection in TA-C is individualized for each case. Tests may include standardized psycho-educational and neuropsychological measures; behavior rating scales completed by parents and teachers; self-report personality and psychopathology measures; and performance-based personality and psychopathology measures, including individually crafted sentence completion tests, stories told to apperception cards, and the Rorschach, typically using extended inquiry methods after the standard inquiry portion is completed.

In collaborative and therapeutic assessment models, tests are approached as tools that can provide access to clients' typical real-world experiences (Fischer, 2000). Handler (1998) asserts that even seemingly objective, straightforward tests such as the Wechsler intelligence tests provide data far beyond what they purport to measure. By observing the child's response to the assessment situation, the assessor can develop a sense of the child's reactions to success and failure, reactions to interpersonal stress, regulation of affect, thought processes, tendencies toward perfectionism, level of anxiety, and defensive and coping strategies. It is important to keep in mind that standard psychological assessment can be an uncomfortable and confusing process for children. The standardized administration procedures for many tests inherently involve "failure experiences," as the assessor is required to continue administering a subtest until the child has answered a string of questions incorrectly, in order to establish a ceiling (Handler, 2007). The assessor generally cannot provide immediate feedback about the child's performance, and this, as well as the assessor's often detached, impersonal stance may arouse anxiety for children. Although it is essential to follow standard procedures so that tests can be properly scored and norm-referenced, in TA the assessor is encouraged to ask about the client's experience of the test, once standardized administration is complete (Finn, 2007).

While this may not be appropriate in all cases, the assessor may also use a "testing of the limits" or "extended inquiry" approach (Handler, 2008), following standardized administration of intelligence and achievement tests, to determine what assistance or modifications are needed for the child to succeed on items that were previously failed. For instance, the assessor may encourage the child to take guesses, walk the child through a problem-solving strategy, or provide small hints (Handler, 2007). Different types of extended inquiry may be used with other tests (Finn, 2007). For example, the child may be invited to make up a story about a character from a Rorschach or TAT response, or asked follow-up questions to contextualize responses to a self-report measure. These procedures can give greater depth and meaning to the understandings construed from test scores, and also provide opportunities for different, more supportive interpersonal interactions with the child. These techniques also assure the "experience-near" level of inference, as responses are explored and associated meanings determined. And these techniques may also inform recommendations for subsequent interventions.

In addition, further opportunities for play, unstructured and structured, may also be incorporated into testing sessions with the child (Tharinger, Christopher & Matson, in press). While this adds to the total time the assessment requires, providing free-play opportunities may be beneficial in several respects. The assessor's invitations to play may contribute to a positive child–assessor alliance, with the possible benefit of increasing the child's comfort during, and cooperation with, the testing. It is likely that the more comfortable and cooperative the child is, the more confident the assessor can be that the child's performance is representative of his or her true abilities and typical behavior.

Furthermore, observing the content and style of the child's play may provide more information and hypotheses about the child's world. In addition, themes and characters that might inform the development of an individualized fable as feedback for the child (discussed later) may arise through play.

In this series of testing sessions, as the child engages in the testing activities, the parents continue to observe from behind the mirror or through the video feed. Parents are encouraged to share comments and ask questions of the assessor who observes with them. As mentioned earlier, this is an extended and active collaborative process with the parents. As appropriate, if a team approach is used, the parents may also meet with both assessors at the end of the session, without the child, for further clarification of their observations. These "checkouts" can be very useful to enhance the parents' understanding of developing answers to their assessment questions.

Development of Initial Case Formulation and Informing the Assessment Questions

During the process of the assessment sessions, and following their completion, the assessment team works to integrate the information that has been gathered, determine if additional data gathering is needed (through tests, interviews, or contacting collateral sources), and starts to put together the case conceptualization. In addition, the assessors reflect on the preliminary feedback that will be given, typically in relation to the assessment questions. In TA-C, this analysis informs the plan for the family intervention session, the next step in the process. Following the family intervention session, the assessment team integrates information learned from this session to arrive at the final case conceptualization, and organizes the feedback to be presented to parents.

Planning and Conducting a Family Intervention Session

Following the completion of the formal testing sessions and tentative case conceptualization, a family intervention session is usually planned and held (Tharinger, Finn, Austin, et al., 2008). The plan and format of this session is individually designed to meet the needs of each family. Typically, the parents and child are guided to interact in a structured or semi-structured family activity. The goals include allowing the assessors to see the child's behavior in the family context, testing systemic hypotheses, and providing parents with the opportunity to experience success in applying new techniques in which they may have been coached by the assessors. Additional goals involve providing the child with a new experience of the parents, assisting the family in gaining insight into how the family contributes to the child's problems (and thus preparing parents to accept systemic feedback), inspiring the family, and imparting new hope.

One of the most creative tasks when planning a family session is deciding on the method or technique to use. When planning a family session, the assessor can choose from a variety of techniques that help move the focus from the child to the family, yet still maintain a common purpose with the assessment process as a whole—to continue to assess factors involved in the child's problems. There are a wide variety of possible methods and activities available for use in a family session; for descriptions and illustrations of parent coaching, semi-structured parent–child play, family drawing, family sculpture, family psychodrama, consensus TAT, and consensus Rorschach methods, see Tharinger, Finn, Austin, et al. (2008). In-depth examples of family intervention sessions also are provided in Hamilton et al. (2009), Tharinger et al. (2007), and Tharinger, Christopher, and Matson (in press). Whatever method is chosen, its implementation must be carefully planned. Special attention is paid to the questions that have guided the assessment, the family's history and patterns of interaction, and the assessors' resulting systemic hypotheses, as well as the assessors' sense of the family's readiness for various levels of intensity that may potentially be evoked during the family session. Of utmost importance is that the activities in the family session be mindfully and uniquely tailored to meet each family's needs, such that the targeted behavior or experience can be invoked "in vivo" and at an appropriate level of intensity considering the family's resources.

Planning Parent Feedback/Summary-Discussion Session: Principles of Case Conceptualization, Organizing Findings by Level of Discrepancy, and Feedback Plan

Throughout all sessions with the parents and the child, and most thoroughly before the feedback sessions, much work is put into an analysis of all information gathered through the interviews, testing sessions, and parental observations and consultations. The analysis of this information is an iterative process that guides and impacts the progression of the assessment from beginning to end. Hypotheses evolve throughout the process until the assessors arrive at the case conceptualization and organization for feedback.

PRINCIPLES OF CASE CONCEPTUALIZATION

In traditional psychological assessment of children, as well as in TA-C, the interpretive task is to make sense of complex information. This includes the child's observed overt behavior, report of conscious experiences and perceptions about self and other, portrayal of unconscious or less conscious dynamics and concerns, and the interpersonal relationship between the child and the assessor (Fowler, 1998; Smith, 1998). As assessment data are usually rich, complex, and often inconsistent, theoretically based interpretations can serve a useful organizing function. Higher-order conceptual constructs often are needed to help "explain" apparent inconsistencies in the findings. Thus, data needs to be understood within the child's cultural context, and examined from multiple theoretical and empirical perspectives, as well as from the assessor's clinical experience and the assessor's experience of the child. The task is to look for meaningful patterns that capture the complexity in the child's thoughts, emotion, behavior, and interpersonal functioning; to understand how the child developed to this point in time; and to figure out what influences help to maintain behavior that is not healthy for the child or the family. In TA-C, these principles are embraced, as well as others discussed below.

In TA-C, it is acknowledged that the information obtained from the child has been given in the present moment, and in the context of the child's interpersonal relationship with the assessor, and thus must be interpreted in that light. In addition, information gathered from the child likely has been influenced by the child's perception of the relationship the assessor has established with the child's parents, so this also needs to be taken into account. Furthermore, if the child's parents have observed the testing sessions, it is safe to assume that the child was consciously or unconsciously communicating to his or her parents, likely making the child's responses more "experience near" and relevant. And finally, it is understood that the assessor is a, if not *the,* central tool in the assessment. The assessor's experience, affect, and counter-transference reactions are essential pieces of information. These must be understood to illuminate potentially important case dynamics and bias in interpretation and communication of the findings. In TA-C, the culminating goal for the assessors is to provide a coherent, individualized portrait of the child, in context, that leads to enhanced understanding and motivation for change for the child, and, perhaps even more importantly, for the parents.

ORGANIZATION OF ASSESSMENT FINDINGS

In TA-C, after interpreting the assessment data and arriving at a case conceptualization, Finn (2007) suggests organizing the findings into three levels, referred to simply as Level 1, Level 2, and Level 3. Level 1 findings are those that are highly consistent with how clients already think about themselves, and that they are likely to agree with and accept easily. These findings should not be surprising to clients. In feedback to parents, of course, the relevant consideration is consistency with how parents view their child, and how they view themselves in relation to their child. Level 2 findings are those that are mildly discrepant from the clients' usual ways of thinking about themselves or their child. Level 2 findings may be reframes of how parents typically see their child. Although parents may be somewhat surprised by Level 2 feedback, they should not be upset by it, or likely to challenge it outright; although they may not immediately accept it without question, they should be able to integrate it into their views of their child fairly easily. Ideally, it is recommended that the majority of information presented during the feedback session be Level 2 information (Tharinger, Finn, Hersh, et al., 2008), as this is the information that parents are most likely to learn from or be changed by.

Level 3 findings are highly discrepant from clients' existing self-views or parents' views of their child. Parents are likely to become anxious upon hearing Level 3 information, and they may challenge or reject these findings. Their views of their child, and in many cases also their related views of themselves, may be threatened by this information. Things that parents suspect but fear may also fall into this category, as they will likely be difficult and anxiety-provoking to hear, even if they are not fully "unknown." Although parents' immediate reaction may be to deny these findings, over a long period of time (e.g., weeks or months after the assessment is completed) they may come to understand and integrate these findings into the way they see themselves. It is important to note that whether the assessors consider a finding to be "positive" or "negative" is not a factor in deciding what level it falls under. What is important are the parents' perceptions and existing views of their child. If these are

negative, then "negative" findings that fit with these existing views are the most likely to be easily accepted by the client—and, thus, are Level 1 feedback. It is equally important to be aware of the idiosyncratic significance some findings may hold for particular parents and families.

These levels determine the order in which findings should be presented to parents during the feedback meeting. Level 1 findings are presented first, followed by Level 2 and then Level 3. Thus, the most self-verifying information is presented first, and then the discussion moves into progressively more discrepant information. Presenting the most self-verifying information first makes parents comfortable, and supports the expectation that the assessment findings will be valid and useful. In contrast, presenting information that parents have trouble grasping is likely to mobilize the clients' defenses, arouse anxiety, and create the expectation that the assessor has not understood or seen them or the child correctly, and will not be able to provide helpful information or suggestions that are connected to their real life challenges. They are then likely to be less engaged and invested in the remainder of the feedback session, and may not optimally benefit even from feedback on other, more self-consistent findings, because they will have already adopted a defensive position and "checked out" to some extent. Or, they may simply remain anxiously preoccupied with the upsetting Level 3 findings, and be unable to focus fully on the remaining feedback.

The assessors' goal in feedback is to help the parents accept and integrate as many of the assessment results as possible. However, in some cases it may not be beneficial to present every single item of information that the assessor believes the assessment reveals about the child. Discussing too much new information at once may be overwhelming for the parents. Furthermore, some Level 3 feedback may be so threatening to the parents that it would not benefit them to hear it at the present time. For example, hearing that their child has a serious depression may be overwhelming for parents to hear, if they have not been somewhat prepared. However, in our experience, if the sequencing of findings is well thought-out, and the discussion of findings is conducted in a collaborative and supportive way, parents may, by the end of the session, be ready to hear Level 3 findings that they may otherwise not have been able to absorb. For example, when parents have been assisted to note their child's depressive affect and irritability, as well as lack of interest in previously enjoyed activities, they are more able to hear the findings related to depression, and be ready to move into ways to help their child.

In addition to careful sequencing, the practice of organizing feedback around parents' assessment questions also increases the likelihood that Level 3 findings will be accepted by the parents. If the information can be framed as an answer to a confounding question, or an explanation for something the parents have long wondered about, the parents may be more motivated to process and consider the information rather than defensively reject it (Finn, 2007). For example, if one of the parents' assessment questions was, "Is my child really sad like her teacher thinks?" feedback addressing depression will likely be easier to hear and respond to. An additional strategy for increasing acceptance of Level 3 information is to give careful consideration to the language used. For instance, if the assessors know that the parents are especially fearful of "depression," it is likely that using this word would immediately arouse significant anxiety. If alternative terms like "lots of sadness" or "feeling down most of the time" can be used instead, the parents may be more able to take in the information and evaluate it against their own self-perceptions and perceptions of their child. In addition to the careful planning and wording of feedback organized around the parents' assessment questions, the entire process of the assessment—particularly the parent observation of the testing sessions, extended inquiries, and family session—is also designed to take potential Level 3 information and make it Level 2. That is, when parents have had the experience along the way of taking in surprising or discrepant information about their child, hearing this information from the assessor at feedback is likely to be much easier.

PREPARING TO PROVIDE FEEDBACK TO PARENTS: GUIDES, RATIONALE, AND RESISTANCE

The literature offers direction for providing oral and written feedback to parents following the assessment of their child (Braaten, 2007). These guides represent a significant advance, as historically psychologists maintained that assessment results were too complex or threatening for clients (Groth-Marnat, 2003) and, as a result, feedback was often withheld or minimized with adults and adolescents, and rarely, if ever, given to children. Fortunately, as ethical codes have evolved, the client's "right to know" has become paramount, requiring assessors to take reasonable steps to provide assessment results

to clients, or to persons acting on the clients' behalf. Many experts have offered guidance for the parent feedback session that occurs at the conclusion of a psychological assessment of a child (for a summary, see Tharinger Finn, Hersh, et al., 2008).

Furthermore, a convincing rationale has developed for the importance of providing feedback to parents and children (Tharinger, Finn, Hersh, et al., 2008). The rationale includes adhering to ethical guidelines (APA, 2002; NASP, 2000); enhancing the involvement of the child and parents; increasing the likelihood that parents will follow through with recommendations (Finn, 2007); and further motivating assessors to clearly conceptualize, understand, integrate, and effectively organize their findings (Finn, 2005). In addition, providing feedback is one of the major ways for the assessment to have a therapeutic impact. Studies have demonstrated that well-formulated feedback with adults leads to a decrease in symptomatology, an increase in self-esteem and hope (Finn & Tonsager, 1997; Newman & Greenway, 1997), enhanced self-related processes such as self-understanding and positive self-regard (Allen et al., 2003), willingness to engage in recommended therapy (Ackerman et al., 2000), and positive alliance to a future psychotherapist (Cromer & Hilsenroth, 2006; Hilsenroth, Ackerman, Clemence, Strassle, & Handler, 2002; Hilsenroth, Peters, & Ackerman, 2004; Weil & Hilsenroth, 2006). Although much less attention has been devoted to investigating the effects of psychological assessment feedback with parents and children, Human and Teglasi (1993) found that parents reported positive changes resulting from feedback from psychoeducational evaluations, such as improved understanding of their child, a better parent–child relationship, and an increase in the child's self-esteem.

Although the rationale for providing feedback is compelling, and the benefits significant, historically there has been and continues to be much professional resistance to providing feedback. Pope (1992) posits that when the fundamental aspects of feedback are carefully considered, the process of feedback can "provide a context of clear communication within which the purpose of an assessment can be achieved;" when neglected, however, it tends to "limit, and sometimes destroy entirely, the usefulness of an assessment" (p. 268). There are a multitude of factors that may explain why, historically, assessment professionals may have regarded the revelation of diagnostic impressions to the client as a "minefield that must be approached with wary caution" (Berg, 1985, p. 55). One contributing factor may be that assessors are often not adequately trained in the task (Butcher, 1992; Pollak, 1988). Standardized assessment is straightforward, manualized, thoroughly taught in training programs, and becomes effectively mastered with practice; the feedback meeting, however, can be a delicate process that requires sensitivity and interpersonal, even therapeutic, skills (Pollak). Perhaps a lack of graduate and professional training contributes to a lack of confidence for some assessors in their ability to translate a psychological conceptualization of a client's performance into words that the client can understand (Pollak, 1998; Lillie, 2007). Theoretically, providing feedback challenges assessors to "build a bridge" between the testing instrument and its clinical utility. Clinical utility can mean anything from pathological diagnoses to "empathic overtures that can bolster self-understanding and self-acceptance" (Quirk, Strosahl, Kreilkamp, & Erdberg, 1995, p. 28).

Resistance to providing feedback may also be fueled by economics. Consistent with many current concerns about resources, "the bureaucratic allocation of time" allows little opportunity to engage in an assessment feedback session in order to address questions and concerns with the client; the clinician may have to donate their free time in order to provide adequate feedback (Pope, 1992, p. 268). Pollak (1988) posits that a clinician with a heavy testing load may view feedback as an imposition, after testing and report writing have been completed. In conclusion, psychologists and psychological training programs have traditionally not given the assessment feedback process much attention. This is unfortunate, considering that "the value of even the most comprehensive and expertly conducted psychological assessment is significantly diminished if findings are misunderstood and recommendations go unheeded" (Pollak, p. 145).

Summary/Discussion (Feedback) Session with Parents in TA-C

A general organization for discussing findings with parents following a TA-C has been offered by Tharinger, Finn, Hersh, et al., (2008) and is summarized here. The assessors begin by acknowledging that parents are often anxious about attending feedback sessions, and check in with the parents about their initial emotional state at the beginning of the session. The assessors then review the plan for the entire session, explaining what will happen and encouraging questions and collaboration. Before beginning the discussion of findings, the assessors thank the parents for participating in the assessment, and particularly acknowledge any factors that may have been especially difficult for the parents. The assessors then move into answering the parents' assessment questions, following Finn's (2007) level-based organization of feedback from least to most self-discrepant, as described above. Because it is likely that the assessors will not have been able to accurately predict all of the parents' reactions, their responses are closely monitored, and if the parents appear to be becoming too overwhelmed, the assessors modify their plan for the session and stop to provide support whenever necessary.

The assessors avoid arguing with parents about assessment findings, and instead encourage them to share their own perspective and how they would explain or make sense of their child's test responses. Although recommendations may have been offered throughout the session, all recommendations are summarized at the end of the session. The parents are encouraged to discuss how feasible the recommendations may be, and whether they have any questions or concerns about how to implement them. Before ending the session, it is recommended that the assessors discuss with the parents how feedback will be communicated to the child. The assessors also thank the parents again, and share genuine statements about what each assessor learned or gained from being involved with the family. See Hamilton, et al. (2009) for a case example.

Preparing to Provide Assessment Feedback to Children

Providing assessment results to children in a way that they can understand, appreciate, and relate to, is not an easy or straightforward process. Tharinger, Finn, Wilkinson, et al., (2008) offer that providing feedback to children is "equally if not more difficult" than providing it to parents or teachers. Additionally, assessors who have attempted to deliver a summary of the findings to a child, perhaps as straightforward as strengths and weaknesses, have likely encountered blank stares and a sense of the child being overwhelmed, or just tuning out. Assessors may then, understandably, feel "ineffective and vulnerable in their relationship with the child," and decide to focus their efforts only on feedback to the parents (Tharinger, Finn, Wilkinson, et al.). However, for practitioners of collaborative and therapeutic assessment with children (Finn, 2007; Fischer, 1985/1994; Handler, 2007; Purves, 2002; Tharinger, Finn, Wilkinson, et al.), it would be considered a rare exception *not* to provide the child with individualized information about his or her assessment performance. These professionals are committed to engaging children in a process that is "respectful and responsive" to their experience, and sharing the results in a child-friendly manner. Indeed, helping children understand the purpose and process of an assessment, inviting their participation in determining the goals of the assessment, and providing an explanation of the results, are important aims of collaborative and therapeutic assessment of children.

Thus, in TA-C it is important to find effective ways to present children with some feedback. As discussed in Tharinger, Finn, Wilkinson, et al. (2008), feedback needs to be given to the child using language as close as possible to that which the child would use. It is a good idea to use images or words the child actually used during the assessment. The tone should be supportive and hopeful, and the assessor should carefully select which findings to share with the child. Although the prior preparation the assessor has completed for the parent feedback is foundational, the child is given much less direct information, perhaps just a single piece or two of the "new story." Typically, appreciations are shared, strengths emphasized, and Level 1 and 2 information included. In almost all cases, providing Level 3 information to the child would be considered only if the parents have indicated strong support for the child in beginning to address these issues. In most instances, it is better for Level 3 information to be addressed over time through ongoing interventions, perhaps by a therapist or teacher.

However, even with this level of awareness and preparation on the part of the assessor, upon reflection it is hardly surprising that many children's ability to absorb highly self-relevant and emotion-laden material during a feedback session is extremely limited. It is our experience that children often tune out when findings from the assessment are presented to them in a direct manner, even when adjusted for level of language and complexity. Fortunately, many assessors (Finn, 2007; Purves, 2002; Tharinger, Finn, Wilkinson, et al., 2008) have successfully overcome the challenge of direct feedback by developing more indirect and engaging methods of explaining assessment findings to children. Drawing from Fischer's (1985/1994) example as well the classic work of Winnicott (1953), these practitioners routinely create individualized fictional or metaphorical stories or fables that incorporate assessment findings into a child-friendly format.

Tharinger, Finn, Wilkinson, et al. (2008) outline the rationale and benefits of providing children with their assessment results through individualized fables. First, the format of a fable presents a more digestible form of information for a child, and gives the child a vehicle to try out new conceptions of the self without becoming overwhelmed. Second, using fables can help children feel validated and understood, and can provide them with an intense experience of positive, accurate mirroring. And, in addition, sharing the fable with the child's parents present enhances their ability to empathize with and construct, or accept, a new story about the difficulties their child is having, how those difficulties might be affected by the systemic functioning of the family, and how the family may be able to intervene.

We have found that children who receive a fable created especially for them, a fable that portrays their functioning and family in an understandable way, often experience a sense of finally being *really* understood for the first time. Furthermore, fables can diminish children's shame and negative self-conceptions, in that the stories can help reframe the child, for instance, from "bad" to sad, or from "dumb" to dyslexic. The fable also serves as a "transitional object" that can be kept, illustrated, and referred to by the child and the parents long after the assessment is over. The child may read the fable numerous times, allowing the child to better internalize the story and be soothed by it over time. Finally, in our experience, parents also find the fable to be a lasting, positive product from the assessment. The child may request that the parent read the story to them again and again, thus promoting the parent and child working together. We have also found that parents are grateful to have the story to refer to themselves, as it serves as a hopeful reminder of the changes to which they have committed.

For the assessor, constructing a fable is both a clinical *and* a creative undertaking. The following steps have been offered for constructing fables (Tharinger, Finn, Wilkinson, et al., 2008).

(1) *Create the individualized storyboard.* The beginning of a fable typically incorporates elements of the child's and family's development and culture. The goal is to bring the story alive with details the child will recognize and be drawn to, thus engaging the child's attention and imagination. This is accomplished through creating a somewhat veiled connection with the child's everyday reality. The child is the main character in the fable, often represented as an animal or a mythical creature that the

child has identified as being his or her favorite, or one he or she wishes to be. Important family members are included as additional characters. In addition, the assessor typically is included in the fable and represented as a figure of wisdom and kindness; for example, as a wise owl, sage, or respected tree in the forest. The parent characters usually have sought assistance from this wise character (as occurred during the assessment).

(2) *Introduce and address the challenge(s).* Following the introduction that sets up the scenario, the child's character is typically confronted with a challenge or conflict that is quite similar to one in the child's past or recent experience, and that in real life has been somewhat overwhelming. The focus of the challenge is based on one of the presenting concerns for the assessment, on the obtained findings, and on the level of change the family appears to be ready for at the time. The goal of a fable is to model a successful step toward constructive change. The steps may be suggested by the wise character in the story, but typically are carried out by the parental characters, representing the parents' commitment to helping the child.

(3) *Be realistic.* It is important to emphasize that if parents are not capable of or willing to implement a certain solution, it should not be incorporated into a fable for the child. In cases where the next steps are unclear at the time the child receives feedback, the fable should indicate that the next steps and solutions are to be worked out, and (if it is true) that the parents have committed to work toward change. Examples of fables from TAP are provided in Hamilton, et al. (2009), Tharinger et al. (2007), Tharinger, Finn, Wilkinson, et al. (2008), and Tharinger, Christopher, and Matson (in press).

Providing Child Feedback

We advise that feedback to the child follow the oral feedback to the parents and, if possible, take place in an entirely separate session, possibly a few days or a week later. This sequence allows the parents time to discuss and absorb the feedback presented to them about their child. This timing also allows the assessors to reflect on how the parents responded to the feedback they received, and what growth steps they have committed to undertaking. As discussed above, this understanding helps the assessors decide what steps to represent in the fable. The child and parents attend this session together, and the assessors start the session by thanking the child for participating in the assessment. Following, it is time to introduce the fable and emphasize how special it is.

The child is told that the assessors, together with the parents' input (if that is the case; parents are often invited to collaborate), wrote the fable particularly for the child. The child is then invited to choose who will read the fable: one of the assessors, a parent, or the child. After the fable has been read and reactions expressed, we suggest that the assessor invite the child to modify it if he or she wishes. This gives the child an active role with the fable, and a chance to impart his or her own sense of what is needed. Many children like the story just the way it was written, but others may choose to change some details such as the name of a character, or the color of an animal's fur. We suggest always asking if the child likes the "ending" (i.e., the resolution) of the story. In our experience it is unusual for a child to ask for major changes, but if that occurs it is very instructive. (The few times this has happened, a child had a different idea of how the fable should end.) The presentation of the fable typically concludes the assessment process with the child and the parents (although in many cases we suggest a follow-up check-in three months later, discussed in an upcoming section). Because the fable may serve as a transitional object, the assessors may wish to remind the child that he or she can read it, or ask the parents to read it, whenever he or she wishes.

Written Feedback for Parents

Most child assessments culminate in the production of a written report, usually intended for the use of other professionals, treatment facilities, or the child's school. The report serves as an enduring, transportable record of the assessment to facilitate communication of the findings. Because reports have historically been used primarily by other professionals for intervention planning purposes, relatively little attention has been given to the usefulness and comprehensibility of written reports to parents. In TA-C, Finn (2007) suggests organizing written feedback for parents to correspond to the assessment questions they generated at the beginning of the process. The format of written feedback in TA-C is typically very similar to the organization of oral feedback, and thus the preparation time put into the oral feedback pays off greatly when it comes to producing a written letter. Findings are organized by assessment question, and presented in the same order as during the feedback session. The written communication typically takes the form of a letter to parents, rather than a traditionally organized psychological report (Finn, 2007), although a formal report may also be provided if needed for other purposes, such as documenting a diagnosis or disability for school accommodations.

In the parent letter, the assessors use first person, colloquial language and active voice, and incorporate comments, examples, or even disagreements that the parents offered during the feedback session. Fischer's (1985/1994) collaborative assessment reports take a similar approach to written feedback. Information about the child is presented in the form of characteristic behaviors, rather than labels or categorizations, and the child and parents are described as having been active participants in the process. The narrative style and tone of the letter communicate that it provides the assessors' subjective impressions rather than some "absolute truth" about the client, but the clear descriptions and examples explain how the assessors arrived at these impressions. Examples of partial parent feedback letters from TAP cases of TA-C can be found in Tharinger et al. (2007) and Tharinger, Christopher, and Matson (in press).

Follow-up Session

If possible, it is highly recommended that an in-person follow-up session occur one to three months after the TA-C has been completed. The assessor(s) typically meet with the parents and the child to discuss progress the child and family have made. This is also a time to explore factors that may be promoting or hindering progress, answer any additional questions the parents and child may have, and problem-solve any difficulties that may be interfering with implementation of the recommendations. New events in the life of the family, both positive and negative, may also be explored as to their impact on the child and the family. In our experience, it is often most useful to use part of the session to check in with the parents, and then invite the child to join at the end. In some cases we have found it useful to reintroduce the fable to the parents and child, and ask them to add the next steps to the fable; that is, the child and family story.

Application of TA-C to School-Based Assessment

Up to this point in the chapter, we have provided a description of the development of collaborative assessment and TA, and reviewed evidence for the efficacy of these assessment approaches and models. We have also presented an in-depth view of the comprehensive model of TA-C used in TAP, as well as the rationale for many of the steps, particularly

the importance of obtaining assessment questions, actively collaborating with parents, and providing meaningful feedback to the parents and the child. As indicated in the introduction, we are well aware that comprehensive TA-C, especially the extensive involvement of parents in observing their child and participating in family intervention sessions, is not readily transportable to school-based assessment practice. In addition, TA-C in its comprehensive form is unlikely to be feasible in most educational settings due to limited time, personnel, and economic resources. Furthermore, the focus of assessments of children in schools is not typically the child in the context of the family, but rather the child in the context of the school, with emphasis on the areas of learning and achievement. However, we are confident that many of the components of TA-C can be adapted successfully into school-based assessments with many benefits for children, teachers, and parents.

We now discuss the components of TA-C that appear to offer the most value and transportability to assessment practice in the schools. We have organized these components into four stages (see Figure 11.1): (1) adopting a new foundational base, which includes embracing a collaborative stance to assessment; (2) utilizing innovative assessment practices, which include constructing assessment questions with the child, parent, and teachers; utilizing process testing techniques, including testing the limits and extended inquiry processes; and being actively collaborative with the child, parents, and teachers throughout the assessment; (3) integrating innovative practices of case conceptualization; and (4) feedback planning and delivery, including an analysis and organization of the findings by assessment questions, and levels of feedback to guide discussions with parents and teachers; developing a fable or other creative method for providing child feedback; and communicating feedback to the parents, child, and teachers in meaningful and collaborative ways. These four stages are sequential, and build on and inform one another. There can be no progression to Stage 2 without Stage 1, no progression to Stage 3 without Stage 2, etc. We also give some consideration to the development of intervention sessions with the assessor and the child, and possibly with the teacher. These sessions have some resemblance to, and may coincide with, Response to Intervention (RTI) strategies or dynamic assessment (Palinscar, Brown & Campione, 1994)

We follow the discussion of the four stages with four case examples to illustrate the application of

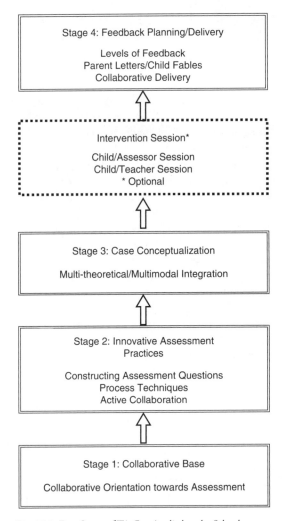

Fig. 11.1 Four Stages of TA-C as Applied to the Schools

Stage 4: Feedback Planning/Delivery

Levels of Feedback
Parent Letters/Child Fables
Collaborative Delivery

Intervention Session*

Child/Assessor Session
Child/Teacher Session
* Optional

Stage 3: Case Conceptualization

Multi-theoretical/Multimodal Integration

Stage 2: Innovative Assessment
Practices

Constructing Assessment Questions
Process Techniques
Active Collaboration

Stage 1: Collaborative Base

Collaborative Orientation towards Assessment

components of TA-C in school based assessment. The examples are drawn from cases that were completed by graduate students in school psychology, who were taking an assessment course (covering social/emotional assessment and TA-C components) under Tharinger in the fall semester of 2006, 2007, or 2008. The students were placed in a number of public school districts for this assessment practicum. The cases involved children referred for assessment due to suspected emotional disturbance (ED), or for reevaluation for an existing ED handicapping condition. All cases included here, with one exception, involved children in elementary and middle school. One, however, completed by the second author, involves an older adolescent, and is included due to its exceptional ability to illustrate the effectiveness of the components of TA in a complex case.

Foundational Base—Embracing a Collaborative Stance and Orientation to Assessment

The use of a collaborative stance by the assessor has the potential to provide a richer assessment experience for children, parents, and teachers than may typically occur in the school setting. By utilizing a collaborative approach, an assessment is done *with* the child, not *to* the child. This collaborative stance generally yields active participation and a positive experience for the child, parents, and teachers involved in the assessment. Generating a collaborative atmosphere includes consistently portraying genuine concern and interest in the input of the child, parents, and teachers. The assessor explicitly conveys the collaborative nature of the assessment, and emphasizes the importance of the perspectives and opinions of those participating in the assessment. Incorporating a collaborative stance into all aspects of the assessment process is a relatively easy way to for an assessor to enhance the assessment process in schools.

The task of establishing a collaborative orientation overlaps with that of establishing a strong working alliance. A strong working alliance involves a sense of connectedness between assessor and child while working towards common goals. Fostering a strong working alliance is highly beneficial, for it can increase a child's investment in the assessment process. This heightened investment can, in turn, result in the collection of a rich sample of the child's emotional, behavioral, cognitive, and academic capabilities. To establish rapport and engender a strong working alliance, the assessor spends time exploring the child's interests and using play and playfulness. The assessor also exhibits respect towards the child based on cultural knowledge, and enhances his/her understanding of the child's cultural context and accompanying cultural beliefs, values, and worldview. These assessor behaviors should occur in an interpersonal climate marked by warmth, acceptance, unconditional positive regard, and appropriate limits.

Innovative Assessment Techniques
CONSTRUCTION OF ASSESSMENT QUESTIONS

The construction of assessment questions with children, parents, and teachers, is a component of TA-C that can be readily incorporated into school based assessment practice. Most school based assessments are guided by questions about special education eligibility and programming, and how to best meet the needs of children in the school context. In addition, assessors can allow additional questions from those involved, to help direct the assessment. The inclusion of this TA-C component is an early demonstration of the assessor's authentic commitment to collaboration, and later facilitates the process of heightening the relevance of the feedback to invested parties. Furthermore, creating assessment questions fosters enhanced motivation to contribute to the assessment by allowing the child, parents, and teachers to take some ownership of the assessment process, and to know that they will receive feedback that is important and meaningful to them.

Assessors can request assessment questions during interviews with children, parents, and teachers. If these individuals have difficulty generating questions, offering examples of assessment questions is beneficial. During interviews, the assessor also listens for other potential underlying questions. The assessor then poses any suspected questions, to discuss whether the questions are of interest to the parent/teacher/child. The co-construction of assessment questions is intended as a collaborative effort, requiring active involvement from both the assessor and those interviewed.

USE OF PROCESS ASSESSMENT METHODS

Process assessment also is easily transported to school based assessments. Although a standard battery may be required in school settings, it can be supplemented with additional assessment instruments that are chosen on an individual basis to address specific assessment questions. Furthermore, rather than administering assessment tools in a way that only seeks answers to each question, the recommendation from TA-C is to intermittently process the testing experience with the child. The assessor is also encouraged to use him- or herself as a key assessment tool, by remaining highly attuned to the child's emotional and behavioral responses throughout administration of the assessment instruments. Recognition and identification of the child's responses to the testing situation are invaluable to gaining a more comprehensive understanding of the child's functioning. The assessor maintains cognizance of counter-transference reactions to the child, as a means of gaining an appreciation for others' experience with the child. For example, if, during testing, a child is easily distracted by external stimuli in the room, has difficulty staying in his seat, and consistently needs redirection, the assessor will experientially understand the energy required to manage his behavior. The assessor will

then be able to gain appreciation for the teacher's dilemma, and subsequent frustration related to managing that child's behavior while simultaneously trying to attend to the needs of the other students in the classroom.

Processing testing is also useful in that it can contribute to the child's expanded awareness of personal strengths and weaknesses, which in itself is an intervention. Of noteworthy importance, the assessor uses creativity and flexibility *without* compromising standardization, which is required for valid interpretation of test results. To conduct process testing with the child, the assessor intersperses brief breaks within the testing protocols to "check in" with the child and to better understand his or her current thoughts and feelings. The assessor also makes reflective statements about the child's verbal and nonverbal responses to various aspects of testing. The assessor asks the child for ideas about what would make particularly challenging aspects of testing easier. The assessor inquires about situations in school and at home that elicit similar negative responses from the child, in order to start making broader connections about the child's interaction with the environment. Including the technique of processing testing with the child is relatively simple and, as an added benefit, can help demystify the assessment process for children in schools.

ACTIVE COLLABORATION

A form of active collaboration with parents is also highly recommended and transportable. Parent collaboration is vital to the therapeutic nature of the process and the systemic change that is possible with TA-C. It is important for parents to feel like part of a team, helping the assessor explore ideas about their child, and thus gaining a level of investment beyond that typically seen in assessment practice as usual. This may be especially important given that parents begin the assessment with their own background and history of school experiences. Navigating the school system may be intimidating for some parents, and so active collaboration can foster greater parental involvement in the assessment process.

Increased collaboration with parents not only has the potential to ease the parent–school relationship, but can also provide important information and produce change both inside and outside of the school context. Collaboration begins by focusing on what the parents would like to learn from the assessment and constructing assessment questions, as detailed earlier. The collaboration continues with check-in phone calls, which help keep parents informed about the progress of the assessment, and also key the assessor in to any major family events or changes outside of school. By providing parents with updates on the assessment, assessors also can begin to connect testing observations to the child's real world, in school and at home. For example, the assessor may share an observation such as, "I know one of the concerns for Johnny is his ability to pay attention and stay on task in the classroom. I noticed that after spending only 1 to 2 minutes on a series of drawings, Johnny became very involved in the last one, taking over 30 minutes. He was highly focused and paid great attention to detail for this last drawing. Have you ever noticed anything similar? Are there some things that Johnny will really get involved in?" These follow-up questions provide the assessor with more information and can help parents start to connect the assessment to their own experiences. Not only does this build the assessor–parent relationship, but it also lays the groundwork for feedback. Based on how the parents are able to integrate some of the assessor's observations, the assessor begins to determine what information may be Level 1, 2, or 3, for feedback.

In translating TA-C components to the school setting, collaboration with teachers is a significantly larger area of focus than in comprehensive TA-C. In comprehensive TA-C, the systemic process generally focuses on the parents' views of the child, whereas in schools *both* the parents' and teacher's views are important. Especially if the referral concern is more academic in nature, the teacher is likely to be the primary focus of TA methodology. Thus, teacher questions should be gathered, and the collaborative stance should be extended to include the teacher. Teachers will most likely be a major source of information regarding the child, and so helping them invest in the assessment process can impact the teachers' openness to feedback. Often, recommendations at the end of a school assessment will ask teachers to make additional modifications or accommodations for a student. An "expert" approach by a school psychologist, where the teacher's views and the realities of the classroom have not been explored, can lead to more resistance in following through with recommendations. However, if the teacher has been involved in the assessment and supported by the assessor, then the recommendations can be tailored to the realities of the teacher's resources; subsequently, he or she is more likely to incorporate suggestions and to reinvest in the student. The collaboration process with teachers should be similar to that with parents, including constructing assessment questions, doing check-ins about the student and the progress of testing, and beginning to collaboratively hypothesize about test results. Checking to see if the testing confirms the teacher's experiences with the student can provide a means of testing the teacher's openness to systemic feedback. Parallel to the parent process, teacher collaboration will heighten the depth and long-term intervention potential of the assessment. Teachers often face the challenging task of managing multiple children with emotional and behavioral difficulties, in addition to the rest of the students in the classroom. Minimal support or advice may be offered to these teachers to assist with this demanding task. The level of parental support may differ for each child, which can be frustrating. Furthermore, teachers may not receive sufficient validation for their hard work and taxing experiences. Therefore, the collaboration, support, and advice from an assessor can be highly valuable to teachers, and has the potential to greatly benefit children because of the significant portion of time children spend with their teachers in school.

Case Conceptualization

The approach used in TA-C to integrating assessment data and developing a case formulation (detailed earlier) can be applied in the school setting. In the TA-C model, information gathered through interviews, testing sessions, and observations, is analyzed in an iterative fashion with appreciation for and awareness of the child's cultural context, and is used to support and refute hypotheses about the child. The data is considered from multiple theoretical perspectives. For example, children are part of multiple systems; therefore, a child's functioning will need to be examined in the family, school, interpersonal, and intrapersonal contexts. A behavioral approach may explain how a behavior is reinforced via attention at school, yet understanding how those needs for attention either are or are not being met at home can help an assessor understand the child more holistically. And although the assessment focuses on the child, it is extremely important to gauge the needs and resources of the major adults—namely, teachers and parents—who may be frustrated or overwhelmed by a child, and thus will need support themselves, in order to create a supportive environment for the child.

The objective for an assessor employing this component of TA-C in a school setting is to integrate the data about the child into a coherent, individualized case conceptualization that is organized by the needs of the school, as well as by the parents', child's, and teacher's assessment questions. A tentative case formulation provides hypotheses that can be addressed in an intervention session, if applicable, which then allows for further refinement of the case conceptualization. Most important, the case formulation is critical in determining how to organize parent, child, and teacher feedback, and how to deliver feedback in such a way that the results can be heard and internalized.

Consideration of an Intervention Session

As discussed earlier, including family intervention sessions in TA-C allows the assessor to test hypotheses, determine the systemic level of change possible, and promote positive solutions/skills before the final feedback meeting (see Tharinger, Finn, Austin, et al., 2008). In TA-C, not only is the assessment itself considered an intervention, but there also is room for the incorporation of an explicit intervention session, which may be extremely beneficial in the school setting. Although intervention sessions in TA-C typically involve parent(s) and child, an assessor in a school setting could potentially create a child–teacher intervention session instead, or even an intervention session with the child alone. Intervention sessions can provide unparalleled information about how the child might respond to new and different ideas, and can allow the testing of these ideas before implementing a fully formalized intervention. Intervention sessions in the schools could help find a "best fit" of intervention practices within the RTI model.

However, it is important to recognize that school resources are limited, and full intervention sessions with parents or teachers may not be feasible for every assessment. Therefore, it is beneficial for the assessor to fully adopt the perspective that the entire assessment is an intervention, and to realize he or she has the potential to do mini-interventions with the child throughout the assessment process. This concept is similar to testing the limits in a standardized test protocol. After administering a standardized test, assessors can return to test the limits to gain more information about the child's strengths and weaknesses. Assessors use their judgment about whether testing the limits could provide new or revealing information. This idea can be translated to the social/emotional components of assessments as well. For example, after administering a Rorschach with very low Human and Popular content, going back through the cards to determine whether or not the child can see the popular responses (after being told what they are) can illuminate important distinctions in the case conceptualization (see Hamilton et al., 2009). For academic assessment, providing the child with additional math problems and a calculator could determine whether the calculator will be helpful, or whether the child will need assistance in learning to use the calculator effectively. Testing how a child responds to positive reinforcement, or to a token system, can also be diagnostic and help inform specific recommendations.

If the assessor is able to create the opportunity for a teacher–child intervention session, this could be an important time to foster a more positive relationship, or to test out new routines and behavior techniques for the teacher–child dyad. For example, in planning and creating family intervention sessions, a variety of activities can be used to foster positive interactions and to help parents feel as though they can become part of the solution. Similarly, a school intervention session could help the teacher gain more empathy and understanding for why a child reacts the way she does, and help the teacher reframe seeing the child as "the problem" in the classroom. A successful intervention session could help a teacher reinvest in a child who may need significant support and understanding. Ideas for the session can be drawn from family therapy exercises, play therapy, or behavioral interventions. In summary, intervention sessions are a component of TA-C that can often be a turning point in creating a new "story" for the child, and for helping adults understand their role in maintaining, and opportunities for changing, problem behaviors. As mentioned above, the intervention session is also a piece of TA-C that fits particularly well within the RTI model, and facilitates the use of RTI to address social/emotional as well as academic issues. Years ago, we even did an intervention session with a teacher in which she tried a different instructional method with a kid—with the assessor present as a coach/observer/consultant. It was very helpful to everyone.

Integrating Innovative Practices of Feedback Planning and Delivery
LEVELS OF FEEDBACK
In order to help assessors provide feedback to parents and teachers in a way that allows for them to understand and integrate as much information as possible, TA-C advocates the use of three levels, as described previously. Organizing feedback by levels can be especially important when determining what "official" feedback will be given to the school as part

of the assessment report, and what feedback can be given to individual parents and teachers. The use of the parents' and teachers' assessment questions to provide an organizational scheme for feedback also furthers the collaborative relationship, provides real-world relevance, and promotes investment in hearing the results.

Level 1 feedback is often what parents or teachers may already know, and therefore functions as confirmation or validation of that information. If the assessor has been able to create a collaborative relationship with the parents, pieces of Level 1 feedback have likely already been shared during check-ins. This can allow for the quick assimilation of Level 1 information during the formal feedback session, and can thus allow assessors to focus on addressing deeper levels of feedback. Level 2 feedback may not be as obvious for parents, or may begin to incorporate systemic feedback that does not focus solely on the child. Ideally, the assessor has already planted the seeds of Level 2 feedback during check-ins and the co-construction of assessment questions. This makes the Level 2 feedback more accessible to the parent or teacher, and can help the long-term intervention potential of the assessment. Lastly, Level 3 feedback is the most difficult for parents to hear, and in some cases may or may not be shared, based on how the parent is able to respond to the previous Levels. It does not help the child when a parent, who may already be low on emotional resources, is overwhelmed by feedback results. Thus, Level 3 feedback that does not bear directly on the child's eligibility for services may not always be appropriate given the family's current situation, including level of emotional or financial stressors. However, the collaborative relationship often helps parents pick up on themes and systemic involvement on their own, which can create a bridge to Level 3 conversations.

It should be noted that levels of feedback may vary by feedback recipient. For example, something that might already be strongly suspected by a teacher (and thus Level 1 or 2 feedback for the teacher) might be highly surprising and upsetting information for the parents (and thus Level 3 for them). If parent and teacher feedback will occur in separate meetings (as is advisable), the assessor may need to plan different organizations of the findings for each party.

PARENT FEEDBACK

Parent feedback is typically a standard part of a psychological assessment of a child. In the school setting, parent feedback for an assessment often happens at the time of a formal special education meeting, where eligibility and services are determined. In this scenario, parents are asked to hear, understand, and then make decisions about services for their child, without much time to truly process the information. Although some assessments may be relatively straightforward, and the results aligned with parent expectations, more complicated cases, especially those surrounding SED qualifications, may require more in-depth parent feedback. Best practice is to provide parents with a separate feedback session, prior to the eligibility meeting, to address their questions and to provide them the space to integrate feedback that may be difficult to hear.

Not only should feedback be provided to parents in a way where they are free to ask questions and process the information, it should also be communicated in a way that is more accessible than a typical school report. We have found the use of parent-friendly letters summarizing the assessment findings to be extremely effective in helping parents return to the themes of the assessment in their own time. These are sent following the parent feedback meeting. A letter also provides a tangible result that can make the assessment seem worthwhile to the parent, especially when it addresses their concerns and assessment questions (see Tharinger et al., 2007).

TEACHER FEEDBACK

Providing teachers with appropriate and useful feedback is essential in a school-based assessment. As it is the teacher who will be implementing recommendations in the classroom, addressing the teacher's questions and concerns is a top priority. Teachers are often understandably concerned about their ability to provide extra services to one child, while also maintaining responsibility for the other students in their class. Thus, feedback should be informed by real world constraints of the teacher and school system, including time and energy. It is also the case that, as with parents, teachers sometimes have inaccurate and distorted "stories" about a child. This is where an intervention session, to test the reality potential of an intervention in the classroom and the teacher's perceptions, could be of great use in generating teacher investment. The collaborative relationship fostered by TA principles enhances the teacher's ability to hear and process feedback. Just as parents may be resistant to more systemic levels of feedback, teachers may also need support in hearing their own role in maintaining a student's behavior. If the collaboration with the teacher(s) has been successful, then feedback according to Levels 1 and 2 should be readily absorbed by teachers. Just as parents should be given time to digest assessment results, teachers should also receive feedback prior to being asked to make significant changes in the classroom for interventions or new services.

CHILD FEEDBACK

Child feedback, especially for elementary-aged children, is often overlooked in the long and detailed process of initiating more specialized services in schools. However, best practice includes providing developmentally appropriate feedback to children as part of an assessment. If the process of the assessment has been collaborative with the child (as explained in previous sections), then the feedback can be an extension of the assessor helping the child process the assessment and what will happen next. Just as we recommend a personalized format for parents, TA-C also uses a personalized format for child feedback, such as a story or fable, as discussed earlier. One of the most creative and rewarding parts of TA with children can be the use of fables to communicate assessment results (Tharinger, Finn, Wilkinson, et al., 2008). Fables provide children with a metaphor they can relate to, and help the assessor communicate results in an interpersonally safe and developmentally appropriate manner. Child feedback does not need to be limited to fables; any medium that the child can relate to would be appropriate (e.g., card, poem, rap song, co-constructed cartoon).

Case Examples of Components of TA-C Applied to School-Based Assessment

As just described, the various components of TA-C work in tandem to create the therapeutic impact of assessment. Although we have delineated the different components of TA that are applicable in schools, case examples that embed components of TA-C applied within the school context can serve as useful illustrative tools. The following four examples show the integration of TA-C techniques across diverse clients and assessment goals. Names have been altered to protect the students' privacy. The case vignettes are arranged from least to most complex, in terms of the extent to which TA components were incorporated into the assessments.

Daniel

Daniel's case highlights the importance of fostering an ongoing collaborative relationship with the parent that can then help shift the parent's "story" of his/her child. Daniel is an 8-year-old, Hispanic second-grader in a primarily Hispanic school district in a large southwestern state. He repeated first grade due to reading difficulties, and has a history of externalizing behaviors, including tearing/crumpling work, refusing to do work, shutting down, crying, throwing chairs, yelling, and leaving the classroom. At the time of referral, Daniel was in a supplemental behavior program and receiving RTI reading services. However, his behavior remained a significant concern, so he was referred for a comprehensive evaluation.

COLLABORATIVE STANCE

As is typical in a large system such as a school, there was already information about Daniel and his family that other adults thought the assessor should know before beginning the assessment. The main concerns expressed were that Daniel reported that his father said Daniel did not have to listen to a female teacher, and that the father was sexist. This information could have damaged the collaborative potential of the assessment before it began. However, the female assessor was encouraged to form her own opinions and embrace a collaborative stance, gather the father's assessment questions, and check in with him throughout the assessment.

CASE CONCEPTUALIZATION

The assessment revealed that Daniel was dealing with an irritable form of depression due to changes in his family system. His mother and father had divorced two years prior, and Daniel had lived with his mother, two half-siblings, and his mother's boyfriend. Daniel's behavior problems and repetition of first grade happened around the time of the divorce. Approximately four months before the evaluation, his mother and the rest of the family moved, leaving Daniel in his father and grandmother's care. Responses to projective measures indicated that Daniel was dealing with conflicting feelings towards his mother (love and abandonment), while his feelings towards his father indicated a lack of emotional availability on his father's part. Cognitive results and academics were average, with reading slightly below average; thus, Daniel did not meet criteria for an LD in reading. Rather, it was determined that his academics were being hindered by his depression.

PLANNING AND PROVIDING FEEDBACK

One of the most therapeutic outcomes of the assessment was helping the father change his view of Daniel from "mad" to "sad." This idea was introduced over the course of the assessment, so that during parental feedback, the father was able to accept his son's depression, rather than solely focusing on Daniel's anger and misbehavior. The father was able to begin understanding what triggered Daniel's outbursts, and why he was better behaved at home, where his father's presence provided a sense of security. In planning the child feedback, the assessor noted how Daniel had communicated especially well via his drawings, in which he created a tree with broken hearts that needed to be planted, and "Dino-Man," a boy who would turn into a dinosaur when he got sad or angry. Daniel's drawings served as the basis for constructing a personalized fable as his feedback. At the end of the process, Daniel was moved to a more structured behavior program for the next school semester. In addition, his father was willing to initiate family therapy to help Daniel with the family changes, and remained committed to attending the sessions.

Overall, in this case, components of TA-C were used to enhance the depth and improve intervention outcomes of Daniel's assessment. It would have been easy for the assessor to have minimized the father's input, or to have been too intimidated by rumors of his sexism to work collaboratively with him. However, collaboration with the father was essential in helping him learn that his son was depressed. Not only was the father able to make this shift; he was also subsequently open to family therapy services. The mismatch between the father's expectations for how Daniel should handle his problems, and Daniel's sensitivity/depression, was a fruitful area for family work, enabled by the collaborative nature of the assessment.

Christina

Christina's case particularly highlights the TA components of collaborative stance of the assessor, the co-construction of assessment questions, working closely with a teacher, the process of sensitively delivering feedback, and the importance of the alliance established between Christina and the assessor. Christina is a 13-year-old White female of low SES in seventh grade, referred for a reevaluation to determine continued eligibility for special education services. She was previously classified as a student with an Other Health Impairment (OHI) due to ADHD, ED, and an LD in math reasoning. She began receiving special education services in fifth grade. At the time of the assessment, she was in a resource math class and was receiving counseling.

COLLABORATIVE STANCE

The assessor developed a strong working alliance with Christina by exploring her interests, particularly in the areas of Anime and Harry Potter. The assessor also sought to understand Christina's strengths, which Christina described as her creativity and imagination. In addition, the assessor was successful in working together with the mother and teacher throughout the assessment. Through collaboration with all these individuals, the assessor was trying to understand Christina and the contexts in which she was developing. Christina's mother explained that the family was under increased stress since the father had lost his job a year ago, and was only able to find another job recently. She mentioned multiple concerns about Christina, including being late to class and social isolation. The mother also reported that Christina's silliness "turns off" other kids, and that she is regularly teased. The teacher expressed various concerns about Christina's behavior. The teacher reported that Christina is often late to class and disorganized, and exhibits odd social behavior, such as laughing for no apparent reason. The teacher described Christina as socially unaware because she was not tuned in to others' feelings or to social cues. The teacher also stated that students consider Christina "weird" and sometimes refuse to work with her in groups.

INNOVATIVE ASSESSMENT TECHNIQUES

The assessor worked with the mother, teacher and Christina to formulate assessment questions. The mother's assessment questions included: (1) "What are your general impressions of Christina?" and (2) "Why has she started being late to classes?" The teacher's assessment questions were: (1) "What are her academic strengths and weaknesses?" and (2) "How much of what she says is real and how much is for attention?" Christina's assessment questions were: (1) "How can I learn more about Anime?" and (2) "How can I do better in front of people?" Answers to these questions were sought during the assessment, along with determination of Christina's eligibility for special education services. Those involved in the assessment seemed to appreciate posing questions that would later be answered during feedback.

Christina was cooperative and friendly during testing, and seemed to be putting forth adequate effort.

The child interview was informative, as Christina explained that she sometimes likes to go into her own fantasy world in her mind. Throughout the interview, she went off on tangents about her interests. The assessor let her do this to learn more about her interests, as well as her thought process. Christina acknowledged that she has a few friends but that most people think she is "weird." She relayed that although she occasionally becomes upset and cries, she uses her imagination to cheer herself up. During testing, Christina sporadically began telling stories about fantasy characters. Occasionally, she would start performing a task correctly and then forget what she was supposed to be doing.

CASE CONCEPTUALIZATION

Testing revealed that Christina's overall intellectual functioning was in the average range. She displayed a weakness in processing speed, the ability to perform simple tasks rapidly, mainly due to inattention. As found previously, she had a weakness in math reasoning, while her other academic achievement areas were commensurate with her overall cognitive functioning. The assessor also learned that Christina's imagination is a coping strategy she has developed to help regulate her negative emotions. Her depressive and anxious symptoms had dramatically decreased since her last evaluation, and Christina indicated that she had learned through counseling to employ her imagination to better manage these symptoms. Although her imagination was an adaptive tool for emotion regulation, it also appeared to function as an impediment to her academic progress and social relationships. The testing showed continued attentional difficulties as well, which, along with her imagination, often worked together to distract her from class work. At the time of this assessment, Christina no longer met the criteria for ED, but qualified for OHI based on her history of ADHD, and for LD in math reasoning. It was recommended that she continue to receive counseling services to help her more effectively use her imagination, as well as other coping strategies, and to improve her social skills. It was also recommended that she continue in a resource math class to improve her math reasoning skills.

PLANNING AND CONDUCTING FEEDBACK

Feedback was organized into levels and delivered to the mother, teacher, and Christina to address their assessment questions, and to provide the other findings from the assessment. Feedback for the mother first involved answering her question about the assessor's general impressions of Christina. For Level 1 feedback, the assessor explained that Christina is very imaginative and likes attention. For Level 2 feedback, the assessor described that Christina talked about wanting more friendships and how, although her imagination has helped with her depression and anxiety, her imagination seems to be affecting her peer relationships. Addressing the mother's second question about why Christina has been late to class was also seen as Level 2 feedback. The assessor connected Christina's increased tardiness to when she stopped taking medication for ADHD. Christina had ceased taking medication because the family was unable to pay for it. The tardiness seemed to be related to Christina's tendency to "wander off" into her imagination, and to the attention she receives from her teachers when she is late to class. The assessor also described the cognitive and achievement findings, Christina's eligibility for special education services, and her recommendations for Christina. The assessor checked in often with the mother during the feedback session to inquire about what she thought of the information provided. Because the feedback was provided gently and in a collaborative manner, the mother was receptive to and appreciative of the feedback.

Feedback for the teacher was organized according to her questions, first starting with a discussion of Christina's academic strengths and weaknesses. This was Level 1 feedback and involved an explanation of Christina's difficulty with math reasoning. An explanation of Christina's processing speed deficit due to ADHD, and her subsequent trouble focusing, was also provided, highlighting how this affects her performance in school. The teacher's second question about what portion of Christina's behavior is real and what part is for attention was answered through Level 1 and Level 2 feedback. The Level 1 feedback for this question was that Christina's behavior is a combination of these. She seeks attention, but also has some difficulty with social skills. For Level 2 feedback, a description of the ways in which Christina's imagination has helped her manage her depressive and anxious symptoms was given. Then, the assessor talked with the teacher about how Christina sometimes overly uses her imagination, which may appear strange to others. The assessor gave the example that Christina might think about something funny in her imagination and then start laughing out loud, which seems odd to others who are not aware of her imaginative thoughts. The teacher had also expressed concern about Christina's tardiness to class. The assessor explained that this was partly related to ADHD and her difficulty planning and organizing, but also due to her desire for attention. The assessor carefully explained that Christina even tried to gain negative attention. She preferred being noticed and scolded for being late, to no attention at all. The assessor checked in with the teacher intermittently throughout the feedback session to remain attuned to how the teacher was receiving the feedback. The teacher thanked the assessor for the feedback, and appreciated the way the feedback answered her assessment questions. Although she was slightly shocked to learn that Christina was enjoying negative attention, she said that this made sense. The teacher agreed to work with the assessor through consultation to try to reduce Christina's tardy behavior. The teacher was grateful for this additional support from the assessor. The teacher reported that she felt more compassionate towards Christina as she began to better understand Christina's social skills deficit from the assessor's feedback.

Feedback was provided to Christina by first giving her some direct feedback from the assessment (i.e., general feedback, and then answers to her assessment questions), and then sharing a fable the assessor had written for Christina. For general Level 1 feedback, the assessor stressed Christina's strengths, specifically her creativity and her imagination. For Level 2 feedback, the assessor suggested that she wonders if Christina is starting to use her imagination a little too much at times (e.g., she started writing a story in the middle of a class). The assessor also explained that it is easier for Christina to get distracted than other kids her age because of her ADHD. The assessor then addressed Christina's assessment questions, with an answer to her question about how to learn more about Anime as Level 1 feedback. The Level 2 feedback encompassed a discussion of Christina's other assessment question about talking in front of others. The assessor said that she wonders if it is sometimes easier for Christina to retreat to her imagination rather than to talk with other kids in school. The assessor stressed that Christina's imagination helps her greatly when she is feeling nervous or sad, but that she might be more comfortable talking in front of others if she gets to know her classmates better. The assessor checked in with Christina as she was providing feedback to find out how she was thinking and feeling about the findings.

The assessor then shared the fable, which was about an Anime character, Kittyama, who loved to dance. Kittyama wanted to show the other Anime kids at school her dance moves, but was worried that they might laugh at her or tease her. Another special thing about Kittyama was that she could transport herself to another world called Imaginoku. When she was there, she could dance as much as she liked. She had many friends in Imaginoku and never worried about being teased. Kittyama enjoyed being in Imaginoku so much that sometimes she would transport herself there when she was supposed to be somewhere else. Kittyama wanted more friends at school, and desired to show them her dance moves. One day, Kittyama met a wise tree who she told about her dilemma with those at school, and how she wanted to demonstrate her dance moves. The wise tree asked if maybe others at school did not get to know her, because she would often go to Imaginoku. The wise tree suggested that she try to stay in school more and talk with other kids, rather than transport herself to Imaginoku so often. Kittyama tried this, and found that she was able to talk with others a little more easily. Although she was not ready to dance for them yet, she thought that she probably would be able to, once she spent more time with them and got to know them better.

Christina appreciated the Level 1 feedback, but was not receptive to the Level 2 feedback or the message of the fable. Instead of considering the fable's message, she focused on the illustration of the Anime character on the cover of the fable. As the assessor was observing Christina's reaction to feedback, she realized that what she anticipated to be Level 2 feedback was, in fact, Level 3 feedback. The assessor understood that Christina was not able to integrate all of the feedback she provided. Therefore, she remained flexible and met Christina at her level without pushing her to process more than she was able to. The assessor had been in close contact with Christina's counselor throughout the assessment process, so she was able to ensure that he would provide Christina with extra support and additional coping strategies that would not negatively affect her social relationships as her imagination had.

During school based collaborative assessments, certain components of TA-C may have more pronounced, positive effects on outcome than others. The most significant TA-C components illustrated through Christina's assessment were the collaborative stance of the assessor, the co-construction of assessment questions, working closely with a teacher, the gentleness of providing feedback, and the alliance established with Christina. Christina had previously suffered from depression and anxiety. She created an imaginative world to soothe herself, which was highly effective. Yet, this world had become a pervasive part of her life that was interfering with her ability to function well in school and in social relationships. The assessor needed to connect with Christina and show acceptance and appreciation for the world she had created, in order to facilitate a disequilibrium that would motivate her openness to trying other coping strategies. Causing such a dramatic change for Christina was understandably going to be a difficult process, requiring a supportive environment beyond the assessment. The assessor's collaboration with the mother, teacher, and counselor helped these people better understand Christina, and enhanced their willingness to support Christina as needed in the future.

Michael

Many TA-C components were applied during Michael's assessment, mainly because of the complexity of the case and the high stakes of needing to determine how to help him progress in the school context. Thus, Michael's story portrays the utility of incorporating a collaborative stance, a strong working alliance, the collection of assessment questions, processing testing, a case formulation, and the delivery of feedback into a school-based evaluation. Michael is a 17-year-old Caucasian male from a family with minimal financial resources. He should have been a twelfth-grader, but was a tenth-grader according to course credits, due to failing multiple classes. The families in the school district where Michael was enrolled were culturally diverse and ranged from middle to low socioeconomic status. Michael had a history of disciplinary problems in school stemming from verbal and physical aggression towards students and teachers. He had previously been sent to alternative educational placements eight times, and had been summoned to court six times. Most recently, Michael was sent to an alternative educational placement for "making a terroristic threat" towards a teacher at his high school. Following this placement, Michael was referred for a comprehensive reevaluation to assess his continued eligibility for special education programming and to determine an appropriate educational setting for him. Michael qualified for special education in the past as a student with ED, and an LD in reading comprehension.

COLLABORATIVE STANCE

The development of a strong working alliance was critical to this evaluation, as Michael had previously undergone numerous unfavorable experiences with assessors and was therefore resistant to cooperating and putting forth effort. Michael initially tried to shock the assessor by interspersing strange, fantastical comments into their conversations so that she would view him negatively and avoid delving deeper. He had successfully elicited this response from others throughout his life. However, the assessor maintained a collaborative, therapeutic stance, as she displayed unconditional positive regard and an unwavering interest in learning more about him. The assessor explored his interests in video games and in writing stories, as they established rapport. Michael slowly became more invested in the assessment process as he realized that the assessor genuinely valued his input and was dedicated to helping him, his mother, and his teachers better understand him.

By collaborating with Michael's teachers, the assessor discovered that Michael failed numerous classes due to a lack of effort, rather than due to insufficient ability. In fact, the teachers explained that Michael was one of the brightest students in their classes. Michael's mother was surprised to find out that he had qualified for a learning disability in reading comprehension in the past, because she reported that he loves to read. This highlighted the importance of providing the mother with accessible feedback from the assessment.

The collaboration with teachers and Michael's mother was also highly beneficial to investigating his behavior. Because of his history of failing classes, Michael was not enrolled in any advanced coursework and, subsequently, was not adequately challenged in his current classes. Teachers informed the assessor that he typically displayed problematic behavior when he finished independent schoolwork before others in the class, and was therefore bored. In those situations, he would try to make others think he was "weird" and "crazy." For example, during one class, after he finished his work he bit into a pen and let the ink drip down his face. His teachers explained that he had no friends in school, and had often been ridiculed by peers. Michael's mother also helped the assessor understand the etiology of Michael's behavioral issues, as she explained that she and Michael had been physically and verbally abused by her husband throughout Michael's life. The husband had recently moved out of the home, which both the mother and Michael reported had a positive impact on them. The mother also described the danger of their neighborhood, as they lived in a trailer home without any security features.

INNOVATIVE ASSESSMENT TECHNIQUES

The assessor co-constructed assessment questions with the teacher and mother, which further increased investment in the assessment process and heightened their interest in the findings. The assessment questions from both the mother and teacher inquired about Michael's peer relationships, and why he constantly exhibited shocking behaviors such as biting the pen. Michael did not generate any assessment questions, as he stated that he already knew everything about himself. The assessor respected Michael's perceived self-awareness, and did not force him to provide assessment questions. Instead, she relayed appreciation for the opportunity to learn about him. With a strong working alliance, the assessor was able to obtain an accurate representation of his current functioning. Extended inquiry was used with the social/emotional assessment tools to gain a more comprehensive understanding of his emotional and behavioral functioning. For example, he quickly completed a standard version of sentence completion items. Yet, he spent significantly more time attempting to complete idiographic sentence completion items. When asked about the difference in completion time, he was aware of the stark contrast. He attributed this discrepancy to the individualized, personal nature of the idiographic items and stated that it was far more difficult for him to complete these than the other items.

CASE CONCEPTUALIZATION

Through integrating the information from teachers and the mother with the testing data, the assessor formulated a case conceptualization. According to test results, Michael's overall cognitive functioning was in the high average range, and all of his academic abilities, including reading comprehension, were commensurate with his cognitive functioning. In addition, Michael shared with the assessor a fictional book he was writing, which provided further evidence of his proficiency in reading comprehension. The test results indicated that he did not qualify for an LD in reading comprehension.

However, Michael was not progressing in obtaining course credits in high school, possibly due to the mismatch between his academic prowess and the level of instruction. The alternative educational placement where he was located during the assessment was a self-paced learning environment that allowed him to earn course credits at an accelerated rate. Michael preferred this environment, and desired to complete the credits required for graduation from high school at the alternative school. Michael's verbally and physically aggressive behavior seemed to be his way of protecting himself by preemptively striking out against those he viewed as threatening. In support of this finding, one of Michael's stories from the Thematic Apperception Test featured a lonely dragon that chomped humans and stole their armor, as it thought that if it could not have friends, it would cover it up with treasure. Michael's constant hypervigilance and defensive stance were also understandable, considering the lack of safety and security present in his neighborhood, and in his home during his formative years, due to his father's abusiveness.

PLANNING AND CONDUCTING FEEDBACK

Feedback was delivered to Michael primarily to shed light on his behavior, and also to examine his willingness to participate in counseling. His openness to receiving feedback and engaging in a counseling intervention was facilitated by the strong working alliance. He appreciated the relationship forged between himself and the assessor. The assessor's persistence in wanting to learn more about him, and her refusal to negatively evaluate him, provided a corrective emotional experience that gradually resulted in the shedding of armor and the subsequent exposure of a lonely boy. While Michael may not have shifted his view of himself, he was struck by the fact that someone had taken the time to know and understand him in a nonjudgmental, caring way, rather than being repulsed by his shocking behavior.

The feedback for the mother and teachers was individualized to address their concerns. The assessor helped these people shift their view of Michael from "bad" to "lonely and scared." This new understanding of Michael was therapeutic, in that it enhanced their sympathy towards him and ultimately altered the way his mother and teachers related to him. During the course of the assessment, Michael began to quickly earn course credits. The assessor and teachers determined that he could complete high school at the alternative school. Over the next few months following the assessment, he completed all credits required for graduation, and graduated on time with the other twelfth-graders.

Damien

Damien's assessment case demonstrates commitment to a collaborative orientation, collection of assessment questions, building a strong alliance with the child, an integrative case conceptualization, organizing feedback according to levels, and the use of a child fable as a successful feedback medium. This case also used an intervention session between the child and assessor that provided a mini-intervention in the area of academics, and informed subsequent recommendations. Damien is a 12-year-old African American boy in the seventh grade. He was originally assessed for ED while in fourth grade, due to depressive symptoms that had been present for over a year. At the time of the assessment, Damien was living with his mother and 17-year-old stepbrother. The reevaluation was conducted to determine Damien's continued eligibility in special education, and the suitability of his current services.

COLLABORATIVE STANCE

Damien is from a low SES family facing serious economic hardship. Damien's father passed away eight months before the assessment, and Damien's depression and irritability had subsequently increased. His mother did not have a car, so a face-to-face interview at the school was not feasible. In TA-C, meeting with parents in person is part of building the collaborative relationship. However, this may not always be possible in a school setting, and phone interviews have been used if needed. In this case, the assessor was able to schedule a home visit to meet with Damien's mother. The assessor's willingness to make a special effort to meet with the mother laid the foundation for a collaborative relationship and strong working alliance with her. The assessor's efforts clearly demonstrated that she valued the mother's input as an important part of the assessment.

During the home visit, the assessor was able to gauge Damien's mother's emotional resources. It became clear that she and the rest of the family were still grieving the loss of her husband, and that the resultant economic hardship was a constant stressor. Her priorities were trying to provide for her boys' basic needs, and helping keep them out of trouble. She reported that she and Damien would argue over chores, and sometimes Damien would become irritable and yell, while at other times he would start crying. Damien's mother was clearly overwhelmed by her circumstances, and in her comments kept focusing on her own struggles to support her family.

Although Damien's depressive symptoms began years ago, it was essential for the assessor to understand the family's coping around the death of his father, and the limited available emotional support at home. By meeting with the mother, the assessor was able to gain important information about her resources and her inability to handle any difficult assessment results that might constitute Level 3 feedback.

INNOVATIVE ASSESSMENT TECHNIQUES

Although Damien was invited to include his own assessment questions, he did not contribute any. When asked about previous assessment experiences, he said, "They just had me fill out a lot of different forms that I didn't really care about.... I feel like I work with so many people I don't even know." Thus, in order to gain Damien's active participation, the assessor had to focus on building rapport and demonstrating to Damien that this assessment could be a different experience. Damien's mother contributed two assessment questions: (1) "Why does Damien argue about chores so much?" and (2) "Why does he lie and make me look like a bad parent?" Although these questions were not as systemically oriented as we often seek in a comprehensive TA-C, they were realistic and genuine questions that could enrich feedback with the mom.

Damien's teacher also contributed assessment questions, and the following is a good summary of her perspective: "I want to learn how to help him understand that it is okay that something is difficult, and that it is okay if he doesn't understand it right away the first time. He's almost afraid to believe in himself. I want to know how to help him realize that he can do a lot of things he says he can't. I also want to understand why he puts so much stress on himself to make things better at home—to make his mom happy." Damien's teacher provided important information about his daily experiences and emotional reactions. Thus, by actively collaborating and seeking questions from Damien's mother and teacher, the primary adults in Damien's network were more personally invested in the assessment. Instead of Damien's reevaluation simply focusing on whether he continued to meet criteria for ED, the assessment process could also be tailored to address the mother's and teacher's concerns.

CASE CONCEPTUALIZATION

Damien's cognitive testing showed average to low average cognitive abilities, with weaknesses in short-term and long-term memory. Damien's achievement results were in the low average range, with an LD in mathematical calculation based on a discrepancy model. Damien was known as a gifted artist, and thus the projective drawings were a good medium for him to express himself. Damien's Draw-a-Person featured an elf warrior woman, who was a character from an online game. He described her as someone who had been hurt emotionally, due to her forest being burned down, but whom he respected because she was strong and loyal. Damien had more difficulty attempting the Kinetic Family Drawing, in that it was harder for him to draw "real" people, especially his family. Damien's illustration showed his mother sleeping in bed with his father's pillow, while Damien played on his computer and his stepbrother playfully did chores. Thus, the assessor was given more support for her conceptualization of his mother as emotionally unavailable and preoccupied with grief about her deceased husband. Damien appeared to be meeting his own needs by seeking out the support and stability of the online game, which he often played for over six hours per day.

The Draw-a-Tree projective provided insight into Damien's functioning. He drew a small oak tree in the desert that only survives by having roots that can get water from deep within the ground. However, behind the small tree was a spirit tree to help the smaller tree grow. When asked what the [smaller] tree needed most, Damien replied unequivocally, "A protector" to keep it safe from wind, storms, and debris. Similar to the elf protecting her forest, Damien appeared to be seeking support and protection, but also relying on himself to be strong.

The case conceptualization indicated three major areas contributing to Damien's depression. First, his frustration and sense of failure in school had resulted in a low sense of self-efficacy. Damien's weaknesses in short- and long-term memory seemed to contribute significantly to his frustration, because he had a difficult time learning and retaining new information. He felt doomed to do poorly, no matter what his effort. Secondly, the grief surrounding the death of his father was a recent and profound stressor that would tax the resources of any child, and most certainly was affecting Damien. And lastly, although his mother was working very hard to provide for Damien and his stepbrother, Damien did not seem to be receiving the emotional support he needed at home, resulting in Damien seeking out other areas in which to feel supported and competent, namely the online game.

Damien had numerous strengths, particularly his solid social skills and average cognitive abilities. Damien also possessed a good sense of humor and was well liked by both teachers and peers. Although Damien was easily frustrated in school and would shut down and withdraw from work, he did not have any acting-out behaviors or discipline concerns. Damien also had a great desire to succeed in school, as he felt this might "make his mom happy." Understanding both Damien's abilities, and his attitudes toward school and himself, were important components of the case conceptualization because they helped explain the underlying mechanisms maintaining his depression.

INTERVENTION SESSION

Observation and teacher report had indicated that one of Damien's biggest struggles in the classroom was avoiding work he felt was difficult. Once Damien began to shut down, the teacher had little success in re-engaging him in an activity or assignment. It was hypothesized that Damien's weaknesses in short- and long-term memory made learning and retaining information challenging. This was especially clear in math, which involves remembering basic math facts and working through multi-step problems. However, the assessor noticed in Damien's achievement testing that although he struggled with basic calculation, his performance in applied reasoning of math concepts was commensurate with his other cognitive abilities. Because the assessor had not been able to give Damien feedback about his performance during standardized administration, Damien was unaware that he did better in math reasoning, including problems with money, time, and fractions, than in calculation.

Thus, the assessor designed a mini-intervention session to determine whether Damien could accept positive feedback about an area of academics, and learn to discriminate his strengths and weaknesses. The assessor prepared for the intervention session and decided to use the math achievement section from a different achievement test than the one previously used. Damien was asked to complete a few calculation problems while being timed. Then, he and the assessor discussed how difficult Damien found those problems. However, the assessor was able to praise Damien's effort and stress that, although he struggled, he was able to do about half of the problems correctly. The assessor was very careful not to push Damien to the point where he would shut down before experiencing success.

The assessor then asked Damien if he would be willing to try a different type of problem, one that the assessor had noticed Damien did not seem to mind as much during prior testing. Damien agreed, and the assessor was able to tell Damien each time he got a question correct on the applied math problems. After getting five in a row correct, the assessor mentioned to Damien how well he seemed to be doing; however, Damien replied that those had been easy questions, so his performance was not a big deal. Damien and the assessor continued and as the questions became harder and Damien continued to do well (getting about 80% correct), the assessor again paused and noted how well Damien was doing. The assessor also reflected that it seemed like Damien truly comprehended the questions that were being asked. Damien gave a shy smile and said that these questions were not as "mathy" as the others, that they were more "common sense." The assessor and Damien engaged in a conversation in which the assessor emphasized that the common-sense problems could actually be harder than the straightforward calculations, for some people.

The assessor then tried to connect his experience in the mini-intervention session to the classroom by asking Damien what it is like for him when he is doing math in class. Damien indicated that normally he just started "tuning out" when math class started. The assessor wondered aloud whether there were parts of math that were hard, but other parts that were easier for him. Damien replied that he just seemed to have it backwards, that he could not complete the "easy" questions, but could sometimes understand the longer word problems. Damien and the assessor ended the session by discussing how Damien and his teacher could work on not letting the basic calculations interfere when trying to do more complex problems.

Although at first Damien defended against his ability to do well in math, the consistent positive feedback during the intervention session allowed the assessor and Damien to better understand Damien's strengths and weaknesses in math. His overgeneralization of negative thoughts, and low frustration tolerance, seemed to be some of the hallmark thoughts and behaviors maintaining his depression around academics. After the intervention session, Damien seemed to have a better sense of his strengths and weaknesses, and how he could start trying to work around them instead of giving up.

PLANNING AND CONDUCTING FEEDBACK
In planning the parent feedback, the assessor was initially concerned that the idea that Damien was not receiving enough positive emotional support at home would be overwhelming, and hence Level 3 feedback for his mother, who was already stressed and needing support of her own. However, after reviewing his mother's questions, the assessor was able to tie the questions to Damien's depression and how he was expressing it at home and school. Her first question of, "Why does he argue with me so much over chores?" was answered by reminding Damien's mother about his depression, and then informing her that especially for adolescents and children, depression may not always be expressed through sadness. The assessor planned to use the "arguing over chores" as an example of irritability, and explain why sometimes Damien would cry and at other times yell when he was upset.

The mother's second question was, "Why does he lie and tell people I am a bad parent?" This question referred to incidents in which Damien would say he did not have a coat, or his mom did not give him lunch money, when in fact she had provided both of those things. The assessor answered this question first by validating how important the mother was to Damien, and that throughout the assessment he spoke of her as his biggest supporter and the person he needs the most. The assessor then wanted to frame Damien's lying as an "acting-out behavior," similar to the irritability just discussed around chores. The assessor planned to do more brief parent education about how adolescents, especially boys, may not know how to deal with uncomfortable feelings, and will often either seek support or act out in ways that elicit negative attention. By bringing up Damien's need for attention, the assessor was able broach the idea that Damien desires positive attention from his mother, and that this can help him deal with some of his negative feelings. Thus, the assessor was able to incorporate into feedback the notion that Damien needed positive attention from his mother, in a way that answered her questions and explained his behavior and needs in terms of his depression, which she already knew about from a previous assessment.

By the end of the assessment, the assessor had a solid conceptualization about what was contributing to Damien's depression, and how that was impacting his home and school life. Thus, the assessor felt that besides the academic feedback, Damien should and could hear that he is capable, and that there are teachers at school who want to help him. Because of Damien's affinity for the online game, the assessor decided to create a fable using some of the characters, skills, and names from the game.

During the student feedback, Damien seemed somewhat blasé as the assessor talked about the actual testing results. Then the assessor told Damien she had written a story using what she had learned about him and some of the characters from the online game. Damien immediately sat up and looked the assessor in the eye as she read the story to him. The fable told the story of a young Orc who struggled with learning the different skills for battleax during school, but who loved alchemy and would often study different potions at home. The Orc story paralleled the events in Damien's life, such as losing his father, having difficulty in academics (battleax skills), and arguing with his mother. The story ends with the Orc meeting a wise elf who helped him begin to understand his feelings of sadness, as well as how to deal with those feelings. The story does not promise a "happily ever after" ending, but rather honors the reality that the young Orc is dealing with some very sad and difficult issues, while providing hope that there are others ready to support the young Orc and help him with those feelings.

After the assessor finished the fable, Damien simply asked her to read it again. Following the second read through, Damien paused, looked at the assessor, and said, "I got it." He clearly realized the Orc story was based on him, and then he and the assessor were able to talk about the different kinds of counseling services he could receive at school, and how they could help him manage his sad feelings. Damien was clearly more engaged with the assessor after the fable and, by the time the feedback session occurred, their collaborative relationship had grown so that Damien was able to be more open about his thoughts and responses than in the first few sessions, where the assessor had still been gaining his trust. The extra time and creativity the assessor put into creating the fable for Damien showed that she really understood him and wanted to communicate in a way that would work for him. The feedback experience was positive for both Damien and the assessor, as they were able to communicate via the fable and feel connected around the assessment experience.

Damien's case demonstrates that an early commitment to collaboration with parent, teacher, and student led to a rich case conceptualization and feedback that was relevant and helpful to the participants. Once in special education, students receive reevaluations every three years; thus, Damien came into the assessment with a typical "let's get this over with" attitude. However, the assessor took the time to understand Damien, his concerns, his strengths, and what his daily life was like for him, which resulted in a

different type of assessment experience. The multi-theoretical case conceptualization went beyond just identifying Damien's continued depression, to understanding the interplay between home and school experiences that were maintaining his symptoms, and appreciating his strengths. He was a student in need of positive attention, and the meetings with the assessor started to provide some of this basic support and led to Damien's receptiveness to feedback. Damien's positive experience with child feedback demonstrates the power of communicating with students in a way that is personalized and relevant to them. The application and integration of TA-C components in this school assessment helped create an enriching and positive experience for all involved.

Summary and Conclusions

TA-C is a relatively new form of psychological assessment that can serve as a collaborative, short-term family intervention. It is designed to engage children and their parents collaboratively in the assessment process, address their questions of interest, provide meaningful and sensitively ordered feedback, and facilitate meaningful change (both during and subsequent to the assessment). In this chapter we have described the development of collaborative assessment and TA, reviewed the extant research addressing their efficacy and effectiveness, and presented the comprehensive model for using TA with children. Initial research findings are encouraging, and offer a beginning evidence base for the use of TA and TA-C. In addition, noting that the implementation of comprehensive TA-C is unlikely in most cases of school based assessment, we have proposed components of TA-C that we see as most likely to transfer well to the school setting and have a significant impact. We also provided four case illustrations of using components of TA-C in school based assessment of children and adolescents, including teacher involvement. We hope these cases have created excitement about the possibilities and benefits of using components of TA-C. As introduced early on, one of the main principles of TA-C is that the assessment in and of itself can be an important intervention for children and parents. Our hope is that incorporating aspects of TA-C into school based assessment will prove to be an important intervention for children, teachers, parents, and schools. We plan to continue our research efforts to test out this possibility.

We also are aware that in contemporary school psychology assessment practice, assessment is viewed as the last step in a series of referral processes. And, in models based on RTI, assessment is seen as a fallback to be used only after all other standard or empirically based interventions have been tested. The principles of TA-C suggest that assessment is not the last step, but rather another potential intervention that can provide an even greater level of detailed, individualized information about the child. Components of TA-C can be incorporated into school assessments to help maximize the information gathering *and* intervention potential of an assessment. While some of the previously discussed components of TA-C are easier to implement than others, each of the components stands to be highly beneficial, and certain components may be more or less applicable depending on the particular school based case. Thus, we encourage assessors in schools to individually tailor the incorporation of these components into their assessments with children, in order to maximize the potential for new understanding and change for all involved parties.

References

Ackerman, S. J., Hilsenroth, M. J., Baity, M. R., & Blagys, M. D. (2000). Interaction of therapeutic process and alliance during psychological assessment. *Journal of Personality Assessment, 75,* 82–109.

Allen, A., Montgomery, M., Tubman, J., Frazier, L. & Escovar, L. (2003). The effects of assessment feedback on rapport-building and self-enhancement processes. *Journal of Mental Health Counseling, 25*(3), 165–181.

Beck, J. S. (1995). *Cognitive therapy: Basics and beyond.* New York: Guilford Press.

Berg, M. (1985). The feedback process in diagnostic psychological testing. *Bulletin of the Menninger Clinic, 49,* 52–69.

Bodin, D., Beetar, J., Yeates, K., Boyer, K., Colvin, A., & Mangeot, S. (2007). A survey of parent satisfaction with pediatric neuropsychological evaluations. *Clinical Neuropsychologist, 21*(6), 884–898.

Braaten, E. B. (2007). Personality assessment feedback with adolescents. In S. Smith & L. Handler (Eds.), *The clinical assessment of children and adolescents: A practitioner's handbook* (pp. 73–83). Mahwah, NJ: Lawrence Erlbaum Associates.

Brenner, E. (2003). Consumer-focused psychological assessment. *Professional Psychology: Research and Practice, 34*(3), 240–247.

Butcher, J. N. (1992). Introduction to the special section: Providing psychological test feedback to clients. *Psychological Assessment, 4,* 267.

Cohen, J. (1997). On the uses and misuses of psychological evaluations. In Flaherty, L. T., & Horowitz, H. A. (Eds.), *Adolescent psychiatry: Developmental and clinical issues* (pp. 253–268). New York: Analytic Press.

Colley, T. E. (1973). Interpretation of psychological test data to children. *Mental Retardation,11* (1), 28–30.

Cromer, T. D., & Hilsenroth, M. J. (2006, March). *Personality predictors of patient and therapist alliance during a collaborative feedback session.* Paper presented at the annual meeting of the Society for Personality Assessment, San Diego, CA.

Finn, S. E. (1994, April). *Testing one's own clients mid-therapy with the Rorschach.* Paper presented at the Society for Personality Assessment annual meeting, Chicago, IL.

Finn, S. E. (1996). *Manual for using the MMPI–2 as a therapeutic intervention.* Minneapolis: University of Minnesota Press.

Finn, S. E. (1998). Teaching Therapeutic Assessment in a required graduate course. In L. Handler & M. Hilsenroth (Eds.), *Teaching and learning personality assessment* (pp. 359–373).

Finn, S. E. (2003). Therapeutic assessment of a man with "ADD". *Journal of Personality Assessment, 80,* 115–129.

Finn, S. E. (2005). How psychological assessment taught me compassion and firmness. *Journal of Personality Assessment, 84*(1), 29–32.

Finn, S. E. (2007). *In our clients' shoes: Theory and techniques of therapeutic assessment.* Mahwah, New Jersey: Lawrence Erlbaum Associates.

Finn, S. E., & Kamphuis, J. H. (2006). Therapeutic assessment with the MMPI–2. In J. N. Butcher (Ed.), *MMPI–2: A practitioners guide* (pp. 165–191). Washington, D.C.: APA Books.

Finn, S. E., & Tonsager, M. E. (1992). Therapeutic effects of providing MMPI–2 test feedback to college students awaiting therapy. *Psychological Assessment, 4,* 278–287.

Finn, S. E., & Tonsager, M. E. (1997). Information-gathering and therapeutic models of assessment: Complementary paradigms. *Psychological Assessment, 9,* 374–385.

Finn, S. E., & Tonsager, M. E. (2002). How therapeutic assessment became humanistic. *The Humanistic Psychologist, 30,* 10–22.

Fischer, C. T. (1970). The testee as co-evaluator. *Journal of Counseling Psychology, 17,* 70–76.

Fischer, C. T. (1985). *Individualizing psychological assessment.* Monterey, CA: Brooks/Cole Publishing.

Fischer, C. T. (1985/1994). Individualizing psychological assessment. Mahwah, NJ: Erlbaum.

Fischer, C. T. (2000). Collaborative, individualized assessment. *Journal of Personality Assessment, 74,* 2–14.

Fowler, J. C. (1998). The trouble with learning personality assessment. In L. Handler & M. J. Hilsenroth (Eds.), Teaching and learning personality assessment (pp. 31–44). Mahwah, NJ: Lawrence Erlbaum Associates.

Groth-Marnat, G. (2003). *Handbook of psychological assessment* (4th ed.). Hoboken, NJ: John Wiley & Sons.

Hamilton, A. M., Fowler, J. L., Hersh, B., Hall, C., Finn, S. E., Tharinger, D. J., et al. (2009). Why won't my parents help me? Therapeutic assessment of a child and her family. *Journal of Personality Assessment, 91,* 108–120.

Handler, L. (1998). Teaching and learning the interpretation of the Wechsler intelligence tests as personality instruments. In L. Handler & M. J. Hilsenroth (eds.), *Teaching and learning personality assessment* (pp. 295–320). Mahwah, NJ: Lawrence Erlbaum.

Handler, L. (2007). The use of therapeutic assessment with children and adolescents. *The clinical assessment of children and adolescents: A practitioner's handbook* (pp. 53–72). Mahwah, NJ: Lawrence Erlbaum.

Handler, L. (2008). Supervision in therapeutic and collaborative assessment. In A. Hess, K. Hess & T. Hess (Eds.), *Psychotherapy Supervision: Theory, Research, and Practice* (2nd ed., pp. 200–222). New York: John Wiley & Sons.

Handler, L., & Meyer, G. J. (1998). The importance of teaching and learning personality assessment. In L. Handler & M. J. Hilsenroth (Eds.), *Teaching and learning personality assessment* (pp. 3–30). Mahwah, NJ: Erlbaum.

Hilsenroth, M. J., Ackerman, S. J., Clemence, A. J., Strassle, C. G., & Handler, L. (2002). Effects of structured clinical training on patient and therapist perspectives of alliance early in psychotherapy. *Psychotherapy: Theory/Research/Practice/Training, 39*, 309–323.

Hilsenroth, M. J., Peters, E. J. & Ackerman, S. J. (2004). The development of therapeutic alliance during psychological assessment: Patient and therapist perspectives across treatment. *Journal of Personality Assessment, 83*(3), 332–344.

Human, M. T., & Teglasi, H. (1993). Parents' satisfaction and compliance with recommendations following psychoeducational assessment of children. *Journal of School Psychology, 31*, 449–467.

Kamphaus, R. W. (2001). *Clinical assessment of child and adolescent intelligence* (2nd ed.). Boston: Allyn and Bacon.

Laine, C. & Davidoff, F. (1996). Patient centered medicine: A professional evolution. *Journal of the American Medical Association, 275*, 152–156.

Lillie, R. (2007). Getting clients to hear: Applying principles and techniques of Kiesler's Interpersonal Communication Therapy to assessment feedback. *Psychology and Psychotherapy: Theory, Research, and Practice, 80*, 151–163.

Michel, D. M. (2002). Psychological assessment as a therapeutic intervention in patients hospitalized with eating disorders. *Professional Psychology: Research and Practice 33*(5), 470–477.

Mosak, H. H. & Gushurst, R. S. (1972). Some therapeutic uses of psychological testing. *American Journal of Psychotherapy, 26*, 539–546.

Mutchnick, M. G. & Handler, L. (2002). Once upon a time…: Therapeutic interactive stories. *The Humanistic Psychologist, 30*, 75–84.

National Association of School Psychologists. (2000). *Professional conduct manual* (4th ed.). Bethesda, MD: Author.

Newman, M. L., & Greenway, P. (1997). Therapeutic effects of providing MMPI–2 test feedback to clients at a university counseling service: A collaborative approach. *Psychological Assessment, 9*, 122–131.

Palinscar, A. S., Brown, A. L., & Campione, J. C. (1994). Models and practices of dynamic assessment. In G. P. Wallach & K. G. Butler (Eds.), *Language learning disabilities in school-age children and adolescents* (pp. 132–144). New York: Merrill.

Pegg, P. O., Auerbach, S. M., Seel, R. T., Buenaver, L. F., Kiesler, D. J., & Plybon, L. E. (2005). The impact of patient-centered information on patients' treatment. *Rehabilitation Psychology, 50*(4), 366–374.

Pollak, J. (1988). The feedback process with parents in child and adolescent psychological assessment. *Psychology in the Schools, 25*(2), 143–153.

Pope, K. S. (1992). Responsibilities in providing psychological test feedback to clients. *Psychological Assessment, 4*(3), 268–271.

Purves, C. (2002). Collaborative assessment with involuntary populations: Foster children and their mothers. *The Humanistic Psychologist, 30*(1), 164–174.

Quill, T. E. & Brody, H. (1996). Physician recommendations and patient autonomy: Finding a balance between physician power and patient choice. *Annals of Internal Medicine, 125*, 763–769.

Quirk, M. P., Strosahl, K., Kreilkamp, T., & Erdberg, P. (1995). Personality feedback consultation to families in a managed mental health care practice. *Professional Psychology: Research and Practice, 26*, 27–32.

Riccio, C. A., & Rodriquez, O. L. (2007). Integration of psychological assessment approaches in school psychology. *Psychology in the Schools, 44*, 243–255.

Richman, J. (1967). Reporting diagnostic test results to patients and their families. *Journal of Projective Techniques and Personality Assessment, 31*, 62–70.

Smith, B.L. (1998). The impossible takes a bit longer: The role of theory in teaching psychological assessment. In L. Handler & M.J. Hilsenroth (Eds.), *Teaching and learning personality assessment* (pp. 69–82). Mahwah, NJ: Erlbaum.

Smith, J. D. & Handler, L. (2009). "Why do I get in trouble so much?" A family therapeutic assessment case study. *Journal of Personality Assessment, 91*, 197–210.

Smith, J. D., Wolf, N., Handler, L., & Nash, M. R. (2009). Testing the effectiveness of family therapeutic assessment: A case study using a time-series design. *Journal of Personality Assessment, 91*, 518–536.

Swann, W. B., Jr. (1990). To be adored or to be known: The interplay of self-enhancement and self-verification. In R. M. Sorrentino & E. T. Higgins (Eds.), *Foundations of Social Behavior*, (Vol. 2, pp. 408–448). New York: Guilford.

Tharinger, D. J., Christopher, G., & Matson, M. (In press). Play, playfulness, and creative expression in therapeutic assessment with children. In S. W. Russ & L. N. Niec (Eds.), *An evidence-based approach to play in intervention and prevention: Integrating developmental and clinical science*. New York: Guilford Press.

Tharinger, D. J., Finn, S. E., Austin, C., Gentry, L, Bailey, E., Parton, V., & Fischer, M. (2008). Family sessions as part of child psychological assessment with children: Goals, techniques, clinical utility, and therapeutic value. *Journal of Personality Assessment, 90*, 547–558.

Tharinger, D., Finn, S., Gentry, L., Hamilton, A., Fowler, J., Matson, M. et al. (2009). Therapeutic assessment with children: A pilot study of treatment acceptability and outcome. *Journal of Personality Assessment, 91*, 238-244.

Tharinger, D. J., Finn, S. E., Hersh, B., Wilkinson, A., Christopher, G. & Tran, A. (2008). Assessment feedback with parents and pre-adolescent children: A collaborative approach. *Professional Psychology: Research and Practice, 39*, 600–609.

Tharinger, D. J., Finn, S. E., Wilkinson, A., DeHay, T, Parton, V.T., Bailey, K. E., & Tran, A. (2008). Providing psychological assessment feedback with children through individualized fables. *Professional Psychology: Research and Practice, 39*, 610–618.

Tharinger, D. J., Finn, S. E., Wilkinson, A. D., & Schaber, P. M. (2007). Therapeutic assessment with a child as a family intervention: Clinical protocol and a research case study. *Psychology in the Schools, 44*, 293–209.

Tharinger, D. & Roberts, M. (In press). Human figure drawings in therapeutic assessment with children: Process, product, life context, and systemic impact. In L. Handler (Ed.), *Projective techniques: Research, innovative techniques, and case studies*.

Weil, M. P., & Hilsenroth, M. J. (2006, March). *Patient experience of a collaborative feedback session: The impact on psychotherapy process across treatment*. Paper presented at the annual meeting of the Society for Personality Assessment, San Diego, CA.

Winnicott, D. W. (1953). Transitional objects and transitional phenomena. *International Journal of Psychoanalysis, 34*, 89–97.

Assessment of Classroom Environments

Maribeth Gettinger, Clarissa Schienebeck, Stephanie Seigel, *and* Laura Vollmer

Abstract

The quality of classroom environments is a central variable in determining behavioral and learning outcomes of students. This chapter reviews learning environment research that links measurable dimensions of teaching and classroom environments to student performance, including effective teaching behaviors, classroom management, teacher–student relationships, academic learning time, emotional climate and support, grouping format, class size, and physical characteristics. A review of three approaches to assessing these dimensions of classroom environments is provided; specifically, classroom observations, classroom environment surveys, and eco-behavioral assessment. Finally, implications for classroom practice and future directions for research are presented.

Keywords: learning environment, eco-behavioral assessment, effective teaching, academic engaged time, classroom climate, functional assessment

Introduction

This chapter focuses on research findings and assessment procedures related to the study of classroom learning environments. The chapter is organized into four main sections. The first section summarizes essential background information, including a rationale for evaluating classroom environments, and review of historical perspectives on learning environment research. Second, a review of literature is presented concerning measurable aspects of classroom environments that are associated with positive student outcomes. Following this discussion of environmental variables, the third section provides a descriptive summary of selected instruments for assessing multiple dimensions of learning environments. Finally, the fourth section discusses implications and future directions for classroom environment research.

Background to Assessment of Classroom Environments
Importance of Evaluating Classroom Environments

Students spend a vast amount of time in classroom settings. The quality of classroom environments is central to defining the character of schools and contributing to student outcomes. Despite the importance of classroom environments, the majority of educational research has focused on the assessment of individual learner characteristics, or family background variables, as determinants of school performance. Extensive research continues to document the effects of students' attitudes, abilities, and behaviors, on their achievement and adjustment in school. Research has also demonstrated the significant influence of family and background variables, such as socioeconomic status, on school performance. Unlike learner abilities or family characteristics, however, classroom environment is viewed as a manipulable factor that contributes to student learning. According to Dorman (2002), classroom environment encompasses the climate or affective tone of classrooms, as well as the structural, organizational, and instructional features. Increasingly, researchers have acknowledged that classroom environment is a strong determinant of student outcomes, similar to learner and background variables. Fraser (2002), for example, reported that students' perceptions of the quality of their classroom environments accounted for a significant increment in achievement, over and beyond general ability. Moreover, students in high-quality classrooms have higher achievement than those in low-quality classrooms, even when they have similar individual characteristics and family backgrounds (Dorman, Aldridge, & Fraser, 2006).

Given these findings, it is not surprising that interest in classroom learning environments has expanded significantly in recent years, particularly among international researchers, educators, and administrators. The study of learning environments continues to be a burgeoning area of inquiry, as is evident in the recent introduction of *Learning Environments Research*, a journal devoted exclusively to research on learning environments, as well as the establishment of the Learning Environments Special Interest Group within the American Educational Research Association.

For the purpose of this chapter, it is important to underscore a distinction between school-level versus classroom-level environments, the latter of which is the focus of the chapter. The effects of classroom and school environments are clearly interdependent and cumulative. Despite the logical linkages between these two areas, school-level and classroom-level environment research have remained somewhat independent (Fraser, 1991). Classroom environment concerns the dynamics, interactions, and behaviors within classrooms or small learning environments, including how students experience the characteristics of the classroom, and what teachers do to establish a productive learning setting for all learners. Whereas classroom environment is usually assessed in terms of students' perceptions and observed classroom characteristics, the school environment is typically measured in terms of staff or parent perceptions, and more global quality indicators (e.g., number of school disciplinary referrals). The classroom-level perspective in this chapter includes a focus on the physical, behavioral, social and psychological, as well as instructional dimensions of classroom environments.

Historical Perspectives on Classroom Environment Research

Prior learning environment research has contributed significantly to current conceptualizations of classroom environment and assessment approaches. In the 1970s, Herbert Walberg and Rudolph Moos initiated independent research programs focusing on the psychosocial dimensions of learning environments.

During this time, Walberg began developing the *Learning Environment Inventory* (Walberg & Anderson, 1968) in conjunction with research and evaluation related to the Harvard Project Physics. Concurrently, Moos developed the *Classroom Environment Scale* (Moos & Trickett, 1974), as part of a comprehensive research program focusing on individuals' perceptions of the overall social climate in hospital, university, and work environments. During the 1980s, the conceptualization and measurement of classroom environments expanded rapidly, primarily through the work of Barry Fraser, including the development of the *My Class Inventory* measure. The findings of these early learning environment researchers demonstrated consistent associations between classroom environment dimensions and a range of student outcomes among diverse samples of learners, using a variety of different measures (Fraser, 1994).

Historically, several terms have been central to an understanding of both the conceptual and methodological issues in classroom environment research and assessment. Murray (1938) first introduced the terms *alpha press* and *beta press* in the study of classroom environments. According to Murray, alpha press describes the learning environment as assessed by an external, objective observer; beta press describes the subjective approach of asking individuals who function within the environment (e.g., students or teachers) to assess the learning environment as they perceive it. Alpha press in the classroom usually requires observers to record specific events according to a categorical coding scheme. Because it involves direct observation, alpha press is considered to be highly objective. By contrast, beta press represents the environment as it is perceived and experienced by an individual. Within a classroom setting, this depends on a subjective assessment by students and/or teachers. According to Murray, beta press may actually exert the greater influence on behavior, because it is interpreted and experienced by individuals within their environment.

In addition to alpha press and beta press, there has also been a distinction between low-inference and high-inference measures for assessing classroom environments. According to Rosenshine (1970), low-inference measures assess specific, observable, relatively objective classroom behavior and events, primarily in terms of the frequency of occurrence, such as the number of questions asked by students or the number of times a teacher offers praise. Perhaps the most notable low-inference classroom research tool of the 1960s and 1970s was the

Flanders Interaction Analysis System (FIAS; Flanders, 1970), which involved recording explicit sequences of teacher and student interactions during classroom instruction. This system was the most sophisticated technique for classroom observation available during the early 1970s. In using the FIAS, teacher behaviors are recorded at 3-second intervals into one of 10 mutually exclusive categories (accepting feelings, praising or encouraging, accepting or using student ideas, asking questions, lecturing, giving ideas, criticizing, student response, student-initiated talk, and silence or confusion). In contrast to low-inference measures such as the FIAS, high-inference measures require respondents to make an inference based on a series of classroom events using specific constructs, such as the level of classroom competition or degree of teacher friendliness. Compared to low-inference measures, high-inference measures focus on the psychological significance or meaning of classroom events for students and teachers.

Consideration of the press type (alpha, beta) and level of inference (high, low) suggests that four possible approaches to the measurement of classroom environments may be used: low-inference alpha, high-inference alpha, low-inference beta, and high-inference beta. The methodological tradition of early classroom environment research was to rely on high-inference beta press measures. In recent years, however, there has been a growing emphasis on low-inference alpha press measures using objective, trained observers to code key dimensions of classroom environments.

A final methodological consideration in learning environment research is the distinction between private and consensual beta press, and the corresponding unit of statistical testing. *Private beta press* refers to the individual's perception of the environment, whereas *consensual beta press* is the shared view that members of a group hold about the environment. In classroom environment studies, consensual beta press often has been measured by using the classroom as the unit of analysis. That is, students in an entire classroom respond to questionnaires about the learning environment, and individual student scores are averaged to form a class mean for each classroom environment dimension. Classroom means (not individual means) are used in subsequent statistical analyses. A characteristic of much learning environment research is that data are often nested (e.g., students within classrooms, classrooms within schools). As discussed in a later section of this chapter, the use of multi-level or hierarchical linear modeling, in which the nested nature of data

can be preserved during analysis, has become widely used in learning environment studies.

Dimensions of Classroom Environments Linked to Student Outcomes

This section focuses on research which identifies classroom environment variables that promote effective learning outcomes for students. By far, the most prolific form of classroom environment research has involved investigating the link between the quality of environment in classrooms and the academic, affective, and behavioral outcomes of students in those classrooms. Results of studies over the last 30 years have demonstrated that specific aspects of classroom environments are important determinants of student performance (Fraser, 2002). In this section, research investigating the effects of eight dimensions of classroom learning environments is reviewed. These dimensions include effective teaching behaviors, classroom management, teacher–student relationships, academic learning time, emotional climate and support, grouping format, class size, and physical characteristics. This section summarizes evidence documenting the influence of classroom environment on multiple educational outcomes. Collectively, the research findings underscore the importance of assessing the quality of classrooms, and using the results of those assessments to create effective, positive, and productive learning environments to promote student success.

The majority of research reviewed in this section has relied primarily on ex post facto designs and correlational data techniques (Fraser, 2002). In general, students perform better when they perceive the classroom environment more positively, and/or when there is evidence (based on direct observation) that classroom environments are high in terms of quality indicators. Across varied samples and measurement procedures, the quality of the classroom environment accounts for significant and appreciable variance in learning outcomes, beyond what is attributed to student characteristics (Goh & Khine, 2002). For example, Goh and Fraser (1998) found that higher cognitive (achievement) and affective (interest, enjoyment) outcomes in elementary students were associated with better teacher leadership, more friendly/helping classroom environments, and teachers' understanding and empathy towards students. Dorman, Adams, and Ferguson (2002) studied 1317 secondary students and found significant positive associations between the quality of classroom environment (assessed through questionnaires and observations) and students' attitudes toward math. Similarly, Dorman (2001) found that in a sample of 3602 secondary students, perceptions of the quality of the learning environment accounted for significant variance in students' academic self-efficacy.

Effective Teaching Behaviors

Within the study of environmental variables that impact student outcomes, considerable attention has been focused on effective teaching behaviors. Effective teaching behaviors encompass a variety of instructional and management practices that have been found to increase student engagement, learning, and achievement, as well as to decrease the occurrence of challenging behaviors in the classroom. Teachers who exhibit certain behaviors are successful in creating productive learning environments for all learners. Specifically, effective teachers (a) have high expectations for students, (b) reinforce students' success and provide informative feedback, (c) ensure a high amount of learning time, (d) organize the classroom to promote engagement in learning, and (e) are knowledgeable about and implement research-supported teaching strategies (Yates & Yates, 1990). Three observable features of effective instructional environments include a high degree of teacher-directed learning, active student involvement, and guided practice with feedback to promote student learning and success (Gettinger & Kohler, 2006).

First, teacher-directed learning, also referred to as active teaching, incorporates a substantial amount of feedback, questions, answers, and explanations from the teacher throughout instruction, and has consistently been linked with increased student engagement and achievement (Brophy & Good, 1986; Gettinger & Stoiber, 1999). To be effective, teacher-directed instruction should be clear, well-structured, and sufficiently redundant (Brophy & Good, 1986). Instruction that is high in clarity proceeds in a coherent, step-by-step manner, relates new information to students' prior knowledge, includes ample illustrations of the content to be learned, and incorporates questioning to ensure that students understand the content (Gettinger & Kohler, 2006; McCaleb & White, 1980). Clear instruction is positively associated with student satisfaction, engagement, and achievement (Hines, Cruickshank, & Kennedy, 1985). Student achievement is also maximized when instruction conveys a strong academic focus (Gettinger & Kohler, 2006). Students learn more from teachers who are task-oriented, and allocate the majority of available instructional time to curriculum-related rather than nonacademic activities (Brophy & Good, 1986).

Effective teaching behaviors also promote a high level of active student involvement, which has been shown to be a strong determinant of achievement (Gettinger, 1986). Teachers can elicit student involvement by asking pupils a lot of questions and by utilizing high-participation activity formats, such as group problem-solving, discussion, peer teaching, and cooperative learning (Gettinger & Ball, 2008).

A third measurable feature of instruction that enhances student learning is guided practice. Guided practice constitutes a crucial time for students to engage in cognitive-processing activities such as organizing, rehearsing, and reviewing, which ultimately aid in the acquisition of new knowledge (Rosenshine, 2002). The use of teacher-guided practice is most effective following brief presentations of new material (Rosenshine, 2002); it involves scaffolding and providing assistance to students so they can work productively and independently to develop new skills (Gettinger & Kohler, 2006). Guided practice should occur on a frequent basis, as students are more likely to retain and apply skills they have practiced repeatedly, rather than skills they have mastered only partially (Brophy & Alleman, 1991).

Guided practice is most useful when it also incorporates timely feedback regarding student performance. Frequent feedback helps learners to perform better, and maintain high levels of engagement in academic activities (Gettinger & Stoiber, 1999). To be effective, feedback should (a) be specific and make explicit reference to the target objective to be achieved, (b) incorporate information about accuracy, or the results achieved in meeting the standard, and (c) provide recommendations about alternate methods for meeting the objective (Kindsvatter, Wilen, & Ishler, 1988).

Classroom Management

Effective classroom management promotes positive academic outcomes and enhances social/emotional growth through the development of a safe, orderly environment. According to Evertson and Weinstein (2006), classroom management consists of "the actions teachers take to create an environment that supports and facilitates both academic and social/emotional learning" (p. 4). Effective classroom management includes four interrelated components: (a) organizing and implementing instruction,

(b) using group management methods to encourage academic engagement; (c) promoting the development of students' social skills and self-regulation; and (d) developing caring, supportive relationships with students. The following discussion is limited to the instructional and organizational aspects of classroom management. The quality of teacher–student relationships, the fourth component of classroom management, is addressed in a separate subsection.

ORGANIZING AND IMPLEMENTING INSTRUCTION

Effective classroom management includes several instructional variables that have been shown to maximize learning for all students (Evertson & Weinstein, 2006; Wang, Haertel, & Walberg, 1993). In their review of process–product research, Gettinger and Kohler (2006) confirmed the link between effective instruction and effective classroom management. Not surprisingly, there is considerable overlap in classroom environment variables that characterize both effective teaching (described previously) and effective management. These include: (a) using teacher-directed instruction in which teachers provide academic-focused instruction and assume responsibility for student achievement; (b) implementing techniques that elicit a high degree of active student involvement or responding; (c) providing guided practice; (d) incorporating into instruction humor, enthusiasm, and motivational strategies such as goal setting; (e) utilizing cooperative learning strategies; and (f) differentiating instruction to match students' needs.

Differentiated instruction is based on the premise that instructional approaches should vary and be adapted to accommodate the diverse needs of students in classrooms. The importance of differentiated instruction has been supported through research examining the adoption of less traditional approaches to instruction within classroom management systems, such as Howard Gardner's multiple intelligence (MI) theory (Gardner, 1995) and Dunn and Dunn's Learning-Style Model (Dunn, Griggs, Olson, & Beasley, 1995). Within an MI approach, students have multiple options for processing information and demonstrating knowledge. Support for organizing and implementing instruction shaped by MI theory has been established through research with diverse students, especially English language learners (ELL). Haley (2004) found that ELL students who received MI-based instruction demonstrated higher proficiency in oral and written skills than did students receiving traditional instruction. Furthermore, these students reported a higher level of satisfaction with their teachers and school, and they displayed fewer behavior problems. Jackson and Veeneman Panyan (2002) stated that viewing instruction within the MI perspective "can provide the basis for rethinking how educators perceive the role of diversity in lesson planning, which can be instrumental in resolving challenging behaviors that have their origins in the manner in which instruction is provided" (p. 34).

Similarly, the positive effects of differentiated instruction have been supported through evaluations of Dunn and Dunn's Learning Style Model (LSM) (see Dunn et al., 1995, for a description of the Learning Style Model). A meta-analysis of 36 experimental studies based on the LSM indicated that students with strong learning style preferences who were taught in environments that matched their preferences, particularly in the physiological category, displayed higher academic outcomes compared to students whose learning environments were not explicitly matched to learning styles (Dunn et al., 1995; Searson & Dunn, 2001).

ENCOURAGING STUDENTS' ENGAGEMENT IN ACADEMIC TASKS

A second component of effective classroom management is the creation of classroom environments that promote active engagement in learning and, simultaneously, prevent behavior and learning problems. In 1970, Kounin's influential work changed the focus of group management strategies from being reactive (responding to behavior problems) to being proactive (preventing challenges). Kounin's observational research revealed that teachers in classrooms with fewer disruptive behaviors and higher student academic engagement were able to effectively manage their classrooms and prevent challenging situations by adjusting their own behaviors (e.g., simultaneous attention to multiple, overlapping events) and instructional strategies (e.g., lesson smoothness, momentum, and stimulating seatwork).

Several additional management strategies have been shown to encourage students' engagement in academics, particularly when implemented at the beginning of the school year. These include clearly explaining, explicitly teaching, and repeatedly practicing classroom rules, procedures, routines, behavioral expectations, and behavioral and transitional cues or signals (Evertson & Smithey, 2001; Gettinger & Ball, 2008). Furthermore, engagement is enhanced when teachers closely monitor students' behaviors, thus allowing them to respond quickly, efficiently, and consistently to inappropriate behaviors and to reinforce appropriate behaviors.

PROMOTING ADJUSTMENT THROUGH SELF-REGULATION

The final component of classroom management involves the actions teachers take to develop students' adaptive skills, and to minimize behaviors which interfere with learning. Examples of such actions include differential reinforcement of alternative behaviors (DRA; Jackson & Veeneman Panyan, 2002) and the development of self-regulation (Zimmerman, 1998) and self-monitoring (Shimabukuro, Prater, Jenkins, & Edelen-Smith, 1999) among students. Differentially reinforcing prosocial alternative behaviors, or DRA, is one way teachers can address behavioral problems while simultaneously teaching students appropriate classroom social skills and behaviors. Through DRA, instead of punishing inappropriate behavior, reinforcement is provided for an alternative prosocial behavior to replace the inappropriate behavior (Jackson & Veeneman Panyan, 2002).

Self-regulation and self-monitoring are examples of successful strategies to aid students in developing adaptive skills to improve their academic and behavioral outcomes. Implementation of self-monitoring strategies for students with behavioral and/or learning difficulties has been shown to increase assignment completion and accuracy across reading, math, and written expression areas (Shimabukuro et al, 1999), on-task behaviors (Shimabukuro et al., 1999), and achievement scores (Cleary & Zimmerman, 2004). Furthermore, self-regulation strategies not only improve student outcomes, they also teach students skills such as goal setting, self-observation, and self-evaluation (Cleary & Zimmerman, 2004; Zimmerman, 1998). Such skills are generalizable throughout school and personal domains (e.g., athletics, health), and allow students to accurately assess and direct their own behavior and achievement (Cleary & Zimmerman, 2004).

Teacher–Student Relationships

"The quality of teacher–student relationships is the keystone for all other aspects of classroom management" (Marzano & Marzano, 2003, p. 6). Caring and supportive teacher–student relationships are proven to have a positive impact on the social/emotional climate of the classroom, and support students' social/emotional growth and academic development (Hamre & Pianta, 2001; Howes, 2000; Murray & Greenberg, 2000).

Research in the area of teacher–student relationships has focused on three types of relationships and their effects on student outcomes (e.g., Birch & Ladd, 1997; Pianta, Steinberg & Rollins, 1995; Thijs, Koomen, & van der Leij, 2008). Specifically, closeness, conflict, and dependency characterize teacher–student interactions, as assessed through teachers' perceptions of a student's relationship-oriented behavior, their observed reactions to students' behavior, and self-reported feelings or beliefs regarding their relationships with students (Pianta et al., 1995). Teacher–student relationships characterized by close interactions indicate a positive and supportive relationship with a high degree of warmth, caring, and open communication (Hamre & Pianta, 2001; Pianta et al., 1995). Conflictual and dependent teacher–student relationships are indicative of lower-quality relationships. Conflictual relationships are characterized by a general negative rapport between the teacher and student, which may include discordant interactions, negativity, and anger (Birch & Ladd, 1997; Hamre & Pianta, 2001). Dependent teacher–student relationships result when students become over-reliant or overly dependent on the teacher for support in the classroom (Birch & Ladd, 1997). Research has consistently documented the influence of teacher–student relationships on student outcomes (Pianta & Stuhlman, 2004). As summarized below, relationship quality affects students' adaptation to the classroom environment within three broad outcome domains (social/emotional, behavioral, and academic).

SOCIAL/EMOTIONAL OUTCOMES

Loneliness, negative attitudes toward school, and avoidance or withdrawal behaviors have all been correlated with low quality teacher–student relationships characterized by conflict and dependency. Birch and Ladd (1997) revealed that kindergarten students assessed as having a dependent relationship with their teachers had a more negative attitude toward school than did their nondependent peers. This was evidenced by high levels of loneliness, dislike for school, and self-reported desire to avoid the classroom environment. Similarly, classroom climates characterized by low levels of closeness and/or high levels of conflict are predictive of social withdrawal behaviors in the classroom (e.g., shy, afraid, or unwilling to play with peers) (Howes, 2000).

Conversely, teacher–student relationships characterized by closeness have been correlated with students' social competence. Social competence refers to students' ability to play cooperatively, follow classroom rules, show empathy toward peers, be assertive and responsible, and display self-control in social situations (Pianta & Stuhlman, 2004). Across varied measures of students' social competence, such as prosocial ratings or observed prosocial behaviors, a significant positive relationship has been found between closeness and social competence. For example, middle school students who reported they had a caring relationship with their teacher displayed high levels of social competence, as evidenced by their efforts to share, help peers, and follow classroom rules (Wentzel, 1997). Furthermore, Howes (2000) found that preschool classroom environments that were low in conflict and high in closeness predicted students' social competence as second graders.

BEHAVIORAL OUTCOMES

Although students' social/emotional outcomes are significantly influenced by each type of teacher–student relationship, conflictual relationships have the greatest impact on students' behavioral outcomes. Kindergarteners with conflictual teacher–student relationships were viewed as displaying low levels of cooperative participation (Birch & Ladd, 1997), and demonstrated high levels of behavioral problems at the end of second grade (Pianta et al., 1995). A comparative study of students who were at risk for special education referral or retention revealed that students who were never referred had less conflictual relationships than did their at-risk peers who were referred or retained (Pianta et al., 1995). Furthermore, positive correlations have been found between observed levels of aggression and disruptive behavior displayed by second graders, and the degree of conflict characterizing the relationship with their teacher (Howes, 2000). Hamre and Pianta (2001) found that students with significant behavioral issues who are able to form relationships low in dependency and conflict, display fewer behavioral problems in their later years of schooling. Interestingly, teachers' perceptions of the type of relationships they have with individual students influence their behavior as well. Teachers reported enforcing higher levels of behavioral regulation for students with whom they perceived having conflictual or dependent relationships (Thijs et al., 2008).

ACADEMIC OUTCOMES

Many factors within the classroom contribute to students' academic outcomes, as previously discussed. The quality of the relationship between the teacher and student is no exception. As would be predicted, high quality teacher–student relationships characterized by closeness contribute positively to academic outcomes. For example, students rated as having relationships high in closeness with their teachers had higher language scores as kindergarteners (Birch & Ladd, 1997), and were rated by their teachers as having higher academic performance and better work habits than did their peers with conflictual relationships (Pianta & Stuhlman, 2004). Furthermore, close teacher–student relationships in kindergarten were predictive of positive academic outcomes in eighth grade for girls (Hamre & Pianta, 2001). Wentzel (1997) also found that adolescents' perceptions of their relationships with teachers predicted their academic effort. Specifically, adolescents who believed their teachers cared for them put forth greater effort in school, paid more attention, and had higher grades compared to students who did not view their teachers as supportive.

Academic Engaged Time

Across all age groups and multiple content domains, the amount of time students devote to active engagement in appropriate learning activities is significantly related to their achievement outcomes (Smith, 2000). Academic learning time has been accorded special significance in learning environment research, because of the well-documented relationship between time and learning, and because time is viewed as a manipulable facet of classroom life. Research has shown that certain teacher behaviors and classroom practices can influence the amount of time students are engaged in learning (Gettinger, 1986).

To understand the link between academic learning time (ALT) and performance, it is important to note that ALT is not merely the amount of time allocated for learning activities. Instead, it is the amount of time a student spends attending to relevant academic tasks while performing those tasks at a high rate of success. Academic learning time is a quality of classroom environments that is directly impacted by the teacher's behaviors in terms of planning, management, and instruction. Small changes in classroom variables can lead to large increases in academic engaged time. Indeed, some experts have argued that academic engaged time has a stronger relationship with academic achievement than any other environmental variable that a teacher can control within the classroom (Gettinger & Ball, 2008; Vockell, 1987).

Academic engaged time is highly associated with multiple positive student outcomes. Actively engaged children demonstrate sustained behavioral involvement, effort and concentration, and positive emotional tone. Additional benefits of increased academic engaged time include higher rates of responsiveness from teachers, better grades and standardized test scores, and improved school performance (Skinner & Belmont, 1993). Active engagement during instructional time is especially important for students who may be at risk for school failure. For example, Taylor, Pearson, Clark, and Walpole (2000) examined levels of engaged learning time in low-income schools; they found that students who have higher engagement in reading activities attain higher levels of reading achievement, compared to peers with lower engagement rates.

Much has been written about classroom practices that promote students' active engagement in learning, including effective classroom management practices, effective teaching behaviors instruction, and student-mediated strategies (Gettinger & Ball, 2008). For example, when instruction is delivered at a brisk pace and enables students to experience a moderate level of success, disruptive behavior is minimized and students' engaged learning time is maximized (Munk & Repp, 1994). Marks (2000) found that the amount of within-classroom time needed for completing an academic task, or mastering certain content, varies among individual students due, in part, to the variable amount of time students spend studying outside of school. Moreover, low-achieving students may need 3–6 times more instructional time than their high-achieving peers to succeed with a given task (Marks, 2000). Therefore, student-mediated strategies also play an important role in optimizing academic engaged time. Students' use of cognitive, self-monitoring, or self-management strategies, for example, has been shown to increase their performance and maintain active engagement.

Emotional Climate and Support

The conclusions from research on classroom climate indicate that learning environments that contribute to positive outcomes are those in which (a) teachers respect and support students, (b) there is a pleasant and orderly atmosphere that promotes coherence and positive relationships, (c) there are positive feelings among students and teachers about learning, and (d) there is a strong sense of community in which students cooperate with each other and contribute to achieving goals (Dorman et al., 2002).

According to Matsumara, Slater, and Crosson (2008), an ideal learning environment is one in which the academic demands are balanced with emotional support and caring about students as individuals. Thus, it is important to assess the emotional climate of classrooms, in that it contributes significantly to student outcomes.

The literature is consistent in identifying measurable characteristics that define the emotional climate of classroom environments. These include the interactions and relationships between students, or between students and teachers, the degree of emotional support from teachers and students, the level of organization and cohesion, the consistency of rules and expectations, and the number of opportunities for leadership, achievement, and cooperative activities (Brand, Felner, Shim, Seitsinger, & Dumas, 2003; Ghaith, Shaaban, & Harkous, 2007; Shapiro, 1993). An emotionally positive and supportive classroom environment is also one that encourages cooperative learning activities.

Emotional support has been defined as the ways in which teachers positively contribute to the overall climate or ambience of a classroom (Buyse, Verschueren, Doumen, Damme, & Maes, 2008). Positive emotional support is characterized as conveying a high degree of warmth and sensitivity, directing learning activities at children's individual interests and needs, and getting to know each student personally (Buyse et al., 2008; Pianta, Hamre, & Stuhlman, 2003; Wilson, Pianta, & Stuhlman, 2007). Examples of negative teacher support, which can have detrimental effects on student outcomes, include hostility, irritability, and comparing students to each other (Shann, 1999).

Interestingly, emotional support from teachers is found to have a stronger influence on student outcomes than support from peers (Ghaith, 2003). The effect is especially large for children who may be at risk for learning challenges. For example, Buyse et al. (2008) found that at-risk children have fewer conflict-filled relationships with peers and other adults in the classroom when they have an emotionally supportive teacher. When teachers provide consistent support for all students in a classroom, students are more likely to value heterogeneity, feel less alienated, and believe that the teacher's grading and evaluation of their performance are fair (Ghaith et al., 2007). Classrooms with positive teacher support also promote the use of self-regulation among students, and students exhibit overall higher levels of positive social functioning (Patrick, Ryan, & Kaplan, 2007).

Classrooms with a positive emotional climate lead to numerous beneficial outcomes for students, academic as well as social/emotional. Shapiro (1993) stated that classrooms in which students are achieving at a high level are characterized by positive interactions between peers, between the students and their teacher, and within the classroom as a whole. When positive interactions are facilitated through cooperative learning, teachers report that students have higher academic self-esteem, and they participate and learn more (Shapiro, 1993). Specific academic outcomes associated with a positive emotional climate include increased achievement in the areas of reading, language, and math (Dunn & Harris, 1998). Conversely, classrooms in which negative interactions and bullying or aggression occur, contribute to depression, alienation, and social anxiety, as well as poor academic performance, especially among secondary students (Juvonen, Nishina, & Graham, 2001; Matsumara et al., 2008).

Beneficial social outcomes are also commonly cited in the literature for students in classrooms with high levels of emotional support. For example, early childhood classrooms with positive emotional climates (e.g., minimal conflict, high teacher support, cooperation) promote prosocial behaviors and decrease negative behaviors toward peers (e.g., Brophy-Herb, Lee, Nievar, & Stollack, 2007). Early elementary classrooms in which teachers display high levels of sensitivity and optimism, provide positive feedback, and offer multiple opportunities for independent and cooperative peer play, have been shown to promote higher levels of social competence among children compared to less nurturing classrooms (Wilson et al., 2007).

Grouping Formats

Research has also demonstrated the influence of student grouping, another feature of classroom environments, on educational outcomes. The composition of groups in which students learn can affect their achievement. Research examining the effects of various instructional contexts has investigated whether, and under what conditions, student participation in learning groups is beneficial to achievement. A comprehensive meta-analysis conducted by Lou and colleagues (1996) found that within-class grouping (i.e., small-group instruction) has multiple positive effects on student learning when compared to individual seatwork and traditional whole-class instruction. Namely, students placed in small groups achieve more, report higher general self-concept, and hold more positive attitudes than

students in classrooms that do not incorporate small-group instruction.

In addition to documenting the general benefits of small-group learning, Lou et al. (1996) described specific conditions that seem to enhance the effectiveness of within-class grouping. First, the optimal number of students per learning group appears to be three to four members. Whereas pairs of students achieve significantly more than do students from classrooms without grouping (yet, not as much as students in 3– or 4-member learning groups), students in groups of 6 to 8 members do not. Second, small-group instruction appears to be particularly beneficial in math and science classes (possibly due to the hierarchical nature of learning tasks), as well as classes that are larger in size. Third, small-group learning is most effective when it involves modified teaching methods and instructional materials. Fourth, the achievement effects of within-class grouping appear to be moderated by the type of small-group instructional method that is used. Specifically, the data suggest that small groups learn more when there is outcome interdependence among group members, as is characteristic of cooperative learning tasks, where all students contribute to the group's goal or outcome.

Cooperative learning, defined as a "teaching strategy that teams students in small groups with different levels of ability, using a variety of learning activities to improve their understanding of a subject" (Wilson-Jones & Caston, 2004, p. 280), incorporates both positive interdependence and individual accountability (Lou, Abrami, & Spence, 2000). Research has linked cooperative learning to improvements in students' academic achievement, behavior, attendance, self-confidence, motivation, and school satisfaction (Wilson-Jones & Caston, 2004). Evidence exists to suggest that cooperative learning leads to greater student achievement than other methods of small-group instruction, such as ability grouping, and unstructured group work in which students are not positively interdependent (Lou et al., 2000). Moreover, cooperative learning has been shown to be effective in enhancing academic engagement and achievement among diverse populations of students, including children with learning disabilities (Gillies & Ashman, 2002), and young antisocial boys (Quinn, 2002).

Another instructional grouping strategy supported by research is classwide peer tutoring. A 12-year longitudinal study found that classwide peer tutoring significantly increases students' engagement during instruction, contributes to gains in student achievement, and is associated with a reduction in the number of students requiring special education services, as well as the number of students dropping out of school by twelfth grade (Greenwood, 1991; Greenwood & Delquadri, 1995). Thus, both classwide peer tutoring and cooperative learning represent effective alternatives to traditional, whole-class instruction, and have been demonstrated to enhance a number of student outcomes.

Class Size

Another observable dimension of classroom environments that contributes to student performance is class size. Class size is defined as the number of students that are regularly present in a teacher's classroom for instruction (Deutsch, 2003). A class size of less than 20 students is considered to be small, and is associated with positive student outcomes; classrooms with more than 20 students are viewed as large (Finn, Pannozzo, & Achilles, 2003).

Despite consistent findings regarding the benefits of small classes, some studies on class size reduction have been criticized because of small sample size, lack of random assignment, and the minimal focus on long-term benefits. For example, in many investigations, students are more likely to be assigned to a small class based on low achievement, rather than being randomly assigned. One notable exception is the Student/Teacher Achievement Ratio program (STAR) in Tennessee, in which students from kindergarten through third grade are randomly assigned to either small classes of 13–17 students, or larger classes of 22–26 students (Hanushek, 1999). Through the influence of Project STAR findings and No Child Left Behind Act (NCLB), a national class size reduction program (CSR) was initiated. The goal of CSR is to hire 100,000 new teachers to aid in reducing kindergarten through third grade classrooms to 18 students per classroom nationwide (Milesi & Gamoran, 2006).

Finn et al. (2003) conducted a comprehensive review of multiple investigations of class size, including studies evaluating Project STAR, and summarized the benefits of reduced class size on three types of outcomes: (a) students' learning behaviors; (b) students' social behaviors; and (c) student–teacher interactions. Compared to students in large classes (more than 20 students), students in small classes were found to display higher levels of academic engagement, which is positively correlated with achievement (Finn et al., 2003). Students who were randomly assigned to small classes in Project STAR also had higher standardized achievement test scores than did students in large classes. Teachers in classrooms with less than 20 students reported that their students participated more often during discussions and question-and-answer sessions (Folger, 1989). Compared to large classes, teachers with small classes give their students more individualized attention, which allows increased opportunities to identify which students are at risk and provide them with individualized instruction (Nye, Hedges, & Konstantopoulos, 2002). Nye et al. (2002) also found that lower-achieving students benefited more from participating in classrooms with fewer than 20 students than did higher-achieving students, particularly in the area of reading.

Children also experience social benefits by being taught in small classes. Researchers for Project Prime Time, a study that looked at small classes of 18 students, found small classrooms to be more manageable, peaceful, and quiet (Mueller, Chase & Walden, 1988). In small classes, teachers are readily available to prevent potential problems and, therefore, have fewer disruptive behaviors to manage (Johnston, 1990). This allows teachers to delegate more time for instruction and less time to discipline prevention. Johnston (1990) reported that teachers of small classes in Project STAR perceived their students to be more cooperative, supportive, and caring towards their peers than those in larger classes. Their pupils, especially lower achievers, were more likely to take risks, encourage each other, and exhibit confidence in their work. Teachers also reported that students were less likely to form social cliques within the classroom, compared to those in larger classes.

Interactions between students and teachers are also positively affected by small class sizes. Students in reduced classes are more likely to initiate contacts and interact more frequently with teachers (Johnston, 1990). During instruction, teachers in smaller classes were more likely to follow up on their questions with specific probes, and they were found to respond more positively overall to students, compared to teachers with large classes (Bourke, 1986). Overall, teachers reported having more enthusiasm, higher morale, and more positive interactions with learners when they taught small classes (Zahorik, 1999).

In sum, despite criticisms to the validity of some studies of class size, the research findings, especially those related to Project STAR, have documented both immediate and long-term benefits linked to reduced class sizes (Nye, Hedges, & Konstantopoulos,

2001). Thus, class size is one observable and malleable dimension of classroom environments that has the potential to benefit all students.

Physical Characteristics of the Classroom

The final dimension of learning environments associated with student outcomes, and often the focus of assessment, encompasses the physical characteristics and arrangement of classrooms. Perhaps the most widely researched physical feature of the classroom is seating arrangement, which has merited attention because it represents an environmental variable that influences student behavior, yet is typically under teacher control. A recent review of research conducted by Wannarka and Ruhl (2008) supports the notion that students' seating position within the classroom is related to a variety of positive behaviors, including compliance with teacher's requests and raising one's hand for assistance (Axelrod, Hall, & Tams, 1979), making eye contact with materials (Wheldall, Morris, Vaughn, & Ng, 1981), and asking questions (Marx, Furher, & Hartig, 2000).

Wannarka and Ruhl (2008) addressed the common question of whether a specific type of seating arrangement is most conducive to on-task behavior and student learning. After reviewing the studies cited above, in addition to several other studies investigating the link between seating arrangement and student behavior, the authors conclude that, "There is no single classroom seating arrangement that promotes positive behavioral and academic outcomes for all tasks, because the available research clearly indicates that the nature (i.e., interactive versus independent) of the task should dictate the arrangement" (p. 93). In other words, it appears that teachers should arrange seats into rows when they want to maximize on-task behavior during independent seatwork, and they should alternatively arrange seats into groups or semicircles when the goal is to facilitate student performance on tasks that are more interactive in nature and/or involve substantial amounts of peer collaboration.

Another physical characteristic of classroom environments that can influence student performance is noise level. Background noise often distracts children, causing them to struggle to listen and concentrate (Martin, 2006). Students exposed to outside noise exhibit increased dissatisfaction with their classrooms, and may experience stress if the noise is excessive (Schneider, 2002). Although there is typically little teachers can do to reduce noise emanating from outside sources such as trains or airplanes, Choi and McPherson (2005) suggest that it may be possible to minimize the effects of within-classroom noise by arranging the classroom such that students are seated away from fans, air conditioners, and other sources of loud noise.

Whereas several studies have demonstrated a link between chronic exposure to excessive noise and diminished student achievement (e.g., Bronzaft & McCarthy, 1975; Evans & Maxwell, 1997; Haines, Stansfeld, Job, Berglund, & Head, 2001), research examining the influence of normal levels of classroom noise in relation to student performance has produced mixed results. Zentall and Shaw (1980), for instance, found that while conversational background noise may interfere with students' abilities to perform some tasks, it can actually facilitate their ability to perform others. The difference seems to lie in the perceived difficulty of the task. That is, moderate levels of classroom noise may enhance performance of highly familiar tasks, yet have an adverse effect on the performance of more difficult tasks. Haines et al. (2001) thus point out that when striving to create ideal conditions for learning, teachers must be cognizant of the differential effects that ambient noise may have on various types of tasks.

Instruments for Assessing Classroom Environments

As noted above, research has identified multiple classroom environment variables as strong predictors of student performance, thus underscoring the need for valid and reliable assessment of classroom learning environments. Despite its importance, the assessment of learning environments is challenging. This is due to the complexity of the phenomena under investigation, the number of possible approaches that can be taken to assess learning environments, and the conceptual and methodological difficulties within each approach.

This section reviews specific techniques and measures for assessing classroom environments. Because numerous measures of learning environments have been developed over the last decades, the intent of this section is to describe only selected measures. Specifically, instruments that are multidimensional in nature, well documented in the psychological and educational literature, and supported by some reliability and validity data, are presented. The literature addresses three general approaches to the assessment of learning environments: (a) the use of trained observers to code classroom environments, usually in terms of explicit, observable phenomena; (b) students' and teachers' perceptions of the learning environment, obtained through the administration of questionnaires; and, (c) ecobehavioral methods. In the following subsections, each general approach to assessment of classroom environments is explained, and exemplary measures or methods within each approach are described.

Few studies have explored the convergent validity of these different methods of environmental assessment by examining the relationship between measures obtained through alternative approaches. Kaye, Trickett, and Quinlan (1976) assessed two classroom environment characteristics, teacher control and teacher support, using three different environmental assessment methods. The methods involved assessment of students' perceptions using subscales from the *Classroom Environment Scale* (Moos & Trickett, 1974), global ratings by outside observers, and direct observation and coding of classroom interactions. Their findings documented both convergence and divergence among different methods of assessment, and underscored the importance of using multiple methods in classroom environment research. Similarly, Schell (1993) investigated the relationship between observed verbal classroom behaviors and students' perceptions of classroom environment, as measured by items from the *Learning Environment Inventory* (Fraser, Anderson, & Walberg, 1982). Schell found statistically significant correlations between the two methods of classroom environment assessment, but also reminded researchers that each method makes a distinct contribution to the assessment of classrooms.

Classroom Observation Assessment Tools

One approach to studying classroom environments is the use of direct observation. Observation tools involve external observers who systematically code classroom interactions, behaviors, and events according to a predetermined category scheme. Classroom observation tools can be used to assess a student's behavior, academic performance, the instructional or emotional classroom environment, or an interaction among all three. Observation techniques are advantageous, in that trained observers are used to record explicit behaviors and events that occur during a specified period of observation. At the same time, however, a disadvantage is that the observers themselves may alter the behavior patterns of both students and teachers in a classroom, such that the observations are not reliable.

Over the past 20 years, several large-scale observational research efforts have identified measurable aspects of classroom environments that promote learning among students, through extensive field testing and validation of observation procedures (Pianta, 2003). The use of classroom observation methods have the potential for improving teaching and learning, by codifying and quantifying specific dimensions of learning environments that are linked to student outcomes. In the following subsections, four observational tools for conducting an assessment of classroom environments are described: (a) *Classroom Assessment Scoring System* (CLASS; Pianta, LaParo & Hamre, 2007); (b) *Classroom Systems Observation Scale* (CSOS; Fish & Dane, 1995); (c) *The Instructional Environment Scale* (TIES; Ysseldyke & Christenson, 1987); and, (d) *Functional Assessment of Academic Behavior* (FAAB; Ysseldyke & Christenson, 2002).

CLASSROOM ASSESSMENT SCORING SYSTEM

The *Classroom Assessment Scoring System* (CLASS; Pianta et al., 2007) is an observational measure used to assess the quality of classroom environments (preschool through secondary) through direct observation and coding of specific classroom dimensions, including teacher–child interactions, classroom climate, teacher and peer sensitivity and support, behavior management, quality of instruction, and level of feedback. The CLASS examines classroom quality within three broad domains: (a) emotional support; (b) classroom organization; and (c) instructional support. Emotional support is evaluated by three scales: positive climate (emotional connection between the teacher and student or between peers); negative climate (level of aggression in the classroom); and teacher sensitivity. Classroom organization is measured by three scales: teacher control (teacher flexibility regarding children's needs); behavior management (preventing and monitoring disruptions); and productivity (how well the classroom functions and maximizes learning time). Finally, the third domain, instructional support, consists of three scales, including: concept development (encouraging critical thinking and problem solving); instructional learning formats (how teachers optimize instruction and activities); and quality of feedback. Each CLASS dimension is rated using a 7-point rating scale (1 = classroom is extremely low on this dimension; 7 = classroom is extremely high on this dimension), based on classroom observations conducted over an extended period of time (i.e., 30-minute cycles over at least 3 hours of observation).

The CLASS is widely used in observational studies of classroom quality (e.g., LaParo, Pianta, Stuhlman, 2004). Mashburn et al. (2008) found that the quality of emotional interactions in early-childhood classrooms examined by the CLASS was positively associated with children's social competence, and negatively associated with problem behaviors in a preschool classroom. Additionally, Howes et al. (2008) found associations between ratings on the Instructional Support Scale on the CLASS and children's literacy and math skills, and between ratings on the Emotional Support Scale and occurrence of classroom behavior problems. Overall, the CLASS is a useful observational tool for measuring the quality of classroom environments, and documenting the relationship between learning environment dimensions and students' academic and social outcomes.

CLASSROOM SYSTEMS OBSERVATION SCALE

The *Classroom Systems Observation Scale* (CSOS) assesses the functioning of an entire classroom (preschool through sixth grade) through a systems-level perspective (Fish & Dane, 1995). As such, the design of the CSOS shifts the focus of traditional classroom observation from the individual child, to the classroom system. A systems perspective posits that all learning environments (e.g., school, family, community) function in the same way, and influence one another. The members within each individual system interact with and affect each other individually, as well as the system as a whole. Typically, the systems perspective is used for evaluating family functioning; however, Fish and Dane (2000) applied the approach to the observation of classroom practices that enhance student achievement, using the CSOS.

Analogous to family systems, the CSOS measures three major dimensions of classroom learning environments: (a) cohesion, (b) flexibility, and (c) communication. Classroom cohesion is defined as feelings of closeness and caring between classroom members. A flexible classroom is one where students and teachers fluidly adapt to changing needs. Finally, the CSOS defines a classroom with good communication as one with open and relevant discussions that engage active listeners (O'Connor & Fish, 1998). The CSOS is comprised of 47 different items which are grouped into three subscales, each representing one of the key dimensions.

In using the CSOS, trained observers focus on verbal and nonverbal interactions and classroom movements to rate the 47 items. Observations are conducted for 45 minutes, and each item is rated using a 4-point scale. The meaning and interpretation of each 4-point scaling vary slightly, depending on which dimension is observed. For example, the Flexibility subscale values range from 1 (rigid), 2 (structured), 3 (flexible), to 4 (chaotic). Item ratings are averaged within each domain to compute a Global Classroom Rating score (Fish & Dane, 2000).

According to the developers of the CSOS, the scale is appropriate for use in preschool through sixth grade classrooms. It provides information for interventions to improve the overall quality of classroom environments, and to strengthen the alignment between the classroom system and family system (Fish & Dane, 2000). The CSOS has been used in learning environment research in recent years. For example, O'Connor, Fish, and Yasik (2004) used the CSOS to assess if a teacher's level of experience (e.g., expert vs. novice) was related to the levels of flexibility, cohesion, and communication in the classroom. The study found that classrooms of expert, or experienced, teachers were observed to be significantly higher on both the flexibility and cohesion dimensions.

THE INSTRUCTIONAL ENVIRONMENT SCALE

TIES (Ysseldyke & Christenson, 1987) is predicated on the assumption that academic problems can be the result of a mismatch between students' individual learning needs and the instructional environment of their classroom. On TIES, the instructional or learning environment represents an interaction of the teacher's instruction and behavior management skills, individual student and group characteristics, and the assigned topic or task (Christenson & Ysseldyke, 1989). For TIES-II (1993 revision of TIES; Ysseldyke & Christenson, 1993), instructional environment was expanded to include both school and home contexts.

TIES and TIES-II are comprehensive measurement tools designed to evaluate the effectiveness of a classroom's instructional environment for individual students (Ysseldyke & Christenson, 1989). Completion of TIES involves three primary information-gathering procedures: (a) direct observation and coding of dimensions of the student's instructional environment; (b) interview with the student's teacher; and (c) interview with the student. TIES provides an assessment of the presence and quality of key components of classroom environments that have been shown to contribute to student performance, including teacher expectations, instructional match, classroom climate, instructional presentation, cognitive emphasis, motivational strategies, relevant practice, informed feedback, academic engaged time, adaptive instruction, progress evaluation, student understanding, expectations and attributions, discipline orientation, home affective environment, parent participation, and structure for learning.

The primary purpose of TIES (and TIES-II) is to allow professionals to evaluate the extent to which a student's academic deficits are due to a potential mismatch with the instructional environment. TIES is also useful in aiding consultation efforts between school service providers and teachers, in progress monitoring of instructional changes, and in comparing an individual student's different classrooms to determine the most beneficial learning environment (Ysseldyke & Christenson, 1987). Recently, TIES II has also been used to evaluate instructional environments of classrooms in schools moving towards the response-to-intervention (RTI) method of services (Case, Speece, & Molloy, 2003).

FUNCTIONAL ASSESSMENT OF ACADEMIC BEHAVIOR (FAAB)

Functional assessment is a multi-method framework for problem solving that is frequently used for assessing behavior problems of individual students (Knoster & McCurdy, 2002). Functional behavior assessment (FBA) guides professionals toward understanding the function of a student's behavior problem or academic difficulty, by using a multi-assessment method to identify setting events, antecedents, and consequences that are related to behavior or learning (Knoster & McCurdy, 2002).

The *Functional Assessment of Academic Behavior* (FAAB) is based on the key principles and goals of FBA, with a specific focus on academic problems (not challenging behaviors). The FAAB was derived from *The Instructional Environment Scale* (TIES). The FAAB consists of forms, checklists, questionnaires, and rating scales that aid in the collection and organization of both observational and interview data, directed at assessing the influence of a child's classroom environment on his or her current level of academic performance (Brassard & Boehm, 2007).

The FAAB provides an assessment of 23 environmental components, which comprise 12 classroom components, 5 home components, and 6 home–school relationship components (Ysseldyke & Christenson, 2002). The classroom components are instructional supports for learning that are significantly related to positive educational outcomes (e.g., instruction matches with the student's needs, positive and supportive classroom environment). The home components include the level of parents' involvement in the child's academics, and the emotional quality of the home environment. Finally, examples of the home–school components include shared standards and expectations between teachers and parents, and a consistent structure for learning at home and in the classroom, provided by parents and teachers (Ysseldyke & Christenson, 2002). The FAAB allows for a comparison of environmental dimensions across the student's classroom and home environments, and analysis of the combined effects of the two environments on students' learning and academic performance.

Classroom Environment Questionnaires

In addition to direct observations of the classroom, another valuable method for assessing learning environments involves the use of classroom environment questionnaires. Much of the early research on learning environments focused on students' perceptions of multiple facets of classroom environments, as measured on student-completed questionnaires. This early research (e.g., Fraser & Fisher, 1982; Haertel, Walberg, & Haertel, 1981) provided strong support for students' perceptions of classroom environments in accounting for significant variance in learning outcomes. As a result of these initial findings, a number of scales for the assessment and evaluation of learning environments have been developed and validated over the last 20 years (Fraser, 1998). Classroom environment questionnaires assess students' perceptions of multiple dimensions of classroom learning environments, such as student cohesiveness or teacher support, that may not be reliably measured through direct observations. Classroom environment measures are typically completed by students and teachers, and thus differ from many classroom observation tools, in that they assess the learning environment through the eyes of the actual participants, rather than an external observer (Fraser, 1987).

According to Fraser and Walberg (1981), the use of student perceptual measures is advantageous for several reasons. First, paper-and-pencil assessments are more cost-effective than classroom observations that involve the expense of trained external observers. Second, perceptual measures reflect students' experiences across several class sessions, whereas observational data are frequently based on a limited number of lessons or classroom situations.

Third, perceptual measures draw upon the collective judgments of all students, whereas observational data typically reflect the impressions of a single observer. Fourth, students' perceptions may be even more important than observed behaviors, because they have a strong impact on student behavior. Fifth, perceptual measures of classroom climate have generally been found to account for more variance in student learning outcomes than have directly observed variables.

Given the many advantages of perceptual measures, and the fact that students' perceptions of the classroom environment are strongly related to learning outcomes (den Brok, Fisher, Rickards, & Bull, 2006), considerable research has been devoted to the development, validation, and administration of classroom environment questionnaires. Although differences exist in the development and validation procedures, typically the same general 3-step strategy has been used. The first step is the identification of salient dimensions of classroom environments that have been shown to predict learning and behavioral outcomes. The second step is writing items that reflect each dimension. In this step, the item pool is typically reviewed by an "expert" panel that provides feedback regarding the face validity and readability of individual items. The third step is field testing and item analysis. Specifically, faulty items are removed, and internal consistency (the extent to which each item in the scale measures the same construct as the rest of the items) and discriminant validity (extent to which each subscale measures a dimension not measured by any other subscale in the battery) are determined. The following paragraphs discuss several of the instruments most commonly used to assess students' and teachers' perceptions of learning environments.

LEARNING ENVIRONMENT INVENTORY AND MY CLASS INVENTORY

The *Learning Environment Inventory* (LEI) was initially developed in the late 1960s as part of the evaluation of the Harvard Project Physics (Anderson & Walberg, 1968; Fraser et al., 1982; Walberg & Anderson, 1968). Following field tests and revisions of the instrument, the final version of the LEI contains 105 statements that describe multiple aspects of the typical school classroom (Fraser et al., 1982). The LEI is designed for use with high school students, and measures students' perceptions of 15 dimensions of the classroom learning environment. These dimensions include cohesiveness, diversity, formality, speed, material environment, friction,

goal direction, favoritism, difficulty, apathy, democracy, cliqueness, satisfaction, disorganization, and competitiveness. Each dimension contains seven statements for which the student may select a response using the following 4-point scale: Strongly Disagree, Disagree, Agree, or Strongly Agree. A sample item from the Goal Direction Scale is, "The objectives of the class are specific." A sample item from the Cohesiveness Scale is, "A student has the chance to get to know all other students in the class."

Following the development and widespread use of the LEI, a simplified version of the instrument was designed for use with children at the elementary school level. The resulting instrument, known as the *My Class Inventory*, differs from the LEI in four important ways (Fraser et al., 1982). First, to prevent fatigue among young students completing the questionnaire, the MCI includes only five of the original 15 classroom environment dimensions assessed by the LEI, specifically cohesiveness, satisfaction, friction, difficulty, and competitiveness. Second, the wording of the items was simplified to make the scale more accessible for young readers. Third, the 4-point response scale has been replaced with a 2-point, yes/no format. Fourth, students respond to the statements on the questionnaire itself, rather than on a separate response sheet, so as to avoid transcription errors. The final version of the MCI consists of 38 items, examples of which include, "Most children say the class is fun" (satisfaction scale), and "Most children can do their schoolwork without help" (difficulty scale).

Due to their psychometrically sound properties and ease of administration, the LEI and MCI have been used in an extensive amount of research assessing students' perceptions of classroom learning environments. Several studies have utilized the instruments to examine the relationship between learning environment variables and student achievement. In a meta-analysis of 12 studies representing the perceptions of 17,805 students from four countries, it was found that student cognitive, affective, and behavioral outcomes were greater in those classes in which students perceived more goal direction, cohesiveness and satisfaction, and less disorganization and friction, as measured by the LEI and MCI (Haertel et al., 1981).

CLASSROOM ENVIRONMENT SCALE

Another widely used questionnaire, the *Classroom Environment Scale* (CES), was developed in the early 1970s by Rudolf Moos at Stanford University (Moos & Trickett, 1974; Trickett & Moos, 1973).

Based on a comprehensive research program involving a variety of human environments, such as hospitals, university residences, and work settings, the original CES contained 242 items representing 13 dimensions of learning environments. After extensive field testing, the scale was modified such that its final version (Moos & Trickett, 1974) includes 90 items with a true–false response format, divided equally among 9 dimensions (involvement, affiliation, teacher support, task orientation, competition, order and organization, rule clarity, teacher control, and innovation).

Like the LEI, the CES is intended for use with high school students. It is distinct from the former, however, in that it is also designed to measure teachers' perceptions of classroom climate (Fisher & Fraser, 1983a). Moreover, the CES includes supplemental forms which may be used to assess respondents' perceptions of ideal or preferred learning environments, in addition to the actual learning environment in which they participate.

According to Fraser and Fisher (1986), researchers have employed the CES in a variety of ways. Within one line of research, several studies have utilized CES dimensions as predictor variables to examine the relationship between elements of the learning environment and student outcomes. Findings from such studies have documented relationships between the classroom environment, and student grades and absences (Moos & Moos, 1978), student mood, achievement, popularity, and adjustment (Wright & Cowen, 1982), student motivation to learn (Knight, 1991), and students' attitudes towards science (Fouts & Myers, 1992).

Additional lines of research involving the CES, as described by Fraser and Fisher (1986), include: (a) studies utilizing CES scores as dependent variables to examine differences between various types of schools and classes (e.g., Trickett, 1978; Hearn & Moos, 1978); (b) studies investigating differences between teachers' and students' perceptions of actual and preferred learning environments (e.g., Fisher & Fraser, 1983b); and (c) studies examining whether students achieve more in their preferred classroom environment, as compared to other learning environments (e.g., Fisher & Fraser, 1983a).

INDIVIDUALIZED CLASSROOM ENVIRONMENT QUESTIONNAIRE

The *Individualized Classroom Environment Questionnaire* (ICEQ), like the CES, is an instrument designed to measure secondary school students' and teachers' perceptions of actual and preferred classroom environments (Wheldall, Beaman, & Mok, 1999). It differs from the CES and other instruments, however, in that it assesses dimensions of the learning environment that distinguish individualized or open classrooms from more conventional ones (Wheldall et al., 1999). The ICEQ consists of five scales (Personalization, Participation, Independence, Investigation, and Differentiation), each of which contains 10 items, for a total of 50 items. Each item has a 5-point response format that includes the options Almost Never, Seldom, Sometimes, Often, and Very Often. Examples of items include, "The teacher takes a personal interest in each student" (personalization scale), and "Students' ideas and suggestions are used during classroom discussion" (participation scale).

In terms of research applications, the ICEQ has been employed in various types of studies comparable to those described above for the CES (Fraser & Fisher, 1986). Namely, studies have investigated the relationship between classroom environment and student outcomes (e.g., Rentoul & Fraser, 1980), differences between student and teacher perceptions of actual and preferred learning environments (e.g., Fisher & Fraser, 1983b), and whether it is possible to make improvements to classroom environments based on feedback from student responses to the ICEQ (e.g., Fraser, Seddon, & Eagleson, 1982).

WHAT IS HAPPENING IN THIS CLASS QUESTIONNAIRE

The *What Is Happening In This Class* (WIHIC) questionnaire (Fraser, Fisher, & McRobbie, 1996) assesses high school students' perceptions of their classroom learning environment. Designed to bring parsimony into the field of classroom environment research, the WIHIC combines salient scales from past questionnaires, with additional scales that address contemporary educational concerns such as equity and constructivism (Fraser, 1998). It contains 56 items that are divided equally among seven scales (Student Cohesiveness, Teacher Support, Involvement, Investigation, Task Orientation, Cooperation, and Equity) and utilizes a 5-point frequency response format (Almost Never, Seldom, Sometimes, Often, Almost Always).

Research has demonstrated that the WIHIC is useful and valid across a number of countries and subjects (den Brok et al., 2006). According to den Brok and others (2006), the instrument has been used to study learning environments in Taiwan, Singapore, Korea, Brunei, Canada, Australia, USA, and Indonesia. In addition to its widespread application in cross-national research, the WIHIC has also been used to investigate associations between learning environments in mathematics classrooms and students' attitudes toward the subject (Rawnsley & Fisher, 1998), the effects of teacher training on students' perceptions of their learning environment (Pickett & Fraser, 2004), and the association between parent and student perceptions of the classroom environment and student outcomes (Allen & Fisher, 2007).

Ecobehavioral Assessment

Ecobehavioral assessment is an observational approach used to directly analyze the interaction between classroom environmental variables and students' behaviors. Observations focus simultaneously on student behaviors proven to enhance learning and developmental outcomes (e.g., academic engagement), as well as the ecological, or environmental features (e.g., instructional procedures, grouping formats, teacher behaviors) that co-occur with, or "set the stage" for such behaviors (Carta & Atwater, 1990; Kontos, Burchinal, Howes, Wisseh, & Galinsky, 2002; Powell, Burchinal, File, & Kontos, 2008). The unique coding systems of ecobehavioral assessments allow for the simultaneous recording of environmental variables and student behaviors, within a momentary time-sampling procedure (Carta & Atwater, 1990). This ability to directly observe the co-occurrence of student behaviors and environmental factors differentiates ecobehavioral assessment from many of the measures discussed above, to assess classroom learning environments (Greenwood, Carta & Atwater, 1991; Kontos et al., 2002; Powell et al., 2008). As such, ecobehavioral assessment can provide an in-depth statistical analysis of specific classroom environmental variables that promote positive student outcomes (Carta & Atwater, 1990).

ACCELERATOR BEHAVIORS AND
ECOBEHAVIORAL CODING SYSTEMS

An ecobehavioral approach to classroom observations requires the identification of student behaviors that are empirically linked to the enhancement of the learning or developmental outcomes of interest (Carta & Atwater, 1990; Kontos et al., 2002; Kontos & Keyes, 1999). Such behaviors are labeled "accelerator behaviors" (Carta & Atwater, 1990; Kontos et al., 2002). Accelerator behaviors (e.g., academic engagement) become the focus of the observation, and determine the type of ecobehav-

ioral coding system utilized. Several observational coding systems have been developed to increase the applicability of ecobehavioral assessment to a variety of ecological settings and accelerator behaviors. These coding systems provide the observer with a set of individual codes, specific to the accelerator behaviors of interest, which relate to the three categories of variables within the ecobehavioral assessment approach: ecological, teacher, and student (Kontos & Keyes, 1999).

The *Code for Instructional Structure and Student Academic Response* (CISSAR), for example, is a coding system which was developed to advance special education research methods beyond traditional observations of one variable across a time-sample (Greenwood, Carta, Kamps, Terry, & Delquadri, 1994). CISSAR provides variable codes, and a momentary time-sampling procedure that enables 53 events, across ecological and student behavior categories, to be recorded during a single observation period (Greenwood, 1991; Greenwood et al., 1994). The adoption and adaptation of CISSAR to address research questions outside of special education resulted in the development of an expanded version, the *Mainstream CISSAR* (MS-CISSAR) (Greenwood et al., 1994). An additional 46 events were added, thus increasing its sensitivity and applicability to (a) both general and special education settings, (b) a variety of teachers within these settings (e.g., paraprofessionals, classroom tutors), (c) teacher behaviors, (d) student behaviors across elementary and middle school levels, and (e) academic activities experienced by students with special needs (Greenwood et al., 1994).

Another widely used ecobehavioral coding system is the *Ecobehavioral System for Complex Analyses of Preschool Environments* (ESCAPE) (Carta & Atwater, 1990). This coding system was developed to specifically assess the effectiveness of preschool instruction and environments (Carta & Greenwood, 1985; Greenwood et al., 1994). It provides codes for 101 individual events, divided into 12 subcategories unique to the preschool setting, preschool teacher events, and the behaviors of 3- to 5-year-old children (Greenwood et al., 1994). Furthermore, computer software for each of these coding systems is available to assist with observer training, data collection, and analysis, as a way to improve the reliability of the observations (Greenwood et al., 1994). These technology-supported coding systems (Greenwood et al., 1994), and the level of statistical analysis they provide

(Carta & Atwater, 1990), make ecobehavioral observations a unique approach to assessing classroom environments.

ASSESSING CLASSROOM ENVIRONMENTS USING AN ECOBEHAVIORAL APPROACH

Researchers have utilized ecobehavioral assessment to address a wide variety of research questions relating to educational environments and student behaviors (Arreaga-Mayer & Perdomo-Rivera, 1996; Carta & Atwater, 1990; Powell et al., 2008). Several of the measurable aspects of classroom environments, discussed above, have been linked to positive student outcomes through research utilizing an ecobehavioral assessment approach. Academic engagement, for example, has been a focal accelerator behavior in numerous studies, thus providing detailed information regarding variables contributing to academic learning time in the classroom.

In a study comparing a preschool classroom for students with disabilities, to a general education kindergarten classroom, Carta and Atwater (1990) discovered that this transition requires students with disabilities to adjust their level of academic engagement. Students attending the special education preschool program spent a greater percentage of their time actively engaged in activities (e.g., manipulating objects), whereas the general education setting required students to spend a larger percentage of their time passively engaged (Carta & Atwater, 1990). Using MS-CISSAR, Kamps, Leonard, Dugan, Boland, and Greenwood (1991) demonstrated the effects of "naturally occurring" procedures, curriculum activities, and teacher behaviors, on the academic engagement of students with autism and other disabilities, in community-based classroom settings. Students displayed a higher probability of responding during math and arts activities, paper-and-pencil tasks, and activities involving the use of manipulatives, flashcards, or pictures. Students also displayed a higher probability of responding when teachers used "academic statements," as opposed to statements requiring students to perform some type of "management" task (Kamps et al., 1991).

Furthermore, ecobehavioral assessment findings have provided information regarding effective instructional and grouping formats for increasing students' academic learning time, engagement, and achievement. The use of peer groups, as opposed to whole-group configurations during preschool academic activities (Powell et al., 2008), classwide peer tutoring and direct instruction for at-risk elementary students (Greenwood, 1991), and interactive, fast-paced small-group formats for students with autism and developmental disabilities (Kamps et al., 1991) have all been supported via ecobehavioral observational procedures as ways to promote engagement and achievement.

Ecobehavioral assessment has also been used within comparative studies designed to measure the effectiveness of various teacher behaviors and instructional formats across different student populations (Arreaga-Mayer & Perdomo-Rivera, 1996) and academic settings (Thurlow, Ysseldyke, Graden & Algozzine, 1983). In a study by Arreaga-Mayer and Perdomo-Rivera (1996), ecobehavioral assessment served as a method to compare the types of teacher behaviors (e.g., instruction, monitoring, listening) displayed in either the general education setting, or an English language learner (ELL) setting. Similarly, Thurlow et al. (1983) used an ecobehavioral assessment approach in their comparison of academic engagement among students with learning disabilities within the special education setting, and the general education setting. Results demonstrated that teachers in the special education setting provided students with 10 to 15 times more individual and small-group instructional time than what they received in the general education setting. In the general education setting, however, students with learning disabilities spent a larger percentage of their academic time in large-group rather than small-group formats. Furthermore, ecobehavioral assessments indicated that students' active engaged time did not differ between the two classroom settings (Thurlow et al., 1983).

Summary and Conclusion

The quality of classroom environments is an important determinant of student achievement. Learning environment research has consistently demonstrated that key dimensions of the classroom environment have an impact on students' learning and behavior in school. The assessment of classroom environments, however, remains a difficult task, given the complex nature of classroom interactions, organization, and instruction. Moreover, learning environments are defined by physical and behavioral, as well as social/emotional characteristics. This chapter has provided a review of eight environmental features of classrooms that are both measurable and amenable to change. Three approaches to systematically assessing the quality of classroom environments were explained, including observations, questionnaires, and ecobehavioral assessment.

Whereas each approach measures unique dimensions of learning environments, information from environmental assessment tools can be used to inform both instruction and management in classrooms.

Future Directions

This final section suggests possible directions for future research and practice related to the assessment of classroom learning environments. Two critical assertions underlie this chapter's focus on learning environments. First, the classroom environment in which students learn can make a difference in their academic achievement and learning behaviors. Second, key dimensions of classroom environments are both measurable and amenable to change. In the following paragraphs, five potential directions for future research and practice that build on these two assertions are presented.

One of the best ways to use information derived from classroom environment assessment tools is in the context of classroom action research. Action research is a process by which teachers reflectively and systematically examine their own classrooms and teaching behaviors, as a basis for improving the learning environment and educational practices (O'Hanlon, 1996). Conducting an assessment of the environment near the beginning of the year can help teachers identify classroom dimensions to improve (e.g., strengthening teacher–student relationships) and, through mid-year and end-of-year assessment, determine whether positive changes have occurred. For example, a fifth grade teacher sought to enhance the quality of the learning environment in her classroom during the literacy and writing block. An assessment of the classroom environment revealed that her students were minimally engaged in writing activities, and that her interactions with students during writing periods were aimed primarily at redirecting students to work. She also noted that the expressive and creative quality of her students' writing, as well as their attitudes toward writing, were below average. Based on this assessment, she incorporated a conferencing component as part of her writing instruction (i.e., peer conferencing and student–teacher conferencing) to increase engagement and improve students' quality of writing and attitudes. Another action-research approach aimed at helping teachers to improve their classrooms is to conduct assessments of students' perceptions of both actual and preferred classroom environment. Once discrepancies between actual and ideal environments are identified, teachers can think about classroom strategies to reduce discrepancies.

A second way in which classroom environment assessment tools can be used is through the enhancement of teacher preparation and professional development. Learning environment research findings can be used as part of professional development programs, to make teachers aware of critical features of their classrooms. Moreover, the use of classroom environment assessment can help to target specific areas for professional development, so that teachers learn the skills necessary to establish productive learning environments for students. In addition, an evaluation of classroom environments, using both observation and questionnaires, can be included as part of formative assessment for students in teacher education programs. Duschl and Waxman (1991) found that the use of classroom environment assessment tools was important for beginning teachers, because it provided explicit guidance for improving their classroom practices. Classroom environment assessment is useful to provide preservice teachers with meaningful information about problem areas, and a tangible basis for improvement. Goh and Khine (2002) emphasized the value of introducing preservice teachers to classroom environment instruments, to sensitize them to important aspects of classroom life and to provide them with explicit feedback to guide improvements in their teaching.

Third, with the expanding use of computers and multimedia technology in classrooms, there is also a growing need to focus on the quality of technologically based learning environments. For example, Zandvliet and Fraser (2005) investigated students' perceptions of the learning environment in technology-based mathematics and sciences classrooms, in which laptop computers were used for teaching. Interestingly, female students indicated a higher preference for direct involvement in learning tasks and less computer usage than did boys, suggesting that the quality of learning environments may be differentially affected for boys and girls when technology is used for instruction. The movement toward technologically based learning environments also underscores the increasing importance of the physical environment of classrooms, and the relationship between student outcomes and aspects of the technological physical environment (e.g., hardware, computer software, technological support, etc.). There is a need to provide more comprehensive evaluations of classrooms and school learning environments, including the quality of physical environments. Even with rapid advances in the use of technology in classrooms, student learning may be limited if the physical environment is substandard in terms of technological hardware, software, or other teaching and learning supports and resources.

Another area of future work involves continued scale development and validation, particularly in three areas. The first is the development of environmental measures that are aligned with contemporary theory and practice related to teaching and learning. For example, Thomas (2003) developed the *Metacognition Orientation Learning Environment Scale–Science* (MOLES-S) based on research and theory related to metacognition and learning environments. Metacognition refers to students' knowledge, control, and awareness of their learning processes. MOLES-S was developed to evaluate whether science classrooms are oriented to the development of students' metacognition; that is, to measure classroom dimensions related to factors that specifically influence such development. According to Thomas (2003), the metacognitive orientation of a science classroom learning environment, as measured by the MOLES-S, is the extent to which that environment supports the development and enhancement of students' metacognition. A second instrument design issue is the development of personal forms, rather than class forms, of existing instruments. Whereas class forms elicit students' judgments of the class as a whole (e.g., "Students find out answers by doing investigations."), personal forms ask students about the individual student's role in the classroom (e.g., "I find out answers by doing investigations."). McRobbie, Fisher and Wong (1998) demonstrated that personal and class forms of the *Science Laboratory Environment Questionnaire* accounted for unique variance in student outcomes that cannot be explained by the other form. In other words, class and personal forms appear to measure different components of classroom environments. Finally, a major goal of comprehensive school reform is to promote the development of safe, nurturing, and healthy learning environments. Therefore, it is important that educators assess whether their teaching practices and behaviors do, in fact, achieve this end. To evaluate their classroom learning environments, teachers require easy-to-use measures that are also reliable and valid. Thus, a third area of scale development research is needed to validate short forms of classroom environment measures for use in a variety of classroom settings.

A final direction for classroom environment research is the use of more robust methods of data analysis. With regard to instrument development, exploratory factor analysis has been employed widely. Researchers should give more attention to the use of confirmatory factor analysis, in which a measurement model is postulated to account for relationships between observed variables and underlying constructs. Whereas most learning environment research has used correlational designs, few investigators have used multilevel analysis that considers the hierarchical nature of classrooms. Researchers should consider the use of structural equation modeling (SEM) to generate more sophisticated models. For example, SEM can be used to establish significant paths between multiple learning environments, as well as other variables (gender, attendance, etc.). Finally, when possible, experimental and quasi-experimental studies are needed, in which aspects of learning environments are deliberately changed to establish more clearly the causal effects of changes on student outcomes. Despite the importance of such quantitative studies, continued progress in using qualitative methods in learning environment research is also warranted. Information derived from classroom visits, student journals, and focus interviews can supplement observations or surveys with rich descriptive data, to enhance an understanding of learning environments and their effects on students' performance.

References

Allen, D., & Fisher, B. J. (2007). Parent and student perceptions of classroom learning environment and its association with student outcomes. *Learning Environment Research, 10,* 67–82.

Anderson, G. J., & Walberg, H. J. (1968). Classroom climate and group learning. *International Journal of Educational Sciences, 2,* 175–80.

Arreaga-Mayer, C., & Perdomo-Rivera, C. (1996). Ecobehavioral analysis of instruction for at- risk language-minority students. *The Elementary School Journal, 96,* 245–258.

Axelrod, S., Hall, R.V., & Tams, A. (1979). Comparisons of two common seating arrangements. *Academic Therapy, 15,* 29–36.

Birch, S. H., & Ladd, G. W. (1997). The teacher–child relationship and children's early school adjustment. *Journal of School Psychology, 35,* 61–79.

Bourke, S. (1986). How smaller is better: Some relationships between class size, teaching practices, and student achievement. *American Educational Research Journal, 23,* 558–571.

Brand, S., Felner, R., Shim, M., Seitsinger, A., & Dumas, T. (2003). Middle school improvement: Development and validation of school level assessment of climate, cultural pluralism, and school safety. *Journal of Educational Psychology, 95,* 570–588.

Brassard, M. R., & Boehm, A. E. (2007). *Preschool assessment: Principles and practices.* New York: Guilford Press.

Bronzaft, A. L., & McCarthy, D. P. (1975). The effect of elevated train noise on reading ability. *Environment and Behavior, 7,* 517–527.

Brophy, J., & Alleman, J. (1991). Activities as instructional tools: A framework for analysis and evaluation. *Educational Researcher, 20*(4), 9–23.

Brophy, J., & Good, T. (1986). Teacher behavior and student achievement. In M. Wittrock (Ed.), *Handbook of research on teaching* (3rd ed., pp. 328–375). New York: MacMillan.

Brophy-Herb, H. E., Lee, R. E., Nievar, M. A., & Stollak, G. (2007). Preschooler's social competence: Relations to family characteristics, teacher behaviors and classroom climate. *Journal of Applied Developmental Psychology, 28,* 134–148.

Buyse, E., Verschueren, K., Doumen, S., Damme, J. V., & Maes, F. (2008). Classroom problem behavior and teacher–child relationships in kindergarten: The moderating role of classroom climate. *Journal of School Psychology, 46,* 367–391.

Carta, J. J., & Atwater, J. B. (1990). Applications of ecobehavioral analysis to the study of transitions across early education settings. *Education & Treatment of Children, 13,* 298–315.

Carta, J. J., & Greenwood, C. R. (1985). Ecobehavioral assessment: A methodology for expanding the evaluation of early intervention programs. *Topics in Early Childhood Special Education Quarterly, 5,* 88–104.

Case, L. P., Speece, D. L., & Molloy, D. E. (2003). The validity of a response-to-instruction paradigm to identify reading disabilities: A longitudinal analysis of individual differences and contextual factors. *School Psychology Review, 32,* 557–582.

Choi, C. Y., & McPherson, B. (2005). Noise levels in Hong Kong primary schools: Implications for classroom listening. *International Journal of Disability, Development, and Education, 52,* 345–360.

Christenson, S. L., & Ysseldyke, J. E. (1989). Assessing student performance: An important change is needed. *Journal of School Psychology, 27,* 409–425.

Cleary, T. J., & Zimmerman, B. J. (2004). Self-regulation empowerment program: A school based program to enhance self-regulated and self-motivated cycles of student learning. *Psychology in the Schools, 4,* 537–543.

den Brok, P., Fisher, D., Rickards, T., & Bull, E. (2006). Californian science students' perceptions of their classroom learning environments. *Educational Research and Evaluation, 12,* 3–25.

Deutsch, F. M. (2003). How small classes benefit high school students. *NASSP Bulletin, 87,* 35–44.

Dorman, J.P. (2001). Associations between classroom environment and academic efficacy. *Learning Environments Research, 4,* 243–257.

Dorman, J.P. (2002). Classroom environment research: Progress and possibilities. *Queensland Journal of Educational Research, 18,* 112–140.

Dorman, J.P., Adams, J.E., & Ferguson, J.H. (2002). Psychosocial environment and student self-handicapping in secondary school mathematics classes: A cross-national study. *Educational Psychology, 22,* 499–511.

Dorman, J.P., Aldridge, J.M., & Fraser, B.J. (2006). Using students' assessment of classroom environment to develop a typology of secondary school classrooms. *International Education Journal, 7,* 906–915.

Dunn, R., Griggs, S.A., Olson, J., & Beasly, M. (1995). A meta-analytic validation of the Dunn and Dunn model of learning style preferences. *Journal of Educational Research, 88,* 353–362.

Dunn, R. J., & Harris, L. G. (1998). Organizational dimensions of climate and the impact on school achievement. *Journal of Instructional Psychology, 25,* 100–114.

Duschl, R.A., & Waxman, H.C. (1991). Influencing the learning environments of student teaching. In B.J Fraser & H.J Walberg (Eds.), *Educational environments: Evaluation, antecedents and consequences* (pp. 255–270). London: Pergamon.

Evans, G. W., & Maxwell, L. (1997). Chronic noise exposure and reading deficits. *Environment and Behavior, 29,* 638–656.

Evertson, C.M., & Smithey, M.W. (2001). Mentoring effects on protégés' classroom practice: An experimental field study. *Journal of Educational Research, 93,* 293–304.

Evertson, C. M., & Weinstein, C. S. (2006). Classroom management as a field of inquiry. In C.M. Evertson, & C.S. Weinstein (Eds.), *Handbook of classroom management: Research,* practice, and contemporary issues (pp. 3–16). Mahwah, N.J.: Lawrence Erlbaum Associates.

Finn, J. D., Pannozzo, G. M., & Achilles, C. M. (2003). The "why's" of class size: Student behavior in small behavior in small classes. *Review of Educational Research, 73,* 321–368.

Fish, M.C., & Dane, E. (1995). *Classroom Systems Observation Scale manual.* New York: Queens College of the City University of New York.

Fish, M. C., & Dane, E. (2000). The Classroom Systems Observation Scale: Development of an instrument to assess classrooms using a systems perspective. *Learning Environments Research, 3,* 67–92.

Fisher, D. L., & Fraser, B. J. (1983a). Validity and use of the Classroom Environment Scale. *Educational Evaluation and Policy Analysis, 5,* 261–271.

Fisher, D. L., & Fraser, B. J. (1983b). A comparison of actual and preferred classroom environments as perceived by science teachers and students. *Journal of Research in Science Teaching, 20,* 55–61.

Flanders, N.A. (1970). *Analyzing teacher behavior.* Reading, MA: Addison-Wesley.

Folger, J. (1989). Project STAR and class size policy. *Peabody Journal of Education, 67,* 382–399.

Fouts, J. T., & Myers, R. E. (1992). Classroom environments and middle school students' views of science. *Journal of Educational Research, 85,* 356–361.

Fraser, B. J. (1987). Use of classroom environment assessments in school psychology. *School Psychology International, 8,* 205–219.

Fraser, B.J. (1991). Two decades of classroom environment research. In B.J. Fraser & H.J. Walberg (Eds.), *Educational environments: Evaluation, antecedents, and consequences* (pp. 3–27). Oxford, UK: Pergamon Press.

Fraser, B.J. (1994). Research on classroom and school climate. In D. Gabel (Ed.), *Handbook of research on science teaching and learning* (pp. 493–541). New York: Macmillan.

Fraser, B. J. (1998). Classroom environment instruments: Development, validity, and applications. *Learning Environments Research, 1,* 7–33.

Fraser, B.J. (2002). Learning environments research: Yesterday, today and tomorrow. In S.W. Goh & M.S. Khine (Eds.), *Studies in educational learning environments: An International perspective* (pp. 1–25). Singapore: World Scientific.

Fraser, B. J., Anderson, G. J., & Walberg, H. J. (1982). *Assessment of learning environments: Manual for Learning Environment Inventory (LEI) and My Class Inventory (MCI).* Perth: Western Australian Institute of Technology.

Fraser, B.J., & Fisher, D.L. (1982). Predicting students' outcomes from the perceptions of classroom psychosocial environments. *American Educational Research Journal*, *19*, 498–518.

Fraser, B. J., & Fisher, D. L. (1986). Using short forms of classroom climate instruments to assess and improve classroom psychosocial environment. *Journal of Research in Science Teaching*, *23*, 387–413.

Fraser, B. J., Fisher, D. L., & McRobbie, C. J. (1996, April). *Development, validation and use of personal and class forms of a new environment instrument.* Paper presented at the Annual Meeting of the American Educational Research Association, New York.

Fraser, B.J., Seddon, T., & Eagleson, J. (1982). Use of student perceptions in facilitating improvement in classroom environment. *Australian Journal of Teacher Education*, *7*, 31–42.

Fraser, B. J., & Walberg, H. J. (1981). Psychosocial learning environment in science classrooms: A review of research. *Studies in Science Education*, *8*, 67–92.

Gardner, H. (1995). Reflections on multiple intelligences: Myths and messages. *Phi Delta Kappan*, *77*, 200–209.

Gettinger, M. (1986). Issues and trends in academic engaged time of students. *Special Services in the Schools*, *2*, 1–17.

Gettinger, M., & Ball, C. (2008). Best practices in increasing academic learning time. In A. Thomas & J. Grimes (Eds.), *Best practices in school psychology–V* (pp. 773–787). Bethesda, MD: National Association of School Psychologists.

Gettinger, M., & Kohler, K. M. (2006). Process-outcome approaches to classroom management and effective teaching. In C. M. Evertson & C. S. Weinstein (Eds.), *Handbook of classroom management: Research, practice, and contemporary issues* (pp. 73–95). Mahwah, NJ: Lawrence Erlbaum Associates.

Gettinger, M., & Stoiber, K. C. (1999). Excellence in teaching: Review of instructional and environmental variables. In C. R. Reynolds & T. B. Gutkin (Eds.), *The handbook of school psychology* (3rd ed., pp. 933–958). New York: John Wiley.

Ghaith, G. (2003). The relationship between forms of instruction, achievement and perceptions of classroom climate. *Educational Research 45*, 83–95.

Ghaith, G. M., Shaaban, K. A., & Harkous, S. A. (2007). An investigation of the relationship between forms of positive interdependence, social support, and selected aspects of classroom climate. *System*, *35*, 229–240.

Gillies, R. M., & Ashman, A. F. (2000). The effects of cooperative learning on students with learning disabilities in lower elementary school. *Journal of Special Education*, *34*, 19–28.

Goh, S.C., & Fraser, B.J. (1998). Teacher interpersonal behavior: Classroom environment and student outcomes in primary mathematics in Singapore. *Learning Environments Research*, *1*, 199–229.

Goh, S.C., & M.S. Khine. (Eds.) (2002). *Studies in educational learning environments: An international perspective.* Singapore: World Scientific.

Greenwood, C. R. (1991). Longitudinal analysis of time, engagement, and achievement in at-risk versus non-risk students. *Exceptional Children*, *57*, 521–535.

Greenwood, C. R., Carta, J. J., & Atwater, J. B. (1991). Ecobehavioral analysis in the classroom: Review and implications. *Journal of Behavioral Education*, *1*, 55–77.

Greenwood, C. R., Carta, J. J., Kamps, D., Terry, B., & Delquadri, J. (1994). Development and validation of standard classroom observation systems for school practitioners: Eobehavioral assessment systems software (EBASS). *Exceptional Children*, *61*, 197–210.

Greenwood, C. R., & Delquadri, J. (1995). Class-wide peer tutoring and the prevention of school failure. *Preventing School Failure*, *39*, 21–25.

Haertel, G., Walberg, H., & Haertel, E. (1981). Social-psychological determinants and learning: Quantitative synthesis. *British Educational Research Journal*, *7*, 27–36.

Haines, M. M., Stansfeld, S. A., Job, R. F. S., Berglund, B., & Head, J. (2001). Chronic aircraft noise exposure, stress responses, mental health and cognitive performance in school children. *Psychological Medicine*, *31*, 265–77.

Haley, M. H. (2004). Learner-centered instruction and the theory of multiple intelligences with second language learners. *Teachers College Record*, *106*, 163–180.

Hamre, B. K., & Pianta, R. C. (2001). Early teacher–child relationships and the trajectory of children's school outcomes through eighth grade. *Child Development*, *72*, 625–638.

Hanushek, E.A. (1999). Some findings from an independent investigation of the Tennessee STAR experiment and from other investigations of class size. *Educational Evaluation and Policy Analysis*, *21*, 143–163.

Hearn, J. C., & Moos, R. H. (1978). Subject matter and classroom climate: A test of Holland's environmental propositions. *American Educational Research Journal*, *15*, 111–124.

Hines, C. V., Cruickshank, D. R., & Kennedy, J. J. (1985). Teacher clarity and its relationship to student achievement and satisfaction. *American Educational Research Journal*, *22*, 87–99.

Howes, C. (2000). Social-emotional classroom climate in child care, child-teacher relationships and children's second grade peer relations. *Social Development*, *9*, 291–204.

Howes, C., Burchinal, M., Pianta, R., Bryant, D., Early, D., Clifford, R., & Barbarin, O. (2008). Ready to learn? Children's pre-academic achievement in pre-kindergarten programs. *Early Childhood Research Quarterly*, *23*, 27–50.

Jackson, L., & Veeneman Panyan, M. (2002). *Positive behavior support in the classroom: Principles and practices.* Baltimore, MD: Paul H. Brookes.

Johnston, J. M. (1990, April). *What are teachers' perceptions of teaching in different classroom contexts?* Paper presented at the Annual Meeting of the American Educational Research Association, Boston, MA. (ERIC Document Reproduction Service No. ED320867).

Juvonen, J., Nishina, A., & Graham, S. (2001). Self views versus peer perceptions of victims status among early adolescents. In J. Juvonen & S. Graham (Eds.), *Peer harassment in school: The plight of the vulnerable and victimized* (pp. 105–124). New York: Guilford Press.

Kamps, D., Leonard, B., Dugan, E., Boland, B., & Greenwood, C. (1991). The use of ecobehavioral assessment to identify naturally occurring effective procedures in classrooms serving students with autism and other developmental disabilities. *Journal of Behavioral Education*, *1*, 367–397.

Kaye, S., Trickett, E.J., & Quinlan, D.M. (1976). Alternative methods for environmental assessment: An example. *American Journal of Community Psychology*, *4*, 367–377.

Kindsvatter, R., Wilen, W., & Ishler, M. (1988). *Dynamics of effective teaching.* New York: Longman.

Knight, S. L. (1991). The effects of students' perceptions of the learning environment on their motivation in language arts. *Journal of Classroom Interaction*, *26*, 19–23.

Knoster, T.P., & McCurdy, B. (2002). Best practices in functional behavioral assessment for designing individual student programs. In A. Thomas & J. Grimes (Eds.), *Best practices in school psychology–IV* (pp. 1007–1027). Bethesda, MD: National Association of School Psychologists.

Kontos, S., Burchinal, M., Howes, C., Wisseh, S., & Galinsky, E. (2002). An ecobehavioral approach to examining the contextual effects of early childhood classrooms. *Early Childhood Research Quarterly, 17*, 239–258.

Kontos, S., & Keyes, L. (1999). An ecobehavioral analysis of early childhood classrooms. *Early Childhood Research Quarterly, 14*, 35–50.

Kounin, J. (1970). *Discipline and group management in classrooms*. New York: Holt, Rinehart and Winston.

La Paro, K. M., Pianta, R. C., & Stuhlman, M. (2004). The Classroom Assessment Scoring System: Findings from the prekindergarten year. *The Elementary School Journal, 104*, 409–426.

Lou, Y., Abrami, P. C., & Spence, J. C. (2000). Effects of within-class grouping on student achievement: An exploratory model. *Journal of Educational Research, 94*, 101–112.

Lou, Y., Abrami, P. C., Spence, J. C., Poulsen, C., Chambers, B., & d'Apollonia, S. (1996). Within-class grouping: A meta-analysis. *Review of Educational Research, 66*, 423–458.

Marks, H. M. (2000). Student engagement in instructional activity: Patterns in the elementary, middle, and high school years. *American Educational Research Journal, 37*, 153–184.

Martin, S. H. (2006). The classroom environment and children's performance: Is there a relationship? In C. Spencer & M. Blades (Eds.), *Children and their environments: Learning, using and designing spaces.* (pp. 91–107). New York: Cambridge University Press.

Marx, A. Furher, U., & Hartig, T. (2000). Effects of classroom seating arrangements on children's question asking. *Learning Environments Research, 2*, 249–263.

Marzano, R. J., & Marzano, J. S. (2003). The key to classroom management. *Educational Leadership, 61*(1), 6–13.

Mashburn, A. J., Pianta, R. C., Hamre, B. K., Downer, J. T., Barbarin, O. A., Bryant, D., Burchinal, M., Early, D. M., & Howes, C. (2008). Measures of classroom quality in prekindergarten and children's development of academic, language, and social skills. *Child Development, 79*, 732–749.

Matsumura, L. C., Slater, S. C., & Crosson, A. (2008). Classroom climate, rigorous instruction, and curriculum, and students' interactions in urban middle schools. *The Elementary School Journal, 108*, 293–312.

McCaleb, J., & White, J. (1980). Critical dimensions in evaluating teacher clarity. *Journal of Classroom Interaction, 15*, 27–30.

McRobbie, C.J., Fisher, D.L., & Wong, A.F.L. (1998). Personal and class forms of classroom environment instruments. In B.J. Fraser & K.L. Tobin (Eds.), *International handbook of science education* (pp. 581–594). Toronto: Kluwer.

Milesi, C., & Gamoran, A. (2006). Effects of class size and instruction on kindergarten achievement. *Educational Evaluation & Policy Analysis, 28*, 287–313.

Moos, R. H., & Moos, B. S. (1978). Classroom climate and student absences and grades. *Journal of Educational Psychology, 70*, 263–269.

Moos, R. H., & Trickett, E. J. (1974). *Classroom Environment Scale Manual.* Palo Alto, CA: Consulting Psychologists Press.

Mueller, D. J., Chase, C. I., & Walden, J. D. (1988). Effects of reduced class size in primary classes. *Educational Leadership, 45*(5), 48–50.

Munk, D. D., & Repp, A.C. (1994). The relationship between instructional variables and problem behavior: A review. *Exceptional Children, 60*, 390–401.

Murray, C., & Greenberg, M. T. (2000). Children's relationship with teachers and bonds with school: An investigation of patterns and correlates in middle childhood. *Journal of School Psychology, 38*, 423–445.

Murray, H.A. (1938). *Explorations in personality.* Oxford, UK: Oxford University Press.

Nye, B., Hedges, L. V., & Konstantopoulos, S. (2001). Are effects of small classes cumulative? Evidence from a Tennessee experiment. *Journal of Educational Research, 94*, 336–345.

Nye, B., Hedges, L. V., & Konstantopoulos, S. (2002). Do low-achieving students benefit more from small classes? Evidence from the Tennessee class size experiment. *Educational Evaluation and Policy Analysis, 24*, 201–217.

O'Connor, E. A., & Fish, M. C. (1998, April). *Differences in the classroom systems of expert and novice teachers.* Paper presented at the Annual Meeting of the American Educational Research Association, San Diego, CA. (ERIC Document Reproduction Service No. ED422314).

O'Connor, E. A., Fish, M. C., & Yasik, A. E. (2004). The influence of teacher experience on the elementary classroom system: An observational study. *Journal of Classroom Interaction, 39*, 11–18.

O'Hanlon, C. (Ed.). (1996). *Professional development through action research in educational settings.* Washington, DC: Falmer Press.

Patrick, H., Ryan, A. M., & Kaplan, A. (2007). Early adolescents' perceptions of the classroom social environment, motivational beliefs, and engagement. *Journal of Educational Psychology, 99*, 83–98.

Pianta, R.C. (2003). *Standardized classroom observations from pre-K to third grade: A mechanism for improving quality classroom experiences during P–3 years.* Charlottesville, VA: University of Virginia, Curry School of Education.

Pianta, R.C., Hamre, B., & Stuhlman, M. (2003). Relationships between teachers and children. In W. Reynolds & G. Miller (Eds.), *Comprehensive handbook of psychology: Vol. 7, Educational psychology* (pp. 199–234). Hoboken, NJ: Wiley.

Pianta, R.C., LaParo, K.M., & Hamre, B.K. (2007). *Classroom Assessment Scoring System.* Baltimore, MD: Paul Brookes.

Pianta, R. C., Steinberg, M. S., & Rollins, K. B. (1995). The first two years of school: Teacher-child relationships and deflections in children's classroom adjustment. *Development and Psychopathology, 7*, 295–312.

Pianta, R. C., & Stuhlman, M. W. (2004). Teacher–child relationships and children's success in the first years of school. *School Psychology Review, 33*, 444–458.

Pickett, L. H., & Fraser, B. J. (2004, April). *An evaluation of a science mentoring program for beginning elementary school teachers in terms of learning environment, student achievement and teacher attitudes.* Paper presented at the Annual Meeting of the National Association for Research in Science Teaching, Vancouver, Canada.

Powell, D. R., Burchinal, M. R., File, N., & Kontos, S. (2008). An ecobehavioral analysis of children's engagement in urban public school preschool classrooms. *Early Childhood Research Quarterly, 23*, 108–123.

Quinn, M. M. (2002). Changing antisocial behavior patterns in young boys: A structured cooperative learning approach. *Education and Treatment of Children, 25*, 380–395.

Rawnsley, D., & Fisher, D. L. (1998, December). *Learning environments in mathematics classrooms and their associations with students' attitudes and learning.* Paper presented at the Australian Association for Research in Education Conference, Adelaide, Australia.

Rentoul, A. J., & Fraser, B. J. (1980). Predicting learning from classroom individualization and actual–preferred congruence. *Studies in Educational Evaluation, 6*, 265–277.

Rosenshine, B. (1970). Evaluation of classroom instruction. *Review of Educational Research, 40*, 279–300.

Rosenshine, B. (2002). Converging findings on classroom instruction. In A. Molnar (Ed.), *School reform proposals: The research evidence* (pp. 175–196). Greenwich, CT: Information Age Publishing.

Schell, J.W. (1993). A framework for learning advanced postsecondary vocational–technical skills. *Community College Journal of Research and Practice, 17*, 357–374.

Schneider, M. (2002). *Do school facilities affect academic outcomes?* Washington, DC: National Clearing House for Educational Facilities.

Searson, R., & Dunn, R. (2001). The learning-style teaching model. *Science and Children, 38*(5), 22–26.

Shann, M. H. (1999). Academics and a culture of caring: The relationships between school achievement and prosocial and antisocial behaviors in four urban middle schools. *School Effectiveness and School Improvement, 10*, 390–413.

Shapiro, S. (1993). Strategies that create a positive classroom climate. *Clearing House, 67*, 91–97.

Shimabukuro, S. M., Prater, M. A., Jenkins, A., & Edelen-Smith, P. (1999). The effects of self-monitoring of academic performance on students with learning disabilities and ADD/ADHD. *Education & Treatment of Children, 22*, 397–414.

Skinner, E. A., & Belmont, M. J. (1993). Motivation in the classroom: Reciprocal effects of teacher behavior and student engagement across the school year. *Journal of Educational Psychology, 85*, 571–581.

Smith, B. A. (2000). Quantity matters: Annual instructional time in an urban school system. *Educational Administration Quarterly, 36*, 652–682.

Taylor, B.M., Pearson, P.D., Clark, K., & Walpole, S. (2000). Effective schools and accomplished teachers: Lessons about primary grade reading instruction in low-income schools. *The Elementary School Journal, 101*, 121–166.

Thijs, J. T., Koomen, H. M. Y., & van der Leij, A. (2008). Teacher–child relationships and pedagogical practices: Considering the teacher's perspective. *School Psychology Review, 37*, 244–260.

Thomas, G.P. (2003). Conceptualisation, development and validation of an instrument for investigating the metacognitive orientation of science classroom learning environments: The Metacognitive Orientation Learning Environment Scale – Science (MOLES-S). *Learning Environments Research, 6*, 175–197.

Thurlow, M. L., Ysseldyke, J. E., Graden, J. L., & Algozzine, B. (1983). What's "special" about the special education resource room for learning disabled students? *Learning Disability Quarterly, 6*, 283–288.

Trickett, E. J. (1978). Toward a social-ecological conception of adolescent socialization: Normative data on contrasting types of public school classrooms. *Child Development, 49*, 408–414.

Trickett, E. J., & Moos, R. H. (1973). Social environment of junior high and high school classrooms. *Journal of Educational Psychology, 65*, 93–102.

Vockell, R. (1987). The computer and academic learning time. *Teaching Exceptional Children, 19*(2), 72–75.

Walberg, H. J., & Anderson, G. J. (1968). Classroom climate and individual learning. *Journal of Educational Psychology, 59*, 414–419.

Wang, M. C., Haertel, G. D., & Walberg, H. J. (1993). Toward a knowledge base for school learning. *Review of Educational Research, 63*, 249–294.

Wannarka, R. & Ruhl, K. (2008). Seating arrangements that promote positive academic and behavioural outcomes: A review of empirical research. *Support for Learning, 23*, 89–93.

Wentzel, K.R. (1997). Student motivation in middle school: The role of perceived pedagogical caring. *Journal of Educational Psychology, 89*, 411–419.

Wheldall, K., Beaman, R., & Mok, M. (1999). Does the Individualized Classroom Environment Questionnaire (ICEQ) measure classroom climate? *Educational and Psychological Measurement, 59*, 847–854.

Wheldall, K., Morris, M., Vaughn, P., & Ng, Y.Y. (1981). Rows versus tables: An example of the use of behavioral ecology in two classes of 11-year-old children. *Educational Psychology, 1*, 171–184.

Wilson, H. K., Pianta, R. C., & Stuhlman, M. (2007). Typical classroom experiences in first grade: The role of classroom climate and functional risk in the development of social competencies. *The Elementary School Journal, 108*, 81–96.

Wilson-Jones, L., & Caston, M. C. (2004). Cooperative learning on academic achievement in elementary African American males. *Journal of Instructional Psychology, 31*, 280–283.

Wright, S., & Cowen, E. L. (1982). Student perception of school environment and its relationship to mood, achievement, popularity, and adjustment. *American Journal of Community Psychology, 10*, 687–703.

Yates, G.C.R., & Yates, S.M. (1990). Teacher effectiveness research: Toward describing user-friendly classroom instruction. *Educational Psychology, 10*, 225–238.

Ysseldyke, J. E., & Christenson, S. L. (1987). *The Instructional Environment Scale.* Austin, TX: PRO-ED.

Ysseldyke, J. E., & Christenson, S. L. (1989). Evaluating students' instructional environments. *Remedial and Special Education, 8*, 17–24.

Ysseldyke, J. E., & Christenson, S. L. (1993). *The Instructional Environment System–II.* Longmont, CO: Sopris West.

Ysseldyke, J. E., & Christenson, S. L. (2002). *Functional Assessment of Academic Behavior.* Longmont, CO: Sopris West.

Zahorik, J. A. (1999). Reducing class size leads to individualized instruction. *Educational Leadership, 57*, 50–53.

Zandvliet, D., & Fraser, B. (2005). Physical and psychosocial environments associated with networked classrooms. *Learning Environment Research, 8*, 1–17.

Zentall, S. S., & Shaw, J. H. (1980). Effects of classroom noise on performance and activity of second-grade hyperactive and control children. *Journal of Educational Psychology, 72*, 830–840.

Zimmerman, B.J. (1998). Developing self-fulfilling cycles of academic regulation: An analysis of exemplary instructional models. In D.H. Schunk & B.J. Zimmerman (Eds.), *Self-regulated learning: From teaching to self-reflective practice* (pp. 1–19). New York: Guilford Press.

Assessment of Externalizing Behavioral Deficits

Robert J. Volpe *and* Sandra M. Chafouleas

Abstract

Given the considerable amount of research attention that has been provided to externalizing behavioral deficits, a wide array of assessment methodologies is available to reliably assess core features. The purpose of this chapter is to provide a guide for the assessment of externalizing behavior problems. The chapter begins with an overview of externalizing problems, with focus on disorders of attention and disruption. Discussion of relevant disorders is based on the *Diagnostic and Statistical Manual of Mental Disorders* (4th Edition, text revision; DSM-IV-TR) and special education law. Next, a five-phase model is presented for school-based assessment of externalizing problems that addresses issues of classification (screening, multimethod assessment, interpretation of results) as well as design and evaluation of the treatment plan.

Keywords: behavior assessment, oppositional defiant disorder, attention deficit hyperactivity disorder, conduct disorder, disruptive behavior, externalizing problems, evaluating behavior response

Introduction

The assessment of externalizing behavioral deficits has received a considerable amount of research attention, affording a wide array of assessment methodologies to reliably assess core features of externalizing problems. The purpose of this chapter is to provide a guide for the assessment of externalizing behavior problems. The chapter begins with an overview of externalizing problems, and relevant disorders are discussed based on the *Diagnostic and Statistical Manual of Mental Disorders* (4th Edition, text revision; DSM-IV-TR) and special education law. Next, a five-phase model is presented for school-based assessment of externalizing problems that addresses issues of classification, as well as treatment planning and evaluation.

Overview of Externalizing Problems

A series of seminal factor analytic studies and comprehensive reviews has established that childhood psychopathology can be delineated into two broad-band dimensions (c.f., Achenbach & Edelbrock, 1978;

Quay, 1977). The *internalizing* dimension (also referred to as overcontrolled) includes withdrawn, anxious, and inhibited symptoms. In contrast, the *externalizing* dimension encompasses symptoms that are outwardly directed, and typically are described by parents and teachers as disruptive and annoying. Other terms for externalizing behavior include acting out, undercontrolled, disruptive, or conduct problems (Hinshaw, 1987; Hinshaw & Lee, 2003). This broad domain includes hyperactive, oppositional, defiant, and aggressive behaviors, all of which can have a negative impact on the social and academic functioning of students (Barkley, 2006), and the school environment in general (Frick, 1998). Furthermore, this class of behavior problems can lead to problems in adolescence and adulthood, including substance abuse (e.g., White, Xie, Thompson, Loeber, & Stouthamer-Loeber, 2001) and antisocial behavior (e.g., Robins, 1991) that result in a high cost to society (e.g., Foster, Jones, and the Conduct Problems Prevention Research Group, 2005).

The most widely accepted system for classifying externalizing behavior problems in the United States and Canada is the *DSM-IV*. The DSM-IV includes a section of "Disorders Usually First Diagnosed in Infancy, Childhood, or Adolescence." Within this section, under the heading of "Attention-Deficit and Disruptive Behavior Disorders," are listed the diagnostic criteria for the three major externalizing disorders of childhood: attention-deficit/hyperactivity disorder (ADHD), conduct disorder (CD), and oppositional defiant disorder (ODD).

Attention-Deficit/Hyperactivity Disorder

ADHD is a psychiatric disorder typified by developmentally inappropriate levels of inattention, response inhibition, and overactivity that result in functional impairment in more than one setting (American Psychiatric Association, 2000). These symptoms tend to appear between the ages of 3 and 5, but can be evidenced as early as the first year of life and are typically of childhood onset (Barkley, Fischer, Edelbrock, & Smallish, 1990). Estimates indicate that 3% to 7% of school-aged children in the United States have ADHD, with 2 to 9 times more boys than girls affected (American Psychiatric Association, 2000). Longitudinal studies have shown ADHD to be chronic, persisting into adolescence and adulthood for a large proportion of affected individuals (Gittleman, Manuzza, Shenker & Bonagura, 1985).

Over the past 20 years that childhood disorders have been included in the DSM (e.g., DSM-II, 1968), considerable controversy has existed over the conceptualization of inattention-hyperactivity-impulsivity disorders (see Hinshaw, 1987). In particular, the primary emphasis on three clusters of symptoms (inattention, hyperactivity, impulsivity) has shifted from one edition of the DSM to the next. For example, in the *Diagnostic and Statistical Manual of Mental Disorders, Third Edition* (DSM-III; American Psychiatric Association, 1980), the principal emphasis was placed on attention and impulsivity, with a secondary emphasis on hyperactivity. However, the *Diagnostic and Statistical Manual of Mental Disorders, Third Edition, Revised* (DSM-III-R; American Psychiatric Association, 1987) eliminated the DSM-III subtype of attention-deficit disorder (ADD) without hyperactivity, returning to a more unidimensional view of the disorder. The current DSM (DSM-IV) conceptualizes ADHD in two dimensions: inattention and hyperactivity/impulsivity (specific diagnostic criteria for ADHD are provided in Table 13.1). For each dimension, nine symptom criteria are provided, which are used to categorize three subtypes of ADHD: predominantly inattentive type (ADHD-I), predominantly hyperactive/impulsive type (ADHD-HI), and combined type (ADHD-C). The three subtypes differ in terms of degree of impairment, age, and gender ratio (e.g., Lahey et al., 1994). Also, significant differences exist between subtypes with regard to prevalence rates. Specifically, ADHD-HI is the least common and is most often diagnosed in preschool or young elementary-aged children (Lahey et al, 1994). It has been speculated that ADHD-HI may be a precursor to ADHD-C. Most prevalence studies have focused on ADHD-C and ADHD-I, with ADHD-C being two to six times more common than ADHD-I (Baumgaertel, Wolraich, & Dietrich, 1995; Szatmari, Offord, & Boyle, 1989). There has been some question as to whether children with ADHD-I exhibit the same attention problems as children with the ADHD-C (e.g., Barkley, DuPaul, & McMurray, 1990), and whether ADHD-I should be considered a subtype of ADHD or indeed should be classified as a separate disorder altogether (Barkley, 2006).

Children with ADHD experience functional deficits in a number of domains. In the peer domain, children with ADHD are both more rejected and less accepted than children without the disorder (see Hinshaw & Melnick, 1995 for a review). The majority of students diagnosed with ADHD experience academic performance problems (Cantwell & Baker, 1991), and a significant minority of affected children demonstrate academic difficulties severe enough meet criteria for a learning disability (Frick et al., 1991; Faraone et al., 1993).

Disruptive Behavior Disorders

Classifications for CD and the predecessor of ODD were introduced in the DSM-III (American Psychiatric Association, 1980). In the revision of the DSM-III (DSM-III-R; American Psychiatric Association, 1987) "oppositional disorder" was renamed oppositional defiant disorder. Although specific criteria for these categories have been modified in the DSM-IV (see Tables 2 and 3 for DSM-IV diagnostic criteria), the names of the disorders themselves have remained unchanged. According to the DSM-IV, CD is marked by a persistent pattern of childhood behavior that infringes on the basic rights of others, or violates major societal norms for the child's age (see Table 13.2). These behaviors can include aggressive behavior that harms or threatens to cause harm to other people or animals (e.g., fighting, bullying), destruction of property (e.g., fire setting, vandalism), deceitfulness or stealing (e.g., lying to obtain goods, shoplifting), and breaking rules that are

Table 13.1   DSM-IV-TR criteria for Attention Deficit Hyperactivity Disorder

A. Either 1 or 2

1. Six or more of the following symptoms of inattention have been present for at least 6 months, to a point that is disruptive and inappropriate for developmental level:

Inattention

    a. Often fails to give close attention to details, or makes careless mistakes in homework, work, or other activities

    b. Often has difficulties sustaining attention in tasks or play activities

    c. Often does not seem to listen when spoken to directly

    d. Often does not follow through instructions and fails to finish schoolwork, chores, or duties in the workplace (not due to oppositional behavior or failure to understand instructions)

    e. Often has difficulties organizing tasks and activities

    f. Often avoids, dislikes, or is reluctant to engage in tasks that require sustained mental efforts

    g. Often loses things necessary for tasks or activities (e.g., toys, school assignments, pencils, books)

    h. Is often easily distracted by extraneous stimuli

    i. Is often forgetful in daily activities

2. Six or more of the following symptoms of hyperactivity-impulsivity have been present for at least 6 months, to an extent that is disruptive and inappropriate for developmental level:

Hyperactivity

    a. Often fidgets with hands or feet or squirms in seat

    b. Often leaves seat in classroom or in other situations in which remaining seated is expected

    c. Often runs about or climbs excessively in situations in which it is inappropriate (in adolescents or adults, may be limited to subjective feelings of restlessness)

    d. Often has difficulty playing or engaging in leisure activities quietly

    e. Is often "on the go" or often acts as if "driven by a motor"

    f. Often talks excessively

Impulsivity

    g. Often blurts out answers before questions have been completed

    h. Often has difficulty awaiting turn

    i. Often interrupts or intrudes on others (e.g., butts into conversations or games)

B. Some symptoms causing impairment were present before age 7

C. Some impairment from the symptoms is present in two or more settings (e.g., at school and at home)

D. There must be clear evidence of clinically significant impairment in social, academic or occupational functioning

E. The symptoms do not happen only during the course of a Pervasive Developmental Disorder, Schizophrenia, or other Psychotic Disorder. The symptoms are not better accounted for by another mental disorder (e.g., Mood Disorder, Anxiety Disorder, Dissociative Disorder, or a Personality Disorder).

Based on these criteria, three types of ADHD are identified:

    ADHD, *Combined Type*: if both criteria 1A and 1B are met for the past 6 months

    ADHD, *Predominantly Inattentive Type*: if criterion 1A is met but criterion 1B is not met for the past six months

    ADHD, *Predominantly Hyperactive-Impulsive Type*: if Criterion 1B is met but Criterion 1A is not met for the past 6 months.

Content adapted and reprinted with permission from: *American Psychiatric Association: Diagnostic and Statistical Manual of Mental Disorders, Fourth Edition, Text Revision*. Washington, DC: American Psychiatric Association, 2004.

Table 13.2   DSM-IV-TR criteria for Conduct Disorder

A. A repetitive and persistent pattern of behavior in which the basic rights of others, or major age-appropriate societal norms or rules, are violated, as manifested by the presence of three (or more) of the following criteria in the past 12 months, with at least one criterion present in the past 6 months:

Aggression to people and animals

1. Often bullies, threatens, or intimidates others
2. Often initiates physical fights
3. Has used a weapon that can cause serious physical harm to others (e.g., a bat, brick, broken bottle, knife, gun)
4. Has been physically cruel to people
5. Has been physically cruel to animals
6. Has stolen while confronting a victim (e.g., mugging, purse snatching, extortion, armed robbery)
7. Has forced someone into sexual activity

Destruction of property

8. Has deliberately engaged in fire setting with the intention of causing serious damage
9. Has deliberately destroyed others' property (other than by fire setting)

Deceitfulness or theft

10. Has broken into someone else's house, building, or car
11. Often lies to obtain goods or favors, or to avoid obligations (i.e., "cons" others)
12. Has stolen items of nontrivial value without confronting a victim (e.g., shoplifting, but without breaking and entering; forgery)

Serious violations of rules

13. Often stays out at night despite parental prohibitions, beginning before age 13 years
14. Has run away from home overnight at least twice while living in parental or parental surrogate home (or once without returning for a lengthy period)
15. Is often truant from school, beginning before age 13 years

B. The disturbance in behavior causes clinically significant impairment in social, academic, or occupational functioning. If the individual is age 18 years or older, criteria are not met for Antisocial Personality Disorder

Code based on age at onset:
Conduct Disorder, Childhood-Onset Type: Onset of at least one criterion characteristic of Conduct Disorder prior to age 10 years
Conduct Disorder, Adolescent-Onset Type: Absence of any criteria characteristic of Conduct Disorder prior to age 10 years
Conduct Disorder, Unspecified Onset: Age at onset is not known

Specify severity:
Mild: few if any conduct problems in excess of those required to make the diagnosis **and** conduct problems cause only minor harm to others
Moderate: number of conduct problems and effect on others intermediate between "mild" and "severe"
Severe: many conduct problems in excess of those required to make the diagnosis **or** conduct problems cause considerable harm to others

For individuals over age 18 years, a diagnosis of Conduct Disorder can be given only if the criteria are not also met for Antisocial Personality Disorder. The diagnosis of Antisocial Personality Disorder cannot be given to individuals under age 18 years.

Content adapted and reprinted with permission from: *American Psychiatric Association: Diagnostic and Statistical Manual of Mental Disorders, Fourth Edition, Text Revision.* Washington, DC: American Psychiatric Association, 2004.

considered serious (e.g., running away from home overnight, skipping school). The DSM-IV lists a total of 15 antisocial behaviors, three of which must have been evident to a degree causing significant impairment in functioning (American Psychiatric Association (APA), 2000). A key issue recognized by the DSM-IV is the distinction between

childhood-onset type and adolescent-onset type. The former requires that only one of the 15 behaviors be present before the age of 10years. The childhood-onset type is associated with more stable patterns of behavior and cognitive problems, and occurs less frequently than the adolescent-onset type of CD. Children with the childhood-onset type are more likely to engage in violent behavior than their adolescent-onset counterparts. In contrast, the adolescent-onset type is much more common, more transient, and is less associated with overall psychopathology (Moffit & Caspi, 2001).

ODD is a less severe disruptive behavior disorder than CD, involving behaviors that are negativistic, hostile, and defiant (American Psychiatric Association, 2004). In Table 13.3, the diagnostic criteria for ODD are listed. These criteria include eight symptoms, four of which must be present to an extent that is considered developmentally extreme and impairing. Much discussion has centered on the relationship between ODD and CD, and whether ODD is in fact a viable diagnostic entity. Critiques of ODD have pointed to relatively low diagnostic reliability, and the preponderance of ODD symptoms in typically developing children, particularly with regard to preschoolers and adolescents (see Hinshaw & Lee, 2003 see also Loeber et al., 2000). Nevertheless, ODD tends to occur earlier in development than CD, and is predictive of CD (Biederman et al, 1996). Because ODD symptoms represent a less severe and more malleable form of antisocial behavior, the identification of children with ODD may prove useful in efforts to prevent CD and adult forms of antisocial behavior (Lahey, Loeber, Quay, Frick, & Grimm, 1992).

Comorbidity of Externalizing Problems

ADHD and the disruptive behavior disorders often do not occur in isolation, and there is a substantial degree of overlap between them. In clinically referred samples, studies have found that over half of children with ADHD-C also meet diagnostic criteria for ODD, and half of clinically referred adolescents with ADHD-C meet diagnostic criteria for CD (Barkley, 1998). The relationship between the hyperactive-impulsive symptoms and aggression

appears to be particularly strong (Hinshaw, 1987), with disruptive behavior disorders more likely to co-occur with the ADHD-HI or ADHD-C types than with the ADHD-I type (Wolraich, Hannah, Pinnock, Baumgaertel, & Brown, 1996).

The relationship between academic underachievement and externalizing behavior is well documented, though complex. A significant minority of children diagnosed with ADHD also is classified with a learning disability (DuPaul & Stoner, 2003; Knivsberg, Reichelt, &Nodland, 1999; Semrud-Clikeman et al., 1992), with up 80% of students with ADHD exhibiting academic performance problems (Cantwell & Baker, 1991). In addition, between 20% and 25% of children with a disruptive behavior disorder experience academic underachievement in at least one subject area (Frick et al., 1991). Studies examining differential developmental outcomes for children with disruptive behavior disorders have found evidence suggesting that the symptoms of ADHD, but not CD, are associated

Table 13.3 DSM-IV-TR criteria for Oppositional Defiant Disorder

A. A pattern of negativistic, hostile, and defiant behavior lasting at least 6 months, during which four (or more) of the following are present:

1. Often loses temper
2. Often argues with adults
3. Often actively defies or refuses to comply with adults' requests or rules
4. Often deliberately annoys people
5. Often blames others for his or her mistakes or misbehavior
6. Is often touchy or easily annoyed by others
7. Is often angry and resentful
8. Is often spiteful or vindictive

Note: Consider a criterion met only if the behavior occurs more frequently than is typically observed in individuals of comparable age and developmental level.

B. The disturbance in behavior causes clinically significant impairment in social, academic, or occupational functioning.

C. The behaviors do not occur exclusively during the course of a Psychotic or Mood disorder.

D. Criteria are not met for Conduct Disorder, and, if the individual is age 18 years or older, criteria are not met for Antisocial Personality Disorder.

Content adapted and reprinted with permission from: *American Psychiatric Association: Diagnostic and Statistical Manual of Mental Disorders, Fourth Edition, Text Revision.* Washington, DC: American Psychiatric Association, 2004.

with later academic problems, whereas the symptoms of CD, but not ADHD, are associated with later delinquency (Farrington, Loeber, & Van Kammen, 1990; Fergusson &Horwood, 1995; Fergusson, Horwood, & Lynskey, 1993; Fergusson, Lynskey, & Horwood, 1997; Frick et al., 1991). These studies notwithstanding, the relationship between ADHD, the disruptive behavior disorders, and academic achievement is likely reciprocal and deterministic (Hinshaw & Lee, 2003). For example, attention problems can lead to academic difficulties or vice versa, which in turn may lead to motivational problems and antisocial behavior, which can have further negative impacts on achievement.

Although it may seem counterintuitive, there is a higher than chance association between externalizing problems and internalizing problems (e.g., Rutter, Giller, & Hagell, 1998), with the rates of comorbidity between ADHD and anxiety and/or depression in epidemiological samples averaging approximately 25% (Angold, Costello, &Erkanli, 1999; Jensen, Martin, & Cantwell, 1997). Likewise, a meta-analysis of children in community samples with CD or ODD found between 2% and 45% to have depression, and 5% to 55% to have an anxiety disorder (Angold et al., 1999).

Special Education Classification
There are several mechanisms for students diagnosed with the DSM disorders listed above to qualify for special education services. First, many students experiencing significant academic difficulties will meet criteria for a specific learning disability (Barkley, 1998). Students with ADHD, in particular, can qualify for services under the "Other Health Impaired" category (see Table 13.4) of the Individuals with Disabilities Education Improvement Act (IDEA, 2004), depending on the severity of impairment. Likewise, students with ADHD may qualify for services under Section 504 of the Rehabilitation Act of 1973, though this does not necessarily include special education services. Students with externalizing behavior disorders may also qualify for special education services if they meet criteria for emotional disturbance (see Table13.4). However, note in the definition that students who are "socially maladjusted" have been excluded from this category within various iterations of state and federal legislation. Although a definition of socially maladjusted is not provided in the IDEA, it has been suggested that a diagnosis of CD serve as a proxy (see Merrell, 2008, for a more detailed review of this topic). However, substantial controversy regarding the defining features and appropriateness

Table 13.4 IDEA criteria for Categories of Emotional Disturbance and Other Health Impaired

Emotional Disturbance

A condition in which one or more of the following characteristics are exhibited over a long period of time and to a marked degree, which adversely affects a child's educational performance:

- An inability to learn that cannot be explained by intellectual, sensory, or health factors
- An inability to build or maintain satisfactory interpersonal relationships with peers and teachers
- Inappropriate types of behavior or feelings under normal circumstances
- A general pervasive mood of unhappiness or depression
- A tendency to develop physical symptoms or fears associated with personal or school problems

The term includes schizophrenia, but does not apply to children who are socially maladjusted, unless it is determined that they have an emotional disturbance.

Other Health Impairment

- Limited strength, vitality, or alertness (or heightened alertness to environmental stimuli that results in limited alertness with respect to the educational environment) that adversely affects a child's educational performance
- The impairment may be caused by a chronic or acute health problem, such as asthma, attention-deficit disorder or *attention-deficit/hyperactivity disorder*, diabetes, epilepsy, a heart condition, hemophilia, lead poisoning, leukemia, nephritis, rheumatic fever, or sickle cell anemia

Note. Definitions were adapted from the Individuals with Disabilities Education Act [IDEA], 2004. Retrieved from: http://idea.ed.gov.

of "social maladjustment" as an exclusionary criteria continues (see, for example, the special issue of *Psychology in the Schools*, Vol. 41, Issue 8, 2004). Although students with a diagnosis of CD may be disqualified from receiving services based on emotional disturbance, they may still qualify for special education services in cases of comorbid ADHD or learning disability.

A Five-Phase Model for School-Based Assessment of Externalizing Problems
Since 1975, when the Education for All Handicapped Children Act (PL 94-142) was passed, the most common assessment role for school psychologists has been to evaluate students for placement into special education. Although the refer–test–place model remains common in school psychology practice

(Reschly, 2000; Curtis, Hunley, & Grier, 2004), over the last several decades the role of school psychologists has expanded to include a greater emphasis on a problem-solving approach, wherein problems are identified, analyzed, and addressed with interventions that are evaluated for effectiveness (Gresham, 2007). Although a referral to a child study team for externalizing problems still requires an evaluation to determine the students' eligibility for services, more often school psychologists are expanding their assessments to incorporate a problem-solving approach. Combining the two general tasks of diagnosis (the traditional approach) and a problem-solving approach, involves four principle assessment goals: (a) screening, (b) diagnosis, (c) treatment planning, and (d) outcome evaluation. Based on the educational decision-making model of Salvia and Ysseldyke (2004), DuPaul (1992) organized these goals into a five-stage diagnostic and problem-solving model of assessment for ADHD. We have expanded this model to include the assessment of the DSM-IV disruptive behavior disorders (ODD and CD), and also discuss a Responseto-Intervention(RTI) approach that more fully integrates assessment goals related to outcome evaluation.

Based on DuPaul (1992), we have organized the aforementioned assessment tasks into a five-stage model following initial teacher referral (See Figure 13.1). It is assumed that prior to teacher referral for comprehensive assessment, pre-referral interventions have been investigated that did not fully address the problem behavior, and/or required resources that could not be sustained without intensive supports such as special education or other additional services. In the following sections, we describe each phase of this model, beginning with critical questions to be answered at each stage. For each stage of the model, recommendations are provided with regard to specific assessment methods and techniques.

Stage I: Screening

Screening of individual students often is the first step in typical school-based referrals for behavior problems. The principle question to be addressed at Stage I of the five-stage model is whether further assessment for an externalizing behavior disorder is warranted. To answer this question, one must establish whether the student exhibits sufficient symptoms to warrant further assessment, and whether these behaviors are likely to be associated with one of the disorders in question—or if, instead, one or more transitory environmental variables might explain the problem. Additionally, in this phase of assessment,

the specific behaviors of concern can be identified, and information can be gathered concerning what factors in the school environment may be maintaining them. Two assessment methods are recommended at this phase of assessment. First, a teacher interview may be conducted to identify the referral concern, and to delineate the topography (frequency, intensity, duration) of the behaviors of concern, and what environmental conditions might be investigated as possible antecedents and consequences of these behaviors. Next, the teacher(s) should complete a broad-band rating scale to establish whether the level of symptomatology justifies a comprehensive assessment. (Various interview formats and behavior ratings scaleswill be described in the Stage II section.)

| Stage I |
| Screening |
| |
| -What is the problem? |
| -Is further assessment required? |

| Stage II |
| Multi-Method Assessment |
| |
| -What are the nature and pervasiveness of the problem? |
| -What environmental factors are maintaining the problem? |
| -What resources are available to address the problem? |

| Stage III |
| Interpreting Results |
| |
| -Does the child meet the symptom criteria for one or more disorder? |
| -What is the trajectory of symptomatologyover time? |
| -Is the child significantly impaired? |
| -Are other factors present that could explain the problem? |
| -Does the child qualify for special services? |

| Stage IV |
| Designing the Treatment Plan |
| |
| -How severe are the problems of interest? |
| -What are the targets for intervention? |
| -What available resources will best address the problem? |

| Stage V |
| Evaluation of the Treatment Plan |
| |
| -Are desired goals being met? |
| -Are modifications to the treatment plan needed? |

Fig. 13.1 Five-Phase Assessment Model

Some authors have advocated for the use of narrow-band rating scales for screening (e.g., DuPaul, 1992); however, such an approach may narrow the window of assessment too early in the assessment process. For example, the symptoms of ADHD, particularly the inattentive symptoms, are notoriously nonspecific, and may indicate a problem relating to any number of factors including internalizing problems or adjustment difficulties. Indeed, problems paying attention in class can be associated with anxiety, depression, or something more transitory (e.g., a parent moving out of the house). Even if a referral for ADHD is valid, the degree of comorbidity with the disruptive behavior disorders is sufficient to justify a broader screening to include such symptoms. Even if one were to use a rating scale that included the symptoms of ODD and CD in addition to ADHD, internalizing problems may often present themselves in the form of inattention and irritability, and may be confused with an externalizing problem. So, the assessment window could still be considered too narrow. A clear advantage of narrow-band scales is that they are significantly shorter than more comprehensive broad-band measures. However, in the case of individual screening, as opposed to systemwide screening, teachers typically will not be asked to complete screening measures for a large number of students at any given time. Thus, the overall time commitment would seem reasonable.

Whether using a narrow-band or a broad-band rating scale for screening, some evaluators will forego the use of standardized scores and instead count the number of items on a DSM-based scale considered to be present to determine if the number of symptoms meets the symptom count criterion for the disorder in question. In the case of ADHD-Inattentive type, for example, if six of the nine inattentive symptoms were rated as "often" or "very often," that might be considered a positive screen. This approach is not recommended, because the overwhelming majority of the data used to develop the cutoffs for the DSM-IV were collected on Caucasian school-aged boys (Lahey, Applegate, McBurnett et al., 1994; Lahey et al., 1994). Thus, the generic DSM symptom cutoff criteria may underestimate or overestimate the severity of the problem depending on the age, gender, and race and ethnicity of the child in question (e.g., Reid, Casat, Norton, Anastopoulos, & Temple, 2001).

When making any kind of binary decision, it should be expected that errors will be made, and so steps must be taken to minimize them by adjusting decision criteria in the appropriate direction based on the purpose and importance of the decision. In the screening stage of assessment, Type I errors (false positives) are more acceptable than Type II errors (false negatives). To ensure that all students who may require further assessment do advance to the next assessment stage, we must accept that some students not needing further assessment will also advance to be further assessed. Therefore, care must be taken to use normative data that is appropriate for the child being assessed, and that liberal cutoffs for screening are employed. It is recommended that, when available, normative data be used that are specific to the age, gender, and race and ethnicity of the child being assessed.

Stage II. Multi-Method Assessment of ADHD and Disruptive Behavior Disorders

For students who are considered to have met screening criteria for externalizing problems, a more comprehensive evaluation is necessary to: (a) determine the characteristics and pervasiveness of the problem; (b) gather further information concerning factors in the environment that maintain the behaviors of concern; and (c) identify what factors in the environment may be brought to bear to address the behaviors of concern and to improve overall child functioning. Although we do not specifically address the assessment of psychiatric problems outside of ADHD and the disruptive behavior disorders here, as noted earlier, a myriad of disorders may co-occur with these disorders and should be assessed where appropriate.

Several assessment methods are employed in this phase of assessment. Typically, a multi-method assessment battery consists of a review of school records, interviews with adults who know the child, a series of broad-band and narrow-band rating scales completed by multiple informants, and direct observations of the child. This multi-method assessment process may seem daunting at first, given all the various forms of data that must be gathered, scored, and interpreted. However, this stage is best conceptualized as an iterative process, wherein one wave of data collection informs the next. We have suggested the use of broad-band rating scales in the screening stage. In addition to the advantages discussed earlier, a key benefit of administering broad-band ratings scales first, is that useful information is provided toward selection of narrow-band rating scales, and can help direct the focus of clinical interviews with parents, teachers and children (cf., McConaughy, 2005. Likewise, anecdotal (informal) observations and interviews can inform the selection of available systematic direct observation codes, or construction of specialized observation codes (Hintze, Volpe, & Shapiro, 2008; Volpe, DiPerna, Hintze, & Shapiro, 2005).

Before discussing specific measures, it is important to discuss what exactly needs to be measured in this stage of assessment in order to address the key questions concerning diagnosis and treatment planning. With regard to diagnosis, information must be gathered concerning not only the frequency or severity of the symptoms of the disorders in question, but also other diagnostic criteria such as age of onset, duration of problems, and functional impairment. It is equally important to assess the degree to which other factors (e.g., medical, environmental) might be responsible for the problems of interest. With regard to treatment planning, the multimethod assessment can be useful in providing information for the selection of target behaviors for intervention efforts, and assessing the viability of various treatment options. These issues are discussed in more detail under Stage IV (Treatment Plan Development).

REVIEW OF SCHOOL RECORDS

Examining a student's school records can provide useful information regardingthe student's level of functioning, and the onset of externalizing problems (DuPaul & Stoner, 2003). Such records provide archival information with regard to student grades, access to services, attendance, tardiness, and office referrals for behavior problems. Report cards often are used by teachers to communicate social, emotional, and behavior difficulties demonstrated by the child in the classroom and other school settings. All of this information can be useful in tracking the onset and trajectory of a student's academic, social, and behavior problems. The School Archival Records Search (SARS: Walker, Block-Pedego, Todis, & Severson, 1991) is one tool that can be useful in organizing information obtained from school records, and also might serve as a template forkey indicators to include (e.g., achievement test scores, number of grade retentions, disciplinary contacts, academic and behavioral referrals).

TEACHER INTERVIEW

Teachers are valuable sources of information concerning child functioning in the school setting, and are the most common source of referrals for externalizing problems. Teachers have the opportunity to observe students under a variety of conditions, and are able to make comparisons between students in the same age range. If the student has been referred for a comprehensive evaluation, it is likely that the teacher already has some experience attempting to

manage the target child's behavior problems alone, or with the help of a consultant.

It is assumed that at this stage of assessment, a brief teacher interview (e.g., Bergan & Kratochwill, 1990) already has been performed, and a broad-band teacher rating scale has been administered and scored. Therefore, prior to the clinical teacher interview, the assessor has some idea of the concerns that should receive the greatest attention. The Semistructured Teacher Interview (STI; see McConaughy, 2005) can be a useful tool for gathering important information from teachers. The STI covers the following content areas: (a) concerns about the child; (b) school behavior problems; (c) academic performance; (d) teaching strategies; (e) school interventions for behavior problems; and (f) special help/services. The STI provides a useful structure for directing interviews with teachers, andit offers sufficient flexibility so that interviews are not mechanical. The format covers most of the areas one would want to address in a teacher interview regarding the identification of behaviors of particular concern, factors in the environment that might maintain the problem, the identification of areas of concern with regard to academic skills and achievement, and the acceptability of relevant interventions and school services. One area that is not addressed explicitly in the STI is student social functioning. Later, we will discuss other methods of obtaining such information. However, the teacher interview is an ideal mechanism for obtaining information about specific social issues the student may be experiencing in the school setting. Hence, supplementing the STI with additional questions about student social functioning is recommended.

PARENT INTERVIEW

Parent interviews are among the most valuable sources of information in the assessment of externalizing problems. It is important to assess parent concerns about child functioning, and determine priorities with regard to which problems are of greatest concern. In addition, parents can provide information about family history of externalizing and internalizing problems, the child's developmental and medical history, including previous attempts to address the problems of concern, the child's responsibilities at home, how parents resolve conflicts in the home, and the child's history withthe problem behaviors of interest. The parent can provide information concerning the presence and severity of symptoms, the onset and duration of problem behaviors, and the child's level of functional impairment, all of which are necessary for a DSM-IV diagnosis.

Fully structured clinical interviews are available to aid in diagnosis, and closely follow the diagnostic criteria of the DSM-IV. Such measures were initially designed for epidemiological research studies, to enable administration by extensively trained lay interviewers as a cost saving measure. The Diagnostic Interview Schedule for Children-Version IV (DISC-IV; Shaffer, Fisher, Lucas, Dulcan, & Schwab-Stone, 2000) is a classic example of a fully structured parent interview, and a youth version is available for interviewing children between 6 and 17 years old. No clinical judgment is required to administer the DISC-IV; the interviewer reads from a script and the informant's responses dictate which questions will be asked. A computer version is available that generates a report summarizing the interview. Although structured interviews have strong psychometric properties, and have been used in school settings, extensive training is required, and each interview may take between one and two hours to administer. Thus, these interviews may not be practical for most school-based practitioners. Furthermore, they focus on diagnostic criteria, and do not provide information relating to the function of problem behaviors.

In contrast, several semistructured interviews are available for interviewing parents. These formats can take less time to administer than structured interviews, and offer greater flexibility. Semistructured parent interviews will be most efficient if information is gathered prior to the interview date. Most schools and clinics have standard parent information forms that are designed to gather information concerning the child's home situation, and his or her family, medical, and developmental history. A good example of a parent information form is provided by McConaughy (2005). Such a form typically is sent out with a cover letter and broad-band rating scales. Reviewing this information prior to the interview can help make the best use of the limited time available for interviewing. Two inexpensive options are the Semistructured Parent Interview (SPI) and the Kiddie Schedule for Affective Disorders or Schizophrenia (K-SADS; Puig-Antich & Chambers, 1978). The SPI is available in McConaughy (2005), and users can copy the form for their own use. The interview is designed to assess (a) parent concerns about the child, (b) the presence and severity of emotional and behavior problems, and environmental factors that may be maintaining the problems, (c) social functioning, (d) school functioning, (e) use of special help and school services, (f) medical and developmental history, and (g) home environment.

The SPI provides a convenient format to guide a parent interview, and is useful for gathering information relevant to diagnosis and treatment planning. A version of the K-SADS, the Kiddie SADS-Present and Lifetime Version (K-SADS-PL; Kaufman, Birmaher, Brent, Rao & Ryan, 1996) currently is available online as a downloadable pdf file (www. wpic.pitt.edu/ksads/default.htm). There are several other versions of the K-SADS (for a review see Ambrosini, 2000). The K-SADS-PL was designed to be administered to both parents and children, and data are used along with other information to achieve summary ratings for each category. In addition to externalizing behavior disorders, a wide array of childhood disorders is assessed with the K-SADS-PL. The K-SADS-PL can take as long as 2.5 hours to administer to both informants when the child is experiencing many problems and, like the DISC-IV, training is required before one should administer the interview (Kaufman & Schweder, 2003).

BEHAVIOR RATING SCALES

A wide array of well validated broad-band and narrow-band behavior rating scales is available to assess domains of interest in the assessment of ADHD and the disruptive behavior disorders. Although at this point in the assessment the practitioner should already have administered a broad-band teacher rating scale for screening, at this stage it is recommended to expand the broad-band assessment by collecting ratings from multiple informants (e.g. additional teachers, one or both parents, child). Examples of broad-band rating scales available for parents can be found in Table 13.5. Ratings from multiple informants may be compared to examine patterns of problem areas indicated by each informant. Consistencies of problem areas across informants clearly indicate areas of concern. However, it is not unexpected to find relatively low agreement between types of raters such as parents and teachers. Such differences may be explained by the different perspectives of informants, or may reflect differences in the child's behavior across settings (Achenbach, McConaughy, & Howell, 1987). Results from broad-band assessments can aid in the selection of appropriate narrow-band measures, which are designed to offer a more detailed analysis of a more restricted set of related constructs than are the broad-band measures.

Typically, narrow-band rating scales have been used to obtain detailed information from multiple informants concerning childhood symptomatology, and social and academic functioning. To select appropriate narrow-band rating scales, one must consider the domains of interest, the informants of interest, child characteristics, and the available psychometric properties for the relevant instruments. Table 13.6 was designed to assist in this decision-making process, but practitioners also should examine technical manuals closely, and should carefully consider each case individually, as opposed to repeatedly using a default battery of rating scales.

A detailed review of relevant rating scales is beyond the scope of this chapter (see Angello et al. 2003 and Pelham, Fabiano, & Massetti, 2005 for reviews of a wide array of relevant rating scales), but Tables 13.5 and 13.6 provide a summary of some of the more commonly used rating scales to assess externalizing problems. Notice that these instruments vary considerably with regard to the number of constructs they have been designed to assess. For example, the 18-item ADHD Rating Scale-IV (DuPaul, Power, Anastopoulos, & Reid, 1998) was designed to measure only the DSM-IV symptoms of ADHD (inattention, hyperactivity/impulsivity), while the 45-item (parent) and 41-item (teacher) short forms of the Conners–Third Edition (Conners, 2008) assess a much wider selection of domains (inattention, hyperactivity/impulsivity, learning problems, executive functioning, aggression, and peer relations). Another instrument worth mentioning is the Impairment Rating Scale (IRS; Fabiano et al., 2006) which is a rating scale designed to obtain information from parents and teachers concerning child impairment across several domains. Using the IRS, parents rate the severity of problems and the need for treatment in the following domains: (a) relationships with peers, (b) relationships with siblings, (c) relationships with parents, (d) academic progress, (e) self-esteem, (f) the child's influence on family functioning, and (g) overall impairment. Teachers are asked to rate the severity of problems and the need for treatment in the following domains: (a) relationships with peers, (b) relationship with the teacher, (c) academic progress, (d) self-esteem, (e) the child's influence on classroom functioning, and (f) overall impairment. The instrument and normative data are available online for free at http://ccf.buffalo.edu/resources.php. One study (Fabiano et al., 2006) provides encouraging findings on the psychometric properties of the IRS, and the measure provides much more detailed information than global impairment instruments such as the Children's Global Assessment Scale (Setterberg, Bird, & Gould, 1992) and the Columbia Impairment Scale (Bird et al., 1993). Furthermore, the IRS is less costly

than these measures, which were designed to be completed by practitioners as opposed to parents and teachers. Other informant rating scales that may be useful for measuring impairment are the Academic Competence Evaluation Scale (DiPerna & Elliott, 2000), the Academic Problems Rating Scale (APRS; DuPaul, Rapport, & Perriello, 1991), the Social Skills Rating System (Gresham & Elliott, 1990, 2008), the Teacher Assessment of Social Behavior (Cassidy & Asher, 1992), and the Walker–McConnell Scale of Social Adjustment (Walker & McConnell, 1988).

SYSTEMATIC DIRECT OBSERVATION

Systematic direct observation (SDO) of student behavior in school settings is an essential component of a multimodal assessment in the diagnosis of ADHD and ODD. However, given the relatively low frequency and duration of aggressive and delinquent behavior in school settings, other assessment methods may be more appropriate for assessments of CD. SDO is a direct method of assessment that is less subject to the bias inherent in informant reports (e.g., Abikoff, Courtney, Pelham, & Koplewicz, 1993; Barkley, 1998). Therefore, SDO is useful in the verification of problems reported by adults. In addition, SDO is an invaluable tool in conducting functional behavioral assessments. Unlike rating scales that ask informants to make summary judgments with regard to the frequency or severity of child behavior, SDO quantifies relatively small samples of behavior, so these instruments are quite sensitive to environmental factors present at any given time. In a traditional approach to assessment wherein one is attempting to measure a relatively stable construct, fluctuations in scores across observations would be viewed as error—but in a functional approach, such fluctuations indeed are the unit of analysis. That is, in functional assessment, one attempts to correlate changes in environmental conditions with changes in behavior (e.g., changes in disruptive classroom behavior with the difficulty of the task assigned to the student). In Table 13.7, a review of general distinctions among various SDO coding schemes is presented, to assist in understanding available options.

SDO has a high degree of face validity, since behaviors are operationally defined and recorded as they occur. However, Merrell (1999) has listed the following six threats to the validity of data obtained via SDO: (a) poorly defined behavior categories; (b) low inter-observer reliability; (c) observee reactivity; (d) situational specificity of target behaviors;

Table 13.5   Example broad-band behavior rating scales

Measure	Scales/Subscales Used	Informant	Comments
Behavior Assessment System for Children, 2nd Ed. (BASC – 2) www.pearsonassessments.com	Primary Scales *Adaptive Skills:* Activities of Daily Living, Functional Communication; *Behavioral Symptoms Index:* Adaptability, Conduct Disorder, Social Skills; *Externalizing Problems:* Attention Problems, Atypicality, Aggression, Hyperactivity, Leadership; *InternalizingProblems:* Anxiety, Depression, Withdrawal; *School Problems:* Learning Problems, Somatization (Study Skills) Optional Scales Anger Control, Bullying, Developmental Social Disorders, Emotional Self-Control, Executive Functioning, Negative Emotionality, Resiliency	Parent Teacher Self (ages 6–25 years)	• Efficient, particularly effective for assessing externalizing behavior problems • Normed using two populations: (1) a general population sample of children and adolescents (N = > 3400); (2) a clinical norm sample of children and adolescents diagnosed with emotional, behavioral, or physical problems (N = 1462) • Moderate inter-rater reliability; moderate to high test-retest reliability; high internal consistency with teacher rating scales; lower reliability with parent rating scales • Adequate construct validity for internalizing and externalizing scales • Satisfactory criterion-related validity • High convergent validity when compared to related assessment tools (CRS-R, CBCL, BASC)
Child Behavior Checklist (CBCL) www.ASEBA.org	Internalizing Problems Anxious/Depressed, Withdrawn, Somatic Complaints Externalizing Problems Delinquent Behavior, Aggressive Behavior Total Problems Attention Problems, Social Problems, Thought Problems	Parent Teacher Self (ages 11–18 years)	• Normed using a racially and socioeconomically diverse sample of American parents (N > 1300) • High test-retest reliability; moderate to high internal consistency reliability • Moderate to high construct and criterion-related validity

Table 13.5 (Cont'd) Example broad-band behavior rating scales

Conners 3rd Edition *www.mhs.com*	*Long and Short Form:* <u>Conners Scales:</u> Inattentive; Aggression; Hyperactive/Impulsive; Peer Relations[2]; Executive Functioning[2]; Learning Problems; Family Relations[3]; <u>Validity Sales:</u> Positive & Negative Impression; Inconsistency Index *Long Form:*<u>DSM-IV Symptom Subscales):</u> ADHD (Inattentive, Hyperactivity-Impulsive); Conduct Disorder, Oppositional Deviant Disorder <u>Conners 3:</u> Global Index; ADHD Index; <u>Screener/Impairment/Critical Items:</u> Anxiety, Depression, Schoolwork/Grades, Friendships/ Relationships, Home Life[1] [1] *Only for Parent Rating Scale;* [2] *Excluded on Self-Report* [3] *Only for Self-Report*	Parent Teacher Self (ages 8–18 years)	• Long version requires more time to administer, yet corresponds better with DSM-IV criteria. • Shorter version is best for repeated administrations • Normed using a large sample of American children (N > 6000) • High internal reliability; subscales enjoy high construct validity • Scale often used for the assessment of ADHD, but can also be used for screening, research, treatment and clinical diagnosis of conduct problems, cognitive problems, anxiety problems, social problems
Child Symptom Inventory–4 (CSI–4) *www.checkmateplus.com*	<u>Parent, Teacher and Youth Rating Scales screen</u> <u>for the following disorders:</u> Attention Deficit/Hyperactivity, Oppositional Defiant, Conduct, Generalized Anxiety, Schizophrenia, Major Depressive, Dysthymic Disorder, Autism Specturm, Asperger's, Social Phobia, Obsessive Compulsive, Pervasive Developmental, Vocal Tics, Motor Tics	Parent Teacher Self (ages 12–18 years)	• Normed using a sample of children attending public elementary schools (N = 551) • Moderate to high test-retest reliability; high internal consistency reliability • Moderate to high sensitivity; moderate to high specificity for most disorders • High convergent validity with other behavior rating scales • Moderate criterion validity

Table 13.6 Narrowband behavior rating scales

Measure	Scales/Subscales Used	Informant	Comments
ADHD Symptom Rating Scale *www.parinc.com*	Inattentive; Hyperactivity-Impulsive	Parent Teacher	Normed on a large sample of US children (N = 2,800), stratified by age, gender, ethnicity, and geographic region. High reliability and validity Requires 10–15 minutes for administration
ADHD Rating Scale IV *www.guilford.com*	Inattentive; Hyperactivity; Impulsivity	Parent Teacher Clinician	Normed using large sample Good internal consistencies Requires 10 minutes for completion
Conners 3rd Edition ADHD Index *www.mhs.com*	Inattentive; Hyperactivity-Impulsive	Parent Teacher Self (ages 8–18 years)	Included in full Conners 3rd Edition test pack Available in Spanish Requires 5–10 minutes for completion Efficient for screening large groups of children

(e) inappropriate code selection; and (f) observer bias. These threats may be minimized through the careful selection of instruments, and adequate training in their use. A special issue of *School Psychology Review* (Volpe & McConaughy, 2005) provides a wealth of information concerning SDO that should aid in its selection and appropriate use. Included in the miniseries are reviews of a wide variety of coding schemes designed for use in classrooms (Volpe, DiPerna, Hintze, & Shapiro, 2005), on playgrounds (Leff & Lakin, 2005), and in testing and interview situations (McConaughy, 2005). In addition, the miniseries includes an article (Hintze, 2005) that provides useful information to aid in the evaluation of the psychometric properties of various coding schemes. In addition to the threats delineated by Merrell, one must also consider the number of observations required to obtain a reliable estimate of behavior. Although few studies have investigated this issue, it seems clear that the practice of performing

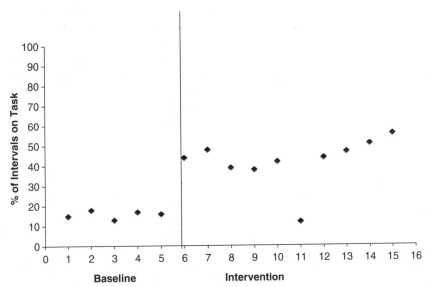

Fig. 13.2 Example Case Study Using SDO to Evaluate Behavioral Response

Case Study: Jack

Over the course of 5 days, Jack's on-task behavior was observed and recorded during language arts class to establish baseline. SDO served as the assessment method, with procedures involving momentary time sampling. On Day 6, Jack began a self-monitoring intervention designed to increase on task behavior. Data points collected were as follows:

Baseline – 15, 18, 13, 17, 16

Intervention – 44, 48, 39, 38, 42, 12, 44, 47, 51, 56

Table 13.7 Summary of options for Systematic Direct Observation Coding Procedures

Type of Procedure	Use when...
Event-Based Recording (Direct recording of each behavior occurrence)	
Frequency – a count of the number of times the target behavior occurs	... the target behavior has a clear beginning and end.
Duration – duration of behavior occurrence	... measurement of elapsed time is of interest.
Latency – time elapsed between signal and response to the signal	... measurement of elapsed time is of interest.
Time-Based Recording (Approximations of behavior occurrence given recording of behavior during specific intervals throughout the observation period)	
Whole Interval – record if behavior occurs throughout the entire duration of an observation interval	... the target behavior is continuous.
Partial Interval – record if behavior occurs at any point within the observation interval	... the target behavior is low-frequency yet lengthy
Momentary Time Sampling – record only if behavior occurs at the end of the observation interval	... several target behaviors are of simultaneous interest and/or peer comparisons are desired.

Adapted from Chafouleas, Riley-Tillman, & Sugai (2007).

one or two observations is not sufficient to obtain a reliable estimate of student behavior (see Hintze & Matthews, 2004; Volpe, McConaughy, & Hintze, 2009).

To verify the extent of off-task and disruptive behaviors in relation to the contextual environment, it is recommended to collect several observations on the target student, in addition to that of a peer. Several methods can be employed. Using the ADHD School Observation Code (Gadow, Sprafkin, & Nolan, 1996) the target child and comparison children are observed in alternating 1-minute segments (four 15-second intervals). Alternatively, in the Direct Observation Form (DOF; McConaughy &

Achenbach, 2009), the target student and comparison children are observed in alternating 10-minute sessions. Using either method provides an estimate of the target student's behavior, and that of one or more peers that can be compared, to provide information concerning just how deviant the target child's behavior is compared to typical peers—ideally of the same age, gender, race and ethnicity.

Stage III. Interpreting Results

In this stage of the assessment model, data gathered during the multi-method assessment is interpreted to determine if one or more of the externalizing disorders (ADHD, ODD, CD) is present, or if some other problem or set of problems better explains the referral concern. The following questions must be addressed: (a) Does the child meet the symptom criteria for one or more disorder? (b) What is the trajectory of symptomatology over time?, (c) Is the child significantly impaired? (d) Are other factors present that could explain the problem behaviors? and (e) Does the child qualify for special services?

SYMPTOM CRITERIA

Rating scales and interviews can provide data concerning whether a child exhibits a sufficient number of symptoms to qualify for ADHD and/or one of the disruptive behavior disorders. If one were to take a pure DSM, or symptom-count approach, one would review responses to interviews and rating scales at the item level, and determine the presence or absence of each DSM symptom. If the number of symptoms present meets the criterion for a particular disorder, then the symptom criterion would be met. For example, the presence of four or more symptoms is required for a diagnosis of ODD. However, as we noted earlier, a strict symptom-count approach is not recommended, as it does not take into account child demographic characteristics such as age and gender. Therefore, it is advisable to take a normative approach, wherein raw scores are converted into standardized scores such as T-scores. Typically, a T-score ≥ 70 (2 standard deviations above the mean) based on normative data for age and gender could be employed to satisfy the symptom criterion. T-scores between 65 and 70 (between 1.5 and 2 standard deviations) typically demarcate the borderline range.

However, one potential problem in a normative approach arises when the demographic characteristics of the child are not adequately represented in the standardization sample of the measures used in the assessment. Rating scales commonly used for the

Table 13.8   Practical resources on functional behavior assessment in schools

Cipani, E. & Schock, K. (2007). *Functional Behavioral Assessment, Diagnosis, and Treatment: A Complete System for Education and Mental Health Settings.* New York: Springer Publishing Company.

Crone, D. & Horner, R.H. (2003). *Building Positive Behavior Support Systems in Schools: Functional Behavioral Assessment.* New York: The Guilford Press.

McDougal, J.L., Chafouleas, S.M., & Waterman, B. (2006). *Functional Behavioral Assessment and Intervention in Schools: A Practitioner's Guide – Grades 1-8.* Champaign, IL: Research Press.

O'Neill, R.E., Horner, R.H., Albin, R.W., Storey, K., & Sprague, J.R. (1997). *Functional Assessment and Program Development for Problem Behavior: A Practical Handbook.* Pacific Grove, CA: Brooks/Cole Publishing Company.

Umbreit, J., Ferro, J., Liaupsin, C.J., & Lane, K.L. (2006). *Functional Behavioral Assessment and Function-Based Intervention: An Effective, Practical Approach.* Upper Saddle River, NJ: Prentice Hall.

Watson, T.S. & Steege, M.W. (2003). *Conducting School-Based Functional Behavioral Assessments: A Practitioner's Guide.* New York: The Guilford Press.

assessment of ADHD and the disruptive behavior disorders typically offer separate normative data for males and females, for several age ranges. However, to our knowledge, no scales offer separate normative data for different races or ethnicities. This is likely due to the expense involved in gathering such comprehensive standardization data. Nevertheless, collapsing standardization data across race and ethnic groups may underestimate or overestimate the severity of problems for certain groups of children. Thus, far more research in this area is needed. However, several studies have indicated that ratings of ADHD and aggression are higher for African American children than for Whites and Hispanics, although these differences are partially explained by differences in socioeconomic status (e.g., Reid, Casat, Norton, Anastopoulos, & Temple, 2001; DuPaul, Power et al., 1998; Reid et al., 1998).

AGE OF ONSET AND THE TRAJECTORY OF SYMPTOMATOLOGY

The ages at which symptoms first appear have important implications in the classification of both ADHD and CD. Typically, such information

is available via parent interview, but also may be obtained through a careful review of school records. With regard to ADHD, to meet diagnostic criteria, some of the symptoms must have caused impairment before the age of 7 years. However, this criterion is controversial, as there appears to be little difference between children meeting this age of onsetcriterion and those who do not (see Barkley & Biederman, 1997). In the diagnosis of CD, the age at which symptoms first occur is used to classify the child into either the child-onset type (at least one symptom present before the age of 10 years) or the adolescent-onset (no symptoms present before the age of 10). As noted earlier, the child-onset type is considered more severe and persistent than the adolescent-onset type.

Information concerning the duration of symptoms typically is obtained via parent interview, but additional information can be obtained from a teacher interview, and a review of school records. All three of the disorders being discussed require that at least some symptoms be present for atleast 6months, although the number of symptoms necessary to satisfy this criterion differs for each disorder. These duration criteria are consistent with other DSM disorders. Although the utility of duration criteria lacks empirical support, they likely reduce the proportion of false positive that would be associated with more transitory problems.

IMPAIRMENT

All of the assessment measures and methods described above can provide useful information concerning the child's level of functional impairment. The question of impairment is perhaps the most central issue in the classification of psychopathology. That is, irrespective of a clear diagnosis, if the child demonstrates significant impairment, treatment is needed. Impairment considerations differ across the diagnostic categories of ADHD, ODD and CD. In the diagnosis of ADHD, some impairment should be demonstrated across two or more settings (e.g., school and home). For the disruptive behavior disorders, significant impairment need only be demonstrated in social, academic, and/or occupational functioning. The rating scales discussed earlier can provide a normative reference as to the level of impairment the child may be experiencing in academic and social domains, and direct measures of academic performance also can be useful in this regard. Furthermore, SDO across multiple settings (e.g., classroom, cafeteria, playground), also can be used to quantify the degree of impairment. Here, peers may be observed for comparison purposes (e.g., the number of positive social exchanges exhibited by the target child compared to one or more peers of the same age, gender, and ethnicity).

ALTERNATIVE EXPLANATIONS FOR PROBLEM BEHAVIORS

Data gathered from the multi-method assessment must be reviewed against DSM guidelines to make a differential diagnosis, and to rule out alternative explanations for the problem behaviors. The evaluator should pay close attention to the rule-out criteria specific to each disorder. In addition, other factors should be examined that may contribute to child behavior problems. Students with learning problems may demonstrate disruptive behavior when asked to perform tasks that are associated with frustration (DuPaul & Stoner, 2003). Such behaviors may be limited to inattention and overactivity, or may include refusal to perform certain tasks or other, more severe interfering behaviors that can result in removal from the classroom. Also, as suggested above, adjustment difficulties also may be lead to ADHD symptoms (DuPaul & Stoner, 2003), or more severe behavioral symptoms such as oppositional behavior or delinquency.

One issue that emerges frequently in this stage of assessment is low agreement across informants (Achenbach, McConaughy, & Howell, 1987). As noted earlier, such differences may relate to differences in the perceptions of various informants, differences in the observation of behavior, or may indeed represent true differences in child functioning across settings. In cases where informants disagree on the frequency and severity of symptoms (particularly in regard to ADHD and ODD symptoms), this may be indicative of poor behavior management in the setting where ratings are higher. Such situations necessitate an assessment of the behavior management practices in place, and the relationship the child has with the adults in those settings.

In taking a medical history, it is useful to determine what medications may currently be prescribed, and to investigate any possible sideeffects with regard to mood and behavior. There is some evidence that medications prescribed for seizure disorders and for asthma may have an impact on the symptoms of ADHD, and lead to increased levels of irritability (see Barkley, 2006). Parents also should be asked whether their child experiences sleep disturbance. Many children with ADHD experience problems falling asleep and staying asleep (Gruber, Sadeh, & Raviv, 2000), and for children with ODD,

there may be conflict with parents around bedtime that also can impact sleep (see Corkum, Moldofsky, Hogg-Johnson, Humphries, & Tannock, 1999). Although it is unclear whether lack of sleep leads to behavior problems, there does appear to be an association between sleep and externalizing symptoms in the school setting (Aronen, Paavonen, Fjallberg, Soininen, & Torronen, 2000).

Whether or not students meet full DSM criteria for ADHD or one of the disruptive behavior disorders, they still may qualify for special services according to the Individuals with Disabilities Education Improvement Act (IDEA, 2004), or Section 504 of the Rehabilitation Act of 1973. These criteria should be reviewed carefully to determine how appropriate accommodations can be provided.

Stage IV. Designing the Treatment Plan

Irrespective of whether the student in question meets diagnostic criteria for an externalizing behavior disorder, or qualifies for special education services, students who have met initial screening criteria will likely require some kind of intervention. It is beyond the scope of this chapter to review specific interventions for students with externalizing behaviors. Rather, we offer here some basic considerations for designing optimal treatment plans. Questions to be addressed in this stage of assessment include: (a) How severe are the problems of interest? (b) What are the targets for intervention? and (c) What available resources will best address these problems?

SEVERITY

The severity of the externalizing problems discussed in this chapter varies widely, andcan be conceptualized several ways. First, for students meeting diagnostic criteria for one of the DSM disorders, the severity of problems can range from borderline to severe. For example, in the DSM-IV, the severity of CD is indicated by the number of symptoms and the degree to which they harm others. The degree of impairment is another important indicator (APA, 2000). Second, the disorders discussed here can be conceptualized as falling along a continuum of severity from ADHD to CD, with CD being the most severe. Third, the co-occurrence of externalizing and learning disorders is an additional consideration. For example, the presence of ADHD in children in children with ODD and CD is associated with more severe and persistent aggressive behaviors, and higher levels of peer rejection (Abikoff & Klein, 1992).

Often, the first line of intervention for school psychologists working with children with externalizing behaviors involves designing interventions wherein antecedent conditions are manipulated, or desired behaviors are reinforced. Functional assessment data gathered via interviews with adults, or via direct observation, can be useful in identifying the environmental variables maintaining problem behaviors (e.g., DuPaul & Stoner, 2003). However, as the severity of behavior problems increases, so does the need to involve a greater number of agents of change. For example, the more severe the case, the more appropriate it is to support referral to a physician for a prescription of medication. Although treatment of ADHD and ODD often involves ongoing collaboration across home, school, and medical settings, the treatment of conduct problems can be far more complicated, and should involve a system of care including multiple professionals and agencies working in collaboration with families (see Clarke & Clarke, 1996).

TARGETS FOR INTERVENTION

Targets for intervention can be identified through problem-identification interviews with adults who know the child well (e.g., Bergan & Kratochwill, 1990), but also can be identified via behavior rating scales and observation. Pelham et al. (2005) have argued that DSM symptoms are not socially valid targets for intervention. However, this may not hold true for all symptoms. Indeed, many individual symptoms seem to mirror common complaints made by parents and teachers in their referrals (e.g., difficulty organizing tasks, out of seat, blurts out answers, argues, bullies etc.). Nevertheless, a sole focus on DSM symptoms for target behaviors would be far too narrow, and areas of functional impairment and adaptive skills also should be considered (DuPaul & Stoner, 2003; Pelham et al., 2005). Identifying appropriate targets for intervention requires thoughtful analysis of which problem behaviors are having the greatest impact on the child's functioning across settings, and which specific skills deficits, if ameliorated, would have the greatest positive impact on child functioning.

AVAILABLE RESOURCES

Part of the process of designing any intervention is an assessment of resources that are available to address the problem. Students with clinically significant externalizing problems require ongoing intervention efforts, involving treatment resources beyond what can be provided in the school setting. It may be necessary to refer the child and his or her family to a physician, or one or more community agencies. Severe cases may require wraparound services that provide integrated systems of care. Although access of such services often originates outside of the school setting, there are several examples of effective school-based wraparound programs (Eber, Sugai, Smith, & Scott, 2002; Eber & Nelson, 1997). School psychologists are uniquely suited to evaluate such intervention efforts, given their training in research methods and measurement (e.g., Power, Atkins, Osborne, & Blum, 1994). Furthermore, school psychology training programs increasingly are focusing on interagency communication and collaboration (e.g., Power, DuPaul, & Shapiro, 2003)

Stage V. Evaluation of the Treatment Plan

Thus far, we have focused our presentation on content related to assessment with regard to screening and diagnostic stages, which certainly form an important piece in assessment of externalizing behavior deficits. That is, we need to first understand the degree to which a problem is present (problem identification) before we can move to analysis as to why the problem is occurring, and then how we might effectively intervene. However, within the problem-solving assessment framework that we have presented in this chapter, assessment only for screening or diagnosis does not comprehensively address our needs. Within a problem-solving assessment framework, data sources relevant to evaluation of student behavior also are needed in order to drive decisions about the effectiveness of our intervention efforts. One approach to assessment of the intervention plan involves use of summative (pre/post) data, to provide an overall evaluation of intervention effectiveness at the end of implementation. Another approach is to include data sources that can provide repeated information about behavior as the intervention is implemented. In this option, once our initial assessments have identified a problem, and a desired change in student behavior has been determined, then progress-monitoring data sources can be put in place to provide a complete assessment picture that informs decisions about behavioral response over time, such as in response to various intervention supports. In this section, we present an overview of various methods of behavior assessment, including discussion of strengths and limitations of each. In particular, we emphasize an approach to assessment of the intervention plan based on formative evaluation, so that data may be used throughout the intervention implementation phase to determine whether desired goals are being met, and/or if modifications to the current plan are needed. Thus, rather than waiting until the end to determine whether an intervention plan worked, we can be proactive in identifying features that require modification, such as intensity or dosage, to improve effectiveness.

SELECTING ASSESSMENT TOOLS

As has been previously reviewed in this chapter, a myriad of options exist with regard to available behavior assessment tools. However, methods of behavior assessment might be considered to fall under four broad categories that include direct observation, behavior rating scales, direct behavior rating, and extant data gleaned from permanent products. In this section, we discuss each of these broad categories in relation to use within assessment and evaluation of the treatment plan. We frame discussion of each category around four desirable characteristics of formative assessment tools that include defensibility, repeatability, efficiency, and flexibility. By *defensible*, we mean a body of evidence supporting the technical adequacy of an assessment method. *Repeatability* refers to the capacity for a method to be administered on a frequent basis, in order to result in a stream of data about behavior. *Efficiency* refers to the feasibility of the method for use in the intended setting, and includes considerations such as required time, materials, cost, and personnel. Finally, *flexibility* is defined as the ability to adapt and modify method instrumentation and procedures to match the assessment situation.

Although distinctions among direct observation instrumentation and procedures were alluded to earlier in this chapter, clarification becomes highly significant in this section, given the implications for progress monitoring. During the initial stages in assessment of externalizing behavior deficits, it can be helpful to conduct informal observation of student behavior to inform further directions. However, when multiple data points are collected (i.e., formative assessment) it becomes critical to standardize the direct observation procedures in order to obtain quantifiable data that can be used to evaluate change in behavior over time. The following characteristics distinguish SDO procedures: a) the purpose of the observation is to measure specific target behavior; b) those behaviors have been defined in measurable terms; c) data are collected under standardized procedures; d) time and place for observation have been selected a priori; and e) data are scored and summarized in a standardized fashion (Salvia & Ysseldyke, 2004).

As previously noted, SDO quantifies relatively small samples of behavior; thus, data are highly sensitive to environmental factors. This sensitivity is precisely what is desirable in formative assessment, and although some have argued that it establishes the defensibility of the method, others have advocated for the relevance and need to apply traditional psychometric approaches (e.g., reliability, validity) to SDO (see Silva, 1993 for a complete discussion). Regardless, such debate has resulted in relatively few psychometric investigations of the method. As noted previously, what is known is that interpretations of student behavior using SDO must include multiple (repeated) data points. Related to the discussion of sensitivity, the flexibility inherent in selecting instrumentation and procedures make SDO highly attractive as a formative behavior assessment method. That is, each characteristic (target behaviors, coding scheme) can be manipulated to create the best match for an assessment situation. Aside from controversy surrounding how to establish defensibility of SDO, the largest limitation of the method stems from questionable efficiency. Resources required to conduct SDO can include significant time and personnel, assuming that the majority of observations are completed by an external observer. Thus, although SDO provides a valuable source of formative data, if instrumentation and procedures cannot be developed which are feasible for use by the direct service provider (e.g. classroom teacher), widespread use of SDO may not be efficient, and might best be restricted to more intense assessments.

As discussed earlier, standardized, norm-referenced behavior rating scales can be useful tools for identifying profiles of strengths and weaknesses related to student behavior, both within an individual and, if available, in comparison to an appropriate reference group. Certainly, technical adequacy of the more widely used scales has been established to justify the defensibility of behavior rating scales (see Tables 13.5 and 13.6 for a brief review). Behavior rating scales generally cast a wider net about behavior over a longer period of time (typically several months) than systematic direct observation procedures, which are designed to record information about relatively few target behaviors during short observation intervals. Thus, behavior rating scales often are touted as providing an efficient way to obtain information about an individual. However, efficiency can be significantly reduced when behavior rating scales are repeatedly administered on a frequent basis. Thus, behavior rating scales might best be used in pre/post evaluation of intervention effectiveness, but can be burdensome in frequent formative assessment. Flexibility of behavior rating scales also is restricted, given that technical adequacy related to modified item content is largely unknown. However, there has been recent interest in understanding how specific items might be grouped to create abbreviated scales that would be defensibly and efficiently used in formative assessment. For example, Volpe, Gadow, Blom-Hoffman, and Feinberg (2009) recently proposed two methods of creating abbreviated rating scales by extracting items from existing instruments. Using items from a DSM-IV-based behavior rating scale, used in a medication titration procedure, these researchers found that 4-item scales created by selecting items with the highest factor loadings, or created by selecting items rated highest by teachers at baseline, performed comparably to the original 9-item scales in terms of reliability and treatment sensitivity. In summary, although behavior ratings scales are likely to be defensible and efficient for infrequent retrospective recording of behavior, in their commercially available form, restrictions related to flexibility and repeatability may limit use for progress-monitoring assessment purposes.

Another assessment method with potential in evaluating response is Direct Behavior Rating (DBR), a method that encompasses a unique expansion on behavior rating scales (Chafouleas, Riley-Tillman, & Christ, 2009; Christ, Riley-Tillman, & Chafouleas, 2009). Similar to indirect behavior rating scales, rating of behavior with DBR is conducted by a person familiar with the student. However, in DBR, rating is more direct, in that ratings are made using shorter time intervals than typically employed with traditional behavior rating scales. For example, whereas a typical rating scale may instruct a teacher to summarize student behavior over the past several weeks or months, DBR procedures require informants to rate behavior based on pre-identified, specific periods. For example, such ratings might occur immediately following hallway transition to assess the degree of disruptive behavior displayed, or might occur daily while monitoring a student's response to supports that attemptto increase positive social behaviors. A number of versions of DBR instrumentation (e.g., number and format of behavior targets) and procedures (e.g., length of observation period) have been studied to date, although certainly much more study is needed to fully evaluate the potential of this method (see Christ et al, 2009, for further review of

work related to the characteristics and distinctions of DBR method). An advantage of DBR over systematic direct observation relates to efficiency, in that it typically takes only a few seconds to complete a rating, which can usually be done by a person present in the setting (e.g., teacher). In addition, DBRs, like other informant ratings, allow for the assessment of behaviors that occur at a relatively low frequency (e.g., hitting or biting), which typically are not a good match for SDO, given the length of observation needed to obtain a reliable estimate of behavior. These characteristics define the broad method, yet it is important to acknowledge the flexible nature of DBR. That is, it has been proposed that a variety of options might be appropriate with regard to DBR instrumentation (e.g., What should the scale look like? How many items should be included?) and procedures (e.g., How often should ratings be completed? How long should the observation interval be?). However, investigations into the defensibility of DBR have occurred for a limited number of versions to date. Although such findings have been positive, much more work is needed to provide thorough evaluation of technical adequacy. In addition, Chafouleas and colleagues (Chafouleas, Riley-Tillman, & Christ, 2009; Christ, Riley-Tillman, & Chafouleas, 2009) have been systematically investigating the defensibility of single-item DBR scales, with results to date demonstrating promise for use in formative assessment. In summary, DBR has been proposed as flexible, efficient, and repeatable for use in formative assessment, yet more research to firmly establish defensibility is needed.

Finally, we review characteristics of extant data gleaned from permanent products in relation to their use in progress monitoring assessment. As defined by Alberto and Troutman (2006), permanent products are "the tangible items or environmental effects that result from a behavior" (p. 62). Many permanent products of student behavior— e.g., academic (grades) and behavior(attendance, suspensions)—are collected on a frequent basis. Determining which data are available, and then organizing it in an efficient fashion, can be a daunting task. However, given that these data are recorded repeatedly and already exist, such sources can fill a valuable role in formative assessment, if the products are contextually relevant for the assessment situation. For example, extant data related to attendance does not inform intervention decisions if attendance is not a problem (and thus not an intervention target). However, data gleaned from a classwide behavior management system (e.g., token economy, self-monitoring sheets) could be highly relevant to formative evaluation of intervention supports. These data are flexible, in that implementation was based on contextual relevance for the specific setting; and data are efficient, assuming that the implementer has not posed concerns related to collection. Again, the biggest challenge relates to how informationcan be summarized to form an efficient stream of data. Perhaps the most commonly used permanent product related to student behavior in schools is the office discipline referral (ODR). Within positive behavior supports (www.pbis.org), ODRs comprise an important source of formative data regarding behavior of not only individual target students, but also schoolwide patterns of behavior (e.g., which behaviors are most evident? where and when are those behaviors most likely to occur?). In fact, researchers at the University of Oregon have created a web-based system for tracking ODRs (see www.swis.org), which is currently utilized by thousands of school across the country as part of the "data" in a schoolwide positive-behavior-supports framework. Although technical adequacy of ODRs has not been thoroughly investigated (Wright & Dusek, 1998), some investigations have supported validity of use in decision making about student behavior (see Irvin, Horner, Ingram, Todd, Sugai, Sampson, et al, 2006; Irvin, Tobin, Sprague, Sugai, & Vincent, 2004). However, it is important to note that extant data sources such as ODRs generally do not have a preventive or prosocial focus (i.e., receiving an ODR means that a significant rule infraction has occurred). Thus, although ODRs might be considered an important measure of social impact (Gresham, 2005), it is likely that less serious behavior, and sensitivity to small change in behavior, would not be captured in the data. In summary, forprogress-monitoring assessment purposes, extant data sources likely possess characteristics of repeatability, efficiency, and flexibility; yet, defensibility of many extant sources is relatively unknown.

EVALUATING BEHAVIORAL RESPONSE

As progress-monitoring data are collected, an essential feature of utility involves evaluation of behavioral response. In other words, how do we use the data to know if an intervention plan is effective toward reducing deviant behavior and/or increasing prosocial behavior? In discussing possible options for evaluating treatment effectiveness, Gresham (2005) has advocated use of a problem-solving approach, such as described within Response to Intervention (RTI) models. Within such an approach, assessment and evaluation of student performance between baseline (pre-intervention) and intervention phases occurs, to determine appropriate action with regard to behavioral response. Strategies for evaluation of behavioral response might be accomplished through a number of approaches. Two of those approaches presented by Gresham (2005) that are relevant for presentation in this chapter involve visual inspection, and quantitative indices for establishing reliable changes in behavior.

As noted by Gresham (2005), visual inspection involves an "interocular" rather than a statistical test of significance, with the underlying logic being that meaningful change should be easily noticeable through viewing of graphed data. Typical visual analysis strategies involve examination of (a) change in level, (b) immediacy of change, (c) change in trend, and (d) variability in data (Chafouleas, Riley-Tillman, & Sugai, 2007; Riley-Tillman & Burns, 2009). In Box 13.1, definitions and example calculations for each can be found. The relevance of each strategy is related to the purpose of the intervention, and the predicted change in target behavior. In addition, the interaction of each of these strategies must be considered. For example, increased variability in the outcome data can minimize the importance of a level change, whereas decreased variability might indicate a small level change to be important.

According to Riley-Tillman and Burns (2009), incorporating visual analysis strategies in the evaluation of behavioral response has two major advantages. First, visual analysis has an extensive history as the preferred method of analysis for single-case design research. As such, this method has been vetted through the review process, and strengths and weaknesses of the method are well understood. The second advantage is related to utility of visual analysis strategies in practice. Simply put, when examining a well-constructed line graph depicting student behavior over time, in response to intervention, visual analysis is a method that makes sense to experts and novices alike. However, as previously mentioned, use of visual analysis strategies isnot without limitations. Drawbacks of exclusive reliance on visual inspection also have been noted. For example, Gresham (2005) noted an absence of standards for determining whether behavior change is educationally significant, as well as concerns about potentially high Type I error rates and interpretation of autocorrelated time series data. Thus, increasing advocacy for use of quantitative methods for evaluation of response has appeared within the literature.

Box 13.1   Metrics for Interpretation of Behavioral Response

Visual Analysis: Examination of meaningful intervention effects through visual consideration of level, variability, and trend in data (see Figure 13.2).

Presentation: Baseline data evidence stable and consistent, responding that is lower than desirable (M = 15.8%). Following introduction of the intervention, Jack's on-task behavior improved (M = 42.1%). Intervention data evidence consistent, responding with a slight upward trend in a positive direction. Overall, data support meaningful improvement to Jack's on-task behavior following introduction to the intervention.

Absolute Level of Change: The difference between mean baseline and intervention scores.

Calculation: Compute the mean score during the baseline phase, and then in the intervention phase. The difference between the means is the absolute change.

42.1% – 26. 3% = 26.3%

Percentage Change: Comparing the mean level of baseline performance in the baseline to the mean level of performance in the intervention phase, through calculation of the percent of change across phases.

Calculation: Compute the mean score during the baseline phase, and then in the intervention phase. Subtract the intervention mean from the baseline mean, and then divide by the baseline mean.

(26.3% – 42.1%)/26.3% = 60%

Percentage of Non-Overlapping Data: An indication of the range of behavior in the intervention phase that is not included in the baseline phase.

Calculation: Identify the number of intervention data points that do not overlap with the baseline data points. Divide by the total number of intervention data points.

1 / 10 = .10 or 10%

Effect Size: A measure of the magnitude of the treatment effect.

Calculation: Although multiple options are available, Cohen's *d* offers a simple calculation and is often used in single subject research. Subtract the intervention mean from the baseline mean. Divide by the standard deviation, pooled across baseline and intervention phases:

$Mean_{intervention} - Mean_{baseline} = 42.1 - 15.8 = 26.3$

$Pooled\ SD_{baseline + intervention} = 16.0$

$ES = 26.3 / 16.0 = 1.64$

Reliable change index (RCI): A metric used to quantify reliable changes from baseline to intervention.

Calculation: Subtract the mean intervention score from the mean baseline score. Divide the difference by the standard error of difference between intervention and baseline scores. Note: An RCI of +1.96 (p<.05) is considered a reliable change in behavior.

$SE = SD / (\sqrt{N})$

$SE_{baseline} = 1.92 / (\sqrt{5}) = 1.92 / 2.2 = .87$

$SE_{intervention} = 11.88 / (\sqrt{10}) = 11.7 / 3.2 = 3.71$

Metrics for quantifying behavioral response have been proposed as a way to address the potential limitations of visual analysis strategies. Gresham (2005) described such metrics as evaluation of reliable changes in behavior, because the strategies allow demonstration that behavioral response should be attributed to the intervention, and not due to chance or extraneous factors. Gresham (2005) summarized the following five possible metrics for examining reliable change in behavior: (a) absolute levels of change, (b) percentage change from baseline, (c) percent of non-overlapping data, (d) effect size, and (e) reliable change indices. Continuing with the example provided above, definitions and calculation procedures for each of these metrics can be found in Box 13.1. It is important to note that limited empirical attention has been paid to evaluating use of these metrics within

the behavioral domain. Recent work initiated has suggested that some metrics may be more useful than others in the evaluation of students at risk for developing emotional or behavioral disorders. Specifically, in a study conducted by Cheney, Flower, and Templeton (2008), the five metrics were examined with regard to evaluation of student response to a large scale behavioral intervention called *Check, Connect, and Expect*. Results suggested that percent of non-overlapping data was not found to be useful due to ceiling effects, but that the other four metrics were potentially useful. Overall, these researchers concluded that percentage of change and effect size may be the most useful quantitative metrics toward understanding student response to behavioral intervention. However, when considering these options, it is also important to note that others have advocated social validity to be the ultimate determinant (see Gresham, 2005, 2007). That is, answering questions related to the social importance of the behavior change, such as whether teachers and parents perceive that the student's behavior now falls within the functional range, determines overall intervention effectiveness.

In conclusion, evaluation of behavioral response presumes that data are used to understand behavior change in response to intervention. The evaluation of quantitative behavioral response to intervention should involve the two-step process advocated by Horner and colleagues (2005). In this process, the first question to ask is whether the target behavior has changed, which can be accomplished through the techniques of visual analysis and reliable change metrics. An additional second question must be answered in order to be confident that observed change was a result of a particular intervention. To effectively answer this question, it is critical that a defensible single-case design has been implemented, to establish acceptable levels of experimental control. It is possible to identify whether this has occurred, if observed changes are consistent with changes predicted at the time of design selection. Further information regarding selection, implementation, and evaluation of single-case design in educational practice can be found in Riley-Tillman and Burns (2009).

Concluding Considerations in the Assessment of Externalizing Behavior Deficits

Once a child or adolescent is referred for evaluation, the first questions to be addressed are, "What is the problem?" and, "What are the goals of this assessment?" We acknowledge that the goals of assessment for school practitioners often include classification for special education placement. However, a key question also to be addressed is, "What can be done to solve the problem?" One key advantage of the model presented in this chapter, which was adapted from DuPaul (1992), is that it encompasses both the goals of assessment for classification, and the goals associated with a problem-solving approach (identifying and solving the problem). Another advantage is that the model provides a useful framework for organizing the myriad of tasks associated with providing a thorough assessment. The model takes a DSM approach to diagnosis, which can be viewed as both an advantage and a disadvantage. On the positive side, DSM-based categories are far more specific than special education service categories, and are widely recognized across service agencies, making them useful for between-agency communications. In addition, DSM categories may help to select appropriate interventions based on research findings involving the group or groups of interest, and are necessary for remuneration outside of the school setting. Finally, information gathered in a DSM-based assessment provides important information in the determination of eligibility for special education services. On the negative side, a DSM approach, as with any taxonomic approach, provides a label which can be stigmatizing, can perpetuate the view that the problem is centered within the child, and so may interfere with case conceptualizations that fully appreciate the environmental influences (DuPaul & Stoner, 2003).

A final concluding comment involves the importance of considering the increasing shift in focus of assessment toward promotion of prosocial skills and, thus, prevention and early intervention of behavior deficits. Our primary focus in this chapter was on assessment of individual students already referred for concerns about externalizing deficits. Although this approach has a long history within school, clinic, and research settings, such an approach can have restricted application within a school-based preventive framework designed to provide early identification of potential for difficulty, and implementation of effective intervention supports. Thus, it is important to also attend to the growing body of literature that has advocated assessment procedures to include universal screening of all students for behavioral difficulties (see Severson, Walker, Hope-Doolittle, Kratochwill, & Gresham, 2007). These screening data can be integrated into a multiple gating assessment approach, which may incorporate steps of the 5-phase assessment model. In conclusion, in this chapter, we have presented a framework for the assessment of externalizing behavior deficits which integrates traditional diagnostic practices, along with a problem-solving approach, in order to facilitate treatment planning and evaluation likely to be effective and usable in school-based settings.

Appendix A
Internet Resources on Externalizing Behavior Deficits

RESOURCE	BRIEF DESCRIPTION
GENERAL RESOURCES	
American Psychiatric Association http://www.psych.org/	The American Psychiatric Association offers an interactive website with information about common issues concerning mental health. Specifically, the site offers diagnostic criteria and treatment strategies. The American Psychiatric Association's website provides specific facts about ADHD.
American Psychological Association http://www.apa.org/	Like the American Psychiatric Association, the American Psychological Association hostsa site with a broad spectrum of information on a variety of mental health concerns. The page devoted to ADHD, however, offers a plethora of recent journal articles, news items, books, and video suggestions, as well as other resources in one centralized location.
National Institute of Mental Health at the National Institute of Health www.nih.gov; http://www.nimh.nih.gov http://www.nimh.nih.gov/health/topics/ child-and-adolescent-mental-health/index. shtml	A resource for addressing broad concerns regarding mental health, with a variety of topics covered concerning child and adolescent mental health.
Institute on Violence and Destructive Behavior (IVDB) www.uoregon.edu/~ivdb/	A resource for information on evidence-based interventions, taken from research and made accessible to parents, teachers, and related service providers among others, for use in applied settings. Also lists original research endeavors aimed at making schools healthier, safer and violence-free.
Technical Assistance Center on Social Emotional Intervention for Young Children (TACSEI) http://www.challengingbehavior.org	A resource of best practice research that promotes social competence for children with disabilities or at risk. Material targets decision makers, caregivers, and service providers.
ADHD-SPECIFC	
National Institute of Mental Health – Book on ADHD http://www.nimh.nih.gov/health/ publications/adhd/nimhadhdpub.pdf	A 49-page overview of ADHD available for download. Chapters cover such topics as symptoms, diagnosis, comorbid disorders, treatment options, and implications for home and family life.
ADHDInfo.com www.adhdinfo.com	A resource for gaining a broad understanding of the signs and symptoms of ADHD, as well as treatment options. Parents and school personnel can peruse articles such as "ADHD and Home Life" and "ADHD and School." Links to external resources send consumers to texts, magazines, and otherorganizations with more information on ADHD.
Children and Adults with Attention Deficit/Hyperactivity Disorder www. chadd.org	The website for a national nonprofit organization whosemission is providing information for, and advocating on behalf of, those affected by ADHD.
National Resource Center on AD/HD: A Program of CHADD http://www.help4adhd.org/	A division of CHADD that offers additional resources for parents, children, teachers, professionals, and others interested in learning more about ADHD.

Attention Deficit Disorder Association (ADDA) http://www.add.org/	The site compiled by ADDA includes information regarding adult and adolescent ADHD. There is a search engine to find local support groups or online support groups for parents or children living with ADHD. Resources such as a weekly blog, relevant news items, and information on ADHD conferences, make this site additionally helpful in lending support.
National Center for Girls and Women with AD/HD http://www.ncgiadd.org/	A site addressing gender issues in ADHD diagnosis and treatment.

CONDUCT DISORDER - SPECIFIC

Children's Mental Health Facts: Children and Adolescents with Conduct Disorder, National Mental Health Information Center at the Substance Abuse and Mental Health Services Administration http://mentalhealth.samhsa.gov	A resource accessible by all interested in gaining more information about the risks, symptoms, and treatments available for conduct disorder. Information is also available about resources in place to help families living with a child with conduct disorder, as well as details regarding what parents can do to help their child.
Conduct Disorder Fact Sheet, Mental Health America http://www.nmha.org/	A brief fact sheet devoted to covering the basics of conduct disorder. A search engine for therapists and support groups offer families options for local resources. A crisis line is also available for emergency information.
American Academy of Child and Adolescent Psychiatry http://www.aacap.org/cs/ODD.ResourceCenter	A site that features clinical resources and a section for frequently asked questions about ODD. Additional resources include books, video clips and links to research journals for those interested in gaining more information about ODD.

References

Abikoff, H. & Klein, R. G. (1992). Attention-deficit hyperactivity and conduct disorder: Comorbidity and implications for treatment. *Journal of Consulting and Clinical Psychology, 60,* 881–892.

Abikoff, H., Courtney, M., Pelham, W. E., & Koplewicz, H. S. (1993). Teachers' ratings of disruptive behaviors: The influence of halo effects. *Journal of Abnormal Child Psychology, 21,* 519–533.

Achenbach, T. M., & Edelbrock, C. S. (1978). The classification of child psychopathology: A review and analysis of empirical efforts. *Psychological Bulletin, 85,* 1275–1301.

Achenbach, T. M., McConaughy, S. H., & Howell, C. T. (1987). Child/adolescent behavioral and emotional problems: Implications of cross-informant correlations for situational specificity. *Psychological Bulletin, 101,* 213–232.

Alberto, P. A., & Troutman, A. C. (2006). *Applied Behavior Analysis for Teachers (7th Ed.).* Upper Saddle River, NJ: Prentice Hall.

Ambrosini, P. J., (2000). Historical development and present status of the Schedule for Affective Disorders and Schizophrenia for school-aged children (K-SADS). *Journal of the American Academy of Child and Adolescent Psychiatry, 39,* 49–58.

American Psychiatric Association (1968). *Diagnostic and statistical manual of mental disorders* (2nd ed.). Washington, DC: Author.

American Psychiatric Association (1980). *Diagnostic and statistical manual of mental disorders* (3rd ed.). Washington, DC: Author.

American Psychiatric Association. (2000). *Diagnostic and Statistical Manual of Mental Disorders* (4th ed. Text Revision). Washington, DC: Author.

Angello, L. M., Volpe, R. J., DiPerna, J. C., Guerasko–Moore, S. P., Guerasko–Moore, D. P., Nebrig, M. R., & Ota, K. (2003). Assessment of attention deficit hyperactivity disorder: An evaluation of six published rating scales. *School Psychology Review, 32,* 241–262.

Angold, A., Costello, E. J., & Erkanli, A. (1999). Comorbidity. *Journal of Child Psychology and Psychiatry, 40,* 57–87.

Aronen, E. T., Paavonen, E. J., Fjallberg, M., Soininen, M., & Torronen, J. (2000). Sleep and psychiatric symptoms in school-aged children. *Journal of the American Academy of Child and Adolescent Psychiatry, 39,* 502–508.

Barkley, R. A. (2006). *Attention deficit hyperactivity disorder: A handbook for diagnosis and treatment* (3rd ed.). New York: The Guilford Press.

Barkley, R. A., & Biederman, J. (1997). Towards a broader definition of the age of onset criterion for attention deficit hyperactivity disorder. *Journal of the American Academy of Child and Adolescent Psychiatry, 36,* 1204–1210.

Barkley, R. A. (1998). Attention-deficit/hyperactivity disorder. In E.J. Mash & R.A. Barkley (Eds.) *Child Psychopathology* (2nd Ed., pp.75–143). New York: The Guilford Press.

Barkley, R. A., DuPaul, G. J., McMurray, M. B. (1990). Comprehensive evaluation of attention deficit disorder with and without hyperactivity as defined by research criteria. *Journal of Consulting and Clinical Psychology, 58,* 775–789.

Barkley, R. A., Fischer, M., Edelbrock, C. S., & Smallish, L. (1990). The adolescent outcome of hyperactive children diagnosed by research criteria: I. An 8-year prospective follow-up study. *Journal of the American Academy of Child and Adolescent Psychiatry, 29,* 546–557.

Baumgaertel, A., Wolraich, M. L. & Dietrich, M. (1995). Comparison of diagnostic criteria for attention deficit disorders in a German elementary school sample. *Journal of the American Academy of Child and Adolescent Psychiatry, 34,* 629–638.

Bergan, J. R., & Kratochwill, T. R. (1990). Behavioral consultation and therapy. New York: Plenum Press.

Biederman, J., Faraone, S. V., Milberger, S., Jetton, J. G. (1996). Is childhood oppositional disorder a precursor to adolescent conduct disorder? Findings from a four-year follow-up study of children with ADHD. *Journal of the American Academy of Child and Adolescent Psychiatry, 35,* 1193–1204.

Bird, H. R., Shaffer, D., Fisher, P., Gould, M. S, et al. (1993). The Columbia Impairment Scale(CIS): Pilot findings on a measure of global impairment for children and adolescents. *International Journal of Methods in Psychiatric Research, 3*(3), 167–176.

Cantwell, D. P., & Baker, L. (1991). Association between attention-deficit hyperactivity disorder and learning disorders. *Journal of Learning Disabilities, 24,* 88–95.

Cassidy, J. & Asher, S. (1992). Loneliness and peer relations in young children. *Child Development, 63,* 350–365.

Chafouleas, S.M., Riley-Tillman, T.C. & Christ, T.J. (2009). Direct Behavior Rating (DBR): An Emerging Method forAssessing Social Behavior within a Tiered Intervention System. *Assessment for Effective Intervention, 34,* 195–200.

Christ, T.J., Riley-Tillman, T.C., & Chafouleas, S.M. (2009). Foundation for the Development and Use of Direct Behavior Rating (DBR) to Assess and Evaluate Student Behavior. *Assessment for Effective Intervention, 34,* 201–213.

Chafouleas, S. M., Riley–Tillman, T. C., & Sugai, G. (2007). *School-based Behavioral Assessment: Informing Instruction and Intervention.* New York: Guilford.

Cheney, D., Flower, A., & Templeton, T. (2008). Applying response to intervention metrics in the social domain for students at risk of developing emotional or behavioral disorders. *The Journal of Special Education, 42,* 108–126.

Christ, T.J., Riley-Tillman, T.C., & Chafouleas, S.M. (2009). Foundation for the development and use of direct behavior rating (DBR) to assess and evaluate student behavior. *Assessment for Effective Intervention, 34,* 201-213.

Clarke, H. B., & Clarke, R. T. (1996). Research on the wraparound process and individualized services for children with multi-system needs. *Journal of Child and Family Studies, 5,* 1–5.

Conners, C. K. (2008).Conners, 3rd Edition. North Tonawanda, NJ: Multi-Health Systems.

Corkum, P., Moldofsky, H., Hogg–Johnson, S., Humphries, T., & Tannock, R. (1999). Sleep problems in children with attention-deficit/hyperactivity disorder: Impact of subtype, comorbidity, and stimulant medication. *Journal of the American Academy of Child and Adolescent Psychiatry, 38,* 1285–1293.

Curtis, M. J., Hunley, S. A., & Grier, J. E. C. (2002). Relationships among the professional practices and demographic characteristics of school psychologists. *School Psychology Review, 31,* 30–42.

DiPerna, J. C. & Elliott, S. N. (2000). *Academic Competence Evaluation Scales.* San Antonio, TX: The Psychological Corporation.

DuPaul, G. J. (1992). How to assess attention-deficit hyperactivity disorder within school settings. *School Psychology Quarterly, 7,* 60–74.

DuPaul, G. J., Rapport, M. D., & Periello, L. M. (1991). Teacher ratings of academic skills: The development of the Academic Performance Rating Scale. *School Psychology Review, 20,* 284–300.

DuPaul, G. J., & Stoner, G. (2003). *ADHD in the schools: Assessment and intervention strategies* (2nd Ed.). New York: The Guilford Press.

DuPaul, G. J., Anastopoulos, A. D., Power, T. J., Reid, R., Ikeda, M. J., & McGoey, K. E. (1998).Parent ratings of attention-deficit/hyperactivity disorder symptoms: Factor structure and normative data.*Journal of Psychopathology and Behavioral Assessment, 20,* 83–102.

DuPaul, G. J., Power, T. J., Anastopoulos, A. D., & Reid, R. (1998). *ADHD Rating Scale–IV: Checklists, Norms, and Clinical Interpretation.* New York, NY: The Guilford Press.

Eber, L., & Nelson, C. M. (1997). School-based wraparound planning: Integrating services for students with emotional and behavioral needs. *American Journal of Orthopsychiatry, 67,* 385–395.

Eber, L., Sugai, G., Smith, C. R., Scott, T. M. (2002). Wraparound and positive behavioral interventions and supports in the schools. *Journal of Emotional and Behavioral Disorders, 10,* 171–180.

Fabiano, G. A., Pelham, W. E., Waschbusch, D. A., Gnagy, E. M., Lahey, B. B. et al. (2006). A practical measure of impairment: Psychometric properties of the Impairment Rating Scale in samples of children with attention deficit hyperactivity disorder and two school-based samples. *Journal of Clinical Child and Adolescent Psychology, 35,* 369–385.

Faraone, S. V., Biederman, J., Lehman, B., Keenan, K., Norman, D. et al. (1993). Evidence for the independent familial transmission of attention deficit hyperactivity disorder and learning disabilities: Results from a family genetic study. *American Journal of Psychiatry, 150,* 891–895.

Farrington, D. P., Loeber, R. & Van Kammen, W. B. (1990). Long-term criminal outcomes of hyperactivity, impulsivity, attention deficit and conduct problems in childhood. In L.N. Robins & M. Rutter (Eds.), *Straight and devious pathways from childhood to adulthood* (pp. 62–81). Cambridge: Cambridge University Press.

Fergusson, D. M., & Horwood, L. J. (1995). Early disruptive behavior, IQ, and later school achievement and delinquent behavior. *Journal of Abnormal Child Psychology, 23,* 183–199.

Fergusson, D. M., Horwood, L. J., & Lynskey, M. T. (1993). The effects of conduct disorder and attention deficit in middle childhood on offending and scholastic ability at age 13. *Journal of Child Psychology and Psychiatry, 34,* 899–916.

Fergusson, D. M., Lynskey, M. T., & Horwood, L. J. (1997). Attentional difficulties in middle childhood and psychosocial outcomes in young adulthood. *Journal of Child Psychology and Psychiatry, 38,* 633–644.

Foster, E. M., Jones, D. E., & The Conduct Problems Prevention Research Group (2005). The high cost of aggression: Public expenditures resulting from conduct disorder. *American Journal of Public Health, 95,* 1767–1772.

Frick, P. J. (1998). Conduct Disorders. In T.H. Ollendick& M. Hersen (Eds.). *Handbook of Child Psychopathology* (3rd ed, pp. 213–237). New York: Plenum Press.

Frick, P. J., Kamphaus, R. W., Lahey, B. B., Loeber, R., Christ, M. A. G., Hart, E. L., & Tannenbaum, L. E. (1991). Academic underachievement and the disruptive behavior disorders. *Journal of Consulting and Clinical Psychology, 59,* 289–294.

Gadow, K. D., Sprafkin, J., & Nolan, E. E. (1996). ADHD School observation code. Stony Brook, NY: Checkmate Plus.

Gittelman, R., Mannuzza, S., Shenker, R., & Bonagura, N. (1985). Hyperactive boys almost grown up. *Archives of General Psychiatry, 40*, 827–83.

Gresham, F. M. (2005). Response to intervention: An alternative means of identifying students as emotionally disturbed. *Education and Treatment of Children, 28*, 328–244.

Gresham, F. M. (2007). Evolution of the response-to-intervention concept: Empirical foundations and recent developments. In S.R. Jimerson, M. K. Burns, & A. M. VanDerHeyden (Eds.) *Handbook of response to intervention: The science and practice of assessment and intervention* (pp. 10–24). New York: Springer.

Gresham, F. M., & Elliott, S. N. (1990). *The Social Skills Rating System*. Circle Pines, MN: American Guidance Service.

Gresham, F. M., & Elliott, S. N. (2008). Social Skills Improvement System. Circle Pines, MN: Pearson Assessment.

Gruber, R., Sadeh, A., & Raviv, A. (2000). Instability of sleep patterns in children with attention-deficit/hyperactivity disorder. *Journal of the American Academy of Child and Adolescent Psychiatry, 39*, 495–501.

Hinshaw, S. P. (1987). On the distinction between attentional deficits/hyperactivity and conduct problems/aggression in child psychopathology. *Psychological Bulletin, 101*, 443–463.

Hinshaw, S. P., & Lee, S. S. (2003). Conduct and oppositional defiant disorders. In E.J. Mash & R.A. Barkley (Eds.) *Child Psychopathology* (2nd ed., pp. 144–198). New York: The Guilford Press.

Hinshaw, S. P., & Melnick, S. M. (1995). Peer relationships in children with attention-deficit hyperactivity disorder with and without comorbid aggression. *Development and Psychopathology, 7*, 627–647.

Hintze, J. M. (2005). Psychometrics of Direct Observation. *School Psychology Review, 34*, 507–519.

Hintze, J. M. & Matthews, W. J. (2004). The generalizability of systematic direct observations across time and setting: A preliminary investigation of the psychometrics of behavioral assessment. *School Psychology Review, 33*, 258–270.

Hintze, J. M., Volpe, R. J., & Shapiro, E. S. (2008). Best practices in systematic direct observation of student behavior. In A. Thomas & J. Grimes (Eds.), *Best practices in school psychology V* (Vol. 2, pp. 319–335). Bethesda, MD: National Association of School Psychologists.

Horner, R. H., Carr, E. G., Halle, J., McGee, G., Odom, S., & Wolery, M. (2005). The use of single-subject research to identify evidence-based practice in special education. *Exceptional Children, 71*, 165–179.

Irvin, L. K., Horner, R. H., Ingram, K., Todd, A. W., Sugai, G., Sampson, N. K., & Boland, J. B. (2006). Using discipline referral data for decision making about student behavior in elementary and middle schools: An empirical evaluation of validity. *Journal of Positive Behavior Interventions, 8*, 10–23.

Irvin, L., Tobin, T., Sprague, J., Sugai, G., & Vincent, C. (2004). Validity of office discipline referral measures as indices of school-wide behavioral status and effects of school-wide behavioral interventions. *Journal of Positive Behavior Interventions, 6*, 131–147.

Jensen, P. S., Martin, D., & Cantwell, D. P. (1997). Comorbidity in ADHD: Implications for research, practice, and DSM–V. *Journal of the American Academy of Child and Adolescent Psychiatry, 36*, 1065–1079.

Kaufman, J., Birmaher, B., Brent, D., Rao, A., & Ryan, N. (1996). Kiddie-SADS-PL, Version 1.0. Pittsburgh, PA: University of Pittsburg, School of Medicine, Department of Psychiatry.

Kaufman, J., & Schweder, A. E. (2003). The Schedule for Affective Disorders and Schizophrenia for School-age Children: Present and Lifetime Version (K-SADS-PL). In Hersen, M., Hilsenroth, M. J. and Segal, D. L. (Eds.), Comprehensive Handbook of Psychological Assessment (Vol. 2, pp. 247–255). New York: John Wiley and Sons.

Knivsberg, A., Reichelt, K. L., & Nodland, M. (1999). Comorbidity, or coexistence, between dyslexia and attention deficit hyperactivity disorder. *British Journal of Special Education, 26*, 42–47.

Lahey, B. B., Applegate, B., Barkley, R. A., Garfinkel, B., McBurnett, K., Kerdyk, L. et al. (1994). DSM–IV field trials for oppositional defiant disorder and conduct disorder in children and adolescents. *American Journal of Psychiatry, 151*, 1163–1171.

Lahey, B. B., Applegate, B., McBurnett, K., Biederman, J., Greenhill, L., Hynd, G. W., et al. (1994). DSM–IV field trials for attention-deficit / hyperactivity disorder in children and adolescents. *American Journal of Psychiatry, 151*, 1673–1685.

Lahey, B. B., Loeber, R., Quay, H., Frick, P. J., & Grimm, J. (1992). Oppositional defiant disorder and conduct disorder. In T.A. Widiger, A.J. Frances, H.A. Pincus, R. Ross, M.B. First, & W. Davis (Eds.), *DSM–IV Sourcebook* (Vol. 3, pp. 189–209). Washington, DC: American Psychiatric Press.

Leff, S. S. & Lakin, R. (2005). Playground-based observational systems: A review and implications for practitioners and researchers. *School Psychology Review, 34*, 475–489.

Loeber, R., Burke, J. D., Lahey, B.B., Winters, A., & Zera, M. (2000). Oppositional defiant and conduct disorder: A review of the last 10 years, part I. *Journal of the American Academy of Child and Adolescent Psychology, 39*, 1468–1484.

McConaughy, S. H. & Achenbach, T. M. (2009). *Manual for the ASEBA Direct Observation Form*. Burlington, VT: University of Vermont, Research Center for Children, Youth, & Families.

McConaughy, S. H. (2005). Clinical interviews for children and adolescents: Assessment to intervention. New York: The Guilford Press.

Merrell, K. W. (2008). Behavioral, social, and emotional assessment of children & adolescents (3rd ed.). Mahwah, NJ: Lawrence Erlbaum Associates.

Merrell, K. W. (1999). Behavioral, social, and emotional assessment of children & adolescents (2nd ed.). Mahwah, NJ: Lawrence Erlbaum Associates.

Moffit, T. E., & Caspi, A. (2001). Childhood predictors differentiate life-course persistent and adolescent limited antisocial pathways among males and females. *Development and Psychopathology, 13*, 355–375.

Pelham, W. E., Fabiano, G. A., Massetti, G. M. (2005). Evidence-based assessment of attention deficit hyperactivity disorder in children and adolescents. *Journal of Clinical Child and Adolescent Psychology, 3*, 449–476.

Power, T. J., Atkins, M. S., Osbome, M. L., & Blum, N. J. (1994). The school psychologist as manager of programming for ADHD. *School Psychology Review. 23*, 279–291.

Power, T. J., DuPaul, G. J., & Shapiro, E. S. (2003). Preparing psychologists to link systems of care in managing and preventing children's health problems. *Journal of Pediatric Psychology, 28*, 147–155.

Puig–Antich, J., & Chambers, W. (1978). *The Schedule for Affective Disorders and Schizophrenia for School-Age Children*. New York, NY: New York State Psychiatric Association.

Quay, H. (1977). Measuring dimensions of deviant behavior: The Behavior Problem Checklist. *Journal of Abnormal Child Psychology, 5*, 277–289.

Reid, R., Casat, C. D., Norton, J.H., Anastopoulos, A. D., & Temple, E. P. (2001). Using behavior rating scales for ADHD across ethnic groups: The IOWA Conners. *Journal of Emotional and Behavioral Disorders, 9*, 210–218.

Reid, R. DuPaul, G. J., Power, T. J., Anastopoulos, A. D., Rogers–Adkinson, D., Noll, M., & Riccio, C. (1998). Assessing culturally different students for attention deficit hyperactivity disorder using behavior rating scales. *Journal of Abnormal Child Psychology, 26*, 187–198.

Reschly, D. J. (2000). The present and future status of school psychology in the United States. *School Psychology Review, 29*, 507–522.

Riley–Tillman, T. C. & Burns, M. K. (2009). *Evaluating Educational Interventions: Single-Case Design for Measuring Response to Intervention*. New York: The Guilford Press.

Robins, L. N. (1991). Conduct Disorder, *Journal of Child Psychology and Psychiatry, 32*, 193–212.

Rutter, M., Giller, H., & Hagell, A. (1998). *Antisocial behavior by young people*. Cambridge, England: Cambridge University Press.

Salvia, J., & Ysseldyke, J.E. (2004). *Assessment* (9th ed.). Princeton, NC: Houghton Mifflin.

Semrud–Clikeman, M., Biederman, J., Sprich–Buckminster, S., Lehman, B. K., Faraone, S. V., & Norman, D. (1992). Comorbidity between ADDH and learning disability: A review and report in a clinically referred sample. *Journal of the American Academy of Child & Adolescent Psychiatry, 31*, 439–448.

Setterberg, S., Bird, H., & Gould, M. (1992). *Parent and Interviewer Version of the Children's Global Assessment Scale*. New York:Columbia University.

Severson, H. H., Walker, H. M., Hope–Doolittle, J., Kratochwill, T. R., & Gresham, F. M. (2007). Proactive, early screening to detect behaviorally at-risk students: Issues, approaches, emerging innovations, and professional practices. *Journal of School Psychology, 45*, 193–223.

Shaffer, D., Fisher, P., Lucas, C. P., Dulcan, M., & Schwab–Stone, M. E. (2000). NIMH Diagnostic Interview Schedule for Children Version, Version IV (NIMH DISC–IV): Description, differences from previous versions and reliability of some common diagnoses. *Journal of the American Academy of Child and Adolescent Psychiatry, 39*, 28–38.

Silva, F. (1993). *Psychometric Foundations and Behavioral Assessment*. Newbury Park, CA: Sage.

Szatmari, P., Offord, D. R., & Boyle, M. H. (1989). Ontario Child Health Study: Prevalence of attention deficit disorder with hyperactivity. *Journal of Child Psychology and Psychiatry, 30*, 219–230.

Volpe, R. J., DiPerna, J. C., Hintze, J. M., & Shapiro, E. S. (2005). Observing students in classroom settings: A review of seven coding schemes. *School Psychology Review, 34*, 454–474.

Volpe, R. J., Gadow, K. D., Blom-Hoffman, J., & Feinberg, A. B. (2009). Factor analytic and individualized approaches to constructing brief measures of ADHD behaviors. *Journal of Emotional and Behavioral Disorders, 17*, 118–128. DOI: 10.1177/1063426608323370.

Volpe, R. J., & McConaughy, S. H. (2005). Introduction to the mini-series: Systematic direct observational assessment of student behavior: Its use and interpretation in multiple settings. *School Psychology Review, 34*, 451–453.

Volpe, R. J., McConaughy, S. H., & Hintze, J. M. (2009). Generalizability of classroom behavior problem and on-task scores from the Direct Observation Form. *School Psychology Review, 38*, 382–401.

Walker, H. M., Block–Pedego, A., Todis, B., & Severson, H. (1991). *School archival records search*. Longmont, CO: Sopris West.

Walker, H. M., & McConnell, S. R. (1988). Walker–McConnell Scale of Social Competence and School Adjustment. Austin, TX: Pro-Ed.

White, H. R., Xie, M., Thompson, W., Loeber, R., & Stouthamer–Loeber, M. (2001). Psychopathology as a predictor of adolescent drug use trajectories. *Psychology of Addictive Behavior, 15*, 210–218.

Wolraich, M. L., Hannah, J. N., Pinnock, T. Y., Baumgaertel, A., & Brown, J. (1996). Comparison of diagnostic criteria for attention-deficit/hyperactivity disorder in a country-wide sample. *Journal of the American Academy of Child and Adolescent Psychiatry, 35*, 319–324.

Wright, J. A., & Dusek, J. B. (1998). Compiling school base rates for disruptive behaviors from student disciplinary referral data. *School Psychology Review, 27*, 138–147.

Assessment of Internalizing Behavioral Deficits

Randy W. Kamphaus *and* Kristen L. Mays

Abstract

The purpose of this chapter is to provide an overview of the assessment of internalizing problems in children and adolescents. The chapter consists of three sections. The first section summarizes the categorical and dimensional systems used to classify social and emotional problems in youth. The second section discusses a variety of assessment techniques (e.g., structured and semistructured interviews and behavioral rating scales) that can be used to evaluate internalizing problems. This section also provides descriptions of several assessment measures including the DISC-IV, K-SADS-PL, ASEBA, BASC-2, BYI-II, CDI, RCMAS-2, and STAIC. Finally, the chapter concludes with a discussion of several practical issues to consider when evaluating the emotional and behavioral status of youth.

Keywords: internalizing, assessment, children, adolescents, school psychology, anxiety, depression, somatization

Introduction

Of the myriad functions school psychologists serve within the educational system, the assessment of youth[1] suspected of having emotional and behavioral problems remains a pivotal role. Internalizing behavioral deficits (or *excesses* depending on one's point of view) are often characterized by symptoms related to depressive mood, anxiety, fearfulness, somatic complaints, and social withdrawal. The purpose of this chapter is to provide an overview of the assessment of internalizing problems in childhood.[2] We begin this chapter with a discussion of the primary systems used to classify psychopathology in youth, followed by an overview of various assessment techniques and instruments that school psychologists commonly use to evaluate students' internalizing behavior. Finally, we conclude with a discussion of several practical issues to consider when evaluating the emotional and behavioral status of youth.

Classification Systems for Internalizing Disorders

Within the psychopathology literature, two primary approaches have been presented for classifying emotional and behavioral problems in youth: categorical and dimensional systems. Categorical systems classify problems in a dichotomous, yes/no fashion. An individual is judged to possess a disorder only if he or she displays the required features of the classification category. For example, according to one of the most commonly used categorical classification systems, the *Diagnostic and Statistical Manual for Mental Disorders, Fourth Edition, Text Revision* (DSM-IV-TR; American Psychiatric Association [APA], 2000), a diagnosis of major depression is made when an individual exhibits *at least* five of nine symptoms specified in Criterion A. However, if an individual only exhibits four of the symptoms, or meets any of the exclusionary criteria, the individual is judged not to have the disorder. This situation is analogous to the medical classification of pregnancy. Just as one is either pregnant or not, one either has a specific anxiety or mood disorder or not.

As opposed to depicting psychopathological manifestations as discrete categories, dimensional classification systems situate empirically derived constructs of behavior (e.g., internalizing behavior) on a continuum of scores or ratings. Consider, for example, a person's height. Height is typically measured on a continuous scale. A person may be identified as "short," "average," or "tall" based upon where a person's "height score" (e.g., 5 feet or 7 feet) falls along the height dimension. Classification of a person's height may also be relative to other factors such sex, age, or cultural group. What is considered tall for a 5-year-old is very different from what is considered tall for an 18-year-old. Similarly, a youth's internalizing behavior "score" may be classified as "elevated" or "normal"depending on his or her age, gender, etc.

Dimensional approaches to classification typically recognize two superordinate, broad-band behavioral domains, referred to as *internalizing/overcontrolled* behavior and *externalizing/undercontrolled* behavior, in addition to several subordinate, narrow-band behavioral dimensions (Achenbach, et al., 1966, 1985, 1988; Achenbach & Edelbrock, 1978; Quay, 1979). Narrow-band behavioral dimensions typically vary across instruments and informants. For example, the internalizing domain of the *Behavioral Assessment System for Children, Second Edition* (BASC-2; Reynolds & Kamphaus, 2004) is subdivided into three narrow-band dimensions termed *depression, anxiety,* and *somatization,* whereas the internalizing domain of the *Achenbach System of Empirically Based Assessment* (ASEBA; Achenbach & Rescorla, 2001) is subdivided into three dimensions labeled *anxious/depressed, withdrawn/depressed,* and *somatic complaints.* The BASC-2 and the ASEBA instruments will be explained in further detail later in the chapter.

The differential value of categorical and dimensional systems continues to be widely debated throughout the psychopathology literature. Proponents of categorical systems assert that categorical classification results in a parsimonious nomenclature that facilitates communication among mental health providers and the public; improves the transmission of information concerning services, treatment, and outcomes for varying disorders; and introduces clear, operationally defined diagnostic standards for forming homogeneous clinical groups for research (Dowdy, Mays, Kamphaus, & Reynolds, 2009).

For example, with regard to professional communication, when two mental health professionals discuss a client diagnosed with major depressive disorder, they both have a general idea of what the client's symptoms look like, the course the client's symptoms may take, and the service or treatment options generally available to support the client. Opponents of categorical systems underscore the substandard reliability and validity evidence for many categorical diagnoses, as well as the failure of these systems to account for differential levels of symptom severity, subsyndromal psychopathology, adaptive behavioral functioning, elevated rates of comorbidity, and atypical presentations of disorders (Dowdy, et al., 2009).

Proponents of dimensional systems emphasize that these methods account for many of the shortcomings of categorical methods, including quantifying levels of symptomatology, increasing the reliability and validity of diagnoses, and minimizing many of the problems associated with comorbidity and atypical, mixed, and not otherwise specified categories (Dowdy, et al., 2009). Unfortunately, a consensus regarding the optimal dimensions to be used for classification purposeshas not been achieved, which limits the ease of communication that is afforded by more commonly used categorical systems. Until agreement exists regarding the optimal way to classify psychopathology (categorical, dimensional, or a hybrid of the two), school psychologists should be familiar with both systems for classifying internalizing problems, and the strengths and weaknesses inherent in each approach.

Categorical Classification Systems
DSM-IV-TR

As mentioned in the previous section, the DSM-IV-TR (APA, 2000) is by far the most commonly used classification system for emotional and behavioral problems in the United States, and remains widely used around the world. While the DSM-IV-TR does not designate a specific internalizing category, anxiety and mood disorders fall within the internalizing domain. Brief descriptions of relevant anxiety and mood disorders described in the DSM-IV-TR are provided in Table 14.1.

Though the majority of school psychologists are not expected (nor sanctioned, based upon many local or state statutes) to make DSM-IV-TR diagnostic decisions, it is important for school psychologists working in schools to be familiar with the diagnoses that commonly occur in youth. First, knowledge of the etiology and developmental

Table 14.1 Characteristics of DSM–IV–TR Internalizing Disorders

Mood Disorders	
Major Depressive Disorder	Persistent depressed mood or anhedonia
Dysthymic Disorder	Chronic depressed mood for at least 2 years
Bipolar Disorder	Occurrence of one or more manic or hypomanic episodes and is usually accompanied by major depressive episodes
Anxiety Disorders	
Generalized Anxiety Disorder	Persistent and excessive worry that is difficult to control and not easily reassured by others
Obsessive Compulsive Disorder	Recurrent obsessions and compulsions
Panic Disorder	Recurrent, unexpected panic attacks
Posttraumatic Stress Disorder	Reexperiencing of an extremely traumatic event
Social Phobia	Excessive fear in social or performance situations
Specific Phobia	Excessive and persistent fear concerning a specific stimulus or situation
Other Disorders of Infancy, Childhood, or Adolescence	
Separation Anxiety Disorder	Developmentally inappropriate fear concerning the separation from home or a major attachment feature
Selective Mutism	Persistent failure to speak in specific social situations

Note: Descriptions of disorders are abbreviated. Complete diagnostic criteria and descriptions can be located in the DSM–IV–TR (APA, 2000).

trajectories of DSM-IV-TR disorders can alert school psychologists to emerging symptomatology in students. Additionally, knowledge of the medical and psychological research literature regarding the treatment for DSM-IV-TR disorders can help guide intervention decisions within the school or classroom. Finally, knowledge of DSM-IV-TR terminology facilitates communication between school psychologists and other mental health care providers (Callahan, Panichelli-Mindel, & Kendall, 1996; McConaughy & Rittner, 2008).

IDEIA

Another important classification system that is frequently used within schools is the Individuals with Disabilities Education Improvement Act of 2004 (IDEIA; P.L.108–476,2004). IDEIA is a federal initiative that requires schools to provide free and appropriate public education, related services, and accommodations for all youth with disabilities. IDEIA stipulates specific sets of criteria that an individual must meet to qualify for disability status under one of the 13 identified disability categories. Youth with internalizing problems are most likely to qualify for special education under the category

of emotional disturbance (ED). The classification criteria for ED are included in Table 14.2. Youth with a DSM-IV-TR medical diagnosis of an anxiety disorder (e.g., post-traumatic stress disorder) or a mood disorder (e.g., major depressive disorder) may also qualify under the category of other health impairment (OHI). The classification criteria for OHI are displayed in Table 14.3.

Assessment Instruments

Assessment is important both in the clinical evaluation of internalizing disorders, and for research designed to enhance our understanding of the nature of internalizing problems in youth. The next section focuses on two general assessment methods that school psychologists commonly use to evaluate youth exhibiting internalizing symptomatology: structured and semistructured interviews, and behavior ratings scales.

Although projective assessment techniques continue to be widely used in school psychologists' assessment practices (Hojnoski, Morrison, Brown, & Matthews, 2006; Shapiro & Heick, 2004), we will not provide a review of these instruments for several reasons. First, multiple researchers

Table 14.2 Criteria for Emotional Disturbance from IDEIA (P.L. 94-142, 2004)

(i) Emotional disturbance means a condition exhibiting one or more of the following characteristics over a long period of time and to a marked degree that adversely affects a child's educational performance:

(A) An inability to learn that cannot be explained by intellectual, sensory, or health factors;

(B) An inability to build or maintain satisfactory interpersonal relationships with peers and teachers;

(C) Inappropriate types of behavior or feelings under normal circumstances;

(D) A general pervasive mood of unhappiness or depression;

(E) A tendency to develop physical symptoms or fears associated with personal or school problems;

(ii) Emotional disturbance includes schizophrenia. The term does not apply to children who are socially maladjusted unless it is determined that they have an emotional disturbance under paragraph (c) (4) (i) of this section.

Note: Taken from the Code of Federal Regulation, Title 34, Section 300.7(c)(4)

---

examining the psychometric properties of projective techniques have concluded that many projective tests have questionable or even poor levels of reliability and validity, especially as diagnostic instruments (Miller & Nickerson, 2007). Moreover, the use of such instruments in conjunction with more valid estimates of functioning may weaken the validity of the entire comprehensive assessment (Kennedy, Faust, Willis, & Piotrowski, 1994). Second, the extent to which projective tests contribute valuable information beyond

---

Table 14.3 Criteria for Other Health Impairment from IDEIA (P.L. 94-142, 2004)

Other health impairment means having limited strength, vitality, or alertness, including a heightened alertness to environmental stimuli, that results in limited alertness with respect to the educational environment, that–

(i) is due to chronic or acute health problems such as asthma, attention deficit disorder or attention deficit hyperactivity disorder, diabetes, epilepsy, a heart condition, hemophilia, lead poisoning, leukemia, nephritis, rheumatic fever, sickle cell anemia, and

(ii) adversely affects a child's educational performance.

Note: Taken from the Code of Federal Regulation, Title 34, Section 300.7(c)(9).

---

other information (incremental validity) remains questionable (Lilienfield, Wood, & Garb, 2000; Miller & Nickerson, 2007). Instruments with poor or null incremental validity add additional cost and time to the assessment process that may be better-spent delivering direct services to youth (Yates & Taub, 2003). Third, research suggests that projective instruments may over-identify psychopathology (Lilienfield, et al., 2000). Finally, many of these instruments have not been demonstrated as appropriate for use with culturally or ethnically diverse populations (Lilienfield).

Page limits prohibit an exhaustive review of all available clinical procedures and instruments appropriate for the assessment of internalizing problems in youth. Consequently, we introduce only a brief selection of tools that are available. Instruments discussed at length were selected for their psychometric support and relative popularity among school, child, clinical, and developmental psychologists. We wish to emphasize that these instruments merely represent examples of tools within each assessment domain. Given the rapid proliferation of new or updated instruments, school psychologists should strive to stay abreast of the most current, empirically supported assessment practices. As colloquially stated, today's accepted practice is tomorrow's malpractice.

Interviews

School psychologists frequently employ structured and semistructured interviews as a component of their evaluation practices for students referred for behavioral and emotional difficulties. According to a study that surveyed the assessment practices of school psychologists with students referred for behavioral and emotional problems, almost 70% of school psychologists reported conducting formal interviews in four or more of their last 10 cases (Shapiro & Heick, 2004). As with most evaluation methods, interviews have both advantages and disadvantages that school psychologists should consider before incorporating them into their assessment practices.

According to Loney and Frick (2003), one advantage of diagnostic interviews is that they can elicit specific information (e.g., duration of a youth's symptomatology, age at which problems began to emerge, etc.) that is difficult or impossible to obtain with more time-efficient methods (e.g., behavior rating scales). Another advantage is that interviews can assess the level of academic, social, or lifestyle impairment associated with each behavioral or emotional symptom. This is important because level of impairment can sometimes be a more important indicator of the need for treatment than symptom severity alone. Finally, interviews allow one to make a diagnosis based on strict adherence to diagnostic criteria.

Loney and Frick (2003) also discuss several limitations for clinical interviews. Although clinical interviews can provide comprehensive and detailed diagnostic information, they can also be costly in terms of clinician and student time. In addition, they are dependent on specific diagnostic categories that may not be well supported by empirical studies. Other weaknesses include their lack of normative data, and the potential attenuation of reported symptoms across repeated administrations.

In the next section, we focus on two types of clinical interviews: structured, respondent-based interviews, and semistructured, interviewer-based interviews. The central difference between structured, respondent-based and semistructured, interviewer-based interviews is the degree of clinical judgment the interviewer must employ when administering the interview. In respondent-based interviews, interviewers ask a set of standardized questions and follow explicit guidelines to score each item. Algorithms establish whether the respondent reported enough symptoms to meet the diagnostic criteria for the disorder (Shaffer, Fisher, & Lucas, 1999). Thus, in respondent-based interviews, diagnostic decisions are determined by the respondent's answers, similar to the way item performance is assessed on formal objective psychological tests. Although respondent-based interviews can be reliably administered by trained laypersons or computer programs, potentially saving valuable clinician time, this format does not allow the interviewer to tailor the interview to specific interviewee characteristics (e.g., developmental level), or ask follow-up questions to ensure that the interviewee fully comprehends each question (Achenbach & Rescorla, 2007; VanDeventer & Kamphaus, 2006).

In contrast to respondent-based interviews, interviewer-based interviews require a higher level of skill and clinical judgment to administer and interpret. During interviewer-based interviews, interviewers ask an initial set of questions and then probe a respondent's answers for more detailed information. The interviewer then uses his or her clinical judgment to determine whether a symptom is present or absent (Shaffer, Fisher, &Lucas, 1999). Although this format allows the interviewer considerable freedom to adapt questions to the specific needs of the respondent, these instruments are more difficult to administer, and may require considerable expertise and training to score properly (Achenbach & Rescorla, 2007; VanDeventer & Kamphaus, 2006).

There are a number of structured and semistructured interviews available that can be used to evaluate anxiety and mood disorders in childhood. Tables 14.4 and 14.5 present a brief summary of the basic characteristics of a selection of these instruments. A more thorough description of the *Diagnostic Interview Schedule for Children, Fourth Edition* (DISC-IV; Shaffer, Fischer, Lucas, Duncan, & Schwab-Stone, 2000) and *Schedule of Affective Disorders and Schizophrenia, School-Age Children–Present and Lifetime* (K-SADS-PL; Puig-Antich & Chambers, 1978) is provided below.

Structured Interviews
DISC-IV

The DISC-IV is a highly structured, respondent-based diagnostic interview for youth ages 9 to17 years (DISC-Y), and parents or caretakers of youth ages 6 to 17 years (DISC-P). Designed to be administered by trained lay interviewers, the DISC-IV assesses DSM-III-R, DSM-IV (APA, 1987, 1994), and the *International Classification of Diseases and Related Health Problems, 10th edition* (ICD-10; World Health Organization, 1993) diagnostic criteria for mental health disorders typically found in youth. Although it was was originally commissioned by the U.S. National Institute of Mental Health (NIMH) in 1983 to serve as a research tool for large-scale epidemiological research, the DISC has subsequently been used in numerous screening projects and research studies, as well as in clinical and community-based service settings (Shaffer, et al., 2000; Shaffer, Fisher, & Lucas, 2004). Additional versions of the DISC, and those currently in preparation, are listed in Table 14.6.

The DISC-IV is organized into six diagnostic modules that can be administered separately or in combination: *anxiety disorders* (e.g., separation anxiety disorder), *mood disorders* (e.g., major depression), *behavior disorders* (e.g., oppositional defiant disorder), *substance abuse disorders* (e.g., alcohol abuse/dependence), and *other disorders* (e.g., anorexia nervosa). Each module assesses the presence of disorders both within the past year, and within the previous 4-week period. Interviewers also have the option to administer a "whole-life" module, which assesses the presence of mental disorders throughout an individual's lifetime.

Table 14.4   Basic characteristics of structured, interviewer-based interview schedules for youth

Instrument	Primary References	Relevant Internalizing Classifications	Informants/ Age Range	Time	Administration Format
Child and Adolescent Psychiatric Assessment (CAPA)	Angold & Costello (1995); Angold, Prendergast, Cox, Harrington, Simonoff & Ruttner(1995); Angold& Costello (2000)	**Mood Disorders:** Major depression Dsythymia **Anxiety Disorders:** Separation anxiety Avoidant Overanxious Panic Social phobia Simple phobia Generalized anxiety Elective mutism Obsessive compulsive	SR/PR: 9–18 years	SR/PR: 1–2 hours	Interviewer
Diagnostic Interview for Children and Adolescents, 4th edition (DICA–IV)	Reich, Welner, & Herjanic (1997); Reich (2000)	**Mood Disorders:** Major depression/ Dsythymia **Anxiety Disorders:** Separation anxiety Panic disorder Agoraphobia Generalized anxiety Social/Specific Phobias Obsession/Compulsive Post–traumatic stress	SR–C: 6–12 years SR–A: 13–18 years PR: 6–17 years	SR/PR: 1–2 hours	Interviewer or Computer
The National Institute of Mental Health Diagnostic Interview Schedule for Children, 4th edition (DISC–IV)	Shaffer et al. (2000); Shaffer, Fischer, & Lucas (2004)	**Mood Disorders:** Dsythymia Major Depression Mania/Hypo-Mania **Anxiety Disorders:** Agoraphobia General Anxiety Obsessive-Compulsive Panic Posttraumatic stress Separation Anxiety Social Phobia Specific Phobia	SR: 9–17 years PR: 6–17 years	SR/PR: 70–120 minutes	Interviewer or Computer

SR = Self-report; PR = Parent report; C = Child; A = Adolescent

The DISC-IV includes nearly 3,000 questions: 358 "stem" questions that are asked to every respondent, and approximately 1,300 contingent questions that are asked if the respondent answers particular stem, or previous contingent, questions affirmatively. An additional 732 questions elicit information concerning the age of onset, type/level of impairment, and previous treatment for reported symptoms. An optional 499 questions assess symptomatology over an individual's lifetime ("whole-life" module).

The majority of questions can be answered with a dichotomous response of either "yes" or "no." Questions that require open-ended responses tend to occur when a description is warranted of an unusual symptom (e.g., delusions, compulsions, tics, etc.), treatment, or a traumatic event (Shaffer, Fisher, & Lucas, 2004).

The DISC-IV can be administered by hand, or using a computer-assisted program (C-DISC-4.0), which is available in both English and Spanish.

Table 14.5 Basic characteristics of semi-structured, respondent-based interview schedules for youth

Instrument	Primary References	Relevant Internalizing Classifications	Informants/ Age Range	Time	Administration Format
Child Assessment Schedule (CAS)	Hodges, Kline, Stern, Cytryn, & McKnew, (1982) Hodges, McKnew, Cytryn, Stern, & Kline (1982)	**Mood Disorders:** Major depressive Dsythymia **Anxiety Disorders:** Separation anxiety Overanxious	SR: 7–16 years	SR/PR: 45–60 minutes	Interviewer
Interview Schedule for Children and Adolescents (ISCA)	Sherrill, & Kovacs (2000)	**Mood Disorders:** Major depression Dysthmia Cyclothymia Bipolar Mood NOS **Anxiety Disorders:** Phobias Obsessive Compulsive Anxiety NOS	SR/PR: 8–17 years	SR: 45–90 min PR: 2–2.5 hours	Interviewer
Schedule for Affective Disorders and Schizophrenia, School-Aged Children–Present and Lifetime Version (K-SADS-PL)	Ambrosini (2000) Kaufman & Schweder (2004)	**Mood Disorders:** Major/Minor depression/ Dsythymia Bipolar **Anxiety Disorders:** Generalized Anxiety Obsessive-Compulsive Simple/Social Phobia Agoraphobia Panic Posttraumatic stress	SR/PR: 6–18 years	SR/PR: 1.5 hours	Interviewer (Computer version under development)

SR = Self-report; PR = Parent report

Although the computer-assisted interview format does not necessarily reduce administration time, it may minimize interviewer and editor error, training time, and data entry costs. Administration of the whole DISC-IV requires approximately 70 to 80 minutes per informant in community populations, and 90 to 120 minutes in clinical populations. Limiting the diagnostic modules to only those relevant to the specific person being evaluated reduces this administration time (Shaffer, Fisher, & Lucas, 2004). School psychologists evaluating internalizing behaviors may wish to focus selectively on the anxiety disorders and the depression disorders-modules. The DISC-IV can be scored by hand (though this is not recommended, due to the instrument's complexity) or using computer algorithms that are programmed in Statistical Analysis System (SAS; SAS Institute, 1990). The DISC-P and DISC-Y can be scored independently, or by integrating the two forms (Shaffer, Fisher, & Lucas, 2004).

The test–retest reliability of the English version of the C-DISC-4.0 was examined in a study of 84 parents and 82 children (ages 9 to 17 years) recruited from youth outpatient clinics (Shaffer, et al., 2000). Updated results using the latest version of the DISC algorithms indicated slight to moderate agreement (kappa coefficients from 0.2 to < 0.8) for specific internalizing diagnoses for the DISC-Y, and fair to moderate agreement (kappa coefficients from 0.4 to < 0.80) for the DISC-P (see Table 14.7). Overall, the DISC-P displayed higher reliability coefficients than the DISC-Y. Studies investigating test–retest reliability of translated versions of DISC-IV have revealed comparable results in both Spanish (Bravo et al., 2001) and Chinese (Ho et al., 2005) speaking clinical populations (Shaffer et al., 2000).

Roberts, Parker, and Dagnone (2005) reported acceptable levels of correspondence between DISC-IV diagnoses and clinical diagnoses made by a multidisciplinary team (kappa = 0.57). The results

Table 14.6 Alternate versions of the DISC

Present State C-DISC4	Computerized instrument that evaluates the presence of current DSM-IV specified symptoms
*Voice DISC	Audio version of the Present State DISC designed for self-administration
*Teacher DISC	Evaluate the presence of DSM-IV diagnostic requirements that may be observable in the school environment
Young Child DISC	Adapted to assess the presence of DSM-IV diagnostic requirements in preschool children
Young Adult DISC	Adapted to assess older adolescents living independently and young adults up to age 24
*DISC Predictive Scales	Screening instrument for DSM-IV diagnoses
*Columbia DISC Depression Scale	Screening instrument for the presence of depression symptomatology
Quick DISC	Designed to shorten administration time

* Indicates versions that may be *particularly* useful for school psychologist working in a school environment

of this study also revealed that the presence of a DISC-IV diagnosis was associated with elevated scores on the *Global Severity Index of the Symptom Check List-Revised* (SCL-90-R; Aronen et al., 1993). Replication of these studies with larger sample sizes and in nonclinical settings is needed.

SEMISTRUCTURED INTERVIEWS
K-SADS-PL
The K-SADS-PL (Puig-Antich & Chambers, 1978) is a semistructured diagnostic interview designed to assess present and lifetime psychopathological episodes, in youth ages 7 to 18 years, according to the DSM-III-R and DSM-IV (APA, 1987, 1994).

The K-SADS-PL contains a systematic, but flexible, set of questions that require the interviewer to use his or her clinical judgment to explore or clarify the interviewee's responses. Interviewers are encouraged to use the language supplied by the parent or child when probing specific symptoms, and adjust their language to the developmental level of the youth (Kaufman & Schweder, 2004).

Administration of the K-SADS-PL child and parent interviews each take approximately 35 to 45 minutes in general populations, to 1.25 hours in clinical populations, and consists of six phases: (1) *Introductory Interview*; (2) *Diagnostic Screening Interview*; (3) *Supplement Completion Checklist*; (4) *Diagnostic Supplements*; (5) *Summary Lifetime Diagnoses Checklist*; and (6) *Children's Global Assessment Scale* (C-GAS) ratings. The *Introductory Interview* takes approximately 10 to 15 minutes to complete. During this section, the interviewer gathers demographic, health, presenting complaint, and prior treatment data, as well as information regarding the youth's school functioning, hobbies, and peer and family relations. The *Diagnostic Screening Interview* is designed to streamline the assessment process. During this phase, the interviewer surveys 82 core symptoms across 20 diagnostic areas. At the conclusion of each diagnostic area, the interviewer uses criteria to determine whether additional interviewing is necessary. Though all sections of the *Diagnostic Screening Interview* must be completed, interviewers have the option of surveying the diagnostic areas in any order. This allows the interviewer the flexibility to initially focus on the relevant diagnoses suggested by the respondent's complaints. After the screening phase, if a youth manifests a designated number of primary symptoms related to specific diagnoses, the interviewer administers appropriate *Diagnostic Supplements* for these disorders. The K-SADS-PL includes five diagnostic supplements: affective disorders, psychotic disorders, anxiety disorders, behavioral disorders, substance abuse, and other disorders. Each supplement contains a list of symptoms, probes, and additional criteria to evaluate the current and most severe past episodes of the disorders. The last two phases are completed by integrating all of the information provided by the respondents. Additional information regarding the use of the K-SADS-PL can be found at http://www.wpic.pitt.edu/ksads/default.htm.

Kaufman and colleagues (1997) evaluated the interrater reliability, test–retest reliability, and concurrent validity of K-SADS-PL using a sample of 55 psychiatric outpatients and 11 controls, ages 7 to 17 years (M = 12.4 years). Interrater reliability for 15 randomly selected subjects (10 outpatients and 5 controls) ranged from 93% to 100% for current diagnoses, and was 100% for past diagnoses. Test–retest reliability kappa coefficients for internalizing diagnoses after a mean of 17.9 days ranged from 0.67 to 1.00 for present diagnosis, and 0.60 to 1.00 for lifetime diagnosis (see Table 14.7).

Table 14.7   Comparison of test–retest reliabilities of the C-DISC-IV and K-SADS-PL

Internalizing Classification	(DISC-Y)[1]		(DISC-P)[1]		K-SADS-Present[2]		K-SADS-Lifetime[2]	
	N	Kappa	*N*	Kappa	*N*	Kappa	*N*	Kappa
Major Depressive Disorder	82	0.78	83	0.69	10	0.90	13	1.00
Any Depression[3]	–	–	–	–	11	0.90	14	1.00
Depressive Disorder NOS	–	–	–	–	2	–	5	0.86
Any Bipolar Disorder[4]	–	–	–	–	5	1.00	5	1.00
Generalized Anxiety Disorder	82	–	83	0.65	8	0.75	8	0.78
Post-traumatic Stress Disorder	–	–	–	–	8	0.67	11	0.60
Specific Phobia	81	0.41	83	0.54	–	–	–	–
Social Phobia	82	0.25	83	0.54	–	–	–	–
Separation Anxiety	82	0.42	83	0.58	–	–	–	–
Any Anxiety Disorder[5]	–	–	–	–	11	1.00	13	0.60

[1] Shaffer, Fisher, and Lucas (2004)
[2] Kaufman, et al.(1997)
[3] Defined as MDD and/or Dysthymia
[4] Defined as Bipolar I or Bipolar NOS
[5] Defined as Panic, Separation Anxiety, Social Phobia, Agoraphobia, Simple Phobia, Generalized Anxiety, or Obsessive-Compulsive

Concurrent validity was assessed by comparing K-SADS-PL generated diagnosis with standardized rating scales. Children who screened positive for current depression scored significantly higher than the other children on the *Child Behavior Checklist* (CBCL) internalizing scale, while those who screened positive for any anxiety disorder scored significantly higher than other children on the parent and child versions of the Screen for *Child Anxiety Related Emotional Disorders* (SCARED; Birmayer et al., 1997) and the CBCL internalizing scales.

Behavior Ratings Scales and Standardized Self-Report Scales

Behavior ratings scales are another popular method for evaluating internalizing problems in youth. Recent decades have seen a dramatic increase in the number of empirically and theoretically developed ratings scales, and their use in multi-method, multi-informant assessment practices. Some rating scales are similar to symptom checklists, which allow the rater to indicate whether a particular symptom is present or absent, in the interest of determining whether or not a child meets DSM or other diagnostic criteria. Other rating scales, while appearing similar in structure and content, assess the extent to which a child possesses the depression or anxiety construct along a continuum of scores. Item responses allow for the assessment of the degree of severity of a symptom, behavior, or emotion. For instance, the BASC-2 allows parents and teachers to rate a student's behavior on a 4-point scale. Thus, each informant can rate a student's behavior as occurring *never, sometimes, often,* or *almost always.*

The widespread use of rating scales stems from the many practical advantages this assessment method provides. First, in comparison to other assessment methods (e.g., clinical interviews, direct observation), rating scales allow information to be obtained from multiple informants in a time- and cost-efficient manner. Second, rating scales also allow for a more objective, systematic collection of data, and tend to produce higher reliability than projective and semistructured interviews. Third, rating scales can measure low-base-rate behaviors that are unlikely to occur during infrequent direct observation (e.g., rule-breaking behavior such as stealing). Fourth, rating scales allow other informants to rate youth who cannot readily provide information about themselves. They also allow informants to provide information, which that they may refrain from disclosing in a face-to-face interview. Fifth, rating scales make it possible to compare data for a particular student across informants (e.g., teachers, parents, students themselves, etc.) and overtime. Finally, standardized rating scales allow an individual's behavior to be compared to a normative sample representative of the general population (Hart & Lahey, 1999; McConaughy & Ritter, 2008; Merrell, 2008).

Despite numerous advantages, rating scales possess several limitations. First, rating scales generally do not provide information related to specific criteria for psychiatric diagnoses (e.g., age of onset, duration of behavior, etc.). Second, they typically do not possess probes designed to clarify qualitative details concerning the reported behavior such as onset, intensity, etc. (Hart & Lahey, 1999). Finally, rating scales may be subject to response bias (e.g., social desirability effects, halo effects, leniency–severity bias, central tendency effects, etc.) and are less likely to detect malingering (Martin, Hooper, & Snow, 1986).

To combat methodological limitations such as careless or untruthful responding, misunderstanding, or other forms of response bias, several rating scales have developed validity indices. For instance, the BASC-2 has four validity indicators: F Index, L Index, V Index, and Response Pattern Index. The F Index assesses the possibility that a respondent rated test items in an exceedingly negative fashion (e.g.,"faking bad"). Alternatively, the L Index identifies response sets that may be inordinately positive (e.g., "faking good"). The V index contains illogical items (e.g., "I eat 100 sandwiches a day") that may be marked due to carelessness, uncooperativeness, or failure to comprehend the questions. Finally, the Response Pattern Index detects patterned responding (e.g., marking all items false or alternately responding T, F, T, F, T, F).

Similar to structured and semistructured interviews, there are a variety of broad- and narrow- band ratings scales that can be used to assess internalizing symptomatology in youth. Tables 14.8 and 14.9 present a brief summary of many of these instruments. More thorough descriptions of the ASEBA, BASC-2, BYI-2, CDI, RCMAS, and STAIC are provided in the sections below.

BROAD-BAND RATING SCALES
ASEBA
The ASEBA School-Age Forms (Achenbach and Rescorla, 2001) is a multi-informant system of instruments for evaluating the behavior and self-perceptions of youth ages 6 to 18 years (see Table 14.8). The ASEBA includes three parallel behavior rating scales (Child Behavior Checklist [CBCL/6-18], Teacher Report Form [TRF], and Youth Self-Report [YSR]), which can be used independently or in combination to measure numerous aspects of youth behavior across both adaptive

and clinical dimensions. Each form is written at the fifth grade level. Interviewers may also read the questions aloud for those respondents who have difficulty reading the forms. Additional translations of one or more of these forms are available in 65 languages (Bérubé & Achenbach, 2003).

The CBCL/6-18 has 120 items, and is designed to be completed by parents or others who view youth in home-like settings (e.g., relatives, foster parents, personnel in residential treatment facilities, etc.). Based on behaviors observed in the preceding six months, respondents rank items on a 0 to 2 scale corresponding to the descriptors "Not True," "Somewhat or Sometimes True," and "Very True or Often True." In addition, the CBCL/6-18 requires the respondent to describe the child's functioning in sports, organizations, jobs and chores, friendships, relationships with significant others, and academic performance, along with any illnesses or disabilities that the youth has, informant concerns regarding the youth, and the youth's strengths.

The TRF possesses120 items and can be completed by teachers, counselors, or other school personnel. Similar to the CBCL, respondents score items on a scale from 0 to 2. Although there is some overlap between items on the TRF and the CBCL/6-18, several items reflect variations in home versus school environments. Also, the CBCL/6-18 competence items are replaced by items that assess aspects of adaptive functioning evident in school (e.g., academic performance, work effort, appropriate school behavior, etc.). Teachers are also asked to provide available achievement and/or ability test data, and respond to open-ended questions about various aspects of the student's functioning (e.g., student's strengths, teacher's primary concerns).

The YSR contains 112 items and targets youth ages 11 to 18 years. The YSR possesses many of the same problem and competence items as the CBCL/6-18, but the items are worded in the first person. Youths are also asked to describe their illnesses and disabilities, concerns about school, and the best things about themselves.

The data provided by each respondent are represented across three separate profiles. The first profile represents competency data and displays scales for *Activities, Social, School,* and *Total Competence.* The second profile depicts eight problem syndromes: anxious/depressed, withdrawn/depressed, somatic complaints, social problems, thought problems, attention problems, rule-breaking behavior, and aggressive behavior. In addition, the subscales of the syndrome profile can be combined to form

Table 14.8 Basic characteristics of broad-band rating scales

Instrument	Primary References	Relevant Scales	Informants/ Age Range	Items/ Response Format	Time	Administration/ Scoring Options
Achenbach System of Empirically Based Assessment (ASEBA)	Achenbach &Rescorla (2007)	All Forms: Internalizing Anxious/ Depressed Withdrawn/ Depressed Somatic Complaints	SR: 11–18 years P/T: 6–18 years	SR: 112 items 3 point scale P/T: 113 items 3 point scale	SR: 20 min P/T: 15–20 min	Administration: Paper and pencil Internet Scoring: Hand score Computer entry
Behavioral Assessment System for Children, 2nd Edition (BASC-2)	Reynolds & Kamphaus (2004)	All Forms: Internalizing Problems Anxiety Depression Somatization Withdrawal (P/T forms only)	SR: (I) 6–7 years (C) 8–11 years (A) 12–21 years P/T: (P) 2–5 years (C) 6–11 years (A) 12–21 years	SR: (I) 64 items (C) 139 items (A) 176 items 4 point scale True/False P: (P) 100 items (C) 139 items (A) 139 items 4 point scale T: (P) 134 items (C) 160 items (A) 150 items 4 point scale	SR: 20–30 min P: 10–20 min T: 10–15min	Administration: Paper and pencil Scoring: Hand score Computer entry Scannable
Beck Youth Inventories, 2nd edition (BYI-2)	Beck, Beck, Jolly, & Steer (2005)	SR: Depression Inventory Anxiety Inventory	SR: 7–18 years	SR: 20 items per inventory 4 point scale	SR: 5–10 min per inventory	Administration: Paper and pencil Scoring: Hand score

SR = Self-report; P = Parent report; T = Teacher Report; (I) = Interview; (P) = Preschool; (C) = Child; (A) = Adolescent

internalizing and externalizing dimensions. Finally, the third profile includes six DSM-oriented scales (affective problems, anxiety problems, somatic problems, attentiondeficit/hyperactivity problems, oppositional defiant problems, and conduct problems) that are consistent with particular diagnostic categories of the DSM-IV (APA, 1994). School psychologists interested in the assessment of internalizing problems should pay particular attention to the *anxious/depressed, withdrawn/depressed, somatic complaints* syndrome scales and the *affective problems, anxiety problems,* and *somatic problems* DSM-oriented scales.

Administration time for the CBCL, TRF, and YRF ranges from 15–20 minutes, depending on the instrument administered. The forms can be scored by hand or by computer entry using ASEBA Windows software. T-scores and percentile ranks can be computed for each scale based on national norms. Additionally, cross-informant comparisons can be generated using the computer software.

According to the technical manual (Achenbach & Rescorla, 2001), the CBCL/6-18, TRF, YSR were normed on samples containing 1,753, 2,319, and 1,057 individuals respectively. Internal consistencies (Cronbach's alpha) for the CBCL/6-18 ranged from 0.63 (*school*) to 0.69 (*activities*) for the Competence and Adaptive scales, from 0.78 (*somatic complaints/thought problems*) to 0.94 (*aggressive problems*) for the Syndrome scales, and from 0.72 (*anxiety problems*) to 0.91 (*conduct problems*) for the DSM-oriented scales. For the YSR, internal consistencies ranged from 0.55 (*social*) to 0.72 (*activities*) for the Competence and Adaptive scales, from 0.71 (*withdrawn/depressed*) to 0.86 (*aggressive behavior*) for the Syndrome scales, and from 0.67

(*anxiety problems*) to 0.83 (*conduct problems*) for the DSM-oriented scales. Finally, internal consistencies ranged for the TRF from 0.72 (*somatic complaints/ thought problems*) to 0.95 (*aggressive behavior*) for the Syndrome scales, and from 0.73 (*anxiety problems*) to 0.94 (*attentiondeficit/hyperactivity problems*) for the DSM-oriented scales.

Test–retest reliabilities at 8 to 16 day intervals for the CBCL/6-18 ranged from 0.82 (*activities*) to 0.93 (*social*) for the Competence and Adaptive scales, from 0.82 (*anxious/depressed*) to 0.92 (*somatic complaints/attention problems*) for the Syndrome scales, and from 0.80 (*anxiety problems*) to 0.93 (*attention deficit/hyperactivity problems*) for the DSM-oriented scales. For the YSR, test–retest reliabilities ranged from 0.83 (*activities*) to 0.91 (*school*) for the Competence and Adaptive scales, from 0.67 (*withdrawn/depressed*) to 0.88 (*aggressive behavior*) for the Syndrome scales, and from 0.68 (*anxiety problems*) to 0.86 (*attention deficit/hyperactivity problems*) for the DSM-oriented scales. Finally, test–retest reliabilities for the TRF ranged from 0.83 (*school*) to 0.93 (*social*) for the Competence and Adaptive Scales, from 0.60 (*withdrawn/ depressed*) to 0.95 (*attention problems/social problems*) for the Syndrome scales, and from 0.62 (*affective problems*) to 0.95 (*attention deficit/hyperactivity problems*) for the DSM-oriented scales.

The technical manual (Achenbach and Rescorla, 2001) provides content, criterion, and construct validity evidence for the ASEBA scales. Item content is supported by decades of research, as well as consultation with mental health and educational professionals, pilot testing, feedback, and refinement. Criterion-related validity is supported by multiple regression analyses, odds ratios, and discriminant analyses that indicate the ability of CBCL, TRF, and YRF to differentiate significantly ($p < .01$) from demographically similar referred and non-referred youth. Finally, construct validity is supported on the basis of moderate to strong correlations with analogous scales on other instruments, including the BASC (Reyonlds & Kamphaus, 2002), the Conner's Rating Scales-Revised (Conners, 1997), and the DSM-IV Checklist (Hudziak, 1998), cross-cultural replications of the empirically based syndromes, genetic and biochemical correlates, and longitudinal outcomes.

BASC-2
The BASC-2 (Reynolds & Kamphaus, 2004) is a multi-informant, multidimensional system for evaluating the behavior and self-perceptions of youth and young adults aged 2 to 25 years (see Table 14.8). The BASC-2 contains three types of behavior rating scales (i.e., parent rating scale [PRS], teacher rating scale [TRS], and self-report of personality [SRP]) that can be used independently or in combination, to measure numerous aspects of a youth's behavior and personality across adaptive and clinical dimensions.

The TRS and the PRS target three age levels (Preschool, 2 to 5 years; Child, 6 to 11 years; and Adolescent, 12 to 21 years), with separate forms and number of items for each. The SRP assesses four age groups (Interview, 6 to 7 years; Child, 8 to 11 years; Adolescent, 12 to 21 years; and College, 18 to 25 years). Depending on the measure, each form is completed by an informant using a true/false format and/or a 4-choice response format, designated by the descriptors *never, sometimes, often,* and *almost always*. The TRS, PRS, and SRP consist of 4 to 5 composite scales, 11 to 16 primary scales, or 1 to 7 optional content scales, depending on the age group and informant used. Administration time varies from 10 to 30 minutes, depending on the component administered. The TRS, PRS, or SRP forms can be scored by hand, computer entry, or scanning, using the BASC-2 Assist software. T-scores and percentile ranks can be computed for each scale based on national norms, in addition to age, gender, or clinical status specific norms. The instruments also include validity scales to detect positive or negative informant response sets, and random or patterned responding.

The BASC-2 PRS, TRS, and SRP scales possess items and subscales intended to assess depression, anxiety, and somatization constructs. The items for these scales were not initially selected empirically, using clinical populations or diagnostic symptomatology, but rather by selecting items associated with these constructs based on psychopathology, personality, neurological, and temperamental research findings (Reynolds & Kamphaus, 2004). Elevated T-scores on these scales reflect high levels of the associated construct, which, although highly correlated with a diagnosis, does not indicate conclusively that a child has a disorder. Analogously, a high "height" score, whether 4 feet or 7 feet, does not necessarily indicate that an individual has a disorder. Rather, that decision is based on many factors, including an individual's age, societal opinions, and/or consensus criteria set by professional bodies and health or regulatory agencies. On the other hand, a depression, anxiety, or somatization T-score at or around the 98th percentile rank indicates that a youth's adjustment in any one of these areas is more impaired than the vast majority of children her or his age. Scores in this range suggest the need for treatment, monitoring, further assessment, or other intervention, regardless of whether or not a diagnosis is applicable.

The BASC-2 manual (Reynolds & Kamphaus, 2004) provides extensive information detailing the technical characteristics of the TRS, PRS, and SRP. Standardization data was collected between 2002 and 2004, from over 375 sites in 257 cities and 40 states. The general norms sample consists of over 13,000 cases for youth ages 2 to 18 years, and is highly consistent to the March 2001 U.S. census data with regard to sex, race/ethnicity, geographic region, socioeconomic status, and inclusion of special populations. The clinical norms sample consists of over 1,700 cases for youth ages 4 to 18 years, and includes individuals identified as having a clinical diagnosis in the following classification categories: Learning Disability, Speech–Language Impairment, Mental Retardation/Developmental Disability, Emotional/Behavioral Disturbance, Hearing Impairment, Attention Deficit/Hyperactivity Disorder, Pervasive Developmental Disorders, and Other.

The BASC-2 manual (Reynolds & Kamphaus, 2004) includes internal consistency and test–retest reliability estimates for the TRS, PRS, and SRP, and interrater reliability for the TRS and PRS. With regard to the TRS, internal consistency coefficients (coefficient alpha) ranged from 0.87 to 0.92 for the Internalizing Problems Composite, from 0.75 to 0.84 for the Anxiety Scale, and from 0.77 to 0.83 for the Somatization Scale. Reliabilities were generally higher for the adolescent age groups compared to the preschool age groups. With an interval of 8 to 65 days between ratings, test–retest reliabilities ranged from 0.81 to 0.85 for the Internalizing Problems Composite, from 0.64 to 0.77 for the Anxiety Scale, from 0.78 to 0.85 for the Depression Scale, and from 0.72 to 0.79 for the Somatization Scale. Finally, interrater reliabilities ranged from 0.48 to 0.61 for the Internalizing Problems Composite, from 0.23 to 0.52 for the Anxiety Scale, from 0.50 to 0.66 for the Depression Scale, and from 0.19 to 0.74 for the Somatization Scale.

For the PRS, internal consistency coefficients (coefficient alpha) ranged from 0.85 to 0.91 for the Internalizing Problems Composite, from 0.71 to 0.85 for the Anxiety Scale, from 0.79 to 0.88 for the Depression Scaleand from 0.79 to 0.84 for the Somatization Scale. Similar to the TRS, reliabilities

were generally higher for the adolescent age groups compared to the preschool age groups. With an interval of 9 to 70 days between ratings, test–retest reliabilities ranged from 0.78 to 0.90 for the Internalizing Problems Composite, from 0.73 to 0.84 for the Anxiety Scale, from 0.73 to 0.87 for the Depression Scale, and from 0.65 to 0.84 for the Somatization Scale. Finally, interrater reliabilities ranged from 0.69 to 0.70 for the Internalizing Problems Composite, from 0.57 to 0.80 for the Anxiety Scale, from 0.59 to 0.78 for the Depression Scale, and from 0.53 to 0.70 for the Somatization Scale.

For the SRP, internal consistency coefficients (coefficient alpha) ranged from 0.95 to 0.96 for the Internalizing Problems Composite, from 0.86 to 0.89 for the Anxiety Scale, from 0.84 to 0.88 for the Depression Scale, and from 0.67 to 0.71 for the Somatization Scale. With an interval of 13 to 66 days between ratings, test–retest reliabilities ranged from 0.70 to 0.86 for the Internalizing Problems Composite, from 0.82 to 0.86 for the Anxiety Scale, from 0.73 to 0.87 for the Depression Scale, and from 0.67 to 0.74 for the Somatization Scale.

The technical manual provides validity support through the scale intercorrelations (divergent and convergent), factor analysis (covariance structure analysis and principle axis analysis), correlations of composite and scale scores with other behavioral measures of similar constructs, and score profiles for various clinical groups. In general, the factorial structures for the composites and scales appear to be robust. Correlations with other instruments including the BASC (Reynolds & Kamphaus, 1992), the Conners Rating Scale-Revised (CRS-R; Conners, 1997), the Behavior Rating Inventory of Executive Functioning (BRIEF; Gioia, Isquith, Guy, & Kenworthy, 2000), Conners-Well's Adolescent Self-Report Scale (CASS; Conners, 1997), CDI (Kovacs, 2003), (RCMAS; Reynolds & Richmond, 1985), Brief Symptom Inventory (BSI; Derogatis, 1993), and the Beck Depression Inventory-II (BDI-II; Beck, Steer, & Brown, 1996) provide evidence for convergent and discriminant construct validity. Profile comparisons of various clinical groups (e.g., anxiety, depression, etc.) to normative mean scores provide additional evidence of construct validity.

BYI-II

The Beck Youth Inventories–2nd Edition for Children and Adolescents (BYI-II; Beck, Beck,

Jolly, & Steer, 2005) is a set of five self-rated inventories that are designed to be used separately or in combination, to assess youth ages 7 to 18 years across five areas: depression, anxiety, anger, disruptive behavior, and self-concept (see Table 14.8). Each inventory consists of 20 items, takes approximately 5 to 10 minutes to complete, and can be administered individually or in groups. Items are written at a second grade level, and reflect statements concerning the thoughts, feelings, and behaviors associated with emotional and social impairment in youth. Youths report how frequently the statement has been true for them during the previous two weeks on a 4-point scale (0 = never, 1 = sometimes, 2 = often, 3 = always). Total raw scores range from 0 to 60 and can be converted to T-scores, cumulative percentages, descriptive classifications, and scale profiles.

The BYI-II manual (Beck et al., 2005) contains specific procedures for the administration, scoring, and interpretation of the inventories, as well as sections describing the instrument's development, standardization, normative sample, reliability, and validity. Internal consistency estimates range from 0.86 to 0.96, and test–retest reliability coefficients range from 0.74 to 0.93, depending on scale and age group. The average correlations coefficients between the BYI-II depression scale and Children's Depression Inventory (CDI; Kovacs, 2003) were reported as 0.70 for a subsample of 128 children (7–14 years) and 0.67 for a subsample of 26 adolescents (15–18 years). Similarly, the average correlations between the BYI-II Anxiety Scale and the Revised Children's Manifest Anxiety Scale (RCMAS, Reynolds & Richmond, 1985) were reported as 0.70 for a subsample of 192 children (7–14 years) and 0.64 for a subsample of 35 adolescents (15–18 years). Future studies are necessary to further evaluate the utility of BYI-II for the assessment of internalizing disorders in youth.

NARROW-BAND RATING SCALES
The Children's Depression Inventory
The Children's Depression Inventory [2003 update] (CDI [2003 update]; Kovacs, 2003) is a multi-informant system of instruments for evaluating the presence and severity of depressive symptoms in youth ages 7 to 17 years (see Table 14.9). The CDI [2003 update] includes the original 27-item self-report instrument (CDI; Kovacs, 1992), a 10-item short version (CDI:S), a 17-item parent version (CDI:P), and a 12-item teacher version (CDI:T). The self-report, parent, and teacher versions can be used individually or in conjunction, to gather perspectives across multiple raters.

The CDI (Kovacs, 1992) was developed as a downward extension of the BDI (Beck, 1967) for use with children and adolescents. The CDI:S was developed to serve as a quick screening measure of depressive symptoms. The CDI and CDI:S both require respondents to identify which of three statements (corresponding to the absence of symptoms, mild symptoms, or definite symptoms) best fits their feelings and ideas during the preceding 2 weeks. Both forms can be administered individually or in a group format. The CDI requires approximately 15 minutes to complete, whereas the CDI:S requires approximately 5 minutes. Scoring can be computer or hand generated. In addition to the *Total Score*, the CDI also produces five subscale scores: *negative mood, interpersonal problems, ineffectiveness, anhedonia*, and *negative self-esteem*. The CDI:S yields a total score only.

Items on CDI: P and CDI:T are similar to the CDI, but reworded to reflect variations in informant, and home and school contexts. Based on behaviors observed over the past 2 weeks, respondents select one response from the descriptors *not at all, some of the time, often*, or *much or most of the time*. The CDI:P and CDI:T yield a total score in addition to two subscales (*emotional problems* and *functional problems*), and can be completed in approximately 10 minutes. Similar to the CDI and CDI:S, scoring can be computer or hand generated.

The CDI and CDI:S standardization data, gathered between 1979 and 1984, included self-reports from 1,266 Florida public school students ages 7 to 17. Data regarding student ethnicity was not reported (Finch, Saylor, and Edwards, 1985). CDI:P and CDI:T standardization data, collected between 1997 and 2003, includes both clinical and non-clinical samples (Freeman, 2007). The nonclinical sample consisted of 1,187 parent and 631 teacher evaluations. Ethnicity for the nonclinical population was reported as 83.4% Caucasian, 4% African American, 3.8% Hispanic, and 2.8% Asian. The clinical sample consisted of 167 parent and 114 teacher evaluations of youth with a variety of psychiatric diagnoses. Ethnicity for the clinical sample was reported as 77.9% Caucasian, 2.9% African American, 3.9% Hispanic, and 4.4% Asian.

Internal consistency of the CDI, as measured by coefficient alpha, ranged from 0.71 in a group of 61 pediatric medical outpatients to 0.87 in a group of 860 Canadian school children. Internal consistencies of the CDI:P and CDI:T ranged from 0.68 to 0.88 for the nonclinical sample, and from 0.76 to 0.89 for the clinical sample. Test–retest reliabilities ranged from 0.38 to 0.87 for intervals of 1 to 4 weeks, and from 0.54 to 0.67 for intervals of 6 weeks (Freeman, 2007) for the CDI.

Research suggests that the factor structure of the CDI varies depending on sample characteristics. For instance, in a study contrasting clinical and control samples, Carey, Faulstich, Gresham, Ruggiero, & Enyart (1987) found two factors (*depressive affect* and *oppositional behavior*) for a clinical sample of psychiatric inpatients, and three factors (*depressive affect, oppositional behavior,* and *personal adjustment*) for the control sample. In contrast, the results of comparing clinic-referred children and adolescent samples suggested a five first-order and one second-order factor structure for the CDI (Weiss, et al., 1991). Differing factor content suggests a developmental effect may exist for this measure.

Although studies report significant relationships of the CDI to other instruments claimed to measure depression and related constructs (Merrell, 2008), and support its ability to distinguish between children with depression compared to nonreferred children (Carey, et al., 1987), multiple studies indicate that the CDI is unable to discriminate between clinical groups of youth with conduct disorders, compared to youth with affective disorders (e.g. Nelson, Politano, Finch, Wendel, & Mayhall, 1987; Saylor, Finch, Baskin, et al., 1984, Saylor, Finch, Spirito, & Bennett, 1984). Doerfler, Felner, Rowlison, and Raley (1988) found that the CDI correlated poorly with parent and teacher ratings of depression. In combination, these findings suggest that the CDI may be more appropriate as a screening instrument for emotional distress, rather than a diagnostic tool for depression.

RCMAS-2

The Revised Children's Manifest Anxiety Scale, 2nd edition (RCMAS-2; Reynolds & Richmond, 2008) is a 49-item self-report instrument of trait anxiety for youth ages 6 to 19 years (see Table 14.9). The instrument uses a Yes/No response format, and consists of 4 anxiety scales (i.e., *total anxiety, physiological anxiety, worry,* and *social anxiety*), 2 validity scales (i.e., *inconsistent responding index* and *defensiveness*), and a 10-item, content-based cluster that focuses on performance anxiety. The RCMAS-2 can be administered individually or in a group format, and can be completed in approximately 10 to 15 minutes. A short-form total score can also be generated by

only administering the first 10 items, which takes about 5 minutes to complete. Raw scores can be converted to subscale and T-score percentile ranks using a scoring worksheet and profile sheet corresponding to the respondent's age (6–10 years; 9–14 years; or 15–19 years).

According to the technical manual (Reynolds & Richmond, 2008), the RCMAS-2 was standardized on a nationally representative sample of 2,369 youth ages 6 to 19 years. Internal consistency reliabilities for scale scores ranged from 0.75 (Physiological Anxiety) to 0.92 (Total Anxiety) for the full reference sample, and 0.70 (Physiological Anxiety) to 0.92 (Total Anxiety) for a clinical sample. Test–retest values for a one week interval ranged from 0.64 (Social Anxiety) to 0.76 (Total Anxiety) for the full form and 0.54 (Total Anxiety) for the short form.

The manual (Reynolds & Richmond, 2008) also provides convergent and divergent validity evidence for the RCMAS-2, using correlational studies between the RCMAS-2 scales and the Children's Measure of Obsessive-Compulsive Symptoms (CMOCS; Reynolds & Livingston, in press), Conners' Rating Scales–Parent and Teacher Forms (CRS-P and CRS-T; Conners, 1989), CDI:S (Kovacs, 2003), and RCMAS (Reynolds & Richmond, 1985). The test authors assert that because the RCMAS-2 scales correlate highly with the RCMAS scales, and due to the substantial item overlap between the two versions, validity research using the RCMAS can be extended to the RCMAS-2. Despite this claim, additional reliability and validity research is needed to further support the inferences drawn from the newly updated RCMAS-2.

STAIC

The State–Trait Anxiety Inventory for Children (STAIC; Speilberger, Edwards, Montuori, & Lushene, 1973) is a self-report assessment of anxiety of children ages 9 to 12 years (see Table 14.9). The STAIC consists of two 20-item scales that can be administered independently or in combination. Each scale requires approximately 10 minutes to complete and may be administered individually or in group format. The State Anxiety Scale provides a measure of the amount of anxiety the respondent is feeling at the time of the inventory administration (e.g., how they feel "right now, in this very moment"), while the Trait Anxiety Scale measures the youth's general level of anxiety (how they "usually feel"). Items are scored as 1, 2, or 3 points, with the higher scores reflecting increasingly severe

Table 14.9 Basic characteristics of narrow-band rating scales for assessing internalizing deficits

Instrument	Primary References	Scales	Informants/ Age Range	Items/ Response Format	Time	Administration/ Scoring Options
Clinical Assessment of Depression (CAD)	Bracken & Howell (2004)	SR: Total Score Depressed Mood Anxiety/Worry Diminished Interest Cognitive/ Physical Fatigue	SR: 8–79 years	SR: 50 items 4 point scale	SR: 10 minutes	Administration: Paper and pencil Scoring: Hand scoring Computer entry
Children's Depression Inventory[2003 update] (CDI)	Kovacs (2003)	SR: Total Score Negative Mood Interpersonal Difficulties Negative Self-Esteem Ineffectiveness Anhedonia P & T: Total Score Emotional Problems Functional Problems SF: Total Score	All forms: 7–17 years	SR: 27 items 3 point scale P: 17 items 4 point scale T: 12 items 4 point scale SF: 10 items 3 point scale	SR: 15 minutes P: 10 minutes T: 10 minutes SF: 5 minutes	Administration: Paper and pencil Scoring: Hand scoring Computer entry
State–Trait Anxiety Inventory for Children (STAIC)	Speilberger, Edwards, Montuori, & Lushene (1973)	SR: State Anxiety Trait Anxiety	SR: 9–12 years	SR: 20 items per scale 3 point scale	SR: 8–20 minutes	Administration: Paper and pencil Scoring: Hand Scoring
Multidimensional Anxiety Scale for Children (MASC)	March, Parker, Sullivan, Stallings, &Conners (1997) Rynn, et al. (2006)	SR: Total Anxiety Physical Symptoms Harm Avoidance Social Anxiety Separation Panic SF: Total Anxiety	SR: 8–19 years	SR: 39 items SF: 10 items	SR: 15 min SF: 5 min	Administration: Paper and pencil Scoring: Hand Scoring
Revised Children's Manifest Anxiety Scale (RCMAS-2)	Reynolds & Richmond (2008)	SR: Total Anxiety Physiological Anxiety Worry Social Anxiety SF: Total Anxiety	All forms: 6–19 years	SR: 49 items Yes/No SF: 10 items Yes/No	SR: 15 min SF: 5 min	Administration: Paper and pencil Audio Scoring: Hand Scoring Computer Entry
Reynolds Child Depression Scale (RCDS)	Reynolds (1989)	SR: Total Score	SR: 8–12 years	SR: 30 items 4 point scale	SR: 10 min	Administration: Paper and pencil Scoring: Hand Scoring

(Continued)

Table 14.9   (Cont'd) Basic characteristics of narrow-band rating scales for assessing internalizing deficits

Instrument	Primary References	Scales	Informants/ Age Range	Items/ Response Format	Time	Administration/ Scoring Options
Reynolds Adolescent Depression Scale, 2nd Edition (RADS-2)	Reynolds (2002) Reynolds (2004)	SR: Total Score Dysphoric Mood Anhedonia/Negative Affect Negative Self-Evaluation Somatic Complaints	SR: 11–20 years	SR: 30 items 4 point scale	SR: 5–10 min	Administration: Paper and pencil Scoring: Hand Scoring

SR = Self-report; P = Parent; T = Teacher; SF = Short Form

symptoms. T scores are derived with a mean of 50 and a standard deviation of 10. Evidence of test–retest reliability, internal consistency, and construct validity is presented in the manual for the STAIC. The STAIC is reported to have good internal consistency (State Anxiety: 0.82 males, 0.87 females; Trait Anxiety: 0.78 for males; 0.81 for females).

According to the technical manual (Speilberger et al., 1973), the STAIC was standardized on 1,554 fourth, fifth, and sixth grade students in the state of Florida. Internal consistency coefficients for both scales have generally been reported in the 0.80s range (Frick, Burns, & Kamphaus, 2009). The test–retest reliability coefficients reported in the manual are higher for the trait anxiety scale (0.65 to .071) than for the state anxiety scale (0.31 to 0.41) at 6-week intervals. Hodges (1990) found the Trait Scale of the STAIC to be valid in differentiating children with anxiety disorders from children with a conduct disorder or depression diagnosis, and children without any diagnosis. In a clinical study of psychiatrically hospitalized children, Hoehn-Saric, Maisami, and Wiegand (1987) found that the Trait Scale of the STAIC failed to differentiate anxiety-disordered from non-anxiety-disordered children. In another study, Strauss and colleagues (1988) found that the State Scale, but not the Trait measure, discriminated between children with anxiety disorders and controls.

Assessment Process

Informant rating scales have become the defacto "gold standard" for the assessment of children's internalizing problems and disorders, alongside use of the DSM-IV-TR diagnostic criteria. Rating scales have become common for two principal reasons: practicality of time and cost, and the ability

to assess deviancy or severity using nationally representative norming samples. Despite its advantages, this dimensional approach does not represent the gold standard for diagnosis; that distinction still belongs to the DSM classification. These scales, however, have become the gold standard for construct assessment, severity assessment, progress monitoring, and assessment or outcomes in treatment efficacy and other research studies.

The popularity of informant rating scales, however, poses a number of additional research and practice questions, including selection of informants, combination of informants, and selection of norming sample comparisons. In fact, much more is unknown than known about selecting and combining informants. Put succinctly by Johnston and Murray (2003), "There is a clear need for more research in this area rather than blind faith in a 'more are better' approach to selecting informants" (p. 500). We do know that the perceptions of informants differ (Achenbach, McConaughy, & Howell, 1987), but any recommendations about the "best" informant are just that. While for many years it was commonly believed that teachers and parents were best suited for the assessment of the core symptoms of ADHD, for example, there is now some evidence to suggest that children from middle childhood on through adolescence report these symptoms relatively accurately on self-report measures (Reynolds & Kamphaus, 2004). In the absence of substantial evidence to guide practice, another practical way to think of information selection is to consider the setting of interest and the referral source. If, for example, impairment is occurring in school, then a teacher rating (or two) seems necessary. If a goal of assessment or diagnosis is to ascertain whether or not there is impairment in more than one setting, parent ratings may provide insight into community and home adjustment, and a self-report may provide an assessment of problems with peer or intrapsychic adjustment. In addition, the referral source that expresses concern may, in fact, be the person who knows the child's problems best and, thus, should likely be included as an informant.

Of course, one of the most important decisions in assessment practice is that of differential diagnosis, which begs the question of which informant is likely to provide the most accurate symptom picture needed to make a "diagnosis." In this regard, not much has changed since Piacentini, Cohen, and Cohen (1992) revealed in their seminal investigation that a single symptom assessment that produces a diagnosis is as efficient as trying to combine informants in some complicated fashion. In other words, if the child, parent, or teacher provides enough information to exceed the threshold for a diagnosis, then a diagnosis is typically warranted, regardless of whether a diagnostic standard requires impairment in two or more settings.

The typical diagnostic question has to do with detection of a disorder by assessing deviance from the norm, be it the presence of abnormal cancer cells, significant arterial plaque, more hyperactivity than is typical, or anxiety that far exceeds that of most children. In all of these medical and psychiatric diagnostic questions, the decision is relatively SES, sex, age, ethnicity, and linguistically blind, although there are exceptions. In other words, the same diagnostic threshold is used to determine whether or not a person has heart disease or depression, regardless of whether it is a man or woman, boy or girl. Thus, most modern psychological tests do not even include subgroup norms like the Wechsler intelligence scales, mathematics tests, or measures of height. On all of these measures, for example, there aresome statistically different results for girls and boys, but separate sex subgroup norms are not provided. This is not the case, however, for some behavior rating scales of internalizing problems where sex-differentiated norms are the only norms available. The effect of using separate sex based norms is that it eliminates sex differences (Reynolds & Kamphaus, 2004), which seems at odds with bountiful research showing that sex differences abound in depression, hyperactivity, and other constructs. Accordingly, we recommend the use of a general national normative sample, inclusive of all sex, SES, ethnic, linguistic, nationality, and other groups, as the norming sample of choice for making a diagnostic decision.

Conclusion

The assessment technology available for assessing internalizing disorders of childhood has improved substantially, in that better informant rating scales are available to assess the construct, and the DSM categorical system continues to improve with each revision. The use of these two classes of measures in tandem, in this case informant rating scales allow for the early detection of children at risk for these disorders, and those subsyndromal cases that may benefit from early intervention, as well. The DSM system allows for better classification of children and adolescents who are syndromal, therefore enhancing the ability of researchers to document the etiologies, comorbidities, courses, and epidemiology of internalizing disorders, with the aim of improving prevention and treatment efforts. Ultimately, better measurement remains a prerequisite for scientific progress and improved treatment of anxiety, depression, and somatization problems.

Future Directions

The many unanswered research questions surrounding internalizing disorders and their assessment were outlined earlier in this chapter. One potential future direction that has not been mentioned is a rapprochement between the dimensional and categorical classification systems, in the form of a new hybrid system that includes the best aspects of both. A new system of this nature is now possible, and being explored, thanks to the advent of item response theory, structural equation modeling, cognitive diagnostic models, and related methods. This hybrid classification model would have the advantage of being able to classify the full range of internalizing problem severity, from the typical to the severe and incapacitating. An assessment and classification system that covers the full range of problems has been predicted for decades and, we hope, will become feasible in the near future. Skinner (1981) foresaw the need for a hybrid system about three decades ago and concluded, "… the debate over dimensions versus categories has generated a heated controversy throughout the history of psychiatry. Hybrid models, such as the class–quantitative structure, may prove fruitful for integrating the distinctive merits of each approach. Perhaps a real breakthrough in our understanding of psychiatric disorders awaits the skillful use of composite models "(p. 72).

Much has changed in measurement science, psychometrics, and psychiatric diagnosis since Skinner made this observation, resulting in new opportunities to improve diagnostic practices. Specifically, the cognitive diagnostic modeling approach espoused by Rupp, Templin, and Henson (2010) may constitute an analytic method and logic model that may allow internalizing disorder diagnosis to better approach Skinner's goals.

Endnotes

1. Children and adolescents are henceforth referred to as *youth*
2. The term *childhood* refers to both childhood and adolescence

Appendix A: Lit of Abbreviations

Achenbach System of Empirically Based Assessment (ASEBA)

American Psychiatric Association (APA)

Beck Depression Inventory-II (BDI-II)

Beck Youth Inventories-2nd Edition for Children and Adolescents (BYI-II)

Behavioral Assessment System for Children (BASC)

Behavioral Assessment System for Children, 2nd Edition (BASC-2)

Behavior Rating Inventory of Executive Functioning (BRIEF)

Brief Symptom Inventory (BSI)

Child and Adolescent Psychiatric Assessment (CAPA)

Clinical Assessment of Depression (CAD)

Child Assessment Schedule (CAS)

Child Behavior Checklist (CBCL)

Children's Depression Inventory (CDI)

Children's Measure of Obsessive-Compulsive Symptoms (CMOCS)

Conners' Rating Scales-Revised (CRS-R)

Conners-Well's Adolescent Self-Report Scale (CASS)

Diagnostic Interview Schedule for Children and Adolescents, 4th edition (DICA-IV)

Diagnostic Interview Schedule for Children, 4th edition (DISC-IV)

Diagnostic and Statistical Manual for Mental Disorders, 3rd edition, revised (DSM-III-R)

Diagnostic and Statistical Manual for Mental Disorders, 4th edition (DSM-IV)

Diagnostic and Statistical Manual for Mental Disorders, 4th edition, text revision (DSM-IV-TR)

Emotional disturbance (ED)

Global Severity Index of the Symptom Check List-Revised (SCL-90-R)

Individuals with Disabilities Education Improvement Act (IDEIA)

International Classification of Diseases, 10th revision (ICD-10)

Interview Schedule for Children and Adolescents (ISCA)

Multidimensional Anxiety Scale for Children (MASC)

Other Health Impairment (OHI)

Reynolds Adolescent Depression Scale, 2nd edition (RADS-2)

Reynolds Child Depression Scale (RCDS)

Revised Children's Manifest Anxiety Scale (RCMAS)

Revised Children's Manifest Anxiety Scale, 2nd edition (RCMAS-2)

Schedule of Affective Disorders and Schizophrenia, School-Age Children-Present and Lifetime version (K-SADS-PL)

Screen for Child Anxiety and Related Emotional Disorders (SCARED)

State-Trait Anxiety Inventory for Children (STAIC)

U.S. National Institute of Mental Health (NIMH)

References

Achenbach, T. M. (1966). The classification of children's psychiatric symptoms: A factor-analytic study. *Psychological Monographs, 80*, Whole No. 615.

Achenbach, T. M. (1985). *Assessment and taxonomy of child and adolescent psychopathology.* Thousand Oaks, CA: Sage Publications, Inc.

Achenbach, T. M. (1988). Integrating assessment and taxonomy. *Assessment and diagnosis in child psychopathology* (pp. 300–343). New York, NY: Guilford Press.

Achenbach, T. M, & Edelbrock, C. S. (1978). The classification of child psychopathology: A review and analysis of empirical efforts. *Psychological Bulletin, 85*(6), 1275–1301.

Achenbach, T., McConaughy, S., & Howell, C. (1987). Child/adolescent behavioral and emotional problems: Implications of cross-informant correlations for situational specificity. *Psychological Bulletin, 101*(2), 213–232.

Achenbach, T. M. & Rescorla, L. A. (2001). *Manual for the ASEBA School-Age Forms and Profiles.* Burlington, VT: Research Center for Children, Youth, and Families.

Achenbach, T., & Rescorla, L. (2007). *Multicultural understanding of child and adolescent psychopathology: Implications for mental health assessment.* New York, NY US: Guilford Press.

Ambrosini, P. J. (2000). Historical development and present status of the schedule for affective disorders and schizophrenia for school-aged children (K-SADS). *Journal of the American Academy of Child and Adolescent Psychiatry, 39*, 49–58.

American Psychiatric Association (1987). *Diagnostic and statistical manual of mental disorders* (3rd ed., text revision). Washington, DC: Author.

American Psychiatric Association (1994). *Diagnostic and statistical manual of mental Disorders* (4th ed.). Washington, DC: Author.

American Psychiatric Association (2000). *Diagnostic and statistical manual of mental disorders* (4th ed., text revision). Washington, DC: Author.

Angold, A., & Costello, E. J. (1995). A test–retest reliability study of child-reported psychiatric symptoms and diagnoses using the Child and Adolescent Psychiatric Assessment (CAPA-C), *Psychological Medicine, 25*, 755–762.

Angold, A., & Costello E. (2000). The Child and Adolescent Psychiatric Assessment (CAPA). *Journal of the American Academy of Child and Adolescent Psychiatry, 39*, 39–48.

Angold, A., Prendergast, M., Cox, A., Harrington, R., Simonoff, E., & Ruttner, M. (1995). The Child and Adolescent Psychiatric Assessment (CAPA), *Psychological Medicine, 25*, 739–753.

Aronen, E. T., Noam, G. G., & Weinstein, S. R. (1993). Structured diagnostic interviews and clinicians' discharge diagnoses in hospitalized adolescents. *Journal of the American Academy of Child and Adolescent Psychiatry, 32*, 674–681.

Beck, A. T. (1967). *Depression.* New York: Hoeber.

Beck, J. S., Beck, A. T., Jolly, J. B., & Steer, R. A. (2005). *Beck Youth Inventories–Second Edition for Children and Adolescents Manual.* San Antonio, TX: Psychological Corporation.

Beck, A. T., Steer, R. A., & Brown, G. K. (1996). *Beck Depression Inventory–II.* San Antonio, TX: The Psychological Corporation.

Bérubé, R. L., & Achenbach, T. M. (2003). *Bibliography of published studies using ASEBA: 2003 edition.* Burlington, VT: University of Vermont, Research Center for Children, Youth, & Families.

Birmaher, B., Khetarpal, S., Brent, D., Cully, M., Balach, L., Kaufman, J., et al. (1997). The Screen for Child Anxiety Related Emotional Disorders (SCARED): Scale construction and psychometric characteristics. *Journal of the American Academy of Child and Adolescent Psychiatry, 36*, 545–553.

Bracken, B. A., & Howell, K. (2004). *Clinical Assessment of Depression: Professional manual.* Odessa, FL: Psychological Assessment Resources.

Bravo, M., Riberia, J., Rubio–Stipec, M., Canino, G., Shrout, P., Ramierez, R., et al. (2001). Test–retest reliability of the Spanish version of the Diagnostic Interview Schedule for Children (DISC–IV). *Journal of Abnormal Child Psychology, 29*, 433–444.

Callahan, S.A., Panichelli-Mindel, S. M., & Kendall, P. C. (1996). DSM–IV and internalizing disorders: Modifications, limitations, and utility. *School Psychology Review, 25*(3), 297–307.

Carey, M. P., Faulstich, M. E., Gresham, F. M., Ruggiero, L., & Enyart, P. (1987). Children's Depression Inventory: Construct and discriminant validly across clinical and non-referred (control) populations. *Journal of Consulting and Clinical Psychology, 55*, 755–761.

Conners, C. K. (1989). Conners' Rating Scales Manual. New York: Multi-Health Systems.

Conners, C. K. (1997). Conners' Rating Scales–Revised Manual. New York: Multi-Health Systems.

Derogatis, L. R. (1993). *Brief Symptom Inventory.* Minneapolis, MN: National Computer Systems.

Doerfler, L. A., Felner, R. D., Rowlison, R. T., & Raley, P. A. (1988). Depression in children and adolescents: A comparative analysis of the utility and construct validity of two assessment measures. *Journal of Consulting and Clinical Psychology, 56*, 769–772.

Dowdy, E., Mays, K. L., Kamphaus, R. W., & Reynolds, C. R. (2009). Roles of diagnosis and classification in school psychology. In T. B. Gutkin & C. R. Reynolds (Eds.). *The Handbook of School Psychology* (4th ed.). New York: John Wiley & Sons.

Finch, A. J., Saylor, C. F., & Edwards, G. L. (1985). Children's Depression Inventory: Sex and grade norms for normal children. *Journal of Consulting and Clinical Psychology, 53*, 424–425.

Freeman, S. J. (2007). Review of the Children's Depression Inventory. In K. F. Geisinger, R. A. Spies, J. F. Carlson, and B.S. Plake (Eds.). *The seventeenth mental measurements yearbook.* Lincoln, NE: Buros Institute of Mental Measurements. Retrieved from Mental Measurements Yearbook database.

Frick, P. J., Burns, C., & Kamphaus, R. W. (2009). *Clinical assessment of child and adolescent personality and behavior (2nd Ed.).* New York, NY: Springer.

Gioia, G. A., Isquith, P. K., Guy, S. C. & Kenworthy, L. (2000). *Behavior Rating Inventory of Executive Function* (BRIEF). Lutz, FL: Psychological Assessment Resources.

Hart, E. L., & Lahey, B. B. (1999). General child behavior rating scales. In D. Shaffer, C.P. Lucas, & J. E. Richters (Eds.). *Diagnostic Assessment in Child and Adolescent Psychopathology* (pp. 3–33). New York: The Guildford Press.

Ho, T., Leung, P. W., Lee, C., Tang, C., Hung, S. Kwong, S., et al., (2005). Test–retest Reliability of the Chinese version of the Diagnostic Interview Schedule for Children–Version 4 (DISC–IV). *Journal of Child Psychology and Psychiatry, 46*(10), 1135–1138.

Hodges, K., Kline, J., Stern, L., Cytyrn, L., & McKnew, D. (1982). The development of a child assessment interview for research and clinical use. *Journal of Abnormal Child Psychology, 10*, 173–189.

Hodges, K., McKnew, D., Cytryn, L., Stern, L., & Kline, J. (1982). The Child Assessment Schedule (CAS) diagnostic interview: A report on reliability and validity. *Journal of the American Academy of Child Psychiatry, 21*, 468–473.

Hodges, K. (1990). Depression and anxiety in children: A comparison of self-report questionnaires to clinical interview. *Psychological Assessment, 2*, 376–381.

Hoehn-Saric, E., Maisami, M., & Wiegand, D. (1987). Measurement of anxiety in children and adolescents using semistructured interviews. *Journal of the American Academy of Child and Adolescent Psychiatry, 26*, 541–545.

Hojnoski, R. L., Morrison, R., Brown, M., & Matthews, W. J. (2006). Projective test use among school psychologists: A survey and critique. *Journal of Pyschoeducational Assessment, 24*(2), 145–159.

Hudziak, J. J. (1998). *DSM–IV Checklist for Childhood Disorders.* Burlington, VT: University of Vermont, Research Center for Children, Youth, and Families.

Individuals with Disabilities Education Improvement Act of 2004, Pub. L. No. 108–476 §1400 et seq. (2004).

Johnston, C., & Murray, C. (2003). Incremental validity in the psychological assessment of children and adolescents. *Psychological Assessment, 15*, 496–507.

Kaufman, J., Birmaher, B., Brent, D., Rao, U., Flynn, C., & Moreci, et al. (1997). Schedule for Affective Disorders and Schizophrenia for School-Age Children–Present and Lifetime version (K-SADS-PL): Initial reliability and validity data. *Journal of the American Academy of Child & Adolescent Psychiatry, 36*(7), 980–988.

Kaufman, J., & Schweder, A. E. (2004). The Schedule for Affective Disorders and Schizophrenia for School-Age Children: Present and Lifetime Version (K-SADS-PL). In Hersen, M. (Ed.), *Comprehensive handbook of psychological assessment* (pp. 247–255). New Jersey: Wiley & Sons.

Kennedy, M. L., Faust, D., Willis, W. G., & Piotrowski, C. (1994). Social-emotional assessment practices in school psychology. *Journal of Psychoeducational Assessment, 12*, 228–240.

Kovacs, M. (2003) *Children's Depression Inventory.* North Tonawanda, NY: Multi-Health Systems.

Kovacs, M. (1992) *Children's Depression Inventory.* North Tonawanda, NY: Multi-Health Systems.

Lilienfeld, S. O., Wood, J. M., & Garb, H. N. (2000). The scientific status of projective techniques. *Psychological Science in the Public Interest, 1*, 27–66.

Loney, B. R., & Frick, P. J. (2003).Structured diagnostic interviewing. In C. R. Reynolds & R. W. Kamphaus (Eds.), *Handbook of Psychological & Educational Assessment of Children* (pp. 235–255). New York: The Guildford Press.

March, J. S., Parker, J., Sullivan, K., Stallings, P., & Conners, C. K. (1997). The Multidimensional Scale for Children (MASC): factor structure, reliability, and validity. *Journal of the American Academy of Child and Adolescent Psychiatry, 36,* 554–565.

Martin, R. P., Hooper, S., & Snow, J. (1986). Behavior rating scale approaches to personality assessment in children and adolescents. In H. M. Knoff (Ed.), *The assessment of child and adolescent personality* (pp. 309–351). New York: Guilford Press.

McConaughy, S. H., & Ritter, D. R. (2002/2008). Best practices in multidimensional assessment of emotional or behavioral disorders. In A. Thomas & J. Grimes (Eds.), *Best practices in school psychology IV* (pp. 1303–1320). Bethesda, MD: National Association of School Psychologists.

Merrell, K. W. (2008). *Behavioral, social, and emotional assessment of children and adolescents* (3rd ed.). New York: Lawrence Erlbaum Associates.

Merrell, K. W., Ervin, R. A., & Gimpel, G. A. (2006). *School psychology for the 21st century: Foundations and practice.* New York: Guilford.

Miller, D. N.,& Nickerson, A. B. (2007). Projective techniques and the school-based assessment of childhood internalizing disorders: A critical analysis. *Journal of Projective Psychology & Mental Health, 14,* 48–58.

Nelson, W. M., Politano, P. M., Finch, A. J., Wendel, N., & Mayhall, C. (1987). Children's Depression Inventory, Normative data and utility with emotionally disturbed children. *Journal of the American Academy of Child and Adolescent Psychiatry, 26,* 430–48.

Piacentini, J. C., Cohen, P., & Cohen, J. (1992). Combining discrepant diagnostic information from multiple sources: Are complex algorithms better than simple ones? *Journal of Abnormal Child Psychology. 20,* 51-63.

Puig-Antich, J., & Chambers, W. (1978). *The Schedule for Affective Disorders and Schizophrenia for School-Age Children.* New York: New York State Psychiatric Association.

Quay, H. C. (1979). Classification. In H. C. Quay & J. S. Werry(Eds.), *Psychopathological Disorders of Childhood* (pp. 1–42). New York: Wiley.

Reich, W. (2000). Diagnostic Interview for Children and Adolescents (DICA). *Journal of the American Academy of Child and Adolescent Psychiatry, 39*(1), 59–66.

Reich, W., Welner, Z., Herjanic, B., & Multi-Health Systems Staff (1997). *User's Manual for the Child/Adolescent and Parent Version.* Toronto, ON: Multi-Health Systems Inc.

Reynolds, C. R, & Kamphaus, R. W. (1992). *Behavior Assessment System for Children.* Circle Pines, MN: AGS.

Reynolds, C. R, & Kamphaus, R. W. (2004). *Behavior Assessment System for Children–Second Edition.* Circle Pines, MN: AGS.

Reynolds, C. R., & Livingston, R. B. (in press). *Children's Measure of Obsessive-Compulsive Symptoms (CMOCS): Manual.* Los Angeles: Western Psychological Services.

Reynolds, C. R., & Richmond, B. O. (1985). *Revised Children's Manifest Anxiety Scale.* Los Angeles: Western Psychological Services.

Reynolds, C. R.,& Richmond, B. O. (2008).*Revised Children's Manifest Anxiety Scale: Second Edition.* Los Angeles, CA: Western Psychological Services.

Reynolds, W. M. (1989). *Reynolds Child Depression Scale.* Odessa, FL: Psychological Assessment Resource.

Reynolds, W. M. (2002). *Reynolds Adolescent Depression Scale: Professional manual-Second Edition.* Psychological Assessment Resources. Odessa, FL.

Reynolds, W. M. (2004). The Reynolds Adolescent Depression Scale–Second Edition (RADS-2). In Hersen, M. (Ed.), *Comprehensive handbook of psychological assessment* (pp. 224–236). New Jersey: Wiley & Sons.

Roberts, N., Parker, K. C. H., & Dagnone, M. (2005). Comparison of clinical diagnoses, NIMH-DISC-IV diagnoses and SCL-90-R ratings in an adolescent psychiatric inpatient unit: A brief report. *Canadian Child and Adolescent Psychiatry Review, 14*(4), 103–105.

Rupp, A., Templin, J., & Henson, R. (2010). Diagnostic Assessment: Theory, Methods, and Applications. New York: Guilford.

Rynn, M. A., Barber, J. P., Khalid-Khan, S., Siqueland, L., Dembiski, M., McCarthy, K.S., et al. (2006). The psychometric properties of the MASC in a pediatric psychiatric sample.

SAS/STAT (1990). *User's guide version 6* (4th ed.). Carey, NC: SAS Institute.

Saylor, C. F., Finch, A. J., Baskin, C. H., Saylor, C. B., Darnell, G., & Furey, W. (1984). Children's Depression Inventory: Investigation of procedures and correlates. *Journal of the American Academy of Child Psychiatry, 23,* 626–628.

Saylor, C. F., Finch, A. J., Spirito, A., & Bennett, B. (1984). The Children's Depression Inventory: A systematic evaluation of psychometric properties. *Journal of Consulting and Clinical Psychology, 52,* 955–967.

Shaffer, D., Fisher, P., & Lucas, C. (1999). Respondent-based interviews. In D. Shaffer, C.P. Lucas, & J. E. Richters (Eds.). *Diagnostic Assessment in Child and Adolescent Psychopathology* (pp. 3–33). New York: The Guildford Press.

Shaffer, D., Fisher, P., & Lucas, C. (2004). The diagnostic interview schedule for children (DISC). In Hersen, M. (Ed.), *Comprehensive handbook of psychological assessment* (pp. 256–270). New Jersey: Wiley & Sons.

Shaffer, D., Fisher, P., Lucas, C., Duncan, M. K., & Schwab-Stone, M E. (2000). NIMH diagnostic interview schedule for children version IV (NIMH DISC–IV): Description, differences from previous versions, and reliability of some common diagnoses. *Journal of the American Academy of Child and Adolescent Psychiatry, 39*(1), 28–38.

Shapiro, E. S., & Heick, P. F. (2004). School psychologist assessment practices in the evaluation of students referred for social/behavior/emotional problems. *Psychology in the Schools, 41,* 551–561.

Sherrill, J., & Kovacs, M. (2000). The Interview Schedule for Children and Adolescents (ISCA). *Journal of the American Academy of Child and Adolescent Psychiatry, 39,* 67–75.

Speilberger, C. D., Edwards, C. D., Montuori, J., & Lushene, R. (1973). *State–Trait Anxiety Inventory for Children.* Redwood City, CA: Mind Garden.

Strauss, C. C., Last, C. G., Hersen, M., & Kazdin, A. E. (1988). Association between anxiety and depression in children and adolescents with anxiety disorders. *Journal of Abnormal Child Psychology, 15,* 57–68.

VanDeventer, M. C., & Kamphaus, R. W. (2006). Assessment and diagnosis of substance use in children and adolescents. In *Psychodiagnostic Assessment of Children* (R. W. Kamphaus

& J. M. *Campbell*, (Eds.). New Jersey: Wiley & Sons, 391–435.

Weiss, B., Weisz, J. R., Politano, M. Carey, M., Nelson, W. M., & Finch, A. (1991). Developmental differences in the factor structure of the Children's Depression Inventory. *Psychological Assessment: A Journal of Consulting and Clinical Psychology, 3*, 38–45.

World Health Organization (1993). *The ICD-10 Classification of Mental and Behavioral Disorders: Diagnostic Criteria for Research*. Geneva: World Health Organization.

Yates, B. T., & Taub, J. (2003). Assessing the costs, benefits, cost-effectiveness, and cost-benefit of psychological assessment: We should, we can, and here's how. *Psychological Assessment, 15*, 478–495.

Learning Disabilities: Assessment, Identification, and Treatment

H. Lee Swanson

Abstract

This chapter provides an overview of definitions, assessment procedures, and instructional treatments for children with learning disabilities. A focus is placed on assessment issues related to reading and math disabilities. Also reviewed are potential causes of learning disabilities, as well as some of the controversies (e.g., role of IQ testing, discrepancy models, RTI) related to assessment practices. An operational definition of LD is discussed that focuses on using cutoff scores from standardized measures related to IQ and specific academic domains (e.g., reading, math).

Keywords: learning disabilities, assessment, treatment, subtypes, reading disabilities, math disabilities

Overview of Definitions

The term learning disabilities (LD) was first coined in a speech that Samuel Kirk delivered in 1963 at the Chicago Conference on Children with Perceptual Handicaps. Clinical studies prior to his 1963 presentation identified a group of children who suffered perceptual, memory, and attention difficulties related to their poor academic performance, but who were not intellectually retarded (see Hallahan & Cruickshank, 1973, for a review). Currently, children (as well as adults) classified with LD are individuals who are of normal intelligence, but suffer mental information processing difficulties that underlie poor academic achievement. Several definitions across the last four decades have referred to children with LD as reflecting a heterogeneous group of individuals with "intrinsic" disorders that are manifested by specific difficulties in the acquisition and use of listening, speaking, reading, writing, reasoning, or mathematical abilities. These definitions (see Hammill, 1990, for a review) assume that the learning difficulties of such individuals are:

(1) Not due to inadequate opportunity to learn, to general intelligence, or to significant physical or emotional disorders, but to basic disorders in specific psychological processes (such as remembering the association between sounds and letters).

(2) Not due to poor instruction, but to specific psychological processing problems that have a neurological, constitutional, and/or biological base.

(3) Not manifested in all aspects of learning. Such individuals' psychological processing deficits depress only a limited aspect of academic behavior. For example, such individuals may suffer problems in reading, but not arithmetic.

To assess LD at the cognitive and behavioral level, school psychologists must employ systematic efforts to detect: (a) normal psychometric intelligence, (b) below normal achievement on standardized measures of achievement (e.g., word recognition), (c) below normal performance on measures of specific cognitive processes (e.g., phonological awareness, working memory), (d) that evidence-based instruction has been presented under optimal conditions, and (e) that academic and/or cognitive processing deficits are not directly caused by environmental factors or contingencies (e.g., socioeconomic status [SES]). In essence, the identification of children with LD requires the documentation of normal intelligence (i.e., individuals do not suffer from mental retardation) and deficient academic performance that persists after best instructional practices have been systematically provided.

Overview of Common Testing Measures

There are several common measurement instruments commonly used to help the school psychologist define LD. These instruments are assumed to evaluate the cognitive and academic weaknesses that may contribute to children's academic difficulties. Tests such as the Wechsler Intelligence Scale for Children, 4th ed. (WISC IV; Wechsler,2003), the Woodcock-Johnson Tests of Cognitive Abilities, 3rd ed. (W-III COG; Woodcock, McGrew, & Mather, 2001), the Das-Naglieri Cognitive Assessment System (CAS; Naglieri & Das, 1997), the Kaufman Assessment Battery for Children, 2nd ed. (KABC-II; Kaufman & Kaufman, 2004), and the Stanford-Binet Intelligence Scales, 5th ed. (SB5; Roid, 2003) are useful for evaluating children's cognitive skills. Academic achievement tests such as the Wechsler Individual Achievement Test, 2nd ed. (WIAT II; Psychological Corporation, 2001), and the Woodcock-Johnson Test of Achievement, 3rd ed. (WJ-III ACH; Woodcock, McGrew, & Mather, 2001) provide standardized methods of evaluating and documenting academic skills. These tools allow for the measurement of specific academic skills and acquired knowledge. If a child is found to have a deficit in these areas, exclusionary factors are evaluated (i.e., limited English proficiency, mild mental retardation, behavioral or emotional disturbance). If these exclusionary factors are not found to be the primary cause of the academic skill deficit, then measurement of cognitive abilities, processes, and aptitudes for learning are indicated. The school psychologist attempts to establish the consistencies between a child's cognitive processing abilities and the academic performance profile that would account for the child's academic underachievement. For example, a child's demonstrated difficulties with phonological awareness, speed of information processing, and working memory, may provide a likely explanation for a child's low basic reading skill level.

Prevalence

Depending on the definition, the incidence of children with LD is conservatively estimated to reflect 2%–5% of the public school population. It is the largest category of children served in special education. There is, of course, state to state variability in the prevalence of learning disabilities. Some states report students identified as LD as high as 8% (Rhode Island), whereas other states report lower incidence rates of 3% (Kentucky; see Hallahan, Keller, Martinez, Byrd, Gelman, & Fan, 2007, for a review); however, the high incidence of LD does not appear to be any more variable than that of low-incidence categories. For example, Hallahan, et al. (2007) showed that the incidence of LD was no more variable than those of low incidence disabilities (e.g., hearing impaired), suggesting that as a group, children with LD are as well defined as those with other handicapping conditions.

Reading disabilities, or dyslexia, are the most common forms of LD; some studies have reported that approximately 80% to 90% of the children served in special education have problems in reading (Lerner, 1989; Kavale & Reese, 1992). Epidemiological data for children suggests that reading disabilities (RD) fits a dimensional model in which proficient reading and RD occurs along a continuum, with RD representing the lower tail of a normal distribution of reading ability (e.g., Gilger, Borki, Smith, DeFries, & Pennington, 1996). Further, longitudinal studies—both prospective (Francis, Shaywitz, Stuebing, Shaywitz, & Fletcher, 1996) and retrospective (Bruck, 1990)—indicate that RD is a persistent chronic condition from childhood to adulthood. For example, in the Connecticut Longitudinal Project approximately 70% of children identified with RD in grade 3 had RD as adults (e.g., Shaywitz, et al, 1999). Thus, over time and age, proficient readers and those with RD maintain their relative position along the spectrum of reading ability (Shaywitz & Shaywitz, 2003; 2005).

Heterogeneity

A great deal of heterogeneity exists within the groups defined as having LD. For example, the 2004 reauthorization of the Individuals with Disabilities Education Act (IDEA) defines "specific learning disability" in a similar manner to previous versions of the law in capturing this heterogeneity, as follows:

" (A) The term 'specific learning disability' means a
disorder in one or more of the basic psychological
processes involved in understanding or in using
language, spoken or written, which a disorder may
manifest itself in the imperfect ability to listen,
think, speak, read, write, spell, or do mathematical
calculations.
(B) Disorders included.—Such term includes such
conditions as perceptual disabilities, brain injury,

minimal brain dysfunction, dyslexia, and developmental aphasia.

(C) Disorders not included.—Such term does not include a learning problem that is primarily the result of visual, hearing, or motor disabilities, of mental retardation, of emotional disturbance, or of environmental, cultural, or economic disadvantage." (P.L. 108-446, Section 602(30)

As can be determined from this definition, there are several areas in which LD may manifest itself. Most researchers attempt to handle this heterogeneity by subtyping or subgrouping children along various dimensions. Although several types of LD have been discussed in the literature, few of these subtypes have been considered valid, because (a) these particular subtypes do not respond differently to instructional programs when compared to other subtypes, and/or (b) the skills deficient in a particular subtype are not relevant to the academic areas important in the school context.

However, there are two subtypes that have been extensively researched and are relevant to the school context: reading disabilities and mathematical disabilities. These subtypes are usually defined by standardized (norm-referenced) and reliable measures of intelligence and achievement (as described above). The most commonly used intelligence tests, however, are from the Wechsler series and common achievement tests that include measures of word recognition or identification (Woodcock-Johnson Psychoeducational Battery, Wide Range Achievement Test, Woodcock Reading Mastery Test, Kaufman Test of Educational Achievement, Peabody Individual Achievement Test) and arithmetic calculation (all the aforementioned tests and the Key Math Diagnostic Test). In general, individuals with intelligence quotient (IQ) scores equal to or more than a full-scale IQ score of 85, reading subtest scores equal to or less than the 25th percentile, and/or arithmetic subtest scores equal to or less than the 25th percentile captures two high incidence disorders within LD: reading (word recognition) and arithmetic (computation, written work).

Reading Disabilities

Several researchers argue that fundamental to evaluating RD is a focus on word recognition measures, because they capture more basic processes and responses than reading comprehension (e.g., Siegel, 2003a). Reading problems are best conceptualized as a continuum with varying degrees of severity

because, as several studies show, children with RD show a remarkable homogeneity in cognitive profiles (e.g., Stanovich & Siegel, 1994). Several authors (e.g., Francis et al., 1996; Grigorenko, 2001; Mann, 2003; Morris, Stuebing, Fletcher, Shaywitz, Lyon, Shankwieler, et al., 1998; Swanson & Siegel, 2001) find in these profiles deficiencies in three critical processes: phonological processing (ability to segment sounds), syntactical processing (ability to understand grammatical structure), and working memory (combination of transient memory and long-term memory) (also see Siegel, 2003a, for a review).

Because not all problems in reading are at the word recognition level, some other types of distinct reading problems have been suggested (e.g., Morris et al., 1998). In their recent examination of the current state and perspectives on learning disabilities, Fletcher, Lyon, Fuchs, and Barnes (2007) proposed the existence of three types of RD. The first type is associated with problems in word recognition and spelling. The second form refers to difficulties in reading comprehension. Finally, the third type includes individuals who experience difficulty in reading fluency and poor automaticity of word reading. The largest numbers of students with reading disabilities demonstrate problems on word level recognition; however, a subset of students with RD who have intact word recognition skills shows deficits in reading comprehension. This type of disability is related to problems in oral language and working memory—the capacity to integrate new information with old information when high demands are made on attention. Finally, a group of students with average word decoding skills differ in reading fluency: these individuals have either slow reading rates, or average rates but low reading accuracy.

Morris, et al (1998) studied the variability of RD subtypes in a large group of 7- to 9-year-old children with reading problems. Based on the results of their study, several reading subtypes emerged: two subtypes without reading disability, five subtypes with specific reading disability, and two categorized as "globally deficient" in the sense that performance across all measures was very low. Five specific reading disability subgroups varied with regard to phonological (working) memory and rapid naming. Six of the reading disability groups exhibited deficits in phonological awareness skills. The authors concluded that children with RD could be differentiated from the "garden variety" poor readers on the basis of their vocabulary level, which was in the average range for children with specific RD. However, Morris and colleagues' work on subtyping reading disabilities is consistent with a phonological processing hypothesis, which postulates that problems in the phonological domain account for reading difficulties. These phonological problems either occur in isolation or co-occur with problems in other cognitive domains.

Other subtype studies tested whether good and poor readers could be differentiated on their performance on memory related measures (e.g., Swanson, 1993a; Katzir, Kim, Wolf, Morris, & Lovett, 2008). For instance, Swanson (1993a) examined individual differences in several forms of memory of students with and without RD. Although several subgroups with different profiles emerged, the results indicated that children with RD had low performance on memory tasks not because of reading, but rather due to inefficient working memory (WM). Swanson concluded, that "the connection between reading and WM operates on a continuum of independence to dependence as reading becomes more skilled." (p.327)

Math Disabilities

In terms of math disabilities, several studies (Badian, 1983; Shalev, Manor, & Gross-Tsur, 1997; Kosc, 1974) estimated that approximately 6% to 7% of the school age population have mathematical disabilities. Although this figure may be inflated because of variations in definition (e.g., Desoete, Roeyers, & De Clercq, 2003, suggest the figure varies between 3% and 8%), a significant number of children demonstrate poor achievement in mathematics. Some studies suggest that math disabilities (MD) are as common as RD and that a similar cognitive deficit may contribute to the co-occurrence of MD and RD in some children (Geary, 1993, 2003). Interestingly, although MD is a common disorder, the majority of research has been directed toward children with RD.

One of the most comprehensive syntheses of the cognitive literature on MD was provided by Geary (1993; also see Geary, 2003, for a review). His review indicated that children with MD are a heterogeneous group and show one of three types of cognitive disorders. One disorder characterizes children with MD as deficient in semantic memory. These children are characterized as having weak fact retrieval and high error rates in recall. Disruptions in ability to retrieve basic facts from long-term memory (LTM), due to inhibition, may be a defining feature of MD (Geary, 1993). Further, Geary's review indicated that the characteristics of these retrieval deficits, such as slow solution times, suggest that children with MD do not experience a simple developmental delay but rather have a more persistent cognitive disorder across a broad age span. However, other studies (e.g., Goldman, Pellegrino, & Merz, 1988) have suggested that some children with MD have a developmental delay related to immature counting knowledge (e.g., use of fingers to count).

Another type of MD is procedural. Children in this category generally use developmentally immature procedures in numerical calculations, and therefore have difficulties in sequencing multiple steps in complex procedures. For example, Gross-Tsur et al. (1996) indicated that children with MD have a basic understanding of numbers and small quantities. However, children with MD have difficulties keeping information in working memory and monitoring the counting process (Geary, Hamson, & Hoard, 2000; Hitch & McAuley, 1991), which creates errors in their counting. Other studies (e.g., Jordan & Montani, 1997) indicate that children with MD have difficulties in solving simple and complex arithmetic problems. These differences are assumed to involve both procedural and memory based deficits. Procedural deficits relate to miscounting or losing track of the counting process.

The third type is a visual/spatial math disorder. These children have difficulties representing numerical information spatially. For example, they may have difficulties representing the alignment of numerals in multicolumn arithmetic problems and rotation of numbers. Further, they have difficulties in areas that require spatial ability, such as geometry and place values. Recent work by Geary, Hoard, Byrd-Craven and DeSoto (2004) suggests that these deficits are not due to poor spatial abilities, but rather to poor monitoring of the sequence of steps of an algorithm, and from poor skills in detecting and then self-correcting errors.

Regardless of the type of disorder for MD, however, the majority of these studies suggest that children with MD have memory deficits. The ability to utilize memory resources to temporarily store numbers when attempting to reach an answer is of significant importance in learning arithmetic. Poor recall of arithmetic facts, of course, leads to difficulties executing calculation procedures and immature problem-solving strategies (Geary, 1993).

Causes of LD

The most researched causes of LD have been in the area of reading. This is because most of the interventions and referral in the assessment of LD in the schools are related to reading problems. Vellutino, Fletcher, Snowling, and Scanlon (2004) provide an overview of research on specific RD and effective interventions across four decades. They conclude that inadequate facility in word identification, due to basic deficits in phonological coding (converting written letters and words into sounds, skills of segmenting and blending sounds associated with letters—what is generally referred to as *phonics knowledge*) underlie RD. These deficits in phonological coding are defined as an inability to use speech codes to represent information in the form of words and parts of words. In short, these individuals have an inability to represent sound units in one's mind. There are some studies that have suggested that there may be some general language deficits in this population (e.g., Mann, 2003; Scarborough, 1990). Some of these general problems have been related to difficulties in attention, naming speed, making association between sounds and visual shapes, processing verbal to auditory information or transfer, and working memory. We will briefly review some of the other research programs that seek to determine the causes of RD.

Naming Speed

Wolf, Bowers, and Biddle (2000) have found a connection between rapid naming of letters, numbers, and objects, and reading disabilities. Slow naming speed marks a core deficit associated with reading disabilities. Rapid naming is associated not only with initial reading fluency, but also whether there are any fluency gains after practice. Some research has investigated the role of rapid naming and reading achievement in languages other than English. The research suggests that slow naming speed is somewhat distinct from phonemic awareness. Some of Wolf's work has focused on subtyping by strengths and weaknesses in rapid naming, as well as phonological awareness. That research suggests a double deficit hypothesis, in which children can vary in terms of difficulty on phonological skills, rapid naming skills, or both of those skills.

Working Memory

Swanson and his colleagues (1993b, 1999; Swanson, Howard, Sáez, 2006) have researched RD by primarily focusing on short-term memory, working memory, and their distinction. Deficits in reading comprehension and problem solving experienced by children with RD are related to memory problems in a speech-based storage system, and/or

memory problems related to specific aspects of a general executive system of working memory. The executive system focuses on the monitoring of information, focusing and switching attention, and activating representations from long-term memory. Problems in the executive system of children with RD are related to the inefficient mental allocation of attention, and the poor inhibition of irrelevant information. Problems in executive processing are described in terms of limitations in attentional capacity rather than processing strategies. Because short-term memory has minimal application to complex academic tasks, the majority of his research on RD focuses on the relationship between working memory and complex cognition (reading comprehension, word problems).

Neurological Correlates

Several Studies have focused on the neurological correlates of reading disabilities (e.g., see Miller, Sanchez, & Hynd, 2003; Pugh, Mencl, Jenner, Lee, Katz, Frost, et al., 2001; Shaywitz, Mody, & Shaywitz, 2006, for review). Neurobiological evidence for reading disabilities is primarily done through postmortem, electrophysiological, family, and functional imaging studies. Evidence from this neurological data suggests the disruption of the neurological system for language in individuals with RD. Brain-based research in RD has focused on the planum temporale, gyral morphology of the perisylvian region, corpus colossum, as well as cortical abnormalities of the tempoparietal region. Although at this point in time it is difficult to summarize this research, the neural biological codes believed to underlie cognitive deficits in the reading disabled are centered on the left temporoparietal region. Differences in the asymmetry of the planum temporale have consistently been found in association with RD (see Miller et al., 2003, for a review). Specifically, asymmetry of the planum temporale is due to a larger right plana. A reversal of normal pattern of left greater than right asymmetry has been found in individuals with developmental dyslexia.

Recent studies by Shaywitz, Shaywitz, Blachman, Pugh, Fulbright, and Skudlarski et al. (2004) have found differences in the tempo-parieto-occipital brain regions between reading disabled and nonimpaired readers. The converging evidence using functional brain imaging in adult reading disabled readers shows a failure in the left hemisphere posterior brain system to function properly during reading. Some brain imaging studies show differences in brain activation in frontal regions in reading disabled compared to non-impaired readers. The majority of this research has focused on the brain regions where previous research has implicated reading and language. The research shows clear activation patterns related to phonological analysis. For example, on nonword rhyming tasks, reading disabled readers experience a disruption of the posterior system that involves activation of the posterior superior temporal gyrus (also known as Wernicke's area, the angular gyrus, and the striate cortex.) The research demonstrates a persistent functional disruption in the left hemispheric neural systems, and indicates that this disorder is lifelong.

Genetic Factors

Several studies have addressed genetic influences on RD. This research suggests that phonological coding abilities have a genetic etiology. The Colorado twin studies support the existence of major gene effects on reading disabilities, although the precise information about the mode of inheritance is less clear (Olson, Forsberg, Gayen, & Defries, 1999). Some of the literature (see Grigorenko, 2001) has found the localization of dyslexic gene sites (some of the gene sites have been attributed to chromosome 1, 2, 6, 15, and 18). Some research suggests that genes contributing to nonword repetition also account for the genetic basis of memory span score. Recent developments have focused on genotype/phenotype correlations, biological consequences of specific genetic changes, and intentional intervention strategy guided by genetic profiles.

Math Disabilities and Causes

As indicated above, more is known about potential causes of RD than MD. Some of the difficulty in the literature is that the primary cognitive mechanisms that separate MD from RD are unclear. Although there is some agreement that children with MD are slower and less efficient at recognizing numerosities, some authors have suggested that memory representations for arithmetic facts are supported in part by the same phonological and semantic memory systems that support decoding words and reading comprehension (see Geary, 1993; Hecht, Torgesen, Wagner, & Rashotte, 2001, for a review). Others challenge this assumption (Jordan, Hanich & Kaplan, 2003).

Unfortunately, there are several reasons why it is difficult to determine from existing literature whether the cognitive processing of children with MD is distinct from other children. One reason is that the operational criteria for measures used in the selection of children with MD and RD vary across studies (Swanson & Jerman, 2006). For instance, measures used to establish MD vary from the 48th percentile to the 8th percentile across studies. Previous studies that have examined math difficulties in groups around the 30th percentile have been described as investigations of learning "difficulties," whereas studies that have examined groups in about the lower 10th percentile have been described as investigations of MD (Mazzocco, 2007). Children with MD who perform in the lower 10th percentile on math tests, and have been exposed to evidence-based math instruction, are likely to have MD with a biological origin, and represent developmental deviance (Mazzocco, 2007).

Another reason is that most studies on math disabilities in terms of brain involvement are done with adults. Cognitive development in children and neurological findings in adults may lead to different conclusions. A casual review of the literature shows that MD in adults has been associated with the left basal ganglia, thalamus, and the left parieto-occipito-temporal areas (e.g., Dehaene & Cohen, 1995; 1997). Damage to these regions may be associated with difficulties in accessing number facts. With adult samples, there is some neurological evidence that the ability to understand numbers is dissociable from language (Cohen, Dehaene, Cochon, Lehericy, & Naccache, 2000), semantic memory, and short-term memory (Cappelletti, Butterworth & Kopelman, 2001). However, when the focus is on children who demonstrate normal cognitive development (e.g., Geary et al., 2000; Hecht, Close, & Sabatisi, 2003; Jordon & Montani, 1997), a different theoretical account of various types of math difficulties emerges. For example, Geary et al. indicated that the mechanisms that underlie this have been related to poor WM, either related to the phonological system or the executive system, such as the inability to inhibit irrelevant information. Jordan indicated that the mechanisms that may underlie MD are related to deficits in fact retrieval, and by extension, calculation and fluency. In contrast, Hecht et al. focus on the conceptual knowledge of children with MD. They find that conceptual understanding is a consistent and important source of variability in estimation, word problem solving, and computation in children with MD.

Swanson and Jerman (2006) completed a quantitative synthesis of the literature that compared children with MD to average achievers, children with RD, and children with comorbid disabilities (RD+MD). Average achievers clearly outperformed children with MD on measures of verbal problem solving, naming speed, verbal and visual-spatial working memory, and long-term memory. The results further indicated that children with MD outperformed children with combined reading and math disabilities on measures of literacy, visual-spatial problem solving, LTM, short-term memory for words, and verbal working memory. Children with MD could only be clearly differentiated from children with RD on measures of naming speed and visual-spatial working memory. These problems were persistent across age and severity of math disability.

Summary

The causes of RD and MD are assumed to have a biological base. In the area of reading, there is some converging evidence that deficits in specific language and memory processes in children with RD have a biological and genetic origin.

Scientifically Based Treatments

As indicated earlier, children with LD are a heterogeneous group; therefore, no general instructional model can be recommended for all of them. However, some common general principles for teaching students with LD have been identified. Although these principles often operate in different ways with different students, in different content areas and different settings, nevertheless they can be used in designing effective remediation programs for such students. We summarize these principles from a comprehensive educational intervention research synthesis for students with LD (Swanson, Hoskyn, & Lee, 1999). Before reviewing these underlying principles, a historical context is necessary.

Trends Related to Instructional Interventions

Wiederholt (1974), in reviewing the history of the LD field, indicated that its unique focus was on identifying and remediating specific psychological processing difficulties. Popular intervention approaches during the 1960s and 1970s focused on visual-motor, auditory sequencing, or visual perception training exercises. Several criticisms were directed at these particular interventions on methodological and theoretical grounds.

By the late 1970s, dissatisfaction with a processing orientation to remediation of learning disabilities, as well as the influence of federal regulations in the United States (Public Law 94-142), remediation

programs focused on basic skills such as reading and mathematics. The focus on basic skills rather than psychological processes was referred to as *direct instruction*. The mid 1980s witnessed a shift from the more remedial/academic approach of teaching, to instruction that included both basic skills and cognitive strategies (ways to better learn new information and efficiently access information from long-term memory). Children with LD were viewed as experiencing difficulty in "regulating" their learning performance. An instructional emphasis was placed on teaching students to check, plan, monitor, test, revise, and evaluate their learning during their attempts to learn or solve problems.

The early 1990s witnessed a resurgence of direct instruction intervention studies, primarily influenced by reading research, which suggested that a primary focus of intervention should be directed to phonological skills. The rationale was that because a large majority of children with LD suffer problems in reading, some of these children's reading problems were exacerbated because of lack of systematic instruction in processes related to phonological awareness (the ability to hear and manipulate sounds in words and understand the sound structure of language). This view gave rise to several interventions that focused heavily on phonics instruction, and intense individual one-to-one tutoring to improve children's phonological awareness of word structures and sequences.

From the turn of the twenty-first century to the present, some interventions have been linked to assessment. A method of identifying school-aged students with LD known as *Response to Intervention* (RTI, to be discussed later) first establishes low academic performance, and then determines if a disability is present. The RTI model is partially based on intervention programs that have distinguished children experiencing academic difficulty due to instructional deficits, from those with disability-related deficits (Al Otaiba & Fuchs, 2002; Vellutino, Scanlon, Sipay, Small, Pratt, Chen et al., 1996). Federal regulations in the United States regarding the Individuals with Disabilities Education Improvement Act of 2004 have influenced the use of RTI by supporting a child's response to scientific, research based intervention as a process for LD identification. In general, the RTI model identifies whether a student's current skill level is substantially lower than instructional level (based on predetermined criteria: e.g., below the 25th percentile). Low academic performance is established using standardized, norm-referenced and/or curriculum based measurements (Compton, Fuchs, Fuchs & Bryant, 2006; Fuchs, Fuchs, & Compton, 2004). After establishing low performance, empirically based interventions are implemented to determine if a disability is present. Student progress is monitored during the intervention. When a student does not respond to high quality intervention, the student may have a learning disability.

Scientifically Based Intervention Programs

The term *intervention* is defined as the direct manipulation (usually assigned at will by the experimenter) of variables (e.g., instruction) for the purposes of assessing learning (1) efficiency, (2) accuracy, (3) and understanding. Swanson et al. (1999) have provided the most comprehensive analysis of the experimental intervention literature on LD to date. Interventions were analyzed at three levels: general models of instruction, tactics used to convey information, and components that were most important to the instructional success.

In terms of general models, methodologically sound studies (those studies with well-defined control groups and clearly identified samples) found that positive outcomes in remediation were directly related to a **combination** of direct and strategy instructional models. Components of direct instruction emphasize fast paced, well-sequenced, highly focused lessons (e.g., Adams & Carnine, 2003 Kame'enui, Jitendra, & Darch, 1995). The lessons are delivered in small groups to students, who are given several opportunities to respond and receive feedback about accuracy and responses. Components related to effective strategy include: advance organizers (provide students with a type of mental scaffolding on which to build new understanding, i.e., consisting of information already in the students' minds, and the new concepts that can organize this information); organization (information or questions directed to students to stop from time to time, to assess their understanding); elaboration (thinking about the material to be learned in a way that connects the material to information or ideas already in the student's mind); generative learning (learners must work to make sense out of what they are learning by summarizing the information); and general study strategies (e.g., underlining, note taking, summarizing, having students generate questions, outlining, and working in pairs to summarize sections of materials (see Wong, Harris, Graham & Butler, 2003, for a review).

The two models included a graduated sequence of steps with multiple opportunities for overlearning the content and skills, cumulative review routines, mass practice, and teaching of all component skills to a level that showed mastery. The interventions involved (a) teaching a few concepts and strategies in depth rather than superficially, (b) teaching students to monitor their performance, (c) teaching students when and where to use the strategy in order to enhance generalization, (d) teaching strategies as an integrated part of an existing curriculum, and (e) providing teaching that includes a great deal of supervised student feedback and practice.

In terms of tactics, Swanson (2000) divided studies into eight models based on key instruction tactics: direct instruction (a focus on sequencing and segmentation of skills), explicit strategy training, monitoring (teaching children strategies), individualized and remedial tutoring, small interactive group instruction, teacher indirect instruction (teacher makes use of homework and peers' help for instruction), verbal questioning/attribution instruction (asking children key questions during the learning phase, and whether they thought what they were learning would transfer), and technology (using computers to present concepts). The results indicated that explicit strategy instruction (explicit practice, elaboration, strategy cuing) and small group interactive settings best improved the magnitude of treatment outcomes.

In terms of components, Swanson (1999b) found that all effective instructional models follow a sequence of events:

1. State the learning objectives and orient the students to what they will be learning, and what performance will be expected of them.

2. Review the skills necessary to understand the concept.

3. Present the information, give examples, and demonstrate the concepts/materials.

4. Pose questions (probes) to students and assess their level of understanding and correct misconceptions.

5. Provide group instruction and independent practice. Give students an opportunity to demonstrate new skills and learn the new information on their own.

6. Assess performance and provide feedback. Review the independent work and give a quiz. Give feedback for correct answers and reteach skills if answers are incorrect.

7. Provide distributed practice and review.

They also found that some instructional components were far more important than others.

For example, in the domain of reading comprehension, key instructional components that contributed significantly to improving the magnitude of outcomes were:

1. Directed Response/Questioning. Treatments related to dialectic or Socratic teaching, the teacher directing students to ask questions, the teacher and a student or students engaging in reciprocal dialogue.

2. Control Difficulty or Processing Demands of Task. Treatments that included short activities, level of difficulty controlled, teacher providing necessary assistance, teacher providing simplified demonstration, tasks sequenced from easy to difficult, and/or task analysis.

3. Elaboration. Treatments that included additional information, or explanation provided about concepts, procedures or steps, and/or redundant text or repetition within text.

4. Modeling by the Teacher of Steps. Treatments that included modeling by the teacher in terms of demonstration of processes and/or steps the students are to follow to solve the problem.

5. Small Group Instruction. Treatments that included descriptions about instruction in a small group, and/or verbal interaction occurring in a small group with students and/or teacher.

6. Strategy Cues. Treatments that included reminders to use strategies or multi-steps, use of "think aloud" models, and/or teacher presenting the benefits of strategy use or procedures.

In contrast, the important instructional components that increased the effect sizes for word recognition were:

1. Sequencing. Treatments included a focus on breaking down the task, fading of prompts or cues, sequencing short activities, and/or using step by step prompts.

2. Segmentation. Treatments included a focus on breaking down the targeted skill into smaller units, breaking into component parts, segmenting and/or synthesizing components parts.

3. Advanced Organizers. Treatments included a focus on directing children to look over material prior to instruction, directing children to focus on particular information, providing prior information about task, and/or the teacher stating objectives of instruction prior to commencing.

The importance of these findings is that only a few components from a broad array of activities were found to enhance treatment outcomes.

Regardless of the instructional focus (math, writing, reading), two instructional components emerged in Swanson et al.'s analysis of treatments for children with LD. One component was *explicit practice*, which included activities related to distributed review and practice, repeated practice, sequenced reviews, daily feedback, and/or weekly reviews. The other component was *advanced organizers*, which included: (a) directing children to focus on specific material or information prior to instruction; (b) directing children about task concepts or events before beginning; and/or (c) the teacher stating objectives of the instruction.

Controversies within the Field of LD

Before discussing some of the controversies in the field, as well as recent trends, areas of some consensus are reviewed. Some consensus statements were developed at a federally funded Learning Disabilities Summit (Bradley, Danielson, & Hallahan, 2002) regarding the nature of specific learning disabilities (SLD). Areas of consensus included the following:

* The concept of SLD is valid, supported by strong converging evidence.
* SLD are neurologically based and intrinsic to the individual.
* Individuals with SLD show intra-individual differences in skills and abilities.
* SLD persist across the life span, though manifestations and intensity may vary as a function of developmental stage and environmental demands.
* SLD may occur in combination with other disabling conditions, but are not due to other conditions, such as mental retardation, behavioral disturbance, lack of opportunities to learn, primary sensory deficits, or multilingualism.
* SLD are evident across ethnic, cultural, language, and economic groups.

Given these consensus statements, we will now address some of the issues within the field.

Using Discrepancy Criteria to Define LD

One impediment to making advances in the field of LD revolves around issues of definition. Traditionally, assessment practices have relied primarily on uncovering a significant discrepancy between achievement in a particular academic domain, and general intellectual ability. The implicit assumption for using discrepancy scores is that individuals who experience reading, writing, and/or math difficulties, unaccompanied by a low IQ, are distinct in cognitive processing from slow or low achievers (e.g., Fletcher, Francis, Rourke, Shaywitz, & Shaywitz, 1992). This assumption is equivocal (e.g., Stuebing, Fletcher, LeDoux, Lyon, Shaywitz, & Shaywitz, 2002). A plethora of studies have compared children with reading disabilities (RD; i.e., children with discrepancies between IQ and reading) with nondiscrepancy defined poor readers (i.e., children whose IQ scores are in the same low range as their reading scores), and found that these groups are more similar in processing difficulties than different (Hoskyn & Swanson, 2000; Stuebing et al., 2002). As a result, some researchers have suggested dropping the requirement of average intelligence, in favor of a view where children with reading problems are best conceptualized as existing at the extreme end of a continuum from poor to good readers (Siegel, 2003b; Stanovich & Siegel, 1994). Although there are operational definitions of individuals with LD provided by researchers that do not rely on discrepancy criteria (e.g., cutoff scores for determining RD on various measures, e.g., Siegel & Ryan, 1989, Swanson, 1993b), there are two issues that limit consensus on defining individuals with LD. One is related to the role of IQ in the assessment process, and the other to whether the cognitive processes that underlie LD are distinct from other poor reading groups. These issues and related research are briefly reviewed.

DETERMINING THE ROLE INTELLIGENCE PLAYS IN THE ASSESSMENT OF LD

Several authors have argued that variations in IQ tell us little about differences in processing when groups are defined at low levels of reading (e.g., Francis, Fletcher, Stuebing, Lyon, Shaywitz & Shaywitz, 2005). In response to these concerns, current legislation (IDEIA, 2004) has allowed alternative procedures to using IQ as a measure of aptitude for determining RD. Thus, the issue on the importance of IQ scores is not clear from current legislation. However, are variations in IQ and reading (former indicators of LD) really irrelevant? The literature on this issue is equivocal when considered in reference to three major meta-analyses (quantitative synthesis of the literature) on the topic.

Three meta-analyses were completed prior to the passing of IDEIA (2004; Fuchs, Fuchs Mathes & Lipsey, 2000; Hoskyn & Swanson, 2000; Stuebing et al., 2002) that addressed the role of IQ in defining RD. The contradictions in the three meta-analyses

are reviewed in Stuebing et al. (2002). Stuebing et al. considered the Hoskyn and Swanson (2000) selection process of studies to be the more conservative of the three, and these findings are highlighted related to the relevance of IQ. Hoskyn and Swanson (2000) analyzed published literature comparing children who are poor readers but either had higher IQ scores than their reading scores, or had IQ scores commensurate with their reading scores. The findings of the synthesis were consistent with previous studies, outside the domain of reading, that report on the weak discriminative power of discrepancy scores. Although the outcomes of Hoskyn and Swanson's synthesis generally supported current notions about comparable outcomes on various measures among the discrepancy and nondiscrepancy groups, verbal IQ significantly moderated effect sizes between the two groups. That is, although the degree of discrepancy between IQ and reading was irrelevant in predicting effect sizes, the magnitude of differences in performance (effect sizes) between the two groups were related to verbal IQ. They found that the effect size differences between discrepancy (reading disabled group) and nondiscrepancy groups (low achievers, in this case) were significantly moderated (influenced the strength and direction of effect sizes) by verbal IQ measures. When the mean verbal IQ of the reading disabled (RD) group was greater than 100, the differences between the low achieving (LA) groups were significantly greater. In contrast, when verbal IQ was less than 100, estimates of effect size between the two groups on various cognitive measures were close to 0. Thus, the farther the RD group moved from IQs in the 80 range to above the 100 range (the cutoff score used to select RD samples), the greater the chances their overall performance on cognitive measures would differ from the low achievers.

Stuebing et al. (2002) in their meta-analysis concluded that IQ was irrelevant to reading. However, their analysis showed (see Table 6) that IQ accounted for a substantial amount of the explainable variance in reading (explainable variance ranges from approximately .47 to .58). Moreover, robust differences on measures between the two groups were found by Fuchs et al. (2000). For example, Fuchs et al. (2000), comparing low achieving students with and without LD, found moderate effect sizes (ES=.61, see p. 94) in favor of low achievers without LD. In general, the three meta-analyses suggest that removing IQ as an aptitude measure in classifying children as LD, especially verbal IQ, is not uniformly supported by the assessment literature.

TREATMENT OUTCOMES AS A FUNCTION OF DEFINITION

One test of the validity of using IQ as part of the identification criteria is whether IQ is related to treatment outcomes. Although some studies have found very little relevance of IQ to treatment outcomes (e.g. Vellutino, Scanlon & Lyon, 2000), the literature on the issue of whether IQ has relevance across an array of intervention studies needs to be considered.

One means of evaluating whether aptitude variations in the LD sample interact with treatment is to compare the relationship between treatment outcomes (treatment vs. control) with multivariate data that include different configurations of how samples with LD are defined. This can be accomplished by placing studies on the same metric (e.g., effect size), and comparing the magnitude of these outcomes as a function of variations in the sample definition (e.g., on measures of intelligence and reading). An analysis of treatment outcomes (as measured by effect size) and IQ has been reported (Swanson & Hoskyn, 1998; Swanson et al., 1999). The analysis shows significant LD definitions x treatment interactions exist across evidence based studies (see Swanson & Hoskyn, 1999, for a review). Variations in IQ and reading level were important moderators of instructional outcomes in both group design (Swanson & Hoskyn, 1998, 1999) and single subject design studies (Swanson & Sachse-Lee, 2000). The general pattern across these results was that studies that failed to report psychometric information on participants with LD yielded significantly higher effect sizes than studies reporting psychometric information. Thus, a poorly defined sample *inflated* treatment outcomes, by introducing greater heterogeneity into the sample when compared to studies that selected samples based on psychometric criteria. Significant effects related to the magnitude of treatment outcomes were isolated to the severity of reading x intelligence interaction. The influence of IQ scores on the magnitude of the treatment outcomes was relevant when reading scores were below the 25th percentile. The effect sizes were moderate (0.52) when intelligence was above 90, but substantial (.95) when IQs were below 90. Thus, the implication of these findings is that variations in IQ and reading cannot be ignored when predicting treatment outcomes and, therefore, are a critical ingredient to the identification process.

Two other important findings emerged, as subsets of the Swanson and Hoskyn (1998) data were analyzed. First, LD adolescent samples with discrepancies in intelligence and reading were more likely to yield lower treatment outcomes (effect sizes) than studies that reported aggregated IQ and reading scores in the same low range (e.g., Swanson, 2001). Second, treatment measures related to reading recognition and comprehension vary as a function of IQ. Effect sizes for word recognition studies were significantly related to samples defined by cutoff scores (IQ > 85 and reading < 25th percentile), whereas the magnitude of effect size for reading comprehension studies were sensitive to discrepancies between IQ and reading, when compared to competing definitional criteria.

SUMMARY AND IMPLICATIONS OF IQ TESTING

IQ has relevance to definitions of LD. Groups of students with LD who have aptitude profiles similar to generally poor achievers or slow learners (low IQ and low reading), produced higher effect sizes in treatment outcomes (in relation to control situations) than those samples with a discrepancy between IQ and reading. Given that there has been very little research on why these discrepancies occur, it is important to recognize that IQ, especially verbal, has a moderating role in assessment and treatment outcomes.

Alternatives to the Discrepancy Model

One currently popular alternative to defining LD based on the IQ–Achievement discrepancy model is referred to as Response to Intervention (RTI). The goal of RTI is to monitor the intensity of instruction, and make systematic changes in the instructional context as a function of a student's overt performance. This is done by considering various tiers of instructional intensity. This approach is compatible with those that attempt to identify the cognitive and neuropsychological (i.e., psychometric) aspects of LD. RTI focuses on a systematic manipulation of the environmental context (i.e., instruction, classroom, school) to determine procedures that maximize learning, whereas cognitive and neurological approaches focus on mapping the internal dynamics of learning. The unique application of cognitive and neurological approaches to the field of LD is (1) to explain "why" and predict "how" individual differences emerge in children at risk for LD after intense intervention and (2) to document whether functional brain anatomy changes emerge as a function of intervention.

Historically, the concept of RTI as a means to further refine the definition of LD has been discussed since the inception of the field (see Haring & Bateman, 1977, and Wiederholt, 1974, for a review). For example, the term itself, "learning disabilities," originated to replace a focus on neurological mechanisms such as minimal brain dysfunction (e.g., Clements, 1966), and thereby place an emphasis on "instruction." In addition, several earlier writings made distinctions between children who fall by the wayside because of poor instruction, and those who are truly "learning disabled." For example, Haring and Bateman (1977), in a text entitled *Teaching the Learning Disabled Child*, differentiated between "instruction disabled" and "learning disabled." As they stated, "although a child may have no clinically observable signs of neurological disorders, he or she certainly may have some learning disabilities that cannot be readily accounted for by poor instruction. These learning problems seem to persist in a very small number of children, even though their curriculum has been individualized and they have received systematic instruction." (p. 4). The authors further call for the use of precision teaching via continuous monitoring and recording of student performance on basic academic tasks. Various forms of RTI that we see today, such as curriculum based measurement and progress monitoring, can be traced to refinements or reformatting of precision teaching procedures, and the provision of instruction in various tiers or intensities reflects a reconfiguration of Deno's (1980) cascade model.

Unfortunately, RTI as an assessment approach to define LD has a weak experimental base. At the time of this writing, there have been no controlled studies randomly assigning children seriously at risk for LD to assessment and/or delivery models (e.g., tiered instruction vs. special education, orresource room placement) to measure outcomes on key variables such as over-identification, stability of classification, and academic and cognitive growth in response to treatment. The few studies that compare RTI with other assessment models (e.g., discrepancy based or low-achievement based models) involve post hoc assessments of children divided at post-test within the same sample. In addition, different states and school districts vary in their interpretations of how RTI should be implemented, thereby weakening any uniformity that could link the science of instruction to assessing children at risk for LD.

Although there is enthusiasm for RTI as a means to provide a contextual (or more ecologically valid) assessment of children at risk for LD when compared to other models (e.g., models based on inferences from behavioral data about internal processing), the use of RTI as a scientific means to identify children at risk for LD has several obstacles to overcome. The first obstacle is that in contrast to standardized formats of testing and assessment, there are no standardized applications of evidence-based instruction. A second obstacle is that teacher effects cannot always be controlled. The teacher variable plays a key role in mediating treatment outcomes for children. Further, this variance cannot be accounted for by merely increasing treatment fidelity. Procedures that control for treatment fidelity in applying evidence-based treatments account for a very small amount of variance in student outcomes (see Simmerman & Swanson, 2001, for discussion). Although the role of teacher effects can be controlled to some degree, there is no "expert teaching model" that has been operationalized and implemented for instructional delivery in evidence-based practices. Another obstacle is that even under the best instructional conditions, individual differences in achievement in some cases will increase. There will be some instructional conditions that vastly improve achievement in both average achievers and children at risk for LD, but these robust instructional procedures will increase the performance gaps between some children. Thus, significant performance differences will remain for some children with LD when compared to their counterparts, even under the most intensive treatment conditions. Perhaps even more fundamental than these three major obstacles, is the lack of consensus about what "nonresponsiveness" entails, and how it should be uniformly measured.

One of the major issues for RTI is the translation of best evidence-based practices to assessment. That is, implementing RTI procedures is predicated on administering best evidence practices. There are two issues related to this translation.

First, individual differences will emerge even under the best intervention conditions. Swanson and several colleagues (e.g., Swanson & Deshler, 2003; Swanson & Hoskyn, 1998; Swanson & Sachse-Lee, 2000) condensed over 3000 effect sizes related to LD treatment versus LD control conditions for group design studies, and found a mean effect size (ES) of .79 for group design studies (Swanson & Hoskyn, 1998) and 1.03 for single subject design studies (Swanson & Sachse-Lee, 2000). According to Cohen's (1988) classification system, the magnitude of the ES is small when the absolute value is at .20 or below, moderate when the ES is .60 and large when the ES is .80 or above.

Thus, on the surface, the results are consistent with the notion that children with LD are highly responsive to intense instruction. However, when children with LD were compared to nondisabled children of the same grade or age, who also were receiving the same best-evidence intervention procedure, effect sizes (M= .97) were substantially in favor of nondisabled children (see Swanson et al., 1999, see p. 162 to 169). More importantly, the mean effect size difference increased in favor of children without LD (ES=1.44; Swanson et al., p. 168) when psychometric scores related to IQ and reading were not included as part of sample reporting. Thus, evidence-based instructional procedures did little to bridge the gap related to performance differences between children with and without LD, with instruction treatments found to be highly effective in samples of children with and without LD. Further, it is important to note that in the regression modeling, the best instructional programs (explicit practice, elaboration, strategy cuing, and small group interactive settings) accounted for less than 15% of the variance in predicting outcomes (Swanson, 1999a). This finding held when controls were made in the analysis for methodology, age, type of research design, and type of academic domain (e.g., reading, math, writing). The finding is consistent with the National Reading Panel's report (2000) that provided an analysis of best practice in reading (teaching of phonics). This procedure accounted for approximately only 10% of the variance in reading treatment outcomes (Hammill & Swanson, 2006). Thus, a tremendous amount of variance is unaccounted for in studies considered the "best" of evidence-based practices.

Second, "best evidence studies" cannot be taken at face value. Simmerman and Swanson (2001) analyzed best evidence studies and found that slight variations in the internal and external validity significantly moderated the magnitude of treatment outcomes. Some violations that were significantly related to treatment outcomes included: teacher effects (studies that used the identical experimenter for treatment and control in administrating treatments yield smaller effect sizes than studies using different experimenters in administering treatments—a condition that may be analogous to 3-tiered instruction); reliance on "non" norm referenced measures (studies that did not use standardized measures had much larger effect sizes than those using standardized measures); and heterogeneous sampling (e.g., studies that included both elementary and secondary students

yielded larger effect sizes than the other age-level conditions).

More importantly, studies that left out critical information commonly used in most neuropsychological test batteries (e.g., IQ and achievement scores) on individual differences data (or aggregated differences) greatly inflated treatment outcomes. For example, the underreporting of information related to ethnicity (studies that reported ethnicity yielded significantly smaller effect sizes than those that did not report ethnicity) and psychometric data (significantly larger effect sizes occurred when no psychometric information was reported, when compared to the other conditions) positively inflated the magnitude of treatment outcomes. The magnitude of effect sizes was also influenced by whether studies relied on federal definitions (studies that did not report using the federal definition [PL-94-142] yielded a larger weighted effect score than those that did), or reported using multiple definitional criteria in selecting their sample (studies that included multiple criteria in defining their sample yielded smaller effect sizes than those that did not use multiple criteria).

In summary, "best evidence" studies are influenced by a host of environmental and individual difference variables that make a direct translation to assessing children at risk for LD based on an RTI-only model difficult. In addition, although RTI relies on evidence based studies in the various tiers of instruction, especially in the area of reading, it is important to note that even under the most optimal instructional conditions for teaching reading (direction instruction), less than 15% of the variance in outcomes is related to instruction (see Table 5, Swanson, 1999b).

SAMPLE OF RTI MODELS
Some RTI models are gaining a research base, and these are briefly reviewed. For example, a 3-tiered model (Fuchs, Mock, Morgan, & Young, 2003; Fuchs & Vaughn, 2005) includes, as a first step, continual monitoring by the classroom teacher of all children's academic performance. Children who are not responding to instruction are moved to the second level, where they are provided with more or different instruction, and progress is monitored. The intervention at this level is administered by the classroom teacher, or in small groups with a learning specialist. Those children who do not demonstrate accelerated growth, despite a well-implemented intervention, move to the third level, where a comprehensive evaluation becomes necessary in order to

make the best determination of whether a specific learning disability exists. Differential diagnosis takes into account the cognitive abilities of the individual child, and attempts to rule out mental retardation (as required by the federal definition of specific learning disabilities), behavioral and emotional factors (such as attention deficit/hyperactivity disorder), and language acquisition (e.g., English language learners).

There are a number of strengths to this approach. First, the approach has the advantage of intervening early, with close monitoring of student achievement and adjustment of curriculum and teaching methodologies that may be more helpful. Frequent monitoring of a child's response to the intervention provided allows the teacher to adjust goals for the child, resulting in improved student achievement (Fuchs, Fuchs, & Hamlett, 1989). Second, monitoring progress in RTI provides the opportunity to assess the rate of development for the child who is at risk. Monitoring of progress may be the domain of the teacher, special educator, or of a psychologist, either inside or outside of the school. It can be done using a variety of methods and at a variety of time intervals. Use of norm-referenced tests, particularly those which provide alternative forms, is optimal when assessing a child's response to intervention over a longer period of time.

A common strategy for routinely assessing RTI over shorter periods of time is the use of academic probes drawn directly from local curricula, referred to as *curriculum based measurement* (CBM). These probes are brief, and vary widely in terms of their reliability. Some common tools include the Dynamic Indicators of Basic Early Literacy Skills (DIBELS: University of Oregon Center for Teaching and Learning, 2007), Monitoring Basic Skills Progress (MBSP; Fuchs, Hamlett, & Fuchs, 1990), and Yearly Progress Pro (McGraw-Hill Digital Learning, 2002; also, see National Center for Student Progress Monitoring, 2006).

Summary

The assessment of LD (in contrast to other learning problems) focuses primarily on: (a) determining achievement difficulties (e.g., reading, math) that are not due to inadequate opportunity to learn, general intelligence, or to physical or emotional/behavior disorders, but to basic disorders in specific cognitive information processes; (b) determining the link between specific information processing deficits and neurological, constitutional, and/or biological correlates; and (c) determining those specific information processing deficits that are limited to aspect of academic behavior (e.g., phonological processing). There is growing consensus among researchers that it is more appropriate to use an absolute definition of learning disabilities (below some cutoff score on achievement), rather than a discrepancy between achievement and IQ. Although there is controversy over what the absolute cutoff should be to determine LD, the majority of researchers rely on cutoff scores on standardized measures at or above 85 on general intelligence measures, and at or below a standard score of 90 on primary academic domains (e.g., reading and mathematics). Researchers distinguish individuals with LD from those with other general handicapping conditions, such as mental retardation, and visual and/or hearing impairments. Further specification is made that bilingualism, socioeconomic status, and conventional instructional opportunity do not account for depressed achievement scores. Such specification allows the scientist to infer that learning problems are intrinsic to the individual.

The scientific research shows that children with LD can be assessed, and significant gains can be made in academic performance as a function of treatment. However, there is considerable evidence that some children with normal intelligence, when exposed to the best instructional conditions, fail to efficiently master skills in such areas as reading, mathematics, and/or writing. Some literature suggests that individuals with LD are less responsive to intervention than individuals with similar primary academic levels but without LD, and that these academic problems persist into adulthood. Finally, these difficulties in academic mastery reflect fundamental cognitive deficits (e.g., phonological process, working memory).

References

Adams, G., & Carnine, D. (2003). Direct instruction. In H.L. Swanson, K. Harris, & S. Graham, (Eds.), *Handbook of learning disabilities.* (pp. 323–344). New York: Guilford Press.

Al-Otaiba, S., & Fuchs, D. (2002). Characteristics of children who are unresponsive to early literacy intervention: A review of the literature. *Remedial and Special Education, 23*(5), 300–316.

Badian, N. A. (1983). Arithmetic and nonverbal learning, In H. R. Myklebust (Ed.), *Progress in learning disabilities* (Vol. 5, pp. 235–264). New York: Grune and Stratton.

Bradley, R., Danielson, L, & Hallahan, D. P. (2002). Specific learning disabilities: building consensus for identification and classification. In R. Bradley, L. Danielson, & D. P. Hallahan (Eds). *Identification of learning disabilities* (pp. 791–804), Mahwah, NJ: Erlbaum.

Bruck, M. (1990). Word recognition skills of adults with childhood diagnoses of dyslexia. *Developmental Psychology, 26,* 439–454.

Cappeletti, M., Butterworth, B., & Kopelamn, M. D. (2001). Spared numerical abilities in a case of semantic dementia. *Neuropsychologia, 39,* 1224–1239.

Clements, S.D. (1966). Learning disabilities–who? In *Special education: Strategies for educational progress-selected convention papers* (44th Annual CEC convention). Washington DC: Council for Exceptional Children.

Cohen, J. (1988). *Statistical power analysis for the behavioral sciences* (2nd ed.). New York: Academic Press.

Cohen, L., Dehaene, S. Cochon, F., Lehericy, S., & Naccache, L. (2000). Language and calculation within the parietal lobe: A cognitive, anatomical and fMRI study. *Neuropsychologia, 38,* 1426–1440.

Compton, D. L., Fuchs, D., Fuchs, L. S., & Bryant, J. D. (2006). Selecting at-risk readers in first grade for early intervention: A two-year longitudinal study of decision rules and procedures. *Journal of Educational Psychology, 98*(2), 394–409.

Dehaene, S., & Cohen, L. (1995). Towards an anatomical and functional model of number processing. *Mathematical Cognition, 1,* 83–120.

Dehaene, S., & Cohen, L. (1997). Cerebral pathways for calculation: Double disassociation between rote verbal and quantitative knowledge of arithmetic. *Cortex, 33,* 2219–2250.

Deno, E. (1980). Special education and developmental capital. *Exceptional children, 37,* 229–237.

Desoete, A., Roeyers, H., & De Clercq, A. (2004). Children with mathematical learning disabilities in Belgium. *Journal of Learning Disabilities, 37,* 50–61.

Edlnformation, Inc. (2007). AIMS web progress monitoring and response to intervention system. Retrieved June 29, 2007, from http://www.aimsweb.com.

Fine, J. G., Semrud-Clikeman, M., Keith, T. Z., Stapleton, L. M., & Hynd, G. W. (2007). Reading and the corpus callosum: An MRI family study of volume and area. *Neuropsychology, 21,* 235–241.

Fletcher, J. M., Lyon, G. R., Fuchs, L. S., & Barnes, M. A. (2007). *Learning disabilities: From identification to intervention.* New York: Guilford Press.

Fletcher, J. M., Francis, D. J., Rourke, B. P., Shaywitz, S. E., & Shaywitz, B. A. (1992). The validity of discrepancy-based definitions of reading disabilities. *Journal of Learning Disabilities, 25,* 555–561.

Francis, D.J., Shaywitz, S.E., Stuebing, K.K., Shaywitz, B.A., & Fletcher, J.M. (1996). Developmental lag versus deficit models of reading disability: A longitudinal, individual growth curves analysis. *Journal of Educational Psychology, 88,* 3–17.

Francis, D. J., Fletcher, J. M., Stuebing, K. K., Lyon, G. R., Shaywitz, B. A., & Shaywitz, S. E. (2005). Psychometric approaches to the identification of LD: IQ and achievement scores are not sufficient. *Journal of Learning Disabilities, 38*(2), 98–108.

Fuchs, L. S., Fuchs, D., & Hamlett, C. L. (1989). Effects of alternative goal structures within curriculum-based measurement. *Exceptional Children, 55,* 429–438.

Fuchs, L.S., Hamlett, C. L., & Fuchs, D. (1990). *Monitoring basic skills progress.* Austin, TX: Pro.Ed.

Fuchs, D., Fuchs, L. S., & Compton, D. L. (2004). Identifying reading disabilities by responsiveness-to-instruction: Specifying measures and criteria. *Learning Disability Quarterly, 27*(4), 216–227.

Fuchs, D., Fuchs, L., Mathes, P.G., & Lipsey, M. (2000). Reading differences between low achieving students with and without learning disabilities. In R. Gersten, E.P. Schiller, & S. Vaughn (Eds.), *Contemporary special education research: Synthesis of knowledge base of critical issues.* Mahwah, NJ: Erbaum.

Fuchs, D. Mock, D., Morgan, P., & Young, C. L. (2003). Responsiveness-to-intervention: Definitions, evidence, and implications for the learning disabilities construct. *Learning Disabilities Research & Practice, 18,* 157–171.

Fuchs, L. S., & Vaughn, S. R. (2005). Response-to-intervention as a framework for identification of learning disabilities. *Trainer's Forum: Periodical of the Trainers for School Psychologists, 25,* 12–19.

Geary, D. C. (1993). Mathematical disabilities: Cognitive, [neuropsychological and genetic components. *Psychological Bulletin, 114,* 345–362.

Geary, D. C. (2003). Math disabilities. In H. L. Swanson, K. Harris, & S. Graham (Eds.), *Handbook of learning disabilities.* New York: Guilford Press.

Geary, D. C., Hoard, M. K., Byrd-Craven, J., & DeSoto, M. C. (2004). Strategy choices in simple and complex addition: Contributions of working memory and counting knowledge for children with math disability. *Journal of Experimental Child Psychology, 80,* 121–151.

Geary, D. C., Hamson, C. O., & Hoard, M. K. (2000). Numerical and arithmetical cognition: A longitudinal study of process and concept deficits in children with learning disability. *Journal of Experimental Child Psychology, 77,* 236–263.

Gilger, J. W., Borecki, I. B., Smith, S. D., DeFries, J. C., & Pennington, B. F. (1996). The etiology of extreme scores for complex phenotypes: An illustration of reading performance. In C. Chase, G.D. Rosen & G.F. Sherman (Eds). *Developmental dyslexia: Neural, cognitive, and genetic mechanisms.* (pp. 63–85). Baltimore MD: York Press.

Goldman, S. R., Pellegrino, J.W., & Mertz, D. L. (1988). Extended practice of basic addition fact: Strategy changes in learning disabled student. *Cognition and Instruction, 5,* 223–265.

Gross-Tsur, V., Manor, O., & Shalev, R.S. (1996). Developmental dyscalculia: Prevalence and demographic features. *Developmental Medicine and Child Neurology, 38,* 25–33.

Grigorenko, E. (2001). Developmental dyslexia: An update on genes, brains, and environments. *Journal of Child Psychology and Psychiatry, 42,* 91–125.

Hallahan, D., & Cruickshank, W.M. (1973). *Psychoeducational foundations of learning disabilities.* Englewood Cliffs, NJ: Prentice Hall.

Hallahan, D. Keller, C., Martinez, E., Byrd, E.S., Gelman, J., & Fan, X. (2007). How variable are interstate prevalence rates of learning disabilities and other special education categories? A longitudinal comparison. *Exceptional Children, 73,* 136–146.

Hammill, D. (1990). On defining learning disabilities: An emerging consensus. *Journal of Learning Disabilities, 23,* 74–84.

Hammill, D. D., & Swanson, H. L. (2006). The national reading panel's meta-analysis of phonics instruction: Another point of view. *The Elementary School Journal., 107,* 17–26.

Haring, N.G., & Bateman, B. (1977). *Teaching the learning disabled child.* Englewood Cliffs, NJ: Prentice Hall.

Hecht, S. A., Close, L., & Sabatisi, M. (2003). Sources of individual differences in fraction skills. *Journal of Experimental Child Psychology, 86,* 277–302

Hecht, S. A., Torgesen, J. K., Wagner, R., & Rashotte, C. (2001). The relationship between phonological processing abilities and emerging individual differences in mathematical computation skills: A longitudinal study of second to fifth grades. *Journal of Experimental Child Psychology, 79*, 192–227.

Hitch, G. J., & McAuley, E. (1991). Working memory in children with specific arithmetical learning disabilities. *British Journal of Psychology, 82*, 375–386.

Hoskyn, M., & Swanson, H. L. (2000). Cognitive processing of low achievers and children with reading disabilities: A selective meta-analytic review of the published literature. *School Psychology Review, 29*, 102–119.

Individuals with Disabilities Education Improvement Act of 2004 (IDEA), Pub. L. No. 108–446,118 Stat. 2647 (2004). [Amending 20 U.S.C. §§ 1400 et. Seq.].

Jordan, N., & Montani, T. (1997). Cognitive arithmetic and problem solving: A comparison of children with specific and general mathematics difficulties. *Journal of Learning Disabilities, 30*, 624–634.

Jordan, N., Hanich, L. B., & Kaplan, D. (2003). A longitudinal study of mathematical competencies in children with specific mathematics difficulties versus children with co-morbid mathematics and reading difficulties. *Child Development, 74*, 834–850.

Kaméenui, E. J., Jitendra, A. K., & Darch, C. B. (1995). Direct instruction reading as contronym and eonomine. *Reading & Writing Quarterly: Overcoming Learning Difficulties, 11*, 3–17.

Katzir, T., Kim, Y., Wolf, M., Morris, R., & Lovett, M. W. (2008). The varieties of pathways to dysfluent reading: Comparing subtypes of children with dyslexia at letter, word, and connected text levels of reading. *Journal of Learning Disabilities, 41*(1), 47–66.

Kaufman, A.S., & Kaufman, N.L. (2004). *Kaufman assessment battery for children* (2nd ed.). Circle Pines, MN: American Guidance Press.

Kavale, K., A., & Reese, L. (1992). The characteristics of learning disabilities: An Iowa profile. *Learning Disability Quarterly, 15*, 74–94.

Kosc, L. (1974). Developmental dyscalculia. *Journal of Learning Disabilities, 7*, 164–177.

Landerl, K., Bevan, A., & Butterworth, B. (2004). Developmental dyscalculia and basic numerical capacities: A study of 8–9 year old students. *Cognition, 99*–125.

Lerner, J. (1989). Educational intervention in learning disabilities. *Journal of the American Academy of Child and Adolescent Psychiatry, 28*, 326–331.

Mann, V. A. (2003). Language processes: Keys to reading disability. In H. L. Swanson, K. R. Harris, & S. Graham (Eds.), *Handbook of learning disabilities* (pp. 213–228). New York: Guilford Press.

Mazzocco, M. M. (2007). Defining and differentiating mathematical learning disabilities and difficulties. In D. Berch & M. M. Mazzocco (Eds). *Why is math so hard for some children.* (pp. 29–48). Baltimore: Brookes.

McGraw-Hill Digital Learning. (2002). Yearly Progress Program. Retrieved June 28, 2007, from www.mhdigitallearning.com/prod_tour.jsp

Miller, C. J., Sanchez, J., Hynd, G. W. (2003). Neurological correlates of reading disabilities. In H. L. Swanson, K. R. Harris, & S. Graham, (Eds.), *Handbook of learning disabilities.* (pp. 242–255). New York: Guilford Press.

Morris, R. D., Stuebing, K. K.; Fletcher, J. M., Shaywitz, S. E., Lyon, G. R., Shankweiler, D. P., et al. (1998). Subtypes of reading disability: variability around a phonological core. *Journal of Educational Psychology, 90*, 347–373.

Naglieri, J. A., & Das, J. P. (1997). Cognitive assessment system. Itasca, IL: Riverside Publishing Co.

National Center for Student Progress Monitoring. (2006). Review of progress monitoring tools. Retrieved June 28, 2007, from www.studentprogress.org/chart/chart.asp

Olson, R., Forsberg, H., Gayen, J., & DeFries, J.C. (1999). A behavioral–genetic analysis of reading disabilities and component processes. In R.M. Klein & P.A. MCMullen (Eds.) *Converging evidence for understanding reading and dyslexia* (pp. 133–153). Cambridge, MA: MIT Press.

Psychological Corporation. (2001). *Wechsler individual achievement test* (2nd ed.). San Antonio, TX: Author.

Pugh, K. R., Mencl, W. E., Jenner, A. R., Lee, J. R., Katz, L., Frost, S. J., et al. (2001). Neuroimaging studies of reading development and reading disability. *Learning Disabilities Research & Practice Special Issue: Emergent and Early Literacy: Current Status and Research Directions, 16*(4), 240–249.

Roid, G. H. (2003). *Stanford–Binet intelligence scales* (5th ed.). Itasca, IL: Riverside.

Scarborough, H. (1990). Very early language deficits in dyslexic children. *Child Development, 61*, 1728–1743.

Shalev, R. S., Manor, O., & Gross-Tsur, V. (1997). Neuropsychological aspects of developmental dyscalculia. *Mathematical Cognition, 3*(2), 105–120.

Shaywitz, S.E., Fletcher, J.M., Holahan, J.M., Schneider, A.E., Marchione, K.E., Stuebing, K.K., Francis, D.J., & Shaywitz, B.A. (1999). Persistence of dyslexia: The Connecticut longitudinal study at adolescence. *Pediatrics, 104*, 1351–1359.

Shaywitz, S. E., Mody, M., & Shaywitz, B. A. (2006). Neural mechanisms in dyslexia. *Current Directions in Psychological Science, 15*, 278–281.

Shaywitz, S.E., & Shaywitz, B. A. (2003). Neurobiological indices of dyslexia. In H. L. Swanson, K. R. Harris, & S. Graham, (Eds.). *Handbook of learning disabilities.* (pp. 514–531). New York: Guilford Press.

Shaywitz, S. E., & Shaywitz, B. A. (2005). Dyslexia (specific reading disability). *Biological Psychiatry, 57*, 1301–1309.

Shaywitz, B. A., Shaywitz, S. E., Blachman, B. A., Pugh, K. R., Fulbright, R. K., & Skudlarski, P. et al. (2004). Development of left occipitotemporal systems for skilled reading in children after a phonologically-based intervention. *Biological Psychiatry, 55*, 926–933.

Shaywitz, S. E., Shaywitz, B. A., Fulbright, R. K., Skudlarski, P., Mencl, W. E., & Constable, R. T. et al. (2003). Neural systems for compensation and persistence: Young adult outcome of childhood reading disability. *Biological Psychiatry, 54*, 25–33.

Siegel, L. S. (2003a). Basic cognitive processes and reading disabilities. In H. L. Swanson, K. R. Harris, & S. Graham (Eds.), *Handbook of learning disabilities* (pp 158–181). New York: Guilford Press.

Siegel, L. S. (2003b). IQ-discrepancy definitions and the diagnosis of LD: Introduction to the special issue. *Journal of Learning Disabilities, 36*, 2–3.

Siegel, L. S., & Ryan, E. B. (1989). The development of working memory in normally achieving and subtypes of learning disabled children. *Child Development, 60*, 973–980.

Simmerman, S., & Swanson, H. L. (2001). Treatment outcomes for students with learning disabilities: How important are internal and external validity? *Journal of Learning Disabilities, 34*, 221–236.

Stanovich, K. & Siegel, L.S. (1994). Phenotypic performance profile of children with reading disabilities: A regression-based test of the phonological-core variable-difference model. *Journal of Educational Psychology, 86,* 24–53.

Stuebing, K. K., Fletcher, J. M., LeDoux, J. M., Lyon, G. R., Shaywitz, S. E., & Shaywitz, B. A. (2002). Validity of IQ-discrepancy classifications of reading disabilities: A meta-analysis. *American Educational Research Journal, 39,* 469–518.

Swanson, H. L. (1993a). Individual differences in working memory: a model testing and subgroup analysis of learning-disabled and skilled readers. Intelligence, *17,* 285–332.

Swanson, H.L. (1993b). Working memory in learning disability subgroups. *Journal of Experimental Child Psychology, 56,* 87–114.

Swanson, H. L. (1999a). Reading comprehension and working memory in learning-disabled readers: Is the phonological loop more important than the executive system? *Journal of Experimental Child Psychology, 72*(1), 1–31.

Swanson, H. L. (1999b). Reading research for students with LD: A meta-analysis in intervention outcomes. *Journal of Learning Disabilities, 32,* 504–532.

Swanson, H. L. (2000). Searching for the best cognitive model for instructing students with learning disabilities: A component and composite analysis. *Educational and Child Psychology, 17,* 101–121.

Swanson, H. L. (2001). Research on interventions for adolescents with learning disabilities: A meta-analysis of outcomes related to higher-order processing. *The Elementary School Journal., 101,* 331–348.

Swanson, H. L., & Deshler, D. (2003). Instructing adolescents with learning disabilities: Converting a meta-analysis to practice. *Journal of Learning Disabilities, 36,* 124–135.

Swanson, H. L., & Hoskyn, M. (1998). Experimental intervention research on students with learning disabilities: A meta-analysis of treatment outcomes. *Review of Educational Research, 68,* 277–321.

Swanson, H. L., & Hoskyn, M. (1999). Definition × treatment interactions for students with learning disabilities. *School Psychology Review, 28,* 644–658.

Swanson, H. L., Hoskyn, M., & Lee, C. M. (1999). *Interventions for students with learning disabilities.* New York: Guilford Press.

Swanson, H. L., Howard, C. B., & Sáez, L. (2006). Do different components of working memory underlie different subgroups of reading disabilities? *Journal of Learning Disabilities, 39,* 252–269.

Swanson, H. L., & Jerman, O. (2006). Math disabilities: A selective meta-analysis of the literature. *Review of Educational Research, 76*(2), 249–274.

Swanson, H. L., & Sachse-Lee, C. (2000). A meta-analysis of single-subject-design intervention research for students with LD. *Journal of Learning Disabilities, 33,* 114–136.

Swanson, H. L., & Siegel, L. (2001). Learning disabilities as a working memory deficit. *Issues in Education, 7,* 1–48.

Torgesen, J.K., Wagner, R.K., & Rachotte, C. (1999). *Test of word reading efficiency.* Austin, TX: Pro-Ed.

U.S. Office of Education. (1977). Assistance to states for education for handicapped children: Procedures for evaluating specific learning disabilities. Federal Register, 42, GI082-G1085.

University of Oregon Center for Teaching and Learning. (2007). Official DIBELS Homepage. Retrieved June 3, 2010 from http://dibels.uoregon.edu

Vellutino, F. R., Fletcher, J. M., Snowling, M. J., & Scanlon, D. M. (2004). Specific reading disabilities (dyslexia): What have we learned in the past four decades? *Journal of Child Psychology and Psychiatry, 45,* 2–40.

Vellutino, F. R., Scanlon, D. M., & Lyon, G. R. (2000). Differentiating between difficult-to-remediate and readily remediated poor readers: More evidence against the IQ-achievement discrepancy. *Journal of Learning Disabilities, 33,* 192–199.

Vellutino, F. R., Scanlon, D. M., Sipay, E. R., Small, S. G., Pratt, A., Chen, R., et al. (1996). Cognitive profiles of difficult-to-remediate and readily remediated poor readers: Early intervention as a vehicle for distinguishing between cognitive and experimental deficits as basic causes of specific reading disability. *Journal of Educational Psychology, 88,* 601–638.

Wechsler, D. (2003). *Wechsler intelligence scale for children: Administration and scoring manual.* (4th ed.). San Antonio: Psychological Corporation.

Wiederholt, L. (1974). Historical perspective on the education of the learning disabled. In L. Mann, D. Sabatino (Eds.) *The second review of special education* (pp. 103–152). Austin: Pro-Ed.

Wolf, M., Bowers, P. G., & Biddle, K. (2000). Naming-speed processes, timing, and reading: A conceptual review. *Journal of Learning Disabilities, 33,* 387–407.

Wong, B., Harris, K., Graham, S., & Butler, D. (2003). Cognitive strategies instruction research in learning disabilities. In H.L. Swanson, K. Harris, & S.Graham (Eds.) *Handbook of learning disabilities* (pp. 383–402). New York: Guilford.

Woodcock, R. W., McGrew, K.S., & Mather, N. (2001). *Woodcock-Johnson III tests of cognitive abilities and tests of achievement.* Itasca, IL: Riverside.

The Clinical Interview in Mathematics Assessment and Intervention: The Case of Fractions

Zheng Zhou

Abstract

Research from both domestic and international assessments has revealed the problematic nature of mathematics instruction and assessment practice. The method of standardized testing is extremely influential in school psychology, dominating the evaluation and study of children's thinking. Although increasing numbers of practitioners are relying on curriculum-based measurement (CBM) as an alternative assessment to standardized testing, the procedure used in CBM is notably similar to testing in previous decades in terms of the types of items and the methods of administration. This type of assessment does not allow in-depth examination of children's dynamic mathematical thinking and development due to its "standardized" assessment procedures. Therefore, the potential for developing effective intervention and instruction to foster children's mathematics learning is limited. The clinical interview, a powerful set of assessment strategies, presents an alternative, or supplementary method, for the study of children's thinking and reasoning. Understanding the underlying cognitive processes in children's problem solving is particularly important in the semantically complex domains in mathematics, such as fractions. Developing the knowledge and skills necessary to conduct clinical interviews are critical in developing evidence-based instruction and intervention in mathematics.

Keywords: clinical interview, dynamic assessment, curriculum-based measurement, fractions, mathematical reasoning, response to intervention

In response to unacceptable levels of mathematics achievement in the U.S., the National Council of Teachers of Mathematics (NCTM, 2000) and National Mathematics Advisory Panel (2008) have put forth compelling proposals for the reform of mathematics education. Research findings from various domestic and international studies, such as Trends in International Mathematics and Science Study (TIMSS) and the Programme for International Student Assessment (PISA), have revealed the problematic nature of mathematics instruction and assessment practice in this country (Ginsburg, 1997; Niemi, 1994; Siegler, 2007; Stevenson, Chen, & Lee, 1993; Stevenson & Stigler, 1992; Stigler & Hiebert, 1999; Stigler & Perry, 1988; Stigler & Stevenson, 1991). According to the *Principles and Standards for School Mathematics* developed by NCTM (a professional organization that oversees the nation's mathematics education of students in pre-kindergarten through grade 12), the "best practice" for understanding children's mathematical learning is to align the assessment strategies with the complex structure of mathematics (NCTM, 2000). The significance of this type of approach is grounded in the belief that all students should "learn mathematical concepts and procedures with understanding." According to Webb & Romberg (1992), "Consideration of the structure of mathematics in constructing assessment methods affects how tasks are designed and chosen, how tasks are administered, the desired form of response, [and] what rules are followed to make judgments about responses" (p.5). Traditional assessments, including those often used by school psychologists, typically involve standardized procedures that have not adequately attended to the structured nature of mathematical understanding; therefore, educational assessment and practice is not linked as yet to the theoretical framework (Ginsburg, 1997; Niemi, 1994; Siegler, 1999, 2007). An *understanding-based* or *meaning-based* instruction (two terms commonly used in mathematics education) demands comprehensive and dynamic assessment strategies that reflect conceptual analyses of key domains in mathematics (Messick, 1989; Siegler, 1998, 1999, 2000, 2007; Rittle-Johnson, Sielger, & Alibali, 2001). Developing the knowledge of how to conduct comprehensive assessments that are sensitive to differences in student understanding is critical in building evidence-based instructional practices in mathematics.

This chapter draws from the literature in the assessment of children's mathematics from three disciplines: school psychology, cognitive psychology, and mathematics education. First, a brief overview of the basic features of current CBM strategies in mathematics is presented, followed by a discussion of some limitations inherent in its "standardized" assessment procedures. Next, the rationale for using a clinical interview, as an alternative or supplemental method to the traditional standardized assessment procedures, is explained. In order to further elucidate the role of clinical interviews in mathematics assessment and intervention, a theoretical discussion of mathematical knowledge structure in general, and rational number concepts (with a focus on fraction concepts) in particular, is presented. Following this discussion, illustrations of how the clinical interview is conducted to assess children's knowledge of fractions is described. Finally, implications for the training of school psychologists and educators in applying clinical interview methods to evidence-based practice in assessing mathematics learning are discussed.

Current Evidence-Based Mathematics Assessment Strategies

The widely practiced curriculum-based measurement (CBM), the foundation for response to intervention (RTI; Clarke, Baker, & Chan, 2008), is an evidence-based practice of determining students' needs through comprehensive assessment practices. CBM is a particular *type* of curriculum-based assessment (CBA; Shinn, 2008) (For more information on distinctions among types of CBM, see Hosp, Hosp, & Howell, 2007; Shinn & Bamonto, 1998; Shinn, Rosenfield, & Knutson, 1989; Tindal, 1993). The purpose of CBM is to provide effective instruction

that meets students' learning needs by regularly monitoring student progress to ensure achievement in various academic areas (Kelley, 2008), including mathematics. Its positive effects in mathematics have been reported by researchers (e.g., VanDerHeyden & Burns, 2005; Stecker & Fuchs, 2005). CBM is implemented in a three-tier problem solving model to conduct both universal screening and progress monitoring (Tilly, 2008). Despite its popularity, even its proponents acknowledge that it lacks "diagnostic power and prescriptive efficacy," and raise concerns about its potential benefits to intervention and instruction since it "does not tell why a child has an academic discrepancy or how to intervene to reduce it" (Shinn, 2008, p. 247). Furthermore, what constitutes "comprehensive" assessment remains undefined (Reynolds & Shaywitz, 2009). This is particularly true in the semantically complex domains in mathematics, since there is no fixed terminus for understanding. Understanding may develop indefinitely with increasing experience and competence; therefore, as Brownell (1967) put it, "it is meaningless to say that any child 'has' this or that concept or understanding. It is more accurate to say that he 'has' the concept or understanding to a greater or lesser degree of completeness and precision" (p.3). The goal of assessment, then, is to ascertain the degree of completeness and precision of conceptual understanding, and to identify different types of understanding (Ginsburg, 1997; Siegler, 1999; 2007).

In the field of school psychology, the method of standardized testing is extremely influential, dominating the assessment and study of children's thinking. Throughout the paper, the term *standardized assessment/testing* refers to *standardized assessment procedures*. Although viewed as an alternative assessment, the CBM assessment procedure is notably similar to testing in previous decades, in terms of the types of items and the methods of administration (Cole, 1986). In fact, CBM's most important feature is "that the testing process is standardized and test materials are of equal difficulty" (Shinn, 2008, p. 244). The measurement procedures are described as "technically sound, quick and easy to administer and interpret" (Thurber, Shinn, & Smolkowski, 2002, p. 499). Typically, CBM math assessment consists of a set of standardized and short duration tests (i.e., 1 to 5 minutes) and is administered by educators or school psychologists, using standardized procedures (Clarke & Shinn, 2004), to evaluate effects of instructional interventions in the basic skills such as reading and math (Shinn, 2008). The core CBM features in mathematics consist of mathematics computation, and mathematics application. In *mathematics computation* CBM, students solve grade-level computation problems on paper in a short duration (usually 2 to 4 minutes; Shinn & Shinn, 2004). The number of correct digits is counted (Foegen, Jiban, & Deno, 2007). In *mathematics applications* CBM, students solve grade-level mathematics application problems on paper (Fuchs, Fuchs, & Hamlett, 1995), and their correct answers are counted (Foegen et al., 2007; Fuchs & Deno, 1994). Problem identification consists of three steps: (1) tests are scored and data are summarized; (2) existing assessment data are reviewed and, if necessary, additional information is obtained; and (3) error patterns identified during problem analysis are used to determine the presumed cause of the student's difficulty. Observations are made during the assessment process, and student interviews are sometimes conducted after the assessment. However, the qualitative data gathered through the observation and interview are rarely discussed and interpreted. The error analysis, though useful, is not adequate in providing insight into children's underlying cognitive processes during problem solving. Following CBM, an instructional plan is developed that consists of a child's present level of academic achievement and functional performance. In addition, a list of instructional goals and objectives are developed, and instructions are subsequently planned and implemented (Greenwood, Carta, Baggett, Buzhardt, Walker, & Terry, 2008).

Clearly, CBM gives principal attention to the correctness of students' responses, therefore giving "mathematical validity" to the CBM method. This assessment practice of children's mathematical ability consists primarily of their accuracy of response under timed test conditions. Within these constraints, the only acceptable interpretation of meaningful understanding and level of academic performance is the test scores, with speed and accuracy as the observable outcome criteria. Quantitative measures are respected, while qualitative ones are essentially ignored (Goldin, 2008).

Limitations in Standardized Assessment Procedures

To provide comprehensive assessment as required by RTI, the traditional methods of standard testing procedures are inadequate. Ginsburg, a prominent researcher in children's mathematical cognition at Teachers College, Columbia Univeristy, argues that standardized methods are based on outmoded

theory and are not effective techniques for providing adequate insight into cognitive function. However, proponents defend standardized testing on both scientific and ethical grounds. On scientific grounds, they argue that if anything is to be learned from investigations, the experimenter must ensure that procedures are fully standardized. As Anastasi (1988) put it, "if the scores obtained by different persons are to be comparable, testing conditions must obviously be the same for all" (p.25). To do otherwise would be to render the data uninterpretable. Similarly, Kamphaus (1993) argues that standardized procedures are crucial because "...the examiner can then feel confident that comparing the child's scores to the norm... is justified" (p. 82). On ethical grounds, Anastasi (1988) asserts that when "prejudices distort interpersonal evaluations, tests provide a safeguard against favoritism and arbitrary or capricious decisions" (p. 67) and "... if standardized tests were eliminated, we would have to fall back on subjective judgment, which is subject to "unreliability, subjectivity, and potential bias." (p.68). These arguments date back to Binet and Simon (1916), who argued that fairness demanded standardized, uniform administration in order to be fair to the child. In essence, the standardized assessment method aims at accurate measurement, unconfounded by variation in test administration, in an effort to ensure fairness in the sense of impartiality.

The method of standardized administration often falls short on both scientific and ethical grounds. Ginsburg (1997) points out some basic flaws in standardized methods. He argues from the scientific perspective that standardized achievement tests are (1) usually based in outmoded assumptions about cognition (2) not suitable instruments for studying complex thinking, (3) inadequate for the kinds of exploration often required in research and practice, (4) not suitable instruments for studying dynamic change, (5) children do not always interpret the questions intended by the examiner, and (6) the cognitive processes involved in solving problems are not clear. From an ethical perspective, he argues that standardized procedures cannot effectively motivate all children, and are "often not suitable for tapping the competence of those who are in some way 'different' by virtue of culture, ethnicity, health status, or other reasons" (p. 10). If evidenced-based practice has to be based on our understanding of the complexity of children's thinking and development, then the standardized procedures we currently use are not adequate. The assessment procedures used in CBM are based on an unfounded psychological theory which views learning as the passive accumulation of facts provided by instruction. Ginsburg (1997) argues, "traditional achievement tests ignore students' construction of psychological knowledge, their thinking, and their underlying conceptions" (p. 16). He goes on to state, "the usual testing situation is devised that students must deal with a narrow problem over a short period of time and are allowed to respond only in limited ways. Tests demand impoverished responses because to permit richness would be to make scoring difficult" (p. 19). These constraints of standardized testing do not allow students to demonstrate what they can do, or for educators to learn from what the students have done.

From the instructional perspective, standardized assessment procedures do not provide information useful for teaching. According to Linn (1986), the test results are more likely to confirm what the teachers already know about the student. The scores do not provide teachers with new insights, nor do they reveal anything about the causes of a particular student's problem or provide any direct indications as to what instructional strategies would be most effective.

Effective instructional interventions depend on the availability of techniques for assessing understanding. As Chevallard (cited in Bodin, 1993, p.132) put it, "… assessment is in fact one of the determining aspects of the learning process—which controls and regulates both the behavior of the teacher and the learning of the students."

When teachers or school psychologists do not have, or do not use, validated methods for discerning whether systematic understanding has been achieved, then the effectiveness of instruction and intervention will be compromised. In such instances, instructional decisions will have to be made on an inadequate diagnosis of whether children understand previously taught concepts, or how they interpret topics under discussion. At present, standardized procedures used in CBM do not adequately assess understanding of specific concepts or conceptual domains and, therefore, are of limited use for decision making in the course of "teaching for understanding." Their validity rests primarily on "face validity," on correlation with similar tests, on "predictive" correlations, and on post-hoc analyses of the factors represented by different items, not on the diagnostic utility or construct validity of the measure itself. Given the considerable evidence on how the power of testing influences curriculum, instruction, and learning, there is an urgent need for validation of assessments aligned with "meaning-based" instructional intervention

(Garcia, Rasmussen, Stobbe, & Garcia, 1990; Goldin, 1992; Hatch & Gardner, 1990; Linn, Baker, & Dunbar, 1991; Fredericksen, 1984). As Messick (1989) noted, assessments that are insensitive to learning can hardly be used to guide and inform instruction.

The Role of the Clinical Interview in Assessing Children's Mathematical Understanding

Despite the limitations inherent in the standardized testing, school psychologists have been reluctant to abandon the methods rendered obsolete by new theoretical developments. Recent theoretical and methodological advances in cognitive psychology have revealed important techniques appropriate for the study of children's thinking and reasoning. One reason for the increasing emphasis on cognitive change process is that discovery of new strategies is constrained by conceptual understanding (Coyle & Bjorklund, 1997; Gelman & Williams, 1998; Granott, 1993; Kuhn, Garcia-Mila, Zohar, & Anderson, 1995; Schauble, 1990, 1996; Zhou, Peverly, Boehm, & Lin, 2000). The phenomenon has been observed in diverse areas such as scientific reasoning, arithmetic, collaborative problem solving, memory strategies, and motor skills (Chen & Siegler, 2000). In order to capture the dynamic changes in children's conceptual development in a knowledge domain, researchers often characterize children's knowledge at the level of rules, strategies, and processing components that underlie their degree of success, the particular error they make, and their solution time, rather than simply indicating that the child "has" the relevant competence or capability. For example, Zhou and her colleagues (Zhou & Peverly, 2004; Zhou, Peverly, Boehm, & Lin, 2000) studied American and Chinese children's understanding of the interrelations among distance, time, and speed concepts in both cross- and within-cultural settings. Using the clinical interview method, Zhou was able to identify three levels of strategies in solving distance-time-speed problems, and the related cross-cultural differences in children's use of these strategies. The findings showed that most children in the United States who gave correct responses to tasks verbalized incorrect reasoning when they were asked to justify their problem solutions. Furthermore, Chinese children reported, at a much earlier age than their U.S. counterparts, the use of the most advanced integration strategy in solving distance-time-speed problems. Lastly, children taught by teachers, who were trained in the theory and practice of the "mathematical thinking" instructional model, reported more frequent use of the most advanced level of strategies, compared to those taught by teachers without such training. The clinical interviews used in the studies by Zhou and her colleagues clearly enabled the researchers to examine, at a conceptual level, children's understanding of distance, time, and speed interrelations.

Lamon (1993) also used clinical interviews to study children's reasoning in solving ratio and proportion problems. In her study, she presented sixth graders the following problem: Ellen, Jim, and Steve bought 3 helium-filled balloons and paid $2.00 for all three. They decided to go back and get enough balloons for all of the students in their class. How much did they pay for 24 balloons? Four levels of reasoning were identified: *random operations* (using whole number operations to combine two of the given numbers at a time), *single unit strategy* (the cost of one item is computed and multiplied by the desired number of items), *building up strategy* (successive multiples of the 3-unit of people and the 2-unit of dollars), and *composite unit strategy* (composite unit whole to get 8 and multiply $2, arriving at $16).

By applying the clinical interview method in both Zhou et al. and Lamon's research, detailed accounts of students' strategies and errors were identified, and various developmental states were distinguished and ordered according to mathematical sophistication. By providing a more refined picture of children's thinking, the researchers help the teachers to recognize proportional reasoning when it occurs, and recognize what the process of learning looks like. The researchers' work demonstrates that many children have a repertoire of powerful strategies at their command. They choose from among these strategies, matching them to specific context and conditions. Many students use metacognitive strategies in evaluating the appropriateness of their existing strategies, the efficiency of their methods, and the reasonableness of their answers. Assessing the underlying cognitive processes during problem solving provides the detailed information that can be useful in informing instructional practices that promote children's mathematical thinking in solving complex math problems.

The microgenetic method developed by Siegler and his colleagues has been used to examine children's thinking and reasoning at an even greater and more refined level (Chen & Siegler, 2000; Kuhn & Phelps, 1982; Siegler, 1999; Siegler, 2000; Siegler, 2007; Siegler & Chen, 1998; Siegler & Crowley, 1991; Siegler & Stern, 1998). Framed in the Overlapping Waves Theory (Siegler, 1996), the microgenetic method focuses on the examination of the mechanisms that underlie learning by using repeated observations and interviews of individual children working on a set of problems over a period of time. Some consistent findings have emerged from research using this method: (1) discovery of new strategies is conceptually constrained; (2) cognitive change tends to be gradual; (3) new strategies are discovered regardless of whether children are succeeding or failing at the task, and (4) the greater the initial variability in thinking, the more likely that children will generate useful new problem solving strategies (Chen & Siegler, 2000). These findings point to new directions in constructing the kinds of measures that are needed to assess cognitive competence, as well as the level of detail at which thought processes should be described.

At the heart of the aforementioned research is the use of the clinical interview that has recently gained popularity in cognitive developmental research and education. The clinical interview has its historic roots in Piaget and Vygotsky. In the 1920s, Piaget observed and interviewed children, presented them with intellectual tasks, and recorded their answers. He reported his sensitive insights into children's thinking in many volumes, among them, *The Origins of Intelligence in Children* (1952), *The Language and Thought of the Child* (1926), *Judgment and Reasoning in the Child* (1928), *The Moral Judgment of the Child* (1932), and *The Child's Conception of the World* (1976). Based on his observations and interviews, Piaget conceptualized intellectual development as having four main stages in its advancement from sensorimotor to formal operational stage.

Russian psychologist, Vygotsky (1986), considered the clinical interview method as "a truly invaluable tool" for studying intellectual development. He has drawn our attention to the "dynamics" of the child's intellect, its flexibility, its learning potential, and its ability to profit from experience and assistance. In Vygotsky's view, a child's learning and development take place at two levels: (1) the child's actual developmental level, by learning about the child's problem solving capability as he or she works without any adult help, and (2) what the child can do with adult guidance. The "zone of proximal development" is the notion that he coined to describe the difference between what a child can do independently (actual developmental level) and what she or he can do when working with a competent adult (potential developmental level).

Despite its renewed popularity, the clinical interview methods are not sufficiently understood in the field of school psychology. Part of the reason is that the method violates the standard paradigm, since it directly challenges the traditional point of view concerning the scientific method in research and practice. According to Ginsburg (1997), psychologists tend to assume that the more "standardized" the assessment, the more "valid" it is. Although the scientifically rigorous approach relies on the method of standardized administration, the approach is often inadequate for gaining insight into the child's mental constructions (Siegler, 1996, 1998, 2007). The method of standardized administration is unsuitable for the measurement of the complexity of thinking; "it is like dipping into the stream in one place all the time with the same little ladle," (Ginsburg, 1997, p. 63). Ginsburg thus concludes that to assess the "river of thought," flexible methods like the clinical interview are required.

The use of the clinical interview strategy is particularly important in assessing knowledge in the complex domains of mathematics, such as rational numbers (fractions, decimal, and percent). The rationale is simple: the scores obtained from the standardized testing procedures do not provide a detailed portrait of children's thinking. Correct and incorrect answers to any single item may result from any number of strategies; therefore, the test provides no direct information about which strategies might have been employed by the child to solve a particular problem. In order to understand the role of clinical interview in the comprehensive assessment of children's mathematical thinking, a theoretical discussion of the structure of mathematical knowledge in general, and fraction in particular, is necessary.

A Theory of Relational Understanding of Mathematical Knowledge

Comprehensive and dynamic assessment of children's mathematics learning difficulties relies on our knowledge of the structure of mathematics. In a seminal discussion of problems in mathematics education, Skemp (1976) differentiated two kinds of mathematical understanding: instrumental and relational. Instrumental understanding centers on knowing which procedures to employ in a problem situation, but not why. The outcome of the instrumental understanding is unconnected learning. A child may know the algorithm for dividing by fractions by applying the rule of "invert and multiply" without knowing why the procedure works, other than the rule has been expressly taught

in class. The relational understanding, on the other hand, refers to "knowing both what to do and why." (Skemp, 1976, p. 20). The process of developing such understanding is like constructing a "mental map." To illustrate his point, Skemp compared instrumental understanding and relational understanding to two ways of getting around a town. One way is to memorize fixed routes for getting from one point to another (instrumental understanding), whereas another way of maneuvering around town is to explore the relations among major landmarks and street layouts (relational understanding). Using fixed plans, one can find the way from each starting point to the destination, just like using Google's MapQuest. However, as many have learned, it only takes one mistake to get lost. A person with a good mental map, on the other hand, can produce many routes for any set of starting points and destinations. A wrong turn is not necessarily disastrous, but may produce new knowledge. Relational understanding may be more difficult to assess, because we not only want to know which procedural "route" the student has memorized, but also their mental maps of the domain. We want to know whether students know the major landmarks, and how well these maps match the domain as experts see it. Herscovics and Bergeron (1993) refer to relational structures in a given concept domain as a "conceptual scheme." Analysis of a concept scheme provides the basis for designing assessment tasks and instructional activities. Valid assessment of understanding for instructional purposes requires that one obtain information on students' knowledge about symbols, concepts, and operations, as well as the relations among them. In other words, to assess children's relational understanding, one should go beyond counting the right and wrong answers and focus on, instead, assessing conceptual understanding. It is important to detect whether children can see that the structure of a task may be the same despite changes in representation, use representations of concepts effectively in problem solving, and be able to explain their meaning and use (Niemi, 1994)

Our current standardized assessment strategies do not match the complex nature of mathematics knowledge, and are limited to the assessment of instrumental understanding but not relational understanding. This is especially true when assessing children's learning in more complex domains such as rational numbers, a domain where many children experience tremendous difficulties. The subsequent section illustrates the multiplicative structures of fractions, to illustrate the need to go beyond the standardized assessment procedures in order to examine children's conceptual understanding of fractions.

Assessing Children's Conceptual Understanding of Fractions

Of all the elementary school mathematics topics, there is considerable agreement that failure to learn rational number concepts (fractions, decimals, and percent) is a serious obstacle in mathematical concept development in children. The difficulty with rational numbers is pervasive (National Mathematics Advisory Panel, 2008). To illustrate the application of the clinical interview, however, this chapter will be limited to the discussion of children's learning of fraction concepts. Fraction knowledge forms a basis for understanding a wide range of related concepts, and is essential to expertise in more advanced topics such as algebra and calculus (Kieren, 1992). Because of their importance and difficulty, fractions occupy a prominent place in school curricula from second grade on. Yet, even the simplest fraction problems vex many students, as analyses of large-scale assessment data show. For example, in one study, only 44% of eleventh graders were able to choose the correct answer for the following item (Carpenter, Lindquist, Brown, Kouba, Silver, & Swafford, 1998, p.40):

$$5\frac{1}{4} \text{ is the same as:}$$

$$a. \ 5+\frac{1}{4} \quad b. \ 5-\frac{1}{4} \quad c. \ 5\times\frac{1}{4} \quad d. \ 5\div\frac{1}{4}$$

In another extensive and widely cited project, fourth through eighth grade students' fraction knowledge was extremely unstable, and susceptible to almost any type of perceptual distortion (e.g., Behr, Harel, Post, & Lesh, 1992; Behr, Lesh, Post, & Silver, 1983; Lesh, Laudau, & Hamilton, 1983). In more complex problem solving situations, where greater understanding is required, performance is much worse. Studies across a range of grade levels confirm that many students report searching among procedures that have almost no meaning to them in order to find one that might lead to an answer, and cannot evaluate or justify their solution procedures (Behr, Lesh, Post, & Silver, 1983; Kerslake, 1986; Kieren, 1988; Nik Pa, 1989; Pandey, 1991; Peck & Jencks, 1981; Post, Behr, & Lesh, 1986; Wearne & Hiebert, 1988). Parallel to the students' poor understanding of the fractions, teachers have been found to have equally poor fraction knowledge in comparison to their international counterparts (Ma, 1999; Zhou, Peverly, & Xin, 2006). Studies by

Ma and Zhou, et al. document profound deficiencies in children's fraction understanding, and the failure of instruction to address those deficiencies.

Research demonstrates that the instructional models, and the assessment strategies built on these models, do not adequately address children's difficulties in fraction learning. For example, research supports the conclusion that use of manipulatives per se is not enough to ensure whether concepts or connections between symbols and concepts will develop (e.g., Hart, 1981; Hiebert & Carpenter, 1992; Lesh, 1981; Resnick & Ford, 1981; Resnick & Omanson, 1987; Wearne & Hiebert, 1988). Seeing a procedure in operation and acting it out with objects is often assumed to provide meaning for that procedure. However, procedures with objects and the marks made on the paper to "represent" actions in those objects are never strictly isomorphic (Ohlsson, 1987). Thus, the illustrations that have been adopted for pedagogical reasons may not be appropriate for the goal of developing mathematically correct fraction concepts. Assessment based on these models may also not accurately reflect levels or types of mathematical understanding. For example, symbolizing fractions as pieces of pie is one type of fraction illustration or model that has dominated elementary mathematics instruction and assessment. For instance, on the Math Reasoning subtest of the Wechsler Individual Achievement Test-Second Edition (WIAT-II; Wechsler, 2002), three out of five questions on fractions use pies as illustrations (Items # 40, 43, & 45). In the pie model, fraction numerators and denominators can be seen as unrelated whole numbers representing two separate counts: number of pieces in the "part" above a fraction line, and the number of pieces in the "whole" below the line. The part–whole model is criticized as being inadequate for fractional quantities because misconceptions can easily arise (Davydov & Tsvetkovich, 1991; Kerslake, 1986; Ohlsson, 1988). Throughout elementary school, it is common for children to come up with diagrams, like the one below, as "proof" (Kerslake, 1986) that demonstrates children's incomplete understanding of the fraction concepts:

$$\frac{a}{b}+\frac{c}{b}=\frac{a+c}{b+b}$$

Thus,

$$\frac{1}{4}+\frac{2}{4}=\frac{3}{8}$$

The data suggest that it is difficult to develop the concept of a fraction as number representing a relation between two numbers (or two quantities) simply by separating, combining, or "shading in" parts of objects (e.g., Kerslake, 1986; Kieren, 1992). These activities tend to lead to perceptions of fractions as pieces of objects—that is, away from, not toward, a more advanced rational number concept (Harris, 1985).

Among the additional problems that children face is that to "understand" a fraction means to see it simultaneously as a pair of numbers and a single quantity. As an interpretation of a rational number, a fraction must be conceived as the result of a relation between two numbers, and at the same time as a single quantity subject to mathematical operations. To grasp this point, even implicitly, requires considerable cognitive restructuring (Gelman, Cohen, & Hartnett, 1989) and new understanding of mathematical units (Davydov & Tsvetkovich, 1991; Piaget, Inhelder, & Szeminska, 1960). To do more advanced mathematical work requires that multiple entities or objects or even parts of entities be taken as units, and new quantifying activities such as measuring and partitioning be mastered. For example (See Figure 16.1), six marbles can be equally divided into two bags with three marbles in each bag (2 three-units), or three bags with two marbles in each bag (3 two-units). The 6, 2, or 3 marbles in each bag are all 1's (one bagful). Thus, the mathematical concepts of oneness and the invariance of the whole are presented in this conceptual and computational scheme for the concept

of "1" as the underlying basis (Zhou & Lin, 2001; Zhang & Liu, 1991). In this sense, "1" can be used to represent an object, a geometric shape, etc. It can also be used to represent a composite unit "1" that consists of many objects or people. "1" as the composite unit can entail large or small number of objects or people. For example (See Figure 16.2), 3 apples is a composite unit of "1"; they can be divided into three equal parts, each part is $\frac{1}{3}$ and has 1 apple; 6 apples is also a composite of "1"; they can also be divided into 3 equal parts. Each part is $\frac{1}{3}$ and has 2 apples; 12 apples is also a composite unit "1." They can be divided into 3 equal parts, and each part has 4 apples. The ability to construct a reference unit or a unit whole, and then to reinterpret a situation in terms of that unit, appears critical to the development of increasingly sophisticated mathematical ideas.

The "unit" concept illustrated thus far is grounded in the part–whole models. The measurement model of fractions conceived by theorists (e.g. Davydov & Tsvetkovich, 1991; Freudenthal, 1983; and Vergnaud, 1983) measures children's understanding of fractional quantities, such as finding fraction "equivalence" and solving fraction addition and other operations. The procedure for adding $\frac{2}{3}$ and $\frac{1}{4}$ can be understood in terms of re-measuring the three quantities (the two fractional quantities and the "whole" to which

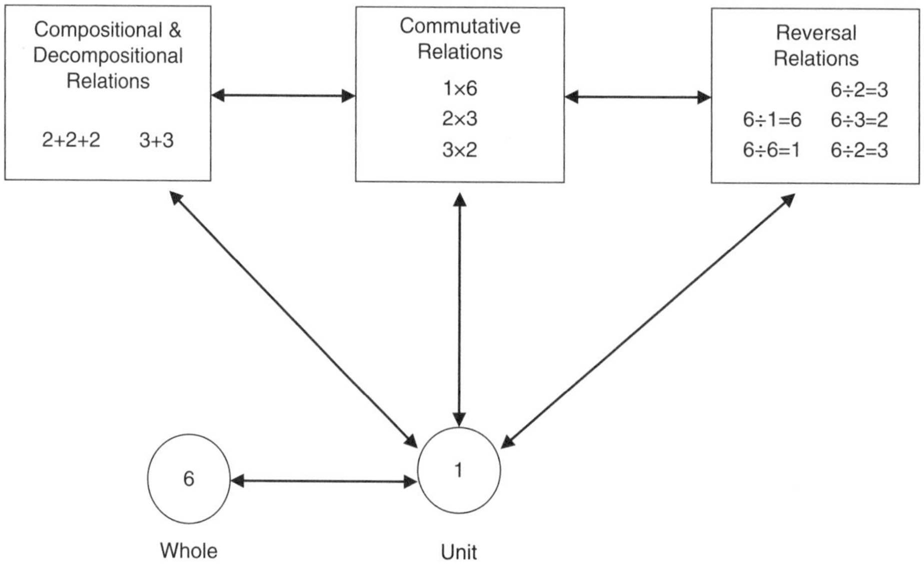

Fig. 16.1 The Conceptual and Computational Scheme for the Concept "1" as an Underlying Basis

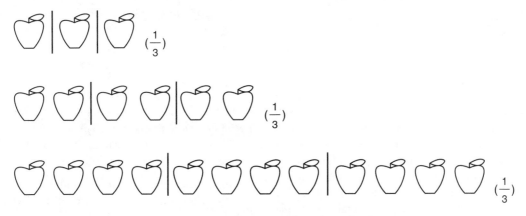

Fig. 16.2 Using "1" as Underlying Basis for Understanding Fractions

they are related) with a smaller unit (i.e., twelfths). Use of the quantitative model implies that assessment should encompass measures of students' understanding of fractional quantities, not just the part–whole models.

Given the complex structure of fraction knowledge, dynamic assessment should involve more than just counting the correct responses on a test. A comprehensive assessment requires assessing a "conceptual field" (Vergnaud, 1983; 1988) that includes identification of situations that give meaning to concepts represented by the defining symbols, or operations performed on the symbols, and comparing situations that are described verbally, pictorially and/or represented graphically. The clinical interview is an assessment tool capable of examining the underlying cognitive processes during children's problem solving. The following section illustrates how clinical interview is used to assess children's conceptual understanding of fraction knowledge.

Clinical Interview as Dynamic and Comprehensive Assessment Techniques

In the educational system, children are not often encouraged enough to think about the logic behind the mathematical operations they use. Many children tend to believe that mathematics is the collection of skills they are tested on, and that mathematics consists of a huge number of procedures and facts to be memorized (Izard, 1993). For example, one of my students, Tracy, conducted the following interview:

Interviewer (I): How much is $\dfrac{2}{3} + \dfrac{3}{4} = ?$

Student (S): Let me think… I want to say that it is

$\dfrac{3}{7}$, but I know something is wrong… I remember Ms. D says that is not right, so I know I can't do that.

I: Is there any reason for that?

S: I don't know. I only know I am not supposed to do that, but I just can't remember how to figure it out.

In Kerslake (1986) study, even when children were able to give correct answers to $\dfrac{2}{3} + \dfrac{3}{4}$, none was able to give any explanation as to why they used the denominator 12. This is illustrated in the following interview segment:

Interviewer (I): Show me how you solve $\dfrac{2}{3} + \dfrac{3}{4}$

Student (S): $\dfrac{2}{3} + \dfrac{3}{4} = \dfrac{8}{12} + \dfrac{9}{12} = 1\dfrac{5}{12}$

I: Would you explain how you did that?

S: I said, "What's the next thing 3 will go into?… that's 12. Then, "What do you do to 3 to make 12?"…Times it by 4, Two 4's are 8 "What do you do to 4 to make it 12?" Times it by 3. Three 3's are 9. Add the two together."

I: Why did you do this bit with the twelves?

S: I am not sure.

I: It's difficult to explain?

S: You're taught something, you're never taught why.

The interviews reveal that the difficulties children have with fractions are conceptual. In these observations, children are going through the motions of operations with fractions (i.e., instrumental understanding) without knowing why the procedures are used (i.e., relational understanding), resulting in unconnected learning. This type of learning is reinforced by assessment methods that emphasize fragmented and memorized knowledge, thus encouraging teachers and students to see mathematics as a collection of a large number of facts and procedures.

Alternatively, the clinical interview probes children's thinking about what they have done and why. It is sensitive to children's understanding, and allows for examination of the complexity and dynamics of the child's mind. In this section, some examples of clinical interviews on children's understanding of fraction concepts are presented to illustrate this method of assessment. Overall, the clinical method is a flexible assessment involving the interviewer as the measuring instrument. It begins with a standard problem of interest that is presented with concrete objects (e.g., hats, dolls, words on a paper). The interviewer presents the child with the initial task, followed by probes to uncover the thoughts and concepts underlying the child's verbalizations. The interviewer observes and interprets what is observed. The interviewer follows the child's lead, and is free to devise new problems on the spot to test hypotheses. The clinical interview provides rich data and a "thick description" of children's underlying cognitive processes during problem solving. Such information forms the foundation on which to build effective instruction and intervention.

The purpose of the first interview is to examine whether the child understands the concept of the unit equivalence. The following excerpt is from an interview conducted by one of my students, Giovanna. She asked a sixth grade student to draw three different sketches or diagrams that illustrate the fraction $\frac{2}{3}$ (See Figure 16.3).

Interviewer (I): Have you learned fractions in school?
Student (S): Yes.
I: Could you draw three different pictures or diagrams that show the fraction $\frac{2}{3}$?
S: Can it be any shape?
I: You have to decide.... Show me what you have.
S: I made a peace sign and shaded two pieces.
I: Show me another picture.

S: I made a rectangle and made some lines and shaded two pieces.
I: Can you think of one more?
S: I made a triangle with three lines and shaded two out of the three.
I: How do you know you are right?
S: Because... I shaded two out of three in all of them!
I: I see...Does the size of each part matter?
S: No... some pieces could be smaller or larger. It all depends.

The problem presented to the student has three major characteristics. First, the basic test was decided upon before hand ("Draw three sketches of $\frac{2}{3}$"). Therefore, the initial presentation of the task is essentially standardized. Second, the task involved "objects" for the child to work with. In this case, it was a pencil and paper. The examiner first made sure that the student had already learned fractions. The question of interest was whether the student understood the unit equivalence, a critical concept in solving fraction problems. Third, a question was asked to elicit the child's account of how he solved the problem ("How do you know?"). Then, the interviewer must interpret the response on the spot. The student's statement that "some pieces could be smaller or larger" is not uncommon among children. He seemed to believe that he could draw any three parts as long as he shaded in two of them to represent "two-thirds." This hypothesis was tested out in the last section of the clinical interview. The interviewer challenged the student by asking "Does the size of each part matter?" which was unplanned, but seemed useful in eliciting the child's thinking. This on-the-spot hypothesis-making and testing is essential to the interview process. Educators generally agree that learning occurs when one challenges, or builds upon, a child's existing conceptions. Having knowledge of children's common

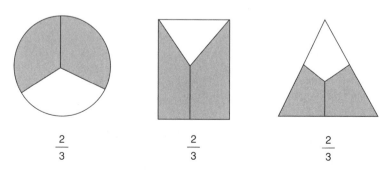

$$\frac{2}{3} \qquad \frac{2}{3} \qquad \frac{2}{3}$$

Fig. 16.3 Example of Incomplete Fraction Concept

conceptions and misconceptions about the subject matter is essential for teaching (Tirosh, 2000). In order to make the appropriate interpretation of the child's common conceptions and misconceptions, the interviewer must possess the domain-specific knowledge under investigation, as well as an understanding of general knowledge of children's problem solving strategies.

Sometimes, children's conceptions of fraction are of insufficient depth to permeate the operations of comparison. For example, in Kerslake's (1986) study, while most of the children were able to identify or construct simple examples of equivalent fractions, there was little evidence of their ability to connect the diagrammatic illustration of equivalent fractions with the algorithm for finding an equivalent by multiplication or division. They simply did not think of producing equivalent fractions to solve the problem. Children's incomplete concepts of fractions prevented them from comparing fractions correctly. However, the clinical interview revealed how a child's thinking could change and develop in response to help from those more knowledgeable than the child. This is illustrated in the following two excerpts from interviews by Kerslake (p.44).

Interviewer (I): "Would you rather have $\frac{2}{3}$ or $\frac{10}{15}$ of a cake you particularly like?

The student (S) was not sure at first…

S: I'd say $\frac{2}{3}$.

I: Could you say why?

S: You'd get more, because with $\frac{10}{15}$ you only have little pieces.

I: Yes, but you would have 10 of them.

S: You'd probably get sick of them after a while.

I: Why?

S: Well, can you imagine eating ten pieces of cake?

I: What, rather than $\frac{2}{3}$?

S: Yep.

I: But you get more cake that way?

S: You'd get more…No, it is the same!

I: What's the same?

S: They're exactly the same.

I: Aha! Why?

S: Because 2 goes into that five times, and that goes into that five times, so they are the same.

Note that the clinical interview presents a sophisticated method for examining conceptual change in children's fraction knowledge. The interview reveals

that the child was first concentrating on the denominator of the fraction $\frac{10}{15}$ and the fact that the pieces would be small. Then, when her attention was drawn to the fact that there would be more of them, she appears uncertain and somewhat confused. Finally, she was able to reconcile both views, and concluded that the fractions were the same, quoting the multiplying factor in support. Such cognitive reconstruction of the fraction concepts (i.e., understanding of equivalence) was achieved through the improvisation during the interview: the interviewer had the freedom to vary questions as seemed necessary without giving away the answers. These questions were unplanned and deliberately nonstandardized, in order to test a specific hypothesis that the interviewer had in mind. The standardized testing procedures could not reveal the same level of complexity in children's thinking. Here is another example by Kerslake (1986, p. 49):

Interviewer (I): Which is bigger $\frac{3}{4}$ or $\frac{4}{5}$?

Student (S): $\frac{3}{4}$ is bigger.

I: How did you know that?

S: If it was $\frac{3}{4}$ of a cake, you'd have one piece left…oh, it is the same.

I: You said, with $\frac{3}{4}$, there'd be one piece left. What fraction would be left?

S: $\frac{1}{4}$…and fifths… $\frac{1}{5}$ left. It isn't the same! $\frac{1}{4}$ is higher than $\frac{1}{5}$.

I: So, what do you think now—which is bigger, $\frac{3}{4}$ or $\frac{4}{5}$?

S: $\frac{4}{5}$.

From this excerpt, we see that a small amount of structuring, that is, placing the question in context without giving away the answer, was sufficient to allow the child to produce a correct response. The interviewer did not give away the answer, but merely provided the means for the child to access preexisting knowledge.

The major features of a clinical interview are summarized below. More detailed descriptions can be found in Ginsburg (1997). Basically the steps include:

Step 1: present the initial task in a standardized form ("How many fourths equal $3\frac{1}{4}$?")

Step 2: use objects (paper & pencil, chips, etc.) for children to demonstrate their thinking

Step 3: ask follow-up questions ("How did you do it?" or "Why?")

Step 4: immediately interpret the child's response

Step 5: engage in on-the-spot hypothesis testing, and

Step 6: improvise whenever necessary (e.g., make up new tasks to further test hypothesis)

By talking and listening to children during the interview, the nature of errors that they made and the strategies that they used are made apparent. This approach involves reshaping of the test situation from a rigidly standardized procedure to a flexible, individualized, and intensely interactive process among the three partners involved: the tasks, the examinee and the examiner (Feuerstein, Rand, Jensen, Kaniel, & Tzuriel, 1987). The clinical interview provides an analysis that is based upon the child's perspective and way of functioning with respect to that task. It provides insight into the child's cognition. Mostly importantly, giving children the opportunity to explain verbally promotes metacognitive skills, because it requires thinking about thinking. Such activities are related to the advancement from concrete to formal thinking, a development that is critical in children's mathematics learning.

Implications for the Training of School Psychologists in Mathematics Assessment

At the present time, a serious mismatch exists between what is assessed by the standardized math achievement tests and the kind of understanding and abilities in mathematics that are needed for success in the twenty-first century. There are number of implications at both theoretical and practical levels.

At the theoretical level, a framework for assessing meaningful mathematics learning and understanding needs to be developed. This assessment framework should be *reflective* in taking into account children's analysis of his or her own cognitive strategies. At the same time, it should also be *descriptive*, so that one can obtain useful profiles of a child's mathematics development, as we evaluate insightful

problem solving and depth of understanding (Goldin, 2008). The assessment strategies should be aligned with theoretical analyses of the construct domain being assessed. Goldin purports that a well designed system for measuring understanding informs, and consequently enhances, the classroom teacher's judgments—enabling the teacher to build on individual students' strengths while addressing cognitive obstacles more effectively.

At the practical level, if a response-to-intervention (RTI) approach is expected to improve student's math performance, school psychologists will need considerable guidance and support in learning how to conduct assessment, and how to link such assessment to effective instructional practices. According to Webb and Romberg (1992) "For an assessment method to be aligned with the field of math means that students are tested on math in a way that is compatible with the structure of math and how math exists within the minds of students" (p. 45). To do so, the psychologist and educators must observe as directly as possible how the child is thinking while performing a criterion task, with the knowledge of the nature of successful reasoning on that task. Many school psychologists currently are very comfortable with the role of an expert in standardized assessment (Greenwood, Carta, Baggett, Buzhardt, Walker, & Terry, 2008). However, when curriculum standards in which high-level mathematical reasoning processes are central and universally expected, school psychologists must develop more rigorous assessment strategies to meet such challenges. That means, they need to step outside of their comfort zone and expand their skills beyond standardized testing to focus on evaluating students' ability in finding patterns, making connections, communicating mathematically, and engaging in real-life and open-ended problem solving. According to Goldin (2008), this type of learning is best assessed through open-ended, authentic, or alternative assessment methods such as clinical interview (and assessed least well through short-answer, standardized skill tests). In this regard, the assessment goal is not so much to contribute to an understanding of the nature of "learning disability" in general, but rather to understand the specific processes that interfere with the child's learning of particular academic content (Ginsburg, 1997).

School psychologists also need to play a vital role in helping teachers to understand what children know and don't know, and how they are learning (Ginsburg, Lee, & Boyd, 2008). To this end, school psychologists must develop expertise in instruction.

This is a role that many are not familiar with, nor comfortably engage in (Greenwood, et al., 2008). To effectively address instruction, school psychologists must have a fundamental knowledge about learning and teaching, as well as practical skills in assisting teachers to investigate the interactions among variables comprising instruction, curriculum, and the student (Gravois & Gickling, 2008). With RTI, school psychologists are expected to be experts in both assessment and instruction in order to bridge these two areas. This presents unique challenges to school psychologists. They not only have to have knowledge of math curriculum and instruction pertaining to a specified domain, but also the domain knowledge to determine what constitutes "sufficient" student progress. To establish the child's competence, assessment strategies need to be guided by hypothesis testing to determine whether the child's response expresses the limits of his or her competence. It will require fundamental revision of current assessment techniques in mathematics to provide relatively sophisticated levels of analysis and interpretation of the nature of the student's understanding. The assessment information gained through such analysis can then be used to enable teachers to build on the strength of each individual student to reach grade-level achievement. Clarke, Baker, and Chan (2008) point out that "student achievement is enhanced when they are given opportunities to verbalize their thinking in solving math problems" (p. 460). A deep understanding of children's mathematical knowledge structure is critical in designing appropriate intervention strategies for children in both Tiers 2 (those below grade level who need additional assistance) and Tier 3 (those who have significant needs for intervention in specific academic areas). School psychologists need to be open to incorporating assessment techniques that go beyond determining deficiencies within the individual students.

With new emphasis placed on mathematics in the U.S., school psychologists are in a unique position to bring about critical changes in mathematics assessment. The clinical interview discussed in this chapter has been demonstrated to contribute to better understanding of the learning difficulties through rigorous developmental analyses of how children learn—and fail to learn. The interview technique is vital in exploring the psychological processes underlying test scores, understanding learning in the classroom, assessing meaningful mathematics learning effectively, and designing effective instruction and intervention to help our

children "gain powerful assess to mathematical ideas" (Skovsmore & Valero, 2008). The paradigm in school psychology has shifted toward a more science based practice (Reschley, 2008); so should the assessment strategies.

References

Anastasi, A. (1988). *Psychological testing* (6th ed.). New York: Macmillan.

Behr, M.J., Lesh, R., Post, T., & Silver, E.A. (1983). Rational number concepts. In R. Lesh & M. Landau (Eds.), *Aquisition of mathematics concepts and processes* (pp. 91–126). New York: Academic Press.

Behr, M.J., Harel, G., Post, T. & Lesh, R. (1992). Rational number, ratio, and proportion. In D.A. Grouws (Ed), *Handbook of research on mathematics teaching and learning* (pp. 296–333). New York: Macmillan.

Binet, A., & Simon, T. (1916). *The development of intelligence in children*. Baltimore, MD: Williams & Wilkins.

Bodin, A. (1993). What does to assess mean? The case of assessing mathematical knowledge. In M. Niss (Ed.), *Investigations into assessment in mathematics education* (pp. 113–141). Dordrecht, Holland: Kluwe Academic Publishers.

Brownell, W.A. (1967). *Arithmetical abstractions: The movement toward conceptual maturity under differing systems of instruction*. Berkeley, C.A: University of California.

Carpenter, T.P., Lindquist, M.M., Brown, C.A., Kouba, V.L., Silver, E.A., & Swofford, J.O. (1988). Results of the fourth NAEP assessment of mathematics: Trends and conclusions. *Arithmetic Teacher, 36*, 38–41.

Chen, Z. & Siegler, R. S. (2000). Overlapping waves theory. *Monographs of the Society for Research in Child Development, 65* (5).

Clarke, B. & Shinn, M.R., (2004) A preliminary investigation into the identification and development of early mathematics curriculum based measurement. *School Psychology Review, 33*(2), 234–248.

Clarke, B., Baker, S., & Chan, D. (2008). Best practices in mathematics assessment and intervention with elementary students. In A. Thomas & J. Grimes (Eds.) *Best practices in school psychology Vol. 2* (453–463). Bethesda, MD: National Association of School Psychologists (NASP).

Cole, N.S. (1986). Future directions for educational achievement and ability testing. In B.S. Plake & J.C. Witt (Eds.), *The future of testing* (pp. 73–88). Hillsdale, NJ: Erlbaum.

Coyle, T.R., & Bjorklund, D.F. (1997). Age differences in, and consequences of, multiple-and variable-strategy use on a multitrial sort-recall task. *Developmental Psychology, 33*, 372–380.

Davydov, V.V., & Tsvetkovich, Z.H. (1991). On the objective origin of the concept of fractions. *Focus on Learning Problems in Mathematics, 13*, 13–61.

Feuerstein, R., Rand, Y., Jensen, M. R., Kaniel, S., & Tzuriel, D. (1987). Prerequisites for assessment of learning potential: The LPAD model. In C. S. Lidz (Ed.), *Dynamic assessment: An interactional approach to evaluating learning potential* (pp. 35–51). New York: Guilford Press.

Foegen, A., Jiban, C., & Deno, S. L. (2007). Progress monitoring measures in mathematics: A review of the literature. *The Journal of Special Education, 41*, 121–139.

Frederiksen, N. (1984). The real test bias: Influences of testing on teaching and learning. *American Psychologist, 39*, 193–202.

Freudenthal, H. (1983). *Didactical phenomenology of mathematical structures*. Dordrecht, Holland: D. Reidel.

Fuchs, L.S., Fuchs, D., & Hamlett, C. L. (1989). Effects of instrumental use of curriculum-based measurement to enhance instructional programs. *Remedial and Special Education, 10*, 43–52.

Fuchs, L. S., & Deno, S. L. (1992). Must instructionally useful performance assessment be based in the curriculum? *Exceptional Children, 58*, 232–243.

Garcia, E., Rasmussen, B., Stobbe, C., & Garcia, E. (1990). Portfolios: Assessment tool in support of instruction. *International Journal of Educational Research, 14*, 431–436.

Gelman, R., Cohen, M., & Hartnett, P. (1989). Proceedings from the Eleventh Annual Meeting of the North American Chapter, International Group for Psychology of Mathematics Education: *To know mathematics is to go beyond thinking that "Fractions aren't numbers."* New Brunswick, NJ.

Gelman, R., & Williams, E. (1998). Enabling constraints for cognitive development and learning: Domain specificity and epigenesist. In D. Kuhn & R. S. Seigler (Eds.), W. Damon (Series Ed.), *Handbook of child psychology: Vol. 2. Cognition, perception, and language* (5th ed). (pp. 575–630). New York: Wiley.

Ginsburg, H.P. (1997). *Entering the child's mind: The clinical interview in psychological research and practice*. New York: Cambridge University Press.

Ginsburg, H. P., Lee, J. S., & Boyd, J. S. (2008). Mathematics education for young children: What it is and how to promote it. *Society for Research in Child Development (SRCD) Social Policy Report: Giving child and youth development knowledge away, 12* (1), 3–23.

Goldin, G.A. (1992). Toward an assessment framework for school mathematics. In R. Lesh & S.J. Lamon (Eds.), *Assessment of authentic performance in school mathematics* (pp. 63–88). Washington, DC: American Association for the Advancement of Science.

Goldin, G. (2008). Perspectives on representation in mathematical learning and problem solving. In L.D. English (Eds.), *Handbook of international research in mathematics education* (2nd ed.), (pp. 176–201). New York: Routledge.

Granott, N. (1993). Patterns of interaction in the co-construction of knowledge; Separate minds, joint effort, and weird creatures. In R. Wozniak & K.W. Fischer (Eds.), *Development in context: Acting and thinking in specific environments* (pp. 183–207). Hillsdale, NJ: Erlbaum.

Gravois T.A., & Gickling, E.E. (2008). Best practice in instructional assessment. *Best practice in school psychology* (pp. 503–518). National Association of School Psychologists (NASP).

Greenwood, C. R., Carta, J. J., Baggrett, K., Buzhardt, J., Walker, D. & Terry B. (2008). Best practice in integrating progress monitoring and response-to-intervention concepts into early childhood systems. *Best practice in school psychology* (pp. 535–547). Bethesda, MD: National Association of School Psychologists (NASP).

Harris, W.T. (1985). Editor's preface. In McLellan, J.A., & Dewey, J. (1895). *The psychology of numbers* (pp. 5–9), New York: Appleton-Century-Crofts.

Hart, K. (1981). *Children's understanding of mathematics: 11–16*. London, England: Murray.

Hatch, T., & Gardner, H. (1990). If Binet has looked beyond the classroom: The assessment of multiple intelligences. *International Journal of Educational Research, 39*(1), 23–41.

Herscovics, N., Bergeron, J.C. (1993). An epistemological study of the child's construction of early arithmetic. *The Alberta Journal of Research, 39*(1), 23–41.

Hiebert, J., & Carpenter, T.P., (1992). Learning and teaching with understanding. In D.A. Grouws (Ed.), *Handbook of research on mathematics teaching and learning* (pp. 65–97), New York: Macmillan.

Hosp, M. K., Hosp, J. L., & Howell, K. W. (2007). *The ABCs of CBM: A practical guide to curriculum-based measurement*. New York: Guilford Press.

Izard, J. (1993). Challenges in the improvement of assessment practice. In M. Niss (Ed.), *Investigations into Assessment in Mathematics Education*. (pp. 185–194). Dordrecht, Holland: Kluwe Academic Publishers.

Kamphaus, R. W. (1993). *Clinical assessment of children's intelligence: A handbook for professional practice*. Boston, MA: Allyn & Bacon.

Kelley, B. (2008). Best practices in curriculum-based evaluation and math. In A. Thomas & J. Grimes (Eds.), *Best practices in school psychology Vol. 2* (pp.419–438). Bethesda, MD: National Association of School Psychologists (NASP).

Kerslake, D. (1986). *Fractions: Children's strategies and errors, a report of the strategies and errors in secondary mathematics project*. Windsor, England: NFER-Nelson.

Kieren, T.E. (1988). Personal knowledge of rational numbers: Its intuitive and formal development. In J. Hiebert & M. Behr (Eds.), *Number concepts and operations in the middle grades* (pp. 162–181). Reston, VA: National Council of Teachers of Mathematics (NCTM).

Kieren, T.E. (1992). Rational and fractional numbers as mathematical and personal knowledge: Implications for curriculum and instruction. In G. Leinhardt, R. Putnam, & R.A. Hattrup (Eds.), *Analysis of arithmetic for mathematics teaching* (pp. 323–371). Hillsdale, NJ: Erlbaum.

Kuhn, D., Garcia-Mila, M., Zohar, A., & Andersen, C. (1995). Strategies of knowledge acquisition. *Monographs of the Society for Research in Child Development, 60* (4, Serial No. 245).

Kuhn, D., & Phelps, E. (1982). The development of problem-solving strategies. In H. Reese & L. Lipsitt (Eds.), *Advances in child development and behavior* (pp. 1–44). San Diego, CA: Academic Press.

Lamon, S. J. (1993). Ratio and proportion: Children's cognitive and metacognitive processes. In T. P. Carpenter, E. Fennema, & T. A. Romberg (Eds.), *Rational numbers* (pp. 131–156). Hillsdale, New Jersey: Lawrence Erlbaum.

Lesh, R. (1981). Applied mathematical problem solving. *Educational Studies in Mathematics, 12*, 235–264.

Lesh, R., Landau, M., & Hamilton, E. (1983). Conceptual models and applied mathematical problem-solving research. In R. Lesh & M. Landau (Eds.), *Acquisition of mathematics concepts and processes* (pp. 263–343). New York: Academic Press.

Linn, R.L. (1986). Barriers to new test designs. In *The redesign of testing for the 21st Century: Proceedings of the 1985 ETS invitational conference* (pp. 69–79). Princeton, NJ: Educational Testing Service.

Linn, R.L., Baker, E.L., & Dunbar, S.B. (1991), Complex performance-based assessment: Expectations and validation criteria. *Educational Researcher, 20* (8), 15–21.

Ma, L.-P. (1999). *Knowing and teaching mathematics: Teachers' understanding of fundamental mathematics in China and the United States*. New Jersey: Erlbaum.

Messick, S. (1989). Validity. In R.L. Linn (Ed.) *Educational measurement, 3rd edition* (pp. 13–104). New York: Macmillan.

National Council of Teachers of Mathematics (NCTM) (2000). *Principles and standards for school mathematics.* NCTM: Reston, Virginia.

National Mathematics Advisory Panel (2008). *Foundations for success: The final report of the national mathematics advisory panel,* U.S. Department of Education: Washington, DC.

Niemi, D.M. (1994). *Assessing fifth grade students' fraction understanding: A conceptual field method for fusing assessment and instruction* (Unpublished Doctoral dissertation, University of California at Los Angeles).

Nik Pa, N.P. (1989). Research on children's conceptions of fractions. *Focus on Learning Problems in Mathematics, 11(3),* 3–25.

Ohlsson, S. (1987). Sense and reference in the design of interactive illustrations for rational numbers. In R.W. Lawler and M. Yazdani (Eds.), *Artificial intelligence and education, volume one* (pp. 307–344). Norwood, NJ: Ablex.

Ohlsson, S. (1988). Mathematical meaning and applicational meaning in the semantics of fractions and related concepts. In J. Hiebert and M. Behr (Eds.), *Number concepts and operations in the middle grades* (pp. 53–92). Reston, VA: National Council of Teachers of Mathematics (NCTM).

Pandey, T. (1991). *A sampler of mathematics assessment.* Sacramento, CA: California Department of Education.

Peck, D.M., & Jencks, S.M. (1981). Conceptual issues in the teaching and learning of fractions. *Journal for Research in Mathematics Education, 12,* 339–349.

Piaget, J. (1926). *The language and thought of the child.* (M. Worden, Trans.). New York: Harcourt, Brace.

Piaget, J. (1928). *Judgment and reasoning in the child.* (M. Worden, Trans). London: Routledge & Kegan Paul.

Piaget, J. (1932). *The moral judgment of the child.* (M. Worden, Trans). New York: Harcourt, Brace.

Piaget, J. (1952). *The origins of intelligence in children.* (M. Cook, Trans). New York: International Universities Press.

Piaget, J. (1976). *The child's conception of the world.* (J. Tomlinson & A. Tomlinson, Trans.). Totowa: NJ: Littlefield, Adams.

Piaget, J., Inhelder, B., & Szeminska, A. (1960). *The child's conception of geometry.* New York: Basic Books.

Post, T.R., Behr, M., & Lesh, R. (1986). Research-based observations about children's learning of rational number concepts. *Focus on Learning Problems in Mathematics, 8,* 39–48.

Reschley, D.J. (2008). School psychology paradigm shift and beyond. In A. Thomas & J. Grimes (Eds.), *Best Practices in School Psychology V, volume one* (pp. 3–15). Bethesda, MD: National Association of School Psychologists (NASP).

Resnick, L.B., & Ford, W.W. (1981). *The psychology of mathematics for instruction.* Hillsdale, NJ: Erlbaum.

Resnick, L.B., & Omanson, (1987). Learning to understand arithmetic. In R. Glaser (Ed.), *Advances in instructional psychology, v. 3* (pp. 41–95). Hillsdalem NJ: Erlbaum.

Reynolds, C. R., Shaywitz, S. E. (2009). Response to intervention: Ready or not, from wait-to-fail to watch-them-fail. *School Psychology Quarterly, 24* (2) 130–145.

Rittle-Johnson, B., Siegler, R. S., & Alibali, M. W. (2001). Developing conceptual understanding and procedural skill in mathematics: An iterative process. *Journal of Educational Psychology, 93*(2), 346–362.

Schauble, L. (1990). Belief revision in children: The role of prior knowledge and strategies for generating evidence. *Journal of Experimental Child Psychology, 49,* 31–57.

Schauble, L. (1996). The development of scientific reasoning in knowledge-rich context. *Developmental Psychology, 32,* 102–119.

Shinn, M.R., (2008). Best practices in using curriculum-based measurement in a problem-solving model. In A Thomas & J. Grimes (Eds.), *Best Practices in School Psychology V volume two,* (pp. 243–261). Bethesda, MD: National Association of School Psychologists.

Shinn, M.R., & Bamonto, S. (1998). Advanced applications in of curriculum-based measurement: "Big ideas" and avoiding confusion. In M.R. Shinn (Ed.) Advanced applications of curriculum-based measurement (pp. 1–31). New York: Guilford Press.

Shinn, M.R., Rosenfield, S., & Knutson, N. (1989). Curriculum-based assessment: A comparison and integration of models. *School Psychology Review, 18,* 299–316.

Shinn, M.R., & Shinn, M.M., (2004). *AIMSweb training workbook administration and scoring mathematics curriculum-based measurement (M-CBM) for use in general outcome measurement.* Eden Prairie, MN: Edformation.

Siegler, R. S. (1996). *Emerging minds: The process of change in children's thinking.* New York: Oxford University Press.

Siegler, R. S. (1998). *Children's thinking.* Upper Saddle River, NJ: Prentice Hall.

Siegler, R. S. (1999). Strategic development. *Trends in Cognitive Sciences, 3*(1), 430–435.

Siegler, R. S. (2000). The rebirth of children's thinking. *Child Development, 71*(1), 26–35.

Siegler, R. S. (2007). Cognitive variability. *Developmental Science, 10* (1), 104–109.

Siegler, R. S. & Chen, Z. (1998). Developmental differences in rule learning: A microgenetic analysis. *Cognitive Psychology, 36,* 273–310.

Siegler, R.S., & Crowley, K. (1991). The microgenetic method: A direct means for Studying cognitive development. *American Psychologist, 46*(6), 606–620.

Siegler, R. S. & Stern, E. (1998). A microgenetic analysis of conscious and conscious strategy discoveries. *Journal of Experimental Psychology: General, 127,* 377–397.

Skemp, R.R. (1976), Relational and instrumental understanding. *Mathematics Teaching, 77,* 20–26.

Skovsmose, O., & Valero, P. (2008). Democratic access to powerful mathematical ideas. In English, L.D., (Eds.), Handbook of International Research in Mathematics Education (2nd ed.). (pp. 415–438). New York: Routledge.

Stecker, P. M., & Fuchs, L. S. (2005). Using curriculum-based measurement to improve student achievement: Review of research. *Psychology in the Schools, 42,* 795–819.

Stevenson, H. W., & Stigler, J. W. (1992). Mathematics classrooms in Japan, Taiwan, and the United States. *Child Development, 58,* 1272–1285.

Stevenson, H. W., Chen, C., & Lee, S. (1993). Mathematics achievement of Chinese, Japanese, and American children: Ten years later. *Science, 259,* 53–58.

Stigler, J. W., & Perry, M. (1988). Mathematics learning in Japanese, Chinese, and American classrooms. *New directions for child development, 41,* 27–54.

Stigler, J. W., & Stevenson, H. W. (1991). How Asian teachers polish each lesson to perfection. *American Educator, 14* (4), 13–20, 43–46.

Stigler, J. W. & Hiebert, J. (1999). *The teaching gap: Best ideas from the world's teachers for improving education in the classroom.* New York: The Free Press.

Thurber, R.S., Shinn, M.R., & Smolowski, K. (2002) What is measured in mathematics tests? Construct validity of curriculum-based mathematics measures. *School Psychology Review, 31*(4), 498–513.

Tilly, W.D. (2008). The evolution of school psychology to science-based practice: Problem solving and the three-tiered model. In A. Thomas and J. Grimes (Eds.), *Best Practices in School Psychology V, volume one* (pp. 17–35). Bethesda, MD: National Association of School Psychologists (NASP).

Tindal, G. (1993). A review of curriculum-based procedures in nine assessment Components. In J. Kramer Ed., *Curriculum-based measurement* (pp. 26–64), Lincoln, NE: Buros Institute of Mental Measurements.

Tirosh, D. (2000). Enhancing prospective teachers' knowledge of children's conceptions: The case of division of fractions. *Journal for Research in Mathematics Education, 31*(1), 5–25.

VanDerHeyden, A.M., & Burns, M.K. (2005). Using curriculum-based assessment and curriculum-based measurement to guide elementary mathematics instruction: Effects on individual and group accountability. *Assessment for Effective Intervention 30*(3), 15–31.

Vergnaud, G. (1983). Multiplicative structures. In R. Lesh & M. Landau (Eds.), *Acquisition of mathematics concepts and processes* (pp. 127–174). New York: Academic Press

Vergnaud, G. (1988). Multiplicative structures. In J. Hiebert & M. Behr (Eds.), *Number concepts and operations in the middle grades* (pp. 220–235). Reston, VA: National Council of Teachers of Mathematics (NCTM).

Vygotsky, L.S. (1986) *Thought and language* (A. Kozulin, Trans.). Cambridge, MA: MIT Press.

Wearne, D., & Hiebert, J. (1988). A cognitive approach to meaningful mathematics instruction: Testing a local theory using decimal numbers. *Journal for Research in Mathematics Education, 19,* 371–384.

Webb, N., & Romberg, T.A. (1992). Implications of the NCTM Standards for mathematics assessment. In T.A. Romberg (Ed.), *Mathematics assessment and evaluation: Imperatives for mathematics educators* (pp. 37–60). Albany, NY: State University of New York Press.

Wechsler, D. (2002). *Wechsler Individual Achievement Test-Second Edition.* San Antonio, TX: The Psychological Corporation.

Zhang, M. –L., & Liu, L. -H (1991). An experiment to promote the development of children's mathematical thinking. *Applied Psychology: An International Review, 40* (1), 27–35.

Zhou, Z., Peverly, S. T., Boehm, A. E., & Lin, C. D. (2000). American and Chinese children's understanding of distance, time, and speed interrelations. *Cognitive Development, 15,* 215–140.

Zhou, Z., & Lin, J. (2001). Developing mathematical thinking in Chinese kindergarten children: The case of addition and subtraction. *International Journal of Educational Policy, Research, and Practice, 2,* 141–155.

Zhou, Z., & Peverly, S. T. (2004) Within- and cross-cultural variations in American and Chinese children's understanding of distance, time, and speed interrelations: A follow-up study. *Journal of Genetic Psychology, 165,* 5–27.

Zhou, Z., Peverly, S. T., & Xin, T. (2006). Knowing and teaching fractions: A cross-cultural study of American and Chinese mathematics teachers. *Contemporary Educational Psychology, 31,* 438–457.

PART 6

Intervention

Prevention as Early Intervention for Young Children at Risk: Recognition and Response in Early Childhood

Cathryn Lehman, Jennifer L. Salaway, Stephen J. Bagnato, Robert M. Grom, *and* Barbara Willard

Abstract

Learning difficulties that typically lead to intervention in the academic setting, such as deficits in language, motor skills, phonological awareness, self-regulation, and executive functioning, are most often manifested in the preschool years. Despite this, appropriate services are not readily available in the early childhood classroom, causing young children to fall behind academically before they even enter kindergarten. Policymakers and educational professionals have begun to advocate for universal screening and early intervention services, as prevention, delivered through a multi-tiered intervention approach. School-age programs have responded to these guidelines by adopting a *Response to Intervention* (RTI) model of service delivery. While recent data has suggested that the RTI model is useful with school-aged populations, it is much less widely used for the universal screening and early intervention recommended by governing institutions of early care and education settings. However, with relatively simple modifications to the school-age model, the Preschool RTI model has the potential to effectively link observation and authentic assessment to early childhood care and instruction. The following chapter proposes a model for Preschool RTI, more appropriately designated as "Recognition and Response," which includes the implementation of evidenced-based interventions that are linked to screening and assessment results, to meet the individual needs of each student. The model emphasizes prevention, mentoring, and consultation aligned with early childhood best practice standards.

Keywords: prevention, early intervention, response to intervention, recognition and response

Young children often demonstrate learning difficulties in preschool, prior to entering kindergarten. Their learning may be affected by problems in a number of developmental areas, such as language, motor skills, phonological awareness, self-regulation, or executive functioning. While some of these developmental variables may be a precursor to subsequent learning disabilities, it is unlikely that these children will qualify for special education services in preschool, and therefore they will not receive support to help them obtain the necessary skills for later school success. However, policymakers and educational professionals have begun to advocate for universal screening and early intervention services delivered through a multi-tiered intervention approach. Both the President's Commission on Excellence in Special Education (United States Department of Education Office of Special Education and Rehabilitative Services, 2002) and the No Child Left Behind Act of 2001 (NCLB; United States Department of Education, 2001) recommend implementation of prevention and intervention programs in early childhood settings for children at risk for academic and behavioral difficulties. The most recent revision of the Individuals with Disabilities Education Improvement Act (2004) describes provisions for prevention, early identification, and early intervention services for addressing young children's learning and social/emotional needs.

School-age programs have responded to these guidelines by adopting a *Response to Intervention* (RTI) model of service delivery. The RTI framework is often used by schools to (1) serve students with academic and behavioral difficulties, and (2) reduce instances of inappropriate identification of learning disabilities and referral to special education. The RTI process allows for functional assessment of children's skills that directly links to intervention planning and progress monitoring.

To date, very few early childhood and early intervention programs have adopted an RTI model for implementation of services. While recent data has suggested that the RTI model is useful with school-age populations, it is arguably equally effective, yet much less widely used, for the universal screening and early intervention recommended by governing institutions of the early childhood setting. By modifying the process to accommodate early childhood sensibilities, standards, and practices, RTI has the potential to effectively link observation and authentic assessment to early childhood care and instruction. This chapter will review the evidence base for RTI in early childhood, describe existing multi-tiered models, and propose a framework for RTI in early childhood that focuses on prevention. The chapter will provide:

- Brief history of school-age RTI movement
- Description of early childhood RTI models
- Present contrast between school-age and preschool RTI models
- Proposed early childhood RTI model
- Conclusions about RTI for preschool

School-Age RTI

In 2004, additions to the Individuals with Disabilities Education Act (IDEA) stated that local education agencies "may use a process that determines if the child responds to scientific, research based intervention as part of the evaluation procedures" (Pub. L. No. 108-446, 614 [b][6][A]; 614 [b][2&3]) when determining eligibility for special education services. This is in sharp contrast to the previously accepted discrepancy model, in which differences between a child's intellectual functioning and achievement were formally assessed, and a diagnosis was made prior to the student receiving intervention. By allowing evidence-based intervention to precede diagnosis in the schools using this new approach, improved identification accuracy for diagnosis and contextualized decision making are realized, students are able to benefit

from intervention in a more timely manner, schools experience improved treatment validity, and students benefit from more accurate and effective intervention (VanDerHeyden & Jimerson, 2005). The model is, therefore, widely accepted as an effective method for identification and intervention.

The RTI movement has roots in the Instructional Support Team (IST) process. The Commonwealth of Pennsylvania implemented a statewide instructional support team process in 1990 to provide pre-referral assessment and intervention for children at risk (Kovaleski, Gickling, Morrow, & Swank, 1999). The IST is composed of core school staff including the principal, teacher, and support teachers, and uses a problem-solving process to assess and provide interventions to students prior to referring them for special education services (Kovaleski, et al., 1999). Elements of the IST process are similar to those of RTI models: linking assessment data to intervention planning, classroom-based intervention, progress monitoring of student outcomes, and evaluation of the planned intervention. The IST process also involves using progress-monitoring data to determine the need for referral to special education services.

Since 2004, a host of models aimed at this goal have been proposed, and in some cases validated for use with school-aged populations. While models may vary, the Response to Intervention terminology and theoretical framework has taken hold. In general terms, school-aged RTI is a tiered system in which progressively intensive levels of evidence-based intervention (EBI) are implemented based on failure to meet expected rates of progress, which is assessed using curriculum based measurement (CBM) tools (Coleman, Buysse & Neitzel, 2006; Fuchs & Fuchs, 2006a; Fuchs & Fuchs, 2006b; Glover & DiPerna, 2007). Common components of RTI models include group problem solving, close monitoring of student progress, implementation of evidence-based interventions, and consideration for special education services only after students do not make adequate progress (Fuchs, Mock, Morgan, & Young, 2003). As demonstrated throughout this chapter, proposed models vary in terms of number of tiers, team roles and responsibilities, and methods of intervention and progress monitoring.

Evidenced-based interventions are an essential piece of the RTI model. The National Association of School Psychologists (NASP, 2008) defines EBIs as "interventions in which empirical evidence links the application of practices with demonstrated outcomes." When interventions are not evidence based, there is an increased chance that the intervention will not result in desired effects, and there is a decreased probability of treatment validity. NASP (2008) states that when choosing an evidence-based intervention it is important to consider if:

- A clear description of the intervention is provided
- There is a complete report of the study sample
- The researcher used valid outcome measures
- There were sufficient controls
- The effect size is discussed
- An explanation of the clinical significance of results is provided
- The EBI is a good fit with the school's needs
- The EBI aligns with the educational philosophy and other programs in place

Another commonality among strong school-age models of RTI is the use of curriculum based measurement for assessing progress. In contrast to the high-stakes testing results that are sometimes used, CBM samples a broad range of skills by sampling each dimension of the annual curriculum using weekly tests, assessing the same constructs by repeating measurement in alternate forms of equivalent difficulty (Fuchs & Fuchs, 2002). This technique can be used to identify nonresponders in an RTI model by determining when a student's CBM growth rate is less then the expected growth rate in a specific area. When this occurs, the teacher may first modify teaching strategies, and if necessary, later implement group or individualized interventions.

Early Childhood RTI Models

It is clear that RTI research has traditionally focused on the academic concerns of school-aged children; however, RTI is increasingly understood among early childhood researchers to be an opportunity for the union of the cautiously accepted statewide early learning standards with authentic assessments, individualized intervention, and ongoing progress monitoring. Most states now utilize early learning standards for children ages 3–5 in the areas of language, literacy, and mathematics. While these standards are intended to provide a framework for early childhood education, they are often criticized for their insensitivity to the variability in growth and development of young children. The RTI model for early childhood works to interweave instruction and assessment, integrating decision-making stages to determine if children are progressing as expected based on age and benchmarks, or if they require

intervention (McCabe & College, 2006). It is therefore possible to utilize the early learning standards in conjunction with evidence-based practices, progress monitoring, and intervention, to identify and assist children at risk for learning difficulties.

Guided by principles specific to early childhood, Coleman, Buysse, and Neitzel (2006) have created a model called the Recognition and Response System. According to the authors, Recognition and Response "emphasizes a systematic approach to responding to early learning difficulties that include assessing the overall quality of early learning experiences for all children and making program modifications, tailoring instruction strategies and providing appropriate supports for individual children who struggle to learn" (Coleman, Buysse & Neitzel, 2006, p.3). The Recognition and Response System has four components:

1. An intervention hierarchy, emphasizing increasing intensity in instruction and intervention based on need.
2. Screening, assessment, and progress monitoring that rely on multimodal and multisource information.
3. Research based curriculum, instruction, and focused interventions.
4. A collaborative problem-solving process for decision making that utilizes information from assessments to inform decisions.

While applying RTI principles to early childhood is a fairly new concept in school psychology, a few models have been proposed and implemented in various early childhood settings. For example, Barnett and colleagues (2007) proposed a general three-tiered integrated model of intervention: (1) classwide support, (2) embedded or small group support, and (3) intensive support and eligibility. Key to this proposed model is the linkage of functional assessment to intervention goals, empirically supported interventions, treatment integrity, and decision rules for moving through the tiers of intervention.

Early Language/Literacy RTI Models

Early childhood RTI models are unique in their intervention goals. Experts estimate that more than one in three children experience significant difficulties in learning how to read (Adams, 1990), and early reading problems are associated with a number of negative developmental outcomes for children (Whitehurst & Lonigan, 2002). Therefore, language and early literacy skills are most often targeted for intervention in early childhood programs. The following section describes elements of existing RTI models applied to target early language and early literacy skills.

Gettinger and Stoiber (2008) implemented an early intervention model using RTI components for promoting the development of emergent literacy skills for Head Start children. Their Early Reading First funded model, the Exemplary Model of Early Reading Growth and Excellence (EMERGE), contains (1) evidence-based early literacy curriculum, instruction, and activities implemented along a three-tiered intervention hierarchy, with increasing intensity; (2) screening, progress monitoring, and assessment to guide decision making and identification of children in need of intense supports; (3) high-quality, print-rich classroom environments; and (4) ongoing professional development. Specifically, Tier 1 instruction consisted of an evidence-based reading curriculum, a print-rich environment, and instructional activities that targeted phonological awareness, oral language, alphabet knowledge, and print awareness. Tier 2 instruction included teacher-directed, small-group instruction of the early literacy skills targeted in Tier 1. Finally, Tier 3 consisted of individual tutoring and explicit instruction of those early literacy skills for children identified as most at risk for developing skills, based on screening assessment results. Preliminary evaluation of this model indicated that children who attended classrooms participating in the EMERGE program demonstrated greater attainment of early literacy skills when compared to a control group. This model is noteworthy in that the intervention tiers were centered on a set of early literacy skills that are fundamental for later school success.

Similarly, Hagans-Murillo (2005) recommended a "standard-protocol" approach to applying RTI elements to preschool. In school settings, the standard-protocol approach is described as a set of brief, intensive, small-group interventions provided to students who display similar skill deficits. Applied to preschool, the standard-protocol approach entails teaching fundamental early literacy skills to preschoolers along a continuum. For example, Hagans-Murillo described the protocol as carefully constructed activities and structured tasks designed to explicitly increase children's literacy skills. Furthermore, data collection informs decision making regarding the intensity, structure, and grouping of intervention in terms of content, duration, interventionist, and children receiving the intervention (Hagans-Murillo, 2005).

Curriculum based measures are often used as screening assessments and progress monitoring tools in RTI models. VanDerheyden and colleagues (2007) examined the utility of using curriculum based early literacy measures as screening tools, and to evaluate whether growth in early literacy skills was detected following intervention for a group of preschool children classified as at-risk. The curriculum based measures in this study included an alliteration probe and a rhyming probe, both developed by the Early Childhood Research Institute for Measuring Growth and Development. When used in combination with a conventional screening measure, the curriculum based measures led to enhanced decision making about children at risk for reading difficulties.

The models and studies described in the preceding section demonstrate promise for the expansion of RTI into early childhood. It is important to define and be able to accurately assess the fundamental early literacy skills children need to obtain prior to entering kindergarten. This skill set can shape the target of instruction and intervention along the tiers of the RTI hierarchy. Perhaps most crucial to early childhood RTI models is the use of authentic and curriculum based measurement to screen and progress-monitor the skills of preschool children, and link those assessment results to tiered interventions.

Social/Emotional RTI Models

Studies show that social/emotional difficulties in early childhood can have lasting effects on the child, if adequate intervention is not provided. For example, children with challenging behaviors in preschool are less likely to be successful in kindergarten, and are at risk for school failure (Kazdin, 1993; Tremblay, 2000). Despite this, according to Kazdin and Kendall (1998), fewer than 10% of children who engage in problem behavior at a young age receive appropriate services.

To meet the needs of the range of children who are served in early childhood settings, a Response to Intervention model is needed that focuses on supporting the social/emotional development of each child, including prevention, and intervention on existing social/emotional difficulties. The model should be jargon-free, teacher-friendly, developmentally appropriate, effective, and efficient.

One proposed option is Hemmeter and colleagues' (2006) *Teaching Pyramid*, which is designed to promote young children's social-emotional development and to address their challenging behavior. The three-tiered Pyramid consists of four components:

- Building positive relationships with children and families
- Designing supportive and engaging environments
- Teaching social and emotional skills
- Developing individualized interventions for children with the most challenging behaviors

The Pyramid can be implemented by classroom teachers with consultation from mental health specialists. The model is effective because it not only focuses on the individual child, but also the family and the environment. Additionally, interdisciplinary collaboration is encouraged.

A second model focused on social/emotional functioning is Brown, Odom and Conroy's (2001) *Hierarchy for Promoting Young Children's Peer Interactions*. The model uses a hierarchy system of intervention, with classroom-wide interventions at the broadest level, including developmentally appropriate practices and inclusion in early childhood programs with socially responsive peers, and effective classwide interventions to influence attitudes. At the second level, naturalistic interventions include friendship activities and incidental teaching of social behaviors. Finally, social integration activities and explicit social skills training are implemented with specific, targeted children. Key aspects of this model include a focus on developmentally appropriate practices and inclusion.

Barnett, Elliot, and Wolsing, et al. (2006) present a Response to Intervention model for preschool programs that is specific to challenging behaviors. The model consists of three tiers—classwide, group and embedded, and intensive and individualized— all focusing on evidence-based practices and intervention. In Tier 1, the teacher implements classwide interventions, including but not limited to a positive behavior support program (PBS). Agency supports are utilized at this level to provide classroom management strategies, to aid in curriculum implementation, and to assist with PBS. At Tier 2, specialized professionals help teachers to plan, monitor, and in some cases implement group and embedded interventions for children who do not show adequate progress based on Tier 1 supports. Examples include small group social curriculums, or small group practice opportunities for specific social skills. Tier 3 involves the most intensive and individualized intervention. In this phase, functional assessments are used by an expanded team of professionals to determine additional need for more immediate, comprehensive programming. Brief intervention trials are used to define intervention plans, and parents are enlisted to provide intervention across settings. Key aspects of the Response to Intervention Model include the use of functional assessments and evidence-based intervention, as well as an emphasis on interdisciplinary collaboration, parent involvement, and the effective use of agency supports.

Finally, the HealthyCHILD model (Bagnato, Blair, Slater, McNally, Matthews, & Minzenberg, 2004) provides a framework for integrating both behavioral health and physical health supports through a continuum of prevention/intervention supports to teachers, parents, and children. The model targets both children with chronic medical conditions, and children with challenging behaviors. The model consists of a developmental healthcare team that collaborates with early childhood programs to deliver supports to children within their natural environment (home, classroom, and childcare settings). Developmental healthcare team members include a developmental healthcare consultant, pediatric nurse, psychologist, and developmental pediatrician. The team offers an array of consultative services and supports that are designed to prevent problems, or to identify and manage specific problems. The team also works to ensure the use of professionally sanctioned recommended standards for early childhood intervention. HealthyCHILD utilizes a tiered consultation model of graduated intervention. The first level consists of education in professional and evidence-based practices in early childhood. The second level of support includes consultation in classroom prevention practices. Specific strategies for building social skills and self-control behaviors are reflective of the third tier, and the fourth level of support is intensive, direct interventions with children.

Aspects of each of the above models are particularly effective and noteworthy, and should be combined when creating a comprehensive preschool Response to Intervention model. They include:

1. An initial focus on the classroom environment
2. The use of developmentally appropriate practices and inclusion
3. Family commitment and parent involvement
4. The use of evidence-based intervention
5. Interdisciplinary collaboration
6. Effective use of agency supports

Contrast between School-age and Preschool RTI Models

While still termed *response to intervention*, it is important to note that the preschool model of RTI differs significantly from the school-age model. In preschool, prevention must be the focus and first level of intervention. When used at this level, intervening services can prevent future academic problems for many students who are experiencing learning difficulties due to external factors such as inadequate instruction (Coleman, Buysse, & Neitzel, 2006). This means that the classroom environment must meet assessment standards using valid and reliable instruments such as the Early Childhood Environmental Rating Scale-Revised (ECERS-R; Harms & Clifford, 1998). Instruction should be evidence based, and child progress should be monitored frequently and consistently to determine additional needs.

Furthermore, early childhood best practice standards such as those of the Council for Exceptional Children, Division of Early Childhood (DEC; Sandall, Hemmeter, Smith, & McLean, 2005) and the National Association for the Education of Young Children (NAEYC; Bredekamp & Copple, 1997) must guide prevention and classroom quality. For example, teaching and instructional strategies should focus on school readiness skills by providing literacy-rich environments and building positive relationships with all children.

Another difference between the preschool and school-age model is the inconsistency of skill performance at the preschool level. Because preschool children do not typically demonstrate skills consistently across time and settings, authentic assessments should be used to measure progress. Authentic assessments are assessments that measure child progress over time in the natural environment, and are completed by individuals who are familiar with the child. This is in contrast to the high-stakes testing that is often used with school-aged students. Authentic assessment measures should be used as universal screening and progress monitoring tools, to accurately and effectively identify children in need of more intensive intervention.

Prevention Focused Early Childhood Response to Intervention Model

The proposed preschool RTI model includes implementation of *evidenced-based* interventions that are *linked to screening and assessment* results to meet the *individual* needs of each student. The model emphasizes *prevention*, *mentoring*, and *consultation* aligned with early childhood best practice standards. The RTI model emphasizes collecting information about children's performance across various domains, and intervening with intentional instruction and support. The model assumes that prevention and early intervention strategies can prevent later learning and behavioral difficulties. An early childhood instructional support team of professionals trained in early childhood education, developmental psychology, and school psychology, collaborate with early childhood programs to implement the model. Parents should also be integral members of the team. Components of the model include systematic screening and student progress monitoring, the use of multiple tiers of increasingly intense evidence-based intervention, and a problem-solving process to facilitate decision making. The model consists of the following elements:

Tier 1

- Focus on classroom quality and teacher's skills in implementing best practices according to early childhood professional organizations (i.e., DEC and NAYEC)
- Consultants and coaches mentor teachers to improve classroom quality to meet state and federal standards
- Consultants and coaches mentor teachers on how to implement evidence-based curriculum and create literacy-rich environments
- Consultants and coaches use authentic classroom measures to guide mentoring activities:
  - Early, Language, and Literacy Observation Toolkit (ELLCO; Smith & Dickinson, 2003)
  - Inventory of Practices for Promoting Children's Social and Emotional Competence (Center on the Social and Emotional Foundations for Early Learning, 2006)
  - Early Childhood Environmental Rating Scale-Revised (ECERS-R; Harms & Clifford, 1998)
- Universal screening across all domains of learning
- Universal screening of all children using authentic measures:
  - Developmental Observation Checklist System (DOCS; Hresko, Miguel, Sherbenou, & Burton, 1994)

o Preschool and Kindergarten Behavior System Second Edition (PKBS-2; Merrill, 2002)
o Basic Schools Skills Inventory Third Edition (BSSI-3; Hammill, Leigh, Pearson, & Maddox, 1998)
o Curriculum-based assessments

Tier 2

• Children receive Tier 2 intervention based on screening assessment scores, teacher report, and consensus team decision making
• Small group instruction for children not meeting Tier 1 benchmarks:
  o Direct instruction
  o Tutoring
  o Social skills groups
  o Social/emotional lessons
• Teachers provide research based interventions for targeted children
• Consultants mentor teachers on how to implement evidence-based interventions
• Progress monitoring through curriculum based assessment and behavioral observations:
  o Dynamic Indicators of Basic Early Literacy Skills–6th Edition (Dibels; Good & Kaminski, 2002)
  o Individual Growth and Development Indicators (IGDIs; Early Childhood Research Institute, 2000)
  o Preschool Observation Code (POC; Bramlett & Barnett, 1993)

Tier 3

• Children receive Tier 3 intervention based on progress monitoring assessment results, teacher reports, and consensus team decision making
• Individual instruction and intervention for children not meeting Tier 2 benchmarks
• Teachers implement more intensive and individualized interventions:
  o Social stories
  o Behavioral contingency plans
  o Behavior charts
  o Response cost interventions
  o Positive reinforcement
  o Direct reading and language instruction
• Consultants mentor teachers on how to implement evidence-based interventions

Tier 4

• Children receive Tier 4 intervention based on progress monitoring assessment results, teacher reports, and consensus team decision making
• Formal evaluation for children not meeting Tier 3 benchmarks
• Linkage to community-based agencies and resources

Movement through the tiers is guided by the data-based decision making of the early childhood instructional support team. The data used to make decisions includes periodic universal screening results, progress monitoring results, and behavioral observations, as well as teacher and consultant feedback. Treatment integrity is also a key component to the model, and must be measured and evaluated at every tier. Figure 17.1 is a visual display of the model.

Under the direction of author Stephen Bagnato, the Early Childhood Partnerships program of Children's Hospital of Pittsburgh of UPMC and the University of Pittsburgh School of Medicine has been implementing principles of Response to Intervention and Recognition and Response since its inception in 1995, through several of its community-based core programs. Table 17.1 outlines features of these core programs—HealthyCHILD (Collaborative Health Interventions for Learners with Differences); COMET (Center on Mentoring for Effective Teaching); and SPECS for Early Reading First (Scaling Progress in Early Childhood Settings)

A Child Vignette Applying Recognition and Response

The following child vignette is presented to highlight how the Response and Recognition model may be applied for providing support for children attending an early childhood community program.

Nathan was a 4-year, 2-month-old male who attended a preschool in an urban region of Western Pennsylvania. Nathan was a charming child who craved attention from adults. He loved dinosaurs and plants, and would engage in extended conversations on these topics.

Nathan's preschool classroom was accredited by The National Association for the Education of Young Children (NAEYC), and followed a Developmentally Appropriate Practice format. Early literacy coaches regularly provided consultation for each classroom in the preschool. Environmental assessments, including the Early Childhood Environmental Rating Scale-Revised (ECERS-R;

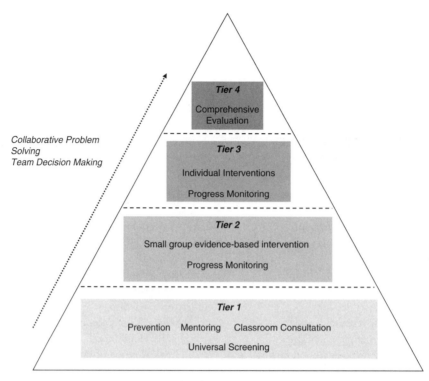

Fig. 17.1 The Four-Tier Model

Harms & Clifford, 1998), were used regularly to assess classroom quality. Individual progress monitoring was also conducted using the Developmental Observation Checklist System (DOCS; Hresko, Miguel, Sherbenou, & Burton, 1994), Preschool and Kindergarten Behavior System Second Edition (PKBS-2; Merrill, 2002), the Basic Schools Skills Inventory Third Edition (BSSI-3; Hammill, Leigh, Pearson, & Maddox, 1998) and a curriculum based assessment.

Table 17.1   Early childhood partnerships core programs

ECP Program	Program Features	Elements of RTI and R&R
HealthyCHILD	• Education in professional and evidence-based practices in early childhood • Consultation in classroom prevention practices • Specific strategies for building social skills and self-control behaviors • Intensive direct interventions with children • Collaborative problem-solving team	• Tiered level of support • Collaborative problem-solving team • Evidence-based interventions
COMET	• Quality mentoring for effective teaching practices • Collaborative problem-solving team	• Collaborative problem-solving team
SPECS for ERF	• Universal screening of early literacy skills • Universal screening of classroom literacy environment • Implementation of evidence-based classroom curriculum • Progress monitoring of early literacy skills • Small group, evidence-based early literacy interventions (i.e., direct instruction) • Individualized learning plans • Collaborative problem-solving team via Early Literacy Support Team	• Universal screening • Evidence-based core curriculum • Collaborative problem-solving • Progress monitoring • Small group interventions • Individual interventions

After over two months in the program, it became apparent that Nathan struggled both behaviorally and academically, and required intervention. His teachers reported restricted patterns of play, difficulty playing cooperatively with peers, defiance, and emotional reactions to everyday events. Nathan frequently refused to participate in classroom activities, consequently missing a large portion of circle time and other teacher-directed activities. When asked to join activities, he would often act aggressively.

Nathan's preschool conducted monthly interdisciplinary team meetings to discuss individual children in need of intervention. Referrals were made by individual teachers by completing a one-page referral form. The team consisted of the preschool director, the child's teacher, a literacy coach, the program's social worker, a contracted psychologist, and the parent of the presenting child.

Nathan's teacher submitted a referral, and an interdisciplinary team meeting was scheduled to discuss his behaviors. Based on the discussion, and using current research, a direct instruction approach was chosen for a small group intervention. Direct instruction is a behavioral approach to teaching, which is strongly teacher-directed and uses small group, face-to-face instruction, and carefully scripted lessons which are sequenced deliberately and taught explicitly in a fast-paced manner. The intervention was chosen based on research involving children with global developmental delays, and individuals from low income neighborhoods. To monitor Nathan's behavior, the Preschool Observation Code (Bramlett & Barnett, 1993) was used in 30-minute intervals on a weekly basis. Baseline and weekly observations were conducted. Additionally, direct measures including the Kaufman Survey of Early Academic and Language Skills (K-SEALS) and Dynamic Indicators of Basic Early Learning Skills (DIBELS) were used on a monthly basis.

After approximately one month in the direct instruction Tier 2 intervention, it was determined that Nathan was not making adequate progress in the small group intervention. The interdisciplinary team reconvened, and individualized interventions were chosen. These interventions consisted of social stories based on social interactions that Nathan found to be difficult, dialogic reading, picture schedules, and an anger-mometer. Each intervention was chosen based on research involving children with similar deficits.

The preschool team worked diligently with Nathan, providing intervention consistently and with integrity. However, progress-monitoring data reflected that Nathan was not meeting behavioral and academic goals. A referral was then made to the county early intervention provider, who conducted a comprehensive evaluation and, with input from the instructional support team, recommended special education services for Nathan.

Conclusion

The field of school psychology holds promise to implement Response to Intervention in early childhood programs. Preschoolers who struggle to learn are at an increased risk of special education referrals, placement, and intensive intervention in subsequent years. Often these young children do not receive the support they need, due to federal and state guidelines. Under a tiered model of support, these children can obtain the necessary skills to succeed throughout their education.

The tiered model of support for Recognition and Response should follow these guidelines.

Essential Guidepoints

- Focus on prevention through quality classroom environments, developmentally appropriate practice, and effective agency supports
- Use evidence-based intervention
- Foster relationships that encourage family commitment and parent involvement
- Use authentic assessment measures to conduct universal screenings and progress monitoring
- Make collaborative decisions as part of an interdisciplinary team

Future Directions

1. Examination of evidence-based preschool interventions linked to assessment
2. Evaluation of the efficacy of current early childhood RTI models
3. Development of collaborative partnerships among community early childhood programs and university training programs to build and implement early childhood RTI models
4. Further integration of early childhood education and the field of school psychology

References

Adams, M.J. (1990). *Beginning to read: Thinking and learning about print*. Cambridge, MA: MIT Press.

Bagnato, S.J., Blair, K., Slater, J., McNally, R., Matthews, J., & Minzenberg, B. (2004). Developmental healthcare partnerships in inclusive early childhood settings: The HealthyCHILD model. *Infants and Young Children*, *17*(4), 301–317.

Barnett, D.W., Elliot, N., Wolsing, L., Bunger, C.E., Haski, H., McKissick, C., & Vander Meer, C.D. (2006). Response to intervention for young children with extremely challenging behaviors: What it might look like. *School Psychology Review*, *35*, 568–582.

Barnett, D.W., VanDerHeyden, A.M., Witt, J.C. (2007). Achieving science-based practice through response to intervention: What is might look like in preschool. *Journal of Educational and Psychological Consultation*, *17*(1), 31–54.

Bramlett, R.K. & Barnett, D.W. (1993). The development of a direct observation code for use in preschool settings. *School Psychology Review*, *22*(1), 49–62.

Bredekamp, S., & Copple, C. (1997). *Developmentally appropriate practice in early childhood programs*. Washington, DC: National Association for the Education of Young Children.

Brown, W.H., Odom, S.L., & Conroy, M.A. (2001). An intervention hierarchy for promoting young children's peer interactions in natural environments. *Topics in Early Childhood Special Education*, *21*, 162–175.

Center on the Social and Emotional Foundations for Early Learning. (2006). *Inventory of Practices for Promoting Children's Social Emotional Competence*. Retrieved August 6, 2006 from Center on Social and Emotional Foundations for Early Learning: http://www.vanderbilt.edu/csefel/modules/module4/handout8.pdf

Coleman, M.R., Buysse, V., & Neitzel, J. (2006). *Recognition and response: An early intervening system for young children at-risk for learning disabilities*. University of North Carolina Child Development Institute.

Early Childhood Research Institute on Measuring Growth and Development. (1998/2000). *Individual Growth and development indicators for preschool children: Picture naming/expressing meaning*. Minneapolis, MN: Center for Early Education and Development, University of Minnesota. Available from: www.getgotgo.net

Fuchs, D., Mock, D., Morgan, P.L., & Young, C.L. (2003). Responsiveness-to-intervention: Definitions, evidence, and implications for the learning disabilities construct. *Learning Disabilities Research & Practice*, *18*, 157–171.

Fuchs, L.S., & Fuchs, D. (2002). Curriculum-based measurement: Describing competence, enhancing outcomes, evaluating treatment effects, and identifying treatment non-responders. *Peabody Journal of Education*, *77*(2), 64–84.

Fuchs, L.S., & Fuchs, D. (2006a). A framework for building capacity for responsiveness to intervention. *School Psychology Review*, *35*, 621–626.

Fuchs, L.S., & Fuchs, D. (2006b). Introduction to response to intervention: What, why, and how valid is it? *Reading research Quarterly*, *41*, 93–99.

Gettinger, M., & Stoiber, K. (2008). Applying a response-to-intervention model for early literacy development in low-income children. *Topics in Early Childhood Special Education*, *27*(4), 198–213.

Glover, T.A., & DiPerna, J.C. (2007). Service delivery for response to intervention: Core components and directions for future research. *School Psychology Review*, *36*, 526–540.

Good, R.H., & Kaminski, R.A. (Eds.). (2002). *Dynamic indicators of basic early literacy skills* (6th ed.). Eugene, OR: Institute for the Development of Education Achievement. Available at: http://dibels.uoregon.edu/.

Hagans-Murillo, K. (2005). Using a response-to-intervention approach in preschool to promote literacy. *The California School Psychologist*, *10*, 45–54.

Hammill, D.D., Leigh, J.E., Pearson, N.A., & Maddox, T. (1998). *Basic school skills inventory, 3rd edition*. Austin, Texas: Pro-Ed.

Harms, T., & Clifford, R.M. (1998). *Early Childhood Environment Rating Scale–Revised*. New York: Teachers College Press.

Hemmeter, M.L., Ostrosky, M., & Fox, L. (2006). Social emotional foundations for early learning: A conceptual model for intervention. *School Psychology Review*, *35*, 583–601.

Hresko, W., Miguel, S., Sherbenou, R., & Burton, S. (1994). *Developmental observation checklist system*. Austin, Texas: Pro-Ed.

Individuals with Disabilities Education Improvement Act of 2004, Pub. L. 108–446, 118 Stat. 2647.

Kazdin, A.E. (1993). Adolescent mental health: Prevention and treatment programs. *American Psychologist*, *48*, 127–141.

Kazdin, A.E., & Kendall, P.C. (1998). Current progress and future plans for developing effective treatments: Comments and perspectives. *Journal of Clinical Child Psychology*, *27*, 217–226.

Kovaleski, J. F., Gickling, E. E., Morrow, H., & Swank, P. (1999). High versus low implementation of instructional support teams: A case for maintaining program fidelity. *Remedial and Special Education*, *20*, 170–183.

McCabe, P.C. & College, B. (2006). Responsiveness to intervention (RTI) in early childhood: Challenges and practical guidelines. *Journal of Early Childhood and Infant Psychology*, *2*, 157–180.

Merrill, K.W. (2002). *Preschool and kindergarten behavior scales* (2nd ed.). Austin, Texas: Pro-Ed.

National Association of School Psychologists (2008). Implementation of EBIs: Tips for school psychologists. *NASP Communique*, *36*(7).

Sandall, S., Hemmeter, M.L., Smith, B.J., & McLean, M.E. (2005). *DEC recommended practices: A comprehensive guide for practical application in early intervention/early childhood special education*. Longmont, CO: Sopris West.

Smith, M.W., & Dickinson, D.K. (2003). *Early language and literacy classroom observation toolkit*. Maryland: Brookes.

Tremblay, R.E. (2000). The development of aggressive behavior during childhood: What have we learned in the past century? *International Journal of Behavioral Development*, *24*, 129–141.

United States Department of Education. (2001). *No child left behind*. Retrieved August 21, 2001, from http://www2.ed.gov/policy/elsec/leg/esea02/107-110.pdf

United States Department of Education Office of Special Education and Rehabilitative Services. (2002). *A new era: Revitalizing special education for children and families*. Washington, DC: Author.

VanDerHeyden, A.M., & Jimerson, S.R. (2005). Using response-to-intervention to enhance outcomes for children. *The California School Psychologist*, *10*, 21–32.

VanDerHeyden, A.M., Snyder, P.A., Broussard, C., & Ramsdell, K. (2007). Measuring response to early literacy intervention with preschoolers at risk. *Topics in Early Childhood Special Education*, *27*(4), 232–249.

Whitehurst, G.J. & Lonigan, C.J. (2002). *Emergent literacy: Development from prereaders to readers*. In S.B. Neuman & D.K. Dickinson (Eds.), *Handbook of Early Literacy Research* (pp. 11–29). New York: Guilford Press.

Externalizing Disorders in Children and Adolescents: Behavioral Excess and Behavioral Deficits

William R. Jenson, Sarah Harward, *and* Julie M. Bowen

Abstract

This chapter is a review of externalizing disorders in youth, with an emphasis on behavioral deficits, behavioral excesses and effective interventions. The term *externalizing disorders* refers to a broad topic that includes several clinically recognized disorders such as attention-deficit/hyperactivity disorder (ADHD), conduct disorder (CD), and oppositional defiant disorder (ODD). While specific chapters elsewhere in this volume cover each of these disorders, this chapter will investigate common similarities across several externalizing disorders, review their origins, and suggest evidence-based interventions for effective treatment. Academic intervention and academic assessment will not be addressed, because they are covered in two separate chapters. An emphasis will be placed on evidence-based practice interventions for externalizing disorders for the practicing school psychologist. It should be noted that by grouping ADHD, CD, and ODD under one label, *externalizing disorders*, the commonalities of these disorders will be highlighted, but in the process, some of their important differences will also be de-emphasized. (Mullin & Hinshaw, 2007).

Keywords: externalizing disorders, tough kid, behavioral excesses, socially maladjusted

Conceptualization of Externalizing Disorders

The term *externalizing disorders* refers to a child or adolescent whose behavior negatively affects persons (i.e., parents, other adults, and peers) who are external to them. The problematic behaviors are directed outward and commonly include noncompliance, aggression, impulsive behaviors, arguing, rule breaking, and property destruction. This is in contrast to *internalizing disordered* children and adolescents who inwardly direct their problematic behaviors, such as anxiety, fears, and somatic complaints.

The clinical term "externalizing disorders" is not found in any commonly accepted classification system such as the *Diagnostic and Statistical Manual of Mental Disorders*—Fourth Edition (DSM-IV-TR) (American Psychiatric Association, 2000), *International Classification of Diseases and Health Related Problems* (ICD-10; World Health Organization, 2005), nor in the definitions for disabilities for the

reauthorization of the Individuals with Disabilities Education Act (IDEA)–2004. The DSM-IV-TR combines externalizing behavior problems under disruptive disorders (e.g., ADHD, CD, and ODD). IDEA-2004 includes both externalizing disorders and internalizing disorders under the category of *seriously emotionally disturbed*; however, it specifically excludes "socially maladjusted" students from receiving services unless they are also severely emotionally disturbed. Some state educational agencies and school districts specifically equate socially maladjusted with externalizing disorders, and thus deny these students special education services (Jenson, Olympia, Farley, & Clark, 2004).

Possibly the best research based origin for the concept of externalizing comes from the development of behavior rating scales such as the Child Behavior Checklist (CBCL; Achenbach & Rescorla, 2001) or the Behavior Assessment System for Children-II (BASC-II; Reynolds & Kamphaus, 2004).

When behavioral items are developed for these rating scales and thousands of children are rated, two broad-band spectrum areas develop. One spectrum is made up of behaviors and sub-factors such as attention, delinquency, hyperactivity, conduct problems, and aggression, that are significantly associated with externally directed problem behaviors. This is as opposed to internally directed problem behaviors with sub-factors of depression, anxiety, withdrawal, and somatic problems. In a sense, with ratings by parents and teachers on thousands of clinically referred children, these individually rated behavior items intercorrelate and form the broad spectrums of externalizing and internalizing disorders.

There is also a clinical definition of externalizing disorders that goes beyond just the label and sub-factors (refer to Table 18.1). This definition describes externalizing disorders as consisting of *behavioral excesses* and *behavioral deficits* (Rhode & Jenson, 2010; Gelfand & Drew, 2003). The behavioral excesses include behaviors frequently associated with externalizing disorders such as aggression (i.e., physical aggression, verbal aggression, revenge-seeking, property vandalism, engaging in bullying, and cruelty to animals), and noncompliance (i.e., not following directions, rule breaking, and arguing). However, this definition also includes substantial behavioral deficits such as lack of rule-governed behavior (i.e., does not internalize societal and behavioral rules that govern behavior) and poor social skills (i.e., has few friends, considered imma-ture and demanding in social situations, constantly seeks attention), as well as deficits in academic skills and behaviors related to school success. These chil-dren are commonly described as "Tough Kids" because they are difficult to manage behaviorally and teach (Rhode et al., 2010). Defining external-izing disorders by describing core behavioral excesses and deficits is advantageous, particularly in design-ing interventions and prevention programs for these children. If only behavioral excesses are highlighted and treated, then the intervention programs for these externalizing students will frequently fail. Even if there is an initial decrease in behavioral excesses, externalizing students will frequently revert back to their old behavioral excesses to escape or avoid environments and situations that require skills they do not posses (Rhode & Jenson, 2010). For example, if noncompliance, arguing, and aggression decrease during a treatment program, and the stu-dent with academic deficits is then placed back into a demanding classroom environment that requires successful academic performance, this student will likely revert back to his old behavioral excesses to escape this setting. Good interventions for external-izing disorders must address both behavioral excesses and behavioral deficits.

Causes of Externalizing Disorders

There is no single cause for externalizing disorders (Gelfand & Drew, 2003; Rutter, 2003). Rather, this disorder has multiple causes that interact to produce externalizing behaviors. These causes include bio-logical factors, genetics, family and parenting issues, learning coercive behaviors, and several other envi-ronmental factors. We do a disservice to students with externalizing disorders when we assume there is one single cause and one single treatment, and exclude other factors. When we do this, we miss the "bigger picture" of this disorder. There are many causes for externalizing disorders, and several ave-nues of treatment that should be recognized.

Genetics and Temperament

Biological factors play an important part in the eti-ology of externalizing disorders. Many researchers believe there is an inherited biological risk for the development of externalizing disorders (Dick, 2007; Hicks, Krueger, Iacono, McGue, & Patrick, 2004; Kendler, Jacobson, Myers, & Eaves, 2007). However, few researchers believe there is a single gene of trans-mission for externalizing behaviors. Rather, it is commonly assumed that there is a reciprocal influ-ence between the genetic makeup and biology of a child, and such factors as inherited temperament, a "goodness of fit" between temperament style and the demands of the environment, parenting style, the community, and several other environmental factors (Carey, 1998; Smith, Barkley, & Shapiro, 2006; Gelfand, & Drew, 2003; McMahon, Wells, & Kotler, 2006; Patterson, 2002; Patterson, Reid, & Dishion, 1992).

The percentage of genetic influence on external-izing behaviors, especially antisocial behavior, is dif-ficult to estimate. In 1994, Mason and Frick conducted a meta-analysis of several studies that included 3795 twin pairs and 338 adoptees, to esti-mate the influence of genetics on antisocial behavior. They concluded that approximately 50% of the vari-ance in measures of antisocial behaviors was proba-bly attributable to genetic effects. Baker, Bezdijan, and Raine (2006) reached a similar conclusion, "Heritability estimates suggest as much as one-half of the variation in propensity toward antisocial behavior can be explained by genetic differences among individuals" (p. 19). Rhee and Waldman

Table 18.1 Practical definition of a tough kid

Behavioral excesses: Too much of a behavior

Non-compliance

Does not do what is requested

Breaks rules

Argues

Makes excuses

Delays

Does the opposite of what is expected

Aggression

Tantrums

Fights

Destroys property

Vandalizes

Sets fires

Teases

Verbally abuses

Is revengeful

Is cruel to others

Behavioral deficits: Inability to adequately perform a behavior

Self-management skills

Cannot delay rewards

Acts before thinking – impulsive

Shows little remorse or guilt

Will not follow rules

Cannot foresee consequences

Social skills

Has few friends

Goes through friends fast

Noncooperative – bossy

Does not know how to reward others

Lacks affection

Has few problem-solving skills

Constantly seeks attention

Table 18.1 (continued)

Academic skills

Generally behind in academics, particularly reading

Off-task

Fails to finish work

Truant or frequently tardy

Forgets acquired information easily

From Rhode and Jenson's *The Tough Kid Book*. Reprinted with permission of Pacific Northwest Publishing.

(2002), in a study of 51 twin and adoption studies, found that the proportion of variance due to additive genetic influence was approximately 32%, with 42% due to nonshared environmental influences. Hicks, et al. (2004), studying 542 families in the Minnesota Twin Family Study, concluded that there was a familial transmission of "highly heritable general vulnerability" for externalizing disorders.

Although the study of general inheritability of externalizing behaviors has made advancements, pinpointing specific genes has been more difficult. Dick (2007) has reviewed the area and concluded there may be predisposition genes (i.e., GABRA2 and CHRM2); others (Beaver, Wright, Delisi, Walsh, Vaughn, Boisvert & Vaske, 2007) have found a gene x gene interaction (DRD2 X DRD4) that is related to the development of antisocial behaviors. These genes are "not specific to one externalizing disorder but will predispose individuals broadly to a spectrum of externalizing pathology" (Dick, 2007, p. 331).

Other researchers have found links with genetics and different levels of physiological arousal associated with thrill seeking, novelty seeking, and a decreased sensitivity to punishment and behavioral inhibition (Atkins, Osborne, Bennett, Hess, & Halperin, 2001; Sharp, Petersen, & Goodyer, 2008). These biological differences in physiological arousal may help explain the impulsive behaviors of externalizing children, and their failure to learn from aversive consequences for these behaviors. In a sense, these genetic differences produce under-arousal in some externalizing children, requiring them to seek exciting situations (e.g., rule breaking, aggression, taking chances) to maintain an optimal level of physiological arousal (Gelfand & Drew, 2003). These genes have been dubbed the "adventure genes" and have been associated with novelty seeking, impulsivity, exploratory behavior, and substance abuse (Ebstein & Belmaker, 1996; Lusher, Chandler & Ball 2001).

Temperament also appears to be an important factor in the development of externalizing disorders of childhood (Rettew, Copeland, Stanger, & Hudziak, 2004). Since the early research of Chess and Thomas (1984), and the publication of their longitudinal study of temperament in children, there has been a great deal of research linking temperament with externalizing disorders. Chess and Thomas studied 133 children from infancy to young adulthood. They found that 65% of the infants (2 to 3 months of age) in their sample could be categorized on nine behavioral characteristics into three distinct categories: easy temperament (40%), slow to warm up (15%), and difficult temperament (10%) infants. Difficult-temperament infants tended to be more emotional, irritable, active, fussy, and to cry more easily than other infants. Patterson et al. (1982) include a difficult temperament as one of several precursors that later leads antisocial behavior in children. Difficult-temperament children are also more vulnerable to abuse, school failure, and showed some of the poorest responses to childhood stressors such as divorce (Chess & Thomas, 1984). Other researchers have linked temperament with externalizing characteristics such as hyperactivity, novelty seeking, and aggression (Berdan, Keane, & Calkins, 2008; Rettew, et al., 2004).

Although temperament has a strong genetic link (Saudino, 2005; Torgerson & Kringlen, 1978), Chess and Thomas (1984) reported that a number of subjects in the population they studied changed temperament categories as they grew older. It is most likely the fit between a child's temperament and the demands of the environment that significantly affect the development of problem behaviors. Chess and Thomas (1984) stated that "These findings suggest that poorness of fit between the child's characteristics (i.e., temperament) and capabilities, and the demands and expectation of the environment, is sufficient to produce a behavior disorder by early childhood" (p. 58). Environmental and familial factors may play a role in changing temperament characteristics as a child grows older. With a good fit, the child is viewed as less difficult temperamentally; with a poor fit the child is viewed as more difficult. Biological factors such as genetic makeup and temperament may predispose a child to a general vulnerability, which is then triggered by a multiple set of familial and environmental factors, thus producing externalizing problem behaviors in children (Patterson et al., 1982; Rutter, 2003).

Family Factors

The role of the parents and family in the development of externalizing disorders is well documented (Frick & Loney, 2002, Kendall, 2000; Patterson, 2002; Patterson, 1982; Snyder & Stoolmiller, 2002). These factors can take several forms, including parental deviance, parental rejection, coercive family interactions, lack of discipline or overly harsh discipline, marital conflict, divorce, and lack of supervision (Hetherington, Law, & O'Connor, 1993; Kendall, 2000; Snyder & Stoolmiller, 2002). Alcoholism, drug abuse, criminality, and psychiatric disorders in parents, all can contribute to the development of aggression, noncompliance, delinquency, and externalizing problems in children (Patterson et al., 1982; McMahon et al., 2006). Parental criminality and antisocial behavior has been linked to conduct disorders and oppositional defiant disorders in children (Frick, Lahey, Loeber, Tannenbaum, Van Horn, Christ 1993; Frick & Loney, 2002). Parental antisocial behavior may interfere with the development of positive parenting practices, while it also models deviant behaviors for their children (Capaldi, DeGarmo, Patterson, & Forgatch, 2002; Patterson et al., 1992). Criminality and antisocial behavior in parents may partially account for the trans-generation of antisocial behavior. In essence, one generation passes it to the next. Substance abuse and alcoholism may also have similar trans-generational effects for children with externalizing disorders (Hicks, et al., 2004; Schuckit, Smith, Pierson, Trim, & Danko, 2007). Alcoholism specifically can affect parenting ability by altering the parent's perceptions of a child's behavior, and contribute to inadequate monitoring and supervision, indulgence, and inconsistent or overly harsh parenting (McMahon et al., 2006).

Other family stressors such as divorce, marital distress, maternal depression, neighborhood risk, and low SES can also influence the development of externalizing disorders in children (Amato & Keith, 1991; Capaldi, et al., 2002; Cummings & Davies, 1994; Igoldsby & Shaw, 2002; Snyder, 2002). Research indicates that boys are more likely to develop the externalizing behaviors of noncompliance and aggression than girls following divorce (Amato, 2001; Amato & Keith, 1991; Malone, Lansford, Castellino, Berlin, Dodge, Bates, & Pettit, 2004). It should be recognized that a child's antisocial behavior may also promote marital disharmony, which contributes to divorce, leads to a lower standard of living, and exacerbates maternal depression. It is a chicken and egg problem. The causal mechanism is unclear, of how much the family factors influence the development of externalizing behaviors in the child, or how much the child's externalizing behaviors affect the discord in a family (Kazdin, 1995; Patterson, 1982; Patterson, et al., 1992).

Child rearing practices have an impact on the development of externalizing behaviors in children. However, these child rearing practices span a spectrum from harsh and abusive practices to inconsistent or negligent parenting practices (Burke, Loeber, & Birmaher, 2002; Patterson et al., 1992). Harsh, abusive, and punitive parenting that models parent aggression is associated with disruptive externalizing behaviors (Patterson, et al., 1992). This type of parenting focuses on what the child has done wrong, rather than teaching the child what he or she should do (Gelfand & Drew, 2003). On the other end of the spectrum are inconsistent parents who habitually have difficulty setting reasonable limits, and establishing family rules and consistent routines (Patterson, 1982; Patterson, et al., 1992). This type of parenting often leaves children confused about the exact limits and consequences for their behaviors. It is interesting to note that parents who use erratic control and are inappropriately permissive often revert to abuse, and are more likely to use aggression to discipline their child (Chamberlain, Reid, Ray, Capaldi, & Fisher, 1997; Jaffee, Caspi, Moffitt, & Taylor, 2004). These deficits in parenting and caregiving can also lead to attachment problems and difficulty with emotional regulation in a developing child (Guttmann-Steinmetz & Crowell, 2006). Some researchers have labeled this type of problem as a pattern of "insecure coercive attachment" (Devito & Hopkins, 2001). Families with high rates of conflict and coercive interactions make their children especially vulnerable to the development of externalizing, antisocial problem behaviors (Patterson, 1982; Patterson et al., 1992).

Coercion: The Aversive Cycle
Understanding the coercive family cycle and the role of noncompliance is essential for the successful treatment of externalizing behaviors in children. The coercion model (Patterson; 1976; Patterson et al., 1992) is an escalating cycle of aversive interactions between a parent and child. In the coercive process, escape from an ever escalating cycle of aversive behaviors is the motivating consequence that fuels externalizing behaviors such as aggression, arguing,

temper tantrums, and noncompliance. For example, in a coercive interaction a parent may ask a child to clean his room. The child responds by ignoring the parent's request. The parent then presses the request, and the child starts to whine. At this point, the parent may yell at the child, who then starts to argue with the parent about the unfairness of the request. Caught in the child's argument, the parent may threaten the child with negative consequences for not following their directions. Next, the child may explode in a tantrum and become aggressive. The parent may then leave the room in frustration and, in effect, withdraw the original request to clean the room. In this model, the child has escaped the parent's request by escalating his behavior from ignoring, whining, arguing, temper tantrumming and finally becoming aggressive. The parent likewise has avoided the child's escalating string of aversive behaviors by walking away and withdrawing the original request. The child learns that his aversive behaviors can turn off the aversive parental behavior (i.e., parent request to clean his room). Both the parent and child are negatively reinforced through the coercive process. Coercion is a gradual learning process, which results in several deleterious consequences for the child. Gerald Patterson has described a child caught in an aversive interaction as a "victim and architect of the coercive system" (Patterson, 1976; Patterson, 1982).

By "victim" Patterson means that, although the child may have escaped an unwanted request from his parent, there were negative long-term consequences for engaging in this process. Patterson, (1982) hypothesized there are basically four progressive stages in the coercive process. The first stage is the learning process, where the child learns to use coercion to control others (i.e., parents, siblings, and other adults). Stage 1 is characterized by poor discipline, lax supervision, and parental inconsistency. It also puts the child at risk for child abuse, family disruption, and lower self-esteem. At Stage 2 the child learns to export the coercive process to peers and other adults such as teachers, thus leading to poor academic performance and rejection by peers. As the child gets older, Stage 3 begins with the coercive child seeking associations with other deviant peers, increased substance abuse, and delinquency. Stage 4 is the adult culmination of the coercive process, with chaotic employment experiences, disrupted marriage, legal problems, and possible institutionalization (i.e., incarceration).

The child is not only the victim in this process, but also the architect in the sense that coercion fundamentally changes family dynamics. However, the coercive child is not the only architect of this system. Both siblings and parents unknowing facilitate coercive family interactions (Patterson, 1982; Snyder, 2002). Overall, families of externalizing children that engage in coercion have much higher rates of aversive interactions such as yelling, threats, aggression, crying, whining, and noncompliance (Patterson, 1982). There does not appear to be a great deal of difference between the coercive child and his siblings. If grouped together, an uninformed observer would have difficulty picking out the clinically referred coercive child among the siblings. In essence, once the coercive cycle is initiated in the family, it tends to reverberate within the family and "once initiated these aversive events tend to snowball and have a life of their own" (Snyder, 2002, p. 73).

The Effects of Deviant Peers and Social Skills Deficits

There are other ramifications for the coercive process, which helps explain the behavioral deficit components (i.e., rule following, social skills and academic deficits) of the definition of externalizing disorders given earlier in this chapter. By learning the coercive process in the home, the externalizing child is likely to export it to the neighborhood and school. Externalizing children who use coercion are more likely to be rejected and disliked by their peers, and develop a negative reputation as being uncooperative, non-rule-following, and aggressive (Dishion, 1990; Coie & Kupersmidt, 1983; Snyder, 2002). These children do not learn the more sophisticated social skills needed to deal with disagreements, conflict, and competition with their peers. Rejection by a normal peer group often results in externalizing children looking for others that share similar behavioral characteristics (Snyder, 2002). Thus, they often form affiliations and friendships with other externalizing children, which add to their social problems. Externalizing children not only need to learn more sophisticated social skills, they also need appropriate contingencies to perform these skills.

It is important to note that the phenomena of seeking other children and adolescents with similar behavioral characteristics can produce a significant risk factor in treatment. Simply grouping externalizing students with each other in a treatment group or classroom setting can inadvertently foster antisocial behavior (Arnold & Hughes 1999). Dishion, McCord, & Poulin (1999) showed that grouping externalizing adolescents for prosocial skills training actually significantly increased their tobacco use and

delinquent behavior as rated by teachers. Dishion et al. (1999) have named this phenomena "deviancy training." When grouped together, through verbal and nonverbal communication, deviant peers positively reinforce each other for antisocial behavior; they learn new forms of deviant behavior; and they form friendships that extend beyond the group. This "iatrogenic" effect of making antisocial behavior worse through grouping occurs mostly with older externalizing youths. It is found more frequently when the groups are relatively unstructured, have little direction, and are poorly managed. This iatrogenic effect has important implications in treatment programs for externalizing youth. Arnold and Hughes (1999) have stated, "First, do no harm..." (p. 99) in reference to the harmful effects that can occur when externalizing students are grouped in treatment or skills training.

Academic and Self-Management Deficits

Academic problems are closely associated with externalizing disorders (Mullin & Hinshaw, 2007). These problems include disorganization, poor study skills, underachievement, grade retention, dropping out of school, and poor reading ability (Gelfand & Drew, 2003; Hinshaw, 1992; Walker, Ramsey, Gresham, 2004). Patterson, DeBaryshe, & Ramsey (1989) have indicated that the family coercive process is a major contributor to academic failure once school begins. Coercive students are at particular risk when their reading ability is low, and they constantly receive the negative message that they are a failure at school (Morgan & Jenson, 1988; Walker et al., 2004). This negative message is compounded each year when their negative reputations have preceded them with peers, teachers, and other school staff (Snyder, 2002). Externalizing students often have a general negative conditioning experience to school and academics, which follows them through each grade during their educational experience. The problem becomes one of not only academic remediation, especially in reading, but also of motivating the student to stay in school and continue to work academically (Rhode & Jenson, in press). Two chapters in this book address the core issues of academic interventions and assessment that are essential to the adjustment of the externalizing student to school.

The inability of externalizing children to self-manage and govern their behavior by following rules, develop empathy, and internalize societal values is a third major area of deficit (Smith et al., 2006; Rhode & Jenson, 2010). Skinner (1953) long ago outlined the developmental process of learning to be self-managed and rule governed by a three-step basic process. First, the child learns to be controlled (i.e., compliance to requests) by the language of others. Second, the child learns self-control through language and private speech. Finally, the child internalizes rules and creates new rules (i.e., problem solving) to govern his or her behavior in new and unsupervised settings. Normal children use internalized rules and problem-solving strategies to govern their behavior in novel situations. Externalizing children, especially coercive and impulsive children, are more contingency governed by the immediate environment, and have difficultly following rules and requests from parents and teachers (Snyder, 2002; Snyder & Stoolmiller, 2002).

This lack of self-management and rule governed behavior becomes a significant problem when externalizing children are not supervised nor monitored (Patterson, 1982).

Externalizing children are impulsive by nature, and controlled directly by what they encounter in their immediate environment. When externalizing children are left unsupervised in high-risk environments with deviant peers, they are far more likely to develop antisocial behaviors (Kilgore, Snyder, & Lentz, 2000; Patterson et al., 1992; Snyder, 2002). For externalizing children with poor rule governed behaviors, a major treatment focus is teaching self-management skills to the child, and increasing both parental and school staff monitoring of behavior. This issue is particularly problematic when externalizing students are unmonitored after school and on weekends. It is also a major argument against the expulsion and suspension of externalizing students (Jenson, Rhode, Evans, & Morgan, 2006). When approximately 200 secondary students in Utah with externalizing problems were asked what type of disciplinary action they preferred, the vast majority indicated they would prefer out of school suspension (Evans, 2008). Simply putting externalizing youth on the streets of a community without supervision is asking for trouble, for the youth and for the community. Alternative positive supervision interventions are needed for externalizing students who are at risk for expulsion and suspension from schools.

The Role of Noncompliance

In discussing the coercive process for externalizing children, and its associated behavioral deficits, it is important to highlight the importance of noncompliance. Noncompliance is one of the most common behavior problems of childhood (Kalb & Loeber,

2003). Simply defined, noncompliance is not following a direction (i.e., from a parent or teacher) within a specific period of time (Forehand, 1977; Kalb & Loeber, 2003; Rhode & Jenson, in press). The reason noncompliance is so important because it is the "basic building block" of antisocial behavior that leads to more severe forms such as aggression and violence (Snyder, 2002). Children usually do not argue, tantrum, talk back, or make excuses in a vacuum. These aversive behaviors are generally exhibited to escape demanding situations, or request or commands from an adult. Thus noncompliance is core to the coercive process, and appears to be a behavior associated with all the major clinical conditions (i.e., ADHD, CD, and ODD) that make up the broad spectrum of behaviors that define externalizing disorders.

Noncompliance may be more than a core, but rather the "kingpin" that is central to coercion and holds the aversive behaviors together in the cycle. The kingpin is like an axle around which all the other behavioral excesses revolve as spokes. The externalizing child's compliance to adult requests is approximately 40% to 50%, whereas normal children respond to approximately 80% to 85% of adult requests (Forehand, 1977; Rhode & Jenson, 2010). Research has shown that interventions focused on improving noncompliance in externalizing children will also collaterally improve the child's aggression, arguing, and temper tantrums (Martinez & Forgatch, 2001; Parrish, Cataldo, Kolko, & Engle, 1986; Russo, Cataldo, & Cushing, 1981; Wells, Forehand, & Griest, 1980). In other words, interventions used to improve a child's noncompliance will also improve other behavioral excesses and deficits, even though they are not the target of an intervention. Once the "kingpin" behavior of noncompliance is reduced, other antisocial behaviors in the coercive cycle will also improve. For externalizing children, a major focus of treatment should be the improvement of noncompliance in the home, in the neighborhood, and at school.

Stability and Developmental Nature of Externalizing Disorders

The changing nature of behavior as the child develops and grows older is an important concept for effective intervention with children with externalizing disorders. Figure 18.1 contains the compilation of hundreds of children ages 6 to 18 that have been rated on the Child Behavior Checklist (CBCL) by parents, self-reported on the Youth Report Form (YSR), and reported by teachers on the Teacher Report Form (TRF)

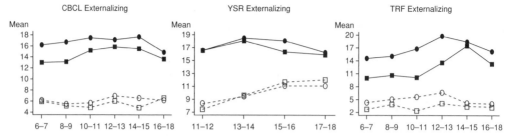

CBCL Externalizing   YSR Externalizing   TRF Externalizing

Fig. 18.1 Ratings on Children and Adolescents for Externalizing Behaviors by their Parents, the Youth Themselves, and their Teachers. From: Achenbach, T. M. & Rescorla, L. A. (2001). Manual for the ASEBA school-age forms & profiles, Burlington, VT: University of Vermont. Copyright by T. M. Achenbach. Reproduced by permission.

(Achenbach & Rescorla, 2001) for externalizing behaviors. Open circles (boys) and squares (girls) represent nonreferred children, and closed circles and squares represent children referred for psychological problems.

It is easy to see from the parent, youth, and teacher ratings that externalizing problems are elevated and remain very stable and consistent across ratings, with teacher ratings more elevated. These data suggest that the behaviors that make up the constellation of externalizing disorders such as noncompliance and arguing are very stable over time, with some problem behaviors (e.g., truancy, substance abuse) gradually getting worse.

However, as children age and develop, there are stability differences between the clinical disorders (i.e., ADHD, CD, and ODD) that make up the externalizing grouping. For both CD and ODD, the problem behaviors appear to be very stable (e.g., boys), or get worse at about age 12 years (ratings of girls). In contrast, ratings for ADHD children (both parent and teacher ratings) appear to improve over time, but never fall within the normal range of nonreferred children.

Similarly, research literature has shown that as ADHD children age, the hyperactive-impulsive behaviors decline (Barkley, 1996). When an ADHD child is a preschooler, they exhibit higher rates of excessive motor activity, inattention, and impulsivity. When they enter school at about age 5–6, they are often recognized as being deviant from nondisabled peers. This is especially true for structured academic tasks that require sustained attention, problem solving, and sitting quietly (Barkely 1996). In adolescence, 43%–80% of these youths continue to have the disorder. When they approach young adulthood, this percentage falls to 30–50% (Barkley, 1996). Young adults with ADHD continue to have poorer outcomes than non-ADHD adults, including higher accident rates, substance abuse, more

sexual partners, poor work histories, and more interpersonal problems (Weiss & Hechtman, 1993). However, the comorbidity of aggression and severe oppositional behavior with ADHD (i.e., 35%–40%) produces significantly poorer outcomes (Smith, et al., 2006).

The stability and developmental issues of behaviors associated with ODD and CD are twofold. One issue is age of onset during childhood for these disorders. The second issue is the changing nature of the behaviors that make up the symptom clusters of ODD and CD as the child gets older. Both onset of the externalizing disorder and the changing nature of the CD and ODD have significant implications for treatment.

Externalizing children who have life-course paths (early starters) for antisocial behavior have a developmental course which persists from early childhood to young adulthood (Moffit, Caspi, Dickson, Silva, & Stanton, 1996). This pathway is similar to the early-onset CD described in the DSM IV-TR. This type of externalizing disorder has many of the problems and risks that were discussed earlier in this chapter. They are identified as being difficult-temperament infants, crying frequently, irritable, and hyperactive. It has been suggested that there may be early neurobiological deficits with these children that interfere with the development of inhibition, language, memory, and self-control (Moffitt, 1993; Moffitt, 2003). These children come from families that engage in coercion, the parents may exhibit antisocial behavior, there is martial distress, and maternal depression is more common, as is abuse (Patterson et al., 1992; McMahon et al., 2006). For life-course externalizers there appears to be a transition in antisocial behavior that moves them from overt ODD type behaviors to more covert CD based behaviors. Life-course pathway children may begin by "biting and hitting at age 4, shoplifting and truancy by age 10, selling drugs and stealing cars by age 16, robbery and rape by age 22, and fraud and child abuse by age 30" (Moffitt, 1993, p. 679). The life-path externalizing youth continue this pattern through childhood and adolescence and are at increased risk for more negative outcomes in adulthood (Moffitt, 2003).

The second basic type of externalizing disorder for children with CD type behaviors is the adolescent-limited pathway. This path generally starts in puberty when the youth is a teenager. The early history of an adolescent-limited externalizer is quite different from a life-path externalizer. Adolescent-limited youth engage in less deviant behavior and aggression in childhood, with less family problems, fewer temperament issues, and less academic failure (Moffitt, 1990; Moffitt, 2003). There is a sex ratio difference between males and females with a 10:1 ratio of males to females for life-course externalizers, and 1.5:1 ratio of males to females for adolescent-limited externalizers (Moffitt, & Caspi, 2001). Adolescent-limited externalizing youth are more susceptible to deviant peer influences that often result in violating societal norms and delinquency (Moffitt, 2003). They usually engage in less violent and aggressive behaviors, and engage in more status offences such as restricted adult privileges (i.e., alcohol, drug abuse, early sexual experiences, curfew violations). Many of the problem behaviors associated with adolescent-limited externalizers are rebellious in nature, and involve asserting independence from their parents (Moffitt, & Caspi, 2001). The long-term outcome in adulthood is much better for adolescent-limited pathway youth than for life-path externalizing youth, especially if the deviant behavior does not include getting caught in a societal "snare." Societal snares are problems such as dropping out of school, substance abuse, incarceration, or arrests that preclude and cut off later adult opportunities, especially employment (McMahon et al., 2006). Many of the delinquent antisocial behaviors peak at around age 17, decrease during the 20s, and are reduced sharply (85%) by age 28.

As there are differences in life-path and adolescent-limited externalizing pathways, there is a difference in the very nature of the behaviors evolving from early childhood through adolescence. Loeber and Schmaling (1985) have proposed a bipolar one-directional development of problematic behaviors, ranging from overt behavior to covert type behaviors. Overt deviant behaviors include those that directly confront others, or cause the disruption of the environment (e.g., aggression, temper tantrums, defiance, and fighting). This is opposed to covert externalizing behaviors, which include

behaviors that usually occur without the immediate awareness on the part of an adult (e.g., lying, vandalism, truancy, stealing, fire setting, and substance abuse) (McMahon et al., 2006). In a further analysis of the dimensions of externalizing behavior, Frick, Lahey, Loeber, Tannenbaum, Van Horn, & Christ (1993) found not only the bipolar dimensions of overt to covert behaviors, but also other dimensions of destructiveness and non-destructiveness. This analysis is given in Figure 18.2, which shows basically four subtypes of externalizing behavior—property violations, aggression, status violations, and oppositional behaviors.

This figure shows the early development of overt externalizing behaviors of opposition and aggression, which are then followed by more covert forms of behaviors of property violations and status violations. It is interesting to note that in this analysis, noncompliance is at the apex, or center, of the four behavior dimensions, indicating its central role as a kingpin behavior in the development of the four conduct problem dimensions (Loeber & Sschmaling, 1985). This finding of noncompliance as an apex or central behavior to the other dimensions of externalizing problem behaviors underscores the need for reducing noncompliance.

Assessment of Externalizing Disorders

Best practice assessment is a structured information gathering technique that leads to decisions about diagnosis, treatment, evaluation of that treatment, and research (Gelfand & Drew, 2003; Sattler, 2008). Structured information gathering means that the assessment instruments have been psychometrically standardized with good reliability and validity characteristics. For example, factor analyzed behavior rating scales, behavioral observations, curriculum based academic measurement, intelligence tests, and functional behavior assessments are all structured assessment approaches. This is opposed to nonstructured approaches such as anecdotal reporting, projective testing, or informal interviewing.

Best practice assessment for externalizing disorders should include multiple standardized assessment measures, multiple informants completing those measures, and the use of assessment measures across multiple environments (Morgan & Jenson, 1990; Rhode & Jenson, 2010). This type of assessment reduces bias, and averages out error that might come from the use of just one type of assessment measure, a biased informant, or missing behavior problems that occur in multiple environments. Best practice assessment can give a school psychologist a

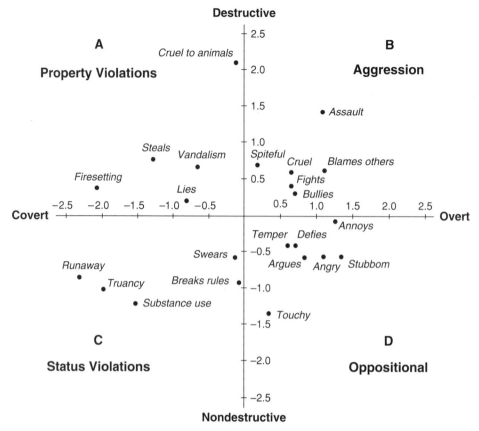

Fig. 18.2 Multi-Dimensions of Child Conduct Problems. Reprinted from Frick, P. J., Lahey, B. B., Lober, R., Tannenbaum, L. E., Van Horn, Y., Christ, M. A. G. (1993). Oppositional defiant disorder and conduct disorders: A meta-analytic review of factors analyses and cross-validation in a clinical sample. *Clinical Psychology Review*, 13, 319–340. p. 327. Reprinted with permission from Elsevier.

good estimate of the severity of the problem behavior, pinpoint problem behaviors for intervention, assess whether an implemented intervention has been effective, and possibly prevent exacerbation of externalizing behaviors.

Behavior Rating Scales

Behavior rating scales are basically checklists, with many items describing specific behaviors. Items are rated as a dichotomy—either the behavior exists "Yes" or it doesn't exist "No." Or, items are rated on a graded Likert Scale, such as *no problem, somewhat of a problem*, or *a significant problem*. When rating scales are developed and normed, hundreds of children are rated by parents or teachers on the individual behavior items or questions. When these behavior-rating scale items have similar structure and meaning, they intercorrelate highly and form broad bands of behaviors such as externalizing and internalizing, as previously described in this chapter. These broad bands

(e.g., externalizing) are then made up of narrower bands or factors such as attention problems, aggressive behaviors, and delinquent behaviors (e.g., CBCL/6-18) (Achenbach & Rescorla, 2001).

One of the earliest behavior checklists was the Behavior Problem Checklist (Quay & Peterson, 1975), which was originally developed by Peterson in 1961. For the BPC, 400 cases referred to child guidance clinics and 831 elementary students were rated by parents and teachers. These items were then statistically intercorrelated (factor analyzed), and formed unitary behavioral dimensions (factors). Since 1961, work has continued on the Revised-BPC (1996), which has broad-band externalizing and internalizing behavior factors that include Conduct Disorder, Socialized Aggression, Attention Problems, Anxiety-Withdrawal, Psychotic Behavior, and Motor Excess. The Conduct Disorder factor is similar to the life-path externalizer; Socialized-Aggression corresponds to the adolescent-limited pathway, and Attentional

Problems and Motor Excess correspond to ADHD. Together, these factors form the broad-band externalizing disorder, and Anxiety and Withdrawal factors form the broad-band internalizing disorder. Psychotic Behavior is a factor by itself.

More recent behavior rating scales can be specific to particular disorders deficit areas such as ADHD (Conners, 1997), oppositional defiant disorder (Hommersen, Murray, Ohan, & Johnson, 2006), autism (Schopler, Reichler, & Renner, 1988), Asperger's syndrome (Gilliam, 2003), depression (Kovacs, 1992), social skills deficits (Gresham and Elliott,1990), and others. Behavior ratings scales have now evolved into comprehensive assessment systems that can include behavior rating scales from preschool through late adulthood, observation systems, and corresponding interviews. For example, the Achenbach System of Empirically Based Assessment (ASEBA; Achenbach & Rescorla, 2001) includes child behavior checklists (i.e., CBCL) from preschool (i.e., age 1½–5), childhood-adolescence (6–18), adulthood (18–59), and older adults (59–90). The child and youth forms can be filled out by parents, teachers, and with some applications, a youth self-report form. This gives the assessment advantage of multiple raters (i.e., parent, teacher, and youth) across multiple environments (i.e., school and home). The individual items are rated on a Likert Scale of 0 = Not a Problem, 1 = Somewhat or Sometimes True, and 2 = Very True or Often True. The ASEBA system has been standardized on numerous cultures in several countries. There is a corresponding Direct Observation Form for classrooms and group activities, which is conducted in 10 minute increments, over 96 problem items, with an emphasis on on-task behavior. There is Semistructured Clinical Interview for Children and Adolescents (McConaughy & Achenbach, 2001) with eight syndrome scales that parallel the child behavior checklist's (CBCL) behavioral factors and DSM IV-TR diagnostic categories.

When the CBCL behavior rating scale is completed by a parent or teacher, the items are scored and transferred to two profile sheets—one profile sheet for a Competence Scale Score, and one profile sheet for a Syndrome Scale Score. Both profile sheets are based on T-scores, with T-score of 50 being average, and with each increase of 10 points being one standard deviation from the mean. It is generally considered for the Syndrome Scale that a score of T-70 (i.e., two standard deviations above average T-50) is clinically significant, and at the 98th percentile. The Competence Scale Score shows adjustment to normal activities, social activities, and school performance. The Syndrome Scale is divided into several clinical factors (e.g., anxious depressed, withdrawal depressed, somatic complaints, social problems, thought problems, attention problems, rule-breaking behavior, and aggressive behavior) depending on the age and sex of the child. The rule-breaking factor and aggressive behavior make up a special externalizing broad-band factor for the CBCL. School psychologists can obtain an estimate of the overall externalizing behavioral excesses of a child by first reviewing the T-score rating of the Externalizing Broad Band on the Syndrome Scale Profile (see Figure 18.3).

The second step is then to identify the narrow-band factors such as rule-breaking that have been scored over T-70. The third step is to review the specific items included under the narrow-band factors that have been individually highly rated with a 1 or 2, such as *truant, bad friends, sets fires,* and *steals.* This Syndrome Scale Profile analysis gives a school psychologist a good estimate of the particular behaviors and severity of the externalizing behavioral excesses of a child (e.g., scores above T-70). A fourth step of reviewing the Competence Scale Score profile gives an estimate of the externalizing child's behavioral deficits, such as deficits in social activities, sports, friends, and school achievement and performance.

The ASEBA system has been used extensively in clinical and research settings for externalizing disorders (Gelfand & Drew, 2003; McMahon, et al., 2006). There are other comprehensive behavior rating systems such as the Behavior Assessment System for Children–Second Edition (BASC-II; Reynolds & Kamphaus, 2004), which is equally useful in assessing externalizing children. For school psychologists interested in an extensive review of available behavior ratings scales, the website (www2.massgeneral.org/schoolpsychiatry/schoolpsychiatry_checklists.asp) at the School Psychiatry Program of Massachusetts General Hospital is an excellent site. This site lists all of the major behavior rating scales as either preliminary screening checklists (i.e., CBCL, BASC-II) or checklists by specific disorders (i.e., ADHD, Aspergers, Depression, etc.), along with the age ranges, who completes the checklist, time to complete, and if there is a free version to view online.

Behavioral Observation Systems
Behavioral observation systems have several distinct advantages for school psychologists, particularly when assessing students with externalizing disorders. This is especially true when compared to

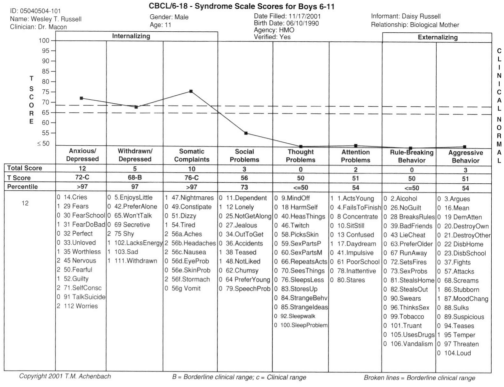

Fig. 18.3 Syndrome Profile for the CBCL. Achenbach, T. M. & Rescorla, L. A. (2001). Manual for the ASEBA school-age forms & policies. Burlington, VT: University of Vermont. p. 65. Copyright by T. M. Achenbach. Reproduced by permission.

anecdotal accounts and informal observations that are often conducted on externalizing-disordered children, but are of limited clinical use. Volpe and McConaughy (2005) discuss several advantages, including the following: they target specific behaviors; the behaviors are operationally defined; they follow standardized coding procedures; they yield quantitative scores; and they can be tested for reliability and validity. The major drawback of structured observation systems is that they seldom include a standardized comparison group, so comparing the severity of a behavior with a norm is difficult. Also, structured observation systems can be time consuming in comparison to other assessment approaches, such as behavior rating scales.

For assessing externalizing students in the classroom setting, there are several structured observations systems (Volpe, Diperna, Hintze, & Shapiro, 2005). These systems include the Behavioral Observation of Students in Schools (BOSS; Shapiro, 2004), ADHD School Observation Code (Gadow, Sprafkin, & Nolan, 1996), Classroom Observation Code (Abikoff & Gittelman, 1985); State-Event

Classroom Observation System (Saudargas, 1997); and the Student Observation System (Reynolds & Kamphaus, 2004). These observation systems have the advantage of giving specific sampling of such externalizing behaviors as aggression (physical and verbal), out-of-seat behavior, talking out, off-task, hyperactive behavior, and noncompliance. Several of these systems are advantageous because the observational data can be directly entered into a laptop computer or handheld device, to collect and summarize.

The Behavioral Observation of Students in School (BOSS; Shapiro, 2004) is an excellent example of a school based observation system. It has been recommended for use with externalizing students (Volpe et al., 2005), and can be used to assess behavioral excesses in the classroom (i.e., leaving seat, throwing objects, talk-outs) and behavioral deficits (i.e., passive inattention, off-task). The BOSS gives a quantitative estimate of a student's active engagement time (AET) when they are directly engaged in appropriate academic activities (i.e., reading aloud) and passive engagement time (PET; i.e., listening to the teacher). The observational data can be easily collected and entered into a handheld device. It also has the advantage that for every fifth interval of recording observational data on a referred child, data are also taken on a comparison peer in the classroom. This allows a direct comparison of the externalizing student's behavior to a nonreferred peer's behavior.

Other formal observation systems have been developed that can be used by school psychologists during test sessions and clinical interviews (McConaughy, 2005), and in clinic settings (McMahon et al., 2006; Roberts, 2001). The Behavioral Coding System (BCS; Forehand & McMahon, 1981) is particularly useful in structured situations (i.e., playroom) in which parents are guided (often with a radio "bug" in the ear) to interact with their child in a free play situation. For externalizing students, direct measures can be made on how parents give their child commands, compliance rates of the child, and the ability of parents to follow through with consequences (e.g., praise, timeout).

A simple approach to measuring one of the core problem behaviors for externalizing disorders, noncompliance, is the Compliance Test (Roberts & Powers, 1988). In a "clean up the toys" analog clinic setting, a parent is given a list of thirty 2-step commands (from an observing therapist behind a one-way mirror, with a radio bug device in the parent's ear) to give to the child. For example, in the first step the parent gives the child the command to "Pick up the toy." If the child complies, the parent then gives a second step command, "Now put it in the box." If the child does not initially comply, the parent says, "Now pick up the toy and put it in the box." Once the command is given by the parent, there is no verbal follow-up or consequence to the child. The child's compliance or noncompliance behaviors are then coded. There is also a classroom version of the Compliance Test in which teachers give 30 common commands to an externalizing student (Jesse, 1989; Rhode et al., 2010). The advantage of either the clinic or school version of the Compliance Test is that is gives a direct estimate of noncompliance of an externalizing child (e.g., 50% compliance to request is considered clinically significant) and can be done in approximately 15 minutes. Research has shown that the Compliance Test accurately identifies and discriminates disruptive externalizing children from typical children (Filcheck, Berry, & McNell, 2004).

Another approach that is useful in observing externalizing students in classroom settings is the response discrepancy observation system (Alessi, 1980). A problem with most behavioral observation systems is that there is generally no comparison group of nondisabled students to use as a comparison standard. One solution for school psychologists using direct observations of externalizing students is the response discrepancy model (Rhode et al., 1992). With this model, during each observational time interval in which the externalizing student is observed, a nondisabled peer is also observed for the same time interval. Figure 18.4 gives an example of a response discrepancy observation sheet. There are ninety 10-second intervals on this sheet for a standard 15-minute observation. The method utilizes a momentary time sampling approach. With this approach, if the referred student exhibits any of the behaviors listed in the behavior code list (see Figure 18.4) that behavior is coded in the last second of the 10-second interval.

At the same time, for the same 10-second interval, a typical peer is also observed and his behavior is also is recorded. In the next 10-second interval, the referred student is observed again, however, now a different typical peer is also observed. At the end of the ninety 10-second observations in the 15-minute period, the observer has a good sample of the problem behaviors exhibited by the referred child. In addition, the school psychologist has a micronorm for comparison on the same problem behaviors exhibited by the typical peers in the same classroom.

The advantages of the response discrepancy observation system listed in Figure 18.4 are the normative comparison to peers, and the problem behaviors coded by the system. This approach focuses on the off-task behavior in the classroom, because off-task is a good index behavior of lower frequency externalizing problem behaviors, such as noncompliance (Barriga, Dorn, Newell, Morrison, Barbetti, & Robbins, 2002). Noncompliance, disruptive behaviors, and aggression occur at much lower rates and are thus harder to observe. However, off-task behaviors occur at a much higher rate and can easily be observed. There is a direct correlation between the occurrence of high-rate off-task behaviors and lower rate externalizing behaviors (e.g., noncompliance and disruption; Barriga et al., 2002; Rhode & Jenson, 2010). Knowing the rate of off-task behaviors is a good indicator of other low-rate externalizing behaviors. In addition, this observation system offers some unique coded behaviors associated with externalizing disorders, such as *playing with an object*, *making noise with body*, and *inactive off task*. The observation system can also be used to assess the

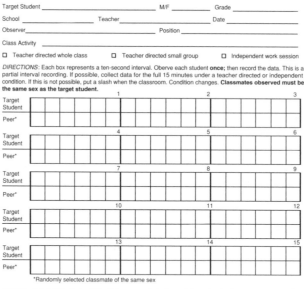

Behavior Observation Form

Target Student _____ M/F _____ Grade _____

School _____ Teacher _____ Date _____

Observer_____ Position _____

Class Activity _____

☐ Teacher directed whole class   ☐ Teacher directed small group   ☐ Independent work session

DIRECTIONS: Each box represents a ten-second interval. Oberve each student **once**; then record the data. This is a partial interval recording. If possible, collect data for the full 15 minutes under a teacher directed or independent condition. If this is not possible, put a slash when the classroom. Condition changes. **Classmates observed must be the same sex as the target student.**

	1	2	3
Target Student			
Peer*			
	4	5	6
Target Student			
Peer*			
	7	8	9
Target Student			
Peer*			
	10	11	12
Target Student			
Peer*			
	13	14	15
Target Student			
Peer*			

*Randomly selected classmate of the same sex

NOTE: To observe class—begin with the first same sex student in row 1. Record each subsequent same sex student in following intervals. Data reflect an average of classroom behavior. **Skip unobservable students.**
ON TASK CODES: Eye contact with teacher or task and performing the requested task.
OFF-TASK CODES:

- **T** = **Talking Out/Noise:** Inappropriate verbalization or making sounds with object, mouth, or body.
- **O** = **Out of Seat:** Student fully or partially out of assigned seat without teacher permission.
- **I** = **Inactive:** Student not engaged with assigned task and passively waiting, sitting, etc.
- **N** = **Noncompliance:** Breaking a classroom rule or not following teacher directions within 15 secondes.
- **P** = **Playing With Object:** Manipulating objects without teacher permission.
- **+** = **Positive Teacher Interaction:** One-on-one positive comment, smiling, touching, or gesture.
- **-** = **Nagative Teacher Interaction:** One-on-one reprimand, implementing negative consequence, or negative gesture.
- **/** = **Neutral Teacher Interaction:** One-on-one expressionless teacher interaction, no approval or disapproval expressed, directions given.

Fig. 18.4 Response Discrepancy Observation Sheet. From Rhode and Jenson's *The Tough Kid Book*. Reprinted with permission of Pacific Northwest Publishing.

positive and negative teacher interactions with the externalizing student, which are valuable when designing effective intervention strategies.

Functional Behavior Assessment and Externalizing Students

Functional behavior assessment (FBA) has gained widespread support for use with students with disabilities (Gelfand & Drew, 2003; March & Horner, 2002). The FBA concept is not new, and was first described by B. F. Skinner in 1953. Functional behavior assessment "is the process of identifying the events that reliably predict and maintain problem behavior" (March & Horner, 2002, p. 158). In essence, functional behavior assessment shows the functional relationship between a problem and the events that precede it (antecedents) and the variables that follow the behavior and maintain it (consequences).

This functional relationship is described as the A (antecedent) B (behavior) C (consequence) model, or *ABC model*. The antecedents in this model set the occasion and precede the problem behavior, and are commonly events (e.g., changing classes, loud distracting sounds, class interruptions, requests), people (e.g., peers, teachers, parents), times (e.g., between classes, after school, late weekend nights), or places (e.g., alone in a car, behind the school with peers, at the shopping mall). The Bs in the ABC model are generally the behavioral excesses exhibited by externalizing students such as aggression, noncompliance, or arguing. However, the externalizing behaviors can also include such behavioral deficits as poor social skills or academic problems. The consequences that motivate and follow the behavior are positive reinforcing events that increase or maintain the behavior (e.g., attention, money, illegal substances), punishing events that suppress or reduce a behavior (i.e., timeout, loss of privileges, criticism), and negative reinforcing events, which increase or maintain a behavior to escape or avoid the consequence. Coercion, where a student increases his arguing, tantrums, and aggression to escape complying with an adult request, is a good example of a negatively reinforcing consequence.

There are several approaches and formal systems that can help a school psychologist collect the information for the ABC model, including interviewing, review of the student's records, filling out ABC event sheets, plotting the behavior as a scatter plot, and direct observations. With a specialized type of FBA, *functional behavior analysis*, a mini-experiment is performed by the clinician in which antecedents and consequences are intentionally manipulated to see if they systematically affect the problem behavior being studied (Alberto & Troutman, 2006). There are formalized, commercially published functional behavior assessment systems that have generated a great deal of research and can be used clinically and educationally (Nelson, Roberts, & Smith, 1998; O'Neill, Horner, Albin, Sprague, Storey, & Newton, 1997; Witt, Daley, Noell, 2000). There is also a computerized functional behavior assessment system (Functional Behavior and Assessment System [FAIP], Jenson, Likins, Hofmeister, Morgan, Reavis, Rhode, & Sweeten, 1999) which guides the ABC interview, assesses and reports the antecedents and consequences, suggests interventions, and compiles a complete FBA report. This system has been shown to be as effective as more formalized FBA systems, and preferred by educators because it takes less time, prepares an FBA report, and suggests interventions for the problem behavior being studied (Hartwig, Tuesday-Heathfield, & Jenson, 2004).

Legislation in the United States (Reauthorization of IDEA-2004) now requires an FBA to be conducted when a student with a disability has been suspended from school for more than 10 days because of a problem behavior that is a direct manifestation of their disability. However, even if an FBA were not legally required, it is still one of the most informative assessment procedures for students with externalizing disorders. FBAs have been used to assess externalizing students for such problem behaviors as aggression and tantrumming (Erickson, Stage, & Nelson, 2006), for ADHD/being off task (Ervin, DuPaul, Kern, & Friman, 1998), running away (Kodak, Grow, & Northrup, 2004), and noncompliance (Wilder, Harris, Reagan, & Rasey, 2007). For externalizing students, some of the most common antecedents for problem behaviors are the presence of peers, or a poorly given command or request from an adult (Rhode et al., 2010). Conversely, some of the most common maintaining consequences are attention from peers, or escape or avoidance of an adult request. A simple approach

for conducting an FBA is the use of ABC event sheets (Rhode et al., 2010). An example of an ABC event sheet is given in Figure 18.5. Multiple copies are made of the ABC event sheet. Each time the problem behavior occurs, the antecedents that precede the behavior and the consequences that follow the behavior are filled in on the ABC sheets.

Over time, when several ABC sheets have been completed, they can be compared to assess common antecedents and consequences for the externalizing student. The most frequently occurring antecedents described on the ABC sheets are the probable events that elicit or set the occasion for the problem behavior. The most frequent consequences that follow the behavior are the probable events that motivate the problem behavior.

Whole School Assessment of Externalizing Disorders

Assessments can be made of whole schools in which screenings are conducted to identify individual students with externalizing problems. In addition to identifying at-risk externalizing students, whole school assessment can pinpoint which types of problem behaviors are occurring most often in a school, where they are occurring, and at what specific times of the school day. Whole school assessments allow a school to be strategic in designing intervention programs. Whole school assessment can also be used to identify externalizing students and design early interventions and prevention programs before the behavior problems become exacerbated and entrenched.

The Systematic Screening for Behavior Disorders (SSBD; Walker & Serverson, 1990) is a multi-gated screening assessment system for children at risk for externalizing and internalizing disorders. Although the SSBD system screens for both externalizing and internalizing students, this discussion will focus only on externalizing students. The SSBD system was first standardized on elementary school children grades 1–6, but has been adapted for a downward extension of preschool students (Feil, Severson, & Walker, 1998), and an upward extension to middle and junior high school students (Caldarella, Young, Richardson, Young, & Young, 2008).

The SSBD system is a multiple gating assessment because it consists of a series of three interrelated assessment steps called gates (Walker, et al. 2004). With the first gate of the assessment process, a teacher is asked to nominate three students who meet the profile of an externalizing student. A written description is given to the teacher of a profile of a typical

ABC-Functional Assessment Event Sheet

Student Name: _____ Date: _____

Rater's Name: _____ Setting: _____

A Antecedent-Something Before The Behavior

Time: _____
People _____
Places: _____
Events _____
Other Behavior _____
Down Time/Transitions _____

B Behavior-Specific, Observable, Objective

Excesses to Decrease _____
Or
Deficits to Increase _____

C Consequence-Something That Follows The Behavior

Punisher _____
Positive Reinforcers _____
Attention
Tangibles
Sensory
Negative Reinforcers _____
Escape
Avoid

Possible Setting Event: _____
Possible Replacement Behavior: _____
Comments

Fig. 18.5 ABC Sheets Event Sheet. From Rhode and Jenson's *The Tough Kid Book*. Reprinted with permission of Pacific Northwest Publishing.

externalizing student who is aggressive, noncompliant, defiant, and argues. Using the written profile as a guide, the teacher lists three students who rank highest on the externalizing dimension in his class. With the second gate, the teacher is asked to rate these three highest ranking externalizing students on two brief rating scales. The first rating scale is the Combined Frequency Index which measures how frequently the student exhibits certain adaptive and maladaptive behaviors. The second scale is the Critical Events Index which includes 33 externalizing behaviors. The teacher is asked to rank the frequency of these behaviors by the student over the past 6 months. Students that exceed the norms on both of these steps in the second gate are referred for a third gate assessment. In the third gate, a professional trained observer, such as a school psychologist, is asked to complete two direct observations of all students who have made it past gates one and two. One observation is of student academic engagement while working on an independent assignment in the classroom. The second observation is of the student's social

behavior at recess or on the playground. Students who are identified, pass through all three gates, and exceed the norms, are those who are at most risk for developing significant externalizing problem behaviors (Caldarella, et al., 2008; Walker, Cheney, Stage, Blum, & Horner, 2005; Walker, Severson, Nicholson, Kehle, Jenson, & Clark, 1994).

Another schoolwide screening approach for externalizing students is based on the Positive Behavior Supports (PBS) model developed at the University of Oregon (Lewis & Sugai, 1999). The PBS system is based on the public health model for disease which includes primary, secondary, and tertiary levels of prevention and care. The PBS model is best visualized as a triangle. The broad base (or first tier) of the triangle represents 80% of the students in the school who are successfully managed with the primary management and discipline techniques already established in the school. The second tier of the triangle represents approximately 15% of the students who are at risk for significant behavior, academic, and social problems. The top tier of the triangle represents those students (5%) who are having significant discipline problems at school. The PBS model is a primary prevention model that emphasizes positive whole school management, the establishment of expectations through universal school rules, data based decision making, and the use of functional behavior assessment.

The data based decision making of the PBS model is based on the University of Oregon's computerized School-Wide Information System (SWIS). With the SWIS system, office discipline referrals (ODRs) are entered into a computer data base. The ODR is the standard unit of measurement for discipline problems in the SWIS system. Over time, this system is capable of summarizing data on individual students, groups of students, or the whole student body. The 15% of students (Tier 2) who are at risk in the PBS triangle generally have two to five ODRs in a year, and about 5% of the students who are at most risk (Teir 3) have six or more ODRs (Scott, 2007). The at-risk students and most-at-risk students generally exhibit externalizing types of behaviors such as noncompliance, inappropriate physical contact, interrupting, etc. (Marchant, Anderson, Caldarella, Fisher, Young, & Young, 2008). Research has shown that PBS school management teams, given SWIS data on at-risk students, can reduce the overall number of ODRs in school in a year by approximately 50% with significant overall improvements in academic achievement (Scott, 2007).

Interventions for Externalizing Disorders: An Evidence Based Practice Approach

The term *evidence-based practice* (EBP) is frequently used today in relation to educational and psychosocial treatments for children and youth. Its frequency may be partially attributable to the reference 111 times to "researched based" or "research proven techniques" in the No Child Left Behind (United States Office of Education, 2002) federal legislation. However, EBP has roots that reach back to 1996 when Division 12 (Clinical Psychology) of the American Psychological Association published a state of the art summation and update of characteristics of empirically supported treatments (Chambless, Sanderson, Shoham, Johnson, Pope, Crits-Christoph, et al.,1996). Since then, EBP position papers and criteria have been published specifically for special education (Odom, Brantlinger, Gersten, Horner, Thompson, & Harris, 2005), behavior analysis (O'Donohue & Ferguson, 2006), school psychology (Stoiber & Kratochwill, 2000), and by the American Psychological Association

(APA Task Force on Evidence-Based Practice, 2006) and the U.S. Office of Education, Institute of Education Science (Coalition Board of Advisors, 2003). There have been several intervention books published that focus exclusively on evidence based treatments and interventions: *Treatments that Work with Children: Empirically supported strategies for managing childhood problems* (Christophersen & Mortweet, 2002); *Interventions: Evidence-Based Behavioral Strategies for Individual Students* (Sprick & Garrison, 2008); *School–Based Interventions for Students with Behavior Problems* (Bowen, Jenson, & Clark, 2004); and *Evidence-Based Psychotherapies for Children and Adolescents* (Kazdin & Weisz, 2003). Recently, a special edition of the *Journal of Child and Adolescent Psychology* (2008) published an update of evidence-based psychosocial treatments for all of the major disorders in children (Silverman & Hinshaw, 2008). For externalizing disorders, there are two review papers of particular interest, one an EBP review of ADHD (Pelham, & Fabiano, 2008) and a second EBP review of disruptive disorders in children (Eyberg, Nelson, & Boggs, 2008).

The basic criteria for EBP include: a series of group or single-subject designed research studies; random assignment of subjects; well defined samples; conducted in independent research settings; statistically superior treatments (e.g., large effect sizes); and the inclusion of treatment manuals (see review by Silverman & Hinshaw, 2008).

Also gaining credence as a method for indentifying EBP treatments are meta-analytic studies. Meta-analyses study a particular intervention, for a specific population, over many years (e.g., 10 years) and yield effect sizes which are easily interpretable and show a magnitude of effect that is not based on the null hypotheses or simple p values (Jenson, Clark, Kircher, & Kritjansson, 2007). The effect sizes produced by meta-analytic studies indicate the magnitude of an effect with .0 = no effect, .2 = small effect, .5 = medium effect, and .8 = a large effect size (Cohen, 1988).

In this section, EBP standards will be used to judge the effectiveness of interventions for children with externalizing disorders. When meta-analytic studies are available, they will be used along with their reported effect sizes to judge the effectiveness and magnitude of specific interventions. The focus of the interventions will not be the traditional treatments associated with ADHD, CD, or ODD, because these are well reported in the literature (Eyberg, et al, 2008; Smith et al., 2006; McMahon, et al., 2006; Pelham, & Fabiano, 2008) and in this volume. Interventions that are associated with externalizing disorders in general, and are consistent with the definition of externalizing disorders given at the beginning of this chapter, will be reported. These include interventions for noncompliance, countering the negative effects of peers in groups, supervision and monitoring, parent training, and social skills training.

Interventions for Noncompliance

Noncompliance is one of the most common behavior problems of childhood, and a leading reason for referrals for intervention and treatment (Gelfand & Drew, 2003; Kalb & Loeber, 2003; Patterson et al., 1992). It is also one of the most common problematic behaviors found across all the major externalizing conditions (e.g., ADHD, ODD, and CD; see McMahon et al., 2006; Smith, et al., 2006). As we have reported earlier, noncompliance is a core characteristic of externalizing disorders, and a kingpin behavior (Patterson, 1982; Forgatch, & DeGarmo, 2002). Improvements in noncompliance will often result in collateral improvements in other non-treated problematic behaviors (Martinez & Forgatch, 2001; Parrish, Cataldo, Kolko, & Engle, 1986; Russo, Cataldo, & Cushing, 1981; Wells, Forehand, & Griest, 1980).

Noncompliance has been defined as the refusal to initiate a requested behavior from another person (generally an adult) within a specific period of time (5 to 10 seconds) (Forehand & McMahon, 1981; Yeager & McLaughlin, 1995; Rhode et al., 2010). The exact normative rates of compliance are difficult to establish because of differences due to the age and sex of the child, clinically versus nonclinically referred children, what type of requests are given, and several other factors. However, in an early review paper, Forehand (1977) reported compliance rates for nonclinically referred children as 70% to 80%, and for clinically referred children as approximately 30% to 40%.

Noncompliance is developmental in nature, frequently starting to increase in the early preschool years and decreasing about age five (Patterson, 1976). Many parents view their toddlers in these early years as "extremely noncompliant" (Kalb & Loeber, 2003). In the Pittsburg Youth Study, noncompliance before school age was not considered to predict later poor outcomes in childhood unless it was accompanied by aggression, impulsivity, and hyperactivity (Kalb & Loeber, 2003). However, by school age, boys at age 7 with persistent noncompliance were at greater risk for developing significant

behavior problems. One study (Hämäläinen & Pulkkinen, 1996) found that noncompliance at age 8 was also correlated with aggression at age 8, and then correlated with aggression and norm-breaking at age 14. By the time a child enters school, noncompliance—especially when associated with aggression, impulsivity, and negativism—can lead to significant social and school adjustment problems. Early effective intervention is important in stemming problems that can lead to school failure, social rejection, family disruption, and delinquency.

Evidence-based interventions for problematic noncompliance can be viewed through an ABC model of antecedent control, consequence control, and approaches that include both antecedent and consequence control. The best predictor of a child's noncompliance to a request is the antecedent event occurring immediately before the child's noncompliant behavior (Williams & Forehand, 1984). This "antecedent event" is generally an adult caregiver (e.g., parent or teacher) who issues the command. The manner in which the request or command is given can affect student compliance rates by 20% to 40% (Hamlet, Axelrod, Kuerschner, 1984; Matheson & Shriver, 2005). Much of the antecedent control research for noncompliant behavior has been pioneered by Forehand and McMahon (Forehand, 1977; McMahon & Forehand, 1981). These antecedents include proximity or closeness to the child (Forehand, 1977; Kalb & Loeber, 2003); giving a direct command rather than indirect request (implied or suggested) (Elrod, 1987; Matheson & Shriver, 2005); specific rather than vague commands (Dumas & Lechowicz, 1989); making eye contact when giving the command (Hamlet et al., 1984; Kapalka, 2004); allowing enough time (e.g., 5 seconds) for compliance (Forehand, 1977; Matheson & Shriver, 2005), not interrupting the initial command in the 5-second window by repeating the command (Forehand, 1977); stating the command in a quiet and positive voice (Matheson & Shriver, 2005); giving fewer commands and waiting for compliance (Forehand, 1977); giving more positive initiation "do" commands than negative cessation "don't" commands (Neef, Shafer, Egel, Cataldo, & Parrish, 1983); not using a question formatted command (e.g., Wouldn't you like to......?) but rather a positive direct command (e.g., Please do...; Faciane, 2005; Reed, 1985); and preceding a low-probability compliance request (40% or lower) with a high-probability compliance request (70% or higher), which is referred to as behavior momentum (Mace, & Belfiore, 1990). A summary of the antecedent events associated with effective request-making is given in Table 18.2.

Some researchers have formalized the antecedent variables listed above into a two-part request with a "signal" or warning word (MacKay, McLaughlin, Kimberly, & Derby, 2001; Musser, Bray, Kehle, & Jenson, 2001; Rhode et al., 2010; Yeager & McLaughlin, 1995). The two-part request is, "Please (request behavior)," allowing a 5-second time period for the child to comply, followed by praise and attention if the child complies. If the child does not comply, the request is followed by a "You *need* to (request behavior)." The word "need" is the discriminative stimulus that if the child does not comply with the original request, then a reductive consequence will follow. Reductive consequences have included timeout, loss of a favored toy, or loss of points (MacKay, et al., 2001; Muesser, et al., 2001; Rhode et al., 2010, Yeager & McLaughlin, 1995). This type of two-part request has been termed *precision requests,* and has been shown to improve compliance rates from baselines of approximately 40% to near average levels of compliance of 70% to 80% (MacKay, et al., 2001; Muesser, et al., 2001; Rhode et al., 2010; Yeager & McLaughlin,

Table 18.2   Strategies for improving compliance

Antecedent strategies

Do not use a question format for a request

Give time for compliance (approximately 3 to 5 seconds)

Get close to the child when giving the request (approximately 3 feet)

Use the child's name when giving a request

Do not give repeated commands (approximately 2 commands)

Look the child in the eye when you give a request

Give a direct request rather than an indirect command (i.e., a suggestion)

Give a clear and specific request rather then a vague request

Give the request in a quiet, positive voice

Give more "Do" requests rather than "Don't" requests

Give high probability compliance request immediately before a low probability request

Socially reward the child for following the request

1995). Additional compliance training programs will be described later in this chapter. Although maximizing antecedent control for improvements in noncompliance is significant, it is also critically important to socially reward the compliance with positive adult attention. Some researchers have estimated that positive social reinforcement from adults for compliance in externalizing students is near chance (Van Acker, Grant, & Henry, 1996) or zero levels (Gunter & Shores, 1994). If only antecedent control such as using precision commands does not also include positive social reinforcement, compliance rates will eventually drop (Rhode et al., 2010). Other treatment approaches utilizing antecedent control combined with parent training will be covered later in this chapter.

Interventions for Inappropriate Peer Influences in Group Settings

As reviewed earlier in this chapter, research has shown (Arnold & Hughes, 1999; Dishion et al., 1999) that grouping externalizing students together in instructional or treatment groups can lead to negative peer deviancy training. In essence, peers in these groups teach and reinforce deviant forms of behavior to each other. With this deviancy training, "adolescents derive meaning and values from the deviancy training process that provides the cognitive basis for motivation to commit delinquent acts in the future…" (Dishion et al., 1999, p. 762). It is estimated (Buehler, Patterson, & Furiness, 1966) that in institutional settings, the peer reinforcement to adult reinforcement rate is 9:1, indicating strong peer influence and an undermining of adult control. When antisocial youth are paired in groups, the training sequence involves the rule-breaking talk of one youth, which is followed by reinforcing laughter from another youth, and then an escalation in antisocial behavior for that pair of youth and others in the group (Dishion, Spracklen, Andrews, & Patterson, 1996). If behavioral control is lost in a group setting, with rule breaking and peer reinforcement for deviant behavior, then the intended purpose of instruction or treatment in the group is defeated.

Several variables can mediate this negative peer influence (Arnold & Hughes, 1999; Dishion et al., 1999). Age of the student is one variable, with younger students showing less of a negative peer effect. The nonhomogeneous grouping of youth, where externalizing youth are mixed with prosocial youth can have a dampening effect on inappropriate peer influences. However mixing prosocial and externalizing youth may be an unrealistic procedure.

Behavior management procedures that control group behavior may have a distinct advantage when the grouping of externalizing students is necessary. A group contingency is a system that delivers an incentive (a reward or reductive consequence) to the entire group based on the behavior of the individuals in that group (Jenson & Reavis, 1996). Evidence-based practice meta-analytic research has shown that group contingencies are the most effective intervention in reducing disruptive behavior in public education settings (Stage & Quiroz, 1997). Group contingencies are particularly effective when there is both overt and covert peer support for inappropriate behavior, and there is a need to foster positive peer cooperation (Morgan & Jenson, 1989).

The effectiveness of group contingencies has been shown to be effective in the control of disruptive classroom behavior (Theodore, Bray, Kehle, & Jenson, 2001), problematic bus riding behavior (Greene, Bailey, & Barber, 1981), inappropriate behavior in lunchroom settings (Fabiano, Pelham, Karmazin, Kreher, Panahon, & Carlson, 2008), disruptive library behavior (Fishbein & Wasik, 1981), class transition times (Campbell & Skinner, 2004), swearing behavior (Kazdin, 2005), and several other areas. There are basically three types of group contingencies: dependent, independent, and interdependent (Litow & Pumroy, 1975). In a dependent group contingency, the whole group's incentive is based on the performance or behavior of one (or a few) individual(s). This is the most pressuring type of group contingency, and adverse effects can occur if the identity of the individual is known. It should be used with extreme caution or not at all with externalizing students. In an independent group contingency, each member of the group who meets a preset criteria is rewarded. The incentive is based on each student's own performance in meeting the criteria. All the students meeting the criteria are rewarded; all the students that do not meet the standard are not rewarded. In an interdependent group contingency, the students in the group receive an incentive dependent upon the behavior or performance of the whole group. The interdependent group contingency is possibly the most powerful in managing inappropriate peer reinforcement and behaviors, because all students are dependent upon each other.

One of the best known and most studied group contingencies is the Good Behavior Game developed by Barrish, Saunders, and Wolf (1969). The Good Behavior Game utilizes team cooperation, peer influ-

ence, and an interdependent group contingency to increase rule following and decrease disruptive behaviors. It is especially effective in reducing inappropriate peer reinforcement for deviant behavior. With the Good Behavior Game, the group is split into teams which compete against themselves or a preset criterion for a reward. In the original study, conducted in a classroom of disruptive students, the team with the lowest number of behavioral infractions (i.e., rule-breaking) or less than 5 rule infractions won a group incentive. In this way, one team could win (i.e., lowest rule infractions) or all the teams could win (i.e., each team with less than 5 infractions). The Good Behavior Game has been well researched in a variety of settings, and its effectiveness documented over a 33-year period of time (Tingstrom, Sterling-Turner, & Wilczynski, 2006). It is especially effective in reducing subtle peer reinforcement for inappropriate and deviant behaviors. As in the original study (Barrish et al., 1969), if a particularly difficult peer refuses to participate and continues to disrupt, that individual is placed on a team by himself.

The randomized group contingency is a new form of group contingency that has been shown to be especially effective in controlling peer deviant behavior in group settings (Coogan, Kehle, Bray, & Chafouleas, 2007). With the mixed group contingency, the type of group contingency (i.e., dependent, independent, or interdependent), the type of problem behavior, the criteria for reinforcement, and the reinforcement to be earned can be all randomized. For example, Kelshaw-Levering, Sterling-Turner, Henry, and Skinner (2000) used a mixed group contingency with a veteran second grade teacher to control her disruptive classroom. The teacher had 27 years of teaching experience and described the class as "the worst class she has ever taught." The mixed group contingency utilized four jars that were placed on the teacher's desk. The first jar contained slips of papers labeled *Behaviors*, which specified the behaviors (e.g., off-task) and criteria that were to be judged for compliance. The second jar was labeled the *Contingency Jar*, with slips of paper with the terms *Whole Class* or *Individual Name*. The third jar was labeled *Names*, and contained all the students' names in the classroom. The fourth jar was labeled *Reinforcers* which contained slips of paper with various reinforcers that could be earned.

Baseline observations in the classroom had shown that disruptive behaviors occurred 60 times during a 75-minute block of time (almost one per minute). The day was divided into three evaluation periods. At the end of an evaluation period a slip was drawn from the Behavior jar, which stated the behavior and criteria to be evaluated. Then a slip was drawn from the second Contingency jar, either a whole class slip or an individual student slip. If it was an individual student slip, then a student's name was drawn from the third jar, Names. That student's performance was then compared to the behavior and criteria selected from the Behavior jar. If the randomly selected slip from the Contingency jar was *Whole Class*, then the whole class' performance was compared for the behavior selected from the Behavior jar. If the criteria were met (either by the whole class, or by an individual student, depending on the contingency), a reinforcer was randomly selected from the fourth Reinforcer jar for the whole class. After using this procedure, disruptive behaviors decreased dramatically from approximately 40% of the measured intervals in the baseline to less than 4% of the intervals in treatment.

In a similar study, Theordore et al., (2001) used a randomized group contingency to control the disruptive behavior of five inner city high school students in a self-contained classroom for students with severe emotional disturbance. The randomized group contingency reduced overall disruptive behavior in this classroom from an average of 42% of the baseline intervals to just 4% of the treatment phase intervals. Both of these studies show that a random mixed group contingency is very effective in reducing disruptive behaviors that are reinforced by deviant peers.

Supervision and Monitoring Externalizing Students

The importance of supervising and monitoring externalizing students has been highlighted earlier in this chapter. Externalizing students left unmonitored often develop problem behaviors, especially if the environment is high risk and populated with deviant peers. The areas that are most problematic in schools include transitions in the hallways, bunching of students near lockers, bathrooms, and stairwells, transition to school, and other areas where students can be easily unmonitored. One of the most high-risk times for students is the period of time right after school, before they reach home (Pettit, Laird, Dodge, & Bates, 1997). It is difficult for school psychologists to monitor all the high-risk areas in a school. However, teachers can be urged to stand by their doors during class transitions, and staff can be assigned times to randomly enter bath-

rooms, to walk in the halls, or stand at the top of stairwells. For externalizing students, there are also researched, structured supervision programs that are positive and effective in monitoring students' high-risk behaviors.

The Check and Connect program was developed at the University of Minnesota to monitor and assist high-risk students (Anderson, Christenson, Sinclair, & Lehr, 2004; Christenson, Sinclair, Thurlow, & Evelo, 1999). The program has two basic components. The *Check* component is a continuous assessment of a student's progress through a set of indicators that includes school attendance, grades, credits, disciplinary problems, and suspensions. The *Connect* component is a regular meeting (at least once a month, and often weekly) with an appointed monitor. During the Connect meeting, the mentor provides social skills instruction, academic support (homework assistance and tutoring), recreational and community service opportunities, and mediation with other school staff on the student's behalf. The Check and Connect program emphasizes the continuous monitoring of at-risk students, and the relationship between the student and appointed mentor. The Check and Connect program has been extensively researched and recognized by the U.S. Office of Education What Works Clearing House (2006) as effective in helping students stay in school and make meaningful academic progress. Todd, Campbell, Meyer, and Horner (2008) have recently reported the effectiveness of the Check and Connect program in significantly lowering problem behaviors in four elementary schools in Oregon.

Another monitoring program is the Behavior Education Program (BEP; Crone, Horner, & Hawken, 2004) developed at the University of Oregon. The BEP is a check-in and check-out program for high-risk students who have received three to five office referrals for discipline problems in one academic year. The BEP program is commonly used with such behaviors as noncompliance, disruptive behavior, inappropriate language, and classroom talk-outs.

With the BEP, a student checks in with a supervising adult at the beginning of the school day and checks out again at the ending of the day. The program emphasizes that the adult checking the student in and out should be positive, supportive, and a person the student trusts. The student initially develops a BEP contract with the supervising adult that lists the behaviors that will be tracked and monitored across the day. During this contracting process, the student also negotiates a list of rewards he can earn by making progress. At the morning check-in, the student picks up his Daily Progress Report (DPR) card with a list of behaviors (e.g., follows directions, keeps hands and feet to self) or academic tasks (e.g., completing work, being prepared). The student then carries the (DPR) card across the day, and his progress is monitored and rated by his teachers. At the end of the day the DPR card is rated by the supervising adult and feedback is given, and the student's progress is graphed. The student has a chance to earn points that are later exchanged for back-up reinforcers.

Over time, the supervising adult enters the student's DPR ratings into a spreadsheet to monitor student progress. The student's progress is regularly monitored by the school's BEP team. If problems occur, or a student does not seem to be making progress, the school's BEP team can suggest program adjustments or conduct a functional behavior assessment (FBA) and develop a formal Behavior Support Plan. Parents are also given an orientation to the BEP program, and receive copies of the DPR card.

The research on the BEP program has documented its effectiveness in reducing problem behaviors with reductions of approximately 50% in office disciplinary referrals (Fairbanks, Sugai, Guardino, & Lathrop, 2007; Filter, McKenna, Benedict, Horner, Todd, & Watson, 2007; Hawken, MacLeod, & Rawlings, 2007). The program is designed for students who are at risk and externalizers, but not for the most extreme violent or destructive students.

Social Skills Training for Externalizing Students

Social skills deficits are a defining deficit of externalizing students. These students are commonly shunned by other youth, and seek other externalizing students for social affiliation (Gresham, 1998; Patterson et al., 1992). These social problems may be a function of not knowing how to perform essential social skills (i.e., a deficit) or performance problems (i.e., knowing how to perform the skill, but not doing so; Gresham, 1986; Gresham, Sugai, & Horner, 2001). Performance problems may be a function of anxiety in performing the skill, negative reactions from other deviant youth, or the inability to generalize the skill from the training environment to actual social situations. Performance problems can undermine the generalization of newly learned social skills from the training environment to the general social environment of the externalizing youth.

There are several different types of social skills training programs which focus on teaching social skills for general social interaction skills, making friends, and using problem solving in social situations. These programs include Skill Streaming the Elementary School Child (McGinnis & Goldstein, 1997), The Prepare Curriculum (Goldstein, 1988), The ASSET Program (Hazel, Bragg, Schumaker, Sherman, & Sheldon-Wildgen, 1981), The ACCEPTS Program: A Curriculum for Children's Effective Peer and Teacher Skills (Walker, McConnell, Holmes, Todis, Walker, & Golden, 1983), and The Tough Kid Social Skills Program (Sheridan, 1995). These general social skills programs are frequently standalone programs, where students are "pulled out" of their regular school activities and placed in a special social skill training group for instruction. This instruction generally includes a rationale for using the social skill, task analysis teaching of the steps involved in the skill, demonstration of the skill through modeling, role playing the skill, and coaching of the skill (Walker, Ramsey, & Gresham, 2004). Some programs include behavior management strategies, homework, and generalization techniques.

The overall effectiveness of general social skills programs for externalizing youth is mixed. Several meta-analytic studies have shown that general social skills programs are ineffectual, with limited supporting research (Forness & Kavale, 1996; Quinn, Kavale, Mathur, Rutherford, & Forness, 1999; Smith & Travis, 2001). The externalizing youth may learn the skills in an instructional environment, but fail to use them in social situations where they are needed. DuPaul and Eckert (1994) have described this phenomena as "the effects of social skills curricula: now you see them and now you don't" (p. 13). DuPaul and Eckert (1994) suggest that the problem of not using newly learned social skills in the general social environment is a "generalization" problem, and gives several suggestions (e.g., train sufficient exemplars, modify consequences, use self-mediated stimuli) to improve generalization. Other researchers (Cook, Gresham, Kern, Barreas, Thornton, & Crews, 2008), in a reanalysis of the meta-analytic research on social skills training for secondary students, have reported more promising results. However, even in this extensive reanalysis of the meta-analytic research, the effect size for treatment effectiveness for general social skills programs is still only a modest .32.

Other specialized social skills programs involve a more comprehensive training program that includes training the externalizing students, their parents, and their teachers. The Incredible Years Parents, Teachers, and Children Training Series (http://www.incredibleyears.com) is one such program (Webster-Stratton & Reid, 2003). This program has an extensive curriculum, video modeling tapes, behavior management, and dinosaur puppets for instruction of toddlers through elementary students diagnosed with ADHD, CD, or ODD. The evaluation of the Incredible Years social skills program (i.e., Dino Dinosaurs) has been extensively researched, with significant reductions in aggression at school and home (Webster-Stratton & Reid, 2003). Another program is the Problem-Solving Skills Training (PSST; Kazdin, 2003), which focuses on teaching problem-solving skills for real-life social problems. The model is based on an information processing model that includes problem identification, generating solutions, making a decision, and evaluating the outcome. This program also includes a parent training component and therapeutically planned activities outside the training session, called "super solvers," for practice and generalization of the problem-solving skills. The PSST has been evaluated compared to placebo controls, a supportive relationship therapy group, and client-centered relationship therapy (Kazdin, Bass, Siegel, & Thomas, 1989; Kazdin, Esveldt-Dawson, French, & Unis, 1987). The PSST approach was significantly superior to the supportive relationship and client-centered relationship therapy groups, as measured by CBCL and the TRF, with maintenance at a one-year follow-up evaluation.

There are specialized social skills training programs that focus on anger management and bullying. These programs are multi-component programs that can include self-management procedures, direct interventions, and prevention components.

Anger Coping Training (Lochman, Barry, & Pardini, 2003) is designed as a social information processing intervention for externalizing elementary children. In the program, children discuss anger-based social encounters with peers, the anger-provoking cues, and the possible motives of the peers. The children are taught cognitive-behavioral techniques to reduce their anger, including anger reducing self-talk, problem solving, negotiation, and other skills. In addition to the school based training program, the Anger Coping Training program also includes a parent training component. Lochman and Wells (2003) have shown that the Anger Control Training leads to a reduction in substance abuse, and improved children's social competence when compared to a no-treatment control group. A similar program is Anger Replacement Training (ART; Goldstein, Glick, Reiner, Zimmerman, Coultry, & Gold, 1987). ART is a multi-component program for externalizing adolescents that involves teaching moral reasoning, basic social skills training, self-coaching, and an ABC-functional assessment model of dealing with anger. The student learns the antecedent cues for their anger (triggers), stress reduction, and anger control strategies, and maintains a Hassle Log of their difficult anger interactions with adults and peers. The effectiveness research on ART has shown improvements in global ratings of anger, and reductions in arrests (Goldstein & Glick, 1994). However, in residential treatment center evaluation of Aggression Replacement Training, there was a reported improvement of the knowledge in how to manage anger, but no significant changes in overt behavior of externalizing adolescents (Coleman, Pfeiffer, & Okland, 1991). In an effort to determine the overall effectiveness of evaluation of cognitive-behavioral interventions for anger management, a meta-analysis was conducted by Sukhodolsky, Kassinove, and Gorman in 2004. This included 51 intervention studies, and yielded only a medium magnitude effect size of .67.

Anit-bullying programs can be viewed as a specialized social skills program to reduce bullying behaviors, primarily from externalizing students. Bullying is often defined as an "intent to do harm, the repeated aspect of the harmful acts, and the power imbalance between bully and victim" (Merrell, Gueldner, Ross, & Isava, 2008, p. 26).

The basic focus of many anti-bullying programs is at the whole-school level, by raising awareness of bullying behavior for students and staff. Other components can include special training for victims, and interventions for identified bullies. The Olweus Bully Prevention Program (Olweus, 1993) from Norway is possibly the best researched anti-bullying program. This program is divided into core components which include several school-level anti-bullying components (e.g., develop schoolwide rules against bullying, form of a Bully Prevention Coordinating Committee, and develop specific consequences for bullying); a classroom-level component (e.g., classroom training to increase knowledge of bullying and empathy for victims, informational meetings with parents); and an individual-level component (e.g., interventions for children who bully and their victims, and discussions with parents of involved students). (See www.clemson.edu/olweus/). This program has been evaluated in several large Norwegian studies, including 2,500 children grades 4–7 in Norway (Olweus, 1991) and in the United

States, including 18 middle schools in South Carolina (Limber, 2004) and 12 elementary schools in Philadelphia (Black, 2003). Reductions in bullying by student self-reports in these studies are approximately 50%. Other bullying programs have been developed in the United States, such as Bully-Proofing Your School (Garrity, Jens, Porter, Sager, Short-Camilli, 1993), the Expect- Respect Program (Whitaker, Rosenbluth, Valle, & Sanchez, 2003), and the Tough Kid Bully Blockers program (Bowen, Ashcraft, Jenson, & Rhode, 2008).

The evidence-based practice research on anti-bullying programs is mixed. One problem with the anti-bullying programs is that the outcome data is primarily based on student and teacher self-reports. Few evaluation studies have actually utilized outcome measures based on behavioral observations, or reductions in disciplinary office referrals for bullying. Smith, Schneider, Smith, and Anaiadou (2004) conducted a meta-analysis of 14 studies and concluded, "the majority of programs evaluated to date have yielded nonsignificant outcomes on measures of self-report victimization" (p. 547). Ferguson, Miguel, Kilburn, and Sanchez (2007) conducted a meta-analysis of 45 anti-bullying studies, reaching the similar conclusion that anti-bullying programs are not practically effective in reducing bullying behavior or violence in the schools. In a third meta-analysis of 16 anti-bullying programs over a 25-year period based on 15,386 students K–12 grades, Merrill et al. (2008) found that only one-third of the effect sizes reflected meaningful and clinically important effects. The majority of effect sizes showed no meaningful positive effects. The authors concluded that bullying programs "are more likely to influence knowledge, attitudes, and self-perception rather than actual bullying behaviors" (p. 26).

Parent Training for Externalizing Students

Behavioral parent training is also known by several other names, such as behavioral family therapy (Griest & Wells, 1983), parent-interaction therapy (Bell & Eyberg, 2002), or parent management training (Patterson, Reid, Jones, & Conger, 1975). Essentially, these programs focus on teaching parents needed skills to effectively manage their child's problem behaviors. These parent programs are not "talk therapy" or communication based programs; rather, they teach specific skills to manage misbehavior.

There are several common skills that are included in most behavior parent training programs. These skills generally involve teaching parents to specifically define and pinpoint target behaviors to be

changed, focusing on positive reinforcement and effective praise; establishing home rules, learning to give effective commands, and learning to effectively use reductive consequences such as timeout and response cost for problem behaviors (Maughan, 2004). Some parent training programs (Jenson, Rhode, & Hepworth, 2003; Patterson, 1974) work exclusively by training the parents without the child being present. The parents learn and practice the skills with the therapist, and then apply the techniques as homework assignments with their child. Other programs (Forehand & McMahon, 1981; 2003; Hanf, 1969) train parents with the child present under controlled clinic conditions, such as one-way mirror training rooms and radio "bug in the ear" with real-time instructions to the parents given by an observing therapist. Both approaches have proven effective in managing externalizing students (McMahon et al., 2006; Eyberg, et al., 2008).

Patterson (1974; 1982) introduced the Parent Management Training Oregon Model to train parents to manage their externalizing children who had been referred for treatment from juvenile courts, schools, and mental health centers. Patterson et al. (1973) used programmed teaching manuals, *Living with Children: New Methods for Parents and Teachers* (Patterson & Gullion, 1968), or *Families: Applications of Social Learning to Family Life* (Patterson, 1971), to train parents to pinpoint behaviors, construct behavioral contracts, and apply contingencies for problem behaviors. In one study with 27 externalizing boys (Patterson, 1974), the program significantly reduced the frequency of deviant behaviors (approximately by 50%) for 2 out of 3 boys, with a time investment of 31.4 hours of training and 1.9 hours for a follow-up booster session.

Forehand and McMahon (1981) developed a treatment model, Helping the Noncompliant Child (Forehand and McMahon, 2003), that was based on the earlier parent training model of Hanf (1969; 1970). This model consists of two phases. In the first phase (differential attention), the parent is trained to break out of the coercive cycle by increasing positive attention to the child's appropriate behaviors while ignoring inappropriate behaviors. The parent learns to positively describe the child's behavior as they play a game in a controlled therapy room with "bug in the ear" instructions from a therapist. In the second phase of the intervention (compliance training), the parent is trained to give precise and direct commands (Alpha Commands) to the child, and refrain from imprecise and vague commands (Beta Commands). If the child complies with the parental command, he or she is socially rewarded and praised. If the child is noncompliant, the parent learns to effectively use reductive consequences such as a timeout procedure. The effectiveness of the Forehand and McMahon (2003) model has been documented and extensively reviewed (Eyberg, et al., 2008; McMahon, et al., 2006). The effects of significantly reduced deviant behaviors generalize over time, and appear independent of the families' socioeconomic levels.

Other training programs for parents of externalizing children appear equally effective, with reductions in problematic behavior for Parent-Child Interaction Therapy (Brinkmeyer & Eyberg, 2003), the Incredible Years Program (Webster-Stratton, 1984), and the Tough Kid Parent Training Program (Jenson, Rhode, & Hepworth, 2003; Kuhn, 2004). The evidence-based practice research for the effectiveness of parent training has been established (Eyberg, et al., 2008). Two meta-analytic studies have also validated the effectiveness of parent training. Serketch & Dumas (1996) analyzed 26 behavioral parent training studies for children with antisocial behaviors (e.g., aggression, temper tantrums, and noncompliance). ADHD children were excluded from this study. The overall effect sizes for the reduction of externalizing behaviors were large (i.e., parent report, .84, independent observer, .85, and teacher report, .73). In essence, 80% of the children improved when their parents were trained. Maughan, Christensen, Jenson, Olympia, and Clark (2005) conducted a meta-analysis of 79 studies on parent training for externalizing children. This study did include ADHD children along with other externalizing children. For group designed research studies (between- and within-group), the effect sizes for reduction of externalizing behaviors ranged between .30 and :69, indicating that 62% and 76% of children whose parent(s) had received training did better than nontreated children. For single subject design studies, the effect size was very large, 1.56, indicating the children of trained parents were 95% better than nontreated children. The differences in meta-analytic studies and effect sizes are probably due to the selection of the externalizing children (i.e., exclusion or not of ADHD), the type of research designs (i.e., between group, within group, or single subject design), and whether the effect sizes were weighted for sample size. From the meta-analytic evaluation studies, it appears that training the parents of externalizing children is an effective intervention. The studies have shown significant

reductions in behavioral excesses and disruptive behavior such as noncompliance, and improvement in positive family interactions and reductions in parent stress (Kuhn, 2004; Maughum et al., 2005).

Conclusions

Externalizing disorders represent one of the largest groups of children and adolescents referred for clinical and educational services. This group commonly includes children labeled as AttentionDeficit/ Hyperactivity Disorder (ADHD), Conduct Disorder (CD), Oppositional Defiant Disorder (ODD), Severely Emotionally Disturbed (SED), and Behavior Disordered (BD). Primarily, these children have behaviors that are directed outward (externally) and affect others such as teachers, adult caretakers, and peers. In this chapter, we have chosen to define an externalizing disorder as a condition with behavioral excesses and behavioral deficits. The behavioral excesses include several behaviors such as noncompliance, aggression, impulsivity, arguing, tantrumming, property destruction, and bullying. The behavioral deficits include such areas as lack of self-control, poor social skills, and deficits in academic skills and school related behaviors. We have emphasized research that shows noncompliance as one of the defining characteristics of externalizing disorders. It is a "kingpin" behavior that is implicated in almost all the other behavior excesses, such as arguing, aggression, and tantrumming. It is also implicated in the causation of many of the behavioral deficits in the academic and social behavior of externalizing children. Research has shown that treatments that lead to significant reductions in noncompliance, collaterally lead to improvements in untreated externalizing behavioral excesses and behavioral deficits.

We have reviewed the literature for externalizing disorders, and have stressed several points about this disorder. First, externalizing disorders have multiple causes that include biological, familial, and environmental factors. The biological factors tend to result in a general vulnerability that put a child at risk for developing externalizing problems. Other factors include the development of the coercive cycle in families, which then leads to the development of more robust externalizing behaviors. This aversive cycle within a family negatively reinforces and shapes externalizing behaviors such as noncompliance and aggression. The child then learns and transfers coercive behaviors to other environments, including school and neighborhood settings. Academic failure and rejection by peers often compounds the problems of the externalizing child. This type of externalizing disorder is considered a "life path" externalizing disorder that starts early in a child's life and then continues throughout adolescence and adulthood, as opposed to an "adolescent path" externalizing disorder that is characterized by a non-affected childhood and an onset in adolescence.

Research has shown for the "life path" externalizing disorder that early in childhood these behaviors are overt (e.g., aggression, opposition, defiance) and easily observed. However, as the child ages and enters adolescence they change into more covert behaviors (e.g., stealing, running away, substance abuse), which are more clandestine in nature. For the "adolescent path" there is a less problematic childhood, which is followed by antisocial behaviors developing in adolescence.

There are other important environmental factors that contribute to externalizing behavior problems. One area of particular concern is the influence of peers in high-risk unsupervised environments. Since externalizing children are commonly shunned and excluded by non-affected peers, they frequently seek other antisocial children for peer associations. These antisocial peers provide deviancy training, and directly reward antisocial behavior in each other. Grouping externalizing students for treatment or instruction without effective behavioral control can exacerbate externalizing problem behaviors.

Successful treatment approaches for children with externalizing disorders must be comprehensive to be successful. By comprehensive we mean that the treatment must successfully manage behavioral excesses and remediate behavioral deficits. We have limited our discussion in this chapter to only evidence-based treatments that can be commonly used with externalizing disorders. Some of the most promising treatments focus on reducing noncompliance, utilizing antecedent interventions such as precision requests. Other treatments emphasize increasing the supervision of externalizing disordered children, such as check-in and check-out monitoring programs. Still other interventions focus on peer management, especially when externalizing students are put into groups for instruction and treatment. Group contingencies that utilize randomized criteria and consequences have been notably successful in reducing deviant and disruptive behaviors in peers when they are grouped.

Some promising approaches such as social skills training, anger management, and bully prevention programs, have only been moderately successful. This is especially true of "pull out" training programs, where children are pulled out of their everyday environments and placed in special groups for social skills training. If social skills training programs are to be successful, then they must include systematic generalization procedures to ensure transfer of the skills to the child's natural environment.

Possibly one of the most successful interventions for externalizing problems is training parents to use specialized behavior management techniques. These techniques include pinpointing and targeting specific behaviors for change, increasing reinforcement and rewards for appropriate behaviors, leaning antecedent control techniques such as making effective requests, and designing consequences for problem behaviors. Research has shown that this type of parent training is effective in reducing such problems as noncompliance and aggression, while improving social behaviors in externalizing children. Parent training is cost effective, focuses on the family, and emphasizes the development of appropriate behaviors and social skills.

References

Abikoff, H., & Gittelman, R. (1985). Classification observation code: A modification of the Stoney Brook code. *Psychopharmacology Bulletin, 21,* 901–909.

Achenbach, T. M. & Rescorla, L. A. (2001). *Manual for the ASEBA school-age forms & profiles.* Burlington, VT: University of Vermont.

Alberto, P. A., & Troutman, A. C. (2006). *Applied behavior analysis for teachers* (7th ed.). Upper Saddle River, NJ: Prentice-Hall.

Alessi, G. J. (*1980*). Behavioral *observation* for the school psychologist: Responsive-discrepancy model. *School Psychology Review, 9*(1), 31–45.

Amato, P. R. (2001). Children and divorce in the 1990s: An update of the Amato and Keith (1991) meta-analysis. *Journal of Family Psychology, 15,* 355–370.

Amato, P. R., & Keith, B. (1991). Parental divorce and the well-being of children: A meta-analysis. *Psychological Bulletin,110,* 26–46.

American Psychiatric Association (2000). *Diagnostic and statistical manual of mental disorders–text revision.* Washington DC: Author.

Anderson, A. R., Christenson, S. L., Sinclair, M. F., & Lehr, C. A. (2004). Check & Connect: The importance of relationships for promoting engagement with school. *Journal of School Psychology, 42,* 95–113.

Arnold, M. E. & Hughes, J. N. (1999). First do no harm – adverse effects of grouping deviant youth for skills training, *Journal of School Psychology, 37,* 99–115.

Atkins, M. S., Osborne, M., Bennett, D., Hess, L., Halperin, J. (2001) Children's competitive peer aggression during reward and punishment. *Aggressive Behavior, 27,* 1–13.

Baker, L. A., Bezdjian, S., & Raine, A. (2006). Behavioral genetics: The science of antisocial behavior. *Law Contemporary Problems, 69,* 7–46.

Barkley, R. A. (1996). Attention-deficit/hyperactivity disorder. In E. J. Mash & R. A. Barkley (Eds.) *Childhood psychopathology* (pp. 63–112). New York: Guildford Press.

Barriga, A. Q., Doran, J. W., Newell, S. B., Morrison, E. M., Barbetti, V., & Robbins, B. D. (2002). Relationships between problem behaviors and academic achievement in adolescents. *Journal of Emotional and Behavioral Disorders, 10*, 233–240.

Barrish, H., Saunders, M., & Wolf, M. M. (1969). Good behavior game: Effects of individual contingencies for group consequences on disruptive behavior in a classroom. *Journal of Applied Behavior Analysis, 2*, 119–124.

Beaver, K. M., Wright, J. P., Delisi, M., Walsh, A., Vaughn, M. G., Boisvert, D., & Vaske, J. (2007). A gene x gene interaction between DRD2 and DRD4 is associated with conduct disorder and antisocial behavior in males. *Behavior and Brain Function, 3*, 30.

Bell, S., & Eyberg, S. M. (2002). Parent–child interaction therapy. In L. VanderCreek, S. Knapp, & T. L. Jackson (Eds.), *Innovations in clinical practice: A source book.* (Vol. 20, pp. 57–74). Sarasota, FL: Professional Resource Press.

Berdan, L. E., Keane, S. P., & Calkins, S. D. (2008). Temperament and externalizing behavior: Social preference and perceived acceptance as protective factors. *Developmental Psychology, 44*, 957–968.

Black, S. (2003). An ongoing evaluation of the bullying prevention program in Philadelphia schools: *Student survey and student observation data.* Paper presented at Centers for Disease Control's Safety in Numbers Conference, Atlanta, GA.

Bowen, J., Ashcraft, P., Jenson, W. R., & Rhode, G. (2008). *Tough Kid bully blockers program.* Eugene, OR: Pacific Northwest Publishing.

Bowen, J., Jenson, W. R., & Clark, E. (2004). *School–Based Interventions for Students with Behavior Problems.* New York, Kluwer Academic/Plenum Publishers.

Brinkmeyer, M. Y., & Eyberg, S. M. (2003). Parent–child interaction therapy for oppositional children. In A. E. Kazdin & J. R. Weisz (Eds.), *Evidence-based psychotherapies for children and adolescents* (pp. 204–223). New York: Guilford Press.

Buehler, R. E., Patterson, G. R., & Furiness, J. M. (1966). The reinforcement of behavior in institutional settings. *Behavior Research and Therapy, 4*, 157–167.

Burke, J. D., Loeber, R., & Birmaher, B. (2002). Oppositional defiant disorder and conduct disorder: A review of the past 10 years, Part II. *Journal of the American Academy of Child Psychiatry, 41*, 1275–1293.

Caldarella, P., Young, E. L., Richardson, M. J., Young, B. J., & Young K. R. (2008). Validation of the systematic screening for behavior disorders in middle and junior high school. *Journal of Emotional and Behavioral Disorders, 16*, 105–117.

Campbell, S., & Skinner, S. H. (2004). Combining explicit timing with an interdependent group contingency program to decrease transition times: An investigation of the timely transition game. *Journal of Applied School Psychology, 20*, 11–27.

Capaldi, D. M., DeGarmo, D. S., Patterson, G. R., & Forgatch, M. S. (2002). Contextual risk across the early life span and association with antisocial behavior. In J. B. Reid & G. R. Patterson & J. Snyder (Eds.), *Antisocial behavior in children and adolescents: A developmental analysis and model for intervention* (pp. 123–145). Washington DC: American Psychological Association.

Carey, W. B. (1998). Temperament and behavior problems in the classroom. *School Psychology Review, 27*, 551–563.

Chamberlain, P., Reid, J. B., Ray, J., Capaldi, D. M., & Fisher, P. (1997). DSM-IV review for Parent Inadequate Discipline (PID). In T. A. Widiger, A. J. Frances, H. A. Pincus, R. Ross, M. B. First, & W. Davis (Eds.), *DSM-IV sourcebook* (Vol. 3., 569–629). Washington, DC: American Psychiatric Association.

Chambless, D. L., Sanderson, W. C., Shoham, V., Johnson, S. B., Pope, K. S., Crits-Christoph, P. et al., (1996). An update on empirically validated therapies. *The Clinical Psychologist, 49*, 5–18.

Chess, S., & Thomas, A. (1984). *Origins & evolution of behavior disorders.* New York: Brunner/Mazel.

Christenson, S. L., Sinclair, M. F., Thurlow, M. L., & Evelo, D. (1999). Promoting student engagement with school using the Check & Connect model. *Australian Journal of Guidance & Counseling, 9*, 169–184.

Christophersen, E. R. & Mortweet, S. L. (2002). *Treatments that work with children: Empirically supported strategies for managing childhood problems.* Washington, DC: American Psychological Association.

Cohen, J. (1988). *Statistical power analysis for the behavioral sciences* (2nd ed.). Hillsdale, NJ: Lawrence Earlbaum Associates.

Coie, J. D., & Kupersmidt, J. B. (1983). A behavioral analysis of emerging social status in boys' groups. *Child Development, 54*, 1400–1416.

Coleman, M. Pfeiffer, S. & Okland, T. (1991). *Aggression replacement training with behavior disordered adolescents.* Unpublished manuscript, University of Texas, Austin.

Conners, K. (1997). *Conners' revised rating scales manual.* North Tonawand, NY: Multi-Health Systems.

Coogan, B. A., Kehle, T. J., Bray, M. A., & Chafouleas, S. M. (2007). Group contingencies, randomization of reinforcers, and criteria for reinforcement, self-monitoring, and peer feedback on reducing inappropriate classroom behaviors. *School Psychology Quarterly, 22*, 540–556.

Cook, C. R., Gresham, F. M., Kern, L., Barreras, R. B., Thorton, S., & Crews, S. D. (2008). Social skills training for secondary students with emotional and/or behavioral disorders. *Journal of Emotional and Behavioral Disorders, 16*, 131–144.

Crone, D. A., Horner, R. H., & Hawken, L. S. (2004). *Responding to problem behavior in schools: The behavior education program.* New York: Guilford Press.

Cummings, E.M. & Davies, P.T. (1994). Maternal depression and child development. *Journal of Child Psychology and Psychiatry, 35*, 73–112.

DeVito, C., & Hopkins, J. (2001). Attachment, parenting, and marital dissatisfaction as predictors of disruptive behavior in preschoolers. *Developmental Psychopathology, 13*, 215–231.

Dick, D. M. (2007). Identification of genes influencing a spectrum of externalizing psychopathology, *Current Directions in Psychological Science, 16*, 331–335.

Dishion, T. J. (1990). The peer context of troublesome child and adolescent behavior. In P. Leone (Ed.). *Understanding troubled and troublesome youth* (pp. 128–153). Beverly Hills, CA: Sage.

Dishion, T. J., McCord, J., & Poulin, K. (1999). When interventions harm: Peer groups and problem behavior. *American Psychologist, 54*, 755–764.

Dishion, T. J., Spracklen, K. M., Andrews, D. W., & Patterson, G. R. (1996). Deviancy training in male adolescent friendships. *Behavior Therapy, 27*, 373–390.

Dumas, J. E., & Lechowicz, J. G. (1989). When do noncompliant children comply? Implications for family behavior therapy. *Child Family and Behavior Therapy*, *11*, 21–38.

DuPaul, G. J., & Eckert, T. L. (1994). The effects of social skills curricula: Now you see them, now you don't. *School Psychology Quarterly*, *9*, 113–132.

Ebstein, R. P., & Belmaker, R. H. (1996). Saga of an adventure gene: Novelty seeking, substance abuse and the dopamine D4 receptor (*D4DR*) exon III repeat polymorphism. *Molecular Psychiatry*, *2*, 381–384.

Elrod, M. M., (1987). *Children's understanding of indirect commands. Journal of Genetic Psychology*, *148*, 63–70.

Erickson, M. J., Stage, S. A. & Nelson, J. R. (2006). Naturalistic study of the behavior of students with EBD referred for functional behavioral assessment. *Journal of Emotional and Behavioral Disorders*, *14*, 31–40

Ervin, R. A., DuPaul, G. J., Kern, L., & Friman, P. C. (1998). Classroom-based functional and adjunctive assessments: Proactive approaches to intervention selection for adolescents with attention deficit hyperactivity disorder. *Journal of Applied Behavior Analysis*, *31*, 65–78.

Evans, C. (personal communication, August, 15, 2008).

Eyberg, S. M., Neslon, M. M., & Boggs, S. R. (2008). Evidence-based psychosocial treatments for children and adolescents with disruptive behaviors. *Journal of Clinical Child and Adolescent Psychology*, *37*, 215–237.

Fabiano, G. A., Pelham, W. E., Karmazin, K. Kreher, J., Panahon, C. J., & Carlson, C. (2008). A group contingency program to improve the behavior of elementary school students in a cafeteria. *Behavior Modification*, *32*, 121–132.

Faciane, S. A. (2005). An investigation into the effects of eye contact on child compliance. Doctoral dissertation, University of Southern Mississippi, 2005). *Dissertation Abstracts International*, 65(10), 5382B.

Fairbanks, S., Sugai, G., Guardino, D., & Lathrop, M. (2005). An evaluation of a collaborative social behavior response to intervention system of behavior support for second grade students. *Exceptional Children*, *73*, 288–310.

Feil, E. G., Severson, H. H., & Walker, H. M. (1998). Screening for emotional and behavioral delays: The Early Screening Project. *Journal of Early Intervention*, *21*, 252–266.

Ferguson. C. J., Miguel, C., Kilburn, J. C., Sanchez, P. (2007). Effectiveness of school-based anti-bullying programs: A meta-analytic review. *Criminal Justice Review*, *32*, 401–414.

Filcheck, H. A., Berry, T. A., McNeil, C. B., & Vincent, J. D. (2004). Preliminary investigation examining the validity of the compliance test and a brief behavioral observation measure for identifying children with disruptive behavior. *The Child Study Journal*, *34*, 1.

Filter, K. J., McKenna, M. K., Benedict, E. A., Horner, R. H., odd, A. W., & Watson, J. (2007). Check in/Check out: A post-hoc evaluation of an efficient, secondary-level targeted intervention for reducing problem behaviors in schools. *Education and Treatment of Children*, *30*, 69–84.

Fishbein, J., & *Wasik*, B. H. (1981). Effect of the good *behavior* game on disruptive *library behavior*. *Journal of Applied* Behavior *Analysis*, *14*, 89–93.

Forehand, R. (1977). Child noncompliance to parental requests: Behavioral analysis and treatment. In M. Hersen, R. M. Eisler, and P. M. Miller (Eds.), *Progress in behavior modification*, Vol. 5. (pp. 295–343), New York: Academic Press.

Forehand, R., & McMahon, R. J. (2003). *Helping the noncompliant child: A clinician's guide to parent training*. New York: Guilford Press.

Forgatch, M. S. & DeGarmo, D. S. (2002). Extending and testing the social interaction learning model with divorce samples. In J. R. Reid, G. R. Patterson, & J. Snyder (Eds.), *Anti-social behavior in children and adolescents: A developmental analysis and model for intervention* (pp. 235–256). Washington, DC: American Psychological Association.

Forness, S. R., & Kavale, K. A. (1996). Treating social skills deficits in children with learning disabilities: A meta-analysis of the research. *Learning Disability Quarterly*, *19*, 2–13.

Frick, P. J., Lahey, B. B., Loeber, R., Tannenbaum, L. E., Van Horn, Y., Christ, M. A. G., Hart, E. A., & Hansen, K. (1993). Oppositional defiant disorder and conduct disorder: A meta-analytic review of factor analyses and cross-validation in a clinic sample. *Clinical Psychology Review*, *13*, 319–340.

Frick, P. J. & Loney, B. R. (2002). Understanding the association between parent and child antisocial behavior. In R .J. McMahon & R. D. Peters (Eds.), *The effects of parental dysfunction on children* (pp. 105–126). New York: Plenum.

Gadow, K. D., Sprafkin, J., & Nolan, E. E. (1996). *ADHD school observation code*. Stoney Brook, NY: Checkmate Plus.

Garrity, C., Jens, K., Porter,W. Sager, N., & Short-Camilli, C. (1994). *Bully-proofing your school*, Longmont, CO: Sopris West.

Gelfand, D. M., & Drew, J. C. (2003). *Understanding childhood behavior disorders*. Belmont, CA: Wadsworth/Thomson Learning.

Gilliam, J. E. (2003). *Gilliam's Asperger's disorder scale*. Lutz, FL: Psychological Assessment Resources.

Goldstein, A. P. (1988). *The prepare curriculum: Teaching prosocial competencies*. Champaign, IL: Research Press.

Goldstein, A. P., & Glick, B. (1994). Aggression replacement training: Curriculum and evaluation. *Simulation and Gaming*, *25*, 9–26.

Goldstein, A. P., Glick, B., Reiner, S., Zimmerman, D. L., Coultry, T. M., & Gold, D. (1987). *Aggression replacement training: A comprehensive intervention for aggressive youth*. Champaign, IL: Research Press.

Greene, B.F., Bailey, J.S., Barber, F. (1981). An analysis and reduction of disruptive behavior on school buses. *Journal of Applied Behavior Analysis*, *14*, 177–192.

Gresham, F. M. (1986). Conceptual issues in the assessment of social competence in children. In P. S. Strain, M. J. Guralnick, & H. M. Walker (Eds.), *Children's social behavior: Development, assessment, and modification* (pp. 143–179). New York: Academic Press.

Gresham, F. M. (1998). Assessment of social skills in students with emotional and behavioral disorders. *Assessment for Effective Intervention*, *26*, 51–58.

Gresham, F. M., & Elliott, S. N. (1990) *Social skills rating system*. Upper Saddle River, NJ: Pearson Publishing.

Gresham, F. M., Sugai, G., & Horner, R. H. (2001). Interpreting outcomes of social skills training for students with high-incidence disabilities. *Exceptional Children*, *67*, 331–344.

Griest, D. L., & Wells, K. C. (1983). Behavioral family therapy with conduct disordered children. *Behavior Therapy*, *14*, 37–53.

Gunter, P. L., & Shores, R. E. (1994). A case study of altering instructional interactions on the disruptive behavior of a child identified with severe behavior disorders. *Education and Treatment of Children*, *17*, 435–445.

Guttmann-Steinmetz, S., & Crowell, J. (2006). Attachment and externalizing disorders: a developmental psychopathology perspective. *Journal of the American Academy of Child Psychiatry*, *45*, 440–451.

Hämäläinen, M., & Pulkkinen, L. (1995). Aggressive and non-prosocial behavior as precursors to criminality. *Studies on Crime and Crime Prevention*, *4*, 6–21.

Hamlet, C. C., *Axelrod, S., & Kuerschner*, S. (1984). Eye contact as an antecedent to compliant behavior. *Journal* of *Applied Behavior Analysis*, 17, 553–557.

Hanf, C. (1969). *A two-stage program for modifying maternal controlling during mother-child (M-C) interaction*. Paper presented at the meeting of the Western Psychological Association, Vancouver, BC.

Hanf, C. (1970). *Shaping mothers to shape their children's behaviors*. Unpublished manuscript, University of Oregon Medical School.

Hartwig, L., Tuesday-Heathfield, L., & Jenson, W. R. (2004). Standardization of the functional assessment and intervention program (FAIP). *School Psychology Quarterly*, *19*, 272–287.

Hawken, L. A., MacLeod, K. S., & Rawlings, L. (2007). Effects of the behavior education program (BEP) on office discipline referrals of elementary school students, *Journal of Positive Behavior Interventions*, *9*, 94–101.

Hazel, S., Bragg, J. Schumaker, J. Sherman J. & Sheldon-Wildgen J. (1981). *A social skills program for adolescents (ASSET)*. Champaign, IL: Research Press.

Hetherington, E. M., Law, T. C., & O'Connor, T. G. (1993). Divorce: Challenges, changes, and new chances. In F. Walsh (Ed.), *Normal family processes*. New York: Guilford Press.

Hicks, B. M., Krueger, R. F., Iacono, W. G., McGue, M., & Patrick, C. J. (2004). Family transmission and heritability of externalizing disorders: A twin-family study, *Archives of General Psychiatry*, *61*, 922–928.

Hinshaw, S. P. (1992). Externalizing behavior problems and academic underachievement in childhood and adolescence: Causal relationships and underlying mechanisms. *Psychological Bulletin*, *111*, 127–155.

Hommersen, P., Murray, C., Ohan, J. L., & Johnston, C. (2006). The Oppositional Defiant Disorder Rating Scale: Preliminary evidence of reliability and validity. *Journal of Emotional and Behavioral Disorders*, *14*, 118–125.

Individuals with Disabilities Education Act (IDEA)–2004. Available at www2.ed.gov/policy/speced/guid/idea/idea2004.html

Ingoldsby, E. M., & Shaw, D. S. (2002). The role of neighborhood contextual factors on early-starting antisocial behavior. *Clinical Child and Family Psychology Review*, *6*, 21–65.

Jaffee, S. R., Caspi, A., Moffitt, T. E., & Taylor, A. (2004). Physical maltreatment victim to antisocial child: Evidence of an environmentally mediated process. *Journal of Abnormal Psychology*, *113*, 44–55.

Jenson, W. R., Clark, E., Kircher, J., & Kristjansson, S. D. (2007). Statistical reform: Evidence-based practice, meta-analyses, and single subject designs. *Psychology in the Schools*, *44*, 483–493.

Jenson, W. R., Likins, M., Brad, R., Hofmeister, A. M., Morgan, D. P., Reavis, J. K., Rhode, G., & Taylor-Sweeten, M. (1999). *Functional assessment and intervention program (FAIP)*. Longmont, CO: Sopris West.

Jenson, W. R., Olympia, D. Farley, M. & Clark, E. (2004) Positive psychology and externalizing students in a sea of negativity, Psychology in the Schools, *41*, 51–66.

Jenson, W. R., & Reavis, K. (1996). Using group contingencies to improve motivation. In K. Reavis, S. J. Kukic, W. R. Jenson, D. Morgan, D. Andrews, D., & S. Fister (Eds.), *Best practices: Behavioral and educational strategies for teachers* (pp. 77–86). Longmont: CO: Sopris West Publishing.

Jenson, W. R., Rhode, G., Evans, C., & Morgan, D. (2006). *Tough kid principal's briefcase: A practical guide to schoolwide behavior management and legal issues*. Longmont, CO: Sopris West Publishing.

Jenson, W. R., Rhode, G., & Hepworth, M. (2003). *Tough kid parent training book*. Longmont, CO: Sopris West.

Jesse, V. (1989). *Compliance training and generalization effects using the compliance matrix and spinner system*. Unpublished doctoral dissertation, University of Utah, Salt Lake City, UT.

Kalb, L. M. & Loeber, R. (2003). Childhood disobedience and noncompliance: A review. *Pediatrics*, *111*, 641–652.

Kapalka, G. M. (2004). Longer eye contact improves ADHD children's compliance with parent's commands. *Journal of Attention Disorders*, *8*(1), 17–23.

Kazdin, A. E. (1995). *Conduct disorders in childhood and adolescence* (2nd ed.), Thousand Oaks, CA: Sage.

Kazdin, A. E. (2003). Problem-solving skills training and parent management training for conduct disorder. In A. E. Kazdin & J. R. Weisz (Eds.), *Evidence-based psychotherapies for children and adolescents* (pp. 241–262). New York: Guilford Press.

Kazdin, A. E. (2005). *Parent training: Treatment for oppositional, aggressive, and antisocial behavior in children and adolescents*. Oxford, England: Oxford University Press.

Kazdin, A. E., Bass, D., Siegel, T. C., & Thomas, C. (1989). Cognitive behavior therapy and relationship therapy in the treatment of children referred for antisocial behaviors. *Journal of Consulting and Clinical Psychology*, *57*, 522–536.

Kazdin, A. E., Esveldt-Dawson, K. French, N. H. & Unis, A. (1987). Problem-solving skills training and relationship therapy in the treatment of antisocial behavior. *Journal of Consulting and Clinical Psychology*, *55*, 76–85.

Kazdin, A. E. & Weisz, J. R., (2003) *Evidence-based psychotherapies for children and adolescents*. New York: Guilford Press.

Kelshaw-Levering, K., Sterling-Turner, H.E., Henry, J.R., & Skinner, C.H. (2000). Randomized interdependent group contingencies: Group reinforcement with a twist. *Psychology in the Schools*, *37*, 523–533.

Kendall, P. C. (2000). *Childhood disorders*. New York: Taylor and Frances.

Kendler, K. S., Jacobson, K., Myers, J. M., & Eaves, L. J. (2007). A genetically informative developmental study of the relationship between conduct disorder and peer deviance in males. *Psychological Medicine*, *38*, 1001–1011.

Kilgore, K., Snyder, J., & Lentz, C. (2000). The contribution of parental discipline, parental monitoring, and school risk to early-onset conduct problems in African-American boys and girls. *Developmental Psychology*, *36*, 1–11.

Kodak, T., Grow, L., & Northup, J. (2004). Functional analysis and treatment of development for a child with attention deficit disorder. *Journal of Applied Behavior Analysis*, *37*(2), 229–232.

Kovacs, M. (1992). *Children's depression inventory*. Upper Saddle River, NJ: Pearson Publishing.

Kuhn, L. (2004). *Validation of the effectiveness of a parent training program for parents of preschool-age children with attention deficit hyperactivity disorder*. Unpublished maters thesis, University of Utah, Salt Lake City.

Lewis, T. J., & Sugai, G. (1999). Effective behavior support: A systems approach to proactive school-wide management. *Focus on Exceptional Children, 31*(6), 1–24.

Limber, S. P. (2004). Implementation of the Olweus bullying prevention program: lessons learned from the field. In D. Espelage & S. Swearer (Eds.) *Bullying in American schools: A social–ecological perspective on prevention and intervention* (pp. 351–363). Mahwah, NJ: Lawrence Erlbaum.

Litow, L., & Pumroy, D. K. (1975). A brief review of classroom group-oriented contingencies. Journal of *Applied Behavior Analysis, 8,* 341–347.

Lochman, J. E., Barry, T. D., & Pardini, D. A. (2003). Anger control training for aggressive youth. In A. E. Kazdin & J. R. Weisz (Eds.), *Evidence-based psychotherapies for children and adolescents* (pp. 263–281). New York: Guilford Press.

Lochman, J. E., Wells, K. C. (2003). A social–cognitive intervention with aggressive children: Prevention effects and contextual implementation issues. In R. D. Peters & R. J. McMahon (Eds.), *Preventing childhood disorders, substance abuse, and delinquency* (pp. 111–143). Thousand Oaks, CA: Sage.

Loeber, R., Schmaling, K. B. (1985). Empirical evidence for overt and covert patterns of antisocial conduct problems: A meta-analysis. *Journal of Abnormal Child Psychology, 13,* 337–352.

Lusher, J. M., Chandler C. J. and Ball, D. (2001) Dopamine D4 Receptor gene (DRD4) is associated with Novelty seeking (NS) and substance abuse: the saga continues. *Molecular Psychiatry, 6,* 497–499.

Mace, F. C., & Belfiore, P. (1990). Behavioral momentum in the treatment of escape-motivated stereotypy. *Journal of Applied Behavior Analysis, 23,* 507–514.

MacKay, S., McLaughlin, T. F., Weber, K., & Derby, M. L. (2001). The use of precision requests to decrease noncompliance in the home and neighborhood: A case study. *Child & Family Behavior Therapy, 23,* 41–50.

Malone, P. S., Lansford, J. E., Castellino, D. R., Berlin, L. J., Dodge, K. A., Bates, J. E., & Pettit, G. S. (2004). Divorce and child behavior problems: Applying latent change score models to life event data. *Structural Equation Modeling, 11,* 401–423.

March R. E., & Horner, R. H. (2002). Feasibility and contributions of functional behavior assessment in schools. *Journal of Emotional and Behavior Disorders, 10,* 158–170.

Marchant, M., Anderson, D., Caldarella, P., Young, B., & Young, K. R. (2008). *School-wide screening and programs of positive behavior support: Informing the universal interventions.* Paper presented at the 5th annual International Conference on PBS, Chicago, IL.

Martinez, C. R., Jr., & Forgatch, M. S. (2001) Preventing problems with boys' noncompliance: Effects of a parent training intervention for divorcing mothers. *Journal of Consulting and Clinical Psychology, 69,* 416–428.

Mason, D. A., & Frick, P. J. (1994). The heritability of antisocial behavior: A meta-analysis of twin and adoption studies. *Journal of Psychopathology and Behavioral Assessment, 16,* 301–323.

Matheson, A. S., & Shriver, M. D. (2005). Training teachers to give effective commands: Effects on student compliance and academic behaviors. *School Psychology Review, 34,* 202–219.

Maughan, D. R., Olympia, D., Jenson, W. R., Clark, E., & Christiansen, E. (2005). Behavioral parent training as a treatment for externalizing behaviors and disruptive behavior disorders: A meta-analysis, *School Psychology Review, 34,* 267–286.

McConaughy, S. H., & Achenbach, T. M. (2001). *Manual for the Semistructured Clinical Interview for Children and Adolescents* (2nd ed.). Burlington, VT: University of Vermont, Center for Children, Youth, & Families.

McConaughy, S, H, (2005). Direct observational assessment during test sessions and child clinical interviews. *School Psychology Review, 34,* 490–506.

McGinnis, E., & Goldstein, A. P. (1997). *Skillstreaming the elementary school child: New strategies and perspectives for teaching prosocial skills.* Champaign, IL: Research Press

McMahon, R. J., Wells, K. C., & Kotler, J. S. (2006). Conduct problems. In E. J. Mash & R. A. Barkley (Eds.), *Treatment of childhood disorders* (pp. 137–270). New York: Guilford Press.

Merrill, K. W., Gueldner, B. A., Ross, S. W. Isava, D. M., (2008). How effective are school bullying intervention programs? A meta-analysis of intervention research. *School Psychology Quarterly, 23,* 26–42.

Moffitt, T. E. (1990). Juvenile delinquency and attention deficit disorder: Boys' developmental trajectories from age 3 to 15. *Child Development, 61,* 893–910.

Moffitt, T. E. (1993). "Life-course persistent" and "adolescent-limited" antisocial behavior: A developmental taxonomy. *Psychological Review, 100,* 674–701.

Moffitt, T. E. (2003). Life-course-persistent and adolescent-limited antisocial behavior: A 10-Year research review and research agenda. In B. B. Lahey, T. E. Moffitt, & A. Caspi (Eds.), *Causes of conduct disorder and juvenile delinquency* (pp. 49–75), New York: Guilford Press.

Moffitt, T. E., & Caspi, A. (2001). Childhood predictors differentiate life-course persistent and adolescent-limited pathways among males and females. *Development and Psychopathology, 13,* 355–375.

Moffitt, T. E., Caspi, A., Dickson, N., Silva, P. A. & Stanton (1996). Childhood-onset versus adolescent-onset antisocial conduct problems in males, Natural history from ages 3 to 18 years. *Developmental Psychopathology, 8,* 399–424.

Morgan, D, & Jenson, W. R. (1989). *Teaching behaviorally disordered students: Preferred practices.* Columbus, OH: Merrill Publishing.

Mullin, B., & Hinshaw, S. P. (2007). Emotion regulation and externalizing disorders in children and adolescents. In J. Gross (Ed.), *Handbook of emotion regulation* (pp. 523–541). New York: Guilford.

Musser, E. H., Bray, M. A., Kehle, T. J., & Jenson, W. R. (2001). Employing precision requests and antecedent strategies to reduce disruptive behavior in students with social and emotional disorders: A replication. *School Psychology Review, 30,* 294–304.

Neef, N. A., Shafer, M. S., Egel, A. L., Cataldo, M. F., & Parrish, J. M. (1983). The class specific effects of compliance training with do and don't requests: Analogue analysis and classroom application. *Journal of Applied Behavior Analysis, 16,* 81–99.

Nelson, J. R., Roberts, M. L., & *Smith.* D. J. (1998). *Conducting functional behavioral assessments: A practical guide.* Longmont, CO: Sopris West.

O'Neill, R. E., Horner, R. H., Albin, R. W., Sprague, J. R., Storey, K., & Newton, J. S. (1997). *Functional assessment and program development for problem behavior: A practical handbook.* Belmont, CA: Wadsworth.

Olweus, D. (1991). Bully/victim problems among schoolchildren: Basic facts and effects of a school based intervention program. In D. J. Pepler & K. H. Rubin (Eds.), *The development and treatment of childhood aggression* (pp. 411–448). Hillsdale, NJ: Erlbaum.

Olweus, D. (1993). *Bullying at school: What we know and what we can do.* Cambridge: Blackwell.

Parrish, J. M., Cataldo, M. F., Kolko. D., Neef, N. A., & Engel, A. (1986). Experimental analysis of response co-variation among compliant and inappropriate behavior. *Journal of Applied Behavior Analysts, 19,* 241–254.

Patterson, G. R. (1971). *Families: Applications of social learning to family life.* Champaign, IL: Research Press.

Patterson, G. R. (1974). Interventions for boys with conduct problems: Multiple settings, treatments, and criteria. *Journal of Consulting and Clinical Psychology, 42,* 471–481.

Patterson, G. R. (1976). The aggressive child: Victim and architect of the coercive system. In L. A. Hamerlynck, L. C. Handy, & E. J. Mash (Eds.), *Behavior modification and families: Theory and research* (Vol. 1) (pp. 267–316), New York: Brunner/Mazel.

Patterson, G. R. (1982). *Coercive family process.* Eugene, OR: Castalia Press.

Patterson, G. R. (2002). The early development of coercive family process. In J. R. Reid, G. R. Patterson, & J. Snyder (Eds.), *Anti-social behavior in children and adolescents: A developmental analysis and model for intervention* (pp. 25–44). Washington, DC: American Psychological Association.

Patterson,G. R.,DeBaryshe, B. D., & *Ramsey,* E. (1989). A developmental perspective on antisocial behavior. *American Psychologist, 44,* 329–335.

Patterson, G. R., & Gullion, M. D. (1968) *Living with children: New methods for parents and teachers*

Patterson, G. R., Reid, J. R., & Dishion, T. J. (1992). *Antisocial boys.* Eugene, OR: Castalia Press.

Patterson, G. R., Reid, J. B., Jones, R. R., & Conger, R. R. (1975). *A social learning approach to family intervention: Families with aggressive children (Vol. 1).* Eugene, OR: Calstalia.

Pelham, W. E., & Fabiano, G. A. (2008). Evidence-based psychosocial treatments for attention-deficit/hyperactivity disorder. *Journal of Clinical Child and Adolescent Psychology, 37,* 184–214.

Peterson, D. R. (1961). Behavior problems of middle childhood. *Journal of Consulting Psychology, 25,* 205–209.

Pettit, G. S., Laird, R. D., Dodge, K. A., & Bates, J. E. (1997). Patterns of after-school care in middle childhood: Risk factors and developmental outcomes. *Merrill-Palmer Quarterly, 43,* 515–538.

Quay, H. C., & Peterson, D. R. (1975). *Manual for the behavior problem checklist.* Coral Gables Fla: University of Miami.

Quinn, M. M. Kavale, K. A., Mathur, S. R., Rutherford, R. B., & Forness, S. R. (1999). A meta-analysis of social skills interventions for students with emotional and behavioral disorders. *Journal of Emotional and Behavioral Disorders, 7,* 54–64.

Reed, K. F. (1985). Child compliance as a function of imperative versus interrogative commands. (Doctoral dissertation, Purdue University, 1985). *Dissertation Abstracts International, 45* (10), 3343.

Rettew, D. C., Copeland, W. E., Stanger, C., Hudziak, J. J. (2004.) Associations between temperament and DSM-IV externalizing disorders in children and adolescents. *Journal of Developmental and Behavioral Pediatrics, 25,* 383–391.

Reynolds, C. R., & Kamphaus, R. W. (2004). *Behavior assessment system for children* (2nd ed.) (BASC-2). Circle Pines, MN: American Guidance System Publishing.

Rhee, S. H., & Waldman, I. D. (2002). Genetic and environmental influences on antisocial behavior: A meta-analysis of twin and adoption studies. *Psychological Bulletin, 128,* 490–529.

Rhode, G. Jenson, W. R. (2010). *The tough kid book: Practical classroom management strategies* (2nd ed.). Eugene, OR: Pacific Northwest Publishing.

Roberts, M. W. (2001). Clinical observations of structured parent–child interaction designed to evaluate externalizing problems. *Psychological Assessment, 13,* 46–58.

Roberts, M. W., & Powers, S. W. (1988). The compliance test. *Behavioral Assessment, 10,* 375–398.

Russo, D. C., Cataldo, M. F., & Cushing, P. J. (1981). Compliance training and behavioral co-variation in the treatment of multiple behavior problems. *Journal of Applied Behavior Analysis,14,* 209–222.

Rutter, M. (2003). Crucial paths from indicator to causal mechanism. In B. B. Lahey, T. E. Moffitt, & A. Caspi (Eds.), Causes of conduct disorder and juvenile delinquency (pp. 3–26), New York: Guilford Press.

Sattler, J. (2008) *Assessment of Children* (5th ed.). San Diego: Sattler Press.

Saudargas, R. A. (1986). State-event classroom observation code (SECOS). Observation Manual. University of Tennessee, Knoxville.

Saudino, K. J. (2005). Behavioral genetics and child temperament. *Journal of Behavioral Pediatrics, 26,* 214–223.

Schopler, E., Reichler, R. J., & Renner, B. R. (1988). Childhood autism rating scale. Los Angeles: Western Psychological Services.

Schuckit, M. A., Smith, T. L., Pierson, J., Trim, R., & Danko, G. P. (2007). Externalizing disorders in offspring from the San Diego prospective study of alcoholism. *Journal of Psychiatric Research, 42,* 644–652.

Scott, T. (2007, June). *School-wide systems of positive behavior support: simplified success strategies across the school.* PBIS Summer Institute, Baltimore, MD.

Serketch, W. J., & Dumas, J. E. (1996). The effectiveness of behavioral parent training to modify antisocial behavior in children: A meta-analysis. *Behavior Therapy, 27,* 171–186.

Shapiro, E. S. (2004). *Academic skills problems workbook (rev.)* New York: Guilford Press.

Sharp, C., Petersen, N., & Goodyer, I.M. (2008). Emotional reactivity and the emergence of conduct problems and emotional symptoms in 7- to 11-year-olds: A 1-year follow-up study. *Journal of American Academy for Child and Adolescent Psychiatry, 47,* 565–573.

Sheridan, S. (1995). *The Tough Kids social skills program.* Longmont,CO: Sopris West.

Silverman, W. K., & Hinshaw, S. P. (2008). The second special issue on evidence-based psychosocial treatments for children and adolescents: A 10-year update. *Journal of Clinical and Child Adolescent Psychology, 37,* 1–7.

Skinner, B. F. (1953). *Science and human behavior.* New York: Macmillan.

Smith, B. H., Barkley, R. A., & Shapiro, C. J. (2006). Attention-deficit/hyperactivity disorder. In E. J. Mash & R. A. Barkley (Eds.), *Treatment of childhood disorders* (pp. 65–136). New York: Guilford Press.

Smith, J. D., Schneider, B. H., Smith, P. K. & Ananiadou, K. (2004). The effectiveness of whole-school antibullying programs: A synthesis of evaluation research. *School Psychology Review, 33,* 547–560.

Smith, S. W., & Travis, P. C. (2001). Conducting social competence research: Considering conceptual frameworks. *Behavioral Disorders, 26,* 360–369.

Snyder J. (2002). Reinforcement and coercive mechanisms in the development of antisocial behavior: Peer relationships. In J. R. Reid, G. R. Patterson, & J. Snyder (Eds.), *Anti-social behavior in children and adolescents: A developmental analysis and model for intervention* (pp. 101–123). Washington, DC: American Psychological Association.

Snyder J., & Stoolmiller, M. (2002). Reinforcement and coercive mechanisms in the development of antisocial behavior: The family. In J. R. Reid, G. R. Patterson, & J. Snyder (Eds.), *Anti-social behavior in children and adolescents: A developmental analysis and model for intervention* (pp. 65–100). Washington, DC: American Psychological Association.

Sprick, R., & Garrison, M. (2008). *Interventions: Evidence-based behavioral strategies for individual students* (2nd ed.). Eugene, OR: Pacific Northwest Publishing.

Stage, S. A. & Quiroz, D. R. (1997). A meta-analysis of interventions to decrease disruptive classroom behavior in public education settings. *School Psychology Review, 26,* 333–368.

Stoiber, K. C., & Kratochwill, T. R. (2000). Empirically supported interventions and School Psychology: Rationale and methodological issues–Part 1. *School Psychology Quarterly, 15,* 75–105.

Sukhodolsky, D. G., Kassinove, H., & Gorman, B. S. (2004). Cognitive–behavioral therapy for anger in children and adolescents: A meta-analysis. *Aggression and Violent Behavior, 9,* 247–269.

Theodore, L. A., Bray, M. A., Kehle, T. J., & Jenson, W. R. (2001). Randomized and group contingencies to reduce disruptive behavior of adolescent students in special education. *Journal of School Psychology, 39,* 267–277.

Tingstrom, D. H., Sterling-Turner, H. E., & Wilczynski, S. M. (2006). The good behavior game: 1969–2002. *Behavior Modification, 30,* 225–253.

Todd, A. W., Campbell, A. L., Meyer, G. G., & Horner, R. H. (2008). The effects of a targeted intervention to reduce problem behaviors. *Journal of Positive Behavior Interventions, 10,* 46–55.

Torgerson, A. M., & Kringlen, E. (1978). Genetic aspects of temperament differences in infants. *Journal of the American Academy of Child Psychiatry, 17,* 433–444.

Van Acker, R., Grant, S. H., & Henry, D. (1996). Teacher and student behavior as a function of risk for aggression. *Education and Treatment of Children, 19,* 316–334.

Volpe, R. J., DiPerna, J. C., Hintze, J. M., & Shapiro, E. S. (2005). Observing students in classroom settings: A review of seven coding schemes. *School Psychology Review, 34*(4), 454–474.

Volpe, R. J., & McConaughy, S. H. (2005). Introduction to the mini-series: Systematic direct observational assessment of student behavior: Its use and interpretation in multiple settings. *School Psychology Review, 34,* 451–453.

Walker, B., Cheney, D., Stage, S., Blum, C. & Horner, R. H. (2005). Schoolwide screening and positive behavior supports: Identifying and supporting students at risk for school failure. *Journal of Positive Behavior Interventions, 7,* 194–204

Walker, H., McConnell, S., Holmes, D., Todis, B., Walker, J., & Golden, N. (1983). *The Walker social skills curriculum: The ACCEPTS program.* Austin, TX: Pro-Ed.

Walker, H. M., Ramsey, E., & Gresham, F. M. (2004). *Antisocial behavior in school.* Belmont, CA: Wadsworth/Thomas Learning.

Walker, H. M., & Severson, H. (1990). *Systematic screening for behavior disorders.* Longmont, CO: Sopris West.

Walker, H. M., Severson, H. H., Nicholson, F., Kehle, T. J., Jenson, W. R., & Clark, E. (1994). Replication of the systematic screening for behavior disorders procedures (SSDB) for the identification of at-risk children. *Journal of Emotional and Behavior Disorders, 2,* 66–77.

Webster-Stratton, C., & Reid, M. J. (2003). Treating conduct problems and strengthening social and emotional competence in young children: The Dina Dinosaur treatment program. *Journal of Emotional and Behavioral Disorders, 11,* 130–143.

Weiss, G., & Hechtman, L. (1993). *Hyperactive children grown up* (2nd ed.). New York: Guilford Press.

Wells, K. C., Forehand, R., & Griest, D. L. (1980). Generality of treatment effects from treated to untreated behaviors resulting from a parent training program. *Journal of Clinical Child Psychology, 9,* 217–219.

Whitaker, D. J. Rosenbluth, B., Valle, L. A., & Sanchez, E. (2003). Expect respect: A school-based intervention to promote awareness and effective responses to bullying and sexual harassment. In D. L. Espelage & S. M. Swearer (Eds.), *Bullying in American schools: A social-ecological perspective on prevention and intervention* (pp. 327–350). Mahwah, NJ: Erlbaum.

Wilder, D. A., Harris, C., Reagan, R. & Rasey, A. (2007). Functional analysis and treatment of noncompliance by preschool children. *Journal of Applied Behavior Analysis, 40,* 173–177.

Williams, C. & Forehand, R. (1984). An examination of predictor variables for child compliance and noncompliance. *Journal of Abnormal Child Psychology, 12,* 491–504.

Witt, J.C., Daly, E. M., & Noell, G. (2000). *Functional Assessments: A step-by-step guide to solving academic and behavior problems.* Longmont, CO: Sopris West.

World Health Organization (2005). *International statistical classification of diseases and related health problems–10th* Geneva: Author.

Yeager, C. & McLaughlin, T. F. (1995). The use of a time out ribbon and precision requests to improve child compliance in the classroom: A case study. *Child & Family Behavior Therapy, 17,* 1–9.

Interventions for Students with Internalizing Behavioral Deficits

Barbara A. Gueldner *and* Kenneth W. Merrell

Abstract

The incidence of depression and anxiety among children is a serious concern, often going unrecognized. This chapter reviews the characteristics of these problems found in children, the enormous cost to society in the adult population when depression and anxiety go untreated, and assessment methods available for early detection in a school setting. School-based prevention and intervention strategies and programs are highlighted, with a focus on the movement toward Social and Emotional Learning (SEL) implemented for all students. Barriers to implementation are discussed, along with strategies known to promote integrated and sustainable practices. The chapter concludes with a discussion of the impact of other ecologies on the development of internalizing problems, highlighting the need for targeted prevention and intervention efforts in other settings. Future directions are proposed regarding areas where additional research and practice are needed.

Keywords: depression, anxiety, prevention, intervention, SEL

Introduction to Internalizing Problems

Awareness is growing that children experience internalizing problems, which include the symptoms of depression, anxiety, social withdrawal, and somatic or physical problems. Children who were previously thought of as highly irritable, resistant to get out of bed and go to school, shy and wary of attending birthday parties, or lethargic and daydreamers are now considered to be potentially experiencing a broader symptomatic spectrum of depressive and/or anxious taxonomies. When these maladaptive behaviors are viewed through a lens that considers the possibility that high levels of irritability may also suggest sadness, irrational thoughts and beliefs about the world, themselves, and the future, or the stressful, reciprocal transactions amongst their ecologies (e.g., the interaction between school bullying and students' fears of attending school), children are better understood and attended to, beyond concerns about their physical and academic development.

Fortunately, steady improvements in research and clinical intervention and prevention efforts are leading to a better understanding of the mental health concerns that affect children and, in turn, help children feel better, lead more productive and enjoyable childhoods, and slow or stop a downward spiral of repeated episodes of depression and anxiety.

The purpose of this chapter is to review childhood internalizing problems and highlight current prevention and intervention strategies and programs that show encouraging evidence for practical utility in the school setting. We discuss methods of assessing internalizing problems and the limitations that exist, especially when monitoring symptoms for signs of alleviating, worsening, and responses to treatment. Common barriers to program implementation in the school setting will be addressed, along with a discussion regarding the role of parents and communities in promoting children's mental health.

An Overview of Internalizing Problems

Depression and anxiety are the hallmark characteristics of internalizing problems. *Internalizing* refers to the "inside" manner in which symptoms are experienced and persist. Reynolds (1992) referred to internalizing problems as a *secret illness*; when a secret is held, generally no one but the secret-keeper knows about it, and often it is difficult for outsiders to see the telltale signs that a secret even exists. Similarly, symptoms of depression and anxiety may be difficult to detect, especially if one is unfamiliar with evidence that is often subtle and easily misunderstood. This is particularly true when children experience incredibly uncomfortable anxious feelings (for example, starting swimming lessons and being afraid of the water), and communicate their fear through externalizing types of behaviors such as crying, screaming, and tantrumming. Often, the anxious feelings are "hiding" behind externalizing behaviors that are thought of as noncompliant, and are disciplined as such. The fact that the unruly behavior may be a sign that the child might be worried and fearful may never be considered, when parents and teachers do not understand that children can experience these feelings. Understanding the child's behavior through a more educated and comprehensive lens can significantly help a child recognize his own behavior, identify his feelings, and use strategies that will help him adapt more easily.

The extent to which children are actually diagnosed with an internalizing disorder (i.e., meets diagnostic criteria in the Diagnostic and Statistical Manual, IV-TR-Fourth Edition) is largely dependent on the number and severity of symptoms that are experienced; most children experience worries and sadness from time to time, without having a diagnosable problem. The extent to which these feelings persist over time and interfere with expected childhood behavior and development will indicate the presence or absence of a disorder (Hughes & Gullone, 2007; Merrell, 2008a, 2008b). Regardless of whether they have a disorder or not, all children can learn skills that they can use to deal with feelings that are uncomfortable.

Types of Internalizing Problems

The primary internalizing problems include depression, anxiety, social withdrawal, and somatic or physical problems (Merrell, 2008a, 2008b; Quay, 1986). Social withdrawal and somatic problems are generally not considered specific diagnostic conditions, but are frequently associated with depression and anxiety. Depression and anxiety are broad classifications that contain subcategoricial diagnoses or classifications. This section will focus on the characteristics of depression and anxiety, and how social withdrawal and somatization often are evident via these classifications.

Depression occurs in many children. Researchers at the Oregon Research Institute collected data on the prevalence of depression throughout childhood, indicating that throughout this course of development, depression afflicts one in five boys, and one in three girls (see Seeley, Rohde, Lewinsohn, & Clarke, 2002). Girls and boys tend to report symptoms of depression at similar rates prior to adolescence. However, symptoms appear to occur more frequently for girls during adolescence. Garber (2006) summarized research linking the risk of developing and having a prolonged experience of depression symptoms to fixed and variable risk factors. Gender is among these risk factors, in addition to and not limited to genetic makeup, parental depression, temperament, and anxiety symptoms. Depression can exist along a continuum of severity, and can include such diagnostic categories such as dysthymia (mild to moderate symptoms for at least one year for children), adjustment disorder, where symptoms occur after a stressful life event, depressive disorder (symptoms are severe enough to interfere with functioning), and bipolar disorders, where depression symptoms are part of a "cycle" between depression and mania, or mood elevation and extreme behavioral activation (Merrell, 2008a). Symptoms of depression include depressed mood, loss of interest in activities, sleep disturbance, fatigue, feelings of worthlessness and/or excessive guilt, difficulties with concentration and decision making, irritability, somatic complaints, and thoughts of death and dying beyond expectations for developmental stages.

Anxiety symptoms frequently co-occur with depression symptoms (Angold, Costello, & Erkanli, 1999). However, anxiety may also stand alone, and can share components of generalized distress, physiological hyperarousal, and low positive affect that are present in depression (see Clark and Watson, 1991 for a discussion on the tripartite model). In childhood, anxiety is a relatively common experience for children, and consequently occurs more frequently than depression. It also is believed to precede depression and be a risk factor for developing depression in childhood and adulthood (see Flannery-Schroeder, 2006 for a summary of this research). The construct of anxiety is somewhat broad, but it tends to include subjective feelings of discomfort, fear, or dread, overt behaviors such as avoidance of stimuli or withdrawal, and physiological responses such as sweating, nausea, and general arousal (Merrell, 2008a). Like depression, anxiety can exist along a continuum of severity; however, it is frequently delineated across subtypes or disorders with specific characteristics. As with a diagnosis of a depressive disorder, the diagnosis of an anxiety disorder is only met when symptoms have persisted over time and interfere with daily functioning. Anxiety disorders most commonly found in children include separation disorder, social phobia, school phobia or school refusal, generalized anxiety disorder, and obsessive-compulsive disorder.

As previously mentioned, social withdrawal and somatic problems are generally not diagnosed as a separate disorder, but frequently are present with anxiety and depression symptoms. Children who withdraw from social situations often do so to avoid being with other children, due to prior negative experiences, cognitive distortions regarding their understanding of and past experiences with social interactions, or patterns of awkward social interactions, often due to gaps in social skills. Social withdrawal and somatic problems may be temporary, due to a developmental phase (e.g., separation anxiety may cause toddlers to withdraw from being held by non-caretaking adults) or an acute contextual issue (e.g., rapid heartbeat prior to giving a speech), or longstanding (e.g., children with an autism spectrum disorder often have difficulty understanding the "rules" of conversation, and consequently may avoid situations where conversation would be expected). These problems can also range from mild to severe in their persistence and impairment. It is important to recognize these characteristics as potential contributors to the manner in which depression and anxiety "play out" in children's daily lives (e.g., anxiety regarding school performance leading to frequent stomachaches and school absences), so that these contributions may be screened during assessment and targeted as part of comprehensive intervention programming.

Differences across Cultural Groups

Although the scope of this chapter does not permit a comprehensive discussion regarding the possible differences among children across diverse ethnic and cultural groupings and their experiences with internalizing problems, acknowledgement of this area is important in order to recognize that differing rates of occurrence may either occur, or be believed to exist, without substantiated evidence.

Professionals should be aware of the evidence and potentially inaccurate perceptions, and to address cultural considerations by applying sensitive assessment and intervention practices. When choosing assessment methods for an evaluation, one must consider normative daily practices and beliefs in the context of culture in order to evaluate whether a problem truly exists. For example, children can exhibit differences in the ages at which they are comfortable with separating from their caregivers for extended periods of time. One facet of this difference can be attributed to the acceptability of encouraging separation from caregivers amongst ethnic and cultural groups. Thus, assessment, interpretation, and resulting case conceptualization must take into consideration the normative separation expectancies within the ethnic and cultural groups associated with the family.

Although research investigating whether certain cultural and/or ethnic groups may differ in the incidence of internalizing problems is still growing, several studies have demonstrated an association between certain ethnic groups and the rates of subtypes of anxiety and depression. For example, African American children have been found to have longer-lasting traumatic stress symptoms when compared to White children (Last & Perrin, 1993). Ginsburg and Silverman (1996) found a greater incidence of childhood separation anxiety and fearfulness to be reported among Hispanic parents as compared with White parents. In a recent study by Austin and Chorpita (2004), Native Hawaiian children were reported to experience more separation anxiety than Filipino American, Japanese American, and White. Chinese Americans reported more social anxiety as compared with Native Hawaiians and Whites. There were no group differences for depression or generalized anxiety across groups. The authors supported the theory that traits associated with ethnicity may *shape* the expression of internalizing characteristics. For example, Native Hawaiians may experience more separation anxiety due to an emphasis on closeness within the family, making separations more difficult. The purpose for highlighting this research is not to inappropriately pathologize one group in comparison to another. To the contrary, we wish to draw attention to the fact that (1) some groups may experience higher or lower incidences of depression and anxiety; (2) these reasons are not well understood at this time; (3) additional research is warranted, with the critical recognition that membership to an ethic group does not automatically map onto cultural affiliation and, within-ethnic differences can greatly shape emotional development when considered in the context of specific cultural affiliations (e.g., religious differences); and (4) clinicians must always be mindful of sources of bias in assessment measurement, and attentive to specific cultural considerations when choosing interventions for the treatment of depression and anxiety.

The Cost of Children Experiencing Internalizing Problems

The monetary cost of children experiencing acute, and especially chronic, episodes of depression and anxiety is substantial. Consider the economic burden of the occurrence of depression among American adults. In 2000, it was estimated to cost a total of $83.1 billion to not only treat this problem, but to also account for the resources that were lost to decreased productivity or premature death (Greenberg, Kessler, Birnbaum, Leong, Lowe, Berglund, et. al., 2003). Among children and adolescents, a recent meta-analysis (Lynch & Clarke, 2006) identified a mere five studies that reviewed the economic cost of depression in this demographic, and whether the interventions used for treatment were cost-effective and beneficial. Although this review indicated that children are increasingly accessing community organizations (e.g., community health clinics, schools) for treatment of depression symptoms, and that prevention and intervention programs can be cost-effective, more study is needed to reliably determine the short and long-term costs associated with internalizing problems, the long-term savings associated with prevention and treatment, and, most importantly, improved quality of life for future adult citizens of the world. Schools have a front-row seat by default to observe and be impacted by children's emotional suffering. Cost-benefit analyses can provide information to guide policies and procedures that publicly funded organizations, such as school districts, will be interested to initiate, fund, and support mental health policies and/or programs that reciprocally influence academic performance. There must be compelling evidence that committed investment in mental health services will generate positive returns.

Regardless of the growth needed to develop and sustain programs and procedures that will address children's mental health issues, methods whereby we can identify children at risk for developing internalizing problems have improved, to catch them when they are in the midst of acute or chronic depression and/or anxiety. This next section will review methods of assessing depression and anxiety in children and adolescents, the limitations of these assessments, and how assessment is used to monitor progress when interventions are initiated to treat existing problems.

Assessing Internalizing Problems

This section provides an overview and discussion of some of the critical issues and recommended practices related to screening and assessing students who have internalizing problems and related behavioral deficits. Although this section is necessarily brief, the topic of assessing internalizing problems is extensive and complex, requiring significantly more space than we can devote in this chapter. For more complete discussions of the assessment process, readers are referred to the following recent works by the second author: Merrell, 2008a; Merrell, 2008b; and Levitt and Merrell, 2008. This section includes comments on the differences between assessment at the universal and indicated levels, a discussion of the areas that are assessed when considering internalizing problems, an overview of the most useful methods of assessment, and some final comments on using assessment data for intervention planning and progress monitoring.

Universal and Indicated Assessment

In planning for assessment within the three-tier model of prevention and student support, it is important to distinguish *screening* from *assessment*. At the universal level of support—where the focus is on all students—screening is a logical procedure to consider. Screening involves narrowing a larger general population down to a smaller population of interest, based on specific characteristics (Merrell, 2008b). The purpose of screening for any social or emotional concern is to identify at-risk students who may need additional support, for the purpose of preventing the occurrence of significant problems in the future. Because screening processes involve dealing with larger groups of students, the procedures that are employed must be simple and quick. Screening may involve some detection errors, but such errors should not be viewed as a problem so long as they are more likely to be false-positive errors rather than false-negative errors: at this stage, it is better to identify students who may not fit the criteria of interest than to fail to identify such students. Because screening should lead to further evaluation and assessment designed to more closely evaluate the screened cases before any further action is taken, "false positive" cases will be sorted out later.

Assessment processes, on the other hand, are necessarily more detailed, involved, and intensive, and are more likely to involve individual students rather than groups. Rather than narrowing a population of interest, assessment should lead to important individual decisions regarding the existence of specific problems or concerns, classification and program eligibility, and, most important, intervention planning. Thus, assessment processes are most likely to be used with students at the indicated level of support—the "top of the triangle" or "the red zone," as this population is sometimes considered.

What is Assessed?

One of the issues often overlooked in considering assessment of students with internalizing problems is the deceptively simple question, "What is to be assessed?" The answer appears to be, "Internalizing problems, of course." This statement is true, or necessary, but not sufficient. Obviously, the focus on assessing internalizing problems requires a focus on pathology, disorders, negative affect, and other problem symptoms. Tools such as problem behavior rating scales, depression and anxiety checklists and self-report measures, and clinical diagnostic interviews are often used for this purpose. These types of assessment tools typically focus on symptoms and characteristics of problem emotions (e.g., sadness, tension, despondency, anxiousness, irritability), problem cognitions (e.g., hopelessness, distorted appraisal and thought processes, poor mental coping skills), and problem behaviors (e.g., social withdrawal, behavioral avoidance, engaging in maladaptive behavior processes, failure to fulfill one's responsibilities). Although a problem-focused assessment may be helpful in making diagnostic decisions and in identifying targeted symptoms for treatment, it is also important to focus on positive assets and affect of individuals who may be experiencing internalizing problems. As a general rule, it is easier and more direct to increase rather than decrease behaviors, and to teach new skills rather than

extinguish maladaptive responses. By focusing on social skills, cognitive and behavioral coping processes, the presence or absence of positive affect, and resiliency skills, it is possible to identify specific deficit targets for intervention, and to build on the student's current strengths as a plan is developed for supporting them (Gueldner & Merrell, 2008; Levitt & Merrell, 2008).

Methods of Assessment

Figure 19.1 (adapted from Merrell, 2008b) depicts the primary recommended methods that are used in empirically based social/emotional assessment, as well as the settings in which assessment may be based, and the sources of information to be gathered in the assessment. These recommended methods include direct behavioral observation, third-party behavior rating scales, self-report instruments, reviews of existing records, sociometric procedures, and interviews. There are other assessment methods available, such as projective/expressive techniques (e.g., drawing tests) and cognitive appraisal techniques (e.g., the Rorschach and similar tests), but we do not recommend them for routine use in school settings because of reliability issues, time and training requirements, and general usefulness for the goals of school based social/emotional assessment.

The six social/emotional assessment methods we generally support for school based practice are not equally valid and reliable for the specific challenges of assessing internalizing problems. Although direct behavioral observation is a true naturalistic assessment method that allows inferences on both the student and the environment, it is notoriously challenging with respect to identifying internalizing problems and related strengths, because they often involve affective and cognitive characteristics that are difficult to detect through external means. In addition, direct behavioral observation of student social/emotional behavior may require as many as

Fig. 19.1 Recommended Components of Social and Emotional Assessment: Methods, Sources, and Settings.

Adapted from *Behavioral, social, and emotional assessment of children and adolescents* (3rd ed.), by K. W. Merrell. Copyright 2008, Taylor & Francis/Routledge. Reprinted with permission.

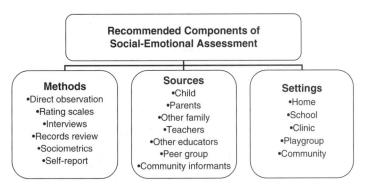

six observational periods over time to gather reliable data (Hintz, 2005; Hintze & Matthews, 2004), a time luxury that few school based clinicians can afford. Likewise, a review of existing records, although it is quick and easy, often misses important internalizing characteristics because they were never noted in the records in the first place. Sociometric assessment has an impressive research base with assessment of depression, but the logistical challenges it creates (including obtaining informed consent from parents of all students in the classroom, and involving all students in the assessment) make it better suited to research than to clinical assessment. The remaining three methods—behavior rating scales, self-report instruments, and interviews—are the methods best suited for assessing students with internalizing problems, and we propose that they have a place in most comprehensive assessments where internalizing problems are a focus. Although behavior rating scales are subject to some of the same false-negative problems as direct observation when secretive internalizing characteristics are considered, they generally have strong technical properties, they provide a quick means to gather parent and teacher perspectives, and many of the most popular scales (such as the Achenbach System of Empirically-Based Assessment, and the Behavioral Assessment System for Children, 2nd Edition) include subscales that are specifically focused on and validated for the internalizing domain. Self-report measures of depression, anxiety, and general internalizing problems (as well as social skills and assets) are appropriate for most children ages 9 or 10 and older. These tools provide the opportunity for insight into the student's own perspective. Interviews—including interviews with the student, and his parents and teachers—provide a relatively direct and focused means of gathering diagnostic information, and have the advantage of being adaptable for gathering information on supports available within the student's environment that can be used in the intervention process.

Linking Assessment to Intervention

Using assessment data in an effective way for intervention planning has often been overlooked in the past. Typical practice in this regard has often consisted of using the assessment data for diagnostic purposes, and then selecting an intervention plan based more on the skills and interests of the interventionist than on any particular aspects of the assessment data. In fact, interventions for social/emotional concerns of children and adolescents have often been developed without being sufficiently informed by assessment data, despite frequent criticism of this approach (Merrell, 2008b).

Fortunately, there is increasing interest in using assessment data systematically in the development and monitoring of interventions, and this interest is particularly apparent in the field of school psychology. One way in which intervention planning can be informed by assessment results is to include a focus on protective factors (such as social skills, social support, and coping skills) in the assessment (rather than focusing exclusively on pathology), and to use this information to identify strengths which can be tapped in the intervention, as well as deficit areas in need of support (Levitt & Merrell, 2008). For example, cognitive-behavioral intervention programs aimed at reducing depression symptoms may include direct instruction around coping strategies such as problem solving. Another way in which the design of the assessment may inform intervention is to systematically gather information on both positive and negative affect of students, and then use that information to identify intervention targets. For example, if a child reports having elevated levels of negative affect and decreased levels of positive affect, intervention strategies could focus on promoting positive affect through behavioral activation strategies, as well as reducing negative affect through teaching coping mechanisms, such as cognitive problem-solving skills (Merrell, 2008a).

Finally, the use of brief self-report and brief teacher or parent rating scale tools, which are based on the assessment results and individualized to the student's intervention targets, appears to have great potential for use in monitoring the progress of intervention and making adjustments as needed (Levitt & Merrell, 2008). We recommend an experimental practice of carefully noting the self-report and teacher rating items where the highest level of problem symptoms are indicated, identifying which of those characteristics will be most directly targeted in the intervention(s) that are to be provided to the student in question, and then using those few items—usually not more than 10—as the basis for creating idiographic, practitioner-developed progress monitoring tools for both self-report and teacher report progress monitoring. Data from these brief monitoring tools can be gathered frequently—weekly, or more often if needed—with very little time required. These data can be plotted on a graph, where the intervention target is clearly visible, to create an "aim line," which may be useful in determining whether intervention progress is on track, or adjustments may be advisable. For more details on linking assessment to intervention for students with internalizing problems, we refer readers to the comprehensive treatment of this topic by Levitt and Merrell.

Prevention and Intervention

We have reviewed the characteristics of internalizing problems, their prevalence in children, and detecting their presence through appropriate assessment methods. It is not enough to identify children with depression and anxiety and "admire" the problem without proactively intervening with effective treatments. As discussed in the previous section regarding the economic consequences of internalizing problems, immediate action is not limited to early intervention, but also can include preventative efforts designed to give all children a chance to build the skills to cope with life stressors.

Promoting Mental Health through Universal Prevention

Responding to children experiencing internalizing problems demands not only increased awareness of the characteristics of these problems, but also an organized and supportive framework from which to respond quickly and effectively. For many children with internalizing problems, it is not until they are glaringly symptomatic, and the symptoms are interfering with daily functioning (e.g., not completing homework, highly irritable, suicidal), that they get the support that they need. As discussed in the last section of this chapter, universal and indicated assessment methods can readily improve the speed and accuracy with which children are identified and directed to effective intervention strategies. Expanding upon this notion is the idea that *all* children would benefit from general social and emotional instruction that could act as an inoculation against inevitable stressors. That is, if all children could learn basic skills such as emotion identification, and general stress and anger management strategies, they may be more apt to engage in proactive and effective problem-solving approaches and thereby offset an exacerbation of internalizing symptoms to the point that targeted assessment and intervention are required. Much like the developmental course of academic instruction and learning, social and emotional instruction and learning can provide students with basic skills upon which they can build, as they mature cognitively and emotionally and interface with increasingly challenging and complex problems.

Many educational settings are increasingly addressing children's social and emotional needs in the school setting, in a way that extends services beyond responding to crises. Specifically, education is increasingly adapting public health models of service delivery, whereby specific assessment, prevention, and intervention efforts are strategically delivered in a school setting (see Merrell and Buchanan, 2006 for an historical review of this conceptual model). These efforts are similar to practices found in pediatric medical settings, whereby children are routinely screened for attaining developmental milestones, parents are given anticipatory guidance regarding circumstances most children will encounter so the risk of injury is minimized (e.g., the importance of wearing seatbelts in motorized vehicles), and prescribed treatment for acute illness is available. The use of *positive behavioral supports* (see Todd, Horner, Sugai, & Sprague, 1999, for a thorough review) is a notable educational application of this model, whereby instructional methods and content are used to teach prosocial behavior to all students, assessment data is collected to monitor their behavioral status (e.g., progress or regression), and targeted interventions are designed when necessary to remediate behavior interfering with behavioral functioning. Together, these components provide a highly structured approach to meeting the behavioral needs of an *entire* student body, and are not limited to those with acute or severely chronic behavioral problems. Although improvements are still needed to identify and implement effective strategies for students experiencing internalizing problems (i.e., these problems largely go undetected or are misunderstood), the innovation in adapting a public health model to education is found in the emphasis on *prevention.* Preventing depression and anxiety symptoms is undeniably linked to the global well-being of students; establishing this link is paramount to understanding the importance of supporting positive mental health in our students—the next step is systematically integrating strategic instruction regarding positive social and emotional development into the normal course of a school day.

Using Social and Emotional Learning to Build Resiliency

Social and Emotional Learning (SEL) provides a structure by which all students can receive attention to their social and emotional needs, regardless of point of occurrence or severity, and is increasingly becoming a prioritized agenda item for educational policy.

This term was initiated in 1994, during a time in which many prevention programs aimed at addressing children's mental health were enthusiastically implemented, but in a manner that was short term, fragmented, and unsystematic in delivery, and were not tested for effectiveness in naturalistic settings. At the time of this writing, several investigative groups, including the Collaborative for Academic, Social, and Emotional Learning (CASEL; see www.casel.org) are proactively working to study the effectiveness of SEL strategies and programs, and the qualities that produce positive results for all children. Greenberg, Weissberg, Utne O'Brien, and colleagues (2003) extensively discussed the rationale behind providing students with coordinated and sustainable social and emotional instruction in an educational setting across grade levels. Although the concept of SEL can include a variety of topic areas crucial to childhood mental health development (e.g., anger management, prevention of substance use and abuse), we will focus on the application of SEL in the context of internalizing problems. The importance of addressing internalizing problems swiftly and accurately cannot be emphasized enough. School attendance, work completion, and peer relationships, all partially depend upon students having the capacity to get out of bed in the morning, concentrate, and appropriately interact with their peers (e.g., laugh, understand others' feelings). Having the social and emotional skills to successfully navigate inevitable developmental, maturational changes can directly impact students' academic performance (Wang, Haertel, & Walberg, 1997). These skills can be taught and learned (CASEL, 2003), and executed in a manner that is feasible for educators and does not detract from the keystone of education—academic learning and performance.

Educational settings are gradually increasing their efforts of implementing SEL strategies in an organized and thoughtful manner; however, challenges abound in establishing sustainable implementation that *all* school players will embrace—teachers, teacher assistants, administrators, students, parents and school board electees, and community members. Experience has more than adequately demonstrated that while there are effective programs available that address a variety of SEL concepts, all too often the manuals and videos collect dust in a cabinet because the program was systemically unsupported, either by insufficient training, funding, and time, or because it failed to produce the expected outcomes of problem remediation. It is unrealistic to expect that a program can be successful in the absence of systemic support for implementation in the manner in which it was intended, and in the absence of plans for sustainability. Elias, Bruene-Butler, Blum, and Schuyler (2000) discussed common barriers to implementation and, in particular, the frustration that schools are increasingly providing this type of instruction when the focus might be better spent on academics. Certainly, it is highly desirable for children to receive social and emotional instruction in their home environments; unfortunately, many caregivers are insufficiently equipped to teach their children effective strategies for healthy coping, in ways that are proven effective. On a positive note, our own research (and that of our colleagues) has demonstrated that classroom teachers are quite capable of delivering SEL interventions that lead to student success (Gueldner & Merrell, in press; Harlacher, 2008; Merrell, Juskelis, Tran, & Buchanan, 2008; Tran, 2007), and also overwhelmingly believe in the link between social and emotional skills and school performance (Buchanan, Gueldner, Tran, & Merrell, 2009). Although the challenges inherent in conducting research in naturalistic settings, with strict adherence to randomized controlled designs, exhausts the scope of this chapter (see Spence and Shortt, 2007, for a review on school-based programs targeting depression), it is important to note that attention to the balance between the need for proven efficacy, and the realistic application of effectiveness research in educational settings, is increasing (see Flannery-Schroeder, 2006, and Merrell & Buchanan, 2007, for this discussion). Related to this issue is the fact that many schools are prioritizing the need to reach federally mandated academic standards, along with protecting students against school violence. These efforts often take precedence over social and emotional learning efforts, especially those focused on preventing depression and anxiety.

There are features of SEL programming that have been found to be easily embedded into academic instruction while respecting and working with the priorities, needs, and challenges of individual school sites. Greenberg, Weissberg, Utne O'Brien, and colleagues (2003) stressed the importance of strategically planning SEL programming to consider the needs and priorities of the district, ensuring that programming will systematically occur over the course of students' education tenure (i.e., minimally, kindergarten through grade 12), utilize assessments to monitor learning and application of concepts, and adjust instruction to accommodate student and classroom needs. Payton and colleagues (2000) additionally highlighted the following strategies as being important to the success of SEL implementation: the instructional concepts should be based on a conceptual framework; the materials are easy to implement; students should actively participate in instructional experiences that are relevant to their lives; teachers should have access to instructional support through trainings or onsite technical assistance; concepts should be taught throughout the course of the school day; and school-to-family and school-to-community partnerships should be developed. These strategies must be strongly considered to be implemented, if SEL is to be successful for the long term and not just a passing trend.

An Example of an SEL Curriculum Promoting Resiliency: The Strong Kids Series

The *Strong Kids* social/emotional learning programs were developed by us and our colleagues at the University of Oregon, with the goal of creating user-friendly, low cost, and carefully structured materials that could be easily implemented by school personnel to promote resiliency and coping for students in pre-kindergarten through the twelfth grades. Five age-specific versions of the Strong Kids programs were created to ensure that the content was developmentally appropriate, and to build upon the concepts in a way that students can have exposure to them across time, to promote maintenance and generalization. These five versions include *Strong Start for Pre-K* (Merrell, Whitcomb, & Parisi, 2009), *Strong Start for Grades K–2* (Merrell, Parisi, & Whitcomb, 2007), *Strong Kids for Grades 3–5* (Merrell, Carrizales, Feuerborn, Gueldner, & Tran, 2007a), *Strong Kids for Grades 6–8* (Merrell, Carrizales, Feuerborn, Gueldner, & Tran, 2007b), and *Strong Teens for Grades 9–12* (Merrell, Carrizales, Feuerborn, Gueldner, & Tran, 2007c). Ten to 12 lessons are included in the volumes (few lessons for younger children), with a focus on teaching social and emotional learning concepts, building resiliency, finding assets and building upon them, setting goals, and learning general coping skills. Skills that can be used to address internalizing problems are specifically reviewed, such as emotion identification, behavioral activation, managing stress and anxiety, social problem solving and anger management, and cognitive restructuring. The curriculum was designed to be used in the classroom during a typical school day, and integrated naturally into academic areas such as language arts, a health and wellness curriculum, and social studies. Research to date has demonstrated positive, promising results with the Strong Kids programs, most notably in the areas of students retaining the content knowledge they have learned, decreasing existing internalizing symptoms, high levels of intervention integrity, and strong social validity (e.g., Gueldner & Merrell, in press; Harlacher, 2008; Merrell, Juskelis, Tran, & Buchanan, 2008; Tran, 2007). Areas of future research include evaluating generalization and maintenance effects across common situations and over time, the use of "booster sessions" facilitate these effects, and supporting school-to-home partnerships to bolster this relationship and promote wellness throughout. For more details about the Strong Kids programs, readers are directed to the official Strong Kids website at http://strongkids.uoregon.edu.

Universal Strategies Useful for Addressing Internalizing Problems

As we discussed in the previous section, using social and emotional learning concepts is a growing technology whereby all students can learn skills to protect against and address a myriad of problems that occur in childhood. For students at risk of developing, and known to experience, depression and anxiety symptoms, what types of strategies are known to be effective specifically for these issues? Treatments focused on improving mental health outcomes in children have been clearly documented over the past decade or so (e.g., Burns & Hoagwood, 2002; Burns, Hoagwood, & Mrazek, 1999; Weisz, Weiss, Han, Granger, & Morton, 1995). This is quite encouraging, and demonstrates the field's focus and commitment to recognizing and treating acute and chronic childhood mental health problems. Although there are many mental health prevention strategies and programs that focus on a variety of facets of children's mental health (e.g., social skills, bullying, self-control, social problem-solving, aggression and antisocial behavior), the field remains in its infancy in terms of the number and quality of effective, universally and easily implemented programs that focus on the prevention of, and early intervention with, anxiety and depression. Reasons for this are comprehensively discussed in Flannery-Schroeder's (2006) call for increased attention to the role of comorbid factors, such as anxiety and its potential prodrome to depression, and in Merrell and Buchanan's (2006) review of the strength and limitations of efficacy and effectiveness research in applied settings. Understanding how anxiety and depression develop in childhood is improving; however, given the multiple contributing factors and their interactions (see Garber, 2006 for an excellent review), the task of implementing and studying prevention programs in one of many ecologies (i.e., the school) known to influence childhood mental health development is often difficult and daunting. We acknowledge the multitude of challenges associated with these issues, and support rigorous efforts to further the research in applied settings. In light of the complexity of these factors, the next section of this chapter focuses on currently used and effective strategies applied to educational settings, either in isolation or as part of a comprehensive curriculum aimed at preventing and reducing internalizing symptoms.

Universal prevention strategies and programs involve whole groups of individuals, not just those who are preselected due to meeting at-risk or clinically indicated criteria for having depression and/or anxiety symptoms. The goal is to expose this group of students (often in a mandated health or language arts course) to instructional content known to boost one's ability to cope with stress, and dissuade anxiety and depression from taking hold. The content is generally focused on cognitive and behavioral techniques that have proven effective with individuals having existing depression and anxiety symptoms. Commonly used content typically includes: developing a vocabulary and understanding of common, more complex emotions (as one becomes older); engaging in behavioral activities that activate known physiological buffers to stress (e.g., exercising), or that can provide distraction from stressful times or just plain enjoyment; learning about one's thoughts accompanied by emotions, and the thinking errors that can be experienced simultaneously and worsen symptoms; treating these thoughts as alterable; and promoting better understanding of other people's feelings and ways to interact in a prosocial manner.

Emotion Education, Behavioral Strategies, and Cognitive Restructuring

Before discussing specific programs or curricula found to be beneficial to students, there are many individual strategies worth mentioning that can be easily implemented during the course of a typical school day. Simply learning about one's emotions is an excellent starting point for most children, particularly young children just starting school. Students learn about a variety of common emotions, their associated facial expressions on themselves and other people, physiological sensations that usually accompany emotion (e.g., a rapid heartbeat often occurs in the context of anxious feeling), whether these emotions are "comfortable" or "uncomfortable," and how

emotions can be complex at times (e.g., feeling surprised might feel comfortable in some situations, but uncomfortable in others). Once students learn about their emotions, they can apply this knowledge to situations that they directly experience. The use of sentence stems may be useful in helping students utilize this technique. For example, students would be prompted by an adult or worksheet to reflect on situations in which they experience an emotion and fill in the blank (e.g., "I feel scared when…" or "I was really nervous when…"). This structure is commonly used to productively communicate emotions throughout a lifetime (e.g., communicating in an adult, romantic relationship) and is an excellent start to learning a lifelong skill.

Once students learn about emotions and positive ways in which they can communicate them, they can learn to engage in activities that can distract them or alleviate uncomfortable feelings. Behaviorally based strategies can be regularly used to effectively offset the negative spiral of depression and anxiety. Students can be taught to identify and generate a list of activities that they enjoy, and can easily engage in on a regular basis. Adults can encourage and give students structure around how to consistently fit these activities into their other daily activities. Another way in which teachers can reinforce behaviors that are incongruent with feeling depressed or anxious is to praise or offer tangible rewards for behaviors such as smiling, giving eye contact, engaging in social interactions that are enjoyable.

As students cognitively mature, they can increasingly take part in learning about their thoughts, and how their thoughts and feelings interact with one another. This will be difficult for younger or lower functioning children, as they may not have the capacity to understand some of these complexities. Beck (1967) is largely credited with the pioneering work in the area of using cognitive strategies to treat depression, and this model greatly shaped its use as applied to youth. A first step in recognizing cognitions is to have students identify situations that evoked a particular emotion, and then consider the intensity of the emotion that they experienced. A common example is the emotion of anger, and considering how it can vary in intensity according the situation, how the event was interpreted (i.e., what were the cognitions?). This helps students understand that most emotions can occur to varying degrees of intensity, and occupy greater or lesser portions of their focus. The next step is to increase awareness that there are thoughts that simultaneously and often *precede* emotions. This idea may be novel to many, depending on their level of prior experience with this concept, and certainly is it still novel to many adults! For example, one student may interpret a poor grade on a test with the thought, "The teacher deliberately gave me this bad grade," and experience a feeling of anger, while another student may interpret the same event with the thought, "I just knew I'd get a D on this assignment because I didn't study enough." Students are prompted to pay attention to their thoughts primarily by being coached to do so, and to keep track of their thoughts via a "Thought Chart" (see Merrell, 2008a for activity ideas and reproducible worksheets). Once students understand that thoughts and emotions co-occur, they learn to identify common thinking errors, beliefs they may have about themselves (e.g., "I just knew I'd get a D on this assignment [thought]…because I *always* do and am really stupid [belief]"), and determine ways of changing the way they think, so these negative or irrational thoughts do not lead to depression and anxiety. We have found through our research that students really enjoy learning about their thoughts, and the notion that there may be ways to look at situations more realistically and perhaps positively. Using journal writing during a language arts instructional block is a popular activity that can be used to guide students through identifying thoughts, feelings, and beliefs, in a structured way in which they can receive support and feedback, as well as learn from each other by sharing their journaling as appropriate.

Programs Designed to Prevent Depression and Anxiety

We have just reviewed the primary components of programs and curricula aimed at preventing or intervening early with depression and anxiety symptoms—emotion identification, understanding the interaction among thoughts, feelings, and beliefs, and using strategies to change negative or irrational thoughts and beliefs and, consequently, improve mood. For some settings and circumstances, these strategies may work best in isolation; however, often they are best used in conjunction with one another, and with multiple opportunities for practice and generalization. There are a few programs that are specifically designed to prevent internalizing problems by universally delivering them in an educational setting. Researching prevention programs aimed to prevent internalizing problems is in its infancy, largely because: (1) few programs have been developed to address this area, and (2) this research demands longitudinal tracking of symptoms over

time, taking into account multiple influential variables. The following programs have recent publications documenting short-term effectiveness on depression and anxiety symptoms.

The *Strong Kids* series is one program that was developed with prevention in mind. As previously discussed, this curriculum has specifically been studied to evaluate the extent to which students are able to retain the content of the curricular materials, and whether existing depression and anxiety symptoms may be reduced. Of course, with any population that represents a "typically functioning" student sample, the base rate of symptoms is often low when considered as a whole. For this reason, measuring *resiliency skills and strengths* rather than symptoms is perhaps more meaningful as an outcome measure (Harlacher, 2008). The *Reaching New Heights* program appears to be in early stages of study (Klein, 2004), and was evaluated with two classrooms consisting of middle-school-age gifted children. Intervention components included learning stress management skills, decreasing social and academic anxiety, and increasing coping skills. Results from this study suggested improvements in problem solving and improvements in frustration tolerance and assertiveness. The *Resourceful Adolescent Program (RAP)* is an 11-session program designed to be implemented as part of the typical school curriculum for typically developing students, as a way of teaching skills known to prevent and intervene with symptoms of depression. Results of a pilot study (Shochet, Dadds, Holland, Whitefield, Harnett, & Osgarby, 2001) suggested the program was able to be implemented with good fidelity, with a high degree of student participation. Student participants showed a decrease in depression symptoms at post-intervention and 10 months follow-up, suggesting a preventative effect over time. Parents were also invited to participate as part of this intervention, but unfortunately, low participation likely contributed to unremarkable findings in this area.

Indicated Programs Useful for Addressing Depression

The literature that addresses intervening with depression symptoms, either because students have been identified to be at risk of developing depression or the symptoms may worsen, is much better developed and encouraging than that reviewed in the last section. Certainly, measuring effects of an intervention used with students known to be acutely experiencing symptoms can be more precise, given the vast use of reliable and valid assessments available (e.g., Children's Depression Inventory) and the ability to measure change. We are also increasingly recognizing the importance of prevention and "retooling" our methodologies so they apply to new, prevention-oriented questions. Additionally, the field continues to struggle with assessing the effects of the intervention in the most comprehensive manner (expanding measurement beyond student self-report to include parent and teacher reports, interviews, observations, and the impact on school performance) *and* making these measurements feasible for participants. That said, there are several programs worthy of note that have documented effects, are organized in their delivery, and comprehensive in scope, in their efforts to intervene with depression symptoms in children.

The most effective interventions for depression in children utilize cognitive and behavioral techniques. We discussed the theoretical background, as well as example strategies, in a previous section in this chapter; this section will focus on specific programs that integrate these principles into comprehensive and coordinated programs. The *Adolescent Coping with Depression* course (Clark, Lewinsohn, & Hops, 1990) is a well researched psychoeducational program that was designed to teach adolescents and their parents cognitive and behaviorally based skills to cope with depression. Skills include education regarding depression, learning how to reduce stress and make life changes, challenging irrational thoughts, learning and applying positive communication and problem-solving strategies, and setting life goals. Sixteen 2-hour sessions comprise this curriculum, with additional sessions held with parents. Classes are taught in small groups in a "classroom" type environment to reduce stigma associated with psychotherapy. Unlike the individual strategies previously discussed in this chapter, the sessions for this program are highly structured and, in fact, scripted for ease of use and standardization. The *Taking ACTION Program* (Stark & Kendall, 1996) is another program that uses cognitive and behaviorally based strategies, to be used with children ages 9 through adolescence, who are coping with depression. Again, this program is structured, well organized, and is delivered via thirty 1-hour sessions. It uses an unscripted curriculum to allow for flexibility, but provides a detailed list of activities and objectives that are pertinent to each lesson. A group format is used to facilitate the program, highlighting the importance of social learning and support, in conjunction with assisting individuals in specific areas of need as necessary.

This program has been field-tested in schools, but would be very appropriate for use in other settings. *Interpersonal family therapy for childhood depression (IFT)* offers an alternative focus on depression intervention by working with families, and the interactions that occur within this system, as a way of improving symptoms and overall functioning (see Schwartz, Kaslow, Racusin, & Carton, 1998, for a review of research documenting the impact of family factors on childhood depression). IFT integrates the use of psychoeducation and cognitive and behavior strategies to ameliorate depression, but also focuses on treating the entire family and changing interactions that may be contributing to depression characteristics. A challenge to the success of this program is retaining parent participation due to busy schedules, but also their own mental health problems, and not having access to or refusing treatment. A final program of note is *interpersonal psychotherapy (IPT)* for use with adolescents. This therapy is best used with children having average or higher intellectual skills, with the goal of improving depression symptoms and their interpersonal functioning. IPT is based on the assumption that treating depression involves addressing interpersonal relationships that may contribute to the development and maintenance of depression, as well as the interaction between the two. As applied to adolescents, the focus is on typical adolescent development, relationships with parents, peers, and teachers, and usual social problems. A treatment manual is available by Mufson and colleagues (1993, 2004) and details the content of the 12 lessons designed to be implemented at a rate of one lesson each week. This program has documented success in treating depression; users should be mindful that to be successful, it is best used with adolescents having good inter- and intrapersonal insight. Of course, implementation of any of these programs must take a variety of factors into consideration, including the age and cognitive maturity of the student, availability of parents, and how the program can fit into the normal course of a school day, or routine in another mental health facility.

Strategies Useful for Addressing Anxiety

Symptoms associated with anxiety are another facet of internalizing problems, and often co-occur or precede depression. Manifestations of anxiety can range from simple fears of insects or a general sense of worrying during most of the day, to refusing to attend school due to social interaction problems and debilitating panic. Behavioral treatments for anxiety are grounded in operant and classical conditioning, with the addition of cognitive strategies similar to those previously discussed. There are three primary intervention techniques that will be discussed in this section; all are systematically applied and tailored to individually specific needs. For example, working with a child with a specific phobia of spiders will follow a general treatment format, but may need alterations if the child is four years old as compared to 15 years old. Structured programs that have also been rigorously evaluated are also available to treat anxiety, and will be discussed in the section following.

Systematic desensitization is a behaviorally based intervention for reducing fears and phobias. Typically, inducing a sense of calm and relaxation is used as a physiological response that is incompatible to anxiety, and is implemented in conjunction with exposure to feared stimuli. In the case of a student who is refusing to go to school, the treatment would start by coaching the student to use a relaxation strategy until it is mastered to the point where the student can fairly independently use the strategy. Next, the student would generate a list or hierarchy of stimuli that produce anxiety, and then imagine the least anxiety-producing item on this list. For example, if a student is experiencing social phobia or anxiety, and subsequently refusing to go to school to avoid all social interactions, the student would be asked to imagine getting ready for school, walking onto the school grounds, going into the school building, walking into the classroom, and so on, and then progressing to in vivo exposure to these same actions. The student would practice relaxation strategies before and during engagement in the imaginary and in vivo exposures. Most students can learn how to engage in this treatment during the course of a school day, with situations that are applicable to school. A trained school professional can teach relaxation strategies that can be practiced during a school group or individual session; a hierarchy of anxiety-producing stimuli may be developed by asking students to rank order their feared situations; desensitization can be invoked with the guidance of the school-based professional—this is usually best done individually, as compared to in a group, since individual fears will differ.

Modeling and *positive reinforcement* can also be used as interventions for behaviors and feelings associated with anxiety. Modeling is based on social learning theory, and posits that by observing the behavior of other students and the outcomes of that behavior, students experiencing anxiety can learn

that it is more likely that there will be positive outcomes associated with engaging in the activity they fear. Students who worry about public speaking may observe others giving speeches, and watch the speaker and audience's behavior. The professional guiding the student through this process might highlight how quickly the time passed, the audience clapping after the speech, and how, regardless of the quality of the speech, it is typically human nature for audience members to not dwell on someone else's speech but rather quickly be engaged by the next task at hand (i.e., audience members do not ruminate about the content and quality of a speech to the extent that speakers generally do!). Younger children benefit from this technique by reading fictional accounts with lively illustrations via children's literature. They watch how facing one's fears typically does not result in feared consequences, but rather some positive outcomes (e.g., the vaccination hurts briefly and the child patient receives a small toy or sticker). Similarly, students can be *differentially reinforced* for behaviors that are not compatible with behaviors associated with anxiety. For example, for a student who refuses to eat lunch in the cafeteria with other children due to the fear of being watched eating in public, the student would be given a desired reinforcer for eating in the cafeteria. Positive reinforcement occurs when the probability that the desired behavior (eating in the cafeteria) increases with each attempt. Paramount to this process is determining the reinforcers that are preferred by students. They can vary from obtaining a tangible object (reward from school store) to nontangible, via verbal praise, earning a privilege, or getting out of something undesired. Simply providing the student with a list of options from which to choose can get this very important part of the intervention started, and motivate toward change.

Cognitive strategies can be combined with behaviorally oriented strategies (as those described in the last section) to form comprehensive programming for students experiencing anxiety. There are five specific programs that have shown promise at being effective. The first is *self-control training,* whereby students are taught to monitor their thoughts and feelings, as well as the outcomes that occur following their thoughts and behaviors. Because students are essentially in charge of doing this themselves after awhile, it is generally recommended that children be at least 10 or 11 years old or older. This strategy can often be used in conjunction with systematic desensitization or modeling, and can be effective at monitoring those self-statements and thoughts that lead to anxiety. *Self-instructional training for anxiety* can be used by children of many ages, by using self-talk to change thoughts and behaviors (Meichenbaum, 1986). Scripted self-talk is modeled to students by an adult, while performing a task that typically elicits anxiety. Students eventually learn through many opportunities for practice to engage in this process with automaticity and application to a variety of situations. A *transfer-of-control approach* is a strategy useful for children having phobias, as well as general anxiety and fears, and uses expert consultation by way of a therapist to "transfer" this expertise to the parent and then to the child. This strategy was developed and implemented in clinical settings, but can be used by mental health consultants (e.g., school psychologists) in the school setting. Exposure is used as the primary mechanism to teach youth how to cope with anxiety and fear. Parents are given specific instructions on how to implement the techniques at home, so that practice may occur across settings and with support. They may need additional coaching to cope with the common parental instinct of protecting their child against uncomfortable feelings elicited from feared stimuli, which is counterproductive to treatment (Merrell, 2008a). Cognitive techniques are also applied during exposure, to identify anxious thoughts and feelings and consider other thoughts or behaviors that are more adaptive.

Indicated Programs Useful for Addressing Anxiety

We just reviewed a variety of behavioral and cognitive strategies that have been successfully applied to students experiencing anxiety. While there are few comprehensive programs that are known to be effective for youth identified as experiencing acute or chronic anxiety, two programming efforts are important for review. First, the *Coping Cat Program* was developed by Kendall and associates for children ages 8 though 17, and offers two versions—one for children and one for adolescents. The program can be used with individuals and with groups, and includes psychoeducation regarding somatic, cognitive, and behavioral characteristics of anxiety, and treatment using cognitive-behavioral techniques to deal with these symptoms. This program includes many of the techniques described in this section, and combines them into a comprehensive program. A second general program is *social skills training*. Many students with anxiety experience symptoms that impact their social functioning (e.g., withdrawal, missing school due to somatic

complaints, fears of speaking in public or with peers), which is a vital part of the human experience. Often these students are deficient in their ability to solve socially oriented problems, and are prone to disengaging in the very interactions that strengthen these skills. Sometimes they have the skills, but do not perform the skill when appropriate due to an anxious cognition that interferes with performing the skill (e.g., knowing how to say "Thank you," but fearing that her voice sounds strange to others).

Merrell and Gimpel (1998) reviewed common social-skills models and programs, and identified the primary components of this skill training. Students identify problems and possible solutions, students are taught how to engage in the social behavior that will best solve the problem by watching an adult model the behavior and then practice it via role-playing situations, and students are given feedback on their performance with praise, correction, and additional modeling. Students are also asked to say aloud the thoughts they are having during practice, so distorted or maladaptive thoughts are identified. Social skills training programs often use behavioral management strategies to minimize inappropriate behavior during this instructional time. A key element of these programs is promoting generalization of these skills across settings, and maintaining their effects over time. In order to do this, students must be given multiple opportunities for practice with supportive coaching along the way.

Remembering Embedded Ecologies

Research and practice have documented promising developments in the way in which internalizing problems are identified and treated in children. Although we have reviewed some of the current trends in assessment, identification, and treatment, this discussion is incomplete without a look at other ecological factors that influence the development and maintenance of depression and anxiety in children. Garber (2006) highlighted known risk factors for the development of internalizing problems, and the importance of linking them to prevention efforts for childhood depression. Ecologies of note include microsystemic issues of the inherited factors that may predispose children to depression, gender, and temperament; living with a parent who is depressed, and the parent–child transactions that shape children's cognitions and behaviors; interpersonal relationships with adults and peers (family and other); stressful life events, which often include meso, exo and macrosystemic community factors such as socioecomonic status, employment opportunities, access to health services, discrimination and cultural disparities, and so on.

In the field of school psychology we are, of course, aware of and concerned with the school as an ecology, whereby we try to improve upon variables that may be altered—some more easily than others—via programming that can support all students (e.g., positive behavior supports, anti-bullying policies and programs). Schools must take into consideration the impact of strong, effective policies and schoolwide initiatives on school climate and children's mental health. Espelage and Swearer (2004) candidly discussed the impact of bullying, peer harassment, and relational aggression on the development of internalizing problems in children. Adopting anti-bullying policies and *diligently observing them* can contribute to making the school ecology a safer place to learn and develop. We strive to support teachers in their efforts to model adaptive, positive coping strategies and problem-solving, as an informal means to teaching students life skills beyond academics. The school ecology is additionally impacted by the value placed on mental health services, noticeable via the number and quality of school based mental health clinics and clinicians. Consideration of these factors is *mandatory* if we are to appropriately attend to the mental health needs of students, both from a prevention and intervention approach. Continued education of professionals both within and outside the field of school psychology is required to ensure these additional factors are not only contemplated, but acted upon.

Conclusion

The field of school psychology is in an incredibly advantageous position to influence the incidence of internalizing problems in a student population. We cannot emphasize enough the importance of prevention and early intervention efforts that can occur in this setting—a virtual front-row seat to this problem and opportunity. Research efforts must continue to rigorously evaluate the effectiveness of new and existing prevention and intervention programs, taking into account cultural factors and the unique circumstances associated with research in applied settings. Our hope is that *all* children may one day possess the skills needed to build their resiliency to face current and, inevitably, ongoing challenges and stressors in life, and we are confident that with tenacious efforts, this is an achievable goal.

Future Directions

1. There is emerging evidence to suggest that implementing school-based prevention efforts to address internalizing problems is a viable strategy. More research is needed to determine the long-term effects of these efforts on students' ability to engage resiliency skills during difficult times.

2. More school based interventions are being implemented in schools. It is imperative that we continue to promote coordinated efforts that are sustainable over time, are naturally embedded into a typical school day, and are found to be cost effective.

3. Home–school collaborative efforts are critically needed for families to support their children in learning, practicing, and applying the social and emotional concepts they learn in school, and transferring this knowledge to everyday situations.

References

Angold, A., Costello, E. J., & Erkanli, A. (1999). Comorbidity. *Journal of Child Psychology and Psychiatry, 40,* 57–87.

Austin, A. A., & Chorpita, B. F. (2004). Temperament, anxiety, and depression: Comparisons across five ethnic groups of children. *Journal of Clinical Child and Adolescent Psychology, 33,* 216–226.

Beck, A. T. (1967). *Depression: Clinical, experimental, and theoretical.* New York: Hoeber.

Buchanan, R., Gueldner, B. A., Tran, O. K., & Merrell, K. W. (2009). Social and emotional learning in classrooms: A survey of teachers' knowledge, perceptions, and practices. *Journal of Applied School Psychology, 25,* 1–17.

Burns, B. J. & Hoagwood, K. (2002). *Community treatment for youth: Evidence-based interventions for severe emotional and behavioral disorders.* New York: Oxford University Press.

Burns, B. J., Hoagwood, K., & Mrazek, P. J. (1999). Effective treatment for mental disorders in children and adolescents. *Clinical Child and Family Psychology Review, 2,* 199–254.

Collaborative for Academic, Social, and Emotional Learning. (2003). *Safe and sound: An educational leader's guide to evidence-based social and emotional learning programs.* Retrieved July 1, 2005 from www.casel.com.

Clark, L. A. & Watson, D. (1991). Tripartite model of anxiety and depression: Evidence and taxonomic implications. *Journal of Abnormal Psychology, 100,* 316–336.

Clark, G., Lewinsohn, P., & Hops, H. (1990). *Coping with adolescent depression course: Leader's manual for adolescent groups.* Eugene, OR: Castalia. Note: This program is no longer available in print, but is available electronically as a free download from the Kaiser Permanente Center for Health Research website, at www.kpchr.org/public/acwd/acwd.html.

Elias, M. J., Bruene-Butler, L., Blum, L., & Schuyler, T. (2000). Voices from the field: Identifying and overcoming roadblocks to carrying out programs in social and emotional learning emotional intelligence. *Journal of Educational and Psychological Consultation, 11,* 253–272.

Espalage, D. L., & Swearer, S. M. (2004). *Bullying in American schools: A social-ecological perspective on prevention and intervention*. Malwah, NJ: Lawrence Erlbaum Associates.

Flannery-Schroeder, E. C. (2006). Reducing anxiety to prevent depression. *American Journal of Preventative Medicine, 31,* 136–140.

Garber, J. (2006) Depression in children and adolescents. Linking risk research and prevention. *American Journal of Preventive Medicine, 31,* 104–125.

Ginsberg, G. S., & Silverman, W. K. (1996). Phobias and anxiety disorders in Hispanic and Caucasian youth. *Journal of Anxiety Disorders, 10,* 517–528.

Greenberg, P. E., Kessler, R. C., Birnbaum, H. G., Leong, S. A., Lowe, S. W., Berglund, P. A., & Corey-Lisle, P. K. (2003). The economic burden of depression in the United States: How did it change between 1990 and 2000? *Journal of Clinical Psychiatry, 64,* 1465–1475.

Greenberg, M. T., Weissberg, R.P., Utne O'Brien, M., Zins, J. E., Redericks, L., Resnik, H., & Elias, M. J. (2003). Enhancing school-based prevention and youth development through coordinated social, emotional, and academic learning. *American Psychologist, 58,* 466–474.

Gueldner, B. A., & Merrell, K. W. (in press). Evaluation of a social-emotional learning program in conjunction with the exploratory application of performance feedback incorporating motivational interviewing techniques. *Journal of Educational and Psychological Consultation, 21*(1).

Gueldner, B. A., & Merrell, K. (2008). Internalizing problems and mental health. In R. S. Sprick & M. Garrison, *Interventions: Evidence-based behavioral strategies for individual students* (2nd. ed.) (pp. 751–791). Eugene, OR: Pacific Northwest Publishing.

Harlacher, J. E. (2008). *Social and emotional learning as a universal level of support: Evaluating the follow-up effect of Strong Kids on social and emotional outcomes*. Unpublished doctoral dissertation, University of Oregon, Eugene.

Hintz, J. M. (2005). Psychometrics of direct observation. *School Psychology Review, 34,* 507–519.

Hintze, J. M., & Matthews, W. J. (2004). The generalizability of systematic direct observations across time and setting: A preliminary investigation of the psychometrics of behavioral observation. *School Psychology Review, 33,* 258–270.

Hughes, E. K. & Gullone, E. (2007). Internalizing symptoms and disorders in families of adolescents: A review of family systems literature. *Clinical Psychology Review, 28,* 92–117.

Klein, S. M. (2004). *Reaching new heights: A primary prevention program for gifted middle school students*. Unpublished Dissertation. Department of Psychology, Graduate College of Bowling Green State University.

Last, C. G., & Perrin, S. (1993). Anxiety disorders in African American and White children. *Journal of Abnormal Child Psychology, 21,* 153–164.

Levitt, V. H., & Merrell, K. W. (2008). *Linking assessment to intervention for internalizing problems of children and adolescents*. Manuscript submitted for publication.

Lynch, F. L. & Clarke, G. N. (2006). Estimating the economic burden of depression in children and adolescents. *American Journal of Preventive Medicine, 31,* 143–151.

Meichenbaum, D. (1986). Cognitive behavior modification. In F. H. Kanfer & A. P. Goldstein (Eds.), *Helping people change* (3rd ed., pp. 390–422). Elmsford, NY: Pergamon Press.

Merrell, K. W. (2008a). *Helping students overcome depression and anxiety: A Practical guide* (2nd ed.). New York: Guilford Publications.

Merrell, K. W. (2008b). *Behavioral, social, and emotional assessment of children and adolescents* (3rd ed.). London: Taylor and Francis/Routledge.

Merrell, K. W. & Buchanan, R. (2006). Intervention selection in school-based practice: Using public health models to enhance systems capacity of schools. *School Psychology Review, 35,* 167–180.

Merrell, K. W., Carrizales, D., Feuerborn, L., Gueldner, B. A., & Tran, O. K. (2007a). *Strong kids for grades 3–5: A social and emotional learning curriculum*. Baltimore: Paul H.Brookes Publishing.

Merrell, K. W., Carrizales, D., Feuerborn, L., Gueldner, B. A., & Tran, O. K. (2007b). *Strong kids for grades 6–8: A social and emotional learning curriculum*. Baltimore: Paul H.Brookes Publishing.

Merrell, K. W., Carrizales, D., Feuerborn, L., Gueldner, B. A., & Tran, O. K. (2007c). *Strong teens for grades 9–12: A social and emotional learning curriculum*. Baltimore: Paul H.Brookes Publishing.

Merrell, K. W. & Gimpel, G. A. (1998) *Social skills of children and adolescents: Conceptualization, assessment, treatment*. Malwah, NJ: Erlbaum.

Merrell, K. W., Juskelis, M. P., Tran, O. K., & Buchanan, R. (2008). Social and emotional learning in the classroom: Evaluation of Strong Kids and Strong Teens on students' social-emotional knowledge and symptoms. *Journal of Applied School Psychology, 24,* 208–224.

Merrell, K. W., Parisi, D., & Whitcomb, S. (2007). *Strong Start for Grades K–2: A social and emotional learning curriculum*. Baltimore: Paul H. Brookes Publishing.

Merrell, K. W., Whitcomb, S., & Parisi, D. (2009). *Strong Start for Pre-K: A social and emotional learning curriculum*. Baltimore: Paul H. Brookes Publishing.

Mufson, L., Dorta, K. P., Moreasu, D., & Weissman, M. M. (2004). *Interpersonal therapy for depressed adolescents* (2nd ed.). New York: Guilford Press.

Mufson, L., Moreau, d., Weissman, M. M., & Klerman, G. L. (1993). *Interpersonal therapy for depressed adolescents*. New York: Guilford Press.

Quay, H. R. (1986). Classificiation. In H. C. Quay & J. S. Werry (Eds.), *Psychopathological disorders of childhood* (3rd ed., pp. 1–34). New York: Wiley.

Payton, J. W., Wardlaw, D. M., Graczyk, P. A., Bloodworth, M. R., Tompsett, C. J., Weissberg, R. P. (2000). Social and emotional learning: A framework for promoting mental health and reducing risk behaviors in children and youth. *Journal of School Health, 70,* 179–185.

Reynolds, W. M. (Ed.). (1992). *Internalizing disorders in children and adolescents*. New York: Wiley.

Schwartz, J. A. J., Kaslow, N. J., Racusin, G. R., & Carton, E. R. (1998). Interpersonal family therapy for childhood depression. In V. B. Van Hasselt & M. Hersen (Eds.), *Handbook of psychological treatment protocols for children and adolescents* (pp. 109–151). Mahwah, NJ: Erlbaum.

Seeley, J. R., Rohde, P., Lewinsohn, P. M., & Clarke, G. N. (2002). Depression in youth: Epidemiology, identification, and intervention. In M. R. Shinn, H. M. Walker, & G. Stoner (Eds.), *Interventions for academic and behavior problems II: Preventative and remedial approaches* (pp. 885–911). Bethesda, MD: National Association of School Psychologists.

Shochet, I. M., Dadds, M. R., Holland, D., Whitefield, K., Harnett, P. H., & Osgarby, S. M. (2001). The efficacy of a universal school-based program to prevent adolescent depression. *Journal of Clinical Child Psychology, 30*, 303–315.

Spence, S. H. & Shortt, A. L. (2007). Research review: Can we justify the widespread dissemination of universal, school-based interventions for the prevention of depression among children and adolescents? *Journal of Child Psychology and Psychiatry, 48*, 526–542.

Stark, K. D., & Kendall, P. C. (1996). *Treating depressed children: Therapist manual for ACTION.* Ardmore, PA: Workbook Publishing.

Todd, A. W., Horner, R. H., Sugai, G., & Sprague, J. R. (1999). Effective behavior support: Strengthening school-wide systems through a team-based approach. *Effective School Practices, 17, 23–27.*

Tran, O. K. (2007). *Promoting social and emotional learning in schools: An investigation of massed versus distributed practice schedules and social validity of the Strong Kids curriculum in late elementary aged students.* Unpublished doctoral dissertation, University of Oregon, Eugene.

Wang, M. C., Haertel, G. D., & Walberg, H. J. (1997). Learning influences. In H. J. Walberg & G. D. Haertel (Eds.), *Psychology and educational practice* (p. 199–211). Berkely, CA: McCatchan.

Weisz, J. R., Weiss, B., Han, S. S., Granlger, D. A., & Morton, T. (1995). Effects of psychotherapy with children and adolescents revisited: A meta-analysis of treatment outcome studies. *Psychological Bulletin, 117*, 450–468.

Classroom Interventions for Attention and Hyperactivity

George J. DuPaul, Jocelyn R. Helwig, *and* Peter M. Slay

Abstract

Problems with inattention and hyperactivity are the core behaviors comprising attention-deficit/hyperactivity disorder (ADHD). Students exhibiting ADHD-related behaviors experience significant difficulties with behavior and academic performance. Thus, classroom interventions can be used to address these difficulties in the context of a three-tiered, data based, problem-solving model. Specific intervention strategies addressing behavioral, academic, and social functioning are described across all three tiers. A case study is provided to demonstrate the implementation of this three-tiered model for a student with ADHD. Alternative classroom interventions with little to no empirical support are also briefly described. Finally, the chapter concludes with a delineation of limitations of the extant treatment literature, and suggestions for future directions.

Keywords: attention-deficit/hyperactivity disorder, ADHD, classroom interventions, school psychology

Problems with attention, impulse control, and/or activity level are relatively common among school-aged youth in the United States. When these difficulties are frequent, chronic, have a childhood onset, and are associated with significant impairment, then students may be diagnosed with attention-deficit/hyperactivity disorder (ADHD; American Psychiatric Association, 2000). ADHD affects between 3% to 10% of children and adolescents with boys outnumbering girls from a 2:1 to 6:1 ratio (American Psychiatric Association, 2000; Barkley, 2006). This disorder is associated with a myriad of other difficulties including academic skills deficits, oppositional and defiant behavior, conduct problems, and symptoms of anxiety disorder or depression (Smith, Barkley, & Shapiro, 2007). In fact, students with ADHD are at higher than average risk for chronic behavior and academic problems that may result in special education placement, school drop-out, and lower rates of completion of post-secondary education (Barkley, Murphy, & Fischer, 2008).

The behavioral symptoms of ADHD (i.e., inattention and hyperactivity-impulsivity) are, by definition, associated with significant impairments in academic and/or social functioning (American Psychiatric Association, 2000). Specifically, students with this disorder exhibit high levels of off-task, disruptive behavior; frequently do not complete assigned tasks, or do so in a hasty, inaccurate fashion; demonstrate below-average academic achievement; and are atrisk for grade retention and/or referral for special education services (Barkley, 2006; DuPaul & Stoner, 2003). Approximately 30% of children with ADHD also have one or more learning disabilities (DuPaul& Stoner, 2003). In the social domain, students with this disorder have difficulty making and keeping friends, particularly among same-aged peers, often are rejected by their peers, and display problematic relationships with authority figures including teachers and other school personnel (American Psychiatric Association, 2000; Barkley, 2006). Thus, interventions addressing their behavioral symptoms and concomitant functional impairments are critical throughout the school years.

The purpose of this chapter is to describe effective classroom interventions for students with ADHD. It is important to note that both expert opinion (e.g., Barkley, 2006) and empirical research (e.g., MTA Cooperative Group, 1999, 2004) support the implementation of a comprehensive treatment approach that may include psychotropic medication (e.g., methylphenidate and atomoxetine) and behavioral strategies in both home and school settings. Thus, the strategies discussed in this chapter typically would be combined with other treatment approaches in order to maximize the probability of successful outcomes.

Classroom strategies for addressing the difficulties exhibited by students with ADHD are presented in the context of a three-tiered, data based, problem-solving model. This model involves using assessment data regarding response to intervention, to make decisions regarding the content, frequency, and intensity of treatment components. Interventions at all three tiers include strategies addressing behavioral, academic, and social functioning. A case study is provided to demonstrate the implementation of this three-tiered model for a student with ADHD. Alternative classroom interventions (i.e., those with little to no empirical support) are discussed briefly, so that practitioners are aware of the limitations of popular but non-research-based "treatments." The chapter concludes with a delineation of limitations of the extant treatment literature, and suggestions for future directions.

Response to Intervention: Tiered Approach to Service Delivery
Overview
In the past, school psychologist' training promoted assessment for the primary purpose of making categorical distinctions to justify the provision of special educational services (Fagan & Wise, 2007). In this way, categorization served a heuristic value in terms of providing professionals with a form of shorthand for understanding the basic needs of students. Unfortunately, categorical distinctions alone provide very imprecise information for ongoing intervention planning targeted at specific students' needs.

With the emergence of research supporting the benefits of tiered approaches to service delivery (Kovaleski, Gickling, Morrow, & Swank, 1999; Marston, Muyskens, Lau, & Canter, 2003), and

the passage of the Individuals with Disabilities Education Improvement Act (IDEIA, 2004), which permits the use of Response to Intervention (RTI) models as one part of a comprehensive assessment process, schools have increasingly moved to assimilate RTI methodologies into standard practice (for review, see Jimerson, Burns, & VanDerHeyden, 2007).

Problem Solving across Domains
RTI and multi-tiered service delivery systems share a number of common components, including universal screening, matching intervention intensity to student's level of need, monitoring progress through an iterative process of systematic assessment, and titrating intervention strength based upon students responsiveness (Brown-Chidsey & Steege, 2005). Although most research on multi-tiered service delivery has been in the academic domain, with the most rigorous implementation being delivered in the area of reading, RTI has been noted to have relevance in the domains of behavior and social relationships (Malecki & Demaray, 2007). Across each domain, the notion that intervention intensity should be systematically monitored and adjusted based on the student's level of need is critical. Framing assessment and intervention planning in terms of a tiered approach to service delivery has a number of benefits (e.g., individualizing interventions, progress-monitoring the effectiveness of interventions, conserving limited teacher resources, and the systematic documentation of children's difficulties over time).

Analyzing the problems children with ADHD face, within the context of an RTI framework, requires that attention be given to student functioning across academic, behavioral, and social relationships. RTI applications to academic, behavioral, and social difficulties require that one think about the tiers in terms of universal prevention for all students (Tier 1), selective intervention for at-risk students (Tier 2), and indicated intervention for students who warrant the most intensive treatments available (Tier 3).

Guidelines for Intervention
The following issues should be considered when designing behaviorally based interventions for classroom problems related to ADHD:

1. The design and selection of the intervention strategy should be guided by a thorough assessment of the presenting problem. This should include a functional assessment.

2. Children with ADHD require frequent feedback to optimize their performance. Specifically, initial phases of interventions should incorporate contingencies that can be delivered in a continuous manner, and at the point of performance of the behavior (Goldstein & Goldstein, 1998). It is necessary to decrease the schedule of reinforcement gradually, as children with ADHD may have difficulty maintaining their behavior (Douglas, 1984).

3. Whenever possible, preferred activities (e.g., choice during free time, access to a classroom computer) should be used as reinforcers, rather than tangible items (e.g., stickers, candy). In addition, reinforcers should be varied or rotated as needed to maintain child interest in them and, as a result, interest in the intervention (DuPaul & Stoner, 2003).

4. A "priming" procedure can be used with the child to enhance the incentive value of possible reinforcers. "Priming" involves the teacher and student reviewing the list of possible reinforcers prior to the student beginning a task. During this time, the student chooses the reinforcer he or she would like to obtain following the work period.

5. The integrity and fidelity of the intervention must be continually monitored (Gresham, 1989). This process of evaluation can serve as the basis for making changes in the intervention components, justification for additional resources, and/or developing and providing additional training regarding the intervention procedures.

Intervention for ADHD
Tier 1

Within an RTI framework, Tier 1 represents the application of empirically based instruction and procedures to all students within a classroom or school (Jimerson et al., 2007). By providing all students with high quality instruction and behavior management founded upon best practice, environmental explanations (e.g., poor instruction and classroom structure) for student's difficulties are effectively neutralized. Tier 1 interventions are geared toward preventing the emergence of learning, behavioral, and social difficulties. In this way, students with a propensity to struggle may not do so when they have been availed high quality instruction and consistent behavior management within a general education environment. When students are provided with an education that conforms to best practice and still struggle, it becomes clear that they

require more intensive interventions. Tier 1 becomes the foundation for all other subsequent intervention approaches. In some instances, students diagnosed with ADHD will be helped greatly when Tier 1 interventions are applied consistently within a given setting. Still other students will need more support, in which case more intensive intervention becomes warranted.

Classroom Structure

The way that a classroom is physically arranged has important implications for student's academic engagement and social relationships. Specifically, classroom structure impacts the degree to which the environment promotes order, predictability, and optimal engagement in a variety of learning tasks (Sugai, Horner, & Gresham, 2002). Research has indicated that the physical layout of desks within a classroom impacts student engagement and behavior (Bennett & Blundell, 1983; Wheldall & Lam, 1987). For example, Bennett and Blundell (1983) noted large increases in the quality and quantity of work completed when student's desks were arranged in rows rather than facing one another. Further, Wheldall and Lam found that when desks were situated in rows rather than in group clusters, students spent more time on task and less time engaging in disruptive behavior. Hastings and Schwieso (1995) further replicated these results, demonstrating that more disruptive children at baseline benefited most from morehighlystructured seating arrangements.

Similarly, classrooms should be arranged in such a manner as to allow the teacher to quickly and efficiently be able to survey each student's behavior (Emmer, Evertson, Clements, &Worsham, 1994). If the teacher is able to see all students, minor student difficulties and misbehavior can be dealt with before they develop into more serious problems. Classrooms should further be arranged to minimize distraction. This could take the form of minimizing the availability of highly stimulating materials (e.g., crayons, art projects) or arranging classroom traffic patterns in such a way as to limit peer interaction (e.g., location of pencil sharpener, bathroom passes).

Classroom Management

How teachers manage their classes in terms of scheduling, preparing for transitions, and supporting positive behavior will have an impact on all children, but especially those with ADHD. It is generally well accepted that children with ADHD benefit when they are provided with a high degree of structure (Pfiffner et al., 2006; Yehl & Wambold, 1998). Tier 1 interventions that provide the basis for this structure include the following:

Establish clear classroom expectations. All children need rules for establishing what constitutes acceptable behavior within a given environment. Rules should be clearly and positively stated to indicate the behavior that is being encouraged, rather than discouraged (DuPaul & Stoner, 2003). For example, if a teacher wants to communicate that it is not okay for students to touch each other, a positively stated rule could state, "Keep your hands to yourself." When possible, students should be permitted to play a role in creating classroom expectations (Sugai & Horner, 2002). This fosters a sense of ownership and classroom community that may reinforce involvement in positive behavior.

Post expectations where children can see them. Rules and classroom expectations should be posted where all children can easily see them. This serves the dual purpose of providing a continual reminder to students, in addition to cuing the teacher to refer to them throughout the course of the school day. The number of classroom rules should be limited to no more than five in order to avoid overwhelming the teacher and students with too many behaviors to monitor and control.

Teach examples and non-examples of expectations. In line with the principles of positive behavior support (PBS; Bambara & Kern, 2005) and antecedent interventions, students need to be actively taught examples and non-examples of expectations. For example, the rule "Keeping your hands to yourself" could be taught by illustrating what it looks like to touch and not touch other people. A period of guided instruction would then give way to modeling behavior and asking children to decide whether they were indeed following the rule or not.

Utilize classroom routines. Routines help children to anticipate what they need to do throughout the course of the school day. Routines increase predictability and classroom structure that may decrease the likelihood that children will engage in problematic behaviors (Mace, Shapiro, & Mace, 1998). Routines during times of transition, such as morning arrival, afternoon departure, and moving from one class to the next, serve to provide clear direction for students regarding what is expected of them.

Praise. Providing students with behavior specific praise has been shown to increase the rate at which children engage in appropriate academic and social behavior (Chalk & Bizo, 2004; Sutherland, Wehby, & Copeland, 2000). Praise that focuses on a specific behavior, particularly behavior consistent with posted classroom rules, can be utilized with an individual student, or with an entire class.

In addition to providing a high quality environment that is well managed, and physically and structurally conducive to learning, it is important that effective teaching practices are also being employed. Utilizing empirically validated curriculum is a necessary starting point within an RTI framework. However, even with the best curriculum, effective teaching practices still need to be implemented. Students benefit when they are provided with direct instruction, brisk pacing, increased opportunities to respond, and opportunities to link new learning with previously learned material (Sugai et al., 2002).

It is presumed that by focusing on providing classroom environments that incorporate high quality teaching with consistent behavior management in Tier 1, some children with ADHD symptoms will exhibit appropriate behavioral, academic, and social functioning. Alternatively, some children with ADHD and associated challenging behaviors will continue to experience difficulties and will require Tier 2 interventions.

Tier 2: Selective Interventions

Tier 2 interventions are implemented for students with ADHD who do not exhibit appropriate levels of behavior control and/or academic achievement when Tier 1 strategies are used. Some Tier 2 interventions are delivered individually (e.g., token reinforcement, daily report card, and computer assisted instruction), while others are classwide strategies (e.g., good behavior game, classwide peer tutoring, and providing task-related choices).

Token Reinforcement and Contingency Contracting

Students with ADHD often require frequent, immediate reinforcement for behavior to conform to teacher expectations (Barkley, 2006; DuPaul & Stoner, 2003). Although contingent praise may be helpful in this regard, many children with this disorder will require more powerful contingencies that go beyond verbal reinforcement. Teachers can provide token reinforcers (e.g., points, poker chips, stickers) on a relatively frequent schedule to students who are meeting behavioral expectations and goals. These tokens can be exchanged for back-up reinforcers (e.g., preferred activities in the classroom or at home) at a later point in the school day. Thus, token reinforcement programs allow for immediate feedback, while also connecting expected behavior to more salient rewards beyond specific praise. A plethora of research studies have demonstrated that classroom-based token reinforcement leads to significant reductions in disruptive behavior, along with concomitant improvements in classwork productivity, among students with ADHD and related disruptive behavior disorders (for review, see Pelham & Fabiano, 2008). In fact, token reinforcement systems are an essential part of classroom behavior modification programs that have been implemented in large-scale clinical trials of psychosocial intervention for this population (e.g., MTA Cooperative Group, 1999) and are considered the cornerstone of school based treatment (Barkley, 2006; DuPaul & Stoner, 2003).

A variant of token reinforcement is the use of contingency contracts with secondary school students with ADHD. Contingency contracts involve the written delineation of student responsibilities (i.e., expected student behaviors and/or levels of achievement) and privileges (i.e., activities or products that can be earned), as well as the circumstances under which privileges are available (DuPaul & Stoner, 2003). Students negotiate the terms of this contract with their teacher(s) and/or parent(s), both at the onset of the program as well as over time, as progress is made. The contingency contract is essentially a more abstract version of a token reinforcement program, in that an explicit connection between expected behaviors and contingent reinforcers is made; however, concrete token reinforcers are not used. Contingency contracts have been found effective for reducing disruptive behaviors of students with externalizing disorders like ADHD, in the context of controlled case study designs (e.g., D'Amico, 2000).

Daily Report Card

There are several parent-mediated intervention strategies that can help improve student performance in the classroom. It is important that educators clearly communicate behavioral and academic expectations of the classroom, and teach strategies that can be used by parents to promote student success in these areas of functioning. Educators should design a system to support ongoing communication between the parent and teacher. This may consist of a simple strategy, such as weekly phone calls, emails, or short conversations when the student is picked up from school. In contrast, daily report cards or home school notes are more formal and concrete strategies that can be used for the

same purpose. Regardless of the design employed, maintaining communication allows the parent to hear about the student's successes and difficulties in the classroom, communicate aspects of the home environment that may impact the student's classroom performance, and build a partnership with the teacher to promote positive classroom behavior and academic achievement.

Daily report cards or school–home notes include several important components (DuPaul & Stoner, 2003; Kelley, 1990). First, three to five specific goals should be set for the student. Goals should be focused on appropriate behavior (e.g., actively participate in class, raise hand before talking) and academic performance (e.g., complete work accurately). These goals should be realistic and attainable, so that the student has a reasonable chance of being successful. Second, the teacher should provide a numerical rating (e.g., 5 = excellent, 1 = poor) with respect to each goal. Preferably, these ratings would be provided several times during the day (e.g., following the completion of each subject period). Third, home-based contingencies or privileges (i.e., preferred activities and products) should be provided based on the points earned during the school day. Parents and students should negotiate the number of points that must be earned in order to gain access to privileges. Finally, it is critical that all three participants (i.e., student, parent, and teacher) in this system have input into the structure and content of the daily report card, as this will increase the probability of all three parties fulfilling their responsibilities. Periodic meetings should be held to make adjustments to the daily report card, either as progress is made or difficulties are encountered. Daily report cards have been found effective in the management of ADHD, particularly when used in the context of school-based behavioral systems (for review, see Pelham & Fabiano, 2008).

Computer Assisted Instruction

Students with ADHD may experience significant academic achievement difficulties due to their inconsistent attention and careless completion of schoolwork (Pfiffner, Barkley, & DuPaul, 2006). Those students who continue to experience academic problems despite the use of Tier 1 strategies will require a more focused intervention approach. One option is to replace or supplement typical drill-and-practice activities (e.g., written class assignments) with computer-based practice or computer-assisted instruction. For example, rather than completing a series of math problems using paper and pencil, the same types of problems can be completed using computer software. Computer-based activities can incorporate several features that are critical to the success of students with ADHD, including exposure to curriculum material that is consistent with the student's level of functioning; provision of frequent, immediate performance feedback; use of salient auditory and visual stimuli; and opportunity for immediate error correction (DuPaul & Stoner, 2003). Given these features, it is not surprising that computer-assisted instruction has been found to enhance the on-task behavior and academic skill acquisition of students with ADHD in the context of several single-subject design studies (Clarfield & Stoner, 2005; Mautone, DuPaul, & Jitendra, 2005; Ota & DuPaul, 2002).

Good Behavior Game

Classwide approaches can be taken to address the behavioral and academic needs of students with ADHD. One classwide strategy to address behavioral functioning is the use of the Good Behavior Game (Embry, 2002). This intervention typically involves dividing the classroom into three teams, with boys and girls evenly divided among teams. The teacher then clearly describes what behaviors are considered "good" (e.g., quietly working, actively participating in class activities) and what activities are deemed disruptive (e.g., talking without permission, physical aggression). Teams receive a check mark on a publicly posted chart whenever a team member exhibits a disruptive behavior. The team with the fewest check marks at the end of the game period, and at the end of the week, receives reinforcement (e.g., tokens, access to preferred activities). This strategy is initially implemented for short periods of time (e.g., 20 to 30 minutes) and then gradually extended to cover the entire school day as the students appear to understand and conform to the game rules. Although not specifically studied for students with ADHD, the Good Behavior Game has been found effective in reducing disruptive behavior and increasing task engagement for a variety of classrooms, including those with disruptive students (e.g., Van Lier, Muthén, van der Sar, & Crijnen, 2004), as well as preventing nicotine use and symptomatic behaviors of conduct disorder (Ialongo et al., 2001).

Classwide Peer Tutoring

One prominent classwide approach to addressing academic difficulties is the use of peer tutoring. Classwide Peer Tutoring (CWPT; Greenwood, Seals, & Kamps, 2010) involves students working in pairs and taking turns tutoring each other. The steps to this strategy include: (a) dividing the class into two teams; (b) assigning students to pairs within each team; (c) setting aside 20 minutes per day for tutoring; (d) providing tutoring pairs with academic scripts (i.e., assigned items in math, reading, or spelling); (e) tutors orally administering items while providing points for correct responses; (f) tutors providing immediate error correction and opportunity for tutees to correct their responses; (g) teachers providing additional points for tutoring pairs that are working effectively with each other; and (h) teachers tallying points earned by each pair, to derive a total score for each of the two class teams. At the end of each week, team totals are compared and the team with the most points is applauded by the other team. Typically, no back-up reinforcers are needed with this system. Greenwood and colleagues have demonstrated the short- and long-term success of CWPT for both low and high achieving students (for review, see Greenwood et al., 2010). More specifically, peer tutoring has been found to enhance task-related attention and academic performance among students with ADHD (DuPaul, Ervin, Hook, & McGoey, 1998; Plumer & Stoner, 2005).

Providing Task-Related Choices

Another potential classwide strategy is to provide students with task-related choices. The strategy of choice-making was originally investigated as an intervention for children with developmental disabilities, and has been found to increase attentive behavior and decrease disruptive behavior among students in this population (Dyer, Dunlap, & Winterling, 1990). This strategy requires students choosing an activity from two or more concurrently presented options. It is important to note that the options provided should result in similar outcomes. For example, students could choose from a menu of classwork assignments. In this example, the assignment students choose isirrelevant, because there will be a similar outcome (i.e., practice of the specific academic skill). Alternatively, students could choose among objects or activities, partners for activities, sequencing steps within a task, scheduling activities, where the activity is performed, amount of assistance given, or working conditions. Presumably, choice-making promotes student initiative and independence, such that increased task engagement results. In fact, Dunlap, dePerczel et al. (1994) found that providing written assignment choices was effective in reducing disruptive behaviors and improving task engagement for students with disruptive behavior disorders, including ADHD. However, it is unclear if this strategy is effective in improving academic performance and, thus, further research is needed to address this important issue.

Tier 3: Indicated Interventions

Tier 3 interventions are delivered to those students with ADHD who do not make adequate behavioral, academic, and/or social progress with Tier 2 strategies. Possible Tier 3 interventions include response cost, time-out from positive reinforcement, self-management, task/instructional modifications and, possibly, strategy training.

Response Cost

An individualized component of the classwide token reinforcement program is known as *response cost*. This is a commonly used strategy in which students earn points for meeting behavioral expectations, and can later exchange points for privileges. In this type of token economy system, students earn points for positive classroom behavior and lose them for inappropriate behavior. Because this approach gives students the opportunity to earn back lost tokens, it increases the probability that they will remain engaged and motivated to display appropriate classroom behavior. Specifically, several studies have supported the use of response cost strategies for students with attention problems (DuPaul, Guevremont, & Barkley, 1992; Rapport, Murphy, & Bailey, 1980, 1982).

Response cost systems require planning and clear communication between the teacher and student before implementation. It is important to teach the rules of the system, and review them with the student on a regular basis. Specifically, the student should understand when the system will be used, how points may be earned and lost, when points may be exchanged for privileges, and what privileges are available at any given time. It may be beneficial to check which privilege a student is working toward prior to beginning an activity, and intermittently change the available privileges to maintain student interest and motivation.

For this approach to be effective, it is essential that the student be involved in the creation of the menu of available privileges, and supported to gain privileges on a consistent basis. An example of an electronic version of response cost is the Attention Training Systen (ATS; Rapport, 1987; available from Gordon Diagnostic Systems, DeWitt, New York, see http://www.gsi-add.com/attentiontraining.htm),

a small electronic device that can be placed on the student's desk, and automatically awards points at a set interval while the student works independently or in a group. When the teacher notices inappropriate classroom behavior, points are deducted via a handheld remote control while continuing to work with other students or the whole class. This tool allows the teacher to provide immediate feedback on student behavior without interrupting classroom activities or instruction.

A second option is the manual version of response cost, which uses numbered cards held together by a binder ring. The teacher awards or deducts points by changing the top card on the teacher's set as the student displays appropriate or inappropriate behavior. As the teacher changes cards, the student changes a set of cards to match the number on the teacher's set of cards. Thus, the response cost strategy provides the student with immediate and frequent feedback on behavioral performance, which is an important factor in helping children with attention problems meet the behavioral expectations of the classroom (DuPaul& Stoner, 2003). This immediate communication of positive or corrective feedback from the teacher has been demonstrated to increase levels of on-task behavior, seatwork behavior, and academic accuracy in this population of students (DuPaul, Guevremont, & Barkley, 1992; Rapport et al., 1980, 1982).

Time-out from Positive Reinforcement

Time-out from positive reinforcement is a type of a mild punishment strategy that may be appropriate for classroom use to minimize problem behaviors. This strategy involves restricting the student's access to positive reinforcement, such as teacher and peer attention. Procedural guidelines in using this strategy include ensuring that it is implemented immediately following inappropriate behavior, applied with consistency, and employed for the smallest amount of time (i.e., one minute for every two years of age of the student) that proves effective. If the student must be moved to the time-out area, this location should be a relatively dull area of the classroom that allows the teacher to monitor the student's activities. Criteria for terminating the time-out period should include: (a) the completion of a time-period deemed effective for a student of that age and severity of the behavior displayed; (b) a short period of calm, during which the student does not engage in inappropriate behavior; and (c) the student's expressed willingness to correct the misbehavior that led to the time-out (Pfiffner,

Barkley, &DuPaul, 2006). A student who prematurely leaves the time-out location should have the time period increased by a predetermined amount for each violation, or lose points if this strategy is employed concurrently with a token economy system.

Although this strategy may be used as an effective response to difficult behaviors, time-out from positive reinforcement procedures must be monitored very carefully, and used only in the context of existing positive reinforcement programming. The teacher must note whether the use of this strategy results in the intended reduction, rather than increase, in rates of inappropriate behavior. This is important because the "time-out" may be reinforcing to some students who may be displaying disruptive behavior to avoid undesirable tasks. In addition, one must be careful to ensure that the continued use of this strategy does not cause the student to miss academic instruction on a regular basis, which could lead to further behavioral and academic problems. Finally, time-out from positive reinforcement is not considered to be a viable ongoing management strategy, and is best conceptualized as a short-term behavior reduction technique.

Self-Management

In cases where students have benefited from externally managed interventions (e.g., response cost, contingency contracting), self-management strategies can be used to promote the maintenance and generalization of obtained behavioral effects. With self-management, students are required to monitor and/or evaluate their own behavior over time. Students are typically required to observe and evaluate their own behavior, while the teacher is responsible for identifying the target behavior and creating behavioral goals (Fantuzzo & Polite, 1990). When developing these types of intervention strategies, it may be beneficial to clearly identify which aspects will be teacher controlled, and which will be managed by the students, basing these decisions on the specific needs and abilities of the individual child. Although self-control training procedures, sometimes referred to as cognitive-behavioral interventions, have been only minimally effective in the treatment of students with ADHD (Abikoff, 1985), self-monitoring and self-evaluation interventions that include a contingency component have become increasingly popular (Shapiro & Cole, 1994) and may be effective tools in improving behavior in the classroom setting (Dunlap & Dunlap, 1989). Further, interventions with a self-management component may be more effective than strategies that are solely managed externally by the teacher (Fantuzzo & Polite, 1990).

Self-monitoring strategies involve training students to recognize and record whether they have demonstrated the target behavior during an identified period of time (Gureasko-Moore, DuPaul, & White, 2006, 2007). This requires observation of one's own behavior, and recording that behavior in some way. For example, a student might be taught to recognize and record instances of on-task behavior during independent seatwork. Typically, an auditory or visual stimulus (e.g., beep from a recording device, a hand signal from the teacher) prompts students to observe their current behavior at various intervals. After recognizing their current behavior, students record whether they were on-task, on a behavior chart taped to their desks. As students display success with the intervention procedures, the involvement of the educator should be faded. Thus, the behavior of students should eventually be entirely self-managed. When choosing behaviors to self-monitor, previous research has indicated that it may be more effective to have students monitor task completion and/or task accuracy, rather than to simply monitor attentive behavior (Lam, Cole, Shapiro, & Bambara, 1994). Additionally, this strategy may be successful when organizational skills are the target behavior (Gureasko-Moore, DuPaul, & White, 2006, 2007).

Self-evaluation strategies incorporate a gradual shift from external to self-reinforcement by allowing students to earn points that can be exchanged for privileges (Rhode, Morgan, & Young, 1983). Prior to implementing this strategy, the teacher clearly defines the target behavior and expected academic performance, provides a written scale to record and evaluate the target behavior, and trains the student to recognize the target behaviors associated with the provided ratings (e.g., 5 = all work completed, 3 = some work completed, 0 = little or no work completed). Subsequently, the teacher and student independently rate the student performance during the specified time period. At the end of this activity, the teacher and student compare ratings. If the student ratings are within one point of the teacher ratings, the student is able to keep all of the points. If the student and teacher ratings match exactly, the student keeps all of the points and earns an additional point as a bonus. If the student and teacher ratings deviate by more than one point, the student is not given any points. The points can then be exchanged for privileges on a daily or weekly basis.

Similar to self-monitoring strategies, the close teacher involvement is eventually faded, and the student becomes responsible for monitoring and evaluating his or her own behavior. For example, the frequency of teacher and student comparisons is gradually reduced. Self-evaluation strategies have been found to improve attention and related behaviors of students with ADHD (e.g., Hoff & DuPaul, 1998).

Some students with attention problems may have difficulty accurately judging their own behavior. In other cases, the process of teaching self-management procedures may be lengthy (e.g., several months to several school years). Nevertheless, a contingency-based, self-evaluation strategy may be a viable option in promoting the maintenance and generalization of behavior change that is influenced by external forces. The goal of this strategy is to train the student to monitor and evaluate his or her behavior in the classroom, without continuous feedback from the teacher.

Task/Instructional Modification

Task or instructional modifications are strategies designed to improve the academic performance of students with ADHD, and involve revising curriculum procedures or aspects of the curriculum in an attempt to reduce problem behaviors and increase attention and academic achievement. These strategies are proactive; meaning, changes are made to the curriculum before the task is presented to the student. Depending on the specific needs of the individual student, these strategies can focus on increasing the amount of structure and/or organization in the environment, altering the goals and academic tasks to appear more manageable to reduce levels of frustration and increase persistence, and decreasing stimulation to help sustain attention.

Several studies have examined the influence of instructional modifications on the learning rate and acquisition of reading skills in students with ADHD. For example, Skinner, Johnson, Larkin, Lessley, and Glowacki (1995) compared fast-taped words (FTW) and slow-taped words (STW) on word reading list performance of students with and without attention problems. Results indicated that relatively higher rates of accurate reading were demonstrated in the STW condition. These results suggest that a slow-taped words intervention could improve reading accuracy rates for students with attention problems. In another study, Dubey and O'Leary (1975) compared oral versus silent reading, on reading comprehension of students with attention problems.

Results indicated that oral reading produced greater comprehension when compared to silent reading. Specifically, silent reading resulted in nearly twice the number of comprehension errors as did oral reading. These results suggest that students with attention problems may benefit from oral reading activities, as opposed to silent reading activities.

Strategy Training

Strategy training involves teaching students to use specific classroom strategy or skill when completing tasks to improve academic performance (Evans, Pelham, & Grudberg, 1995). These strategies, or sets of procedures, specifically address the demands of an academic situation. Strategy training gives added responsibility and ownership of academic performance to the student, thereby lessoning the burden on the teacher and parent. In addition, if the strategy taught is applicable to a variety of academic situations, there may be increased opportunities for generalization.

Students with attention problems may have increased difficulty understanding and synthesizing material from classroom lectures. A directed note-taking activity (DNA) created by Spires and Stone (1989) has been shown to decrease off-task behavior and improve study habits of students with ADHD (Evans, Pelham, & Grudberg, 1995). Specifically, the teacher instructs students to divide notes into main ideas and supporting details, through lectures and model notes that students can compare to their own. Gradually, the number of teacher prompts is faded, until the student can create an outline independently, based on presented lecture material. A second type of strategy training can be used to help students prepare and study for tests, or to complete long-term projects. The teacher should break long-term, abstract assignments into a series of short-term, concrete, and brief tasks that can be completed on a daily basis. In addition, students should be provided with feedback and contingencies, for motivation to complete these steps. Specifically, long-term projects should be broken into a series of small steps, daily goals for completing each step should be set, feedback should be provided to the student upon completion of short-term steps, and reinforcement should be contingent upon the completion of each daily step.

Case Example
Danny

From the time that Danny was in preschool, his mother reported that he had had difficulty attending to tasks for extended periods of time. Although he had consistently struggled to attend to instruction and stay seated during independent seatwork through the years, his previous teachers were always more than willing to accommodate these difficulties by providing him with extra attention and giving him shorter assignments. In third grade, Danny began to struggle in math, and was exhibiting more behavioral difficulties (e.g., walking around the classroom for extended periods of time, calling out, and getting into fights with classmates). His third grade teacher had high expectations for her students, and prided herself on running a highly organized classroom. Despite continued attempts to impress upon Danny the value of conforming to classroom rules, Danny continued to struggle.

Having been trained in a multi-tiered service delivery model, the school psychologist was called in to evaluate Danny and to determine what constituted an appropriate level of support. Examination of the classroom revealed that the teacher was using an empirically validated curriculum, had a high degree of structure and routine within the classroom, and generally went out of her way to praise students for engaging in positive behaviors. Seemingly, Danny's teacher was doing all that she could do within a Tier 1 framework. To put this theory to the test, the psychologist engaged in a number of direct observations that revealed that Danny's desk was situated in the front of the classroom, pushed up against the blackboard. In addition, Danny seemed to become overwhelmed when given math assignments, immediately getting out of his seat to ask peers for help. Not wanting to get into trouble, other students would either ignore Danny or make nasty comments to him. This really upset Danny and caused him to go around the room trying to find help. In order to make sure that Danny was getting the most out of Tier 1 strategies, the psychologist recommended that Danny's seat be moved back in line with the rest of the class. It was further recommended that a classwide peer tutoring procedure be initiated to provide all students with a peer that they could work with during math to ask questions of, if they were having difficulties. Lastly, the teacher was advised to increase her use of praise when she saw students engaged in appropriate behaviors and following classroom rules.

After a period of time, Danny's behavioral excesses declined, but he was still struggling when it came to work production and developing positive peer relationships. Having satisfactorily employed Tier 1 interventions, the psychologist recommended that Danny be provided with Tier 2 intervention supports, consisting of small group interventions to provide remedial support in math and social skills development. After five weeks of Tier 2 intervention, Danny's work production was much improved and his relationships with peers were becoming much more positive.

This case example highlights the need to examine the quality and quantity of support students are receiving at each tier. In Danny's case, there was clear benefit in maximizing Tier 1 interventions by moving his seat (i.e., classroom structure), and by encouraging increased use of praise for all students. Despite these improvements, Danny continued to struggle to complete his work and to engage in prosocial interactions with peers. The application of Tier 2 interventions (e.g., classwide peer tutoring) proved to be sufficient in addressing these needs. By using a tiered approach, services were tailored to the point of student need. This proved to be a much more effective and efficient use of teacher and classroom resources than implementing Tier 3 interventions for a child who clearly did not require this level of support.

Alternative Classroom Interventions

Unfortunately, in some venues, the treatment of ADHD is characterized by skepticism and debate. Despite a developed literature on what constitutes effective intervention within classrooms, there remains no shortage of alternative interventions promulgated through the media, Internet, and social support networks claiming the importance of novel alternative interventions. Low-sugar diets (Wolraich, et al., 1994), nutritional supplements (Sternberg, 1996), eye movement desensitization (Tinker & Wilson, 1999), and biofeedback (Lubar & Shouse, 1977) are just some of the alternative interventions promoted in the popular media. Moreover, a number of common interventions employed within schools are intuitively appealing but have minimal empirical support, such as providing extra time on assignments, utilizing study carrels, and using earphones to reduce auditory distractions. When parents and teachers entertain the idea of employing these interventions, they must carefully assess the degree to which there is empirical support for their use. The use of unproven interventions may have adverse ramifications for student outcomes, parent–teacher relationships, and the misappropriation of valuable resources that could be channeled to more productive intervention efforts.

The following guidelines are provided to help practitioners discern the best possible course for intervention planning. Interventions that have been deemed to be effective have undergone controlled experimentation with no-treatment controls, stringent peer review, have been published in professional journals, and have replicated these results across numerous studies (for review of effective interventions for ADHD, see Pelham & Fabiano, 2008). When a proposed intervention has not been subjected to the aforementioned guidelines, teachers and parents are strongly encouraged to seek out other interventions.

Summary and Future Directions

Students with ADHD experience significant academic and behavioral difficulties as a function of their symptoms of inattention, impulsivity, and/or hyperactivity. Although these symptoms can be reduced with psychotropic medication, functional impairments are rarely "normalized" by pharmacotherapy alone (Brown et al., 2008). Thus, school based interventions are a necessary component to the multimodal treatment of this disorder. This chapter described effective strategies that can be implemented in the context of a three-tiered, data based, problem-solving model. At Tier 1, high quality instruction and behavior management used on a classwide basis can ameliorate some of the symptomatic behaviors of ADHD. Stated differently, good teaching and good behavior management can help all students, including those with ADHD, to attain academic and behavioral success. For those students who do not respond adequately to Tier 1 strategies, various classwide (e.g., good behavior game) or individual (e.g., daily report card) interventions may be helpful. Finally, some students with ADHD will require highly individualized treatments addressing behavioral (e.g., response cost) and/or academic (e.g., direct instruction) functioning. Importantly, the effect sizes for behavior change associated with school based interventions are nearly equivalent to those obtained for psychotropic medication (Pelham & Fabiano, 2008).

Despite the success of school based interventions for students with ADHD, there are important limitations to extant clinical practice and research literature. First, most treatment outcome studies for ADHD have included samples that are predominantly white, middle class, and male. Thus, we have limited knowledge regarding the impact of interventions on nonwhite, poorer, and female populations. Second, current practice and research almost exclusively emphasize school based strategies that are appropriate for elementary school students. Stated differently, we know very little regarding how best to treat symptoms of this disorder in secondary school settings. Third, a critical gap in the school based intervention literature is a lack of information on how psychotropic medication and classroom behavioral intervention can be combined in an optimal fashion. For example, we know very little about how these treatments should be sequenced (i.e., should behavior management precede medication, or vice versa?). Finally, most interventions as implemented in applied and research settings have focused on symptom reduction (i.e., behavioral improvement) rather than enhancement of academic and social functioning. Thus, although best practices for addressing behavioral symptoms of this disorder are well established, currently available interventions have much weaker effects on areas that are critical to school success. For example, DuPaul and Eckert (1997) found small effect sizes for academic outcomes associated with school based interventions for ADHD.

Given these limitations to research and clinical practice, future investigations of school based interventions for ADHD must focus on several critical issues. First, treatment outcome studies should go beyond evaluating whether interventions reduce ADHD symptoms and/or disruptive behavior. It is clear that students with ADHD suffer from extensive deficits across multiple areas of functioning. Thus, strategies focused on reducing physical activity and disruptiveness only address one aspect of school adjustment difficulties. Second, the degree to which treatment needs to be modified to address the unique status of students from diverse backgrounds with ADHD should be determined through careful empirical research. It is critical to identify strategies that can be effective for girls, for those from ethnically and/or linguistically diverse backgrounds, and for secondary school students. Finally, factors that can enhance the translation of research findings into real-world implementation need to be identified. Stated differently, how can school psychologists effectively introduce and maintain evidence-based best practice into classrooms, given the myriad complexities and resource limitations of these settings? Issues related to feasibility, acceptability, and treatment integrity will be important foci of this line of investigation.

The effective treatment of students with ADHD has come a long way over the past several decades.

Not only do we know of effective psychotropic medications, but an impressive array of school-based behavioral and academic interventions have been developed and evaluated. It is assumed that when these evidence-based strategies are implemented in the context of a data based, problem-solving model, students with this disorder will show more successful outcomes. In order to realize these outcomes, school psychologists must collaborate with school personnel, mental health professionals, and parents, to bring evidence-based best practice into the school setting.

References

Abikoff, H. (1985). Efficacy of cognitive training interventions in hyperactive children: A critical review. *Clinical Psychology Review, 5*, 479–512.

American Psychiatric Association. (2000). *Diagnostic and statistical manual of mental disorders* (4th ed.–Text revision). Washington, D.C.: Author.

Bambara, L. M., & Kern, L. (2005). *Individualized supports for students with problem behaviors.* New York: Guilford.

Barkley, R.A. (Ed.). (2006). *Attention-deficit/hyperactivity disorder: A handbook for diagnosis and treatment* (3rd ed.). New York: Guilford.

Barkley, R.A., Murphy, K.R., & Fischer, M. (2008). *ADHD in adults: What the science says.* New York: Guilford.

Bennett, S. N., & Blundell, D. (1983). Quantity and quality of work in rows and classroom groups. *Educational Psychology, 20*, 431–446.

Brown, R.T., Antonuccio, D., DuPaul, G.J., Fristad, M., King, C.A., Leslie, L.K., McCormick, G., Pelham, W.E., Piacentini, J., & Vitiello, B. (2008). *Childhood mental health disorders: Evidence base and contextual factors for psychosocial, psychopharmacological, and combined interventions.* Washington, DC: American Psychological Association.

Brown-Chidsey, R. & Steege, M. W. (2005). *Response to intervention: Principles and strategies for effective practice.* New York: Guilford.

Chalk, K., & Bizo, L. A. (2004). Specific praise improves on-task behavior and numeracy enjoyment: A study of year four pupils engaged in the numeracy hour. *Educational Psychology in Practice, 20*, 335–374.

Clarfield, J., & Stoner, G. (2005). The effects of computerized reading instruction on the academic performance of students identified with ADHD. *School Psychology Review, 34*, 246–254.

D'Amico, P.J. (2000). A behavior analytic approach. *Cognitive and Behavioral Practice, 8*, 189–195.

Douglas, V.A. (1984). The psychological processes implicated in ADD. In L. M. Bloomingdale (Eds.), *Attention deficit disorder: Diagnostic, cognitive, and therapeutic understanding* (pp. 147–162). New York: Spectrum.

Dubey, D.R., & O'Leary, S.G. (1975). Increasing reading comprehension of two hyperactive children: Preliminary investigation. *Perceptual Motor Skills, 41*, 691–694.

Dunlap, G., dePerczel, M., Clarke, S., Wilson, D., Wright, S., White, R., & Gomez, A. (1994). Choice making to promote adaptive behavior for students with emotional and behavioral challenges. *Journal of Applied Behavior Analysis, 27*, 505–518.

Dunlap, L.K., & Dunlap, G. (1989). A self-monitoring package for teaching subtraction with regrouping to students with learning disabilities. *Journal of Applied Behavior Analysis, 22*, 309–314.

DuPaul, G.J., & Eckert, T.L. (1997). School-based interventions for children with attention-deficit/hyperactivity disorder: A meta-analysis. *School Psychology Review, 26*, 5–27.

DuPaul, G. J., Ervin, R. A., Hook, C. L. & McGoey, K. E. (1998). Peer tutoring for children with Attention Deficit Hyperactivity Disorder: Effects on classroom behavior and academic performance. *Journal of Applied Behavior Analysis, 31*, 579–592.

DuPaul, G.J., Guevremont, D.C., & Barkley, R.A. (1992). Behavioral treatment of attention deficit hyperactivity disorder in the classroom: The use of the Attention Training System. *Behavior Modification, 16*, 204–225.

DuPaul, G.J., & Stoner, G. (2003). *ADHD in the schools: Assessment and intervention strategies* (2nd ed.). New York: Guilford.

Dyer, K., Dunlap, G., & Winterling, V. (1990). Effects of choice making on the serious problem behaviors of students with severe handicaps. *Journal of Applied Behavior Analysis, 23*, 515–524.

Embry, D.D. (2002). The good behavior game: A best practice candidate as a universal behavioral vaccine. *Clinical Child and Family Psychology Review, 5*, 273–297.

Emmer, E. T., Evertson, C. M., Clements, B. S., & Worsham, M. E. (1994). *Classroom management for secondary teachers* (3rd ed.). Needham Heights, MA: Allyn & Bacon.

Evans, S.W., Pelham, W.E., & Grudberg, M.V. (1995). The efficacy of note taking to improve behavior and comprehension of adolescents with attention-deficit hyperactivity disorder. *Exceptionality, 5*, 1–17.

Fagan, T. K., & Wise, P. S. (2007). *School psychology: Past, present, and future.* White Plains, NY: Longman.

Fantuzzo, J.W., & Polite, K. (1990). School-based, behavioral self-management: A review and analysis. *School Psychology Quarterly, 5*, 180–198.

Goldstein, S. & Goldstein, M. (1998). *Managing attention deficit hyperactivity disorder in children: A guide for practitioners* (2nd ed.). New York: Wiley.

Greenwood, C. R., Seals, K., & Kamps, D. (2010). Peer teaching interventions for multiple levels of support. In M. R. Shinn&H. M. Walker (Eds.), *Interventions for achievementand behavior problems in a three-tier model including RTI.* (pp. 633–676). Bethesda, MD: National Association of School Psychologists.

Gresham, F.M. (1989). Assessment of treatment integrity in school consultation and prereferral intervention. *School Psychology Review, 20*, 23–36.

Gureasko-Moore, S., DuPaul, G.J., & White, G.P. (2006). The effects of self-management in general education classrooms on the organizational skills of adolescents with ADHD. *Behavior Modification, 30*, 159–183.

Gureasko-Moore, S., DuPaul, G.J., & White, G.P. (2007). Self-management of classroom preparedness and homework: Effects on school functioning of adolescents with attention-deficit/hyperactivity disorder. *School Psychology Review, 36*, 647–664.

Hastings, N., & Schwieso, J. (1995). Tasks and tables: the effects of seating arrangements on task engagement in primary classrooms. *Educational Research, 37*, 279–291.

Hoff, K., & DuPaul, G.J. (1998). Reducing disruptive behavior in general education classrooms: The use of self-management strategies. *School Psychology Review, 27*, 290–303.

Ialongo, N., Poduska, J., Werthamer, L., & Kellam, S. (2001). The distal impact of two first-grade preventive interventions on conduct problems and disorder in early adolescence. *Journal of Emotional and Behavioral Disorders, 9*, 146–160.

Individuals with Disabilities Education Improvement Act of 2004. Pub. L. No. 108,446.

Jimerson, S. R., Burns, M. K., &VanDerHeyden, A. M. (2007). *Handbook of response to intervention: The science and practice of assessment and intervention.* New York, NY: Springer Science+Business Media, LLC.

Kelley, M. L. (1990). *School-home notes: Promoting children's classroom success.* New York: Guilford.

Kovaleski, J. F., Gickling, E. E., Morrow, H., & Swank, P. R. (1999). High versus low implementation of instructional support teams: A case for maintaining program fidelity. *Remedial and Special Education, 20*, 170–183.

Lam, A.L., Cole, C.L., Shapiro, E.S., & Bambara, L.M. (1994). Relative effects of self monitoring on-task behavior, academic accuracy, and disruptive behavior in students with behavior disorders. *School Psychology Review, 23*, 44–58.

Lubar, J. F., & Shouse, M. N. (1977). Use of biofeedback in the treatment of sizure disorders and hyperactivity. In A. E. Kazdin (Ed.) *Advances in clinical psychology* (Vol. 1, pp. 203–265). New York: Plenum Press.

Mace, A. B., Shapiro, E. S., & Mace, F. C. (1998). Effects of warning stimuli for reinforcer withdrawal and task onset on self-injury. *Journal of Applied Behavior Analysis, 1*, 139–150.

Malecki, C. K., & Demaray, M. K. (2007) Social behavior assessment and response to intervention. In S. R. Jimerson, M. K. Burns, & A. M. VanDerHeyden (Eds.), *Handbook of response to intervention: The science and practice of assessment and intervention.* (pp. 161–171). New York, NY: Springer Science & Business Media.

Marston, D., Muyskens, P., Lau, M., & Canter, A. (2003). Problem-solving model for decision making with high-incidence disabilities: the Minneapolis experience. *Learning Disabilities Research & Practice, 18*, 187–200.

Mautone, J. A., DuPaul, G. J., & Jitendra, A. K. (2005). The effects of computer-assisted instruction on the mathematics performance and classroom behavior of children with attention-deficit/hyperactivity disorder. *Journal of Attention Disorders, 8*, 301–312.

MTA Cooperative Group. (1999). A 14-month randomized clinical trial of treatment strategies for attention-deficit/hyperactivity disorder. *Archives of General Psychiatry, 56*, 1073–1086.

MTA Cooperative Group (2004). National Institute of Mental Health multimodal treatment study of ADHD Follow-up: 24-month outcomes of treatment strategies for attention-deficit/hyperactivity disorder. *Pediatrics, 113*, 754–761.

Ota, K.R., & DuPaul, G.J. (2002). Task engagement and mathematics performance in children with attention deficit hyperactivity disorder: Effects of supplemental computer instruction. *School Psychology Quarterly, 17*, 242–257.

Pelham, W.E. Jr., & Fabiano, G.A. (2008). Evidence-based psychosocial treatments for attention-deficit/hyperactivity disorder. *Journal of Clinical Child and Adolescent Psychology, 37*, 184–214.

Pfiffner, L.J., Barkley, R.A., & DuPaul, G.J. (2006). Treatment of ADHD in school settings. In R.A. Barkley (Ed.), *Attention-deficit hyperactivity disorder: A handbook for diagnosis and treatment* (3rd ed., pp. 547–589). New York: Guilford.

Plumer, P. J., & Stoner, G. (2005). The relative effects of class-wide peer tutoring and peer coaching on the positive social behaviors of children with ADHD. *Journal of Attention Disorders, 9*, 290–300.

Rapport, M.D. (1987). *The Attention Training System: User's manual.* DeWitt, NY: Gordon Systems.

Rapport, M.D., Murphy, A., & Bailey, J.S. (1980). The effects of a response cost treatment tactic on hyperactive children. *Journal of School Psychology, 18*, 98–111.

Rapport, M.D., Murphy, A., & Bailey, J.S. (1982). Ritalin vs. response cost in the control of hyperactive children: A within subject comparison. *Journal of Applied Behavior Analysis, 15*, 205–216.

Rhode, G., Morgan, D.P., & Young, K.R. (1983). Generalization and maintenance of treatment gains of behaviorally handicapped students from resource rooms to regular classrooms using self-evaluation procedures. *Journal of Applied Behavior Analysis, 16*, 171–188.

Shapiro, E.S., & Cole, C.L. (1994). *Behavior change in the classroom: Self-management interventions.* New York: Guilford.

Skinner, C.H., Johnson, C.W., Larkin, M.J., Lessley, D.J., & Glowacki, M.L. (1995). The influence of rate of presentation during taped-words interventions on reading performance. *Journal of Emotional and Behavior Disorders, 4*, 214–223.

Smith, B.H., Barkley, R.A., & Shapiro, C.J. (2007). Attention-deficit/hyperactivity disorder. In E.J. Mash & R.A. Barkley (Eds.), *Assessment of childhood disorders* (4th ed.) (pp. 53–131). New York: Guilford.

Spires, H. A., & Stone, D. P. (1989). The directed notetaking activity: A self-questioning approach. *Journal of Reading, 33*, 36–39.

Sternberg, E. M. (1996). Paathogenesis of L-tryptophan eosinophilia-myalgia syndrome. *Advances in Experimental Medicine and Biology, 398*, 325–330.

Sugai, G., & Horner, R. H. (2002). The evolution of discipline practices: School-wide positive behavior supports. *Child & Family Behavior Therapy, 24*, 23–50.

Sugai, G., Horner, R. H., & Gresham, F. M. (2002). Behaviorally effective school environments. In M. R. Shinn, H. M. Walker, & G. Stoner (Eds.), *Interventions for academic and behavior problems II: Preventative and remedial approaches.* (pp. 315–350). Bethesda, MD: National Association of School Psychologists.

Sutherland, K. S., Wehby, J. H., & Copeland, S. R. (2000). Effect of varying rates of behavior-specific praise on the on-task behavior of students with EBD. *Journal of Emotional Behavioral Disorders, 8*, 2–8.

Tinker, R. H., & Wilson, S. A. (1999). *Through the eyes of a child: EMDR with children.* New York: Norton Professional Books.

Van Lier, P.A.C., Muthén, B.O., van der Sar, R.M., & Crijnen, A.A.M. (2004). Preventing disruptive behavior in elementary schoolchildren: Impact of a universal classroom-based intervention. *Journal of Consulting and Clinical Psychology, 72*, 467–478.

Wheldall, K., & Lam, Y. Y. (1987). Rows versus tables II: The effects of two classroom seating arrangements on classroom disruption rate, on-task behavior and teacher behavior in three special school classes. *Educational Psychology, 7*, 303–312.

Wolraich, M. L., Lindgren, S. D., Stumbo, P. J., Stegnik, L. D., Applebaum, M. I., &Kiritsy, M. C. (1994). Effects of diets high in sucrose or aspartame on the behavior and cognitive performance of children. *New England Journal of Medicine, 330*, 301–307.

Yehl, A. K., &Wambold, C. (1998). An ADHD success story: Strategies for instructors and students. *Teaching Exceptional Children, 30*, 8–13.

Social Skills Assessment and Intervention

Richard J. Cowan

Abstract

In a culture driven by legislation such as the Individuals with Disabilities Education Improvement Act and No Child Left Behind, indices of accountability often focus on student performance in traditional academic subject areas such as reading, mathematics, writing, and spelling. However, over 40 years of research has informed parents, educators, and other professionals that social competence is correlated with academic performance, as well as other success indicators throughout the lifespan. This chapter addresses social skills assessment and intervention for school-aged children across grade and ability levels. Within the context of a three-tiered positive behavior support (PBS) approach to assessment and intervention, this chapter describes evidence-based approaches to addressing social skills related behaviors to promote success for all students. Following a brief review of this literature, the chapter concludes with a discussion of implications for the role of the practicing school psychologist.

Keywords: social skills, positive behavior support, multidimensional assessment, social validity, generalization

When it comes to developing a comprehensive understanding of everyday social skills functioning in school-aged children, there are many questions to be considered by school psychologists, teachers, and other professionals in the school setting. To begin: What are *social skills*? What is *social competence*? How are these terms related? Furthermore, how do children learn social competence? That is, where do they learn behaviors that allow them to be socially competent across a variety of settings? Is it necessary to systematically teach social skills to *all* students? If so, how do educators determine a social skills curriculum applicable to a variety of students across several settings? What are some valid approaches to progress monitoring, such that data are sensitive enough to detect change to guide instruction? These and related questions have guided over 40 years of research focusing on the education and treatment of school-aged children demonstrating poor or limited social competency. This line of inquiry has resulted in studies extending across the home,

school, and community settings (e.g., clinics, community mental health facilities), involving parents, educators, counselors, clinicians, and other concerned parties as treatment facilitators and research participants.

Unfortunately, despite the wide attention this line of inquiry has received in the literature, outcomes associated with social skills training have been moderate, at best (Bellini, Peters, Benner, & Hopf, 2007; Forness & Kavale, 1996; Gresham, 2002; Gresham, Sugai, & Horner, 2001; Kavale et al., 1997; Kavale & Forness, 1995; Landrum & Lloyd, 1992; Mathur, Kavale, Quinn, Forness, & Rutherford, 1998). Yell, Meadows, Drasgow, and Shriner (2009) offer several plausible explanations for poor outcomes associated with social skills research. One explanation is that those behavioral skills targeted for social skills research may lack social validity. More specifically, researchers are not targeting for intervention those skills deemed appropriate by key stakeholders. A potentially powerful remedy for this scenario is for research–practitioners to select behavioral skills identified as important by key stakeholders, including teachers, parents, and peers. If the perceptions of these individuals are not considered when selecting skills related to the curriculum, students may continue to be perceived by others as socially incompetent, even in cases where new skills are acquired. This has to do with but one aspect of social validity (i.e., the social significance of the target behaviors). In addition to considering the social significance of the target behaviors, social validity as a construct is concerned with perceptions of consumers (e.g., teachers) regarding the appropriateness of the procedures (i.e., treatment acceptability), and the social importance of the intervention (Kazdin, 1980; Wolf, 1978). All three elements are critical in social skills assessment and intervention.

Another explanation for the limited outcomes is that researchers sometimes assume that students are demonstrating *skills* deficits when they are actually demonstrating *performance* deficits (Yell et al., 2009). In an effort to resolve this matter, in addition to teaching (sometimes re-teaching) specific behavioral skills, school based practitioners are encouraged to reinforce the demonstration of new and emerging skills in applied settings. This will help students recognize those specific behaviors deemed appropriate in these settings, and increase the likelihood that they recur under similar conditions. In addition to reinforcing specific skills in applied settings, educators are encouraged to assess those features of the environment that may naturally reinforce adaptive responses as they emerge (Gresham, 2002). Ultimately, it is the natural reinforcers (e.g., positive peer attention and sustained engagement in enjoyable interactions) that are hypothesized to capture and maintain adaptive behaviors in applied settings (Alberto & Troutman, 2009; Gresham).

Another limitation in this body of research, according to Yell et al. (2009), is that participants may not be exposed to enough direct instruction and practice time associated with emerging skills (i.e., training lacks sufficient intensity). One of the defining characteristics of effective interventions is the provision of multiple opportunities to practice new and emerging skills in relevant contexts (Cowan & Allen, 2007; Maag, 1999; Yell et al.). An additional explanation for relatively poor outcomes is that those skills targeted for intervention may have been taken from preexisting curricula, as opposed to the practice of developing a custom-tailored curriculum (Yell et al.). This may impact the intensity of

observed gains in cases where baseline levels for some adaptive skills were within the "average" range. Yell et al. also observed that researchers frequently fail to identify the function of disruptive, maladaptive social behaviors to guide in the development of functionally relevant replacement behaviors (i.e., "new" social skills). Effective social skills intervention involves teaching new skills while simultaneously extinguishing disruptive social behaviors (Gresham, 2002; Yell et al.).

A final explanation offered by Yell et al. is that researchers often fail to plan for the generalization of specific skills from the teaching setting to criterion settings. Lack of generalization in social skills training is perhaps one of the most frequently cited limitations in the social skills literature (Gresham, 2002; Landrum & Lloyd, 1992). Indeed, many studies in the treatment literature rely on a "train and hope" approach, wherein research teams *train* in an artificial (i.e., non-criterion) setting and *hope* those skills transfer, or generalize, to other critical settings without requiring additional instruction (Stokes & Baer, 1977). An alternative to "train and hope" is to plan for generalization at the onset of social skills intervention. Solutions to the problem of failing to address generalization training have been addressed repeatedly in the literature (e.g., Edelstein, 1989; Kendall, 1989; Stokes & Baer, 1977; Stokes & Osnes, 1989). Although a number of strategies have been proposed for promoting generalization, they may be grouped into three general categories: *use natural consequences, train diversely,* and *incorporate mediators* (Allen & Cowan, 2008; Stokes & Osnes). As related to skills development and enhancement, natural consequences include things that occur naturally in the environment, as the result of a particular behavior, that increase the likelihood of behavior recurrence (e.g., social praise, desired behavioral responses from peers). It is recommended that as training takes place in applied settings, practitioners utilize natural consequences as often as possible to enhance the likelihood of behavior change over time. Training diversely is concerned with teaching skills through multiple means, across a variety of settings, and through the utilization of several instructors, which in turn helps the student learn to recognize a variety of stimuli likely to elicit the same behavioral response across a variety of learning conditions (Allen & Cowan). Finally, incorporating mediators involves the use of objects or conditions that readily transfer from the learning environment to a variety of criterion settings (e.g., prompts).

Although a review of the social skills intervention literature indicates that there have been poor-to-limited outcomes for a variety of students exposed to a wide range social skills training curricula, careful contemplation of the procedures and limitations associated with this line of inquiry provides researchers and school based practitioners with a variety of considerations when seeking to improve outcomes for students demonstrating limited social competency. These implications were briefly discussed earlier in this section, and are further addressed throughout the remainder of this chapter.

The purpose of this chapter is to address social skills assessment and intervention for school-aged children in educational settings. Following definitional considerations related to the term *social skills*, the chapter provides a brief overview of how ecological theory (Bronfenbrenner, 1979) and the positive behavior support (PBS) model (Lewis & Sugai, 1999) can serve as a foundation from which to consider social skills assessment and intervention. Following a discussion of a comprehensive approach to assessment and an overview of promising approaches to social skills intervention, the chapter concludes with a discussion of implications for the role of the practicing school psychologist.

Definitional Considerations and Guiding Theoretical Models
Defining "Social Skills"

When attempting to establish an agreed-upon definition of *social skills* as a construct, it may be helpful to make a distinction between *social skills* and *social competence* (Sheridan & Walker, 1999; Sheridan, Hungelmann, & Poppenga Maughan, 1999). Whereas *social skills* may be defined as "discrete learned behaviors exhibited by an individual for the purpose of performing a [social] task" (Sheridan & Walker, 1999, p. 686), *social competence* is concerned with the evaluative judgments and opinions of significant others (e.g., parents, teachers, peers; Gresham, 1986), thus being interpreted in accordance with the standards of *social validity* (i.e., the degree to which a specific social behavior is relevant for a particular child within a specific context; Sheridan & Walker).

If social skillfulness is perceived to be a combination of both (a) the traditional social skills definition (i.e., a discrete set of learned social behaviors), and (b) the social competence (i.e., social validity) criterion, *social skills* may be defined as "goal-directed, learned behaviors that allow one to interact and function effectively in a variety of

social contexts" (Sheridan & Walker, 1999, p. 687). That is, in addition to possessing discrete adaptive social skills (e.g., how to initiate a social interaction with a peer), individuals who are socially skillful are able to consider a range of specific contexts (e.g., lunchroom, playground, homeroom) and determine which skills to use to experience success within these respective environments. Demonstrating social competence involves both (a) the active demonstration of situation-relevant skills, and (b) the ability to refrain from demonstrating socially inappropriate behaviors (Sheridan, 1995). As such, students demonstrating difficulty with social competence are often seen by others as demonstrating too few socially appropriate behaviors (e.g., greeting others, initiating conversations, tactfully responding to being teased) or too many socially maladaptive behaviors (e.g., fighting, teasing, disrupting others). This chapter considers strategies for monitoring and modifying both behavioral deficits and behavioral excesses, as related to social competency within the school setting.

Potential Causes of Poor Social Skills Functioning in Students

Research and practice to date has been guided by two theories regarding the cause of poor social skills competency in children: (a) poor social functioning is related to *internal deficits*, and (b) poor social functioning is the result of *external variables* (Gresham, 1997; Sheridan & Walker, 1999; Sheridan et al., 1999). The "internal deficits" theory is grounded in the hypothesis that poor social functioning is caused by either (a) an *internal social skills deficit* (i.e., the child does not possess those skills necessary to achieve social competence), or (b) *an internal performance deficit* (i.e., although the child possesses specific social skills, s/he does not demonstrate confidence due to characteristics such as impulsivity or social anxiety). The primary hypothesis behind the "external variables" theory is that poor social functioning is related to *external variables* (i.e., antecedents, consequences, setting events) related to the demonstration of particular social behaviors (Carey & Stoner, 1994; Gresham, 1997; Sheridan et al., 1999).

The interventionist's hypothesis regarding the cause of poor social functioning is critical in guiding social skills curriculum for children in the educational setting (Gresham, 1997; Mathur & Rutherford, 1996; Sheridan & Gutkin, 2000). For example, if the internal-deficit model is used, and it is hypothesized that a child lacks the skills necessary to perform a specific social task (i.e., a skills deficit), intervention will likely focus on direct instruction. Using an applied example, if a child were to consistently demonstrate difficulty making adaptive decisions in the face of challenging situations (i.e., demonstrates a problem solving skill deficit), the intervention may consist of teaching the child the problem solving sequence of problem identification, solution generation, consequential analysis, response selection, and evaluation (Sheridan, 1995, 1998). On the other hand, if external variables are identified as potential contributing factors to a lack of skills demonstration, intervention might target external variables that may be causing or maintaining poor social performance. For example, if a functional assessment determined that a child may be getting significant amounts of peer attention (i.e., reinforcement) for demonstrating physical aggression towards others, intervention may consist of manipulating the levels of peer attention in the environment so more attention is given for socially appropriate behavior than for physical aggression. In an example with a slightly different behavioral target, if it were determined that a child may not be getting enough reinforcement from others when attempting to initiate social interactions, the environment might be changed so peers are taught to positively respond to initiations made by the child, in an effort to increase the likelihood that the child continues to reach out to others within that social context.

Two Theoretical Models to Guide Research and Practice

ECOLOGICAL THEORY

Although it may be helpful to separate the skills-deficit approach from the performance-deficit approach for the sake of illustration, given what we know about human behavior (i.e., all behavior is learned *and* behavior is governed by antecedent and consequential conditions; Skinner, 1953), it may be more helpful to inherit an approach guided by ecological theory (Bronfenbrenner, 1979), wherein human behavior is conceptualized "as a function of ongoing interactions between the characteristics of individuals and the multiple environments within which they function" (Sheridan & Gutkin, 2000, p.489). When one assumes an ecological approach to behavior change, four assumptions are inherent (Apter & Conoley, 1984; Sheridan & Gutkin). First, "each child is an inseparable part of a small social system" (Apter & Conoley, p. 87). The implication here is that research–practitioners must gain

an understanding of each child's social systems in order to conduct assessment, intervention, and progress monitoring. Second, "disturbance is not viewed as a disease located within the body of the child but, rather, as discordance… in the system" (Apter & Conoley, p. 89). This means that research–practitioners must look beyond the child to consider the environment when searching for hypotheses to guide intervention associated with either the child's demonstration of disruptive behavior, or the child's failure to demonstrate an adaptive response. Third, "discordance may be defined as a disparity between an individual's abilities and the demands or expectations of the environment" (Apter & Conoley, p. 91). When adopting this lens, practitioners appreciate that inadequate performance is the result of a mismatch between the individual's skills repertoire and the behavioral responses observed in most individuals in a particular environment. And finally, "the goal of any intervention is to make the system work" (Apter & Conoley, p. 92). This may be interpreted to mean that one of the primary roles of the school psychologist is to promote positive change that improves the system and is sustainable beyond his or her immediate involvement in that system (Sheridan & Gutkin). These four assumptions may serve as helpful guidelines to school based practitioners charged with the task of developing a comprehensive approach to social skills assessment that lends to data-driven, evidence-based social skills intervention. The remainder of this chapter will assume an ecological approach to understanding behavior, as discussed within the context of the positive behavior support service delivery model described next.

THE POSITIVE BEHAVIOR SUPPORT MODEL

A review of the social skills literature reveals that the majority of earlier research focused almost exclusively on children demonstrating characteristics associated with specific disability categories, such as emotional disturbance, specific learning disabilities, autism spectrum disorders, and the like. More recently, the literature has shifted its focus toward the investigation of social and behavioral skills assessment and intervention within the context of a three-tiered service delivery model, commonly referred to as positive behavior supports (PBS; Lewis & Sugai, 1999). The PBS model addresses the needs of *all* students by concurrently addressing the comprehensive needs of the school as a system, as well as the individualized needs of students who require more intensive levels of support (Cowan & Sheridan, 2008).

As such, PBS encourages researchers and practitioners to focus on both prevention and intervention for *all* students—not only those students with severe behavioral excesses and/or deficits. The PBS model has been used to enhance adaptive social and behavioral skills in children, reduce disruptive behaviors observed in the classroom, and promote academic success in a variety of students across grade levels.

Positive behavior support encompasses three distinct levels of intervention: (a) *universal intervention programs* (formerly referred to as primary intervention) delivered at the schoolwide or classwide tier, which are generally effective for the majority of students (approximately 80%) who exhibit mild behavioral concerns; (b) *targeted interventions* (formerly described as secondary interventions) aimed at approximately 10%–15% of students for whom the universal behavioral approach is insufficient to remediate maladaptive behaviors; and (c) *intensive intervention* programs (formerly tertiary intervention) for approximately 1%–5% of students whose chronic behavioral problems require individualized functional assessment and intervention planning, given their lack of responsiveness to more global, less intensive behavioral programming (Lewis & Sugai, 1999; Walker et al., 1996).

As indicated above, a major advantage of the PBS model is its promotion of both prevention and intervention, through implementation across the universal, targeted, and intensive levels. An indicator of effective instruction is the provision of multiple opportunities to practice new and emerging skills commensurate with level of need (Maag, 1999; Yell et al., 2009). Within the PBS framework, individuals at the universal level of intervention who do not necessarily need extra practice are still afforded access to reinforcement when universal interventions offer direct skills instruction coupled with reinforcement for the demonstration of appropriate skills (Lewis & Sugai, 1999). Perhaps more importantly, individuals at the targeted and intensive levels of intervention are provided with systematically increased opportunities to practice skills and receive reinforcement for the demonstration of adaptive social and behavioral skills in applied settings. The PBS approach relies on actively teaching and reinforcing skills, as opposed to relying on punishment alone to promote behavior change.

One major concern with relying exclusively on punishment is that it extinguishes socially maladaptive behavior without actively teaching the student an adaptive replacement behavior. Alberto and Troutman (2009) remind practitioners that the additional pitfalls associated with the use of punishment include the potential for learned helplessness, emotional reaction, increased aggression (especially in cases where physical punishment is administered), and response substitution (e.g., replacing one inappropriate or undesired behavior for another, such as biting with hitting). It is highly recommended that to the greatest extent possible, positive interventions are incorporated to enhance learning. If punishment procedures are deemed necessary, it is recommended that they be used in combination with positive interventions (e.g., the use of differential reinforcement, a token economy with a response cost feature), and that they be planned in advance to ensure proper implementation and to avoid overpunishment (Alberto & Troutman; Cowan & Sheridan, 2008; Maag, 1999).

Social Skills Assessment

An ecological approach to addressing social skills in school-aged children reminds educators and related services personnel of the importance of seeking comprehensive data to inform practice. When the assessment of social skills is viewed through the PBS lens, practitioners are encouraged to follow an assessment protocol that includes screening, classification, target behavior selection, and functional assessment to inform data-based intervention within the school setting (Gresham, 2002). This helps ensure that *all* students receive the appropriate level of treatment and progress monitoring. As indicated earlier, approximately 80% of all students in a given school respond to universal intervention, wherein quality instruction and primary prevention are sufficient to teach students those behavioral expectations—including social skills—prerequisite to continued success in the educational setting. It is recommended that school psychologists and other members of educational teams identify a common metric for selecting those students for whom targeted intervention may be warranted. Although originally developed as a screening instrument to identify students with behavior or emotional disorders, the *Systematic Screening for Behavior Disorders* protocol (Walker & Severson, 1992) contains guidelines and elements (e.g., teacher ratings, the Peer Social Behavior [PSB] coding system) that may be useful for identifying students who may benefit from participation at the targeted or intensive levels of intervention. Additional guidelines for screening students for more intensive levels of social skills intervention are offered by Sheridan (1995, 1998) and the OSEP Technical Assistance Center on Positive Behavioral Interventions and Supports (NDA).

Whereas the initial screening process involves the use of more universal instrumentation, assessment at the targeted and intensive levels of intervention require more thorough assessment, including the use of instruments sensitive enough to develop baseline levels of behavior performance. Depending on the practices of the school system and/or the needs of individual students, the school based practitioner will need to develop a protocol that best suits the educational objective(s) and research question(s). Regardless of the level of application (i.e., individual or group), the goals of social skills assessment generally include identifying social skills strengths, acquisition deficits, performance deficits, and fluency deficits (Gresham, 2002). Furthermore, assessment includes the consideration of competing or interfering behavior, conducting functional behavioral assessment, determining the social validity of target behaviors, and ultimately selecting target behaviors (Gresham). Following is an overview of a comprehensive approach to assessment that may be used as a framework to guide school based practitioners as they develop assessment protocols to meet the needs of their school systems and individual students.

The multidimensional assessment protocol (McConaughy & Ritter, 2002) involves gathering multisource data (i.e., data from several key stakeholders, including parents, teachers, and other professionals) through multiple means (e.g., utilizing ratings scales, interviews, direct observations, records review) across a variety of settings (e.g., home, school, community treatment organization), in an effort to gain a comprehensive baseline of student performance across settings. As related to the assessment of social behaviors in students, a multidimensional approach may involve teacher interviews, direct observations, rating scales, and a review of records (e.g., disciplinary logs, grades, etc.). Following is a brief description of these elements coupled with some examples of specific instruments that may be used for assessment.

Teacher Interviews

There are a variety of approaches to interviewing teachers for the purpose of informing behavior modification programs, including published interview forms that are either semistructured or structured in format. Given that social behaviors are learned and heavily influenced by the environment, it is recommended that school psychologists adopt and employ a functional assessment approach to interviewing. According to Gresham (2002), the functional assessment interview (FAI) is governed by four goals: (a) to clearly identify and operationalize social skills difficulties; (b) to assist in differentiating between acquisition and performance deficits; (c) to identify those conditions in the environment that compete with and/or interfere with social skills acquisition and performance; and (d) to obtain preliminary data to guide the development of hypotheses regarding what may be causing and/or maintaining interfering behaviors. The interview should also be geared toward gathering information that allows the practitioner to identify which elements may be missing in the environment that, if present, might well support the display of socially appropriate behaviors. In the end, this interview should lend to data that inform the assessment process, as well as guide in the development of the intervention plan.

Direct Observations

A prerequisite to the systematic observation of social behaviors in applied settings is the development of an operational definition of the target behavior(s) that lends itself to concrete, reliable data collection. Given that the PBS model fosters equal attention to disruptive behaviors and adaptive replacement behaviors, it is important for the team to develop operational definitions of disruptive behaviors as well as positive, adaptive behaviors. Regardless of whether a social behavior is disruptive in nature (e.g., teasing others) or not happening frequently enough (e.g., initiating conversations with peers), members of the educational team may select from the following approaches to data collection: event recording, interval recording/time sampling, duration recording, and latency recording (Alberto & Troutman, 2009).

Event recording directly measures the number of times a particular behavior occurs in a particular setting. Specifically, the observer tallies the number of incidents of a particular behavior during a specified time period and/or setting. Another approach to monitoring the number of times a behavior occurs is interval recording/time sampling. There are three forms of interval recording: partial interval, whole interval, and momentary time sampling (Alberto & Troutman, 2009). A partial interval recording system monitors whether or not a behavior occurs at all during the prescribed interval; a whole interval recording system measures whether or not a behavior occurs for the entire duration of the prescribed interval; and the momentary time sampling approach allows the observer to record a simple "yes" or "no" to indicate whether or not a behavior occurs at the end of the prescribed time interval.

An example of an interval recording system related to social behaviors is the *Peer Social Behavior Code* (PSB; Walker & Severson, 1992), one of many components contained in the *Systematic Screening for Behavior Disorders* protocol (SSBD; Walker & Severson, 1992). The PSB interval recording system was designed to assess an individual student's behavioral adjustment to his or her peer group within the context of social settings, and has proven to be reliable and highly sensitive to "discriminating among the social behavior patterns of Externalizing, Internalizing, and Normal control students in the 1–6 grade range" (Walker & Severson, 1992, p. 1). Specifically, the PSB incorporates an interval recording system that allows the observer to code the following categories of social behavior: Social Engagement (SE), Participation (P), Parallel Play (PLP), Alone (A), and No Codeable Response (N). In addition, it allows the observer to code the percent intervals of Social Engagement and Participation as either positive (+) or negative (–). Although the SSBD–PSB coding system contains some normative data, it is a limited population sample. Practitioners may use the system to develop local norms to allow for peer comparisons in the spirit of social validity (Kazdin, 1982).

Duration recording is used to measure how long a particular behavior occurs. For example, it may be helpful in monitoring the duration of a conversation between two or more students. Alternatively, latency recording is used to measure the amount of time that expires between a cue to perform a behavior and the execution of a response to that cue. A common example here is the amount of time it takes a student to respond to a teacher directive or command. Both time-related measures are readily applicable to a variety of social contexts.

In addition to gathering information about the frequency, intensity, and/or duration of specific social behaviors through the use of any of the data collection systems described above, it is important to gather supplementary data to monitor the antecedents and consequences surrounding social behaviors, to inform hypotheses through functional behavioral assessment (FBA). If this occurs following the teacher interview, these data may be used to confirm, enhance, or oppose information provided

by the teacher. A comprehensive lens is critical when considering data to inform practice.

Behavior Rating Scales

There are a number of behavior rating scales that may be completed by adults (e.g., teachers, parents, paraprofessionals) and students to inform intervention across settings. Some of the more common broad-band instruments that contain scales sensitive to social skills functioning include the Behavior Assessment System for Children, Second Edition (BASC-2; Reynolds & Kamphaus, 2004) and the Achenbach System of Empirically-Based Assessment (ASEBA; Achenbach & Rescorla, 2001). Both of these broad-band instruments result in standardized scale scores, which lend to comparisons with a national sample of school-aged children.

Gresham (2002) suggests using behavior rating scales prior to teacher and parent interviews to guide topics addressed in the interview. It is important to note that, as compared to data obtained through direct behavioral observations (which tend to be more objective than any other assessment method), data obtained through interviews and rating scales tend to be more subjective in nature. As such, neither teacher interviews nor behavior rating scales should be used alone in the assessment process. This is one of many reasons multidimensional approaches to behavioral assessment are encouraged in the literature (McConaughy & Ritter, 2002).

Review of Existing Records

A final source of data that may be helpful in further informing a comprehensive understanding of a student's past and recent history as related to social skills functioning involves those elements contained in the student's permanent records (e.g., report cards, office referrals, records of disciplinary action, attendance records, and the like). While these types of records may vary across schools and individual students in their completeness and accuracy, they may contain invaluable information to inform treatment. For example, a review of a report card not only provides data on level of academic performance, it often provides a score or ranking indicative of relative "citizenship" in the academic setting. Although a student may be making good grades in the traditional academic domains, a citizenship grade or ranking demonstrating poor attendance, as related to truancy or suspension, may prove useful in building the case for additional supports. In another example, a review of a depressed adolescent female's student records may offer data to support that she is frequently absent, failing many of her classes, and rarely participates in extracurricular activities. This information may prove helpful when developing an intervention protocol geared toward enhancing social and coping skills in a potentially isolated student.

Social Skills Intervention

Social skills interventions are wide and varied in their objectives, scope, intensity, and fidelity. Within the context of the PBS model, social skills curricula are delivered at the universal, targeted, and intensive levels of intervention. Regardless of the level of intervention implementation, sound social skills training programs and curricula are designed to promote skill acquisition, enhance skill performance, remove competing behaviors, and facilitate generalization (Gresham, 1997, 2002). Skill acquisition is facilitated through some combination of direct instruction, modeling, guided practice with feedback, and coaching (Gresham, 2002; Sheridan, 1995, 1998; Yell et al., 2009). Enhancing skill performance is facilitated through the manipulation of antecedents and consequences (Gresham). There are several means of enhancing skill performance through antecedent manipulation. For example, one can involve peers through peer initiation activities, peer coaching, and peer tutoring (Gresham). Another means of fostering social and behavioral skill performance through antecedent manipulation is the use of proactive classroom management strategies (e.g., teaching and posting classroom rules, and reinforcing students for demonstrating them) and precorrection (Colvin, Sugai, Good, & Lee, 1997; Gresham). Examples of fostering skills performance through the manipulation of consequences include the use of behavioral contracting, verbal praise, tangibles as rewards, access to primary reinforcers (e.g., food, beverages), activity reinforcers, token economy systems, and home–school notes (Gresham; Sheridan, 1995, 1998). The use of positive reinforcement for positive social behaviors may be overlooked in many school settings. However, in addition to presenting multiple opportunities to review and practice emerging skills, reinforcing appropriate behavioral responses in applied settings is a critical element in effective instruction (Alberto & Troutman, 2009; Maag, 1999).

Gresham (2002) suggests the use of the following means of removing competing behavior problems: differential reinforcement, overcorrection procedures, time-out, systematic desensitization, or flooding. Differential reinforcement may be particularly effective, because it combines the application of both planned ignoring (i.e., extinction) and positive reinforcement (i.e., rewarding students when they demonstrate positive social skills). The interested reader is referred to Alberto and Troutman (2009) for procedural details and a brief overview of the research to support this approach. Overcorrection and time-out are among the most punitive approaches in this listing. Although they may yield favorable outcomes associated with extinguishing disruptive behaviors, if used alone they will likely fail to teach adaptive behavioral responses. As such, they should be used sparingly and with caution. Systematic desensitization and flooding are evidence-based approaches to anxiety-based competing behaviors. The interested reader is referred to Miltenberger (2003) for procedural details and a brief overview of the research to support these approaches. As indicated earlier, generalization is concerned with the transfer of newly learned skills from the instructional setting to a variety of naturalistic settings. One of the greatest limitations of the social skills literature is its failure to systematically address generalization through its application as a dependent variable (Landrum & Lloyd, 1992). It is recommended that school based practitioners actively plan for generalization, through bringing the world into training (i.e., bringing elements of applied settings into the instructional setting) as well as bringing social skills instruction into a variety of applied settings (Sheridan et al., 1999).

Applications across the Universal, Targeted, and Intensive Levels

When planning social skills training and instruction, many school based practitioners develop applications across the universal, targeted, and intensive levels of intervention. At the universal level, intervention might include the following basic components: clearly defining 3–5 universal behavioral expectations, teaching expectations to students through direct instruction and other means, extensively communicating the universal expectations on a schoolwide level, implementing a comprehensive schoolwide positive reinforcement system, and evaluating progress to inform practice (Sugai, Sprague, Horner, & Walker, 2000). For individuals who fail to respond favorably to this level of intervention, targeted intervention generally includes additional opportunities to learn and practice emerging adaptive social and behavioral skills. For example, students at this level may participate in a social skills training group (e.g., "lunch bunch" or "friendship group") made up of the following sequential components: (1) *verbal skill instruction* (i.e, introducing the step-by-step sequence of a behavior); (2) *modeling* (either live, where the target children observe a behavior in the desired setting, or symbolic, where the children observe a film or videotape); (3) *skill performance/practice* (i.e., the children perform the skill, often through role-plays); and (4) *feedback,* whereby the skills trainer responds with specific, constructive feedback (Cartlege & Milburn, 1995; Sheridan & Walker, 1999). In addition, generalization elements might include the use of self-monitoring forms and behavioral contracts for new or emerging skills (Sheridan, 1995). Within the PBS model, it is assumed that children at the targeted level of intervention receive two layers of support (i.e., access to both universal and targeted intervention) until progress monitoring data indicate that two layers are no longer warranted (i.e., the students have made clinically significant gains in their social skills performance).

There are many factors to consider when grouping students together for targeted social skills instruction. For example, it may be helpful to consider the age, skill level, and cognitive ability of students when pairing them to maximize outcomes. In some cases, it may be beneficial to incorporate prosocial peers into social skills instruction. For example, there is a growing body of literature to suggest that for children with autism, the use of well trained, prosocial peer confederates is beneficial (Odom & Strain, 1986; Rogers, 2000). It is equally as important to consider potential harm associated with certain combinations of students. For example, whereas it appears to be the norm to combine children demonstrating emotional disturbance (ED) into small groups for direct intervention (Kavale et al., 1997), an emerging body of literature suggests that combining children with ED characteristics may be more harmful than helpful (Ang & Hughes, 2002; Arnold & Hughes, 1999; Dishion, McCord, & Poulin, 1999). Specifically, a handful of published research has concluded that in some cases, deviant youth targeted for intervention worsened as a result of intervention involving groups of deviant peers (Arnold & Hughes). Similarly, Dishion et al. report that long-term research data indicate peer intervention for deviant youth may result in increases in adolescent problem behavior and negative life outcomes (i.e., adulthood maladjustment). This body of literature reminds school based practitioners of the importance of anticipating outcomes associated with specific pairings of students, when developing targeted interventions in the school.

For the limited number of students who fail to respond to targeted intervention, additional assessment and instructional supports are warranted as they enter intensive intervention. At this level of intervention, it is critical that the educational team allows the comprehensive assessment data to drive individualized intervention geared toward the student's demonstrated strengths and needs. Over 40 years of research has produced a variety of procedures that have proven to be at least moderately effective in enhancing social skills in children demonstrating significant excesses in disruptive behaviors and/or deficiencies in positive, adaptive social skills. The majority of these procedures can be classified into three major categories: operant conditioning/behavioral, social learning, and cognitive-behavioral (Elliott & Gresham, 1993; Sheridan & Walker, 1999). *Operant conditioning* techniques are primarily concerned with discrete, observable behaviors, and the antecedents and consequences surrounding these behaviors (Elliott, Sheridan, & Gresham, 1989; Elliott & Gresham). This approach to intervention assumes that a child possesses discrete, observable social behaviors, but fails to perform them due to contingencies within the environment (Morgan, 1993). Interventions subsumed under this category most often use reinforcement or punishment, contingent on the display of a particular behavior. According to Bandura's (1977) *social learning* theory, social behavior is learned through reinforced and observational learning. *Reinforced learning* occurs when an individual demonstrates a social behavior that is reinforced in a social setting, and consequently increases the future use of this behavior. *Observational learning* occurs when individuals gain social skills through observing the behavior of others, and performing those behaviors that are reinforced (for the model they are observing) in social settings. Based on observational learning theory, modeling is the most common approach in social learning interventions. In this case, modeling is broken down into those four common sequential components described above, under targeted interventions: verbal instruction, modeling, skill performance/practice, and feedback.

Finally, *cognitive-behavioral social skills interventions* are concerned primarily with the child's internal cognitions (e.g., thoughts, self-statements, and self-regulation), and include coaching and social problem solving. Coaching generally consists of three steps: (1) the child is presented with the rules and standards of a behavior (i.e., skills instruction); (2) the child behaviorally rehearses the social skill (usually with a parent or social skills instructor); and (3) the child receives specific feedback with recommendations for future performance (Elliott & Gresham, 1993; Sheridan, 1998). Although coaching and modeling (described earlier) are similar in practice, the following distinction may be made: Coaching refers to child participants being encouraged to use a skill within a training or applied setting, whereas modeling is primarily concerned with having the target child observe peers and/or group leaders engaging in a particular skill (i.e., usually within the context of direct instruction).

The majority of research has investigated these approaches within the context of larger, multimodal intervention programs (Jones, Sheridan, & Binns, 1993). Specifically, most social skills training research programs are comprised of training a number of generic skills (e.g., initiating socialization with others, controlling anger, solving problems) through a variety of procedures (i.e., operant conditioning/behavioral, social learning, and cognitive-behavioral strategies). This makes it difficult for researchers to determine which components promote meaningful change across settings (Mathur & Rutherford, 1996). However, as compared to "monomodal" intervention, "multimodal" intervention packages generally result in higher efficacy (Beelmann, Pfingsten, & Losel, 1994). These findings have been interpreted to indicate that because of the efficacy of multimodal interventions, they should be used in an effort to capitalize on the combined effects of various social skills training techniques (Barton, 1986; Erwin, 1994). Similarly, it could be argued that social skills interventions comprising components from all three treatment approaches (i.e., operant conditioning/behavioral, social learning, and cognitive-behavioral) are better able to address both internal (i.e., skill related) and external (i.e., reinforcement in natural settings) hypotheses regarding poor social functioning. Multimodal approaches also appear congruent with intensive intervention as described within the context of the PBS model.

As school based practitioners consider the needs of the students they are serving, to develop intensive level interventions, it is critical to custom-tailor intervention to both the needs of the students and the social contexts in which they must function on a regular basis. There is a subtle, yet critical, difference between comprehensive intervention and eclectic intervention. Whereas *comprehensive* intervention is designed to meet the pervasive instructional needs of children at the intensive level of intervention through the use of multiple evidence-based, skill-specific strategies, an *eclectic* approach to intervention incorporates a variety of procedures while paying little attention to the behavioral goals of the student and the relative efficacy of the intervention components (i.e., it is somewhat haphazard in nature).

Implications for the Role of the School Psychologist

A review of the social skills literature reveals many implications related to the role of the practicing school psychologist. Perhaps the most significant implication is the increasingly popular assumption that school systems can and should address social behaviors in *all* children—not only those students demonstrating clinically significant social skills difficulties. An ecological approach, when coupled with the PBS model, provides an intricate framework from which to operate regarding comprehensive social skills assessment and intervention, in and across a variety of educational settings. This requires the practicing school psychologist to have competencies beyond initial assessment and data analysis. Specifically, school psychologists should be competent in their ability to conduct and oversee systematic screening for internalizing and externalizing difficulties, ongoing data collection procedures to inform practice across levels, intervention strategies for use across levels, and comprehensive consultation and program evaluation, as well as systems-level change through interactions with both general education and special education teachers. These competencies are congruent with those domains of practice addressed in *Standards for Training and Field Placement Programs in School Psychology* (National Association of School Psychologists, 2000). In addition, there is much overlap of these training standards and competencies outlined in *The Blueprint for Training and Practice III* (Yselldyke et al., 2006).

Another consideration for school psychologists engaged in social skills assessment and intervention is the importance of attending to social validity throughout the process. As indicated earlier, social validity is concerned with: (a) the social significance of the goals of the intervention; (b) the social appropriateness of the procedures involved; and (c) the social importance of the intervention (Wolf, 1978). At the heart of social validity is the consideration of the following critical question: "So what?" That is, what will significant others in the environment (e.g., parents, teachers, peers) think of the behavioral skills selected for intervention, the procedures used to foster skills development and enhancement, and the outcomes associated with intervention? If any of these elements are overlooked, treatment fidelity and the overall level of successful outcomes for students may be compromised.

School psychologists and other practitioners may address the "So what?" as related to the social significance of the goals by involving key stakeholders (e.g., parents, teachers, and peers) in assessment, student nominations and screenings, target skills selection, and related procedures. School-based practitioners may address the "So what?" as related to the social appropriateness of the procedures through assessing *treatment acceptability*. Treatment acceptability may be defined as "judgments about the treatment procedures by nonprofessionals, lay persons, clients and other potential consumers of treatment regarding whether treatments are appropriate, fair, reasonable, and intrusive, and whether treatments meet with conventional notions about what treatments should be" (Kazdin, 1980, p. 259). The *Behavior Intervention Rating Scale* (BIRS; Von Brock & Elliott, 1987) is an example of an instrument that may be used to assess parent and teacher treatment acceptability ratings, and the *Children's Intervention Rating Profile* (CIRP; Witt & Elliott, 1985) offers a valid measure of student treatment acceptability ratings. Assessing treatment acceptability may have implications from the beginning of treatment implementation. Witt and Elliott hypothesize that if consumers deem an intervention to be acceptable, they are more likely to implement the intervention with fidelity. If one assumes that positive behavior change is the result of treatment, treatment integrity is a necessary prerequisite to positive intervention outcomes (Witt & Elliott). The important principle here is that if consultants, researchers, and intervention teams fail to monitor treatment fidelity, and the intervention results in low-to-moderate outcomes, it is difficult to determine whether poor outcomes are associated with a weak intervention, or merely the failure to implement a potentially powerful intervention with adequate fidelity.

Finally, school based practitioners may address social validity as related to outcomes via two mechanisms: social comparison, and subjective evaluation (Kazdin, 1982). The social comparison approach to assessing is concerned with gathering objective, normative data on the performance of peers who are functioning adequately within the social environment, and comparing the performance of children targeted for more intensive intervention with that of their peers (Kazdin). Assessing goal attainment has been identified as an effective means of assessing consumers' subjective evaluations of overall treatment efficacy, as related to student progress (Sladeczek, Elliott, Kratochwill, Robertson-Mjaanes, & Stoiber, 2001). An example of such an approach is *Goal Attainment Scaling* (GAS; Kiresuk, Smith & Cardillo, 1994) wherein significant others rate the child's progress toward goal attainment. Frequent subjective ratings can provide insight to the clinical meaningfulness of the child's progress toward treatment goals. The interested reader is referred to Roach and Elliott (2005) for a succinct overview of goal attainment scaling.

A final implication for the role of the practicing school psychologist has to do with planning for and incorporating generalization procedures throughout social skills intervention. As indicated earlier, there exists a comprehensive social skills intervention literature to document low-to-moderate outcomes associated with multimodal social skills training as the independent variable (Kavale et al., 1997). There are at least three major limitations related to generalization in the current literature: (a) researchers rarely examine the generalization of behavior in social skills research; (b) those studies that do provide generalization data often rely on the least analytic approaches; and (c) generalization is seldom considered a dependent variable in social skills training research (Landrum & Lloyd, 1992). Unfortunately, the maintenance and generalization of treatment gains, when assessed, generally result in poor long-term outcome data (DuPaul & Eckert, 1994; Landrum & Lloyd, 1992). Although more research is needed to address this large gap in the literature, there is an emerging line of inquiry that has identified many procedures that may prove effective in enhancing the generalization of new and emerging skills to multiple applied settings. For example, it may be beneficial to incorporate key stakeholders into training and generalization settings as co-facilitators and behavioral coaches (Sheridan, 1998). Roles for behavioral coaches may include observing students in applied settings, seeking out and actively creating situations through which targeted students may practice using new and emerging positive social skills, and providing reinforcement (e.g., the use of a token or access to immediate rewards) for successes and successive approximations of the desired behavioral response.

It has also been suggested that the use of behavioral contracts, coupled with self-monitoring, may be beneficial for students to transfer skills more readily into applied settings (Sheridan, 1995, 1998). These and other procedures may be incorporated to help ensure that to the greatest extent possible, the intervention team employs generalization procedures grounded in the use of natural consequences, training diversely, and incorporating mediators (Allen & Cowan, 2008; Stokes & Osnes, 1989). Incorporating generalization procedures from the beginning of treatment is likely to enhance the overall maintenance and generalization of treatment gains in students across settings and levels of intervention.

Conclusion

Despite over 40 years of research investigating outcomes associated with various social skills training interventions for a wide variety of students, the fields of education and psychology remain in need of more definitive answers to many of the questions posed at the beginning of this chapter. It could be argued that the complex nature of social competency itself remains the biggest challenge to developing more conclusive guidelines for "best practices" in the education and treatment of students demonstrating too few adaptive social skills and/or excessive amounts of disruptive, maladaptive social behaviors. The literature to date has resulted in helpful guidelines related to social skills assessment and intervention. For example, it appears most logical to subscribe to a multi-method approach to assessment that is flexible, comprehensive, and lends to multilevel applications. Furthermore, a review of the literature reveals that there exist several promising treatment approaches that, when used as part of a multimodal approach, may lend to moderate outcomes in the school setting. In addition, the literature provides some guidelines to enhance the overall effectiveness and utility of intervention (e.g., attending to social validity and generalization considerations). Given the evolving nature of social skills research, it is important for school based practitioners to remain informed regarding newly emerging research to guide practice. It is also critical for school based personnel to remain cognizant that regardless of the level of intervention or the nature of the curriculum being implemented, it is essential to gather ongoing progress-monitoring data to inform practice. The accumulation of continuous data allows practitioners and other members of educational teams to make data-based decisions regarding the continuation, modification, or termination of social skills intervention in applied settings.

References

Achenbach, T. M., & Rescorla, L. A. (2001). *Manual for the ASEBA school-age forms and profiles.* Burlington, VT: University of Vermont.

Alberto, P. A., & Troutman, A. C. (2009). *Applied behavior analysis for teachers* (8th ed.). Upper Saddle River, NJ: Merrill.

Allen, K. D., & Cowan, R. J. (2008). Using naturalistic procedures to educate children with autism. In J. K. Luiselli, D.C. Russo, W.P. Christian, & S.M. Wilczynski (Eds.), *Effective practices for children with autism: Educational and behavior support interventions that work* (pp. 213–240). New York: Oxford University Press.

Ang, R. P., & Hughes, J. N. (2002). Differential benefits of skills training with antisocial youth based on group composition: A meta-analytic investigation. *School Psychology Review, 31,* 164–185.

Apter, S. J., & Conoley, J. C. (1984). *Childhood behavior disorders and emotional disturbance: An introduction to teaching troubled children.* Englewood Cliffs, NJ: Prentice-Hall.

Arnold, M. E., & Hughes, J. N. (1999). First do no harm: Adverse effects of grouping deviant youth for skills training. *Journal of School Psychology, 35,* 99–115.

Bandura, A. (1977). *Social learning theory.* Englewood Cliffs, NJ: Prentice Hall.

Barton, E. J. (1986). Modification of children's prosocial behavior. In P.S. Strain, M. J. Guralnick, & H.M. Walker (Eds.), *Children's social behavior: Development, Assessment, and Modification.* Orlando, FL: Academic Press.

Beelmann, A. Pfingsten, U., & Losel, F. (1994). Effects of training social competence in children: A meta-analysis of recent evaluation studies. *Journal of Clinical Child Psychology, 23,* 260–271.

Bellini, S., Peters, J. K., Benner, L., & Hopf, A. (2007). A meta-analysis of school-based social skills interventions for children with autism spectrum disorders. *Remedial and Special Education, 28,* 153–162.

Bronfenbrenner, U. (1979). *The ecology of human development.* Cambridge, MA: Harvard University Press.

Carey, S. P., & Stoner, G. (1994). Contextual considerations in social skills instruction. *School Psychology Quarterly, 9,* 137–141.

Cartlege, G., & Milburn, J. F. (1995). *Teaching social skills to children: Innovative approaches* (3rd ed.). Boston: Allyn & Bacon.

Colvin, G., Sugai, G., Good, R. H., & Lee, Y. Y. (1997). Using active supervision and precorrection to improve transition behaviors in an elementary school. *School Psychology Quarterly, 12,* 344–363.

Cowan, R. J., & Allen, K. D. (2007). Using naturalistic procedures to enhance learning in individuals with autism: A focus on generalized teaching within the school setting. *Psychology in the Schools, 44,* 701–716.

Cowan, R. J., & Sheridan, S. M. (2008). Evidence-based approaches to working with children with disruptive behavior. In T. Gutkin & C. Reynolds (Eds.), *The handbook of school psychology* (4th ed.) (pp. 569–590). New York: Wiley & Sons.

Dishion, T. J., McCord, J., & Poulin, F. (1999). When interventions harm: Peer groups and problem behavior. *American Psychologist, 54,* 755–764.

DuPaul, G. J., & Eckert, T. L. (1994). The effects of social skills curricula: Now you see them, now you don't. *School Psychology Quarterly*, *9*, 113–132.

Edelstein, B. A., (1989). Generalization: Terminological, methodological and conceptual issues. *Behavior Therapy*, *20*, 311–324.

Elliott, S. N., & Gresham, F. M. (1993). *Social skills intervention guide*. Circle Pines, MN: American Guidance Service.

Elliott, S. N., Sheridan, S. M., & Gresham, F.M. (1989). Assessing and treating social skills deficits: A case study for the scientist-practitioner. *Journal of School Psychology*, *27*, 197–222.

Erwin, E. J. (1994). Social competence in young children with visual impairments. *Infants and Young Children*, *6*, 26–33.

Forness, S. R., & Kavale, K. A. (1996). Training social skills deficits in children with learning disabilities: A meta-analysis of research. *Learning Disability Quarterly*, *19*, 2–13.

Gresham, F. M. (1986). Conceptual issues in the assessment of social competence in children. In P.S. Strain, M.J. Guralnick, & H.M. Walker (Eds.), *Children's social behavior: Development, assessment, and modification* (pp. 143–179). New York: Academic Press.

Gresham, F. M. (1997). Social competence in children with behavior disorders: Where we've been, where we are, and where we should go. *Education and Treatment of Children*, *20*, 233–249.

Gresham, F. M. (2002). Teaching social skills to high-risk children and youth: Preventive and remedial strategies. In M. Shinn, H. Walker, & G. Stoner (Eds.), *Interventions for academic and behavior problems II: Preventive and remedial approaches* (pp. 403–432). Bethesda, MD: National Association of School Psychologists.

Gresham, F. M., & Elliott, S. N. (1990). *Social skills rating system manual*. Circle Pines, MN: American Guidance Service.

Gresham, F. M., Sugai, G., & Horner, R. (2001). Interpreting outcomes of social skills training for students with high-incidence disabilities. *Exceptional Children*, *67*, 331–344.

Jones, R. N., Sheridan, S. M., & Binns, W. R. (1993). Schoolwide social skills training: providing preventive services to students at-risk. *School Psychology, Quarterly*, 57–80.

Kavale, K. A., & Forness, S. R. (1995). Social skills deficits and training: A meta-analysis of the research in learning disabilities. In T. E. Scruggs & M.A. Mastropieri (Eds.), *Advances in learning and behavioral disabilities* (Vol. 11, pp. 1–26). Greenwich, CT: JAI.

Kavale, K. A., Mather, S. R., Forness, S.R., Rutherford, R. B., & Quinn, M. M. (1997). Effectiveness of social skills training for students with behavior disorders: A meta-analysis. *Advances in Learning and Behavioral Disabilities*, *11*, 1–26.

Kazdin, A. E. (1980). Acceptability of alternative treatments for deviant child behavior. *Journal of Applied Behavior Analysis*, *13*, 259–273.

Kazdin, A. E. (1982). *Single case research designs: Methods for clinical and applied settings*. New York: Oxford University Press.

Kendall, P. C. (1989). The generalization and maintenance of behavior change: Comments, considerations, and the "no cure" criticism. *Behavior Therapy*, *20*, 357–364.

Kiresuk, T. J., Smith, A., & Cardillo, J. E., (Eds.) (1994). *Goal attainment scaling: Applications, theory, and measurement*. Hillsdale, NJ: Lawrence Erlbaum.

Landrum, T. J., & Lloyd, J. W. (1992). Generalization in social behavior research in children and youth who have emotional or behavioral disorders. *Behavior Modification*, *16*, 593–616.

Lewis, T. J., & Sugai, G. (1999). Effective behavior support: A systems approach to proactive school-wide management. *Effective School Practices*, *17*(4), 47–53.

Maag, J. W. (1999). *Behavior management: From theoretical implications to practical applications*. San Diego, CA: Singular Publishing Group.

Mathur, S. R., & Rutherford, R. B. (1996). Is social skills training effective for students with emotional or behavioral disorders? Research issues and needs. *Behavioral Disorders*, *22*, 21–28.

Mathur, S. R., Kavale, K. A., Quinn, M. M., Forness, S. R., & Rutherford, R. B. (1998). Social skills interventions for students with emotional or behavioral disorders: A meta-analysis of the single-subject research. *Behavioral Disorders*, *23*, 149–152.

McConaughy, S. H., & Ritter, D. (2002). Best practices in multidimensional assessment of emotional and behavioral disorders. In A. Thomas & J. Grimes (Eds.), *Best practices in school psychology-IV* (pp. 1303–1320). Bethesda, MD: National Association of School Psychologists.

Miltenberger, R. (2003). *Behavior modification: Principles and procedures* (3rd ed.). New York: Wadsworth Publishing.

Morgan, J. C. (1993). *Analog assessment of the effectiveness of social skills training with ADHD boys*. Masters thesis proposal, University of Utah, Salt Lake City, UT.

National Association of School Psychologists. (2000). *Standards for training and field placement programs in school psychology*. Bethesda, MD: Author.

Odom, S. L., & Strain, P. S. (1986). A comparison of peer-initiation and teacher-antecedent interventions for promoting reciprocal social interaction of autistic preschoolers. *Journal of Applied Behavioral Analysis*, *19*, 59–71.

OSEP Technical Assistance Center on Positive Behavioral Interventions and Supports (NDA). *Overview of tertiary intervention*. Retrieved December 10, 2008, at http://www.pbis.org/school/tertiary-level/default.aspx

OSEP Technical Assistance Center on Positive Behavioral Interventions and Supports (NDA). *School-wide positive behavior support: Implementer's blueprint and self-assessment*. Retrieved June 1, 2009 at: http://pbis.org/common/pbisresources/publications/SWPBS_implementation_Blueprint.pdf

Reynolds, C. R., & Kamphaus, R. W. (2004). *Behavior assessment system for children* (2nd ed.). Circle Pines, MN: American Guidance Service.

Roach, A. T., & Elliott, S. N. (2005). Goal attainment scaling: An efficient and effective approach to monitoring student progress. *Teaching Exceptional Children*, *37*, 8–17.

Rogers, S. J. (2000). Interventions that facilitate socialization in children with autism. *Journal of Autism and Developmental Disorders*, *30*, 399–409.

Sheridan, S. M. (1995). *The tough kid social skills book*. Longmont, CO: Sopris West.

Sheridan, S. M. (1998). *Why don't they like me? Helping your child make and keep friends*. Longmont, CO: Sopris West.

Sheridan, S. M., & Gutkin, T. B. (2000). The ecology of school psychology: Examining and changing our paradigm for the 21st century. *School Psychology Review*, *29*, 485–502.

Sheridan, S. M., & Walker, D. (1999). Social skills in context: Considerations for assessment, intervention, and generalization. In C.R. Reynolds & T.B. Gutkin (Eds.), *The handbook of school psychology* (3rd ed., pp. 686–708). New York: Wiley & Sons.

Sheridan, S. M., Hungelmann, A., & Poppenga Maughan, D. (1999). A contextualized framework for social skills assessment, intervention, and generalization. *School Psychology Review, 28*, 84–103.

Skinner, B.F. (1953). *Science and human behavior.* New York: Macmillan.

Sladeczek, I. E., Eilliott, S. N., Kratochwill, T. R., Robertson-Mjaanes, S., & Stoiber, K. C. (2001). Application of goal attainment scaling to a conjoint behavioral consultation case. *Journal of Educational and Psychological Consultation, 12*, 45–58.

Stokes, T. & Baer, D. (1977). An implicit technology of generalization. *Journal of Applied Behavior Analysis, 10*, 349–367.

Stokes, T. F., & Osnes, P. G. (1989). The operant pursuit of generalization. *Behavior Therapy, 20*, 337–355.

Sugai, G., Sprague, J. R., Horner, R. H., & Walker, H. M. (2000). Preventing school violence: The use of office discipline referrals to assess and monitor school-wide discipline interventions. *Journal of Emotional and Behavioral Disorders, 8*, 94–101.

Von Brock, M., & Elliott, S. N. (1987). Influence and treatment effectiveness information on the acceptability of classroom interventions. *Journal of School Psychology, 25*, 131–144.

Walker, H. M., & Severson, H. H. (1992). Systematic *screening for behavior disorders.* Longmont, CO: Sopris West.

Walker, H. M., Horner, R. H., Sugai, G., Bullis, M., Sprague, J. R., Bricker, D., & Kaufman, M. J. (1996). Integrated approaches to prevention anti-social behavior patterns among school-age children and youth. *Journal of Emotional and Behavioral Disorders, 4*, 194–209.

Witt, J. C., & Elliott, S. N. (1985). Acceptability of classroom intervention strategies. In T. R. Kratochwill (Ed.), *Advances in school psychology* (Vol. 4, pp. 251–288). Hillsdale, NJ: Lawrence Erlbaum.

Wolf, M. M. (1978). Social validity: The case for subjective measurement or how applied behavior analysis is finding its heart. *Journal of Applied Behavior Analysis, 11*, 203–214.

Yeaton, W. H., & Sechrest, L. (1981). Critical dimensions in the choice and maintenance of successful treatment: Strength, integrity, and effectiveness. *Journal of Consulting and Clinical Psychology, 49*, 156–167

Yell, M. L., Meadows, N. B., Drasgow, E., & Shriner, J. G. (2009). *Evidence-based practices for educating students with emotional and behavioral disorders.* Upper Saddle River, NJ: Merrill.

Ysseldyke, J., Morrison, D., Burns, M., Ortiz, S., Dawson, P., Rosenfideld, S., et al. (2006). *School psychology: A blueprint for training and practice III.* Bethesda, MD: National Association of School Psychologists.

Challenging Gifted and Talented Learners with a Continuum of Research-Based Interventions Strategies

Sally M. Reis *and* Joseph S. Renzulli

Abstract

An overview of definitions of giftedness, special populations of gifted and talented children, methods of identification, and a continuum of services are summarized in this chapter. These services include organizational strategies (such as instructional grouping options), instructional strategies (such as acceleration and enrichment options), and a variety of talent development opportunities that should be included in a continuum of services that will engage and challenge all gifted and talented students. Also included in this chapter are some social and emotional challenges that may affect gifted and high potential children, such as the potential underachievement of children who do not encounter sufficient challenge in school. The chapter ends with a summary of research about the effectiveness of grouping, instructional, and talent development strategies, as well as recommendations for the creation of a continuum of services in each school district that will challenge and engage all students.

Keywords: gifted and talented students, curriculum enhancement, grouping strategies, enrichment, acceleration, talent development, differentiation, continuum of services, underachievement

Introduction

The study of gifts and talents in children continues to fascinate teachers and educators who watch with wonder as a 3-year-old reads without any instruction, or a child composes elegant poetry, or a young person writes compelling original music. This chapter addresses three questions that have long intrigued and perplexed researchers, psychologists, educators, and parents interested in developing the gifts and talents of high potential children: how do we define giftedness in children; how do we identify giftedness or the potential for giftedness in these students; and what interventions work best to help develop the gifts and talents of students with high potential? In an ideal world, researchers and educators would respond to each question with definitive answers, citing research-based strategies that work in diverse school settings; however, in the real world we know that personality, environment, school, and home factors interact with potential and the ability to translate that potential into demonstrated gifts and

talents (Renzulli, 1978, 1986, 2006). Accordingly, the reality is somewhat more complex.

Current research shows that some children who are identified as gifted and talented excel in school, attend competitive colleges, complete their bachelor's degree with honors, head to outstanding graduate schools where they excel, and pursue distinguished careers in which they make a difference in the lives of others (Hébert, 1993; Westberg, 1999). Other research demonstrates that some gifted students, who excel in elementary and middle school, underachieve in high school and eventually drop out of school (Reis & McCoach, 2000; Reis et al., 1995). One recent study using a national database found that 5% of gifted students drop out of high school (Renzulli & Park, 2000). Another study shows that half of the identified gifted students in an urban high school were underachieving by the time they entered their sophomore year (Reis et al., 1995). Research about gifted and talented learners points to the great diversity among this heterogeneous group of young people (Neihart, Reis, Robinson, & Moon, 2001), and the fact that many do not realize their potential, in part, due to school factors that contribute to their underachievement, halted development, and failure to develop gifted behaviors (Reis & McCoach, 2000).

Traits, Characteristics, and Definitions of Giftedness

Despite the diversity in this population, research suggests that some traits occur with greater frequency in gifted and high potential learners than in the general population (Frasier & Passow, 1994; Renzulli, 1986). In this chapter, some of these traits are discussed, as are the definitions of giftedness that accompany these traits. However, it is not our intention to provide an absolute definition or checklist of students as either "gifted" or "not gifted"; rather, we will discuss some characteristics that may be present in some gifted and high ability students, and illustrate how these characteristics will vary based on a variety of factors, including gender, sociocultural group, the presence of a hidden or overt disability, age, and/or level of achievement. Our hope is that by discussing the heterogeneity of gifted and talented learners, this chapter will enable both educators and psychologists to understand that more diverse and flexible conceptions of giftedness and talent, extending beyond IQ, must be considered in a broad spectrum of children and young adults. Our ultimate goal is to help educators develop a continuum of services that will contribute to the development of the gifts and talents of children and young people. We begin the chapter with two case studies that illustrate the diverse behaviors demonstrated by young people identified as gifted and talented, and the need that exists for talent development opportunities for students like them.

Keisha

Keisha was a shy, quiet fifth grader who had been identified as gifted in second grade, in a school that used a cutoff on aptitude scores to qualify for the gifted program. An avid reader and introvert, she displayed few characteristics related to most traditional notions of giftedness. She was so quiet that her teachers failed to see the high level of creative potential which she subsequently displayed in school and life. Her verbal skills were hard to identify because she was shy. Although she read avidly, she did not initially appear to display verbal precocity. Her current teachers had not observed any indications of problem solving, reasoning,

insight, or other commonly acknowledged characteristics of academic giftedness. Keisha was primarily known for being quiet and kind, and an advanced reader who did not like to discuss or share what she was reading, perhaps due to her shyness.

Keisha did well in school, but was not considered the most advanced student in any of her classes between second and fifth grade. In the beginning of fifth grade, however, she developed a closer relationship with her new classroom teacher, who had some coursework in gifted education and talent development and understood Keisha's shyness. Her teacher spent time getting to know her, found books in her interest area, took an interest in what Keisha was doing at home, and asked Keisha about some of her aspirations and hopes for the future. Over the next few months, Keisha's affect and attitudes in school changed, and she began to excel in all content areas. She became involved in an in-depth independent study project and started, with the support of her teacher, a book drive in the school for a nearby community center for children of poverty with little access to books at home. Interestingly enough, few of the characteristics that Keisha displayed when she was working on her book project had been apparent to her teachers prior to this time. The circumstances that emerged with her new teacher and her book project gave Keisha the opportunities, resources, and encouragement (Renzulli & Reis, 1997) to actively demonstrate and further develop her latent gifts and talents.

Peter

Although he had been identified as gifted in third grade, Peter's schoolwork had frustrated both his parents and teachers for years. Always a child of remarkably high potential, his grades fluctuated in elementary, middle, and senior high school. In elementary school, Peter was identified as gifted in a district that required an IQ of above 130, in addition to evidence of high achievement, for entrance to the gifted program. He enjoyed discussing his ideas with others and was highly verbal, but had poor work habits in required subjects in technology and math, his two areas of interest. As the years progressed, Peter's work became less and less impressive, and his teachers questioned his identification as gifted. His writing was considered below average, and the only class in which he consistently excelled was math.

Peter disliked reading anything that was unrelated to his interests. His grades varied, from top marks in math and technology to failing grades in subjects that did not interest him. Although he took advanced math classes in middle and high school, and achieved a near perfect score on the math section of the SAT, during his junior year of high school, Peter had become an "underachiever" because of his varying attitudes toward school. He rarely displayed characteristics of a gifted student in classes in which he did not have an interest. His technology and math teachers realized his potential and saw his talents in problem solving, persistence, and creativity. Few other teachers noted any positive characteristics, and he continued to underachieve in school. Over time, a pattern emerged. If Peter liked his teacher, he would do well in class, regardless of the content. If Peter liked the content of the class, but not his teacher, he would do enough to get by with marginal grades, usually Cs. But if Peter did not like either his teacher or the content, or the content was well below his ability level, Peter usually failed the class or earned a grade of D. He always did well on his exams, even when he had done none of the assigned work in class. He simply lost credit for the homework and class work that he failed to complete.

The problem was not that Peter was lazy. In fact, his parents usually had to plead with him to go to bed on time because he was reading books about artificial intelligence, or pursuing his own interests, designing software and building computers. In his senior year, Peter got recruitment letters from the best colleges in the country because his SAT scores were nearly perfect but, unfortunately, he did not graduate from high school, failing both English and history. He did not like his teachers, and the work was too easy in the lower-track classes to which he had been assigned because of his lackluster effort and low grades in earlier years. Not graduating from high school was, for Peter, the lesser of two fates. The worse fate, in his opinion, was pretending to be interested in boring, non-inspiring classes taught by teachers he believed did not care about him or their teaching practices. Despite the many creative and motivational characteristics that Peter displayed at home or in content areas in which he had a sincere interest, his teachers failed to see the traits associated with his gifts and talents.

Characteristics and Operational Definitions of Giftedness and Talents

These case studies illustrate the difficulty in relying on one definition to describe diverse gifted behaviors. The overlapping definitions of giftedness in educational research underlie the complexity of defining

with absolute certainty who is and who is not gifted (Sternberg & Davidson, 2005). In describing this heterogeneous group of learners, current educators may interchangeably use more expanded definitions of giftedness and talent. This was not always the case, for in decades past, researchers and psychologists, following in the footsteps of Lewis Terman, equated "giftedness" with high IQ (Terman, 1925). In practice, this legacy survives to the present day, with some researchers, educators, and parents equating a high psychometric score on an intelligence test as equivalent to "giftedness." However, more recently, most definitions of giftedness or talent have become more multidimensional, and include the interplay of culture and values on the development of talents and gifts (Sternberg & Davidson, 2005). The most current research offers multiple perspectives on conceptions of giftedness by many different researchers ranging from general, broad characterizations to more targeted definitions of giftedness identified by *specific* actions, products, or abilities within domains (Sternberg & Davidson, 1986; Sternberg & Davidson, 2005). This research, conducted during the last few decades, supports a broader conception of giftedness that includes various combinations of multiple qualities such as motivation, self-concept, and creativity, in addition to intellectual potential (Sternberg & Davidson, 2005).

The Federal Definition, The Renzulli Three-Ring Definition, and Gagne's Conception

Following the seminal research conducted by Terman and his associates almost a century ago, researchers have expanded upon this one-dimensional conception of giftedness as equating with high IQ. A consensus in more recent research defines giftedness as a multidimensional construct incorporating a variety of traits, skills, and abilities. This expanded conception is particularly evident in two separate scholarly examinations of giftedness in Sternberg and Davidson's (1986, 2005) edited volumes of conceptions of giftedness, in which most contributors propose conceptions of giftedness that extend beyond IQ. This philosophical stance is an even stronger theme in most second edition chapters (Sternberg & Davidson, 2005) in which characteristics such as rapid learning as compared to others in the population, attention control, memory efficiency, perception, desire to develop one's gifts, and task commitment are all proposed as aspects of giftedness (Heller, Perleth, & Lim, 2005; Reis, 2005; Renzulli, 2005).

In research on characteristics of diverse groups of gifted and talented learners, Frasier and Passow (1994) synthesized traits, aptitudes, and behaviors identified by researchers as common to gifted students (Table 22.1), noting that these basic elements of giftedness appear to be similar across cultures (though each is not displayed by every student). Their research found that these traits, aptitudes, and behaviors may be manifested in various ways in different students, and educators should be especially careful in attempting to identify these characteristics in students from diverse backgrounds (i.e., economically disadvantaged, ethnically or racially diverse, etc.), as specific behavioral manifestations of the characteristics may vary across cultures (Frasier & Passow, 1994).

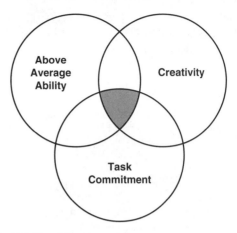

Fig. 22.1 Three-Ring Conception

Renzulli's Three-Ring Conception

One of the earliest theorists to propose a multifaceted conception of giftedness was Renzulli (1978), whose research resulted in his three-ring conception. The theory, which has gained widespread research and popular appeal, supports the idea that "gifted behaviors" result from the interaction among distinct intrapersonal characteristics, as outlined in the excerpt below.

> Gifted behavior consists of behaviors that reflect an interaction among three basic clusters of human traits—above average ability, high levels of task commitment, and high levels of creativity. Individuals capable of developing gifted behavior are those possessing or capable of developing this composite set of traits and applying them to any potentially valuable area of human performance. Persons who manifest or are capable of developing an interaction among the three clusters require a wide variety of educational opportunities and services

that are not ordinarily provided through regular instructional programs.
(*Renzulli & Reis*, 1997, p. 8)

Characteristics that are often manifested in Renzulli's three clusters are presented in Table 22.2.

Other Definitions of Giftedness

The United States Department of Education's current federal definition of giftedness also represents a multidimensional approach that is widely used in school districts and states across the country (1993):

> Children and youth with outstanding talent perform or show the potential for performing at remarkably high levels of accomplishment when compared with others of their age, experience, or environment. These children and youth exhibit high performance capability in intellectual, creative, and/or artistic areas, possess an unusual leadership capacity, or excel in specific academic fields. They require services or activities not ordinarily provided by the schools. Outstanding talents are present in children and youth from all cultural groups, across all economic strata, and in all areas of human endeavor.
(U.S. Department of Education, 1993, p. 26)

Francois Gagné's conception of giftedness differentiates between giftedness and talent, hypothesizing that talent is a skill within a single domain that must be systematically developed, as opposed to giftedness, which represents innate abilities in and across multiple domains (Gagné, 1985, 1999, 2000). Gagné proposes that giftedness is the manifestation of natural abilities to a level that places the student in the top 10% of their chronological peers. These abilities, often called *aptitudes* or *gifts*, appear in at least one of five natural

Table 22.1 Frasier & Passow's common attributes of giftedness

• motivation	• advanced interests
• communication skills	• problem-solving ability
• well-developed memory	• inquiry
• insight	• reasoning
• imagination/creativity	• sense of humor
• advanced ability to deal with symbol systems	

Adapted with permission from The National Research Center on the Gifted and Talented.

Table 22.2   Taxonomy of behavioral manifestations of giftedness according to Renzulli's "Three-ring" definition of gifted behaviors

Above Average Ability (general)
- high levels of abstract thought
- adaptation to novel situations
- rapid and accurate retrieval of information

Above Average Ability (specific)
- applications of general abilities to specific area of knowledge
- capacity to sort out relevant from irrelevant information
- capacity to acquire and use advanced knowledge and strategies while pursuing a problem

Task Commitment
- capacity for high levels of interest and/or enthusiasm
- hard work and determination in a particular area
- self-confidence and drive to achieve
- ability to identify significant problems within an area of study
- setting high standards for one's work

Creativity
- fluency, flexibility, and originality of thought
- open to new experiences and ideas
- curious
- willing to take risks

From Renzulli & Reis, 1997. Adapted with permission of Creative Learning Press.

aptitude domains: intellectual, creative, socioaffective, sensorimotor, and others. Talents, as defined in this model, emerge from the systematic development and nurturance of these aptitudes into skills that characterize a particular field. Similar to Renzulli, Gagné's definition of giftedness focuses on the role that talent development plays in transforming natural abilities into systematically developed skills, as he discusses the role played by interpersonal factors, environmental factors, and chance (Tannenbaum, 1983, 1986).

There is no single agreed upon definition of giftedness at the national or even the state level. Thus, the research-based interventions discussed in this chapter will differ based on various conceptions of giftedness. For example, if intellectual giftedness with characteristics such as attention control, memory efficiency, advanced reasoning, and rapid processing and retrieval of information are used as the basis for identification, the use of acceleration and advanced content would be an appropriate program choice. Characteristics and definitions should always lead to corresponding identification

procedures, as well as the program services selected, a concept we call *internal consistency*.

Creativity and Creative Productive Definitions of Giftedness and Talent

Creativity is an area of interest to many scholars, but there is no universally accepted definition of creativity (Treffinger, Young, Selby, & Shepardson, 2002), and characteristics of creativity vary within and among people and across disciplines (Renzulli, 1978). Academic giftedness and creative giftedness may be two separate concepts, as per Sternberg and Lubart's assertion that the "academically successful children of today are not necessarily the creatively gifted adults of tomorrow" (1993, p. 12). Individuals with high intelligence may or may not have high creative ability as well (Renzulli & Reis, 1997). Some evidence, however, suggests that a relationship exists between the constructs. A "threshold concept" discussed by MacKinnon in 1978, includes a base level of intelligence (an IQ of about 120) that is essential for creative productivity. Beyond that threshold, no relationship between creativity and intelligence appears to be measured by IQ tests (Sternberg & Lubart, 1993).

Teachers try to identify the potential for creative productivity of children in general areas, as children with high potential for creativity often demonstrate fluency, flexibility, originality, and elaboration, as well as the abilities to think in creative or divergent ways (Guilford, 1950; Torrance, 1988). What defines a child with high creative potential? Gardner (1993) defines a creative individual as one who *"regularly* solves problems or fashions products in a *domain*, and whose work is considered both novel and acceptable by knowledgeable members of a field" (p. xvii). Creativity should not be regarded as a construct in the mind or personality of an individual; rather it is something that emerges from the interactions of intelligence (personal profile of competences), domain (disciplines or crafts within a culture), and field (people and institutions that judge quality within a domain; Gardner, 1993).

What "resources" and environments might children need in school to enable their gifts and talents to be nurtured and developed? We believe that the use of certain enrichment opportunities included in our work on the Schoolwide Enrichment Model (Renzulli & Reis, 1997) can result in the creation of an environment that nurtures creativity in children. Teachers who want to develop creatively gifted children enable them to create, formulate, and plan ideas and projects, while also processing information through abstract thinking and generalizing (Renzulli & Reis, 1997). Teachers and parents who hope to develop creativity in children must nurture a belief in self and creative ideas; this should be done in an environment in which children are allowed to work on creative tasks, and one in which creativity is rewarded and creative ideas are celebrated. Our work (Renzulli & Reis, 1985, 1997) focuses on a developmental three-ring conception of giftedness, and the ways in which we nurture students' interests, learning, and product styles. Our goal is to provide opportunities, resources, and encouragement for children to develop these potentials and creative products, through a continuum of services (Renzulli & Reis, 1997). A series of broad and diverse opportunities described later in this chapter in the Schoolwide Enrichment Model (Renzulli & Reis, 1997) are considered to be positive forces in the development of creative potential, and academic gifts and talents, in children.

Special Populations of Gifted Learners

The last two decades have been marked by an increasing interest in diverse gifted students (Briggs, Reis, & Sullivan, 2008; Tomlinson, Ford, Reis, Briggs, & Strickland, 2003). These students may include children from ethnic, racial, and linguistic minorities, as well as those from economically disadvantaged homes. Literature and research conducted on gifted girls (Reis, 1998), gifted underachievers (Reis & McCoach, 2000), gifted gay, lesbian, or bisexual students (Cohn, 2003), and gifted students with disabilities (Baum & Owen, 2004) suggests that the underrepresentation of these groups in gifted programs is consistent and pervasive. With increased awareness of this issue, some policymakers and educators have sought ways to ensure that diverse groups of gifted students receive opportunities similar to those that other gifted students enjoy (Ford, 1998; Ford & Harris, 1999; Tomlinson et al., 2003). Complicating the process, however, is the reality that many current identification and selection procedures may be ineffective and inappropriate for the identification of these young people (Briggs et al., 2008; Ford, 1998). Certainly, limited referrals and nominations of culturally, linguistically, and economically diverse (CLED) students affect their low placement in programs (Ford, 1998; Ford & Harris, 1999; Ford, Howard, Harris, & Tyson, 2000; Frasier & Passow, 1994; Briggs et al., 2008).

Part of the problem may be that gifted students in these populations demonstrate characteristics that are different from those of "typical" gifted students (Briggs et al., 2008; Ford, 1998). Recognizing the need to acknowledge characteristics of different cultures in the identification of talent among diverse groups, Ford (1998) urged educators to avoid assessments that are culture-blind when working with students of color and, instead, favor identification procedures that may be more sensitive to cultural differences. In this section of the chapter, a brief overview is presented on several of these populations.

Gifted Students with Learning Disabilities

The potential frustrations experienced by students with both high potential and learning disabilities may place them at risk for social and emotional problems (Baum & Owen, 2004; Reis, 1995). Identifying traits and characteristics of gifted and talented students with disabilities is complicated by the fact that the abilities of gifted students often mask their disabilities and, in turn, their disabilities may disguise their giftedness. As a result, students who are gifted and also have disabilities are at risk of under identification or exclusion both from programs for students with learning disabilities, and programs for gifted and talented students (Baum & Owen, 2004; Reis, Neu, & McGuire, 1995). This dual exclusion is also true of gifted students with other exceptionalities such as ADHD (Moon, 2002) and Asperger's syndrome (Neihart, 2000).

Gifted/LD students require unique educational programs and services for both their academic and affective development. According to research by Baum and Owen (2004) and Gerber and Ginsberg (1990), behaviors contributing to success can be cultivated and shaped, and strategies exhibited by successful adults with learning disabilities can be reasonably applied to the education of gifted/LD students. Baum (1990) makes these recommendations for working with gifted students with learning disabilities: encourage compensation strategies, cultivate awareness of strengths and weaknesses, focus on developing the child's gift, and provide an environment that values individual differences.

Gifted Students with ADHD

Children with ADHD (Attention Deficit Hyperactivity Disorder) and gifted children may exhibit similar behaviors (e.g., inattention, high energy level, and impulsivity), and mounting evidence suggests that many children diagnosed with ADHD are also particularly bright and creative (Cramond, 1995; Leroux, 2000; Moon, 2002). Likewise, evidence suggests that many gifted children exhibit symptoms similar to those of ADHD when they are unchallenged. Bright students may experience inattention when bored, while also demonstrating a high energy level in areas of intense interest (Reis & McCoach, 2000).

Baum and Owen (2004) found that when schools implement comprehensive programs that identify and develop individual gifts and talents, twice-exceptional students begin to behave socially, emotionally, and academically more like gifted students without disabilities than like nongifted students with learning disabilities. These findings, corroborated by Bender and Wall (1994), indicate that as educators diminish the attention to, and importance of, the disability, and concentrate instead on the gifts, many twice-exceptional students can become creatively productive.

Gifted Students with Behavioral Problems

Gifted students with emotional and behavioral problems are rarely referred for gifted programs, or are terminated from programming due to disruptive actions (Reid & McGuire, 1995). These children often experience periods of underachievement (Reid & McGuire, 1995), are frequently underchallenged in school, and experience high frustration with "dead time" as they wait for their peers to finish their work (Neu, 1993). In a review of the sparse research on this population, Reid and McGuire (1995) found that as a result of their emotional and behavioral disorders, these students may disengage from learning opportunities, resulting in inconsistencies in both academic skills and content knowledge, and high dropout rates.

Underachieving Gifted Learners

Student performance that falls noticeably short of potential, especially for young people with high ability, is bewildering and perhaps the most frustrating of all challenges that teachers and parents face (Reis & McCoach, 2000). According to a 1990 national needs assessment survey conducted by The National Research Center on the Gifted and Talented, educators of gifted students identified the problem of underachievement as their number one concern (Renzulli, Reid, & Gubbins, 1991). Too often, students who show great academic potential fail to perform at levels commensurate with their abilities. Gifted students who underachieve do so for different reasons (Reis & McCoach, 2000). Some have not learned to work; others students may have poor self-regulation skills, or low self-confidence

or self-efficacy. Other low achievers may have either obvious or hidden disabilities, including psychological and/or psychiatric disorders. Some students underachieve or fail in school for obvious reasons: excessive absences from school, poor performance, disruptive behavior, family problems, and poverty (Reis & McCoach, 2000). Underachievement in gifted or high potential students is often the result of their interaction with an inappropriate curriculum and simplistic content. However, underachievement can be reduced, and even eliminated in some students, with the right types of challenge and interest-based programs, as documented by Baum, Renzulli, and Hébert (1999).

Identification of Gifted, Talented and High Potential Students

Identification of gifted, talented, and high potential children continues to be an area of interest and concern to educators and psychologists (Callahan, Hunsaker, Adams, Moore, & Bland, 1995; Ford, 1998; Gagné, 1994; Renzulli & Delcourt, 1994). Questions are often raised about the appropriate age at which children should be identified, what should be included in an assessment, and which tests are most accurate and effective. Although these are important questions, they are not the central issue that relates to the identification of gifted and talented students—namely, for what purpose are we identifying students. In other words, for what *programs* and *services* are we identifying students? The methods educators should use to identify an intellectually advanced child in math will be different from those used for a highly creative child, and the programs that are developed to meet the needs of either of these children should be linked to both the definitions and identification procedures used.

How, Why, and When to Identify Gifted and High Potential Students

Differing views exist regarding how, why, and when to identify as child as gifted or talented, as well as the utility of different types and forms of assessment. Most researchers who study identification agree that the primary goal of assessment is to identify a pattern of abilities in and across specific domains (Renzulli & Delcourt, 1994). The rationale for assessment should also be based on how educators and parents can better understand a child's relative strengths and deficits, and how these relate to both educational and social settings. Comprehensive assessment of children's abilities and achievement levels should also focus on determining the level and type of services each student needs. Because there is no perfect test to determine giftedness, we recommend the use of a variety of tests and assessments, rather than the use of IQ testing alone, for a comprehensive examination of children's talents (Renzulli & Delcourt, 1994).

When should we begin the process of identifying gifted and talented students? Generally, testing is believed to be most reliable and most predictive between the ages of six and nine years. Consensus exists among professionals that there is rarely a need to test before the child is ready to enter school, and that testing at younger ages may not provide reliable results (Renzulli, Reis, & Smith, 1981; Robinson, 1987). Most comprehensive assessments conducted by private or school psychologists include some form of developmental history with examples of children's work, as well as a broad battery of assessments. Many tests are used to measure intelligence, aptitude, and achievement, but little consensus exists about which tests are most effective. Because of the flawed options available for testing talented and gifted children, we recommend the use of a variety of tests or test sections for the most comprehensive combination of skills assessments. Most researchers believe that the primary goal of assessment should be to identify a pattern of abilities in and across specific domains (Plucker, Callahan & Tomchin, 1996; Renzulli & Delcourt, 1994; Renzulli, Smith, White, Callahan, Hartman, & Westberg, 2002).

Twenty or thirty years ago, identification of gifted and talented students was usually completed primarily through the use of standardized test scores and intelligence tests. During the 1980s, for example, teacher recommendations were most widely used in identification, followed by achievement tests, and then the use of IQ tests (Cox, Daniel, & Boston, 1985). Two decades later, students are most often identified by the use of standardized achievement tests, as they are so readily available. This method of identification has resulted in disproportionately smaller numbers of culturally diverse, learning disabled, or economically disadvantaged students being identified for gifted programs, even though the American population was increasing in diversity, and the number of minority students has increased in schools (Ford, 1998). Accordingly, researchers interested in diverse gifted students are increasingly concerned about how to identify underrepresented populations for gifted program services (Ford, 1998). More equitable methods have subsequently been developed, focusing on the use of multiple criteria (Renzulli & Reis, 1997). Tests remain a part of most identification processes, but teacher nominations and rating scales, as well as students' grades and work, are now included in newer, multiple criteria approaches (Renzulli & Reis, 1997; Renzulli, Smith, White, Callahan, Hartman, & Westberg, 2002).

Research Based Interventions for Gifted and Talented Students

This section of the chapter includes a comprehensive review of research related to the need for, and efficacy of, different types of interventions for gifted and talented students. We begin this section with an overview of the Schoolwide Enrichment Model, one of the most researched interventions available to challenge academically talented learners (Renzulli, 1977; Renzulli & Reis, 1997; Van Tassel-Baska & Brown, 2007). Then, we provide an overview of research findings that establish the groundwork for other programmatic recommendations in this chapter, including the well documented research finding that high potential, above average, and gifted students have not fared well in current school settings in which the focus is on students with deficits, as mandated by current policies related to the No Child Left Behind legislation.

The Schoolwide Enrichment Model

The Schoolwide Enrichment Model (SEM) (Renzulli & Reis, 1985, 1997) was created to encourage and develop both academic talents and creative productivity in young people. The SEM, based on Renzulli's Enrichment Triad, has been implemented in thousands of schools across the country and has continued to expand internationally. Separate studies on the SEM and the Triad Model have demonstrated its effectiveness in schools with widely differing socioeconomic levels and program organization patterns (Burns, 1998; Olenchak, 1988; Olenchak & Renzulli, 1989). The effectiveness of the model has been studied in over 20 years of research and field testing about (a) student creative productivity (Delcourt, 1993; Hébert, 1993; Westberg, 1999); (b) personal and social development (Olenchak, 1991); (c) the use of SEM with culturally diverse or special needs populations (Baum, Renzulli, & Hébert, 1999; Olenchak, 1991); (d) student self-efficacy (Schack, Starko, & Burns, 1991; Starko, 1988); (e) the SEM as a curricular framework (Karafelis, 1986; Reis, Gentry, & Park, 1995); (f) learning styles and curriculum compacting (Reis & Purcell, 1993); and (g) longitudinal research on the SEM (Delcourt, 1993; Hébert, 1993; Westberg, 1999). This research on the SEM suggests that the model is effective at serving high ability students, and providing enrichment in a variety of educational settings including schools serving culturally diverse and low socioeconomic populations.

Theoretical Background of the SEM

The SEM is based on Renzulli's three-ring conception of giftedness that defines gifted behaviors rather than gifted individuals, as well as a series of interventions based on the Enrichment Triad Model. The SEM is currently used as the basis for many gifted programs, enrichment programs, and magnet, charter, and theme schools. The original Enrichment Triad Model, with three types of enrichment (Renzulli, 1977), is the core of the SEM. Type I enrichment is designed to expose students to a wide variety of disciplines, topics, occupations, hobbies, persons, places, and events that would not ordinarily be covered in the regular curriculum. Type II enrichment includes materials and methods designed to promote the development of thinking and affective processes that promote original inquiry and creative explorations. Some Type II enrichment is general, consisting of training in areas such as creative thinking and problem solving, learning how to learn skills such as classifying and analyzing data, and advanced reference and communication skills. Type III enrichment occurs when teachers work collaboratively to encourage students to become interested in pursuing a self-selected area, and are willing to commit the time necessary for advanced content acquisition and process training in which they assume the role of a first-hand inquirer. These three types of enrichment will be discussed in greater detail later in the chapter.

The SEM focuses on the development of both academic and creative-productive giftedness. Creative-productive giftedness describes those aspects of human activity and involvement where a premium is placed on the development of original material and products that are purposefully designed to have an impact on one or more target audiences. Learning situations designed to promote creative-productive giftedness emphasize the use and application of information (content) and thinking skills in an integrated, inductive, and real-problem-oriented manner. In the SEM, academic gifts are developed by transforming the role of the student from that of a learner of lessons, to one in which she or he uses the modus operandi of a firsthand inquirer to

experience the joys and frustrations of creative productivity. This approach is quite different from other approaches that tend to emphasize deductive learning, advanced content and problem solving, and the acquisition, storage, and retrieval of information. In other words, creative-productive giftedness enables children to work on issues and areas of study that have personal relevance to the student, and can be escalated to appropriately challenging levels of investigative activity.

Identification in the SEM

Translating theory into practice is always challenging. Although our work on a conception of giftedness has dealt with theory development, equal attention has been given to how the theory can guide practical strategies for the identification of *all* students who can benefit from special services. This constitutes one of the greatest challenges in the SEM, because a more flexible approach to identification oftentimes is at odds with traditional state or local regulations that require precision, names on lists signifying who is gifted, and resource allocations that make sharp distinctions between the work of special program personnel, and other teachers who may be able to contribute to a school's total talent development mission. These practical realities have resulted in our identification plan that, while still maintaining a degree of flexibility, is a compromise between a totally performance-based system, and a system that targets certain students.

The goal of identification within the SEM is to form a talent pool of students who are targeted because of strengths in particular areas that will serve as a primary (but not total) rationale for the services that the special program will provide. Before listing the six steps involved in this identification system, three important considerations will be discussed. First, talent pool size will vary in any given school, depending upon the general nature of the total student body. In schools with unusually large numbers of high achieving students, it is conceivable that talent pools will be larger than in lower scoring schools. But even in schools where achievement levels are below national norms, there still exists an upper level group of students who need services above and beyond those provided for the majority of the school population. Some of our most successful programs have been in urban schools that serve disadvantaged and bilingual youth. Even though these schools were below national norms, talent pools of approximately 15% of students needing supplementary services were still identified.

Talent pool size is also a function of the availability of resources (both human and material), and the extent to which the general faculty is willing (a) to make modifications in the regular curriculum for above average ability students; (b) to participate in various kinds of enrichment and mentoring activities; and (c) to work cooperatively with any and all personnel who may have special program assignments. It is very important to determine beforehand the number of students who can be served in ways that make a difference when program accountability is considered, such as curriculum compacting and the use of advanced content. Since teacher nomination plays an important role in this identification system, a second consideration is the extent of orientation and training that teachers have had, about both the program and procedures for nominating students. A third consideration is, of course, the type of program for which students are being identified. The identification system is based on models that combine both enrichment and acceleration, whether or not they are carried out in self-contained programs, inclusion programs, pull-out programs, or any other organizational arrangement. Regardless of the type of organizational model used, it is also recommended that a strong component of curriculum compacting (Reis, Burns, & Renzulli, 1992) be a part of the services offered to high achieving talent pool students.

Once a target number or percent of the school population is established, that number should be divided in half. For example, if the target talent pool is 15% talent pool, approximately half of the students will be selected using test scores, thus guaranteeing that the process will not discriminate against traditionally high scoring students. Step Two uses a research-based teacher nomination scale (Renzulli et al., 2002) for students not included in Step One. Again, the above-mentioned training helps to improve the reliability of ratings. With the exception of teachers who are habitually under- or over-nominators, these ratings are treated on a par value with test scores. Our experience has shown that the vast majority of talent pool nominees result from the first two steps.

Step Three enables the use of other criteria (e.g., parent, peer, or self nomination, previous product assessment) that a school may or may not want to consider—but in this case, a selection committee reviews the information in a case study fashion. Step Four enables previous year teachers to recommend students who were not nominated in the first three steps. This "safety valve" guards against bias or incompatibility on the part of the nominator in Step Two, and it allows for consideration of student potential that may be presently unrecognized because of personal or family issues, or a turn-off to school. Step Five provides parents with information about why their son or daughter was nominated for the talent pool, the goals and nature of the program as it relates to their child's strength areas, and how a program based on the Three-Ring Conception of Giftedness differs from other types of programs. Step Six is a second safety valve, in which teacher nomination enables the consideration of targeted services for a young person who may show a remarkable display of creativity, task commitment, or a previously unrecognized need for highly challenging opportunities.

Overview of the SEM

The SEM (1997) was designed to challenge and meet the needs of high potential, high ability and gifted students, and at the same time, provide challenging learning experiences for all students. In the SEM, using the identification steps discussed previously, a talent pool of 10%–20% of above average ability/high potential students is identified and eligible for three services: the Total Talent Portfolio, Curriculum Modification and Differentiation, and Enrichment (See Figure 22.2). These three services are delivered across the regular curriculum, a continuum of services, and a series of enrichment clusters.

In the SEM, teachers encourage students to better understand four dimensions of their own learning: their abilities, interests, learning styles, and preferred modes of expression. This information, focusing on their strengths rather than deficits, is compiled into a "Total Talent Portfolio" which can be subsequently used to make decisions about talent development opportunities in regular classes, enrichment clusters, and/or in the continuum of special services. The ultimate goal of learning that is guided by these principles and the SEM is to replace dependent and passive learning with independence and engaged learning.

Curriculum differentiation using compacting and other forms of curriculum modification are also provided to all eligible students for whom the regular curriculum must be adjusted. Curriculum compacting is the elimination or streamlining of curriculum to enable above average students to avoid repetition of previously mastered work. The compacting process guarantees mastery, while simultaneously finding time for more appropriately

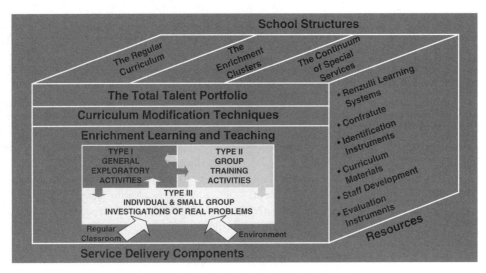

Fig. 22.2 The Schoolwide Enrichment Model (SEM)

challenging activities. A form, entitled the Compactor, is used to document which content areas have been compacted and what alternative work has been substituted (See Figure 22.3)

Third, a series of enrichment opportunities organized around the Enrichment Triad Model offers three types of enrichment experiences through various forms of delivery, including the regular curricular and enrichment clusters. The Triad Model

(Renzulli, 1977)—the curriculum and instructional basis of the Schoolwide Enrichment Model—was originally designed as a gifted program model to (a) encourage creative productivity in young people by exposing them to various topics, areas of interest, and fields of study and (b) further train them to *apply* advanced content, process-training skills, and methodology training to self-selected areas of interest using three types of enrichment. Types I, II,

INDIVIDUAL EDUCATIONAL PROGRAMMING GUIDE
The Compactor

Prepared by: Joseph S. Renzulli
Linds M. Smith

NAME_____ AGE _____ TEACHER(S) _____ | Individual Conference Dates And Persons Participating in Planning Of IEP

SCHOOL_____ GRADE_____ PARENT(S) _____ | ___ ___ ___ ___ ___

CURRICULUM AREAS TO BE CONSIDERED FOR COMPACTING Provide a brief description of basic material to be covered during this marking period and the assessment information or evidence that suggests the need for compacting	PROCEDURES FOR COMPACTING BASIC MATERIAL Describe activities that will be used to guarantee proficiency in basic curricular areas.	ACCELERATION AND/OR ENRICHMENT ACTIVITIES Describe activities that will be used to provide advanced level learning experiences in each area of the regular curriculum.

Check here if additional information is recorded on the reverse side.

Fig. 22.3 The Compactor

and III enrichment are offered to all students; however, Type III enrichment is usually more appropriate for students with higher levels of ability, interest, and task commitment.

Type I enrichment is designed to expose students to a wide variety of disciplines, topics, occupations, hobbies, persons, places, and events that would not ordinarily be covered in the regular curriculum. In schools using this approach, an enrichment team of parents, teachers, and students often organizes and plans Type I experiences by contacting speakers, arranging minicourses, conducting overviews of enrichment clusters, demonstrations, performances, or by ordering and distributing films, slides, videotapes, or other print and nonprint media.

Type II enrichment includes materials and methods designed to promote the development of thinking and feeling processes. Some Type II enrichment is general, consisting of training in areas such as creative thinking and problem solving, learning how to learn skills such as classifying and analyzing data, and advanced reference and communication skills. Type II training is usually carried out both in classrooms and in enrichment programs, and includes the development of (1) creative thinking and problem solving, critical thinking, and affective processes; (2) a wide variety of specific learning-how-to-learn skills; (3) skills in the appropriate use of advanced level reference materials; and (4) written, oral, and visual communication skills. Other Type II enrichment is specific, as it cannot be planned in advance and usually involves advanced instruction in an interest area selected by the student. For example, students who become interested in botany after a Type I on this topic would pursue advanced training in this area by reading advanced content in botany, compiling, planning and carrying out plant experiments, and, eventually, using more advanced methods training for those who choose to pursue a Type III in this area.

Type III enrichment involves students who become interested in pursuing a self-selected area, and are willing to commit the time necessary for advanced content acquisition and process training when they assume the role of a firsthand inquirer. The goals of Type III enrichment are providing opportunities for applying interests, knowledge, creative ideas, and task commitment to a self-selected problem or area of study; acquiring advanced level understanding of the knowledge (content) and methodology (process) that are used within particular disciplines, artistic areas of expression, and interdisciplinary studies; developing

authentic products that are primarily directed toward bringing about a desired impact upon a specified audience; developing self-directed learning skills in the areas of planning, organization, resource utilization, time management, decision making, and self-evaluation; and the development of task commitment, self-confidence, and feelings of creative accomplishment. Type III products can be completed by individuals or small groups of students, and are always based on students interests.

The three service delivery components of the SEM (Total Talent Portfolio, Curriculum Compacting, and Enrichment Teaching and Learning) are applied to three school structures: the regular curriculum, enrichment clusters, and a continuum of services developed as a part of the SEM.

The Regular Curriculum
The regular curriculum includes the predetermined goals, learning outcomes, and delivery systems of the school. The regular curriculum might be traditional, innovative, or in the process of transition, but its predominant feature is that policymakers, school councils, or textbook adoption committees have determined that the regular curriculum should be the "centerpiece" of student learning. Application of the SEM influences the regular curriculum in three ways: through processes such as curriculum compacting and differentiation and modification procedures; the replacement of easier content with in-depth learning experiences; and the types of enrichment recommended in the Enrichment Triad Model (Renzulli, 1977).

The Enrichment Clusters
Enrichment clusters, a second component of the Schoolwide Enrichment Model, are nongraded groups of students who share common interests and are grouped together during specially designated time blocks, to work with an adult who shares their interests and has some degree of advanced knowledge and expertise in the area. Enrichment clusters usually meet for a block of time each week during the semester, and all students in the school participate, therefore enabling some enrichment services to be given to all students in the school. All students complete an interest inventory developed to assess their interests, and an enrichment team of parents and teachers tally all of the major families of interests. Adults from the faculty, staff, parents, and community are recruited to facilitate enrichment clusters based on these interests, which might include creative writing, drawing, sculpting, archeology,

and other areas. Training is provided to the facilitators who agree to offer the clusters, and a brochure is developed and sent to all parents and students with descriptions of enrichment clusters. Students select their top three choices for the clusters, and scheduling is completed to place all children into their first, or in some cases, second choice. Like extracurricular activities and programs such as 4-H and Junior Achievement, the main rationale for participation in one or more clusters is that *students and teachers want to be there.* All teachers (including music, art, physical education, etc.) are involved in facilitating the clusters, and their involvement in any particular cluster is based on the same type of interest assessment that is used for students in selecting clusters of choice.

The Continuum of Special Services

A broad range of special services is the third school structure targeted by the model (See Figure 22.4). Although the enrichment clusters and the SEM-based modifications of the regular curriculum provide a broad range of services to meet individual needs, a program for total talent development still requires supplementary services that challenge our most academically talented young people, who are capable of working at the highest levels of their special interest and ability areas. These services, which cannot ordinarily be provided in enrichment clusters or the regular curriculum, typically include individual or small group counseling, various types of acceleration, direct assistance in facilitating advanced level work, arranging for mentorships with faculty members or community persons, and making other types of connections between students, their families, and out-of-school persons, resources, and agencies.

Direct assistance also involves setting up and promoting student, faculty, and parental involvement in special programs such as creative problem solving competitions (such as Future Problem Solving, Odyssey of the Mind), state and national essay competitions, and mathematics, art, and history contests. Another type of direct assistance consists of arranging out-of-school involvement for individual students in summer programs, on-campus courses, special schools, theatrical groups, scientific expeditions, and apprenticeships at places where advanced level learning opportunities are available. Provision of these services is one of the responsibilities of the enrichment specialist, or an enrichment team of teachers and parents who work together to provide options for advanced learning.

New Directions: Using Renzulli Learning to Implement the SEM

Renzulli Learning (RL) is an interactive online program that assists with the implementation of SEM

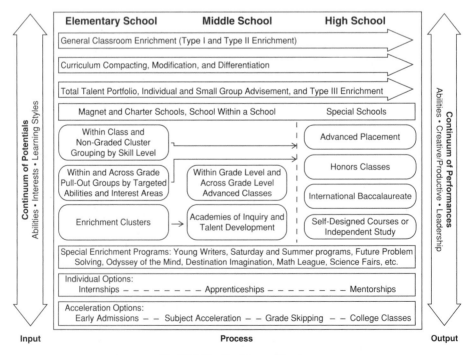

Fig. 22.4 The Continuum of Services

by matching student interests, expression styles, and learning styles with a vast array of enrichment activities and resources designed to engage and challenge all students. RL helps students independently explore, discover, learn, and create using the SEM and the most current technology resources, independently and in a safe environment.

RL has easy-to-use online tools that help with the implementation of SEM, including an interactive profiler assessment tool to identify students' talents, strengths, interests, preferred learning and expression styles. Following the completion of their profile, students are matched to resources from the Renzulli Enrichment Database, containing over 36,000 carefully screened, grade-level appropriate, child-safe enrichment opportunities, which are regularly monitored, updated, enhanced and expanded. They also have access to the Wizard Project Maker, an online project tool that helps students to create their own high interest projects and store them in their own Talent Portfolio. Over 150 Super Starter Projects have been added to the Project Maker, enabling students to have the scaffolding to begin the process of selecting and independently completing projects in their areas of interest.

Collectively, the components of RL correlate with the SEM to provide both students and teachers with unique educational experiences, which are directly suited to their unique learning profiles, while simultaneously giving parents insights about their child's enrichment needs. RL also helps all teachers better understand and know their students and meet their diverse needs. Perhaps the most significant aspect of the RL is its emphasis on students' strengths. Many adjunct educational programs focus on finding and correcting weaknesses and liabilities. RL celebrates and builds upon students' strengths, abilities, and interests, in the tradition of SEM. This web-based online program matches students' interests, learning styles, expression styles, abilities, and grade level to thousands of opportunities designed to provide enriched and challenging learning.

Few instructional practices or curriculum are currently being implemented to challenge gifted and talented students in American classrooms. The SEM is one instructional and programmatic service that can encourage the talents and develop the gifts of high potential students. The next part of the chapter includes a research-based summary of the reasons that gifted programs should be implemented, as well as a compilation of strategies, in addition to SEM, that have also been demonstrated to develop high potentials in children.

Demonstrated Lack of Challenge for Gifted Students in Regular Classrooms

Why are programs for talented and gifted students needed in schools? According to several well designed studies, the needs of gifted and high ability students are generally not addressed or met in American classrooms, where the focus is most often on struggling learners and where most classroom teachers have not had the training necessary to meet the needs of gifted students (Archambault et al.,1993; Fordham, 2008; Moon, Tomlinson, & Callahan, 1995; Reis et al., 2004, Reis & Purcell, 1993; Westberg et al., 1993). This is the major reason that programs and services such as the SEM and acceleration remain so important for gifted and talented students. Archambault and colleagues (1993) found that 61% of approximately 7300 randomly selected third and fourth grade teachers in public and private schools in the United States reported that they had never experienced any training in teaching gifted students. In their classroom practices studies, a broad and diverse sample of classroom teachers admitted that they made, on a very irregular basis, only minor modifications to the regular curriculum to meet the needs of gifted students. This result was consistent for all types of schools sampled, and for classrooms in various parts of the country and for various types of communities.

Westberg, Archambault, Dobyns, and Salvin (1993), in a follow-up to the Classroom Practices Study, conducted systematic observations in 46 third or fourth grade classrooms with two students: one high ability student, and one average ability student. They found little differentiation in the instructional and curricular practices, including grouping arrangements and verbal interactions, for gifted students in the regular classroom. In all content areas over 92 observation days, gifted students rarely received instruction in homogeneous groups (only 21% of the time), and targeted gifted students experienced no instructional or curricular differentiation in 84% of the instructional activities in which they participated. A recently released Fordham Institute report found that low-achieving students made gains under NCLB, advanced learners did not. These students may be failing to make progress because teachers believe that they need to spend the majority of their time with struggling students, even though they know that others in the classroom need attention as well (Fordham, 2008). In a study by Reis and colleagues (2004), talented readers in urban and suburban schools were found to have received very little reading instruction at all, and little purposeful or meaningful differentiated reading instruction was provided for talented readers in any of the classrooms. Above-grade-level books were rarely available for these students in their classrooms, and they were not often encouraged to select more challenging books from the school library. Talented readers seldom encountered challenging reading material during regular classroom instruction. Even less advanced content and instruction was made available for urban students than for suburban. Attention in almost all classrooms was directed primarily at students who read well below grade level, while talented readers received little reading instruction and differentiation.

Reis, Westberg, Kulikowich, and Purcell (1998), in an analysis of content elimination and strategies used by elementary classroom teachers in the curriculum compacting process, found that the use of curriculum compacting could be used to modify the curriculum and eliminate previously mastered work for high ability/gifted students. Classroom teachers could eliminate between 40%–50% of the previously mastered regular curriculum for high ability students, and when they eliminated that content, no differences were found between students whose work was compacted and students who did *all* the work in reading, math computation, social studies, and spelling. Almost all classroom teachers learned to use compacting, but they needed coaching and support to substitute appropriately challenging options.

Moon, Tomlinson, and Callahan (1995) studied gifted students in middle schools, finding similar patterns of results: both teachers and principals readily admitted that academically diverse populations receive very little, if any, targeted attention in their schools. Teachers reported the use of little differentiation for gifted middle school students. This study demonstrated that both principals and teachers held strong beliefs that may deny challenge to advanced middle school students. The overwhelming majority believed that these students' needs are more social than academic. Half of all middle school principals and teachers surveyed actually stated that they believed that middle school students were in a plateau learning period, where little new learning takes place.

In summary, during the last decade or two, several research studies have found little differentiation of curriculum and instruction for gifted and talented students in regular classrooms (Archambault et al., 1993; Fordham Institute, 2008; Moon, Tomlinson, & Callahan, 1995; Reis et al., 2004; Reis & Purcell, 1993; Westberg et al., 1993). Although this differentiation can and will be implemented with strong support and professional development, it occurs much less often than it should, due to a lack of training, resources, and materials to assist teachers.

Demonstrated Underachievement in Academically Talented Students

Identified populations of gifted students underachieve or fail in school. For example, Hébert and Reis (1999) and Reis and Diaz (1999) studied academically talented urban students who either achieved or underachieved in high school, finding that half of the 35 students who participated in this longitudinal study underachieved in school. Academically talented students who achieved in school acknowledged the importance of being grouped together in honors and advanced classes with other academically talented and motivated students. The findings in these studies strongly suggested that underachievement began in elementary school, where these high potential students were not provided with appropriate levels of challenge, and never learned to work.

Gifted students are also among the 8000 students who drop out each day in our country. Renzulli and Park (2000) found that approximately 5% of a large, national sample of gifted students dropped out of high school. These students leave school for many reasons, including poor grades, failure to engage, need for employment, pregnancy, and/or other related reasons. Many gifted students who dropped out of school participated in fewer extracurricular activities. Many of these students were from low SES families and culturally diverse groups, and had parents with low levels of education.

Current research also suggests that high ability and gifted students from high poverty backgrounds often face the greatest challenges in continuing to make academic progress in school. In a recent report released by the Jack Kent Cooke Foundation, *Achievement Trap: How America is Failing 3.4 Million High-Achieving Students from Lower-Income Families,* found that millions of lower-income, high achieving students fail to make progress in school. The report highlights troubling statistics showing that only 28% of students in the top quarter of their first grade class are from lower income families, while 72% come from higher income families. This decrease worsens over time; as during the period between first to fifth grade, nearly half of the lower income students in the top 25% of their class in reading fell out of this high quartile. The trend continues in high school, where another quarter of the lower income students who ranked in the top 25% of their class in eighth grade math fell out of this top ranking by twelfth grade. It is critical to note that upper income students maintain their places in the top quartile of achievement at significantly higher rates than lower income students, again suggesting that poverty has a negative developmental outcome on the development of gifts and talents in this population.

Other Research Based Services to Challenge Gifted and Talented Students

What instructional and programmatic services can benefit gifted and high potential students whose needs are so seldom addressed? What services and programs can be implemented, in addition to the SEM, to encourage the talents and develop the gifts of high potential students? The following research based strategies have been demonstrated to contribute to the development of students' gifts and talents.

Instructional Grouping Practices

A volume of research has demonstrated that instructional grouping practices that enable high potential and gifted students to be grouped together, result in higher achievement for these students (Gentry & Owen, 1999; Kulik, 1992; Rogers, 1991). Several different methods can be used to implement instructional grouping in and across classrooms. Cluster grouping across classrooms is the purposeful reduction in the range of instructional levels by clustering groups of learners in similar levels of achievement together in one classroom. In a study of cluster grouping, Gentry and Owen (1999) found that elementary aged students of all achievement levels (high, medium, and low) benefited from cluster grouping, and other forms of instructional grouping accompanied by differentiated instruction and content. Students in cluster group classrooms scored significantly higher than students who were not grouped, and increasing numbers of students were identified as high achieving during the three years that cluster grouping was used in the school.

Kulik's (1992) research synthesis on instructional and ability grouping showed that achievement is increased when gifted and talented students are grouped together for enriched or accelerated learning. Instructional grouping without curricular acceleration or enrichment produced little or no differences in student achievement in Kulik's

research. Bright, average, and struggling students all benefitted from being grouped with others in their ability/instructional groups when the curriculum was adjusted to the aptitude levels of the group. Kulik found that when gifted students were grouped together, and received advanced enrichment or acceleration, they outperformed control group students, who were not grouped and did not receive enrichment or acceleration, by five months to a full year on achievement tests.

Rogers also conducted a meta-analysis (1991) on the benefits of using grouping to meet the needs of academically talented and gifted students, and found that grouping gifted and talented students together for instruction improved their academic achievement. Full-time ability/instructional grouping produced substantial academic gains in these students. Pull-out enrichment grouping options produced substantial academic gains in general achievement, critical thinking, and creativity. Within-class grouping and regrouping for specific instruction options also produced substantial academic gains, when the instruction was differentiated. Cross-grade grouping also resulted in substantial academic gains.

Tieso (2002) also studied instructional grouping in math with 645 students elementary and middle school students, and found significant differences on math achievement for treatment group students (who were grouped for an enriched math lesson and exposed to an enhanced unit) when compared to the comparison groups. Results indicated significant differences favoring the group that received a modified and differentiated curriculum in a grouped class.

Instructional grouping with differentiated content has been repeatedly found to benefit this population, resulting in increased achievement for gifted and talented students, and in some cases, also for students who are achieving at average and below average levels (Gentry & Owen, 1999; Kulik, 1992; Rogers, 1991; Tieso, 2002). Grouping students, however, without changing the curriculum after the grouping has occurred, results in few to no academic gains (Kulik, 1992; Rogers, 1991).

ACCELERATION

Acceleration of various types enables academically talented and gifted students to move more rapidly than usual through the regular curriculum, and results in exposing students to curriculum at a younger age than usual (Colangelo, Assouline, & Gross, 2004). Various forms of acceleration are used in many schools—grade skipping (the most common form), as well as early entrance to kindergarten or first grade; content-level acceleration, which enables students who are advanced in reading to work at an advanced level that is commensurate with their reading comprehension level; and curriculum compacting. Research over the last few decades has demonstrated that acceleration practices have positive effects on academic achievement (Colangelo, Assouline, & Gross, 2004; Kulik, 1992), and limited or nonexistent negative effects on psychosocial adjustment (Brody & Benbow, 1987; Kulik, 1992).

A report funded by The Templeton Foundation entitled *A Nation Deceived* (Colangelo, Assouline, & Gross, 2004) identified many forms of acceleration that enabled students to complete traditional school curriculum at much faster rates. The report summarized research finding that students who were accelerated tended to be more ambitious and earn graduate degrees at higher rates than other students. Interviewed years later, an overwhelming majority of accelerated students say that acceleration was an excellent experience for them. The report also summarized research documenting the fact that accelerated students believed they were both academically challenged and socially accepted, and did not fall prey to boredom, as did so many highly capable students who are forced to follow the curriculum for their age peers. Acceleration of high potential and gifted students has been studied for decades, and research about this standard practice has been uniformly positive (Colangelo, Assouline, & Gross, 2004; Kulik, 1992). In summary, a strong research base demonstrates that the use of acceleration results in higher achievement for gifted and talented learners (Colangelo, Assouline, & Gross, 2004; Kulik, 1992; Rogers, 1991).

Enrichment and Curricular Enhancement

Enrichment experiences are usually given to advanced students to spark their interests, engage them in more challenging content, and extend and enrich their school experiences so that they are more challenged and interested (Renzulli & Reis, 1997). Enrichment can be constructed around the interests and talents of children, and can also be based on what teachers and other professionals determine to be appropriate content and curriculum, such as extensions of the regular curriculum, or more advanced curriculum in areas of talent and strengths. Enrichment should also be provided to all students, but the depth, pace, and level of enrichment for academically talented students should be differentiated to meet their individual needs.

Enrichment has been shown to have strong, positive effects on the achievement of academically talented students. Curricular enhancement and enrichment occur in many different ways. Classroom teachers can differentiate curriculum and instruction in their regular classroom situations, and can substitute eliminated work by extending gifted education strategies and pedagogy to other content areas (Gavin et al., 2007; Reis et al., 2007; Reis, Westberg, Kulikowich, & Purcell, 1998; Tieso 2002).

Enrichment includes work given to students that extends beyond the regular classroom, and may include predetermined, academically challenging units of enriched instruction in areas that extend the regular curriculum. Academically talented students may be able to participate in an enriched unit that enables them to delve more deeply into some area of the prescribed curriculum with more depth and complexity (Kaplan, 1999). Depth and complexity can be applied to the regular curriculum in many ways. While other students learn about the pilgrims landing at Plymouth, MA, identified gifted students may, for example, use primary sources from the Plimoth Plantation online archives to examine and study of artifacts of the daily life of seventeeth-century residents, comparing the life experiences of the Indians to those of the pilgrims.

Other forms of enrichment enable teachers and/or specialists with a background in enrichment and gifted education pedagogy to work collaboratively with classroom teachers to co-teach and/or design special activities. They may also work with small groups of students on extensions of the regular curriculum, or pursue independent or small group projects that either extend the regular curriculum or give opportunities for independent study or self-selected investigations of problems that students identify. The focus of many enrichment programs is on creative and critical thinking, problem solving, and opportunities for leadership, talent development in both intellectual/academic areas and the arts, and the creation of products and investigation of problems of personal interest to students (Renzulli & Reis, 1997).

Curriculum enhancement in programs or classes for gifted and talented students is usually organized around more complex ideas, problems, and themes that integrate knowledge across content areas (Renzulli, 1977, 1988; Van Tassel-Baska et al., 1998). Curriculum for this population should also enable students to develop and apply critical and creative thinking skills that may lead to the generation of new knowledge. Curriculum for the gifted/talented also enables students to understand that knowledge changes constantly, and that individuals are responsible for their own learning and understanding. Renzulli (1988) also suggested that curriculum for the gifted involves the opportunity for independent learning, the pursuit of real problems, and the chance to use the methods of practicing professionals including authentic inquiry.

Research on the use of enrichment and curriculum enhancement has also shown that these forms of gifted programming result in higher achievement for gifted and talented learners, as well as other students (Field, 2009; Gavin et al., 2007; Gentry & Owen, 1999; Gubbins et al., 2007; Renzulli & Reis, 1994; Reis et al., 2007;). Some enrichment pedagogy and strategies (i.e., choice, interest, independent study) can benefit struggling and special needs students when implemented in a variety of settings (Baum, 1988; Reis & Renzulli, 2003; Reis et al., 2007). Vaughn, Feldhusen, and Asher (1991), in a meta-analysis of research on pull-out programs in gifted education, evaluated the effectiveness of these programs, using experimental studies that investigated self-concept, achievement, critical thinking, and creativity. The results indicated that enrichment models in gifted education have significant positive effects on achievement, critical thinking, and creativity.

Differentiation of the Regular Curriculum for Gifted and Talented Students

A strong body of research also suggests that although the process is challenging, differentiated curriculum and instruction in regular classroom situations resulted in higher levels of challenge and engagement for both gifted and talented students, as well as other students who may not have been identified as talented, but who have potential in one or more content areas (Colangelo, Assouline, & Gross, 2004; Field, in press; Reis, Gentry, & Maxfield, 1998; Reis et al., 2007; Reis, Westberg, Kulikowich, & Purcell, 1998).

Field (2009 conducted an experimental study using Renzulli Learning to help teachers differentiate instruction. She investigated reading fluency and comprehension, as well as social studies achievement, in 383 elementary and middle school students, finding that after 16 weeks, students who participated in differentiated programs using Renzulli Learning for 2–3 hours each week demonstrated significantly higher growth in reading comprehension than

control group students who did not participate in the program. Students who participated in Renzulli Learning demonstrated significantly higher growth in oral reading fluency and in social studies achievement than those students who did not participate.

Gifted education programs and strategies have also been found to be effective at serving gifted and high ability students in a variety of educational settings and in schools serving diverse ethnic and socioeconomic populations, and in reversing underachievement in these students (Baum, 1988; Baum, Renzulli, & Hébert, 1999; Colangelo, Assouline, & Gross, 2004; Gavin et al., 2007; Hébert, & Reis 1999; Reis et al., 2007).

Content Area Enrichment and Curriculum Enhancement

Gavin et al. (2007) investigated methods of providing enriched math curriculum on math achievement in elementary students using Project M^3: Mentoring Mathematical Minds. Enriched curriculum units were developed for mathematically talented students. This enriched, challenging math curriculum resulted in significant gains in achievement in math concepts, computation, and problem solving, each year over a 3-year period, for talented math students in grades 3, 4, and 5. Students using the curriculum outperformed a comparison group of students of like ability from the same schools. Significant gains were found on challenging open-ended problems, adapted from international and national assessments, in favor of students using the enriched curriculum over the comparison group. Students receiving the advanced math achieved significant gains in all mathematical concepts across grade levels.

Little, Feng, VanTassel-Baska, Rogers, and Avery (2007) studied the use of an enriched social studies curriculum with 1200 students, using quasi-experimental methods to examine curriculum designed to respond to the needs of high ability students in elementary and middle school social studies. Results demonstrate significant differences between treatment and comparison groups in the area of content learning, favoring the treatment group; but no significant differences were found for the small subsample of gifted students. Continuing with the use of quasi-experimental designs, VanTassel-Baska, Bass, Ries, Poland, and Avery (1998) studied the effectiveness of an enriched science curriculum for high ability students, and found small but significant gains for students using a unit on the dimension of integrated science process skills, when compared to equally able students not using the units. In another quasi-experimental study, Van Tassel-Baska, Zuo, Avery, and Little (2002) investigated the use of the William and Mary Language Arts and Science Curriculum, with gifted students in grades 3 to 5 in language arts, critical reading, persuasive writing, and scientific research design skills, through the use of the curriculum across individual academic years finding significant increases for students using the program.

Reis and colleagues (2007, 2008) investigated the use of the Schoolwide Enrichment Model in Reading (SEM-R) in experimental designs to compare performances of students who used the SEM-R as opposed to control group students who participated in basal reading programs. The SEM-R is an enriched and accelerated program that targets talented readers, but is usually implemented in regular classrooms. Students who participated in the SEM-R had significantly higher scores in reading fluency, comprehension, and attitudes toward reading than students in the control group, who did not participate (Reis & Fogarty, 2006; Reis et al., 2007, 2008). Students in the SEM-R treatment group scored statistically significantly higher than those in the control group in reading fluency and comprehension. Results demonstrated that talented readers, as well as average and below average readers, benefited from the SEM-R intervention (Reis et al., 2005; Reis et al., 2007; Reis, Eckert, et al., 2008).

Social and Emotional Counseling and Support

A recent research synthesis was conducted by scholars in the field to address the social and emotional needs of gifted and high ability students, suggesting that children so identified are typically at least as well adjusted as any other group of children (Neihart, Reis, Robinson, & Moon, 2001). Nevertheless, these students face a number of issues that, while not unique to them, can constitute sources of risk to their social/emotional development. Some of these issues emerge because of the mismatch with educational environments not responsive to the pace and level of gifted students' learning and thinking. Some seem to arise from the creativity, energy, intensity, and advanced abilities of these students, as well as the developmental internal asynchronies they experience. Still other issues emanate from the difficulty many gifted students experience in finding compatible friends, and the pressures they feel to conform.

The aspects of gifted children's life experiences that result from their differences from other children, and the fact that most of them demonstrate greater maturity in some domains than others, may put them at risk for specific kinds of social and emotional difficulties if their needs are not addressed through counseling and support from teachers, parents, psychologists and counselors. These needs include ways to adjust to issues deriving from students' advancement compared with age peers; problems deriving from internal asynchronies in development; common areas of psychological vulnerability, such as underachievement; and being labeled as a member of a group of gifted children and youth with special needs, such as those who underachieve (Neihart, Reis, Robinson, & Moon, 2001). Some counseling and support strategies to support these students would be necessary for them to realize their potential.

Longitudinal Research on Programs

Several different longitudinal studies have been conducted on gifted students. Subotnik and Arnold (1994) published a volume summarizing some of this work, and other researchers have continued to do work in this area with compelling findings. Hébert (1993), in studying the long-term impact of elementary school experiences in creative productivity, found that participation in gifted programs had a positive effect on the subsequent interests of students and also positively affected their postsecondary plans. In the same study, early advanced project work served as important training for later productivity, and nonintellectual characteristics with students remained consistent over time.

In a similar longitudinal study, Westberg (1999) studied participants in a program based on Renzulli's (1977) Enrichment Triad Model, and found that students maintained interests and were still involved in both interests and creative productive work after they finished college and graduate school. Delcourt (1993) also studied participants in a longitudinal study investigating creative productivity among secondary school students, finding several benefits of gifted programs. She learned that students maintained interests over time, and were still involved in creative productive work a decade after they left their gifted programs. Students who had participated in gifted programs maintained the interests they developed in these programs. These interests, in turn, influenced their career aspirations in college. Students' gifts and talents could be predicted by their elementary school creative/productive behaviors. Taylor (1992) studied the effects of the use of the Enrichment Triad Model on the career development of 60 vocational/technical school students, finding that students' involvement in gifted programs in high school enabled them to explore potential career interests, allowed them to see themselves in the role of practicing professionals, and helped them visualize a different sense of self. Students had increased post-secondary education plans that had expanded from obtaining an associate's degree to graduating from a 4-year college program. Moon, Feldhusen, and Dillon (1994) conducted a retrospective study investigating the effects on students and their families of an elementary pull-out gifted program, based on the Purdue Three-Stage Model, and most families indicated the program had a long-term positive impact on the cognitive, affective, and social development of participating students.

Compelling research has also documented the benefits of acceleration. Lubinski, Webb, Morelock, and Benbow (2001) conducted follow-up studies with 320 gifted students identified as highly gifted adolescents. These students pursued doctoral degrees at over 50X the base rate expectations. In a similar study, Lubinski, Benbow, Webb, and Bleske-Rechek (2006) investigated talent-search participants who scored in the top .01% on cognitive ability measures, and were identified before age 13 and tracked over 20 years. Their creative, occupational, and life accomplishments were compared with those of graduate students (299 males, 287 females) enrolled in top-ranked U.S. mathematics, engineering, and physical science programs in 1992 and tracked over 10 years. By their mid-30s, the two groups achieved comparable and exceptional success (e.g., securing top tenure-track positions) and reported high and commensurate career and life satisfaction. Park, Lubinski, and Benbow (2007) studied a sample of 2,409 intellectually talented adolescents (top 1%) who were assessed on the SAT by age 13 and tracked longitudinally for more than 25 years. The creative accomplishments of this group, with particular emphasis on literary achievement and scientific/technical innovation, were examined. The results showed that the distinct ability patterns identified by age 13 suggested subsequent similar and complimentary creative expression by middle age.

Developing a Continuum of Services to Challenge All Gifted and Talented Students

We recommend, as part of the SEM approach described earlier (1997), the development of a continuum of services to challenge the diverse learning and affective needs of gifted and talented students. These services should be targeted for high potential and gifted and talented students across all grade levels. A broad range of both cognitive and affective services should be implemented to ensure that children have access to areas such as curriculum and instructional differentiation to meet their rapid, advanced learning needs. These include both advanced content, to enable all students to make continuous progress in all content areas, as well as the availability of opportunities for individualized research for students who are highly creative and want the chance to pursue advanced interests (Renzulli, 1977; Renzulli & Reis, 1997) For students with gifts and talents who are underachieving or have learning disabilities, counseling and other services are recommended to address their special affective needs (Baum & Owen, 2004; Reis & McCoach, 2000).

Two considerations exist when a districtwide continuum of services is developed (Renzulli & Reis, 1997). The first is organizational, relating to where and when students will be provided with services to meet their advanced learning needs. Gifted and talented students can be grouped by instructional level in both elementary and middle schools. They can be cluster grouped in one or more content areas across classrooms, and assigned to classes with teachers who have had professional development and use strategies to meet their learning needs (Gentry & Owen, 1999). Separate classes can be provided for gifted students at any grade level. Interventions to attempt to reverse underachievement can be incorporated into counseling options, either during or after school, at the high school level. Students can have opportunities for advanced project work after school, or during a time that their curriculum has been compacted.

The second consideration in the development of a districtwide continuum of services relates to types of curriculum and learning opportunities, as decisions must be made about what will be taught and why (Renzulli & Reis, 1997). Educators must consider what they will do to adjust the curriculum and learning opportunities for advanced students. Will acceleration opportunities be made available? Will the regular curriculum be extended with enrichment, or will it be compacted and replaced with teacher-selected advanced content? Will students have the opportunity to pursue their personal interests using independent study?

Both of these considerations should be addressed when a continuum of services is developed in a district or school. If organizational structures are the only component addressed in a districtwide continuum of services, little thought will have been extended to essential instructional and curricular decisions. If students are grouped into a separate class for gifted students without any advanced or accelerated curriculum or instruction, little justifiable reason exists for that instructional grouping, as research has demonstrated that minimal gains will be made by those students (Gentry & Owen, 1999; Kulik, 1992). If a large percentage of gifted students are underachieving and are not able to participate in advanced classes, or are dropping out of school, an expansion of a district continuum of services should be considered to include more affective and counseling services to address their underachievement (Reis & McCoach, 2000).

Services in a Continuum Targeted for High Potential and Gifted Students

Some of the services that might be targeted for gifted and talented students are relatively inexpensive, some involve considerable time and funds, and others involve no cost at all, since they involve strategies for grouping and regrouping students based on their interests, ability, and achievement levels. Establishing opportunities for enrichment across the grade levels, and differentiation in all classrooms, constitute the first steps in the development of a continuum of services. This continuum can range from a minimal level of service in the regular classroom setting, to a series of advanced opportunities in the regular classroom, advanced learning opportunities in content, independent self-selected study, counseling for underachievers, and separate classes, a school, or a center for gifted learners (Renzulli & Reis, 1997).

School based gifted programs can offer diverse learning opportunities. The presence of enrichment specialists enable teachers to send students from their regular classrooms to spend time with other high potential students, giving them the opportunity for in-depth, advanced independent study projects and group projects in their interest areas (Renzulli & Reis, 1997). In some districts, students have the opportunity to travel to a center one day each week to work with other identified gifted and talented students on advanced curriculum, or to pursue individual interests. These types of centers supplement the regular school program by providing differentiated educational opportunities for academically gifted students. In some centers, students spend one day each week at the center studying advanced content and exploring personal interests through independent study. When in their home/sending schools, these same students receive enrichment and acceleration experiences from their regular classroom teachers, who have been trained in gifted education pedagogy such as curriculum compacting (Reis, Burns, & Renzulli, 1992), acceleration (Colangelo, Assouline, & Gross, 2004; Kulik, 1992) independent study (Renzulli & Reis 1997) and advanced content (Little, Feng, VanTassel-Baska, Rogers, & Avery, 2007; Reis et al., 2007; Renzulli, 1988; VanTassel-Baska, Zuo, Avery, & Little, 2002), and mentorship opportunities in which an academically talented student is paired with an older student or adult with both an interest and expertise in the same area. As noted previously, cluster grouping and other forms of instructional grouping, with differentiated instruction and content, benefits gifted and talented students and helps also to challenge other students across all levels of achievement (Gavin et al., 2007; Gentry & Owen, 1999; Reis, Gentry, & Maxfield, 1998; Reis et al., 2007; Gubbins et al., 2007; Tieso, 2002). Many principals and superintendents urge classroom teachers to use differentiated instruction and curriculum compacting across all grade levels, to ensure sufficient challenge to all students and to eliminate content that students already have mastered (Tieso, 2002; Reis, Westberg, Kulikowich, & Purcell, 1998). Some schools provide after-school enrichment programs, or send academically talented students to advanced content Saturday programs offered by museums, science centers, or local universities.

A continuum of services for gifted and high potential learners can also include a number of challenging curriculum content options implemented in classrooms. Several research-based curriculum and instructional options have been developed in reading, science, social studies, and mathematics (Gavin et al., 2007; Reis & Renzulli, 2003; Reis et al., 2007; Little, Feng, VanTassel-Baska, Rogers, & Avery, 2007; VanTassel-Baska, Zuo, Avery, & Little, 2002).

National programs that engage students in creative thinking and problem solving are also included on some continuums of service. These programs have enabled hundreds of thousands of students to apply problem-solving techniques to real-world problems in society, and in their communities. Although not intended solely for academically talented and advanced students, opportunities such as Future Problem Solving are widely used in gifted programs because of the curricular freedom and academic challenge associated with the problems that students pursue. Many gifted students have the opportunity to participate in National History Day, where they work individually or in small groups on an historical event, person from the past, or invention related to a theme that is determined each year. Using primary source data such as diaries or other archives gathered in libraries, museums, and interviews, students prepare research papers, projects, media presentations, or performances, as entries. Many school districts and states also have developed innovative programs that include a variety of services for high potential and gifted learners, such as mentorships, Saturday programs, and summer internships.

A recent innovation to challenge gifted and talented learners in classrooms, and in separate gifted programs, is a new online system designed to use strength-based assessment and differentiated learning experiences for gifted and talented students (Renzulli & Reis, 2007). Renzulli Learning can be used independently of SEM, and provides a computer-based diagnostic assessment to create an individual profile of each student's academic strengths, interests, learning styles, and preferred modes of expression. The online assessment, which takes about 30 minutes, results in a printed profile that highlights individual student strengths. The profile is then matched to a differentiation search engine that selects hundreds of resources that relate specifically to each student's interests, learning styles, and product styles. The search engine matches student strengths and interests to an enrichment database of 35,000 enrichment activities, materials, resources, contests and competitions, independent studies, and opportunities for research and follow-up. A project management tool, called the Wizard Project Maker, guides students and teachers to use specifically selected resources for assigned curricular activities, independent or small group investigative projects, and research studies. Students' work can be saved in an electronic portfolio. The system also offers many tools for teachers to more easily differentiate instruction and curriculum, and to group students by interests, abilities, and learning styles.

Summer programs also exist, such as the Talent Search at the Center for Talented Youth at Johns Hopkins University and Northwestern University, that actively recruit and provide program opportunities for academically talented youth. These students generally have scored highly on standardized tests and are recommended by teachers or counselors to participate in early assessment. They may be eligible for multiple options, including summer programs, acceleration, and college courses.

In most states, advanced, intensive summer programs are provided by Governor's Schools in specific content areas. The Pennsylvania Governor's Schools of Excellence, for example, offer different 5-week-long summer residential programs on college campuses. These programs are committed to meeting the educational needs of artistically or academically talented high school students. Many larger school districts also offer challenging summer programs for advanced and gifted learners. The National Association for Gifted Children has a comprehensive list of summer programs for academically talented students on their web page, as well as a comprehensive list of parent recommendations and research findings that district administrators can recommend to parents of talented students. Several states have created separate schools for academically talented students in math and science, such as the North Carolina School for Science and Mathematics, the Illinois School for Mathematics and Science, and the more recently created Kentucky School, which also targets mathematically talented students. Some large school districts have established magnet schools to serve the needs of academically talented students.

Summary

The research summarized in this chapter strongly supports the effectiveness of various interventions to challenge gifted and talented students. Unfortunately, current research also finds that gifted and talented students are often unchallenged in their classrooms (Archambault et al., 1993; Fordham Institute, 2008; Moon, Tomlinson, & Callahan, 1995; Reis et al., 2004; Reis & Purcell, 1993; Westberg et al., 1993). This lack of challenge and programming can result in underachievement (Hébert & Reis, 1999; Reis & Diaz, 1999), suggesting a need for gifted education programs using both enrichment (Renzulli & Reis, 1997) and acceleration (Colangelo, Assouline, & Gross, 2004; Kulik, 1992) to help these students make continuous progress in school. An absence of teacher training and professional development in gifted education and curriculum and instructional differentiation strategies for classroom teachers results in fewer challenges, less differentiation, and lower achievement for groups of students (Archambault et al., 1993; Westberg et al., 1993). Teachers can learn how to differentiate and compact curriculum to provide more challenge to all students, when they have the professional development, time, and support to learn how to effectively implement these skills and strategies. Longitudinal research (Delcourt, 1993; Hébert, 1993; Lubinski, Benbow, Webb, & Bleske-Rechek, 2006; Subotnik & Arnold, 1994) demonstrates the effectiveness of gifted education programs. Research also supports the use of curriculum enhancement and differentiated curriculum, in raising student achievement (Gavin et al., 2007; Little, Feng, VanTassel-Baska, Rogers, Avery, 2007; Reis et al., 2007; Tieso, 2002; Reis, Westberg, Kulikowich, & Purcell, 1998), as well as helping students to develop interests, creativity, productivity, and career goals (Renzulli & Reis, 1994, 1997). Current research has also found that some types of enrichment pedagogy and strategies (i.e., choice, interest, independent study) can be extended to and benefit all students when implemented in a variety of settings (Baum, 1988; Reis et al., 2005, 2007). A body of research on underachievement has found that some gifted students do underachieve and drop out of school, but this process can be reversed when students are provided with challenging enriched learning opportunities in areas of interest (Baum, Renzulli, & Hébert, 1999).

A goal for school psychologists, teachers, and administrators, is to work with parents in the development of a continuum of services that takes into consideration the unique learning needs of all students, and that targets the advanced needs of gifted and talented students. It is essential to carefully assess the programs and services already in place, and develop programs in every school that will challenge every student, even those at the highest range of achievement. Every child deserves the opportunity to make continuous progress in learning each year in school.

Defining and Developing Gifts and Talents in Young People

In the last few years, perhaps related to the negative consequences due to lack of challenges for gifted students since the advent of No Child Left Behind, we have seen a resurgence of interest in the study of gifted children and related efforts to provide services for identified students, those who underachieve, and those placed at-risk due to poverty and other factors that thwart their achievement (Fordham Institute, 2008). Some high potential young people may show their potential in ways that are not always recognized in traditional school programs. Some of the interest in gifted and high potential children has emerged from research that has investigated the

paths of talented individuals, to study what has contributed to the development of their talents. For example, Benjamin Bloom's study of talent development investigated young people who excelled in areas such neurology, swimming, and sculpture (1985). Bloom and his colleagues closely examined 120 individuals who excelled in an area before the age of 35, to determine the factors that were significant in the development of their talents. The researchers investigated the ways in which home and school contributed to an international level of accomplishment by individuals in three areas: academic talents (research mathematicians and neurologists); artistic talents (concert pianists and sculptors); and athletic talents (Olympic swimmers and tennis players). Bloom and his colleagues found that the development of talent occurred most often when a positive family environment existed, as parents or other family members had a personal interest in the talent field and gave strong support, encouragement, and rewards for developing the talent. In fact, most families assumed that the talent would be developed as part of the family's life. Other environmental and educational components were also found to be associated with high levels of talent, including specialized instruction from teachers in the talent field, both at home and in an instructional setting, which was usually individualized and personalized.

In another longitudinal study of talented teenagers, Mihaly Csikszentmihalyi, Kevin Rathmunde, and Samuel Whalen investigated, over a 5-year period, the process of how teenagers remain committed to, or became disengaged from, the development of their talent (1993). This seminal research identified commonalities and differences among teens that developed their talents, as opposed to those who failed to do so, as well as specific factors that influenced talent development. They learned the importance of identification, as teens had to be recognized as talented in order to develop a talent. These researchers also found that personality traits such as concentration, endurance, and being open to experience, awareness and understanding, spending time in challenging pursuits with friends instead of wasting time, focused attention, and being comfortable with spending time alone, were more conducive to talent development. Talent development was easier for those teens that had already developed habits about how to expend effort. Talented teens were also more aware of the possible conflict between productive work and relationships, and had families that provided both support and challenge to enhance the development of talent. Talented teenagers were positively influenced by teachers who were supportive and modeled enjoyable involvement in a field. Talent development, according to this study, was found to be a process that required both expressive (evoking positive feelings) and instrumental (useful to future goals) rewards. The last finding in this study relates to a theme that has emerged across multiple studies reviewed in this chapter; that is, talent development is more likely to occur if it produces optimal experiences in teenagers. Memories of peak moments motivated these talented students to continue to work to improve, in the hopes of achieving or replicating the same intense experience again.

Future Directions

We sincerely hope that some degree of renewed interest, as well as important research, will result in the emergence of new and innovative theories about the development of gifts and talents, producing a greater variety of strategies that will give us better insights and more defensible approaches to identification and programming. Conflicting theoretical explanations abound, and various interpretations of research findings add an element of excitement and challenge that can only result in greater understanding of what makes giftedness, and how we develop it in children and young adults. In this chapter, we have attempted to provide a summary of conceptions of giftedness and talent, as well as research based strategies to identify and serve diverse populations of high potential youth. The information presents a practical, educational perspective based on research that is relevant to educators and psychologists, about conceptual definitions that are aligned to services that are both realistic and defensible.

The task of providing better services to our most promising youth can't wait much longer. The needs and opportunities to improve educational services for these young people exist in countless classrooms every day of the week, where few, if any, programs and services are being provided to these students. Some students are already underachieving, some are considering dropping out, and many are learning how to expend minimal effort in school. All need some types of programming to achieve at high levels. What is needed in each school is a continuum of services that takes into account the unique learning needs of the students, the continuation of programs and services already in place, and a better understanding of what is needed to challenge every child and give each the opportunity to make continuous progress.

Questions for Future Research

- How can the needs of gifted and talented students be served in most classrooms, when teachers continue to focus on students who are achieving well below grade level?
- What is currently happening, and what might happen in the future, to challenge gifted and talented students in most regular classroom settings?
- In what ways might school psychologists be able to help gifted and talented students who are underachieving in school?
- Why is the identification of gifted students with disabilities so challenging?
- What is the Schoolwide Enrichment Model, and why is it a flexible plan for both identification and programming?
- What components should be included in a continuum of services for gifted and talented learners?
- Why is instructional grouping one strategy that should be implemented for gifted learners?

References

Archambault, F. X., Jr., Westberg, K. L., Brown, S., Hallmark, B. W., Emmons, C., & Zhang, W. (1993). *Regular classroom practices with gifted students: Results of a national survey of classroom teachers* (RM93102). Storrs, CT: The National Research Center on the Gifted and Talented, University of Connecticut.

Baum, S. M. (1988). An enrichment program for gifted learning disabled students. *Gifted Child Quarterly, 32,* 226–230.

Baum, S. M. (1990). *Gifted but learning disabled: A puzzling paradox.* ERIC Digest #E479. Reston, VA: Council for Exceptional Children.

Baum, S. M., Renzulli, J. S., & Hébert, T. P. (1999). Reversing underachievement: Creative productivity as a systematic intervention. *Gifted Child Quarterly, 39,* 224–235.

Baum, S. M., & Owen, S. V. (2004). *To be gifted and learning disabled: Strategies for helping bright students with LD, ADHD, and more.* Mansfield Center, CT: Creative Learning Press.

Baum, S. M., Renzulli, J. S., & Hébert, T. P. (1999). Reversing underachievement: Creative productivity as a systematic intervention. *Gifted Child Quarterly, 39,* 224–235.

Bender, W. N. & Wall, M. E. (1994). Social–emotional development of students with learning disabilities. *Learning Disabilities Quarterly, 17,* 323–341.

Bloom, B. S. (Ed.) (1985). *Developing talent in young people.* New York: Ballantine Books.

Briggs, C. J., Reis, S. M., & Sullivan, E. E. (2008). A national view of promising practices and programs for culturally, linguistically, and ethnically diverse gifted and talented students. *Gifted Child Quarterly. 52* (2), 131–145.

Brody, L. E., & Benbow, C. P. (1987). Accelerative strategies: How effective are they for the gifted? *Gifted Child Quarterly, 31,* 105–110.

Burns, D. (1998). *The SEM directory of programs*. Storrs, CT: Neag Center for Gifted Education and Talent Development, University of Connecticut.

Callahan, C. M., Hunsaker, S. L., Adams, C. M., Moore, S. D., & Bland, L. C. (1995). *Instruments used in the identification of gifted and talented students* (Research Monograph 95130). Storrs, CT: The National Research Center on the Gifted and Talented, University of Connecticut.

Cohn, S. (2003). The gay gifted learner: Facing the challenge of homophobia and anti-homosexual bias in schools. In J. A. Castellano (Ed.), *Special populations in gifted education: Working with diverse gifted learners* (pp. 123–134). Boston: Allyn and Bacon.

Colangelo, N., Assouline, S., & Gross, M. (Eds.). (2004). *A nation deceived: How schools hold back America's brightest students* (pp. 109–117). Iowa City, IA: University of Iowa Press.

Cox, J., Daniel, N., & Boston, B.O. (1985). *Educating able learners: Programs and promising practices*. Austin, TX: University of Texas Press.

Cramond, B. (1995). *The coincidence of attention deficit hyperactivity disorder and creativity*. Storrs, CT: The National Research Center on the Gifted and Talented, University of Connecticut.

Csikszentmihalyi, M., Rathunde, K., & Whalen, S. (1993). *Talented teenagers: The roots of success and failure*. Cambridge, England: Cambridge University Press.

Delcourt, M. A. B. (1993). Creative productivity among secondary school students: Combining energy, interest, and imagination. *Gifted Child Quarterly, 37*, 23–31.

Field, G. B. (2009). The effects of using Renzulli Learning on student achievement: An investigation of internet technology on reading fluency, comprehension, and social studies. *International Journal of Emerging Technologies in Learning, 4*(1), 29-39.

Ford, D. Y. (1998). The underrepresentation of minority students in gifted education: Problems and promises in recruitment and retention. *Journal of Special Education, 32*(1), 4–14.

Ford, D. Y., & Harris, J. (1999). *Multicultural gifted education*. New York: Teachers College Press.

Ford, D. Y., Howard, T. C., Harris, J. J., & Tyson, C. A. (2000). Creating culturally responsive classrooms for gifted African American students. *Journal for the Education of the Gifted, 23*, 397–427.

Fordham Institute Report (2008). *High-achieving students in the age of NCLB*. Available at: http://www.edexcellence.net/doc/20080618_high_achievers.pdf, accessed June 6, 2010.

Frasier, M. M., & Passow, A. H. (1994). *Towards a new paradigm for identifying talent potential*. Storrs, CT: The National Research Center on the Gifted and Talented, University of Connecticut.

Gagne, F. (1985). Giftedness and talent: Re-examining and reexamination of the definition.

Gagné, F. (1994). Are teachers really poor talent detectors? Comments on Pegnato and Birch's (1959) study of the effectiveness and efficiency of various identification techniques. *Gifted Child Quarterly, 38*, 124–126.

Gagne, F. (1999). My convictions about the nature of abilities, gifts, and talents. *Journal for the Education of the Gifted, 22*(2), 109–136.

Gagne, F. (2000). Understanding the complex choreography of talent development. In K. A. Heller, F. J. Monks.

R. J. Sternberg, & R. F. Subotnik (Eds.), *International handbook of giftedness and talent* (pp. 67–79). Amsterdam: Elsevier.

Gardner, H. (1993). *Frames of mind: The theory of multiple intelligences* (10th anniversary ed.). New York: Basic Books.

Gavin, M. K., Casa, T. M., Adelson, J. L., Carroll, S. R., Sheffield, L. J., & Spinelli, A. M. (2007). Project M³: Mentoring mathematical minds: Challenging curriculum for talented elementary students. *Journal of Advanced Academics, 18*, 566–585.

Gentry, M. L., & Owen, S. V. (1999). An investigation of the effects of total school flexible cluster grouping on identification, achievement, and classroom practices. *Gifted Child Quarterly, 43*, 224–243.

Gerber, P. J., & Ginsberg, R. J. (1990). *Identifying alterable patterns of success in highly successful adults with learning disabilities: Executive summary*. Washington, DC: U.S. Department of Education, Educational Information Center. (ERIC Document No. ED342168).

Gubbins, E. J., Housand, B., Oliver, M., Schader, R., & De Wet, C. (2007). *Unclogging the mathematics pipeline through access to algebraic understanding*. Storrs, CT: The National Research Center on the Gifted and Talented, University of Connecticut.

Guilford, J.P. (1950). Creativity. *American Psychologist, 5*, 444–454.

Hébert, T. P. (1993). Reflections at graduation: The long-term impact of elementary school experiences in creative productivity. *Roeper Review, 16*, 22–28.

Hébert, T. H., & Reis, S. M. (1999). Culturally diverse high-achieving students in an urban high school. *Urban Education, 34*, 428–457.

Heller, K.A., Perleth, Ch. & Lim, T.K. (2005). The Munich model of giftedness designed to identify and promote gifted students. In R.J. Sternberg & J.E. Davidson (Eds.), *Conceptions of giftedness* (2nd ed., pp. 172–197). New York: Cambridge University Press.

Kaplan, S. N. (1999). Teaching up to the needs of the gifted English language learner. *Tempo, 14*(2), 20.

Karafelis, P. (1986). *The effects of the tri-art drama curriculum on the reading comprehension of students with varying levels of cognitive ability*. Unpublished doctoral dissertation, University of Connecticut, Storrs.

Kulik, J. A. (1992). *An analysis of the research on ability grouping: Historical and contemporary perspectives* (RBDM 9204). Storrs, CT: The National Research Center on the Gifted and Talented, University of Connecticut.

Leroux, J. A. (2000). The gifted child with attention deficit disorder: An identification and intervention challenge. *Roeper Review, 22*(3), 171–176.

Little, C. A., Feng, A. X., VanTassel-Baska, J., Rogers, K., & Avery, L. D. (2007). A study of curriculum effectiveness in social studies. *Gifted Child Quarterly. 51*(3), 272–284.

Lubinski, D., Webb, R. M., Morelock, M. J., & Benbow, C. P. (2001). Top 1 in 10,000: A 10 year follow-up of the profoundly gifted. *Journal of Applied Psychology, 4*, 718–729.

Lubinski, D., Benbow, C. P., Webb, R. M., Bleske-Rechek, A. (2006). Tracking exceptional human capital over two decades. *Psychological Science. 17*(3). 194–199.

MacKinnon, D. W. (1978). *In search of human effectiveness*. Buffalo, NY: Creative Education Foundation.

Moon, S. M. (2002). Gifted children with attention-deficit/hyperactivity disorder. In M. Neihart, S. M. Reis, N. Robinson, & S. M. Moon, (Eds.). (2002). *The social and emotional development of gifted children. What do we know?* (pp. 193–204). Waco, TX: Prufrock Press.

Moon, S. M., Feldhusen, J. F., & Dillon, D. R. (1994). Long-term effects of an enrichment program based on the purdue three-stage model. *Gifted Child Quarterly, 38*, 38–48.

Moon, T. R., Tomlinson, C. A., & Callahan, C. M. (1995). *Academic diversity in the middle school: Results of a national survey of middle school administrators and teachers* (Research Monograph 95124). Storrs, CT: The National Research Center on the Gifted and Talented, University of Connecticut.

Neihart, M. (2000). Gifted children with Asperger's syndrome. *Gifted Child Quarterly, 44*, 222–230.

Neihart, M., Reis, S. M., Robinson, N., & Moon, S. M. (Eds.). (2001). *The social and emotional development of gifted children. What do we know?* Waco, TX: Prufrock Press.

Neu, T. W. (1993). *Case studies of gifted students with emotional or behavioral disorders.* Unpublished doctoral dissertation, University of Connecticut, Storrs.

Olenchak, F. R. (1988). The Schoolwide Enrichment Model in the elementary schools: A study of implementation stages and effects on educational excellence. In J. S. Renzulli (Ed.), *Technical report on research studies relating to the revolving door identification model* (2d ed., pp. 201–247). Storrs: Bureau of Educational Research, University of Connecticut.

Olenchak, F. R. (1991). Assessing program effects for gifted/learning-disabled students. In R. Swassing & A. Robinson (Eds.), *NAGC 1991 research briefs* (pp. 86–89). Washington, DC: National Association for Gifted Children.

Olenchak, F. R., & Renzulli, J. S. (1989). The effectiveness of the schoolwide enrichment model on selected aspects of elementary school change. *Gifted Child Quarterly, 33*, 36–46.

Park, G., Lubinski, D., & Benbow, C. P. (2007) Contrasting intellectual patterns predict creativity in the arts and sciences: Tracking intellectually precocious youth over 25 years. *Psychological Science, 18*, 948–95.

Plucker, J. A., Callahan, C. M., & Tomchin, E. M. (1996). Wherefore art thou, multiple intelligences? Alternative assessments for identifying talent in ethnically diverse and low income students. *Gifted Child Quarterly, 40*(2), 81–92.

Reid, B. D. & McGuire, M. D. (1995). *Square pegs in round holes—these kids don't fit: high ability students with behavioral problems.* Storrs, CT: The National Research Center on the Gifted and Talented, University of Connecticut

Reis, S. M. (1995). Talent ignored, talent diverted: The cultural context underlying giftedness in females. *Gifted Child Quarterly, 39*(3), 162–170.

Reis, S. M. (2005). *The scales for rating the behavioral characteristics of superior students: Reading.* Mansfield Center, CT: Creative Learning Press.

Reis, S. M. (1998). *Work Left Undone: Compromises and Challenges of Talented Females.* Mansfield Center, CT: Creative Learning Press.

Reis, S. M., Burns, D. E., & Renzulli, J. S. (1992). *Curriculum compacting: The complete guide to modifying the regular curriculum for high ability students.* Mansfield Center, CT: Creative Learning Press.

Reis, S. M., & Diaz, E. I. (1999). Economically disadvantaged urban female students who achieve in school. *The Urban Review, 31*, 31–54.

Reis, S. M., Eckert, R. D., McCoach, D. B. Jacobs, J. K., Coyne, M. (2008). Using enrichment reading practices to increase reading fluency, comprehension, and attitudes. *Journal of Educational Research. 101* (5) 299–314.

Reis, S. M., Eckert, R. D., Schreiber, F. J., Jacobs, J. K., Briggs, C., Gubbins, E. J., & Coyne, M. (2005). *The Schoolwide Enrichment Model reading study* (RM05214). Storrs: The National Research Center on the Gifted and Talented, University of Connecticut.

Reis, S. M. & Fogarty, E. (2006). Savoring reading, schoolwide. *Educational Leadership.* October, 32–36.

Reis, S. M., Gentry, M., & Maxfield, L. R. (1998). The application of enrichment clusters to teachers' classroom practices. *Journal for Education of the Gifted, 21*, 310–324.

Reis, S. M., Gentry, M., & Park, S. (1995). *Extending the pedagogy of gifted education to all students* (RM95118). Storrs: National Research Center on the Gifted and Talented, University of Connecticut.

Reis, S. M., Gubbins, E. J., Briggs, C., Schreiber, F. R., Richards, S., & Jacobs, J. (2004). Reading instruction for talented readers: Case studies documenting few opportunities for continuous progress. *Gifted Child Quarterly, 48*, 309–338.

Reis, S. M., Hébert, T. P., Díaz, E. I., Maxfield, L. R., & Ratley, M. E. (1995). *Case studies of talented students who achieve and underachieve in an urban high school* (Research Monograph No. 95120). Storrs, CT: The National Research Center on the Gifted and Talented, University of Connecticut.

Reis, S. M., & McCoach, D. B. (2000). The underachievement of gifted students: what do we know and where do we go? *Gifted Child Quarterly, 44*(3), 152–170.

Reis, S. M., McCoach, D. B., Coyne, M., Schreiber, F.J., Eckert, R.D., Gubbins, E.J. (2007). Using Planned Enrichment Strategies with Direct Instruction to Improve Reading Fluency, Comprehension, and Attitude toward Reading: An Evidence-Based Study. *The Elementary School Journal. 108* (1). 3–24.

Reis, S. M., Neu, T. W., & McGuire, J. M. (1995). *Talent in two places: Case studies of high ability students with learning disabilities who have achieved.* Storrs, CT: The National Research Center on the Gifted and Talented, University of Connecticut.

Reis, S. M., & Purcell, J. H. (1993). An analysis of content elimination and strategies used by elementary classroom teachers in the curriculum compacting process. *Journal for the Education of the Gifted, 16* (2), 147–170.

Reis, S, M., & Renzulli, J. S. (2003). Research related to the schoolwide enrichment triad model. *Gifted Education International, 17*(1), 15–39.

Reis, S. M., Westberg, K. L., Kulikowich, J. M., & Purcell, J. H. (1998). Curriculum compacting and achievement test scores: What does the research say? *Gifted Child Quarterly, 42*, 123–129.

Renzulli, J. S. (2005). The three-ring conception of giftedness: A developmental model for promoting creative productivity. In R. J. Sternberg & J. Davidson (Eds.), *Conceptions of giftedness* (2nd ed.). Boston, MA: Cambridge University Press, pp. 217–245.

Renzulli, J. S. (1977). *The Enrichment Triad Model: A guide for developing defensible programs for the gifted and talented.* Mansfield Center, CT: Creative Learning Press.

Renzulli, J. S. (1978). What makes giftedness? Reexamining a definition. *Phi Delta Kappan, 60*, 180–184.

Renzulli, J. S. (1986). The three-ring conception of giftedness: A developmental model for creative productivity. In R. J. Sternberg & J. E. Davidson (Eds.), *Conceptions of Giftedness*, 53–92.

Renzulli, J. S. (1988). The multiple menu model for developing differentiated curriculum for the gifted and talented. *Gifted Child Quarterly, 32*, 298–309.

Renzulli, J. S., & Delcourt, M. A. B. (1986). The legacy and logic of research on the identification of gifted persons. *Gifted Child Quarterly, 30*, 20–23.

Renzulli, J. S., & Park, S. (2000). Gifted dropouts: The who and the why. *Gifted Child Quarterly, 44*, 261–271.

Renzulli, J. S., Reid, B. D., & Gubbins, E. J. (1991). *Setting an agenda: Research priorities for the gifted and talented through the year 2000.* Storrs, CT: The National Research Center on the Gifted and Talented, University of Connecticut.

Renzulli, J. S., & Reis, S. M. (1985). *The schoolwide enrichment model: A comprehensive plan for educational excellence.* Mansfield Center, CT: Creative Learning Press.

Renzulli, J. S., & Reis, S. M. (1994). Research related to the Schoolwide Enrichment Triad Model. *Gifted Child Quarterly, 38*(1), 7–20.

Renzulli, J. S., & Reis, S. M. (1997). *The schoolwide enrichment model: A comprehensive plan for educational excellence* (2nd ed.). Mansfield Center, CT: Creative Learning Press.

Renzulli, J. S. & Reis, S.M. (2007). A technology based program that matches enrichment resources with student strengths. *International Journal of Emerging Technologies in Learning, 2*, 3.

Renzulli, J. S., Reis, S. M., & Smith, L. H. (1981). *Revolving door identification model guidebook.* Mansfield Center, CT: Creative Learning Press.

Renzulli, J. S., Smith, L. H., White, A. J., Callahan, C. M., Hartman, R. K., & Westberg, K. L. (2002). Scales for rating the behavioral characteristics of superior students. (Revised). Mansfield Center, CT: Creative Learning Press.

Robinson, N. M. (1987). The early development of precocity. *Gifted Child Quarterly, 31* (4), 161–164.

Rogers, K. B. (1991). The relationship of grouping practices to the education of the gifted and talented learner (RBDM 9102). Storrs, CT: The National Research Center on the Gifted and Talented, University of Connecticut.

Schack, G. D., Starko, A. J., & Burns, D. E. (1991). Self-efficacy and creative productivity: Three studies of above-average ability children. *Journal of Research in Education, 1*(1), 44–52.

Starko, A. J. (1988). Effects of the revolving door identification model on creative productivity and self-efficacy. *Gifted Child Quarterly, 32*, 291–297.

Sternberg, R. J., & Davidson, J. E. (Eds.) (1986). *Conceptions of giftedness.* Cambridge, England: Cambridge University Press.

Sternberg, R. J. & Davidson, J. (Eds.). (2005). *Conceptions of giftedness* (2nd ed.).Boston, MA:

Sternberg, R. J., & Lubart, T. I. (1993). Creative giftedness: A multivariate investment approach. *Gifted Child Quarterly, 37*(1), 7–15.

Subotnik, R. F., & Arnold, K. D. (Eds.). (1994). *Beyond Terman: Contemporary longitudinal studies of giftedness and talent.* Norwood, NJ: Ablex.

Tannenbaum, A. J. (1983). *Gifted children: Psychological and educational perspectives.* New York: Macmillan.

Tannenbaum, A. J. (1986). Giftedness: A psychosocial approach. In R. J. Sternberg & J. E. Edwards (Eds.), *Conceptions of giftedness* (pp. 21–52). Cambridge, England: Cambridge University Press.

Taylor, L. A. (1992). *The effects of the Secondary Enrichment Triad Model and a career counseling component on the career development of vocational–technical school students.* Storrs, CT: The National Research Center on the Gifted and Talented, University of Connecticut.

Terman, L. M. (1925–1959). *Genetic studies of genius* (5 vols.). Stanford, CA: Stanford University Press.

Tieso, C. L. (2002). The effects of grouping and curricular practices on intermediate students' math achievement (RM02154). Storrs, CT: The National Research Center on the Gifted and Talented, University of Connecticut.

Tomlinson, C. A., Ford, D. H., Reis, S. M., Briggs, C. J., & Strickland, C. A. (2003). *In search of the dream: Designing schools and classrooms that work for high potential students from diverse cultural backgrounds.* Washington, DC: The National Association for Gifted Children and The National Research Center on the Gifted and Talented.

Torrance, E.P. (1988). The nature of creativity as manifest in its testing. In R. J. Sternberg (Ed.), *The nature of creativity: Contemporary psychological perspectives* (pp. 43–75). New York: Cambridge University Press.

Treffinger, D. J., Young, G. C., Selby, E C., & Shepardson, C. (2002). *Assessing creativity: A guide for educators.* RM02170. Storrs, CT: The National Research Center on the Gifted and Talented, University of Connecticut.

United States Department of Education, Office of Educational Research and Improvement (1993). *National excellence: A case for developing America's talent.* Washington, DC: U.S. Government Printing Office.

Van Tassel-Baska, J., Bass, G. M., Ries, R. R., Poland, D. L., & Avery, L. D. (1998). A national pilot study of science curriculum effectiveness for high ability students. *Gifted Child Quarterly, 42*, 200–211.

Van Tassel-Baska, J. & Brown, E. F. (2007). Toward best practice: An analysis of the efficacy of curriculum models in gifted education. *Gifted Child Quarterly, 51*, 342–358.

Van Tassel-Baska, J., Zuo, L., Avery, L. D., & Little, C.A. (2002). A curriculum study of gifted student learning in the language arts. *Gifted Child Quarterly, 46*, 30–44.

Vaughn, V. L., Feldhusen, J. F., & Asher, J. W. (1991). Meta-analyses and review of research on pull-out programs in gifted education. *Gifted Child Quarterly, 35*, 92–98.

Westberg, K. L. (1999, Summer). What happens to young, creative producers? *NAGC: Creativity and Curriculum Divisions' Newsletter, 3*, 13–16.

Westberg, K. L., Archambault, F. X., Jr., Dobyns, S. M., & Salvin, T. J. (1993). *An observational study of instructional and curricular practices used with gifted and talented students in regular classrooms.* (RM93104). Storrs, CT: The National Research Center on the Gifted and Talented, The University of Connecticut.

Interventions to Address School Crises and Violence

Steven G. Little, Angeleque Akin-Little, *and* Natasha S. Medley

Abstract

The following chapter provides detailed information on interventions for school crises and violence. The interventions are placed in the context of the three-tier model, and promoting wellness in the schools. Further, the interventions are conceptualized along the primary, secondary, and tertiary continuum. Intervention specifics are provided for individual aggressive students, gang violence, and bullying. The emerging phenomenon of cyber-bullying, and how to intervene, is also detailed in the section on bullying. Trauma is also discussed, with trauma-focused cognitive behavior therapy (TF-CBT) featured as the most efficacious intervention. Empirical support for each intervention is presented, along with a rationale for the importance for primary prevention whenever possible.

Keywords: intervention, crisis, violence, trauma, bullying, gangs, school psychology

Recent years have witnessed an increased focus on school violence and crises as a result of tragic events in locations such as Red Lake, Minnesota; Littleton, Colorado; Paducah, Kentucky; and Jonesboro, Arkansas. These high profile shootings have heightened public concern about school violence (Larson, Smith, & Furlong, 2002) in spite of the fact that little reported violence involving children and youth are reported in schools (Heaviside, Rowand, Williams, & Farris, 1998), school violence has decreased over the past decade (Cornell, 2006; DeVoe, Peter, Noonan, Snyder, & Baum, 2005), and students are safer at school than away from school (DeVoe et al; Dusenbury, Falco, Lake, Brannigan, & Bosworth, 1997; Hyman & Perone, 1998).

This does not mean that children in schools are immune from the effects of violence and crises in their environments. A survey of high school students in Los Angeles revealed that approximately one-half of the boys and one-third of the girls sampled reported witnessing severe forms of violence such as a shootings or stabbings in their communities during the year prior to the study (O'Keefe, 1997). Similarly, the 2007 Youth Risk Behavior Surveillance Survey reported that 5.5% of high school students did not go to school at least one day in the past month due to feeling unsafe at school, or in transit to or from school (Centers for Disease Control and Prevention, 2008a). In addition, estimates suggest that at least 3.3 million children witness domestic violence in the United States annually (Schewe, 2008), an estimated 3.5% of children under the age of 18 in the United States have experienced the death of a parent (Haine, Ayers, & Sandler, 2008), and according to FEMA (2008), an average of 54.1 major disasters have occurred in the United States annually from 1998 to 2007. While schools may be safe, children and youth are not immune from the effects of violence and crises.

National reports indicate that homicides in schools are extremely rare events (DeVoe et al., 2005). Results of the School-Associated Violent Death (SAVD) study found that school-associated homicides accounted for less than 1% of all homicides among students, with a rate of only 0.03 per 100,000 students (Centers for Disease Control and Prevention, 2008b). Similarly, current crime statistics do not support the claim that school-based violence has increased in recent years (DeVoe et al.). For example, carrying weapons at school among high school students decreased from 12% in 1993 (Kann et al., 1995) to 7% in 1999 (Kann et al, 2000) to 5% in 2005 (Eaton et al., 2006). Between 1992 and 1998, the rate of serious violent crimes at school remained relatively stable at about 8 to 13 per 1,000 students (Kaufman et al., 2000), and dropped to 6 per 1,000 students by 2001, and 5 per 1,000 students by 2005 (Dinkes, Cataldi, & Lin-Kelly (2007).

While the above statistics present good news for schools, the numbers are not as optimistic for bullying. Bullying can take the form of overt or covert behaviors intended to physically harm or ostracize a particular student. While fewer schools reported weekly occurrences of student bullying in 2005 than in 2000 (24.5 % and 29.3%, respectively), in 2005, 28% of students reported having been bullied during the last 6 months (Dinkes et al, 2007). Additionally, the last 3 to 4 years have seen an increase in the occurrence of cyber-bullying. There are reports of 20% to 40% of middle and high school students being bullied at least one time online (Stover, 2006). While our schools may be relatively safer that public perception in terms of the threat of physical harm, the rate of bullying remains disturbingly high.

Regardless of the current incidence of school violence, efforts need to be made to insure that schools are safe environments for all students. School psychologists can play a key role in efforts to prevent school violence and crises, and in responding to their aftermath. They have the knowledge and skills that make them a useful resource for prevention, intervention, and crisis response. They receive training in psychological processes that enables them to understand the issues of risk, resiliency, prevention, and intervention associated with school safety (Morrison, Furlong, & Morrison, 1994). School psychologists are skilled practitioners, and can take the leading role in preventing school violence and promoting mental health.

Furlong, Morrison, and Pavelski (2000) propose that the ongoing concerns regarding school violence and crises interventions provide the profession of school psychology an opportunity to reinvent itself. Traditionally, school psychologists have served two primary roles, referred to by Fagan (2002) as the "sorter" and the "repairer." The function of the sorter is to provide psychoeducational assessment of children, to see who belongs in special education programs. The repairer provides group and individual interventions. In the past, these roles were often restricted to certain activities, but in recent decades have broadened due to factors such as legislation, improvements in training, and a shift in thinking toward the provision of greater mental health services to children (Fagan). It is the intent of this chapter to illustrate how school psychologists can contribute to the broadening of the profession by providing a summary of evidenced-based interventions that can be used to address school crises and violence.

School Violence

School violence has many negative effects on students, school staff, and society in general. Violence within the school environment has a direct impact on school climate and the quality of education provided, and can lead to physical as well as emotional harm of students and staff. Victims experience a range of reactions including fear, worry, anxiety, avoidance of high-risk situations, truancy and dropping out, reduced self-confidence, negative self-identity, declining achievement, gang membership, anger, and violence (Benjamin, Little, & Akin-Little, 2007). Students who fear for their safety will often avoid school, or certain areas of the school, and may even engage in illegal activities such as bringing weapons into the schools (Batsche & Knoff, 1994). To combat these detrimental effects, school psychologists must provide effective response, and these responses should include efficacious prevention, intervention, and crisis response programs.

The Three Tier Model and Promoting Wellness in the Schools

Schools have become increasingly interested in identifying factors to reduce disruptive and violent behaviors and raise prosocial behaviors in students. Although severe behavioral problems are caused by only 5% to 10% of the school population, these children often utilize 50%–60% of the school's resources (Sugai, Horner, & Gresham, 2003). In order to address the concerns created by these at-risk children, the 1997 amendments to the Individuals with Disabilities Education Act (IDEA) mandated that schools create functionally based behavioral intervention plans for students with disabilities exhibiting severe behavior problems. These function-based interventions are built on the practices and systems of positive behavior support (PBS;

Ingram, Lewis-Palmer, & Sugai, 2005). Positive behavior support is an alternative to aversive interventions, and applies positive behavioral interventions and systems to increase appropriate behavior (Sugai et al., 2000). PBS has been found to be effective in decreasing problem behavior and increasing academic achievement in at-risk and adjudicated youth (Scott et al., 2002).

SCHOOLWIDE POSITIVE BEHAVIOR SUPPORT

Schoolwide positive behavior support has been proposed as a proactive and preventive method to reduce problematic behavior in schools (Walker, 2004, Walker et al., 1996; Walker & Shinn, 2003). Under this approach, educators and administrators seek to create a school environment that fosters prosocial behavior, and attempts to systematically deter problem behaviors before they occur. An effective schoolwide program comprises six major components: (a) the purpose of the program, (b) a list of positively stated behavioral expectations, (c) procedures to teach expectations and appropriate skills to students, (d) various strategies for encouraging expectations, (e) a continuum of strategies to prevent rule violations, and (f) procedures for monitoring behavior (Colvin, Kame'enui, & Sugai, 1993; Gresham, 1998; Walker & Shinn). Traditional approaches to problem behavior are often reactionary, requiring the child to misbehave prior to adult response (Crone & Horner, 1999–2000). In the traditional reactionary model, the focus is not teaching the student appropriate behavior, but utilizing punishment strategies such as suspension and expulsion to reduce the undesirable behavior. Despite their widespread implementation in primary and secondary educational institutions, the effectiveness of reactive policies has not been proven valid (Sugai & Horner, 2002). Furthermore, these reactive strategies, (e.g., suspension, referrals to the principal's office) may actually indirectly reinforce the negative behavior by either providing attention (albeit negative attention) or escape from an undesirable task demand (Sugai & Horner, 2002).

Positive behavior support (PBS) is a proactive model that utilizes preventive strategies at three levels to reduce problematic behavior across multiple school settings (e.g., classroom; playground, cafeteria; Anderson & Kincaid, 2005; Eber, Sugai, Smith, & Scott, 2002; Sugai & Horner, 2008). The three-tier model employs empirically based interventions to promote prosocial behavior in (a) the general school population who lack chronic behavior problems (primary prevention); (b) students that

are at risk of developing chronic behavior problems (secondary prevention); and (c) students with major behavioral problems (tertiary prevention). The interventions within the PBS program come out of the applied behavior analysis literature. The goal of schoolwide PBS is to (a) prevent problem behavior from occurring; (b) decrease existing behavioral problems; and (c) increase prosocial behavior in the school population (Safran & Oswald, 2003; Sugai & Horner, 2008). PBS strategies are applied universally across the setting, and become more individualized as needed, based on the student's behavior (Scott et al., 2002). Under the schoolwide framework, the intensity of the intervention is equal to the severity of the problem behavior, and the effectiveness of the intervention system is highly related to the overall efficiency of the school system (Sugai et al., 2003). When viewed holistically, PBS provides a behavior support continuum characterized by four change elements: (a) systems change; (b) environmental changes; (c) behavioral changes in students and adults; and (d) an increased appreciation of appropriate behavior by all members of the educational environment (Sugai et al., 2003). Success at all levels of a schoolwide PBS system is dependent upon the capacities or support capabilities of the host environment (Scott et al., 2002).

The primary prevention level, or first tier in a schoolwide PBS model, focuses on providing a school environment that fosters learning by reducing the number of future cases of problem behavior and addressing minor behavior problems that could escalate, thus requiring the use of resources that are often scarce (Scott et al., 2002; Scott, Liauspin, Nelson, & McIntyre, 2005). Universal interventions are provided for the general population of children that have not been identified as at risk for developing behavioral problems. According to Sugai and colleagues (2003) these children enter school with adequate social skills and are able to respond to universal interventions teaching social skills. It is suggested that these students are the basis for creating a positive school climate. The focus of the primary prevention strategy is to enhance protective factors to minimize the number of students that become at risk (Walker et al., 1996). Early intervention plays a key role in preventing students from obtaining maladaptive behaviors. Kazdin (2007) suggests that if comprehensive early intervention is not provided by grade 3 or 4, the chances of positively changing the problem behavior is low. Tier 1 interventions are generally sufficient in initiating and maintaining positive behaviors in 75% to 85%

of the school's student population. At this level, children are taught appropriate social skills and explicitly told expectations regarding behavior in multiple settings. All staff maintain unified expectations and focus on reinforcing positive behavior, rather than on punishing negative behavior.

Second Step (Fitzgerald & Edstrom, 2006) offers an example of a primary prevention intervention. Nationally, over 15,000 schools have implemented the Second Step program from preschool to eighth grade (Walker & Shinn, 2003), and it has been judged to meet criteria for strong evidence of program effectiveness (Carey, Dimmitt, Hatch, Lapan, & Whiston, 2008). The curriculum teaches four important skills to all students to prevent school violence. Students receive lessons on: (a) empathy, (b) impulse control, (c) problem solving, and (d) anger management/conflict resolution. Second Step requires extensive staff training prior to and during implementation. All staff are provided with developmentally appropriate curricular activities. Teachers instruct students with the materials each day for 30 minutes over a 3- to 6-month period. Parent involvement is also integrated into the intervention. A recent evaluation of the Second Step program with elementary school students (Cooke et al., 2007) found improvement on a number of variables, including caring-cooperative behavior and suppression of aggression, but no changes in aggressive-antisocial behaviors.

Secondary Prevention

The secondary level targets the needs of 10% to 15% of the school population for whom tier one interventions were ineffective. This at-risk population enters school with backgrounds containing several risk factors, such as poverty, dysfunctional families, or illness (Sugai et al., 2003). The goal of this stage is to use specific behavioral techniques to reduce the current observed problematic behavior, as well as to prevent the escalation of serious behavioral challenges (Scott, McIntire et al., 2005). The focus is to remove or reduce the number of risk factors that may negatively impact student behavior, and create programs that protect students against negative environmental factors. These interventions are typically applied on an individual or group basis. Secondary prevention goals are often referred to as "selective" because students select themselves out by not responding to the primary intervention. In order to create effective interventions at this level, educators and administrators must be able to ascertain the antecedents, or setting events, that may

influence student behavior. Interventions at this level could be academic and/or behavioral. Examples of possible interventions are mentoring, skill development, social skills training, self-management, and scheduling changes (Walker & Shinn, 2003).

An example of an empirically based secondary prevention program is Walker et al's (1997) First Step to Success program. First Step to Success is an early intervention program designed for children in kindergarten that are at risk for developing disruptive and aggressive behavior. The program includes (a) universal behavioral screening tools; (b) a school intervention targeted at students identified as at risk, that teaches appropriate, prosocial school behavior; and (c) a home intervention focus that provides parents with skills to help increase their child's school success (Walker & Shinn, 2003). A First Step consultant works with students, teachers, and parents for approximately 50–60 hours over a 3-month period to implement the program. Research on First Step to Success has yielded inconsistent results (excellent to poor), which has been attributed mainly to uneven treatment integrity (Walker, Golly, McLane, & Kimmich, 2005).

Tertiary Prevention

The tertiary level targets those students that did not benefit from interventions at both the primary and secondary level. This is generally 5%–10% of the population. Despite comprising only a small portion of the school population, these students are typically responsible for 40%–50% of the behavioral disruptions on campus (Sugai et al., 2003). Students at this level display chronic behavior problems, and demonstrate a developmental trajectory marked with consistent patterns of antisocial and destructive behavior (Walker & Shinn, 2003). Successful interventions at this level must begin early, and must incorporate all environments (i.e., home, school). Wraparound services are critical at the tertiary level. School administration, teachers, parents, and even community members must be involved in intervention development and implementation (Eber et al., 2002). The goal of this stage is to prevent present levels of problem behavior from escalating into behaviors that overwhelm the school environment, therefore leading to school failure and exclusion (Scott, Liaupsin et al., 2005; Scott et al., 2002).

Multisystemic Therapy (MST) offers an example of a wraparound tertiary intervention (Heggeler, Schoenwald, Borduin, Rowland, & Cunningham, 1998; Schoenwald, Brown, & Heggeler, 2000).

MST is designed to change the social environment of adolescents who display antisocial behavior, and their families, such that positive adjustment and functioning are advanced. The MST assessment focuses on understanding the child's identified problems and the broader systemic context (Walker & Shinn, 2003). Interventions target high frequency behaviors in multiple settings, and are designed to require participation by all family members. Curtis, Ronan, and Borduin (2004) conducted a meta-analysis of MST outcome studies and found an effect size of .55 following treatment, and that youths and families who receive MST were functioning better than 70% of youths and families who received other treatment. A more in-depth discussion of MST will follow.

School-Based Interventions for Violence

In spite of the fact that schools are relatively safe places, and the rate of school violence has been decreasing for a number of years, incidents do occur, and interventions are needed in response to these incidents. This section will include a short description of programs designed for individuals who perpetrate violent and aggressive behavior, followed by a longer section on interventions designed for individuals exposed to violent and aggressive behavior.

INTERVENTIONS FOR VIOLENT AND AGGRESSIVE STUDENTS

Prevention, early intervention, and intensive services can reduce violence and other troubling behaviors in schools. While prevention activities are the first course of action for schools, aggressive and disruptive behavior will occur, and the earlier these students are identified and provided intervention, the less likely other students will suffer trauma as a result of their actions. While schools are generally safe, incidents do occur. For example, in 2007, 26.5% of high school girls and 44.4% of high school boys reported being involved in a physical fight (Centers for Disease Control and Prevention, 2008a).

Wilson and Lipsky (2007) conducted a meta-analysis evaluating the effectiveness of school-based psychosocial programs for reducing aggressive and disruptive behavior (249 studies). Seventy-seven studies were found which delivered classroom-wide programming (primarily cognitively oriented). The weighted mean effect size on aggressive/disruptive behavior outcomes was .21. Also of interest was that two student variables were significantly associated with effect size. Younger students demonstrated

larger effect sizes than older students, and lower socioeconomic status students had larger effect sizes than middle class students. Specific programs targeting individually identified children ($N = 108$ studies) were also examined and found to have an overall effect size of .29. Programs utilizing behavioral strategies (e.g., rewards, token economies, contingency contracts, etc.) were found to be more effective than other modalities. Programs where students were placed outside of their regular classrooms in a self-contained environment ($N = 43$) were examined and found to have a more modest effect size ($d = .11$). Finally, 21 studies that involved multiple treatment components were studied, with a nonsignificant overall effect size of .05. The authors conclude that school based programs for aggressive and disruptive behaviors generally have positive effects, but that schools should probably give priority in program selection to those that are easiest to implement well.

As was mentioned previously, Multisystemic Therapy (MST) (Heggeler et al., 1998, Schoenwald et al., 2000) is an example of an evidence-based (SAMHSA, 2007) tertiary intervention to address school violence, and has been used with both children (ages 6–12) and adolescents (age 13–17). MST focuses on the individual, family, and extrafamilial systems and their interrelations, as a way to reduce symptoms and to promote prosocial behavior. (Kazdin, 2007). Its goal is to give caregivers (e,g., parents and teachers) the skills needed to address behavior problems and associated challenges, as well as to develop prosocial behaviors. Treatment using MST is provided in the individual's natural environment (i.e., home, school, and neighborhood) and typically lasts 3–5 months. Therapists are available for consultation 24 hours per day, 7 days per week, and therapist contact is greatest in the early stages of treatment. Burns, Schoenwald, Burchard, Faw, and Santos (2000) offer nine principles that guide the assessment and intervention process:

1. The primary purpose of assessment is to understand the fit between the identified problems and their broader systemic context.

2. Therapeutic contacts emphasize the positive, and should use systemic strengths as levers for change.

3. Interventions are designed to promote responsible behavior and decrease irresponsible behavior among family members.

4. Interventions are present-focused and action-oriented, targeting specified and well-defined problems.

5. Interventions target sequences of behavior within and between multiple systems that maintain the identified problems.

6. Interventions are developmentally appropriate and fit the developmental needs of the youth.

7. Interventions are designed to require daily or weekly effort by family members.

8. Intervention effectiveness is evaluated continuously from multiple perspectives, with providers assuming accountability for overcoming barriers to successful outcomes.

9. Interventions are designed to promote treatment generalization and long-term maintenance of therapeutic change, by empowering caregivers to address family members' needs across multiple systemic contexts (pp. 286–287).

Intervention focuses on a number of factors including parental disciplinary practices, family interactions, and communication between school and home, while attempting to decrease the child or adolescent's association with deviant peers. Also a focus of intervention are social skills, school performance, and vocational training. Individual therapy is included when needed, but tries to always include input from family members (Burns et al., 2000). A complete description of MST is beyond the scope of this chapter, but interested individuals can find more details about MST and an extensive list of references supporting the efficacy of this intervention at http://www.mstservices.com/index.php.

Teacher behavior is an important variable in managing and modifying disruptive and aggressive behavior in the classroom (McMahon, Wells, & Kotler, 2006). Classroom management practices such as the use of clear and unambiguous rules, student-directed pace in programmed instructional materials, positive and corrective feedback, classroom token economies, and possibly the use of response cost or time-out, have all been found to be effective (McMahon et al.). Walker, Ramsey, and Gresham (2004) do caution, however, that praise alone may not be effective with this population because of a history of negative interactions with adults. They recommend pairing praise with other incentives.

In a meta-analysis investigating interventions designed to reduce inappropriate behaviors in public schools, Stage and Quiroz (1997) found that group-oriented contingencies yielded the largest effect size ($d = 1.02$) of any intervention studied. This was followed by self-management ($d = .97$), differential reinforcement ($d = .95$), token economies ($d = .90$), and stimulus cues (.83). It is clear that behavioral interventions are effective in reducing a number of inappropriate behaviors in the classroom. In fact, the past 40 years have witnessed the success of the use of reinforcement procedures in the classroom (Akin-Little, Eckert, Lovett, & Little, 2004). Why then are they not used more consistently? Akin-Little and colleagues point out the cognitivist position that extrinsic reinforcement may negatively affect a student's intrinsic motivation to perform a reinforced task, once the reinforcer for that task is withdrawn. They conclude, however, that little detrimental effect is found with the use of external reinforcement when studies examining this effect are well designed.

One class of interventions that have met with a high degree of success in motivating behavioral change within the classroom is the group contingency system. Group contingency systems possess several advantages that recommend them for classroom use. Group contingency systems are documented to be cost-effective, time efficient, easily implemented, and highly acceptable to teachers and students (Moore, Waguespack, Wickstrom, Witt, & Gaydos, 1994).

Several types of group contingency programs, including dependent, independent, and interdependent, have been utilized successfully within the classroom to modify a large variety of social and academic behaviors. However, interdependent group contingency systems, in which the entire group is reinforced for collectively meeting a group goal, are particularly well suited to the classroom setting and have been found to reduce disruptive behavior (Campbell & Skinner, 2004; Kelshaw-Levering, Sterling-Turner, Henry, & Skinner, 2000; Theodore, Bray, Kehle, & Jenson, 2001). In addition, Skinner, Cashwell, and Skinner (2000) used an interdependent group contingency management program to increase prosocial behavior of fourth grade students.

Unfortunately, interdependent group contingencies contain some potential disadvantages that have deterred their widespread use in the classroom setting. These difficulties can include reinforcement satiation effects, unequal reinforcer strength, and difficulties arising from unequal contributions of group members to the group goal (Litow & Pumroy, 1975). However, several methodological solutions have been suggested in order to address these disadvantages and better adapt interdependent group contingencies for classroom use.

One proposed solution that has received recent attention is randomized reinforcement. Randomization of reinforcement addresses several of the disadvantages typically associated with interdependent contingency systems. Randomizing the type of reinforcer provided decreases the probability of reinforcer satiation, by making available a variety of different reinforcers in a random manner. The potential effects of unequal reinforcer strength are also addressed, as the class remains unaware of which reinforcer they are receiving until after they have already met the required criteria. By randomizing the reinforcer, students are effectively working toward the chance of receiving a preferred reinforcer, rather than the specific reinforcer itself. Interdependent group contingency systems employing randomized reinforcement have been previously applied to the problem of disruptive and inappropriate classroom behavior (Kelshaw-Levering et al., 2000; Theodore et al., 2001).

Intervening with Gang Violence

Most aggressive gang behavior is committed by male youths between 14 and 18 years of age. It has been suggested that schools, by not fully addressing the needs of the children and their families, could cultivate conditions that lead to gang involvement and antisocial behavior (Dishion, Nelson, & Yasu, 2005). One hypothesis contends that aggression is the normative behavior for these groups which leads to support and encouragment for violence (Vigil, 2003). While deviant to mainstream society, these norms guide gang members in their reactions to slights and threats (real or imagined) to themselves or fellow gang members. Violence becomes expected and required, or a gang member risks being disrespected by others in the gang and suffers a loss of honor.

Communities and police agencies across the country have made attempts to address gang-related problems, frequently without success. Initial attempts tend to emphasize prevention, in an attempt to keep youth from joining gangs. As these attempts fail and gangs grow more organized and violent, the focus tends to shift more to police suppression. Alone, neither of these approaches has demonstrated much effectiveness in addressing gang problems. As a result, a more comprehensive approach is more likely to be used (Office of Juvenile Justice and Delinquency Prevention, OJJDP, 2007). Most community based approaches are based on work done at the University of Chicago (see Spergel, 1995). This model is based on survey responses from 254 law enforcement and social service agencies that were part of the National Youth Gang Suppression and Intervention Research and Development Project. The comprehensive approach includes these five components (OJJDP):

- **Community Mobilization**: Involvement of local citizens, including former gang youth, community groups and agencies, and the coordination of programs and staff functions within and across agencies.
- **Opportunities Provision**: The development of a variety of specific education, training, and employment programs targeting gang-involved youth.
- **Social Intervention**: Involving youth-serving agencies, schools, grassroots groups, faith-based organizations, police and other juvenile/criminal justice organizations in "reaching out" to gang-involved youth and their families, and linking them with the conventional world and needed services.
- **Suppression**: Formal and informal social control procedures, including close supervision and monitoring of gang-involved youth by agencies of the juvenile/criminal justice system, and also by community-based agencies, schools, and grass roots groups.
- **Organizational Change and Development**: Development and implementation of policies and procedures that result in the most effective use of available and potential resources, within and across agencies, to better address the gang problem (p. 2).

Gang Resistance Education and Training Program (G.R.E.A.T., Esbensen, 2004) is a 13-session classroom based course taught by law enforcement officers designed to discourage children and young adolescents from joining gangs, which is delivered by law enforcement to middle school students. Developed by the U.S. Bureau of Alcohol, Tobacco and Firearms (ATF) and the Phoenix Police Department, the program highlights the dangers of gang life and provides information on the dangers of gang involvement, attempts to assist students in developing peaceful conflict resolution skills, offers techniques in resisting pressure to join gangs, and encourages adolescents to develop a positive relationship with law enforcement. Unlike most efforts to reduce gang involvement, this program is given to an entire classroom, rather than focusing on adolescents who appear to be most at risk for gang membership. Overall results, while positive, have been modest. Esbersen reported that when compared to nonparticipants, G.R.E.A.T. participants reported 7% lower levels of victimization, a 5% difference in negative perceptions about gangs, a 5% difference in favorable attitudes toward the police, a 5% difference in risk-seeking behaviors, and a 4% difference in prosocial activities with peers

Bullying

Mouttapa, Valente, Gallaher, Rohrback, and Unger (2004) defined bullies as those who repeatedly physically or emotionally harm another student. They also noted that this behavior among 8 to 15 year olds was considered to be a bigger problem than using drugs and alcohol. Coolidge, DenBoer, and Segal (2004) defined bullying behavior as physical or verbal abuse, the use of power, and using physical acts such as hitting, kicking, pushing, and taunting. Orpinas and Horne (2006a) add that for bullying to take place, the bully must be stronger and more powerful than the victim. Houbre, Tarquinio, Thuillier, and Hergott (2006) noted that serious and less serious bullying affects about 5% and up to 30%, respectively, of students in Europe and the United States. The following are some facts about bullying:

- Bullying is any type of negative behavior that a child is subjected to repeatedly and over time (Piskin, 2003).
- Bullying is not just physical or verbal abuse. Relational bullying, which includes social exclusion, spreading rumors, and withholding friendship, can have a lasting effect on children's social and psychological adjustments into adulthood (Bauman & Del Rio, 2006).
- Victims of bullying can experience emotional damage long term (Wessler & De Andrade, 2006).
- Research has shown a correlation between having legal or criminal issues in adulthood and students who used to bully other students (Piskin, 2003).
- Most bullying occurs on the school playground (Hirschstein, Edstrom, Frey, Snell, & MacKensie, 2007)
- Detection and researched estimates of school bullying is mostly a result of self-reports from the victim (Piskin, 2003).

- It is estimated that one of five students identifies themselves as being a bully, while one of four children is the target of being bullied (Whitted & Dupper, 2005).

Interventions to Prevent Bullying

Bullying is different from simple aggression, because there is an implied power differential between the bully and the victim. As such, the victim is frequently unable to protect him/herself or engage in other activities that may reduce the incidence of the bullying behavior. It is therefore imperative that adults in the lives of children take actions to prevent and/or reduce the incidence of bullying (Orpinas & Horne, 2006a). Olweas (1995) developed the first comprehensive schoolwide intervention for bullying in Norway in the 1980s. Core components of the program included increasing adult awareness and involvement, increased student supervision during recess and lunch time, class rules against bullying, and individual communication with bullies and their parents (Olweas, 1995). While Olweas reported impressive results (50% reduction in bullying) similar results have not been observed in subsequent studies (Orpinas & Horne).

Merrell, Gueldner, Ross, and Isava (2008) recently published a meta-analysis of intervention research in school bullying. Surveying the published literature for a 25-year period from 1980 to 2004, they identified 16 studies with a total of 15,386 student participants from six countries. Results indicated a small but meaningful reduction in students' reports of being bullied ($ES = .27$). The only other variable with an average effect size of .20 or greater (minimum n of two studies) was student self-report of witnessing bullying ($ES = .35$). When all studies are combined, however, the authors concluded that there is some support for school bullying interventions in improving students' social competence, self-esteem, and peer acceptance, in improving teachers knowledge of effective practices, and in responding to bullying. What was less clear was how much the interventions actually reduced the incidence of bullying.

Orpinas and Horne (2006a) and Limper (2000) offer suggestions on strategies to reduce bullying, the majority of which are systemic in nature. First, there needs to be an awareness of the problem by all relevant school personnel, including the principal, other administrators, and teachers. Only by understanding the magnitude of the problem can a commitment develop to take action to prevent and reduce bullying. Orpinas and Horna (2006b) suggest accomplishing this by surveying students and teachers regarding bullying, and presenting the data to teachers, administrators, parents, and student representatives in a meeting of the school community. Addressing misconceptions about bullying such as "boys will be boys" or "students need to stand up for themselves" should be a part of this meeting.

POLICIES AND RULES

School policies that address all types of bullying need to be developed. Included are a good set of school rules. In helping schools develop a set of rules that can be applied in each classroom, there are certain assumptions that need to be conveyed to school personnel. First and foremost is the idea that good rules are the backbone of behavior management. With rules in place, other behavior management techniques will be much easier to implement. There should also be a minimum expectation for behavior for every student in the school. All students should be expected to follow the rules, even special education students. Once rule exceptions are made, a double standard exists and rules become worthless. Next, it is essential that students understand the resulting consequences (both positive and privilege loss) of the rules. Finally, the rules should posted in every classroom in a visible spot, as well as other key locations in the school (Little & Akin-Little, 2009). There are a number of characteristics that have been found associated with good rules (McGinnis, Frederick, & Edwards 1995; Rhode, Jenson, & Reavis, 1993; Wilke, 2003). These include:

- *Number*: The number of rules should be kept to a minimum, with five rules considered the maximum. Compliance is greatest when students can readily recall all of the rules.
- *Simplicity*: The wording of rules should be kept as simple as possible and should convey exactly what behavior is expected. Pictures or icons depicting the rules may help younger students understand the rules.
- *Positive*: Keep the wording of the rules positive if at all possible. Most rules can be stated in a positive manner; some rules cannot. However, the majority of rules should be positive. It is much better to have rules that convey the behavior that is expected of the students, rather than a list of don'ts.

- *Specific*: The rules should be very specific. The more ambiguous the rules are, the more difficult they are to understand. If there are loopholes in the rules, students will find them. Operational definitions of expected behavior are the best.
- *Observable*: The rules should describe behavior that is observable. The behavior must be observable so that teachers can make an unequivocal decision as to whether or not the rule has been followed.
- *Measurable*: Rules describe behavior that is measurable. That is, behavior must be able to be counted and quantified in some way for monitoring purposes.
- *Consequences*: Following the rules should be connected to consequences. Spell out what happens positively if students follow the rules, and what they lose if they do not follow the rules.
- *Compliance*: A compliance rule should always be included. If you want to improve compliance in the classroom, a rule such as "Do what your teacher asks immediately" should be included.

Schools also need to provide a means by which bullying and incidents of violence can be reported, including anonymous reports. Orpinas and Horne (2006a) suggest the use of a reporting box which can be placed in classrooms and in other central locations throughout the school. They also suggest the development of bullying prevention teams to receive and review complaints. Finally, teacher training in classroom and behavior management can help promote prevention efforts and enhance teacher skill in responding to incidents of violence (Little & Akin-Little, 2009).

POSITIVE SCHOOL CLIMATE

Earlier in this chapter, a discussion of the importance of prevention and early intervention efforts was provided. The best way to reduce incidents of bullying is to develop a positive school climate through the use of positive behavioral supports and other proactive methods. Teachers should treat students with respect, and attempt to develop positive relationships with students. This does not mean that teachers strive to be their students' friend, but that positive student behaviors are recognized via praise and other methods of providing positive feedback, and that negative consequences are applied fairly and consistently. There are times when even the most proactive educator must follow through with a negative consequence for an inappropriate behavior. Remember, however, that the worst time to select a punishment is during an episode with a student. In instances such as these, the teacher may be tempted to use a punishment that is too severe for the behavior. Also, it is important to understand each student for whom punishment will be used, because in some cases the intention to punish a behavior results in the behavior being inadvertently reinforced. Additionally, even in those localities where corporal punishment is legal, it is not recommended as an effective behavior management technique. For a detailed discussion of this and other important issues, see Hyman and Snook (1999).

SUPERVISION

Adults are most likely a discriminative stimulus to refrain from bullying activities (Glover, Gough, Johnson, & Cartwright, 2000). In other words, the more adult supervision in school related activities, the less likely students are to bully other students. Schools should develop a practical supervision plan so that adults are present in hallways, lunchrooms, playgrounds, buses, and other critical locations throughout the school. These adults also need to be prepared to intervene in the event aggressive and bullying behavior is observed.

STUDENT EDUCATION

Students need to be educated on a regular basis, at least once per semester, that bullying is not acceptable (Orpinas & Horne, 2006a). In addition to targeting the behavior of the bully, victims need to know that they can and should ask their teachers and parents for help. Practice in positive prosocial behaviors, managing negative emotions, and conflict resolution should also be included (Orpinas & Horne, 2006b). Finally, it is important to address students who are neither the bully nor the victim. The vast majority of bullying occurs when nonparticipant student observers are present; however, fewer than 20% do anything to defend the victim (Hawkins, Pepler, & Craig, 2001). Students should be taught to not reinforce the bullying by laughing or cheering; students should speak out against bullying; and students should inform adults when bullying occurs (Orpinas & Horne, 2006a).

PARENT EDUCATION

Finally, parents need to be educated as to what bullying is, and school policies on bullying. They also need to understand what parental behaviors both encourage and discourage bullying. They need to understand signs of victimization, and what to do if they suspect their child is being bullied (Orpinas & Horne, 2006a).

CYBER BULLYING

Cyber-bullying involves the exploitation of information and socialization technologies such as email, cell phones, text messaging, instant messaging, and personal/social cyber-community web sites (e.g., MySpace), to encourage harsh and repetitive actions by one person or group upon another person or group, with the intent of causing harm and/or humiliation (Anderson & Sturm, 2007). Cyber-bullying is a relatively new form of harassment, and has not been extensively researched. One of the first and very popular documented occurrences of online harassment that was downloaded by millions was the self-made film by a 15-year-old Quebec boy imitating a Star Wars fight, which earned him the title as the Star Wars Kid (Snider & Borel, 2004). Another incident that helped generate attention to cyber-bullying was a picture posted on the Internet of an overweight boy, shot on a personal camera phone while he was changing in a locker room (Campbell, 2005).

Cynics of cyber-bullying think that it is not as harmful to the victims as face-to-face bullying because there is no direct physical damage; yet, the psychological damage that is happening gets disregarded (Anderson & Sturm, 2007). There are reports of 20% to 40% of middle and high school students that have been bullied at least one time online (Stover, 2006). Research has shown that one out of four students is bullied, and of those students 61% do not tell their parents what happened. In addition, 53% of students admit that they have done something nasty or inappropriate to another person online, while one in three of those go on to be repeat abusers (Hitchcock, 2007). This information from past research and studies provides evidence that there are numerous victims and abusers of cyber-bullying.

Recommendations regarding cyber-bullying include teachers and school administrators recognizing its existence and impact, taking it seriously, and educating parents, students, and the entire school community about what it is, and the consequences of engaging in this type of behavior. It is crucial that there are strict disciplinary policies placed in schools to help reduce the incidence of these types of behaviors (Wolfsberg, 2006). Students also need to be aware of how to protect themselves from online predators; for example, placing all of their settings to "private" on social networking websites (Hitchcock, 2007). It is crucial that parents are involved in their children's lives, so they are aware of what they are doing online.

Interventions in Response to Crises

Schools face a number of crisis situations, including suicide, violence, natural disasters, and child abuse and neglect, that may impact individual students or create schoolwide crises (Collins & Collins, 2005). As crises can impact individual students and overall school safety and functioning, swift and specific responses are needed. In addition to the potential physical threat of these situations, they also can take an emotional toll on students and school personnel. Despite the prevalence of crisis situations in schools, there are minimal empirical data addressing specific strategies to prepare and respond to crises in schools (Jimerson, Brock, & Pletcher, 2005).

There are many critical components of school crisis preparation. The first step is the development of a crisis team, which includes the identification of appropriate personnel for crisis response. Effective preparation is important, because structure is essential so that the response to a crisis is timely and efficient (Brock & Poland, 2002). System-level administrative support is critical for school systems attempting to develop and implement comprehensive crisis intervention plans. Developing these plans and training potential team members takes time and resources that likely need to be allocated at a district level (Brock, 2002). Administrative support is also necessary at the building level, as principals and other administrators play a critical role in leading crisis preparation and response efforts (Poland, Pitcher, & Lazarus, 2001).

Identifying and organizing the core group of individuals responsible for responding is an important first step in crisis team development (Dwyer & Jimerson, 2002). There are a number of models for organizing crisis response teams, including the use of school based teams, district and/or regional school system teams, and combined school–community teams. However, a hierarchical model that includes school based, district, and regional response teams working in conjunction as needed, is usually recommended (Brock, 2002; Trump, 2000). This hierarchical structure emphasizes using school based teams as primary responders, with regional and district level teams providing additional support and expertise when necessary.

The composition of the crisis team may differ from school to school, but usually will consist of school psychologists, school counselors, school social workers, principals, teachers, nurses, and security officers and administrative staff (Heath & Sheen, 2006; Sprague & Walker, 2005). The crisis team evaluates each crisis situation and develops and implements a specific plan as necessary. The functions of the team include: (a) determine if a crisis exists; (b) determine if the crisis response team should be activated; (c), evaluate risk factors for students, faculty, and the school; (d) develop and implement specific intervention plans; (e) communicate and coordinate with school administration and staff; (f) communicate and coordinate with community agencies; (g) communicate with and provide support to students, staff, and families; (h) help return the school to normalcy after the crisis; (i) provide follow-up support to students and staff; (j) review actions and provide recommendations for improvements following incidents (Heath & Sheen; Knox & Roberts, 2005; Sprague & Walker).

The National Organization for Victim Assistance (NOVA) uses a team model for crisis management. While this model is designed for community crises, it is very adaptable to schools and the crises they may experience. Their model, based roughly on Maslow's need hierarchy, includes three essential tasks to reestablishing functioning within the school (Jimerson et al., 2005). The first involves establishing safety and security. This includes taking care of victims' immediate needs for safety, medical care, food, etc. It also involves connecting individuals (students and school personnel) with their loved ones. When the crisis counselor is communicating with victims, it is important to give them privacy to express emotions and to let them know that their reactions and emotions are acceptable. It is important, however, to recognize that individuals respond to crises in different ways, and the counselor should not impart his or her preconceived notion of how to react on any individual. The second task is to allow ventilation and validation. Let the individual tell her or his story (ventilate) and insure them that their reaction is normal, and their experience unique. Recognize, however, that this approach may be contraindicated in psychically injured acute crisis victims (Jimerson et al.). The third task (prediction and preparation) involves predicting issues that will be faced by victims in the near future, and helping them make preparations. This includes the likelihood of future emotional responses. The next section discusses an individual approach for working with children in the aftermath of trauma.

Trauma

Children and adolescents may experience a number of different types of trauma. These can include direct experience of abuse (e.g., sexual, physical), grief, domestic and community violence, natural disasters, or a combination of the above. In a retrospective study of over 17,000 adults, Felitti and colleagues (1998) reported that more than one-half of their sample had experienced at least one adverse event in childhood, with approximately one-quarter reporting having experienced two or more. This included 10.6% who experienced emotional abuse, 28.3% who experienced physical abuse, and 20.7% who experienced sexual abuse. In 2005, 13.8 per 1000 children aged 12–17 were victims of serious violent crimes (aggravated assault, rape, robbery, and homicide). This was down from a rate of 43.8 per 1000 in 1993, but it still represents 350,649 adolescents in the United States (Bureau of Justice Statistics, 2006). And, this figure does not include children and adolescents who may have been traumatized by witnessing violent acts. Finally, increasing numbers of children and adolescents have been victims of natural disasters. For example, more than one million people were displaced, at least temporarily, by Hurricane Katrina in 2005, and many remain displaced today (Akin-Little & Little, 2008). It is clear that exposure to traumatic events is not uncommon in childhood and adolescence, and psychologists working in schools should have some training in meeting the needs of this segment of the population.

One intervention which has been empirically supported in the trauma field is Trauma-Focused Cognitive Behavior Therapy (TF-CBT). While most of the research (i.e., controlled, randomized trials) has supported the efficacy of TF-CBT with sexually abused children (e.g., Cohen, Deblinger, Mannarino, & Steer, 2004; Cohen, Mannarino, & Knudsen, 2005), this intervention has also proved efficacious for other types of trauma (Cohen, Mannarino, & Deblinger, 2006; Cohen, Mannarino, & Staron, 2006).

While there is a clear need for services for children and adolescents who have experienced a single or repeated traumatic event(s), most mental health professionals have not received training in this, or any empirically validated therapeutic technique for working with individuals with traumatic stress (Courtois, 2001). To ameliorate this need, and to attempt to provide additional training, the National Crimes Treatment and Research Center at the Medical College of the University of South Carolina developed, with the award of a grant from Substance Abuse and Mental Health Services Administration (SAMSHA), a 10-hour, web-based, multimedia distance education course for mental health professionals seeking to learn TF-CBT. The only requirements for participating in the training are that individuals have a master's degree or higher in a mental health discipline, or are currently enrolled in a graduate training program in a mental health discipline. Interested individuals can find the training program at http://tfcbt.musc.edu/ (Medical University of South Carolina, 2005).

Further, while there is mandated training on crisis intervention in many school psychology programs, at both the specialist and doctoral level, there is little training provided specifically addressing the needs of children who have suffered a trauma (Benjamin et al., 2007). Of course, crisis intervention skills are very important (National Association of School Psychologists, 2000), but obtaining the skills to ensure these children and adolescents receive effective services post-crisis is also important. As with other medical and psychological ailments, if left unchecked, symptoms do worsen. So, while school psychologists may not be receiving this specific training, the need for it is clear. This is supported by data discussed above, and is further buttressed by the newly created Trauma Division (Division 56) and the Childhood Trauma Special Interest Group of the American Psychological Association.

Psychological Impact of Trauma

Unfortunately, stressful events are not an unusual occurrence in child and adolescent development. Parents divorce, grandparents die, children and others in their lives get injured. These may not be considered extreme trauma, however. According to the *Diagnostic and Statistical Manual of Mental Disorders–Fourth Edition, Text Revision* (*DSM-IV-TR*; American Psychiatric Association [APA], 2000), an extreme traumatic stressor is one that involves "direct personal experience of an event that involves actual or threatened death or serious injury, or other threat to one's physical integrity; or witnessing an event that involves death, injury, or threat to the physical integrity of another person; or learning about unexpected or violent death, serious harm, or threat of death or injury experienced by a family member or other close associate" (p. 463).

Examples include sexual or physical abuse, severe accidents, cancer or other life threatening illness, natural or manmade disasters, war, terrorism, or the sudden death of a parent, sibling, or peer (Cohen, Mannarino, & Deblinger, 2006). However, it should also be noted that not every child exposed to a traumatic event will develop trauma symptoms. Many children demonstrate resiliency, the ability to thrive and excel even when exposed to severe stressors (Leckman & Mayes, 2007).

Cohen, Mannarino, and Deblinger (2006) divide trauma symptoms into four main categories: affective, behavioral, cognitive, and physical. Affective symptoms include fear, depression, anger, and mood dysregulation (e.g., frequent mood changes). Behavioral symptoms center on the avoidance of things that remind the individual of the traumatic experiences. While this may be an effective short-term coping mechanism, if these behaviors generalize, it may have a severe negative impact on the child's participation in normal, age-appropriate activities. This type of coping in turn may exacerbate the affective symptoms. Cognitive symptoms involve distorted cognitions the child may have about themselves, others, the event, or the world (e.g., "the event is my fault"). There is not always a rational explanation for why bad things happen, so in an attempt to provide an explanation for the traumatic event, it is common for irrational beliefs to occur. These beliefs are generally dogmatic, rigid musts (e.g., "this must be my fault") and imperative demands (Dryden, DiGiuseppe, & Neenan, 2003). Most probably this type of coping appears in order to help the child develop a sense of control or predictability over their environment. Cohen and colleagues report that the most common irrational belief in children is blaming themselves. Finally, physical symptoms are related to the chronic stress these children are experiencing. They include elevated resting pulse rates and blood pressure, greater physical/muscle tension, and hypervigilance. It has also been found that prolonged exposure to trauma and maltreatment can decrease brain size and functioning (DeBellis et al., 1999).

Trauma-Focused Cognitive Behavior Therapy: The Core Values

Trauma-Focused Cognitive Behavior Therapy (TF-CBT) is one of only three interventions that have been identified as meeting the criteria for evidence-based practice by the Kauffman Best Practices Project (Chadwick Center for Children and Families, 2004), and is the only trauma treatment

for children with a scientific rating of 1, meaning it is well supported, effective practice according to the California Evidence-Based Clearinghouse for Child Welfare (2006-2007). TF-CBT consists of six core values (Cohen, Mannarino, & Deblinger, 2006). First, it is components based, meaning that it consists of a collection of core skills that build on one another. It is not a rigid session-by-session treatment approach, but rather is designed to match the needs of the individual child and family. The second value is respect. For treatment to be effective it must be consistent with the family's religious, community, and cultural values. The TF-CBT therapist works with the family to determine the optimal course of treatment. Third is adaptability, which denotes the need for flexibility and creativity on the part of the therapist in selecting and implementing TF-CBT components. The fourth core value is family involvement. Parents are a key component in treatment, and improving parent–child interactions, communication, and intimacy, is a major focus. Fifth is the idea that the therapeutic relationship is a key factor in restoring trust and functioning in the child. To accomplish this, the therapist must model trust, empathy, and acceptance throughout the course of treatment. The final core value is self-efficacy. The goal of TF-CBT is an optimally functioning individual and family well after treatment has been terminated. To accomplish this, the therapist attempts to establish a sense of self-efficacy in the client's affect, behavior, and cognitions.

TF-CBT: The Specific Components

TF-CBT is a short-term treatment that involves individual sessions with children and parents, as well as joint parent–child sessions. It has been empirically validated for children ages 4 to 18 who have behavioral and emotional problems related to traumatic life events. The main components of TF-CBT include psychoeducation, parenting skills, relaxation, affective modulation, cognitive coping and processing, trauma narrative, in vivo mastery of trauma reminders, conjoint child–parent sessions, and enhancing future safety and development. While this paper will summarize these components, a more complete description of each component can be found in Cohen, Mannarino, and Deblinger (2006).

Psychoeducation is the first component of the TF-CBT package, and it continues for the duration of therapy for both the child and parent. It is important to provide information about trauma, its effects, and its treatment. There is not any one set list of information that needs to be provided, however. It is important to individualize the information so that it is specific to the type of trauma that was experienced, and the child's developmental level. Educating parents and children about what they should expect from treatment helps to enlist their cooperation and to prepare them for the types of activities that will be conducted during therapy.

Working with a child who has experienced a traumatic event can be difficult for even the most competent parents. The parenting skills included in TF-CBT have been found to be effective in helping parents with their child's behavior problems (Cohen, Deblinger, Mannarino, & Steer, 2004; Deblinger, Lippmann, & Steer, 1996). Parenting skills taught include the use of praise, selective attention, time-out, and contingency management.

Relaxation techniques are taught to the child in an effort to help him/her reduce the physiological symptoms of stress such as autonomic nervous system arousal, and to help the child sleep and manage other behavioral manifestations of stress. There is no one relaxation technique that is recommended. Cohen, Mannarino, and Deblinger (2006) do, however, recommend some combination of focused breathing, meditation, and progressive muscle relaxation. They also recommend training parents in the relaxation techniques, so that they can practice and reinforce these skills in their children. The authors also have found the relaxation program developed by Cautela and Groden (1978) useful when working with children and adolescents.

Affective expression and modulation involves teaching children to manage their emotions and deal with their anxiety. Children who have experienced a traumatic event frequently have difficulty with these skills. They may find it hard to identify emotions, differentiate between emotions, or express their feelings appropriately. Additionally, if the child is able to express and control their feelings, they may be less likely to use avoidance as a coping strategy. Techniques that are used during this component include thought interruption techniques, positive imagery, positive self-talk, and social skills building.

Cognitive coping and processing involves teaching children and parents about the relationships among thoughts, feelings, and behavior, and how they can identify and correct unhelpful thoughts. Initially the focus is on thoughts and beliefs in general, and dealing with trauma-related cognitions comes later. The first step is recognition and sharing of internal dialogs, with the focus changing to inaccurate and unhelpful thoughts once they have developed initial skills in this area.

Helping children create and discuss a narrative version of their traumatic experiences is essential in helping them cope. It is the most important step in helping to control intrusive and upsetting trauma-related imagery. The goal of the trauma narrative is to separate unpleasant associations between thoughts, reminders, or discussion of the trauma, from overwhelming negative emotion. Over the course of several sessions, the child is encouraged to describe more and more details about what happened before, during, and after the trauma, as well as the child's thoughts and feelings through these times. Eventually the child will share this narrative with his or her parent(s) or caregiver.

In vivo mastery of trauma reminders is designed to help resolve generalized avoidant behaviors. Frequently, innocuous cues in the environment remind the child of the trauma. They bring up unpleasant emotions, and one way of dealing with them is through avoidance. For example, a child who was abused in the basement of one home may avoid going into the basement of any home. This does not mean you want to desensitize the child to all perceived trauma cues. Many are legitimate and serve to help the child from being retraumatized. Part of this component is getting them to distinguish important cues from innocuous, conditioned cues.

TF-CBT also includes conjoint child–parent sessions to review information, read the child's trauma narrative, and facilitate communication. The goal is to get the child comfortable in talking with their parent or caregiver about their traumatic experiences and other significant events that happen in their life. These sessions tend to occur toward the end of therapy, as the child needs adequate time to cognitively process the trauma; however, there are times when it may be advisable to involve the parents earlier.

The final component of TF-CBT is designed to enhance the child's future safety and development. In many cases the child will be unlikely to face a similar trauma in the future. While it is acceptable to stress this, the therapist should never assure any child that he/she will not experience trauma again. Our goal, however, is to insure that they have the skills to minimize the likelihood of future trauma and cope with trauma effectively should it occur again.

Empirical Support for TF-CBT

As mentioned previously, TF-CBT has been empirically validated and is recognized by multiple sources as an empirically based intervention. The following section summarizes a representative sample of studies on TF-CBT for both trauma and grief. TF-CBT has consistently been demonstrated as an efficacious treatment for PTSD, depression, anxiety, and other related symptoms. There is also an abundance of evidence to support the efficacy of TF-CBT over treatments such as nondirective play therapy and supportive therapies for children who were the victims of sexual abuse (Cohen, Deblinger, & Mannarino, 2004). In addition, while the majority of studies have focused on child sexual abuse, evidence also suggests that it is effective for children exposed to other types of trauma, as well as children who are multiply traumatized (Cohen, 2005).

Cohen and Mannarino (1996) conducted the first treatment outcome study for sexually abused children using TF-CBT. In this study, TF-CBT was compared to a nondirective supportive therapy (NST) for 67 sexually abused preschool children and their parents. Treatment consisted of 12 individual sessions for both the child and parent. Results indicated that while the NST group did not change significantly with regard to symptomology, the TF-CBT group demonstrated improvement on most outcome measures. These findings provided strong preliminary evidence for the effectiveness of TF-CBT for sexually abused preschool children and their parents. In a follow-up to their 1996 study, Cohen and Mannarino (1997) evaluated treatment outcome 6 and 12 months after initial treatment. Results indicated that the TF-CBT group exhibited significantly more improvement over time than the NST group. Results also indicated the superior effectiveness of TF-CBT over NST in reducing sexually inappropriate behavior.

Cohen, Deblinger, Mannarino, and Steer (2004) compared the efficacy of TF-CBT with Child Centered Therapy (CCT) for the treatment of PTSD and related emotional and behavioral problems in children who have been sexually abused. A total of 203 children ages 8 to 14 years of age who had a verified case of sexual abuse were included in the study. Participants were randomly assigned to a manualized treatment consisting of TFCBT or CCT. Therapists were trained in the modality they provided, and received supervision. Treatment integrity was assessed by video and audiotape recording. Results indicated that parents in the TF-CBT reported lower levels on each of the outcome measures (except on parental support) than those who received CCT. That is, children and parents in the TF-CBT group reported improvement

in PTSD symptoms, depression, shame, behavioral problems, and dysfunctional abuse attributions. Results also indicated that two times as many children in the CCT group continued to have PTSD, based on *DSM-IV-TR* (APA, 2000) criteria. TF-CBT also appeared to improve children's feelings of trust, perceived credibility, and shame. This study is important because it supports the use of a shorter version of TF-CBT.

Deblinger, Mannarino, Cohen, and Steer (2006) conducted a follow-up study to assess the maintenance effects of TF-CBT and CCT on participants in the Cohen, Deblinger, Mannarino, and Steer (2004) study, as well as to determine predictors of treatment responsiveness using sex, race, age, relationship to perpetrator, total number of traumas experienced before treatment, and pretreatment scores on psychological measures. Participants from the Cohen, Deblinger et al. study were followed for 6 additional months while being provided with booster sessions. Results indicated that children in the TF-CBT group maintained the gains made at posttreatment (6 months of maintenance with booster sessions). That is, the children who received TF-CBT continued to show fewer PTSD symptoms and fewer symptoms of shame compared to children in the CCT group. In addition, parents in the TF-CBT group reported less emotional distress than parents in the CCT group. This study is important because it provides support that a shortened version of the TF-CBT protocol has benefits that persist (at least for 6 months) after treatment has concluded. That children experienced less abuse related shame during follow-up is also important to note, as shame may mediate the impact of sexual abuse in hindering long term recovery.

Cohen, Mannarino, and Knudsen (2004) examined a 16-session (8 sessions trauma based and 8 sessions grief based) trauma focused cognitive-behavioral therapy for childhood traumatic grief (CTG). Traumatic grief occurs when trauma symptoms interfere with a child's ability to successfully deal with the normal grieving process. Twenty-two children and their primary caretakers received the CTG intervention. Results indicated that children experienced significant improvements in CTG, PTSD, depression, and anxiety symptoms, and a reduction in behavior problems. PTSD symptoms improved only during the trauma focused treatment components, while CTG improved during both trauma focused and grief focused components. In addition, parents also experienced significant improvement in PTSD and depressive symptoms.

In a follow-up study to Cohen, Mannarino, and Knudsen (2004), Cohen, Mannarino, and Staron (2006) examined the effectiveness of a 12-session cognitive-behavioral therapy/childhood traumatic grief model (CTG) in treating trauma and grief symptoms. Despite the relative effectiveness of the 16 session approach, this study sought to examine the impact of a shortened version of the CBT-CTG protocol used in Cohen, Mannarino, and Knudsen, to match shorter bereavement treatment protocols serving children with trauma and grief. Participants included 39 children and adolescents ranging in age from 6 to 17 years who had experienced a loss of a parent or sibling due to accidental death, medical reasons, homicide, suicide, or drug overdose. Significant improvement in children's self-reported symptoms of CTG, PTSD, depression, and anxiety were reported. In addition, parents reported improvement in their child's PTSD, internalizing and externalizing symptoms, and total behavior problems, but they themselves did not report improvement in their depressive symptoms. Similar to Cohen, Mannarino, and Knudsen, a decline in PTSD symptoms and improvement in adaptive functioning was observed only during the trauma focused phase of CBT, while CTG symptoms improved for both the traumatic and grief focused CBT interventions. The authors conclude that a protocol that is trauma focused together with a shortened version of a grief focused CBT protocol is effective at reducing PTSD and CTG, and anxiety, behavioral problems, and depressive symptoms. This study has practical utility because it demonstrated that a shortened version of a trauma and grief focused CBT can be effective at improving childhood trauma and grief symptoms. This study also involved a collaborative approach with children and parents. so the information gained from therapy can be transferred between home and clinic, and potentially improve generalization and maintenance.

Kitchiner, Phillips, Roberts, and Bisson (2007) conducted a pilot study to evaluate the effectiveness of a Trauma-Focused Cognitive Behavior Therapy (TF-CBT) educational training package, coupled with a mental health practitioner (MHP) clinical group supervision (CGS) component for the treatment of PTSD. Ten professionals ranging in experience levels from certified psychiatrists to a midwife with no experience participated as therapists. Therapists received between 6 and 23 sessions of TF-CBT training (e.g., education, case discussions, role plays, and manualized training). Each therapist provided services to at least one participant for a range of 5 to 16 hours of time spent in a dyad. Results indicated that PTSD symptoms improved significantly on the Beck Depression Inventory and a secondary measure. In addition, participants also reported slight increases in adjustment related to being alone and at work. Despite the improvements reported in the pilot study, these may need to be viewed with a cautious eye due to minimal control and comparison groups. One would want, potentially, to assess the relative impact of the TF-CBT+CGS against TF-CBT alone, to determine if CGS adds more strength to TF-CBT. In addition, this study did not provide the ages and gender of the participants and therapists. Further exploration should be conducted to assess the benefit of coupling GCS with TFCBT. Schools often do not provide students with appropriate and necessary mental health services because they do not have the appropriate resources, or students are not triaged as needing such services (Walker et al., 2004). Indeed, TF-CBT should be evaluated with much more scrutiny to determine its relative effectiveness and practical utility with school aged children, as well as the social acceptability and habilitative properties for the student, teacher, and family members.

In the only published study to date in schools, Kataoka et al. (2003) used group TF-CBT with Latino immigrant students who have been exposed to community violence. Participants included 198 students in grades 3–8 with trauma related depression and/or PTSD symptoms. The therapy was delivered in Spanish. Results indicated that students in the intervention group ($n = 152$) had significantly greater improvement in PTSD and depressive symptoms, compared with waitlist controls ($n = 47$) at 3-month follow-up. Findings suggest that this program can be implemented in school settings, and is associated with a decline in trauma related mental health problems.

Clearly, as discussed earlier, children and adolescents are experiencing traumatic events. However, most school psychologists are not receiving specific training in efficacious service delivery. Trauma-Focused Cognitive Behavior Therapy is an effective therapeutic technique that can be utilized in many different types of traumatic situations (e.g., natural disaster; see Akin-Little & Little, 2006; Akin-Little & Little, 2008). So, it behooves school psychologists to take advantage of this free training in order to be able to meet the needs of children who may have been victim to a traumatic event—and, in this way, insure the best possible prognosis for all children.

Relaxation

Studies have demonstrated that relaxation techniques with children can be efficacious components of stress reduction following a traumatic event (e.g., Möhlen, Parzer, Resch, & Brunner, 2005; Scheeringa et al., 2008). Cautela and Groden (1978) offer a comprehensive relaxation program for children and adolescents. The following summarizes their recommended procedures. The relaxation procedures used with children are similar to procedures used with adults, although there are some necessary modifications to the techniques employed. Specific changes include: (a) gross motor areas of the arms and legs need to be covered first, before moving on to more difficult areas in the face and neck; (b) more sessions are needed to go through each muscle group to ensure learning; (c) reinforcers for success (tangible, tokens, activities, and social) are more important than with adults; (d) it is necessary to do more touching and manipulation with the client; (e) special apparatus such as squeeze toys, whistles, or pinwheels may be needed; (f) instructions need to be simplified, and more discrete steps employed; (g) modeling procedures are needed to a greater extent; (h) sometimes prerequisite skills may need to be taught; (i) more guidance and prompting is needed, especially in naturalistic environments, to ensure compliance; and (j) sessions are usually shorter than with adults due to lower attention span, fatigue, etc. It is also very important to consider generalization when doing relaxation with children. Just because a child is able to employ relaxation techniques in the controlled environment of an office does not mean that they will successfully employ these techniques when needed in their natural environment. To increase the likelihood of generalization you can teach relaxation in a number of positions, and a number of different places around the school and community, if possible. It is also important to have different people in the child's life learn the procedures so that they can assist the child in various environments. This should include both the teacher and parent. It is also helpful to have teachers and parents identify cues to anxiety and tension for the child, and prompt him/her to relax. If child is at a level where they can do this themselves, then you can gradually switch responsibility to child. Finally, you want to start reinforcement on a very rich schedule (continuous) each time a muscle group, environment, or adult prompt changes, and gradually thin the reinforcement schedule. You may also want to vary reinforcers so child doesn't satiate.

Summary

Schools are, for the most part, safe environments for children and adolescents. In spite of the relative calm that exists in most schools, aggression, bullying, and traumatic events do occur, and all schools should be prepared to deal with them. The best approach to take is a proactive one. There is validity to old clichés, and one that stands true is "an ounce of prevention is worth a pound of cure." This chapter, therefore, focused on prevention and early intervention, positive behavioral supports, the three-tier model, and promoting wellness in schools. Even the best efforts at prevention and early intervention will not work 100% of the time, however. Therefore, this chapter also discussed interventions for dealing with aggressive behavior, gang activity, and school-wide and individual response to trauma.

When behaviors occur that need a response, it is best to remember that identifying the functional relationship between stimuli and responses can have a significant impact on outcome. While a functional analysis rarely identifies all factors that influence behavior, it will lead to a greater understanding of the relationships between behaviors, their antecedent conditions, and their maintaining effects (Follette & Naugle, 2006). There is no "one size fits all" approach, because there are different antecedent and consequent conditions from individual to individual, event to event, school to school, and community to community. This chapter summarized the most common approaches, but recognizing the unique characteristics of each situation should make adapting the approaches discussed in this chapter more efficacious.

References

Akin-Little, K. A., & Little, S. G. (2006). Our Katrina experience. *The School Psychologist, 60,* 82–86.

Akin-Little, K. A., & Little, S. G. (2008). Our Katrina experience: Providing mental health services in Concordia Parish, Louisiana. *Professional Psychology: Research and Practice, 39,* 18–23.

Akin-Little, K. A., Eckert, T. L., Lovett, B. J., & Little, S. G. (2004). Extrinsic reinforcement in the classroom: Bribery or best practice. *School Psychology Review, 33,* 344–362.

American Psychiatric Association (2000). *Diagnostic and statistical manual of mental disorders* (4th ed., Text Revision). Washington, DC: Author.

Anderson, C. M., & Kincaid, D. (2005). Applying behavior analysis to school violence and discipline problems: Schoolwide positive behavior support. *Behavior Analyst, 28,* 49–63.

Anderson, T., & Sturm, B. (2007). Cyberbullying from playground to computer. *Young Adult Library Services, 5*, 24–27.

Batsche, G. M., & Knoff, H. M. (1994). Bullies and their victims: Understanding a pervasive problem in the schools. *School Psychology Review, 23*, 165–174.

Bauman, S., & Del Rio, A. (2006). Preservice teachers' responses to bullying scenarios: Comparing physical, verbal, and relational bullying. *Journal of Educational Psychology, 98*, 219–231.

Benjamin, R. M., Little, S. G., & Akin-Little, K. A. (2007). The preparation of school psychologists to provide services related to school violence: A survey of current training programs. *The Trainers Forum, 26*, 11–18.

Brock, S. E. (2002). Preparing for the school crisis response. In J. Sandoval (Ed.), *Handbook of crisis counseling, intervention, and prevention in the schools* (2nd ed., pp. 25–38). Mahwah, NJ: Lawrence Erlbaum Associates.

Brock, S. E., & Poland, S. (2002). School crisis preparedness. In S. E. Brock, P. J. Lazarus, & S. R. Jimerson (Eds.), *Best practices in school crisis prevention and intervention* (pp. 273–288). Bethesda, MD: National Association of School Psychologists.

Bureau of Justice Statistics (2006). National crime victimization survey: Violent crime trends, 1973–2005. U.S. Department of Justice Office of Justice Programs. Retrieved September 14, 2007 from http://www.ojp.usdoj.gov/bjs/glance/tables/viortrdtab.htm.

Burns, B. J., Schoenwald, S. K., Burchard, J. D., Faw, L., & Santos, A. B. (2000). Comprehensive community-based interventions for youth with severe emotional disorders: Multisystemic therapy and the wraparound process. *Journal of Child and Family Studies, 9*, 283–314.

California Evidence-Based Clearinghouse for Child Welfare (2006–2007). *Trauma treatment for children.* Retrieved September 13, 2007 from http://www.cachildwelfareclearinghouse.org/search/topical-area/7.

Campbell, M. A. (2005). Cyber bullying: An old problem in a new guise. *Australian Journal of Guidance & Counseling, 15*, 68–76.

Campbell, S., & Skinner, C. H. (2004). Combining explicit timing with an interdependent group contingency program to decrease transition times: An investigation of the Timely Transitions Game. *Journal of Applied School Psychology, 20*, 11–27.

Carey, J. C., Dimmitt, C., Hatch, T. A., Lapan, R. T., & Whiston, S. C. (2008). Report of the national panel for evidence-based school counseling: Outcome research coding protocol and evaluation of student success skills and second step. *Professional School Counseling, 11*, 197–206.

Cautela, J. R., & Groden, J. (1978). *Relaxation: A comprehensive manual for adults, children, and children with special needs.* Champaign, IL: Research Press.

Centers for Disease Control and Prevention (2008a). Youth risk behavior surveillance — United States, 2007. *Morbidity and Mortality Weekly Report, 57*, SS–4.

Centers for Disease Control and Prevention (2008b). School-associated student homicides — United States, 1992–2006. *Morbidity and Mortality Weekly Report, 5*, 33–36.

Chadwick Center for Children and Families. (2004). *Closing the quality chasm in child abuse treatment: Identifying and disseminating best practices.* San Diego, CA: Author.

Cohen, J. A. (2005). Treating traumatized children: Current status and future directions. In E. Cardeña & K. Croyle (Eds.), *Acute reactions to trauma and psychotherapy: A multidisciplinary and international perspective* (pp. 109–121). New York: Haworth Press.

Cohen, J. A., & Mannarino, A. P. (1996). A treatment outcome study for sexually abused preschool children: Initial findings. *Journal of the American Academy of Child and Adolescent Psychiatry, 35*, 42–50.

Cohen, J. A., & Mannarino, A. P. (1997). A treatment study for sexually abused preschool children: Outcome during a one-year follow-up. *Journal of the American Academy of Child and Adolescent Psychiatry, 36*, 1228–1235.

Cohen, J. A., Deblinger, E., & Mannarino, A. P. (2004, September). Trauma-focused cognitive-behavioral therapy for sexually abused children (pp. 109–121). *Psychiatric Times, 21*(10). Retrieved from http://www.psychiatrictimes.com/p040952.html.

Cohen, J. A., Deblinger, E., Mannarino, A. P., & Steer, R. A. (2004). A multi-site, randomized controlled trial for sexually abused children with PTSD symptoms. *Journal of the American Academy of Child and Adolescent Psychiatry, 43*, 393–402.

Cohen, J. A., Mannarino, A. P., & Deblinger, E. (2006). *Treating trauma and traumatic grief in children and adolescents.* New York: The Guilford Press.

Cohen, J. A., Mannarino, A. P., & Knudsen, K. (2004). Treating childhood traumatic grief: A pilot study. *Journal of the American Academy of Child and Adolescent Psychiatry, 43*, 1225–1423.

Cohen, J. A., Mannarino, A. P., & Knudsen, K. (2005). Treating sexually abused children: One year follow-up of a randomized controlled trial. *Child Abuse and Neglect, 29*, 135–145.

Cohen, J., Mannarino, A. P., & Staron, V. R. (2006). A pilot study of modified cognitive–behavioral therapy for childhood traumatic grief (CBT-CTG). *Journal of the American Academy of Child and Adolescent Psychiatry, 45*, 1465–1473.

Collins, B. C., & Collins, T. M. (2005). *Crisis and trauma: Developmental–ecological intervention.* Boston: Lahaska Press.

Colvin, G., Kameenui, E. J., & Sugai, G. (1993). Reconceptualizing behavior management and school-wide discipline in general education. *Education and Treatment of Children, 16*, 361–381.

Cooke, M. B., Ford, J., Levine, J., Bourke, C., Newell, L., & Lapidus, G. (2007). The *effects* of city-wide implementation of 'Second Step' on elementary school students' prosocial and aggressive behaviors. *Journal of Primary Prevention, 28*, 93–115.

Coolidge, F. L., DenBoer, J. W., & Segal, D. L. (2004). Personality and neuropsychological correlates of bullying behavior. *Personality and Individual Differences, 36*(7), 1559–1569.

Cornell, D. G. (2006). *School violence: Fears versus facts.* Mahwah, NJ: Lawrence Erlbaum Associates.

Courtois, C. A. (2001). Traumatic stress studies: The need for curriculum inclusion. *Journal of Traumatic Practice, 1*, 33–57.

Crone, D. A., & Horner, R. H. (1999–2000). Contextual, conceptual and empirical foundations of functional behavioral assessment in schools. *Exceptionality, 8*, 161–172.

Curtis, N. M., Ronan, K. R., & Borduin, C. M. (2004). Multisystemic treatment: A meta-analysis of outcome studies. *Journal of Family Psychology, 18*, 411–419.

De Bellis, M. D., Keshavan, M. S., Clark, D. B., Casey, B. J., Giedd, J. N., Boring, A. M., Frustaci, K., & Ryan, N. D. (1999). Developmental traumatology: II. Brain development. *Biological Psychiatry, 45*, 1271–1284.

Deblinger, E., Lippmann, J., & Steer, R. (1996). Sexually abused children suffering posttraumatic stress symptoms: Initial treatment outcome findings. *Child Maltreatment, 1,* 310–321.

Deblinger, E., Mannarino, A. P., Cohen, J. A., & Steer, R. A. (2006). A follow-up study of a multisite, randomized, controlled trial for children with sexual abuse-related PTSD symptoms. *Journal of the American Academy of Child and Adolescent Psychiatry, 45,* 1474–1484.

DeVoe, J. F., Peter, K., Noonan, M., Snyder, T. D., & Baum, K. (2005). *Indicators of school crime and safety: 2005* (NCES 2006–001/NCJ 210697). U.S. Departments of Education and Justice. Washington, DC: U.S. Government Printing Office.

Dinkes, R., Cataldi, E. F., & Lin-Kelly, W. (2007). *Indicators of school crime and safety: 2007* (NCES 2008-021/NCJ 219553). National Center for Education Statistics, Institute of Education Sciences, U.S. Department of Education, and Bureau of Justice. Statistics, Office of Justice Programs, U.S. Department of Justice. Washington, DC.

Dishion, T. J., Nelson, S. E., & Yasu, N. (2005) Predicting early adolescent gang involvement from middle school adaptation. *Journal of Clinical Child and Adolescent Psychology, 34,* 62–73.

Dryden, W., DiGiuseppe, R., & Neenan, M. (2003). *A primer on rational emotive behavior therapy* (2nd ed.). Champaign, IL: Research Press.

Dusenbury, L, Falco, M., Lake, A., Brannigan, R., & Bosworth, K. (1997). Nine critical elements of promising violence prevention programs. *Journal of School Health, 67,* 409–415.

Dwyer, K., & Jimerson, S. R. (2002). Enabling prevention through planning. In S. E. Brock, P. J. Lazarus, & S. R. Jimerson (Eds.), *Best practices in school crisis prevention and intervention* (pp. 23–46). Bethesda, MD: National Association of School Psychologists.

Eaton, D. K., Kann, L., Kinchen, S., Ross, J., Hawkins, J., Harris, W. A., Lowry, R., McManus, T., Chyen, D., Shanklin, S., Lim, C. Grunbaum, J., & Wechsler, H. (2006). *Youth risk behavior surveillance—United States, 2005.* Atlanta, GA: Centers for Disease Control and Prevention.

Eber, L., Sugai, G., Smith, C. R., & Scott, T. M. (2002). Wraparound and positive behavioral interventions and supports in the schools. *Journal of Emotional and Behavioral Disorders, 10,* 171–180.

Esbensen, F. A. (2004). *Evaluating G.R.E.A.T.: A school-based gang prevention program.* Washington, DC: U.S. Department of Justice.

Fagan, T. K. (2002). Trends in the history of school psychology in the United States. In A. Thomas & J. Grimes (Vol. Ed.), *Best Practices in School Psychology-IV:* Vol 1. (pp. 209–221). Bethesda, MD: The National Association of School Psychologists.

Felitti, V. J., Anda, R. F., Nordenberg, D., Williamson, D. F., Spitz, A. M., Edwards, V., Koss, M. P., & Marks, J. S. (1998). Relationship of childhood abuse and household dysfunction to many of the leading causes of death in adults. The Adverse Childhood Experiences (ACE) Study. *American Journal of Preventive, 14,* 245–258

FEMA (2008). *Declared disasters by year or state.* Retrieved July 15, 2008 from http://www.fema.gov/news/disaster_totals_annual.fema.

Fitzgerald, P. D., & Edstrom, L. V. (2006). Second Step: A violence prevention curriculum. In S. Jimerson & M. Furlong (Eds.), *The handbook of school violence and school safety: From research to practice.* Mahwah, NJ: Erlbaum.

Follette, W. C., & Naugle, A. E. (2006). Functional analytic clinical assessment in trauma treatment. In V. M. Follette & J. I. Ruzek (Eds.), *Cognitive-behavioral therapies for trauma* (2nd ed., pp. 17–33). New York: The Guilford Press.

Furlong, M., Morrison, G., & Pavelski, R. (2000). Trends in school psychology for the 21st century: Influences of school violence on professional change. *Psychology in the Schools, 37,* 81–90.

Glover, D., Gough, G., Johnson, M., & Cartwright, N. (2000). Bullying in 25 secondary schools: Incidence, impact, and intervention. *Educational Research, 42,* 141–156.

Gresham, F. M. (1998). Social skills training: Should we raze, remodel, or rebuild? *Behavioral Disorders, 24,* 19–25.

Haine, R. A., Ayers, T. S., & Sandler, I. N. (2008). Evidence-based practices for parentally bereaved children and their families. *Professional Psychology: Research and Practice, 39,* 113–121.

Hawkins, D. L., Pepler, D. J., & Craig, W. M. (2001). Naturalistic observations of peer interventions in bullying. *Social Development, 10,* 512–527.

Heath, M. A., & Sheen, D. (2005). *School-based crisis intervention: Preparing all school personnel to assist.* New York: Guilford Press.

Heaviside, S., Rowand, C, Williams, C., & Farris, E. (1998). *Violence and discipline problems in U. S. public schools: 1996–1997.* (NCES 98-030). Washington D.C.: U.S. Department of Education, National Center for Education Statistics.

Heggeler, S. W., Schoenwald, S. K., Borduin, C. M., Rowland, M. D., & Cunningham, P. B. (1998). *Multisystemic treatment of antisocial behavior in children and adolescents.* New York: The Guilford Press.

Hirschstein, M. K., Edstrom, L. V. S., Frey, K. S., Snell, J. L., & MacKensie, E. P. (2007). Walking the talk in bullying prevention: Teacher implementation variables related to initial impact of the Steps to Respect program. *School Psychology Review, 36,* 3–21.

Hitchcock, J. A., (2007). Cyber bullies, online predators, and what to do about them. *MultiMedia & Internet @ Schools, 14,* 13–15.

Houbre, B., Tarquinio, C., Thuillier, I., & Hergott, E. (2006). Bullying among students and its consequences on health. *European Journal of Psychology of Education, 21*(2), 183–208.

Hyman, I. A., & Perone, D. C. (1998). The other side of school violence: Educator policies and practices that may contribute to student misbehavior. *Journal of School Psychology, 36,* 7–27.

Hyman, I. A., & Snook, P. A. (1999). *Dangerous schools: What we can do about the physical and emotional abuse of our children.* San Francisco: Jossey-Bass.

Individuals with Disabilities Education Act Amendments of 1997, Public Law 105-17, 20, U. S. C. Chapter 33, Section 1415 et seq.

Ingram, K., Lewis-Palmer, T., & Sugai, G. (2005). Function-based intervention planning: Comparing the effectiveness of FBA function-based and non-function-based intervention plans. *Journal of Positive Behavior Interventions, 7,* 224–236.

Jimerson, S. R., Brock, S. E., & Pletcher, S. W. (2005). An integrated model of school crisis preparedness and intervention: A shared foundation to facilitate international crisis intervention. *School Psychology International, 26,* 275–296.

Kann, L., Kinchen, S. A., Williams, B. I., Ross, J. G., Lowry, R., Grunbaum, J. A., Kolbe, L. J., & State, Local YRBSS Coordinators. (2000). Youth risk behavior surveillance

United States, 1999. *Morbidity and Mortality Weekly Report CDC Surveillance Summary, 49*, 1–96.

Kann, L., Warren, C. W., Harris, W. A., Collins, J. L., Douglas, K. A., Collins, M. E., Kinchen, S. A., Williams, B. I., Ross, J. G., Kolbe, L. J., & State, Local YRBSS Coordinators. (1995). Youth risk behavior surveillance United States, 1993. *Morbidity and Mortality Weekly Report CDC Surveillance Summary, 44*, 1–56.

Kataoka, S. H., Stein, B. D., Jaycox, L. H., Wong, M., Escudero, P. Tu, W., Zaragoza, C., & Fink, A. (2003). A school-based mental health program for traumatized Latino immigrant children. *Journal of the American Academy of Child Psychiatry, 42*, 311–318.

Kaufman, P., Chen, X., Choy, S. P., Ruddy, S. A., Miller, A. K., Fleury, J. K., Chandler, K. A., Rand, M. R., Klaus, P., & Planty, M. G., (2000). *Indicators of school crime and safety, 2000* (NCES 2001-017/NCJ-184176). Washington, DC: U.S. Department of Education, U.S. Department of Justice.

Kazdin, A. E. (2007). Psychosocial treatments for conduct disorder in children and adolescents. In P. E. Nathan & J. M. Gorman (Eds.), *A guide to treatments that work* (3rd ed.). New York: Oxford University Press.

Kelshaw-Levering, K., Sterling-Turner, H. E., Henry, J. R., & Skinner, C. H. (2000). Randomized interdependent group contingencies: Group reinforcement with a twist. *Psychology in the Schools, 37*, 523–533.

Kitchiner, N. J., Phillips, B., Roberts, N., & Bisson, J. I. (2007). Increasing access to trauma focused behavioural therapy for post traumatic stress disorder through a pilot feasibility study of a group clinical supervision model. *Behavioural and Cognitive Psychotherapy, 35*, 251–254.

Knox, K. S., & Roberts, A. R. (2005). Crisis intervention and crisis team models in schools. *Children and Schools, 27*, 93–100.

Larson, J., Smith, D. C., & Furlong, M. J. (2002). Best practices in school violence prevention. In A. Thomas & J. Grimes (Eds.), *Best practices in school psychology IV*: Vol. 2. (pp. 1081–1097). Bethesda, MD: The National Association of School Psychologists.

Leckman, J. F., & Mayes, L. C. (2007). Nurturing resilient children. *Journal of Child Psychology and Psychiatry, 48*, 221–223.

Limper, R. (2000). Cooperation between parents, teachers, and school boards to prevent bullying in education: An overview of work done in the Netherlands. *Aggressive Behavior, 26*, 125–134.

Litow, L., & Pumroy, D. K. (1975). A brief review of classroom group oriented contingencies. *Journal of Applied Behavior Analysis, 8*, 341–347.

Little, S. G., & Akin-Little, A. (2009). Classroom management. In W. O'Donohue, & J. Fisher, (Eds.), General principles and *empirically supported techniques of cognitive behavior therapy* (pp. 325–333). Hoboken, NJ: Wiley.

McGinnis, J. C., Frederick, B. P., & Edwards, R. (1995). Enhancing classroom management through proactive rules and procedures. *Psychology in the Schools, 32*, 220–224.

McMahon, R. J., Wells, K. C., & Kotler, J. S. (2006). Conduct problems. In E. J. Mash & R. A. Barkley (Eds.), *Treatment of childhood disorders* (3rd ed.) (pp. 153–225). New York: The Guilford Press.

Medical University of South Carolina (2005). *A web-based learning course for trauma-focused cognitive-behavioral therapy.* Web site: http://tfcbt.musc.edu.

Merrell, K. W., Gueldner, B. A., Ross, S. W., & Isava, D. M. (2008). How effective are school bullying intervention programs? A meta-analysis of intervention research. *School Psychology Quarterly, 23*, 26–42.

Möhlen, H., Parzer, P., Resch, F., & Brunner, R. (2005). Psychosocial support for war-traumatized child and adolescent refugees: Evaluation of a short-term treatment program. *Australian and New Zealand Journal of Psychiatry, 39*, 81–87.

Moore, L. A., Waguespack, A. M., Wickstrom, K .F., Witt, J. C., & Gaydos, G. R. (1994). Mystery motivator: an effective and time efficient intervention. *School Psychology Review, 23*, 106–118.

Morrison, R. L., Furlong, M. J., & Morrison, G. M. (1994). Knocking the wheels off the school violence bandwagon. *Educational Leadership, 24*, 6–9.

Mouttapa, M., Valente, T., Gallaher, P., Rohrbach, L A., & Unger, J. B. (2004). Social network predictors of bullying and victimization. *Adolescence, 39*(154), 315–334.

National Association of School Psychologists (2000). *Standards for training and field placement programs in school psychology.* Bethesda, MD: Author.

Office of Juvenile Justice and Delinquency Prevention (2007). *Best practices to address community gang problems: OJJDP's comprehensive gang model.* Retrieved August 11, 2008 from http://www.iir.com/nygc/publications/gang-problems.pdf.

O'Keefe, M. (1997). Adolescents' exposure to community and school violence: Prevalence and behavioral correlates. *Journal of Adolescent Health, 20*, 368–376.

Olweas, D. (1995). Bullying or peer abuse at school: Facts and interventions. *Current Directions in Psychological Science, 4*, 196–200.

Orpinas, P., & Horne, A, M. (2006a). Bullies and victims: A challenge for schools. In J. R. Lutzker (Ed.), *Preventing violence: Research and evidence-based intervention strategies* (pp. 147–165). Washington, DC: American Psychological Association.

Orpinas, P., & Horne, A, M. (2006b). *Bullying prevention: Creating a positive school climate and developing social competence.* Washington, DC: American Psychological Association.

Piskin, M. (2003). School bullying: Definition, types, related factors, and strategies to prevent bullying problems. *Educational Sciences: Theory & Practices, 2*, 555–563.

Poland, S., Pitcher, G., & Lazarus, P. M. (2001). Best practices in crisis prevention and management. In A. Thomas & J. Grimes (Eds.), *Best practices in school psychology IV* (pp. 1057–1080). Bethesda, MD: National Association of School Psychologists.

Rhode, G., Jenson, W. R., & Reavis, H. K. (1993). *The tough kid book: Practical classroom management strategies.* Longmont, CO: Sopris West.

Safran, S. P., & Oswald, K. (2003). Positive behavior supports: Can schools reshape disciplinary practices? *Exceptional Children, 69*, 361–373.

SAMHSA (2007). *National registry of evidence-based programs and practices: Multisystemic therapy (MST) for juvenile offenders.* Retrieved August 1, 2008 from http://www.nrepp.samhsa.gov/programfulldetails.asp?PROGRAM_ID=102.

Scheeringa, M. S., Salloum, A., Arnberger, R. A., Weems, C. F., Amaya-Jackson, L., Cohen, J. A. (2007). Feasibility and effectiveness of cognitive-behavioral therapy for posttraumatic stress disorder in preschool children: Two case reports. *Journal of Traumatic Stress, 20*, 631–636.

Schewe, P. A. (2008). Direct service recommendations for children and caregivers exposed to community and domestic violence. *Best Practices in Mental Health: An International Journal, 4*, 31–47.

Schoenwald, S., Brown, T., & Heggeler, S. (2000). Inside multisystemic therapy: Therapist, supervisory and program practices. *Journal of Emotional and Behavioral Disorders, 8,* 113–127.

Scott, T. M., Liaupsin, C., Nelson, C. M., & McIntyre, J. (2005). Team-based functional behavior assessment as a proactive public school process: A descriptive analysis of current barriers. *Journal of Behavioral Education. Special Issue: Functional Behavioral Assessment, 14,* 57–71.

Scott, T. M., McIntyre, J., Liaupsin, C., Nelson, C. M., Conroy, M., & Payne, L. D. (2005). An examination of the relation between functional behavior assessment and selected intervention strategies with school-based teams. *Journal of Positive Behavior Interventions, 7,* 205–215.

Scott, T. M., Nelson, C. M., Liaupsin, C. J., Jolivette, K., Christle, C. A., & Riney, M. (2002). Addressing the needs of at-risk and adjudicated youth through positive behavior support: Effective prevention practices. *Education & Treatment of Children, 25,* 532–551.

Skinner, C. H., Cashwell, C .S., & Skinner, A. L. (2000). Increasing tootling: The effects of a peer monitored group contingency program on students' reports of peers' prosocial behaviors. *Psychology in the Schools, 37,* 263–270.

Snider, M., & Borel, K. (2004). Stalked by a cyberbully. *Maclean's, 177,* 76–77.

Spergel, I. A. (1995). *The Youth Gang Problem.* New York, NY: Oxford University Press.

Sprague, J. R., & Walker, H. M. (2005). *Safe and healthy schools: Practical prevention strategies.* New York: Guilford Press.

Stage, S. A., & Quiroz, D. R. (1997). A meta-analysis of interventions to decrease disruptive behavior in public education settings. *School Psychology Review, 26,* 333–368.

Stover, D. (2006). Treating cyberbullying as a school violence issue. *Education Digest, 72,* 40–42.

Sugai, G., & Horner, R. (2002). The evolution of discipline practices: School-wide positive behavior supports. *Child and Family Behavior Therapy, 24,* 23–50.

Sugai, G., & Horner, R. H. (2008). What we know and need to know about preventing problem behavior in schools. *Exceptionality, 16,* 67–77.

Sugai, G., Horner, R. H., & Gresham, F. M. (2003). Behaviorally effective school environments. In M.R. Shinn, H.M. Walker, & G. Stoner (EDS.), *Interventions for academic and behavior problems II: Preventative and remedial approaches* (pp. 315–351). Bethesda, MD: National Association of School Psychologists.

Sugai, G., Horner, R. H., Dunlap, G., Hieneman, M., Lewis, T. J., & Nelson, C. M. et al. (2000). Applying positive behavior support and functional behavioral assessment in schools. *Journal of Positive Behavior Interventions, 2,* 131–143.

Theodore, L. A., Bray, M. A., Kehle, T. J., & Jenson, W. R. (2001). Randomization of group contingencies and reinforcers to reduce classroom disruptive behavior. *Journal of School Psychology, 39,* 267–277.

Trump, K. S. (2000). *Classroom killers? Hallway hostages? How schools can prevent and manage school crises.* Thousand Oaks, CA: Corwin Press.

Vigil, J. D. (2003). Urban violence and street gangs. *Annual Review of Anthropology, 32,* 225–243.

Walker, H. M. (2004). Use of evidence based interventions in schools: Where we've been, where we are, and where we need to go. *School Psychology Review, 33,* 398–407.

Walker, H. M., & Shinn, M. R. (2003). Structuring school-based interventions to achieve integrated primary, secondary, and tertiary prevention goals for safe and effective schools. In M. R. Shinn, H. M. Walker, & G. Stoner (Eds.), *Interventions for academic and behavior problems II: Preventative and remedial approaches* (pp. 315–351). Bethesda, MD: National Association of School Psychologists.

Walker, H. M., Golly, A., McLane, J. Z., & Kimmich, M. (2005). The Oregon first step to success replication initiative: Statewide results of an evaluation of the program's impact. *Journal of Emotional and Behavioral Disorders, 13,* 163–172.

Walker, H. M., Horner, R. H., Sugai, G., Bullis, M., Sprague, J.R, Bricker, D., & Kaufman, M. (1996). Integrated approaches to preventing antisocial behavior patterns among school-age children and youth. *Journal of Emotional and Behavioral Disorders, 4,* 194–209.

Walker, H. M., Ramsey, E., & Gresham, F. M. (2004). *Antisocial behavior at school: Evidence-based practices.* Belmont, CA: Wadsworth/Thompson Learning.

Walker, H. M., Stiller, B., Golly, A., Kavanagh, K., Severson, H. H., & Feil, E. (1997). *First Step to Success: Helping young children overcome antisocial behavior.* Longmont, CO: Sopris West.

Wessler, S. L., & De Andrade, L. L. (2006). Slurs, stereotypes, and student interventions: Examining the dynamics, impact, and prevention of harassment in middle and high school. *Journal of Social Issues, 62,* 511–532.

Whitted, K. S., & Dupper, D. R. (2005). Best practices for preventing or reducing bullying in schools. *Children and Schools, 27,* 164–175.

Wilke, R. L. (2003). *The first days of class: A practical guide for the beginning teacher.* Thousand Oaks, CA: Corwin Press

Wilson, S. J., & Lipsey, M. W. (2007). School-based interventions for aggressive and disruptive behavior: Update of a meta-analysis. *American Journal of Preventive Medicine, 33* (Supplement 2), S130–S143.

Wolfsberg, J. S. (2006). Student safety from cyberbullies, in chat rooms, and in instant messaging. *The Educational Digest, 72,* 33–37.

Promoting Subjective Well-Being

Shannon M. Suldo, E. Scott Huebner, Jessica Savage, *and* Amanda Thalji

Abstract

Considerable research has investigated the relationship between positive emotions and attitudes (i.e., subjective well-being) and important life processes and outcomes among adults. Although the specific nature of the mechanisms that account for linkages between subjective well-being (SWB) and its consequences remains to be clarified, researchers have demonstrated strong links between adults' positive SWB and important outcomes in a variety of contexts. For example, SWB has been found to facilitate good interpersonal behavior and relationships, job performance, creativity, physical health, and even a longer life (Lyubormirsky, King, & Diener, 2005). Furthermore, most people report that high SWB is desirable in and of itself (Diener & Oishi, 2006). Finally, King (2008) argues cogently that the desire to maintain SWB promotes personal growth through the revision of goals and behavior in response to the loss of SWB during adverse life circumstances. Lyubomirsky (2007) concludes that "empowering people to develop a positive state of mind—to live the most rewarding and happiest lives that they can—is just as important as psychology's traditional focus on repairing their weakness and healing their pathologies" (p. 3). The purposes of this chapter are thus threefold. First, we review the extant research on the benefits of positive SWB in youth. Second, we discuss strategies and interventions to promote SWB in youth. Finally, we discuss implications for future research and practice efforts.

Keywords: school psychology, subjective well-being, adolescents, interventions

Recent work on positive emotions and attitudes has been subsumed within the overarching field of subjective well-being (SWB) research as summarized by Diener (1984). According to Diener, Scollon, and Lucas (2004), SWB "emphasizes an individual's own assessment of his or her own life—not the judgments of experts—and includes satisfaction (both general, and satisfaction with specific domains), pleasant affect, and low negative affect" (p. 189). More specifically, pleasant or positive affect is defined as the frequency of positive emotions (e.g., joy, excitement) and negative affect is defined as the frequency of negative emotions (e.g., sadness, anger). Life satisfaction has been defined as a "cognitive judgmental process in which individuals assess the quality of their lives on the basis of their own unique set of criteria" (Pavot & Diener, 1993, p. 164). Life satisfaction judgments can be made with respect to a student's "overall" or global life, and with respect to specific domains (e.g., school, family, peers). SWB has also been defined as "a pervasive sense that life is good" (Myers, 1992, p. 23), reflecting its longer-term perspective in contrast to momentary emotions or moods. It should be noted that these definitions are all consistent with the current positive psychology perspective, in which mental health is not viewed as simply the absence of mental illness, but also the presence of positive indicators of functioning such as SWB (Seligman & Csikszentmihalyi, 2000).

The scientific study of SWB of adults has grown rapidly (see Eid & Larsen, 2008). Although much remains to be learned, considerable progress has been made in understanding the antecedents and consequences of individual differences in adult SWB. Research on children's SWB has lagged behind, but it has increased during the last decade. Whereas substantial research has been conducted for many years on negative affect (e.g., anxiety, depression) in youth, research on positive emotions and life satisfaction awaited the development of psychometrically sound measures appropriate for children and youth. Studies of positive affect in youth remain sparse; nevertheless, studies of life satisfaction have especially increased, and a reasonable body of literature supports its construct validity for children between the ages of 8–18 (Huebner, 2004; Huebner, Suldo, & Gilman, 2006).

Studies reveal that most children and youth are satisfied with their overall lives and with the important domains of their lives (Gilman et al. 2008; Huebner, Drane, & Valois, 2000). Although most children report levels of satisfaction above a neutral point, few report the highest levels of life satisfaction. Nevertheless, despite some concerns that very high life satisfaction may be dysfunctional (Schwartz & Garmamoni, 1986), life satisfaction appears to be a necessary, but not sufficient, condition for the good life (Diener, 2003). Youth who report that they are *very* satisfied with their lives show pervasive positive functioning across intrapersonal, interpersonal, and school-related domains (Gilman & Huebner, 2006; Suldo & Huebner, 2006). For example, in Gilman and Huebner's (2006) study, relative to students with average life satisfaction, students with very high life satisfaction reported higher scores on measures of intrapersonal functioning and attitudes toward teachers, and lower scores on stress. Also, no students in the very high life satisfaction group demonstrated clinical levels of psychopathology symptoms, whereas 7% of the average group and 42% of the very low group reported clinical levels of symptoms.

Importance of Subjective Well-Being in Youth

The historical preoccupation of most psychologists, educators, and researchers' interest in negative indicators of mental health (i.e., psychopathology) belies the growing body of literature that demonstrates the salience of SWB to healthy development in childhood and adolescence. The studies reviewed next illustrate some of the many desirable youth outcomes that are linked to SWB, and demonstrate that SWB not only predicts healthy development

but also serves functional roles (specifically, as a mediator and/or moderator) in understanding how environmental circumstances are linked to children's outcomes. Recent literature that demonstrates the importance of SWB as an independent and unique indicator of mental health is presented first, in part to make the case that professionals who are interested in complete mental health should examine SWB in addition to more traditional indicators of psychological functioning, such as mental illness.

Relationship between SWB and Psychopathology

Given the premise that mental health is not simply the absence of mental illness, the importance of differentiating SWB and childhood psychopathology should be apparent. Such a distinction is manifested in the dual-factor model of mental health (cf. Greenspoon & Saklofske, 2001), in which positive indicators of SWB are included with traditional negative indicators of psychopathology (i.e., internalizing and externalizing behavior problems) in a comprehensive assessment of child well-being. In a powerful demonstration of the importance of differentiating SWB and pathology, Suldo and Shaffer (2008) identified the existence of four distinct groups of middle school students: 57% of the sample had "complete mental health" (i.e., high SWB and low pathology), 13% were "vulnerable" (low SWB and low pathology), 13% were "symptomatic but content" (high SWB and high pathology), and 17% were "troubled" (low SWB and high psychopathology). Although the means of all four groups differed significantly on a variety of outcome variables (described in detail later in this section), most importantly, the "vulnerable" group had lower standardized test scores, academic self-concepts, valuing of school, and social support from classmates and parents, as well as more school absences, self-perceived physical health problems, and social problems, compared to the students with complete mental health. The identification of a group of students who are nonsymptomatic of psychopathology but relatively low in SWB, and who are clearly differentiable in terms of academic, physical, and interpersonal functioning, provides strong support for the additional utility of the inclusion of positive psychology measures (i.e., SWB) in comprehensive youth assessments.

Other recent research demonstrating the independent contribution of positive SWB data to comprehensive assessments involved the evaluation of the incremental validity of positive assessment data

(Lewis, Huebner, Reschly, & Valois, 2009). Using the Positive and Negative Affect Scale for Children (PANAS-C; Laurent et al., 1999), this study specifically investigated the incremental validity of positive affect (joy, excitement) relative to negative affect (e.g., anxiety, sadness) in predicting adaptive school functioning, with a sample of middle and high school students. Results indicated that positive affect demonstrated significant incremental validity in predicting school satisfaction, adaptive coping, and student engagement, but not self-reported GPA. Taken together, the approach of Suldo and Shaffer (2008) and Lewis et al. (2009) provide substantial support for the notion that measures of positive SWB provide important, incremental information in comprehensive assessments of child and youth functioning.

Outcomes Correlated with SWB
Developmental tasks of youth involve productivity in educational pursuits, ultimately geared toward preparing a young person for gainful and meaningful employment (Berk, 2006). Formation of healthy interpersonal relationships is also crucial, in part because social support from classmates engenders achievement motivation and self-esteem, as well as lowers one's risk for suicide attempts and depressive symptoms (Hall-Lande, Eisenberg, Christenson, & Neumark-Sztainer, 2007; Nelson & DeBacker, 2008). In addition to positive social adjustment and attainment of educational outcomes, good physical health is a necessary outcome that facilitates students' capacities to meet their personal goals, as well as developmental tasks pertinent to social/emotional functioning and academic achievement (Blackman & Gurka, 2007; Luster & Small, 1994; Schwimmer, Burwinkle, & Varni, 2003).

SOCIAL RESOURCES
A landmark study of very happy people found that the happiest adults were distinguished from people in the average range of happiness primarily by their high sociability and strong interpersonal relationships, including healthy relationships with close friends, romantic partners, and family members (Diener & Seligman, 2002). Since this study was published, research with adolescents in Ireland and America has identified the same trend, such that youth reporting the highest SWB also perceive significantly higher levels of social support from significant adults (i.e., parents, teachers) and same-age youth (i.e., classmates, close friends; Nevin, Carr, Shevlin, Dooley, & Breaden, 2005; Suldo &

Huebner, 2006; Suldo & Shaffer, 2008), and hold more positive attitudes towards their teachers (Gilman & Huebner, 2006). In addition to perceiving more extant social resources, higher life satisfaction in adolescence co-occurs with greater confidence in one's social abilities needed to relate to and get along with peers (Suldo & Shaffer, 2007), suggesting the endurance of continued positive social outcomes.

ACADEMIC PERFORMANCE
Studies of American students in middle and high school have yielded small to moderate, but statistically significant, correlations ($r = .21–.32$) between students' life satisfaction and their grade point averages (Gilman & Huebner, 2006; Suldo, Shaffer, & Riley, 2008). Recent research with middle school youth found that students with complete mental health (i.e., high SWB, low psychopathology) earned higher scores on statewide assessments of reading skills than their peers with low SWB (Suldo & Shaffer, 2008). In addition to this trend toward better academic performance among youth with high SWB, a strong link exists between students' life satisfaction and their beliefs salient to achievement, such that high SWB co-occurs with more confidence in one's academic abilities, and more positive attitudes about the value of education (Leung, McBride-Chang, & Lai, 2004; Suldo & Shaffer, 2007; Suldo, Shaffer, & Riley, 2008).

OCCUPATIONAL STATUS
Comprehensive examinations are needed of SWB in youth in relation to their subsequent occupational attainment and job performance. Preliminary support for the salience of SWB to gainful employment can be drawn from extant research on career indecision during adolescence, positive affect during adolescence as a predictor of job satisfaction and pay in adulthood, and ties between SWB and occupational performance in adulthood. First, a longitudinal study that underscored the negative impact of being undecided about one's future career at a relatively young age (i.e., eighth and tenth grades) on adolescents' career development activities and self-esteem, found that higher life satisfaction among eighth grade students was associated with more decisiveness about future careers, both concurrently and during high school, while students who were undecided at either time point reported significantly lower life satisfaction during eighth grade (Creed, Prideaux, & Patton, 2005). The only study to link SWB in youth to subsequent occupational-related outcomes in adulthood found that higher levels of

positive affect at age 18 predicted greater work satisfaction, financial security, and intellectual stimulation through job responsibilities at age 26 (Roberts, Caspi, & Moffitt, 2003). Regarding research with adults, indicators of superior occupational performance (e.g., higher pay, better supervisor-rated performance) are predicted by greater experiences and expressions of positive affect while at work (Staw, Sutton, & Pelled, 1994), higher life satisfaction (Jones, 2006), and greater psychological well-being (Wright & Cropanzano, 2000). These ties between SWB and desirable occupational outcomes have led to increased interest in promoting employees' SWB (Hartung & Taber, 2008; Russel, 2008).

PHYSICAL HEALTH
Although preliminary research does not support the presence of diminished SWB among youth with chronic illness such as cancer (Hexdall & Huebner, 2007), SWB is associated with better health among general samples of children and adolescence. For instance, studies of large samples of students in middle school (Suldo & Shaffer, 2008) and high school (Piko, 2006; Zullig, Valois, Huebner, & Drane, 2005) found that high SWB was associated with better self-rated health (e.g., less illness, more positive perceptions of overall health) and fewer disruptions in activities of daily living (e.g., family activities, work, self-care) due to health problems. During youth, life satisfaction is also inversely associated with many risky behaviors associated with health problems, such as use of alcohol, cigarettes, and drugs (Zimmerman, Salem, & Maton, 1995), involvement in serious fights that warrant medical attention (Valois, Paxton, Zullig, & Huebner, 2006), suicide attempts (Kim & Kim, 2008), and high-risk sexual behaviors such as unprotected sex, sexual intercourse during childhood, and multiple lifetime partners (Valois, Zullig, Huebner, Kammermann, & Drane, 2002).

Functions of SWB
In addition to direct associations with the desirable outcomes discussed above, life satisfaction has also demonstrated functional roles in youth development, reflecting its importance as more than a simple byproduct of positive experiences. Life satisfaction has been shown to play a mediational role in the relationship between stressful environmental experiences and youth behavior problems (McKnight, Huebner, & Suldo, 2002). Furthermore, life satisfaction mediates the relationship between authoritative parenting practices and adolescent

behavior problems (Suldo & Huebner, 2004a). Finally, high life satisfaction also appears to serve a moderator function; that is, it operates as a buffer against the development of future externalizing behavior problems that adolescents may manifest when faced with increased stressful life events (Suldo & Huebner, 2004b).

Promoting SWB: Extending Implications of Research on Predictors and Correlates
Guidance for psychologists and educators interested in promoting SWB in youth can be gleaned from two bodies of literature. The first pertains to studies that have identified potentially malleable factors within the environment (e.g., peers, family, and school) as well as within individuals (e.g., cognitions and activities) that are correlated with increased life satisfaction among children and adolescents. Although the bulk of these studies have been cross-sectional and thus the directionality of associations is unknown, efforts to increase the positive correlates of SWB may contribute to elevations in SWB. The second area of research involves results of controlled-trial intervention studies that specifically target SWB through manipulating subjects' circumstances. While implementing interventions that have support for efficacy is typically the most logical route for those interested in increasing SWB, several caveats about the literature on empirical interventions for SWB are warranted. First, this research is relatively recent (i.e., only begun in the past decade) and has not yet been subjected to replication by independent research teams. Second, the growing body of published studies has been limited to samples of adult participants; studies in which youth participated have only been disseminated within the past few years. As such, generalizing results of intervention studies largely requires a leap of faith that what works with adults will also work with youth. The following sections thus summarize results of the two literature bases on correlates of SWB, and intervention studies that have targeted SWB as an outcome.

Enhancing Systems-Level Factors that are Correlated with SWB
POSITIVE FAMILY RELATIONSHIPS
Satisfaction with family members, as well as with friendships and schooling experiences (discussed later in this section), are among the five domains of life originally identified as comprising children's general life satisfaction (Huebner, 1994). Recent qualitative research in which Mexican-American

high school students were asked to identify the "factors [that] contribute to life satisfaction and happiness" yielded three themes, the primary of which pertained to the importance of family in providing support, encouragement, care, and love (Edwards & Lopez, 2006). The salience of healthy parent–child relations has been confirmed by quantitative studies that yielded large correlations between adolescents' life satisfaction and their attachment relationship to parents, such that high life satisfaction co-occurred in the presence of a strong sense of trust (i.e., perceived security and understanding) in one's parents (Ma & Huebner, 2008; Nickerson & Nagle, 2004).

Qualitative and quantitative studies that have identified specific family interactions and circumstances associated with higher life satisfaction in youth provide guidance for those interested in arranging family environments to foster SWB. These desirable family-related factors include a loving and harmonious atmosphere among family members, particularly one in which warmth, encouragement, and concern is conveyed from parents to children; open and trusting communication; involved parents who are aware of their children's activities and whereabouts; minimal parent–child conflict; a comfortable physical home environment; permission for children to have a life outside of the family; and a sense of being irreplaceable, significant, and worthy within the family (Chang, McBride-Chang, Stewart, & Au, 2003; Flouri & Buchanan, 2002; Joronen & Astedt-Kurki, 2005; Leung, McBride-Chang, & Lai, 2004; Shek, 1997; Vera et al., 2008; Young, Miller, Norton, & Hill, 1995; Zimmerman, Salem, &Maton, 1995). Authoritative parenting, which involves parental provision of high levels of acceptance/involvement, strictness/supervision, and granting of psychological autonomy, is an approach to childrearing that captures many of these parenting behaviors. Adolescents who perceive their parents to convey high levels of authoritative parenting behaviors report greater life satisfaction (Milevsky, Schlechter, Netter, & Keehn, 2007; Suldo & Huebner, 2004a).

POSITIVE PEER RELATIONSHIPS

In Edwards and Lopez's (2006) qualitative research, a second prominent theme that emerged during discussions of factors crucial to adolescents' life satisfaction involved the importance of friends' provision of help and fun. Similar findings have emerged in quantitative studies in which adolescents' satisfaction with their friendships yielded

moderate to strong correlations with their global life satisfaction (Gilman, Easterbrooks, & Frey, 2004; Park & Huebner, 2005). Attachment theory research identified consistent links between higher quality attachment relationships with peers, and elevated life satisfaction among early adolescents (Nickerson & Nagle, 2004; Ma & Huebner, 2008). Although attachment to peers is not as strong a predictor as attachment to parents, Ma and Huebner's research demonstrated that it serves as a mediator through which parent attachment is associated with life satisfaction, particularly for girls, suggesting that intervening with peer relationships may offset the more distal influence of negative parent relationships. The aspect of peer attachment most salient to life satisfaction involves a trusting, committed relationship with one's peers, which is characterized by mutual caring, liking, and loyalty (Nickerson & Nagle, 2004).

Similarly, global life satisfaction is strongly and inversely associated with negative social interactions, including chronic stress experienced when interacting with others (Gilman & Huebner, 2006), loneliness (Buelga, Musitu, Murgui, & Pons, 2008), rejection and alienation from peers (Nickerson & Nagle, 2004), overt, reactive, and instrumental aggression enacted toward peers (Buelga et al., 2008), and perceptions of overt aggressive acts in which other students have harmed or threatened to harm a student's physical well-being (Martin & Huebner, 2007). Martin and Huebner's research with middle school students found that another facet of SWB, negative affect, was associated with higher levels of both overt aggression and a more covert type, deemed relational aggression. Logically, promoting students' SWB would involve attempts to ameliorate these social risk factors, as well as to increase protective factors such as receipt of prosocial acts (supportive acts enacted by peers; Martin & Huebner, 2007) and, in the case of immigrant youth, integration with peers from diverse ethnic backgrounds. Support for the latter comes from Neto's (2001) investigation of ethnically diverse high school students in Portugal, one-third of whom were born in a different country, which found that more out-group social interaction (i.e., free time spent with peers from other ethnic groups) was significantly related to higher life satisfaction, whereas frequency of interactions with peers of one's same ethnic group was not associated with life satisfaction.

HEALTHY SCHOOL CLIMATE

International studies have underscored the salience of a positive school climate to students' SWB.

For instance, a study of more than one thousand Norwegian adolescents identified perceived emotional support from teachers as the psychosocial predictor most strongly related to an increase in the odds of students feeling happy (Natvig, Albrektsen, & Qvarnstrom, 2003). Research with over 7,000 youth ages 11–15, from over 200 schools in northeast Italy, found that life satisfaction reports were higher among students who perceived a stronger sense of school community; specifically, greater levels of belongingness and acceptance at their school, fulfillment of academic needs, and a shared emotional connection to their school among students (Vieno, Santinello, Pastore, & Perkins, 2007). Of note, both of these studies are limited by use of a one-item indicator of SWB.

Research using a more comprehensive and valid indicator of life satisfaction found that perceptions of school climate explained 14% of the variance in high school students' global life satisfaction (Suldo, Shaffer, & Riley, 2008). This study identified significant bivariate relationships between life satisfaction and all six aspects of school climate that were examined, such that higher life satisfaction was associated with more positive perceptions of interpersonal relations among students, student–teacher relations, parental involvement in schooling, order and discipline, equal student access to school resources and activities, and the physical appearance of the school building. Two aspects of school climate—parental involvement and student–teacher relations—emerged as most strongly and uniquely associated with life satisfaction.

The likely positive effects of facilitating supportive student–teacher relationships, particularly emotional and instrumental support, to promote SWB in youth is also supported by a recent study of middle school students that found student perceptions of teacher support accounted for 16% of the variance in students' SWB (Suldo et al., 2009). While quantitative analyses in this study found that higher perceptions of emotional support (i.e., care, trust) and instrumental support (i.e., helping behaviors) were associated with increased SWB in a similar manner for both girls and boys, a qualitative follow-up portion of the study, in which students described teacher behaviors they felt conveyed support, suggests that teachers' efforts to promote SWB should be tailored to gender groups. Specifically, girls were particularly likely to perceive their teachers as supportive when they contributed to improving students' moods and emotional states, via such means as creating a positive emotional environment in the classroom and/or treating students respectfully—for instance, by being honest and maintaining student privacy. Boys, on the other hand, were much more likely to perceive teachers as supportive when they provided access to treats, pleasurable activities, a manageable (vs. overwhelming) academic workload, and/or better grades, as well as encouraged students to ask questions in class.

In sum, a growing body of literature confirms strong and consistent links between SWB and factors within youths' families, peer groups, and schools. Psychologists and educators can strive to promote SWB in children and adolescents by facilitating positive interactions with the important people with whom youth interact, as well as within the institutions in which youth function. While the importance of environmental-level health promotion efforts cannot be overstated, efforts to foster SWB must also address the important role of within-child states and individual-level child activities that are correlated with SWB. The intrapersonal correlates of life satisfaction discussed next (e.g., student engagement and activities, adaptive cognitive approaches such as hopeful and optimistic thinking) were selected for discussion because they all represent constructs that have the potential to be changed; intrapersonal correlates such as impulsivity, temperament, and personality characteristics are omitted from the subsequent review, because of their presumed stability.

Enhancing Child-Focused Factors that are Correlated with SWB

ENGAGEMENT AND ACTIVITIES

Life satisfaction is associated with how students spend their afterschool time, such that increased engagement (i.e., participation in extracurricular activities; being with others after school) is associated with higher life satisfaction compared to youth who are alone at home or with friends without adult supervision (Shek, 2007), or participate in fewer structured extracurricular activities (SEAs) during high school (Gilman, 2001). Gilman (2001) found that youth who participated in a greater number of SEAs (i.e., seven or more) were particularly satisfied with their schooling experiences relative to youth who participated in three or fewer SEAs. Involvement in SEAs at school can be conceptualized as a behavioral indicator of student engagement in schooling. Reschly and colleagues' (2008) recent research found consistent links between two other forms of student engagement (specifically, cognitive and psychological) and the affective component of SWB, such that students' frequent experiences of positive emotions at school co-occurred with (a) greater perceived relevance of schoolwork and future aspirations (i.e., cognitive engagement), and (b) more emotional support for learning from family and peers, as well as more positive student–teacher relationships (i.e., psychological engagement). In addition to these direct effects, greater positive affect (but not negative affect) was also linked to student engagement indirectly, through influencing students' use of adaptive coping strategies. Reschly et al. (2008) also found that students who reported less engagement in school experienced more frequent negative emotions while in the school setting.

Students' behavioral, cognitive, and psychological engagement with academic pursuits and extracurricular activities may be linked to their SWB because it enables them to derive a sense of personal meaning from their daily activities. This notion is consistent with results of a study of a diverse group of Australian youth (e.g., homeless teenagers, students at public and alternative schools), which found adolescents' sense of personal meaning (i.e., greater direction in life as well as a more coherent understanding of self, others, and life) to be the strongest predictor of their subjective quality of life (Bearsley & Cummins, 1999). In sum, assisting youth to use their time during and after school constructively, such that they (a) are engaged in their schooling, (b) participate in extracurricular activities that, ideally, are consistent with their personal interests and values, and (c) are cognizant of the fit between their daily activities and ultimate goals, should provide a fruitful avenue for promoting SWB in children and adolescents.

ADAPTIVE COGNITIONS

Even youth recognize the salience to their SWB of their interpretations of events and purposeful thinking. For instance, high school students in Edwards and Lopez's (2006) qualitative study frequently discussed the role of a positive attitude towards life and problems (e.g., being optimistic, trying your hardest) in maintaining high life satisfaction and happiness. Similar findings were obtained from a more covert, quantitative study of predictors of SWB among urban middle school students from minority racial and ethnic backgrounds, in which hope and optimism predicted over one-third of the variance in adolescents' global life satisfaction and positive affect (Vera et al., 2008). Just as it co-occurs with higher levels of optimism (i.e., the tendency to expect positive outcomes), life satisfaction is inversely

associated with dispositional pessimism (i.e., expectations for negative outcomes) in adolescents (Extremera, Duran, & Rey, 2007). Regarding the link between hope and SWB in youth, a growing body of literature has defined hope consistent with Snyder and colleagues' (2005) conceptualization, in which high hope entails being able to envision plausible routes to one's goals (i.e., pathways thinking) and to initiate and sustain movement toward these goals (i.e., agency thinking). These studies have confirmed that greater levels of hope predict increases in life satisfaction (Valle, Huebner, & Suldo, 2006) and positive affect (Ciarrochi, Heaven, & Davies, 2007) among adolescents, as well as co-occur with elevated life satisfaction and/or positive affect among samples of youth who are Mexican American (Edwards, Ong, & Lopez, 2007), primarily Caucasian (Gilman, Dooley, & Florell, 2006), and majority African American (Valle, Huebner, & Suldo, 2004).

Other cognitive dispositions that predict SWB include attributional styles and locus of control. Among high school students, an adaptive attributional style, in which one attributes positive events to internal causes and undesirable events to external causes, predicts subsequent decreases in negative affect, specifically fear and hostility (Ciarrochi, Heaven, & Davies, 2007), and is associated with higher concurrent levels of global life satisfaction (Rigby & Huebner, 2005) and elevated SWB (Nevin et al., 2005). Conversely, a maladaptive attributional style (i.e., the tendency to make internal, stable, and global attributions for negative events and external, unstable, and specific attributions following positive outcomes) is inversely correlated with life satisfaction (Rigby & Huebner, 2005). Youth with a more internal locus of control perceive higher life satisfaction (Ash & Huebner, 2001), such that adolescents who perceive a greater sense of mastery and control over their lives (i.e., an ability to influence their current and future circumstances) are more satisfied with their lives (Neto, 2001).

The extent to which youth expect, strive for, and attain lofty goals is correlated with their SWB, and some types of such perfectionistic thinking are adaptive. For instance, setting high standards for oneself and striving for personal excellence are associated with higher life satisfaction and/or positive affect among samples of gifted students in China (Chan, 2007), as well as among typical school-age youth in Croatia and America (Gilman & Ashby, 2003; Gilman, Ashby, Sverko, Florell, & Vargas, 2005). On the other hand, forms of maladaptive perfectionism, including a rigid adherence to one's high standards, avoidance of mistakes, and a discrepancy between one's high standards and actual performance, co-occur with more frequent negative emotions (Chan, 2007) and reduced global life satisfaction (Gilman et al., 2005).

Taken together, results suggest that promoting SWB among youth through enhancing child-focused correlates likely entails helping children and adolescents develop (a) more positive expectations about the potential to experience positive things in life (e.g., look on the bright side, expect good things to come from bad situations); (b) multiple methods to obtain one's future goals, as well as the confidence and motivation to follow these plans; (c) more adaptive attributions regarding the causes of positive and negative events; (d) a sense of personal control over situations; and (e) reasonably high yet flexible personal standards for performance.

Promoting SWB: Results of Empirical Studies that Target SWB

Due to evidence that an absence of mental illness is not sufficient for optimal mental health, interventions designed to increase children's happiness are necessary tools to use when addressing social/emotional functioning. In effect, an enhancement of SWB and the factors with which it is correlated may serve as protective factors against the occurrence of such negative outcomes as social/emotional difficulties and school failure. To date, however, most controlled-trial studies of the efficacy of specific interventions intended to increase SWB have been limited to samples of adults. Multiple happiness-increasing interventions for this population have now gained efficacy, demonstrating that intentional and/or goal directed activities can lead to sustainable gains in SWB. Specific interventions (i.e., experimenter facilitated, purposeful changes in behaviors and/or cognitions) shown to increase adults' SWB include communicating gratitude to others, identifying and using one's character strengths, performing acts of kindness, cultivating hope, and problem-solving/goal setting strategies. Two preliminary studies of targeted methods for manipulating children's cognitions and behaviors in order to increase SWB have provided promising results; these interventions have focused on gratitude and hope. Each of these areas of research will be discussed next, in order to provide the reader with an understanding of possible interventions that may yield a positive indirect or direct effect on SWB in youth.

Studies with Adults
GRATITUDE

According to Seligman (2002), positive and negative emotions related to the past are driven by thoughts and interpretations of past events, actions, and relationships. When one dwells on past events that have been interpreted negatively, negative emotion is increased. When negative evaluations are no longer the focus of thought, the adverse impact of negative evaluation on mood is extinguished. Similarly, focusing thoughts on positive interpretations of past events can hold emotion in the upper range of positive intensity. Gratitude, defined as one's perception that a positive event is the result of another's actions for oneself, and appreciation of those actions (Emmons & McCullough, 2003), works to increase SWB because it amplifies the intensity and frequency of positive memories. Furthermore, Sheldon and Lyubomirsky (2006) assert that the act of purposeful grateful thinking creates a state of savoring the moment in which all possible pleasurable feelings are maximized. In effect, hedonic adaptation (i.e., adaptation to positive changes in one's life causing a return to baseline happiness level from a temporarily elevated level) is prevented, in that the act of taking for granted positive events is incompatible with the expression of gratitude for them. This same concept of incompatibility can be taken further to include inhibition of excessive negative emotions, as well (e.g., anger, jealousy, greed; Sheldon & Lyubomirsky, 2006). It follows that grateful thinking could be conceptualized as an ability to appreciate life circumstances, as well as a mechanism of coping through reinterpretation of negative appraisals of events (Sheldon & Lyubomirsky, 2006). For example, one might initially interpret having a flat tire as an entirely negative experience, perseverating on the inconvenience and cost. However, grateful thinking might lead to a reevaluation in which one expresses gratitude for having an insurance company that offers roadside assistance at no extra cost, or a co-worker who gladly went the extra mile to cover the workload until the situation was resolved.

Emmons and McCullough (2003) found that daily attention to grateful thoughts significantly and noticeably increased positive affect and life satisfaction among adults. Practicing grateful thinking entailed "counting one's blessings," in that participants were asked to write down up to five things in their lives for which they felt grateful each day, for 2 or 3 weeks (termed a "grateful list"). Results showed that college undergraduates (N=166) and older adults with neuromuscular disease (N=65) who turned in a grateful list each week, rated their lives better and reported more positive affect than adults in control conditions (e.g., reflecting on stressors, no intervention). It is notable that Emmons and McCullough conducted this intervention initially utilizing a once-per-week basis for 10 weeks to reflect on and write down things for which one was grateful. However, they found that counting one's blessings on a *daily* basis for 2–3 weeks lead to greater increases in positive affect and life satisfaction, which was hypothesized by the researchers to be related to a presumed higher intensity of intervention inherent in more frequent implementation.

Additional studies of college students have suggested that the positive effect of contemplating the things for which one is grateful may be moderated by the duration and frequency with which grateful thinking is completed. Sheldon and Lyubomirsky (2006) modified the gratitude exercise described in the above study for an investigation involving 67 university undergraduates. Over the course of four weeks, participants in the gratitude exercise condition were asked to "cultivate a sense of gratitude" through identifying parts of life for which one is grateful, but had yet to express or act on such appreciation. Although students were asked to continue this line of thought over the course of the intervention, they were asked to write down their thoughts only once, while participating in a small group laboratory session with the researchers. In comparison, participants in the control condition were asked to generally think about the typical details and events of their day. As in the gratitude condition, participants were asked to write down their thoughts only during the laboratory session, and continue to mentally review their daily activities for the duration of the four weeks. Results showed that completion of the gratitude exercise on one occasion did not appear to significantly increase positive affect relative to control conditions, possibly due to the relative lack of intensity over time in accordance with the findings of Emmons and McCullough (2003). These findings are supportive of the "sustainable happiness" model, which suggests sustained effort is necessary in order to gain long-lasting increases in emotional wellness (Lyubomirsky, Sheldon, & Schkade, 2005). In contrast, counting one's blessings once per week for six weeks (vs. three times per week over the course of six weeks) resulted in short boosts of increased positive emotion from pre- to post-intervention in a previous study by the same researchers (Lyubomirsky et al., 2005). Considering this contrast with Emmons and McCullough (2003), possible satiation as well as intensity of activity may need to be balanced as factors relevant to the most effective intervention dose.

Seligman, Steen, Park, and Peterson (2005) conducted a study in which five interventions based on positive psychology theories of activities that should boost SWB were implemented via online registration and participation through the Internet. Over the course of six months, 411 adult participants (ages 35 to 54) completed exercises consistent with their randomly assigned intervention or control condition. The control condition consisted of writing about one's early memories, while two of the intervention conditions included exercises intended to increase gratitude (via either performance of a gratitude visit or gratitude journaling). Completion of a gratitude visit (i.e., writing and delivering a letter in person to someone who has been especially kind, but has never been properly thanked), and writing about three good things that went well each day, both resulted in positive changes in happiness. Interestingly, participants who wrote down three good things that went well each day, and their causes, over the course of one week experienced increases in happiness that only began one month after the intervention concluded, but lasted for at least five more months, suggesting that grateful thinking may have a delayed and long-term effect. Furthermore, those who completed gratitude visits showed the largest immediate positive gains compared across conditions, lasting through a one-month follow-up. However, the positive effects of the gratitude visit had diminished by three months. These results, coupled with outcomes of studies on creating grateful lists, suggest that varied methods of increasing grateful thinking are valuable avenues toward promoting positive short- and long-term effects on SWB.

CHARACTER STRENGTHS

According to Seligman (2002), positive emotions within the present include joy, zest, ecstasy, calm, pleasure, and ebullience. Typically, these are the emotions that people refer to when they discuss "happiness." There are two distinct types of present positive emotions, including pleasures (i.e., raw sensory feelings) and gratifications (i.e., full engagement or absorption in activities that are enjoyed through thinking, interpreting, and tapping into strengths and virtues). Since pleasures are fleeting, momentary, and of short duration, the focus of intervention research is on increasing gratifications, which are more highly related to long-term happiness outcomes (Seligman, 2002). Gratifications require identification and development of character strengths, challenging those strengths, and absorbing oneself into strength-related activities. Character strengths are moral virtues that are used voluntarily, in differing degrees, by individuals. An important distinction is necessary: *strengths* are dispositions to act that require judgment and enable people to thrive, whereas *talents* are qualities that one is born with but may be improved somewhat by purposeful actions (e.g., perfect pitch in one's singing voice, rhythm in dance, running speed). Therefore, character strengths (e.g., integrity, kindness, fairness, originality) are moral virtues that are developed and used by choice. For a complete list of character strengths, see Peterson and Seligman (2004).

In the previously described Internet-based study comparing interventions aimed at increasing happiness, Seligman and colleagues (2005) included two conditions involving identification of signature character strengths. In both conditions, participants completed the Values in Action (VIA; Peterson, Park, & Seligman, 2005) inventory of character strengths online, and received individualized feedback regarding their top five character strengths, termed *signature strengths*. The difference between conditions was based on behaviors that participants were asked to complete over one week, including either to take note of or use their signature strengths more often, or to choose one of their signature strengths and use it in a new and different way each day. Participants who used their signature strengths in new ways showed greater increases in happiness compared to participants involved in other positive psychology interventions, including the condition in which participants simply identified and used signature strengths in the same ways, but with increased frequency; moreover, the gains in happiness that were associated with using strengths in new ways were also marked by a longer duration (i.e., gains were maintained at one, three, and six months post-intervention). Seligman and colleagues hypothesized that the increased effort in creating new ways to utilize signature strengths may be related to the lasting impact on happiness. The behavior change component of this intervention seems crucial, as simply learning about one's character strengths did not cause changes in happiness.

ACTS OF KINDNESS

Lyubomirsky and colleagues (2005) discussed acts of kindness as a method for temporarily boosting moods, and contributing to long-lasting well-being through satisfying basic human needs of relatedness. Acts of kindness were defined as "behaviors that benefit other people or make others happy, usually at some cost to oneself (e.g., donating blood, helping a friend with a paper, writing a thank you note)" (Lyubomirsky et al., 2005, p. 125). They state that those who perform greater numbers of helping, prosocial behaviors tend to express higher ratings of happiness. This outcome was hypothesized by the researchers to be caused by several functions, including that performing acts of kindness (a) fosters a sense of community, cooperation, and interdependence; (b) initiates recognition of one's own good fortune; (c) creates expression of gratitude from others; (d) causes a greater sense of being liked by others; and (e) enhances social supports. Whereas Lyubomirsky et al. describe kindness in terms of social behavior, Park, Peterson, and Seligman (2004) defined kindness as a character strength, or virtue of humanity, which is a stable trait one can develop and utilize to impact well-being. By either frame of reference, the research bears out that adults' performance of kind acts is associated with their SWB.

In addition to investigating gratitude, Lyubomirsky et al. (2005) asked college undergraduates to perform five acts of kindness each week for a duration of six weeks. Students chose to perform these acts all in one day, or spread them over the course of the week. Results showed that those who performed five acts of kindness in one day each week showed a significant increase in SWB compared to a control condition; however, no increases were seen in students who spread the five acts over the course of the week. It was suggested that minor acts of kindness spread over time may have lost strength of impact among usual behaviors, whereas the concentration of kind acts in one day created a distinction with lasting impact.

In a study of Japanese undergraduates, a positive relationship between happiness and motivation to perform, enactment of, and recognition of kind behaviors was found (Otake, Shimai, Tanaka-Matsumi, Otsui, & Fredrickson, 2006). A "counting kindnesses" intervention was intended to increase participant awareness of their preexisting kind behaviors toward others. Each day for one week, 71 female undergraduate students kept track of every act of kindness they performed, and reported the daily total number of acts. Results found that simply counting the acts of kindness a person typically performs over one week's time reportedly increased happiness through one month follow-up, relative to students in a no-treatment control condition. Importantly, students with the greatest increase in happiness performed three times as many acts of kindness as their peers who experienced smaller gains. Taken together, these two studies of kindness suggest that frequency and amount of kind acts impact well-being.

HOPE

Snyder, Rand, and Sigmon (2005) discuss hope theory in terms of a "belief that one can find pathways to desired goals and become motivated to use those pathways" (p. 257). In the face of an obstacle, a person with a hopeful frame of mind would believe that another method to accomplish goals is accessible, and would devise potential avenues for successful outcomes. Motivation is defined as the belief that one can reach one's goals due to having the abilities in demand, and being able to obtain the resources necessary (Snyder et al., 2005). For example, if a student desired to play basketball but did not make the school's team, he might organize a recreational team in his neighborhood with the assistance of trusted adults as another path toward his goal. In this way, hope is conceptualized in terms of an expectation of, and motivation for, goal accomplishment.

Because they emphasize desired goals, potential paths to take to achieve such goals, and motivation for future success, studies on the positive outcomes of writing about life goals provide empirical tests of hope theory. King (2001) found that focusing on life goals in the form of an exercise known as one's "best possible self (BPS)" was highly associated with increased life satisfaction and optimism, as well as decreased negative affect. Eighty-one college students were assigned to one of four conditions, in which they were asked to write on one of the following topics for four consecutive days: (a) BPS in the future (i.e., the realization of all of your life dreams); (b) traumatic events personally experienced; (c) these topics in combination; or (d) detailed plans for the day (i.e., control condition). More specifically, those participants in the BPS condition were asked to imagine that they have accomplished all of their life goals, and write in detail about their perception of that experience. The traumatic events condition involved writing in detail about "some traumatic event or traumatic loss" personally experienced, and encouraged participants to express all emotions and thoughts related to that experience as well. Participants in the combination condition were

provided the instruction to write about traumatic events during the initial two days of implementation, whereas the final two days were dedicated to the BPS activity. Each controlled writing session lasted 20 minutes over four consecutive days. Measures of positive and negative affect were completed both before and after each session. Life satisfaction and optimism were measured three weeks post-intervention. Results found an immediate effect of intervention condition, such that participants who wrote narrative descriptions about their BPS in the future experienced increased positive affect, decreased negative affect, and increased physiological well-being (i.e., reduced number of health center visits for illness). Relative to students who wrote about traumatic experiences only, the BPS, alternating writing, and control groups all showed significantly higher levels of positive affect but did not differ substantially from one another. However, at 3-week follow-up, SWB (life satisfaction and optimism) increased only for participants in the BPS condition. King hypothesized that the latter result is possibly related to visualization of goal attainment, prompting motivation and actual efforts to reach goals, similar to the description of hope theory.

Additionally, results of a study by Sheldon and Lyubomirsky (2006) suggest that envisioning one's best possible self (i.e., a version of the future self having accomplished desired goals) is potentially beneficial to maintaining increased positive affect. In addition to the gratitude ($n=21$) and control conditions ($n=23$) described previously, these researchers asked 23 university students to "visualize and write [in detail] about their best possible selves" during the one-time research lab session, and then continue to do the exercise on their own over the course of the 4-week study (p. 75–77). These instructions were adapted from King (2001). Results showed an immediate increase in positive affect compared to the control conditon, but these gains in happiness were only maintained in participants who continued to perform the exercise on their own during the four weeks of the study (Sheldon & Lyubomirsky, 2006). Similar to hope theory, the researchers suggested that some participants continued the BPS exercise over the four weeks due to identification with goals imagined and desire to participate in goal planning. It could be the case that the more individuals identified with their imagined fulfilled goals, the more confident they became in terms of ability and resources to actually accomplish their goals. Overall, both studies found written expressions of hope to increase aspects of SWB (i.e., positive affect, life satisfaction) with the potential for gains to be maintained over time.

GOAL SETTING AND ATTAINMENT

Whereas the research related to hope focused on the belief that one can attain goals, there is evidence regarding positive outcomes of interventions focused on actual goal setting and attainment. Sheldon, Kasser, Smith, and Share (2002) developed a goal-training program aimed at improving participant ownership of their own goals, and actual ability to make efforts toward goal attainment. These researchers hypothesized that actual efforts made in the pursuit of goals would positively impact psychological functioning due to goal representation of action to create positive change, and further development of a purposeful, meaningful life. Initiated during the first week of the academic semester, the intervention included 90 university undergraduates who were randomly assigned to the goal training or control condition (i.e., an empirical investigation unrelated to personal goals). At three time points (prior to and completion of intervention, follow-up at the end of the university semester) all participants completed questionnaires of affect and well-being (specifically, adjustment and satisfaction in six psychosocial domains: autonomy, mastery, relationships, purpose, growth, and meaning). Participants in the goal training condition attended a single scripted 60-minute group session (held two weeks after pretest) and a single scripted 30-minute individual counseling session (held one week after group session). During these training periods, participants were directed to take ownership over their goals (i.e., reflect on meaningfulness of goals), develop a hierarchy of small to large goals, balance goals (i.e., equally divide effort among goals), and ensure an element of pleasurable activity in goal enactment. Analyses controlled for initial participant expectation for goal attainment, in order to ascertain the impact of actual progress on outcomes.

Participants who demonstrated progress toward their respective goals by mid-semester experienced significant increases in well-being and positive affect, as well as reduced negative affect, whereas expectancies did not impact SWB. Consequently, Sheldon et al. asserted that the experience of goal pursuit and attainment influence positive change, not simply motivation or positive attitude. This conclusion is contradictory to research supporting the construct of hope as described by Snyder and colleagues (2005). Taken together, it may be that individual differences exist in terms of the level of intensity needed for changes in self-perception of well-being and mood, in that some individuals may benefit from a hopeful frame of reference alone, while others experience greater impact through the physical pursuit of goals.

Research by MacLeod, Coates, and Hetherton (2008) demonstrated that both belief in, and actual progress toward, goals increases SWB. The specific intervention tested was comprised of teaching goal setting and planning (GAP) skills through participant selection of goals that are sought-after due to interest or pleasure, positive engagement with goals, and specific plan development for goal attainment. The investigation included two experimental conditions (group-based teaching of GAP skills, self-administered GAP training with telephone support) and a waitlist control condition comprised of adult and university student participants matched on age, gender, and community vs. student status. The 29 participants in the group-based teaching of GAP skills took part in one of three small group (i.e., 5–7 participants per group) training sessions for the duration of an hour, in the following sequence: first session, one week off; second session, two weeks off; and third session. The time between sessions was designed to accommodate participant enactment of assigned exercises on their own time. Sessions were based on manualized procedures and exercises, with the latter provided to the participants in personalized manuals that included both in-group and between-group exercises. In the self-administered condition of GAP training with minimal counselor support, a detailed, self-contained GAP manual based upon the group version was provided to 9 adults, who were instructed to read, follow, and complete the manualized exercises over five weeks. Researchers made four phone calls to each participant spread over the intervention implementation timeline. Relative to the control groups, participants trained in GAP skills through either modality experienced significant increases in positive affect, as well as greater self-efficacy for goal attainment. The group-based teaching of GAP skills yielded a significant increase in life satisfaction, and a nonsignificant trend toward increased life satisfaction was noted among participants in the self-administered GAP training condition. The self-administered condition was also associated with decreases in negative affect. Although results should be interpreted with caution due to the relatively small sample sizes, this research lends further support toward the utility of goalbased interventions for enhancing SWB.

PROBLEM SOLVING

Taking the literature a step further from goal creation and pursuit, Ayres and Malouff (2007) investigated the impact of increased control over one's life through enhanced problem-solving skills as a method for increasing life satisfaction and positive affect. Consistent with social cognitive theory (Bandura, 1997), Ayres and Malouff hypothesized that training in problem-solving skills would encourage more successful enactment of problem-solving steps that would lead to improved self-efficacy and perceived control over one's life, due to realization that issues and dissatisfactions can be resolved favorably, thereby improving SWB. Participants included 120 Australian flight attendants who had described their work environment as prescribing them little control or decision making allowance in daily activities. Participants randomly assigned to the intervention condition were trained in a multistep problem-solving procedure that included problem identification and definition, goal setting, generation and evaluation of potential solutions, plan implementation, and evaluation of one's belief in ability to put forth the effort needed for problem solving. Problem solving skills were taught in the context of goals that participants had previously identified, and pertinent barriers currently inhibiting goal attainment. For four weeks, participants maintained a twice-weekly journal in which they described efforts taken toward reaching goals. Intervention integrity checks were completed by phone calls to participants twice during the course of the intervention. Intervention group participants experienced growth in problem solving self-efficacy, life satisfaction, and positive affect relative to participants in a no-treatment control condition.

The goal-centered procedure for problem solving (i.e., identification of goals prior to learning and implementation of the problem-solving method) utilized in Ayres and Malouff's (2007) research suggests problem solving as a method of making progress toward goals. As described in the previous section, goal-based interventions have been empirically supported in promoting positive outcomes in terms of both the belief that one can attain goals (i.e., hope theory) as well as increasing actual ability to do so (i.e., goal planning/enactment). Considering these studies together, there are strong implications for the relevance of developing a hopeful frame of reference and viable skills to make positive change in one's life, as an avenue for increased well-being.

Studies with Children and Adolescents

GRATITUDE

In line with Emmons and McCullough's (2003) investigation into outcomes of grateful thinking, Froh, Sefick, and Emmons (2008) asked early adolescents to increase attention to areas of life for which they were grateful. In this study, gratitude was conceptualized as a state of emotion resulting from the realization that a positive impact on oneself was the result of a source beyond the self. The aim of the investigation was to elucidate the relationship between grateful thinking and SWB in adolescents, as a continuation of this line of research from the adult population, in part to determine if gratitude may be experienced differently by developmental stage, thereby impacting adolescents in a unique manner. Froh and colleagues asserted that since adolescence is a period of change as one transitions into adulthood, it may be an opportunistic time to enhance psychological growth through fostering strengths and buffering against negative outcomes.

Froh et al. (2008) duplicated the Emmons and McCullough (2003) methodology for increasing grateful thinking, and measured adolescents' SWB at multiple time points, including post-intervention (i.e., the last day of active participation in the experimental conditions) and three-week follow-up. Eleven sixth and seventh grade classes (N = 221 students) were randomly assigned to one of three conditions, including gratitude, hassles, or control groups. Students in the gratitude and hassles conditions completed activities specific to these conditions for a duration of two weeks. The four classes assigned to the gratitude condition were asked to think about the events of the past day, and list up to five things for which they were grateful (i.e., "count their blessings"). Conversely, the four classes assigned to the hassles conditions were asked to think about things that annoyed them over the past day, and write up to five hassles that occurred (i.e., "count their burdens"). The three classes in the control group completed the outcome measures and no activities. A notable difference in the implementation of this study methodology with adolescents included the use of teachers as intervention agents. Whereas adults are typically asked to complete exercises on their own time, students completed assigned exercises during class instructional time, as initiated and monitored by the classroom teacher. Random integrity checks were completed by the first author and school psychologist at the data collection site.

Students in the gratitude condition reported significantly less negative affect relative to students in the hassles condition at post-intervention, and maintained this difference at follow-up. Additionally, students enacting grateful thinking reported greater satisfaction with important domains of life. Specifically, they reported higher levels of school satisfaction at post-intervention as well as follow-up, compared to students in the hassles and control conditions, as well as greater satisfaction with their living environment than students in the hassles group at follow-up. Consistent with the positive outcomes of gratitude interventions previously identified with adults (Emmons & McCullough, 2003), Froh and colleagues (2008) found that exercises aimed at increasing gratitude were related to both short- and long-term changes in affect and domains of life satisfaction. Considering that the schooling experience is a major focus of adolescence, the particular finding related to increases in satisfaction with school is a notable outcome relative to optimized wellness in youth.

HOPE

As discussed earlier in this chapter, cross-sectional studies demonstrate that hope is correlated with multiple aspects of SWB during childhood and adolescence. To date, only one known intervention study has been conducted utilizing hope as a mechanism to increase well-being in this age group. Marques, Pais-Ribeiro, and Lopez (2007) developed an intervention for middle school students based on Snyder et al.'s (2005) hope theory with the aim of impacting life satisfaction, self-worth, level of hope, and mental health outcomes. Participants included 62 students assigned to either an intervention group or no-treatment control group comparison that was matched on demographics and pretest measures of the outcome variables. The intervention condition was divided into small groups of 6–8 students who participated in five weekly sessions of the "Building Hope for the Future" program, each lasting 50 minutes. Marques and colleagues' intervention was based on the unpublished hope intervention entitled, "Making Hope Happen" developed by Lopez and colleagues (2000), and modified for use with Portuguese youth. The Building Hope for the Future program included the following components: (a) developing and refining clear goals; (b) generating several pathways toward goals; (c) creating and maintaining motivation and energy for goal pursuit; and (d) framing potential obstacles as challenges that can be faced and succeeded.

As is described by Lopez, Floyd, Ulven, and Snyder (2000), the researchers incorporated a hopeful therapeutic relationship, and utilized cognitive-behavioral, solution focused, and narrative therapy techniques. To help promote goal setting and pursuit by students in the intervention condition, their parents and teachers were also provided with intervention manuals, and guided through intervention principles and procedures during a single one-hour session that occurred before the commencement of the small-group hope training with the students. Students who completed the hope intervention significantly increased life satisfaction, hope, and self-worth relative to the control group. The outcomes of this study indicate that goal-based interventions may be similarly useful for adolescents, as they have been found for adults.

Considered together, these two intervention studies with youth suggest that goal direction and belief in one's ability to attain goals, coupled with appreciation for events and people who help one successfully pursue goals, may comprise a powerful pathway toward optimized SWB in children and adolescents. In addition to replication of these preliminary results with additional samples of children and adolescents, studies with youth are clearly needed to evaluate the efficacy of other potentially SWB-increasing interventions that target kindness, character strengths, and problem solving.

Attending to SWB in School Psychology Professional Roles

The implications of the literature on SWB for the field of school psychology are enormous. The practice of school psychology has long been operationalized in many schools by a refer–test–place model, characterized by a search for pathology (Reschly & Ysseldyke, 1999). In this model, school psychologists become involved with students only after referrals are made from teachers or others. Following the receipt of the referral, presumably after a "problem" has already become serious, the task of the school psychologist is to "test" the child to determine the nature and determinants of the problems, and whether or not she or he is eligible for individualized interventions (e.g., special education). According to Clonan, Chafouleas, McDougal, & Riley-Tillman (2004), "such a deficit-oriented focus leads to treatment services that are primarily reactive, limited in scope (i.e., help only the disordered), and also delays the provision of services until a diagnosable disorder is manifest-thereby missing a critical window wherein more positive services that are potentially more efficient (e.g., of shorter duration) could be offered" (p. 102). In contrast, a focus on positive psychology incorporates a search for strengths, such as positive SWB, positive character traits, and characteristics of environments and institutions that facilitate positive SWB and character.

Assessment

In this manner, psychoeducational assessments that address negative (e.g., deficits) and positive (e.g., assets) aspects of children's behavior, emotions, and environments, provide a more comprehensive lens through which to understand, predict, and promote children's adaptation. Including measures, observations, and interview questions that focus on positive behaviors and emotions, personal strengths, and environmental assets, may enhance rapport with clients as well as client caregivers. Although most such methods are currently nonstandardized, informal methods related to personal strengths are elaborated upon in Epstein et al. (2003), while methods related to environmental strengths are elaborated upon in Huebner, Nagle, and Suldo (2003).

The inclusion of measures of positive emotions and life satisfaction enables assessments that estimate higher levels of SWB beyond a neutral point, differentiating among individuals who may be "mildly" happy versus those who may be "moderately" or "very" happy. To reiterate, given that the absence of a diagnosis is not equivalent to optimal functioning, such differentiations have been shown to be useful in cross-sectional studies (Gilman & Huebner, 2006; Suldo & Huebner, 2006) and may be useful in predictive studies as well (Haranin, Huebner & Suldo, 2007; Lewinsohn, Redner, & Seely, 1991). Students who show declines in SWB may be reflecting prodromal indicators of psychopathological conditions, or relapses, that may be amenable to early interventions to prevent such occurrences. Similarly, increases in SWB may afford more sensitive indicators of optimal levels of functioning as a result of naturally occurring or planned life changes (e.g., transition to secondary school, systematic psychosocial interventions). Whatever the case, large scale monitoring efforts (e.g., national monitoring systems of child well-being, school-wide assessments) as well as individual case studies should benefit from the inclusion of measures of SWB that include positive indicators reflecting the full range of functioning from "very low" to "very high" levels. Measures of positive emotions, such as the PANAS-C (Laurent et al., 1999), and of life satisfaction, such as the SLSS (Huebner, 1991),

MSLSS (Huebner, 1994), and the BMLSS (Huebner et al., 2003), should be helpful in this regard. A case study demonstrating the usefulness of measures of SWB and environmental assets is provided in Huebner, Gilman, and Suldo (2007).

Interventions

Positive SWB research supplements traditional deficit-focused intervention services, as well. In his Quality of Life Therapy approach, Frisch (2006) elucidates how a conjoint focus on symptoms and SWB data can inform a more comprehensive approach to treatment for individuals with psychological difficulties. Furthermore, Seligman, Rashid, and Parks (2006) demonstrated that clinically depressed individuals experience significant decreases in symptoms by participating in group or individual positive psychotherapy sessions that include positive SWB interventions (e.g., recalling three positive experiences during each day, expressing gratitude), and in some cases experience increasing levels of SWB even after the intervention has been terminated. Also, Beaver (2008) offers useful suggestions for how to focus on developing skills in children with internalizing disorders that may "better aid the family in helping children be happier and more fully engaged in their lives rather than settle for reduction in symptoms" (p. 134).

Suldo, Shaunessy, and Hardesty's (2008) research suggests the importance of amplifying positive coping skills (in particular, positive appraisal of challenging situations; communication with family members), in addition to decreasing negative coping skills (i.e., expressing anger and venting; substance use). Nevertheless, as noted by Lazarus (2003), scholars and practitioners should avoid an exclusive emphasis on positive characteristics of students and their lives, because an appreciation of the negative is necessary to fully experience the good. Also, Lazarus cautions that interpretations of positive SWB and behaviors must always be contextualized. Positive emotions may be adaptive in one situation but not in another, just as negative emotions may be maladaptive in one situation but not another. Similarly, King (2008) argues that long-term positive SWB should not reflect continuous positive emotions, but rather frequent positive emotions in the context of a rich emotional life. Although positive mean levels of SWB over time appear to promote healthy functioning, further research is needed to understand the complex interplay of specific emotions, moods, and longer-term SWB in various intervention contexts.

Nevertheless, the perceived benefits of sustained happiness has led some educators (e.g., Noddings, 2003) to propose that the promotion of children's positive SWB during their school years, and the development of the knowledge and skills essential to leading satisfying lives as adults, should be central aims of schooling for *all* children. To quote Noddings, "the best homes and schools are happy places. The adults in these happy places recognize that one aim of education is happiness. They also recognize that happiness serves as both means and end" (p. 261). Thus, effective school psychologists recognize the need to consider expanded conceptualizations of direct and indirect intervention services aimed at enhancing the SWB of children in the home, school, and community (Huebner, Suldo, Smith, & McKnight, 2004).

Conclusions

In a thought provoking book chapter, King (2008) raises the question, "Should we enhance subjective well-being?" (p. 432). Given the many individually and socially valued benefits associated with positive SWB, she concludes that efforts to enhance SWB are worthwhile. However, she cautions that "because of the problem of adaptation, however, it is important to focus not on the attainment of happiness, per se, but on engagement in life, particularly through the pursuit of important goals" (p. 443). Furthermore, recent research by Oishi, Diener, and Lucas (2007) suggests that optimal levels of SWB may vary for different outcomes. Specifically, they found that adults with the highest levels of SWB reported the highest levels of success in terms of social relationships, whereas those with slightly lower levels of SWB reported the highest levels of income, academic success, and political participation. Thus, the response to King's question may differ as a function of an individual or group's goals and values. Given the developmental differences among children, adolescents, and adults, the response may also vary as a function of age. Additional research is needed to clarify the conditions under which it is desirable to develop systematic interventions to promote positive SWB for specific children, and for specific purposes. Nevertheless, the growing body of studies summarized in this chapter that demonstrate the desirable educational, social, and physical health outcomes associated with high SWB in youth, suggests that promotion of children and adolescents' SWB is likely to be associated with a multitude of benefits.

References

Ash, C., & Huebner, E. S. (2001). Environmental events and life satisfaction reports of adolescents: A test of cognitive mediation. *School Psychology International, 22*, 32–336.

Ayres, J., & Malouff, J. M. (2007). Problem-solving training to help workers increase positive affect, job satisfaction, and life satisfaction. *European Journal of Work and Organizational Psychology, 16*, 279–294.

Bandura, A. (1997). *Self-efficacy: The exercise of control.* New York: Freeman.

Bearsley, C., & Cummins, R. A. (1999). No place called home: Life quality and purpose of homeless youths. *Journal of Social Distress and Homelessness, 8*, 207–226.

Beaver, B. R. (2008). A positive approach to children's internalizing problems. *Professional Psychology: Research and Practice, 39*, 129–136.

Berk, L. E. (2006). *Child Development* (7th ed.). Boston, MA: Pearson Education.

Blackman, J. A., & Gurka, M. J. (2007). Developmental and behavioral comorbidities of asthma in children. *Journal of Developmental and Behavioral Pediatrics, 28*, 92–99.

Buelga, S., Musitu, G., Murgui, S., & Pons, J. (2008). Reputation, loneliness, satisfaction with life, and aggressive behavior in adolescence. *The Spanish Journal of Psychology, 11*, 192–200.

Chan, D. W. (2007). Positive and negative perfectionism among Chinese gifted students in Hong Kong: Their relationships to general self-efficacy and subjective well-being. *Journal for the Education of the Gifted, 31*, 77–102.

Chang, L., McBride-Chang, C., Stewart, S. A., & Au, E. (2003). Life satisfaction, self-concept, and family relations in Chinese adolescents and children. *International Journal of Behavioral Development, 27*, 182–189.

Ciarrochi, J., Heaven, P. C. L., & Davies, F. (2007). The impact of hope, self-esteem, and attributional style on adolescents' school grades and emotional well-being: A longitudinal study. *Journal of Research in Personality, 41*, 1161–1178.

Clonan, S. M., Chafouleas S. M., McDougal, J. L., & Riley-Tillman, T. C. (2004). Positive psychology goes to school: Are we there yet? *Psychology in the Schools, 41*, 101–110.

Creed, P., Prideaux, L., & Patton, W. (2005). Antecedents and consequences of career decisional states in adolescence. *Journal of Vocational Behavior, 67*, 397–412.

Diener, E. (1984). Subjective well-being. *Psychological Bulletin, 95*, 542–575.

Diener, E. (2003). What is positive about the positive psychology: The curmudgeon and Pollyanna. *Psychological Inquiry, 14*, 115–120.

Diener, E., Scollon, C.M., & Lucas, R.E. (2004). The evolving concept of subjective well-being: The multifaceted nature of happiness. In P.T. Costa & I.C. Siegler (Eds.), *The psychology of aging: Vol. 15* (pp. 187–220). Amsterdam: Elsevier Science.

Diener, E., & Seligman, M. E. P. (2002). Very happy people. *Psychological Science, 13*, 81–84.

Edwards, L. M., & Lopez, S. J. (2006). Perceived family support, acculturation, and life satisfaction in Mexican American youth: A mixed-methods exploration. *Journal of Counseling Psychology, 53*, 279–287.

Edwards, L. M., Ong, A. D., & Lopez, S. J. (2007). Hope measurement in Mexican American youth. *Hispanic Journal of Behavioral Sciences, 29*, 225–241.

Eid, M., & Larsen, R. J. (2008). *The science of subjective well-being.* New York, NY: Guilford Press.

Emmons, R. A., & McCullough, M. E. (2003). Counting blessings versus burdens: An experimental investigation of gratitude and subjective well-being in daily life. *Journal of Personality and Social Psychology, 84(2)*, 377–389.

Epstein, M. H., Harniss, M. K., Robbins, V., Wheeler, L., Cyrulik, S., Kriz, M., Nelson, J. R. (2003). Strengths-based approaches to assessment in schools. In M. D. Weist, S. W. Evans, & N. A. Lever (Eds.), *Handbook of school mental health: Advancing practice and research* (pp. 285–299). New York: Kluwer.

Extremera, N., Duran, A., & Rey, L. (2007). Perceived emotional intelligence and dispositional optimism-pessimism: Analyzing their role in predicting psychological adjustment among adolescents. *Personality and Individual Differences, 42,* 1069–1079.

Flouri, E., & Buchanan, A. (2002). Life satisfaction in teenage boys: The moderate role of father involvement and bullying. *Aggressive Behavior, 28,* 126–133.

Frisch, M. B. (2006). *Quality of Life Therapy: Applying a life satisfaction approach to positive psychology and cognitive therapy.* New York: John Wiley & Sons Ltd.

Froh, J. J., Sefick, W. J., & Emmons, R. A. (2008). Counting blessings in early adolescents: An experimental study of gratitude and subjective well-being. *Journal of School Psychology, 46,* 213–233.

Gilman, R. (2001). The relationship between life satisfaction, social interest, and frequency of extracurricular activities among adolescent students. *Journal of Youth and Adolescence, 30,* 749–767.

Gilman, R., & Ashby, J. S. (2003). A first study of perfectionism and multidimensional life satisfaction among adolescents. *Journal of Early Adolescence, 23,* 218–235.

Gilman, R., Ashby, J. S., Sverko, D., Florell, D., & Varjas, K. (2005). The relationship between perfectionism and multidimensional life satisfaction among Croatian and American youth. *Personality and Individual Differences, 39,* 155–166.

Gilman, R., Dooley, J., & Florell, D. (2006). Relative levels of hope and their relationship with academic and psychological indicators among adolescents. *Journal of Social and Clinical Psychology, 25,* 166–178.

Gilman, R., Easterbrooks, S. R., & Frey, M. (2004). A preliminary study of multidimensional life satisfaction among deaf/hard of hearing youth across environmental settings. *Social Indicators Research, 66,* 143–164.

Gilman, R., & Huebner, E. S. (2006). Characteristics of adolescents who report very high life satisfaction. *Journal of Youth and Adolescence, 35,* 311–319.

Gilman, R., Huebner, E.S., Lili, T., Park, N., Langknecht, H., O'Byrne, J., Sverko, D., & Schiff, M. (2008). Cross-national adolescent multidimensional life satisfaction reports: Analyses of mean scores and response style differences. *Journal of Youth and Adolescence, 37,* 142–154.

Greenspoon, P. J., & Saklofske, D. H. (2001). Toward an integration of subjective well-being and psychopathology. *Social Indicators Research, 54,* 81–108.

Hall-Lande, J. A., Eisenberg, M. E., Christenson, S. L., & Neumark-Sztainer, D. (2007). Social isolation, psychological health, and protective factors in adolescence. *Adolescence, 42,* 265–286.

Haranin, E. C., Huebner, E. S., & Suldo, S. M., (2007). Predictive and incremental validity of global and domain-based adolescent life satisfaction reports. *Journal of Psychoeducational Assessment, 25,* 127–138.

Hartung, P. J., & Taber, B. J. (2008). Career construction and subjective well-being. *Journal of Career Assessment, 16,* 75–78.

Hexdall, C. M., & Huebner, E. S. (2007). Subjective well-being in pediatric oncology patients. *Applied Research in Quality of Life, 2,* 189–208.

Huebner, E. S. (1991). Initial development of the Students' Life Satisfaction Scale. *School Psychology International, 12,* 231–240.

Huebner, E. S. (1994). Preliminary development and validation of a multidimensional life satisfaction scale for children. *Psychological Assessment, 6,* 149–158.

Huebner, E. S. (2004). Research on assessment of life satisfaction of children and adolescents. *Social Indicators Research, 66,* 3–33.

Huebner, E.S., Drane, W.J., & Valois, R.F. (2000). Levels and demographic correlates of adolescent life satisfaction reports. *School Psychology International, 21,* 281–292.

Huebner, E. S., Gilman, R., & Suldo, S. M. (2007). Assessing perceived quality of life in children and youth. In S. R. Smith & L. Handler (Eds.), *Clinical assessment of children and adolescents: A practitioner's guide* (pp. 347–363) Mahwah, NJ: Lawrence Erlbaum Associates, Inc.

Huebner, E. S., Nagle, R. J., & Suldo, S. M. (2003). Quality of life assessment in child and adolescent health care: The Multidimensional Students' Life Satisfaction Scale (MSLSS). In M. L. Sirgy, D. Rahtz, & A. C. Samli (Eds.), *Advances in quality of life theory and research.* Dordrecht, Netherlands: Kluwer.

Huebner, E. S., Suldo, S. M., & Gilman, R. (2006). Life satisfaction. In G. G. Bear & K. M. Minke (Eds.), *Children's needs III: Development, prevention, and intervention.* Washingon, DC: National Association of School Pschologists.

Huebner, E. S., Suldo, S. M., Smith, L. C., & McKnight, C. G. (2004). Life satisfaction in children and youth: Empirical foundations and implications for school psychologists. *Psychology in the Schools, 41,* 81–93.

Huebner, E.S., Suldo, S.M., Valois, R.F., Drane, W.J., & Zullig, K.J. (2003). Brief Multidimensional Students' Life Satisfaction Scale: Gender, race, and grade effects. *Psychological Reports, 94,* 351–356.

Jones, M. D. (2006). Which is a better predictor of job performance? Job satisfaction or life satisfaction. *Journal of Behavioral and Applied Management, 8,* 20–42.

Joronen, K., & Astedt-Kurki, P. (2005). Familial contribution to adolescent subjective well-being. *International Journal of Nursing Practice, 11,* 125–133.

Kim, H. S., & Kim, H. S. (2008). Risk factors for suicide attempts among Korean adolescents. *Child Psychiatry & Human Development, 39,* 221–235.

King, L. A. (2001). The health benefits of writing about life goals. *Personality and Social Psychology Bulletin, 27,* 798–807.

King, L.A. (2008). Interventions for enhancing subjective well-being: Can we make people happier and should we? In M. Eid & R.J. Larsen (Eds.), *The science of subjective well-being* (pp. 431–448). New York: Guilford.

Laurent, J., Catanzaro, S. J., Joiner, T. E., Rudolph, K. D., Potter, K. I., & Lambert, S. et al. (1999). A measure of positive and negative affect for children: Scale development and preliminary validation. *Psychological Assessment, 11,* 326–338.

Lazarus, R. S. (2003). Does the positive psychology movement have legs? *Psychological Inquiry, 14,* 93–109.

Leung, C. Y., McBride-Chang, C., & Lai, B. P. (2004). Relations among maternal parenting style, academic competence, and life satisfaction in Chinese early adolescents. *Journal of Early Adolescence*, *24*, 113–143.

Lewinsohn, P., Redner, J., & Seely, J. (1991). The relationship between life satisfaction and psychosocial variables: New perspectives. In F. Strack, M. Argyle, & N. Schwartz (Eds.), *Subjective well-being* (pp. 193–212). New York: Plenum.

Lewis, A. J., Huebner, E. S., Reschly, A. L., & Valois, R. F. (2009). The incremental validity of positive emotions in predicting school functioning. *Journal of Psychoeducational Assessment*, *27*, 397–408.

Lopez, S. J., Bouwkamp, J., Edwards, L. E., & TerramotoPedrotti, J. (2000). *Making hope happen via brief interventions*. Paper presented at the Second Annual International Positive Psychology Summit, Washington, D. C.

Lopez, S. J., Floyd, R. K., Ulven, J. C., & Snyder, C. R. (2000). Hope therapy: Helping clients build a house of hope. In C. R. Snyder (Ed.). *Handbook of hope: Theory, measures, and applications* (pp. 123–150). San Diego: Academic Press.

Luster, T., & Small, S. A. (1994). Factors associated with sexual risk-taking behaviors among adolescents. *Journal of Marriage the Family*, *56*, 622–632.

Lyubomirsky, S. (2007). *The how of happiness: A scientific approach to getting the life you want*. New York: Plenum Press.

Lyubomirsky, S., Sheldon, K. M., & Schkade, D. (2005). Pursuing happiness: The architecture of sustainable change. *Review of General Psychology*, *9*, 111–131.

Lyubomirsky, King, & Diener (2005). The benefits of frequent positive affect: Does happiness lead to success? *Psychological Bulletin*, *13*, 803–855

Ma, C. Q., & Huebner, E. S. (2008). Attachment relationships and adolescents' life satisfaction: Some relationships matter more to girls than boys. *Psychology in the Schools*, *45*, 177–190.

MacLeod, A. K., Coates, E., & Hetherton, J. (2008). Increasing well-being through teaching goal-setting and planning skills: Results of a brief intervention. *Journal of Happiness Studies*, *9*, 185–196.

Marques, S. C., Pais-Ribeiro, J. L., & Lopez, S. J. (2007, December). *Hope intervention and psychological benefits in middle-school students*. Paper presented at the International Society for Quality-of-Life Studies Annual Conference, San Diego, CA.

Martin, K. M., & Huebner, E. S. (2007). Peer victimization and prosocial experiences and emotional well-being of middle school students. *Psychology in the Schools*, *44*, 199–208.

McKnight, C. G., Huebner, E. S., & Suldo, S. M. (2002). Relationships among stressful life events, temperament, problem behavior, and global life satisfaction in adolescents. *Psychology in the Schools*, *39*, 677–687.

Milevsky, A., Schlechter, M., Netter, S., & Keehn, D. (2007). Maternal and paternal parenting styles in adolescents: Associations with self-esteem, depression, and life satisfaction. *Journal of Child and Family Studies*, *16*, 39–47.

Myers, D.G. (1992). *The pursuit of happiness: Who is happy and why*. New York: William and Morrow.

Natvig, G. K., Albrektsen, G., & Qvarnstrom, U. (2003). Associations between psychosocial factors and happiness among school adolescents. *International Journal of Nursing Practice*, *9*, 166–175.

Nelson, R. M. & DeBacker, T. K. (2008). Achievement motivation in adolescents: The role of peer climate and best friends. *The Journal of Experimental Education*, *76*, 170–189.

Neto, F. (2001). Satisfaction with life among adolescents from immigrant families in Portugal. *Journal of Youth and Adolescence*, *30*, 53–67.

Nevin, S. Carr, A., Shevlin, M., Dooley, & Breaden, C. (2005). Factors related to well-being in Irish adolescents. *The Irish Journal of Psychology*, *26*, 123–136.

Nickerson, A. B., & Nagle, R. J. (2004). The influence of parent and peer attachments on life satisfaction in middle childhood and early adolescence. *Social Indicators Research*, *66*, 35–60.

Noddings, N. (2003). *Happiness and education*. Cambridge, UK: Cambridge University Press.

Oishi, S., Diener, E., & Lucas, R.E. (2007). The optimum level of well-being: Can people be too happy? *Psychological Science*, *2*, 346–360.

Otake, K., Shimai, S., Tanaka-Matsumi, J., Otsui, K., & Fredrickson, B. L. (2006). Happy people become happier through kindness: A counting kindnesses intervention. *Journal of Happiness Studies*, *7*, 361–375.

Park, N., & Huebner, E. S. (2005). A cross-cultural study of the levels and correlates of life satisfaction among adolescents. *Journal of Cross-Cultural Psychology*, *36*, 444–456.

Park, N., Peterson, C., & Seligman, M. E. P. (2004). Strengths of character and well-being. *Journal of Social and Clinical Psychology*, *23*, 603–619.

Pavot, W., & Diener, E. (1993). The review of the Satisfaction with Life Scale. *Psychological Assessment*, *5*, 164–172.

Peterson, C., Park, N., & Seligman, M.E.P. (2005). Assessment of character strengths. In G.P. Koocher, J.C. Norcross, & S.S. Hill III (Eds.), *Psychologists' desk reference* (2nd ed., pp. 93–98). New York: Oxford University Press.

Peterson, C., & Seligman, M.E.P. (2004). *Character strengths and virtues: A handbook and classification*. Washington, DC: American Psychological Association.

Piko, B. F. (2006). Satisfaction with psychological health and materialism among Hungarian youth. *Journal of Health Psychology*, *11*, 827–831.

Reschly, A. L., Huebner, E. S., Appleton, J. J., & Antaramian, S. (2008). Engagement as flourishing: The contribution of positive emotions and coping to adolescents' engagement at school and with learning. *Psychology in the Schools*, *45*, 419–431.

Reschly, D. J., & Ysseldyke, J. E. (1999). Paradigm shift: The past is not the future. In T. Gutkin & C. R. Reynolds (Eds.), *The handbook of school psychology* (3rd ed.; pp. 3–20). New York: Wiley.

Rigby, B. T., & Huebner, E. S. (2005). Do causal attributions mediate the relationship between personality characteristics and life satisfaction in adolescence? *Psychology in the Schools*, *42*, 91–99.

Roberts, B. W., Caspi, A., & Moffitt, T. E. (2003). Work experiences and personality development in young adulthood. *Journal of Personality and Social Psychology*, *84*, 582–593.

Russel, J. E. A. (2008). Promoting subjective well-being at work. *Journal of Career Assessment*, *16*, 117–131.

Schwartz, R., & Garmamoni, S. (1986). Structural model of positive and negative states of mind: Asymmetry in the internal dialogue. In P. C. Kendall (Ed.), *Advances in cognitive-behavioral research and therapy* (5th ed.) (pp. 1–62). New York: Academic Press.

Schwimmer, J. B., Burwinkle, T., & Varni, J. W. (2003). Health-related quality of life of severely obese children and adolescents. *Journal of the American Medical Association*, *289*, 1813–1819.

Seligman, M. E. P. (2002). *Authentic Happiness: Using the New Positive Psychology to Realize Your Potential for Lasting Fulfillment.* New York: Free Press.

Seligman, M. E. P., & Csikszentmihalyi, M. (2000). Positive psychology introduction. *American Psychologist, 55,* 5–14.

Seligman, M. E. P., Rashid, T., & Parks, A. C. (2006). Positive psychology. *American Psychologist, 61,* 774–788.

Seligman, M. E. P., Steen, T. A., Park, N., & Peterson, C. (2005). Positive psychology progress: Empirical validation of interventions. *American Psychologist, 60,* 410–421.

Shek, D. T. L. (1997). The relation of parent-adolescent conflict to adolescent psychological well-being, school adjustment, and problem behavior. *Social Behavior and Personality, 25,* 277–290.

Shek, D. T. L. (2007). After-school time and perceived parental control processes, parent-adolescent relationship qualities, and psychological well-being in Chinese adolescents in Hong Kong. *Family Therapy, 34,* 107–126.

Sheldon, K. M., Kasser, T., Smith, K., & Share, T. (2002). Personal goals and psychological growth: Testing an intervention to enhance goal attainment and personality integration. *Journal of Personality, 70,* 5–31.

Sheldon, K. M., & Lyubomirsky, S. (2006). How to increase and sustain positive emotion: The effects of expressing gratitude and visualizing best possible selves. *The Journal of Positive Psychology, 1,* 73–82.

Snyder, C. R., Rand, K. L., & Sigmon, D. R. (2005). Hope theory: A member of the positive psychology family. In C. R. Snyder & S. J. Lopez (Eds.), *Handbook of Positive Psychology* (pp. 257–276). New York: Oxford University Press, Inc.

Staw, B. M, Sutton, R. I., & Pelled, L. H. (1994). Employee positive emotion and favorable outcomes at the workplace. *Organization Science, 5,* 51–71.

Suldo, S. M., Friedrich, A. A., White, T., Farmer, J., Minch, D., & Michalowski, J. (2009). Teacher support and adolescents' subjective well-being: A mixed-methods investigation. *School Psychology Review, 38,* 67–85.

Suldo, S.M., & Huebner, E.S. (2004a). The role of life satisfaction in the relationship between authoritative parenting dimensions and adolescent behavior problems. *Social Indicators Research, 66,* 165–195.

Suldo, S.M., & Huebner, E.S. (2004b). Does life satisfaction moderate the effects of stressful life events on psychopathological behavior during adolescence? *School Psychology Quarterly, 19,* 93–105.

Suldo, S. M., & Huebner, E. S. (2006). Is extremely high life satisfaction during adolescence advantageous? *Social Indicators Research, 78,* 179–203.

Suldo, S. M., & Shaffer, E. J. (2007). Evaluation of the self-efficacy questionnaire for children in two samples of American adolescents. *Journal of Psychoeducational Assessment, 25,* 341–355.

Suldo, S. M., & Shaffer, E. J. (2008). Looking beyond psychopathology: The dual-factor model of mental health in youth. *School Psychology Review, 37,* 52–68.

Suldo, S. M., Shaffer, E. J., & Riley, K. N. (2008). A social-cognitive-behavioral model of academic predictors of adolescents' life satisfaction. *School Psychology Quarterly, 23,* 56–69.

Valle, M. F., Huebner, E. S., & Suldo, S. M. (2004). Further evaluation of the Children's Hope Scale. *Journal of Psychoeducational Assessment, 22,* 320–337.

Valle, M.F., Huebner, E.S., & Suldo, S.M. (2006). An analysis of hope as a psychological strength. *Journal of School Psychology, 44,* 393–406.

Valois, R. F., Paxton, R. J., Zullig, K. J., & Huebner, E. S. (2006). Life satisfaction and violent behaviors among middle school students. *Journal of Child and Family Studies, 15,* 695–707.

Valois, R. F., Zullig, K. J., Huebner, E. S., Kammermann, S. K., & Drane, W. J. (2002). Association between life satisfaction and sexual risk-taking behavior among adolescents. *Journal of Child and Family Studies, 11,* 427–440.

Vera, E., Thakral, C., Gonzales, R., Morgan, M., Conner, W., Caskey, R. et al. (2008). Subjective well-being in urban adolescents of color. *Cultural Diversity and Ethnic Minority Psychology, 14,* 224–233.

Vieno, A., Santinello, M., Pastore, M., & Perkins, D. D. (2007). Social support, sense of community in school, and self-efficacy as resources during early adolescence: An integrative model. *American Journal of Community Psychology, 39,* 177–190.

Wright, T. A., & Cropanzano, R. (2000). Psychological well-being and job satisfaction as predictors of job performance. *Journal of Occupational Health Psychology, 5,* 84–94.

Young, M. H., Miller, B. C., Norton, M. C., & Hill, E. J. (1995). The effect of parental supportive behaviors on life satisfaction of adolescent offspring. *Journal of Marriage and the Family, 57,* 813–822.

Zimmerman, M. A., Salem, D. A., & Maton, K. I. (1995). Family structure and psychosocial correaltes among urban African-American adolescent males. *Child Development, 66,* 1598–1613.

Zullig, K.J., Valois, R. F., Huebner, E. S., & Drane, J. W. (2005). Adolescent health-related quality of life nd perceived satisfaction with life. *Quality of Life Research, 14,* 1573–1584.

Efficacy of Special Education

Kenneth A. Kavale *and* Lucinda S. Spaulding

Abstract

This chapter discusses effective practices for improving special education student achievement outcomes. The early special education emphasis on process training (e.g., perceptual–motor training, psycholinguistic training) whose goal was to "fix" and "cure" students with disabilities is shown to be ineffective for improving student learning. Realizing that process training had limited efficacy, special education shifted emphasis to a teaching–learning paradigm, focused on academic instruction guided by research-based practices that permit student gains across content areas. This positive shift in emphasis is traced through the accumulated findings from quantitative research syntheses (i.e., meta-analyses) which themselves have been combined (i.e., mega-analysis) to inform the field about "what works" in special education.

Keywords: special education, process training, research-based practices, academic interventions, meta-analysis, mega-analysis, strategy instruction, direct instruction, school psychology

Introduction

Modern special education is usually traced to the work of Jean-Marc-Gaspard Itard with Victor, the Wild Boy of Aveyron (Itard, 1806/1962). In 1799, a "wild boy" was found in southeast France and, in 1800, was transferred to Paris where Itard developed a program for Victor's "mental and moral education" (p. 10). Although the carefully conceived educational activities enhanced sensory development, Victor did not develop speech and language skills, and his mental development stagnated with the onset of puberty leading Itard to terminate the program (Shattuck, 1994).

Although there has been the perception that Itard "failed" (e.g., Kirk & Johnson, 1951), in reality the outcomes attained by Victor were significant, and Itard "left us procedures which are still among the best we have after 170 years of practices and innovation. Few current educational interests fail to be illuminated by his single slender volume" (Gaynor, 1973, p. 445). The case of the "wild boy"

demonstrates that judging the efficacy of special education is often a subjective process. When special education is unable to "cure" children or "fix" disabilities, a disillusionment develops which soon leads to pessimism about the possibility for successful special education. The pessimism remains until the next new "solution" is offered, and its efficacy is less than promised. Slavin (1989) referred to this phenomenon as the "pendulum" of educational change: the enthusiastic adoption of an intervention, the initiation of research efforts, the dampening of enthusiasm due to inconclusive or insignificant findings, and the eventual abandonment of the intervention quickly followed by the enthusiastic adoption of another new intervention.

The cyclical nature of perceptions about the worth of special education has fostered the perception that there is little that is "new" in special education, because change often comes in the form of earlier solutions in a new guise that invariably fails. The consequences are evidenced by the view that special education is harmful, not helpful; evil, not good (Hallahan & Kauffman, 1994). The debate then shifts to answering the enduring question, "Is special education special?" (see Milofsky, 1974). Unfortunately, answers are too often provided at an ideological rather than an empirical level, leading to significant misunderstanding and misrepresentation about the meaning of special education (Hockenbury, Kauffman, & Hallahan, 1999–2000). For example, special education has been perceived as possessing no truly *special* instructional practices, but rather simply representing little more than good general education. Lost in this perception is the fact that "special education is about providing specially designed instruction that meets the needs of individual students. These individuals have disabilities that vary in complexity and severity" (Zigmond, Jenkins, Fuchs, Deno, & Fuchs, 1995, p. 306).

The picture, however, may not be as bleak as portrayed (see Fuchs & Fuchs, 1995a, 1995b). Over the past 25 years, special education research has made significant contributions and "these developments can be linked to the Individuals with Disabilities Education Act [(IDEA) which provided] not only educational services [but] also paved the way for dramatically altering the knowledge base about effective instructional practices" (Vaughn, Klingner, & Hughes, 2000, p. 163). The focus of this chapter is on synthesizing the available quantitative syntheses to demonstrate that special education can, in fact, be "special."

Special Education Research Traditions

Special education has long embraced the "scientific method" (Kauffman, 1987), and most special education research demonstrates an implicit recognition of the scientific method, as reflected in the way the research process is structured and findings are disseminated. Nevertheless, use of the scientific method has been criticized (e.g., Eisner, 1983) because it often produces findings that are seen as "obvious" (Gage, 1991). The "awful reputation" of educational research (Kaestle, 1993) has led to "counsels of despair" over the failure to produce long-lasting generalizations (Gage, 1996). Berliner (2002), however, suggested that the fault lies not in the scientific method but rather in the failure to recognize the complexity of scientific work in education—which too often fails to acknowledge the wide array of contexts wherein students find themselves, the ambiguity of interactions, and the possibility that earlier findings become negated by social, cultural, and intellectual changes.

Paradigm Wars

In discussing research on teaching, Gage (1989) described "paradigm wars" which led to a decline in empirical research on teaching. Special education has experienced similar paradigm wars with calls to replace the "Newtonian mechanistic paradigm" with a holistic paradigm (Heshusius, 1989). Similarly, Poplin (1988) advocated strongly for the elimination of the reductionistic foundation of special education, while Iano (1986) called for the replacement of the "natural science-technical model" with a human science model. These calls for radical change, however, have not gone unchallenged (e.g., Forness & Kavale, 1987; Kimball & Heron, 1988; Licht & Torgesen, 1989; Ulman & Rosenberg, 1986).

The paradigm wars in special education are best illustrated in two competing volumes *Challenging Orthodoxy in Special Education: Dissenting Voices* (Gallagher, Heshusius, Iano, & Skirtic, 2004) and *Challenging the Refusal of Reasoning in Special Education* (Mostert, Kavale, & Kauffman, 2008). From their postmodern base, Gallagher et al. (2004) suggested that "the untenable assumptions of the empiricist paradigm have literally produced the very problems that empiricist special education scholars have sought to resolve" (pp. 23–24). As suggested by Sasso (2001), however, the problem is that postmodernism offers only polemics, which only "reassures aspiring cultural critics that they can play a significant role in the treatment of disabilities without having to do anything" (p. 190).

Nevertheless, Gallagher et al. (2004) questioned the knowledge base in special education by suggesting that "there is no question the concepts of objectivity, predictability, certainty, and control have been completely undermined" (p. 364). When postmodernists use concepts like *justice* and *liberation* to support their views, it is erroneous to believe that such concepts have anything to do with judging the efficacy of special education. For example, Kauffman and Sasso (2006b) demonstrated that support for whole-language instruction in reading was based on ideology, not evidence. They maintained that empirical evidence is what counts, which means their view of reality rejects the postmodern view, even though the postmodernists reject theirs. In essence, there is no common ground in these positions—but the real world of special education demands that searching for a single truth at least be attempted: "Philosophical speculation about the nature of objectivity and reality may be personally fascinating, but it is not helpful in the face of everyday demands in dealing with what most people consider real children and real problems (Kauffman & Sasso, 2006a, p.117).

New Research Paradigms

The reauthorization of the Individuals with Disabilities Education Act (IDEA, 2004) stipulated that special education use teaching practices with proven effectiveness obtained from "scientifically based research" (see Eisenhart & Towne, 2003). For the National Research Council (Shavelson & Towne, 2002), the randomized control trial (also termed the *randomized experimental group design*) represents the "gold standard" in research design for demonstrating the effectiveness of an instructional technique. Like many other areas, however, there is presently a dearth of special education research employing the "gold standard" design (see Gersten, Baker, Flojo, & Hagan-Burke, 2004; Seethaler & Fuchs, 2005).

Nevertheless, special education has endorsed the "gold standard" as well as a strong commitment to other valid research methodologies (Odom, Brantlinger, Horner, Thompson, & Harris, 2005). These include nonrandomized group designs (Gersten, Fuchs, Greenwood, & Innocenti, 2004), correlational studies (Thompson, Diamond, McWilliam, Snyder, & Synder, 2004), single subject research (Horner et al., 2004), and qualitative research (Brantlinger, Jimenez, Klingner, Pogach, & Richardson, 2005). The goal is to stimulate rigorous "scientific" research in special education to create a reliable and valid knowledge base (see Feuer, Towne, & Shavelson, 2002). Nevertheless, postmodern critics continue to view the knowledge base in special education as irrelevant (Brantlinger, 1997). Forness (2005) suggested that special education does possess a strong research base, but the problem has been one of presenting these "evidence-based practices in a default mode. Rather than specifying substantive criteria for our evidence-based practices, and delineating those practices that meet criteria, we have been offering up such practices primarily as rebuttals or refutations to special education critics" (p. 312).

Research Synthesis

Traditionally, the narrative review is the most common method for research synthesis. In reality, the narrative review provides limited accumulation of knowledge, and tends to keep individual findings independent and isolated, which means knowledge tends to be neither corroborated nor refuted. Similarly, research synthesis sometimes employs numerical (vote-counting) methods based on classification of study outcomes (e.g., statistical significance or nonsignificance) but the vagaries of statistical inference make outcomes problematic for deciding subject matter issues (see Morrison & Henkel, 1970). In fact, Hedges and Olkin (1980) found that, "the power of this procedure decreases as the number of studies reviewed increases" (p. 359).

Meta-analysis offers the possibility for a systematic and rigorous summarization of individual study findings, which permits the empirical generalizability of findings rather than solely the logical methods common in the behavioral sciences (Glass, 1976). The techniques of meta-analysis have been comprehensively reported (e.g., Cooper & Hedges, 1994; Glass, McGaw, & Smith, 1981; Hunter, Schmidt, & Jackson, 1982). The essential feature of meta-analysis is the "effect size" (ES) statistic which transforms study data into a z-score (standard deviation [SD]) representing the magnitude of treatment effects (Kavale, 2001b). Among the advantages of meta-analysis is the flexibility afforded in ES interpretation (Cook et al., 1992). As an SD, the meaning of an ES may be conveyed through notions of overlapping distributions and comparable percentiles. For example, suppose an intervention reveals an ES = 1.00 for the treated group. This 1 SD advantage indicates that a student at the 50th percentile of the comparison group would gain 34 percentile ranks as a result of the intervention, and rise to the 84th percentile of the comparison group distribution. The relationship suggests that a student receiving the intervention would be better off than 84% of the control group, whereas only 16% of the control group would be better off than a student receiving the intervention.

In some instances, ESs are themselves meaningful; e.g., zero and negative (group not receiving the intervention does better). Based on notions of statistical power, Cohen (1988) provided "rules of thumb" whereby ES can be classified as small (0.20), medium (0.50), or large (> 0.80). Rosenthal and Rubin (1983) offered the "binomial effect size display" (BESD) that addresses the question: What is the percentile increase in the number of successful responses when using a new practice? Based on converting ES to r, the BESD for intervention X (ES = 1.16, for example) would show an increase in success rate from 25% to 75%. The 50-percentage-point spread between treatment (75%) and comparison (25%) success rate indicates that intervention X possesses not only statistical significance, but also *practical* significance (Kirk, 1996). Another alternative ES interpretation was provided by McGraw and Wong (1992) in the "common language effect size" (CLES) which converts ES into a probability indicating that a score sampled from one distribution will be greater than a score sampled from another. For example, a sample of studies investigating intervention Y that produces a CLES of 0.83 indicates that 83 out of 100 subjects would show improvement with the use of intervention Y. Thus, the ES metric imparts a clarity and explicitness to empirical findings, which produces synthesized evidence that is more objective and verifiable for making decisions about "what works" (Kavale, 2001a).

Meta-analysis thus affords the opportunity to summarize research findings and provide the empirical evidence necessary to judge efficacy (Forness, 2001). Even more insight may be gleaned by combining the findings from individual meta-analyses into what may be termed a "mega-analysis" (Forness, Kavale, Blum, & Lloyd, 1997). Special education has produced a significant number of meta-analyses (see Appendix A), which served as the basis for the mega-analyses presented in this chapter.

In discussing evidence-based practice (e.g., Chambless & Hollon, 1998; Hoagwood, 2003–2004), the primary problem is how to determine what practices are properly deemed to be evidence based. It is our contention that mega-analyses meet the criterion for evidence-based practice: "organization of research domains, identification of research studies, review of studies, evaluation and analysis to develop a research synthesis, and a summarization of findings that involves interpretation, presentation, and dissemination of information in [evidence based interventions]" (Kratochwill & Shernoff, 2004, p. 35). By synthesizing existing quantitative research syntheses, it is possible to organize large

numbers of primary research studies into a structure that provides insights into the nature of effective special education practices.

Process Training: Special Education's Intervention of Choice

From the time of Itard and his student Edouard Séguin (see Séguin, 1866), process training dominated practice in special education. The emphasis on process training reflected special education's commitment to the medical model; academic problems were regarded as a "disease" and interventions were aimed at "curing" the disease (i.e., removing the pathology; Kauffman & Hallahan, 1974). The dominance of process training was based on the assumption that the goal of special education was correcting or reversing altered learning functions. The aim was to enhance cognitive processes so students in special education might then be able to learn in the same way as students in general education. Mann (1979) traced the history of process training, and demonstrated that special education retained a strong belief that process training allowed "the precise delineation of cognitive processes and the equally precise fitting of developmental and remedial stratagems and tactics to children's individual needs" (p. 440). Following the work of Strauss and Kephart (1955), process training remained a major form of intervention in special education. Although a predominant intervention, it nevertheless remains important to ask: Is process training effective? The efficacy of major process training approaches is shown in Table 25.1.

Perceptual-Motor Training

Perceptual motor training represented a major process intervention until about 1975. During the

Table 25.1 Effectiveness of process training

Method	Mean ES	Percentile Rank Equivalent	Power Rating
Irlen Lenses	–0.02	49	Negative
Perceptual-Motor Training	0.08	53	Negligible
Diet Modification (Feingold)	0.12	55	Small
Modality-Matched Instruction	0.14	56	Small
Social Skills Training	0.23	64	Small
Psycholinguistic Training	0.39	65	Small–Medium
Frostig Visual Perceptual Training	0.10	54	Negligible–Small

1960s, the nature of process deficits was explicated in theoretical formulations offered by Kephart (1960), Frostig (see Frostig & Horne, 1964) and Barsch (1967), among others. These theoretical speculations were often accompanied by training programs aimed at enhancing the processes that were assumed to underlie learning failure. Thus, process training possessed a powerful intuitive appeal, captured in the assumption that what is most fundamental is training of the mind and its processes (powers, abilities, capacities, faculties).

A number of clinical reports popularized perceptual motor training as a favored intervention for the new category of "specific learning disability" (SLD; e.g., Arena, 1969; Barsch, 1967; Van Witson, 1967). The emerging empirical evaluations, however, did not appear to favor perceptual–motor training (e.g., Balow, 1971; Goodman & Hammill, 1973; Hammill, Goodman, & Weiderholt, 1974). Yet, the unfavorable empirical evidence was interpreted to suggest that, "although no persuasive empirical evidence has been brought to the fore in support of perceptual–motor training, neither has there been solid negative evidence" (Hallahan & Cruickshank, 1973, p. 216). Besides debate about empirical research findings, there were increasingly heated ideological debates (see Kephart, 1972; Mann, 1970) which led to reorganization of the major SLD organizations (i.e., Council for Learning Disabilities, Division of Learning Disabilities) because of disagreement over the nature of SLD and the preferred approach to remediation.

Using the methods of meta-analysis, Kavale and Mattson (1983) synthesized the findings from 180 investigations examining the effectiveness of perceptual–motor training. The average ES was 0.08, which, using Cohen's (1988) rules of thumb, is deemed "very small." If two distributions (intervention versus no intervention) separated by 0.08 standard deviations, the difference indicates that a student who is not better off than average (i.e., at the 50th percentile) rises to the 53rd percentile, for a minimal 3 percentile gain on an outcome measure. Among the ES measurements, 48% were negative, suggesting that almost half the time, students *not* receiving perceptual–motor training revealed enhanced performance. By any comparative standard, perceptual–motor training does not appear to be an efficacious intervention.

Although it is possible that a single ES (0.08) may mask particular instances where perceptual–motor training might be effective, further analyses spanning a diverse assortment of outcome assessments, student classifications, and grade levels also revealed "small" ES. The average expected yearly academic progress for the average student is ES = 1.00 which makes perceptual–motor training approximately 10 times *less* effective than teacher-delivered instruction. For example, the effects associated with the most popular perceptual–motor programs were "small" and produced gains ranging from 2 (Kephart) to 6 (Barsch) percentile ranks. In fact, the programs used most often (Kephart & Frostig) produced the smallest effects (ES = 0.06 and 0.10, respectively).

Perceptual–motor training revealed no indications of being an effective intervention, but seductive clinical reports and positive anecdotal evidence have supported its continued use. Although the Kavale and Mattson (1983) meta-analysis appeared to offer unequivocal negative evidence, historical tradition and intuitive appeal prevents the acceptance of negative evidence because, "it is injudicious to decide wholeheartedly that perceptual–motor training deserves or does not deserve approval" (Hallahan & Cruickshank, 1973, p. 216). Fundamental belief in perceptual–motor training is thus difficult to dislodge, and new forms like *Brain Gym* (Dennison & Dennison, 1994) continue to appear (see also Hyatt, 2007). As suggested by Mann (1979):

> Process training has always made the phoenix look like a bedraggled sparrow. You cannot kill it.
> It simply bides its time in exile after being dislodged by one of history's periodic attacks upon it and then returns, wearing disguises or carrying new *noms de plume*, as it were, but consisting of the same old ideas doing business much in the same old way. (p. 539)

Psycholinguistic Training

The controversy over process training is also illustrated by psycholinguistic training. Based on a theoretical model developed by the psychologist Charles Osgood (1957), Samuel A. Kirk developed the Illinois Test of Psycholinguistic Abilities (ITPA; Kirk, McCarthy, & Kirk, 1968) whose findings were assumed to reveal intra-individual deficits which would then be treated with a variety of remedial programs. The assumption that discrete psychological and linguistic abilities can be identified and trained, initiated debate evidenced by differing interpretations about the efficacy of psycholinguistic training.

Hammill and Larsen (1974) summarized the findings from 39 studies based on statistical significance or nonsignificance. This "vote-counting" methodology led to the conclusion that "researchers have been unsuccessful in developing those skills which would enable their subjects to do well on ITPA [and] the idea that psycholinguistic construct, as measured by ITPA, can be trained by existing techniques remains invalidated" (pp. 10–11).

Minskoff (1975) critiqued the Hammill and Larsen (1974) review and concluded that psycholinguistic deficits could respond to training. Newcomer, Larsen, and Hammill (1975) challenged Minskoff's (1975) conclusions and suggested that "psycholinguistic training based on the Kirk-Osgood model is unsuccessful because it does not help children improve their ability to speak or understand language, nor apparently does it aid them in academic skills such as reading, writing, or spelling" (p. 147).

The next interpretation came 3 years later when Lund, Foster, and McCall-Perez (1978) reevaluated the 39 studies analyzed by Hammill and Larsen (1974) and reported:

> Our analysis indicated that some studies show significant positive results as measured by ITPA, some studies show positive results in the areas remediated, and some do not show results from which an conclusion can be drawn. It is, therefore, not logical to conclude either that all studies in psycholinguistic training are effective or that all studies in psycholinguistic training are not effective. (p. 317)

The debate continued with Hammill and Larsen's (1978) reaffirmation of their original position by concluding that "the overwhelming consensus of research evidence concerning the effectiveness of psycholinguistic training is that it remains essentially non-validated" (p. 412). They then went on to suggest that "regardless of the reevaluations by pro-psycholinguistic educators, the current state of research strongly questions the efficacy of psycholinguistic training and suggests that programs designed to improve psycholinguistic functioning need to be viewed cautiously and monitored with great care" (p. 413).

After 5 years, a fundamental question remained: What is really known about the efficacy of psycholinguistic training? Kavale (1981) conducted a meta-analysis on 34 studies investigating psycholinguistic training and found an ES of 0.39, indicating that the average subject gained approximately 15 percentile ranks on the ITPA. Using Cohen's rules of thumb, 0.39 ES falls slightly above the midpoint between "small" (0.20) and "medium" (0.50).

Because of the emphasis on subtest analysis, the 0.39 ES for total ITPA score may not be informative. Table 25.2 displays ES data classified by ITPA subtest. Five of the ten regularly administered ITPA subtests reveal small, albeit positive, effects, making it questionable whether these psycholinguistic abilities respond to training, or whether they should be trained at all. For four subtests, however, training was found to be more effective: Auditory and Visual Association, and Verbal and Manual Expression. Psycholinguistic Training of these psycholinguistic abilities improved functioning from 15 to 24 percentile ranks on the ITPA. Thus, the average trained

Table 25.2 Average effect size for psycholinguistic training by Illinois Test of Psycholinguistic Abilities (ITPA) subtest

ITPA Subtest	Mean Effect Size	Percentile Equivalent
Auditory Perception	0.21	58
Visual Reception	0.21	58
Auditory Association	0.44	67
Visual Association	0.39	65
Verbal Expression	0.63	74
Manual Expression	0.54	71
Grammatic Closure	0.30	62
Visual Closure	0.48	68
Auditory Sequential Memory	0.32	63
Visual Sequential Memory	0.27	61

subject would be better off than approximately 65% to 74% of untrained subjects with respect to these associative and expressive abilities.

Kavale's (1981) findings indicated that, although some ITPA subtests do not respond to remedial efforts, a majority revealed a positive response to training. The gains realized on most ITPA subtests would appear to contravene the conclusion that "neither the ITPA subtests nor their theoretical constructs are particularly ameliorative" (Hammill & Larsen, 1974, p. 12). The benefits of psycholinguistic training for Verbal Expression were particularly noteworthy since they embodied the "linguistic" aspects of the ITPA and the tangible skill of productive language behavior critical for academic success. Practically, for a basic skill area like language, the average elementary-level student would gain approximately one year on a language achievement measure (ES = 1.00) after one year of schooling. After about 50 hours of psycholinguistic training, the ITPA Verbal Expression subtest revealed benefits (ES = 0.63) that actually exceeded those expected from one-half year of school-based language instruction (ES = 0.50). Unlike perceptual–motor training, psycholinguistic training appears to produce selected benefits.

Effective Special Education

With the realization that process training was ineffective, special education began to focus on the instructional process and improving the teaching-learning process for students with disabilities. Special education thus became better aligned with its formal definition as "specially designed individualized or group instruction or special services or programs...to meet the unique needs of students with disabilities" (U. S. Department of Education, 2006, p. 223). The increased focus on enhancing the education of students with disabilities was also necessitated for legal reasons. Over the past 35 years, special education policy has shifted from "whether students with disabilities should receive a special education" to concerns about "what constitutes a free and appropriate public education (FAPE)." The Rowley case (Board of Education of the Henrik Hudson Central School District vs. Rowley, 1982) indicated that a FAPE consists of "specially designed instruction" and related services that are "individually designed to provide educational benefit." The educational benefit criterion was interpreted to mean that schools need not provide an ideal education seeking to maximize potential but rather a beneficial one that provides "meaningful progress"

(Huefner, 1991), which is defined by academic progress: "Although no court has established any one standard for all students with disabilities, there are standards that require a measure of academic progress" (Laski, 1997, p. 79). Thus, academic instruction became a significant marker in judging whether a FAPE yields benefits.

To aid the FAPE process, special education identified critical features of instruction to ensure that students with high-incidence disabilities (SLD, Intellectual Disability [ID], emotional/behavioral disorder [E/BD]) received the best possible FAPE. For example, Christenson, Ysseldyke, and Thurlow (1989) listed 10 essential factors shown in Table 25.3. These instructional factors have been repeatedly reinforced. For example, Meese (2001) listed empirically validated instructional practices and grouping arrangements, which are displayed in Table 25.4. In extending this work, Kame'enui and Carnine (1998) discussed basing instructions on six design principles: big ideas, mediated scaffolding, conspicuous strategies, strategic integration, primed background knowledge, and judicious review.

Generally, it was concluded that good special education parallels good general education, but requires a more individualized and comprehensive perspective. For example, Polloway and Patton (1997) provided an instructional model based on

Table 25.3 Instructional factors for students with mild disabilities factors

- The degree to which classroom management is effective and efficient
- The degree to which there is a sense of "positiveness" in the school environment
- The degree to which there is an appropriate instructional match
- The degree to which teaching goals and teacher expectations for student performance and success are stated clearly and are understood by the student
- The degree to which lessons are presented clearly and follow specific instructional procedures
- The degree to which instructional support is provided for the individual student
- The degree to which sufficient time is allocated to academics and instructional time is used efficiently
- The degree to which the student's opportunity to respond is high
- The degree to which the teacher actively monitors student progress and understanding
- The degree to which student performance is evaluated appropriately and frequently

Table 25.4 Effective approaches for students with mild disabilities instructional practices

- Explicit, well-structured lessons
- Tasks defined by sequenced steps
- Providing clear examples
- Direct measurement of student progress
- Clear feedback
- Repetition to mastery
- Supervised and independent practice
- Strategies to insure maintenance and generalization
- Modifications to accommodate unique learner characteristics

Grouping Arrangements

- Cooperative learning
- Flexible grouping based on need and skill
- Peer tutoring
- Collaborative teaching

three dimensions of effective practice: management considerations, instructional practices, and evaluative and collaborative activities. The model thus emphasizes activities that precede instruction, the actual instructional procedures and activities after instruction, which are viewed as interactive and necessary for effective special education.

Undoubtedly, a major difference between general and special education is the emphasis on the individual, which requires judgments about the rate, amount, and manner of presentation for a particular student, rather than a larger group of students. Additionally, successful learning for students with disabilities requires more feedback, as well as efforts directed at maintenance and generalization of learned knowledge (see Bos & Vaughn, 2002; Mastropieri & Scruggs, 2004).

Accessing General Education

Syntheses of special education intervention research have identified effective instructional practices that include *explicit* instruction for skill building, as well as the development of particular instructional strategies for reading, mathematics, and writing (Swanson, Hoskin, & Lee, 1999; Vaughn, Gersten, & Chard, 2000). The problem, however, is in implementing effective *special education* practices in often very different *general education* settings. King-Sears (2001) suggested three steps for improving the academic learning for students with disabilities in the general education classroom: a) analyze the general education curriculum to identify accessible resources; b) enhance areas of the general education curriculum as required; and c) identify and implement modifications to make curriculum access easier.

General education often has inappropriate resources that lack design features to support learning for students with disabilities. For example, reviews of programs and textbooks suggest they are often not accessible to students with disabilities (e.g., Harniss, Dickson, Kinder, & Hollenbeck, 2001; Jitendra et al., 2001). Smith et al. (2001), in an analysis of the phonological awareness component of four kindergarten reading programs, found that they lacked validated instructional design features like systematically sequencing tasks, increasing opportunities to produce sounds at the phoneme level, and providing suggestions for scaffolding tasks and materials. Similar deficiencies were found for math programs (Jitendra, Salmento, & Haydt, 1999) and writing programs (Gleason & Isaacson, 2001). Consequently, implementation of good instruction requires teachers to include missing material, and add supports such as modeling and explicit instruction, providing scaffolds, and developing background conceptual knowledge.

Special Education and the Intensity of Instruction

Efforts to enhance general education curriculum should focus on increasing the level of intensity with which instruction is provided (Foorman & Torgesen, 2001). Besides intensity, Kame'enui and Carnine (1998) described "big ideas" for reading instruction including phonemic awareness, phonics, fluency, vocabulary, and constructing meaning for reading (see Coyne, Kame'enui, & Simmons, 2001). In the math area, number sense, geometric thinking, computational proficiency, and problem solving represent "big ideas" (Cawley, Parmar, Foley, Salmon, & Roy, 2001), while big ideas for writing include mechanics, writing genre, spelling, and handwriting (Graham, Harris, & Larsen, 2001).

Access to the general education curriculum usually begins with efforts aimed at the prevention of future difficulties. The preventative instruction is delivered to a whole class, with the goal of providing students with disabilities the opportunity to master fundamental skills in the context of general education. These efforts have been shown to be effective for reading (O'Connor, 2000), mathematics (L. Fuchs & D. Fuchs, 2001), and written expression (Graham et al., 2001). Fuchs and Fuchs suggested that sound prevention practices are those that a) have demonstrated effectiveness, b) are research-based, and c) contain *universal design* features, which means that the elements of instruction enhance learning for students with disabilities, but are also appropriate for students without disabilities.

Nevertheless, preventive practices are often not enough, and more intensive instruction is required, which may be achieved by increasing instructional time and reducing group size (Foorman & Torgesen, 2001). Additionally, more explicit instruction may be required that is achieved when students with disabilities are taught the strategies used by more effective learners. To enhance explicit instruction, strategies need to be identified and modeled, students need to demonstrate their use in isolation, students need to explain why and how they use a strategy, and students need to be provided with substantial feedback (Gersten, 1998). In addition to making instruction more explicit and intensive, increased efficacy has also been shown to be associated with aligning task difficulty and student level, providing follow-up instruction to ensure mastery, providing access to the lower-level skills needed to use higher-level skills, and providing opportunities for students to self-regulate learning (Vaughn et al., 2000). The goal is to provide instruction that supports not only the acquisition of basic skills, but also allows for the acquisition of more complex skills and strategies that enhance achievement.

Levels of Instruction

In a general education setting, special education usually delivers instruction within a "tiered approach" (Vaughn & Linan-Thompson, 2003). The first tier is aimed at prevention, and parallels general education instruction that aligns with universal design features. If unsuccessful, successive tiers increase the intensity and explicitness of instruction. For example, L. Fuchs and D. Fuchs (2001) developed a model where peer-assisted learning strategies (PALS) were used to provide quick paced instruction where students worked in pairs and had the opportunity to be both tutor and tutee. Features of effective instruction like mediated verbal rehearsal, feedback, modeling strategic behavior, and frequent interactions were also incorporated. If students did not make gains, Fuchs and Fuchs designed two additional tiers. The second tier incorporated additional instructional features: goal setting, self-monitoring, computer assisted instruction, and concrete representation of number concepts. If necessary, a third tier provided greater individualization with intensive instruction and explicit skills-based instruction.

In the area of early reading, O'Connor (2000) attempted to reduce failure by providing instruction across four levels that varied in length and duration. Tier 1 consisted of whole class, teacher-led lessons about phonological awareness. At Tier 2, students received one-on-one instruction in 12-minute sessions, three times a week for ten weeks. Tier 3 targeted first grade students who received 30-minute sessions four times a week for fourteen weeks in small groups. By the end of first grade, it was found that reading failure among these at-risk students declined by about 25%.

The Nature of Special Education

For a relatively long period of time, special education appeared to focus on the adjective "special," that is, interpreting the purpose of special education to be the use of unique and exclusive methods providing a distinct identity. Although such unique and exclusive methods would not routinely be used in general education, they fit special education's goal of correcting or reversing the altered learning functions of the students with disabilities—but these unique and exclusive methods (process training) were found to be ineffective (see Table 25.1). Process training appears to demonstrate the inherent difficulties in attempting to ameliorate hypothetical constructs (see Cronbach & Meehl, 1955). The outcomes of training (products) are the only observable component, while the means by which those products were attained (process) are not observable. A prime example is found in the case of social skills training (SST), where the measured skills represent products (i.e., behaviors) that may only be presumed to represent the hypothetical construct of social competence (Gresham, 1986). With a mean ES of 0.23, it appears that SST does not enhance social competence. This appears to be the case for both students with learning disabilities (ES = 0.21; Forness & Kavale, 1996) and students with emotional and behavioral disorders (ES= 0.20; Quinn, Kavale, Mathur, Rutherford, & Forness, 1999). Further confirmation of these findings is found in a meta-analysis of single-subject research whose PND (a metric of treatment effectiveness based on the percentage of nonoverlapping data point) was 62% (Mathur, Kavale, Quinn, Forness, & Rutherford, 1998). A PND of 62% would be in the "small-medium" ES range (Scruggs, Mastropieri, & Casto, 1987).

The converging evidence suggests that social skills training demonstrates limited efficacy, but questions remain about whether or not SST should be recommended (see Gresham, 1998; Maag, 2005, 2006). Why did such a widely used intervention produce rather disappointing findings about its efficacy? An examination of the research base points out several possibilities. The first involves intensity of training, where the average allotted time for SST was 30 hours or less (i.e., fewer than 3 hours per week for less than 10 weeks). The possibility exists that longer interventions might be required to produce more positive results.

A second possibility surrounds measurement issues (Maag, 1989). The problems include poor rationale for selection of items, dubious psychometric properties of instruments developed, failure to account for contextual variables that influence the expression of social skills, and lack of differentiation between skill and performance deficits. Finally, a third possible reason involves the training packages themselves, which were almost exclusively designed for research purposes with no clear rationale, and limited pilot testing beforehand. Although a number of potentially effective social skills training programs exist (e.g., Hazel, Schumaker, Sherman, & Sheldon-Wildgen, 1981; McGinnis, Goldstein, Sprafkin, & Gershaw, 1984; Walker. H., McConnell, Holmes, Todis, Walker., & Golden 1983), they were not often used in the research studies synthesized.

Effective Special Education Practice: The Problem of Unique and Exclusive Methods

The unique and exclusive methods developed by special education to enhance student performance do not paint an optimistic picture about their efficacy (see Table 25.1). With an average gain of 1 year (ES = 1.00) for the average student on achievement measures, the process training methods used in special education (Mega ES = 0.11) do not compare favorably since, on average, the special education student would gain only about 2 months growth on an achievement measure. Process training methods thus represent less advantage than one-quarter year's worth of schooling, and do not appear to accelerate the rate of academic gain necessary for students with disabilities to eliminate decrepancies in their eduational performance. Yet, the strong clinical tradition and deep historical roots continue to provide positive perceptions about process training. Negative research evidence is often dismissed as inconclusive, and questions about efficacy fail to achieve closure.

A prime example is found for modality-matched instruction. The research evidence in both general education (Cronbach & Snow, 1977) and special education (Lloyd, 1984), however, has not supported the idea that aptitude-treatment interactions

(ATI) have a positive influence on learning. Whether termed the *modality model, learning styles*, ATI, or *differential programming*, the benefits are widely believed (e.g., Dunn & Dunn, 1978), even though research reviews have revealed few benefits (e.g., Arter & Jenkins, 1979; Larrivee, 1981; Tarver & Dawson, 1978).

Kavale and Forness (1987) found a "small" ES of 0.14 for modality-matched instruction. The ES translates into a modest 6-percentile rank improvement and, in a practical sense (i.e., BESD), translates into only an 8% increase in success rate. The small effects were found across modalities: auditory (ES = 0.18), visual (ES = 0.09), and kinethestic (ES = 0.18). Across 205 ES measurements, 35% were negative, suggesting that comparison subjects not receiving modality-based instruction performed better. Across reading skills, modality-matched instruction produced small improvments ranging from 2 (comprehension) to 7 (vocabulary and spelling) percentile ranks. Modality-matched instruction was not effective, leading Kavale and Forness to conclude that "Learning appears to be really a matter of substance over style" (p. 228).

Dunn (1990) challenged the findings from the Kavale and Forness (1987) meta-analysis by suggesting that the "correct" body of literature was not synthesized. Although additional points were contested (see Kavale & Forness, 1990), the exchange demonstrated that even precise and dispassionate findings associated with meta-analysis are sometimes not convincing when they encounter irresistible appeal and strong advocacy in the form of the less-than-disinterested view of Rita Dunn, who has a substantial stake in modality based instruction (R. Dunn & K. Dunn, 1978; R. Dunn, K. Dunn, & Price, 1979).

The issue resurfaced when Dunn, Griggs, Olson, Beasley, and Gorman (1995) produced a meta-analysis with the "correct" body of literature investigating the Dunn and Dunn Model of Learning-Style Preferences (DDMLSP) and concluded that, "providing educational interventions that are compatible with students' learning-style preferences is beneficial" (p. 357). Kavale, Hirshoren, and Forness (1998) criticized the Dunn et al. (1995) meta-analysis for potentially biased sampling: "The Dunn et al. meta-analysis seems to have a dearth of published literature [i.e., peer-reviewed journal articles] because 35 of the 36 studies included were dissertations" (p. 76). Without peer review, it is not possible to determine the reliability of dissertation findings.

The possibility for bias increases "when it is realized that 21 (58%) of the 36 studies were completed at St. John's University, where Dunn heads the Center for the Study of Learning and Teaching Styles. Some tangible proof that no bias exists is absolutely necessary under such circumstances" (Kavale, Hirshoren, & Forness, 1998, p. 77).

A decade later, Lovelace (2005) published a meta-analysis similar to Dunn et al. (1995) and suggested that the findings "were consistent and robust…[and] the data overwhelmingly supported the position that matching students' learning style preferences with complementary instruction improved academic achievement and student attitudes toward learning" (p. 181). The Lovelace (2005) meta-analysis is, however, also open to criticism about sampling (Kavale & LeFever, 2007). Although ostensibly conducting a comprehensive literature search, 96% of the included studies were dissertations (i.e., unpublished literature). Also, 70% of the included dissertations were completed at St. John's University, which again increases the potential for "home-team" bias.

When the sampling timeframe of the Lovelace (2005) meta-analysis is examined, additional problems arise. Lovelace found 76 studies that met the stipulated inclusion criteria for the years 1980–2000. Of the 76 studies, however, 36 were used previously in the Dunn et al. (1995) meta-analysis whose sampling timeframe was 1980–1990. Thus, the Lovelace literature base included only 53% "new" studies ($n = 40$) which, given the 47% overlap makes for the unsurprising (but relatively uninformative) conclusion that, "the effect-size values and general findings were similar in both the previous and the current meta-analyses" (p. 180). With almost one-half of the findings already known, it is difficult to determine the extent to which the Lovelace meta-analysis provided enhanced understanding of the DDMLSP.

The Nature of Effective Special Education

During special education's process training period, basic skill instruction was a secondary consideration, but the limited efficacy of process training directed attention at finding ways to enhance basic skill instruction for students with disabilities. The goal was to make academic learning more efficient by modifying the way instruction was delivered. In essence, special education moved toward a general education teaching–learning model, and away from reliance on "special" interventions.

Effective Instructional Practices

A number of effective instructional practices have been identified and are shown in Table 25.5. The mega-analytic findings revealed an overall ES of 1.26 for strategy instruction (e.g., self-monitoring, mnemonic instruction, self-questioning, and repeated reading). Examining the influence of teacher practices (e.g., systematic instruction, reinforcement, strategy instruction) yielded an average ES of 0.93. These findings demonstrate the move of special education away from reliance on "special" interventions (e.g., process training) and toward a general education teaching–learning model that relies on effective instructional practices (see Forness, 2001; Swanson, 2001).

META-COGNITIVE STRATEGIES

Many highly effective instructional strategies involve the development of meta-cognition, the ability to think about thinking. Meta-cognition is improved by developing strategies such as self-monitoring (ES = 1.74) and self-questioning (ES = 1.04), both serving to improve students' ability to self-regulate their learning and behavior, ultimately improving academic outcomes (see L. Fuchs et al., 2003; Santangelo, Harris, & Graham, 2008). The value of self-regulated strategy instruction was demonstrated in a study examining the contribution of self-regulated learning strategies on 3rd graders' mathematical problem solving when combined with problem-solving transfer instruction (see L. Fuchs et al., 2003). The findings indicated that self-regulated learning strategies positively affected performance as demonstrated by ESs of 1.43, 0.95, and 0.58, respectively, for immediate, near, and far transfer measures. The self-regulated learning strategies included self-scoring problems using a key specific to the unit's problem structure, charting daily scores, evaluating charts and setting goals, self-scoring homework prior to submission, reporting how the unit's problem structure was transferred to another topic, and constructing a class graph recording homework turn-in rates and reports of transfer events.

Teaching self-regulation strategies was also an effective instructional practice for writing. *Self-Regulated Strategy Development* (SRSD) is an instructional model used to help students explicitly learn the steps and strategies used by highly skilled writers (Santangelo et al., 2008). In three meta-analyses, SRSD produced average ES of 1.14 or greater, by emphasizing procedures for "teaching

Table 25.5 Effective instructional practices

Practice	Mean ES	Common Language ES	Percentile rank equivalent	Binomial ES display Success rate increase	
				From (%)	To (%)
Strategies	1.26	0.81	90	23	77
Self-Monitoring	1.74	0.89	96	17	83
Mnemonic Devices	1.51	0.86	93	20	80
Self-Questioning	1.04	0.77	85	27	73
Repeated reading	0.76	0.71	78	32	64
Teacher Practices	1.20	0.75	82	25	75
Systematic Instruction	2.18	0.94	99	13	87
Reinforcement	1.17	0.80	88	25	75
Drill & Practice	0.99	0.76	84	28	72
Strategy Based Instruction	0.98	0.75	84	28	72
Feedback	0.97	0.75	83	28	72
Direct Instruction	0.93	0.75	82	29	71
Behavioral Interventions	0.98	0.75	84	28	72
Self-regulation	1.38	0.84	92	22	78
Applied Behavior Analysis	0.93	0.75	82	29	71
Peer Mediation	0.64	0.67	74	35	65
Instructional Aids	0.89	0.74	81	30	70
Visual Displays	0.90	0.74	82	29	71
Computer-Assisted Instruction	0.87	0.73	81	30	7
Grouping Practices	0.59	0.66.	72	36	64
Groups	1.01	0.76	84	27	73
Peer Tutoring	0.58	0.66	72	36	64
Partners	0.40	0.61	66	40	60
Multiple Group Formats	0.36	0.60	64	41	59
Instructional Arrangements	0.58	0.66	72	36	64
Tutoring (tutors/paraprofessionals)	0.76	0.71	78	32	68
Co-teaching	0.40	0.61	66	40	60

students how to brainstorm and organize ideas, generate substantial content, and edit and revise their work" (p. 79). The SRSD instructional model includes six stages: (1) Develop background knowledge: at this stage the primary goal is ensuring students understand, learn, and apply the strategy; (2) Discuss it: to ensure students are motivated to use the new strategy; (3) Model it: students are shown explicitly how to use the new strategy; (4) Memorize it: students should become familiar enough that they can use the strategy automatically; (5) Support it: through scaffolded instruction, students resume responsibility for using the new strategy; and (6) Independent performance: consistent use over time, with a variety of tasks in multiple settings (Santangelo et al., 2008).

MNEMONIC DEVICES

Because many special education students possess memory deficits, efforts have been directed at improving memory through the use of strategies (Kavale & Forness, 1999). Mnemonic instruction (MI) is an example of a highly effective instructional strategy (ES = 1.51) used to transform difficult-to-remember facts into more memorable forms through recording, relating, and retrieving information. A common method is the keyword approach, which reconstructs unfamiliar verbal stimuli into acoustically similar representations and elaborates the reconstructed stimuli with response information (Atkinson, 1975). For example, to teach that the mineral *apatite* is No. 5 on Moh's hardness scale, is *brown* in color, and is used for making *fertilizer*, students are first taught a "key word" for apatite, a familiar and concrete word that is orthographically or phonetically similar. In this case, *ape* is the key word. Then, students are taught rhyming "peg words" for recalling the numbers 1 through 10 (e.g., 1 is *bun*, 2 is *shoe*, 3 is *tree*). In the case of apatite, 5 is *hive*. Finally, students are shown an interactive illustration of a *brown ape* pouring a bag of *fertilizer* on a *beehive*. Hence, students are provided with a direct retrieval route for all factual information associated with the mineral apatite.

In a meta-analysis investigating the effectiveness of mnemonic approaches for vocabulary instruction, Jitendra, Edwards, Sacks, and Jacobson (2004) reported a mean ES of 1.93 favoring keyword mnemonic approaches over traditional methods for aiding the memorization and free recall of key vocabulary items. Findings from inclusive high school social studies classes showed that, when compared to direct instruction, mnemonic instruction was associated with higher levels of academic engagement and was generally preferred by both students and teachers (Fontana, Scruggs, & Mastropieri, 2007). Furthermore, when compared to traditional geographical map reading symbols, the use of mnemonic keywords resulted in higher student recall of feature locations on maps (ES = 1.25; Gajira, Jitendra, Sood, & Sacks, 2007). Mnemonic illustrations have also been demonstrated to enhance student learning and performance in the acquisition of science concepts (ES = 1.78), and to aid in the comprehension of nonfiction texts (ES = 0.97).

Mnemonic devices are an important element of *recall routines* used to "enhance the concreteness and meaningfulness of information presented during a lesson or unit of study, thereby making the information easier to recall" (Deshler et al., 2001, p. 99). Recall routines involve memory tools such as mnemonic devices, and involve a series of steps: (1) reviewing the importance of the content, (2) co-creating or teaching students a mnemonic device to remember the information, and (3) reviewing the content and mnemonic device.

DIRECT INSTRUCTION

Direct instruction (ES = 0.93) has also been shown to be an effective instructional practice. The term *direct instruction* (DI) began as a general description of effective teaching behaviors (e.g., Rosenshine, 1976), and developed into a comprehensive system including not only effective instruction, but also curriculum design, classroom management, and teacher preparation (Gersten, Woodward, & Darch, 1986). DI is characterized by "fast-paced, well-sequenced, and highly focused lessons" (Swanson, 2001, p. 3) emphasizing student acquisition of isolated skills (as opposed to strategy instruction which focuses on rules). Furthermore, the most effective form of DI generally involves intensive instruction in small groups (ES = 1.01), with ample opportunity for teacher feedback (ES = 0.97) and error correction (ES = 0.72; see Swanson, 2001).

Programs based on DI are generally structured around six critical features (see Gersten, Carnine, & Woodard, 1987): (1) an explicit step-by-step strategy; (2) development of mastery at each step in the process; (3) strategy (or process) corrections for student errors; (4) gradual fading from teacher directed activities toward independent work; (5) use of adequate systematic practice with a range of examples; and (6) cumulative review of newly learned concepts.

White (1988) synthesized 25 studies investigating the efficacy of DI and found an average ES of 0.84, indicating that students taught with DI procedures were better off than 80% of students taught with comparison instructional methods. Math and reading outcomes revealed average ESs of 0.50 and 0.85 respectively.

A highly effective component of DI is systematic instruction (ES = 2.18). Systematic instruction involves explicit, sequential instruction, and has been validated for instruction in phonics (see Ehri, Nunes, Stahl, & Willows, 2001) and basic math skills (see Browder, Spooner, Ahlgrim-Delzell,

Harris, & Wakeman, 2008). Summarizing the National Reading Panel's meta-analysis (see Ehri et al., 2001) on phonemic awareness, Foorman and Torgesen (2001) reported the following:

> (1) systematic phonics instruction produces significant benefits for students with reading disabilities regardless of socio-economic status (SES); (2) the impact is strongest in kindergarten and first grade; and (3) phonics must be integrated with instruction in phonemic awareness, fluency, and comprehension. (p. 204)

For the improvement of basic math skills, Browder et al. (2008) found that systematic instruction involving explicit conceptual demonstrations were highly effective (PND = 92%). Specifically, highly effective instruction included the use of systematic prompting with an explicit fading procedure to decrease support as ability increased, as well as the application of math skills to real settings.

Swanson (1999) found that DI was effective for improving word recognition (ES = 0.98). Swanson then identified important instructional components for teaching word-recognition skills: (1) *sequencing*: breaking down the task, step-by-step prompts, fading of prompts and cues; (2) *segmentation*: breaking down targeted skill into smaller units, components, or parts; and (3) *advanced organizers*: providing prior information, previewing material prior to instruction, stating objectives in advance. These teacher practices (sequencing, segmenting, and use of advanced organizers) were positive elements for both direct (ES = 0.93) and systematic instruction (ES = 2.18).

Another important element of DI is ongoing and cumulative review of acquired skills and concepts. Drill tasks (ES = 0.99)—defined as "rehearsal or practice, which consists of all other tasks such as computation, writing, spelling, and subskills of reading; for example, word attack and sight-word recognition" (Burns, 2004, p. 167)—have been found important for academic remediation. In a meta-analytic comparison of drill task outcomes using different ratios (e.g., < 50% known words, 50–60% known words, 70–80% known words), Burns reported an overall mean ES of 0.82, with effects increasing as drill ratios increased. These findings suggested that the provision of an appropriate level of challenge is necessary for improving academic outcomes through drill tasks, and support Swanson and Sachse-Lee's (2001) finding that effective teaching included the instructional components of drill/repetition/practice/review.

BEHAVIORAL INTERVENTIONS

Skiba and Casey (1985) used meta-analysis to investigate the efficacy of applied behavior analysis techniques for enhancing academic and behavioral outcomes of students in special education. Across 41 studies, 26 ES measurements yielded an ES of 0.93, indicating an almost 1 standard deviation advantage for students receiving the behavioral intervention. For improving behavior, intervention produced an average ES of 0.77, while an ES of 1.57 was found when intervention targeted basic achievement skills, amounting to about a 44 percentile-rank improvement on achievement measures. Skiba and Casey's (1985) robust ES of 0.93 was confirmed by L. Fuchs and D. Fuchs' (1986) meta-analysis examining the effects of behavior modification techniques when used in conjunction with formative evaluation (ES = 1.12).

Stage and Quiroz (1997) used meta-analysis to examine 99 studies that used behavior interventions to decrease disruptive classroom behavior. They reported an average ES of 0.72, suggesting that behavior modification was successful in reducing disruptive classroom behavior for 78% of the students receiving intervention in public education classrooms when compared to nontreated students. Reid, Trout, and Schartz (2005) synthesized findings from studies investigating behavioral interventions for increasing student self-regulation. Overall, self-regulation interventions reduced inappropriate/disruptive behavior (ES = 1.82) and significantly increased on-task behavior (ES = 2.25).

GROUPING PRACTICES

Although the optimal teacher/student ratio is one-on-one, this is rarely possible or practical (Vaughn, Gersten, & Chard, 2000); consequently, teachers use different grouping practices that have demonstrated effectiveness, including small groups (ES = 1.01), peer tutoring (ES = 0.58), and partnering (ES = 0.40). The use of students as instructional agents has a long history (e.g., Allen, 1976) and offers a variety of academic and social benefits. Academic benefits for tutors often include learning more than the tutees, while the social benefits include improving attitudes about school, increasing responsibility, and improved self-confidence and self-esteem (see Scruggs & Richter, 1985).

In a meta-analytic review evaluating the effects of peer tutoring on students with mild disabilities in secondary settings (seventh through twelfth grade), Stenhoff and Lignugaris/Kraft (2007) found an ES of 0.46 across groups. Heterogeneous peer tutoring (i.e., tutees are taught by tutors in the same grade with higher skills or knowledge) was most effective, and prior peer–tutor training significantly improved outcomes.

To determine the efficacy of grouping practices for reading instruction, Elbaum, Vaughn, Hughes, and Moody (1999) conducted a meta-analysis contrasting different grouping formats. They reported a mean ES of 0.40 for students working in pairs, 1.61 for students working in small groups (i.e., 3 to 10 students), and 0.36 for multiple groups formats (i.e., a combination of small groups and pairs implemented systematically). It also appeared that students with disabilities found tutoring younger children a useful experience. Although it was easier to facilitate in special education than in general education classrooms, it was also found that educators must monitor arrangements closely to ensure that both tutors and tutees gain maximum advantage from the activity.

INSTRUCTIONAL ARRANGEMENTS

Special education has seen an increasing emphasis on serving students with disabilities in the general education setting. The Individuals with Disabilities Education Act (IDEA, 1990) and subsequent amendments (1997, 2004) emphasized the *least restrictive environment* (LRE) which was interpreted to mean serving students in settings more like those of their non-disabled peers. Co-teaching (ES = 0.40) is a service delivery option designed to meet the needs of students being served in the general education classroom. Cook and Friend (1995) defined co-teaching as "two or more professionals delivering substantive instruction to a diverse or blended group of students in a single physical space" (p. 2). Murawski and Swanson (2001) reviewed 89 studies investigating co-teaching, but only 6 provided adequate quantitative information for calculating ES, which averaged 0.40 (range = 0.24 to 0.95). Thus, more research is necessary before co-teaching can be considered among the effective service delivery options.

To support the inclusion of students with disabilities in the general education curriculum, general and special education classrooms are often supported by tutors and paraprofessionals. Meta-analytic findings demonstrated that early interventions were effective when implemented by tutors and paraprofessionals (ES = 0.76; Ehri et al., 2001). Scammacca, Vaughn, Roberts, Wanzek, and Torgesen (2007) reported that early reading intervention can be effective when provided by relatively low-cost implementers (paraprofessionals; ES range: 0.21 to 1.18). These paraprofessionals, however, should be trained and provided structured lesson plans and instructional routines, working one-on-one or in small groups of 2 to 3 students. Investigating the effectiveness of nonprofessional tutors in a phonologically based reading intervention, Vadasy, Jenkins, and Pool (2000) reported that tutored students outperformed students in the control (i.e., untutored) group in reading, spelling, and decoding, with effects ranging from moderate to strong (ES = 0.42 through 1.24).

Effective Instruction

The primary objective when implementing effective instructional practices is to increase student achievement, and the possibilities for enhanced academic performance across content areas are shown in Table 25.6. The findings appear to demonstrate the potential for significant achievement gains across the curriculum with the implementation of effective instruction. Instruction is most effective when delivered by a combination of direct instruction (e.g., systematic instruction, reinforcement, feedback, error correction) and strategy instruction (e.g., meta-cognitive strategies, repeated reading, mnemonic instruction; see Swanson, 2001).

MATHEMATICS

Students in special education represent widespread and heterogeneous deficits in mathematics. Over 50% of students in the category of specific learning disability (SLD) have IEP goals in math (Kavale & Reese, 1992), and research has demonstrated that students with SLD progress at a rate of about 1 year for every two years in school (Cawley & Miller, 1989).

L. Fuchs and D. Fuchs (2001) identified four principles necessary for effective math intervention: (1) quick pace and varied instructional activities and high levels of engagement; (2) challenging standards of achievement; (3) self-verbalization methods; and (4) physical and visual representations of number concepts or problem-solving situations. Many of the identified effective instructional practices (see Table 25.5) are reflected in these four practices: direct instruction (ES = 0.93), systematic instruction (ES = 2.18), self-monitoring (ES = 1.74)/self-questioning (ES = 1.04), and visual displays (ES = 0.90). Furthermore, mnemonic instruction (ES = 1.51) has been demonstrated to effectively remediate mathematics deficits, specifically in teaching multiplication facts to elementary and middle school students (Greene, 1999).

Table 25.6 Effective special education instruction

Subject area	Mean ES	Percentile Rank Equivalent	Common language ES	Binomial ES display Success rate increase	
				From (%)	To (%)
Mathematics	1.51	93	0.86	20	80
Basic Skills	2.18	99	0.94	13	87
Problem Solving	0.83	80	0.72	31	69
Writing	1.03	85	0.77	27	73
Handwriting	1.32	91	0.82	22	78
Expository Writing	1.02	85	0.76	27	73
Process	0.98	84	0.75	28	72
Narrative Writing	0.97	83	0.75	28	72
Spelling	0.87	81	0.73	30	70
Reading	1.03	85	0.74	27	73
Oral Reading	1.31	91	0.82	22	78
Language	1.27	90	0.82	22	78
Comprehension	1.04	85	0.77	27	73
Word Recognition	0.98	84	0.75	28	72
Vocabulary	0.85	80	0.73	30	70
Phonics	0.70	76	0.69	33	67

Instructional practices emphasizing text organizers and visual displays are not only effective in primary-grade math instruction, but also serve to enhance conceptual understanding in older students. Ives (2007) investigated the effectiveness of using graphic organizers for instructing students with SLD in secondary algebra. The obtained ESs ranged from "medium" to "large" and findings "consistently showed that students who worked with the graphic organizers had a stronger grasp of the conceptual foundations for solving systems of linear equations than did the students who did not work with the graphic organizers" (p. 117).

WRITING

Writing problems, along with reading deficits, lead to the largest number of referrals and placements in special education (Hallahan & Kauffman, 2006). Furthermore, writing problems develop early and tend to persist throughout school (Isaacson, 1995). Students with high incidence disabilities often struggle with the task of planning and organizing their writing, but instructional practices involving

both direct and strategy instruction have been demonstrated to enhance writing skills (ES = 1.03).

Gersten and Baker (2001) reported a mean ES of 0.81 across 13 studies that *systematically* taught organizational and mechanical aspects of writing in addition to social and creative aspects. Summarizing the findings from meta-analyses investigating expressive writing, Vaughn et al. (2000) reported that best practices in expressive writing instruction included: (a) explicit teaching of critical steps in the writing process, supported by a "think sheet"; (b) explicit teaching of the conventions of a writing genre, providing "text structures" to guide the writing task (i.e., expository [ES = 1.02] or narrative [ES = 0.86]); and (c) guided feedback to students on aspects of quality, strengths, and missing elements of work. These findings confirmed the efficacy of direct (e.g., explicit) instruction, meta-cognitive strategies (e.g., a "think sheet"), mnemonic devices, reinforcement, and feedback (see Table 25.2). Large improvements in handwriting (ES = 1.32) and spelling (ES = 0.87) were attained with direct instruction, while Baker, Gersten, and Graham (2003) highlighted the importance of systematic instruction in handwriting and spelling, since difficulty mastering these skills slows students' progress and undermines their ability to use other writing processes such as planning and revising.

READING

Reading difficulties often represent the primary area of academic difficulty for students with high-incidence disabilities. Reading deficits often include a failure to recognize words and associate them with concepts, or a failure to recognize and interpret sentences, ultimately hindering comprehension. Remedial reading efforts have focused on improving decoding skills by enhancing phonological processing abilities (see Ehri et al., 2001). Students with SLD, however, often continue to demonstrate significant deficits in reading comprehension even when level of decoding skill is controlled (Vaughn, Gersten, & Chard, 2000). Although representing a heterogeneous assortment of problems, students who struggle with reading comprehension generally demonstrate poor recall, difficulty identifying main ideas and supporting details, and have problems making inferences and relating new information to prior knowledge (Gajira, Jitendra, Sood, & Sacks, 2007).

Consequently, there has been increasing recognition that reading comprehension skills also need to be taught, with efforts focusing on cognitive interventions (e.g., specific problem solving skills, advanced organizers, and strategy instruction), cognitive-behavioral interventions (e.g., self-monitoring behavior during reading, self-questioning about text), vocabulary interventions (e.g., correcting oral reading errors, pronunciation and meaning of words in context and isolation), pre- and mid-reading (e.g., story previews, questions about the story, background knowledge), and direct instruction interventions (programmed materials, rapid oral responding, ongoing assessment and correction, error analysis, and reinforcement; Kavale & Forness, 1999).

Gajira et al. (2007) synthesized findings from 29 studies designed to improve comprehension of expository text for students with SLD. Interventions were categorized as either content enhancement or cognitive strategy instruction. Content enhancement interventions included the use of advanced and graphic organizers, visual displays, mnemonic illustrations, and computer assisted instruction, and had a mean ES of 1.06. Cognitive strategy instruction involved emphasis on text structure, main idea identification, summarization, questioning, cognitive mapping, and reciprocal teaching. Large effects were found for approaches that stressed the identification of main ideas and paraphrasing or summarizing passages (ES = 2.56).

Gajira et al's. (2007) findings supported earlier conclusions from Swanson's (1999) meta-analysis of 54 studies examining measures of word recognition and reading comprehension, indicating that "a combined instructional model that includes both strategy and direct instruction positively influences reading comprehension performance" (p. 521). Specifically, strategy cueing, small-group instruction, and meta-cognitive strategies significantly improved reading comprehension.

To determine the efficacy of reading comprehension interventions for students with SLD, Talbott, Lloyd, and Tankersley (1994) synthesized findings from 48 studies, and across 255 measurements found an ES of 1.13, while Mastropieri, Scruggs, Bakken, and Whedon (1996), in a similar meta-analysis, reviewed 68 studies investigating reading comprehension instruction and found an overall reading comprehension intervention mean ES of 0.98.

These two meta-analyses investigating reading comprehension demonstrate the possibility of judging the magnitude of "real" effects. The two meta-analyses (Talbot et al., 1994; Mastropieri et al., 1996) produced ESs of 1.13 and 0.98, a modest 3-percentile rank difference in outcomes (87 vs 84). When comparing specific methods for improving reading comprehension, the two meta-analyses reveal similar patterns of findings. The largest effects (ES = 1.60 and 1.33) were found for meta-cognitive techniques (e.g., self-monitoring, self-questioning). Text enhancement procedures (e.g., advanced organizers, mnemonics) produced ES of 1.09 and 0.92. The least powerful (but nevertheless effective) techniques involved skill-training procedures (e.g., vocabulary, repeated reading) with ES of 0.79 and 0.62. The consistency of findings across these two meta-analyses indicates reading comprehension can be enhanced with effective instruction.

Thus, effective reading comprehension interventions generally involve a combination of direct and strategy instruction, followed by opportunities for practice while being supported by correction and feedback (Vaughn, Gersten, & Chard, 2000). Moreover, meta-analytic findings suggest that, on average, the 'real' effect of reading comprehension instruction is ES = 1.04, a level comparable to one year's worth of reading comprehension instruction in general education (ES = 1.00). Thus, methods adapted for the purposes of special education produced the same effect as one year of general education instruction.

Reading fluency—the ability to read with speed and accuracy—has been shown to have a significant influence on reading comprehension (Therrien, 2004). Poor readers expend a considerable amount of cognitive resources on decoding, leaving little for comprehension, while fluent readers decode quickly and accurately, reserving resources for comprehension. Repeated reading was demonstrated to be an effective strategy (ES = 0.76) for improving both the fluency (ES = 0.77) and comprehension (ES = 0.59) of students with SLD (Therrien, 2004).

Vocabulary knowledge is also a major contributor to reading comprehension. Although developing proficient reading skills has been found to be the most effective word learning strategy, students who struggle to read often do not engage in the independent reading levels needed to improve vocabulary development and acquire necessary levels of vocabulary knowledge (Jitendra et al., 2004). Vocabulary knowledge, however, can be improved with intervention (ES = 0.85), with the most effective methods including keyword or mnemonic approaches that emphasize explicit phonetic and imagery links promoting definition recall (ES = 1.93); cognitive strategy instruction providing students with a framework and strategies for understanding and categorizing related words (ES = 1.10); direct instruction including an explicit and systematic presentation of the word and its meaning (ES = 9.78); constant time delay, involving a statement of the vocabulary word followed immediately by its definition, and repeating with increased pauses before responses; and activity based methods involving vocabulary instruction within the context of discipline-specific activities (ES = 0.45; Jitendra et al., 2004).

Reading research syntheses continue to validate the effectiveness of strategy instruction (ES = 0.98 to 1.26). Summarizing the report, *Reading Next: A Vision for Action and Research in Middle and High School Literacy* (Biancarosa & Snow, 2004), Biancarosa (2005) listed nine key instructional strategies found to improve literacy for older students: (1) direct, explicit instruction; (2) effective instructional principles embedded in content (e.g., using informational and content-area texts in reading instruction); (3) motivation and self-directed learning; (4) text-based collaborative learning (i.e., performing reading and writing tasks with a small group or a partner); (5) strategic tutoring (recognizing and targeting individual needs, focusing on fostering independence); (6) diverse texts; (7) intensive writing; (8) technology components (e.g., multimedia instruction including audio, animations, text); and (9) ongoing formative assessment of students (often informal and occurring daily). Biancarosa was careful to point out that this list of nine instructional strategies should not be viewed as a "menu from which to order one thing, but as a list of ingredients that they will want to mix with care, depending on their schools' strengths and needs" (p. 21).

These conclusions about reading instruction were confirmed by Swanson (1999), who demonstrated that certain instructional components increased the predictive power of the treatment across multiple models of instruction. These components included: (1) directed response/questioning: dialectic or Socratic teaching; (2) controlling difficulty of processing demands of task: simplified demonstration, sequencing tasks from simple to more complex; (3) elaboration: additional information or explanation about concepts, steps, and procedures; (4) modeling by the teacher: demonstrating processes or steps; (5) group instruction: verbal interaction occurring in a small group with students and/or teacher; and (6) strategy cues: teacher verbalizing steps or procedures, using "think aloud models."

Since phonological processing abilities have been identified as the underlying reason for success or failure in early reading, attention has been directed at developing effective interventions for improving the phonological processing abilities of young children (e.g., Catts, Gillespie, Leonard, Kail, & Miller, 2002; Nelson, Benner, & Gonzalez, 2003; Wagner, Torgesen, Laughon, Simmons, & Rashotte, 1993). Research findings have validated the use of systematic and direct instruction for teaching phonics to young children (ES = 0.70). In one study, three interventions were evaluated to determine their effectiveness in preventing reading disabilities in young children with weak phonological skills. The first involved direct and intensive instruction in phonemic decoding strategies; the second emphasized the development of phonemic skills but was more "balanced" in its use of word and text level instruction; the third was designed to resemble the child's regular reading instruction in the classroom. Analysis revealed that the students receiving systematic and direct phonics instruction had significantly stronger skills in phonological awareness, phonemic decoding, word level reading skills, and untimed, context-free reading (Torgesen, Wagner, Rashotte, Rose, Lindamond, & Conway, 1999).

Summary

Although the findings from meta-analyses are useful in demonstrating the efficacy of special education instructional practices, such findings must be converted into real world practice in order to positively influence student performance and improve academic outcomes. Swanson and Deshler (2003) provided an example of how meta-analyses can inform instruction through the process of identifying the "instructional principles that underlie the most effective intervention programs" (p. 124). From their synthesis of intervention research, Swanson and Deshler identified "the big picture"—the instructional factors that captured the majority of intervention programs investigated (i.e., questioning, sequencing, segmentation, skill modeling, organization and explicit practice, small-group setting, indirect teaching activities, technology, and scaffolding). They follow by asserting, "In short, to be effective, the instruction provided to students with LD must be delivered in a fashion that employs these factors in combination" (p. 129).

When special education focuses on the teaching–learning process, several instructional practices consistently translated into effective instruction across the curriculum (i.e., mathematics, reading, writing). These include: meta-cognitive strategy instruction (i.e., self-monitoring, self-questioning, self-regulating); mnemonic instruction; direct and systematic instruction, preferably in small groups, with opportunity for error correction, feedback, reinforcement, and review; and instructional aids (i.e., visual displays, graphic organizers, computer assisted instruction). However, there is no "one-size-fits-all" and, in keeping with the historical nature of special education, strategies must be selected and practices implemented to meet the "unique" and "special" needs of students with disabilities.

Early Intervention

Casto and Mastropieri (1986) synthesized 74 studies to produce an ES of 0.68, suggesting that a child receiving early intervention could be expected to gain about 25 percentile ranks on a variety of IQ, motor, language, and academic achievement outcomes. Although intervention effects did not vary greatly with respect to age at which the intervention began, effects varied greatly by intensity and duration of intervention. Interventions lasting 500 hours or more (ES = 0.86) produced larger effects than interventions totaling less than 50 hours (ES = 0.56).

Pre-referral intervention models (PIM; e.g., child study teams, student assistance teams, instructional support teams) were developed to intervene early with students struggling to learn, but not receiving special education. PIMs were generally defined as, "any multi-disciplinary problem solving team that develops interventions to meet the needs of students in general education that are difficult to teach" (Burns & Symington, 2002, p. 438). The PIMs generally follow 5 steps—(1) request for consultation, (2) consultation, (3) observation, (4) conference, and, if needed, (5) formal referral for special education eligibility—and have been found to improve student outcomes (ES = 1.15) and reduce referrals to special education (ES = 0.90; Burns & Symington, 2002). Although PIMs initially developed to support general education as an alternative to special education, there is a renewed interest in early intervention and PIMs because of the response-to-intervention (RTI) regulations in the reauthorized Individuals with Disabilities Education Act (IDEA, 2004).

Effective Special Education Related Services

A hallmark of special education is the provision for additional services to be provided when deemed appropriate for augmenting the instructional program. A sample of these adjunct activities are shown in Table 25.7. Most related services produce "medium" ES, which in 68 out of 100 cases reveals that a positive response to a related service was attained (CLES = 0.68).

Special education has long debated the issue of placement. Where should students with disabilities be educated? Beginning with the passage of PL 94-142, students with disabilities were placed in more integrated settings. During the 1990s, the mainstreaming movement became more radicalized with the rise of the inclusive schools movement (D. Fuchs & L. Fuchs, 1994). Kavale and Forness (2000) demonstrated how discussions about inclusion were based more on ideology than evidence. In fact, the empirical evidence suggests "caution," and any generalizations about the efficacy of inclusion remain tentative (MacMillan, Gresham, & Forness, 1996).

Greater perspective about inclusion is provided when it is realized that placement per se has little influence on academic performance (ES = 0.12). (The ES was arranged so that a positive ES favored the special class, while a negative ES favored the general education class [see Carlberg & Kavale, 1980]). The success rate associated with placement increases only 6% (47% to 53%). The "small" ES appears to suggest that "where" (that is, placement)

Table 25.7 Effective special education related services and activities

Subject area	Mean ES	Common language ES	Binomial ES display Success rate increase	
			From (%)	To (%)
Memory Training	1.12	0.79	25	75
Prereferral	1.10	0.78	26	74
Cognitive Behavior Modification	0.74	0.70	32	68
Stimulant Medication	0.62	0.67	35	65
Counseling	0.60	0.66	35	65
Consultation	0.55	0.65	36	64
Rational-Emotive Therapy	0.50	0.64	38	62
Attribution Training	0.43	0.62	39	61
Placement	0.12	0.53	47	53

is clearly not as important as the "what" (that is, nature of instruction provided). This view is supported by the positive ES associated with prereferral activities (ES = 1.10) where the CLES (0.78) indicates that in 78 out of 100 cases, prereferral activities produce positive outcome. Prereferral "works" because it is predicated on modifications of instructional activities, and its 48% increase in success rate means that almost half of students provided with prereferral activities will not need to be referred for further evaluation.

Although placement does not appear to be a significant factor, differences related to special education classification (ID, SLD, EBD) emerged that suggest a general education setting may not be appropriate for *all* students with disabilities. The meta-analytic findings showed that students with ID did better in general education settings (ES = -0.14) while students with SLD or EBD did better in a special class setting (ES = 0.29). These findings may reflect differences in teacher attitudes. For students with ID in special classes, academic instruction may be accompanied by lowered expectations (conscious or unconscious) that may result in less effort on the teacher's part and less learning by the students. On the other hand, teachers in special classes for students with SLD or EBD may take a more optimistic view about the ability of their students, and thus focus on designing the most effective programs of academic remediation for overcoming academic difficulties. Nevertheless, where the student is placed is not the salient variable

determining academic success, but debate has focused on placement to such an extent that setting has come to be equated with intervention. What happens in any setting (i.e., the nature of instruction) is the major influence in outcomes.

The Nature of Special Education

Special education can "work" (i.e., students with disabilities can achieve positive academic gains). The focus, however, must be providing *instruction* based on effective practices, which has not always been the case as evidenced by special education's tradition of using unique and exclusive methods. The prime example was process training, whose goal was to "fix" impaired learning processes with academic instruction placed in a secondary position until process deficits were remediated. When intervention is focused on "special" (i.e., singular and different) methods, and basic skill instruction is subordinate, the nature of special education can be conceptualized as SPECIAL *education*. Such SPECIAL *education*, however, reveals limited efficacy (see Table 25.1), suggesting that process deficits are difficult to "fix" with little benefit accruing from attempts to make learning more efficient by remediating processes.

The recognition that "special" interventions did not produce desired outcomes led special education in the direction of emphasizing "education" to enhance academic outcomes. When intervention efforts shift to an emphasis on instructional activities, the nature of special education can be conceptualized as *special* EDUCATION. The instructional techniques employed usually originated in general education, and were modified to accommodate the learning needs of students with disabilities, with the goal being the more efficient acquisition and assimilation of basic skill and content area knowledge. Thus, the emphasis on instruction permits a more direct remedial approach, rather than the more indirect approach found with "special" approaches. The *special* EDUCATION conceptualization demonstrates significant success (see Table 25.5) and produces improved achievement outcomes (see Table 25.6).

The difference between the two conceptualized forms of special education (i.e., SPECIAL *education* and *special* EDUCATION) is seen in the mega ES (mean of the means) where *special* EDUCATION (mega ES = 0.85) is almost six times more effective than SPECIAL *education* (mega ES = 0.15). The emphasis on education (i.e., instruction) results in achievement outcomes (mega ES = 1.19) that exceed one year's worth of general education instruction (ES = 1.00) by almost two months of achievement credit. These substantial gains stand in sharp contrast to SPECIAL *education* that provides only a 6% advantage (56%) which is an improvement level only slightly above chance (i.e., 50%). In contrast, *special* EDUCATION produces a 30% advantage, which is significantly above the chance level at 80%. The SPECIAL *education* meta-analyses also produced about 25% negative ES, indicating that students *not* receiving the "special" intervention sometimes performed better.

Clearly, *special* EDUCATION methods provide a foundation for designing effective academic programs. The contrasts between the two conceptualizations of special education can be stark. For example, Direct Instruction (DI), the explicit step-by-step teaching strategy (ES = 0.93) is 6.5 times more effective than the intuitively appealing modality-matched instruction that attempts to enhance learning by capitalizing on learning style differences (ES = 0.14). Students with disabilities taught with DI would be better off than 87% of students not receiving DI, and would gain over 11 months credit on achievement measures, compared to about one month for modality-matched instruction. With its grounding in effective instruction, *special* EDUCATION can sometimes be up to 25 times more effective than SPECIAL *education*.

Effective Special Education
Lipsey and Wilson (2001) suggested three advantages for meta-analysis: (1) it provides a disciplined process of summarizing research findings; (2) it represents study findings in a more differentiated metric; and (3) it provides a way of finding effects or relationships that may be obscured in other approaches to summarizing research. The purpose of this chapter was to extend these advantages by synthesizing meta-analyses to produce what were termed *mega-analyses*. The mega-analytic findings related to *special* EDUCATION methods and techniques appear to place them in the realm of "evidence-based practice" (EBP) wherein instructional activities are grounded in findings that demonstrate empirically that certain actions performed are likely to produce predictable, beneficial, and effective results (Odom et al., 2005).

Although EBP is desirable, extraneous factors like tradition ("We have always used it") and history ("It has worked before") represent powerful barriers to EBP implementation. Vaughn and Dammann (2001) discussed the importance of scientific development for special education, but then demonstrated how special education really developed as a craft, which is defined as a goal-oriented body of knowledge developed through trial and error. The major disadvantage of developing as a craft is significant inefficiency in creating a knowledge base that is rigorous and systematic. Without an objective knowledge base, little consensus has emerged about the nature of effective special education intervention. Consequently, intervention decisions are often predicated on inappropriate factors like cash validity (i.e., the program sells well), or the promise of being "doctor-tested" (even though no empirical evidence of effectiveness was ever provided). The consequences are found in the creation of "bandwagons" whereby interventions gain sudden popularity and, as they gain momentum, possess significant influence on practice (Blatt, 1979).

The negative impact of extraneous influences like bandwagons means that advocacy, not science, often drives decisions in special education (Brigham, Gustashaw, & Brigham, 2004). Under such circumstances, research findings "are embraced by some, ignored by others, and modified to suit the routines and preferences of still others" (Gersten, Vaughn, Deshler, & Schiller, 1997, p. 46). Thus, until recently, science and scientific thinking did not have a significant impact on practice in special education (Landrum & Tankersley, 2004), which fostered the development of a number of faulty notions about special education that have only served to hinder effective service delivery (Heward, 2003).

The tenuous relationship between science and special education is seen in the enduring research-to-practice gap (Carnine, 1997). The problem is *not* that a reliable research base does not exist, but rather that the instructional implications that might be drawn from the research base have neither been recognized, agreed upon, nor implemented in classrooms (Gersten, Vaughn, Deshler, & Schiller, 1997). Greenwood and Abbott (2001) suggested unique aspects of the research to practice gap in special education, including the separation of the research and practice communities, the limited relevance of educational research as perceived by teachers and administrators, and the failure of research to produce innovations appropriate for "real" classrooms. When queried, special education teachers believed that being "research-based" was not an important selection criteria, and, instead, sought instructional practices that were perceived to be feasible and appropriate for students, as well as amenable to individualization in multilevel classrooms (Boardman, Arguelles, Vaughn, Hughes, & Klingner, 2005).

The failure to implement EBP is a major contributor to the problem of sustainability, the continued use of an instructional practice supported by evidence of improved outcomes for students with disabilities (Gersten, Vaughn, & Kim, 2004). Investigations of sustainability (e.g., Gersten, Chard, & Baker, 2000; Klingner, Arguelles, Hughes, Vaughn, 2001; Klingner, Vaughn, Hughes, & Arguelles, 1999) revealed low rates because teachers believe that their practices are, at least, moderately effective, that the moderate success of present practice does not provide motivation for change, and that change becomes problematic when initiated by district professionals and administrators. For special education, if sustainability of research-based practices is not attained, then the effectiveness of even the best practices may be compromised.

The individualized instruction that defines special education makes instructional design decisions critically important. Such decisions, however, are complex because of the introduction of "uncertainty" (i.e., the program may not work) and "risk" (i.e., negative outcomes; Glass, 1983). In meta-analysis, uncertainty and risk can be described by the standard deviation (SD), a measure of dispersion around the mean ES representing an index of variability. Taken together, the ES and SD provide a theoretical expectation about the possible magnitude of intervention efficacy (i.e., ES ± SD).

For example, the process training interventions demonstrate larger SDs than mean ES. Psycholinguistic training (0.39 ± 0.54) spans a theoretical range (-0.15 to 0.93) including negative ES ("risk") to "large" ES. The problem: no features associated with psycholinguistic training (e.g., age of students, trainer experience, type of training materials) correlate substantially with ES, meaning that is not possible to predict where or when psycholinguistic training will be effective. Thus, special education interventions may demonstrate effectiveness by producing replicable benefits, on average, but those benefits vary greatly in an essentially unpredictable manner.

The mega ES for SPECIAL *education* (0.15) is associated with a larger mega SD (0.48) making "special" interventions actually more variable than effective (0.15 ± 0.48). The associated theoretical range for SPECIAL *education* includes the possibility of producing modestly positive ("medium") effects but also the possibility of significant risk (i.e., negative ES) where those *not* receiving the intervention perform better. Thus, the unique and exclusive methods which once defined special education introduce considerable uncertainty and risk to the special education teaching–learning process.

In contrast, methods focusing on *instruction* provide a different uncertainty and risk scenario. For example, the use of mnemonic devices (ES = 1.51) eliminates the possibility of risk and reduces uncertainty (1.51 ± 0.82). Although positive effects may possibly decline to a "medium-large" level (ES = 0.69), the ES magnitude is still greater than even the best case scenario for "special" interventions (ES = 0.63). With a mega ES of 0.84 and a mega SD of 0.79, the interventions emphasizing *special* EDUCATION reveal themselves to be more effective than variable (0.84 ± 0.79). Although the theoretical range shows that *special* EDUCATION may not "work" in some instances (ES = 0.05), there is also the possibility that it may be almost twice as effective (ES = 1.63). Thus, an emphasis on the acquisition and assimilation of knowledge (i.e., instruction) rather than efforts directed at "fixing" hypothetical entities, significantly reduces the "uncertainty" and "risk" associated with special education.

Conclusion

This chapter traced the positive shift in special education practice from a medical model perspective aimed at "fixing" and "curing" students with disabilities through process training procedures, to a teaching–learning model focused on research-based instruction for ameliorating achievement deficits. Accumulated findings from quantitative research syntheses (i.e., meta-analyses) were combined to demonstrate the nature of effective practice in special education across content areas.

Nevertheless, the special education teaching–learning process remains a capricious enterprise (that is, variable and unpredictable) that cannot be approached in a prescriptive manner (that is, do A in circumstance X or Y, and do B in circumstance Z). Teachers remain the central characters in the special education instructional process, and their decision making should be based on knowledge about the most effective options (that is, practices with "large" ES). The evidence suggests that special education teachers are, in fact, making rational choices about "what works" (e.g., Mather, Bos, & Babur, 2001; McCutchen et al., 2002; Rankin-Erickson & Pressley, 2000). The increased emphasis on evidence based practice brings a greater scientific element to special education, but empirical knowledge alone is not sufficient because "using science to achieve practical ends requires artistry—the artistry that enters in knowing when to follow the implications of the laws, generalizations, and trends, and especially, when not to" (Gage, 1978, p. 18).

Thus, the essential task of the special education teacher is to narrow the gap between the state of the art (what has been demonstrated to be possible) and the state of the practice (current ways of providing instruction) "because quality education for special education students will always be based on the artful application of science" (Kavale & Forness, 1999, p. 93).

References

Allen, V. L. (1976). The helping relationship and socialization of children: Some perspectives on tutoring. In V. L. Allen (Ed.), *Children as teachers: Theory and research on tutoring* (pp. 9–25). New York, NY: Academic Press.

Arena, J. I. (Ed.). (1969). *Teaching through sensory-motor experiences.* San Rafael, CA: Academic Therapy Publications.

Arter, J. A., & Jenkins, J. R. (1979). Differential diagnostic–prescriptive teaching: A Critical appraisal. *Review of Educational Research, 49,* 517–555.

Atkinson, R. C. (1975). Mnemotechnics in second-language learning. *American Psychologist, 30,* 821–828.

Baker, S., Gersten, R., & Graham, S. (2003). Teaching expressive writing to students with learning disabilities: Research-based applications and examples. *Journal of Learning Disabilities, 36*(2), 109–123.

Balow, B. (1971). Perceptual-motor activities in the treatment of severe reading disability. *Reading Teacher, 25,* 513–525.

Barsch, R. H. (1967). *Achieving perceptual-motor efficiency: A space-oriented approach to learning.* Seattle, WA: Special Child Publications.

Berliner, D. C. (2002). Educational research: The hardest science of all. *Educational Researcher, 31,* 18–20.

Biancarosa, G. (2005). After third grade. *Educational Leadership,* 16–22.

Biancarosa, G., & Snow, C. E. (2004). *Reading next—a vision for action and research in middle and high school literacy: A report from Carnegie Corporation of New York.* Washington, DC: Alliance for Excellent Education.

Blatt, V. (1979). Bandwagons also go to funerals. *Journal of Learning Disabilities, 12*(5), 288–291.

Board of Education of the Henrik Hudson Central School District vs. Rowley, 458 (U.S. 176 1982).

Boardman, A. G., Arguelles, M. E., Vaughn, S., Hughes, M. T., & Klingner, J. (2005). Special education teachers views of research based practices, *Journal of Special Education, 37,* 168–180.

Bos, C. S., & Vaughn, S. (2002). *Strategies for teaching students with learning and behavior problems (5th Ed.).* Boston: Allyn & Bacon.

Brantlinger, E. (1997). Using ideology: Cases of non-recognition of the politics of research and practice in special education. *Review of Educational Research, 67,* 425–459.

Brantlinger, E., Jimenez, R., Klingner, J., Pogach, M., & Richardson, V. (2005). Qualitative studies in special Education. *Exceptional Children, 71,* 195–207.

Brigham, F. J., Gustashaw, W. E., Brigham, M. S. P. (2004). Scientific practice and the tradition of advocacy in special education. *Journal of Learning Disabilities, 37,* 200–206.

Browder, D. M., Spooner, F., Ahlgrim-Delzell, L., Harris, A. A., & Wakeman, S. (2008). A meta-analysis on teaching mathematics to students with significant cognitive disabilities. *Exceptional Children, 74*(4), 407–432.

Burns, M. K. (2004). Empirical analysis of drill ratio research: Refining the instructional level for drill tasks. *Remedial and Special Education, 25*(3), 167–173.

Burns, M. K., & Symington, T. (2002). A meta-analysis of pre-referral intervention teams: Student and systemic outcomes. *Journal of School Psychology, 40,* 437–447.

Carlberg, C., & Kavale, K. (1980). The efficacy of special versus regular class placement for exceptional children: A meta-analysis. *Journal of Special Education, 14,* 296–309.

Carnine, D. (1997). Bridging the research-to-practice gap. *Exceptional Children, 63,* 513–521.

Casto, C. & Mastropieri, M. A. (1986). The efficacy of early intervention programs: A meta-analysis. *Exceptional Children, 52,* 417–424.

Catts, H. W., Gillispie, M., Leonard, L., B., Kail, R. V., & Miller, C. A. (2002). The role of speed of processing, rapid naming, and phonological awareness in reading achievement. *Journal of Learning Disabilities, 35*(6), 509–524.

Cawley, J. F., & Miller, J. H. (1989). Cross-sectional comparisons of the mathematics performance of children with learning disabilities: Are we on the right track toward comprehensive programming? *Journal of Learning Disabilities, 22,* 250–254.

Cawley, J., Parmar, R., Foley, T., Salmon, S., & Roy, S. (2001). Arithmetic performance of students: Implications for standards and programming. *Exceptional Children, 67,* 311–328.

Chambless, D. L., & Hollon, S. D. (1998). Defining empirically supported therapies. *Journal of Consulting and Clinical Psychology, 66,* 7–18.

Christenson, S. L., Ysseldyke, J. E., & Thurlow, M. L. (1989). Critical instructional factors for students with mild Handicaps: An integrative review. *Remedial and Special Education 10,* 21–31.

Cohen, J. (1988). *Statistical power analysis for the behavioral sciences (2nd Ed.).* Hillsdale, NJ: Erlbaum.

Cook, T. D., Cooper, H., Cordray, D. S., Hartman, H., Hedges, L. V., Light, R. J., Louis, T. A., & Mosteller, F. (1992). *Meta-analysis for explanation: A casebook.* New York, NY: Russell Sage Foundation.

Cook, L., & Friend, M. (1995). Co-teaching: Guidelines for creating effective practices. *Focus on Exceptional Children, 28*(3), 1–16.

Cooper, H., & Hedges, L. V. (1994). *The handbook of research synthesis.* New York: Russell Sage Foundation.

Coyne, M. D., Kame'enui, E. J., Simmons, D. (2001). Prevention and intervention in beginning reading: Two complex systems. *Learning Disabilities Research & Practice, 16,* 62–73.

Cronbach, L. J., & Meehl, P. E. (1955). Construct validity in psychological tests. *Psychological Bulletin, 52,* 281–301.

Cronbach, L. J. & Snow, R. E. (1977). Aptitudes and instructional methods: A handbook for research on interactions. New York, NY: Irvington.

Dennison, P. E., & Dennison, G. E. (1994). *Brain gym teacher's edition – revised.* Ventura, CA: Edu-Kinesthetics.

Deschler, D. D., Schumaker, J. B., Lenz, B. K., Bulgren, J. A., Hock, M. F., Knight, J., & Ethren, B. J. (2001). Ensuring content-area learning by secondary student with learning disabilities. *Learning Disabilities Research & Practice, 16*(2), 96–108.

Dunn, R. (1990). Bias over substance: A critical analysis of Kavale and Forness' Report on Modality-Based Instruction. *Exceptional Children, 56,* 352–356.

Dunn, R., & Dunn, K. J. (1978). *Teaching students through their individual learning styles.* Englewood Cliffs, NJ: Prentice-Hall.

Dunn, R., Dunn, K., & Price, G. (1979). *Learning Style Inventory.* Lawrence, KS: Price Systems.

Dunn, R., Griggs, S. A., Olson, J., Beasley, M., & Gorman, B. S. (1995). A Meta-Analytic Validation of the Dunn and Dunn model of learning-style preferences. *The Journal of Educational Research, 88,* 353–362.

Ehri, L.C., Nunes, S. R., Stahl, S. A., & Willows, D. M. (2001). Systematic phonics instruction helps students learn to read: Evidence from the National Reading Panel's meta-analysis. *Review of Educational Research, 71*(3), 393–447.

Eisenhart, M., & Towne, L. (2003). Contestation and change in national policy on "Scientifically Based" education research. *Educational Researcher, 32,* 31–38.

Eisner, E. (1983). Anastasia might still be alive, but the monarchy is dead. *Educational Researcher, 12,* 13–24.

Elbaum, B., Vaughn, S., Hughes, M., & Moody, S. W. (1999). Grouping practices and reading outcomes for students with disabilities. *Exceptional Children, 65*(3), 399–415.

Feuer, M. J., Towne, L., & Shavelson, R. J. (2002). Scientific culture and educational research. *Educational Researcher, 31,* 4–14.

Fontana, J. L., Scruggs, T., & Mastropieri, M. A. (2007). Mnemonic strategy instruction in inclusive secondary social studies classes. *Remedial and Special Education, 28*(6), 345–355.

Foorman, B. & Torgesen, J. (2001). Critical elements of classroom and small-group instruction promote reading success in all children. *Learning Disabilities Research & Practice, 16*(4), 203–212.

Forness, S. R. (2001). Special education and related services: What have we learned from meta-analysis? *Exceptionality, 9*(4), 185–197.

Forness, S. R. (2005). The pursuit of evidence-based practice in special education for children with Emotional or Behavioral Disorders. *Behavioral Disorders, 30,* 311–330.

Forness, S. R., & Kavale, K. A. (1987). Holistic inquiry and the scientific challenge in special education: A reply to Iano. *Remedial and Special Education, 8,* 47–51.

Forness, S. R., & Kavale, K. A. (1996). Treating social skills deficits in children with learning disabilities: A meta-analysis of the research. *Learning Disabilities Quarterly, 19,* 2–13.

Forness, S. R., Kavale, K. A., Blum, I. M., & Lloyd, J. W. (1997). Mega-analysis of meta-analyses: What works in speical education and related services. *Teaching Expectional Children, 29,* 4–11.

Frostig, M., & Horne, D. (1964). *The Frostig program for the development of visual perception.* Chicago, IL: Follett.

Fuchs, D., & Fuchs, L. S. (1994). Inclusive schools movement and the radicalization of special education reform. *Exceptional Children, 60,* 294–309.

Fuchs, D., & Fuchs, L. S. (1995a). Special education can work. In J. M. Kauffman, J. W. Lloyd, D. P. Hallahan, & J. A. Astuto, *Issues in Educational Placement: Students with Emotional and Behavioral Disorders* (pp. 363–377). Hillsdale, NJ: Lawrence Erlbaum.

Fuchs, D., & Fuchs, L. S. (1995b). What's "Special" about Special Education? *Phi Delta Kappan, 76,* 522–530.

Fuchs, L. S., & Fuchs, D. (1986). Effects of systematic formative evaluation: A meta-analysis. *Exceptional Children, 53,* 199–208.

Fuchs, L. S., & Fuchs, D. (2001). Principles for the preventions and intervention of mathematics difficulties. *Learning Disabilities Research and Practice, 16*(2), 86–95.

Fuchs, L.S., Fuchs, D., Prentice, K., Burch, M., Hamlett, C. L., & Owen, R. et al. (2003). Enhancing third-grade students' mathematical problem solving with self-regulated learning strategies. *Journal of Educational Psychology, 95*(2), 306–315.

Gage, N. L. (1978). *The scientific basis of the art of teaching.* New York, NY: Teachers College Press, Columbia University.

Gage, N. L. (1989). The paradigm wars and their aftermath: A "historical" sketch of research on teaching since 1989. *Educational Researcher, 18,* 4–10.

Gage, N. L. (1991). The obviousness of social and educational research. *Educational Researcher, 20,* 10–16.

Gage, N. L. (1996). Confronting counsels of despair for the behavioral sciences. *Educational Researcher, 25,* 5–15, 22.

Gajira, M., Jitendra, A. K., Sood, S., & Sacks, G. (2007). Improving comprehension of expository text in students with LD: A research synthesis. *Journal of Learning Disabilities, 40*(3), 210–225.

Gallagher, D. J., Heshusius, L., Iano, R. P., & Skirtic, T. M. (2004). *Challenging orthodoxy in special Education: Dissenting voices.* Denver: Love Publishing Co.

Gaynor, J. (1973). The "failure" of J.M.G. Itard. *Journal of Special Education, 7,* 439–445.

Gersten, R. (1998). Recent Advances in Instructional research for Students with Learning Disabilities: An Overview. *Learning Disabilities Research and Practice, 13,* 162–170.

Gersten, R., & Baker, S. (2001). Teaching expressive writing to students with learning disabilities: A meta-analysis. *The Elementary School Journal, 101*(2), 251–

Gersten, R., Baker, S. K. J., Flojo, J. R., & Hagan-Burke, S. (2004). A tale of two decades: Trends in support for federally funded experimental research in special Education. *Exceptional Children, 70*, 323–332.

Gersten, R., Carnine, D., & Woodard, J. (1987). Direct instruction research: The third decade. *Remedial and Special Education, 8*, 48–56.

Gersten, R., Chard, D., & Baker, S. (2000). Factors enhancing sustained use of research-based instructional practices. *Journal of Learning Disabilities, 43*, 445–457.

Gersten, R., Fuchs, L. S., Greenwood, C., & Innocenti, M. S. (2004). Quality indicators for group experimental and quasi-experimental research in special education. *Exceptional Children, 71*, 149–164.

Gersten, P., Vaughn, S., Deshler, D., & Schiller, E. (1997). What we know about using research findings: Implications for improving special education practice. *Journal of Learning Disabilities, 30*, 466–476.

Gersten, R., Vaughn, S., & Kim, A. H. (2004). Introduction: Special issue on sustainability. *Remedial and Special Education, 25*(1), 3–4.

Gersten, R., Woodard, J., & Darch, C. (1986). Direct instruction: A research-based approach to curriculum design and teaching. *Exceptional Children, 53*, 17–31.

Glass, G. V. (1976). Primary, secondary, and meta-analysis of research. *Educational Researcher, 5*, 3–8.

Glass, G. V. (1983). Effectiveness of special education. *Policy Studies Review, 2*, 65–78.

Glass, G. V., McGaw, B., & Smith, M. L. (1981). *Meta-analysis in social research.* Beverly Hills, CA: Sage.

Gleason, M. M., & Isaacson, S. (2001). Using the new basals to teach the writing process: modifications for students with learning problems. *Reading and Writing Quarterly, 17*, 75–92.

Goodman, L., & Hammill, D. (1973). The effectiveness of the Kephart-Getman activities in developing perceptual motor and cognitive skills. *Focus on Exceptional Children, 4*, 1–9.

Graham, S., Harris, K. R., & Larsen, L. (2001). Prevention and intervention of writing difficulties for students with learning Disabilities. *Learning Disabilities Research and practice, 16*, 78–84.

Greene, G. (1999). Mnemonic multiplication fact instruction for students with learning disabilities. *Learning Disabilities Research & Practice, 14*(3), 141–148.

Greenwood, C. R, & Abbott, M. (2001). The research to practice gap in special education. *Teacher Education and Special Education, 24*, 276–289.

Gresham, F. M. (1986). Conceptual and definitional issues in the assessment of social skills: Implications for classification and training. *Journal of Clinical Child Psychology, 15*, 16–25.

Gresham, F. M. (1998). Social skills training: Should we raze, remodel, or rebuild? *Behavioral Disorders, 24*, 19–25.

Hallahan, D. P., & Cruickshank, W. M. (1973). *Psychoeducational foundations of learning disabilities.* Englewood Cliffs, NJ: Prentice-Hall.

Hallahan, D. P., & Kauffman, J. M. (1994). Toward a culture of disability in the aftermath of Deuo and Dunn. *The Journal of Special Education, 27*, 496–508.

Hallahan, D. P., & Kauffman, J. M. (2006). *Exceptional learners: An introduction to special education* (10th ed.). Boston, MA: Allyn & Bacon.

Hammill, D. P., Goodman, L., & Wiederholt, J. L. (1974). Visual–motor processes: Can we train them? *Reading Teacher, 27*, 469–478.

Hammill, D. P., & Larsen, S. C. (1974). The effectiveness of psycholinguistic training. *Exceptional Children, 41*, 5–14.

Hammill, D. P., & Larsen, S. C. (1978). The effectiveness of psycholinguistic training: A reaffirmation of position. *Exceptional Children, 44*, 402–414.

Harniss, M. K., Dickson, S. V., Kinder, D., & Hollenbeck, K. L. (2001). Textual problems and instructional solutions: Strategies for enhancing learning from published history textbooks. *Reading and Writing Quarterly, 17*, 127–150.

Hazel, J. S., Schumaker, J. B., Sherman, J. A., & Sheldon-Wildgen, J. (1981). ASSET: *A social skills program for adolescents.* Champaign, IL: Research Press.

Hedges, L. V., & Olkin, I. (1980). Vote-counting methods in research synthesis. *Psychological Bulletin, 88*, 359–369.

Heshusius, L. (1989). The Newtonian mechanistic paradigm, special education, and contours of alternatives: An overview. *Journal of Learning Disabilities, 22*, 403–415.

Heward, W. L. (2003). Ten faulty notions about teaching and learning that hinder the effectiveness of special education. *Journal of Special Education, 36*, 186–205.

Hoagwood, K. (2003–2004). Evidence-based practice in child and adolescent mental health: Its meaning, application, and limitations. *Emotional and Behavioral Disorders in Youth, 4*, 7–8.

Hockenbury, J. C., Kauffman, J. M., & Hallahan, D. P. (1999–2000). What is Right about Special Education. *Exceptionality, 8*, 3–11.

Horner, R., Carr, E. G., Halle, J., McGee, G., Odom, S., & Wolesy, M. (2004). The use of single-subject design research to identify evidence-based practice in special education. *Exceptional Children, 71*, 165–179.

Huefner, D. S. (1991). Judicial review of the special education program requirements under the Education for All Handicapped Children Act: Where have we been and where should we be going? *Harvard Journal of Law and Public Policy, 14*, 483–516.

Hunter, J. E., Schmidt, F. L., & Jackson, G. B. (1982). *Meta-Anaylsis: Cumulating research findings across studies.* Beverly Hills, CA: Sage.

Hyatt, K. J. (2007). Brain Gym: Building stronger brains or wishful thinking? *Remedial and Special Education, 28*, 117–124.

Iano, R. P. (1986). The study and development of teaching: With implications for advancement of special education. *Remedial and Special Education, 7*(5), 50–61.

Individuals with Disabilities Education Improvement Act (IDEA), Public Law 108—446, 118 Stat. 2647 (2004), [Amending 20 U.S.C. § § 1400 et seq.]

Isaacson, S. (1995, February). *A comparison of alternative procedures for evaluating written expression.* Paper presented at the annual Pacific Coast Research Conference, Laguna Beach, CA.

Itard, J.M.G. (1806/1962). *The wild boy of Aveyron (G. Humphrey & M. Humphrey, trans.).* New York: Appleton-Century-Crofts.

Ives, B. (2007). Graphic organizers applied to secondary algebra instruction for student with learning disorders. *Learning Disabilities Research and Practice, 22*(2), 110–118.

Jitendra, A. K., Edwards, L. L., Sacks, G., & Jacobson, L. A. (2004). What research says about vocabulary instruction for students with learning disabilities. *Exceptional Children, 70*(3), 299–322.

Jitendra, A. K., Notel, V., Xiu, Y. P., Gomez, D. I., Renouf, L. I., & DaCosta, J. (2001). An analysis of middle school geography textbooks: Implications for students with learning problems. *Reading and Writing Quarterly, 17*, 151–173.

Jitendra, A. K., Salmento, M. M., & Haydt, L. A. (1999). A case analysis of fourth-grade subtraction instruction in basal mathematics programs: Adherence to important instructional design criteria. *Learning Disabilities Research and Practice, 14*, 69–79.

Kaestle, C. F. (1993). The awful reputation of education research. *Educational Researcher, 22*, 25–31.

Kame'enui, E. J., & Carmine, D. W. (1998). *Effective teaching strategies that accommodate diverse learners.* Upper Saddle River, NJ: Merrill/Prentice Hall.

Kauffman, J. M. (1987). Research in special education: A commentary. *Remedial and Special Education, 8*, 57–62.

Kauffman, J. M., & Hallahan, D. P. (1974). The Medical Model and the Science of Special Education. *Exceptional Children, 41*, 97–102.

Kauffman, J. M., & Sasso, G. M. (2006a). Certainty, doubt, and the reduction of uncertainty. *Exceptionality, 14*, 109–120.

Kauffman, J. M., & Sasso, G. M. (2006b). Toward ending cultural and cognitive relativism in special education. *Exceptionality, 14*, 65–90.

Kavale, K. A. (1981). Functions of the Illinois Test of Pscyholinguistic Abilities (ITPA): Are they trainable? *Exceptional Children, 47*, 496–510.

Kavale, K. A. (2001a). Decision-making in special education: The function of meta-analysis. *Exceptionality, 9*, 245–268.

Kavale, K. A. (2001b). Meta-analysis: A primer. *Exceptionality, 9*, 177–183.

Kavale, K. A., & Forness, S. R. (1987). Substance over style: Assessing the efficacy of modality testing and teaching. *Exceptional Children, 56*, 228–239.

Kavale, K. A., & Forness, S. R. (1990). Substance over style: A rejoinder to Dunn's animadversions. *Exceptional Children*, 357–361.

Kavale, K. A., & Forness, S. R. (1999). *Efficacy of special education and related services.* Washington, DC: American Association on Mental Retardation.

Kavale, K. A., & Forness, S. R. (2000). *History, rhetoric, and reality. Analysis of the inclusion debate. Remedial and special education, 21*, 279–296.

Kavale, K. A., Hirshoren, A., & Forness, S. R. (1998). Meta-analytic validation of the Dunn and Dunn model of learning-style preferences: A critique of what was Dunn. *Learning Disabilities Research and Practice, 13*, 75–80.

Kavale, K. A., & LeFever, G. B. (2007). Dunn and Dunn Model of Learning Style Preferences: Critique of Lovelace meta-analysis. *The Journal of Educational Research, 101*(2), 94–97.

Kavale, K. A., & Mattson, P. D. (1983). One jumped off the balance beam: Meta-analysis of perceptual-motor training. *Journal of Learning Disabilities, 16*, 165–173.

Kavale, K. A., & Reese, J. H. (1992). The character of learning disabilities. *Learning Disability Quarterly, 15*, 74–94.

Kephart, N. C. (1960). *The slow learner in the classroom.* Columbus, OH: Merrill.

Kephart, N. C. (1972). On the value of empirical data in learning disability. *Journal of Learning Disabilities, 4*, 393–395.

Kimball, W. H., & Heron, T. E. (1988). A behavioral commentary on Poplin's discussion of reductionistic fallacy and holistic/constructivist principles. *Journal of Learning Disabilities, 21*, 425–428.

King-Sears, M. (2001). Three steps for gaining access to the general education curriculum for learners with disabilities. *Intervention in School and Clinic, 37*, 67–76.

Kirk, R. E. (1996). Practical significance: A concept whose time has come. *Educational and Psychological Measurement, 36*, 746–759.

Kirk, S. A., & Johnson, G. O. (1951). *Educating the retarded child.* Boston, MA: Houghton Mifflin.

Kirk, S. A., McCarthy, J. J., & Kirk, W. D. (1968). *Illinois Test of Psycholinguistic Abilities* (rev. ed.). Urbana, IL: University of Illinois Press.

Klingner, J. K., Arguelles, M. E., Hughes, M. T., & Vaughn, S. (2001). Examining the schoolwide "spread" of research-based practices. *Learning Disability Quarterly, 24*, 221–234.

Klingner, J.K., Vaughn, S., Hughes, M. T., Arguelles, M. E. (1999). Sustaining research-based practices in reading: A 3-year follow-up. *Remedial and Special Education, 20*, 263–274, 287.

Kratochwill, T. R., & Shernoff, E. S. (2004). Evidence-based practice: Promoting evidence-based interventions in school psychology. *School Psychology Review, 33*, 34–48.

Landrum, T. J., Tankersley, M. (2004). Science in the schoolhouse: An uninvited guest. *Journal of Learning Disabilities, 37*, 207–212.

Larrivee, B. (1981). Modality preference as a model for differentiating beginning reading instruction: A review of the issues. *Learning Disability Quarterly, 4*, 180–188.

Laski, F. (1997). IDEA, amended or not, the past is prologue. *Journal of the Association for Persons with Severe Handicaps, 22*, 77–79.

Licht, B. K., & Torgesen, J. K. (1989). Natural science approaches to questions of subjectivity. *Journal of Learning Disabilities, 22*, 418–419, 421.

Lipsey, M. W., & Wilson, D. B. (2001). *Practical meta-analysis.* Thousand Oaks, CA: Sage.

Lloyd, J. W. (1984). How shall we individualize instruction–or should we? *Remedial and Special Education, 5*, 7–15.

Lovelace, M. K. (2005). Meta-analysis of experiemental research based on the Dunn and Dunn model. *The Journal of Educational Research, 98*, 176–183.

Lund, K. A., Foster, G. E., & McCall-Perez, G. C. (1978). The effectiveness of psycholinguistic training: A reevaluation. *Exceptional Children, 44*, 310–319.

Maag, J. W. (1989). Assessment in social skills training in general education classrooms: Issues and tactics for collaborative consultation. *Remedial and Special Education, 53*, 519–569.

Maag, J. W. (2005). Social skills training for youth with emotional and behavioral disorders and learning disabilities: Problems, conclusions, and suggestions. *Exceptionality, 13*, 155–172.

Maag, J. W. (2006). Social skills training for students with emotional and behavioral disorders: A review of reviews. *Behavioral Disorders, 32*, 5–17.

MacMillan, D. L., Gresham, F. M., & Forness, S. R. (1996). Full inclusion: An empirical perspective: *Behavioral Disorders, 21*, 145–159.

Mann, L. (1970). Perceptual training: Misdirections and redirections. *American Journal of Orthopsychiatry, 40*, 30–38.

Mann, L. (1979). *On the trail of process.* New York, NY: Grune & Stratton.

Mastropieri, M. A., & Scruggs, T. E. (2004). *The inclusive classroom: Strategies for effective instruction (2nd Ed.).* Upper Saddle River, NJ: Pearson Education.

Mastropieri, M. A., Scruggs, T. E, Bakken, J. P., & Whedon, C. (1996). Reading comprehension: A synthesis of research in learning disabilities. In T. E. Scruggs & M. A. Mastropieri (Eds.), *Advances in learning and behavioral disabilities* (vol. 10, pp. 277–303). Greenwich, CT: JAI Press.

Mather, S. R., Bos, C., & Babur, N. (2001). Perceptions and knowledge of preservice and inservice teachers about early literacy instruction. *Journal of Learning Disabilities, 34*, 472–482.

Mathur, S. R., Kavale, K. A., Quinn, M. M., Forness, S. R. & Rutherford, R. B. (1998). Social skills interventions with students with emotional and behavioral problems: A quantitative synthesis of single-subject research. *Behavioral Disorders, 23*, 1993–2001.

McCutchen, D., Abbott, R. D., Green, L. B., Beretvas, S. N., Cox, S., Potter, N. S., Quiroga, T., & Gray, A. L. (2002). Beginning literacy: Links among teacher knowledge, teacher practice, and student learning. *Journal of Learning Disabilities, 35*, 69–86.

McGinnis, E., Goldstein, A., Sprafkin, R., & Gershaw, N. (1984). *Skill streaming the elementary school child: A guide for teaching prosocial skills.* Champaign, IL: Research Press.

McGraw, K. O., & Wong, S. P. (1992). A common language effect size. *Psychological Bulletin, 111*, 361–365.

Meese, R. L. (2001). *Teaching learners with mild disabilities: Integrating research and practice (2nd Ed.).* Belmont, CA: Wedswort/Thomson Learning.

Milofsky, C. (1974). Why special education isn't special. *Harvard Educational Review, 44*, 437–458.

Minskoff, E. (1975). Research on psycholinguistic training: Critique and guidelines. *Exceptional Children, 42*, 136–144.

Morrison, D. E., & Henkel, R. E. (1970). *The significance test controversy: A reader.* Chicago: Aldine.

Mostert, M. P., Kavale, K. A., & Kauffman, J. M. (2008). *Challenging the refusal of reasoning in special education.* Denver: Love Publishing Co.

Murawski, W. W., & Swanson, H. L. (2001). A meta-analysis of co-teaching research: Where are the data? *Remedial & Special Education, 22*(5), 258–267.

Nelson, J. R., Benner, G., Gonzalez, J. (2003). Learner characteristics that influence the treatment effectiveness of early literacy interventions: A meta-analytic review. *Learning Disabilities Research & Practice, 18*(4), 255–267.

Newcomer, P., Larsen, S., & Hammill, D. (1975). A response. *Exceptional Children, 42*, 144–148.

O'Connor, R. E. (2000). Increasing the intensity of intervention in kindergarten and first grade. *Learning Disabilities Research and Practice, 15*, 43–54.

Odom, S. L., Brantlinger, E., Horner, R. H., Thompson, B., & Harris, K. R. (2005). Research in special education: Scientific methods and evidence-based practices. *Exceptional Children, 72*, 137–148.

Osgood, C. E. (1957). *Motivational dynamics of language behavior.* In M. R. Jones (Ed.), *Nebraska symposium on motivation.* Lincoln: University of Nebraska Press.

Polloway, E. A., & Patton, J. R. (1997). *Strategies for teaching learners with special needs (6th Ed.).* Upper Saddle River, NJ: Prentice Hall.

Poplin, M. S. (1988). The reductionist fallacy in learning disabilities: Replicating the past by reducing the present. *The Journal of Learning Disabilities, 21*, 389–400.

Quinn, M. M., Kavale, K. A., Mathur, S. R., Rutherford, R. B., & Forness, S. R. (1999). A meta-analysis of social skills

interventions for students with emotional or behavioral disorders. *Journal of Emotional and Behavioral Disorders, 7*, 54–64.

Rankin-Erickson, J. L., & Pressley, M. (2000). A survey of instructional practices of special education teachers nominated as effective teachers of literacy. *Learning Disabilities Research and Practice, 15*, 206–225.

Reid, R., Trout, A. L., & Schartz, M. (2005). Self-regulation interventions for children with Attention Deficit/Hyperativity Disorder. *Council for Exceptional Children, 71*(4), 361–377.

Rosenshine, B. (1976). Classroom instruction. In N. L. Gage (Ed.), *The psychology of teaching methods: The seventy-fifth yearbook of the National Society for the Study of Education* (pp. 109–143). Chicago, IL: University of Chicago Press.

Rosenthal, R., & Rubin, D. B. (1983). A simple, general purpose display of magnitude of experimental effect. *Educational Psychology, 74*, 166–169.

Santangelo, T., Harris, K. R., & Graham, S. (2008). Using self-regulated strategy development to support students who have "trubol giting thangs into werds." *Remedial and Special Education, 29*(2), 78–89.

Sasso, G. M. (2001). The Retreat from inquiry and knowledge in special education. *Journal of Special Education, 34*, 178–193.

Scammacca, N., Vaughn, S., Roberts, G., Wanzek, J., & Torgesen, J. K. (2007). *Extensive reading interventions in grades K–3: From research to practice.* Portsmouth, NH: RMC Research Corporation, Center on Instruction.

Scruggs, T. E., Mastropieri, M. A., & Casto, G. (1987). The quantitative synthesis of single-subject research: Methodology and validation. *Remedial and Special Education, 8*, 24–33.

Scruggs, T. E., & Richter, L. (1985). Tutoring learning disabled students: A critical review. *Learning Disability Quarterly, 8*, 286–298.

Seethaler, P. M., & Fuchs, L. (2005). A drop in the bucket: Randomized controlled trials testing teading and math interventions. *Learning Disabilities Research and Practice, 20*, 98–102.

Seguin, E. (1866). *Idiocy and its treatment by the physiological method.* New York, NY: William Wood.

Shattuck, R. (1994). *The forbidden experiment: The story of the Wild Boy of Aveyron.* New York: Farra, Strauss, & Giroux.

Shavelson, R. J., & Towne, L. (Eds.). (2002). *Scientific research in education.* Washington, DC: National Academy Press.

Skiba, R., & Casey, A. (1985). Interventions for behaviorally disordered students: A quantitative review and methodological critique. *Behavioral Disorders, 10*, 239–252.

Slavin, R. E. (1989). PET and the pendulum: Faddism in education and how to stop it. *Phi Delta Kappan, 70*, 752–758.

Smith, S. B., Simmons, D. C., Gleason, M. M., Kame'enui, E. J., Baker, S., & Sprick, M., et al. (2001). An analysis of phonological awareness instruction in four kindergarten basal reading programs. *Reading and Writing Quarterly, 17*, 25–51.

Stage, S. A., & Quiroz, D. R. (1997). A meta-analysis of interventions to decrease disruptive classroom behavior in public education settings. *School Psychology Review, 26*(3), 333–368.

Stenhoff, D. M., & Lignugarisk/Kraft, B. (2007). A review of the effects of peer tutoring on students with mild disabilities in secondary settings. *Exceptional Children, 74*(1), 8–30.

Strauss, A. A., & Kephart, N. C. (1955). *Psychopathology and education of the brain-injured child: Vol. II. Progress in theory and clinic.* New York, NY: Grune & Stratton.

Swanson, H. L. (1999). Reading research for students with LD: A meta-analysis of intervention outcomes. *Journal of Learning Disabilities, 32*(6), 504–532.

Swanson, H. L. (2001). Searching for the best model for instructing students with learning disabilities. *Focus on Exceptional Children, 34*(2), 1–14.

Swanson, H. L., & Deschler, D. (2003). Instructing adolescents with learning disabilities: Converting a meta-analysis to practice. *Journal of Learning Disabilities, 36*(2), 124–135.

Swanson, H. L., Hoskin, M., & Lee, S. (1999). *Interventions for Students with Learning Disabilities: A Meta-Analysis of Treatment Outcomes.* New York: Guilford.

Swanson, H. L., & Sachse-Lee, C. (2001). A meta-analysis of single-subject-design intervention research for students with LD. *Journal of Learning Disabilities, 33*(2), 114–136.

Talbot, E., Lloyd, J. W., & Tankersley, M. (1994). Effects of reading comprehension interventions for students with learning disabilities. *Learning Disability Quarterly, 17,* 223–232.

Tarver, S. G., & Dawson, M. M. (1978). Modality preference and the teaching of reading: A review. *Journal of Learning Disabilities, 1,* 5–17.

Therrien, W. J. (2004). Fluency and comprehension gains as a result of repeated reading. *Remedial and Special Education, 25*(4), 252–261.

Thompson, B., Diamond, K., McWilliam, R., Snyder, P., & Synder, S. (2004). Evaluating the quality of evidence from correlational research for evidence-based practice. *Exceptional Children, 71,* 181–194.

Torgesen, J. K., Wagner, R. K., Rashotte, C. A., Rose, E., Lindamond, P., & Conway, T. (1999). Preventing reading failure in young children with phonological processing disabilities: Group and individual responses to instruction. *Journal of Educational Psychology, 91*(4), 579–593.

Ulman, J. D., & Rosenberg, M. S. (1986). Science and superstition in special education. *Exceptional Children, 52,* 459–460.

U.S. Department of Education. (2006). Assistance to states for the education of children with disabilities and preschool grants for children with disabilities; final regulations. *Federal Register, 71*(156), 34 CFR 300 and 301.

Vadasy, P. F., Jenkins, J. R., & Pool, K. (2000). Effects of tutoring in phonological and early reading skills on students at risk for reading disabilities. *Journal of Learning Disabilities, 33*(6), 579–590.

Van Witsen, B. (1967). *Perceptual training activities handbook.* New York, NY: Teachers College Press.

Vaughn, S., & Dammann, J. E. (2001). Science and sanity in special education. *Behavioral Disorders, 27,* 21–29.

Vaughn, S., & Linen-Thompson, S. (2003). What is special about special education for students with learning disabilities? *The Journal of Special Education,* 140–147.

Vaughn, S., Gersten, R., & Chard, D. J. (2000). The underlying message in LD intervention research: Findings from research syntheses. *Exceptional Children, 67,* 99–114.

Vaughn, S., Klingner, J., & Hughes, M. (2000). Sustainability of research-based practices. *Exceptional Children, 66,* 163–171.

Wagner, R. W., Torgesen, J. K., Laughon, P., Simmons, K., & Rashotte, C. A. (1993). Development of young readers' phonological processing abilities. *Journal of Educational Psychology, 85*(1), 83–103.

Walker, H. M., McConnell, S., Holmes, D., Todis, B., Walker, J., & Golden, N. (1983). *The Walker social skills curriculum: The ACCEPTS program.* Austin, TX: Pro-Ed.

White, W. A. T. (1988). A meta-analysis of effects of direct instruction in special education. *Education and Treatment of Chidren, 11,* 364–374.

Zigmond, N., Jenkins, J., Fuchs, D., Deno, S., & Fuchs, L. (1995). When students fail to achieve satisfactorily. *Phi Delta Kappan, 77,* 303–306.

Appendix A Primary Effect Size Sources

Adams, G. L, & Carnine, D. (2003). Direct Instruction. In H. L. Swanson, K. R. Harris, & S. Graham (Eds.), *Handbook of learning disabilities* (pp. 403–416). New York: Guilford Press.

Adams, G. L., & Englemann, S. (1996). Research on Direct Instruction: 25 years beyond DISTAR. Seattle, WA: Educational Achievement Systems.

Browder, D. M., & Xin, Y. P. (1998). A meta-analysis and review of sight word research and its implications for teaching functional reading to individuals with moderate and severe disabilities. *Journal of Special Education, 32,* 130–153.

Browder, D. M., Spooner, F., Ahlgrim-Delzell, L., Harris, A. A., & Wakeman, S. (2008). A meta-analysis on teaching mathematics to students with significant cognitive disabilities. *Exceptional Children, 74*(4), 407–432.

Burns, M. K. (2004). Empirical analysis of drill ratio research: Refining the instructional level for drill tasks. *Remedial and Special Education, 25,* 167–173.

Burns, M. K., & Symington, T. (2002). A meta-analysis of pre-referral intervention teams: Student and systemic outcomes. *Journal of School Psychology, 40,* 437–447.

Bus, A. G., & van Ijzendoorn, M. H. (1999). Phonological awareness and early reading: A meta-analysis of experimental training studies. *Journal of Educational Psychology, 91*(3), 403–414.

Carlberg, C., & Kavale, K. (1980). The efficacy of special versus regular class placement for exceptional children: A meta-analysis. *Journal of Special Education, 14,* 296–309.

Carlson, M. (1987). *Social and academic outcomes of cooperative learning in the mainstreamed classroom: A meta-analysis.* Unpublished manuscript, Claremont Graduate School, CA.

Casto, G., & Mastropieri, M. A. (1986). The efficacy of early intervention programs: A meta-analysis. *Exceptional Children, 52,* 417–424.

Conners, F. A. (1992). Reading instruction for students with moderate mental retardation: Review and analysis of research. *American Journal on Mental Retardation, 96,* 577–597.

Cook, S. B., Scruggs, T. E., Mastropieri, M. A., & Casto, G. C. (1985–1986). Handicapped students as tutors. *Journal of Special Education, 19,* 483–492.

Crenshaw, T. M., Kavale, K. A., Forness, S. R., & Reeve, R. E. (1999). Attention deficit hyperactivity disorder and the efficacy of stimulant medication: A meta-analysis. In T. E. Scruggs & M. A. Mastropieri (Eds.), *Advances in learning and behavioral disabilities* (Vol. 13, pp. 135–165). Stamford, CT: JAI Press.

Durlak, J. A., Fuhrman, J., & Lampman, C. (1991). Effectiveness of cognitive-behavior therapy for maladapting children: A meta-analysis. *Psychological Bulletin, 110,* 204–214.

Elbaum, B., Vaughn, S., Hughes, M., & Moody, S. W. (1999). Grouping practices and reading outcomes for students with disabilities. *Exceptional Children, 65,* 399–415.

Elbaum, B., Vaughn, S., Hughes, M., Moody, S. W., & Schumm, J. S. (2000). How reading outcomes of students with disabilities are related to instructional grouping formats: A meta-analytic review. In R. Gersten, E. Schiller, & S. Vaughn (Eds.), *Contemporary Special Education Research* (pp. 105–135). Mahwah, NJ: Erlbaum.

Engles, G. I., Garnefski, N., & Diekstra, R. F. W. (1993). Efficacy of rational emotive therapy: Aquantitive analysis. *Journal of Consulting and Clinical Psychology, 61,* 1083–1090.

Forness, S. R. (2001). Special education and related services: What have we learned from meta-analysis? *Exceptionality, 9,* 185–198.

Forness, S. R., Kavale, K. A., Blum, I. M., & Lloyd, J. W. (1997). Mega-analysis of meta-analysis: What works in special education and related services. *Teaching Exceptional Children, 29,* 4–9.

Forness, S. R., & Kavale, K. A. (1993). Strategies to improve basic learning and memory deficits in mental retardation: A meta-analysis of experimental studies. *Education and Training in Mental Retardation, 28,* 99–110.

Forness, S. R., & Kavale, K. A. (1996). Treating social skill deficits in children with learning disabilities: A meta-analysis of the research. *Learning Disability Quarterly, 19,* 1–13.

Fuchs, L. S., & Fuchs, D. (1986b). Effects of systematic evaluation. A meta-analysis. *Exceptional Children, 53,* 199–208.

Gajira, M., Jitendra, A. K., Sood, S., & Sacks, G. (2007). Improving comprehension of expository text in students with LD: A research synthesis. *Journal of Learning Disabilities, 40*(3), 210–225.

Gersten, R., & Baker, S. (2001). Teaching expressive writing to students with learning disabilities: A meta-analysis. *Elementary School Journal, 101,* 251–272.

Gonzalez, J. E., Nelson, J. R., Gutkin, T. B., Saunders, A., Galloway, A., & Shwery, G. S. (2004). Rational emotive therapy with children and adolescents: A meta-analysis. *Journal of Emotional and Behavioral Disorders, 12,* 222–235.

Graham, S., & Harris, K. R. (2003). Students with learning disabilities and the process of writing: A meta-analysis of SRSD studies. In H. L. Swanson, K. R. Harris, & S. Graham (Eds.), *Handbook of learning disabilities* (pp. 323–344). New York: Guilford Press.

Hillocks, G. (1984). What works in teaching composition: A meta-analysis of experimental treatment studies. *American Journal of Education, 93,* 133–170.

Horn, W. F., & Packard, T. (1985). Early identification of learning problems: A meta-analysis. *Journal of Educational Psychology, 77,* 597–607.

Innocenti, M. S., & White, K. R. (1993). Are more intensive early intervention programs more effective? A review of the literature. *Exceptionality, 4,* 31–50.

Jitendra, A. K., Edwards, L. L., Sacks, G., & Jacobson, L. A. (2004). What research says about vocabulary instruction for students with learning disabilities. *Exceptional Children, 70,* 299–322.

Johnson, D.W., Johnson, R. T., & Maruyama, G. (1983). Interdependence and interpersonal attraction among heterogeneous and homogeneous individuals: A theoretical formulation and meta-analysis of the research. *Review of Education Research, 53,* 5–54.

Kavale, K. (1981). Function of the Illinois Test of Psycholinguistic Abilities (ITPA). Are they trainable? *Exceptional Children, 47,* 496–510.

Kavale, K. (1982a). The efficacy of stimulant drug treatment for hyperactivity: A meta-analysis. *Journal of Learning Disabilities, 15,* 280–289.

Kavale, K. (1982b). Psycholinguistic training programs: Are there differential treatment effects? *The Exceptional Child, 29,* 21–30.

Kavale, K. A. (1984). A meta-analytic evaluation of the Frostig test and training program. *The Exceptional Child, 31,* 134–141.

Kavale, K. A. (1990). Variances and verities in learning disability interventions. In T. E. Scruggs & B. Y. L. Wong (Eds.), *Intervention research in learning disabilities* (pp. 3–33). New York: Springer-Verlag.

Kavale, K. A., & Dobbins, D. A. (1993). The equivocal nature of special education interventions. *Early Child Development and Care, 86,* 23–37.

Kavale, K. A., & Forness, S. R. (1983). Hyperactivity and diet treatment: A meta-analysis of the Feingold hypothesis. *Journal of Learning Disabilities, 16,* 324–330.

Kavale, K. A., & Forness, S. R. (1987). Substance over style: Assessing the efficacy of modality testing and teaching. *Exceptional Children, 54,* 228–239.

Kavale, K. A., & Forness, S. R. (2000). Policy decisions in special education: The role of analysis. In R. Gersten, E. Schiller, & S. Vaughn (Eds.), *Contemporary special education research* (pp. 281–326). Mahwah, NJ: Erlbaum.

Kavale, K. A., & Glass, G. V. (1982). The efficacy of special education interventions and practices: A compendium of meta-analysis findings. *Focus on Exceptional Children, 15*(4), 1–14.

Kavale, K. A., & Glass, G. V. (1984). Meta-analysis and policy decisions in special education. In B. K. Keogh (Ed.), *Advances in special education* (Vol. IV, pp. 195–247), Greenwich, CT: JAI.

Kavale, K. A., & Mattson, P. D. (1983). "One jumped off the balance beam": Meta-analysis of perceptual-motor training. *Journal of Learning Disabilities, 16,* 165–173.

Kavale, K. A., & Mostert, M. P. (2005). Somewhere over the rainbow: A meta-analysis of Irlen lenses/color overlays for improving reading. Unpublished manuscript, Regent University, Virginia Beach, VA.

Kroesbergen, E. H., & VanLuit, J. E. H. (2003). Mathematics interventions for children with special educational needs: A meta-analysis. *Remedial and Special Education, 24,* 97–114.

Lapadat, J. C. (1991). Pragmatic language skills of students with language and/or learning disabilities: A quantitative synthesis. *Journal of Learning Disabilities, 24,* 147–158.

Lipsey, M. W., & Wilson, D. B. (1993). The efficacy of psychological, educational, and behavioral treatment. *American Psychologist, 48,* 1181–1209.

Mastropieri, M. A., Bakken, J. P., & Scruggs, T. E. (1991). Mathematics instruction for individuals with mental retardation: A perspective and research synthesis. *Education and Training in Mental Retardation, 26,* 115–129.

Mastropieri, M. A., & Scruggs, T. E. (1985–1986). Early intervention for socially withdrawn children. *Journal of Special Education, 19,* 429–441.

Mastropieri, M.A., & Scruggs, T. E. (1989). Constructing more meaningful relationships: Mnemonic instruction for special populations. *Educational Psychology Review, 1,* 83–111.

Mastropieri, M. A., Scruggs, T. E., Bakken, J.P., & Whedon, C. (1996). Reading comprehension: A synthesis of research in learning disabilities. In T. E. Scruggs & M. A. Mastropieri (Eds.), *Advances in learning and behavioral disabilities* (Vol. 10, pp. 227–303). Greenwich, CT: JAI Press.

Mastropieri, M. A., Spencer, V., Scruggs, T. E., & Talbott, E. (2000). Students with disabilities as tutors: An updated research synthesis. In T. E. Scruggs & M. A. Mastropieri (Eds.),

Advances in learning and behavioral disabilities: Educational interventions (Vol. 14, pp. 247–279). Stamford, CT: JAI Press.

Mathur, S. R., Kavale, K. A., Quinn, M. M., Forness, S. R., & Rutherford, R. B. (1998). Social skills interventions with students with emotional and behavioral problems: A quantitative synthesis of single-subject research. *Behavioral Disorders, 23,* 193–201.

Nye, C., Foster, S. H., & Seaman, D. (1987). Effectiveness of language intervention with the language/learning disabled. *Journal of Speech and Hearing Disorders, 52,* 348–357.

Quinn, M. M., Kavale, K. A., Mathur, S., Rutherford, R. B., & Forness, S. R. (1999). A meta-analysis of social skill interventions for students with emotional or behavioral disorders. *Journal of Emotional and Behavioral Disorders, 7,* 54–64.

Reddy, L., Barboza-Whitehead, S., Files, T., & Rubel, E. (2000). Clinical focus of consultation outcome research with children and adolescents. *Journal of Applied School Psychology, 16,* 1–22.

Robinson, T. R., Smith, S. W., Miller, M. D., & Brownell, M. T. (1999). Cognitive behavior modification of hyperactivity–impulsivity and aggression: A meta-analysis of school-based studies. *Journal of Educational Psychology, 91,* 195–203.

Santangelo, T., Harris, K. R., & Graham, S. (2008). Using self-regulated strategy development to support students who have "trubol giting thangs into werds." *Remedial and Special Education, 29*(2), 78–89.

Schmidt, M., Weinstein, T., Niemic, R., & Walberg, H. J. (1985–1986). Computer-assisted instruction with exceptional children. *Journal of Special Education, 19,* 494–501.

Schumm, J. S., Moody, S. W., & Vaughn, S. (2000). Grouping for reading instruction: Does one size fit all? *Journal of Learning Disabilities, 33,* 477–488.

Scruggs, T. E., Mastropieri, M. A., Cook, S., & Escobar, C. (1986). Early intervention for children with conduct disorders: A quantitative synthesis of single-subject research. *Behavioral Disorders, 11,* 260–271.

Scruggs, T. E., Mastropieri, M. A., Forness, S. R., & Kavale, K. A. (1988). Early language intervention: A quantitative synthesis of single-subject research. *Journal of Special Education, 22,* 259–283.

Shonkoff, J. P., & Hauser-Cram, P. (1987). Early intervention for disabled infants and their families: A quantitative analysis. *Pediatrics, 80,* 650–658.

Skiba, R. J., & Casey, A. (1985). Interventions for behaviorally disordered students: A quantitative review and methodological critique. *Behavioral Disorders, 10,* 239–252.

Stenhoff, D. M., & Lignugarisk/kraft, B. (2007). A review of the effects of peer tutoring on students with mild disabilities in secondary settings. *Exceptional Children, 74*(1), 8–30.

Stevens, R. J., & Slavin, R. E. (1991). When cooperative learning improves the achievement of students with mild disabilities: A response to Tateyama-Sniezck. *Exceptional Children, 57,* 276–280.

Swanson, H. L. (1999). Interventions for students with learning disabilities: A meta-analysis of treatment outcomes. New York: Guilford.

Swanson, H. L. (1999). Reading research for students with LD: A meta-analysis of intervention outcomes. *Journal of Learning Disabilities, 32,* 504–532.

Swanson, H. L. (2001). Research on interventions for adolescents with learning disabilities: A meta-analysis of outcomes related to higher-order processing. *Elementary School Journal, 101,* 331–348.

Swanson, H. L., Carson, C., & Sachse-Lee, C. M. (1996). A selective synthesis of intervention research for students with learning disabilities. *School Psychology Review, 25,* 370–391.

Swanson, H. L., & Hoskyn, M. (1998). Experimental intervention research on students with learning disabilities: A meta-analysis of treatment outcomes. *Review of Educational Research, 68,* 277–321.

Swanson, H. L., & Hoskyn, M. (2000). Intervention research for students with learning disabilities: A comprehensive meta-analysis of group design studies. In T. E. Scruggs & M. A. Mastropieri (Eds.), *Advances in learning and behavioral disabilities* (Vol. 14, pp. 1–153). Stamford, CT: JAI Press.

Swanson, H. L., O'Shaughnessy, T. E., McMahon, C. M., Hoskyn, M., & Sachse-Lee, C. M. (1998). A selective synthesis of single subject design intervention research on students with learning disabilities. In T. E. Scruggs & M. A. Mastropieri (Eds.), *Advances in learning and behavioral disabilities* (Vol. 12, pp. 79–126). Greenwich, CT: JAI Press.

Talbott, E., Lloyd, J. W., & Tankersley, M. (1994). Effects of reading comprehension interventions for students with learning disabilities. *Learning Disability Quarterly, 17,* 223–232.

Therrien, W. J. (2004). Fluency and comprehension gains as a result of repeated readings: A meta-analysis. *Remedial and Special Education, 25,* 252–261.

Thurber, S., & Walker, C. E. (1983). Medication and hyperactivity: A meta-analysis. *Journal of General Psychology, 108,* 79–86.

Vaughn, S., Gersten, R., & Chard, D. J. (2000). The underlying message in LD intervention research: Findings from research syntheses. *Exceptional Children, 67,* 99–114.

Vaughn, S, Klingner, J., Hughes, M. (2000). Factors enhancing sustained use of research-based instructional practices. *Journal of Learning Disabilities, 33,* 445–457.

Walberg, H. J. (1984). Improving the productivity of America's schools. *Educational Leadership, 41,* 19–30.

Wang, M. C., & Baker, E. T. (1985–1986), Mainstreaming programs: design features and effects, *Journal of Special Education, 19,* 503–521.

Waxman, H. C., Wang, M. C., Anderson, K. A., & Walberg, H. J. (1985). Adaptive education and student outcomes: A quantitative synthesis. *Journal of Educational Research, 78,* 228–236.

White, K. R. (1985–1986). Efficacy of early interventions. *Journal of Special Education, 19,* 401–416.

White, W. A. T. (1988). A meta-analysis of the effects of direct instruction in special education, *Education and Treatment of Children, 11,* 364–374.

Xin, Y. P., & Jitendra, A. K. (1999). The effects of instruction in solving mathematical word problems for students with learning problems: A meta-analysis. *Journal of Special Education, 32,* 207–225.

Academic Interventions: What School Psychologists Need to Know for Their Assessment and Problem Solving Consultation Roles

Virginia W. Berninger, Michel Fayol, *and* Nicole Alston–Abel

Abstract

This chapter provides an overview of critical concepts about academic interventions that school psychologists can apply in their assessment (prevention and diagnosis) and problem solving consultation roles. Topics covered include (a) general principles from research on reading, writing, math, and science instruction and learning; (b) home–school relationships; and (c) issues of diversity, motivation, and interpersonal relationships. School psychologists are encouraged to read widely and deeply the research literature on academic instruction and learning, to which many disciplines have contributed. School psychologists are also encouraged to practice and master the artful transformation of that research knowledge to the individual case at hand within a specific social context, including the family, classroom, school, community, and culture.

Keywords: reading, writing, math, science, home–school relationships, diversity

In an era of accountability in education, with high expectations for student learning outcomes, school psychologists are expected to partner with teachers and other educational professionals to raise academic achievement. In the United States, the federal government has issued a clear mandate that teachers should use evidence-based instructional practices to improve student learning outcomes. In this chapter we discuss other issues that school psychologists need to consider, along with research knowledge of teaching methods, to help students better learn academic skills.

The job responsibility of school psychologists is not to teach students academic skills directly. School psychologists contribute to improved student learning outcomes through indirect services—assessment and problem-solving consultation—which are their job roles (Peverly, 2009). Assessment may include screening for early intervention, progress monitoring to assess response to intervention (RTI), and testing to determine if students qualify for special education (eligibility decisions) or meet criteria for specific learning disabilities that have instructional implications (diagnostic decisions). Problem-solving consultation includes discussions with other professionals about a referred student to identify the student's problem, plan intervention to modify the program that is not working, monitor the response to the intervention (RTI), and, if the student does not respond to that intervention, design an alternative plan. For both the assessment and consultation roles, knowledge of evidence-based academic interventions is highly relevant for generating academic intervention plans based on the assessment information, and increasing the probability that students will respond to the intervention. See Berninger (2007) for further discussion of these issues with applications to practice.

However, the amount and nature of preservice preparation school psychologists receive regarding academic interventions vary greatly. Some programs, especially those with an exclusively behavioral or special education orientation, may not cover the comprehensive body of research generated since the mid-twentieth century in fields ranging from mainstream reading, writing, math, and science research to linguistics, cognitive psychology, developmental psychology, and cognitive neuroscience. Moreover, inservice school psychologists may not have the time to keep up with, and become knowledgeable consumers of, an ever growing and evolving body of research relevant to academic learning. Consequently, they tend to rely on some of the following sources to obtain their information about evidence-based academic intervention practices: professional development presentations that offer continuing education credits, chapters in books that review the research, results of meta-analyses of multiple research studies, and testimony of publishers that a product is evidence-based.

Moreover, the emphasis in these secondary sources is often on what the teacher should do and what works for students, without sufficient attention to individual differences or systems variables (family and home–school relationships, interpersonal relationships in classrooms, school, community, and cultural issues, etc). Although knowledge of evidence-based practices based on research samples is necessary and desirable, such knowledge may not be sufficient; considerable clinical expertise is required for effectively translating that knowledge into educational practice (see Rosenfield & Berninger, 2009). Because school psychologists are the individual-differences specialists in schools, they are in an ideal position to help educators custom tailor academic instructional programs to the needs of individual learners.

The main goals of this chapter are, therefore, to provide for school psychologists (a) references to access recent reviews, syntheses, and meta-analyses of research findings about effective instruction in reading, writing, math, and science; (b) offer general principles based on the accumulating research evidence from many relevant research traditions that provide a conceptual framework for transforming research knowledge about academic learning into educational practice (planning, implementing, and evaluating academic interventions); and (c) discuss other important issues beyond instruction per se, for which research also exists, such as learning processes from the perspective of the student who is expected to respond to the instruction. To address these issues beyond teaching behaviors, we adopt a *systems approach* and apply it to (a) the individual learner's *response to instruction* across the domains of academic learning—reading, writing, math, and science; and (b) the social context in which learning occurs at school and home across cultures.

A theme that has been supported by meta-analyses of research across these academic domains is that children respond best to *explicit instruction*. However, what counts as evidence-based, explicit instruction is far ranging and includes (a) instructional activities to develop conscious awareness of the relevant aspects of domain-specific learning; (b) teacher modeling of procedural knowledge for how to perform specific academic skills; (c) teacher-guided lessons that lead students to articulate conclusions, generate summaries, and/or answer questions that require inferential thinking; (d) direct explanations; and (e) strategy instruction for self-regulated learning (see Berninger, 2007; Cartwright, 2008; Graham, Harris, & Zito, 2005; Mayer & Wittrock, 2004; Rosenfield & Berninger, 2009, Part I; Swanson & Deschler, 2003).

Reading
Accessing Research on Effective Reading Instruction
Many reviews and meta-analyses of effective reading instruction have been conducted in the recent past (for an overview of these, see McCardle & Miller, 2009). In this chapter we focus on instructional and learning issues, for which evidence exists, but that were not covered in the influential National Reading Panel Report (NICHD, 2000), which has had major impact on instructional practices in the United States. The instructional components recommended by the National Reading Panel included phonological awareness, phonological decoding (alphabetic principle), fluency, vocabulary, and reading comprehension. To illustrate that research-generated knowledge is ever expanding, we propose that four additional kinds of evidence-based instruction should also be recommended for best practices: linguistic awareness that includes orthographic and morphological awareness as well as phonological awareness; teaching predictable decoding for written English words that draws on multiple knowledge sources including the three kinds of linguistic awareness; teaching oral language to facilitate learning of written language; and integrating writing and reading. Then, we discuss, from a systems perspective, the complexities of the skills that the learner must orchestrate in responding to reading instruction.

Linguistic Awareness
The ability to store words in working memory and reflect upon their constituent parts is critical to the acquisition of written language (Mattingly, 1972).

However, three kinds of linguistic awareness play a role, but only the first kind was reviewed by the National Reading Panel: (1) phonological awareness of the sounds in spoken words; (2) orthographic awareness of letters and multi-letter units in written words; and (3) morphological awareness of the base word, plus or minus affixes in both spoken and written words that underlie the formation of longer, complex words, refine meaning and, in the case of suffixes, mark grammatical information linking words to higher levels of language. For evidence supporting *orthographic awareness*[1], see Berninger (1987), Caravolas, Kessler, Hulme, and Snowling, (2005), Cassar and Trieman (1997), Olson, Forsberg, and Wise (1994), Seymour (1997), Pacton, Perruchet, Fayol, and Cleeremans (2001), Pacton, Fayol, and Perruchet (2005), and Varnhagen et al. (1999). For evidence supporting *morphological awareness*[1], see Bourassa, Treiman, and Kessler (2006), Carlisle and Nomanbhoy (1993), Fayol, Totereau, and Barrouillet (2006), Leong, (2000), Nagy, Berninger, and Abbott (2006), Nunes and Bryant (2006), Pacton et al. (2005), and Pacton and Deacon (2008).

All three kinds of linguistic awareness, especially the interrelationships among phonological, orthographic, and morphological awareness, predict reading (and writing) outcomes of typically developing children and children with dyslexia (Berninger et al., 2008). See Henry (2003) for evidence-based approaches to teaching the phonology, orthography, and morphology of English words of Anglo-Saxon, Romance (French and Latin), and Greek origin, all of which are needed for reading achievement, from the beginning but especially after the first three grades. After the third-to-fourth-grade transition from oral to silent reading, the silent orthography and silent morphology of written words (which do not always correspond to phonological units of the same size), become increasingly important in languages with deep morphologies that code not only letter-sound correspondence, but also spelling-morphology correspondences (Jaffré & Fayol, 2006).

Teaching Regularities for Decoding in Morphophonemic Orthographies

English has a deep morphophonemic orthography, which means that even though it is not perfectly regular in pronunciation in terms of a single letter and a single phoneme, it is predictable when all three knowledge sources (orthography, morphology, and phonology) are taken into account (Venezky, 1970, 1999). For example, in English, the predictable correspondences in alphabetic principle tend to be between 2-letter (and not just-1-letter) spelling units and one phoneme, or a small set of phonemes called alternations, which can be applied strategically to decoding words until a match with a meaningful word in the mental dictionary is made. Moreover, alphabetic principle is not the only knowledge source that is relevant to decoding words in English, because pronunciation can also be based on multi-letter units corresponding to a rime unit (the part of a syllable left when the onset phoneme or blend is deleted), which often contains multiple phonemes; these correspondences are referred to by teachers as a *word family* (e.g., *ould* in could and would). Multi-letter units may also correspond to morphemes units with predictable spelling and pronunciation (see Nunes & Bryant, 2006). For example, tion and sion, which both contain the -ion morpheme, but the former has ti and the latter has si to stand for the alternate spellings of /sh/ in words of Latinate origin and in both cases the whole unit is pronounced /shun/ despite the unaccented /o/ vowel that does not have regular grapheme-phoneme correspondence.

Thus, teachers (or psychologists) should never tell children who are learning to read English that they should sound out unfamiliar words letter by letter, or that English is hopelessly irregular. Instead, an evidence-based approach teaches children the multiple ways units of written language (not just single letters) are related to units of spoken language within the word parts that mark meaning and grammar, so that the relationships among spelling, pronunciation, and meaning are evident. No words are completely irregular when the multiple connections underlying written and spoken language are taught explicitly to children. In addition, synthetic phonics alone, as recommended by the National Reading Panel, may not be effective if children cannot apply phonics rules learned as declarative knowledge (rules) to the decoding process. It may be necessary to teach alphabetic principle and other strategies for translating units of written language into units of spoken language as *procedural knowledge*; that is, how to produce the corresponding unit of language during the actual reading process. For school psychologists not familiar with the research from linguistic science, cognitive science, and instructional science that has provided the evidence supporting these general principles of reading instruction, which were not covered in the National Reading Panel Report, see the Table of Contents in Berninger (2007), with instructional resources from interdisciplinary research on word decoding along with explanations of the rationale underlying these word learning concepts. Berninger and Wolf (2009-a, 2009-b) also illustrate with practical examples how these general principles can be implemented in instruction.

Role of Oral Language in Learning Written Language

Many mistakenly believe that children have already learned oral language skills prior to school entry, and that the sole purpose of elementary education is to teach written language skills (reading and writing), that is, literacy. Mainstream educational research has long recognized that oral language is an important part of the instructional program for learning to read and write; many research studies have pointed to the conclusion that reading instruction benefits from oral discussion before and after reading text (e.g., Reznitskaya, Anderson, McNurlen, Nguyen-Jahiel, Archodidou, & Kim, 2001). However, children show considerable intra-individual differences in their oral language (listening and speaking) and written language (reading and writing) skills (Berninger et al., 2006), and some may have instructional needs in oral language if they are to learn written language.

Just as importantly, children have to learn from teacher talk (instructional language), which has two unique characteristics. First, although oral language in conversation typically has considerable contextual support from the conversational partner to support the conversation (Garvey & Berninger, 1980), children listening to instructional language must extract the message from longer stretches of talk without such frequent support from interacting with the speaker. Second, even though instructional language is typically oral, it often uses vocabulary and grammar that characterize the academic register rather than the oral register, and children need to learn to understand the unique patterns of language use in the academic register (see Silliman & Scott, 2009). Moreover, children who have language learning disabilities originating in the preschool years that interfere with development of syntactic awareness and inferential thinking about text may have extreme difficulty in learning to process the language teachers use (Silliman & Scott). Also, children who are dialect users and do not speak mainstream English (Washington and Thomas-Tate, 2009), or for whom English is not the first language, may also have difficulty in learning to understand instructional language and participate in oral language discussions. The importance of teaching oral language along with written language skills was not adequately addressed by the National Reading Panel, but see Berninger and Wolf (2009-a) for practical suggestions about how to do so.

Integrating Reading and Writing

To be successful in the reading program, children have to be able to write. They write to show that they understand what they read, for example, answering questions on independent seatwork, writing summaries, or composing book reports. As they get older, they are increasingly expected to read source material, take notes, and convert those notes into written reports in the content areas. These activities require executive functions (Altemeier, Abbott, & Berninger, 2008) to integrate reading and writing so that children become writing-readers (Altemeier, Jones, Abbott, & Berninger, 2006). The National Reading Panel did not examine the relationship of writing to development of reading skills. See Rieben, Ntamakiliro, Gonthier, and Fayol, (2005) for a review of research showing that including writing instruction in the kindergarten reading program can benefit reading development, for example, through opportunity to invent spellings that represent speech sounds and also receive feedback about conventional spellings.

System Issues

Teaching does not cause learning apart from the mind of the learner, which mediates response to intervention (Berninger & Richards, 2009). For example, the learner must *plan* (set goals for reading based on the purpose—to skim for an answer to a specific question, or to read carefully for the main idea and supporting details), *translate* (turn the written squiggles on the page into identified *words*, *syntactic structures*, and *discourse structures* drawing on both what is stated in the text, and what must be inferred based on activated background knowledge about the topic/s and metaknowledge about language), and *review* (self-monitor) *and revise* (reread if translation does not make sense). All this mental activity that supports the reading comprehension process takes place in working memory, which has limited capacity and resources to support the processing and complex temporal coordination required to orchestrate all the component processes involved in reading (cf., Fayol, 1999; Bourdin & Fayol, 1994, 1996). Comprehensive assessment of response to instruction should take into account all these components of the functional system that support reading—not just the automatic ones, but also the controlled, strategic ones (also see Cartwright, 2008).

If the teacher is guiding the reading process, explicit cues from the teacher help the student to regulate (manage) the complex process. If the child is reading independently, the reading success may depend on the individual's executive functions (mental self-government) for self-regulating the complex process involving all the components, from planning to translating to reviewing and revising, which collectively serve as the higher order executive functions that guide the cognitive processes in processing and producing written language (cf., Fayol, 1999; Hayes & Flower, 1980). When a student fails to respond to reading instruction, school psychologists should help the teacher figure out where in the complex system of many components the difficulty is, and then devise modified instructional approaches to overcome this difficulty in group instruction and/or independent work settings, as needed.

Writing
Accessing Research on Effective Writing Instruction

For a meta-analysis of effective writing instruction in students in fourth grade and above, see Graham and Perin (2007a, 2007b). For a review of evidence-based writing instruction, with focus on early and middle childhood, see Berninger (2008) and Hooper, Knuth, Yerby, Anderson, and Moore (2009). For an overview of evidence-based instructional practices for struggling writers in general, see Troia (2009), and for writers in general, including general and special education, see Graham, MacArthur, and Fitzgerald (2007).

Writing Components from an Instructional Perspective

Much instructional research on writing has focused on specific skills taught in the curriculum; for example, handwriting, spelling, and composing. Although earlier in the history of education in the United States, handwriting and spelling were often overemphasized and not taught in relationship to composing, currently relatively more emphasis is placed on composing (for a review of changes in instructional practices and overview of current approaches to writing instruction, see Wong & Berninger, 2004). Recent surveys of teacher practices in handwriting (Graham, Harris, Mason, Fink-Chorzempa, Moran, & Saddler, 2008a) and spelling (Graham et al., 2008b)

document variability among teachers in what and how they are teaching these skills. School psychologists in schools that have not adopted systematic, explicit programs of handwriting and spelling instruction might, in their consultation role, volunteer for participation on the district curriculum committee to help adopt such a program, given clear research evidence for the importance of explicit, systematic instruction in these skills (Berninger, 2008; Graham & Perin, 2007a, 2007b; Hooper et al., in press).

Phonological, orthographic, and morphological awareness, which contributes to learning to read words, as discussed in an earlier section, also contributes to learning to spell words. However, they are interrelated in different directions for spelling (spoken to written words) and for reading (written to spoken words). In addition to these three kinds of linguistic awareness, other knowledge sources have been identified that contribute to spelling (and contribute to word reading, too): *phonotactic* (knowledge of permissible sound sequences and positions; e.g., Bernstein & Treiman, 2001; Kessler, & Treiman, 1997), *orthotactic* (knowledge of permissible letter sequences and positions; e.g., Apel, Wolter, & Masterson, 2006; Pacton et al., 2001, 2005), *vocabulary* meaning (e.g., Stahl & Nagy, 2005), and *spelling rules* (e.g., Chliounaki & Bryant, 2007). See Berninger and Fayol (2008) for instructional methods for teaching spelling that draw on these seven knowledge sources that contribute to spelling. In addition, grammatical knowledge (e.g., the possessive, contractions, inflectional suffixes that mark tense and number, derivational suffixes that mark part of speech, function words for prepositions, conjunctions, pronouns, and articles, and compounding of base words) contribute to spelling (e.g., Bryant, Nunes, & Bindman, 1997, 2000; Fayol et al., 2006; Kemp & Bryant, 2003; Nagy et al., 2006) and may facilitate the application of spelling knowledge during composing text (e.g., Carlisle, 1994).

Writing Components from an Individual Differences Perspective

Multivariate cross-sectional and longitudinal research have identified skills that are not writing per se, but contribute uniquely to specific writing skills within the same grade level or across adjacent grade levels (e.g., see Berninger, 2007; Hooper et al., 2009). In this chapter we focus on one writing-related skill that contributes unique variance in predicting writing achievement; namely, working memory (e.g., Swanson & Berninger, 1996), which supports the written language production system discussed next.

Writing Components from an On-Line Processing Perspective

In other programmatic research on writing, experiments have been conducted to study the on-line processing of the writer during the writing production process. According to Fayol (1999), who has been a leader in this line of research, most language production models include three components, which are orchestrated in working memory, for (a) conceptual planning to generate and organize ideas for a particular topic, writing goal, and audience; (b) translation of the ideas into units of language—words, syntax, and discourse; and (c) production of the language via speech or transcription (letter writing and word spelling by hand or keyboard). Two features of the production system, and the working memory system that supports it, influence how efficiently its components are orchestrated: (a) its limited capacity and resources; and (b) its temporal coordination, that is, executive management of the component processes. Because of the capacity limitation feature, the more resources any one component needs, the fewer resources are available for the other components. To the degree that any component is automatic[2]—that is, it can be performed quickly and effortlessly outside conscious awareness—the fewer resources it will use, and the more resources will be available for the other components. However, resources are still needed for the executive management of the system that orchestrates the component parts. The executive management requires controlled, strategic processing for smooth coordination; that is, fluency,[2] and is resource-draining. If the sum of the resources needed for each component and for the executive management of the system exceeds the available resources, the system is said to be on overload.

On-line experiments have investigated the executive management of the component writing processes. Initially, writing processes are orchestrated serially—one process at a time—because parallel execution of multiple processes exceeds capacity limitations. For example, the number of ideas that can be generated and coherence of text are greater for oral production, which does not require handwriting, than for written production, which does (Bourdin & Fayol, 1994, 1996). Before handwriting is automatic in beginning writers, the amount that can be copied within a constant time limit is reduced (Bourdin & Fayol, 2000) compared to adults who have automatized their handwriting (Bourdin & Fayol, 2002).

On-line experiments have also shown that when writers experience difficulty in integrating component writing skills in real time, they adjust their writing speed or increase pause duration. For example, Chanquoy, Foulin, and Fayol (1990) found that adults, but not eight-year-olds, modified their pause durations between clauses. Beginning writers are unable to modify their handwriting speed, as skilled writers are, in response to changing conceptual or linguistic requirements of the writing task, probably because their handwriting is not yet automatic (Bourdin & Fayol, 1994, 1996). Recent studies (in preparation) extend this work by showing that skilled writers can carry out two writing-related tasks at a time in parallel—for example, planning the next clause while still writing the current clause—but beginning writers carry out these same two writing tasks serially, and complete the transcription of one clause before planning the next clause.

Systems Issues

Many times when students do not start or finish writing assignments it is not because they are unmotivated, lazy, or have emotional problems; rather, their written language system may be on overload. Two ways to overcome overload are to (a) automatize transcription skills, and (b) combine tasks (Fayol, 1999). Not only does automating transcription free up resources for other writing components, but also automating one component makes it possible for other components to be executed in parallel; for example, choosing words and spelling words simultaneously, rather than serially (Fayol, Hupert, & Largy, 1999). Sentence combining, which has been shown to be an effective method of writing instruction (Graham & Perin, 2007a, 2007b), may be so because combining the two sentences teaches students more efficient executive management. Another way to overcome overload is to increase knowledge related to the writing topic (Bourdin & Fayol, 2002).

Instructional methods that have been validated in the University of Washington writing instruction studies for overcoming capacity limitations and facilitating executive management systems during writing include the following: (a) teach a plan for automatic writing of letters, and practice each of the alphabet letters once during a warm-up at the beginning of a lesson; (b) teach automatic phoneme–spelling correspondence and reflective coordination of phonological, orthographic, and morphologic awareness for word spelling; (c) teach for transfer of transcription skills to independent, self-regulated, authentic composing; (d) teach to all levels of language (subword, word, and text) close in time, so that they are coordinated in time for executive management; and (e) use a variety of brief instructional activities to avoid habituation by prolonged practice in any one skill—less is more! (See Berninger, 2007, Table of Contents, Instructional Resources; Berninger & Wolf, 2009-a, 2009-b).

Math

Accessing Research on Effective Math Instruction

For meta-analyses on effective math instruction, see Swanson (2009) and Swanson and Jerman (2006). Also, see the conclusions and recommendations of the recently issued National Math Report (United States Department of Education, 2008). This report, which recommended that students should master Algebra II for high school graduation in the United States, concluded that the evidence does not support the use of handheld calculators as a substitute for explicit instruction and practice in math fact retrieval and computation.

Evidence-Based Instructional Approach

Overall, Mayer's (2004) review of the history of math instruction in the United States supported guided discovery in math learning, with explicit instructional guidance, rather than pure discovery, with unstructured exploration as advocated by the constructivist philosophy of instruction, which has dominated teacher education for over a decade. The meta-analyses of Swanson and colleagues (e.g. Swanson, 2009; Swanson & Jerman, 2006) also found that explicit strategy instruction was the most effective for math learning. However, as discussed in the introduction, explicit instruction can provide a balance between automating skills and guiding students in reflective activities.

Math Disabilities

Children with math disabilities (MD) may have problems in math fact retrieval, computation, or visual spatial representation (Geary, 2003), or math fact retrieval, computation, and problem solving (Andersson, 2008).

Math Fact Retrieval and Computational Operations

Experimental studies have shown that early in schooling, children apply counting or other algorithms to find the answers to addition and subtraction problems,

but later in schooling, when math fact retrieval is automated, use direct retrieval of math facts for addition and subtraction (Barrouillet & Fayol, 1998). That is why children who do not have automatic math fact retrieval may benefit from counting forwards and backwards by variable increments along a number line taped to their desk in learning their basic additional and subtraction number facts (Berninger, 2007). In contrast, problems in learning math facts for multiplication were related to inefficiencies in inhibiting incorrect responses, rather than in direct memory retrieval (Barrouillet, Fayol, & Lathulière, 1997). Perhaps activities in which children are timed for choosing the correct products among foils will help them become more efficient in inhibiting incorrect responses.

Problem Solving

Children benefit from explicit instruction in schema for math word problems (Fuchs & Fuchs, 2003). Mayer (2004) contrasted these well-defined, routine math problems and the ill-defined problems, which are more likely to characterize math problems in the real world. His review of the research identified four cognitive processes that contribute to math problem solving, including representations (nature of the problem to be solved and strategies for doing so), planning/monitoring (executive management), executing, and self-regulation. He also identified seven effective instructional methods for problem solving including load-reducing, structure-based, schema-activation, generative, guided discovery, modeling, and teaching thinking.

Systems Issues

As for reading and writing, multi-component production systems underlie math problem solving. Children make plans (represent the problem and construct or choose strategies for solving the problem), translate underlying number concepts into written numerals, number facts, or written computations (sequential steps of arithmetic algorithms for addition, subtraction, multiplication, and division), and review and, when errors are detected, revise. Although much arithmetic instruction teaches math fact retrieval, computation, and problem solving as separate processes, real-world math often requires the integration of these three processes. Executive functions are needed for integration of components in math problem solving, and monitoring (self-checking) and revising.

Children who do not have automatic math retrieval may benefit from multimodal practice (listen–say, listen–write, look–say, look–write) rather than look–say drill alone. Computation can break down because of problems in representing numerals in visual spatial arrays, in applying the sequential steps of calculation algorithms, in retrieval of math facts during calculation, misunderstanding the place value concept underlying the problem representation itself during the steps of the calculation or in expressing an answer, or momentary breakdowns in any step of the process, and failure to monitor and self-correct the errors that result. Children with problems in learning fractions or telling time benefit from explicit instruction in part–whole relationships. As with reading and writing, limited working memory resources and timing constraints can interfere with efficient math problem solving; however, including mental math activities at the beginning of each math lesson may improve the efficiency of working memory during math problem solving. For further discussion of all these issues, see Berninger (2007).

Science

Although relatively little research exists on effective instruction for science, what does exist supports the same conclusion Mayer reached for more general problem solving: guided inquiry, including some direct explanation, is superior to unstructured discovery learning (Klahr & Nigram, 2004; Li & Klahr, 2006). Case studies have shown that teacher-guided inquiry is also effective with students with learning disabilities (Palincsar, Collins, Marano, & Magnusson, 2000). Progress is being made in improving teaching of vocabulary in the science content domain for students with a variety of language learning needs (see Silliman & Scott, 2009). Science can be a motivating part of writer or writing-readers workshops for struggling readers and writers (Berninger, 2009-b).

Home–School Relationships
Home Literacy

Literacy knowledge construction takes place both at home and at school (Purcell-Gates, 1996). Most children become acquainted with written language well before entering formal schooling, through observing and participating in literacy activities in their homes (van Steensel, 2006), both informal and formal (Senechal, LeFevre, Thomas, and Daley, 1998). Informal home literacy practices, which include interactions with print, such as storybook reading for the purpose of learning the message contained in print, are related to the development of

language skills (Senechal & LeFevre, 2002). Formal home literacy practices, which include interactions focused on the print itself, for example, using an alphabet book to talk about letters and letter sounds (Senechal et al., 1998), are related to emergent literacy skills (Senechal & LeFevre, 2002; Evans et al., 2000). Senechal and colleagues found that all parents in their samples reported using informal home literacy activities, whereas only some reported formal ones. Not surprisingly, parents had differing ideas about the appropriate means for teaching their students early literacy skills (Fitzgerald, Spiegal, & Cunningham, 1991; Senechal et al.; Stipek, Milburn, Clements, & Daniels, 1992).

Parental Contribution to Academic Learning

Parental involvement enhances academic development (Leslie & Allen, 1999; Lonigan & Whitehurst, 1998; McWayne, Hampton, Fantuzzo, Cohen, & Sekino, 2004) through home literacy practices (Boudreau, 2005; Evans, Shaw, & Bell, 2000). Early home and childcare experiences were indirectly related to reading achievement through their influence on language development, and language and phonological knowledge were both directly related to acquisition of reading skills (Poe, Birchinal, & Roberts, 2004). The way in which parents view themselves within the framework of children's academic success has been positively linked to indicators of student achievement, including student grades, achievement test scores, and teacher ratings of student competence (Hoover-Dempsey, et al., 2005).

A variety of parental beliefs and behaviors influence children's academic socialization and school-related development (Taylor, Clayton, & Rowley, 2004). Rashid, Morris, and Sevcik (2005) found that, after maternal education level and children's IQ were accounted for, parental indicators such as obtaining a library card for their child accounted for a significant amount of the variance in children's reading comprehension and spelling performance. In contrast, direct measures of children's literacy activities did not. Parental expectations for their children's educational attainment and socialization practices, while not classified as a literacy activity, have also influenced children's academic achievement (Lee & Bowen, 2006). Socialization practices can include both home literacy and other activities such as monitoring and structuring children's time, discussing school and education, and holding educational expectations (Suizzo & Soon, 2006).

However, most of the research on parent involvement in academic learning has focused on reading rather than writing, math, or science.

Parent–School Relationships

Children benefit from positive collaboration between schools and families (Patrikakou, Weissberg, Redding, & Walberg, 2005). Hoover-Dempsey et al. (2005) frames the construct of parental involvement in terms of parental role construction and parental sense of self-efficacy. Parental role construction, which is how parents view what they are supposed to do in relation to their children's education, and the patterns of behavior that follow those beliefs, is important because it establishes a basic range of activities that parents will construe as important, necessary, and permissible for their own actions with and on behalf of their children (Hoover-Dempsey & Sandler, 1997). Parental self-efficacy, which is the belief that what one does makes a difference, requires experiences of success in helping the child learn, opportunities to observe other parents successfully helping their children with academic tasks, encouragement from important others (e.g., teachers), and support for positive feelings gained from success, or encouragement when doubts emerge (Hoover-Dempsey et al., 2005). If parents feel that their actions matter, they will become involved, but if they think their efforts are useless, they will avoid involvement for fear of confronting their perceived inadequacies (Hoover-Dempsey & Sandler, 1997).

Diversity Issues Related to Home Variables
Family, Race, Socioeconomic, Culture

Children's early experiences within their family, and aspects of family structure, are consistently strong predictors of emergent literacy skills and later academic achievement (Downer & Pianta, 2006). The quality and quantity of those experiences are often mediated through the demographic factors of race, ethnicity, and socioeconomic status. Lack of material resources often place ethnic minority families at a disadvantage in terms of the home literacy environments they create for their children, and their relationships with the schools that educate them.

Parent academic involvement has been found to function differently across ethnicity and SES. In their study on the demographic characteristics of parenting, Hill et al. (2004) found several differences related to parental involvement. These included the finding that African Americans had higher levels of involvement in educational activities at home,

whereas European Americans were more likely to be involved at school. Hill and Craft (2003) found differential pathways for African American and European American parents with regard to behavioral control and child outcomes. Jeynes (2003) found that parental involvement in school was more influential for African American and Latino students than for Asian American students.

Parents' efficacy levels have been associated with their levels of education, which are often included as a measurement of socioeconomic status (Kohl, Lengua, & McMahon, 2000), with parents who have lower educational attainment tending to have lower efficacy than parents with higher levels of education (Hoover-Dempsey & Sandler, 1997). Higher parental education has been associated with more stimulating learning environments (Parcel & Menaghan, as cited in Manguson & Duncan, 2002). Alternatively, parents with lower levels of education may be less involved with school because they feel less comfortable communicating with school personnel, as a result of the differences in education (Lee & Bowen, 2006). Kohl et al. (2000) found that parental education level was related to the quality and amount of parent–teacher contact, parental involvement in school and at home, and teacher's perceptions of the parent's valuing of education. These findings held true across ethnic lines. Burchinal et al. (2002) found that maternal education and parent's practices and attitudes were strong predictors of child outcomes. Hoover–Dempsey and Sandler (1997) cited research that parents with less education expressed doubts about their abilities to help their children in school, and their hope that teachers would assume responsibility for teaching needed skills.

The role of parents' beliefs about parenting practices and sense of efficacy in terms of their involvement with their children's development varies according to social class and ethnic background, but each of these constructs has been linked to achievement outcomes (Burchinal, Peisner-Feinberg, Pianta, & Howes, 2002). Lee and Bowen (2006) framed the relationship among race, SES, and parental education in terms of cultural or social capital, which has been defined as (a) features of a social organization that facilitate cooperation for mutual benefit, and include mechanisms such as mutual trust among individuals, and community participation (Garcia Coll & Pachter, 2002), and (b) personal dispositions, attitudes and knowledge gained from experience, connections to education related objects (i.e., books, academic credentials, technology), and connections to education-related institutions (Lee and Bowen, 2006). According to Lee and Bowen, the greater an individual's cultural capital, the more likely the individual is to obtain benefits for themselves and their families. The less cultural capital available, the more constrained and restricted the family becomes with regard to resources (2006). For example, European American and middle class parents are more likely to share the school culture and feel comfortable with the school, whereas African American, Latino, and low-income parents usually do not share cultural backgrounds with the school and may be more reluctant to initiate contact (Desimone, 1999).

Parents from higher SES backgrounds are more likely to see themselves as in partnership with schools, and tend to presume they are more entitled to be involved in their child's education (Hill et al., 2004). The results of shared culture for European American and middle income families is that there is congruence between home and school culture, which has been found to be advantageous to student outcomes (Lee & Bowen, 2006). Alternatively, parents with lower cultural capital are less likely to have access to information about school systems which could inform their practices at home, which, in turn, could relate to their children's academic outcomes.

Biologically Based Learning Disabilities

Another source of diversity that cuts across socioeconomic and racial groups is genetic and neurological (Berninger et al., 2008). Because other family members in the current or past generations are likely to be affected when a learning disability has a genetic basis, school psychologists are encouraged to reach out proactively to parents of children with developmental and learning problems, who may fear their children will experience the same school struggles they did. See Berninger (2007) for practical ways to do so early in schooling.

Interpersonal Relationships, Multicultural Factors, and Systems Variables

Interpersonal relationships between teachers and students, and among peers in the same classrooms, can influence academic learning and response to instruction as much as cognitive variables can (Pianta, 1999). Multicultural factors can influence how the child responds to instruction at school, or the kind of home–school relationships that are established. See Jones (2009) for an overview of multicultural research that is relevant to school psychology practice. Motivation variables such as

creating interest, hope, and self-efficacy, setting goals, and graphing progress toward meeting goals, also contribute to learning and affect response to instruction (Berninger & Hidi, 2006). Other systems variables in the classroom, school, family and community may also influence a child's learning at school.

Conclusions

Knowledge of what research has found about effective instruction is valuable for the school psychologist who assesses children and consults with teachers and parents on behalf of children. However, equally important for improving a student's academic learning is broader knowledge of the cognitive and motivational processes in learning, individual differences among students due to language, cultural, socioeconomic, or biological diversity, knowledge of the student's interpersonal relationships within the classroom and relevant family issues, and the school psychologist's relationship with other professionals in the school and the family. Compassionativity (caring about the student who struggles with academic learning, see Berninger & Richards, 2002) can be just as important as research knowledge in helping students respond to instruction and improve their learning outcomes, behavior, and mental health.

Notes

1. Because of space limitations, these are examples of research articles with evidence rather than exhaustive review of the literature.

2. Please note that automaticity is not the same as fluency. When cognitive processes become automatic, the previously controlled, strategic processing, which requires relatively more working memory resources, is transformed to rely on direct retrieval of a single item, which requires fewer working memory resources. In contrast, fluency refers to the executive coordination of serial items over time that is controlled and strategic, but after practice becomes fast, coordinated, and smooth, and thus requires fewer working memory resources than it did when it was first being learned. Fluency may also be enhanced by flexibility, and not only automaticity (Cartwright, 2008).

References

Altemeier, L., Abbott, R., & Berninger, V. (2008). Executive functions for reading and writing in typical literacy development and dyslexia. *Journal of Clinical and Experimental Neuropsychology, 30*, 588–606.

Altemeier, L., Jones, J., Abbott, R., & Berninger, V. (2006) Executive factors in becoming writing-readers and reading-writers: Note-taking and report writing in third and fifth graders. *Developmental Neuropsychology, 29*, 161–173.

Andersson, U. (2008). Mathematical competencies in children with different types of learning difficulties. *Journal of Educational Psychology, 100*, 48–66.

Apel, K., Wolter, J., & Masterson, J. (2006). Effects of phonotactic and orthotactic probabilities during fast mapping on 5-year-olds' learning to spell. *Developmental Neuropsychology, 29*(1), 21–42.

Barrouillet, P., & Fayol, M. (1998). From algorithmic computing to direct retrieval: Evidence from number and alphabetic arithmetic in children and adults. *Memory & Cognition, 26,* 355–368.

Barrouillet, P., Fayol, M., & Lathulière, E. (1997). Selecting between competitors in mulitiplication tasks: An explanation of the errors produced by adolescents with learning difficulties. *International Journal of Behavioral Development, 21,* 253–275.

Berninger, V. (1987). Global, component, and serial processing of printed words in beginning readers. *Journal of Experimental Child Psychology, 43,* 387–418.

Berninger, V. (2007). *Process assessment of the learner II user's guide.* San Antonio, TX: Harcourt/PsyCorp. (CD format) ISBN 0158661818 Second Revision issued August, 2008.

Berninger, V. (2008). Evidence-based written language instruction during early and middle childhood. In R. Morris & N. Mather (Eds.) *Evidence-based interventions for students with learning and behavioral challenges* (pp. 215–235). Mahwah, NJ: Lawrence Erlbaum Associates (LEA).

Berninger, V. Abbott, R., Jones, J., Wolf, B., Gould, L., Anderson-Youngstrom, M. et al. (2006). Early development of language by hand: Composing-, reading-, listening-, and speaking-connections, three letter writing modes, and fast mapping in spelling. *Developmental Neuropsychology, 29,* 61–92.

Berninger, V., & Fayol, M. (2008). Why spelling is important and how to teach it effectively. Encyclopedia of Language and Literacy Development (pp. 1-13). London, ON: Canadian Language and Literacy Research Network. http://www.literacyencyclopedia.ca/pdfs/topic.php?topId=234

Berninger, V., & Hidi, S. (2006). Mark Twain's writers' workshop: A nature–nurture perspective in motivating students with learning disabilities to compose. In S. Hidi, & P. Boscolo (Eds). *Motivation in writing* (pp. 159–179). Amsterdam, Elsevier.

Berninger, V., Raskind, W., Richards, T., Abbott, R., & Stock, P. (2008). A multidisciplinary approach to understanding developmental dyslexia within working-memory architecture: Genotypes, phenotypes, brain, and instruction. *Developmental Neuropsychology, 33,* 707–744.

Berninger, V., & Richards, T. (2002). *Brain literacy for educators and psychologists.* New York: Academic Press.

Berninger, V. & Richards, T. (2009). Brain and learning. In E. Anderman & L. Anderman (Eds.), *Psychology of classroom learning: An encyclopedia,* Vol. 1 (pp. 15-22). Detroit: Macmillan Reference USA.

Berninger, V., & Wolf, B. (2009-a). *Teaching students with dyslexia and dysgraphia: Lessons from teaching and science.* Baltimore: Paul H. Brookes.

Berninger, V., & Wolf, B. (2009-b). *Helping students with dyslexia and dysgraphia make connections: Differentiated instruction lesson plans in reading and writing.* Baltimore: Paul H. Brookes.

Bernstein, S., & Treiman, R. (2001). Learning a novel grapheme: Effects of positional and phonemic context on children's spelling. *Journal of Experimental Child Psychology, 79,* 56–77.

Boudreau, D. (2005) Use of parent questionnaire in emergent and early literacy assessment of preschool children. *Language, Speech, and Hearing Services in Schools, 36,* 33–47.

Bourassa, D., Treiman, R., & Kessler, B. (2006). Use of morphology in spelling by children with dyslexia and typically developing children. *Memory and Cognition, 34*(3), 703–714.

Bourdin, B. & Fayol, M. (1994). Is written language production really more difficult than oral language production? *International Journal of Psychology, 29,* 591–620.

Bourdin, B. & Fayol, M. (1996). Mode effects in a sentence production task. *Current Psychology of Cognition, 15,* 245–264.

Bourdin, B. & Fayol, M. (2000). Is graphic activity cognitively costly? A developmental approach. *Reading and Writing, 13,* 183–196.

Bourdin, B. & Fayol, M. (2002). Even in adults, written production is still more costly than oral production. *International Journal of Psychology, 37,* 219–222.

Bryant, P., Nunes, T., & Bindman, M. (1997). Children's understanding of the connection between grammar and spelling. In B. Blachman (Ed.), *Foundations of reading acquisition and dyslexia: Implications for early intervention* (pp. 219–240). Mahwah, NJ: Erlbaum.

Bryant, P., Nunes, T., & Bindman, M. (2000). The relations between children's linguistic awareness and spelling: The case of the apostrophe. *Reading and Writing: An Interdisciplinary Journal, 12,* 253–276.

Burchinal, M., Peisner-Feinberg, E., Pianta, R. & Howes, C. (2002) Development of academic skills from preschool through second grade: Family and classroom predictors of developmental trajectories. *Journal of School Psychology, 40*(5), 415–436.

Caravolas, M., Kessler, B., Hulme, C., & Snowling, M. (2005). Effects of orthographic consistency, frequency, and letter knowledge on children's vowel spelling development. *Journal of Experimental Child Psychology, 92*(4), 307–321.

Carlisle, J. (1994). Morphological awareness, spelling, and story writing. Possible relationships for elementary-age children with and without learning disabilities. In N.C. Jordan, & J. Goldsmith-Phillips (Eds.), *Learning disabilities. New directions for assessment and intervention* (pp. 123–145). Boston: Allyn Bacon.

Carlisle, J., & Nomanbhoy, D. (1993). Phonological and morphological awareness in first graders. *Applied Psycholinguistics, 14,* 177–195.

Cartwright, K. (Ed.), (2008). *Flexibility in literacy processes and instructional practice: Implications of developing representational ability for literacy teaching and learnin*g NY: Guilford.

Cassar, M., & Treiman, R. (1997). The beginnings of orthographic knowledge: Children's knowledge of double letters in words. *Journal of Educational Psychology, 89*(4), 631–644.

Chanquoy, L., Foulin, J.N. & Fayol, M. (1990). The temporal management of short text writing by children and adults. *European Bulletin of Cognitive Psychology, 10,* 513–540.

Chliounaki, K., & Bryant, P. (2007). How children learn about morphological spelling rules. *Child Development, 78,* 1360–1373.

Desimone, L. (1999) Linking parent involvement with student achievement: Do race and income matter? *Journal of Educational Research, 93*(1), 11–30.

Downer, J., & Pianta, R. (2006) Academic and cognitive functioning in first grade: Associations with earlier home and child care predictors and with concurrent home and classroom experiences. *School Psychology Review, 35*(1), 11–30

Evans, M.A., Shaw, D., & Bell, M. (2000) Home literacy activities and their influence on early literacy skills. *Canadian Journal of Experimental Psychology, 54*(2), 65–75.

Fayol, M. (1999). From on-line management problems to strategies in written composition. In M. Torrance & G. Jeffery (Ed.), *The cognitive demands of writing*. Amsterdam: Amsterdam University Press.

Fayol, M., Hupet, M. & Largy, P. (1999). The acquisition of subject–verb agreement in written french. From novices to experts errors. *Reading and Writing*, 11, 153–174.

Fayol, M., Totereau, C. & Barrouillet, P. (2006). Disentangling the impact of semantic and formal factors in the acquisition of number inflections. Noun, adjective and verb agreement in written French. *Reading and Writing*, 19, 717–736.

Fitzgerald, Spiegal, & Cunningham (1991) The relationship between parental literacy level and perceptions of emergent literacy. *Journal of Reading Behavior*, 23, 191–213.

Fuchs, L., & Fuchs, D. (2003). Enhancing the mathematical problem solving of students with math difficulties. In Swanson, H. L. Harris, K., & Graham. S. (Eds.) *Handbook of learning disabilities* (pp. 306–322). New York: Guilford.

Garcia Coll, C. & Pachter, L. (2002) Ethnic minority parenting. In M.C. Bornstein (Ed.) *Handbook of Parenting*, Vol. 4: *Social and Applied Parenting* (2nd ed., pp. 1–20). Mahwah, NJ: Lawrence Erlbaum Associates.

Garvey, C., & Berninger, G. (1980). Timing and turn-taking in children's conversations. *Discourse Processes*, 4, 27–57.

Geary, D. C. (2003). Math disabilities. In H. L. Swanson, K. Harris, & S. Graham (Eds.), *Handbook of learning disabilities*. New York: Guilford.

Graham, S., Harris, K.R., Mason, L., Fink-Chorzempa, B., Moran, S., & Saddler, B. (2008a). How do primary grade teachers teach handwriting: A national survey. *Reading & Writing: An Interdisciplinary Journal*, 21, 49–69.

Graham, S., Harris, K. R. & Zito, J. (2005). Promoting internal and external validity: A synergism of laboratory-like experiments and classroom-based self-regulated strategy development research. In G. Phye, D. Robinson, & J. Levin (Eds.) *Empirical methods for evaluating interventions*. (pp. 85–112). San Diego: Elsevier Academic Press.

Graham, S., MacArthur, C., & Fitzgerald, J. (2007). *Best practices in writing instruction*. NY: Guilford.

Graham, S., Morphy, P., Harris, K., Fink-Chorzempa, B., Saddler, B., Moran, S. et al. (2008b). Teaching spelling in the primary grades: A national survey of instructional practices and adaptations. *American Educational Research Journal*, 45, 796–825.

Graham, S., & Perin, D. (2007a). *Writing next: Effective strategies to improve writing of adolescents in middle and high schools— A report to Carnegie Corporation of New York*. Washington, DC: Alliance for Excellent Education.

Graham, S., & Perin, D. (2007b). A meta-analysis of writing instruction for adolescent students. *Journal of Educational Psychology*, 99, 445–476.

Hayes, J. R., & Flower, L. (1980). Identifying the organization of the writing process. In L. W. Gregg & E. R. Sternberg (Eds.), *Cognitive processes in writing* (pp 3–30). Hillsdale, NJ: Erlbaum.

Henry, M. K. (2003). *Unlocking literacy: Effective decoding and spelling instruction*. Baltimore: Paul S. Brookes Publishing.

Hill, N. Castellino, D. Lansford, J., Nowlin, P., Dodge, K., Bates, J., et al. (2004) Parent academic involvement as related to school behavior, achievement, and aspirations: Demographic variations across adolescence. *Child Development*, 75(5), 1491–1509.

Hill, N., & Craft, S., (2003) Parent-school involvement and school performance: Mediated pathways among socioeconomically comparable African-American and Euro-American families. *Journal of Educational Psychology*, 95(1), 74–83.

Hooper, S., Knuth, S., Yerby, D., Anderson, K., & Moore, C. (2009). A review of science supported writing instruction with implementation in mind. In S. Rosenfield & V. Berninger (Eds.), *Implementing evidence-based interventions in school settings* (pp. 49-83). New York: Oxford University Press.

Hoover-Dempsey, K., & Sandler, H. (1997). Why do parents become involved in their children's education? *Review of Educational Research*, 67(1), 3–42.

Hoover-Dempsey, K. Walker, & J. Sandler (2005) Parents' motivations for involvement in their children's education. In E. Patrikakou, R. Weissberg, S. Redding, & H. Walberg (Eds.) *School-Family Partnerships for Children's Success* (pp. 40–56). New York: Teachers College Press.

Hoover-Dempsey, K. Walker, J., Sandler, H., Whetsel, D., Green, C., Wilkins, A., et al. (2005). Why do parents become involved? Research findings and implications. *The Elementary School Journal*, 106(2), 105–130.

Jaffré, J-P. & Fayol, M. (2006). Orthography and literacy in French. In R.M. Joshi & P.G. Aaron (Eds.), *Handbook of orthography and literacy* (pp. 81–104). Mahwah, NJ: Laurence Erlbaum.

Jeynes, W. (2003) A meta-analysis: The effects of parental involvement on minority children's academic achievement. *Education and Urban Society*, 35(2), 202–218.

Jones, J.M. (Ed.) (2009). *The psychology of multiculturalism in the schools: A primer for practice, training, and research*. Bethesda, MD: National Association of School Psychologists.

Kemp, N., & Bryant, P. (2003). Do beez buzz? Rule-based and frequency-based knowledge in learning to spell plural -s. *Child Development*, 74, 63–74.

Kessler, B., & Treiman, R. (1997). Syllable structure and the distribution of phonemes in English syllables. *Journal of Memory and Language*, 37, 295–311.

Klahr, D., & Nigram, M. (2004). The equivalence of learning paths in early science instruction: Effects of direct instruction and discovery learning. *Psychological Science*, 15, 661–667.

Kohl, G.O., Lengua, L.J., & McMahon, R.J. (2000) Parent involvement in school: Conceptualizing multiple dimensions and their relations with family and demographic risk factors. *Journal of School Psychology*, 38(6), pp. 501–523.

Lee, J-S., & Bowen, N. (2006) Parent involvement, cultural capital, and the achievement gap among elementary school children. *American Educational Research Journal*, 43, 193–218.

Leong, C. (2000). Rapid processing of base and derived forms of words and grades 4, 5 and 6 children's spelling. *Reading and Writing: An Interdisciplinary Journal*, 12, 277–302.

Leslie, L. & Allen, L., (1999) Factors that predict success in an early literacy intervention project. *Reading Research Quarterly*, 34, 404–424.

Li, I., & Klahr, D. (2006). The psychology of scientific thinking: Implications for science teaching and learning. In J. Rhoton, & P. Shane (Eds.), *Teaching science in the 21st century*. National Science Teachers Association and National Science Education Leadership Association: NSTA Press.

Lonigan, C.J., & Whitehurst, G.J., (1998) Relative efficacy of parent and teacher involvement in a shared-reading intervention for preschool children from low-income backgrounds. *Early Childhood Research Quarterly*, 13, 262–290.

Magnuson, K., & Duncan, G. (2002) Parents in poverty. In M.H. Bornstein (Ed.) *Handbook of parenting:* Volume 4: *Social conditions and applied parenting.* (2nd ed., pp. 95–121). Mahwah, NJ: Lawrence Erlbaum Associates

Mattingly, I. (1972). Reading, the linguistic process, and linguistic awareness. In J. Kavanagh & I. Mattingly (Eds.), *Language by ear and by eye: The relationship between speech and reading* (pp. 133–147). Cambridge, MA: MIT Press.

Mayer, R. (2004). Should there be a three-strikes rule against pure discovery learning? *American Psychologist, 59,* 14–19.

Mayer, R., & Wittrock, M. (2004). Problem solving, In P.A. Alexander, & P. Winne (Eds.), *Handbook of educational psychology* (pp. 287–303). Washington, DC: The American Psychological Assocation (Division 15).

McCardle, P., & Miller, B.(2009).Why we need evidence-based practices in reading and where to find that evidence. In S. Rosenfield & V. Berninger (Eds.), *Implementing evidence-based interventions in school settings* (19-48). New York: Oxford University Press.

McWayne, C., Hampton, V., Fantuzzo, J., Cohen, H., & Sekino, Y. (2004). A multivariate examination of parent involvement and social and academic competencies of urban kindergarten children. *Psychology in Schools, 41*(3), 363–377.

Nagy, W., Berninger, V., & Abbott, R. (2006). Contributions of morphology beyond phonology to literacy outcomes of upper elementary and middle school students. *Journal of Educational Psychology, 98,*134–147.

National Institute of Child Health and Human Development (NICHD). (2000). *Report of the National Reading Panel. Teaching children to read: An evidence-based assessment of the scientific research literature on reading and its implications for reading instruction: Reports of the subgroups (NIH Publication No. 00–4754).* Washington, DC: U.S. Government Printing Office.

Nunes, T., & Bryant, P. (2006). *Improving literacy by teaching morphemes (Improving learning series).* New York: Routledge.

Olson, R., Forsberg, H., & Wise, B. (1994). Genes, environment, and the development of orthographic skills. In V. W. Berninger (Ed.), *The varieties of orthographic knowledge I: Theoretical and developmental issues* (pp. 27–71). Dordrecht, Netherlands: Kluwer Academic Press.

Pacton, S. & Deacon, S.H. (2008). The timing and mechanisms of children's use of morphological information in spelling: Evidence from English and French. *Cognitive Development, 23,* 339–359.

Pacton, S., Fayol, M., & Perruchet, P. (2005). Children's implicit learning of graphotactic and morphological regularities, *Child Development, 76,* 324–329.

Pacton, S., Perruchet, P., Fayol, M., & Cleeremans, A. (2001). Implicit learning out of the lab: The case of orthographic regularities. *Journal of Experimental Psychology: General, 130,* 401–426.

Palincsar, A., Collins, K., Marano, N., & Magnusson, S. (2000). Investigating the engagement and learning of students with learning disabilities in guided inquiry science teaching. *Language, Speech, and Hearing Sciences in Schools, 31,* 240–251.

Patrikakou, E., Weissberg, R, Redding, S., & Walberg, H. (2005). School–family partnerships: Enhancing the academic, social, and emotional learning of children. In E. Patrikakou, R. Weissberg, S. Redding, & H. Walberg (Eds.) *School–family partnerships for children's success* (pp. 1–17). New York: Teachers College Press.

Peverly, S. (2009). Beyond monitoring of students' progress in classrooms: The assessment of students, curriculum, and teachers. In S. Rosenfield & V. Berninger (Eds.), *Implementing evidence-based interventions in school settings* (pp. 575–600). New York: Oxford University Press.

Pianta, R. (1999). *Enhancing relationships between children and teachers.* Washington, DC: American Psychological Association.

Poe, M., Burchinal, M., & Roberts, J. (2004). Early language and the development of children's reading skills. *Journal of School Psychology, 42*(4), 315–332.

Purcell-Gates, V. (1996) Stories, coupons, and the TV Guide: Relationships between home and literacy experiences and emergent literacy knowledge. *Reading Research Quarterly, 31,* 406–428.

Rashid, F., Morris, R., & Sevcik, R. (2005) Relationship between home literacy environment and reading achievement in children with reading disabilities. *Journal of Learning Disabilities, 38*(1), 2–11.

Reznitskaya, A., Anderson, R., McNurlen, B., Nguyen-Jahiel, K., Archodidou, A., & Kim, S. (2001). Influence of oral discussion on written argument. *Discourse Processes, 32,* 155–175.

Rieben, L., Ntamakiliro, L., Gonthier, B. & Fayol, M. (2005). Effects of various early writing practices on reading and spelling. *Scientific Studies of Reading, 9,* 145–166.

Rosenfield, S., & Berninger, V. (Eds.) (2009). *Implementing evidence-based interventions in school settings.* New York: Oxford University Press.

Senechal, M., & LeFevre, J. (2002) Parental involvement in the development of children's reading skill: A five year longitudinal study. *Child Development, 73*(2), 445–460.

Senechal, M., LeFevre, J., Thomas, E. M., & Daley, D, K. E. (1998). Differential effects of home literacy experiences on the development of oral and written language. *Reading Research Quarterly, 33*(1), 96–116.

Seymour, P. (1997). Foundations of orthographic development. In C. Perfetti, L. Rieben, & M. Fayol (Eds,), *Learning to spell. Research, theory, and practices across languages* (pp. 319–337). Mahwah, NJ: Lawrence Erlbaum Associates.

Silliman, E., & Scott, C. (2009). Research-based oral language intervention routes to the academic language of literacy: Finding the right road. In S. Rosenfield & V. Berninger (Eds.), *Implementing evidence-based interventions in school settings* (pp. 107-145). New York: Oxford University Press.

Stahl, S., & Nagy, W. (2005). *Teaching word meaning.* Mahwah, NJ: Lawrence Erlbaum.

Stipeck, D., Milburn, S., Clements, D., & Daniels, D.H. (1992). Parents beliefs about appropriate education for young children. *Journal of Applied Developmental Psychology, 13,* 293–310.

Suizzo, M-A, & Soon, K. (2006) Parental academic socialization: Effects of home-based parental involvement on locus of control across U.S. ethnic groups. *Educational Psychology, 26*(6), 827–846.

Swanson, H. L. (2009). Science-supported math instruction for children with math disabilities: Converting a meta-analysis to practice. In S. Rosenfield & V. Berninger (Eds.), *Implementing evidence-based interventions in school settings.* New York: Oxford University Press.

Swanson, H.L., & Berninger, V. (1996). Individual differences in children's working memory and writing skills. *Journal of Experimental Child Psychology, 63,* 358–385.

Swanson, H.L., & Deshler, D. D. (2003). Instructing adolescents with learning disabilities: Converting meta-analysis to practice. *Journal of Learning Disabilities, 36,* 124–135.

Swanson, H.L., & Jerman, O. (2006). Math disabilities: A selective meta-analysis. *Review of Education Research, 76,* 249–274.

Taylor, L., Clayton, J., & Rowley, S. (2004) Academic socialization: Understanding parental influences on children's school related development in the early years. *Review of General Psychology, 8*(3), 163–178.

Troia, G. (Ed.). (2009). *Writing instruction and assessment for struggling writers: From theory to evidence based practices.* New York: Guilford.

United States Department of Education (2008). *Final report of the national mathematics advisory panel. Foundations for success.* Available at: www.ed.gov/MathPanel/.

van Steensel, R. (2006) Relations between socio-cultural factors, the home literacy environment and children's literacy development in the first years of primary education. *Journal of Research in Reading, 29*(4), 367–382.

Varnhagen, C. K., Boechler, P. M., & Steffler, D. J. (1999). Phonological and orthographic influences on children's vowel spelling. *Scientific Studies of Reading, 3*(4), 363–379.

Venezky, R. (1970). The *structure of English orthography.* The Hague: Mouton.

Venezky, R. L. (1999). *The American way of spelling: The structure of origins of american english orthography.* New York: Guilford Press.

Washington, J., & Thomas-Tate, S. (2009). How research informs cultural–linguistic differences in the classrooms: The bidialectal African-American child. In S. Rosenfield & V. Berninger (Eds.), *Implementing evidence-based interventions in school settings* (pp. 147-163). New York: Oxford University Press.

Wong, B., & Berninger, V. (2004). Cognitive processes of teachers in implementing composition research in elementary, middle, and high school classrooms. In B. Shulman, K. Apel, B. Ehren, E. Silliman, & A. Stone (Eds.), *Handbook of language and literacy development and disorders* (pp. 600–624). New York: Guilford.

Evidence-Based Practice and Autism Spectrum Disorders

Susan M. Wilczynski, Laura Fisher, Leslie Sutro, Jennifer Bass, Dipti Mudgal,
Victoria Zeiger, Lauren Christian, *and* Jesse Logue

Abstract

This chapter provides an overview of Autism Spectrum Disorders (ASD) and reviews a number of
interventions for ASD that are well supported in the research literature. The informed practitioner
must understand both the defining symptoms of ASD and the importance of careful differential
diagnosis. A description of the diagnostic process is followed by a careful analysis of seven educational
and behavioral interventions that have been found to be effective through well-controlled research.
These interventions include: early intensive behavioral intervention, behavioral package, naturalistic
teaching strategies such as incidental teaching or pivotal response treatments, joint attention, modeling,
peer training, and self-management. The importance of selecting research-supported treatments in
conjunction with other essential information (e.g., professional judgment and data-based clinical
decision making, family values and preferences, and capacity) is addressed. Even among these
empirically supported interventions, research must be extended to additional age groups, treatment
targets, or diagnostic subgroups. Suggestions for future research are provided.

Keywords: behavioral intervention, naturalistic teaching, modeling, peer training, self, management,
joint attention, school psychology

Introduction

In recent years, there has been an increased interest
in autism spectrum disorders (ASD), or Pervasive
Developmental Disorders (PDD) as they are called
in the current edition of the Diagnostic and Statistical
Manual (DSM-IV-TR). According to major autism
research groups, the prevalence of autism today is
one in 110 children Center for Disease Control &
Prevention 2009). Autism is a universal disorder that
does not discriminate based on race, as it is seen in
all cultures around the world (Wong, Hui, & Lee,
2004; Howlin & Asgharian, 1999). Unfortunately,
the numbers of autism cases appear to be increasing
worldwide (Fombonne, 2003). Years ago, teachers
were unlikely to have a student with ASD. Today,
not only do special education teachers regularly serve
children with ASD, but general education teachers
increasingly teach this population, as well.

The diagnosis of autism and its closely related disorders have been around since the middle of the last
century, when first discussed by Leo Kanner in 1943.
Kanner had observed symptoms in children that
included delays in speech development and other
forms of communication, social interaction deficits,
and repetitive or ritualized behavior. He noticed that
these children did not appear to adapt to change the
same way that their same-aged peers did. Kanner
also recognized that some children appeared to
regress, or lose skills, over time.

Initially, there were few treatment options for ASD.
Professionals often blamed parents for their child's
symptoms, referring to parents, especially mothers, as
"refrigerator mothers" (Bettleheim, 1967), implying
that mothers who were cold and distant from their
children were causing ASD. Professionals now know
that this is not the case, but it is unfortunate that

parents sometimes still experience this type of discrimination. For example, a popular radio host recently suggested ASD was caused by poor and absentee parenting. As professionals, we need to make certain that the community understands that ASD is a neurobiological disorder, believed to be caused by a combination of genetic and environmental factors, although the specifics of these factors are yet unknown (Folstein & Rosen-Sheidley, 2001).

The diagnostic process has changed dramatically over the years. When autism was first a recognized diagnosis, the diagnostic classification for autism was very narrow. A child needed to meet a strict set of criteria to receive an autism diagnosis. These children were often profoundly impaired and unable to speak. Families were often advised to have their children institutionalized. However, in 1994 (American Psychiatric Association), the diagnostic nomenclature changed in ways that expanded our understanding of these disorders. In part, this was due to a recurrence of research published by Hans Asperger that had previously been lost or neglected (Wing & Gould, 1979). Asperger's work focused on children who appeared to exhibit some of the symptoms seen in children with autism; however, these children often did not have cognitive delays, or delays in their adaptive functioning. In addition, researchers and clinicians began to identify a small group of children who presented with symptoms of classic autism that also did not have cognitive delays, although their speech and adaptive functioning was affected. These children were described as having "high functioning autism" (Ozonoff, Dawson, & McPartland, 2002). Therefore, the psychological community reworked its definition of ASD in the 1994 revision of the Diagnostic and Statistical Manual to better capture and define the symptoms seen in each of these subgroups of children.

Currently, there are five professionally accepted diagnoses that fall under the Pervasive Developmental Disorder (PDD) as listed in the DSM-IV: Autistic Disorder, Asperger's Disorder, Pervasive Developmental Disorder–Not Otherwise Specified, Rett's Disorder, and Childhood Disintegrative Disorder. Two of these (Rett's Disorder and Childhood Disintegrative Disorder) are not usually considered when the phrase "Autism Spectrum Disorder" is used, due to the differences in expected developmental trajectories associated with these disorders. Interested readers are encouraged to read Van Acker, Loncola, and Van Acker (2005) and Volkmar, Koenig, and State (2005) for details on these rare disorders.

ASD are classified as lifelong disorders beginning in childhood and progressing through adulthood. These disorders have no cure; however, researchers have found ways to intervene and produce remarkable improvements in nearly half of the children who receive early intensive behavioral intervention (EIBI; Lovaas, 1987). ASD affect a child's ability to communicate, socialize, and engage in meaningful play and work. In order for a child to be diagnosed with ASD, symptoms must be present in one of the core domains before the age of three, and the symptoms must negatively affect a child's functioning in more than one area of their life (e.g., home, school, community). These symptoms cannot be better explained by another disorder—although a large percentage of children with ASD do have comorbid symptoms of cognitive delays congruent with intellectual disabilities (Chakrabarti & Fombonne, 2005).

Autistic disorder is characterized by impairments in three core domains: communication, socialization, and repetitive and restricted interests or behaviors (Klinger, Dawson, & Renner, 2003). In order to meet criteria for autistic disorder, a child must meet 6 of 12 set symptoms, two of which fall in the social domain. Children with autistic disorder often do not use nonverbal strategies (e.g., facial expressions, body posturing, gestures) to communicate their intention. They also do not appear to engage in social reciprocity such as turn-taking, conversational banter, or indicating shared emotional experiences with others. Often, they do not show or share things of interest with loved ones, and do not appear to take pride in or ownership of their accomplishments. Finally, they often have difficulty initiating social interactions, or, when initiated, they have difficulty maintaining these interactions. Therefore, friendships can be limited and, unfortunately, once friendships are established they are difficult to maintain.

Deficits may be observed both in verbal and nonverbal methods. In terms of speech, the child with ASD may not utter their first words by age two, develop phrase speech by age three, or engage in social exchanges by preschool years. When speech is present, it may not involve functional exchanges. Children with autistic disorder may not be able to start, maintain, or stop conversations appropriately. They may not understand social nuances of language. They often do not understand jokes or metaphors, and can be quite literal in their interpretation of language. For instance, if a parent said, "It's raining cats and dogs out there!" a child with autistic disorder may be looking for cats and dogs falling from the sky. Sometimes, children's speech is peppered with nonfunctional language such as echolalia. Echolalia is defined as repeating phrases heard by another speaker, or repeating previously heard scripts that were delivered live or via media (e.g., television, DVD, etc). The play skills of children on the autism spectrum are often delayed, including imitation and make-believe play skills. Also, children with ASD often prefer playing alone, or with children much younger or older than themselves.

The final core domain of difficulty involves restricted, repetitive, nonfunctional patterns of behavior, interests, or activity. Sometimes, children with autistic disorder flap their hands or tense their bodies when excited or upset. Other times, they play with a toy in a circumscribed way, such as repetitively opening and closing the doors of a car, watching the wheels of a truck from a close distance, or spinning toys over and over. Some children line up their toys, or organize their items into specific categories (e.g., all cars by color). Other children play with one toy functionally, but in a repetitive manner and to the exclusion of all other toys. Children with autistic disorder often seek routines or rituals. They may not respond well if their schedules are altered, and they can become extremely upset with basic changes in routines. At times, these same children will engage in self-injury such as head banging, hand biting, or throwing themselves onto the floor. Finally, some children can become preoccupied with a specific interest, such as dinosaurs, train schedules, or maps. Each of these behaviors in isolation does not necessarily indicate that a child has autistic disorder; however, when multiple symptoms cluster together, it is more concerning and diagnostically indicative.

Asperger's disorder is very similar to autistic disorder, in that children can exhibit the same deficits in the core areas of social and behavioral functioning. However, by definition, children with Asperger's disorder do not have a delay in speech and language functioning. In fact, children with Asperger's disorder are often reported as hyperverbal, and demonstrate advanced language skills very early in their development. Some of these children have hyperlexia, or the ability to read or decode words above what would be expected for the child's age, typically without understanding what they have read. Children with Asperger's disorder may display incredible memory for facts and other forms of data, and can surprise people with their knowledge of circumscribed areas of interest. However, they may struggle engaging in a back and forth exchange about a topic that they know very little about. In fact, they are likely to change the topic back to their circumscribed interest.

Another key difference between autistic disorder and Asperger's disorder is that children with Asperger's disorder do not have delays in their adaptive functioning. These children are able to tie their shoes, feed themselves with forks and spoons, and can dress themselves without assistance. Children with Asperger's disorder often attend regular education classrooms in school, complete high school with same-aged peers, and work in the greater community. Some go on to lead very productive lives, although they may always appear "quirky" and may need extra support in social situations over time. However, we should not assume that individuals with Asperger's disorder will attain this level of successful functioning without sufficient support throughout their formative school years. Indeed, some individuals with Asperger's Disorder may experience debilitating anxiety or depression that will further limit their participation in their communities.

Pervasive Developmental Disorder–Not Otherwise Specified (PDD–NOS) is a broad category of classification (Walker et al., 2004). Children who do not meet full criteria for an autistic disorder would fall under the diagnosis of PDD–NOS. Also, children who have atypical presentations of ASD may be given this diagnosis. For instance, a child who does not display delays prior to the age of three, or experiences regressions in skills after that age, may demonstrate symptoms matching the criteria for autistic disorder. The idea that PDD–NOS is a milder form of autistic disorder is a common misperception. Children exhibiting four or five severe symptoms of ASD would be more developmentally delayed than a child who had six mild symptoms of autistic disorder.

Identification

Diagnosis and screening of ASD is evolving. Researchers and clinicians strive to find better and more accurate ways to address subtle aspects of ASD. This is particularly necessary with children under the age of three, as ASD are more difficult to diagnose in young children and we know that early intervention is key to long-term success with these children (Harris & Handleman, 2000). The currently accepted gold standard of autism diagnosis is based on a combination of results gleaned from a diagnostic interview and clinical judgment of an autism expert, in combination with the Autism Diagnostic Observation Schedule (ADOS), a developmental play-based assessment protocol involving the systematic observation of key features associated with ASD (Lord & Risi, 2001). In some cases, the Autism Diagnostic Interview–Revised (ADI–R) serves as the diagnostic interview. However, this instrument is most often used in research, and requires lengthy training and validation of clinicians' administration and interpretation skills, making it less likely to be used in the school and clinical setting. We provide further description on the ADOS later in this section.

Screening

Recent guidelines for pediatricians published by the American Academy of Pediatrics (2007) encourage all pediatricians to screen for autism at least two times prior to the age of 2. This means that school psychologists should increasingly receive autism screening results before children enter preschool. There are many different types of screening and diagnostic instruments available at this time. Some checklists are specifically focused on primary detection, and therefore are appropriate as first line screeners (pediatricians), such as the Modified Checklist for Autism in Toddlers (M-CHAT; Robins, Fein, Barton, & Green, 2001). Pediatricians often ask parents to complete the M-CHAT at a child's 24-month well visit. It requires individuals to answer 23 yes/no questions about a child's behavior, following a short direct observation period. It was normed on 1,293 children, and is based on critical items found on the Checklist for Autism in Toddlers (CHAT), which is completed by pediatricians at the child's 18-month well visit. If a child fails two critical items, or three items altogether, the child is considered "at risk" for ASD and should be referred on for further evaluation. This checklist has good research support and has been translated into many different languages. It takes approximately two minutes to score, and is appropriate for children between the ages of 16 and 30 months old.

Other checklists are more nuanced, and are appropriate for children who are already deemed at risk for the disorder or are being evaluated for ASD. The Childhood Autism Rating Scale (CARS) is one of the most well known screening tools for ASD (Schopler, Reichler, DeVillis, & Daly, 1980). The CARS can be used with children as young as two years of age, is appropriate for children in the school setting, and provides a cutoff score that is indicative of autism risk. The screening tool comprises 15 questions that a school psychologist should rate based on direct observation of the child, review of records, and interview with the parents. The tool was standardized on 1500 children who were suspected of having an ASD. School professionals can easily be trained on administration of the CARS. It is effective, quick, and well supported in the research literature as a solid screening tool for autism. It is important to note, however, that it is not a diagnostic instrument and should not be used in isolation to establish an ASD diagnosis, irrespective of the fact it enjoys strong psychometric support.

Another tool that is useful in identifying school-aged children at risk of ASD is the Social Responsiveness Scale (SRS; Constantino et al., 2003). The SRS comprises a longer checklist consisting of 65 items normed on a population of 1600 children. Parents answer a list of questions in response to their child's presenting symptoms. This checklist can also be given to teachers who interact with the child on a day-to-day basis. In fact, when results from both a parent report and teacher report coincide, the chance of a child being accurately screened for an ASD significantly increases. This checklist provides cutoff scores for at-risk children, and provides an indication of severity of symptoms. This checklist discriminates between autistic disorder, pervasive developmental disorder–not otherwise specified, and Asperger's disorder. It is appropriate for children between the ages of 4 and 18, and takes approximately 15–20 minutes for parents and/or teachers to complete, depending on reading ability. Although it has solid psychometric support, the SRS cannot be used to definitively diagnosis an ASD.

Another popular screening tool used by school psychologists is the Gilliam Autism Rating Scale (GARS; Gilliam, 1995), which was recently revised to reflect updated norms (1,107 children from 48 states). This screening tool can be used with children as young as 3 years old, but is often utilized with school-aged children. Along with a cutoff score, it provides an indicator of severity of symptoms a child demonstrates. It also discriminates between children who have autism, and children who are displaying symptoms of intellectual disabilities. This screening tool consists of 42 items that describe a child's behavior in the following areas: stereotyped behaviors, communication, and social interaction. Items are based on known DSM-IV criteria, and established symptoms provided by the Autism Society of America. It takes 5–10 minutes to complete. The GARS also has a parent and teacher rating form, so that school psychologists can gather data from two different sources. There is modest psychometric support for the GARS, so additional research is necessary before it is well established as a screening instrument.

A final checklist to consider using is the Social Communication Questionnaire (SCQ; Berumert et al., 1999). This 40-item screening tool provides cutoff scores for at-risk children. It takes approximately 10 minutes to complete. There are two forms available for use—a form that looks at current symptoms, and a lifetime form that analyzes symptoms over time. The SCQ is appropriate for children with a mental age of at least 2, and a chronological age of 4 or older. Therefore, it may be useful for school psychologists who work directly with children who have an intellectual disability. The SCQ is based on critical items from the ADI–R. This checklist is available in both English and Spanish. Additionally, this checklist can also be utilized as a screening tool for Asperger's disorder. Although the SCQ has adequate psychometric support for screening for ASD, it is less likely to effectively rule out other disorders.

There are not as many screening tool options specifically examining Asperger's disorder. This may be due to the subtle nature of Asperger's disorder, and its confounding presentation with other disorders such as attention-deficit/hyperactivity disorder (ADHD) or obsessive compulsive disorder (OCD). Two previously mentioned screening tools, the SRS and SCQ, are best at differentiating between autistic disorder and Asperger's disorder; however, these screening tools presume that a child has already been deemed "on the spectrum." One promising option to screen for Asperger's disorder is the Autism Spectrum Screening Questionnaire (ASSQ). This screening tool consists of 27 questions that are based on symptom presentation commonly seen in children with Asperger's disorder or high functioning autism (HFA). It is appropriate for children between the ages of 7–16 who have mild intellectual disabilities to average intelligence. Cutoff scores are provided, and the screening tool has good psychometric support (Elhers, Gillberg, & Wing, 1999).

Another option for screening Asperger's disorder is the Childhood Aspergers Screening Test (CAST) developed by Scott, Baron-Cohen, & Brayne (2002). This screening test is appropriate for children between 4-11 years of age. It was initially normed on 1150 children in a primary school setting. Preliminary research supports this screener as an effective tool to isolate children with Asperger's disorder. The screener comprises 37 questions in the areas of social communication, physical issues, cognitive functioning, and coping skills, that are answered directly by children suspected of Asperger's disorder. If a child scores high on the CAST, a parental version of the test can be administered for collaboration of data.

A final screening option is the Asperger Syndrome Diagnostic Scale (ASDS; Myles, Bock, & Simpson, 2001). A school psychologist, or a teacher who is familiar with the student, completes the 50-question form. It is appropriate for children ages 5–18 and addresses symptoms such as social development, cognition, sensory issues, and motor problems. It takes 10–15 minutes to complete. Of note, this screener was normed on only 115 children, and should be utilized with caution until more robust research support is established.

Diagnosis and/or Verification

Developmental play assessments may be useful for school psychologists who work with very young children. There are a number of play-based assessments available. The most well known play assessment is the Autism Diagnostic Observation Schedule (ADOS), which requires extensive training for practitioners. The ADOS is a structured play assessment that looks at core deficits seen in ASD (communication, social interaction, play skills, and behavior problems) through a variety of activities. This assessment takes between 45 minutes to an hour to complete. The ADOS can be administered to individuals as young as 18 months through adulthood. A child or adult does not need functional language to participate in the assessment. Algorithm results indicate whether a child or adult meets a standard cutoff score for "autism" or an "autism spectrum disorder." The ADOS has been extensively studied for psychometric support, and is considered a robust instrument in identifying core symptoms of autism, especially when paired with a comprehensive developmental interview with the child's parents (Lord et al, 2000).

Another developmental play assessment option is the Screening Tool for Autism in Two-Year-Olds (STAT; Stone, Coonrod, & Ousley, 2000). Like the ADOS, the STAT requires additional training and certification. This instrument is based on a variety of skills that are often delayed in children with autism (e.g., directing attention, turn-taking behavior, imitation, and requesting). It provides a score for children "at risk" of autism, and therefore in need of further evaluation. The STAT has solid psychometric support. It is appropriate for children between the ages of 14 months and 33 months, and takes approximately 20 minutes to complete.

Before a child is diagnosed with or verified as having an ASD, a diagnostic interview should occur. Without a complete history it is impossible to accurately diagnose or verify an ASD. The screening process provides a snapshot of current symptoms (Miesels, 1989). Yet, the age at which symptoms first appear makes a clear difference in whether or not a specific ASD should be diagnosed and/or verified. The history of general developmental delays should be considered, in addition to the defining features of ASD. Further, the extent to which difficulties with academics, cognitive functioning, motor skills, adaptive functioning, problem behaviors, and sensory or emotional regulation are present, should be determined. In addition to the proper identification of comorbid conditions (see below), a history should rule out alternative explanations for symptom presence (e.g., the child has been extremely isolated in an abusive/neglectful home).

In addition to the diagnostic interview, a review of records may prove useful. It is not uncommon for older children to have a history strewn with misdiagnoses. These misdiagnoses often yield inappropriate interventions and frustration on the part of the child with ASD, as well as the adults with whom the child interacts. Further, individuals with ASD may also have comorbid conditions that must be considered when providing educational recommendations.

Differential Diagnoses/Accurate Verification
Often, children who exhibit with symptoms of ASD also present symptoms that can look like other disorders, such as ADHD, OCD, bipolar disorder, or even oppositional defiant disorder (ODD). This is especially true for older children, among whom there is a higher propensity for anxiety and/or depression symptoms. For instance, does a child in middle school who is acting out in class, associating with a negative peer group, and demonstrating difficulty in academic achievement have an ASD, ODD, or a learning disability? Similarly, does a teenager who isolates from others, refuses to speak up in class, and exhibits poor hygiene, have depression, prodromal schizophrenia, or an ASD? Many symptoms exhibited by children with ASD mimic other disorders. A child who insists on routine and ritualized behavior may have an ASD, or may have OCD. Furthermore, the explosive behavior frequently seen in younger students with ASD has often been misconstrued as bipolar disorder. Therefore, as part of a comprehensive evaluation for ASD, it is important for school psychologists to consider various competing diagnoses when looking at the presentation of a child suspected of having ASD.

One way to effectively and easily accomplish differential diagnosis is by screening for the "other" disorders outside of ASD. There are two well known

and well established screening devices that examine a constellation of symptoms in children and adolescents: the Child Behavior Checklist (CBCL; Achenbach, 1999) and the Behavior Assessment System for Children (BASC; Gladman & Lancaster, 2003). Each of these screening tools assesses children for anxiety, depression, learning difficulties, oppositional behavior and conduct concerns, attention, and somatic complaints, among other things. Both the CBCL and the BASC allow school psychologists to gather information from both caregivers and teachers who are working closely with the child. In addition, these instruments are also available in a self-report form for children who are older and can accurately report on their current symptoms. However, given children with ASD's literal interpretation of statements, further investigation may be necessary even when these screening tools are used. The first author once assessed an adolescent with ASD who reported that "she heard voices when no one was there." She was not psychotic; instead, she reported this because the speaker was seated in the next room and she could not see him! Both the CBCL and BASC are available in English and Spanish versions, which is important for accurate capturing of symptoms for bilingual students and their families. These screening tools are effective at looking at symptoms of children as young as 18 months, and as old as 22 years. The completion time varies based on reading ability of the respondent, but usually can be completed within 30 minutes. There is solid psychometric support for both of these measures, and they are frequently used in schools across the country today.

Highly specific screening tools can be used if a specific behavioral presentation is noted. For instance, if a school psychologist suspects that an adolescent (either never diagnosed or holding a formal diagnosis for years) is exhibiting symptoms of depression, a screening tool such as the Reynold's Adolescent Depression Scale (RADS; Reynolds, 2002) can be administered. This 30-item screening test, which is completed by the student directly, provides cutoff scores for adolescents based on age and gender. It also breaks down symptoms of depression into more specific symptom presentations, such as somatic complaints or lowered self-esteem. Reliability and validity were established through population studies with over 9,000 school-aged students. The RADS is considered a robust screening tool based on over 20 years of collective research.

Students who may be exhibiting symptoms of anxiety can be effectively screened for most anxiety-based disorders utilizing the Multidimensional Anxiety Scale for Children (MASC; March, 1997). This 39-item assessment tool is appropriate for children ages 8–19 years. It examines symptoms such as social phobia, perfectionism, separation and panic disorder, and somatic concerns associated with anxiety-based disorders. Children with at least a fourth grade reading level can complete this test without assistance. This screening tool allows for re-administration to look at symptom presentation over time. It takes approximately 10 minutes to complete. The MASC has moderate to strong psychometric support (Baldwin & Dadds, 2007).

Final Diagnostic/Verification Considerations

A final word on the difference between screening and diagnosis—each of the aforementioned screening and diagnostic tools is designed to indicate that a child *may* have an ASD. Only when information derived from these instruments is used in conjunction with a strong diagnostic interview by a qualified professional, who has extensive training and experience with ASD, should a diagnosis ever be rendered. It is unfortunate that professionals in a wide range of settings are now providing diagnoses based on insufficient information or an incomplete understanding of ASD. Given how broadly disparate the presentation of ASD can be, simply having exposure to a few children with ASD does not make someone qualified to make a diagnosis. Although screening tools can be very important to early identification, and, therefore, early intervention, they should never be substituted for a comprehensive evaluation (Ozonoff, Goodlin-Jones, & Solomon, 2005). Ideally, the comprehensive evaluations are completed at a specialty clinic that focuses on autism diagnosis and treatment. These specialty clinics should actively seek input from parents and school professionals before a diagnosis is rendered or treatment recommendations are made. Also, professionals who participate in the verification process should not only receive sufficient training in the tools used to verify ASD, but also obtain adequate supervision as they gain the experience necessary to properly verify ASD.

Treatment of ASD
Evidence-Based Practice

In recent decades, an ever growing number of children have been diagnosed with an ASD, and these children need access to effective treatments in order to reach their potential. As the number of children diagnosed on the autism spectrum increases, so to do the treatment options proliferate. Certainly, no one would argue that all of these treatments are equally effective—to have hundreds of treatments come in at a statistical dead heat would defy logic and even the best Las Vegas odds! The question becomes, how do we select among the myriad treatment choices? We argue that evidence-based practice should guide our treatment selection process.

Evidence-based practice involves the integration of research findings with (a) professional judgment and data-based clinical decision making, (b) values and preferences of families, and (c) assessment and improvement of the capacity of the delivery system to implement the intervention with a high degree of procedural accuracy (Wilczynski & Christian, 2008). Each of these components is critical, and none should be easily dismissed. First, practitioners must determine which treatments have strong evidence of effectiveness. Clinical guidelines in the treatment of ASD have been developed in the recent past. The New York Department of Health Guidelines (1999) and the National Research Council's *Educating Children with Autism* (2001) involved an extensive review of the literature by experts who identified treatments that enjoyed strong research support. Unfortunately, these guidelines are now out of date. The National Autism Center (NAC) released an exhaustive review of the educational and behavioral treatment literature in the fall of 2009. This document identifies the strength of evidence for comprehensive approaches to treatment as well as focused interventions. The National Standards Report (NAC; 2009) can be used to identify research support that is critical in treatment selection when practitioners engage in evidence-based practice.

Professional judgment must play a critical role in decision making. First, when selecting treatments, it is highly advisable to be familiar with the strength of evidence for a treatment involving a broader population, in addition to the data presented in the National Standards Report. For example, knowing the research support for treatments involving individuals with developmental disabilities, or literature for affective problems such as anxiety and depression, may be necessary to supplement the outcomes reported in the National Standards Report (NAC, 2009). Professional judgment is also important in understanding unique factors that can impact treatment selection for individual students. School psychologists, for example, may be able to advocate for or advise against a treatment based on their knowledge about the function of the behavior. If a treatment is not well matched to the function of the behavior, it is not going to be a good choice, even if it enjoys the strongest level of research support. Further, the school psychologist may have data to show that a treatment has been ineffective in the past, even if it is identified as having strong research support. The school psychologists' professional role in advocating for data-based clinical decision making should be central, irrespective of the treatment selected.

The values and preferences of families can often be overlooked, or are undermined if we do not recognize the role family input should play in the treatment selection process. Families are in a unique position to inform us whether or not a treatment can be implemented in the home. When selecting treatments for critical skills like communication, the practical utility of the system needs to be given serious consideration. An expensive communication device may not be appropriate if the family cannot afford it in their home, and a less expensive alternate should seriously be considered. In some cases, we need to get input from the individual with ASD. An adolescent with ASD might prefer a less intrusive intervention like "Social Stories" over a pull-out program social skills package. Finally, we need to be concerned about the capacity to implement interventions with a high degree of treatment fidelity. It may take time to get the training, materials, and/or staff to implement the intervention. Once training has been obtained, treatment fidelity must be maintained with ongoing feedback. It might be necessary to select an interim treatment that that has slightly less research support, but can be implemented with a high degree of treatment fidelity while the school builds its capacity to implement an intervention with stronger research support. This is not to suggest that building schoolwide capacity should not be aggressively pursued; it is merely recognizing that capacity building is a process that may take some time to do properly. Implementing an intervention that, in practice, bears little or no resemblance to the treatment that was investigated empirically, is not engaging in evidence-based practice. A review of evidence-based practice in treatment follows.

Comprehensive Approaches

An ever growing number of comprehensive approaches to treatment are offered every day. At first blush, this is a very desirable outcome. More choices give school systems and families more flexibility in the treatment selection process, right? Unfortunately, many of these comprehensive approaches have not yet been studied with sufficient scientific rigor that we can draw firm conclusions about their effectiveness. We are legally and ethically obligated to select evidence-based practices. At present, the only treatment approach that enjoys strong evidence of effectiveness at this time is EIBI, based in the principles of applied behavior analysis (ABA).

Applied Behavior Analysis (ABA) is a scientific practice, guided by empirically based behavior principles and used to improve people's lives by helping them make positive behavioral changes. ABA aspires to create lasting improvements in a person's functioning by using empirically sound behavioral principles to assess, analyze, describe, and measure behavior while systematically manipulating antecedent variables and consequences in an effort to reduce problem behaviors (Baer, Wolf, & Risley 1968). Currently, ABA is used in classrooms, homes, and therapy centers to inform a variety of educational and therapeutic interventions for children with a range of diagnoses and problem behaviors.

ABA has produced a number of treatment programs, some of which have contributed to the scientific literature. Examples of these treatment programs include but are not restricted to: Children's Toddler School, Project LEAP, The Lovaas Institute, May Institute, and Princeton Child Development Institute. There are differences across these treatment programs. For example, some of these treatment programs occur in more restrictive educational environments, and others are integrated models relying heavily on parent and/or peer involvement. However, all of these programs are based on the principles of applied behavior analysis.

The most well known ABA approach is an EIBI program that was initially developed by Ivar Lovaas in the 1960s. In 1987, Lovaas published a seminal work on the early intensive behavioral approach to the treatment of children with ASD. In this study, 19 young children (under the age of 4) with ASD were provided intensive treatment (40 hours per week) for a prolonged period of time (2–3 years). A control group of children with ASD received approximately 10 hours of special education services per week. The children receiving Lovaas' ABA program performed significantly better. Specifically, 47% of the children had IQ scores falling in the average range at the conclusion of the study. In contrast, none of the children receiving special education services achieved this level of cognitive functioning. Importantly, teachers reported that children benefiting from Lovaas' treatment were considered indistinguishable from their peers. These children were followed over time, and the beneficial treatment effects were sustained for the children receiving Lovaas' ABA treatment.

An important question emanating from this research is, "Were the differences simply due to the number of hours treatment was provided?" The answer was provided by research published almost 20 years after Lovaas' original work. Howard, Sparkman, Cohen, Green, & Stanislaw (2005) compared three intervention programs. The first intervention group involved 25–40 hours of EIBI. The second intervention group received a 30-hour eclectic intervention. The last group received a 15-hour traditional preschool program. There were no significant differences in outcomes between the 30-hour eclectic group and the 15-hour traditional preschool program group. However, the EIBI group showed significant improvements in terms of cognitive functioning, nonverbal skills, communication (both receptive and expressive skills), as well as adaptive skills. This finding was further supported by research conducted by Eikeseth, Smith, Jahr, & Eldevik (2002; 2007). Again, socially important outcomes (e.g., IQ, communication, adaptive skills) were improved for the children receiving EIBI over those receiving an eclectic treatment, and these differences were sustained at a 3-year follow-up.

Additional research has been conducted since Lovaas's (1987) groundbreaking work, and these studies have also demonstrated substantial improvement following treatment (Cohen, Amerine-Dickens, & Smith, 2006; Smith, Groen, & Wynn, 2000). It is important to note, however, that although these ABA-based programs were the only ones that produced clinically and educationally relevant improvements, important considerations remain. For example, the comprehensive programs described here all involved EIBI. ABA is often used to increase developmentally appropriate and socially relevant outcomes throughout the lifetime. No comprehensive treatment programs using ABA have yet published large-scale studies demonstrating effectiveness across the lifespan. Indeed, numerous studies (Fenske et al., 1985; Luiselli, Cannon, Ellis, & Sisson, 2000) have shown that intervention prior to 5 years of age is critical in producing the substantial gains reported here. Importantly, data providing strong evidence of effectiveness for focused interventions based on applied behavior analysis have been published (see **Focused Interventions** below).

Another concern often raised about the effectiveness of ABA-based programs is the absence of sustained data regarding the complex skills associated with social/pragmatic communication. Improvements in social skills have been noted in the literature (Lovaas, 1987), but additional research will be necessary to establish that children maintain the level of social sophistication required to navigate the complex social world of adolescence and adulthood.

Focused Interventions

Although evidence has been forwarded about the effectiveness of comprehensive approaches, the vast majority of the treatment literature falls into the area of focused interventions. Studies falling in the area of focused interventions typically target one or more specific skill deficits or behavioral excesses, and do not meet the rigid criteria for comprehensive approaches. These interventions target (or focus on) one or more specific domains (e.g., communication, interpersonal, play, self-regulation, problem behaviors, etc.), or on a subset of a comprehensive approach. With changes in the Individuals with Disabilities Education Act of 1997 (IDEA, 1997), school districts have become increasingly responsible for providing interventions that not only address the academic needs of children with autism, but also those that target deficits related to communication, social skills, motor ability, sensory disturbances, and adaptive functioning (Weber, Killu, Derby, & Barretto, 2005). In many cases, a child's school district is responsible for and oversees a program to address individualized education plan IEP goals that may be conducted in the child's home and/or community as well as the school setting. We review a small number of focused interventions for which there is strong evidence of effectiveness, below.

Behavioral Package

As noted earlier in this chapter, increasing empirical support for treatments based on ABA principles has influenced our concept of best practice for ASD (National Research Council, 2001; NAC, 2009; New York State Department of Health 1999). Behaviorally based autism treatments can be divided into two broad categories: comprehensive programs, and focused treatments (NAC, 2009). Although myriad focused treatments are used in schools and treatment facilities, autism interventions are most often combined and delivered as part of a "behavioral package" that combines a number of teaching strategies and methods to bring about behavior change. Behavioral treatment packages are most effective if they are created for an individual student's needs, and not offered as a "one-size-fits-all" solution. Before a set of behavioral interventions can be implemented, several determinations first need to be made. Is the goal of intervention to teach a new behavior or skill, or is it to shape an existing one? Does the target behavior require a prerequisite skill set that may need to be taught first? How will prompts be faded to avoid prompt-dependent responding? Have effective reinforcers been identified for this child? What type of reinforcement schedule will be used? How will generalization of the skill or behavior be determined? These are just a few of the questions that should be asked prior to treatment implementation. Despite popular beliefs to the contrary, behavioral packages do not involve simply choosing between M & Ms and stickers!

The following example of a behavioral package further clarifies these approaches. In a recent study (Pelios, MacDuff, & Axelrod, 2003), a treatment package including contingent or delayed reinforcement for correct responses, fading of prompts and teacher presence, a response-cost system for incorrect responses, and a pattern of unpredictable appearance of a supervising teacher, was successfully implemented in a school setting to increase the on-task and on-schedule behavior of three children with autism. At the end of the intervention, students who had previously required high levels of supervision and prompting to stay on task and follow their picture schedules were consistently (95%-99%) staying on task with minimal adult supervision. Not only did the target behaviors increase substantially during treatment, but these results were maintained over time for the two students on whom maintenance data were collected.

Additional strategies commonly used in a behavioral package include, but are not limited to, antecedent interventions (e.g., environmental modification, noncontingent reinforcement, high-probability request sequences), imitation, behavioral rehearsal, chaining procedures, token economy systems, extinction procedures, discrete trial teaching (DTT), and errorless learning (Alberto & Troutman, 2003; Carr & Carlson, 1993; Cooper, Heron, & Heward, 2007). Various combinations of these behaviorally based teaching strategies are commonly used in focused treatments and comprehensive programs to effectively teach new skills, and manage interfering behaviors in the home and classroom, for children with ASD.

Naturalistic Teaching Strategies
Behavioral research suggests that when children are provided 1:1 individualized instruction that

(a) is highly structured and teacher-directed, (b) utilizes prompting procedures for correct responses and delivery of immediate consequences, and (c) is conducted in an environment with minimal distractions, effective learning can take place and considerable progress can be made. However, once these provisions have been made, the teaching environment inevitably becomes much different from the child's natural environment. As a result, the child may have difficulty using a new skill taught under such tightly controlled conditions in other, less structured settings, unless directly taught to do so. For example, a child who learns to identify his numbers written on index cards by working one-on-one with a teacher in a partitioned area of the classroom may not be able to identify those same numbers during a calendar activity at circle time, sitting with his peers. In this case, the child with ASD has failed to use the skill he learned, within the natural environment, during the usual time of the day in which this skill should be used. This difficulty is referred to as *generalization*, which is defined as the ability to learn a skill and then demonstrate that skill in multiple environments (other than the teaching environment), with multiple people, and with multiple materials or exemplars. While typically developing children are able to generalize newly acquired skills somewhat easily without additional teaching, children with ASD experience great difficulty with generalization.

One option is to teach the child with ASD under highly controlled conditions, and then carefully plan for generalization of each skill across different situations (e.g., with multiple individuals, using multiple stimuli, in multiple locations). Alternatives to teaching a child under a highly controlled situation do exist. That is, it is possible to address generalization at the outset of treatment by teaching a child in the natural environment, during the usual times of the day in which a particular skill should be demonstrated. This process is referred to as *naturalistic teaching*. Naturalistic teaching procedures embed teaching opportunities in naturally occurring events throughout the day (e.g., snack, recess, circle time). For example, a child who is unable to open a milk carton at lunch is taught to request "help" at this time; a child who cannot identify his colors is taught this skill during various art activities; or a child who does not initiate interactions with his peers is taught to greet five peers as they arrive in the classroom each morning. Teaching occurs during the times of the day when the opportunities naturally present themselves (i.e., when it makes sense for the child to demonstrate the targeted skill) rather than during a separate "work" time. In this manner, generalization becomes part of the intervention from the initial teaching interactions.

Naturalistic teaching strategies employ three basic principles for promoting generalization: using natural consequences, training diversely, and incorporating mediators (Stokes & Osnes, 1989). Generalization of behaviors is more likely to occur when direct reinforcers are used, rather than consequences that are preprogrammed by a teacher. Often, "reinforcers" selected by teachers are selected based on convenience, may not be related to the specific behavior being reinforced, and may not actually serve to increase the skills being targeted for improvement! In the examples above, the child learning to identify colors during art might be given the desired color paint once the child has correctly named the color. This would provide a more direct relationship between the activity and the reinforcer than if he correctly identified a color and was then given a favorite toy to play with for a predetermined amount of time. It is important, however, to make certain that the item that is delivered actually serves as a reinforcer (i.e., it increases the target behavior).

Training diversely refers to the use of different materials and contexts to teach a particular skill. A child with ASD might be able to identify a picture of a red car, but be unable to select the red plastic car from the toy bin, or the red car in the parking lot. By using many different materials during teaching, this difficulty with generalization can often be addressed.

Incorporating mediators refers to the use of stimuli during teaching that are likely to be encountered in other settings or conditions. By allowing for these variations, teaching becomes less rigid, and generalization is embedded within the teaching procedures. Thus, the child who is learning his colors during art activities is also being taught his colors during free play with different colored blocks or other toys, and during snack time, to request an item of a particular color.

Naturalistic teaching strategies share many common characteristics. These characteristics include: (a) incorporating loosely structured teaching sessions; (b) capitalizing on teaching opportunities that result from the child's initiation; (c) teaching across multiple settings with multiple exemplars; (d) using a variety of prompts and accepting a variety of responses; and 5) incorporating naturalistic reinforcers (Cowen & Allen, 2007). These characteristics

will be illustrated below, in the descriptions of the most common naturalistic teaching approaches: Incidental Teaching, Natural Language Paradigm, and Pivotal Response Training.

INCIDENTAL TEACHING

Incidental teaching was originally developed to guide the generalization and spontaneous use of language in disadvantaged preschoolers (Hart & Risley, 1968). This approach involves arranging an environment with preferred items, toys, and/or activities that are visible to the child, but unavailable to him or her (e.g., they are out of reach). Teaching occurs when the child initiates an interaction with the adult in order to gain access to a desired item. Following this initiation, the adult uses the opportunity to teach more elaborate language by prompting the child to request, for example, the particular color, size, or amount of the desired item. Once the child responds with this new response, the child is given the item along with the adult's attention. This approach can be modified and individualized for children ranging in verbal ability. For example, if the child is not yet speaking in sentences, the adult may prompt the child to simply name the item before providing access to the item. Features of incidental teaching that distinguish it as a naturalistic procedure include: (a) teaching opportunities are facilitated by the child's interests and initiations, (b) natural settings and direct consequences are used, and (c) multiple stimuli are incorporated across teaching opportunities.

When structured teaching approaches are compared to incidental teaching, incidental teaching has resulted not only in greater generalization, but also equal-to-greater spontaneous verbal responses of children with autism (McGee, Krantz, & McClannahan, 1985). Schepis, Reid, Behrmann, and Sutton (1998) trained classroom staff to use incidental teaching procedures to increase use of a voice output communication aid (VOCA) in four children with autism. The main strategies used included using child-preferred stimuli during natural daily routines, teaching only after a child initiated with the staff, and using verbal and/or gestural prompts, thus minimizing physical guidance whenever possible. All children demonstrated an increase in their communicative behaviors, using the VOCA in a variety of ways (e.g., to request items, respond to questions, and comment) during the two targeted natural routines of snack and play time.

NATURAL LANGUAGE PARADIGM

Developed by Koegel, O'Dell, & Koegel (1987), the Natural Language Paradigm (NLP) is a teaching approach that seeks to improve communication. By focusing on student motivation, higher levels of active engagement and less resistance to teaching may occur. Strategies for targeting child's motivation in teaching include, but are not restricted to: (a) following the child's choice when selecting stimuli; (b) using direct reinforcers; (c) providing task variation (i.e., mixing teaching trials for mastered skills with teaching trials for emerging skills); and (d) reinforcing communicative attempts. The final two strategies help to distinguish NLP from other naturalistic procedures. A child's motivation to persist in the midst of challenging, unmastered acquisition tasks can be enhanced by interspersing easier, previously mastered tasks with these more difficult items. Additionally, reinforcement is not delivered exclusively when a task has been completed perfectly. Instead, a child's *attempt* to communicate is rewarded and the response is gradually shaped over time.

Smith and Camarata (1999) examined the effectiveness of naturalistic language teaching strategies for three children with ASD in their general education classroom setting. General education teachers were trained to implement naturalistic language procedures to encourage the children to interact with others. Once the teachers were adequately trained in the use of these procedures, a consultative model was adopted, with the teachers and the trainers meeting twice weekly for a brief period of time for feedback and questions. General education teachers were taught to implement the following strategies in the classroom: (1) the use of items of high interest to the children, chosen by the children; (2) the progression of language, from naming the item to phrases and sentences embedded in conversational play; (3) the modeling words for high-interest items and subsequent play with items involving interactions between the teacher and the children; (4) reinforcement of correct attempts and responses; and (5) the use of both natural and social reinforcers (e.g., opportunity to play with the item, and teacher attention). All three children demonstrated an increase in the intelligibility of their verbalizations. In addition, amount of time spent speaking either increased to, or was maintained at "near typical levels." Implementation in a classroom by general education teachers (as opposed to highly trained clinicians) are benefits to naturalistic language procedures.

PIVOTAL RESPONSE TRAINING (PRT)

PRT is an extension of NLP to all goals that must be addressed for children with ASD. In addition to motivational strategies, central features of PRT include the development of skills that could be a watershed for a broad number of subskills. The goals of PRT are to (a) teach the child to appropriately respond to multiple teaching opportunities occurring in the natural environment, (b) decrease the child's dependence on others to coach or direct his/her behavior, and (c) decrease the amount of time a child is removed from natural settings (Koegel, Koegel, Harrower, & Carter, 1999). Motivation is considered one of four identified pivotal behaviors. The following procedures are used to increase motivation during teaching: (1) child selection of materials, (2) natural reinforcers linked directly to the task, (3) the interspersal of mastered tasks with learning tasks, and (4) reinforcement for attempts.

In addition to outlining specific strategies for how to teach, PRT identifies what to teach, through the identification of the remaining three pivotal behaviors. First, children should be taught to respond to multiple cues in any environment. This is important because children with ASD have a tendency to become overselective in their response patterns, responding to only one person or aspect of a given stimulus. A second pivotal response is self-initiation. This is an essential skill to teach because once a child learns to self-initiate, opportunities for further learning are made available. This is achieved by teaching children to query for information, a skill individuals typically perform in order to initiate social interactions and/or to obtain information. Finally, self-management is considered a pivotal response. This involves teaching children to monitor their own behavior and to self-administer consequences (see the **Self-Management** section of this chapter for further details).

In a study conducted by Harper, Symon, and Frea (2008), typically developing peers were trained in the application of the motivation techniques of PRT to help increase the social interactions during recess of two children with ASD. Peers participated in seven training sessions (20 minutes each) focusing on how to gain attention, vary activities, narrate play, reinforce attempts, and take turns when interacting with children with ASD. Peers also received training on how to handle potential aggressive behavior from a child with ASD. Peer implementation of these PRT techniques led to improvements in social interactions for the two children with ASD. Following the intervention (i.e., when training strategies were removed) the target children maintained the improvements in initiating and responding.

PRT has also been used to increase play skills in children with ASD. Stahmer (1995) used PRT strategies to teach symbolic play to seven children with ASD. Prior to intervention, none of the targeted children engaged in symbolic play. Following symbolic play training, all children demonstrated an increase in symbolic play and play complexity, to levels similar to those of language-matched typical peers. In most cases, generalization of these play behaviors to different toys, environments, and play partners occurred. In a related study, Thorp, Stahmer, and Schreibman (1995) used PRT strategies to teach sociodramatic play to three children with ASD. Although all target children had language skills of at least 3 years 6 months, none exhibited sociodramatic play prior to treatment. Following 16 hours of training, all children substantially increased their role-playing behavior, which generalized across settings and play partners. In addition, all children demonstrated an increase in their ability to carry out a play theme from beginning to end, although they experienced some difficulty generalizing this skill following training. Make-believe play also increased for all three children post-training.

In sum, incidental teaching, PRT and NLP are all effective naturalistic teaching strategies for teaching skills to children with ASD. By using stimuli of interest to the child, waiting for the child to initiate an interaction, teaching the child in the natural environment with different materials and across different contexts, and delivering direct reinforcers, children with ASD can not only learn new skills, but generalize these skills and maintain them over time.

An added advantage of naturalistic teaching procedures is the ability to individualize teaching for a specific child. As noted previously, materials are child-specific and child-selected. In addition, targeted responses are determined by the child's level of functioning (e.g., words, phrases, conversations, etc.). Many naturalistic teaching procedures emphasize a child-directed approach, with the teacher or adult waiting for the child to initiate an interaction, a behavioral deficit for many children with ASD. As a result, naturalistic procedures can be modified to include an adult directive. The mand-model procedure (Rogers-Warren & Warren, 1980) was developed specifically to decrease the reliance on child initiations. Similarly, the time-delay procedure, which utilizes a nonverbal cueing approach, is an alternative for children who tend to become overly dependent on verbal prompts (Halle, Marshall, & Spradlin, 1979).

Joint Attention

Joint attention occurs when two individuals share a common focus on objects or events in their surrounding area. Skills required to engage in joint attention include but are not restricted to pointing to objects, showing objects to another person, following another individual's eye gaze, and responding to invitations to engage in social interaction. Given the critical role joint attention plays in the development of complex social, communication, and play skills, interventions targeting this skill set have recently been developed. Although few joint attention intervention studies have been published, the evidence from well-controlled studies is compelling.

Joint attention studies often use multiple behavioral strategies. Whalen and Schreibman (2003) briefly taught joint attention skills using discrete trial training. Skills were then transferred to a more naturalistic setting. Prompting, maintenance interspersal (i.e., intermingling novel tasks with those that have already been mastered), choice, modeling, and reinforcement with a direct response/reinforcer relationship (i.e., stimulus serving as a reinforcer was directly related to the task/behaviors targeted) were techniques used to improve joint attention skills. Four young children (aged 4) with ASD participated in the study involving two phases: response training and initiation training. Response training involves teaching children to respond to a variety of joint attention bids from adults. Examples include: (a) adult puts child's hand on an object; (b) adult taps an object; (c) adult shows an object; (d) adult seeks eye contact; (e) adult points at a proximal or distant object; and (f) adult uses eye gaze to regulate the attention of the child. Whalen and Schreibman (2003) successfully demonstrated significant gains in joint attention responding with this brief intervention (16–23 days with 3 sessions per day). All children showed improvements in responding to adult pointing or shifting of eye gaze.

Initiation training was implemented in phase two of the joint attention training. Initiation training involves teaching the child to make bids to engage in joint attention with others. Strategies involved coordinating eye gaze and protodeclarative pointing (i.e., pointing to share an experience, as opposed to pointing for the purpose of requesting). Improvements in joint attention initiations were evidenced for all participants, with more substantial gains in coordinated eye gaze. Gains in responding to and initiating joint attention bids were generally sustained at a 3-month follow-up, with some reduction in responding for pointing (Whalen & Schreibman, 2003).

Whalen and Schreibmen's (2003) generalization data were not quite as strong. Generalization across settings was demonstrated, but gains were not consistently maintained during follow-up evaluation. Although some improvements were noted with parents, consistent improvements in joint attention skills were not reported. This would suggest generalization across multiple individuals should be planned. For most preschool-aged children, parents would seem to be an excellent agent for improving joint attention skill. This pattern should not eliminate our use of joint attention training, however; based on video clips, half of the participants were rated as equally "normal" compared to their typically developing peers by the undergraduates.

In 2006, Martins and Harris also implemented a behaviorally based joint attention intervention to target joint attention responding. In this case, discrete trial training procedures were combined with maintenance interspersal, prompting, and time delays. Adults signaled the joint attention bid by securing the child's attention and then using nonverbal strategies (e.g., turning head, eye gaze) to regulate the child's behavior. Probes were collected in the child's classroom, and generalization data were collected in an unfamiliar room in the same building. At the completion of the training, all children responded to joint attention bids from adults at a much higher rate in the absence of additional training. Further, the generalization data indicated these high rates of responding to joint attention bids were sustained across settings. Although not targeted directly, data were also collected on joint attention initiations. Unfortunately, joint attention initiations did not appear to be a collateral gain when joint attention responding was taught, suggesting joint attention initiations must be taught directly.

Joint attention training has been directly compared to alternate treatments for preschool children (Kasari, Freeman, & Paparella, 2006). Three groups of preschool-aged boys with ASD participated in treatment for 30 minutes per day for a 5–6 week period. Both treatments were similar, in that they incorporated developmental procedures into treatments emerging from the field of applied behavior analysis. Like the previous studies described, skills were taught directly using discrete trial training before the same skill was addressed in a less structured setting (i.e., on the floor). Prompting, reinforcement, child-directed strategies, imitation of child's toy use, and use of child's play activities were employed with each of these treatment approaches. Whereas the joint attention intervention focused on coordinated joint looking, showing, giving to share, pointing (proximal and distal), and following pointing, the symbolic play

intervention focused on combining objects in increasingly symbolic ways. Each treatment was associated with improvements in comparison to the no-treatment control group. Both treatment conditions improved initiations involving showing objects to experimenters, and coordinated joint looks. The joint attention intervention group also improved responding to joint attention bids, giving and showing to parents, and high rates of initiations with parents. The only gain noted exclusively in the symbolic play group was greater overall play activity with an improved variety in symbolic play. Once again, strong evidence for joint attention training was provided, but it is noteworthy that additional targeted treatment in the area of symbolic play may be necessary to build this unique set of skills.

Finally, Rocha, Schreibman, and Stahmer (2007) provided a compelling reason to use a behavior analytic approach to teach joint attention. Three young (under 5 years of age) children diagnosed with ASD, and their parents, participated in the study. Parents were taught to use joint attention strategies at a university clinic. Strategies parents used included physically handing their child preferred toys, tapping objects, showing objects, following a pointing gesture, and following the eye gaze of another person. Parents were able to use these strategies effectively, and children's joint attention responding increased. Indeed, participants often responded at approximately the same level as typically developing children. Further, two-thirds of the children showed demonstrable gains in their use of joint attention skills during the generalization probes in the home. Parent use of the strategies did not change significantly for the child who did not show gains in joint attention responding during the home generalization probes. Given the brief nature of this treatment (a minimum of 17 hours over a span of 6 weeks), these improvements are considerable. It is certainly promising to see joint attention interventions be effectively implemented by parents in a way that produces gains in this crucial skill domain because young children spend the majority of their waking hours in contact with their parents.

In summary, joint attention is a critical skill deficit identified in children with ASD. Although research has only recently been conducted on joint attention training, clear and compelling evidence has been forwarded to support the usefulness of this focused intervention. Given the brief time commitment required for joint attention training, this is undoubtedly a treatment individuals serving preschool-aged individuals with ASD should consider pursuing.

Modeling/Video Modeling

In practice, modeling involves the process of showing a student how to successfully complete a specified task. This "demonstration" should serve as a prompt to the students so they know the exact steps to imitate. Often, modeling is combined with multiple other behavioral techniques (Gena, Krantz, McClannahan, & Poulson, 1996). For example, extra-modeling prompts and reinforcement are almost universally used when modeling procedures are employed.

Qualitative impairments in communication are one of the defining features of ASD, and schools across the country are working to improve these critical skills for the children with ASD. Communication involves an extraordinarily broad and complex set of skills, making it particularly difficult to target effectively. Studies supporting the use of modeling to improve communication have been published (Jahr, 2001). For example, it is essential that children learn to answer 'wh' questions in order to fully benefit from the teaching processes often used in general education classes. Young children (ages 3 to 7) were successfully taught to answer questions like "What do you like to drink (eat)?" or "Where do you play (swim)?" Not only did the students acquire the ability to respond to 'wh' questions, but they were able to generalize this to another part of their kindergarten classrooms with adults who did not participate in the original training. Also, these skills were maintained over time.

Another core deficit in ASD is a qualitative impairment in social interaction. Appropriate affective responding that is matched to the social context is an important aspect of regulating and maintaining social interactions. Gena, Krantz, McClannahan, and Poulson (1996) successfully demonstrated that modeling could be used to improve the affective behavior of middle and high school aged students. Affective behaviors included making appropriate eye contact and statements, smiling or laughing as appropriate, and use of nonverbal strategies (e.g., shaking head). Not only was affective behavior considerably and meaningfully improved, but these changes were also noted with multiple individuals (generalization across people) and were sustained at a one-month follow-up.

The vast majority of recently published work in the area of modeling has been on the topic of video modeling. Like other forms of modeling, video modeling involves a demonstration in order to show a child exactly how to perform an action, behavior, or activity (LeBlanc, Coates, Daneshvar, Charlop-Christy, Morris, & Lancaster, 2003). However, video modeling relies on the use of technology, in that the demonstration occurs via videotape or DVD presentation. Video modeling has been used to target a broad range of skill deficits or behavioral excesses.

There are disadvantages and advantages to video modeling. Certainly, video modeling requires the technology (e.g., video camera, television, playback device) to develop and present the demonstration. Developing the video may require time and technical expertise to ensure sufficient quality in the video presentation, such that the observer can benefit from the activity. Although these disadvantages exist, the advantages far outweigh the disadvantages. First, once the video has been developed, the same demonstration can be displayed repeatedly at the convenience of the teacher without spending the time required to (a) secure necessary materials and (b) provide models when competing demands, such as teaching other children, may be present. Second, video may be a medium that allows for greater attention to the requisite steps necessary to complete the target task (Charlop-Christy, Le, & Freeman, 2000). Third, video modeling can be cost effective, in that the video can be presented to more than one child during more than one time period. Fourth, parents and professionals often report that children with ASD prefer videos to live modeling, and may be more likely to respond to video demonstrations (Charlop-Christy, Le, & Freeman). Finally, when comparing live and video models, video modeling has sometimes been demonstrated to yield faster acquisition of target skills. In one study, skill acquisition was associated with higher generalization (Charlop-Christy, Le, & Freeman). It is noteworthy, however, that these differences have not always emerged when these demonstration modalities have been directly compared. We review a small sample of the video modeling literature below, to highlight the range of skills/behaviors and age groups for whom video modeling has successfully led to acquisition and generalization of targets.

An early demonstration of the effectiveness of video modeling involved young adults (20 years of age) who were taught to purchase materials in community settings (Haring, Kennedy, Adams, Pitts-Conway, 1987). Treatment began with direct training of skills. However, training alone did not produce generalization of purchasing skills across different community settings. When a video modeling treatment was introduced, video modeling skills not only improved but generalized to three different stores.

Given the paucity of research with older individuals on the autism spectrum, this early investigation is important not only because it highlights the value of video modeling as a useful intervention, but also because it is a clear demonstration that video modeling can be effective with older students.

Teaching adaptive or daily living skills has not been restricted to older children. Using a rigorous single-case design methodology, Shipley-Benamou, Lutzker, and Taubman (2002) established the effectiveness of video modeling with 5-year-olds with ASD, who were identified as having deficits in daily living skills (e.g., making orange juice, setting a table, cleaning a fish bowl, etc.). Point-of-view video modeling (i.e., video taken from the perspective of the individuals performing the task) that focused on an adult's hands as the daily living skills were performed was used. Not only did video modeling produce meaningful improvements in daily living skills, but these skills were maintained one month after the last video presentation. Further, although the intervention was implemented in the school settings, probes were collected in the homes of the participants which showed that children generalized the skills across settings.

As noted previously, video modeling may be associated with improved outcomes in comparison to traditional modeling demonstrations, but this finding has not been consistently demonstrated. An early comparison of in vivo and video modeling targeted developmentally appropriate skills ranging from communication and play, to self-help skills, to elementary and middle school children (Charlop-Christy, Le, & Freeman, 2000). Both approaches to modeling improved performance for all children; however, skill acquisition occurred more rapidly for several participants in the video modeling condition. Further, video modeling more successfully produced generalized effects across stimuli than did in vivo modeling for the majority of participants. In contrast, Gena, Couloura, and Kymissis (2005), used similarly rigorous methodology and did not show differences when using live (i.e., in vivo) versus video modeling. In this study, appropriate affective responding was targeted for preschool-aged individuals. Improvements in affective responding were noted with both approaches to modeling, with no approach clearly superior in acquisition or generalization. These effects were maintained at one- and three-month follow-up evaluations. The differences between these two studies may simply be due to chance. However, the possibility exists that the type of behaviors or skills targeted, or the age at which

these treatments are introduced, could influence the outcomes. Further investigation from similarly well-controlled studies is necessary.

An inability to understand the perspective of another individual will certainly undermine the quality of social interactions shared by two people (Robert-McComb & Barker, 2008). Given that individuals with ASD have been demonstrated to have impairments in perspective-taking, it is imperative for researchers to identify treatments that can effectively improve this important skill. Using a well controlled single-case design methodology, Charlop-Christy and Daneshvar (2003) clearly demonstrated that perspective-taking skills could be improved for 3 elementary school-aged boys with ASD. Further generalization of skills was significantly improved for two of the three participants. Although other approaches to teaching perspective-taking have been proposed, they often do not show this level of improvement in the area of generalization.

In addition to teaching developmentally appropriate skills, video modeling has successfully been used to reduce problem behaviors (Schreibman, Whalen, & Stahmer, 2000). Video demonstrations were presented prior to transitions which had been associated with problem behavior previously. In this case, problem behaviors included whining, crying, screaming, aggression, pulling, verbal resistance, and dropping to the ground. These brief videos served to "prime" appropriate responding during transition activities. Generalization data were collected to determine if responding continued to improve when the video was no longer presented immediately prior to the transition activity, or when irrelevant videos were presented in lieu of the video demonstration. Overall, significant reductions in disruptive behaviors were evidenced and maintained at a one-month follow-up. Given the class- and schoolwide impact of disruptive behaviors in school settings, video modeling should be considered as a means of priming appropriate behavior.

Most often adults and peers have served as the models when video model treatments have been used. Once video modeling was identified as an effective treatment, researchers attempted to identify whether having the target child participate in the video could improve skills as well. This method may be more difficult because, if the child performed the skill fluently enough to make development of the video an easy process, then video modeling would not be necessary. Although video self-modeling has been demonstrated to effectively improve skills for elementary and middle school-aged students

(Buggey, Toombs, Gardener, & Cervetti, 1999), no improved benefit to video self-modeling has been reported over video modeling in general (Sherer et al., 2001). Given the likelihood that producing the video will be much easier with an adult or peer model, individuals new to using video modeling may want to avoid video self-modeling when they first begin using this approach.

In sum, a substantial number of well controlled studies have been published demonstrating the effectiveness of modeling in general, and video modeling in particular. It is noteworthy that these treatment approaches have been used both to effectively increase a broad range of developmentally appropriate skills, and to decrease behavioral excesses that can interfere with social interactions and classroom participation. Without question, the fact that these skills were maintained over time, and generalized across materials or people, supports the broad use of modeling and video modeling with children on the autism spectrum.

Peer Training

Without successful intervention, social deficits tend to become more pronounced as children with ASD get older (Strain, 1981). One strategy for improving social interactions involves integrating children with ASD into classrooms with typically developing peers. In practice, this process often amounts to hoping that close physical proximity to peers will lead to acquisition of necessary social interaction skills as a result of modeling and increased opportunities for social exchanges. Despite the intended logic of integration, typically developing peers tend to play with one another, often ignoring or rejecting children with ASD unless they have been directly taught more effective skills. In turn, children with ASD remain isolated. Simply put, children with ASD who are merely placed in close proximity to typically developing peers often fail to learn effective social interaction skills.

One strategy that has successfully improved social interactions of children with ASD involves the use of peer-mediated interventions. In peer-mediated interventions, typically developing peers are directly taught ways to interact more effectively with children with ASD, which will in turn result in social gains by the children with ASD themselves. Modifying typically developing peers' behavior can affect the social behavior of the children with ASD. These peer-mediated interventions share many common components. Such interventions usually involve training typically developing peers, who are chosen by teachers based on qualities such as demonstrating age-appropriate social skills, overall compliance with instructions, regular school attendance, willingness to participate in training, and ability to imitate a model.

Small groups of typically developing peers participate in training that focuses on a range of social interaction skills. Examples include attention getters, play organizers, shares, responses, assists, affection, compliments (Strain, 1987), and how to be a good "buddy" (e.g., stay with your buddy, play with your buddy, and talk to your buddy; English, Goldstein, Shafer, & Kaczmarek, 1997; Laushey & Heflin, 2000). Peer training typically involves a multiple-step training process with skills being taught one at a time until mastered. Strategy training typically includes: (1) a discussion of why it is important to play with friends, (2) an introduction and description of the target skill for the day, with questions asked to determine understanding, (3) modeling of the skill, and (4) role-play, with the instructor providing feedback and prompting as necessary (Strain & Odom, 1986). Training gets progressively more difficult, with the instructor introducing some of the challenges that may be encountered when interacting with children with ASD (e.g., including their self-stimulatory stereotypic behavior and tendency to ignore peers). Visual supports, such as posters illustrating the target skill, are sometimes used as prompts. Peers are often provided reinforcers throughout training to improve skill acquisition. If children with ASD are included in peer training, it is usually during the last step of training in which typically developing peers practice their skills with a target child as a partner.

Once strategy training is completed, typically developing peers are instructed to play with their classmates with ASD in a structured play setting. It is important to include materials that are of interest to the child with ASD in the play setting, in order to keep him/her motivated. If social interactions are not initiated at a sufficient rate, the instructor provides prompts to typically developing peers and/or children with ASD as needed. Reinforcement is typically implemented throughout, in order to increase the use of social interaction strategies.

There is a growing body of research suggesting that stereotypic behavior and impaired social interaction may be related; stereotypic behavior may be decreased by engaging children with ASD in social interaction. Lee, Odom, and Loftin (2007) established this to be the case by implementing a peer-mediated social intervention with three elementary students with ASD. With strategy training involving modeling, practice, and feedback, typically developing peers were asked to "get their friends to play with them," using four social skills concepts (i.e., sharing, suggesting play ideas, assisting, and being affectionate). Social interactions were observed during a structured play activity, and peers were verbally prompted if interactions were insufficiently frequent. The children with ASD did not engage in social interaction with typically developing peers until after the peer-initiation training began. Their increase in social engagement was also accompanied by a decrease in stereotypic behavior for all of the children, with simultaneous motor and vocal/oral stereotypic behavior being most directly decreased.

The effectiveness of peer-mediated strategies in improving social interactions of children with ASD is increasingly being recognized. However, one of the largest criticisms of peer-mediated approaches is that teacher prompts may inadvertently lead to prompt dependency by both the children with ASD and the typically developing peers. Improvements in interaction strategies have generally been exhibited only when encouraged or prompted by teachers or researchers. Sainato, Goldstein, and Strain (1992) addressed this concern by developing a visual strategy and self-evaluation procedure to decrease reliance on teacher prompting. Following strategy training with visual supports, six typically developing preschoolers participated in self-evaluation training. The peers were trained to self-evaluate whether or not they were successful in their interactions during training with the instructor. Preschool-aged peers did not use the facilitative strategies until the self-evaluation component was added to the intervention. Similarly, the social behavior of the children with ASD did not increase until their corresponding typically developing peer partner was trained in the self-evaluation strategy. On a positive note, teacher prompting was somewhat reduced following the self-evaluation procedure. This finding suggests two strategies (i.e., visual supports depicting social skills and self-evaluation training) may lead to increased use of social initiation strategies, and less reliance on teacher prompts.

Interventions designed to improve social interaction skills of children with ASD may be most successful if both the children with ASD and their typically developing peers are taught social initiation/responding skills. Children with ASD are often excluded from play groups with their typically developing peers due to their difficulties entering into playgroups (Wolfberg, 1995). Nelson, McDonnell, Johnston, Crompton, and Nelson (2007) combined

a visual strategy for initiation called "Keys to Play" with a peer-mediated strategy, in an attempt to increase the play initiations and time spent engaged in playgroups of four preschoolers with ASD. Children with ASD and their typically developing peers wore laminated paper "keys" that they could use to initiate play. Peers were taught how to use the keys, and were prompted to show their keys to their peers with ASD and initiate play during learning centers. An incidental teaching model was used to teach children with ASD how to use and respond to the keys. This model involved prompting the child to approach the playgroup, modeling the use of the key with verbal statements such as "I want to play," giving verbal recommendations such as "You can use your key to say you want to play," and physical prompting. Although all of the children significantly increased time spent engaged in playgroups following intervention, their interest in the play of others and their use of strategies to initiate entrance into playgroups was variable, and often dependent on how interested they were in the activity or play materials, again highlighting the importance of providing a play setting that is likely to enhance motivation.

Thiemann and Goldstein (2004) also recognized that peer-mediated training alone may not be sufficient to improve social communication skills of elementary-aged children with ASD. They incorporated a different visual strategy (i.e., a written text cueing strategy) into peer training. Given that verbal social communication skills are a critical component of social interactions in elementary-aged children, typically developing peers were taught a variety of communication skills (e.g., "look, wait, and listen," "answer question," "keep talking," "say something nice," and "start talking"). In addition to peer training, children with ASD were taught three communication skills including: (1) initiating requests for actions/objects, (2) initiating requests for information, and (3) initiating compliments using a written text treatment (WTT). WTT involved a variety of visual supports, such as using a skill sheet with the target skill listed, scripts, and monitoring/feedback forms. Training for both children with ASD and typically developing peers consisted of introduction to the target skill, generation of appropriate verbalizations incorporated into the topic bubbles, role-play of scripts, and goal setting of target skill use. The children with ASD were provided feedback regarding their use of the social communication skills, and prompts were faded as training continued. The children with ASD increased their use of targeted social communication skills following WTT, and were reported to have improved social skill development, acceptance, and friendship ratings.

The majority of studies that have attempted to increase social interaction skills of children with ASD have been conducted in classroom settings, with typically developing peers serving as change agents. Fewer studies have involved typically developing siblings, despite the fact that the children with ASD often spend the majority of their time with similar-aged siblings at home and in the community. Siblings have been taught to promote play and play-related speech, praise play behaviors, and prompt their siblings with ASD to respond to initiations (Celiberti & Harris, 1993). Classroom-based social skills intervention packages have been adapted for home use, with family members training typically developing siblings to engage in social overtures toward their siblings with ASD (Strain & Danko, 1995). More recently, Tsao and Odom (2006) investigated the effectiveness of a sibling-mediated intervention that included elements of several previously used classroom based, peer-mediated interventions. Like other peer-mediated studies cited previously, typically developing peers (in this case siblings) increased their social behavior toward the child with ASD. Similar increases were noted in the social behavior of children with ASD, as well as their frequency of joint attention (see joint attention section for further details) toward their typically developing siblings. Although siblings were able to direct social behavior toward their siblings with ASD, the children with ASD had significant difficulty responding to social initiations in a setting outside of the home.

In summary, peer-mediated approaches have successfully increased social interactions between children with ASD and their peers. Benefit has been clearly noted both when peers are taught specific strategies to promote positive social interactions with children with ASD, and children with ASD have been taught skills directly. More research is needed on interventions that combine teaching skills to both the children with ASD and their typically developing peers, given the need of children with ASD to have direct interventions. It is also clear that improvements may be found when these strategies are combined with additional supports (e.g., visual supports). The degree to which multi-component treatments are necessary to facilitate high levels of social interaction will require more exploration, despite this promising beginning.

Irrespective these successes, a number of limitations still exist regarding the use of such approaches.

Although peer-mediated approaches have resulted in social improvements, these skills have rarely generalized to other settings and peers. This difficulty generalizing social interaction skills is not surprising, given the overall difficulty that children with ASD have in generalizing most skills. Similarly, we must all be concerned that when a skill is developed it can be maintained over time, with minimal environmental modifications. Strategies such as the self-evaluation and written text treatment techniques described earlier provide a viable way to reduce prompting that may lead to further maintenance and generalization of results.

Self-Management

The more a person is independent, the greater the likelihood they will succeed in most situations and settings. A dependent individual is often limited in the range of social and life experiences available to them. Parents, teachers, and employers often strive to help children, students, and employees become less dependent on them, at least for simple, rote, everyday and necessary tasks. Self-management is a widely used procedure when the goal is to foster independence with tasks in which adult supervision is not needed, accepted, and/or expected.

Self-management is actually one of those strategies that is usually automatic for typically developing individuals, but in the context of students with developmental disabilities, like ASD, such strategies need to be programmatically implemented and evaluated. Self-management techniques have been strongly supported by research, and are encouraged for use with individuals who do not typically learn on their own to adapt and change their behavior based on naturally occurring cues in the environment. Cues to adapt or modify our behavior are abundant in our environment, and failure to alter our behavior and/or to recognize such cues can impede success in various situations. Therefore, researchers have explored the use of self-management techniques in a wide range of situations and behaviors for individuals with ASD (e.g., Newman et al., 1995; Pierce & Schreibman, 1994; Strain, Kohler, Storey, & Danko, 1994). The goal of self-management techniques is to teach students with ASD to function successfully without adult supervision. Self-management can (a) help the individual with ASD reach their full potential, (b) give them skills that are more consistent with those demonstrated by their peers, and (c) facilitate the smooth running of the classroom.

Often, self-management components entail students independently selecting a reinforcer, monitoring their own behavior, evaluating their own performance, and getting access to reinforcement when a task is completed (Pierce & Schreibman, 1994). In studies evaluating self-management, the participants appear to mirror a teacher's role, wherein they are trained to identify target behaviors, discriminate between correct and incorrect responses, record occurrences of target behaviors, and initiate contact with the identified reinforcers (Koegel & Frea, 1993). When put together, these steps support independence with various tasks.

Researchers have used self-monitoring alone to foster observing and recording one's own behavior (Todd & Reid, 2006). By self-monitoring, students become aware of their behavior and are accountable for carrying out the self-monitoring procedure. Self-monitoring enables the student to receive direct and immediate feedback when recording data. Feedback then helps students modify their behavior to meet the stated criterion. Receiving self-feedback can potentially increase the likelihood that children will exhibit the same or improved levels of the target behaviors, as compared to receiving overt feedback from an adult.

If a desirable change in behavior can be achieved simply through self-monitoring, it should be preferred over prompts from instructors. Not only does it foster independence, it also decreases the likelihood of social stigma that may come from adult prompting with tasks in which adult supervision is not accepted and/or expected. Self-management procedures also foster multitasking required to manage one's own behavior.

APPLICATIONS OF SELF-MANAGEMENT SYSTEMS

Self-management for students with ASD has been evaluated across various domains and age groups. Newman et al. (1995) sought to support adolescent students with ASD in transitioning between activities like their typical developing peers, who used cues such as clocks, bells, or other transition-signaling devices. Self-management techniques were used to successfully improve all students' ability to follow a schedule and transition between activities. The self-management procedure employed involved training students to use a token system for accurate transitioning. Adult prompting occurred initially, but teacher cues were later removed. All students responded to the procedure with varying levels of progress, but meaningful increases in transition were eventually noted for all students.

Self-management has also been used to teach elementary school-aged children with ASD to complete daily-living tasks (e.g., setting the table, getting dressed) in home and clinic settings (Pierce & Schreibman, 1994). Following a task analysis, pictures of each step were arranged in a sequential order in a photo album, with the last picture designed to signal reinforcement delivery. Each student was trained systematically in each step of the process, using just one picture initially and then eventually achieving autonomy on the entire task (task materials, task steps, and contacting reinforcers) without adult supervision. All three children were able to complete the tasks using the self-management procedure. Just as was the case with peer training, use of visual support can be important in facilitating independent performance of key tasks.

Self-management has also resulted in improved academic performance. Academic tasks (e.g., written language) were improved when adolescents with ASD received instruction on a writing strategy and watched a video of themselves performing the task (i.e., video self-modeling; Delano, 2007). Although the effects of the two procedures in isolation were not available, the use of self-management on academic performance is noteworthy.

Physical activity represents another domain in which self-management has been successfully applied. A lack of exercise has been noted as a serious concern for children all over the country, and children with ASD are no exception. Teenagers with ASD have been trained to track their physical activity and to access reinforcers for reaching the established criterion. These self-management strategies effectively increased physical activity (snowshoeing and walking/jogging; Todd & Reid, 2006). Of course, overeating or having a poor diet are also health concerns that should be taken into consideration when developing any reinforcement-based system. Managing one's own dietary requirements and/or following a health regimen could be an avenue to utilize self-management for children with ASD.

Social skill deficits represent a major area of concern, and are almost always a target of ASD intervention. Self-management as a means to improving social skills is well documented in the literature (Koegel & Frea, 1993; Koegel, Koegel, Hurley, & Frea, 1992; Strain et al, 1994). Strain et al. (1994) taught preschool boys with ASD to engage in social interactions including initiations (organizer, share, assistance, compliments, and affection), and responses to initiations in a play context, by using a self-management technique (see peer training section for greater detail). Students were taught to place tokens in a container after engaging in an appropriate target behavior, and then to contact the reinforcer independently, contingent upon meeting a preset criterion. Although this strategy was used in conjunction with other adult-directed techniques and adult prompts throughout the investigation, results were encouraging and supportive of self-management technique for young children. (Strain et al.)

Social behaviors have successfully been targeted for a larger age group, as well. Elementary to middle school-aged students have been taught to use appropriate verbal responses (Koegel et al., 1992) and high school-aged students have been taught pivotal social behaviors such as appropriate facial expression and affect, nonverbal mannerisms, voice volume, avoiding perseveration of topic, and eye gaze (Koegel & Frea, 1993) through the use of self-management procedures. Koegel et al. noted that the use of self-management not only increased appropriate social behaviors but decreased disruptive behaviors, suggesting that tasks may have been perceived as positive by students, thereby decreasing the likelihood of escape or avoidance disruptive behaviors. Importantly, teachers will be thrilled to find that reductions in their direct efforts will be required, but socially appropriate behaviors and decreases in disruptive behavior in the classroom will still be evidenced.

DESIGNING SELF-MANAGEMENT SYSTEMS

Prior to establishing a self-management system, it is important to know if the student can perform the targeted behaviors and procedures. It should be predetermined if prompting and/or additional interventions will be used in conjunction with self-management procedures. Finally, the division of responsibility (adult versus child) should be ascertained prior to implementation.

Some studies have eliminated the need for instructor prompts altogether (e.g., Pierce & Schreibman, 1994), whereas others aimed for partial independence by including adult prompts (e.g., Strain et al., 1994; Todd & Reid, 2006). Although it is ideal to strive for complete independence, it may be acceptable to involve some adult prompts, especially if an adult's presence with a task is likely. For example, striving for complete autonomy while getting dressed is ideal, but allowing some adult prompts when grocery shopping is certainly fine for most children.

Dependence on programmed prompts has resulted in errors or complete absence of the target behavior when prompts were not delivered (Pierce & Schreibman, 1994). Systematic plans to fade any external, overt cues used during self-management should be developed. However, there might be situations where planned fading of prompts may be possible only to a limited extent. In such cases, it may be better to continue using prompts as long as a desirable level of self-management continues to exist across novel behaviors. Some studies have faded adult prompts by gradually increasing the duration of adult absence (starting with the adult leaving the room/area for few seconds, to the adult just "checking in" for few seconds); whereas others have started with decreasing adult proximity to the student (Pierce & Schreibman).

Some researchers have used tangible or environmental cues/prompts to manage/record self-behavior. Wrist counters, paper and pencil data sheets, tokens (card, foam disks), cards with smiley faces, pictures, and clocks have been used as recording devices (Koegel et al., 1992; Newman et al., 1995; Strain et al., 1994). Target behaviors will not only need to be operationally defined, they will need to be described using language that can be easily understood by the students. Researchers have utilized videos of target behaviors (Delano, 2007), modeled correct and incorrect responses (Koegel & Frea, 1993), demonstrated data collection procedures (Mithaug & Mithaug, 2003), and provided verbal explanations as strategies to train students to identify target behavior, and to explain the self-management system prior to the initiation of the procedure. Pierce and Schreibman (1994) established mastery criteria to allow students to advance through each stage of the procedure (identifying picture, discriminating between pictures, getting required task materials, turning picture book, contacting reinforcer) before moving to the next stage, and before combining all stages of a task.

Data collection should occur, to ensure that the students are correctly understanding and completing all steps of the procedure as planned (Koegel et al., 1992). In some instances, students recorded their own behaviors but relied on teachers to provide reinforcement (Todd & Reid, 2006), whereas in others, students performed the entire self-management procedure with no adult present (Pierce & Schreibman, 1994). When students evaluate their own behavior, a contingency is typically set such that student's self-evaluation reports must match the teacher's evaluation or else they cannot access the reinforcers (Mithaug & Mithaug, 2003).

Reinforcers used in these systems have been individualized, and often selected prior to the tasks. It should be a goal to systematically thin the schedules of reinforcement to match the schedule naturally existing in a student's environment. Finally, generalization of such procedures should be systematically evaluated to ensure that students will be able to self-manage their behavior in untrained and novel situations across different materials, prompting levels, and personnel (Pierce and Schreibman, 1994).

Conclusions

ASD represent the fastest growing developmental disabilities in the world. Not only are the lives of individuals with ASD strongly influenced by the symptoms they experience, but the lives of parents, siblings, educators, service providers, and members of our communities are also impacted. Early intervention can produce rather staggering improvements in life functioning. This EIBI is only possible when children receive a diagnosis at the youngest possible ages. Diagnosis and verification often involve a number of professionals who require considerable expertise in ASD. Physicians should provide screenings, and psychologists should provide diagnosis, in conjunction with speech language pathologists and other allied health professionals who can identify levels of communication, sensory, and motor impairments. It is critical that each of these professionals be familiar with the appropriate instruments that can assist in this important process. A comprehensive evaluation yields the best recommendations that allow the entire intervention team to move forward.

Severe impairments in communication and social interaction, as well as behavioral excesses such as restricted, repetitive, nonfunctional patterns of behavior, interests, or activity, represent a huge challenge to everyone who shares the life of an individual with ASD. Years ago, parents were told that children with ASD could not be helped, and educators were given no direction on how best to serve children with ASD. Fortunately, there is a growing body of literature that identifies interventions that have strong evidence of effectiveness. As noted previously, EIBI has resulted in striking improvements for children with ASD that have been sustained over a protracted period of time. These treatments are intensive in nature (e.g., a minimum of 25 hours per week) and require a high level of student engagement. EIBI requires a high teacher-to-student ratio and targets.

In addition to the strong research support for EIBI at the comprehensive level, a number of behavioral interventions have strong evidence of effectiveness at the focused intervention level. Very often, these behavioral interventions involve a combination of two or more therapeutic approaches emerging from the field of applied behavior analysis and/or positive behavior supports. Collectively, these behavioral methods have strong evidence of effectiveness.

For the youngest children on the autism spectrum, joint attention training represents one of the first focused interventions that should be considered. Joint attention involves some of the most basic social interaction skills that set the foundation for complex social relationships. Joint attention training often involves teaching children to follow the gaze or point of another individual so that an item of interest can be shared, showing objects to another person, and responding when another person initiates a joint attention bid with the child with ASD. Given the importance of developing these foundational social interaction skills, preschool teachers should consider incorporating this intervention into their teaching.

Peer-mediated strategies enjoy strong research support with young children, but have also been used to effectively improve social interaction skills among elementary school-aged students. Peer-mediated approaches to treatment involve training typically developing peers how to facilitate social interactions with children with ASD. These peer-mediated interventions often involve modeling, prompting, and reinforcement, which are applied in naturalistic settings (e.g., play settings). Peer-mediated treatments may be most effective when they are combined with direct teaching of the social interaction skills to children with ASD, and visual supports for both children with ASD and their peers.

Given the importance of modeling in peer-mediated approaches, it should come as no great surprise that modeling and video modeling procedures independently enjoy strong evidence of effectiveness. These modeling procedures have been used with students of all ages. Modeling simply involves providing a demonstration of a particular task to facilitate observational learning. Modeling may be in vivo or in a video format. Video modeling may be preferable over in vivo modeling because it can be cost and time effective. However, both modeling approaches have produced impressive gains in skill acquisition and generalization with a broad number of treatment targets (e.g., communication, social interaction, play, perspective-taking skills, etc.).

Interestingly, peer-mediated treatments occur in naturalistic settings just as naturalistic teaching strategies do. Incidental teaching, Natural Language Paradigm, and Pivotal Response Teaching each represent naturalistic teaching strategies that benefit children with ASD. Not only do these strategies result in skill acquisition in critical domains, but they are also often associated with greatly improved generalization of skills to new situations. Further, these skills are maintained over time.

Finally, self-management is one of the most important skills any of us can use to regulate our own activities and meet our personal goals. By learning self-management strategies, children with ASD can learn to meet the expectations of others, or their own goals, while simultaneously becoming less dependent on others. As noted previously, these self-management strategies are often combined with other treatments (see video supports description in the **Peer Training** section).

There has been an explosion in the number of treatment options available. Unfortunately, this proliferation of treatment options has not always been accompanied by high quality research designed to identify if these interventions are effective. On a positive note, we now have strong evidence that multiple treatment options are effective. Ideally, preschool-aged individuals with ASD will obtain access to comprehensive EIBIs. School systems should seek to develop the capacity to provide this type of programming with a high degree of intensity.

EIBI is not always feasible, or may not be appropriate for children that present with few symptoms of ASD. In this case, school psychologists should make certain the educators with whom they consult are in a position to use focused interventions that have strong evidence of effectiveness, such as the ones described in this chapter. Although it is exciting to know that a number of focused interventions enjoy strong evidence of effectiveness, it is also true that these treatment options may not meet every need that educators identify. As a result, school psychologists must become familiar with additional treatments that are not described in this chapter. Irrespective of the level of research support for different treatment options, school psychologists should encourage the use of data collection so that informed decisions can be made about the continuation or modification of the selected treatment. We argue that data should be collected very frequently when less research supported treatments are selected, so that decisions to alter treatment directions can be made quickly. As a concluding remark, we encourage school psychologists to use evidence-based practice guidelines like the National Standards Report (NAC, 2009) as they support families and educators in selecting treatments.

Future Directions

1. Research has yet to be conducted with older children with respect to joint attention training. Given that joint attention is a core deficit affecting social communicative progress, future research should focus on determining if older children with this deficit benefit from joint attention interventions.

2. Investigators need to conduct further research to better identify if video modeling or in vivo (live) modeling produce better outcomes.

3. Most peer-mediated social interventions have been conducted within a classroom setting involving brief sessions. It is possible that providing more intensive interventions that are distributed throughout the day would result in more drastic social gains that can be generalized and maintained.

4. Further investigation is needed to target prompt fading during the use of self-management techniques, to better foster complete independence with target tasks.

5. Future research is needed regarding which children are likely to benefit most from naturalistic teaching procedures, and which children may require more traditional forms of teaching (and which may benefit from a combination of approaches). This work is currently underway.

References

Achenbach, T. M. (1999). Child behavior checklist and related instruments. In M.E. Maruish (Ed.), *The use of psychological testing for treatment planning and outcomes assessment* (2nd ed.). Hillsdale, NJ: Erlbaum.

Alberto, P. A., & Troutman, A. C. (2003). *Applied behavior analysis for teachers* (6th ed.). Upper Saddle River, NJ: Pearson Education.

American Academy of Pediatrics, Committee on Children with Disabilities: Developmental surveillance and screening of infants and young children. (2007). *Pediatrics*, (*108*), 192–196.

American Psychiatric Association (APA) 1994. Diagnostic and Statistical Manual of Mental Disorders, 4th Edition (DSM-IV). Washington, D.C.: APA.

Baer, D. M., Wolf, M. M., & Risley, T. R. (1968). Some current dimensions of applied behavior analysis. *Journal of Applied Behavior Analysis*, 1, 91–97.

Baldwin, J. S., & Dadds, M. R. (2007). Reliability and validity of parent and child versions of the multidimensional anxiety scale for children in community samples. *Journal of American Academy of Child and Adolescent Psychiatry*, 46(2), 252–260.

Scott, F., Baron-Cohen, S., Bolton, P., & Brayne, C. (2002). The CAST (Childhood Asperger Syndrome Test): Preliminary development of a UK screen for mainstream primary-school-age children. *Autism*, 6(1), 9–31.

Berumert, S. K., Rutler, M., Lord, C., Pickles, A. & Bailey, A. (1999). Autism screening questionnaire: Diagnostic validity. *British Journal of Psychiatry*, 175, 444–451.

Bettelheim, B. (1967). *The empty fortress: infantile autism and the birth of the self*. New York: Plenum Press.

Buggey, T., Toombs, K., Gardener, P., & Cervetti, M. (1999). Training responding behaviors in students with autism: Using videotaped self-modeling. *Journal of Positive Behavior Interventions, 1*(4), 205–214.

Carr, E. G., & Carlson, J. I. (1993). Reduction of severe behavior problems in the community using a multicomponent treatment approach. *Journal of Applied Behavior Analysis, 26,* 157–172.

Center for Disease Control & Prevention. (2009). Prevalence of autism spectrum idosrders - autism and developmental disabilities monitoring network, United States, 2006 [Surveillance Summaries]. *Morbidity & Mortality Weekly Report*, 58 (SS-10).

Celiberti, D. A., & Harris, S. L. (1993). Behavioral intervention for siblings of children with autism: A focus on skills to enhance play. *Behavior Therapy, 24,* 573–599.

Chakrabarti, C., & Fombonne, E. (2005). Pervasive developmental disorders in preschool children: Confirmation of high prevalence. *American Journal of Psychiatry, 162,* 1133–1141.

Charlop-Christy, M., & Daneshvar, S. (2003). Using video modeling to teach perspective taking to children with autism. *Journal of Positive Behavior Interventions, 5*(1), 12–21

Charlop-Christy, M. H., Le, L., & Freeman, K. A. (2000). A comparison of video modeling with in vivo modeling for teaching children with autism. *Journal of Autism and Developmental Disorders, 30*(6), 537–552.

Cohen, H., Amerine-Dickens, M., & Smith, T. (2006). Early intensive behavioral treatment: replication of the UCLA model in a community setting. *Journal of Developmental and Behavioral Pediatrics, 27*(2), 145–155.

Constantino, J. N., Davis, S. A., Todd, R. D., Schindler, M. K., Gross, M. M., Brophy, S. L., Metzger, L. M., Shoushtari, C. S., Splinter, R., & Reich, W. (2003). Validation of a brief qualitative measure of autistic traits: Comparison of the SRS with the Autism Diagnostic Interview-Revised. *Journal of Autism and Developmental Disorders, 33*(4), 427–433.

Cooper, J. O., Heron, T. E., & Heward, W. L. (2007). *Applied behavior analysis*, 2nd ed. Upper Saddle River, N.J.: Pearson Prentice Hall.

Cowan, R., and Allen, K.D. (2007). Using naturalistic procedures to enhance learning in individuals with autism: A focus on generalized teaching within the school setting. *Psychology in the Schools*, 44 (7), 701–715.

Delano, M. (2007). Improving written language performance of adolescents with Asperger syndrome. *Journal of Applied Behavior Analysis, 40,* 345–351.

Eikeseth, S., Smith, T., Jahr, E., & Eldevik, S. (2002). Intensive behavioral treatment at school for 4- to 7-year-old children with autism: A 1-year comparison controlled study. *Behavior Modification, 26*(1), 49–68.

Eikeseth, S., Smith, T., Jahr, E., & Eldevik, S. (2007). Outcome for children with autism who began intensive behavioral treatment between ages 4 and 7. *Behavior Modification, 31*(3), 264–278.

Ehlers, S., Gillberg, C., & Wing, L. (1999). A screening questionnaire for Asperger syndrome and other high-functioning autism spectrum disorders in school age children. *Journal of Autism and Developmental Disorders, 29*(2), 129–141.

English, K., Goldstein, H., Shafer, K., & Kaczmarek, L. (1997). Promoting interactions among preschoolers with and without disabilities: Effects of a buddy skills-training program. *Exceptional Children, 63,* 229–243.

Fenske, E. C., Zalenski, S., Krantz, P. J., & McClannahan, L. E. (1985). Age at intervention and treatment outcome for autistic children in a comprehensive intervention program. *Analysis & Intervention in Developmental Disabilities, 5*(1–2), 49–58.

Folstein, S. E., & Rosen-Sheidley, B. (2001). Genetics of Autism: Complex etiology for a heterogeneous disorder. *Nature Reviews Genetics, 2* (12), 943–955.

Fombonne, E. (2003). Epidemiological surveys of autism and other pervasive developmental disorders: An update. *Journal of Autism and Developmental Disorders, 33*(4), 365–382.

Gena, A., Krantz, P., McClannahan, L., & Poulson, C. (1996). Training and generalization of affective behavior displayed by youth with autism. *Journal of Applied Behavior Analysis, 29*(3), 291–304.

Gena, A., Couloura, S., & Kymissis, E. (2005). Modifying the affective behavior of preschoolers with autism using in-vivo or video modeling and reinforcement contingencies. *Journal of Autism and Developmental Disorders, 35*(5), 545–556.

Gilliam, J. E. (1995). Gilliam Autism Rating Scale. Austin, TX: Pro Ed.

Gladman, M., & Lancaster, S. (2003). A review of the Behaviour Assessment System for Children. *School Psychology International, 24*(3), 276–291.

Halle, J. W., Marshall, A. M., and Spradlin, J. (1979). Time-delay: A technique to increase language use and facilitate generalization in retarded children. *Journal of Applied Behavior Analysis*, 1, 109–120.

Haring, T. G., Kennedy, C. H., Adams, M. J., & Pitts-Conway, V. (1987). Teaching generalization of purchasing skills across community settings to autistic youth using videotape modeling. *Journal of Applied Behavior Analysis, 20*(1), 89–96.

Harper, C. B., Symon, J. B. G., and Frea, W. D. (2008). Recess is time-in: Using peers to improve social skills of children with autism. *Journal of Autism and Developmental Disabilities,* 38, 815–826.

Harris, S. L., & Handleman, J. S. (2000). Age and IQ at intake as predictors of placement for young children with autism: A four to six year follow-up. *Journal of Autism and Developmental Disorders, 30*(2), 1447–1453.

Hart, B. M., and Risley, T. R. (1968). Establishing use of descriptive adjectives in the spontaneous speech of disadvantaged preschool children. *Journal of Applied Behavior Analysis,* 1, 109–120.

Howard, J. S., Sparkman, C.R., Cohen, H. G., Green, G., & Stanislaw, H. (2005). A comparison of intensive behavior analytic and eclectic treatments for young children with autism. *Research in Developmental Disabilities, 26*(4), 359–383

Howlin, P., & Asgharian, A. (1999). The diagnosis of autism and asperger syndrome: Findings from a systematic survey. *Developmental Medicine and Child Neurology,* 4, 834–839.

Jahr, E. (2001).Teaching children with autism to answer novel wh-questions by utilizing a multiple exemplar strategy. *Research in Developmental Disabilities, 22,* 407–423.

Kanner, L. (1943). Autistic disturbances of affective contact. *Nervous Child, 2,* 217–250.

Kasari, C., Freeman, S., & Paparella, T. (2006). Joint attention and symbolic play in young children with autism: a randomized controlled intervention study. *Journal of Child Psychology and Psychiatry, and Allied Disciplines, 47*(6), 611–620.

Klinger, L. G., Dawson, G., & Renner, P. (2003). Autistic Disorder. In E. Mash & R. Barlkey (Eds.), *Child psychopathology* (2nd edition) (pp. 409–454). New York: Guilford Press.

Koegel, L. K., Koegel, R. L., Hurley, C., & Frea, W. D. (1992). Improving social skills and disruptive behavior in children with autism through self-management. *Journal of Applied Behavior Analysis, 25,* 341–353.

Koegel, R. L., O'Dell, M. C., and Koegel, L. K. (1987). A natural language paradigm for teaching nonverbal autistic children. *Journal of Autism and Developmental Disabilities, 17,* 187–199.

Koegel, R. L., & Frea, W. D. (1993). Treatment of social behavior in autism through the modification of pivotal social skills. *Journal of Applied Behavior Analysis, 26,* 369–377.

Koegel, R. L., Koegel, L. K., Harrower, J. K., & Carter, C. M. (1999). Pivotal teaching interactions for children with autism. *School Psychology Review, 28*(4), 576–594.

Laushey, K. M., & Heflin, L. J. (2000). Enhancing social skills of kindergarten children with autism through the training of multiple peers as tutors. *Journal of Autism and Developmental Disorders, 30,* 183–193.

LeBlanc, L. A., Coates, A. M., Daneshvar, S., Charlop-Christy, M. H., Morris, C., & Lancaster, B. M. (2003). Using video modeling and reinforcement to teach perspective-taking skills to children with autism. *Journal of Applied Behavior Analysis, 36*(2), 253–257.

Lee, S., Odom, S. L., & Loftin, R. (2007). Social engagement with peers and stereotypic behavior of children with autism. *Journal of Positive Behavior Interventions, 9*(2), 67–79.

Lord, C., & Risi, S. (2001). Diagnosis of autism spectrum disorders in young children. In A.M. Wetherby & B.M. Prizant (Eds.), *Autism Spectrum Disorder: A transactional developmental perspective* (pp. 11–30). London: Paul H. Brooks.

Lovaas, O. I. (1987) Behavioral treatment and normal educational and intellectual functioning in young autistic children. *Journal of Consulting and Clinical Psychology, 55*(1), pp. 3–9.

Luiselli, J. K., Cannon, B. O. M., Ellis, J. T., & Sisson, R. W. (2000). Home-based behavioral interventions for young children with autism/pervasive developmental disorder: A preliminary evaluation of outcome in relation to child age and intensity of service delivery. *Autism, 4*(4), 426–438.

March, J. S. (1997). *Multidimensional anxiety scale for children.* North Tonawanda, NY: Multi-Health Systems, Inc.

Martins, M. P., & Harris, S. L. (2006). Teaching children with autism to respond to joint attention initiations. *Child & Family Behavior Therapy, 28*(1), 51–68.

McGee, G. G., Krantz, P. J., and McClannahan, L.E. (1985). The facilitative effects of incidental teaching on preposition use by autistic children. *Journal of Applied Behavior Analysis, 18,* 17–31.

Miesels, S. J. (1989). *Screening Assessment Guidelines for Identifying Young Disabled and Developmentally Vulnerable Children & their families.* Washington, D.C.: National Center for Clinical Infant Programs.

Mithaug, D. K., & Mithaug, D. E. (2003). Effects of teacher-directed versus student-directed instruction on self-management of young children with disabilities. *Journal of Applied Behavior Analysis, 36,* 133–136.

Myles, B. S., Bock, S. J., & Simpson, R. L. (2001). *Asperger's Syndrome Diagnostic Scale.* Austin, TX: Pro-Ed.

National Autism Center. (2009). *National Standards Report: National Standards Project - Addressing the need for evidence-based practice guidelines for autism spectrum disorders.* Randolph, MA: National Autism Center, Inc.

National Research Council. (2001). *Educating children with autism.* Committee on Educational Interventions for Children with Autism, Division of Behavioral and Social Sciences and Education. Washington, D.C.: National Academy Press.

Nelson, C., McDonnell, A.P., Johnston, S. S., Crompton, A., & Nelson, A. R. (2007). Keys to play: A strategy to increase the social interactions of young children with autism and their typically developing peers. *Education and Training in Developmental Disabilities, 42*(2), 165–181.

Newman, B., Buffington, D. M., O'Grady, M., McDonald, M. E., Poulson, C. L., & Hemmes, N. S. (1995). Self-management of schedule following in three teenagers with autism. *Behavioral Disorders, 20,* 190–196

New York State Department of Health Early Intervention Program. (1999) *Clinical practice guideline: Report of recommendations. Autism/pervasive developmental disorders: Assessment and intervention for young children (age 0–3years).* Albany, NY: New York State Department of Health Early Intervention Program.

Ozonoff, S., Dawson, G., & McPartland, J. (2002). *A parent's guide to asperger syndrome & high- functioning autism: How to meet the challenges and help your child thrive.* New York, NY: The Guilford Press

Ozonoff, S., Goodlin-Jones. B. L., & Solomon, M. (2005). Evidence based assessment of autism spectrum disorders in children and adolescents. *Journal of Clinical Child and Adolescent Psychology, 34*(3), 523–540.

Pelios, L. V., MacDuff, G. S., & Axelrod, S. (2003). The effects of a treatment package in establishing independent academic work skills in children with autism. *Education & Treatment of Children, 26*(1), 1–21.

Pierce, K. L., & Schreibman, L. (1994). Teaching daily living skills to children with autism in unsupervised settings through pictorial self-management. *Journal of Applied Behavior Analysis, 27,* 471–481.

Reynolds, W.M. (2002). *Reynolds Adolescent Depression Scale* (2nd ed.). Lutz, Fl.: Psychological Assessment Resources, Inc.

Robert-McComb, J., & Barker, C. (2008). *Exercise guidelines for children and adolescence. The active female: Health issues throughout the lifespan* (pp. 241–245). Totowa, NJ, US: Humana Press. Retrieved July 29, 2008, from PsycINFO database.

Robins, D. L., Fien, D., Barton, M. L., & Green, J. A. (2001). The modified checklist for autism in toddlers: An initial study investigating the early detection of autism and pervasive developmental disorder. *Journal of Autism and Pervasive Developmental Disabilities, 3*(2), 131–144.

Rocha, M. L., Schreibman, L., & Stahmer, A. C. (2007). Effectiveness of training parents to teach joint attention in children with autism. *Journal of Early Intervention, 29*(2), 154–172.

Rogers-Warren, A., & Warren, S. (1980). Facilitating the display of newly trained language in children. *Behavior Modification, 4,* 361–382.

Sainato, D.M., Goldstein, H., & Strain, P.S. (1992). Effects of self-evaluation on preschool children's use of social interaction strategies with their classmates with autism. *Journal of Applied Behavior Analysis, 25,* 127–141.

Schepis, M. M., Reid, D.H., Behrmann, M. M. & Sutton, K. A. (1998). Increasing communicative interactions of young children with autism using a voice output communication aid and naturalistic teaching. *Journal of Applied Behavior Analysis, 31*, 561–578.

Schopler, E., Reichler R. J., DeViellis, R., & Daly, K. (1980). Towards objective classification of childhood autism: Childhood autism rating scale (CARDS). *Journal of Autism and Developmental Disorders, 10*(1), 91–103.

Schreibman, L., Whalen, C., & Stahmer, A. C. (2000). The use of video priming to reduce disruptive transition behavior in children with autism. *Journal of Positive Behavior Interventions, 2*(1), 3–11.

Sherer, M., Pierce, K. L., Paredes, S., Kisacky, K. L., Ingersoll, B., & Schreibman, L. (2001). Enhancing conversation skills in children with autism via video technology. Which is better, "self" or "other" as a model? *Behavior Modification, 25*(1), 140–158.

Shipley-Benamou, R., Lutzker, J. R., & Taubman, M. (2002). Teaching daily living skills to children with autism through instructional video modeling. *Journal of Positive Behavior Interventions, 4*(3), 165–175.

Smith, A. E. & Camarata, S. (1999). Using teacher-implemented instruction to increase language intelligibility of children with autism. *Journal of Positive Behavior Interventions, 1*(3), 141–151.

Smith, T., Groen, A. D., & Wynn, J. W. (2000). Randomized trial of intensive early intervention for children with pervasive developmental disorder. *American Journal on Mental Retardation, 105* (4), 269–285.

Stahmer, A. C. (1995). Teaching symbolic play skills to children with autism using pivotal response training. *Journal of Autism and Developmental Disabilities,* 25(2), 123–141.

Stokes, T. F., & Osnes, P. G. (1989). The operant pursuit of generalization. *Journal of Applied Behavior Analysis, 20*, 337–355.

Stone, W. L., Coonrod, E. E., & Ousley, O. Y. (2000). Brief report: Screening tools for autism in two year olds (STAT): Developmental and preliminary data. *Journal of Autism and Pervasive Developmental Disabilities, 30*(6), 607–612.

Strain, P. S. (1981). Modification of sociometric status and social interaction with mainstreamed developmentally disabled children. *Analysis and Intervention in Developmental Disabilities, 1*, 157–169.

Strain, P. S. (1987). Comprehensive evaluation of intervention for young autistic children. *Topics in Early Childhood Special Education, 7*, 97–110.

Strain, P. S., Kohler, F. W., Storey, K., & Danko, C.D. (1994). Teaching preschoolers with autism to self-monitor their social interactions: An analysis of results in home and school settings. *Journal of Emotional and Behavioral Disorders, 2*, 78–88.

Strain, P. S., & Odom, S. L. (1986). Peer social initiations: Effective intervention for social skills development of exceptional children. *Exceptional Children, 52*, 543–551.

Strain, P. S., & Danko, C. D. (1995). Caregivers' encouragement of positive interaction between preschoolers with autism and their siblings. *Journal of Emotional and Behavioral Disorders, 3*, 2–13.

Thiemann, K. S., & Goldstein, H. (2004). Effects of peer training and written text cueing on social communication of school-age children with pervasive developmental disorder. *Journal of Speech, Language, and Hearing Research, 47*, 126–144.

Thorp, D. M., Stahmer, A. C., and Schreiman, L. (1995). Effects of sociodramatic play training on children with autism. *Journal of Autism and Developmental Disabilities, 25*(3), 265–282.

Todd, T., & Reid, G. (2006). Increasing physical activity in individuals with autism. *Focus on Autism and Other Developmental Disabilities, 21*, 167–176.

Tsao, L., & Odom, S. L. (2006). Sibling-mediated social interaction intervention for young children with autism. *Topics in Early Childhood Special Education, 26*(2), 106–123.

U. S. Department of Education (1997). *IDEA '97: The Individuals with disabilities act amendments of 1997.* Accessed from http://www.ed.gov/offices/OSERS/Policy/IDEA/index.html. (Retrieved July 29, 2008).

Van Acker, R., Loncola, J. A., & Van Acker, E. Y. (2005). Rett syndrome: A pervasive developmental disorder. In F.R. Volkmar, R. Paul, A. Klin, & D.Cohen (Eds). *Handbook of autism and pervasive developmental disorders: Assessment, interventions, and policy* (2nd ed.). Hoboken, NJ: John Wiley & Sons.

Volkmar, F. R., Koenig, K., & State, M. (2005). Childhood disintegrative disorder. In F.R. Volkmar, R. Paul, A. Klin, & D.Cohen (Eds). *Handbook of autism and pervasive developmental disorders: Assessment, interventions, and policy* (2nd ed.). Hoboken, NJ: John Wiley & Sons.

Walker, D. R., Thompson, A., Zwaigenbaum, L., Goldberg, J., Bryon, S. E., & Mahoney, W. J. (2004). Specifying PDD-NOS, Asperger Syndrome, and Autism. *Journal of the American Academy Child and Adolescent Psychiatry, 43*(2), 172–180.

Weber, K. P., Killu, K., Derby, K. M., & Barretto, A. (2005). The status of functional behavioral assessment (FBA): Adherence to standard practice in FBA methodology. *Psychology in the Schools, 42*(7), 737–744.

Whalen, C., & Schreibman, L. (2003). Joint attention training for children with autism using behavior modification procedures. *Journal of Child Psychology and Psychiatry, and Allied Disciplines, 44*(3), 456–468.

Wilczynski, S. M. & Christian, L. E. (2008). The National Standards Project: Promoting evidenced-based practice in autism spectrum disorders. In J. K. Luiselli, D. C. Russo, W. P. Christian, & S. M. Wilczynski (Eds), *Effective practices for children with autism: Educational and behavior support interventions that work.* New York: Oxford University Press.

Wing, L., & Gould J. (1979). Severe impairments of social interaction and associated abnormalities in children: epidemiology & classification. *Journal o f Autism and Developmental Disorders, 9*(1), 11–29.

Wolfberg, P. J. (1995). Enhancing children's play. In K.A. Quill (Ed.), *Teaching children with autism: Strategies to enhance communication and socialization* (pp. 193–218). New York: Delmar.

Wong, V., Hui, L., & Lee, W. (2004). A modified screening tool for autism (Checklist for autism in toddlers [Chat-237]) for chinese children. *Pediatrics, 114*(2), 166–176.

The ClassMaps Framework for Data-Based, Classwide Classroom Management

Beth Doll, Kristin Jones, Allison Champion, Allison Osborn, Sharon Zumbrunn, Alyssa Collaro, *and* Chelsie Guerrero

Abstract

Educators in the United States have met the challenge of simultaneously teaching large groups of students using a factory analogy, grouping and tracking strategies, applying principles of behavior modification and behavior consultation, and, most recently, data-based problem solving. This chapter describes a data-based problem solving program that forges adaptive classroom communities that promote positive discipline and prevent misbehavior throughout a classroom or school. The strategy targets six characteristics that contribute to students' success: (1) strong teacher–student relationships; (2) effective peer relationships including friendships between students and their classmates, and conflict management; (3) strong home–school relationships; (4) high levels of academic efficacy; (5) a good sense of self-determination; and (6) behavioral self-control. Data from anonymous student surveys are used to engage teachers and their students in systematic problem solving to strengthen these characteristics of their class. Resources are provided for educators who implement this framework for classroom management.

Keywords: discipline, classroom management, effective classrooms, ClassMaps Consultation, school psychology

From the moment that groups of children were gathered together to learn, teachers have struggled to "manage" their classroom learning environments so that these maximize student achievement and minimize the disruptions that interrupt students' concentration. Students' misbehavior is one of the most common classroom disturbances. All students misbehave from time to time and, when their behavior interrupts the work of the class, teachers will act to end the misbehavior and restore order to the classroom (Goldstein & Brooks, 2007; Bear, Cavalier, & Manning, 2005). Chronic, disturbing misbehavior makes it difficult for students to learn, limits teachers' ability to teach, and jeopardizes the safety of classrooms. Misbehaving students often lag behind their peers academically, and have difficulty maintaining their friendships. Clearly, preventing student misbehavior is an important aspect of classroom management.

It is tempting to equate classroom management with the management of student misbehavior, but disciplined learning is much more than simple compliance with classroom rules. Disciplined learners are self-directed and intellectually curious, mindful of their social responsibilities, and considerate of classmates. Effective classroom management strategies promote these kinds of positive student discipline, as well as maintain safety and order within the classroom environment (Eggen & Kauchak, 1997; Goldstein & Brooks, 2007). Thus, as Goldstein and Brooks (2007) aptly note, the ideal classroom is "not necessarily the environment in which grades are highest or behavior best, but rather a miniature community in which values, ideas, and curriculum are sustainable" (p. 30). Elsewhere, we have argued that the most adaptive classroom communities are those with ample, natural supports for students' healthy interpersonal relationships and autonomous self-regulation (Doll, Zucker,

& Brehm, 2004; Doll, LeClair, & Kurien, 2009). We have described the ClassMaps strategy that uses systematic, data-based problem solving to promote classwide routines and practices that support competent social interactions and self-managed learning, in addition to preventing student misbehavior. In this chapter, we will first trace the concepts underlying classroom management as these have evolved in U. S. schools. Then, we will describe the conceptual underpinnings of classroom management practices that forge adaptive classroom communities. Next, we will specify the ClassMaps goals for classroom management that are implicit in the promotion of positive discipline, as well as the prevention of misbehavior. Fourth, we will describe the ClassMaps data-based classwide classroom management strategy that engages teachers and their students in the creation and maintenance of adaptive classroom communities. Finally, we will describe resources and references that are readily available for interested teachers and other educators who implement this framework for classroom management.

Our ClassMaps framework for classroom management proceeds from the assumption that school classrooms are innately difficult settings for teaching and learning. Grouping many children into a class, with one or few adult instructors, minimizes the immediacy of feedback that students can receive during learning and distorts the influence that adults can exert over the children's behavior and motivation. Given the individuality of students, their optimal learning environments differ from one student to the next, and adults' capacities for accommodating these differences is greatly reduced when they are teaching multiple children simultaneously. Further, learning is an inherently challenging activity in which students engage in activities and practice skills that they do not altogether know how to do. When this learning occurs within a large group of peers, it can easily become an opportunity for students to display their incompetence—something that few students want to do, and that most students will avoid at all costs. Despite these difficulties, and also because of them, classroom instruction requires that teachers balance the intellectual, social, and emotional demands of instruction in ways that harmonize each student's unique differences with those of their classmates.

This harmony is challenged by many factors external and internal to the classroom. Children and adolescents are predisposed toward curiosity, enthusiasm, and high levels of energy, and it requires effort for them to sit quietly at a desk and concentrate for extended periods of time. Innovative teachers frequently foster student understanding and learning through active and sometimes noisy classwork that capitalizes on students' natural inquisitiveness. For some students, learning is impaired by restricted opportunities associated with poverty, difficult family interactions, limited English language proficiency, neighborhood violence, inadequate health care, and biological and psychological vulnerabilities (Adelman & Taylor, 2006). Effective teachers allow for these differences by providing class work of different complexity, reflecting different interests, drawing upon different strengths, and accommodating different learning histories of students. Current teacher preparation programs regularly emphasize curriculum and instruction, with particular attention to rising educational standards and high-stakes testing, but give only limited attention to pre-service teachers' understanding of how to keep students' attention throughout the day, control angry student outbursts, calm a distressed child, foster competent interactions, and promote self-regulation by learners. Committed teachers must often learn "on the job" to use creative instructional practices that keep students engaged and learning despite the risks that accompany them into the classroom.

Brief History of Classroom Management

To address the inherent challenges of classrooms, educators in the United States have experimented with many different reforms that changed the ways that classrooms were organized and students were taught. As one of the earliest examples, mid-nineteenth century schools and classrooms were viewed with a factory analogy, in which students represent raw materials who are passed through assembly lines of instruction (teachers and curriculum) with the goal of producing uniform products (graduates) who satisfy specific quality standards (employability; Field, 1976). This analogy is founded upon a flawed assumption that classrooms are precise and identical assembly lines (when they are not), and neglects the fact that students are diverse rather than anonymous "widgets" passing through "production." Remnants of this factory analogy persist into the present when educational policymakers still expect that all students will arrive at school with very similar learning readiness, should receive very similar educational experiences, and should graduate from public schools with very similar competencies.

One way that the factory analogy persisted into the twentieth century was in grouping and tracking practices. To ensure the success of all children while maintaining age-homogenous grades and classes, students of differing abilities were tracked into very specific instructional groups that differed in their task complexity, instructional methods, the pace of instruction, and ultimately in the instructional goals. Such tracking practices maintained the factory model of classroom instruction while establishing different production "lines" for different kinds of students. Research ultimately demonstrated that tracking was largely ineffective and promoted student inequity (Kulik & Kulik, 1982). Today, tracking and grouping has largely been replaced by cooperative or flexible grouping practices, in which students are closely monitored and continuously reassessed and reassigned to different instructional groups based upon their growth and progress (Marzano, Pickering, & Pollock, 2001).

While these first two educational reforms were examples of instructional practices, they illustrate the intricate interrelations that exist between academic learning and students' curiosity, motivation, and ultimately their personal discipline. A subsequent reform related more specifically to classroom behavior. In the 1960s and 1970s, the principles of behavior modification were moved out of the psychology laboratories and into the schools. Then, these principles were used to shape desirable classroom behaviors by reducing behavioral excesses (e.g., reducing blurt-outs), strengthening behavioral deficits (e.g., increasing words read per minute), and rearranging environmental reinforcements or punishments (Kratochwill & Shapiro, 2000; Miltenberger, 2008). Almost immediately, heated tensions were evident between teachers who were told to use the behavioral principles to manage their students' behavior and administrators and researchers who advocated for behavioral classroom management. Many teachers thought that behavioral strategies bribed or punished students into compliance without strengthening students' personal discipline, and that the use of external consequences ultimately limited the students' intrinsic motivation in the classroom (Steege, Mace, & Brown-Chidsey, 2007; Witt & Elliot, 1982). They believed that behaviorism was effective in managing and changing disruptive behaviors, but did not address the underlying causes of those behaviors. Indeed, in their early form, the majority of classroom behavioral interventions incorporated positive and negative reinforcement, as well as punishment, but did not attempt to address the cause of the misbehavior (Bergan, 1977; Steege et al., 2007; Winett & Winkler, 1972).

Behavioral frameworks were subsequently refined in response to these criticisms by examining why a particular behavior occurred (the motivating variables, antecedents, and consequences that maintain behaviors), broadening the impact of successful behavioral interventions to new settings or behaviors, and emphasizing the use of positive and reinforcing contingencies in lieu of punishment (Bear et al., 2005; Gettinger & Seibert, 2000; Steege et al., 2007). Students' misbehavior was understood to be purposeful, and to often occur for one of three reasons: positive reinforcement (a student who stole a favorite toy from another student gained possession of the toy); negative reinforcement (a student who threw a tantrum before math time was able to avoid participating in math instruction); or social attention (a student who blurted out inappropriate comments was reinforced by her classmates' laughter; Miltenberger, 2008). From the hypothesized functions of the behaviors, interventions were developed to change the conditions that motivated the behavior, teach the child appropriate replacement behaviors, restrict access to reinforcers of problem behaviors, or increase reinforcers for appropriate behavior (Crone & Horner, 2003; Steege & Brown-Chidsey, 2005). Data continued to be collected during the intervention to assess its effectiveness, and to confirm or disprove the initial hypothesis (Lee & Jamison, 2003). Depending on its effectiveness, the intervention would then be generalized to other times or settings, adjusted to be more effective, or removed completely to investigate another possible function of the behavior (Lee & Jamison, 2003). These second-generation behavioral procedures frequently built upon and strengthened students' self-management skills, in that behavioral competence was not simply imposed upon the students but was managed with them. Refined behavioral strategies with their concomitant use of data-based problem solving have become the basis of much of the science underlying behavior management strategies in schools (Erchul & Martens, 2002).

By the 1980s, behavioral consultation emerged as a strategy to help teachers apply behavioral principles in situations where students' misbehavior was particularly difficult or intractable. In behavioral consultation, teachers worked in collaboration with a consultant to devise behavioral interventions that targeted behavioral excesses or deficits (Kratochwill & Bergan, 1990; Rybski Beaver & Busse, 2000). Through a series of consultative meetings, the consultant and teacher worked together to understand the problem, define the problem in behavioral terms, collect baseline data, design and implement an intervention, collect data to judge the effectiveness of the intervention, and make changes to the intervention as needed. In some cases, the "consultant" in behavioral consultation was a Student Assistance Team (SAT), typically comprising regular and special education teachers, administrators, and school psychologists (Noell, Gilbertson, VanDerHeyden, & Witt, 2004). Behavioral consultation was quickly criticized as an impractical and time-consuming technique for addressing behavioral problems in schools (Witt, Gresham, & Noell, 1996). Still, in a series of small-n designs, researchers demonstrated that high-fidelity behavioral consultation is a very effective intervention for classroom behavior problems and, as a result, it remains an important tool that school psychologists use to help teachers manage particularly difficult student behaviors (Kratochwill & Bergan, 1990).

Behavioral consultation, Student Assistance Teams, and second-generation behavioral interventions are all examples of data-based decision making procedures in which schools use carefully structured data collection, data-based problem solving, and empirical data interpretation rules to make sound decisions about strategies to manage students' behavior (Haynes & O'Brien, 1999; Lee & Jamison, 2003; Yetter & Doll, 2007). The integration of practical data collection into daily activities of schools represents a breakthrough contribution of behavioral analysis to school practice. The collection and examination of useful data makes it possible for schools to systematically refine those practices that are instrumental in strengthening students' school success.

Conceptual Underpinnings of Data-Based, Classwide Classroom Management

In this chapter, we describe the current generation of classroom management that applies these same principles of data-based service delivery, but with two important modifications: first, a broader framework defines classroom management as the promotion of positive discipline in addition to the prevention of misbehavior; and second, classroom management strategies are provided classwide, or even schoolwide, using a population-based service delivery model. Thus, data-based classwide classroom management uses data to assess the collective discipline of all students in the class, defined as strong social and self-regulatory competence and minimal misbehavior. Then, classwide management plans are implemented to strengthen those practices

that data show to be lacking, while data continues to be collected so that the plan can be refined as necessary in response to evidence of its impact (Doll & Cummings, 2008; Doll et al., 2004).

Classwide classroom management strategies are typically multi-tiered, including universal interventions that promote the social competence and self-regulation of all students in the class (the first tier), specialized management strategies for selected students who present a special risk for disrupted behavior and learning (the second tier), and intensive, individualized behavior management plans for students with very challenging behaviors that do not respond to interventions at the first two tiers (the third tier; Bear, 2008; Doll & Cummings, 2008). Thus, the most supportable classwide classroom management plans are amalgamations of multiple strategies that address needs that have been documented through the data-based assessments.

There are many advantages to shifting the target of classroom management strategies from individual students to the collective enrollment of all the students in the class. It acknowledges the interdependence among the discipline of all students in the class, makes it easier to notice the causes of management difficulties when these are related to classroom settings or classwide practices, is more manageable for teachers than a collection of multiple individual student behavior plans, and it can lead to deceptively simple modifications with important outcomes. A special advantage for school psychologists is that classwide perspectives fully integrate the mission of school mental health professionals (with their expertise in students' developing social, emotional, and behavioral competence) with schools' core instructional mission: the promotion of competence for all students.

The starting point for data-based classwide management strategies is developmental research describing critical classroom competencies, over and above cognitive or intellectual ability, that promote students' success in school. The operational objectives of any classroom management plan are to strengthen these critical competencies. In particular, substantial evidence demonstrates that successful students show high levels of on-task behavior such as completing assignments, complying with teacher requests, working independently, seeking help when appropriate, volunteering to answer questions, and engaging in assigned tasks during instruction (Greenwood, 1991; Liaupsin, Umbreit, Ferro, Urso, & Upreti, 2006). Students who put this kind of effort into their work are said to be "academically engaged," and their effort can be documented through direct behavioral observations that their eyes are on their work, their pencils are in hand, and their gaze is on the teacher whenever directions are given (Greenwood, 1991).

Still, this is only the simplest form of academic engagement, and may not differentiate between students who are passively following classroom rules and those who are making committed efforts to learn (Finn, 1989; Fredricks, Blumenfeld, & Paris, 2004; Reschly & Christenson, 2006). Some students may appear to be participating in classroom work without really thinking about the material, while others may be diligent because they are "teacher pleasing" even though they have no real interest in the work. Thus, students who are not only diligent but interested in their classroom work are not only behaviorally engaged but are also cognitively engaged. As Fredricks et al. (2004) very appropriately note, cognitive investment in learning is partially task dependent, because students will not demonstrate the same investment in memorizing rote knowledge and terms as they do in confirming hypotheses, discovering important principles, or understanding new relations. Consequently, classroom instructional practices and classwide management strategies are inevitably interdependent.

Students show even higher levels of school success if they are not only on-task and interested, but strive for knowledge and take charge of their classroom learning by setting personal goals for success, and regulating their concentration and effort to achieve these goals (Pintrich, 2003). In this instance, the students can be identified as "autonomously engaged." Even higher levels of academic engagement have been identified when students are emotionally entranced with learning (They're loving it!), are part of a strong social network within the school (They belong!), or when they move into leadership roles in their school that allow them to strengthen schoolwide conditions for learning (They take charge!). Within this tiered model of academic engagement, adaptive classroom communities encompass attitudinal and emotional aspects as well as behavioral elements, such that effective classroom management efforts will require cognitive, emotional, and behavioral components.

Promising research has identified important alterable features of classrooms that promote autonomous academic engagement in students: relatedness, or the degree to which teachers and classmates form a socially supportive learning community; perceived competence, or the degree to which the classroom's students expect to be successful in their learning; and autonomy, or the degree to which classroom learning incorporates choices, shared decision making, and intrinsic controls (Fredricks et al., 2004; Furrer & Skinner, 2003; National Research Council, 2004). Not surprisingly (because they emerge from the same body of developmental research), these three engagement-promoting factors parallel the characteristics of effective learning environments that underlie the ClassMaps framework for data-based classwide classroom management (Doll, Kurien et al., 2009; Doll, Leclair, & Kurien, 2009). The ClassMaps framework incorporates three aspects of classroom relatedness: teacher–student relationships, peer relationships, and relationships that exist between students' families and their classrooms. Perceived competence is parallel to the ClassMaps factor of *academic self-efficacy*, and autonomy is represented by the two ClassMaps factors of *academic self-determination* and *behavioral self-control*.

Classwide Goals for Classroom Management

Within ClassMaps' data-based classroom management, these engagement-promoting factors are systematically evaluated and strengthened through classwide assessments and interventions. Integral to ClassMaps are six classroom characteristics that can be rewritten as goals to strengthen classwide supports for students' success: (1) strong teacher–student relationships; (2) effective peer relationships, including friendships between students and their classmates, and conflict management; (3) strong home–school relationships; (4) high levels of academic efficacy; (5) a good sense of self-determination; and (6) behavioral self control. The relevance of each of these goals for promoting students' personal discipline has been demonstrated through existing research in education and child development, while the importance of each goal for a particular classroom depends upon the current status of these factors. It is more important to strengthen features that are deficient than to focus energy and attention on those features that are already strong in a classroom. Over the past ten years, classroom assessments from rural and urban schools in Nebraska, Illinois, and New Jersey have provided some information about typical classroom strengths and weaknesses (Doll, LeClair et al., 2009; Doll, Kurien et al., 2009). In the remainder of this section, we will briefly summarize the research supporting the relevance and importance of each goal in typical classrooms.

Of the three relatedness factors, *teacher–student relationships* have shown the strongest relation to students' classroom success (Birch & Ladd, 1998; Hamre & Pianta, 2005; Murray & Malmgren, 2005). Effective relationships between teachers and their students are very caring, enjoyable, respectful, and empowering (Walker, 2008). These relationships are just as important for students' academic success and personal discipline as the curriculum and instructional strategies that are used, and are especially important for students who are not excelling academically or who have trouble with peers (Brooks & Goldstein, 2007). For these students in particular, teachers' high expectations of their students can help them feel encouraged and support their sense of self-worth and self-discipline (Bear et al., 2005). Fortunately, students generally rate their relationships with their teachers to be one of the strongest ClassMaps features in their classrooms (Doll, LeClair et al, 2009), and so teacher–student relationships are rarely identified as a goal for classroom change. Still, when student ratings suggest that teachers' relationships are unsupportive or even negative, the goal of improving these relationships becomes essential for effective classroom management.

Peer relationships are also critical for classroom relatedness. Students' friendships with each other act as a tether that binds students to the school, provides them with a sense of belonging, and are a source of assistance and personal support (Doll, 1996). Peer conflicts are particularly disturbing for students who worry about the possibility of peer aggression or, more worrisome for students, the possible loss of valued friendships (Doll, Murphy, & Song, 2003; Ladd, Birch, & Buhs, 1999). Of these two distinct aspects of peer relationships, not having friends is more troubling for students than is the presence of frequent peer aggression. Still, the availability of peer friendships is generally rated by students to be one of the stronger features of their classrooms, and so this aspect of peer relationships rarely needs to be targeted as a goal for classroom change (Doll, LeClair et al., 2009). Alternatively, distressing peer conflicts are frequently reported by classrooms' students and are often identified as a classroom goal. Subsequent classroom meetings have suggested that it is not the frequency or the severity of peer conflicts that shapes student perceptions, but whether students believe that they are unable to cope with and resolve instances of peer aggression when these occur.

While *home–school relationships* are not consistently emphasized as a predictor of academic engagement, they are of central importance within the ClassMaps framework. To the degree that families and teachers endorse shared goals for students' learning, and common expectations for students' success, students' personal discipline will be influenced by a clear value system that reinforces the importance of school and their efforts to learn. Student ratings of their home–school relationships generally fall in the midrange, and so these are frequently identified as moderately important goals for classroom changes.

Second only to teacher–student relationships, another powerful predictor of students' school success is their perception that they are academically capable (Schunk & Pajares, 2005). Perceived competence is represented by the ClassMaps construct of *academic self-efficacy*. Students who believe that they are capable are more likely to act in ways that foster competence: they will persist when faced with difficult tasks, work harder, work smarter, and ask for help when they need it. Importantly, this sense of competence is contagious across students in a class, and when a majority of students within a classroom expect to be successful, their confidence "rubs off" on their classmates. Ratings of shared efficacy in typical classrooms vary from moderately low to moderately high, and when student ratings are low, efforts to strengthen students' expectations of success are very important goals for classroom change.

Finally, autonomy is captured by the ClassMaps features of academic self-determination and behavioral self control. Of these, behavioral self control describes the rule-following behaviors that are traditionally understood to comprise classroom management. To some extent, students' rule following is teacher controlled: classroom behavior is more orderly when teachers consistently employ positive reinforcement for following the classroom rules, and ignore students' undesirable behaviors (Bear et al., 2005; Campbell, 1999; Erchul & Martens, 2002; Miltenberger, 2008). Rules are more effective when there are fewer rules, described in words that the students can understand, and phrased positively so that they are a list of things "To Do" and not a list of things "Not to Do." Still, rule following is most effective when it is self-controlled by students—when students take an active role in creating the classroom rules, self-monitor their rule-following behaviors, and actively and thoughtfully manage their own behavior so that it is consistent with these expectations (Doll et al., 2004). In this respect, then, students' rule-following behavior can be influenced by classroom routines and their classmates. For example, classroom meetings where rules are agreed upon together promote students' ownership of the classroom's deportment (Bear et al., 2005). Students often rate their classmates' rule-following behavior to be quite low, and so this is frequently a goal for classroom change.

Ultimately, autonomy is supported by students' emerging sense of self-determination and its component skills of goal setting, decision making, self-monitoring, and self-control. Students with strong self-determination clearly understand the purpose of their learning, and the relevance of the daily tasks that fill their school days. They are able to moderate their own actions in order to achieve their personal goals and the shared goals of the classroom. Self-determination is threatened in classrooms where all learning goals are externally imposed rather than chosen. (Indeed, a frequent criticism of state and national curriculum standards is that these impose goals on students and their teachers without regard to their personal judgments of the goals' relevance.) Moreover, self-determination is the most developmental of the six classroom goals, since competence for self-management emerges with age and experience, and societal expectations for decision making and goal setting also grow with age. Student ratings in both self-control and self-determination vary from moderately low to moderately high, and are sometimes chosen as important goals for classroom change.

The ClassMaps strategy for classroom management is predicated on the assumption that, when these characteristics of classrooms are optimized, students will be more fully engaged in the task of learning, and disturbances that interrupt learning will be minimized.

Data Based Classroom Management

The familiar data-based problem solving procedures can be used to systematically work toward these six goals for classroom management (Doll et al., 2004; Doll, LeClair et al., 2009). This is a cyclical process that begins with a needs assessment to identify classwide management strengths and weaknesses, the information from which leads to the development of an intervention plan to build upon the strengths and correct the weaknesses, which is implemented even while data continues to be collected to evaluate the plan's effectiveness and refine it as necessary. We will first describe the four steps of this cycle in general terms, and then we will elaborate on each step in more detail.

The first step in data-based classroom management is to identify aspects of the classroom routines and practices that should be strengthened. The ClassMaps conceptual framework has identified the classroom characteristics that are related to effective classroom management. The purpose of the ClassMaps Survey is to measure the six characteristics reliably and carefully, so that the data-based portrait can be used as an accurate representation of the present classroom and as an index against which to measure change once interventions are implemented. Other options exist for collecting useful classwide management data: Walker et al. (2010) describe one example where the Systematic Screening for Behavior Disorders (SSBD) was used to describe schoolwide behavior management goals for a southern school district. As population-based models become more prominent, new screening techniques will be developed, and many of these will be strength based (promoting positive discipline) instead of, or in addition to, being problem based (describing misbehavior).

The second step is to create a change plan that preserves the classroom strengths while strengthening classroom weaknesses. Because classrooms are social systems, with teachers and students as important members, systems change will require collaborative efforts on the part of both to create classroom management systems that support learning. Responding to the data that has been collected, teachers and students can brainstorm possible changes in classroom practices that are likely to address the weaknesses that they have identified. Selecting from their list of ideas, they can design a classroom-change plan that they judge to be very likely to succeed, and practical to implement given existing classroom resources.

While the class implements their plan, data continues to be gathered to evaluate the impact of the intervention: Was it possible to follow the plan reliably? If so, did the classroom's behaviors improve? Were there any unintended consequences of the plan, positive or negative? Were the classroom improvements worth the extra effort that it required to make the changes? Without careful data describing classroom changes, teachers and students will be unable to isolate the causes of any changes and build upon those successes in the future.

Classroom changes that prove to be effective can be "routinized" or integrated into the ongoing practices of the classroom and, even then, classroom data should be collected and analyzed periodically to verify the ongoing wellness of the classroom. If the planned classroom changes are not effective, teachers and students can discuss the data and modify the plan until data show that the intervention has resulted in a satisfactory classroom learning climate.

Assessing Classroom Strengths and Needs

To assess the management needs of a classroom, we have developed the ClassMaps Survey (Doll et al., 2004; Doll, Kurien, LeClair, Spies, Champion, Osborn, 2009), a 55-item student rating scale that provides a brief, relevant, and conceptually simple evaluation of important classroom characteristics related to students' academic engagement. The survey's original content was carefully planned from a comprehensive review of developmental research describing academic engagement and the correlates of students' school success (Doll et al., 2004), and it was refined in a series of studies with elementary and middle school-aged students, so that the subscale reliability was strengthened and survey items were clear and easy to understand (Doll, Kurien et al., 2009).

Each ClassMaps Survey item describes a characteristic of the classroom or its students, and students respond using a 4-point Likert scale (Never, Sometimes, Often, Almost Always). Items describing positive attributes are coded with a value of '0' for Never and '3' for Almost Always, and negatively worded items are reverse coded so that higher scores always represent more positive judgments of the classroom. The 55 items are organized into eight subscales. Five subscales describe relational aspects of the classroom, including teacher–student relationships (*My Teacher*, 7 items), peer friendships (*My Classmates*, 7 items), peer conflict (*Kids in this Class*, 5 items), worries about peer aggression (*I Worry That*, 8 items), and home–school relationships (*Talking With My Parents*, 7 items.) Three of the subscales describe self-regulatory characteristics including academic self-efficacy (*Believing in Me*, 8 items), self-determination (*Taking Charge*, 8 items), and behavioral self-control (*Following Class Rules*, 6 items.) Evidence that the surveys factor cleanly into these subscales and have strong internal consistency reliabilities (.79 to .93) is available from a middle school study with 466 students (Doll et al., 2004), an elementary school study with 1,615 students (Doll & Siemers, 2004); and an elementary school study with 388 students (Doll & Spies, 2007). Item values are averaged across all items in a subscale to represent a subscale score.

Despite the brevity of each subscale (ranging from 5 to 8 items in length), the ClassMaps subscales have repeatedly shown strong internal consistency reliability. One study of 420 elementary-aged students (grades 3 through 5) showed coefficient alphas ranging from .86 to .96 for the ClassMaps Survey subscales (Doll & Spies, 2007). A second study of 345 elementary aged students (grades 3 through 5) showed subscale coefficient alphas ranging from .78 to .93 (Doll, Kurien, et al., 2008). A third study of 1056 fifth through eighth grade science students showed coefficient alphas ranging from .88 to .91 (Doll, Champion, & Kurien, 2008). Given three replications showing very solid subscale reliabilities, it is possible to administer any subscale of the ClassMaps Survey in isolation, and use those results as a basis for classroom planning. Preliminary evidence from intervention studies using a small-n design suggests that the subscale scores are responsive to classroom interventions (Murphy, 2002; Nickolite & Doll, 2008).

Concurrent validity evidence comparing subscales of the ClassMaps Survey and related measures is also within the adequate range. Parallel scales of ClassMaps and the Yale School Development Program School Climate Survey were significantly correlated (.47 to .80; Paul, 2005). Correlations between the Friendship Features Scale and the peer relationships subscales of the ClassMaps Survey were significant and robust (r = .81 with *My Classmates* and .28 with *Kids in This Class*; Doll, Spies, Strasil, LeClair, Fleissner, & Kurien, 2006). A third study demonstrated significant correlations between all subscales of the ClassMaps Survey subscales, and the degree to which middle school science students valued their science instruction (Doll, Champion, & Kurien, 2008).

The ClassMaps Survey acts as a checklist of the classroom attributes that are most relevant for effective classroom management. Results are displayed in bar graphs showing the frequency of student responses to each set of items. Using practical decision rules, teachers and students can identify strengths when the majority of students in a class endorse positive classroom attributes by checking "often" or "almost always" and or when a majority does not endorse negative classroom attributes by checking "never" or "only sometimes."

Planning for Classroom Intervention

Based on this data-based needs assessment, teachers select weaknesses (paired with goals for change) that could guide classroom planning efforts. The goal should be specific enough to be measured easily, but not so specific that it limits the importance or breadth of change (Doll et al., 2004). In many cases, a subscale of the ClassMaps Survey, or even an item, could define a classroom's goal for change, and the survey was designed with this purpose in mind. Next, teachers include students in a comprehensive planning meeting in which they share the ClassMaps Survey data, and discuss with students. Is the data accurately describing the situation? What do the students believe is causing the problem? And, what could be done (by adults and by the students) to make things better?

This student voice is essential for capturing the kid-perspective in understanding engagement problems. In many instances, these student perspectives have differed substantially from adult perspectives. For example, eighth graders were enmeshed in multiple, serious disagreements with peers during the lunch break that resulted in disciplinary suspensions (and in some cases, in dropping out of school). Teachers believed that the solution would lie in strengthening supervision over the lunch break, but students suggested that more games and activities be made available to provide students with something other than arguing to occupy their time. As another example, third graders were unruly and inattentive during a post-recess social studies class. The teacher planned to directly teach the rules and raise the negative consequences for off-task behaviors. The students suggested, instead, that they needed a warning prompt so that they noticed when the class was getting too boisterous.

Given their shared understanding of the possible causes of, and solutions for, the classroom's weakness, teachers and students work together to create a plan outlining the steps towards change. For example, the plan could include rearranging the physical features of the classroom, altering a classroom routine, or implementing an evidence-based, manualized intervention. The plan needs to be implemented with integrity, and students can contribute to the work required to implement the plan. For example, it may be feasible to give students responsibility for keeping records of the class's activities, collecting simple data to document daily changes, or prompting each other to follow the plan.

Classroom Changes to Strengthen Classroom Management

Three kinds of strategies are useful for enhancing classroom management: setting modifications that alter the physical features of the classroom, changes in classroom routines and practices, and manualized classroom intervention programs. Students' concentration and motivation can be affected by large class sizes, small classrooms, the ways in which desks are organized, lighting, and the availability of textbooks and other materials (Bear et al., 2005; Campbell, 1999; Doll et al., 2004; Goldstein & Brooks, 2007).

If classrooms are too small or crowded, teachers and students may not have ample space to organize their belongings and maintain their personal space. When this occurs, students and teachers are more likely to feel stressed and irritable, which may lead to an increase in student misbehavior. In one classroom, when students' desks were positioned in rows, they were twice as productive as they had been when desks were in groups of three or four (Wheldall & Lam, 1987).

Other efforts to strengthen classroom management involve modifications in the routines and practices of the classroom. For example, the enhancement of teacher–student relationships occurs transactionally when *students* are taught to behave in ways that develop and sustain supportive relationships with their teachers, and *teachers* are helped to understand the significance of their relationships with students and to act in ways that encourage formation of the bond (Consortium on the School-based Promotion of Social Competence, 1994; Pianta, 1999). Peer relationships can be facilitated by providing frequent opportunities for students to have fun together (working together, learning together, or performing classroom chores; Doll, 1996) and friendships also increase when cooperative learning strategies are used in the classroom (Johnson, Johnson, Buckman, & Richards, 1998). Perceived competence is strengthened when students are frequently encouraged and guided in evaluating their work, and in practicing self-regulatory skills under conditions of strong support and encouragement, and when feedback is immediate, frequent, and focuses on effort (Pajares & Schunk, 2001; Pintrich, 2003). Students can be taught a self-monitoring system that increases their on-task behaviors in the classroom and raises their work completion (Brooks, Todd, Tofflemoyer, & Horner, 2003). Learning becomes more autonomous when classroom goals are specific (e.g., describing the number of problems to be completed), proximal (e.g., having deadlines of tomorrow or next week), and attainable (Pajares & Schunk, 2001), and if students are helped to understand the purpose and importance of the learning (Assor, Kaplan, & Roth, 2002).

The data-based problem solving framework emphasizes continued collection of monitoring data, even while changes are being made, so that it is apparent whether modified routines strengthen students' classroom discipline. Progress toward the goal can be assessed by periodically re-administering the ClassMaps Survey, or by monitoring other indicators of these characteristics of classrooms. If the classroom goals have been met, then the classroom changes should be "routinized" or permanently embedded into the classroom practices, in order to maintain the success (Doll, et al. 2004). If the goals have not been met, or were only partially met, it may be necessary to revise the plan so that it is stronger, implemented for a longer period of time, or discontinued and replaced with a comprehensive, manualized intervention.

A few evidence-based interventions have been demonstrated to strengthen students' academic engagement. For example, the Check and Connect program strengthened the school engagement of students with disabilities through regular tracking of tardies, truancies, and behavioral referrals (Sinclair, Christenson, Evelo, & Hurley, 1998). Through ongoing consultation, the at-risk students were given regular information about the monitoring system, provided with regular feedback about their educational progress, reminded frequently of the importance of staying in school, and were helped to solve some of the problems that placed them at risk for dropping out. The Coca-Cola Valued Youth Program (VYP) has used community service activities with demonstrated success in reducing school dropout among Latino students who speak English as their second language (Fashola & Slavin, 1998). The Achievement for Latinos through Academic Success (ALAS) program assigned an advocate who worked directly with the student, and also fostered and coordinated efforts of the school, family and community to keep the student in school (Rumberger & Larson, 1994). The ACT-REACT program (Rock & Thead, 2007) teaches students to use self-monitoring procedures to strengthen their own academic engagement and work completion.

A Classroom Example

The following example describes the application of ClassMaps data-based classroom management strategy in one fourth grade classroom:

This had been a difficult year for the classroom. As a result of a major asbestos removal project, all students and teachers had been moved to a sports center that would be their temporary school for the year. Facilities were "make do" and classrooms were separated by temporary walls that stretched halfway up to the ceiling. The noise in the building bounced off of the steel roof, and classroom doorways were covered with hanging sheets rather than solid doors. The temporary playground was a large flat field—absent such amenities as the tetherball, four-square courts, and concrete pad for jumping rope. With few other

choices, most fourth graders spent the recess playing soccer.

The ClassMaps Survey was completed by all students in the class in November, two weeks before the Thanksgiving holiday break. Results showed high rates of peer conflict on the playground (*Kids in this Class*) and somewhat limited academic efficacy in the classroom (*Believing in Me*). On the other hand, the teacher–student relationship was strikingly strong (*My Teacher*), children described satisfying friendships (*My Classmates*), and the classroom self-control was rated as appropriate (*Following Class Rules.*) The teacher decided to focus her attention on the playground conflict, because this was a particularly strong value for the class.

Since these fourth graders were very accustomed to sitting together in classroom meetings, the discussion of the ClassMaps results was rich and useful. It was clear from the survey results and the students' discussion that most of the conflict involved verbal aggression—teasing, arguing, and name-calling. Most of it happened on the playground, but occasionally it followed the students back into the classroom. The students' comments kept returning to the lunchtime soccer game that they held, and the arguments involving picking teams, disagreeing about rules, and negotiating the rule violations that occurred. Ultimately, the class settled on a plan for change with several parts. First, they decided to choose soccer teams once each week, and then use those same teams for the rest of the week. That way, they would have more time to play soccer if they were spending less time figuring out how to divide themselves into teams. They added some "fairness" rules for choosing teams: certain "really good" soccer players had to be divided evenly among the two teams, and everyone who wanted to play had to be chosen for one team or the other. Next, they decided to research the rules for soccer and write these into their own fourth grade soccer rule book (an exercise that the teacher integrated into an expository writing unit that was already in the class's curriculum). To adjudicate violations quickly and fairly, they decided that students would take turns acting as the referee for the soccer game, and only students who passed a knowledge test on the rules could act as a referee. Finally, because the teacher was still concerned about arguments that followed students into their classroom, they developed a "teasing worksheet" that students would complete after any teasing incident. The student who did the teasing would complete the left side, and the one who was teased would complete the right side, so both would have to talk through the incident while they worked.

Four weeks later, the class re-completed the ClassMaps Survey and met together to talk about how well their plan was working. Their discussion and the survey results showed that rates of playground conflict had dropped, and the students reported having much more fun during their recess. The soccer rulebook and team-selecting strategy had worked so well that several other classes were adopting them. On the other hand, the teasing worksheet had not been used even once—although students did report that rates of teasing had fallen as well, and they thought that they were talking through some of the worksheet steps even when they did not sit down together and complete it. Rather than belabor the teasing worksheet, the students and the teacher decided to focus their attention on the next goal—raising the levels of academic efficacy in the classroom.

Summary and Other Resources

This chapter's discussion differs from traditional classroom management frameworks in several important respects: it broadens the purpose of classroom management to include promoting positive discipline as well as preventing misbehavior; it applies familiar problem solving steps toward the development of classwide management plans; it strengthens and focuses the problem solving by incorporating data collection and interpretation into the planning strategy; and it builds these features upon a framework describing the features of effective classrooms that has been derived from developmental research and operationalized in the ClassMaps Survey. We have argued that the origins of these modifications are evident in the early history of classroom management strategies, and that this data-based classwide classroom management is the logical next step in the profession's progression toward increasingly effective models of classroom management.

Putting the unfamiliar aspects of this framework into practice can be challenging, but there are resources and references that can ease the transition. First, this chapter's definition focuses on classroom characteristics that have not traditionally been linked to classroom management including teacher–student relationships, peer relationships, and academic efficacy. This requires that schools broaden their curriculum beyond the topics that are readily available in schools' scope and sequence charts. Fortunately, an increasing number of curricula have been developed to teach these skills within classroom settings. For example, peer relationships, academic efficacy and self-determination are all integrated into Merrill, Gueldner, and Tran's (2008) Strong Kids curricula, and components of social problem solving are incorporated into Shure's (2001) curriculum in social problem solving. Other programs and practices addressing social and emotional competence are referenced on the website of the Collaborative for Academic, Social, and Emotional Learning (www.casel.org) and on the website of the UCLA Center for Mental Health in the Schools (http://smhp.psych.ucla.edu/).

Many school psychologists may be unfamiliar with this chapter's emphasis on data collection and data interpretation, and the use of data in action research that supports practice. Chapters describing action research strategies can be found in the Doll et al. (2004) reference on classroom-based consultation, as well as the Doll and Cummings (2008) reference on population-based services. As an example, the application to school change efforts of the Systematic Screening for Behavior Disorders (SSBD) can be found in a Walker et al. (2010) chapter on the prevention of behavior disorders. In addition, examples of practical measures for school reform are available at no cost on the website of the Annenberg Institute for School reform (www.annenberginstitute.org) as well as on the CASEL website (www.casel.org).

Perhaps the most challenging aspect of this chapter is its focus on classroom management strategies that are implemented classwide and schoolwide, rather than one difficult child at a time. In actuality, this population-based framework is already integrated into many of the practices of school psychologists (Doll & Cummings, 2008). For example, theories and practices of the profession already emphasize the importance of normative development and typical performance on educational tasks, acknowledges the functional role played by environment and setting in determining children's behavior, and values the contributions of multiple school professionals within collaborative and consultative teams. Combined with school psychologists' thorough grounding in measurement statistics, behavioral intervention, and consultation, it is clear that practicing school psychologists are well prepared to implement a classwide, data-based classroom management strategy.

References

Adelman, H. S. & Taylor, L. (2006). *The school leader's guide to student learning supports: New directions for addressing barriers to learning.* Thousand Oaks, CA: Corwin Press.

Assor, A., Kaplan, H., & Roth, G. (2002). Choice is good, but relevance is excellent: Autonomy-enhancing and suppressing teacher behaviours predicting students'engagement in schoolwork. *British Journal of Educational Psychology 72*, 261–278.

Bear, G. (2008). School-wide approaches to behavior problems. In B. Doll & J. A. Cummings (Eds.), *Transforming school mental health services: Population-based approaches to promoting the competency and wellness of children* (pp. 103–141). Thousand Oaks, CA: Corwin Press in cooperation with the National Association of School Psychologists.

Bear, G. C., Cavalier, A. R., Manning, M. (2005). Developing self-discipline and preventing and correcting misbehavior. Boston: Pearson/Allyn & Bacon.

Bergan, J. R. (1977). *Behavioral consultation.* Columbus, OH: Merrill.

Birch, S. H., & Ladd, G. W. (1998). Children's interpersonal behaviors and the teacher-child relationship. *Developmental Psychology, 34*, 934–946.

Brooks, A., Todd, A.W., Tofflemoyer, S. & Horner, R.H. (2003). Use of functional assessment and a self-management system to increase academic engagement and work completion. *Journal of Positive Behavior Interventions, 5*(3), 144–152.

Brooks, R. B., & Goldstein, S. (2007). Developing the mindset of effective teachers. In S. Goldstein, & R. B. Brooks (Eds.), *Understanding and managing children's classroom behavior: Creating sustainable, resilient classrooms* (2nd Ed.), (pp. 189–207). Hoboken, NJ: John Wiley & Sons.

Campbell, J. (1999). *Student discipline and classroom management: Preventing and managing discipline problems in the classroom.* Springfield, IL: Charles C Thomas, Publisher.

Consortium on the School-based Promotion of Social Competence. (1994). The school-based promotion of social competence: Theory, research, practice, and policy. In R.J. Haggerty, L.R. Sherrod, N. Garmezy, & M. Rutter (Eds.), *Stress, risk, and resilience in children and adolescents* (pp. 268–316). New York: Cambridge University Press.

Crone, D. A., & Horner, R. H. (2003). *Building positive behavior support systems in schools: Functional behavior assessment.* New York: Guilford Press.

Doll, B. (1996). Children without friends: Implications for practice and policy. *School Psychology Review, 25*, 165–183.

Doll, B., Champion, A., & Kurien, S. (2008, February). Social and psychological context for high quality classrooms. A poster presented at the 2008 Annual Convention of the National Association of School Psychologists, New Orleans.

Doll, B., & Cummings, J. (2008). *Transforming school mental health services: Population-based approaches to promoting the competency and wellness of children.* Thousand Oaks, CA: Corwin Press in cooperation with the National Association of School Psychologists.

Doll, B., Kurien, S., LeClair, C., Spies, R., Champion, A., & Osborn, A. (2009). The ClassMaps Survey: A framework for promoting positive classroom environments. In R. Gilman, S. Huebner, and M. Furlong (Eds.), *Handbook of positive psychology in the schools* (pp. 213–227). New York: Routledge.

Doll, B., Kurien, S., LeClair, C., Spies, R., Osborn, A., Champion, A., Collaro, A., & Jones, K. (2008, August). Mixed-methods portrait of a school's learning environment. A poster presented at the 116th Convention of the American Psychological Association, Boston.

Doll, B., LeClair, C., & Kurien, S. (2009). Effective classrooms: Classroom learning environments that foster school success, (pp. 791–807). In T. Gutkin & C. Reynolds (Eds.),

The handbook of school psychology. Hoboken, NJ: John Wiley & Sons.

Doll, B., Murphy, P., & Song, S. (2003). The relation between children's self-reported recess problems, and peer acceptance and friendships. *Journal of School Psychology, 41*, 113–130.

Doll, B., & Siemers, E. (2004, April). *Assessing instructional climates: The reliability and validity of ClassMaps.* A poster presented at the annual convention of the National Association of School Psychologists, Dallas, TX.

Doll, B., & Spies, R. A. (2007, March). *The ClassMaps Survey.* A paper presented at the Annual Convention of the National Association of School Psychologists, New York.

Doll, B., Spies, R., Strasil, E., LeClair, C., Fleissner, S., & Kurien, S. (2006, March). *Successful student study: precursors to academic, social and behavioral success.* A paper presented at the Annual Convention of the National Association of School Psychologists, Anaheim, CA.

Doll, B., Zucker, S., & Brehm, K. (2004) *Resilient classrooms: Creating healthy environments for learning. A text in the series, Practical interventions in schools.* New York: Guilford Publications.

Eggen, P., and Kauchak, D. (1997). *Educational psychology: Windows on classrooms.* Upper Saddle River, N. J.: Prentice Hall.

Erchul, W. P., & Martens, B. K. (2002). *School consultation: Conceptual and empirical bases of practice* (2nd ed). New York: Kluwer Academic/Plenum Publishers.

Fashola, O. S., & Slavin, R. E. (1998). Effective program prevention and college attendance programs for students placed at risk. *Journal for the Education of Students Placed At Risk, 3*, 159–183.

Field, A. J. (1976). Educational expansion in mid-nineteenth-century Massachusetts: Human capital formation or structural reinforcement? *Harvard Educational Review, 46*, 521–552.

Finn, J. D. (1989). Withdrawing from school. *Review of Educational Research, 59*, 117–142.

Fredricks, J. A., Blumenfeld, P. C., & Paris, A. H. (2004). School engagement: Potential of the concept, state of the evidence. *Review of Educational Research, 74*, 59–109.

Furrer, C., & Skinner, C. (2003). Sense of relatedness as a factor in children's academic engagement and performance. *Journal of Educational Psychology, 95*, 148–162.

Gettinger, M. & Seibert, J. K. (2000). Analogue assessment: Research and practice evaluating academic skills problems. In E. S. Shapiro, & T. R. Kratochwill (Eds.), *Behavioral assessment in schools: Theory, research, and clinical foundations* (pp. 139–167). New York: Guilford Press.

Goldstein, S. & Brooks, R. B (2007). Creating sustainable classroom environments: The midsets of effective teachers, successful students, and productive consultants. In S. Goldstein, & R. B. Brooks (Eds.), *Understanding and managing children's classroom behavior: Creating sustainable, resilient classrooms* (2nd Ed.), (pp. 22–39). Hoboken, NJ: John Wiley & Sons.

Greenwood, C. R. (1991). Longitudinal analysis of time, engagement and achievement in at-risk versus nonrisk students. *Exceptional Children, 57*, 521–535.

Hamre, B. & Pianta, R. (2005). Can instructional and emotional support in the first-grade classroom make a difference for children at-risk for school failure? *Child Development, 76*, 949–967.

Haynes, S. N., & O'Brien, W. H. (1999). *Principles and practice of behavioral assessment.* New York: Kluwer.

Johnson, D. W., Johnson, R. T., Buckman, L. A., & Richards, P. S. (1998). The effect of prolonged implementation of cooperative learning on social support within the classroom. *The Journal of Psychology, 119,* 405–411.

Kratochwill, T. R., & Bergan, J. R. (1990). *Behavioral consultation in applied settings: An individual guide.* New York: Plenum Press.

Kratochwill, T. R. & Shapiro, E. S. (2000). Conceptual foundations of behavioral assessment in schools. In E. S. Shapiro, & T. R. Kratochwill (Eds.), *Behavioral assessment in schools: Theory, research, and clinical foundations,* (pp. 3–15), New York: Guilford Press.

Kulik, C. L. C., & Kulik, J. A. (1982). Effects of ability grouping on secondary school students: A meta-analysis of evaluation findings. *American Educational Research Journal, 19,* 415–428.

Ladd, G.W., Birch, S.H., & Buhs, E. S. (1999). Children's social and scholastic lives in kindergarten: Related spheres of influence? *Child Development, 70,* 1373–1400.

Lee, S. W. & Jamison, R. T. (2003). Including the FBA process in student assistance teams: An exploratory study of team communications and intervention selection. *Journal of Educational and Psychological Consultation, 14,* 209–293.

Liaupsin, C., Umbreit, J., Ferro, J., Urso, A., & Upreti, G. (2006). Improving Academic Engagement through Systematic, Function-Based Intervention. *Education and Treatment of Children, 29,* 573–591.

Marzano, R.J., Pickering, D. J., & Pollock, J. E. (2001). *Classroom instruction that works: Research-based strategies for increasing student achievement.* Alexandria, VA: Association for Supervision and Curriculum Development.

Merrell, K. W., Gueldner, B. A., & Tran, O. K. (2008). Social and emotional learning: A school-wide approach to intervention for socialization, friendship problems, and more. In B. Doll and J. Cummings (Eds.), *Transforming school mental health services: Population-based approaches to promoting the competency and wellness of children* (pp. 165–185). Bethesda, MD: National Association of School Psychologists.

Miltenberger, R. G. (2008). *Behavior modification: Principles and procedures* (4th ed). Belmont, CA: Thomson Wadsworth.

Murphy, P. (2002). *The effect of classroom meetings on the reduction of recess problems: A single case design.* Unpublished doctoral dissertation, University of Denver, Denver, CO.

Murray, C. & Malmgren, K. (2005). Implementing a teacher–student relationship program in a high-poverty urban school: Effects on social, emotional, and academic adjustment and lessons learned. *Journal of School Psychology, 43,* 137–152.

National Research Council and the Institute of Medicine. (2004). *Engaging schools: Fostering high school students' motivation to learn.* Committee on Increasing High School Students' Engagement and Motivation to Learn; Board on Children, Youth, and Families; Division of Behavioral and Social Sciences and Education. Washington, DC: The National Academies Press.

Nickolite, A., & Doll, B. (2008). Resilience applied in school: Strengthening classroom environments for learning. *Canadian Journal of School Psychology, 23,* 94–113.

Noell, G. H., Gilbertson, D. N., VanDerHeyden, A. M., & Witt, J. C. (2004). Eco- behavioral assessment and intervention for culturally diverse at-risk students. In, C. Frisby, & C. R. Reynolds (Eds.) *Comprehensive handbook of multicultural school psychology,* (pp. 904–927), New York: John Wiley & Sons.

Pajares, F., & Schunk, D. H. (2001). Self-beliefs and school success: Self-efficacy, self-concept, and school achievement. In R. J. Riding & S. G. Rayner (Eds.), *Self perception* (pp. 239–265). Westport, CT: Ablex Publishing.

Paul, K. (2005). SchoolMaps: *A reliability and validity study for a secondary education school climate instrument.* Unpublished doctoral dissertation, University of Nebraska Lincoln.

Pianta, R.C. (1999). *Enhancing relationships between children and teachers.* Washington, DC: American Psychological Association.

Pintrich, P. (2003). A motivational science perspective on the role of student motivation in learning and teaching contexts. *Journal of Educational Psychology, 95.* 667–686.

Reschly, A., & Christenson, S. (2006). Prediction of dropout among students with mild disabilities: A case for the inclusion of student engagement variables. *Remedial and Special Education, 27,* 276–292.

Rock, M.L., & Thead, B.K. (2007). The effects of fading a strategic self-monitoring intervention on students' academic engagement, accuracy and productivity. *Journal of Behavioral Education, 16,* 389–412.

Rumberger, R. W., & Larson, K. A. (1994). Keeping high-risk Chicano students in school: Lessons from a Los Angeles middle school dropout prevention program. In R. J. Rossi (Ed.). *Schools and students at risk: Context and framework for positive change* (pp. 141–162). New York: Teachers College Press.

Rybski Beaver, B., & Busse, R. T. (2000). Informant reports: Conceptual and research bases of interviews with parents and teachers. In E. S. Shapiro, & T. R. Kratochwill (Eds.), *Behavioral Assessment in Schools: Theory, Research, and Clinical Foundations,* (pp. 257–287), New York: The Guilford Press.

Schunk, D. H., & Pajares, F. (2005). Competence perceptions and academic functioning. In A. J. Elliot & C. S. Dweck (Eds.), *Handbook of competence and motivation* (pp. 85–104). New York: Guilford Publications, Inc.

Shure, M. B. (2001). *I can problem solve: An interpersonal cognitive problem-solving program* (2nd ed.). Champaign, IL: Research Press.

Sinclair, M. F., Christenson, S. L., Elevo, D. L., Hurley, C. M., (1998). *Dropout prevention for youth with disabilities: Efficacy of a sustained school engagement procedure. Exceptional Children, 65,* 7–21.

Steege, M. W., & Brown-Chidsey, R. (2005). Functional behavioral assessment: The cornerstone of effective problem solving. In R. Brown-Chidsey, (Ed.), *Assessment for intervention: A problem-solving approach,* (pp. 131–154). New York: Guilford Press.

Steege, M. W., Mace, C. B., & Brown-Chidsey, R. (2007). Functional behavioral assessment of classroom behavior. In S. Goldstein, & R. B. Brooks (Eds.), *Understanding and managing children's classroom behavior: Creating sustainable, resilient classrooms* (2nd ed., pp. 43–63). Hoboken, NJ: John Wiley & Sons.

Walker, T.W. (2008). Looking at teacher practices through the lens of parenting style. *The Journal of Experimental Education, 76*(2), 218–240.

Walker, H. M., Severson, H., Naquin, G., D'Atrio, C., Feil, E. G., Hawken, L., & Seeley, C. (2010). Implementing universal screening systems within an RtI-PBS context. In Doll, B., Pfohl, W., & Yoon, J. (Eds.). *Handbook of youth prevention science* (pp. 96-120. New York: Routledge.

Wheldall, K., & Lam, Y. Y. (1987). Rows versus tables. II. The effect of two classroom seating arrangements on classroom disruptive rate, on–task behavior and teacher behavior in three special school classes. *Educational Psychology, 7*, 303–312.

Winett, R., & Winkler, R. (1972). Current behavior modification in the classroom: Be still, be quite, be docile. *Journal of Applied Behavior Analysis, 5*, 499–504.

Witt, J. C., & Elliott, S. N. (1982). The response cost lottery: A time efficient and effective classroom intervention. *Journal of School Psychology, 20*, 155–161.

Witt, J. C., Gresham, F. M., & Noell, G. H. (1996). The consultant's corner: What's behavioral about behavioral consultation? *Journal of Educational and Psychological Consultation, 7*, 327–344.

Yetter, G., & Doll, B. (2007). The impact of logistical resources on prereferral team acceptability. *School Psychology Quarterly, 22*, 340 –357.

Response to Intervention: Conceptual Foundations and Evidence-Based Practices

Frank M. Gresham

Abstract

Response to intervention (RTI) is based on the notion of determining whether an adequate or inadequate change in academic or behavioral performance has been accomplished by an intervention. In an RTI approach, decisions regarding changing or intensifying an intervention are based on how well or how poorly a student responds to an evidence-based intervention that is implemented with integrity. RTI is used to make important educational decisions about services for children in schools, including (but not exclusively) special education and related services. RTI has three defining features: (a) delivery of high-quality interventions that are evidence-based, (b) assessment of the rate and level performance using data-based practices, and (c) making important educational decisions about children and youth. RTI typically takes place in a three-tier model that includes universal, selected, and intensive interventions. Two basic approaches to RTI practice are problem solving approaches and standard protocol approaches, with the former approach being emphasized in this chapter. This chapter concludes with a discussion of treatment strengths and how it might be operationalized in the delivery of RTI-based approaches in schools.

Keywords: RTI, 3-tier model, standard protocol, problem solving

Students' academic and behavioral difficulties are addressed in school settings using a predictable three-stage process of referral, testing, and placement. Historically, school psychologists have engaged in a process whereby they receive referrals from teachers, conduct comprehensive assessments, and make special education eligibility recommendations based on established criteria (Bocian, Beebe, MacMillan, & Gresham, 1999). Teacher referrals are based primarily on a student's performance relative to the modal performance of a given classroom, and thus the guiding principle is one of *relativity*. The testing stage of this process is based primarily on norm-referenced tests, and the guiding principle is one of *acceptability*—is the performance acceptable relative to normative standards? Placement recommendations are based on the principle of *profitability*, which reflects the collective perception that special education services at a given school site will benefit the child.

More often than not, the assessment data used to make these placement recommendations have little, if anything, to do with recommended intervention strategies (Gresham & Witt, 1997; Reschly, 2008). Despite a longstanding tradition, the "refer–test–place" approach to the identification of students with disabilities has several drawbacks. The procedures used by schools to identify students with learning and/or behavioral difficulties are often confusing, logically inconsistent, and fraught with much "diagnostic error" (Gresham, 2002; 2008; MacMillan & Siperstein, 2002; Ysseldyke & Marston, 1999).

There are two different routes whereby children become qualified as being eligible for special education (MacMillan, Gresham, Bocian, & Siperstein, 1997). Children qualified via route 1 include children with sensory (deaf or blind), physical (orthopedic), medical (chronic illnesses), or mental (moderate-severe-profound mental retardation) disabilities. The overwhelming majority of these cases are diagnosed by physicians employing medical histories, physical examinations, and laboratory tests to determine the correct diagnosis. Most children with these disabilities are identified prior to school entry (often shortly after birth), and there is little disagreement among medical or educational professionals concerning the validity of the diagnosis. The reason for this high level of agreement is that these children display highly visible or salient characteristics, about which there is little room for disagreement.

Children deemed eligible for special education via route 2 create much consternation and disagreement among educational, psychological, and medical professionals. These children may be identified as having a specific learning disability, mild mental retardation, emotional disturbance, or attention-deficit/hyperactivity disorder. Unlike children with sensory or physical impairments, children with these so-called "mild" or high-incidence disabilities are deemed eligible using procedures that are plagued with much diagnostic error (Gresham, 2008). Children functioning around the margin of a disability group create special problems in assessment, measurement, and special education eligibility determination. It is difficult to know the precise point where low academic achievement becomes a "specific learning disability," or when a behavior problem becomes an "emotional disturbance." This is because these disabilities are measurement bound, and hence are identified based on the *degree* of impairment rather than the *kind* of impairment (e.g., deaf, blind, or orthopedic impairment).

There are two basic types of diagnostic error for high-incidence disabilities: *false positive errors* and *false negative errors*. False positive errors ("false alarms") occur when children are identified as having a disability (e.g., specific learning disability) when in fact they do not have a disability. False negative errors ("misses") occur when children are not identified as having a disability when in fact they do have a disability. False positive and false negative errors may also occur among various disability categories. For example, children meeting well-established criteria for mild mental retardation may be incorrectly identified as having a specific learning disability. In these cases, two diagnostic errors occur. Failure to identify a child with mental retardation is a false negative error (a "miss"), and instead classifying the child as having a specific learning disability is a false positive error (a "false alarm").

A typical error in this process occurs when school psychologists attempt to differentiate children with learning disabilities (discrepant low achievers) from students who are "garden-variety" low achievers (nondiscrepant low achievers). In fact, attempts to differentiate learning disabled from discrepant and nondiscrepant low achiever populations are futile, based on a large body of research showing that these children share salient characteristics making them part of the same population (Fletcher, Francis, Shaywitz, Lyon, Foorman, Steubing, et al., 1998; Gresham, 2002; Gresham, MacMillan, & Bocian, 1996; Steubing, Fletcher, LeDoux, Lyon, Shaywitz, & Shaywitz, 2002).

Research by Gresham and colleagues suggested that schools frequently do not base their classification and placement decisions on state or district guidelines for high-incidence disabilities of mild mental retardation or specific learning disabilities (Gresham, MacMillan, & Bocian, 1998). Numerous interviews of these schools' placement committees indicated that they were basing their eligibility decisions based on their perceptions of what is best for a given child in terms of educational needs and supports, and not based on some equivocal and arbitrary authoritative definition of a mild disability. Based on these problems with the traditional "refer–test–place" approach, an alternative approach based on response to intervention is recommended.

Response to Intervention: An Alternative Approach

The notion of response to intervention, or RTI, is based on the concept of determining whether an adequate or inadequate change in academic or behavioral performance has been achieved by an intervention (Gresham, 2002). In an RTI approach, decisions regarding changing or intensifying an intervention are made based on how well or how poorly a student responds to an evidence-based intervention that is implemented with integrity. RTI logic is used to select and/or modify interventions, based on how the child responds to that intervention. RTI assumes that if a child shows an inadequate or weak response to the best intervention available and feasible within a given setting, then that child can and should be eligible for additional assistance, including special education and related services. RTI is *not* used exclusively to make special education entitlement decisions, although it can be used for that purpose. RTI is a philosophy of behavior change based on treatment response, rather than diagnostic assessment of unobservable and highly inferential psychological or emotional processes.

RTI logic is not a new concept in other fields. The field of medicine provides a useful example of how physicians use RTI principles in their everyday practice to treat physical problems. Physicians assess weight, blood pressure, and heart rate every time they see a patient, because these three factors are important indicators of general physical health, and have scientifically established benchmarks for typical and atypical functioning. If these weight and blood pressure measurements exceed benchmark criteria, then a physician may recommend that the patient diet, exercise, and quit smoking. The next time the patient sees the physician, these same indicators are measured; if the indicators show no change, then the physician may place the patient on a special diet and exercise regimen, and tell the patient to stop smoking. The next time the patient sees the physician, these same indicators are measured, and if they still show nochange, the physician may put the patient on medication, refer to a dietician, and send the patient to a smoking cessation clinic. Finally, the next time the physician sees the patient, and the same indicator data are in the atypical range, then upon further assessment the patient may require surgery to prevent mortality.

Several important points should be recognized in considering the above example. First, intervention intensity was increased only after the data suggested that the patient showed an inadequate response to intervention. Second, treatment decisions were based on objective data collected continuously over time (data-based decision making). Third, the data that were collected were well-established indicators of general physical health. Finally, decisions about treatment intensity were based on the collection of more and more data, as the patient moved through each stage of treatment intensification. RTI can and should be used in schools in a parallel manner, to make important educational decisions for children and youth.

The concept of RTI can also be found in the experimental analysis of behavior literature that has studied the conditions under which behavior shows "resistance to extinction" (Nevin, 1988). Gresham (1991) applied this literature to the field of behavior disorders in describing how and why certain behaviors are highly resistant to change (i.e., they do not respond to intervention efforts). Using an analogy to Newtonian physics, Nevin (1988) used the term *behavioral momentum* to explain a behavior's resistance to change. That is, a moving body possesses both mass and velocity, and will maintain constant velocity under constant conditions. The velocity of an object will change only in proportion to an exter-

nal force, and in inverse proportion to its mass. Considering the momentum metaphor, an effective intervention ("force") will result in a high level of momentum ("responsiveness") for the behavior in question.

For example, an intervention designed to decrease rates of disruptive and oppositional behavior in a classroom would be considered successful if it rapidly decreased these problem behaviors, and reliably, during intervention, and if these behavioral decreases persisted after the intervention was withdrawn. In contrast, if disruptive and oppositional behaviors returned to baseline levels after the intervention was withdrawn, teachers would not be satisfied with the intervention no matter how well the student behaved during intervention. Many behaviors are highly resistant to intervention efforts, and therefore require strong and consistent applications of powerful interventions (i.e., those with a large amount of "force").

Evolution of the RTI Concept

The historical basis of RTI, at least in special education, can be traced to the National Research Council (NRC) report (Heller, Holtzman, & Messick, 1982) in which the validity of the special education classification system was evaluated on the basis of three criteria: (a) the quality of the general education program, (b) the value of the special education program in producing important outcomes for students, and (c) the accuracy and meaningfulness of the assessment process in the identification of disability. Vaughn and Fuchs (2003) suggested that the first two criteria emphasized the quality of instruction, whereas the third criterion involved judgments of the quality of instructional environments, and the student's response to instruction delivered in those environments. The third criterion described in the NRC Report is consistent with Messick's (1995) notion of evidential and consequential bases of test *use* and *interpretation*. That is, there must be evidential and consequential bases for using and interpreting tests in a certain way. If these bases do not exist, then we may conclude that there is insufficient evidence for the validity of a given assessment procedure.

An important aspect in the evolution of the RTI concept is the notion of *treatment validity* (sometimes called *treatment utility of assessment*). Treatment validity can be defined as the extent to which any assessment procedure contributes to beneficial outcomes for individuals (Cone, 1989; Fuchs & Fuchs, 1998; Hayes, Nelson, & Jarrett, 1987). A central feature of treatment validity is that there must be a clear and unambiguous relationship between the assessment data collected and the recommended intervention.

For any assessment procedure to have treatment validity, it must lead to the identification of relevant areas of concern (academic or behavioral), inform treatment planning, and be useful in evaluating treatment outcomes. Traditionally, many assessment procedures in school psychology have failed to demonstrate treatment validity because they do not inform instructional or behavioral intervention practices (Cronbach, 1975; Gresham, 2002; Gresham & Witt, 1997; Reschly, 2008). The concept of RTI depends largely on the treatment validity of measures used to determine adequate or inadequate treatment response. In short, assessment procedures having treatment validity not only inform the selection of intervention procedures, they also are used to evaluate treatment outcomes.

The RTI concept further evolved as a viable alternative to the IQ–achievement discrepancy approach to identifying learning disabilities from the *LD Initiative,* which was a working group meeting held in Washington, D.C. and sponsored by the Office of Special Education Programs in May, 1999. Based on the LD Initiative, a national conference was held in Washington, D.C. in August, 2001, entitled the *LD Summit*. Nine white papers were written and presented over a 2-day period to a group of LD professionals and stakeholders from all over the United States. One paper (Gresham, 2002) specifically addressed the literature on *responsiveness to intervention* that was responded to by four well-known professionals in the field of LD (Fuchs, 2002; Grimes, 2002; Vaughn, 2002; Vellutino, 2002). Gresham's paper argued that a student's inadequate response to an empirically validated intervention, implemented with integrity, can and should be used as evidence of the presence of LD, and should be used in eligibility decisions. RTI was viewed as a viable and superior alternative to defining LD on the basis of IQ–achievement discrepancy approaches, which have a myriad of conceptual and measurement difficulties.

Subsequent to the LD Summit, the President's Commission on Excellence in Special Education (2002) emphasized RTI as a viable alternative to IQ–achievement discrepancy in the identification of LD. In December, 2004, President Bush signed into law the reauthorization of the Individuals with Disabilities Education Improvement Act (IDEIA, 2004). The law states that a child may be determined to have a specific learning disability based on how that child *responds to a scientific, research based intervention* or RTI.

Features of RTI

RTI involves the provision of high quality interventions matched to student need, frequent progress monitoring to guide decisions about changes in interventions, and using student data to guide important educational decisions. RTI models have three defining characteristics: (a) delivery of high quality interventions that are evidence based, (b) rate and level of performance, and (c) important educational decisions. High quality interventions are those that are matched to student need, scientifically based, and individually based. Rate and level of student performance involves the assessment of the rate of change in behavior over time, the relative standing of student behavior on important academic or behavioral dimensions, and data-based decision making on student response to interventions. Important educational decisions are those that are based on student response to intervention across multiple tiers of intervention, differing in intensity. These decisions might be made about changes in the intensity of intervention, special education eligibility, and/or exiting special education (Gresham, 2002, 2006).

The effectiveness of schoolbased interventions is based on several interrelated factors that must be considered in the design, implementation, and evaluation process. It is unfortunate that some school based professionals engage in a fruitless search for "silver bullet" interventions that will be universally effective with all students, will work every time, will be easy to implement, and will maintain their effectiveness over a long period of time. Such interventions do not exist. Interventions implemented in schools often do not enjoy empirical support, and are chosen for reasons such as personal appeal, popularity, acceptability, and/or ease of implementation rather than research supporting their use.

The following medical analogy illustrates the above logic. If surgeons adopted a procedure that has a 20% mortality rate over one that has a 10% mortality rate because: (a) it is easier to do, (b) the surgeon was trained in it, and (c) the surgeon just likes it better, such a practice would not be tolerated. However, intervention strategies in schools are often driven by a similar logic. Intervention practices in schools are based, in part, on the fact that many educators have not been trained in empirically supported intervention methods, and/or they simply may be invested in philosophical or theoretical approaches that are at odds with more effective intervention strategies (Gresham, 2004).

RTI and the Three-Tier Model

Perhaps the most important concept in a RTI approach to service delivery in schools is the notion of matching the intensity of the intervention to the intensity and severity of the presenting problem behavior. One approach adopted by the U.S. Public Health Service describes three levels of "prevention" outcomes: primary prevention, secondary prevention, and tertiary prevention. This approach considers prevention as an outcome, rather than simply a means to an end. Primary prevention efforts seek to *prevent* harm, whereas secondary prevention efforts seek to *reverse* harm. Tertiary prevention efforts target the most severe academic and/or behavior difficulties and attempt to *reduce* harm (Walker, Ramsay, & Gresham, 2004).

This prevention model has subsequently been recast in terms of types of interventions that differ in the nature, comprehensiveness, and intensity of the interventions, as well as the degree of unresponsiveness of an individual's behavior to a given intervention. This model of intervention typically is composed of three tiers of intervention intensity: universal interventions, selected interventions, and targeted/intensive interventions.

Universal Interventions

These interventions are designed to target and affect all students, and are delivered in the same manner and under the same conditions. These interventions are delivered in a classwide, schoolwide, or districtwide level, with each student receiving the same "dosage" of the intervention. Some examples of universal interventions are vaccinations, schoolwide discipline plans, districtwide bully prevention programs, and districtwide adopted reading, mathematics, and language arts curricula.

Universal interventions accomplish two major goals of education: the academic and social development of students. Implementing best practice, evidence-based interventions focuses on reducing or eliminating academic or behavioral difficulties before they become more severe. Estimates suggest that universal interventions will be effective with *80%–90%* of any given school population. This figure may be higher or lower depending on the severity level of academic and behavioral challenges in any given school or school district, as well as on the quality of the particular universal intervention that is implemented.

Selected Interventions

These interventions focus on the weak or nonresponders to universal interventions. It is estimated that approximately 5%–10% of the school population may require some form of selected interventions. These students are at risk for severe academic or behavioral difficulties if more intense interventions are not implemented. Many of these students will respond to relatively simple, individually focused academic and behavioral interventions. These interventions are delivered in general education classrooms, and are typically developed in a consultation framework between general education teachers and support personnel (e.g., school psychologists or school counselors).

The goal of selected interventions is to provide more intense, individually prescribed intervention strategies to remediate academic and/or behavioral difficulties. These strategies are not complicated or comprehensive, but should be evidence based. Numerous examples of these types of interventions can be found in the area of academics (see Daly, Chafouleas, & Skinner, 2005) and social behavior (see DuPaul& Stoner, 2003; Miltenberger, 2004).

Targeted/Intensive Interventions

The most intense level of intervention focuses on students that are the most resistant to change, and who exhibit chronic academic or behavioral difficulties. It is estimated that this group of students constitutes about 1%–5% of any given school population. In terms of behavioral difficulties, these students are responsible for 40%–50% of behavioral disruptions in schools, and they drain 50%–60% of school building and classroom resources (Walker et al., 2004). In the area of reading, these students are weak responders to universal and selected intervention efforts, and will require very intensive phonics-based reading instruction (Vaughn, Linan-Thompson, & Hickman, 2003; Vellutino, 1987).

For behavioral difficulties, these interventions usually are based on a functional behavioral assessment (FBA) to determine the consequent events maintaining problem behaviors. FBA is defined as a collection of methods for collecting information regarding antecedents, behaviors, and consequences, to determine the *function* (purpose or "cause") of problem behavior (Gresham, Watson, & Skinner, 2001). Once behavioral function is determined, this information is used to design interventions to reduce competing problem behaviors, and to increase positive replacement behaviors that serve the same behavioral function.

For academic difficulties, intense remedial efforts are typically delivered in a small group pull-out setting, and involve a relatively large number of hours of instruction. For example, intensive reading interventions by Vellutino and colleagues (Vellutino, Scanlon, Sipay, Small, Pratt, Chen et al., 1996), Torgesen and colleagues (Torgesen, Alexander, Wagner, Rashotte, Voeller, & Conway, 2001), and Vaughn et al. (2003) require anywhere from 35 to 68 hours of intense, phonics-based reading instruction. Even despite these intense intervention efforts, approximately 25% of the poor reader population will show an inadequate or weak response to intervention (Torgesen, Wagner, Rashotte, Rose, Lindamood, Conway, et al., 1999).

Response to Intervention Models

Two basic approaches are used to deliver interventions in a RTI approach: (a) problem-solving approaches, and (b) standard protocol approaches (Fuchs, Mock, Morgan, & Young, 2003). Some RTI models combine these two approaches, particularly within a multi-tier model of service delivery described earlier (see Barnett, Daly, Jones, & Lentz, 2004; Duhon, Noell, Witt, Freeland, Dufrene, & Gilbertson, 2004; VanDerHeyden, Witt, & Naquin, 2003). These particular models are best described as multi-tier RTI approaches to intervention. Despite these two basic RTI approaches, this chapter will concentrate on problem-solving RTI, because this approach is the most commonly used by school psychologists.

Problem Solving Approaches

Problem solving can be traced back to the behavioral consultation model first described by Bergan (1977), and later revised and updated by Bergan and Kratochwill (1990). Behavioral consultation takes place in a sequence of four phases: (a) problem identification, (b) problem analysis, (c) plan implementation, and (d) plan evaluation. The goal in behavioral consultation is to define the problem in clear, unambiguous, and operational terms, to identify environmental conditions related to the referral problem, to design and implement an intervention plan with integrity, and to evaluate the effectiveness of the intervention (Bergan & Kratochwill, 1990). More recently, the behavioral consultation model was described by Tilly (2002) in the form of four fundamental questions governing the identification and intervention of school based academic and behavioral problems: (a) What is the problem? (b) Why is the problem happening? (c) What should be done about it?, and (d) Did it work? Each of these steps is described briefly in the following sections.

PROBLEM IDENTIFICATION

Problems are defined, in a problem solving approach, as a *discrepancy* between current and desired levels of performance. As such, the larger this discrepancy, the larger the problem. For example, if a student's current rate of oral reading fluency is 50 words correct per minute, and the desired rate is 100 words correct per minute (based on a benchmark standard), then there is a 50%, or 50-word discrepancy between current and desired levels of performance. This same logic can be applied to any type of referral problem (academic or behavioral) as the first step in a problem solving approach.

A critical aspect of problem identification is the *operational definition* of the referral problem into specific, measurable terms that permit direct, objective assessment of the behavior or skill in question. Operational definitions are objective, clear, and complete. These definitions are objective if they can be read, repeated, and paraphrased by others. Operational definitions are clear if two or more observers of a behavior or skill are able to read the definition and use it to record and measure the behavior or skill. Operational definitions are complete if they specify the boundary conditions for inclusion of behaviors that are not part of the definition. For example, an operational definition of noncompliance might be as follows: *Noncompliance is defined as the student not complying with a verbal request or directive from the teacher within 5 seconds after the request or directive has been given. Examples of verbal requests or directives are being told to sit down, begin work, copy from the board, come to the teacher's desk, and so forth.* Any other behaviors that do not meet this operational definition are not considered to be part of the response class of noncompliance.

PROBLEM ANALYSIS

Another important aspect of problem solving is to determine why the problem is occurring. At this stage, the distinction between "can't do" (acquisition or skill deficits) and "won't do" (motivational or performance deficits) is critical (Gresham, 1981; VanDerHeyden & Witt, 2008). "Can't do" problems are considered to be acquisition deficits, meaning that the child does not have the skill or behavior in his or her repertoire. For example, if the child does not engage in appropriate social interactions with peers on the playground, then it may be because the child lacks appropriate peer group entry strategies.

In this case, the acquisition deficit should be remediated by directly teaching the child appropriate peer group entry strategies.

"Won't do" problems are considered to be performance or motivational deficits, meaning that the child knows how to perform the skill or behavior, but does not do so. Reasons for not performing the behavior or skill may be due to the lack of opportunities to perform the skill or behavior, or the lack of or low rate of reinforcement for performing the behavior or skill. In cases like these, remedial interventions would involve providing multiple opportunities to perform the behavior or skill, and increasing the rate of reinforcement for skill or behavioral performance.

PLAN IMPLEMENTATION

The implementation of an intervention plan, designed in the problem analysis state of problem solving, is a critical aspect of the RTI enterprise. All RTI approaches argue for the implementation of scientific, evidence-based interventions; however, this is only part of the task in plan implementation. A fundamental principle of any intervention in a problem solving approach, particularly interventions delivered by third parties such as teachers or parents, is that the intervention will be delivered as intended or planned (Gresham, 1989). This is known as *treatment integrity* or *treatment fidelity*. From a research perspective, it must be demonstrated that changes in a dependent variable (behavior or skill) can be attributed to systematic, manipulated changes in the independent variable (i.e., the treatment). From a practice perspective, consultants collaboratively designing and assisting in the implementation of interventions must take steps to ensure that the intervention is implemented as intended. Poorly implemented interventions are likely to be ineffective in changing behavior. Treatment integrity, therefore, becomes a cornerstone of any RTI model.

Treatment integrity focuses on the *accuracy* and *consistency* with which interventions are delivered in schools or classrooms. Accuracy refers to the degree to which an intervention is implemented according to an established set of procedures. Consistency refers to the degree to which the intervention is implementedwhen it is supposed to be implemented (each subject period, on the half hour, daily). The ineffectiveness of many interventions designed in a problem solving approach may be due to the poor integrity with which these interventions are implemented, and poor integrity can result from inaccuracy, inconsistency, or both (Gresham, 1997). Deviations from an agreed-upon intervention plan or protocol explain why many interventions delivered in schools are not used, and are rendered ineffective. Without assessment of treatment integrity in an RTI approach, one cannot know if a given treatment was simply ineffective, or if the treatment would have been effective had it been implemented with good integrity.

PLAN EVALUATION

An essential component of the RTI approach is the determination of what constitutes an adequate or inadequate response to intervention. This determination is somewhat easier for academic performance than it is for social behavior. For academic performance, curriculum based measurement (CBM) typically is used to index response to intervention. CBM has the most well-established empirical history, and close connection to problem solving based assessment practices (Deno, 2005; Shinn, 2008). CBM measures are considered to be among the most highly regarded assessment tools for continuous progress monitoring to quantify student performances in reading, mathematics, and written language in short-term interventions. To be useful in formative evaluations, progress monitoring tools must meet technical adequacy standards (reliability and validity), must be sensitive to short-term changes in academic performance, and must be time-efficient so that teachers can monitor student performance frequently (1–2 times per week). CBM indices are ideal in an RTI approach because there are well-established benchmarks for both *level* and *trend* (growth) in the basic areas of academic performance (see Shinn, 2008).

Unfortunately, there is no CBM analogue for dependably measuring students' response to short-term interventions in the area of social behavior. Progress monitoring for students' social behavior is important, because educators need to determine whether a student's rate of progress in a social-behavioral intervention is adequate to reach an acceptable criterion of proficiency in a reasonable period of time. The purpose of progress monitoring of social behavior is to establish students' rates of improvement, to identify students who are not responding to an intervention, and to use these data to make decisions about continuing, altering, or terminating intervention based on how students are responding.

For students' social behavior, several methods have been proposed and used, to determine whether a student is showing an adequate or acceptable response to intervention. These methods include: (a) absolute change in behavior, (b) percent change from baseline, (c) reliable change index, (d) effect size estimates, and (e) social validation of behavior change (see Gresham, 2005). Each of these methods has advantages and disadvantages, and will be described briefly in the following section.

Absolute change in behavior is the degree or amount of change an individual makes that does not involve comparison to other groups. Absolute change can be calculated in one of three ways: (a) the amount of change from baseline to post-intervention levels of performance; (b) an individual no longer meeting established criteria for a diagnosis (e.g., classification of emotionally disturbed or DSM-IV diagnoses); and (c) the total elimination of behavior problems. Absolute change is straightforward, intuitively logical, and easy to calculate. It is also consistent with a problem solving approach to defining problems as *the discrepancy between expected and desired levels of performance* described earlier. Using this approach, a problem is considered "solved" if the degree of absolute change is large relative to the three criteria described above.

There are some problems with using metrics of absolute change. For instance, an individual might show a relative large amount of absolute change from baseline to post-intervention levels of performance, but this change may not be large enough to allow that individual to function successfully within a general education setting. Absolute change also interacts with tolerance levels for problem behavior at the classroom and school levels. That is, even though a change in behavior is large, the behavior pattern still might not be tolerated by significant others in the school environment. Also, an individual may no longer meet the diagnostic criteria for an emotional disturbance, but this may be due to biases operating in the diagnostic and eligibility decision-making process.

Percent change from baseline is another metric that can be used to index response to intervention. This metric involves comparing the median level of performance in baseline to the median level of performance in intervention. For example, if the median frequency of a behavior in baseline is 8, and the median frequency of behavior after intervention is 2, then the percent change from baseline would be 75% (8–2/8=75%). The advantage of this metric is that outliers or aberrant data points, or floor and ceiling effects, do not greatly affect this metric, mainly because the median rather than the mean is used in its calculation. Percent change is commonly used in medicine to evaluate the effects of medical treatments, such as drugs to reduce cholesterol or blood pressure.

There are well established medical benchmarks for desirable levels of blood cholesterol (<200 *dl*) and blood pressure (120/80) indexed to important medical outcomes (e.g., cardiovascular disease or mortality rates). Unfortunately, there are no such benchmarks for many behaviors targeted for intervention. There are no clear guidelines for determining the magnitude of behavior change that is sufficient to indicate an individual has demonstrated an adequate response to intervention. As such, this metric should be supplemented by other measures or indicators or response to intervention.

The *reliable change index* (RCI) is based on the notion that an individual's behavior during intervention is sufficiently large to have surpassed the margin of measurement error. RCI is calculated by subtracting an individual's mean score after baseline (posttest score) from the pretest score, and dividing this difference by the standard error of difference between posttest and pretest scores (Jacobson, Follette, & Revenstorf, 1988). The standard error of difference represents the variability in the distribution of change scores if no change had occurred, and is based on the standard deviation of pretest scores and the test/retest reliability of the measure used to index behavior change. An RCI of 1.96 (*p*<.05) would be considered a statistically reliable change in behavior.

RCI has the advantage of quantifying reliable changes from baseline to post-intervention levels of performance, and confidence intervals can be placed around change scores to avoid overinterpretation of results. The RCI is affected by the reliability (stability) of outcome measures used. If a measure is highly reliable (stable), then small changes in behavior might be considered statistically reliable, but not educationally significant or important. In contrast, if a measure has relatively low reliability (stability), then large changes in behavior may be educationally important but statistically unreliable.

Perhaps the most serious drawback of RCI is that it cannot be used to estimate reliable changes in behavior using direct observations of behavior. No "test-retest" reliability coefficient is calculated in using direct observations of behavior. "Reliability" in direct observations is typically calculated by interobserver agreement indices. This is not the same as stability of behavior over time, in the traditional use of that term, and thus cannot be used to calculate RCI.

Two types of *effect size* estimates for the individual case are typically used to gauge response to intervention. The first estimate is a modification of

Cohen's *d* that is used in meta-analytic research. This effect size is calculated by subtracting the intervention mean from the baseline mean, and dividing by the standard deviation of baseline data points (Busk & Serlin, 1992). A drawback of this effect size estimate is that it can yield large effect size estimates that cannot be interpreted in the same way as effect sizes calculated in meta-analytic research.

A second effect size metric is the *percent of nonoverlapping data points* (PND) computed by calculating the percentage of nonoverlapping data points between baseline and intervention phases (Mastropieri & Scruggs, 1985–1986). If the goal of an intervention is to decrease behavior, one computes PND by counting the number of intervention data points exceeding the *highest* data point in baseline, and dividing by the total number of data points in the intervention phase. For example, if 8 of 10 data points in intervention exceeded the highest baseline data point, the PND would be 80%. Alternatively, if the goal of intervention is to increase behavior, then one calculates PND by counting the number of intervention data points that are below the *lowest* baseline data point, and dividing by the total number of data points in the intervention phase.

PND was proposed to provide a quantitative index to document the effects of an intervention that is easy to calculate. There are, however, some drawbacks of using this method that should be noted. One, PND often does not reflect the magnitude of behavior change in an intervention. That is, one can have 100% nonoverlapping data points in the treatment phase, yet have an extremely weak treatment effect. Two, unusual baseline trends (high and low data points) can skew the interpretation of PND. Three, PND is greatly affected by floor and ceiling effects. Four, aberrant or outlier data points can make interpretation of PND difficult (see Strain, Kohler, & Gresham, 1998 for a discussion). Five, there are no well-established guidelines for what constitutes a large, medium, or small effect using PND.

Perhaps the most essential and relevant means of determining adequate response to intervention is *social validation*. Social validity addresses three fundamental questions with respect to intervention: What should we change? How should we change it? How will we know it was effective? There are often disagreements among professionals and treatment consumers on these three fundamental questions (see Hawkins, 1991; Schwartz & Baer, 1991). Wolf (1978) described the social validation process as involving the *social significance* of intervention goals, the *social acceptability* of intervention procedures,

and the *social importance* of intervention outcomes. This last aspect of the social validation process is the most relevant in quantifying and evaluating treatment effectiveness in a RTI approach.

Establishing the social importance of the effects of intervention attests to the practical or educational significance of behavior change. Do the quantity and quality of the changes in behavior make a difference in the student's behavioral functioning and adjustment? In short, do the changes in behavior have *habilitative validity* (Hawkins, 1991)? Is the student's behavior now in the functional range, subsequent to the intervention? These questions capture the essence of establishing the social importance of intervention effects.

A way of establishing the social importance of intervention effects is to view behavioral functioning (academic or social) as belonging to either a functional or dysfunctional distribution. An example might be socially validating a behavioral intervention by showing the student's behavior moved from a dysfunctional to a functional range of performance. Using teacher and/or parent ratings on nationally normed behavior rating scales is one means of quantifying the social importance of intervention outcomes (Gresham & Lopez, 1996). Moving a student's problem behavior ratings from the 95th percentile to the 50th percentile would represent a socially important change. Similarly, changing a target behavior problem measured by direct observations into the range of nonreferred peers would also corroborate the behavior ratings, and therefore could be considered socially important.

Social importance can also be conceptualized and evaluated on several levels: proximal effects, intermediate effects, and distal effects (Fawcett, 1991). Proximal effects are changes in target behaviors produced by the intervention such as increases in social skills, decreases in aggressive behavior, or increases in oral reading fluency. Proximal effects can be evaluated by visual inspection of graphed data, percent change from baseline, and/or the reliable change index. Intermediate effects can be evaluated by more molar assessments, such as substantial changes in ratings on normed behavior rating scales, teacher ratings of academic performance, or standardized tests of academic achievement. Distal effects can be evaluated by changes on *social impact* measures such as office discipline referrals, suspension/expulsion rates, school attendance, promotion/retention status, or incarceration rates.

It should be noted that social impact measures are not particularly sensitive in detecting short-term changes in behavior produced by interventions. Many treatment consumers may consider these social impact measures to be the most important metrics in gauging successful intervention outcomes; however, exclusive reliance on these measures might ignore or mask a great deal of behavior change (see Kazdin, 2003).

It is often the case that rather large and sustained changes in behavior are required before these changes are reflected on social impact measures. A method based on *just noticeable differences* (JNDs) has been recommended to index intervention outcomes (Sechrest, McKnight, & McKnight, 1996). A JND approach answers the question: How much of a difference in behavior is required before it is "noticed" by significant others (teachers, parents, school personnel), or reflected on other social impact measures? For example, how much of a decrease in aggressive/disruptive behavior in the classroom and on the playground is required, before it is reflected in a decrease and subsequent elimination of office discipline referrals? Similarly, how much of an increase in oral reading fluency is necessary before it is reflected in a student's performance on a high-stakes achievement test?

Conclusion and Future Directions

RTI is a process of providing high quality interventions that are matched to student need, and uses frequent progress monitoring of student response to interventions to assist in making important educational decisions. At the most basic level, all RTI approaches share three common features: (a) use of evidence-based interventions, (b) assessing the rate and level of student performance in those interventions, and (c) use of individual student responsiveness data to make educational decisions. The key concept in any RTI approach is that the intensity of an intervention is matched to the intensity and severity of academic or behavioral difficulties. RTI is typically conceptualized in a three-tier model that describes three levels of prevention: primary prevention, secondary prevention, and tertiary prevention. These three levels of prevention seek to prevent, reverse, and reduce harm, respectively.

An important and unresolved concept in RTI is treatment strength (see Yeaton & Sechrest, 1981). What makes a given intervention or treatment strong? In pharmacological interventions, more of a drug necessarily makes it stronger (e.g., 100 milligrams is twice as strong as 50 milligrams—assuming no drug tolerance effects). However, in education or psychology, administering more of a treatment does not necessarily make it stronger. For example,

doubling the amount of an ineffective treatment would have nothing to do with its strength in changing behavior, because the treatment does not have the active ingredients necessary to change behavior.

Another dimension of treatment strength is *duration* of the treatment. Are longer treatments stronger than those delivered with shorter durations? This depends on the inherent properties of the treatment that constitutes its ability to change behavior. For example, is a 3-month treatment stronger than a 1-month treatment? Again, administering a longer duration of treatment would not necessarily result in larger changes in behavior if the treatment contains few or no active ingredients to promote behavior change. In fact, there are cases in which longer treatments may lose their effectiveness over time. A good example is the concept of reinforcer*satiation* in which a reinforcer loses its effectiveness over time (i.e., children get tired of the reinforcer).

A third dimension of treatment strength is the *intensity* of the treatment. Treatment intensity can refer to how many times the treatment is delivered (e.g., twice a day, once per day, once per week). Treatment intensity can also be conceptualized as the consistency with which a treatment is delivered. This concept captures the notion of treatment integrity, or the degree to which a treatment is implemented as planned or intended.

In an RTI approach to intervention service delivery, the strength of educational or psychological interventions cannot be reliably defined a priori, because there is not a one-to-one correspondence between the "dosage" of a treatment and subsequent response to a treatment. Several assumptions may be helpful in considering the notion of treatment strength. One, stronger treatments often result in greater behavior change than weaker treatments. It is unclear, however, what makes a treatment "strong." A defensible approach to determining treatment strength can be found in the meta-analytic literature on academic and behavioral interventions. That is, treatments producing larger effect sizes can legitimately be considered stronger than treatments producing smaller effect sizes. In other words, evidence-based treatments are de facto stronger than treatments having little or no empirical evidence to support their use. For example, a treatment that produces an effect size of $d=.80$ will be much stronger than another treatment that produces an effect size of $d=.20$.

Another assumption in treatment strength is the effect of treatment integrity. That is, treatment strength may be diluted or enhanced by the level of treatment integrity. For example, an evidence-based treatment delivered with 100% integrity should be stronger than that same treatment delivered with only 50% integrity. However, treatment integrity does not necessarily result in stronger treatments (i.e., 100% of a weak treatment may not equal 50% of a strong treatment). Moreover, each component of a treatment may not be equally strong in producing behavior change (Gresham, 1989).

This chapter discussed RTI from the perspective of a three-tier approach to service delivery in schools. Instead of diagnosing within-child conditions (e.g., specific learning disabilities or emotional disturbance), the RTI approach focused on four stages of a problem solving process: problem identification, problem analysis, plan implementation, and plan evaluation. Each of these steps in the problem solving process takes place at each of three levels of intervention: universal, selected, and intensive. This chapter concluded with a discussion of how strength of treatments can moderate treatment outcomes, and discussed unresolved issues in conceptualizing and operationalizing treatment strength.

References

Barnett, D., Daly, E., Jones, K., Lentz, F.E. (2004). Response to intervention: Empirically-based special service decisions for increasing and decreasing intensity using single case designs. *The Journal of Special Education, 38,* 66–79.

Bergan, J. (1977). *Behavioral consultation.* Columbus, OH: Merrill.

Bergan, J., & Kratochwill, T.R. (1990). *Behavioral consultation and therapy.* New York: Plenum.

Bocian, K., Beebe, M., MacMillan, D., & Gresham, F.M. (1999). Competing paradigms in learning disabilities classification by schools and variations in the meaning of discrepant achievement. *Learning Disabilities Research and Practice, 14,* 1–14.

Busk, P., & Serlin, R. (1992). Meta-analysis for single case research. In T. Kratochwill & J. Levin (Eds.), *Single-case design and analysis* (pp. 187–212). Hillsdale, NJ: Erlbaum.

Cone, J. (1989). Is there utility for treatment utility? *American Psychologist, 44,* 1241–1242.

Cronbach, L. (1975). Beyond two disciplines of scientific psychology. *American Psychologist, 30,* 116–127.

Daly, E., Chafouleas, S., & Skinner, C. (2005). *Interventions for reading problems: Designing, and evaluating effective strategies.* New York: Guilford.

Deno, S. (2005). Problem-solving assessment. In R. Brown-Chidsey (Ed.), *Assessment for intervention: A problem-solving approach* (pp. 10–40). New York: Guilford.

Duhon, G., Noell, G., Witt, J., Freeland, J., Dufrene, B., & Gilbertson, D. (2004). Identifying academic skill and performance deficits: The experimental analysis of brief assessments of academic skills. *School Psychology Review, 33,* 429–443.

DuPaul, G., & Stoner, G. (2003). *ADHD in the schools: Assessment and intervention strategies.* New York: Guilford.

Fawcett, S. (1991). Social validity: A note on methodology. *Journal of Applied Behavior Analysis, 24,* 235–239.

Fletcher, J., Francis, D., Shaywitz, S., Lyon, G.R., Foorman, B., Stuebing, K., et al. (1998). Intelligent testing and the discrepancy model for children with learning disabilities. *Learning Disabilities Research & Practice, 13,* 186–203.

Fuchs, D., Mock, D., Morgan, P., & Young, C. (2003). Responsiveness to intervention: Definitions, evidence, and implications for the learning disabilities construct. *Learning Disabilities Research and Practice, 18,* 157–171.

Fuchs, L. (2002). Three conceptualizations of "treatment" in a responsiveness-to-treatment framework for LD identification. In R. Bradley, L. Danielson, & D. Hallahan (Eds.), *Identification of learning disabilities; Research to practice* (pp. 521–529). Mahwah, NJ: Erlbaum.

Fuchs, L., & Fuchs, D. (1998). Treatment validity: A unifying concept for reconceptualizing the identification of learning disabilities. *Learning Disabilities Research and Practice, 13,* 204–219.

Gresham, F.M. (1981). Social skills training with handicapped children: A review. *Review of Educational Research, 51,* 139–176.

Gresham, F.M. (1989). Assessment of treatment integrity in school consultation and prereferral intervention. *School Psychology Review, 18,* 37–50.

Gresham, F.M. (1991). Conceptualizing behavior disorders in terms of resistance to intervention. *School Psychology Review, 20,* 23–36.

Gresham, F.M. (1997). Treatment integrity in single-subject research. In R. Franklin, D. Allison, & B. Gorman (Eds.), *Design and analysis of single-case research* (pp. 93–118). Mahwah, NJ: Erlbaum.

Gresham, F.M. (2002). Responsiveness to intervention: An alternative approach to the identification of learning disabilities. In R. Bradley, L. Danielson, & D. Hallahan (Eds.), *Identification of learning disabilities: Research to practice* (pp. 467–519). Mahwah, NJ: Erlbaum.

Gresham, F.M. (2004). Current status and future direction of school-based behavioral interventions. *School Psychology Review, 33,* 326–343.

Gresham, F.M. (2006). Responsiveness to intervention. In G. Bear & K. Minke (Eds.), *Children's needs III: Development, prevention, and intervention* (pp. 525–540). Bethesda, MD: National Association of School Psychologists.

Gresham, F.M. (2008). Best practices in diagnosis in a multitier problem-solving approach. In A. Thomas & J. Grimes (Eds.), *Best practices in school psychology V* (vol. 2, pp. 281–294). Bethesda, MD: National Association of School Psychologists.

Gresham, F.M., & Lopez, M. (1996). Social validation: A unifying concept for school-based consultation research and practice. *School Psychology Quarterly, 11,* 204–227.

Gresham, F.M., MacMillan, D.L., &Bocian, K. (1996). Learning disabilities, low achievement, and mild mental retardation: More alike than different? *Journal of Learning Disabilities, 29,* 570–581.

Gresham, F.M., MacMillan, D.L., &Bocian, K. (1998). Agreement between school study team decisions and authoritative definitions in classification of students at-risk for mild disabilities. *School Psychology Quarterly, 13,* 181–191.

Gresham, F. M., Watson, T.S., & Skinner, C. (2001). Functional behavioral assessment: Principles, procedures, and future directions. *School Psychology Review, 30,* 156–172.

Gresham, F.M., & Witt, J.C. (1997). Utility of intelligence tests for treatment planning, classification, and placement decisions: Recent empirical findings and future directions. *School Psychology Quarterly, 12,* 249–267.

Grimes, J. (2002). Responsiveness to interventions: The next step in special education identification, service, and exiting decision making. In R. Bradley, L. Danielson, & D. Hallahan (Eds.), *Identification of learning disabilities: Research to practice* (pp. 531–547). Mahwah, NJ: Erlbaum.

Hawkins, R. (1991). Is social validity what we are interested in? Argument for a functional approach. *Journal of Applied Behavior Analysis, 24,* 205–213.

Hayes, S., Nelson, R., & Jarrett, R. (1987). The treatment utility of assessment: A functional approach to evaluating assessment quality. *American Psychologist, 42,* 963–974.

Heller, K., Holtzman, W., & Messick, S. (Eds.) (1982). *Placing children in special education: A strategy for equity.* Washington, DC: National Academy Press.

Individuals with Disabilities Education Improvement Act (2004). Pub. L 108–446.

Jacobson, N., Follette, W., & Revenstorf, D. (1988). Statistics for assessing clinical significance of psychotherapy techniques: Issues, problems, and new developments. *Behavioral Assessment, 10,* 133–145.

Kazdin, A. (2003). Clinical significance: Measuring whether interventions make a difference. In A. Kazdin (Ed.), *Methodological issues & strategies in clinical research* (3rd ed., pp. 691–710). Washington, DC: American Psychological Association.

MacMillan, D.L., & Siperstein, G.N. (2002). Learning disabilities as operationally defined by schools. In R. Bradley, L. Danielson, & D. Hallahan (Eds.), *Identification of learning disabilities: Research to practice* (pp. 287–333). Mahwah, NJ: Erlbaum.

MacMillan, D.L., Gresham, F.M., & Bocian, K. (1997). The role of assessment in qualifying students as eligible for special education: What is and what's supposed to be. *Focus on Exceptional Children, 30,* 1–20.

Messick, S. (1995). Validity of psychological assessment: Validation of inferences from persons' responses and performances as scientific inquiry into score meaning. *American Psychologist, 50,* 741–749.

Mastropieri, M., & Scruggs, T. (1985–1986). Early intervention for socially withdrawn children. *The Journal of Special Education, 19,* 429–441.

Miltenberger, R. (2004). *Behavior modification: Principles and procedures* (3rd ed.). Belmont, CA: Wadsworth/Thomson Learning.

Nevin, J. (1988). Behavioral momentum and the partial reinforcement effect. *Psychological Bulletin, 103,* 44–56.

President's Commission on Excellence in Special Education (2004). *A new era: Revitalizing special education for children and families.* Washington, DC: United States Department of Education, Author.

Reschly, D.J. (2008). School psychology paradigm shift and beyond. In A. Thomas & J. Grimes (Eds.), *Best practices in school psychology V* (Vol. 2, pp. 3–16). Bethesda, MD: National Association of School Psychologists.

Schwartz, I., & Baer, D. (1991). Social validity assessment: Is current practice state of the art? *Journal of Applied Behavior Analysis, 24,* 189–204.

Sechrest, L., McKnight, P., & McKnight, K. (1996). Calibration of measures for psychotherapy outcome studies. *American Psychologist, 51,* 1065–1071.

Shinn, M. (2008). Best practices in using curriculum-based measurement in a problem-solving model. In A. Thomas & J. Grimes (Eds.), *Best practices in school psychology V* (vol. 2, pp. 243–261). Bethesda, MD: National Association of School Psychologists.

Strain, P., Kohler, F., & Gresham, F.M. (1998). Problems in logic and interpretation of quantitative synthesis of single case research: Mather and colleagues as a case in point. *Behavioral Disorders, 24,* 74–85.

Steubing, K., Fletcher, J., LeDoux, J., Lyon, G.R., Shaywitz, S., & Shaywitz, B. (2002). Validity of IQ-discrepancy classification in reading disabilities: A meta-analysis. *American Educational Research Journal, 39,* 469–518.

Tilly, W.D. (2002). Best practices in school psychology as a problem-solving enterprise. In A. Thomas & J. Grimes (Eds.), *Best practices in school psychology IV* (pp. 21–36). Bethesda, MD: National Association of School Psychologists.

Torgesen, J., Alexander, A., Wagner, R., Rashotte, C., Voeller, K., & Conway, T. (2001). Intensive remedial instruction for children with severe reading disabilities: Immediate and long-term outcomes from two instructional approaches. *Journal of Learning Disabilities, 34,* 33–58.

Torgesen, J., Wagner, R., Rashotte, C., Rose, E., Lindamood, P., Conway, T., et al. (1999). Preventing reading failure in young children with phonological processing disabilities; Group and individual response to instruction. *Journal of Educational Psychology, 91,* 579–593.

Van DerHeyden, A., & Witt, J.C. (2008). Best practices in can't do/won't do assessment. In A. Thomas & J. Grimes (Eds.), *Best practices in school psychology V* (vol. 2, pp. 131–140). Bethesda, MD: National Association of School Psychologists.

Van DerHeyden, A., Witt, J.C., & Naquin, G. (2003). The development and validation of a process for screening referrals to special education. *School Psychology Review, 32,* 204–227.

Vaughn, S. (2002). Using response to treatment for identifying students with learning disabilities. In R. Bradley, L. Danielson, & D. Hallahan (Eds.), *Identification of learning disabilities: Research to practice* (pp. 549–554). Mahwah, NJ: Erlbaum.

Vaughn, S., & Fuchs, L. (2003). Redefining learning disabilities as inadequate response to instruction: The promise and potential problems. *Learning Disabilities Research & Practice, 18,* 137–146.

Vaughn, S., Linan-Thompson, S., & Hickman, P. (2003). Response to instruction as a means of identifying students with reading/learning disabilities. *Exceptional Children, 69,* 391–409.

Vellutino, F.R. (1987). Dyslexia. *Scientific American, 256,* 33–41.

Vellutino, F.R. (2002). On the role of intervention in identifying learning disabilities. In R. Bradley, L. Danielson, & D. Hallahan (Eds.), *Identification of learning disabilities: Research to practice* (pp. 555–564). Mahwah, NJ: Erlbaum.

Vellutino, F.R., Scanlon, D., Sipay, E., Small, S., Pratt, A., Chen, R., et al. (1996). Cognitive profiles of difficult-to-remediate and readily remediated poor readers: Early intervention as a vehicle for distinguishing between cognitive and experiential deficits as basic causes of special reading disabilities. *Journal of Educational Psychology, 88,* 601–638.

Walker, H.M., Ramsay, E., & Gresham, F.M. (2004). *Antisocial behavior in school: Evidence-based practices* (2nd ed.). Belmont, CA: Wadsworth/Thomson Learning.

Wolf, M.M. (1978). Social validity: The case for subjective measurement or how applied behavior analysis is finding its heart. *Journal of Applied Behavior Analysis, 11,* 203–214.

Yeaton, W., & Sechrest, L. (1981). Critical dimensions in the choice and maintenance of successful treatments: Strength, intensity, and effectiveness. *Journal of Consulting and Clinical Psychology, 49,* 156–167.

Ysseldyke, J., & Marston, D. (1999). Origins of categorical special education services in schools and a rationale for changing them. In D. Reschly, W.D. Tilly, & J. Grimes (Eds.), *Special education in transition: Functional assessment and noncategorical programming* (pp. 1–18). Longmont, CO: Sopris West.

Counseling in the Practice of School Psychology

Tony D. Crespi *and* Denise E. Laramboise

Abstract

Counseling services, including individual counseling and group counseling, can serve as an invaluable service provision by school psychologists. While individual psychological assessment services and teacher and parent consultation often occupies the bulk of a workday, a wide spectrum of psychological problems affecting children has increasingly amplified the importance of individual and group counseling initiatives. Given the complexity of individual and group counseling interventions, though, and given the complex nature of counseling practices when applied within the schools, many school psychologists find contemporary counseling challenging. This article reviews mental health issues impacting children's mental health, considers differing individual and group counseling models, examines contemporary legal issues inherent in school practice, and considers future directions.

Keywords: counseling, school counseling, counseling and school psychology; individual counseling, group counseling, family counseling, therapeutic alliance, client-centered therapy, motivational interviewing, cognitive behavioral therapy, solution focused therapy, microskills.

Psychological problems in children are significant and widespread. Power, Eiraldi, Clarke, Mazzuca, and Krain (2005) reported, for instance, that mental health problems are common in children. Of course, this not new; in fact, more than a decade ago the Carnegie Council on Adolescent Development (1996) observed that more than 8 million children are in need of psychological services, yet Ringel and Sturm (2001) estimate that 75% of children with emotional disorders do not receive services. Tolan and Dodge (2005) suggest that a serious crisis is evident in children's mental health.

Looking within this broad perspective, the situation is quite dire. Duchnowski, Kutash, and Friedman (2002) reported that approximately 10% of adolescents have moderate to severe mental health problems necessitating intervention, and 20% have mental health problems creating at least mild problems.

Indeed, though, what are the issues impacting children? Root and Resnick (2003) estimate that 3%

to 7% of children have attention-deficit/hyperactivity disorder (ADHD), and Pope and Hudson (1992) noted that as many as 67% of children experience sexual abuse. Still, this only offers a glimpse of a much larger problem. Unfortunately, as many as 1 in 7 adolescents has no health insurance, and is therefore unable to receive third-party reimbursable mental health services in the private sector (Crespi and Howe, 2002). Thus, while the need for mental health services and counseling is significant and growing, access to affordable services in the community appears to be shrinking, creating growing numbers of children in the school system with unmet needs. Thus, in fact, mental health services offered in the school are often the only services available to students (Auger, 2005).

Fortunately for the 52 million children attending public schools, as noted by Jamieson, Curry, & Martinez (2001), school psychologists are in a key position to address this pressing issue. In many ways, the school environment is well suited for the provision of counseling services (Leaf et al., 1996). Students spend at least 6 hours a day at school, in a context which places cognitive, social and emotional demands on them, and school personnel are in a unique position to identify and evaluate problems soon after they develop, and to intervene quickly to prevent more serious problems. Indeed, Roberts, et al. (2003) note that children with severe psychological and behavioral disorders pose significant challenges for teachers, and that school psychologists are frequently requested to identify, diagnose, and design interventions for these youth.

As an added benefit, while attrition rates for youth services in community clinics can be as high as 60% (Ambruster & Kazdin, 1994), the school provides an environment where children already show up, and a structure through which regular contact is easily maintained.

Overall, then, with the average child spending approximately 6 hours each day in school, and given that academic performance and behavioral adjustment are correlated, school based counseling is becoming an increasingly important role for school psychologists.

Putting this together, this article provides a brief overview on psychological issues impacting children, and reviews major models of individual and group counseling. The overall intention is to provide a resource and reference for practitioners interested in providing school based counseling services.

Psychological Issues Supporting Counseling in School Psychology

Children are in need of counseling to a greater degree than at any time in history. Huang et al. (2005) noted that 1 in 5 children have a diagnosable mental disorder. In an earlier work, Crespi (1997) noted that such issues as parental divorce, alcoholism in the home, depression, suicide, and physical, sexual, and emotional abuse represent a sampling of problems which children bring to school, and which can be addressed in school based counseling. In addition, school psychologists are commonly called on to intervene in cases of student behavioral problems in the classroom, such student aggression, defiance, or bullying, for problems with motivation, and diverse interpersonal problems.

Sadly, school psychologists facilitating individual and group counseling have a large array of issues available that can nicely serve as topics for counseling. Looking at home–school concerns, as an example, Crespi and Howe (2002) noted that only 7%

of youth actually live in traditional families, with varying family configurations creating issues that can affect classroom attention and overall adjustment. Still, this only partially glimpses the issues. Approximately 80% of children witness spousal abuse, and problems including sexual abuse and aggression highlight the pictures of families in turmoil (Crespi & Howe, 2002). Parental abuse is also an important area of focus. One in seven children report having been punched, kicked, or choked by a parent (Moore, 1994). Fortunately, and of note, school professionals can socialize children to different behaviors to decrease the chances of their emulating aggressive and violent behavior learned at home (Dworetzky, 1996).

Individual Counseling

One-on-one counseling approaches represent the most commonly practiced psychological interventions in general clinical practice, and even in the school environment these approaches are used more often by school psychologists than any other intervention modality (Prout et al., 1993). Although individual counseling is more time and resource intensive than other intervention modalities, such as group counseling or classroom-based interventions, it offers a number of advantages to those alternatives. Individually based interventions allow for a treatment approach uniquely tailored to each student's particular issues, needs, and goals. In addition, one-on-one counseling affords the opportunity to develop a strong therapeutic relationship between the school psychologist and the student, which can be called upon in the future should the need arise.

School based individual counseling, however, presents unique challenges that arise out of the demands and constraints inherent in the school environment. Prout et al. (1993) found that practicing school psychologists reported individual counseling sessions were typically 30–40 minutes, and individual cases lasted an average of ten sessions. Thus, the constraints of the school-day schedule, and limited resources, necessitate briefer sessions and a shorter course of treatment than typical of traditional clinical environments. Another unique challenge to the school based practitioner is the ambiguous nature of the client. That is, although the identified client is ostensibly the student, in treating a case, school psychologists are also meeting the needs of teachers, parents, and even administrators, and may work extensively with any of these individuals. Lastly, students can be challenging clients. Students are rarely self-referred, but are more commonly sent to school psychologists by teachers, administrators, or parents. As such, students may not recognize or acknowledge problems, or may feel misunderstood, wrongly blamed, or stigmatized by the referral (Shirk and Karver, 2003). The nature of the referral may result in poor motivation for treatment, or outright hostility or defiance. This stance may be particularly common among adolescents referred for work with school psychologists (Lambie, 2004).

Given the above considerations, it might be understandable to question how effective individual counseling can be when offered in the schools. Reviews of outcome studies of psychotherapy interventions with children and adolescents indicate that there is sound empirical support for the effectiveness of counseling with youth. Several meta-analytic studies have found that children and adolescents in distress who receive counseling or psychotherapy fare better than those who do not receive these services, that the interventions are moderately successful at their targeted goals, and that the benefits of counseling are lasting (Roberts et al, 2003). The good news for school psychologists is that despite the challenges of working in school settings, school based psychotherapy and counseling shows moderate effectiveness, on par with results found in the research literature on psychotherapy outcomes for adults in general clinical environments (Prout & DeMartino, 1986).

Given the demonstrable benefits of individual school based counseling for children and adolescents, the question becomes not *whether* school psychology practices should include individual counseling, but the methods to adopt to optimize counseling outcomes. School psychologists have historically described themselves as "eclectic pragmatists" in their practice of counseling (Sandoval, 1993), and they have traditionally adopted a wide range of therapeutic approaches. For instance, Prout et al. (1993) found that school psychologists tended to report cognitive-behavioral orientations as most useful, but endorsed a variety of orientations as *occasionally* or *often* useful, including multimodal therapy, reality therapy, family systems, social learning, and client-centered approaches. Consideration of the psychotherapy outcome literature from the past 15 years, and the unique parameters of school based counseling interventions, suggest several principles and approaches as worthy of particular attention for school psychologists in their individual therapeutic work with students.

The Primacy of the Therapeutic Relationship

One consistent finding which has emerged from psychotherapy outcome research is that while psychotherapy is found to be generally effective, outcomes tend to be similar across widely divergent therapeutic approaches (Lambert and Ogles, 2004). These results have stimulated examination of the factors that are common across all counseling and psychotherapy approaches. One of the common factors research has pointed to is the critical role that the therapeutic relationship plays in therapy effectiveness. In fact, it is estimated that the therapeutic relationship accounts for 30% of the variance in psychotherapy outcomes, or twice what is accounted for by technique or therapeutic orientation (Asay & Lambert, 1999). The importance of the therapeutic relationship has been hypothesized as possibly even more critical to success in work with children and adolescents (Murphy, 1999). Shirk and Karver (2003) carried out a meta-analysis of the research linking the therapeutic relationship with outcomes in child and adolescent therapy, and found that relationship variables were modestly but consistently correlated with outcome across diverse types and modes of therapy for children and adolescents.

Based on this work, we know that a simple but powerful therapeutic tool that school psychologists can use to effect favorable counseling outcomes is the development of warm, positive therapeutic relationships, and a shared sense of goals and active collaborations often referred to as the *therapeutic alliance* (Lambert and Ogles, 2004). Simply stated, when children feel respected, heard, and understood by someone they feel they can trust, they will be more open, self-disclosing, and motivated to change, and more receptive and responsive to interventions.

The techniques and strategies used to foster positive therapeutic relationships are based on the humanistic orientation of client-centered psychotherapy, and hinge on the foundational techniques of active listening and reflection taught in most introductory counseling courses. Broken down into its most basic elements, Ivey and Ivey (2006) identify the microskills involved in listening and empathic understanding, including: attending behavior; use of open questions; observation skills; encouraging, paraphrasing, and summarizing; and noting and reflecting feelings. All told, then, the use of a broadly humanistic approach, emphasizing a warm caring relationship and exploration of client feelings and experiences, may be sufficient to provide substantial improvement in some cases seen by school psychologists (Auger, 2005).

Motivation Enhancement Approaches

As noted above, students referred for counseling or psychotherapy in the school setting often come to the table denying problems, or lacking motivation for treatment. Fortunately, clinicians have available empirically supported strategies for enhancing insight and increasing motivation for change. *Motivational interviewing* is a set of techniques and strategies originally developed for use with substance abusers, another population often considered resistant to treatment, or unmotivated for change (Miller & Rolnick, 2002). However, the approach uses many of the principles from client-centered and cognitive orientations, and can be used successfully in school-based individual counseling (Lambie, 2004). These strategies are primarily intended as very brief interventions (one to three sessions, typically) to facilitate greater problem recognition and motivation for change at the beginning stages of counseling, after which work can shift to change-focused approaches (Miller & Rolnick, 2002).

Lambie (2004) reviews the basic principles and strategies of motivational enhancement approaches as applied to school settings. First, ambivalence and resistance to change is viewed as a normal response. It is understood that when pushed for change from outside, individuals often feel as though their autonomy and personal control are being challenged, and react with a "push back" response. Therefore, motivational enhancement approaches seek to use active listening and gentle feedback approaches instead of confrontation strategies, in order to encourage problem recognition from the student. These strategies allow students to explore all aspects of the problem issue, focusing on the perceived positives as well as negatives of their behavior or problem, and what they have to gain or lose by changing. A "decisional balance sheet" technique can be used, in which the student lists the pros and cons of changing, as well as the pros and cons of staying the same.

Throughout the process, the clinician emphasizes the student's control and personal choice in the issue. However, the clinician listens for and emphasizes "change talk," or insight and acknowledgement that a problem may exist, and that change may be beneficial (Lambie, 2004; Miller and Rollnick, 2002). Further, the clinician emphasizes the student's ability to confront the problem and successfully negotiate change, as individuals will only move toward change when they believe there is a viable pathway, and a reasonable chance for success.

Cognitive Behavioral Approaches

Among school psychologists, behavioral and cognitive-behavioral approaches have traditionally been popular and viewed as useful (Prout et al., 1993; Sandoval, 1993). These approaches seem tailor-made for the kind of counseling conducted in school settings: they tend to be oriented toward work on specific, concrete problems, symptoms, and disorders; they are present-focused, structured, and geared toward short-term treatment. Indeed, their efficacy for in these contexts is borne out empirically. While Prout and DeMartino's (1986) meta-analysis of school based psychotherapy found that all therapy orientations were effective generally, they found the largest effect sizes for behavioral and cognitive approaches. These authors also found that the problems treated most successfully were observable behaviors, and problem-solving skills. Roberts et al. (2003) conducted a review of the evidence-based support for therapeutic approaches across specific problem domains. Their review determined that cognitive-behavioral therapy (CBT) approaches were unequivocally the most effective treatments for anxiety disorders, including obsessive-compulsive disorder and post-traumatic stress disorder. Their findings replicate strong empirical support for CBT approaches with youth in traditional clinical settings (Braswell & Kendall, 2001), and in general, mirror the treatment outcome literature for adults, which consistently find CBT to be highly effective for treating anxiety disorders. While findings supporting CBT are not as robust for depressive disorders, CBT continues to be a viable and effective treatment approach (Roberts et al., 2003; Auger, 2005).

Given the strong evidence supporting CBT as the most effective treatment approach for anxiety in children and adolescents, and the high prevalence of anxiety disorders among children and adolescents (McLoone et al., 2006), all school psychologists who provide individual counseling should have some acquaintance with the basic arsenal of cognitive-behavioral techniques and strategies. Fortunately, CBT techniques are relatively straightforward to learn, since they are based on a very structured approach for which a number of step-by-step manuals are available (McLoone et al., 2006; Roberts et al., 2003). Roberts et al. (2003) advise that school psychologists invest in a number of CBT treatment programs such as Philip Kendall's "Coping Cat" program, a manualized individual treatment for anxiety in 9- to 13-year-olds.

Solution-Focused Brief Therapy

A relatively new but increasingly popular addition to the battery of school psychology therapy approaches is *solution-focused brief therapy* (SFBT). This approach seems ideally suited to school-based individual counseling for a number of reasons: it is even briefer than cognitive behavioral approaches, fitting well into the brief time frames afforded individual interventions in the school; it is present and future oriented; and it is limited in scope to addressing a single, specific problem or issue (Mostert et al., 1997).

In addition, SFBT has the unique and appealing perspective of a strengths-based approach. That is, clients' positive behavior is emphasized, and clients are seen as capable of solving their own problems through their strengths and positive qualities. In this spirit, the student's problem is not the focus of treatment so much as what are called "exceptions"— times when the problem is not present, or is present to a lesser degree. Through this positive lens, the focus of treatment is not on decreasing or eliminating negative behavior or the problem, but *increasing* positive behavior, or exceptions to the problem. This positive focus engenders hope, and enhances self-efficacy and self-esteem in students (Newsome, 2005).

Although not yet as extensive as support for CBT, solution-focused brief therapy appears quite promising, and is accumulating a body of evidence supporting its efficacy in general clinical use, as well as in schools (Franklin et al., 2008; Newsome, 2005). Murphy (1994) provides a useful overview of the approach, emphasizing the SFBT principle that it is easier to get students to increase successful behaviors and strategies than to eliminate negative behaviors or problems. He goes on to describe the "5-E" method utilized in SFBT:

- Task One, Eliciting: Allow client to thoroughly describe his or her concerns and problems while being alert to possible exceptions to the problem pattern.
- Task Two, Elaborating: Instances of times of exception to the problem or symptoms are explored through questions about the client's experiences and circumstances, in order to understand the necessary conditions for the exceptions.
- Task Three, Expanding: The task of treatment focuses on increasing instances of exception (times when the problem is not present or less severe) through generalizing

exceptions to more situations, and increasing the frequency of exceptions. Clients are encouraged to "do more of" what's already working for them.
- Task Four, Evaluating: Effectiveness of the efforts is evaluated based on predetermined goals. Scaled questions (ratings on a scale of 1 to 10, for instance) are frequently used in SFBT
- Task Five, Empowering: Encourage the client to take ownership of the changes they have made in order to increase self-efficacy and maintain the changes over time. This includes strategies such as asking questions like, "How were you able to make that change?" or "What will you do to continue with these successes?"

In sum, individual counseling interventions offer a host of options for helping students with mental health and behavioral problems which are backed up by strong research evidence for their effectiveness. While more time and resource intensive than alternative modes of intervention, individual counseling also offers distinctive advantages in its ability to allow a treatment approach to be uniquely tailored to the individual student's needs and goals, and to foster a more intensive, positive relationship between student and school. In all cases the development of this strong therapeutic bond forms the basic foundation to successful intervention, and in some instances the general person-centered approach, which has as its centerpiece the therapeutic relationship, is enough to support and encourage students, leading to successful outcomes. In more challenging cases, treatment approaches such as motivational enhancement techniques, cognitive-behavioral strategies, and solution-focused brief therapy offer proven strategies for addressing specific challenges successfully.

Group Counseling

Group counseling represents an important model for addressing children's psychological needs. In fact, Littrell and Peterson (2002) observed that groups afford the opportunity to positively impact the school. Unfortunately, while the National Association of School Psychologists addresses a need for counseling training, specialty training in group counseling is not specifically required (Fleming, 1999). Elsewhere, Schaefer (1999) observed that on an individual level, short-term counseling can be most effective in helping children develop adaptive processes for coping with a range of problems. Overall, groups can be positive. Still, what types of groups are generally used? What "stages" characterize group process? What programmatic issues need to be considered in initiating group counseling services?

Shechtman (2002) outlined major group types:

- Educational Groups: Typically these groups are targeted toward the normal population, and may address social skills issues including classroom behavior, school performance, and peer relations.
- Counseling Groups: Typically these groups are targeted toward children with developmental challenges, with the groups often addressing self-esteem and social challenge issues.
- Therapy Groups: Typically these groups are targeted at severe adjustment and behavioral difficulties in children, ranging from aggressive and violent behavior to eating disorders and severe psychological disorders including depression and suicide.

Group Stages

For professionals involved in facilitating groups, five stages can serve as a theoretical foundation for understanding group development. These stages follow:

- The Forming Stage: This stage is characterized by an initial orientation to the group with initial dependence and structure formation. Polite discourse, rules, and silences are typical of this stage.
  - Courtesy: Meet, greet, and develop rapport.
  - Confusion: Following basic instructions, members operate with little direction.
  - Caution: Concern about statements outside boundaries.
  - Commonality: Bonds of similarity among members emerge.
- The Storming Stage: This stage is characterized by conflict and competition, as group members interact and struggle with individual and group dynamics. Disagreements over process, anger, critical discourse on rules and ideas, and basic hostility often mark this stage.
  - Concern: No member should harm another.
  - Conflict: As bonds of similarity arise, dissimilarity appears.

- Confrontation: Members learn how to confront others.
- Criticism: As lack of progress occurs, criticisms emerge.

- The Norming Stage: This stage is characterized by a beginning sense of cohesiveness, as members experiment with new roles. Basic harmony, established rules and roles, and a beginning sense of support are characteristic of this stage.
  - Cooperation: Members address basic rules.
  - Collaboration: As rules emerge, agreement is needed on process.
  - Cohesion: Togetherness emerges.
  - Commitment: As a group unit, they move forward.

- The Performing Stage: This stage is characterized by supportive process, as basic conflicts have been resolved and as members are able to "perform." High task orientation, productivity, decreased emotionality, and enhanced problem solving mark this stage.
  - Challenge: Members feel increased responsibility for the group.
  - Creativity: New methods of communication emerge.
  - Consciousness: With increased openness, member self-recognition increases.
  - Consideration: Increased awareness of self and others merges.

- The Adjourning Stage: This stage is characterized by general termination and closure, as the group ends its meetings and plans for participants to utilize learned skills elsewhere.
  - Compromise: Members recognize unresolved issues and strive for balance.
  - Communication: An awareness of changes through communication occurs.
  - Consensus: Members deal with conflict through compromise.
  - Closure: Reluctantly at times, members face closure and termination.

Legal Issues in School Practice

Schools possess unique structural dimensions. This section overviews key legal issues impacting counseling.

Consent. Consent, informed consent, involves a patient or legal guardian's consent to treatment, or for release of treatment information. All minors must have parent permission to participate in counseling. Further, school psychologists might consider securing consent from participants as well as legal guardians, thereby securing emotional commitments from both parties.

Notification. Notification is generally a lower standard for practice than the acquisition of informed consent. Unfortunately, many students do not read student handbooks, student handouts, nor mailings provided in the course of a school year. Because many students do not read such materials, written notification alone may not be adequate. Signed consents are preferable.

Confidentiality. Confidentiality involves the legal obligation not to disclose information surrounding treatment. While adults in counseling own "privilege" and, thus, confidentiality, parents, not minors, actually own privilege. As such, participants should be appropriately informed about limits of confidentiality and disclosure issues. Appropriate safeguards should be implemented to maximize confidentiality through careful selection of setting and through participant and parent contracts.

Dangerous Behavior. How should one proceed if a concern arises regarding danger to self or others? Schools should develop policies and procedures for such situations in order to adequately protect both counseling participants as well as practitioners. While there may be situations where suicidal risk, as example, may seem so eminent that an emergency room visit may be required, or a risk to safety so evident that police must be contacted immediately, more commonly a student may simply make a comment worthy of concern but not evidenced by behavior necessarily supportive of a concurrent threat? An immediate consultation and interview by another school mental health professional is one viable option with a consensus guiding decision making.

Disclosure. How should a practitioner proceed, if a parent or teacher requests details from counseling? Must a practitioner disclose confidential information? Unfortunately, while disclosure may compromise therapeutic progress and basic trust, parents "own" privilege related to a minor's confidentiality. While it makes sense to explain to a parent that breaking confidentiality may compromise a child's trust and progress, it is also true that a school psychologist must share counseling content details if requested, as the parent, not the child, owns privilege and confidentiality.

In contrast, a practitioner must protect a child's privilege and confidentiality with a teacher and, therefore, cannot disclose nor discuss a child's involvement, nor progress. A school psychologist might proactively explain about confidentiality to staff and colleagues prior to initiating counseling.

Summary and Conclusions

Behavior, adjustment, and psychological problems have increased in children. Issues including family discord, parental neglect and abuse, sexual abuse, attention disorders, and violence in the home, all impact children's adjustment (American Psychiatric Association, 2000). Unfortunately, large numbers of children exhibit multiple disorders. Riddle and Bergin (1997) noted, for instance, that 28.6 million children live within an alcoholic family; Pope and Hudson (1992) estimated that as many as 67% of children may experience sexual abuse and, more globally, the Carnegie Council on Adolescent Development (1996) reported that there are more than 8 million children in need of psychological services.

In a basic way, then, school based counseling initiatives offer ample issues and topics from which to develop counseling programs. With 1 in 7 children having been punched, kicked, or choked by a parent (Moore, 1994), with children from violent homes demonstrating violent behavior at school (Crespi & Howe, 2002), and with the knowledge that school professionals can socialize children to different behaviors to decrease the chances of emulating aggressive and violent behavior learned at home (Dworetzky, 1996), group counseling programs are of increasing importance.

It makes sense, then, to offer comprehensive counseling programs in the schools. Crespi and Rigazio-DiGilio (1996) noted that school-based early intervention programs can decrease delinquent behaviors in youth, and universally it has been noted that schools function as a vital resource for psychological services. Yet, counseling often is not the focus of training in school psychology graduate education.

Looking to the future, coursework guided by evidenced-based practice will likely become more commonplace in counseling training. One especially difficult area in school practice, yet to be fully addressed, involves parental requests for disclosure of counseling content. With legal mandates necessitating breaches in confidentiality, students cannot be expected to be completely forthcoming. Changes in legal standards for consent and disclosure could ultimately address this highly complex issue.

Key questions to be addressed follow:

1) Should practitioners advocate for the elimination of parental consent for participation in counseling? Since it is reasonable to assume that not all students wish to have parental figures know their interest in counseling, parental consents can actually reduce participation. Future directions could, though, modify these requirements.

2) Should school psychologists be required to disclose counseling content to parents? Since parents own "privilege," disclosure is required at present. At the same time, this can reduce trust in the therapeutic process. Future initiatives might massage this issue to more effectively encourage candid participation by clients.

3) Should training standards mandate specific hours of client contact during training? At present, training standards do not specify the degree of counseling experience required in training. Future standards might create minimum hourly requirements in individual and group counseling by school psychologists in training.

This article has been constructed to serve as a resource. In a broad way, while children are coping with an extraordinary array of problems and stressors, school psychologists have the opportunity to offer students an array of positive interventions. Individual and group counseling can be useful intervention models that can positively impact children. The challenge, from this point forward, is helping practitioners and schools begin to implement the model.

References

Ambruster, P., & Kazdin, A. E. (1994). Attrition in child psychotherapy. *Advances in Clinical Child Psychology, 16*, 81–108.

American Psychiatric Association. (2000). *Diagnostic and statistical manual of mental disorders* (4th ed). Washington, DC: Author.

Asay, T. P. & Lambert, M. J. (1999). The empirical case for common factors in therapy: Quantitative findings. In M. A. Hubble, B. L. Duncan, & S. D. Miller (Eds.) *The heart and soul of change: What works in therapy* (pp. 23–55). Washington, DC: American Psychological Association.

Auger, R. W. (2005). School-based interventions for students with depressive disorders. *Professional School Counseling, 8*(4), 344–352.

Barke, L.A. & Adilman, H.S. (1994). Mental health and help-seeking among ethnic minority adolescents. *Journal of Adolescence, 17*, 251–263.

Braswell, L. & Kendall, P. C. (2001). Cognitive–behavioral therapy with youth. In Dobson, K. S. (Ed.), *Handbook of cognitive behavioral therapies*. New York: Guilford Press.

Carnegie Council on Adolescent Development. (1996). *Great transitions: Preparing adolescents for a new century*. New York: Author.

Crespi, T.D. (1997). Bridging the home-school connection: Family therapy and the school psychologist. *Family Therapy, 24*, 209–215.

Crespi, T.D., & Howe, E.A. (2002). Families in crisis: Considerations for special service providers in the schools. *Special Services in the Schools, 18*, 43–54.

Crespi, T.D., & Rigazio-DiGilio, S.A. (1996). Adolescent homicide and family pathology: Implications for research and treatment with adolescents. *Adolescence, 31*, 353–367.

Duchnowski, A.J., Kutash, J., & Friedman, R.M. (2002). Community-based interventions in a system of care and outcomes framework. In B.J. Burns & K. Hoagwood (Eds.), *Community treatment for youth: Evidenced-based interventions for severe emotional and behavioral disorders* (pp. 16–37). New York: Oxford University Press.

Dworetzky, J.P. (1996). *Introduction to child development* (Sixth Edition). St. Paul, MN: West Publishing.

Fleming, V.M. (1999). Group counseling in the schools: A case for basic training. *Professional School Counseling, 2*, 409–414.

Franklin, C., Moore, K., & Hopson, L. (2008). Effectiveness of solution-focused brief therapy in a school setting. *Children and Schools, 30*(1), 15–26.

Huang, L., Stroul, B., Friedman, R., Mrazek, P., Friesen, B., Pires, S., & Mayberg, S. (2005). Transforming mental health care for children and their families. *American Psychologist, 60*, 615–627.

Ivey, A. E., & Ivey, M. B. (2006). *Intentional interviewing and counseling: Facilitating client development in a multicultural society* (6th ed.). Pacific Grove, CA: Brooks/Cole.

Jamieson, A., Curry, A., & Martinez, G. (2001). *School enrollment in the United States – Social and economic characteristics of students* (Current Population Report No. P20–533). Washington, DC: U.S. Bureau of the Census.

Lambert, M. J., & Ogles, B. M. (2004). Efficacy and Effectiveness of Psychotherapy. In Lambert, M. J. (Ed.), *Bergin and Garfield's handbook of psychotherapy and behavior change* (pp.139–193). New York: John Wiley & Sons.

Lambie, G. W. (2004). Motivational enhancement therapy: A tool for professional school counselors working with adolescents. *Professional School Counseling, 7*(4), 268–276.

Leaf, P.J., Alegria, M., Cohen, P., Goodman, S.H., Horwitz, S.M., Hoven, C.W., Narrow, W.E., Vanden-Kiernan, M., & Regier, D.A.(1996). Mental health service use in the community and schools: Results from the four-community MECA study. *Journal of the American Academy of Child and Adolescent Psychiatry, 35*, 889–897.

Littrell, J.M., & Peterson, J.S. (2002). Establishing a comprehensive group work program in an elementary school: An in-depth case study. *Journal For Specialists In Group Work, 27*, 161–172.

McLoone, J., Hudson, J.L., & Rapee, R.M. (2006). Treating anxiety disorders in a school setting. *Education and Treatment of Children, 29*(2), 219–242.

Miller, W. R. & Rollnick, S. (2002). *Motivational interviewing: Preparing people to change addictive behavior.* (2nd ed.). New York: Guilford Press.

Moore, D.W. (1994). One in seven Americans are victims of child abuse. *The Gallup Poll Monthly*, 18–22.

Mostert, D. L., Johnson, R., & Mostert, M. P., (1997). The utility of solution-focused brief counseling in schools: Potential from an initial study. *Professional School Counseling, 1*(1), 21–24.

Murphy, J. J. (1994). Working with what works: A solution-focused approach to school behavior problems. *School Counselor, 42*(1), 59–65.

Murphy, J. J. (1999). Common factors of school-based change. In M. A. Hubble, B. L. Duncan, & S. D. Miller (Eds.) *The heart and soul of change: What works in therapy* (pp. 361–386). Washington, DC: American Psychological Association.

Newsome, W. S. (2005). The impact of solution-focused brief therapy with at-risk junior high school students. *Children & Schools, 27*(2). 83–90.

Pope, H.G., & Hudson, J.I. (1992). Is childhood sexual abuse a risk factor for bulimia nervosa? *American Journal of Psychiatry, 4,* 455–463.

Power, T.J., Eiraldi, R.B., Clarke, A.T., & Mazzzuca, A.L. (2005). Improving mental health service utilization for children and adolescents. *School Psychology Quarterly, 20,* 187–205.

Prout, H. T., Alexander, S. P., Fletcher, C. E. M., Memis, J. P. & Miller, D. M. (1993). Counseling and psychotherapy services provided by school psychologists: An analysis of patterns in practice. *Journal of School Psychology, 31,* 309–316.

Prout, H. T., & DeMartino, R. A. (1986). A meta-analysis of school-based studies of psychotherapy. *Journal of School Psychology, 24,* 285–292.

Riddle, J., & Bergin, J.J. (1997). Effects of group counseling on the self-concept of children of alcoholics. *Elementary School Guidance and Counseling, 31,* 192–204.

Ringel, J., & Sturm, R. (2001). National estimates of mental health utilization and expenditure for children in 1998. *Journal of Behavioral Health Services and Research, 28,* 319–332.

Roberts, M.C., Jacobs, A.K., Puddy, R.W., Nyre, J.E., & Vernberg, E.M. (2003). Treating children with serious emotional disturbances in schools and community: The intensive mental health program. *Professional Psychology: Research and Practice, 34,* 519–526.

Roberts, M. C., Lazicki-Puddy, T. A., Puddy, R. W. & Johnson, R. J. (2003). The outcomes of psychotherapy with adolescents: A practitioner-friendly review. *JCLP/In Session, 59*(11), 1177–1191.

Root, R.W., & Resnick, R.J. (2003). An update on the diagnosis and treatment of attention-deficit/hyperactivity disorder in children. *Professional Psychology: Research and Practice, 34,* 34–41.

Sandoval, J. (1993). The history of interventions in school psychology. *Journal of School Psychology, 31,* 195–217.

Schaefer, C.E. (1999). *Short-term psychotherapy groups for children: Adapting group processes for specific problems.* Northvale, NJ: Aronson.

Shechtman, Z. (2002). Child group psychotherapy in the school at the threshold of a new millennium. *Journal of Counseling and Development, 80,* 293–299.

Shirk, S.R. & Karver, M. (2003). Prediction of treatment outcome from relationship variables in child an adolescent therapy: A meta-analytic review. *Journal of Consulting and Clinical Psychology, 71*(3), 452–464.

Tolan, P.H., & Dodge, K.A. (2005). Children's mental health as a primary care and concern: A system for comprehensive support and service. *American Psychologist, 60,* 601–614.

Systems-Based Service Delivery in School Psychology

Susan G. Forman *and* Jeffrey S. Selman

Abstract

This chapter examines the meaning of systems-based service delivery, the knowledge base that provides the underpinnings of this approach to professional functioning, and examples of how school psychologists have used this approach in educational settings. The nature and processes of social systems are described as they relate to schools and the lives of children and youth. Systems-based service delivery is a complex process that involves knowledge and skill in changing the behaviors of the adults who inhabit the social systems of children and youth, and changing the way these social systems function. Literature on organizational change and innovation implementation is reviewed as a basis for understanding how to incorporate new practices and programs in classrooms, schools, and school districts. Examples of approaches to systems change, and programs involving systems-based service delivery in school psychology, are presented. The core of systems-based service delivery is the recognition that in order to prevent and treat problems of children and youth, the various systems that surround them must be the targets of professional practice.

Keywords: systems-based service delivery, systems intervention, implementation, innovation implementation, organizational change, school psychology

Introduction

Systems-based service delivery is identified as a primary domain of professional functioning in the most recent school psychology *Blueprint for Training and Practice* (Ysseldyke et al., 2008). In this document, the domain of systems-based service delivery is described as follows: "School psychologists should provide leadership in developing schools as safe, caring, and inviting places in which there is a sense of community, in which contributions of all persons are valued, in which there are high expectations of excellence for all students, and where home–school–agency partnerships are valued" (p.49). Over several decades, school psychology literature has called for a systems orientation to service delivery and, as a foundation of this approach, for an understanding of the change agent role (Magary, 1967; Sarason, 1971; Shaughency & Ervin, 2006). School psychology practice has traditionally tended to emphasize work with individuals or small groups of children and adolescents. However, a systems approach to service delivery focuses on building the capacity of systems that provide the environmental context to support academic, social, and emotional development for children and adolescents. This chapter will examine the meaning of systems-based service delivery, the knowledge base that provides the underpinnings of this approach to professional functioning, and some examples of how school psychologists have used this approach in educational settings.

Systems Concepts and Theory
What is a System?
In order to understand systems-based service delivery in school psychology, it is important to first understand what systems are and how they work.

A lack of understanding of systems functioning and systems change principles has been cited as a major reason for the failure of program implementation and school reform efforts (Curtis, Castillo, & Cohen, 2008; Sarason, 1990). Systems concepts and theory were initially developed in the biological and physical sciences. Systems theory is a broad theory of nature that describes relationships. The universe can be conceived as systems within systems. A systems approach assumes that everything is interrelated and interdependent.

A system is conceptualized as parts or components that interact to produce a product or outcome. A system is composed of parts that are related to and dependent on one another, and that when in interaction form a unitary whole. Systems can be mechanical or living. A social system, which is of most interest to psychologists, has been defined as "an orderly combination of two or more individuals whose interaction is intended to produce a desired outcome" (Curtis, et al., 2008; p. 889). An organization is a large social system consisting of a number of people in a patterned relationship, established to carry out a purpose based on a perceived need.

Schools can be viewed as social systems and as organizations because they consist of individuals such as teachers, principals, students, and special services providers, who are interacting and engaging in activities with the goal of increasing student knowledge and skill, so that children and youth can grow into productive members of society. A systems perspective can help one understand how systems such as schools function. Systems theory explains how changes in parts of the system impact other parts of the system, as well as how changes in the system's environment have an impact on the system.

What are the Components and Characteristics of Systems?

All systems are thought to have certain characteristics in common (Berrien, 1968). In addition to *components* that interact with each other, systems have *boundaries* that serve to separate one system from another, and to define the membership of a social system. For example, the staff and student rosters of a school would define the boundaries of that school as a social system. Sometimes, interface regions or *interfaces* connect systems. For example, an interagency coordinating council may connect various agencies that deal with mental health issues, while each of these individual agencies can be conceptualized as a system with a boundary.

All systems process *inputs* and produce *outputs* that are different from the inputs. Inputs are the material, energies, or information that the system works with to produce an outcome. In systems theory, that outcome is also called an *output*. In a school that has child study teams to process referrals for potential placement in special classes, the child study team can be viewed as a system. The inputs are the student referrals, the outputs are the individualized education plans (IEPs) and other reports. with recommendations generated by the members of the team who are the components of that system. These outputs are discharged from the system into the *suprasystem*. In the case of the child study team, the suprasystem is the school in which it operates. In order to survive, every system must deliver outputs that are acceptable to its environment or suprasystem. If the outputs are unacceptable to the environment, the system may be forced to change significantly, or may be destroyed. For example, if the actions of the child study team result in what is deemed by the state education department to be too many placements in special education classes, the school district special services director may work to change the way the team goes about its work.

In social systems, individuals have *roles*. The role is the part, function, or pattern of behavior an individual has in a social system. In a school, the role of the principal consists of a set of behaviors designed to manage school functions, while the role of the teacher is direct interaction with students for the purpose of increasing student knowledge and skill. Social systems also have *norms*, which are established ways of behaving and working in the system, or the expectations for the members of the system. The practice of teachers discussing significant school events in the teachers' lounge is a norm in many schools. *Values* are general justifications for roles and norms. For example, a school district may hold the value that "emotional and social growth is as important as academic growth in students." This value would provide the rationale for the fact that in this school, teachers implement social and emotional learning programs in their classrooms, and teachers see this as an important part of the curriculum.

Systems Functioning

Systems are considered *open systems* because they exchange materials, energies, or information with their surroundings. Open systems operate under the principle of *reciprocal influence* (Miller, 1955). Reciprocal influence implies an interaction between different parts of a system, as well as with the environment.

The various parts of a system influence each other, and a social system is influenced by its environment and also influences its environment. For example, a family may be viewed as an open system. The members of a family may consist of one or two parents and children. An ailing grandparent who can no longer live independently may need to join this family system. Siblings may now be required to share a room, the parent may need to be home more to provide care for the grandparent, and family finances may be strained. A school may also be viewed as an open system. If a teacher has difficulty with classroom management, and uses referral of students for evaluation for special education as a potential solution to her problem, she will influence the work of the school psychologist in her school. One can think of a school as a system, and a state department of education as a suprasystem. Decreases in state funding for schools may lead to termination of some school programs. At the same time, decreases in state funding for schools may lead to decreased achievement levels of students in school districts, and the state may find itself with compliance problems related to federal requirements. Understanding interrelationships has been seen as the essence of systems thinking (Senge, 1990).

Social systems, as open systems, are dependent on other social systems. In general, social systems are subsystems of one or more larger systems. The manner in which a social system links to larger systems impacts the way it functions. For example, when the principal of a school has a close relationship with the superintendent of the school district, that school is likely to have activities and programs that are closely related to the agenda of the superintendent. An open system must continuously monitor the external environment, so that it can manage the environment's demands and the changes that it imposes (Goodstein, 1990). For example, a school district must monitor proposed changes in state funded programs so that it can manage its own budget well.

Open systems that are successful are thought to have permeable boundaries that allow for communication and the flow of information (Senge, 1990). Permeable boundaries allow a system to acquire important information in the environment that may affect system functioning. When boundaries are impermeable, systems do not acquire the information needed about potential contextual changes that may affect the ability of the system to meet its goals. For example, within some school districts, special education and regular education function as separate systems, with separate staffs, roles, and operating procedures. If there is little communication and flow of information between these systems, the school district may be unable to work effectively on reducing disproportionality in special education, after being identified by the state education agency as in need of remediation in this area.

Open systems function through a recurring cycle of input, *transformation* (sometimes called *throughput*) and output. Schools enroll new students each year (input) and engage them in a variety of educational activities and programs (transformation) so that they become individuals who can function as productive members of society who possess a range of knowledge and skills (output). *Feedback mechanisms* allow a system to monitor and control inputs and system functioning through examination of outputs. For example, when a school monitors the academic achievement levels of its students, it can make adjustments in the curriculum if these levels are not deemed to be adequate. *Adaptation* refers to the modifications made in a system over time to ensure success and survival.

Similar to living organisms, social systems and organizations such as schools seek to maintain a steady state, or *homeostasis*. Organizations such as schools have norms and values that guide behavior in the system. When an innovation is introduced that is incongruent with a system's norms and values, the system resists (Stollar, Poth, Curtis, & Cohen, 2006). For example, in a school district in which traditionally parents and teachers have seen special education classes as positive ways to provide specialized services for students with disabilities, efforts to mainstream students with disabilities may meet with protests to administrators and the board of education.

Schools as Social Systems

Schools are recognized as social systems because people come together in schools to perform specific tasks in order to yield student learning. People in schools, like components of any system, interact in regular and predictable ways. As social systems and organizations, schools have boundaries, roles, norms, values. In addition, they coexist with subsystems and suprasystems that influence their functioning. By recognizing schools as social systems, those interested in making change in schools can have a better understanding of how, where, with whom, and at what level to act (Ervin & Schaughency, 2008).

The concept of nested social ecology (Glisson, 2002) explains that individuals working in human service organizations, such as schools, work in a social system in which they are members of one or more subsystems nested within broader systems. A teacher may be part of a grade level group of teachers, as well as part of a group based on curriculum area (such as math), and is also part of the school, which is part of the school district, the local community, and the state. Each of the systems of which the teacher is a member will have an influence on her attitudes and behaviors, and thus on her willingness to engage in change efforts.

Two dimensions of the school context, culture and climate, are thought to be instrumental to the manner in which schools function (Glisson & Green, 2006). *Culture* is "the way things are done around here" and involves shared norms, patterns of behavior, behavioral expectations and basic assumptions and beliefs that are held by the organization's members (Hemmelgarn, Glisson, & James, 2006). Two types of organizational culture have been identified as having qualities that either promote or inhibit change (Hemmelgarn et al., 2006). Constructive cultures have norms that result in a greater likelihood of innovation, addressing challenging tasks, and developing staff potential. Organizations with defensive cultures tend to resist change. *Climate* is the positive or negative psychological impact of the work environment on staff well-being. Positive climate involves openness, trust, and confidence that disagreements can be raised safely and discussed productively within the organization. Negative climate includes role conflict, overload, depersonalization, emotional exhaustion, and the perception that the work environment is "bad" for one's well-being (Hemmelgarn, et al., 2006).

Glisson, Dukes and Green (2006) suggest that culture influences climate, which influences performance. Both culture and climate are aspects of organizations such as schools that need to be understood, in order to work effectively to change individual and system functioning. Knowledge of culture and climate in a school will help a change agent understand if a proposed change is congruent with current system functioning, and the steps that will need to be taken to bring the proposed system change to fruition. For example, if a school has a *culture* that includes being "tough on discipline issues," using reactive rather than preventive approaches and having a negative attitude toward use of incentives with students, and a *climate* that includes teacher perceptions of being a threatening and unsupportive place to work, implementation of a schoolwide positive behavior support program will present significant difficulties. Much effort will need to be invested in attempts to change this culture and climate prior to initial implementation of this type of program.

Children and Systems

The lives of children and adolescents may also be viewed from a systems perspective. Both Bandura (1978) and Bronfenbrenner (1979) have suggested that children should be viewed from a systems, or ecological, framework, in which a child influences and is influenced by the systems of which he or she is a part. Bronfenbrenner (1979) states that children develop within a set of embedded contexts of influence, and that we cannot understand their development without understanding the forces that operate in each of these contexts.

This ecological framework for development can be thought of in terms of the multiple systems that surround the individual child. The *microsystem* includes relationships between the child and the immediate environment, such as the family, daycare center, or school. The *mesosystem* is the connection between elements of the child's microsystem, such as the relationship between the parent and the teacher. The *exosystem* refers to social systems that do not directly interact with the child, but that affect one of the child's microsystems, such as the parent's workplace. The *macrosystem* includes values, laws, customs, and larger cultural settings in which the microsystems and exosystems are embedded, such as socioeconomic status, family ethnic identity, public policy, and federal government. The *chronosystem* refers to the ever-changing dynamic nature of the child's environment. These different systems interact with each other and impact the child's development and well-being in many ways.

To illustrate this point, consider a child living in poverty. At the microsystem level, the child may come from a single-parent home without the means to support educational growth, and may attend a school district with scarce resources. At the exosystem level, the child's single parent may have a job that requires long hours away from home with little opportunity to take time off to deal with personal or family issues. At the mesosystem level, the relationship between the child's parent and teacher may be strained, because the parent does not come to meet with the teacher due to the parent's work situation. At the macrosystem level, the child may be influenced by the mainstream culture's negative views and expectations of impoverished individuals and families. When considering an intervention for this child, a systems or ecological framework implies that we must look beyond the individual child to the multiple systems that surround him. For example, this could occur at the mesosystem level, where open and active communication and support from school personnel with the family can be essential to helping the child. A child's problem is not viewed as occurring within him- or herself, but as the result of a systemic problem, or the interaction between the child and the environment (Sheridan & Gutkin, 2000).

School Psychologists and Systems Change

There are several implications of systems theory and systems perspectives of schools and the lives of children and adolescents for schools psychologists. First, in order to improve student outcomes, school psychologists may be required to create interventions that address systemic barriers to academic, behavioral, and social/emotional learning (Curtis, et al., 2008). Such interventions may need to be tied to the classroom, the school building, the school district, and to students' families and communities, with the goal of building systems that can support academic, social, and emotional growth. Student development and achievement must be viewed as occurring within multiple systems, rather than only at the individual student level. Such systems-based service delivery is a complex process that involves knowledge of, and skill in changing, the behaviors of the adults who inhabit the child's various social systems, and in changing the way these social systems function. The following sections will address the knowledge base that provides the underpinnings for systems change skills and systems-based service delivery.

Systems Change
Leadership and the Change Agent Role

As stated above, functioning in the domain of systems-based service delivery requires school psychologists to provide "leadership" (Ysseldyke et al., 2008). What is leadership, and what does it mean in the context of the school psychologist? The organizational psychology and management literature are filled with definitions of leadership, but all definitions share the view that leadership involves the process of influence, and that all leaders have one or more followers.

Early research on leadership conceptualized it as a personal trait. Although there is now awareness that traits interact with a context, and that they are malleable and not fixed, some universal traits associated with effective leadership have been identified. These include: persistence, tolerance for ambiguity, self-confidence, drive, honesty, integrity, internal locus of control, achievement motivation, and cognitive

ability (Avolio, 2007). Other approaches to the study of leadership have focused on leaders' actions (Lowin & Craig, 1968). These include: *situational theory*, in which traits and behaviors of leaders are viewed as mediating variables between structural antecedents and organizational outcomes (Perrow, 1970); *contingency theory*, which focuses on the interaction of leader and situational characteristics (Fiedler, 1967); and normative and descriptive models, which deal with the form in and degree to which the leader involves subordinates in decision making (Vroom & Jago, 1988).

A contemporary definition of leadership that has particular relevance for school psychology has been advanced by Vroom & Jago (2007), who define leadership as "a process of motivating people to work together collaboratively to accomplish great things" (p. 18)—a definition that is consistent with the tasks of developing schools as positive environments for academic, social, and emotional learning. Using this definition, leadership is a process as opposed to a property of a person, indicating the potential of many individuals to be leaders. Also notable is that use of particular types of incentives are not part of the definition. Thus, using this definition, we see that a school psychologist can provide leadership even if their formal job does not include direct reporting responsibility for other staff members, or budgetary control. In addition, the particular form of influence that this definition advances is "motivating" for the purpose of collaborating to pursue a common goal. The emphasis on collaboration is consistent with the historically collaborative nature of the school psychology role.

An additional contemporary approach to leadership that speaks to school psychology is Sternberg's WICS model of leadership (Sternberg, 2007) which views leadership as how one formulates, makes, and acts on decisions. According to this model, the three key components of leadership are wisdom, intelligence, and creativity, synthesized. Wisdom, intelligence, and creativity are viewed as modifiable attributes, and their use is seen as dependent upon how situations interact with an individual's skills.

Creativity refers to skills and dispositions needed for generating ideas that are relatively novel, high in quality, and appropriate for a given situation. Successful *intelligence* is the skills and dispositions needed to succeed in life, given the individual's own notion of success. *Wisdom* is the use of successful intelligence, creativity, and knowledge mediated by values to reach a common good. "An effective leader needs creative skills and dispositions to come up with ideas, academic skills and dispositions to decide whether they are good ideas, practical skills and dispositions to make the ideas work and convince others of the value of the ideas, and wisdom based skills and dispositions to ensure that the ideas are in the service of the common good rather than just the good of the leader, or perhaps some clique of family members or followers." (Sternberg, 2007; p. 40). For those who work to advance the profession of school psychology, the components identified in this model of leadership define the key attributes that can and should be developed as a basis for high level functioning in the profession.

The role of change agent for school psychologists, which has been encouraged in school psychology literature (Merrell, Ervin, & Gimpel, 2006), is consistent with the contemporary notions of leadership described above. School psychologists who are working to make changes in schools, to develop positive contexts for students, will need to use intellectual and creative assets to motivate others to collaborate with them in working toward this common good. Literature on the change agent (Rogers, 2003) identifies facilitating the flow of innovations from one social system to another as a primary role. Change agents typically provide a link between a resource system with some kind of expertise (such as intervention/program developers) and a client system (such as a school). Change agents usually possess a high degree of expertise regarding innovations that can be of use to a client system in meeting certain goals. In this respect, the school psychologist—who is likely the most highly knowledgeable member of a school or school district staff regarding behavioral, social, and emotional issues and the manner in which they intersect with learning, as well as the functioning of students with disabilities—emerges as a most appropriate potential change agent for issues related to improving the school context for learning, especially with regard to how good social and emotional development supports academic growth.

Rogers (2003) identifies seven roles of change agents who work to bring an innovation to a client system such as a school or school district. These roles provide a blueprint of activities that must be undertaken for the process of bringing a new practice or program to an organization to be effective.

1) Develop a need for change—the change agent helps clients become aware of the need to alter their behavior by raising awareness of problems and pointing out alternatives to these problems.

2) Establish an information exchange relationship—the change agent develops credibility and rapport with clients.

3) Diagnose problems—the change agent analyzes problems to determining why existing alternatives are not working.

4) Create an intent to change—the change agent seeks to motivate client interests in the innovation.

5) Translate intent into action—the change agent seeks to work with social/interpersonal networks in the system to influence implementation of the innovation.

6) Stabilize adoption and prevent discontinuance—the change agent stabilizes implementation of the innovation through use of reinforcing messages.

7) Achieve a terminal relationship—the change agent shifts the responsibility to the client for continued implementation of the innovation.

Innovation Implementation

DEFINITION

Virtually all current examples of systems-based delivery of school psychology services involve assuming a change agent role for the school psychologist. This implies engaging in efforts to incorporate new practices and/or programs in classrooms, schools and/or school districts that will support the academic, emotional, and social growth of children and adolescents. Given the emphasis of this type of activity in systems-based service delivery, literature in the areas of innovation implementation and innovation diffusion have much to offer the school psychologist. An innovation is something that is perceived as new. Innovation implementation is an effort to incorporate a new program or practice in the functioning of an organization, group, and/or individual.

INNOVATION DIFFUSION AND SOCIAL SYSTEMS

Some who have contributed to this literature use the term *innovation diffusion*. Innovation diffusion is defined as a more comprehensive process that includes innovation implementation. Innovation diffusion is the planned and spontaneous spread of new ideas; it is a type of social change, in which alteration occurs in the structure and function of a social system (Rogers, 2003). In writing about the elements in the diffusion of new ideas, Rogers (2003) emphasizes the importance of the social system and identifies: (a) an innovation—something that is perceived as new; (b) communication about the innovation, in which individuals share information with one another to reach a mutual understanding; c) time—the innovation process occurs over time, and may occur at different times for different individuals in a system; and (d) a social system. Similar to the definitions above, Rogers (2003) describes a social system as a set of interrelated units (which may be individuals, groups or organizations) that are engaged in joint problem solving to accomplish a common goal. It is the sharing of the common goal that binds the systems together. Thus, the notions of innovation diffusion and implementation, and the concept of a social system, are intertwined.

DEGREES OF IMPLEMENTATION

Literature about innovation implementation identifies a number of degrees of implementation that are typically seen in organizational settings, which should alert the school psychologist working in the area of systems-based service delivery to the difficulty, complexity, and pitfalls of this type of professional role. Hernandez and Hodges (2003) have described three degrees of implementation: paper implementation, process implementation, and performance implementation. *Paper implementation* involves putting new written policies and procedures in place in policy and procedure documents and manuals. They point out that paper implementation may occur when outside groups are mandating or monitoring implementation. They also point out that having such documents is not the same as using innovations with clients. *Process implementation* involves putting new operating procedures in place, such as conducting training workshops, providing supervision, and changing reporting requirements. Again, these alterations alone will not necessarily lead to using the innovation with clients. *Performance implementation* involves putting processes in place so that an innovation is used with positive impact on clients. Many efforts to bring new practices and programs to schools have resulted in paper or process implementation only. As Fixsen et al. (2005) state, having "the trappings of evidence-based practices and programs plus lip service do not equal putting innovations into practice with benefits for consumers" (p. 6).

STAGES OF IMPLEMENTATION

Another concept essential for effective systems-based service delivery is that there are stages to the implementation process. The nature of each stage will necessitate different actions on the part of the school psychologist change agent to assist in moving the implementation process to the next stage.

Understanding of the stages of implementation will provide a roadmap for professional action as the implementation process progresses. Fixsen et al. (2005) have identified six stages:

1) Exploration and adoption. The match between individual and/or organizational needs, innovation needs, and individual/organizational resources are assessed. A decision is made to proceed (or not) with the innovation. Information about the innovation is acquired; the need for the innovation and the fit between the innovation and the client is explored; information about the innovation is spread in the organization to mobilize support for it.

2) Program installation. There is preparation for doing things differently. Structural supports for the innovation such as funding, staff development, new staff, new staff responsibilities, space, equipment, supplies, new policies, new procedures are put in place.

3) Initial implementation. The new practice or program begins. Implementers deal with fear of change, inertia, investment in the status quo, and the difficulty of doing something new.

4) Full operation. The new practice or program is fully operational, and clients are receiving it. There is appropriate staffing for it, it is carried out with proficiency, administrators support it, and it has been integrated into individual and organizational practices.

5) Innovation. The new program or practice is refined to better fit the conditions under which it is being implemented; some of the changes may be desirable, but some may be undesirable.

6) *Sustainability*. The new program is implemented in years subsequent to the first full implementation. There may be staff and leadership turnover, and changes in champions, funding, and the social/environmental context.

In their conceptualization of innovation in schools, the Concerns Based Adoption Model, Hall and Hord (1987) point out that different issues and actions are important at different stages of the implementation process. In this model, in the preadoption stage it is important that potential adopters are aware of the innovation, have information about what it does and how to use it, and understand how the innovation will affect them personally. During early use of an innovation, success is more likely if implementers have continuing access to information about what the innovation does, and to sufficient training and support on how to fit the innovation to their daily tasks. Later in implementation, success is more likely if adequate feedback is provided about the consequences of implementation, and if the implementer has sufficient opportunity and support to adapt the innovation. This model provides direction for school psychologists who are leaders for systems change by specifying the issues that will likely be of concern at each stage of implementation, pointing to potential actions that can be taken to address these issues.

Implementation Effectiveness

Research related to innovation implementation has revealed that implementation success is related to three major factors: (a) characteristics of the innovation, (b) characteristics of the implementer, and (c) characteristics of the organization in which the potential implementer works, and its environmental context. The next sections will explore each of these areas.

INNOVATION CHARACTERISTICS

Literature on innovation characteristics provides direction for examining the types of innovative practices and programs that may yield successful implementation, given the individual and organizational context within which a school psychologist is working. A significant body of multidisciplinary literature has been amassed concerning the characteristics that affect implementation of innovations, as perceived by individuals., In a review of this literature, Rogers (2003) indicates that innovations that are perceived by individuals as having greater relative advantage, compatibility, trialability and observability, and less complexity, will be adopted more rapidly than other innovations. *Relative advantage* is the degree to which an innovation is perceived as better than what exists. *Compatibility* is the degree to which an innovation is perceived as being consistent with existing values, past experiences, and needs of adopters. *Complexity* is the degree to which an innovation is perceived as difficult to understand and use. *Trialability* is the degree to which an innovation may be experimented with, or tried out. *Observability* is the degree to which the results of an innovation are visible to others. Additional attributes of innovations that have been found to influence adoption include riskiness and task relevance (Greenhalgh, Robert, Macfarlane, Bate, & Kyriakidou, 2004). If an innovation is perceived as risky, it is less likely to be adopted. If the innovation is relevant to the performance of the user's work and improves work performance, it is more likely to be adopted.

Studies of school reform have resulted in identification of three characteristics that seem to influence implementation: locus of development, targeted versus whole-school change, and structure versus teacher knowledge and curriculum content (Glennan, Bodilly, Gallagher, & Kerr, 2004). *Locus of development* refers to whether an intervention is developed internally by teachers and administrators in a school, or externally by developers. Externally developed interventions are easier and less costly to implement, and have a greater likelihood of implementation success. However, even if an intervention is developed externally, teachers and administrators can still have a role in making decisions about how it will be carried out, and adapting it to a specific school context. *Targeted versus whole-school change* refers to whether the intervention is targeted toward specific populations or curricular areas, or is implemented broadly across a site. There is some evidence to indicate that whole-school reforms are more effective than interventions that target a particular segment of the student population, a specific part of the curriculum, or only a few classrooms in a school. The relative importance of structural or organizational changes versus changes that focus on improving teacher knowledge and the content of curricula has been the subject of debate in literature on schools. *Structural changes* include such things as altering student grouping, establishing team teaching, or changing budget and personnel responsibilities. Evidence suggests that reforms should focus on both curriculum, or teaching techniques, *and* structural changes, as opposed to structural changes alone.

IMPLEMENTER CHARACTERISTICS

Types of implementers. Organizational research has led to the development of ways of classifying members of a social system on the basis of their innovativeness, or the degree to which an individual or group is relatively early in adopting new ideas. Rogers (2003) defines five adopter/implementer categories:

1) Innovators—they are the earliest adopters, who tend to be venturesome;

2) Early adopters—they tend to be more integrated in the local social system than are innovators; they also tend to have the highest degree of opinion leadership;

3) Early majority—they are deliberate, and adopt new ideas just before the average member of a social system; they interact frequently with peers, but seldom hold positions of opinion leadership;

4) Late majority—they adopt new ideas just after the average member of a social system; they tend to be skeptical;

5) Laggards—they are the last in a social system to adopt an innovation; they are traditional.

The differences among the adopter categories suggest that change agents should use different approaches in communicating with, and attempting to motivate, individuals in each category.

Social systems also have individuals who function as opinion leaders. These are typically not the most innovative members of a social system, who are often perceived as deviant by the average members of the system. Opinion leaders are those who influence others' attitudes and beliefs. Opinion leaders typically have gained this status because of their competence, social accessibility, and conformity to system norms (Rogers, 2003). For the school psychologist engaging in systems-based service delivery, these individuals are important to identify and work with, even when they are not directly involved in implementation of a new practice or program.

A *champion* is a final category of individuals who are important in the success of innovation implementation efforts. A champion is a charismatic individual who puts his or her support behind an innovation. Champions do not necessarily have formal power in an organization, but are skillful at persuasion and negotiation. The champion, once identified, can help the innovation fit with the organizational context (Rogers, 2003).

Implementer attitudes and beliefs. Although, as stated above, innovation characteristics have a significant impact on individuals' willingness to implement new practices and programs, individuals may judge the attributes or characteristics of an innovation differently from one another, and what is easy for one person to use may be difficult for another to use. Although the meaning attached to an intervention has a strong influence on the initial decision to use an intervention, this meaning is not necessarily fixed and can be reframed through discourse (Greenhalgh et al., 2004). Thus, school psychologists should be prepared to work to establish perceptions, attitudes, and beliefs in implementers and other stakeholders that will support implementation success, through means such as presentations, workshops, formal and informal discussion, and consultation.

Literature on decision making (Plous, 1993) can provide some guidance about dealing with perceptions, attitudes, and beliefs of implementers and other stakeholders in innovative programs and practices in schools. *Loss aversion* is the tendency for individuals to attempt to avoid losses, or situations in which change is negative. Research in this area tells us that losses loom larger than gains; that in making a decision, a possible loss will be considered more than a possible gain. This points to the importance of emphasizing the negatives of *not using* a proposed innovative program or practice, as well as the positives of using it. Research on vividness, or the perceived intensity of information, tells us that decisions are affected by how emotionally interesting information is. Thus, using anecdotes, rather than only data and statistics to develop a rationale and make a case for an innovation will be important.

The phenomenon of cognitive dissonance (Festinger, 1957), which occurs when people try to reduce inconsistency when they have two thoughts that are psychologically inconsistent, has implications for dealing with potential adopter/implementer attitudes and beliefs. Having potential implementers, other stakeholders, and relevant others in the implementers' and stakeholders' social networks, participating in the selection of a new practice or program will be important in building a solid base for effective implementation. When individuals are involved in selection of an innovation, they are more likely to be supportive when implementation begins and proceeds.

Diffusion investigation studies have shown that most individuals do not evaluate innovations based on scientific studies of their consequences. Instead, they depend on the subjective evaluations of other individuals like themselves—the experiences of near peers (Rogers, 2003). Thus, innovation diffusion and implementation is a social process that emphasizes interpersonal communication, with most people making decisions about innovations based on their knowledge of what others like themselves think about the innovation. This implies that in addition to working with potential implementers of new practices and programs, it is essential for the school psychologist in the context of systems intervention to work with individuals who have relationships with implementers, as these individuals may influence the attitudes and beliefs of those implementers.

Rogers (2003) describes an innovation decision process through which an individual forms attitudes about an innovation, and makes decisions about whether to adopt and implement the innovation. In the *knowledge* stage, the individual obtains information about the innovation, and before progressing to the next stage, must define that information as relevant to him or her. In the *persuasion* stage, the individual forms a favorable or unfavorable attitude toward the innovation, seeking the opinions of peers in evaluating the innovation's advantages and disadvantages to their situation. The *decision* stage takes place when the individual engages in activities that lead to a choice to adopt or reject an innovation. A demonstration or a small-scale trial of the innovation is helpful for the individual in this stage. In the *implementation* stage, the individual puts the innovation to use and may make adaptations to the innovation to better fit it to his or her situation (reinvention). Finally, in the *confirmation* stage, the individual seeks reinforcement for the decision they have made. Again, opinions of peers are important in this stage, as well as evaluation feedback about the outcomes of the innovation.

ORGANIZATIONAL CHARACTERISTICS

An organization is a type of social system in which individuals work together to achieve common goals through prescribed roles, an authority structure with a hierarchy of ranks, rules and regulations, and informal practices, norms, and social relationships. Organizations handle tasks through patterns of regularized human relationships (Katz & Kahn, 1966). Schools are organizations with the goal of educating children and adolescents. A number of organizational characteristics have been found to affect innovation implementation.

In literature on innovation implementation in the business workplace, implementation has been seen as a function of two factors (Klein & Sorra, 1996). The first factor is the organization's climate for implementation of the innovation. This refers to staff members' perceptions of the extent to which the innovation is rewarded, supported, and expected. Thus, in attempting to implement new practices and programs in schools, the school psychologist should consider if and how the innovation fits with the philosophy, mission, goals, policies, and existing programs of the school, and should communicate those connections with stakeholders. In addition, garnering teacher and administrative support, especially principal support, will be essential (Forman, 2009). The second factor is the organizational members' perceptions of the fit of the innovation to their values. Staff members who perceive the innovation to be consistent with their values are more likely to be committed and enthusiastic in their use. Understanding stakeholders' values, and communicating the connections between those values and proposed innovations, can serve to enhance effectiveness.

Greenhalgh et al. (2004) reviewed literature on system readiness for innovation in human service organizations and found a number of essential elements that can be used to gauge whether an innovation implementation effort is likely to be effective. These elements include:

1) Tension for change—staff must feel that the current situation is problematic or intolerable.

2) Innovation-system fit—the innovation must fit with the organization's existing values, norms, strategies, goals, skill mix, supporting technologies, and ways of working.

3) Assessment of implications—the potential effects of the innovation should be fully assessed and anticipated.

4) Support and advocacy—supporters of the innovation should outnumber and be more strategically placed than opponents.

5) Dedicated time and resources—budget and other resources should be adequate and continuing.

6) Capacity to evaluate—the organization should be able to monitor and evaluate the impact of the innovation.

Rogers (2003) has outlined an innovation-decision process that takes place in organizations, which consists of initiation and implementation subprocesses. In the initiation subprocess, agenda setting and matching occur, during which there is identification of needs and problems and a search for innovations that can address these needs and problems. The organization's members then attempt to establish the feasibility of a proposed innovation in solving the organization's problems. In the implementation subprocess, the innovation is reinvented or adapted to accommodate the organization, and the organization's structure may be modified to fit the innovation. The innovation begins to be put into widespread use in the organization, and organizational members seek to gain an understanding of the new practice or program. "What does it do?" and "How does it affect me?" are some of the questions that people in the organization discuss with each other as they develop a common, socially constructed view of the innovation. Finally, the innovation becomes incorporated into the regular activities of the organization, and may lose its separate identity.

In the innovation implementation process both the innovation and the organization usually change. An innovation almost never fits in an organization perfectly, so the innovation may be modified and/or the structure of the organization may be changed

(Van de Ven, 1986). In a review of school reform, sponsored by the Rand Corporation, successful implementation efforts were viewed as a process of interaction, feedback, and adaptation among teachers, program developers/providers, schools, districts, and state administrators. Implementation sites were not viewed as receivers of new programs, but as active participants in an iterative process (Glennan et al., 2004).

EXTRA-ORGANIZATIONAL FACTORS

The external environment and suprasystems of an organization will impact the success of attempts to implement innovations. In the case of schools and school districts, state and federal policy have a major impact on functioning and must be considered in innovation implementation planning. State standards and accountability policies and procedures have encouraged schools to improve their practice. State standards and accountability policies and procedures are typically of great importance to individual schools and school districts, in part because adherence to standards and policies may have financial implications. It is, therefore, important to align new practices and programs with these standards and policies in order to facilitate their implementation. On the federal level, most of the policies, regulations, and initiatives that affect school functioning come from the U.S. Department of Education and the Department of Health and Human Services. The Individuals with Disabilities Act and the No Child Left Behind Act are particularly relevant to school psychologists, as they contain language, guidelines, and regulations aimed at meeting the mental health needs of school-age children and youth, and the educational needs of children and youth with disabilities. Again, federal policies and regulations may be linked to funding for school districts, so compatibility of new interventions with these policies and regulations will affect implementation efforts. In addition, in many cases state and federal agencies provide grant funding as incentives to improve school functioning. These grant programs can be important vehicles for financial support of new programs.

In many locales, most school funding is determined at the local level. Locally based funding, combined with local school district governance, points to the importance of local community culture, norms, and politics in school functioning. It is therefore important to recognize the influence of the local community context on efforts to improve schools through new programs and practices.

Systems-Based Service Delivery: Examples from School Psychology

Over the past few years, a number of examples of systems-based service delivery in school psychology practice have emerged. Some of these examples focus on the process of facilitating this type of school psychological service, while others focus on particular types of programs or approaches that use a systems framework and an understanding of systems processes in the delivery of services to students in school. This section describes a number of these efforts.

Systems-Based Service Delivery Processes

COLLABORATIVE STRATEGIC PLANNING

Colloborative Strategic Planning (CSP) (Stollar, Poth, Curtis, & Cohen, 2006) is a team-based approach that uses collaborative planning and problem solving to address student problems and system issues. When CSP is used, a school-based planning team is developed that is composed of building and district administrators, teachers, special services providers, parents, community members, and other stakeholder groups. The CSP process is based on the following five-step problem solving model.

1. Problem identification. This step focuses on the question, "How effective is the school at promoting positive outcomes for students?" It involves using data-based problem identification, which means that expectations for student performance must be defined, and information about actual student performance must be obtained, in order to determine if there is a discrepancy between what is desired and what is occurring.

2. Problem analysis. This step consists of generating questions about how and why the identified discrepancy or problem may be occurring, and collection of data to answer the questions. In order to complete this step effectively, it is important that the questions are phrased so that potential answers can be clearly defined, observable, and measurable.

3. Goal setting. In this step, a clear goal for system-level change is developed which, according to information yielded in the problem analysis, is likely to address the identified discrepancy.

4. Plan development and implementation. This step involves development and implementation of an action plan which is likely to result in attainment of goals that have been identified. Each reason for an identified problem should be matched with a research-based strategy,

and strategies should be adapted to fit the context of the school. In addition, it is suggested that the team generate a list of potential barriers to success, and prepare plans to address those barriers.

5. Plan evaluation. In this step, implementation is evaluated, as well as student outcomes, with the intention of using evaluation information to make adjustments to strategies in order to yield better outcomes.

THE PARTICIPATORY INTERVENTION MODEL

The Participatory Intervention Model (PIM) (Nastasi, Varjas, Schensul, Silva, Schensul, & Ratnayake, 2000) is an approach to planning and implementation that integrates theory and research in the development of culture- or context-specific interventions. It is designed to promote ownership and empowerment among stakeholders who are responsible for sustaining an intervention after support by change agents, consultants, or university-based teams, has terminated. The goal of this approach is sustainability of implementation efforts, and institutionalization or integration of the intervention in the organizational context. PIM has roots in the process of participatory action research, developed by applied anthropologists.

PIM has three phases: participatory generation of intervention design, natural adaptation or implementation, and essential changes or evaluation of effectiveness. Throughout these phases, change agents in partnership with stakeholders are continually engaged in data collection and analysis to ensure acceptability and cultural specificity of the intervention, to adapt the intervention to the demands of the context, and to monitor change related to intervention goals. There is continual attention to issues of acceptability, integrity, and effectiveness. Building on a sense of partnership, change agents and stakeholders together design the intervention, monitor its implementation, and evaluate its effectiveness. There is an expectation that stakeholders will assume responsibility for continuing and institutionalizing the new intervention.

This process, which emphasizes partnership, begins with formative research to identify and examine individual and cultural variables relevant to the change process, such as individual competencies, cultural practices, norms, and resources. This information is used to generate culture-specific theory, culture-specific goals, intervention strategies, and a culture-specific intervention. Intervention implementation involves modifying an evidence-based intervention to fit the needs and resources of the target population and stakeholders, in their context. Alterations in the intervention are made to achieve an optimal fit with the recipients and the context. Continual monitoring of intervention integrity occurs. This involves preservation of the critical elements of the intervention (identified in program theory and research), while allowing variation in noncritical elements. Documentation of change addresses the progress that has been made toward achieving the goals of the intervention, as well as the extent to which change efforts have persisted, and whether stakeholders have developed strategies for extending use of the intervention. Throughout this process, change agents, such as school psychologists, can facilitate sustainability and institutionalization by helping stakeholders develop skills and confidence, helping them access needed resources, and helping them create an infrastructure that will support the intervention.

PROBLEM SOLVING PROCESS FOR DECISION MAKING AND CHANGE

Ervin and Schaughency (2008) indicate that a problem solving perspective should guide all professional practice, and that specific emphases in this process can facilitate systems-level change. The basic problem solving process consists of posing four questions: What is the problem? Why is it happening? What should be done about it? Did it work? When working toward system change, Ervin and Schaughency (2008) contend that it especially important to include an emphasis on measurable outcomes, a focus on targets amenable to change, and use of formative feedback to guide decision making.

The discrepancy between current and desired outcomes is at issue in the first question in the problem solving process (What is the problem?) Developing a common answer to the question among stakeholders is important, and that answer must include clearly defined outcomes or goals. In addressing the second (Why is it occurring?) and third questions (What should be done about it?) it is important to identify variables that are related to the problem, and ones that can be altered or are amenable to change. In addressing the fourth question (Did it work?) both implementation evaluation and outcomes evaluation are important. When both are used, program managers and stakeholders can determine if new interventions are yielding needed changes, and if not, can gain clues about how the interventions should be adjusted in order yield more positive outcomes.

SYSTEMIC AND STRUCTURED PLANNING AND PROBLEM SOLVING

An additional model for addressing systems level issues, Systemic and Structured Planning and Problem Solving, has been advanced by Curtis, et al. (2008). This model emphasizes the importance of identifying and dealing with organizational issues that might impact the success of attempts to implement new interventions. The model consists of eight steps to be used by a problem solving team:

1. Describe the problem in as much detail as possible, and identify the desired outcome in concrete, descriptive terms.

2. Analyze the problem to determine the factors that might help to reduce it, as well as factors that might serve as barriers to problem resolution. This involves members of the problem solving team using brainstorming to generate a list of resources and barriers.

3. In the third step, the problem solving team selects one identified barrier for initial discussion.

4. The team brainstorms strategies than can be used to reduce or eliminate the barrier identified in Step 3.

5. Multiple action plans are designed to reduce or eliminate the barrier identified in Step 3. Each plan should specify who, what and when (who will carry out what activity, by when?).

6. The sixth step consists of developing a plan to monitor implementation of each action plan and intervention.

7. A plan is developed that specifies how data will be collected regarding reduction of the barrier identified in Step 3, and progress toward attainment of the outcome identified in Step 1.

8. In the final step, the team decides on a process and timeline for using the data collected through Step 7 to decide if progress toward eliminating the barrier and attaining the desired outcome is satisfactory. In addition, the next steps in the problem solving process are determined. The team determines if the intervention should be adjusted, if a new intervention should be tried, and/or if additional barriers should be addressed.

Systems-Based Service Delivery Programs

POSITIVE BEHAVIOR SUPPORT

School-Wide Positive Behavior Support (SWPBS) is an approach to improving school conduct and discipline that has gained wide support among school psychologists and other educators during the past few years. This approach is based on theory and research in applied behavior analysis and behavior modification (Mayer, 1998). SWPBS provides a systems-based approach to using effective behavior management strategies in schools. The goal of SWPBS is to improve adoption, implementation, and sustained use of evidence-based practices to improve student behavior (Sugai, Horner, & McIntosh, 2008). Important characteristics of SWPBS include: (a) use of evidence-based interventions to support behavioral and academic success of students; (b) use of data to guide decision making about, and selection of, interventions; (c) use of measurable social and academic outcomes; and (d) use of systems supports to improve implementation (Sugai & Horner, 2002). While behavior modification and applied behavior analysis strategies have been used to improve behaviors of individual students for many years, SWPBS represents an approach for supporting improvements in student behavior for entire schools, and recognizes the systemic nature of student and school functioning.

SWPBS emphasizes prevention through a three-tiered model (Crone & Horner, 2003). At the primary prevention, or universal level, all students in a school are exposed to a common, instructionally oriented way of developing appropriate and constructive behaviors. A major strategy at the primary level is the setting of schoolwide behavioral expectations. At the secondary, or targeted level, group oriented evidence-based interventions are provided for students whose behaviors are not responsive to the strategies used at the universal level. At the tertiary, or intensive level, individualized, intensive evidence-based and function-based interventions are used for students who are not responsive to primary and secondary level interventions.

The systems perspective of SWPBS includes an emphasis on capacity-building of schools. In this respect, the approach emphasizes establishing competent coordination of activities, use of coaching, use of ongoing progress monitoring and evaluation, and use of related procedures and programs that have common goals. High fidelity of implementation is a priority (Sugai, et al., 2008).

As a result of the dissemination and technical assistance efforts of the National Center on Positive Behavioral Interventions and Supports (PBIS), Sugai et al. (2008) have identified several factors related to the accurate and sustained use of evidence-based assessment and intervention. These factors are consistent with the systems and innovation implementation concepts described previously. They emphasize the importance of a leadership team, of commitment by the entire school staff to the initiative, of administrator support, of adequate data and information management systems, and of commitment to sustained implementation.

A school leadership team with several characteristics has been found to be related to successful implementation and sustainability. These characteristics include: high status related to school improvement planning; representation from key school groups; active administrator participation and support; representation from students, family, and community members; behavioral knowledge and capacity; and the means for communication and effective decision making.

The importance of the commitment of school staff to SWPBS is illustrated by the common practice of requiring 80% of the school faculty to commit or agree to implement before moving forward. It is suggested that commitments be made in terms of having prevention as a priority, teaching students prosocial behavior, establishing behavior as a top school improvement goal, and engaging in self-assessment and data-based planning and decision making. Implementation of SWPBS activities is discouraged until such commitments are secured from the leadership team and from other school staff.

The active participation of administrators has also been found to be important. Active participation is defined as including good management of human, material, and financial resources, as well as effective scheduling of activities, with the goal of successful implementation of SWPBS. In addition, administrators who are effective supporters of SWPBS are expected to be implementation models, using the processes and procedures in their own work and interactions in their school.

Data and information systems have been found to be essential to effective implementation of SWPBS. They are used to guide selection of interventions, to evaluate implementation fidelity and effectiveness, and to assist in efforts to adapt interventions to make them more effective. Such data systems should be easy to use, and should be built around clearly specified evaluation questions. These questions guide what data will be collected, who will collect it, and the timeframe for data collection.

Finally, Sugai, et al. (2008) have found that for implementation to be effective, a commitment must be made to "multiyear, multicomponent systems implementation" (p. 769). They stress the importance of a 3 to 4 year implementation commitment. They contend that this type of commitment will lessen the documented tendency of schools to organize one-shot professional development programs, and then hope that implementation will occur (Greenwood, Delquadri, & Bulgren, 1993).

Understanding of the manner in which systems function and influence each other has also been shown by recognition of the importance of involving school districts in implementation of SWPBS (Center on PBIS, 2004). An SWPBS Implementers' Blueprint emphasizes the role of school-district-level leadership in helping individual schools successfully implement SWPBS (Center on PBIS, 2004). District level leadership is defined as: development of a district-level leadership team; support for capacity-building at the school level through coaching, training, and evaluation; provision of funding (for at least three years); visibility (documentation and dissemination of outcomes and showcasing of exemplars of success with SWPBS); and political support (through policy decisions, public endorsement of SWPBS, and participation in SWPBS activities).

Further use of a systems perspective in the implementation of SWPBS can be seen in suggestions for and examples of state level implementation (Knoff, 2008). At this systems level, state leadership teams guide school districts in SWPBS implementation efforts. This is seen as especially useful for small-sized districts, or other districts that may not have the capacity in terms of coordination, coaching, training, and evaluation to launch their own implementation efforts with all the components needed for success. In order to scale up and sustain use of SWPBS in individual schools, Sugai, et al. (2008) call for recognition of systems functioning by looking beyond the school as the unit of implementation, to state and national levels. State and national level efforts would focus on development of policy, funding, coordination, and local implementation capacity. Recommendation of these efforts recognizes the profound impact suprasystems can have on individual schools.

Preventive Mental Health Programs – Social and Emotional Learning

Over the past several years, a number of school-based preventive mental health programs have been designated as "evidence-based" by a variety of federal agencies and other organizations that engage in vetting of programs developed to improve the social and emotional capacities of children and youth (Forman & Burke, 2008). Mental health has been found to be integral to success in school (Zins, Bloodworth, Weissberg, & Walberg, 2004), and some contend that in order to be effective, school reform efforts must include efforts to improve the emotional and social functioning of students (Adelman & Taylor, 2006).

These programs, frequently called social and emotional learning (SEL) programs, help students understand and cope with their own emotions, manage their own behavior, and develop and maintain constructive relationships with others. The Collaborative for Academic, Social, and Emotional Learning (CASEL) defines SEL as "the process of acquiring the skills to recognize and manage emotions, develop caring and concern for others, establish positive relationships, make responsible decisions, and handle challenging situations effectively" (Devaney, O'Brien, Resnik, Keister, & Weissberg, 2006, p. 11). SEL competencies include self-awareness, self management, social awareness, relationship skills, and responsible decision making (CASEL, 2003). Effective SEL programs generally use cognitive-behavioral and behavioral procedures to teach students self-control and social competency (Wilson, Gottfredson, & Najaka, 2001).

In recognition of the importance of a thorough understanding of the process of implementation to high quality SEL programs, CASEL has published an implementation guide (Devaney, et al., 2006). This guide is designed to provide direction for administrators and planning teams concerning how to implement and sustain high quality SEL programs. The guide is based on a review of the research on school leadership, comprehensive school reform, SEL and prevention program implementation, and reflects an understanding of how schools function as organizations, and of the systemic nature of schools and their impact on students. The guide emphasizes the idea that SEL is a process as opposed to a program, and that the goal is to create a safe, healthy, caring school community. The guide sets forth a rubric for implementation that includes three phases: readiness, planning, and implementation.

The readiness phase underscores the importance of administrative leadership, and of involvement of stakeholders. In the readiness phase, the school principal must commit to a schoolwide SEL initiative. In addition, in this phase the principal shares information about SEL with stakeholder groups, and creates an SEL steering committee.

In the planning phase the steering committee, of which the principal is a member, creates a vision of student social, emotional, and academic development. The vision is shared schoolwide. In addition, in this phase the steering committee conducts a needs and resources assessment of current SEL programs and practices, the local and state policy context,

student and staff needs, school climate, readiness to make SEL a schoolwide priority, and potential barriers to implementation. An action plan is developed that is based on the needs and resources assessment, and that considers the importance of planning for sustainability. Evidence-based SEL programs that meet identified SEL goals are reviewed and selected.

In the implementation phase, initial professional development is provided to school staff, so that they are knowledgeable about the selected evidence-based SEL program's theory, principles, and strategies. Teachers begin implementing the SEL program in classrooms, and have opportunities to reflect on the implementation process. Necessary program adaptations are made, and SEL practices are integrated into other school activities. The steering committee reviews SEL activities on a regular basis to determine if changes are needed.

The importance of attention to factors that will support sustainability is emphasized in the guide. It is recommended that planning for sustainability begin early in the process, during the planning phase. These factors include the need for: ongoing professional development for implementers; ongoing evaluation and monitoring; a supportive school infrastructure, including policies, funding, time and personnel; integration of the selected SEL program with other school activities, including academics; family and community involvement; and ongoing communication with the entire school community.

Consistent with these implementation guidelines, Forman and Burke (2008) recommend that school psychology practitioners engage in planning and action in a number of areas in order to support successful implementation of evidence-based programs, based on a review of literature on innovation implementation:

1. identification of potential implementers and stakeholders;
2. consideration of implementer and stakeholder perceptions of program characteristics;
3. development of positive implementer and stakeholder attitudes and beliefs;
4. development of administrator and stakeholder support;
5. provision of effective training for implementers and stakeholders;
6. provision of technical assistance for implementers;
7. provision of necessary resources and infrastructure;
8. alignment with school reward structure;

9. alignment with school mission, policies, procedures and other school programs;

10. development of procedures to ensure fidelity; and

11. development of capacity to monitor and evaluate the new program.

These areas recognize the systemic nature of schools, and the importance of understanding characteristics and processes of systems when attempting to implement and sustain new programs.

RESPONSE TO INTERVENTION (RTI)

Response to Intervention (RTI) is a schoolwide process that ensures high quality instruction and supplemental individualized support based on needs of students. RTI integrates evidence-based instruction, assessment, and intervention, and offers a framework within which educators can identify and respond to students at risk for learning and behavior difficulties, and those who are failing to make educational progress. There are several key components of an RTI approach: (a) implementation of multiple tiers of assessment and intervention services; (b) schoolwide screening, assessment, and progress monitoring, and use of data-based decision making; c) evidence-based instruction and intervention; (d) maintenance and adherence to established protocols (i.e., procedural integrity); and (e) creating and sustaining systems-level capacity (Glover & DiPerna, 2007).

Similar to School-Wide Positive Behavior Support, RTI relies on a multi-tiered model of service delivery, which targets all students and provides them with a continuum of services (Johnson & Smith, 2008). Tier 1 instruction (primary prevention level) is delivered to everyone in the general education classroom, and it is estimated that 80% to 85% of students should be successful, without additional services or interventions. Through assessment and progress monitoring, students who are identified as at risk are delivered Tier 2 services (secondary prevention level) which typically consist of accommodations, differentiated instruction, and/or small group programs designed to address student risk and protective factors, deficits, and problems. Tier 3 (tertiary prevention) addresses the needs of students with disabilities in an intensive, individualized fashion, and may be done through special education placement. It is believed that a benefit of using a three-tiered model of prevention and early intervention is that the number of students referred for special education services will be significantly reduced (Johnson & Smith, 2008). At all levels, scientifically based interventions are used in instruction and intervention.

To date, RTI has been used most frequently to distinguish students who are struggling academically from those who have specific learning disabilities and should be considered for special education placement (Shinn, 2007), and in attempts to improve students' reading skills (Wanzek & Vaughn, 2007). It has been used as an alternative to the traditional model for identifying learning disabled students, which requires a discrepancy between ability and achievement documented by test data. Through its emphasis on prevention, RTI seeks to limit the number of students referred for special education by providing evidence-based support, and monitoring student response and progress (Danielson, Doolittle, & Bradley, 2007).

As indicated above, the RTI model recognizes the importance of understanding the school within a systems framework, and building capacity at systems level in order to implement and sustain effective service delivery (Glover & DiPerna, 2007). Systems-related issues that are emphasized in RTI literature include the importance of professional development (Kratochwill, Volpiansky, Clements, & Ball, 2007), use of collaborative, schoolwide teams, and the importance of administrative support (Danielson, et al., 2007). Professional development has received special attention, as it must address the need for training of school personnel in new assessment procedures, prevention-intervention procedures, and methods of successfully adopting, implementing and sustaining effective services. Kratochwill, et al. (2007) contend that RTI is dependent on both the skills of school personnel and the system in which it occurs, and that high quality professional development, which includes multiple sessions, definition of learning outcomes, and measurement of mastery (Brown-Chidsey & Steege, 2005), is essential to successful RTI implementation. These authors also point out that professional development must be viewed within a systems-change perspective, in which other aspects of the school structure and functioning are considered in implementation efforts.

Conclusions

Systems-based service delivery recognizes the systemic nature of schools, and the fact that children and youth live within multiple systems which impact their development, achievement, and functioning. The core of systems-based service delivery is the recognition that in order to prevent and treat the academic, social, behavioral, and emotional problems of children and youth, the various systems that surround them must be the targets of professional practice. The potential for school psychologists to have a positive impact on the lives of children and youth can be greatly increased by understanding and working with the components and processes of the systems that affect students' lives. Several authors contend that school psychologists are in an excellent position to assume a systems change role, because their training is grounded in the study of human behavior and the application of this knowledge to the context of educational settings (Curtis, et al., 2008; Merrell, et al., 2006).

However, in order to successfully engage in systems-based service delivery and systems change, a number of training areas need to receive additional emphasis to support a systems-based approach, rather than an individual-based approach to practice. The training of school psychologists, although steeped in the study of human behavior, tends to focus on individuals and individual differences, with little emphasis on context and systems issues. Forman (2009) has described a course for school psychology doctoral students—"Implementing Innovations in Educational and Human Service Settings"—that addresses theory and research on implementing innovations in schools and other organizational settings, emphasizing the process of bringing psychological and educational research to professional practice with the goal of improving the various systems that surround the lives of children and adolescents. The course addresses the manner in which the process of innovation implementation proceeds, and the individual, group, and organizational factors that influence implementation success. A primary goal of the course is to develop student understanding that potential implementers of new practices and programs operate within a context of social and organizational systems that influence their attitudes, beliefs, and behaviors about interventions, and that a successful plan for implementation will address the various systems that may impact potential implementers. This type of course addresses some of the core areas of knowledge and skill that are necessary for professional competency in systems-based service delivery. Other areas include organizational psychology, community psychology, family systems, adult learning, group dynamics, and program planning and evaluation (Forman & Zins, 2007).

Additional research will also be required to provide the knowledge base for successful engagement in systems-based service delivery, and systems change in school psychology practice. As indicated in the section above, there are several emerging approaches and models for the process of systems-based service delivery. These approaches and models, however, remain largely untested, and research related to their effectiveness is sorely needed. These studies should focus on the effects of these approaches and models on implementation integrity, sustainability, and on student outcomes.

In addition to studies that evaluate overall effectiveness of these approaches and models on implementation and student outcomes, studies that focus on determination of essential or core components are called for. Most of the approaches and models consist of a number of complex steps. Studies are needed to determine which steps or components are essential to successful systems change and improved outcomes for students.

The literature cited above specifies a number of factors that influence the success of innovation implementation and organizational change, including characteristics of the innovation, implementer characteristics, organizational characteristics, and extra-organizational characteristics. However, we do not know the relative impact of these factors on change efforts in school settings. It will be important for future studies to determine this, in order to provide direction for potential change agents so that they can evaluate their probability of success in a change effort, and use their time and resources wisely.

Finally, although a substantial percentage of practicing school psychologists wish to change their role and decrease their time spent in assessment activities with individual students, some have managed to make the shift to engaging in systems-based service delivery. We know little about how this relatively small segment of the profession has managed to accomplish this. Research designed to determine the personal and organizational factors that contribute to the ability of school psychologists to take on this role would be beneficial for the profession.

References

Adelman, H.S. & Taylor, L. (2006). *The school teacher's guide to student learning supports*. Thousand Oaks, CA: Corwin.

Avolio, B.J. (2007). Promoting more integrative strategies for leadership theory-building. *American Psychologist, 62,* 25–33.

Bandura, A. (1978). The self-system in reciprocal determination. *American Psychologist, 33,* 344–358.

Berrien, F.K. (1968). *General and social systems.* New Brunswick, NJ: Rutgers University Press.

Bronfenbrenner, U. (1979). *The ecology of human development.* Cambridge, MA: Harvard University Press.

Brown-Chidsey, R. & Steege, M.W. (2005). *Response to intervention: Principles and strategies for effective practice*. New York: Guilford.

Collaborative for Academic, Social, and Emotional Learning (CASEL). (2003). *Safe and sound: An educational leader's guide to evidence-based social and emotional learning (SEL) programs*. Chicago, IL: CASEL.

Center on Positive Behavioral Interventions and Supports. (2004). *School-Wide Positive Behavior Support: Implementers' blueprint and self-assessment*. Washington DC: Office of Special Education Programs, U.S. Department of Education.

Crone, D.A. & Horner, R.H. (2003). *Building positive behavior support systems in schools: Functional behavioral assessment*. New York: Guilford Press.

Curtis, M.J., Castillo, J.M., & Cohen, R.M. (2008). Best practices in system-level change. In A. Thomas and G. Grimes (Eds.) *Best Practices in school psychology V*. (pp. 887–902). Washington, DC: National Association of School Psychologists.

Danielson, L., Doolittle, J., & Bradley, R. (2007). Professional development, capacity building, and research needs: Critical issues for response to intervention implementation. *School Psychology Review, 36*, 632–637.

Devaney, E., O'Brien, M., Resnick, H. Keister, S., & Weissberg, R.P. (2006). *Sustainable schoolwide social and emotional learning (SEL):Implementation Guide*. Chicago, IL: Collaborative for Academic, Social, and Emotional Learning, University of Illinois at Chicago.

Ervin, R.A. & Schaughency, E. (2008). Best practices in accessing the systems change literature. In A. Thomas and G. Grimes (Eds.) *Best practices in school psychology V*. (pp. 853–874). Washington, DC: National Association of School Psychologists.

Festinger, L. (1957). *A theory of cognitive dissonance*. Stanford, CA: Stanford University Press.

Fielder, F. (1967). *A theory of leadership effectiveness*. New York: McGraw-Hill.

Fixsen, D.L., Naoom, S. F., Blasé, K.A., Friedman, R.M., & Wallace, F. (2005). *Implementation research: A synthesis of the literature*. Tampa, FL: University of South Florida.

Forman, S.G. (2009). Innovation implementation: Developing leadership for evidence-based practice. In S. Rosenfeld & V. Berninger (Eds.) *Translating science-supported instruction into evidence-based practices: Understanding and applying the implementation process* (pp. 655–676). New York: Oxford University Press.

Forman, S.G. & Burke, C.R. (2008). Best practices in selecting and implementing evidence-based school interventions. In A. Thomas and G. Grimes (Eds.) *Best practices in school psychology V*. (pp. 799–812). Washington, DC: National Association of School Psychologists.

Forman, S.G., Olin, S.S., Hoagwood, K.E., Crowe, M., & Saka, N. (2009). Evidence-based interventions in schools: Developers' views of implementation barriers and facilitators. *School Mental Health, 1*, 26–36.

Forman, S.G. & Zins, J.E. (2008). Evidence-based consultation: The importance of context and the consultee. In W.P. Erchul and S.M. Sheridan (Eds.) *Handbook of research in school consultation* (pp. 361–371). New York: Taylor and Francis.

Glennan, T.K., Bodilly, S.J. Gallagher, J. R., & Kerr, K.A. (2004). *Expanding the reach of education reforms: Perspectives from leaders in the scale-up of educational interventions*. Santa Monica, CA: Rand Corporation.

Glisson, C. (2002). The organizational context of children's mental health services. *Clinical Child and Family Psychology Review, 5*, 233–253.

Glisson, C., Dukes, D., & Green, P. (2006). The effects of the ARC organizational intervention on caseworker, climate, and culture in children's service systems. *Child Abuse & Neglect, 30*, 855–880.

Glisson, C. & Green, P. (2006). The effects of organizational culture and climate on the access to mental health care in child welfare and juvenile justice systems. *Administration and Policy in Mental Health and Mental Health Services Research, 33*, 433–448.

Glover, T.A., & DiPerna, J.C. (2007). Service delivery for response to intervention: Core components and directions for future research. *School Psychology Review, 36*, 526–540.

Goodstein, L.D. (1990). A case study in effective organizational change toward high involvement management. In D.B. Fishman & C. Cherniss (Eds.) *The human side of corporate competitiveness* (pp. 171–200). Thousand Oaks, CA: Sage.

Greenhalgh, T., Robert, G. Macfarlane, F., Bate, P., & Kyriakidou, O. (2004). Diffusion of innovations in service organizations: Systematic review and recommendations. *The Milbank Quarterly, 82*, 581–629.

Greenwood, C.R., Delquadri, J., & Bulgren, J. (1993). Current challenges to behavioral technology in the reform of schooling: Large-scale, high quality implementation and sustained use of effective educational practices. *Education and Treatment of Children, 16*, 401–404.

Hall, G.E. & Hord, S.M. (1987). *Change in schools: Facilitating the process*. Albany, NY: State University of New York Press.

Hemmelgarn, A.L., Glisson, C., & James, L.R. (2006). Organizational culture and climate: Implications for service and interventions research. *Clinical Psychology: Science and Practice, 13*, 73–89.

Hernandez, M. & Hodges, S. (2003). Building upon the theory of change for systems of care. *Journal of Emotional and Behavioral Disorders. 11*, 19–26.

Johnson, E.S., & Smith, L. (2008). Implementation of response to intervention at middle school: Challenges and potential benefits. *Teaching Exceptional Children, 40*, 46–52.

Katz, D. & Kahn, R.L. (1966). *The social psychology of organizations*. New York: John Wiley & Sons.

Klein, K.J., & Sorra, J.S. (1996). The challenge of innovation implementation. *Academy of Management Review, 21*, 1055–1080.

Knoff, H.M. (2008). Best practices in implementing statewide positive behavioral support systems. In A. Thomas and G. Grimes (Eds.) *Best practices in school psychology, V*. (pp. 749–764). Washington, DC: National Association of School Psychologists.

Kratochwill, T.R., Volpiansky, P., Clements, M., & Ball, C. (2007). Professional development in implementing and sustaining multitier prevention models: Implications for response to intervention. *School Psychology Review, 36*, 618–631.

Lowin, A. & Craig, J.R. (1968). The influence of level of performance on managerial style: An experimental object-lesson in the ambiguity of correlational data. *Organizational Behavior and Human Performance, 3*, 440–458.

Magary, J.F. (1967). *School psychological services*. Englewood Cliffs, NJ: Prentice Hall.

Mayer, R.G. (1998). Constructive discipline for school personnel. *Education and Treatment of Children, 22*, 36–54.

Merrell, K.W., Ervin, R.A. & Gimpel, G.A. (2006). *School psychology for the 21st century*. New York:Guilford Press.

Miller, J.G., (1955). Toward a general theory for the behavioral sciences. *American Psychologist, 10,* 513–531.

Nastasi, B.K., Vargas, K, Schensul, S.L., Silva, K.T., Schensul, J.J. & Ratnayake, P. (2000). The participatory intervention model: A framework for conceptualizing and promoting intervention acceptability. *School Psychology Quarterly, 15,* 207–232.

Perrow, C. (1970). *Organizational analysis: A sociological view.* Belmont, CA: Wadsworth.

Plous, S. (1993). *The psychology of judgment and decision making.* Philadelphia: Temple University Press.

Rogers, E.M. (2003). *Diffusion of innovations.* New York: The Free Press.

Sarason, S.B. (1990). *The predictable failure of school reform.* San Francisco: Jossey-Bass.

Sarason, S.B. (1971). *The culture of the school and the problem of change.* Boston: Allyn and Bacon.

Senge, P.M. (1990). *The fifth discipline.* New York: Doubleday.

Schaughency, E. & Ervin, R. (2006). Building capacity to implement and sustain effective practices to better serve children. *School Psychology Review, 35,* 155–166.

Sheridan, S.M., & Gutkin, T.B. (2000). The ecology of school psychology: Examining and changing our paradigm for the 21st century. *School Psychology Review, 29,* 485–502.

Shinn, M.R. (2007). Identifying students at risk, monitoring performance, and determining eligibility within response to intervention: Research on educational need and benefit from academic intervention. *School Psychology Review, 36,* 601–617.

Sternberg, R.J. (2007). A systems model of leadership: WICS. *American Psychologist, 62,* 34–42.

Stollar, S.A., Poth, R.L., Curtis, M.J., & Cohen, R.M. (2006). Collaborative strategic planning as illustration of the principles of systems change. *School Psychology Review, 35,* 181–197.

Sugai, G. & Horner, R.H. (2002). The evolution of discipline practices: School-wide positive behavior supports. *Child and Family Behavior Therapy, 24,* 23–50.

Sugai, G., Horner, R., & McIntosh, K. (2008). Best practices in developing a broad-scale system of school-wide positive behavior support. In A. Thomas and G. Grimes (Eds.) *Best practices in school psychology V.* (pp. 765–779). Washington, DC: National Association of School Psychologists.

Van de Ven, A. (1986). Central problems in the management of innovation. *Management Science, 32,* 590–607.

Vroom, V.H. & Jago, A.G. (2007). The role of the situation in leadership. *American Psychologist, 62,* 17–24.

Vroom, V. H. & Jago, A.G. (1988). *The new leadership: Managing participation in organizations.* Englewood Cliffs, NJ: Prentice Hall.

Wanzek, J., & Vaughn, S. (2007). Research-based implications from extensive early reading interventions. *School Psychology Review, 36,* 541–561.

Wilson, D.B., Gottfredson, D. C., & Najaka, S.S. (2001). School-based prevention of problem behaviors: A meta-analysis. *Journal of Quantitative Criminology, 17,* 247–272.

Ysseldyke, J. Burns, M., Dawson, P., Kelly, B., Morrison, D., Ortiz, S., Rosenfield, S. & Telzrow, C. (2006). School psychology: A blueprint for training and practice. In A. Thomas and G. Grimes (Eds.) *Best practices in school psychology V.* (pp. 37–69). Washington, DC: National Association of School Psychologists. Bethesda, MD: National Association of School Psychologists.

Zins, J.E., Bloodworth, M.R., Weissberg, R.P., & Walberg, H.J. (2004). The scientific base linking social and emotional learning to school success. In J.E. Zins, R.P. Weissberg, M.C. Wang, and H.J. Walberg (Eds.) *Building academic success on social and emotional learning: What does the research say?* (pp. 3–22). New York: Teachers College Press.

Positive Behavioral Supports

Lisa M. Hagermoser Sanetti *and* Brandi Simonsen

Abstract

Positive behavior support (PBS) is the application of positive behavioral interventions and systems to achieve socially important outcomes valued by relevant stakeholders. Over the past decade, PBS has evolved from an approach solely focused on the individual behavioral needs of students with disabilities, to an approach also focused on schoolwide systems and the behavioral needs of all students. The purpose of this chapter is threefold. First, we provide an overview of the evolution of PBS including the (a) theoretical, scientific, philosophical, and legal foundations; (b) unique features of PBS; and (c) evolution of PBS from an approach applied to individual students to a systems-level approach. Second, we provide an overview of schoolwide PBS, including the (a) tiers of support in SWPBS, (b) critical features of SWPBS, and (c) implementation of schoolwide PBS (SWPBS). Finally, we provide a synthesis of the empirical support for PBS across public school, alternative school, and juvenile justice settings.

Keywords: positive behavior support, schoolwide positive behavior support, prevention, discipline, behavior intervention, schoolwide intervention, systems change, school psychology

Introduction

"Positive behavior support (PBS) is an applied science that uses educational methods to expand an individual's behavior repertoire and systems change methods to redesign an individual's living environment to first enhance the individual's quality of life and, second, to minimize his or her risk of problem behavior" (Carr et al., 2002, p. 4). Although initially developed as an alternative to application of aversive intervention strategies with students with significant disabilities, PBS has been implemented successfully across a variety of students and contexts (Durand & Carr, 1985; OSEP Center on Positive Behavioral Interventions and Supports, 2000). In this chapter, we provide (a) a discussion of the evolution of PBS, (b) an overview of schoolwide PBS, and (d) a synthesis of the empirical support for PBS across settings.

Evolution of PBS

To set a context for the evolution of PBS, we first discuss its scientific, theoretical, philosophical, and legal foundations. Next, we discuss the unique features of PBS and the evolution of PBS, from an approach solely applied to individual students to an approach also applied at the systems-level.

Scientific, Theoretical, and Philosophical Foundations of PBS

Applied behavior analysis, the normalization/inclusion movement, and person-centered values are the three primary theoretical and philosophical foundations of PBS (Carr et al., 2002). Applied behavior analysis (ABA), an extension of behaviorism, provides the scientific basis of PBS (Dunlap, 2006). Baer, Wolf and Risely (1968) proposed the following seven defining characteristics of ABA: applied, behavioral, analytic, technological, conceptually systematic, effective, and generality.

- *Applied* refers to researchers and practitioners selecting target behaviors that are socially significant to the participant.

- *Behavioral* refers to three interrelated points. First, the target behavior is the behavior in need of improvement, not a proxy. Second, the target behavior must be measurable. Third, when behavior change occurs, one must determine whose behavior changed (i.e., the researcher, practitioner, or participant).
- *Analytic* studies are those in which the experimenter demonstrates a functional relationship between experimental events and the occurrence or nonoccurrence of the target behavior.
- *Technological* research reports describe the study procedures in sufficient detail such that a consumer could replicate them with similar results.
- *Conceptually systematic* research reports describe the behavior change procedures, and any discussion of why the procedures were effective in terms of the relevant behavioral principles from which they were derived.
- *Effective* behavioral techniques result in a practically meaningful level of behavioral improvement.
- *Generality* is demonstrated when change in a target behavior is (a) maintained over time, (b) demonstrated across environments other than the one in which the intervention was implemented, or (c) extended to behaviors not directly targeted by the intervention (Baer et al., 1968).

The results of years of research in ABA provided empirical support for behavioral principles, as well as assessment and intervention strategies that are incorporated within PBS (Carr et al., 2002; Simonsen, Sugai, & Fairbanks, 2007). More specifically, ABA provided the concept of the three-term contingency, setting events, establishing operations, stimulus control, generalization, and maintenance, all of which have allowed for "the elaboration and development of PBS" (Carr et al., p. 5). With regard to assessment strategies, functional assessment and analysis of behavior originated in ABA as a method for first determining the purpose of target behaviors, and then facilitating intervention planning (Iwata, Dorsey, Slifer, Baurman, & Richman, 1982). Finally, ABA was influential in developing numerous educational and intervention strategies, such as shaping, fading, chaining, prompting, and reinforcement contingencies, that are incorporated

within PBS (Carr et al.; Simonsen et al., 2007). Thus, ABA serves as the primary scientific and theoretical foundation of PBS.

The normalization and inclusion movements serve as the philosophical foundation of PBS (Carr et al., 2002). Both of these movements are based on the notion that individuals with disabilities should be able to (a) live in the same settings as others, (b) access the same opportunities as others across all areas of their life (e.g., family, education, work, recreation, socialization), and (c) assume "valued social roles" (Carr et al., p. 5). Closely related to these movements is the philosophy of person-centered values, which is also embraced by PBS. This values perspective is evidenced by, for example, a focus on empowering an individual by increasing choice and decision-making, goal-setting, self-management, and self-advocacy, as well as careful consideration of an individual's specific characteristics, needs, and goals in the development of an intervention plan. As a result of this philosophical foundation, PBS represents "a melding of values and technology, in that strategies are judged not only with respect to efficacy (a technological criterion), but also with respect to their ability to enhance personal dignity and opportunities for choice (a values criterion)" (Carr et al., p. 6). This blending of values and technology is in concert with and reinforced by the relationship between PBS and the ABA tradition of focusing on socially significant target behaviors in real-world settings, while collaborating with local stakeholders (e.g., parents, teachers, students; Simonsen et al., 2007; Sugai & Horner, 2002).

Legal Foundation of PBS

When the amendments to the Individuals with Disabilities Education Act (IDEA) became law in June of 1997, new concepts were introduced related to the education of children who demonstrate behaviors in violation of school codes of conduct or norms of socially acceptable behavior (OSEP Center on Positive Behavioral Interventions and Supports, 2000). More specifically, in Section 1414(d)(3)(B)(i), Congress explicitly provided for the use of "positive behavior interventions, strategies, and supports" when a student's behavior impedes his or her learning (for complete discussions see Wilcox, Turnbull, & Turnbull, 2000; Turnbull, Wilcox, Stowe, Raper, & Hedges, 2000). Also at this time, the term *Positive Behavior Interventions and Supports* (PBIS) was introduced, and the National Technical Assistance Center on PBIS (www.pbis.org) was created (Simonsen et al., 2007). In the most recent reauthorization, the Individuals with Disabilities Education Improvement Act (IDEIA) of 2004, PBIS was referenced eight times (see Table 32.1). Inclusion of PBS in both the 1997 amendments and the 2004 revisions represents an important effort at the federal level to increase the quality of behavior supports provided to all students, especially students with disabilities (OSEP Center on Positive Behavioral Supports and Interventions, 2000). As a result of their training and range of responsibilities, school psychologists have the foundation knowledge, skills, and competence to implement PBS, and thus are in a position to put best practices and legally sound behavioral interventions into practice to benefit students.

Unique Features of PBS

Although PBS evolved from ABA and the normalization and inclusion movements, as discussed above, PBS has a core set of unique features that differentiate it from any other approach to behavioral intervention (Carr et al., 2002). Carr and colleagues (2002) identified the following nine features of PBS, at the individual and systems levels, as those that distinguish PBS from other intervention approaches: (a) comprehensive lifestyle change and quality of life, (b) lifespan perspective, (c) ecological validity, (d) stakeholder participation, (e) social validity, (f) systems change and multi-component intervention, (g) emphasis on prevention, (h) flexibility with respect to scientific practices, and (i) multiple

Table 32.1   References to PBS within IDEA 2004

Location within IDEA 2004	Reference to PBS
§ 1401(c)(5)(F)	PBS is an effective intervention
§ 1411(e)(2)(B)(iii)	PBS is an activity for which states can receive federal funds
§ 1412(a)(22)(B)	When states are reviewing their suspension and expulsion rate data for state eligibility, PBS practices must be reviewed
§ 1414(d)(3)(c)	PBS is an area in which the regular education teacher should assist in determining appropriate strategies.
§ 1454(a)(3)(B)(iii) (I) § 1462(a)(6)(D) § 1465(b)(1)(B-C)	PBS training should be provided as part of professional development of school personnel.

theoretical perspectives. Each of these is discussed in more detail below.

COMPREHENSIVE LIFESTYLE CHANGE AND QUALITY OF LIFE

Perhaps the defining feature of PBS is its focus on improving all participants' quality of life in socially important domains (e.g., social relationships, personal satisfaction, employment, self-determination, recreation, leisure, community integration; Carr et al., 2002). At the individual level, the focus is on lifestyle change that will improve the quality of life for both individuals with disabilities and those who support them. At the systems level, the focus is on broad changes to the system that result in improved outcomes for everyone involved in the system.

LIFESPAN PERSPECTIVE

In PBS, intervention is considered an ongoing systemic process that maintains improvements and addresses new challenges across time. At the individual level, PBS strategies may be adopted and altered, as necessary, as a student with a disability transitions from preschool to elementary and high school, and then to vocational settings. At the systems level, school-wide PBS is being implemented not only in elementary and middle schools, but is also being implemented and evaluated in high schools, alternative schools, and juvenile justice settings (see Empirical Evidence Supporting SWPBS, below).

ECOLOGICAL VALIDITY

In alignment with its foundation in the normalization and inclusion movements, the PBS approach focuses on balancing internal validity issues with applying the behavioral science in real-world settings so as to achieve ecological validity. Toward this end, PBS efforts at the individual and systems levels involve (a) utilizing local intervention agents (e.g., teachers, parents) as opposed to researchers; (b) intervening in typical settings (e.g., home, school, community) as opposed to analogue (e.g., lab) settings; and (c) intervening for extended periods of time across all relevant settings as opposed to brief demonstrations of effectiveness in optimal environments (Carr et al., 2002).

STAKEHOLDER PARTICIPATION

In stark contrast to traditional models of assessment and intervention that have been primarily expert-driven, PBS emphasizes the equal and collaborative participation of all stakeholders in all assessment and intervention practices. At the individual level, all relevant members of the support team, such as parents, siblings, friends, teachers, and the person with disabilities, work with professionals to provide unique perspectives for assessment purposes, and to develop an intervention plan that addresses the most challenging behaviors across all relevant settings in a manner that fits the individual's support network (Carr et al., 2002). At the systems level, teams that work to develop the vision and action plans necessary to implement SWPBS include a broad range of representatives. More specifically, district-level leadership teams may have representatives from special education, curriculum and instruction, families, and administration. Likewise, school-level teams may have teachers, administrators, administrative support staff, sanitary engineers, cafeteria staff, mental health professionals, and hall monitors as representatives (OSEP Center on Positive Behavioral Interventions and Supports, 2004).

SOCIAL VALIDITY

A logical result of the critical features discussed above, social validity is a central factor in designing and implementing PBS strategies. More specifically, at both the individual and systems levels, increased attention is paid to an intervention's (a) practicality, (b) desirability, (c) goodness of fit, and (d) subjective effectiveness regarding both problem behavior and quality of life (Carr et al., 2002).

SYSTEMS CHANGE AND MULTI-COMPONENT INTERVENTION

One of the hallmarks of PBS is its focus on addressing problem environments, not solely problem behaviors. By restructuring environments, PBS promotes behavior change that can be sustained over time. Addressing the numerous facets of an individual's context that are problematic requires a comprehensive approach that incorporates multi-component interventions (Carr et al., 2002). Likewise, implementation at the systems level incorporates multi-component interventions to address numerous contexts including, but not limited to, the community in which the schools are located, students' homes, school buildings, classroom settings, and non-classroom settings (e.g., cafeteria, hallways, bus, playground, parking lot; OSEP Center on Positive Behavioral Interventions and Supports, 2000).

EMPHASIS ON PREVENTION

PBS is a proactive and preventative approach that embraces the idea that the best time to intervene in a serious problem behavior is before the behavior occurs. Methodologically, at both the individual and systems levels, the PBS emphasis on prevention is apparent in the focus on skill building (e.g., preventing the recurrence problem behavior, increasing communicative skills, developing self-management skills) and systems change (e.g., increasing opportunities to make choices, modifying setting events that increase the effectiveness of reinforcers for appropriate behaviors, altering the curricula; Carr et al., 2002).

FLEXIBILITY WITH RESPECT TO SCIENTIFIC PRACTICES

PBS research, in line with the approach's focus on ecological validity, is conducted in community based locations such as schools, homes, and job sites. In such settings, it is nearly impossible to assert the level of experimental control available in analogue settings. Thus, the PBS approach allows for more flexibility with regard to assessment and intervention practices than found in traditional ABA research. For example, although functional analysis is a powerful method of determining functional relationships when implemented by researchers in institution settings, it is typically not feasible in community settings. Likewise, according to a strictly scientific perspective, it is necessary to implement only one intervention at a time to evaluate effectiveness; however, when attempting to address multiple behavioral concerns within complex systems, multi-component interventions are nearly always necessary. The realities of implementing PBS in natural settings, with natural implementers, require adoption of multiple research methodologies (e.g., correlational analyses, naturalistic observations, case studies), assessment approaches (e.g., qualitative measures, interviews, questionnaires, logs, self-report), and multi-component interventions (Carr et al., 2002)

MULTIPLE THEORETICAL PERSPECTIVES

As discussed above, ABA provides the primary theoretical foundation of, and was instrumental in shaping, the development of PBS (Carr et al., 2002; Dunlap, 2006). However, the systematic and community based aspects of PBS led to consideration of other theoretical perspectives. More specifically, systems analysis, ecological psychology, environmental psychology, community psychology, cultural psychology, anthropology, and sociology have all made significant contributions to the evolution of PBS at the individual and systems levels (Carr et al.).

SUMMARY OF UNIQUE FEATURES

The features described above are not new, and many are present, individually, in other approaches to addressing problem behavior (Carr et al., 2002). For example, an emphasis on stakeholder participation is central to person-centered planning. Collectively, however, these nine features distinguish PBS from other approaches, as PBS is the only approach to addressing problem behavior that not only incorporates all of the features described above, but also emphasizes the *integration* of these features.

Evolution of PBS: From Individuals to Systems

As discussed above, PBS emerged from the scientific and theoretical contributions of ABA, and is evaluated against the social validity standards inherent in the normalization and inclusion movements, and person-centered values. When PBS initially emerged from ABA, it was primarily applied to individuals with disabilities and their families (e.g., Horner et al., 1990). Likewise, application at the individual level was mandated in the 1997 amendments to IDEA, and is present in the 2004 revision to this law. However, as the PBS approach evolved, it expanded from addressing the behavioral needs of students with disabilities who receive special education services to addressing the behavioral needs of *all* students. The systems-level application of PBS is typically referred to as *school-wide PBS* (SWPBS) and has been defined as "the application of positive behavioral interventions and systems to achieve socially important behavior change" (OSEP Center on Positive Behavioral Interventions and Supports, 2000, p. 133). Over the past decade, SWPBS has been adopted by numerous school districts interested in addressing students' problem behavior in a proactive and preventative manner (www.pbis.org, 2008). As of 2008, the OSEP Center on PBIS has provided training and technical assistance in implementing SWPBS to over 7500 schools across more than 40 states; many additional schools and districts have adopted SWPBS policies and practices without support from the OSEP Center (www.pbis.org, 2008).

Overview of SWPBS

Now that you have an understanding of the foundations and unique aspects of PBS, as well as the evolution of PBS from application at the individual to the systems-level, we will provide an overview of SWPBS. More specifically, in this section, we review: (a) tiers of support in SWPBS, (b) critical features of SWPBS, and (c) implementation of SWPBS. Interested readers may also refer to the following sources for additional detailed descriptions of the characteristics and procedures of SWPBS: Lewis and Sugai, 1999; OSEP Center on Positive Behavioral Interventions and Supports, 1998, 2000; Safran and Oswald, 2003; Simonsen et al., 2007.

Tiers of Support in SWPBS

As mentioned above, one of the critical features of PBS is its emphasis on prevention. At the systems level, SWPBS is based on the public health model of prevention (Caplan, 1964), which is typically operationalized in a continuum of interventions with three tiers or levels: primary or universal, secondary or group, and tertiary or individual (see Figure 32.1; Simonsen et al., 2007). As is discussed in more detail below, these tiers exist on two continua: the "scope of students involved" and the "intensity" of supports provided (Turnbull et al., 2002, p 378).

PRIMARY TIER

At the primary tier, interventions are delivered to all students, across all settings (i.e., classroom and non-classroom), and involve all relevant stakeholders (i.e., all school personnel, family members, community members; Sugai & Horner, 2006). These interventions tend to be the least intense supports provided. The emphasis of primary-level interventions within SWPBS is teaching contextually relevant social skills, establishing a schoolwide reinforcement system, and arranging teaching and learning environments that encourage appropriate and discourage inappropriate behavior (Simonsen & Sugai, 2009; Sugai & Horner). Data collected across 1,010 elementary, 312 middle/junior, and 104 high schools implementing SWPBS indicate that when primary level support is implemented with a high level of fidelity, approximately 84% of students will be referred to the office for a major rule violation one or fewer times during a school year (Horner, 2007).

SECONDARY TIER

At the secondary tier, more intensive interventions are applied to a relatively small proportion of students who require more than primary-tier supports to reduce the severity of the occurrence of program behavior (Sugai & Horner, 2006). Typical characteristics of secondary support include increasing (a) structure and prompts, (b) explicit social skills instruction, (c) active monitoring, (d) the frequency

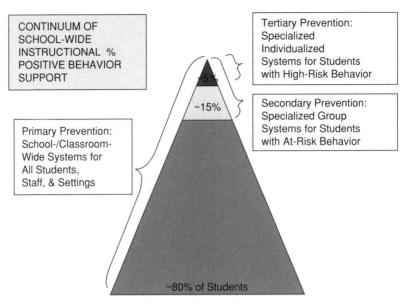

CONTINUUM OF
SCHOOL-WIDE
INSTRUCTIONAL %
POSITIVE BEHAVIOR
SUPPORT

Tertiary Prevention:
Specialized
Individualized
Systems for Students
with High-Risk Behavior

~5%

~15%

Secondary Prevention:
Specialized Group
Systems for Students
with At-Risk Behavior

Primary Prevention:
School-/Classroom-
Wide Systems for
All Students,
Staff, & Settings

~80% of Students

Fig. 32.1 Three-Tiered Continuum of Positive Behavior Support. Reprinted with Permission from OSEP Center on Positive Behavioral Interventions and Supports

or strength of reinforcement provided for appropriate behavior, or (e) a combination of the above (Simonsen & Sugai, 2009). Most schools implementing SWPBS will adopt one or two standardized secondary-tier behavioral interventions, such as check-in/check-out or social skills instruction, that can be applied to all students who require more intensive supports in a similar manner. This approach provides an efficient, feasible, and cost effective method of providing students with supports that match their level of need (Simonsen & Sugai). Approximately 11% of students who do not respond to primary level supports will require secondary support (Horner, 2007).

TERTIARY TIER

At the tertiary tier, intensive, individualized interventions are provided to the small number of students who do not respond to primary or secondary level supports. The hallmark of tertiary level interventions is a function-based approach to behavior assessment and intervention planning (Crone & Horner, 2003). First, a functional behavioral assessment (FBA) is conducted to determine the common antecedent conditions that occasion, and the consequence conditions that maintain, the undesired behavior. In other words, data resulting from the FBA identify the situations in which the behavior is most likely to occur, and the type of reinforcement (i.e., positive or negative) or "function" that

maintains the behavior. This information is utilized to develop an individualized positive behavior intervention plan. Such a plan typically includes strategies to (a) change antecedent conditions, thereby decreasing the likelihood of the behavior being occasioned; (b) teach replacement behaviors that provide the student with a more socially acceptable, efficient, and effective manner of obtaining the same function; and (c) provide function-consistent reinforcement contingent on demonstration of the replacement behavior(s). Approximately 5% of all students will require tertiary level supports (Horner, 2007).

SWPBS AND RESPONSE TO INTERVENTION

Recent education legislation, such as the No Child Left Behind Act of 2001 and the Individuals with Disabilities Education Improvement Act of 2004, encourages schools to change their approach to supporting students, from more reactive traditional approaches to preventative approaches that match supports to the students' needs. In response to the need for more preventative intervention approaches, *response to intervention* (RTI), a general problem-solving framework, has evolved. Although numerous specific RTI models have been proposed, the following six characteristics are common to a majority: (a) universal screening, (b) data-based decision making, (c) progress monitoring, (d) focus on student performance, (e) continuum of evidence-based interventions, and (f) treatment integrity (Brown-Chisdey & Steege, 2005; Christ, Burns, & Yesseldyke, 2005; Fuchs & Deschler, 2007; Fuchs & Fuchs, 2007; Fuchs, Mock, Morgan, & Young, 2003; Gresham, 2005; Gresham et al., 2005; Kame'enui, 2007; Severson, Walker, Hope-Doolittle, Kratochwill, & Gresham, 2007; Sugai, 2008). Each of these characteristics is defined below.

- *Universal screening* requires that all students' performance is reviewed on a regular basis to identify students who are (a) making adequate progress, (b) at some risk of failure, or (c) at high risk of failure.
- *Data-based decision making* requires that information that is a direct measure of student learning and outcomes in the relevant area is used to make decisions about instructional effectiveness, student responsiveness, and intervention effectiveness.
- *Continuous progress monitoring* requires that student progress is assessed regularly to determine the adequacy of growth trends and inform instructional decisions.
- *Continuum of evidence-based practices* requires that an integrated set of interventions be available such that (a) all students receive a core curriculum,

(b) a modification of the core curriculum is provided to students who are nonresponsive to the core, and (c) a more intensive and individualized curriculum is created for students who are nonresponsive to the modified core.

- *Treatment integrity* requires that structures and procedures are in place to coordinate and ensure the accurate, complete, and sustained implementation of the full continuum of evidence-based practices.

Due to the inclusion of RTI in the discussion of eligibility determination for students with learning disabilities in the 2004 revision of the Individuals with Disabilities Education Improvement Act, RTI is often considered a new approach, associated with special education and students with academic problems. However, RTI is neither new, nor limited to a category of educators or students. In fact, SWPBS is compatible with the core principles of RTI (Sandomierski, Kincaid, Algozzine, 2007; Sugai, 2008). Table 32.2 provides an example of how both a schoolwide early literacy and a social behavior (i.e., SWPBS) program align with these core principles. Moreover, Figure 32.2 illustrates how the three-tiered prevention logic, discussed above, has direct applications to a continuum of evidence-based academic and social behavior practices.

Table 32.2   Core features of RTI problem solving model across early literacy and behavior examples

Core Feature of RTI	Early Literacy	Social Behavior
Universal Screening:	Curriculum-based measurement	SSBD; records review; gating
Data-Based Decision Making	Student study team reviews schoolwide literacy data (e.g., CBM benchmark measures), adjustments to literacy curriculum based on data	SWPBS team review of review of schoolwide data, adjustments to implementation based on data
Continuous Progress Monitoring:	Curriculum-based measurement	Office discipline referrals, suspensions, behavior incidents
Student Performance:	Curriculum-based measurement	Office discipline referrals, suspensions, behavior incidents
Continuum of Evidence-Based Practices:	Strategies related to 5 specific reading skills: phonemic awareness, phonics, fluency, vocabulary, comprehension	Direct social skills instruction, positive reinforcement, token economy, behavioral contracting, function-based support
Treatment Integrity	Planning and Evaluation Tool (PET), school-based measures of implementation	SET, Benchmarks of Quality, school-based measures of implementation

From Sugai, G., (August 1, 2007). School-wide positive behavior support and responsiveness-to-intervention. Keynote presentation to and paper for the Southern Maryland PBIS Summer Regional Conference. Waldorf, MD. Adapted with permission.

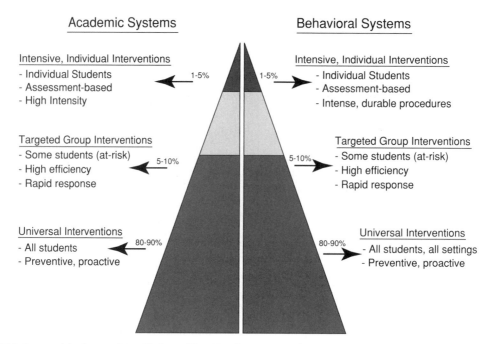

Academic Systems

Intensive, Individual Interventions
- Individual Students
- Assessment-based
- High Intensity

Targeted Group Interventions
- Some students (at-risk)
- High efficiency
- Rapid response

Universal Interventions
- All students
- Preventive, proactive

Behavioral Systems

Intensive, Individual Interventions
- Individual Students
- Assessment-based
- Intense, durable procedures

Targeted Group Interventions
- Some students (at-risk)
- High efficiency
- Rapid response

Universal Interventions
- All students, all settings
- Preventive, proactive

1-5%   1-5%
5-10%   5-10%
80-90%   80-90%

Fig. 32.2 Integrated Academic snd Social Behavior Three-Tiered Continuum of Support. Reprinted with permission from OSEP Center on Positive Behavioral Interventions and Supports.

Similar to RTI, SWPBS provides a continuum of interventions, implemented with a high level of treatment integrity, that are provided to students based on their level of need. Determinations of students' level of need and intervention effectiveness are based on formative data. Consistent with its roots in ABA, SWPBS focuses on modifying the environment to improve behavior problems (Sandomierski et al., 2007; Sugai, 2008). Undoubtedly, SWPBS is well aligned with the RTI problem solving model, and should be considered part of an RTI approach to supporting students, not a competing initiative.

Critical Features of SWPBS

There are four key elements of SWPBS: outcomes, practices, data, and systems. The relationships among these elements are briefly defined in Table 32.3 and illustrated in Figure 32.3 (e.g., OSEP Center on Positive Behavioral Interventions and Supports, 2004). PBS is guided by consideration of outcomes (e.g., academic achievement, social skill development), which are chosen and valued by local stakeholders (e.g., students, families, educators, employers); appropriate to the cultural and regional context and customs; aligned with federal, state, and district mandates and priorities; and feasible within available resources (Simonsen & Sugai, 2009; Sugai & Horner, 2002).

To maximize these outcomes, SWPBS is founded on the long-term implementation of evidence-based practices (i.e., interventions, strategies, supports). This requires not only identifying, adopting, and maintaining research-validated practices that are preventative, aligned with outcomes, and positive, but also rejecting new, less well-established initiatives, curricula, and strategies (Sugai & Horner, 2002). Questions to consider when adopting a new practice are provided in Table 32.4.

Decisions within SWPBS are based on data. Data are used to make decisions regarding the adoption of new practices, areas to be prioritized, effectiveness of practices, quality of implementation of practices,

Table 32.3   Definitions of the four critical features of SWPBS

- *Outcomes* are the academic and behavioral targets chosen and valued by students, families, and educators.
- *Practices* are the evidence-based interventions, strategies, and supports that are implemented to achieve the desired outcomes.
- *Data* the information utilized to determine the need for intervention as well as intervention effectiveness.
- *Systems* supports are utilized to ensure the accurate implementation of PBS over time.

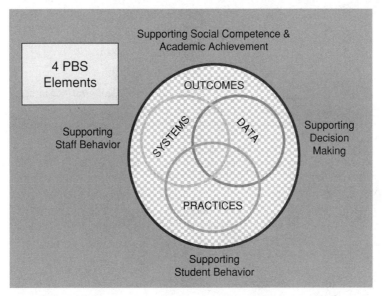

Fig. 32.3 Critical Features of SWPBS. Reprinted with permission from OSEP Center on Positive Behavioral Interventions and Supports.

and student or system progress. Data-based decision making in SWPBS can occur at multiple levels (e.g., individual, classroom, school), include multiple stakeholders (e.g., family, students, educators), address multiple contexts (e.g., home community, school, job site), and be related to multiple outcomes (e.g., academic, behavioral, social, vocational; Sugai & Horner, 2002).

Table 32.4   Questions to consider when adopting a new practice within PBS

"Are educationally and/or socially relevant outcomes specified?"
"Will the efficiency of outcome achievement be improved (e.g., time, effort)?"
"Is research accessible and supportive?"
"Are adoption costs (e.g., training, purchase) justifiable?"
"Are sound conceptual and theoretical foundations indicated?"
"Are successful local applications available?"
"Does evidence exist to support a change in current practice?"
"Have previous practices been implemented with high fidelity?"
"Are supports in place to occasion and sustain implementation?"

From *Behavior Psychology in the Schools: Innovations in Evaluation, Support, and Consultation*, by Sugai and Horner. Copyright 2002 by Haworth Press/Taylor & Francis Books. Reproduced with permission of Haworth Press/Taylor & Francis.

Finally, SWPBS addresses the systems necessary to support the sustained implementation of the evidence-based practices and decision-making procedures, to maximize the identified outcomes. Addressing systems issues includes consideration of, for example, the effectiveness, efficiency, and significance of organizational processes, routines, structures, policies, and activities. As Horner (2003) emphasized, organizations do not behave; rather, individuals within the organization behave. Thus, an organization is defined by the extent to which its membership moves it toward a common goal; promoting such goal-directed behaviors requires the type of systems-level supports promoted within SWPBS (Sugai & Horner, 2006).

Implementation of SWPBS

At this point, you should have a clear understanding of the critical features of the SWPBS model. Now, we will describe the process by which schools implement primary tier, or universal, SWPBS. To implement universal SWPBS, schools typically: (a) engage in activities to meet readiness requirements; (b) participate in professional development activities; (c) develop a data-based action plan; (d) adopt evidence-based practices; (e) develop and invest in systems; and (f) implement, monitor, and revise their data-based action plan (see Figure 32.4). Each of these steps will be explored in the next sections.

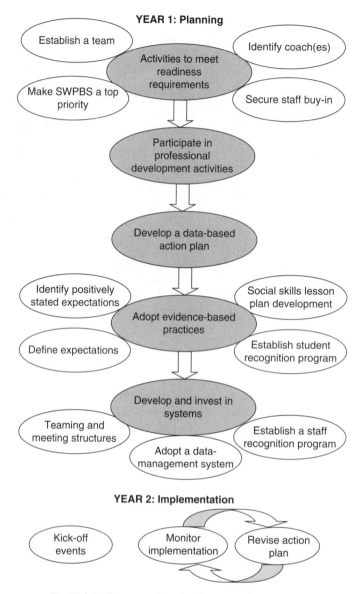

YEAR 1: Planning

Establish a team

Identify coach(es)

Activities to meet readiness requirements

Make SWPBS a top priority

Secure staff buy-in

Participate in professional development activities

Develop a data-based action plan

Identify positively stated expectations

Social skills lesson plan development

Adopt evidence-based practices

Define expectations

Establish student recognition program

Develop and invest in systems

Teaming and meeting structures

Establish a staff recognition program

Adopt a data-management system

YEAR 2: Implementation

Kick-off events

Monitor implementation

Revise action plan

Fig. 32.4 Implementation Timeline for Universal-Level SWPBS

ENGAGE IN ACTIVITIES TO MEET READINESS REQUIREMENTS

When members of a school faculty express interest in SWPBS, the first step is to contact their state PBS coordinator. The state PBS coordinator will share the readiness requirements that must be met prior to the school participating in professional development activities. Individuals who are approved, by the Office of Special Education Program's National Technical Assistance Center on Positive Behavior Interventions and Supports, to function as state coordinators are listed on the National Technical Assistance Center's website

(www.pbis.org). Although readiness requirements may vary by state, typical requirements include: establishing a team, identifying coach(es), securing staff buy-in, and making SWPBS a top priority (e.g., OSEP Center on Positive Behavioral Interventions and Supports, 2004).

ESTABLISH A TEAM.

SWPBS should be planned, developed, implemented, and monitored by a representative team of individuals. Typically, the team comprises (a) an administrator who is able to commit school resources; (b) general education teachers who represent (by grade, content, or both) the certified general education faculty; (c) one or more members of special support services (e.g., special educator, counselor, school psychologist, social worker) with behavioral expertise; (d) a member of noncertified staff (e.g., paraprofessional, administrative assistant, janitor); (e) one or more stakeholders (i.e., family and community members) who represent outside perspectives; and (f) one or more students, if appropriate, based on maturity. Members should be selected on the basis of supporting SWPBS implementation at the school, having expertise in one or more areas (e.g., behavioral interventions), and having social influence (i.e., being respected by peers and colleagues such that they are able to impact behavior). The SWPBS team should be large enough to be representative, but small enough to be functional (i.e., to effectively communicate and make decisions at team meetings). In general, teams are made up of 8–12 individuals.

IDENTIFY ONE (OR MORE) COACH(ES).
After team members are selected, one (or more) team member(s) is identified to perform coaching functions. Coaching functions include facilitating team meetings, managing the data-based action plan (described in a subsequent section), ensuring that team members obtain faculty input on all critical decisions, staying true to SWPBS content, and other similar tasks. Thus, coaches should be individuals who are comfortable in a leadership role (i.e., facilitating, communicating, and presenting information) and who have time allocated to performing coaching functions.

SECURE STAFF BUY-IN.
Staff support, or buy-in, is critical to the success of any schoolwide initiative, including SWPBS. To obtain staff support, most school-level SWPBS teams will present an overview of SWPBS to their staff, and conduct a vote of staff members to determine how many support (i.e., are willing to learn more and implement SWPBS) and do not support implementing SWPBS in their school. The typical rule-of-thumb is that at least 80% of staff should vote in support of SWPBS before team members invest in professional development activities.

MAKE SWPBS A TOP PRIORITY.
For SWPBS to be implemented with fidelity and success, it should be one of the top three priorities for the school. Typically, school priorities are articulated in a school or district improvement plan or a similar document used for strategic planning. When SWPBS is not a top priority, schools often find that team members are pulled in multiple directions, and the required planning, implementation, and monitoring activities are not conducted with fidelity.

PARTICIPATE IN PROFESSIONAL DEVELOPMENT ACTIVITIES
After schools have met the readiness requirements specified by their state PBS coordinator, they are able to participate in professional development activities. Schools should anticipate spending one year preparing to implement SWPBS (i.e., planning). During the planning year, professional development activities typically include three 2-day team training events (6 days total) and three half-day coaching events. Throughout training activities, the state-approved trainer will (a) share the conceptual framework supporting SWPBS (i.e., an overview of the behavioral theory and applied behavior analysis, similar to that presented earlier in this chapter); (b) describe how to implement practices, establish systems, and use data to make decisions across all settings of the school (i.e., classroom and nonclassroom); (c) provide instruction in how to create a data-based action plan and other products required to implement contextually appropriate evidence-based practices and systems; and (d) give school teams an opportunity to work collaboratively during structured action planning sessions. In other words, school team members receive the information required to complete the remaining implementation steps. During the implementation year, school teams continue to participate in ongoing professional development focused on addressing specific issues related to implementation (e.g., issues with implementation fidelity).

DEVELOP A DATA BASED ACTION PLAN
Throughout and following professional development activities, school teams develop, evaluate, and revise an action plan. The action plan specifies the action items to be completed, by one or more team members, on or before a specified date. Action items include activities required to plan, develop, implement, monitor, and revise SWPBS at each school. More specifically, action items include (a) steps required to create and implement contextually appropriate evidence-based practices, (b) actions involved in developing and sustaining systems, and (c) other activities required to implement SWPBS. The action plan is a "living" document; that is, it is

developed during professional development activities, reviewed at each team meeting, and modified based on data.

ADOPT EVIDENCE-BASED PRACTICES

As you can infer from the description of the critical features of the SWPBS model, SWPBS is not a curriculum or packaged program. Instead, each school is guided to identify, adopt, and implement evidence-based practices that align with their outcomes. In particular, schools identify a small number of positively stated expectations, define each expectation within each school routine, develop and deliver explicit social skills lesson plans to teach each expectation within each routine, and establish a schoolwide student recognition program to reward expectation-following behavior (e.g., OSEP Center on Positive Behavioral Interventions and Supports, 2004). Although the SWPBS team members will perform most of the work for each of these tasks, it is important that team members recruit feedback from all staff members to maintain staff buy-in.

IDENTIFY A SMALL NUMBER OF POSITIVELY STATED EXPECTATIONS.

Rather than enforcing a list of rules specifying what students *should not* do, schools implementing SWPBS select a small number of positively stated expectations that specify what students *should* do. These expectations, or rules, should be broadly stated (to encompass a variety of distinct behaviors) and mutually exclusive (such that each behavior fits within only one expectation). For example, a school may adopt three expectations: Be Safe, Be Respectful, and Be Responsible. At this school, the discrete behaviors of "walk in the hallway" and "bring materials to class" would fall under the expectations Be Safe and Be Responsible, respectively.

DEFINE EXPECTATIONS WITHIN SCHOOL SETTINGS AND ROUTINES.

After SWPBS team members have identified the expectations, they provide operational definitions of each expectation within each setting or routine. That is, they describe what it "looks like" to engage in expectation-following behavior within each setting or routine. One way to do this is to develop an expectations-within-routines matrix, or table. Using this format, they write expectations as row headings, settings and routines as column headings, and use short bulleted statements to define the expectation within each routine (in the appropriate box in the matrix). For example, the team members may

write "keep hands, feet, and objects to self"; "walk on the right side of the hallway"; and "report unsafe objects and behavior to a teacher" at the intersection of the expectation "Be Safe" and the setting "Hallway."

DEVELOP AND DELIVER EXPLICIT SOCIAL SKILLS LESSON PLANS.

Next, SWPBS team members develop lesson plans to teach each expectation within each routine; that is, they write a separate lesson plan for each box in the matrix. Each lesson plan should include (a) an introduction that identifies, describes, and defines each expectation within each routine; (b) a clearly stated lesson objective; (c) a list of positive and negative examples, which sample the range of variations in expected behavior and progress from minimally to maximally different; (d) lesson activities that explicitly teach (model, lead, and test) students the expectation-following behavior; and (e) strategies to prompt, monitor, reinforce, correct, and evaluate expectation-following behavior after instruction. Because all teachers within a school will deliver lesson plans, the lesson plans should be scripted to facilitate consistent and systematic social skills instruction.

In addition to creating lesson plans, SWPBS team members develop a schedule to ensure that all teachers consistently deliver lesson plans in the natural context (i.e., lessons on hallway behavior are taught in the hallway). Some schools will opt to schedule all of their lesson plans during the first week of school, acknowledging that giving priority to social behavior instruction will likely improve student behavior during subsequent academic instruction. Other schools will schedule social skills lessons during homeroom or morning periods across the school year. Regardless of schedule, SWPBS team members should anticipate scheduling additional review and re-teaching sessions prior to times when problem behaviors are likely to escalate based on data. For example, a school staff who delivered intensive social skills instruction during the first week of school may need to provide booster sessions before November, March, and May (months that preceded or included major schedule disruptions during which office discipline referrals were the highest across the past 3 years).

ESTABLISH A SCHOOLWIDE STUDENT RECOGNITION PROGRAM.

To increase the likelihood that students will engage in expectation-following behavior, SWPBS team members should design a schoolwide student recognition system. There are a variety of strategies that schools may choose to recognize student behavior, including specific and contingent praise and a continuum of other positive strategies to "catch students being good." For example, many schools elect to use positive behavior tickets or coupons that specify which expectation a student was "caught" following, in which routine or setting. At the beginning of the year, when students are learning how to follow the expectations, positive tickets would be delivered frequently to ensure that most students experience success. After most students have demonstrated that they are able to engage in expectation-following behavior, positive tickets would be given less often and reserved for exemplary behavior. Once earned, students may enter tickets or coupons into a lottery for a prize drawing, or students may use them as money in a school store. Regardless of the configuration, the schoolwide student recognition system should ensure that school staff members: (a) recognize students immediately for expectation-following behavior, (b) tell students specifically why they are being recognized, (c) employ a continuum of procedures to ensure that all students (i.e., students who enjoy adult attention, students who like to escape work, and students who prefer peer attention) will benefit from the recognition, and (d) use data to monitor the effectiveness of the system and adjust as necessary.

DEVELOP AND INVEST IN SYSTEMS

As stated previously, SWPBS team members invest in systems to ensure that practices are implemented with fidelity and sustained across time. Systems are the supports put in place for staff and typically include teaming and meeting structures, data management systems, and a schoolwide staff recognition program (e.g., OSEP Center on Positive Behavioral Interventions and Supports, 2004).

TEAMING AND MEETING STRUCTURES.

To ensure that SWPBS is implemented and monitored consistently, the SWPBS team should be given priority status in the school. Specifically, team meetings should be scheduled on the master calendar for the school, and attendance at meetings should be expected (i.e., mandatory). School administrators should ensure that conflicting meetings and events are not scheduled, and the administrator who is assigned to the team should attend each meeting for the full time.

The individual(s) designated as coach(es) should facilitate each meeting, using a structured agenda that includes timelines for discussing and deciding on each item. A typical meeting agenda includes the following items: review of schoolwide data, adjustments to implementation based on data, review of action plan, and modification of action plan based on data and adjustments to implementation. During the meeting, the coach ensures that each item on the agenda is discussed, team members are held accountable for items assigned to them on the action plan, and a specific plan of action is created and documented for any future tasks.

In addition to SWPBS team meetings, team members should request time during the larger faculty meetings to communicate with all staff members. To ensure that this time is protected, team members should ask the school administrator responsible for leading faculty meetings to add SWPBS to the standard agenda. Throughout both the planning and implementation phases, it is critical to share information and ask for staff input to maintain staff support for SWPBS.

DATA MANAGEMENT SYSTEM.

SWPBS team members should invest in a data management system that allows for (a) efficient data input and (b) effective and flexible output (i.e., meaningful graphs of schoolwide data). Schools typically rely on office discipline referral (ODR) data as an indicator of problematic social behavior. Currently, there are commercially available, web-based products (e.g., www.swis.org; May et al., 2000) that facilitate data input and output. Schools should also develop a system to track their schoolwide student recognition program (e.g., track the number of positive tickets or coupons distributed by each staff member). In addition, schools should use other schoolwide data (e.g., percentage of students meeting benchmarks on state- and district-wide tests, progress on AYP) to measure progress toward relevant outcomes (e.g., Simonsen & Sugai, 2007).

Along with developing a data management system to track outcome data, schools should invest in a data system to track the fidelity of implementation of SWPBS practices, or the degree to which the practices are implemented as intended. In many states, there are evaluation structures that provide schools with annual (or semi-annual) evaluations of fidelity, using the Schoolwide Evaluation Tool (SET; Todd et al., 2004); trained outside evaluators (i.e., district- or state-level administrators) administer the SET.

Schools should also consider developing their own systems to monitor fidelity. For example, a school may examine data that are already being collected (e.g., the number of positive tickets distributed by each teacher) as an indicator of the fidelity with which a certain component of SWPBS (e.g., the student recognition system) is being implemented. Regardless of the system chosen, schools should ensure that fidelity data are being collected and used to make decisions.

In addition to investing in data-management systems (for outcome and fidelity data), SWPBS team members need to ensure that the necessary support structures (i.e., staffing resources, technical support) are in place. In general, this requires that the school designate one or more individuals to enter data, one or more individuals to summarize data in a user-friendly format (i.e., print graphs), and one or more individuals to share data with other team members and the larger school faculty. In addition, SWPBS team members and other school administrators should ensure that data are reviewed and used to make all major school decisions. For example, an assistant principal may share school-wide ODR and positive ticket data before asking staff to make a decision about increasing the frequency with which they give positive tickets in a particular setting (e.g., a hallway where problem behaviors currently occur at higher rates and fewer coupons are currently given).

SCHOOLWIDE STAFF RECOGNITION PROGRAM.
At this point, it should be clear that implementing SWPBS requires a great deal of staff behavior change. Therefore, it is important to call for and recognize staff accomplishments by developing a staff recognition program. Like the schoolwide student recognition program, the specific features of the staff recognition program will be determined by the context of the school. For example, one school may implement a system where staff members write positive (or thank you) notes to each other, which are read at a faculty meeting to provide social recognition. A different school may choose to recognize staff based on data (e.g., the highest ratio of positive coupons to ODRs), and provide rewards such as a free designated parking space, an opportunity to come into school late one day, or other similar privileges. Regardless of the specific makeup, the staff recognition system should have the following key features: (a) staff behavior is recognized immediately, (b) a variety of strategies are used to provide recognition to account for variations in staff preference, and

(c) data are used to monitor the effectiveness and fairness (i.e., ensuring that recognition is spread among all deserving staff) of the system.

IMPLEMENT, MONITOR, AND REVISE ACTION PLAN

After spending an entire year participating in professional development activities, engaging in action planning, and developing the products required to implement SWPBS practices (e.g., expectations-within-routines matrix, social skills lesson plans, student recognition program) and systems (e.g., data management system, staff recognition program), the school is ready to implement SWPBS. Typically, implementation is "kicked off" by a staff event and a student event. For example, a school may have a staff event during the orientation and training week before the start of school. At this event, members of the SWPBS team may remind the staff about critical features of SWPBS, provide instruction on how to deliver social skills lessons according to the schedule, and introduce the staff recognition system. Then, the school may introduce SWPBS to the students at an initial assembly, where members of the SWPBS team present the expectations and introduce the schoolwide student reinforcement system. Following this assembly, staff members deliver social skills lessons according to the agreed-upon schedule, and they catch students following the expectations and provide recognition (e.g., specific praise and a positive behavior ticket).

Throughout the year (i.e., after the initial kick-off events), SWPBS team members continue to meet regularly (i.e., once or twice per month on the dates specified on the school meeting calendar) to monitor implementation. At each meeting, the coach prompts team members to follow the agenda; that is, team members review schoolwide data and their progress on their action plan, make adjustments to their implementation based on data, and update their action plan to reflect the adjustments. SWPBS team members gather faculty input for each major change, and they communicate any decisions made (e.g., to increase student recognition in a particular setting) at the next faculty meeting. In addition, fidelity data are taken and reviewed on a regular basis to ensure that (a) most staff members are implementing SWPBS practices as intended, and (b) additional support is provided to faculty who require (or request) it.

In sum, implementing SWPBS, or any similarly comprehensive schoolwide initiative, is a large undertaking. School teams should anticipate spending a year planning (i.e., participating in professional development and developing an action plan and related products) prior to implementing SWPBS. Then, schools should expect to spend one or more years working with staff to ensure that most staff members implement with fidelity, and once desired fidelity is achieved, schools should expect to work to maintain it. Throughout implementation, SWPBS team members should meet regularly, review data on outcomes and fidelity, use data to make decisions, review and adjust their action plan, and recruit feedback from the larger school faculty to maintain staff support. When SWPBS is implemented well across years, many schools experience positive results. The next section describes the empirical support for SWPBS.

Empirical Evidence Supporting SWPBS

SWPBS is a well-documented approach to effecting meaningful behavior change in a school setting. In this section, we review the literature supporting the implementation of the SWPBS model in public school, alternative school, and juvenile justice settings.

Public School Setting

The majority of research on SWPBS was conducted in public school settings. Studies have focused on both *schoolwide* (i.e., whole-school implementation of SWPBS) and *setting specific* (i.e., implementation of interventions in one or more settings within a school) PBS implementation.

SCHOOLWIDE PBS

Much of the early literature supporting SWPBS involved descriptive or quasi-experimental studies of the model within or across a small number of schools or settings. For example, case studies were conducted to investigate the impact of SWPBS, and descriptive data indicated that interventions within each of the three tiers (i.e., primary, secondary, and tertiary) were related to positive changes in (a) the overall performance of students within the school (i.e., increases in positive interactions, decreases in ODRs; Netzel & Eber, 2003; Turnbull et al., 2002) and (b) the performance of an individual student with chronic problem behavior (i.e., being able to state schoolwide expectations, increases in self-management; Turnbull et al., 2002). In addition, researchers demonstrated that implementation of SWPBS is associated with (a) decreases student problem behavior, as documented by ODRs and other disciplinary actions (e.g., suspensions,

expulsions), and (b) increases in student academic performance (for school-age students) in the following public, or typical, school settings:

- Preschool (e.g., Muscott, Mann, & Lebrun, 2008),
- Elementary School (e.g., McCurdy, Manella, & Eldrige, 2003; Muscott et al., 2008),
- Middle School (e.g., Lassen, Steele, & Sailor, 2006; Metzler, Biglan, Rusby, & Sprague, 2001; Muscott et al., 2008), and
- High School (e.g., Bohanon et al., 2006; Muscott et al., 2008).

More recently, researchers have conducted randomized control trials (RCTs), the "gold standard" for experimental research, to document the impact of implementing SWPBS across groups of schools. In a recently conducted RCT, Horner and colleagues (2009) randomly assigned 90 elementary schools to treatment (SWPBS) or wait list (control) conditions. Initial results indicate that schools assigned to SWPBS implemented the model with fidelity and experienced positive outcomes (improved perceptions of school safety and potential increases in academic performance). Similarly, Bradshaw, Reinke, et al. (2008) conducted a RCT with 37 elementary schools; 21 schools participated in SWPBS training and 16 agreed to postpone training. Preliminary results suggest that schools that participated in training were able to implement with fidelity and experienced positive outcomes (i.e., reductions in office discipline referrals and suspensions, increases in indicators of organizational health). In sum, initial RCT data provide support for considering SWPBS an evidence-based practice. However, additional experimental studies are necessary to confirm that SWPBS is an evidence-based practice, especially for middle and high school settings.

SETTING-SPECIFIC PBS

In addition to demonstrations of the entire SWPBS model, researchers have demonstrated the effectiveness of setting-specific interventions, which are based on SWPBS logic (e.g., indicated by data, evidence-based) and implemented in SWPBS schools. For example, Kartub, Taylor-Green, March, and Horner (2000) implemented a simple intervention to address excessive cafeteria noise in a public middle school, and they documented the effects in a nonexperimental single subject case study (AB design). The intervention included the following components: (a) modeling quiet behavior; (b) signaling when voices were too loud; (c) teaching the rule "when you see the light (blinking light), lips stay tight" (p. 180); and (d) reinforcing quiet behavior. Following implementation of this noise reduction intervention, cafeteria noise decreased by an average of 7.6, 9.3, and 9.0 decibels across sixth, seventh, and eighth grades, respectively, from baseline to follow-up.

Similarly, other researchers (e.g., Lewis, Powers, Kelk, & Newcomer, 2002; Haydon & Scott, 2008) have developed and implemented simple interventions (e.g., teaching and reinforcing expected behavior, increasing active supervision and precorrection), which have systematically reduced the frequency of observed problem behavior in the targeted common areas (e.g., playground, morning gym). Thus, emerging evidence suggests that schools implementing SWPBS are able to design and implement effective setting-specific interventions.

In sum, SWPBS is associated with positive outcomes (i.e., decreases in recorded problem behavior and increases in academic achievement) in typical public school settings. When students' needs cannot be met within a typical school environment, they may be served in other educational environments, including alternative school and juvenile justice settings. The next sections review the literature supporting implementation of SWPBS in each of these settings.

Alternative School Settings

To date, there is a very limited evidence base supporting SWPBS or similar proactive schoolwide interventions in alternative school settings. Miller, George, and Fogt (2005) implemented a schoolwide positive preventative approach at the Centennial School at Lehigh University. Although they did not call their intervention "SWPBS," they stated that they implemented "systemic change," which included Effective Behavior Support (a predecessor of SWPBS; Lewis & Sugai, 1999). In particular, they identified outcomes (i.e., goals and vision), used data to drive decision making, implemented evidence-based practices (e.g., social skills instruction and reinforcement programs), and invested in systems (e.g., established a schoolwide team, reorganized staffing patterns). As a result of implementing this proactive schoolwide intervention, Centennial School reduced the rate of physical restraints from 1,064 in one year (an average of 14 per student) to near-zero levels (Miller et al.).

Similarly, Miller, Hunt, and Georges (2006) demonstrated positive effects when a proactive systemwide intervention was introduced into two

residential treatment facilities that each included a residential and a school unit. Specifically, they documented a 59% reduction in physical restraints following the implementation of the systemwide intervention. Simonsen, Britton, and Young (2010) also demonstrated positive effects after introducing SWPBS into one alternative school in a descriptive case study. Thus, several studies have documented positive effects when SWPBS or a similar systemwide intervention was implemented in an alternative school setting. However, no studies have employed experimental methodology, and additional research is needed before SWPBS is considered an evidence-based approach for alternative school settings.

Juvenile Justice Settings

Like alternative school settings, there is a limited evidence base that supports implementation of SWPBS in juvenile justice settings. Although there have been no experimental studies conducted to date, Scott and colleagues (2002) described how each of the three tiers of SWPBS can support adjudicated youth, and they argued that SWPBS may be an effective form of prevention and intervention for this population. Subsequently, Houchins, Jolivette, Wessendorf, McGlynn, and Nelson (2005) conducted focus groups with stakeholders in a juvenile justice facility that had implemented systemwide PBS for a year and a half: the Iowa Juvenile Home/Girls State Training School.

Using qualitative methodology, Houchins and colleagues (2005) identified themes related to stakeholders' perceptions of implementing SWPBS in a juvenile justice setting. In particular, they noted that implementing PBS represented a significant shift from traditional models of service delivery in juvenile justice settings. For example, SWPBS required staff members to change the way they interacted with youth (i.e., teaching and reinforcing rather that forcing compliance), changes that were sometimes met with resistance. Stakeholders also identified that implementing SWPBS required knowledge of and access to evidence-based practices that could be adapted to juvenile justice settings. In some instances, this proved challenging; for example, stakeholders stated that it was difficult to identify effective reinforcers that were not prohibited in the setting. In addition, stakeholders shared the difficulty with maintaining communication and consistency across the various environments (e.g., cottages, school) and shifts of staff. Despite the identified barriers, Houchins and colleagues assert that SWPBS can be an effective service delivery model within juvenile justice settings, especially when the goal is to "merge" SWPBS with more traditional correctional practices. Clearly, additional empirical research is needed before SWPBS can be considered an evidence-based program for juvenile justice settings.

Conclusion

Over the past decade, central elements of SWPBS, such as (a) a continuum of support operationalized by three tiers of support; (b) a focus on outcomes, systems, practices, and data; and (c) a process for implementation, have been defined, implemented, and studied. At this point, experimental evidence indicates that implementation of SWPBS in public elementary schools resulted in positive outcomes (Bradshaw, Koth, et al., 2008; Bradshaw, Reinke et al., 2008). In addition, descriptive and quasi-experimental data support implementation of SWPBS in public preschool, middle school, and high school settings (Bohanon et al., 2006; Lassen et al., 2006; McCurdy et al., 2003; Metzler et al., 2001; Muscott et al., 2008). Descriptive case studies also indicate that SWPBS may be effective in alternative education settings (Miller et al. 2005, 2006; Simonsen et al., 2008), and researchers have suggested implementing SWPBS in juvenile justice facilities (Scott et al., 2002; Houchins et al., 2005).

Future Directions

Additional research is needed to document that SWPBS is an evidence-based practice across the range of school settings. More specifically, data from RCT studies would be beneficial to support available evidence from descriptive and quasi-experimental studies regarding the effectiveness of SWPBS in public preschool, middle school and high school settings. Furthermore, systematic lines of research are needed to understand how SWPBS can be effectively adapted and applied within alternative education settings and juvenile justice facilities.

References

Baer, D. M., Wolf, M. M., & Risely, T. R. (1968). Some current dimensions of applied behavior analysis. *Journal of Applied Behavior Analysis, 1*, 91–97.

Bohanon, H., Fenning, P., Carney, K. L., Minnis-Kim, M. J., Anderson-Harris, S., Moroz, K. B., et al. (2006). Schoolwide application of positive behavior support in an urban high school: A case study. *Journal of Positive Behavior Interventions, 8*, 131–145.

Bradshaw, C., Koth, C., Bevans, K., Ialongo, N., & Leaf, P. (2008). The impact of school-wide positive behavioral interventions and supports (PBIS) on the organizational health of elementary schools. *School Psychology Quarterly, 23*, 462–473.

Bradshaw, C., Reinke, W., Brown, L., Bevans, K., & Leaf, P. (2008). Implementation of school-wide positive behavioral interventions and supports (PBIS) in elementary schools: Observations from a randomized trial. *Education and Treatment of Children, 31*, 1–26.

Brown-Chisdey, R., & Steege, M. W. (2005). *Response to intervention: Principles and strategies for effective practice.* New York: Guilford Press.

Caplan, G. (1964). *Principles of preventive psychiatry.* New York: Basic Books.

Carr, E. G., Dunlap, G., Horner, R. H., Koegel, R. L., Turnbull, A. P., Sailor, W. et al. (2002). Positive behavior support: Evolution of an applied science. *Journal of Positive Behavior Interventions, 4*, p.4–16.

Christ, T. J., Burns, M., K., & Yesseldyke, J. E. (2005). Conceptual confusion within response-to-intervention vernacular: Clarifying meaningful differences. *Communique, 34*, 1–8.

Crone, D. A., & Horner, R. H. (2003). *Building positive behavior support systems in schools: Functional behavioral assessment.* New York: Guilford Press.

Dunlap, G. (2006). The applied behavior analytic heritage of PBS: A dynamic model of action-oriented research, *Journal of Positive Behavior Interventions, 8*, 58–60.

Durand, M. V., & Carr, E. G. (1985). Self-injurious behavior: Motivating conditions and guidelines for treatment. *School Psychology Review, 14*, 171–176.

Fuchs, D., & Deschler, D. D. (2007). What we need to know about responsiveness to intervention (and shouldn't be afraid to ask). *Learning Disabilities Research & Practice, 22*, 129–136.

Fuchs, D., & Fuchs, L. S. (Eds.). (2007). Responsiveness to intervention [Special issue]. *Teaching Exceptional Children, 39*.

Fuchs, D., Mock, D., Morgan, P. L., & Young, C. L. (2003). Responsiveness-to-intervention: Definitions, evidence, and implications for the learning disabilities construct. *Learning Disabilities Research and Practice, 18*, 157–171.

Gresham, R. M. (2005). Responsiveness to intervention: An alternative means of identifying students as emotionally disturbed. *Education and Treatment of Children, 28*, 328–344.

Gresham, F. M., Reschly, D. J., Tilly, W. D., Fletcher, J., Burns, M., Prasse, D., et al. (2005). A response to intervention perspective. *The School Psychologist, 59*, 26–33.

Haydon, T. & Scott, T. M. (2008). Using common sense in common settings: Active supervision and precorrection in the morning gym. *Intervention in School and Clinic, 43*, 283–290.

Horner, R. H. (2003, March 27). *Extending positive behavior support to whole schools: Sustainable implementation.* Keynote address, First International Conference on Positive Behavior Support, Orlando, FL.

Horner, R. (2007). Discipline Prevention Data. Eugene, OR: OSEP Center on Positive Behavior Interventions and Supports, University of Oregon.

Horner, R. H., Dunlap, G., Koegel, R. L., Carr, E. G., Sailor, W., Anderson, J., et al. (1990) Toward a technology of "nonaversive" behavioral support. *Journal of The Association for Persons with Severe Handicaps, 17*, 125–132.

Horner, R. H., Sugai, G., Smolkowski, K., Todd, A., Nakasato, J., & Esperanza, J., (2009). A randomized control trial of schoolwide positive behavior support in elementary schools. *Journal of Positive Behavior Interventions, 11*, 133–144.

Houchins, D. E., Jolivette, K., Wessendorf, S., McGlynn, M., & Nelson, C. M. (2005). Stakeholders' view of implementing positive behavioral support in a juvenile justice setting. *Education and Treatment of Children, 28*, 380–399.

Individuals with Disabilities Education Act (IDEA) Amendments of 1997. Public L. No. 105-17. 111 Stat.37 (1997a).

Individuals with Disabilities Education Improvement Act (2004), 20 U.S.C. § 1400 Et. Seq.

Iwata, B. A., Dorsey, M. F., Slifer, K. J., Baurman, K. E., & Richman, G. S. (1982). Toward a functional analysis of self-injury. *Analysis and Intervention in Developmental Disabilities, 2*, 3–20.

Kame'enui, E. J. (2007). A new paradigm: Responsiveness to intervention. *Teaching Exceptional Children, 39*, 6–7.

Kartub, D. T., Taylor-Greene, S., March, R. E., & Horner, R. H. (2000). Reducing hallway noise: A systems approach. *Journal of Positive Behavior Interventions, 2*, 179–182.

Lassen, S. R., Steele, M. M., & Sailor, W. (2006). The relationship of school-wide positive behavior support to academic achievement in an urban middle school. *Psychology in the Schools, 43*, 701–712.

Lewis, T. J., Powers, L. J., Kelk, M. J., Newcomer, L. L. (2002). Reducing problem behaviors on the playground: An investigation of the application of schoolwide positive behavior supports. *Psychology in the Schools, 39*, 181–190.

Lewis, T. J., & Sugai, G. (1999). Effective behavior support: A systems approach to proactive schoolwide management. *Focus on Exceptional Children, 31*, 1–24.

May, D. C. S., Ard, W. I., Todd, A. W., Horner, R. H., Glasgow, A., Sugai, G., et al. (2000). *School-wide information system.* Eugene, OR: Educational and Community Supports. University of Oregon.

McCurdy, B. L., Manella, M. C., & Eldrige, N. (2003). Positive behavior support in urban schools: Can we prevent the escalation of antisocial behavior? *Journal of Positive Behavior Interventions, 5*, 158–170.

Metzler, C. W., Biglan, A., Rusby, J. C., & Sprague, J. R. (2001). Evaluation of a comprehensive behavior management program to improve school-wide positive behavior support. *Education and Treatment of Children, 24*, 448–479.

Miller, D. N., George, M. P., & Fogt, J. B. (2005). Establishing and sustaining research-based practices at Centennial School: A descriptive case study of systemic change. *Psychology in the Schools, 42*, 553–567.

Miller, J. A., Hunt, D. P., & Georges, M. A. (2006). Reduction of physical restraints in residential treatment facilities. *Journal of Disability Policy Studies, 16*, 202–208.

Muscott, H. S., Mann, E. L., & LeBrun, M. R. (2008). Positive behavioral interventions and supports in New Hampshire: Effects of large-scale implementation of school-wide positive behavior support on student discipline and academic achievement. *Journal of Positive Behavior Interventions, 10*, 190–205.

Netzel, D. M., & Eber, L. (2003). Shifting from reactive to proactive discipline in an urban school district: A change of focus through SWPBS implementation. *Journal of Positive Behavior Interventions, 5*, 71–79.

No Child Left Behind, 20 U.S.C. § 16301 Et Seq.

OSEP Center on Positive Behavioral Interventions and Supports. (1998). Office of Special Education Programs, U. S. Department of Education (#H326S980003). Washington D. C. (www.pbis.org).

OSEP Center on Positive Behavioral Interventions and Supports. (2000). Applying positive behavior support and functional behavioral assessment in schools. *Journal of Positive Behavior Interventions, 2*, 131–143.

OSEP Center on Positive Behavioral Interventions and Supports. (2004). *School wide positive behavior support: Implementers' blueprint and self-assessment.* Eugene: University of Oregon Press.

Safran, S. P., & Oswald, K. (2003). Positive behavior supports: Can schools reshape disciplinary practices? *Exceptional Children, 69*, 361–373.

Sandomierski, T., Kincaid, D., & Algozzine, B. (2007). Response to intervention and positive behavior support: Brothers from different mothers or sisters with different misters? *Positive Behavioral Interventions and Supports Newsletter, 4.*

Scott, T. M., Nelson, C. M., Liaupsin, C. J., Jolivette, K., Christle, C. A., & Riney, M. (2002). Addressing the needs of at-risk and adjudicated youth through positive behavior support: Effective prevention practices. *Education and Treatment of Children, 25*, 532–551.

Severson, H. H., Walker, H. M., Hope-Doolittle, J., Kratochwill, T. R., & Gresham, F. M. (2007). Proactive, early screening to detect behaviorally at-risk students: Issues, approaches, emerging innovations, and professional practices. *Journal of School Psychology, 45*, 193–223.

Simonsen, B., Britton, L., & Young, D. (2010). School-wide positive behavior support in a non-public school setting: A case study. *Journal of Positive Behavior Interventions, 12*, 180-191. doi:10.1177/1098300708330495

Simonsen, B., & Sugai, G. (2007). Using school-wide data systems to make decisions efficiently and effectively. *School Psychology Forum, 1*, 46–58.

Simonsen, B., & Sugai, G. (2009). School-wide positive behavior support: A systems-level application of behavioral principles. In A. Akin-Little, S. G. Little, M. Bray., & T. Kehle (Eds.), *Handbook of Behavioral Interventions in Schools* (pp. 125–140). Washington, DC: American Psychological Association.

Simonsen, B., & Sugai, G., & Fairbanks, S. (2007). School-wide positive behavior support Preventing the development and occurrence of problem behavior. In S. W. Evans, M. D. Weist, Z. N. Serpell (Eds.), *Advances in school-based mental health interventions: Best practices and program models, Vol II.* (pp. 1–17). Kingston, NJ: Civic Research Institute.

Sugai, G., (August 1, 2007). *Schoolwide positive behavior support and responsiveness-to-intervention.* Keynote presentation to and paper for the Southern Maryland PBIS Summer Regional Conference. Waldorf, MD.

Sugai, G. (2008). School-wide positive behavior support and response to intervention. *RTI Action Network.* Retrieved July 7, 2007, from http://www.rtinetwork.org/Learn/Behavior/ar/SchoolwideBehavior

Sugai, G., & Horner, R. (2002). The evolution of discipline practices: Schoolwide positive behavior supports. *Behavior Psychology in the Schools, 24*, 23–50.

Sugai G., & Horner, R. (2006). A promising approach for expanding and sustaining schoolwide positive behavior support. *School Psychology Review, 35*, 245–259.

Todd, A. W., Lewis-Palmer, T., Horner, R. H., Sugai, G., Sampson, N. K., & Phillips, D. (2004). *School-wide Evaluation Tool.* Eugene, OR: ECS.

Turnbull, A.P., Edmonson, H., Griggs, P., Wickham, D., Sailor, W., Freeman, R., et al. (2002). A blueprint for school-wide positive behavior support: Implementation of three components. *Exceptional Children, 68,* 377–402.

Turnbull, H. R., Wilcox, B. L., Stowe, M., Raper, C., & Hedges, L. P. (2000). Public policy foundations for positive behavioral interventions, strategies, and supports. *Journal of Positive Behavior Interventions, 2,* 218–230.

Wilcox, B. L., Turnbull, R., & Turnbull, A. P. (2000). Behavioral issues and IDEA: Positive behavioral interventions and supports and the functional behavioral assessment in the disciplinary context. *Exceptionality, 8,* 173–187.

Problem Solving Consultation: Applications in Evidence-Based Prevention and Intervention

Caroline N. Racine Gilles, Thomas R. Kratochwill, Jacquelyn N. Felt, Clarissa J. Schienebeck, *and* Cara A. Vaccarello

Abstract

Problem solving consultation has been identified as a practice guideline in the delivery of evidence-based interventions (EBIs). This mandate is likely to advance the current initiatives of implementing EBIs and incorporating multi-tiered prevention models within the school setting. The purpose of this chapter is to review the most prominent models of consultation (mental health, behavioral, organizational development, instructional, and technology training) and discuss the associated features of each model. While differences exist among the models, all involve problem solving expertise of the consultant (conceptualized as an individual or team) within the context of a triadic relationship. The remainder of the chapter is devoted to the concept of problem solving consultation (PSC), which is a broad term that incorporates and draws on the aforementioned models. Finally, we offer some recommendations for the professional practice of PSC within the context of evidence-based practice.

Keywords: problem-solving consultation, models of consultation, evidence-based interventions, evidence-based practice

Introduction

Consultation has been a longstanding approach to service delivery within school settings. Over the years, the hallmarks of the consultation process, regardless of model, have been its method of indirect service delivery and the utilization of a problem solving approach to ameliorate problems and support students, parents, staff, and systems. School psychologists typically spend 16% of their professional time engaged in consultation activities, second only to assessment (Bramlet, Murphy, Johnson, Wallingsford, & Hall, 2002). With the advent of some recent initiatives in prevention science and response to intervention (RTI), it is likely that psychologists working in schools will participate in consultation with even greater frequency.

Most recently, problem solving consultation has been identified as a practice guideline in the delivery of evidence-based interventions (EBIs) (Frank &

Kratochwill, 2005). This mandate is likely to advance the current initiatives of implementing EBIs and incorporating multi-tiered prevention models within the school setting. The purpose of this chapter is to review the most prominent models of consultation (mental health, behavioral, organizational development, and instructional) and discuss the associated features of each model. While differences exist among the models, all involve problem-solving expertise of the consultant (conceptualized as an individual or team) within the context of a triadic relationship. The remainder of the chapter is devoted to the concept of *problem solving consultation*, which is a broad term that incorporates and draws on the aforementioned models. Finally, we offer some recommendations for the professional practice of problem solving consultation within the context of evidence-based practice in the schools.

Models of Consultation
Mental Health Consultation

Mental health consultation originated as a method for providing indirect services to clients by consulting with community mental health workers (Caplan, 1963; 1995). Caplan's original model of mental health consultation, however, has since been adopted within settings outside of the mental health community. Specifically, this model has proved to be useful within the school setting due to its prevention-oriented framework, focus on collaborative nonhierarchical relationships, and emphasis on individual and ecological factors (Caplan, Caplan, & Erchul, 1995). As such, it has been redefined and refined to improve its applicability to the school setting and differentiate it from other consultation models (Caplan, et al., 1995; Knotek & Sandovol, 2003; Kratochwill & Pittman, 2002).

In response to the adoption of mental health consultation within schools, Caplan et al. (1995) reformulated the model to accommodate this alternative use. This new model, called *Mental Health Collaboration,* was designed to account for the structural and relational differences that exist among schools and community mental health settings— the basis for the design of mental health consultation (Caplan et al., 1995). According to Caplan et al. (1995), mental health collaboration allows for the consultant and consultee relationship to exist between professionals employed within the same setting or institution who share direct responsibility for the outcome of the client. Due to this shared responsibility, the consultant may at times need to switch between direct and indirect service delivery to the client. Therefore, in this form of consultation, the relationship between the consultant and consultee may not always be nonhierarchical, whereby the consultee can accept or reject the consultant's advice. Although these characteristics assist in the adoption of a consultative approach to service delivery within school based systems, the framework has continued to evolve with a focus on consultee-centered case consultation.

In the original model, Caplan (1963) described four main types of Mental Health Consultation: (a) client-centered case consultation, (b) program-centered administrative consultation, (c) consultee-centered case consultation, and (d) consultee-centered administrative consultation. Of these, consultee-centered case consultation has been the most widely utilized and adapted mental health consultation model within the school psychology field. Over the past 40 years, consultee-centered

case consultation has evolved beyond its original use for clients with mental health needs, to a more general consultation approach that allows for use within a variety of settings (Knotek & Sandoval, 2003). The core components of the consultee-centered case consultation framework include (a) establishing a collaborative consultant-consultee relationship that remains nonhierarchical, regardless of the differences in expertise of the dyad members (Knotek & Sandoval, 2003); and (b) increasing the knowledge and skills of parents and/or teachers through indirect and direct consultation whereby the consultant models and coaches the consultee throughout the stages of the problem solving process (Kratochwill & Pittman, 2002). This indirect service-delivery model of consultee skill development has also been referred to as technology training consultation within problem-solving consultation models (Kratochwill & Pittman, 2002). Here, the consultative process focuses specifically on training teachers and/or parents throughout all phases of consultation.

Consultee-centered consultation was previously viewed as having many distinctions from the widely used behavioral consultation framework (Knotek & Sandoval, 2003). Recent developments in research and practice have led to the expansion of the definition of behavioral consultation to include theories, assessments, and intervention strategies from areas outside of the behavior modification discipline (Kratochwill, 2008; Kratochwill, Elliott, & Stoiber, 2002). Thus, behavioral consultation has evolved into "problem solving consultation" as a way to account for an expanded view of consultative school-based services (Kratochwill, 2008; Kratochwill & Pittman, 2002). Accordingly, consultee-centered case consultation can serve as a framework for providing school-based problem solving consultation services, such as training and professional development for parents and teachers, i.e., technology training consultation (Kratochwill & Pittman, 2002).

MENTAL HEALTH CONSULTATION EFFECTIVENESS RESEARCH

Despite the improved applicability of consultee-centered case consultation to school based services, there is limited empirical evidence to support its effectiveness within the school setting. In general, mental health consultation "has been the least empirically supported consultation model" (Knotek, Kaniuka, & Ellingsen, 2008, p. 129). The majority of mental health consultation literature has focused on theory and interpersonal variables, rather than outcome measures validating its effectiveness. Although consultee-centered case consultation has become a well-defined mental health consultation model suited for use within the schools, it currently does not meet the criteria for an evidence-based practice; and thus, continued research regarding the efficacy and effectiveness of its outcomes is required. (Knotek et al., 2008).

Behavioral Consultation

Behavioral consultation and its variations, perhaps the most widely practiced form of consultation, have been identified as best practice in problem solving and EBI delivery within school psychology and the educational setting (Kratochwill, 2008). Behavioral consultation is a case-specific and case-centered process that involves a triadic relationship between a consultant, a consultee, and a client. In this process, the consultee presents with a problem concerning the client. The consultant and consultee engage in a problem-solving process to develop a plan to serve the client. While the consultant–consultee relationship can exist anywhere on a continuum of collaboration to hierarchy (see Gutkin, 1999; Kratochwill & Pittman, 2002; Sheridan, Meegan, & Eagle, 2002; Witt, 1991), the consultant is often seen as the process facilitator. Within this process, the consultee implements the plan with the client to effect behavior change. Thus, the consultee serves as a mediator in service delivery to the client by the consultant. In addition, consultees receive services (i.e., increased knowledge, skill development, and so forth) themselves, throughout the consultation process. Therefore, the consultant can be seen as serving two entities, both the consultee and the client.

GOALS OF BEHAVIORAL CONSULTATION

Two major goals have been identified as outcomes for the behavioral consultation process (Bergan & Kratochwill, 1990; Kratochwill, 2008). The first and most obvious goal is to effect change in the client. Because the process begins with the presentation of a problem, it is hoped that consultation will end in successful implementation of a plan that remediates the problem behavior. Secondly, behavioral consultation aims to create change in the consultee. Through knowledge dissemination from the consultant, it is hoped that consultation will result in the consultee possessing greater service-delivery competencies, expertise, and knowledge with which to meet future problem behaviors.

Behavioral consultation has historically followed a four-stage process (Bergan & Kratochwill, 1990), although a fifth initial phase has been identified as best practice (Kratochwill, 2008). These stages are fluid and often overlap in practice, and the consultant and consultee may return to a previous stage prior to concluding the consultation process. These five stages are:

1) Establishing relationships
2) Needs (or problem) identification
3) Needs (or problem) analysis
4) Plan implementation
5) Plan (or problem) evaluation

Establishing relationships. The first stage in behavioral consultation involves the establishment of a relationship between the consultant and the consultee. Establishing a productive relationship through trust, openness, flexibility, and positive communication dynamics has been studied extensively in the literature (e.g., see Dinnebeil, Hale, & Rule, 1996), and research has demonstrated that these elements are essential in facilitating collaboration during later stages of the problem solving process. Thus, overtly focusing on the establishment of a positive and productive relationship has been deemed important to the process of behavioral consultation (Kratochwill, 2008).

Needs identification. The second stage in behavioral consultation is needs identification. Sometimes referred to as *problem identification*, needs identification focuses on operationally defining the presenting problem behavior and its discrepancy from the desired behavior. In addition, this identification phase strives to create an understanding of social and academic needs. This step in the consultation process is considered the most critical, as appropriate needs identification is an important predictor of effective planning and implementation (Bergan & Tombari, 1975; 1976). Bergan and Kratochwill (1990) originally defined five steps within needs identification:

1. Establish objectives.
2. Establish measures for performance objectives.
3. Establish and implement data collection procedures.
4. Display the data.
5. Define the problem by establishing the discrepancy between current performance, as reflected in the data collected, and the desired performance, as indicated in the performance objectives (p. 82).

Needs identification typically takes place through a consultee interview with the consultant, coupled with direct data collection procedures.

Needs analysis. The third stage in the behavioral consultation process is to analyze the client's needs. During this phase, the intervention plan is developed collaboratively between the consultant and the consultee through an interview process, which leads to a hypothesis about the problem behavior, for which a solution can then be generated. Bergan and Kratochwill (1990) identified five steps for this stage of the process as well:

1. Choose an analysis procedure (analyze conditions or skills related to the problem).
2. Conduct conditions and/or skills analysis.
3. Develop plan strategies (general courses of action).
4. Develop plan tactics (specific tactics used to implement strategy).
5. Establish procedures for assessing performance during implementation (p. 140).

Throughout the process, the consultant offers expertise in psychological and educational principles and strategies, and the consultee provides insight into whether the intervention is a good fit for the client, whether he or she feels competent to implement the intervention, and other variables that may influence problem outcomes (Bergan & Kratochwill, 1990). The intervention must be evidence-based and effective, as well as acceptable in regards to consultee skills, resources and preferences, and contain parameters for data collection (Kratochwill, 2008). Depending on the information covered in this stage, the consultant and consultee may enhance or redefine the original problem and/or goals developed in the second stage (Kratochwill, 2008).

Plan implementation. The intervention plan is implemented during the fourth stage of the process. However, this stage entails much more than simply delivering an intervention to the client. Prior to intervention, materials must be assembled and skills must be taught and/or developed. Throughout implementation, progress must be monitored, data collected, and procedures may need to be revised, depending on the perceived intervention effectiveness. Throughout this stage, the consultant checks in with the consultee, or observes implementation to ensure treatment integrity and to assist with any unforeseen problems. The consultant may also choose to review consultee records to monitor progress and assess any movements toward behavior change. Bergan and Kratochwill (1990) outline three steps during the plan implementation stage: (1) develop consultee's skills; (2) monitor plan implementation process; and (3) make plan revisions, if necessary.

Plan evaluation. The final stage, although not necessarily the end of consultation, is plan evaluation. In this stage, goal attainment and plan effectiveness are assessed, through a formal plan evaluation interview. In this interview, the consultant and consultee determine the next steps for the client. Three decisions are available: (1) the problem has been resolved, the client's needs met, and the consultation completed; (2) the problem was not adequately analyzed and consultation must return to that stage; or (3) the problem has been resolved and a new goal must be developed to meet another client need. In the case of the first option, the consultant and consultee must then consider behavior maintenance and generalizability, and decide whether to leave the intervention in place, introduce a new plan, or remove the intervention. In the second or third case, consultation returns to the appropriate respective stage. Finally, post-implementation recording procedures and post-implementation planning for reducing problem reoccurrence must be considered.

Variations of Behavioral Consultation
TEACHER-MEDIATED BEHAVIORAL CONSULTATION
Teacher-mediated consultation is the most traditional form of behavioral consultation. In this problem-solving consultation model, the teacher serves as the consultee. The teacher–school psychologist relationship is particularly well suited to consultation, as teacher availability, knowledge of the student, and educational role lend themselves well to the consultation process (Kratochwill & Pittman, 2002). Most of the research literature devoted to behavioral consultation has been conducted with teachers (Kratochwill & Pittman, 2002), and thus is most applicable to this specific form of consultation.

PARENT-MEDIATED BEHAVIORAL CONSULTATION
In parent-mediated consultation, one, or sometimes both, parents serve as the consultees throughout the problem solving process. While the term "parent consultation" is typically not found in consultation literature, school psychologists often discuss child needs, interventions, and progress with parents, and provide indirect services to children by creating intervention plans to be implemented at home and advising parents on child behavior (Kratochwill & Pittman, 2002). When parent consultation is cited in research studies, it is often within the context of *conjoint behavioral consultation*, which includes both

parents and teachers as consultees. Parent consultation is a growing area of research, with current evidence suggesting its importance in fostering home and school partnerships and promoting parental engagement (Christenson & Cleary, 1990; Sheridan & Kratochwill, 2008).

CONJOINT BEHAVIORAL CONSULTATION

This extended form of consultation combines both home and school spheres of influence to maximize positive outcomes for the child. In conjoint behavioral consultation (CBC), parents and teachers share joint responsibility and input as mediators in service delivery, and all consultation stages are conducted simultaneously with both parents and teachers. Thus, needs must be analyzed and prioritized across settings to the satisfaction of both consultees, and attention must be paid to clear, effective, and relationship-building communication (Sheridan & Kratochwill, 2008). Like parent-mediated consultation, CBC seeks to strengthen home–school partnerships and promote parental involvement, in addition to problem-solving for the client.

CBC is rated by parents, teachers, and children as "very acceptable" to "highly acceptable" (Cowan & Sheridan, 2003), and has been reported to be the most preferred option by both teachers and parents for behavioral, socio-emotional, and academic problems (Freer & Watson, 1999). A growing body of research has been devoted to CBC, and meta-analyses have found CBC to be a generally effective service-delivery model across home and school settings (Sheridan, Eagle, Cowan, & Mickelson, 2001). Garbacz, Woods, Swanger-Gagne, Taylor, Black, and Sheridan (2008) have extended the CBC approach by adding a partnership orientation (e.g., fostering strengths, being sensitive and responsive, being resourceful and helpful) to the problem solving process.

CHILD-MEDIATED BEHAVIORAL CONSULTATION

Child-mediated behavioral consultation has also been suggested as a viable form of consultation (Kratochwill & Pittman, 2002), but in this case, the child serves as consultee and the adult as client. Research has shown effects of child behavior on teacher behavior, such as attention and assistance and negative contacts, through behavior reinforcement contingencies (Graubard, Rosenberg, & Miller, 1971). While the usefulness of child-mediated consultation has yet to be determined, Kratochwill and Pittman (2002) suggest this form

of consultation may, for example, be promising in dealing with teacher resistance issues. Unfortunately, little research is being conducted in this area.

PEER-MEDIATED BEHAVIORAL CONSULTATION

In this final form of consultation, a student's peers serve as consultees, delivering interventions to the peer client. Peer-assisted learning has long been seen as useful in dealing with academic and behavioral problems in the classroom (e.g., Ginsburg-Block, Rohrbeck, & Fantuzzo, 2006). Peer-assisted learning can include peer tutoring, peer modeling, peer monitoring, peer assessment, peer reinforcement, and peer generalization assistance (Kratochwill & Pittman, 2002). Hence, the use of students as consultees through peer-mediated consultation has been suggested as a framework that would reduce demands on teacher time, allow the clients individual attention, and possibly provide a less threatening behavior change process (Kratochwill & Pittman, 2002; Topping & Ehly, 2001).

BEHAVIORAL CONSULTATION EFFECTIVENESS RESEARCH

Traditionally, behavioral consultation has been reported to be an effective treatment delivery system, with positive results in approximately 75% of cases (MacLeod, Jones, Somers, & Havey, 2001; Sheridan, Welch, & Orme, 1996), and conjoint behavioral consultation has been demonstrated to be effective across both home and school settings (Sheridan, Eagle, Cowan, & Mickelson, 2001; Guli, 2005) with positive effect sizes, regardless of diversity (Sheridan, Eagle, & Doll, 2006). A recent review of research on the effectiveness of behavioral consultation found it to be both a popular and effective practice in schools, leading to decreased numbers of children referred for special education placement, and increased placement rates for children who were referred (Martens & DiGennaro, 2008). Prereferral programs, including behavioral consultation problem-solving processes and consultants, were found to be more effective than other programs. With regards to CBC as a specific form of behavioral consultation, a review by Sheridan, Clarke, and Burt (2008) found CBC to demonstrate the strongest evidence for effectiveness among all parent consultation models, with average effect sizes of 1.10, retaining generally high effect sizes with diverse populations. CBC was also found to be socially valid and acceptable to parents, teachers, and practicing school psychologists, and to demonstrate effectiveness in creating positive, collaborative relationships, as well as positive student outcomes.

Instructional Consultation

Instructional Consultation (IC) is an indirect consultee-centered approach to providing consultative services to staff (e.g., teachers) and students within school systems (Rosenfield, 2008). Through the use of a stage-based problem solving process (Kratochwill, Elliott, & Stoiber, 2002), IC provides collaborative support to teachers and enhances their knowledge and skills to improve students' academic achievement within the classroom setting (Rosenfield, 2008). Such services can be provided by either an individual practitioner within the school system, or through a schoolwide multidisciplinary team approach: IC Teams (Rosenfield & Gravois, 1996). (See Organizational Development Consultation Model for discussion of IC Teams).

IC's ecological approach to assessing student concerns places the focus of the problem solving process on the identification of alterable instructional variables within the classroom, as opposed to the identification of an internal student deficit, as has been the focus of traditional referral processes (Rosenfield, 2002). Furthermore, IC utilizes data-based decision making processes (Rosenfield, 2002) and evidence-based assessment and intervention strategies (Rosenfield, 2008) throughout the process. Thus, IC provides schools with a problem solving approach designed to aid in achieving accountability standards within least-restrictive environments, as set forth by IDEA and NCLB, while also being compatible within an RTI service delivery system (Kratochwill, 2008; Rosenfield, 2008).

Ecological Approach: The Instructional Triangle

The problem solving stages that comprise the IC approach are set within the context of a collaborative relationship focused on identifying and evaluating three key ecological components within the classroom. These components form what Rosenfield (2002) has termed the *instructional triangle* and consist of (a) the current behavior and entry-level skills of the student, (b) the tasks the student is asked to perform in the classroom, and (c) the teacher's instructional and/or management strategies. The assessment of variables within the instructional triangle guide the IC process in achieving the goal of determining whether there is "an instructional match that facilitates student learning" or "if there is a gap between the student's current and expected performance that requires intervention" (Rosenfield, 2008, p. 1655). Whether the teacher's concern is regarding a student's academic performance or behavioral performance, IC concentrates on understanding the "goodness of fit" between the components of the instructional triangle (Rosenfield, 2008).

IC Problem Solving Stages

In general, the problem solving stages within IC closely follow those outlined as being "best practices" in providing school-based problem solving consultative services (see Kratochwill, 2008). Components essential to IC include: (a) establishing a collaborative consultation relationship, (b) identifying and analyzing the problem, (c) designing and planning the intervention, (d) implementing and evaluating the intervention, and (e) resolving or terminating the IC process (see Rosenfield, 2008).

Instructional Consultation Effectiveness Research

The effectiveness of IC within real-world school settings has been supported by program evaluation data, as well as quasi-experimental and qualitative research studies. Such analyses provide evidence supporting the influence of IC teams on (a) decreasing special education referrals and increasing appropriate referral placements of all children; (b) reducing special education referrals for culturally and linguistically diverse students, specifically; (c) assisting students in goal attainment in specific academic and behavioral areas; and (d) influencing teacher outcomes. Teachers working with IC teams reported high levels of satisfaction in collaborating with the teams. They reported increased efficacy regarding their own abilities in the problem solving process, and using data to guide their decisions. Furthermore, teachers also reported having learned skills and strategies from the IC team and an improved ability to generalize these skills to other students in their classrooms. Current research demonstrates the effectiveness of IC in practice; however, the efficacy and causal relationship between IC and practice outcomes has yet to be established through randomized experimental study (Rosenfield, Silva, & Gravois, 2008.)

Organizational Development Consultation

Organizational development consultation, or system-based consultation, can be conceptualized as large-scale systems change for the purposes of providing academic, socio-emotional, and behavioral support to all students in the school community (e.g. Ikeda, Tilly, Stumme, Volmer, & Allison, 1996; Sugai & Horner, 2006). Rosenfield (1992) remarks that school change is not an event, but rather the process by which individuals and situations within the system are transformed. "It is not only a process of developing new skills to the point of routine use, but of experiencing a sense of meaning and satisfaction in new ways of doing things" (Rosenfield, 1992, p. 32). Organizational development consultation requires collaborative efforts among stakeholders across multiple levels of the school community in effective prevention, identification, and intervention for students facing difficulties in school. The professional literature has evidenced increased support for ecologically-based procedures (e.g., school-wide positive behavior support; Crone & Horner, 2003) that consider the relationship of students with their learning environment, and facilitate positive learning communities.

A traditional lack of coordinated efforts in schools has created complex barriers to consultation at the system level (Kratochwill & Pittman, 2002). The field of school psychology has conventionally focused on teachers as primary consultees (i.e., teacher-mediated behavioral consultation), and often an individual student serves as the unit of analysis. This scope ignores other important stakeholders in the problem solving process, such as parents, students, and the "system" as consultees (Kratochwill & Pittman, 2002). In this traditional educational model, learning, innovation, and school improvement are approached at the individual rather than system level (O'Neil, 1995). Ineffective components of the system (e.g., curriculum components, teachers) are identified, removed and replaced (Wald & Castleberry, 2000). Likewise, problem solving is approached from an individual-deficit perspective, in which individual students are identified and targeted for improvement (Rosenfield, 1992). Alternatively, organizational development consultation considers the school as the unit of analysis, and achievement of system-wide goals is determined by the collective actions of individuals within the school (Sugai & Horner, 2006). System-based consultation serves broader issues than those addressed by traditional, case-centered approaches by integrating concepts of organizational structure and group problem solving (Kratochwill & Pittman, 2002). Additionally, system-based consultation considers how teachers learn and incorporates procedures that promote ongoing professional development and reflection of progress towards system-level goals (O'Neil, 1995). (See Models and Stages of Systems Change section).

The traditional organization of school systems naturally separates students, faculty, administrators, and parents by numerous features such as grade, location, needs and abilities, and presence in school (Kratochwill & Pittman, 2002). Organizational development consultation is a community-building approach; aimed at creating a culture that supports relationships and collaboration among students, parents, teachers, and their school (Kratochwill & Pittman, 2002). Wald and Castleberry (2000) describe this type of school culture as one that simultaneously supports individual and organizational growth through its focus on *school as a community* and *collaborative learning*. Creating this cultural change at the system level requires a focus on collective learning so that individuals at multiple levels share common goals, work to accomplish these goals, and receive support in their efforts (O'Neil, 1995). "It demands that individuals shed the expert role and adopt a collaborative approach that recognizes the values, knowledge, and expertise of all community members" (Wald & Castleberry, 2000, p.4).

Models and Stages of Systems Change
Rosenfield's concept of instructional consultation teams provides an example of systems-level consultation. Rosenfield (1992) outlines the implementation of instructional consultation teams (IC teams) as part of school-wide consultation service models. IC team efforts are intended to achieve two major outcomes at the system level: (a) "a conceptual and behavioral shift" in the referral process; and (b) a school management system with a collaborative problem-solving orientation and support from a school-based team. The goals of IC team models challenge traditional approaches to defining and treating student difficulties. These goals move beyond the narrow assumption that the problem lies within the child, to a broader practice that considers the role of student strengths and environmental supports in addressing student success (Rosenfield, 1992). The model is based on three assumptions:

1. All students can learn.
2. The student–teacher relationship is a critical setting for change.
3. Schools work best when operating within a collaborative problem-solving orientation.

Rosenfield describes three stages of systems change (i.e., initiation, implementation, and institutionalization) as it applies to her model for organizational change.

INITIATION

During the initiation stage, a plan is adopted, followed by the development, organization, and allocation of resources. A clearly defined vision for future change is established, and a commitment to achieving these goals through the plans of the model is understood by all relevant stakeholders. Another critical component to this stage is the incorporation of an effective training plan that provides staff development in the areas of knowledge, skills, and program vision. Schools may decide to assign roles of change facilitators, whose tasks include introducing the model to the school system and supporting its implementation. (Rosenfield, 1992)

IMPLEMENTATION

At the second stage of the change process, system stakeholders put the plan, along with evaluative procedures, into practice. Outcomes are measured against implementation integrity—that is, goal attainment and progress are evaluated with respect to how well the model was put into practice. "Outcome evaluation of the implemented innovation is usually multidimensional and requires that the goals for change are clear in advance" (Rosenfield, 1992, p. 33). Staff development and training at this stage of change is focused on the development of critical skills. Staff is provided with guided practice, feedback, and continued onsite support for the development of skills in consultation, classroom-based assessment and intervention, and progress monitoring. To facilitate the ongoing development of skills, a model outlining competency levels, areas of growth, and techniques for self-evaluation also may be provided to staff (Rosenfield, 1992).

INSTITUTIONALIZATION

At the third stage of the change process, the change initiative has a sustainable framework within the school, reflected by the routine use and support of its components. As Rosenfield (1992) remarks, schools adopt frequent and sometimes brief initiatives, leaving school personnel without a meaningful understanding of, or connection to, their school's educational innovations. At the institutionalization stage of systems change, school staff understands the roles they serve within their school's plan, and can competently carry out the goals of the initiative. An effective systems change model progresses through each stage with ongoing evaluation of plan implementation, training outcomes, plan institutionalization and students outcomes. Adaptations to the plan are made to better fit the needs of the system (Rosenfield, 1992).

Organizational Development Consultation Effectiveness Research

Organizational development is a consultation-focused, multidisciplinary practice that uses numerous theoretical frameworks for achieving fundamental change in school functioning (Illback & Pennington, 2008). The school psychology literature is rife with examples of school-based initiatives and system-level strategies; yet, because these practices vary considerably, the research on the efficacy and effectiveness of consultation-based organizational development approaches is limited.

A customary lack of experimental design in organizational development implementation has resulted in gaps between outcomes and the processes behind the change. Recently, however, there has been increased use of data-driven models that (a) seek to identify complex variables related to change, (b) ascertain general effectiveness across studies, and (c) identify core indicators of change (See Illback & Pennington, 2008). One system-wide initiative with growing evidential support is Positive Behavioral Interventions and Supports (PBIS). PBIS is a systems-level change initiative with theoretical and empirical underpinnings. PBIS efforts shape school environments to support positive behaviors, reduce challenging behaviors, and facilitate student success (Sugai & Horner, 2006). PBIS approaches link research-validated practices to a hierarchy of systems that influence student learning and behavior (i.e., school-wide systems, classroom systems, non-classroom systems, and individual student support systems). The systematic use of data-based decision making is an essential practice within PBIS models. Empirical studies have documented both the efficacy and effectiveness of school-wide PBIS models in promoting change; however, PBS-related studies fall short of or identifying consultation processes or consultant behaviors related to PBIS outcomes (Illback & Pennington, 2008).

Problem Solving Consultation: Applications in Prevention

Current legislative and fiscal mandates (IDEIA, 2004; NCLB, 2001), call for educational practices that will teach children to meet specified academic benchmarks, as well as to be responsible and positive contributors to society. Unfortunately, many children come to school lacking the necessary resources that would allow them to benefit from common educational practices. Additionally, the student population continues to be increasingly diverse with respect to ethnicity, socioeconomic status, disability, and non-English speaking status. Current school policies may also dictate zero tolerance for behavioral infractions. Most discipline practices are reactive, punitive, and exclusionary. There needs to be recognition that schools play a major role in the development of social behavior (March, Hawken, & Green, 2003). In addition, research has shown that academic and social/emotional behaviors are interrelated (Diperna & Elliott, 2000), and likely influence each other reciprocally, indicating that if there is a problem in one domain it is likely to lead to a problem in the other arena (Algozinne & Kay, 2002). Comprehensive systems change initiatives are designed to create a web of supports and services that "wrap around" children and families in an effort to disrupt current fragmentation and categorical separation of school programs (Sugai & Horner, 1999). The movements that include PBIS and RTI discussed above are designed to enhance the much-needed system change efforts and school reform.

Problem solving consultation (PSC), which has recently replaced the term *behavioral consultation* (see Kratochwill, 2008), is a set of skills and processes that goes beyond traditional behavioral consultation. PSC is a strength-based process whereby teams or individual consultants invoke specific consultation models and problem solving processes to achieve a resolution of identified need. These identified needs can be at the macro- and/or micro-level within a school or school system. PSC utilizes a broad conceptualization of designating the consultant, consultee, and client roles. PSC aids in the facilitation of PBIS and RTI frameworks (herein referred to as the *blended model*) and in the advancement of incorporating evidence-based interventions (EBI) into school-based practice contexts (Auster, Feeney-Kettler, & Kratochwill, 2006; Frank & Kratochwill, 2005; Kratochwill, 2008). The theorized result of effective PSC is increased positive student outcomes (both academic and behavioral) and an increase in overall school functioning. PSC can be utilized along a continuum of supports that is reflective of our current systemic, multi-tiered prevention and intervention models. PSC is now discussed within the context of the three-tiered, blended model (See Table 33.1 for an overview).

Tier I: Universal Level

PSC is utilized at the universal level to ensure that schools have incorporated and can sustain effective, research-based practices that often involve environmental and instructional redesign. The "consultant" at this tier takes the form of a problem solving team consisting of variety of members such as teachers, support personnel, students, parents, and community members. The PSC team utilizes several different consultation models, such as organizational development and instructional consultation, to accomplish the goals at this level. Additionally, an individual consultant (internal or external to the system), who holds expertise in the blended model and the process of consultation, can be a consultant to a system or PSC team, ensuring a foundation of support is in place. The "consultee" includes key stakeholders (e.g., staff, parents, caregivers, community members) that are involved with the school. The client is the system, or whole school. Here again, the PSC team needs to rely on the concepts utilized in organizational development consultation, as macro-level change rests squarely on systems change theory. The problematic context of the system is the focus of change.

The universal level targets all students, and uses proactive practices and interventions known to be effective in preventing most behavior and academic problems. The expectation (hope) is that approximately 80% of all students will respond favorably to these practices. Here, the PSC team proceeds through the typical phases seen in the behavioral consultation process. The PSC team identifies the needs of the system, assesses and analyzes problems and needs, uses data-based decision making procedures, makes recommendations for the consultee (system or school) to put evidence-based practices into place, and evaluates the effects of the school-wide interventions. The result is meaningful and durable change, as evidenced by incorporating effective school-wide practices.

At this level, care should be taken to support all aspects of the system. Ongoing support to staff, parents, and community is critical. In this process, the PSC team may rely on the central tenets of mental health consultation, whereby the clinician targets staff, families, or community members to be the recipients of additional training on skill development, coping skills, or adapting to change.

Tier II: Selected Level

At this level, a PSC team or consultant is useful in analyzing the school-wide data with an eye toward what is working for some students, but not for others. Approximately 15% of all students will need additional instruction or services beyond universal supports and practices. The PSC team helps to

Table 33.1 Problem-solving consultation across a continuum of support mediating variables: intervention integrity, acceptability, transportability, and efficacy

Level of Support	Consultation Components and/or Process Features	Possible Consultation Model Utilized	Role Definition
Tier I	Prerequisites: collective capacity, investment in the system, and stakeholder buy-in 1. Identify needs of system and subsystems(i.e., classroom, nonclassroom, etc.) 2. Analyze needs based on ongoing progress monitoring data or targeted assessment (i.e., universal screeners, CBA, office discipline referrals, incident reports, suspensions, etc.) 3. Based on data obtained in steps 1 and 2, select target (typically: environment / instructional redesign, academic or behavior enablers) for intervention / change. Select intervention based on evidence base, skills, and resources available. 4. Evaluate plan through identified ongoing progress monitoring procedures and plan for sustainability.	Organizational Development Instructional Consultation	Consultant: PSC Team; Individual Consultee: Key Stakeholders Client: System; Whole school
Tier II	Prerequisites: Same as Tier I 1. Identify groups of individuals who are nonresponsive to Tier I interventions. 2. Analyze needs through available data. 3. Select intervention plan based on evidence, resources, and options for support 4. Evaluate plan through predetermined data collection procedures. Adhere to components of EBP as outlined in chapter	Organizational Development Technology Training Instructional Consultation Mental Health	Consultant: PSC Team; Individual Consultee: Teacher(s) Parent(s) Individual Stakeholders Client: Students
Tier III	Prerequisite: well-established relationship between the consultant and consultee. 1. Identify specific individuals who are nonresponsive to Tier I and II interventions. 2. Analyze needs through available and a functional behavioral analysis (FBA) 3. Select intervention based on evidence, skills and resources available, and options for support. Adhere to components of EBP as outlined in chapter.	Behavioral Consultation Mental Health	Consultant: Team Individual Consultee: Key stakeholders Client: Student

identify needs, to analyze the discrepancies between actual performance and benchmark criteria, to suggest appropriate EBIs to meet the identified needs, and to evaluate the EBIs in an ongoing fashion. The *technology training consultation model* guides the practitioner or team during this level of PSC. Professionals must consider what is needed to implement a particular EBI. Are there particular training needs at this level? What is the target population? What support is necessary to sustain the needed practices? The PSC team assumes responsibility for ensuring that the needs of those who deliver the EBIs are met.

Tier III: Targeted Level

Approximately 5% of all students will need more intensive and specialized support that goes well beyond what is offered by the first two tiers. These are individual students who need a more comprehensive assessment that targets their specific needs. The EBIs will need to be individualized based on identified need, have high intensity, and demonstrate durability. The model of behavioral case-centered consultation can be most useful model at this level. The consultant (individual or team) will need a strong foundation in functional behavioral assessment and wraparound procedures, to ensure that the school can meet a student's targeted needs. At this level, the student is likely to need a comprehensive system of care that will utilize resources beyond the school setting. For example, a school district and its community mental health center(s) might partner to offer expedited access to services for students who have not responded to previous levels of prevention and intervention. The school and community stakeholders could work jointly within the context of a PSC team to brainstorm ideas, services, and resources to wrap around the student in need. Barriers to services and programming would be explored and overcome.

Problem Solving Consultation and Evidence-Based Practice

With the advent of the evidence-based practice movement, there has been increased interest in using the process of consultation in the delivery of EBIs. Indeed, consultation represents an excellent service delivery model for the transfer of intervention technology to educational settings. In this regard, the process of PSC can serve as a practice guideline for this venue (Frank & Kratochwill, 2005).Given these developments as a backdrop for PSC in the schools, we can address the components in this evidence-based practice (Kratochwill, 2008). These components include the following: (a) adoption of an intervention that carries designation as "evidence-based" by a professional group, organization, task force, government unit, etc.; (b) use of a well-developed manual or guide that provides an overview of the intervention; (c) assessing and developing of the skill level of individuals who implement the intervention; (d) documentation of the integrity of the intervention; (e) use of a basic evaluation structure such as an A/B design that can be use to document that the intervention was responsible for the observed outcomes; and (f) use of high-quality progress monitoring procedures across phases of the intervention evaluation.

DESIGNATION OF THE INTERVENTION AS "EVIDENCE-BASED" BY A PROFESSIONAL GROUP, ORGANIZATION, TASK FORCE, AND/OR GOVERNMENT UNIT

Consultants have access to a variety of programs, practices, and procedures that have been designated as *evidence-based* by some professional organization (see Kratochwill, 2007). One example is the What Works Clearinghouse (http://www.whatworks.ed. gov/) that provides a variety of options in both academic and social/emotional prevention and intervention programs. We do not review these programs in detail here, as they have been presented in previous publications and are widely known in school psychology.

The consultant and/or PSC team should check to determine if the program or practice adopted in the school is among those that are evidence-based in one of these or other resources (e.g., What Works Clearinghouse). When the consultant examines the various resources for the evidence base for an intervention, a number of different designations are possible including, for example, "empirically supported," "evidence-based," or "model program," among other designations. Some programs with less support may have designations such as "promising," but can still be used in the school if they are part of a listed evidence-based program.

A WELL DEVELOPED MANUAL OR GUIDE

Most of the programs that the consultant will be considering will include some kind of manual or guide that was part of the original research on the intervention program, developed during the research trials. In fact, one of the requirements for a designation as an EBI is that there is a manual or guide that outlines the program implementation. The consultant should document that a manual, guide, or curriculum can be used to implement the program in the school, and what modifications and/or adaptations are necessary for implementation.

In many cases it will be necessary to modify or deviate from the manual that is recommended for implementation of the intervention. This will certainly be an acceptable practice, but it will be important for the consultant to document the modifications that were made. Documenting the modifications allows consideration of cost and logistical challenges in their school.

PROFESSIONAL DEVELOPMENT AND TRAINING FOR INDIVIDUALS WHO IMPLEMENT THE INTERVENTION

The majority of EBIs require at least some professional development or training of consultees for appropriate implementation (including the consultant). The professional development leads to a knowledge base and set of skills that will promote correct implementation of the intervention program with integrity (see section below on intervention integrity). The professional development will range from reading a manual or curriculum, to having several days of workshop training in implementation. The primary rationale for training in the intervention is that it will promote integrity during implementation. In addition, many programs fail to show positive outcomes because the implementer, or consultee, does not have the skill level to successfully implement the program. Sometimes EBIs are dismissed as delivering poor outcomes due to intervention characteristics, when, in fact, inadequate implementation was uncovered as the basis for poor outcomes.

One important role that the consultant can play in EBP is to ensure that professional development is part of the system of consultation services in the school. As noted in one of the models of problem solving in behavioral consultation, technology training is critical focus for skill development (Kratochwill & Pittman, 2002). Further information on the importance of professional development and models of professional development is available (see Kratochwill, Volpiansky, Clements, & Ball, 2008). Most successful models require systemic change, and integration of skill development into the psychological services provided.

DOCUMENTATION OF THE INTEGRITY OF THE INTERVENTION

In consultation problem-solving models, the consultee is most often the primary implementer of the intervention, and in some cases the consultant will assist in implementation and/or supervision of the intervention. Once the consultee has acquired the knowledge and skills for implementation of the intervention, it will be necessary to monitor and ensure the integrity of the intervention. The *integrity* refers to the degree to which the intervention was implemented as originally designed (O'Donnell, 2008; Sanetti & Kratochwill, 2005).

There are two important features of integrity that the consultant must consider. First, the program/intervention developer may have some suggestions for how integrity should be monitored and how often. These recommendations should be followed as closely as possible. For example, the developer may have a record form that specifies the method (i.e., ratings scales or direct observations) of monitoring integrity, and with what frequency (i.e., daily, weekly) these assessments should occur. Second, when it is determined that integrity is compromised, it will be necessary to determine the cause and correct the problem(s). The reasons for failed integrity are many and include, for example, low skill level of the consultee(s), poor acceptability of the intervention,

and variables that surround the logistics of the implementation process, such as time, cost, resources, and other variables. Durlak and DuPre (2008) reviewed various factors that could influence the integrity of implementation of prevention programs (see Table 33.2). Once these variables have been identified, steps can be taken to address them. (e.g., through professional development, supervision, etc.), and the program can move forward to successful implementation with integrity.

A BASIC EVALUATION STRUCTURE TO DOCUMENT THE INTERVENTION

In accord with the scientist-practitioner models of consultation problem solving, EBP should address ongoing evaluation of the intervention. Some suggestions (e.g., Hayes, Barlow, & Nelson, 1999) are for the use of single-case design where replication and functional relationships are established, such as through ABAB and multiple-baseline designs. However, these strategies may be challenging in typical practice. Another option is to use the basic A/B design in which there is a comparison between the baselines to the intervention phases. This baseline-to-intervention comparison allows an examination of the change in mean level, variability, and trend in the data series between these two phases. The most common option to make a determination that the intervention was working is to visually analyze the data, taking into account these aforementioned characteristics across phases. Detailed strategies for this process can be found in Stoiber and Kratochwill (2002).

In addition to the various characteristics of the data observed that we noted above, social validation criteria can be used by consultants and/or PSC teams to make decisions about intervention effectiveness (Stoiber & Kratochwill, 2002). Social validation consists of two features: social comparison, and subjective evaluation. Social comparison consists of a normative framework in which the outcomes of an intervention (at the student, group, or system) are compared to a peer or group of peers. A peer standard can be established in a variety of ways, such as actual comparison of the intervention target to a peer group, classroom academic or behavioral benchmarks, or through various standardized assessment measures (e.g., achievement tests, rating scales, and checklists).

As a complementary criterion, subjective evaluation involves a consensus in which professional judgment of school professionals is used to determine outcomes. For example, if a team establishes an

Table 33.2 Factors affecting the implementation process

I. Community Level Factors
    A Prevention Theory and Research
    B Politics[a,b]
    C Funding[a,b,c]
    D Policy[a,b]

II. Provider Characteristics
    A Perceived Need for Innovation[b,c]
      Extent to which the proposed innovation is relevant to local needs
    B Perceived Benefits of Innovation[b]
      Extent to which the innovation will achieve benefits desired at the local level
    C Self-efficacy
      Extent to which providers feel they are will be able to do what is expected
    D Skill Proficiency[a,b,c]

III. Characteristics of the Innovation
    A Compatibility (contextual appropriateness, fit, congruence, match)[b,c]
      Extent to which the intervention fits with an organization's mission, priorities, and values.
    B Adaptability (program modification, reinvention)[b]
      The extent to which the proposed program can be modified to fit provider preferences, organizational practices, and community needs, values, and cultural norms

IV. Factors Relevant to the Prevention Delivery System: Organizational Capacity
    A General Organizational Factors
      1. Positive Work Climate[a,b,c]
         Climate may be assessed by sampling employees' views about morale, trust, collegiality, and methods of resolving disagreements
      2. Organizational norms regarding change (a k a, openness to change, innovativeness, risk-taking)[b]
         This refers to the collective reputation and norms held by an organization in relation to its willingness to try new approaches as opposed to maintaining the status quo
      3. Integration of new programming[b,c]
         This refers to the extent to which an organization can incorporate an innovation into its existing practices and routines
      4. Shared vision (shared mission, consensus, commitment, staff buy-in)[b]
         This refers to the extent to which organizational members are united regarding the value and purpose of the innovation
    B Specific Practices and Processes
      1. Shared decision-making (local input, community participation or involvement, local ownership, collaboration)[a,b,c]
         The extent to which relevant parties (e.g., providers, administrators, researchers, and community members) collaborate in determining what will be implemented and how
      2. Coordination with other agencies (partnerships, networking, intersector alliances, multidisciplinary linkages)[a,b,c]
         The extent to which there is cooperation and collaboration among local agencies that can bring different perspectives, skills, and resources to bear on program implementation
      3. Communication[b]
         Effective mechanisms encouraging frequent and open communication
      4. Formulation of tasks (workgroups, teams, formalization, internal functioning, effective human resource management)[a,b,c]
         Procedures that enhance strategic planning and contain clear roles and responsibilities relative to task accomplishments
    C Specific Staffing Considerations
      1. Leadership[a,b,c]
         Leadership is important in many respects, for example, in terms of setting priorities, establishing consensus, offering incentives, and managing the overall process of implementation
      2. Program champion (internal advocate)[a,b,c]
         An individual who is trusted and respected by staff and administrators, and who can rally and maintain support for the innovation, and negotiate solutions to problems that develop

(continued)

Table 33.2   (Cont'd) Factors affecting the implementation process

      3. Managerial/supervisory/administrative support[a,b,c]
         Extent to which top management supervisors clearly support and encourage providers during implementation
V. Factors Related to the Prevention Support System
    A Training[a,b,c]
      Approaches to insure provider proficiencies in the skills necessary to conduct the intervention and to enhance providers' sense of self-efficacy
    C Technical Assistance[a,b,c]
      This refers to the combination of resources offered to providers once implementation begins, and may include retraining in certain skills, training of new staff, emotional support, and mechanisms to promote local problem solving effects

[a] Factors also identified by Fixsen et al. (2005)
[b] Factors also identified by Greenhalgh et al. (2005)
[c] Factors also identified by Stith et al. (2006)
Note: A detailed listing of the studies supporting the importance of each factor is available from the first author on request.
Reprinted with kind permission from Springer Science+Business Media: Durlak, J.A., & DuPre, E. P. (2008). Implementation matters: A review of research on the influence of implementation on program outcomes and the factors affecting implementation. *American Journal of Community Psychology, 41*, 327–350. Copyright 2008.

academic goal for the student, they have embraced a subjective evaluation criterion. Subjective evaluation enters into all decisions about the effects of an intervention, and will always feature professional judgment in the process. Of course, virtually all intervention outcome criteria at the student, classroom, or system level will be improved with a combination of the two approaches. The reader is referred to Stoiber and Kratochwill (2002) for more detailed information on outcome evaluation and various measures that can be used in this process (see next section on progress monitoring).

Progress Monitoring Procedures in Evaluation of Outcomes

Our final category of consideration for EBP is related to monitoring outcomes. Progress monitoring across phases of the evaluation is important to document the intervention outcomes. There are several considerations in this regard (Cone, 2001; Stoiber & Kratochwill, 2002). First, progress monitoring measures must be selected that represent the construct of interest in evaluating intervention outcomes. For example, when evaluating the outcomes of a program designed to reduce behavior problems, some direct assessment of disruptive classroom behavior is preferred, but can be supplemented with other proxy outcomes (e.g., office disciplinary referrals).

Second, progress monitoring measures should be selected that can be assessed repeatedly across time. Curriculum-based assessment measures are a good example of assessments that can easily be repeatedly

assessed across time, without problems of practice effects or reactivity of measurement, among other problems encountered with traditional tests such as intelligence and achievement. They can also be developed to be part of the system of assessment in the school, and used for the dual purpose of screening and progress monitoring.

Third, progress monitoring measures must be consistent across phases of the evaluation design structure (i.e., the A and B phases). That is, one must not change the type of measures used across the baseline to intervention phases of the evaluation, because the outcome may be due to the change in measuring the target issue. For example, if reading fluency measures are selected for progress monitoring in the baseline assessment, one should not switch to comprehension measures during the intervention phase(s).

Fourth, the consultant should give some consideration to evaluating performance beyond the domain selected for outcome assessment (given that the aforementioned issues are addressed). There is growing evidence that academic and behavioral problems are linked, and may even influence the development of each other (Algozzine, Putnam, & Horner, 2008). For example, a child who exhibits disruptive classroom behavior might typically be monitored on number of talk-outs, episodes of aggressive behavior, and out-of-seat behavior. However, the assessment of academic outcomes (completion of assignments, reading skill) also should be considered part of the evaluation, when possible.

Current Issues and Conclusions

Although research indicates the importance of adopting a problem solving process in consultation across multi-tiered prevention and intervention models, little to no research has examined the adherence to a particular problem-solving consultation model. Typically, the problem solving process revolves around the five stages typically seen in various forms of consultation: establishing the relationship, problem identification, problem analysis, plan implementation, and plan evaluation (Frank & Kratochwill, 2005). Unfortunately, little research exists on the adherence to a particular problem solving model and its ability to produce the identification and adoption of EBIs. Just as systems need to be more flexible and responsive to student needs, so does the consultation process need to be able to serve one or many uses. Just as our schools have become compartmentalized, so have our service delivery models. PSC, as we propose here, seeks to combine useful consultation models to meet the needs of students and systems across all levels, by ensuring effective practices (core curriculum, universal screening, systematic data collection, data-based decision making, and effective instructional techniques) are used at all levels of prevention and intervention.

The purpose of this chapter was twofold: (1) to review prominent consultation models and their defining features; and (2) to articulate a comprehensive model of problem solving consultation that addresses EBPs. In particular, we recommended the following components for "best practice" for consultants to engage in EBP: (a) use of an intervention that has a designation as "evidence-based" by a professional group, organization, task force, government unit, etc.; (b) use of a well-developed manual or guide that provides an overview of the intervention; (c) assessing and developing the skill level of individuals who implement the intervention; (d) documentation of the integrity of the intervention; (e) use of a basic evaluation structure such as an A/B design that can be use to document that the intervention was responsible for the observed outcomes; and (f) use of high quality progress monitoring procedures across phases of the intervention evaluation. Embracing these components will facilitate the success of interventions in the school, and improve the outcomes for teachers, parents, and children.

References

Algozinne, B. & Kay, P. (Eds.) (2002). *Preventing Problem Behaviors: A Handbook of Successful Prevention Strategies.* Thousand Oaks: CA: Corwin Press.

Algozzine, B., Putnam, B., & Horner, R. (2010). What comes first-the achievement or the behavior (problem)? Charlotte, NC: Behavior and Reading Improvement Center. Retrieved from http://education.uncc.edu/bric/reports/whatcomesfirst.pdf

Auster, E.R., Feeney-Kettler, K.A., & Kratochwill, T.R. (2006). Conjoint behavioral consultation: Application to the school-based treatment of anxiety disorders. *Education and Treatment of Children, 29(2),* 243–256.

Bergan, J. R., & Kratochwill, T. R. (1990). *Behavioral consultation in applied settings.* New York: Plenum.

Bergan, J. R., & Tombari, M. L. (1975). The analysis of verbal interactions occurring during consultation. Journal of School Psychology, 13, 209–226.

Bergan, J. R., & Tombari, M. L. (1976). Consultant skill and efficiency and the implementation of outcomes of consultation. *Journal of School Psychology, 14,* 3–14.

Bramlet, R. K., Murphy, J. J., Johnson, J., Wallingsford, L., & Hall, J. D. (2002). Contemporary practices in school psychology: A national survey of roles and referral problems. *Psychology in the Schools, 39,* 327–335.

Caplan, G. (1995). Types of mental health consultation. *Journal of Educational and Psychological Consultation, 6*(1), 7–21.

Caplan, G., Caplan, R. B., & Erchul, W. P. (1995). A contemporary view of mental health consultation: Comments on ' types of mental health consultation' by Gerald Caplan (1963*). Journal of Educational & Psychological Consultation, 6*(*1*), 23.

Christenson, S. L., & Cleary, M. (1990). Consultation and the parent–educator partnership: A perspective. *Journal of Educational and Psychological Consultation, 1,* 219–241.

Cone, J. D. (2001). *Evaluating outcomes: Empirical tools for effective practice.* Washington, DC: American Psychological Association.

Cowan, R. J., & Sheridan, S. M. (2003). Investigating the acceptability of behavioral interventions in applied conjoint behavioral consultation: Moving from analog conditions to naturalistic settings. *School Psychology Quarterly, 18,* 1–21.

Crone, D. A., & Horner, R. H. (2003). *Building positive behavior support systems in schools: Functional behavioral assessment.* New York: Guilford.

Crone, D. A., Horner, R. H., & Hawken, L. S. (2004). *Responding to problem behavior in schools: The Behavior Education Program.* New York: Guilford.

Dinnebeil, L. A., Hale, L. M., & Rule, S. (1996). A qualitative analysis of parents' and service coordinators' descriptions of variables that influence collaborative relationships. *Topics in Early Childhood Special Education, 16,* 322–347.

DiPerna, J.C. & Elliott, S.N. (2000). *ACES Academic Competence Evaluation Scales Manual K–12.* The Psychological Corporation.

Durlak, J.A., & DuPre, E. P. (2008). Implementation matters: A review of research on the influence of implementation on program outcomes and the factors affecting implementation. *American Journal of Community Psychology, 41,* 327–350.

Fixsen, D.L., Naoom, S.F., Blasé, K.A., Friedman, R.M., & Wallace, F. (2005) Implementation research: A synthesis of the literature. Tampa: University of South Florida, Louis de la Parte Florida Mental Health Institute.

Frank, J. L., & Kratochwill, T. R. (2005). School-based problem-solving consultation: Plotting a new course for evidence-based research and practice in consultation. In W.P. Erchul & S. M. Sheridan (Eds.), *Handbook of research in school consultation* (pp. 13–30). New York, NY: Lawrence Erlbaum Associates.

Freer, P., & Watson, S. (1999). A comparison of parent and teacher acceptability ratings of behavioral and conjoint behavioral consultation. *School Psychology Review, 28*, 672–684.

Garbacz, A.S., Woods, K.E., Swanger-Gagne, M.S., Taylor, A.M., Black, K.A., & Sheridan, S. (2008). The effectiveness of a partnership-centered approach in conjoint behavioral consultation. *School Psychology Quarterly, 23(3)*, 313–326.

Ginsburg-Block, M. D., Rohrbeck, C. A., & Fantuzzo, J. W. (2006). A meta-analytic review of social, self-concept, and behavioral outcomes of peer-assisted learning. *Journal of Educational Psychology, 98*, 732–749.

Graubard, P. S., Rosenberg, H., & Miller, M. B. (1971). Student applications of behavior modification to teachers and environments or ecological approaches to social deviancy. In E. A. Ramp & B. L. Hopkins (Eds.), *A new direction for education: Behavior analysis*. Lawrence, KS: The University of Kansas Support and Development Center for Follow Through.

Guli, L. A. (2005). Evidence-based parent consultation with school-related outcomes. *School Psychology Quarterly, 4*, 455–472.

Gutkin, T. B. (1999). The collaboration debate: Finding our way through maze: Moving forward into the future: A response to Erchul (1999). *Journal of School Psychology, 37*, 229–241.

Hayes, S. C., Barlow, D. H., & Nelson-Gray, R. O. (1999). *The scientist practitioner: Research and accountability in the age of managed care*. Boston: Allyn and Bacon.

IDEIA (2004). *Individuals with Disabilities Education Improvement Act.* Pub.L 108-446.

Ikeda, M. J., Tilly, W. D., Stumme, J., Volmer, L., & Allison, R. (1996). Agency-wide implementation of problem solving consultation: Foundation and current implementation and future directions. *School Psychology Quarterly, 11*, 228–243.

Illback, R.J., & Pennington, M.A. (2008). Organizational development and change in school settings. In W.P. Erchul & S. M. Sheridan (Eds.), *Handbook of research in school consultation* (pp. 225–265). New York, NY: Lawrence Erlbaum Associates.

Knotek, S. E., Kaniuka, M., & Ellingsen, K. (2008). Mental health consultation and consultee-centered approaches. In W. P. Erchul & S. M. Sheridan (Eds.), *Handbook of research in school consultation* (pp. 127–145). New York: Lawrence Erlbaum Associates.

Knotek, S. E., & Sandoval, J. (2003). Current research in consultee-centered consultation. *Journal of Educational & Psychological Consultation, 14(3)*, 243–250.

Kratochwill, T. R. (2007). Preparing psychologists for evidence-based school practice: Lessons learned and challenges ahead. *American Psychologist, 62*, 826–843.

Kratochwill, T. (2008). Best practices in school-based problem-solving consultation: Applications in prevention and intervention systems. In A. Thomas, & J. Grimes (Eds.), *Best practices in school psychology* (5th ed., pp. 1673–1688). Bethesda, MD: National Association of School Psychologists.

Kratochwill, T. R., Clements, M. A., & Kalymon, K. M. (2007). Response to intervention: Conceptual and methodological issues in implementation. In S. R. Jimerson, M. K. Burns, & A. M. VanDerHeyden (Eds.), *The handbook of response to intervention: The science and practice of assessment and intervention.* New York: Springer.

Kratochwill, T. R., Elliott, S. N., & Stoiber, K. (2002). Best practices in school-based problem-solving consultation.

In A. Thomas, & J. Grimes (Eds.), *Best practices in school psychology* (4th ed., pp. 583–608). Bethesda, MD: National Association of School Psychologists.

Kratochwill, T. R., & Pittman, P. H. (2002). Expanding problem-solving consultation training: Prospects and frameworks. *Journal of Educational and Psychological Consultation, 13*, 69–95.

Kratochwill, T. R., Volpiansky, P., Clements, M., & Ball, C. (2008). The role of professional development in implementing and sustaining multi-tier prevention and intervention models: Implications for response-to-intervention. *School Psychology Review, 36*, 618–631.

MacLeod, I. R., Jones, K. M., Somers, C. L., & Havey, J. M. (2001). An evaluation of the effectiveness of school-based behavioral consultation. *Journal of Educational and Psychological Consultation, 12*, 203–216.

March, R., Hawken, L. & Green, J. (2003). Schoolwide behavior support: Creating urban schools that accommodate diverse learners. *Journal of Special Education Leadership, 16(1)*, 15–22.

Martens, B. K., & DiGennaro, F. D. (2008). Behavioral consultation. In W. P. Erchul & S. M. Sheridan (Eds.), *Handbook of research in school consultation* (pp. 147–170). New York: Lawrence Erlbaum Associates.

O'Donnell, C. L. (2008). Defining, conceptualizing, and measuring fidelity of implementation and its relationship to outcomes in K 12 curriculum intervention research. *Review of Education Research, 78*, 33–84.

O'Neil, J. (1995). On schools as learning organizations: A conversation with Peter Senge. *Educational Leadership, 52*, 20–23.

Rosenfield, S. (1992). Developing school-based consultation teams: A design for organizational change. *School Psychology Quarterly, 7*, 27–46

Rosenfield, S. (2002). Best practices in instructional consultation. In A. Thomas, & J. Grimes (Eds.), *Best practices in school psychology* (4th ed., pp. 609–623). Bethesda, MD: National Association of School Psychologists.

Rosenfield, S. (2008). Best practice in instructional consultation and instructional consultation teams. In A. Thomas, & J. Grimes (Eds.), *Best practices in school psychology* (5th ed., pp. 1645–1660). Bethesda, MD: National Association of School Psychologists.

Rosenfield, S. A., & Gravois, T. A. (1996). *Instructional consultation teams: Collaborating for change*. New York, NY: The Guilford Press.

Rosenfield, S. A., Silva, A., & Gravois, T. A. (2008). Bringing instructional consultation to scale: Research and development of IC and IC teams. In W. P. Erchul & S. M. Sheridan (Eds., *Handbook of research in school consultation* (pp. 203–223). New York: Lawrence Erlbaum Associates.

Sanetti, L. H., & Kratochwill, T. R. (2005). Treatment integrity assessment within a problem-solving model. In R. Brown-Chelsey (Ed.), *Assessment for intervention: A problem-solving approach* (pp. 304–325). New York: Guilford Press.

Sheridan, S. M., Clarke, B. L., & Burt, J. D. (2008). Conjoint behavioral consultation: What do we know and what do we need to know? In W. P. Erchul & S. M. Sheridan (Eds.), *Handbook of Research in School Consultation* (pp. 171-202). New York: Lawrence Erlbaum Associates, Inc.

Sheridan, S. M., Eagle, J. W., Cowan, R. J., & Mickelson, W. (2001). The effects of conjoint behavioral consultation: Results of a four-year investigation. *Journal of School Psychology, 39*, 361–385.

Sheridan, S. M., Eagle, J. W., & Doll, B. (2006). An examination of the efficacy of conjoint behavioral consultation with diverse clients. *School Psychology Quarterly, 21*, 396–417.

Sheridan, S. M., & Kratochwill, T. R. (2008). *Conjoint behavioral consultation: Promoting family-school connections and interventions, 2nd ed.* New York: Springer.

Sheridan, S. M., Meegan, S. P., & Eagle, J. W. (2002). Assessing the social context in initial conjoint behavioral consultation interviews: An exploratory analysis investigating processes and outcomes. *School Psychology Quarterly, 17*, 299–324.

Sheridan, S. M., Welch, M., & Orme, S. F. (1996). Is consultation effective? A review of outcome research. *Remedial and Special Education, 17*, 341–354.

Stith, S., Pruitt, I., Dees, J., Fronce, M., Green, N., Som, A. et al. (2006). Implementing community-based prevention programming: A review of the literature. *Journal of Primary Prevention, 27*, 599–617

Stoiber, K.C. & Kratochwill, T.R. (2002). *Outcomes: Planning, monitoring, and evaluating.* San Antonio, TX: The Psychological Corporation.

Sugai, G., & Horner, R. (2006). A promising approach for expanding sustaining school-wide positive behavior support. *School Psychology Review, 35*, 245–259.

Topping, K. J., & Ehly, S. W. (2001). Peer assisted learning: A framework for consultation. *Journal of Educational and Psychological Consultation, 12*, 113–132.

Wald, P. J., & Castleberry, M. S., (2000). *Educators as learners: Creating a professional learning community in your school.* Alexandria, VA: Association for Supervision and Curriculum Development.

Witt, J. C. (1991). Collaboration in school-based consultation: Myth in need of data. *Journal of Educational and Psychological Consultation, 1*, 367–370.

PART 7

Medical Problems

Pediatric Health-Related Disorders: Prevention and Early Intervention

LeAdelle Phelps

Abstract

The prevalence of chronic medical conditions in children has nearly doubled in the last several decades. Both Division 16 of the American Psychological Association (APA) and the National Association of School Psychologists (NASP) advocate that school psychologists play a primary role in consulting and collaborating with other professionals for the health and wellness of children. It is imperative that school psychologists look beyond assessment and general academic functioning in the service provision for such children, and instead encourage prevention, early diagnosis, and health promotion. This chapter provides specific recommendations for such services related to the pediatric health issues of childhood obesity, prenatal cocaine exposure, and lead exposure.

Keywords: childhood obesity, evidence-based interventions, health promotion, lead exposure, prenatal cocaine exposure, prevention models, wellness

Introduction

It has been estimated that at least one in five youth have developmental, physical, or mental disabilities (U.S. Department of Health and Human Services, 2005a). This results in approximately one million children in this country who have a chronic illness that affects their daily functioning. The identification and treatment of children and adolescents with such disorders is a major health incentive in the United States. For example, the *Surgeon General's Call to Action to Improve the Health and Wellness of Persons with Disabilities* was released on July 26, 2005 (full text is available at http://surgeongeneral. gov/library/disabilities/index.html). One of the goals of this initiative was to increase the knowledge of health care professionals, for the improvement of services for this population.

In direct alignment with this goal, both Division 16 (School Psychology) of the American Psychological Association (APA) and the National Association of School Psychologists (NASP) advocate that school psychologists play a primary role in consulting and collaborating with other professionals for the health

and wellness of children (www.indiana.edu/~div16/ goals.html, 1) (NASP, 2006) Not only can school psychologists interact with medical personnel to better link home and school health care services, they can also provide school based personnel with much needed information about the etiology, diagnostic indicators, and biopsychosocial outcomes of specific disorders. By increasing knowledge and facilitating the coordination of medical treatments, educational services, and social/emotional interventions, school psychologists are responding to the Surgeon General's initiative.

Chronic Illnesses in Children

Chronic conditions are those that have a protracted course of treatment, and often result in compromised physical, cognitive, and psychosocial functioning (Phelps, 2006). The prevalence of chronic medical conditions in children has nearly doubled in the last several decades (U.S. Department of Health and Human Services, 2005a). This increased prevalence has been attributed to the significant decrease in infant mortality rates in lower socioeconomic sectors of the country (National Institute of Child Health and Human Development, 2000). Yet, children from low income and ethnic minority backgrounds remain at significant risk for health related difficulties because postnatal care is often inadequate, and exposure to neurotoxins is not unusual (Covington, Nordstrom-Klee, Ager, Sokol, & Delancy-Black, 2002; Phelps, 2005).

There are a wide variety of etiological models for chronic illnesses. Some childhood disorders originate solely from prenatal or postnatal environmental events (e.g., deaf-blindness in the offspring caused by the pregnant mother contracting rubella, exposure to toxic chemicals such as PCBs [polychlorinated biphenyls], occurrence of a traumatic head injury), but others are related to a defective gene transmitted through the generations (e.g., albinism, hemophilia, sickle cell anemia, Tay-Sachs). Many health conditions appear to result from genetic susceptibility coupled with prenatal or postnatal stressors (e.g., stuttering, Tourette's syndrome).

Regardless of etiology, medical issues common to the pediatric population may be protracted and continue throughout childhood because of the lack of early diagnosis and appropriate treatment. School psychologists are familiar with such chronic issues as learning disabilities, attention-deficit/hyperactivity disorder (ADHD), and developmental disorders. Less understood are chronic medical conditions that impact every aspect of the lives of affected children, but are overlooked for the simple reason that the disorder is so widespread. One such example is obesity in the pediatric population. Another reason health issues may be disregarded is the faulty assumption that because the outcomes are not readily apparent, the disorder has few long-lasting consequences. Several types of visual impairment (e.g., amblyopia, strabismus) and lead poisoning are good illustrations of this phenomenon. Nonetheless, these are inaccurate suppositions, and the resulting delays in treatment may have prolonged effects.

It is no longer acceptable to view medical conditions as beyond the purview of educational institutions (Shaw & Paez, 2002). The Individuals with Disabilities Act specifies that children with health impairments are eligible for services when the medical condition adversely affects her or his educational performance (IDEA, 34 U.S.C 300.7 (c) (9), 2004). Section 504 of the Rehabilitation Act of 1973 (20, C.F.R. Part 104) ensures equal access to educational activities, and additional supportive services when appropriate for children with a disability that limits major life activities (e.g., walking, hearing, seeing,

breathing, learning). Although some chronic health related issues may not impact a child's educational attainment or day-to-day activities, it is incumbent upon school psychologists to look beyond the rudiments of general academic functioning and to determine what, if any, additional services may be most beneficial (Lee & Janik, 2006).

Health Related Prevention and Wellness

There is an emerging service model within psychology that focuses on prevention and wellness within the context of comprehensive programming (i.e., educational, health, social/emotional interventions; Phelps & Power, 2008). The emphasis on health promotion is highly appropriate and much needed. School psychology as a profession has been driven for much of its history by a deficit model that focused on the clear presence of a disorder (e.g., discrepancy model for the diagnosis of a learning disability). Recently, the fields of school psychology in general, and pediatric health psychology in particular, are starting to embrace a preventive service model. As an illustration, one of the guiding principles of the 2002 School Psychology Futures Conference stated: "Prevention and early intervention will be necessary to achieve positive outcomes for children, families, and schools" (Harrison et al., 2003, p. 381).

Editors of journals that focus on school psychology have facilitated the health related prevention, early intervention, and wellness movement by supporting the publication of special issues on the topic. For example, several prevention approaches were described in the *School Psychology Review* four-part series entitled, "Emerging Models for Promoting Children's Mental Health: Linking Systems for Prevention and Intervention" that was guest edited by Power (2003, 23[1–4]). The topic of promoting wellness was highlighted in the *Psychology in the Schools* special issue: "Positive Psychology and Wellness in Children" edited by Chafouleas and Bray (2004, 4[1]). "School-based Health Promotion," edited by Walcott and Chafouleas (2008), further explicated measures that can be taken to integrate mental and physical health services into the schools.

Effective psychosocial prevention programming is dependent upon the identification of specific risk and protective factors. Risk catalysts are associated with higher probability of onset, greater severity, and longer duration of the disorder, whereas protective variables are affiliated with improved resistance and resilience. After successful identification of such factors, highly specific strategies can then be developed with the prevailing intent to reduce risk factors while enhancing protective factors. Using this model, prevention efforts with children are particularly important when environmental factors place them at risk. An excellent example is the prevention of lead exposure. As with most chemical substances, lead contamination is entirely preventable. Working with parents to ensure the provision of appropriate county health services reduces lead poisoning in preschool children (Phelps, 2005).

Review of Several Common Childhood Disorders

Following are extensive reviews of several disorders that have chronic and pervasive negative outcomes for children. All are issues that respond well to prevention, early diagnosis, and health promotion interventions. Prevalence rates, probable etiology, psychoeducational outcomes, prevention models, and evidence-based interventions will be reviewed. Specific risk and/or protective factors will be elucidated. Of primary importance with all these disorders is the close collaboration between schools, medical professionals, and health services.

Childhood Obesity

Obesity in children, defined as a body mass index (BMI) at or above the 95th percentile, has increased to 17% of the population (Ogden et al., 2006). Recent prevalence rates are especially high among African American girls (24%) and Mexican American boys (22%). Although many studies support a genetic predisposition for excess weight (e.g., Herbert, Gerry, & McQueen, 2006; Saunders et al., 2007), children are surrounded by the food their parents select, and inundated with delectable fare advertised on television. Although it is apparent that maternal obesity is associated with earlier onset and more severe weight problems in adolescent offspring (Gordon-Larsen, Adair, Suchindran, 2007), parental eating habits (e.g., type and portions of foods served at mealtime, availability of high caloric snacks, frequent consumption of sugar-sweetened sodas) provide strong social modeling. Hence, there is little doubt that a complex interplay of genetic risk and environmental factors result in the current obesity epidemic. Yet, because rates of obesity in children have more than tripled in the last 40 years (Ogden et al.), it is likely that specific alterations in the environment are most accountable for these changes.

The rapid increase in childhood obesity has alarmed the public health sector and resulted in several government and organizational initiatives. One such project was the campaign launched by the U.S. Department of Health and Human Services (2005a) with the logo: "Eat well, play hard, make it balance" (www.healthychildrencoalition.org/about. html). Focusing on the importance of matching caloric intake (e.g., food selections and portions) with physical output (e.g., participation in organized sports and/or afterschool activities), the campaign used multimedia ads featuring NFL players who encouraged children to "get up and play an hour a day" (U.S. Department of Health and Human Services, 2007;). http://www.hhs.gov/news/press/2007pres/10/20071009a.html

RESEARCH ON RISK AND PROTECTIVE FACTORS Another initiative was the expert committee convened by the American Medical Association (AMA), the Centers for Disease Control and Prevention (CDC), and the U.S. Health Resources and Services Administration (HRSA). Hereafter referred to as the AMA/CDC/HRSA Expert Committee, the group reviewed evidence-based research and made recommendations regarding the prevention and treatment of child and adolescent obesity (Barlow & Expert Committee, 2007). Given the difficulty of successful weight loss, and then the subsequent maintenance of weight within normal boundaries, prevention of pediatric obesity is the obvious choice (Wang, Chyen, Lee, & Lowry, 2008). The AMA/CDC/HRSA Expert Committee recommended that interventions to assist children and youth in maintaining appropriate weights start early in life (Barlow & Expert Committee). The Committee identified specific risk and protective factors that have consistent empirical support. By using these findings, prevention and early intervention programming can be planned and implemented in school systems. Schools are natural sites because of the amount of time children and youth spend there, the structured physical education offerings, the administrative control of food selections in the lunchroom cafeteria, health classes that can implement the recommended curriculum, and the availability of facilities for afterschool activities (e.g., gyms, swimming pools, weight rooms, locker rooms).

Three environmental factors that have consistent data-based evidence for placing children at risk for weight gain are: poor food selection (e.g., drinking sugar-sweetened soda, eating larger portions, snacking on high calorie foods, having meals at fast food restaurants); inadequate physical exertion (e.g., spending less time in physical activities both in and out of school); and increased sedentary activities (e.g., watching television, playing video games;

Barlow & Expert Committee, 2007; Davis et al., 2007). In addition, the AMA/CDC/HRSA Expert Committee identified protective factors that may assist in the maintenance of normal weight. These protective factors are: eating breakfast daily, having family meals in which the parents and children eat together, engaging in moderate to vigorous physical activity for at least 60 minutes a day, and consuming a balanced diet that includes fiber, fruits, and vegetables (Barlow & Expert Committee, 2007).

The American Dietetic Association (ADA) Childhood Overweight Evidence Analysis Project (2006) supported these conclusions (www.adaevidencelibrary.com). That report provided evidence that participation in family meals, intake of fruits and vegetables, and increased physical activity promoted the prevention of childhood obesity, whereas the intake of sugar-sweetened beverages (including soft drinks), skipping breakfast, eating at fast food establishments, eating large portions, and sedentary behaviors increased the risk for weight problems (Davis et al., 2007).

PREVENTION AND EARLY INTERVENTION PROGRAMS

Inclusion of parents in prevention and early intervention efforts is vital (Epstein, Pulauch, Roemmich, & Beecher, 2007; Institute of Medicine, 2005). For younger children, the regularity of exercise, the frequency of eating at fast food establishments, and the availability of high caloric snacks and soft drinks are all choices dictated by parental choices. Although the effects of parental discretion decrease with the age of the offspring, and the peer group becomes more of an intervening factor, habits established throughout childhood have an impact on adolescent behaviors (Cleland, Venn, Fryer, Dwyer, & Blizzard, 2005; Davison & Birch, 2001, Epstein, Paluch, Gordy, & Dorn, 2000).

Summarizing the evidence-based research, prevention/early intervention programming should assist the pediatric population in balancing energy intake with energy output. To accomplish this, school based initiatives could include five components: (a) availability of healthy food and limited access to soft drinks, candy, and snacks in the cafeteria and from vending machines; (b) health curriculum with instruction, discussion, and goal setting regarding food selection and physical activity; (c) increased vigorous activity during recess (elementary schools) or physical education classes (secondary schools); (d) increased availability to afterschool activities and organized sports; and (e) parent programs that focus on encouraging exercise,

limiting sedentary behaviors (e.g., watching television, playing video games, instant messaging), and providing healthy food choices for their children.

Prenatal Cocaine Exposure

Although cocaine in various forms has been in use for some 15 centuries, crack (a mixture of cocaine with water and baking soda) was introduced in the late 1980s. Selling for $5 to $20 a "hit," crack cocaine has resulted in the drug being more readily available to a multitude of consumers. As a consequence, approximately 375,000 infants are born every year with gestational exposure to cocaine (Frank, Augustyn, Knight, Pell, & Zuckerman, 2001).

Beginning in the early 1990s, the popular press published reports, based largely on single case studies, suggesting that children exposed in utero to cocaine exhibited severe and irreversible damage. At the time, there was little definitive evidence specifically linking intrauterine cocaine exposure to adverse long-term developmental outcomes. Subsequent research documented that the public, as well as health organizations, had overreacted. As illustrated by a review of 99 data-based studies that evaluated prenatal exposure and child outcomes, Lester, Lagasse, and Brunner (1997) concluded that most of the early data were compromised, and that multiple risk factors such as concurrent use of other drugs, postnatal parenting characteristics, and environmental lifestyle issues (e.g., continued drug usage) were seldom taken into consideration.

RESEARCH ON RISK AND PROTECTIVE FACTORS

Research using multivariate analyses, careful matching of comparison groups having no, single-drug, or multi-drug usage, and meta-analyses, generally confirms only marginal intrauterine growth retardation (e.g., lower birth weight, infant length, and smaller head circumference) and neurobehavioral abnormalities (e.g., tremors, irritability, sleep pattern disturbances, excessive crying, and diminished responsiveness) in newborns that can be linked specifically to chronic fetal cocaine exposure (Phelps & Cottone, 1999). Growth impediments are viewed primarily as a function of the concurrent polydrug use of alcohol, tobacco, and marijuana that is ubiquitous in cocaine users, as well as inadequate prenatal care (Cornelius, Goldschmidt, Day, & Larkby, 2002). The neurobehavioral effects that are frequently present appear to be transitory, and reflect the pharmacological actions of cocaine present in the infant's system (Behnke, Eyler, Garvan, Wobie, & Hou, 2002). There is consensus in the literature that as the infant matures, general development and motor skills (as measured by the *Bayley Scales of Infant Development, 2nd Edition*; Bayley, 1993) are not adversely affected by prenatal cocaine exposure. For example, Frank et al. (2002) completed a prospective, longitudinal study of 203 urban infants divided into 3 groups (unexposed, light exposure, heavy exposure). At 24 months of age, there were no significant differences on the Bayley Index scores between the three groups.

Well-controlled studies with preschool and school-age children indicate few long-term neurodevelopmental consequences that can be linked to cocaine exposure. In the best meta-analysis to date, Frank et al. (2001) evaluated 74 empirical articles that studied children with cocaine exposure. Using rigorous criteria (e.g., prospective studies utilizing a comparison group, and masked assessment), the authors identified 36 studies meeting the specifications for inclusion in the meta-analysis. The authors concluded:

> Among children aged 6 years or younger, there is no convincing evidence that prenatal cocaine exposure is associated with developmental toxic effects that are different in severity, scope, or kind from the sequelae of multiple other risk factors. Many findings once thought to be specific effects of in utero cocaine exposure are correlated with other factors, including prenatal exposure to tobacco, marijuana, or alcohol, and the quality of the child's environment (p.1614).

Additional studies published after the Frank et al. meta-analysis continue to support their conclusion. For example, Bennett, Bendersky, and Lewis (2002) compared 85 four-year-old children with gestational cocaine exposure, to 138 children without exposure. After controlling for environmental and demographic risk variables (e.g., poverty, race, maternal education, maternal verbal IQ, quality of caretaking), the researchers reported that there were no significant differences between the two groups on intellectual ability, as measured by the *Stanford-Binet, 4th Edition* (Thorndike, Hagen, & Sattler, 1986), or behavior as reported by the mother on the Child Behavior Checklist (Achenbach, 1991). Similarly, Frank et al. (2005) evaluated the intellectual functioning of 91 children who had a history of prenatal exposure to 79 children who did not. At four years of age, cocaine exposure was not associated in bivariate or multivariate models in decrements in IQ scores on the Wechsler Preschool and Primary Scale of Intelligence–Revised (WPPSI-R; Wechsler, 1989). Evaluating 7-year-old inner city children, Kilbride, Castor, Fuger, and

Kilbride (2006) found no significant differences between exposed vs. non-exposed groups in growth, behavior, cognitive, or verbal functioning. Likewise, Accornero, Anthony, Morrow, Xue, and Bandstra (2006) found no significant differences on the Child Behavior Checklist (Achenbach, 1991) in a prospective, longitudinal study of 210 cocaine-exposed and 197 non-exposed 7-year-olds. Thus, the findings from vigorous studies suggest that many developmental difficulties ascribed to prenatal cocaine exposure may well reflect the myriad prenatal, postnatal, socioeconomic, and environmental factors that place these children at considerable risk.

Recognizing the importance of postnatal confounding variables such as parenting skills, medical care, and continued parental drug usage is imperative. Infants and preschoolers with prenatal cocaine exposure often experience a postnatal environment that includes a primary caretaker who continues to abuse substances, as well as the related issues of poverty, dysfunctional parenting, and inadequate medical care. These factors almost certainly exacerbate the effects of prenatal cocaine exposure (Mayes, 2002). For example, Singer et al. (2004) completed a longitudinal, prospective, masked comparison group (exposed/non-exposed) and reported that a better home environment was associated with improved cognitive functioning at 4 years of age. Likewise, Claussen, Scott, Mundy, and Katz (2004), as well as Lewis et al. (2004) concluded that an enriched environment decreased language delays assessed at age 4. These results continue to be evident as children mature. For example, Hurt et al. (2005) followed 135 inner-city children (62 with gestational cocaine exposure and 73 without) until the end of the fourth grade, and found that better home environments resulted in higher academic success.

In addition to the many confounding factors that affect child outcomes, there is a notable tendency among laypersons and professionals alike for stereotyping and negative attributions that distort perceptions. For example, Rose-Jacobs, Cabral, Posner, Epstein, and Frank (2002) reported that masked professional evaluators misclassified nearly all children in a sample of 163 4-year-olds. In the sample, 37% of the children who were exposed to cocaine were misclassified as unexposed (false negatives), whereas 74% of those children unexposed were incorrectly classified as exposed (false positives). This study illustrates the harmful labeling and false ascriptions that often occur with this population.

PREVENTION PROGRAMS

Although gestational cocaine exposure does not *directly* affect child outcomes, prevention of cocaine use during pregnancy is an important first step. The identification of variables predictive of *drug usage among females of childbearing age* would aid significantly in the development of prevention programs designed to intervene *before* any such exposure has occurred. It is generally hypothesized that multilevel (i.e., primary, secondary, and tertiary prevention) comprehensive programs that target specific populations and focus on precise risk/protective factors would be most efficacious in the prevention of intrauterine drug exposure.

To date, residential and outpatient programs directed at reducing/eliminating consumption by pregnant women who abuse drugs have seldom been successful (e.g., Haller, Miles, & Dawson, 2003; Svikis, Silverman, Haug, Stitzer, & Keyser-Marcus, 2007; Winhusen et al., 2008). Likewise, knowledge of the negative consequences of prenatal exposure among minority women of childbearing age is alarmingly poor (Haller et al.). It seems evident that prenatal prevention instruction may be more successful if directed toward adolescents and young adults who have yet to experiment with cocaine.

Two significant limitations of previously published primary prevention efforts with adolescents/young adult populations are the reliance upon didactic presentations of factual information, and the exclusive focus on risk factors. For example, alcohol and drug abuse prevention programs have frequently relied on dissemination of factual information in an effort to increase knowledge, change attitudes, and effectuate behavior change. Often relying on arousal of fear, such didactic approaches have been shown to affect knowledge and attitudes, but have little impact in reducing current use, altering projected intentions, or changing future actions (for two excellent reviews of this literature, refer to Kim, Crutchfield, Williams, & Hepler, 1998; and Tobler et al., 2000). As the old adage goes, "Insight seldom changes behavior."

More recent approaches have focused primarily on the social mores and psychological factors presumed to encourage drug use. Such activities as increasing student awareness of peer norms promoting drug use (i.e., social influence model), providing specific skills and techniques to resist inappropriate use (i.e., cognitive-behavioral model), and enhancing general self-esteem (i.e., life skills model) have been implemented with limited success. (Only studies that provided longitudinal follow-up data and

utilized a control/experimental group design are cited.) A good example is the popular prevention program, Project DARE (Drug Abuse Resistance Education), which is designed to affect 6th–12th grade students' attitudes, beliefs, social skills, and drug use behaviors. Although evaluations completed shortly after the conclusion of the program indicated positive effects on students' knowledge, attitudes, resistance to peer pressure, self-esteem, and opposition to risky behaviors, the results faded over time (Birkeland, Murphy-Graham, & Weiss, 2005; Ullman, Stein, & Dukes, 2000). For example, using multilevel analyses (i.e., random-effects ordinal regressions) conducted over 6 years, Rosenbaum and Hanson (1998) reported no long-term effects on a wide range of drug use measures, and no lasting effects on hypothesized protective factors. Unfortunately, all the previously documented short-term effects had dissipated by the conclusion of the 6-year follow-up.

On the positive side, a drug abuse prevention program offered in southern California (Project Towards No Drug Abuse) involving youth who were at *high risk for drug abuse* (i.e., alternative high school placement) did show significant preventive effects for alcohol and hard drug use at 1, 2, and 5-year follow-up (Sun, Skara, Sun, Dent, & Sussman, 2006; Sussman, Dent, & Stacy, 2002; Sussman, Sun, McCuller, & Dent, 2003). In the analyses, the researchers reported that the effects were present only when delivered in a highly interactive version led by a teacher (Sussman, Rohrbach, Patel, & Holiday, 2003). When students led the interactions, a peer environment that supported substance abuse actually *accelerated* drug usage (Valente et al., 2007). Hence, explicit monitoring of classroom discussions by an adult, and targeting individuals who are at *significantly higher risk* for alcohol/cocaine abuse versus global efforts appear promising.

Lead Exposure

Inner-city homes containing severely decaying lead-based paint are the source of most lead poisoning for low-income children. As lead paint deteriorates, house dust and yard soil become contaminated. Lead then easily enters the body through normal hand to mouth activity. (Ingestion of non-edible substances such as paint chips, sand, hair, and plaster is quite common in infants and young children as they explore their environment and mouth objects.) When the primary source of exposure is lead-containing dirt, dust, and paint chips, childhood blood lead levels peak around 2 years of age. To rid older homes and the surrounding yard of lead dust, meticulous professional cleaning of floors, windowsills, window wells, and outside soil is required (Ettinger et al., 2002).

Until the late 1960s, acceptable upper limits in blood lead levels were 80 micrograms (ug) per deciliter (dl) for adults and 60 ug/dl for children. At these levels, overt signs of lead poisoning become apparent (e.g., excessive fatigue, persistent vomiting, convulsions, coma). Evidence indicated, however, that more covert neurological effects were evident at lower levels, In 1971, the Surgeon General specified 40 ug/dl as the criterion blood lead level requiring treatment, and encouraged the identification and remediation of exposure sources. Over the next 20 years, the government lowered the criterion blood lead level to 30, then 25, and finally to 10 ug/dl (Centers for Disease Control [CDC], 1991). The government currently monitors children's blood lead levels via the National Health and Nutrition Examination Surveys (NHANES) that requires states to report results to CDC annually. Current data indicate that the number of children with lead levels of > 10 ug/dl has steadily decreased because of county and state cleanup efforts (CDC, 2003).

RESEARCH ON RISK AND PROTECTIVE FACTORS
Methodological issues have plagued the lead investigatory field since inception (Kaufman, 2001a, 2001b; Phelps, 1999). As with cocaine exposure, it is essential to implement a prospective research design wherein blood lead levels are assessed numerous times, and the independent effects of lead exposure are isolated by controlling for confounding developmental variables. Unfortunately, numerous studies purporting to verify the negative impact of *low-level* (< 25 ug/dl) lead exposure have been neither prospective nor designed to control for critical confounding variables. Another essential consideration is the correction for type I errors (false positives) when a single prospective data set is analyzed multiple times. Running analyses year after year on the same children is a common practice in toxicology explorations; yet, few scientists attempt to correct for false positives by requiring a more stringent alpha level or using more parsimonious analyses. In addition, it is not unusual for researchers to draw generalized conclusions about lead's harmful effects based upon a large number of analyses, of which only a few are statistically significant.

When appropriate research designs are followed, it appears that most psychoeducational outcomes are more affected by: (a) child factors such as initial birth weight and age at testing; (b) parental factors such as IQ and education; and (c) environmental issues such as socioeconomic status (SES), quality of early caretaking, and preschool program attendance, than by low levels of lead exposure (Kaufman, 2001b; Phelps, 1999). For example, there is agreement among well-designed prospective studies that low-level prenatal or early postnatal (1–18 months of age) lead exposure has only transient effects. By 2 and 3 years of age, no significant negative developmental outcomes from early exposure are evident. (Dietrich et al., 1990; Ernhart, Morrow-Tlucak, Marler, & Wolf, 1987; Wasserman et al., 1992; Wolf, Jimenez, & Lozoff, 1994). As summarized by Ernhart et al., "Variations in low level lead added nothing to the strong impact that patterns of caretaking had on early measures of child development and intelligence" (p. 268). Likewise, as toddlers mature, the relationship between low level (<25 ug/dl) lead exposure and neurodevelopmental outcomes alters little. From 4 to 7 years of age, most studies reported no significant independent effects of such exposure (e.g., Conney, Bell, McBride, & Carter, 1989; Dietrich, Berger, & Succop, 1990; Ernhart, Morrow-Tlucak, Wolf, Super, & Drotar, 1989; McMichael et al., 1992). It needs to be stated, however, that these results reflect low blood lead levels, not moderate to high exposure. At elevated levels, distinctions in cognitive, academic, and behavioral outcomes become apparent (Phelps, 1999).

In spite of numerous prospective studies in which the researchers controlled for important confounding variables, the controversy surrounding low-level lead exposure has continued. In an attempt to provide further clarity, Lanphear, Dietrich, Auinger, and Cox (2000) used a data subset of 13,944 children from the National Health and Nutrition Examination Survey III (NHANES III). Based on these data, the authors concluded that cognitive and academic deficits were apparent at lower levels of exposure. Seeking to replicate these findings, Stone and Reynolds (2003) completed a series of empirical analyses and concluded that missing data, lack of control for notable confounding variables, and odd distributions of blood lead levels resulted in the NHANES III data being unsuitable to answer questions of causality. A key to all the low-level lead research is that the confounding social (particularly poverty) and biological variables accounted for far more variance in the outcome variables than did blood lead levels.

PREVENTION PROGRAMS
As with most chemical substances, lead contamination is entirely preventable. Providing parents with information about hand to mouth transmission, the

necessity of thorough housecleaning, the advisability of new paint, and the services provided through the county health agency, are essential. Most of the data on such community outreach programs, however, are not positive. That is, families most at risk are unlikely to come to the school or community center for lectures or discussion groups on prevention (Dilworth-Bart & Moore, 2006). Racial disparities are abundantly evident, with over 50% of African American children living in low-income housing (National Center for Children in Poverty, 2007), placing them at higher risk for lead exposure. Having lead screening available by parental request does not seem to be the answer, as the General Accounting Office (2001) reported that only 19% of children between the ages of 1–5 whose families were receiving Medicaid received testing. Therefore, personalized outreach services via home visits to at-risk families, who are unlikely to actively seek assistance, are necessary. Communications in the primary language of the family must be completed in an appropriate manner, with sensitivity to cultural differences (Dowling, Miranda, & Galaviz, 2008).

Nowhere may the need for prevention services and early identification be greater than at the preschool level. Because the primary method of lead exposure is hand to mouth activity, infants and toddlers residing in substandard housing need to be carefully monitored. Evidence of fatigue, irritability, or persistent vomiting should receive an immediate referral to the appropriate health care facility. Recall, however, that such overt signs of lead poisoning are usually not evident until higher levels (e.g., 60 ug/dl) of exposure. It has, therefore, been suggested by the Center for Disease Control (CDC, 1991) that venous (from a vein) blood sampling of all children ages 6 months through 6 years of age occur. Although this recommendation is viewed as far beyond the monetary resources of most county health agencies, advocating for such screening with at-risk children living in dilapidated housing is highly recommended. This is in keeping with the CDC (1991) requirement that all children less than 5 years of age from families with income less than twice the poverty level be tested. As indicated earlier, early detection and appropriate medical intervention can greatly reduce the negative psychoeducational outcomes.

Recall that environmental cleanup is essential to avoid recontamination (Ettinger et al., 2002). As most of these families reside in lower-income rental units, assisting the parents in advocating for environmental cleanup is essential. Unfortunately, soil rehabilitation and residential repairs seldom occur without concentrated attention by county health officials (Environmental Protection Agency, 2000). Such efforts are reaping positive results, for the number of children with blood levels > 10 ug/dl has been dropping notably from 1997 through 2001 (CDC, 2003). Nonetheless, there are still approximately 250,00 children in the U.S. with blood lead levels greater than this cutoff (CDC, 2010; http://cdc.gov/lead/).

Conclusion and Future Directions

Chronic medical conditions may impact every aspect of the lives of affected children. Although some health related issues may not affect a child's educational attainment, it is incumbent upon school psychologists to learn about chronic illnesses, and advocate such that these children receive appropriate services. School psychologists are in an ideal position to play a primary role in consulting and collaborating with other professionals for the health and wellness of these children. Not only can school psychologists interact with medical personnel to better link home and school health care services, they can also provide school based personnel with much-needed information, and guide evidence-based intervention planning and prevention/wellness promotion.

Future research will no doubt identify additional risk and protective factors for childhood chronic illnesses that will enhance prevention and intervention efforts. In the meantime, school psychologists may help mitigate negative stereotypes and overreactions expressed in laypersons and professionals alike. Childhood issues such as obesity, a history of cocaine exposure, or past treatment for lead exposure, need to be viewed as opportunities to provide appropriate individualized services. In summary, training school psychologists in the area of chronic health related disorders is essential if we, as a profession, are going to effectively serve these children.

References

Accornero, V.H., Anthony, J.C., Morrow, C. E., Xue, L., Bandstra, D. S. (2006). Prenatal cocaine exposure: An examination of childhood externalizing and internalizing behavior problems at age 7 years. *Edpidmiologia d Psichiatria Sociale*, *15*, 20–29.

Achenbach, T. (1991). *Child Behavior Checklist*. Burlington: University of Vermont.

American Dietetic Association (2006). *Childhood overweight evidence analysis project*. Retrieved September 13, 2008 from http://www.adaevidencelibrary.com.

Barlow, S.E., & Expert Committee (2007). Expert committee recommendations regarding the prevention, assessment, and treatment of child and adolescent overweight and obesity: Summary report. *Pediatrics, 120,* (Supp. 4), 164–192.

Bayley, N. (1993). *Bayley scales of infant development* (2nd ed.). San Antonio: Psychological Corporation.

Behnke, M., Eyler, F. D., Garvan, C. W., Wobie, K., & Hou, W. (2002). Cocaine exposure and developmental outcomes from birth to 6 months. *Neurotoxicology and Teratology, 24,* 283–295.

Bennett, D. S., Bendersky, M., & Lewis, M. (2002). Children's intellectual and emotional behavioral adjustment at 4 years as a function of cocaine exposure: Maternal characteristics, and environmental risks. *Developmental Psychology, 38,* 648–658.

Birkeland, S., Murphy-Graham, E., & Weiss, C. (2005). Good reasons for ignoring good evaluations: The case of the drug abuse resistance education (DARE) program. *Evaluation and Program Planning, 28,* 247–256.

Centers for Disease Control (CDC) (1991). Preventing lead poisoning in young children: A statement by the Centers for Disease Control (Rep. No. PB92- 155076). Atlanta, GA: Author.

Centers for Disease Control (CDC) (2003). Surveillance for elevated blood lead levels among children in the United States: 1997–2001. *Surveillance Summaries: Morbidity and Mortality Weekly Report, 52* (10), 1–21.

Centers for Disease Control (CDC) (2010). Childhood lead poisoning. Retrieved June 21, 2010 from http//www//cdc.gov/lead/default.html

Chafouleas, S. M., & Bray, M. A. (Guest Eds.). (2004). Positive psychology and wellness in Children [Special issue]. *Psychology in the Schools, 41*(1).

Claussen, A.H., Scott, K. G., Mundy, P. C., & Katz, L. F. (2004). Effects of three levels of early Intervention services on children prenatally exposed to cocaine. *Journal of Early Intervention, 26,* 204–220.

Cleland, V., Venn, A., Fryer, J., Dwyer, T., & Blizzard, L. (2005). Parental exercise is associated with Australian children's extra-curricular sports participation and cardiorrespiratory fitness: A cross-sectional study. *International Journal of Behavior, Nutrition, and Physical Activity,* 2, 3.

Conney, G. H., Bell, A., McBride, W., & Carter, C. (1989). Low-level exposures to lead: The Sydney lead study. *Developmental Medicine and Child Neurology, 31,* 640–649.

Cornelius, M. D., Goldschmidt, L., Day, N. L., & Larkby, C. (2002). Alcohol, tobacco, and marijuana use among pregnant teenagers: 6-year follow-up of offspring growth effects. Neurotoxicology and Teratology, 24, 703–710.

Covington, D. Y., Nordstrom-Klee, B., Ager, J., Sokol, R., & Delancey-Black, V. (2002). Birth to age 7 growth in children prenatally exposed to drugs: A prospective cohort Study. *Neurotoxicology and Teratology, 24,* 489–496.

Davis, M.M., Gance-Cleveland, B., Hassink, S., Johnson, R., Paradis, G., & Resnicow, K. (2007). Recommendations for prevention of childhood obesity. *Pediatrics, 120,* S229–S253.

Davison, K.K., & Birch, L.L. (2001). Child and parent characteristics as predictors of change in girls' body mass index. *International Journal of Obesity and Related Metabolic Disorders, 25,* 1834–1842.

Dietrich, K. N., Berger, O. G., & Succop, P. A. (1993). Lead exposure and the motor developmental status of urban six-year-old children in the Cincinnati prospective study. *Pediatrics, 91,* 301–307.

Dietrich, K. N., Succop, P. A., Bornschein, R. L., Krafft, K. M., Berger, O., Hammond, P. B., & Buncher, C. R. (1990). Lead

exposure and neurobehavioral development in later infancy. *Environmental Health Perspectives, 89,* 13–19.

Dilworth-Bart, J.E., & Moore, C. F. (2006). Mercy mercy me: Social injustice and the prevention of environmental pollutant exposures among ethnic minority and poor children. *Child Development, 77,* 247–265.

Dowling, K.C., Miranda, V., & Galaviz, V.E. (2008). Improved participation in blood test Screening with in-home phlebotomy. *Journal of Primary Prevention, 29,* 323–330.

Environmental Protection Agency (2000). *America's children and the environment.* Retrieved October 10, 2008 from http://www.epa.gov/envirohealth/children/

Epstein, L.H., Paluch, R. A., Gordy, C.C., & Dorn, J. (2000). Decreasing sedentary behaviors in treating pediatric obesity. *Archives of Pediatric and Adolescent Medicine, 154,* 220–226.

Epstein, L.H., Paluch, R.A., Roemmich, J.N., & Beecher, M.D. (2007). Family-based obesity treatment, then and now: Twenty-five years of pediatric obesity treatment. *Health Psychology, 26,* 381–391.

Ernhart, C. B., Morrow-Tlucak, M. M., Marler, M. R., & Wolf. A. W. (1987). Low level lead exposure in the prenatal and early preschool periods: Early preschool development. *Neurotoxicology and Teratology, 9,* 259–270.

Ernhart, C. B., Morrow-Tlucak, M. M., Wolf, A. W., Super, D., & Drotar, D. (1989). Low level lead exposure in the prenatal and early preschool periods: Intelligence prior to school entry. *Neurotoxicology and Teratology, 11,* 161–170.

Ettinger, A. S., Bornschein, R. L., Farfel, M., Campbell, C., Ragan, B, & Rhoads, G. G. (2002). Assessment of cleaning to control lead dust in homes of children with moderate lead poisoning: Treatment of lead-exposed children trial. *Environmental Health Perspectives, 110,* 773–780.

Frank, D. A., Augustyn, M., Knight, W. G., Pell, T., & Zuckerman, B. (2001). Growth, development, and behavior in early childhood following prenatal cocaine exposure: A systematic review. *Journal of the American Medical Association, 285,* 1613–1625.

Frank, D. A., Rose-Jacobs, R., Beeghly, M., Augusty, M., Bellinger, D., Cabral, H., & Heeren, T. (2002). Level of prenatal cocaine exposure and scores on the Bayley Scales of Infant Development: Modifying effects of caregiver, early intervention, and birth weight. *Pediatrics, 110,* 1143–1152.

Frank, D.A., Rose-Jacobs, R., Beeghly, M., Wilbur, M., Bellinger, D., & Cabral, H. (2005). Level of prenatal cocaine exposure and 48-month IQ: Importance of preschool environment. *Neurotoxicology and Teratology, 27,* 15–28.

General Accounting Office (2001). *Medicaid: Stronger effects needed to ensure children's access to health screening services. GAO-01-749.* Retrieved September 23, 2008 from http://www.gao.gov/

Gordon-Larsen, P., Adair, L.S., & Suchindran, C.M. (2007). Maternal obesity is associated with younger age at obesity onset in U.S. adolescent offspring followed into adulthood. *Obesity, 15,* 2790–2796.

Haller, D.L., Miles, D.R., & Dawson, K.S. (2003). Factors influencing treatment enrollment by pregnant substance abusers. *American Journal of Drug and Alcohol Abuse, 29,* 117–131.

Harrison, P. L., Cummings, J.A., Dawson, M., Short, R. S., Gorin, S., & Palomares, R. (2003). Responding to the needs of children, families, and schools. The 2002 multisite conference on the future of school psychology. *School Psychology Quarterly, 18,* 358–388.

Herbert, A., Gerry, N.P., & McQueen, M.R. (2006). A common genetic variant is associated with adult and childhood obesity. *Science, 312,* 279–283.

Hurt, H., Brodsky, N.L., Roth, H., Malmud, E., & Giannetta, J.M. (2005). School performance of children with gestational cocaine exposure. *Neurotoxicology and Teratology, 27,* 203–211.

Individuals with Disabilities Education Improvement Act of 2004, 20 U.S.C 1401 (2004).

Institute of Medicine Committee on Prevention of Obesity in Children and Youth, Food and Nutrition Board, Board on Health Promotion, and Disease Prevention (2005). *Prevention of childhood obesity: Health in the balance.* Washington, DC: National Academics Press.

Kaufman, A.S. (2001a). Do low levels of lead produce IQ loss in children? A careful examination of the literature. *Archives of Clinical Neuropsychology, 6,* 303–342.

Kaufman, A.S. (2001b). How dangerous are low (not moderate or high) doses of lead for children's intellectual development? *Archives of Clinical Neuropsychology, 6,* 403–431.

Kilbride, H.S., Castor, C.A., Fuger, K.L., & Kilbride, H.W. (2006). School-age outcomes of children with prenatal cocaine exposure following early case management. *Journal of Developmental and Behavioral Pediatrics, 27,* 181–187.

Kim, S., Crutchfield, C., Williams, C., & Hepler, N. (1998). Toward a new paradigm in substance abuse and other problem behavior prevention for youth: Youth development and empowerment approach. *Journal of Drug Education, 28,* 1–17.

Lanphear, B.P., Dietrich, K., Auinger, P., & Cox, C. (2000, November). Cognitive deficits associated with blood lead concentrations < 10 ug/dl in United States' children and adolescents. U.S. Department of Health and Human Services; Public Health Reports. Public Health Report 2000 (Vol. 115, pp. 521–529).

Lee, S. W., & Janik, M. (2006). Provision of psychoeducational services in the schools: IDEA, Section 501, and NCLB. In Phelps, L. (Ed.). *Chronic health-related disorders in children: Collaborative medical and psychoeducational interventions.* Washington, DC: American Psychological Association.

Lester, B. M., Lagasse, L., & Brunner, S. (1997). Data base of studies on prenatal cocaine exposure and child outcome. *Journal of Drug Issues, 27,* 487–499.

Lewis, B.A., Singer, L.T., Short, E.J., Minnes, S., Arendt, R., Klein, N., & Min, M.D. (2004). Four-year language outcomes of children exposed to cocaine in-utero. *Neurotoxiology and Teratology, 26,* 617–627.

Mayes, L. C. (2002). A behavioral teratogenic model of the impact of prenatal cocaine exposure on arousal regulatory system. *Neurotoxicology and Teratology, 24,* 385–395.

McMichael, A. J., Baghurst, P. A., Vimpani, G. V., Robertson, E. F., Wigg, N. R., & Tong, S. (1992). Sociodemographic factors modifying the effect of environmental lead on development in early childhood. *Neurotoxicology and Teratology, 14,* 321–327.

National Association of School Psychologists (2006). *School psychology: A Blueprint for training and practice III.* Bethesda, MD.: Author

National Center for Children in Poverty (2007). *Low-income children in the United States: National and state trend data, 1996–2006.* Retrieved October 11, 2008 from http://www.nccp.org/publications/pub_761.html.

National Institute of Child Health and Human Development. (2000). *Health disparities: Bridging the gap.* Rockville,MD.: Author.

Ogden, C.L., Carroll, M.D., Curtin, L.R., McDowell, M.A., Tabak, C.J., & flegal, K.M. (2006). Prevalence of overweight and obesity in the United Stated: 1999–2004. *Journal of the American Medical Association, 295,* 1549–1555.

Phelps, L. (1999). Low-level lead exposure: Implications for research and practice. *School Psychology Review, 28,* 477–492.

Phelps, L. (2005). Health-related issues among ethnic minority and low-income children: Psychoeducational outcomes and prevention models. In C.L. Frisby & C. R. Reynolds (Eds.). *Comprehensive handbook of multicultural school psychology.* Hoboken, N.J.: Wiley & Sons.

Phelps, L. (Ed.). (2006). *Chronic health-related disorders in children: Collaborative medical and psychoeducational interventions.* Washington, D.C.: American Psychological Association.

Phelps, L., & Cottone, J. W. (1999). Long-term developmental outcomes of prenatal cocaine exposure. *Journal of Psychoeducational Assessment, 17,* 343–353.

Phelps, L. & Power, T. J. (2008). Integration of educational and health services through comprehensive school-based service delivery. *Psychology in the Schools, 45,* 88–90.

Power, T. J. (Ed). (2003). Emerging models of promoting children's mental health: Linking systems for prevention and intervention [Special series]. *School Psychology Review, 32* (1–4).

Rehabilitation Act of 1973, 20 C.F.R. Part 104 (1973).

Rose-Jacobs, R., Cabral, H., Posner, M. A., Epstein, J., & Frank, D. A. (2002). Do "we just know"? Masked assessors' ability to accurately identify children with prenatal cocaine exposure. *Journal of Developmental and Behavioral Pediatrics, 23,* 340–347.

Rosenbaum, D. P., & Hanson, G. S. (1998). Assessing the effects of school-based drug education: A six-year multilevel analysis of Project DARE. *Journal of Research in Crime and Delinquency, 35,* 381–412.

Saunders, C.L., Chiodini, B.D., Sham, P., Lewis, C.M., Abkevich, V., Adeyemo, A.A., Arya, R.,Berenson, G.S., Price, R., & Turner, S. (2007). Meta-analysis of genome-wide studies in BMI and obesity. *Obesity, 15,* 2263–2275.

Shaw, S. R., & Paez, D. (2002). Best practices in interdisciplinary service delivery to children with chronic medical issues. In A. Thomas and J. Grimes (Eds.). *Best practices in school psychology IV.* Bethesda, MD: National Association of School Psychologists.

Singer, L.T., Minnes, S., Short, E., Arendt, R., Farkas, K., Lewis, B., Klein, N., Russ, S., Min, M.O., & Kirchner, H.L. (2004). Cognitive outcomes of preschool children with prenatal cocaine exposure. *Journal of the American Medical Association (JAMA), 29,* 2448–2456.

Stone, B.M., & Reynolds, C. R. (2003). Can the national health and nutrition examination survey III (NHANES III) data help resolve the controversy over low blood lead levels and neuropsychological development in children? *Archives of Clinical Neuropsychology, 18,* 219–244.

Sun, W., Skara, S., Sun, P., Dent, C.W., & Sussman, S. (2006). Project towards no drug abuse: Long-term substance use outcomes evaluation. *Preventive Medicine: An International Journal Devoted to Practice & Theory, 42,* 188–192.

Surgeon General (2005). *Surgeon General's call to action to improve the health and wellness of persons with disabilities.* Retrieved Mune 21, 2010 from : http://surgeongeneral.gov/library/disabilities/index.html

Sussman, S., Dent, C.W., & Stacy, A. W. (2002). Project Towards No Drug Abuse: A review of findings and future directions. *American Journal of Health Behavior, 26,* 354–364.

Sussman, S., Rohrbach, L.A., Patel, R., & Holiday, K. (2003). A look at an interactive classroom-based drug abuse prevention program: Interactive contents and suggestions for research. *Journal of Drug Education, 33,* 355–368.

Sussman, S., Sun, P., McCuller, W.J., & Dent, C. W. (2003). Project Towards No Drug Abuse: Two-year outcomes of a trial that compares health educator delivery to self-instruction. *Preventive Medicine: An International Journal Devoted to Practice and Theory, 37,* 155–162.

Svikis, D.S., Silverman, K., Haug, N.A., Stitzer, M., & Keyser-Marcus, L. (2007). Behavioral strategies to improve treatment participation and retention by pregnant drug-dependent women. *Substance Use and Misuse, 42,* 1527–1535.

Thorndike, R. L., Hagen, E. P., & Sattler, J. M. (1986). *Stanford-Binet Intelligence Scale: 4th Ed.* Chicago: Riverside Publishing.

Tobler, N.S., Roona, M.R., Ochshorn, P., Marshall, D. G., Streke, A.V., & Stackpole, K.M. (2000). School-based adolescent drug prevention programs: 1998 meta-analysis. *Journal of Primary Prevention, 20,* 275–336.

Ullman, J.B., Stein, J.A., & Dukes, R.L. (2000). Evaluation of DARE with latent variables In context of a Solomon four group design. In J.S. Rose, L. Chassin, C.S Presson, & S.J. Sherman (Eds.). *Multivariate applications in substance abuse research: New methods for new questions.* (pp. 203–231). Mahwah, NJ: Erlbaum Associates Publishers.

U.S. Department of Health and Human Services (2005a). *Call to action on disability: A report from the Surgeon General.* Washington, DC: Author.

U.S. Department of Health and Human Services (2005b). *Healthy children coalition.* Retrieved September 2, 2008 from http://www.healthychildrencoalition.org/about.html

U.S. Department of Health and Human Services (2007). *U.S. Department of Health and Human Services and ad council join NFL to combat childhood obesity.* Retrieved December 11, 2007 from : http://www.hhs.gov/news/press/2007pres/10/20071009a.html

Valente, T.W., Ritt-Olson, A., Stacy, A., Unger, J.B., Okamoto, J., & Sussman, S. (2007). Peer acceleration: Effects of social network tailored substance abuse prevention program among high-risk adolescents. *Addiction, 102,* 1804–1815.

Walcott, C.M., & Chafouleas, S.M. (Guest Editors). (2008). The practitioner's edition on school-based health promotion [Special issue]. *Psychology in the Schools, 45,* 1–90.

Wang, L.Y., Chyen, D., Lee, S., & Lowry, R. (2008). The association between body mass index in adolescence and obesity in adulthood. *Journal of Adolescent Health, 42,* 512–518.

Wasserman, G. A., Graziano, J. H., Factor-Litvak, R., Popovac, D., Morina, N., Musabegovic, A., Vrenezi, N., Capuni-Paracka, S., Lekic, V., Preteni-Redjepi, E., Hadzialjevic, S., Slavokovich, V., Kline, J., Shrout, P., & Stein, Z. (1992). Independent effects of lead exposure and iron deficiency anemia on developmental outcomes at age 2 years. *Journal of Pediatrics, 121,* 695–703.

Wechsler, D. (1989). *Preschool and Primary Scale of Intelligence–Revised.* San Antonio: Psychological Corporation.

Winhusen, T., Knopp, F., Babcock, D., Erickson, S.J., Renz, C., Rau, L., Lewis, D., & Leimberger, J. (2008). Motivational enhancement therapy to improve treatment utilization and outcome in pregnant substance abusers. *Journal of Substance Abuse Treatment, 35,* 161–173.

Wolf, A. W., Jimenez, E., & Lozoff, B. (1994). No evidence of developmental ill effects of low-lead exposure in a developing country. *Journal of Developmental and Behavioral Pediatrics, 15,* 224–231.

Pediatric Psychopharmacology

Thomas Kubiszyn

Abstract

This chapter informs school psychologists about recent growth in the use of psychotropic drugs with children and adolescents, and related controversies (e.g., polypharmacy, off-label prescribing, drug industry marketing practices, and publication biases). It describes a potential role as "knowledge brokers" for school psychologists with appropriate competencies to assist decision-makers in selecting drug, psychosocial, or combination treatments. The chapter reviews safety concerns, including U.S. Food and Drug Administration (FDA) warnings and advisories, and common drug side effects and interaction effects. It reviews efficacy evidence, including FDA drug indications and approvals, randomized controlled clinical trials (RCTs) and meta-analyses of RCTs. The chapter identifies several future research directions which school psychologists may be uniquely qualified to pursue.

Keywords: pediatric psychotropics, school psychology, safety, efficacy, controversies, future research, knowledge broker, disorders, polypharmacy, FDA warnings, FDA indications

Introduction

This chapter is intended to inform school psychologists about the growing use of psychotropic drugs with children and adolescents, related controversies and safety concerns, extant research support, and future research directions. But, why would school psychologists, who are primarily concerned with learning, behavior, and development need to be informed about pediatric psychotropic drugs? The answer is at least fourfold: (a) in spite of recent controversies, more and younger children are now taking one or more drugs that can affect learning, behavior, and development; (b) school psychologists will inevitably work with many of these pupils and their teachers, parents, and prescribers; (c) school psychologists informed about pediatric psychopharmacology can facilitate better informed consideration of the potential risks and benefits of drug, psychosocial, and combined treatments by decision-makers; and (d) although relevant research has increased over the last decade, significant gaps remain, and informed

school psychologists with appropriate competencies may be uniquely positioned to advance needed research.

This chapter is targeted toward school psychologists, not pediatric psychotropic prescribers. The primary intents of this chapter are to enhance awareness about important safety issues, and to review the randomized, controlled research, where it exists. Before doing so, several important contextual issues will be reviewed. These include the expansion of pediatric psychotropic prescribing and research over the last decade, involvement of school psychologists in this arena, and several recently emerging concerns and controversies.

Pediatric Psychotropic Prescribing: A Rapidly Growing Phenomenon

In spite of growing safety concerns and controversy regarding efficacy, the prescribing of psychotropic drugs to school-aged children continues to increase (Olfson, Blanco, Liu, Moreno & Laje, 2006; Vitiello,

Zuvekas, & Norquist, 2006; Zito et al., 2003). Patel et al. (2002) and Olfson et al. (2006) documented a 500% increase over the last decade in the prescribing of atypical (second generation) antipsychotics to youth, with the greatest proportional increases evident in younger children (ages 2–4 and 5–9; Patel et al., 2005). Some reasons for these increases may include greater awareness of mental health disorders in children; pharmaceutical marketing campaigns that increasingly include direct to consumer advertising in popular magazines and on television; gift-giving, in-office meals, dinners and other continuing education events sponsored by pharmaceutical manufacturers for prescribers; the effectiveness of some drugs for managing some symptoms; the perceived cost-effectiveness of drug treatment compared to psychosocial treatment; and our societal tendency to seek a "quick fix" to what may be complex developmental, family, school, and systemic issues. Another likely factor is increased media attention, such as a recent one-hour episode of the public television series, *Frontline*, entitled "The Medicated Child" (Gaviria, 2008, January 8), and a cover story in the weekly magazine *Newsweek*, entitled "Growing up Bipolar" (Carmichael, 2008, May 26).

Pediatric Psychotropic Research: Less Rapid Growth

Although pediatric psychotropic drug research has increased in the last decade, prescribing practices exceed the empirical support base (Brown et al., 2008). Randomized controlled trials (RCTs) were scarce through the 1990s because drug manufacturers were reluctant to include pediatric patients in their studies for a number of financial, ethical, legal, and practical reasons. Recognizing the need to stimulate pediatric drug development research, the federal government enacted the Food and Drug Administration Modernization Act (FDAMA) as federal policy in 1997. The FDAMA granted an additional 6 months "exclusivity" or patent protection to drug manufacturers who voluntarily included pediatric subjects in their drug development studies. Although 6 months of patent protection may not seem like much of an incentive, it proved to be a powerful stimulus, since the protection extended to adult sales of the drug as well as pediatric sales. Another incentive followed; in 1998 the federal "Pediatric Rule" gave the FDA the authority to require the inclusion of pediatric subjects in studies for new drugs, and certain existing drugs if a new indication, form of dosage, dosage regimen, or route of administration is requested by the drug manufacturer.

A parallel development also spurred research growth and sophistication: the establishment of the Research Units in Pediatric Psychopharmacology (RUPP), sponsored by the National Institute of Mental Health (NIMH). RUPP teams in more than a dozen sites now collaborate to conduct increasingly sophisticated and methodologically complex (e.g., a placebo washout phase to minimize placebo responders in the trial, crossover designs, long-term follow-ups), government sponsored (sometimes with support from drug manufacturers), large scale, multisite RCTs to assess the relative effectiveness of psychotropic drug treatments, psychosocial treatments, and combinations of drug and psychosocial treatments that have proven too challenging for individual research teams to undertake. To date, RUPP teams have completed several treatment studies that compare and contrast drug, psychosocial, combined treatments, and placebo for pediatric attention-deficit/hyperactivity disorder (ADHD), including a recent preschool ADHD study, major depressive disorder (MDD), obsessive-compulsive disorder (OCD), autism spectrum disorders (ASD), and non-OCD anxiety disorders, with similar studies for other disorders underway (e.g., pediatric bipolar disorder).

Are School Psychologists Involved?

Several surveys indicate that school psychologists have been and continue to be involved in discussions about drug and psychosocial treatment approaches and their safety and effectiveness (Carlson, Demaray & Hunter-Oehmke, 2006; Gureasko-Moore, DuPaul & Power 2005; Kubiszyn & Carlson 1995). These surveys indicate that school psychologists regularly consult with school staff, parents and caretakers, children, and even prescribers about drug treatment and psychosocial alternatives. Many prescribers are primary care physicians (pediatricians and family practitioners) or physician extenders (nurse practitioners, physician assistants) who have little or no expertise in education, psychiatric or mental health diagnostic training, or psychotropic prescribing training (DeLeon & Wiggins, 1996; Lavoie & Barone, 2006; MacGillivray et al., 2003). Thus the reality is that parents, teachers, and others commonly bring questions about pediatric psychopharmacology to school psychologists. Reflecting school psychology's increasing involvement, models and rationales have been developed recently that clarify the important role that school psychologists can also play in the evaluation of drug treatment effectiveness (Power, DuPaul, Shapiro, & Kazak, 2003; Volpe, Heick, & Gureasko-Moore, 2005).

The Knowledge Broker: A Potential Role for School Psychologists

Clearly, it would be beyond the scope of practice and competency of most school psychologists to directly make medication treatment decisions or recommendations (unless, of course, they possess appropriate postdoctoral training and competencies). Yet, by virtue of their research training, their training as scientist-practitioners, and their training in evidence-based diagnosis, intervention and consultation around pediatric learning, behavioral, and developmental issues, school psychologists may be uniquely positioned among school based professionals to assist drug treatment decision-makers (Kubiszyn, 1994). School psychologists with these competencies, and with additional, balanced knowledge about drug, psychosocial, and combination treatment safety and efficacy should be well positioned to become "knowledge brokers" (Phillips, 1999, p.66) in pediatric psychopharmacology, thereby helping decision-makers to evaluate potential risks and benefits of different types of treatment.

In the role of knowledge broker, school psychologists must accept the responsibility of understanding and communicating the strength and relevance of research findings to decision-makers (Phillips, 1999). In the context of pediatric psychopharmacology, the school psychologist functioning as a knowledge broker could serve several useful functions. These could include (a) facilitating better informed, collaborative treatment decision making among parents, school staff, and prescribers (b) identifying and sharing the relative risks and benefits associated with pediatric drug, psychosocial, and combination treatments, and (c) directing decision-makers to reliable, balanced sources of information (e.g., peer-reviewed literature reviews, non-drug industry sponsored websites, etc.) about the safety and efficacy of drug, psychosocial, and combination treatments. This last function may be particularly important today, because decision-makers can be confused and overwhelmed by sometimes exaggerated and contradictory claims that are available on the internet and in other media about the safety and efficacy of psychotropic drugs and psychosocial alternatives.

Yet, identifying, comprehending, and disseminating balanced data about the rapidly growing body of pediatric psychotropic drug research has become a daunting task. For example, in 1992, the author chaired a Task Force on Psychopharmacology in the Schools for Division 16 (School Psychology) of the American Psychological Association (APA). At that time, the task force identified only a few dozen randomized, controlled trials of psychotropic drugs that included children and adolescents. Today, the number of relevant, controlled pediatric studies has grown into the hundreds, and their methodologies have become increasingly sophisticated. Furthermore, these studies are typically reported in medical and psychiatric journals that may be difficult to locate and comprehend, because school psychologists may be unfamiliar with drug terminology, or medical research design, procedures, and methodology. To fulfill the knowledge broker function, school psychologists need access to research findings that are organized in ways that they are more accustomed to. This chapter is intended to help address this need by identifying and disseminating balanced drug safety and efficacy data and their sources.

Controversies

Many controversies have emerged in recent years around trends in contemporary pediatric prescribing practice, pharmaceutical industry marketing practices, potential conflicts of interest, and medical journal publication practice. Because these controversies raise vexing questions about practice, research, and public policy, they provide an important contextual backdrop against which drug safety and efficacy data must be considered. Although pediatric drug efficacy research has increased over the last decade (Vitiello, 2006), current prescribing practice outstrips the empirical support base (Brown et al., 2008) and is commonly extrapolated from adult prescribing practice (Vitiello & Jensen, 1997; Martin, Van Hoof, Stubbe, Sherwin & Scahill, 2003). Much concern has been generated by recent FDA warnings about suicidality, weight gain, sudden death, and other adverse events associated with commonly prescribed psychotropic drugs for youth (e.g., U.S. Food and Drug Administration, 2003a; 2003b; 2004a; 2004b; 2005a; 2005b; 2005c; 2005d; 2005e; 2005f; 2006a; 2006b; 2006c; 2007a; 2007b; 2007c; 2008a; 2008b). Other pediatric psychopharmacology controversies involve "off-label" prescribing, polypharmacy, pharmaceutical corporate funding and conflicts of interest, and selective publication of research findings.

Many pediatric drugs are routinely prescribed "off-label," including psychotropic drugs (Efron et al., 2005; Novak & Allen, 2007; Zito et al., 2000). Off-label prescription means that a drug is approved (i.e., is issued an FDA indication) by the FDA for one disorder (e.g., an anticonvulsant is approved for pediatric epilepsy), but the drug is then prescribed for another disorder (e.g., the anticonvulsant is prescribed for pediatric bipolar disorder) and/or for a different population (e.g., a drug is approved for adult use but is then prescribed for children). Although off-label prescribing is not necessarily dangerous or ineffective, it is not necessarily safe or effective, either. If a drug lacks a pediatric indication, this may mean that the manufacturer has not submitted a drug approval application for pediatric use or has, but research failed to demonstrate efficacy or safety.

Polypharmacy is the prescription of more than one psychotropic drug to augment monotherapy (i.e., single-drug treatment) in an attempt to enhance effectiveness or to counteract side effects of another drug or drugs. Pediatric polypharmacy is increasing, in spite of a nearly complete absence of published studies of the safety and efficacy of pediatric polypharmacy, including polypharmacy with off-label drugs (Efron et al., 2005; Zonfrillo, Penn & Henrietta, 2005). Julien, Advocat and Comaty (2008) reported that an estimated 1.6 million youths were taking two or more psychotropics in 2006, and that about 280,000 of the children were under 10 years of age.

The influence of the pharmaceutical industry on psychotropic research has become a major source of concern. For example, potential conflicts of interest have arisen because of financial relationships between pharmaceutical manufacturers and those individuals who are critical to the integrity of drug research: prominent researchers, peer reviewers, journal editors, and members of FDA advisory committees. Controversy also surrounds the influence on prescribing behavior of various incentives provided to prescribers by drug representatives (e.g., industry sponsored continuing education seminars and dinner lectures, lunches provided in prescribers' offices, medication samples, coffee cups, notepads, pens, etc.; Campbell, Gruen, Mountford, Miller, Cleary & Blumenthal, 2007; Pachter, Fox, Zimbardo & Antonuccio, 2007; Avorn, 2007). Additional and disturbing controversy has recently emerged involving the selective publication of positive drug outcome studies, a practice that may lead prescribers, the media, and consumers to conclude that research support for pediatric psychotropic drug treatment is more robust than it may actually be. Published psychotropic drug studies overwhelmingly reflect positive drug study outcomes, while nonsignificant or negative outcomes are much less frequently published. Whether this publication bias results from a failure to submit manuscripts on the part of authors

and drug manufacturers, from decisions by journal editors and reviewers not to publish nonsignificant findings, or both, is unclear (Turner, Matthews, Linardatos, Tell, & Rosenthal, 2008). Finally, other research studies have been suppressed by drug manufacturers until disclosed in legal proceedings because they reflected negatively on a drug's safety and efficacy (Jureidini, Leemon & Mansfield, 2008).

Evaluating Pediatric Drug Risk and Benefit: Safety First (in most cases)

In most risk–benefit analyses, a conservative "safety first" approach appears warranted. Youth central nervous systems (CNS), where these drugs putatively exert their effects, are "works in progress," so these drugs may exert differential effects on the youth and the adult CNS. For example, although tricyclic antidepressants (TCAs) have demonstrated efficacy for major depressive disorder (MDD) in many adult studies, Ambrosini, Bianchi, Rabinovich and Elia (1993) failed to find a single positive finding in 13 RCTs with TCAs for youth with MDD. In addition to efficacy differences, differential CNS development across youth may place some youth at greater risk for harm than others. Brown et al (2008) concluded that children with autism spectrum disorders (ASD) may be at increased risk for drug-induced side effects because their "brains are likely to be more sensitive to pharmacological intervention" (p. 110). A recent multisite RCT speaks to this proposition. Eighteen percent of the youth with ASD experienced adverse events with stimulants, compared to about 2% of non-ASD youth (Research Units in Pediatric Psychopharmacology Autism Research Network, 2005). Late-emerging effects may not be evident until months, years, or decades later, such as birth defects linked to thalidomide in the 1960s, and heart attacks and stroke more recently linked to Vioxx, Celebrex and Bextra. Yet, long-term pediatric psychopharmacology follow-up studies are lacking, or have only recently begun to be reported (e.g., MTA Cooperative Group 2004a, 2004b). Questions about the long-term safety and efficacy of most psychotropic drugs remain unanswered, and likely will for years or decades to come, especially with regard to polypharmacy and off-label prescribing. Thus, it appears that in all but the most acute, severe cases, a "safety first" approach to risk–benefit analysis is the most appropriate approach.

Risk–benefit analysis is difficult enough when the child's disorder is only mildly to moderately impairing and when evidence-based alternative treatment options exist (e.g., attention deficit/hyperactivity disorder, or ADHD, when behavioral parent training and behavioral classroom management is available). Yet, the burden may be almost unbearably heavy when the impairment is acute and severe, and escalating to the point that the child's safety is at stake, and when effective psychosocial or other alternatives (e.g., hospitalization) do not exist (or are unavailable). Should a drug treatment that may suppress self-destructive behavior (e.g., sexual promiscuity during a manic episode) be withheld because of the drug's possible adverse events? In such situations, the risk of withholding drug treatment could be judged to be unacceptably high, even if there is no FDA indication, efficacy data are lacking, and adverse events have been reported for the drug (through an FDA warning or advisory, research findings, or clinical experience). In this example, which perspective on safety should be primary? Is it more appropriate to protect the teen from the potential harm associated with the drug, or the potential harm associated with the manic behavior? Although extreme, this example is not beyond comprehension. Under more common circumstances the potential for harm to the developing child is arguably the reason why safety, not efficacy, should be given primary consideration by decision-makers in pediatric risk–benefit analysis.

The safety issues discussed above and in the remainder of this chapter should be considered to be suggestive rather than exhaustive, or even comprehensive, because the emergence of unintended outcomes is highly idiosyncratic; it is one of the ever-present risks associated with all drug treatments, regardless of age. Thus, whether a child will experience a serious adverse event, or less serious side effects (many of which are transient or can be eliminated or reduced through dosage adjustment), and what the impact of the drug may be on learning, behavior, or development, simply cannot be predicted at this time. If we cannot predict adverse events or side effects for an individual drug (i.e., monotherapy, or prescribing a single drug), the task becomes even more complex when two or more drugs are prescribed (i.e., polypharmacy, or prescribing multiple drugs). Decision-makers must consider many uncertainties in evaluating the risks and benefits of drug treatment.

Next, the factors driving the recent growth of pediatric psychopharmacology and the controversies that have emerged in recent years are described. Safety issues identified in FDA warnings and advisories will then be presented, followed by common side effects and interaction effects for the drug categories.

Organization of this Chapter

To emphasize that safety generally should be the first consideration in pediatric psychotropic decision making, FDA warnings, advisories, and known drug side effects and interaction effects will then be presented, organized by drug category. Presenting safety information first should also reduce redundancy in this chapter. Today, the same drug is often prescribed for multiple disorders. A drug's category (e.g., antidepressant, antipsychotic) no longer necessarily indicates the disorder the drug is used for. For example, although antidepressants were once used almost exclusively to treat depression, today they are commonly used to treat depression, various anxiety disorders including obsessive-compulsive disorder, aggression and disruptive behaviors, and autism spectrum disorders. Similarly, antipsychotics are used to treat aggressive and disruptive behavior, mania, and depression, as well as schizophrenia and psychosis. Thus, antidepressant safety issues, for example, would have to be reviewed in almost every disorder category if the chapter was entirely organized by disorder. Drug efficacy research will follow the safety section, organized by disorder. Because diagnostic criteria and descriptions of the various disorders are readily available in the DSM-IV (American Psychiatric Association, 2000) and other sources, these criteria and descriptions will not be included in the disorder sections. The chapter concludes with a discussion of future research directions.

Drug Safety Issues, by Drug Category

In this section, FDA warnings and advisories, common side effects, and drug–drug interactions for different categories of drugs will be reviewed. The FDA warnings and advisories typically affect a small percentage of patients (e.g., less than 1%–4%); and are very low probability (one in one million) but they may be very serious and must be considered seriously (e.g., liver failure, life-threatening rash, sudden unexplained death). Side effects, on the other hand, occur much more frequently but are typically less serious.

Stimulants

Stimulants include methylphenidate (MPH) and amphetamine (AMP) formulations. The various MPH formulations are marketed under the trade names of Ritalin, Concerta, Metadate and Daytrana. AMP formulations are marketed under the trade names of Dexedrine, Dextrostat, and Adderall (mixed amphetamine salts), and a unique AMP formulation, lisdexamfetamine (d-amphetamine prodrug), or Vyvanse.

Stimulants are classified as Schedule II drugs by the Drug Enforcement Agency (DEA) and are tightly regulated. Depending on state regulations, each MPH and AMP prescription must be completed in duplicate or triplicate, phone refills are not allowed, and no more than 30- to 60-day prescriptions may be filled at a time. When Vyvanse is crushed, a protein molecule deactivates the amphetamine, eliminating its abuse and diversion potential. Nevertheless, Vyvanse is still considered a Schedule II drug, and is tightly regulated, just like the other AMP and MPH formulations.

STIMULANTS: FDA WARNINGS AND ADVISORIES

In recent years there have been a number of FDA warnings and advisories about both stimulant and non-stimulant ADHD drug treatments (e.g., atomoxetine or Straterra). The stimulant warnings will be reviewed in chronological order in this section, and the atomoxetine warnings will be reviewed in the antidepressant section, because the chemical structure of atomoxetine is more comparable to that of the antidepressants than it is to the stimulants.

In 1999, the FDA issued a black box warning for pemoline (Cylert) warning of possible liver damage and liver toxicity in the pediatric population (U. S. Food and Drug Administration, 1999). The FDA identified 15 reports of liver failure resulting in liver transplant or death, usually within four weeks of onset of signs and symptoms of liver failure. Although the absolute number of reported cases of liver failure with pemoline was not large, the reporting rate for liver failure with pemoline was 4 to 17 times greater than the rate of liver failure in the general population. In October 2005, Abbott Laboratories chose to stop sales and marketing of Cylert, and all manufacturers of generic pemoline also agreed to stop sales and marketing (U.S. Food and Drug Administration, 2005e). Thus, pemoline is no longer recommended for ADHD treatment.

In February 2005, shortly after Health Canada (the Canadian equivalent of the FDA) suspended the marketing and sale of Adderall products (mixed amphetamine salts) in Canada, the FDA issued a public health advisory noting that there were 12 reported cases of sudden unexplained death (SUD) associated with the use of Adderall products between 1999 and 2003 (U.S. Food and Drug Administration, 2005a). The FDA advisory noted that that the 12 deaths occurred in the context of 30 million prescriptions written for Adderall between 1999 and 2003, and that SUD rate for Adderall was only slightly greater than the number reported for methylphenidate (MPH) products.

Yet, the FDA did not ban Adderall and the advisory was not extended to MPH products. The FDA noted that the deaths occurred in pediatric patients with structural cardiac abnormalities. By August 2005, Health Canada rescinded its ban, cautioning that Adderall products should not be used in patients with structural cardiac abnormalities.

In February 2007 the FDA required that a medication guide be issued by all manufacturers of all categories of ADHD drugs (stimulants and non-stimulants) indicating that there is an increased risk of significant cardiovascular events (e.g., SUD), and for the possible emergence of psychotic/manic symptoms, even where there was no prior history of psychotic/manic symptoms (U. S. Food and Drug Administration, 2007a). The FDA advised close monitoring, and recommended that prescribers of ADHD drugs complete an evaluation of current health status and a careful health history, with particular attention given to the child's and family's cardiovascular history. Next, the side effects and interaction effects associated with stimulant use will be reviewed.

STIMULANTS: SIDE EFFECTS AND INTERACTION EFFECTS

Common acute side effects of stimulants include appetite reduction, insomnia, nervousness, abdominal pain, headache, mood liability, nausea, and vomiting (Connor & Meltzer, 2006). These side effects occur in 4% to 10% of patients and tend to resolve when the stimulants are discontinued or the dosages decreased. A multisite, government sponsored study reported that continued use of stimulants is associated with steady growth suppression of about 1 centimeter per year in both school-aged (MTA Cooperative Group 2004b; Swanson et al., 2007) and preschool subjects (Swanson et al., 2006). Although the development or worsening of tics has been attributed to stimulant use, a recent study by Palumbo, Spencer, Lynch Co-Chien and Faraone (2004) indicated that stimulants do not cause or worsen tics. The use of stimulants for ADHD has been considered by some to be a "gateway" to later substance abuse. In their review, Brown et al. (2008) reported equivocal findings with regard to risk for later substance abuse.

In the National Institute of Mental Health (NIMH) sponsored multisite Preschool ADHD Treatment Study (PATS) study, Greenhill et al. (2006) and Wigal et al (2006) reported that loss of appetite, sleep disturbance, stomachache, social withdrawal and lethargy were more common at higher stimulant doses (for this sample) in 3- to 5-year-olds. They also reported a higher dropout rate for stimulant treatment than was evident in prior studies with school-aged children. However, this finding may have been inflated somewhat because parents of children in the placebo group had the option of leaving their assigned group and entering the drug treatment arm of the study at any time.

Although rare, life-threatening hypertensive crises have been reported when stimulant treatment is offered concurrently with furazolidone (Furoxone), an antibiotic, and also with monoamine oxidase inhibitors (MAOIs), a class of drug used primarily for treatment of adult depression and anxiety. Concurrent treatment with furazolidone should be avoided, and if the stimulant has been prescribed it should be terminated at least two weeks before the MAOI is initiated, and vice-versa (Connor & Meltzer, 2006). In addition, three cases of SUD were reported by Cantwell, Swanson & Connor (1997) in children treated for ADHD with a combination of methylphenidate (Ritalin) and clonidine (Catapres), an antihypertensive. Although there is no direct evidence that this medication combination directly resulted in these deaths, close monitoring of vital signs is recommended if this treatment is used.

Antidepressants (ADs)

The antidepressant (AD) category includes tricyclic antidepressants (TCAs), selective serotonin reuptake inhibitors (SSRIs), serotonin-norepinephrine reuptake inhibitors (SNRIs), and atypical antidepressants. Because the section on ADHD safety and efficacy was just completed, this section begins with a discussion of atomoxetine (Strattera) because it is far more commonly used for treatment of ADHD than for treatment of depression.

ATOMOXETINE (STRATTERA): FDA WARNINGS AND ADVISORIES

Multiple FDA warnings and advisories have been issued for atomoxetine or Strattera, a non-stimulant, antidepressant typically used for ADHD treatment. In December 2004, the FDA issued a warning for atomoxetine cautioning about potential liver damage in pediatric patients (U. S. Food and Drug Administration, 2004b). Specifically, the FDA warned about the potential for jaundice and reported that there were two cases of reversible liver damage reported for the 2 million prescriptions that had been filled.

In September 2005, the FDA issued a public health advisory for atomoxetine indicating that atomoxetine use was associated with increased risk for suicidality (suicidal ideation or action; U. S. Food and Drug Administration, 2005d). This advisory was an extension of an October 2004 FDA black box warning about suicidality associated with pediatric AD use (discussed in more detail later in this section). This is not particularly surprising, because atomoxetine is very similar in its chemical structure to many of the ADs implicated in the October 2004 FDA warning (U. S. Food and Drug Administration, 2004a).

In October 2006, the FDA issued another warning indicating increased risk for cardiac and psychiatric events with atomoxetine (U. S. Food and Drug Administration, 2006b). The reported events included sudden unexplained death (SUD) in children and adolescents with structural cardiac abnormalities or serious heart conditions, and psychotic/manic symptoms, even in children with no prior history of psychotic or manic illness. This warning was extended to all ADHD drugs in February 2007 (U. S. Food and Drug Administration, 2007a).

ATOMOXETINE (STRATTERA): SIDE EFFECTS AND INTERACTION EFFECTS

Common side effects for atomoxetine include gastrointestinal disturbances, nausea, decreased appetite, rash, headache, and mild weight loss in children and younger adolescents, and constipation, dry mouth, lethargy, decreased appetite, insomnia, sexual dysfunction, and urinary difficulty in older adolescents (Connor & Meltzer, 2006). Sedation is also common unless atomoxetine is titrated (i.e. adjusted) slowly. Atomoxetine has commonly been shown to increase heart rate by approximately five beats per minute, and to increase both systolic and diastolic blood pressure by approximately 1.5 mmHg. Because of potential interaction effects, treatment with a monoamine oxidase inhibitor (MAOI) should not be considered until two weeks following cessation of atomoxetine treatment (Conner & Meltzer).

ANTIDEPRESSANTS OTHER THAN ATOMOXETINE: FDA WARNINGS AND ADVISORIES

There have been several FDA warnings and advisories issued for ADs other than atomoxetine since 2002. In January 2002 the FDA issued a black box warning for nefazodone (Serzone) warning of potential liver abnormalities and liver failure (U.S. Food and Drug Administration, 2002). Although Serzone is no longer marketed, generic nefazodone may still be obtained. The FDA reported a rate of liver failure about 3–4 times the estimated average rate of liver failure. The FDA also noted that this rate may be an underestimate because of underreporting, and that the true risk could be greater.

In October 2003 an FDA Public Health Advisory warned about possible increases in suicidality associated with the use of selective serotonin reuptake inhibitors (SSRIs), and other ADs (mirtazapine or Remeron, nefazodone, and venlafaxine or Effexor) for pediatric MDD (U. S. Food and Drug Administration, 2003a). The advisory stated that although the data did not clearly indicate an association between the drugs and suicidality, the risk could not be ruled out. The advisory also clarified that only fluoxetine was demonstrated to be effective for pediatric major depressive disorder (MDD).

In October 2004, the FDA issued a black box warning for all ADs, informing prescribers and consumers about an increased risk of suicidality associated with pediatric AD use, and emphasizing the need for close management especially at the onset and termination of treatment, and subsequent to dosage adjustments (U. S. Food and Drug Administration, 2004a). This black box warning did not prohibit pediatric AD use, and was based on the FDA's analysis of nine ADs across 24 RCTs with an aggregated sample size of over 4400 children and adolescents. This analysis indicated that the rate of occurrence (4%) of suicidality was roughly twice as high in the active drug treatment group as opposed to the placebo group (Hammad, Laughren & Racoosin, 2006). In 2007 the FDA included young adults in an extension of this warning about increased suicidality associated with ADs.

In November 2006, an FDA advisory was issued warning that concurrent ingestion of triptans (drugs used to treat migraine headaches) with either SSRIs or SNRIs could lead to a potentially life-threatening serotonin syndrome, caused by elevated serotonin levels (U.S. Food and Drug Administration, 2006c). Serotonin syndrome symptoms include restlessness, hallucinations, loss of coordination, fast heartbeat, rapid changes in blood pressure, increased body temperature, overactive reflexes, nausea, vomiting, and diarrhea. Serotonin syndrome may be more likely to occur when starting or increasing the dose of a triptan, SSRI or SNRI.

In spite of these public health advisories and warnings, many questions remain regarding the appropriateness of prescribing ADs for pediatric MDD. Among the more prominent issues is the direction of causality. In other words, do pediatric ADs cause an increase in suicidality, or does suicidality cause an increase in pediatric AD use? Brent (2007) concluded that "it is much more likely that suicidal behavior leads to treatment than that treatment leads to suicidal behavior" (p. 991).

ANTIDEPRESSANTS OTHER THAN ATOMOXETINE: SIDE EFFECTS AND INTERACTION EFFECTS

Tricyclic Antidepressants (TCAs)

TCAs are no longer recommended for any of the internalizing disorders because of their significant anticholinergic effects, potential cardiotoxicity, and lethality in overdose (Birmaher and Brent, 2003; LaBellarte & Ginsburg, 2003). Anticholinergic effects include dry mouth, urinary retention, constipation, nausea, blurred vision, memory impairment and confusion. Cardiotoxic effects include syncope (loss of consciousness with interruption of awareness of oneself and one's surroundings), and QTc prolongation (a delay in normal heart rhythms that may lead to arrhythmia and sudden death). Desipramine (Norpramin) has been associated with at least six sudden pediatric deaths, and imipramine (Tofranil) has been associated with at least three sudden deaths in the pediatric population (Green, 2007). Amitai and Frischer (2006) compared the lethality of several TCAs in accidental or intentional overdose in the pediatric population. They concluded that desipramine was more lethal than amitriptyline, imipramine, nortriptyline, and doxepin, and recommended that restriction should be placed on the pediatric use of desipramine. To date, however, no such restriction has been issued by the FDA.

Connor and Meltzer (2006) reported that TCAs also have the potential for significant drug interactions. A hypertensive crisis can occur when TCAs and MAOIs are taken concurrently. Serum levels of TCAs can also reach toxic levels when taken concurrently with other drugs (e.g., cimetidine or Tagamet, antipsychotics, SSRIs, and oral contraceptives). When taken concurrently with buproprion, there is an increased risk of seizures. In spite of these concerns, TCAs continue to be prescribed for a variety of childhood and adolescent disorders, including enuresis, OCD, MDD, ADHD, and non-OCD anxiety disorders.

Selective Serotonin Reuptake Inhibitors (SSRIs)

SSRIs include fluoxetine (Prozac), fluvoxamine (Luvox), sertraline (Zoloft), paroxetine (Paxil), citalopram (Celexa), and escitalopram (Lexapro). Compared with the TCAs, SSRIs tend to be well tolerated and are less toxic in overdose than the TCAs

(Emslie, Walkup, Pliszka & Ernest, 1999). Most side effect data have emerged from the adult literature, or are based on case reports. Antonuccio, Danton, De Nelsky, Greenberg, & Gordon (1999) listed common SSRI side effects including agitation, sleep disturbance, gastrointestinal complaints, and sexual dysfunction. Connor and Meltzer (2006) identify gastrointestinal complaints, headache, anxiety and nervousness, agitation, insomnia, sexual dysfunction, sweating, weight loss and rash as common SSRI side effects. In their review of animal and human studies, Brown et al. (2008) raised concerns "about the possibility that antidepressants can alter the course of pubertal growth and development in adolescents" (p. 80). They noted case studies indicating that sexual dysfunction can persist even after medication cessation (Csoka & Shipko, 2006), and other case studies indicate that growth suppression also may be associated with SSRI use in children (Weintrob, Cohen, Klipper-Aurbach, Zaadik & Dickerman, 2002). Other side effects include behavioral activation or mania (Preda, MacLean, Mazure & Bowers, 2001) and a serotonin withdrawal syndrome (Rosenbaum, Fava, Hoog, Ashcroft & Krebs, 1998) that is most commonly associated with paroxetine discontinuation (Connor and Meltzer, 2006).

It is important to note that although SSRIs are relatively safe compared to the TCAs, SSRIs can interfere with the metabolism and excretion of a variety of drugs by inhibiting the activity for the cytochrome (CYP) liver enzyme family. As a result of this CYP enzyme inhibition, serum levels of drugs that are normally metabolized by CYP enzymes may reach toxic levels. Both fluoxetine and fluvoxamine are potent CYP enzyme inhibitors, and if concurrently administered can lead to toxicity for TCAs, thioridazine (Mellaril), benzodiazepines, carbamazepine, phenytoin, warfarin, buproprion, lithium, and melatonin (Connor and Meltzer, 2006). Finally, although the SSRIs are not nearly as toxic in overdose as are the TCAs, Connor and Meltzer note that there have been fatalities in pediatric patients associated with SSRI overdose, alone and in combination with other agents.

Serotonin–Norepinephrine Reuptake Inhibitors (SNRIs)
SNRIs include venlafaxine (Effexor), duloxetine (Cymbalta), and mirtazapine (Remeron). Rubino, Roskell, and Tennis (2007) found that suicidal ideation was much more common with venlafaxine than with fluoxetine. In their study of Effexor-XR (extended-release venlafaxine) Emslie, Yeung and Kunz

(2007) were concerned enough about suicidal ideation and attempts in their sample that they characterized venlafaxine as "a third-line antidepressant in children and adolescents" (p. 223). Green (2007) reported that common side effects associated with venlafaxine include anxiety, insomnia, nausea, anorexia, weight loss, constipation, sweating, dry mouth, dizziness, and sexual dysfunction. In addition, Green noted the possibility of serious, life-threatening reactions if venlafaxine is taken concurrently with an MAOI.

Green (2007) reported that nausea, dry mouth, constipation, fatigue, decreased appetite, sweating, and sexual dysfunction are common side effects associated with duloxetine (Cymbalta). Like other drugs that affect the CYP liver enzyme systems, duloxetine has potential for drug–drug interactions and should also not be taken concurrently with an MAOI (Connor and Meltzer, 2006; Green, 2007). Serum concentrations of duloxetine will increase if taken concurrently with fluvoxamine, fluoxetine or SSRI antidepressants. Concurrent administration of the TCAs or phenothiazines (first generation, typical antipsychotics) with duloxetine will also lead to increased serum concentration of these drugs. Connor and Meltzer report that there is a risk of QTc prolongation (the cardiac ventricular polarization–depolarization interval) and arrhythmia if duloxetine and thioridazine (Mellaril) are taken concurrently.

Sedation and somnolence are the most common side effects associated with mirtazapine (Remeron). Other common side effects include weight gain, dizziness, dry mouth, abnormal dreams, constipation, and increases in cholesterol and triglycerides (Connor and Meltzer, 2006). However, because mirtazapine does not affect the CYP liver enzyme systems there is less potential for drug–drug interactions than with the SSRIs (Green, 2007).

Atypical Antidepressants
Atypical ADs include buproprion (Wellbutrin), trazodone (Desyrel) and nefazodone (Serzone). Connor and Meltzer (2006) report that common side effects of buproprion include agitation, anxiety, confusion, auditory and visual disturbances, constipation, dry mouth, gastrointestinal disturbances, dizziness, headache, hostility, hypertension, rapid heart rate, sleep difficulties, rash, sweating, weight change, and tremor. Buproprion's therapeutic dosage window is limited due to increased seizure risk, especially if the dosage is greater than 450 mg per day (therapeutic level is 300 mg per day). The seizure risk in such cases is 0.4%,

which is about four times the seizure risk associated with other ADs (Green, 2007). In addition, in rare cases, psychosis and mania may occur, along with cardiac arrhythmias

Connor and Meltzer (2006) and Green (2007) reported that the side effects of trazodone (Desyrel) include drowsiness, dizziness, decreased appetite, dry mouth, nausea and vomiting, blurred vision, sweating, lethargy, and memory impairment. Priapism (a prolonged, inappropriate erection) is a rare (one in 15,000) but serious side effect that may require surgical intervention and can result in subsequent sexual impairment. Potentially serious arrhythmias and hypo- or hypertension have also been associated with trazodone treatment (Connor and Meltzer).

As was noted earlier, nefazodone has a black box warning issued by the FDA in 2002 for liver abnormalities and potential liver failure. Connor and Melzer (2006) note that nefazodone typically has fewer cardiovascular, anticholinergic, sedating, and sexual side effects than the other ADs. Nevertheless, common side effects of nefazodone include abnormal vision, cough, headache, confusion and memory impairment, constipation, dry mouth, nausea, dizziness, somnolence, and blurred vision. In addition, Connor and Meltzer report that nefazodone has more potential for drug–drug interactions than venlafaxine or trazodone because it inhibits the CYP liver enzyme family.

Monoamine Oxidase Inhibitors (MAOIs)

Monoamine oxidase inhibitors (MAOIs) include phenelzine (Nardil), tranylcypromine (Parnate), and selegiline, or L-deprenyl. Because of their significant side effect profiles, MAOIs are not recommended for pediatric patients (Connor and Meltzer, 2006). Green (2007) reported that dizziness, headache, orthostatic hypotension (dizziness and fainting when quickly standing after being seated), insomnia, sedation, fatigue, dry mouth, and gastrointestinal disturbances have all been reported with MAOIs. A potentially life-threatening hypertensive (high blood pressure) crisis can occur if foods containing tyramine are ingested concurrent with MAOI treatment. Such foods include cheese, some types of beans, yeast derivatives, and alcohol. Hypertensive crises and seizures can also occur if MAOIs are taken concurrently with TCAs, amphetamines, methylphenidate or Ritalin, and other compounds, including common cold medicines.

Antipsychotics (APs)

APs are also referred to as neuroleptics. Typical or first-generation APs began to be used in the 1950s and were referred to as "major tranquilizers" at that time. They include chlorpromazine (Thorazine), thioridazine (Mellaril), trifluoperazine (Stelazine), thiothixene (Navane), fluphenazine (Prolixin), perphenazine (Trilafon), haloperidol (Haldol), and pimozide (Orap) and other similar compounds. In 1989 clozapine (Clozaril) became the first of the atypical, or second-generation APs approved for use. Atypical APs also risperidone (Risperdal), olanzapine (Zyprexa), ziprasidone (Geodon), quetiapine (Seroquel), and aripiprazole (Abilify).

TYPICAL (FIRST GENERATION) APS: FDA WARNINGS AND ADVISORIES

In June 2000, the FDA required that a black box warning be added to the packaging for thioridazine (Mellaril) indicating that there was a dose-related association between thioridazine and QTc prolongation, which is associated with cardiac arrhythmias and possible sudden death (U. S. Food and Drug Administration, 2000). The warning also stated that thioridazine was contraindicated in combination with fluoxetine, fluvoxamine, propranolol, and any other agents known to prolong the QTc interval, and that thioridazine was also contraindicated in patients known to have reduced levels of the CYP liver enzymes, as well as in patients with congenital long QTc syndrome or a history of cardiac arrhythmias.

In September 2007, the FDA issued a warning for haloperidol (Haldol) cautioning about potentially serious cardiotoxic effects, including QTc prolongation (U. S. Food and Drug Administration, 2007b). In June 2008, an FDA black box warning was issued for haloperidol, pimozide, and a variety of other typical APs, warning about the possibility of death in the elderly population when given to patients with dementia (U. S. Food and Drug Administration, 2008b). A similar FDA warning was issued for all the atypical or second-generation APs in 2005 (U. S. Food and Drug Administration, 2005b).

TYPICAL APS: SIDE EFFECTS & INTERACTION EFFECTS

Connor and Meltzer (2006) report that typical APs "have many side effects in children and adolescents." (p.169) and that "the use of thioridazine for the treatment of childhood severe behavior problems, explosive aggression, ADHD and conduct problems, mood liability, and for poor frustration tolerance, is no longer approved by the FDA" (p. 164). The most troubling side effects associated with typical APs include sedation, cognitive impairments and extrapyramidal symptoms (involuntary movements), including tardive dyskinesia—a serious, irreversible orofacial movement disorder. Other typical AP side effects include weight gain and metabolic disturbances, allergic effects, hypertension and sexual dysfunction, anticholinergic effects (described in the TCA side effects section), cardiovascular effects including QTc prolongation with an increased risk of arrhythmias and sudden death, elevated prolactin levels and menstrual irregularities, liver abnormalities, and ophthalmologic difficulties.

ATYPICAL (SECOND-GENERATION) APS: FDA WARNINGS AND ADVISORIES

In 1994 an FDA warning for clozapine cautioned about an increased risk (about 1%–2% of all patients) for agranulocytosis (a potentially fatal blood disorder) and seizures. In April 2005 the clozapine warning was updated to note an increased risk of myocarditis (an inflammation of the heart muscle), and other adverse cardiac and respiratory events (U. S. Food and Drug Administration, 2005f). In November 2003, the FDA required manufacturers of atypical APs to relabel their package inserts to include an additional warning about increased risk of hyperglycemia and diabetes mellitus associated with the use of atypical antipsychotics (U. S. Food and Drug Administration, 2003b)

Although targeted toward geriatric rather than pediatric use, two FDA warnings should give us pause because of their seriousness, and because both children and the elderly may be at greater overall risk than those of other ages. A public health advisory was issued by the FDA in April 2005 warning about treatment of behavioral disorders in elderly patients with dementia with second-generation atypical APs because of an increased risk of death (U. S. Food and Drug Administration, 2005b). This advisory was issued for aripiprazole (Abilify), risperidone (Risperdal), olanzapine (Zyprexa), quetiapine (Seroquel), clozapine (Clozaril), ziprasidone (Geodone), and Symbyax, a unique combination of olanzapine and fluoxetine (Prozac), an SSRI antidepressant. In June 2008, this warning was extended to include first-generation or typical APs, as well (U. S. Food and Drug Administration, 2008b).

ATYPICAL APS: SIDE EFFECTS AND INTERACTION EFFECTS

Although the overall risk of extrapyramidal symptoms is somewhat less for atypical APs and than for typical APs, the atypicals are often associated with

greater weight gain and more metabolic disturbances. Brown et al. (2008) note that most studies of APs are of limited duration (eight weeks or less) and therefore may not be of sufficient duration to identify the full range of significant side effects, especially late emerging extrapyramidal side effects.

Connor and Meltzer (2006) report that atypical APs are associated with a wide range of side effects in the pediatric population. These can include various metabolic effects including significant weight gain, insulin resistance, and the development of type II diabetes (American Diabetes Association, American Psychiatric Association, American Association of Clinical Endocrinologists, North American Association for the Study of Obesity, 2004). Connor and Meltzer report that the risk of metabolic effects may be especially true for children with a positive family history for diabetes. Of the atypicals, clozapine and olanzapine carry the greatest risk of weight gain and associated metabolic disturbances such as Type II diabetes, and ziprasidone and aripirazole may have the lowest risk (Allison et al., 2001; Julien et al., 2008). Neurological side effects include sedation, seizures, and extrapyramidal symptoms at higher doses. Endocrine side effects (except for clozapine) include prolactin elevation, especially for risperidone, and related menstrual irregularities and amenorrhea, as well as gynecomastia (development of abnormally large breasts in males), sexual dysfunction, and cardiovascular effects including QTc prolongation, which can lead to arrhythmias and fatalities.

Clozapine (Clozaril)

As noted in the FDA warning, agranulocytosis (a potentially fatal blood disorder) occurs in approximately 1%–2% of patients. Seizure risk also is increased with clozapine, particularly at higher doses (Green, 2007), with up to 5% of patients developing seizures at higher doses. Weight gain, insulin resistance, hyperglycemia and type II diabetes and sedation are common. For pediatric use, Green recommends a baseline EEG and periodic EEG monitoring. Serum concentrations of clozapine increase when taken concurrently with fluvoxamine (Luvox), and serum levels of clozapine decrease when taken concurrently with carbamazepine, barbiturates, and phenytoin.

Risperidone (Risperdal)

Green (2007) notes that significant weight gain, insulin resistance, hyperglycemia and type II diabetes are all potential side effects of risperidone therapy.

In addition, risperidone may cause elevations of pro-lactin, which may in turn lead to unwanted endo-crine related sexual side effects (e.g. menstrual irregularity or cessation, pubertal delay, enlarged male breasts). Green also notes that risperidone treatment is associated with orthostatic hypotension, dizziness, tachycardia, QTc prolongation, somnolence, consti-pation, rhinitis, and other undesirable effects. Aman et al. (2005) reported that somnolence and weight gain were the side effects of greatest concern in a 6-month study of risperidone safety for a sample of youth with autism and serious behavioral disorders.

Olanzapine (Zyprexa)
Common side effects associated with olanzapine include weight gain, insulin resistance, hyperglyce-mia and type II diabetes, somnolence, insomnia, orthostatic hypotension, rapid heart rate, and liver enzyme elevations. When taken concurrently with carbamazepine, serum levels of olanzapine may decrease, necessitating a dosage increase of olanzap-ine (Green, 2007).

Quetiapine (Seroquel)
Green (2007) reports that orthostatic hypotension, dizziness, weight gain, tachycardia, somnolence, con-stipation, dry mouth, and indigestion have all been reported as common side effects of quetiapine. When quetiapine is taken concurrently with carbamazepine, barbiturates, or phenytoin, serum levels of quetiapine decrease, necessitating a dosage increase.

Aripiprazole (Abilify)
Compared to other atypical APs aripiprazole is asso-ciated with less weight gain. Green (2007) reports a median increase in heart rate of about four beats per minute. If taken concurrently with fluoxetine or peroxidine (Vitamin B6), serum levels of aripipra-zole increase and the AP dosage should be reduced to at least one half of the usual dose, according to Green. He also reports that quinine can double serum levels of aripipazole, necessitating a reduced AP dosage.

Ziprasidone (Geodon)
QTc prolongation (and possible arrhythmia and sudden death) is greatest for ziprasidone among the atypical APs, although less than for some typical APs (Green, 2007). Nevertheless, Blair, Scahill, State and Martin (2005) were concerned enough that they rec-ommended baseline and follow-up EKGs when using ziprasidone in the pediatric population. Less weight gain and reduced likelihood of insulin resistance,

hyperglycemia and type II diabetes are associated with ziprasidone (Allison et al., 2001).

Mood Stabilizers
Through the 1990s, the term *mood stabilizers* was lim-ited to lithium carbonate and various anticonvulsants (anti-epileptics) used in the treatment of bipolar dis-order. More recently, some have also begun to include atypical APs in this category. Connor and Meltzer (2006) note that "no single definition of mood stabi-lizers has been agreed upon, and, in fact, the Food and Drug Administration (FDA) does not recognize the term" (p. 111). For purposes of this review, we will include only lithium carbonate and the anticonvul-sants in this category. Safety information relative to the atypical APs is included in the previous section of this review. Anticonvulsant mood stabilizers include valproate (valproic acid or Depakote), lamotrigine (Lamictal), topiramate (Topamax), carbamazepine (Tegretol), oxcarbazepine (Trileptal), felbamate (Felbatol), gabapentin (Neurontin), levetiracetam (Keppra), pregabalin (Lyrica), tiagabine (Gabitril), and zonisamide (Zonegran).

MOOD STABILIZERS: FDA WARNINGS AND ADVISORIES
FDA warnings and advisories have been issued for several of the mood stabilizers. These include lithium carbonate, lamotrigine (Lamictal), and Divalproex (valproic acid or Depakote).

Lithium Carbonate
An FDA warning in the 1980s required that each package of lithium carbonate include a boxed warn-ing that states "Lithium toxicity is closely related to serum lithium levels, and can occur at doses close to therapeutic levels. Facilities for prompt and accurate serum lithium determinations should be available before initiating therapy" (U. S. Food and Drug Administration, 1986).

Anticonvulsants
In March 1997 the FDA issued a black box warning for lamotrigine (Lamictal; U. S. Food and Drug Administration, 1997) stating that lamotrigine is not indicated for use in children below 16 years of age. This warning was generated in response to reports of potentially life-threatening, severe rash (Stevens-Johnson syndrome and toxic epidermal necrolysis). The warning indicated that the incidence of life-threatening rash in the pediatric population was approximately one in 50 to 100, as compared to one in 1000 in the adult population.

In October 2005, the FDA issued an alert about serious, potentially life threatening dermatological complications (Stevens-Johnson Syndrome and toxic epidural necrolysis) of oxcarbazepine (Trtileptal) treatment in children and adults (U. S. Food and Drug Administration, 2005c). The rate of these complications is 3 to 10 times higher than in the untreated population, and has occurred with both initial administration and reintroduction of the drug; thus, the FDA advises that if these complications occur the drug should not be reintroduced later. Multiorgan sensitivity also was noted, often preceded by fever and rash.

In July 2006, the FDA issued a black box warning for valproic acid (divalproex, Depakote) warning about potentially fatal liver damage, especially in children under the age of two who are treated with multiple anticonvulsants, who have congenital metabolic disorders, who have mental retardation along with seizures, and in those who have an organic brain syndrome (U. S. Food and Drug Administration, 2006a). The fatalities were preceded in some cases by overall malaise, weakness, lethargy, facial swelling, nausea and vomiting, and anorexia. In the same warning, the FDA also warned about possible cases of fatal pancreatitis in both children and adults treated with valproic acid. The course of the pancreatitis was described as hemorrhagic with a rapid progression from initial symptoms to death, and the FDA warned that symptoms of abdominal pain, nausea, vomiting, and anorexia can be symptoms of fatal pancreatitis and that immediate medical evaluation should be sought.

In December 2007, an FDA warning was issued for carbamazepine (Tegretol) that described an increased risk (about 10 times higher) of Stevens-Johnson syndrome and toxic epidermal necrolysis when used to treat individuals of Asian descent (U. S. Food and Drug Administration, 2007c). The warning encourages patients of Asian descent to undergo genetic testing to determine whether they possess the antigen that has been implicated in the development of these disorders before carbamazepine treatment is initiated. This warning also strengthened an earlier FDA warning about increased risk of agranulocytosis and aplastic anemia, both of which are rare but serious blood disorders. The new warning indicates that the rate of these disorders is 5 to 8 times higher in individuals taking carbamazepine compared to the untreated population.

In January 2008, the FDA issued a warning about an approximate doubling of the risk of suicidality (ideation and actions) for patients taking any one or more of 11 anticonvulsant/antiepileptic drugs (U. S. Food and Drug Administration, 2008a). The increase suicidal risk emerged from a review of RCTs involving the 11 drugs. The increased risk for suicidality emerged as early as one week into treatment and continued for as long as 24 weeks. There was no evidence of increased or decreased suicidality across various age groups, including children and adolescents. The suicidality risk was elevated for patients who were treated for psychiatric disorders, epilepsy, or other disorders with the anticonvulsants, but was highest for patients who had epilepsy. The drugs included carbamazepine (Tegretol), felbamate (Felbatol), gabapentin (Neurontin), lamotrigine (Lamictal), levetiracetam (Keppra), oxcarbazepine (Trileptal), pregabalin (Lyrica), tiagabine (Gabitril), topiramate (Topamax), valproate (valproic acid or Depakote), and zonisamide (Zonegran).

MOOD STABILIZERS: SIDE EFFECTS AND INTERACTION EFFECTS
Lithium Carbonate
The required FDA warning indicates that lithium is a drug with a low threshold of toxicity. This means that when the serum levels exceed therapeutic levels by relatively minimal amounts (compared to other drugs) clinically significant side effects may be expected to appear. Side effects associated with lithium are numerous. Green (2007) notes that these can include tremor, polyurea (excreting larger than average amounts of urine), nausea and gastrointestinal complaints, weight gain, and headache early in treatment. Later emerging side effects can include these side effects as well as thyroid and renal (kidney) abnormalities, dermatologic abnormalities, fatigue, and leukocytosis (an abnormal increase in white blood cells).

Lithium also has potential for interactions with a number of medications. Connor and Meltzer (2006) report that lithium will increase serum levels of TCAs, valproic acid and alcohol, thereby increasing the risk that toxic serum levels of these drugs may be obtained. When concurrent nonsteroidal anti-inflammatory drugs (NSAIDs) or calcium channel blockers are taken, these drugs increase the risk for lithium induced neurological side effects. Diuretics may increase or decrease lithium serum levels dependent on the chemical structure of the diuretic. Patients taking lithium must be particularly cautious during hot weather or periods of vigorous physical activity because of increased risk of salt loss and dehydration.

Among the various psychotropic drugs, lithium may be the most difficult to manage because dosing is driven by serum levels rather than body weight, necessitating frequent blood draws. Connor and Meltzer (2006) also recommend several laboratory tests at 3-month intervals for the first year, and 6-month intervals thereafter. These include renal function tests, complete blood counts with differentials, thyroid function tests, electrocardiograms, electrolytes, and collection of serum calcium and phosphorus levels. Because of lithium's low toxicity threshhold, careful adherence to medication dosing by caregivers is also necessary.

Anticonvulsants

Divalproex (valproic acid, or Depakote). Connor and Meltzer (2006) indicate that common divalproex side effects include nausea, sleep difficulty, dizziness, hair loss, a variety of gastrointestinal complaints, tremor and ataxia (a loss of coordination of muscle movements), headache, sedation, and blurred vision and other ophthalmologic difficulties. A more serious potential side effect is polycystic ovary syndrome, which is associated with a variety of reproductive and endocrine abnormalities. Isojarvi, Laatikainen, Pakarinen, Juntunen, and Myllyla (1993) noted an association between divalproex use and polycystic ovary syndrome that was more pronounced in women who begin treatment with divalproex before the age of 20 than was the case for those who begin treatment after the age of 20. Because these women were being treated for epilepsy, it was not clear whether the association was the result of the epilepsy or the divalproex. A recent study by Joffe et al. (2006) implicated divalproex. They found the risk of developing polycystic ovary symptoms was seven to eight times higher for subjects taking divalproex compared to other mood stabilizers in a non-pediatric sample of 230 women (ages 18–44) with bipolar disorder.

Drug interactions are common with divalproex. An increased risk of neurotoxicity exists when it is taken concurrently with lithium and phenytoin, an antiepileptic. When taken concurrently with TCAs, increased TCA serum levels can result in the likelihood of TCA-related side effects. When taken concurrently with anticoagulants (e.g., aspirin and warfarin or Coumadin) excessive bleeding may result. Green (2007) also noted that divalproex may potentiate central nervous system depression when taken with alcohol and benzodiazepines, and that when taken with clonazepam (Klonopin), absence seizures may be induced in patients with a history of absence seizures.

Carbamazepine (Tegretol). Green (2007) reports that the most frequently reported side effects

of carbamazepine include dizziness, drowsiness, nausea and vomiting, and unsteadiness. In addition to these side effects, Connor and Meltzer (2006) also report dry mouth, constipation, urinary difficulty, blurred vision, confusion, and loss of appetite. Although rare, liver inflammation and hematological problems are possible. Rash also occurs more frequently with carbamazepine than with divalproex (Connor and Meltzer, 2006).

Carbamazepine interacts with numerous medications. Carbamazepine serum levels increase when taken with fluoxetine (Prozac), certain antibiotics, and valproic acid. When taken concurrently with lithium there is an increased risk of neurotoxicity. When taken with TCAs there is an increased risk of cardiac arrhythmias, even though serum TCA serum levels may decline. Asthmatic symptoms may also increase when carbamazepine is taken concurrently with theophylline, an asthma medication.

Lamotrigine (Lamictal). Common side effects include minor skin rash, headache, nausea and vomiting, ataxia (poor coordination), visual disturbances, dizziness and drowsiness. Lamotrigine has also been associated with an increased risk of potentially life-threatening, serious rashes (see the FDA warning section). The mortality rate for these rashes ranges between 1% and 3%, and these include Stevens-Johnson syndrome and toxic epidural necrolysis. The risk of these serious rashes increases when lamotrigine is taken concurrently with divalproex (Connor and Meltzer, 2006).

Connor and Meltzer (2006) report that lamotrigine also has several other potential drug–drug interactions. When taken concurrently with sertraline (Zoloft) lamotrigine serum levels increase and carry with them an increased risk for side effects. Concurrent administration of carbamazepine (Tegretol), oxcarbazepine (Trileptal), and primidone, an anticonvulsant, result in decreased lamotrigine serum levels. Phenobarbital and phenytoin result in more rapid clearance of lamotrigine from the patient.

Oxcarbazepine (Trileptal). Green (2007) reports that common side effects of oxcarbazepine include fatigue, nausea and vomiting, headache, somnolence, dizziness, ataxia, various ophthalmologic difficulties, and emotional lability. Green also noted that with oxcarbazepine the risk of rash, blood disorders, and drug–drug interactions is less than with carbamazepine.

Topiramate (Topamax). Green (2007) identified several topiramate side effects. These included anorexia and weight loss, paresthesias (feeling pins and needles), diarrhea, mood problems, difficulty with concentration and attention, fever, and hair loss. Like the other anticonvulsants, topiramate has a number of potential interactions, but because it has been less well studied than older anticonvulsants, little information about such interactions is currently available.

Other anticonvulsants. Systematic identification of side effects and safety issues with newer anticonvulsants has not yet been completed.

Antihypertensives

The antihypertensives most commonly prescribed to pediatric patients include clonidine, or Catapres, and guanfacine, or Intuniv (also marketed as Tenex). These agents have been prescribed for symptoms of ADHD, disruptive behavior disorders, and autism spectrum disorders.

ANTIHYPERTENSIVES: FDA WARNINGS AND ADVISORIES

There have been no FDA warnings or advisories for either clonidine or guanfacine for pediatric use. It should be noted, however, that only guanfacine (Intuniv) has a pediatric ADHD indication and this indication was only issued recently (i.e. in 2009). Clonidine only has a pediatric indication for treatment of hypertension in patients 12 years of age and older.

ANTIHYPERTENSIVES: SIDE EFFECTS AND INTERACTION EFFECTS

Common side effects of both clonidine and guanfacine include sedation, irritability, depression, hypertension if abruptly discontinued, hypotension and slowed heart rate Conner & Meltzer; 2006; Zinner, 2004). Cantwell et al. (1997) reported three sudden deaths in children taking methylphenidate (Ritalin) in combination with clonidine, and Connor and Meltzer reported four deaths with the same medication combination. In each of these cases, Connor and Meltzer reported that the specific cause of death could not be determined because "previous cardiac disease and concomitant use of other medications" (p. 219) was noted in each case. They also noted that no instances of sudden death have been reported for methylphenidate and guanfacine combination treatment, and that in general, guanfacine tends to be associated with fewer side effects than clonidine. Next, the efficacy data for pediatric drug treatments for various disorders will be reviewed.

Drug Efficacy Findings by Disorder

Drug efficacy findings are presented by disorder, after any FDA indications are reported. Only randomized

controlled trials (RCTs), or meta-analyses of RCTs, are included in this review because the RCT continues to be the highest standard of rigor in drug research. It should be noted that non-RCT studies like open label studies (i.e., either the patient/parent, the prescriber, the researcher, or all concerned parties knew whether the patient was receiving the active drug or the placebo) can make important contributions in emerging research areas, but their outcomes are not considered to be as robust as those that emerge from RCTs. The RCT is characterized by random assignment to treatment and control conditions and is appropriately blinded (i.e., neither the individual administering the drug or placebo, the researcher, the subject, nor the subject's caretakers know whether the active drug or a placebo is being administered). The decision to include only RCTs in this review is a conservative one, and an extension of the "safety first" approach. It should be noted that the absence of RCT support does not necessarily mean the treatment is ineffective. The treatment may be so new that studies have yet to be published, it may be that methodological issues compromised the ability of the treatment to separate from placebo, or there may be measurement or other factors that masked the treatment's efficacy (McClure, Kubiszyn, & Kaslow, 2002).

When available, efficacy findings from large, nonindustry sponsored, multisite RCTs that contrast drug, psychosocial, combination, and placebo arms are presented first, followed by large-scale studies and then small-scale, preliminary studies. Sample sizes are included for each study to enable the reader to separate preliminary or small size studies from the larger and typically more generalizable and sophisticated studies.

Attention-Deficit/Hyperactivity Disorder (ADHD)

FDA PEDIATRIC INDICATIONS

Several drugs carry FDA indications for the treatment of ADHD symptoms. Table 35.1 includes the trade or patent name for each medication, its generic name, and the ages for which the drug has been approved by the FDA for ADHD treatment. The table includes stimulant medications, arranged alphabetically by trade name, and the only non-stimulant medication with an FDA indication for ADHD.

Next, the randomized controlled trials (RCTs) that have demonstrated the efficacy of ADHD drug treatments will be reviewed.

STIMULANT EFFICACY

Stimulants have been demonstrated to be superior to placebo and psychosocial intervention in one

Table 35.1. ADHD drugs with FDA pediatric indications

Trade Name	Generic Name	Approved Age
Stimulus Medications		
Adderall	amphetamine	3 and older
Adderall XR	amphetamine (extended release)	6 and older
Concerta	methylphenidate (long acting)	6 and older
Dexedrine	dextroamphetamine	3 and older
Dextrostat	dextroamphetamine	3 and older
Metadate/Metadate ER	methylphenidate (extended release)	6 and older
Ritalin/Ritalin SR	methylphenidate (sustained release)	6 and older
Daytrana	methylphenidate	6–12
Vyvanse	lisdexamphetamine	6–12
Non-Stimulant Medication		
Straterra	atomoxetine	6 and older
Intuniv	guanfacine	6 and older

large NIMH sponsored multisite study (MTA Cooperative Group, 1999a, 1999b). Furthermore, a 24-month follow-up indicated that discontinuation of stimulant treatment was associated with clinical deterioration, and initiation of stimulant treatment to the placebo group was associated with clinical improvements (MTA Cooperative Group, 2004a). Both the American Academy of Child and Adolescent Psychiatry (2007) and the American Academy of Pediatrics (2001) recommend that stimulants should be the first-choice medication for the treatment of ADHD symptoms in children and adolescents. Brown et al. (2008) and Greenhill et al. (2006) reported that the effect size for stimulants for treating ADHD symptoms has ranged from 0.7 to more than 1.0 (moderate to strong) in most studies, with improvements in attention and task completion, along with reductions in disruptive behavior and aggression commonly reported (MTA Cooperative Group, 1999a). Recently, Greenhill et al. reported on the findings from an NIMH sponsored multisite RCT for preschoolers ranging from 3 to 5.5 years old. The Preschool ADHD Treatment Study (PATS) found a smaller effect size (effect size = 0.4 – 0.8) than is typical for school-aged children (effect size = 0.7 to more than 1.0). However, the smaller effect size may be attributable to the lower dosages used in this study, which were lower than they typically were in prior studies of school-aged children.

Stimulants are effective in 80% of cases (1999a, 1999b), and a consensus-driven algorithm was developed recently by the Texas Medication Algorithm Project to guide prescribers in making drug treatment selections when an initial stimulant trial fails (Pliszka et al. 2006). Because of the superior efficacy of stimulants over non-stimulants, this algorithm recommends a trial of a second stimulant before consideration is given to a non-stimulant. It should be noted, however, that this strategy is consensus driven, and awaits controlled study. Although stimulants are effective in treating the symptoms of ADHD, therapeutic gains dissipate when stimulant treatment is terminated (Brown et al., 2008).

NON-STIMULANT EFFICACY

Non-stimulant treatments for ADHD include atomoxetine (Strattera), guanfacine (Inuniv), buproprion (Wellbutrin), TCAs, the antihypertensive clonidine (Catapres), and occasionally monoamine oxidase inhibitors (MAOIs). Although the strength of the evidence supporting the use of these drugs is varied in RCTs, none is as strong as the evidence that exists for the stimulants. Atomoxetine is the most promising compared to the stimulants, based on several large RCTs (Michelson et al., 2001, 2002 [n=297]; Spencer et al. 2002 [n = 291]; Weiss et al. 2005 [n=153]). The FDA issued an indication for guanfacine (Intuniv) in 2009 based on two large, short-term studies (n = 325 in an eight week study and n = 324 in a nine week study).

Atomoxetine has unique advantages over the stimulants. Because it is not a stimulant it has little or no abuse or diversion potential. It also has the advantage of 24-hour effectiveness, although there is generally a lag of one week or more before its therapeutic effects are noted. There is some evidence that higher than average doses may be needed for therapeutic effectiveness for children with ADHD with comorbid oppositional defiant disorder (Newcorn et al., 2005 [n=141]). Similarly, guanfacine does not have the abuse potential associated with stimulants. On the other hand, it does not appear to be as effective in symptom remediation as are the stimulants and sedation and nausea are more common with guanfacine than with other ADHD drugs. Unlike the stimulants and atomoxetine, neither buproprion, the TCAs, clonidine, or the MAOIs carry FDA indications for pediatric ADHD. Buproprion (Wellbutrin) has been demonstrated to be superior to placebo in large ADHD multisite studies, but is less effective than is typical for the stimulants (Connors et al. 1996 [n=109]). As with atomoxetine, there is a lag of one or more weeks with buproprion before a therapeutic response may be expected. Although TCAs have RCT support for ADHD treatment, they too are not as efferctive as the stimulants (Pliszka, 1987). In a meta-analysis, clonidine was judged to be moderately effective for ADHD symptoms (Connor, Fletcher and Swanson, 1999). Monoamine oxidase inhibitors (MAOIs) have limited RCT support, but also trail the stimulants in efficacy (Zametkin et al., 1985 [n=14]; Feigin et al., 1996 [n=24]) and have undesirable safety and side effect profiles (see the AD safety section).

Tourette's Syndrome and Tic Disorders
FDA PEDIATRIC INDICATIONS
Two typical antipsychotics (APs) carry pediatric FDA indications. Haloperidol (Haldol) carries an FDA indication for Tourette's syndrome, psychotic disorders, and explosive aggression in children ages 3 and above when psychosocial interventions and other APs have proven ineffective. Pimozide (Orap) also carries an indication for severe Tourette's syndrome in children 2 years and older who have not responded adequately to other APs. Thioridazine (Mellaril) has sometimes been used in the treatment of Tourette's and tic disorders. However, thioridazine only carries an FDA indication for the treatment of schizophrenia in children 2 years of age or older who have failed to adequately respond to treatment with at least two other APs. The FDA warnings and safety and side effects section of this chapter should be reviewed for additional information about thioridazine (Mellaril) and haloperidol. None of the other psychotropic drugs used to treat Tourette's syndrome or tic disorders carry FDA indications for these disorders in the pediatric population.

DRUG EFFICACY
In their recent review, Brown et al. (2008) reported that several small RCTs have demonstrated "at least moderate treatment effects for the typical and atypical APs and guanfacine, with more equivocal support for clonidine." (Page 48). They noted that the strongest effects have been found for haloperidol (Haldol), a typical AP, and risperidone (Risperdal), an atypical AP. Brown et al. noted that both agents were superior to placebo in at least two controlled trials each. Risperidone was also demonstrated to be superior to clonidine (Gaffney et al., 2002 [n=21]), and pimozide (Orap), a typical AP (Gilbert, Batterson, Sethuraman & Sallee, 2004 [n=19]). Finally, Brown et al. concluded that atomoxetine as well as clonidine have also demonstrated modest benefits for tic disorder that is comorbid with ADHD.

Disruptive Behavior Disorders (DBD)
FDA PEDIATRIC INDICATIONS
Disruptive Behavior Disorders (DBD) is not a DSM-IV diagnosis. It generally includes youth diagnosed with DSM-IV diagnoses of conduct disorder (CD) or oppositional defiant disorder (ODD), and also includes those without these diagnoses who exhibit socially unacceptable behavior (e.g., aggressiveness, temper tantrums, defiance, destructiveness, criminal behavior, disobedience). There are currently no FDA- indicated medications for the treatment of pediatric disruptive behaviors (DBD) for the general population. Risperidone (Risperdal) and aripiprazole (Ability), bothatypical APs, were given FDA indications in 2006 and 2009, respectively for aggression, irritability, and self-injury for youths ages six and older with autism spectrum disorders (ASD), based on samples with below average intellectual ability. Nevertheless, risperidone, aripiprazole and other atypical APs are often prescribed off-label for children without ASD and with normal intelligence. Several typical APs also carry indications for treatment of pediatric psychosis and schizophrenia only, but are used to treat pediatric DBD off label.

Although lithium, APs (both typical and atypical), anticonvulsants, stimulants, and antihypertensives have been used to treat DBD, atypical APs have become the drug of choice in recent years (Olfson et al., 2006). Once prescribed exclusively for low incidence disorders like psychosis and schizophrenia, atypical APs are now commonly prescribed off-label for disruptive, aggressive behavior, regardless of diagnosis, and for pediatric bipolar disorder (Julien et al., 2008). In recent years, prescriptions of pediatric atypical APs have increased 500% or more (Patel et al., 2002; 2005 Olfson et al., 2006).

DRUG EFFICACY

Connor and Meltzer (2006) report that "ODD and CD are not considered robustly medication-responsive disorders." (p .324). The few RCTs that have yielded positive findings for lithium, both types of APs, stimulants, anticonvulsants, and antihypertensives, in children and adolescents with DBD who have intellectual ability in the average range or above, will be reviewed next.

Lithium

Malone, Delaney, Leubbert, Cater, and Campbell (2000) demonstrated that lithium was superior to placebo in reducing aggressive behavior for children and adolescents with conduct disorder in an inpatient setting (n = 40). An RCT completed by Campbell et al. (1995) also revealed that lithium was more effective than placebo in treating hospitalized aggressive children with conduct disorder (n = 50).

Typical Antipsychotics

In an RCT, Campbell et al. (1984) reported that both haloperidol and lithium were superior to placebo in managing hospitalized, aggressive children aged 5 to 13 years (n = 61).

Atypical Antipsychotics

One small RCT supports the efficacy of risperidone for DBD in youth with at least average intelligence ability. Findling et al. (2000) demonstrated that risperidone was superior to placebo in reducing symptoms of CD in youth (n = 20) with average IQs or higher. Two large RCTs have demonstrated that risperidone is superior to placebo for aggressive behavior, but with samples of either below average IQ youth, youth with autism spectrum disorders, or both (Aman et al., 2002 [n=118]; McCracken et al, 2002 [n =101]). Two small RCTs also demonstrated that risperidone was superior to placebo for aggressive children and adolescents with subaverage intellectual ability (Buitelaar et al., 2001 [n=38]; Van Bellinghem & DeTroch, 2001 [n=13]).

Anticonvulsants

Steiner et al. (2003) demonstrated a decrease in aggressive behavior for divalproex (Depakote) compared to placebo in an RCT (n = 58). In a smaller RCT (n = 20) Donovan et al. (2000) found that divalproex was effective for youth with the explosive aggression.

Stimulants

Stimulant medication alone has no empirical support suggesting it is effective for DBD, unless comorbid ADHD is present (Brown et al., 2008). For example, Jensen et al. (2001) (n=579) reported that children with comorbid ADHD and ODD responded to methylphenidate. Klein, Abikoff, Ganeles, Seese and Pollack (1997) also found an improvement in both CD and ADHD symptoms in an RCT (n = 84).

Antihypertensives

Similar to the stimulants, a combination of methyphenidate and clonidine (Hazell & Stuart, 2003) reduced conduct disorder symptoms in an RCT involving a sample (n = 38) of youth with diagnoses of either CD or ODD with comorbid ADHD.

Bipolar Disorder (BPD)

FDA PEDIATRIC INDICATIONS

Although many medications are prescribed for pediatric bipolar disorder (BPD), only five carry FDA indications specific for pediatric mania associated with BPD; lithium for children 12 and older, risperidone (Risperdal), aripiprazole (Abilify), and quetiapine (Seroquel) all atypical antipsychotics (APs), for children aged 10 to 17, and another atypical antipsychotic, olanzapine (Zyprexa), is now FDA indicated for mania in PBD for children ages 13-17. All four of the atypicals, risperidone, aripiprazole, quetiapine, and olanzapine are also FDA indicated for pediatric schizophrenia in children ages 13-17. Although none of the anticonvulsants currently carry FDA indications for pediatric BPD or mania, several have FDA indications for pediatric epilepsy. Prescribers often prescribe these drugs off label for pediatric BPD, and often in combination with atypical antipsychotics and/or other psychotropic medications.

DRUG EFFICACY

The diagnosis and treatment of childhood bipolar disorder is controversial and inconsistent (Brown et al., 2008). There are several areas of diagnostic disagreement that include debate about the core symptoms, discrete episodes, and the definition and duration of cycling (Kowatch & Fristad, 2006). This lack of diagnostic agreement may be one of the factors that has contributed to the recent "epidemic" of pediatric BPD diagnoses. For example, Moreno, Laje, Blanco, Jiang, Schmidt, and Olfson (2007) documented a 4000% increase in pediatric BPD diagnoses between 1993 and 2003, although they noted that they could not determine whether this meant that pediatric BPD was significantly underdiagnosed in the 1990s, or whether it is significantly overdiagnosed today.

Controversy also exists with regard to treatment of pediatric BPD. Smarty and Findling (2007) reviewed the pediatric BPD treatment literature published between 1995 and 2006. They concluded that lithium, atypical APs, and some anticonvulsants may be useful, but limited, as acute monotherapy for youth with BPD. Because of the limited efficacy of drug monotherapy for pediatric BPD, they argued that this justified increased use of polypharmacy for pediatric BPD. Given the diagnostic controversies, safety concerns, and the absence of research support for pediatric polypharmacy with this population, this conclusion is arguable, at best. The evidence that exists for various categories of drugs used to treat pediatric BPD is reviewed next.

Lithium Carbonate
Although lithium carries an FDA indication for youth aged 12 years and older, and is one of the better studied medications for pediatric BPD, Kowatch et al. (2005) note that the RCTs that support its use are characterized by small sample sizes and methodological limitations. One example of this is the use of crossover designs, which limit the generalizability and interpretability of findings for cyclical disorders like pediatric BPD; symptom exacerbations or decreases may correspond to the disorder's cycle rather than a treatment effect. Recent findings and opinions also raise questions about lithium's efficacy. For example, an RCT (n = 40) conducted by Kafantaris et al. (2004) failed to demonstrate a significant difference between lithium and placebo. Furthermore, Julien et al. (2008) concluded that lithium's clinical effectiveness is less than is predicted by its clinical trials.

Anticonvulsants
Kowatch, Findling, Scheffer and Stanford (2007) recently reported findings from the Pediatric Bipolar Collaborative Mood Stabilizer Trial. This was an 8-week, multisite, NIMH sponsored comparison of lithium, divalproex (Depakote or valproic acid) and

placebo in 7- to 17-year-olds (n = 157). Only divalproex was associated with a significant reduction in scores on the Young Mania Rating Scale (YMRS), and on clinical global improvement (CGI) ratings. Few other studies support the efficacy of anticonvulsants in the treatment of bipolar disorder in children (Brown et al., 2008). Wagner, Kowatch et al. (2006) (n=116) reported no difference from placebo for oxcarbazepine (Trileptal) in a multisite RCT for children 7 to 18 years old with BPD. DelBello et al. (2006) (n=50) compared divalproex and quetiapine (Seroquel), an atypical AP, in children and adolescents with BPD. Results showed that quetiapine produced a quicker onset and was at least as effective as divalproex. An RCT (n =56) for topiramate (Topimax) was discontinued early when findings from the adult arm of the study were inconclusive (DelBello et al., 2005). RCTs are lacking for lamotrigine (Lamictal), and carbamazepine (Tegretol), and for newer ACV formulations; evetiracetam, zonisamide, and tiagabine.

Atypical Antipsychotics (APs)
Risperidone (Risperdal), aripiprazole (Abilify), quetiapine (Seroquel), and olanzapine (Zyprexa), are all now FDA indicated for pediatric mania associated with BPD, with quetiapine and olanzapine receiving FDA indications in 2009. The efficacy of aripiprazole in pediatric patients with BPD was established in a 4-week RCT with 296 pediatric patients aged 10–17 (Chang et al., 2007). The efficacy of Risperdal in the treatment of manic or mixed episodes in children or adolescents with BPD was demonstrated in a 3-week, multicenter RCT in patients (n = 197) who were experiencing a manic or mixed episode at the time of entry into the study. Treated patients generally had fewer symptoms, including a decrease in their elevated mood and hyperactivity, and other symptoms of their disorder (Pandina et al., 2007). According to the FDA for prescribing data quetiapine was demonstrated to be superior to placebo in a three-week RCT (n = 284) and olanzapine was demonstrated to be superior to placebo in a three-week RCT (n = 161). No other RCTs demonstrating the efficacy of atypical APs for pediatric BPD were located, other than the DelBello et al. (2006) study that indicated that quetiapine produced a quicker onset and was at least as effective as divalproex.

Obsessive Compulsive Disorder (OCD)
FDA PEDIATRIC INDICATIONS
Three selective serotonin reuptake inhibitors (SSRIs) carry FDA indications for treatment of pediatric

obsessive-compulsive disorder (OCD). These include fluvoxamine (Luvox) for children aged 8 and older, sertraline (Zoloft) for children aged 6 and older, and fluoxetine (Prozac) for children aged 7 and older. A fourth drug, clomipramine (Anafranil), a TCA, also carries an FDA indication for pediatric OCD in children aged 10 and older.

DRUG EFFICACY

Because SSRIs are better tolerated, they have become the predominant psychotropic medication used in treating pediatric OCD today. However, the first drug to receive FDA approval for pediatric OCD was clomipramine (Anafranil). Clomipramine is no longer used as a first or second line of treatment in pediatric OCD (Brown et al., 2008) because of its significant adverse side effects. Although only flu-voxamine (Luvox), sertraline (Zoloft), and fluoxetine (Prozac) are FDA indicated, others such as parox-etine (Paxil), escitalopram (Lexapro), and citalopram (Celexa) are commonly prescribed off label.

Selective Serotonin Reuptake Inhibitors (SSRIs)
A recent multisite RCT sponsored by the National Institute of Mental Health (NIMH) compared drug, psychosocial, combined drug and psychosocial treatment, and placebo. The Pediatric OCD Treatment Study (POTS) included 97 subjects aged 7 to 17 and compared the effects of cognitive behavior therapy (CBT) alone, sertraline (Zoloft) alone, CBT and ser-traline, and placebo (pill). Results showed that OCD remission rates were as follows: 53.6% for combined, 39.3% for CBT and 21.4% for sertraline. The effect sizes were 1.4 for combined treatment, .97 for CBT alone, and .67for sertraline alone. The authors concluded that children with OCD should begin treatment with CBT alone or CBT plus an SSRI (Pediatric OCD Treatment Team (2004).

Geller et al. (2003) (n = 1,044) included 12 RCT medication trials in a meta-analysis of the efficacy of four SSRIs (paroxetine or Paxil, fluoxetine or Prozac, fluvoxamine or Luvox, and sertraline or Zoloft) and clomipramine. This meta-analysis concluded that clomipramine was significantly superior to all of the SSRIs studied, and that all four SSRIs were similarly effective in comparison.

The efficacy of SSRIs for pediatric OCD has been researched in several large RCTs for fluoxetine (n = 103; Geller et al., 2001), sertraline (n=187; March et al., 1998), and fluvoxamine (n=120; Riddle et al., 2001). An earlier review by March & Curry (1998) concluded that the efficacy of any medication for the treatment of pediatric OCD is considered modest.

In fact, treatment with medication only showed a 30% to 40% decrease in OCD symptoms.

Another SSRI, paroxetine (which is not FDA indicated for pediatric OCD) was reported to be superior to placebo, however, it had more adverse side effects in the younger population (ages 7–11; Geller et al., 2004 [n=207]). The newer SSRIs (citalopram or Celexa and escitalopram or Lexapro) continue to lack RCT-based support (Brown et al., 2008).

Tricyclic Antidepressants (TCAs)
Although TCAs are no longer recommended for internalizing disorders such as OCD (Birmaher & Brent, 2003; Labellarte & Ginsburg, 2003), the efficacy of one TCA, clomipramine (Anafranil), was demonstrated to be superior to placebo in several RCTs (Flament et al., 1985 [n = 19]; Leonard et al., 1991 [n = 48]) and superior to the SSRIs in a meta-analysis (Geller et al., 2003 [n = 1044]). Because of potential cardiotoxicity, and because of the anticho-linergic effects associated with TCAs (see the safety section of this chapter), it is not suggested as either a first- or second-line treatment today (March, Frances, Carpentar, & Kahn, 1997).

Non-OCD Anxiety disorders (GAD, SAD, SoP)

In this section we will limit our discussion to the drug treatment of three non-OCD anxiety disorders, generalized anxiety disorder (GAD), separation anxi-ety disorder (SAD), and social phobia (SoP), also referred to as social anxiety disorder. A variety of categories of drugs have been used to treat pediatric non-OCD anxiety. These include the selective serotonin reuptake inhibitors (SSRIs), tricyclic antidepressants (TCAs), serotonin-norepinephrine reuptake inhibitors (SNRIs), benzodiazepines (BZs), monoamine oxidase inhibitors (MAOIs), and other drugs (buspirone, antihistamines, clonidine, beta-blockers, antipsychotics, and sedatives).

FDA PEDIATRIC INDICATIONS

Two drugs carry pediatric indications for non-OCD anxiety disorders, although they are rarely if ever prescribed today. These drugs are meprobamate (Miltown), a barbiturate and CNS depressant, and doxepin (Sinequan), a TCA. Although Miltown is no longer marketed as a patent drug, meprobamate is still available and carries an FDA indication for anxiety for children 6 years of age and older. Doxepin carries an indication for anxiety in adoles-cents aged 12 and older. However, both formula-tions have significant side-effect and adverse event potential, and are rarely prescribed for pediatric use today. Thus, these indications may be of more historical than practical interest. No other medications carry FDA indications for pediatric non-OCD anxiety disorders.

DRUG EFFICACY

Selective Serotonin Reuptake Inhibitors (SSRIs)
The Child/Adolescent Anxiety Multimodal Treatment Study (CAMS) was a large (n = 112), recently completed NIMH-sponsored multisite RCT (Walkup et al., 2008). The CAMS study compared the effects of sertraline (Zoloft), cognitive behavior therapy (CBT), and their combination for pediatric GAD, SOP, and SAD. On the Clinical Global Impression of Improvement Scale subjects rated as improved or very much improved included 80.7% for combined treatment, 59.7% for CBT alone, and 54.9% % for sertraline alone. Other RCTs have demonstrated the effectiveness of fluvoxamine (Luvox), paroxetine (Paxil), fluoxetine (Prozac), and sertraline (Zoloft) for pediatric non-OCD anxiety. A large (n = 128) NIMH funded multisite RCT found that fluvoxamine was superior to placebo for GAD, SOP, or SAP (Research Units on Pediatric Psychopharmacology Anxiety Study Group, 2001). The overall effect size of 1.1 was indicative of a strong effect, and was comparable to effect sizes for stimulants with ADHD. However, subjects diagnosed with social phobia, and those with greater disorder severity at baseline, were significantly less likely to improve regardless of treatment condition. In a large (n=322) multisite NIMH funded RCT, Wagner et al. (2004) found that paroxetine was superior to placebo for social phobia. Birmaher et al. (2003) found that fluoxetine was superior to placebo for GAD, SOP, or SAP. However this was a relatively small study (n= 37). Sertraline was demonstrated to be superior to placebo for GAD by Rynn, Siqueland and Rickles (2001) in a small study (n= 22). Another small study (n=14) by Black and Uhde (1994) also found that fluoxetine was superior to placebo for selective mutism, which is generally considered to be equivalent to social phobia.

Tricyclic Antidepressants (TCAs)
Gittelman-Klein and Klein (1971) found that imipramine (Tofranil) was superior to placebo for school avoidance, but not for SAD (Klein, Koplowitz & Kanner, 1992 [n=20]).

Benzodiazepines (BZs)
In controlled studies of benzodiazepines, including alprazolam (Xanax) and clonazepam (Klonopin)

drug treatment was not superior to placebo (Bernstein, Garfinkel and Borchardt, 1990 [n = 9]; Simeon et al., 1992 [n=30]; Graae. Milner, Rizotto & Klein, 1994 [n=15]).

Other Drugs
None of the other drugs used for pediatric non-OCD anxiety disorders have been demonstrated effective in RCTs, or have not been studied in RCT trials (i.e., serotonin-norepinephrine reuptake inhibitors (SNRIs), monoamine oxidase inhibitors (MAOIs), buspirone, antihistamines, clonidine, beta-blockers, antipsychotics, and sedatives).

Major Depressive Disorder (MDD)

A wide range of drugs have been used to treat pediatric MDD. These include the tricyclic antidepressants (TCAs), selective serotonin reuptake inhibitors (SSRIs), selective serotonin-norepinephrine reuptake inhibitors (SNRIs), atypical antidepressants, and monoamine oxidase inhibitors (MAOIs).

FDA PEDIATRIC INDICATIONS

Fluoxetine (Prozac) carries an FDA indication for major depression in 8-17 year olds and escitalopram (Lexapro) was recently indicated for 12-17 year olds. A monoamine oxidase inhibitor (MAOI), phenelzine (Nardil), has FDA approval for MDD in adolescents aged 16 years and older, although MAOIs are not recommended for pediatric use because of their significant side effect profiles (Connor & Meltzer, 2006; Green 2007; Julien et al., 2008).

DRUG EFFICACY

Tricyclic Antidepressants (TCAs)
The TCAs include imipramine (Tofranil), desipramine (Norpramin), amitriptyline (Elavil), nortriptyline (Pamelor) and clomipramine (Anafranil). In at least 13 RCTs the TCAs have been demonstrated to be no better then placebo in the treatment of pediatric depression (Birmhaer & Brent, 2003; Brown et al., 2008).

Selective Serotonin Reuptake Inhibitors (SSRIs)
The SSRIs include fluoxetine (Prozac), sertraline (Zoloft), paroxetine (Paxil), fluoxetine (Luvox), citalopram (Celexa), and escitalopram (Lexapro). Research into the efficacy of the SSRIs for pediatric MDD has been characterized by methodological difficulties and a relative lack of clear findings. For example, Jureidini et al. (2004) noted the high placebo response rate associated with drug treatment of pediatric MDD (often more than 50%), and they questioned the clinical

significance of the statistically significant, but modest improvements associated with SSRI treatment. For example, a recent meta-analysis of SSRIs by Bridge et al. (2007) focused on SSRI treatment for major depressive disorder (MDD), obsessive-compulsive disorder (OCD) and non-OCD anxiety disorders. The total number of participants aggregated from 13 RCTs was 2,910. For MDD, the SSRI response rate was 61%, in contrast to a placebo response rate of 50%. Jureidini et al. also noted that positive findings tended to emerge much more frequently from clinician ratings than from parent or patient ratings.

Interestingly, the 61% SSRI response rate reported by the Bridge et al. (2007) meta-analysis is consistent with the 61% response rate for fluoxetine demonstrated in the Treatment of Adolescent Depression Study (TADS), a large (n=432), NIMH sponsored RCT completed by the Research Units in Pediatric Psychopharmacology (RUPP; Treatment of Adolescents with Depression Team, 2004). This is the largest study to date that contrasted drug (fluoxetine), cognitive-behavior therapy (CBT), a combination of fluoxetine and CBT, and placebo. The results indicated that the combination of fluoxetine and CBT yielded a 71% improvement in symptoms of MDD, while fluoxetine alone was associated with a 61% improvement and CBT alone was associated with a 43% improvement. In addition, clinically significant suicidal ideation improved the most in the combination fluoxetine and CBT treatment group.

The FDA indication for fluoxetine was based on significant improvement on most, but not all, outcome measures reported by, Emslie, Rush, Weinberg, Guillion, Rintlemann and Hughes (1997) (n=96) and Emslie et al. (2002) (n=219). Promising results from a follow-up relapse prevention study (Emslie et al., 2008) also support fluoxetine treatment of pediatric MDD, as do the findings from the TADS study for adolescents (TADS, 2004). A recent escitalopram study (n = 264) was published by Wagner, Jonas, Findling, Ventura and Khalil (2006). Their study included youth from 6 to 17 years of age, and found no significant difference between escitalopram and placebo for the overall sample. However, when the findings were disaggregated, a significant improvement for the adolescents was noted. Other large studies also found positive outcomes for the SSRIs on some but not all measures. These included a paroxetine study (Keller et al., 2001 [n=275]), a sertraline study (Wagner et al., 2003 [n=366]), and a citalopram study (Wagner et al., 2004 [n=174]).

On the other hand, several large studies of the SSRIs for MDD failed to demonstrate the superiority of drug over placebo. These included a sertraline study by Rynn et al. (2006 [n=364]), and paroxetine studies by Millin et al. (1999) and Emslie et al. (2006 [n=206]). Braconnier, Le Coent, and Cohen (2003) failed to find a difference when they contrasted paroxetine with clomipramine in a multicenter RCT (n=121). In a large (n= 286) international, adolescent, multisite (33 sites) RCT of paroxetine, Berard, Fong, Carpenter, Thomason and Wilkinson (2006) reported mixed results, with paroxetine superior to placebo on one of two outcome measures, and with results generally more favorable for older adolescents than younger adolescents. Overall, the largely equivocal nature of the published findings, the marginal clinical significance of those findings that were statistically significant, and the methodological concerns described by Jureidini et al. (2004) and others, indicate that empirical support for the efficacy of drug treatments of pediatric MDD is limited, with the strongest support evident for fluoxetine.

Serotonin–Norepinephrine Reuptake Inhibitors (SNRIs) and Atypical Antidepressants
In a large study (n=334) of a venlafaxine (Effexor), a serotonin-norepinephrine reuptake inhibitor (SNRI), Emslie et al. (2007) failed to find significant improvements over placebo. Other SNRIs, buproprion or Wellbutrin, trazodone or Desyrel, and nefazodone, or Serzone, have all failed to differ significantly from placebo in RCTs, or have not been studied in RCTs.

Monoamine Oxidase Inhibitors (MAOIs)
As was noted above, one of the MAOIs (phenelzine, or Nardil), carries an FDA indication for use with adolescents with MDD aged 16 and above. However, because of safety and side effect concerns, MAOIs are not currently recommended for pediatric use (Conner & Melzer, 2006; Green 2007; Julien et al., 2008).

Autism Spectrum Disorders
Autism spectrum disorders (ASD) include children diagnosed with autism, pervasive developmental disorder (PDD), Asperger's disorder, Rett's disorder, and childhood disintegrative disorder. Drug treatments of youth with ASD have focused on correcting core social and communication and language deficits, and on reducing troublesome behaviors. Although, Filipek et al. (2000) reported that there are no clear guidelines regarding psychopharmacology treatment of youth with ASD, fenfluramine, naltrexone, secretin, antipsychotics (APs), antidepressants (ADs),

stimulants, anticonvulsants, and antihypertensives have all been used off-label to treat disruptive and dangerous behaviors in the ASD population, and their use continues to increase. Aman, Lam, and Van Bourgondien (2005) reported that AD use for youth with ASD more than tripled between 1993 and 2001, primarily due to the use of selective serotonin reuptake inhibitors (SSRIs) for the management of perseverative disorders in this population. In addition, they reported that prescription of APs, stimulants, and antihypertensives also increased for this population. Oswald and Sonenklar (2007) sampled a large commercial database (MedStat). Their sample consisted of 2390 individuals diagnosed with an ASD under the age of 21, who completed a visit with an outpatient or inpatient provider in 2002. Eighty-three percent of the sample (n = 1985) had at least one psychotropic prescription filled during 2002, and an average of 5.8 different psychotropic drugs were prescribed. It should be noted, however, that in some cases multiple prescriptions included different preparations of the same drug. Although the drugs came from 125 different therapeutic classes, the most common were ADs, stimulants, APs, anticonvulsants, antihypertensives, sedatives, and benzodiazepines (BZs).

FDA PEDIATRIC INDICATIONS

he FDA issued a pediatric indication for risperidone (Risperdal) in 2006 and aripiprazole (Abilify) to treat aggression, self-injury, and temper tantrums in children ages six and older with ASD. Currently, there are no other FDA indications for the use of psychotropic drugs, either to treat the core deficits of ASD, or the associated disruptive and/or repetitive behaviors.

DRUG EFFICACY

Fenfluramine, Naltrexome, and Secretin

Aman, Lam & Collier-Crespin (2003) and Witwer & Lecavalier (2005) reviewed more than a dozen RCTs and concluded that fenfluramine, naltrexone, and secretin have been ineffective in remediating the core deficits associated with ASD.

Atypical Antipsychotics

In a large multisite RCT, risperidone (Risperdal) was demonstrated to be effective in decreasing severe aggressive and irritable behaviors in 5- to 17-year-old children with ASD and a mental age of at least 18 months (Aman et al. 2002 [n=118]; McCracken et al., 2002 [n=101]). More than 60% of children with ASD were rated improved at the end of an 8-week trial, compared with 12% on placebo. McDougle et al.

(2005) reported that risperidone treatment resulted in improvements in repetitive stereotypical behavior, but did not alter deficits in communication or social interactions. Two additional large multicenter RCTs demonstrated that risperidone was superior to placebo for highly disruptive, sub-average IQ youth (Pandina et al., 2006 [n=228]; Snyder et al., 2002 [n = 110]). Pandina et al. (2006) concluded that the use of risperidone seems to be safe and effective in children with sub-average IQs who display disruptive behaviors. Three small RCTs also demonstrated that risperidone was superior to placebo for aggressive children and adolescents with sub-average IQs. (Buitelaar et al., 2001[n=38]; Findling et al., 2000 [n=10]; Van Bellingham & De Troch, 2001[n=13]). The FDA prescribing information for aripiprazole indicates that superiority to placebo was demonstrated in two 8 week RCTs children between the ages of 6 and 17 diagnosed with autism spectrum disorder with tantrums, aggression, self-injurious behavior, or a combination of these problems (n = 98, n = 218).

Antidepressants

In a small study Gordon, State, Nelson, Hamburger and Rapoport (1993) found that clomipramine (Anafranil) and desipramine (Norpramine) (both TCAs) were superior to placebo for ASD symptoms, but TCAs are no longer recommended for pediatric use because of their significant side-effect potential. In a larger study (n=45) Hollander et al. (2005) demonstrated that liquid fluoxetine (Prozac), an SSRI, was efficacious in managing perseverative behaviors and stereotypical behaviors in children with ASD. Fluoxetine appears to be the best tolerated of the SSRIs (Brown et al., 2008).

Stimulants

According to the DSM–IV (APA, 2000), diagnosis of ADHD in the context of an ASD is not appropriate. Nevertheless, a recently completed multisite, NIMH-sponsored RCT found that methylphenidate (MPH) was significantly more efficacious than placebo for children with ASD who exhibit ADHD symptoms. However, compared to youth diagnosed with ADHD but without ASD, MPH efficacy and tolerability were more limited for those with ASD (Research Units in Pediatric Psychopharmacology Autism Research Network, 2005). Approximately 50% of the ASD sample had a therapeutic response to MPH compared to 70%–80% of non-ASD subjects, and 18% of the ASD sample experienced adverse events, compared to about 2% of non-ASD subjects.

Mood Stabilizers/Anticonvulsants

Although both divalproex (Depakote) and lithium have been used to treat aggressive behavior and tantrums in the ASD population, no RCTs support the use of these treatments with this population.

Antihypertensives

Both clonidine (Catapres) and guanfacine (Tenex) have been used with children with ASD in efforts to control hyperactivity and aggression/severe tantrums. However, no RCTs support the use of these interventions.

Conclusion

This chapter provides school psychologists with balanced information about the prescription of psychotropic drugs for children and adolescents, and suggests that school psychologists with appropriate competencies may be well suited to function as knowledge brokers to assist pediatric treatment decision-makers. The growth of pediatric psychopharmacology, associated controversies, concerns about safety and side effects, and the research support that exists for this practice were reviewed. In conclusion, it is clear that pediatric psychotropic prescribing practice has expanded more rapidly than has supporting research over the last decade. Furthermore, this expansion has occurred in spite of many emerging safety issues, financial and professional controversies, and limited research support for the efficacy of pediatric drug treatment (with the exception of stimulants for short-term treatment of the core symptoms of ADHD), and especially for polypharmacy. Nevertheless, it appears likely that prescription of psychotropic drugs, including polypharmacy, will only increase in the foreseeable future. All this suggests that if school psychologists choose to function as knowledge brokers around pediatric psychotropic treatment decision making, they must commit to staying current with rapidly evolving developments in this controversial arena.

Future Directions

Because current pediatric prescribing practice exceeds the empirical support base (Brown et al., 2008) much additional research is needed around both the short- and long-term safety and efficacy of drug treatments (especially polypharmacy), psychosocial alternatives, integrated treatments, and sequencing of treatments. These directions will be discussed in order. School psychologists with appropriate competencies will be well suited to contribute to these research needs, particularly with regard to the effects of drugs on achievement and behavior.

Safety

Safety issues are of paramount concern. Unlike adults, children and adolescents are "works in progress." The structures, processes, and functions of their developing central nervous systems can be affected by these drugs. Indeed, alteration of the central nervous system is the putative mechanism of action for psychotropic drugs. Because we lack long-term, systematic, controlled study of the safety and impact of psychiatric drugs on development, we do not know whether the effects of these drugs on various aspects of development are advantageous, disadvantageous, or innocuous. Longitudinal, long-term studies are clearly needed to identify potential late-emerging safety issues, and the effects of these drugs on development, behavior, and achievement

Polypharmacy

The FDA warnings and advisories typically refer to a single drug or category of drug treatment (i.e., monotherapy), a practice that has been commonly supplanted by the prescription of multiple drugs (polypharmacy) in efforts to enhance drug treatment efficacy. This practice raises serious safety issues. Many psychiatric drugs are prone to interact with other drugs, psychiatric or not, in ways that may elevate serum levels of one drug or another to toxic levels, thereby increasing the probability of serious adverse events. How much of an increase in toxicity may be expected for polypharmacy compared to monotherapy, and whether such increases are additive or multiplicative in the pediatric population, is unclear. Studies are needed to determine both the short and long-term safety and efficacy of polypharmacy, and its long-term effects on development, behavior and achievement.

Efficacy

The efficacy of stimulants for the short-term treatment of the core symptoms of ADHD has been demonstrated in multiple RCTs completed by multiple independent research teams. By comparison, RCT support for the drug treatment of other pediatric disorders, and for the long-term treatment of the core symptoms of ADHD (as well as functional outcomes of ADHD) may be characterized as limited, emerging, or nonexistent. Studies of the efficacy of polypharmacy in the pediatric population are nonexistent. School psychologists may be particularly well suited to make research contributions to behavioral and achievement efficacy research utilizing single-subject, multiple baseline designs within a response-to-intervention framework.

Psychosocial Alternatives

Effective psychosocial alternatives to drug treatments exist, and many have been demonstrated to meet well established, and probably efficacious, psychological criteria (Silverman & Hinshaw, 2008) and accepted levels of methodological rigor (Nathan & Gorman, 2007). Furthermore, the risks and safety issues that accompany drug treatments are not characteristic of psychosocial treatments, and the effect sizes associated with some pediatric psychosocial treatments not only meet but exceed the effect sizes for drug treatments (e.g., see Brown et al., 2008 for comparisons for various disorders). For example, although strong empirical support for the short-term drug treatment of ADHD symptoms exists, equally strong empirical support for behavioral treatments for ADHD also exists, and the psychosocial treatments appear to be more beneficial than drugs for functional outcomes such as school functioning, home functioning, and social functioning (Brown et al., 2008). Space limitations preclude more detailed description of psychosocial treatment research, but comprehensive, recent reviews have been published for ADHD by Pelham and Fabiano (2008), DBD by Eyberg, Nelson and Boggs (2008), OCD by Barrett, Farrell, Pina, Peris and Piacentini (2008), non-OCD anxiety disorders by Silverman, Pina and Viswesvaran (2008), depressive disorders by David-Ferdon and Kaslow (2008), and ASD by Rogers and Vismara (2008). Although these reviews of psychosocial treatments are encouraging, further research is needed to identify both moderators and mediators, as is the dissemination of psychosocial research findings to decision-makers.

Integrated Drug and Psychosocial Treatments

Government-sponsored multisite treatment studies completed within the last decade have demonstrated improved efficacy of combined drug and psychosocial social treatments, over drug or psychosocial treatment alone, for adolescent depression (Treatment of Adolescents with Depression Team, 2004), obsessive-compulsive disorder (Pediatric OCD Treatment Team, 2004), and non-OCD anxiety disorders (Walkup et al., 2008). Although the superiority of integrated treatment for ADHD was less potent (MTA, 1999a) than was combination treatment for OCD and non-OCD anxiety, this finding may have been due to a "ceiling" effect, illustrating the difficulty inherent in demonstrating an improvement above and beyond that attributable to strong individual treatments (Abikoff et al.,

2004). Other studies have indicated that for ADHD, reductions in stimulant dosage may be achieved when concomitant behavioral interventions are provided (Fabiano et al. 2007). Future integrated treatment research is needed to extend these studies to other disorders, and evaluate outcomes on school based behavior and achievement.

Sequencing of Treatment

Future research should begin to consider contextual variables (e.g., client preferences, ethnic, cultural, setting) that may affect the sequencing of treatment implementation. For example, parents generally prefer behavioral to drug treatments (Krain, Kendall & Power, 2005; MTA, 1999b), and parents, especially African American parents, are more likely to adhere to behavioral treatment recommendations (Krain et al.). Yet, Pelham and Fabiano (2008) note that, in spite of comparable efficacy to stimulant treatment, practice guidelines differ significantly in terms of how strongly, or even whether, behavioral treatments are recommended for initial treatment of ADHD. Because treatment acceptability and adherence likely affect treatment effectiveness, the decision about whether to begin with a drug, a psychosocial, or a combination treatment may be enhanced if preferences and the influence of cultural or other variables are better understood and considered. Identifying the individual and contextual variables that may affect treatment acceptability and adherence, and therefore efficacy, is another area where school psychologists may make an important contribution to future research.

References

Abikoff, H., Hechtman, L., Klein, R. G., Weiss, G., Fleiss, K., Etcovich, J. et al. (2004). Symptomatic improvement in children with ADHD treated with long-term methylphenidate and multimodal psychosocial treatment. *Journal of the American Academy of Child and Adolescent Psychiatry, 43* 802–811.

Allison, D. B., Mentore, J. L., Heo, M., Chandler, L. P., Cappelleri, J. C., Infante, M. C. et al. (2001). Antipsychotic-induced weight gain: A comprehensive research synthesis. *American Journal of Psychiatry, 158,* 501–512.

Aman, M.G., Arnold, L. E., McDougle, C. J., Vitiello, B., Scahill, L., Davies, M., et al. (2005). Acute and long-term safety and tolerability of risperidone in children with autism. *Journal Child Adolescent Psychopharmacology 15,* 869–884.

Aman, M. G., De Smedt, G., Derivan, A., Lyons, B., Findling, R. L. & the Risperidone Disruptive Behavior Study Group (2002). Double-blind, placebo-controlled study of risperidone for the treatment of disruptive behaviors in children with subaverage intelligence. *American Journal of Psychiatry, 159,* 1337–1346

Aman, M. G., Lam, K. S., & Collier-Crespin, A. (2003) Prevalence and patterns of use of psychoactive medicines among individuals with autism in the Autism Society of Ohio. *Journal of Autism and Developmental Disorders, 33,* 527–534.

Aman, M. G., Lam, K. S. L., & Van Bourgondien, M. E. (2005). Medication patterns in patients with autism: Temporal, regional, and demographic influences. *Journal of Child and Adolescent Psychopharmacology, 15,* 116–126.

Ambrosini, P. J., Bianchi, M. D., Rabinovich, H. & Elia, J. (1993). Antidepressant treatment in children and adolescents: I. Affective disorders. *Journal of the American Academy of Child and Adolescent Psychiatry, 32,* 1–6.

American Academy of Child and Adolescent Psychiatry. (2007). Practice parameter for the assessment and treatment of children and adolescents with attention-deficit/hyperactivity disorder. *Journal of the American Academy of Child and Adolescent Psychiatry, 46,* 894–921.

American Academy of Pediatrics (2001). Clinical Practice Guideline: Treatment of the School-Aged Child with Attention-Deficit/Hyperactivity Disorder. *Pediatrics, 108,* 1033–1044.

American Diabetes Association, American Psychiatric Association, American Association of Clinical Endocrinologists, North American Association for the Study of Obesity. (2004) Consensus development conference on antipsychotic drugs and obesity and diabetes. *Journal of Clinical Psychiatry, 65,* 267–72.

American Psychiatric Association (2000). Diagnostic and Statistical Manual of Mental Disorders, 4th edition, Text Revision (DSM-IV-TR). Washington, DC: American Psychiatric Association.

Amitai, Y. & Frischer, H. (2006). Excess fatality from desipramine in children and adolescents. *Journal of American Academy of Child and Adolescent Psychiatry, 45,* 54–60.

Antonuccio, D. O., Danton, W. G., DeNelsky, G. Y., Greenberg, R. P. & Gordon, J. S. (1999). Raising questions about antidepressants. *Psychotherapy and Psychosomatics, 68,* 3–14.

Avorn, J. (2007). Paying for drug approvals – Who's using whom? *New England Journal of Medicine, 356,* 1697–1700.

Barrett, P. M., Farrell, L., Pina, A., Peris, T. S., & Piacentini, J. (2008). Evidence-based psychosocial treatments for child and adolescent obsessive-compulsive disorder. *Journal of Clinical Child and Adolescent Psychology, 37,* 131–155.

Berard, R., Fong, R., Carpenter, D. J., Thomason, C. & Wilkinson, C. (2006). An international, multicenter, placebo-controlled trial of paroxetine in adolescents with major depressive disorder *Journal of Child and Adolescent Psychopharmacology, 16,* 59–75.

Bernstein, G. A., Garfinkel, B. D., & Borchardt, C. M. (1990). Comparative studies of pharmacotherapy for school refusal. *Journal of the American Academy of Child and Adolescent Psychiatry, 29,* 773–781.

Birmaher B., & Brent, D.A. (2003). Depressive Disorders. In Martin, A., Scahill, L.,Charney, D. S. & Leckman, J. F. (Eds.). *Pediatric Psychopharmacology: Principles and Practice.* New York: Oxford University Press.

Birmaher, B, Axelson, D, Monk, K, Kalas, C, Clark, D. B., Ehmann, M. et al. (2003). Fluoxetine for the Treatment of Childhood Anxiety Disorders. *Journal of the American Academy of Child and Adolescent Psychiatry, 42,* 415–423.

Black, B., & Uhde, T. W. (1994). Treatment of elective mutism with fluoxetine: A double-blind, placebo-controlled study. *Journal of the American Academy of Child and Adolescent Psychiatry, 33,* 1000–1006.

Blair, B. S., Scahill, L., State, M. & Martin, A. (2005). Electrocardiographic changes in children and adolescents treated with ziprasidone: A prospective study. *Journal of the American Academy of Child and Adolescent Psychiatry, 44,* 73–79.

Braconnier A, Le Coent R, & Cohen D. (2003) Paroxetine versus clomipramine in adolescents with severe major depression: A double-blind, randomized, multicenter trial. *Journal of the American Academy of Child and Adolescent Psychiatry 42,* 22–29.

Brent, D. (2007). Antidepressants and suicidal behavior: Cause or cure? *American Journal of Psychiatry, 164,* 898–991.

Bridge, J. A., Iyengar, S., Salary, C. B., Barbe, R. P., Birmaher, B., Pincus, H. A., et al. (2007). Clinical response and risk for reported suicidal ideation and suicide attempts in pediatric antidepressant treatment. *The Journal of the American Medical Association, 297,* 1683–1696.

Brown, R. T., Antonuccio, D. O., DuPaul, G. J., Fristad, M. E., King, C. E., Leslie, L. K., McCormick, G. S., Pelham Jr., W. E., Piacentini, J. C. & Vitiello, B. (2008) *Childhood mental health disorders: Evidence base and contextual factors for psychosocial, psychopharmacological, and combined interventions.* Washington, DC: American Psychological Association.

Buitelaar, W.G., van der Gaag, R. J., Cohen-Kettenis P., & Meloman C. T. M., (2001). A randomized controlled trial of risperidone in the treatment of aggression in Hospitalized adolescents with subaverage cognitive abilities. *Journal of Clinical Psychiatry, 62,* 239–248.

Campbell, E. R. G., Gruen, R. L., Mountford, J., Miller, L. G., Cleary, P. D. & Blumenthal, D. (2007). A national survey of physician–industry relationships. *New England Journal of Medicine, 356,* 1742–1750.

Campbell, M., Small, A.M., Green, W.H., Jennings, S.J., Perry, R., Bennett, W.G., et al. (1984). Behavioral efficacy of haloperidol and lithium carbonate. A comparison in hospitalized aggressive children with conduct disorder. *Archives of General Psychiatry, 41,* 650–656.

Campbell M, Adams PB, Small AM, Kafantaris V, Silva RR, Shell J, Perry R, Overall JE. (1995) Lithium in hospitalized aggressive children with conduct disorder: a double-blind and placebo-controlled study. *Journal of the American Academy of Child and Adolescent Psychiatry, 34,* 445–453.

Cantwell, D. P., Swanson J., & Connor, D. F. (1997). Case study: adverse response to clonidine. *Journal of the American Academy of Child and Adolescent Psychiatry, 36,* 539–544.

Carlson, J. S., Demaray, N. K., & Hunter-Oehmke, H. (2006), S. A survey of school psychologists' knowledge and training in child psychopharmacology. *Psychology in the Schools, 43,* 623–633.

Carmichael, M. (2008, May 26). Growing up bipolar. *Newsweek.*

Chang, K. D., Nyilas, M., Aurang, C., et al. (2007). Efficacy of aripiprazole in children (10–17 years old) with mania. Poster presented at American Academy of Child and Adolescent Psychiatry Annual Meeting, Boston, Massachusetts

Connor, D., Fletcher, K., & Swanson, J. (1999). A meta-analysis of clonidine for symptoms of attention-deficit hyperactivity disorder. *Journal of the American Academy of Child and Adolescent Psychiatry. 38,* 1551–1559.

Connor, D. F. & Meltzer, B. M. (2006). *Pediatric psychopharmacology: Fast facts.* Norton: New York.

Conners, C. K., Casat, C. D., Gualtieri, C. T., et al. (1996), Bupropion hydrochloride in attention deficit disorder with hyperactivity. *Journal of the American Academy of Child and Adolescent Psychiatry, 35*, 1314–1321.

Csoka, A.B. & Shipko, S. (2006). Persistent sexual side effects after SSRI discontinuation. *Psychotherapy and Psychosomatics, 75*, 187–188.

David-Ferndon, C. & Kaslow, N. J. (2008). Evidence-based psychosocial treatments for child and adolescent depression. *Journal of Clinical Child and Adolescent Psychology, 37*, 62–104.

DelBello, M., Findling, R. L., Kushner, S., Wang, D., Olson, W. H., Capece, J. A., et al. (2005). A pilot controlled trial of topiramate for mania in children and adolescents with bipolar disorder. *Journal of the American Academy of Child and Adolescent Psychiatry, 44*, 539–546.

DelBello, M.A., Kowatch, R.A., Adler, C.M., Stanford, K.E., Welge, J.A., Barzman, D.H., et al. (2006). A double-blind randomized pilot study Comparing quetiapine and divalproex for adolescent mania. *Journal of American Academy of Child and Adolescent Psychiatry, 45(3)*, 305–313.

DeLeon, P. H. & Wiggins, J.G. (1996) Prescription privileges for psychologists. *American Psychologist, 51*, 225–229.

Donovan, S. J., Stewart, J. W., Nunes, E. V., Quitkin, F. C., Parides, M. er al (2000). Divalproex treatment for youth with explosive temper and mood lability: A double-blind, placebo-controlled crossover design. *American Journal of Psychiatry 157*, 818–820.

Efron, D., Hiscock, H., Sewell, J. R., Cranswick, N. E., Alasdair, L., Vance, A. et al. (2005). Prescribing of psychotropic medications for children by Australian pediatricians and child psychiatrists. *Pediatrics, 111*, 372–375.

Emslie, G. J., Findling, R. J., Yeung, P., Kunz, N. & Li, Y. (2007). Venlafaxine ER for the treatment of pediatric subjects with depression: results of two placebo-controlled trials. *Journal of the American Academy of Child & Adolescent Psychiatry. 46*, 479–488.

Emslie, G. J., Helligstein, J. H., Wagner, K. D., Hoog, S. L., Ernest, D. E., Brown, E. et al (2002). Fluoxetine for treatment of depression in children and adolescents: A randomized placebo-controlled clinical trial. *Journal of the American Academy of Child & Adolescent Psychiatry. 41*, 1205–1215.

[My paper][My paper]Emslie, G. J., Kennard, B. D., Mayes, T. L., Nightingale-Teresi, J., Carmody, T. Hughes, C. W. et al. (2008). Fluoxetine versus placebo in preventing relapse of major depression in children and adolescents. *American Journal of Psychiatry, 165*, 459–467.

Emslie, G. J., Rush, A. J., Weinberg, W. A., Guillion, C. M., Rintlemann, J. & Hughes, C. W. (1997). A double-blind placebo controlled trial of fluoxetine in children and adolescents with depression. *Archives of General Psychiatry, 54*, 1031–1037.

Emslie, G. J., Wagner, K.D., Kutcher, S., Krulewicz, S., Fong, R., Carpenter, D. J. et al. (2006). Paroxetine treatment in children and adolescents with major depressive disorder: a randomized, multicenter, double-blind, placebo-controlled trial. *Journal of the American Academy of Child and Adolescent Psychiatry, 45*, 709–719.

Emslie, G. J., Walkup, J.T., Pliszka, S.R., & Ernest, M. (1999). Nontricyclic antidepressants: Current trends in children and adolescents. *Journal of the American Academy of Child and Adolescent Psychiatry, 38*, 517–528.

Emslie G. J., Yeung P. P. & Kunz N. R. (2007). Long-term, open-label venlafaxine extended-release treatment in children and adolescents with major depressive disorder. *CNS Spectrums, 12*, 223–233.

Eyberg, S. M., Nelson, M. M. & Boggs, S. R. (2008). Evidence-based psychosocial treatments for children and adolescents with disruptive behavior. *Journal of Clinical Child and Adolescent Psychology, 37*, 215–237.

Fabiano, G. A., Pelham, W. E., Gnagy, E. M., Burrows-MacLean, L., Chacko, A., Coles, E. K., et al. (2007). The single and combined effects of multiple intensities of behavior modification and multiple intensities of methylphenidate in a classroom setting. *School Psychology Review, 36*, 195–216.

Feigin, A., Kurlan, R., McDermott, M. P., Beach, J., Dimitsopulos, T., Brower, C. A. et al. (1996). A controlled trial of deprenyl in children with Tourette's syndrome and attention deficit hyperactivity disorder. *Neurology, 46*, 965–968.

Filipek, P. A., Accardo, P.J., Ashwal, S., Baranek, G. T., Cook, E. H. Jr., Dawson, G., et al. (2000). Practice parameter: Screening and diagnosis of autism. *Neurology, 55*, 468–479.

Findling, R. L., McNamara, N. K., Branicky, L. A., Schluchter, M. D., Lemon, E., & Blumer, J. L., (2000). A double-blind pilot study of risperidone in the treatment of conduct disorder. *Journal of the American Academy of Child and Adolescent Psychiatry, 39*, 509–516.

Flament, M. F., Rapoport, J. L., Berg, C. J., Sceery, W., Kilts, C., Mellstrom, B., et al. (1985). Clomipramine treatment of childhood obsessive-compulsive disorder: A double-blind controlled study. *Archives in General Psychiatry, 42*, 977–983.

Gaffney, G. R., Perry, P. J., Lund, B. C., Bever-Stille, K. A., Arndt, S. & Kuperman, S. (2002). Risperidone versus clonidine in the treatment of children and adolescents with Tourette's syndrome. *Journal of the American Academy of Child and Adolescent Psychiatry, 41*, 330–336.

Gaviria, M. (Producer). (2008, January 8). The Medicated Child [Television series episode] In M. Gaviria (Producer), *Frontline*: Public Broadcasting System.

Geller, D. A., Biederman, J., Stewart, S. E., Mullin, B., Martin, A., Spencer, T., et al. (2003). Which SSRI? A meta-analysis of pharmacotherapy trials in pediatric obsessive-compulsive disorder. *American Journal of Psychiatry, 160*, 1919–1928.

Geller, D. A., Hoog, S. L., Heiligenstein, J. H., Ricardi, R. K., Tamura, R., Kluszynski, S., (2001). Fluoxetine treatment for obsessive-compulsive disorder in children and adolescents: A placebo-controlled clinical trial. *Journal of the American Academy of Child and Adolescent Psychiatry, 40*, 773–779.

Geller, D. A., Wagner, K. D., Emslie, G., Murphy, T., Carpenter, D., Wetherhold, E., et al. (2004). Paroxetine treatment in children and adolescents with obsessive-compulsive disorder: A randomized, multicenter, double-blind, placebo-controlled trial. *Journal of American Academy of Child and Adolescent Psychiatry, 43*, 1387–1396.

Gilbert, D. L., Batterson, J. R., Sethuraman, G. & Sallee, F. R. (2004). Tic reduction with risperidone versus pimozide in a randomized, double-blind, crossover trial. *Journal of the American Academy of Child and Adolescent Psychiatry, 43*, 206–214.

Gittelman-Klein, R. & Klein, D. (1971). Controlled imipramine treatment of school refusal. *Archives of General Psychiatry, 25*, 204–207.

Gordon, C., State, R., Nelson, J. E., Hamburger, S. D., & Rapoport, J.L. (1993). A double blind comparison of clomipramine, desipramine, and placebo in the treatment of autistic disorder. *Archives of General Psychiatry, 50*, 441–447.

Graae, F., Milner, J., Rizzotto, L., & Klein, R. G. (1994). Clonazepam in childhood anxiety disorders. *Journal of the*

American Academy of Child and Adolescent Psychiatry, 33, 372–376.

Green, W. H. (2007). *Child and adolescent clinical psychopharmacology* (4th ed.). Philadelphia: Lippincott Williams & Wilkins.

Greenhill L., Kollins S., Abikoff, H., McCracken J., Riddle M., Swanson J., et al. (2006). Efficacy and safety of immediate-release methylphenidate treatment for preschoolers with ADHD. *Journal of the American Academy of Child and Adolescent Psychiatry, 45,* 1284–1293.

Gureasko-Moore, D., DuPaul, G. J., & Power, T. J. (2005). Stimulant treatment for ADHD: Medication monitoring practices of school psychologists. *School Psychology Review, 34,* 232–245.

Hammad, T. A., Laughren, T. & Racoosin, J. (2006). Suicidality in pediatric patients treated with antidepressant drugs. *Archives of General Psychiatry, 63,* 332–339.

Hazell, P. L., & Stuart, J. E. (2003). A randomized controlled trial of clonidine added to psychostimulant medication for hyperactive and aggressive children. *Journal of the American Academy of Child and Adolescent Psychiatry, 42,* 886–894.

Hollander, E., Phillips, A., Chaplin, W., Zagursky, K., Novotny, S., Wasserman, S., et al. (2005). A placebo controlled crossover trial of liquid fluoxetine on repetitive behaviors in childhood and adolescent autism. *Neuropsychopharmacology, 30,* 582–599.

Isojarvi, J., Laatikainen, T. L., Pakarinen, A. J., Juntunen, K., & Myllyla, V. V. (1993). Polycystic ovaries and hyperandrogenism in women taking valproate for epilepsy. *New England Journal of Medicine, 329,* 1383–1388.

Jensen, P. S., Hinshaw, S. P., Kraemer, H. C., Lenora, N., Newcorn, J. H., Abikoff, H. B., et al., (2001). ADHD comorbidity findings from the MTA study. Comparing comorbid subgroups. *Journal of the American Academy of Child and Adolescent Psychiatry, 40,* 147–158.

Joffe, H., Cohen, L. S., Suppes, T., McLaughlin, W. L., Lavori, P., Adams, J. M. et al (2006). Valproate is associated with new-onset oligoamenorrhea with hyperandrogenism in women with bipolar disorder. *Biological Psychiatry, 59,* 1078–1086.

Julien, R. M., Advocat, C. D. & Comaty, J. E. (2008). *A primer of drug action: A comprehensive guide to the actions, uses, and side effects of psychoactive drugs* (11th ed.). New York: Worth Publishers.

Jureidini, J. N., Doecke, C. J., Mansfield, P. R., Haby, M. M., Menkes, D. B., & Tonkin, A. L. (2004). Efficacy and safety of antidepressants for children and adolescents. *British Medical Journal, 328,* 879–883.

Jureidini, J. N., Leemon B. M. & Mansfield, P.R. (2008). Clinical trials and drug promotion: Selective reporting of study 329. *The International Journal of Risk and Safety in Medicine, 20,* 73–81.

Kafantaris, V., Coletti, D. J., Dicker, R., Padula, G., Pleak R.R. & Alvir, J. M. (2004). Lithium treatment of acute mania in adolescents: a placebo-controlled discontinuation study. *Journal of the American Academy of Child and Adolescent Psychiatry, 43,* 984–993.

Keller, M., Ryan, N., Strober, M., Klein, R., Kutcher, S., Birmaher, B., et al. (2001). Efficacy of paroxetine in the treatment of adolescent major depression: A randomized, controlled trial. *Journal of the American Academy of Child and Adolescent Psychiatry, 40,* 762–772.

Klein, R. G., Abikoff, H., Ganeles, D., Seese, L. M. & Pollack, S. (1997). Clinical efficacy of methylphenidate in conduct disorder with and without attention deficit hyperactivity disorder. *Archives of General Psychiatry, 54,* 1073–1080.

Klein, R. G., Koplowicz, H., & Kanner, A. (1992). Imipramine treatment of children with separation anxiety disorder. *Journal of the American Academy of Child and Adolescent Psychiatry, 31,* 21–28.

Kowatch, R. A., Findling, R. L., Scheffer, R. E. & Stanford, K.E. (2007). *Placebo-controlled trial of divalproex versus lithium for bipolar disorder.* Poster presented at American Academy of Child and Adolescent Psychiatry Annual Meeting. Boston, Massachusetts.

Kowatch, R. A. & Fristad, M. A. (2006). Pediatric bipolar disorders. In R. T. Ammerman, M. Hersen, & J. C. Thomas (Eds.), *Comprehensive handbook of personality and psychopathology, vol. iii: Child psychopathology.* NY: John Wiley & Sons.

Kowatch, R. A., Fristad, M. A., Birmaher, B.W., Wagner, K. D., Findling, R. L., Hellander, M. et al. (2005). Treatment guidelines for children and adolescents with bipolar disorder. *Journal of the American Academy of Child and Adolescent Psychiatry, 44,* 213–235.

Krain A. L., Kendall P. C & Power T. J. (2005). The role of treatment acceptability in the initiation of treatment for ADHD. *Journal of Attention Disorders, 9,* 425–434.

Kubiszyn, T. (1994) Pediatric psychopharmacology and prescription privileges: Implications and opportunities for school psychology. *School Psychology Quarterly, 9,* 26–40.

Kubiszyn, T. & Carlson, C. I. (1995). School psychologists' attitudes toward an expanded health care role: Psychopharmacology and prescription privileges. *School Psychology Quarterly, 10,* 247–270.

Labellarte, M.J., & Ginsburg, G.S. (2003). Anxiety disorders. In Martin, A., Scahill, L., Charney, D.S. & Leckman, J.F. (Eds.). *Pediatric psychopharmacology: Principles and practice* (pp. 497–510). New York: Oxford University Press.

Lavoie, K. & Barone, S. (2006). Prescription privileges for psychologists: A comprehensive review and critical analysis of current issues and controversies. *CNS Drugs, 20,* 51–66.

Leonard, H. L., Swedo, S. E., Lenane, M. C., Rettew, D. C., Cheslow, D. L., Hamburger, S. D., et al. (1991). A double-blind desipramine substitution during long-term clomipramine treatment in children and adolescents with obsessive-compulsive disorder. *Archives of General Psychiatry, 48,* 922–927.

MacGillivray S. Arroll B. Hatcher S. Ogston S. Reid I. Sullivan F. et al. (2003). Efficacy and tolerability of selective serotonin reuptake inhibitors compared with tricyclic antidepressants in depression treated in primary care: Systematic review and meta-analysis. *British Medical Journal. 326,* 1014–1017.

Malone, R. P., Delaney, M. A., Leubbert, J. F., Cater, J., & Campbell, M. (2000). A double-blind, placebo-controlled study of lithium in hospitalized aggressive children and adolescents with conduct disorder. *Archives of General Psychiatry, 57,* 649–654.

March, J.S., Frances A., Carpenter, D., & Kahn, D.A. (1997). The expert consensus guidelines series: Treatment of obsessive–compulsive disorder. *Journal of Clinical Psychiatry, 58, 1–72*

March, J. S., Biederman, J., Wolkow, R., Safferman, A., Mardekian, J., Cook, E. H., et al. (1998). Sertraline in children and adolescents with obsessive-compulsive disorder: A multicenter randomized control trial. *Journal of the American Medical Association, 280,* 1752–1756.

March, J.S. & Curry, J. (1998). Predicting the outcome of treatment. *Journal of Abnormal Child Psychology*, 58, 1–72.

Martin, A., Van Hoof, T., Stubbe, D., Sherwin, T., & Scahill, L. (2003). Multiple psychotropic pharmacotherapy among child and adolescent enrollees in Connecticut medicaid managed care. *Psychiatric Services*, 54, 72–77.

McClure, E., Kubiszyn, T. & Kaslow, N. (2002). Evidence-based assessment of childhood mood disorders. *Professional Psychology: Research and Practice*, 33, 125–134.

McCracken, J. T., McGough, J., Shah, B., Cronin, P., Hong, D., Aman, M. G., et al. (2002). Risperidone in children with autism and serious behavioral problems. *New England Journal of Medicine*, 347, 314–321.

McDougle, C. J., Scahill, L., Aman, M. G., McCracken, J. T., Tierney, E., Davies, M., et al. (2005). Risperidone for the core symptom domains of autism: Results from the RUPP autism network study. *American Journal of Psychiatry*, 162, 1142–1148.

Michelson, D., Allen. A. J., Busner, J., et al. (2002). Once-daily atomoxetine treatment for children and adolescents with attention-deficit/hyperactivity disorder: a randomized placebo-controlled study. *American Journal of Psychiatry*, 159, 1896–1901.

Michelson, D., Faries, D., Wernicke, J. et al. (2001). Atomoxetine in the treatment of children and adolescents with attention-deficit/hyperactivity disorder: a randomized placebo-controlled, dose-response study. *Pediatrics*, 108, 83–87.

Millin, R. P., Simeon, J. & Spenst, W. P. (1999). Paroxetine in the treatment of children with major depression. Poster presented at the 46th annual meeting of the American Academy of Child and Adolescent Psychiatry, Chicago, IL.

Moreno C., Laje G., Blanco C., Jiang H., Schmidt A. B., & Olfson M. (2007). National trends in the outpatient diagnosis and treatment of bipolar disorder in youth. *Archives of General Psychiatry*, 64, 1032–1039.

MTA Cooperative Group. (1999a). 14 month randomized clinical trial of treatment strategies for attention deficit hyperactivity disorder. *Archives of General Psychiatry*, 56, 1073–1086.

MTA Cooperative Group. (1999b). Moderators and mediators of treatment response for children with attention-deficit/hyperactivity disorder. *Archives of General Psychiatry*, 56, 1088–1096.

MTA Cooperative Group. (2004a). National institute of mental health multimodal treatment study of ADHD follow-up: 24 month outcomes of treatment strategies for attention-deficit/hyperactivity disorder. *Pediatrics*, 113, 754–761.

MTA Cooperative Group (2004b). National Institute of Mental health multimodal treatment study of ADHD follow-up: Changes in effectiveness and growth after the end of treatment. *Pediatrics*, 113, 762–769.

Nathan, P. E. & Gorman, J. M. (Eds.). (2007). *A guide to treatments that work*. New York: Oxford University Press.

Newcorn, J. H., Spencer, T. J., Biederman, J., Milton, D. R., & Michelson, D. (2005). Atomoxetine treatment in children and adolescents with attention deficit/hyperactivity disorder and comorbid oppositional defiant disorder. *Journal of the American Academy of Child and Adolescent Psychiatry*, 44, 240–248.

Novak, E. & Allen, P. J. (2007).Prescribing medications in pediatrics: Concerns regarding FDA approval and pharmacokinetics. *Pediatric Nursing*, 33, 64–70.

Olfson, M., Blanco, C., Liu, L., Moreno, C., & Laje, G. (2006). National trends in the outpatient treatment of children and adolescents with antipsychotic drugs. *Archives of General Psychiatry*, 63, 679–685.

Oswald, D. P & Sonenklar, N. A. (2007). Medication use among children with autism-spectrum disorder. *Journal of Child and Adolescent Psychopharmacology*, 17, 348–355.

Pachter, Fox, Zimbardo & Antonuccio, (2007). Corporate funding and conflicts of interest: A primer for psychologists. *American Psychologist*, 62, 1005–1015.

Palumbo, D., Spencer, T., Lynch, D., Co-Chien, H. & Faraone, S. V. (2004). Emergence of tics in children with ADHD: Impact of once-daily OROS methylphenidate therapy. *Journal of Child and Adolescent Psychopharmacology*, 4, 185–194.

Pandina, G. Bossie, C. Youssef, E. Zhou, Y., & Dunbar, F. (2006). Risperidone improves behavioral symptoms in children with autism in a randomized, double-blind, placebo-controlled trial. *Journal of Autism and Developmental Disorders*, 24, 170–196.

Pandina, G. J., DelBello M. P., Kushner S., et al. (2007). Risperidone for the treatment of acute mania in bipolar youth. Poster presented at American Academy of Child and Adolescent Psychiatry Annual Meeting, Boston, Massachusetts

Patel, N. C., Sanchez, R. J., Johnsrud, M. T., & Crimson, M. L. (2002). Trends in antipsychotic use in a Texas Medicaid population of children and adolescents: 1996 to 2000. *Journal of the American Academy of Child and Adolescent Psychiatry*, 12, 221–229.

Patel, N. C., Crimson, M. L., Hoagwood, K., Johnsrud, M. T., Rascati, K. L., Wilson, J. P., et al. (2005). Trends in the use of typical and atypical antipsychotics in children and adolescents. *Journal of the American Academy of Child and Adolescent Psychiatry*, 44, 548–556.

Pediatric OCD Treatment Team. (2004). Cognitive-behavior therapy, sertraline, and their combination for children and adolescents with obsessive-compulsive disorder: The pediatric OCD treatment study (POTS) randomized controlled trial. *Journal of the American Medical Association*, 292, 1969–1976.

Pelham, W. E. & Fabiano, G. A. (2008). Evidence-based psychosocial treatments for Attention Deficit/Hyperactivity Disorder, *Journal of Clinical Child and Adolescent Psychology*, 37, 184–214.

Phillips, B. (1999). Strengthening the links between science and practice: Reading, evaluating and applying research in school psychology. In C. Reynolds & T. Gutkin, (Eds.). *The Handbook of School Psychology* (3e), (pp. 56–77), New York: Wiley.

Pliszka, S. R. (1987). Tricyclic antidepressants in the treatment of children with attention deficit disorder. *Journal of the American Academy of Child and Adolescent Psychiatry*, 26, 127–132.

Pliszka, S. R., Crismon, M. L., Hughes, C. W., Conners, C. K., Emslie, G. J., Jensen, P. S., et al. (2006). The Texas Children's Medication Algorithm Project: Revision of the algorithm for pharmacotherapy of attention-deficit/hyperactivity disorder. *Journal of the American Academy of Child & Adolescent Psychiatry*, 45, 642–657.

Power, T. J., DuPaul, G. J., Shapiro, E. S., & Kazak, A. (2003). Preparing psychologists to linksystems of care in managing and preventing children's health problems. *Journal of Pediatric Psychology*, 28, 147–155.

Preda, A., MacLean, R. W., Mazure, C. M., & Bowers. (2001). Antidepressant-associated mania and psychosis resulting in psychiatric admissions. *Journal of Clinical Psychiatry*, 62, 30–33.

Research Units on Pediatric Psychopharmacology Anxiety Study Group (2001). An eight-week placebo-controlled trial of fluvoxamine for anxiety disorders in children and adolescents. *New England Journal of Medicine, 344,* 1279–1285.

Research Units on Pediatric Psychopharmacology Autism Network. (2005). A randomized, double-blind, placebo-controlled, crossover trial of methylphenidate in children with hyperactivity associated with pervasive developmental disorders. *Archives of General Psychiatry, 62,* 1266–1274.

Riddle, M. A., Reeve, E. A., Yaryura-Tobias, J. A., Yang, H. M., Claghorn, J. L., Gaffney, G., et al. (2001). Fluvoxamine for children and adolescents with obsessive-compulsive disorder: A randomized, controlled, multicenter trial. *Journal of the American Academy of Child and Adolescent Psychiatry, 40,* 222–229.

Rogers, S. J. & Vismara, L. A. (2008). Evidence-based comprehensive treatments for early autism. *Journal of Clinical Child and Adolescent Psychology, 37,* 8–38.

Rosenbaum, J. F., Fava, M., Hoog, S. L., Ashcroft, R. C., & Krebs, W. (1998). Selective serotonin reuptake inhibitor discontinuation syndrome: A randomized clinical study. *Biological Psychiatry, 44,* 77–87.

Rubino, A., Roskell, N., & Tennis P. (2007). Risk of suicide during treatment with venlafaxine, citalopram, fluoxetine, and dothiepin: retrospective cohort study. *British Medical Journal, 334,* 242–247.

Rynn, M. A., Siqueland, L., & Rickels, K. (2001). Placebo-controlled trial of sertraline in the treatment of children with generalized anxiety disorder. *American Journal of Psychiatry, 158,* 2008–2014.

Rynn, M., Wagner, K. D., Donnelly, C., Ambrosini, P., Wohlberg, C. J., Landau, P. et al. et al. (2006). Long-term sertraline treatment of children and adolescents with major depressive disorder. *Journal of Child and Adolescent Psychopharmacology, 16,* 103–116.

Silverman, W. K. & Hinshaw, S. P. (2008). The second special issue on evidence-based psychosocial treatments for children and adolescents. *Journal of Clinical Child and Adolescent Psychology, 37,* 1–7.

Silverman, W. K., Pina, A. & Viswesvaran, C. (2008). Evidence-based psychosocial treatments for phobic and anxiety disorders in children and adolescents, *Journal of Clinical Child and Adolescent Psychology, 37,* 105–130.

Simeon, J. G., Ferguson, H. B., Knott, V., Roberts, N., Gauthier, B., DuBNois, C. et al. 1992). Clinical, cognitive, and neurophysiological effects of alprazolam in children and adolescents with overanxious and avoidant disorders. *Journal of the American Academy of Child and Adolescent Psychiatry, 31,* 29–33.

Smarty, S. & Findling, R.L. (2007). Psychopharmacology of pediatric bipolar disorder: a review. *Psychopharmacology, 19,* 39–54.

Snyder, R., Turgay A., Binder C., Fisman S., Carrol, A. & the Risperidone Conduct Study Group (2002). Effects of risperidone on conduct and disruptive behavior disorders in children with subaverage IQs. *Journal of the American Academy of Child and Adolescent Psychiatry, 41,* 1026–1036.

Spencer, T., Heiligenstein, J. H., Biederman J., Fairies, D. E., Kratochvil, C. J., Connors, C. K. et al. (2002). Results from 2 proof-of-concept, placebo-controlled studies of atomoxetine in children with attention-deficit/hyperactivity disorder. *Journal of Clinical Psychiatry, 63,* 1140–1147.

Steiner, H., Petersen, M.L., Saxena, K., Ford, S., & Matthews, Z. (2003). Divalproex sodium for the treatment of conduct disorder: A randomized controlled clinical trial. *Journal of Clinical Psychiatry, 64,* 1183–1191.

[My paper]Swanson, J. M., Elliot, G., Greenhill, L., Wigal, T., Arnold, L., Vitiello, B. et al (2007). Effects of stimulant medication on growth rates across 3 years in the MTA follow-up. *Journal of the American Academy of Child Adolescent Psychiatry, 46,* 1015–1027.

Swanson J., Greenhill L., Wigal T., Kollins S., Stehli A., Davies M., et al. (2006). Stimulant-related reductions of growth rates in the PATS. *Journal of the American Academy of Child Adolescent Psychiatry, 45,* 1304–1313.

Treatment of Adolescents with Depression Team (TADS). (2004). Fluoxetine, cognitive-behavioral therapy, and their combination for adolescents with depression. *Journal of the American Medical Association, 292,* 807–820.

Turner, E. H., Matthews, A. M., Linardatos, E., Tell, R. A., Rosenthal, R. (2008). Selective publication of antidepressant trials and its influence on apparent efficacy. *New England Journal of Medicine, 358,* 252–260.

U. S. Food and Drug Administration Labeling Change (1986, May 9). Important drug information; lithium carbonate. Retrieved June 6, 2007 from http://www.fda.gov/cder/foi/appletter/2001/18421s16ltr.pdf

U. S. Food and Drug Administration Dear Health Professional Letter (1997, March 11). Important lamotrigine (lamictal) warning. Retrieved September 11, 2008 from http://www.fda.gov/medwatch/safety/1997/lamict.htm

U. S. Food and Drug Administration Dear Health Professional Letter (1999, March 11). Alert for healthcare professionals pemoline tablets and chewable tablets (marketed as Cylert). Retrieved June 6, 2008 from http://www.fda.gov/cder/foi/label/2003/016832s022_017703s018lbl.pdf

U. S. Food and Drug Administration Dear Health Professional Letter (2000, June 30). Important drug warning: Thioridazine (Mellaril) and QTc prologationhttp://www.fda.gov/medwatch/safety/2000/mellar.htm

U. S. Food and Drug Administration Dear Health Professional Letter (2002, January 8). Serzone (nefazodone) and hepatic failure. Retrieved September 6, 2007 from http://www.fda.gov/cder/foi/appletter/2002/20152s29ltr.pdf

U. S. Food and Drug Administration Public Health Advisory (2003a, October 27). Reports of suicidality in pediatric patients being treated with antidepressant medications for major depressive disorder (MDD). Retrieved November 30, 2003 from http://www.fda.gov/cder/drug/advisory/mdd.htm

U. S. Food and Drug Administration Dear Health Professional Letter (2003b, November 10). Important drug information: Hyperglycemia, diabetes mellitus and atypical antipsychotics. Retrieved October 6, 2008 from http://www.fda.gov/CDER/warn/2004/12195Risperdal.pdf

U. S. Food and Drug Administration Public Health Advisory (2004a, March 22). Worsening depression and suicidality in patients being treated with antidepressant medications. Retrieved June 15, 2004 from http://www.fda.gov/cder/drug/antidepressants/AntidepressanstPHA.htm

U. S. Food and Drug Administration (FDA) Talk Paper (2004b, December 17). New warning for strattera. Retrieved November 29, 2005 from http://www.fda.gov/bbs/topics/ANSWERS/2004/ANS01335.html

U. S. Food and Drug Administration (FDA) Public Health Advisory (2005a, February 9). Public health advisory for adderall and adderall xr. Retrieved November 28, 2005 from http://www.fda.gov/cder/drug/advisory/adderall.htm

U. S. Food and Drug Administration Public Health Advisory (2005b, April 11). Deaths with antipsychotics in elderly patients with behavioral disturbances. Retrieved July 6, 2006 from http://www.fda.gov/cder/drug/advisory/antipsychotics.htm.

U. S. Food and Drug Administration Dear Health Professional Letter (2005c, April 18). Important drug warning for oxcarbazapine (trileptal). Retrived on June 15, 2010 from http://www.fda.gov/downloads/Safety/MedWatch/SafetyInformation/SafetyAlertsforHumanMedicalProducts/UCM164881.pdf http://www.fda.gov/medwatch/safety/2005/trileptal_hcp.pdf

U. S. Food and Drug Administration (FDA) News (2005d, September 30). FDA Issues Public Health Advisory on Strattera (atomoxetine) for Attention Deficit Disorder. Retrieved October 28, 2005 from http://www.fda.gov/bbs/topics/news/2005/new01237.html

U. S. Food and Drug Administration (FDA) News (2005e, October 24). Alert for Healthcare Professionals, Liver Injury Risk and Market Withdrawal: Pemoline Tablets and Chewable Tablets (marketed as Cylert). Retrieved March 16, 2006 from http://www.fda.gov/Cder/drug/InfoSheets/HCP/pemolineHC.html

U. S. Food and Drug Administration Dear Health Professional Letter (2005f, December). Important Clozapine (Clozaril) Drug Warning and New Information. Rtetrieved on September 16, 2008 from http://www.fda.gov/MEDWATCH/SAFETY/2006/Clozaril_chart_letter_final12-2005.pdf

U. S. Food and Drug Administration Labeling Change (2006a, July 20). Hepatic failure, teratogenicity and pancreatitis with valproic acid formulations. Retrieved from http://www.fda.gov/MEDwatch/safety/2006/Oct_PIs/DepakoteDRTabs_PI.pdf4

U. S. Food and Drug Administration Labeling Change (2006b, October 30). Required labeling change for atomoxetine. Retrieved August 1, 2007 from http://www.fda.gov/cder/foi/label/2006/021411s018lbl.pdf.

U. S. Food and Drug Administration Public Health Advisory (2006c, November 24). Combined Use of 5-Hydroxytryptamine Receptor Agonists (Triptans), Selective Serotonin Reuptake Inhibitors (SSRIs) or Selective Serotonin/Norepinephrine Reuptake Inhibitors (SNRIs) May Result in Life-threatening Serotonin Syndrome. Retrieved June 15, 2010 from http://www.fda.gov/Drugs/DrugSafety/PublicHealthAdvisories/ucm124349.htm

U. S. Food and Drug Administration (FDA) News (2007a, February 21). FDA Directs ADHD Drug Manufacturers to Notify Patients about Cardiovascular Adverse Events and Psychiatric Adverse Events. Retrieved October 12, 2007 from http://www.fda.gov/bbs/topics/NEWS/2007/NEW01568.html.

U. S. Food and Drug Administration (FDA) Alert (2007b, September 17). Information for Healthcare Professionals Haloperidol (marketed as Haldol, Haldol Decanoate and Haldol Lactate). retrieved March 16, 2008 from http://www.fda.gov/cder/drug/InfoSheets/HCP/haloperidol.htm

U. S. Food and Drug Administration (FDA) Alert (2007c, December 12). Information for Healthcare Professionals: Carbamazepine (marketed as Carbatrol, Equetro, Tegretol, and generics). Retrieved January 26, 2008 from http://www.fda.gov/cder/drug/InfoSheets/HCP/carbamazepineHCP.htm

U. S. Food and Drug Administration (FDA) News (2008a, January 31). FDA Alerts Health Care Providers to Risk of Suicidal Thoughts and Behavior with Antiepileptic Medications. Retrieved February 1, 2008 from http://www.fda.gov/cder/drug/infopage/antiepileptics/default.htm

U. S. Food and Drug Administration (FDA) News (2008b, June 16). FDA Requests Boxed Warnings on Older Class of Antipsychotic Drugs. Retrieved June 23, 2008 from http://www.fda.gov/bbs/topics/NEWS/2008/NEW01851.html.

Van Bellinghen, M., & De Troch, C. (2001) Risperidone in the treatment of behavioral disturbances in children and adolescents with borderline intellectual functioning: a double-blind, placebo-controlled pilot trial. Journal of Child and Adolescent Psychopharmacology, 11, 5–13.

Vitiello, B. (2006). An update on publicly funded, multisite trials in pediatric psychophramacolopgy. Child and Adolescent Psychiatric Clinics of North America, 15, 1–12.

Vitiello, B. & Jensen, P. S. (1997). Medication development and testing in children and adolescents: Current problems, future directions. Archives of General Psychiatry, 54, 871–876.

Vitiello, B., Zuvekas, S. H. & Norquist, G. S. (2006). National estimates of antidepressant medication use among U.S. children. Journal of the American Academy of Child and Adolescent Psychiatry, 45, 271–279.

Volpe, R. J., Heick, P. F., & Guerasko-Moore, D. (2005). An agile behavioral model for monitoring the effects of stimulant medication in school settings. Psyhcology in the Schools, 42, 509–523.

Wagner, K. D., Adelaide S. R., Findling, R. L., Jianqing J., Gutierrez, M. M. & Heydorn, W. E. (2004). A randomized, placebo-controlled trial of citalopram for the treatment of major depression in children and adolescents. American Journal of Psychiatry, 161, 1079–1083

Wagner, K. D., Ambrosini, P., Rynn, M., Wohlberg, C., Yang, R., Greenbaum, M. S. et al. (2003). Efficacy of sertraline in the treatment of children and adolescents with major depressive disorder. Journal of the American Medical Association, 290, 1033–1041.

Wagner, K. D., Jonas, J. Findling, R. L., Ventura, D. & Khalil S. (2006). A double-blind, randomized, a placebo-controlled trial of escitalopram in the treatment of pediatric depression. Journal of the American Academy of Child and Adolescent Psychiatry, 45, 280–288.

Wagner, K. D., Berard, R., Stein, M.B., Wetherhold, E., Carpenter, D. J., Perera, J. et al. (2004). A multicenter, randomized, double-blind, placebo-controlled trial of paroxetine in children and adolescents with social anxiety disorder. Archives of General Psychiatry, 61,1153–1162.

Wagner, K.D., Kowatch, R.A., Emslie, J.G., Findling, R.L., Wilens, T.E., McCague,K., et al. (2006). A double-blind, randomized, placebo-controlled trial of oxcarbazepine in the treatment of bipolar disorder in children and adolescents. American Journal of Psychiatry, 163, 1179–1186.

Walkup, J. T., Albano, A. M., Piacentini, J., Birmaher, B., Compton, S. N., Sherrill, J. T. et al. (2008). Cognitive behavioral therapy, sertraline, or a combination in childhood anxiety. The New England Journal of Medicine, 359, 2753–2766.

Weintrob, N., Cohen, D., Klipper-Aurback, Y., Zadik, Z., & Dickerman, Z. (2002). Decreased growing during therapy with selective serotonin reuptake inhibitors. Archives of Pediatric Adolescent Medicine. 156, 696–701.

Weiss, M., Tannock, R., Kratochvil, C., Dunn, D., Velez-Borras, J., Thomason, C., et al. (2005). A randomized, placebo-controlled study of once-daily atomoxetine in school setting in children with ADHD. Journal of the American Academy of Child and Adolescent Psychiatry, 44, 647–655.

Wigal T., Greenhill L., Chuang S., McGough J., Vitiello B., Skrobala A., et al. (2006). Safety and tolerability of methylphenidate in preschool children with ADHD. *Journal of the American Academy of Child and Adolescent Psychiatry*, 45, 1294–1303.

Witwer, A. & Lecavalier, L. (2005). Treatment rates and patterns in young people with autism spectrum disorders. *Journal of Child and Adolescent Psychopharmacology*, 15, 671–681

Zametkin, A., Rapoport, J. L., Murphy, D. L., Linnoila, M. & Ismond, D. (1985). Treatment of hyperactive children with monoamine oxidase inhibitors. I. Clinical efficacy. *Archives of General Psychiatry*, 42, 962–966.

Zinner, S. (2004). Tourette syndrome-much more than tics: Management tailored to the entire patient. *Contemporary Pediatrics*, 21, 38–49.

Zito, J.M., Safer, D. J., dosReis, S., Gardner, J.F., Boles, M & Lynch, J. (2000). Trends in the prescribing of psychotropic medications to preschoolers. *Journal of the American Medical Association*, 283, 1025–1030.

Zito, J.M., Safer, D. J., dos Reis, S., Gardner, J.F., Magder, L., Soeken, K. et al., (2003). Psychotropic practice patterns for youth. *Archives of Pediatrics and Adolescent Medicine*, 157, 17–25.

Zonfrillo, M. R., Penn, J. V., & Henrietta, L. L. (2005, August). Pediatric psychotropic polypharmacy. *Psychiatry*, 2, 14–19.

Psychologically Based Treatments for Children with Medical Problems

Laura B. Allen, Jennie C. I. Tsao, Caryn Freeman, *and* Lonnie K. Zeltzer

Abstract

This chapter describes and reviews the evidence for a range of psychological treatments to assist children with medical problems. The interventions discussed in this chapter are designed to address the distress associated with a range of medical problems in children by reducing stress and anxiety, improving patients' abilities to cope with their illness, and by encouraging developmentally appropriate behaviors to promote social, academic and family functioning. The focus of this chapter is on the treatment of chronic, nonmalignant pain, since this condition involves the complex interaction of biological, psychological and social aspects and is thus well suited to psychosocial intervention. This biopsychosocial model is at the core of psychological interventions for chronic medical problems in children which aim to promote active, adaptive coping with symptoms and illness-related disability.

Keywords: psychological treatments, medical problems, children and adolescents, school psychology

Health problems in children and adolescents can have a significant impact on social, family, and academic functioning. Short-term effects of significant medical problems include missed school, withdrawal from social and physical activities, and family stress and tension. However, long-term effects of health problems in youth may be even more deleterious. In addition to placing them at risk for future health problems, significant medical conditions can also lead to chronic illness, premature death, emotional disorders, and other maladaptive behaviors such as violent or risk-taking behaviors (Power, DuPaul, Shapiro, & Parrish, 1998). Medical problems such as chronic nonmalignant pain are associated with poor academic performance and school attendance (Logan, Simons, Stein, & Chastain, 2008). This chapter will focus largely on psychosocial interventions for chronic nonmalignant pain, since there is a comprehensive literature of empirical trials of treatments targeting this condition. Moreover, it is recognized that chronic pain involves the interaction of biological, psychological and social aspects (Gatchel, Peng, Peters, Fuchs, & Turk,

2007) and is thus well suited to psychosocial intervention. This biopsychosocial model is at the core of psychosocial approaches to address the distress associated with chronic medical problems in children, and to promote active, adaptive coping with symptoms and illness-related disability (cf. Zeltzer & Schlank, 2005)

Chronic pain, including functional disorders such as Complex Regional Pain Disorder Type 1 (CRPS-1), chronic daily headaches, fibromyalgia, myofascial pain disorders, and recurrent abdominal pain, is a significant medical problem among youth. Chronic pain has been defined as recurrent or continuous pain lasting more than 3 months (Perquin et al., 2000). Epidemiological work indicates more than 45% of children aged 10–18 report chronic pain, most commonly headaches, abdominal pain, limb pain, and back pain (Perquin et al., 2000; Roth-Isigkeit, Thyen, Raspe, Stoven, & Schmucker, 2004). These youth can exhibit patterns of "doctor-seeking" and over-utilization of medications, as well as high levels of psychosocial distress, particularly symptoms of anxiety and depression (Palermo,

Krell, Janosy, & Zeltzer, 2008; Zeltzer & Krell, 2007).

There are also significant economic costs associated with medical problems such as chronic pain. For example, use of healthcare services is higher in adolescents with chronic pain, resulting in significant financial burdens to families and government programs. One study of 70 adolescents with juvenile rheumatoid arthritis found the mean annualized direct cost per child was $7,905, with extra school costs estimated at $1,449 and family costs at $1,524/year (Allaire, DeNardo, Szer, Meenan, & Schaller, 1992). More recently, annual costs for each child with chronic pain in the United Kingdom (UK) are estimated at £8000 ($14,000), resulting in a yearly nationwide cost of £3840 million (Sleed, Eccleston, Beecham, Knapp, & Jordan, 2005).

As a result of the increasing demand placed on the healthcare system, school psychologists and other treatment providers are increasingly utilized as a method for delivery of psychosocial support to children with medical problems. Although some school psychologists provide consultation and assessment services, many also provide direct psychological services to students with medical problems. School psychologists, in particular, are in a unique position to be able to provide varied levels of psychosocial treatment, depending on the particular needs of each student (Brown & DuPaul, 1999). This chapter will review several psychologically based treatments for children with various medical conditions that would be applicable to psychologists providing interventions in a school based setting.

Cognitive-Behavioral Therapy (CBT)
Background
The origins of CBT began in the 1960s, when psychologists attempted to modify behavioral responses to situations in a systematic manner. Behavioral strategies such as "systematic desensitization" (Wolpe, 1958) were introduced and applied to patients with phobias, resulting in occasional mild relief of anxiety symptoms. Wolpe (1958) hypothesized that this strategy was helpful because of "reciprocal inhibition"—the concept that inhibiting the fear response (i.e., through relaxation techniques) during exposure to a phobic stimulus will alter the conditioned fear response, and subsequently result in decreased anxiety. Although this technique was not helpful for individuals with more widespread fears and phobias, Wolpe's attempts to expose the individual to feared stimuli nonetheless represented the

beginnings of exposure-based behavioral treatments. Future research began to explore situational exposure for extensive phobic behavior, such as agoraphobia (i.e., fear of places where escape may be difficult, such as crowded places, due to concerns of experiencing severe anxiety), with more success (e.g., Agras, Leitenberg, & Barlow, 1968; Marks, 1971).

The introduction of cognitive therapy (CT; Beck, 1972; Beck, 1976; Beck, Rush, Shaw, & Emery, 1979) in the 1970s, originally for the treatment of depression, was a tremendous advancement in effectiveness of psychotherapy for a variety of emotional problems. CT assumes that an individual's maladaptive, automatic thoughts lead to more problematic thoughts, feelings, and behaviors; thus, CT strategies focus on identifying these thoughts and "restructuring" or changing them to be more adaptive and objective. When used in combination with behavioral modification strategies, results from clinical trials in the 1980s suggested individualized CBT protocols for anxiety, depression, and other disorders were highly efficacious (Barlow, 2002).

In contrast to the adult literature's emphasis on disorder-specific approaches to psychopathology (e.g., CBT for panic disorder only), research in children and adolescents supports the benefit of non-disorder-specific approaches. In youth, CBT approaches must also consider the child's internal and external environment, as well as developmental stage (Kendall, 1993). Some CBT protocols have included a family-based component (Barrett, Dadds, & Rapee, 1996; Shortt, Barrett, & Fox, 2001), although recent evidence suggests that there are no significant advantages to include family, in at least the treatment of anxiety-disordered youth (Kendall, Hudson, Gosch, Flannery-Schroeder, & Suveg, 2008).

Now, there is strong support for the efficacy of CBT techniques in youth for a variety of emotional and related problems. An initial randomized clinical trial (RCT) of CBT for children and adolescents with anxiety disorders suggested the cognitive and behavioral strategies could be useful in significantly reducing anxiety symptoms in youth (Kendall, 1994). Subsequently, numerous studies have confirmed the superiority of CBT for treating anxious youth (e.g., Barrett, Rapee, Dadds, & Ryan 1996) as compared to waitlist control (Compton et al., 2004), with gains maintained for several years following treatment (Barrett, Duffy, Dadds, & Rapee, 2001). Kendall, Brady, and Verduin (2001) demonstrated a positive impact of CBT for a range of principal anxiety disorders, including generalized anxiety disorder (GAD), separation anxiety disorder, and social phobia, on other comorbid anxiety disorders in children aged 8–13 years. Other studies of anxious youth have found significant decreases in depression following CBT for anxiety (Barrett et al., 1996; Kendall et al., 1997; Mendlowitz et al., 1999). Moreover, a CBT-based universal prevention program for children at risk for anxiety disorders led to improved anxiety and depression symptoms (Lowry-Webster, Barrett, & Dadds, 2001). Recently, a review of ten RCTs examining CBT for child and adolescent anxiety disorders reported a significantly higher remission rate for the CBT groups (56.5%) as compared to the control groups (34.8%), suggesting that CBT for youth anxiety has a strong effect (Cartwright-Hatton, Roberts, Chitsabesan, Fothergill, & Harrington, 2004). In addition to anxiety disorders, CBT principles have also been applied to youth with depression (e.g., Stark, Rouse, & Livingston, 1991) and anger/aggression (e.g., Kazdin, 2007).

A particularly interesting application of CBT involves using these principles when working with children and adolescents with medical problems (Kendall & Braswell, 1986). A significant portion of research in this area has focused on chronic pediatric pain, because CBT approaches are ideally suited to addressing two specific aspects of the pain experience: pain perception (cognition) and pain coping (behavior; (Varni, 1991). In addition, at least for chronic pain sufferers, appropriate pain management is rarely achieved by standard medical care (Eccleston & Malleson, 2003). When chronic pain cannot be fully alleviated, the optimal goal is for the patient to learn effective ways to continue functioning and to self-manage pain. CBT seeks to mediate behavioral change through cognitive relearning, and changing behavioral responses to pain.

CBT has been shown to be effective for a variety of chronic pain syndromes in children, including recurrent abdominal pain (Robins, Smith, Glutting, & Bishop, 2005; Sanders, Shepherd, Cleghorn, & Woolford, 1994) and pediatric migraine (Fentress, Masek, Mehegan, & Benson, 1986). In the first published RCT of CBT for adolescents (ages 10–17) with chronic fatigue syndrome (CFS), results indicated that patients who received CBT reported significantly lower fatigue severity and functional impairment as compared to patients in the waitlist control condition (Stulemeijer, de Jong, Fiselier, Hoogveld, & Bleijenberg, 2005), and some gains

were further improved at follow-up (Knoop, Stulemeijer, de Jong, Fiselier, & Bleijenberg, 2008). A pilot study of a cognitive-behavioral intervention for a sample of eight adolescents with various pain problems suggested that this type of program improves mastery of pain and improved quality of life, while being feasible for patients and their families (Merlijn et al., 2005). An interdisciplinary group cognitive-behavioral intervention for adolescents with chronic pain has also demonstrated improved functioning and decreased anxiety both immediately after and three months following treatment (Eccleston, Malleson, Clinch, Connell, & Sourbut, 2003).

Description and Application of CBT

In common with CBT for mental disorders, CBT for chronic pain incorporates methods such as education, verbal reinforcement for positive cognitions and actions, and cognitive reframing of negative thoughts, to help the patient develop positive expectations of behavior change, minimize negative expectations, and internalize the conviction of his/her own ability to overcome barriers and effectively self-manage medical problems. In effect, the patient becomes the agent of change (Turk, 2002, 2003). To this end, CBT sessions are often structured and symptom-focused, but may be conducted either individually or in a group setting. Although it is beyond the scope of this chapter to describe in detail the various CBT protocols for different medical conditions, we will review the basic elements of a CBT protocol as it is applied to adolescent chronic pain.

PSYCHOEDUCATION

The first phase of treatment involves providing the patient (and family, if possible) with psychoeducation about chronic pain and the social, environmental, and biological factors that contribute to the pain experience. The clinician will also want to identify maladaptive thoughts and feelings that exacerbate pain, and how the patient copes with and responds to pain (i.e., withdrawal from activities, isolation, etc.). Psychoeducation is a critical step in the treatment process that will assist in building rapport with the clinician, allowing the patient (or family) to openly discuss thoughts and feelings (Roy-Byrne, Wagner, & Schraufnagel, 2005). The interaction between three components of pain (thoughts, feelings, and behaviors), and how the treatment will address each component, is then reviewed.

SELF-MONITORING

Monitoring of pain and emotional states outside of the therapy session is an essential component of any CBT protocol. Self-monitoring typically begins following the first session, so that the patient (1) develops the habit early, and (2) is able to recognize external (situations) and internal (thoughts, feelings) concomitants/triggers associated with pain. Objective monitoring of events over the course of the week is also helpful in developing an "observer's perspective" for the adolescent, which can be used to track progress and it is an excellent tool for the clinician to gain a more detailed perspective of functioning over the week.

PROBLEM SOLVING

Problem solving skills assist the patient with decision making, and taking action to correct a situation that may be contributing to the patient's physical or emotional distress (D'Zurilla, 1986). As the patient's functioning improves, he/she may encounter new challenges where a direct application of skills to the problem itself is needed. This is different than the coping skills taught to manage pain and related emotions in other parts of the protocol, where the focus is on changing *internal* events. Problem solving steps include identifying triggers for pain, stress, and related emotions, reviewing past solutions and their outcomes, exploring new solutions, and implementing these solutions (Lipchik, Smitherman, Penzien, & Holroyd, 2006).

COGNITIVE RESTRUCTURING

Cognitive restructuring techniques assist the patient in identifying automatic, maladaptive (and often negative) thoughts or predictions about a situation. Cognitions are considered maladaptive if they: (1) occur automatically, without full consideration of the situation or the evidence for the thought; (2) they lead to increased discomfort or distress beyond what would be expected from the situation; or (3) they result in behaviors that are also maladaptive, such as withdrawal. The patient is first asked to monitor thoughts during episodes of pain, stress, anxiety, or any other emotion. Next, common cognitive distortions/errors are reviewed (e.g., catastrophizing, probability overestimation, black and white thinking), and the patient is asked to identify the cognitive distortion present in the automatic thought. Once the distortion is identified, the clinician assists the patient in challenging the thought by reviewing evidence supporting the validity of the thought, and by assessing the patient's ability to cope with the situation, if the thought were true. Based on this procedure, alternative, adaptive thoughts are generated.

BEHAVIORAL ASSIGNMENTS, ACTIVATION, AND EXPOSURES

Behavioral strategies used in CBT protocols aim to reduce the conditioned, maladaptive behavior patterns that occur in response to a particular event or emotion. These maladaptive behaviors are typically habitual and have been maintained through the principles of negative reinforcement. For example, if even minimal relief is attained by withdrawing from activity, the behavior (withdrawal) will become powerfully conditioned to the pain experience because of its ability to minimize the pain, even if only briefly (Turk, Swanson, & Tunks, 2008). Behavioral assignments and behavioral activation strategies include setting specific active, behavioral goals for each week, such as exercising daily (doing a specified exercise for a predetermined length of time), adhering to a sleep schedule, or changing eating habits. Behavioral strategies can also focus on medication compliance, if that is an issue. Again, self-monitoring is a critical aspect of behavior change, so that the patient can see his/her progress, and potential obstacles to completing the behavioral plan can be identified and eliminated.

In addition to a behavioral plan to improve functioning, behavioral assignments may also include "exposing" the patient to thoughts, emotions, physical sensations, or situations that are distressing. A clear example of this is in the treatment of phobias, where a CBT approach would include helping the patient approach and confront the feared stimulus, rather than avoiding it (Antony & Barlow, 2002). Among children with chronic pain, fear of pain following activity can be addressed in a similar fashion by assisting the patient in gradually engaging in the feared activity. Increasing activity level is particularly important because avoidance of activity contributes to strength deconditioning and, ultimately, increased pain.

Certainly, behaviorally based exposures can prove challenging with more complex, widespread medical and emotional disorders, but the essential target of change remains the same. Exposure-based treatments are conducted in a controlled manner, with full cooperation of the patient at every step. The negative effects of avoidance of situations and feelings are highlighted, to increase motivation and compliance with exposures. Next, a situational hierarchy is created to identify a range of uncomfortable situations for future exposure planning. Ideally, the clinician and the patient work progressively up the hierarchy and eventually conduct exposures in the most difficult situations. For an adolescent with chronic pain, exposure-based treatments might include visiting places where he/she experiences strong pain memories, doing exercises that cause some discomfort without causing any injury, or specifically recalling pain-related memories that are distressing.

Therapists do not need to obtain a particular license or certification to administer CBT. However, training workshops, seminars, and manuals are available to assist clinicians with implementing the concepts in session. Because CBT is highly structured, it may be more easily administered by even somewhat inexperienced therapists. However, supervision and training in various protocols will certainly facilitate the application of more complex strategies such as cognitive restructuring, and designing and implementing exposures.

Studies have supported the use of master-level clinicians in successfully implementing CBT protocols for panic disorder in adults, although recent evidence suggests some benefit to therapist experience, at least when treating panic disorder with agoraphobia with a highly structured CBT protocol (Huppert et al., 2001). However, distance approaches with minimal therapist contact are now gaining support. A recent pilot of a CD-ROM based CBT intervention for pediatric headache has showed that children who received the CD-ROM intervention showed greater improvement in headache activity than those who received treatment as usual (TAU) (Connelly, Rapoff, Thompson, & Connelly, 2006). Similar results have been obtained using a CD-ROM for children with cystic fibrosis (Davis, Quittner, Stack, & Yang, 2004), and using Internet- and telephone-based interventions for pediatric pain (Hicks, von Baeyer, & McGrath, 2006; Palermo, Wilson, Peters, Lewandowski, & Somhegyi, 2009).

Biofeedback
Background
Biofeedback is a technique that improves self-regulation of physiological responses (such as pain or anxiety) by using a computer or other feedback device to promote awareness and voluntary control of physiology. As early as the 1970s, research was emerging on the use of biofeedback in patients with headache. Prior research had used electromyographic (EMG) integration circuits to evaluate physiology associated with headache, and this technique

was subsequently evaluated as a treatment by providing headache patients with feedback about their stress response, so that they could control their levels of relaxation (Budzynski, Stoyva, Adler, & Mullaney, 1973). This method is known as electromyographic biofeedback (EMG-BFB). Another technique commonly used is thermal biofeedback (TFB), which teaches the patient to control the heat of the body by providing feedback on the temperature of the skin (Hermann & Blanchard, 2002). Other monitored changes can include muscle tension, sweat gland response, brain wave activity, or breathing rate, with the goals of giving the patient a sense of control and mastery over his/her physiology, and increasing relaxation.

Biofeedback is especially popular for the treatment of migraine and headaches, although it may be used for other medical conditions, such as asthma (Bray, Kehle, Grigerick, Loftus, & Nicolson, 2007). Numerous studies have documented improvement in both frequency and intensity of headaches in adults, and early meta-analyses have confirmed that biofeedback can result in up to 65% improvement in pain (Blanchard & Andrasik, 1987; Blanchard, Andrasik, Ahles, Teders, & O'Keefe, 1980). In addition, in a recent comprehensive review of the efficacy of biofeedback for headaches in adults, Nestoriuc, Martin, Rief, and Andrasik (2008) found medium to large effect sizes for adult patients with migraine or tension type headaches. Furthermore, significant improvements in perceived self-efficacy, anxiety and depression, and medication consumption were observed.

However, the efficacy of biofeedback in children is less clear. One study (Scharff, Marcus, & Masek, 2002) examined two types of TBF (handwarming biofeedback – HWB and, handcooling biofeedback - HCB) and a waitlist control in 36 children with migraine, and found that a significantly greater proportion of the HWB group (53.8%) achieved clinically significant improvement (i.e., greater than 50% reduction in symptoms) compared with the HCB group (10%) at post-treatment, and at 3- and 6-month follow-ups. The waiting list group did not show significant changes. However, because TBF was part of a treatment package that included many other components (i.e. progressive muscle relaxation, imagery training of warm places and vasodilation, and instruction in deep breathing), it is not possible to attribute the improvement in headache symptoms solely to the TBF.

Other studies examining BFB for pediatric tension headache have reported high success rates

(80%–90%) (Grazzi, Leone, Frediani, & Bussone, 1990; Kroner-Herwig, Mohn, & Pothmann, 1998; Kroner-Herwig, Plump, & Pothmann, 1992), although two of these studies were conducted by the same research group, and the generalizability of the findings are limited by small cell sizes and large variation in treatment outcome (Hermann & Blanchard, 2002). In addition to EMG–BFB, two additional studies have examined the addition of BFB to relaxation strategies in children with tension headaches. Only one of these studies (Bussone, Grazzi, D'Amico, Leone, & Andrasik, 1998) used a randomized controlled design, comparing EMG–BFB with relaxation in 35 children (aged 11–15 years). Results indicated that although the groups were equivalent at one month post-treatment, by 6- and 12-month follow-ups, the EMG–BFB group achieved significantly greater reductions in symptoms compared with controls. Furthermore, in a recent meta-analysis of psychological treatments for children with recurrent headache, Trautmann, Lackschewitz, and Kroner-Herwig (2006) found that over 50% of children who received biofeedback demonstrated clinically significant change; however, the change in actual headache intensity, duration, and frequency yielded only small to medium effect sizes. Although these data are promising, further research is needed to determine the efficacy of different types of biofeedback for different pediatric populations, and carefully controlled, randomized studies are essential.

Description and Application of BFB

During a biofeedback session, electrodes are attached to the patient's skin on the area of the body that the biofeedback will be measuring. These electrodes then feed physiological information to a box that translates this information into a tone that varies in

pitch, a visual meter that varies in brightness, or a computer screen that varies the lines moving across a grid, depending on the type of biofeedback used. As previously mentioned, EMG–BFB measures muscle tension, and can be used to help the patient identify when his/her muscles are relaxed, so that relaxation can be induced outside of the session. It is also possible to monitor the body's temperature (TFB), sweat gland response, brain wave activity, or breathing or heart rate. The clinician then leads the patient in various mental exercises to assist with modifying the signal in the desired direction (e.g., lowering the tone by relaxing one's muscles). Whichever modality is used, the patient is provided with feedback about physiological responding during stress; then, he/she can use this information to become more aware of stress-related physical sensations, and implement relaxation strategies to combat the stress. Through trial and error, patients can soon learn to identify and control the activities that will bring about the desired physical changes. Eventually, these new relaxation responses can be used in a variety of situations, so that overall levels of stress (and pain) are reduced. Biofeedback sessions typically last 30 to 60 minutes and can be conducted in any type of treatment setting, with the appropriate equipment.

No specific license is required to perform for biofeedback. Most practitioners have other licenses such as R.N. (Registered Nurse), M.F.T (Marriage and Family Therapist), L.I.C.S.W. (Licensed Independent Clinical Social Worker), or are physical therapists or psychologists. However, biofeedback certification is available, and may be required by some states. No clinician should practice biofeedback without first receiving proper training.

Yoga
Background

Yoga was first developed in ancient India as a physical activity designed to incorporate principles of meditation, posture, and breathing to promote physical and psychological health and well-being. Many forms of yoga exist, including *Iyengar yoga*—a form of yoga commonly used to treat chronic pain conditions (Evans, Subramanian, & Sternlieb, 2008). Iyengar yoga is a form of *Hatha yoga*, which is a branch of yoga that deals with the physical body and is frequently practiced in the United States. The yoga poses are intended to correct health related problems, both in body structure and in internal organ function, and to promote a sense of mastery over the body through a series of specific *asanas*

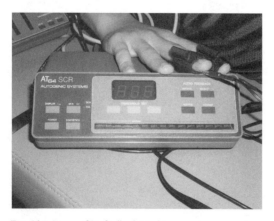

Fig. 36.1 Image of Biofeedback Machine

(body postures), *pranayama* (prescribed breathing patterns), and meditation. The poses allow patients to look at the underlying causes and habits that may contribute to their pain problems, and learn how to change them.

Most research studies evaluating the efficacy of yoga for treating medical conditions have been conducted with adults. Reduced pain and disability, and increased quality of life have been reported in RCTs of yoga for migraine and headaches (John, Sharma, Sharma, & Kankane, 2007; Latha & Kaliappan, 1992), rheumatoid arthritis (Garfinkel et al., 1998), osteoarthritis (Garfinkel, Schumacher, Husain, Levy, & Reshetar, 1994), asthma (Jain & Talukdar, 1993), and chronic low back pain (Williams et al., 2005). A review of the literature on yoga for cancer (Bower, Woolery, Sternlieb, & Garet, 2005) concluded that yoga interventions consistently yield modest improvement across a range of outcomes, including psychological (mood, distress, stress) and somatic (e.g., sleep disturbance) symptoms. Other reviews of yoga for pain, disability and quality of life (Evans et al., 2008), as well as depression (Pilkington, Kirkwood, Rampes, & Richardson, 2005) and anxiety (Kirkwood, Rampes, Tuffrey, Richardson, & Pilkington, 2005), have noted that yoga appears to enhance physical and psychological functioning, although much of the literature is limited by methodological problems, including small sample sizes, unclear description of randomization, and lack of appropriate control groups.

Empirical research on the specific effects of yoga among children and adolescents is lacking, although the available research suggests yoga is promising as a treatment for medical problems in children and adolescents. Jain and colleagues (1991) examined the efficacy of yoga in 46 adolescents ages 11–18 with asthma, and found that daily yoga was associated with improved lung function and exercise capacity. In addition, one recent RCT of 25 adolescents (ages 11–18) with irritable bowel syndrome (IBS) compared a home-based yoga intervention (guided by video) to a waitlist control group. Post-treatment data revealed significantly lower levels of functional disability, decreased use of emotion-focused avoidance, and lower anxiety for individuals in the yoga condition, as compared to the control condition (Kuttner et al., 2006). Although further research in younger populations is warranted, Bray and colleagues (Bray et al., 2007) as well as others (e.g., Evans et al., 2008) suggest that yoga is a calming activity that can promote stress reduction and self-efficacy, so it may be very useful for children with medical concerns.

Description and Application of Yoga

Iyengar yoga is a traditional form of yoga taught in the lineage of BKS Iyengar, who is known for his prominent texts on yoga, his influence on the practice of yoga, and his innovative teaching techniques (Iyengar, 1966, 2001, 2005). Iyengar yoga is an ideal form of activity for people with health needs, as the emphasis on alignment in this practice protects muscles, organs and joints, yet involves sufficient movement to increase circulation and breathing capacity. Young children or adolescents with medical problems, who may experience pain or discomfort, can perform postures with the support of props (blocks, bolsters, chairs, straps, and blankets) that allow postures to be held without stress. Yoga postures are designed to promote circulation and stimulate the hormonal and lymphatic systems through body position and muscle activity. The use of props allows postures to be held for long periods of time without fatigue, so that relevant systems are activated without strain.

Yoga sessions are typically conducted 1 to 2 times per week, with at-home practice encouraged. Both private and group lessons are typically offered, although the poses can be challenging at the beginning, which is why private lessons may be preferable for someone who is unfamiliar with the practice.

It is best for children to learn yoga with a qualified teacher. Such teachers may be brought into schools or other settings, for individual or group sessions. Iyengar yoga is renowned for its extensive teacher training, and instructors study for at least seven years before being certified to work with students who have therapeutic needs. They must pass several certification tests before an impartial national board. These tests include teaching, performance of

Fig. 36.2 Image of Patient in a Yoga Pose

poses and breathing techniques, anatomy, and therapeutic sequences. It is important that a yoga exercise program is developed by a qualified individual who knows human physiology and can tailor the yoga program to the needs of the child with medical problems.

Relaxation and Guided Imagery
Background
Relaxation and guided imagery (RGI) combination interventions include two components: (a) a relaxation component to reduce stress and sympathetic arousal, and (b) a guided imagery component that helps the patient form a mental picture of healing his/her medical condition (Zahourek, 1988). RGI is a self-regulatory strategy aimed to promote improvement in medical conditions through deactivation of the sympathetic nervous system and the stress response. Although relaxation strategies alone have been shown to be beneficial for a variety of medical complaints, including adolescents with headaches (Larsson, Carlsson, Fichtel, & Melin, 2005), it is believed that the addition of the guided imagery component may provide added benefit, particularly for children with pain (Weydert et al., 2006). Weydert et al. (2006) state that RGI allows for the patient to tap into the subliminal mind to access and change aspects of the autonomic nervous system. The authors propose that, through imagining and communicating with the images generated during the practice, it is possible to activate aspects of the body that can facilitate deep relaxation, decrease anxiety, and improve healing. It has also been thought that imagery promotes a greater sense of control and mastery over undesirable physical sensations and illnesses (Neparstek, 1994). Sodergren's (1992) extensive review of 44 early studies using RGI suggest that this strategy is useful in helping adult patients manage a variety of symptoms including pain, anxiety, depression, hypertension, and problem solving. Giedt (1997) also suggests that RGI can assist with immune function, to help patients with diseases such as cancer and HIV.

However, far less empirical research has been carried out in younger populations, despite the notion that children are ideally suited to RGI because of their active imaginations (Rusy & Weisman, 2000). In one study of children with recurrent abdominal pain (RAP), 18 patients were treated with RGI, and across a mean of 4.3 sessions (Youssef et al., 2004). Follow-up data indicated that abdominal pain improved in 89% of patients, and significant decreases in weekly pain episodes, pain intensity,

and missed school days, were also observed. However, the study did not include a control group, so it is difficult to directly attribute these improvements to RGI. A pilot study of RGI for children with RAP found that the patients experienced a 67% decrease in pain during the therapy (Ball, Shapiro, Monheim, & Weydert, 2003). A follow-up to this study compared RGI with breathing exercises in 22 children with RAP (ages 5–18; (Weydert et al., 2006). Although the children in the RGI group had significantly more days of pain at baseline, follow-up data revealed the RGI group experienced a significantly greater decrease in the number of days with pain (67%) as compared to the breathing exercise group (21%). Children in the RGI group also had significantly fewer days with missed activities, and a greater proportion had less than 5 days per month of pain in comparison to children in the breathing exercise group. RGI has also been shown to be efficacious in reducing the length of symptomatic episodes in adolescents with recurrent upper respiratory tract infections, as compared to a control group (Hewson-Bower & Drummond, 2001). In addition, in a multiple baseline design of four children with asthma, Peck, Bray, and Kehle (2003) found that a school-based RGI program improved lung function and decreased anxiety in the majority of the students. Taken together, these data suggest that RGI is a safe and probably efficacious treatment for medical conditions in children and adolescents.

Description and Application of RGI
Imagery is the "deliberate formation of a mental representation while in a deeply relaxed state" and can have "visual, auditory, olfactory, gustatory, or tactile-proprioceptive" qualities (Giedt, 1997, p. 115). Guided imagery refers to the use of any device to promote imagery, such as a story, particular scents, visual cues, or a therapist's voice. During a guided imagery session, the patient begins by getting in a relaxed state through the use of meditation or breathing exercises. He/she may be sitting or lying down, with eyes open or closed. The focus is on promoting comfort and relaxation for the patient.

Once relaxation has been attained, the patient is asked to visualize a safe, comfortable place, and focus on the qualities of that place to enhance the imagery. The particular place – real or imaginary – is not important; rather, it is important that the patient focus on the specific qualities of the image to further enhance the strength of the image–feeling connection. Next, the patient is asked to form a visual representation of his/her illness or physical symptoms (e.g., nausea, pain, discomfort). The representation may consist of various colors, shapes, or objects, or it may be a single object. The therapist asks the patient to describe the illness (or physical sensation) in detail, and then identify how the patient would like it to change. For example, the patient may envision the illness or sensation being destroyed by an outside force, or slowly shrinking until it is no longer present. Again, the specific manner in which the illness or symptom is eliminated is not important. Depending on the distress level of the patient, the clinician may ask the patient to then return to the image of the safe, comfortable place, after several minutes or longer. The session is concluded by focusing on the safe, comfortable place to promote further relaxation. Once the patient becomes more comfortable with the process, sessions may last longer, or include several images. Audio recordings may also be helpful for use at home.

Unlike biofeedback treatment, therapists performing RGI typically do not require specialized training, although such training is available through private companies. Clinicians practicing RGI include nurses, L.I.C.S.W.s, M.F.T.s, and psychologists. If a clinician has not ever conducted an RGI session, it is advisable that he/she obtain some supervision from an experienced practitioner to ensure the treatment is implemented correctly.

Hypnotherapy
Background
Like many of the therapies described earlier, hypnotherapy is based upon a mind-body approach to healing, where the focus is on helping the mind heal the body when the body may not be able to be healed directly. Hypnosis was initially developed over 200 years ago as a method to treat medical conditions when other effective treatment modalities were not available (Stewart, 2005). However, it wasn't until the 1950s that hypnosis was recognized as a possible treatment by both the British and American Medical Associations. Despite these advances, existing literature on hypnosis has suffered from a paucity of well-controlled, randomized studies (Gold, Kant, Belmont, & Butler, 2007) and lack of agreement over what specific techniques constitute "hypnosis" (Tsao & Zeltzer, 2005). This lack of consistency in definition is evident in that terms such as hypnotherapy, imagery, and relaxation that have been used interchangeably to describe hypnotic techniques. In response to this criticism, the American Psychological Association's Division

of Hypnosis stated that hypnosis has occurred when a person responds to another person's suggestions, as evidenced by changes in subjective perception, including thoughts, feelings, behavior, or sensations (Green, Barabasz, Barrett, & Montgomery, 2005).

Neuroimaging research is now emerging that provides support for deactivation (and activation) of brain areas associated with arousal, visual imagery, and perceptual experiences (Rainville, Hofbauer, Bushnell, Duncan, & Price, 2002), which corroborates clinical and research reports that hypnosis is highly effective in treating a variety of psychological and medical complaints. A recent meta-analysis of 22 studies explored the efficacy of hypnotherapy for psychosomatic complaints (Flammer & Alladin, 2007). The studies included in this meta-analysis focused primarily on adults (although four studies focused on children, or both children and adults) and were categorized into classical hypnosis, modern hypnosis, or mixed. Classical hypnosis consisted of interventions with direct suggestions for relaxation, imagination, or elimination of symptoms, whereas modern hypnosis included interventions with more implicit methods such as metaphors (e.g., using the analogy of a burning flame dying down with less air, to describe pain that diminishes with less stress) or age regression. Results indicated that, overall, hypnotherapy produced a medium effect size for the treatment of psychosomatic complaints, although when analyzed separately, modern and mixed hypnotherapies produced better outcomes than classical hypnosis. Interestingly, the authors also found that the number of treatment sessions was not related to treatment outcome.

A consistent body of literature supports the use of hypnotherapy for treating both acute and chronic pain in adults (for a review, see Patterson, 2004). There is also some evidence that self-hypnosis can be a helpful adjunctive treatment for hay fever. In an RCT, 24 patients with hay fever received hypnosis plus TAU, and 28 patients with hay fever received TAU alone over the course of one year (Langewitz et al., 2005). During the second year, the hypnosis group continued to receive hypnosis (and TAU), and the control group also received hypnosis plus TAU. Generally, results indicated that individuals in the hypnosis group retrospectively reported fewer symptoms during the previous pollen season, although this finding was not supported when comparing the daily symptom logs kept by patients during this time. However, following hypnosis, there was evidence of decreased medication use and increased tolerance to allergen exposure.

In children, hypnosis has been used to treat various medical conditions, including dyspnea (difficulty breathing; (Anbar, 2001a), cystic fibrosis (Belsky & Khanna, 1994), and dermatological conditions such as eczema (Sokel et al., 1993). Hypnotherapy is also a promising treatment for asthma in children (Hackman, Stern, & Gershwin, 2000). The first controlled study of hypnosis for asthma in 25 children showed no improvement in symptoms at post-treatment or one-month follow-up (Smith & Burns, 1960); however, future studies including waitlist of treatment controls reported outcomes that were more favorable (cf. Brown, 2007). Kohen (1995) reported that hypnosis resulted in improved quality of life for children with asthma, although no evidence of physiological improvements in lung functioning were evident. Another study found no changes in asthma attacks, although parental reports indicated decreased doctor visits and emergency room visits as a result of hypnosis (Kohen & Wynne, 1997). Some authors have suggested that hypnosis may be particularly useful for children with asthma because hypnotherapy promotes awareness of physical functioning, and a greater sense of self-efficacy and competency for dealing with and responding to asthma attacks (Bray et al., 2007). Although the exact mechanisms underlying improvement in asthmatic children as a result of hypnosis remain unclear, it is nonetheless a safe, effective, and useful adjunct to other medical and psychological treatments (Kohen, 1995).

Hypnotherapy has also been used in children and adolescents with chronic pain. A review of 11 studies testing the use of hypnosis for pediatric headaches indicated relaxation/self-hypnosis to be a well established and efficacious treatment, with evidence of gains being maintained over time (Holden, Deichmann, & Levy, 1999). Vlieger, Menko-Frankenhuis, Wolfkamp, Tromp, and Benninga (2007) tested the efficacy of hypnotherapy in a sample of pediatric patients (ages 8–18) with functional abdominal pain (FAP). Twenty-eight patients were randomized to receive six sessions of gut-directed hypnotherapy (a hypnotherapy directed specifically at sensations in the gut) over a 3-month period; 25 received standard medical treatment and six sessions of supportive therapy (SMT). Results indicated that pain scores decreased significantly for both groups from baseline to 12 months post-treatment, although the hypnotherapy group evidenced a significantly greater decline in pain scores than the SMT group. Furthermore, 85% of individuals in the hypnotherapy group were considered successfully treated

at the one-year follow-up, as compared to only 25% in the SMT group. Another study of children with FAP ages 8–16 also found that 80% of patients were able to successfully eliminate their pain within a 3-week period by engaging in self-hypnosis daily (Anbar, 2001b).

Description and Application of Hypnosis

During hypnosis, modification or enhancement of sensation and perception often occurs, and it is been suggested that children's increased susceptibility to hypnosis makes them ideal candidates for this treatment modality (Tsao & Zeltzer, 2005). However, depending on the age of the child, specific modifications of the hypnotherapy may be required to be more developmentally appropriate. As the child gets older, cognitive abilities develop and more adult language can be used. However, for younger children, concrete examples and language should be employed. For these reasons, it is important that a hypnotherapist be familiar with a variety of techniques. In addition, most hypnotherapy treatments require daily practice to be successful, so the child must not feel "forced" to do the practice, or it is likely to be unsuccessful (Olness, 2008).

A hypnotherapy session is typically conducted once per week or less frequently. These sessions are essentially training session in self-hypnosis, so that the patient can then practice the self-hypnosis at home daily. During a session, the therapist helps the patient attain a state of relaxation, which can be done through breathing exercises, a guided meditation, or having the patient focus on a specific visual point. Once in this relaxed state, the therapist will make either specific or general directions designed to modify particular symptoms. The patient may be asked specifically to recall times when the symptom was not present, or he/she may recall generally feeling strong or healthy. The therapist and patient focus on that feeling or modification of symptom during the hypnosis. The therapist may also tell a story that incorporates the change in behavior or symptoms that the patient desires. Following the session, the patient is asked to continue practicing on his/her own.

Hypnotherapists can obtain varying levels of certification through state boards, and the requirements for practicing vary by state. Hypnosis board examinations are given in areas such as psychology, medicine, and social work, and the American Society of Clinical Hypnosis offers a certification program for professionals (Olness, 2008). Training courses and private certification are available in most locations.

Again, it is best to receive supervision from an experienced clinician prior to practicing hypnotherapy independently.

Future Directions

Psychologically based treatments are an essential component to helping children with medical problems (cf. Evans & Zeltzer, 2008). However, few studies to date have been conducted within the school setting. Thus, there is little information on *which* psychosocial interventions are most suitable to the school environment, as well as *how* these treatments may best be delivered and by *whom*. Whereas the existing literature indicates that several psychosocial approaches, including CBT, hypnosis, and biofeedback, have demonstrated efficacy in reducing distressing symptoms including pain, other modalities such as yoga have not been the subject of sufficient research. Moreover, there is a dearth of information regarding the patient, family and environmental factors that may impact treatment response. Thus, additional studies are needed to specify which patients are most likely to benefit from psychosocial approaches, and how the family as well as the school contexts may be modified to achieve optimal therapeutic results.

Generally speaking, research on psychological interventions for children with medical problems would benefit from a more systematic approach to developing a supportive evidence base. As discussed by Wild and Espie (2004) many studies in the hypnosis literature have compared an unproven intervention to an already-established treatment, without first showing that the intervention is superior to a no-treatment control or standard medical care. Thus, these authors recommend that investigators first compare the new approach to a no-intervention or "care as usual" condition. Pending successful completion of these initial studies, the results should then be replicated in large-scale, randomized studies, perhaps drawing from multiple settings in order to provide sufficient sample sizes. Only if the results of these first-step studies show that the new intervention yields benefits exceeding that of standard care or no-intervention, should further work be undertaken to compare the new intervention to established therapies and/or an attention-control/placebo condition. Another important consideration is isolating the therapeutic ingredient(s) that leads to change. Given that many of the psychological interventions discussed above have been studied within the context of an overall treatment package that includes many different treatment components,

careful treatment dismantling studies testing the efficacy of each individual component should also be conducted, if the overall package is shown to be efficacious.

Several additional recommendations may be incorporated into future work. First, the psychological intervention to be tested should be standardized using a treatment manual or its equivalent. Use of a manual will allow assessments of the degree of adherence to the treatment protocol on the part of therapists, and will also allow the replication of results by independent research groups. The lack of standardization appears to be particularly problematic in the hypnosis literature, which has a relatively large body of studies dating back over 20 years. However, it should be noted that more recent hypnosis research has incorporated manualized treatment (Liossi & Hatira, 2003). Second, increased attention should be paid to methodological confounds that may lead positive findings to be attributable to nonspecific effects, rather than specific effects of the intervention. Among the most important considerations include: (1) randomization of group assignment; (2) use of valid and reliable outcome measures; (3) inclusion of sufficient sample sizes to achieve adequate statistical power to detect between-group differences; and (4) use of an appropriate control condition. Finally, even though mechanisms of action in psychosocial interventions may not be well understood, systematic testing of existing mechanistic models should be pursued (Wild & Espie, 2004). Hermann and Blanchard (2002) pointed out that if the beneficial effects of biofeedback on pain are found to be mediated by psychological (e.g., self-efficacy) rather than physiological (e.g., muscle tension) factors, this would increase the likelihood that biofeedback will be studied in relation to other pain problems (e.g., recurrent abdominal pain) rather than headache alone.

However, all of these research considerations need to take into account what is actually feasible within the school setting. The role of teachers and school principals in supporting the implementation and success of such approaches for children with medical problems should also be carefully considered. One possibility that has yet to be explored in large-scale studies is the implementation of psychosocial interventions such as relaxation/guided imagery on a schoolwide basis with trained teachers leading entire classrooms in these practices. The advantage of such an approach is that all students, including those without any identifiable medical problems, would be able to participate. This approach would also lessen the stigma of engaging in a psychological treatment since the goal would be to promote the general health and well-being of all students. It is our hope that additional and much-needed research in the school setting will be conducted in order to promote safe, efficacious, and cost-effective psychosocial interventions for children with medical problems.

Authors' note

This research was supported by 1F32MH084424 awarded by the National Institute of Mental Health (PI: Laura B. Allen), 2R01DE012754, awarded by the National Institute of Dental and Craniofacial Research (PI: Lonnie K. Zeltzer), and by UCLA General Clinical Research Center Grant MO1-RR-00865 (PI: Lonnie K. Zeltzer).

References

Agras, W. S., Leitenberg, H., & Barlow, D. H. (1968). Social reinforcement in the modification of agoraphobia. *Archives of General Psychiatry, 19*, 423–427.

Allaire, S. H., DeNardo, B. S., Szer, I. S., Meenan, R. F., & Schaller, J. G. (1992). The economic impacts of juvenile rheumatoid arthritis. *Journal of Rheumatology, 19*(6), 952–955.

Anbar, R. D. (2001a). Self-hypnosis for management of chronic dyspnea in pediatric patients. *Pediatrics, 107*, e21.

Anbar, R. D. (2001b). Self-hypnosis for the treatment of functional abdominal pain in childhood. *Clinical Pediatrics, 40*, 447–451.

Antony, M. M., & Barlow, D. H. (2002). Specific phobias. In D. H. Barlow (Ed.), *Anxiety and its disorders: The nature and treatment of anxiety and panic* (2nd ed., pp. 380–417). New York: Guilford Press.

Ball, T. M., Shapiro, D. E., Monheim, C. J., & Weydert, J. A. (2003). A pilot study of the use of guided imagery for the treatment of recurrent abdominal pain in children. *Clinical Pediatrics, 42*, 527–532.

Barlow, D. H. (2002). *Anxiety and its disorders: The nature and treatment of anxiety and panic* (2nd ed.). New York: The Guilford Press.

Barrett, P. M., Dadds, M. R., & Rapee, R. M. (1996). Family treatment of childhood anxiety: A controlled trial. *Journal of Consulting and Clinical Psychology, 64*, 333–342.

Barrett, P. M., Duffy, A. L., Dadds, M. R., & Rapee, R. M. (2001). Cognitive-behavioral treatment of anxiety disorders in children: Longterm (6-year) follow-up. *Journal of Consulting and Clinical Psychology, 69*, 135–141.

Barrett, P. M., Rapee, R. M., Dadds, M. M., & Ryan, S. M. (1996). Family enhancement of cognitive style in anxious and aggressive children. *Journal of Abnormal Child Psychology, 24*, 187–203.

Beck, A. T. (1972). *Depression: Causes and treatment*. Philadelphia: University of Pennsylvania Press.

Beck, A. T. (1976). *Cognitive therapy and the emotional disorders*. Oxford, England: International Universities Press.

Beck, A. T., Rush, A. J., Shaw, B. F., & Emery, G. (1979). *Cognitive therapy of depression*. New York: Guilford Press.

Belsky, J., & Khanna, P. (1994). The effects of self-hypnosis for children with cystic fibrosis: A pilot study. *American Journal of Clinical Hypnosis, 36*, 282–292.

Blanchard, E. B., & Andrasik, F. (1987). Biofeedback treatment of vascular headache. In J. P. Hatch, J. G. Fisher & J. Rugh (Eds.), *Biofeedback: Studies in clinical efficacy* (pp. 1–49). New York: Plenum Press.

Blanchard, E. B., Andrasik, F., Ahles, T. A., Teders, S. J., & O'Keefe, D. (1980). Migraine and tension headache: A meta-analytic review. *Behavior Therapy, 11*, 613–631.

Bower, J. E., Woolery, A., Sternlieb, B., & Garet, D. (2005). Yoga for cancer patients and survivors. *Cancer Control, 12*, 165–171.

Bray, M. A., Kehle, T. J., Grigerick, S. E., Loftus, S., & Nicolson, H. (2007). Children with asthma: Assessment and treatment in school settings. *Psychology in the Schools, 45*, 63–73.

Brown, D. (2007). Evidence-based hypnotherapy for asthma: A critical review. *International Journal of Clinical and Experimental Hypnosis, 55*, 220–249.

Brown, R. T., & DuPaul, G. J. (1999). Introduction to the miniseries: Promoting school success in children with chronic medical conditons. *School Psychology Review, 28*, 175–181.

Budzynski, T. H., Stoyva, J. M., Adler, C. S., & Mullaney, D. J. (1973). EMG biofeedback and tension headache: A controlled outcome study. *Psychosomatic Medicine, 35*, 484–496.

Bussone, G., Grazzi, L., D'Amico, D., Leone, M., & Andrasik, F. (1998). Biofeedback-assisted relaxation training for young adolescents with tension-type headache: A controlled study. *Cephalalgia, 18*, 463–467.

Cartwright-Hatton, S., Roberts, C., Chitsabesan, P., Fothergill, C., & Harrington, R. (2004). Systematic review of the efficacy of cognitive behaviour therapies for childhood and adolescent anxiety disorders. *British Journal of Clinical Psychology, 43*, 421–436.

Compton, S., March, J., Brent, D., Albano, M., Weering, R., & Curry, J. (2004). Cognitive-behavioral therapy for anxiety and depressive disorders in youth: An evidence-based medicine review. *Journal of the American Academy of Child and Adolescent Psychiatry, 43*, 930–959.

Connelly, M., Rapoff, M. A., Thompson, N., & Connelly, W. (2006). Headstrong: A pilot study of a CD-ROM intervention for recurrent pediatric headache. *Journal of Pediatric Psychology, 31*, 737–747.

D'Zurilla, T. (1986). *Problem solving therapy*. New York, NY: Springer Publishing Co.

Davis, M. A., Quittner, A. L., Stack, C. M., & Yang, M. C. (2004). Controlled evaluation of the STARBRIGHT CD-ROM program for children and adolescents with Cystic Fibrosis. *Journal of Pediatric Psychology, 29*, 259–267.

Eccleston, C., & Malleson, P. (2003). Managing chronic pain in children and adolescents. *BMJ, 326*, 1408–1409.

Eccleston, C., Malleson, P. N., Clinch, J., Connell, H., & Sourbut, C. (2003). Chronic pain in adolescents: Evaluation of a programme of interdisciplinary cognitive behaviour therapy. *Archives of Disease in Childhood, 88*, 881–885.

Evans, S., Subramanian, S., & Sternlieb, B. (2008). Yoga as treatment for chronic pain conditions: A literature review. *International Journal on Disability and Human Development, 7*, 25–32.

Evans, S., & Zeltzer, L. K. (2008). Complementary and alternative approaches for chronic pain. In G. A. Walco & K. R. Goldschneider (Eds.), *Pain in children: A practical guide for primary care* (pp. 153–162). Totowa, NJ: Humana Press.

Fentress, D. W., Masek, B. J., Mehegan, J. E., & Benson, H. (1986). Biofeedback and relaxation-response training in the treatment of pediatric migraine. *Developmental Medicine and Child Neurology, 28*, 139–146.

Flammer, E., & Alladin, A. (2007). The efficacy of hypnotherapy in the treatment of psychosomatic disorders: Meta-analytical evidence. *International Journal of Clinical and Experimental Hypnosis, 55*, 251–274.

Garfinkel, M. S., Schumacher, H. R., Jr., Husain, A., Levy, M., & Reshetar, R. A. (1994). Evaluation of a yoga based regimen for treatment of osteoarthritis of the hands. *Journal of Rheumatology, 21*, 2341–2343.

Garfinkel, M. S., Singhal, A., Katz, W. A., Allan, D. A., Reshetar, R., & Schumacher, H. R., Jr. (1998). Yoga-based intervention for carpal tunnel syndrome: A randomized trial. *JAMA, 280*, 1601–1603.

Gatchel, R. J., Peng, Y. B., Peters, M. L., Fuchs, P. N., & Turk, D. C. (2007). The biopsychosocial approach to chronic pain: Scientific advances and future directions. *Psychological Bulletin, 133*, 581–624.

Giedt, J. F. (1997). Guided Imagery. A psychoneuroimmunological intervention in holistic nursing practice. *Journal of Holistic Nursing, 15*, 112–127.

Gold, J. I., Kant, A. J., Belmont, K. A., & Butler, L. D. (2007). Practitioner review: Clinical applications of pediatric hypnosis. *Journal of Child Psychology and Psychiatry, 48*, 744–754.

Grazzi, L., Leone, M., Frediani, F., & Bussone, G. (1990). A therapeutic alternative for tension headache in children: Treatment and 1-year follow-up results. *Biofeedback and Self-Regulation, 15*, 1–6.

Green, J. P., Barabasz, A. F., Barrett, D., & Montgomery, G. H. (2005). Forging ahead: The 2003 APA Division 30 definition of hypnosis. *International Journal of Clinical and Experimental Hypnosis, 53*(3), 259–264.

Hackman, R. M., Stern, J. S., & Gershwin, M. E. (2000). Hypnosis and asthma: A critical review. *Journal of Asthma, 37*, 1–15.

Hermann, C., & Blanchard, E. B. (2002). Biofeedback in the treatment of headache and other childhood pain. *Applied Psychophysiology and Biofeedback, 27*, 143–141S162.

Hewson-Bower, B., & Drummond, P. D. (2001). Psychological treatment for recurrent symptoms of colds and flu in children. *Journal of Psychosomatic Research, 51*, 369–377.

Hicks, C. L., von Baeyer, C. L., & McGrath, P. J. (2006). Online psychological treatment for pediatric recurrent pain: A randomized evaluation. *Journal of Pediatric Psychology, 31*, 724–736.

Holden, E. W., Deichmann, M. M., & Levy, J. D. (1999). Empirically supported treatments in pediatric psychology: Recurrent pediatric headache. *Journal of Pediatric Psychology, 24*, 91–109.

Huppert, J. D., Bufka, L. F., Barlow, D. H., Gorman, J. M., Shear, M. K., & Woods, S. W. (2001). Therapists, therapist variables, and cognitive-behavioral therapy outcome in a multicenter trial for panic disorder. *Journal of Consulting and Clinical Psychology, 69*, 747–755.

Iyengar, B. (1966). *Light on Yoga.* New York: Schocken Books.

Iyengar, B. (2001). *The Path to Holistic Health:* DK.

Iyengar, B. (2005). *Light on Life:* Rodale.

Jain, S. C., Rai, L., Valecha, A., Jha, U. K., Bhatnagar, S. O., & Ram, K. (1991). Effect of yoga training on exercise tolerance in adolescents with childhood asthma. *Journal of Asthma, 28*, 437–442.

Jain, S. C., & Talukdar, B. (1993). Evaluation of yoga therapy programme for patients of bronchial asthma. *Singapore Medical Journal, 34*, 306–308.

John, P. J., Sharma, N., Sharma, C. M., & Kankane, A. (2007). Effectiveness of yoga therapy in the treatment of migraine without aura: A randomized controlled trial. *Headache, 47*, 654–661.

Kazdin, A. E. (2007). Psychosocial treatments for conduct disorder in children and adolescents. In P. E. Nathan & J. M. Gorman (Eds.), *A guide to treatments that work* (3rd ed., pp. 71–104). New York: Oxford University Press.

Kendall, P. C. (1993). Cognitive-behavioral therapies with youth: Guiding theory, current status, and emerging developments. *Journal of Consulting and Clinical Psychology, 61*, 235–247.

Kendall, P. C. (1994). Treating anxiety disorders in children: Results of a randomized clinical trial. *Journal of Consulting and Clinical Psychology, 62*, 100–110.

Kendall, P. C., Brady, E. U., & Verduin, T. L. (2001). Comorbidity in childhood anxiety disorders and treatment outcome. *Journal of the American Academy of Child and Adolescent Psychiatry, 40*, 787–794.

Kendall, P. C., & Braswell, L. (1986). Medical applications of cognitive-behavioral interventions with children. *Journal of Developmental and Behavioral Pediatrics, 7*, 257–264.

Kendall, P. C., Flannery-Schroeder, E., Panichelli-Mindel, S. M., Southam-Gerow, M., Henin, A., & Warman, M. (1997). Therapy for youths with anxiety disorders: A second randomized clinical trial. *Journal of Consulting and Clinical Psychology, 65*, 366–380.

Kendall, P. C., Hudson, J. L., Gosch, E., Flannery-Schroeder, E., & Suveg, C. (2008). Cognitive-behavioral therapy for anxiety disordered youth: A randomized clinical trial evaluating child and family modalities. *Journal of Consulting and Clinical Psychology, 76*, 282–297.

Kirkwood, G., Rampes, H., Tuffrey, V., Richardson, J., & Pilkington, K. (2005). Yoga for anxiety: A systematic review of the research evidence. *British Journal of Sports Medicine, 39*, 884–891.

Knoop, H., Stulemeijer, M., de Jong, L. W., Fiselier, T. J., & Bleijenberg, G. (2008). Efficacy of cognitive behavioral therapy for adolescents with chronic fatigue syndrome: Long-term follow-up of a randomized, controlled trial. *Pediatrics, 121*, 619–625.

Kohen, D. (1995). Applications of relaxation/mental imagery (self-hypnosis) to the management of childhood asthma: Behavioral outcomes of a controlled study. *HYPNOSIS: The Journal of the European Society of Hypnosis in Psychotherapy and Psychosomatic Medicine, 22*, 132–144.

Kohen, D. P., & Wynne, E. (1997). Applying hypnosis in a preschool family asthma education program: Uses of storytelling, imagery, and relaxation. *American Journal of Clinical Hypnosis, 39*, 169–181.

Kroner-Herwig, B., Mohn, U., & Pothmann, R. (1998). Comparison of biofeedback and relaxation in the treatment of pediatric headache and the influence of parent involvement on outcome. *Applied Psychophysiology and Biofeedback, 23*, 143–157.

Kroner-Herwig, B., Plump, U., & Pothmann, R. (1992). Progressive relaxation and EMG biofeedback in the treatment of chronic headache in children: Results of an explorative study. *Schmerz, 6*, 121–127.

Kuttner, L., Chambers, C. T., Hardial, J., Israel, D. M., Jacobson, K., & Evans, K. (2006). A randomized trial of yoga for adolescents with irritable bowel syndrome. *Pain Research and Management, 11*, 217–223.

Langewitz, W., Izakovic, J., Wyler, J., Schindler, C., Kiss, A., & Bircher, A. J. (2005). Effect of self-hypnosis on hay fever symptoms - A randomised controlled intervention study. *Psychotherapy and Psychosomatics, 74,* 165–172.

Larsson, B., Carlsson, J., Fichtel, A., & Melin, L. (2005). Relaxation treatment of adolescent headache sufferers: Results from a school-based replication series. *Headache, 45,* 692–704.

Latha, D., & Kaliappan, K. V. (1992). Efficacy of yoga therapy in the management of headaches. *Journal of Indian Psychology, 10,* 41–47.

Liossi, C., & Hatira, P. (2003). Clinical hypnosis in the alleviation of procedure-related pain in pediatric oncology patients. *International Journal of Clinical and Experimental Hypnosis, 51,* 4–28.

Lipchik, G. L., Smitherman, T. A., Penzien, D. B., & Holroyd, K. A. (2006). Basic principles and techniques of cognitive-behavioral therapies for comorbid psychiatric symptoms among headache patients. *Headache, 46*(Suppl 3), S119–132.

Logan, D. E., Simons, L. E., Stein, M. J., & Chastain, L. (2008). School impairment in adolescents with chronic pain. *Journal of Pain, 9,* 407–416.

Lowry-Webster, H. M., Barrett, P. M., & Dadds, M. R. (2001). A universal prevention trial of anxiety and depressive symptomatology in childhood: Preliminary data from an Australian study. *Behaviour Change, 18,* 36–50.

Marks, I. M. (1971). Phobic disorders four years after treatment: A prospective follow-up. *British Journal of Psychiatry, 129,* 362–371.

Mendlowitz, S. L., Manassis, K., Bradley, S., Scapillato, D., Miezitis, S., & Shaw, B. F. (1999). Cognitive-behavioral group treatments in childhood anxiety disorders: The role of parental involvement. *Journal of the American Academy of Child and Adolescent Psychiatry, 38,* 1223–1229.

Merlijn, V. P., Hunfeld, J. A., van der Wouden, J. C., Hazebroek-Kampschreur, A. A., van Suijlekom-Smit, L. W., Koes, B. W., et al. (2005). A cognitive-behavioural program for adolescents with chronic pain - a pilot study. *Patient Education and Counseling, 59,* 126–134.

Neparstek, B. (1994). *Staying well with guided imagery.* New York: Warner Books.

Nestoriuc, Y., Martin, A., Rief, W., & Andrasik, F. (2008). Biofeedback treatment for headache disorders: A comprehensive efficacy review. *Applied Psychophysiology and Biofeedback, 33,* 125–140.

Olness, K. (2008). Helping children and adults with hypnosis and biofeedback. *Cleveland Clinic Journal of Medicine, 75*(Suppl 2), S39–S43.

Palermo, T. M., Krell, H., Janosy, N., & Zeltzer, L. K. (2008). Pain and somatoform disorders. In M. Wolraich, D. Drotar, P. Dworkin & E. Perrin (Eds.), *Developmental and behavioral pediatrics: Evidence and practice* (pp. 711–741). Philadelphia, PA: Mosby, Inc.

Palermo, T. M., Wilson, A. C., Peters, M., Lewandowski, A., & Somhegyi, H. (2009). Randomized controlled trial of an Internet-delivered family cognitive-behavioral therapy intervention for children and adolescents with chronic pain. *Pain, 146*(1-2), 205–213.

Patterson, D. R. (2004). Treating pain with hypnosis. *Current Directions in Psychological Science, 13,* 252–255.

Peck, H. L., Bray, M. A., & Kehle, T. J. (2003). Relaxation and guided imagery: A school-based intervention for children with asthma. *Psychology in the Schools, 40,* 657–675.

Perquin, C. W., Hazebroek-Kampschreur, A. A., Hunfeld, J. A., Bohnen, A. M., van Suijlekom-Smit, L. W., Passchier, J.,

et al. (2000). Pain in children and adolescents: A common experience. *Pain, 87,* 51–58.

Pilkington, K., Kirkwood, G., Rampes, H., & Richardson, J. (2005). Yoga for depression: The research evidence. *Journal of Affective Disorders, 89,* 13–24.

Power, T. J., DuPaul, G. J., Shapiro, E. S., & Parrish, J. M. (1998). Role of the school-based professional in health-related services. In L. Phelps (Ed.), *Health-related disorders in children and adolescents.* Washington, DC: American Psychological Association.

Rainville, P., Hofbauer, R. K., Bushnell, M. C., Duncan, G. H., & Price, D. D. (2002). Hypnosis modulates activity in brain structures involved in the regulation of consciousness. *Journal of Cognitive Neuroscience, 14,* 887–901.

Robins, P. M., Smith, S. M., Glutting, J. J., & Bishop, C. T. (2005). A randomized controlled trial of a cognitive-behavioral family intervention for pediatric recurrent abdominal pain. *Journal of Pediatric Psychology, 30,* 397–408.

Roth-Isigkeit, A., Thyen, U., Raspe, H. H., Stoven, H., & Schmucker, P. (2004). Reports of pain among German children and adolescents: An epidemiological study. *Acta Paediatrica, 93,* 258–263.

Roy-Byrne, P. P., Wagner, A. W., & Schraufnagel, T. J. (2005). Understanding and treating panic disorder in the primary care setting. *Journal of Clinical Psychiatry, 66*(Suppl 4), 16–22.

Rusy, L. M., & Weisman, S. J. (2000). Complementary therapies for acute pediatric pain management. *Pediatric Clinics of North American, 47,* 589–599.

Sanders, M. R., Shepherd, R. W., Cleghorn, G., & Woolford, H. (1994). The treatment of recurrent abdominal pain in children: A controlled comparison of cognitive-behavioral family intervention and standard pediatric care. *Journal of Consulting and Clinical Psychology, 62,* 306–314.

Scharff, L., Marcus, D. A., & Masek, B. J. (2002). A controlled study of minimal-contact thermal biofeedback treatment in children with migraine. *Journal of Pediatric Psychology, 27,* 109–119.

Shortt, A. L., Barrett, P. M., & Fox, T. L. (2001). Evaluating the FRIENDS Program: A cognitive-behavioral group treatment for anxious children and their parents. *Journal of Community Psychology, 30,* 525–535.

Sleed, M., Eccleston, C., Beecham, J., Knapp, M., & Jordan, A. (2005). The economic impact of chronic pain in adolescence: Methodological considerations and a preliminary costs-of-illness study. *Pain, 119*(1-3), 183–190.

Smith, J. M., & Burns, C. L. (1960). The treatment of asthmatic children by hypnotic suggestion. *British Journal of Diseases of the Chest, 54,* 78–81.

Sodergren, K. M. (1992). Guided imagery. In M. Snyder (Ed.), *Independent nursing interventions* (2nd ed., pp. 95–109). Albany, NY: Delmar.

Sokel, B., Christie, D., Kent, A., Lansdown, R., Atherton, D., Glover, M., et al. (1993). A comparison of hypnotherapy and biofeedback in the treatment of childhood atopic eczema. *Contemporary Hypnosis, 10,* 145–154.

Stark, K. D., Rouse, L. W., & Livingston, R. (1991). Treatment of depression during hcildhood and adolescence: Cognitive-behavioral procedures for the individual and family. In P. C. Kendall (Ed.), *Child and adolescent therapy: Cognitive-behavioral procedures* (pp. 165–206). New York: Guilford Press.

Stewart, J. H. (2005). Hypnosis in contemporary medicine. *Mayo Clinic Proceedings, 80,* 511–524.

Stulemeijer, M., de Jong, L. W., Fiselier, T. J., Hoogveld, S. W., & Bleijenberg, G. (2005). Cognitive behaviour therapy for adolescents with chronic fatigue syndrome: Randomised controlled trial. *BMJ, 330,* 14.

Trautmann, E., Lackschewitz, H., & Kroner-Herwig, B. (2006). Psychological treatment of recurrent headache in children and adolescents - A meta-analysis. *Cephalalgia, 26,* 1411–1426.

Tsao, J. C., & Zeltzer, L. K. (2005). Complementary and alternative medicine approaches for pediatric pain: A review of the state-of-the-science. *Evidence-Based Complementary and Alternative Medicine, 2,* 149–159.

Turk, D. C. (2002). A cognitive–behavioral perspective on treatment of chronic pain patients. In D. Turk & R. Gatchel (Eds.), *Psychological approaches to pain management: A practitioner's handbook* (pp. 138–158). New York: Guilford.

Turk, D. C. (2003). Cognitive–behavioral approach to the treatment of chronic pain patients. *Regional Anesthesia and Pain Medicine, 28,* 573–579.

Turk, D. C., Swanson, K. S., & Tunks, E. R. (2008). Psychological approaches in the treatment of chronic pain patients – when pills, scalpels, and needles are not enough. *Canadian Journal of Psychiatry, 53,* 213–223.

Varni, J. W. (1991). Behavioral management of pediatric pain. *Journal of Pediatric Oncology Nursing, 8,* 82.

Vlieger, A. M., Menko–Frankenhuis, C., Wolfkamp, S. C., Tromp, E., & Benninga, M. A. (2007). Hypnotherapy for children with functional abdominal pain or irritable bowel syndrome: A randomized controlled trial. *Gastroenterology, 133,* 1430–1436.

Weydert, J. A., Shapiro, D. E., Acra, S. A., Monheim, C. J., Chambers, A. S., & Ball, T. M. (2006). Evaluation of guided imagery as treatment for recurrent abdominal pain in children: A randomized controlled trial. *BMC Pediatrics, 6,* 29.

Wild, M. R., & Espie, C. A. (2004). The efficacy of hypnosis in the reduction of procedural pain and distress in pediatric oncology: A systematic review. *Journal of Developmental and Behavioral Pediatrics, 25,* 207–213.

Williams, K. A., Petronis, J., Smith, D., Goodrich, D., Wu, J., Ravi, N., et al. (2005). Effect of Iyengar yoga therapy for chronic low back pain. *Pain, 115,* 107–117.

Wolpe, J. (1958). *Psychotherapy by reciprocal inhibition.* Stanford, CA: Stanford University Press.

Youssef, N. N., Rosh, J. R., Loughran, M., Schuckalo, S. G., Cotter, A. N., Verga, B. G., et al. (2004). Treatment of functional abdominal pain in childhood with cognitive behavioral strategies. *Journal of Pediatric Gastroenterology and Nutrition, 39,* 192–196.

Zahourek, R. P. (1988). Imagery. In R. P. Zahourek (Ed.), *Relaxation and imagery: Tools for therapeutic communication and intervention* (pp. 53–83). New York: Plenum Press.

Zeltzer, L. K., & Krell, H. (2007). Pain management in children. In R. E. Behrman, R. M. Kliegman, H. B. Jenson & B. F. Stanton (Eds.), *Nelson textbook of pediatrics* (18th ed., pp. 475–484). Philadelphia, PA: Saunders.

Zeltzer, L. K., & Schlank, C. B. (2005). *Conquering your child's chronic pain: A pediatrician's guide for reclaiming a normal childhood.* New York: Harper Collins.

PART 8

Professional Issues

The Influence of Legislation on the Practice of School Psychology

Angie Dahl, Kathryn E. Hoff, Gretchen Gimpel Peacock, *and* Ruth A. Ervin

Abstract

This chapter provides an overview of the manner in which the practice of school psychology has been influenced by U.S. legislation over the past 30+ years. Relevant federal statutes, regulations, and case law are reviewed, with an emphasis on the ways that federal legislation has impacted both the practice of school psychology and the provision of educational services for students with disabilities. Early legislation in the 1970s focused on creating access to education for children with disabilities. Later legislation focused on increasing access as well as defining educational parameters, including increased access to the regular education environment and increased parental rights. Most recently, legislation has emphasized educational outcomes and school accountability. With these changes in legislation, the role of school psychologists has shifted from simply one of gatekeeper to one of prevention, intervention, and assessment specialist. In the future, the practice of school psychology will continue to evolve, molded, in part, by federal statutes, regulations, and case law.

Keywords: school psychology law, special education law, school psychologist, special education, IDEA

The term *school law* loosely encompasses a patchwork of statutes, regulations, and case law that govern the duties and obligations of schools in the modern educational landscape. It would be difficult to overstate the influence of legal mandates and relevant court cases (i.e., case law) on the practice of school psychology today. Such laws are implicated in the day-to-day practice of every school psychologist, and as laws have evolved over time, so too has the practice of school psychology.

In this chapter, our aim is to provide an overview of relevant legislation and case law, and to describe the manner in which the practice of school psychology has been influenced by the major educational laws. In order to narrow the scope of our review, we have limited this chapter to legislation and case law within the United States. Specifically, we review the U.S. federal statutes and regulations, as well as select court decisions, all of which have influenced the provision of education for children with disabilities. We further provide an overview of how these statutes and legal

decisions have impacted educational services for students with disabilities over time, including: (1) initially creating access to education for children with disabilities; (2) expanding access to include more children and defining parameters for educational programs, including increased access to the regular education environment and increased parental rights; and (3) most recently, emphasizing educational outcomes and school accountability. We also describe how this shift in focus has affected the day-to-day practice of school psychology. Before turning to specific pieces of legislation, and in order to provide readers unfamiliar with the structure and workings of the legal system with some context for understanding how educational issues fit within our legislative and legal system, we begin an overview of the this system.

The Legal System: A Basic Overview

Guiding legal principles affecting school psychology arise from three major sources: (1) the United States Constitution; (2) legislative action (including statutes and regulations); and (3) case law (court decisions). A brief description of these three major sources of law follows.

United States Constitution

The legal system of the United States was born more than 200 years ago with the June 21, 1788 ratification of the U.S. Constitution. The U.S. Constitution (along with its 27 amendments) supersedes any other source of law in the United States, including any conflicting state or federal law.

The federal government is one of "limited powers," meaning that it possesses only those specific powers granted to it by the U.S. Constitution. Interestingly, the U.S. Constitution lacks any mention of the words *school* or *education*. The founding fathers did not bestow the power of "education" to the federal government by the Constitution, but instead reserved such power to the states via the Tenth Amendment to the Constitution, which specifies that "powers not delegated to the United States by the Constitution, nor prohibited by it to States, are reserved to the States respectively, or to the people." Thus, individual states provide education to children as an entitlement. Despite the fact that the Constitution does not specifically cover education, various aspects of the U.S. Constitution are relevant to the provision of education. For example, if a state provides a K–12 education to its citizens, that state must abide by various constitutional provisions in implementing and conducting the education. Notable examples of U.S. Constitutional impacts on state schools include the Fourteenth Amendment's guarantees of equal protection (i.e., states cannot "deny to any person within its jurisdiction the equal protection of the laws") and the additional prohibition that states cannot make or enforce laws that "abridge the privileges" of citizens or "deprive any person of life, liberty, or property, without due process of law." Although education is not specifically mentioned in this Amendment, education is considered a "property" right and is therefore covered under this Amendment. Thus, states cannot enact laws that would infringe on an individual's right to an education. Furthermore, if an individual's educational rights are to be removed then *due process* must be followed.

Legislative Laws (Statutes and Regulations)

Although the Constitution clearly plays an important role in ensuring access to education, the bulk of federal intervention in schools is based upon federal lawmaking, which takes the form of statutes and regulations.

Statutes. At the federal level, a statute is a law passed by both houses of Congress (the House and Senate) and signed into law by the President.[1] Thereafter, the laws are codified in the U.S. Code. The scope of a federal statute is limited only by the U.S. Constitution and the power of the federal government to enact laws. State statutes/laws are passed by a state legislative body and signed into law by a state governor. Due to the federal Constitution's supremacy clause, state laws are generally not permitted to conflict with federal laws or the federal Constitution.

Although the federal government does not have the power of education under the U.S. Constitution, Congress does rely upon the so-called "power of the purse" to insert its far reaching policy goals into education. Simply put, the federal government provides an enormous amount of money to schools, but conditions the acceptance of such money on schools following the federal regulations, guidelines, and requirements that accompany the funds. The Supreme Court has established that although the federal government has no power to regulate in a certain area (like education), "it does have power to fix the terms on which its money allotments to states shall be disbursed" (*Oklahoma v. United States Civil Service Commission*, 330 U.S. 127, 143 [1947]). The amount and impact of federal money in schools continues to grow and, as such, the strings that come attached to federal money (in the form of federal laws and regulations) are now a part of public school systems throughout the country.

Regulations. After a statue has been passed at the federal level, Congress often delegates its lawmaking authority to a government department or agency, which is then able to issue regulations (or "rules") that have the force of law. When an agency has been given rulemaking authority by Congress, the agency has to go through a process called *notice and comment* to promulgate regulations. The process that is required of an agency before issuing rules is to publish its intent to issue regulations, take public comments on the proposed regulations, and respond to the public comments before the regulations are permitted to go into effect. Once the regulations are final and effective, they are given the force of law. Regulations are codified at the federal level in the Code of Federal Regulations (C.F.R.). Frequently, both statutes and regulations must be consulted in a particular topical area to get the full picture of applicable laws.

Case Law

Case law is a collection of written opinions issued by a judicial body (e.g., U.S. Supreme Court, U.S.

district courts, State supreme courts) that interpret and construe what various legislative and constitutional provisions mean. Legislative laws (statutes and regulations) are constitutionally tested by the judiciary, where the courts are charged with the duty to determine when laws passed by Congress run afoul of constitutional provisions. Courts also preside over lawsuits where the court is asked to decide when and whether certain actions are impermissible under the law (e.g., whether a school's refusal to desegregate violates the equal protection clause of the U.S. Constitution). Courts also award damages against parties who have been found by the court to have violated laws, as well as issuing injunctions that force parties to take a particular action, or refrain from engaging in illegal behavior.

Although originally seen as the weakest of the branches of government, the judicial system has been instrumental in shaping school policy and protecting educational rights for many different groups. One notable example of court influence over education is the U.S. Supreme Court's landmark decision in *Brown v. Board of Education* in 1954. The landscape of the southern schools in the first half of the twentieth century was a tale of segregation and two school systems, one system for African American students and one for Caucasian students. Southern states billed this as "separate but equal" education. The Supreme Court concluded in *Brown* that if the state provides a free public education, then this education must be provided on an equal basis to all children regardless of race, under the Equal Protection Clause of the Fourteenth Amendment to the Constitution. The Court further held that the separate educational settings for racially diverse children were "inherently unequal." With this ruling, and the ensuing injunction that forced desegregation of schools, the Court largely accomplished what the U.S. Congress was unable to do: racially integrate the schools of the South.

Creating Access to Education for Children with Disabilities

Educational services were bleak for children with disabilities through the mid 1970s, and no state provided educational services to all its children with disabilities (Martin, Martin, & Terman, 1996). During this time, students with disabilities were routinely excluded from school because of their disability, placed in inappropriate education programs, subjected to different admission standards, and at times could not physically access the classrooms due to poor facilities (Turnbull & Turnbull, 2000).

Psychological assessments and subsequent placement in special classrooms were conducted without parents' permission, and parents had little recourse when they disagreed with school decisions (Fagan & Wise, 2007). The school psychologist's role during this time was primarily one of an evaluator. Although the role of clinical psychologists expanded in the mid-1900s following the Boulder Conference in 1949, the role of school psychologists remained much the same, with limited time for services other than those related to evaluation services (Fagan & Wise, 2007). While the role of the school psychologist changed minimally during this time, educational opportunities for students with disabilities expanded gradually as state laws requiring local school districts to provide special education services to children with disabilities were passed. However, problems remained, such as insufficient funds to provide special education services, requirements that only specific children were eligible for the funds, and non-enforcement by state agencies (Martin et al., 1996).

Court Cases: Accessing Education

Parents of children with disabilities turned to the courts to redress their concerns with education for students with disabilities. Using a similar basis to *Brown*—that exclusion of children with disabilities from the public school system violated the 14th Amendment—lawsuits were filed by groups of parents asserting that children with disabilities were being excluded from public schools because of their disabilities, and were being denied their due process and equal protection rights.

The first of two significant cases to address these issues was *Pennsylvania Association for Retarded Children (PARC) v. Pennsylvania* (1971, 1972). In this case, the parents of 13 children with intellectual disabilities filed a lawsuit to contest a state law that allowed schools to deny access to students who had "not attained a mental age of five years" by first grade. In a consent decree (a court order agreed to by both sides of the case), the state agreed to locate all school-age children who were excluded from school, and provide all children with intellectual disabilities access to a free public education. The court also ordered that the educational services should be "appropriate to the child's capacity," and parents should be given notice and an opportunity for a hearing before changes in educational assignments were made.

A second significant case was *Mills v. Board of Education of the District of Columbia* (1972). *Mills* was filed on behalf of seven children (aged 8–16 and identified with a variety of behavioral and learning concerns) who alleged they were eligible for a free public education but were nonetheless excluded on the basis of their disabilities. The U.S. district court found that the school district had deprived the plaintiffs of a public education because of their disabilities, and that the students were excluded without being afforded the due process of law. The court decision required the District of Columbia to provide a free and appropriate public education to all children, regardless of disability or financial capability of the school. In other words, lack of funding could not be used to deny access to education for students with disabilities. The court decision also required schools to evaluate the educational needs of students with disabilities and prepare a "suitable education program" for youth ages 3–21. Further, the court mandated that students with disabilities were entitled to "due process" when there was a change in their status (e.g., labeling, placing, or excluding a child from school), such as providing written notice to parents, access to records, and the right to a hearing.

Cases like *Brown, PARC,* and *Mills* brought the role of the courts to the forefront in education law, and caused an escalation in right-to-education cases. By 1973, more than 30 federal court decisions were made that upheld the same equal protection and due process standards of *PARC* and *Mills* (Martin et al., 1996). This increased judicial intervention, coupled with significant new financial responsibilities from the states and local schools (where responsible agencies were unprepared, and could not handle increased costs required by court decisions and new state laws), as well as increasing political pressure to provide services to children with disabilities, sent the message to Congress that there was a profound need for uniform federal laws to assist and protect children with disabilities. Congress reacted, and legislation followed (Martin et al., 1996; Turnbull & Turnbull, 2000).

Federal Legislation: Accessing Education

Various pieces of federal legislation passed with the intent of providing educational services to students with disabilities, through both amendments of existing federal legislation and antidiscrimination legislation (Jacob & Hartshorne, 2007). In 1965, P.L. 89-10, the Elementary and Secondary Education Act, was signed into law by President Lyndon Johnson. While children with disabilities were not specifically mentioned within this piece of legislation, the act provided financial assistance for the education of children who

were economically disadvantaged, and provided the foundation by which early special education legislation was drafted (Jacob & Hartshorne, 2007). In 1966, P.L. 89-750, the Elementary and Secondary Education Act Amendments of 1966 included a Title VI that provided grant funding opportunities to help states create educational programs for students with disabilities, and established the National Advisory Council (now called the National Council on Disability) and the Bureau of Education of the Handicapped (BEH). It is important to note, however, that this funding was only provided to those states that took initiative to create educational programs for children with disabilities. In 1970, P.L. 91-230, The Education of the Handicapped Act replaced Title VI of the Elementary and Secondary Education Act, and provided funding for special education personnel and related resources. A 1974 reauthorization, P.L. 93-380, The Educational Amendments of 1974, provided an increase in financial assistance for services to children with disabilities, but continued to rely upon the states to enact educational programs for students with disabilities. Within Section 513 of P.L. 93-380, the Family Education Rights and Privacy Act (1974) protected the rights and privacy of all students and their parents. Specifically, the act gave parents and students the "right" to access the student's file, request changes/corrections, and restricted file access to those with a "legitimate interest."

Amendments to civil rights law at a federal level also provided some of the foundational tenets for educational access to students with disabilities. In 1973, the Rehabilitation Act was passed (an amendment to Title VI of the Civil Rights Act of 1964), which prohibited discrimination on the basis of a disability for those programs receiving federal funding. Specifically, Section 504 subpart D addressed the equal right to a free and appropriate public education for "handicapped persons." The definition of an individual with a disability under Section 504 is broad, and includes individuals with physical and/or mental impairments which hinder one or more life activities, individuals with "a record" of impairment or those "regarded as having such impairment." With the passage of Section 504, schools that received federal funding were required to provide a free and appropriate public education to students meeting the definition of the "handicapped person." In so doing, schools were and continue to be required to appoint a Section 504 coordinator, create written plans for students who qualify, and create a free and appropriate education for students with disabilities. However, states were slow to respond to this law—in part due to a lack of funding associated with Section 504, and in part due to confusion regarding how to implement this law, due to a lack of specificity in the law. Although there were a number of court cases related to schools' failure to comply with Section 504, it was not until 1991, when a memo regarding Section 504 services was issued from the U.S. Department of Education, that these services became more commonplace in schools. This memo addressed classification of students with attention-deficit/hyperactivity disorder (ADHD), and clarified that such students may be eligible for special education services in certain categories (including *Other Health Impaired*), and also outlined Section 504 services that schools should provide to students with ADHD (Jacob & Hartshorne, 2007). Thus, the import of Section 504 to the educational system grew, and indeed the full impact of Section 504 was not realized until many years after its passage.

By 1975, Congress estimated that there were eight million children with disabilities in the United States, with more than half of these children lacking appropriate educational services. Further, one million children were completely excluded from public school education (Pub. L. No. 94-142, § 601[b]). Congress recognized the necessity of federal laws to address the educational needs of children with disabilities (Jacob & Hartshorne, 2007), and also the need to provide funding to supplement special education costs (Martin et al., 1996).

Thus, in 1975 Congress enacted P.L. 94-142, the Education for All Handicapped Children Act (EAHCA), landmark legislation in the provision of educational services to students with disabilities. P.L. 94-142 extended the educational services of children with disabilities by providing federal funds to states, and implementing regulations designed to provide a free and appropriate public education (FAPE) in the least restrictive environment (LRE) regardless of the child's disability. Specifically, the purpose of the Act was to "assure that all handicapped children have available to them…a free appropriate public education which emphasizes special education and related services designed to meet their unique needs, to assure that the rights of handicapped children and their parents or guardians are protected, to assist States and localities to provide for the education of all handicapped children, and to assess and assure the effectiveness of efforts to educate handicapped children" (Pub. L. No. 94-142, § 601[9][c]). P.L. 94-142 resulted in significant changes in the education of students with disabilities, guaranteeing access for millions of children previously underserved in the educational environment.

With the passage of P.L. 94-142, and its emphasis on providing access to services for students with disabilities, there was an increase in need for school psychologists to assist with eligibility determinations. In response to this need, the number of training programs, and subsequently the number of practicing school psychologists, grew tremendously in the years following P.L. 94-142 (Fagan & Wise, 2007; Merrell, Ervin, & Gimpel, 2006). Fagan and Wise estimate that the number of school psychologists grew from 5,000 in 1970 to 20,000 in 1988, and to over 30,000 by 2005. Although the number of school psychologists increased during this timeframe, the role of the school psychologist did not broaden as one might expect. Instead, and largely due to the need to determine eligibility for services based on the criteria set forth in P.L. 94-142, the role of the school psychologist became even more assessment focused, with many school psychologists essentially serving as "gatekeepers" in determining who met the criteria to access special education services (Merrell et al., 2006). In a national survey of 856 practicing school psychologists in the early 1980s, Goldwasser, Meyers, Christenson and Graden (1983) found school psychologists spent approximately 70% of their time in assessment activities (pretesting, testing, and post-diagnostic feedback), 20% of their time in consultation, and 10% in direct intervention services. Similarly, 91% and 84% of school psychologists reported membership on evaluation teams and pupil placement teams, respectively, while only 45% of school psychologists consistently served on Individualized Educational Program (IEP) Teams in their schools. Other researchers at the time found similar results, noting the primary role of a school psychologist as "diagnostician," though many school psychologists desired an expanded role, inclusive of assessment, consultation and intervention services (e.g. Smith, 1984; Stevenson-Hicks, 1980).

In addition to the school psychologist being seen as a gatekeeper to special education services, broader school psychology services were often limited to students who were eligible and/or receiving special education services, and there were limited opportunities to work with students in general education. Goldwasser et al. (1993), for example, noted that school psychologists spent the majority of their time (71%) with students with disabilities, while working only 10% of their time in direct intervention or consultation for students without disabilities.

Further, school psychologists stated they believed their role would become more closely intertwined with special education as a result of P.L. 94-142 (Stevenson-Hicks, 1980), while noting a preference to provide services to students in both special education and regular education (Smith, 1984).

In the years since the passage of PL 94-142, the general purpose and core concepts of special education law have remained the same. These include (Turnbull & Turnbull, 2000):

1) *Zero Reject/Free Appropriate Public Education.* Children cannot be excluded from educational services, and all children have a right to a free, appropriate public education.

2) *Nondiscriminatory Identification and Evaluation.* When children are evaluated for special education services, this must be done in a nonbiased manner.

3) *Providing an Individualized Education Program (IEP).* Students must receive an education that is appropriate for them. Goals should be formulated that are specific to the child's current functioning and future needs.

4) *Least Restrictive Environment (LRE).* Students with disabilities should be educated with their peers without disabilities, to the maximum extent possible.

5) *Due Process.* Parents of children, as well as individual children, have rights related to changes in the educational setting or plan. A child's placement and plan cannot be changed unilaterally by the school. If parents disagree with a proposed change, or with the child's IEP, there is a mechanism through which concerns can be heard.

6) *Parental Participation.* Parents are key individuals in a child's life, and as such have significant rights related to decision making with regard to a student's educational plan and placement.

Although these core concepts have remained the same, there have been multiple amendments and reauthorizations of special education law as discussed throughout this chapter. These amendments have, over time, strengthened the rights of students with disabilities and their parents, and helped to shift the school psychologist's role from that of simply a "gatekeeper" (determining which students could access special education services) to more of a prevention/intervention specialist, with the most recent reauthorization of this law. That being said, even more recent surveys of school psychologists suggest that the profession is still very tied to the

assessment role, with school psychologists spending approximately half of their time in assessment related activities (e.g., Hosp & Reschly, 2002). However, it is important to note that even though assessment related activities have remained a prominent part of school psychologists' roles, there has been a substantial reduction in time spent in these activities over the years.

Expanding Access and Defining Parameters for Educational Programs

The evolution of PL 94-142 was coupled with a changing role of the school psychologist, which had become increasingly tied to special education services. This combination of factors helped create a second shift in focus in the school psychologist's role, moving from simply accessing services for typical school-age children to greater support for effective educational programming in the context of a FAPE for individuals with disabilities from birth through age 21. With this change, school psychologists became more involved in service planning, but continued to be highly involved in access determinations (i.e., eligibility), particularly as the law expanded to include preschool-age children. Specifically, educational facilities, courts, parents and school psychologists alike, asked not only "for whom should services be provided?" but also "what is a *free and public appropriate education* under P. L. 94-142?" Since its inception, both court cases and federal legislation have provided interpretation of P.L. 94-142 and guidance for all involved, including school psychologists, school administrators, and parents. In the sections below, we review legislation and court cases that helped shape the focus of special education law as it evolved and questions of programming became more central. In these sections we also discuss how these changes impacted the roles of school psychologists.

Expanding Access and Defining Services: Federal Legislation

While P.L. 94-142 provided the groundwork granting access to education for children and adolescents with disabilities, several pieces of legislation that followed expanded on services provided, offering further directives for school psychologists. In 1983, Congress passed PL 98-199, the Education of the Handicapped Act Amendments. These amendments established services to transition students with disabilities from school to post-school commitments (e.g. work), and provided initial financial incentives for the development of both parenting information centers and research on early-intervention special education. The initial changes were clarified and expanded upon in P.L. 99-457, the Education of the Handicapped Act Amendments, which passed in 1986. P.L. 99-457 mandated the establishment by 1991 of special education services for preschool children with disabilities, aged 3–5 years. The 1986 amendments also established a new program under Part H (which later became Part C), which provided financial incentives for states to develop comprehensive, multidisciplinary early intervention services for infants and toddlers ages birth–3 years. Up until this point, infants and toddlers with disabilities had been serviced by various agencies (e.g. social services, public health, education) in the state and private sector (Jacob & Hartsthorne, 2007), with no federal mandate that these individuals be provided with services. As a result of these two amendments, children, adolescents, and young adults with disabilities, aged 3–21 years of age, were now guaranteed access to a free and appropriate public education. Additionally, services to aid the transition for both "entry" and "dismissal" from special education were clarified. Furthermore, mechanisms were put in place to facilitate states' delivery of services to infants and toddlers (children up to age 3) with disabilities, although this population was not guaranteed a FAPE.

A major reauthorization of special education law took place in 1990 with the passage of P.L. 101-476, the Individuals with Disabilities Education Act (IDEA, 1990). The reauthorization provided further clarification on FAPE and expanded services to individuals with disabilities. In this 1990 reauthorization, the term "handicap" was changed to "disability" and thirteen disability categories were outlined for inclusion in special education, including both autism and traumatic brain injury added as new disability categories. This reauthorization continued to mandate that schools receiving federal funding were to provide a FAPE to children with disabilities ages 3–21 years in the least restrictive environment, mandating inclusion to the maximum extent possible. The FAPE must be designed to meet the individual needs of the student, provide full educational opportunity, and be outlined in the student's IEP. Additionally, IDEA (1990) mandated transition services for individuals in special education, from high school to adult living. Namely, students' IEPs must address transitional plans and needed training to make the transition from high school to adult living. Specifically, IDEA mandated that the team should meet to determine required community services,

vocational training, job placement, and post-school adult living objectives for students starting at age 16. Additionally, assistive technology and related services were defined under this reauthorization. In 1992, P.L. 102-119, the Individuals with Disabilities Education Act Amendments, was passed. These amendments primarily addressed Part H, the provision of services to both infants and toddlers with disabilities. In order to receive funds for early intervention services, states were required to develop statewide, comprehensive systems of service for infants and toddlers with disabilities.

Providing increased access to individuals with disabilities was pertinent not only in the domain of public education, but in wider public and private services as well. While the Rehabilitation Act of 1973 prevented discrimination based on disability for programs receiving federal funding, the 1990 passage of P.L. 101-336, the Americans with Disabilities Act (ADA), prohibited discrimination against individuals with disabilities by both public and private organizations, regardless of whether they receive federal funding. Within the realm of education, ADA is consistent with Section 504 of the Rehabilitation Act of 1973, expanding to include those schools which do not receive federal funding. Congress noted "some 43,000,000 Americans have one or more physical or mental disabilities, and this number is increasing as the population as a whole is growing older" (P.L. 101-336 § 2[a][1]), highlighting discrimination experienced by individuals with disabilities in the spheres of public and private services, accommodations, employment, and transportation. The ADA defined disability similarly to section 504 of the Rehabilitation Act, as having record of or being regarded as an having "a physical or mental impairment that substantially limits one or more major life activities of an individual" (28 C.F.R. § 35.104), and prohibited discrimination based on disability. Said differently, individuals with disabilities gained equal access and opportunity with the passage of ADA in the arenas of employment, transportation, public services, state and local governments, and telecommunications. Title II of the ADA is most pertinent to education, as it states "no qualified individual with a disability shall, by reason of such disability, be excluded from participation in or be denied the benefits of services, programs, or activities of a public entity, or be subjected to discrimination by any such entity." (28 C.F.R. § 35.130). The Department of Justice has designated the Office of Civil Rights for the Department of Education for enforcement within the schools. For school psychologists, an understanding of ADA and related services is beneficial in meeting the needs of students transitioning from special education (Jacob & Hartshorne, 2007).

Court Cases: Free and Appropriate Public Education and Least Restrictive Environment

While PL 94-142 and its reauthorizations guaranteed all students the right to a FAPE, the legislation lacked any actual definition of FAPE, and so it fell to the courts to judicially construe the term. One of the earliest cases that addressed this issue was the 1982 Supreme Court decision *Board of Education of the Hendrick Hudson Central School District v. Rowley*. The subject of this case, Amy Rowley, was a Deaf student who had minimum residual hearing but was an excellent lipreader, understanding approximately 50% of spoken language. In creating Amy's IEP, the school had tested out various supports with her during her kindergarten year, and had determined that the use of an FM hearing aid, three weekly hours of speech therapy services, and one hour daily of a tutor for the Deaf was adequate in providing an appropriate educational plan for Amy's first grade year. While Amy's parents agreed with the provisions outlined by the school, they insisted a sign language interpreter was necessary for optimal school progress. Upon seeking mediation with an independent examiner, it was determined that Amy was making adequate social, educational, and academic progress without an interpreter. As a result, the school and mediator determined an interpreter was not needed. Amy's parents instituted the case in federal district court. The court found Amy to be a well-adjusted child, who interacted well with both peers and teachers and performed academically better than other students her age. At the same time, the court noted Amy was not achieving her full potential, as she did not understand everything verbally that was occurring in the classroom. The court sided with the parents and found that the school had not provided Amy with the opportunity to maximize her potential, and as a result, determined that Amy was not receiving a FAPE. The case went to the Court of Appeals, and then finally to the U.S. Supreme Court, where the Court interpreted FAPE as designed to meet the individual needs of the child, supported by necessary supplemental services for the student to benefit from instruction. Furthermore, the Court determined the school must encourage school progress for the child, but is not responsible to provide the best possible education or maximize the potential of the student. In the end, the Supreme Court found in favor of the

school. In this first interpretation of P.L. 94-142, the Supreme Court offered a two-part test for defining a FAPE: first, are the procedures set forth in the law being followed? And secondly, is the IEP "reasonably calculated" to encourage educational achievement? This initial ruling and two-part test provided the groundwork for subsequent court cases.

Court cases following the *Rowley* decision have generally concluded that services must be provided to allow students to receive educational benefits—although these services do not have to rise to the level of being the very best. While there is a "medical exclusion" clause in special education law (i.e., services that can only be provided by a physician do not have to be provided as part of a child's IEP), several court cases have addressed the question of what constitutes related medical services that school districts would be required to provide as part of FAPE. In several cases, the courts have ruled in favor of parents seeking certain medical services (e.g., the provision of clean intermittent catheterization in *Irving Independent School District v. Tatro*, 1984; nursing care for a ventilator dependent student in *Cedar Rapids v. Garrett F.*, 1999) and concluded that such services must be provided by the schools if they are needed for the child to be able to access his/her educational environment, and can be provided by the school nurse or another trained school professional.

In 1989, *Daniel R.R. v. State Board of Education* provided further interpretation of a FAPE for students with disabilities, namely a FAPE in the LRE. This landmark case provides a blueprint for determining appropriate educational placement for students with disabilities, highlighting placement in the LRE. At the time the case arose, Daniel was a 6-year-old boy with Down Syndrome who exhibited a developmental age of 2–3 years. While the school originally placed Daniel in half-time regular pre-kindergarten class and half-time early childhood resource services upon the parents' request, the admissions, review and dismissal committee revisited Daniel's placement in November of his kindergarten year and recommended full-time special education placement due to difficulties Daniel was exhibiting in the regular education classroom. In disagreement with the committee's decision, Daniel's parents sought mediation and the hearing officer agreed with the school placement. According to the officer, Daniel did not seem to be benefitting from the regular education placement, and was disrupting the other students in the pre-kindergarten class. Ultimately, the case was heard by the U.S. Court of Appeals, which found in favor of the school. The court provided valuable interpretation of an LRE, determining the educational placement for students with disabilities was not an all-or-nothing placement that required the student to be in all mainstream *or* special education. Rather, schools were required under P.L. 94-142 to provide education as appropriate for the student, providing regular education to the maximum extent possible. The Court provided a two-part test when determining the educational placement of a student: (1) Can education be achieved satisfactorily in the regular education environment with supplementary aids and services? And, (2) if special education is required, has the child been integrated into the mainstream setting to the maximum extent possible? In making its decision, the court noted that mainstreaming benefits need not be solely educational in nature and that children may benefit from "nonacademic experiences in the regular education environment." The court also opined that the effect of the placement on the regular education environment could be considered when determining the most appropriate placement.

The case of *Oberti v. Board of Education of the Borough of Clementon School District* (1993) provided placement decision protocols for schools when determining appropriate levels of inclusion in regular education for students with disabilities. In this case, the Borough of Clementon School District wanted Rafael Oberti, a child with Down Syndrome, to be placed in a more restrictive special educational setting in a neighboring school district. Rafael's parents requested mainstreaming in a regular education class. After filing for a due process hearing, the school district and Obertis agreed to mediation. Following mediation, the team decided to place Rafael in a special education setting while actively pursuing mainstreaming possibilities. However, as no attempts toward mainstreaming were made, the Obertis filed again for a due process hearing. Ultimately, the courts ruled in favor of the parents, stating the school had failed to establish that Rafael could not be educated in the regular education classroom with supplemental aids and services. The 3rd Circuit Court outlined three factors relevant to inclusion of the student in the mainstream classroom: (1) whether the school district made reasonable accommodations using supplemental aids and services for the student; (2) educational benefits of regular classroom placement in contrast to special education placement; and (3) the effect of the student with disabilities on the education of students in the regular education classroom. The court

concluded that if full inclusion was not appropriate for the student's educational placement, the student should be mainstreamed to the "maximum extent possible."

Similarly, both *Board of Education, Sacramento City Unified School District v. Holland* (1992) and its appeal, *Sacramento City Unified School District v. Rachel H.* (1994) established mainstream education as the presumed starting point for education of children with disabilities. In this case, the school placed Rachel, a student with an intellectual disability, in half-time regular education and half-time special education. Rachel's parents wanted Rachel placed in full-time regular education and appealed the school's decision. The state hearing officer sided with the parents, and required the school to provide a regular educational placement supplemented with appropriate aids and services. The school appealed this decision to both the district court (1992) and later the circuit court (1994). In the end, the appeals court sided with the parents. In doing so, the 9th Circuit Court established a four-part test to determine whether or not a school district is providing the least restrictive environment. First, the IEP team should examine the educational benefits of placing a child in regular education with supplemental aids and services. Secondly, the nonacademic benefits (e.g., social, communication) should be considered. Third, the team should consider the effects of the student with disabilities on the other students and teacher in the regular education classroom. Finally, the costs of supplementary aids and services associated with this placement should be considered. The court ruled that cost can emerge as a relevant factor only if it adversely effects the education of other students. This four-part test provided school personnel with further directives when determining the most appropriate educational placement for a student.

The aforementioned cases offer further guidelines for administrators, teachers, school psychologists and parents in the provision of FAPE in the LRE. Namely, schools are required to provide a "reasonably calculated" individualized educational plan for the student, but are not necessarily required to maximize the potential of the student. Secondly, in determining appropriate educational placement in the LRE (e.g. special education and/or regular education), the school must consider the academic, social, and emotional benefits of the individual child, as well as possible negative outcomes on both the student with disabilities as well as other students, of both a regular education and special education placement.

Changes in School Psychologists' Roles

Between the initial passage of PL 94-142 through the mid-1990s, both court cases and federal legislation were instrumental in providing access to FAPE for children and adolescents with disabilities, as well as guidance defining FAPE, and requiring an IEP in the LRE for individuals ages 3–21 with necessary supplemental services. During this time, the role of the school psychologist slowly expanded. While the school psychologist remained a "gatekeeper" by determining special education eligibility, there was a slowly increasing emphasis on the role of both interventionist and consultant for both regular education and special education students. Reschly and Wilson (1995) found that school psychologists in 1986 and 1991–1992 continued to be heavily involved in assessment, with approximately one-half of their time being filled by assessment activities. During this time, Reschly (2000) stated that school psychologists reported primarily working with students "who are suspected of or who are diagnosed with disabilities" (p. 513). However, they also noted one-quarter of school psychologists reporting spending less than half of their time in special education related services. Consistent with previous surveys (Smith, 1984; Stevenson-Hicks, 1980), school psychologists continued to prefer less time devoted to assessment with more time being allocated for intervention and consultation activities (Reschly & Wilson, 1995, Reschly, 2000). We next turn to the legislation that followed, providing a third major shift in both legislation and the practice of school psychology and emphasizing not only access and programming, but educational outcomes, procedural safeguards, and accountability as well.

Increased Focus on Educational Outcomes and School Accountability

Most recently, special education law has focused on educational outcomes, school accountability, and increasing parental rights. Since 1997, two reauthorizations of IDEA and the implementation of No Child Left Behind have contributed to this focus. In response, these changes have been linked to an expanded role for school psychologists. In 2000, Reschly predicted that while traditional assessment roles with special education students would continue to dominate the time of school psychologists, the practitioner's role would expand to include intervention services, less standardized assessment procedures, and greater involvement in consultation services. In conjunction with the following pieces of legislation, these assertions are slowly being realized.

IDEA Reauthorizations

INDIVIDUALS WITH DISABILITIES ACT AMENDMENTS OF 1997

P.L. 105-17 (IDEA 97) was the reauthorization of P.L. 101-476. In this reauthorization, key changes increased accountability in providing FAPE for students with disabilities. To increase accountability and focus on the individual student's needs, new statutory requirements were made to the IEP. In particular, IDEA 97 included an increased focus on using the IEP to increase children's involvement in the regular education curriculum. IDEA-97 required the development of goals and short-term IEP objectives for students incorporating both the student's present level of educational performance and influence of the student's disability on classroom success in regular education. Further, goals and objectives were to be written in relation to the general education curriculum. Needed modifications and accommodations were to be specified in the student's IEP, as well as transitional educational needs beginning at age 14. Interestingly, as discussed below, some of these provisions were modified by IDEA 2004, in which short-term objectives are no longer required and the age at which transition needs to begin was moved to 16. IDEA-97 also required regular education teachers on IEP teams for students with disabilities who were partially or completely mainstreamed, to ensure "meaningful access to general curriculum."

Increased focus on accountability in IDEA-97 was reflected in part by requiring students with disabilities to be included in statewide assessments (with needed supports and modifications). Reports from the testing were required to be made available to parents and stakeholders at the same frequency as those reported to parents of regular education students.

Additional changes in IDEA-97 involved discipline issues, including guidelines on how long a child could be removed from the educational environment, as well as provisions to address problematic behavior. Under IDEA-97, students could be removed for up to 10 days without special education services. However, for longer-term removal from the student's current placement (generally into a more restrictive placement) the school must conduct a functional behavioral assessment (FBA) and make modifications to (or develop) the student's behavior intervention plan to ensure the plan addresses the behaviors of concern. A manifestation determination was required for any change of placement.

Other changes in IDEA-97 related to increasing access for additional populations. Notably, provisions were made to include attention-deficit/hyperactivity disorder as a disorder that could qualify a child under the *Other Health Impairment* special education classification. In addition, the age for a *Developmental Delay* classification was increased, from 3–5 years to 3–9 years of age. Services for Infants and Toddlers, formally Part H services, were changed to Part C services and required coordinated, statewide, interagency efforts for the delivery of services to infants and toddlers. IDEA-97 also placed increased emphasis on the need to provide services to infants and toddlers in children's natural environments.

As a result of these amendments, and increased focus on accountability in providing an individualized FAPE education with the regular education environment in mind, the school psychologist role also shifted. Certainly, school psychologists were equipped to provide guidance for both IEP goals and accommodations, tailoring the IEP to the individual student. Additionally, school psychologists now possessed a key role in developing and implementing FBA processes and procedures to adhere to IDEA-97. At this point, school psychologists and administrators indicated many educators were unaware of and had not received training in FBA (Nelson, Roberts, Rutherford, Mathur, & Aaroe, 1999). As a result, school psychologists were needed to provide training and support to teachers for the implementation of FBA under IDEA-97, providing an avenue for the expansion of the school psychologists' role into intervention-related activities (Reschly, 2000). Unfortunately, many school psychologists also knew little about FBA procedures, and the school psychology literature lacked significant discussion of such procedures. Following IDEA-97, the field of school psychology began focusing attention to this area with a great increase in the number of publications and presentations on the topic (Merrell at el., 2006). For today's school psychologists, knowledge of FBA processes and behavioral intervention plan procedures is an important part of both training and practice.

INDIVIDUALS WITH DISABILITIES EDUCATION IMPROVEMENT ACT (2004)

The most recent reauthorization of special education law (P.L. 108-446) further highlights school accountability by increasing the focus on whether students with disabilities are benefitting from the services they receive. Schools are required to monitor the implementation of IDEA and develop performance plans to evaluate how they are doing in terms of that implementation. States must also report outcome data on an annual basis. Regulations indicate that the primary focus of states' monitoring activities should be on: "(1) Improving educational results and functional outcomes for all children with disabilities; and (2) Ensuring that public agencies meet the program requirements under Part B of the Act (which applies to children ages 3-21), with a particular emphasis on those requirements that are most closely related to improving educational results for children with disabilities" (34 C.F.R. § 300.600) States must include students with disabilities in their accountability reporting systems, and publicly report outcome data on an annual basis.

The general provisions of Part B (Assistance for Education of all Children with Disabilities) and Part C (Infants and Toddlers with Disabilities) of IDEA 2004 are outlined below. Because this is the most recent version of special education law we provide a more detailed overview of IDEA 2004 than we have of its predecessors. However, this overview is still brief and we encourage readers to refer to idea.ed.gov and their local state laws regarding its implementation for a more comprehensive overview of IDEA 2004.

Part B mandates that each state educational agency develop a plan to provide a FAPE for children with disabilities. Specifically, the law describes a child with a disability as possessing one of thirteen disabilities: autism, cognitive impairment, deafness, deaf-blindness, emotional disturbance, other health impairment, hearing impairment, learning disability, multiple disabilities, orthopedic impairment, speech/language impairment, traumatic brain injury, visual impairment/blindness, which require special education and related services (P. L. 108-466 § 602 [3] [A]). Additionally, students can qualify under developmental delay from ages 3–9 in the areas of: physical, cognitive, emotional/social, communication or adaptive development who require special education services (34. C.F.R. § 300.8). The obligation to provide a FAPE is from ages 3–21 or until the student meets regular graduation criteria, no longer meets eligibility requirements, or parents refuse special education placement. The FAPE must occur in the LRE with or near same-aged peers and as close to the home school of attendance if possible (34 C.F.R. § 300.116).

Further, each state must implement a plan (Child Find) to actively seek children with disabilities and provide them with full educational opportunity, regardless of the severity of disability. School districts must have a Child Find plan, coordinated with other agencies, and a public awareness campaign to screen and locate children with disabilities in need of special education, including those currently enrolled in public education (34 C.F.R. § 300.111).

In determining qualification for special education services, a three-pronged inquiry is undertaken: A) Does the student meet diagnostic criteria? B) Does the disability cause an adverse effect on the student's educational performance? and C) Does the student require special education intervention? In the assessment phase, multiple sound assessment measures and strategies to determine the student's level of abilities must be used to provide relevant information for educational intervention (34 C.F.R. § 300.304). After completing a thorough evaluation, a meeting is held with the parents (34 C.F.R. § 30.501) to interpret the evaluation data and determine eligibility criteria for special education. Special guidelines and flexibility are outlined for reevaluation. With parental agreement, full assessment is not required if the IEP team determines the current testing is still valid (34 C.F.R. § 300.305). School psychologists, as discussed in more detail below, have a key role in the identification, assessment and qualification of students for special education classification.

In the definition of a learning disability and qualification in one of its eight categories, IDEA 2004 does not require the discrepancy model as previously required. Rather, school districts can use response to intervention (RTI) strategies, as outlined by their state guidelines, to qualify students for special education, provided they rule out lack of appropriate instruction and conduct observations of the learning environment both before and after referral (34 C.F.R. § 300.309). This change in the legislation provides school psychologists with more flexibility in the classification and provision of services for students with learning disabilities. Additionally, up to 15% of the special education budget may be allocated for general education pre-referral interventions. School psychologists may play a key role in the pre-referral intervention process, finding learning strategies that "work" for students, keeping them in the least restrictive educational environment, the regular education classroom. Although many school psychologists are embracing the RTI concept and it certainly seems as though the field of school psychology is poised to more fully integrate this model into its services, it is worth noting that the RTI model is a new one with many current school psychologists not having received training in this model. As when the FBA requirements were added to IDEA-97 and the research and training on this topic increased dramatically, a similar phenomenon is occurring with RTI procedures.

The IEP team must be composed of the parents of the child, a regular education teacher (if the student is participating in any regular education), at least one special education teacher, a representative of the Local Educational Agency (LEA), an individual who can interpret the implications of the evaluation results (e.g. school psychologists), individuals who have knowledge of the child (e.g. related services personnel) and the child, when appropriate (34 C.F.R. § 300.321). Detailed guidelines regarding appropriate notice and meeting components are further outlined by IDEA. The task of the IEP team is the development of an individualized education plan outlining empirically supported intervention strategies for the student with special consideration of behavioral interventions, required related services, language proficiency, and required assistive technology (34 C.F.R. § 300.324). The IEP must explain the extent to which the student will not participate in the regular classroom or with the regular curriculum, and students may be removed from regular education placement only when the severity of the disability prohibits success in the regular classroom with supplemental supports. Additional requirements for the IEP are outlined by IDEA 2004 (see 34 C.F.R. § 300.320). Placement must be reviewed annually or when a student is not progressing and/or exhibiting behavior problems. Additionally, the IEP must have goals (but not necessarily benchmarks as outlined in IDEA 97) and must address transitional services starting at age 16 (rather than 14 as outlined in IDEA 97).

Parental rights are outlined in a booklet of procedural safeguards. These must be provided to parents at least once a year. The safeguards outline many parental rights and school responsibilities, including: consent and notice requirements, evaluation procedures, right to an independent evaluation, IEP and LRE requirements, discipline provisions, mediation procedures, due process hearing, educational records and placement requirements (34 C.F.R. § 300.503-520).

Additional guidelines are outlined which may also be relevant to school psychologists. For example, school personnel cannot require students to obtain prescriptions in order to attend school, be evaluated, or receive special education services (34 C.F.R. § 300.174). IDEA 2004 provided more flexibility for schools to review manifestation determinations for students with severe behavioral difficulties on an individual, case by case basis. Schools can remove a student to an interim alternative education setting for 45 school days for possession of weapons or drugs on school property regardless of manifestation determination (34 C.F.R. §300.530-535).

Although the final regulations for Part C have yet to be issued, Part C appears to be very similar to previous authorizations, providing grants to states for the development of early intervention services. Specifically, services are provided to children with disabilities up to age 3 who exhibit delays in cognitive, social/emotional, physical, communicative and adaptive development. Services are to be provided by a service coordinator in the home environment when possible and may include: family training, speech/language services, occupational therapy, physical therapy or counseling services. As with previous regulations regarding birth to 3 services, the requirement of a *free* appropriate public education is not present. States are not required to provide Part C services (although all currently do) and states are allowed to charge parents fees for services.

While it is yet to be fully realized, changes in IDEA 2004 have the capacity to substantially shift the role of the school psychologist, from that of primary diagnostician to a more evenly distributed, broader role, focusing on consultation, intervention, and assessment. Throughout the entire process of pre-referral intervention, assessment and intervention development, school psychologists are uniquely situated to provide assistance with the implementation of IDEA 2004. With a focus on RTI, school psychologists can play vital roles in pre-referral interventions with regular education students, as they possess the training to track data on the use of empirically supported assessments and interventions to pinpoint the individual student's specific educational difficulty. Of course, with the increased focus on RTI and progress monitoring it is incumbent on school psychology graduate programs to include training on curriculum based measurement, behavioral observations, single subject design methodology and other techniques that allow for the reliable and valid use of data in making educational decisions. If school psychologists can "show" that students respond to regular education intervention, students can remain in the least restrictive educational environment. Similarly, school psychologists are well trained in multimodal quality assessment, which is a requirement for evaluation and qualification under IDEA 2004. For the evaluation of students with specific learning disabilities (SLD), research is continually being conducted to support teachers, school psychologists and administrators in implementing RTI methods (e.g. Gilbertson, Maxfield & Hughes, 2007; Hale, Kaufman, Naglieri & Kavale, 2006; Ofiesh, 2006; VanDerHeyen, Witt & Gilbertson, 2007). As over one-half of students with disabilities are qualified under SLD (Reschly, 2000),

an expanded implantation of RTI will dramatically change the role of the school psychologist from not only administering but also interpreting assessment data, providing the link from assessment to quality, empirically based interventions.

School psychologists can play a vital role as "problem solving consultants" for academic problems (Berninger, 2006) in working with students referred for special education assessment and intervention. School psychologists are also needed to keep abreast of empirically supported interventions and support their implementation in the school setting (Berninger, 2006).

As student and parental rights become more salient in the IEP process, school psychologists can act as advocates for parents and their child(ren), ensuring access to a high quality educational plan which meets the individual needs of the students. From assessment interpretation to the individualized development of the student's IEP, school psychologists should work to ensure that IDEA 2004 is being implemented and the interventions included in the student's IEP are empirically supported and validated to meet the unique needs of the individual child.

No Child Left Behind Act

In addition to accountability being an increasing focus of special education law, accountability was made very prominent in general education with the 2001 passage of P.L. 107-110, the No Child Left Behind Act (NCLB), which was signed into law on January 8, 2002. NCLB was the reauthorization of the Elementary and Secondary Education Act of 1965 and focuses on increased accountability within America's school districts. Specifically, the bill necessitates outcome accountability, scientifically researched teaching methods, student and parental rights, and school flexibility in an attempt to close the academic achievement gap between both minority students and students with disabilities and their peers. In essence, NCLB is an attempt to ensure that all schools are maximizing the learning of all students, including those with disabilities. Although the increased accountability required by NCLB certainly has positive aspects, the manner in which progress has been defined and assessed has created significant challenges for school personnel, including school psychologists.

With the passage of NCLB, school districts are required to demonstrate adequate yearly progress (AYP) on assessments in the areas of math, reading and science. Starting in 2005–2006, NCLB required school districts to test in reading and math annually throughout grades 3–8, and once during the students' high school years. Additionally, beginning in 2007–2008, testing in science was mandated once in each student's elementary, middle and high school years. The law states schools are required to assess 95% of their students using standardized assessment tools, with the option to use other achievement standards for 1% of their students (i.e., students with severe disabilities). Students not proficient in English are also targeted by NCLB, which states that all students with limited English proficiency will become proficient in English. While the assessments and standards themselves may be selected by individual states, the schools must meet the state standards (AYP) to receive federal funding. Further, the law requires 100% proficiency in the areas of reading and math by the school year 2013–2014. Currently, the data regarding student proficiency is bleak, indicating additional progress is needed. In 2006–2007, the United States Department of Education published data regarding nationwide student proficiency. At this time, 34% of fourth graders and 27% of eighth graders achieved reading scores below the basic level in annual testing, and 32% of fourth graders and 29% of eighth graders achieved scores at or above reading proficiency. Similarly, 29% of fourth graders and 34% of eighth graders scored below the basic level in math testing, and 39% of fourth graders and 32% of eighth graders achieved scores at or above the proficiency level in math. Despite the fact that proficiency standards are not being achieved, and a larger portion of students are not meeting the basic or proficient levels on both reading and math skills, 2008 data suggests 70% of America's 98,905 schools were making adequate yearly progress (USDOE, 2008).

To record and publicize school progress, districts must publicize an annual school progress report with data aggregated by ethnicity, gender, and disability, for policymakers, stakeholders and parents. For Title I schools who fail to meet AYP for two years in a row, schools must notify parents of their option for open enrollment, and begin a remediation plan. After three years' failure to meet AYP, schools are required to provide additional instructional programs such as tutoring and afterschool classes. With four years' failure to meet AYP, the state is required to put corrective measures in place. While these are to be determined by the individual state, they may include a staff or curriculum change, reduction in management authority, or extended school day/year. If a school fails to meet AYP for five years, major changes, such as a school takeover, total school staff replacement, or charter

school conversion may be implemented, according to NCLB. All decisions regarding failure to meet AYP are made and implemented by the state in which the school district resides.

NCLB also outlined requirements for teacher qualifications, requiring teachers to be highly qualified (both certified and proficient) in their teaching area by 2005–2006. As of 2006–2007, 95.76% of classrooms in low poverty elementary schools were taught by highly qualified teachers as compared to 90.42% of classrooms in high poverty elementary schools. Similarly, 93.76% of classrooms in low poverty secondary schools were taught by highly qualified teachers as compared to 90.42% of classrooms in high poverty secondary schools (USDOE, 2008). Additionally, paraprofessionals must also be highly qualified, having two years of study at an institution of higher education or having passed a formal assessment, demonstrating knowledge in math, reading and writing.

Several other items were included in NCLB which impacted students, parents and schools. For instance, a provision for military recruitment was included, and schools are now required to give names and contact information of students to the military (parents have the option to opt out). Additionally, schools that make AYP are given the option to use up to 50% of their federal monies for alternative educational programs. Finally, research-based teaching methods must be employed. Specifically, the act outlined curriculum selection requirements, highlighting the use of strong evidence-based interventions such as 1:1 tutoring and direct instruction. School psychologists are knowledgeable about research-based instructional techniques, and may play a key role in their implementation.

Since its inception, NCLB has been a source of both criticism and praise, and remains a highly controversial piece of legislation. Several items included in NCLB are debated. First, concerns abound over the possible reduction of effective instruction. Specifically, critics worry that teachers will "teach to the test," resulting in reduced quality of instruction for students. Secondly, students with disabilities and English-language learners are included in the 100% proficiency requirement. Many schools believe this requirement is too inflexible and does not account for the unique learning needs of each individual student, and fails to consider the length of time it takes for students with disabilities and English-language learners to approach proficiency. Third, several commentators point to the use of standardized testing as inherently problematic, providing only one index of student achievement (e.g. Roach & Frank, 2007). With that said, proponents of NCLB highlight increased test scores, greater exposure of regular education curriculum to special education students, lowered achievement gaps, greater accountability, and increased attention to minority students and students with disabilities, as support for the Act (USDOE, 2006).

Most recently, NCLB was up for reauthorization in 2007. However, Congress did not agree upon reauthorization during either 2007 or 2008. Rather, on October 29, 2008, then Secretary of Education Margaret Spelling and the Department of Education offered new guidelines and regulations for NCLB (34 C.F.R. § 200). First, schools were given directives on how to calculate high school graduation rates; namely, the percentage of students graduating within four years of entering high school. These graduation rates must be calculated as a whole, as well as aggregated by disability, ethnicity, and gender, and are to be included in defining AYP (34 C.F.R. § 200.19). Secondly, to offer further clarification of the school choice provision for parents of students whose schools failed to meet AYP for two or more years, school districts are now required to notify parents in writing prior to the start of the new school year (34 C.F.R. § 200.32). Third, states were directed to reevaluate the minimum number of students in each demographic subgroup (e.g. gender, disability), to ensure both statistical accuracy and privacy of the individual students included (34 C.F.R. § 200.7). Fourth, an additional 2% of students can take an alternate assessment based on modified achievement standards, provided the school can provide evidence that their individual disability prohibits the student(s) from achieving at mainstream levels of proficiency (34 C.F.R. § 200.13).

Certainly, NCLB has impacted teachers, staff, and administrators: the educational environment is now one that must produce positive results. School psychologists have a role as "instructional change agents" for the implementation of NCLB (Elliot, 2007). School psychologists should be knowledgeable and well versed in the standards assessed, and unique implementation of NCLB in their state. Specifically, Elliot (2007) suggested school psychologists provide assistance to students in two ways. First, school psychologists should work to individualize accommodations for students with disabilities in order to ensure "equal footing" for success on standardized assessments. School psychologists should work with individual students to tailor unique accommodations, and train the student in the utilization of these accommodations. Second, school psychologists can work with all students to provide preparation for test taking (e.g., problem solving, coping with test-taking anxiety). As students undoubtedly experience pressure to perform on these high-stakes tests, school psychologists can work to equip students with needed "tools" to succeed on the standardized assessments.

Additionally, school psychologists should support teachers by identifying effective, evidence-based instructional techniques to meet the demands of NCLB. Equally important, school psychologists can assist the evaluation of the "big picture"—the educational goals, curricular needs, and testing demands across the school district, ensuring evidence-based instruction and curriculum which meets the goals and testing requirements. As standardized assessment offers only one piece of data regarding instructional effectiveness and student achievement, school psychologists can aid in the tracking of multiple forms of student data to track both achievement and teaching effectiveness (Elliot, 2007; Roach & Frank, 2007). Finally, school psychologists can also provide training and education for teachers on the use of effective accommodations, behavior management strategies, and creation of positive academic and social classroom environments.

Chapter Summary

Over the last several decades, federal legislation has influenced the role of school psychologists, with both the "intended" and "unintended" consequences of these legislative changes being difficult to predict (Reschly, 2000). With P.L. 94-142 in 1975, the number of school psychologist positions tripled as schools were required to provide educational programming for students with disabilities (Merrell et. al, 2006; Reschly, 2000). As a result, the "gatekeeper" role of school psychologists was strengthened, as they were heavily involved in assessment and educational placement decisions for students with disabilities. While school psychologists at the time vocally stated a preference for a wider job role (e.g., Smith, 1984; Stevenson-Hicks, 1980;), the role of diagnostician and provider of services for students with disabilities was primary. Over the years, the school psychologist's role has changed from simply one of gatekeeper to one of prevention, intervention, and assessment specialist. In part, this is in reaction to court decisions and changes in federal legislation—but it is also important to note that preferences of school psychologists and research by school psychologists helped lead the way for some of the changes in legislation that then resulted in practice changes. In this chapter we have focused on the influence of changes in legislation on the role of the school psychologist, but it is important to note that these changes are not necessarily unidirectional, as laws and legislation are influenced by, and often preceded by changes in practice and research on promising methods (e.g., FBA and RTI). It seems that the "preferences" of school psychologists are slowly being realized, as the role of the school psychologist has recently begun to broaden. As we look to the future, changes to federal, state and local legislation will undoubtedly continue to shape and define the role of school psychologists. Similarly school psychologist practitioners and researches would do well to be proactive in advocating for expansion of the role of the school psychologist.

Endnotes

1. A statute can also be enacted without the President's signature if Congress overrides a presidential veto with a two-thirds vote in both the House of Representatives and the Senate.

References

Americans with Disabilities Act of 1990, Pub. L. No. 101-336, 104 Stat. 327 (1990).

Berninger, V. W. (2006). Research supported ideas for implementing reauthorized IDEA with intelligent professional psychological services. *Psychology in the Schools*, 781–796.

Board of Education v. Rowley. 458 U.S. 176 (1982)

Brown v. Board of Education, 347 U.S. 483 (1954).

Cedar Rapids Community School District v. Garrett F., 526 U.S. 66 (1999).

Civil Rights Act of 1964, Pub. L. 88–352, 78 Stat. 241 (1964).

Daniel R. R. v. State Board of Education. 874 F.2d 1036 (5th Cir. 1989).

Education of the Handicapped Act of 1970, Pub. .L. No. 91-230, 84 Stat. 154 (1970).

Education of all the Handicapped Children Act of 1975, Pub.L. No. 94-142, 89 Stat. 773 (1975).

Education of the Handicapped Act Amendments of 1983, Pub. L. No. 98-199, 97 Stat. 1357 (1983).

Education of the Handicapped Act Amendments of 1986, Pub. L. No. 99-457, 100 Stat. 1145 (1986).

Educational Amendments of 1974, Pub. L. No. 93-380, Pub. L. 93-380, 88 Stat. 484 (1974).

Elementary and Secondary Education Act of 1965, Pub. L. No. 89-10, 79 Stat. 27 (1965).

Elementary and Secondary Education Act Amendments of 1966, Pub. L. No. 89-750, 80 Stat. 1191 (1966).

Elliot, J. (2007). Providing academic support for teachers and students in high stakes learning environments. *Journal of Applied School Psychology (23)*, 87–107.

Fagan, T. K., & Wise, P. S. (2007). School psychology: Past, present, and future (3rd ed.). Bethesda, MD: National Association of School Psychologists.

Gilbertson, D., Maxfield, J., & Hughes, J. (2007). Evaluating responsiveness to intervention for English language learners: A comparison of response modes on letter naming rates. *Journal of Behavioral Education, 16*, 259–279.

Goldwasser, E., Meyers, J., Christenson, S. & Graden, J. (1983). The impact of PL 94-142 on the practice of school psychology: A national survey. *Psychology in the Schools, 20*, 153–165.

Hale, J., Kaufman, A., Naglieri, J., & Kavale, K. (2006). Implementation of IDEA: Integrating response to intervention and cognitive assessment methods. *Psychology in the Schools, 43*, 753–770.

Hosp, J. L. & Reschly, D. J. (2002). Regional differences in school psychology practice. *School Psychology Review, 31*, 11–29.

Individuals with Disabilities Education Act of 1990, Pub. .L. No. 101-476, 104 Stat. 1142 (1990).

Individuals with Disabilities Education Act Amendments of 1992, Pub. L. No. 102-119, 105 Stat. 587 (1991).

Individuals with Disabilities Act Amendments of 1997. P.L. 105-17, 111 Stat. 37 (1997).

Individuals with Disabilities Education Improvement Act of 2004, Pub. L. No. 108-446, 118 Stat. 2647 (2004)

Irving Independent School District v. Tatro, 468 U.S. 883 (1984).

Jacob, S., & Hartshorne, T. S. (2007). Ethics and law for school psychologists, fifth edition. New Jersey: Wiley, John & Sons

Martin, E. W., Martin, R., & Terman, D. L. (1996). The legislative and litigation history of special education. *The Future of Children: Special Education for Students with Disabilities, 6*, 25–39.

Merrell, K. W., Ervin, R. A., & Gimpel, G. A. (2006). School psychology for the 21st century: Foundations and practices. New York: Guilford Press.

Mills vs. District of Columbia Bd. of Educ., 348 F. Supp. 866 (D.D.C. 1972), *contempt proceedings*, EHLR 551:643 (D.D.C. 1980).

Nelson, J. R., Roberts, M. L., Rutherford, R. B., Mathur, S. R. & Aaroe, L. A. (1999). A statewide survey of special education administrators and school psychologists regarding functional behavioral assessment. *Education and Treatment of Children, (22)*, 267–279.

No Child Left Behind Act of 2001, Pub. L. No. 107-110, 115 Stat. 1425 (2002).

Oberti v. Board of Education of the Borough of Clementon School District., 995 F.2d 1204 (3rd Cir. 1993).

Ofiesh, N. (2006). Response to intervention and the identification of students with specific learning disabilities: Why we need comprehensive evaluations as part of the process. *Psychology in the Schools, 43*, 883–888.

Oklahoma v. United States Civil Service Commission, 330 U.S. 127, 143 (1947).

Pennsylvania Association for Retarded Children (PARC) v. Pennsylvania, 334 F. Supp. 1257 (E.D. Pa. 1971); *amended consent agreement*, 343 F. Supp. 279 (E.D. Pa. 1972).

Rehabilitation Act Amendments of 1973, Pub. L. 93-516, 88 Stat. 1617 (1973).

Reschly, D.J. (2000). The present and future status of school psychology in the United States. *School Psychology Review, 29*, 507–522.

Reschly, D. J. & Wilson, M. S. (1995). School psychology practitioners and faculty: 1986 to 1991–92 trends in demographics, roles, satisfaction, and system reform. *School Psychology Review, 24*, 62–81.

Roach, A. T., Frank, J. L. (2007). Large-scale assessment, rationality, and scientific management: the case of No Child Left Behind. *Journal of Applied School Psychology (23)*, 7–25.

Sacramento City Unified School District. v. Rachel H., 14 F.3d 1398 (9th Cir. 1994).

Smith, D. K. (1984). Practicing school psychologists: Their characteristics, activities and populations served. *Professional Psychology, 15*, 798–810.

Stevenson-Hicks, R. (1980). Public-law 94-142: Practicing school psychologists' perceptions of how this law affects them. *Psychology in the Schools, 17,* 491–496.

Turnbull, H. R., & Turnbull, A. P. (2000). Free appropriate public education: The law and children with disabilities (6th ed.). Denver, CO: Love Publishing.

United States Department of Education (May, 2006). *No Child Left Behind is Working.* Retrieved from: http://www.ed.gov/nclb/overview/importance/nclbworking.html.

United States Department of Education (June, 2008). *Mapping America's Educational Progress, 2008.* Retrieved from: http://www.ed.gov/nclb/accountability/results/progress/nation.html.

VanDerHeyen, A. M., Witt, J. C., & Gilbertson, D. (2007). A multi-year evaluation of the effects of a response to intervention (RTI) model on identification of children for special education. *Journal of School Psychology, 45,* 225–256.

Ethical Considerations in the Practice of School Psychology

Kathleen M. McNamara

Abstract

Cross-national variations in the role and function of school psychologists, the organization of schools, and cultural norms require flexibility in applying standards and procedures for ethically sound practice. However, a set of universal ethical principles exists, and serves as a framework within which decisions about ethical matters can be made. In this chapter, four general principles are described—respect for the dignity of persons; responsible caring; integrity in professional relationships; and responsibility to society. Their applications are explored in the context of common and emerging ethical themes and dilemmas, including administrative pressures, unsound educational practices, informed consent, privacy, fairness and nondiscrimination, use of technology, response-to-intervention models, and conflicts of interest. Various models for ethical decision making also are discussed.

Keywords: ethics, ethical principles, school psychology, code of ethics, international school psychology

Introduction: Sources of Guidance for Ethical Practice
Universal Ethical Principles

Although the manner in which school psychology is practiced varies across the world, the profession is founded on a set of core *competencies*, including assessment, consultation, and direct intervention (Oakland & Cunningham, 1997). In contrast, differences in national economies, laws, and customs make it difficult to identify core expectations for professional conduct, since the appropriateness of particular behaviors is judged against local or regional standards. For example, in the United States, autonomy and the interests of the individual are highly valued, as reflected in both public policy and interpersonal conduct. In Arab culture, on the other hand, membership in social systems is of primary importance, and standards for public and private behavior are based on a collectivist orientation (Buda & Elsayed-Elkhouly, 1998). It is easy to understand how this contrast might be reflected in

different standards regarding privacy, access to and consent for professional services, conflicts of interest, and inter-professional relationships.

Nevertheless, there exists a set of universal principles, adopted in 2008 by the International Union of Psychological Science, the International Association of Applied Psychology, and the International Association for Cross-Cultural Psychology. Although these principles pertain to the broad practice of psychology (rather than the more specific practice of school psychology), they provide a flexible and useful framework for exploring and understanding ethical issues encountered by school psychologists.

The preamble to the *Universal Declaration of Ethical Principles for Psychologists* explains that the document "articulates principles and related values that are general and aspirational rather than specific and prescriptive. Application of the principles and values to the development of specific standards or conduct will vary across cultures, and must occur locally or regionally in order to ensure their relevance to local or regional cultures, customs, beliefs, and laws" (2008, p. 1). The ethical code of the International School Psychology Association (ISPA) is similarly noteworthy for its emphasis on the importance of standards that traverse geographic and national boundaries, while acknowledging that universal ethical principles are subject to interpretation in light of norms, values, and traditions that may differ across countries.

The values that describe universal ethical principles in the *Universal Declaration of Ethical Principles for Psychologists* include respect for the dignity of persons and peoples; competent caring for the well-being of persons and peoples; integrity; and professional and scientific responsibilities to society. These are essentially the same as the four general principles of the Canadian Code of Ethics for Psychologists (Sinclair, 1998), which places the principles in hierarchical order, such that "respect for the dignity of persons" precedes and supersedes other principles when there is conflict among them. The universal principles as expressed in the language of the Canadian Code of Ethics will be further explored and employed as a framework for discussing ethical issues later in this chapter: *Respect for the Dignity of Persons; Responsible Caring; Integrity in Relationships*; and *Responsibility to Society* (Canadian Psychological Association, 1986).

Ethical Codes in School Psychology

The adoption of an ethical code is a hallmark of a maturing profession, representing not only a form of self-regulation, but also a social contract through which members of the profession agree to certain standards for professional conduct, as a means of safeguarding the public welfare (Fagan & Wise, 2007). Although school psychology has been a recognized discipline in the United States for decades (numbered among the original "divisions" of the American Psychological Association, established in the late 1940s), it was not until the founding of the National Association of School Psychologists (NASP) in the United States in1969 that consideration was given to the need for a code of ethics pertaining specifically to the practice of school psychology.

While the Universal Declaration of Ethical Principles for Psychologists, and the ethical codes of the American Psychological Association and the Canadian Psychological Association, clearly speak to the responsibilities of school psychologists, the profession differs in several important ways from other subdisciplines within the broader field of psychology. Indeed, the National Association of School Psychologists in the United States was founded because school psychologists were frustrated by the APA's failure to adequately serve their interests (Fagan & Wise, 2007). The practice of school psychology encompasses services not only to children, but to parents, teachers, school administrators, and the community as well. It is a profession in which consultation, rather than direct service, may well be the primary mode of practice (Gutkin & Close-Conoley, 1990), and it is heavily influenced by legislative and institutional contexts. However, ethical principles in psychology were modeled largely on the practice of clinical psychology, so that issues related to parental consent, autonomy of students, assessment, confidentiality of communication and records, advocacy for children's rights, and conflicts of interest—despite being encountered by school psychologists on a daily basis—were not adequately addressed until the publication, for the first time in 1974, of the NASP *Principles for Professional Ethics*. Since issuing its first ethical code, NASP has published revisions in 1984, 1992, 1997, 2000, and 2010.

The International School Psychology Association (ISPA) adopted a code of ethics in 1990, which was approved by the membership in 1991. The ISPA code outlines ethical standards in the areas of professional responsibilities, confidentiality, professional growth, and professional limitations. It further describes appropriate practice in terms of professional relationships, assessment, and research.

Evolution and Change in Expectations for Professional Conduct

Across and within nations and cultures, the practice of school psychology undergoes change as a result of evolving social and educational trends, as well as new interpretations of the rights of children and minors. For example, in the United States, consumer-focused interpretations of the rights of children and parents in recent decades have eclipsed the longstanding doctrine of *in loco parentis*, which shielded educators from liability for harm by asserting that they act in place of parents, and are assumed to make decisions that are in children's best interests. The emergence of technology-based information storage and retrieval systems presents novel challenges to professionals, including school psychologists, who are responsible for the accuracy and confidentiality of their records. In this climate of change, ethical principles can serve as enduring standards guiding decision making, especially when legal provisions are unclear or inadequate.

Apart from ethical codes promulgated by organizations such as ISPA, NASP, APA, and the Canadian Psychological Association, guidance regarding appropriate professional conduct can be found in position statements issued by professional associations. Typically, the topics addressed by position statements reflect emerging trends that may not have been anticipated when ethical codes were last revised. For example, in recent years, NASP has published position statements on corporal punishment; early intervention services; the needs of gay, lesbian, bisexual, transgender, and questioning youth; mental health services in schools; school violence, grade retention and social promotion; and recruitment of minorities into the profession.

Finally, service delivery standards serve as an important source of information and guidance for school psychology practitioners. APA offers "Specialty Guidelines for the Delivery of Services by School Psychologists" (1981), while NASP has published several revisions of its "Guidelines for the Provision of School Psychological Services" (2000). While they are not intended to serve as a standard to which professional association members will be held as a condition of membership (as is the case with ethical standards), service delivery guidelines represent a "best practice" orientation to administrative structures and professional activities involved in the practice of school psychology.

A useful distinction has been drawn between ethical codes and ethical conduct. While ethical codes present a set of standards or rules governing professional behavior, conformance with these rules is inadequate to guarantee ethical conduct. Limitations on ethical codes include the fact that they express broad, sometimes ambiguous principles that may be difficult to interpret; their provisions may sometimes conflict with one another; and, they often fail to address issues of contemporary significance (Jacob & Hartshorne, 2007). Consequently, the ability to *think* ethically has been cited as a key ethical competency (Ford, 1995); that is, school psychologists must be able to recognize situations with ethical implications, identify ethical principles involved, and make decisions that honor the rights and responsibilities of all parties. However, even the most careful deliberation sometimes results in solutions that are less than perfect, underscoring the complex nature of the ethical decision-making process.

Responding to Ethically Troubling Situations

In a review of the literature on ethical decision making, Cottone and Claus (2000) reported that mental health practitioners rely on several factors when confronted with ethical dilemmas, including their understanding of the values of employing institutions, their own convictions, and practical considerations. Of particular concern is research cited by Cottone and Claus demonstrating that practitioners are affected by social influence variables, and that they make the poorest decisions when under pressure. Although feelings or intuition may provoke unease signaling an ethical dilemma, they should not serve as the sole or primary basis for ethical decision making, nor should religious or cultural norms be used for this purpose (Hundert, 1987). Each of these bases is subject to limitations. For example, cultures may accept practices that are later acknowledged as unacceptable, or that violate standards for behavior in other cultures. Instead, a systematic, deliberative approach to decision making is recommended. Unfortunately, research has shown that, while school psychologists typically receive ethics training in professional preparation programs, many do not apply a systematic decision-making procedure, with as few as 16% reporting that they do so (Tryon, 2001; Dailor, 2007). Table 38.1 presents strategies commonly employed by school psychologists when faced with ethically troubling situations. Note that the technique reported by the greatest percentage of school psychologists (66%) involved consulting with colleagues and peers, rather than consulting published or written codes for guidance, which was reported by only 42% of respondents. This finding underscores the importance of educating school psychologists to "think ethically," as Ford suggested, since there is a substantial likelihood that they will be approached by colleagues for information and help in making decisions about ethically appropriate conduct.

There are several models for making decisions in ethically troubling situations. Forester-Miller and Davis (1996) describe a process that is characteristic of many approaches, consisting of problem identification, specification of possible courses of action and their likely outcomes, selection of a course of action, implementation of the selected action, and evaluation of the outcome. Forester-Miller and Davis further recommend a 3-question formula for determining whether a course of action is appropriate: (a) whether the proposed action is fair, (b) whether the practitioner would recommend it to

Table 38.1. Common methods cited by U.S. school psychologists for responding to ethically troubling situations (N = 208)

Method of Responding	Percentage Who Reported Using Method	N
Consulting with colleagues and professional peers	66	137
Consulting codes of ethics, relevant law, or other written practice guidelines	42	88
Thinking about possible benefits and risks associated with various courses of action	41	85
Applying a systematic decision-making model	16	33
Contacting a local or regional professional association for guidance	6	12
Contacting the national professional association for guidance	2	4

Adapted from information in Dailor, A. N. (2007).

a peer, and (c) whether the practitioner would want his or her behavior made public. Hundert (1987) refers to this as "the scale of... conscience" (p. 839).

Koocher and Keith-Spiegel (1998) proposed a model for decision making that has been adapted by Jacob and Hartshorne (2007). In this model, the school psychologist first describes the parameters of the situation, and then defines the potential legal–ethical issues involved. Then, existing legal and ethical guidelines and codes are consulted, and the rights, responsibilities, and welfare of all parties are considered. The next several steps are similar to those presented by Miller and Davis (1996)— generating alternatives, considering their possible consequences, and estimating the likelihood that particular consequences actually would occur. A similar model proposed by McNamara (2008) offers a streamlined version of the decision-making process, treating ethical dilemmas as likely to fall into one of three general categories: conflicting interests of involved parties, competing ethical standards, or unclear ethical standards. Whatever procedure has been used, once a decision has been made, Jacob and Hartshorne emphasize the importance of following through and monitoring the consequences of the action that has been taken.

In a survey of school psychologists in the United States (Dailor, 2007), 24% of respondents said that having to confront a colleague with concerns about unethical practice was among their top three concerns, and only 38% said that they felt well prepared to do so. This is consistent with other research showing that this is a major concern among psychologists (American Psychological Association, 2006), and especially among supervisors, who have to deal with difficult personalities and conflicts (Hunley, et. al, 2000). Typically, school psychologists should approach these situations in a spirit of collegiality, aware of the obligation to assist other school psychologists in improving their professional performance. Moreover, they should avoid a judgmental tone or language, clearly and specifically cite the behavior of concern, and state an expectation for alternative behavior. In some cases, it may be advisable to consult a supervisor or other authority who can offer guidance, or even include a supervisor in the conversation with the colleague in question. Ultimately, the emphasis should be on correcting the misbehavior, especially when the welfare of others is at stake, and it may be necessary to refer the matter to administrative or professional authorities for corrective action.

Common Ethical Concerns in School Psychology

In 2007, a survey was conducted of a representative sample of school psychologists in the United States (Dailor, 2007). The purpose of the survey was to examine the types of dilemmas most frequently reported by school psychologists, and to determine the most common strategies employed to respond to such dilemmas. The question posed by the author asked respondents to report their "top three" concerns related to professional ethics (see Table 38.2). Forty-three percent of school psychologists surveyed (n = 208) said that "administrative pressure to behave unethically" was among their top three ethics-related concerns. Examples of administrative pressure to behave unethically include:

- Failing to recommend a particular service or intervention requiring additional school resources, despite the school psychologist's belief that it would be helpful to the child;
- Failing to disclose evaluation results that might contradict a decision favored by the school.

The second most frequently cited concern among the top three reported by school psychologists in the

Table 38.2. Top three ethical concerns reported by school psychologists in the United States (N = 208)

Concern	Percentage Reporting Concern Within "Top 3"	N
Administrative pressure to act unethically	43	89
Unsound educational practices	41	86
Assessment-related issues	27	56
Confronting colleagues about unethical conduct	24	50
Storage and disposal of confidential records	22	45

Adapted from information in Dailor, A. N. (2007).

U.S. (41%) was "unsound educational practices." This term refers to:

- Awareness that an intervention plan is not being implemented, despite agreement to provide the intervention;
- Awareness that school personnel are engaging in detrimental or unsafe practices;
- Awareness that curriculum and instructional activities are inconsistent with research-based practice.

Third, 27% of respondents reported concerns related to assessment practices, which might include:

- Using only the battery of tests specified by the administration, rather than selecting tests on an individual basis to suit the child's characteristics;
- Using tests with outdated norms, or tests whose psychometric properties are inadequate;
- Using tests that may be inappropriate given the child's characteristics, or in a manner inconsistent with the publisher's instructions;
- Having test results entered into a team or group report, without having had the opportunity to interpret and explain such results.

An earlier survey that had been conducted by Jacob-Timm (1999) also examined U.S. school psychologists' top three ethical concerns, but did so by asking respondents to describe ethically troubling situations they had encountered. Although findings from the two studies are not directly comparable because of differences in methodology, it does appear that there have been changes in the "top three" ethics-related concerns reported by school psychologists between 1999 and 2007. While "administrative pressure to behave unethically" still tops the list, unsound educational practices have become a greater concern. This is probably related to the increased emphasis on intervention, where school psychologists are engaged in planning and evaluating interventions for children in general education settings.

The types and frequency of ethical dilemmas facing school psychologists are also reflected in data describing how often certain kinds of problems have been witnessed by school psychologists, whether they or another person were involved. As presented in Table 38.3, Dailor (2007) found that, of her 208 respondents, 178 (or 86%) had witnessed problematic situations related to assessment. The next most commonly witnessed problem situations involved questionable intervention practices, especially a lack of follow-up (79%), and administrative pressure to behave unethically, commonly reflected in a failure to recommend services and interventions because of their cost (76%). Ethical issues associated with school psychologists' increased involvement in intervention practices will be explored more fully later in this chapter.

Table 38.3. Incidents experienced or witnessed by school psychologists in the United States (N = 208)

Categories of Ethical Misconduct	Percentage Who Experienced or Witnessed Incident	N
Assessment	86	178
Intervention	79	165
Administrative Pressure	76	157
Informed Consent	51	105
Parent Conflicts	48	100
School Records	38	79
Job Competence	36	74
Confidentiality	33	69
Conflicts of Interest	20	42

Adapted from information in Dailor, A. N. (2007).

Guidance in Matters of Professional Ethics: Principles and Applications
Respect for the Dignity of Persons

This principle represents a commitment to "the belief that each person should be treated primarily as a person or an end in him/herself, not as an object or a means to an end", and that "this worth is not dependent upon their… age, or any other preference or personal characteristic, condition, or status" (Canadian Psychological Association, 2000, p. 8). It is considered to be the superordinate principle; that is, if two or more of the four general ethical principles are in conflict, respect for the dignity of persons always prevails, and should not be sacrificed to uphold any other principle.

SELF-DETERMINATION AND AUTONOMY

Depending on laws enacted in various jurisdictions, children have only limited rights to initiate, consent to, or refuse professional services, including those of school psychologists; those legal rights are typically held and asserted by parents or guardians in the form of "informed consent." To ensure that consent is freely given and fully informed, school psychologists provide clear information about the purpose and nature of proposed activities, responsibilities of involved parties, confidentiality safeguards and exceptions, alternatives to the proposed service, likely risks and benefits of the service, possible consequences if services are declined, and the client's right to refuse or withdraw from service at any time. Ethics codes recognize the importance of obtaining children's assent for services, and acknowledge circumstances in which a child's need for professional assistance outweighs the parent or guardian's right to deny permission for such assistance. These provisions reflect an understanding of *self-determination and autonomy* as essential aspects of the principle of respect for the dignity of persons. When children request services from a school psychologist in the absence of a legal right to authorize such services, school psychologists must—as an ethical matter—decide how to proceed. The overriding consideration in these circumstances has to do with whether the requested service is likely to be of direct and significant benefit to the child. Assuming that this is the case, the Canadian Psychological Association (2000) offers a procedure that can be used for decision making, paraphrased as follows:

- Consider whether right to self determination is *developmentally appropriate* for this child (i.e., do the child's age and/or circumstances suggest that s/he is capable of making a responsible decision to obtain school psychological services?);

- Consider impact on the child's welfare (i.e., how might the child's welfare be positively and negatively affected by the provision, or non-provision, of requested services?);

- Seek willing and adequately informed consent from person of diminished capacity (i.e., does the child understand the implications and possible outcomes, both positive and negative, of the decision to obtain school psychological services?).

PRIVACY AND CONFIDENTIALITY

The principle of respect for the dignity of persons also is reflected in the treatment of personal information obtained during the course of service delivery. The duty to honor privacy cautions school psychologists against soliciting sensitive or personal information (whether about the student or others) without good reason, while the promise of confidentiality protects information from unauthorized disclosure to others. Both are designed to encourage candid disclosure of relevant information, since school psychologists who observe these standards are more likely to be viewed as trustworthy.

There is little disagreement about the importance of disclosing to students that there are limits to confidentiality; these limits are imposed not only by statutory law, but by other ethical obligations safeguarding client welfare, and should be disclosed at the outset of a professional relationship (Jacob & Hartshorne, 2007). In most jurisdictions, laws specify circumstances under which confidential information must be disclosed; these typically include situations in which there is the potential for harm to others, or where child abuse is suspected. In general, it is advisable to inform students (in a manner appropriate to their age) that information may need to be disclosed in certain circumstances, but that the school psychologist will not do so without first discussing the disclosure and its implications with the student. When working with adolescents, many school psychologists invite the student to participate with them in the disclosure to parents or guardians, so there is an opportunity to address any adverse reactions that may occur.

Respect for students' privacy and the confidentiality of information also pertains to disclosures to other parties, including teachers and administrators, whether deliberate or inadvertent. When a school psychologist unexpectedly encounters a teacher in the school hallway, or is asked about matters that are not directly relevant to the questioner's role relative to the student, he or she must clarify the boundaries of appropriate communication, and arrange to meet at a time when information can be shared in a more responsible manner. Information should be disclosed orally or in writing only to legitimate authorities, and disclosure should be limited only to information that is needed by the authority, preferably in the form of generalizations (rather than specific confidences shared by the student; Jacob, 2008).

A growing concern among school psychologists is related to the use of web-based reporting and record-storage procedures, as well as electronic transmission of confidential information. School psychologists have queried the NASP Ethics and Professional Practices Committee about measures they should take to safeguard the privacy and integrity of records when unauthorized persons have access to, and even can alter, records that have been created or stored online, or when records are lost due to hardware or software failures (McNamara & Jacob, 2007). It has been recommended that school psychologists avoid the use of networked computers, and disguise personal identifiers in records, but these safeguards are not always possible. Similarly, password access and encryption, while affording some degree of protection, are not failsafe (Harvey & Carlson, 2003). When electronic submission of client records is required for accountability or financial reasons (i.e., reimbursement for services by government agencies), the identity and qualifications of those who might review such information is unknown, so it is impossible to guarantee confidentiality. At minimum, and despite these limitations, school psychologists are advised to minimize the use of personally identifiable information in electronic records (especially in email, which can easily be accessed and altered by others), and should inform clients (and parents) when records are stored or transmitted electronically, including an explanation of the threats to confidentiality that may ensue. In addition, school psychologists should work with school administrators to develop procedures that safeguard the privacy of students and families to the greatest extent possible.

Finally, privacy considerations require school psychologists to seek and use information only from reliable and responsible sources, using appropriate methods. In contemporary terms, this means that information posted by a student on a personal Internet webpage should not be used for evaluative purposes, both because it may be unreliable, and because the school psychologist has not been authorized to access this information.

FAIRNESS AND NON-DISCRIMINATION

Ethical standards require school psychologists to be fair and to avoid discrimination in assessment, consultation, and intervention activities. Traditionally, the standard of fairness has been applied to questions involving specific tests, especially individual intelligence tests. There are three types of bias that are related to the properties of the tests themselves. *Content bias* exists when tests are more difficult for members of a particular group, and there is no accepted theoretical rationale for the difference. When membership in a particular group affects the validity of predictions for that group, but not for other groups, *predictive validity bias* exists. Tests should predict a criterion equally well for all students, regardless of group membership. *Construct validity bias* occurs when a test either measures a different trait for one group than for another, or when the trait is measured with different degrees of accuracy for different groups. In addition to bias inherent in tests, bias can exist in the clinical applications of tests, as well as the consequences of their use. This occurs when there is decision-making bias, or testing circumstances adversely affecting student performance, or when a test results in outcomes that unfairly or disproportionately target members of a specific group. School psychologists are responsible to ensure that they use tests that are free of bias, appropriate to student characteristics, and valid for the purpose for which they are being used. Moreover, they should minimize threats to the reliability of results, and interpret tests in context of other information about the student. Finally, school psychologists should monitor the impact of tests on student outcomes, especially those that involve selecting students into particular programs or services.

The obligation to be fair extends also to school psychologists' attitudes and behavior toward members of other ethnic, religious, and cultural groups, as well as persons of varying sexual orientations. This not only means that school psychologists must educate themselves about the characteristics of various groups that may affect communication, assessment, or intervention services, but they also must be aware of their own values and attitudes toward differences, and provide service only when they can do so competently and free of bias.

Responsible Caring

The principle of "responsible caring" requires school psychologists to attain and maintain competence in the delivery of professional services, and to guard against practices that may result in harmful or damaging consequences. In providing professional services, school psychologists must employ reliable and valid measurement techniques, and recommend or apply interventions that are supported by an adequate research base.

The availability of computer-assisted assessment poses challenges to school psychologists, who benefit from more sophisticated and convenient analysis of test results, but who must ensure that client- and context-specific information is incorporated in reports that contain software-produced narratives. Moreover, ethical codes emphasize the responsibility of practitioners for the technical adequacy of scoring and interpretive aids (Harvey & Carlson, 2003). Interventions facilitated by computer technology include interviewing, counseling, cognitive-behavioral therapy, mediation, and online support groups. Harvey and Carlson, in an extensive review of issues associated with the uses of computer technology by school psychologists (2003), suggest that intervention services are fraught with ethical problems, including the lack of regulation of services or providers, absence of face-to-face contact, and compromised ability to warn of danger to others or to intervene effectively with suicidal ideation. The speed with which technological innovations have been introduced has clearly outpaced the ability of school psychologists and other mental health practitioners to develop and enforce appropriate ethical guidelines. Consequently, this is an area requiring special attention and caution, as reliance on technology does not relieve school psychologists of responsibility for its reliability and validity, or for outcomes resulting from its use.

Intervention-Oriented Services in School Psychology

The profession of school psychology was founded on a psychometric knowledge and skill base and, throughout its history, has been most closely associated with assessment and diagnosis (Fagan & Wise, 2007). While assessment continues to be the central function served by most school psychologists, its characteristics and focus have changed in recent years. In the United States, this transition is best reflected in the adoption of the *response-to-intervention* model (RTI), which employs formative assessment to periodically measure students' academic skills to determine the adequacy of instruction (rather than to diagnose learning disorders). Students whose skills fall short of expected levels are provided with more intensive instruction (i.e., intervention), and brief performance measures are administered to monitor

its impact. In this model, school psychologists' assessment role extends beyond the "tertiary prevention" audience served under the more traditional framework of service delivery, to include the "primary" and "secondary" prevention audiences of students receiving instruction in general (rather than special) education settings. While research supports RTI's potential as a meaningful, more effective, and less biased method of identifying at-risk students and providing them with needed intervention, a number of challenging ethical issues have emerged (Burns, et. al, 2008).

First, the ethical principle of "responsible caring" obliges school psychologists to achieve competency in the technical skills and knowledge needed to implement RTI in an appropriate manner. In some jurisdictions, accreditation and approval standards help to ensure that preservice preparation programs adequately address these needs. However, practicing school psychologists must obtain continuing or inservice education, a daunting prospect when one considers the sweeping and significant differences in knowledge and skills required for implementing RTI. For example, the area on which traditional training focused most sharply—individual psychometric evaluation and diagnosis—plays a relatively trivial role in the RTI model, where it is employed only with those few students (estimated at only 5% of the population) who have not responded adequately to instruction targeted to all students, including those at risk for failure (Reschly, 2008). Even when evaluation and diagnosis are indicated, the RTI model recommends an approach less focused on pinpointing characteristics of the student (e.g., the presence of a learning disability), than on aspects of the instructional environment that need to be modified. Consequently, many practicing school psychologists find that their training has not prepared them for the role they are expected to play as consultants for developing and analyzing universal screening and progress-monitoring measures, and for helping to devise interventions that can be provided by teachers in general education.

The principle of responsible caring requires school psychologists not only to monitor their own practices and decisions for competency and appropriateness, but also to assist schools in identifying and adopting evidence-based educational practices. Since commercial publishers of instructional materials routinely cite a "research base" in advertising materials for sale, the responsibility for evaluating these claims rests on educators themselves, many of whom lack the knowledge needed to evaluate the adequacy of research. In general, the claim of an "evidence base" requires publication of supporting research in a peer-reviewed journal, or approval by independent experts employing a rigorous and objective review process. A number of Internet sites were created to disseminate information about evidence-based educational practices, including the Institute of Education Sciences' *What Works Clearinghouse* (http://ies.ed.gov/ncee/wwc), and the Coalition for Evidence-Based Policy's *Social Programs that Work* (www.evidencebasedprograms.org). Kratochwill has compiled a comprehensive resource that describes standards for determining the adequacy of the research base supporting specific intervention practices, entitled *Evidence-Based Interventions: A Resource Guide*; it is accessible online at http://webspace.umd.edu/mspa/slides/Spring06Handouts/EBI_Res_Guide4-6-06.doc.

The United State Department of Education (2003) summarized standards for evidence-based intervention as follows:

1. The intervention must be supported by "strong" evidence of its effectiveness, exemplified by research of acceptable quality (i.e., randomized, controlled trials that are well designed and implemented) and quantity (i.e., more than one study in typical settings appropriate to the population with which the intervention will be used); *or*

2. Though not supported by "strong" evidence of its effectiveness, the intervention is supported by "possible" evidence of effectiveness (i.e., there were some flaws in the randomized controlled trial designs, but the intervention is supported by research using several well designed and implemented, but nonrandomized, designs).

Apart from the validity of intervention practices, school psychologists must consider the integrity or fidelity with which they are implemented, usually by classroom teachers (Burns et. al, 2008). Especially when used for high-stakes decisions such as determining eligibility for specialized resources and services, interventions must be documented as having occurred as often, and in the same form, as intended. Many interventions fail not because they are inappropriate, but because of inadequate dosage. This requirement raises thorny issues associated with professional relationships, especially with teachers, who may (rightfully) point out that school psychologists have no authority over teachers, nor are they in a position to evaluate teachers' performance. Gansle and Noell (2007) have opened a promising line of research into the value of performance feedback, praise, prompts, negative reinforcement, and reminders of accountability as methods to increase the fidelity with which interventions are implemented; school psychologists can use these methods to support implementation efforts without putting their relationships with teachers at risk.

In addition to concerns about the evidence base for assessment and intervention practices in RTI, questions have been raised about the legitimacy of using this model for diagnosing disorders, especially learning disabilities. Kavale, Kauffman, Bachmeier, & LeFever (2008) offer a comprehensive analysis of the problems associated with an operational definition of "specific learning disability" as inadequate response to (presumably) adequate instruction, including the failure to employ a comprehensive evaluation of child characteristics that would provide affirmative evidence of a disability, rather than of "uncomplicated" underachievement. This is not an insignificant issue, as it is directly related to high-stakes decisions such as assigning disability labels and allocating limited educational resources. As this scholarly debate continues, school psychologists are ethically obliged to follow and weigh the merit of the arguments in light of their evidence base, rather than their popularity or one's personal opinion or bias.

Integrity in Relationships

The third general principle, *integrity in professional relationships*, describes school psychologists' responsibilities to those with whom they work, including clients, parents, colleagues, employers, administrators, and community-based resources. Where *responsible caring* obligates school psychologists to practice at accepted levels of competence, the principle of *integrity* requires openness and honesty about the level and scope of one's competence, as well as credentials and training.

With respect to client relationships, school psychologists must be respectful of physical, mental, emotional, political, economic, social, cultural, ethnic, and racial characteristics, as well as gender, sexual orientation, and religion (NASP, 2000). Apart from issues of fairness and nondiscrimination discussed earlier, client customs and beliefs should be honored, and if these place the client at risk (e.g., refusal to allow services needed by a student), the school psychologist should apply a careful decision-making process to determine an appropriate course of action. The principle of integrity also requires school psychologists to fully inform clients (including students themselves) of the nature of services to be provided, and to obtain consent (of the parent or legal guardian) and assent (from the student, if not legally entitled to give informed consent) prior to the delivery of services.

Current trends in school psychology emphasizing involvement in prevention and intervention activities may give rise to problems related to informed consent. At what point does a school psychologist's involvement in a student's case become a professional service requiring informed consent? In the United States, the growing popularity of the RTI model (discussed earlier) has led to school psychologists' involvement in data collection for screening and progress-monitoring purposes, as well as intervention for academic and behavior problems. These activities are conducted with large groups of students, and only when earlier efforts have proven ineffective are students "referred" for school psychological services, which are then provided in accordance with individual needs. According to Burns, et al. (2008), conditions under which school psychologists should obtain informed consent include (a) when ongoing involvement with a particular student is anticipated; (b) when the school psychologist's activities may involve intrusion on the student or family's privacy beyond what might typically occur in a classroom; or (c) when a disability is suspected. For example, if a school psychologist facilitates a support group for students who are displaying behavior problems, intrusions on students' privacy are likely to occur, and student participation would therefore require informed consent. If a school psychologist participated as a consultant in weekly meetings of a team of teachers, at which a particular student's progress was a continuing topic of discussion, informed consent also would be required. Thus, the question of the need for informed consent for school psychologists' involvement in intervention-related activities (whether direct or indirect in nature) can be answered by examining the nature of the intervention, the manner and extent of the school psychologist's involvement, and the degree to which assessment and intervention depart from typical general education practices.

The principle of integrity in relationships also must be considered in situations where a potential conflict of interests exists (e.g., when a school psychologist has a financial interest in a service or product from which student-clients or their families might benefit), or when there is a dual relationship (e.g., when the school psychologist is related to or involved with clients outside of the professional context). In these circumstances, school psychologists should explicitly acknowledge the conflict of interest or dual relationship, and take steps to ensure that financial or personal considerations do not influence the nature or quality of professional services provided to the client. Acceptable solutions to these situations might include arranging for services to be provided by another professional, or enacting a policy clarifying whether, and in what manner, services can be provided to students and their families outside of the school setting.

Integrity in relationships applies to interactions between school psychologists and community-based professionals, including therapists providing services to students. Among other things, this standard requires school psychologists to be familiar with available resources, refer students and families to such resources, and cooperate in the provision of a comprehensive plan of service. Many school psychologists serve as supervisors or trainers of students and interns; in accepting these responsibilities, they must balance the needs and interests of their student trainees with the rights and welfare of persons receiving services, ensuring that trainee-provided services meet prevailing professional standards. At the same time, trainers and supervisors are obligated to provide timely, appropriate, and comprehensive instruction and feedback to their student trainees (Harvey & Struzziero, 2000).

Responsibility to Society

The fourth and final principle speaks to the role of school psychologists as citizens and advocates for high standards in education and mental health services. This role is enacted in several ways, including involvement in research and public policy initiatives, as well as membership in professional associations. At the local level, school psychologists must be engaged in efforts to create and maintain a school climate that supports children's health and development. They can be especially helpful in assisting school officials to select and implement evidence-based practices, whether for assessment or intervention, and to evaluate the effectiveness of those practices.

At the same time, school psychologists have an ethical responsibility to draw attention to, and, if feasible, to correct circumstances that adversely affect students' welfare (Jacob, 2008). This is of particular importance in light of information obtained in a survey of U.S. school psychologists by Dailor (2007) indicating that "administrative pressure to act unethically" and "unsound educational practices" are among the top three concerns cited by

43% and 41%, respectively, of her respondents. However, laws in specific jurisdictions may define the nature and context of acceptable "whistle-blowing" activities, in which school psychologists might publicize information about unsound or questionable educational practices. In the United States, for example, recent case law restricts the freedom of educators to criticize the actions of school authorities in schools where they are employed, but protects them when the actions were of an unlawful or detrimental nature (Jacob, 2008).

Conclusions

Ethical standards for the practice of school psychology cannot be separated from their environmental context, whether of a cultural, political, social, or economic nature. However, there are four enduring principles that are widely accepted as universal, and can be used to inform local standards as well as individual conduct. These standards—respect for the dignity of persons, responsible caring, integrity in professional relationships, and responsibility to community and society—find expression in the codes of ethics of numerous organizations, including the International School Psychology Association and the (U.S.) National Association of School Psychologists.

The challenges of contemporary practice, including the rapid pace of social change and technological innovation, as well as the changing role of school psychologists, demand not only familiarity with relevant ethical codes, but also the ability to "think ethically." In so doing, school psychologists can respond in a constructive and appropriate manner to dilemmas created by unclear or competing ethical standards, and honor the profession's covenant to balance self-interest with that of consumers of school psychological services.

Future Directions

Several prominent challenges face the profession of school psychology as it moves further into the twenty-first century, including problems associated with rapidly expanding information technology. How should school psychologists respond to demands for electronic record storage and transmission, given concern about maintaining the integrity and confidentiality of information contained in such records? In addition, school psychologists need to consider how best to make use of available resources for computer-assisted assessment and intervention, including ways to evaluate the technical adequacy of these resources.

A second area in which further study is needed is related to the increasing emphasis on school psychologists' contributions to primary and secondary prevention, including assessment and intervention for students at risk for academic and behavior problems. Questions raised in this chapter addressed issues of practitioner competence, informed consent, and evidence-based practice, as well as the adequacy of "response-to-intervention" models as methods for diagnosing educational disorders.

Finally, this chapter has emphasized the need for a thoughtful, deliberative approach to solving ethical dilemmas. However, because relatively few school psychologists report using a systematic decision-making procedure, preservice and inservice training should focus on practical applications of available models, including those proposed by Jacob and Hartshorne (2007), McNamara (2008), and Williams, et al. (2008). Clearly, familiarity with ethical principles and codes is a necessary but insufficient condition for the development of "ethical competence," and opportunities for students and practitioners to engage in simulated problem-solving activities are needed.

References

American Psychological Association, Board of Professional Affairs' Advisory Committee on Colleague Assistance. (2006, February). *Advancing colleague assistance in professional psychology*. Washington, DC: Author.

Buda, & Elsayed-Elkhouly. (1998). Cultural differences between Arabs and Americans: Individualism and collectivism revisited. *Journal of Cross-Cultural Psychology, 29*, 487–492.

Burns, M. K., Jacob, S., & Wagner, A. R. (2008). Ethical and legal issues associated with using response-to-intervention to assess learning disabilities. *Journal of School Psychology, 46*, 263–279.

Canadian Psychological Association (2000). Canadian code of ethics for psychologists, Third edition. Available at http://www.cpa.ca.

Cottone, R. R., & Claus, R. E. (2000). Ethical decision-making models: A review of the literature. *Journal of Counseling and Development, 78*, 275–283.

Dailor, A. N. (2007). A national study of ethical transgressions and dilemmas reported by school psychology practitioners. Unpublished Master's Thesis: Central Michigan University.

Fagan, T., & Wise, S. (2007). School psychology: Past, present, and future (3rd ed.). Bethesda, MD: National Association of School Psychologists.

Ford, G. F. (1995, June). *Teaching psychology students to reason ethically*. Poster presented at the annual meeting of the American Psychological Society, New York.

Forester-Miller, H., & Davis, T. (1996). *A practitioner's guide to ethical decision making* (Practitioner's Guide to Ethics). Alexandria, VA: American Counseling Association.

Gansle, K. A., Noell, G. H. (2007). The fundamental role of intervention implementation in assessing response to intervention. In S. Jimerson, M. Burns, & A. VanDerHeyden

(Eds.), *Handbook of response to intervention: The science and practice of assessment and intervention* (pp. 244–251). New York: Springer.

Gutkin, T. B., & Conoley, J. C. (1990). Reconceptualizing school psychology from a service delivery perspective: Implications for practice, training, and research. *Journal of School Psychology, 28,* 203–223.

Harvey, V. S., & Carlson, J. (2003). Ethical and professional issues with computer related technology. *School Psychology Review, 32,* 92–107.

Harvey, V. S., & Struzziero, J. A. (2000). Professional development and supervision of school psychologists: From intern to expert. Thousand Oaks, CA: Corwin Press.

Hundert, E. M. (1987). A model for ethical problem solving in medicine, with practical applications. *American Journal of Psychiatry, 144,* 839–846.

Hunley, S., Harvey, V., Curtis, M., Portnoy, L., Chesno Grier, E., & Helffrich, D. (2000). School psychology supervisors: A national study of demographics and professional practices. *Communiqué, 28* (8).

Jacob, S. (2008).Best practices in developing ethical school psychological practice. In A. Thomas & J. Grimes (Eds.), *Best practices in school psychology, 5th edition* (pp. 1921–1932). Bethesda, MD: National Association of School Psychologists.

Jacob, S., & Hartshorne, T. (2007). Ethics and law for school psychologists (5th ed.). Hoboken, NJ: John Wiley & Sons.

Kavale, K. A., Kauffman, J. M., Bachmeier, R. J., & LeFever, G. B. (2008). Response to intervention: Separating the rhetoric of self-congratulation from the reality of specific learning disability identification. *Learning Disability Quarterly, 31,* 135–151.

Koocher, G. P., & Keith-Spiegel, P. (1998). *Ethics in psychology* (2nd ed.). New York: Oxford University Press.

McNamara, K. (2008). Best practices in the application of professional ethics. In A. Thomas & J. Grimes (Eds.), *Best practices in school psychology, 5th edition* (pp.1933–1942). Bethesda, MD: National Association of School Psychologists.

McNamara, K., & Jacob, S. (2007, May). *Ethics and professional standards committee activity report.* Bethesda, MD: National Association of School Psychologists.

National Association of School Psychologists (2000). *Professional conduct manual.* Bethesda, MD: Author.

Oakland, T., & Cunningham, J. (1997). International School Psychology Association definition of school psychology. *School Psychology International, 18,* 195–200.

Reschly, D.J. (2008). School psychology paradigm shift and beyond. In A. Thomas & J. Grimes (Eds.), *Best practices in school psychology, 5th edition* (pp. 3–15). Bethesda, MD: National Association of School Psychologists.

Sinclair, C. (1998). Nine unique features of the Canadian code of ethics for psychologists. *Canadian Psychology, 39,* 167–176.

Tryon, G. S. (2001). School psychology students' beliefs about their preparation and concern with ethical issues. *Ethics and Behavior, 11,* 375–394.

United States Department of Education, Institute of Education Sciences, National Center for Education Evaluation and Regional Assistance (2003, December). *Identifying and implementing educational practices supported by rigorous evidence: A user-friendly guide.* Washington, DC: The Council for Excellence in Government.

Williams, B. B., Armistead, L., & Jacob, S. (2008).*Professional ethics for school psychologists: A problem-solving model casebook.* Bethesda, MD: National Association of School Psychologists.

Emerging Trends in the Preparation of School Psychologists for Practice

Rich Gilman, Kristen Missall, *and* Ryan Macks

Abstract

Although school psychology roles and functions have often been shaped by federal, state, and local educational policies, forces *within* school psychology have contributed essential information that has helped shape the discipline in its current form. This chapter focuses on areas within school training programs that may influence how the profession is practiced and how it is perceived by key stakeholders (i.e., teachers, school administrators) in the future. The chapter first provides a brief overview of the current state of school psychology training programs, followed by three specific emerging areas of training that often complement core training emphases on assessment, intervention, consultation, ethics, and other roles. These areas are evidence-based practice, practice in nonschool settings, and student advocacy. Other suggested areas for school psychology training programs conclude the chapter.

Keywords: training, evidence-based practice, nontraditional, advocacy

At the turn of the twentieth century, efforts were made to understand the learning capacities of children, who by that time were required in most states to receive basic education services (Geisinger, 2000; Katz, 1976). The creation of the first child guidance clinic in the United States was one of the first examples of how psychology could be applied to this end. Services that were provided in that clinic, such as working with children having educational difficulties, providing school consultation, helping teachers understand how a child could best learn under a general curriculum and how to offer a child remedial help, remain as the primary functions of school psychologists today (Merrill, Ervin, & Gimple, 2006).

Over the past three decades, a number of federal, state, and local educational policies have directly or indirectly shaped the scope of school psychology practice significantly, requiring (among other things) knowledge of both individual and systems-level interventions. Competence in areas such as (a) academic interventions, (b) crisis intervention,

(c) applied behavior analysis and behavior modification techniques, (d) parent, teacher, and systems consultation, (e) individual and group counseling, (f) psychoeducational evaluation, and (g) program evaluation, are just some of the areas in which school psychologists have been expected to perform.

Yet, it would be incorrect to presume that the roles and functions of school psychologists have always occurred in response to legislative mandates. Borrowing from general systems theory, which has been applied to various aspects of psychology (Barton, 1994; Gunn, Haley, & Lyness, 2007), any system consists of interacting subunits, all of which contribute unique information and perspective that shapes the identity and functioning of the larger entity. Thus, roles and tasks performed by members within the system are often shaped by reciprocal and fluid (rather than unidirectional and static) dynamics (Dooley & Van de Ven, 1999). It often has been the case that mental health and educational needs identified within specific environments (e.g., rural versus urban school settings), or for a number of conditions (e.g., diagnosing learning disabilities, pervasive developmental disorders), are initially revealed in school psychology training programs and professional practice, prior to being codified into policy (Grimes & Tilly, 1996; Merrill, Ervin, & Gimpel, 2006). Thus, and applying systems theory to school psychology, forces *within* school psychology have contributed essential information that has helped shape the discipline in its current form (see Figure 39.1).

Many chapters in this handbook focus on the influences of school psychology practice to the overall identity and value of the discipline to schools and the community. However, the unique contributions that school psychology training programs offer to the development of school psychology roles and functions are often minimized. This chapter will provide an overview of emerging areas of training, and how these areas potentially might help shape how the profession is perceived in the twenty-first century.

As noted elsewhere (Curtis, Grier, Chesnow, & Hunley, 2004; Davis, McIntosh, Phelps, & Kehle, 2004; Fagan & Sachs-Wise, 2007; Reschly, 2000), the dearth of available school psychologists in many school districts, as well as the overall "graying" of the profession make current times particularly promising for school psychology graduate students. By the same token, linguistic, ethnic, and cultural changes witnessed in today's society call for far more comprehensive and extensive training curricula than that required even relatively recently to address the mental health and educational needs of children, families, and schools (Fagan, 2004; Fagan & Sachs-Wise, 2007). Numerous published papers, as well as current guidelines necessary for program accreditation, attest to the importance that the field places on training (e.g., National Association of School Psychologists, 2000; Wnek, Klein, & Bracken, 2008; Ysseldyke, Burns, Dawson, Kelley, Morrison, Ortiz et al., 2006). The intent of this chapter is not to replicate what has been reported elsewhere, but to extend the content into areas that have not, or only have recently been mentioned. These areas are: (a) the inclusion of evidence-based practices in training; (b) diversity of training experiences to include practice in multiple settings; and (c) advocacy to promote school psychology to future recruits into school psychology programs, and to key stakeholders such as teachers and administrators. This chapter concludes with some suggestions for other areas that training programs could consider that would further expand the scope of training.

We note up front that this chapter is not meant to reflect practices that are universally endorsed or observed in training programs. With almost 300 doctoral and subdoctoral (i.e., masters or specialist level) training programs today, and between 20,000 to 30,000 practitioners worldwide (Van Voorhis & Levinson, 2006), there is considerable flexibility in the expectancies of training programs—despite common training standards necessary for accreditation. Nor will this chapter address the ongoing debate on whether the depth or breadth of training differs with respect to educational level (doctorate versus subdoctorate). Clearly there are quantitative differences in the amount of training students receive within certain domains across levels of training (e.g., research). However, whether these differences differentially impact the quality of services provided by trainees remains unclear. This chapter avoids this controversy by focusing on training experiences that can transcend degree level.

Fig. 39.1 Systems Theory and School Psychology

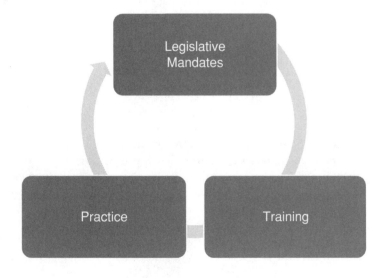

Brief Overview of Education and Training in School Psychology

Students entering graduate programs often face a difficult dilemma in choosing whether to pursue a subdoctoral degree, or to pursue a degree at the doctoral level. The decision is often based on economic factors, time constraints, and location of practice. As noted by Fagan (2005), the majority of school districts and schools continue to honor subdoctoral training as the minimum requirement to practice in schools, and in many systems there is little financial incentive to pursue the doctoral degree. In fact, the differences in pay often amount to a few thousand dollars between levels of training. Such minor differences in salary often do not make up for the additional time needed to obtain a doctorate (see below). In many respects the choice is often primarily based on the students' preference of where they wish to practice as school psychology professionals. For example, for students who wish to pursue careers in research, practice psychology in nonschool settings, or teach as a core faculty member in training programs, the doctoral level is the minimum requirement. In addition, many higher-level administrative positions in school districts (such as director of pupil personnel services or as a superintendent) also require the doctorate. Conversely, students who wish to practice school psychology in schools, with little interest in pursuing higher-level administrative positions, or who have limited time or financial resources, often find little incentive to pursue the doctorate.

Training Differences across Program Levels

As noted by Tharinger, Pryzwansky, and Miller (2008), school psychology has long been recognized as a subspecialty at the doctoral level within professional psychology. (Along with counseling and clinical psychology, it was one of the three original subspecialties eligible for licensure by the American Psychological Association [APA]). Training programs accredited by the APA must adhere to specific standards of training, and must cover specific curriculum components, which include knowledge of psychological foundational skills and developing advanced skills in professional psychology, as well as those specific to practice in schools (e.g., knowledge of educational policies and curriculum instruction). Over 60% of doctoral training programs are APA accredited (APA, 2010), although this number is expected to increase as more state psychology boards require graduation from an APA-accredited program or its equivalent (Tharinger, Pryzwansky, and Miller). Given its more extensive coursework

(which may include a number of advanced predoctoral practicum experiences), a one-year predoctoral internship, and perhaps a 1– 2-year postdoctoral residency, the total time to receive the doctoral degree typically is between 4–7 years.

Professional training at the subdoctoral (and the doctoral) level is also granted by the National Association of School Psychologists (NASP). The difference between the APA and NASP accrediting bodies is that the former represents doctoral-level practitioners only, while NASP was created to represent practitioners at the masters and specialist level. The APA does indirectly recognize subdoctoral training by a provision that allows masters- or specialist-level school psychology practitioners to maintain the title "psychologist" as long as services are provided within schools. Nevertheless, this provision has had a long and often contentious history within APA, and between APA and NASP. Further, the use of the title may also depend on permission from the state. For example, in Texas, the term *licensed specialist in school psychology* is used for subdoctoral practitioners. At any rate, similar to criteria necessary for APA accreditation, NASP-approved programs must also follow specific training criteria.

Given that the time to receive a subdoctoral degree is approximately half of the time required for the doctoral degree (approximately two to three years, including an internship), most of the subdoctoral training curricula focus on learning and applying skills that are necessary to comply with state and federally mandated psychological services in schools. As most programs are located in their respective universities' colleges of education, which themselves often must comply with the National Council for the Accreditation of Teacher Education (NCATE), NASP has established a conjoint approval process where program accreditation suffices for key criteria required for the colleges' NCATE accreditation approval. Thus, the vast majority of subdoctoral (and many doctoral) school psychology programs are NASP approved (see NASP, 2009).

Credentialing

Doctoral-level school psychologists find themselves holding two types of credentials. In almost all states, school psychologists are required by the state board of education to be credentialed for employment in the schools, which usually necessitates passing an examination and maintaining an adequate degree of training. Further, many doctoral-level practitioners choose to become licensed, granted by the state board of psychology, which allows them to practice independently across multiple areas. Credentialing at the subdoctoral level is granted by state boards of education, which historically have recognized the masters level as the base requirement to practice in schools. However, two-thirds of the states now require a specialist degree (a degree that requires more course credits and practicum experiences) as the entry-level criterion to practice in schools (Merrell, Ervin & Gimpel, 2006). Given the number of credit hours now required by most subdoctoral training programs (see Thomas & Grimes, 2008), more programs (and states) will likely follow suit, and grant the specialist degree as the entry-level criterion.

Emerging Areas of School Psychology Training Programs
Evidence-Based Practice

The majority of school psychology training programs adopt the scientist-practitioner model, but specific programs often fall along a continuum, in which some programs emphasize aspects of science while others emphasize aspects of practice (Fagan & Sachs-Wise, 2007). Although the relevance of the model continues to be debated (see Huber, 2007), it is established (and mandated by accrediting bodies) that school psychology students must have an adequate research background. Nevertheless, school psychologists have historically engaged in practices that lacked empirical support. In response, a task force was created in 2002, jointly sponsored by Division 16 (APA) and the Society for the Study of School Psychology, to identify and disseminate information regarding evidence-based practices (EBP) for application in school settings (Kratochwill & Stoiber, 2002).

The term *evidence-based*, which has long been used in medicine but has received less attention in psychology and education (White & Kratochwill, 2005), denotes that selected interventions meet specific criteria. Common criteria that must be met include that the intervention: (a) uses an experimental or quasi-experimental design; (b) occurs for a length of time; (c) incorporates multiple outcome measures; (d) is based on studies that have a sufficient sample and use appropriate statistics; and (e) demonstrates continued effectiveness some time after the intervention is no longer applied (Song & Stoiber, 2008; Stoiber & Waas, 2002). Kratochwill (2007) outlined four reasons why the use of EBP is especially critical for practitioners who work in schools. First, unlike other settings, school psychologists have almost unlimited access to children and families. Second, given this access, school psychologists

have the capacity to deliver services across multiple levels (ranging from prevention to intervention), for multiple conditions. Third, schools offer unique opportunities to deliver services that target—often simultaneously—behavioral, psychological, and social functioning. Finally, school psychologists have greater access to follow children developmentally across the early lifespan, which allows opportunities to gather efficacy data across multiple time points.

A number of school based interventions have been highlighted as evidence-based over the past decade, including trauma (Cohen, Jaycox, Walker, Mannarino, Langley, & DuClos, 2009), drug use prevention (Ringwalt, Vincus, Hanley, Ennett, Bowling, & Rohrbach, 2009), and positive behavioral intervention (Aken-Little, Little, Bray, & Kehle, 2009). Yet, EBP is not specific to behavioral treatments, as the practice has been endorsed in education, particularly around Response to Intervention (RTI) and school based psychotherapy. Each of these areas are briefly described.

RESPONSE TO INTERVENTION
Implementation and evaluation of RTI models and practices has taken center stage in the field of school psychology over the past 5 years. Often, RTI is used as a synonym for any academic intervention, rather than a term reserved for a complex, multi-tiered, data-based, decision-making model. Indeed, to fully understand, implement, and manage an RTI model, an in-depth understanding of the tenets of single-subject design, curriculum based measurement, instructional consultation, curriculum design and implementation, and evidence-based intervention practices are required (see Brown-Chidsey & Steege, 2005; Fuchs, Mock, Morgan, & Young, 2003; Shapiro, 2004; Shinn, 1998; Vaughn & Fuchs, 2003).

Schools using RTI typically follow a three-tiered model for decision making: Tier 1 includes screening, classroom instruction, and monitoring responsiveness to classroom instruction in general education settings by general educators; Tiers 2 and 3 include, respectively, supplementary or specialized instruction, and monitoring responsiveness to instruction in a variety of settings by general and special educators (Brown-Chidsey & Steege, 2005; Fuchs & Fuchs, 2005). Curriculum based measurement (CBM) is commonly used within RTI to monitor intervention effectiveness, given that the method is sensitive to small changes in academic skill (Deno, 1985; Shinn, 1998). Much discussion continues about the interface of RTI and special education eligibility;

some argue that traditional, or slightly modified, eligibility testing should occur after instructional modifications at Tiers 2 and 3, merging traditional assessment models with RTI, and others suggest that eligibility is confirmed by failure to demonstrate academic growth in response to specialized interventions within the tiers of RTI (see Fuchs & Young, 2006; Marston, 2005).

Although an increasing number of graduate programs cover the fundamentals of RTI, mastering all the elements of RTI requires at least one comprehensive class, complete with a practicum experience, in order to allow students to understand the nuances of the process. RTI has demonstrated the potential to be an EBP (Daly, Martens, Barnet, Witt, & Olsen, 2007), although many schools and school districts, under local and state mandates to implement RTI, often implement the process imperfectly, or find themselves in a position where the data are not fully captured or are used illogically. At the very least, most programs offer students a broad understanding of the Tier 1 process; understanding the importance of using evidence-based intervention in conjunction with assessment, and being aware of the pitfalls when interpreting progress data. Knowledge and application of Tiers 2 and 3 are contingent on the level of training, philosophy of the program, and number of credit hours needed for degree, among other factors.

SCHOOL BASED PSYCHOTHERAPY

Various epidemiological studies report rates of emotional, behavioral, or developmental issues among school-aged youth that range anywhere between 17% to 22%, and higher (United States Public Health Service, 2000). It is also well documented that children and adolescents with mental health or behavioral issues represent an underserved population, and community resources in many parts of the United States are lacking, inadequate, or delivered haphazardly (American Academy of Child and Adolescent Psychiatry, 2008). Although indirect services such as consultation, program development, and fostering effective home–school collaborations are essential roles of school psychologists, direct services—which include both individual and group psychotherapy—are also commonly reported by school psychologists (Gilman & Gabriel, 2004; Jimerson, Graydon, Curtis, & Staskal, 2007). Considering the needs of youth, and the lack of appropriate mental health services, many school psychologists will continue to be asked to provide therapy to students in schools.

School psychologists are in an ideal position to provide treatments for a number of conditions experienced by schoolchildren. For example, given their visibility, school psychologists are familiar to, and often trusted by, parents, teachers, and students. Further, school psychologists are aware of contextual variables that may influence the psychological and behavioral functioning of the child, such as the overall supportive climate of the school. Moreover, school psychologists have access to information about the student over the course of treatment, which can include objective data (tests or rating scales) and frequent reports by teachers and administrators. In this way, school based treatments can reduce the overreliance on parents, and reduce the influence of factors associated with parent involvement as it relates to treatment adherence, completion, and monitoring (Storch & Crisp, 2004).

Training standards for both subdoctoral and doctoral levels require students to have at least a basic understanding of counseling skills. Most programs at the specialist level and higher also require students to practice their counseling skills through a practicum experience. Until recently, many of the methods applied to treating psychological and psychosocial issues lacked sufficient empirical evidence. Nevertheless, over the past decade there has been a concerted effort to transfer specific methods into more manualized treatments, which can be taught in a systematic fashion, thus increasing treatment adherence and fidelity. School based treatments that have demonstrated empirical support include those that target depression (Caron & Mufson, 2007); anxiety (Kendall, Aschenbrand, & Hudson, 2003), externalizing disorders (see DuPaul & Weyandt, 2009) and trauma (see Little & Akin-Little, 2009), although the numbers of conditions experienced by children in school dictate the need for more EBPs that can be applied in schools.

SUMMARY

In spite of these and other promising treatments, empirically supported interventions as a whole have rarely been applied in schools. As the number of EBPs expands for potential use in schools, the importance of understanding the research behind the philosophy of EPB is paramount. Shernoff, Kratochwill, and Stoiber (2003) noted a number of challenges for training programs, including the competency of faculty, costs of materials, and differences in program training philosophy. Nevertheless, many training programs provide the foundation for a formal EBP course by requiring at least one research methodology course, and some experience in research (up to and including a dissertation), with the focus of having students become active research producers. Subdoctoral programs require methods and statistics classes designed to have students become active research consumers. In both cases, facility with research design and statistical analysis allows graduates to effectively evaluate potentially viable schoolwide and individually based EBPs.

The Diversity of Training Experiences

Previous assertions by some authors (e.g., Matarazzo, 1987) have noted that skills obtained in most training programs transcend psychology subspecialty. That is, accreditation boards such as the APA specify and monitor training criteria regardless of whether the program is school, clinical, or other applied fields in psychology. This is not to imply that all specialties receive equivalent amounts of training in each area; by virtue of its professional identity, school psychology training programs often provide unique didactic and practicum experiences for their graduate students, to prepare them for school practice. Knowledge of school laws, crisis intervention, and school-based consultation are some areas that would not necessarily be learned in other subspecialties (Tharinger, Pryzwansky, & Miller, 2008). Yet, it is also noted that the broad application of skills learned in school psychology training programs make graduates less defined by a particular setting, and more by the competencies they hold.

Although the numbers of practitioners in "nontraditional" (i.e., nonschool) settings are far less than those who work in schools (Curtis, Hunley, Walker, & Baker, 1999), a number of practitioners have opted to work in nontraditional settings. As reviewed by Gilman and Teague (2005), some of the most prominent settings are private practice, residential treatment settings, neuropsychological centers, and early intervention centers. The advantages to working in nontraditional settings are many. For example, while the majority of a school based psychologist's time is likely spent in assessment activities in schools (Curtis et al., 2004), school psychologists in nontraditional settings may have greater flexibility to spend comparably more time providing other services (e.g., counseling, parent consultation). Further, working in a specific nontraditional setting may allow the school psychologist to assume additional roles and responsibilities not available in school settings. However, there are challenges to working in nontraditional settings that may not be experienced by school based psychologists, including job security, the pressure to secure external funding, and understanding of third-party reimbursements.

Two specific nontraditional settings have been the focus of recent attention in the school psychology literature. One setting most generally applicable to students is as a program trainer. Working in an academic setting typically necessitates a doctoral degree. Those working in a tenure track have a finite amount of time in which to demonstrate competency in three common core areas: teaching, research, and service. Depending on the institution and the training level, teaching loads can range anywhere from one course and higher per semester. Further, and again depending on a multitude of factors (e.g., location of program, philosophy of department/college, level of training), academic research productivity requirements must be met in order to be promoted and tenured. Service requirements typically include serving on student committees, mentoring student research and/or practice requirements, serving on academic program committees, and contributing more broadly to the field.

In many respects, the advantages of joining a training program as faculty after graduation are similar to those found in other nontraditional settings, such as flexibility of roles and assuming higher positions of responsibility as one advances (Stark, Perfect, Simpson, Schnoebelen, & Glenn, 2004). Yet, these advantages are balanced against lower initial salary, and lack of opportunities to practice specific skills (e.g., academic and cognitive testing; Nagle, Suldo, Christenson, & Hansen, 2004; Rosenfield, 2004). Due in part to these concerns, school psychology training programs continue to face serious faculty shortages, with approximately 25% of all training programs advertising positions in any given year (Demaray, Carlson, & Hodgson, 2003; Little & Akin-Little, 2004). Although the number of open positions parallels what has been noted in other subspecialty training programs, the concern that chronic faculty shortages in school psychology programs may limit the number of graduates, comes at a time when school districts are clamoring to hire practitioners.

It has been recommended that training programs devote greater interest to mentoring individuals who are considering a career in academia (Kratochwill, Shernoff, & Sanetti, 2004). Specific suggestions include: (a) emphasizing curriculum and program materials that feature positive aspects of an academic career; (b) shaping, mentoring, and nurturing scholarship that extends beyond term papers, theses, and dissertations; (c) helping interested students establish connections at conferences; and (d) positive role modeling by faculty members. Nevertheless, the effectiveness of these suggestions await empirical study.

Another nontraditional setting of potential interest to students is pediatric hospitals. There are a number of advantages to working in pediatric settings. For example, the roles and types of conditions are broader, salaries are usually higher, and hours are more flexible than in school settings. Nevertheless, these advantages should be balanced against situations that may not be faced in schools, such as productivity requirements and pressures to secure external funds.

Advantages and disadvantages of working in a pediatric setting aside, such settings offer a wide array of training opportunities for school psychology students—even for those who do not wish to apply their knowledge of pediatric issues in schools after graduating. For example, many settings have a sizeable number of staff psychologists with different training backgrounds, which allows for more intensive supervision, a greater variety of didactic instruction and practicum experiences, and exposure to complex cases that may not be seen in school-based practicum experiences. Further, pediatric settings are multidisciplinary in nature, consisting of medical personnel, speech-language clinicians, special educators, physical therapists, and social workers among other personnel. Thus, students get access to a number of didactic and training experiences, allowing them to better identify, assess, and treat a number of developmental, social, physical, and psychological conditions. In this regard, the school psychology student is afforded unique opportunities to learn and practice competencies such as treatment adherence, parent consultation, and parent interviewing. Finally, many pediatric settings are also engaged in research projects, allowing school psychology students to be mentored and participate in medically focused research projects that have direct implications to learning.

Some final training considerations are of note for students who wish to consider working in nontraditional settings, the most important of which is the availability of opportunities for students. Currently, most training programs offer general, broad-based training primarily in school systems. Interested students often have to either design their own independent practicum experience, or enroll in programs that have affiliations in nontraditional settings. For students interested in pediatric settings, there are several programs offering didactic courses and practicum experiences in "pediatric school psychology" (see Brown, 2004; Shaw, 2003), and many others have direct connections to faculty in these settings. Further, the number of courses that must be covered to fulfill accreditation obligations often leaves programs with little flexibility to offer additional courses that would allow students to pursue nontraditional practicum experiences. Unless explicitly written into the curriculum, many students are forced to take additional courses or sign up for independent study credits, which can lead to additional costs and/or lengthen the time to graduate. Finally, students interested in pursuing practicum experiences in nontraditional settings should be mentored by both a field supervisor and a faculty supervisor. Unless faculty supervisors understand the nuances of school psychology as it is applied to nontraditional settings, the quality of supervision is diminished at best, or inadequate at worst.

Advocating for the Field

Various authors have emphasized the need for school psychologists to advocate for reforms that would promote the entire range of school psychology roles and functions, and offset the limited perceptions that are often held by key stakeholders (e.g., Sheridan & Gutkin, 2000). Typically, calls for advocacy have been directed at school psychology practitioners. However, as noted in the introduction, school psychology as seen from a systems perspective consists of multiple interactive units, each of which lends unique opportunities to advocate for reform. Training programs and their students can be equally influential toward influencing the perceptions of how others view the field.

Studies by Gilman and colleagues (Gilman & Gabriel, 2004; Gilman & Handwerk, 2001; Gilman & Medway, 2007) have consistently reported a number of misperceptions held not only by teachers and administrators, but also (and perhaps more disturbing) by potential recruits into school psychology training programs. For example, among a sample of over 600 undergraduate students from five large universities, Gilman and Handwerk found that the majority of students who wished to pursue graduate studies in psychology chose clinical and counseling psychology over school psychology, with the primary reason that they wanted to work with children(!). Follow-up analyses revealed that most undergraduates, while claiming that they were knowledgeable of the field, nevertheless held a rather limited perspective of school psychology roles over those of clinical and counseling psychologists. For example, students as a whole believed that clinical psychologists provided a significantly wider range of services than school psychologists, and that whatever knowledge they learned of school psychology came from either firsthand experiences, or because they knew of someone who worked with a school psychologist. Students were aware of clinical and counseling psychology through many sources, including information obtained from the media, textbooks and journals, and information shared by instructors.

Given these findings, several recommendations were made in order to replace the traditional "finding school psychology through serendipity" (that many practitioners report) with more proactive and effective strategies. Recommendations included placing information about school psychology into the hands of professionals most likely to come into contact with potential graduate students (practitioners working in schools, undergraduate faculty advisors, etc.); providing shadowing opportunities, whereby undergraduate students would be allowed to follow advanced graduate students during portions of their practicum; and having graduate students sponsor undergraduate career planning seminars.

In addition to changing the perceptions of undergraduate students, school psychology graduate students may also play a key role in helping change perceptions held by many teachers and administrators. For example, Gilman and Gabriel (2004) and Gilman and Medway (2007) conducted separate surveys of over 1600 education professionals (i.e., teachers and administrators) from eight districts in four states, comparing their perceptions of school psychological services to that of school counselors. These responses were also compared to school psychologists working in the same districts. Results found that education professionals had a more favorable view of school counselors than of school psychologists, but these views were influenced in turn by the amount of contact the education professionals had with each group. Further, similar to what was found among undergraduate students asked to differentiate roles between clinical and school psychologists, education professionals tended to perceive school psychologists in more limited roles (primarily as test experts) than school counselors. Although the recommendations from the studies were geared more toward professional school psychologists, they could easily be directed to school psychology students, as well. For example, sponsoring inservices that could, in part, explicate the range of roles that school psychologists can perform, could

easily be led by students. Other suggestions, such as (a) forming or being part of the school's pre-referral team, (b) working on projects that directly involve an active collaboration with an administrator, and (c) establishing daily "check-ins" with targeted teachers, could also be written into a formal practicum plan for students.

Other Emerging Trends

The last section of this chapter will discuss several elements central to modern practice that may not be presented as standalone courses in common school psychology curricula. To be sure, school psychology training models could be enhanced by developing a scope and sequence of coursework specifically focused on several key issues outlined in subsequent paragraphs that are relevant to practice in contemporary schools. We focus on just three of them that are increasingly being emphasized in training programs: (1) providing more of a focus on children across the entire early developmental lifespan, (2) emphasizing more family-centered care, and (3) emphasizing services through the lens of multiculturalism.

Focus on P–12

Among school psychologists, discussion about "early skills" and "young children," often refers to kindergarten and early elementary school, even though child development and experience from birth to age 5 greatly impacts and molds children into the kindergartners who enter the doors of formal education. It is no longer disputed that children require cognitive, linguistic, and social/emotional stimulation at a high intensity, high quality level, long before kindergarten (Shonkoff & Phillips, 2000). Research related to achievement gap and social justice issues for increasingly diverse groups of children all point to the importance of the years prior to kindergarten (e.g., Hart & Risley, 1995; Slavin, Karweit, & Wasik, 2004; Zigler & Styfco, 2004). Yet, most school psychology programs only offer explicit training experiences in kindergarten through twelfth grade (K–12), and do not provide a framework for expanding roles and functions to prekindergarten (Hojnoski & Missall, 2007).

Although many states and school districts do not engage (or require engagement of) school psychologists in prekindergarten or early childhood activities, school psychologists are perfectly poised to address critical issues related to early development and transition into formal school. To work effectively in early childhood settings, school psychologists need specialized training related to early development, assessment, identification for services, intervention, family-centered service, and seamless service delivery from prekindergarten into early elementary school (see Hojnoski & Missall, 2007). However, the unique capacity of school psychologists to work throughout the life span and across settings makes them especially well suited to service delivery for young children. By acting as a liaison between K–12 schools and early childhood settings, school psychologists can assist schools in preparing to meet the diverse needs of their youngest students, and can assist early childhood educators in better preparing children for school entry (Carlton & Winsler, 1999).

Family-Centered Service

Taking a page from early childhood special education, school psychology training program, and educational systems more generally would benefit from a family-centered approach to service delivery (see Baily, 2004; Dunst, Trivette, & Deal, 1988; Turnbull & Turnbull, 2000). A family-centered approach is grounded in building a relationship between families and professionals by focusing first on a family's needs, concerns, and priorities. The goal is to develop a positive relationship to support and enhance intervention planning, delivery, and effectiveness. By focusing first on the family, services for the child/student are more targeted, helpful, streamlined and, often, more effective. If the family participates actively in planning intervention, they are more likely to participate in related efforts required for improvement and maintenance.

Although the connection between a family-centered focus and delivery of school psychological services may seem more direct for work with very young children, the principles translate to work with youth of all ages. All youth live in a home environment under the guidance of an adult, even though this relationship can take many forms. Regardless of whether the context of service provision with a youth is focused on prevention or specialized intervention, an excellent starting point for establishing support and trust is consulting with a family to gain understanding of their perspective of their own needs, values, and resources.

Despite federal legislation mandating parental involvement in special education evaluation and intervention efforts, all too often they are not. Sadly, school psychologists tend to observe this in their training, and then come to expect it in their own practice. If training programs were to prime students to expect and invite parent/guardian involvement, and operate from a family-centered perspective,

a multitude of hurdles in service provision and child outcomes might be avoided.

Multicultural Issues

Because youth enrolled in schools are increasingly coming from a variety of cultural backgrounds, training programs would be remiss not to address issues in working with diverse populations. Training programs also need to be firm about openly adopting a broad definition of "culture," including age, gender, socioeconomic status, sexual orientation, family heritage and traditions, race, ethnicity, ability, place of residence (urban/rural), geographic location (native/international), and so on. Training models of old tended to emphasize group differences, and offer specific strategies for working with students from a certain background or race. More contemporary approaches suggest awareness of personal identity (e.g., cultural, racial, sexual), open discussion about differences and identification of common ground, individual issues related to acculturation and worldview, avoidance of terminology like "tolerance," and celebration of a broad range of value systems.

Summary

The purpose of this chapter was to present some emerging areas of school psychology training programs that have complemented core training emphases on assessment, intervention, consultation, and ethics. School psychology as a discipline has matured into a dynamic and complex system much different than even a decade ago. The roles of school psychologists are expanding such that the focus of practice is now more commonly on the contexts of systems, rather than on individuals. Opportunities are more readily available for helping groups of children, rather than diagnosing pathology or working toward eligibility for single children. Professional expectations have moved more toward intervention and away from assessment. Practices are requiring data-based support and decision making. Given the more complex issues that youth face in schools, the task of incorporating these emerging trends into a cohesive training framework makes these quite exciting, yet challenging times. It is hoped that enhancing the scope of training curriculum to include evidence-based practices, work experiences in multiple settings, advocacy in promoting the field, and other emergent areas will continue to keep school psychology on the forefront of best practices for children and their families, and will contribute important information in future educational and mental health reform efforts.

References

Akin-Little, A., Little, S. G., Bray, M. A., & Kehle, T. J. (Eds.) (2009). *Behavioral interventions in schools: Evidence-based positive strategies.* Washington, DC: American Psychological Association.

American Psychological Association (2010). Accredited programs in school psychology [online], author. Available: http://www.apa.org/ed/accreditation/programs/accred-school.aspx.

American Academy of Child and Adolescent Psychiatry (AACAP). 2008. *Health Care Reform Principles.* Washington, DC: American Academy of Child and Adolescent Psychiatry.

Bailey, D. B. (2004). Assessing family resources, priorities, and concerns. In M. McLean, M. Wolery, & D. Bailey (Eds.), *Assessing infants and preschoolers with special needs* (pp. 173–203). Upper Saddle River, NJ: Pearson Prentice Hall.

Barton, S. (1994). Chaos, self-organization, and psychology. *American Psychologist, 49,* 5–14.

Brown, R. T. (2004). *Handbook of pediatric psychology in school settings.* Mahwah, NJ: Lawrence Erlbaum Associates.

Brown-Chidsey, R., & Steege, M. W. (2005). *Response to intervention: Principles and strategies for effective practice.* New York: Guilford.

Carlton, M. P., & Winsler, A. (1999). School readiness: The need for a paradigm shift. *School Psychology Review, 28,* 338–352.

Caron, A., & Mufson, L. (2007). School-based treatment of depression. In S. W. Evans, M. D. Weist, & Z. N. Serpell (Eds), *Advances in school-based mental health interventions: Best practices and program models, (Volume 2)* (pp. 1–17). Kingston, NJ: Civic Research Institute.

Cohen, J. A., Jaycox, L. H., Walker, D. W., Mannarino, A. P., Langley, A. K., & DuClos, J. L. (2009). Treating traumatized children after Hurricane Katrina: Project Fleur-de lis™. *Clinical Child and Family Psychology Review, 12,* 55–64.

Curtis, M. J., Grier, J., Chesno, E., & Hunley, S. A. (2004). The Changing Face of School Psychology: Trends in Data and Projections for the Future. *School Psychology Review, 33,* 49–66.

Curtis, M. J., Hunley, S. A., Walker, K. J., & Baker, A. C. (1999). Demographic characteristics and professional practices in school psychology. *School Psychology Review, 28,* 104–116

Daly, E. J., Martens, B. K., Barnett, D., Witt, J.C.,& Olson, S. C. (2007). Varying intervention delivery in response to intervention: Confronting and resolving challenges with measurement, instruction, and intensity. *School Psychology Review, 36,* 562–581.

Davis, A. S., McIntosh, D. E., Phelps, L., & Kehle, T. J. (2004). Addressing the shortage of school psychologists: A summarative overview. *Psychology in the Schools, 41,* 489–495.

Demaray, M. K., Carlson, J. S., & Hodgson, K. K. (2003). Assistant professors of school psychology: A national survey of program directors and job applicants. *Psychology in the Schools, 40,* 691–698.

Deno, S. L. (1985). Curriculum-based measurement: The emerging alternative. *Exceptional Children, 52,* 219–232.

Dooley, K. J., & Van de Ven, A. D. (1999). Explaining complex organizational dynamics. *Organization Science, 10,* 358–372.

DuPaul, G. J., & Weyandt, L. L. (2009). Behavioral interventions with externalizing disorders. In A. Akin-Little, S. G. Little, M. A. Bray, & T. J. Kehle (Eds) *Behavioral interventions in schools: Evidence-based positive strategies.* (p. 265–280). Washington, DC: American Psychological Association.

Dunst, C. J., Trivette, C. M., & Deal, A. G. (Eds.). (1988). *Enabling and empowering families: Principles and guidelines for practices.* Cambridge, MA: Brookline Books.

Fagan, T. K. (2004). School psychology's significant discrepancy: Historical perspectives on personnel shortages. *Psychology in the Schools, 41,* 419–430

Fagan, T. K. (2005). The 50th anniversary of the Thayer Conference: Historical perspectives and accomplishments. *School Psychology Quarterly, 20,* 224–251

Fagan, T. K., & Sachs-Wise, P. S. (2007). *School psychology: Past, present, and future* (3rd ed.). Bethesda, MD: National Association of School Psychologists.

Fuchs, D., & Fuchs, L. S. (2005). Responsiveness-to-intervention: A blueprint for practitioners, policymakers, and parents. *Teaching Exceptional Children,* Sept/Oct, 57–63.

Fuchs, D., Mock, D., Morgan, P. L., & Young, C. L. (2003). Responsiveness–to-intervention: Definitions, evidence, and implications for the learning disabilities construct. *Learning Disabilities Research and Practice, 18,* 157–171.

Fuchs, D., & Young, C. L. (2006. On the irrelevance of intelligence in predicting responsiveness to reading instruction. *Exceptional Children, 73,* 8–30.

Geisinger, K. F. (2000). Psychological testing at the end of the millennium: A brief historical review. *Professional Psychology: Research and Practice, 31,* 117–118.

Gilman, R., & Gabriel, S. (2004). Perceptions of school psychological services by education professionals: Results from a multi-state survey pilot study. *School Psychology Review, 33,* 271–286.

Gilman, R., & Handwerk, M. L. (2001). Undergraduate students' perceptions of school psychology: Findings and implications. *School Psychology Review, 30,* 120–134.

Gilman, R., & Medway, F. J. (2007). Teachers' perceptions of school psychology: A comparison of regular and special education teacher ratings. *School Psychology Review, 22,* 145–161.

Gilman, R., & Teague, T. L. (2005). School Psychologists in Nontraditional Settings: Alternative Roles and Functions in Psychological Service Delivery. In R. D. Morgan, T. L. Kuther, & C. J. Habben (Eds.), *Life after graduate school in psychology: Insider's advice from new psychologists* (pp. 167–180). New York: Psychology Press.

Grimes, J., & Tilly, W. D. (1996). Policy and process: Means to lasting educational change. *School Psychology Review, 25,* 465–476.

Gunn, W. B., Haley, J., & Lyness, A. M. P. (2007). Systemic approaches: Family therapy. In H. T. Prout and D. T. Brown (Eds.), *Counseling and psychotherapy with children and adolescents: Theory and practice for school and clinical settings* (4th ed., pp. 388–418). Hoboken, NJ: John Wiley & Sons, Inc.

Hart, B., & Risley, T. (1995). *Meaningful differences in the everyday experiences of young American children.* Baltimore, MD: Brookes.

Hojnoski, R. L., & Missall, K. N. (2006). Addressing school readiness: Expanding school psychology in early education. *School Psychology Review, 35*(4), 602–614.

Huber, D. R. (2007). Is the scientist-practitioner model viable for school psychology practice? *American Behavioral Scientist, 50,* 778–788.

Jimerson, S. R., Graydon, K., Curtis, M. J., & Staskal, R. (2007). The international school psychology survey: Insights from school psychologists around the world. In S. R. Jimerson, T. D. Oakland, & P. T Farrell (Eds.), *The handbook of international school psychology.* (pp. 481–500). Thousand Oaks, CA: Sage Publications.

Katz, M. S. (1976). *A history of compulsory education laws.* Bloomington, IN: Phi Delta Kappa Educational Foundation.

Kendall, P. C., Aschenbrand, S. G., & Hudson, J. L. (2003). Child-focused treatment of anxiety. In A. E. Kazdin & J. R. Weisz (Eds), *Evidence-based psychotherapies for children and adolescents* (pp. 81–100). New York: Guilford.

Kratochwill, T. K. (2007). Preparing psychologists for evidence-based school practice: Lessons learned and challenges ahead. *American Psychologist, 62,* 829–843.

Kratochwill, T. R., Shernoff, E. S., & Sanetti, L. (2004). Promotion of academic careers in school psychology: A conceptual framework of impact points, recommended strategies, and hopeful outcomes. *School Psychology Quarterly, 19,* 342–364.

Kratochwill, T. R., & Stoiber, K. C. (2002). Evidence-based interventions in school psychology: Conceptual foundations of the procedural and coding manual of division 16 and the society for the study of school psychology task force. *School Psychology Quarterly, 17,* 341–389.

Little, S. G., & Akin-Little, A. (2004). Academic school psychologists: Addressing the shortage. *Psychology in the Schools, 41,* 451–459.

Little, S. G., & Akin-Little, A. (2009). Trauma-focused cognitive behavior therapy. In A. Akin-Little, S. G. Little, M. A. Bray, & T. J. Kehle (Eds.), *Behavioral interventions in schools: Evidence-based positive strategies.* (p. 325–333). Washington, DC: American Psychological Association.

Marston, D. (2005). Tiers in intervention in responsiveness to intervention: Prevention outcomes and learning disabilities identification patterns. *Journal of Learning Disabilities, 38,* 539–544.

Matarazzo. J. D. (1987). There is only one psychology, no specialties, but many applications. *American Psychologist, 42,* 893–903.

Merrill, K. W., Ervin, R. A., & Gimpel, G. A. (2006). *School psychology for the 21st century: Foundations and practices.* New York, NY: Guilford.

Miller, D. C., DeOrnellas, K., & Maricle, D. (in press). What is so special about the specialist degree? In E. García-Vázquez, T. Crespi and C. Riccio (Eds.). *Handbook of education, training and supervision of school psychologists in school and community – Volume I: Foundations of professional practice.* United Kingdom: Routledge.

Nagle, R. J., Suldo, S. M., Christenson, S. L., & Hansen, A. L. (2004).Graduate students' perspectives of academic positions in school psychology. *School Psychology Quarterly, 19,* 311–326.

National Association of School Psychologists (2000). *Standards for training and field placement programs in school psychology.* Bethesda, MD: Author.

National Association of School Psychologists (2009). *NASP approved/nationally recognized graduate programs in school psychology* (pp. 3–25). Information obtained by accessing http://www.nasponline.org/certification/NASPapproved.aspx.

Reschly, D. J. (2000). The present and future status of school psychology in the United States. *School Psychology Review, 29,* 507–522.

Ringwalt, C., Vincus, A. A., Hanley, S., Ennett, S. T., Bowling, J. M., & Rohrbach, L. A. (2009). The prevalence of evidence-based drug use prevention curricula in U.S. middle schools in 2005. *Prevention Science, 10,* 33–40.

Rosenfield, S. (2004). Academia: It's a wonderful life–isn't it? *School Psychology Quarterly, 19,* 398–408.

Shapiro, E. S. (2004). *Academic skills problems: Direct assessment and intervention* (3rd ed.). New York: Guilford

Shaw, S. R. (2003). Professional preparation of pediatric school psychologists for school-based health centers. *Psychology in the Schools, 40,* 321–330.

Sheridan, S. M., & Gutkin, T. B. (2000). The ecology of school psychology: Examining and changing our paradigm for the 21st Century. *School Psychology Review, 29,* 485–501.

Shernoff, E. S., Kratochwill, T. R., & Stoiber, K. C. (2003). Training in evidence-based interventions (EBIs): What are school psychology programs teaching? *Journal of School Psychology, 41,* 467–483.

Shinn, M. R. (1998). (Ed.), *Advanced applications of curriculum-based measurement.* New York: Guilford.

Slavin, R. E., Karweit, N. L., & Wasik, B. A. (2004) (Eds.), *Preventing early school failure: Research, policy, and practice* (pp. 78–101). Boston, MA: Allyn & Bacon.

Song, S. Y., & Stoiber, K. C. (2008). Children exposed to violence at school: An evidence-based intervention agenda for the "real" bullying problem. *Journal of Emotional Abuse, 8,* 235–253.

Stark, K. D., Perfect, M., Simpson, J., Schnoebelen, S., & Glenn, R. (2004). Encouraging academic careers: one of many desirable career options for doctoral school psychologists. *School Psychology Quarterly, 19,* 382–397.

Stoiber, K. C., & Waas, G. A. (2002). A contextual and methodological perspective on the evidence-based movement within school psychology in the United States. *Educational and Child Psychology, 19,* 7–21.

Storch, E. A., & Crisp, H. L. (2004). Introduction: Taking it to the schools–Transporting empirically supported treatments for childhood psychopathology to the school setting. *Clinical Child and Family Psychology Review, 7,* 191–193.

Tharinger, D. J., Pryzwansky, W. B., & Miller, J. A. (2008). School psychology: A specialty of professional psychology with distinct competencies and complexities. *Professional Psychology: Research and Practice, 39,* 529–536.

Thomas, A., & Grimes, J. (Eds.). (2008). *Best practices in school psychology* (5th ed.). Bethesda, MD: National Association of School Psychologists.

Turnbull, A. P., & Turnbull, H. R. (2000). *Families, professionals, and exceptionality: Collaborating for empowerment* (4th ed.). Upper Saddle River, NJ: Pearson Prentice Hall.

United States Public Health Service. 2000. *Report of the surgeon general's conference on children's mental health: A national action agenda.* Washington, DC: Department of Health and Human Services.

VanVoorhis, R. W., & Levinson, E. M. (2006). Job satisfaction among school psychologists: A meta-analysis. *School Psychology Quarterly, 21,* 77–90.

Vaughn, S., & Fuchs, L. S. (2003). Redefining learning disabilities as inadequate response to instruction: The promise and potential problems. *Learning Disabilities Research and Practice, 18,* 137–148.

White, J. L., & Kratochwill, T. K. (2005). Practice guidelines in school psychology: Issues and directions for evidence-based interventions in practice and training. *Journal of School Psychology, 43,* 99–115.

Wnek, A. C., Klein, G., & Bracken, B. A. (2008). Professional development issues for school psychologists: What's hot, what's not in the United States. *School Psychology International*, *29*, 145–160.

Ysseldyke, J., Burns, M., Dawson, P., Kelley, B., Morrison, D., Ortiz, S., Rosenfield, S., & Telzrow, C. (2006). *School psychology: A blueprint for training and practice III*. Bethesda, MD: National Association of School Psychologists.

Zigler, E., & Styfco, S. J. (2004) (Eds.), *The head start debates*. Baltimore, MD: Brookes.

Program Planning and Evaluation

Laura M. Crothers, Lea A. Theodore, *and* Tammy L. Hughes

Abstract

In recognition of the challenges facing domestic school systems, and a history of "hastily conceived, poorly implemented innovations or programs" (Trachtman, 1981, p. 141), school psychologists have increasingly acknowledged the need for program planning and evaluation as a part of their role functioning. Program planning and evaluation is a discipline arising from the field of educational research, resulting from a commitment to improving education, a value of sound measurement and methodology, and the emphasis upon theory building and theory-based inquiry (D'Agostino, 2001). Organizational or systems consultation is a framework that may be used to assist school psychologists in designing, developing, and evaluating educational programs. In this chapter, the topics of program planning and evaluation are reviewed, including methods and techniques, potential difficulties, and assessing and interpreting results. Case studies of program planning and evaluation are provided to encourage reflection and application of the concepts presented in the chapter.

Keywords: program planning, development, evaluation, organizational and systems consultation

Introduction

As the United States moved into the twenty-first century, concerns were expressed by the nation's citizens, educators, business and industry representatives, and political leaders regarding children's academic achievement, and whether they were being equipped by the public school system with the skills necessary to succeed in employment and/or post-secondary education settings. Thus, the No Child Left Behind Act(P.L.107-110)was enacted in 2001 to raise educational standards to ensure that all children, regardless of race, ethnicity, income, and disability status are able to read and calculate at grade level or above. As a result of the establishment of P.L. 107-110, a renewed emphasis was placed upon the necessity of developing alternative methods for providing educational services to students with special needs (Zins & Ponti, 1990), in response to problems associated with traditional special education programs that often fail to individualize instruction, use curriculum that is diluted, nonexistent, or

is not empiricallyvalidated, and implement models of service delivery that are poorly directed and fragmented (Fuchs & Fuchs, 1994; Wasburn-Moses, 2006; Winzer, 2000).

Unfortunately, issues of quality of instruction are not limited to special education but are often pervasive throughout school systems. As an example, Kehle and Bray (2007) cite concerns raised by Trachtman (1981) in a seminal article regarding faddism in school psychology—which he characterizes as an inundation of "hastily conceived, poorly implemented innovations or programs, the failure to achieve anticipated goals, and consequent disillusionment with the original idea, or backlash" (p. 141)—that serves to perpetuate the mediocrity in schools that so greatly concerns the nation's citizens,educators, business and industry representatives, and political leaders. Kehle and Bray (2007) contend that in school psychology, and perhaps in the field of education as a whole, evolution will be the result only when theory, research, and practice inform one another and improve practitioners' expertise in promoting the well-being of children. Increasing the rigor of educational research, including developing and evaluating programs, relies upon abandoning solely the subjective, such as measures of knowledge and attitudes (Durlak, 2002), and embracing the objective to the greatest extent possible, in terms of the use of effect sizes, confidence intervals, and independent replication of treatment results to guide decisionmaking (Durlak, 2002; Kehle & Bray, 2007).

In moving away from inferential conclusions that existing educational curricula is functional or successful in advancing children's or adolescents' skill development, or that an intuitive collection of ideas sans empirical evidence will constitute an efficacious program, educators such as school psychologists have increasingly acknowledged the need for objective, rigorous program development, planning, and evaluation as a part of their role functioning. Traditionally, practitioners and researchers within the discipline of psychology have been encouraged to be positivists, believing that knowledge can only come from practices that have been empirically validated (Staats, 1991). Despite this orientation, school psychologists and other educators have too often settled for insufficient empirical evidence in the development and evaluation of programs.

A critical mass of researchers and trainers in the field of school psychology has always contended that children and adolescents could not be adequately served without data-based problem solving to guide educational programming, and the call for action in increased rigor in the development and evaluation of curricula began to reach educators throughout the country during the last few decades. In university training programs, school psychologists are taught to be critical-thinking educational researchers, who use objective data and appropriate statistical analyses to determine the success of interventions or programs. When random sampling and experimental designs are not pragmatic, or are ethically unfeasible, school psychologists know to utilize the most rigorous design available, such as a merging of quasi-experimental methodological approaches to determine whether a program has met its goals (de Anda, 2007). In keeping with this orientation, program planning and evaluation (PPE) is a discipline arising from the field of educational research, resulting from a commitment to improving education, a value of sound measurement and methodology, and an emphasis upon theory building and theory-based inquiry(D'Agostino, 2001).

An historic, yet pressing problem that PPE efforts must consider,is the failure to implement evidence-based practices (EBPs) in schools. One reason posited as to why EBPs are not sufficiently used in schools is a research-to-practice gap, in which researchdriven, empirically based interventions have limited transportability to the school setting (Auster, Feeney-Kettler, & Kratochwill, 2006). However, in order for educators to best serve the children and adolescents with whom they work, it is important to design educational programs based upon EBPs, and to consistently, accurately, and comprehensively evaluate existing programs to ensure that these delivery models are reflective of practices that have been recognized as facilitating the learning of children and adolescents. Pragmatically, it may seem daunting to engage in program development and evaluation, even when EBPs guide the process, since many educational systems lack a procedural mechanism for such activities. Because program planning, development, and evaluation often are conducted over a series of years, targeting a number of different services and consumers, it may be helpful to view such activities as processes and not events (Fairchild & Seeley, 1996). Following this paradigm, the question that may be posed is, how does this process begin?

Organizational/Systems Consultation in Program Planning and Evaluation

Given the time-intensive nature of program planning and evaluation, a framework that may be useful in assisting school psychologists in the process of designing, planning, and evaluating educational programs, is organizational or systems consultation (OSC). Consultation in schools—a service delivery model in which a clinician, serving as a consultant, uses problem-solving strategies (in order to alter an existing set of circumstances to become a desired set of circumstances) to address the needs of a consultee and a client—has become a necessary competency for school psychologists (Kratochwill & Bergan, 1990).An expanding body of evidence supports the process of consultation (Gutkin & Curtis, 1990) as an avenue of facilitation for the implementation of data-based interventions, as an organizing framework to increase continuity and coordination among interventions (Gutkin, 1986; Zins & Ponti, 1990), and as a means of developing and evaluating programs to determine whether they are meeting their goals (Zins & Ponti, 1990).

Several theorists in the field of school psychology— including Zins, Curtis, Graden, and Ponti (1988),

Zins and Ponti (1990), Schmuck (1995), Illback and Zins (1995), and Zins and Illback (1995), among others—have advocated for OSC in promoting organizational developmental change, which includes program development and evaluation, in educational settings. In addition to promoting the use of EBPs in the development of programs, the use of OSC may also help avoid Type III error, which is concluding that a program is not effective, when in fact the measurement of program effectiveness was affected by inadequate implementation of the program. Consultants can utilize OSC to determine whether programs are truly ineffective, or whether there is a relationship between levels of program implementation and program outcomes (Kalafat, Illback, & Sanders, 2006). Consultation can increase the use of EBPs by facilitating the transmission of information from consultants to other schoolbased professionals, as well as reducing barriers to EBP implementation, such as intervention complexity, since consultants can provide training, guidance, and supervision to consultees to improve intervention integrity (Auster et al., 2006).

One form of OSC, organizational development consultation (ODC), is particularly appropriate for use in facilitating program planning and evaluation. Organizational development (OD) is a purposeful, continuous effort in which systems study themselves in order to promote improvement in system norms, structures, and procedures (Schmuck, 1995). Frequently, problems in schools that seem to be childfocused are actually building, systems, or community problems that need to be addressed at multiple levels using a problem-solving process to encourage systematic, multifaceted intervention and substantive change (Knoff, 2000). Organizational development consultative (ODC) approaches can be used to assist schools in clarifying their overall problems and their rationale in supporting intervention strategy choices, selecting explicit standards in order to support strength and fidelity of implementation, developing programs designed to deliver empiricallyvalidated interventions, monitoring standards and evaluating feedback regarding implementation quality, analyzing the organizational obstacles impeding high-quality implementation, choosing strategies to overcome such impediments, and evaluating the success of the programs implemented (Gottfredson, 1993).

In essence, ODC may be used as a delivery system for program planning, design, development, and evaluation. Theorists such as Gottfredson and colleagues (Gottfredson,1984, 1993;Gottfredson,

Rickert, Gottfredson, &Advani,1984) have developed an ODC approach, *program development evaluation* (PDE), through which school systems can begin by defining a problem and following a process that culminates in implementing organizational innovations for lasting change through program development and evaluation. This process includes problem definition, assessment, diagnosis, development of implementation standards, measurement, and evaluation of implementation standards (Gottfredson, 1993), all of which can be applied to both program planning and evaluation. Interested readers are encouraged to consult the original articles for greater detail in using this consultative model.

Although the school psychologist may decide to use OSC methods as the vehicle for service delivery, he or she must also understand the particulars of program planning and evaluation before working as a change agent. Consequently, in the next portion of this chapter, the topic of program development will be explored, including its methods, potential obstacles, and evaluation of goals. Following this review, a case study of program planning will be presented in order for readers to understand the application of the concepts to a scenario that might be experienced by school psychologists working in school systems.

Program Planning and Development
What is Program Planning?
Program planning is the act of designing effective programs for children. In the era of accountability introduced by P.L.107-110, schools are required to show that the experiences designed to educate children are selected because of their evidence base, and that the expected learning outcomes for students are meaningful and measurable (Felner, Seitsinger, Brand, Burns, & Bolton, 2008). However, the ability to select interventions for use in the school setting based on empirical findings presents a serious challenge for educators (e.g., Goldfried & Wolfe, 1996; Hunsley, 2007; Kratochwill & Stoiber, 2000; Ringeisen, Henderson,& Hoagwood, 2003).

In regard to program planning, there is often too little time afforded to determining the appropriateness of an intervention. That is, although there has been an increased awareness of the need to select interventions that have evidence of their usefulness, there has been less attention paid to determining the viability of the intervention in its particular setting (Forman & Burke, 2008). The context of an individual school system can compromise not only the selection of an EBP, but also how the intervention is implemented and the interpretation of the conclusions drawn from its findings (Shapiro, 2006). For example, although there may be empirical validation for a particular intervention, the nature of the school, classroom, or child may dissuade its use, or require significant adjustments so that it can be implemented at a specific site. If educators have not spent time examining how their school systems would be able to support an intervention, these otherwise adequate interventions may fail (Forman & Burke, 2008). Further, in the case of implementation in which adjustments have been required, it becomes unclear if these alterations meaningfully change the intervention to a degree that the conclusions gathered in the current setting are no longer comparable to the original evidence-recommended practice (Hunsley, 2007; Ringeisen et al., 2003). As such, if there is a need to make ongoing changes to a modified intervention, the use of the extant literature base to determine the next steps may prove to be of limited use.

Program Planning and Cultural Factors

Regardless of applicability of the relevant literature base, there is a clear need to adjust interventions based upon the context of the school setting (Kratochwill & Stoiber, 2000; Ringeisen et al., 2003). For example, socioeconomic status (SES), race, ethnicity and setting variables (e.g., rural, suburban, urban) should be considered. In fact, because the impact of culture may not be fully realized by the school setting, organizations should examine their cultural competence in an effort to remove barriers that negatively impact minorities (Whealin & Ruzek, 2008). In terms of program planning, this would require the intentional examination of the way in which cultural issues are integrated in the planning, implementation, and evaluation of programs. Whealin and Ruzek (2008) describe ten steps to help organizations plan programs that are sensitive to and reflective of multiculturalism. These steps are designed to move all types of organizations (e.g., culturally incompetent, monoculturallyfocused, or nondiscriminatory) to the state of valuing diversity as an asset at the multicultural stage, andare presented in Table 40.1.

When organizations are committed to developing their cultural competence, efforts on this behalf will help to improve the access of intervention services for minority students and their families. A wellintegrated cultural evaluation process should permeate decisions made at all levels of intervention program planning in the school district.

Factors in Selecting Interventions

Including stakeholders in the development of programs is both pragmatically and ethically advantageous, since there is evidence to suggest that treatment acceptability—including whether individuals believe an intervention will be effective, whether they like the intervention, and whether they perceive the intervention as having a reasonable cost-benefit ratio (Kazdin, 1981; Shapiro, 1987; Wolf, 1978)—is related to the effectiveness of the intervention (Truscott, Cosgrove, Meyers, & Eidle-Barkman, 2000). Stakeholders are individuals who are a part of and affected by the program that is being evaluated (Gall, Borg, & Gall, 1996), and may include students, parents, teachers, administrators, community members, school districts, and state and federal education agencies. In addition to consulting the stakeholders prior to planning a program, however, issues of practicality must also be considered.

Merrell and Buchanan (2006) have suggested that the RE-AIM framework originally developed by Russell Glasgow for implementing large scale public health interventions are useful in determining if an evidence-based intervention under consideration is practical in a particular school system. The RE-AIM model is used to increase the reach, efficacy, adoption, implementation, and maintenance of an intervention. As described by Glasgow, Klesges, Dzewaltowski, Bull, and Estabrooks (2004), _reach_is defined as determining the number of people in the target group. _Effectiveness_describes the change that is (appropriately) related to the target problem. When considering the data regarding intervention outcomes, the school psychologist should examine both the _efficacy_ (e.g., the empirical support showing measurable outcome differences) and the _effectiveness_ (e.g., usefulness of the intervention when it is applied in the real world setting) of the intervention (Hunsley, 2007). Early questions to consider include:

- Does this program reach those who are at highest risk?
- Is this program appropriate for those who are atrisk?
- How can this program be implemented to reach the greatest number of people?
- Can the school system ensure that the program will reach those who will benefit the most?

Adoption refers to the percent of people who are prepared to participate in, faithfully implement,

Table 40.1 Steps in establishing multiculturally sensitive programs

Step	Description
One: Obtain organizational support	Staff may need to better understand potential cultural barriers.
Two: Review and update mission and policies	Because the mission provides a framework for organizing decision making, and policies reflect implementation, each needs to reflect the values of cultural diversity.
Three: Improve staff knowledge about community populations	School personnel need to know the composition of the community they serve, including cultural routines, communication styles, and sociopolitical beliefs common to the culture.
Four: Evaluate and enhance cross-cultural skills	Increase the staff's sensitivity to cross-cultural information by examining the needs of both the school personnel and community, which can be accomplished through a needs assessment.
Five: Build cultural diversity among staff	Increase the number of diverse staff to help the broader faculty gain more exposure to varied cultural experiences.
Six: Assess needs and beliefs	Determine the needs of stakeholders.
Seven: Adapt procedures, infrastructure, and the physical environment	Some cultures prefer high levels of community support rather than individual help in addressing a child's difficulties. Schools should plan to adjust the levels of support required for a student's success. Artwork and other reminders of support should include diverse groups.
Eight: Facilitate verbal and written communication	Communication about the role of intervention programming for a child should be provided in oral and written formats. In some cases, video delivery of what parents can expect may be useful.
Nine: Collaborate with spiritual leaders and traditional healers	Schools can increase the acceptability and reinforcement of their efforts by acknowledging the support system already present.
Ten: Evaluate findings, identify goals, and and disseminate recommendations	Multiple audiences require multiple formats for delivering program results. Informationshould be prepared in formats that directly speak to the various cultural audiences.

Taken from "Program Evaluation of Organizational Cultural Competence in Mental Health Practices," by J. M. Whealin and J. Ruzek, 2008, *Professional Psychology: Research and Practice, 39,* 320-328. Copyright 2008, American Psychological Association. Reprinted with permission.

and maintain the intervention program. Being prepared to participate requires that the practical considerations of implementing the program are known and agreed upon, with questions including:

- What is the cost of the program?
- What type of training and expertise are required for staff to implement the program?
- What are the ongoing supports that are needed for implementation?
- Do we have the capacity to implement the intervention in a manner that will result in the desired measurable outcomes?

Once these questions have been fully evaluated, the information derived from them will help to determine whether the program selection is appropriate.

Currently, schools address academic and social difficulties using three general categories of intervention—primary, secondary, and tertiary. Primary prevention programs often occur at the school or building level, are applied to all students in the environment, and are generally educational in nature. The focus is on supporting the ongoing development of social and cognitive skills. In this type of programming, developmental milestones of children and adolescents are highlighted as the aim for intervention outcomes. For example, school psychologists can conduct school safety lessons with students in order to facilitate development of appropriate communication skills, assertiveness, and conflict resolution. Parents, classroom teachers, or administrators can reinforce students who practice or approximate behaviors that are consistent with healthy skills in these areas.

Secondary intervention programs can include larger scale, schoolbased curricula or interventions that may include a classroom-level or grade-level assembly. Anti-bullying programs are often delivered in this manner, and include interventions that focus on educating students on the different forms of bullying, the various ways to manage bullies, and the school policies relevant to bullying behaviors. The primary difference between primary and secondary interventions is the explicit and comprehensive focus on identifying and coping with undesirable behavior at the secondary level. These approaches are similar in their focus on prosocial problem-solving skills that accompany typical development.

Finally, tertiary prevention programs provide intervention to those who are atrisk or already experiencing academic or social difficulties. This often includes individualized interventions tailored to prompt new skill development for the child or adolescent, occurring in either the general or special education environments. An example of a tertiary intervention would be with a student who has not benefited from the primary or secondary programming regarding appropriate peer development, and who persists in instigating conflict with her peers. She may participate in an individual counseling intervention focused on understanding the viewpoint of others (e.g., perspective-taking), the role of empathy in governing behaviors, and identifying what thoughts guide her social skill difficulties, among others.

With these levels of intervention in mind, school psychologists need to gather the relevant information in order to determine the goals the school is trying to accomplish by implementing itsprogram. Often, the school psychologist may find himself or herself in the position of helping a school district operationalize general sentiments, such as "we want to address bullying" into outcome goals that are subject to measurement. However, in order to determine the needs of both the school system as well as the group targeted for intervention, a needs assessment, in addition to other methods of program planning, may be conducted. In the next section of this chapter, methods of program planning, including needs assessments, will be reviewed.

What Are Methods of Program Planning?

The term *program* may be used to describe a functional unit (e.g., national honor society or alternative education center), a series of activities (e.g., bullying prevention programs), or a onetime event (e.g., employment or college application workshop) in a school system (Barr et al., 1985). In order to effectively implement these programs, individual,

group, and environmental information needs to be gathered. As described by Cooper and Saunders (2000), individual or group-level information should be solicited regarding the skills, knowledge, attitudes, and beliefs of individuals who will attend (e.g., students) or take part (e.g., administrators, teachers, support staff) in the programming initiative. At the environment level, information regarding the culture, norms, politics, stakeholders, and organizational structure needs to be collected.

Data collected to aid in program planning falls under the general term of a *needs assessment.* In an educational setting, *needs* are those factors, conditions, services, and resources that are necessary for a student to achieve educational goals and objectives (Upcraft & Schuh, 1996). This is in contrast to *wants,* which are those experiences that students and faculty may desire, but may not be directly related to obtaining educational goals. In fact, some programming in schools may be implemented for reasons other than achieving educational goals. Any program could qualify as a desire if it is implemented where no need is present. Veteran educators are likely familiar with the experience in which a new program is announced (e.g., computer-assisted career development services) at a faculty assembly, and participation is mandated. The rationale provided may be "we have a grant for that," or "Dr. X thought it would be a good idea to do this for everyone," or "the middle school faculty believed this would be helpful." Although there may be many desires, the purpose of most program planning (e.g., needs) assessment is to ensure that the organizational mission and goals are addressed as a means for students to achieve their educational goals and objectives (Cooper & Saunders, 2000).

NEEDS ASSESSMENT

A needs assessment is simply the process of identifying gaps between the desired results and the current conditions of individual and or organizational performance. Although there is no single method for gathering data (Witkin, 1984), collaboration is often emphasized so that all relevant stakeholders can provide input. A primary purpose of needs assessment procedures is formative evaluation, in which program planners gather data to provide a picture of what currently exists, so that modifications can be made to the operational processes of a program (Marrs & Helge, 1978). Such planning enables program managers such as school psychologists to identify potential problems early on, thereby remedying issues before they become difficult to manage. A comprehensive needs assessment typically includes setting standards, focusing data gathering, selecting means for collecting data, reporting data, and using the data yielded from the needs assessment (see Table 40.2).

FOCUS GROUPS

While the use of focus groups in program evaluation will be discussed later in the chapter, Wyatt, Krauskopf, and Davidson (2008) discuss the value of this methodology in program planning. Focus groups are structured discussions among participants with similar experiences. The questions posed in focus groups allow for open-ended responses about the participants' emotional and cognitive perceptions regarding their shared experiences (Wyatt et al., 2008). Focus group processes differ from a group interview, in that the former encourages discussion among group members whereas the latter does not encourage interaction (Webb &Kevern, 2001). Since focus groups allow the facilitator to assess both cognitive and emotional responses of participants, the information gathered complements data garnered through quantitative methodological approaches. Wyatt et al. (2008) suggest that the information derived from a focus group is highly valid, and can thus be used for program development for individuals who have similar characteristics to the focus group participants.

In school systems, focus groups are useful in determining how stakeholders (e.g., children, parents, teachers, administrators, school board members, and community groups, among others) perceive the discrepancy between an actual and

Table 40.2 Steps in conducting a needs assessment

Step	Description
Establishing standards:	Diagnosing strengths and weaknesses in an organization and by doing so identifying the standards that will be used to guide the future state of an organization's environment. It is recommended that school districts create a standard development team and appoint a liaison between the team and the personnel responsible for implementing the standards (Cooper & Saunders, 2000)
Focusing data gathering:	Data should be collected on the following variables: ○ Organization's philosophies and attitudes ○ Environmental elements (e.g., geographical setting, population characteristics, change patterns, social characteristics of the school's environment, economic factors) ○ Organizational variables (e.g., change patterns within the school system) ○ Attitudinal variables ○ Knowledge base of personnel (Cooper & Saunders, 2000)
Determining means for collecting data:	Data gathering instruments will vary according to the size and scope of the school and assessment, and may include: ○ Questionnaires ○ Interviews ○ Structured observation in classrooms ○ Formal or informal discussions ○ Records review ((Cooper & Saunders, 2000; Marrs & Helge, 1978)
Data reporting:	Data should be collected, with results compared to the previously-identified standards. Resulting discrepancies can be discussed in terms of program or project needs. The two kinds of reporting systems include: ○ Reporting data in terms of findings (e.g., providing a picture of currently existing practices, attitudes, etc.) ○ Reporting data in terms of program standards, with judgments made about observed needs (Cooper & Saunders, 2000)
Using needs assessment data:	Once discrepancies have determined, decisions may be made to a) alter standards or b) change implementation of standards in order to reduce discrepancies between observed conditions and established standards (Cooper & Saunders, 2000)

desired performance or state within the school system (Forman & Burke, 2008). A well-planned focus group is timed to gather the most information in a short time period. Therefore, questions should be prepared in advance. A grouping of four to six individuals is optimal; however, groups of six to ten yield similar (content and style) results (Kennedy, Kools,& Krueger, 2001). Group members should be selected based on the shared experience that the examiner seeks to understand (Horner, 2000). Moreover, issues of SES, age, race, ethnicity and gender should be held constant if those variables are related to the topic of interest (e.g., gender conflict, discrimination).

When children are solicited to be focus group members, their participation should be voluntary and parent permission should be obtained in advance. Additionally, for children who agree to participate, issues of confidentiality should be explained in age-appropriate language. When focus groups include adults, there should be an acknowledgement of the leadership and gatekeeper roles that some in the group hold (e.g., by virtue of the position that a person holds, his or her input may have more influence over the group's participation). Thus, encouragement of diverse feedback should be explicitly welcomed early in the process. It is also important to recognize internal power brokers such as administrative assistants and highly respected teachers, whose influence can impact the success of a program. Finally, because teachers are always at the ground level of implementation, their participation in a focus group is essential (Curtis, Castillo & Cohen, 2008). The information regarding the strengths and weaknesses of focus group methodology is summarized in Table 40.3.

Problems and Pitfalls of Program Planning

Unfortunately, school systems often do not adequately prepare for the process of designing and implementing programs. The need for a particular program may arise by way of failed exemplars that are often the focus of public outrage. As such, program design may occur in the context of internal (e.g., school personnel) and external (e.g., parent, community groups) pressure to identify a solution. In such cases, the primary risk negatively impacting the ability to gather relevant data in focus groups for program design is groupthink.

Groupthink is the process of poor decisionmaking as a consequence of peer pressure to reduce conflict among members to arrive at a decision (Janis, 1972; 1982). When there is considerable pressure to come to a decision, the probability of groupthink increases. Groupthink occurs when individuals ignore alternative explanations for the cause of events, as well as alternative opportunities for solutions. A group is especially vulnerable to groupthink when its members are similar in background, when the group is insulated from outside opinions, and when there are

Table 40.3   **Strengths and weaknesses of using focus groups**

Strengths	Weaknesses
Allows the examination of attitudes regarding specific behaviors (e.g., drug and alcohol use) that would not be readily provided in one-to-one discussions (Wyatt et al., 2008)	Individuals need adequate expressive language and social skills to participate in the group effectively (Ansay et al., 2004).
The process is a free-flowing naturalistic conversation in which participants respond to each other in real time (Horner, 2000).	Some individuals may be intentionally or unintentionally overshadowed by other participants (Ansay et al., 2004).
The dynamic nature of the sessions extends the responsibility for providing information to the group rather than burdening one person to explain his or her feelings, thus increasing quantity and quality of information (Horner, 2000).	Moderators require training in managing group dynamics in order to gather information from all of the participants and decrease the opportunity for groupthink (Ansay et al., 2004; Peterson-Sweeney, 2005).
When focus groups are conducted with those similar to the intended program audience, researchers have improved ability to make authentic decisions to increase success (Heary & Hennessy, 2002) as well as to streamline program development (Ansay, Perkins, & Nelson, 2004).	

no clear rules for decision making (Janis, 1972). Thus, as presented in Table 40.3, the strength of a focus group (e.g., members are selected because of their shared experiences and background) can also become a weakness of the program planning process if moderators are not prepared to address these experiences in their data gathering. Janis (1972, 1982) has described eight symptoms of groupthink for which moderators should prepare:

1. Illusion of invulnerability – members experience excessive optimism that encourages taking extreme risks.

2. Collective rationalization – members conclude that the wisdom of the group is so persuasive that they discount warnings and do not reconsider their assumptions.

3. Belief in inherent morality – highly dedicated and impassioned members believe in the rightness of their cause and therefore ignore the ethical or moral consequences of their decisions.

4. Stereotyped views of out-groups – negative views of the forces working against them (e.g., "the enemy") allow members to conclude that there is no need to design effective responses to the conflict.

5. Direct pressure on dissenters – when members of the group are under pressure not to express arguments against any of the group's views, the risk of ill-considered decision making is increased.

6. Self-censorship – doubts and deviations from the perceived group consensus are not expressed.

7. Illusion of unanimity – the majority view and judgments are assumed to be unanimous.

8. Self-appointed "mind-guards" – members protect the group and the leader from information that is problematic or contradictory to the group's cohesiveness, view, and/or decisions.

Decisions shaped by groupthink have low probability of achieving successful outcomes; as such, moderators should note when these processes occur and emphasize the importance of diversity in participants' feedback during the sessions. If groupthink is not corrected, this phenomenon can curtail appropriate program development efforts, thereby prematurely dooming a program that might otherwise have been successful.

Organizational change in educational systems tends to occur slowly, and must, since there is evidence that efforts to promote rapid systemic changes in organizations often result in resistance and failure (Derr, 1976; Illback & Zins, 1995).Adelman and Taylor (1997) describe four phases that are necessary to enable real change to be sustained in an organization, including creating readiness, initial implementation, institutionalization, and ongoing evaluation.Of these four stages, the second major challenge in program planning often occurs at the implementation phase, which will be subsequently described.

First, becoming ready for a change is accomplished by creating a psychological climate that helps to generate interest in the program, formally negotiating how the new program will be implemented, and aligning the program with existing infrastructure (Adelman & Taylor, 1997).

Even when educators recognize why a program change needs to take place, and they have participated in its development through focus groups and providing feedback, the climate within the school system has to be prepared to begin the implementation process.

Second, initial implementation is the process designed to start and sustain a program. This stage should welcome formative feedback, and use this information to make program adjustments. Earl and Fullan (2002) caution that conducting a summative evaluation, in which accountability is emphasized, is not appropriate at this time. Too often schools expect immediate outcomes when intervention effects have not yet had time to develop. Even after a program is adopted, the ability to commit fiscal and manpower resources, develop organizational structures, and implement policies needed for treatment fidelity,all sustained at the appropriate level of intensity, is difficult (Forman & Burke, 2008). A comprehensive effort in which each individual's role is clearly defined, and ongoing support is available, is required for success (Knoff, 2008). Moreover, schools with a strategic plan devoted to comprehensive reform are better equipped to address program implementation than those who do not have such a blueprint in place (Knoff, 2008).

Third, institutionalization refers to the school's acceptance of the program as a part of its infrastructure (Adelman & Taylor, 2003). Effective program implementation is possible when each team member has an identified role, along with a clear understanding of his or her responsibilities. The team should include members who deliver the intervention (e.g., school psychologist), others who support the intervention (e.g., parents and teachers rewarding appropriate behaviors), and those dedicated to communicating outcome to stakeholders (e.g., teachers conducting progress monitoring and reporting results to parents and administrators). Disseminating outcomes is useful not only to evaluate progress, but also to provide reinforcement for the efforts of the staff (or an opportunity to make adjustments if needed; Eckert & Hintze, 2000) and to gather any ongoing resources requested from administration (Forman & Burke, 2008). As such, the process of providing program feedback is essential to all involved in the process.

Finally, ongoing evaluation is the process for monitoring outcomes and making changes based on the ongoing needs of the system. Opportunities for change are often derived from the data generated by the program evaluation, but may also be required as new information regarding evidence-based practice emerges. In either case, educators should expect that alterations will be required, as will access to resources to make adjustments (Earl & Fullan, 2002).

Evaluation of Results of Program Planning

Program planning is ultimately evaluated by the formal data collected in the program evaluation, which will be discussed in the next portion of the chapter. These evaluation procedures systematically consider the initial data from focus groups, how those data were used for planning purposes, and, ultimately, the outcomes of the desired change. However, it is important to note that the results from focus groups and any data collected in the needs assessment are the foundation upon which all subsequent development and intervention implementation rest. If the programming does not highlight the authentic needs of children in their school systems, no matter how positive the individuals in the system feel about the intervention (e.g., teachers or students really *like* the program), meaningful change will not occur. Similarly, a program that functions as an island that is not well integrated into the overall school system is at risk for failure when there are organizational shifts that may disrupt the current distribution of resources (Adelman & Taylor, 2003).

Once a program is implemented, focus groups may once again be used to determine the usefulness of the interventions at a planned midpoint (formative) as well as at the point of an outcome (summative). Formative evaluation findings should be examined to determine if new data warrants changes in the program. Summative evaluation data used to make conclusions about the program's effectiveness can also inform educators about the type of changes

that have not yet been accomplished (Wyatt et al., 2008). A case study of program planning is now provided as an example of the principles discussed in the previous section.

Once programs have been designed, developed, and implemented, as discussed previously, there is need to evaluate whether the interventions used are resulting in desired outcomes. Consequently, the remainder of the chapter will be largely devoted to the topic of program evaluation, including methods and techniques, possible and expected difficulties, and assessing and interpreting results. After this portion of the chapter, a case study of program evaluation will be provided to encourage reflection and application of the concepts presented in the chapter.

Program Evaluation

Although it has been the recipient of increased attention within the last decade, the topic of program evaluation in school psychology is actually one that has been discussed in the source literature for roughly the last quarter century. Deno (1986) presented the topic of program evaluation in his article regarding formative evaluation of individual student programs, stating that although formative evaluation was likely helpful in determining the quality of an intervention, summative evaluation, such as program evaluation, was necessary at annual review to determine whether adequate progress was being made (Deno, 1986). This prescient focus on accountability foreshadowed the priority placed on the necessity for empirical evidence in intervention studies conducted by academicians and practitioners in grant research.

The advent of program evaluation for educational programs that receive federal funding more recently illuminated the importance of accountability in education (Gall et al., 1996), with the notion that educational programs must demonstrate that they meet standards of student performance. As discussed earlier in the chapter in the section regarding EBPs, the emphasis of accountability in the realization of student competencies for educational outcomes is increasingly a critical role of school psychologists. The intent of program evaluation is to assess the effectiveness of a program, with the ultimate objective of enhancing academic and social/emotional outcomes so that children may realize their maximum potential (D'Agostino, 2001). In order to make this determination, a systematic process of collecting data about a program needs to be conducted, in order to make valid and reliable conclusions regarding its efficacy.

Box 40.1. Case Study of Program Planning

While attending the monthly school consultation meeting, Ms. SP, the school psychologist at Progressive High School, learns from a few teachers that several of the female students in their classes have been distracted and not focusing on their schoolwork for some time now. Once the topic was raised, other teachers reported that they, too, had noticed that a number of female students had been focused on social issues rather than on the academic concepts being presented and discussed in their classes. When questioned, these students reported that they were having trouble with their friendships. Specifically, a particular group of girls who were seen as very socially powerfulwere spreading rumors, gossiping about, and excluding some of their female peers. The girls who were being excluded and harassed expressed feelings of depression and social isolation, with the problem appearing to becoming more severe over time. The educators at the consultation meeting concluded that there was a culture of this kind of bullying, known as relational aggression, at Progressive High School, and that it needed to be addressed. Ms. SP volunteered to do some research, and to suggest a course of action when the group reconvened during the following month.

While consulting the relevant source literature on this topic, Ms. SP finds that the school staff must make a decision regarding how to intervene in an effective, developmentally and systemically appropriate manner. As with bullying in general, she finds that addressing relational and social aggression at school may fall into three categories: primary, secondary, and tertiary intervention. Primary prevention programs occur in a school environment and are generally educational in nature. The focus is on the development of social and cognitive skills through educational programming to reduce relationally and socially aggressive behaviors. Secondary intervention programs include larger scale, school based, antiviolence curricula to address children's and adolescents' social competence, through the development of empathy and perspective-taking, social problem solving, assertiveness, emotion regulation, and anger management skills. Finally, tertiary prevention programs provide intervention to those who are at risk, or already involved in relationally aggressive behaviors or conflicts. This may include victims and perpetrators, with individual interventions tailored to address new skill development for the child or adolescent.

Ms. SP presents the findings of her research to the educators during the following monthly school consultation meeting. The educators review the recommendations made by Ms. SP, and decide to appoint a team to develop a relational aggression program to include the primary, secondary, and tertiary intervention levels recommended by the source literature. The team consists of Ms. SP, the school counselor, the school social worker, the assistant principal, and a group of representative teachers from different grades and subject areas.

The team decides to undertake a needs assessment in order to understand the multiple stakeholders' perceptions of the problem of relational aggression, so that the program developed will be effective. As a part of the needs assessment, focus group interviews are planned with students, teachers, parents, administrators, and community members. In evaluating the data from the needs assessment, the team is careful to avoid the problem of groupthink. Plans are developed in keeping with the primary, secondary, and tertiary model of intervention, and the program is implemented. During the implementation phase of the program, the team reminds school staff not to expect immediate outcomes when intervention effects have not yet had time to develop. Finally, the team begins to make plans for program evaluation to occur once the interventions have been fully implemented and sufficient time has passed.

Implicit in this mandate is the responsibility of schools to promote effective educational programs. Program evaluation determines the extent to which a program has met its stated goals and objectives, demonstrates the impact of a particular program on individuals and institutions, describes strengths and weaknesses, and potentially identifies how to improve the quality of a program (McNamara, 2006). Evaluation of educational programs also provides valuable information regarding the costs and benefits of a program by yielding data that suggest whether the benefits justify the costs, whether they be in time or money. The data that are collected then facilitate decisionmaking regarding the worth of a program, resources, and budget (Gall et al., 1996). Thus, by having goals and objectives, individuals focus their time and resources to meeting these goals, which resultsin more efficient and productive school staff. These evaluation data subsequently inform problemsolving and decisionmaking regarding programs.

Standards for Sound Evaluation

The process of program evaluation is guided by the principles set forth by the Joint Committee on Standards for Ethical Evaluation (1994). These standards are a conceptual framework for evaluating educational interventions, and were developed as a result of evaluations that evidenced poor technical quality and were biased and served self-interests in the absence of standards. Thus, the purpose of these standards was to improve professionalism of evaluations in the field of education (Gall et al., 1996). According to the Joint Committee, a high-quality evaluation comprises 30 criteria subsumed under four categories (see Table 40.4). These categories include utility, feasibility, propriety, and accuracy. *Utility* standards refer to reports that are timely, comprehensive, and beneficial to the individuals affected by the evaluation. *Feasibility* standards emphasize the appropriateness of the design to the setting, as well as the cost-effectiveness of the evaluation. *Propriety* standards ensure the ethical treatment and welfare of those involved in the evaluation. Finally, the standards of *Accuracy* concern the gathering and reporting information that is reliable and valid, allowing for judgments regarding the worth of a program.

Forms of Program Evaluation

As reported earlier in research conducted by Deno (1986), program evaluation may be categorized as formative and summative (Jarosewich, 2005). Formative evaluation is the process of collecting data during program implementation to determine the likelihood of program success, so that the program may be modified or changed as needed in order to achieve the intended result. This type of evaluation incorporates ongoing feedback to make adjustments and improvements based on data collected about a program. Summative evaluation, also known as outcomes assessment, occurs upon completion of the program, and its purpose is to evaluate the extent to which the program was successful as evidenced by outcome indicators (Jarosewich, 2005). Heller and Reimann state, "The formative evaluation, in contrast to the summative evaluation, attempts to optimize ongoing innovative school program...These reports point out where the

negative effects and weak points of the program can be seen and indicate where modifications in the model conditions would be most effective" (2002, p. 238). Both of these types of evaluations are central to documenting meaningful change and facilitating enhanced programming for students.

A fundamental purpose in documenting meaningful change is having confidence in the data that are obtained. Since the research design selected is crucial to determining whether a program has realized its goals and objectives, rigor in research design is essential in the development of a program evaluation. Although a true experimental design would be ideal in evaluating program effectiveness, it is not a practical reality for schools for several reasons (deAnda, 2007). First, children who are randomly selected would miss instructional time, which would result in an interruption of student learning. Second, artificial groupings that may be intended for schoolwide programming results in poor generalizability of results. Third, obtaining a sufficient control group may be problematic, because some students will be selected for the study and others not, therefore making it difficult to justify to parents why some children were excluded from a program that could potentially benefit them. Finally, it is challenging to ensure that there are an adequate number of staff who are adequately trained. Therefore, quasi-experimental and single-subject designs are typically better suited for the school setting (deAnda, 2007).

Steps in Program Evaluation

The first step of the evaluation process is to focus the evaluation (see Table 40.5). The evaluator, in

---

Table 40.4 Joint committee on standards for ethical evaluation

Utility Standards

U1. *Stakeholder Identification.* Identification of the individuals involved who may be affected by the evaluation.

U2. *Evaluator Credibility.* Individuals who are deemed as competent and honorable should conduct the evaluation.

U3. *Information Scope and Selection.* Information collected should be employed to address questions as well as meet the needs of stakeholders.

U4. *Values Identification.* The evaluators' basis for decision-making from the data collected should be clear.

U5. *Report Clarity.* Evaluation reports should be thorough, comprehensive, and clear.

U6. *Report Timeliness and Dissemination.* Evaluation reports and interim findings should be provided to stakeholders in a timely fashion.

U7. *Evaluation Impact.* Evaluations should be conducted in a manner whereby findings will be utilized by stakeholders.

(continued)

Table 40.4   (Con'd) Joint committee on standards for ethical evaluation

Feasibility Standards

F1. *Practical Procedures.* Evaluation procedures should be practical and minimally disruptive so as to obtain information.

F2. *Political Viability.* Obtain the cooperation of interest groups who are affected by the evaluation in order to circumvent bias or sabotage of the results.

F3. *Cost Effectiveness.* The evaluation should be efficient in order to justify resources utilized for the evaluation.

Proprietary Standards

P1. *Service Orientation.* Evaluations should be designed to meet the needs of the stakeholders and the larger community as well.

P2. *Formal Agreements.* Formal parties involved in the evaluation should sign a written agreement to follow-through in a contract.

P3. *Rights of Human Subjects.* Evaluations should protect and respect the welfare of human subjects.

P4. *Human Interactions.* Evaluators should be respectful of individuals in the evaluation.

P5. *Complete and Fair Assessment.* Strengths and weaknesses of a program should be presented in a complete and fair manner.

P6. *Disclosure of Findings.* Individuals affected by the evaluation as well as those with legal rights are to receive a full evaluative report.

P7. *Conflict of Interest.* If conflicts occur, they should be dealt with open and honestly so as not to compromise evaluative findings.

P8. *Fiscal Responsibility.* Expenditure of resources should be done in a prudent and ethical manner.

Accuracy Standards

A1. *Program Documentation.* The program being evaluated should be described in detail.

A2. *Context Analysis.* The context of the program that impact the evaluation should be clearly described.

A3. *Described Purposes and Procedures.* The evaluation's purposes and procedures should be monitored and described in detail.

A4. *Defensible Information Sources.* Sources of information for the evaluation should be described in detail so that adequacy can be determined.

A5. *Valid Information.* The data collected during the evaluation should result in valid findings.

A6. *Reliable Information.* The data collected during the evaluation should results in reliable findings.

A7. *Systematic Information.* The data collected during the evaluation should be reviewed systematically to correct for errors.

A8. *Analysis of Quantitative Information.* Quantitative data should be systematically analyzed and to effectively address evaluative questions.

A9. *Analysis of Qualitative Information.* Qualitative data should be systematically analyzed and to effectively address evaluative questions.

A10. Justified Conclusions. Conclusions yielded by the evaluation are explicitly justified.

A11. *Impartial Reporting.* Evaluation reports do not reflect any bias or distortion by those associated with the evaluation.

A12. *Meta-evaluation.* The evaluation is formatively and summatively assessed.

From: *The program evaluation standards: How to assess evaluations of educational programs.* Joint Committee on Standards for Educational Evaluation, 1994. Reprinted by permission of SAGE Publications. Copyright 1994.

Table 40.5   Steps in program evaluation

Step	Description
Step One: Focus the Evaluation	- Evaluator defines purpose of evaluation, including goals and objectives.
Step Two: Identify Evaluation Questions	-Identify stakeholders. -Structure questions to address stakeholder needs, including what will be evaluated, what is the purpose of the evaluation, who benefits from the evaluation. -Identify a deadline or timeline for completion.
Step Three: Determine Research Design	- Consider the timeline for completion.
and Collection/Analysis of Data	-Consider types of data to be collected. -Consider who will collect the data. -Consider how the data will be collected. -Determine what resources are needed to conduct the evaluation.
Step Four: Data Collection	- Implement data collection procedures.
Step Five: Analyze and Interpret Data and	- Report should address goals set for evaluation.
Develop a Report Based on Findings	-Report should document methods employed to answer questions. -Report should present findings of the evaluation. -Report should include implications of results and recommendations for enhancing the program and its outcomes.

Taken from McNamara, C. (2006). *Field guide to nonprofit program design, marketing and evaluation* (4th ed.). Copyright 2006. Reprinted with permission.

conjunction with stakeholders of the project, defines the purpose of the evaluation, including goals and objectives, and set limits to the evaluation to make it manageable. Stakeholders are individuals who are involved in and affected by the program that is being evaluated (Gall et al., 1996). These individuals may include students, parents, teachers, administrators, community members, school districts, and state and federal education agencies.

The next step is to identify evaluation questions. In determining the questions that need to be addressed, it is important to consult stakeholders, as they are influential in the process and outcome of the evaluation. Thus, questions should be structured to address stakeholder needs. For instance, they may clarify and enumerate the reasons and questions for the evaluation or, conversely, may sabotage an evaluation or discredit findings if they feel that their needs and concerns were not addressed (Gall et al., 1996). The evaluation questions should include what will be assessed, the purpose of the evaluation, who will benefit from the evaluation and how, and a deadline or timeline for completion of the evaluation. Once these questions are formulated and finalized, they

require prioritization to ensure the most efficient allocation of time and resources.

Subsequently, the third step of the evaluation process requires determining an appropriate research design and a plan for the collection and analysis of data. The design of the evaluation necessitates consideration of the time frame for completing the evaluation, the types of data to be gathered to answer the questions developed in the first stage, identifying who and how data will be collected, and identifying the resources needed to conduct the evaluation.

The fourth step involves the actual data collection process. In gathering data to answer the questions identified in the first step, assessors should attempt to follow the information-gathering plan, noting any impediments or unexpected problems along the way. Careful recordkeeping and documentation of findings are critical to ensuring a rigorous data-gathering process; Heller and Reimann (2002) discuss the importance of systematic documentation when conducting both formative and summative program evaluation.

The fifth step is to analyze and interpret the data and develop a report based upon the findings.

Generally, the report should address the goals set forth for the evaluation, methods employed to answer the questions, the findings of the evaluation, implications of the results, and recommendations for enhancing the program and its outcomes. Finally, the findings generated by the report should be placed into effect to improve the program (McNamara, 2006).

There are a variety of methods that may be employed to collect data. The decision primarily depends upon the issue that is being investigated, as well as matters of cost and feasibility. Important considerations include determining what information is needed, which method will yield the greatest information, whether any additional methods will be needed to obtain the desired information, the accuracy of the information, credibility of the data, and whether the information may be collected and analyzed in a cost-efficient manner (McNamara, 2006). Ultimately, the method that is selected should provide relevant information, be implemented by individuals who are skilled and knowledgeable, should be within the budgetary restrictions, and yield credible, accurate, and reliable information. Ideally, a combination of methods should be employed in order to collect as much information as possible from a variety of sources (McNamara, 2006).

Methods of Program Evaluation

Methods employed for data collection can be qualitative or quantitative. Qualitative research emphasizes narrative descriptions in the interpretation and understanding of a particular experience, yielding rich, expansive information. In contrast, quantitative research is a more objective manner of data collection, whereby individuals evaluate and apply methodological techniques to answer research questions. In quantitative designs, there is careful control of the research, which is systematically evaluated using operational definitions, isolated variables, quantification of constructs, and statistical analyses of data (Kazdin, 2003). Table 40.6 provides a summary of the methods of program evaluation, including their strengths and weaknesses.

OBSERVATIONS

Observations entail the use of checklists, charts, rating scales or narrative descriptions in which the occurrences of specific, pre-identified behaviors, events, and programs are monitored. These assessments can take two forms, *structured* and *unstructured*. A structured observation is one that involves gathering quantitative information, such as frequency,

duration, and nature of a behavior, whereas unstructured observation involves gathering qualitative information while a set of behaviors are occurring.

Observational assessment has both strengths and weaknesses. This method is particularly beneficial in determining antecedents and consequences that occur in a natural setting. Thus, observations allow individuals to view a program *in vivo* as it is happening. Direct observational methods can be used to provide unbiased analyses of focal participants' behavior in certain circumstances, and such methods are objective when definitions are clearly articulated and interrater reliability is established (McEvoy, Estrem, Rodriguez, & Olson, 2003). However, there are some drawbacks to this method including costs of time, difficulty in interpreting behaviors, a change in the behavioral comportment of those being observed (Hawthorne Effect), having different observers recording events differently, and observer bias, which may occur when the evaluator who lacks objectivity due to bias takes part in the observations. Observational measures do not usually correlate well over time, perhaps because of limited samples of observations and situational specificity of behavior. These weaknesses can be minimized by sampling behavior in multiple settings over long periods of time (Crothers & Levinson, 2004; Pellegrini & Bartini, 2000). Cole, Cornell, and Sheras (2006) have also noted that observation is time-intensive, and even impractical, due to the need to conduct observations over lengthy periods and across different settings.

INTERVIEWS

This method involves the collection of information from an individual or individuals who have specialized knowledge. In quantitative research, the interviews may be structured or unstructured, whereas qualitative research typically involves the use of an informal conversational interview. Interviews may be conducted facetoface, via the telephone, or through the use of a computer. Noteworthy strengths of the interview method include the ability to obtain a wide range of information as well as to probe and/or clarify information as necessary (Gall et al., 1996). Disadvantages include the expense in time and money, as well as potential bias that the interviewer may impose on the responses received (McNamara, 2006). Another limitation of qualitative assessment techniques such as interviewing is that validity may be compromised because of the self-selected nature of the data. However, information from qualitative measures may be used to

Table 40.6 Methods of program evaluation

Method	Strengths	Weaknesses
Observations	• Determines antecedents and consequences in natural setting (Kazdin, 2003; McNamara, 2006). • Objective when definitions are provided and interrater reliability is established (McEvoy et al., 2003).	• Time costs. • Difficulty in interpreting behaviors. • Hawthorne Effect. • Different observers may record events differently. • Observer bias. • Multiple observers' data does not correlate well over time (Kazdin, 2004; McNamara, 2006).
Interviews	• Ability to obtain wide range of information. • Ability to probe and clarify information as necessary (Gall et al., 1996).	• Time costs. • Monetary costs. • Interviewer bias. • Self-selected nature of data (Casey-Cannon et al., 2001; McNamara, 2006).
Focus Groups	• Time-efficient. • Cost-efficient. • Creativity and depth created from the focus group dialogue. • Easy to set up (Gall et al., 1996; Krueger, 1995; McNamara, 2006; Wyatt et al., 2008).	• Easily misused. • Require skill to moderate. • Tedious data interpretation. • Capturing issues while avoiding bias is difficult. • Poor generalizability of results with unlike populations (Gall et al., 1996; Krueger, 1995; McNamara, 2006; Wyatt et al., 2008).
Document Review	• Ability to provide comprehensive historical information. • Avoids disrupting a program that is already in place (McNamara, 2006).	• Evaluators are restricted to reviewing already-existing data that may be incomplete. • Research is limited to answering questions that fit the existing data (McNamara, 2006).
Questionnaires/Surveys	• Easy to administer. • Cost-efficient. • Yields a large amount of data in a short time. • Easy to reach participants. • Provides direct assessment of participants' functioning in various situations (Gall et al., 1996; Kazdin, 2003).	• Questions may result in biased or artificial answers. • Wording and appearance of survey may influence responses (Kazdin, 2003).
Case Studies	• Depth of insight allows data to be persuasive and motivational (Kazdin, 2003).	• Subjectivity of information. • Evaluator bias. • Alternative explanations may be provided for findings. • Generalizability of data is limited to individuals or groups with similar characteristics (Kazdin, 2003).
Expert Opinion	• Experts are knowledgeable about topic matter (Gall et al., 1996).	• May be time- and cost-intensive (Gall et al., 1996).

supplement and validate responses to quantitative measures (Casey-Cannon, Hayward, & Gowen, 2001).

Individuals considering using an interview method as a form of data collection should take into account the following guidelines when conducting a research interview: (a) insuring confidentiality prior to the interview (this may entail clarifying the intent of the interview, benefits of the study, as well as the procedures that will be employed to protect the anonymity of their responses); (b) establishing rapport with the participant to make him or her feel more comfortable and increase the likelihood that all pertinent information will be revealed; (c) querying when appropriate; and (d) asking questions in a clear and direct manner (Gall et al., 1996).

FOCUS GROUPS

As mentioned earlier in the chapter, focus groups essentially are an interview that typically includes 7 to 10 participants who have certain common characteristics that relate to the subject matter of the group. Heary and Hennessey (2002) describe a focus group as a thoughtful, planned discussion among participants with similar experiences. The group should be large enough to allow for a variety of different views, but small enough so that everyone has an opportunity to contribute. Through the use of such methodology, a synergistic effect occurs, in which participants build upon each other's responses, developing a richness and complexity of concepts and constructs through sharing and collaboration of ideas.

In order for the group to engage in an active dialogue, the interviewer needs to cultivate a nurturing environment that is open to various different points of view, to encourage individuals to be relaxed, comfortable, active participants (Krueger, 1995). The hope is that by creating such an atmosphere, participants will freely interact with one another and express thoughts, feelings, beliefs, and perceptions that may not have been shared if interviewed individually (Krueger, 1995). There are several advantages to focus groups, including feasibility with respect to time and money, and the potential creativity and depth created from the dialogue among participants. On the other hand, focus group interviews are very easily misused. They are easy to set up, but require skill to moderate. Data interpretation is tedious, and capturing the major issues surfaced without bias is often difficult. Further, results may not generalize to the target population.

DOCUMENTATION REVIEW

Documentation review is a form of analysis of records in order to provide documentation of a program or an individual. Types of documentation include applications, minutes from meetings, memos, participant records, critical events, and financial statements. The strengths of documentation review include the ability to provide comprehensive historical information while avoiding disruption of a program already in place. However, evaluators are restricted to reviewing already-existing data that may be incomplete; thus, the research is limited to answering questions that fit the data that has been gathered (McNamara, 2006).

QUESTIONNAIRES/SURVEYS

Questionnaires and surveys are a widely used method of collecting data, chiefly because this methodology yields a large amount of data in a relatively short amount of time. Such instruments can be designed to assess a specified domain of functioning in order to measure individuals' opinions, attitudes, beliefs, and behaviors in response to specific questions (Kazdin, 2003). Surveys may be administered through the mail, via the internet, by telephone, or in a group setting.

Assessors using questionnaires and surveys are able to evaluate multiple characteristics by having respondents answer various items. These assessment tools are appealing because respondents are self-reporting their own unique thoughts and feelings, thus providing a direct assessment of their functioning in various situations. Moreover, surveys are easy to administer, making it relatively easy to reach large numbers of individuals (Kazdin, 2003). They are also cost efficient (Gall et al., 1996).

Interestingly, the characteristic of self-report that allows for direct assessment may also be a drawback to survey research, since questions are reactive in nature and require respondents to endorse certain behaviors that may result in biased and/or artificial answers. A common problem in survey research is that individuals tend to favor the endorsement of socially appropriate behaviors, rather than reporting on true behaviors. In addition, the structure of the survey, including wording and order of appearance, may influence responses (Kazdin, 2003).

CASE STUDIES

This method of data collection provides in-depth information of an individual, group, or unit. Case studies focus intensely on providing a detailed contextual analysis of a contemporary phenomenon in real-life circumstances (Kazdin, 2003). This may be accomplished using a variety of methods including interviews, observations, questionnaires and a permanent product review. Because of the depth of insight of this method of data collection, information that is gathered may be persuasive and motivational in nature. Disadvantages to case studies include the subjectivity of information, since this type of design relies a great deal on judgment and interpretation, which may result in evaluator bias. In addition, alternative explanations may be provided for the findings, and generalizability of the data islimited to individuals or groups with similar characteristics.

EXPERT OPINION

Expert opinion as a method of data collection requires having individuals with expertise make judgments regarding the worth and merit of a program. Typically, experts are asked questions, and theiropinions are collected and summarized and used to make decisions regarding program outcomes (Gall et al., 1996). The strengths of using expert opinion as a method of data collection include confidence in the knowledge base of the reviewer(s), while weaknesses may be the costs in time and money.

Problems and Pitfalls of Program Evaluation

One of the historic difficulties educators have encountered in conducting intervention research or evaluating intervention programs in school settings, is that it is often impossible to meet the demands of the ideal experimental research design, which requires randomization and the use of a control group (de Anda, 2007). Instead, de Anda (2007) advocates for the use of quasi-experimental designs such as a paired comparison design, in which an individual serves as his or her own control, in conjunction with a separatesample pretest-posttest control group design, in order to increase internal and external validity while overcoming the problems associated with implementing a true experimental design.

Cigularov, Chen, Thurber, and Stallones (2008) similarly argue that nonexperimental designs can be a part of rigorous evaluation when random assignment control group designs are not feasible due to practical and ethical reasons. These researchers utilized three methodological approaches (a rolling group design, an internal referencing strategy, and a minimum competency approach) to evaluate the efficacy of a schoolbased suicide education program, and assert that their study demonstrates the utility and practicality of applying three methodological approaches under ethical challenges and practical restraints (Cigularov et al., 2008). Therefore, although there are often statistical challenges to evaluating educational programs, there are opportunities for school psychologists to be creative and accountable in solving such dilemmas.

Evaluating the Results of a Program Evaluation

Once the data are collected, the next step of the evaluation is to analyze the information gathered. This includes tabulating, summarizing, organizing, and interpreting the data in order to answer the evaluation questions. The intent of data analysis is to place the information into perspective with respect to program goals and objectives, discussed in the section on program planning earlier in the chapter (McNamara, 2006). As mentioned previously, data may be either quantitative or qualitative, and consequently require different kinds of analyses.

Quantitative approaches emphasize quantifying relationships between variables and subsequently subjecting them to statistical analysis, which should be conducted by individuals who have the requisite skills for accurate calculation and interpretation. Data may be analyzed by employing descriptive statistics which describe the data, such as the frequency, percentile, standard deviation, and range, as well as measures of central tendencies (e.g., mean, median, mode). Inferential statistics may also be employed in the statistical analysis,andmay include but are not limited to correlation coefficients indicating the linear relationship between two variables; t-tests determining whether the means of two groups are statistically significant; and analysis of variance (ANOVA), which determines similarities or differences between two or more groups.

Qualitative data include information collected from interviews, observations, surveys and questionnaires, and focus groups. This evaluation approach elucidates the meaning and interpretation of programs, but may be more timeconsuming than quantitative methodologies because data need to be organized by themes and categories in order to identify patterns and relationships (McNamara, 2006). Moreover, this type of evaluation is highly subject to the values and perspectives of the evaluators. However, qualitative data helps to provide insights regarding the program (Gall et al., 1996). Program evaluations typically include both quantitative and qualitative data methods, with data often complemented with graphs, charts, figures, etc., to supplement the results. When interpreting the results, it is important to place the data into context and address evaluation goals as well as program strengths and weaknesses. After all, these data inform decision-making that influences the program, and will guide recommendations for program improvement (McNamara, 2006).

Evaluation Reports

An important aspect of a program evaluation is communicating the findings. In writing a program evaluation report, it is important to remember the audience so that the level and scope of the report is appropriate. Writing should be clear and direct, and should highlight the most salient points of the evaluation. Evaluation findings are usually documented in the form of an evaluation report. Reports should be tailored to address the specific questions and concerns that were delineated in the first step of the evaluative process. The results from good evaluations are used by stakeholders to decide whether and how to continue or modify a program, based on the findings (McNamara, 2006).

The following serves as a rubric and functional blueprint for reporting evaluation results (see Table 40.7). First, the report should describe the program, including its goals and objectives as well as the steps in the evaluation process. The report should also include a rationale for why the evaluation was

Table 40.7   Rubric for reporting program evaluation results

Step	Description
Step One	- Describe the program, including goals,objectives, and steps in the evaluation process. - Include a rationale for the evaluation and the evaluative questions.
Step Two:	- Provide a detailed explanation of the procedure and methods used in the evaluation.
Step Three:	- Present the evaluation results.
Step Four:	Describe methodological limitations, conclusions, recommendations for program improvement, and implications of the results

From McNamara, C. (2006).*Field guide to nonprofit program design, marketing and evaluation* (4th ed.). Copyright 2006. Reprinted with permission.

conducted, and list the evaluative questions that were developed. Second, a detailed explanation of the procedures and methods employed in the evaluation should be discussed. Third, the results of the evaluation should be presented. Fourth, methodological limitations, conclusions, recommendations for program improvement, and implications of the results should be presented and discussed (McNamara, 2006). In the next section of this chapter, a case study of program evaluation will be presented in order to encourage reflection and application of the methods and steps of program evaluation.

Conclusions

Throughout the chapter, the reader has been exposed to information regarding OSC, which was presented as a mechanism for engaging in PPE, both of which were described in detail so as to supply school psychologists with the necessary information for engaging in such activities. Organizational and systems consultation (OSC) was portrayed as a time-efficient, systems-conscious method that can be used to positively impact upon large numbers of students when it is used for PPE. The current emphasis upon standards-based accountability has resulted in a demand for vigilance in establishing goals, developing programs, maintaining routine record keeping, and consistently documenting intervention designs and outcomes in order to provide evidence of program effectiveness.

Although PPE were discussed primarily in relation to academic programming, there is ample research suggesting that EBPs are not limited to academics, but extend to social/emotional curricula, as well. Systems level applications of programs such as positive behavior support (PBS; Sugai et al., 2000) and social and emotional learning (SEL; Zins & Elias, 2006), in which OSC plays a vital role, are being used increasingly in multi-tiered service delivery. Program planning and evaluation are necessary elements to developing and implementing intervention programs that allow all children, regardless of disability status, to participate fully in and benefit from their educational experiences. Concluding remarks regarding the topics of program planning and program evaluation specific to school psychology will now be provided in order to highlight the necessity of these activities in the role functioning of school psychologist practitioners.

Program Planning and School Psychology

School psychologists are educators who work toward the central goal of facilitating children's mastery of

Box 40.2. Case Study of Program Evaluation

Mr. SP, the school psychologist, has been called to a meeting with the superintendent, Dr. Administrator (A). Upon meeting with Dr. A, Mr. SP learns that a parent of a high school student diagnosed with a learning disability has lodged a complaint with the school district regarding her son's educational progress. Although the student receives special education support services in a resource room setting for four periods a day, the youngster's parent feels as though the special educators are not effectively delivering the program developed by the Individualized Education Program (IEP) Team. In fact, the parent is questioning the cost-effectiveness of the resource room delivery model, believing that the taxpayers of the community are investing large amounts of money in paying educators that are, in essence, doing very little. The parent has requested that the special education program be assessed in order to determine its effectiveness. Thus, Dr. A has asked Mr. SP to conduct an evaluation of the district's special education program.

Mr. SP decides to consult the source literature regarding the process of a program evaluation, and finds that the steps include: (1) Focusing the evaluation (defining the purpose of the evaluation, including goals and objectives; (2) Identifying the evaluation questions (identifying stakeholders and structuring questions to address stakeholder needs, including what will be evaluated, what is the purpose of the evaluation, who benefits from the evaluation, and identifying a timeline for completion); (3) Determining the research design, collection, and analysis of data (considering the timeline for completion, types of data to be collected, who will collect the data, how the data will be collected, and what resources are needed to conduct the evaluation); (4) Collecting the data (implementation of data collection procedures), and; (5) Analyzing and interpreting the data and developing a report based upon the findings of the evaluation (report should address goals set for evaluation, the methods employed to answer questions, should present findings of the evaluation, should include implications of results, and should offer recommendations for enhancing the program and its outcomes; McNamara, 2006).

In accordance with the suggestions of the source literature, Mr. SP decides to use a mixed methods approach to the program evaluation design, employing the use of questionnaires and surveys as well as interviews with stakeholders, including teachers, parents, students, administrators, and community and business leaders. Mr. SP follows the process of program evaluation described in the previous paragraph. After the datahas been collected, Mr. SP begins the process of tabulating, summarizing, organizing, and interpreting the data in order to answer the evaluation questions, using appropriate statistical analyses when necessary, along with constructing graphs, charts, figures, etc., to supplement the results. When interpreting the results, Mr. SP is careful to place the data into context, and to address evaluation goals as well as program strengths and weaknesses (McNamara, 2006). Finally, Mr. SP writes an evaluation report, describing the program, including its goals and objectives, as well as describing the steps in the evaluation process. The report includes a rationale for why the evaluation was conducted, and lists the evaluative questions that were developed. A detailed explanation of the procedures and methods employed in the evaluation are discussed. The results of the evaluation are presented, and methodological limitations, conclusions, recommendations for program improvement, and implications of the results are presented and discussed (McNamara, 2006). The superintendent arranges for the report to be disseminated at a school board meeting, with a presentation made to the public. As expected, the findings are thought-provoking.

reading, writing, math, and science, and their development of a good understanding of history, literature, the arts, foreign languages, and diverse cultures (Greenberg et al., 2003). Additionally, Greenberg and colleagues (2003) argue that, "A comprehensive mission for schools is to educate studentsto be knowledgeable, responsible, socially skilled, healthy,caring, and contributing citizens" (p. 466). Yet another important point to be made is that school psychologists are increasingly being recognized as pivotal personnel in developing programs to help build schools' capacity to meet the needs of an increasingly diverse population (Wizda, 2004). Important programmatic needs in school systems include establishing research-based programs that are responsive to the needs of diverse students and

their families (Rogers, 2000). Because it is imperative that we not fail at these tasks, school psychologists and their educational colleagues must work to develop empiricallysound programs that are successful in facilitating the learning and healthy development of children. Although this mission is clear, there remain obstacles to impede our progress.

Lenihan (2005) emphasizes that program planning is a practice-based disciplinewithout a welldeveloped theoretical foundation. Because of this, program planning approaches must be sensitive to the institutional priorities and values of a school system, since these affect the purpose and function of such activities (Cooper & Saunders, 2000; Upcraft & Schuh, 1996). Second, responding to needs within school systems often involves suggesting that changes should be made, which can be difficult for individuals and the system itself. Before planning new programs in a school system, McDougal, Clonan, and Martens (2000) and Adelman and Taylor (2007) report that there must be some *organizational readiness,* or a willingness to receive change. School psychologists can be helpful in assisting their colleagues in recognizing that organizational change and strategic planning, particularly in the form of program development, is natural, healthy, and ongoing in educational systems (Knoff, 2000).

Although school psychologists cannot change the current educational landscape on their own, they can position themselves as systems change agents who work to gain administrators' and stakeholders' support to design and implement evidence-based intervention programs in schools. In discussing the role of school psychologists in developing school programs that are responsive to issues of safety, discipline, and crisis prevention, Knoff (2000) implores practitioners to "(a) to plan and embrace an organizational development and strategic planning perspective, (b) to see themselves as part of the school *system* and as *systems change agents,* and (c) to position themselves to be *seen by others* as experts who understand both the pragmatics and the necessity of implementing effective programs at the school system, school, grade, classroom, and individual student levels" (p. 18).

The school psychology literature is replete with references documenting that it is easier to prevent rather than to respond to problems. Indeed, once programs are established, it becomes increasingly difficult to make changes, even considering evaluation evidence that reveals major limitations of the established program (Cronbach et al., 1985; D'Agostino, 2001). Considering the role of school psychologists in promoting children's learning and development, the ability to plan effective programs is of great consequence and is a competency that school psychologist must purposefully seek. Moreover, it is necessary for colleges and university school psychology programs to emphasize this important task in the curriculum of graduate training. As the role of the school psychologist continues to evolve, it is likely that practitioners will only increase their program planning activities in the future.

Program Evaluation and School Psychology

The role of school psychology is continually evolving, with a shift toward a problem-solving focus and away from the role of performing traditional testing and placement into special education (Hawken, 2006). In an age of increasing accountability, particularly given the federal government's involvement in decisionmaking with respect to funding, schools are under increased pressure to document student performance. Understanding the implications and impact of increased accountability for student performance outcomes is crucial. Educators need to be aware of and responsive to the growing demand for evaluations to document effective programs.

Despite the need for program evaluation to be viewed as an essential competency for school psychologists, this topic is often not emphasized in school psychology graduate training programs, because it is not seen as a primary job function of school psychologists. Although the core curriculum of graduate programs includes research methods and statistics, very few offer coursework in program evaluation (Jarosewich, 2005). Noteworthy is that school psychologists are typically the only individuals within the educational milieu that have any background in research and measurement, and are often delegated the task of evaluating programs, given their unique knowledge of research. Because of the increased accountability that is demanded from our nation's schools, and the specialized methodological knowledge of school psychologists, it behooves trainers to prepare students to effectively conduct program evaluations, as these accountability issues are likely to increase over time.

Within the educational setting, program evaluations may include evaluating individualized education programs (IEP's), classroom, schoolwide, and district-level initiatives that address mental health and social services (Carlson, Tharinger, DeMers, Bricklin, & Paavola, 1996), and academic instruction. In addition, these evaluations may entail attending to difficulties such as addressing unmet goals and effectively utilizing resources (Fetterman, Kaftarian, & Wandersman, 1996). Unfortunately, many application fields, including education, are often lacking in evaluation of programs (Heller & Reimann, 2002), likely due to the notion that program evaluations are time-consuming, and the potential threat that findings may highlight less than stellar outcomes (Callahan, 1993). Although professional and practical challenges regarding program evaluation exist, it is a service that appears to be one that will increase due to necessity, and will have wideranging implications for students, schools, and staff alike.

Future Directions

Questions regarding future directions for the field, difficult problems to be solved, or topics that remain to be addressed:

1. Will using organizational and systems consultation as a vehicle for conducting program planning and evaluation make these activities easier to complete?

2. Is the role of the school psychologist changing to become more of a systems change agent?

3. How does a school psychologist go about developing a program for a problem that has not been extensively investigated in the source literature, with little or no empirical evidence to guide him or her?

4. Do university training programs for school psychologists need to devote more class time to such activities as conducting a needs assessment?

5. With the push toward requiring statistical evidence to conclude that a program is effective, will some programs that are difficult to measure, yet thought to be valuable, cause some to be reluctant to use them?

6. Are quasi-experimental designs seen as riskier by grant funders because of poorer internal validity of the research design?

References

Adelman, H. S., Taylor, L. (1997). Toward a scale-up model for replicating new approaches to schooling. *Journal of Educational and Psychological Consultation, 8*,197–230.

Adelman, H. S.,& Taylor, L. (2003). Rethinking school psychology. *Journal of School Psychology, 41*,83–90.

Adelman, H. S., & Taylor, L. (2007). Systemic change for school improvement. *Journal of Educational and Psychological Consultation, 17*,55–77.

Ansay, S. J., Perkins, D. F., & Nelson, J. (2004). Interpreting outcomes: Using focus groups in evaluation research. *Family Relations, 53*, 310–316.

Auster, E. R., Feeney-Kettler, K. A., & Kratochwill, T. R. (2006). Conjoint behavioral consultation: Application to the school-based treatment of anxiety disorders. *Education and Treatment of Children, 29*,243–256.

Barr, M. J., Keating, L. A., & Associates (1985). *Developing effective student services programs.* San Francisco: Jossey-Bass.

Callahan, C. M. (1993). Evaluation programs and procedures for gifted education: International problems and solutions. In K. A. Heller, F. J. Monks, & A. H. Passow (Eds.), *International handbook of research and development of giftedness and talent* (pp. 605–618). Oxford: Pergamon Press.

Carlson, C. I., Tharinger, D. J., DeMers, S. T., Bricklin, P. M., & Paavola, J. C. (1996). Health care reform and psychological practice in schools. *Professional Psychology: Research and Practice, 27*,14–23.

Casey-Cannon, S., Hayward, C., & Gowen, K. (2001). Middle-school girls' reports of peer victimization: Concerns, consequences, and implications. *Professional School Counseling, 5*, 138–147.

Cigularov, K., Chen, P., Thurber, B. W., & Stallones, L. (2008). Investigation of the effectiveness of a school-based suicide education program using three methodological approaches. *Psychological Services, 5*,262–274.

Cole, J. C. M., Cornell, D. G., & Sheras, P. (2006). Identification of school bullies by survey methods. *Professional School Counseling, 9*,305–313.

Cooper, D. L.,& Saunders, S. A. (2000). Assessing programmatic needs. In D. Liddell and J. P. Lund (Eds.), *Powerful programming for student learning: Approaches that make a difference: New directions for student services*(No. 90, pp. 5–20). San Francisco: Jossey-Bass.

Cronbach, L., Ambron, S., Dornbusch, S., Hess, R., Hornik, R., Phillips, D.,Walker, D., & Weiner, S. (1985). *Toward reform of program evaluation.*San Francisco: Jossey-Bass.

Crothers, L. M., & Levinson, E. M. (2004). Assessment of bullying: A review of methods and instruments. *Journal of Counseling and Development, 82*,496–503.

Curtis, M. J., Castillo, J. M., & Cohen, R. M. (2008). Best practices in system level change.In A. Thomas & J. Grimes (Eds.), *Best practices in school psychology V*(pp. 887–902). Bethesda, MD: National Association of School Psychologists.

D'Agostino, J. V. (2001). Increasing the role of educational psychology theory in program development and evaluation. *Educational Psychologist, 36*,127–132.

de Anda, D. (2007). Intervention research and program evaluation in the school setting: Issues and alternative research designs. *Children and Schools, 29*,87–94.

Deno, S. L. (1986). Formative evaluation of individual student programs: A new role for school psychologists. *School Psychology Review, 15*,358–374.

Derr, C. (1976). "OD" won't work in schools. *Brooklyn Education and Urban Society, 8*,227–241.

Durlak, J. A. (2002). Evaluating evidence-based interventions in school psychology. *School Psychology Quarterly, 17*, 475–482.

Earl, L.,& Fullan, M. (2002). Using data in leadership for learning. *Cambridge Journal of Education, 33*,383–394.

Eckert, T. L.,& Hintze, J. M. (2000). Behavioral conceptions and applications of acceptability: Issues related to service delivery and research methodology. *School Psychology Quarterly, 15*,123–148.

Fairchild, T. N., & Seeley, T. J. (1996). Evaluation of school psychological services: A case illustration. *Psychology in the Schools, 33*,46–55.

Felner, R. D., Seitsinger, A. S., Brand, S., Burns, A., & Bolton, N. (2008). Creating a statewide educational data system for accountability and improvement: A comprehensive information and assessment system for making evidence-based change at school, district, and policy levels. *Psychology in the Schools, 45*, 235–256.

Fetterman, D. M., Kaftarian, S. J., & Wandersman, A. (Eds.) (1996). *Empowerment evaluation: Knowledge and tools for self-assessment and accountability.* Thousand Oaks, CA: Sage.

Forman, S. G.,& Burke, C. R. (2008). Best practices in selecting and implementing evidence- based school interventions. In A. Thomas & J. Grimes (Eds.), *Best practices in school psychology V*(pp. 799–812). Bethesda, MD: National Association of School Psychologists.

Fuchs, D., & Fuchs, L. S. (1994). Inclusive schools movement and radicalization of special education reform. *Exceptional Children, 60*,294–309.

Gall, M. D., Borg, W. R., & Gall, J. (1996). *Educational research: An introduction* (6th ed.). New York: Longman Publishers USA.

Glasgow, R.E., Klesges, L.M., Dzewaltowski, D.A., Bull, S.S., &Estabrooks, P. (2004). The future of health behavior change research: What is needed to improve translation of research into health promotion practice? *Annals of Behavioral Medicine 27*, 3–12.

Goldfried, M.R., & Wolfe, B.E. (1996). Psychotherapy practice and research: Repairing a strained alliance. *American Psychologist, 51*, 1007–1016.

Gottfredson, D. C. (1984). A theory-ridden approach to program evaluation: A method for stimulating researcher-implementer collaboration. *American Psychologist, 39*, 1101–1112.

Gottfredson, D. C. (1993). Strategies for improving treatment integrity in organizational consultation. *Journal of Educational and Psychological Consultation, 4*,275–279.

Gottfredson, G. D., Rickert, D. E., Gottfredson, D. C., & Advani, N. (1984). Standards for program development evaluation plans. *Psychological Documents, 14*,32.

Greenberg, M. T., Weissberg, R. P., O'Brien, M. U., Zins, J. E., Fredericks, L., Resnik, H., & Elias, M. J. (2003). Enhancing school-based prevention and youth development through coordinated social, emotional, and academic learning. *American Psychologist, 58*,466–474.

Gutkin, T. B. (1986). Consultees' perceptions of variables relating to the outcomes of school-based consultation interactions. *School Psychology Review, 15*,375–382.

Gutkin, T. B., & Curtis, M. J. (1990). School-based consultation: Theory, techniques, and research. In T. B. Gutkin & C. R. Reynolds (Eds.), *The handbook of school psychology* (2nd ed., pp. 577–611). New York: Wiley.

Hawken, L. (2006). School psychologists as leaders in the implementation of a targeted intervention: The behavior education program. *School Psychology Quarterly, 21*,91–111.

Heary, C. M., & Hennessy, E. (2002). The use of focus group interviews in pediatric health care research. *Journal of Pediatric Psychology, 27*,47–57.

Heller, K. A., & Reimann, R. (2002). Theoretical and methodological problems of a 10-year follow-up program evaluation study. *European Journal of Psychological Assessment, 18*, 229–241.

Horner, S. D. (2000). Using focus group methods with middle school children. *Research in Nursing and Health, 23*, 510–517.

Hunsley, J. (2007). Addressing key challenges in evidence-based practice in psychology. *Professional Psychology: Research and Practice, 39*, 113–121.

Illback, R. J., & Zins, J. E. (1995). Organizational interventions in educational settings. *Journal of Educational and Psychological Consultation, 6*,217–236.

Janis, I. L. (1972). *Victims of groupthink*. New York: Houghton Mifflin.

Janis, I. L. (1982). *Groupthink: Psychological studies of policy decisions and fiascoes*(2nd ed.).New York: Houghton Mifflin.

Jarosewich, T. (2005). Program evaluation. In S. W. Lee (Ed.), *Encyclopedia of school psychology* (pp. 409–412). New York: Macmillan.

Joint Committee on Standards for Educational Evaluation (1994). *The program evaluation standards: How to assess evaluations of educational programs*. Thousand Oaks, CA: Sage.

Kalafat, J., Illback, R. J., & Sanders, D. Jr. (2006). The relationship between implementation fidelity and educational outcomes in a school-based family support program: Development of a model for evaluating multidimensional full-service programs. *Evaluation and Program Planning, 30*,136–148.

Kazdin, A. E. (1981). Acceptability of treatment techniques: The influence of treatment efficacy and adverse side effects. *Behavior Therapy, 12*,493–506.

Kazdin, A. E. (2003). *Research design in clinical psychology* (4th ed.). Boston: Allyn and Bacon.

Kehle, T. J., & Bray, M. A. (2007). On such a full sea and we are still not afloat: Introduction to statistical reform in school psychology. *Psychology in the Schools, 44*,415.

Kennedy, C., Kools, S., & Krueger, R. (2001). Methodological considerations in children's focus groups. *Nursing Research, 50*, 184–187.

Knoff, H. M. (2000). Organizational development and strategic planning for the millennium: A blueprint toward effective school discipline, safety, and crisis prevention. *Psychology in the Schools, 37*,17–32.

Knoff, H. M. (2008). Best practices in strategic planning, organizational development and school effectiveness. In A. Thomas &J. Grimes (Eds.), *Best practices in school psychology V*(pp. 903–916). Bethesda, MD: National Association of School Psychologists.

Kratochwill, T. R., & Bergan, J. R. (1990). *Behavioral consultation in applied settings: An individual guide*. New York: Plenum Press.

Kratochwill, T. R., & Stoiber, K. C. (2000). Empirically supported interventions and school psychology: Conceptual and practice issues – Part II. *School Psychology Quarterly, 15*, 233–253.

Krueger, R.A. (1994). *Focus groups: A practical guide for applied research* (2nd ed.). Thousand Oaks, CA: Sage.

Lenihan, P. (2005). MAPP and the evolution of planning in public health practice. *Journal of Public Health Management and Practice, 11*,381–386.

Marrs, L. W., & Helge, D. I. (1978). The role of needs assessment in program planning and evaluation. *The Journal of Special Education, 12*,143–151.

McDougal, J. L., Clonan, S. M., & Martens, B. K. (2000). Using organizational change procedures to promote the acceptability of prereferral intervention services: The school- based intervention team project. *School Psychology Quarterly, 15*,149–171.

McEvoy, M. A., Estrem, T. L., Rodriguez, M. C., & Olson, M. L. (2003). Assessing relational and physical aggression among preschool children: Intermethod agreement. *Topics in Early Childhood Special Education, 23*,53–63.

McNamara, C. (2006). *Field guide to nonprofit program design, marketing, and evaluation* (4th ed.). Minneapolis, MN: Authenticity Consulting, LLC.

Merrell, K. W., & Buchanan, R. (2006). Intervention selection in school-based practice: Using public health models to enhance systems capacity of schools. *School Psychology Review, 35*, 167–180.

No Child Left Behind Act of 2001, Pub. L. No. 107-110, 115 Stat. 1425 (2002).

Pellegrini, A. D., & Bartini, M. (2000). An empirical comparison of methods of sampling aggression and victimization in school settings. *Journal of Educational Psychology, 92*, 360–366.

Peterson-Sweeney, K. (2005). The use of focus groups in pediatric and adolescent research. Journal of Pediatric Health Care, 19, 104–110.

Ringeisen, H., Henderson, K., & Hoagwood, K. (2003). Context matters: Schools and the "Research to Practice Gap" in children's mental health. School Psychology Review, 32, 153–168.

Rogers, M. R. (2000). Examining the cultural context of consultation. School Psychology Review, 29, 414–418.

Schmuck, R. A. (1995). Process consultation and organization development today. Journal of Educational and Psychological Consultation, 6, 207–215.

Shapiro, E. S. (1987). Intervention research methodology in school psychology. School Psychology Review, 16, 290–305.

Shapiro, E. S. (2006). Are we solving the big problems? School Psychology Review, 35, 260–265.

Staats, A. W. (1991). Unified positivism and unification psychology: Fad or new field? American Psychologist, 46, 899–912.

Sugai, G., Horner, R. H., Dunlap, G., Hieneman, M., Lewis, T. K., Nelson, C. M., Scott, T., Liaupsin, C., Sailor, W., Turnbull, A. P., Turnbull, H. R. III, Wickham, D., Wilcox, B., & Ruef, M. (2000). Applying positive behavior support and functional behavioral assessment in schools. Journal of Positive Behavior Interventions, 2, 131–143.

Trachtman, G. M. (1981). On such a full sea. School Psychology Review, 10, 138–181.

Truscott, S. D., Cosgrove, G., Meyers, J., & Eidle-Barkman, K. A. (2000). The acceptability of organizational consultation with prereferral intervention teams. School Psychology Quarterly, 15, 172–206.

Upcraft, M. L., & Schuh, J. H. (1996). Assessment in student affairs: A guide for practitioners. San Francisco: Jossey-Bass.

Wasburn-Moses, L. (2006). Obstacles to program effectiveness in secondary special education. Preventing School Failure, 50, 21–30.

Webb, C., & Kevern, J. (2001). Focus groups as a research method: A critique of some aspects of their use in nursing research. Journal of Advanced Nursing, 33, 798–805.

Whealin, J. M., & Ruzek, J. (2008). Program evaluation of organizational cultural competence in mental health practices. Professional Psychology: Research and Practice, 39, 320–328.

Winzer, M. A. (2000). The inclusion movement: Review and reflections on reform in special education. In M. A. Winzer & K. Mazurek (Eds.), Special education in the 21st century: Issues of inclusion and reform (pp. 5–26). Washington, DC: Gallaudet University.

Witkin, B. R. (1984). Assessing needs in educational and social programs. San Francisco: Jossey-Bass Inc.

Wizda, L. (2004). An instructional consultant looks to the future. Journal of Educational and Psychological Consultation, 15, 277–294.

Wolf, N. M. (1978). Social validity: The case for subjective measurement or how applied behavior analysis is finding its heart. Journal of Applied Behavior Analysis, 11, 203–214.

Wyatt, T. H., Krauskopf, P. B., & Davidson, R. (2008). Using focus groups for program planning and evaluation. The Journal of School Nursing, 24, 71–77.

Zins, J. E., Curtis, M. J., Graden, J., & Ponti, C. R. (1988). Helping students succeed in the regular classroom: A guide for developing intervention assistance programs. San Francisco: Jossey-Bass.

Zins, J. E., & Elias, M. J. (2006). Social and emotional learning: Promoting the development of all students. In G. G. Bear, K. M. Minke, & A. Thomas (Eds.), Children's needs III: Development, problems, and alternatives (pp. 1–13). Bethesda, ND: National Association of School Psychologists.

Zins, J. E., & Illback, R. J. (1995). Consulting to facilitate planned organizational change in schools. Journal of Educational and Psychological Consultation, 6, 237–245.

Zins, J. E., & Ponti, C. R. (1990). Strategies to facilitate the implementation, organization, and operation of system-wide consultation programs. Journal of Educational and Psychological Consultation, 1, 205–218. Laura M. Crothers, Lea A. Theodore, and Tammy L. Hughes

International Development of School Psychology

Bonnie Kaul Nastasi *and* Kris Varjas

Abstract

The chapter explores converging international forces that provide the context for future development of school psychology, examines the current status of school psychology internationally, and proposes a model for guiding future development of the profession on a global level. A primary reason for universal insufficiency of mental health services for children and adolescents is shortage of mental health professionals such as school psychologists, due in part to the shortage or lack of professional development programs. Critical to the advancement of school psychology internationally is development of a theoretical and empirical basis for training and practice that addresses cultural and contextual diversity. Drawing on models for international development and prior work of the authors, a model for the cultural construction of international school psychology is proposed. Key features of the model include ongoing research and evaluation, and partnership with local stakeholders to facilitate capacity building and sustainability of local programming.

Keywords: international, school psychology, cultural construction, professional development, capacity building, mixed methods research

The new millennium is a propitious time for school psychology to examine its role in the global community. The World Health Organization (WHO; 2005a, 2005b, 2008) provides evidence of significant gaps between the mental health needs of children and adolescents and access to mental health services worldwide. Approximately 20% of children and adolescents worldwide suffer from some type of mental health problem, with approximately 5% severe enough to warrant clinical intervention (WHO, 2005a). Even in high income countries (e.g., U. S.), mental health services are insufficient to meet documented need (WHO, 2005a). One of the major barriers to providing mental health services is the shortage of qualified mental health professionals, including school psychologists (see also Jimerson, Oakland, & Farrell, 2007; Jimerson, Skokut, Cardenas, Malone & Stewart, 2008). In response to these gaps, the United Nations and World Health Organization have called for

stakeholders (government, funders, public health organizations, mental health professionals, community organizations, consumers) to work together to achieve universal mental health (e.g., U. N. Secretary-General, 2008; WHO, 2008a, 2008b).

The documented need for child and adolescent mental health services and calls for universal promotion of mental health provide an opportune context for envisioning the future of school psychology internationally. The purpose of this chapter is to explore the converging international forces that set the stage for future development of school psychology, examine the current status of school psychology internationally, and propose a model for guiding future development of the profession on a global level.

Global Influences on School Psychology Internationally

The World Health Organization (WHO) has documented significant need for development of new approaches to mental health service delivery world-wide. Compiling available data on child and adolescent mental health needs and resources, primarily from the 192 Member States of the United Nations, the WHO presents a clear picture of unmet psychological needs (2005a; Table 41.1 summarizes the related mental health facts compiled by WHO).

Across all countries, including high income countries such as the United States (see U.S. Department of Health & Human Services [USDHHS], 1999, 2001), the need for mental health services is consistent, ranging between 5% and 20% (WHO, 2005a). The needs are universal, irrespective of geographic location, economic status, or culture; however, the manifestation and awareness of needs may vary as a function of these factors (USDHHS; WHO).

Although access to child and adolescent mental health services varies across countries (20% to 80%), service delivery is *not sufficient in any country* to meet documented need (WHO, 2005a). Recent reports by the Surgeon General support such shortages in the U.S. (USDHHS, 1999). Service provision is highest (approaching 80%) in European countries, particularly the Scandinavian region, and Israel (WHO). Some countries lack basic clinical mental health services, including 23% of European countries and 26% of countries in the Americas (WHO). The majority of countries outside of the Americas and Europe lack a system of services for child and adolescent mental health, and more than two-thirds of all countries lack identifiable entities that are responsible for child and adolescent mental health programs (WHO). Although over 90% of countries have nongovernmental organizations devoted to child and adolescent mental health, most are involved in advocacy and policy work rather than service provision (WHO). Neither primary care nor public education institutions are equipped to provide the necessary mental health services to children and adolescents in need, although both have been identified as potential sites for universal access (WHO, 2005a, 2005b, 2008a, 2008b). Moreover, "countries with the higher proportion of children in the world are the ones that lack both mental health policy addressing the needs of children and adolescents and services for the population" (WHO, 2005a, p. 16).

The shortage of service providers has been cited as one of the major barriers to mental health care, in part due to lack of appropriate training for professionals. For example, appropriately trained child and adolescent psychiatrists are uncommon in low-income countries (WHO, 2005a). In addition, other potential providers in the health and education sectors (e.g., pediatricians, educators, social workers, psychologists, speech and language pathologists) lack relevant mental health training (i.e., in child and adolescent mental health). This dearth of mental health professionals in general (as reported by the WHO) is consistent with findings for school psychologists worldwide. In a recent survey of the Member States of the United Nations, Jimerson and colleagues (Jimerson, Skokut, Cardenas, Malone & Stewart, 2008) found evidence of school psychologists (broadly defined by "identifiable professionals employed to fulfill duties characteristic of 'school psychologists'", p. 137) in less than half of the countries (83 of 192; 43%). Furthermore, only 29% of all countries had university training programs that prepared 'school psychologists', and only 10% provided doctoral level preparation.

Other reasons cited for gaps in service provision include insufficient or nonexistent government funding, lack of relevant policies mandating and/or governing mental health service delivery, lack of information or awareness among the general public as well as professionals, and stigma associated with mental health problems (also, at general public and professional levels; WHO, 2005a). These factors are indicative of the need for efforts that bring together the full range of stakeholders (funders, policymakers, professionals, consumers).

Concurrent with recent international concerns about mental health of children and adolescents, the United Nations has identified several *Millennium Development Goals* (MGDs; see Table 41.1) which are reflected in current work of the World Health Organization (e.g., WHO, 2008a, 2008b). The range of issues addressed by MGDs—health, educational, social, environmental—are consistent with global issues identified by community-oriented psychologists as potential targets for domestic and international work (Kolbe, Collins, & Cortese, 1997; Leviton, 1996; Marsella & Pederson, 2004; Nelson & Prilleltensky, 2005). MGDs also are consistent with emerging directions for school psychology in the U.S. (Gutkin, 2008; Harrison et al., 2004; Lakin & Mahoney, 2006; Schaughency & Ervin, 2006; Sheridan & Gutkin, 2000; Stollar, Poth, Curtis, & Cohen, 2006; Ysseldyke et al., 2006), calls for a public health perspective in school psychology (DeJong, 2000; Kubiszyn, 1999; Nastasi, 2000, 2004; Power, 2000, 2003), and international efforts to promote psychological well-being among adolescents (e.g., WHO, 2008). Particularly important for school psychology is the focus of

Table 41.1 World Health Organization (WHO)'s 10 facts on mental health

Fact 1	About half of mental disorders begin before the age of 14. Around 20% of the world's children and adolescents are estimated to have mental disorders or problems, with similar types of disorders being reported across cultures. Yet, regions of the world with the highest percentage of population under the age of 19 have the poorest level of mental health resources. Most low- and middle-income countries have only one child psychiatrist for every 1 to 4 million people. (Source: http://www.who.int/features/factfiles/mental_health/mental_health_facts/en/index.html)
Fact 2	Depression is characterized by sustained sadness and loss of interest along with psychological, behavioural and physical symptoms. It is ranked as the leading cause of disability worldwide. (Source: http://www.who.int/features/factfiles/mental_health/mental_health_facts/en/index1.html)
Fact 3	On average about 800 000 people commit suicide every year, 86% of them in low- and middle-income countries. More than half of the people who kill themselves are aged between 15 and 44. The highest suicide rates are found among men in eastern European countries. Mental disorders are one of the most prominent and treatable causes of suicide. (Source: http://www.who.int/features/factfiles/mental_health/mental_health_facts/en/index2.html)
Fact 4	War and other major disaster have a large impact on the mental health and psychosocial well-being. Rates of mental disorder tend to double after emergencies. (Source: http://www.who.int/features/factfiles/mental_health/mental_health_facts/en/index3.html)
Fact 5	Mental disorders are among the risk factors for communicable and non-communicable diseases. They can also contribute to unintentional and intentional injury. (Source: http://www.who.int/features/factfiles/mental_health/mental_health_facts/en/index4.html)
Fact 6	Stigma about mental disorders and discrimination against patients and families prevent people from seeking mental health care. In South Africa, a public survey showed that most people thought mental illnesses were related to either stress or a lack of willpower rather than to medical disorders. Contrary to expectations, levels of stigma were higher in urban areas and among people with higher levels of education. (Source: http://www.who.int/features/factfiles/mental_health/mental_health_facts/en/index5.html)
Fact 7	Human rights violations of psychiatric patients are routinely reported in most countries. These include physical restraint, seclusion and denial of basic needs and privacy. Few countries have a legal framework that adequately protects the rights of people with mental disorders. (Source: http://www.who.int/features/factfiles/mental_health/mental_health_facts/en/index6.html)
Fact 8	There is huge inequity in the distribution of skilled human resources for mental health across the world. Shortages of psychiatrists, psychiatric nurses, psychologists and social workers are among the main barriers to providing treatment and care in low- and middle-income countries. Low-income countries have 0.05 psychiatrists and 0.16 psychiatric nurses per 100 000 people, compared to 200 times more in high-income countries. (Source: http://www.who.int/features/factfiles/mental_health/mental_health_facts/en/index7.html)
Fact 9	In order to increase the availability of mental health services, there are five key barriers that need to be overcome: the absence of mental health from the public health agenda and the implications for funding; the current organization of mental health services; lack of integration within primary care; inadequate human resources for mental health; and lack of public mental health leadership. (Source: http://www.who.int/features/factfiles/mental_health/mental_health_facts/en/index8.html)
Fact 10	Governments, donors and groups representing mental health workers, patients and their families need to work together to increase mental health services, especially in low- and middle-income countries. The financial resources needed are relatively modest: US$ 2 per person per year in low-income countries and US$ 3-4 in lower middle-income countries. (Source: http://www.who.int/features/factfiles/mental_health/mental_health_facts/en/index9.html)

Note: These facts were downloaded 5 July 2010, from World Health Organization website, http://www.who.int/features/factfiles/mental_health/mental_health_facts/en/index.html. World Health Organization.

millennium goals on universal primary education, gender equality and empowerment, poverty, child mortality, and diseases such as HIV. These goals encompass the context of school psychology practice (i.e., education), ethical responsibilities (e.g., social justice) of school psychologists, and social morbidities (i.e., health problems related to behavioral, social, and environmental factors that influence individual lifestyle; DiClemente, Hansen, Ponton, 1996; Nastasi et al., 2004) that fall into

Table 41.2 United Nations Millennium Development Goals (MGDs)

- Eradicate extreme poverty and hunger
- Achieve universal primary education
- Promote gender equality and empower women
- Reduce child mortality
- Improve maternal health
- Combat HIV/AIDS, malaria, and other diseases
- Ensure environmental sustainability
- Develop a global partnership for development

Source: http://www.un.org/millenniumgoals/poverty.shtml

the purview of school psychology, such as suicide, poverty, violence, HIV and other sexual risks, substance abuse, and diet.

In summary, concerns about the mental health of children and adolescents and related advocacy for universal services stem from efforts of various international organizations and professionals. These different sources share common concerns and propose a range of solutions, but are not necessarily working together. International organizations (WHO, U. N.) are attempting to facilitate more concerted efforts, and perhaps provide the most promise for coordination. The profession of school psychology, especially through its major national, regional, and international organizations (e.g., International School Psychology Association and its national affiliates), is uniquely positioned to advocate for and facilitate collaborative efforts to address the mental health needs of children and adolescents. In subsequent sections, we examine the current status of professional school psychology (especially in terms of its presence in the global community) and propose a process for facilitating planning, advocacy, and action. We conclude with recommendations for action by school psychologists collectively and individually.

Current Status of School Psychology Internationally

The major sources of information about the status quo of school psychology internationally reflect collaborative efforts by researchers from 43 countries, initiated in 2002 under the leadership of Shane Jimerson, and the auspices of the Research Committee of the International School Psychology Association (ISPA; *www.ispaweb.org*). The Research Committee developed the International School Psychology Survey, which was then implemented by researchers within their own countries. The primary outlets for dissemination of this work have been the *School Psychology International* (journal of ISPA;

e.g., Jimerson, Graydon et al., 2004; Jimerson et al., 2006; Jimerson, Graydon et al., 2008) and a recently published international handbook (Jimerson et al., 2007). Most recently, Jimerson and colleagues (Jimerson, Skokut et al., 2008) examined available evidence from the 192 U.N. Member States to provide updated information about the presence of school psychology worldwide. The findings of these studies provide the foundation for our current discussion of international school psychology. Additionally, we highlight current efforts by ISPA to facilitate international development in school psychology.

The International School Psychology Survey (ISPS) was designed to gather information in five areas, including demographic characteristics of school psychologists, their roles and responsibilities, professional preparation and regulation, challenges for the profession, and research foundations (Jimerson, Graydon et al., 2006). Recognizing the wide variations in titles (e.g., counselor, educational/school psychologist, psychologist in schools/education, psychopedagogue) and sites of practice (e.g., schools, clinics, hospitals, universities), researchers defined the specialty of school psychology on the basis of the following responsibilities (or duties) of practitioners:

> individual assessment of children who may display cognitive, emotional, social, or behavioral difficulties; develop and implement primary and secondary intervention programs; consult with teachers, parents, and other relevant professionals; engage in program development and evaluation; conduct research; and help prepare and supervise others (*Jimerson* et al., 2007, p. 1)

To situate the work of Jimerson et al. (2007) within an historical context, we present the internal and external conditions proposed by Oakland (2003) as potential influences on the future development of school psychology. The conditions external to professional school psychology included: (a) legislation to institutionalize and fund school psychological services; (b) a country's economy (Gross National Product); (c) English language use; and (d) the incorporation of diverse cultural perspectives in the field of psychology. The internal conditions included: (a) the development of a national school psychology association; (b) the public statements of the nature of school psychological services; (c) expansion of the role of school psychological services in countries restricted to working with students with special needs; (d) connection between education and school psychology; and (e) the availability of nationally developed tests to assess the areas of cognition, academic achievement, and social, emotional, and behavioral development. These propositions relied on earlier work such as Oakland and Cunningham's (1992) survey of school psychology in 54 countries, which, as the sole international data base prior to the research initiated in 2002 (Jimerson et al., 2007), served as the extant foundation for elucidating the status of school psychology within specific countries.

The *Handbook of International School Psychology* (Jimerson et al., 2007) provides detailed findings for each of the 43 countries that participated in ISPS. Farrell, Jimerson, and Oakland (2007) synthesized the findings across countries and identified characteristics of countries in which school psychology is considered (by Jimerson and colleagues) to be more well developed or "better established"; for example, Israel, most Western European countries, Australia, New Zealand, United States, and Canada. The countries in which the profession was considered well established were characterized by (a) higher gross national product, (b) highly developed and legally mandated educational system (including higher education), (c) special education services, and (d) a well-developed discipline of psychology. Also associated with the strength of professional school psychology were the presence of a national organization representing the profession, and credentialing bodies (e.g., for licensing and certification). University preparation of school psychologists varied widely, and included 4- to 5-year undergraduate degree (e.g., Albania, Estonia, Italy); 6- to 7-year combination of undergraduate and graduate (e.g, 4-year undergraduate plus 2- to 3-year master's or specialist degree, e.g., Australia, China, Cyprus, Germany, Italy, U. S.; 3-year undergraduate plus 3–4 years of graduate study for countries in the European Union); and doctoral degrees (5 to 6 years of graduate work; primarily in U.S., England, Brazil, Wales, Germany). Despite the variations in length of training, the program curriculum varied minimally, and typically included coursework in assessment, intervention, child development, individual differences and disabilities, and research and statistics. Programs also typically included supervised field experiences (practicum and/or internship).

Of particular relevance to the development of the field of school psychology are findings related to the role of standardized tests and research. Farrell et al. (2007) reported that standardized tests play an important role in development of the profession. In particular, the availability of locally developed standardized tests (e.g., normed and standardized on local populations) was associated with the growth and strength of school psychology within a country. This trend likely reflects the importance of standardized tests in U.S. and Western European countries, where the development of school psychology has been closely tied to assessment and diagnosis related to special education eligibility. However, there are exceptions. Jimerson et al. cite examples of countries (e.g., Italy, Hungary, Albania) in which school psychology development has been associated with promoting mental health or psychological well-being of children and adolescents, rather than with assessment; these countries also had minimal testing resources.

As a follow-up to the previous proposals of Oakland (2003), Oakland and Jimerson (2007) presented a revised list of factors or conditions relevant to the development of school psychology. The internal conditions (i.e., internal to school psychology) included the legal status of the field, degree of professionalism (defined by presence of national association and credentialing bodies), the definition of scope and function, the relationship with the field of education, and the scholarly and technical contributions of the field. In addition, the level of development (professionalism) of the general discipline of psychology was identified as an important influence on the specialty of school psychology. External factors (e.g., related to the conditions within the respective country) included cultural history and current conditions, the economy, geographic location (e.g., region or proximity to other countries with established school psychology), language (particularly fluency in English which affects access to scholarly journals), and national needs and priorities (e.g., congruence with priority given to education and public health).

The development of a theoretical and empirical basis for school psychology practice is especially critical to the advancement of the profession. Few school psychology practitioners engage in research, and research relevant to school psychology is published primarily in English (Farrell et al., 2007). This is attributable in part to the roles of school psychology practitioners; their roles do not typically include research activities, thus, limiting research to those working in university settings (Farrell et al.). Other issues that need to be considered, however, include research expertise, which is more likely to be a function of degree (i.e., more likely tied to doctoral-level training; Farrell et al.). The lack of published research in languages other than English, of course, restricts access to the knowledge base for school psychologists in many countries. Furthermore, the bulk of school psychology research has been conducted in the U.S. and Western European countries, raising critical questions about the cultural relevance of our current knowledge base. In response to such concerns, ISPA, in partnership with the Society for the Study of School Psychology (SSSP), began international research initiatives in 2005, which are ongoing. Current initiatives include two projects, *Exploring Student Engagement in Schools Internationally* (Lam & Jimerson, 2008) and *Promoting Psychological Well-Being Globally* (Nastasi et al., 2008). Both projects involve researchers from several different countries working as partners to gather data on respective topics. Such efforts hold promise for advancing the theoretical and empirical basis of school psychology beyond the extant Western perspective, and respond to calls in psychology more generally, such as the following:

> If psychology is to advance significantly as a science . . .
> psychologists around the world must work together
> to understand human development and mental
> health and intervene accordingly
> (*Leong & Ponterotto*, 2003, p. 383).

Future of School Psychology Internationally

We turn now to discussion of future initiatives to advance professional school psychology internationally. To inform future efforts, we draw from models of international development by organizations such as Oxfam, a British nongovernmental organization with extensive international development work (Eade, 1997), and of the World Health Organization (2005b, 2008a). The efforts of these organizations focus on capacity building, or the development of sustainable programs for enhancing the lives of individuals (e.g., eliminating poverty through economic development efforts, or promoting physical and mental health). A necessary component of such programs is the development of infrastructure for continued programming; thus, efforts focus on both individual and ecological or systems change. Within school psychology, Nastasi et al. (2004) have discussed the application of capacity building to development of sustainable, comprehensive school-based mental health programs, with a particular focus on developing programs that are culturally and contextually relevant.

In this section, we introduce a model for development, or cultural construction, of professional school psychology internationally (building on prior work of Nastasi, Varjas, and colleagues; Nastasi,

2000, 2004; Nastasi, Varjas, Bernstein, & Jayasena, 2000; Nastasi et al., 2004). We use the term *cultural construction* to refer to the process of negotiating program models that encompass both professional cultural realities (i.e., existing theoretical-empirical models, individual program developer concepts) with local cultural and contextual realities (i.e., of the target setting, local professional and lay stakeholders; cf. Kleinman, Eisenberg, & Good, 1978). The model, depicted in Figure 41.1, has several characteristics:

1. The use of research, both formative and evaluative, to guide program development and modification.
2. The involvement of key stakeholders in guiding development of the program.
3. In-depth understanding of cultural and contextual conditions (i.e., the ecology) of the target site/country.
4. The development of local capacity for sustaining and institutionalizing program efforts, including institutional infrastructure and professional skills.
5. Commitment to translation or scaling up of local efforts through a similar process of formative and evaluative research.

The proposed model encompasses traditional approaches to program development that typically include examining existing models, identifying goals and/or mission statement, and designing, implementing, and evaluating the program. To these are added several other steps which help to insure development of culturally and contextually relevant (i.e., culturally constructed) programs, promotion of sustainability and institutionalization, translation to other contexts, and dissemination to facilitate international development of school psychology. The model provides the process for ascertaining the current status of the country-specific external and internal conditions (i.e., through formative research) identified by Oakland and Jimerson (2007), and developing plans for advancing school psychology research, training, and practice based on current status and identified mission and goals. Finally, the mechanisms underlying the proposed model are consistent with current conceptions of organizational or system-level consultation in school psychology (Meyers, Meyers, Proctor, & Graybill, 2008; Nastasi et al., 2000). Thus, we might characterize program developers as systems change agents or consultants who engage in a participatory process of organizational/institutional development.

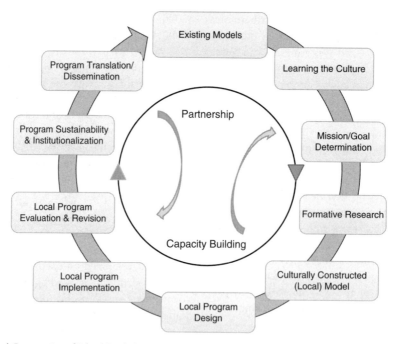

Fig. 41.1. Cultural Construction of School Psychology
Adapted with permission from Nastasi, B.K., Moore, R. B., & Varjas, K. M. School-based mental health services: Creating comprehensive and culturally specific programs. American Psychological Association, Washington, DC, 2004.

The model depicted in Figure 41.1 involves ten (10) phases, intended to be recursive, and two (2) central components, partnership and capacity building. The participatory (i.e., in full partnership with stakeholders) model applies to initial program development, ongoing evaluation and modification to meet changing cultural and contextual needs, and sustainability and institutionalization through capacity building. Briefly, the recursive process begins with examining models for effective capacity building (e.g., from international development or community development work), and existing program models related to school psychology research, training, and practice. Program developers then engage in efforts to gain an in-depth understanding of the cultural context (learning the culture; e.g., through qualitative or mixed-methods research) as they form necessary partnerships and gain entry into the relevant systems. This is followed by a participatory process of determining mission and goals for school psychology development, and formative research to identify relevant needs and resources (e.g., mental health needs of students, existing mental health and educational services), understand local conceptions and language relevant to psychological well-being of children and facilitative environments (e.g., school, communities, homes), and the nature and objectives of school psychological services (i.e., to facilitate psychological well-being of

children). Findings from formative research are used to develop a culturally constructed model for development of school psychology, which in turn informs program design, implementation, and evaluation. The process concludes with ensuring necessary conditions for sustaining and institutionalizing the program, efforts to translate the program to similar sites (e.g., other regions within a country), and dissemination of information to professionals, policymakers, and the public. An outcome of dissemination includes contributions to existing program models that in turn can influence future efforts by others, thus completing the cycle. In this chapter, we discuss application to new program development in countries where school psychology is nonexistent or emerging as a profession. The process of cultural construction also can be applied to revising existing programs, for example, to facilitate internationalization of programs in the U. S. (Olson, Evans, & Shoenberg, 2007; Olson, Green, & Hill, 2008)

Partnership and Capacity Building
Central to the cultural construction model (Figure 41.1) are partnership and capacity building. *Partnership* refers to the involvement of key stakeholders (those with vested interests and/or resources), including policymakers, funders, university administrators, relevant professionals (e.g., relevant to higher [tertiary] education, primary and secondary

education, and health or mental health service provision), and consumers (e.g., potential applicants for tertiary education, community leaders, parents, students). In this model, establishing partnerships occurs early in the process of program development, so that stakeholders can become full participants in decision making. Partnerships are important for two reasons. First, the engagement of stakeholders can help to ensure that program decisions consider culturally and contextually relevant needs and resources. Second, partnerships can contribute to sustainability and institutionalization of programs once the external consultants depart, or, more broadly, to capacity building.

Eade (1997) describes *capacity building* as a means, a process, and an end. As a means, it refers to "strengthening the capacity of primary stakeholders to implement defined *activities*" (Eade, p. 35; emphasis in the original); for example, enhancing the capabilities or skills of faculty to deliver a program of study in school psychology. As a process, capacity building refers to "fostering *communication*: processes of debate, relationship building, conflict resolution" (Eade, p. 35; emphasis in the original); for example, the process of negotiation within a collaborative consultation relationship. As an ends, capacity building refers to "strengthening capacity of primary stakeholders to participate... according to *objectives* defined by them" (Eade, p. 35; emphasis in the original); for example, enhancing the skills of faculty or other institutional stakeholders to develop programs of study that meet their own objectives. Evident across these applications of capacity building is the focus on developing or enhancing the capabilities of stakeholders to engage in the process of, for example, cultural construction of professional school psychology. Thus, a primary goal of external consultants (program developers/planners) is ensuring that local stakeholders have the capacity (skills, capabilities, processes) to independently engage in program development efforts (i.e., to foster self-reliance and autonomy).

Effective partnerships are essential to capacity building. Partnerships provide the context for skill development, communication, and stakeholder ownership of program goals and processes. Facilitating such partnerships requires moving beyond traditional notions of collaboration or collaborative consultation (Nastasi et al., 2000, 2004; Serrano-Garcia, 1990), in which stakeholder roles are limited based on decisions by the external consultants (e.g., stakeholders implement programs developed by consultants). Instead, we prefer the term *participation* or

participatory consultation, which refers to engagement of stakeholders as full partners in all steps of the process (e.g., the 10 phases of the cultural construction process depicted in Figure 41.1). Thus, stakeholders are viewed as members of the team that examines existing models, formulates mission and objectives, plans and conducts formative research, etc. In order for stakeholders to participate fully in such processes, development of relevant skills and expertise (i.e., capacity building) is necessary.

APPLICATION: PARTNERSHIPS IN THE INTERNATIONAL ARENA

The concept of partnership in the development of school psychology internationally has several applications: (a) cross-cultural professional relationships such as those between faculty from well-established and emerging school psychology training programs; (b) cross-disciplinary professional relationships such as those between academic psychologists (e.g., from foundation areas of developmental, educational, cognitive, social, etc.; research and measurement methodologists) and applied psychologists (e.g., school, clinical), between psychology and medical/health (physicians, psychiatrists, public health specialists) or other social science disciplines (e.g., anthropology, sociology), between psychologists and educators (educational researchers, teachers, administrators at local and national levels); and (c) relationships of professionals with private and public stakeholders such as consumers (parents, community members, students), funders, policymakers, nongovernmental organizations (NGOs), and other community organizations. Applied broadly, partnerships refer to the full range of stakeholders whose commitment and participation are necessary to carrying out the activities related to program development and capacity building. Achieving successful partnerships requires leaders and/or external consultants who can facilitate a participatory process of problem solving and decision making, and provide training for stakeholders in skills related to building and maintaining relationships, effective communication, collaborative problem solving, consensus building, resolution of disagreements, and ongoing self-evaluation (see Friend & Cook, 1996; Nastasi et al., 2004; Rosenfield & Gravois, 1996). Moreover, effective partnerships that lead to ownership and capacity building require a sense of equality and humility among members in terms of power and perceived value to the process. Indeed, external consultants who achieve stakeholder ownership should be prepared for being viewed as obsolete by partners, by the end of the process.

APPLICATION: BUILDING CAPACITY IN INTERNATIONAL ARENAS

The capacity to develop and sustain school psychology as a profession is likely to be one of the major challenges in settings where school psychology is nonexistent or emerging. For example, establishing school psychology services requires professionals with relevant skills (e.g., intervention, research, assessment, consultation). As suggested by the data from Jimerson et al. (2007), the pool of professionals is limited or insufficient in some countries. Preparing sufficient numbers of qualified school psychologists requires relevant training programs, and the faculty to staff university programs. Thus, capacity building may require not only developing curriculum for training programs in school psychology, but also building capacity among existing faculty (e.g., facilitating professional development and respecialization of academic psychologists) and building capacity within the university for ongoing professional development of faculty. As we discuss in subsequent sections, capacity building is not equivalent to transporting existing models (e.g., school psychology training in Western countries) to new contexts. Instead, capacity building in new settings requires careful attention to the unique cultural and contextual variables. Existing models, however, do provide a starting point. As we proceed through the 10 phases of program development, we articulate the process of building culturally constructed models from existing models.

Phase 1. Existing Models

Developing school psychology in settings where it is nonexistent or emerging begins with examining existing models for practice and training, such as national or regional training and practice standards developed in the U.S. (National Association of School Psychologists, NASP, 2010a, 2010b; Blueprint III, Ysseldyke et al., 2006; documents available at *www.nasponline.org*) and Europe (European Federation of Psychologists Association, EFPA; *www.efpa.edu*), respectively, or the international training standards developed by International School Psychology Association (ISPA, *www.ispaweb.org*). Program developers might gather examples of training programs from other universities throughout the world, and especially those from similar cultures or contexts. Similarly, program developers might examine models for delivery of school psychological services from other countries and contexts. These examples provide a basis for identifying common competencies (knowledge, attitudes, skills), training experiences (e.g., coursework, field experiences),

and services (e.g., assessment, consultation, prevention). Furthermore, professional literature provides the basis for identifying evidence-based practices (i.e., those supported by research or empirical evidence) such as approaches to intervention and assessment. A key consideration for evidence-based practice, of course, is the cultural and contextual relevance of supportive evidence. Program developers must ask themselves whether practices developed and tested in specific countries or cultures can be generalized to target settings; for example, whether the evidence from U.S.-based programs is sufficient to guide interventions in South Asia or the Middle East. Nevertheless, it is important for program developers to be knowledgeable about the existing evidence base relevant to school psychology.

Although the existing standards and programs provide a starting point for considering essential components of emerging programs, these are insufficient for guiding culturally constructed program development. Thus, program developers would benefit from models for international development or capacity building within school psychology or other disciplines. For example, the respective histories of school psychology in Greece (Hatzichristou, 1998; Hatzichristou, Polychroni, & Georgouleas, 2007) and Hong Kong (Lam, 2007; Jennings, Ehrhardt, & Poling, 2008) provide examples of recent developments in professional preparation and service delivery. The *Handbook of International School Psychology* (Jimerson et al., 2007) provides information on the history and current status of school psychology in 43 countries. Jennings et al. offer a cross-regional comparison in three countries (China, Hong Kong, Taiwan) which are similar in language, culture and values, but differ in history and professional practice of school psychology; this comparison provides insights on factors that contributed to development of alternative models. Current efforts are underway in low-income countries such as Bangladesh (Sayeed & Robinson, 2008), where, until very recently, school psychology was nonexistent. Forthcoming descriptions of the evolutions of these programs are expected to provide insights for other countries interested in introducing school psychology.

Outside of school psychology are models for community development exemplified by the work of Nelson and Prilleltensky (2005), and models for international development such as those of Oxfam (Eade, 1997) and the World Health Organization (2005b, 2008a). These approaches reflect concerted efforts to address issues related to poverty, public education, public health, inequity, and oppression. Evident across these models is the commitment to *social justice* on an international level, *empowerment* of local stakeholders as agents of sustained development, *partnerships* on local and global levels, *capacity building* in governmental and nongovernmental arenas, and *cultural construction* through grassroots involvement and understanding of local needs and resources.

Phase 2. Learning the Culture

The existing models identified in Phase 1 provide the basis for understanding the broad *professional culture*, in this case, conceptual models for school psychology training, models for international development and capacity building, and theoretical-empirical foundations of school psychology practice. The professional culture also includes the conceptual foundations of external consultants or program developers. Thus, understanding culture requires articulation of the personal theories of those professionals guiding the process. Nastasi et al. (2004) define *personal theory* as

. . . the theoretical or philosophical perspective that guides the work and actions of individuals. Personal theory is continuously evolving and represents the accumulated integration of education, professional experience, and personal and cultural experiences into a coherent framework for making sense of the world. (p. 82)

For professionals, developing personal theory requires engaging in reflective practice, or the ongoing examination of the links among theory, research, and practice (c.f., Brammer, Shostrom, & Abrego, 1989). Nastasi et al. provide strategies for facilitating articulation of personal theory by consultants and program developers, as well as local stakeholders (readers are referred to that source for more information).

The cultural construction process also requires in-depth understanding of the local *cultural and contextual realities*. These include the conceptual foundations or personal theories specific to local stakeholders, including policymakers, program planners, academics, administrators, practitioners (e.g., mental health and health service providers, educators), and consumers such as community members, parents, and the school-age population. In addition, cultural/contextual realities include characteristics, needs, and resources of the target setting (country, community, university, public health and educational resources, etc.). Thus, *learning the culture* encompasses investigation of cultural realities (knowledge, beliefs, attitudes, practices,

normative behaviors) of the local population and setting (thus, yielding an *emic,* or insider, perspective), as well as the cultural realities of the external and internal professional community (*etic*, or outsider, perspective). The process of learning the culture begins as one enters the system (organization, community, country), and continues throughout the program development process. In Phase 4, Formative Research, we discuss the use qualitative and mixed-methods research for gaining an understanding of the cultural and contextual factors relevant to the development of school psychology within diverse international settings.

Phase 3. Mission/Goal Determination

This phase of program development involves the identification of mission or goals. Using a participatory approach, program developers work with local stakeholders to identify the purpose or mission of school psychology within the given context. At this point, the focus should be broad and long-term, as data from formative research (Phase 4) are used subsequently to delineate more specific short-term and intermediate goals and objectives. The basis for discussion should include outcomes of Phases 1 and 2. Data on existing models, for example, might include exemplars of the missions of other school psychology training programs or professional school psychology organizations such as ISPA, or social, health, and educational goals of community and international development efforts (see discussion in earlier sections on Global Influences and Current Status). Moreover, data from Phase 2 can assist stakeholders in initial identification of cultural and contextual needs.

Using the available information (integrated and summarized for stakeholders), program developers guide stakeholders through a participatory problem-solving approach. This approach involves stakeholders in brainstorming key concerns and desired outcomes, and reaching consensus through a facilitated discussion and negotiation process. Once goals are agreed upon, the stakeholder group (i.e., partners or planning team) then generates a set of questions to guide formative research in the next phase.

Phase 4. Formative Research

Research plays a key role in this cultural construction process. Data about cultural conceptions related to goals/mission proposed in Phase 3, context-specific needs and resources, prevalence of physical and mental health or educational concerns among the school-age population, and potential facilitators and barriers to program development are necessary to guide decision making and construction of a local model. Decisions specific to conducting formative research include (a) generating research questions, (b) identifying research methods, (c) securing and/or training research staff, and (d) establishing systems for data monitoring, analysis, and dissemination.

RESEARCH QUESTIONS

The specific questions that guide research in this phase are based on the goals identified in Phase 3. For example, assume the stakeholder team identified national goals relevant to ensuring access to public education, and promoting physical and psychological well-being of all children and adolescents (regardless of gender, ethnicity, religion, etc.), and generated "research" questions such as the following:

1. *What is the current status of public education within the country?* Who has access? What is the nature of educational curriculum? What are the qualifications of teachers? What is the teacher–student ratio?

2. *What are the facilitators and barriers to access to public education?* Are particular groups denied access (e.g., based on gender, socioeconomic status)? Are the number of schools and teachers insufficient in some communities (e.g., rural vs. urban)? What are the national and local laws governing public education? What are the perceptions of the community members and parents about need for and access to education?

3. *How do stakeholders define "psychological well-being"?* What does it mean to policymakers, educators, parents, health professionals, children and adolescents? How do these conceptions differ? How do stakeholders define "psychologically healthy" environments (e.g., families, communities, schools that facilitate mental health of children and adolescents)? How do parents, teachers, and peers contribute to psychological well-being of children and adolescents? What are the key stressors for children and adolescents? How do children and adolescents cope with personal, social, and environmental stressors? What are the primary support systems for children and adolescents? (A similar set of questions can be posed to examine cultural conceptions of *physical health*, or to examine *well-being* as a general concept that encompasses both physical and psychological health.)

4. *What are the primary concerns regarding physical health and psychological well-being of children and adolescents?* What are the concerns from the multiple perspectives of parents, teachers, medical professionals, mental health professionals, children and adolescents, policymakers, school administrators, community leaders?

5. *Who are the health and mental health providers?* Are they accessible to all segments of the population? What services do they provide—are services available at primary (prevention), secondary (early intervention, risk reduction), and tertiary (treatment) levels? What services are available in schools or in the community to address physical/medical, learning, behavioral, social, and emotional needs of children and adolescents? Are there professional psychologists available? Are there psychologists specifically prepared to work with children, adolescents, and families? To work in schools? Are nurses or consulting physicians available in schools? Are there medical personnel who specialize in adolescents? What are the barriers and facilitators related to providing health care (physical and mental health) to children, adolescents, and families?

6. *What is the status of school psychology as a profession in country?* Are training (professional preparation) programs available? What is the nature of those programs (curriculum, field experiences, level of preparation)? Is school psychology a recognized profession? Are there professional organizations for school psychologists? Is there a body of literature that provides the theoretical and empirical basis for the practice of school psychology? Is there ongoing research that addresses the culture-specific needs of the population? Is there a culturally relevant evidence base for practice (assessment, intervention, etc.)? (See also the list of external and internal conditions identified by Oakland & Jimerson, 2007.)

The first step in the research process is to review the questions generated by the planning team, and make sure they are stated in researchable terms (and revise accordingly). The resulting questions form the basis for initial data collection; consistent with the recursive nature of the process, other questions are likely to emerge during this phase and through subsequent phases of this process.

RESEARCH METHODS

The next step in the process is to identify the target population and specify the methods for sampling and data collection. To facilitate the recursive process and achieve cultural and contextual specificity, we recommend *participatory action research using mixed qualitative–quantitative methods.*[1] Action research (AR), derived from applied anthropology (Greenwood, Whyte, & Harkavy, 1993; J. J. Schensul & S. L. Schensul, 1992) and consistent with data-based problem solving in school psychology, involves a recursive theory–research–action/practice process to achieve social and cultural change. In AR, existing theory and formative research guide action (community change, program development, psychological practice); subsequent research (evaluation) informs adaptations to practice and contributes to existing theory and research. Participatory action research (PAR) requires involvement of key stakeholders as partners in the theory–research–action process. The mixed-methods approach is best characterized as a recursive use of qualitative and quantitative research methods to inform program development and adaptation (Nastasi, et al., 2004; Nastasi, Hitchcock, Sarkar et al., 2007). Qualitative research methods (e.g., participant observation, in-depth interviews, document/archive review, particularly within ethnographic or grounded theory tradition; see Appendix) are used to identify culture- and context-specific factors, generate local (context-specific) or grounded (i.e., based in the experiences of the target population or culture) theory, formulate and modify culture- and context-specific interventions, and document program implementation. Quantitative methods are used to establish prevalence rates (e.g., in communities, schools), assess and diagnose individuals, and evaluate program effectiveness. Whereas qualitative methods can contribute to the in-depth understanding of key constructs and identification of factors specific to the context (e.g., community) or culture (e.g., country, region, ethnic), quantitative methods can provide a normative perspective and validate program-related changes at individual and population levels.

RESEARCH STAFF

Researchers with relevant expertise should take leadership for research activities and provide consultation regarding the hiring and/or training of research staff. Training stakeholders in data collection and analysis techniques is an important step in capacity building. With appropriate preparation and supervision, paraprofessional research staff can develop necessary expertise for participation in subsequent efforts. In addition, involving representatives of key stakeholder groups as research team members can facilitate access to target populations and settings.

DATA MONITORING, ANALYSIS, AND DISSEMINATION

Professional researchers should take leadership in decision making about data monitoring, analysis, and dissemination. Stakeholders can take multiple roles, for example, as research staff (trained by lead researchers) and as partners in dissemination. The analysis and presentation of data are driven by the research questions, intended audiences, and program goals. We return to the earlier example of goals focused on public education and promoting psychological and physical well-being, and the related research questions that address status of public education and physical and mental health care, school psychology as a profession, and cultural conceptions (definitions, language, perceptions, etc.) related to psychological and physical well-being (see section on Phase 4). Table 41.3 provides a matrix to guide decisions about data analysis and dissemination using the previous example. Each of the three major domains (education, physical health, mental health) could encompass several subdomains such as policy level, physical infrastructure, personnel, information technology, service delivery, and target population. Data also can be organized by source (e.g., interviews with teachers, observations in community clinics, statistics on prevalence of specific diseases or mental health concerns). Intended audience would encompass the full range of stakeholder groups with vested interests or resources; for example, policymakers, national and regional ministers of health and education, teachers, parents, adolescents, and community leaders. Selection of the specific categories for inclusion in the table is driven by the goals of the development team, with content dependent on the data sources and intended audiences. Once data are compiled, decisions about dissemination involve considerations of the interests and educational levels of consumers, and potential outlets for reaching consumers. Stakeholders can help program planners make decisions about specific messages and media outlets. To address the needs of diverse stakeholder groups, dissemination takes multiple forms; for example, written briefings for policymakers, oral presentation at town meetings, and technical presentations to university administrators. At this stage in program development, the purpose of dissemination is to inform consumers, gather feedback, and engage consumers (stakeholders) in decision making.

Table 41.3 Sample matrix for planning data analysis and dissemination

Domain	Needs	Resources	Facilitators	Barriers	Cultural Conceptions	Intended Audience
Education						
Physical Health						
Mental Health						

Phase 5. Culturally Constructed (Local) Model

During this phase, program developers work in partnership with stakeholders (specifically, the planning team) to develop a model that guides cultural construction of school psychology within the given country, region, and/or community. The team has available the data or outcomes from the prior phases: existing theory, research, conceptual models (Phase 1); culture-specific needs and resources relevant to population (Phase 2); proposed mission/goals and research questions (Phase 3); and formative research data (Phase 4). Through a process of participatory problem solving (discussion, negotiation, consensus building, resolving discrepancies), the planning team develops a local model for school psychology that addresses the relevant cultural and contextual factors. The local model provides direction for the work of the subsequent phases.

At a minimum, the model should include mission, goals and objectives, professional competencies for school psychologists, and components of a comprehensive service delivery model. Although existing models can provide guidance, the aim of this phase is to construct a model that is culturally and contextually relevant. Program planners should avoid duplicating extant systems and processes from other countries or communities without due consideration of the current local conditions (e.g., needs of population, status of public education) and the current state of the art/science (e.g., models for comprehensive mental health, evidence base for practice, technology).

Based on the historical trajectory of established school psychology programs in the U.S. and Western European countries (during the last half of the twentieth century), Oakland (2003) and Oakland and Jimerson (2007) proposed that certain existing conditions may be necessary to establish professional school psychology, such as an established system of public education that includes special education (i.e., for individuals with identified learning and emotional/behavioral problems), presence of a general discipline of psychology, and availability of standardized tests. Perhaps these conditions are not necessary to develop new programs in the twenty-first century. Alternatively, we propose that future efforts to develop professional school psychology consider the current and emerging models of practice; for example, as evident in NASP's Blueprint III (Ysseldyke et al., 2006), recommendations from the 2002 Multisite Conference on the Future of School Psychology (which included international representatives; Harrison et al., 2004), recent training and practice standards proposed by the European Federation of Psychologists' Associations (EFPA; www.efpa.eu), and emerging models for promoting psychological well-being of youth in Europe (WHO, 2008a).

Rather than recreating the trajectory that began 50 years ago (Fagan, 2002), it behooves program planners to take advantage of current thinking and technology, and engage in a creative process of constructing school psychology of today. Instead of waiting for the development of public education, stakeholders might propose a model in which psychological services become an integral part of efforts to develop public education. Additionally, instead of restricting school psychologists to limited diagnostic and prescriptive roles (which psychologists in the U.S. are still struggling to overcome; Fagan, 2002; Reschly, 2000), planners could propose a model in which school psychologists become mental health service providers and partners in joint efforts to integrate comprehensive health programs in government-funded schools. Or, instead of duplicating a system in which standardized tests have been central to school psychology practice (such as the system in the U.S.), planners could examine alternatives to assessment that are more directly tied to intervention and evaluation. Thus, school psychological services could encompass a continuum of services, ranging from mental health promotion as part of general education, to consultation with parents and teachers for students at risk for learning or behavior problems, to direct service provision through individual and group therapy, to coordination of research and evaluation that inform program monitoring and development, to advocacy work at systems and policy levels. Working in settings where school psychology is nonexistent or newly emerging provides a prospect for creating a different system of service provision that benefits from current knowledge, and addresses specific cultural and contextual needs. Developing programs that move beyond the boundaries of school psychology and education, however, requires partnerships with stakeholders from a range of disciplines (e.g., medicine, public health, community development) and sectors of society (government, nongovernmental organizations, informal community networks). Models for such partnerships can be found in community and international development work (e.g., Eade, 1997; J. J. Schensul, & S. L. Schensul, 1992; S. L. Schensul, Nastasi, & Verma, 2006).

Phases 6 through 8. Local Program Design, Implementation, Evaluation/Revision

Decisions about program model provide the direction for subsequent activities related to program design, implementation, and evaluation. A full articulation of the considerations and activities related to Phases 6 through 8 are beyond the scope of this chapter. We briefly address these three phases concurrently, and refer readers to other sources for more detail (Kratochwill & Stoiber, 2000a, 2000b; Nastasi et al., 2004; Schaughency & Ervin, 2006; Stollar et al., 2006; WHO, 2005b, 2008a).

Key considerations in program design include specifying long- and short-tem objectives, identifying local needs and resources, establishing timelines, securing and training staff, identifying key stakeholders for involvement in planning, implementation, and oversight (e.g., as part of a leadership team), and identifying and securing necessary external resources (e.g., professional expertise, technology, funding). Broad-based programming (e.g., integrated public education/health) requires bringing together representatives from different disciplines and different sectors of society, formulating leadership teams, securing the necessary political and community support, and identifying sources of financial support (e.g., government, private, local, international). Program design also includes plans for program implementation, oversight, evaluation, and modifications to meet diverse cultural and contextual needs.

Establishing school psychology training and practice in new settings will likely require developing culture-specific assessment and intervention technology, and documenting effectiveness of program components. A systemic plan for formative and summative evaluation is critical, and should include a participatory action research and mixed-method approach consistent with the model of formative research in Phase 3. Thus, program implementation and evaluation is recursive, with evaluation data informing program monitoring and modification. In addition, stakeholders are involved as partners in review of evaluation data and decision making about program changes. Systematic documentation of this data-based decision making process is necessary for facilitating sustainability and translation to other settings.

Phase 9. Program Sustainability and Institutionalization

Ensuring that programs continue once local stakeholders assume full responsibility (e.g., after external consultants depart or initial funding expires) is dependent on the local capacity to both sustain efforts and develop new efforts. Thus, initial program planning should address long-term goals related to sustainability (continuing initial efforts) and institutionalization (ensuring the local infrastructure necessary for sustainability). Drawing on work of international development organizations such as Oxfam (Eade, 1997), Nastasi et al. (2004) discuss capacity building for comprehensive school-based mental health service delivery. The key principles highlighted by Nastasi and colleagues include:

1. Capacity building goes beyond the initial program and requires preparation for sustainable program development.

2. Change efforts occur within an evolving physical, social, cultural, and historical context (ecology). Local capacity to respond to the changing nature of the ecology is critical for sustainability.

3. Social/cultural change is a long-term goal, and dependent on capacity for sustainability in the context of changing needs.

4. Empowerment of stakeholders is critical to sustainable social/cultural change, and is influenced by the sense of ownership and relevant skill development.

5. Capacity building is not a specific strategy, but rather a long-term process of developing necessary resources, infrastructure, and people-power.

6. The fundamental goal of social/cultural change and capacity building is *people-centered* (Eade, 1997). For school psychology, the ultimate

measure of success is well-being of children, adolescents, and families; and professional school psychology is the mechanism.

Phase 10. Program Translation/Dissemination

As depicted in Figure 41.1, the cycle is completed through program translation and dissemination, which in turn contributes to existing models based on theory, research, and practice. Consistent with participatory action research, the theory–research–practice cycle is continual. At the local level, ongoing data collection informs the local conceptual model that in turn guides local practices. This cycle is important to the sustainability of conceptually driven, evidence-based programming, and to the changing nature of the local ecology, whether applied to school psychology training or practice. This final phase, however, takes the theory–research–practice cycle to a more global level of informing the translation to other, similar settings (e.g., establishing psychological services in different school districts, or developing school psychology training programs in other regions or countries). Furthermore, through dissemination to professional audiences (e.g., through international journals, conferences, program development manuals), lessons learned within one setting can contribute to development in other settings.

Consistent with dilemmas related to translation of evidence-based practices (e.g., educational or psychological interventions; Kratochwill & Stoiber, 2000a, 2000b; Nastasi & Schensul, 2005), translation of school psychology program development requires consideration of the cultural and contextual similarities between the original and intended application sites. Thus, a program of training and service delivery that works in South Africa may not work in Southern India. To ensure the cultural construction of school psychology, program planners in the new setting need to repeat the cycle of participatory data-based decision making depicted in Figure 41.1. However, planners can learn from the experiences of others. The extent to which we can translate practices across settings and populations is dependent on in-depth documentation of program development (design, implementation, evaluation), so that consumers can determine the degree of transferability that is possible. Thus, systematic documentation and in-depth reporting (detailed descriptions of the conditions surrounding program implementation) via program manuals can facilitate translation to other settings.

Conclusions

In his message on Mental Health Day (10 October 2008), the Secretary-General of the United Nations highlighted the challenges in providing mental health services, and urged all stakeholders (e.g., government, funders, public health organizations, mental health professionals, consumers) to work in partnership to advocate for, and bring about action to ensure, mental health on a global level. In addition, he emphasized the importance of mental health to overall well-being: "Mental health is of paramount importance for personal well-being, family relationships, and an individual's ability to contribute to society. On this World Mental Health Day, let us recognize that there can be no health without mental health" (For full text, see *http://www.who.int/mental_health/mhgap/ UN_speech_mhgap_english.pdf*).

Similarly, the U.N. Millennium Development Goals (see Table 41.1), which have influenced WHO priorities for the millennium, called attention to the social, health, and educational priorities for international development. One of the MGDs is to achieve universal primary education. The potential intersection of public health and public education as the context for addressing these international priorities provides an exceptional opportunity for international school psychology.

Concurrent with efforts by the U.N. and the WHO, professional organizations in psychology are calling for international development. For example, ISPA is engaged in efforts to support development of new training programs (Farrell, 2008) and multi-country research projects (Lam & Jimerson, 2008; Nastasi et al., 2008). Moreover, in recognition of the need for a more global perspective in American psychology, the Education Directorate of the American Psychological Association (APA) convened a conference on internationalizing the psychology curriculum in the U.S. (Internationalizing Psychology Education, Washington, DC, September 6–9, 2008; *http://www.apa.org/ed/ governance/elc/2008/index.aspx*). Within the conference context, "internationalizing" psychology was broadly defined as integrating a global focus into curriculum of existing post-secondary (university-level undergraduate and graduate) programs of psychology, providing study-abroad opportunities for students, facilitating international exchange (faculty and students) across universities in different countries, and expanding the current conceptions of multicultural education in the U.S. to encompass an international perspective.

Marsella (2008), one of the invited speakers to the aforementioned APA conference, reiterated the significance of internationalizing psychology for expanding our current understanding of multiculturalism and multicultural competencies, developing technology that increases the educational interactions of individuals globally (e.g., distance education), and addressing global challenges such as war, ethnic conflicts, terrorism, poverty, well-being and mental health, racism, sexism, substance abuse, migration and refugees, and the status of universal education (see also Marsella, 1998; Marsella & Pederson, 2004). Achieving these goals requires more extensive international research to better understand the cultural and contextual factors that influence psychological well-being. This research is likely to require expanding the longstanding tradition of quantitative research methods to include qualitative and mixed-methods approaches as foundational to research in psychology. Researchers (e.g., Leong & Ponterotto, 2003; Marsella, 1998), for example, have called for the use of qualitative research (e.g., ethnography, phenomenology, narrative, grounded theory) to develop *global-community psychology*[2], and to provide a voice (*emic* perspective) to culturally diverse populations who have been previously silenced; and for the use of mixed-methods research (Hitchcock et al., 2005, 2006; Nastasi, Hitchcock, Burkholder et al., 2007; Nastasi, Hitchcock, Sarkar et al., 2007) to facilitate development of culturally specific constructs, assessment measures, and interventions.

To capitalize on the current global concerns relevant to psychology and education, we propose the following recommendations for actions by school psychologists collectively and individually.

1. Communicate with school psychologists in other countries to share information (learn from each other) and collaborate on cross-cultural projects focused on research, training, and practice.

2. Engage in international collaborative research efforts, such as the recent efforts sponsored by ISPA.

3. Broaden the focus of school psychology to include global social issues that influence psychological well-being (e.g., war, poverty, discrimination, migration, marginalization, and oppression).

4. Collaborate with professionals in other disciplines, including public health, education, and other social scientists, in order to expand the knowledge base and expertise relevant to school psychology.

5. Promote partnerships of school psychologists and school psychology professional associations with government and nongovernmental agencies to facilitate policy change (Mpfou, Peltzer, Shumba, Serpell & Mogaji, 2005).

6. Position school psychology solidly within the intersection of public education and public health (Nastasi, 2004).

7. Capitalize on international public health efforts such as those of the WHO, especially with reference to inclusion of mental health as integral part of primary health care.

8. Within specific countries, expand school psychology programs to encompass a global perspective.

At no period in history has the profession of school psychology been in a better position to actively participate in global efforts to enhance the lives of children, adolescents, and their families. The intersection of international priorities, current technology for communication, emerging methodologies for collaboration and research, and existing models for international development, makes for optimal conditions to engage in meaningful partnerships to address social issues and promote psychological well-being on a global level. With systematic, coordinated efforts, perhaps the twenty-first century can become the era of *global-community*[2] *school psychology*.

Endnotes

1. Articulation of mixed methods designs and specific qualitative and quantitative methods goes beyond the scope of this chapter. A list of suggested articles and texts are provided in the Appendix.
2. Marsella (1998) proposed the term *global-community psychology* to represent foundations across the multiple cultures, nations, disciplines, and sectors that represent the global community.

Appendix
Suggested Readings on Research Designs and Methods
QUALITATIVE RESEARCH

Camic, P. M., Rhodes, J. E., & Yardley, L. (Eds.). (2003). *Qualitative research in psychology: Expanding perspectives in methodology and design.* Washington, DC: APA.

Denzin, N. K., & Lincoln, Y. S. (Eds.). (2000). *Handbook of qualitative research* (2nd ed.). Thousand Oaks, CA: Sage.

Leech, N. L., & Onwuegbuzie, A. J. (2008). Qualitative data analysis: A compendium of technique and a framework for selection of school psychology research and beyond. *School Psychology Quarterly, 23,* 587–604.

Lincoln, Y. S., & Guba, E. G. (1985). *Naturalistic inquiry.* Thousand Oaks: CA. Sage.

Nastasi, B. K. (2008). Advances in qualitative research. In T. B. Gutkin & C. R. Reynolds (Eds.), *The handbook of school psychology* (4th ed.; pp. 30–53). NY: Wiley.

Nastasi, B. K., & Schensul, S. L. (2005). Contributions of qualitative research to the validity of intervention research. Special issue of *Journal of School Psychology, 43* (3), 177–195.

Schensul, J. J., & LeCompte, M. D. (Eds.). (1999). *Ethnographer's toolkit* (Volumes 1–7). Walnut Creek, CA: AltaMira Press.

Strauss, A., & Corbin, J. (1990). *Basics of qualitative research: Grounded theory procedures and techniques.* Thousand Oaks, CA: Sage.

Spradley, J. P. (1979). *The ethnographic interview.* NY: Holt, Rinehart, Winston.

Spradley, J. P. (1980). *Participant observation.* NY: Holt, Rinehart, Winston.

MIXED METHODS RESEARCH

Nastasi, B. K., Hitchcock, J., Sarkar, S., Burkholder, G., Varjas, K., & Jayasena, A. (2007). Mixed methods in intervention research: Theory to adaptation. *Journal of Mixed Methods Research, 1,* 164–182.

Tashakkori, A., & Teddlie, C. (2010). *Handbook of mixed methods in social and behavioral research.* (2nd ed.) Thousand Oaks, CA: Sage.

EXPERIMENTAL DESIGNS

Flay, R.B., Biglan, A., Boruch, R.F., Castro, F.G., Gottfredson, D., Kellam, S., Moscicki, E.K., Schinke, S., Valentice, J.C., & Ji, P. (2005). Standards of evidence: Criteria for efficacy, effectiveness and dissemination. *Prevention Science, 6(3),* 151–175.

Shadish, W.R., Cook, T.D., & Campbell, D.T. (2002). *Experimental and quasi-experimental designs for generalized causal inference.* Boston: Houghton- Mifflin.

EVALUATION RESEARCH

Chatterji, M. (2004–2005). Evidence on "What Works": An argument for extended-term mixed-method (ETMM) evaluation designs. *Educational Researcher, 33(9),* 3–13. [Corrected version reprinted in 2005, Educational Researcher, 34(5), 14–24]

Fetterman, D., & Wandersman, A. (2005). *Empowerment evaluation principles in practice.* New York: Guilford.

Nastasi, B. K., & Hitchcock, J. H. (2008). Evaluating quality and effectiveness of population-based services. In B. J. Doll & J. A. Cummings (Eds.), *Transforming school mental health services: Population-based approaches to promoting the competency and wellness of children* (pp. 245–276). Thousand Oaks, CA: Corwin Press with National Association of School Psychologists.

Nastasi, B. K., & Hitchcock, J. (2009). Challenges of evaluating multi-level interventions. *American Journal of Community Psychology, 43,* 360–376.

References

Brammer, L. M., Shostrom, E. L., & Abrego, P. J. (1989). *Therapeutic psychology: Fundamentals of counseling and psychotherapy* (5th ed.). Englewood Cliffs, NJ: Prentice-Hall.

DeJong, T. (2000). The role of the school psychologist in developing a health-promoting school. *School Psychology International, 21,* 339–357.

DiClemente, R. J., Hansen, W. B., & Ponton, L. E. (1996). *Handbook of adolescent health risk behavior.* NY: Plenum.

Eade, D. (1997). *Capacity-building: An approach to people-centered development.* Oxford, England: Oxfam.

Fagan, T. K. (2002). School psychology: Recent descriptions, continued expansion, and an ongoing paradox. [Special issue] *School Psychology Review, 31,* 5–10.

Farrell, P. T., Jimerson, S. R., & Oakland, T. D. (2007). School psychology internationally: A synthesis of findings. In S. R. Jimerson, T. D. Oakland, & P. T. Farrell (Eds), *The handbook of international school psychology* (pp. 501–510). Thousand Oaks, CA: Sage.

Friend, M., & Cook, L. (1996). *Interactions: Collaboration skills for school professionals* (2nd ed.). White Plains, NY: Longman.

Greenwood, D. J., Whyte, W. F., & Harkavy, I. (1993). Participatory action research as a process and as a goal. *Human Relations, 46,* 175–192.

Gutkin, T. B. (2008). Ecological school psychology: A personal opinion and a plea for change. In T. B. Gutkin & C. R. Reynolds (Eds.), *The handbook of school psychology* (4th ed.). NY: Wiley.

Harrison, P. L., Cummings, J. A., Dawson, M., Short, R. J., Gorin, S., & Palomares, R., (2004). Responding to the needs of children, families, and schools: The 2002 Multisite Conference on the Future of School Psychology. [special issue] *School Psychology Review, 33,* 12–33.

Hatzichristou, C. (1998). Alternative school psychological services: Development of a databased model. *School Psychology Review, 27,* 246–259.

Hatzichristou, C., Polychroni, F., & Georgouleas, G. (2007). School psychology in Greece. In S. R. Jimerson, T. D. Oakland, & P. T. Farrell (Eds.), *The handbook of international school psychology* (pp. 135–146). Thousand Oaks, CA: Sage.

Hitchcock, J. H, Nastasi, B. K., Dai, D. C., Newman, J., Jayasena, A., Bernstein-Moore, R., Sarkar, S., & Varjas, K. (2005). Illustrating a mixed-method approach for identifying and validating culturally specific constructs. *Journal of School Psychology, 43(3),* 259–278.

Hitchcock, J. H., Sarkar, S., Nastasi, B. K., Burkholder, G., Varjas, K., & Jayasena, A. (2006). Validating culture- and gender-specific constructs: A mixed-method approach to advance assessment procedures in cross-cultural settings. *Journal of Applied School Psychology, 22,* 13–33.

Jennings, R. L., Ehrhardt, K., & Poling, A. (2008). A bibliometric analysis of *School Psychology International* 1995–2007. *School Psychology International, 29,* 515–528.

Jimerson, S. R., Graydon, K., Farrell, P., Kikas, E., Hatzichristou, C., Boce, E., Bashi, G., & International School Psychology Association Research Committee. (2004). The International School Psychology Survey: Development and data from Albania, Cyprus, Estonia, Greece and Northern England. *School Psychology International, 25,* 259–286.

Jimerson, S. R., Graydon, K., Skokut, M., Alghorani, M. A., Kanjaradze, A., Forster, J., & the International School Psychology Association Research Committee. (2008). The International School Psychology Survey: Data from Georgia, Switzerland and the United Arab Emirates. *School Psychology International, 29,* 5–28.

Jimerson, S. R., Graydon, K., Yuen, M., Lam, S.-F., Thurm, J.-M., Klueva, N., Coyne, J., Loprete, L. J., Phillips, J., & International School Psychology Association Research Committee (2006). The International School Psychology Survey: Development and data from Australia, China, Germany, Italy and Russia. *School Psychology International, 27,* 5–32.

Jimerson, S. R., Oakland, T. D., & Farrell, P. T. (Eds.) (2007). *The handbook of international school psychology*. Thousand Oaks, CA: Sage.

Jimerson, S. R., Skokut, M., Cardenas, S., Malone, H., & Stewart, K. (2008). Where in the world is school psychology? Examining evidence of school psychology around the globe. *School Psychology International, 29*, 131–144.

Kleinman, A., Eisenberg, L., & Good, B. (1978). Culture, illness, and care: Critical lessons from anthropological and cross-cultural research. *Annals of Internal Medicine, 88*, 251–258.

Kolbe, L. J., Collins, J., & Cortese, P. (1997). Building the capacity of schools to improve the health of the nation: A call for assistance from psychologists. *American Psychologist, 52*, 256–265.

Kratochwill, T. R., & Stoiber, K. C. (2000a). Empirically supported interventions and school psychology: Rationale and methodological issues—Part I. *School Psychology Quarterly, 15*, 75–106.

Kratochwill, T. R., & Stoiber, K. C. (2000b). Empirically supported interventions and school psychology: Rationale and methodological issues—Part II. *School Psychology Quarterly, 15*, 233–253.

Kubiszyn, T. (1999). Integrating health and mental health services in schools: Psychologists collaborating with primary care providers. *Clinical Psychology Review, 19*, 179–198.

Lakin, R., & Mahoney, A. (2006). Empowering youth to change their world: Identifying key components of a community service program to promote positive development. *Journal of School Psychology, 44*, 513–531.

Lam, S.-F. (2007). Educational psychology in Hong Kong. In S. R. Jimerson, T. D. Oakland, & P. T. Farrell (Eds.), *The handbook of international school psychology* (pp. 147–158). Thousand Oaks, CA: Sage.

Lam, S., & Jimerson, S. R. (2008). Exploring student engagement in schools internationally. *World Go Round* (newsletter of International School Psychology Association), *35* (2), 7–8.

Leong, F. T. L., & Ponterotto, J. G. (2003). A proposal for internationalizing counseling psychology in the United States: Rationale, recommendations, and challenges. *The Counseling Psychologist, 31*, 381–395.

Leviton, L. C. (1996). Integrating psychology and public health: Challenges and opportunities. *American Psychologist, 51*, 42–51.

Marsella, A. J. (1998). Toward a "global-community psychology": Meeting the needs of a changing world. *American Psychologist, 53*, 1282–1291.

Marsella, A. J. (2008, Sept). *Psychology in a global era: Foundations, issues, directions.* Presentation at the 2008 APA Education Leadership Conference: Internationalizing Psychology Education, Washington, DC.

Marsella, A. J., & Pederson, P. (2004). Internationalizing the counseling psychology curriculum: Toward new values, competencies, and directions. *Counselling Psychology Quarterly, 17*, 413–423.

Meyers, J., Meyers, A. B., Proctor, S. L., & Graybill, E. C. (2008). Organizational consultation and systems intervention. In T. B. Gutkin & C. R. Reynolds (Eds.), *The handbook of school psychology* (4th ed.; pp. 921–940). NY: Wiley.

Mpfou, E., Peltzer, K., Shumba, A., Serpell, R., & Mogaji, A. (2005). School psychology in Sub-saharan Africa: Results and implications of a six-country survey. In C. L. Frisby & C. R. Reynolds (Eds.), *Comprehensive Handbook of Multicultural School Psychology* (pp. 1128–1150). Hoboken, NJ: Wiley.

Nastasi, B. K. (2000). School psychologists as health-care providers in the 21st century: Conceptual framework, professional identity, and professional practice. *School Psychology Review, 29*, 540–554.

Nastasi, B. K. (2004). Meeting the challenges of the future: Integrating public health and public education for mental health promotion. *Journal of Educational and Psychological Consultation, 15*, 295–312.

Nastasi, B. K., Hitchcock, J. H., Burkholder, G., Varjas, K., Sarkar, S., & Jayasena, A. (2007). Assessing adolescents' understanding of and reactions to stress in different cultures: Results of a mixed-methods approach. *School Psychology International, 28*(2), 163–178.

Nastasi, B. K., Hitchcock, J., Sarkar, S., Burkholder, G., Varjas, K., & Jayasena, A. (2007). Mixed methods in intervention research: Theory to adaptation. *Journal of Mixed Methods Research, 1*(2), 164–182.

Nastasi, B. K. et al. (2008, July). *Promoting Psychological Well-Being Globally Project: Updates from research partners.* Symposium presented at the 30th annual ISPA Conference, Utrecht, The Netherlands.

Nastasi, B. K., Moore, R. B., & Varjas, K. M. (2004). *School-based mental health services: Creating comprehensive and culturally specific programs.* Washington, DC: American Psychological Association.

Nastasi, B. K., & Schensul, S. L. (2005). Contributions of qualitative research to the validity of intervention research. [Special issue] *Journal of School Psychology, 43*, 177–195.

Nastasi, B. K., Varjas, K., Bernstein, R., & Jayasena, A. (2000). Conducting participatory culture-specific consultation: A global perspective on multicultural consultation. *School Psychology Review, 29*, 401–413.

National Association of School Psychologists. (2010a). *NASP Professional Standards: Model for Comprehensive and Integrated School Psychological Services* (formerly Guidelines for the Provision of School Psychological Services). Bethesda, MD: Author.

National Association of School Psychologists. (2010b). *NASP Professional Standards: Standards for the Graduate Preparation of School Psychologists.* Bethesda, MD: Author.

Nelson, G., & Prilleltensky, I. (2005). *Community psychology: In pursuit of liberation and well-being.* New York, NY: Palgrave Macmillan.

Oakland, T. (2003). International school psychology: Psychology's worldwide portal to children and youth. *American Psychologist, 58*, 985–992.

Oakland, T. D., & Cunningham, J. L. (1992). A survey of school psychology in developed and developing countries. *School Psychology International, 13*, 99–129.

Oakland, T. D., & Jimerson, S. R. (2007). School psychology internationally: A retrospective view and influential conditions. In S. R. Jimerson, T. D. Oakland, & P. T. Farrell (Eds), *The handbook of international school psychology* (pp. 453–462). Thousand Oaks, CA: Sage.

Olson, C. L., Evans, R., & Schoenberg, R. F. (2007). *At home in the world: Bridging the gap between internationalization and multicultural education.* Washington, DC: American Council on Education.

Olson, C. L., Green, M. F., & Hill, B. A. (2008). *Building a strategic framework for comprehensive internationalization.* Washington, DC: American Council on Education.

Power, T. J. (2000). Commentary. The school psychologist as community-focused, public health professional: Emerging challenges and implications for training. *School Psychology Review, 29,* 557–559.

Power, T. J. (2003). Promoting children's mental health: Reform through interdisciplinary and community partnerships. [Special issue] *School Psychology Review, 32,* 3–16.

Reschly, D. J. (2000). The present and future status of school psychology in the United States. *School Psychology Review, 29,* 507–522.

Rosenfield, S. A., & Gravois, T. A. (1996). *Instructional Consultation Teams: Collaborating for change.* New York: Guilford.

Sayeed, S., & Robinson, M. (2008). Training programs: University training Bangladesh Educational Psychology training initiative. *World Go Round* (newsletter of International School Psychology Association), *35* (2), 10–11.

Schaughency, E., & Ervin, R. (2006). Building capacity to implement and sustain effective practices to better serve children. [Special Issue] *School Psychology Review, 35,* 155–166.

Schensul, S. L., Nastasi, B. K., & Verma, R.K. (2006). Community-based research in India: A case example of international and interdisciplinary collaboration. *American Journal of Community Psychology, pp 1–17,* [online version] DOI 10.1007/s10464-006-9066-z, URL *http://dx.doi.org/10.1007/s10464-006-9066-z.*

Schensul, J. J., & Schensul, S. L. (1992). Collaborative research: Methods of inquiry for social change. In M. D. LeCompte, W. L. Millroy, & J. Preissle (Eds.). *The handbook of qualitative research in education* (pp. 161–200). San Diego, CA: Academic.

Serrano-Garcia, I. (1990). Implementing research: Putting our values to work. In P. Tolan, C. Keys, F. Chertok, & L. Jason (Eds.), *Researching community psychology: Issues of theory and methods* (pp. 171–182). Washington, DC: American Psychological Association.

Sheridan, S. M., & Gutkin, T. B. (2000). The ecology of school psychology: Examining and changing our paradigm for the 21st century. *School Psychology Review, 29,* 485–502.

Stollar, S. A., Poth, R. L., Curtis, M. J., & Cohen, R. M. (2006). Collaborative strategic planning as illustration of the principles of systems change. *School Psychology Review, 35,* 181–197.

U.S. Department of Health and Human Services (1999). *Mental health: A report of the Surgeon General.* Rockville, MD: U.S. Department of Health and Human Services, Substance Abuse and Mental Health Administration, Center for Mental Health Services, National Institutes of Health, National Institute of Mental Health.

U.S. Department of Health and Human Services (2001). *Mental health: Culture, race, and ethnicity—A supplement to mental health: A report of the Surgeon General.* Rockville, MD: U.S. Department of Health and Human Services, Substance Abuse and Mental Health Administration, Center for Mental Health Services.

United Nations Secretary-General (2008). *Message on World Mental Health Day, 10 October 2008. http://www.who.int/mental_health/mhgap/UN_speech_mhgap_english.pdf;* downloaded 1/6/09)

World Health Organization. (2005a). *Atlas: Child and adolescent mental health. Global concerns: Implications for the future.* Geneva: WHO.

World Health Organization. (2005b). *Promoting mental health: Concepts, emerging evidence, practice.* Geneva: WHO.

World Health Organization. (2008a). *Mental Health Gap Action Programme (mhGAP): Scaling up care for mental, neurological, and substance abuse disorders.* Geneva, WHO.

World Health Organization. (2008b). *Social cohesion for mental well-being among adolescents.* Copenhagen: WHO Regional Office for Europe.

Ysseldyke, J., Burns, M., Dawson, P., Kelley, B., Morrison, D., Ortiz, S., Rosenfiled, S., & Telzrow, C. (2006). *School psychology: A blueprint for training and practice III.* Bethesda, MD: National Association of School Psychologists.

PART 9

Conclusions and Future Directions

Technology in the Practice of School Psychology: The Future is Past Tense

Jack A. Cummings

Abstract

The Internet and advances in computer hardware and software have been transforming the way school psychologists work. How does technology make psychologists' time more efficient, or allow psychologists to do things that would have not been possible or would have been more time consuming without computers and the Internet? Internet search engines, e-book readers, podcasts, blogs, webinars, email, and electronic forums are among the current tools that school psychologists use. These digital tools are covered in the first section of the chapter. The second and third sections examine how various technologies facilitate and/or contribute to improvements in the delivery of psychological interventions and psychological assessment/report writing. The fourth section addresses digital tools and how they have increased opportunities for professional development and the capacity of university professors in school psychology training programs to work with students. Another issue examined in the fourth section is open access to scientific findings and practice–research networks. Finally, concluding comments are offered on technology diffusion and ethical issues associated with the new technologies.

Keywords: assessment technology, computer-based assessment, search engines, school psychology

Society has been profoundly changed as a function of recent technological developments. The World Wide Web (Web), Internet, and personal computer have added a powerful dimension to the way people interact with each other, with businesses, and educationally. Few could have imagined that the Internet, a hardware and software infrastructure that supports communication across the world, could develop into a powerful network of interlinked computers that transmit written text, voice, video and combinations thereof. Nor could anyone have predicted that computers would become commonplace at home, school, and work. The Internet would be a nonentity if it were not for the availability of relatively affordable computers. Just 40 years ago, mainframe computers were the province of universities and large corporations. In the early 1970s desktop microprocessor computers came in kit form, and sold in small numbers. The Apple II+ came out in 1977, and IBM-PC

four years later in 1981. Memory was severely limited, and floppy disks were used to save information. Improvements in processor speed and storage capacity have played a key role in the digital revolution ushering in the information age.

The high speed of information transmission that comes with broadband access has been a factor in making video part of the Internet experience. In June, 2000, less than 5% of American adults had broadband access to the Internet from home, but 8 years later, in April of 2009, the figure was 63%. (Horrigan, 2009). Approximately two-thirds of online Americans have purchased a product over the Internet. According to the Pew Internet and American Life Project, in 2010 59% of all Americans have access to a wireless network through a cell phone or laptop. (Smith, 2010). In December of 2009, 93% of children between ages 12 and 17 reported use of the Internet (Jones & Fox 2009). They used it for online games, videos, virtual worlds, and social networks. The median percent usage by parents of elementary through secondary students was 83%. The penetration of the Internet is increasing for older Americans. In 2005, 25% of those aged 70–75 reported Internet use, while in 2008 it was 45%. For Americans 76 and older in 2005, the Internet was used by 17% but that figure increased to 27% in 2008. Google has become a verb, and when one wants to find information about something, we "google it." The information age has arrived, and we live in an increasingly digital world.

To illustrate the transformation underway: *Education Week* was a print-based weekly newsletter that covered preK–16 topics; with the addition of a website (www.edweek.org), it has expanded to live chats with experts on No Child Left Behind, blogs on the various topics ranging from motivation, special education, school law, to the national presidential campaign, an audio gallery with topics such as single-sex schools, immigration, race plans, and "unschooling," and a video gallery with links to YouTube videos including comments by a school administrator about the operation of their principals' academy, comments by Muslim students about their experiences in schools in the United States, and comments by a Jordanian educator about the influx of 24,000 Iraqi students to his schools. The Internet has allowed the creative team at *Education Week* to develop more dynamic and interactive options, as opposed to a static print-based weekly newsletter.

If the present *Oxford Handbook of School Psychology* had been conceived at the time of the 1979 Spring Hill conference (Ysseldyke and Weinberg, 1981), there would not have been a chapter on technology. The participants at that conference never would have imagined the ease with which information could be accessed and transferred via the Internet. There is an endless array of activities conducted over the Internet. The last quarter-century has been an exciting time. The purpose of this chapter will be to capture the transformations of traditional practice that are changing the way school psychologists work. How does technology make psychologists' time more efficient, or allow psychologists to do things that would have not been possible or would have been more time consuming without computers and the Internet?

The chapter is divided in five sections. The first section will provide a review of current electronic tools, and how access to resources has been greatly facilitated. The digital tools covered in the first section will be technologies that we have access to now. The second and third sections will examine how various technologies facilitate and/or contribute to improvements in the delivery of psychological interventions and psychological assessment/report writing, respectively. The fourth section will be an examination of how digital tools have increased opportunities for professional development, and the capacity of university professors in school psychology training programs to work with students. The fourth section will address open access to scientific findings and practice–research networks. Finally, concluding comments will be offered on technology diffusion and how school psychologists will benefit from new advances in technology.

Access to Resources

Internet search engines, podcasts, blogs, web conferencing software, and discussion forums are electronic tools that permit access to resources and vehicles for interaction.

Resource Gateways: Internet Search Engines

Google, Yahoo!, and Bing search engines are familiar tools that may be used to find websites, images, maps, news and shopping information. Google Scholar (www.scholar.google.com) is a tool for locating journal articles and books. Google Scholar uses an approach similar to the basic Google search engine. Google Scholar ranks articles and books by how often they are found in reference lists of other journal articles and books. The assumption is that if a given work is frequently referenced by others, it is an important article or book. For instance, a Google Scholar search for works on "social learning theory" reveals that Albert Bandura's 1977 book, *Social Learning Theory*, has been cited 8,479 times, so it appears at the top of the list since it is the most cited work on social learning theory. Another option with Google Scholar is to reorder the results of the search and place recent works at the top of the list. When the results for "social learning theory" are reordered, Mischel's 2007 chapter, "Toward a cognitive social learning reconceptualization of personality" appears at the top of the list, with 856 citations. Google Scholar does an excellent job of quickly locating links to current and up-to-date sources. The links typically lead to journal publishers' websites. The publishers often provide the basic bibliographic citation and the abstract, but require a fee to obtain full text access to the journal article. For university faculty and students, the access to full text articles is usually covered by the subscription fee negotiated with the university library.

PsycINFO, PsycARTICLES, Academic Search Elite, and ERIC (EBSCO) are resource gateways to their respective databases of articles. The advantage of these search tools is they provide full text access to journal articles. A major advantage of Internet access to Google Scholar and other scholarly resource gateways is that most scholarly information is available remotely, without regard to where in the world the information seeker may be.

E-Book Readers

The first version of the Kindle was released November 19, 2007. The Kindle is an electronic book reader that uses Amazon's Whispernet wireless service. Books and newspapers are available as downloads. The service uses Sprint's 3G high speed data network via cell phone towers to transfer files to the handheld e-reader, so there is no need for an Internet connection. A book downloads within a minute. Downloads of newspapers may be scheduled by paid subscription. The most recent version is the Kindle DX International 2 and was announced July 1, 2010. It will hold 3,500 books, has an e-ink screen (9.7 inches measured diagonally), and uses the 3G data network. The Barnes & Noble Nook is a competitor to the Kindle and likewise uses a 3G network to allow consumers to download books. It has a smaller screen, 6 inches measured diagonally. Sony and others have e-readers, but an Internet connection is required to download items.

The iPad from Apple is more than e-book reader. It is a tablet computer that allows the user to browse the Internet, stream media, word process, create presentations and edit database files. Within 80 days of the release of the iPad, more than 3 million were sold. The popularity of the iPad will result in comparable products from other manufactures.

Podcasts

On July 14, 2008, the homepage of NASP, www. nasponline.org, had the following announcement, "Download NASP's first-ever podcast and audio versions of selected NASP articles and handouts." At the NASP website one can download a podcast (audio recording as an MP3 file) of a roundtable, hosted by Dan Florell on the topic of homophobia and bullying, that was recorded on June 27, 2008. One can obtain podcasts of selected articles from the *Communiqué* and *School Psychology Review*, as well as a primer for parents on response to intervention, and David Schonfeld's 2008 NASP Conference keynote address, "Supporting Children in the Aftermath of Crisis."

Blogs

Florell (2008) noted that NASP was looking for potential bloggers to post material on the NASP website every three or four days. The Wikipedia definition of blog states:

> A blog (a contraction of the term "Web log") is a Web site, usually maintained by an individual, with regular entries of commentary, descriptions of events, or other material such as graphics or video.

Florell was hoping to find three to four writers to share writings on three topics: early career practice; establishing RTI in a district; and school psychologists on the job. A feature of the blog is that NASP members can comment on the blog and have a dialogue with the blogger.

On August 28, 2008, Kristy Watts started a blog on the NASP website (http://blog.nasponline.org/early_career/index.php). It has her insights on everything from using a sports watch as a stopwatch, to the dilemma of dressing for professional meetings with parents while in the same afternoon sitting on the floor with a preschooler. Her writings provide the human perspective on issues that interns and new psychologists face, but are certainly relevant for experienced psychologists as well. After reading Forrell's (2008) article, I did a Google search for "school psychology blogs." I found a number of informative blogs. The first was Erin King's http://schoolpsychologist-files.blogspot.com. Her blog is oriented to parents. On July 29, 2008, she posted "back to school" suggestions for parents whose children find school difficult. On August 5, 2008 she addressed the differences between an IEP and 504 plan. I was looking at her blog on September 8, 2008 at 3:45pm, and earlier that day she had posted a compilation of comments and links to articles and resources on parent–teacher interactions.

Another school psychologist blog I found with the Google search was Dr. Gaston Weisz' http://drweisz.blogspot.com. His most recent posting was not yet 24 hours old when I visited his blog. He includes links to podcasts he has made that are oriented to teachers. In his podcasts, he emphasizes the importance of evidence-based practices that are founded in scientific literature, but he also addresses teacher Web tools. As of September 24, 2008, he had a series of 33 podcasts.

The Corporate Relations and Business Strategy Staff of American Psychology Association Practice Organization (Corporate Relations and Business Strategy Staff, 2008) advocated the use of blogs as a low-cost strategy to market the practice of psychologists. They note that a "variety of formats lend themselves to blog posts, including topical summaries, quick tips, short anecdotes, commentary on current issues and descriptions of and links to additional sources for information." They emphasize the importance of timely updates to encourage return visitors to the blog. They suggest blogging will help visitors to the site make decisions on whether to seek psychological services. The Corporate Relations and Business Strategy Staff also advocate the use of a website in conjunction with a blog. The blog can feed the website, and vice versa.

As demonstrated by King's and Weisz' blogs, marketing psychological services should not be limited to the province of private practice psychologists. Rather, the same efforts have payoffs for psychologists working in public schools. Sharing comments on timely research findings, providing resources about disability types, and connecting teachers and parents to resources about positive mental health are valuable blog topics appreciated by parents and teachers.

I was surprised to learn that there are many bloggers who list *school psychologist* as their profession. On **www.blogger.com** there are 1,100 bloggers (as of July 21, 2010) who identify themselves as school psychologists. In a period of two years the number of school psychologist bloggers increased more than fivefold.Although, most chronicle family life and document activities of their children, the potential exists for marketing psychological services by targeting blogs to our clients. The websites www.wordpress.com, www.blogger.com, and www.thefreesite.com/Free_Blog_Resources host blogs at no charge.

Webinars

A *webinar* is a form of web conferencing that is conducted live. It can be unidirectional, where audience members use their Internet connection to link to a presentation. Or, it may be interactive by adding email or messaging capability so viewers can ask questions of the presentation, or comment on the points made. The first wide-scale use of an interactive webinar for school psychologists was at the 2002 Multi-site Conference on the Future of School Psychology (Cummings et al, 2004a; Cummings et al, 2004b). The most powerful form of webinar allows the speaker or speakers to interact directly with the audience. The speaker would be able to hear and see the audience member wishing to ask a question or make a comment.

Adobe Connect (formerly called Macromedia Breeze) is an example of an interactive tool for audio and video conferencing on the web. Conference participants log on to a website that the presenter controls. The presenter can place multiple windows on the screen that participants see. The presenter can show a PowerPoint presentation in a window, place a live video of himself or herself in a box next to the PowerPoint, have a list of conference participants in a box, and have an instant chat box all on the screens simultaneously. The boxes may be moved on and off the screen by simply clicking and dragging. Unlike a podcast or video that one would watch, there is genuine participation from the audience. For instance, at a recent webinar I attended, the speaker mentioned the merits of a specific website. A member of the audience, who was across the state from the presenter, searched the Web and posted the website in the instant chat box. The speaker then grabbed the link and replaced the PowerPoint with an Internet browser that was opened to the link found by the audience member. This all took place in a matter of seconds. In much the same way a speaker in a live class makes momentary adjustments to react to points made by the audience, the Adobe Connect presenter can monitor the live chat box and respond in real time. At Indiana University we have used Adobe Connect as a tool to have intern meetings. In the current academic year, we have interns in Florida, Illinois, and Indiana, and had virtual meetings in combination with postings in an online forum, Oncourse, which is similar to Blackboard.

Another positive feature of a Web-based conference is the capacity to record and save it for subsequent viewings. By placing a link to an archived webinar on a website, individuals may watch the previously recorded webinar. Any links to websites, PowerPoints, PDF documents, or Word documents would be accessible to the individual viewing the archived webinar. The difference between the live and archived versions is that in the archived version, the viewer would not have the live experience of being able to ask questions.

While Adobe Connect requires a licensing fee and server space, Skype (www.skype.com) offers video conferencing at no charge. Users have to register with a username and password, but there is no fee involved. Skype allows both parties to see and hear each other, and has chat capabilities. Pfohl (personal communication, October 22, 2008) reported that he has experimented with the use of Skype with interns at Western Kentucky University. In the past two years, at Indiana University we have used Adobe Connect to meet simultaneously with interns in Colorado, Georgia, Florida, Illinois, Indiana, Tennessee, and Texas.

In order to see and hear all participants, they are promoted to "presenters" as they enter the conference. The audio works well if everyone uses headphones. However, if someone forgets to bring headphones an annoying echo will make it difficult to interact. One issue that confounded our use was an intermittent problem with the cameras built into Mac notebooks. Adobe Connect at times would not recognize the Mac user's camera. Regardless of occasional problems, the value of Web-based conferencing tools is great. They provide a vehicle for individuals separated by distance to see and hear each other, view documents, and collaborate.

Threaded Discussion Forums and Online Communities

A threaded discussion forum allows individuals to have a dialogue online. An individual may react to points made by someone who had previously posted a response. Individuals with minimal computer savvy can participate, because all that is required is typing the comment or question in a textbox and clicking the reply button. That comment or question then becomes part of the dialogue. On the NASP website (www.nasponline.org), one has access to online communities by clicking the "Communities" button on the left sidebar. On July 17, 2008, the Forum had three sections: Online Events & Current Discussions, Member Resources, and Interest Groups. In the first section there was a discussion of whether NASP should recognize subspecialties within school psychology. There were four replies, but the discussion strand had been viewed 462 times (463 after I visited). The following introduction was presented by John Desrochers, editor of *Communiqué*:

> Welcome to our first foray into online discussions about articles recently featured in Communiqué. We plan to make this a regular feature of NASP Communities and hope that you find the discussions lively and informative. Please join in; the more of us who participate the richer the experience will be. The article to be discussed this time is from the February 2008 issue of *Communiqué*. It was written by Dan Miller, Kathy DeOrnellas, and Denise Maricle and is entitled, *Is It Time for NASP to Recognize Subspecialties within School Psychology?*.

As noted by Dr. Desrochers, there is a link that provides the text of the article to be discussed. A nice feature of the discussion is that the authors of the article can react to points made by those that reply to the strand. By pressing the "add reply" button at the bottom of the discussion, an individual may comment on the initial posting, or points made by those who replied previously. Another option is to subscribe using an RSS feed. By clicking the RSS feed button, when a new reply is added to the strand, you are notified of the change. You may be notified by email, or an option can be added to your Internet browser.

Email

It is hard to believe that we once communicated without email. I almost left this paragraph out, but the pervasiveness of email merits at least brief mention. It was not but 30 years ago that "high tech" was a letter typed with an IBM Selectric II typewriter, a typewriter that had a backspace key that would erase a previous mistyped letter. That was when a "CC" or carbon copy was produced by placing a sheet of carbon paper between the original and a blank sheet of paper. In the early 1980s it was exciting to check email and have a message. Imagine now going a couple of days without a message. Suffice to say that we have been transformed to a 24/7 world where email communication is constant. The ability to add an attachment to an email message made collaboration and access to materials a reality for distant individuals. Two researchers can write and edit a manuscript whether they are in adjacent offices or on opposite sides of the world. A tool within Microsoft Word, *track changes*, made collaborative writing easier by allowing collaborators to see modifications in the text. Remotely stored documents represent the next logical step in collaborative work. Google Docs (docs.google.com) allows multiple contributors to access a document stored on a secure Google server. When a contributor edits a document, the new version is saved along with all previous versions. The document may be a Word file, spreadsheet, or presentation file. Instead of receiving an email with an attachment, the contributors are alerted by email that a new version of the shared document is available online. Users of Google Docs have control of who is able to see and revise their documents.

The ability to use email, join virtual communities of psychologists, search the Internet for podcasts, track down scholarly articles, and gain perspective on the use of various digital tools means informed decisions can be made about how technology can improve interventions.

Technology and Interventions

How can technology contribute to the design and implementation of an intervention? The initial phase of an intervention involves understanding the problem in terms of the frequency, duration, and intensity of the problem(s). Three observational software programs will be used to illustrate how use of either a handheld device or laptop may facilitate systematic observation for collecting baseline data, as well as data collection during the treatment and maintenance phases. Then, a Web-based program designed to provide insights to discipline problems, School-Wide Information System (SWIS; May et al., 2003), will be described. Advances in digital video and editing software have put video self-modeling intervention within the reach of psychologists in the schools. The research on video self-modeling will be reviewed. The section on technology and interventions will conclude with consideration of CD-ROM interventions developed by pediatric psychologists and, finally, with a review of programs for reducing children's anxiety disorders. Although the CD-ROM applications developed for children with various chronic illnesses are unlikely to be used by school psychologists on a wide scale, the game type format of the programs can generalize to address common problems that are endemic to schools and the learning process. Programs developed for anxiety reduction will illustrate the incredible potential for CD and online programs to deliver and support therapy.

How can technology be used to facilitate the process of systematic behavioral observation?

Several computer-assisted systems to observe behavior have been developed in the past ten years. These systems are flexible because they are designed to be customized to observe event and interval behaviors. The three observation recording systems reviewed below run on laptops or personal digital assistants (PDAs) This means the observer may use the observational software in whatever setting is needed—classroom, lunchroom, or at recess.

The Portable Observation Program (POP) is one of the components of the well known Behavior Assessment System for Children–2 (BASC-2; Reynolds & Kamphaus, 2004). It was designed for use on a Palm Pilot or laptop computer with a Windows or Mac operating system. The BASC-POP will allow an observer to record behaviors of more than one student. This is useful when collecting normative peer comparison data. There are 18 buttons that can be customized. If there are six behavior codes that are being observed, one set of six buttons could be used for the target student, and the two remaining sets of six buttons could be used to track two other students in the setting. The program will

produce single-session reports, or up to five multiple-session reports. The reports can be saved as either RTF or PDF files. When saved as an RTF, the file may be imported into a Word file, which can later be saved as a PDF file. The advantage of the PDF is that the file cannot be modified. With many school districts moving to Web-based special education records, there is a real advantage to the ability to save a report as a PDF file.

The publisher of the POP reports that approximately one hour is needed to learn the program. Of course, this assumes the user has knowledge and background using event and interval behavior recording strategies. It should be noted that one hour is a relatively short time to learn the use of the tool, especially when one considers the many hours required to become familiar and proficient with common standardized cognitive, achievement or social/emotional measures. A demo disk with five uses is available from Pearson Education; see http://ags.pearsonassessments.com/Group.asp?nGroupInfoID=a38206. Once the POP system is purchased, it comes with an unlimited number of uses, meaning the user does not pay the publisher a fee for each observation.

The Behavioral Observation of Students in Schools (BOSS; Shapiro, 2003) software (http://pearsonassess.com/HAIWEB/Cultures/en-us/Productdetail.htm?Pid=015-8048-601&Mode=summary) was designed for monitoring intervention success. The BOSS has a behavioral template that allows the user to customize it. The templates are designed to allow observation of a normative peer, as well as teacher behaviors. The BOSS operates on the Windows platform, and the Palm operating system 3.1 and higher. If observations are recorded on a personal digital assistant (PDA), the data may be uploaded to either a laptop or desktop computer. Descriptive statistics and frequency counts are generated to summarize observations in a given setting. Similar to the POP, the BOSS comes with an unlimited number of observations once the initial fee has been paid.

!Observe (www.psycsoft.com) was designed to capture both event and momentary time sampling observations. In the event mode, when a given behavior is seen, the time of the event is recorded. In the event mode it is also possible to turn on a stopwatch function to capture the duration of the behavior. Similar to other computer-based observation systems, templates may be tailored to specific behaviors of a child. A template would include a list of behaviors that would be expected to be seen during the observation period. !Observe is compatible with Windows, Mac and Palm operating systems.

These computer-based (or Palm-based) observation recording systems provide a superior alternative to the traditional use of paper, pencil, and stopwatch. With minimal time required to master the features of the programs, they offer the observer flexibility and accuracy. Unlike norm-referenced tests that require new standardization samples because the norms become dated, computer-based observation systems do not become dated because the reference standards are other peers in the setting, or baseline behavior of the target child.

How can psychologists monitor and plan interventions for problem behaviors that lead to disciplinary referrals to the principal's office?

The School-Wide Information System (SWIS; May et al., 2003) was designed to collect information on office discipline referrals and to provide insights on patterns of problem behavior. Irwin et al. (2006) argue that effective schools are those that collect data on students, analyze it, make informed decisions and act on the information. It is in the context of collecting and analyzing office disciple referrals that the SWIS was created. It is a Web-based system that allows teachers and administrators to enter information on the day, time, location, name(s) of student(s) involved, and nature of the behavior problems. It is reported on the SWIS website (www.swis.org) that data entry for a single incident takes roughly 30 seconds.

According to Irwin et al. (2006) there are five standard reports: office referrals in a given time period (by day, by month); referrals by problem type; referrals for an individual student; referrals by where in the school the problem occurred; and referrals by 15-minute time intervals of the day. As with most management software, multiple options exist for customized reports. For instance, one may generate reports by grade level, classroom, school within a district, or to examine year-to-year changes in the patterns of referrals.

Irwin et al. (2006) conducted a single group, non-experimental evaluation of the SWIS. They examined the usage of the SWIS in 22 elementary schools and 10 middle schools. They were interested in how and why the SWIS was used, the extent of use, the perceived consequences of using the SWIS, and suggestions for improvement. At the elementary level, 80% of the respondents indicated that entry of referral events was done weekly, while 90%

at the middle school reported weekly entry. The median time required for entry fell in the range of 10–30 minutes a week for the elementary, and 30–60 minutes for middle school. Schoolwide behavior support teams and administrators were the most frequent users of the report function. It is the report function that provides insight into when and where on school grounds problems are reported. It also breaks down problems by type, grade level, etc. Secondary users of reports included psychologists, counselors and social workers, individual behavior support teams, and individual teachers.

Among the reported uses of the SWIS by the respondents from 22 elementary and 10 middle schools was early identification of problem behaviors, examination of specific types of problem behaviors, problem solving for the purpose of developing an intervention, and monitoring the effectiveness of interventions (Irwin et al., 2006). The respondents reported being either very satisfied (50%) or satisfied (40%). Two improvements were recommended by the respondents of Irwin et al.'s study. First was a set of user interface suggestions, and second was to allow schools/districts to customize the application. Irwin et al. noted the limitation of self-report data, and suggested that future research examine the degree to which implementation of the SWIS results in improved interventions, and changes in the classroom/school climate.

How can technology facilitate tracking of academic interventions as measured by curriculum based measurement?

The AIMSweb program (www.aimsweb.com) and *Dynamic Indicators of Basic Early Literacy Skills (DIBELS) Data System* (dibels.uoregon.edu) are the two most common systems for monitoring the academic progress of students. The AIMSweb program will be described first. Students' names and demographic data already in the district's database are initially uploaded to the server of the Web-based AIMSweb system. This saves the time associated with hand entry of each student's information by teachers. Teachers may then enter raw CBM scores and generate reports for an individual, a selected group of individuals, or an entire class. Comparisons can be charted with individuals' past and current scores. Likewise, a student may be compared to national norms. There is also a scheduling function built into the *progress monitor*. For instance, a child could be scheduled for progress monitoring to occur on a specified date on a biweekly basis. It should be noted that the AIMSweb CBM probes are not administered by computer; rather, scores are entered into the system. In this sense it is similar to the WISC-IV or Woodcock-Johnson, which require the examiner to administer and enter the scores into the program. One of the features of the program is AIMSonline, which is a user forum that serves as a resource of questions and answers about the use of AIMSweb. An AIMSweb user can post questions to the forum, or conduct a search of the forum to see if the question has been answered previously. Another feature to assist the novice user is the download tab, which provides access to training materials. Workbooks, administration and scoring guides, PowerPoint presentations, and software information are all available in the form of downloads.

Similar to the AIMSweb, the DIBELS Data System (dibels.uoregon.edu) will provide reports with graphs and charts that nicely summarize the data on students. A variety of sample reports are available at: dibels.uoregon.edu/samples/index.php#other_pdf. The progress-monitoring charts for individual students have target goals, and aimlines to evaluate whether a student's progress is on track. Falling below the aimline is cause for adjusting the student's intervention.

How can digital video cameras and computers contribute to effective interventions?

Digital video cameras have the advantage of being able to download recorded video to desktop or laptop computers. Once the video file is on the computer hard drive, editing programs may be used to manipulate the video. As basic video editing functions are being packaged with both Windows and Mac operating systems, there is no need for special video editing equipment. An individual with no video editing experience can learn to do straight cuts in 15 minutes. The availability of digital cameras and ease of editing have made the production of video a realistic option for school psychologists.

Sansosti and Powell-Smith (2008) used computer-presented social stories along with video models to increase the communication skills of children with autism. A multiple baseline across participants design was used to test the effects of the treatment on three elementary-aged boys with autism. Sansosti and Powell-Smith created video models with same-aged peers. The peers were shown engaged in the target behavior. The videos were brief, lasting only 45 seconds to a minute. Sansosti and Powell-Smith then created an enhanced PowerPoint presentation. To increase treatment fidelity, the PowerPoint slides advanced

at timed intervals. Upon transitioning to a new slide, the child would hear a voiceover reading the social story. When the social story ended, the child was presented a slide that said "Show Me How" and heard the narrator say "show me how to do it" (p. 166). Then a video clip of a same-aged peer engaged in appropriate communication was presented.

Sansosti and Powell-Smith were eventually able to establish experimental control, and increase the children's communication skills. However, two of the participants needed supplementary intervention in the form of teacher prompts and assistance from peers. Sansosti and Powell-Smith had the teachers complete the Intervention Rating Profile (Martens, Witt, Elliot & Darveaux, 1985) to assess the acceptability of the enhanced PowerPoint presentations. They indicated the intervention was appropriate for the classroom, and that other teachers would find it useful. They also felt the intervention could be used to teach other social skills, as well.

In a study of five children with autism, Charlop-Christy, Le and Freeman (2000) found that video modeling was more effective, placed less demands on the teacher, and required less time. The cumulative time for in vivo modeling was 635 minutes, while the time required for the video modeling was 170 minutes. For further information on the use of video for students with autism see Ayres and Langone (2004).

Hitchcock, Dowrick, and Prater (2003) noted that nearly 200 studies of video self-modeling had been done in the last 30 years. Dowrick (1986, 1991, 1999) defined video self-modeling as an approach where an individual sees video of his or her positive adaptive behaviors. Miscues and errors are edited out of the video. Video self-modeling contrasts with conventional videotape review, where an instructor would critique a video with a student and point out positive and negative behaviors. Video self-modeling allows individuals to view instances of them engaged in a behavior that is beyond their current level of functioning.

Feed forward is a technique which creates a reality that did not actually happen. In a study of two preschool children with autism, Bellini, Akullian and Hopf (2007) used feed forward to create intervention videos. They videotaped approximately 90 minutes of raw footage over three days. While taping, they encouraged the children's teacher to prompt social interactions. The following are illustrative of the prompts used, "Dylan, say 'Hi, Krista,'" or "Dylan, say 'Krista, play with me,'" or "Dylan, push Krista in the wagon." (Bellini et al., 2007, p. 84). The video footage was edited to take out the teachers' prompts and any inappropriate behaviors of the child. Prompted interactions were made to appear unprompted. Three 2-minute videos of each child were created and used for 17 days, over a 4-week period. Bellini et al. noted that one child's social engagement went from a baseline of 3% to a mean of 43% with a slightly increasing trend during the intervention phase. The other child's social engagement was 6% during baseline, and averaged 24% during the intervention phase. During the maintenance phase, the mean percent of social engagement was observed to be 33%.

An important question with any intervention, and especially those that involve technology, is the degree to which the teachers are satisfied with the intrusion into their classrooms. As both children in the Bellini et al. study were in the same class, there was just one teacher. To assess the social validity of their intervention, Bellini et al. monitored the teacher's reactions once a week using a 5-item questionnaire. The teacher reported the intervention did not interfere with typical classroom activities, was easy to implement, and was beneficial for the students. She also reported enjoying the process.

Video self-modeling, alternatively labeled video self-feedback and video self-observation, has been used to create interventions for elective mutism (Kehle, Madaus, Baratta & Bray, 1998; Kehle, Owen, & Cressy, 1990; Pigott & Gonzalez, 1987), physical disabilities including spina bifa and cerebral palsy (Dowrick & Dove, 1980; Dowrick & Raeburn, 1995), parent training (Meharg & Lipsker, 1991), and language skills (Buggey, 1995, 2007; Whitlow & Buggey, 2003).

One of the eminent researchers in video self-modeling, Buggey (2007, p. 157) stated, "We have never encountered a student who did not enjoy the taping process and viewing the videos." Recently there have been several useful reviews of video modeling and video self-modeling (cf Bellini et al., 2007; Buggey, 2007; McCoy & Hermansen, 2007).

How can working memory be improved with computer training?

Klingberg et al. (2005) used the program, Robo-Memo (www.cogmed.com), to determine if working memory could be improved by a computer-presented series of training exercises. A total of 53 children with ADHD, from ages 7–12, were randomly assigned to either the computer treatment condition or a comparison program. None of the children were on stimulant medication. Of the 53 children, 44 completed 20 days of training. Klingberg et al. were able to follow up and check maintenance effects three

months after the intervention phase. They used a span-board task as their dependent measure to determine if the effects of training would generalize to tasks administered in vivo, rather than having them use the computer and a mouse to answer memory tasks. They reported a robust effect size of .93 for the span board tasks. They also found significant differences between the treatment and controls on a digit span task, Stroop test, and Raven's measure. Teacher ratings were not significant, but parents did report fewer ADHD symptoms for those children in the treatment condition.

How can computer technology contribute to cognitive-behavior therapy?

Computer-assisted cognitive-behavior therapy (CCBT) is an exciting area of development. Consider the advantages of CCBT, and the fact that today's children and adolescents have only lived in a digital world. Proportionally, their age group has the highest percentage of Internet users. Children and adolescents are accustomed to interacting with digital devices. Besides the comfort level of children and adolescents interacting with technology, there are multiple other advantages of computerized delivery of therapy. A greater degree of treatment fidelity may be achieved, since the principles of the theoretical model guide the design of the program. A greater degree of standardization does not suggest that everyone would pass through an identical sequence of steps. To the contrary, a strength of the computer is that the software can customize the presentation based on the client's responses (Khanna & Kendall, 2008). Khanna and Kendall also note that the cost of treatment is reduced by decreasing therapist time, and that CCBT may be delivered in multiple settings (home, school, etc.) and in locales where therapists are unavailable. This latter point is especially important given the unacceptably high percentage of children with anxiety and other disorders that go untreated. Spek, Cuijpers, Nyklíček, Riper, Keyzer, and Pop (2007) point out that anonymity and accessibility are important advantages of CCBT. Access is available via the Internet 24 hours a day, well beyond the conventional psychologist's office hours.

Baer, Greist and Marks (2007) reported that clients prefer the confidentiality, a reduced level of stigma, and time savings, since they do not need to travel to the therapist's office. Proudfoot (2004) noted the power of the computer to store, analyze, and report data to the client and the therapist. While there are advantages to CCBT, there are disadvantages relative to conventional face-to-face therapy. Loss of the therapist–client alliance, and the inability to read the client's nonverbal behaviors, are limitations of CCBT (Proudfoot). March, Spence, and Donovan (2009) reported problems with treatment compliance. In a study of an Internet-based CBT program to reduce anxiety, they noted that only 60% of the parents and 33% of the children completed all treatment sessions. Another challenge is noted by Cunningham (2008), who states the 5-year timeframe that is required to develop and run randomized control trials of a new intervention program, plus the rapid evolution of computer hardware and software, present a significant challenge to developers.

Two programs will be used to illustrate CCBT: BRAVE-ONLINE (Spence et al, 2008); and Camp Cope-a-Lot: The Coping Cat CD-ROM (Kendall & Khanna, 2008).

The BRAVE-ONLINE program was developed from a clinic-based CBT anxiety reduction treatment (Spence et al. 2008). One version of the program is designed for children ages 8 to 12, and the other is for teenagers (age 13–17). Both have 10 weekly sessions of approximately 60 minutes. The sessions address recognizing physiological symptoms, relaxation strategies, restructuring thoughts, graded exposure, problem-solving approaches, and self-reinforcement for engaging in feared behaviors. Homework includes engaging in "extreme challenges." In the child version, parents complete six sessions, while in the teenager version the parents complete five sessions. The parent sessions include information about child anxiety, arranging contingencies for behavior, graded exposure, and problem-solving strategies.

Before initiating the 10-session treatment, the Internet therapist engages the family in a 15-minute phone call to brief them about the course of treatment. Over subsequent weeks, email is the primary mode of communication. There is a mix of automated emails generated before and after sessions are completed, as well as personalized emails that are customized by the Internet therapist to support their progress through the program. At the fifth session of the program, phone contact is made to construct an exposure hierarchy. Spence et al. (2008) reported that monitoring the weekly progress requires 10–15 minutes of the Internet therapist's time, as contrasted to 60–90 minutes for the conventional face-to-face treatment.

To maximize the therapist–client alliance, Spence et al. (2008) avoid the term "therapist" and instead the clients refer to their *BRAVE trainer*. Clients

are given the trainer's picture, a brief biography, and together they respond to a set of questions that are designed to get to know each other. Two 60-minute booster sessions follow, 1 and 3 months after the 10-week treatment is completed.

Spence et al. documented two detailed case studies of BRAVE-ONLINE, while March et al. (2008) reported encouraging findings from a comparison of BRAVE-ONLINE to a waitlist control. March et al. had 73 participants (age 7 to 12) who were randomly assigned to either the BRAVE-ONLINE program ($n=40$) or the waitlist control ($n=33$). Small differences between the two groups were reported after the 10-week treatment; however, 6 months following the termination of treatment 75% of the BRAVE-ONLINE participants did not qualify for their initial anxiety diagnosis.

Kendall and Khanna's (2008) Camp Cope-a-Lot: The Coping Cat CD-ROM was designed as a 12-week "computer-*assisted*" (italics from the original) program for children age 7 to 12 with separation anxiety, social phobia, and generalized anxiety disorder. The first six weeks are independent and designed to be completed without the assistance of a therapist. Similar to the BRAVE-ONLINE program, the Camp Cope-a-Lot online mental health professional is not called a therapist, but rather is known to the client as a *coach*. In Camp Cope-a-Lot, the client faces the challenges of a residential summer camp. Interactive experiences provide a context for learning about "anxiety and the physiological features of anxiety, relaxation, and coping and problem-solving strategies for managing anxiety" (Khanna & Kendall, 2008, p. 162). Preliminary evaluations of the program have led to including more interactivity, speeding up the pace, and increasing the energy level of the program. A clinical trial is underway of Camp Cope-a-Lot with 55 children and 15 therapists (Khanna & Kendall).

See Table 42.1 for links to a variety of Internet and CD based programs designed for adolescent anxiety reduction.

Further information on computer-based therapy may be found in a special issue of the *E-Journal of Applied Psychology* 4(2), (http://ojs.lib.swin.edu.au/index.php/ejap/issue/view/19).

The evidence base for computer-based cognitive behavior programs .for anxiety is developing. However, Spek, Cuijpers, Nyklíček, Riper, Keyzer, and Pop's (2007) meta-analysis of 12 randomized controlled CCBT trials with adult clients, age 18 and greater, revealed impressive CCBT effect sizes for the treatment of depression and anxiety. They

Table 42.1 Recently developed computer-based programs for adolescents[1]

Program	Delivery	Age[2]	Research or Product Website
BRAVE-ONLINE	Web	13–17	http://www2.psy.uq.edu.au/webexp/kidscoping/
CAVE	CD	10–17	http://www.medicine.utas.edu.au/research/mentalhealth/
CLIMATE Schools	Web	Students	http://www.climateschools.tv/
Cool Teens	CD	14–18	http://www.psy.mq.edu.au/MUARU/child/highschool.htm
Coping Cat	CD	8–13	http://www.cope-a-lot.com/
MoodGYM[3]	Web	15–16	http://www.moodgym.anu.edu.au
Reach Out! Central	Web (both)	16–25	http://www.reachout.com.au/default.asp?ti=2011
Stress and Anxiety in Teenagers.com	Both	Under 18	http://www.stressandanxietyinteenagers.com
Stressbusters[3]	CD	12–16	N/A
Why Me?	Both	11–16	http://www.ocdaction.org.uk/ocdaction/index.asp?id=296
Working Things Out	CD-DVD	13–15	http://www.workingthingsout.ie

1 Reprinted from Cunningham, M. (2008). Overview of design approaches in The Cool Teens CD and other computer programs for adolescent anxiety. *E-Journal of Applied Psychology, 4(2)*, 6–11. Reprinted with kind permission.
2 Target age stated in program or being studied
3 Primarily (or also) a depression programNeil and Christensen (2007)

concluded "internet-based interventions, especially those with therapist support, are effective" (Spek et al., 2007, p. 327).

How have pediatric psychologists used computerized interventions?

Pediatric psychologists have tested the efficacy of programs targeted for children with various chronic illnesses: cancer (Kato, Cole, Bradlyn, & Pollock, 2008), recurrent headaches (Connelly, Rapoff, Thompson, & Connelly, 2006), cystic fibrosis (Davis, Quittner, Stack & Yang, 2004), and asthma (Bartholomew, Gold, Parcel, Czyzewski, Sockrider, & Fernandez, 2000).

Kato et al. (2008) tested the efficacy of *Re-Mission* (www.re-mission.net) with 375 aged 13–29 individuals who had a malignancy diagnosis (new or relapse) and were undergoing treatment that was expected to last 4 or more months. Re-Mission is available as a download from the website listed above. It has a game format with Roxxi, a nanobot who is on a mission to destroy cancer cells in various parts of the body. The player can select among 20 different missions. For instance, one mission has as its goal targeting severe mucositis and infections that developed in the mouth 4 days after chemotherapy. The user helps Roxxi to target the infection with antibiotics, and to apply an anesthetic medication to the mouth sores.

The participants in Kato et al.'s (2008) study received a computer loaded with either the Re-Mission CD treatment, or to the control condition in which they received *Indiana Jones and the Emperor's Tomb*. Kato et al. collected the computers after the study, and were able to analyze the use of the games. Playing Re-Mission resulted in a 16% increase in compliance with oral antibiotic medication. For those on oral chemotherapy, there was a significant difference reported in favor of the treatment group. The participants in the treatment condition also evidenced significantly higher scores on their cancer-related knowledge and self-efficacy. These gains were maintained over 1- and 3-month follow-ups. They sum up the importance of the computerized intervention:

> These improvements in adherence to therapy are clinically relevant because patients who have cancer and are adherent to oral antibiotic prophylactic regimens have a lower incidence of fevers and infections, and increased survival, and those who adhere to oral 6-MP chemotherapy regimens show improved survival outcomes. (Kato et al., 2008, p. e314)

In another test of a pediatric computerized intervention, Connelly et al. (2006) used a CD-ROM intervention called *Headstrong,* with children who had recurrent headaches. The intervention was designed to be used with minimal therapist contact. Participants (n=37) were aged 7–12 and were randomly assigned to the Headstrong CD treatment group or a waitlist control which received conventional medical care. Those in the CD-ROM treatment also received medical care, so the experimental aspect was the addition of the CD-ROM treatment. Headache records from both child and parent were completed during baseline and treatment phases.

The Headstrong CD treatment consisted of four modules, with one module completed per week. The first module included an orientation to the program and conveyed educational information on the types, prevalence, diagnosis and treatment of headaches. The homework that accompanied the first module was a quiz and a headache-triggers assignment. The second module focused on guided imagery, deep breathing, and progressive relaxation. Logs of relaxation practice sessions were the homework for the second module. The third module addressed the rationale for coping, thought changing, and problem solving. Worksheets on thought changing and problem solving constituted the homework. The final module addressed positive and negative pain behaviors, management, and a review of previous content. The homework required submission of pain behavior sheets. Significant differences were observed between the treatment and controls groups for headache frequency, durations, and severity. These differences were maintained in a 1-month follow-up. The gains made by the treatment group were also followed two and three months following the treatment. In general, the gains were sustained. Connelly et al. cautioned that it was a pilot study, and further study was needed.

Davis et al. (2004) tested the efficacy of the STARBRIGHT Fitting Cystic Fibrosis into Your Life Everyday CD-ROM (available at www. STARBRIGHT.org) with 47 children and adolescents with cystic fibrosis, aged 7–17 years. After completing a cystic fibrosis knowledge questionnaire, and the school-age and adolescent versions of the Role Play Inventory of Situations and Coping Skills, participants were randomly assigned to the STARBRIGHT treatment or the waitlist control. The Role Play Inventory of Situations and Coping Skills is a series of context-specific vignettes that include situations often confronted by children with cystic fibrosis. Unlike the Re-Mission and the Headstrong programs, STARBRIGHT is a brief program requiring only 30 minutes. STARBRIGHT has three modules: Eating, Breathing and Cystic Fibrosis Questions and Answers. Reasons for breathing treatments, the value of exercise,

the importance of taking enzymes, peer relations, and coping with hospitalization are among the topics covered in the CD. Participants in the treatment condition had more knowledge after the program, and significantly more knowledge than those in the control condition. A small effect was noted in the quality of coping-skill problem solutions developed by those in the treatment condition. Davis et al. recommended further study to assess the maintenance of effects, and determine if the program leads to improved *in vivo* social interactions.

Bartholomew, Gold, Parcel, Czyzewski, Sockrider, and Fernandez (2000) used a computer game format to teach self-management skills to urban children with asthma. As was the case with other CD programs designed for children with chronic illnesses, they reported significant effects. Their findings were important because they observed behavioral changes; the program resulted in fewer hospitalizations, and improvement in self-management behaviors.

The video game format has also been employed to foster problem solving in a socially conscious manner.

Video Games to Foster Social Change

Given the pervasive use of video games (Lenhart et al., 2008) by adolescents, psychologists should be aware of games that are socially responsible. Quest Atlantis (http://inkido.indiana.edu/barab/rsrch_qa. html) is a multiuser game that was designed to be socially responsible, educational, and entertaining (Barab, Thomas, Dodge, Cartieaux, & Tuzun, 2005). There are seven social commitments that are built into Quest Atlantis; compassionate wisdom, creative expression, environmental awareness, personal agency, healthy communities, social responsibilities, and affirmation of diversity. The user goes on an educational quest to help heal the problems found in the mythical Atlantis. The quests are structured to fit within state and local academic standards.

Games for Change (www.gamesforchange.org) is an organization dedicated to using digital games for social change. Their websites include nine categories of games that address domestic issues, the environment, global conflict, politics, poverty, and youth-produced digital games. Among the games are found at their website are: *3rd World Farmer* (www.3rdworldfarmer.com). A player confronts the obstacles and dilemmas associated with a small farm in a third world country.

Play the News (www.playthenewsgame.com). The player takes an active role in the news, making predictions that parallel fantasy sport games.

ICED - I Can End Deportation (www.icedgame. com). The player assumes the role of an immigrant and learns about immigration statutes that deny immigrants due process and human rights.

Consent! (http://www.gamesforchange.org/main/ gameprof/668. *Consent!* Is played in Second Life, a virtual world where the user's avatar interacts with others' avatars. Consent! simulates the life and challenges of an African prisoner who faces 50 years of medical racism.

Food Force (http://www.foodforce2.com/. The player grapples with the global hunger and learns the importance of humanitarian aid.

Most of the games at the Games for Social Change website are available as free downloads.

In summary, technology has been applied to all phases of intervention, from behavioral observation and data collection in the baseline phase, to varied types of computerized interventions and analysis of intervention outcomes. Similar technological creativity has been applied to the domain of psychological assessment.

Assessment, Psychological Report Writing and Technology

Beyond the use of word processing, the most pervasive use of technology by school psychologists is the use of scoring programs to convert raw scores to standard scores. Most major measures used by school psychologists have computerized scoring assistants. Beyond scoring a test, the next challenge for the psychologist is making meaning of the findings and writing a report. The *Score and Report* program will be examined as an illustration of a tool that can aid in the efficient preparation of a psychological report.

What are the advantages of computerized test scoring assistants?

Test scores generated by computer scoring programs are more accurate than those that are hand scored (Butcher, Keller, & Bacon, 1985; Jackson, 1985). Scoring software also saves the psychologist the time it takes to find raw scores in a table. Since most measures have multiple subtests, the process of looking up a raw score needs to be repeated for each subtest. When subtests are clustered in domains, subtest scores then need to be added, and yet more tables have to be consulted. Besides saving time, scoring software also eliminates potential table reading errors. Another advantage of scoring software is that the programs often produce tables and graphs that may be pasted into a word-processed report.

Tables and graphs serve as a visual aid to the psychologist to conceptualize a child's performance, as well as to explain the child's performance to a teacher or parent.

The Wechsler Intelligence Scale for Children– Fourth Edition (WISC-IV) has two computerized programs; the WISC-IV Scoring Assistant, and the WISC-IV Writer. The user enters raw scores, and the WISC-IV Scoring Assistant generates scaled and index scores, strength and weakness discrepancies, and tables and graphs. Whereas the chart wizard in Excel provides easy graph construction, the WISC-IV Scoring Assistant includes a band to represent the standard error of measurement around the observed score. The WISC-IV Writer is built on top of the Scoring Assistant and provides interpretative text for a psychological report. The WISC-IV Writer uses a successive-levels approach to interpretation, beginning with the most global interpretation and moving to more specific, skill-based interpretations. One may choose from a list of potential recommendations to include the psychological report. Both the WISC-IV Scoring Assistant and the WISC-IV Writer are add-on programs, and are not included in the price of the WISC-IV.

Two other frequently used measures are the Woodcock-Johnson III Tests of Cognitive Abilities (Woodcock, McGrew & Mather, 2001a) and the Woodcock-Johnson III Tests of Achievement (Woodcock, McGrew & Mather, 2001b). Purchase of each measure includes the cost of the Compuscore and Profiles Program. Similar to the WISC-IV scoring program, the WJ-III Compuscore and Profiles Program generates subtest, cluster and discrepancy scores. If a given discrepancy is statistically significant, a column on the table indicates a significant difference. Graphs can be generated with profiles based on age/grade or standard score/percentile. Scores are represented as bands that indicate the standard error of measurement. A parent report contains a table that graphically represents the child's performance on clusters and individual subtests. Descriptive labels are provided across the range from *negligible, very limited, limited, limited to average, average to advanced, advanced*, to *very advanced*. Percentile ranks for each cluster and subtest score are given, along with a lucid definition of a percentile rank. On the second page of the parent report is a brief explanation of what is measured by each cluster and subtest.

The Achenbach System of Empirically Based Assessment, which includes the Child Behavior Checklist (CBCL/6–18), the Youth Self-Report(YSR/11–18 and the Teacher's Report Form

(TRF/6–18), provides an illustration of multiple ways technology has changed the way the Achenbach measures are administered and scored. The websites, http://www.aseba.org and http://www.web-link.org, offer various options on protocols. The traditional paper-based protocol that is hand scored may be purchased in packages of 50. Another option is the Assessment Data Manager, which allows entry, scoring, and comparisons across respondents' reports. There is also an option to administer the Achenbach measures online. An Internet connection is necessary, but this option allows secure access from any location. Parents, teachers and other caregivers can access the forms and respond to the individual items as they would on a conventional printed version. Then the Assessment Data Manager may be used to score and create reports.

Can computers save time in the administration of psychological tests?

When the question is asked broadly, and not narrowed to psychologists practicing in school settings, the answer is clearly yes. Butcher, Perry and Hahn (2004) reviewed historical developments in the use of computers in clinical assessment, and noted that computer-based tests have found most use in personality and neuropsychological assessment. The computerized version of the MMPI has been extensively studied. Finger and Ones (1999) reported the results of a meta-analysis that examined the question of whether the paper version of the MMPI leads to different scores than the computerized version. Their conclusion was that the two forms of assessment were psychometrically equivalent.

Computerized versions of tests also can save time for examinees. Adaptive testing has been shown to be a viable tool to shorten testing time (Weiss, 1985). Adaptive testing using item response theory allows the examinee's response-to-first-question to change the path of the examinee through the test items. The result is that many fewer test items are administered (Embretson & Reise, 2000). In a sense, a primitive version of adaptive testing occurs when a routing subtest is used to select a starting point in a test. However, since school psychologists have not, by and large, adopted computer-administered measures, applications of sophisticated models of computerized adaptive testing have not found their way into school psychologists' diagnostic batteries. Nevertheless, the potential exists to apply adaptive testing.

The exception is the Computer-Optimized Multimedia Intelligence Test (COMIT; TechMicro, 1999), which uses adaptive testing to limit the time required of the examinee. The typical administration time for the COMIT is 30 minutes, rather than more than one hour with conventional intelligence measures. Fontanini and Masters (2001) commended the effort to develop a computer administered intelligence test for children, but note that the psychologist is required to observe the testing, and is essentially passive. Unlike a conventional intelligence test, in which the psychologist closely monitors the examinee's motivation and gives appropriate encouragement at appropriate moments, the COMIT examiner/observer is more removed from the interaction. Fontanini and Masters stated that a limitation of the COMIT is that the examiner does not receive a record of responses to individual items; as such, it would be difficult to analyze the errors made by the child. They conclude that the COMIT "breaks new ground in an exciting field" (p. 285). However, in the years since its publication we have failed to see the COMIT penetrate the market owned by the major cognitive assessment instruments.

How can a Web-based program contribute to the writing of psychological reports?

Score and Report (www.scoreandreport.com) is a Web-based tool with menu driven features that prompt inclusion of legally required parts of the psychological report. Unlike test scoring software that is installed on your computer, Score and Report is Web-based. Hence, the user logs into the Score and Report website with a username and password. A district-level license allows a designated administrator to see all psychological reports in progress, whereas individual psychologists would only be able to see their own.

Pull-down menus are used throughout. If a psychologist wants to begin a new report, the first choice would be to decide on the type of report. Among the options would be initial evaluation, 3-year reevaluation, RTI report, etc. Depending on what was selected, different report templates would be presented. If it is a new report, demographic information is entered. For instance, if the child is African American and the report is being written for a California school district, there are cognitive measures that are not legal to administer. Thus, access to those measures would not be included in the template.

Score and Report is not a mindless report generator. You do not plug in scores and the report comes out the other end. However, through access to community narratives, the psychologist can find multiple alternative wordings for describing a child's performance. As there can be many options under the community narratives, there is a star rating system that combines past users' ratings, and the frequency with which the text has been included in past reports. Another option beside community narratives is archived text that the individual psychologist has used in previous reports. Hence, the program helps the psychologist craft the report, but does not automatically interpret the test scores.

If scoring software is used for a given test, the user merely saves the file to the desktop and imports the file to Score and Report, which automatically populates the fields. When scores are imported it is not necessary to hand-enter the scores. Another timesaving device is the ability to set up templates that can be reused. One can have a template for reports at a high school, and another template for reports at a given elementary school. One can personalize templates for different types of referrals. These templates would include tests that are typically used.

Score and Report generates graphs from the scores. Rather than producing individual graphs for each measure, the program graphs similar constructs next to each other. For example, if two achievement measures were administered, and both include reading comprehension subtests, they would be graphed side by side. This facilitates comparison of performance on subtests designed to assess the same domain. The inclusion of side-by-side comparisons means the psychologist has visual data to analyze patterns of strengths and weaknesses. J. Brockman (personal communication August 8, 2008) noted that the graphical presentations of data from Score and Report were well received by parents and teachers.

There are considerable advantages to Score and Report over the typical practice of block copying text from previous reports. There would be no gender pronoun errors from copying text from a boy's report and reusing it in a girl's report. Likewise, there would be no instances of another child's name slipping into the report. As would be expected, there is upfront time involved in becoming proficient with the system. However with the time savings per report, it would not take many reports to offset the upfront learning effort. Over 21,000 psychological reports have been written with Score and Report.

When word processors were in the early phase of being adopted by psychologists for report writing, there were many psychologists who preferred to rely on the typewriter because it was comfortable and did not require learning how to use the computer. I think Score and Report and similar Web-based report writing systems will eventually supplant simple word processors such as Word for writing psychological reports.

Access to Score and Report is also sold as a stand-alone program, or as a part of the SEAS Special Education Management System by Computer Automation Systems www.computerautomation.com/products.asp). Besides the management of the psychological reports, the other functions that can be handled by SEAS would be IEP management, forms management, timeline compliance, messaging and workflow management, customized forms, goals, and Medicaid claim generation. Due to the complexity of state and national special education statutes, it is a safe prediction that special education management systems similar to SEAS, and more sophisticated report writing programs, will be in our collective future.

How may access to psychological reports and special education records be more tightly monitored and at the same time increase the accessibility of records from different locations?

With recent increases in the availability of broadband Internet access, school districts and special education cooperatives have sought more efficient ways to store the accumulated volumes and volumes of paper. With the complexity of federal and state special education regulations, Web-based special education management software permits tracking of notices sent to parents, case conferences, IEPs, annual case reviews, and triannual evaluations. A powerful feature of special education management software is the capacity to generate reports. For any given time period, a report may be generated showing the number of children served by grade, disability category, race/ethnicity, etc. Information is instantly available on the status of a referral.

Special education management software is typically menu driven. For example if a teacher wishes to initiate a referral, the system would first require notification of the parent/guardian that an intervention will be tried to address the concern. If the intervention is unsuccessful, then documentation would be required to be entered in the system. Once the preliminary steps have been completed, the system would then permit the notice of a referral for a special education evaluation to go out to a parent.

If a student moves to another school district and the original school district uses the same special education management software, the student records can be transferred at the click of a mouse. This is an incredible advantage for students whose records too often take months to find their way to a new school district.

Time associated with the entry of redundant information is eliminated. Information from the database with the total student population of a school district can be merged or imported. This means that a student's address would only have to be updated in one place. For the many notifications that go out during the process of determining a student's eligibility for special education, there would be no need to retype the name or address, as that would automatically be inserted in the various forms.

Another advantage of web-based special education data management systems is that there is no need to travel to the central office to see a file. Whether the psychologist is at a school, home, or away at a conference, it is possible to access files. It is only a matter of going to a login Web page and entering a username and password. Depending on whether the user is a teacher, psychologist, special educator, or administrator, different levels of access to data would be provided. Thus, the director of special education would have clearance to access data across the entire system. Regular education teachers would be able to see records of students they referred, and those in their class.

Exceed (http://www.spectrumk12.com/exceed/iep//) is a Web-based system for storing and monitoring special education records. *Exceed* will be used to illustrate some of the features of special education management software. When a psychologist signs into the *Exceed* system, the names of all those on that individual's caseload appear. Clicking on a name reveals a timeline of events from the initiation of the referral to present and future required items. Each event is marked as "locked" or "draft" status. Once all the requirements for an event are completed, it is locked. If it is draft status, it means further activity needs to take place. For instance, while in a given student's file, the user sees that the annual IEP meeting is in draft status. By clicking on the "Annual IEP Meeting," the user learns which parts have been completed—an invitation, prior written notice, current levels of performance, accommodations, services, and signatures. Digging further into the student's file, one can click on "Current Levels of Performance." This would take the user to a form that would indicate area of disability assessed, present level of performance, source of information, date, and whether special education is needed. Also built into the form are compliance items, such as primary language of the child, whether Braille is needed, if a functional analysis of behavior was done, etc. *Exceed* provides a comprehensive list of IEP goals by skill area, and allows state standards and local goal banks to be imported. When each required piece is submitted to the system, a diamond changes from red to green. Rights to different aspects of the system are customized to the needs of the district, to comply with state regulations.

Technology and the Preparation of School Psychologists

Digital technology has made possible the transformation of conventional college classes. It has provided opportunities to reach students who previously would have been disadvantaged by distance. Distance as a barrier has been overcome for both in-service and pre-service school psychologists.

How can conventional courses be made richer through the use of technology?

Cummings, Bonk, and Jacobs (2002) did an analysis of education courses listed on the World Lecture Hall to discover ways faculty use technology to interact with their classes, with other instructors, and with practitioners. They note that for most of the twentieth century, university professors distributed paper-based syllabi at the first class, and the remainder of the sessions were lectures with discussions sprinkled in. With the exception of students reading the textbook, doing homework, and studying for tests, most of the class business took place within the walls of the classroom

It was in the twenty-first century that greater opportunities came about as a function of Internet technology. Cummings, Bonk and Jacobs (2002) developed a 3 x 3 matrix that captured the ways interactions took place. See Table 42.2 for an updated version of the original 2002 table. In updating the table, the most notable changes are in the last column. Whereas university resources provided server space to faculty to publish Web pages and add material to the Web, the opportunities are now wide open for everyone to create their own blogs, videos, and Web pages. Previously, university professors were creating the bulk of opportunities for interaction, but that has changed with the availability of inexpensive server space and advertisers who will to cover the cost of hosting the website.

How can professional development be delivered at a distance?

Assessing One and All was a federally supported project (U.S. Department of Education Office of Special Education and Rehabilitative Services, Projects

Table 42.2 An updated version of Cummings, Bonk, and Jacobs' (2002) matrix of communication flow among instructors, students, and practitioners/experts

	To Students	To Instructors	To Practitioners/Experts
From Instructor	Assignment schedule Lecture notes/PowerPoints Audio/Video podcasts via *ITunes U* or *YouTube University* Blogs where the focus is on the learning process Public/private feedback Online tutorials Course website with links to articles Online tools/downloadable tools (test analysis software; Observation software Office hours with instantaneous messaging	Online syllabi (World Lecture Hall, MERLOT.org) Audio/Video podcasts Blogs with a focus on the learning process Course website with links to articles Online tools (test analysis software; Observation software Listserv's Online tutorials	Learning communities Audio/Video podcasts via *ITunes U* or *YouTube University* Blogs with reflections on practice/school cultural issues Online tools/downloadable tools Webcasts Web pages with links to full text articles
From Students	Exemplary work from past semesters Within course discussions on Virtual debates Contributions to electronic forum discussions Sharing portfolios of work	Journal reflections Online quizzes/tests Balloting (before, during, or after class) Electronic minute papers Sessions evaluation Anonymous feedback Unsolicited email feedback Instantaneous mail messages	Audio/Video podcasts via *ITunes U* or *YouTube University* Blogs with reflections on practice/school cultural issues Online tools/downloadable tools Webcasts Web pages
From Practitioners/ Experts	Teleapprenticeships Online mentoring Virtual field trips Live and archived virtual meetings	Syllabus and course feedback Contributions of usable real-world scenarios and case illustrations	Virtual professional development Listservs Blogs with reflections on practice/school cultural issues

Original material reprinted with permission of Elsevier. Copyright 2002.

of National Significance) that took an integrated approach to professional development at a distance (Braden, 2008; Braden, Huai, White, & Elliott, 2005; Braden & Elliot, 2001). Braden et al. (2005) point out that the traditional one-shot workshop, or the "train and hope" model of professional development, has failed to result in behavior change among educators. More effective forms of in-service training require active engagement on the part of the learner, adequate time, either massed or spread out over weeks or months, interaction with other educators in the setting, and attention to context and relevance.

With consideration of the above parameters of effective professional development, Braden et al. (2005) created a case-based approach to situate learning about assessment in context. The units included: Educational Assessment Principles and Practices; Large Scale Assessment; and Accommodations and Alternate Assessment. Beyond video case examples

and documents that could be accessed online, an activity book and a print-based text were available. The text, *Assessing One and All: Educational Accountability for Students with Disabilities* (Elliot, Braden & White, 2001) is available in two versions, print-based and online as a PDF file.

Based on use of the program, Braden et al. reported effect sizes of .73 in knowledge gains and .94 for self-efficacy. These were based on 29 educators in the instructional group, and 26 in the control group. Because there was a site-based collaborative component to the program, it meant individuals could not be randomly assigned to groups. Rather, clusters of groups were randomly assigned.

Braden et al. (2005) conducted focus groups to identify features that the participants believed supported their learning. The participants identified the cases as a strength of the program. The video, PDF files, and hypertext access to information were cited as strengths of the program. The participants also appreciated exercises in the activities booklet, and opportunities for informal collaboration with colleagues. While the hypertext nature of the program came out as a strength, it also was identified as a weakness. In the latter case, some of the participants preferred a linear, instructor-directed approach to acquiring course content; in other words, the traditional format of a college course. Connection speed or time associated with downloads was cited as a weakness. It should be noted that the data were collected from January 2002 to February 2003, and access to broadband has grown exponentially since that time. Thus, download times would not currently be an issue for the majority of educators.

Two of the task force groups from the 2002 Futures Conference developed websites that provide access to resources that are oriented to in-service school psychologists. The website of the Task Force on Improved Academic Competence and School Success for All (http://www.usm.maine.edu/cehd/future/index.htm) has excellent links to online resources, training modules, and videos. There are three modules which consist of PowerPoint presentations on the importance of the problem-solving model, the process of problem solving, and research-based academic interventions. There are eight videos that include an introduction to, demonstration of, and interpretation of curriculum-based assessment, while there are 11 videos of reading instructional strategies.

The University of Nebraska Center for Research on Children, Youth, Families and Schools hosts the website of the Task Force on Family–School Partnerships (http://fsp.unl.edu/). There are six modules that were designed as a toolkit to promote evidence-based family–school partnerships. The set of modules is extensive, with PowerPoint presentations, handouts, reference lists, links to online resources, and video. In the first module alone, there are links to 29 multipage handouts on topics ranging from a teacher's perspective on communicating with families, to conjoint behavioral consultation. The online links in just the first module provide access to 34 different sites with information on family–school partnerships.

Six training modules also exist at the original Futures Conference website (www.indiana.edu/~futures) in the Resources section. These modules (Harrison & Cummings, 2006) were designed for both in-service and pre-service use, and cover topics such as the school psychologist shortage, children's needs, the needs of schools, family–school partnerships, and translating ideas to action. Each module is divided into three sections: (1) Resources for Reading and Review; (2) Questions for Group Discussion/Individual Reflection; and (3) Action Plan Review and Implementation. Ideally, the modules are to be used by groups of psychologists, and are designed to facilitate discussion and planning. Instructions and individual reflection activities are also included if an individual wishes to use the modules alone. Links are provided to presentations made at the conference, and to other reading materials and resources developed during and after the conference.

Another tool that serves an in-service function is the online journal, *School Psychology Forum: Research in Practice* (http://nasponline.org/publications/spf/index.aspx). The journal is refereed and published electronically by NASP. The journal began in 2007 with two issues, and as of July 21, 2010, there have been seven issues published. Ray Christner serves as Editor and Timothy C. Riley-Tillman as Associate Editor. The goals of the *School Psychology Forum* are to see scholarly advances put into practice, and to facilitate dialogue between researchers and practitioners.

How can university professors extend their reach beyond the walls of the classroom?

iTunes U is an approach that Arizona State, Duke, University of California-Berkeley, Wisconsin, and Vanderbilt have adopted to put class content out to students. iTunes U is being used as a vehicle to disseminate audio and video podcasts of lectures and class material. The universities opted to go to where the students are, and deliver course content to their iPods. This allows students 24/7 access to instructional material that they may play back while riding a bus, exercising at the gym, or walking on campus.

YouTube University is another outlet that the University of California/Berkeley is using to disseminate lectures. While there are series of course lectures such as Integrative Biology, Political Science, and Physics, there are also videos of guest speakers. One such video is SIMS 141 – *Search, Google and Life: Sergey Brin* (cofounder of Google).

Both iTunes U and YouTube University represent efforts to take learning to where the students are. They are creative examples of meeting students on their own turf. Distance education delivered as a program represents another application of technology.

What if distance is prohibitive and relocation is not realistic for an individual to pursue graduate studies in school psychology?

Rural communities often have difficulty attracting graduates of traditional school psychology programs.

Often there are teachers who would like to become school psychologists, but can't afford to relocate their families, or their work schedules overlap with the times that courses are offered. Online school psychology programs provide an avenue to education for location-bound students who live a prohibitive distance from traditional university site based programs. Online programs also offer an alternative to those with schedules that do not permit them to attend classes at the times they are offered at their local university.

The University of Calgary (http://education. ucalgary.ca/apsy/med-school-child-psych) offers an online Master of Education degree in school and applied child psychology (Drefs & Ryba, 2008). The courses follow the traditional university schedule, with each course being a semester in duration. The expectation is that students will devote 15 hours per week to each course. The program minimum is 3 years with 6 years being the upper limit. Six advantages to studying online are listed on the website:

1. You can study from wherever you live in the comfort of your own home.

2. You can fit your study schedule with your work and family schedule.

3. You can orient your studies toward your personal and professional interests.

4. You can meet interesting professional colleagues from other places.

5. You will meet with some of the key professional in the field.

6. You will be a participant in a supportive professional community of practice.

Various technologies are used in the delivery of courses. Elluminate Live, a Web-based audio conferencing system, provides a vehicle for live classes. It allows class members to hear each other, as well as to see an interactive whiteboard, text input from text messages in an instant chat box, and to see PowerPoint presentations. E-forums or discussion forums, podcasts, and interactive e-texts are other forms of technology used. As would be the case with traditional courses, students are assigned group projects, but instead of a physical meeting of group members the collaborative work is carried out at a distance.

As with the traditional school psychology program, there are practica required. For the University of Calgary's program, three practicum courses are required. Students access psychoeducational instruments from their local schools. Peer and university supervision is accomplished via videotape and/or CD. The internship is the conventional 1200-hour,

fulltime experience supervised by a local site-based school psychologist and a university-based supervisor.

In online and conventional courses, school psychology faculty members across the country extol the virtues of research and evidence-based practices. Unfortunately, best practices are not immediate adopted as quickly as many would hope.

Research to Practice
Across disciplines, a ubiquitous challenge is the infusion of new research-based knowledge into practice (Bero et al., 1998). School psychology is likewise faced with the difficult task of finding ways to integrate cutting edge knowledge into everyday practices. Part of the problem is limited interaction, because academics are housed in university offices and practitioners work in public and private school settings. The lack of proximity results in fewer interactions. It also should be recognized that there are different role expectations and contingencies for academic school psychologists and school psychologists in K–12 schools, mental health centers, and hospital settings. Before addressing the role of technology as a support in the bridge between practice and research, it is important to acknowledge the scope of relevant research.

Kratochwill (2007) advocates broadening the scope of research by including four types of research. Technology can play a facilitative role in each of the four types of research. For Type I efficacy studies, where tight experimental control is required, labs across locations may collaborate through Web-based conferencing, shared video for checking intervention fidelity, and email. Type II transportability studies test the generalizability of an intervention to the practice setting. These studies examine the degree to which an intervention will function in the real world context. Input on the acceptability of an intervention can be sought through online surveys of teachers, parents, students and administrators. These studies offer the opportunity to test the adequacy of the training for the interventionist. The constraints and assets of the varied contexts where the intervention may be applied will be revealed.

Type III dissemination studies use personnel that are part of the setting to test the degree to which the intervention may be faithfully implemented. Like transportability studies, dissemination studies are characterized by manualized treatment, and contact with the researcher in the form of supervision and oversight. Web resources would be accessible in the form of text-based document sharing, audio podcasts, and video illustrations. Type IV system evaluation studies reduce the formal contact with researcher, but retain the formal evaluation protocols. For system evaluation studies, the access to Web materials would continue. In each stage of research the Web resources would expand. At various points, the status of the project could be included in gateway websites that serve as portals to comprehensive coverage of that type of intervention, and the populations appropriately served.

Practice–research networks have been successfully used by several professional groups. The Practice Research Network of the American Psychiatric Institute for Research and Education has 700 members, and has functioned over the past 15 years. Two goals for the Network were to make research more generalizable, and more relevant to practice.

The Pennsylvania Action Research Network (PAARN; Kuhne & Welrauch, 2001) is another example of a practice research network that promotes practitioner research. The PAARN brings practitioners to a 2-day workshop during the summer. Workshop participants learn the basics of the action research model, share perceptions of the problems they face, generate ideas about new procedures, collaborate on the design of potential studies, and go through a formal process of project approval.

The ideal practice–research network is one where the ideas flow in both directions. While academic psychologists may have more advanced research design and statistical knowledge, this does not mean that practitioners merely follow the marching orders of the academics. This would be a recipe for continuing to spread the gap between research and practice. What is needed is a dynamic interaction, where practitioners and academics collaboratively first frame the problem, then together conceptualize all aspects of the intervention, and finally, design the evaluation to determine the success of the project. Such a partnership would increase the likelihood of interventions that recognize the realities of contemporary schools.

The National Technical Assistance Center on Positive Behavioral Interventions and Supports (PBIS; www.pbis.org) is a good example of a highly successful collaboration across universities and public school settings. The research collaboration is co-directed by George Sugai at the University of Connecticut and Robert Horner at the University of Oregon. In addition, seven other universities are collaborating as research partners. On the implementation side, the collaborators are Sheppard Pratt, the Illinois State Board of Education, Mountain Plains Regional Resource Center, and the May Institute. Contacts are listed for all 50 states.

The PBIS website has a wealth of resources on positive behavior support, including definitions, rationale, and implementation steps. Besides an online library of journal and book citations, a section of the website has links to tools. Among the tools are: Schoolwide Positive Behavior Support Evaluation Template; School-Wide PBS Blueprint; Effective Behavior Support Team Implementation Checklists; Benchmarks Scoring Guide; Benchmarks Team Member Rating; Benchmarks Scoring Form; Functional Behavior Support Plan; Self-Assessment of Contextual Fit in Schools.

The Laboratory for Instructional Consultation Teams at the University of Maryland (www.icteams.umd.edu) is another example of practice–research networking. School partnerships exist with schools in Delaware, Maryland and Virginia. The project is "An Experimental Study of the Effectiveness of Instructional Consultation Teams" founded by the U.S. Department of Education's Institute for Education Sciences .

Howard Adelman and Linda Taylor have collaborated on the UCLA (http://smhp.psych.ucla.edu) Center for Mental Health in Schools. Through the website they offer strategies to remove barriers to learning and promote school mental health. The resources available are extensive and detailed: practitioner toolkit, guides for practice, a listserv, a "Net Exchange" for practitioners to post and respond to questions, and their online book, *Mental Health in School & School Improvement: Current Status, Concerns, and New Directions* (http://smhp.psych.ucla.edu/mhbook/mhbookintro.htm).

The Collaborative for Academic, Social and Emotional Learning (CASEL; www.casel.org) is a group of researchers who compile evidence-based practices to advance social and emotional learning in schools. Their website has full text publications, an e-newsletter, videos, PowerPoint presentations, a searchable database, and extensive training materials.

How can technology be used to provide information to parents, teachers, administrators, and students?

For the most part, public school based psychologists have not taken advantage of Web pages to disseminate information or promote their services. In 2004, Cummings, McDermott, Noble, Loftin and Vitzum-Komanecki reported that four of the five largest school districts in the United States had no Web pages that referred to school psychological services or school psychologists. School districts without Web pages on school psychological services miss the opportunity for school psychologists to tell about their services, share resources, and/or respond to questions. As the Internet has become a common tool for finding information, it is a significant omission if school psychological services are not found on a district's website.

There are numerous topics that should be covered by the psychologists on their portion of the school district website. First would be the mission of the school psychological services unit. Innovative school districts should tell teachers and parents the nature of psychological services offered in terms of assessment, consultation, counseling, in-service presentations, research service, RTI, etc. From the Web page, contact information for individual school psychologists and schools they serve should be available. Since most individual schools also have websites, the psychologists' links should be available there as well. As parents and teachers often have questions about the nature of various disabilities, they would appreciate links to information about ADHD, LD, autism, statutory regulations, programs, etc.

As with any communication, it is essential to consider the potential audiences. Parents, teachers, and school administrators are the most likely visitors to the psychologists Web page. It is especially critical that the language be free of jargon and acronyms. Cummings et al. (2004) noted that one of the innovative features of the School District of Dade County, Florida, website was the inclusion of pictures and background of the individual psychologists. Besides information on the professional preparation of the psychologists, there were details about their outside hobbies. The effect was to make the psychologists seem approachable as human beings, not just professionals with impressive credentials.

The psychologists' website may also serve as a portal to resources. For instance, on the psychological services homepage may be a link to "Helpful Topics for Parents." When that link is clicked on, a page opens up with links to "How to prepare for a home–school conference," "Stress and Children," "Bullying: Not just kids being kids," "Play: Your child's key to learning," etc. These resources can be written or adapted by local psychologists, or they may be links to external sources off the school district website. Depending on the time of year, different resources may be highlighted.

One of the most important advantages of the Web is that resources do not have to be created from scratch. To the contrary, links may be placed on the local website that connect to outside resources. For instance, during the summer and early fall months, back-to-school resources may be highlighted, as well as suggestions for homework and motivation. See below for a partial list of topics that appeared on the NASP families website in July, 2010 (http://www.nasponline.org/families/)

- Back-to-School Transitions: Tips for Parents
- Homework: A Guide for Parents
- Motivating Learning in Young Children
- Home–School Conferences—A Guide for Parents
- Anxiety and Anxiety Disorders in Children: Information for Parents
- Anxiety and Anxiety Disorders in Children: Information for Parents (Spanish)
- School Refusal: Information for Educators

It is unfortunate that many psychologists employed by school districts have not embraced the Web as a powerful tool. Hopefully, as a new generation of psychologists are trained and hired by school districts, this will change. When I have asked psychologists about how they are portrayed on the school district website, I often have heard a reluctance to develop a Web presence. Sometimes they will say that they have all the business they can handle, and fear that more requests for service would be generated. Other times, the fear of more referrals from parents is not directly stated, but reading between the lines, that's the concern. To their credit, some psychologists see the value of marketing their services with the Web, providing a portal to resources to parents and teachers, and using the Web page as a vehicle to funnel questions to them. School psychologists often speak of expanding their role beyond special education. Creating a local portal for resources that teachers, parents, and administrators would find valuable, is a relatively low-cost way to increase psychologist visibility and market needed services.

Although the school psychology practitioners have, by and large, failed to develop portals to access resources, there are exceptions. Two impressive websites will be highlighted. The first is the work of Jim Wright a school psychologist in Syracuse, New York. His website is www.interventioncentral.org. One of the sections of his Web pages includes tools for educators. Among the educator tools are: a *Behavior Reporter,* an online tool to create behavior report cards that can be printed; *Jackpot,* an online tool for creating a reinforcer survey; *ChartDog 2.0* for CBM progress monitoring; and *OKAP* for developing reading probes, etc.

Another feature of Intervention Central is a strong and deep focus on Response to Intervention (RTI). There are links to resources developed by Jim Wright, but also to National Center on Student Progress Monitoring; the RTI symposium held by the National Research Center on Learning Disabilities; DIBELS Phonological Awareness Probes; *Curriculum-Based Measurement: A Manual for Teachers;* and manuals for the administration and scoring of AIMSweb CBM probes, and various graphing tools for summarizing CBM data. These are useful links for educators, but also for psychologists who are contributing to the implementation of RTI in their schools.

Among the links on the Intervention Central homepage are a list of favorite downloads. The ADHD evaluation manual was the first item listed. It was followed by a bully prevention booklet, the curriculum-based measurement warehouse, *Classroom Behavior Report Card Manual*, and others. Videos are also available for download: Academic Intervention Ideas that Any Teacher Can Use and Defiant Kids: Communication Tools for Teachers. Both are AVI files that are less than 10 MB.

Another school psychologist's website is Sandra Steingart's *School Psychology Resources Online* (www.schoolpsychology.net). There are links to information on various disabilities (anxiety disorders, attention deficit disorder autism, behavior disorders, deafness, dissociative disorders, etc.). Hers was among the first school psychology sites to appear on the Web.

Trainers have developed a number of noteworthy websites. Jeffery Miller's Multimodal Functional Assessment (http://mfba.net) has PDF and Word files of FBA forms, PowerPoint presentations, and links to specific online journal articles.

Kevin McGrew's Institute for Applied Psychometrics website has evolved into two blogs: Tic Toc Talk: The IQ brain clock (http://www.ticktockbraintalk.blogspot.com/) and Intelligent Insights on Intelligence Theories and Tests (aka IQ's Corner) (http://www.iqscorner.com/). There is a wealth of information on the Cattell-Horn-Carroll theory of intelligence and the *Woodcock-Johnson III*. An innovative feature of the site is EWOK's or Evolving Webs of Knowledge. An EWOK is a visual–graphic representation of information that has clickable links. In contrast, books are traditional linear forms of knowledge representation. A Link to a W-J EWOK is: http://www.iapsych.com/wj3ewok/map.htm.

The IQ brain clock EWOK addresses temporal processing (see http://www.iapsych.com/iqclock2/map.htm).

Dawn Flanagan and Kevin McGrew initiated the cross-battery assessment site (www.crossbattery.com), which has been refined with the assistance of Samuel Ortiz and Vincent Alfonso. It provides a substantive set of PowerPoint presentations on cross-battery assessment, from guiding principles to interpretation within the context of IDEA 2004 and cross battery interpretation with diverse children.

Ron Dumont and John Willis created the popular Dumont-Willis site (http://alpha.fdu.edu/~dumont/psychology/). An excellent feature of the site is the download section that offers a series of tools for test interpretation. An Excel workbook, CHC Cross-Battery Worksheet Templates for the ATDR-II, with multiple sheets is provided as a download. Additionally there are various test reviews and samples of a variety of psychological reports, with good and bad exemplars.

Louis Kruger created the Global School Psychology Network (www.globalschoolpsychology.org). The network provides an opportunity for school psychologists to communicate about issues they confront while working in school settings. It is noted that the Global School Psychology Network is a way to circumvent differing schedules and distance.

Access to Scientific Knowledge

Traditional print publishers were quick to add electronic options to what were once only paper-based journals. Since publishers are for profit businesses, they devised ways to charge libraries and individual subscribers fees for electronic access via the Internet to journals. When a search engine identifies a specific article for someone without a subscription, the publisher typically accepts a credit card and charges the customer a fee for access to the full text version of that single article. In contrast to traditional publishers, which expect a fee for access to information, is an open access policy that was passed at Stanford University.

On June 10, 2008, the School of Education faculty at Stanford University voted unanimously to make scholarly articles available to the public for free. It is a mandatory policy, meaning faculty members are required to provide copies of their refereed works to the administration, who then have the responsibility to post the material on the Web. What this means is that when Stanford University faculty sign a publication agreement with a publisher, they are required to append a signed copy of an Author Addendum, establishing "a prior, nonexclusive license granted to Stanford University to post an open access copy of the version that the journal has accepted following peer review" (Stanford University School of Education, 2008, p. 1).

This is a major change, not so much for academics that typically have access to articles through contracts between their institutional library and publishers, but for teachers, administrators, and school psychologists working in the preK–12 settings. Parents, legislators and public policymakers will likewise have access to the latest research.

The Directory of Open Access Journals (http://www.doaj.org) lists 91 psychology and 241 education journals (as of July 28, 2008) that have granted open access to articles. By open access they mean users may read, download, copy, distribute, print, search, or link to the full text versions of articles. The list of journals is truly international, with heavy representation from Europe, South America, and Australia. Even when the country of origin is not English speaking, the contents are often available in English. For instance, the *Anales de Psicología* is published by the Universidad de Murcia (Spain), and the journal is available in Spanish, English, and French.

A search for journals with "school psychology" in the title yielded "no matches" in the Directory of Open Access Journals. However, I was able to find *Behavior and Social Issues* (www.uic.edu/htbin/cgiwrap/bin/ojs/index.php/bsi), the *International Journal of Behavioral Consultation and Therapy* (*http://www.baojournal.com/IJBCT/IJBCT-index.html),* and, the *Journal of Behavior Assessment and Internvention in Children* (formerly the *Journal of Early and Intensive Behavioral Intervention)* (http://www.baojournal.com/JEIBI/jeibi-index.html), and other journals of interest to school psychologists.

As most psychology journals published in the United States derive income from the sale of print-based versions as well as electronic forms of the articles, publishers, including the American Psychological Association and the National Association of School Psychologists, will have tough decisions to make on the open access question. The question will be one of priorities. Do the members of the association value open access more than a potential increase in dues to cover losses from journal revenues? It may be, if enough institutions follow the lead of Harvard and Stanford, the question will be moot. The public will have access to the articles via a search engine such as www.scholar.google.com.

How can psychologists share their scientific knowledge and increase their influence in the political process?

Legislative alerts allow instant notification to list-servs and distribution email lists. The following was widely distributed across the practice divisions of American Psychological Association.

With the June 30 deadline just days away, the Senate is poised to consider the Medicare Improvements for Patients and Providers Act of 2008 (H.R. 6331) on Thursday, June 26. H.R. 6331 is the same bill that passed the House yesterday, and it is critically important to psychology. The Medicare bill would restore for 18 months $45 million to psychotherapy and related services cut as a result of the 5-year review, halt the 10.6% Sustainable Growth Rate (SGR) cut, provide a 1.1% update for 2009, and phase in Medicare coinsurance parity.

Key Senators in these targeted states need to hear from their constituents as soon as possible to vote to pass H.R. 6331.

Targets:

Alaska – Lisa Murkowski (R) and Ted Stevens (R)

Kansas – Pat Roberts (R)

Minnesota – Norm Coleman (R)

Mississippi – Thad Cochran (R) and Roger Wicker (R)

New Hampshire – John Sununu (R)

New Mexico – Pete Domenici (R)

North Carolina – Richard Burr (R) and Elizabeth Dole (R)

Ohio – George Voinovich (R)

Pennsylvania – Arlen Specter (R)

Virginia – John Warner (R)

Action (to targeted Senators):

Call (202) 224-3121, ask to speak with your Senator's office and urge the Senator to vote to pass H.R. 6331

Phone Call:
I am a psychologist and constituent in _____ (state) and I am calling to urge the Senator to vote to pass H.R. 6331. The Medicare bill is critically important to my practice and my patients.

While the above example encourages psychologists to use the telephone to express their opinion on a bill, legislative alerts also request action in the form of email. Responses are facilitated by providing a Web link uses the respondent's zip code to identify the congressional member for the district and the senators for the state. Sample text is provided and usually has the option to customize the message to the legislator.

Both NASP and APA use www.capwiz.com. In the two months of January and February, 2009, almost five million constituent messages were delivered to state and federal elected officials and media contacts. These messages were delivered in the form of emails, faxes, phone messages or conventional postal letters.

Ethical Issues that Come with Technology

Knauss (2001) noted that, "Tests can now be administered, scored, and interpreted without human contact" (p. 237). In an article on ethical issues associated with psychological assessment in school settings, she warned that computerized test interpretations should not be accepted blindly. The psychologist signing the report has responsibility for not only the selection and administration of a measure, but also for the interpretation. While the test software publishers should be accountable for the validity of the algorithms used to generate the interpretations, the psychologist using the software must consider the interpretations in the context of the unique characteristics of the examinee, the referral question(s), and the environmental circumstances of the classroom, home, and community. Before using such software, it is incumbent on the psychologist to determine if the publisher has evidence to support the interpretations made by the software. In much the same way as a psychologist does due diligence by reviewing the reliability and validity evidence of a newly published test, the psychologist should carefully examine the theoretical and empirical evidence for the generation of interpretations.

Another important caution raised by Knauss (2001) was that computer-administered tests should not be used to extend the competence of psychologists to an area in which they are not qualified. The same boundaries of competence for the use of conventional tests apply to computerized measures. Knauss points out that the ease of administration, scoring and interpretation of computerized tests should not lead to use by untrained non-psychologists. Again, psychological tests, including computerized tests, should only be used by those who are qualified. These points were captured in the 2002 *Ethical Principles of Psychologists and Code of Conduct*.

A portion of the section on assessment is reprinted below (APA, 2002, p. 14).

9.09 Test Scoring and Interpretation Services

(a) Psychologists who offer assessment or scoring services to other professionals accurately describe the purpose, norms, validity, reliability, and applications of the procedures and any special qualifications applicable to their use.

(b) Psychologists select scoring and interpretation services (including automated services) on the basis of evidence of the validity of the program and procedures as well as on other appropriate considerations. (See also Standard 2.01b and c, Boundaries of Competence.)

(c) Psychologists retain responsibility for the appropriate application, interpretation, and use of assessment instruments, whether they score and interpret such tests themselves or use automated or other services.

Keeping Confidential Information Confidential

The 2002 *Ethical Principles of Psychologist and Code of Conduct* (APA, 2002) states under the Privacy and Confidentiality principle that "Psychologists have a primary obligation and take reasonable precautions to protect confidential information obtained through or stored in any medium"(p. 7). Information stored on networked computers presents special challenges. Just as paper records are stored in secure files, so must digital files. One might assume as much when a file is deleted it is gone; however, the data from a file may still remain. What has been deleted is the information that tells the hard drive where the file data are. Hence, when disposing of a computer, it is essential that the hard drive be completely erased, not just the directory to the file data. Pfohl (2008a, 2008b, 2008c) developed a series of suggestions for computer security and recommended Darik's Boot and Nuke (www.dban.org) to completely erase hard drives and other media.

Schulenberg and Yutrzenka (2004) recommended seeking expert advice on how to secure files so they won't be accessible to unauthorized individuals. Reading Pfohl's (2008a, 2008b, 2008c) suggestions provides a good context for asking the right questions about security. Schulenberg and Yutrzenka recommend a confidentiality agreement be signed with the organization employing the psychologist.

Laptops, portable hard drives, and USB flash drives pose special challenges because they can be lost or stolen. An option to limit access to files whether stored on a desktop, laptop, external drive, or USB flash drive, is to encrypt the file before it is saved. TrueCrypt (www.truecrypt.org) is an open-source, free, software program that creates on-the-fly encrypted files before they are saved. The program is invisible to the user, so the same procedure for saving a document in Word, or Excel would apply. However, to access the files a password is needed. Thus, if a laptop is stolen, the information on the hard drive stays encrypted and inaccessible to an individual without the password.

In practicum and internship, students are frequently emailing psychological reports to site- and university-based supervisors. At Indiana University we require psychological reports to be encrypted and password protected. It is a simple two-step process that can be learned by clicking on help (question mark icon on the upper right of the screen) in Word, and searching for "encrypt." Encryption and password protection are available in both the PC and Mac versions of Word. Since we often use PowerPoint to present cases, besides changing the name of the child, we also encrypt and password-protect PowerPoint files. The steps are the same for Word and PowerPoint.

Personal Information on the Web?

Packard (2008) states that social networks, such as MySpace and blogs, pose ethical questions. For instance, is it appropriate for training directors of either graduate programs or internship programs to check the online presence of prospective students or interns? Packard endorses open disclosure of the training program's policy on whether prospective students' online behavior will be searched. A prerequisite is that the program have a policy that addresses online searches of applicants.

Packard (2008) also advises students against posting party pictures, or any material that one would not want to be available when interviewing with potential employers. For school psychologists the question would be how the personal material posted on the Web would appear to parents, teachers, school administrators, and students. A situation that occurred in a school psychology practicum at Indiana University involved an adolescent male client asking one of the school psychology graduate clinicians to add him as a friend on Facebook. This drove home the point that at least the picture and social network of friends was visible to anyone who joins Facebook. For the boy to get to her full profile on Facebook, she would have had to agree to add

him as friend, but he could view her initial profile picture, and the initial profile pictures of all her friends.

I signed up for a Facebook account primarily because I was writing this chapter. I did not expect to use Facebook. However, once one graduate of the Indiana University School Psychology program found me, I was able to connect with others who graduated 20 years ago. From a distance it was enjoyable to connect with individuals I had lost contact with over the years. Professional associations are even catching on to Facebook. The National Association of School Psychologists has a group. As a member of the group I receive notice of online learning events and conferences.

Should public schools monitor social networks?

Before answering the question, consider a September 3, 2008 article on Facebook in the Washington post by Rachel Beckman. She wasn't sure why, when she opened her Facebook account, the targeted ads assumed she was overweight. Was it that her profile indicated her gender and her age? Perhaps it was what the data miners used to uncover information in the text of messages? For instance, mining software is used to identify ads from content of an individual's Gmail (Google mail) email messages.

> Facebook spokesman Matt Hicks summed up the appeal to advertisers thus: "If you're a wedding photographer, do you want to waste your money advertising to a general audience? Or do you want to reach those that are engaged?" (Beckman, 2008, p. C1).

A serious question that school psychologists and school administrators should ask is whether they should employ data miners in electronic social networks to discover problems such as cyber-bullying, suicide threats, etc. Targeted ads or links to interventions could be delivered to such individuals.

Conclusion

While some technologies addressed in this chapter have been adopted by some school psychologists, as a group, school psychologists have not sought out new technologies or been quick to warm to new possibilities. Word processing, email, and to a lesser extent, search engines to find resources are the primary electronic tools of school psychologists. Unlike pediatric psychologists, we have not explored the potential of CD programs to promote academic, social or emotional goals for students. In an article on technology diffusion, Geroski (2000) states, "it seems to take an amazedly long period of time for new technologies to be adopted by those who seem most likely to benefit from their use" (p. 604).

It is worth considering some of the reasons for the use of patience in adopting new technologies. Early adopters risk time lost on programs that fail to capture the market. When a new innovation is developed, there is often more than one variation introduced to the market. A good example of competing technologies, with one eventually dominating the market, is what has been referred to as the Blue-ray vs. HD-DVD war (or VHS vs. BetaMax, for those that remember those days). The early adopters that choose HD-DVD were disappointed to learn that in February of 2008, Toshiba and other manufacturers announced they would no longer make the HD-DVD players/recorders.

Another reason for reluctance to adopt new technology is that the first release of new software often contains bugs. When new versions of a certain computer operating system have been released, there have been difficulties that resulted in work lost in cyberspace with the computer locked up and needing to be rebooted. Hence, many universities and public schools wait a year to allow others to work out the problems of a new operating system, before adopting it. Pfohl (2007a) recommended waiting to adopt the Vista version of Windows until the first service pack was available. Another difficulty is that the user manuals that accompany software programs are typically inadequate for most people to successfully operate the tool.

Geroski (2000) characterized the technology adoption process as following an S-curve—an initial burst of early adopters, a period of stagnation, then rapid and pervasive adoption. Geroski offered several explanations for the nonlinear path that technological adoption follows. Although his analysis is focused on technology adoption by corporations/firms, there are sufficient parallels to adoption of technologies within public school settings and by psychologists. The epidemic model is one that he used to explain the S-curve of adoption. He suggested the experience of using a program is what leads to mastery, and personal contact is often necessary for the late adopters. It is word of mouth that allows the information diffusion process to accelerate quickly. Probit models offer another perspective on technology diffusion. Here, a combination of expertise, expected gain, and switching costs drive the diffusion of technology. A third explanation of the S-curve of adoption, the information cascade model, ties directly to the example of Blue-ray and HD-DVD. From the information cascade perspective, the initial phase of adoption is actually one of competing alternative technologies trying to accomplish the same goal. It is during this period that early adopters use the competing technologies. Eventually, one of the technologies prevails. Once this happens, everyone jumps on the bandwagon. Those that adopted the wrong technology suffer by having to endure switching costs on top of the costs of acquiring the technology that prevailed.

One might think the question is whether school psychologists should wait for the technology to shake out, or be among the early adopters. My sense is that we have moved past the early adoption phase on all the technologies reviewed in this chapter. The future is not now, but can be cast as past tense. As Pfohl noted (2007, p. 42) "To be computer illiterate today is a handicap, not a badge of honor as it once was." We are in the slow growth phase of the S-curve. Hopefully the use of blogs, CD's, video, virtual professional communities, and electronic records will increase the capacity of school psychologist to better serve children, parents, teachers, and school administrators.

Author's Note

Appreciation goes to Drs. William Pfohl, Raymond Christner, Mike Cunningham, and Lou Kruger, who read earlier drafts of the chapter and pointed me in new and interesting directions. Their insights were valuable in expanding coverage of selected topics in the chapter.

References

American Psychological Association. (2002). *Ethical Principles of Psychologists and Code of Conduct.* Washington, DC: Author. Retrieved September 18, 2008, from http://www.apa.org/ethics/code/index.aspx.

Ayres, K.M. & Langone, J. (2004). Intervention and instruction with video for students with autism: A review of the literature. *Education and Training in Developmental Disabilities. 40,* 183–196.

Baer L, Greist J, Marks IM., (2007). Computer-aided cognitive behaviour therapy. *Psychotherapy and Psychosomatics, 70,* 193–195.

Barab, S., Thomas, M., Dodge, T., Cartieaux, R. & Tuzun, H. (2005). Making learning fun: Quest Atlantis, a game without guns. *Educational Technology Research and Development, 53,* 86–107.

Bartholomew, L. K., Gold, R. S., Parcel, G. S., Czyzewski, D. I., Sockrider, M. M., & Fernandez, M., (2000). Watch, Discover, Think, and Act: Evaluation of Computer-Assisted Instruction To Improve Asthma Self-Management in Inner-City Children. *Patient Education and Counseling, 39,* 269–280.

Beckman, R. (2008). Facebook ads target you where it hurts. *Washington Post*. Retrieved September 15, 2008, from http://www.washingtonpost.com/wp-dyn/content/article/2008/09/02/AR2008090202956.html?sub=new.

Bellini, S., Akullian, J. & Hopf, A. (2007). Increasing Social Engagement in Young Children With Autism Spectrum Disorders Using Video Self-Modeling. *School Psychology Review, 36*, 80–90.

Bero, L., Grilli, R. Grimshaw, J., *Harvey*, E., Oxman, A.D., Mary Ann Thomson, M.A. (1998) Closing the gap between research and practice: An overview of systematic reviews of interventions to promote the implementation of research findings, *BMJ ,317*, 465–468.

Braden, J.P. & Elliott, S.N. (2001). *Assessing one and all (web course)*. Retrieved September 20, 2008, from http://www.wcer.wisc.edu/archive/aoa/index.html.

Braden, J.P. (February, 2008). *Professional development and distance education*. Paper presented February 8, 2008 at the annual meeting of the Trainers of School Psychologists. New Orleans, LA.

Braden, J.P., Huai, N., White, J.L. & Elliott, S.N. (2005). Effective professional development to support inclusive large-scale assessment practices for all children. *Assessment for Effective Intervention, 31*, 63–71.

Buggey, T. (1995) An examination of the effectiveness of videotaped self-modeling in teaching specific linguistic structures to preschoolers. *Topics in Early Childhood Special Education*, 15, 434–458.

Buggey, T. (2007). A picture is worth. . . Video self-modeling applications at school and home. *Journal of Positive Behavior Interventions, 9*, 151–158.

Butcher, J. N., Keller, L. S., & Bacon, S. F. (1985). Current developments and future directions in computerized personality assessment. *Journal of Consulting and Clinical Psychology*, 53, 803–815.

Butcher, J. N., Perry, J. & Hahn, J. (2004). Computers in clinical assessment: Historical developments, present status, and future challenges. *Journal of Clinical Psychology, 60*, 331–345.

Chartop-Christy, M.H., Le, L. & Freeman, K.A, (2000). A comparison of video modeling with in vivo modeling for teaching children with autism. *Journal of Autism and Developmental Disorders, 30*, 537–552.

Connelly, M., Rapoff, M.A., Thompson, N., & Connelly, W. (2006). Headstrong: A pilot study of a CD-ROM intervention for recurrent pediatric headache. *Journal of Pediatric Psychology, 31*, 737–747.

Corporate Relations and Business Strategy Staff of APApractice. org (2008). *Practice marketing: Are you using a blog?* Retrieved September 9, 2008, from http://www.apapracticecentral.org/update/2008/06-18/using-blog.aspx.

Cummings, J. A., Bonk, C. J., & Jacobs, F. R. (2002). Twenty-first century college syllabi: Options for online communication and interactivity. *The Internet and higher education, 5*, 1–19.

Cummings, J. A., Harrison, P.L., Dawson, M., Short, R.J., Gorin, S., & Palomares, R. (2004a) Follow-up to the 2002 futures conference: Collaborating to serve all children, families and schools. *Journal of Educational and Psychological Consultation, 15*, 335–344.

Cummings, J. A., Harrison, P.L., Dawson, M., Short, R.J., Gorin, S., & Palomares, R. (2004b). The 2002 conference on the future of school psychology: Implications for consultation, intervention, and prevention services. *Journal of Educational and Psychological Consultation, 15*, 239–256.

Cummings, J.A., McDermott, E., Noble, J. Loftin, R., & Vitztum-Komanecki, J. (July, 2004) *School psychological services as portrayed by school districts' internet pages*. Poster presented July 28, 2004 at the Annual Meeting of the American Psychological Association, Honolulu, HI.

Cunningham, M. (2008). Overview of design approaches in The Cool Teens CD and other computer programs for adolescent anxiety. *E-Journal of Applied Psychology, 4(2)*, 6–11.

Davis, M.A., Quittner, A.L., Stack, C.M. & Yang, M.C.K. (2004). Controlled evaluation of the STARBRIGHT CD-ROM program for children and adolescents with cystic fibrosis. *Journal of Pediatric Psychology 29*, 259–267.

Dowrick, P.W., 1986. *Social survival for children*, Brunner-Mazel: New York, NY.

Dowrick, P. W. (1991). *Practical guide to using video in the behavioral sciences*. New York: Wiley Interscience.

Dowrick, P. W. (1999). A review of self modeling and related interventions. *Applied and Preventive Psychology, 8*, 23–39.

Dowrick, P. W., & Dove, C. (1980). The use of self-modeling to improve the swimming performance of spina bifida children. *Journal of Applied Behavior Analysis, 13*, 51–56.

Dowrick, P.W. & Raeburn, J.M. (1995). Elf-modeling: Rapid skill training for children with physical disabilities. *Journal of Developmental and Physical Disabilities, 7*, 25–37.

Drefs, M. & Ryba, K. (February, 2008). *University of Calgary: Delivering an online school psychology program*. Paper presented February 8, 2008 at the annual meeting of the Trainers of School Psychologists. New Orleans, LA.

Elliot, S.N., Braden, J.P., & White, J. L. (2001). *Assessing one and all: Educational accountability for students with disabilities*. Arlington, VA: Council for Exceptional Children. Also available online at: http://eric.ed.gov/ERICWebPortal/custom/portlets/recordDetails/detailmini.jsp?_nfpb=true&_&ERICExtSearch_SearchValue_0=ED458746&ERICExtSearch_SearchType_0=no&accno=ED458746.

Embretson, S.E. & Reise, S.P. (2000). *Item response theory for psychologists*. Hillsdale, NJ: Lawrence Erlbaum.

Finger, M.S. & Ones, D.S. (1999). Psychometric equivalence of the computer and booklet forms of the MMPI: A meta-analysis. *Psychological Assessment, 11*, 58–66.

Fontanini A., & Masters, E.M. (2001) Test review: Computer-optimized multimedia intelligence test. *Journal of Psychoeducational Assessment, 19*, 279–285.

Florell, D. (2008) New web initiatives at NASP. *NASP Communiqué, 36(8)*, Retrieved September 8, 2008, from http://www.nasponline.org/publications/cq/mocq368webinitiative.aspx.

Geroski, P.A. (2000) Models of technology diffusion. *Research Policy, 29*, 603–625.

Harrison, P. L. & Cummings, J. A. (2006). The future of school psychology: Online learning modules. Retrieved September 24, 2008, from http://www.indiana.edu/~futures/resources.html.

Hitchcock, C.H., Dowrick, P.W. & Prater, M.A. (2003). Video self-modeling intervention in school-based settings. *Remedial and Special Education, 24*, 36-45.

Horrigan, J. B. (2008) *Home broadband adoption 2009*. Retrieved July 23, 2010 from http://www.pewinternet.org/Reports/2009/10-Home-Broadband-Adoption-2009.aspx.

Irvin, L.K., Horner, R.H., Ingram, K., Todd, A.W., Sugai, G., Sampson, N.K., & Boland, J.B. (2006) Using office discipline referral data for decision making about student behavior in elementary and middle schools: an empirical evaluation of validity. *Journal of Positive Behavior Interventions, 8,* 10–23.

Jackson, D. (1985). Computer-based personality testing. *Computers in Human Behavior, 1,* 255–264.

Jones, S. & Fox, S. (2009). *Generations online in 2009: Pew Internet project data memo.* Retrieved February 27, 2009, from http://www.pewinternet.org/pdfs/PIP_Generations_2009.pdf.

Kato, P.M., Cole, S.W., Bradley, A.S., &. Pollock, B.H. (2008). A video game improves behavioral outcomes in adolescents and young adults with cancer: A randomized trial. *Pediatrics, 122,* e305–e317.

Kehle, T.J. Madaus, M.R., Baratta, V.S. & Bray, M.A. (1998). Augmented self-modeling as a treatment for children with selective mutism. *Journal of School Psychology, 36,* 247–260.

Kehle, T.J., Owen, S.V., & Cressy, E.T. (1990). The use of self-modeling as an intervention in school psychology: A case study of an elective mute. *School Psychology Review 19,* 115–121.

Kendall, P.C. & Khanna, M.S. (2008). Camp *Cope-a-Lot: The coping Cat CD-ROM (software).* Available from http://www.workbookpublishing.com/camp-cope-a-lot.html, retrieved March 29, 2009.

Khanna, M.S., & Kendall, P.C. (2008). Computer-assisted CBT for child anxiety: The Coping Cat CD-ROM. *Cognitive and Behavioral Practice, 15,* 159–165.

Klingberg, T., Fernell, E., Olesen, P.J., Johnson, M., Gustafsson, P., Dahlström, K., Gillberg, C.G., Forssberg, H., Westerberg, H.L.P. (2005). Computerized training of working memory in children with ADHD-A randomized, controlled trial. *Journal of the American Academy of Child and Adolescent Psychiatry, 44,* 177–186.

Knauss, L.K. (2001) Ethical issues in psychological assessment in school settings. *Journal of Personality Assessment, 77,* 231–242.

Kuhne, G.W. & Welrauch, D. (2001). The Pennsylvania Action Research Network (PAARN): A synopsis of findings from five years of practitioner action research in Pennsylvania. *PAACE Journal of Lifelong Learning, 10,* 1–9.

Kratochwill, T.R. (2007) Preparing psychologists for evidence-based school practice: Lessons learned and challenges ahead. *American Psychologist. 62,* 826–843.

Lenhart, A. Kahne, J. Middaugh, E., Macgill, A.R., Evans, C., Vitak, J. (2008). Teens, video games and civics. Pew/Internet & American Life Project. Retrieved September 17, 2008, from http://www.pewinternet.org/pdfs/PIP_Teens_Games_and_Civics_Report_FINAL.pdf.

March, S. Spence, S.H., & Donovan, C.L. (2009). The Efficacy of an Internet-Based Cognitive-Behavioral Therapy Intervention for Child Anxiety Disorders. *Journal of Pediatric Psychology, 34,* 474–487.

Martens, B. K., Witt, J.C., Elliott, S.N., & Darveaux, D.X. (1985). *Professional Psychology: Research and Practice, 16,* 191–198.

May, S., Ard, W., Todd, A., Horner, R.H., Glasgow, Sugai, G., et al. (2003) *School Wide Information System.* Eugene, OR: Educational and Community Supports, University of Oregon.

McCoy, K. & Hermansen, E. (2007). Video modeling for individuals with autism: A review of model types and effects. *Education and Treatment of Children, 30,* 183–213.

Meharg, S.S., & Lipsker, L. E. (1991). Parent training using videotape self-modeling. *Child and Family Behavior Therapy, 13,* 1–27.

Packard, E. (2008) Prizewinner explores the ethics of posting personal information on the Web. *gradPSYCH, 6.* Retrieved September 25, 2008, from http://gradpsych.apags.org/jan08/prizewinner.html.

Pfohl, B. (2007a). Tech corner. *Communiqué, 36(1),* 52.

Pfohl, B. (2007b). Tech corner: The future of technology is now. *Communiqué, 36(3),* 42.

Pfohl, B. (2008a). Tech corner: Security – Part 1. *Communiqué, 36(6),* 36.

Pfohl, B. (2008c). Tech corner: Security – Part 2. *Communiqué, 36(7),* 44.

Pfohl, B. (2008c). Tech corner: Security – Part 3. *Communiqué, 36(8),* 44.

Pogue, D. (2009). The Kindle: Good before, better now. Retrieved February 27, 2009, from http://www.nytimes.com/2009/02/24/technology/personaltech/24pogue.html?_r=1&scp=7&sq=kindle%202&st=cse.

Proudfoot JG. Computer-based treatment for anxiety and depression: is it feasible? Is it effective? *Neuroscience and Biobehavioral Reviews, 28,* 353–363.

Reynolds, C.R., & Kamphaus, R.W. (2004). *BASC-2 behavior assessment system for children, 2nd edition.* Circle Pines, MN: American Guidance Service.

Sansosti , F. J. and Powell-Smith, K. A. (2008). Using computer-presented social stories and video models to increase the social communication skills for children with high-functioning autism spectrum disorders. *Journal of Positive Behavior Interventions, 10,* 162–178.

Schulenberg S.E., Yutrzenka, B.A. (2004). Ethical issues in the use of computerized assessment. *Computers and Human Behavior, 20,* 477–490.

Shapiro, ES (2003). Behavioral Observation of Students in Schools (BOSS). San Antonio, TX: Pearson Education Inc.

Smith, A. (2010, July 7) Mobile Access 2010. Retrieved July 23, 2010, from http://pewinternet.org/Reports/2010/Mobile-Access-2010.aspx.

Spence, S. H., Donovan, C. L. March, S., Gamble, A., Anderson, R., Posser, S., Kercher, A. & Kenardy, J. (2008). Online CBT in the treatment of child and adolescent anxiety disorders: Issues in the development of BRAVE-ONLINE and two case illustrations. Behavioural and Cognitive Psychotherapy, 23, 1-20.

Spek, V., Cuijpers, P., Nyklíček, I., Riper, H., Keyzer, J., & Pop, V. (2007), Internet-based cognitive behaviour therapy for symptoms of depression and anxiety: a meta-analysis. *Psychological Medicine, 37,* 319–328.

Stanford University School of Education (2008). How to Comply with the Open Access Motion. Retrieved July 28, 2008, from http://suse-www.stanford.edu/suse/faculty/open-access-qa.html.

Stelter, B. (2008). Griping Online? Comcast Hears and Talks Back Retrieved July 28, 2008, from http://www.nytimes.com/2008/07/25/technology/25comcast.html?_r=1&scp=2&sq=comcast&st=cse&oref=slogin.

Sugai, G, Sprague, J.R., Horner, R.H., & Walker, H.M. (2000). Preventing school violence: The use of office discipline referrals to assess and monitor school-wide discipline interventions. *Journal of Emotional & Behavioral Disorder, 8,* 94–101.

TechMicro, Inc. (1999). *Computer-optimized multimedia intelligence test.* New York: TechMicro.

Weiss, D.J. (1985). Adaptive testing by computer. *Journal of Consulting and Clinical Psychology, 53,* 774–789.

Whitlow, C.K. & Buggey, T. (2003) Video self-modeling: An effective intervention for a preschooler with language delays.

Journal of Research in Special Education Needs. 3(1). Retrieved September 4, 2008, from http://bert.lib.indiana.edu:2176/cgi-bin/fulltext/120188050/HTMLSTART.

Woodcock, R. W, McGrew, K. S., & Mather, N. (2001a). *Woodcock-Johnson III tests of achievement.* Itasca, IL: Riverside.

Woodcock, R. W, McGrew, K. S., & Mather, N. (2001b). *Woodcock-Johnson III tests of cognitive abilities.* Itasca, IL: Riverside.

Ysseldyke, J. E.,&Weinberg, R. A. (Eds.). (1981). The future of psychology in the schools: Proceedings of the Spring Hill symposium [Special Issue]. *School Psychology Review, 10.*

Conclusion: Evolution of School Psychology

Tanya L. Eckert

Abstract

The chapter reviews the historical developments in the field of school psychology over the last quarter-century, including a review of how the current status of children in the United States has influenced federal legislation and educational reform movements. The chapter also discusses indirect and direct initiatives related to improving the educational, behavioral, and mental health outcomes of children and youth. Two key developments in the field of school psychology, data-based decision making and the multi-tiered problem-solving model, have allowed the field to evolve in order to more effectively serve children, families, and schools in the twenty-first century.

Keywords: school psychology, evolution, history, reform, science-based practice

Introduction

Fagan and Wise (2007) provide the preeminent chronological record of the history of school psychology. Many of the significant events and landmarks detailed in their work have affected the development of the field of school psychology. For example, the *hybrid years* were associated with the field's origins of practice (1890–1969), expansion and acceptance (1910–1929), emerging regulation (1930–1939), organizational (1940–1949) and professional identity (1950–1959), and training and practitioner growth (1960–1969). By the end of this period, school psychology represented a profession that coexisted with other fields including education, psychology, and medicine (Fagan & Wise, 2007). Beginning in 1970, the *thoroughbred years* of the profession were linked with increased regulation, association identity and growth, and profession division (1970–1979), professional reorganization (1980–1989), and stable growth, reform, and identity reconsidered (1990–1999). A key distinguishing feature of the thoroughbred years is the increased regulation of training (Fagan, 1999), which continues to shape and evolve the field today (Fagan, Gorin, & Tharinger, 2000).

Although the field remains situated in the thoroughbred years, the decade that is currently unfolding (2000–present) has been associated with prosperity as well as a broadening identity and practice (Fagan, 2008). For example, Reschly and Ysseldyke (1995, 2002) predicted a paradigm shift in the provision of school psychological services from a correlational model (i.e., refer–test–place) that is largely based on standardized testing, to an experimental model (i.e., problem solving) that is based on the science of interventions designed to improve children's educational outcomes. This paradigm shift would necessitate schoolwide system reform and allow the profession to become more effective in improving the outcomes of *all* children, families, and schools. To date, there is substantial verification that the paradigm shift predicted by Reschly and Ysseldyke (1995, 2002) has come to fruition, as evident by legal requirements directly tied to the provision of school psychological service delivery (Reschly, 2008).

Despite the advances in the field of school psychology, a number of significant challenges confront the continued development and professionalization of the field (Fagan, 2007; Reschly, 2008). Some of these issues relate to a longstanding tension inherent in the belief systems and values of psychologists that was initially identified by Kimble (1984). In their review of the historical context of school psychology, Merrell, Ervin, and Gimpel (2006) describe these conflicts within the context of the field, which include: (a) objective science versus human values; (b) determinism versus indeterminism; (c) objectivism versus intuitionism; (d) laboratory versus field methods; (e) nomothetic versus idiographic methods of inquiry; and (f) elementism versus holism. Although these conflicts are less controversial than in other fields of psychology, Merrell and colleagues highlight the importance of reconsidering these issues as the field continues to evolve.

Other challenges facing the field of school psychology are specific to the discipline, and have caused significant apprehension. Most notably, the continued policy conflicts between the American Psychological Association (APA) and the National Association of School Psychologists (NASP) regarding training and licensure requirements for professional practice in school settings have been perceived as threatening the professional identity and practice of the field (Fagan, 2007; Tharinger & Palomares, 2004; Worrell, 2007). A pending revision to the APA Model Act for State Licensures of Psychologists (1987; i.e., removal of exemption) may prohibit nondoctoral, and perhaps nonlicensed, school psychologists from referring to themselves as "psychologists." The title of "psychologist" would be reserved for professional psychologists who have earned a doctorate and obtained professional licensure in their respective states. In the event that the exemption is removed from the APA Model Act for State Licensures of Psychologists, a very robust division may be established between professional psychologists and nonlicensed, school based practitioners (Short, 2002).

Further contributing to the entry level issue in the field of school psychology, is the predicted personnel shortage of school psychologists until the year 2020, with the most significant shortages expected through 2010, assuming no increased demands for school psychologists (Curtis, Grier, & Hunley, 2004). Although personnel shortages have existed for many years (Fagan, 2002), it is estimated that there will be more than 14,000 unfilled positions through 2020(Curtis, Hunley, & Grier, 2004), with some predictions suggesting the shortage will continue indefinitely (Fagan, 2002). Ethnic minority representation in the field (Zhou et al., 2004), and

practice settings that require a doctoral degree (e.g., school psychology training programs) are predicted to be most significantly affected (Curtis, Grier et al., 2004). In addition, the current and projected shortage of school psychology faculty has been of significant concern (Curtis, Grier et al., 2004), with more than one in four faculty positions remaining unfilled at the conclusion of a hiring cycle (Clopton & Haselhuhn, 2009). As a result, some scholars have argued that these projected trends may impede or reverse the advances previously discussed in this chapter, specifically in terms of the demands placed on school psychologists and the amount of time available for service provision (Davis, McIntosh, Phelps, & Kehle, 2004; Fagan, 2004). Other scholars have argued that this challenge may result in a reconceptualization of the field (Curtis, Grier et al., 2004; Tharinger & Palomares, 2004).

In summary, many historical events influenced the development of school psychology, and a number of issues currently challenge the field's evolution. As duly noted by Fagan and Wise (2007):

> The historical study of school psychology reveals three things: that service origins, innovations, and reforms never occur as a result of universal agreement; that change is better appreciated as a well-intended effort at improvement; and that change never occurs uniformly across settings. (p. 69)

Chapter Overview

In the remaining sections of this chapter, I will review the current status of children, families, and schools in the United States. This review will provide a rationale for the importance of improving the educational, behavioral, and mental health outcomes of children and youth in the United States. Addressing these critical factors has become a priority for the field of school psychology, with numerous federal and policy reform initiatives being advocated or proposed. Next, two sections of the chapter will discuss indirect and direct initiatives that have attempted to improve the outcomes of children, families, and schools. A very strong case can be made that scientific advances in the last decade have directly affected the field of school psychology, serving as a primary catalyst for evolving school psychology practice. Specifically, these improvements have allowed the field of school psychology to dramatically progress into providing evidenced-based services that directly improve the outcomes of children, families, and schools (Eckert, 2005). The chapter will conclude with a review of two key developments in the field of school psychology—data-based decision making and the multi-tiered problem-solving model, which have allowed the field to evolve and shift service delivery paradigms in order to more effectively serve children, families, and schools.

Current Status of Children, Families, and Schools

Demographics. There are more than 73 million children under the age of 18 living in the United States and this figure is projected to increase to 80 million in 2020 (Federal Interagency Forum on Child and Family Statistics, 2007). The racial and ethnic diversity of children in the United States has changed, with increasing numbers of children coming from diverse racial and ethnic backgrounds. The proportion of Hispanic children has increased faster than any other racial and ethnic group (Federal Interagency Forum on Child and Family Statistics, 2007). Related to this trend, there are more children residing with one parent who is foreign born, and almost 20% of children will speak at least one language other than English at home (Federal Interagency Forum on Child and Family Statistics, 2007). The percentage of children speaking another language has increased each year (Federal Interagency Forum on Child and Family Statistics, 2007). These findings suggest that households of children are increasingly diverse, including the nationality of parents and the family structure.

Of those 73 million children residing in the U.S., approximately 12.5 million children (17%) are living in poverty. Although the poverty figure varies greatly by family structure, children residing in female-householder families with no husband present were at the greatest risk of experiencing poverty (Federal Interagency Forum on Child and Family Statistics, 2007). Higher poverty rates exist for Black/African American (36%), American Indian and Alaskan Native (32%), and Hispanic/Latino (32%) children, than non-Hispanic white children (11%; Annie E. Casey Foundation, 2007).

In 2008, it was estimated that more than 49 million children and youth were enrolled in public schools in the United States (Snyder, Dillow, & Hoffman, 2008). This enrollment figure represented a 26% increase since 1985, with the fastest public school enrollment growth observed in the elementary grades (from 27 million to 34.6 million; Snyder et al., 2008). The increased growth at the elementary grades is partly due to the expansion of prekindergarten programs (Snyder et al., 2008). The percentage of children enrolled in private schools remained stable, accounting for approximately 11% of the total elementary and secondary school enrollment figure (Snyder et al., 2008). It was projected that approximately 6.2 million elementary and secondary students were enrolled in private schools (Snyder et al., 2008).

An increasing percentage of children are served under the Individuals with Disabilities Education Improvement Act (IDEA) of 2004 (IDEA, 2004). Based on enrollment figures for the 2005–2006 school year (U.S. Department of Education, 2009), 8.7% of the total student population was served under IDEA. This percentage has increased since 1976, with the total special education expenditures increasing at an annual growth rate of 0.7%. Direct instruction and related services accounted for more than 80% of the total special education expenditures (U.S. Department of Education, 2009). Based on data reported in 2001, approximately 40% of students ages 6–12 receiving special education services had at least one additional disability diagnosed besides their primary disability, and 10% had two or three additional disabilities (U.S. Department of Education, 2009). The most recent reports on school completions (2003–2004) indicated 54.5% of students ages 14–21 graduated with a high school diploma and 14.4% received a certificate of completion (U.S. Department of Education, 2009). A total of 31.1% of students ages 14–21 dropped out of high school (U.S. Department of Education, 2009).

For children ages 6 to 21 years who were eligible for special education services, states reported serving more than 5 million students, representing an increase of 28.4% from the previously measured time period (U.S. Department of Education, 2009). Services were most frequently provided in a regular school building (95.9%), with educational instruction occurring outside of the regular classroom for less than 21% of the school day (U.S. Department of Education, 2009). A small percentage of school-aged children and youth received educational services in separate facilities (3%), residential facilities (0.7%), or home/hospital settings (0.5%; U.S. Department of Education, 2009). The most prevalent disability categories in this age group included specific learning disability (28.5%), speech and language impairments (18.9%), mental retardation (10.6%), and emotional disturbance (8.2%; U.S. Department of Education, 2009). In school settings, referral patterns for special education eligibility determination paralleled these national data. In 2002, Bramlett, Murphy, Johnson, and Wallingsford reported that the most frequent reason for a referral for additional services included reading difficulties (57%), written expression difficulties (43%), task completion difficulties (39%), and mathematics difficulties (27%).

For children ages 3–5 who were eligible for special education services, states reported serving more than 600,000 children. This figure represented an increase of 31.7% from the previously measured time period (U.S. Department of Education, 2009). Three-year-old children experienced the greatest growth in eligibility for services. Across all three age groups, the most prevalent disabilities were speech and language impairments (55.2%) and developmental delays (24.9%; U.S. Department of Education, 2009). Most services were provided in either early childhood settings (36.2%) or early childhood special education settings (34%); services were less frequently provided in part-time early childhood or early childhood special education settings (12.9%; U.S. Department of Education, 2009).

Among infants and toddlers (birth–age 2) who were eligible for special education services, states reported providing services to more than 230,000 young children, representing an increase of 40% from the previously measured time period (U.S. Department of Education, 2009). Of all three age groupings examined (birth–2 years, 3–5 years, 6–21 years), the greatest growth in service provision was observed among infants and toddlers (U.S. Department of Education, 2009), with most services provided at home (68%) and a smaller percentage of services provided in specific programs for children with developmental delays or disabilities (14%) or service provider settings (9%; U.S. Department of Education, 2009).

Educational Outcomes

The early learning experiences for many young children are not encouraging. Data collected by the U.S. Department of Education (2003b) suggest that increasingly more children enter kindergarten displaying physical activity/attention difficulties, speech difficulties, and health problems that require additional educational support or medical services during the school day. A recent analysis of the Early Childhood Longitudinal Study reported that almost 56% of the kindergarten students displayed a delay in at least one of three areas including: health, cognitive achievement, and social and emotional development (Wertheimer, Croan, Anderson Moore, & Hair, 2003). Parents' and kindergarten teachers' perceptions of young children's early learning experiences further corroborate these epidemiological findings. In a summary of the National Transition Study (Love, Logue, Trudeau, & Thayer, 1992), many parents reported that their children entered kindergarten unprepared, and kindergarten teachers estimated that 30% of their students were not ready to learn. Statistics on school retentions and delayed school entries in kindergarten further support these findings. For example, each year 5% of children enrolled in kindergarten are retained, and 6% are delayed in their school entry by one year or more (U.S. Department of Education, 2005).

Many children enrolled in elementary and secondary public schools experience significant difficulty learning to read, write, and compute. This conclusion is largely based on the latest reports from the National Assessment of Educational Progress, which indicated that more than half of the school-age children had not mastered fundamental skills (i.e., proficient achievement level) in reading, mathematics, and written expression. For example, in reading, more than 65% of fourth and eighth grade students could not read at the proficient level (Lee, Grigg, & Donahue, 2007). In the area of mathematics, more than 60% of fourth and eighth grade students could not apply computational and problem-solving skills at the proficient level (Lee, Grigg, & Dion, 2007). Furthermore, in the area of writing, 70% of fourth and eighth grade students could not write at the proficient level (Persky, Daane, & Jin, 2003).

When demographic factors (e.g., ethnicity, eligibility for free and/or reduced price lunch) or additional educational factors (e.g., English language learners, eligibility for special education services) were taken into account, these trends in children's educational achievement were more disconcerting. For example, the greatest reading achievement level disparities were observed among fourth grade children who were identified as English language learners (93% could not read at the proficient level) or who were eligible for special education services (87% could not read at the proficient level; Lee, Grigg, & Donahue, 2007). It is therefore unsurprising that many adults experience difficulties with literacy. In a recent longitudinal study, Kutner, Greenberg, and Baer (2005) compared adult literacy skills in three areas: (a) prose (e.g., search, read, and comprehend a paragraph); (b) document (e.g., search, read, and comprehend a prescription label); and (c) quantitative (e.g., use numbers embedded in printed material) across two time periods (i.e., 1992, 2003). Although an improvement was reported in the adults' quantitative literacy skills, the prose and document literacy skills remained essentially the same from 1992 to 2003. Most notable, however, was the finding that only 13% of adults demonstrated proficiency in all three literacy domains assessed.

Behavioral Outcomes

In addition to the educational outcomes previously described, a number of behaviors can negatively influence the educational experiences of children and youth. One behavioral outcome, school crime and violence, has received increased attention because of the significant impact it can have on the welfare of children, families, and schools (Henry, 2000).

Some aspects of school crime and violence, such as victimization, fighting, bullying, and weapon possession, occur on a frequent basis. For example, during the 2005–2006 school year, an estimated 2.2 million crimes were reported in public school settings, with 86% of public schools reported one or more serious violent incident, nonserious violent incident, theft, or other crime (Dinkes, Cataldi, Lin-Kelly, & Snyder, 2007).Of students ages 12–18, 3% reported theft, 1% reported a violent crime (serious violent crimes and simple assault), and less than 1% reported a serious violent crime (rape, sexual assault, robbery, aggravated assault; Dinkes et al., 2007). Male students, as well as students attending urban schools, were more likely to report victimization and theft than female students and students attending rural schools (Dinkes et al., 2007).

During the 2005–2006 school year, preliminary data indicated a total of 35 school-associated violent deaths that included students and school staff (Dinkes et al., 2007). Although this figure represents a decrease from the previous school year (i.e., 48 homicides; Dinkes, Cataldi, Kena, Baum, & Snyder, 2006), children and youth attending public schools were the victims of more nonfatal crimes than the previous year (Dinkes et al., 2006; Dinkes et al., 2007). Specifically, more than 860,000 thefts and 628,000 violent crimes were reported during 2005 (Dinkes et al., 2007). Further, a total of 51% of schools reported an incident (e.g., vandalism, possession of weapon) to the police, 38% of schools reported at least one violent crime to the police, and 28% of schools reported at least one theft to the police (Dinkes et al., 2007).

There are substantial data supporting the contention that schools provide a safer environment for children and youth than nonschool settings (DeVoe, Peter, Noonan, Synder & Baum, 2005). The percentage of youth homicides occurring at school constituted less than 2% of the total number of youth homicides (Dinkes et al., 2007). Moreover, there are some data suggesting that school safety has improved. Between 1992 and 2005, the victimization rate of youth ages 12–18 declined, as well as the theft rate (Dinkes et al., 2007). However, despite this decrease, students ages 12–18 were more likely to experience theft at school (33 thefts per 1,000 students) than away from school (23 thefts per 1,000; Dinkes et al., 2007). Since 1999, no change has been reported in the percentage of students who reported carrying a weapon (Dinkes et al., 2007). In 2005, approximately 19% of students in grades 9–12 reported carrying a weapon, and approximately 6% reported carrying a weapon on school property (Dinkes et al., 2007). Male students (10%) were more likely to carry weapons than female students (3%; Dinkes et al., 2007). Approximately 7%–9% of students in grades 9–12 reported being threatened or injured with weapons on school property from 1993 to 2005 (Dinkes et al., 2007). Similar to findings reported for carrying a weapon, male students (10%) were more likely to be threatened with or injured by a weapon than female students (6%; Dinkes et al., 2007).

In addition to direct estimates of violent behaviors and crime occurring in school settings, increasing attention has focused on bullying at schools (Espelage & Swearer, 2008; Nickerson & Martens, 2008). These subtle forms of peer victimization are associated with a number of violent crimes (Nansel, Overpeck, Haynie, Ruan, & Scheidt, 2003), including carrying weapons and fighting. In one of the landmark national surveys of youth, Nansel and colleagues (2001) reported that that 29.9% of youth attending secondary schools in the U.S. indicated moderate or frequent involvement in bullying. In 2005, a similar percentage of students ages 12–18 reported being bullied at school within the past 6 months (Dinkes et al., 2007). Approximately 37% of sixth grade students, 28% of ninth grade students, and 20% of twelfth grade students reported being bullied at school (Dinkes et al., 2007). White (30%) and Black students (29%) were more likely to be bullied than Hispanic students (22%) or other racial/ethnic groups (25%; Dinkes et al., 2007).

Of those students reporting being bullied at school in 2005, most students indicated they were bullied inside the school (79%) versus on school property (28%; Dinkes et al., 2007). The type and frequency of bullying also varied, with 19% of students experiencing bullying in the form of teasing, 15% experiencing bullying in the form of gossip or rumors, and 9% experiencing a physical form of assault (e.g., pushing, spitting; Dinkes et al., 2007).

Of those students experiencing a physical form of assault, 24% reported sustaining an injury (e.g., bruise, broken bone, bloody nose; Dinkes et al., 2007). More recently, Swearer, Turner, Givens, and Pollack (2008) reported that males who were bullied in relation to gender nonconformity issues experienced greater psychological distress, increased verbal and physical bullying, and more negative perceptions of school climate than males who were bullied for other reasons.

School violence, crime, and bullying constitute discipline problems for school settings, as well as other school safety factors. During the 2005–2006 school year, principals reported that the most frequently occurring school discipline problems included student bullying (24.5%), student acts of disrespect for teachers (18.3%), and student verbal abuse of teachers (9.5%; Dinkes et al., 2007). Less frequently occurring school discipline problems included student sexual harassment of other students (3.5%), student racial tensions (2.8%), and widespread disorder in the classroom (2.3%; Dinkes et al., 2007). As part of school discipline procedures, students may be temporarily suspended or permanently expelled from school. During the 2002–2003 school year, it was reported that more than 3 million students were suspended from school and more than 89,000 students were expelled from school (U.S. Department of Education, 2002). However, the most recent annual attendance report prepared for the National Educational Welfare Board indicated significantly lower suspensions (n = 133) and expulsions (n = 15,429) in primary and secondary settings during the 2005–2006 school year (Aogain, 2008). Among prekindergarten students, the expulsion rate was 6.7 per 1,000 enrolled, representing a rate three times greater than the national expulsion rate for elementary and secondary students (Gilliam, 2005). Interestingly, prekindergarten teachers who had access to consultants providing classroom-based behavioral consultation reported the lowest expulsion rates (Gilliam, 2005)

Mental Health Outcomes

There is substantial evidence to suggest that children's mental health problems are prevalent and begin at a young age (Knitzer & Lefkowitz, 2006; New Freedom Commission on Mental Health, 2003). It has been estimated that 10% of children and youth suffer from mental health problems that cause significant impairment in functioning (U. S. Public Health Service, 2000). Children and youth living in poverty (57%) are at the greatest risk for experiencing mental health problems, followed by children and youth residing in low-income households (21%; Costello, Compton, Keeler, & Angold, 2003; Howell, 2004). Moreover, Kessler and colleagues (2005) reported that 50% of adults in the U.S. meet the criteria for a mental health disorder in their lifetime, and the first onset occurred during childhood or adolescence. Disorders that consistently demonstrated a younger median age of onset included anxiety disorders (age 11 years) and impulse-control disorders (age 11 years; Kessler et al., 2005).

The importance of improving the mental health outcomes of children and youth has been repeatedly emphasized (Harrison et al., 2004; Ysseldyke et al., 2006), given the findings that mental health is critical to children's academic success (Adelman & Taylor, 2006; Doll & Cummings, 2008; Hoagwood & Johnson, 2003). One mental health challenge that has been significantly underemphasized is suicide and suicidal behaviors (Centers for Disease Control [CDC], 2006a; Institute of Medicine, 2002). According to the CDC, suicide is the third leading cause of death among young people in the U.S. (CDC, 2006a). Moreover, despite decreases in the overall suicide rates among youth ages 10–19 over a 15-year period (1990–2004), the suicide rates for females ages 10–19 and males ages 15–19 increased significantly from 2003 to 2004 (CDC, 2007). Further, between 1981 and 2004, the number of children ages 10–14 committing suicide has increased 51% between (American Association of Suicidology, 2006).

The scope of the problem of youth suicidal behavior becomes even more pressing when considering the prevalence of suicidal ideation and suicide attempts in addition to suicide completion. According to the most recent results of the Youth Risk Behavior Survey, approximately 17% of students in grades 9–12 seriously considered suicide in the previous 12 months, 8.4% reported making at least one suicide attempt, and 2.3% reported making at least one attempt that required medical attention (CDC, 2006b). Collectively, these findings suggest that approximately 1 out of 6 high school students will engage in serious suicidal ideation and that 1 in 12 will make a suicide attempt (Miller & Eckert, 2009).

Despite the prevalence of mental health problems among children and youth, most children and adolescents do not receive services (Kataoka, Zhang, & Wells, 2002). Specifically, in a study of three nationally representative household studies, it was reported that 75% of children and adolescents requiring mental health services had not accessed care in the past year (Kataoka et al., 2002). Only a small percentage of children and adolescents (6%–7.5%) received mental health services, with more White and insured children being able to access care (Kataoka et al., 2002).

Summary of the Current Status of Children, Families, and Schools

The demographic characteristics of children and youth, as well as the educational, behavioral, and mental health outcomes of children and youth, have substantial implications for the evolution of school psychology. First, there will continue to be an increasing demand for educational services to children and youth, as enrollment figures for public elementary and secondary schools estimate increases until 2020 (Federal Interagency Forum on Child and Family Statistics, 2007). Increasing numbers of these students will reside in diverse households with a substantial number living in poverty (Annie E. Casey Foundation, 2007). Second, there will continue to be a need for special education services for children and youth as the percentage served under IDEA (IDEA, 2004) continues to increase across all age groups (U.S. Department of Education, 2009). It appears that the greatest need will occur among infants and toddlers and children ages 3–5 (U.S. Department of Education, 2009). Third, educational outcomes suggest that many children and youth enrolled in American public schools experience significant difficulty learning to read, write, and compute. Given that specific demographic factors (i.e., age, race/ethnicity, poverty) appear to be related to the academic competence of children and youth, it is critical that additional attention be focused on improving the academic competencies of these at-risk children and youth (Eckert, Truckenmiller, Rheinheimer, Perry, & Koehler, 2008). Fourth, although schools provide a safer environment for children and youth than nonschool settings (DeVoe et al., 2005), increased efforts need to be directed at reducing school crime and violence (Dinkes, et al., 2007), addressing bullying (Espelage & Swearer, 2008), and other school discipline problems (U.S. Department of Education, 2002). Fifth, increased mental health services need to be provided to children and youth who suffer from mental health problems (New Freedom Commission on Mental Health, 2003), and more attention needs to focus on the prevention of suicide and suicidal behaviors (Miller & Eckert, 2009). The current status of children and youth in the U.S. provides a compelling rationale for improving the educational, behavioral,

and mental health outcomes of children and youth. Toward this goal, numerous federal and policy reform initiatives have been advocated to improve the outcomes of children, youth, and families.

Indirect Initiatives to Improve the Outcomes of Children, Youth, and Families

Within the past 10 years, a number of reform movements have targeted the educational, behavioral, and mental health outcomes of children and youth. For example, the No Child Left Behind Act (NCLB) of 2001 attempts to improve educational outcomes by linking federal funds to schools that demonstrate academic proficiency in the areas of mathematics, reading or language arts, and science. As discussed by Reschly (2008), four critical features of NCLB had immediate consequences for the provision of educational and school psychological services. These features included: (a) improving the educational achievement of students receiving general, remedial, and special education; (b) advocating the use of scientifically based instruction; (c) preventing achievement and antisocial behavior problems; (d) improving general outcomes for all children and youth; and (e) reporting their students' educational outcomes with respect to various demographic factors including race/ethnicity, economic, language, and disability status (Reschly, 2008). The reauthorization of the Individuals with Disabilities Improvement Act (IDEA) in 2004 provided the legal basis for a number of provisions that denote key advancements in the field of school psychology and include: (a) supporting the use of schoolwide systems (e.g., positive behavioral supports) to promote appropriate school behaviors and improve the behavioral outcomes of children and youth; (b) permitting response-to-intervention as one method for the identification of specific learning disabilities; and (c) requiring data-based assessment and progress monitoring for students suspected of having high incidence disabilities, such as specific learning disabilities or serious emotional disturbance (Reschly, 2008).

Improving children's early learning experiences has also received increased attention (National Research Council, 2000; U.S. Department of Health and Human Services, 2001). For example, *A Nation of Learners* emphasized the importance of all young children having access to developmentally appropriate educational programs (National Education Goals Panel, 1995). Similarly, the National Education Goals Panel (1997) stated that by the year 2000, all young children would start school ready to learn. Reforms were suggested by key policy groups including the National Research Council reading report (Snow, Burns, & Griffin, 1998) and minority representation report (Donovan & Cross, 2002), the National Reading Panel (2000), and the President's Commission on Excellence in Special Education (2002). Similar to the federal and legislative initiatives previously reviewed, these reports emphasized the importance of providing systematic and direct instruction, using scientifically based intervention, and using data-based decision making and progress monitoring to assess the outcomes of children and youth in U.S. schools (Reschly, 2008).

Recent reports by the U.S. Health and Human Services Office of the Surgeon General (1999) and the President's New Freedom Commission on Mental Health (2003) have also emphasized the need to improve mental health services for children and youth. Moreover, increased attention has been directed at addressing youth suicide prevention (U. S. Department of Health and Human Services, 1999; New Freedom Commission on Mental Health, 2003). For example, the U.S. Congress in passing the nation's first suicide prevention bill (Garrett Lee Smith Memorial Act of 2004) noted that "youth suicide is a public health tragedy linked to underlying mental health problems and [that] youth suicide early intervention and prevention activities are national priorities" (p. 1). These directives, coupled with increased attention on improving students' transition to postsecondary educational settings (National Alliance for Secondary Education and Transition, 2005) have rapidly altered the conceptualization of, and practice in, the field of school psychology.

Within the field of school psychology, similar demands have been made (Christenson, 2000; Shapiro, 2000; Sheridan & Gutkin, 2000). For example, the proceedings of the 2002 Conference on the Future of School Psychology (Dawson et al., 2004), identified a shared professional and scientific agenda for the field (Kratochwill & Shernoff, 2004). The results of this conference prioritized five areas: (a) improved academic competence for all children; (b) improved social/emotional functioning for all children; (c) enhanced family–school partnerships and parental involvement in schools; (d) more effective education and instruction for all learners; and (e) increased child and family services in schools that promote health and mental health and are integrated with community services (Dawson et al., 2004).

Accounting for the changes in the field, as well the recommendations from the 2002 Conference on the Future of School Psychology, NASP revised and updated the training and practice standards for the profession (Ysseldyke et al., 2006). In this document, commonly referred to as the *Blueprint III*, the overarching goals were to improve the competencies for all children and youth, as well as to build and maintain services to meet their needs. (Ysseldyke et al., 2006). Specific training and practice and practice components were defined in terms of (a) domains of competence (i.e., foundational and functional competencies), (b) delivery systems (i.e., intensive, targeted, universal), and (c) outcomes (i.e., build capacity of systems, improved competencies for all students).

The recommendations from the 2002 Conference on the Future of School Psychology (Dawson et al., 2004) and the Blueprint III (Ysseldyke et al., 2006) are consistent with recommendations made by leaders in the field of school psychology to shift from an individualized service delivery model to a population-based (Doll & Cummings, 2008), public health approach (Hoagwood & Johnson, 2003; Nastasi, 2004; Power, 2000; Power, DuPaul, Shapiro, & Kazak, 2003; Strein, Hoagwood, & Cohn, 2003) that is more proactive in the prevention of mental health problems (Power, 2003) and youth suicide (Mazza & Reynolds, 2008). Further, Blueprint III (Ysseldyke, 2006) placed an increased emphasis on the functional competencies of school psychologists, which included: (a) enhancing the developmental of cognitive and academic skills; (b) data-based decision making and accountability; (c) enhancing the development of wellness, social skills, mental health, and life competencies; and (d) systems-based service delivery.

Direct Initiatives to Improve the Outcomes of Children, Youth, and Families

Although the previously described reform efforts are, in theory, related to changes in school psychology, none can *directly* or *causally* result in improved outcomes for children, families, and schools (Eckert, 2005). Rather, recent empirical findings and scientific reform initiatives have served as the primary catalyst for improving these outcomes by explicitly determining what works, for whom, and under what conditions (Raudenbush, 2005). These empirical findings and scientific reform initiatives can be grouped into three categories: (1) empirically validated assessment; (2) evidenced-based practice; and (3) advanced methodological and statistical approaches.

Empirically Validated Assessment
Advances have been made in our standards for testing and assessment (AERA, APA, & NCME, 1999).

One method of assessment that has received considerable attention is curriculum based measurement (CBM). CBM is a method of assessment designed to make instructional decisions and evaluate student progress in basic academic skills. This method of assessment involves the use of repeated, brief measurements of academic behaviors taken from the instructional curriculum as a means of assessing student performance over time (Deno, 1985; Deno, Marston, & Mirkin, 1982; Deno, Marston, & Tindal, 1986; Fuchs, Deno, & Mirkin, 1984). The majority of research examining the use of CBM progress-monitoring procedures has employed oral reading fluency as the outcome measure (see Shinn, 1998 for review), and has consistently been determined to be a reliable and valid assessment measure of reading for use with elementary-aged students (Deno et al., 1982; Fuchs, Fuchs, & Maxwell, 1988; Marston & Magnussen, 1985; Shinn, Good, Knutson, Tilly, & Collins, 1992). In addition, studies assessing students' academic skills growth using CBM progress-monitoring procedures have demonstrated that change in student performance over time on CBM passages correlate with changes on standardized measures of reading (see Marston, 1989 for review). Further, a number of studies have demonstrated that CBM procedures are more sensitive to detecting change over short periods of time than standardized measures (Fuchs & Fuchs, 1986; Fuchs, Fuchs, Hamlett, Walz, & Germann, 1993; Hintze, Daly, & Shapiro, 1998; Shinn, Gleason, & Tindal, 1989). As a result of the early psychometric work on CBM, this method of formative assessment has been recommended in national reading reports (e.g., National Reading Panel, 2000), and the National Center on Student Progress Monitoring (2009) provides a review of CBM measures (e.g., AIMSweb, 2009; DIBELS, Good & Kaminski, 2009; iSTEEP, 2009) that have been evaluated across foundational psychometric standards (i.e., reliability, validity), as well as formative evaluation standards (e.g., sensitivity to student improvement, specified rates of student improvement) during four annual evaluations by a technical review committee.

Similar advances have been made with the types of assessment that can be used to inform school-based decision making. For example, a large empirical basis supports the functional assessment of child and youth behavior (Ervin et al., 2001). Functional assessment is defined as a broad set of procedures that examine the function or relationship between problem behaviors and environmental events (Gresham, Watson, & Skinner, 2001). These procedures can be used to identify antecedent and contextual factors, as well as the maintaining contingencies that directly influence behavior (Martens, Eckert, Bradley, & Ardoin, 1999). Most of the research has focused on students diagnosed with low-incidence disabilities exhibiting high-frequency problem behaviors (Ervin et al., 2001), although a considerable number of studies have examined the use of functional assessment in school based settings (Boyajian et al., 2001; Broussard & Northup, 1995; Cooper et al., 1992; Dunlap, Kern-Dunlap, Clarke, & Robbins, 1991; Ervin, DuPaul, Kern, & Friman, 1998; Northup et al., 1991; Umbreit, 1995). The results of these studies suggest that school-based functional assessment can be a valuable assessment approach to identify factors that directly influence the behavior of children and youth, as well as to assist in the development of effective classroom based interventions (Eckert, Martens, & DiGennaro, 2005).

Within the past five years, a framework for extending functional assessment procedures to academic skills has emerged. In a conceptual paper, Daly, Witt, Martens, and Dool (1997) proposed a model for conducting a functional assessment of academic problems. Based on a review of the empirical literature addressing academic performance problems, Daly and colleagues identified common sources of problems (e.g., students do not want to do it, students perceive it as too difficult) and developed eight hypotheses related to the presumed function of academic behavior problems. Potential interventions for each hypothesis were generated, and an efficient design for rapidly examining the effectiveness of interventions (i.e., brief experimental analysis) was proposed. The use of brief experimental analysis, combined with Daly et al.'s conceptual model for examining academic problems, to develop effective reading interventions is incipient (Ervin et al., 2001). However, a small number of research studies using this methodology as an alternative strategy for empirically identifying effective reading fluency interventions studies have recently been published (see Eckert, Dunn, Rosenblatt, & Truckenmiller, 2008 for a review). In addition, two recent meta-analyses (Burns & Wagner, 2008; Morgan & Sideridis 2006), provide additional support for these procedures to improve children's educational outcomes.

Evidenced-Based Practice

Our knowledge of what constitutes effective educational practice (U.S. Department of Education, 2003), empirically validated treatment (Task Force on Promotion and Dissemination of Psychological Procedures, 1995, 1998), evidenced-based treatment (Kratochwill & Stoiber, 2000), and evidence-based practice, have dramatically increased (American Psychological Association, 2002; APA Presidential Task Force on Evidence-Based Practice, 2006). In the field of school psychology, the Task Force on Evidence-Based Interventions in School Psychology Procedural developed a procedural and coding manual (Kratochwill & Stoiber, 2002) to be used to establish evidence-based standards for the field. Eight methodological indicators (i.e., measurement, comparison group, statistically significant outcomes, educational/clinical significant, identifiable components, implementation fidelity, replication, site of implementation) are examined on a four-point Likert type scale (0 = no evidence; 1 = marginal or weak evidence; 2 = promising evidence; and 3 = strong evidence). To date, these standards have been systematically applied to evaluate evidence-based parent and family interventions in school psychology (Bates, 2005; Cox, 2005; Fishel & Ramirez, 2005; Validez, Carlson, & Zanger, 2005), as well as school based suicide prevention efforts (Miller, Eckert, & Mazza, 2009).

Although significant concerns remain regarding the criteria for determining whether practices or treatments are evidence based or empirically supported (Hunsley, 2007), along with concerns about the uniform application of treatments across groups or situations (Kazdin, 2008), there is considerable best research evidence to support the use of various practices and treatments to improve the adaptive behaviors of children, youth, and families while reducing maladaptive behaviors (Office of Special Education Program Center on Positive Behavior Interventions and Supports, 2004). For example, there are empirically validated treatments for children diagnosed with attention-deficit/hyperactivity disorder (Dulcan, 1997; Pelham, Wheeler, & Chrois, 1998), conduct disorder (Brestan & Eyberg, 1998; Steiner, 1997), mood disorder (Birmaher & Brent, 1998), and anxiety disorders (Bernstein & Shaw, 1997). Further, research syntheses (National Reading Panel, 2000; Snow et al., 1998) on effective practices for children with specific learning disabilities have informed instructional practices.

Advanced Methodological and Statistical Approaches

Enhanced methodological and statistical practices have improved the communication of scientific findings (Fidler et al., 2005) and contributed to improved practices for children, families, and schools. Published guidelines for statistical reporting (Wilkinson & the Task Force on Statistical Inference, 1999) and recommendations for the application of multiple research designs (e.g., qualitative research, randomized controlled trials) to address different empirical questions (American Educational Research Association, 2006) have allowed researchers to engage in extensive scientific verification. Similar advances have been made to improve the effectiveness of scientific communications by requiring researchers to follow reporting standards for experimental (Altman et al., 2001), nonexperimental (Des Jarlais, Lyles, Crepaz, & the TREND group, 2004), and alternative empirical designs such as longitudinal research or meta-analysis (APA Publications and Communications Board Working Group on Journal Article Reporting Standards, 2008). Empirical methodologies have also broadened to include the use of case-based time series studies for evaluating treatment effects in applied settings (Borckardt et al., 2008), and engaging in more systematic evaluations of the mechanisms and moderators of change to inform applied practice (Kazdin, 2008).

In addition, alternative statistical or methodological approaches have been proposed to further evaluate the clinical significance of research findings. For example, Killeen (2005, 2006) has advocated for the computation of replication statistics (i.e., the probability of successful replication, p_{rep}) to more expansively evaluate research in applied settings. In comparison to traditional null hypothesis testing, this statistic allows researchers to evaluate the probability of replicating an effect and reduces the emphasis on a binary evaluation of producing an effect (i.e., statistically significant effect versus nonsignificant effect). Sanabria and Killeen (2007) argue that replication statistics allow practitioners to make more informed decisions regarding the cost-effectiveness of educational and psychological practices, thereby reducing reliance on null hypothesis testing.

One of the most significant advancements is the statistical treatment of group administered treatments, which is a common approach in educational research. Although methods for dealing with nested data have been discussed since the mid 1980s (Kenny & Judd, 1986), the influence group membership can have on study outcomes has largely been ignored in educational research. This is especially problematic given the hierarchical structure of education experiences, wherein (a) individual student growth occurs, (b) individual student growth may be affected by personal characteristics and individual experiences that affect student learning, and

(c) all of these characteristics may influence the classroom, teacher behavior, and characteristics of the other students (Raudenbush & Bryk, 2002). A number of statistical corrections have been recommended to control for the increase in Type I errors (Baldwin, Murray, & Shadish, 2005). However, one analytical approach, hierarchical modeling, provides a general statistical framework for appropriately estimating the treatment effects associated with nested studies (Morris & Normand, 1992; Raudenbush & Bryk, 1986; Raudenbush, 2005).

Summary of the Influence of Indirect and Direct Initiatives on the Evolution of School Psychology

The previously reviewed indirect and direct initiatives have been related to improvements in educational, behavioral, and mental health outcomes of children and youth. First, the legislative reforms (e.g., IDEA, NCLB) have major implications for the provision of educational and school psychological services, including using scientifically based instruction and intervention to improve the educational achievement and behavioral outcomes of all children and youth, while preventing and remediating achievement and behavioral problems. The use of data-based decision making, and formative assessment of the educational, behavioral, and mental health outcomes of children and youth are also critical components that increase accountability in school settings as well as preschool and postsecondary settings. Second, training and practice recommendations from the field of school psychology have rapidly altered the conceptualization and practice of the field. Emphasis on shifting school psychological service delivery to a more proactive, population-based approach increases the likelihood that the educational, behavioral, and mental health of children and youth can be improved. Third, recent scientific advances in the areas of empirically validated assessment, evidenced-based practice, and advanced methodological and statistical approaches, have provided the field of school psychology with the tools for improving the educational, behavioral, and mental health of children and youth.

The Evolution of School Psychology: Data-Based Decision Making and Multi-Tiered Problem Solving

Advances in empirically validated assessment and evidenced-based practice have allowed school psychologists to significantly alter their service delivery models in an effort to link assessment to intervention

(Batsche, Castillo, Dixon, & Forde, 2008). Embedded in this approach of linking assessment results to the selection of appropriate interventions is data-based decision making. The use of data-based decision making has a longstanding history in the field of school psychology beginning with the behavioral consultation approach advocated by Bergan and Kratochwill (1990). The key steps in this model address four questions: (1) Is there a problem and what is it? (2) Why is the problem happening? (3) What can be done about the problem? and (4) Did the intervention work? This decision-making approach allows school psychologists to rigorously evaluate the effects of school based interventions on the educational, behavioral, and mental health outcomes of children and youth, while taking into consideration individual differences in responding to intervention components. This approach affords data-based judgments that increase accountability efforts (Daly, Chafouleas, & Skinner, 2005).

Given the educational, behavioral, and mental health difficulties that many children and youth may experience, one alternative service delivery model, multi-tiered problem-solving, has been identified as a key evolution in school psychological service delivery (Reschly, 2008; Tilly, 2008). This model is best illustrated by Walker et al.'s (1996) three-tiered problem solving model, which has been represented visually through the use of a triangle. Three overlapping tiers are included in the triangle, which "collectively represent a continuum of interventions that increase in intensity based on the corresponding responsiveness" of individuals (Sugai, 2007, p. 114). The first tier, represented as the base of the triangle, is referred to as the *universal* or *primary* level, because all students in classrooms receive a universal set of interventions designed to prevent particular emotional, behavioral, or academic problems. The second tier of the triangle, referred to as the *targeted* or *secondary* level, consists of more intensive interventions for those students who do not adequately respond to universal interventions. The third and last tier, referred to as the *indicated* or *tertiary* level, is characterized by highly individualized and specialized interventions for those students who do not adequately respond to universal and targeted levels of prevention and intervention (Sugai, 2007; Walker et al., 1996).

School psychology is increasingly embracing this perspective, in part due to the fact that a continuum of interventions can more broadly meet the needs academic, behavioral, and mental health needs of children and youth in schools (Doll & Cummings,

2008). Specific aspects that have particular relevance for school psychology include (a) applying scientifically derived evidence to the delivery of school based services, (b) strengthening student performance rather than focusing exclusively on decreasing problem behavior, (c) emphasizing community collaboration and linked services, and (d) using appropriate research strategies to improve the knowledge base and effectively evaluate school psychological services (Strein et al., 2003).

The multi-tiered problem solving model is associated with one approach, schoolwide positive behavior support, which has been demonstrated to be highly effective in reducing antisocial behavior among students in schools (Horner, Sugai, Todd, & Lewis-Palmer, 2005). This approach is based on empirically validated strategies to promote appropriate behavior of all students in school settings, and has been adopted in numerous school settings (McKevitt & Braaksma, 2008). Key features of schoolwide positive behavior support include: (a) establishing and defining clear and consistent schoolwide expectations; (b) teaching the expectations to students; (c) acknowledging students for demonstrating expected behaviors; (d) implementing a consequence system to respond to inappropriate behaviors; and (e) using data to evaluate the effects of the support system (Office of Special Education Programs Center on Positive Behavioral Interventions and Supports, 2004).

Another example of the multi-tiered problem solving model is the responsiveness to intervention (RTI) approach, which provides multi-tiered intervention support to children experiencing academic skills problems. Key characteristics of this approach include: (a) providing all students with high quality, research-based instruction; (b) implementing small-group, high-intensity interventions for students demonstrating inadequate progress; and (c) implementing individualized, high-intensity interventions for students continuing to demonstrate inadequate progress (Fuchs, Mock, Morgan, & Young, 2003; McMaster, Fuch, Fuchs, & Compton, 2005; Mellard, Byrd, Johnson, Tollefson, & Boesche, 2004). Recently, the Institute of Education Sciences published practice guidelines for implementing response to intervention and multi-tier intervention in the primary grades (Gersten et al., 2009).

Conclusion

The historical developments in the field of school psychology over the last quarter century coupled with federal legislation and educational reform movements, have attempted to influence the current status of children and youth in the U.S. A number of indirect and direct initiatives have further propelled improvements to the educational, behavioral, and mental health outcomes of children and youth. In addition, these provisions have affected the field of school psychology, and rapidly transformed school psychological practice to include a more preventative, population-based approach to improve the educational, behavioral, and mental health of children and youth. Scientific advances in empirically validated assessment, evidenced-based practice, and advanced methodological and statistical approaches, have allowed the field to evolve so that school psychology is now better positioned to identify, select, and implement appropriate strategies to address the diverse needs of children and youth in school settings (Merrell & Buchanan, 2006).

References

Adelman, H. S., & Taylor, L. (2006). *The school leader's guide to student learning supports: New directions for addressing barriers to learning.* Thousand Oaks, CA: Corwin Press.

AIMSweb. (2009). Retrieved on February 1, 2009 from http://www.aimsweb.com/

Altman, D. G., Schulz, K. F., Moher, D., Egger, M., Davidoff, F., Elbourne, D., Gotzsche, P. C., & Lang, T. (2001). The revised CONSORT statement for reporting randomized trials: Explanation and elaboration. *Annals of Internal Medicine, 134 (8),* 663–694.

American Association of Suicidology. (2006). *Youth suicide fact sheet.* Retrieved May 13, 2008 from http://www.suicidology.org

American Educational Research Association. (2006). Standards for reporting on empirical social science research in AERA publications. *Educational Researcher, 35 (6),* 33–40.

American Educational Research Association [AERA], American Psychological Association [APA], & National Council on Measurement in Education [NCME]. (1999). *Standards for educational and psychological testing.* Washington, DC: American Educational Research Association.

American Psychological Association. (2002). Criteria for evaluating treatment guidelines. *American Psychologist, 57,* 1052–1059.

Annie E. Casey Foundation. (2007). *2007 KIDS COUNT data book: State profiles of child well-being.* Baltimore, MD: Annie E. Casey Foundation.

Aogain, E. M. (2008). *Analysis of school attendance data in primary and post-primary schools, 2003/4 to 2005/6: Report to the National Educational Welfare Board.* Retrieved on February 1, 2009 from http://www.newb.ie/school/attendance_data.asp

APA Model Act for State Licensures of Psychologists. (1987). *American Psychologist, 42,* 696–703.

APA Presidential Task Force on Evidence-Based Practice. (2006). Evidence-based practice in psychology. *American Psychologist, 61,* 271–285.

APA Publications and Communications Board Working Group on Journal Article Reporting Standards. (2008). Reporting standards for research in psychology: Why do we need them? What might they be? *American Psychologist, 63,* 839–851.

Baldwin, S. A., Murray, D. M., & Shadish, W. R. (2005). Empirically-supported treatments or type I errors? Problems with the analysis of data from group-administered treatments. *Journal of Consulting and Clinical Psychology, 73*, 924–935.

Bates, S. L. (2005). Evidence-based parent and family interventions in school psychology: Overview and procedures. *School Psychology Quarterly, 20*, 345–351.

Batsche, G. M., Castillo, J. M., Dixon, D. N., & Forde, S. (2008). Best practices in linking assessment to intervention. In A. Thomas A. J. Grimes (Eds.), *Best practices in school psychology V* (vol. 2, pp. 177–194). Bethesda, MD: National Association of School Psychologists.

Bergan, J. R., & Kratochwill, T. R. (1990). *Behavioral consultation and therapy.* New York: Plenum.

Bernstein, G. A. & Shaw, K. (1997). Practice parameters for the assessment and treatment of children and adolescents with anxiety disorders. *Journal of the American Academy of Child and Adolescent Psychiatry, 36*, 69S–84S.

Birmaher, B., & Brent, D. (1998). Practice parameters for the assessment and treatment of children and adolescents with depressive disorder. *Journal of the American Academy of Child and Adolescent Psychiatry, 37*, 63S–83S.

Borckardt, J. J., Nash, M. R., Murphy, M. D., Moore, M., Shaw, D., & O'Neil, P. (2008). Clinical practice as natural laboratory for psychotherapy research. *American Psychologist, 63*, 77–95.

Boyajian, A. E., DuPaul, G. J., Wartel Handler, M., Eckert, T. L., & McGoey, K. E. (2001). The use of classroom-based brief functional analyses with preschoolers at-risk for attention deficit hyperactivity disorder. *School Psychology Review, 30*, 278–293.

Bramlett, R. K., Murphy, J. J., Johnson, J., & Wallingsford, L. (2002). Contemporary practices in school psychology: A national survey of roles and referral problems. *Psychology in the Schools, 39*, 327–335.

Brestan, E. V. & Eyberg, S. M. (1998). Effective psychosocial treatments of conduct-disordered children and adolescents: 29 years, 82 studies, and 5,272 kids. *Journal of Clinical Child Psychology, 27*, 180–189.

Broussard, C. K., & Northup, J. N. (1995). An approach to functional assessment and analysis of disruptive behavior in regular education classrooms. *School Psychology Quarterly, 10*, 151–164.

Burns, M. K., & Wagner, D. (2008). Determining an effect intervention within a brief experimental analysis for reading: A meta-analytic review. *School Psychology Review, 37*, 126–136.

Centers for Disease Control and Prevention. (2006a). *Suicide prevention scientific information: Consequences.* Retrieved March 27, 2008, from http://www.cdc.gov/ncipc/dvp/Suicide/Suicide-conque.htm

Centers for Disease Control and Prevention. (2006b). *Youth risk behavior survey – United States, 2005.* Retrieved May 13, 2008 from http://www.cdc.gov/mmwr/preview/mmwrhtml/SS5505al.htm

Centers for Disease Control and Prevention. (2007). Suicide trends among youths and young adults aged 10–24 years – United States – 1990 - 2004. *Morbidity and Mortality Weekly Review, 56*, 905–908.

Christenson, S. L. (2000). Commentary: School psychologists as health-care providers: A means to success for all. *School Psychology Review, 29*, 555–556.

Clopton, K. L., & Haselhuhn, C. W. (2009). School psychology trainer shortage in the USA: Current status and projections for the future. *School Psychology International, 30*, 24–42.

Cooper, L., Wacker, D., Thursby, D., Plagmann, L., Harding, J., Millard, T., & Derby, M. (1992). Analysis of the effects of task preferences, task demands, and adult attention on child behavior in outpatient and classroom settings. *Journal of Applied Behavior Analysis, 25*, 823–840.

Costello, E., J., Compton, S. N., Keeler, G., & Angold, A. (2003). Relationships between poverty and psychopathology. *Journal of the American Medical Association, 290*, 2023–2064.

Cox, D. D. (2005). Evidence-based interventions using home-school collaboration. *School Psychology Quarterly, 20*, 473–497.

Curtis, M. J., Grier, E. C., & Hunley, S. A. (2004). The changing face of school psychology: Trends in data and projections for the future. *School Psychology Review, 33*, 49–66.

Curtis, M. J., Hunley, S. A., & Grier, E. C. (2004). The status of school psychology: Implications of a major personnel shortage. *Psychology in the Schools, 41*, 431–442.

Daly, E. J. III, Chafouleas, S., & Skinner, C. (2005). *Interventions for reading problems: Designing and evaluating effective strategies.* New York: Guilford Press.

Daly, E. J. III, Witt, J. C., Martens, B. K., & Dool, E. J. (1997). A model for conducting a functional analysis of academic performance problems. *School Psychology Review, 26*, 554–574.

Davis, A. S., McIntosh, D. E., Phelps, L., & Kehle, T. J. (2004). Addressing the shortage of school psychologists: A summative overview. *Psychology in the Schools, 41*, 489–495.

Dawson, M., Cummings, J. A., Harrison, P. L., Short, R., J., Gorin, S., & Palomares, R. (2004). The 2002 multisite conference on the future of school psychology: Next steps. *School Psychology Quarterly, 18*, 497–509; School Psychology Review, 33, 115–125.

Deno, S. L. (1985). Curriculum-based measurement: The emerging alternative. *Exceptional Children, 52*, 219–232.

Deno, S. L., Marston, D., & Mirkin, P. K. (1982). Valid measurement procedures for continuous evaluation of written expression. *Exceptional Children, 48*, 368–371.

Deno, S. L., Marston, D., & Tindal, G. (1986). Direct and frequent curriculum-based measurement: An alternative for educational decision making. *Special Services in the Schools, 2*, 5–27.

Des Jarlais, D. C., Lyles, C., Crepaz, N., & the TREND Group. (2004). Improving the reporting quality of nonrandomized evaluations of behavioral and public health interventions: The TREND statement. *American Journal of Public Health, 94*, 361–366.

DeVoe, J. F., Peter, K., Noonan, M., Snyder, T. D., & Baum, K. (2005). *Indicators of school crime and safety: 2005.* Washington, DC: U.S. Government Printing Office.

Dinkes, R., Cataldi, E. F., Kena, G., Baum, & Snyder, T. D. (2006). *Indicators of school crime and safey: 2006.* Washington, DC: U.S. Government Printing Office.

Dinkes, R., Cataldi, E. F., Lin-Kelly, W., & Snyder, T. J. (2007). *Indicators of school crime and safey: 2007.* Washington, DC: U.S. Government Printing Office.

Doll, B., & Cummings, J. A. (2008). (Eds.). *Transforming school mental health services.* Thousand Oaks, CA: Corwin Press.

Donovan, M. S. & Cross, C. T. (2002). *Minority students in special and gifted education.* Washington, DC: National Academies Press.

Dulcan, M. (1997). Practice parameters for the assessment and treatment of children, adolescents, and, adults with attention-deficit/hyperactivity disorder. *Journal of the American Academy of Child and Adolescent Psychiatry, 36*, 85S–121S.

Dunlap, G. Kern-Dunlap, L., Clarke, S., & Robbins, F. R. (1991). Functional assessment, curricular revision, and severe behavior problems. *Journal of Applied Behavior Analysis, 24*, 823–840.

Eckert, T. L. (2005). Improving children's educational outcomes by advancing assessment and intervention practices: An overview of the special series. *School Psychology Review, 34*, 4–8.

Eckert, T. L, Dunn, E. K., Rosenblatt, M. A., & Truckenmiller, A. J. (2008). Identifying effective school-based reading interventions: A review of the brief experimental analysis literature. *School Psychology Forum, 2*, 16–28.

Eckert, T. L., Martens, B. K., & DiGennaro, F. D. (2005). Increasing the accuracy of functional assessment methods: Describing antecedent-behavior-consequence relations using conditional probabilities. *School Psychology Review, 4*, 520–528.

Eckert, T. L., Truckenmiller, A. J., Rheinheimer, J. L., Perry, L. J., & Koehler, J. L. (2008). Improving children's academic performance: Benefits and barriers associated with fluency-based interventions (pp. 327-343). In D. H. Molina (Ed.), *School Psychology: 21st Century Issues and Challenges.* Hauppauge, NY: Nova Sciences.

Ervin, R. A., DuPaul, G. J., Kern, L., & Friman, P. C. (1998). Classroom-based functional assessment: A proactive approach to intervention selection for adolescents diagnosed with attention deficit hyperactivity disorder. *Journal of Applied Behavior Analysis, 31*, 65–78.

Ervin, R. A., Radford, P. M., Bertsch, K., Piper, A. L., Ehrhardt, K. E., & Poling, A. (2001). A descriptive analysis and critique of the empirical literature on school-based functional assessment. *School Psychology Review, 30*, 193–210.

Espelage, D. L. & Swearer, S. M. (2008). Addressing research gaps in the intersection between homophobia and bullying. *School Psychology Review, 37*, 155–159.

Fagan, T. K. (1999). Training school psychologists before there were school psychologist training programs: A history, 1890–1930. In C. R. Reynolds & T. B. Gutkin (Eds.), *The handbook of school psychology* (3rd ed.) (pp. 1–33). NY: Wiley.

Fagan, T. K. (2002). School psychology: Recent descriptions, continued expansion, and an ongoing paradox. *School Psychology Review, 31*, 5–10.

Fagan, T. K. (2004). School psychology's significant discrepancy: Historical perspectives on personnel shortages. *Psychology in the Schools, 41*, 419–430.

Fagan, T. K. (2007). In my opinion: Challenges to the continued success of school psychology. *Communique, 35 (8)*, 45–46.

Fagan, T. K. (2008). Trends in the history of school psychology in the United States. In A. Thomas & J. Grimes (Eds.), *Best practices in school psychology V* (pp. 209–222). Bethesda, MD: National Association of School Psychologists.

Fagan, T. K., Gorin, S., & Tharinger, D. (2000). The National Association of School Psychologists and the Division of School Psychology – APA: Now and beyond. *School Psychology Review, 29*, 525–535.

Fagan, T. K., & Wise, P. S. (2007). *School psychology: Past, present, and future* (3rd ed.). Bethesda, MD: National Association of School Psychologists.

Federal Interagency Forum on Child and Family Statistics. (2007). *America's Children: Key National Indicators of Well-Being, 2007.* Washington DC: U.S. Government Printing Office.

Fidler, F., Cumming, G., Thomason, N., Pannuzzo, D., Smith, J., Fyffe, P., et al. (2005). Toward improved statistical reporting. *Journal of Consulting and Clinical Psychology, 73*, 136–143.

Fishel, M. & Ramirez, L. (2005). Evidence-based parent involvement interventions with school-aged children. *School Psychology Quarterly, 20*, 371–402.

Fuchs, L. S., Deno, S. L., & Mirkin, P. K. (1984). The effects of frequent curriculum-based measures and evaluation on pedagogy, student achievement, and student awareness of learning.

Fuchs, L.S., & Fuchs, D. (1986). Effects of systematic formative evaluation on student achievement: A meta-analysis. *Exceptional Children, 53*, 199–208.

Fuchs, L. S., Fuchs, D., Hamlett, C. L., Walz, L., & Germann, G. (1993). Formative evaluation of academic progress: How much growth can we expect? *School Psychology Review, 22*, 27–48.

Fuchs, L.S., Fuchs, D., & Maxwell, L. (1988). The validity of informal reading comprehension measures. *Remedial and Special Education, 9*, 20–28.

Fuchs, D., Mock, D., Morgan, P. L., & Young, C. L. (2003). Responsiveness-to-intervention: Definitions, evidence, and implications for the learning disabilities construct. *Learning Disabilities Research & Practice, 18*, 172–186.

Garrett Lee Smith Memorial Act of 2004, Pub. L. No. 108-355, 118 Stat. 1404 (2004).

Gersten, R., Compton, D., Connor, C. M., Dimino, J., Santoro, L., Linan-Thompson, S., & Tilly, W. D. (2008). *Assisting students struggling with reading: Response to Intervention and multi-tier intervention for reading in the primary grades. A practice guide.* Washington, DC: National Center for Education and Evaluation and Regional Assistance, Institute of Education Sciences, U. S. Department of Education. Retrieved on February 18, 2009 from http://ies.ed.gov/ncee/wwc/publications/practiceguides

Gilliam, W. S. (2005). Prekindergartners left behind: Expulsion rates in state prekindergarten programs. New York: Foundation for Child Development.

Good, R. H., & Kaminski, R. A. (2009). *Dynamic Indicators of Basic Early Literacy Skills.* Retrieved on February 1, 2009 from http://dibels.uoregon.edu

Gresham, F. M., Watson, T. S., & Skinner, C. H. (2001). Functional behavioral assessment: Principles, procedures, and future directions. *School Psychology Review, 30*, 156–172.

Harrison, P. L., Cummings, J. A., Dawson, M., Short, R. J., Gorin, S., & Palomares, R. (2004). Responding to the needs of children, families, and schools: The 2002 Multisite Conference on the Future of School Psychology. *School Psychology Review, 33*, 12–33.

Henry, S. (2000). What is school violence? An integrated definition. *Annals of the American Academy of Political and Social Science, 567*, 16–29.

Hintze, J. M., Daly, E. J., & Shapiro, E. S. (1998). An investigation of the effects of passage difficulty level on outcomes of oral reading fluency progress monitoring. *School Psychology Review, 27*, 433–445.

Hoagwood, K., & Johnson, J. (2003). School psychology: A public health framework I. From evidence-based practices to evidence-based policies. *Journal of School Psychology, 41*, 3–21.

Horner, R. H., Sugai, G., Todd, A. W., & Lewis-Palmer, T. (2005). School-wide positive behavior support. In L. Bambara & L. Kern (Eds.), *Individualized supports for students with problem behaviors: Designing positive behavior support plans* (pp. 359–390). New York: Guilford.

Howell, E. (2004). *Access to children's mental health services under Medicaid and SCHOP*. Washington, DC: Urban Institute.

Hunsley, J. (2007). Addressing key challenges in evidence-based practice in psychology. *Professional Psychology: Research and Practice, 38,* 113–121.

Individuals with Disabilities Education Improvement Act of 2004. 20 U.S.C. § 1400 et seq.

Institute of Medicine. (2002). *Reducing Suicide: A National Imperative*. Washington, DC: National Academies Press.

iSTEEP. (2009). Retrieved on February 1, 2009 from http://www.isteep.com/

Kataoka, S. H., Zhang, L., & Wells, K. B. (2002). Unmet need for mental health care among U.S. children: Variation by ethnicity and insurance status. *American Journal of Psychiatry, 159,* 1548–1555.

Kazdin, A. E. (2008). Evidence-based treatment and practice: New opportunities to bridge clinical research and practice, enhance the knowledge base, and improve patient care. *American Psychologist, 63,* 146–159.

Kenny, D. A. & Judd, C. M. (1986). Consequences of violating the independence assumption in analysis of variance. *Psychological Bulletin, 99,* 422–431.

Kessler, R. C., Beglund, P., Demler, O., Jin, R., Merkiangas, K. R., & Walters, E. E. (2005). Lifetime prevalence and the age-of-onset distributions of DSM-IV disorders in the National Comorbidity Survey Replication. *Archives of General Psychiatry, 62,* 593–602.

Killeen, P. R. (2005). Replicability, confidence, and priors. *Psychological Science, 16,* 1009–1012.

Killeen, P. R. (2006). Beyond statistical inference: A decision theory for science. *Psychonomic Bulletin & Review, 13,* 549–569.

Kimbel, G. A. (1984). Psychology's two cultures. *American Psychologist, 39,* 833–839.

Knitzer, J., & Lefkowitz, J. (2006). *Helping the most vulnerable infants, toddlers, and their families*. New York: National Center for Children in Poverty, Columbia University Mailman School of Public Health.

Kratochwill, T. R., & Shernoff, E. S. (2004). Evidence-based practice: Promoting evidence-based interventions in school psychology. *School Psychology Quarterly, 18,* 389–408.

Kratochwill, T. R., & Stoiber, K. C. (2000). Diversifying theory and science: Expanding boundaries of empirically supported interventions in schools. *Journal of School Psychology, 38,* 349–358.

Kratochwill, T. R., & Stoiber, K. C. (2002). Evidence-based interventions in school psychology. Conceptual foundations of the Procedural and Coding Manual of Division 16 and the Society for the Study of School Psychology. *School Psychology Quarterly, 17,* 341–389.

Kutner, M., Greenberg, E., & Baer, J. (2005). *A first look at the literacy of America's adults in the 21ˢᵗ century*. Washington, DC: U. S. Government Printing Office.

Lee, J., Grigg, W., & Dion, G. (2007). *The Nation's Report Card: Mathematics 2007* (NCES 2007–494). Washington, DC: National Center for Education Statistics, Institute of Education Sciences, U.S. Department of Education.

Lee, J., Grigg, W., & Donahue, P. (2007). *The Nation's Report Card: Reading 2007* (NCES 2007-496). Washington, DC: National Center for Education Statistics, Institute of Education Sciences, U.S. Department of Education.

Love, J. M., Logue, M. E., Trudeau, J. V., & Thayer, K. (1992). *Transitions to Kindergarten in American Schools*. (Contract No. LC88089001). Portsmouth, New Hampshire: U.S. Department of Education.

Marston, D. B. (1989). A curriculum-based measurement approach to assessing academic performance: What is it and why do it? In M.R. Shinn (Ed.), *Curriculum-based measurement: Assessing special children*. New York: Guilford.

Marston, D. & Magnusson, D. (1985). Implementing curriculum-based measurement in special and regular education settings. *Exceptional Children, 52,* 266–276.

Martens, B. K., Eckert, T. L., Bradley, T. A., & Ardoin, S. P. (1999). Identifying effective treatments from a brief experimental analysis: Using single-case design elements to aid decision-making. *School Psychology Quarterly, 14,* 163–181.

Mazza, J. J., & Reynolds, W. M. (2008). School-wide approaches to prevention of and intervention for depression and suicidal behaviors. In B. Doll & J.A. Cummings (Eds.), *Transforming school mental health services* (pp. 213–241). Thousand Oaks, CA: Corwin Press.

McKevitt, B. C. & Braaksma, A. D. (2008). Best practices in developing a positive behavior support system at the school level. In A. Thomas A. J. Grimes (Eds.), *Best practices in school psychology V* (vol. 3, pp. 735–747). Bethesda, MD: National Association of School Psychologists.

McMaster, K. L., Fuchs, D., Fuchs, L. S., & Compton, D. L. (2005). Responding to nonresponders: An experimental field trial of identification and intervention methods. *Exceptional Children, 71,* 445–463.

Mellard, D. F., Byrd, S. E., Johnson, E., Tollefson, J. M., & Boesche, L. (2004). Foundations and research on identifying model responsiveness-to-intervention sites. *Learning Disabilities Quarterly, 27,* 243–256.

Merrell, K. W., & Buchanan, R. (2006). Intervention selection in school-based practice: Using public health models to enhance systems capacity of schools. *School Psychology Review, 35,* 167–180.

Merrell, K. W., Ervin, R. A., & Gimpel, G. A. (2006). *School Psychology for the 21ˢᵗ Century*. New York: Guilford.

Miller, D. N., & Eckert, T. L. (2009). Youth suicidal behavior: An introduction and overview. *School Psychology Review, 38,* 153-168.

Miller, D. N., Eckert, T. L., & Mazza, J. J. (2009). Suicide prevention programs in the schools: A review and public health perspective. *School Psychology Review, 38,* 168-188.

Morgan, P. L., & Sideridis, G. D. (2006). Contrasting the effectiveness of fluency interventions for students with or at risk for learning disabilities: A multilevel random coefficient modeling meta-analysis. *Learning Disabilities Research, 21,* 191–210.

Morris, C. & Normand, S. (1992). Hierarchical models for combining information and for meta-analysis. *Bayesian Statistics, 4,* 321–344.

Nansel, T. R., Overpeck, M. D., Haynie, D. L., Ruan, W. J., & Scheidt, P. C. (2003). Relationship between bullying and violence among U.S. youth. *Archives of Pediatric and Adolescent Medicine, 157,* 348–353.

Nansel, T. R., Overpeck, M., Pilla, R. S. Ruan, W. J., Simons-Morton, B., & Scheidt, P. (2001). Bullying behaviors among US youth: Prevalence and association with psychosocial adjustment. *Journal of the American Medical Association, 285,* 2094–2100.

Nastasi, B. K. (2004). Meeting the challenges of the future: Integrating public health and public education for mental health promotion. *Journal of Educational and Psychological Consultation, 15,* 295–312.

National Alliance for Secondary Education and Transition. (2005). *National standards and quality indicators: Transition toolkit for systems improvement*. Minneapolis, MN: University of Minnesota, National Center on Secondary Education and Transition.

National Center on Response to Intervention. (2009). Response to intervention. Retrieved February 1, 2009, from http://www.rti4success.org/

National Center on Student Progress Monitoring. (2009). Review of progress monitoring tools. Retrieved February 1, 2009, from www.studentprogress.org/chart/chart.asp

National Education Goals Panel. (1995). National education goals report executive summary: Improving education through family–school–community partnerships. Washington, DC: Author.

National Education Goals Panel. (1997). *Getting a good start in school*. Washington, DC: Author.

National Reading Panel. (2000). *Report of the National Reading Panel: Teaching children to read: An evidence-based assessment of the scientific research literature on reading and its implications for reading instruction*. Washington, DC: Author.

National Research Council. (2000). *From neurons to neighborhoods: The science of early childhood development*. Washington, DC: National Academy Press.

New Freedom Commission on Mental Health. (2003). *Achieving the Promise: Transforming Mental Health Care in America*. Rockville, MD: Department of Health and Human Services.

Nickerson, A. B. & Martens, M. P. (2008). School violence: Associations with control, security/enforcement, educational/therapeutic approaches, and demographic factors. *School Psychology Review, 37*, 228–243.

No Child Left Behind Act of 2001 (Pub. L. No. 107-110). Available at http://www.ed.gov/policy/elsec/leg/esea02/107-110.pdf

Northup, J., Wacker, D., Sasso, G., Steege, M., Cigrand, K., Cook, J., & DeRaad, A. (1991). A brief functional analysis of aggressive and alternative behavior in an outclinic setting. *Journal of Applied Behavior Analysis, 24*, 509–522.

Office of Special Education Programs Center on Positive Behavioral Interventions and Supports. (2004). School-wide positive behavior support implementers' blueprint and self-assessment. Eugene, OR: University of Oregon.

Pelham, W. E., Jr., Wheeler, T., & Chronis, A. (1998). Empirically supported psychosocial treatments for attention deficit hyperactivity disorder. *Journal of Clinical Child Psychology, 27*, 190–205.

Persky, H. R., Daane, M. C., & Jin, Y. (2003). *The Nation's Report Card: Writing 2002* (NCES 2003-529). Washington, DC: National Center for Education Statistics, Institute of Education Sciences, U.S. Department of Education.

Power, T. J. (2000). The school psychologist as community-focused, public health professional: Emerging challenges and implications for training. *School Psychology Review, 29*, 557–559.

Power, T. J. (2003). Promoting children's mental health: Reform through interdisciplinary and community partnerships. *School Psychology Review, 32*, 3–16.

Power, T. J., DuPaul, G. J., Shapiro, E. S., & Kazak, A. E. (2003). *Promoting children's health: Integrating school, family, and community*. New York: Guilford Press.

President's Commission on Excellence in Special Education. (2002). *A new era: Revisiting special education for children and their families*. Washington DC: U.S. Department of Education.

Raudenbush, S. W. (2005). *Learning from attempts to improve schooling: The contribution to methodological diversity*. Retrieved February 1, 2009, from http://nationalacademies.org./cfc/Multiple Methods Workshop.html

Raudenbush, S. W., & Bryk, A. S. (1986). A hierarchical model for studying school effects. *Sociology of Education, 59*, 1–17.

Raudenbush, S. W. & Bryk, A. S. (2002). *Hierarchical linear models: Applications and data analysis methods* (2nd ed.). Thousand Oaks, CA: Sage.

Reschly, D. J. (2008). School psychology paradigm shift and beyond. In A. Thomas & A. J. Grimes (Eds.), *Best practices in school psychology V* (vol. 1, pp. 3–15). Bethesda, MD: National Association of School Psychologists.

Reschly, D. J. & Ysseldyke, J. E. (1995). School psychology paradigm shift. In A. Thomas & A. J. Grimes (Eds.), *Best practices in school psychology III* (pp. 17–32). Bethesda, MD: National Association of School Psychologists.

Reschly, D. J. & Ysseldyke, J. E. (2002). Paradigm shift: The past is not the future. In A. Thomas & A. J. Grimes (Eds.), *Best practices in school psychology III* (pp. 3–20). Bethesda, MD: National Association of School Psychologists.

Sanabria, F., & Killeen, P. R. (2007). Better statistics for better decisions: Rejecting null hypotheses statistical tests in favor of replication statistics. *Psychology in the Schools, 44*, 471–481.

Shapiro, E. S. (2000). School psychology from an instructional perspective: Solving big, not little problems. *School Psychology Review, 29*, 560–572.

Sheridan, S. M., & Gutkin, T. B. (2000). The ecology of school psychology: Examining and changing our paradigm for the 21st century. *School Psychology Review, 29*, 485–502.

Shinn, M. R. (1998). *Advanced applications of curriculum-based measurement*. New York: Guilford.

Shinn, M. R., Gleason, M. M. & Tindal, G. (1989). Varying the difficulty of testing materials: Implications for curriculum-based measurement. *The Journal of Special Education, 23*, 223–233.

Shinn, M. R., Good, R. H., Knutson, N., Tilly, W. D., & Collins, V. L. (1992). Curriculum-based measurement of oral reading fluency: A confirmatory analysis of its relations to reading. *School Psychology Review, 21*, 459–479.

Short, R. J. (2002, Summer). School psychology as a separate profession: An unsupportable direction. *The School Psychologist, 56*, 111–117.

Snow, C. E., Burns, M. S., & Griffin, P. (Eds.) (1998). *Preventing reading difficulties in young children*. Washington, DC: National Academies Press.

Snyder, T. D., Dillow, S. A., & Hoffman, C. M. (2008). *Digest of Education Statistics 2007* (NCES 2008-022). Washington, DC: National Center for Education Statistics, Institute for Education Sciences, U. S. Department of Education.

Steiner, H. (1997). Practice parameters for the assessment and treatment of children and adolescents with conduct disorder. *Journal of the American Academy of Child and Adolescent Psychiatry, 36*, 122S–139S.

Strein, W., Hoagwood, K., & Cohn, A. (2003). School psychology: A public health perspective II. Prevention, populations, and systems change. *Journal of School Psychology, 41*, 23–38.

Sugai, G. (2007). Promoting behavioral competence in schools: A commentary on exemplary practices. *Psychology in the Schools, 44*, 113–118.

Swearer, S. M., Turner, R. K., Given, J. E., & Pollack, W. S. (2008). "You're so gay!": Do different forms of bullying matter for adolescent males? *School Psychology Review, 37*, 160–173.

Task Force on Promotion and Dissemination of Psychological Procedures. (1995). Training in and dissemination of empirically-validated psychological treatments: Report and recommendations. *Clinical Psychologist, 48*, 3–23.

Task Force on Promotion and Dissemination of Psychological Procedures. (1998). Update on empirically supported therapies II. *Clinical Psychologist, 51*, 3–16.

Tharinger, D. J. & Palomares, R. S. (2004). An APA-informed perspective on the shortage of school psychologists: Welcome licensed psychologists into the schools (and did we mention xeriscape gardening together?) *Psychology in the Schools, 41*, 461–472.

Tilly, D. W. (2008). The evolution of school psychology to science-based practice: Problem-solving and the three-tiered model. In A. Thomas A. J. Grimes (Eds.), *Best practices in school psychology V* (vol. 1, pp. 17–36). Bethesda, MD: National Association of School Psychologists.

Umbreit, J. (1995). Functional assessment and intervention in a regular classroom setting for the disruptive behavior of a student with attention deficit hyperactivity disorder. *Behavioral Disorders, 20*, 267–278.

U. S. Department of Education. (2002). *Elementary and secondary school survey, state and national projections for enrollment and selected items by race/ethnicity, and sex.* Washington, DC: Author.

U. S. Department of Education. (2003a). *Identifying and implementing educational practices supported by rigorous evidence: A user friendly guide.* Washington, DC: Author.

U.S. Department of Education. (2003b). *Projections of education statistics to 2013* (NCES 2004–013). Washington, DC: Author.

U.S. Department of Education. (2005). *The condition of education, 2005 national center for education statistics.* Washington, DC: Author.

U. S. Department of Education. (2009). *28th Annual report to congress on the implementation of the individuals with disabilities education act, 2006, volume 1.* Washington, DC: U. S. Government Printing Office.

U.S. Department of Health and Human Services. (1999). *The surgeon general's call to action to prevent suicide.* Washington, DC.

U.S. Public Health Service. (2000). *Report of the surgeon general's conference on children's mental health: A national action agenda.* Washington, DC.

Validez, C. R., Carlson, C., & Zanger, D. (2005). Evidence-based parent training and family interventions for school behavior change. *School Psychology Quarterly, 20*, 403–433.

Walker, H. M., Horner, R. H., Sugai, G., Bullis, M., Sprague, J. R., Bricker, D., & Kaufman, M. J. (1996). Integrated approaches to preventing antisocial behavior patterns among school-age children and youth. *Journal of Emotional and Behavioral Disorders, 4*, 193–256.

Wertheimer, R., Croan, T., Anderson Moore, K., & Hair, E. C. (2003). *Attending kindergarten and already behind: A statistical portrait of vulnerable young children.* Washington, DC: Child Trends.

Wilkinson, L. & the Task Force on Statistical Inference. (1999). Statistical methods in psychology journals: Guidelines and explanations. *American Psychologist, 54*, 594–604.

Worrell, F. C. (2007, Fall). Professional psychology, school psychology, and psychological science: Distinctiveness, deindividuation, or separation? *The School Psychologist, 61*, 96–101.

Ysseldyke, J., Burns, M., Dawson, M., Kelly, B., Morrision, D., Ortiz, S., et al. (2006). *School psychology: A blueprint for training and practice III.* Bethesda, MD: National Association of School Psychologists.

Zhou, Z., Bray, M. A., Kehle, T. J., Theodore, L. A., Clark, E., & Jenson, W. R. (2004). *Psychology in the Schools, 41*, 443–450.

INDEX

Note: Page numbers followed by "*f*" and "*t*" denote figures and tables, respectively.

Curriculum based measurement (CBM), 347
Curriculum differentiation, 465
Curriculum enhancement, for gifted students, 472–73
Cutts, N. E., 17, 18*t*
CVAF. *See* Consequence Variables Assessment Form (CVAF)
CWPT. *See* Classwide Peer Tutoring (CWPT)
Cyber-bullying, 492–93

D

Daily report cards, for students with ADHD, 432
D'Amato, R., C., 17, 18–19*t*
DARE. *See* Drug Abuse Resistance Education (DARE)
Darwin, C., 75, 85
Data based action plan, SWPBS and, 657–58
Data-based classroom management, 599–602
  assessing classroom strengths and needs, 600
  conceptual underpinnings of, 596–97
  planning for classroom intervention, 600–601
Data collection decisions, 141–42
  alpha value, 144
  chi-square value, 144
  conditional probability, 144
  confirmatory factor analysis (CFA), 154
  general linear models (GLM), 146
  inferential statistical procedures, 142–43
  intervention program, 145–46
  linear models, 147–48
  multilevel structure models, 151–52
  nonlinear models, 148–50
  parameter estimation, 144–46
  path analysis, 153
  proportionate reduction, in error (PRE) statistics, 142
  pros and cons of various models, 157–58
  sample statistic values, 143
  sampling fluctuation hypothesis, 143, 145
  significance testing, 143–44
  standard normal distribution, 145
  stratified sampling, 142
  structural equation modeling (SEM), 152–53
  type I and type II errors, 144
  worst-case scenario hypothesis, 143
  z-test, 144
  zero relationship/difference, 144
Data management system, SWPBS and, 659–60
Data Recognition Corporation, 215
Decision-making. *See also* Data collection decisions; Statistical methods, for informed decisions
  data for, 103

Dendrites, 172
Dendritic spines, 172
Deno, S. L., 211
Depression, 69
Derby, K. M., 197
Descriptive statistics, 127*t*, 131*t*
  for reading comprehension test, 145–46*t*
Developmental Observation Checklist System (DOCS), 376
Diagnostic and Statistical Manual of Mental Disorders–Fourth Edition, Text Revision (DSM-IV-TR), 494
Diagnostic Interview Schedule for Children-Version IV (DISC-IV), 291
DIBELS. *See* Dynamic Indicators of Basic Early Learning Skills (DIBELS)
Direct instruction (DI), 535–36
Direct observation, of student behavior, 207–10
Disabilities factors
  instructional factors for students with mild, 529*t*
Disabilities instructional practices
  effective approaches for students with mild, 530*t*
DISC-IV, 316–19. *See* Diagnostic Interview Schedule for Children-Version IV (DISC-IV)
DISC-P, 316, 318
DISC-Y, 316, 318
Disruptive behavior disorders
  drug efficacy in, 714
  FDA pediatric indications for, 713–14
Disruptive behavior disorders, 285–88
  adolescent-onset type, 288
  childhood-onset type, 288
  conduct disorder, 285–88
  DSM-IV-TR criteria for, 287*t*
  ODD, 285–88
Dittmer-McMahon, K. I., 198
Divalproex
  side effects of, 710
Diversity issues, in academic interventions, 561–62
Diversity issues, related to home variables, 561–62
DNA methylation, 70–72
DNA sequence, 72
DOCS. *See* Developmental Observation Checklist System (DOCS)
Doctoral and subdoctoral level training, in school psychology, 23–25
Doggett, R. A., 197
Drug Abuse Resistance Education (DARE), 690
Drug efficacy findings
  in ADHD, 711–13
  in attention-deficit/hyperactivity disorder (ADHD), 711–13
  in autism spectrum disorders, 718–20
  in bipolar disorder, 714–16

  in disruptive behavior disorders, 713–14
  in major depressive disorder, 717–18
  in non-OCD anxiety disorders, 716–17
  in obsessive compulsive disorder, 715–16
  in Tourette's syndrome and Tic disorders, 713
Drug safety issues
  antidepressants, 703–6
  antihypertensives, 711
  antipsychotics, 706–8
  mood stabilizers, 708–11
  stimulants, 702–3
DSM-IV, 322
Dufrene, B. A., 197
Dynamic Indicators of Basic Early Learning Skills (DIBELS), 347, 377
Dynamic Indicators of Basic Early Literacy Skills (DIBELS) Data System, 835
Dyslexia, 172, 174–75, 335

E

E-BASS. *See* Ecological behavioral (E-BASS)
E-book readers, in school psychology, 831
E-Journal of Applied Psychology, 838
Early childhood partnerships core programs, 376*t*
Early intensive behavioral intervention (EIBI)
  ASD and, 568
Ecobehavioral approach, to classroom observations, 276
Ecobehavioral assessment, 276–77
Ecobehavioral System for Complex Analyses of Preschool Environments (ESCAPE), 276
Ecological approach, instructional consultation and, 671
Ecological behavioral (E-BASS), 209–10
Ecological theory, social skills, 445
Ecological validity, PBS and, 649
ED. *See* Emotional disturbance (ED)
Educating Children with Autism, 573
Education and school psychology, 31
  continuing, 59
Education for All Handicapped Children Act (PL 94-142), 289
Education licensure, in school psychology
  state board of psychology, 25
  state department, 25
Educational and psychological applications, individual differences, 73–76
Educational outcomes, focus on
  in IDEA 97, 754–55
  in IDEA 2004, 755–57
  in No Child Left Behind Act (NCLB), 757–59
Educational programs
  expanding access and defining parameters for, 750

Focused interventions, for ASD, 575–88
  behavioral package, 575–76
  joint attention, 579–80
  modeling/video modeling, 581–83
  naturalistic teaching strategies,
      576–79
    incidental teaching, 577
    natural language paradigm, 577–78
    pivotal response training, 578–79
  peer training, 583–85
  self-management, 585–88
    applications of, 586–87
    designing of, 587–88
Food Force, 841
Formal operational stage, 94
Frasier & Passow's attributes, of giftedness
      and talent, 459t
Free and appropriate public education
      (FAPE), 529
FTW. *See* Fast-taped words (FTW)
Fuchs, L. S., 211, 217
Functional Assessment Informant Record
      for Teachers (FAIR-T), 191–92,
      200–203
Functional behavioral assessment
      (FBA), 611
  A-B-C/behavioral stream recording, 194
  basic principles, 190
  brief, 195–98
  brief history, 188–89
  categories and subcategories of
      reinforcers, 189t
  conditional probability recording, 195
  direct descriptive, 193–94
  errors committed during, 196–97
  essential components of, 190–91
  functional behavior assessment
      observation form (FBAOF), 195
  indirect procedures, 191–93
  interval recording procedure (IRP), 195
  questions about, 197–98
  SMIRC model, 189–90
  task difficulty antecedent analysis,
      194–95
Functional Behavioral Assessment
      Screening Form (FBASF),
      191–92, 199
Functional MRI (fMRI) scans, 171, 175
Furazolidone, side effects, 703
"Futures Conference" (2002), 37–39, 39t

G
G-coefficient, 160
G factor theory of intelligence, 26
Gagné's conception, giftedness and talent,
      459–60
Gallo, L. C., 69
Galton, Sir Francis, 26, 85
Gang Resistance Education and Training
      Program (GREAT), 489
Gang violence, interventions for, 489–90
Gardner, H., 93
Gardner, M. K., 90

GARS. *See* Gilliam Autism Rating Scale
      (GARS)
GAS. *See* Goal Attainment Scaling (GAS);
      Goal attainment scaling (GAS)
Gaussian curve and individual differences, 3
Gender, 4
General cognitive ability (g)
  g-loaded attainment, 65–66, 73
  individual differences, 64–65
  and job performance, 66–67, 73
  Spearman's g factor, 81–82
General linear models (GLM), 146
General outcome measurement
      (GOM), 210
Generalizability Theory (G-theory), 160
Gf-Gc theory, 26–27
Gifted/talented students, 68
  with ADHD, 461–62
  with behavioral problems, 462
  content area enrichment and curriculum
      enhancement for, 473–74
  development of continuum of services
      to challenge, 475–77
    school based gifted programs, 476
    services in, 476–77
  differentiation of regular curriculum
      for, 473
  enrichment and curricular enhancement
      for, 472–73
  future prospects for, 479
  identification of high potential and,
      462–63
  instructional grouping practices for,
      471–72
  lack of challenges in regular classrooms,
      469–70
  with learning disabilities, 461
  longitudinal research on programs,
      474–75
  research based interventions for, 463–68
    continuum of special services,
      468, 468f
    enrichment clusters, 467–68
    regular curriculum, 467
    SEM, 463–67
  social and emotional counseling and
      support, 474
  special populations of, 461–62
  underachievement in academically,
      470–71
  underachieving, 462
Giftedness and talent
  case study, 457–58
  definition of, 457–61
    characteristics and operational, 458
    creativity and creative productive,
      460–61
    federal, 458–59
    Frasier & Passow's attributes of, 459t
    Gagné's conception, 459–60
    Renzulli's three-ring conception,
      459, 459f
  overview, 456–57

Gilliam Autism Rating Scale (GARS), 570
Glass, G. V., 163
Glial cells, 172
Global Classroom Rating score, 272
Global Severity Index of the Symptom
      Check List-Revised
      (SCL-90-R), 317
Glucose metabolism rate (GMR), 95–96
Goal Attainment Scaling (GAS), 452
Goal Direction Scale, 274
Goddard, H. H., 27
GOM. *See* General outcome measurement
      (GOM)
Good behavior game, students with
      ADHD and, 433
"Good-enough" principle, 125
Goodness-of-fit method, 144
Google Docs, 833
Google Scholar, 830
GORT 4. *See* Gray Oral Reading Test,
      4th Edition (GORT 4)
Gottesman, I. I., 65
Gottfredson, L. S., 64, 66
Gottman, J. M., 163
Graden, J., 210
Graduate training, in school psychology,
      56–59
Gratitude, SWB and
  with adults, 511–12
  with children and adolescents, 516–17
Gray Oral Reading Test, 4th Edition
      (GORT 4), 214
GREAT. *See* Gang Resistance Education
      and Training Program (GREAT)
Great Debate, 175
Greeley-Weld Independent School
      District #6, 35
Greenwood, C. R., 210
Gross domestic product (GNP), 67
Gross state product (GSP), 67
Group counseling, 623–24
Grouping practices, in effective
      instruction, 536–37
Guilford, J. P., 84

H
Haier, R. J., 95–96
*Handbook of International School
      Psychology,* 818
Handcooling biofeedback, 733
Handwarming biofeedback, 733
Hartmann, P., 67
Hauck, W. W., 126, 130
Health, 74
  individual differences, 68–69
  problems in youth, long-term effects
      of, 729
  related prevention and wellness, 686–87
Healthy school climate, SWB and, 508–9
Heick, P. F., 208
Helmholtz Association, 11
Hendrickson, D. E., 95
Henington, C., 197

neural development throughout lifespan, 172–73

potential benefits of combining models and methods, 178–79

practical difficulties, 175–76

RTI model, 177–78

specific learning disability (SLD), 176–77

Neuronal myelination, 172

Neurons, 172

Neuroticism, 67

Neurotransmitters, 172

NHANES. *See* National Health and Nutrition Examination Surveys (NHANES)

NLP. *See* Natural language paradigm (NLP)

No Child Left Behind Act (NCLB), 48, 176, 214, 269, 369, 757–59, 786, 864

Non-cognitive traits, 67

Non-OCD anxiety disorders

drug efficacy in, 717

FDA pediatric indications for, 716–17

Nondirective supportive therapy (NST), 497

Nonlinear models, 148–50

Nontraditional school psychology, 31–33, 32*t*

Norm-referenced standardized tests (NRSTs), 216–17

Northup, J., 196

NOVA. *See* National Organization for Victim Assistance (NOVA)

NRP. *See* National Reading Panel (NRP)

NRST. *See* Norm-referenced standardized tests (NRSTs)

NST. *See* Nondirective supportive therapy (NST)

Null hypothesis significance testing (NHST), 104

for balanced case, 111

of cluster randomized designs, 111

Fisher's approach, 110

Neyman-Pearson approach, 110–11

one-way ANOVA model, 111

type I and type II errors, 109–10, 109*t*, 126

using computer software, 111

Nyborg, H., 64, 67

O

Obesity, childhood, 687–88

prevention and early intervention programs, 688

research on risk and protective factors, 687–88

Observational learning, social skills assessment, 450

!Observe, 834–35

Obsessive compulsive disorder

drug efficacy in, 716

FDA pediatric indications for, 715–16

Occipitotemporal pathway, 174

Occupational status, SWB and, 506–7

Occupational therapist, 29

Off-label prescribing, 699–700

Office of Juvenile Justice and Delinquency Prevention (OJJDP), 489

Olanzapine, side effects of, 708

Olympia Conference (1981), 14*t*, 17

Online communities, in school psychology, 833

Oppositional defiant disorder (ODD), 285–88, 288*t*, 316

Oral language, role in learning written language, 556

Oral reading fluency (ORF), 211

Organizational development consultation, 671–74

effectiveness research, 673–74

models and stages of systems change, 672–73

Organizational development (OD), 788

Organizational development consultation (ODC), 30, 788

Organizational or systems consultation (OSC), 787–88

Orthographic awareness, 555, 557

Oxcarbazepine

FDA warnings and advisories for, 709

side effects of, 710

P

p-value, 125, 127, 130

p-regressor, 106

PAARN. *See* Pennsylvania Action Research Network (PAARN)

PALS. *See* Peer-assisted learning strategies (PALS)

Panacea mongers, 3

PANAS-C. *See* Positive and Negative Affect Scale for Children (PANAS-C)

Paradigm shift," in school psychology, 216

Paradox of, 9

Parameter estimation

confidence interval approach in, 144–46

data collection decisions, 144–46

individual assessment, 160

statistical modeling, 146

Parent education, to prevent bullying, 492

Parent-mediated behavioral consultation, 669–70

Parent-school relationships, 560–61

Parental cocaine exposure, 688–90

prevention programs, 690

research on risk and protective factors, 688–89

Parental contribution. to academic learning, 560–61

Participatory Intervention Model (PIM), 639

Partnership, 816–18

defined, 816

in international arena, application, 817

Passive engaged time (PET), 208

Path analysis, 153

Pavlov, I. P., 188

PBS. *See* Positive behavior support (PBS)

PDD-NOS. *See* Pervasive developmental disorder-not otherwise specified (PDD–NOS)

Pearson, Karl, 142, 144

goodness-of-fit method, 144

Pediatric drugs, "safety first" approach, 700–701

Pediatric psychologists, use computerized interventions, 839–40

Pediatric psychopharmacology, 698

Pediatric psychotropic research

controversies, 699–700

future directions in, 720

growth of, 698

school psychologists role in, 698–99

Peer-assisted learning strategies (PALS), 531

Peer-mediated behavioral consultation, 670

Peer relationships

classroom management and, 598

Peer relationships, SWB and positive, 508

Peer Social Behavior Code (PSB), 448

Peer training, for ASD, 583–85

written text treatment, 584–85

Pembrey, M. E., 72

Pemoline side effects, 702

Pennsylvania Action Research Network (PAARN), 848

Pennsylvania System of School Assessment (PSSA), 215

Percent of nonoverlapping data points (PND), 615

Perceptual motor training, special education and, 526–27

Performance components, 89, 92

Performance deficits, 443

Personality factors, 67

Pervasive developmental disorder-not otherwise specified (PDD–NOS), 569

PET. *See* Passive engaged time (PET)

Petition Package for school psychology, 22

Pharmaceutical industry

influence on psychotropic research, 700

Phelps, L., 17

Phonological awareness, 557

Physical health, SWB and, 507

Physical therapist, 29

Piaget's stage theory of development, 93–94

PIM. *See* Participatory intervention model (PIM); Pre-referral intervention models (PIM)

PISA. *See* Programme for International Student Assessment (PISA)

Pivotal response training (PRT)

for ASD, 578–79

PKBS-2. *See* Preschool and Kindergarten Behavior System Second Edition (PKBS-2)

SEM-R. *See* Schoolwide Enrichment Model in Reading (SEM-R)
Semistructured Parent Interview (SPI), 293
Sensorimotor stage, 94
Serlin, R. C., 125–26, 130
Seroquel. *See* Quetiapine
Serotonin–norepinephrine reuptake inhibitors (SNRIs)
efficacy in major depressive disorder, 718
side effects of, 705
SES. *See* Socioeconomic status (SES)
Setting-specific PBS, 661–62
Sex-specific effects, 72
SFBT. *See* Solution-focused brief therapy (SFBT)
Shapiro, E. S., 208, 218
Shaw, J. H., 270
Shaywitz, Sally, 174–75
Sheridan, S., M., 17
Shivpuri, S., 68
Shooting Stars program, 35*t*
Short-term memory (Gsm), 27
Significance testing, 143–44
Simon, Theodore, 27
Simple/choice reaction time, 86–87, 96
Simple sensory testing, 85
Situational theory, and systems change, 632
Skills deficits, 443
Skinner, M., 75
SLD. *See* Specific learning disability (SLD); specific learning disability (SLD)
Slow-taped words (STW), 436
Small-group learning, 268
Snow, R. E., 65
Social and emotional learning (SEL) programs, 642
Social behavior, influencing factors, 72
Social change
video games role in, 840–41
Social Communication Questionnaire (SCQ)
for ASD, 571
Social competence, defined, 443
Social counseling, for gifted students, 474
Social learning
preventive mental health programs and, 641–43
Social learning theory, 450, 830
Social maladjustment, 69
Social resources, SWB and, 506
Social Responsiveness Scale (SRS), 570
Social significance, 125
Social skills
deficits, self-management of ASD and, 586–87
definition of, 444
external variable theory, 444
functioning in students, potential causes, 444–45
multidimensional assessment protocol, 447
overview, 442–44
and role of school psychologist, 451–53

theoretical models to guide research and practice, 445–46
ecological theory, 445
positive behavior support model, 445–46
Social skills assessment, 446–49
behavior rating scales, 448
direct observations, 447–48
operant conditioning techniques, 450
review of existing records, 448–49
teacher interviews for, 447
Social skills interventions, 449–51
Social systems
innovation diffusion and, 633–34
schools as, 630–31
Social validity, PBS and, 650
Socioeconomic issues, in academic interventions, 561–62
Socioeconomic status (SES), 3, 68, 70
levels of cortisol, 73
Solution-focused brief therapy (SFBT), 623
Spatial intelligence, 93
Spearman, Charles, 26, 80–81
Spearman-Brown prophecy formula, 159
Spearman's Two Factor theory, 80–81
Special education
accessing general education, 530
early intervention, 541
effective. *See* Effective special education
instruction. *See* Instruction, special eduction and
and intensity of instruction, 530–31
nature of, 531–32, 542–44
overview, 523–24
process training, 526–29
effectiveness of, 526*t*
perceptual motor training, 526–27
psycholinguistic training, 527–29, 528*t*
research traditions in, 524–26
new research paradigms, 525
paradigm wars, 524–25
research synthesis, 525–26
services, 33
Special education teacher, 29
Special populations, of gifted/talented students, 461–62
Specific learning disability (SLD), 48, 176–77, 342, 527
Three-Tier Identification Model, 178
Specific subskill (SS) mastery, 210
Speech therapist, 29
Speed of processing, 90
SPI. *See* Semistructured Parent Interview (SPI)
Spiritual intelligence, 93
Spring Hill Symposium (1980), 14*t*, 16–17
SRS. *See* Social Responsiveness Scale (SRS)
SRSD. *See* Self-regulated strategy development (SRSD)

SSBD protocol. *See* Systematic Screening for Behavior Disorders (SSBD) protocol
S.S.P. (Specialist in School Psychology), 24
STAIC. *See* State-Trait Anxiety Inventory for Children (STAIC)
Stakeholder participation, PBS and, 649–50
Standard error estimates, of model, 156, 157*t*, 166–67
Standard errors, 145
Standard normal distribution, 145
Standardized coefficients, 147
Standardized item alpha, 159
Standardized measures, of academic achievement, 212–17
Standardized root mean square residual (SRMR), 156
Standards for Training and Field Placement Programs in School Psychology, 451
Stanford Achievement Test Battery, 10th edition (SAT-10), 214
Stanford Revision of the Binet-Simon Intelligence Scale, 26
STAR. *See* Student/Teacher Achievement Ratio program (STAR)
STARBRIGHT program, 840
STAT. *See* Screening Tool for Autism in Two-Year-Olds (STAT)
State-Event Classroom Observation System (SECOS), 209
State–Trait Anxiety Inventory for Children (STAIC), 326–28
Statistical Analysis System (SAS), 318
Statistical methods, for informed decisions
analysis of variance (ANOVA) design, 106–7
Bayesian framework of analysis, 132–37
cluster randomized design, 108–9, 111
coding schemes, 107
concept of effect size, 114–19
confidence interval, 112–14
equivalence hypotheses testing, 129–32
general linear model formulation, 107
inferential statistical procedures, 105–9
notion of hypothesis testing, 109–12
null hypothesis significance testing (NHST), 104, 109–12
population standard deviation, 106
power calculations, 119–25
random effects model, 108
range null hypothesis testing (RNHT), 125–29
sampling distribution, of a statistic, 105
sampling distribution of mean difference, 106
standard deviation of sampling distribution, 105
two-group posttest comparison, 131*t*
Statistical significance testing, 104
Steege, M. W., 195–96
Sternberg, Robert J., 89–91